The New York Times EVERYDAY DICTIONARY

The New York Times EVERYDAY DICTIONARY

Thomas M. Paikeday, Editor

Times BOOKS

Published by TIMES BOOKS, a division of
Quadrangle/ The New York Times Book Co., Inc.
Three Park Avenue, New York, N.Y. 10016

Library of Congress Cataloging in Publication Data

Main entry under title:

New York times everyday dictionary.

1. English language—Dictionaries. I. Paikeday, Thomas M.
PE1628.N464 1982 423 81-84903
ISBN 0-8129-0910-0

Manufactured in the United States of America

10 9 8 7 6 5 4 3 2 1

ACKNOWLEDGMENTS

The editor wishes to thank the following persons for their valuable help at various stages of the compilation of *The New York Times Everyday Dictionary:*

LEXICOGRAPHICAL POLICIES

Prof. Robert L. Chapman, Drew University, Madison, N.J.
Prof. Philip W. Cummings (deceased), Trenton State College, Trenton, N.J.
Prof. J. Edward Gates, Indiana State University, Terre Haute, Ind.
Prof. Samuel C. Monson, Brigham Young University, Provo, Utah
Prof. B. Hunter Smeaton, University of Calgary, Calgary, Alberta, Can.

MANUSCRIPT PREPARATION

Harold E. Niergarth, consultant and chief copy-editor
Eugene F. Shewmaker, copy-editor
Felice Levy, proofreader
Brad Inwood, assistant editor
Janet M. Allen, Gail Ross, Debby Schaufele: editorial assistants

DATA COLLECTION & PROCESSING

Marc Abdel-Malek, Donald R. Bingley, Julia Gidman, Vic Kass, Anthony Paikeday

PUBLISHER'S NOTE

The New York Times Everyday Dictionary, appropriately enough, is the only dictionary based on a citation file derived principally from *The New York Times* and its electronic edition. Acknowledged as one of the world's leading daily publications in English, *The New York Times* provides an especially authoritative base for current usage.

PREFACE

by Raven I. McDavid, Jr.

Professor Emeritus of English,
University of Chicago

For three centuries, dictionaries of the English language have been best sellers. Originally designed to interpret hard words for the perplexed, they have become, in various ways, rules of conduct, road maps, and historical records. The numbers and kinds multiply in response to special needs. I own at least five dozen.

For a long time dictionaries were made by anonymous publishers' hacks, by entrepreneurs like Noah Webster, or by literary dictators like Samuel Johnson. Now their making is a profession. Editors learn the craft in universities before the years of on-the-job training that develop the industry, artisanship, and artistry that mark the successful lexicographer. Furthermore, though dictionary-makers were once as secretive as the makers of proprietary medicines, editors now fraternize easily at professional gatherings and discuss plans and problems. The resources of the language are available to everyone. Each editor decides how these resources are to be used.

Thomas Paikeday is one of the new school of lexicographers; he is active in meetings of lexicographers and willing to try new ideas. *The New York Times Everyday Dictionary* is evidence of his industry, originality, and ability.

This dictionary of modest size replicates an old model. While Johnson was preparing his monumental dictionary, John Wesley, who prepared a series of pocket books (perhaps we should call them saddlebag books) for circuit riders, edited a small *Compleat English Dictionary* [1753] which he modestly assured the readers was the best in the world. *The New York Times Everyday Dictionary,* somewhat longer than Wesley's, does not make the claims that Wesley made. But like Wesley's it is that rarity among dictionaries—a small book, genuinely unabridged, not cut down from a larger work, but designed afresh and aimed at the common needs of the general reader.

A dictionary of this size cannot provide all the apparatus of the *Oxford,* and, coming down the line, the *Merriam International* series, the *Webster's New World,* or the *Thorndike Barnhart Desk Dictionary.* Realistic editorial decisions are to omit etymologies, indicate pronunciations only when not self-evident, reduce the number of synonyms, eliminate most definitions dealing with special regional and social variants, and sharply curtail the number of encyclopedic entries, both biographical and geographic. Inflectional forms are generally not dignified with independent entries but consolidated under the base form.

These economies allow a somewhat larger word stock than is found in competing works. Though the editor does not disdain the computer, he recognizes its limitations. In the end, human beings must still decide which meanings and words to include. For the audience to which this work is directed Paikeday has chosen well. Explanatory front matter, often ignored by readers, sets a standard for clarity and economy. The typography is clean and attractive. The pronunciation key is simple and useful. From looking at sample pages I find the definitions clear and accurate.

The proof of a dictionary is in its use. I do not know as yet how often I will consult this work, since many other often larger and more specialized dictionaries are at my immediate disposal. But it will hold an honorable place on my shelves.

EXPLANATORY NOTES

The editors have endeavored to make this dictionary as self-explanatory as possible. Answers to questions on spelling, meaning, pronunciation, grammar, and usage may be readily found in the dictionary itself without recourse to a guide, list of abbreviations, or pronunciation key. However, a detailed statement of the principles and practice of our lexicography is provided here for the benefit of dictionary enthusiasts, reviewers, and other specialists.

CONTENTS

I. HOW TO FIND AN ENTRY

Entries are the boldfaced words in alphabetical order at the head of and inside each paragraph.

All entries are printed in boldface type and grouped into convenient paragraphs. A new paragraph normally begins where an entry word is not connected by etymology with the one preceding it. However, the main criterion of paragraphy in this dictionary is not etymology but ease of reference compatible with conservation of dictionary space and convenience of organization of the material.

A. Alphabetical Order

All main entries in this dictionary appear in strict alphabetical order. (See Section C dealing with the listing of subentries under their key words.) Alphabetization is done letter by letter without regard to spaces, hyphens, or punctuation marks.

Alphabetization of entries containing arabic numerals and symbols such as "&" is done as in the pronunciation of the entry. Thus we have:

four-flush	**plod**	**rand**	**Wed.**
fourfold	**PL/1**	**R & B**	**we'd**
4-H (club)	**plop**	**R & D**	**wed**
Four Hundred	**plot**	**random**	**wedding**

Compound names of persons and places are alphabetized by their most frequently used components. Thus:

Man, Isle of.
Michigan —Lake Michigan
Peter, St.
Webster 1 Daniel.
2 Noah.
Whitney, Mount.

Note the different treatment of "St.," based on written usage, in indivisible names such as:

Saint Bernard (dog)
Saint Valentine's Day
St. Lawrence River
St. Louis (city)

B. Main Entries

Main entries start with a boldfaced headword and are followed by a formal definition. Main entries may be at the head of a paragraph or inside it.

The following are the types of main entries to be found in strict alphabetical order:

1. solidly written and hyphenated forms:

time ***n.***
—*v.*
—*adj.*
time-honored
timekeeper

2. inflected forms and derivatives with specialized meanings:

timeless
timely
timer
times
timing

3. open noun compounds referring to a single concept or unit such as the following:

master of ceremonies
negative income tax
nice Nelly
no man's land
piece of eight
Saturday night special
time sharing
X ray

Open compounds are distinguished from phrases which, together with idioms (see Section C) always form subentries. Note the distinction between a compound such as **piece of eight** and phrases such as **piece of one's mind** and **piece of the action**.

C. Subentries Under Key Words

Subentries are the less important entries in the dictionary, entered under the main entries to which they belong grammatically or semantically, hence not necessarily in strict alphabetical order. Groups of subentries such as verb phrases follow alphabetical order within the group, as **get along** through **get up** under the main entry **get**.

If the entry you are looking for is not in its strict alphabetical place, it is probably a subentry entered a few lines above or below, under its key word. Thus **soupspoon** will be found under **soup**, *n.* **1** (not between **soupçon** and **soupy**); **piece of one's mind** is under **piece**, *n.* **1** (not between **piece of eight** and **piecework**), and **stick one's neck out** is under **neck**, *n.* (not between **stickler** and **stickpin**).

The key words for inflectional forms and derivatives are their base words. Thus **aging** and **rosiness** should be looked for under **age** and **rosy** respectively. Frequently, the location of a subentry under the key word to which it belongs has been used to indicate its precise meaning without going the way of a formal definition. Thus **admittance** is distinguished from **admission** by its placement under **admit**, *v.* **1**. The entry **saloonkeeper** follows **saloon**, *n.* **1** to show that it is not applicable to **saloon**, *n.* **2** as in "dining saloon."

Subentries are of the following types:

(a) inflected forms and derivatives

subentry	*key word*
cagier, cagiest	**cagey**
espies, espied	**espy**
ordines	**ordo**
sagged, sagging	**sag**
solvency	**solvent**
tetanic	**tetanus**
thalami	**thalamus**
thematic	**theme**
warier, wariest	**wary**

(b) phrases and idioms

subentry	*key word*
take care of	**care**
diamond in the rough	**diamond**
go ape	**go**
go the whole hog	**hog**
in the negative	**negative**
rest on one's oars	**oar**
pat on the back	**pat**
piece of one's mind	**piece**
take place	**place**

take cover	**take**
on time	**time**
go to waste	**waste**

(c) words defined in context (see also IV, B)

subentry	*key word*
coconut milk	**coconut**
" **oil**	"
" **palm**	"
employment agency	**employment**
exhilarating	**exhilarate**
noise pollution	**noise**
oral history	**oral**
outboard motor	**outboard**
sleeping car	**sleeper**
slot car	**slot**, *n.* & *v.* **1**
soupspoon	**soup**, *n.* **1**
talcum powder	**talc**

Note that all noun compounds are entered under their first components.

The meaning of many combinations of words established by usage, treated as collocations rather than compounds and phrases, may be gathered from the italicized sentences and phrases illustrating their components.

subentry	*key word*
double whammy	**whammy**
hamburger with the works	**hamburger**
hand in the till	**till**
objective test	**objective**
organic architecture	**organic**
out of tune	**tune**
overhead projector	**overhead**
peace offensive	**offensive**
public works department	**works**
sign of the zodiac	**zodiac**
stock option	**option**
take up the slack	**slack**
team teaching	**team**
textured vegetable protein	**textured**
time loan	**time**
triple jump	**triple**
twin bill	**twin**

D. Cross-References

Cross-references help in locating main entries and subentries when they are too far removed from their alphabetical places to be easily spotted by a consulter.

apices see APEX.
dying See DIE.
extrovert same as EXTRAVERT.
millpond, millrace, millstone, millstream, mill wheel See [1]MILL, *n.* 1.
packsaddle See PACK, *n.* 1.
pied See [3]PIE.
pine nut See PIÑON.
slily same as SLYLY.
those *pl.* of THAT.

E. Sound-Spelling Chart

If you still cannot find the entry word you want, and you happen to know the word only by its pronunciation, then check its spelling using the sound-spelling chart on page xvi. A. word that you hear as (KEE) may be actually spelled **quay**, what sounds like (ILE) may be **aisle** or **isle** depending on context, and the animal's name heard as (LEP.urd) is listed before **leotard**, not after **leper**, as one might expect.

II. SYLLABICATION AND SPELLING

1. Entry words of more than one syllable are divided into syllables at their first entry in the dictionary as a boldfaced word, using centered dots except where a hyphen is part of the spelling. Open compounds and phrases follow the syllabication shown for their component words in their own alphabetical places. Abbreviations and word parts such as affixes and combining forms are normally not syllabicated.

Ne·an·der·thal
neanderthal
Ne·a·pol·i·tan
Neapolitan ice cream

socio-
sociol·
so·ci·ol·o·gy

talk
talk·a·tive
talking book
talk·ing-to

2. When two spellings separated by "or" are given for the same entry, they should be considered nearly equal in currency and frequency of usage.

extraversion or **extroversion**
Medicaid or **medicaid**
saltpeter or **saltpetre**

3. A less frequently used form is usually placed at the end of its entry or definition.

naiveté or **naïveté** . . . also **naivety**.
No . . . also **Noh**.
sluice . . . also **sluice gate**.
splenetic 1 . . . also **splenic**.
wintry . . . also **wintery**.

4. Parentheses are sometimes used to abbreviate equal variants which should be read as shown in the following examples:

enlarge (up)on = **enlarge on** or **enlarge upon**
enrol(l) = **enrol** or **enroll**
entom(ol). = **entom.** or **entomol.**
equals, equal(l)ed, equal(l)ing = **equals, equaled** or **equalled, equaling** or **equalling**
in (or **out of**) **order** (not) working properly = **in order** working properly; **out of order** not working properly
permanent (wave) = **permanent** or **permanent wave**
salvo(e)s = **salvos** or **salvoes**
savio(u)r = **savior** or **saviour**
vacuum bottle (or **flask** or **jug**) = **vacuum bottle, vacuum flask**, or **vacuum jug**
wait at (or **on**) = **wait at** or **wait on**
Wilton (rug or **carpet)** = **Wilton, Wilton rug**, or **Wilton carpet**

5. Inflected forms of nouns, verbs, adjectives, and certain derived entries are frequently shortened using a hyphen. The shortened forms should be read as shown to the right below:

aes·thet·ic or **-i·cal** *adj.* = **aes·thet·i·cal**
cap·il·lar·y *n., pl.* **-il·lar·ies** = **cap·il·lar·ies**
per·mis·si·ble·ness or **-bil·i·ty** *n.* = **per·mis·si·bil·i·ty**
war·y *adj.* **war·i·er, -i·est** = **war·i·est**
wea·ry *adj.* **-ri·er, -ri·est** = **wea·ri·er, wea·ri·est**
weath·er·ize *v.* **-iz·es, -ized, -iz·ing** = **weath·er·iz·es, weath·er·ized, weath·er·iz·ing**

III. PRONUNCIATION

This dictionary uses pronunciation respellings that require no key or decoding because the respellings simply use the most typical spellings of English words that you learned to recognize for their regular sound values when you learned to read English.

The syllabication given for each boldfaced entry word is the first clue to its correct pronunciation. Thus if **Xanthippe** is a new word to you, the syllabified form **Xan·thip·pe** shows the word is pronounced as three syllables, which would rule out a pronunciation such as (ZAN·thip). (An English reader will not normally use the "ks" sound of X in the beginning of a word.) Possible English pronunciations then would include (ZAN·thip·ay), (ZAN·thip·ee), and (zan·THIP·ay). But the dictionary respelling (zan·TIP·ee) settles the question beyond a doubt for the average dictionary user.

As in the examples above, the capitalized syllable in a pronunciation respelling shows the stressed syllable. However, since it is a natural and normal tendency for speakers of English to stress the initial syllable of words of more than one syllable, an initial stress is usually not shown in our respellings. Thus, for **Soc·ra·tes**, the partial respelling (-ruh·teez) should suffice. But **So·crat·ic** has a change of stress which is indicated by (-CRAT).

The pronunciation of only those parts of a word that do not follow regular patterns of English spelling is indicated within parentheses. A word such as **pros·ta·glan·din** (-GLAN-) needs only the indication of the stressed syllable for its correct pronunciation. On the other hand, **sin·is·ter** needs no pronunciation respelling at all, the syllabication alone being sufficient. The partial respelling occasionally given for a particular entry may be completed if necessary by glancing back at a preceding entry on which it may be based, often as a derivative. Thus the pronunciation given for **pre·fec·ture** (-chur) implies that the first two syllables of the word are pronounced as in **pre·fect** (PREE-).

More than one respelling given within parentheses and separated by commas indicates more than one acceptable pronunciation of the same word. Thus **sta·tus** (STAY-, STAT-) means the word may be pronounced (STAY·tus) or (STAT·us). Note that the syllabication of pronunciation does not necessarily correspond to that of the spelling.

No pronunciation is given for affixes, abbreviations, symbols, etc. that have no distinctive pronunciations of their own. Derivatives and obvious compounds whose pronunciation may be derived from their component parts are also not respelled within parentheses.

The key spellings most frequently used in the pronunciations are listed in the second column below. The other typical spellings given for each sound are less frequently used; their main purpose is to help in determining the written form of a word from its spoken form.

SOUND-SPELLING CHART

The Alphabet	Key Spellings Illustrating English Sounds	Other Typical English Spellings
A	pa*i*d	pa*y*, ta*k*e, *ei*ght, br*ea*k, h*ey*, buff*et*, ga*u*ge, ga*o*l

	p*a*t	*au*nt, pl*ai*d, p*a*th, l*au*gh
	p*air*	p*a*rent, wh*ere,* th*eir,* w*ear,* pr*ayer,* m*arr*y
	p*ar*t, *ah*	h*ear*t, s*er*jeant, f*a*ther, *a*dios
B	*b*ed	ru*bb*er
C	*ch*ip	ca*tch,* *c*ello, righ*te*ous, ques*ti*on, na*tu*re, ni*che*
D	*d*id	la*dd*er, lov*ed,* cou*ld*
E	p*ee*l	b*ee*r, *e*qual, *ea*sy, *ei*ther, *ae*gis, p*eo*ple, k*ey,* qu*ay,* bus*y*
	p*e*nd	br*ea*d, *a*ny, fr*ie*nd, b*u*ry, gu*e*st, *ae*sthetic, s*ai*d, s*ay*s
	p*er*il	. . .
F	*f*un	pu*ff,* rou*gh,* *ph*oto, cal*f*
G	*g*one	*gu*ess, e*gg,* rog*ue,* *gh*ost
H	*h*at	*wh*ole
	"hw"	*wh*eat
I	d*ye,* *i*ce	f*i*re, *eye,* *ai*sle, h*ei*ght, d*ie,* gu*i*le, b*uy,* b*y,* *aye,* h*igh*
	d*i*d, "di-"	*e*ffect, cour*a*ge, b*ee*n, s*ie*ve, w*o*men, h*y*mn, b*ui*ld, b*u*sy
J	*j*ob	*g*em, exa*gg*erate, ju*dge,* sol*di*er, ver*du*re
K	*k*it, *c*at	a*cc*ord, *ch*oir, yo*lk,* sa*ck,* la*cqu*er, a*cq*uire, li*q*uid, anti*que*
L	*l*ot	te*ll,* *ll*ama, is*l*et
M	*m*an	ha*mm*er, du*mb,* hy*mn,* sa*lm*on, phle*gm,* dra*chm*
N	*n*ip	ru*nn*er, *kn*ight, *gn*u, *mn*emonic, *pn*eumatic
	si*ng*	to*ngu*e, thi*n*k
O	*oh*	h*oe,* *oa*k, *o*ver, *ow*n, b*eau,* s*ew,* y*eo*men, th*ough,* br*oa*ch, ch*au*ffeur
	p*o*t	w*a*ter
	p*or*t	r*oar,* p*our,* d*oor*
	P*au*l, p*aw*	*a*ll, w*a*lk, l*aw*, *ough*t, br*oa*d, Ut*ah,* *o*ff, *au*to
	*oi*l, b*oy*	. . .
	*ou*t, *ow*l	b*ough,* fr*au*
P	*p*in	pe*pp*er
Q	"kw"	*qu*ick
R	*r*un	mer*r*y, *rh*yme, *wr*ist
S	*s*un	mi*ss,* *c*ent, *sc*ent, i*ce,* *ps*alm, *sch*ism
	*sh*e	mi*ssi*on, na*ti*on, *s*ure, *ch*ic, *sch*ist, o*ce*an, con*sci*ence, man*si*on, ra*ci*al, fu*chsi*a, *psh*aw
T	*t*on	ma*tt*er, kiss*ed,* *th*yme, *pt*omaine
	*th*in	. . .

	"dh"	*th*is, ba*the*
U	l*oo*	*ou*sel, r*u*le, dr*ew,* man*eu*ver, can*oe,* m*o*ve, bl*ue,* fr*ui*t, thr*ough*
	l*oo*k	p*u*t, c*ou*ld, w*o*lf, p*oo*r
	h*ue,* "yoo"	*u*se, *you*th, *eu*logy, *ewe, yu*le, b*eau*ty, f*ew,* q*ueue,* ad*ieu,* v*iew*
(unstressed)	*uh,* alb*u*m	er*a,* mount*ai*n, rec*e*nt, nat*io*n, graci*ou*s, at*o*m
(stressed)	b*u*m	*o*ther, bl*oo*d, d*ou*ble, d*oe*s
(stressed)	m*ur*mur	*ear*th, f*er*n, *ir*k, w*or*d, j*our*nal, m*yr*tle, mass*eur*
(unstressed)	murm*ur*	coug*ar,* moth*er,* tap*ir,* hon*or,* glam*our,* zeph*yr*
V	*v*ine	do*v*e, sal*v*e, o*f,* Ste*ph*en, fli*vv*er
W	*w*ine	ch*oi*r, req*ui*re
X	"ks"	bo*x*
Y	*y*et	on*i*on, hallelu*j*ah
Z	*z*oo	bu*zz, x*ylophone, wi*s*e, sci*ss*ors, dog*s,* ha*s,* di*sc*ern
	"zh"	*j*abot, a*z*ure, lo*g*e, lei*su*re, vi*si*on, gla*zi*er

IV. MEANING

A. Formal Definitions

Most of the definitions in the dictionary are formal definitions such as:

sling *n.* a device consisting of a strip of leather for throwing a stone held in its loop; hence, a fling or throw.
smoke *n.* **1** fumes given off by something burning; also, mist, fog, or anything resembling smoke. **2** (a smoking of) a cigar, cigarette, etc.
orthography *n.* (study or system of) spelling.

Note "hence" and "also" used in the definitions of **sling** and **smoke** to add a different but logically connected sense to the main definition instead of numbering it separately. The use of parentheses to avoid wordiness is illustrated by the second definition of **smoke** which telescopes "the thing smoked" and "the action of smoking" without strain on lucidity or readability. Similarly, the definition of **orthography** should be read as "study of spelling," "system of spelling," and "spelling." The following examples illustrate the same device used to define two parts of speech with one gloss:

snack *n.* & *v.* (eat) a light meal.
slapdash *adj.* & *adv.* hurried(ly) or haphazard(ly).

B. Informal Definitions

When there is sufficient context in the definition of one entry to supply the meaning of another word that is closely connected with it, a separate entry and definition are not provided if the second word can be placed as a subentry within the eye span of a consulter looking for it in its strict alphabetical place. Note the completeness as well as compactness of the following groups of definitions:

piston *n.* a flat, round device used in pumps and engines, that moves back and forth by the pressure of a fluid inside a cylinder in which it is fitted tightly by **piston rings**, the resulting motion being transmitted by a **piston rod** attached to the piston.
shower 3 (a bathroom fixture for) an overhead spray of water; also, a wash taken under a shower, or **shower bath**.
sperm whale the best-known of the whales, a thickset animal with paddlelike flippers and an enormous blunt-snouted head that yields **sperm oil** used for lubricating.
squash 3 a game like handball but played with rackets in a walled court, in full **squash racquets**, distinguished from **squash tennis** played in a similar court with larger rackets and an inflated ball.

Sometimes an entry is defined in the context provided by an illustrative phrase or sentence, as in the following:

exhilarate *v.* fill with high spirits: *Riding the roller coaster is very* **exhilarating**.
employment *n.* an employing or being employed, esp. a job: *a housewife who has no problem finding (outside) ~; An* **employment agency** *places workers and bills employers for the service.*
oral *adj.* of or having to do with the mouth: . . . ~ (i.e. spoken) *and written language; an* **oral history** *in the form of tape-recorded interviews with people of the time.*
special *adj.* of a different or particular kind: *as a ~ favor; ~ permission to watch a late movie; a ~ edition; an extra charge for* **special delivery** *by postal messenger;* **special education** *for handicapped children; Green Berets are* **Special Forces** *soldiers trained in guerrilla warfare; lobbying by* **spe.cial-in.ter.est groups** *trying to influence legislation in their favor.*

An informal definition, whether included in a definition group or embodied in an illustrative sentence or phrase, supplies all the essentials of a dictionary definition (i.e. syllabication, spelling, pronunciation where needed, and essential meaning) with only some of the formalities such as formal wording and the explicit enumeration of genus and differentiae omitted. Thus, the formal definition of **piston rod** would be:

piston rod a rod that transmits the motion of a piston.

However, all the information in the entry as above is contained in our definition group, our **piston rod** being also placed in its full context, viz. the complete system of which the piston rod is a part. Again, the formal definition of **exhilarating** would be:

exhilarating *adj.* that exhilarates: *Riding the roller coaster is very ~.*

Such a definition merely refers the reader to the entry for **exhilarate**. Our informal style places the entry in its proper semantic and grammatical setting, showing also that **exhilarating**, albeit a full-fledged adjective (note our use of the modifier "very"), is a development from the present participle of the verb.

C. Meaning by Illustration

Illustrative sentences and phrases normally supplement formal definitions. In this dictionary they are also used independently of definitions because a verbal illustration, like a picture, is worth a thousand words of definition, especially when definition becomes a formality or the routine repetition of another definition in slightly modified phraseology to suit a different part of speech. Note the effectiveness and economy of the illustrations of **siphon** and **tip** as verbs and those of **spring** in its adjectival uses. The formal definitions that have been omitted in the dictionary as self-evident and space-consuming are supplied here within parentheses alongside the illustrations.

	DEFINITION THAT IS UNDERSTOOD
siphon *n.* a bent-tube . . . barrier; *v.*: *Gasoline was ~ed out of the gas tank.*	(to draw off through a siphon)
tip *n.* **1** an end part, esp. a pointed or tapering end: *the ~ of the tongue, nose, toe.* **2** a light stroke or glancing blow; tap. **3** a piece of secret information; also, a useful hint or suggestion. **4** a small gift of money; gratuity. **5** a tilt or slope. —*v.* **tips, tipped, tip·ping** [corresponding to the *n.* senses]	
1: *a cane ~d with brass; a filter- ~d cigarette.*	(to cover the tip of or furnish with a tip)
2: *The ball was ~d into the basket.*	(to tap)
3: *was* **tipped off** *by an anonymous phone call.*	(to give a piece of secret information to)
4: *never forgot to ~ the waiter.*	(to give a gratuity to)
5: *the habit of ~ing his hat to ladies; A boat ~s over when loaded unevenly.*	(to tilt)
spring *n.* **1** a springing: *a sudden ~.* **2** an elastic device or quality: *cars with coil ~s and leaf ~s; the ~ of her step.* **3** the growing season, following winter.	

4 a natural stream rising from under the ground: *mineral* ~*s.*
5 source or origin; also, motive.
—adj. [corresponding to the *n.* senses]
2: *a* ~ *device, lock.* (elastic or springy)
3: ~ *cleaning, rains.* (of the season of spring)
4: *fresh* ~ *water.* (issuing from a spring)

D. Meaning by Paraphrase

Paraphrases within parentheses are supplied wherever needed to elucidate extended meanings of an entry that is defined in context or by illustration, as in the following examples:

nod *n.* a nodding of the head: *A project is given the* ~ (to go ahead).
over-the-counter *adj.* sold directly: ~ *trading* (of securities not listed on a stock exchange).
shred *v.* **shreds, shred·ded, shred·ding** cut or tear into narrow strips or fragments: *a paper* ~*ing machine;* ~*d wheat* (molded into biscuits for use as a breakfast food).
sit *v.* **2** occupy a place or remain in a position: *to* ~ *for a portrait; A hen* ~*s on its eggs (until they are hatched);*
slip *v.* **2** escape (from): *Names* ~ *(from) my mind.*
spring *v.* **3** cause to spring: *a trap that is easily sprung; wanted to* ~ *the news on* (i.e. make it known suddenly to) *her parents.*
static *adj.* **1** of or having to do with rest or equilibrium, not motion: *the* **static** (i.e. not flowing) **electricity** *on a comb run th.ough the hair.*
tension *n.* **1** a stretched or strained condition; hence, stress: *the* ~ *of a violin string; Chewing gum helps relieve (nervous)* ~.
to *adv.* [indicating the direction of an action or movement toward something implied]: *A door swings* ~ (the shut position).
utility beef (of the lowest grade).

Note that "i.e." is used when the parentheses involve a syntactical interruption. A parenthetical word or phrase that can form part of the illustrative phrase or sentence without redundancy or violence to idiom is given without change of type. Thus, in the entry for **space**, *outer* paraphrases the meaning of **space** in the illustration *visitors from space,* but *visitors from outer space* is a locution that is idiomatic in its own right.

space *n.* **1** the boundless expanse or extent which physical objects may occupy: *exploration of* ~*; visitors from (outer)* ~.

V. GRAMMAR AND USAGE

A. Parts of Speech and Inflections

Parts-of-speech labels in italics are provided for all main entries except phrases and open noun compounds.

A part-of-speech label in boldface italics standing alone is a different part of speech of the main entry or definition preceding it.

> **onward** (-wurd) *adv.* forward; also **onwards.—*adj*.**: the ~ *march of events; an ~ journey.*

Note that *adj.* usually means "adjective" but should be read as "adjectival" when its function is merely modifying (e.g. *quality,* as in "quality ice cream") or predicative (e.g. *aghast,* as in "She stood aghast at the sight.")

The same applies to "verb" and "noun" forms. The part-of-speech label *v.* should be read as "verbal" to include participial uses such as *disordered, ingrained,* and *ranging.* The label *n.* includes the use of verbal nouns ending in *-ing.*

Inflectional labels such as *sing., pl., pt., pp., comp.,* and *superl.* are used only where considered necessary or helpful, as before a non-English plural, when a plural form needs to be explicitly pointed out, or when alternate inflected forms of irregular verbs need sorting out.

B. Restrictive Labels

Usage labels such as *Informal, Slang, Archaic, Poetic, Substandard, Regional,* and *British* and field or subject labels such as *Medicine, Music, Latin, French, Trademark,* and *Military* have been used wherever judged necessary to show restrictions in meaning and usage.

C. Usage

Brief notes bearing on usage are provided within square brackets in the following styles:

> **Hoosier** *n.* [nickname] a native or resident of Indiana.
> **¹mine** *adj. Archaic* [used before a vowel or "h" or after the qualified noun]: ~ *eyes; sister ~.*
> **sir(r)ee** *interj.* [used after "Yes" or "No" for emphasis] Sir!
> **sis** *n. Informal* [used as a form of address in speech] sister.
> **skinny** *adj.* [unfavorable] lean or thin-looking.
> **tectonics** *n.pl.* [with *sing. v.*] the study of the earth's crust.
> **than** *conj.* [used to introduce the second term of a comparison]: *Jack is taller ~ Jill.*

very *adv.* [used for emphasis before adverbs, adjectives, and participles except participles with clearly verbal meaning]: *a* ~ *great idea; at* ~ *much reduced prices.*
villain *n.* **2** [used jokingly] rascal.

D. Syntax

1. Parentheses are used in definitions to indicate *transitive-intransitive* distinctions. Thus, the definition of **organize**, "form (into) a union or organization," which is to be read as "form a union or organization" or "form into a union or organization," contains the transitive and intransitive definitions respectively.

2. The characteristic or most usual *objects of verbs and the prepositions that usually follow verbs* are shown in parentheses within their definitions. Examples:

early on at or during an early stage (*in* a period or activity).
oodles *n.pl.* a great amount (*of* something).
opine *v.* express the opinion *(that).*
skilled *adj.* having or showing skill (*in* something).
slice *v.* **1** cut into slices or cut *(off, into, away)* as a slice. **2** hit (a ball) so that it goes off course or into a backspin.
spirit *v.* carry (a person *away*) secretly.
stack up measure up or compare (*with* or *against* a standard).
²tap *v.* **2** choose (someone) *for* a post, membership, etc.
weekend *v.* spend the weekend (*at* or *in* a place, *with* a person, etc.).

3. *Sentence structure* involving the entry word is often shown by illustrative phrases and sentences.

none *pron.* not one; not any: ~ *of them is* (or *are*) *here.*
notwithstanding *prep., conj.,* & *adv.* in spite of: ~ *the lateness of the hour; the lateness of the hour* ~; ~ (i.e. although) *it is late.*
opposite *n.* & *adj.* (anything) set against or contrary (*to* something): *Truth is the* ~ *of lying; . . . the house* ~ *to ours* (across the street); ***prep*.** & ***adv*.**: *the house* ~ *ours; the tree standing* ~ . . .
wire *v.: a house* ~*d for electricity; broken pieces* ~*d together; Students* ~ (i.e. telegraph) *home;* ~ *parents for money;* ~*d congratulations.*
yoke *n.: two* ~ (i.e. pairs) *of oxen.*

4. *Idiomatic collocations* of words are shown wherever possible by illustrative phrases and sentences, as in the examples below:

occasional *adj.* happening now and then, not regularly: *a forecast of* ~ *showers;* ~ *references, music* (for special occasions), *chairs* (for auxiliary use).
wanton *adj.* **1** lacking in restraint; frolicsome: *a* ~ *child;* ~ *winds; in* ~ *profusion; a* ~ (i.e. loose) *woman;* ~ (i.e. sensual) *thoughts.* **2** unprovoked; unjustified: *a* ~ *insult, attack;* ~ *damage, mischief;* ~ (i.e. merciless) *cruelty.*

wisp *n.* a small bunch (of straw, hay, etc.); hence, one that is small or slight: *a ~ of hair, smoke; a ~ of a girl, smile.*

youthful *adj.* young, esp. having to do with a young person's qualities: ~ *audiences, enthusiasm, hopes, impatience, indiscretions, pranks, vigor.*

A

A or **a** (AY) *n.* **A's** or **a's** **1** the first letter of the English alphabet. **2** [used to indicate the first, highest, or best of a group]: *to get an A on a test; grade A eggs; an A1 student.* **3** *Music.* the sixth tone in the scale of C major. ***—adj.*** shaped like an "A": *an A-frame house; an A-line skirt.* **—a.** acre; alto; answer; **a** are(s). **—A.** ammeter; angstrom unit; **A** ampere(s). **—a** (AY, uh) *indef. art.* **1** a single (thing) but not a particular one: *a boy; a jar.* **2** a single (group): *a few books; a lot of apples.* **3** [used with *many* before singular nouns for plural meaning]: *many a ship.* **4** [used with *of* to mean *the same*]: *birds of a feather.* ***—prep.*** each; every: *twice a week.* **—a-** *prefix.* **1** on; in the process of; in condition of: as in *gone a-hunting; to be a-building; ashore; aclutter; asway.* **2** without; lacking; not; non-: as in *amoral, asexual.*

A.A. Alcoholics Anonymous; Associate in Arts; Automobile Association (Brit.).

A.A.A. American Automobile Association.

A. and R. artists and repertory: *an ~ man.*

aard•vark (ARD–) *n.* a S. African anteater with long ears, a pointed snout, and strong claws for digging.

ab. about. **—A.B.** able-bodied seaman; Bachelor of Arts.

A.B.A. American Bar Association.

a•back (uh·BAC) *adv.* **taken aback** surprised.

ab•a•cus (AB·uh–) *n.* **-cus•es** or **-ci** (–sye) a frame of parallel rods holding beads, used for calculating.

a•baft (uh·BAFT) *adv.* at or toward the back part (of a ship). ***—prep.*** behind.

ab•a•lo•ne (ab·uh·LOH·nee) *n.* a large, edible shellfish whose ear-shaped shell is used for making ornaments.

a•ban•don (uh·BAN·dun) *v.* give up or yield; desert: *~ one's car in a snowstorm.* ***—n.*** a carefree manner: *singing with wild ~.* **—a•ban•doned** *adj.* **1** deserted: *an ~ house.* **2** unrestrained; shameless: *an ~ sinner.* **—a•ban•don•ment** *n.*

a•base (uh·BAIS) *v.* **-bas•es, -based, -bas•ing** lower (often, oneself); humble. **—a•base•ment** *n.*

a•bash (uh·BASH) *v.* make ashamed; embarrass. **—a•bash•ed•ly** *adv.* **—a•bash•ment** *n.*

a•bate (uh·BAIT) *v.* **-bates, -bat•ed, -bat•ing** make or become less: *The storm ~d; ~ a nuisance; drugs to ~ pain.* **—a•bate•ment** *n.: a tax ~.*

ab•a(t)•tis (AB·uh·tis) *n. sing. & pl.* a barricade of felled trees with sharpened branches pointing at the enemy.

ab•at•toir (AB·uh·twar) *n.* a place for killing animals for market; slaughterhouse.

ab•ba•cy (AB·uh·see) *n.* **-cies** (the term of) office of an abbot. **—ab•bé** (AB·ay) *n.* any French priest, originally only an abbot. **—ab•bess** (AB·is) *n.* the head, or Mother Superior, of a convent or group of nuns. **—ab•bey** (AB·ee) *n.* **ab•beys** (the church of) a monastery or convent. **—ab•bot** (AB·ut) *n.* the head, or Father Superior, of a group of monks, usu. living in an abbey.

abbr. abbreviation; also **abbrev.** **—ab•bre•vi•ate** (uh·BREE·vee–) *v.* **-ates, -at•ed, -at•ing** make (a word, visit, story, etc.) short(er). **—ab•bre•vi•a•tion** (–AY–) *n.: A.B. is an ~ for Bachelor of Arts.*

ABC *n.* **ABC's** the alphabet; hence, basics or fundamentals: *the ~'s of driving a car.* **—ABC** American Broadcasting Company.

ab•di•cate (AB·di–) *v.* **-cates, -cat•ed, -cat•ing** give up (a position, power, right, etc.): *~d the throne.* **—ab•di•ca•tion** (–CAY–) *n.*

ab•do•men (AB·duh·mun, ab·DOH–) *n.* **1** the belly. **2** in insects, the last of the body segments. **—ab•dom•i•nal** (–DOM–) *adj.;* **ab•dom•i•nal•ly** *adv.* **—ab•dom•i•nous** (–nus) *adj.* having a potbelly.

ab•duct (ab·DUCT) *v.* take away (a woman, child, etc.) by force; kidnap. **—ab•duc•tion** *n.* **—ab•duc•tor** *n.* **—abductor muscle** a muscle that moves a limb away from its natural position.

a•beam (uh·BEEM) *adv.* by the side (of a ship); abreast: *~ of us.*

a•be•ce•dar•i•an (ay·bee·see·DAIR·ee·un) *adj.* of the ABC's; hence, rudimentary. ***—n.*** one learning the basics.

a·bed (uh·BED) *adv.* & *adj.* in bed.

Ab·er·deen An·gus (ab·ur·deen·ANG·gus) a black, hornless beef cattle.

ab·er·rant (–ER·unt) *adj.* not normal, esp. in behavior; deviant. **—ab·er·ra·tion** (–uh·RAY–) *n.* **1** *a mental ~;* also **ab·er·rance; ab·er·ran·cy, -cies. 2** an optical distortion.

a·bet (uh·BET) *v.* **-bets, -bet·ted, -bet·ting** encourage in doing wrong: *aid and ~ a thief.* **—a·bet·tor** or **a·bet·ter** *n.* **—a·bet·ment** *n.*

a·bey·ance (uh·BAY·unce) *n.* suspension: *hold in ~; fall into ~.*

ab·hor (ub·HOR) *v.* **-hors, -horred, -hor·ring** hate: *I ~ flattery.* **—ab·hor·rence** *n.: hold sinners in ~.* **—ab·hor·rent** *adj.: Lying is ~ to his nature.* **—ab·hor·rer** *n.*

a·bide (uh·BIDE) *v.* **-bides,** *pt.* & *pp.* **-bode** or **-bid·ed, -bid·ing 1** bear: *I can't ~ him, he's so nasty.* **2** await: *I ~ your decision.* **3** stay; remain: *You can rely on him to* **abide by** (i.e. keep) *his promise; ~ing* (i.e. lasting) *happiness is difficult in this life.*

Ab·i·djan (ah·bi·JAHN) capital of Ivory Coast.

a·bil·i·ty (uh·BIL–) *n.* **-ties** power; skill; talent: *~ to perform well; a man of great ~.*

ab·ject *adj.* miserable; degraded; wretched; base: *~ poverty; ~ submission; make an ~ apology.* **—ab·ject·ly** *adv.* **—ab·ject·ness** or **ab·jec·tion** (–JEC–) *n.*

ab·jure (–JOOR) *v.* **-jures, -jured, -jur·ing** renounce; solemnly give up: *~ one's faith.* **—ab·ju·ra·tion** (–AY–) *n.* **—ab·jur·a·tor·y** (–JOOR·uh·tor·ee) *adj.* **—ab·jur·er** *n.*

abl. ablative. **—ab·late** (–LATE) *v.* **-lates, -lat·ed, -lat·ing** remove; carry or wear away. **—ab·la·tion** *n.* **—ab·la·tive** (AB·luh·tiv) *n.* a grammatical form in some languages meaning "from, by, away from, etc." something; ***adj.:*** *~ case.*

a·blaze (uh·BLAZE) *adj.* on fire: *a house set ~; ~ with anger.*

a·ble (AY·bl) *adj.* having the means or power; also, skillful; talented: *~ to walk about; an ~ ruler; an ~ lawyer;* **a·bly** *adv.* **—-able** or **-ible** *adj. suffix.* **1** that can or may be: as in *eatable, bearable, collectible.* **2** suitable for: as in *saleable.* **3** inclined to: as in *peaceable.* Hence **-ably** or **-ibly** *adv. suffix.* **—able-bod·ied** *adj.* having a healthy body: *an ~ man.*

a·bloom *adj.* in flower.

ab·lu·tion (–LOO–) *n.* a usu. ceremonial washing or bathing.

ABM antiballistic missile.

Ab·na·ki (–NAH·kee) *n.* (a member of) an American Indian tribe formerly centered in Maine, now living in S. Quebec; also, their Algonquian language.

ab·ne·gate (AB·nuh·gate) *v.* **-gates, -gat·ed, -gat·ing** surrender; deny to oneself. **—ab·ne·ga·tion** (–GAY–) *n.: the ~ of a claim.*

ab·nor·mal (–NOR·mul) *adj.* differing from the normal, average, or regular: *~ behavior; ~ weather.* **—ab·nor·mal·ly** *adv.* **—ab·nor·mal·i·ty** (–MAL–) *n.* **-ties:** *a congenital ~.*

a·board (uh·BORD) *adv.* & *prep.* on, onto, or in (a ship, train, plane, etc.): *All ~!*

a·bode (uh–) *pt.* & *pp.* of ABIDE. ***—n.*** a dwelling; home.

a·bol·ish (uh·BOL–) *v.* do away with; end. **—ab·o·li·tion** (ab·uh·LISH·un) *n.* an abolishing, esp. the ending of slavery in the U.S.; **ab·o·li·tion·ist** *n.* & *adj.* **—ab·o·li·tion·ism** *n.* **—ab·o·li·tion·ar·y** *adj.: an ~ agitator.*

A-bomb (–bom) *n.* an atomic bomb.

a·bom·i·na·ble (–BOM·i·nuh·bl) *adj.* hated; loathsome; disgusting; **Abominable Snowman** a manlike, hairy beast said to live in the Himalayas. **—a·bom·i·na·bly** *adv.* **—a·bom·i·nate** *v.* **-nates, -nat·ed, -nat·ing** hate intensely. **—a·bom·i·na·tion** (–NAY–) *n.*

ab·o·rig·i·nal (ab·uh·RIJ·uh·nl) *adj.* primitive; native. ***—n.*** a member of the oldest native people, not a later settler; also **ab·o·rig·i·ne** (–nee).

a·born·ing (–BORN–) *adv.* while being produced.

a·bort (uh–) *v.* **1** terminate before completion, as a pregnancy, plan, etc. **2** miscarry; fail: *a plan that ~ed.* **—a·bor·tion** *n.* **—a·bor·tion·ist** *n.* one who effects the abortion of a fetus. **—a·bor·tive** (–tiv) *adj.: ~ efforts.*

a·bound (uh–) *v.* exist or have in large numbers: *The lake ~s in fish.*

a·bout (uh–) *prep.* **1** in or to (various places): *going ~ the town; books scattered ~ the room.* **2** concerning; regarding: *Tell me ~ her; How ~ that?* ***—adv.* 1** *I saw the boy wandering ~; girls sitting ~ on the lawn.* **2** near (to); nearly: *~ a mile; I saw him ~ here.* **3** ***—adj.* 1** stirring: *He is up and ~ at 6 a.m.* **2** ready: *~ to leave.* **—a·bout-face** *n.* a reversing, esp. of attitude; ***v.* -fac·es, -faced, -fac·ing** turn to face the opposite way.

a·bove (uh·BUV) *prep.* **1** higher, greater, earlier, more than: *~ the clouds; He is directly ~ me; Value honor ~ wealth;* ***adv.:*** *See page 10 ~; high ~ the earth.* **2** too good, great, high, etc. for: *He is ~ corruption; ~ suspicion.* ***—adj.:*** *the ~ statements.* **—above all** more than anything. **—a·bove·board** *adj.* & *adv.* without dishonesty: *~ in one's actions.*

abp. archbishop.

abr. abridged; abridgment.

ab·ra·ca·dab·ra (ab·ruh·kuh·DAB·ruh) *n.* a word or speech supposed to have magical effect; hence, jargon; gibberish.

a·brade (uh·BRAID) *v.* **a·brades, a·brad·ed, a·brad·ing** wear (off) by rubbing.

A·bra·ham (AY·bruh·ham) the first patriarch of the Hebrews.

ab·ra·sion (–BRAY–) *n.* an abrading or rubbing away; also, a scraped spot or area. **—ab·ra·sive** (–siv) *n.* & *adj.;* **ab·ra·sive·ly** *adv.;* **ab·ra·sive·ness** *n.*

a·breast (uh·BREST) *adv.* & *adj.* side by side. **—(keep) abreast of** (keep) informed of: ~ *of current news.*

a·bridge (uh·BRIJ) *v.* **a·bridg·es, a·bridged, a·bridg·ing** shorten; lessen; abbreviate; curtail. **—a·bridg·er** *n.* **—a·bridg(e)·ment** *n.*

a·broad (uh·BRAWD) *adv.* & *adj.* **1** out of one's country: *He has been ~ ten years; traveling ~.* **2** widespread: *A rumor is ~ about his death.*

ab·ro·gate (AB·ruh–) *v.* **-gates, -gat·ed, -gat·ing** repeal (a law), abolish (a treaty), etc.; **ab·ro·ga·tor** *n.* **—ab·ro·ga·tion** (–GAY–) *n.*

a·brupt (uh–) *adj.* not slow or smooth: *an ~ turn in the road; an ~ manner; an ~ descent.* **—a·brupt·ly** *adv.* **—a·brupt·ness** *n.*

abs. absolute.

ab·scess (AB·ses) *n.* a collection of pus in inflamed tissue. **—ab·scessed** (–sest) *adj.: an ~ tooth.*

ab·scis·sa (ab·SIS·uh) *n.* **-scis·sas** or **-scis·sae** (–see) the distance of a point along a horizontal axis. **—ab·scis·sion** (–SIZH–, –SISH–) *n.* surgical removal of a body part.

ab·scond (ab–) *v.* sneak off and hide: *~ed with the money.* **—ab·scond·er** *n.*

ab·sent *adj.* (AB·sunt) not present; missing; lost in thought. **—*v.*** (ab·SENT): *He ~ed himself from work for 3 days.* **—ab·sence** (AB–) *n.* **—ab·sent·ly** (AB–) *adv.* **—ab·sen·tee** (–TEE) *n.* & *adj.* (one) who is absent: *an ~ landlord;* **ab·sen·tee·ism** (–TEE–) *n.* habitual or customary absence. **—ab·sent-mind·ed** (–MINE–) *adj.* not attentive; forgetful; **ab·sent-mind·ed·ly** *adv.;* **ab·sent-mind·ed·ness** *n.*

ab·sinth(e) (AB·sinth) *n.* a strong green licorice-flavored liqueur.

ab·so·lute (AB·suh·loot) *adj.* perfect; complete: ~ *trust;* ~ *proof; an ~ ruler* (i.e. with unlimited power); ~ (i.e. pure) *alcohol.* **—absolute value** numerical value regardless of the sign. **—absolute zero** the lowest temperature possible, −273.15° C. **—ab·so·lute·ly** *adv.* **—ab·so·lute·ness** *n.* **—ab·so·lut·ism** *n.* government with unlimited power; despotism.

ab·solve (–ZOLV) *v.* **-solves, -solved, -solv·ing** free from guilt or obligation; grant pardon from sin. **—ab·so·lu·tion** (–LOO–) *n.* **—ab·solv·a·ble** *adj.*

ab·sorb (–ZORB) *v.* take in, as a sponge does a liquid; take up; engross (attention): *Rugs ~ sound; an ~ing chess game.* **—ab·sorb·ent** *adj.: ~ paper towels;* also ***n.*** **—ab·sorb·en·cy** *n.* **—ab·sorp·tion** *n.* **—ab·sorp·tive** (–tiv) *adj.*

ab·stain (–STAIN) *v.* **1** refrain *(from): Many ~ed from voting;* **ab·sten·tion** *n.* **2** do without (food, smoking, etc.); **ab·stain·er** *n.* **—ab·sti·nence** (AB–) *n.;* **ab·sti·nent** *adj.*

ab·ste·mi·ous (–STEE–) *adj.* moderate in eating, drinking, etc. **—ab·ste·mi·ous·ly** *adv.* **—ab·ste·mi·ous·ness** *n.*

abstention, abstinence, abstinent See ABSTAIN.

abstr. abstract.

ab·stract (–STRACT) *v.* **1** take out; remove; steal: ~ *the idea of greenness from green objects; A pickpocket ~s money from your purse.* **2** make a summary of (a book, speech, etc.). **—*n.*** (AB–) summary; ***adj.*** removed from the real or the concrete: ~ *ideas;* ~ *art;* distinguished from CONCRETE. **—abstract expressionism** art characterized by self-expression in nonrepresentational forms. **—ab·strac·tion** *n.* **—ab·stract·ly** *adv.* **—ab·stract·ness** *n.* **—ab·stract·ed** *adj.* absent-minded; preoccupied; **ab·stract·ed·ly** *adv.*

ab·struse (–STROOS) *adj.* hard to understand. **—ab·struse·ly** *adv.* **—ab·struse·ness** *n.*

ab·surd (–SURD) *adj.* not sensible; ridiculous. **—the absurd** the pointlessness of human life as seen by existentialists: *theater of the ~.* **—ab·surd·i·ty** *n.* **-ties. —ab·surd·ly** *adv.*

A·bu Dha·bi (ah·boo·DAH·bee) capital of United Arab Emirates.

a·bun·dant (uh·BUN·dunt) *adj.* plentiful; copious: ~ *food supplies.* **—a·bun·dance** (–dunce) *n.* **—a·bun·dant·ly** *adv.*

a·buse *v.* (uh·BYOOZ) **-bus·es, -bused, -bus·ing** **1** use badly; misuse: ~ *a position of trust;* ~ *a tool; Don't ~ your pets.* **2** insult: ~ *an enemy.* Also ***n.*** (uh·BYOOS). **—a·bu·sive** (–siv) *adj.;* **a·bu·sive·ly** *adv.*

a·but (uh–) *v.* **-buts, -but·ted, -but·ting** have a common border or end: *a house ~ing on the lot.* **—a·but·ment** *n.* a structure supporting an arch, bridge, etc. **—a·but·tals** (–tlz) *n.pl.* land boundaries common with other properties.

a·bysm (uh·BIZM) or **a·byss** (uh·BIS) *n.* a bottomless hole; hence, anything too deep to measure: *the ~ of ignorance.* **—a·bys·mal** (uh·BIZ·ml) *adj.: an ~ failure.* **—a·bys·mal·ly** *adv.: ~ poor.* **—a·bys·sal** *adj.: the ~ depths of the sea.*

Ab·ys·sin·i·a (ab·i·SIN·ee·uh) same as ETHIOPIA. **—Ab·ys·sin·i·an** *adj.* & *n.*

-ac *suffix.* indicating relation to: as in *cardiac, demoniac.* **—Ac** actinium. **—a/c** or **A/C** account; account current. **—a.c.** or **A.C.** alternating current. **—A.C.** before Christ.

a·ca·cia (uh·CAY·shuh) *n.* a thorny tree of warm regions that yields gum arabic.

acad. academic; academy. **—ac·a·deme** or **Ac·a·deme** (AC·uh·deem) *n.* the world of scholars: *the groves of ~;* also **ac·a·de·mi·a** (–DEE·mee·uh). **—ac·a·dem·ic** (ac·uh·DEM·ic) *adj.* having to do with schools; also, pedantic; theoretical; ***n.*** a professor; **ac·a·dem·i·cal·ly** *adv.;* **ac·a·dem·i·cism** *n.* **—a·cad·e·mi·cian** (–MISH·un) *n.* a member of an academy. **—a·cad·e·my** (–CAD·uh·

mee) *n.* **-mies** **1** a society of learned people. **2** a school.

A·ca·di·a (uh·CAY·dee·uh) Nova Scotia and New Brunswick as named by French settlers; also, a parish of Louisiana settled by deportees from there. —**A·ca·di·an** *adj.* & *n.*

a·can·thus (uh·CAN–) *n.* **-thus·es** or **-thi** (–thye) an architectural representation of the leaves of a Mediterranean plant; also, this plant.

a cap·pel·la (ah·kuh·PEL·uh) *adj.* & *adv. Music.* without instrumental accompaniment.

acc. accelerate; account; accusative.

ac·cede (ac·SEED) *v.* **-cedes, -ced·ed, -ced·ing** **1** consent: *I ~d to his request; to ~* (i.e. agree) *to a treaty.* **2** assume: *to ~ to an office, position.* —**ac·ced·ence** *n.* —**ac·ced·er** *n.*

ac·cel·er·an·do (ac·sel·uh·RAHN·doh) *adv.* & *adj. Music.* gradually faster in tempo. —**ac·cel·er·ate** (–SEL–) *v.* **-ates, -at·ed, -at·ing** (make) go faster; speed up: *to ~ an engine; ~ to 50 m.p.h.;* **ac·cel·er·a·tive** (–tiv) *adj.;* **ac·cel·er·a·tion** (–RAY–) *n.* —**ac·cel·er·a·tor** (–SEL–) *n.* **1** anything that causes a machine, process, etc. to go faster; esp., the gas pedal of an automobile. **2** a machine, such as a betatron or cyclotron, that increases the speed and energy of atomic particles or nuclei; atom smasher; particle accelerator. —**ac·cel·er·om·e·ter** (–ROM·i·tur) *n.*

ac·cent *n.* (AC·sent) **1** an emphasis given to a syllable by stress, pitch, or duration; also, a mark for such an emphasis: *an acute ~ (´); a grave ~ (`).* **2** a distinctive, esp. foreign manner of speech: *a French ~.* —***v.*** (–SENT) stress a syllable in pronunciation; hence, emphasize: *~ the first syllable; ~s the flavor of good food;* also **ac·cen·tu·ate** (–SEN·choo–) *v.* **-ates, -at·ed, -at·ing.** —**ac·cen·tu·a·tion** (–AY–) *n.* —**ac·cen·tu·al** (–SEN·choo·ul) *adj.*

ac·cept (ac·SEPT) *v.* receive willingly; agree to; approve: *~ a gift; The council ~ed the proposal; ~ed in high society; an* **accepted** (i.e. generally approved) *fact.* —**ac·cept·a·ble** *adj.;* **ac·cept·a·bil·i·ty** (–BIL–) *n.;* **ac·cep·ta·bly** *adv.* —**ac·cept·ance** (–unce) *n.* —**ac·cep·ta·tion** (–TAY–) *n.* the usual meaning: *the common ~ of a word.*

ac·cess (AC·ses) *n.* **1** a way to a place; approach; also right to approach; admittance: *grant her ~ to our records.* **2** an outburst: *an ~ of fury.* —**ac·ces·sa·ry** (–SES–) *adj.* & *n.* **-ries** same as ACCESSORY. —**ac·ces·si·ble** (–SES–) *adj.* easy to approach: *an ~ leader;* **ac·ces·si·bly** *adv.;* **ac·ces·si·bil·i·ty** (–BIL–) *n.* —**ac·ces·sion** (–SESH·un) *n.* **1** the attainment of power or office: *~ to the throne.* **2** something added; an increase: *new ~s* (i.e. books) *in a library.* —**ac·ces·so·ry** (–SES·uh·ree) *n.* **-ries** **1** an item added to complement or complete an outfit: *clothing ~s; Whitewall tires are an auto ~.* **2** a helper: *an ~ to a crime.* —***adj.*** helping as a subordinate. —**accessory after** (or **before**) **the fact** a helper of an accused after (or before) the commission of a crime, not during it.

ac·ci·dence (AC·si·dunce) *n.* the grammar of word inflections, such as case forms. —**ac·ci·dent** (AC·si·dunt) *n.* **1** an unexpected happening; a mishap: *an auto ~;* **ac·ci·dent-prone** *adj.* **2** chance: *I met him* **by accident.** —**ac·ci·den·tal** (–DEN·tl) *adj.;* also ***n.*** a change in a musical key, as a sharp or flat note. —**ac·ci·den·tal·ly** *adv.*

ac·claim (uh·CLAIM) *v.* applaud; hail; also, elect by an overwhelming voice vote; ***n.:*** *He won ~ with his exploits.* —**ac·cla·ma·tion** (ac·luh·MAY–) *n.*

ac·cli·mate (AC·li–) *v.* **-mates, -mat·ed, -mat·ing** accustom or become accustomed to a new climate, environment, or situation; also **ac·cli·ma·tize** (uh·CLIME·uh–) *v.* **-tiz·es, -tized, -tiz·ing;** **ac·cli·ma·ti·za·tion** (–ZAY–) or **ac·cli·ma·tion** (ac·luh·MAY–) *n.*

ac·cliv·i·ty (uh·CLIV·i·tee) *n.* **-ties** an uphill slope.

ac·co·lade (AC·uh–) *n.* praise; tribute.

ac·com·mo·date (uh·COM·uh–) *v.* **-dates, -dat·ed, -dat·ing** **1** adapt; adjust: *~ to new surroundings.* **2** lodge. **3** oblige; do a favor for: *I ~d him with a loan; an ~ing neighbor.* —**ac·com·mo·dat·ing·ly** *adv.* —**ac·com·mo·da·tion** (–DAY–) *n.* an accommodating; **accommodations** *pl.* lodgings; also, a berth, seat, etc.

ac·com·pa·ny (uh·CUM·puh·nee) *v.* **-nies, -nied, -ny·ing** **1** go along (with). **2** play or sing supporting a solo; **ac·com·pa·nist** *n.* —**ac·com·pa·ni·ment** *n.: a piano ~.*

ac·com·plice (uh·COM·plis) *n.* a companion in wrongdoing; confederate; abettor.

ac·com·plish (uh·COM·plish) *v.* **1** succeed in doing; finish; complete. **2** achieve; fulfill: *~ an objective.* —**ac·com·plished** (–plisht) *adj.* **1** finished. **2** skilled; talented: *an ~ actor.* —**ac·com·plish·ment** *n.: a great ~; sewing, dancing, and other ~s.* —**ac·com·plish·er** *n.*

ac·cord (uh–) *v.* **1** grant: *~ him a warm welcome.* **2** agree; be in harmony: *His actions do not ~ with his words.* —***n.*** an agreement; also, harmony: *a peace ~; living in perfect ~;* **of one's own accord** willingly. —**ac·cord·ing** *adj.* in harmony; **according as** to the extent that; depending on how or whether: *You'll be punished ~ as you sin;* **according to** by the word of: *~ to the Bible;* **according to Hoyle** by the rules. —**ac·cord·ing·ly** *adv.* therefore; in agreement: *These are the rules; act ~.* —**ac·cord·ance** (–unce) *n.;* **ac·cord·ant** (–unt) *adj.*

ac·cor·di·on (uh·COR·dee·un) *n.* a reed musical instrument with a boxlike bellows and a keyboard at each end. —***adj.*** like an accordion: *~ pleats.* —**ac·cor·di·on·ist** *n.*

ac·cost (uh–) *v.* approach uninvited or aggressively: *~ed by beggars.*

ac·count (uh–) *v.* reckon; consider: *I ~ him a fool.* **—n. 1** a reckoning; a list or record; a narrative: *an expense ~.* **2** a business arrangement involving money, credit, etc.: *a bank ~; a charge ~; an advertising ~.* **3 accounts** business records. **—account for 1** explain: *~ for one's absence.* **2** be responsible for: *~ for the funds.* **—on account of** because of. **—on no account** not ever for any reason. **—on (someone's) account** on behalf of (someone). **—take into account** take into consideration. **—ac·count·a·ble** *adj.* answerable; **ac·count·a·bly** *adv.;* **ac·count·a·bil·i·ty** (–BIL–) *n.: public ~.* **—ac·count·ant** *n.* bookkeeper. **—account executive** an executive in charge of a client's account, as in an advertising firm. **—ac·count·ing** or **ac·count·an·cy** (–un·see) *n.* the systematic keeping of business records.

ac·cou·ter (uh·COO·tur) *v.* equip, esp. for military duty; **ac·cou·ter·ments** *n.pl.* a soldier's military trappings. Also *Brit.* **ac·cou·tre** *v.;* **ac·cou·tre·ments** *n.pl.*

Ac·cra (uh·CRAH, AC·ruh) capital of Ghana.

ac·cred·it (uh·CRED–) *v.* **1** authorize; approve; certify: *an ~ed school of architecture.* **2** attribute: *a discovery ~ed to Einstein.* **—ac·cred·it·a·tion** (–TAY–) *n.*

ac·cre·tion (uh·CREE–) *n.* a growth or increase by gradual addition. **—ac·cre·tive** (–tiv) *adj.*

ac·crue (uh·CROO) *v.* **-crues, -crued, -cru·ing** add on gradually: *interest ~ing on a loan.* **—ac·cru·al** or **ac·crue·ment** *n.*

acct. account.

ac·cul·tu·ra·tion (uh·cul·chuh·RAY–) *n.* adaptation to another culture. **—ac·cul·tu·rate** (–CUL–) *v.* **-rates, -rat·ed, -rat·ing.**

ac·cu·mu·late (uh·CUE·myuh–) *v.* **-lates, -lat·ed, -lat·ing** heap up; pile up. **—ac·cu·mu·la·tion** (–LAY–) *n.* **—ac·cu·mu·la·tive** (–CUE·myuh·lay·tiv) *adj.* **—ac·cu·mu·la·tor** *n. Brit.* storage battery.

ac·cu·rate (AC·yuh·rit) *adj.* having no errors; correct; exact. **—ac·cu·ra·cy** (–ruh·see) or **ac·cu·rate·ness** *n.* **—ac·cu·rate·ly** *adv.*

ac·curs·ed (uh·CURST, –CUR·sid) *adj.* under a curse; detestable: *that ~ war;* also **ac·curst.** **—ac·curs·ed·ly** *adv.* **—ac·curs·ed·ness** *n.*

ac·cu·sa·tive (–KEW–) *n. & adj.* (grammatical case) indicating a verb's direct object or the object of a preposition; **ac·cu·sa·tive·ly** *adv.* **—ac·cu·sa·to·ry** *adj.* accusing: *~ looks.* **—ac·cuse** (uh·KEWZ) *v.* **-cus·es, -cused, -cus·ing** blame; charge with an offense: *~d of treason;* **ac·cus·er** *n.* **—ac·cus·al** or **ac·cu·sa·tion** (–ZAY–) *n.*

ac·cus·tom (uh·CUS·tum) *v.* make familiar or used; habituate. **—ac·cus·tomed** *adj.: He is ~ to a warm climate; in his ~ position.*

ace *n.* **1** a playing card with one large marking, often the highest; hence, an expert, esp. a fighter pilot; ***adj.:*** *an ~ reporter.* **2** a domino or die of the lowest value, with one spot; hence, the smallest amount: *He was* **within an ace of** *defeat when he rallied.* **—ace in the hole** or **ace up one's sleeve** a hidden advantage.

a·cerb (uh·SURB) or **a·cer·bic** *adj.* bitter; acidic; sharp-tasting: *an ~ medicine.* **—ac·er·bate** (AS·ur–) *v.* **-bates, -bat·ed, -bat·ing** exasperate; irritate. **—a·cer·bi·ty** (–SUR–) *n.* **-ties.**

a·ce·tic (uh·SEE·tic) **acid** a colorless acid found in vinegar; hence **acetic** *adj.* **—ac·et·an·i·lid(e)** (as·i·TAN–) *n.* a drug derived from acetic acid and aniline, used to check pain and fever. **—ac·e·tate** (AS·i–) *n.* a fiber, plastic film, or fabric made from cellulose and acetic acid. **—a·cet·i·fy** (uh·SEE–) *v.* **-fies, -fied, -fy·ing** turn into vinegar. **—ac·e·tone** (AS·i–) *n.* a colorless, volatile, flammable liquid used as a solvent. **—a·ce·tyl·cho·line** (uh·see·tl·COH·leen) *n.* a substance important in the transmission of nerve impulses. **—a·cet·y·lene** (uh·SETL·een) *n.* a colorless flammable gas used in welding and cutting. **—ac·e·tyl·sal·i·cyl·ic** (uh·SEE·tl·sal·i·SIL·ic) **acid** aspirin.

ache (AIK) *v.* **aches, ached, ach·ing 1** suffer a continuous pain in a part of the body: *my ~ing back.* **2** *Informal.* yearn. **—n.:** *~s and pains.* **—ach·y** *adj.*

a·chieve (uh·CHEEV) *v.* **-chieves, -chieved, -chiev·ing** accomplish; attain; gain by effort: *~ one's goal.* **—a·chiev·a·ble** *adj.* **—a·chieve·ment** *n.* **—a·chiev·er** *n.*

A·chil·les (uh·KIL·eez) a legendary Greek, hero of the *Iliad.* **—Achilles' heel** a weak point; mortal weakness. **—Achilles' tendon** the tendon linking the calf muscle and the heel.

ach·ro·mat·ic (ac·ruh·MAT·ic) *adj.* **1** *Music.* diatonic. **2** free of color separation in light refraction: *an ~ lens.* **—ach·ro·mat·i·cal·ly** *adv.*

ac·id (AS·id) *n.* **1** a sour substance that turns litmus paper red; ***adj.:*** *an ~ solution; an ~* (i.e. sharp) *tongue.* **2** *Slang.* LSD; **ac·id·head** *n.* one who uses LSD to go on an acid trip. **—ac·id·ly** *adv.* **—a·cid·ic** (–SID–) *adj.* **—a·cid·i·fy** *v.* **-fies, -fied, -fy·ing** make or become sour or acid; **a·cid·i·fi·er** *n.;* **a·cid·i·fi·ca·tion** (–CAY–) *n.;* **a·cid·i·ty** (–SID–) *n.* **—ac·i·do·sis** (–DOH–) *n.* the condition of having too much acid in the blood. **—acid rain** rain or snow containing acids formed by windborne industrial pollutants, esp. sulfur dioxide, reacting with atmospheric water vapor and causing harm to crops, wildlife, buildings, etc. **—acid test** a decisive test. **—acid trip** *Slang.* an hallucinatory experience caused by LSD. **—a·cid·u·late** (–SIJ·oo–) *v.* **-lates, -lat·ed, -lat·ing** make slightly acid or sour-tasting; **a·cid·u·la·tion** (–LAY–) *n.;* **a·cid·u·lous** (–SIJ·uh·lus) *adj.*

ack. acknowledg(e)(ment).

ack-ack *n.* an antiaircraft gun or gunfire.

ac·know·ledge (–NOL·ij) *v.* **-ledg·es, -ledged, -ledg·ing** **1** admit the truth, existence, authority, etc. of: ~ *defeat.* **2** admit to receiving: ~ *a letter.* **—ac·know·ledg(e)·ment** *n.: a receipt issued in ~ of a payment.*

A.C.L.U. American Civil Liberties Union.

ac·me (AC·mee) *n.* the highest or best point: *the ~ of her perfection as a dancer.*

ac·ne (AC·nee) *n.* a skin disease causing pimples.

ac·o·lyte (AC·uh·lite) *n.* a helper or attendant, esp. in a church service.

A·con·ca·gua (ah·cawn·CAH·gwah) the highest mountain in the W. Hemisphere, in Argentina.

ac·o·nite (AC·uh–) *n.* any of several poisonous plants, esp. the monkshood; also, a drug made from one of them.

a·corn (AY–) *n.* the nut of an oak tree. **—acorn squash** an acorn-shaped, dark-green, winter squash.

a·cous·tic (uh·COO·stic) or **-ti·cal** *adj.* **1** relating to or affecting sounds: ~ *tiles absorb sound.* **2** not electrically amplified: *an ~ guitar.* **—acoustics** *n. pl.* **1** [takes *pl. v.*] the qualities of an enclosed space affecting the perception of sound: *An auditorium without echoes has good ~s.* **2** [takes *sing. v.*] the science of sound. **—a·cous·ti·cal·ly** *adv.*

ac·quaint (uh·KWAINT) *v.* **1** familiarize; inform: *The newcomer soon ~ed himself with our office.* **2 be acquainted with** know or know of: *I am ~ed with his work.* **—ac·quaint·ance** *n.* personal knowledge; also, a person one has met: *not a friend, only an ~;* **make one's acquaintance** meet one. **—ac·quaint·ance·ship** *n.*

ac·qui·esce (ac·wee·ES) *v.* **-esc·es, -esced, -esc·ing** agree passively: *He ~d in the referee's decision.* **—ac·qui·es·cence** *n.* **—ac·qui·es·cent** *adj.;* **ac·qui·es·cent·ly** *adv.*

ac·quire (uh·CWIRE) *v.* **-quires, -quired, -quir·ing** gain for oneself; get: *One ~s a taste for classical music; an ~d, not inherited characteristic;* **ac·quire·ment** *n.* **—ac·qui·si·tion** (ac·wi·ZISH·un) *n.: the ~ of a new car; The new painting was a fine ~ for the museum.* **—ac·quis·i·tive** (–CWIZ·i·tiv) *adj.* eager to get; greedy; **ac·quis·i·tive·ly** *adv.;* **ac·quis·i·tive·ness** *n.*

ac·quit (uh·CWIT) *v.* **-quits, -quit·ted, -quit·ting** **1** free of a charge; **ac·quit·tal** (–CWITL) *n.* **2** free of an obligation; **ac·quit·tance** *n.* **3** conduct (oneself): *He ~d himself well at the interview.*

a·cre (AY·cur) *n.* **1** a unit of area of 4,840 sq. yds. (4,046.9 m²). **2 acres** *pl.* lands; estate. **—a·cre·age** (–ij) *n.* number of acres; amount of land.

ac·rid (AC–) *adj.* harsh and biting: ~ *smoke; Peter made ~ remarks about his former friend.* **—a·crid·i·ty** (–CRID–) or **ac·rid·ness** (AC–) *n.;* **ac·rid·ly** *adv.* **—ac·ri·mo·ny** (–moh·nee) *n.* **-nies** animosity; harshness of temper, esp. as in speech; asperity; **ac·ri·mo·ni·ous** (–MOH·nee·us) *adj.;* **ac·ri·mo·ni·ous·ly** *adv.;* **ac·ri·mo·ni·ous·ness** *n.*

acro- *comb. form.* height, summit, etc. **—ac·ro·bat** *n.* one who performs on a tightrope, trapeze, etc.; also, a gymnast; **ac·ro·bat·ic** (–BAT–) *adj.;* **ac·ro·bat·i·cal·ly** *adv.;* **ac·ro·bat·ics** *n.pl.* **1** [takes *pl. v.*] feats of an acrobat; also, feats of agility: *verbal ~s.* **2** [takes *sing. v.*] acrobatic skill. **—ac·ro·nym** (–nim) *n.* a word formed from the first letters of a phrase, as *NATO; radar* (*ra*dio *d*etection *a*nd *r*anging), etc. **—ac·ro·pho·bi·a** (–FOH·bee·uh) *n.* an abnormal fear of high places. **—a·crop·o·lis** (–CROP·uh·lis) *n.* the fortified crowning part of an ancient Greek city, esp. **the Acropolis** of Athens.

a·cross (uh–) *prep.* from one side to the other of; on, at, to, or from the other side of: *She lives ~ the street; The school is* **across from** (i.e. opposite) *our house;* **adv.:** *Go ~; The river is 100 yards ~.* **—run** (or **come**) **across** meet: *I ran ~ an old friend while shopping.* **—a·cross-the-board** *adj.* applying to all categories: *an ~ pay raise.*

a·cros·tic (uh·CROS–) *n.* an arrangement of verses or words in which a new word or motto can be read by taking corresponding letters together, as *NEWS* from North, East, West, and South when arranged in a column; **adj.:** *an ~ anagram.* **—a·cros·ti·cal·ly** *adv.*

a·cryl·ic (uh·CRIL·ic) *n.* a synthetic paint, textile fiber such as Acrilan and Orlon, or a transparent, thermoplastic resin such as Lucite and Plexiglass.

act. active; actual.

act *n.* **1** a thing done; a doing. **2** a law. **3** a performance; also, division of a play. **4** *Informal.* a pose: *The child is putting on an ~ to get sympathy.* **—v.** **1** do something: ~ *quickly to put out a fire.* **2** perform; behave; appear to be: *~ing the fool.* **—act up** *Informal.* misbehave; give trouble.

A.C.T. Australian Capital Territory.

actg. acting.

ACTH "*a*dreno-*c*ortico-*t*ropic *h*ormone," which stimulates cortisone production in the adrenal cortex.

ac·tin *n.* a protein that acts in muscles.

act·ing *adj.* temporary: *an ~ superintendent.*

ac·tin·ic (–TIN–) *adj.* causing a chemical change by radiation, as ultraviolet rays or X rays do. **—ac·tin·i·cal·ly** *adv.* **—ac·tin·ism** (AC–) *n.* **—ac·ti·nide** (AC–) *n.* any of a series of radioactive chemical elements, from **ac·tin·i·um** (–TIN–) through Lawrencium in the periodic table.

ac·tion *n.* **1** a doing; state of doing; deed: *The police took early ~ to stop smuggling;* **in, into** (or **out of**) **action:** *Gas shortages have put some big cars out of ~.* **2** a lawsuit: *bring an ~ against someone;* **ac·tion·a·ble** *adj.* **3** combat: *killed in ~.* **4 actions** *pl.* conduct; behavior. **5** *Slang.* activity: *a piece of the ~; where the ~ is.* **—action painting** a style of abstract expressionism using paint dripped, thrown, or smeared on a canvas. **—ac·ti·vate** *v.* **-vates, -vat·ed, -vat·ing** make active; **ac·ti·va·tion** (–VAY–) *n.* **—ac·tive** (AC·tiv) *adj.* **1** moving; functioning; energetic: *Tennis is an ~ sport; an ~ business account.* **2** causing change; not passive; **on active duty** fully serving; not on reserve or retired status; **ac·tive·ly** *adv.* **—active voice** a form of sentence in which the doer is the subject of the verb; e.g. "John eats supper" as opposed to "Supper is eaten by John" (PASSIVE VOICE). **—ac·tiv·ism** *n.* the theory or practice of direct action to achieve an end; **ac·tiv·ist** *n.* **—ac·tiv·i·ty** (–TIV–) *n.* **-ties** **1** the state of being active; movement; liveliness: *mental ~.* **2 activities** *pl.* occupations: *Jane's social ~.*

act of God an earthquake, flood, storm, etc. beyond human control. **—ac·tor** (AC·tur) *n.* **1** a performer in a play or movie; *fem.* **ac·tress.** **2** one who plays a role: *a key ~ in Watergate.*

ac·tu·al (AC·choo·ul) *adj.* existing; real; not merely potential: *the ~, not the estimated cost.* **—ac·tu·al·ly** *adv.* **—ac·tu·al·i·ty** (–choo·AL–) *n.* **-ties.** **—ac·tu·al·ize** (AC·choo–) *v.* **-iz·es, -ized, -iz·ing** make actual; bring into being: *~ his plans.*

ac·tu·ar·y (AC·choo·er·ee) *n.* **-ar·ies** a person who calculates insurance risks, premiums, annuities, etc. **—ac·tu·ar·i·al** (–AIR·ee·ul) *adj.: ~tables.*

ac·tu·ate (AC·choo–) *v.* **-ates, -at·ed, -at·ing** impel to action; motivate; also, put in operation; **ac·tu·a·tor** *n.* **—ac·tu·a·tion** (–AY–) *n.*

a·cu·i·ty (uh·CUE·i·tee) *n.* sharpness or keenness, esp. of perception: *visual ~.* **—a·cu·men** *n.* acuteness of insight; also, accuracy of judgment. **—ac·u·punc·ture** (AC·yoo·punk·chur) *n.* a Chinese medical technique using needles to pierce specific parts of the body to relieve pain or treat disease; **ac·u·punc·tur·ist** *n.* **—a·cute** (uh·CUTE) *adj.* **a·cut·er, a·cut·est** **1** pointed. **2** severe; critical: *an ~ shortage of water; an ~ heart condition.* **3** keen; sharp: *a dog's ~ hearing; an ~ thinker.* **—acute accent** an accent mark slanting left to right, as in *blasé.* **—acute angle** an angle less than 90°.

ad *n. Informal.* an advertisement: *a want ~ seeking a typist.*

ad- *prefix.* to; toward: as in *adjoin, advert.*

A.D. Anno Domini, i.e. in the year of the Lord; after Christ's birth: *A.D. 1492*

ad·age (AD·ij) *n.* a proverb; maxim; e.g. "Look before you leap."

a·da·gio (uh·DAH·joh) *adj.* & *adv. Music.* in slow time. **—*n.*** **1** an adagio movement. **2** a slow ballet duet.

Ad·am (AD·um) in the Bible, the first man: *I would* **not know him from Adam** (i.e. not recognize him).

ad·a·mant (AD·uh·munt) *adj.* unchangeable in one's decision; unyielding. **—*n.*** an extremely hard, unbreakable substance; **ad·a·man·tine** (–MAN–) *adj.* **—ad·a·mant·ly** (AD–) *adv.*

Ad·ams, **1 John.** 1735–1826, second U.S. President (1797–1801). **2 John Quincy.** 1767–1848, sixth U.S. President (1825–29). **—Adam's apple** a projection of cartilage in the front of the neck, seen esp. in men.

a·dapt (uh–) *v.* adjust; make fit; accommodate (oneself) to different conditions: *a play ~ed for the cinema; It is hard to ~ to a new climate.* **—a·dapt·a·ble** *adj.;* **a·dapt·a·ble·ness** or **a·dapt·a·bil·i·ty** (–BIL–) *n.* **—a·dap·ted** (–DAP–) *adj.* suited; fitted: *well ~ for its purpose;* **a·dapt·er** or **a·dap·tor** *n.;* **a·dap·tive** (–tiv) *adj.;* **a·dap·tive·ly** *adv.*

add *v.* **1** join (something) to another: *~ sugar to coffee; ~ books to a library.* **2** find the sum of; do sums: *~ 1, 2, 3, and 4 to get 10; able to ~ and subtract.* **—add up to** amount to: *Those smiles ~ up to deceit.* **—add·er** *n.* **—ad·dend** *n.* a number to be added, as 3 in 3 + 2 = 5. **—ad·den·dum** (uh·DEN–) *n., pl.* **-da** something to be added, esp. to a book; appendix.

ad·der *n.* **1** any of several poisonous Old World vipers. **2** any of several harmless North American snakes.

ad·dict *n.* (AD·ict) one habitually and compulsively doing something, esp. using narcotics. **—*v.*** (uh·DICT) devote (oneself) or cause to be devoted to such use; **ad·dic·tion** *n.;* **ad·dic·tive** *adj.: ~ drugs.*

Ad·dis A·ba·ba (AD·is·AB·uh·buh) capital of Ethiopia.

Ad·di·son's (AD·i·sunz) **disease** a serious disease of the cortex of the adrenals.

ad·di·tion (uh·DISH·un) *n.* **1** the act or process of adding. **2** something added: *a new ~ to the house.* **—in addition to** as well as. **—ad·di·tion·al** *adj.: ~ supplies to last the winter;* **ad·di·tion·al·ly** *adv.* **—ad·di·tive** (AD·i·tiv) *adj.: an ~ ingredient;* ***n.*** an added substance: *Color is often an ~ in foods.*

ad·dle (ADL) *v.* **ad·dles, ad·dled, ad·dling** make or become confused; hence **ad·dle·brained, ad·dle·head·ed** or **ad·dle·pat·ed** *adj.* **—addled egg** a rotten egg.

addn. addition; **addnl.** additional.

ad·dress (uh·DRES) *v.* **1** speak or write to. **2** write the destination on (mail). **3** apply (oneself) to. **—*n.*** **1** an elaborate speech. **2** manners; social skill: *a man of pleasing ~.* **3** (*also* AD·res) the location of a person, business, or bit of information in a computer memory. **—ad·dress·ee** (ad·res·EE) *n.* one to whom something is addressed.

ad·duce (uh–) *v.* **ad·duc·es, ad·duced, ad·duc·ing** give as an example or evidence.

ad·duc·tor (uh·DUC·tur) *n.* a muscle that pulls a limb toward a neighboring part.

-ade *n. suffix.* **1** an action done, thing produced, etc.: as in *blockade, tirade.* **2** a drink: as in *lemonade.*

Ad·e·laide (ADL·aid) capital of the state of South Australia.

A·den (AY·dn) capital of Yemen (Aden). **—Gulf of Aden** a part of the Arabian Sea between Yemen (Aden) and Somalia.

ad·e·nine (ADN·een) *n.* a crystalline base found in some glands, tea, beets, etc. **—ad·e·noids** (AD·uh–) *n.pl.* lymphoid tissue growths in the throat behind the nose; **ad·e·noi·dal** (–NOY·dl) *adj.* **—a·den·o·sine tri·phos·phate** (uh·DEN·uh·seen·try·FOS·fate) an ester that releases energy in muscle cells.

ad·ept (uh·DEPT) *adj.* proficient; skilled: ~ *in* (or *at*) *auto repair;* also ***n.*** (AD·ept). **—ad·ept·ly** *adv.* **—ad·ept·ness** *n.*

ad·e·quate (AD·i·kwit) *adj.* enough to satisfy a need; sufficient; satisfactory. **—ad·e·qua·cy** (–kwuh·see) or **ad·e·quate·ness** *n.* **—ad·e·quate·ly** *adv.*

ad·here (–HERE) *v.* **-heres, -hered, -her·ing** **1** stick; be attached: *Glue helps things ~ to one another.* **2** cling; be devoted: ~ *to a plan.* **—ad·her·ent** (–HEER·unt) *adj.* & *n.: an ~ of the civil rights movement;* **ad·her·ence** (–unce) *n.* **—ad·he·sion** (–HEE·zhun) *n.* **1** continuing allegiance. **2** the fact or condition of sticking together; **ad·he·sive** (–HEE·siv) *adj.* & *n.* sticky (substance): *Gum is an ~;* **adhesive tape** *used on bandages;* **ad·he·sive·ness** *n.*

ad hoc for a specified purpose only: *an ~ committee.* **—ad hoc·(c)er·y** (–HOK·ur·ee) *n. Slang.: the ~ of diplomatic bargaining.*

a·dieu (uh·DEW) *interj.* & *n.* **-dieus** or **-dieux** (–DEWZ) farewell.

ad in·fi·ni·tum (–NYE–) *Latin.* without limit; endlessly. **—ad in·te·rim** (–IN–) *Latin.* temporarily; ***adj.*** temporary.

a·di·os (ad·ee·OSE) *interj.* goodbye.

ad·i·pose *adj.* having to do with fat: *Animal fat is stored in* **adipose tissue. —ad·i·pos·i·ty** (–POS–) or **ad·i·pose·ness** *n.* obesity.

Ad·i·ron·dack (ad·uh·RON·dak) **Mountains** or **Adirondacks** a part of the Appalachian Mountains in N.E. New York.

adj. adjective; adjacent; adjutant.

ad·ja·cent (uh·JAY·snt) *adj.* near or next (to); adjoining: *the ~ room.* **—ad·ja·cen·cy** *n.* **—ad·ja·cent·ly** *adv.*

ad·jec·tive (AJ·ik·tiv) *n.* a word that qualifies or limits a noun or other substantive. **—ad·jec·ti·val** (–TYE·vul) *adj.* **—ad·jec·ti·val·ly** *adv.*

ad·join (uh–) *v.* be next to: *My property ~s his.* **—ad·join·ing** *adj.: ~ rooms.*

ad·journ (uh·JURN) *v.* **1** suspend (a meeting or session); close: *We ~ed for lunch.* **2** *Informal.* move (to another place): *Shall we ~ to the drawing room?* **—ad·journ·ment** *n.*

ad·judge (uh·JUJ) *v.* **-judg·es, -judged, -judg·ing** **1** decide according to law; award: *property ~d to his former wife.* **2** deem.

ad·ju·di·cate (uh·JOO–) *v.* **-cates, -cat·ed, -cat·ing** **1** settle (a claim, etc.) judicially. **2** serve as a referee or judge (*on* a case, issue, etc.). **—ad·ju·di·ca·tion** (–CAY–) *n.* **—ad·ju·di·ca·tive** (–kuh·tiv) *adj.* **—ad·ju·di·ca·tor** *n.*

ad·junct (AJ–) *n.* something attached and depending on something else; appendage. **—ad·junc·tive** (–JUNK–) *adj.*

ad·jure (uh·JOOR) *v.* **-jures, -jured, -jur·ing** ask solemnly or earnestly. **—ad·ju·ra·tion** (aj·uh·RAY–) *n.*

ad·just (uh·JUST) *v.* **1** change so as to regulate: ~ *the dial to "Low."* **2** settle (a claim). **3** get used; adapt: ~ *to a new climate.* **—ad·just·a·ble** *adj.* **—ad·just·er** or **ad·jus·tor** *n.* **—ad·just·ment** *n.*

ad·ju·tant (AJ·uh·tunt) *n.* **1** an officer who helps a commander as an administrative assistant. **2** a large stork of Asia and Africa.

ad lib *Informal.* in a free style. **—ad-lib** (–LIB) *v.* **-libs, -libbed, -lib·bing** improvise; speak without a script; ***n.*** an improvised remark; something said in an inventive manner; **ad-lib·ber** *n.* **—ad lib·i·tum** (–LIB–) *Music.* as one wishes.

ad loc. in or to the place.

adm. administration; admitted. **—Adm.** admiral.

ad·man *n.* a man in the advertising business.

admin. administration. **—ad·min·is·ter** (–MIN–) *v.* **1** manage: ~ *an estate.* **2** give out; tender: ~ *a medicine;* ~ *an oath of allegiance;* ~ *the sacrament.* **—ad·min·is·tra·ble** (–truh·bl) *adj.* **—ad·min·is·trant** (–trunt) *adj.* & *n.* **—ad·min·is·tra·tion** (–TRAY–) *n.* **1** act or art of administering. **2** group or team of managers or ruling government officials. **—ad·min·is·tra·tive** *adj.: ~ red tape.* **—ad·min·is·tra·tor** *n.: the ~ of an estate; school ~s.*

ad·mi·ra·ble (AD·muh·ruh·bl) *adj.* deserving admiration. **—ad·mi·ra·bly** *adv.*

ad·mi·ral (AD·muh·rul) *n.* one who commands a fleet; also, a naval officer ranking above a captain. **—ad·mi·ral·ty** *n.* **-ties** a court having jurisdiction in maritime cases. **—Admiralty (Board)** the navy department of the U.K.

ad·mire (ud–) *v.* **-mires, -mired, -mir·ing** regard with wonder, esteem, or approval. **—ad·mir·er** *n.* **—ad·mir·ing·ly** *adv.* **—ad·mi·ra·tion** (–muh·RAY–) *n.*

ad·mis·sion (–MISH·un) *n.* **1** an act of admitting; also, something admitted. **2** a fee for being admitted. **—ad·mis·si·ble** *adj.* worthy of being admitted, esp. as evidence in a trial. **—ad·mis·si·bly** *adv.* **—ad·mis·si·bil·i·ty** (–BIL–) *n.* **—ad·mit** (–MIT) *v.* **-mits, -mit·ted, -mit·ting** **1** allow to enter (a place); **ad·mit·tance** *n.* **2** allow entrance (to a class, privilege, etc.). **3** acknowledge; concede: *I ~ my mistake.* **—admit to** confess to (having done something). **—admit of** leave room for; allow. **—ad·mit·ted·ly** *adv.*

ad·mix (–MIX) *v.* mix together; mix in. **—ad·mix·ture** *n.*

ad·mon·ish (–MON–) *v.* reprimand mildly but seriously; warn. **—ad·mo·ni·tion** (–NISH·un) *n.* **—ad·mon·i·to·ry** (–MON–) *adj.*

ad nau·se·am (–NAW·zee·um) to a sickening degree.

a·do (uh·DOO) *n.* fuss; bother.

a·do·be (uh·DOH·bee) *n.* **1** a structure of sun-dried bricks. **2** the clay for these bricks; also, such a brick. ***—adj.:*** *~ houses.*

ad·o·les·cence (ad·uh·LES–) *n.* the period between childhood and maturity. **—ad·o·les·cent** *adj. & n.: ~ shyness; Teenagers are ~s.*

Ad·o·nai (ad·oh·NYE) a Hebrew name for God.

A·don·is (uh·DON·is) in Greek myth, a beautiful youth.

a·dopt (uh–) *v.* **1** receive (a child) into one's family by law. **2** take as one's own; approve and accept: *~ a foreign costume; ~ the resolution.* **—a·dop·tion** *n.* **—a·dop·tive** *adj.: her ~ son; a child's ~ parents.*

a·dore (uh–) *v.* **-dores, -dored, -dor·ing** **1** worship; consider as divine. **2** *Informal.* be extremely fond of: *A mother ~s her baby.* **—a·dor·a·ble** *adj.* **—a·dor·a·bly** *adv.* **—ad·o·ra·tion** (ad·uh·RAY–) *n.*

a·dorn (uh–) *v.* decorate with ornaments; beautify. **—a·dorn·ment** *n.*

ad·re·nal (uh·DREE·nl) *adj.* of either of two glands **(adrenal glands),** one above each kidney, that secrete **ad·ren·al·in(e)** (uh·DREN·uh·lin), cortisone, and other hormones: *~ cortex; ~ secretion.* ***—n.*** an adrenal gland. **—ad·re·nal·ly** *adv.*

A·dri·at·ic (Sea) (ay·dree·AT·ic) the sea separating Yugoslavia and Italy.

a·drift (uh–) *adv. & adj.* floating without mooring or anchor; drifting; hence, without aim or guidance: *young people ~ in our school system.*

a·droit (uh–) *adj.* **1** skillful; dexterous: *an ~ workman.* **2** shrewd; cunning; ingenious: *an ~ statesman.* **—a·droit·ly** *adv.* **—a·droit·ness** *n.*

ad·sorb (ad·SORB, –ZORB) *v.* take up and hold a substance, called an **ad·sor·bate** (–bait), such as a gas, steam, etc. on the surface, as charcoal does. **—ad·sor·bent** *adj. & n.* **—ad·sorp·tion** *n.* **—ad·sorp·tive** (–tiv) *adj.*

ad·u·la·tion (aj·uh·LAY–) *n.* servile praise; flattery. **—ad·u·late** (AJ·uh–) *v.* **-lates, -lat·ed, -lat·ing. —ad·u·la·tor** *n.* **—ad·u·la·to·ry** (–luh–) *adj.*

a·dult (uh·DULT, AD·ult) *n.* a mature living being; also, a person of legal age. ***—adj.:*** *an ~ movie* (that is not suitable for children); *~ butterflies.* **—a·dult·hood** *n.*

a·dul·ter·ate (uh·DUL–) *v.* **-ates, -at·ed, -at·ing** make impure by adding something inferior or foreign; corrupt; **a·dul·ter·ant** *n.: Water may be an ~ in wine;* also ***adj.;*** **a·dul·ter·a·tor** *n.;* **a·dul·ter·a·tion** (–AY–) *n.* **—a·dul·ter·y** (–DUL–) *n.* **-ter·ies** a married person's sexual relationship with someone other than the spouse; **a·dul·ter·er** *n.; fem.* **a·dul·ter·ess; a·dul·ter·ous** (–us) *adj.;* **a·dul·ter·ous·ly** *adv.*

ad·um·brate (AD·um–, uh·DUM–) *v.* **-brates, -brat·ed, -brat·ing** foreshadow; suggest in advance or in an incomplete way. **—ad·um·bra·tion** (–BRAY–) *n.*

adv. adverb.

ad val. *Abbrev.* for **ad va·lo·rem** (–vuh·LOR·um) according to the value: *an ~ property tax.*

ad·vance (–VANCE) *v.* **-vanc·es, -vanced, -vanc·ing** **1** come, go, move, put, or help forward: *The army is ~ing against us; ~ an unwanted opinion; the ~d countries of the West.* **2** increase; promote; lend: *Prices ~ with inflation; ~d to a higher pay category; ~ someone money till payday.* **3** work as an **advance man,** one who prepares a tour ahead of a political candidate. ***—n.*** **1** an advancing; something advanced: *an ~ of $50.* **2** an improvement; progress. **3** the work of an advance man. **4** usu. **advances** *pl.* a personal approach or wooing. ***—adj.*** prior: *~ information.* **—in advance** ahead of time. **—ad·vance·ment** *n.*

ad·van·tage (–VAN·tij) *n.* a benefit or superiority derived from a favorable position, circumstance, result, etc.: *the ~s of wealth; He wouldn't* **take advantage of** (i.e. exploit) *a person's goodness; use public office to personal ~.* **—ad·van·ta·geous** (ad·vun·TAY·jus) *adj.* **—ad·van·ta·geous·ly** *adv.: an ~ situated harbor.*

ad·vent (AD·vent) *n.* **1** an arrival, esp. an expected one: *the ~ of computer technology; the ~ of space travel.* **2 Advent** the coming of Christ; also, the period before Christmas starting from the Sunday nearest to November 30; **Ad·vent·ist** *n.* one who believes that Christ's second coming is near. **—ad·ven·ti·tious** (–TISH·us) *adj.* added externally; acquired; accidental: *~ roots growing down from branches;* **ad·ven·ti·tious·ly** *adv.;* **ad·ven·ti·tious·ness** *n.*

ad·ven·ture (ad·VENCH·ur) *n.* a risky, dangerous, exciting, or challenging experience, enterprise, or undertaking: *a spirit of ~; an ~ in outdoor living;* also ***v.*** **-tures, -tured, -tur·ing.** **—ad·ven·tur·er** *n.* **1** one who undertakes adventures. **2** one who seeks his fortune by soldiering or unscrupulous means; **ad·ven·tur·ess** *n.* a woman who plays fast and loose for wealth and rank. —**ad·ven·tur·ous** or **ad·ven·ture·some** *adj.* —**ad·ven·tur·ous·ly** *adv.* —**ad·ven·tur·ous·ness** *n.*

ad·verb (AD·vurb) *n.* a word modifying a verb, adjective, or another adverb. —**ad·ver·bi·al** (–VUR·bee·ul) *adj.;* **ad·ver·bi·al·ly** *adv.*

ad·ver·sa·ry (AD·vur·ser·ee) *n.* **-ries** opponent; foe; ***adj.:*** *an ~ role.* —**ad·ver·sa·tive** (–VUR·suh·tiv) *adj.* denoting opposition: *"But" is an ~ conjunction;* **ad·ver·sa·tive·ly** *adv.* —**ad·verse** (–VURCE, AD·vurce) *adj.* **1** opposed; hostile. **2** unfavorable; unfortunate: *~ working conditions.* —**ad·verse·ly** *adv.* —**ad·ver·si·ty** (–VUR–) *n.* **-ties 1** misfortune; hardship. **2** calamity.

ad·vert (–VURT) *v.* direct one's attention *(to).* —**ad·ver·tise** (AD·vur·tize) *v.* **-tis·es, -tised, -tis·ing** announce (a product, service, etc.) through journals, TV, radio, etc., esp. for sale: *an ~d bargain; ~ for an editor; ~ing on radio;* **ad·ver·tis·er** *n.* —**ad·ver·tise·ment** (–TIZE·munt, –VUR·tis–) *n.* a notice designed to announce something; an ad. —**ad·ver·tis·ing** *n.* **1** advertisements. **2** the preparation and publishing of advertisements.

ad·vice (ud·VICE) *n.* **1** opinion; counsel; recommendation: *I need your ~ on a problem.* **2** information. —**ad·vis·a·ble** *adj.* recommended; prudent; **ad·vis·a·bil·i·ty** (–BIL–) *n.;* **ad·vis·a·bly** *adv.* —**ad·vise** (–VIZE) *v.* **-vis·es, -vised, -vis·ing** give advice; **ad·vis·er** or **ad·vi·sor** *n.* —**ad·vis·ed·ly** (–id·lee) *adv.* after consideration. —**ad·vise·ment** *n.: We will* **take** *the matter* **under advisement** (i.e. consider it carefully). —**ad·vi·so·ry** (–VYE·zuh·ree) *adj.* that gives advice: *an ~ body, opinion;* ***n.*** a report: *a weather ~.*

ad·vo·cate *n.* (AD·vuh·kit) **1** one who defends or supports a person or cause: *an ~ of nonviolence.* **2** a lawyer. —***v.*** (–cate) **-cates, -cat·ed, -cat·ing:** *~ing changes in foreign policy.* —**ad·vo·ca·cy** (–kuh·see) *n.*

advt. advertisement.

adz(e) (ADZ) *n.* a tool for dressing wood, with the blade edge at right angles to the handle.

A.E.A. Actors' Equity Association.

A.E.C. Atomic Energy Commission.

A.E.F. American Expeditionary Force(s).

Ae·ge·an (Sea) (ee·JEE·un) the sea between Turkey and Greece.

ae·gis (EE·jis) *n.* **1** protection; patronage; auspices: *under the ~ of the U.N.* **2** originally, the shield of Zeus, a Greek god.

Ae·ne·as (ee·NEE·us) the Trojan hero of Virgil's epic poem the **Ae·ne·id;** legendary ancestor of the Romans.

ae·o·li·an (ee·OH·lee·un) *adj.* having to do with the wind; **aeolian harp** a stringed box that produces musical sounds when a current of air blows over it.

ae·on (EE·on) same as EON.

aer·ate (AIR–) *v.* **-ates, -at·ed, -at·ing** expose to or infuse with air or a gas, as blood with oxygen in the lungs or soda water with carbon dioxide; **aer·a·tor** *n.;* **aer·a·tion** (–RAY–) *n.* —**aer·i·al** (AIR·ee·ul) *adj.* **1** of, in, or by air or an airplane: *an ~ survey.* **2** unreal; imaginary: *~ creatures.* —***n.*** a TV or radio antenna; **aer·i·al·ly** *adv.* —**aer·i·al·ist** *n.* a circus performer of feats on the trapeze, tightrope, etc.

aer·ie (AIR·ee) *n.* a nest, as an eagle's, placed high.

aero- *comb.form.* of the air, aircraft, or gases. —**aer·o·bat·ics** (air·oh·BAT–) *n.pl.* [takes *sing. v.*] stunt-flying; **aer·o·bat·ic** *adj.* —**aer·obe** *n.* a bacterium or other organism that lives on the oxygen of the air; **aer·o·bic** (–OH–) *adj.;* **aer·o·bic·al·ly** *adv.* —**aer·o·bics** *n. pl.* exercises which develop the body's use of oxygen. —**aer·o·drome** *n. Brit.* airport; airfield. —**aer·o·dy·nam·ics** (–NAM–) *n.pl.* [takes *sing. v.*] the mechanics of the forces exerted by gases in motion; **aer·o·dy·nam·ic** or **-i·cal** *adj.;* **aer·o·dy·nam·i·cal·ly** *adv.* —**aer·ol·o·gy** (–OL·uh·jee) *n.* meteorology, esp. as concerned with the air a mile or more above the earth; **aer·o·log·ic** (–LOJ–) *adj.;* **aer·ol·o·gist** (–OL–) *n.* —**aer·o·naut** (AIR·uh·nawt) *n.* one who operates an airship, balloon, etc.; **aer·o·nau·tic** (–NAW–) or **-ti·cal** *adj.;* **aer·o·nau·ti·cal·ly** *adv.* **aer·o·nau·tics** *n.pl.* [takes *sing. v.*] the science of the design, manufacture, and operation of aircraft. —**aer·o·pause** *n.* the altitude above the earth at which the air is too thin for airplanes to fly. —**aer·o·plane** *n. Brit.* airplane. —**aer·o·sol** *n.* fine particles of a liquid or a solid suspended in a gas and sprayed in air under pressure; ***adj.:*** *an ~ bomb; ~ deodorant; ~ insecticide.* —**aer·o·space** *n.* the earth's atmosphere and the space outside in which aircraft, rockets, etc. travel; ***adj.:*** *~ research; ~ industry.* —**aer·o·train** *n.* a train that rides on an air cushion on a single rail. —**aer·y** (AIR·ee) *adj.* ethereal; ***n.*** same as AERIE.

Aes·chy·lus (ES·ki–) 525–456 B.C., a Greek tragic poet. —**Aes·chy·le·an** (es·kuh·LEE·un) *adj.*

Aes·cu·la·pi·us (es·kyoo·LAY·pee·us) the Roman god of medicine.

Ae·sop (EE·sop) a Greek fable writer, reputedly of the 6th c. B.C. —**Ae·so·pi·an** (ee·SOH·pee·un) *adj.*

aes·thete (ES·theet) *n.* one who has or affects a taste for artistic beauty. —**aes·thet·ic** (–THET–) or **-i·cal** *adj.* relating to the taste for the beautiful, esp. in art. —**aes·thet·i·cal·ly** *adv.* —**aes·thet·ics** *n.pl.* [takes *sing. v.*] the philosophy of the beautiful, esp. of the fine arts.

aet. or **aetat.** aged; of age.

aether same as ETHER.

a.f. or **A.F.** audio frequency.

A.F. air force; Anglo-French.

a·far (uh–) *adv.* & *n.* far away; at, to, or from a distance: *Three Wise Men came from ~.*

AFB air force base.
A.F.C. automatic frequency control.
af·fa·ble (AF·uh·bl) *adj.* pleasant in manner; easy to talk to. **—af·fa·bly** *adv.* **—af·fa·bil·i·ty** (–BIL–) *n.*
af·fair (uh·FAIR) *n.* **1** a concern; business: *my ~, not yours.* **2** any matter or event: *an ~ of state.* **3** a temporary love relationship.
af·fect (uh·FECT) *v.* **1** do something to; have an influence on: *not ~ed by heat and cold; Smoking ~s your health.* **2** move the emotions of: *much ~ed by the tragedy;* **af·fect·ing** *adj.;* **af·fect·ing·ly** *adv.* **3** pretend (to have, feel, like, etc.): *He ~s ignorance; She ~ed an air of innocence; an* **affected** (i.e. artificial) *British accent;* **af·fect·ed·ly** *adv.;* **af·fect·ed·ness** *n.;* **af·fec·ta·tion** (af·ec·TAY–) *n.* behavior or an attitude that is put on for effect. **—af·fec·tion** *n.* **1** a feeling of fondness for someone; love; tenderness; **af·fec·tion·ate** *adj.;* **af·fec·tion·ate·ly** *adv.* **2** a disease: *TB is an ~ of the lungs.*
af·fer·ent (AF·uh·runt) *adj.* bringing (usu. impulses) to a central organ: *~ nerves* (leading to the brain).
af·fi·ance (uh·FYE·unce) *v.* **-an·ces, -anced, -anc·ing** pledge to marry: *~d his daughter to the lawyer; a newly ~d couple.*
af·fi·da·vit (af·i·DAY–) *n.* a sworn declaration made in writing.
af·fil·i·ate (uh·FIL·ee–) *v.* **-ates, -at·ed, -at·ing** associate or connect as a member or branch: *They ~d two clubs.* **—*n.*** (–ee·it): *an ~ of the parent company.* **—af·fil·i·a·tion** (–AY–) *n.: a school in ~ with the university.*
af·fin·i·ty (uh·FIN–) *n.* **-ties** an attraction, kinship, or relationship between two people or things: *~ between Canadian and American English; Dutch ~ for English words.*
af·firm (uh·FIRM) *v.* **1** say firmly: *~ one's innocence.* **2** confirm. **3** declare as true. **—af·fir·ma·tion** (af·ur·MAY–) *n.* **—af·firm·a·tive** (uh·FIR·muh·tiv) *n.* **1** a "yes" answer: *replied in the ~.* **2** the side in a debate that supports the proposition. Also ***adj.:*** *an ~ response;* **af·firm·a·tive·ly** *adv.* **—affirmative action** policy of favoring candidates from minority groups to compensate for past discrimination in employment, school admissions, etc.
af·fix (uh·FIX) *v.* attach; fasten; also, add: *~ a signature to a document.* **—*n.*** (AF·ix) something affixed, esp. a prefix or suffix.
af·fla·tus (uh·FLAY–) *n.* inspiration; creative impulse.
af·flict (uh–) *v.* torment; cause suffering to; also, make miserable: *~ed with gout.* **—af·flic·tion** *n.* **—af·flic·tive** *adj.* **—af·flic·tive·ly** *adv.*
af·flu·ent (AF·loo·unt) *adj.* well-to-do; abundant: *~ society; ~ times.* **—af·flu·ent·ly** *adv.* **—af·flu·ence** *n.*
af·ford (uh–) *v.* **1** have the means for; also, spare the time or money for; be able (to): *Can we ~ two cars? can't ~ to miss school.* **2** provide; yield: *Music ~s me pleasure.* **—af·ford·a·ble** *adj.*
af·for·est·a·tion (uh·for·is·TAY–) *n.* the conversion of land into forest. **—af·for·est** *v.*
af·fray (uh–) *v.* a noisy fight; brawl; fray.
af·front (uh·FRUNT) *v.* insult; offend. **—*n.:*** *an ~ to his dignity.*
Af·ghan (AF·gan) *n.* **1** a person of or from Afghanistan. **2** the Pashto language; also ***adj.*** **3 afghan** a woven, knitted, or crocheted shawl or coverlet with a geometric pattern. **—Afghan (hound)** a hunting dog with a long head, large ears, and a thick silky coat. **—af·ghan·i** (–GAN·ee) *n.* the basic monetary unit of Afghanistan, equal to 100 puls. **—Af·ghan·i·stan** a republic in C. Asia; 250,-000 sq.mi. (647,497 km²); *cap.* Kabul.
a·fi·cio·na·do (uh·fish·uh·NAH·doh) *n.* a devotee, enthusiast, or fan.
a·field (uh–) *adv.* & *adj.* on the field; away from home; astray: *He wandered far ~ and was lost.*
a·fire (uh–) *adv.* & *adj.* on fire: *The house was set ~; ~ with patriotic love.* Also **a·flame** *adv.* & *adj.*
AFL-CIO American Federation of Labor and Congress of Industrial Organizations.
a·float (uh–) *adj.* & *adv.* **1** floating; also, on board ship. **2** awash, as a ship's deck. **3** going around: *There are rumors ~.*
a·flut·ter (uh–) *adj.* & *adv.* fluttering; excited: *John was all ~ at the exam.*
a·foot (uh–) *adj.* & *adv.* on foot; also, under way: *A scheme is ~ to raise a million dollars.*
afore- *comb. form.* before; previously: as in **a·fore·men·tioned** *adj.* and **a·fore·said** *adj.* **—a·fore·thought** *adj.* deliberate; premeditated: *murder, with malice ~.*
a for·ti·or·i (ay·for·tee·OR·ee) *Latin.* with even greater reason.
a·foul (uh·FOWL) *adj.* & *adv.* entangled; **run** (or **fall**) **afoul of** be in conflict with (the law, etc.).
Afr. Africa; African.
a·fraid (uh–) *adj.* **1** filled with fear: *She is not ~ of the dark.* **2** regretful: *I am ~ I don't understand.*
A-frame *n.* a building with steep roofs overhanging the sides and meeting in a steep A-like point; an A-shaped structure; ***adj.:*** *an ~ cottage.*
a·fresh (uh–) *adv.* again; anew: *Let's start ~.*
Af·ri·ca (AF·ri·kuh) the continent south of Europe, largest after Asia. **—Af·ri·can** *adj.* & *n.: Swahili is an ~ language; an ~ by birth.* **—African violet** a house plant of African origin with velvety leaves and usu. purple flowers. **—Af·ri·kaans** (af·ri·KAHNS) *n.* a Dutch-derived language that is one of South Africa's official languages; ***adj.*** having to do with Afrikaans or Afrikaners. **—Af·ri·ka·ner** (–KAH·nur) *n.* a South African of European descent, esp. one speaking Afrikaans. **—Af·ro** (AF·roh) *n.* a style of doing the hair in a dense,

bushy mass; ***adj.*** of Africa, Afros, etc.; **Af·ro-A·mer·i·can** *adj.* & *n.* Black American: ~ *studies.*

aft. afternoon.

aft *adj.* & *adv.* to, at, or near the stern or rear: *an* ~ *sail; Let's go* ~.

af·ter (AF–) *adv.* behind; following; later: *and Jill came tumbling* ~. —***prep.*** **1** following: *the day* ~ *tomorrow.* **2** in the manner or style of: *Name the child* ~ *her mother; a woman* ~ *my own heart; The boy takes* ~ (i.e. resembles) *his father.* **3** in pursuit of: *The police are* ~ *the thief.* —***adj.*** later: *In* ~ *years he became an alcoholic.* —***conj.:*** *He stayed* ~ *the others went home.* —**after all** in spite of everything. —**af·ter·birth** *n.* the placenta and fetal membranes expelled from the uterus after a birth. —**af·ter·burn·er** *n.* an auxiliary burner in a jet engine for increasing the plane's thrust. —**af·ter·care** *n.* the treatment following discharge of a person from a hospital or prison. —**af·ter·damp** *n.* dangerous gases that remain after an explosion in a mine. —**af·ter·deck** *n.* the part of a ship's deck toward the rear. —**af·ter·ef·fect** *n.* a secondary or later effect: *Some drugs have* ~*s.* —**af·ter·glow** *n.* the glow seen in the sky after a sunset; hence, a pleasant feeling remaining after some experience: *the* ~ *of a long weekend.* —**af·ter·heat** *n.* the excess heat produced by a nuclear reactor. —**af·ter·im·age** *n.* a visual sensation that continues after its object has passed. —**af·ter·life** *n.* life after death. —**af·ter·math** *n.* a second crop, esp. of hay; hence, a consequence, outcome, result: *the* ~ *of war.* —**af·ter·most** *adj.* nearest the stern; also, hindmost; last. —**af·ter·noon** *n.* the time between noon and evening. —**af·ter-shave** *n.* a scented lotion to dab on the face after shaving. —**af·ter·taste** *n.* a taste remaining in the mouth after eating or drinking something; also, a lingering feeling of a previous experience. —**af·ter·tax** *adj.* after taxes are deducted: ~ *profits.* —**af·ter·thought** *n.* something that comes to mind after an occasion has passed. —**af·ter·ward(s)** *adv.* later; subsequently.

Ag silver.

A.G. adjutant general; attorney general.

a·gain (uh·GEN) *adv.* **1** once more. **2** moreover; on the other hand. —**again and again** often. —**and (then) again** on the other hand: *She might say yes, and then* ~ *she might not.* —**as many** (or **much**) **again:** *I got $20; first $10 and then as much* ~ *as a bonus.* —**now and again:** *Now and* ~ (i.e. from time to time) *our next-door neighbor offers to mow our lawn.* —**time and time again:** *Must I tell you time and time* ~ (i.e. repeatedly) *to turn down the radio?* —**a·gainst** (uh–) *prep.* **1** opposed to; in opposition to: *I am* ~ *a picnic today; swim* ~ *the current.* **2** in(to) contact with: *Don't lean* ~ *the wall.* **3** as a defense from or preparation for: *Take an umbrella* ~ *the chance of rain.* —**over against** facing: *two houses over* ~ *each other.*

Ag·a·mem·non (ag·uh·MEM·non) legendary Greek hero and commander at Troy in the *Iliad.*

¹a·gape (uh–) *adj.* & *adv.* (with mouth) wide open: ~ *with wonder.*

²ag·a·pe (AG·uh·pay) *n.* **1** selfless love, esp. Christian love. **2** a common meal betokening this.

a·gar (AH·gar) *n.* a jellylike substance derived from seaweed and used as a bacterial growth medium *(nutrient* ~*),* in cooking and as a laxative; also **a·gar-a·gar.**

ag·ate (AG·it) *n.* **1** a semiprecious stone colored in patches or bands. **2** a playing marble made of or resembling this.

a·ga·ve (uh·GAH·vee) *n.* any of several tropical plants with thick fleshy leaves and a long flower stalk: *Some* ~*s yield fiber used in making rope.*

agcy. agency.

-age *n. suffix.* **1** a collection of: as in *leafage.* **2** a condition: as in *bondage.* **3** an action or result: as in *breakage, cartage.*

age *n.* **1** the length of one's existence: *ten years of* ~. **2** a certain period or stage of life: *At 18 you are* **of age** (i.e. legally an adult) *in many states; He has reached the* **age of discretion** (i.e. legal responsibility); *He is* **under age** (i.e. too young) *for drinking;* **over age** *for military service; 16 is below the* **age of consent** *for marriage.* **3** a period of culture or civilization; era: *the* ~ *of automation.* **4** *Informal.* a long time: *It seems* ~*s since we last met.* —***v.*** **ag·es, aged, ag(e)·ing** grow old; advance in age: *Some* ~ *faster than others.* —**age-** *comb. form.: an* **age-old** *custom; the* **age-long** *tyranny.* —**aged** *adj.* **1** (AIJD) having the age of: *a child* ~ *five.* **2** (AY·jid) advanced in age: *an* ~ *pensioner; the sick and* **the aged** (i.e. old people). —**age·less** *adj.: an* ~ (i.e. always young) *beauty; the* ~ (i.e. eternal) *genius of Shakespeare.*

a·gen·cy (AY·jun·see) *n.* **-cies** **1** a means or instrument for doing something; also, activity; operation: *Miracles are beyond human* ~. **2** a business office; also, a government division: *a travel* ~*; the Central Intelligence Agency.*

a·gen·da (uh·JEN·duh) *n.* **-das** a list of topics for a discussion; a program: *next item on the* ~.

a·gent (AY·junt) *n.* **1** one who acts for another, esp. in business: *a shipping* ~*; a literary* ~. **2** a government official or emissary: *a secret* ~. **3** a means or instrument: *a chemical* ~*;* **a·gent pro·vo·ca·teur** (proh·voc·uh·TUR), *pl.* **a·gents pro·vo·ca·teurs** (–TUR) one sent to infiltrate a suspected group and provoke them to illegal actions.

age of consent, age of discretion See AGE.

ag·er·a·tum (aj·uh·RAY–) *n.* a garden flower of the composite family bearing clusters of blue, pink, or white flowers.

ag·gior·na·men·to (uh·jor·nuh·MEN·toh) *n.* a modernizing, esp. of the Roman Catholic Church by the Vatican Council, 1962–1965.

ag·glom·er·ate (uh·GLOM–) *v.* **-ates, -at·ed, -at·ing** form into a mass, esp. a rounded mass. **—*adj.*** (–uh·rit): *an ~ flower head;* ***n.*** *an ~ of volcanic rock.* **—ag·glom·er·a·tive** (–tiv) *adj.* **—ag·glom·er·a·tion** (–RAY–) *n.*

ag·glu·ti·nate (uh·GLOO–) *v.* **-nates, -nat·ed, -nat·ing** cause to adhere or clump together, as bacteria or blood cells. **—*adj.*** (–nit): *~ words like "arrowheadmaker"; ~ spores;* also ***n.*** **—ag·glu·ti·na·tive** (–nuh·tiv) *adj.* **—ag·glu·ti·na·tion** (–NAY–) *n.*

ag·gran·dize (uh·GRAN–) *v.* **-diz·es, -dized, -diz·ing** make (esp. oneself) greater in power, wealth, or position; **ag·gran·diz·er** *n.* **—ag·gran·dize·ment** (–diz·munt) *n.: personal ~.*

ag·gra·vate (AG·ruh–) *v.* **-vates, -vat·ed, -vat·ing** **1** make more serious or offensive: *His excuses only ~d the quarrel.* **2** *Informal.* imitate; annoy: *~ing behavior.* **—ag·gra·va·tion** (–VAY–) *n.*

ag·gre·gate *v.* (AG·ruh·gate) **-gates, -gat·ed, -gat·ing** collect together in a mass or cluster. **—*adj.*** (–git): *The blackberry and the raspberry are ~ fruits;* ***n.*** the total amount; **in the aggregate** collectively. **—ag·gre·ga·tive** (–tiv) *adj.* **—ag·gre·ga·tion** (–GAY–) *n.: an ~ of museum exhibits.*

ag·gress (uh·GRES) *v.* begin an attack or quarrel. **—ag·gres·sor** *n.* **—ag·gres·sion** *n.* **—ag·gres·sive** (uh·GRES·iv) *adj.: ~ military powers; an ~* (i.e. enterprising or assertive) *salesman.* **—ag·gres·sive·ly** *adv.: The lawyer made his case ~.* **—ag·gres·sive·ness** *n.*

ag·grieve (uh·GREEV) *v.* **-grieves, -grieved, -griev·ing** cause grief or hurt to: *Jane feels ~d about not getting a raise.*

a·ghast (uh–) *adj.* horrified: *She stood ~ at the sight.*

ag·ile (AJ·ul) *adj.* quick and nimble: *an ~ beast like the leopard; her ~ wit.* **—ag·ile·ly** *adv.* **—a·gil·i·ty** (–JIL–) *n.*

ag·i·tate (AJ·i–) *v.* **-tates, -tat·ed, -tat·ing** **1** move or shake: *the sea ~d by strong winds.* **2** disturb; stir up: *She seems ~d by the delay; It is time to* **agitate** (i.e. try to stir people up) **for** *minority rights.* **—ag·i·ta·tion** (–TAY–) *n.* **—ag·i·ta·tor** (AJ·uh·tay·tur) *n.: a new ~ for the washing machine; a socialist ~.* **—ag·it·prop** (AJ·it·prop) *n.* pro-Communist propaganda using drama, literature, leaflets, etc.

a·gleam (uh·GLEEM) *adj.* gleaming.

a·gley (uh·GLEE) *adv. Scot.* askew; awry.

a·glit·ter (uh–) *adj.* glittering.

a·glow (uh–) *adj.* glowing.

ag·nail (AG–) *n.* a sore about a fingernail or toenail; hangnail.

ag·no·men (–NOH–) *n., pl.* **-min·a** in ancient Rome, a title added to a notable's name in honor of some exploit, as Marcus Aurelius Claudius *Gothicus.*

ag·nos·tic (–NOS–) *n.* one who doubts that truths beyond this world (such as the existence of God) can be known; ***adj.:*** *an ~ position.* **—ag·nos·ti·cism** *n.*

Ag·nus De·i (ahg·nus·DAY·ee) **1** a figure of a lamb that represents Christ. **2** a prayer addressed to Christ beginning with these words.

a·go (uh–) *adj. & adv.* in the past: *years ~.*

a·gog (uh–) *adj. & adv.* eager and excited: *The whole town was ~ at the news.*

a go-go (uh·GOH–) in the latest style; also, abundant; galore: *psychotherapy ~;* also ***n.*** a discotheque.

ag·o·nize *v.* **-niz·es, -nized, -niz·ing** be in agony: *Tim is ~ing over his homework;* **ag·o·nized** *adj.: an ~ expression;* **ag·o·niz·ing** *adj.: an ~ time in a hijacked plane;* **ag·o·niz·ing·ly** *adv.* **—ag·o·ny** (AG·uh·nee) *n.* **-nies** intense pain or suffering in body or mind: *the ~ of suspense; an accident victim in ~.* **—agony column** a section of a newspaper carrying ads about missing persons.

[1]**a·go·ra** (ah·guh·RAH) *n., pl.* **-rot** (–ROHT) a coin of Israeli currency worth 1/100 of a shekel.

[2]**ag·o·ra** (AG·uh·ruh) *n.* **-ras** or **-rae** (–ree) in ancient Greece, a market place as a place of popular assembly. **—ag·o·ra·pho·bi·a** (ag·uh·ruh·FOH·bee·uh) *n.* an abnormal fear of open places. **—ag·o·ra·pho·bic** *adj. & n.* **—agorot** *pl.* of [1]AGORA.

a·gou·ti (uh·GOO·tee) *n.* **-tis** a rabbitlike rodent of tropical America that has grizzled fur; also **a·gou·ty, -ties.**

agr. or **agric.** agricultural; agriculture.

a·grar·i·an (uh·GRAIR·ee·un) *adj.* having to do with land ownership, farms, or agricultural interests: *an ~ party.* **—*n.*** a supporter of **a·grar·i·an·ism** *n.* a movement for agricultural or land reform.

a·gree (uh·GREE) *v.* **-grees, -greed, -gree·ing** **1** say yes; consent; approve of; concede: *It is hard to ~ on the terms of the contract; I ~d to go; We ~d that it was a good book.* **2** [takes *with*] match; correspond; be in harmony; be suitable or healthful: *John's story doesn't ~ with his friend's; The verb must ~ with the subject; Seafood rarely ~s with me.* **—a·gree·a·ble** *adj.* pleasant; ready to agree; suitable: *an ~ smile; an ~ negotiator.* **—a·gree·a·bly** *adv.* **—a·gree·a·ble·ness** or **a·gree·a·bil·i·ty** (–BIL–) *n.* **—a·gree·ment** *n.: The argument ended when we reached an ~; The labor union signed the new ~.*

ag·ri·busi·ness (AG·ruh·biz·nis) *n.* the farming industry, including also the production of farm equipment, fertilizers, and related services. **—ag·ri·cul·ture** (AG·ri·cul·chur) *n.* the science of farming; husbandry. **—ag·ri·cul·tur·al** (–CUL–) *adj.* **—ag·ri·cul·tur·al·ly** *adv.* **—ag·ri·cul·tur·(al·)ist** *n.* **—agro-** *comb. form.* land; crops; agricultural: as in **ag·ro·chem·i·cals** *n.pl.;* **ag·ro-in·dus·try** *n.* **-tries.**

—a·grol·o·gy (–GROL–) *n.* a branch of agriculture dealing with soils; **ag·ro·log·ic** (–LOJ–) or **-i·cal** *adj.;* **a·grol·o·gist** (–GROL–) *n.* **—a·gron·o·my** (–GRON–) *n.* the science of land management and production of crops; also **ag·ro·nom·ics** (–NOM–); **ag·ro·nom·ic** *adj.;* **a·gron·o·mist** (–GRON–) *n.*

a·ground (uh–) *adj.* & *adv.* to the ground; stuck or dragging on the bottom shore; stranded: *a ship fast ~; to run ~ in shallow water.*

agt. agent.

a·gue (AY·gyoo) *n.* a usu. malarial fever with periodic chills and sweating. **—a·gu·ish** *adj.*

ah or **a·ha** (ah·HAH) *interj.* indicating surprise, pain, triumph, etc.

a·head (uh·HED) *adj.* & *adv.* in or toward the front or a better position; forward: *Look ~ when driving; trying to get ~ in life; Go ~ and tell us.* **—get ahead of** outdo: *get ~ of the competition.* **—full speed ahead!** go at full speed.

a·hem (uh–) *interj.* [like a clearing of the throat] used to attract attention.

a·hoy (uh–) *interj.* used by sailors to warn or hail: *Ship ~!*

aid *n.* help; assistance: *TV is an audio-visual ~; a collection in ~ of the Red Cross;* **v.** help. **—aide** *n.* a helper: *a nurse's ~.* **—aide-de-camp** *n.* **aides-de-camp** a military officer who is an assistant to a commander. **—aid·man** *n.* **-men** a medical aide in a field unit.

AID Agency for International Development.

ai·gret(te) (AY·gret, ay·GRET) *n.* a tuft of plumes or jewelry worn usu. on a hat.

ail *v.* be or make ill. **—ail·ing** *adj.*

ai·lan·thus (ay·LANTH·us) *n.* **-thus·es** a deciduous tree of Asiatic origin with small, greenish flowers and reddish-brown fruits.

ai·le·ron (AY·luh–) *n.* a movable section of the rear edge of an airplane's wing that helps it to turn right or left.

ail·ment *n.* illness.

aim *v.* point or direct (a weapon, remark, or action): *~ your gun at the target; remarks ~ed at the whole group; She ~s to be a doctor.* **—n.** an aiming; object; purpose; goal: *take ~ carefully before firing; Money is his ~ in life.* **—aimless** *adj.: an ~ life.* **—aim·less·ly** *adv.* **—aim·less·ness** *n.*

ain't Nonstandard form of *am not, are not, is not, has not, have not;* used informally in the question form *Ain't I?* (i.e. Am I not?).

Ai·nu (EYE·noo) *n.* a member of a light-skinned aboriginal people of Japan; also, their language.

air *n.* **1** a mixture of gases forming the atmosphere. **2** a breeze; wind. **3** appearance; manner; impression: *an ~ of dignity; putting on* **airs** (i.e. unnatural and affected ways). **4** radio or television: *The program is* **on** (or **off**) **the air** (i.e. being or not being broadcast). **5** a melody or tune. **—v.** expose to the air; hence, go public with: *~ one's grievances;* **air·ing** *n.* **—in the air** going around: *There is a rumor in the ~.* **—take the air** go out for a walk or ride. **—up in the air** uncertain. **—walk on air** be elated. **—air·bag** *n.* a protective bag designed to inflate in front of an automobile passenger in a crash. **—air base** an operating headquarters for military aircraft. **—air bladder** in most fishes, a sac containing air that helps to maintain buoyancy and aid respiration. **—air boat** a propeller-driven, flat-bottomed boat used esp. in swamps. **—air·borne** *adj.* flying; carried by air. **—air brake** a brake worked by compressed air. **—air·brush** *n.* a compressed-air device for touching up artwork; **v.:** *Blemishes on a photo can be ~ed away.* **—air castle** daydream. **—air cavalry** a body of reconnaissance, security, or combat troops trained for air transport. **—air cleaner** air filter. **—air-con·di·tion** *v.* control humidity and temperature by means of a device called an **air conditioner. —air·craft** *n. sing.* & *pl.* any machine for traveling in the air, as a balloon, airplane, or helicopter. **—aircraft carrier** a warship with a deck for aircraft to land and take off. **—air cushion vehicle** a vehicle that travels on a cushion of air by means of jets or fans blowing downward and raising it a few feet above ground or water. **—air·drome** *n. Brit.* airport. **—air·drop** *n.* a delivery of cargo by parachute; also **v. -drops, -dropped, -drop·ping.**

Aire·dale (terrier) (AIR–) a large terrier with a rough, wiry coat.

air express *Service mark.* the shipping of parcels by air. **—air·field** *n.* an airport, esp. its landing field. **—air filter** a device for filtering out dust, pollen, etc. from an automobile engine, air conditioner, etc. **—air·foil** *n.* a controlling part of an airplane such as a wing, rudder, or aileron. **—air force** the air arm of a country's armed forces. **—air·frame** *n.* the structure of an airplane without the engine. **—air gun** a gun worked by compressed air. **—air hole** a hole in the ice covering a pond or river. **—air lane** a path regularly used by airplanes. **—air·less** *adj.* without fresh air; without movement of air. **—air letter** a sheet of paper designed to be airmailed as a letter when folded and sealed. **—air·lift** *n.* the transporting of men and supplies by air; also **v.** **—air·line** *n.* a regular passenger service by air; **air·lin·er** *n.* an airline's passenger plane. **—air lock** **1** a blockage caused by air, as in a water pipe. **2** a chamber having airtight doors to maintain pressure in an enclosure, as of a caisson. **—air·mail** *n.* the transporting of mail by air; also **v.** **—air·man** *n.* **-men** a man in the lower ranks of an air force; also, any aviator. **—air mattress** a pad that is inflated for use as a mattress. **—air mile** 6,076.115 feet, or *nautical mile;* 1.852 kilometers. **—air·mo·bile** (AIR·moh·bl) *adj.* of ground troops, that are moved to combat areas by air, usu. helicopter. —**air piracy** aircraft hijacking; hence **air pirate.** —**air·plane** *n.* a heavier-than-air machine with fixed wings and powered by a propeller or jet. —**air plant** a plant that grows on another plant, drawing nourishment from air and rain, as mosses and lichens. —**air pocket** a partial vacuum or other atmospheric condition that makes an aircraft lose altitude while in flight. —**air pollution** contamination of the air by industrial gases, automobile exhausts, etc. —**air·port** *n.* a place with established facilities for planes, passengers, and cargo. —**air pump** a piece of equipment for compressing or removing air. —**air raid** an attack by armed aircraft on a ground target. —**air·ship** *n.* a lighter-than-air craft equipped with power for propulsion and steering; dirigible. —**air·sick** *adj.* nauseated from the movements of an aircraft; **air·sick·ness** *n.* —**air·space** *n.* the space above a country considered as within its territorial jurisdiction. —**air·speed** *n.* the speed of an aircraft relative to the air through which it flies. —**air strike** an attack from the air. —**air strip** a strip of ground that is used as an airfield; a landing strip. —**air·tight** *adj.* **1** too tight for air to get out or in. **2** flawless; inescapable: *an ~ argument.* —**air-to-air** *adj.* directed from an aircraft to a target in the air. —**air-to-ground** *adj.* directed from an aircraft to a ground target. —**air waves** the medium of transmission of radio and TV. —**air·way** *n.* a route used by airplanes. —**air·wor·thy** *adj.* fit to be flown; **air·wor·thi·ness** *n.* —**air·y** *adj.* **air·i·er, -i·est** **1** of or having to do with the quality of the air; light; lively; delicate; breezy. **2** immaterial. —**air·i·ly** *adv.;* **air·i·ness** *n.*

aisle (ILE) *n.* a passageway between two rows of seats, counters, etc. as in an auditorium or supermarket. —**aisled** *adj.*

a·jar (uh·JAR) *adj.* of a door, hinged window, etc., partly open.

AK Alaska.

a.k.a. also known as.

A.K.C. American Kennel Club.

a·kim·bo (uh–) *adj.* & *adv.* with the hands on the hips and the elbows pointing outward: *Standing with arms ~.*

a·kin (uh–) *adj.* related; similar: *"Three" is ~ to the German "drei."*

Ak·ron (AK·run) a city of Ohio.

Al aluminum. —**AL** Alabama. —**A.L.** American League; American Legion. —**-al** *suffix.* **1** *adj.* of, like, or suited to: as in *theatrical, colossal.* **2** *n.* the action or process: as in *recital, refusal.*

Ala. Alabama. —**A.L.A.** American Library Association.

à la or **a la** (AH·lah) in the style or after the manner of: *tragedy ~ Shakespeare.*

Al·a·bam·a (al·uh·BAM·uh) a S. state of the U.S.; 51,609 sq. mi. (133,667 km²); *cap.* Montgomery. —**Al·a·bam·(i·)an** *adj.* & *n.*

al·a·bas·ter (AL·uh–) *n.* a soft, white, stone that resembles marble, used for vases, ornaments, etc. —***adj.*** made of or like alabaster: *an ~ vase; ~ skin;* also **al·a·bas·trine** (–BAS·trin).

à la carte (ah·luh·CART) *adj.* & *adv.* ordered from a menu item by item, not as a complete meal: *~ dinner.*

a·lac·ri·ty (uh·LAC·ri·tee) *n.* eager liveliness.

à la king *adj.* diced and served in a cream sauce with chopped peppers, mushrooms, etc.: *chicken ~.*

Al·a·mo (AL·uh·moh) a Spanish mission in San Antonio, Texas, the site of a battle against Mexico in 1836.

à la mode (al·uh·MODE) *adj.* **1** in the latest fashion. **2** served with ice cream: *apple pie ~.*

a·larm (uh–) *n.* **1** sudden fear. **2** a warning, esp. of danger: *Sound the fire ~.* **3** a warning signal: *the ~ of an* **alarm clock** *that wakes you in the morning.* —***v.*** frighten; also, alert of imminent danger: *Don't be ~ed; an* **alarming** *state of affairs.* —**a·larm·ist** (–LAR–) *n.* & *adj.* (one) inclined to be needlessly alarming: *~ views on the Communist menace.*

a·las (uh·LAS) *interj.* indicating regret, anxiety, sorrow, etc.

A·las·ka (uh·LAS·kuh) a U.S. state in N.W. North America; 586,412 sq. mi. (1,518,800 km²); *cap.* Juneau. —**A·las·kan** *adj.* & *n.*

alb (ALB) *n.* a long, white robe of linen worn by a priest during ceremonies.

al·ba·core (AL·buh–) *n.* any of several fishes of the tuna group.

Al·ba·ni·a (–BAY–) a Balkan country on the Adriatic Sea; 11,100 sq.mi. (28,748 km²); *cap.* Tirana. —**Al·ba·ni·an** *n.* **1** a person from Albania. **2** their language. Also ***adj.***

Al·ba·ny (AWL·buh·nee) capital of New York State.

al·ba·tross (AL·buh–) *n.* **-tross(·es)** any of several large-winged seabirds related to the petrel.

al·be·it (awl·BEE·it) *conj.* although.

Al·ber·ta (al·BUR·tuh) a Prairie Province of W. Canada; 255,285 sq.mi. (661,185 km²); *cap.* Edmonton. —**Al·ber·tan** *adj.* & *n.*

al·bi·no (al·BYE·noh) *n.* a human or animal with white skin and hair and pink eyes due to lack of normal coloration, a deficiency called **al·bi·nism** (AL·buh–). —**al·bum** *n.* **1** a blank book for keeping collections of stamps, photographs, etc. **2** a long-playing record or tape recording or a set of such records. —**al·bu·men** (al·BYOO·mun) *n.* **1** the white of an egg. **2** the protein substance which forms egg white, found also in many plant and animal tissues and juices, and better known as **al·bu·min.** —**al·bu·min·ous** (–nus) *adj.*

Al·bu·quer·que (AL·buh·cur·kee) a city of New Mexico.

alc. alcohol.

al·cal·de (al·CAL·dee) *n.* in Spanish or Spanish-American towns, a mayor with some judicial power. **—al·caz·ar** (AL·cuh·zar) *n.* a fort or palace in Spain, built by the Moors.

al·che·my (AL·cuh·mee) *n.* the medieval chemistry which directed its efforts to the changing of base metals into gold; hence, a miraculous change of the ordinary into something precious. **—al·che·mist** *n.* **—al·chem·ic** (–KEM–) or **-i·cal** *adj.*

Al·ci·bi·a·des (al·si·BYE·uh·deez) 450?–404 B.C., an Athenian politician.

al·co·hol (AL·kuh·hawl) *n.* **1** the pure, colorless liquid forming the intoxicating element in drinks such as beer, wine, and whiskey; also, such a drink. **2** any chemical compound similar to alcohol, such as wood alcohol. **—al·co·hol·ic** (–HOL–) *adj.;* also ***n.*** one who suffers from **al·co·hol·ism** (AL–), the chronic and excessive use of alcohol.

al·cove (AL·cohv) *n.* **1** a recess in a room; nook. **2** a bower in a garden.

ald. alderman.

al den·te (ahl·DEN·tay) firm to the teeth (when cooked); not soft.

al·der (AWL·dur) *n.* any of various trees and shrubs of the birch family.

al·der·man (AWL·dur·mun) *n.* **-men** a member of a municipal council.

ale *n.* a liquor brewed from malt and hops, but paler in color, heavier, and more bitter than beer.

a·le·a·to·ry (AIL·ee·uh·tor·ee) or **a·le·a·tor·ic** (–TOR–) *adj.* **1** depending on chance. **2** of music, random and improvised. **—a·le·a·tor·ism** *n.*

a·lee (uh–) *adv.* & *adj.* leeward.

ale·house *n.* a place where ale is sold and served; saloon.

a·lem·bic (uh·LEM–) *n.* a device formerly used for distilling; hence, something which purifies.

a·lert (uh·LURT) *adj.* **1** awake to danger. **2** lively; quick to perceive. ***—n.*** a signal warning of danger; also, a period of danger: *an air raid* ~. ***—v.*** warn. **—on the alert** on the lookout: *always on the* ~ *for new developments.* **—a·lert·ly** *adv.* **—a·lert·ness** *n.*

A·leut (uh·LOOT) *n.* an aboriginal of the Aleutian Islands; also, the language of the Aleuts; also **A·leu·tian** (uh·LOO·shun) *n.* & *adj.* **—Aleutian Islands** a chain of islands forming an arc westward from Alaska.

ale·wife *n.* **-wives** a herringlike fish used for food, fertilizer, etc.

Al·ex·an·der the Great (al·ig·ZAN·dur) 356–323 B.C. king of Macedonia and conqueror of lands as far east as India. **—Al·ex·an·dri·a** (–dree·uh) a city of Egypt. **—Al·ex·an·dri·an** (–un) *adj.* having to do with Alexander the Great, Alexandria, or Hellenistic Greece. **—al·ex·an·drine** *n.* an iambic hexameter verse; also ***adj.***

a·lex·i·a (uh·LEX·ee·uh) *n.* inability to read caused by brain damage.

al·fal·fa (–FAL–) *n.* a cloverlike plant used as fodder.

Al·fred (AL·frid) **the Great** A.D. 849–899, king of England.

al·fres·co (–FRES–) *adj.* & *adv.* outdoors: *an* ~ *lunch.*

alg. algebra.

al·ga (AL·guh) *n.,pl.* **-gae** (–jee) a primitive form of plant life such as seaweeds or pond scum. **—al·gal** (–gul) *adj.*

al·ge·bra (AL·juh·bruh) *n.* a branch of mathematics that uses symbols in place of quantities. **—al·ge·bra·ic** (–BRAY–) or **-i·cal** *adj.* **—al·ge·bra·ic·al·ly** *adv.* **—al·ge·bra·ist** (AL·juh·bray–) *n.*

Al·ge·ri·a (al·JEER·ee·uh) a country of N. Africa; 919,595 sq.mi. (2,381,741 km²); *cap.* **Al·giers. —Al·ge·ri·an** *adj.* & *n.*

ALGOL or **Algol** (AL·gol) an algebraic computer language.

Al·gon·qui·an (al·GONG·kee·un) *n.* **1** a large family of Amerindian languages. **2** an Indian of an Algonquian tribe. Also **Al·gon·ki·an. —Al·gon·quin** (–GONG–) *n.* (a member of) any of certain tribes that lived in the Ottawa River valley; also, their Algonquian language.

al·go·rithm (AL·guh–) *n.* a set of rules in a mathematical operation for solving a problem; also **al·go·rism.**

a·li·as (AY·lee·us) *adv.* also called: *Jones,* ~ *Johnson.* ***—n.*** an assumed name.

al·i·bi (AL·i·bye) *n.* **1** a claim that one was elsewhere when a crime of which one is accused was committed. **2** *Informal.* an excuse; also ***v.*** **-bis, -bied, -bi·ing.**

al·ien (AIL·yun) *n.* a foreigner. ***—adj.*** **1** foreign; of aliens: ~ *registration.* **2** of a different character; contrary: *Communism is* ~ *to the American way of life.* **—al·ien·ate** *v.* **-ates, -at·ed, -at·ing** **1** transfer to a new owner; **al·ien·a·ble** *adj.* **2** cause to be withdrawn, estranged, or separated: *youth* ~*d from society.* **—al·ien·a·tion** (–NAY–) *n.* a transferring; withdrawal: *A third party is sued for* **alienation of affection** *between spouses.* **—al·ien·ist** *n.* a psychiatrist testifying in court.

a·light (uh–) *v.* **-lights,** *pt.* & *pp.* **-light·ed** or **a·lit** (uh·LIT), **-light·ing** **1** descend: *to* ~ *from a cab.* **2** set down; land; perch: *The bird* ~*ed on a branch.* ***—adj.*** lit; on fire; bright.

a·lign (uh·LINE) *v.* **1** arrange in a line. **2** line up with: *He* ~*ed himself with the Republicans.* Also **a·line, a·lines, a·lined, a·lin·ing.** **—a·lign·ment** or **a·line·ment** *n.*

a·like (uh–) *adj.* similar: *They are all* ~. ***—adv.*** similarly; in the same way: *The law treats everyone* ~. **—a·like·ness** *n.*

al·i·ment (AL·i·munt) *n.* food for the body. **—al·i·men·ta·ry** (al·i·MEN·tuh·ree) *adj.;* **ali-**

mentary canal the digestive system, which extends from the mouth to the anus; also called **alimentary tract.** —**al·i·men·ta·tion** (–TAY–) *n.* nourishment. —**al·i·mo·ny** (AL·i·moh·nee) *n.* **-nies** an allowance paid by one spouse (usu. the husband) to the other in case of separation or divorce.

aline, alinement See ALIGN.

al·i·phat·ic (al·i·FAT·ic) *adj.* pertaining to a class of hydrocarbons in which the carbon atoms are joined in open chains instead of rings.

al·i·quot (AL·i·kwut) *adj.* dividing evenly into another number: *3 is an ~ part of 27.*

alit a *pt.* & *pp.* of ALIGHT.

a·live (uh·LIVE) *adj.* **1** living: *keeping a patient ~.* **2** active: *A claim must be kept ~.* **3** lively. —**alive to** conscious of. —**alive with:** *a town ~ with tourists.* —**a·live·ness** *n.*

alk. alkali(ne).

al·ka·li (AL·kuh·lye) *n.* **-li(e)s** a substance such as soda or potash that combines with acids to form salts. —**al·ka·line** *adj.: ~ soil;* **al·ka·lin·i·ty** (–LIN–) *n.* —**al·ka·lize** or **al·ka·lin·ize** *v.* **-(l)iz·es, -(l)ized, -(l)iz·ing** make alkaline. —**al·ka·loid** *n.* a bitter, nitrogenous organic compound of vegetable origin, such as morphine or quinine; **al·ka·loid(·al)** (–LOID·ul) *adj.*

al·kyd (–kid) *n.* a synthetic resin used in protective coatings such as paints and lacquers.

all (AWL) *adj.* the whole number, amount, extent, etc.: *~ men are mortal; Why punish her, of ~ people? They came with ~ possible speed.* —***pron.*** the whole; everyone: *~ of them are hard workers; ~ (of) the boys were hiding;* **in all** altogether. —***n.:*** *You must give your ~ for this cause.* —***adv.*** wholly; quite: *a child left ~ by himself; I said ~ along not to come; I'm ~ for the idea.* —**all but** almost: *The job is ~ but done.* —**all in** *Informal.* very tired. —**all in all** as a whole: *~ in ~, it was a fair deal.* —**all out** with full effort: *They went ~ out to help the refugees.* —**all over** *Informal.* characteristically: *That's her mother ~ over.* —**all the** so much: *I feel ~ the worse for the medication.* —**all told** altogether: *The trip cost me $100 ~ told.*

Al·lah (AL·uh, AH·luh) *n.* in Islam, the supreme being; God.

all-A·mer·i·can *adj.* **1** wholly American. **2** the best American: *an ~ team; ~ quarterback.* —**all-a·round** same as ALL-ROUND.

al·lay (uh·LAY) *v.* **1** make less; alleviate; lighten. **2** put to rest: *~ one's fears.*

all-clear *n.* a signal indicating the end of an air raid or other danger.

al·lege (uh·LEJ) *v.* **al·leg·es, al·leged, al·leg·ing** **1** to state without proof. **2** put forward as an accusation, claim, or excuse: *He ~d poverty for not paying his bills.* —**al·le·ga·tion** (al·i·GAY·shun) *n.* —**alleged** *adj.: The motive ~ is not convincing; The ~ thief is missing.* —**al·leg·ed·ly** (–id–) *adv.*

Al·le·ghe·ny (al·uh·GAY·nee) **Mountains** a mountain range extending from Pennsylvania to Virginia; also **Al·le·ghe·nies.**

al·le·giance (uh·LEE·junce) *n.* fidelity or loyalty to one's country, a government, person, or cause: *an oath of ~ to the United States.*

al·le·go·ry (AL·uh·gor·ee) *n.* **-ries** a story or description of which the persons, places, and events stand for abstract ideas or moral truths such as patience and purity. —**al·le·gor·ic** (–GOR–) or **-i·cal** *adj.* —**al·le·gor·i·cal·ly** *adv.* —**al·le·go·rist** (AL·uh–) *n.* one who writes an allegory.

al·le·gro (uh·LEG·roh) *adj.* & *adv.* *Music.* in quick time. —***n.,*** *pl.* **-os** a musical passage played in quick time. —**al·le·gret·to** (al·uh·GRET·oh) *adj.* & *adv.* slower than allegro; also ***n.***

al·le·lu·ia (al·uh·LOO·yuh) *interj.* same as HALLELUJAH.

Al·len·town (AL–) a city in Pennsylvania.

al·ler·gy (AL·ur·jee) *n.* **-gies** an abnormal sensitivity to the point of sickness to particular things such as foods, smoke, dust, or insect venom. —**al·ler·gic** (uh·LUR·jic) *adj.* sensitive; hence, disinclined: *He seems ~ to math.* —**al·ler·gen** (AL·ur·jun) *n.* something that causes an allergy; **al·ler·gen·ic** (–JEN–) *adj.* —**al·ler·gist** (AL·ur·jist) *n.* an allergy specialist.

al·le·vi·ate (–LEE–) *v.* **-ates, -at·ed, -at·ing** make (pain, suffering, etc.) more bearable; lessen; relieve: *to ~ misery.* —**al·le·vi·a·tive** (–uh·tiv) or **-a·to·ry** *adj.* —**al·le·vi·a·tion** (–AY–) *n.*

al·ley (AL·ee) *n.* **al·leys** **1** a narrow passage or lane between rows of buildings; also **al·ley·way.** **2** a long narrow lane along which balls are rolled in the game of bowling. —**up** (or **down**) **one's alley** *Informal.* in one's area of special interest. —**alley cat** a stray cat.

all-fired *adj.* & *adv.* *Slang.* extreme(ly): *His ~ nerve!* —**All Fools' Day** April 1, April Fools' Day. —**All·hal·lows** (–HAL·oze) *n.* same as ALL SAINTS' DAY.

al·li·ance (uh·LYE·unce) *n.* a union, association, or relationship. —**allied** See ALLY.

al·li·ga·tor (AL·i·gay·tur) *n.* a reptile similar to the crocodile, found in certain lakes and rivers. —**alligator pear** an avocado.

all-im·por·tant *adj.* of the greatest importance. —**all-in·clu·sive** *adj.* inclusive of everything: *an ~ charge.*

al·lit·er·ate (uh·LIT–) *v.* **-ates, -at·ed, -at·ing** have or use the same initial sound in successive words, as in "Cossack commanders cannonading came." —**al·lit·er·a·tive** (–uh·tiv) *adj.: ~ verse;* **al·lit·er·a·tive·ly** *adv.;* **al·lit·er·a·tor** *n.* —**al·lit·er·a·tion** (–AY–) *n.*

all-night·er *n.* something lasting all night: *He studied in ~s and cram sessions.*

al·lo·cate (AL·uh–) *v.* **-cates, -cat·ed, -cat·ing** set aside; assign; allot: *~ funds for educa-*

tion. **—al·lo·ca·tion** (–CAY–) *n.* **—al·lo·ca·ble** (AL·uh·kuh·bl) *adj.*

al·lot (uh–) *v.* **al·lots, al·lot·ted, al·lot·ting** apportion or assign; also, distribute: *Ten minutes were ~d to each candidate.* **—al·lot·ment** *n.*

all-out *adj.* using all resources: *an ~ effort to win.* **—all·o·ver** *adj.* covering the whole surface: *an ~ pattern.*

al·low (uh·LOU) *v.* **1** permit; let have, be, or do: *No visitors ~ed after 5 p.m.; He ~s his son $2 a week.* **2** agree to; grant; concede: *The judge ~ed the claim.* **—allow for** make concession for: *~ for his age in judging his guilt.* **—allow of** admit of: *This rule ~s of no exception.* **—al·low·a·ble** *adj.* **—al·low·ance** *n.* **—al·low·ed·ly** (–id–) *adv.*

al·loy (AL·oy, uh·LOY) *n.* **1** a combination of two metals; also, the degree of purity of a metal. **2** anything added that lowers quality. ***—v.*** mix with something (as another metal) of lower quality; hence, debase.

all right **1** in good order; adequately; satisfactory: *I felt sick, but I'm ~ now; doing ~ in school.* **2** yes, certainly. Hence **all-right** *adj. Slang.* **—all-round** *adj.* good in every way: *an ~ student.* **—All Saints' Day** November 1, a day to commemorate Christian saints; Allhallows. **—All Souls' Day** November 2, a day of prayer for the dead. **—all·spice** *n.* the spice obtained from the berry of a West Indian tree of the myrtle family. **—all-time** *adj. Informal.* never surpassed: *an ~ record.*

al·lude (uh·LOOD) *v.* **al·ludes, al·lud·ed, al·lud·ing** refer indirectly: *The speaker ~d to his past.* **—al·lu·sion** (uh·LOO·zhun) *n.* **—al·lu·sive** (–siv) *adj.;* **al·lu·sive·ly** *adv.;* **al·lu·sive·ness** *n.*

al·lure (uh·LOOR) *v.* **al·lures, al·lured, al·lur·ing** entice by charm; fascinate. ***—n.*** charm; fascination: *the ~ of riches;* also **al·lure·ment.** **—al·lur·ing** *adj.* fascinating: *an ~ portrait.* **—al·lur·ing·ly** *adv.*

allusion, allusive See ALLUDE.

al·lu·vi·um (uh·LOO·vee·um) *n.* **-vi·ums** or **-vi·a** (–vee·uh) deposit of sand or mud left by flowing water, as on a river bed; also **al·lu·vi·on.** **—al·lu·vi·al** *adj.: ~ soil; an ~ deposit.*

al·ly (uh·LYE, AL·eye) *v.* **al·lies, al·lied, al·ly·ing** unite by some relationship or bond. ***—n., pl.*** **al·lies** one united to another: *The U.S. and Britain were the chief* **Allies** *in World War II.* **—allied** *adj.: English and Dutch are ~ languages; ~ interests.*

al·ma ma·ter (AL·muh·MAH·tur) the school, college, or university where one was educated; also, its official anthem.

al·ma·nac (AWL·muh–) *n.* an annual publication giving information geared to the calendar about the sun, moon, and tides and miscellaneous other data.

al·might·y (awl·MYE·tee) *adj.* all-powerful. **—the Almighty** God.

al·mond (AH·mund, AL–) *n.* an edible nut of a tree related to the plum and peach; also, the tree itself. ***—adj.*** having the shape of an almond, oval with pointed ends: *an ~-eyed Oriental beauty.*

al·mon·er (AL·muh·nur, AH–) *n.* one whose job is to distribute alms.

al·most (AWL·mohst, –MOHST) *adv.* **1** nearly: *I am ~ finished.* **2** [with a negative] scarcely any; practically: *She said ~ nothing of importance in the lecture.*

alms (AHMZ) *n.pl.* money, clothes, food, etc. given to the poor as charity. **—alms·house** *n.* a home for poor people.

al·oe (AL·oh) *n.* **al·oes** **1** a fleshy South African plant of the lily family: *The century plant is often called "American ~."* **2** **aloes** [with *sing. v.*] a purgative prepared from the juice of this plant.

a·loft (uh–) *adv.* up high; in the air.

a·lo·ha (uh·LOH·huh) *interj.* Hawaiian greeting or farewell.

a·lone (uh·LONE) *adj.* **1** by oneself; solitary: *He stood ~.* **2** only: *God ~ knows what happened; She lives for money ~.* Also ***adv.*** **—let alone** not to mention: *He can't even afford a car, let ~ a house.* **—let** (or **leave**) **alone** not meddle with. **—let well enough alone** leave things as they are.

a·long (uh·LONG) *adv.* & *prep.* **1** from one end to the other: *Cars parked ~ the street.* **2** onward; on: *We were driving ~ the highway.* **3** together: *Bring your friends ~ (with you).* **—along about** *Informal.* of time, approaching: *~ about noon.* **—all along** all the time: *knew about her all ~.* **—be along** *Informal.* be there: *Tell them I'll be ~.* **—a·long·shore** *adv.* by the shore. **—a·long·side** *adv.* & *prep.* side by side (with): *a bike driven ~ (of) a car.*

a·loof (uh·LOOF) *adj.* **1** at a distance. **2** reserved; apart: *He keeps ~ in company; an ~ manner.* Also ***adv.*** **—a·loof·ly** *adv.* **—a·loof·ness** *n.*

al·o·pe·ci·a (–PEE·shee·uh) *n.* baldness.

a·loud (uh–) *adv.* so as to be heard: *Read ~; to call ~* (i.e. loudly) *for help.*

alp *n.* a high mountain. See also ALPS.

al·pac·a (–PAC–) *n.* a South American animal that yields wool; also, its wool or a cloth made from it.

al·pen·glow (–gloh) *n.* a reddish glow on mountain peaks at sunrise and sunset. **—al·pen·horn** *n.* a long horn used in the Alps by herdsmen. **—al·pen·stock** *n.* an iron-tipped stick used in mountain-climbing.

al·pha (AL·fuh) *n.* the first letter of the Greek alphabet. **—alpha and omega** the beginning and the end. **—al·pha·bet** *n.* the letters used to write a language; the ABC. **—al·pha·bet·ic** (–BET–) or **-i·cal** *adj.* using an alphabet; in the order of the letters of the alphabet; **al·pha·bet·i·cal·ly** *adv.* **—al·pha·bet·ize** (AL–) *v.* **-iz·es, -ized, -iz·ing** put in alphabetical order;

al·pha·bet·iz·er *n.* **—al·pha·nu·mer·ic** (–MER–) *adj.* pertaining to letters and numbers: *an ~ code.* **—alpha particle** a positively charged particle, consisting of two protons and two neutrons, given off by a radioactive substance, a rapid stream of which is an **alpha ray. —alpha rhythm** the rhythmic activity of the brain as observable on an electroencephalograph, normally at between 8 and 13 cycles per second; also called **alpha wave.**

alp·horn *n.* same as ALPENHORN.

al·pine *adj.* of or having to do with high mountains: *an ~ hut.* **—al·pin·ism** *n.* mountain-climbing, esp. in the Alps; **al·pin·ist** *n.* **—Alps** a mountain system of Europe extending from S. France to Yugoslavia; **Al·pine** *adj.*

al·read·y (awl·RED·ee) *adv.* by now; before a specified time: *When I reached the station, the train had ~ left.*

al·right (awl·RITE) *adj.* & *adv. Nonstandard.* all right.

Al·sace (al·SAS) a region of N.E. France bordering on Germany. **—Al·sa·tian** (–SAY–) *adj.* pertaining to Alsace; also **n. 1** a person from Alsace. **2** *Brit.* a German shepherd dog.

al·so (AWL·soh) *adv.* too; as well. **—al·so-ran** *n. Informal.* a defeated candidate, contestant, etc.

alt. alteration; alternate; altitude; alto.

Alta. Alberta.

al·tar (AWL·tur) *n.* a raised structure or table used in divine worship. **—altar boy** a boy who assists a priest at ceremonies. **—al·tar·piece** *n.* a painting or other work of art at the back of an altar.

al·ter (AWL–) *v.* change; modify; become different: *to ~ clothes to suit a fashion.* **—al·ter·a·ble** (–uh·bl) *adj.* **—al·ter·a·tion** (–RAY–) *n.*

al·ter·ca·tion (awl·tur·CAY–) *n.* a noisy argument; quarrel.

al·ter e·go (AWL·tur·EE·goh) a second self; also, an intimate friend.

al·ter·nate (AWL–) *v.* **-nates, -nat·ed, -nat·ing** occur, arrange, or do by turns. ***—adj.*** (–nit) **1** following each other by turns: *John and I do the dishes on ~ days.* **2** alternative: *switching from gas and oil to* **alternate energy** *sources such as the sun, wind, water, and wood power.* ***—n.*** (–nit) a substitute. **—al·ter·nate·ly** *adv.* in turn: *As she told the story of her escape, she cried and laughed ~.* **—alternating current** an electric current whose direction changes at regular intervals. **—al·ter·na·tion** (–NAY–) *n.* **—al·ter·na·tive** (awl·TUR·nuh·tiv) *n.* an option between two possibilities: *He had no ~ but to resign his position;* ***adj.:*** *an ~ plan;* **al·ter·na·tive·ly** *adv.* **—al·ter·na·tor** (AWL–) *n.* a generator that produces alternating current.

al·though (awl·DHOH) *conj.* in spite of the fact that.

al·tim·e·ter (al·TIM·i·tur) *n.* a barometer for showing altitude. **—al·ti·tude** *n.* height above sea level; also, a place of high elevation: *There is little vegetation at these ~s.* **—al·ti·tu·di·nal** (–TUE–) *adj.*

al·to (AL·toh) *n.* **-tos** the lowest female voice; also, a singer or instrument in this range of voice.

al·to·geth·er (awl·tuh·GEDH·ur) *adv.* entirely; wholly; on the whole. **—in the altogether** *Informal.* in the nude.

al·tru·ism *n.* selfless concern for the welfare of others; opposed to EGOISM. **—al·tru·ist** *n.* **—al·tru·is·tic** (–IS–) *adj.* **—al·tru·is·ti·cal·ly** *adv.*

¹al·um *n.* a colorless crystalline compound of aluminum used medically and in manufacturing. **—a·lu·mi·na** (uh·LOO·mi·nuh) *n.* an oxide of aluminum used in abrasives and ceramics. **—a·lu·mi·num** (–LOO–) *n.* a silvery white malleable and ductible metal widely used in alloys; also, *Brit.* **al·u·min·i·um** (–MIN–). **—a·lu·mi·nize** (–LOO–) *v.* **-niz·es, -nized, -niz·ing** cover or treat with aluminum.

²a·lum (uh·LUM) *n. Informal.* alumnus or alumna. **—a·lum·na** (uh·LUM·nuh) *n., pl.* **-nae** (–nee) a former female student of a particular school; **a·lum·nus** *n.,pl.* **-ni** (–nye) a former male student.

al·ve·o·lus (al·VEE–) *n.,pl.* **-li** (–lye) a small cavity or hollow, as a tooth socket. **—al·ve·o·lar** (–lur) *adj.* pertaining to a hollow, esp. of the sockets of the teeth; *t, d, and s are ~ sounds made by touching the tongue tip to the ridges of the teeth.*

al·ways (AWL·waze, –wiz) *adv.* at all times; forever; also, repeatedly: *He is ~ late; She is ~ asking to go to the movies.*

am first person sing. pres. indic. of BE. **—Am** Americium. **—Am.** America; American. **—AM** amplitude modulation; ante meridiem (also **a.m.**). **—A.M.** Master of Arts.

A.M.A. American Medical Association.

a·mah (AH·muh) *n.* in the East, a maidservant, esp. a nursemaid.

a·main (uh–) *adv. Archaic.* at full speed; hastily; with full strength.

a·mal·gam (uh·MAL·gum) *n.* a mercury alloy; hence, any blending or union, esp. of organizations. **—a·mal·ga·mate** *v.* **-mates, -mat·ed, -mat·ing** unite; combine; **a·mal·ga·ma·tor** *n.* **—a·mal·ga·ma·tion** (–MAY–) *n.*

a·man·u·en·sis (uh·man·yoo·EN–) *n., pl.* **-ses** (–seez) a secretary.

am·a·ranth *n. Poetic.* a flower that never fades. **—am·a·ranth·ine** (–RANTH·in) *adj.*

Am·a·ril·lo (am·uh·RIL·oh) a city of Texas.

am·a·ryl·lis (am·uh·RIL·is) *n.* any of a large family of often lilylike flowers.

a·mass (uh·MAS) *v.* heap up; accumulate. **—a·mass·ment** *n.*

am·a·teur (AM·uh·chur, –tur) *n.* one who engages in a hobby, sport, or other activity for the love of it rather than for money; a nonprofessional. —***adj.:*** ~ *sport;* ~ *painter.* —**am·a·teur·ism** *n.* —**am·a·teur·ish** (–TUR–) *adj.* unskilled; **am·a·teur·ish·ly** *adv.;* **am·a·teur·ish·ness** *n.*

am·a·tive (AM·uh·tiv) *adj.* disposing to love or sex; amorous. —**am·a·tive·ly** *adv.* —**am·a·tive·ness** *n.* —**am·a·to·ry** *adj.* pertaining to sexual love: ~ *poems.*

a·maze (uh–) **a·maz·es, a·mazed, a·maz·ing** surprise; cause wonder; astonish. —**a·maze·ment** *n.* —**a·maz·ing** *adj.* —**a·maz·ing·ly** *adv.*

Am·a·zon (AM·uh·zon) **1** *n.* in Greek myths, one of a warriorlike race of women; **amazon** a strong aggressive woman. **2** a river of South America that flows through Brazil into the Atlantic. —**Am·a·zo·ni·an** (–ZOH·nee·un) *adj.*

amb. ambassador. —**am·bas·sa·dor** (–BAS–) *n.* the resident representative of a foreign government. —**am·bas·sa·do·ri·al** (–DOR–) *adj.* —**am·bas·sa·dor·ship** *n.*

am·ber *n.* a yellowish-brown fossil resin used in jewelry. —***adj.*** of the color of amber: *an* ~ *traffic light.* —**am·ber·gris** *n.* a waxy substance from the intestines of sperm whales that is used as a fixative in perfume-making.

ambi- *comb.form.* both: as in *ambivalent.* —**am·bi·dex·trous** (–DEX·trus) *adj.* able to use both hands equally well; hence, skillful or versatile; also, deceitful or double-dealing; **am·bi·dex·trous·ly** *adv.;* **am·bi·dex·ter·i·ty** (–TER–) *n.* —**am·bi·ence** or **am·bi·ance** (–bee·unce) *n.* a surrounding atmosphere or environment; **am·bi·ent** *adj.: a summit concealed by* ~ *clouds.* —**am·big·u·ous** (–BIG–) *adj.* having more than one meaning; vague; dubious; **am·big·u·ous·ly** *adv.;* **am·bi·gu·i·ty** (–GYOO–) or **am·big·u·ous·ness** (–BIG·yoo–) *n.* —**am·bit** *n.* **1** a sphere of influence or authority. **2** circuit; bounds. —**am·bi·tion** (–BISH–) *n.* a strong desire to achieve a goal; also, the goal, object, or purpose desired; **am·bi·tious** *adj.: an* ~ *young man;* **am·bi·tious·ly** *adv.;* **am·bi·tious·ness** *n.* —**am·biv·a·lence** (–BIV–) *n.* the existence of contrary feelings toward the same object or person; **am·biv·a·lent** *adj.*

am·ble *n.* a leisurely, easy gait, as of a horse. —***v.*** **-bles, -bled, -bling** move at an amble; saunter; **am·bler** *n.*

am·bro·sia (am·BROH·zhuh) *n.* in classical myths, the food of the gods; also, anything delicious. —**am·bro·sial** *adj.* delicious; divine; also **am·bro·sian.** —**Ambrosian** *adj.* pertaining to **St. Ambrose,** a bishop of Milan in the fourth century: ~ *chant;* ~ *hymn.*

am·bu·lance (AM·byuh·lunce) *n.* a vehicle equipped to transport the sick or wounded. —**am·bu·lant** *adj.* walking about. —**am·bu·la·to·ry** *adj.* pertaining to walking: ~ *medical care;* ***n., pl.*** **-ries** a sheltered place for walking, as in a cloister.

am·bus·cade (AM–) *n.* same as **am·bush** *n.* a lying in wait to attack by surprise. Also ***v.*** **-cades, -cad·ed, -cad·ing** or **-bush·es, -bushed, -bush·ing:** *The enemy was* ~*d and defeated.*

a·me·ba, a·me·bic, a·me·boid (uh·MEE–) same as AMOEBA, AMOEBIC, AMOEBOID.

a·mel·io·rate (uh·MEEL·yuh–) *v.* **-rates, -rat·ed, -rat·ing** become or cause to become better; improve; **a·mel·io·ra·tive** (–tiv) *adj.* —**a·mel·io·ra·tion** (–RAY–) *n.*

a·men (ay·MEN, ah–) *interj.* used to express agreement, esp. to a prayer.

a·me·na·ble (uh·MEE·nuh·bl, uh·MEN–) *adj.* **1** responsive; tractable; agreeable: *a child* ~ *to reason.* **2** responsible: ~ *to the law.* —**a·me·na·bly** *adv.;* **a·me·na·ble·ness** or **a·me·na·bil·i·ty** (–BIL–) *n.*

a·mend (uh–) *v.* **1** make free from flaws; improve: *to* ~ *one's life.* **2** change the wording of or revise a law or other document. —**a·mend·ment** *n.* —**a·mends** *n.pl.* [takes *sing.* or *pl. v.*] compensation for harm or hurt; reparation: *His later conduct was* ~ *enough for the past; made* ~ *for his misdeeds.*

a·men·i·ty (uh·MEN–, –MEEN–) *n.* **-ties 1** agreeableness; pleasantness; also, something that makes life pleasant or easy: *a hotel with sauna, color TV, and such* ~*s.* **2 amenities** *pl.* niceties of social behavior; civilities; courtesies.

Amer. America; American. —**Am·er·a·sian** (–uh·RAY–) *adj.* of mixed Asian and American parentage; also ***n.***

a·merce (uh·MURCE) *v.* **a·merc·es, a·merced, a·merc·ing** impose a fine on; hence, punish: *The criminal was* ~*d $50 by the court.* —**a·merce·ment** *n.*

A·mer·i·ca (uh·MER·i·cuh) the United States of America; also, North America or South America. —**the Americas** North, Central, and South America. —**A·mer·i·can** (–cun) *n.* **1** a person of or from North or South America, esp. a United States citizen. **2** English as used in the U.S.; also **American English.** —**American** *adj.* pertaining to America, the Americas, or their peoples or cultures. —**A·mer·i·can·a** (–CAN·uh) *n.pl.* things characteristic of American civilization or culture: *a treasure house of* ~. —**American Indian** a member of any of the aboriginal peoples of the Americas, excepting Eskimos; also, any of their languages. —**A·mer·i·can·ism** *n.* **1** something typically American, esp. a word or usage originating in or peculiar to American English. **2** loyalty to the U.S. or devotion to its traditions and institutions. —**A·mer·i·can·ize** *v.* **-iz·es, -ized, -iz·ing; A·mer·i·can·i·za·tion** (–ZAY–) *n.* —**American Legion** an organization of U.S. war veterans, founded in 1919. —**American plan** a hotel charging rate that includes room and meals; cf. EUROPEAN PLAN. —**American Revolution** the war (1775–1783) between Britain and her

North American colonies by which the U.S. won her independence; Revolutionary War. —**American Samoa** a U.S. territory in the South Pacific, consisting of seven islands; 76 sq. mi. (197 km^2); *cap.* Pago Pago. —**am•er•ic•i•um** (am·uh·RISH·ee·um) *n.* a white radioactive metallic element. —**Am•er•ind** (AM·uh–) *n.* an American Indian or Eskimo. —**Am•er•ind•i•an** (–IND–) *n.* & *adj.* American Indian.

am•e•thyst (AM·uh·thist) *n.* a purple or violet quartz or corundum used as a gem; also, its color. —**am•e•thys•tine** (–THIS·tin) *adj.*

Am•ex (AM·eks) American Stock Exchange.

a•mi•a•ble (AY·mee·uh·bl) *adj.* friendly; good-natured. —**a•mi•a•bil•i•ty** (–BIL–) or **a•mi•a•ble•ness** *n.* —**a•mi•a•bly** *adv.* —**am•i•ca•ble** (AM·i·cuh–) *adj.* showing good will; peaceable: *an ~ settlement.* —**am•i•ca•bly** *adv.* —**am•i•ca•bil•i•ty** (–BIL–) *n.*

a•mid (uh–) *prep.* in the midst of; among.

am•ide *n.* an organic compound derived from ammonia, such as acetamide or sodamide.

a•mid•ships (–MID–) *adv.* toward the middle of a ship (between bow and stern); also **a•mid•ship.** —**a•midst** same as AMID.

a•mi•go (uh·MEE·goh) *n.* **-gos** (–goze) *Spanish.* a friend.

a•mi•no (uh·MEE·noh) **acid** any of various complex organic compounds that combine to form proteins.

A•mish (AH–, AM–) *n.pl.* a Mennonite sect founded in the 17th century by the Swiss Jacob Ammann; ***adj.:*** *an ~ community.*

a•miss (uh–) *adj.* & *adv.* out of place; wrong; wrongly: *Something went ~ with the arrangements.* —**to take amiss** be offended by: *Don't take my remarks ~.*

am•i•ty (–tee) *n.* **-ties** friendly relations: *to live together in ~.*

Am•man (AH·mahn) capital of Jordan.

am•me•ter (AM·ee·tur) *n.* an instrument for measuring an electric current.

am•mo (AM·oh) *n. Slang.* ammunition.

am•mo•nia (uh·MOH·nyuh) *n.* a strong-smelling, colorless gaseous compound of hydrogen and nitrogen, used in refrigeration and in making fertilizers and explosives; also, this dissolved in water, called **ammonia water** or **am•mo•ni•um** (–nee·um) **hydroxide.**

am•mu•ni•tion (am·yuh·NISH·un) *n.* **1** projectiles such as bullets, shells, grenades, and rockets, with their fuzes, charges, and primers. **2** material for attack or defense: *The scandal provided ~ for press attacks against the government.*

am•ne•sia (am·NEE·zhuh) *n.* loss of memory. —**am•ne•si•ac** or **am•ne•sic** (–zik) *adj.* & *n.*

am•nes•ty (–tee) *n.* **-ties** a general pardon granted by a government, esp. to political offenders. —***v.*** **-ties, -tied** (–teed), **-ty•ing** pardon.

am•ni•o•cen•te•sis (am·nee·oh·sen·TEE·sis) *n.* a test for detecting abnormalities of a fetus by drawing and examining a sample of the **am•ni•ot•ic** (–OT–) **fluid** from the **am•ni•on** (AM·nee·un), a membranous sac enclosing the fetus in the womb.

a•moe•ba (uh·MEE·buh) *n.* **-bas** or **-bae** (–bee) a microscopic, one-celled organism that multiplies by fission and is found in soil and water. —**a•moe•bic** *adj.* pertaining to or caused by amoebas: *~ dysentery.* —**a•moe•boid** *adj.* like an amoeba, esp. in changing shape.

a•mok (uh·MUK, –MOK) *adv.* **run amok** rush about wildly in a murderous frenzy.

a•mong (uh·MUNG) *prep.* **1** in the middle of: *a town nestled ~ the hills.* **2** one of: *Einstein is ~ the greatest men of science.* **3** to, with, by, etc. (a group): *to share $100 ~ five people.* **4** with (one another): *Discuss it ~ yourselves.* Also **amongst.**

a•mon•til•la•do (uh·mon·tuh·LAH·doh) *n.* **-dos** a pale dry sherry.

a•mor•al (ay·MOR·ul) *adj.* neither moral nor immoral; nonmoral. —**a•mo•ral•i•ty** (ay·mo·RAL–) *n.* —**a•mor•al•ly** *adv.*

am•o•rous (–uh·rus) *adj.* of or pertaining to love, esp. sexual: *~ verse; ~ glances.* —**am•o•rous•ly** *adv.* —**am•o•rous•ness** *n.*

a•mor•phous (uh·MOR·fus) *adj.* **1** with no definite shape or form. **2** not crystalline: *~ glass, minerals.* —**a•mor•phous•ly** *adv.* —**a•mor•phous•ness** *n.*

am•or•tize (AM·ur·tize, uh·MOR·tize) *v.* **-tiz•es, -tized, -tiz•ing** end (a mortgage, debt, etc.) by installment payments. —**am•or•ti•za•tion** (–ZAY–) *n.*

A•mos (AY·mus) *n.* book of the Old Testament attributed to the prophet Amos, 8th century B.C.

a•mount (uh–) *n.* the total, aggregate, or entire number or quantity: *$1 million is a large ~ of money; No ~ of discussion will help.* —***v.*** add up (to); be equal (to): *His debts ~ to $1,000; disloyalty ~ing to treason.*

a•mour (uh·MOOR) *n.* a love affair, esp. one that is illicit. —**amour pro•pre** (–PROH·pruh) *French.* self-respect.

amp. *Abbrev.* for **am•pere** (AM·peer) *n.* a unit of electric current, equal to one coulomb per second. —**am•per•age** (–puh·rij) *n.* the strength of an electric current in amperes.

am•per•sand *n.* the character "&" meaning "and."

am•phet•a•mine (am·FET·uh·meen, –min) *n.* a drug composed of carbon, hydrogen, and nitrogen, or one of its derivatives, used as a nasal decongestant or as a stimulant.

amphi- *comb.form.* on both sides; on all sides: as in *amphitheater, amphibious.* —**am•phib•i•an** (am·FIB·ee·un) *n.* an animal such as a frog or seal that can live in water and on land; also, a vehicle such as an aircraft, tank, or truck that can operate on land and water; also ***adj.***

—**am·phib·i·ous** (–us) *adj.* adapted for or carried out on land and water: *an ~ attack by ~ troops;* **am·phib·i·ous·ly** *adv.;* **am·phib·i·ous·ness** *n.* —**am·phi·bole** *n.* a rock-forming mineral such as asbestos or hornblende composed mainly of silica, calcium, magnesium, and iron. —**am·phi·bol·ic** (–BOL–) *adj.* —**am·phib·o·lite** (–FIB·uh–) *n.* an igneous or metamorphic rock consisting chiefly of amphibole. —**am·phi·the·a·ter** (AM·fi·thee·uh·tur) *n.* a building with an arena or stage in the middle and rows of seats rising around it. —**am·pho·ra** (–fuh·ruh) *n.* **-ras** or **-rae** (–ree) a jar with a narrow neck and two handles, used by the ancient Greeks and Romans for holding wine, oil, grain, etc.

am·pi·cil·lin (–CIL–) *n.* an antibiotic similar to but effective against more infections than penicillin.

am·ple *adj.* **-pler, -plest** large in size, capacity, amount, etc.; abundant; plentiful: *~ room for four passengers; an income that is ~ for all his needs; a man of ~ resources.* —**am·ple·ness** *n.* —**am·pli·fy** (–fye) *v.* **-fies, -fied, -fy·ing** make larger or stronger: *~ a narrative with details; ~ a voice or an electric current;* **am·pli·fi·ca·tion** (–CAY–) *n.* —**am·pli·fi·er** (–fye·ur) *n.* a device that amplifies. —**am·pli·tude** *n.* **1** breadth; largeness. **2** the extent to which a pendulum or a wave oscillates. —**amplitude modulation** or *AM,* changing of a radio wave's amplitude according to the signal to be transmitted; also, a broadcasting system using this; cf. FREQUENCY MODULATION. —**am·ply** (–plee) *adv.* in an ample manner.

am·pul(e) or **am·poule** (AM·pule,–pool) *n.* a small sealed glass vessel that holds a hypodermic injection solution.

am·pu·tate (AM·pyuh–) *v.* **-tates, -tat·ed, -tat·ing** cut off (a limb) by surgery. —**am·pu·ta·tion** (–TAY–) *n.* —**am·pu·tee** (–tee) *n.* one who has had a limb cut off.

Am·ster·dam the constitutional capital of the Netherlands.

amt. amount.

Am·trak a public U.S. corporation running intercity passenger trains.

amu or **AMU** atomic mass unit.

a·muck (uh·MUK) *adv.* same as AMOK.

am·u·let (AM·yuh·lit) *n.* something worn on one's person as protection against evil; charm; talisman.

a·muse (uh·MEWZ) *v.* **a·mus·es, a·mused, a·mus·ing** **1** provide diversion for; entertain. **2** make laugh, smile, etc. —**a·muse·ment** *n.* —**amusement park** a place of outdoor entertainment equipped with rides, booths for games, snack bars, etc.

AMVETS (AM·vets) an organization of American veterans, founded in 1944.

am·yl·ase (AM·uh–) *n.* the enzyme of saliva, pancreatic juice, and plant tissue that helps convert starch into sugar.

an (AN, 'n) *indef.art.* the form of A used when a vowel sound follows: *an honor; an event; an American.*

An·a·bap·tist (an·uh·BAP–) *n.* one of a Protestant sect opposed to infant baptism that originated in Switzerland about 1520.

a·nab·o·lism (uh·NAB·uh·lizm) *n.* the biological process by which food is converted into living tissue. —**an·a·bol·ic** (–BOL·ic) *adj.*

a·nach·ro·nism (uh·NAC·ruh·nizm) *n.* **1** an error of putting persons, things, or events together that are too far removed in time, e.g. *Alexander the Great cabled Washington.* **2** a person or thing that is out of its proper time. —**a·nach·ro·nis·tic** (–NIS–) or **-ti·cal** *adj.* —**a·nach·ro·nis·ti·cal·ly** *adv.*

an·a·con·da (an·uh·CON·duh) *n.* a large South American tropical snake that crushes its prey in its coils.

a·nad·ro·mous (uh·NAD·ruh·mus) *adj.* coming up from the sea to rivers for breeding, as salmon and shad do.

a·nae·mi·a (–NEE–) same as ANEMIA.

an·aer·obe (AN·uh·robe) *n.* an organism that can survive without oxygen, as bacteria. —**an·aer·o·bic** (–ROH–) *adj.*

an·aes·the·sia, etc. same as ANESTHESIA, etc.

an·a·gram (AN·uh–) *n.* a word formed by rearranging the letters of another word.

An·a·heim (AN·uh·hime) a city of S.W. California.

a·nal (AY·nul) *adj.* of or pertaining to the anus.

anal. analogous; analogy; analysis; analytic.

an·a·lects or **an·a·lect·a** (–LEC·tuh) *n.pl.* a collection of literary passages or sayings: *Confucian ~.*

an·al·ge·si·a (an·ul·JEE·zhuh) *n.* absence of the sense of pain. —**an·al·ge·sic** *adj.* painkilling; ***n.*** a pain-killing agent, such as a drug or ointment.

an·a·log(ue) (AN·uh·log) *n.* something similar or parallel to something else in certain respects: *The gill of a fish is the ~ of a lung; a meat ~ made from soya beans.* —**analog(ue) computer** a calculating device in which numbers correspond directly to quantities such as weights or lengths, as on a slide rule. —**a·nal·o·gous** (uh·NAL·uh·gus) *adj.* similar or comparable: *The wing of an insect is ~ to a bird's.* —**a·nal·o·gy** (uh·NAL·uh·jee) *n.* **-gies** **1** likeness or similarity between things. **2** a process of reasoning based on similarity. **3** a process of word formation based on similarity, as *cows* which replaced the earlier *kine.* Hence **an·a·log·i·cal** (–LOJ–) *adj.;* **an·a·log·i·cal·ly** *adv.*

a·nal·y·sis (uh·NAL·uh–) *n., pl.* **-ses** (–seez) **1** the separation of something into its parts; also, a statement of the result of doing this: *a chemical ~; an ~ of a poem.* **2** psychoanalysis. —**an·a·lyst** (AN·uh·list) *n.* one who makes an analysis, as a systems analyst or psychoanalyst. —**an·a·lyt·ic** (–LIT–) or **-i·cal**

adj. —**an·a·lyt·i·cal·ly** *adv.* —**an·a·lyze** (AN·uh–) *v.* **-lyz·es, -lyzed, -lyz·ing** make an analysis of; psychoanalyze. —**an·a·lyz·a·ble** (–LYE–) *adj.* —**an·a·lyz·er** *n.*

an·a·pest *n.* a foot of verse made up of two short or unaccented syllables followed by a long or accented one, as in "I am lord of the fowl and the brute"; also, a line of such verse. —**an·a·pest·ic** (–PEST–) *adj.*

an·ar·chy (AN·ur·kee) *n.* **-chies** absence of law and order; disorder. —**an·ar·chic** (uh·NAR·kic) or **-chi·cal** *adj.* —**an·ar·chism** *n.* abolition of government in favor of extreme personal liberty. —**an·ar·chist** *n.;* **an·ar·chis·tic** (–KIS–) *adj.*

anat. anatomical; anatomist; anatomy.

a·nath·e·ma (uh·NATH·uh·muh) *n.* a formal curse invoking damnation; also, an accursed person or thing; anything detestable. —**a·nath·e·ma·tize** *v.* **-tiz·es, -tized, -tiz·ing** curse.

An·a·to·li·a (–TOH–) Asia Minor. —**An·a·to·li·an** *n.* a group of languages of ancient Anatolia that includes Hittite; also ***adj.***

a·nat·o·mist (–NAT–) *n.* an anatomy expert. —**a·nat·o·mize** *v.* **-miz·es, -mized, -miz·ing** dissect; analyze. —**a·nat·o·my** (uh·NAT·uh·mee) *n.* **-mies** the science of the structure of animal bodies and their parts; also, a structure; an analysis: *the ~ of a murder.* —**an·a·tom·ic** (an·uh·TOM·ik) or **-i·cal** *adj.;* **an·a·tom·i·cal·ly** *adv.*

anc. ancient.

-ance or **-ence** *n. suffix* [indicating action, state, quality, or amount]: as in *dependence, resistance, abundance;* also **-ancy** or **-ency:** *truancy, consistency.*

an·ces·tor (AN·ses·tur) *n.* a person from whom one is descended; forebear; forerunner; *fem.* **an·ces·tress.** —**an·ces·tral** (–SES–) *adj.* —**an·ces·try** (AN·ces·tree) *n.* **-tries** lineage; line of ancestors.

an·chor (ANG·cur) *n.* a heavy object, usu. of metal, lowered by a cable to the bottom to hold a ship in place. —***v.*** secure or be secured, as a ship or balloon. —**ride at anchor** float while anchored. —**weigh anchor** take up the anchor. —**an·chor·age** (–ij) *n.* a place to anchor. —**An·chor·age** (ANG·cuh·rij) a city of Alaska.

an·cho·rite (ANG·cuh–) or **an·cho·ret** *n.* a hermit; *fem.* **an·cho·ress.**

anchor (man) a person in a sensitive or responsible position in a team, as the last one in a relay or the coordinator of a telecast.

an·cho·vy (AN·choh·vee) *n.* **-vies** or **-vy** a small herringlike fish.

an·cien re·gime (ahn·SYAHN·ray·ZHEEM) *French.* the old order, esp. of France before the Revolution.

an·cient (AYN·shunt) *adj.* belonging to olden days; also, very old. —***n.*** an aged person; **the ancients** people of ancient times, esp. of Greece and Rome. —**an·cient·ly** *adv.* —**an·cient·ness** *n.*

an·cil·lar·y (AN·si·ler·ee) *adj.* subsidiary; accessory; auxiliary: *Logic is ~ to philosophy.*

-ancy See -ANCE.

and *conj.* used to join words, phrases, clauses, sentences, etc.

an·dan·te (ahn·DAHN·tay) *Music. adj.* & *adv.* in moderately slow time; ***n.*** a musical passage in such time. —**an·dan·ti·no** (ahn·dahn·TEE·noh) *adj.* & *adv.* slightly quicker than andante; ***n.,*** *pl.* **-nos** a musical passage in this tempo.

An·des (Mountains) (AN·deez) a mountain range of W. South America, connected with the Rockies and extending from Venezuela to Tierra del Fuego. —**An·de·an** (AN·dee·un) *adj.*

and·i·ron (AN·dye·urn) *n.* one of a pair of metal holders for keeping logs in a fireplace.

and/or *conj.* used when *and* or *or* may be read as the connective: *cream and/or sugar* (i.e. either or both).

An·dor·ra (an·DOR·uh) a republic in the E. Pyrenees; 175 sq. mi. (453 km²); *cap.* **Andorra la Vella.**

andro- *comb.form.* male; masculine. —**an·dro·gen** (AN·druh·jun) *n.* a hormone that induces masculine characteristics; **an·dro·gen·ic** (–JEN–) *adj.* —**an·drog·e·nous** (–DROJ–) *adj.* producing male offspring. —**an·drog·y·nous** *adj.* having male and female characteristics; **an·drog·y·ny** (–nee) *n.* hermaphroditism. —**an·droid** *adj.* having human shape; ***n.*** such a creature, as a robot or automaton.

an·ec·dote (AN·ic–) *n.* a short humorous account of an incident in a person's life. —**an·ec·dot·al** (–DOH·tul) *adj.* —**an·ec·dot·ist** (AN·ic·doh–) *n.* a collector of anecdotes.

an·e·cho·ic (an·i·COH·ic) *adj.* free from echoes.

a·ne·mi·a (uh·NEE·mee·uh) *n.* weakness resulting from lack of red corpuscles in the blood. —**a·ne·mic** *adj.*

an·e·mom·e·ter (an·uh·MOM·i·tur) *n.* an instrument for measuring the force and speed of winds.

a·nem·o·ne (uh·NEM·uh·nee) *n.* a plant of the buttercup family, having showy, usu. white flowers; windflower: *The "sea anemone" is a marine animal.*

a·nent (uh–) *prep. Archaic* or *Regional.* concerning; regarding: *~ your query.*

an·er·oid (AN·uh–) *adj.* not using fluid. —**aneroid barometer** one which indicates air pressure by means of an elastic metal disk connected to a needle.

an·es·the·sia (an·is·THEE·zhuh) *n.* loss of the sense of pain, cold, touch, etc. —**an·es·the·si·ol·o·gy** (–zee·OL·uh·jee) *n.* the branch of medicine that deals with anesthesia; **an·es·the·si·ol·o·gist** (–jist) *n.* —**an·es·**

thet·ic (–THET·ic) *adj.* causing anesthesia; ***n.*** an anesthetic agent such as ether; **an·es·thet·i·cal·ly** *adv.* **—an·es·the·tist** (uh·NES·thuh–) *n.* one who administers anesthetics; **an·es·the·tize** *v.* **-tiz·es, -tized, -tiz·ing; an·es·the·ti·za·tion** (–ZAY–) *n.*

a·new (uh–) *adv.* once more; in a new way: *Fighting broke out ~.*

an·gel (AIN·jul) *n.* **1** a spiritual being, usu. in the role of a heavenly messenger; also, a similar evil spirit. **2** one regarded as good and lovely: *You're an ~!* **3** *Informal.* a financial backer. **—an·gel·ic** (an·JEL·ic) or **-i·cal** *adj.* **—an·gel·i·cal·ly** *adv.* **—angel dust** *Slang.* PCP used as a hallucinogen. **—an·gel·fish** *n.* a bright-colored tropical freshwater fish with a laterally compressed body. **—angel (food) cake** a white fluffy cake made with egg whites. **—an·gel·i·ca** (an·JEL·i·cuh) *n.* any of a number of plants of the parsley family used in medicine and cooking. **—an·ge·lus** (AN·juh–) *n.* a Roman Catholic prayer said morning, noon, and night; also, a bell announcing this.

an·ger (ANG·gur) *n.* a strong feeling of hurt or displeasure; wrath; ire. **—*v.* an·gers, an·gered, an·ger·ing** make or be angry: *Foul play ~s him.*

an·gi·na (an·JYE·nuh) *n.* any illness characterized by spasmodic pain, esp. **angina pec·to·ris** (–PEC·tuh–), a heart ailment accompanied by sudden bursts of chest pain. —**an·gi·nal** *adj.*

angi(o)- *comb.form.* of or having to do with a vessel, esp. blood vessel: as in **an·gi·ol·o·gy** (–OL–) , a branch of anatomy that studies blood and lymph vessels; **an·gi·o·sperm** (AN·jee·uh–), a plant such as the orchid or the rose that bears seeds in a closed ovary; cf. GYMNOSPERM.

Angl. Anglican.

[1]an·gle *n.* **1** the shape formed by the meeting of two lines or surfaces; also, the space in between: *the ~ of a roof; an ~ of 60°.* **2** a point of view: *two stories from different ~s:* **—*v.* -gles, -gled, -gling** direct or proceed at an angle; slant: *an ~d account.* **—angle iron** an L-shaped piece of iron or steel used to join or strengthen beams, masonry, etc. **—an·gu·lar** *adj.* of or having to do with angles; also, stiff; bony; **an·gu·lar·i·ty** (–LAIR–) *n.* **-ties; an·gu·lar·ly** *adv.*

[2]an·gle *v.* **-gles, -gled, -gling** fish with a hook; also, act indirectly; scheme: *to ~ for compliments.* **—an·gler** *n.* **—an·gle·worm** *n.* an earthworm used as bait.

An·gles (–glz) one of the Germanic tribes (with Jutes and Saxons) that settled in Britain in the fifth century. **—An·gli·an** *adj.: an ~ dialect;* also ***n.*** **—An·gli·can** *n.* a member of the Church of England or a related church; ***adj.:*** *The Episcopal Church is in the ~ communion;* **An·gli·can·ism** *n.* **—An·gli·cism** *n.* a typically English expression, trait, etc.; Briticism; also **anglicism. —an·gli·cize,** *v.* **-ciz·es, -cized, -ciz·ing** make (something) English; also **an·gli·fy, -fies, -fied, -fy·ing; an·gli·ci·za·tion** (–ZAY–) *n.* **—An·glo** *n.* **-glos** an English-speaking white North American. **—Anglo-** or **anglo-** *comb.form.* of England; English: as in **An·glo-A·mer·i·can** *adj.* & *n.* **—An·glo·ma·ni·a** *n.* excessive admiration for things English. **—An·glo·phile** *n.* an admirer of England and things English; **An·glo·phobe** *n.* one who hates or fears England and things English; hence **An·glo·pho·bi·a** (–FOH·bee·uh) *n.* **—An·glo·phone** *n.* a speaker of English in a bilingual or multilingual country; **An·glo·phon·ic** (–FON–) *adj.* **—An·glo-Sax·on** *n.* a member of any of the Germanic peoples that settled in Britain in the 5th and 6th centuries; also, their language, Old English; hence, plain English; ***adj.:*** *the ~ people.*

An·go·la (ang·GO·luh) a country in S.W. Africa; 481,354 sq.mi. (1,246,701 km²); *cap.* Luanda.

An·go·ra (ang·GOR·uh) *n.* a goat, rabbit, or cat with long, silky hair; also, the wool or cloth made from the hair of Angora goats or rabbits; mohair.

an·gry (ANG·gree) *adj.* **-gri·er, -gri·est** **1** full of anger; also, stormy; threatening: *~ sea.* **2** inflamed; red: *an ~ wound.* **—an·gri·ly** *adv.* **—an·gri·ness** *n.*

angst (AHNGST) *n.* anxiety.

ang·strom (ANG·strum) *n.* a unit of length equal to one ten-billionth of a meter; also **Angstrom.**

an·guish (ANG·gwish) *n.* intense pain, esp. of the mind. **—*v.:*** *to ~ over trifles.* **—an·guished** *adj.: She wore an ~ expression.*

angular, angularly, angularity See [1]ANGLE.

An·gus (ANG–) *n.* a Scottish breed of black hornless beef cattle.

an·hy·dride (an·HIGH–) *n.* a chemical compound from which water has been removed. **—an·hy·drous** (–drus) *adj.* without water, esp. water of crystallization.

an·i·line (AN·i·lin) *n.* a colorless, poisonous, oily liquid got from benzene, used in making dyes, drugs, explosives, etc.

an·i·mad·vert (an·i·mad·VURT) *v.* make adverse comments (*on* or *upon* someone). **—an·i·mad·ver·sion** *n.*

an·i·mal (–mul) *n.* **1** a living being that has sensation and can move about. **2** a living being as distinguished from man; irrational creature. **3** an inhuman person; brute. —***adj.:*** *Food is one of man's ~ needs; ~ fats; the ~ kingdom, as opposed to the vegetable.* **—an·i·mal·cule** (–MAL–) *n.* a microscopic organism. **—an·i·mal·ism** *n.* the belief in and practice of sensuality as a way of life; **an·i·mal·ist** *n.;* **an·i·mal·is·tic** (–IS–) *adj.* **—an·i·mal·i·ty** (–MAL–) *n.* **—an·i·mal·ize** *v.* **-iz·**

es, -ized, -iz·ing cause to become like an animal; **an·i·mal·i·za·tion** (–ZAY–) *n.* —**animal spirits** lively exuberance. —**an·i·mate** (AN·i–) *v.* **-mates, -mat·ed, -mat·ing** **1** give life, vigor, or interest to: *an ~d discussion.* **2** make a moving picture of with drawings: *to ~ a story;* hence **animated cartoon.** —***adj.*** (AN·i·mit) living; active: *Plants are part of ~ nature.* —**an·i·mat·ed** *adj.;* **an·i·mat·ed·ly** *adv.* —**an·i·ma·tion** (–MAY–) *n.* —**an·i·ma·tor** *n.* —**a·ni·ma·to** (ah·nee·MAH·toh) *adv.* & *adj. Music.* in a lively manner. —**an·i·mism** (AN·i·mizm) *n.* the belief that inanimate things such as rocks, winds, and rivers have souls; **an·i·mist** *n.;* **an·i·mis·tic** (–MIS–) *adj.* —**an·i·mos·i·ty** (an·i·MOS–) *n.* **-ties** hatred; enmity; ill will; also **an·i·mus** (AN·i–) *n.*

an·i·on (AN·eye·un) *n.* a negatively charged ion; cf. CATION. —**an·i·on·ic** (–ON·ic) *adj.* —**an·i·on·ic·al·ly** *adv.*

an·ise (AN·is) *n.* an herb of the parsley family with sweet-smelling seeds called **an·i·seed** that are used in medicine and in flavoring, esp. in **an·i·sette** (·-SET), a liqueur.

An·ka·ra (ANG·kuh·ruh) capital of Turkey.

ankh *n.* an ancient Egyptian emblem of life in the shape of a cross with a loop for its upper vertical arm.

an·kle (ANG·kl) *n.* the part of a leg that links the foot to the calf. —**an·klet** (ANG·klit) *n.* an ankle ornament, as a band or chain; also, a short sock.

ann. annals; annual; annuity.

an·nals (AN·ulz) *n.pl.* a year-by-year narrative or account; history. —**an·nal·ist** *n.*

An·nap·o·lis (uh·NPA·uh–) capital of Maryland.

an·neal (uh·NEEL) *v.* toughen and temper glass, metal, etc. by slow cooling after heating.

an·ne·lid (AN·uh–) *n.* any of a group of animals such as earthworms and leeches that have bodies composed of ringlike segments; ***adj.:*** *an ~ worm.*

an·nex (uh·NEX) *v.* attach: *A city ~es a suburb.* —***n.*** (AN·ex) something attached, as an appendix to a document, an addition to a building, etc.: *a hospital ~ for outpatients.* —**an·nex·a·tion** (–AY–) *n.*

an·ni·hi·late (uh·NYE·uh–) *v.* **-lates, -la·ted, -la·ting** destroy completely. —**an·ni·hi·la·tor** *n.* —**an·ni·hi·la·tion** (–LAY–) *n.*

an·ni·ver·sa·ry (an·uh·VUR·suh·ree) *n.* **-ries** the yearly recurring date of an event: *a wedding ~;* ***adj.:*** *an ~ dinner.* —**an·no Dom·i·ni** (an·oh·DOM·uh·nee) *Latin.* See A.D.

an·no·tate (AN·uh–) *v.* **-tates, -tat·ed, -tat·ing** provide (a text) with notes: *an ~d edition of Shakespeare.* —**an·no·ta·tor** *n.* —**an·no·ta·tion** (–TAY–) *n.*

an·nounce (uh·NOUNCE) *v.* **an·nounc·es, an·nounced, an·noun·cing** **1** proclaim; also, make known the arrival of. **2** act as announcer. —**an·noun·cer** *n.* one who announces, esp. one who reads news, programs, etc. on radio or TV. —**an·nounce·ment** *n.*

an·noy (uh·NOY) *v.* irritate; vex; disturb. —**an·noy·ing** *adj.* —**an·noy·ing·ly** *adv.* —**an·noy·ance** *n.* a being annoyed; also, a source of annoyance; nuisance.

an·nu·al (AN·yoo·ul) *adj.* of a year; every year: *your ~ income; Birthdays are ~ events; Marigolds and zinnias are ~ plants* (that live only one year). —***n.*** **1** an annual plant. **2** a yearbook. —**an·nu·al·ly** *adv.* —**annual ring** a year's growth of wood as seen in concentric rings on a cross section. —**an·nu·i·tant** (uh·NEW·i·tunt) *n.* one who receives an **an·nu·i·ty** (uh·NEW–) *n.* **-ties** a fixed sum of money paid yearly on an investment.

an·nul (uh·NUL) *v.* **an·nuls, an·nulled, an·nul·ling** make void; cancel. —**an·nul·la·ble** *adj.* —**an·nul·ment** *n.*

an·nu·lar (AN·yoo·lur) *adj.* ringlike; **annular eclipse** one in which the rim of the sun's disk is seen as a ring. —**an·nu·lar·ly** *adv.* —**an·nu·lus** *n.* **-lus·es** or **-li** (–lye) a ringlike part, marking, or formation.

an·nun·ci·ate (uh·NUN·see–) *v.* **-ates, -at·ed, -at·ing** announce. —**the An·nun·ci·a·tion** (–AY·shun) *n.* the commemoration, on March 25, of the Virgin Mary's motherhood, as announced by the angel Gabriel. —**an·nun·ci·a·tor** (–NUN–) *n.* a signal board that indicates the source of a call, as at a hotel desk or elevator control; **an·nun·ci·a·to·ry** *adj.*

an·ode (AN–) *n.* the positively charged electrode of an electrolytic cell or electron tube or the negative terminal of a primary cell. —**an·od·ic** (–OD–) or **an·o·dal** (–OH–) *adj.;* **an·od·i·cal·ly** or **an·o·dal·ly** *adv.* —**an·o·dize** (AN·uh–) *v.* **-diz·es, -dized, -diz·ing** coat (a metal) with a protective film as in electroplating; **an·o·di·za·tion** (–ZAY–) *n.*

an·o·dyne (AN·uh–) *n.* a drug that lessens pain; also, anything similar: *Time is the ~ of sorrow.*

a·noint (uh·NOINT) *v.* **1** apply oil or ointment to; also, to do so as a rite: **Anointing of the Sick** *is a sacrament.* **2** consecrate: *to ~ a king.* —**a·noint·er** *n.* —**a·noint·ment** *n.*

a·nom·a·ly (uh·NOM·uh·lee) *n.* **-lies** (–leez) something irregular or abnormal, as stairs that lead nowhere. —**a·nom·a·lous** (–lus) *adj.* —**a·nom·a·lous·ly** *adv.* —**a·nom·a·lous·ness** *n.*

a·non (uh·NON) *adv. Archaic.* soon; again. —**ever and anon** again and again.

anon. *Abbrev.* for **a·non·y·mous** (uh·NON·i·mus) *adj.* with no name given: *an ~ author; An ~ caller warned us.* —**a·non·y·mous·ly** *adv.* —**a·non·y·mous·ness** or **an·o·nym·i·ty** (an·uh·NIM–) *n.*

a·noph·e·les (uh·NOF·uh·leez) *n.* a malaria-carrying mosquito.

an·o·rex·i·a (–uh·REX·ee·uh) *n. Med.* loss of appetite.

an·oth·er (uh·NUDH·ur) *pron.* an additional, different, or similar one: *This cup is broken, give me* ~. **—*adj.*:** *a brilliant physicist,* ~ *Einstein; have* ~ *drink.*

ans. *Abbrev.* for **an·swer** (AN·sur) *n.* a reply to a question; solution to a problem. **—*v.*** say or act in reply: *No one* ~*ed the door;* **an·swer·er** *n.* **—answer back** *Informal.* reply impertinently; talk back. **—answer for** be responsible for; **an·swer·a·ble** *adj.*: *We are* ~ *to our superiors for our work.* **—answer to:** *This dog* ~*s to the description of the missing dog;* ~*s to the name "Tiger."* **—answering service** a service that handles telephone calls for clients.

ant *n.* any of a family of small insects related to bees that live in colonies.

ant. antonym; antenna. **—Ant.** Antarctica. **—ant-** same as ANTI-. **—ant** or **-ent** *n. suffix.* one that acts or is used (in a specified way): as in *refrigerant, deodorant, referent;* ***adj.*:** as in *dependent, salient, benignant.*

ant·ac·id (an·TAS·id) *n.* a chemical such as magnesia or baking soda that neutralizes acidity. ***adj.*:** *an* ~ *agent.*

an·tag·o·nism (an·TAG·uh·nizm) *n.* opposition; hostility; **an·tag·o·nist** *n.* adversary. **—an·tag·o·nis·tic** (–NIS–) *adj.;* **an·tag·o·nis·ti·cal·ly** *adv.* **—an·tag·o·nize** (–TAG–) *v.* **-iz·es, -ized, -iz·ing** make (someone) hostile.

An·ta·nan·a·ri·vo (–REE·voh) same as TANANARIVE.

Ant·arc·tic (–ARC–, –AR–) **the.** *n.* the ice-covered region of the South Pole; also **Ant·arc·ti·ca.** **—*adj.*** of the south polar regions. **—Antarctic circle** the parallel at 66°33′ S that encloses the S. Frigid Zone. **—Antarctic Ocean** the ocean surrounding Antarctica.

An·tar·es (an·TAIR·eez) *n.* the brightest star in the constellation Scorpio.

ant bear a large anteater of South America; great anteater; also called "giant anteater." **—ant cow** an aphid that produces a honeydew that ants feed on.

an·te (AN·tee) *n.* a stake put up by a poker player. **—*v.* -tes,** *pt.* & *pp.* **-te(e)d, -te·ing** put up an ante; **ante up** *Informal.* to pay. **—ante-** *prefix.* before; prior: as in *antechamber, antedate.*

ant·eat·er *n.* a long-snouted mammal that feeds on ants, as the aardvark or the ant bear.

an·te·bel·lum (an·ti·BEL·um) *adj.* of the period before the U.S. Civil War. **—an·te·ce·dence** (–SEE–) *n.* priority; **an·te·ce·dent** *n.* **1** something that precedes, esp. a word or phrase to which a pronoun refers; ***adj.*:** ~ *circumstances.* **2 antecedents** *pl.* one's earlier life; also, predecessors; ancestry: *a nonentity with no* ~. **—an·te·ce·dent·ly** *adv.* **—an·te·cham·ber** *n.* a side room leading into a larger room. **—an·te·date** (AN·ti–) *v.* **-dates, -dat·ed, -dat·ing 1** date (a document, check, etc.) earlier than the actual date. **2** happen earlier than another event. **—an·te·di·lu·vi·an** (an·tee·di·LOO·vee·un) *adj.* very ancient; antiquated; obsolete; ***n.*:** *He is an* ~ *in his attitude toward movies.*

an·te·lope (AN·tuh–) *n.* any of a group of deerlike animals such as the chamois, eland, gazelle, gnu, and pronghorn.

an·te me·rid·i·em (an·tee·muh·RID·ee·um) *adj. Latin.* in the forenoon; a.m. **—an·te·na·tal** (an·tee·NAY·tl) *adj.* before-birth.

an·ten·na (–TEN·uh) *n.* **1.** *pl.* also **-ten·nae** (–nee), any of the slender hornlike projections on the head of an insect, centipede, lobster, etc.; feeler. **2** a system of wires and rods used in sending or receiving TV and radio signals.

an·te·pe·nult (–ti·PEE–) *n.* the third syllable from the end of a word. **—an·te·pen·ul·ti·mate** (–pi·NUL·ti·mit) *n.* antepenult; ***adj.*:** *The* ~ *syllable of "opportunity" is "tu."* **—an·te·ri·or** (–TEER·ee·ur) *adj.* coming before in position or time. **—an·te·room** (AN·ti–) *n.* a small room opening into one larger; waiting room.

an·them (ANTH·um) *n.* a hymn of praise, devotion, or triumph: *college* ~*; national* ~.

an·ther (AN·thur) *n.* the tip of a flower's stamen containing the pollen.

ant·hill *n.* a pile of earth thrown up by ants at the entrance to their nest.

an·thol·o·gy (an·THOL·uh·jee) *n.* **-gies** (–jeez) a collection of writings, usu. by many authors on one theme. **—an·thol·o·gist** *n.* **—an·thol·o·gize** *v.* **-iz·es, -ized, -iz·ing** make into an anthology; include in an anthology.

an·thra·cite (AN·thruh–) *n.* a hard coal that is mostly carbon and burns with great heat and little smoke. **—an·thra·cit·ic** (–SIT–) *adj.* **—an·thrax** *n.* an infectious, often fatal, disease of cattle and sheep, caused by a bacillus.

anthrop. anthropological; anthropology. **—anthropo-** *comb.form.* man; human. **—an·thro·po·cen·tric** (an·thruh·puh·CEN–) *adj.* having man as the center of the universe and interpreting reality in relation to human values. **—an·thro·poid** (AN·thruh–) *adj.* of apes, similar to humans; ***n.*:** *Chimpanzees, gibbons, gorillas, and orangutans are* ~*s;* **an·thro·poi·dal** (–POY–) *adj.* **—an·thro·pol·o·gy** (–POL·uh·jee) *n.* the study of man's origin, physical and social characteristics, and cultural development; **an·thro·po·log·ic** (–LOJ–) or **-i·cal** *adj.;* **an·thro·po·log·i·cal·ly** *adv.;* **an·thro·pol·o·gist** (–POL·uh·jist) *n.* **—an·thro·pom·e·try** (–POM·uh·tree) *n.* a branch of anthropology that deals with body measurements; **an·thro·po·met·ric** (–MET–) or **-ri·cal** *adj.* **—an·thro·po·mor·phic** (–MOR·fic) *adj.* attributing human form or characteristics to gods, animals, things, etc.; **an·thro·po·mor·phism** *n.;* **an·thro·po·mor·phize** *v.* **-phiz·es, -phized, -phiz·ing** humanize: *to attribute wrath to God is to ~ Him.*

ant(i)- *comb.form* [indicating opposition, hostility, prevention, reverse effect, etc.]: as in *antacid, anti-American, anticapitalist.* **—an·ti** (AN·tye, –tee) *n.* **-tis** *Informal.* one who opposes (something); ***prep.:*** *She is ~ everything imported.* **—an·ti·air·craft** (an·tee·AIR–) *adj.* for use against aircraft: *an ~ gun.* **—an·ti·bac·te·ri·al** (–bac·TEER·ee·ul) *adj.* that checks or protects from bacteria. **—an·ti·bal·lis·tic** (–LIS–) **missile** a missile for destroying a ballistic missile in flight. **—an·ti·bi·ot·ic** (–bye·OT·ic) *n.* a substance such as penicillin or tetracycline that is capable of destroying or preventing the growth of harmful microorganisms; ***adj.:*** *an ~ substance.* **—an·ti·bod·y** *n.* **-bod·ies** any of various substances produced in the blood to react against disease germs, poison, etc.

an·tic *n.* a clownish act; caper. ***—adj.*** ludicrous; odd. ***—v.*** **-tics, -ticked, -tick·ing:** *A buffoon ~s on the stage.*

An·ti·christ Christ's adversary, as foretold in the Bible; **antichrist** *n.* an impostor or opponent of Christ.

an·tic·i·pate (–TIS–) *v.* **-pates, -pat·ed, -pat·ing** foresee something; also, take steps in advance; forestall: *to ~ trouble during a strike; I ~d the rain by taking an umbrella;* **an·tic·i·pant** *adj.* & *n.* **—an·tic·i·pa·tion** (–PAY–) *n.* expection; apprehension. **—an·tic·i·pa·to·ry** (–TIS·uh·puh–) *adj.*

an·ti·cli·max (an·ti·CLYE–) *n.* a sudden descent from the serious to the trivial in something said, done, or in a happening, esp. at the close of a series; **an·ti·cli·mac·tic** (–clye·MAC–) *adj.;* **an·ti·cli·mac·ti·cal·ly** *adv.* **—an·ti·cline** (AN–) *n.* a stratified rock formation in which the layers arch downward from a crest in opposite directions; cf. SYNCLINE; **an·ti·cli·nal** (–CLYE·nl) *adj.* **—an·ti·clock·wise** *adj.* & *adv.* counterclockwise. **—an·ti·co·ag·u·lant** (–co·AG·yuh·lunt) *n.* a substance that prevents blood from clotting. **—an·ti·cy·clone** (–SYE–) *n.* a rotating system of winds originating from a center of high pressure; **an·ti·cy·clon·ic** (–CLON–) *adj.* **—an·ti·de·pres·sant** (–PRES·unt) *adj.* tending to prevent emotional depression; ***n.*** an antidepressant drug. **—an·ti·dote** (AN·ti–) *n.* a remedy against poison, evil, or any harm; **an·ti·dot·al** (–DOH·tul) *adj.;* **an·ti·dot·al·ly** *adv.* **—an·ti·freeze** *n.* a substance added to gasoline, radiator coolant, etc. to prevent freezing. **—an·ti·gen** (ANT·i·jun) *n.* a foreign substance such as a virus or pollen that, on entering the body, stimulates the production of antibodies; **an·ti·gen·ic** (–JEN–) *adj.;* **an·ti·gen·i·cal·ly** *adv.;* **an·ti·ge·nic·i·ty** (–juh·NIS–) *n.*

An·ti·gua (–TEE·gwuh, –guh) one of the self-governing Commonwealth states of the West Indies.

an·ti·he·ro *n.* **-roes** the protagonist in a novel or play who lacks the traditional virtues of a heroic character. **—an·ti·his·ta·mine** (–HIS·tuh·meen) *n.* a medicine that is used to relieve the symptoms of colds and allergies; **an·ti·his·ta·min·ic** (–MIN·ic) *adj.* **—an·ti·knock** (an·ti·NOK) *n.* a fuel additive that reduces the noise of too rapid combustion in an engine.

An·til·les (an·TIL·eez) a chain of islands of the West Indies group separating the Caribbean Sea from the Atlantic, consisting of the **Greater Antilles** (Cuba, Jamaica, Puerto Rico, etc.) and the **Lesser Antilles** (Leeward Islands, Windward Islands, etc.). **—An·til·le·an** *adj.*

an·ti·log·a·rithm (–LOG·uh–) *n.* the number (as 10, 100, or 1000) that corresponds to a logarithm (as 1, 2, or 3); also **an·ti·log. —an·ti·ma·cas·sar** (–muh·CAS·ur) *n.* a small covering for the back or arms of a piece of furniture to protect it from soiling. **—an·ti·mag·net·ic** (–mag·NET·ic) *adj.* esp. of a watch, made with nonmagnetic metals to ensure constant movement of parts. **—an·ti·mat·ter** *n.* a theoretical form of matter composed of antiparticles.

an·ti·mo·ny (AN·ti·moh·nee) *n.* a silver-white metallic element used in alloys to make them harder. **—an·ti·mo·ni·al** (–MOH·nee·ul) *adj.*

an·ti·neu·tri·no (–new·TREE·noh) *n.* the antiparticle of the neutrino. **—an·ti·neu·tron** (–NEW·tron) *n.* the antiparticle of the neutron. **—an·tin·o·my** (an·TIN·uh·mee) *n.* **-mies** a contradiction inherent in the same law or between laws. **—an·ti·no·mi·an** (–NOH·mee·un) *n.* one who believes that faith alone, without adherence to moral laws, is necessary for salvation; also ***adj.:*** *the ~ position.* **—an·ti·ox·i·dant** (–OX·i·dunt) *n.* a substance that inhibits oxidation and thus deterioration. **—an·ti·par·ti·cle** *n.* an elementary atomic particle identical in mass with, but opposite in electric charge and magnetic properties to an ordinary atomic particle: *A positron is the ~ of an electron.*

an·ti·pas·to (–PAS·toe) *n.* **-tos** an hors d'oeuvre.

an·tip·a·thy (–TIP·uh·thee) *n.* **-thies** an aversion or dislike; also, an object of such aversion: *Lotteries were a life-long ~ of his;* **an·ti·pa·thet·ic** (–tip·uh·THET·ic) *adj.* **—an·ti·per·son·nel** (–NEL) *adj.* designed for use against humans rather than materials: *an ~ bomb.* **—an·ti·per·spi·rant** (–PUR·spuh·runt) *n.* a cosmetic preparation for checking perspiration. **—an·ti·phon** (AN·ti·fon) *n.* a psalm or chant sung responsively or in alternate parts; **an·tiph·o·ny** (–TIF–) *n.* **-nies** responsive or alternate singing, sounds, etc.; **an·tiph·o·nal** (–TIF·uh·nl) *adj.:* ~ *verse;* **an·tiph·o·nal·ly** *adv.* —**an·ti·pode** (AN·ti·pode) *n.* an exact opposite; **an·tip·o·des** (–TIP·uh·deez) *n.pl.* diametrically opposite parts of the earth; hence, any two opposites; **an·tip·o·dal** (–dl) or **an·tip·o·de·an** (an·tip·uh·DEE·un) *adj.* exactly opposite: *an* ~ *location.* —**an·ti·pol·lu·tion** (–puh·LOO–) *adj.* designed to counteract or prevent pollution: ~ *measures;* **an·ti·pol·lu·tion·ist** *n.* —**an·ti·pope** (AN·ti–) *n.* a rival of an officially chosen pope. —**an·ti·pro·ton** (–PROH·tahn) *n.* the antiparticle of the proton. —**an·ti·py·ret·ic** (–pye·RET·ic) *n.* a fever remedy; ***adj.:*** *an* ~ *drug.*

an·tique (an·TEEK) *n.* an object of artistic or cultural value, as a piece of furniture, pottery, costume, etc. that is at least 100 years old. ***adj.:*** ~ *furniture;* also, ancient; very old: *an* ~ *city;* ~ *heroes.* —***v.*** **-tiques, -tiqued, -tiqu·ing** make look like an antique; **an·tique·ly** *adv.;* **an·tique·ness** *n.* —**an·tiq·ui·ty** (–TIK·wuh·tee) *n.* **-ties** **1** great age. **2** former times: *great men of* ~. **3** *pl.* ancient remains: *Greek and Roman* ~*s.* —**an·ti·quar·y** (AN·ti·kwer·ee) *n.* **-quar·ies** one who collects or studies antiquities; also **an·ti·quar·i·an** (–KWAIR·ee·un) *n.* & *adj.: a vast* ~ *collection.* —**an·ti·quate** (AN·ti–) *v.* **-quates, -quat·ed, -quat·ing** render out-of-date or old-fashioned: *a man of* ~*d ideas.*

an·ti-Sem·ite (–SEM–) *n.* one who hates Jews; **an·ti-Se·mit·ic** (–MIT–) *adj.;* **an·ti-Sem·i·tism** (–SEM–) *n.* —**an·ti·sep·sis** (–SEP·sis) *n.* prevention or stopping of infection by destroying disease germs. —**an·ti·sep·tic** *adj.* **1** : *Carbolic acid and alcohol are* ~ *agents.* Also ***n.*** **2** extremely clean; also, lifeless; sterile; austere. —**an·ti·sep·tic·al·ly** *adv.* —**an·ti·se·rum** (–SEER·um) *n.* **-se·rums** or **-se·ra** (–ruh) a serum effective against a specific disease. —**an·ti·so·cial** (–SOH·shul) *adj.* not sociable; also against the good of society: *Stealing is* ~; **an·ti·so·cial·ly** *adv.*

an·tith·e·sis (–TITH·uh–) *n., pl.* **-ses** (–seez) **1** opposition or contrast; also, something opposite. **2** a contrasting idea or expression, as "Give me liberty or give me death"; **an·ti·thet·ic** (–THET–) or **-i·cal** *adj.;* **an·ti·thet·i·cal·ly** *adv.* —**an·ti·tox·in** *n.* a natural antibody in the blood or a serum injected against a disease such as tetanus or diphtheria. —**an·ti·trades** *n. pl.* winds blowing in an opposite direction to the trade winds. —**an·ti·trust** *adj.* pertaining to laws against business monopolies: *an* ~ *suit.* —**an·ti·ven·in** *n.* an antitoxin or a serum for use against snake venom.

ant·ler *n.* a branched horn of any animal of the deer family. —**ant·lered** (–lurd) *adj.*

ant lion an insect resembling a dragonfly whose larva, the doodle bug, feeds on ants trapped in a conical pit in which it awaits its prey.

an·to·nym (AN·tuh·nim) *n.* a word that means the opposite of another. —**an·ton·y·mous** (–TON·i·mus) *adj.*

an·trum (AN–) *n., pl.* **-tra** (–truh) a bony cavity, esp. a sinus.

Ant·werp (ANT–) a city of Belgium.

an·u·re·sis (an·yoo·REE–) *n.* **1** inability to urinate. **2** failure in the secretion of urine from the kidneys; also **an·u·ri·a** (uh·NEW·ree·uh).

a·nus (AY·nus) *n.* the excretory opening at the end of the alimentary canal.

an·vil *n.* a heavy block on which to hammer metals into shape.

anx·i·e·ty (ang·ZYE·uh·tee) *n.* **1** fear in thinking of what may happen: *a mother's* ~ *about her child's safety.* **2** *pl.* **-ties** an instance of such fear: *the* ~*s of unemployment.* **3** strong wish; eagerness: *a pupil's* ~ *to please his teacher.* —**anx·ious** (ANGK·shus) *adj.* worried; troubled; eager: *many* ~ *hours of waiting for a dear one;* ~ *for a safe return.* —**anx·ious·ly** *adv.* —**anx·ious·ness** *n.*

an·y (EN·ee) *adj.* **1** one or some out of many, much, etc.: ~ *oranges left?* ~ *fruit will do.* **2** [with implied negative]: *without* ~ *hesitation; Hardly* ~ *time remains.* **3** every: *as* ~ *child could tell you.* —***pron.:*** *I have no money. Have you* ~*?* —***adv.*** [implying degree]: *Is she* ~ *better today? Is he* ~ *good at all?* —**at any rate** in whatever case; at least. —**in any case** (or **event**) whatever happens. —**an·y·bod·y** *pron.* anyone: ~ *home?* Also ***n.*** a person of any importance: *Is she* ~*?* —**an·y·how** *adv.* any way; nevertheless. —**an·y·more** *adv.* any longer. —**an·y·one** *pron.* —**an·y·place** *adv.* —**an·y·thing** *pron., n.* & *adv.* —**anything but** not at all. —**an·y·time** *adv.* —**an·y·way** *adv.* —**an·y·where** *adv.* —**an·y·wise** *adv.* in any manner.

A/o or **a/o** account of.

A-OK *adj.* & *adv. Informal.* quite all right.

A1 or **A one** *adj. Informal.* excellent.

a·or·ta (ay·OR·tuh) *n.* **-tas** or **-tae** (–tee) the main artery carrying blood from the heart to the rest of the body. —**a·or·tal** or **a·or·tic** *adj.*

a·ou·dad (AH·oo–) *n.* a type of wild sheep of N. Africa.

Ap. Apostle; April. —**A.P.** Associated Press.

A.P.A. American Philosophical Association; American Psychiatric Association.

a·pace (uh–) *adv.* quickly.

A·pach·e (uh·PACH·ee) *n.* (a member of) a tribe of Indians of S.W. United States and Mexico; also, their Athapascan language. —**a·pache** (uh·PASH) *n.* a Parisian gangster or ruffian.

ap·a·nage (AP·uh·nij) *n.* same as APPANAGE.

a·part (uh–) *adv.* **1** separately; aside; away from each other: *Two houses three miles* ~; *I took him* ~ *for a private chat; tear a thing* ~. **2** being excepted: *Joking* ~, *I want to go to the moon.* —***adj.:*** *They are a class* ~. —**apart from** besides:

~ *from errors, the book is also out-of-date.* —**a·part·heid** (uh·PAR·tate) *n.* South Africa's policy of racial segregation. —**a·part·ment** *n.* a suite of rooms for living in; flat; esp. as part of a building, or **apartment house** (or **building**), containing many such suites; **apartment hotel** a hotel containing apartments with housekeeping facilities for guests on a temporary or permanent basis.

ap·a·thy (AP·uh·thee) *n.* absence of feeling or interest; indifference. —**ap·a·thet·ic** (–THET·ic) *adj.;* **ap·a·thet·i·cal·ly** *adv.*

ap·a·tite (AP·uh–) *n.* a crystalline mineral containing calcium phosphate.

APB all-points bulletin.

ape *n.* **1** a large tailless primate, i.e. a chimpanzee, gorilla, gibbon, or orangutan. **2** any monkey. **3** an imitator; mimic; also, a clumsy person. —***v.*** **apes, aped, ap·ing** imitate (someone).

Ap·en·nines (AP·uh–) [with *pl.v.*] a mountain range extending from N. to S. in Italy.

a·pe·ri·tif (ah·per·i·TEEF) *n.* an alcoholic drink taken before a meal. —**ap·er·ture** (AP·ur·chur) *n.* an opening or hole, as of a camera.

a·pex (AY–) *n.* **a·pex·es** or **ap·i·ces** (AP·i·seez) the highest point; summit; climax: *the ~ of her fortunes.* —**ap·i·cal** *adj.;* **ap·i·cal·ly** *adv.*

a·pha·sia (uh·FAY·zhuh) *n.* loss of the ability to use or understand language, resulting from brain damage. —**a·pha·si·ac** (uh·FAY·zee·ac) or **a·pha·sic** (–FAY–) *adj.* & *n.*

a·phe·li·on (uh·FEE·lee·un) *n., pl.* **-li·a** (–lee·uh) the point in a solar orbit that is farthest from the sun.

a·phid or **a·phis** (AY–, AF–) *n.* **-phids** or **-phi·des** (–fi·deez) any of various small insects that live on the juices of plants.

aph·o·rism (AF·uh–) *n.* a short pithy saying expressing a general truth; maxim. —**aph·o·ris·tic** (–RIS–) *adj.* —**aph·o·ris·ti·cal·ly** *adv.*

a·pho·tic (ay·FOH·tic) *adj.* without light: *lifeless, ~ depths of the sea.*

aph·ro·dis·i·ac (af·ruh·DIZ·ee·ac) *n.* a food, drug, etc. that excites sexual desire. —***adj.:*** *an ~ charm;* also **aph·ro·di·si·a·cal** (–di·ZYE·uh·cul). —**Aph·ro·di·te** (af·ruh·DYE·tee) the Greek goddess of love and beauty.

A·pi·a (ah·PEE·ah) capital of Western Samoa.

a·pi·ar·y (AY·pee·er·ee) *n.* **-ar·ies** a place for keeping bees. —**a·pi·ar·i·an** (–AIR·ee·un) *adj.* pertaining to beekeeping; ***n.*** beekeeper; also **a·pi·a·rist.** —**a·pi·cul·ture** (AY·pi–) *n.* beekeeping.

apical(ly), apices See APEX.

a·piece (uh·PEECE) *adv.* each.

a·plomb (uh·PLOM) *n.* assurance; self-confidence: *She spoke with her usual ~.*

A.P.O. Army Post Office.

Apoc. Apocalypse; Apocrypha(l). —**a·poc·a·lypse** (uh·POC·uh·lips) *n.* **1 the Apocalypse** the last book of the Bible; Book of Revelation. **2** any revelation or prophecy. —**a·poc·a·lyp·tic** (–LIP–) or **-ti·cal** *adj.* —**A·poc·ry·pha** (uh·POC·ruh·fuh) [with *sing. v.*] **1** books of the Old Testament that are not considered authentic. **2 apocrypha** *n.pl.* any writings of dubious authenticity. —**a·poc·ry·phal** *adj.: an ~ story;* **a·poc·ry·phal·ly** *adv.* —**ap·o·cyn·thi·on** (–SIN·thee·un) *n.* same as APOLUNE. —**ap·o·gee** (AP·uh·jee) *n.* the point in an orbit around the earth that is farthest from the earth; **ap·o·ge·an** (–JEE·un) *adj.*

a·po·lit·i·cal (ay·puh·LIT–) *adj.* not concerned with politics. —**a·po·lit·i·cal·ly** *adv.*

A·pol·lo (uh·POL·oh) **1** the Greek sun god and patron of poetry, music, and medicine. **2 apollo** *n.* a handsome youth.

a·pol·o·get·ic (uh·pol·uh·JET·ic) *adj.* making an apology: *an ~ smile;* **a·pol·o·get·i·cal·ly** *adv.* —**ap·o·lo·gi·a** (ap·uh·LOH·jee·uh) *n.* a formal defense of one's position. —**a·pol·o·gist** (–POL·uh·jist) *n.* one who speaks or writes in defense of a cause; **a·pol·o·gize** (–jize) *v.* **-giz·es, -gized, -giz·ing** make an apology: *He ~d for his rudeness.* —**a·pol·o·gy** (–jee) *n.* **-gies** **1** an expression of regret for an offense. **2** a formal defense. **3** a poor specimen or substitute.

ap·o·lune (AP·uh·loon) *n.* the point in a lunar orbit that is farthest from the moon.

ap·o·phthegm (AP·uh·them) *n.* same as APOTHEGM.

ap·o·plex·y (AP·uh–) *n.* a stroke caused by injury to blood vessels in the brain resulting in partial paralysis of the body; **ap·o·plec·tic** (–PLEC–) *adj.*

a·port (uh–) *adv.* to the port or left side of a ship.

a·pos·ta·sy (uh·POS·tuh·see) *n.* **-sies** a giving up of one's religious faith, political party, or other allegiance. —**a·pos·tate** (uh·POS·tate, –tit) *n.* one guilty of apostasy; ***adj.:*** *an ~ priest.*

a pos·te·ri·o·ri (ah·poh·steer·ee·OH·ree) *adj.* & *adv.* of reasoning, proceeding from effect to cause; distinguished from A PRIORI.

a·pos·tle (uh·POSL) *n.* **1** any of the 12 disciples of Christ; also, a first missionary: *the ~ to the Indies.* **2** a reformer; leader of a movement: *an ~ of women's rights.* —**ap·os·tol·ic** (ap·uh·STOL·ic) *adj.* of or having to do with Christ's disciples: *~ times; an ~ church.*

a·pos·tro·phe (uh·POS·truh·fee) *n.* **1** a punctuation mark used to indicate possession *(John's),* omission of a letter *(isn't),* and plurals *(3 A's).* **2** a rhetorical passage addressed to an imaginary person or personified object, e.g. "Milton! thou shouldst be living at this hour." —**a·pos·tro·phize** *v.* **-phiz·es, -phized, -phiz·ing:** *The speaker ~d the spirit of 76.*

a·poth·e·car·y (uh·POTH·uh·ker·ee) *n.* **-car·ies** a pharmacist; druggist. —**apothecar-**

ies' measure the pharmacist's system of measuring volumes. —**apothecaries' weight** the pharmacist's system of weights.

ap·o·thegm (AP·uh·them) *n.* a short, pithy saying or maxim such as "Honesty is the best policy."

a·poth·e·o·sis (uh·poth·ee·OH–) *n., pl.* **-ses** (–seez) divinization; glorification; also, a perfect ideal: *He was the ~ of chivalry.*

app. apparatus; appendix; apprentice.

Ap·pa·la·chians (ap·uh·LAY·chuns) *n.pl.* a chain of mountains of E. North America, extending from Quebec south to Alabama; also **Appalachian Mountains.**

ap·pal(l) (uh·POL) *v.* **ap·pal(l)s, ap·palled, ap·pall·ing** fill with horror, shock, and dismay. —**ap·pall·ing** *adj.: the ~ condition of the slums.*

Ap·pa·loo·sa (ap·uh·LOO·suh) *n.* a hardy Western breed of saddle horse, distinguished by a spotted rump.

ap·pa·nage (AP·uh·nij) *n.* a grant of property, an endowment, or other benefit that one gets by virtue of birth or official position; perquisite; adjunct.

ap·pa·ra·tus (ap·uh·RAT·us, –RAY–) *n.* **-tus(·es)** equipment or materials organized for a specific task; machinery; organization: *a laboratory ~; a party's election ~.*

ap·par·el (uh·PAIR·ul) *n.* clothing, esp. outer; attire. —***v.* -els, -el(l)ed, -el·(l)ing:** *brightly ~d children; Nature "~d in celestial light."*

ap·par·ent (uh·PAIR·unt) *adj.* **1** visible; evident: *His limp is quite ~; It soon became ~ who was lying.* **2** seeming; not real: *an ~ contradiction; an ~ advantage.* —**ap·par·ent·ly** *adv.* —**ap·pa·ri·tion** (ap·uh·RISH·un) *n.* a supernatural vision; ghost; specter.

ap·peal (uh·PEEL) *n.* **1** an earnest call for help or other consideration. **2** a sending of a case to a higher court for a new hearing; also, an application for it. **3** power of interesting or attracting: *The show has lost its ~.* —***v.*** [corresponding to the *n.* senses] **1:** *The convict ~ed to the President for clemency.* **2:** *The decision was ~ed to the Supreme Court.* **3:** *a movie ~ing to man's baser instincts.* —**ap·peal·ing** *adj.: A picture is more ~ than words;* **ap·peal·ing·ly** *adv.*

ap·pear (uh·PEER) *v.* become visible; arrive; be in public view; be published; seem: *The sun ~s on a clear day; The boss hadn't ~ed by 11 a.m.; A book ~s on the market; to ~ dejected.* —**ap·pear·ance** *n.* [besides verbal senses] **1** an outward show: *Even though bankrupt, he is* **keeping up appearances. 2** presence: *He* **puts in an appearance** *even on his days off.*

ap·pease (uh·PEEZ) *v.* **ap·peas·es, ap·peased, ap·peas·ing** placate; pacify; conciliate. —**ap·pease·ment** *n.: Chamberlain's policy of ~ of the Nazis.* —**ap·peas·er** *n.*

ap·pel·lant (uh·PEL·unt) *n.* one who appeals to a higher court. —**ap·pel·late** (uh·PEL·it) *adj.* having power to hear appeals: *an ~ court; ~ jurisdiction.* —**ap·pel·la·tion** (ap·uh·LAY–) *n.* the act of naming; a designation. —**ap·pel·lee** (ap·uh·LEE) *n.* one appealed against in a higher court.

ap·pend (uh·PEND) *v.* add at the end; affix. —**ap·pend·age** (–ij) *n.* an added part; esp. of a body, a subsidiary part, as an arm, tail, fin, etc. —**ap·pen·dec·to·my** (ap·un·DEC·tuh·mee) *n.* **-mies** surgical removal of the appendix; its inflammation is **ap·pen·di·ci·tis** (–SYE–). —**ap·pen·dix** (–PEN–) *n.* **-dix·es** or **-di·ces** (–di·seez) **1** a section added at the end of a book or other document. **2** a short tubelike appendage of the large intestine.

ap·per·tain (AP·ur–) *v.* belong rightfully; relate: *duties ~ing to one's office.*

ap·pe·tite (AP·uh–) *n.* a natural desire of the body, esp. for food; also, any other craving: *sexual ~.* —**ap·pe·ti·tive** (–TYE·tiv) *adj.: an animal's ~ behavior.* —**ap·pe·tiz·er** (–tye·zur) *n.* a food or drink meant to stimulate the appetite. —**ap·pe·tizing** *adj.: an ~ smell;* **ap·pe·tiz·ing·ly** *adv.: food served ~.*

appl. applied.

ap·plaud (uh·PLAWD) *v.* express approval, esp. by clapping hands: *His election was ~ed by everyone; The audience ~ed loudly.* —**ap·plause** (–PLAWZ) *n.* the act of applauding: *Loud ~ greeted the winner.*

ap·ple *n.* a round fleshy fruit with a core of seeds; also, the tree bearing this fruit. —**apple of one's eye** a dear one. —**ap·ple·jack** *n.* a liquor distilled from cider. —**apple-pie order** excellent condition; perfect order. —**ap·ple-pol·ish** *v. Informal.* curry favor (with). —**ap·ple·sauce** *n.* **1** stewed apples in pulp form. **2** *Slang.* nonsense.

ap·pli·ance (uh·PLY·unce) *n.* a piece of equipment for a particular use, as a refrigerator, vacuum cleaner, or air conditioner.

ap·pli·ca·ble (AP·li·cuh·bl, uh·PLIC–) *adj.* capable of being applied; suitable: *a law ~ to everyone;* **ap·pli·ca·bil·i·ty** (–BIL–) *n.;* **ap·pli·ca·bly** *adv.* —**ap·pli·cant** (–unt) *n.* one who applies; **ap·pli·can·cy** (–cun·see) *n.* —**ap·pli·ca·tion** (–CAY–) *n.* [corresponding to the senses of APPLY] **1** : *~ of an ointment.* **2** : *~ of a new method.* **3** : *a discovery with many ~s in daily life.* **4** : *close ~ to detail.* **5** : *His ~ was not granted.* —**ap·pli·ca·tor** (AP·luh·cay·tur) *n.* an applying device. —**ap·pli·qué** (ap·li·KAY) *n.* a decorative design or ornament cut out for attaching to something; ***v.* -qués, -quéd, -qué·ing:** *an ~d floral design.* —**ap·ply** (uh·PLY) *v.* **ap·plies, ap·plied, ap·ply·ing** **1** put on; lay on: *~ brakes to stop a vehicle; ~ glue to paper.* **2** to put into practice or use: *~ a rule; ~d physics.* **3** have a bearing on; refer: *This rule ~s in all cases; it ~s to me.* **4** devote (to some end): *~ oneself to studies.* **5** make a request: *to ~ for a job.* —**ap·pli·er** (–PLY–) *n.*

ap·point (uh–) *v.* **1** fix; set (time or place): *We met at the ~ed place.* **2** name; set up: *John was ~ed to the vacancy; ~ed manager.* **3** furnish; equip: *a well-~ed office.* **—ap·poin·tee** (–TEE) *n.* one who is appointed. **—ap·poin·tive** (–POIN·tiv) *adj.: an ~, not elective office.* **—ap·point·ment** *n.* **1** an appointing or being appointed: *an ~ with the doctor.* **2 ap·pointments** *pl.* furnishings.

Ap·po·mat·tox (ap·uh·MAT·ox) a town in Virginia where Lee surrendered to Grant, April 9, 1865.

ap·por·tion (uh·POR–) *v.* assign as a share; allot. **—ap·por·tion·ment** *n.*

ap·pose (uh·POZE) *v.* **ap·pos·es, ap·posed, ap·pos·ing** place side by side or next (to). **—ap·po·site** (AP·uh·zit) *adj.* appropriate: *an ~ comment;* **ap·po·site·ly** *adv.;* **ap·po·site·ness** *n.* **—ap·po·si·tion** (ap·uh·ZISH·un) *n.* the juxtaposing of a noun or phrase with another as an explanation: *In "Jack the giant-killer," "the giant-killer" is in ~ with "Jack," or is an* **ap·pos·i·tive** (uh·POZ·i·tiv) *n.;* also ***adj.:*** *an appositive phrase;* **ap·po·si·tion·al** (–ZISH–) *adj.* **—ap·pos·i·tive·ly** or **ap·po·si·tion·al·ly** *adv.*

ap·praise (uh·PRAIZ) *v.* **ap·prais·es, ap·praised, ap·prais·ing** judge the value of. **—ap·prais·al** *n.* **—ap·prais·er** *n.*

ap·pre·ci·a·ble (uh·PREE·shuh·bl) *adj.* considerable enough to be measured or experienced; **ap·pre·ci·a·bly** *adv.* **—ap·pre·ci·ate** (uh·PREE·shee–) *v.* **-ates, -at·ed, -at·ing** **1** understand the value of something (fully, highly, gratefully, etc.): *Not educated enough to ~ poetry; Everyone likes to be ~d; I ~ your help.* **2** rise (in value): *Property values ~ each spring.* **—ap·pre·ci·a·tion** (–AY–) *n.* **—ap·pre·cia·tive** (–shuh·tiv) *adj.: an ~ glance.*

ap·pre·hend (ap·ri·HEND) *v.* **1** arrest: *to ~ a burglar.* **2** grasp; understand; **ap·pre·hen·si·ble** *adj.;* **ap·pre·hen·si·bly** *adv.;* **ap·pre·hen·si·bil·i·ty** (–BIL–) *n.* **3** expect anxiously; fear: *In the darkness of the forest he ~ed danger.* **—ap·pre·hen·sion** *n.* **—ap·pre·hen·sive** (–siv) *adj.;* **ap·pre·hen·sive·ly** *adv.;* **ap·pre·hen·sive·ness** *n.*

ap·pren·tice (uh·PREN·tis) *n.* **1** a learner in a trade or profession: *a law ~.* **2** a novice or beginner in any occupation. **—*v.* -tic·es, -ticed, -tic·ing** take or bind for service in return for training in something: *He ~d his son to a tailor.* **—ap·pren·tice·ship** *n.*

ap·prise (uh·PRIZE) *v.* **ap·pris·es, ap·prised, ap·pris·ing** inform; tell: *~d of danger, he fled.*

ap·proach (uh·PROHCH) *v.* **1** move near or nearer (to): *The plane ~ed New York; Night is fast ~ing.* **2** go to (someone) with a specific aim: *to ~ the bank for a loan.* **—*n.*** the act of approaching; a manner or means of approach; access: *The police sealed all ~es to the city; the spurned ~es of an unsuccessful lover.* **—ap·proach·a·ble** *adj.: an ~ and friendly neighbor.* **—ap·proach·a·bil·i·ty** (–BIL–) *n.*

ap·pro·ba·tion (–ruh·BAY–) *n.* approval; praise.

ap·pro·pri·ate *v.* (uh·PROH·pree–) **-ates, -at·ed, -at·ing.** **1** make one's own: *He ~s the books he borrows.* **2** assign to a specific purpose: *to ~ funds for education.* **—*adj.*** (-it) proper; suitable; **ap·pro·pri·ate·ly** *adv.;* **ap·pro·pri·ate·ness** *n.;* **ap·pro·pri·a·tor** *n.* **—ap·pro·pri·a·tion** (–AY–) *n.* money authorized for a purpose: *Senate Appropriations Committee.*

ap·prove (uh·PROOV) *v.* **ap·proves, ap·proved, ap·prov·ing** **1** think or feel favorably about (something or someone). **2** ratify; sanction. **—ap·prov·al** *n.;* **on approval** to be returned if not approved: *goods shipped on ~.* **—ap·prov·ing·ly** *adv.*

approx. approximate(ly). **—ap·prox·i·mate** *adj.* (uh·PROX·i·mit) nearly accurate or exact: *her ~ age; the ~ time.* **—*v.*** (–mate) **-mates, -mat·ed, -mat·ing** bring or come near to: *John's record ~s the champion's.* **—ap·prox·i·mate·ly** *adv.* **—ap·prox·i·ma·tion** (–MAY–) *n.*

appt. appoint(ed); appointment.

ap·pur·te·nance (uh·PUR·tn·unce) *n.* an appendage, accessory, or adjunct: *A company car is an ~ of his office.* **—ap·pur·te·nant** *adj.*

Apr. April.

a·près-ski (ah·pray·SKEE) *n.* & *adj.* (of) the relaxation period after skiing: *~ clothes, parties.*

ap·ri·cot (AP·ri–, AY–) *n.* an orange-colored oval fruit similar to the peach.

A·pril (AY–) *n.* the fourth month of the calendar, having 30 days. **—April fool** a victim of a practical joke on April 1, or **April Fool's Day.**

a pri·o·ri (ah·pree·OR·ee) *adj.* & *adv.* of reasoning, proceeding from cause to effect; cf. A POSTERIORI.

a·pron (AY·prun) *n.* a garment worn in front to protect one's clothes while working; also, anything similar to an apron in form or function, as the front part of a stage: *a man* **tied to** *his wife's* **apron strings** (i.e. dependent on her).

ap·ro·pos (ap·ruh·POH) *adj.* relevant. **—*adv.*** opportunely; also, by the way; incidentally. **—apropos of** with regard to.

apse (APS) *n.* a recessed and vaulted part of a building, esp. one at the end of a church.

apt. apartment; aptitude.

apt *adj.* **1** appropriate: *an ~ observation.* **2** naturally suited; likely to or inclined: *~ at solving problems; ~ to work too hard.* **—apt·ly** *adv.* **—apt·ness** *n.* **—ap·ti·tude** *n.* **1** aptness. **2** natural ability; talent: *a scholastic ~ test.*

aq·ua (AK·wuh) *n., pl.* **-uae** (–wee) or **-uas** **1** water. **2** a greenish-blue color. **—aq·ua·cade** *n.* a water entertainment spectacle featuring swimmers and divers. **—aquaculture, aquafarm** See AQUICULTURE. **—Aq·ua-Lung** *Trademark.* an underwater breathing apparatus; scuba; also **aq·ua·lung** *n.* **—aq·ua·ma·rine** (–muh·REEN) *n.* a bluish-green beryl; also, its color. **—aq·ua·naut** *n.* a scuba diver trained in underwater exploration. **—aq·ua·plane** *n.* a board pulled by a motorboat, which one rides on water standing up; ***v.*** **-planes, -planed, -plan·ing. —aqua re·gi·a** (–REE·jee·uh) a mixture of hydrochloric and nitric acids for dissolving platinum and gold. **—a·quar·i·um** (uh·KWAIR·ee·um) *n.* **-i·ums** or **-i·a** a container for keeping or displaying water animals and plants; also, an establishment with a collection of such exhibits; its keeper is an **a·quar·ist** (uh·KWAIR–). **—A·quar·i·us** (uh·KWAIR·ee·us) *n.* a S. constellation and the 11th sign of the zodiac. **—a·quat·ic** (uh·KWOT·ic, –KWAT–) *adj.* of, in, or on water: ~ *plants;* **aquatics** *n.pl.* water sports; **a·quat·i·cal·ly** *adv.* **—aq·ua·tint** (AK·wuh–) *n.* a method of etching a plate so that the print made with it resembles watercolor; also, a picture thus printed; ***v.:*** *an ~ ed picture.* **—aq·ua·vit** (AK·wuh·veet) *n.* a Scandinavian liquor flavored with caraway seed. **—aqua vi·tae** (–VYE·tee) alcohol or a strong liquor. **—aq·ue·duct** (AK·wuh–) *n.* an inclined, usu. elevated channel for bringing water from a distance; also, the structure supporting such a channel. **—a·que·ous** (AY·kwee·us, AK–) *adj.* dissolved in water; watery: *an ~ solution of ammonia;* **aqueous humor** a fluid that fills the space between the cornea and the lens of an eye. **—aq·ui·cul·ture** (AK·wi·cul·chur) *n.* **1** the cultivation of fish and water plants, usu. in an artificial stream, pond, etc. called an **aq·ua·farm. 2** same as HYDROPONICS. Also **aq·ua·cul·ture. —aq·ui·fer** (AK·wi·fur) *n.* a water-containing layer of porous rock, ·ınd, or gravel.

Aq·ui·la (AK·wi·luh) *n.* a northern constellation in the Milky Way. **—aq·ui·line** (AK·wi–) *adj.* similar to an eagle; **aquiline nose** one shaped like an eagle's beak.

A·qui·nas (uh·KWYE·nus), **Saint Thomas.** 1225–1274, an Italian scholastic philosopher and theologian.

ar. arrival; arrive. **—-ar** *adj. suffix.* of or having to do with; like: as in *globular, lunar, stellar.* **—Ar** Arabic; argon. **—AR** Arkansas. **—A/R** account receivable.

Ar·ab (AIR·ub) *n.* a member of any of the Arabic-speaking Semitic peoples of the Near East; ***adj.*** Arabian: *the ~ League.* **—ar·a·besque** (air·uh·BESK) *n.* a design with intertwining flowers, foliage, and geometric figures, ***adj.:*** *an ~ style.* **—A·ra·bi·a** (uh·RAY·bee·uh) the peninsula between the Red Sea and the Persian Gulf; **A·ra·bi·an** *adj.* & *n.;* **Arabian Sea** the part of the Indian Ocean that lies to the west of India. **—Ar·a·bic** (AIR·uh–) *n.* the S.W. Semitic language of the Arabs, in its classical form as used in the Koran and as dialects spoken mainly in Arabia, Jordan, Syria, Iraq, Palestine, Egypt, and N. Africa; ***adj.*** of or having to do with the language and culture of the Arabs: **Arabic numeral** any of the symbols 1,2,3,4,5,6,7,8,9,0.

ar·a·ble (AIR·uh·bl) *adj.* suitable for tillage and cultivation: ~ *land.* **—ar·a·bil·i·ty** (–BIL–) *n.*

a·rach·nid (uh·RAC–) *n.* an eight-legged insect of a group that includes spiders, scorpions, mites, and ticks.

Ar·a·ma·ic (air·uh·MAY·ic) *n.* a N.W. Semitic language that was widely spoken over S.W. Asia between 300 B.C. and A.D. 650. ***—adj.:*** *the ~ alphabet.*

Ar·a·wak (AIR·uh·wak) *n.* (a member of) an Indian people now living in the Guianas; also, their language. **—Ar·a·wak·an** (–WAK·un) *n.* **1** a South American Indian language group. **2** an Arawak; ***adj.*** pertaining to Arawakans or their languages.

ar·ba·lest (AHR·buh·list) *n.* a medieval military weapon for throwing missiles; also **ar·ba·list.**

ar·bi·ter (AHR·bi·tur) *n.* one who has power to make a binding decision: *Usage is the ~ of language.* **—ar·bi·tra·ble** (AHR·bi·truh·bl) *adj.* capable of being arbitrated. **—ar·bit·ra·ment** (–BIT–) *n.* the deciding of a dispute; also, a decision or award. **—ar·bi·trar·y** (–trer–) *adj.* not based on reason; despotic; **ar·bi·trar·i·ly** *adv.;* **ar·bi·trar·i·ness** *n.* **—ar·bi·trate** *v.* **-trates, -trat·ed, -trat·ing 1** judge between disputing parties. **2** decide. **3** refer to an arbitrator: *When talks failed, the rival factions ~d the dispute.* **—ar·bi·tra·tion** (–TRAY–) *n.* **—ar·bi·tra·tor** (AHR–) *n.* a judge or referee in a dispute.

ar·bor (AHR·bur) *n.* a shady nook or bower formed by overhanging vegetation. **—ar·bo·re·al** (–BOR·ee·ul) *adj.* pertaining to trees; living in trees: *Monkeys are ~ creatures.* **—ar·bo·re·tum** (ahr·buh·REE·tum) *n.* **-tums** or **-ta** a place where trees and shrubs are grown and displayed. **—ar·bor·vi·tae** (ahr·bur·VYE·tee) *n.* any of various trees of the pine family that have scalelike leaves.

ar·bu·tus (–BYOO–) *n.* a plant of the heath family with fragrant pink or white flowers and red berries; also called "trailing arbutus."

arc *n.* anything shaped like a bow, as a segment of a circle or an electrical discharge across two electrodes. ***—v.*** **arcs, arc(k)ed, arc(k)·ing** form or move in an arc.

A.R.C. American Red Cross.

ar·cade (ahr–) *n.* **1** a covered passageway lined with shops. **2** a series of arches with columns supporting them.

ar·cane (ahr–) *adj.* hidden; mysterious.

[1]arch *n.* a curved structure built over a passage, as in gateways and bridges, supporting what is above it; also, any similar structure or formation: *a triumphal ~; the ~ of the foot.* ***—v.:*** *eye-*

brows ~ed in amazement; a rainbow ~ing over a field.

[2]arch *adj.* **1** also *comb.form.* chief; principal; extreme: *the archenemy; archdeacon; an ~ rogue;* also **archi-**: *~-episcopal.* **2** playfully saucy: *her ~ smile;* **arch·ly** *adv.;* **arch·ness** *n.* **—arch** *n. suffix.* ruler; leader: as in *heresiarch, matriarch.* **—arch.** archaic; architect; architectural; architecture. **—ar·chae·ol·o·gy** (ahr·kee·OL·uh·jee) *n.* the scientific study of man's past usu. involving the excavating and examining of fossils, tombs, artifacts, etc.; **ar·chae·ol·o·gist** *n.* **—ar·chae·o·log·i·cal** (–LOJ–) *adj.;* **ar·chae·o·log·i·cal·ly** *adv.* **—ar·chae·op·ter·yx** (ahr·kee·OP–) *n.* an extinct bird that represents a stage of evolution between reptiles and birds. **—Ar·chae·o·zo·ic** (–kee·uh·ZOH–) same as ARCHEOZOIC. **—ar·cha·ic** (ahr·CAY·ic) *adj.* **1** ancient; antiquated: *~ laws.* **2** of words, usage, etc. belonging to the language of an earlier period. **—ar·cha·i·cal·ly** *adv.* **—ar·cha·ism** (AHR·kee–) *n.* an archaic word, usage, etc.: *"Forsooth" is an ~ for "truly";* **ar·cha·ist** *n.* **—arch·an·gel** (ARK·ain·jul) *n.* an angel of the highest order. **—arch·bish·op** (arch·BISH·up) *n.* a bishop of the highest rank; **arch·bish·op·ric** *n.* an archbishop's jurisdiction or his position. **—arch·dea·con** (–DEE·kun) *n.* esp. in the Anglican Church, a church official who assists a bishop. **—arch·di·o·cese** (–DYE·uh·sis) *n.* the diocese of an archbishop. **—arch·duke** (–DUKE) *n.* a prince of the former royal family of Austria; his wife or widow is an **arch·duch·ess** (–DUTCH–); their territory is an **arch·duch·y, -chies; arch·du·cal** (–DEW–) *adj.* **—arch·en·e·my** (ARCH–) *n.* **-mies** a chief enemy, esp. Satan. **—ar·che·ol·o·gy** (–kee·OL–) same as ARCHAEOLOGY. **—Ar·che·o·zo·ic** (–kee·uh·ZOH·ic) *adj.* pertaining to the earliest geological era, some 2,300 million years ago.

arch·er *n.* one who uses a bow and arrow. **—arch·er·y** *n.* the art of shooting with a bow and arrows.

ar·che·type (AHR·ki–) *n.* the original model or pattern on which things of the same type are based; prototype; **ar·che·typ·al** (–TYE·pul) or **ar·che·typ·i·cal** (–TIP–) *adj.* **—arch·fiend** (–FEEND) *n.* a chief fiend, esp. Satan. **—archi-** same as [2]ARCH, *adj.* 1. **—ar·chi·e·pis·co·pal** (–kee·i·PIS·cuh·pul) *adj.* pertaining to an archbishop. **—ar·chi·man·drite** (–ki·MAN–) *n.* in Eastern churches, a cleric ranking below a bishop; esp., the head of a monastery or convent.

Ar·chi·me·des (–ki·MEE·deez) 287?–212 B.C. Greek mathematician and inventor. **—Ar·chi·me·de·an** (–MEE·dee·un) *adj.*

ar·chi·pel·a·go (–ki·PEL·uh·go) *n.* **-go(e)s** a group of islands; also, a sea dotted with islands. **—ar·chi·tect** (AHR·ki–) *n.* one who designs buildings and oversees their construction. **—ar·chi·tec·ton·ic** (–tec·TON·ic) *adj.* of or having to do with architectural principles; **architectonics** *n.pl.* [with *sing.* or *pl. v.*] the science of architecture; structural design. **—ar·chi·tec·ture** (AHR·ki·tec·chur) *n.* the art or science of building; also, the design of a building; **ar·chi·tec·tur·al** (–TEC–) *adj.: an ~ beauty;* **ar·chi·tec·tur·al·ly** *adv.* **—ar·chi·trave** (AHR·ki–) *n.* in classical architecture, the beam resting immediately on top of a column or row of columns. **—ar·chive** (AHR·kive) *n.* usu. **archives** *pl.* a historical document or public record; also, the place where such materials are kept; **ar·chi·val** (ahr·KYE·vul) *adj.;* **ar·chi·vist** (AHR·ki–) *n.* **—ar·chon** (AHR·con) *n.* one of the chief magistrates of classical Athens.

arch·way *n.* a passageway with an arch over it; also, the arch itself.

-archy *comb.form.* rule; government: as in *monarchy, oligarchy.*

arcked, arck·ing See ARC.

arc lamp an electric lamp that gives a brilliant light from an arc struck between two incandescent electrodes enclosed in a gas; also **arc light.**

arc·tic (ARC–, AR–) *n.* **1 the Arctic** the polar region north of the **Arctic Circle** which is a parallel of latitude at 66° 33′N. **2** a warm waterproof overshoe. ***—adj.*** **1** of or having to do with the Arctic region: *the ~ fox; an ~ plant.* **2** bitterly cold; frigid: *an ~ disposition.* **—Arctic Ocean** the waters north of the Arctic Circle. **—Arctic Zone** the region north of the Arctic Circle.

Arc·tu·rus (arc·TOOR·us) *n.* the brightest star of the constellation Boötes.

-ard or **-art** *n.suffix.* one who does (something) to excess: as in *braggart, drunkard.*

ar·dent (AR·dunt) *adj.* burning; zealous; passionate: *an ~ lover; an ~ champion of the feminists;* **ardent spirits** strong liquors; **ar·dent·ly** *adv.* **—ar·den·cy** *n.* **—ar·dor** (AHR·dur) *n.* warmth of feeling; enthusiasm; zeal.

ar·du·ous (AHR·joo·us) *adj.* requiring much energy and effort: *an ~ climb uphill;* **ar·du·ous·ly** *adv.;* **ar·du·ous·ness** *n.*

[1]are (AHR) the form of BE used with *you, we, they.*

[2]are (AIR, AHR) *n.* a metric unit of area; 100 sq. meters. **—ar·e·a** (AIR·ee·uh) *n.* **1** the extent of a surface or its measure: *a vast ~; an ~ of 3 acres.* **2** a geographical region; also, a section: *the desert ~s of Africa; a play ~.* **3** sphere of knowledge or activity; field: *the ~ of one's specialty.* **—area code** a usu. three-digit number designating a telephone area. **—ar·e·al** (–ul) *adj.* **—ar·e·a·way** (AIR·ee·uh–) *n.* a small sunken area for light and air or for access to a basement.

a·re·na (uh·REE·nuh) *n.* the central area of the ancient Roman amphitheatre used as the stage; hence, any sphere of struggle or activity: *the political ~.* **—arena theater** one with the stage in the center; theater-in-the-round.

aren't (ARNT) are not.

Ar·e·op·a·gus (air·ee·OP·uh–) *n.* the highest court of ancient Athens.

Ar·es (AIR·eez) the Greek god of war.

ar·gent (AHR·junt) *adj. Rare.* of or like silver. **—*n.*** silver. **—ar·gen·tine** (–tyne) *adj.* silvery. **—ar·gen·tite** *n.* an important ore of silver.

Ar·gen·ti·na (ahr·jun·TEE·nuh) a South American republic; 1,072,163 sq.mi. (2,776,-889 km²); *cap.* Buenos Aires; also called **the Argentine. —Ar·gen·tine** (–teen) or **Ar·gen·tin·e·an** (–TIN·ee·un) *n. & adj.*

Ar·go (AHR–) *n.* a southern constellation.

ar·gon (AHR–) *n.* an inert gaseous element found in the atmosphere and used as a filler for electric bulbs.

ar·go·sy (AHR·guh·see) *n.* **-sies** a fleet of merchant ships; also, rich cargo.

ar·got (AHR·goh, –gut) *n.* the language of a particular group, esp. that of the underworld.

ar·gue (AHR–) *v.* **-gues, -gued, -gu·ing 1** give reasons in order to persuade, attack, or defend: *Salesmen ~ us into buying a product; a lawyer ~s a case; He ~s soundly; to ~ for justice to the poor; to ~ that all are equal.* **2** quarrel; dispute: *They are always ~ing.* **3** indicate; prove: *John's decision ~s a lot of maturity.* **—ar·gu·a·ble** *adj.* **—ar·gu·ment** *n.* a reasoning; dispute; quarrel. **—ar·gu·men·ta·tion** (–TAY–) *n.* the process of reasoning. **—ar·gu·men·ta·tive** (–MEN·tuh·tiv) *adj.* fond of disputing.

Ar·gus (AHR·gus) *n.* in Greek myths, a hundred-eyed monster; **Ar·gus-eyed** *adj.* vigilant.

ar·gyle (AHR·guile) *n.* a varicolored knitting pattern composed of diamonds; also **argyll.**

ar·i·a (AH·ree·uh) *n.* a vocal solo with accompaniment, forming part of an opera, oratorio, or cantata.

-arian *n.suffix.* one who believes in, or promotes: as in *humanitarian, Unitarian, vegetarian.*

ar·id (AIR·id) *adj.* dry; parched; also dull: *an ~ desert; ~ discourse.* **—a·rid·i·ty** (uh·RID–) *n.*

Ar·ies (AIR·eez) a N. constellation and the first sign of the zodiac; also called "the Ram."

a·right (uh·RITE) *adv.* correctly; rightly.

a·rise (uh·RIZE) *v.* **a·ris·es, a·rose, a·ris·en** (uh·RIZ·un), **a·ris·ing 1** get up. **2** result; come to be: *If the need ~s, phone for help.*

ar·is·toc·ra·cy (–TOC·ruh·see) *n.* **-cies 1** nobility; also, government by the nobility. **2** an elite group. **—a·ris·to·crat** (uh·RIS·tuh–) *n.* **—a·ris·to·crat·ic** (–CRAT–) *adj.;* **a·ris·to·crat·i·cal·ly** *adv.*

Ar·is·toph·a·nes (ar·is·TOF·uh·neez) 450?–380? B.C., Greek comic dramatist.

Ar·is·tot·le (AIR·is·totl) 384–322 B.C., Greek philosopher.

arith. arithmetic(al). **—a·rith·me·tic** (uh·RITH·muh–) *n.* computation with numbers, using addition, subtraction, multiplication, and division. **—ar·ith·met·ic** (air·ith·MET·ic) or **-i·cal** *adj.;* **ar·ith·met·i·cal·ly** *adv.* **—a·rith·me·ti·cian** (uh·rith·muh·TISH·un) *n.*

-arium *n.suffix.* a place for; a thing related to: as in *herbarium, honorarium.*

Ariz. *Abbrev.* for **Ar·i·zo·na** (air·i·ZOH·nuh) a S.W. state of the U.S.; 113,909 sq. mi. (295,-023 km²); *cap.* Phoenix. **—Ar·i·zo·nan** *adj.* & *n.*

ark *n.* **1** the boat in which Noah and his family survived the Flood. **2** the chest in which the ancient Hebrews carried the tablets of the law; also called **ark of the covenant.**

Ark. *Abbrev.* for **Ar·kan·sas** (AHR·kun·saw) a S. state of the U.S.; 53,104 sq.mi. (137,539 km²); *cap.* Little Rock. **—Ar·kan·san** (–KAN·zun) *adj.* & *n.*

¹arm *n.* either of one's two upper limbs; also, anything resembling it: *the ~s of a chair; ~s* (i.e. sleeves) *of a shirt; an ~ of the sea; an ~ of the military* (i.e. infantry, artillery, army, navy, etc.). **—the arm of the law** power; authority. **—at arm's length** at a distance. **—with open arms** warmly. **—arm·less** *adj.*

²arm *n.* **1 arms** *pl.* weapons: *the ~s race between the superpowers;* **take up arms** fight; **up in arms** ready to fight. **2 arms** *pl.* a heraldic or other pictorial design used as insignia, esp. on a shield; also called *coat of arms.* **—*v.*** be or get ready for action; equip with weapons; prepare for war: *to ~ a bomb; ~ing the citizenry;* **armed** *adj.* ready or equipped to fight; military: *the ~ services; an ~ camp.* **—ar·ma·da** (–MAH·duh) *n.* a fleet of warships. **—ar·ma·dil·lo** (ahr·muh·DIL·loh) *n.* **-los,** a small, toothless, burrowing tropical animal having a protective covering of bony plates.

Ar·ma·ged·don (ahr·muh·GED·un) *n.* the final conflict between good and evil, as foretold in the Bible.

ar·ma·ment (AHR·muh·munt) *n.* **1** military force; weapons and supplies. **2** the process of arming for war. **—ar·ma·ture** (AHR·muh·chur) *n.* **1** the rotating part of a dynamo or motor, in which current is produced. **2** a protective covering. **—arm·chair** *n.* a chair with armrests. **—armed forces** the military, naval, and air forces of a country.

Ar·me·ni·a (ahr·MEE·nee·uh) an ancient kingdom of Asia Minor, now forming the **Armenian Soviet Socialist Republic** (*cap.* Yerevan) and parts of Turkey and Iran. **—Ar·me·ni·an** *n.* a person of or from Armenia; also, the Indo-European language of the Armenians; ***adj.:*** *the ~ church.*

arm·ful *n.* **-fuls** as much as can be held in one arm or in both together. **—arm·hole** *n.* an opening in a garment for the wearer's arm. **—ar·mi·stice** (AHR·muh·stis) *n.* stoppage of fighting by agreement on all sides; truce; **Armistice Day** Nov. 11, observed as the anniversary of the end of World War I: celebrated since 1954 as Veterans Day on the 4th Monday in October. **—arm•let** (–lit) *n.* a band worn on an arm around the sleeve. **—arm•lock** *n.* hammerlock. **—ar•mor** (AHR·mur) *n.* a usu. metal protective covering, as a soldier's *suit of armor,* the steel plating of ships and tanks, etc.; **ar•mored** *adj.: an ~ car.* **—ar•mor•er** *n.* **1** one who makes or repairs weapons. **2** an army man in charge of firearms. **—ar•mo•ri•al** (–MOR·ee·ul) *adj.* pertaining to heraldry; **armorial bearings** coat of arms. **—ar•mor•y** (AHR·muh·ree) *n.* **-mor•ies** a place for storing arms; also, an arms factory. **—arm•pit** *n.* the hollow under the arm where it joins the body. **—arm•rest** (ARM–) *n.* a support for the arm or elbow. **—arm-twist•ing** *n.* coercive pressure; **arm-twist•er** *n.* **—ar•my** (AHR·mee) *n.* **-mies** **1** an organized body of men trained in warfare. **2** any organized group; multitude; *the Salvation Army; an ~ of ants.* **—army ant** a variety of ants that move and attack in colonies. **—army worm** the caterpillar of a variety of moth that attacks crops in vast numbers.

ar•ni•ca (AHR·ni·kuh) *n.* a tincture applied to sprains and bruises, prepared from a composite herb with bright-yellow ray flowers; also, the plant itself.

Ar•nold (AHR·nuld) *n.* **1 Benedict.** 1741–1801, American general in the Revolutionary War who later became a traitor. **2 Matthew.** 1822–1888, English poet and critic.

a•ro•ma (uh·ROH·muh) *n.* the agreeable spicy smell of foods, certain vegetables, etc.: *the ~ of coffee.* **—ar•o•mat•ic** (air·uh·MAT·ic) *adj.: an ~ tobacco.*

arose *pt.* of ARISE.

a•round (uh–) *adv. & prep.* **1** in a circle (of): *to drive ~ (the block); 30 inches ~ (the waist).* **2** here and there (in); about: *to browse ~ (in a library).* **3** *Informal.* near; approximately: *Hang ~ (here); a car costing ~ $10,000.* **4** on the other side (of): *He went ~ (the corner).* **5** in the opposite way: *Turn ~ !*

a•rouse (uh·ROWZ) *v.* **a•rous•es, a•roused, a•rous•ing** **1** awaken. **2** stir up; excite: *The patient gets violent when ~d.* **—a•rous•al** *n.*

ar•peg•gi•o (ahr·PEJ·ee·oh) *n.* **-os** in music, a chord whose notes are to be played in rapid succession.

arr. arranged; arrival; arrive(d).

ar•raign (uh·RAIN) *v.* call before a court to answer a charge; also, charge or accuse. **—ar•raign•ment** *n.*

ar•range (uh·RAINJ) *v.* **-rang•es, -ranged, -rang•ing** **1** put in order: *~ books on a shelf.* **2** set up; plan; prepare: *She ~d a meeting between them; to ~ with the bank for a loan.* **3** adapt (music) to suit other voices or instruments. **—ar•range•ment** *n.* **—ar•rang•er** *n.*

ar•rant (AIR·unt) *adj.* downright; utter: *~ nonsense!*

ar•ras (AIR·us) *n. sing. & pl.* tapestry, esp. as a wall hanging or screen.

ar•ray (uh–) *n.* an arrangement that is imposing or splendid: *an army in battle ~; an ~ of jewelry; beautiful in her bridal ~; an ~ of facts and figures.* **—v.:** *~ed like a queen; troops ~ing for battle.*

ar•rears (uh·REERZ) *n.pl.* **1** overdue debts or other unfulfilled obligations: *~ of work.* **2 in arrears** behind (in discharging some obligation): *His rent is in ~.*

ar•rest (uh–) *v.* **1** stop or check. **2** seize and hold legally. **3** capture the attention; **ar•resting** *adj.: an ~ view of the lake.* **—n.:** *The police made several ~s;* **under arrest** legally detained.

ar•rière-pen•sée (ar·ee·air·pahn·SAY) *n.* *French.* ulterior motive.

ar•rive (uh–) *v.* **ar•rives, ar•rived, ar•riv•ing** **1** reach somewhere or some conclusion: *to ~ in Paris; to ~ at a decision.* **2** come: *The time for departure has ~d.* **3** be successful in one's career: *Votes showed that the young politician had ~d.* **—ar•ri•val** (uh·RYE·vul) *n.: A crowd awaited the hero's ~; These rooms are for late ~s.*

ar•ro•gance (AIR·uh·gunce) *n.* a haughty manner or attitude. **—ar•ro•gant** (–gunt) *adj.* excessively and unpleasantly sure of oneself; **ar•ro•gant•ly** *adv.* **—ar•ro•gate** *v.* **-gates, -gat•ed, -gat•ing** take or claim without right: *He ~d too much authority to himself;* **ar•ro•ga•tive** *adj.;* **ar•ro•ga•tion** (–GAY–) *n.*

ar•row (AIR·oh) *n.* a slender, pointed shaft used as a missile to be shot from a bow; also, a figure (→) used to point somewhere, as on a sign or a map. **—ar•row•head** *n.* **1** the pointed tip of an arrow. **2** a marsh plant whose leaves resemble the tips of arrows. **—ar•row•root** *n.* a starch made from the roots of a tropical American plant; also, the plant.

ar•roy•o (uh·ROY·oh) *n.* **-os** *Southwestern U.S.* a channel cut by an intermittent flow of water; gully; also, a flowing rivulet.

arse (AHRS) same as ASS, *n.* 2.

ar•se•nal (AHR·suh·nul) *n.* a place where arms and ammunition are made or stored; hence, a storehouse: *A dictionary is an ~ of words.*

ar•se•nic (AHR·suh–) *n.* a chemical element which forms poisonous compounds with oxygen and is used in insecticides, weed-killers, etc. **—adj.:** *an ~ compound;* also **ar•sen•i•cal** (–SEN–) or **ar•se•ni•ous** (–SEE·nee·us).

ar•son (AHR·sun) *n.* the wrongful burning of property. **—ar•son•ist** *n.*

[1]art *n.* **1** creation or expression of beauty; also, products of beauty: *That painting is a work of ~.* **2** skilled activity: *the ~ of sewing.* **3** usu. **arts** *pl.* the humanities, as distinguished from science. **4** artfulness; cunning; tricks.

²art *Archaic.* the form of BE used with *thou.* **—art.** article; artificial; artillery. **— -art** same as -ARD.

art dec·o (–DEC·oh) a style of design characterized by geometric forms, used in furnishings, architecture, fashions, etc; also **Art Deco.**

ar·te·fact same as ARTIFACT.

Ar·te·mis (AHR·tuh–) in Greek myths, the goddess of hunting, wildlife, and the moon.

ar·ter·y (AHR·tuh·ree) *n.* **-ter·ies** **1** any of a system of tubular vessels that carry blood from the heart to every part of the body. **2** any main channel or route of transportation or communication: *the ~s of the Mississippi River.* **—ar·te·ri·al** (–TEER·ee·ul) *adj.* of or like an artery: *~ blood; ~ railways;* ***n.*** a through street or expressway. **—ar·te·ri·al·ly** *adv.* **—ar·te·ri·ole** (–TEER·ee–) *n.* any of an artery's branches leading to capillaries; **ar·te·ri·o·lar** (–OH·lur) *adj.* **—ar·te·ri·o·scle·ro·sis** (–teer·ee·oh·skluh·ROH–) *n.* a chronic disease in which hardening of the arteries impairs blood circulation; **ar·te·ri·o·scle·rot·ic** (–ROT·ic) *adj.*

ar·te·sian (ahr·TEE·zhun) **well** a well bored deep to a source of water that gushes up because of its pressure.

art·ful *adj.* **1** showing art or skill. **2** crafty; cunning. **—art·ful·ly** *adv.* **—art·ful·ness** *n.*

ar·thri·tis (ahr·THRYE–) *n.* inflammation of the joints. **—ar·thrit·ic** (–THRIT·ic) *adj.;* also ***n.*** an arthritic patient.

ar·thro·pod (AHR·thruh–) any of a large group of backboneless animals (including insects, spiders, and crabs) that have segmented bodies and jointed antennae and limbs.

Ar·thur (AHR·thur) **1 King.** a British king of the 6th century, hero of the **Ar·thu·ri·an** (ahr·THOOR·ee·un) romances of the Knights of the Round Table. **2 Chester A.** 1830–1886, 21st U.S. President (1881–85).

ar·ti·choke (AHR·ti–) *n.* a tall thistlelike herb of the composite family with a large flower head that is used as a vegetable.

ar·ti·cle *n.* **1** a particular thing, item, or object: *an ~ of food or clothing.* **2** a clause or section of a document: **Articles of Confederation** (i.e. the 1781 U.S. Constitution). **3** a nonfiction essay or story: *a newspaper ~.* **4** either of two grammatical items, the *definite article* (THE) or the *indefinite article* (A, AN). ***—v.*** **-cles, -cled, -cling** bind by a contract: *an ~d apprentice.* **—ar·tic·u·lar** (–TIC·yuh·lur) *adj.* of or having to do with body joints: *~ membrane; ~ cartilage.* **—ar·tic·u·late** (–lit) *adj.* **1** jointed. **2** of speech, clear and distinct; intelligible. **3** of a person, able to express thoughts clearly: *So excited, he was barely ~.* ***—v.*** (–late) **-lates, -lat·ed, -lat·ing** **1** join together. **2** express or speak distinctly. **—ar·tic·u·late·ly** *adv.;* **ar·tic·u·late·ness** *n.* **—ar·tic·u·la·tion** (–LAY–) *n.*

ar·ti·fact (AHR·ti–) *n.* something made or formed by human hands, esp. an item of archaeological interest. **—ar·ti·fice** (AHR·ti·fis) *n.* **1** skillfulness; also, a skillful device. **2** ingenuity; trickery. **—ar·ti·fi·cer** (–TIF·i·sur) *n.* a skilled craftsman. **—ar·ti·fi·cial** (–FISH·ul) *adj.* **1** made by man rather than by nature; also, imitative of something natural: *an ~ leg; ~ silk; ~ light.* **2** affected; not natural: *an ~ smile.* **—artificial insemination** introduction of semen into a female without sexual contact. **—artificial respiration** a forced breathing method, such as mouth-to-mouth resuscitation, used on a person whose lungs are not working. **—ar·ti·fi·ci·al·i·ty** (–ee·AL–) *n.* **—ar·ti·fi·cial·ly** (–FISH·uh·lee) *adv.* **—ar·ti·fi·cial·ness** *n.*

ar·til·ler·y (ahr·TIL·uh·ree) *n.* mounted guns of large caliber; also, a branch of an army equipped with these. **—artilleryman, -men** or **ar·til·ler·ist** *n.*

ar·ti·san (AHR·ti·zun) *n.* a manually skilled craftsman, as a tailor or carpenter. **—art·ist** *n.* one who practices any of the fine arts, esp. painting or sculpture. **—ar·tiste** (–TEEST) *n.* a professional entertainer, esp. singer, actor, or dancer. **—ar·tis·tic** (–TIS–) *adj.;* **ar·tis·ti·cal·ly** *adv.* **—art·ist·ry** (AHR·tis·tree) *n.* an artist's skill or quality. **—art·less** *adj.* **1** free from guile; not artful; candid: *a child's ~ questions.* **2** not artificial; natural: *the ~ grace of gazelles.* **3** lacking artistic qualities. Hence **art·less·ly** *adv.;* **art·less·ness** *n.* **—art·sy** *adj.* **art·si·er, -si·est** arty; also **art·(s)y-craft·(s)y.** **—art·work** *n.* **1** artistic work: *Eskimo ~ on display.* **2** the graphic portions of a printed text. **—art·y** *adj.* **art·i·er, -i·est** *Informal.* artistic in a showy, dilettantish, or imitative way; **art·i·ly** *adv.;* **art·i·ness** *n.*

arty. artillery.

ar·um (AIR·um) *n.* a type of plant similar to the calla lily with large leaves and tiny flowers on a fleshy spike enveloped in a white hoodlike spathe, as the jack-in-the-pulpit.

A.R.V. American (Standard) Revised Version (of the Bible), published in 1901.

-ary *n. suffix.* one connected with: as in *functionary.* ***—adj.:*** as in *parliamentary.*

Ar·y·an (AIR·ee·un) *n.* a member or descendant of a prehistoric people that spoke a language from which modern Indo-Iranian and European languages are descended; Indo-European; also, the language of the Aryans. ***—adj.:*** *English is an ~ language.*

as (AZ) *adv.* **1** in the same degree; equally: *~ tall as an oak.* **2** for instance: *felines, ~ lions and leopards.* ***—conj.*** **1** in the same way as: *She did ~ promised.* **2** during the time that; while: *She wept ~ she told the story.* **3** because: *They stopped work ~ it was getting dark.* **4** though: *Tall ~ John is, he is shorter than Jim.* **5** with the result that: *Worried so much ~ to lose sleep.* ***—prep.*** **1** in the character or position of: *Speaking ~ a lawyer, he was against it.* **2** like: *cool ~ a cucumber.* **—as . . . as:** *~ good ~ gold; ~ busy ~ a bee; ~ white ~ a sheet.* **—as if** or **as though:** *It looks ~ though it might rain.* **—as for, as to:** *~ for me, I don't mind working on the holiday; indifferent ~ to money.* **—as is** unchanged: *a scratched chair sold ~ is at a reduced price.*

As arsenic.

AS Anglo-Saxon; antisubmarine.

as·a·fet·i·da (as·uh·FET·i·duh) *n.* a strong-smelling gum obtained from a group of Asiatic plants used in medicine and as a seasoning.

as·bes·tos (as·BES·tus) *n.* a nonburning fibrous mineral containing magnesium silicate, used for fireproofing; also **as·bes·tus.**

A.S.C. American Society of Cinematographers.

as·cend (uh·SEND) *v.* move upward; climb; go higher up: *~ a mountain; ~ a river.* **—ascend the throne** become king (or queen). **—as·cen·dant** (uh·SEND·unt) *adj.* rising in influence or power: *His star is* **in the ascendant;** also **as·cen·dent.** **—as·cend·an·cy** (uh·SEN·dun·see) *adj.* dominance; also **as·cend·en·cy.** **—as·cen·sion** *n.* the act of ascending; **the Ascension** Christ's departure for Heaven: *The Thursday 40 days after Easter is observed as* **Ascension Day.** **—as·cent** (uh–) *n.* **1** the act of climbing upward; also, the way up: *a steep ~.* **2** the rate of ascending; slope or elevation: *an ~ of 15°.*

as·cer·tain (–ur·TAIN) *v.* find out with certainty: *~ the facts of a story.* **—as·cer·tain·a·ble** (–TAY·nuh·bl) *adj.*

as·cet·ic (uh·SET·ic) *adj.* self-denying, esp. with a religious motive; austere; also **as·cet·i·cal.** **—*n.*:** *an ~'s regimen of life.* **—as·cet·i·cal·ly** *adv.* **—as·cet·i·cism** *n.*

a·scor·bic (uh·SCOR–) **acid** Vitamin C, used against scurvy.

as·cot (AS·cut, –cot) *n.* a neck scarf for men, worn looped under the chin, with the ends overlapping and lying flat.

as·cribe (uh·SCRIBE) *v.* **-cribes, -cribed, -crib·ing** attribute: *~ bad motives to somebody; He ~s his success to luck.* **—as·crib·a·ble** *adj.* **—as·crip·tion** (–SCRIP–) *n.*

a·sep·sis (uh·SEP–) *n.* the condition of wounds, dressings, etc. being free from germs. **—a·sep·tic** *adj.*

a·sex·u·al (ay·SEK·shoo·ul) *adj.* sexless; without sexual activity: *~ reproduction* (as in budding and cell division).

ash *n.* **1** the soft, gray, powdery substance left after burning: *a house burned to ~es.* **2** **ashes** *pl.* the remains of a cremated person. **3** a tree of the olive family with compound leaves and tough wood; also, the wood. **—ash·en** *adj.* **1** of the color of ashes; pale: *a face turned ~ with fear;* also **ash·y, ash·i·er, -i·est:** *an ~ deposit.* **2** of the ash tree.

a·shamed (uh·SHAIMD) *adj.* feeling shame; reluctant: *~ to beg.*

ash can **1** a can for trash. **2** *Slang.* a depth charge.

ash·lar (ASH·lur) *n.* squared stone for building; also **ashler.**

a·shore (uh·SHORE) *adv.* & *adj.* to or on the shore; aground.

ash·ram (ASH·rum) *n.* **1** a Hindu hermitage. **2** a religious retreat.

ash·tray (ASH–) *n.* a small dish for tobacco ash, cigar butts, etc.

Ash Wednesday the first day of Lent.

ashy See ASH.

A·sia (AY·zhuh) the land mass east of Europe; largest of the continents. **—Asia Minor** the W. peninsula of Asia, extending from the Black Sea to the Mediterranean, including most of Turkey; formerly, Anatolia. **—A·sian** *n.* & *adj.*: *Europeans and ~s; ~ Review* (since 1953). **—A·si·at·ic** (–AT–) *n.* & *adj.* [considered offensive in ref. to Asians]: *~ cholera; ~ Review* (i.e. *Asian Review* before 1953).

a·side (uh·SIDE) *adv.* to one side; away; apart: *Push a chair ~; put doubts ~; set ~ a court decision; Joking ~, I remain firm;* **aside from** besides; except for. **—*n.*** **1** an actor's words that other actors are supposed not to hear. **2** a digression.

as·i·nine (AS·uh–) *adj.* stupid. **—as·i·nin·i·ty** (as·uh·NIN–) *n.*

ask v. **1** call for an answer to: *I ~ a question.* **2** request someone *(for, about, to* do) something: *Sheila ~ed Jane her name; ~ for a loan; ~ about John's health; Smith is outside, please ~ him in; I ~ed her out to lunch.* **3** request something *(of, from)* someone: *to ~ leave of company; You're* **asking for** (i.e. looking for) *trouble.* **—ask·ing** *n.*: *A free sample is yours for the ~;* **asking price** the maximum price desired by a seller.

a·skance (uh·SKANCE) *adv.* with disapproval or distrust: *He* **looked askance at** *my suggestion;* also **askant** *Archaic.*

a·skew (uh·SKEW) *adj.* & *adv.* awry; to one side.

a·slant (uh·SLANT) *adj.* & *adv.* in a slanting direction; obliquely. **—*prep.*:** *the rain beating ~ the window.*

a·sleep (uh·SLEEP) *adj.* & *adv.* in(to) a state of sleep: *to fall ~ at one's desk; She's fast ~.*

a·so·cial (ay·SOH·shul) *adj.* not liking society; not social.

asp *n.* a small venomous snake.

as·par·a·gus (uh·SPAIR·uh–) *n.* a plant of the lily family whose tender shoots are used as a vegetable; also, the shoots.

A.S.P.C.A. American Society for the Prevention of Cruelty to Animals.

as·pect (AS–) *n.* **1** the appearance of a person or thing, esp. from one point of view: *a man of solemn ~; to study a subject in all its ~s.* **2** the facing (of a building, window, etc.) in a particular direction: *a church with a southern ~.* **—as·pec·tu·al** (–PEK·choo·ul) *adj.*

as·pen (AS–) *n.* any of several kinds of poplar whose leaves flutter in the slightest wind because of their flat stalks: *the quaking* ~.

as·per·i·ty (–PER–) *n.* **-ties** roughness; coarseness; harshness; also, an instance of these qualities: *~s of life in the Arctic.*

as·perse (uh·SPURCE) *v.* **-pers·es, -persed, -pers·ing** slander. **—as·per·sion** *n.* a slandering; a slanderous remark: *cast ~s on someone's character.*

as·phalt (AS·fault) *n.* a mixture of sand or gravel with a brownish black bituminous substance, that is used in paving streets. **—*v.*** pave with asphalt. **—as·phal·tic** (–FAUL–) *adj.* **—asphalt jungle** a crowded city viewed as a place hard to survive in.

as·pho·del (AS·fuh–) *n.* a plant of the lily family with white or yellow flowers.

as·phyx·i·a (as·FIX·ee·uh) *n.* suffocation caused by a lack of oxygen. **—as·phyx·i·ate** *v.* **-ates, -at·ed, -at·ing** suffocate or be suffocated, as by carbon monoxide poisoning, electric shock, or strangulation; **as·phyx·i·a·tion** (–AY–) *n.*

as·pic (AS–) *n.* **1** a jelly made with fish or meat stock. **2** *Archaic.* asp.

as·pi·rate (AS·puh–) *v.* **-rates, -rat·ed, -rat·ing** utter with an "h" sound; ***adj.*** (–rit) aspirated. **—as·pire** (uh·SPIRE) *v.* **-pires, -pired, -pir·ing** have a desire (to attain a goal); seek after: *to ~ to be President.* **—as·pi·rant** (AS·puh·runt) *n.* one who aspires: *an ~ to the priesthood.* **—as·pi·ra·tion** (–RAY–) *n.* **1** a breathing in or out; the use of an "h" sound. **2** a desire to achieve a goal; also, an instance of it: *Medicine was one of his early ~s.* **—as·pi·ra·tor** (–RAY·tur) *n.* a suction device for removing fluids from a space or cavity.

as·pi·rin (AS·puh–) *n.* a white crystalline drug for relieving pain and fever; also, a tablet of this: *a couple of ~(s).*

ass *n.* **1** a braying animal related to the horse but smaller; donkey; also, a stupid person. **2** *Vulgar.* buttocks; also, anus.

assagai same as ASSEGAI.

as·sail (uh·SAIL) *v.* attack violently, either with blows or verbally. **—as·sail·a·ble** *adj.* **—as·sail·ant** *n.*

as·sas·sin (uh·SAS·in) *n.* a murderer, esp. one hired to kill a prominent person. **—as·sas·si·nate** *v.* **-nates, -nat·ed, -nat·ing; as·sas·si·na·tion** (–NAY–) *n.*

as·sault (uh·SAWLT) *n.* **1** an attack with violence or words. **2** *Law.* a physical threat: *~ and battery.* **3** rape. **—*v.:*** *A policeman was ~ed in the street.* **—as·sault·er** *n.*

as·say (AS·ay, as·AY) *n.* a test or analysis (of a precious metal, ore, drugs, etc.) to determine quality or composition. **—*v.*** analyze or test; evaluate; estimate.

as·se·gai or **as·sa·gai** (AS·uh·guy) *n.* a light wooden spear with an iron tip used by tribesmen in S. Africa.

as·sem·blage (–SEM·blij) *n.* **1** act or process of assembling; assembly. **2** an assembled group. **3** (*also* ahs·ahm·BLAZH) an artistic composition using odds and ends; **as·sem·blag·ist** *n.* an artist who makes assemblages. **—as·sem·ble** (uh·SEM·bl) *v.* **-bles, -bled, -bling** **1** gather together; congregate: *The principal addressed the ~d staff.* **2** put together: *~ an automobile;* **as·sem·bler** *n.* **—as·sem·bly** (–SEM·blee) *n.* **-blies** **1:** *a school ~; a gear ~; a military ~ in ranks; an unlawful ~ of people.* **2** a legislative body: *a State Assembly; the U.N. General Assembly.* **—assembly line** a factory system in which each worker does a specific operation in assembling a product. **—as·sem·bly·man** *n.* **-men** or **as·sem·bly·wom·an, -wom·en** a member of a legislative body.

as·sent (uh·SENT) *v.* agree; consent; concur. **—*n.:*** *an ~ given to a proposal; a nod of ~.* **—as·sent·er** *n.*

as·sert (uh·SURT) *v.* say positively; defend (one's rights or claims). **—assert oneself** be forthright or bold, esp. to insist on one's rights. **—as·sert·er** *n.* **—as·ser·tion** *n.*: an ~ of innocence. **—as·ser·tive** (uh·SUR·tiv) *adj.* inclined to assert oneself: *an ~ young woman;* **as·ser·tive·ly** *adv.;* **as·ser·tive·ness** *n.*: *a course in* **assertiveness training** *to help one act with confidence in interpersonal relations and get positive results out of frustrating situations.*

as·sess (uh·SES) *v.* **1** fix the rate or amount of (a levy, fine, damages, etc.); also, impose (a payment): *Each member was ~ed $20.* **2** estimate (property, income, etc.) for taxation; also, evaluate: *to ~ the merit of a thesis.* **—as·sess·a·ble** *adj.* **—as·sess·ment** *n.* **—as·ses·sor** (–sur) *n.*

as·set (AS·et) *n.* **1** anything valuable or useful; advantage: *Experience is an ~ for a job applicant.* **2 assets** *pl.* property that may be used to pay one's debts, as real estate, securities, trademarks, good will, etc.

as·sev·er·ate (uh·SEV·uh·rate) *v.* **-ates, -at·ed, -at·ing** declare solemnly. **—as·sev·er·a·tion** (–RAY–) *n.: an ~ of faith.*

as·sid·u·ous (uh·SIJ·oo·us) *adj.* diligent; unremitting: *~ application to detail.* **—as·sid·u·ous·ly** *adv.;* **as·sid·u·ous·ness** or **as·si·du·i·ty** (as·i·DEW–) *n.*

as·sign (uh·SINE) *v.* **1** give out as someone's share: *A teacher ~s work.* **2** appoint to a post or duty: *A reporter is ~ed to a story.* **3** name; specify: *to ~ an hour for a ceremony; to ~ a motive for a murder.* **4** *Law.* transfer ownership of: *to ~ a book's copyright.* **—*n.*** an assignee. **—as·sign·a·ble** *adj.* **—as·sig·na·tion** (as·ig·NAY–) *n.* **1** allotment. **2** a lovers' tryst. **—as·sign·ee** (uh·sye·NEE) *n.* one to whom an ownership or right is legally assigned; also **as·sign.** **—as·sign·ment** *n.* **1** an act of assigning, esp. a transfer of ownership. **2** a task or duty assigned: *a math ~; an*

~ *to a foreign embassy.* —**as·sign·or** or **as·sign·er** *n.*

as·sim·i·late (uh·SIM·i–) *v.* **-lates, -lat·ed, -lat·ing** make or become similar: **a** by digestive or similar absorption: *Food is ~d in the body; the mind ~s knowledge.* **b** because of closeness of sounds: *the "p" in "cupboard" is ~d to "b."* **c** by cultural adaptation: *Immigrants ~ with the rest of a nation.* —**as·sim·i·la·ble** (–luh·bl) *adj.* —**as·sim·i·la·tion** (–LAY–) *n.*

as·sist (uh·SIST) *v.* **1** *Formal.* help; aid. **2 assist at** attend (a function or ceremony). —***n.*** an instance of helping; in baseball, ice hockey, and soccer, the action of a player that helps a teammate to make a putout or score a goal. —**as·sis·tance** (–tunce) *n.* —**as·sis·tant** (–tunt) *n.* one who helps: *a marketing ~;* ***adj.:*** *an ~ manager.*

as·size (uh·SIZE) *n.* **1** an inquest by judge and jury. **2 assizes** *pl.* periodic sessions of High Court judges in the counties of England and Wales, since 1971 replaced by Crown Courts. —***adj.:*** *an ~ town; ~ sessions.*

assn. association. —**assoc.** associate; association. —**as·so·ci·ate** (uh·SOH·shee·ate, –see·ate) *v.* **-ates, -at·ed, -at·ing** **1** of persons, join or be connected: *Jones and Smith are ~d in a law firm; to ~ with bad characters.* **2** link in the mind: *A red light is usually ~d with danger.* —***n.*** (*also* –shee·it, –see·it) companion; colleague; ***adj.:*** *an ~ judge.* —**associate professor** one ranking above an assistant professor but below a full professor. —**as·so·ci·a·tion** (–AY–) *n.* the act of associating; also, a union or group; **association football** soccer. —**as·so·ci·a·tive** (–AY·tiv, –uh·tiv) *adj.* in mathematics, having the property of not changing the result of an operation in whichever order the elements are grouped, as addition and multiplication.

as·so·nance (AS·uh·nunce) *n.* resemblance of vowel sounds that gives the effect of a partial rhyme, as in "seen—feel." —**as·so·nant** *adj.*

as·sort (uh·SORT) *v.* distribute (usu. things) into groups; classify. —**as·sort·ed** *adj.* of various kinds; miscellaneous: *a box of ~ Christmas cards.* —**as·sort·ment** *n.*

A.S.S.R. Autonomous Soviet Socialist Republic.

asst. assistant.

as·suage (uh·SWAIJ) *v.* **-suag·es, -suaged, -suag·ing** make (feelings, desires, etc.) less; ease; satisfy. —**as·suage·ment** *n.*

as·sume (uh·SOOM) *v.* **as·sumes, as·sumed, as·sum·ing** **1** suppose: *Let's ~ there is life on Mars.* **2** take (a responsibility, right, etc.) as one's own: *The junta ~d dictatorial powers.* **3** seem to take on; put on: *The problem ~s awesome proportions; to ~ an air of indifference.* —**assuming** *adj.* presumptuous; arrogant: *a very ~ young man.* —**as·sump·tion** *n.* **1** an act of assuming. **2 the Assumption** the taking up into Heaven of the Virgin Mary; also, a Church celebration of this on August 15.

as·sure (uh·SHOOR) *v.* **as·sures, as·sured, as·sur·ing** **1** make (someone) sure or confident of (something); tell confidently; convince: *John being out of the race, I was ~d of first place; This car is quite safe, I can ~ you.* **2** make certain: *Her future is ~d, thanks to the inheritance.* —**as·sur·ance** (uh·SHOOR·unce) *n.* **1** confidence; certainty. **2** promise; pledge. —**assured** *adj.* confident: *Rest ~ that your child will recover;* ***n.*** an insured person; **as·sur·ed·ly** (uh·SHOOR·id·lee) *adv.;* **as·sur·ed·ness** *n.*

As·syr·i·a (uh·SEER·ee·uh) an ancient empire that extended from the Nile to the Caspian Sea with Nineveh as capital. —**As·syr·i·an** *adj.* & *n.*

As·tar·te (uh·STAR·tee) *n.* the ancient Phoenician goddess of fertility.

a·stat·ic (ay·STAT·ic) *adj.* not static; having no tendency to assume any particular position or direction: *a galvanometer's ~ needle.* —**as·ta·tine** (AS·tuh·teen) *n.* a very unstable radioactive chemical element.

as·ter *n.* a plant of the composite family, bearing daisylike flowers of varying color. —**as·ter·isk** *n.* a star-shaped figure (*) used in printing as a reference mark or to indicate omission of letters; ***v.:*** *an ~ed footnote.* —**as·ter·ism** (AS·tuh–) *n.* a cluster or group of stars; a constellation; also, a starlike figure of light seen in some crystals.

a·stern (uh·STERN) *adj.* & *adv.* at or toward the rear of (a ship); behind: *The boat came up ~ of the ship.*

as·ter·oid (AS·tuh·roid) *n.* one of the many small planets orbiting around the sun between Mars and Jupiter. —***adj.*** star-shaped; also **as·ter·oi·dal** (–ROY·dul).

asth·ma (AZ·muh) *n.* a chronic disease of the chest marked by coughing, wheezing, and other breathing difficulties. —**asth·mat·ic** (–MAT–) *n.* an asthma patient; ***adj.:*** *an ~ attack.*

a·stig·ma·tism (uh·STIG·muh–) *n.* a focusing defect in a lens, esp. of the eye which results in blurred vision. —**as·tig·mat·ic** (–MAT–) *adj.*

a·stir (uh–) *adv.* & *adj.* **1** in an excited state: *a town ~ with the news of victory.* **2** out of bed; up.

as·ton·ish (uh·STON–) *v.* amaze; surprise greatly. —**as·ton·ished** *adj.* stunned: *an ~ audience.* —**as·ton·ish·ing** *adj.: The acrobat's feats were ~;* **as·ton·ish·ing·ly** *adv.* —**as·ton·ish·ment** *n.: Everyone stared in ~.*

as·tound (uh·STOWND) *v.* fill with sudden wonder. —**as·tound·ing** *adj.;* **as·tound·ing·ly** *adv.*

a·strad·dle (uh·STRADL) *adv.* & *prep.* astride: *to ride ~; ~ her horse.*

as·tra·khan (AS·truh·can) *n.* the curly fur made from the young lambs of a breed of Asian sheep from **Astrakhan,** a city in the U.S.S.R.; karacul. ***—adj.:*** *an ~ cap.*

as·tral (AS·trul) *adj.* pertaining to the stars; starry; stellar: *~ influences.*

a·stray (uh·STRAY) *adj.* & *adv.* away from the right course: *led ~ by bad company.*

a·stride (uh·STRIDE) *adj., adv.* & *prep.* with legs on either side (of): *to ride a horse ~; ~ riding seems safer; ~ a banister.*

as·trin·gent (uh·STRIN·junt) *adj.* tending to contract (blood vessels, tissues, etc.). ***—n.:*** *Shaving lotions contain ~s.* **—as·trin·gen·cy** *n.*

astro- *comb. form.* of the stars; of outer space: as in *astronaut, astrophysics.* **—astrol.** astrologer; astrological; astrology. **—as·tro·labe** (AS·truh–) *n.* a medieval instrument used like the modern sextant to determine the positions of heavenly bodies. **—as·trol·o·gy** (uh·STROL·uh·jee) *n.* the study of the positions of the stars in order to predict their influence on human affairs; **as·trol·o·ger** *n.;* **as·tro·log·i·cal** (as·truh·LOJ·i·kl) *adj.;* **as·tro·log·i·cal·ly** *adv.* **—astron.** astronomer; astronomical; astronomy. **—as·tro·naut** (AS·truh–) *n.* a person trained for space flights; cosmonaut; **as·tro·nau·tic** (–NAW–) or **-ti·cal** *adj.;* **as·tro·nau·tics** *n.pl.* [takes *sing. v.*] the science of making and operating spacecraft. **—as·tro·nom·i·cal** (–truh·NOM–) or **-nom·ic** *adj.* **1** pertaining to astronomy. **2** extraordinarily large: *an ~ price;* **astronomical unit** the mean radius of the earth's orbit, used as a unit of distance in astronomy. **—as·tron·o·my** (uh·STRON·uh·mee) *n.* **-mies** the science of the dimensions, constitution, motions, etc. of heavenly bodies; **as·tron·o·mer** *n.* **—as·tro·phys·ics** (–FIZ–) *n.pl.* [takes *sing. v.*] the science of the physical properties and chemical composition of heavenly bodies; **as·tro·phys·i·cist** *n.;* **as·tro·phys·i·cal** *adj.*

as·tute (–STEW–) *adj.* shrewd; sharp: *an ~ lawyer.* **—as·tute·ly** *adv.* **—as·tute·ness** *n.*

A·sun·ción (ah·soon·SYAWN) capital of Paraguay.

a·sun·der (uh·SUN·dur) *adj.* & *adv.* separated; in parts: *families torn ~ by war.*

ASV American (Revised) Standard Version of the Bible, published in 1901.

a·sy·lum (uh·SYE–) *n.* **1** protection; sanctuary: *political ~ for refugees.* **2** a place of safety; refuge; also, a mental institution.

a·sym·me·try (ay·SIM·uh·tree) *n.* lack of symmetry. **—a·sym·met·ric** (–MET–) or **-ri·cal** *adj.;* **a·sym·met·ri·cal·ly** *adv.*

as·ymp·tote (AS·im–) *n.* a straight line that is tangential to a curve but never meeting it within a finite distance, as the ordinate of a hyperbola. **—as·ymp·tot·ic** (–TOT·ic) *adj.;* **as·ymp·tot·i·cal·ly** *adv.*

¹at *prep.* [indicating] **1** position in time, place, etc.: *I met her ~ school; See you ~ noon.* **2** direction, movement, rate, degree, etc.: *aim ~ a target; driving ~ top speed; men ~ work; nations ~ war.* **3** manner, condition, state, etc.: *a body ~ rest; sold ~ auction; happy ~ his victory.*

²at (AHT) *n. sing.* & *pl.* a money unit in Laos, equal to 1/100 of a kip.

At astatine.

At·a·brine (AT·uh·brin) *Trademark.* a drug used in treating malaria; quinacrine; also **atabrine** *n.*

at·a·vism (AT·uh–) *n.* reappearance of a hereditary characteristic after a gap of several generations; **at·a·vis·tic** (–VIS–) *adj.;* **at·a·vis·ti·cal·ly** *adv.*

ate *pt.* of EAT.

-ate *suffix.* **1** *v.* make; become; cause to become (as specified): as in *invalidate, consecrate.* **2** *n.* one made or become (as specified); also an office or function: as in *mandate, episcopate.* **3** *adj.* characterized by (as specified): as in *moderate, precipitate.*

at·el·ier (ATL·yay) *n.* a workshop or studio, esp. an artist's.

a tem·po (ah·TEM·poh) *Music.* in regular time.

Ath·a·pas·can or **Ath·a·pas·kan** (ath·uh·PAS·kun) *n.* an Amerindian language family of western U.S. and Canada, including the Navaho and Apache languages; also, one of a people speaking any of these languages. ***—adj.:*** *an ~ tribe.* Also **Athabascan, Athabaskan.**

a·the·ism (AY·thee–) *n.* the denial of God's existence. **—a·the·ist** *n.* **—a·the·is·tic** or **-ti·cal** *adj.* **—a·the·is·ti·cal·ly** *adv.*

A·the·na (uh·THEE·nuh) the Greek goddess of wisdom. **—ath·e·n(a)e·um** (ath·uh·NEE·um) *n.* an institution of learning; a literary or scientific club; a library. **—Ath·ens** (ATH·unz) capital of Greece; **A·the·ni·an** (uh·THEE·nee·un) *n.* & *adj.*

ath·er·o·scle·ro·sis (ath·uh·roh·scluh·ROH–) *n.* a thickening of arterial walls because of fatty accumulations inside them; **ath·er·o·scle·rot·ic** (–ROT–) *adj.*

a·thirst (uh·THIRST) *adj.* longing (*for* freedom, glory, adventure, news, etc.)

ath·lete (ATH·leet) *n.* one trained for competing in physical exercises, sports, and games, i.e. **ath·let·ics** (ath·LET–) *n.pl.* [takes *sing. v.*] **—ath·let·ic** *adj.: an ~ event; a man of ~ build.* **—athlete's foot** a contagious skin disease of the feet.

a·thwart (uh·THWORT) *adv.* & *prep.* from side to side (of): *riding ~ the path of an army.*

a·tilt (uh·TILT) *adj.* & *adv.* in a tilted position.

-ation *n. suffix.* action, state, result, etc. of: as in *regulation, civilization, coloration.*

-ative *adj. suffix.* of or having to do with: as in *affirmative, creative;* also ***n.:*** as in *narrative, purgative.*

Atl. Atlantic. —**At·lan·ta** (at·LAN·tuh) capital of Georgia. —**At·lan·tic** (–LAN–) *adj.* of or having to do with the Atlantic Ocean; ***n.*** the Atlantic Ocean, the ocean lying between the Americas in the west and Europe and Africa in the east. —**At·lan·tis** a legendary continent supposed to have sunk in the Atlantic Ocean. —**At·las** (AT·lus) **1** in Greek myths, a Titan punished by Zeus by being forced to hold up the heavens on his shoulders. **2** **atlas** *n.* a book of maps. —**Atlas Mountains** the mountains lying across Morocco, Algeria, and Tunisia in N.W. Africa.

ATM automated teller machine.

atm. atmosphere; atmospheric. —**at·mos·phere** (AT·mus·feer) *n.* **1** the air surrounding the earth; also, the similar gaseous envelope around any heavenly body. **2** the air or environment of any place; general mood; also a distinctive effect or quality: *That restaurant has real ~.* —**at·mos·pher·ic** (–FEER–, –FER–) *adj.;* **at·mos·pher·i·cal·ly** *adv.* —**atmospherics** *n.pl.* disturbances caused in radio reception by natural phenomena, as during a storm.

at·oll (AT·ol) *n.* a ring of coral reefs and islands enclosing a lagoon.

at·om (AT·um) *n.* **1** a tiny bit; jot: *There's not an ~ of evidence.* **2** the smallest particle of an element that may be involved in chemical reactions. **3 the atom** atomic energy. —**a·tom·ic** (uh·TOM·ic) *adj.;* **a·tom·i·cal·ly** *adv.* —**atom(ic) bomb** a very destructive weapon using energy **(atomic energy)** released by the splitting of atomic nuclei. —**atomic clock** a precise clock that is regulated by the atomic vibrations of certain substances. —**atomic number** the number of protons in the atomic nucleus. —**atomic pile** or **atomic reactor** a nuclear reactor. —**atomic weight** the weight of an atom of an element as compared with that of an atom of another element chosen as the standard with a number assigned to it, usu. carbon, at. wt. 12. —**at·om·ism** (AT·uh·mizm) *n.* the philosophical theory that the universe is ultimately composed of indestructible atoms; **at·om·ist** *n.* —**at·om·ize** (AT·uh·mize) *v.* **-iz·es, -ized, -iz·ing** reduce (a liquid, esp. a medicine or perfume) into a fine spray using a device called an **at·om·iz·er; at·om·i·za·tion** (–ZAY–) *n.* —**atom smasher** *Informal.* accelerator (*n.* 2).

a·ton·al (ay·TOH·nul) *adj.* of music, not based on a key; **a·ton·al·ly** *adv.* —**a·to·nal·i·ty** (ay·toh·NAL·uh·tee) *n.*

a·tone (uh·TONE) *v.* **a·tones, a·toned, a·ton·ing** make up (for a wrong): *He ~d for past misdeeds by philanthropy.* —**a·tone·ment** *n.* reparation; amends; esp. **Atonement,** the reconciliation of man with God through Christ's sufferings.

a·top (uh·TOP) *prep.* & *adv.* on top (of): *landed ~ a building; perched ~ of a tower.*

-ator *n. suffix.* agent: as in *creator, translator.*

ATP See ADENOSINE TRIPHOSPHATE.

a·tri·um (AY·tree·um) *n., pl.* **a·tri·a** (–uh) or **a·tri·ums** the main room or entrance hall of an ancient Roman house; hence, an entrance chamber or cavity of a body part, as the auricles of the heart and the cavity behind the eardrum.

a·tro·cious (uh·TROH·shus) *adj.* **1** wicked; cruel. **2** *Informal.* terribly bad: *~ manners; an ~ necktie.* —**a·tro·cious·ly** *adv.* —**a·tro·cious·ness** *n.* —**a·troc·i·ty** (–TROS–) *n.* **-ties** something atrocious: *Nazi ~s against Jews; the ~s of bad spellers.*

at·ro·phy (AT·ruh·fee) *n.* the wasting away or stop in growth of a body part or tissue, as in polio. —***v.*** **-phies, -phied, -phy·ing:** *an ~d limb; A skill ~s from lack of practice.*

at·ro·pine (AT·ruh·peen) *n.* a belladonna extract used to control spasms and to dilate the pupil of the eye for examination.

att. attached; attention; attorney.

at·tach (uh·TACH) *v.* **1** join; fasten; connect with; be bound to: *A label is ~ed to a parcel; I ~ my signature to a petition; a garage ~ed to a house; a school ~ed to a university; Do you ~ any political significance to the mayor's speech? Two friends deeply ~ed to each other; No blame ~es to his wife for John's behavior.* **2** take away by legal writ: *A debtor's property is ~ed;* **at·tach·a·ble** *adj.* —**at·ta·ché** (at·uh·SHAY, uh·TASH·ay) *n.* a diplomatic official: *a press ~.* —**attaché (case)** a thin suitcase for business papers. —**at·tach·ment** *n.*

at·tack (uh·TAK) *n.* **1** an offensive action (against someone): *~ is the best form of defense.* **2** an aggressive speech or writing: *a newspaper ~.* **3** an affliction: *a mild ~ of measles.* **4** a start of an activity: *a fresh ~ on a problem.* —***v.*** make an attack. —**at·tack·er** *n.*

at·tain (uh·TAIN) *v.* reach (a state, position, goal, etc.): *~ the age of 21; ~ success by hard work;* **attain to** arrive at: *~ to great power and glory; ~ to man's estate.* —**at·tain·a·ble** *adj.* —**at·tain·a·bil·i·ty** (–BIL–) *n.* —**at·tain·der** *n.* an attainting: *The U.S. Constitution forbids* **bills of attainder.** —**at·tain·ment** *n.* an attaining or thing attained: *a position difficult of ~; a woman of great cultural ~s.* —**at·taint** (uh·TAINT) *v. Law.* deprive one (usu. on conviction for treason) of all property and civil rights: *Political foes used to be ~ed by bills of Parliament.*

at·tar (AT·ur) *n.* a fragrant oil obtained from flowers: *Roses yield* **attar of roses.**

at·tempt (uh·TEMT) *n.* & *v.* (make) an effort; try: *an ~ at winning first place; an ~* (i.e. attack) *on the governor's life.*

at·tend (uh·TEND) *v.* **1** be present at: *a well-~ed meeting.* **2** accompany: *a speech ~ed by shouts from the audience.* **3** give thought to; wait on; care for: *~ to your chores; Nurses ~ the sick; Do you ~* (i.e. listen) *in class?* **—at·ten·dance** (–TEN·dunce) *n.: No doctor is in ~ on Sundays; ~ is compulsory at the first lecture; ~ is not taken before noon.* **—at·ten·dant** (–dunt) *n.* one who attends to give service: *a parking-lot ~;* also ***adj.*** attending: *the ~ nurse; evils ~ on a war.* **—at·ten·tion** *n.* **1** act of attending (def. 3): *a letter for the boss's ~; A wound requires immediate ~; ~, ladies! Soldiers stand at ~.* **2 attentions** *pl.* courtesies: *The youngster liked the ~s he received.* **—at·ten·tive** (–tiv) adj.: *Teachers like ~ pupils; Be ~ to your escort's needs;* **at·ten·tive·ly** *adv.;* **at·ten·tive·ness** *n.*

at·ten·u·ate (uh·TEN·yoo–) *v.* **-ates, -at·ed, -at·ing** make or become thin; weaken; ***adj.*** (–yoo·it) : *an ~ limb.* **—at·ten·u·a·tion** (–AY–) *n.*

at·test (uh·TEST) *v.* **1** certify: *~ a signature by witnessing it.* **2** manifest. **3 attest to** bear witness to. **—at·tes·ta·tion** (at·uh·STAY–) *n.*

Att. Gen. attorney general.

at·tic (AT·ic) *n.* a room or space just under a roof; garret.

At·tic (AT·ic) *adj.* of or having to do with Attica, Athens, or Athenians; hence, classical: *~ architecture;* ***n.*** the Attic dialect. **—At·ti·ca** Greek province in S.E. Greece.

At·ti·la (AT·uh·luh) A.D. 406?–453, king of the Huns.

at·tire (uh·TIRE) *n.* clothing; dress. **—*v.* at·tires, at·tired, at·tir·ing:** *~d in regal splendor.*

at·ti·tude (AT·uh–) *n.* the way one feels or thinks about something; also, a posture expressing this: *a cooperative ~; standing in the doorway in a threatening ~;* **strike an attitude** assume a posture. **—at·ti·tu·di·nal** (–TUE–) *adj.* **—at·ti·tu·di·nize** *v.* **-niz·es, -nized, -niz·ing** take an affected attitude: *Is this philosopher merely ~ing in his writings?*

attn. attention.

at·tor·ney (uh·TUR·nee) *n.* **-neys** legal authority to act for another; power of attorney; hence, a person with this authority; lawyer **(attorney at law). —attorney general,** *pl.* **attorneys general** or **attorney generals** chief lawyer in a government's service; **Attorney General** head of the U.S. Department of Justice; also, a minister of justice in other countries.

at·tract (uh·TRACT) *v.* draw toward one: *Honey ~s bees; Dick feels ~ed to Jane.* **—at·trac·tant** *n.* an attracting substance. **—at·trac·tion** *n.: magnetic ~; a city's many ~s.* **—at·trac·tive** (–tiv) *adj.: a beautiful and ~ girl; an ~ bargain;* **at·trac·tive·ly** *adv.;* **at·trac·tive·ness** *n.* **—at·trac·tor** or **at·tract·er** *n.* one that attracts.

attrib. attributive. **—at·trib·ute** *n.* (AT·ri·byoot) an inherent characteristic: *Being all-powerful is an ~ of God.* **—*v.*** (uh·TRIB·yoot) **-utes, -ut·ed, -ut·ing** consider as due to; ascribe: *He ~s his successes to luck;* **at·trib·ut·a·ble** (–TRIB·yuh–) *adj.* **—at·tri·bu·tion** (–BYOO–) *n.* **—at·trib·u·tive** (uh·TRIB·yuh·tiv) *adj.* of a word, coming before and modifying, as in "*Bible* story" and "*good* book"; ***n.*** an attributive word: *In "The book is good," "good" is a predicative adjective, not an ~;* **at·trib·u·tive·ly** *adv.*

at·tri·tion (uh·TRISH·un) *n.* **1** a wearing away; gradual weakening: *A war of ~ could destroy both sides.* **2** reduction in personnel by resignations, retirements, and deaths.

at·tune (uh·TUNE) *v.* **-tunes, -tuned, -tun·ing** bring into harmony; tune (to): *a mother's ears ~d to her children's voices.*

atty. attorney; **Atty. Gen.** Attorney General.

ATV *pl.* **ATVs** "all-terrain vehicle," an amphibious motor vehicle.

a·twit·ter (–TWIT–) *adj.* & *adv.* twittering; excited.

at. wt. atomic weight.

a·typ·i·cal (ay·TIP·i·cl) *adj.* not typical; unusual.

Au gold.

au·burn (AW–) *n.* a reddish brown; ***adj.:*** *~ hair.*

Auck·land (AWK·lund) a city and the largest seaport of New Zealand.

au cou·rant (oh·coo·RAHN) *adj. French.* of a person, up-to-date.

auc·tion (AWK–) *n.* sale by bidding. **—*v.*** esp. **auction** (something) **off** sell at auction. **—auction bridge** a bridge game in which tricks made in excess of the bid have score value. **—auc·tion·eer** (–shuh·NEER) *n.* one who conducts an auction.

auc·to·ri·al (awk·TOR·ee·ul) *adj.* authorial.

aud. audit; auditor.

au·da·cious (aw·DAY·shus) *adj.* bold; insolent; **au·da·cious·ly** *adv.* **—au·da·cious·ness** or **au·dac·i·ty** (aw·DAS–) *n.*

au·di·ble (AW·di–) *adj.* loud enough to be heard. **—*n.*** in football, a play called by a quarterback at the line of scrimmage. **—au·di·bil·i·ty** (–BIL–) *n.* **—au·di·bly** *adv.* **—au·di·ence** (AW·dee·unce) *n.* **1** the people listening to a communication, as the gathering in an auditorium or theater and those that can be reached by the media: *a TV show with high ~ ratings.* **2** a formal interview: *a papal ~; received in ~ by the Queen.* **3** an opportunity to be heard. **—au·di·o** (AW·dee·oh) *n.* the audible part of a TV broadcast or film; also, the equipment used to handle sound signals; also, such signals; cf. VIDEO; ***adj.:*** *an ~ amplifier; ~ components;* **audio** (i.e. audible) **frequencies** *range from 20 to 20,000 hertz;* **audio-** *comb. form.* as in **au·di·o·lin·gual** *adj.* using speech and hearing: *~ education.* **—au·di·ol·o·gy** (–OL·uh·jee) *n.* the science of hearing; **au·**

di·ol·o·gist *n.;* **au·di·o·log·i·cal** (–LOJ–) *adj.* —**au·di·om·e·ter** (–OM·i·tur) *n.* an instrument for measuring hearing. —**au·di·o·phile** (–file) *n.* one who is fond of hi-fi equipment. —**au·di·o·vis·u·al** (–VIZH·oo·ul) *adj.* of or having to do with both audio and visual communication, esp. of an educational nature; **audiovisuals** *n.pl.* teaching aids such as film strips, record players, and slides.

au·dit (AW–) *n.* an official checking and verification of books of account; also, a report made after such a checking. —*v.* **1** officially examine books of account. **2** attend a course of study, but not for credit. —**au·di·tion** (aw·DISH·un) *n.* hearing; also, act of hearing, esp. a trial hearing given to an actor, singer, etc. before hiring; ***v.:*** *The director was ~ing actors yesterday; Three girls ~ed today for the leading part.* —**au·di·tor** (–tur) *n.* **1** a listener. **2** one who audits. —**au·di·to·ri·um** (–TOR·ee·um) *n.* **-ri·ums** or **-ri·a** (–ree·uh) a building or a part of one, as a hall or theater, for seating audiences. —**au·di·to·ry** (AW·di·tor·ee) *adj.* pertaining to hearing: *~ nerves connect the ear to the brain.*

auf Wie·der·se·hen (owf·VEE·dur·zay·un) *German.* farewell!

aug. augmentative. —**Aug.** August.

au·ger (AW·gur) *n.* any of various tools for boring holes in wood, in the earth, etc.

aught (AWT) *n.* a cipher; zero; ought.

aug·ment (awg·MENT) *v.* make or become larger: *to ~ one's income with a sideline; a stream ~ed by rain.* —**aug·men·ta·tion** (–TAY–) *n.*

au gra·tin (oh·GRAH·tin) *French.* of dishes, with a light crust of bread crumbs or grated cheese: *egg and spinach ~.*

au·gur (AW·gur) *n.* one who foretells the future; soothsayer. —*v.* **1** foretell, esp. from signs and omens. **2** be a sign of: *A long drought does not ~ well for a good harvest.* —**au·gu·ry** (AW·gyuh·ree) *n.* **-ries** divination; also, a sign or omen.

au·gust (aw·GUST) *adj.* majestic: *an ~ personage;* **au·gust·ly** *adv.;* **au·gust·ness** *n.* —**Au·gust** (AW·gust) *n.* the 8th month of the year. It has 31 days. —**Au·gus·ta** (aw·GUS·tuh) capital of Maine. —**Au·gus·tan** (aw·GUS·tun) *adj.* of or having to do with the reign of Augustus Caesar; hence, classical: *the Augustan age* (i.e. early 1700's) *of English literature.* —**Au·gus·tine** (–GUS·tin), **Saint.** A.D. 354–430, a N. African bishop and philosopher; **Au·gus·tin·i·an** (–TIN·ee·un) *n.* a member of a religious order named for St. Augustine; ***adj.:*** *the ~ rule.*

au jus (oh·ZHOO) *French.* of cooked meat, served with its own juices.

auk (AWK) *n.* any of various oceanic birds including razor-bills and puffins that have short tail and wings, webbed feet, and a chunky body: *the flightless "great auk" extinct since 1844.*

auld *adj. Scot.* old, as in **auld lang syne** (awld·lang·zyne), the good old days.

au na·tu·rel (oh·nah·too·REL) *French.* in the natural state; nude; also, of food, plainly cooked.

aunt (ANT, AHNT) *n.* one's father's or mother's sister; the wife of one's uncle; also **aun·tie, aunt·y,** *Informal.*

au pair (oh·PAIR) a domestic arrangement for exchange of services; also, a person involved in one, as an American student living in a French home doing light housework while learning French; ***adj.:*** *an ~ girl.*

au·ra (AW·ruh) *n.* **-ras** or **-rae** (–ree) a distinctive atmosphere or quality of something, esp. about a person: *an ~ of mystery.* —**¹au·ral** *adj.*

²au·ral (AW·rul) *adj.* of the ear or sense of hearing: *an ~ surgeon.* —**au·ral·ly** *adv.*

aurar *pl.* of EYRIR.

au·re·ate (AW·ree·it) *adj.* gilded; golden; also, ornate: *an ~ style or diction.* —**au·re·ole** (AW·ree–) *n.* a halo; aura; circle of light; also **au·re·o·la** (aw·REE·uh·luh).

Au·re·o·my·cin (aw·ree·oh·MY·sin) *Trademark.* an antibiotic.

au re·voir (oh·ruh·VWAR) *n.* & *interj.* goodbye.

au·ri·cle (AW·ri–) *n.* the external ear; also, the earlike part of any other organ, as the upper chambers of the heart. —**au·ric·u·lar** (aw·RIK·yoo·lur) *adj.* of or pertaining to an auricle: *~ confession* (made in the ear of a priest).

au·rif·er·ous (aw·RIF·uh·rus) *adj.* gold-bearing.

Au·ri·ga (aw·RYE·guh) a constellation in the N. Hemisphere.

au·ro·ra (uh·ROR·uh) *n.* **-ras** or **-rae** (–ree) flashes of light seen in night skies, esp. near the poles. —**aurora aus·tra·lis** (–aw·STRAY–) aurora seen in S. regions. —**aurora bo·re·al·is** (–bor·ee·AL·is) aurora of N. skies. —**au·ro·ral** (–rul) *adj.*

A.U.S. Army of the United States.

aus·cul·ta·tion (aw·skul·TAY–) *n.* a listening, esp. with a stethoscope, to the sounds of the internal organs to determine their condition.

aus·pice (AWS·pis) *n.* usu. **aus·pic·es** *pl.* **1** patronage: *a meeting held* **under the auspices** *of the Y.M.C.A.* **2** omens; signs. —**aus·pi·cious** (aws·PISH·us) *adj.* having good omens; propitious: *an ~ day for starting on a journey;* **aus·pi·cious·ly** *adv.;* **aus·pi·cious·ness** *n.*

Aus·sie (AW·see) *n.* & *adj. Informal.* Australian.

Aus·ten (AWS·tun), **Jane.** 1775–1817, English novelist.

aus·tere (aw·STEER) *adj.* strict in manner of style; showing self-discipline: *an ~ monk; an ~, unadorned style.* —**aus·tere·ly** *adv.* —**aus·ter·i·ty** (aw·STER–) *n.*

Aus·tin (AWS–) capital of Texas.

aus·tral (AWS·trul) *adj.* southern. —**Aus·tral·a·sia** (aws·truh·LAY·zhuh) Australia, New Guinea, New Zealand, and nearby islands; **Aus·tral·a·sian** *n.* & *adj.* —**Aus·tral·ia** (aw·STRAIL·yuh) the island continent to the S.E. of Asia between the Pacific and Indian oceans; also, the country, **Commonwealth of Australia,** including this island and Tasmania; 2,967,909 sq.mi. (7,686,848 km²); *cap.* Canberra. —**Aus·tral·ian** *n.* & *adj.*

Aus·tri·a (AW·stree·uh) a country of C. Europe; 32,374 sq.mi. (83,849 km²); *cap.* Vienna. —**Aus·tri·an** *n.* & *adj.*

Aus·tro·ne·sia (aw·stroh·NEE·zhuh) the islands and the region between Madagascar in the west and Hawaii and Easter Island in the east. —**Aus·tro·ne·sian** *n.* & *adj.*

auth. authentic; author; authority; authorized.

au·then·tic (–THEN–) *adj.* genuine; real: *an ~ signature;* **au·then·ti·cal·ly** *adv.* —**au·then·ti·cate** *v.* **-cates, -cat·ed, -cat·ing** prove or determine to be authentic: *an ~d Picasso;* **au·then·ti·ca·tion** (–CAY–) *n.* —**au·then·tic·i·ty** (–TIS–) *n.*

au·thor (AW·thur) *n.* one who makes or originates something, esp. something written; also such writings: *translating a Latin ~; the ~ of a plot;* ***v.:*** *Shakespeare ~ed many plays;* **au·thor·ship** *n.* —**au·tho·ri·al** (–THOR–) *adj.* pertaining to an author. —**au·thor·i·tar·i·an** (–TAIR–) *n.* one who believes in submission to authority more than in individual freedom; ***adj.:*** *an ~ government;* **au·thor·i·tar·i·an·ism** *n.* —**au·thor·i·ta·tive** (–THOR·i·tay·tiv) *adj.* having authority: *an ~ source of information;* **au·thor·i·ta·tive·ly** *adv.* —**au·thor·i·ty** (–THOR–) *n.* **-ties** the power or right to do something; also, a person or institution with power or expert knowledge; a decision or opinion of such a person: *Which dictionary is your ~? an order issued under the ~ of a judge; a minister officiating without proper ~; to report a crime to the ~s; Jesus taught with ~.* —**au·thor·ize** (AW–) *v.* **-iz·es, -ized, -iz·ing** permit or allow officially: *a budget spending ~d by Congress;* **au·thor·i·za·tion** (–ZAY–) *n.* —**Authorized Version** a translation of the Bible published in 1611, authorized by King James I.

au·tism (AW–) *n.* a mental disorder of children that is characterized by daydreaming and other signs of withdrawal from reality. —**au·tis·tic** (–TIS–) *adj.: ~ children are often mute.* —**auto.** automatic. —**auto-** *comb. form.* of or by oneself; self. —**au·to** (AW·toh) *n.* **-tos** an automobile. —**au·to·bahn** (–bahn) *n.* a German superhighway. —**au·to·bi·og·ra·phy** (–OG–) *n.* **-phies** an author's own life history; **au·to·bi·og·ra·pher** *n.;* **au·to·bi·og·raph·i·cal** (–GRAF–) *adj.* —**au·toch·tho·nous** (–TOK·thuh·nus) *adj.* of flora, fauna, minerals, etc., indigenous or aboriginal. —**au·toc·ra·cy** (aw·TOC·ruh·see) *n.* **-cies** government by a single person, or **au·to·crat,** one having absolute power; **au·to·crat·ic** (–CRAT–) *adj.;* **au·to·crat·i·cal·ly** *adv.* —**au·to·gi·ro** or **au·to·gy·ro** (–JYE·roh) *n.* **-ros** an early form of the helicopter. —**au·to·graph** *n.* a person's signature; also, an original manuscript; ***v.:*** *an ~ed picture of a movie star.* —**au·to·in·tox·i·ca·tion** *n.* poisoning by toxins produced in one's body. —**au·to·mat** *n.* a cafeteria that sells food through coin-operated machines. —**au·to·mate** *v.* **-mates, -mat·ed, -mat·ing** operate or control (a process, equipment, system, etc.) automatically. —**au·to·mat·ic** (–MAT–) *adj.* self-acting; ***n.*** any self-acting machine; **au·to·mat·i·cal·ly** *adv.* —**automatic pilot** an aircraft control mechanism; **automatic rifle** a machine gun. —**au·to·ma·tion** (–MAY–) *n.* the automatic control and operation of a process: *~ replaces much unskilled labor.* —**au·tom·a·tism** (–TOM–) *n.* involuntary activity, as in sleepwalking, digestion, etc. —**au·tom·a·tize** (–TOM–) *v.* **-tiz·es, -tized, -tiz·ing** make automatic; **au·tom·a·ti·za·tion** (–ZAY–) *n.* —**au·tom·a·ton** (–TOM·uh·tun) *n.* **-tons** or **-ta** a robot or a similar mechanism. —**au·to·mo·bile** (aw·tuh·moh·BEEL) *n.* a self-propelled, usu. four-wheeled passenger vehicle; also ***adj.;*** also **au·to·mo·tive** (–MOH·tiv) *adj.: ~ engine; ~ parts; Detroit's ~ workers.* —**au·to·nom·ic** (–NOM–) *adj.* governing involuntary actions: *~ nervous system.* —**au·ton·o·mous** (–TON·uh·mus) *adj.* having autonomy; **au·ton·o·mous·ly** *adv.* —**au·ton·o·my** (–TON–) *n.* **-mies** (a state or region with) self-government. —**au·to·pi·lot** *n.* automatic pilot. —**au·top·sy** (AW·top·see) *n.* **-sies** the examination of a corpse to determine cause of death; post-mortem; ***v.*** **-sies, -sied, -sy·ing:** *Those dead of unknown causes are ~d.* —**au·to·stra·da** (–STRAH·duh) *n.* an Italian expressway. —**au·to·sug·ges·tion** (–JES–) *n.* mental suggestion to oneself; self-hypnosis.

au·tumn (AW·tum) *n.* the season between summer and winter; fall. —**au·tum·nal** (–TUM·nl) *adj.;* **autumnal equinox** Sept. 22 or 23, when days and nights are equally long in the N. Hemisphere.

aux. or **auxil.** *Abbrev.* for **aux·il·ia·ry** (awg·ZIL·yuh·ree) *adj.* & *n.* **-ries** (one) in a helping, subordinate, or supplementary function: *An* **auxiliary verb** *such as "be," "can," "do," "must," or "shall" is used with another verb; an ~* (bishop); *a women's ~* (i.e. organization).

aux·in (AWK·sin) *n.* a plant hormone affecting growth.

av. avenue; average; avoirdupois. —**a.v.** ad valorem. —**A.V.** Authorized Version; audiovisual.

a·vail (uh–) *v.* be of advantage; help: *A last-minute effort will ~ us nothing; He bought a house* **to avail himself** *of a tax deduction.* —***n.*** **to**

(or **of**) **no** (or **little**) **avail:** *The strike was of little ~ in forcing a settlement; living off the* **avails** (i.e. proceeds) *of prostitution.* —**a·vail·a·ble** (–VAY·luh·bl) *adj.* obtainable; reachable: *tickets not ~ to the public; too busy to be ~ for an interview;* **a·vail·a·ble·ness** or **a·vail·a·bil·i·ty** (–BIL–) *n.*

av·a·lanche (AV·uh·lanch) *n.* a massive descent of loose earth, snow, rock, or something similar: *an ~ of mail from an enraged public.* —***v.*** **-lanch·es, -lanched, -lanch·ing:** *~d with questions from reporters.*

a·vant-garde (ah·vahnt·GARD) *n.* the front line or vanguard of a movement, esp. in the arts; ***adj.:*** *Dada was an ~ art form.*

av·a·rice (AV·uh·ris) *n.* greed for money. —**av·a·ri·cious** (–RISH·us) *adj.: Shylock was ~;* **av·a·ri·cious·ly** *adv.*

a·vast (uh·VAST) *interj. Naut.* halt! cease!

av·a·tar (AV·uh–) *n.* in Hinduism, a god's incarnation in human or animal form.

a·vaunt (uh·VAWNT) *interj. Archaic.* away!

avdp. avoirdupois.

ave. or **Ave.** avenue.

A·ve Ma·ri·a (AH·vay·muh·REE·uh) the Hail Mary.

a·venge (uh·VENJ) *v.* **a·veng·es, a·venged, a·veng·ing** take vengeance for (a wrong) or on behalf of (the wronged one); **a·veng·er** *n.*

av·e·nue (AV·uh·new) *n.* **1** a wide street. **2** an approach: *Explore all ~s to a peaceful settlement.*

a·ver (uh·VUR) *v.* **a·vers, a·verred, a·verr·ing** assert confidently; **a·ver·ment** *n.*

av·er·age (AV·uh·rij) *n.* **1** the arithmetic mean: *7 is the ~ of 2, 3, 5, 8, 11, and 13; This car gives you 20 m.p.g.* **on the average.** **2** an ordinary level of achievement: *well above ~ in her class.* —***adj.:*** *The ~ American is of a practical turn of mind; She has an ~ I.Q.* —***v.*** **-ag·es, -aged, -ag·ing:** *Losses and gains* **average out** *to a small profit each year.*

a·verse (uh–) *adj.* opposed; disinclined: *a late sleeper ~ to early rising.* —**a·ver·sion** (uh·VUR·zhun) *n.: a built-in ~ to smoking; TV is one of his pet ~s;* **Aversion therapy** *makes a patient's habit repugnant to him.* —**a·vert** (uh·VURT) *v.* **1** turn away: *The child ~ed her eyes from the scary picture.* **2** prevent: *A strike was ~ed at the last minute.*

A·ves·ta (uh·VES·tuh) *n.* the Zoroastrian scriptures; **A·ves·tan** *adj.;* also ***n.*** the Old Iranian language of the Avesta.

avg. average.

av·gas (AV·gas) *n.* gasoline for aircraft. —**a·vi·an** (AY·vee·un) *adj.* of birds: *an ~ enthusiast.* —**a·vi·ar·y** (–air·ee) *n.* **-ar·ies** a cage; a house for birds, as in a zoo. —**a·vi·a·tion** (–AY–) *n.* flying as an art, science, or industry: **Aviation medicine** *deals with illnesses peculiar to flyers and astronauts.* —**a·vi·a·tor** (–ay·tur) *n.* an airplane pilot; *fem.* **a·vi·a·trix.**

av·id (AV–) *adj.* eager; ardent: *Midas was ~ for gold; an ~ reader of romances;* **av·id·ly** *adv.* —**a·vid·i·ty** (–VID–) n.

a·vi·on·ics (–ON–) *n.pl.* [takes *sing. v.*] electronics applied to aviation and astronautics; **a·vi·on·ic** *adj.*

av·o·ca·do (av·uh·CAH·doh) *n.* **-do(e)s** a greenish, pear-shaped tropical fruit; also, the tree bearing the fruit or its color.

av·o·ca·tion (av·uh·CAY–) *n.* a side occupation or hobby; **av·o·ca·tion·al** *adj.*

av·o·cet (AV·uh–) *n.* a wading bird with long legs and a slender, upturned bill.

a·void (uh·VOID) *v.* keep away from; shun: *Drive on the right to ~ collisions.* —**a·void·a·ble** *adj.* —**a·void·a·bly** *adv.* —**a·void·ance** *n.*

av·oir·du·pois (av·ur·duh·POIZ) *n.* **1** the weight system based on pounds, ounces, and drams. **2** *Informal.* one's weight: *a man of great moral ~.*

a·vouch (uh·VOWCH) *v.* vouch for.

a·vow (uh·VOW) *v.* acknowledge openly: *an ~ed Communist.* —**a·vow·al** *n.* —**a·vow·ed·ly** (–id·lee) *adv.* admittedly.

a·vun·cu·lar (uh·VUNG·kyuh·lur) *adj.* of an uncle: *an ~ manner.*

a·wait (uh–) *v.* wait for: *Death ~s us.*

a·wake (uh–) *adj.* roused from sleep; aware; alert: *a new recruit ~ to his duties.* —***v.*** **a·wakes,** *pt.* **a·woke** or **a·waked,** *pp.* **a·waked, a·woke** or **a·wok·en, a·wak·ing** wake up; be roused. Also **a·wak·en,** *pt.* & *pp.* **a·wak·ened.** —**a·wak·en·ing** *n.* a waking up: *the new ~ about women's rights;* ***adj.:*** *a bugle's ~ call.*

a·ward (uh·WORED) *v.* give officially, as a court ruling, prize, etc. —***n.*** a judgment; prize: *an Academy ~ for a movie.*

a·ware (uh·WAIR) *adj.* conscious; knowing: *Are you ~ of your rights?* **a·ware·ness** *n.*

a·wash (uh·WOSH) *adj.* & *adv.* being washed; flowing; flooded: *a speech ~ with self-pity.*

a·way (uh·WAY) *adv.* **1** from (a place, person, etc. referred to); to or at a distance: *The church is 10 miles ~; Get ~ from the fire; far ~ in China;* ***adj.*** removed; absent: *The boss is ~ on business.* **2** far: *She's ~ down on the list; ~ back in 1926.* **3** on; along: *He is grinding ~ at his tasks; Time is ticking ~.* **4** [in exclamations]: *~ with the nuisance!* —**do away with** get rid of; kill. —**far** (or **out**) **and away** very much. —**right** (or **straight**) **away** at once.

awe (AW) *n.* a mixed emotion of fear, respect, wonder, reverence, etc., esp. as felt toward a supernatural being: *The heavens are ~-inspiring.* —***v.*** **awes, awed, aw·ing:** *pupils* **awed into** *submission; The faithful are ~d by God's wonders.* —**awe·some** (AW·sum) *adj.* causing awe: *an ~ oath of office; an ~ sight.* —**awe·strick·en** or **awe·struck** *adj.* filled with awe. —**aw·ful** *adj.* **1** terrible: *an ~ murder.* **2** *Informal.* very (bad, great, etc.): *~ manners; an ~ load of work;* **aw·ful·ly** *adv. Informal: 100°F is ~* (i.e. very) *hot; You're ~ good to me.*

a·wear·y (uh·WEER·ee) *adj. Poetic.* tired: ~ *of the world.*

a·weigh (uh·WAY) *adj.* suspended: *With anchors ~, the boat put out to sea.*

a·while (uh–) *adv.* for some time: *Stay ~, have a coffee.*

a·whirl (uh–) *adj.* & *adv.* in a whirl.

awk·ward (AWK·wurd) *adj.* **1** clumsy; graceless; also, uncomfortable: ~ *movements; an ~ posture.* **2** hard to handle; embarrassing: *a lawyer dealing with ~ facts.* **—awk·ward·ly** *adv.;* **awk·ward·ness** *n.*

awl *n.* a pointed tool for piercing holes in leather, wood, etc.

awn *n.* a bristle or bristles on the head of a grass or cereal grain; beard. **—awned** *adj.: Barley, oats, and some fruits and leaf-tips are ~.*

awn·ing *n.* an overhanging, often canvas shelter above a door, window, etc.

awoke(n) See AWAKE.

A·WOL (AY·wall) *adj.* absent without leave. **—a·wol** *n.* one who is AWOL.

a·wry (uh·RYE) *adj.* & *adv.* askew; amiss: *a scheme that went ~.*

ax(e) (AKS) *n., pl.* **ax·es** (–siz) a tool with a heavy cutting blade fitted parallel to the handle. **—*v.* ax·es, axed, ax·ing —get the ax** *Informal.* be dismissed from a job. **—have an ax to grind** *Informal.* have a private, selfish motive.

axes *pl.* of AX or AXIS. **—ax·i·al** (AK·see·ul) *adj.* of or on an axis: ~ *symmetry;* **axial skeleton** one of the head and trunk alone; **ax·i·al·ly** *adv.*

ax·i·om (AK·see·um) *n.* a basic truth or principle; also, a proposition that is or is accepted as self-evident: *the ~s of conventional wisdom; a geometrical ~.* **—ax·i·o·mat·ic** (–MAT–) *adj.;* **ax·i·o·mat·i·cal·ly** *adv.*

ax·is (AK·sis) *n., pl.* **ax·es** (–seez) **1** a straight line around which an object rotates or may rotate, or is symmetrical: *The earth revolves on its ~.* **2** a reference line, as on a graph: *where the x ~ meets the y ~.* **3 the Axis** the alliance of Germany, Italy, Japan, etc. in World War II.

ax·le (AK·sl) *n.* **1** a shaft on which a wheel or wheels turn. **2** a shaft with wheels that turn on bearings on either end, as of an automobile or the **ax·le·tree** of a wagon or carriage.

ax·o·lotl (AX·uh·lotl) *n.* a dark salamander of Mexico and S.W. United States that breeds in the larval stage.

ay·ah (AH·yuh) *n.* in India, a native nurse or maid.

a·ya·tol·lah (ah·yuh·TOH·luh) *n.* an honorific title for a distinguished Islamic clergyman, esp. in Iran; also **a·ya·tul·lah.**

ay(e) *adv.* **1** (AY) *Poetic.* forever. **2** (AYE) yes; ***n.*** a yes vote or one who gives it: *The ~s have it.*

az. azimuth. **—AZ** Arizona.

a·zal·ea (uh·ZAIL·yuh) *n.* any of a group of flowering shrubs of the genus Rhododendron.

Az·er·bai·jan (ah·zur·bye·JAHN) **Soviet Socialist Republic** a republic in southwestern U.S.S.R.; *cap.* Baku.

az·i·muth (AZ–) *n.* the distance in degrees from due north or south to an object, usu. measured clockwise along the horizon; **az·i·muth·al** (–MUTH·ul) *adj.*

A·zores (AY–) a group of Portuguese islands in the N. Atlantic.

Az·tec (AZ–) *n.* (a member of) a highly advanced people in Mexico before the Spanish invasion; also, their language; ***adj.:*** ~ *culture.* **—Az·tec·an** *adj.*

az·ure (AZH·ur) *n.* sky blue; also, *Poetic.* the clear sky. Also ***adj.***

B

B or **b** (BEE) *n.* **B's** or **b's** the second letter of the English alphabet; hence, second in a series; second highest: *received a B (grade) in math.* —**b.** or **B.** bachelor; base; basso; Bible; book; born. —**B** **1** boron. **2** the seventh note of the C major scale.

Ba barium.

B.A. Bachelor of Arts; British Academy.

baa (BAH) *v.* **baas, baaed, baa·ing** bleat, as a sheep does; also ***n.***

Ba·al (BAY·ul) *n., pl.* **Ba·al·im** or **Ba·als** an ancient Semitic god; hence, an idol or false god; **Ba·al·ism** *n.;* **Ba·al·ist** *n.*

Bab·bitt (BAB·it) *n.* an uncultured, materialistic, self-satisfied member of the middle class; **Bab·bitt·ry** *n.* —**Babbitt metal** an alloy of antimony, copper, and tin, used to line bearings.

bab·ble *v.* **bab·bles, bab·bled, bab·bling** talk foolishly or indistinctly like a baby; talk too freely; hence, murmur: *a ∼ing brook;* ***n.:*** *a baby's ∼; the ∼ at a bazaar.* —**bab·bler** *n.*

babe *n.* **1** a baby: *a ∼ in arms.* **2** *Slang.* a girl or woman. —**babe in the woods** a helpless innocent.

ba·bel (BAY·bl, BAB·ul) *n.* a noisy confusion: *a ∼ of voices; ∼ of dialects.*

ba·boon (–BOON) *n.* a big African monkey with a long snout and large canines.

ba·bush·ka (buh·BOOSH·kuh) *n.* a usu. triangular head scarf.

ba·by (BAY·bee) *n.* **-bies** **1** an infant or one very young; the youngest of a group. **2** a childish person. **3** *Slang.* a girl or woman. —***adj.*** young; small; of or for a baby. —***v.*** **ba·bies, ba·bied, ba·by·ing** treat with excessive care. —**baby beef** beef from a calf slaughtered at one or two years of age. —**baby carriage** or **baby buggy** one for pushing infants in. —**baby grand piano** one five to six feet (1.5 to 1.8 m) long. —**ba·by·ish** *adj.* —**ba·by·hood** *n.*

Bab·y·lon (BAB·i·lun) the wealthy and luxurious capital city of **Bab·y·lo·ni·a** (–LOH·nee·uh), an ancient Mesopotamian empire. —**Bab·y·lo·ni·an** *adj. & n.: ∼ splendor.*

baby's breath any of several plants with many small, usu. white flowers. —**ba·by-sit** *v.* **-sits, -sat, -sit·ting** look after child(ren) while the parents are away; **ba·by-sit·ter.** Also **ba·by·sit, ba·by·sit·ter.**

bac·ca·lau·re·ate (–LOR·ee·it) *n.* the bachelor's degree; hence, an address to a graduating class.

bac·ca·ra(t) (BAC·uh·rah) *n.* a card game used for gambling.

bac·cha·nal (bac·uh·NAL) *n.* **1** a drunken revel, originally in honor of **Bac·chus,** Greek wine god; also **bac·cha·na·li·a** (–NAY·lee·uh) *n.pl.* **2** a reveler. —**bac·cha·na·li·an** (–NAY–) *adj.: ∼ orgies.*

Bach (BAHK) **Johann Sebastian.** 1685–1750, German composer.

bach·e·lor (BACH·uh·lur) *n.* **1** an unmarried man; **bach·e·lor·hood** or **bach·e·lor·ship** *n.* **2** one who has received an undergraduate degree from a university or college, as the **Bachelor of Arts** or **Bachelor of Science.** —**bachelor girl** *Informal.* an independent single woman. —**bachelor's button** any of several plants with buttonlike flowers, esp. the cornflower.

ba·cil·lus (buh·SIL·us) *n., pl.* **-cil·li** (–SIL·eye) a bacterium, esp. one that is rod-shaped or causes disease. —**ba·cil·la·ry** (BAS·i·ler·ee) *adj.*

back *n.* **1** the rear part of the human body, from the neck to the base of the spine; also, the spine itself; hence, the corresponding part in other animals. **2** anything that supports or covers the back: *the ∼ of a dress; the ∼ of a chair.* **3** the part that is opposite, behind, or furthest from the front, esp. if less important or visible: *the ∼ of his head; the ∼ of a card.* **4** *Sports.* a player stationed in the backfield. —**(in) back of** *Informal.* behind; **behind one's back** in one's absence; **be on one's back** harass; **get** (or **put**) **one's back up** make (or become) angry; **have one's back to the wall** be in a desperate situation; **on one's back** sick in bed. —***adj.*** **1** in, at, or toward the rear: ∼

fence; ~ country. **2** of the past: *a periodical's ~ issues* (that are no longer on sale); *~ rent* (i.e. in arrears). ***—adv.*** **1** at or toward the rear: *Stand ~!* **2** in reserve or restraint: *Hold ~ your best card.* **3** in, at, or toward an earlier time, state, or position: *Bring the book ~; ~ in 1910.* **4** in return: *He hit me, so I hit him ~.* ***—v.*** **1** move backward or to the rear. **2** bet on; support: *~ the right horse;* **back·er** *n.* **3** form the back of; provide backing for: *a beach ~ed by cliffs.* **4** have the back in a certain place: *Our house ~s on a park.* **—back down** withdraw from a stand one has taken. **—back off** (or **out** or **away**) withdraw. **—back up** **1** support. **2** accumulate and clog. **3** move in reverse. **—back·ache** *n.* a dull pain in the lower back. **—back·bite** *v.* **-bites, -bit, -bit·ten, -bit·ing** slander; **back·bit·er** *n.* **—back·board** *n.* in basketball, the upright rebound board behind the basket. **—back·bone** *n.* **1** the spinal column. **2** courage; resolution. **3** main support. **—back burner** usu. **on the back burner,** in a position of low priority. **—back country** unsettled area behind a settled one. **—back·drop** *n.* **1** a usu. painted cloth hung at the back of a stage. **2** background: *seen against the ~ of current events.* **—back·field** *n.* (football players in) positions behind the line of scrimmage. **—back·fire** *n.* **1** a controlled fire set to check a forest or prairie fire by depriving it of its fuel. **2** an improperly timed fuel explosion in an internal-combustion engine; ***v.*** **-fires, -fired, -fir·ing** blow up with a backfire; hence, turn out opposite to one's intent: *a plan that ~d.*

back·gam·mon (BAC·gam·un) *n.* a board game with counters moved according to throws of the dice.

back·ground *n.* **1** the less important parts forming the setting for the main interest, as distant scenery in a painting or music for a movie; **in the background** in a less visible or important place. **2** events that influence something else, as experience *(He has no ~ for the job)* or general conditions *(the ~ of the war).* **—back·hand** *adj.* done with the hand in the position opposite to the usual one: *a* **backhand stroke** *in tennis* (i.e. with the back of the hand forward); *~ writing* (slanting from upper left to lower right); also ***n.*** & ***adv.*** **—back·hand·ed** *adj.* **1** backhand. **2** concealing an opposite intent: *a ~* (i.e. sarcastic) *compliment.* Also ***adv.*** **—back·ing** *n.* **1** support. **2** a thing placed behind to strengthen. **—back·lash** *n.* **1** hostile reaction. **2** any sharp backward motion or reaction. **—back·log** *n.* an accumulation of supplies or of things to do; ***v.*** **-logs, -logged, -log·ging** accumulate. **—back order** a purchase order waiting to be filled. **—back·pack** *n.* a knapsack, esp. on a metal frame; ***v.*** hike with or carry in a backpack; **back·pack·er** *n.* **—back·ped·al** (BAC·pedl) *v.* turn a bicycle's pedals backward; also, retreat. **—back·side** *n.* the buttocks. **—back·slap·per** *n.* an effusively friendly person; hence **back·slap** *v.* **-slaps, -slapped, -slap·ping.** **—back·slide** *v.* **-slides,** *pt.* **-slid,** *pp.* **-slid** or **-slid·den, -slid·ing** fall back into moral laxity; **back·slid·er** *n.* **—back·spin** *n.* a spin on a ball inclining it to slow down or bounce backward. **—back·stage** *adv.* in or to the area behind the stage, not seen by the audience; hence, privately; behind the scenes; also ***adj.*** **—back·stair(s)** *adj.* sordid and secret: *~ intrigue.* **—back·stop** *n. Sports.* a fence or screen to stop balls from getting away. **—back·stretch** *n.* the racetrack straightaway opposite the homestretch. **—back·stroke** *n.* a swimming stroke made with the swimmer on his back. **—back talk** an impudent retort. **—back-to-back** *adj. Informal.* consecutive. **—back·track** *v.* go back the way one came; hence, retreat; back down. **—back·up** *n.* a standby or replacement; ***adj.:*** *a ~ computer; ~ supplies.* **—back·ward** (BAC·wurd) or **back·wards** *adv.* **1** to the back or past; with the rear leading. **2** in the wrong way; to a worse condition. **—back·ward** *adj.* **1** turned or done the wrong way. **2** shy; slow in development: *a ~ region;* **back·ward·ness** *n.* **—back·wash** *n.* air or water thrown back, esp. by a propeller; hence, a resulting situation; aftermath. **—back·wa·ter** *n.* a stretch of water, as a lagoon or inlet, that is backed up, and thus without currents; hence, an unprogressive area. **—back·woods** *n.pl.* thinly populated forest land; hence, a remote and backward area; also ***adj.;*** **back·woods·man** *n.* **-men.**

ba·con (BAY·cun) *n.* cured and smoked side or back pork. **—bring home the bacon** *Informal.* provide for one's family; also, win; succeed. **—save one's bacon** *Informal.* escape from danger or trouble.

Ba·con, Francis. 1561–1626, English philosopher and statesman; **Ba·co·ni·an** (bay·COH·nee·un) *adj.: a ~ theory.*

bac·te·ri·um (–TEER·ee·um) *n., pl.* **-ri·a** any of a large number of microscopic organisms that cause fermentation, disease, etc. **—bac·te·ri·al** *adj.: ~ canker;* **bac·te·ri·al·ly** *adv.* **—bac·te·ri·cide** *n.* a substance that kills bacteria; **bac·te·ri·cid·al** (–SYE·dul) *adj.* **—bac·te·ri·ol·o·gy** (–OL·uh·jee) *n.* the study of bacteria; **bac·te·ri·ol·o·gist** *n.;* **bac·te·ri·o·log·ic** (–LOJ–) or **-i·cal** *adj.;* **bac·te·ri·o·log·i·cal·ly** *adv.* **—bac·te·ri·o·phage** (–faij) *n.* a virus that kills bacteria.

bad *adj., comp.* **worse** (WURSE), *superl.* **worst** (WURST) **1** having undesirable qualities; esp., morally objectionable: *~ language; a ~ boy* (i.e. one who misbehaves). **2** improper; unhealthy; not valid; *~ plumbing; Smoking is ~ for you; ~ eggs; a ~ check.* **3** severe: *a ~ cold.* **4** unfavorable: *~ news.* **5** unwell: *He looks ~.* **6** sorry; causing sorrow: *I feel ~ for*

you; Too ~! —**bad blood** ill will. —**bad·ly** *adv.* —**bad·ness** *n.*
bade *pt.* of BID.
badge *n.* **1** an emblem or device worn to show one's membership or rank: *a policeman's ~.* **2** a symbol.
badg·er *n.* a flesh-eating, burrowing member of the weasel family. —**v.** tease cruelly; harass.
bad·i·nage (bad·i·NAZH) *n.* banter.
bad·lands *n.pl.* dry barren land, esp. if eroded into strange shapes.
bad·min·ton *n.* a racket game in which a shuttlecock is hit back and forth over a net.
Bae·de·ker (BAY·duh·kur) *n.* a guidebook.
baf·fle *v.* **baf·fles, baf·fled, baf·fling** thwart; perplex: *a ~ing mystery;* **baf·fle·ment** *n.;* **baf·fler** *n.* —**n.** a device for slowing or redirecting the flow of air, water, etc.
bag *n.* **1** an open-topped container made of paper, cloth, etc.; also, a purse; suitcase. **2** *Sports.* the amount of game shot or caught. **3** *Slang.* what one likes to do or is good at. —**v. bags, bagged, bag·ging** **1** put into a bag; also, hang loosely. **2** shoot or catch (game). —**in the bag** assured; successfully completed.
ba·gasse (buh·GAS) *n.* sugar-cane pulp left after the juice is extracted.
bag·a·telle (–uh·TEL) *n.* **1** a trifle, esp. a short musical composition. **2** a board game played with a cue and balls.
ba·gel (BAY·gl) *n.* a hard, leavened, ring-shaped roll.
bag·gage (BAG·ij) *n.* **1** suitcases, personal effects, etc. carried when traveling. **2** *Informal.* a saucy or pert young woman.
bag·gy (BAG·ee) *adj.* **bag·gi·er, bag·gi·est** loose; sagging; bulging: *~ pants.* —**bag·gi·ly** *adv.* —**bag·gi·ness** *n.*
Bagh·dad (BAG·dad) capital of Iraq.
bag·man *n.* **-men** *Slang.* a collector or distributor of illegally acquired money.
bagn·io (BAN·yoh) *n.* a brothel.
bag of waters same as AMNION. —**bag·pipe** *n.* [often in *pl.*] a wind instrument consisting of a bag with pipes attached to it, played by air blown in through a mouth tube and by means of holes on a melody pipe.
ba·guette (ba·GET) *n.* a gem cut into a long rectangle.
bah *interj.* expressing contempt, disgust, etc.
Ba·ha·ma (buh·HAH·muh) **Islands** a Commonwealth country formed by islands S.E. of Florida; 5,380 sq.mi. (13,935 km²); *cap.* Nassau. Also called **the Bahamas.** —**Ba·ha·mi·an** (–HAY·mee·un) *adj.* & *n.*
Bah·rain or **Bah·rein** (bah·RAIN) a group of islands forming a nation in the Persian Gulf; 240 sq.mi. (622 km²); *cap.* Manama. —**Bah·rain·i** or **Bah·rein·i** (–RAY·nee) *adj.* & *n.*
baht *n., pl.* **baht(s)** the basic unit of currency in Thailand, equal to 100 satang.
bail *n.* **1** a scoop, bucket, etc. for bailing a boat; also, the semicircular handle of a kettle or pail. **2** a security of money posted by a bondsman to ensure a released prisoner's appearance at trial. —**v.** **1** empty (a boat) of water by dipping. **2** [often *bail out*] grant or get someone's release on bail. **3 bail out** parachute from an airplane. —**bail·a·ble** *adj.: a ~ person, offense.* —**bail·iff** *n.* **1** an official who assists in a courtroom. **2** *Brit.* a sheriff's assistant; a landowner's representative or steward; a minor magistrate. —**bail·i·wick** *n.* a bailiff's jurisdiction; hence, one's own area of ability or activity. —**bails·man** *n.* **-men** a bondsman.
bairn *n. Scot.* a child.
bait *n.* an enticement, esp. food placed in a trap or on a hook to catch animals or fish. —**v.** **1** put bait on or in (a trap, hook, etc.); lure. **2** torment mercilessly for fun, as in bearbaiting; persecute. —**bait·er** *n.*
baize *n.* a feltlike cloth used esp. to cover billiard tables.
bake *v.* **bakes, baked, bak·ing** cook, dry, or harden by dry heat, as in an oven or kiln: *~ a cake; sun-~d bricks.* —**n.** a social event at which, usu., baked food is served. —**bak·er** *n.* one who bakes and sells bread, rolls, cakes, etc. in a **bak·er·y, -er·ies.** —**baker's dozen** a dozen plus one. —**bake·shop** *n.* bakery. —**baking soda** bicarbonate of soda used as a leavening agent and in **baking powder,** a leavening agent that contains also a starch and an acid.
bak·sheesh (bak·SHEESH) *n. sing.* & *pl.* in India, Egypt, Turkey, etc., a tip or alms.
Ba·ku (bah·KOO) capital of the Azerbaijan S.S.R. in Russia.
bal. balance.
bal·a·lai·ka (bal·uh·LYE·kuh) *n.* a guitarlike Russian stringed instrument.
bal·ance (–unce) *n.* **1** a centrally pivoted weighing instrument in which the thing to be weighed is made to equal a known weight placed at the opposite end; **in the balance** still to be determined. **2** equilibrium; steadiness, mental or physical; hence, a state in which both sides (as credit and debit columns) are equal; also, what makes both sides equal; remainder: *the ~ of nature; The rider lost his ~ and fell; The books are in ~; ~ of account.* **3** harmony; proportion. **4** a balance wheel. —**v. -anc·es, -anced, -anc·ing** **1** bring, come, or be in balance: *~ a budget.* **2** keep steady while unsupported: *~ a book on your head.* **3** consider the relative merits of: *~ing the pros and cons.* **4** counterbalance. **5** bring into proportion or harmony: *a ~d diet.* —**balance of payments** the difference between payments and receipts for the goods and money entering and leaving a country. —**balance of trade** the difference in value between a country's exports and imports. —**balance sheet** a financial statement showing assets, liabilities, and net worth. —**balance wheel** a wheel that regulates the movement of a clock or watch.
bal·bo·a (–BOH·uh) *n.* the basic unit of money in Panama, equal to 100 centesimos.

bal·brig·gan (–BRIG·un) *n.* a cotton fabric used esp. for underwear and hosiery.

bal·co·ny (BAL·cuh·nee) *n.* **-nies** an overhanging gallery in a theater, auditorium, etc.; also, an outside projecting platform with a railing around it.

bald (BAWLD) *adj.* **1** without its usual covering, esp. of hair on a head: *A ~ tire has no tread left; The* **bald eagle** *has a white head.* **2** plain; blunt: *a ~ style.* **—*v.*** become bald: *a ~ing man.* **—bald·ly** *adv.* **—bald·ness** *n.*

bal·da·chin or **bal·da·quin** (BAL·duh·kin, BAWL–) *n.* a canopy over an altar; also, a kind of brocade.

bal·der·dash (BAWL–) *n.* nonsense.

bal·dric (BAWL–) *n.* a belt to hold a sword or horn, worn diagonally from shoulder to waist.

bale *n.* a large package of goods or material, compressed and bound: *a ~ of hay; ~s of cotton;* also ***v.*** **bales, baled, bal·ing. —bal·er** *n.*

Bal·e·ar·ic (–ee·AIR·ic) **Islands** a W. Mediterranean island group belonging to Spain; *cap.* Palma de Mallorca.

ba·leen (buh·LEEN) *n.* whalebone.

bale·ful *adj.* evil; threatening; deadly. **—bale·ful·ly** *adv.*

Ba·li (BAH·lee) an island in S. Indonesia. **—Ba·li·nese** *adj.* & *n.*

balk (BAWK) *v.* **1** thwart. **2** refuse to proceed; recoil: *He ~ed at the idea of murder;* **balk·y** *adj.* **balk·i·er, -i·est:** *a ~ mule.* **—*n.*** **1** an obstacle. **2** in baseball, an illegal hesitation by the pitcher.

Bal·kan (BAWL·cun) *adj.* pertaining to the **Balkans,** or **Balkan States,** the countries in the **Balkan Peninsula** in S.E. Europe, i.e. Bulgaria, Greece, Albania, and Yugoslavia.

¹ball (BAWL) *n.* **1** a formal dancing party. **2** *Slang.* a good time: *We had a ~.*

²ball *n.* **1** a round or ovoid object, esp. one used in sports: *a tennis ~; the ~ of the foot.* **2** a game played with a ball; in baseball, a hit or pitched ball, esp. a pitched ball that is neither a hit nor a strike: *foul ~; fast ~; ~ four!* **—*v.*** form into a ball. **—ball up** confuse; ruin. **—on the ball** efficient; keen.

bal·lad (BAL·ud) *n.* a narrative song in stanzas, esp. a folk song; also, a popular love song. **—bal·lad·eer** (–DEER) *n.* a ballet singer; also, a composer; **bal·lad·ry** *n.* the balladeer's art.

ball-and-sock·et joint a joint, as of the hip or shoulder, having a knoblike part fitting into a hollow.

bal·last (BAL·ust) *n.* **1** heavy material carried to stabilize a ship, aircraft, etc. **2** crushed stone used to hold in place railroad ties or to make concrete. **—*v.*** load with ballast.

ball bearing a bearing with small steel balls turning to reduce friction; also, such a ball.

bal·le·ri·na (bal·uh·REE·nuh) *n.* a female ballet dancer. **—bal·let** (BAL·ay) *n.* an elaborate, graceful, stylized form of dance used in usu. narrative musical performances; **bal·let·ic** (–LET–) *adj.* **—bal·let·o·mane** (ba·LET·uh–) *n.* a ballet enthusiast; **bal·let·o·ma·ni·a** (–MAY·nee·uh) *n.*

bal·lis·tic (buh·LIS·tic) *adj.* pertaining to the flight of a projectile or to **bal·lis·tics** *n.pl.* [takes *sing.v.*] the study of the motion and behavior of bullets, rockets, bombs, etc.: *a police ~s laboratory.* **—ballistic missile** a missile that is powered only while ascending, and reaches its target in free flight.

bal·loon (buh·LOON) *n.* **1** an airtight bag filled with helium, hot air, etc. and often used to lift loads into the atmosphere. **2** a thin rubber bag inflated with air, used as a toy. **—*v.*** **1** swell like a balloon; increase. **2** ride in a balloon; **bal·loon·ist** *n.* **—balloon tire** a wide pneumatic tire at low pressure to cushion bumps.

bal·lot (BAL·ut) *n.* **1** a piece of paper used in secret voting; also, a list of the candidates in an election: *Cast your ~.* **2** the act, method, or right of voting. **3** all of the votes cast. **—*v.*** vote.

ball·park *n.* a baseball field; **ballpark figure** a figure that is a reasonable estimate. **—ball-point pen** a pen with a ball bearing for a point, which rolls ink from a cartridge onto the paper.

ball·room *n.* a large hall for social dancing.

bal·ly·hoo (BAL·ee·hoo) *n.* extravagant and noisy advertising. **—*v.*** **-hoos, -hooed, -hoo·ing** praise or publicize with ballyhoo.

balm (BAHM) *n.* **1** an aromatic medicinal ointment or lotion; hence, something soothing. **2** any of several aromatic herbs: *~ tea.* **—balm·y** *adj.* **balm·i·er, -i·est** **1** soothing; mild: *a ~ breeze.* **2** *Slang.* insane. **—balm·i·ness** *n.*

ba·lo·ney (buh·LOH·nee) *n.* **1** bologna sausage. **2** *Slang.* false and worthless talk; bunk.

bal·sa (BAWL·suh) *n.* the lighter-than-cork wood of a tropical American tree.

bal·sam (BAWL·sum) *n.* **1** the fragrant resin of several trees, used esp. in medicines. **2** a garden flower, also called IMPATIENS. **—bal·sam fir** a North American evergreen valued for its pulpwood and as a Christmas tree.

Balt (BAWLT) *n.* a native or resident of one of the Baltic States. **—Bal·tic** (BAWL–) *adj.* **1** pertaining to the **Baltic Sea** between Sweden and the U.S.S.R. or to the **Baltic States,** a part of Russia, made up of Estonia, Lithuania, and Latvia. **2** pertaining to an Indo-European language group including Old Prussian, Latvian, and Lithuanian. **—*n.*** **1** the Baltic Sea. **2** the Baltic language group. **—Bal·to-Sla·vic** (–SLAH–) *n.* a subfamily of Indo-European including the Baltic and Slavic groups.

Bal·ti·more (BAWL–) the largest city in Maryland; **Bal·ti·mo·re·an** (–MOR–) *adj.* & *n.* —**Baltimore oriole** an American songbird whose male has bright orange, black, and white plumage.

bal·us·ter *n.* a post supporting a railing. —**bal·us·trade** *n.* a row of balusters and the rail on top of them as an ornamental parapet, esp. on a balcony or terrace.

Bal·zac (BAWL–), **Honoré de.** 1799–1850, French novelist.

Ba·ma·ko (bah·mah·COH) capital of Mali.

bam·boo (bam·BOO) *n.* a tall, woody, often hollow-stemmed grass used for building, fishing poles, etc. —***adj.:*** *a ~ hut.* —**bamboo curtain** the ideological barrier between Communist Asia and the West.

bam·boo·zle (–BOO–) *v.* **-zles, -zled, -zling** **1** cheat; deceive: *~d into buying an old encyclopedia.* **2** perplex. —**bam·boo·zler** *n.*

ban *v.* **bans, banned, ban·ning** officially forbid (shows, books, organizations, or activities). —***n.*** **1** an official prohibition: *the nuclear test ~.* **2** a solemn curse. **3** (BAHN), *pl.* **ba·ni** (BAH·nee) a Romanian coin worth 1/100 of a leu.

ba·nal (buh·NAHL, BAY·nl) *adj.* trite; commonplace: *~ romanticism.* —**ba·nal·i·ty** (–NAL–) *n.* **-ties.**

ba·nan·a (buh·NAN·uh) *n.* a thin, curved, edible tropical fruit with a thick yellow or reddish peel. —**banana republic** any small Latin American country. —**banana split** a dessert of ice cream with split banana.

band *n.* **1** a thin strip of material that encircles and binds together or forms a decoration; a colored stripe: *a rubber~; a hat~.* **2** a range of values, radio frequencies, etc.: *a citizens' ~ radio.* **3** a group of people or animals: *a ~ of thieves; an Indian ~.* **4** a group of musicians: *a jazz ~.* —***v.*** **1** put a band around, esp. to identify (birds, etc.): *the* **banded** (i.e. striped) *rattlesnake.* **2** gather together for a common purpose: *~ed together for self-defense.* —**band·age** (–ij) *n.* a strip of gauze or cloth used to bind or cover an injured part of the body; ***v.*** **-ag·es, -aged, -ag·ing** put a bandage on. —**Band-Aid** *Trademark.* a small adhesive gauze bandage used to cover cuts; **band-aid** *adj.* stop-gap; patched up; temporary.

ban·dan·(n)a (–DAN·uh) *n.* a large brightly colored handkerchief or scarf.

Ban·dar Ser·i Be·ga·wan (–buh·GAH·wun) capital of Brunei.

band·box *n.* a light, round or oval box for holding hats or collars.

ban·de·rol(e) (BAN·duh·role) *n.* a narrow flag or streamer with a forked end, as on a knight's lance.

ban·di·coot *n.* **1** a ratlike marsupial of Australia. **2** a large destructive rat of India and Sri Lanka.

ban·dit *n.* **-dits** or **-dit·ti** (–DIT·ee) an outlaw, esp. one of a band of highwaymen. —**ban·dit·ry** *n.*

ban·do·leer or **ban·do·lier** (–duh·LEER) *n.* a cartridge belt worn across the chest and over one shoulder.

band saw a power saw whose cutting edge is a toothed endless steel belt.

band·stand *n.* a raised platform for a musical band, usu. a roofed one outdoors.

b. and w. or **B. and W.** black and white.

band·wag·on *n.* a large, decorated wagon used to carry a band in a parade. —**(hop, jump,** or) **climb on the bandwagon** support a cause when it is winning, esp. in a political campaign.

ban·dy *v.* **-dies, -died, -dy·ing** knock back and forth; exchange (gossip, insults, etc.), esp. frivolously or in anger: *All they did was ~ words about.* —***adj.*** curved outwards; **ban·dy-leg·ged** *adj.* bowlegged.

bane *n.* a cause of death or woe; also, a poison. —**bane·ful** *adj.* evil: *the ~ influence of drugs on society.*

[1]bang *v.* **1** strike hard or with a loud noise; also, make a loud noise: *She ~ed her elbow on the door; Don't let the door ~ behind you.* **2** handle roughly or noisily. —***n.*** **1** a sudden loud noise; a noisy blow. **2** *Slang.* a thrill: *You'll get a ~ out of this.* —***adv.*** directly; precisely; with a bang: *ran ~ into the wall.*

[2]bang *n.* [usu. in *pl.*] fringe of hair cut squarely across the forehead; ***v.*** cut in bangs.

Bang·kok capital of Thailand.

Ban·gla·desh a nation between Burma and India on the Bay of Bengal; 55,126 sq.mi. (142,776 km^2); *cap.* Dacca.

ban·gle *n.* a rigid bracelet worn on the wrist or ankle; also, an ornament hanging from this.

Ban·gui (BAHN·ghee) capital of the Central African Republic.

bang-up *adj. Informal.* first-rate: *a ~ job.*

bani *pl.* of BAN, *n.* 3.

ban·ish *v.* **1** expel from a country; exile. **2** send away, esp. from the mind: *~ care and woe.* —**ban·ish·ment** *n.: a king overthrown and sent into ~.*

ban·(n)is·ter *n.* **1** the railing along a set of stairs: *sliding down the ~.* **2** a baluster.

ban·jo *n.* **-jo(e)s** a usu. five-stringed musical instrument with a long neck and a round, hollow, skin-covered body. —**ban·jo·ist** *n.*

Ban·jul capital of Gambia.

[1]bank *n.* **1** a pile or heap; also, a shallow area under water; also, a slope, esp. the edge of a body of water: *a ~ of snow; a ~ of clouds; the opposite ~s of a river.* **2** the inward tilt of a vehicle, esp. an aircraft, as it turns; also, the slant in a road or railbed at a curve: *The pilot put the plane into a steep ~.* **3** a row or tier, as of oars, organ keys, etc. —***v.*** **1** put a bank around; pile up; also, heap fuel, ashes, etc. on a fire to slow its burning: *The camper ~ed the fire and went to sleep.* **2** tilt: *This turn is too steeply*

~ed for ordinary drivers. **3** in billiards, hit (the ball) so that it rebounds from the cushion. **4** arrange in tiers, as typewriter keys.

²bank *n.* **1** a business establishment that deals in money deposits, loans, etc.; hence, any fund or pool of money. **2** a reserve or supply for future use: *a blood ~.* **—v.** put (money) in a bank; do business at a bank; **bank on** rely on. **—bank·book** *n.* a depositor's record of deposits and withdrawals. **—bank card** a credit card issued by a bank. **—bank·er** *n.* one who owns or manages a bank. **—bank·ing** *n.* the work or occupation of a banker. **—bank note** a note issued by a bank guaranteeing payment of a stated sum to bearer. **—bank·roll** *n. Informal.* a supply of ready money; **v.:** *a new joint ~ed by the underworld.* **—bank·rupt** *n.* **1** a person or business legally declared unable to pay creditors fully; **v.** make bankrupt. **2** one totally lacking in usefulness or some other quality: *a moral ~.* Also **adj.:** *a ~ corporation; a government ~ of sound leadership.* **—bank·rupt·cy** *n.* **-cies:** *driven into ~ by a recession.*

ban·ner *n.* **1** a flag; standard; esp., a large strip of cloth with a slogan on it. **2** an idea as a symbol or rallying point. **3** an across-the-page newspaper headline. **—adj.** outstanding: *a ~ year for the Democrats.*

bannister same as BANISTER.

ban·nock *n.* a usu. unleavened griddle cake of barley or oatmeal.

banns *n.pl.* the announcement in church of an intended marriage.

ban·quet *n.* an elaborate feast, usu. in honor of a person or event: *a wedding ~.* **—v.** take part in or honor with a banquet.

ban·quette (bang·KET) *n.* **1** a platform for gunners behind a parapet or inside a trench wall. **2** an upholstered bench along a wall.

ban·shee *n.* in Irish and Scottish folklore, a female spirit whose wail foretells a death in the house: *screaming like a ~.*

ban·tam *n.* **1** a dwarfish but aggressive breed of domestic fowls. **2** a small aggressive person. **3** also **ban·tam·weight,** a boxer weighing between 113 and 118 lbs. (52 and 54 kg for Olympics). **—adj.** small and aggressive.

ban·ter *n.* playful teasing. **—v.** tease good-humoredly; also, joke playfully *(with).*

bant·ling *n.* a young child.

Ban·tu (BAN·too) *n.* any of many related Negroid peoples of C. and S. Africa; also, any of their related languages, including Swahili. Also **adj.** **—Ban·tu·stan** *n.* a South African homeland.

ban·yan (–yun) *n.* a fig tree of India with aerial shoots that grow into the soil forming new trunks.

ban·zai (bahn·ZYE) *interj.* a Japanese cheer or battle cry. **—banzai attack** a usu. suicidal mass attack.

ba·o·bab (BAY·oh–) *n.* a tropical tree with a thick trunk, large edible fruit, and medicinally useful bark and leaves.

Bap. or **Bapt.** Baptist. **—bap·tism** *n.* **1** a baptizing. **2** an initiation; **baptism of fire** a soldier's first experience of combat. **—bap·tis·mal** (–TIZ·ml) *adj.: ~ font.* **—bap·tis·ter·y** (BAP·tis·tree) *n.* **-ter·ies** a place or a tank of water for baptizing; also **bap·tis·try** *n.* **-tries.** **—Bap·tist** *n.* a member of any of several Protestant denominations practicing the baptism of mature believers by immersion; **adj.:** *a ~ congregation.* **—bap·tize** *v.* **-tiz·es, -tized, -tiz·ing** **1** admit (a person) to a Christian church by sprinkling with or immersing in water; hence, give a Christian name **(baptismal name)** to. **2** initiate; also, purify.

bar *n.* **1** a regular oblong object, esp. such a piece of wood or metal: *an iron ~; a ~ of slap; a chocolate ~.* **2** a bar used to block a passage or fasten a door or gate; hence, an obstacle: *a ~ to progress;* **behind bars** in prison. **3** a band, as of color. **4** a counter for serving food or drink, esp. alcoholic drink; also, a business with such a counter; hence, one for sales of any kind: *Joe's ~ and grill; a cosmetics ~.* **5** the legal profession; also, a law court or place of judgment: *admitted to the ~; before the ~ of conscience.* **6** a vertical line dividing a staff of music into measures; also, a portion so divided. **—v. bars, barred, bar·ring** **1** fasten with a bar: *~ the door.* **2** forbid; block; exclude: *The heckler was ~d from all future meetings.* **—prep.** excepting: *~ none.*

bar. barometer; barrel; barrister.

barb *n.* a backward-turning point, as on a fishhook or arrow; hence, anything sharp or cutting, as criticism or sarcasm: *~s of wit.* **—barbed** *adj.: a ~ comment.*

Bar·ba·dos (–BAY·doze) a country that is the most easterly of the West Indies; 166 sq.mi. (431 km²); *cap.* Bridgetown. **—Bar·ba·di·an** (–BAY·dee·un) *adj.* & *n.*

bar·bar·i·an (–BAIR·ee·un) *n.* **1** a member of a primitive or less developed culture. **2** an uncultured person; a cruel brute. Also **adj.:** *~ peoples; a ~ custom.* **—bar·bar·ic** (bar·BAIR·ic) *adj.* primitive; wild: *the ~ splendor of a temple's interior.* **—bar·ba·rism** (BAHR·buh–) *n.* **1** a primitive level of civilization; also, a cruel or savage act or trait. **2** the use of nonstandard words. **—bar·bar·i·ty** (–BAIR–) *n.* **-ties** **1** a cruel or savage act or custom. **2** a crude taste, manner, or action. **—bar·ba·rous** (BAHR·buh·rus) *adj.* **1** savage; brutal; uncivilized. **2** of words and expressions, nonstandard; **bar·ba·rous·ly** *adv.*

bar·be·cue (BAHR·buh·cue) *n.* an outdoor pit, fireplace, or portable grill for roasting meats; also, a party at which such food is served. **—v. -cues, -cued, -cu·ing** cook on a barbecue; also, cook with a seasoned sauce, or

barbecue sauce, made with tomatoes and vinegar.

barbed wire wire with sharp points along it, used for fences or barricades; also **barb•wire** *n.*

bar•bell *n.* a metal rod or bar with variable weights on both ends, lifted for exercise.

bar•ber *n.* one who cuts hair, shaves men's beards, etc. as a trade; also ***v.;*** **bar•ber•shop** *n.: A* **barbershop quartet** *has four harmonized voices singing popular songs.*

bar•ber•ry *n.* **-ber•ries** a low thorny shrub with red berries.

bar•bi•can (BAHR·bi·cun) *n.* a fortified approach to a city, esp. a tower over a gate.

bar•bi•tal (–taul) *n.* a white crystalline powder containing barbituric acid. **—bar•bi•tu•rate** (–BICH·uh·rit) *n.* any of a group of potentially addictive sedative or sleep-inducing drugs. **—bar•bi•tu•ric** (–TYOOR–, –TOOR–) **acid** an organic acid used in making barbiturates.

barbwire same as BARBED WIRE.

bar•ca•rol(l)e (BAHR·cuh·role) *n.* a Venetian gondolier's song; also, a similar piece of music with a beat suggestive of the rhythm of rowing.

Bar•ce•lo•na (–suh·LOH·nuh) a Mediterranean seaport in N.E. Spain.

bar code a code such as the UNIVERSAL PRODUCT CODE for use in computerized checkout and inventory systems.

bard *n.* a minstrel; tribal poet; **Bard of Avon** Shakespeare. **—bard•ic** *adj.*

bare *adj.* **bar•er, bar•est** **1** without its usual covering, contents, or equipment; plain without elaboration: *sunburned on his ~ legs; the cupboard was ~; the ~ facts.* **2** just sufficient; no more than; mere: *the ~ necessities of life.* ***—v.*** **bares, bared, bar•ing** reveal; lay bare: *The lion growled and ~d its teeth.* **—bare•ly** *adv.: a ~* (i.e. scantily) *furnished apartment; She had ~* (i.e. scarcely) *met him before he proposed; ~ survived the fire.* **—bare•ness** *n.* **—bare•back(ed)** *adj.* & *adv.* without a saddle. **—bare•faced** *adj.* shameless: *a ~ lie.* **—bare•foot(•ed)** *adj.* & *adv.* without shoes: *seen walking ~ in the park.* **—bare•hand•ed** *adj.* without a weapon. **—bare•head•ed** *adj.* & *adv.* with head exposed; hatless. **—bare•leg•ged** *adj.* & *adv.: ~ children shivering on street corners.*

bar•fly *n.* **-flies** *Slang.* one who regularly drinks in bars.

bar•gain (BARG·in) *n.* **1** an agreement or deal to buy, sell, trade, etc.; **strike a bargain** make a deal. **2** something bought or sold for a low price; **in** (or **into**) **the bargain** in addition. ***—v.*** negotiate a bargain or terms, as of a contract. **—bargain on** (or **for**) expect. **—bar•gain•er** *n.*

barge (BARJ) *n.* **1** a big flat-bottomed freight boat used on canals, rivers, etc. **2** a finely decorated ceremonial boat: *Cleopatra's ~ on the Nile.* ***—v.*** **barg•es, barged, barg•ing** **1** transport by barge. **2** *Informal.* move or intrude clumsily or rudely: *always ~ing in where he's not wanted.* **—barge•man** *n.* **-men.**

bar•i•tone (BAIR–) *n.* a male singing voice lower than tenor and higher than bass.

bar•i•um (BAIR·ee·um) *n.* a soft, silver-white metallic chemical element.

[1]bark *n.* the short gruff sound made by a dog; "bow-wow": *His ~ is worse than his bite.* (i.e. is frightening but harmless). ***—v.*** utter a bark; hence, speak sharply or hoarsely; **bark up the wrong tree** proceed with one's efforts, criticisms, etc. misdirected; be on the wrong track.

[2]bark *n.* the tough outer covering of woody stems and roots. ***—v.*** **1** take the bark off. **2** *Informal.* scrape the skin of: *He fell and ~ed his shin.*

[3]bark *n.* a sailing ship with the after mast rigged fore-and-aft and the others rigged square; also **barque.**

bar•keep•er *n.* a bartender; also, the owner of a bar serving liquor; also **bar•keep.**

bark•er *n.* one who loudly calls out to attract people, esp. to a sideshow or sale.

bar•ley (–lee) *n.* a grain used for food and in making beer and whiskey.

bar•maid *n.* a woman who serves drinks in a bar. **—bar•man** *n.* **-men** a bartender.

bar mitz•vah (–MITS·vuh) a ceremony marking the taking on of religious responsibility by a 13-year-old Jewish boy; also, such a boy.

barn *n.* a large building for sheltering farm equipment, animals, crops and feed, etc.; also, a similar building for buses, trucks, etc.

bar•na•cle (–nuh·kl) *n.* a marine shellfish that fastens itself firmly to rocks, timbers, ship hulls, etc.

barn•storm *v.* tour the countryside giving plays, speeches, or exhibitions of stunt flying. **—barn•storm•er** n. **—barn•yard** *n.* a yard near a barn; ***adj.*** earthy: *low ~ humor.*

bar•o•graph (BAIR·uh·graf) *n.* a self-recording barometer. **—ba•rom•e•ter** (buh·ROM·i·tur) *n.* **1** an instrument for measuring atmospheric pressure. **2** an indicator of change. **—bar•o•met•ric** (bair·uh·MET·ric) *adj.: ~ pressure;* **bar•o•met•ri•cal•ly** *adv.*

bar•on (BAIR·un) **1** a peer of the lowest inherited rank; *fem.* **bar•on•ess.** **2** a magnate: *a beef ~; a mining ~.* **—bar•on•et** (BAIR·uh·net) *n.* a member of a titled order ranking below baron; **bar•on•et•cy** *n.* **-cies.** **—ba•ro•ni•al** (buh·ROH·nee·ul) *adj.* of a baron: *~ privilege; ~* (i.e. large) *dimensions.*

ba•roque (buh·ROAK) *adj.* of art, music, literature, and esp. architecture, in a style prevalent in the 17th and 18th centuries, noted for contrasts and florid ornamentation; hence, flamboyantly ornate.

ba•rouche (buh·ROOSH) *n.* a four-wheeled, four-seater, carriage with a collapsible top.

barque See [3]BARK.

bar·racks (BAIR·uks) *n.pl.* [takes *sing.* or *pl.v.*] a building or a group of buildings housing soldiers: *a school built like a ~; refugee ~.*
bar·ra·cu·da (bair·uh·COO·duh) *n.* a thin-bodied, fierce fish of tropical seas.
bar·rage *n.* **1** (BAH·rij) a man-made blockage in a watercourse to raise its level for irrigation. **2** (buh·RAHZH) heavy, sustained burst of artillery fire; hence, a continuous stream, as of questions, abuse, etc.: *Anchored* **barrage balloons** *are used to block enemy aircraft.* **—v. bar·rag·es, bar·raged, bar·rag·ing:** *a speaker ~d with questions.*
bar·ra·try (BAIR·uh·tree) *n.* **1** fraud or negligence by a captain or crew resulting in loss to a shipowner. **2** the incitement of vexatious lawsuits. **3** the purchase and sale of church or state offices. **—bar·ra·tor** or **bar·ra·ter** (BAIR·uh·tur) *n.*
barred *adj.* having bars: *a* **barred owl** (with brown stripes on its chest); *a ~ window.*
bar·rel (BAIR·ul) *n.* **1** a round wooden cask with bulging sides; drum; hence, any of several measures of capacity. **2** a cylindrical part of an apparatus or machine, esp. the firing tube of a gun. **3** *Informal.* a great amount: *a ~ of laughs.* **—v. bar·rels, bar·rel(l)ed, bar·rel·(l)ing 1** pack in a barrel. **2** *Slang.* travel at high speed. **—over a barrel** *Informal.* at someone's mercy. **—barrel organ** a street musician's hand organ that is worked by cranking a cylinder in a box containing pipes. **—barrel roll** a complete longitudinal revolution of an aircraft in flight.
bar·ren (BAIR·un) *adj.* **1** incapable of bearing offspring or fruit; of land, unproductive. **2** lacking in interest, useful results, etc. **3** devoid: *Animals are not ~ of intelligence.* **—n.** a tract of barren ground. **—bar·ren·ness** *n.*
bar·rette (bah·RET) *n.* a small hair clasp.
bar·ri·cade (BAIR·i–) *n.* a hastily built rampart or barrier, esp. one blocking a street; hence, any barrier: *Man the ~s, citizens!* **—v. -cades, -cad·ed, -cad·ing** block, obstruct, or protect, esp. with a barricade.
bar·ri·er (BAIR·ee·ur) *n.* something that blocks, hinders, or separates, esp. a fence or wall: *social ~s; the booms of supersonic planes breaking the sound ~.* **—barrier reef** a coral reef parallel to and separated by a channel from a coast.
bar·ring *prep.* except in case of: *They will arrive at noon, ~ accidents.*
bar·ri·o (BAH·ree·oh) *n.* **-os** a Spanish-speaking part of an American city.
bar·ris·ter (BAIR·is·tur) *n. Brit.* a lawyer qualified to plead in all courts; cf. SOLICITOR.
bar·room *n.* a room with a bar for selling liquor.
bar·row (BAIR·oh) *n.* **1** an ancient mound over a grave site. **2** a wheelbarrow; also, a handbarrow. **3** a castrated boar.
bar·stool *n.* a high stool used at a bar.
Bart. baronet.
bar·ten·der *n.* one who serves alcoholic beverages at a bar.
bar·ter *v.* trade without using money: *The trapper ~ed his furs for a rifle.* **—n.:** *~ precedes a money economy.*
bas·al (BAY·sul) *adj.* being or pertaining to the base or basis; basic; minimal. **—basal metabolism** the minimal amount of energy used by an organism for cell activity, respiration, and circulation, as when at rest.
ba·salt (buh·SAWLT, BAY–) *n.* a dark, hard, often glassy volcanic rock.
¹base *adj.* **1** ignoble; demeaning: *~ cowardice.* **2** not precious: *a* **base coin** *is alloyed with ~ metals.* **—base·ly** *adv.* **—base·ness** *n.*
²base *n.* **1** the lower or supporting part, as of a statute; esp. in geometry, the side on which a figure rests. **2** the number on which a numeration system is based: *10 is the ~ of the decimal system.* **3** a starting point; also, a camp or town supplying food, equipment, etc. for a military or other operation: *their ~ of operations; a naval ~; the ~ camp of the expedition.* **4** the main ingredient: *a paint with an oil ~.* **5** the foundation or beginning of a plan, theory, line of reasoning, etc. **6** a substance that reacts with an acid to form a salt. **7** in baseball, one of the four points to be touched for a run to count; **off base** *Informal.* mistaken or unprepared. **8** the part of a word to which affixes are added; stem. **—v. bas·es, based, bas·ing 1** place at a base: *a Marine ~d at Camp Pendleton.* **2** have or provide a base or basis: *a story ~d on fact; a film ~d on a book.* **—base·ball** *n.* a game played by two teams of nine players on a diamond-shaped field with a bat and ball; also, the ball. **—base·board** *n.* a molding at the base of a wall.
base·born *adj.* of low or illegitimate birth; ignoble.
base hit in baseball, a hit allowing a batter to get on base without the help of an opponent's error or the forcing out of a teammate. **—base·less** *adj.* groundless; without foundation. **—base·line** *n.* **1** a line serving as a base, esp. in surveying. **2** in baseball, one of the four lanes connecting the bases. **—base·man** *n.* **-men** an infielder playing at first, second, or third base. **—base·ment** *n.* the foundation of a building; also, the lowest story, at least partly underground. **—base on balls** a baseball batter's advance to first base after being pitched four balls. **—base pay** pay exclusive of overtime and other additions. **—base runner** a baseball player on the team at bat who has reached or is trying to reach a base.
bases *pl.* of BASIS.
bash *v. Informal.* hit very hard; smash. **—n.** *Slang.* a party.
bash·ful *adj.* shy; sensitive and timid. **—bash·ful·ly** *adv.* **—bash·ful·ness** *n.*

bas•ic (BAY–) *adj.* **1** fundamental: *a ~ outline of the course;* **bas•i•cal•ly** *adv.* **2** *Chemistry.* pertaining to or containing a base; **ba•sic•i•ty** (–SIS–) *n.* —**bas•ic** *n.* something basic: *The negotiators got down to ~s.* —**BASIC** a computer language using common English terms. —**Basic English** simplified English with an 850-word vocabulary.

bas•il (BAZ–) *n.* an aromatic cooking herb of the mint family.

ba•sil•i•ca (buh·SIL·i·cuh) *n.* **1** a rectangular building with an apse and side aisles used as a church, esp. by early Christians. **2** a Roman Catholic church with certain ceremonial rights.

bas•i•lisk *n.* a mythical lizard with a fatal breath and glance.

ba•sin (BAY·sn) *n.* **1** an open, shallow, rounded vessel for water; also, a sink. **2** a usu. enclosed body of water, as a harbor or pond; also, the area passed through by a river: *the Colorado River ~.* **3** a broad, rounded depression in a land mass.

ba•sis (BAY–) *n., pl.* **ba•ses** (–seez) **1** reason or grounds for a decision, expectation, etc.; principle: *Common interests are a good ~ for friendship.* **2** fundamental part. **3** footing: *We are on a first-name ~; put the company on a sound economic ~.*

bask *v.* expose oneself luxuriatingly to warmth, love, admiration, etc.: *sunbathers ~ing on the beach.*

bas•ket *n.* **1** a container made of usu. interwoven strips of wood, cane, fiber, etc.; also, anything similar; **bas•ket•ful** *n.* **2** an elevated round hoop fitted with an open, hanging net that forms the goal in basketball; also, a throw of the ball through it that counts as a score. —**bas•ket•ball** *n.* a game played with an inflated round ball by two teams of five players each; also, the ball. —**basket weave** a type of interlaced cloth weave.

bas mitz•vah (bahs·MITS·vuh) same as BATH MITZVAH.

Basque (BASK) *n.* a member of a culturally distinct people of the French and Spanish Pyrenees; also, their unique native language. —***adj.:*** *the ~ Provinces* (in N. Spain).

bas-re•lief (bah·ri·LEEF) *n.* a form of sculpture in which figures stand out slightly from their flat background.

[1]bass *n.* any of a group of freshwater and marine game fishes.

[2]bass (BAYCE) *adj.* of the lowest pitch. —***n.*** **1** a male singer or an instrument with a bass range. **2** the lowest part in harmonic arrangements.

bas•set (hound) (BAS·it) a short-legged, long-eared breed of dog.

bas•si•net (–NET) *n.* a hooded, basketlike baby's bed.

bas•so (BAS·oh) *n.* **bas•sos** a singer with a bass voice. —**bas•soon** (buh·SOON) *n.* a double-reed wind instrument with a bass range. —**bass** (BAYCE) **viol** same as DOUBLE BASS.

bass•wood *n.* the North American linden tree.

bast *n.* a bark fiber used to make rope, matting, etc.

bas•tard (–turd) *n.* **1** an illegitimate child. **2** anything spurious, of low quality, hybrid, etc. **3** *Slang.* [abusive epithet] an offensive person. —***adj.:*** **bastard** (i.e. inferior) **mahogany; bastard title** (i.e. a book's half-title page). —**bas•tard•ly** *adj.: a ~ trick.* —**bas•tard•ize** *v.* **-iz•es, -ized, -iz•ing** make or declare bastard; debase: *He spoke a ~d French.* —**bas•tard•y** *n.* **-tard•ies** illegitimacy.

baste *v.* **bastes, bast•ed, bast•ing** **1** fasten with large stitches. **2** beat or scold soundly. **3** pour drippings, sauce, etc. over (meat or fish) while it is cooking: *~d turkey.*

bas•ti•na•do (–NAH·doh) *n.* **-does** a beating, esp. on the soles of the feet.

bas•tion (BAS·chun) *n.* a fortified projection of a wall or rampart; hence, a strong position: *the last ~ of conservatism.* —**bas•tioned** *adj.: a ~ fort.*

[1]bat *n.* **1** a stick or racket for hitting a ball in baseball, cricket, table tennis, etc.; **at bat** taking one's turn as a hitter in baseball; **right off the bat** *Informal.* immediately. **2** a blow. **3** *Slang.* a binge. —***v.*** **bats, bat•ted, bat•ting** **1** hit, esp. with a bat; take a turn at bat. **2** flutter; wink: *She didn't* **bat an eye** *at the news* (i.e. showed no surprise).

[2]bat *n.* any of a large group of nocturnal mammals, including vampires and flying foxes, that fly by means of membranous wings: *blind as a ~.*

batch *n.* things or people forming a group and attended to at one time: *a fresh ~ of bread; a new ~ of trainees.*

bate *v.* **bates, bat•ed, bat•ing** make smaller or less forceful: *with ~d breath.*

ba•teau (ba·TOH) *n., pl.* **ba•teaux** (–TOZE) a flat-bottomed light boat, usu. with narrow bow and stern.

bath *n.* **1** an immersion of an object in a liquid, esp. the washing of the body in water; also, the water, tub, room, or building used. **2 baths** *pl.* a building with large rooms and pools for washing: *Turkish ~s.* —**bathe** (BAIDH) *v.* **bathes, bathed, bath•ing** **1** take or subject to a bath; also, go swimming. **2** soak: *meadows ~d in sunlight.* —**bath•er** *n.*

ba•thet•ic (–THET–) *adj.* characterized by bathos.

bath•house *n.* a building for bathing; also, one for swimmers to change clothes in. —**bathing suit** swimming apparel.

bath mitz•vah (baht·MITS·vuh) a ceremony for a girl similar to the bar mitzvah.

bath•o•lith *n.* a subterranean mass of igneous rock intruding into other strata.

ba•thos (BAY–) *n.* **1** a sudden transition from the sublime to the trivial. **2** overdone or insincere pathos.

bath•robe *n.* a loose robe worn for lounging, going to and from a bath, etc. —**bath•room** *n.* a room for taking baths, usu. having also a toilet and washbasin. —**bath•tub** *n.* a tub for bathing.

bath•y•scaph(e) (–skaf, –skayf) *n.* a manned, submersible ship for deep-sea exploration. —**bath•y•sphere** *n.* a manned steel sphere lowered by cable to great depths for undersea observation.

ba•tik (buh·TEEK, BAT·ik) *n.* a technique for dyeing cloth by coating with wax the parts to remain uncolored.

ba•tiste (buh·TEEST) *n.* a soft, lightweight cloth of wool, cotton, or rayon.

bat•man *n.* **-men** *Brit.* an officer's orderly.

ba•ton (buh·TAHN) *n.* a light stick used by the conductor of an orchestra; also, any of various other rods, staves, etc.: *~-twirling drum majorettes.*

Bat•on Rouge (batn·ROOZH) capital of Louisiana.

bats•man *n.* **-men** *Brit.* the batter in cricket.

bat mitz•vah (baht·MITS·vuh) same as BATH MITZVAH.

ba•tra•chi•an (buh·TRAY·kee·un) *n.* a frog, toad, or other tailless amphibian.

bat•tal•ion (buh·TAL·yun) *n.* a military unit made up of two or more companies, batteries, etc.; hence, army: *~s of census takers.*

bat•ten (BATN) *n.* a long thin board used for flooring or to fasten other boards in place. —*v.* **1 batten down the hatches** secure a ship's hatch covers, esp. before a storm. **2** thrive or grow fat; overfeed.

[1]**bat•ter** *n.* in baseball, one whose turn it is to bat.

[2]**bat•ter** *n.* a beaten mixture for cooking, fluid enough to be poured: *pancake ~.* —*v.* strike or pound heavily or repeatedly: *a badly ~ed child;* **battering ram** a heavy, metal-tipped log used to batter down walls, doors, etc.

bat•ter•y *n.* **bat•ter•ies 1** a device for storing or generating electricity: *a storage ~; flashlight ~.* **2** a set of similar things used together, esp. artillery guns: *a ~ of searchlights; a ~ of tests.* **3** *Baseball.* the pitcher and catcher. **4** *Law.* a beating, esp. the illegal striking of a person: *assault and ~.*

bat•ting *n.* flat wads of the fibers of cotton, wool, etc.: *cotton ~* (used in bandages).

bat•tle *n.* a conflict, esp. a large armed combat: *the ~ of Waterloo; "The first blow is half the ~."* —*v.* **bat•tles, bat•tled, bat•tling** fight; also **give** (or **do) battle.** —**bat•tle-ax(e)** *n.* **-ax•es 1** a heavy ax used as a weapon. **2** *Slang.* an aggressive domineering woman. —**battle cry** a slogan or cry used as encouragement in a conflict. —**bat•tle•field** *n.* the site of a battle. —**bat•tle•ment** *n.* a parapet or top of a defensive wall. —**bat•tle•ship** *n.* a warship of the most heavily armed class; also **bat•tle•wag•on** *Slang.*

bat•ty (BAT·ee) *adj.* **bat•ti•er, bat•ti•est** *Slang.* eccentric; crazy: *He's gone ~ from the strain.*

bau•ble (BAW·bl) *n.* a worthless, showy trinket.

Baude•laire (bode·LAIR), **Charles.** 1821–1867, French poet.

baux•ite *n.* the claylike ore of aluminum. —**baux•it•ic** (–SIT–) *adj.*

Ba•var•i•a (buh·VAIR·ee·uh) a S. state in West Germany; *cap.* Munich. —**Ba•var•i•an** *adj.* & *n.*

bawd *n.* a female brothel-keeper. —**bawd•y** *adj.* **bawd•i•er, -i•est** obscene; lewd: *~ jokes;* **bawd•i•ly** *adv.;* **bawd•i•ness** *n.*

bawl *v.* shout, cry, or weep loudly: *~ing like a baby;* also ***n.*** —**bawl out** *Informal.* scold vigorously.

[1]**bay** *n.* **1** a deep, continuous barking, esp. of hunting dogs. **2** the position of a cornered animal or one that is checked: *a wild boar* **brought to bay** *by hounds; The sniper held the police* **at bay. 3** a separate compartment, esp. for storage: *a bomb ~ in an aircraft; a sick ~* (i.e. infirmary on a ship). **4** a recess in an outer wall, esp. one with a window, i.e. **bay window.** —*v.* **1** give repeated, prolonged barks: *dogs ~ing at the moon.* **2** pursue with barking; corner.

[2]**bay** *n.* a body of water extending into the land, usu. smaller than a gulf, sometimes an estuary: *Delaware Bay; "Bay State"* (i.e. Massachusetts).

[3]**bay** *n.* **1** a kind of laurel whose leaves are used dried in cooking **(bay leaf)** and to weave garlands; **bays** *pl.* fame and honor. **2** a similar tree or shrub.

[4]**bay** *adj.* reddish-brown. —***n.*** an animal of this color, esp. a horse.

bay•ber•ry *n.* **-ber•ries 1** a tropical American tree whose oil-bearing leaves are used in **bay rum,** a fragrant liquid used in soothing skin lotions. **2** any of several shrubs, as the wax myrtle.

bay•o•net (–uh–) *n.* a heavy knife made to be attached to a rifle barrel for hand-to-hand combat. —*v.* **-nets, -net•(t)ed, -net•(t)ing** stab with a bayonet.

bay•ou (BY·oh, –oo) *n.* in Louisiana, Mississippi, and Texas, a shallow, usu. sluggish channel, tributary, or offshoot of a body of water.

bay rum See BAYBERRY; **bay window** See [1]BAY.

ba•zaar (buh·ZAR) *n.* **1** in the Orient, a marketplace. **2** a sale of assorted goods, usu. for charity. Also **ba•zar.**

ba•zoo•ka (buh·ZOO·kuh) *n.* a portable firing tube for launching armor-piercing rockets.

bb or **b.b.** base on balls. —**BB** shot of .18 in. (0.4572 cm) diameter, as used in a BB gun.

B.B.A. Bachelor of Business Administration.

B.B.B. Better Business Bureau.

B.B.C. British Broadcasting Corporation.

BB gun an air rifle.

bbl. barrel(s).

B.C. before Christ; British Columbia. —**bc** or **bcc** blind (carbon) copy.
B.C.E. Bachelor of Civil Engineering.
bd. board; bond; bound. —**B.D.** Bachelor of Divinity; bills discounted.
bdl(e). bundle.
bdrm. bedroom.
be (BEE) *auxiliary v.* (I) **am;** (you, we, they) **are;** (he, she, it) **is;** *pt.* (I, he, she, it) **was,** (you, we, they) **were;** *pp.* **been** (BIN); **be·ing** **1** exist as real; live: *There is no such thing as a unicorn; Old Pete is no more.* **2** occupy some place: *It was in the corner.* **3** go: *I've been to London to visit the Queen.* **4** occur: *The party was a week ago.* **5** continue; stay: *I will be here for a month.* **6** stand for; mean: *Let "c" be the speed of light.* **7** [used to join subject and predicate]: *To work is to pray; This is my dress; The sky is blue; The dog is a mammal.* **8** [used with a present participle to show continued action]: *He was sitting on the fence.* **9** [used with a past participle to form the passive voice]: *They were hit by a car.* **10** [used with *to* to show futurity, expectation, duty, etc.]: *He was to come to the party.*
be- *prefix.* **1** around; thoroughly: as in *bespatter.* **2** cover, furnish, or treat with: as in *bewitch, befog.* **3** make or make seem: as in *befoul.* **4** off; away: as in *behead, betake.* **5** about: as in *bewail.* —**Be** beryllium. —**b.e.** or **B/E** bill of exchange. —**B.E.** Bachelor of Education; Board of Education.
beach (BEECH) *n.* a shallowly sloping shore usu. covered with sand or small stones. —***v.*** bring or force (a vessel) onto a beach. —**beach buggy** dune buggy. —**beach·comb·er** *n.* one who lives on what he finds along the beach. —**beach flea** a small leaping crustacean found on beaches. —**beach·head** *n.* a fortified advance position on a beach, held by invading soldiers.
bea·con (BEE·kn) *n.* a fire, lighthouse, buoy, radio signal, or other device used to guide or warn ships, aircraft, etc.
bead (BEED) *n.* **1** a small globular object or an ornament of glass, wood, etc. pierced for stringing together: *~s* (i.e. droplets) *of dew;* **draw a bead on** take aim at. **2 beads** *pl.* a string of beads; a rosary; **say** (or **tell**) **one's beads** say prayers with a rosary. **3** a narrow, semicircular molding. —***v.*** ornament with or form beads: *a ~ed dress.* —**bead·y** *adj.* **bead·i·er, -i·est** small, round, and shiny: *~ eyes.*
bea·dle (BEE·dl) *n.* a parish official keeping order in church.
bea·gle (BEE·gl) *n.* a small, long-eared hound with a smooth coat.
beak (BEEK) *n.* **1** a hard, sharp, often hooked mouth structure, esp. a bird's bill. **2** *Informal.* the human nose. —**beaked** *adj.*
beak·er (BEE·kur) *n.* a broad-mouthed vessel with a pouring lip and no handle, used in laboratories; also, a goblet.
beam (BEEM) *n.* **1** a long, heavy piece of wood, steel, etc. used esp. in building; also, a crosspiece, as of a ship, of a balance, etc. **2** a directed bundle of light rays, electromagnetic waves, particles, etc.; esp., a radio signal used to guide aircraft; **off** (or **on**) **the beam** *Informal.* off or on the right track. —***v.*** **1** broadcast on or send a beam: *~ing radio shows via satellites.* **2** smile radiantly: *a face ~ing with joy.*
bean (BEEN) *n.* **1** the seed or seed pod of several plants of the pea family: *green ~s; lima ~s;* **spill the beans** *Informal.* reveal a secret. **2** any similar seed: *coffee ~s.* **3** *Slang.* the head; ***v.*** hit on the head. —**bean·ball** *n.* a baseball pitched at a batter's head. —**bean curd** a soybean cheese. —**bean·ie** (-ee) *n.* a small skullcap.
[1]**bear** (BAIR) *n.* **1** a large, thick-furred, short-tailed mammal: *grizzly ~; polar ~.* **2** a gruff or clumsy person: *Grandpa was an old ~.* **3** an investor who sells securities in expectation of a drop in price. —**bear·like** or **bear·ish** *adj.*
[2]**bear** *v.* **bears,** *pt.* **bore,** *pp.* **borne** or **born** (def. 2), **bear·ing** **1** carry; endure; support; tolerate: *the right to ~ arms; can't ~ the pain; The mule ~s a heavy load; Can we ~ this insolence? angels ~ing glad tidings; He ~s all the blame; ~ the mark of slavery;* **bear·a·ble** *adj.* **2** [*pp.* **born** in passive sense without "by"] give birth to; yield: *a tree ~ing nuts; a man born in 1703; born of immigrant parents; 11 children borne by the same mother.* **3** give: *Do not ~ false witness.* **4** be fit for; require: *This case ~s looking into.* **5** go or turn: *~left.* **6** exert pressure or influence; relate to: *Guilt ~s heavily on his mind; a detail that ~s on the case.* —**bear out** confirm. —**bear with** tolerate patiently. —**bear·er** *n.*
beard (BEERD) *n.* the hair on a man's face; hence, a similar bristly growth on a plant or animal; **beard·ed** *adj.: a ~ seal.* —***v.*** defy face to face: *We must ~ the lion in his den.*
bear·ing *n.* **1** one's comportment or demeanor: *a man of noble ~.* **2** birth; yielding. **3** a part supporting a machine's moving part: *a ball ~.* **4** relation: *This has no ~ on the issue.* **5** direction; **bearings** *pl.* orientation, esp. to one's surroundings: *We lost our ~s in the fog.*
bear·skin (BAIR-) *n.* a rug, blanket, or tall fur cap made from a bear's skin or similar fur.
beast (BEEST) *n.* **1** an animal, esp. a four-legged one: *The camel is a* **beast of burden** (i.e. one used to carry loads). **2** a cruel, coarse, disgusting person or these characteristics in a person: *She brings out the ~ in him.* —**beast·ly** *adj.* **-li·er, -li·est:** *~ savagery; ~ manners;* ***adv.*** *Brit.* very: *It is ~ cold outside.* —**beast·li·ness** *n.*
beat (beet) *v.* **beats,** *pt.* **beat,** *pp.* **beat** or **beat·en, beat·ing** **1** strike hard or repeat-

edly, esp. to injure, to mark rhythm or make sound, to mix or shape: *a man robbed and ~en; ~time; ~ the drum; ~ eggs in a cup; ~en gold; The sun ~ down.* **2** defeat; outdo: *I ~ him at chess; She ~ him to the corner* (by arriving there first); *This ~s* (*Informal.* puzzles) *me; was ~en* (*Informal.* tricked) *for $5; It ~s* (*Informal.* is preferable to) *walking.* **3** pulsate regularly, as a flying bird's wings, a heart, etc. **4** travel with difficulty, repeatedly, or to find something: *~ing the woods for game;* **off the beaten track** (or **path**) not following others; unusual. ***—n.*** **1** a regular stress in music or poetry. **2** a stroke, blow, pulsation, etc. **3** a path traveled or job done regularly: *a policeman walking his ~.* **4** a beatnik. ***—adj.*** **1** *Informal.* tired; exhausted. **2** pertaining to the **beat generation** of social rebels of the 1950's, called **beat•niks,** who expressed themselves in distinctive speech, clothing, music, and literature: *beat poetry.* **—beat around the bush** avoid coming to the point. **—beat it** *Slang.* leave quickly. **—beat up** *Informal.* thrash soundly. **—beat•er** *n.*

be•a•tif•ic (bee·uh·TIF·ic) *adj.* indicating or causing bliss: *a ~ vision* (of God). **—be•at•i•fy** (bee·AT·i·fye) *v.* **-fies, -fied, -fy•ing** **1** make blissful. **2** declare (a dead person) to be blessed in heaven; **be•at•i•fi•ca•tion** (–CAY–) *n.* **—be•at•i•tude** (–AT–) *n.* **1** supreme joy or blessedness. **2 Beatitude** one of Christ's statements beginning "Blessed are. . . ."

beat•nik (BEET–) See BEAT, *adj.* 2.

beau (BOH) *n.* **beaus** or **beaux** (BOZE) a fine-looking dandy; also, a woman's escort or suitor. **—beau geste** (–ZHEST), *pl.* **beaux gestes** or **beau gestes** (–ZHEST) a noble or generous gesture. **—beau i•de•al** (–eye·DEE·ul), *pl.* **beau ideals** the perfect model of its type.

Beau•jo•lais (boh·zhoh·LAY) *n.* a French red wine.

beau monde (–MOND), *pl.* **beaux mondes** or **beau mondes** (boh·MOND) fashionable society.

Beau•mont (BOH·mont) a city in S.E. Texas.

beaut (BYOOT) *n. Slang.* a beauty; anything superlative: *Your new car is a real ~!* **—beau•te•ous** (BYOO·tee·us) *adj. Poetic.* beautiful; **beau•te•ous•ly** *adv.* **—beau•ti•cian** (–TISH·un) *n.* one who cuts or styles women's hair. **—beau•ti•ful** (BYOO–) *adj.* having beauty; pleasing to the mind or senses: *a ~ day, girl, song;* **beautiful people** wealthy and fashionable members of international high society; **beau•ti•ful•ly** *adv.* **—beau•ti•fy** (–fye) *v.* **-fies, -fied, -fy•ing** make or become beautiful; ornament; **beau•ti•fi•er** (–fye·ur) *n.;* **beau•ti•fi•ca•tion** (–CAY–) *n.* **—beau•ty** *n.* **-ties** **1** a combination of aesthetically, intellectually, or morally pleasing qualities. **2** a person or thing having beauty, esp. an attractive woman. **—beauty shop** (or **parlor** or **salon**) a business establishment giving cosmetic care to women's hands, skin, and esp. hair.

beaux arts (boh·ZAHR) *pl.* the fine arts.

bea•ver (BEE·vur) *n.* a large amphibious rodent with a flat tail and strong incisors used to fell trees; also, its valuable fur: *works like a ~* (i.e. very hard).

be•calmed *adj.* motionless through lack of wind: *a ship ~ in the South Seas.*

became *pt.* of BECOME.

be•cause (bi·KAWZ, –KUZ) *conj.* for the reason that; **because of** on account of.

Bech•u•a•na (bech·oo·AH·nuh) *n.* one of a Bantu-speaking people of Botswana, formerly **Bech•u•a•na•land;** also, their language.

beck *n.* a summoning gesture. **—at one's beck and call** ready to obey on command. **—beck•on** (–un) *v.* summon, esp. with a gesture; hence, entice; also ***n.***

be•cloud (bi·CLOWD) *v.* cover with clouds; confuse; obscure.

be•come (bi·CUM) *v.* **-comes, -came, -come, -com•ing** **1** come to be; develop into. **2 become of** happen to. **3** be suitable for; hence **be•com•ing** *adj.: a ~ing dress;* **be•com•ing•ly** *adv.*

bed *n.* **1** a place, esp. a piece of furniture, for sleeping. **2** a flat area underneath; foundation: *the ~ of the sea; miners approaching a ~ of coal.* **3** a piece of cultivated land: *a flower ~; a seed ~.* ***—v.*** **beds, bed•ded, bed•ding** **1** put or go to bed; plant in a bed; embed. **2** lay out or form in layers. **—(have) got up on the wrong side of the bed** be in a bad mood. **—make the bed** prepare or tidy up the bedclothes.

be•daub (bi·DAWB) *v.* smear; smudge: *~ed with mud.*

be•daz•zle (bi·DAZL) *v.* **-daz•zles, -daz•zled, -daz•zling** dazzle; confuse; blind with brightness.

bed•bug *n.* a bloodsucking insect often infesting beds.

bed•clothes *n.pl.* sheets and blankets used on a bed. **—bed•ding** *n.* **1** bedclothes. **2** a building foundation.

be•deck (bi·DEK) *v.* decorate.

be•dev•il (bi·DEVL) *v.* **-ils, -il(l)ed, -il(l)ing** plague; confuse. **—be•dev•il•ment** *n.*

be•dew (bi·DEW) *v.* wet or sprinkle, esp. with dew.

bed•fast *adj.* forced to stay in bed.

bed•fel•low (BED·fel·oh) *n.* one sharing a bed: *"Politics makes strange ~s"* (i.e. unlikely associates).

be•dim (bi·DIM) *v.* **-dims, -dimmed, -dim•ming** make dim.

be•diz•en (bi·DYE·zn) *v.* adorn gaudily.

bed•lam (–lum) *n.* uproarious confusion.

Bed•ou•in (BED·oo·in) *n.* an Arab nomad of the Middle East or North Africa.

bed•pan *n.* a pan used in bed or by the bedside as a toilet.

be·drag·gled (bi·DRAGLD) *adj.* wet, limp, and dirty: *~ clothes.*

bed·rid·den *adj.* confined to bed by age or illness. —**bed·rock** *n.* solid rock under soil, loose rock, etc.; hence, something fundamental. —**bed·roll** *n.* a roll of portable bedding, as a sleeping bag, for camping out. —**bed·room** *n.* a room for sleeping. —**bed·side** *n.* the area beside a bed, esp. of a sick person; ***adj.:*** *a doctor's fine ~ manner; ~ books.* —**bed·sore** *n.* a skin irritation or ulcer caused by being bedridden. —**bed·spread** (–spred) *n.* a decorative cover over the bedclothes. —**bed·stead** (–sted) *n.* a frame for the springs and mattress of a bed. —**bed·time** *n.* the time one goes to bed: *past your ~.*

bee *n.* **1** a small, four-winged stinging insect that gathers nectar from flowers. **2** a social gathering for work or competition: *a quilting ~; a spelling ~.* —**have a bee in one's bonnet** be preoccupied with a notion.

beech *n.* a hardwood tree with silvery gray bark and edible nuts.

beef *n.* **1** *pl.* **beeves** (BEEVZ) a full-grown bovine raised for slaughter; also, its flesh as food. **2** brawn; strength; **beef·y** *adj.* **beef·i·er, -i·est:** *a ~ bodyguard.* **3** *pl.* **beefs** *Slang.* a complaint. —***v.*** *Slang.* complain. —**beef up** *Slang.* strengthen. —**beef·eat·er** *n.* a yeoman of the guard in England. —**beef·steak** (–stake) *n.* a thick slice of beef for broiling, frying, etc.

bee·hive *n.* **1** a natural or man-made hive for bees. **2:** *The campaign office was a ~ of activity.* —**bee·keep·er** *n.* one who tends domesticated bees for their honey; **bee·keep·ing** *n.* —**bee·line** *n.* shortest route: *The students* **make a beeline for** *the cafeteria at the lunch hour.*

Be·el·ze·bub (bee·EL·zi·bub) Satan.

been *pp.* of BE.

beep *n.* & *v.* (make) a short, high-pitched tone as a signal; **beep·er** *n.* a beeping device.

beer *n.* **1** an alcoholic drink, usu. made from malted barley and hops; **beer·y** *adj.* **beer·i·er, -i·est:** *a ~y flavor.* **2** a soft drink made from extracts of roots, bark, etc.: *root ~.*

bees·wax (BEEZ–) *n.* wax made by bees for honeycombs.

beet *n.* any of several plants grown for their edible red or white roots; *The red ~ is used as a vegetable, the white is a source of sugar.*

Bee·tho·ven (BAY·toh·vun), **Lud·wig van.** 1770–1827, German composer.

[1]**bee·tle** *n.* a wooden tool for beating or mashing.

[2]**bee·tle** *n.* any of a large group of insects with hard forewings covering the flying wings when at rest. —***v.*** **bee·tles, bee·tled, bee·tling** overhang; project: *~ing cliffs;* **bee·tle-browed** *adj.* having overhanging eyebrows; also, frowning.

beeves *pl.* of BEEF, *n.* 1.

B.E.F. British Expeditionary Force.

be·fall (bi·FAWL) *v.* **be·falls, be·fell, be·fall·en, be·fall·ing** happen (to): *What strange fate befell him?*

be·fit (bi·FIT) *v.* **-fits, -fit·ted, -fit·ting** be appropriate to: *as ~s a person of that stature.* —**be·fit·ting** *adj.* proper; appropriate; **be·fit·ting·ly** *adv.*

be·fog (bi·FOG) *v.* **-fogs, -fogged, -fog·ging** cover with fog; confuse; obscure: *wits ~d with drink.*

be·fore (bi·FOR) *adv.* **1** previously; earlier: *a joke I've heard ~.* **2** in front. —***prep.*** **1** earlier than; ahead of; in preference to: *on or ~ October 12; Death ~ dishonor.* **2** in the presence of; being considered by: *a case ~ the court.* **3** in front of: *on your knees ~ the king.* —***conj.*** previous to the time that; sooner than: *He would beg ~ he would steal.* —**be·fore·hand** *adv.* & *adj.* in advance; ahead of time: *Prepare for trouble ~.*

be·foul (bi·FOWL) *v.* make dirty; foul: *a stream ~ed by city wastes.*

be·friend (bi·FREND) *v.* act as a friend to; help.

be·fud·dle (bi·FUD–) *v.* **-fud·dles, -fud·dled, -fud·dling** confuse, esp. with drink; muddle. —**be·fud·dle·ment** *n.*

beg *v.* **begs, begged, beg·ging** ask for, as charity *(So desperate, he would ~, borrow, or steal)* or formally *(I ~ your pardon)* or earnestly *(Don't risk your life, I ~ you!).* —**beg the question** assume the truth of the point in question.

began *pt.* of BEGIN.

be·get (bi·GET) *v.* **-gets,** *pt.* **-got,** *pp.* **-got·ten** or **-got, -get·ting** be father of; hence, cause: *Poverty ~s crime.*

beg·gar (BEG·ur) *n.* one who begs for a living; poor person. —***v.*** impoverish: *The sight of Everest ~ed description* (i.e. was too great for words). —**beg·gar·ly** *adj.* very poor; contemptible: *The miners were paid a ~ wage.* —**beg·gar·y** *n.* great poverty.

be·gin (bi·GIN) *v.* **-gins, -gan, -gun, -gin·ning** **1** start to do or exist: *~at page ten; ~on our new job; ~ at the beginning.* **2** bring into being. **3** be or have as first part: *The alphabet ~s with A; A ~s the alphabet.* —**be·gin·ning** *n.*: *In the ~ was God.* —**be·gin·ner** *n.*

be·gone (bi·GON) *interj.* go away: *~ dull care!*

be·gon·ia (bi·GOH·nyuh) *n.* any of a group of decorative plants with attractive leaves and flowers.

begot, begotten See BEGET.

be·grime (bi–) *v.* **-grimes, -grimed, -grim·ing** to soil.

be·grudge (bi–) *v.* **-grudg·es, -grudged, -grudg·ing** envy or resent: *Don't ~ him his good fortune.* —**be·grudg·ing·ly** *adv.*

be·guile (bi·GUILE) *v.* **be·guiles, be·guiled, be·guil·ing** **1** deceive: *~d into betraying his plans.* **2** pass (time) pleasantly; also, charm: *a pretty tale to ~ fools.* —**be·guile·ment** *n.* —**be·guil·er** *n.*

be·guine (bi·GEEN) *n.* a lively West Indian dance.

be·gum (BEE·gum) *n.* a Moslem woman of high standing.

begun *pp.* of BEGIN.

be·half (bi·HAF) *n.* interest; support: *a lawyer acting* **in** *Mrs. Smith's* **behalf;** *spoke* **on behalf of** *his client.*

be·have (bi·HAIV) *v.* **-haves, -haved, -hav·ing** act, function, conduct (oneself), etc.; esp., comport (oneself) properly: *Billy, ~ yourself! The machine ~d well during the tests.* **—be·hav·ior** *n.: The drugged man showed strange ~; Be on your best ~!* (i.e. Behave properly). **—be·hav·ior·al** *adj.: Psychology and sociology are* **behavioral sciences. —be·hav·ior·ism** *n.* a branch of psychology based solely on the observation and analysis of objective behavior; **be·hav·ior·ist** *n.;* **be·hav·ior·is·tic** (–RIS–) *adj.*

be·head (bi·HED) *v.* cut off the head (of): *~ed traitors.*

beheld *pt.* & *pp.* of BEHOLD.

be·he·moth (bi·HEE·muth) *n.* a large, monstrously powerful beast or thing.

be·hest (bi·HEST) *n.* a command or urgent request: *We act at your ~.*

be·hind (bi·HINED) *adv.* **1** in, to, or at the rear, a previous place or time, etc.: *the child he left ~.* **2** slow; not advanced enough; in arrears: *a pupil falling ~ in school.* **—prep. 1** later or less advanced than: *He finished three seconds ~ the leader; Don't fall ~ the class.* **2** in or to the rear of; on the far side of; hidden by: *~ your back; ~ the wall; What is ~ this clever facade?* **3** supporting: *We are ~ you all the way.* **—be·hind·hand** *adv.* & *adj.* in arrears; slow: *~ with the rent.*

be·hold (bi·HOLED) *v.* **-holds, -held, -hold·ing** gaze upon: *~, great wonders!* **—be·hold·en** *adj.* obligated: *~ to you for your kindness.*

be·hoof (bi·HOOF) *n. Rare.* benefit: *acting solely for his own ~.*

be·hoove (bi·HOOV) *v.* **-hooves, -hooved, -hoov·ing** be necessary or proper for: *It ~s us to be modest.*

beige (BAIZH) *n.* a yellowish brown; also ***adj.***

be·ing (BEE–) *n.* **1** existence; life: *called into ~ by God.* **2** a living or existing thing: *a human ~.* **3** one's nature: *She loved with her whole ~.*

Bei·rut (BAY·root) capital of Lebanon.

be·la·bor (bi·LAY·bur) *v.* **1** attack with blows or words. **2** harp on: *The speaker ~ed his point for two hours.*

be·lat·ed (bi·LAY·tid) *adj.* coming too late: *Happy New Year and a ~ Merry Xmas!* **—be·lat·ed·ly** *adv.*

be·lay (bi·LAY) *v.* **-layed, -lay·ing 1** secure a rope around a cleat or pin, called **belaying pin** on a ship. **2** secure (a mountain climber) by a rope. **3** *Nautical.* stop: *~there!*

belch *v.* send out something noisily or violently, esp. gas from the stomach: *industrial chimneys ~ing smoke.* **—*n.*** *The volcano released a great ~ of fire.*

bel·dam(e) (BEL·dum) *n.* an old, usu. ugly woman.

be·lea·guer (bi·LEE·gur) *v.* **-guers, -guered, -guer·ing** beseige; persecute; harass: *the ~d diplomats abroad.*

Bel·fast (BEL·fast) capital of Northern Ireland.

bel·fry (BEL·free) *n.* **-fries** a chamber in a steeple or tower where bells are hung; also, the steeple or tower. **—have bats in one's belfry** be crazy.

Belg. Belgian; Belgium. **—Bel·gium** (–jum) a monarchy on the North Sea in W. Europe; 11,781 sq. mi. (30,513 km²); *cap.* Brussels. **—Bel·gian** *adj.* & *n.*

Bel·grade (BEL–) capital of Yugoslavia.

be·lie (bi·LYE) *v.* **-lies, -lied, -ly·ing 1** prove false; also, give a false idea of: *Facts ~d her tale; His face ~d his true feelings.* **2** disappoint: *Chance ~d our hopes.* **—be·li·er** *n.*

be·lieve (bi·LEEV) *v.* **-lieves, -lieved, -liev·ing 1** accept as true or truthful; also, suppose; opine: *I did not ~ the story; I ~ that is so.* **2** have religious faith; also, have confidence in the value, existence, etc. of: *Do you ~ in God?* **—be·liev·a·ble** *adj.: a ~ story.* **—be·liev·er** *n.: the fellowship of true ~s.* **—be·lief** *n.: ~ in someone's story; firm religious ~s.*

be·lit·tle (bi·LITL) *v.* **-lit·tles, -lit·tled, -lit·tling** cause to seem or represent as smaller, less important, etc.: *Don't ~ the merits of free enterprise; a ~ing* (i.e., disparaging) *remark.* **—be·lit·tle·ment** *n.*

Be·lize (buh·LEEZ) a self-governing British colony on the Caribbean coast of Central America; 8,867 sq. mi. (22,965 km²); *cap.* Belmopan.

bell *n.* **1** a hollow, usu. metal vessel which rings when struck: *a door ~; a church ~.* **2** something with a bell's flaring shape. **3** a stroke of a bell to indicate time on ships: *Eight ~s and all's well.* **—*v.* 1** flare like a bell: *a ~ed skirt.* **2** provide with a bell: *to ~ the cat.*

bel·la don·na (bel·uh·DON·uh) *n.* a bushy plant of the nightshade family yielding a poisonous drug; also, this drug; atropine.

bell-bot·tom *adj.* flaring at the bottom of the leg; also bell-bottomed. **—bell-bottoms** *n.pl.* bell-bottom trousers.

bell·boy or **bell·hop** *n.* a club or hotel employee who carries patrons' luggage, runs errands, etc.; their supervisor is a **bell captain.**

belle (bel) *n.* an attractive and popular woman: *~ of the ball.* **—belles-let·tres** (bel·LET·ruh) *n.pl.* [takes *sing.v.*] literature as one of the fine arts; **bel·let·rist** (bel·LET·rist) *n.;* **bel·le·tris·tic** (–TRIS–) *adj.*

bellhop same as BELLBOY.

bel·li·cose (BEL·i·cose) *adj.* always ready to fight or quarrel: *~ nations;* **bel·li·cos·i·ty** (–COS–) *n.* **—bel·lig·er·ent** (–LIJ–) *adj.*

1 at war: *the ~ powers in the Middle East.* **2** bellicose; hostile: *a ~ swaggering bully.* Also ***n.:*** *The U.N. condemned the ~s.* **—bel·lig·er·ent·ly** *adv;* **bel·lig·er·ence** or **bel·lig·er·en·cy** *n.*

bell·man *n.* **-men** a bellhop.

bel·low (BEL·oh) *v.* **1** make a deep, loud roar, like a bull. **2** shout in this way: *~ing out orders; ~ing with pain.* Also ***n.***

bel·lows (BEL·oze) *n. sing. & pl.* a usu. hand-operated device for pumping and directing air, as to fan a fire; also, anything resembling a bellows, as the folding part of a camera.

bells *n.pl. Informal.* bell-bottom trousers.

bell·weth·er *n.* a usu. belled male sheep leading a flock; hence, a person or thing considered as leader: *Is the New Hampshire primary the ~ for presidential hopefuls?*

bel·ly (BEL·ee) *n.* **bel·lies** **1** the abdomen, esp. if roundly bulging; also, the stomach: *a pain in the ~; a slave to one's ~.* **2** the underside of an animal, aircraft, etc.; also, the insides of something: *the ~ of a ship.* ***—v.*** **bel·lies, bel·lied, bel·ly·ing** swell out: *a sail ~ing in the wind.* **—bel·ly·ache** *n.* an abdominal pain. ***—v.*** **-aches, -ached, -ach·ing** *Slang.* complain. **—bel·ly·but·ton** *n. Informal.* navel. **—belly dance** a usu. solo dance with erotic abdominal motions; also ***v.;*** **belly dancer. —bel·ly·ful** *n. Informal.* all that one wants or can stand: *The soldiers had had their ~ of war.* **—belly laugh** a deep, hearty laugh.

be·long (bi·LONG) *v.* **1** be the property or a member or part of: *The house ~s to Jack; Bill ~s to the Rotary Club.* **2** have a proper place: *It ~s in the corner.* **—be·long·ings** *n.pl.* possessions: *personal ~s.*

be·lov·ed (bi·LUV·id) *adj.* loved very much. — ***n.:*** *Dearly ~!*

be·low (bi·LOH) *prep.* **1** lower than: *20 ~ zero; just ~ the hilltop.* **2** unworthy of: *insults ~ his notice.* ***—adv.*** **1** in, to, or at a lower level; esp. **here below,** on earth. **2** further on: See *page 35 ~.*

belt *n.* **1** a band of material, usu. leather, worn about the waist; hence, any endless strip used to transfer motion (as a *fan ~*) or move things (as a *conveyor ~*). **2** an area distinct in some way: *a ~ of trees; a green ~* (of parkland); *the Cotton Belt* (where cotton is grown). **3** *Slang.* a blow; also, a drink of liquor. ***—v.*** **1** encircle, support, strike, or mark with a belt. **2** *Slang.* beat; hit; also **belt (out)** sing forcefully. **—below the belt** unfair(ly). **—tighten one's belt** adjust to austerity; hence **belt tightening. —belt line** a circular transportation route. **—belt·way** *n.* a highway bypassing a city.

be·lu·ga (buh·LOO·guh) *n.* a white sturgeon whose roe is used for caviar.

bel·ve·dere (BEL·vuh·deer) *n.* a structure providing a fine view, as an open gallery or a summerhouse.

be·mire (bi·MIRE) *v.* **-mires, -mired, -mir·ing** soil with or sink in mud.

be·moan (bi·MOHN) *v.* mourn over; show sorrow for.

be·muse (bi·MYOOZ) *v.* **-mus·es, -mused, -mus·ing** confuse; cause to be lost in thought: *a distant, ~d smile.*

bench *n.* **1** a long seat for two or more people. **2** a long, sturdy work table. **3** the office of a judge; also, judges collectively. ***—v.*** **1** provide with a bench. **2** put or keep on a bench. **—on the bench** **1** acting as judge. **2** not playing in the game. **—bench mark** a precisely located point of reference for surveyors; hence, any standard for measuring. **—bench warrant** a court order to arrest someone.

bend *v.* **bends, bent, bend·ing** **1** make, be, or become crooked or curved: *~ a steel bar; trees ~ing in the wind.* **2** submit or cause to submit: *I ~ before my master.* **3** turn; direct; apply: *~ one's efforts to a task; He ~s him to his own purposes.* ***—n.*** **1** a curved or crooked part: *a ~ in the road.* **2 the bends** same as DECOMPRESSION SICKNESS. **—bend over backwards** try very hard, esp. to please. **—bent on** (or **upon**) intending or resolved on: *a gang of thugs ~ on robbery.* **—bend·er** *n. Slang.* a spree, esp. of drinking.

be·neath (bi·NEETH) *prep.* **1** below; underneath: *~ the old apple tree;* ***adv.:*** *gazing at the valleys ~.* **2** unworthy of; inferior to: *Is it ~ you to go to work?*

ben·e·dict *n.* a longtime bachelor recently married. **—ben·e·dic·tion** (–DIC–) *n.* a blessing, esp. one at the end of a church service. **—ben·e·fac·tion** (–FAC–) *n.* a charitable gift, given by a **ben·e·fac·tor** or **ben·e·fac·tress** *fem.* **—ben·e·fice** (–fis) *n.* a church office with an income-producing endowment. **—be·nef·i·cent** (–NEF–) *adj.* doing good, esp. charitable things; also, beneficial; **be·nef·i·cent·ly** *adv.;* **be·nef·i·cence** *n.* **—ben·e·fi·cial** (–FISH·ul) *adj.* helpful; favorable; **ben·e·fi·cial·ly** *adv.* **—ben·e·fi·ci·ar·y** (–FISH·ee·er·ee) *n.* **-ar·ies** one who receives benefits, esp. from an insurance policy or a trust. **—ben·e·fit** *n.* **1** anything conducive to someone's betterment; advantage: *No real ~ comes from war; Because of insufficient evidence, the accused was given the* **benefit of the doubt** *and acquitted.* **2** often **benefits** *pl.* payments made by an insurance or welfare agency, as in sickness, retirement, etc. **3** a social event, entertainment, sale, etc. for a charitable cause: *Hamlet was staged as a ~.* ***—v.*** **1** do good to: *Inflation ~s no one.* **2** derive good (from): *Have we ~ed from social legislation?* **—be·nev·o·lence** (–NEV·uh·lunce) *n.* **1** a tendency to do good deeds. **2** a charitable act. **—be·nev·o·lent** *adj.;* **be·nev·o·lent·ly** *adv.*

Ben·gal (ben·GAWL) **1 Bay of,** the N. part of the Indian Ocean, E. of India. **2** a region N. of the Bay of Bengal, now divided into

West Bengal in India and East Bengal (i.e. Bangladesh). —**Ben·gal·i** (–GAW·lee) *n.* a person from or the language of Bengal; ***adj.:*** *a ~ Brahmin; a ~ poem.*

Ben·g(h)a·zi or **Ben·ga·si** (ben·GAH·zee) a seaport and, with Tripoli, one of Libya's two capitals.

Ben-Gu·ri·on (ben·GOOR·ee·un), **David.** 1886–1973, statesman and first prime minister of Israel.

be·night·ed (bi·NIGHT·id) *adj.* unenlightened. —**be·night·ed·ly** *adv.*

be·nign (bi·NINE) or **be·nig·nant** (bi·NIG·nunt) *adj.* **1** gentle and kind; helpful. **2** not malignant: *a ~ tumor.* —**be·nig·ni·ty** *n.* **-ties** or **be·nig·nan·cy** *n.* **-cies.**

Be·nin (beh·NEEN) a republic of W. Africa; 43,484 sq.mi. (112,622 km²); *cap.* Porto-Novo.

ben·i·son *n.* a blessing.

ben·ny *n.* **ben·nies** *Slang.* an amphetamine pill.

bent *adj.* **1** curved or crooked. **2 bent on** (or **upon**) See BEND. —***n.*** an inclination or talent: *a natural ~ for acting.*

ben·thos *n.* the plant and animal life of the bottom of a body of water. —**ben·thic, ben·thal** or **ben·thon·ic** (–THON–) *adj.*

ben·ton·ite (BEN·tuh·nite) *n.* an absorbent clay used in paints, medicines, etc. —**ben·ton·it·ic** (–NIT·ic) *adj.*

bent·wood *adj.* of furniture, made of wood bent into shape: *a ~ chair.*

be·numb *v.* deaden the feelings of: *hands ~ed with cold; the ~ing effect of sorrow.*

Ben·ze·drine (BEN·zuh·dreen) *Trademark.* an amphetamine.

ben·zene (BEN·zeen) *n.* an aromatic, colorless liquid hydrocarbon used in making solvents, dyes, etc. Its carbon atoms are arranged in a closed hexagon, or **benzene ring.** —**ben·zine** (–zeen) *n.* a volatile, colorless liquid used as a cleaning solvent and as a motor fuel. —**ben·zo·ate** *n.* a salt or ester of benzoic acid; **ben·zo·ic** (–ZOH–) **acid** the active ingredient of benzoin, used as an antiseptic and a food preservative. —**ben·zo·in** (BEN·zoe·in) *n.* any of a group of fragrant resins obtained from some Asiatic trees, used in medicines and perfumes. —**ben·zol** *n.* benzene.

Be·o·wulf (BAY·uh·woolf) the legendary hero of an Old English poem of the same name.

be·queath (bi·KWEETH) *v.* hand down or leave, esp. in a will. —**be·quest** *n.* **1** the act of bequeathing. **2** something bequeathed.

be·rate (bi·RATE) *v.* **-rates, -rat·ed, -rat·ing** scold severely: *a watchman ~d for sleeping on the job.*

Ber·ber *n.* a member of one of the indigenous tribes of N. Africa; also, their Hamitic language.

ber·ceuse (bur·SOOZ) *n.* **-ceus·es** a lullaby; also, a lulling piece of music.

be·reave (bi·REEV) *v.* **-reaves,** *pt.* & *pp.* **-reaved** or **-reft, -reav·ing** **1** deprive of: *a life bereft of all joy.* **2** leave lonely, as by a death: *The ~d husband wept by his wife's coffin.* —**be·reaved** *n.: The ~ stood around the grave.* —**be·reave·ment** *n.*

be·ret (buh·RAY) *n.* a flat, round cloth or felt cap.

berg *n.* an iceberg.

ber·i·ber·i (BER·ee–) *n.* a disease caused by a lack of thiamine, leading to muscular stiffness or paralysis and great weakness.

Ber·ing Sea the N. Pacific between Alaska and Kamchatka, joined to the Arctic Ocean by the **Bering Strait.**

Berke·ley (BURK·lee) a city in California.

Berke·li·um (BURK·lee·um) *n.* a synthetic radioactive element.

Ber·lin (bur·LIN) a city in eastern Germany, divided into **West Berlin** and **East Berlin,** capital of East Germany. —**Ber·lin·er** *n.*

Ber·mu·da(s) (bur·MYOO·duh, –duz) a British group of islands about 600 miles E. of North Carolina; *cap.* Hamilton. —**Ber·mu·dan** or **Ber·mu·di·an** *adj.* & *n.* —**Bermuda shorts** or **Bermudas** knee-length shorts.

Bern(e) capital of Switzerland. —**Ber·nese** (–NEEZ) *adj.* & *n.*

ber·ry (BER·ee) *n.* **ber·ries** a usu. small, fleshy fruit with many seeds, as a blueberry, a strawberry, or a tomato; hence, a dried seed, as a coffee bean. —***v.*** **ber·ries, ber·ried, ber·ry·ing** gather or bear berries.

ber·serk (bur·SURK) *adj.* & *adv.* in or into a destructive frenzy: *went ~ and shot his family.*

berth *n.* **1** a place to sleep on a ship, railroad car, etc. **2** a place for a ship to anchor. **3** a positon; job. —***v.*** occupy or put into a berth. —**give a wide berth to** avoid.

ber·yl (ul) *n.* a hard, lustrous mineral of various colors used as a gem (e.g. emerald and aquamarine) and as a source of **be·ryl·li·um** (buh·RIL·ee·um), a hard, rare, metallic element used in alloys.

be·seech (bi–) *v.* **-seech·es,** *pt.* & *pp.* **-seeched** or **-sought** (–SAWT), **-seech·ing** entreat; ask for earnestly: *Mercy, I ~ you!*

be·seem (bi–) *v.* *Archaic.* be suitable for: *It hardly ~s you to beg.*

be·set (bi·SET) *v.* **-sets, -set, -set·ting** **1** trouble or attack on all sides: *a traveler ~ by thieves.* **2** harass constantly: *Pride is the king's ~ing sin.* —**be·set·ment** *n.*

be·side (bi–) *prep.* **1** at or near the side of: *The garage is ~ the house.* **2** compared with. —**beside the point** irrelevant. —**beside oneself** agitated and distraught. —**besides** *prep.* other than; in addition to: *No one is left ~ father;* **adv.:** *He owns a house and a cottage in the country ~* (i.e. in addition).

be·siege (–SEEJ) *v.* **-sieg·es, -sieged, -sieg·ing** lay siege to; crowd; harass, esp. with requests: *a ~d city; employment agencies ~d by applicants.* **—be·sieg·er** *n.*

be·smear (bi·SMEER) *v.* smear; sully: *a wall ~ed with paint; a ~ed reputation.*

be·smirch (bi–) *v.* dirty; sully: *~ing her good name.*

be·som (BEE·zum) *n.* a broom.

be·sot (bi·SOT) *v.* **-sots, -sot·ted, -sot·ting** make infatuated; stupefy, esp. with alcohol.

besought a *pt.* & *pp.* of BESEECH.

be·span·gle (bi·SPANG·gl) *v.* **-gles, -gled, -gling** decorate with spangles: *a star-~d sky.*

be·spat·ter (bi·SPAT·ur) *v.* spatter with dirt, calumny, etc.

be·speak (bi·SPEEK) *v.* **-speaks, -spoke, -spok·en, -speak·ing** **1** claim or ask for in advance. **2** indicate; foretell: *an omen ~ing good fortune.*

be·sprin·kle (bi·SPRING·kl) *v.* **-kles, -kled, -kling** sprinkle: *a lawn ~d with dew.*

best *adj.* [*superl.* of GOOD] **—adv.** [*superl.* of WELL] **—*v.*** outdo: *a boxer ~ed in a fair fight.* **—as best one can** as well as possible. **—at best** under the most favorable conditions. **—for the best** good after all. **—get the best of** defeat; outwit. **—had best** should. **—make the best of** do as well as possible despite (something unfavorable). **—the best part of** almost all of. **—with the best (of them)** as well as any.

bes·tial (BES·chul) *adj.* pertaining to or like beasts; savage: *~ cruelty;* **bes·tial·ly** *adv.* **—bes·ti·al·i·ty**(–chee·AL·i·tee)*n.* **-ties.—bes ti·ar·y** (BES·chee·er·ee) n. **-ar·ies** a moralizing description of beasts and their behavior.

be·stir (bi–) *v.* **-stirs, -stirred, -stir·ring** make active: *It is morning, ~ yourself!*

best man a bridegroom's male attendant.

be·stow (bi·STOH) *v.* give as an honor or gift; devote: *~ great praise on the war hero;* **be·stow·al** (–ul) *n.*

be·stride (bi–) *v.* **-strides, -strode, -strid·den, -strid·ing** get, sit, stand, etc. astride: *The knight bestrode his horse.*

bet *n.* **1** an agreement that one who is wrong about an outcome will give something to one who is right; wager: *We made a $50 ~ on the election.* **2** that on which a bet is made: *His team was a safe ~ to win.* **—*v.* bets,** *pt.* & *pp.* **bet** or **bet·ted, bet·ting** **1** make a bet; wager (usu. money): *~ting on horse races.* **2** claim as though betting: *I ~ he'll never come back.* **—bet·tor** or **bet·ter** *n.*

bet. between.

be·ta (BAY·tuh) *n.* the second letter of the Greek alphabet. **—beta particle** an electron or positron emitted by a radioactive substance, a stream of which is called a **beta ray.** **—be·ta·tron** (–tron) *n.* an electron accelerator.

be·take (bi–) *v.* **-takes, -took, -tak·en, -tak·ing** cause (oneself) to go: *They betook themselves to school.*

be·tel (BEE·tl) *n.* a tropical vine whose leaf is chewed as a stimulant with lime and **betel nuts** (from the **betel palm** tree) by people of S. Asia.

bête noire (BAIT·nwar), *pl.* **bêtes noires** (BAIT·nwarz) a person or thing that one abhors.

beth·el *n.* a chapel or church, usu. one for sailors.

be·think (bi–) *v.* **-thinks, -thought, -think·ing** make (oneself) recall or consider: *~ yourself of your duty.*

Beth·le·hem (BETH·luh·hem) the town in Palestine where Jesus was born.

be·tide (bi–) *v.* befall: *Woe ~ the sinner on Judgment Day.*

be·times (bi–) *adv.* early; on time.

be·to·ken (bi·TOH–) *v.* be a sign of: *preparations ~ing war.*

betook *pt.* of BETAKE.

be·tray (bi–) *v.* **1** be disloyal to; act against: *~ one's nation; Don't ~ my confidence in you.* **2** reveal, esp. unwittingly: *A sneeze ~ed our presence; Trembling hands ~ed his fear.* **3** lead astray; esp., seduce and forsake. **—be·tray·al** *n.* **—be·tray·er** *n.*

be·troth (bi·TROTHE) *v.* promise to marry or give in marriage. **—be·trothed** *adj.* & *n.* **—be·troth·al** (–ul) *n.*

bet·ter (BET·ur) *adj., comp.* of GOOD. **—*adv.*** *comp.* of WELL. **—*n.*** (one's) superior: *Listen to your elders and ~s.* **—*v.*** **1** improve; **bet·ter·ment** *n.: for the ~ of mankind.* **2** outdo. **—better half** *Informal.* one's spouse, esp. wife. **—better off** happier; more prosperous. **—get the better of** outdo; overcome. **—go one better** outdo. **—had better** should. **—no better than one should be** of loose morals. **—the better part of** more than half of. **—think better of** reconsider.

bettor or **better** See BET.

be·tween (bi·TWEEN) *prep.* [indicating]: **1** an intermediate position, place, time, degree, etc.: *~ these walls; the road ~ here and Boston; ~ 7 and 8 p.m.* **2** joint or related ownership, action, connection, etc.: *We own 400 acres ~ the two of us; the War ~ the States; just ~ you and me* (i.e. confidentially). **3** things to choose from: *He can't choose ~ the two ties.* **—*adv.:*** *lunch and supper, with snacks in ~.* **—few and far between** widely scattered.

be·twixt (bi·TWIXT) *prep. Archaic.* between; **be·twixt and between:** *neither in the city nor in the suburbs but ~ and between.*

bev·el (BEV·ul) *n.* **1** an angle other than 90°, as of a sloping surface, edge, etc. **2** an adjustable ruler for marking angles. **—*v.* bev·els, bev·el(l)ed, bev·el·(l)ing** cut to, set at, or have a bevel. **—bevel gear** one of a pair of gearwheels meshing at an angle so as to transmit motion with a change of direction.

bev·er·age (BEV·rij) *n.* a drink other than water.

bev·y (BEV·ee) *n.* **bev·ies** a group (of quail, deer, or females): *a ~ of beauties.*
be·wail (bi·WAIL) *v.* lament. —**be·wail·ment** *n.* —**be·wail·er** *n.*
be·ware (bi–) *v.* be careful or cautious (of): *Let the buyer ~; ~ of the dog.*
be·wil·der (bi·WIL–) *v.* confuse, esp. by complication. —**be·wil·der·ment** *n.*
be·witch (bi–) *v.* **1** cast a magic spell on. **2** charm: *a ~ing beauty.* —**be·witch·ing·ly** *adv.*
bey (BAY) *n.* a Turkish governor or ruler, as in the Ottoman Empire.
be·yond (bi·YOND) *prep.* **1** on the far side of; later than: *~ the horizon; Don't stay ~ midnight.* **2** outside the limits of: *His deeds are ~ praise; living ~ one's means.* —***adv.*** farther on; besides. —**the (great) beyond** the hereafter.
bez·el (BEZ·ul) *n.* **1** a sloping surface, as the edge of a chisel or a side on a cut gem. **2** a grooved rim holding a watch crystal or a gem in its place.
bf. or **b.f.** boldface. —**B/F** brought forward.
B.F.A. Bachelor of Fine Arts.
bg. bag. —**B.G.** Brigadier General.
bhang (BANG) *n.* an intoxicating drug made from hemp; also, the plant.
b.hp. or **bhp** brake horsepower.
Bhu·tan (boo·TAHN) a monarchy between India and Tibet; 18,147 sq. mi. (47,000 km^2); *cap.* Thimphu. —**Bhu·tan·ese** (boo·tn·EEZ) *n. sing.* & *pl.* a person from or the language of Bhutan; also ***adj.***
Bi bismuth. —**bi-** *comb. form* [indicating] two, twice, etc.: as in *bifocal, bimonthly;* **bi·an·nu·al** (bye·AN·yoo·ul) *adj.* occurring twice a year; **bi·an·nu·al·ly** *adv.*
bi·as (BYE·us) *n.* **bi·as·es** **1** a slanting line across the weave of a cloth; ***adj.* & *adv.:*** *a ~ seam:* **on the bias** diagonally. **2** a prejudice or inclination for or against something. —***v.*** **bi·as·(s)es, bi·as(s)ed, bi·as·(s)ing** give a bias to: *The juror was rejected because he seemed very* **biased** (i.e. prejudiced).
bi·ath·lon (bye·ATH·lun) *n.* a combined skiing and rifle-shooting contest.
bib *n.* **1** a cloth tied under a child's chin at meals. **2** the upper part of a pair of overalls or an apron.
Bib. Bible; Biblical.
bi·be·lot (BEE·buh·loh) *n.* a small but valued object; trinket.
Bi·ble (BYE·bl) *n.* **1** the sacred scriptures of Christians; also, the scriptures of Judaism or other religions. **2 bible** any authoritative book. —**Bib·li·cal** (BIB–) or **bib·li·cal** *adj.* —**Bib·li·cal·ly** or **bib·li·cal·ly** *adv.* —**biblio-** *comb. form.* book; of books. —**bib·li·og·ra·phy** (–OG·ruh·fee) *n.* **-phies** **1** the study of editions, history, etc. of published works. **2** a list of books and articles on one topic or by one author; **bib·li·og·ra·pher** *n;* **bib·li·o·graph·ic** (–GRAF–) or **-i·cal** *adj.* —**bib·li·o·phile** (BIB·lee·uh·file) *n.* a lover or collector of books.
bib·u·lous (BIB·yoo·lus) *adj.* **1** given to alcoholic drink. **2** absorbent. —**bib·u·lous·ly** *adv.* —**bib·u·lous·ness** *n.*
bi·cam·er·al (bye·CAM·uh·rul) *adj.* having two houses of legislature: *Congress is ~.*
bi·car·bon·ate (bye·CAR·buh·nit) *n.* an acid salt of carbonic acid. —**bicarbonate of soda** same as SODIUM BICARBONATE.
bi·cen·te·nar·y (bye·sen·TEN·uh·ree) *adj.* & *n.* **-nar·ies** same as **bi·cen·ten·nial** (–TEN·ee·ul) *n.* a 200th anniversary; also, the celebration of it; ***adj.:*** *the ~ celebrations of 1976.*
bi·ceps (BYE·seps) *n. sing.* & *pl.* a muscle that attaches at two points on one end, esp. the one at the front of the upper arm.
bi·chlo·ride (bye·CLOR–) *n.* any of several chlorine compounds, esp. **bichloride of mercury,** or **mercuric chloride,** a poisonous chemical used in photography, as an insecticide, etc.
bick·er *v.* squabble; quarrel over trivialities; also ***n.***
bi·con·cave (bye·con·CAVE) *adj.* concave on both sides: *a ~ lens.* —**bi·con·cav·i·ty** (–CAV·i·tee) *n.*
bi·con·vex (bye·con·VEX) *adj.* convex on both sides. —**bi·con·vex·i·ty** *n.*
bi·cus·pid (bye·CUS–) *adj.* having two points: *a ~ tooth; a ~ valve* (in the heart). —***n.*** a premolar.
bi·cy·cle (BYE·sicl) *n.* a two-wheeled vehicle driven usu. by pedals, having a seat and handlebars. —***v.*** **-cles, -cled, -cling** ride a bicycle. —**bi·cy·clist** or **bi·cy·cler** *n.*
bid *v.* **bids,** *pt.* **bid** or **bade** (BAD), *pp.* **bid** or **bid·den, bid·ding** **1** command; also, express: *They bade her be silent; They have ~en us farewell.* **2** offer a price: *She ~ $5 for the chair.* **3** declare the trump suit and how many points or tricks one will make: *His bridge partner had ~ 3 hearts.* **4** try to get, win, etc. —***n.:*** *Six firms made ~s for the airport construction; 3 hearts is a bad ~; a ~ for support at the polls.* —**bid fair to** seem likely to. —**bid·der** *n.* —**bid·da·ble** *adj.* **1** obedient. **2:** *a ~ hand in bridge.*
b.i.d. *Medicine.* twice a day.
bid·dy (BID·ee) *n.* **bid·dies** **1** a hen, esp. a young one. **2** a gossipy or shrewish old woman.
bide *v.* **bides,** *pt.* **bode** or **bid·ed,** *pp.* **bid·ed, bid·ing** wait; remain. —**bide one's time** patiently await one's chance.
bi·det (bi·DAY) *n.* a low basin for washing the genitals and anal area.
bi·en·ni·um (bye·EN·ee·um) *n.* **-en·ni·ums** or **-en·ni·a** a two-year period. —**bi·en·ni·al** *adj.* **1** occurring every two years: *a ~ convention.* **2** lasting or living for two years: *a ~ plant;* ***n.:*** *The beet and carrot are ~s.* —**bi·en·ni·al·ly** *adv.*

bier (BEER) *n.* a stand for a coffin or corpse.

bi·fo·cal (bye·FOH·cul) *adj.* having two focal lengths. —**bi·fo·cals** *n. pl.* spectacles with divided lenses for distant and close vision.

bi·fur·cate (BY–) *v.* **-cates, -cat·ed, -cat·ing** divide into two branches. —**bifurcate(d)** *adj.* forked. —**bi·fur·ca·tion** (–CAY–) *n.*

big *adj.* **big·ger, big·gest** **1** large; swelling; also, important: *a ~ wind; a ~ man on campus.* **2** full-grown; older: *You're a ~ boy, now.* **3** boastful; generous: *~ talk; a ~-hearted man.* —**adv.** *Informal.* **1** on a grand scale: *Think ~.* **2** boastfully: *talking ~.* —**big·ness** *n.* —**too big for one's boots** (or **breeches**) too cocky.

big·a·my (BIG·uh·mee) *n.* the crime of being married to two people. —**big·a·mist** *n.* —**big·a·mous** (–mus) *adj.*

big bang a primeval explosion of cosmogonic matter supposed to have caused our present universe. —**big brother** **1** a man who befriends a disadvantaged boy. **2 Big Brother** the all-powerful leader of an authoritarian state; **Big Broth·er·ism.** —**big deal** *Informal* [also used ironically] a matter of importance; also, a great fuss: *Don't make such a ~ deal out of your promotion.* —**Big Dipper** the seven stars of the constellation Ursa Major. —**big·horn** *n.* a wild sheep of the Rocky Mountains having large horns.

bight *n.* **1** a gently curving bay. **2** the slack or looped part of a rope.

big name a well-known, popular person, esp. an entertainer. —**big-name** *adj.: a ~ actor.*

big·ot (BIG·ut) *n.* an intolerant, blindly prejudiced person. —**big·ot·ed** *adj.: ~ attitudes.* —**big·ot·ry** *n.*

big shot *Slang.* an important person. —**big time** *Slang.* the top level of any field, esp. entertainment: *The singer hit the ~ time;* **big-time** *adj.: a ~ operator.* —**big top** the main circus tent; hence, *Informal.* a circus. —**big·wig** *n. Informal.* an important person.

bike *n. Informal.* **1** a bicycle. **2** a motorcycle; **bik·er** *n.* —**v. bikes, biked, bik·ing** ride a bike.

bi·ki·ni (bi·KEE·nee) *n.* a woman's scanty two-piece bathing suit.

bi·lat·er·al (bye·LAT·uh·rul) adj. made by or affecting both sides equally: *a ~ agreement; the* **bilateral symmetry** *of the human body.* —**bi·lat·er·al·ly** *adv.*

bile *n.* a greenish-yellow fluid produced in the liver that helps in digesting fats; also, bad temper.

bilge (BILJ) *n.* **1** the bottom of the inside of a ship; also, the water that collects there. **2** *Slang.* nonsense.

bi·lin·gual (bye·LING·gwul) *adj.* pertaining to, speaking, or written in two languages: *a ~ country; ~ education for students whose first language is not English.* —**bi·lin·gual·ism** *n.*

bil·ious (BIL·yus) *adj.* **1** pertaining to the bile; also, suffering from a disorder of the bile. **2** ill-tempered: *a ~ old man.* —**bil·ious·ness** *n.*

bilk *v.* cheat, esp. by avoiding payment; **bilk·er** *n.*

¹bill *n.* the hard mouth parts of a bird; beak; hence, something similar; also **v.; bill and coo** kiss and caress.

²bill *n.* **1** a list of payments due: *a doctor's ~.* **2** a list of items, as on a menu, theater program, etc.; **fill the bill** fulfill the requirements. **3** an advertising poster or public notice. **4** a piece of paper money: *a ten-dollar ~.* **5** a proposed law: *a ~ before Congress.* **6** a certificate or other document: *~ of health.* —**v.** **1** enter in or present with a bill: *~ me at the end of the month.* **2** advertise with bills: *~ed as a famous actor.* —**bill·board** *n.* a signboard for posters, notices, etc. —**bil·let** (BIL·it) *n.* **1** an order for a civilian to lodge a soldier in his house; hence, such a lodging. **2** a job. —**v.** quarter (troops) by billet: *a platoon ~ed in the village.* —**bil·let-doux** (bil·ee·DOO) *n., pl.* **bil·lets-doux** (–ee·DOOZ) a love letter. —**bill·fold** *n.* a wallet. —**bill·head** *n.* a printed form for making out bills. —**bil·liards** (–yurdz) *n.* any of several games played by striking hard balls with a cue on a rectangular, cloth-covered **billiard table; billiard** *adj.: ~ ball; ~ player.* —**bill·ing** *n.* the display of performers' names according to their importance: *a big star who gets top ~ in New York.*

bil·lings·gate *n.* vulgar abuse.

bil·lion (–yun) *n.* **1** a thousand millions (1,000,000,000). **2** *Brit.* a million millions (1,000,000,000,000). —**bil·lionth** *n.* & *adj.* —**bil·lion·aire** (–NARE) *n.* someone whose wealth comes to at least a billion dollars, francs, etc.

bill of exchange a document requiring the payment of a sum to a named person; draft. —**bill of fare** a menu. —**bill of health** a certificate about diseases among a ship's crew: *A disease-free ship gets a* **clean bill of health.** —**bill of lading** a document listing goods received for shipment. —**bill of rights** a statement of the fundamental rights of a people, as in the American **Bill of Rights,** the first 10 amendments to the U.S. Constitution, adopted in 1791.

bil·low (BIL·oh) *n.* a swelling or surging mass, esp. a large wave of water. —**v.** rise, swell, or roll in billows: *Smoke ~ed from the chimney.* —**bil·low·y** *adj.: the ~ ocean.*

bil·ly (BIL·ee) *n.* **bil·lies** a short wooden club; also called **billy club.** —**billy goat** a male goat.

bi·met·al·lic (bye·muh·TAL·ic) *adj.* **1** made of two metals: *a ~ thermostat;* also **bi·met·al** (bye·MET·ul) *adj.* & *n.: a bimetal(lic) strip.* **2** pertaining to **bi·met·al·ism,** the simultaneous use of gold and silver as monetary standards; **bi·met·al·list** *n.*

bi·month·ly (bye·MUNTH·lee) *adj.* **1** occurring once every two months. **2** loosely, occurring twice a month. Also ***adv.***

bin *n.* a large box, container, etc. for storage: *a coal ~; a grain ~.*

bi·na·ry (BYE·nuh·ree) *adj.* **1** having two parts: *a ~ chemical compound;* **binary fission** the asexual division of protozoans. **2** pertaining to **binary notation,** the writing of numbers using only the **binary digits** 0 and 1. **—*n.,*** *pl.* **-ries** something binary; a pair. **—binary star** two stars revolving around each other.

bin·au·ral (bye·NOR·ul) *adj.* **1** pertaining to or used with both ears: *a ~ stethoscope.* **2** having to do with a two-source system of sound reproduction giving a stereophonic effect: *~ transmission.*

bind (BINED) *v.* **binds, bound** (BOWND), **bind·ing** **1** tie or hold together; bandage: *~ sheafs of wheat; She ~s her hair with ribbons; The nurse bound up their wounds.* **2** obligate or constrain by law, duty, love, etc.: *an apprentice bound to serve for 7 years; a ~ing contract.* **3** stick together or cause to cohere: *Cement ~s gravel well.* **4** strengthen or decorate an edge with braid, tape, etc.; also, fasten a book's pages together or into a cover, as done in a **bind·er·y.** **—*n.*** *Informal.* a difficult situation: *Losing his job put him in a financial ~.* **—bind·er** *n.* a thing or person that binds, esp. a cover which holds loose paper. **—bind·ing** *n.* something that binds, esp. the covers and back of a book, the boot fastenings on skis, etc.

binge (BINJ) *n. Informal.* a spree, as of drinking, shopping, etc.

bin·go (BING·go) *n.* **-gos** a gambling game played on cards with numbered squares, won by covering five of these in a row as matching numbers are drawn.

bin·na·cle (BIN·uh·cl) *n.* a case or stand for a ship's compass.

bin·oc·ul·ar (bye·NOK·yuh·lur, bi–) *adj.* using or for use by both eyes at once: *~ vision; a ~ microscope.* **—*n.*** usu. **binoculars** *pl.* an optical instrument, pair of opera glasses, etc. with two lens tubes, esp. field glasses. **—bin·oc·ul·ar·ly** *adv.* **—bin·oc·ul·ar·i·ty** (–LAIR·i·tee) *n.*

bi·no·mi·al (bye·NOH·mee·ul) *n.* **1** a mathematical expression consisting of two terms linked by a + or – sign; e.g. 3x – 4xy. **2** a two-word scientific name indicating genus and species, as *Equus caballus* (horse), *Equus asinus* (ass). Also ***adj.***

bio- *comb. form.* life; living things; biology. **—bi·o·as·tro·nau·tics** (bye·oh·as·truh·NAU–) *n.* the study of the biological reactions to space travel, a branch of which is "space medicine." **—bi·o·chem·is·try** (–KEM–) *n.* a branch of chemistry dealing with living organisms and their chemical processes; **bi·o·chem·i·cal** *adj.;* **bi·o·chem·ist** *n.* **—bi·o·cide** *n.* a substance which can destroy life; also, the destruction of life; **bi·o·cidal** (–SYE·dul) *adj.* **—bi·o·clean** *adj.* free from microorganisms, esp. harmful ones. **—bi·o·de·grad·a·ble** (–GRAY–) *adj.* able to be broken down by biological agents, esp. bacteria; **bi·o·de·grad·a·bil·i·ty** (–duh·BIL–) *n.;* **bi·o·deg·ra·da·tion** (–deg·ruh·DAY–) *n.;* **bi·o·de·grade** (–GRADE–) *v.* **-grades, -grad·ed, -grad·ing** **—bi·o·feed·back** *n.* the facilitation of mental control of the body by making bodily processes (as brainwaves) perceptible (as with an oscilloscope). **—bi·o·ge·og·ra·phy** (–jee·OG·ruh·fee) *n.* the study of the geographical distribution of living organisms; **bi·o·ge·og·ra·pher** *n.;* **bi·o·ge·o·graph·ic** (–jee·uh·GRAPH·ic) or **-i·cal** *adj.* **—bi·og·ra·phy** (–OG·ruh·fee) *n.* **-phies** the story of someone's life as written by another; also, the branch of literature comprising such stories; **bi·og·ra·pher** *n.* **—bi·o·graph·ic** (–GRAPH–) or **-i·cal** *adj.* **—bi·ol·o·gy** (–OL·uh·jee) *n.* the science of living organisms and life processes; also, a group of organisms or their life processes; **bi·ol·o·gist** *n.;* **bi·o·log·ic** (–LOJ–) or **-i·cal** *adj.;* **bi·o·log·i·cal·ly** *adv.;* **biological clock** an inborn mechanism controlling timed or cyclical behavior in organisms; **biological warfare** the use of destructive or toxic germs, insects, poisons, etc. in war. **—bi·o·mass** *n.* total amount of living organisms in a given place: *renewable energy from ~ fuels such as wood, garbage, and other biological wastes.* **—bi·o·med·i·cine** (–sin) *n.* the medical study of reactions to abnormal environments, esp. in space travel; **bi·o·med·i·cal** *adj.* **—bi·on·ics** (–ON–) *n.pl.* the study and design of electronic devices modeled on living things; **bi·on·ic** *adj.* **—bi·o·phy·sics** (–FIZ·ics) *n.* the study of life processes using the principles and methods of physics; **bi·o·phys·i·cal** *adj.;* **bi·o·phys·i·cist** *n.* **—bi·op·sy** (–OP·see) *n.* **-sies** the removal of living fluid or tissue for diagnostic examination. **—bi·o·sat·el·lite** (–SATL·ite) *n.* a satellite carrying a living thing for scientific research. **—bi·o·sphere** (BY·uh–) *n.* that part of the earth and its surroundings which supports any form of life. **—bi·o·te·lem·e·try** (–tuh·LEM·uh·tree) *n.* the remote sensing and recording of vital functions; **bi·o·tel·e·met·ric** (–MET–) *adj.* **—bi·ot·ic** (–OT·ic) *adj.* caused by or pertaining to living things. **—bi·o·tin** (BYE·uh–) *n.* a growth-promoting vitamin in the B complex, found in yeast, egg yolk, etc. **—bi·o·tite** (BYE·uh–) *n.* a dark-colored form of mica.

bi·par·ti·san (bye·PAR·ti·zn) *adj.* of or supported by two sides or parties: *a ~ committee;* **bi·par·ti·san·ship** *n.* **—bi·par·tite** (–PAR–) *adj.* having or divided into two parts; **bi·par·ti·tion** (–TISH–) *n.* **—bi·ped** (BYE–) *n.* a two-footed animal; ***adj.:*** *Man is a ~ (animal).* **—bi·plane** *n.* an airplane with two main wings, usu. one above the other. —**bi·po·lar** (bye·POH·lur) *adj.* **1** having two poles. **2** of or living in the two polar regions: *a ~ species;* **bi·po·lar·i·ty** (–poh·LAIR–) *n.* —**bi·ra·cial** (–RAY·shul) *adj.* of or having to do with two races: *a ~ society;* **bi·ra·cial·ism** *n.*

birch *n.* **1** any of about 40 kinds of deciduous trees whose smooth bark peels off in layers; also, its hard wood. **2** a bunch of birch twigs used to give a whipping; ***v.:*** *The schoolboy was ~ed for lying.* —**birch(·en)** *adj.* —**Birch·er** *n.* a member of an extreme right-wing group, the **John Birch Society; Birch·ism** *n.;* **Birch·ite** *n.* & *adj.: ~ policies.*

bird *n.* **1** any of a class of two-legged, feathered, winged, warm-blooded vertebrates. **2** *Slang.* a person, esp. an eccentric: *a wise old ~.* **3 the bird** *Slang.* a scornful rejection; a hissing: *They gave the juggler the ~.* **4 for the birds** *Slang.* absurd; worthless. —**bird·bath** *n.* a shallow outdoor basin for birds to bathe in. —**bird·house** *n.* an outdoor artificial nesting box for birds. —**bird·ie** (–ee) *n. Golf.* a one-under-par score on a hole. —**bird·lime** *n.* a sticky stuff smeared on twigs to catch small birds. —**bird of paradise** any of several beautifully plumed birds of New Guinea. —**bird of passage** a migrating bird. —**the birds and the bees** *Informal.* the rudimentary facts about sex. —**bird·seed** *n.* an assorted mixture of seeds for feeding usu. caged birds. —**bird's-eye** *adj.* **1** seen from high up; quick or general: *a ~ view.* **2** with markings like a bird's eye: *a ~ pattern; ~ maple.*

bi·ret·ta (buh·RET·uh) *n.* a square clerical cap.

Bir·ming·ham (BUR–) **1** (–ham) a city in Alabama. **2** (–um) a city in C. England.

birth *n.* **1** the act of being born or bringing forth a child: *He weighed 7 lbs. at ~; a difficult ~.* **2** beginning: *the ~ of a new idea.* **3** inheritance; descent: *a man of noble ~.* —**give birth to** bring forth; cause or originate. —**birth control** control over the number of births by contraceptive measures. —**birth·day** *n.* the day or anniversary of a birth. —**birth·place** *n.* the place of birth. —**birth·mark** *n.* a mark on the skin present from birth. —**birth·rate** *n.* the ratio of births to total population in an area. —**birth·right** *n.* a privilege had from the circumstances of birth, as inheritance, citizenship, etc. —**birth·stone** *n.* a gemstone symbolizing the month of one's birth.

bis·cuit (BIS·kit) *n.* **1** a small bread or roll leavened without yeast. **2** *Brit.* a cracker or cookie.

bi·sect (bye·SECT) *v.* **1** divide into two usu. equal parts. **2** bifurcate. —**bi·sec·tion** *n.: the ~ of an angle.* —**bi·sec·tor** *n.*

bi·sex·u·al (bye·SEK·shoo·ul) *adj.* **1** of or having organs of both sexes. **2** sexually attracted to both sexes. Also ***n.*** —**bi·sex·u·al·i·ty** (–AL–) *n.*

bish·op (–up) *n.* **1** a Christian clergyman who supervises a diocese, other clergymen, etc. **2** a chess piece which moves diagonally. —**bish·op·ric** *n.* the rank, office, or jurisdiction of a bishop.

Bis·marck (BIZ·mark) **1 Otto von.** 1815–1898, German statesman. **2** capital of North Dakota.

bis·muth (BIZ–) *n.* a brittle, whitish metallic element used in drugs and alloys. —**bis·muth·al** or **bis·mu·thic** (–MYOO–) *adj.*

bi·son (BYE·sun) *n.* a wild, oxlike North American bovine, having a large head and shaggy mane; also, a European wild ox.

bisque (BISK) *n.* a creamy thick soup often made with shellfish.

Bis·sau (–SOW) capital of Guinea-Bissau.

bis·tro (BIS·troh) *n.* a small restaurant, bar, or nightclub.

bit *n.* **1** the cutting edge of a tool; esp., a tool for boring or drilling: *a brace and ~.* **2** the part of a bridle held in a horse's mouth. **3** a small portion, amount, interval, etc.; **a bit** slightly: *a ~ too big;* **a bit of** somewhat: *a ~ of a fool;* **bit by bit** little by little. **4** *Informal.* the amount of 12½ cents: *2 ~s; 4 ~s; 6 ~s.* **5** in entertainment, a short routine; ***adj.*** small: *a ~ part.* **6** *Informal.* a stereotyped behavior, speech, etc.: *Her husband did the jealousy ~.* **7** a binary digit. —**do one's bit** do one's fair share.

bitch *n.* **1** the female of the dog or other canine. **2** *Slang.* a hated woman: *that "son of a bitch!"* —***v.*** *Slang.* complain. —**bitch·y** *adj.* **bitch·i·er, -i·est** *Slang.* spiteful; ill-tempered.

bite *v.* **bites,** *pt.* **bit,** *pp.* **bit·ten** or **bit, bit·ing** seize, pierce, or cut with or as if with the teeth, as a dog, snake, or mosquito: *mailmen ~n by dogs; Fish ~ at baits; They aren't ~ing today; She likes to ~ into an apple; bit off a large piece; tires that ~ into snow; fingers ~n by frost; his* **biting** *sarcasm;* **bite the bullet** suffer stoically; **bite the dust** be killed in battle; be vanquished; **bit·ing·ly** *adv.* —***n.*** an act of biting, a biting or stinging quality, a wound or sting, or what is bitten off: *just enough time for a ~* (*Informal.* light meal); *the tax ~* (*Informal.* deduction); **put the bite on** *Slang.* press for money or some favor.

bit·ter *adj.* **1** having an unpleasant, sharp taste: *~ medicine.* **2** harsh; unpleasant, esp. to the mind: *~ weather; ~ news to hear.* **3** expressing sorrow or grief: *~ tears.* **4** full of hatred or resentment: *~ enemies.* —***n.*** something bitter, esp. **bit·ters** *pl.* a usu. alcoholic bitter liquid used as a tonic or cocktail flavoring. —**bit·ter·ly** *adv.: ~ cold.* —**bit·ter·ness** *n.*

bit·tern (BIT·urn) *n.* a heronlike marsh bird with a booming cry.

bit·ter·sweet *adj.* both bitter and sweet; painful and pleasant: *a ~ memory.* —***n.*** **1** a climbing vine with orange seed pods. **2** a climbing vine of the nightshade family with poisonous berries.

bi·tu·men (bi·TUE·mun) *n.* any of various tar-like hydrocarbons, esp. asphalt, used esp. to surface roads. —**bi·tu·mi·nous** (–nus) *adj.;* **bituminous coal** soft coal, which burns smokily with a yellow flame.

bi·valve (BY·valv) *n.* any mollusk with two hinged shells, as a clam. —***adj.*** having two movable parts, like a clamshell: *The pea has a ~ pod.*

biv·ou·ac (BIV·uh·wac) *n.* a temporary camp in the open, esp. for soldiers. —***v.*** **-acs, -acked, -ack·ing:** *The platoon ~d in the woods.*

bi·week·ly (bye–) *adj.* & *adv.* **1** once every two weeks. **2** loosely, twice a week. —***n.,*** *pl.* **-lies** a biweekly publication. —**bi·year·ly** (bye–) *adj.* & *adv.* **1** once every two years. **2** loosely, twice a year.

bi·zarre (bi·ZAR) *adj.* strikingly odd, eccentric, or fantastic. —**bi·zarre·ly** *adv.* —**bi·zarre·ness** *n.*

Bi·zet (bee·ZAY), **Georges.** 1838–1875, a French composer.

bk., *pl.* **bks.** bank; book. —**Bk** berkelium.

bkcy. bankruptcy.

bkg. banking.

bkgd. background.

bkpg. bookkeeping.

bks. or **Bks.** barracks.

bkt. basket.

bl. bale; barrel; black; blue.

blab *v.* **blabs, blabbed, blab·bing** talk foolishly; reveal a secret by talking. —***n.*** one who blabs; also, such chatter.

black *n.* **1** the color opposite to white, reflecting very little light; also, a pigment, clothing, etc. of this color: *The widow wore ~ in mourning;* **in the black** making a profit; cf. IN THE RED. **2** a dark-skinned, esp. Negro person; also **Black.** —***v.*** make or become black; blacken: *The shoeshine boy ~ed his boots;* **black out 1** lose consciousness temporarily. **2** extinguish all the lights. —***adj.*** **1** very dark; of the color black: *a ~ flag; the ~est night.* **2** dirty: *hands ~ with grease.* **3** wicked; gloomy; angry; disastrous; morbid: *a ~ depression; a ~ future; He gave his sister a ~ look; ~ Friday left many investors bankrupt.* **4** of or having to do with blacks: *a ~ family.* —**black·ish** *adj.;* **black·ly** *adv.;* **black·ness** *n.* —**black-and-blue** *adj.* darkly bruised, as from beating. —**black art** witchcraft. —**black·ball** *n.* a negative vote, esp. against a prospective member; ***v.*** exclude or ostracize; **black·ball·er** *n.* —**black bass** any of several freshwater game fish of E. North America. —**black belt 1** the highest rating in judo or karate; also, a person thus rated. **2** an area inhabited by many Negroes. —**black·ber·ry** *n.* **-ber·ries** the fleshy but seedy fruit of any of several bramble bushes. —**black·bird** *n.* any of various North American birds whose males are black. —**black·board** *n.* a dark, smooth board for writing on with chalk. —**black·bod·y** *n.* **-bod·ies** a body or surface that absorbs all radiation striking it. —**black box** a complex electronic device, as the flight recorder in an aircraft, whose mode of operation is unknown to the user. —**black coffee** coffee without cream, milk, etc. —**black·en** *v.* to black; hence, sully: *came out of the scandal with his name ~ed.* —**black eye** a dark bruise around the eye. —**black-eyed Susan** the yellow daisy, a plant with yellow flowers around a dark center. —**Black·foot** *n., pl.* **-foot** or **-feet** (a member of) any of three Algonquian peoples now living in Montana and W. Canada; also, any of their languages. —**black·guard** (BLAG·urd) *n.* a villainous or foul-mouthed person. —**black·head** *n.* a dark clog of oil and dirt in a skin pore. —**black hole** a region supposedly formed in outer space by the collapse of a massive star and of such great density and gravity that even light cannot escape from it. —**black humor** comedy stressing the morbid and the absurd.—**black·ing** *n.* a substance for blackening something, esp. shoes. —**black·jack** *n.* **1** a short bludgeon with a flexible handle; also ***v.*** **2** a card game in which one wins by having cards that total more than the dealer's and that add up to 21 or less. —**black light** ultraviolet or infrared radiation. —**black·list** *n.* a list of people who are disapproved of; ***v.*** put on such a list. —**black lung** a lung disease caused by breathing coal dust. —**black magic** witchcraft. —**black·mail** *n.* payment extorted, esp. by a threat of discreditable exposure; also, such an extortion; also ***v.;*** **black·mail·er** *n.* —**black market** buying and selling against government regulations; also ***v.*** **black marketer** (or **marketeer**). —**Black Mass** a satanic parody of the Christian Mass. —**Black Muslim** a member of an Islamic Negro group advocating a separate Negro community. —**black nationalism** a movement urging a separate black nation; **black nationalist.** —**black·out** *n.* a blacking out, as in the absence of light, consciousness, etc. —**Black Panther** a member of a radical Negro political group, the **Black Panther Party.** —**Black Power** a movement for Negro rights based on black solidarity. —**Black Sea** a large sea linked to the Mediterranean and lying between Russia and Turkey. —**black sheep** a person considered disgraceful by the rest of his group. —**black·smith** *n.* one who works with iron, esp. one who shoes horses. —**black·thorn** *n.* **1** a thorny European bush producing dark plums. **2** an American hawthorn. —**black tie** a tuxedo or the black bow tie that is worn with it. —**black·top** *n.* asphalt or a similar material for surfacing roads; ***v.*** **-tops, -topped, -top·ping:** *a freshly ~d driveway.* —**black widow** a spider of which the female is large, dark, and poisonous.

blad·der *n.* **1** a membranous bag in an animal, esp. the receptacle for urine. **2** any similar object.
blade *n.* **1** the thin, flat cutting part of a sword, knife, ax, skate runner, etc; a similar part on a propeller, oar, paddle, etc. **2** the long flat leaf of a grass or cereal. **3** a spirited young man: *a gay ~.*
blain *n.* an inflamed or blistered patch of skin.
Blake, William. 1757–1827, English poet and artist.
blame *v.* **blames, blamed, blam·ing** consider (someone) responsible, esp. for a failure: *They ~d the pitcher for the loss; Don't ~ it on me! Who's* **to blame** (i.e. at fault)? **—*n.*** responsibility; also, the resultant criticism: *John* **took the blame** *for the broken window.* **—blam·a·ble** *adj.* **—blame·less** *adj.;* **blame·less·ly** *adv.;* **blame·less·ness** *n.* **—blame·wor·thy** *adj.*
blanch *v.* make or become pale or white: *His face ~ed with fear.* **—blanc·mange** (bluh·MAHNZH) *n.* a sweet, jellylike dessert made with milk, starch, etc.
bland *adj.* **1** pleasing; soothing: *a ~ smile; a ~ diet.* **2** dull; undistinguished: *a ~ report; a ~ character.* **—bland·ly** *adv.* **—bland·ness** *n.* **—blan·dish** *v.* cajole; persuade with flattery. **—blan·dish·er** *n.* **—blan·dish·ment** *n.*
blank *adj.* **1** without writing or marks *(a ~ page; a ~ space),* decoration *(a ~ window),* expression *(a ~ stare),* thought or memory *(a ~ mind),* etc. **2** absolute: *~ terror.* **—*n.* 1** something blank or empty, esp. a space left empty for writing in; hence, a form having such blanks: *fill in the ~s.* **2** an unfinished part or object: *The key was an uncut ~.* **3** a gun cartridge with no bullet. **—*v.* 1** delete: *He ~ed out the offending words.* **2** keep scoreless: *~ed the Bruins 2-0.* **—draw a blank** *Informal.* be unsuccessful. **—blank check** a signed check with the amount to be filled in by the recipient; hence, freedom of action. **—blan·ket** (BLANG·kit) *n.* **1** a large cloth covering used for warmth, esp. on a bed. **2** a covering: *a ~ of snow.* **—*v.:*** *A fog ~ed the coast.* **—*adj.*** applying to all cases: *a ~ rule; ~ authorization.* **—blank verse** unrhymed iambic pentameter.
blare *v.* **blares, blared, blar·ing** sound or call out loudly and brashly: *The radio ~d out the news.*
blar·ney (BLAHR·nee) *n.* **1** smooth, coaxing flattery, a gift for which is reputedly gained by kissing the **Blarney Stone** in Blarney Castle, Ireland. **2** nonsense. Also ***v.***
bla·sé (blah·ZAY) *adj.* bored by too much of something: *T.V. viewers are ~ about violence.*
blas·pheme (–FEEM) *v.* **-phemes, -phemed, -phem·ing 1** speak impiously about (God or something sacred); curse. **2** utter blasphemy; **blas·phem·er** *n.* **—blas·phe·mous** (BLAS·fuh·mus) *adj.;* **blas·phe·mous·ly** *adv.* **—blas·phe·my** (BLAS·fuh·mee) *n.* **-mies** contemptuous talk about God.
blast *n.* **1** a powerful gust of air, gases, etc.: *a ~ of cold air; the trumpet's ~;* **at full blast** at full capacity. **2** an explosion; also, the shock wave from it. **3** a blight that withers plants. **4** a critical or abusive attack. **5** *Slang.* a wild good time. **—*v.* 1** explode: *Danger: ~ing!* **blast off** of rockets, missiles, etc., take off with an explosion; **blast·off** *n.* **2** wither: *~ed flowers.* **3** criticize violently. **4** damn: *You ~ed idiot!* **—blast furnace** one that uses blasts of air to improve combustion for smelting.
bla·tant (BLAY·tunt) *adj.* **1** offensively noisy. **2** obtrusively obvious. **—bla·tant·ly** *adv.* **—bla·tan·cy** *n.* **-cies.**
blath·er *v.* talk foolishly; also ***n.*** **—blath·er·er** or **blath·er·skite** *n.* a talkative fool.
blaze *n.* **1** a large hot flame; also, a bright, usu. hot light: *the ~ of the tropical sun.* **2** **blazes** hell: *Go to ~!* **3** an outburst; also, a showy, brilliant display: *a ~ of fury; the ~ of fall colors.* **4** a light-colored mark on an animal's face, one cut into a tree (as a trail marker), etc. **—*v.* blaz·es, blazed, blaz·ing 1** burn or shine brightly. **2** break out, esp. emotionally: *~ing with anger.* **3** be showily bright. **4** mark (a tree) with a blaze; hence **blaze a trail** mark out a new path. **5 blaze away** shoot repeatedly. **—blaz·er** *n.* a light, usu. single-breasted sports jacket, often blue with metal buttons. **—bla·zon** (BLAY·zun) *n.* **1** a showy display. **2** a coat of arms or the description of it. **—*v.* 1** publicize widely: *a billboard ~ing forth our product.* **2** display; adorn.
bld. boldface.
bldg. building.
bleach *v.* make or become pale or white: *sun-~ed bones.* **—*n.*** a substance used to bleach: *laundry ~.* **—bleach·ers** *n.pl.* tiers of usu. roofless seats for spectators.
bleak *adj.* **1** barren and windswept: *~ cliffs.* **2** cold and raw: *a ~wind.* **3** gloomy: *a ~ future.* **—bleak·ly** *adv.* **—bleak·ish** *adj.* **—bleak·ness** *n.*
blear·y (BLEER·ee) or **blear** *adj.* esp. of eyes, blurred or unclear from fatigue, tears, etc.; **blear·y-eyed** or **blear·eyed** *adj.* **—blear·i·ly** *adv.;* **blear·i·ness** *n.*
bleat *v.* make the cry of a calf, goat, or sheep; also ***n.***
bleed *v.* **bleeds, bled, bleed·ing 1** shed blood; also, of plants, lose sap from a wound. **2** feel sympathy: *My heart ~s for you.* **3** draw blood, gas, etc. from; force money from: *The blackmailers* **bled him white** (i.e. took all his money). **—bleed·er** *n.* a hemophiliac. **—bleeding heart 1** any of several plants with pink, heart-shaped flowers. **2** a person overly sympathetic to the disadvantaged.
blem·ish *n.* a disfigurement or flaw. **—*v.*** mar.
blench *v.* **1** flinch; draw back. **2** turn pale.
blend *v.* **1** mix thoroughly. **2** combine varieties into one product: *~ed whiskey.* **3** harmonize; merge by degrees: *A chameleon ~s into*

his surroundings; voices ~ing. **—n.** something blended. **—blend·er** *n.*

bless *v.* **bless·es,** *pt.* & *pp.* **blessed** or **blest, bless·ing** **1** make holy: *The bishop ~ed the wine.* **2** revere as holy. **3** ask divine favor for: *The minister ~ed his flock.* **4** make happy; protect: *God ~ you!* **5** favor; endow: *a man ~ed with the gift of gab.* **—bless·ed** (–id) *adj.* **1** holy: *the* **Blessed Virgin** *Mary.* **2** fortunate: *~ are the meek.* **3** beatified: *the ~ martyrs.* **—bless·ed·ly** *adv.;* **bless·ed·ness** *n.* **—bless·ing** *n.* **1** a prayer for divine favor or before a meal. **2** a grant of divine favor; hence, anything causing happiness; boon: *the apparent misfortune that turns out to be a* **blessing in disguise.**

blew *pt.* of BLOW.

blight *n.* **1** any of various diseases or pests causing withering or death in plants. **2** anything causing destruction, impairment, etc.; also, its result: *Slums are a ~ on the landscape.* **—v.** affect with or have blight: *~ed hopes; a ~ed apple tree; ~ed neighborhoods.*

blimp *n.* a nonrigid dirigible.

blind (BLINED) *adj.* **1** unable to see: *~ as a bat.* **2** not using vision: *a ~ landing.* **3** unable to perceive: *~ to his own foolishness.* **4** lacking reason, judgment, forethought, etc.: *~ faith; ~ chance.* **5** hidden; with one open end; with no openings: *a ~ intersection; a ~ alley; the ~* (i.e. windowless) *side of a house.* **6** involving the unknown: *a ~ purchase; a ~ date.* **—adv.:** *a pilot flying ~ in the storm.* **—v.** make blind; dazzle; confuse: *a ~ing light; with ~ing speed.* **—n.** **1** something to shut out light: *Venetian ~s.* **2** a hunter's place of concealment. **—blind·ly** *adv.;* **blind·ness** *n.* **—blind date** a date between people who have never met; also, either partner. **—blind·er** *n.* one of a pair of leather flaps blocking a horse's sideways vision. **—blind·fold** *v.* tie a cloth over the eyes of; also **n.** a cloth so used. **—blind spot** **1** the point where the optic nerve joins the retina, insensitive to light. **2** a place one cannot see. **3** a topic in which one is ignorant or prejudiced: *Religion was his one ~ spot.* **—turn a blind eye to** ignore tactfully.

blink *v.* **1** shut and open (the eyes) quickly; hence, flicker, flash (lights) on and off, etc.; **blink·er** *n.* a flashing light; also, a blinder. **2 blink at** ignore: *~ing at minor illegalities.* **—n.** an act of blinking; hence, a glimmer. **—on the blink** *Slang.* out of order.

blintz or **blin·tze** (BLINT·suh) *n.* a thin pancake rolled around a usu. cheese filling.

blip *n.* a dot of light on a radar screen.

bliss *n.* complete, serene happiness: *heavenly ~; "Ignorance is ~."* **—bliss·ful** *adj.;* **bliss·ful·ly** *adv.*

blis·ter *n.* **1** a patch of skin raised and filled with fluid, as from a burn, irritation, etc. **2** a similar bulging, as on paint or metal; **v.:** *Her new shoes ~ed her heel; My hands ~ easily.* **—blister beetle** a beetle such as the Spanish fly or cantharis that is dried and powdered for use in raising blisters in medical treatment.

blithe *adj.* cheerful and carefree: *~ spirit;* also **blithe·some.** **—blithe·ly** *adv.;* **blithe·ness** *n.*

blitz *n.* **1** a lightning-fast military attack; also **blitz·krieg** (–kreeg). **2** an intensive campaign: *a public relations ~.* Also **v.**

bliz·zard (BLIZ·urd) *n.* a severe snowstorm driven by high winds.

blk. black; block; bulk.

bloat (BLOHT) *v.* swell, as with fat, gas, vanity, etc.: *a ~ed ego.* **—bloat·er** *n.* a smoked and salted mackerel or herring.

blob *n.* a shapeless mass or spot of color: *a ~ of paint; a ~ of grease.* Also **v.**

bloc *n.* a combination of parties, nations, etc. for one purpose, usu. political: *the Soviet ~.* **—block** *n.* **1** a mass of wood, stone, metal, etc., usu. with at least one flat side: *a concrete ~; a chopping ~; an engine ~.* **2** a hindrance or stoppage. **3** a building with many units: *an office ~.* **4** an urban area bounded by consecutive streets on all four sides; also, the length of one side of this. **5** a number of shares in a company, contiguous seats, etc. **6** an auction platform; **on the block** up for sale. **7** a case containing pulleys, used with ropes, or **block lines,** in a **block and tackle** arrangement for lifting or pulling. **8** *Slang.* the head. **—v.** **1** hinder; obstruct; clog: *A fallen tree ~s the road.* **2** support with a block. **—block·age** *n.* **—block·er** *n.* **—block out** sketch or plan in outline. **—block·ade** *n.* **1** a blocking off of the access to a city, harbor, etc. **2** a fleet or other force forming a blockade. Also **v.** **—block and tackle** See BLOCK, *n.* 7. **—block·bust·er** *n.* *Informal.* **1** a very powerful bomb. **2** something with a powerful impact. **—block·head** *n.* a dolt. **—block house** *n.* a reinforced building for observation or protection in a dangerous operation. **—block letter** a printed capital letter. **—block line** See BLOCK, *n.* 7.

blond *adj.* **1** light or pale; of hair, yellowish or light brown: *~ wood.* **2** with blond hair. **—n.** a blond person; *fem.* **blonde** *adj.* & *n.: a ~ bombshell* (i.e. an attractive blonde woman).

blood (BLUD) *n.* **1** the red fluid in veins and arteries; hence, life, vigor, etc.: *Younger employees put new ~ into the company.* **2** temper; passion; hence BAD BLOOD; **make someone's blood boil** (or **run cold**) make someone angry (or frightened). **3** family background and ties; descent, esp. if noble: " *~ is thicker than water"; a horse of good ~.* **4** violence; bloodshed. **5** a foppish or dashing young man. **—blood·less** *adj.: a ~ coup; a ~, cerebral poem;* **blood·less·ly** *adv.;* **blood·less·ness** *n.* **—blood and thunder** violent melodrama. **—blood bank** a place where blood is stored for use in transfusions. —**blood·bath** *n.* a massacre. —**blood count** the number of red and white cells in an amount of blood. —**blood·cur·dling** *adj.* terrifying; **blood·cur·dling·ly** *adv.* —**blood·ed** *adj.* **1** of fine pedigree: ~ *horses.* **2** *comb. form.* with a certain kind of blood: *cold-~ animals.* —**blood·hound** *n.* a large, long-eared, keen-scented tracking dog. —**blood·let·ting** *n.* **1** bloodshed. **2** the therapeutic bleeding of a person. —**blood·line** *n.* a line of direct descent. —**blood·mobile** (–moh·beel) *n.* a truck, van, etc. outfitted for collecting blood donations. —**blood poisoning** any blood disease caused by toxins, infections, etc. —**blood pressure** the pressure of the blood on the blood-vessel walls. —**blood relative** one related by birth, not marriage. —**blood·root** *n.* a wildflower whose root yields a red juice. —**blood·shed** *n.* the violent shedding of blood; killing. —**blood·shot** *adj.* of the eyes, red from inflammation. —**blood·stain** *n.* a dark stain made by blood; **blood·stained** *adj.* —**blood·stone** *n.* a red-flecked green quartz. —**blood stream** the flow of blood in the blood vessels, i.e. veins, arteries, capillaries, etc. —**blood·sucker** *n.* a leech or other creature that sucks blood; **blood·suck·ing** *adj.* —**blood test** the clinical testing of a blood sample. —**blood·thirst·y** *adj.* eager to kill. —**blood·y** *adj.* **blood·i·er, -i·est** **1** of, containing, or stained with blood; bleeding: *a ~ sword; a ~ nose.* **2** involving bloodshed; also, cruel; bloodthirsty: *a ~ persecution; a ~ tyrant.* **3** *Brit. Slang.* damned; also ***adv.*** very. —**Bloody Mary** a vodka-and-tomato-juice cocktail.

bloom *n.* **1** a flower; **in bloom** flowering. **2** a flourishing condition; a rosy glow, esp. in the cheeks. —***v.*** **1** of plants and trees, have flowers. **2** flourish; glow with health. —**bloom·er** *n.* **1** one that flowers. **2** blooper. —**bloom·ing** *adj. Informal.* thorough: *a ~ nincompoop.*

bloom·ers *n.pl.* baggy women's trousers gathered at the knee; also, women's underpants of this style.

bloop·er *n. Informal.* **1** a stupid mistake. **2** in baseball, a fly ball falling between the infield and the outfield.

blos·som (BLOS·um) *n.* a flower, esp. of a fruit tree: *apple ~s.* —***v.*** bloom. —**in blossom** flowering. —**blos·som·y** adj.

blot *n.* **1** a stain, esp. of spilled ink. **2** a disgrace: *a ~ on the family name.* —***v.*** **blots, blot·ted, blot·ting** **1** put a blot on; stain. **2** absorb (esp. spilled ink) with absorbent paper; **blot out** cover over; also, destroy. —**blotch** *n.* an irregular discoloration or stain, esp. a skin blemish; also ***v.;*** **blotch·y** *adj.* **blotch·i·er, -i·est:** *a ~ complexion.* —**blot·ter** *n.* **1** a sheet of blotting paper. **2** a daily record sheet: *the police ~* (of arrests, charges, etc.). —**blotting paper** a soft paper used to dry ink after writing.

blouse *n.* **1** a loose shirtlike garment, esp. for women. **2** a short military coat. **3** a kind of smock.

¹blow (BLOH) *v.* **blows, blew** (BLOO), **blown, blow·ing** bloom. —***n.*** a bunch of blooms.

²blow (BLOH) *v.* **blows, blew** (BLOO), **blown, blow·ing** **1** of air, be in motion: *The wind is ~ing.* **2** make a stream of air with the mouth or nose; also, pant; of whales, eject air and water in a spout: ~ *the candle out* (i.e. extinguish it); ~ *one's nose* (to clear it); *puffing and ~ing; There she* (i.e. the whale) *~s!* **3** move or be moved by wind: *a paper ~ing down the street.* **4** make or do by blowing; sound (a whistle, trumpet, etc.) esp. by blowing: *a child ~ing bubbles; ~ the horn.* **5** burst, as a fuse, tire, etc.; explode. **6** *Informal.* spend extravagantly: *Charlie blew $75 at the races.* **7** *Slang.* bungle: *The actress blew her lines.* **8** *Slang.* leave. **9** *Informal.* boast; also **blow one's own horn.** —***n.*** **1** a blowing; esp. a heavy storm. **2** a hard stroke; hence, an emotional shock; **come to** (or **exchange**) **blows** fight. —**blow·er** *n.* —**blow over** pass. —**blow up** **1** explode. **2** inflate; make larger. **3** *Informal.* get very angry. —**blow-by-blow** *adj.* detailed: *a ~ report of a quarrel.* —**blow dryer** an electric blower for drying the hair. —**blow·gun** *n.* a tube for shooting a dart by blowing. —**blow·out** *n.* the bursting of a tire. —**blow·pipe** *n.* a tube for blowing in, as to fan a fire, blow glass, etc. —**blow·torch** *n.* a portable torch for shooting a gasoline flame under pressure. —**blow·up** *n.* **1** an explosion. **2** an enlarged photograph. **3** a fit of anger. —**blow·y** *adj.* **blow·i·er, -i·est** windy.

blow·zy (BLOWZ·ee) *adj.* **-zi·er, -zi·est** untidy and coarse; also **blow·sy.**

BLS Bureau of Labor Statistics. —**B.L.S.** Bachelor of Library Science.

BLT bacon, lettuce, and tomato (in a sandwich).

blub·ber *n.* fat, esp. of whales, seals, etc.; **blub·ber·y** *adj.* —***v.*** weep noisily; **blub·ber·er** *n.*

blu·cher (BLOO·chur) *n.* a shoe having the vamp and tongue of one piece.

bludg·eon (BLUJ·un) *n.* a short heavy club. —***v.*** beat with a bludgeon; hence, bully.

blue (BLOO) *n.* **1** the color of a cloudless daytime sky; something of or wearing this color. **2** **the blue** the sky; the ocean; **out of the blue** unexpectedly. **3** **blues** *pl.* a melancholy mood; also, a slow, sad style of jazz. —***adj.*** **blu·er, blu·est** **1** of the color blue. **2** gloomy: *I'm feeling ~.* **3** puritanical. **4** noble: *~ blood.* **5** *Informal.* off-color; risqué: *~ jokes, movies.* —**blu·ish** *adj.* —**blue baby** a baby born with a bluish skin from a heart defect. —**blue·bell** *n.* any of several plants with blue, bell-shaped flowers. —**blue·ber·ry** *n.* **-ber·ries** the small, edible dark-blue fruit of a wild or cultivated shrub. —**blue·bird** *n.* any of several small, North American songbirds whose male is bright blue. —**blue·bon·net** *n.* any of several blue wild flowers of the S.W. United States. —**blue·bot·tle** *n.* any of several flies with blue bodies. —**blue box** an electronic device for bypassing telephone circuits and making toll-free calls. —**blue cheese** cheese having veins of blue mold. —**blue chip** an expensive, secure investment stock. —**blue-col·lar** *adj.* pertaining to manual or industrial workers: ~ *trades;* cf. WHITE-COLLAR. —**blue·fish** *n.* any of several bluish, fierce, edible fishes. —**blue·grass** *n.* **1** any of several pasture grasses grown esp. in Kentucky (nicknamed "Bluegrass State"). **2** Southern country music played on string instruments. —**blueing** same as BLUING. —**blue·jack·et** *n.* a common sailor in the navy. —**blue jay** a blue, crested North American bird. —**blue jeans** jeans of stout blue denim. —**blue·nose** *n.* a puritan. —**blue-point** *n.* a small edible oyster. —**blue·print** *n.* a kind of photographic reproduction of building plans, maps, etc.; hence, a detailed plan: *a ~ for progress;* also ***v.*** —**blue·stock·ing** *n.* a woman having literary or intellectual interests. —**blue streak** a rapid stream of words: *talking a ~ streak.* —**blu·et** (BLOO·it) *n.* a small wildflower with bluish, four-lobed blooms.

¹bluff *v.* mislead or intimidate by a deceptive show of confidence or strength; also ***n.*** —**bluff·er** *n.*

²bluff *n.* a steep, flat-fronted cliff or bank. —***adj.*** **1** : *a ~ shoreline.* **2** blunt and good-natured: ~ *King Hal.* —**bluff·ly** *adv.* —**bluff·ness** *n.*

blu(e)·ing *n.* a blue laundering additive used to prevent the yellowing of clothes.

blun·der *v.* 1 move clumsily. **2** make a foolish mistake; also ***n.*** —**blun·der·buss** *n.* **1** a short, old-fashioned gun with a wide muzzle. **2** one who blunders.

blunt *adj.* **1** without a sharp edge: *a ~ object.* **2** plainspoken: *a ~ man.* **3** dull; insensitive. —***v.*** make or become blunt: *He ~ed his ax on the rock.* —**blunt·ly** *adv.* —**blunt·ness** *n.*

blur *v.* **blurs, blurred, blur·ring** **1** smear. **2** make or become indistinct or dim: *~d vision.* —***n.*** **1** a smear: *a ~ on the page.* **2** something indistinct: *The cars raced past in a ~.* —**blur·ry** *adj.: a ~ photograph;* **blur·ri·ness** *n.*

blurb *n.* a publisher's write-up of a book, printed on its dust jacket.

blurt *v.* say (something) without thinking: *~ed out a secret.* Also ***n.***

blush *v.* turn red, esp. in the face from shame, modesty, etc.: *a ~ing bride.* —***n.*** a reddening of the face; also, a pinkish color: *the ~ of dawn in the morning sky.* —**blush·ful** *adj.*

blus·ter *v.* **1** blow in heavy gusts. **2** speak or act in noisy threats or boasts. —***n.:*** *a bully's empty ~.* —**blus·ter·er** *n.* —**blus·ter·y** *adj.: a ~ day.*

blvd. boulevard.

b.m. bowel movement.

BMR basal metabolic rate.

bn. battalion.

B'nai B'rith (buh·NAY–) an international Jewish service organization.

B.O. body odor; box office; branch office.

bo·a (BOH·uh) *n.* **1** any of several tropical snakes, as the **boa constrictor,** which crush and swallow their prey. **2** a long scarf of feathers of fluffy fur.

boar *n.* **1** a male pig. **2** a fierce Old World wild pig.

board *n.* **1** a long, thin, rectangular piece of wood, as for building. **2** a rectangular upright surface used for notices, writing, etc.: *a bulletin ~.* **3** a table for serving food; hence, meals, esp. at hired lodgings: *room and ~.* **4** a flat surface for playing games on: *a chess ~.* **5** pasteboard, as for book covers. **6** an official council: *the ~ of directors.* **7 the boards** the stage: *an actor* **treading the boards** (i.e. acting in a play). —***v.*** **1** get on (a ship, bus, train, etc.). **2** receive or provide with meals and often a room; also, assign to such lodgings: *The landlady ~s 7 men; I ~ed my horse while on vacation.* **3** cover or shut with boards; usu. **board up.** —**above board** open and honest. —**go by the board** become forgotten, abandoned, lost, etc. —**on board** aboard. —**board·er** *n.* one who receives meals and often a room for pay, as at a **board·ing·house.** —**board·walk** *n.* a sidewalk of boards; also, a beach promenade.

boast (BOHST) *v.* **1** speak of (one's abilities, deeds, etc.) with too much pride. **2** be proud to have: *The town ~s a new concert hall.* —***n.*** a boasting; also, that which one boasts about. —**boast·ful** *adj.;* **boast·ful·ly** *adv.;* **boast·ful·ness** *n.*

boat (BOHT) *n.* **1** a vessel for water travel, esp. a small, open one. **2** a dish for serving sauces: *a gravy ~.* —***v.*** travel or carry in a boat. —**in the same boat** in the same circumstances. —**miss the boat** miss one's opportunity. —**boat·er** *n.* **1** one who boats. **2** a flat-topped hard straw hat. —**boat·man** *n.* **-men** one who operates, works with, or deals in boats. —**boat·swain** (BOH·sn) *n.* a ship's petty officer in charge of the deck, hull, anchor, etc.

¹bob *v.* **bobs, bobbed, bob·bing** **1** jerk up and down; also, try to grab with one's teeth something floating or hanging: *~ for apples.* **2** come up or in suddenly: *a cork ~ing up in water; ~d into the room.* **3** cut short: *a horse with a ~d tail.* —***n.*** **1** a rapid up-and-down movement: *a ~ of the head.* **2** a float for a fishing line. **3** a woman's short hair style. **4** a small weight, as on a plumb line.

²bob *n. sing.* & *pl. Brit. Slang.* shilling.
bob·bin *n.* a spool for thread or yarn on a machine.
bob·ble *v.* **bob·bles, bob·bled, bob·bling** fumble, as with a ball in sports; also ***n.***
bob·by *n.* **bob·bies** *Brit. Informal.* a policeman.
bobby pin a small, ridged hair clip. —**bob·by-sox·er** *n. Informal.* a teen-age girl of the 1940's, esp. one who wore ankle-high **bobby socks** (or **sox**).
bob·cat *n.* a spotted, tan or reddish brown North American wildcat.
bob·o·link (–uh–) *n.* a North American songbird.
bob·sled *n.* **1** a joined pair of short sleds. **2** a heavy racing sled with two sets of runners, a steering wheel, and brakes. —***v.*** **-sleds, -sled·ded, -sled·ding.**
bob·white *n.* any of several North American quails.
Boc·cac·cio (boh·CAH·chee·oh), **Gio·van·ni.** 1313–1375, an Italian author.
boc·cie, boc·ce, boc·ci (BOCH·ee) *n.* an Italian form of lawn bowling.
bock (beer) *n.* a dark, sweetish beer.
¹bode *pt.* of BIDE.
²bode *v.* **bodes, bod·ed, bod·ing** portend.
bod·ice (BOD·is) *n.* the fitted upper portion of a woman's dress; also, a usu. laced woman's vest.
bod·ied *adj.* & *comb. form.* having a body (of specified kind): *an able-~ sailor; a full-~ wine.* —**bod·i·ly** *adj.* physical; of the body; ***adv.*** **1** in person. **2** as a whole: *The group walked out ~.* —**bod·i·less** *adj.*
bod·kin *n.* any of several pointed instruments, as a stiletto, a kind of awl, an ornamental hairpin, a blunt needle for pulling tape or ribbon, etc.
bod·y *n.* **bod·ies** **1** the physical part of an organism: *She loved him* **body and soul** (i.e. totally). **2** a corpse. **3** the trunk of an animal; hence, the main part of anything: *the ~ of an essay; an automobile ~* (i.e. exclusive of chassis and engine). **4** a bounded mass: *a ~ of water.* **5** a group: *The workers protested* **in a body** (i.e. all together). **6** *Informal.* a person. **7** of wine, paint, hair, etc., thickness, richness, consistency, or texture. —**body English** body movements reflecting a player's desire to control a ball after throwing it. —**bod·y·guard** *n.* one or more guards protecting a person. —**body language** postures, gestures, etc. as they express feelings, thoughts, reactions, etc. —**body politic** the people as a political unit under a government. —**body rub** a massage, as given in a massage parlor. —**body snatcher** one who illegally digs up corpses, esp. for dissection. —**body stocking** a close-fitting light garment covering the trunk and often the legs and arms.
Boer (BOHR, BOOR) *n.* a South African of Dutch descent; also ***adj.:*** *the* **Boer War** (1899–1902) *between England and the Boers.*
bof·fo (BOF·oh) *adj. Slang.* successful, as a box-office hit.
bog *n.* an area of wet marshy ground. —***v.*** impede or get stuck in or as if in a bog: *a student* **bogged down** *with homework.*
bo·gey (BOH·gee) *n.* **-geys** **1** Also **bo·gie,** one stroke over par on a hole in golf; ***v.*** make this score. **2** Also **bo·gy** or **bo·gie,** *pl.* **-gies** a frightening spirit; also, something feared unnecessarily: *Final examinations were his ~;* **bo·gey·man, bo·gy·man, boo·gie·man** *n.* **-men** a bogey, esp. as used to frighten children.
bog·gle *v.* **bog·gles, bog·gled, bog·gling** **1** be startled or hesitate (at): *~d at a talking horse; Theories of space and time ~ my mind.* **2** bungle.
Bo·ga·tá (boh·guh·TAH) capital of Colombia.
bo·gus (BOH·gus) *adj.* fake: *a ~ twenty-dollar bill.*
bogy(man) See BOGEY.
Bo·he·mi·a (boh·HEE·mee·uh) a region in W. Czechoslovakia. —**Bo·he·mi·an** *n.* **1** a native of Bohemia, also ***adj.*** **2** often **bohemian,** a person, esp. an artist, who lives unconventionally; ***adj.:*** *~ life-styles.*
¹boil *n.* a swollen and pus-filled bacterial infection of the skin.
²boil *v.* **1** cause to bubble and vaporize by heating to its **boiling point,** as 100°C for water; also, be heated to such a temperature or be very hot: *The water is ~ing.* **2** cook or sterilize in boiling water: *~ed onions.* **3** seethe with anger: *I'm ~ing (mad)!* **4** churn: *~ing rapids.* —***n.*** the state of boiling: *at a gentle ~.* —**boil down** **1** condense by boiling. **2** be or mean basically: *It all ~s down to greed.* —**boil·er** *n.* a tank, pot, etc. in which water is boiled, as for steam power or cooking. —**boil·er·mak·er** *n. Informal.* whiskey with a beer as chaser.
Boi·se (–see) capital of Idaho.
bois·ter·ous (–us) *adj.* **1** rowdy: *a ~ party.* **2** noisily exuberant: *~ good humor.* —**bois·ter·ous·ly** *adv.* —**bois·ter·ous·ness** *n.*
Bol. Bolivia.
bo·la (BOH·luh) *n.* a weapon thrown at animals to entangle and catch them, consisting of weighted balls on the end of long cords; also **bo·las** (–lus).
bold *adj.* **1** courageous; daring: *a ~ adventurer.* **2** impudent: *a ~ young man.* **3** distinctly visible: *a ~ outline.* **4** steep: *a ~ cliff.* —**make bold to** dare to. —**bold·ly** *adv.* —**bold·ness** *n.* —**bold·face** *n.* a heavy, dark style of type. —**bold·faced** *adj.* **1** impudent. **2** in boldface.
bole *n.* a tree trunk.
bo·le·ro (buh·LAIR·oh) *n.* **1** a short, open-fronted jacket with or without sleeves and collar. **2** a Spanish dance in 3/4 time.
Bol·i·var (BOL·i·ver), **Simon.** 1783–1830, South American statesman and revolutionary. —**bol·i·var** *n.* **-vars** or **-var·es** (–VAH·res) the basic unit of currency in Venezuela, equal

to 100 centimos. —**Bo·liv·i·a** (buh·LIV·ee·uh) a land-locked South American republic; 424,165 sq.mi. (1,098,581 km²); *caps.* La Paz and Sucre. —**Bo·liv·i·an** *adj.* & *n.*

boll *n.* a round seed pod, as of cotton, flax, etc. —**boll weevil** a small beetle that attacks cotton bolls. —**boll·worm** *n.* any of several moth larvae that feed on cotton bolls, corn ears, etc.

bo·lo (BOH·loh) *n.* a kind of machete used in the Philippines.

bo·lo·gna (sausage) (buh·LOH·nee) *n.* a large sausage of smoked mixed meats. —**Bo·lo·gna** (buh·LOH·nuh) a N. Italian city.

Bol·she·vik (BOHL·shuh·vik) *n.* **-viks** or **-vi·ki** (–vik·ee) a member of the communist party that came to power in Russia in 1917; hence, any radical or communist; also ***adj.*** —**Bol·she·vism** *n.* —**Bol·she·vist** *adj.* & *n.*

bol·ster (BOHL·stur) *n.* a long, thin, firm pillow, cushion, etc.; hence, a support. —***v.*** reinforce; prop up: *His speech ~ed our sagging spirits.*

bolt *n.* **1** a rod or bar used to fasten a door, window, etc.; also, a metal fastener with threads on one end and a head at the other: *nuts and ~s.* **2** a roll of cloth. **3** a blast of lightning; **bolt from the blue** an unforeseen shock. **4** a dash: *made a ~ for the door.* —***v.*** **1** fasten with a bolt: *~ the door.* **2** dash away; hence, refuse to support (a political party, candidate, etc.): *The horse ~ed from the barn.* **3** swallow (food) rapidly. **4** sift (flour, grain, etc.) —**bolt upright** rigidly erect.

bo·lus *n.* a round lump to be swallowed, as a ball of chewed food or a large pill.

bomb (BOM) *n.* **1** a projectile filled with explosives, gas, incendiary material, etc.; **the Bomb** the atomic bomb: *Ban the ~!* **2** an aerosol spray can. **3** *Slang.* a total failure. —***v.*** **1** destroy or attack with bombs. **2** *Slang.* be a total failure. See also BOMBED. —**bom·bard** (–BARD) ***v.*** **1** attack with artillery guns, bombs, etc.; hence, harass persistently: *a Congressman ~ed with protests.* **2** send atomic particles, rays, etc. at (a nucleus); —**bom·bard·ment** *n.* —**bom·bar·dier** (bom·buh·DEER) *n.* the crew member who releases bombs from an aircraft.

bom·bast (BOM·bast) *n.* pretentious and lofty writing, speech, etc.; **bom·bas·tic** (–BAS–) *adj.;* **bom·bas·ti·cal·ly** *adv.*

Bom·bay (–BAY) a west-coast seaport and city of India.

bom·ba·zine (–buh·ZEEN) *n.* a usu. black twilled cloth of silk or rayon and worsted.

bomb bay a compartment on the underside of a bomber from which bombs are released. —**bombed** *adj. Slang.* intoxicated. —**bomb·er** *n.* an airplane designed to drop bombs. —**bomb·proof** *adj.* resisting a bomb explosion: *a ~ basement.* —**bomb·shell** *n.* a bomb; hence, something or someone stunning or shocking. —**bomb·sight** *n.* a bomb-aiming device used in aircraft.

bo·na fi·de (BOH·nuh·fide, –FYE·dee) **1** in good faith; sincere. **2** genuine.

bo·nan·za (buh·NAN·zuh) *n.* something yielding a very great profit, esp. a large pocket of gold or silver, a prosperous farm, a successful movie, etc.

Bo·na·parte (BOH·nuh·part), **Napoleon.** 1769–1821, Napoleon I of France.

bon·bon (BON·bon) *n.* a candy, esp. with a soft center and chocolate coating.

bond *n.* **1** something which unites, ties, obliges, etc.; **bonds** *pl.* fetters: *the ~s of friendship.* **2** a state of being united. **3** a pledge or a guarantee secured by a financial penalty; esp., an insurance agreement to pay an employer for loss caused by a certain employee. **4** one who provides bail or surety; bondsman. **5** a pledge by a government or corporation to repay a loan plus interest on a specific date to the owner of the bond **(bond·hold·er).** **6** the state of goods held pending payment of taxes. **7** a strong, superior paper; also called **bond paper.** —***v.*** **1** join; unite: *two boards ~ed by glue.* **2** guarantee (a worker) with a bond. **3** place (goods) in bond. —**bond·age** (–ij) *n.* slavery; serfdom. —**bond·man** *n.* **-men** a slave or serf; *fem.* **bond·maid** or **bond·wom·an, -wom·en.** —**bond·ser·vant** *n.* bondman. —**bonds·man** *n.* **-men** **1** one who provides bail; surety. **2** bondman.

bone *n.* **1** the hard substance of vertebrate skeletons; also, a piece of this; **a bone to pick** something to argue about; **make no bones about** *Informal.* do or admit to without hesitation. **2** a similar material, as whalebone. **3** something made of bone; esp. **bones** *pl. Informal.* dice. —***v.*** **bones, boned, bon·ing** take the bones out of: *~ing a fish;* **bone up on** study (a subject) intensively. —**bone black** a pigment made from charred bones. —**bone-dry** *adj.* very dry. —**bone·less** *adj.: a ~ roast.* —**bone meal** crushed bone used as feed or fertilizer. —**bon·er** *n. Slang.* a blunder.

bon·fire *n.* a large fire built outdoors.

bon·go (BONG·go) **drums** a joined pair of small drums of different pitch, each of which is a **bongo,** *pl.* **-gos.**

bon·ho(m)·mie (bon·uh·MEE) *n.* good-natured amiability. —**bon·ho·mous** (BON·uh·mus) *adj.: a ~ salesman.*

bo·ni·to (buh·NEE·toh) *n., pl.* **-to** or **-to(e)s** any of several tunalike fishes.

bon mot (bohn·MOH), *pl.* **bons mots** (–MOHZ) a witty remark.

Bonn capital of the Federal Republic of Germany.

bon·net *n.* a head covering for women and children that is tied under the chin; hence, any hood or covering, as an Indian's feathered headdress.

bon·ny or **bon·nie** *adj.* **bon·ni·er, bon·ni·est** *Scot.* & *Brit.* healthy and good-looking: *a ~ lass.*

bon·sai (bone·SYE) *n. sing.* & *pl.* **1** an ornamental dwarf tree. **2** the art of growing these.

bo·nus (BOH·nus) *n.* **-nus·es** something paid or given that is extra: *a $25 Christmas ~.* **—bon vi·vant** (–vi·VAHNT) one who likes good food, drink, and other luxuries. **—bon voy·age** (–voi·AZH) farewell; (have a) pleasant trip!

bon·y (BOH·nee) *adj.* **bon·i·er, -i·est** **1** of bone; having many bones: *a ~ fish.* **2** thin; having prominent bones: *~ knees.* Also **bon·ey.**

boo *interj.* & *n., pl.* **boos** a sound made to show disapproval or to frighten. **—*v.* boos, booed, boo·ing:** *an actor ~ed off the stage.* **—boob** *n. Slang.* **1** a dolt. **2** a woman's breast. **—boo-boo** *n. Slang.* **-boos** a blunder. **—boob tube** *Slang.* TV. **—boo·by** (–bee) *n.* **-bies** a doltish person. **—booby hatch** *Slang.* a mental institution. **—booby prize** a prize given to the loser in fun. **—booby trap** a deceptive object that explodes when touched.

boo·dle *n. Slang.* **1** caboodle. **2** money, esp. as a bribe or loot.

boogieman See BOGEY.

book *n.* **1** a set of paper or similar sheets bound along one edge; also, a literary, historical, etc. composition of some length; hence, a main division of such a work: *the third ~ of the Aeneid.* **2 the (Good) Book** the Bible. **3 books** financial records: *balancing the ~s.* **4** a bound package of tickets, paper matches, etc. **5** a betting record. **—*v.* 1** engage in advance: *~ a room; ~ a night club tour.* **2** make a charge against: *~ed for murder.* **—by the book** correctly or properly. **—make book** make or take bets. **—book·case** *n.* a piece of furniture having bookshelves. **—book club** a company that sells books at a discount to members who have to buy a minimum number annually. **—book·end** *n.* something put at one end to keep a line of books upright. **—book·ie** (–ee) *n. Slang.* a bookmaker. **—book·ish** *adj.* fond of reading books; hence, pedantic or literary: *a ~ style.* **—book jacket** same as DUST JACKET. **—book·keep·er** *n.* one who keeps business records and accounts; **book·keep·ing** *n.* **—book·let** *n.* a small, usu. paperbound book. **—book·mak·er** *n.* one who accepts bets, usu. on races. **—book·mark** *n.* something put in a book to mark a place. **—book·mo·bile** (–moh·beel) *n.* a truck equipped as a mobile library or book store. **—book·plate** *n.* a label in a book identifying its owner. **—book·sell·er** *n.* one who runs a bookstore. **—book·shelf** *n.* **-shelves** a shelf to keep books on. **—book·shop** or **book·store** *n.* a place where books are sold. **—book·worm** *n.* **1** any of several insects that eat book bindings. **2** an avid reader or student.

¹boom *n.* **1** a long horizontal pole, as one used to hold out the bottom edge of a sail, support a load on a derrick, hold a microphone, etc. **2** a barrier of connected logs used to contain floating timber: *a log ~.* **—lower the boom** *Informal.* crack down.

²boom *v.* **1** make or utter with a deep resonant sound: *guns ~ing in the distance.* **2** make or become suddenly prosperous, famous, active, etc.: *Industry ~ed after World War II.* **—*n.* 1** a booming sound. **2** a sudden increase or prosperity: *the post-war baby ~; the ~-and-bust cycle* (of prosperity and depression).

boom·er·ang *n.* **1** a curved flattish stick thrown as a weapon by Australian aborigines; it returns if it misses its target. **2** something which rebounds to its author's disadvantage; ***v.:*** *The politician's dirty tricks ~ed on him.*

boom town a suddenly prosperous town.

boon *n.* **1** something helpful. **2** a favor: *Grant me one ~.*

boon companion a close convivial friend.

boon·docks *n.pl. Informal.* a rural or backwoods area.

boon·dog·gle *v.* **-dog·gles, -dog·gled, -dog·gling** *Informal.* waste time by doing pointless work. **—*n.*** pointless work. **—boon·dog·gler** *n.*

Boone, Daniel. 1734–1820, American frontiersman.

boor *n.* a rude or clumsy person, esp. a rustic. **—boor·ish** *adj.: ~ bad manners.* **—boor·ish·ly** *adv.*

boost *v.* **1** raise; esp., help up from below: *a compliment to ~ his morale.* **2** promote or support. **—*n.:*** *Give me a ~ up the tree.* **—boost·er** *n.: civic ~s attracting industry to town;* a **booster rocket** (for launching a spacecraft); **booster shot** a supplementary dose of vaccine or antigen.

¹boot *v. Archaic.* avail: *What ~s it to labor long?* **—to boot** as well: *a drunkard and a liar to ~.*

²boot *n.* **1** heavy footwear covering some part of the leg: *rubber ~s; work ~s.* **2** a kick; hence, *Informal.* a thrill. **3** *Brit.* the trunk of an automobile. **4** a navy or marine recruit, esp. one in a training camp **(boot camp).** **—*v.*** kick; hence, *Informal.* dismiss, esp. from a job: *He got* **the boot** (i.e. got fired) *after only a week on the job.* **—lick (someone's) boots** toady to. **—boot·black** *n.* one who cleans and shines shoes and boots. **—boot·ee** or **boot·ie** *n.* a baby's shoe made of soft cloth.

Bo·ö·tes (boh·OH·teez) *n.* a N. constellation containing the star Arcturus.

booth *n.* a small enclosed area, esp. a stall for displaying goods at a fair, a private compartment *(a voting ~),* a partly enclosed table with two bench seats in a restaurant, etc.

boot·leg *v.* **-legs, -legged, -leg·ging** make or deal in liquor illegally. **—*adj.* & *n.:*** *~ gin; We bought some ~.* **—boot·leg·ger** *n.*

boot·less *adj. Formal.* useless. **—boot·less·ly** *adv.* **—boot·lick·er** *n.* a toady.

boo·ty *n.* **-ties** goods seized or stolen, as in a war, by pirates, etc.

booze *n. Informal.* alcoholic drink. **—*v.* booz·es, boozed, booz·ing** drink to excess. **—booz·er** *n.* **—booz·y** *adj.: a ~ old sot.*
bop *v.* **bops, bopped, bop·ping** *Informal.* hit. **—*n.:*** *a ~ on the head.*
Bo·phu·that·swa·na (–SWAH–) a homeland of the Tswana people of South Africa; 15,610 sq.mi. (40,430 km²); *cap.* Mmabatho.
bor. borough.
bo·rac·ic (buh·RAS·ic) **acid** a white, water-soluble compound of boron used as an antiseptic, in glass-making, and to produce borax. **—bo·rate** (BOR–) *n.* a salt or ester of boric acid. **—bo·rax** (BOR–) *n.* a white powder that is a compound of sodium and boric acid, used in cleaning, medicines, enamels, etc.
Bor·deaux (–DOH) a seaport in S.W.France. **—*n.*** a wine from the Bordeaux region.
bor·del·lo (–DEL·oh) *n.* a brothel.
bor·der *n.* **1** an edge or boundary, esp. between states, countries, etc. **2** a strip outlining an edge: *a lace ~ on a cuff.* **—*v.*** provide with a border; **border on** be next to; be very similar to: *His actions ~ on the insane.* **—bor·der·land** *n.* land near a border; hence, an uncertain, intermediate condition. **—bor·der·line** *n.* a line marking a border; ***adj.*** marginal, esp. marginally acceptable, competent, etc.: *a ~ pass in a test.*
¹bore *v.* **bores, bored, bor·ing** **1** make a usu. long, narrow hole, esp. by drilling or digging: *to ~ a tunnel; ~ through a piece of wood.* **2** pierce. **3** weary by being repetitive, dull, etc.: *I won't ~ you with the details.* **—*n.*** **1** a hole made by boring; also, the hollow inside a pipe, gun, etc.; hence, caliber: *a large-~ rifle.* **2** a boring person or thing. **—bor·er** *n.*
²bore *pt.* of BEAR.
³bore *n.* a tidal wave with a steep front.
bo·re·al (BOR·ee·ul) *adj.* northern: *~ regions.*
bore·dom *n.* the condition of being bored.
bo·ric acid same as BORACIC ACID.
born *pp.* of BEAR. **—*adj.*** **1** brought forth by birth. **2** natural: *a ~ loser.* **—in all my born days** *Informal.* in all my life. **—born-a·gain** *adj.* reborn spiritually; regenerate: *a ~ Baptist.*
borne *pp.* of BEAR.
Bor·ne·o (BOR·nee·oh) a large island S.W. of the Philippines, belonging to Indonesia and Malaysia.
bo·ron (BOR·on) *n.* a nonmetallic element used in alloys and to control nuclear reactions.
bor·ough (BUR·oh) *n.* **1** an incorporated town in some states; also, one of the five divisions of New York City. **2** *Brit.* a town that elects one or more members to Parliament.
bor·row (BOR·oh) *v.* **1** receive from another and agree to return or replace: *May I ~ $5 until payday?* **2** adopt as one's own: *English has ~ed many words from Spanish.* **—bor·row·er** *n.*
borsch (BORSH) or **borscht** (BORSHT) *n.* a kind of Russian beet soup.
Bosch (BOS), **Hieronymus.** 1450?–1516, a Dutch painter.
bosh *n. Informal.* nonsense!
bosk·y *adj.* **bosk·i·er, -i·est** wooded; shaded: *~ hills.*
bos'n or **bo's'n** See BOSUN.
bos·om (BOOZ·um) *n.* **1** the chest or breasts; also, the part of the clothing covering this. **2** a position of close relationship: *in the ~ of the church; the ~ of one's family;* ***adj.:*** *my ~* (i.e. close) *buddy;* **-bos·omed** *comb. form.: flat-~.* **—bos·om·y** *adj.* big-breasted.
Bos·po·rus (BOS·puh–) the strait joining the Black Sea and the Sea of Marmara.
¹boss *n.* a knoblike projecting ornament or stud. **—*v.*** provide with a boss.
²boss *n.* one who gives orders; esp. an employer, a foreman, etc.: *corrupt party ~es.* **—*v.:*** *His older brother ~ed him around.* **—boss·y** *adj.* overbearing; **boss·i·ly** *adv.;* **boss·i·ness** *n.*
Bos·ton (BAW·stun, BOS·tun) capital of Massachusetts. **—Bos·to·ni·an** (–TOH·nee·un) *adj.* & *n.*
bo·sun (BOH·sn) *n.* boatswain. Also **bos'n, bo's'n,** or **bo'sun.**
Bos·well (BOZ–), **James.** 1740–1795, the biographer of Samuel Johnson.
bot. botany; botanist; bottle. **—bo·tan·i·cal** (–TAN–) *adj.* having to do with botany: *~ gardens.* **—bot·a·nize** *v.* **-niz·es, -niz·ed, -niz·ing** collect or study plants: *students ~ing in the woods.* **—bot·a·ny** (BOTN·ee) *n.* the science of plants; **bot·a·nist** *n.*
botch *v.* do clumsily; ruin by carelessness. Also ***n.*** **—botch·y** *adj.*
both (BOHTH) *adj.* the one as well as the other: *bread buttered on ~ sides;* ***pron.*** the two: *~ of us.* **—both . . . and . . .:** *~ clumsy and careless; He ~ sang and danced.*
both·er (BODH·ur) *v.* **1** disturb; trouble: *little boys ~ing their mother; always ~ing himself about money.* **2** take the trouble: *Don't ~ to come.* **—*n.*** trouble; concern; also, a source of this: *Babies are a lot of ~.*
Bot·swa·na (bot·SWAH·nuh) a S. African republic; 231,805 sq. mi. (600,372 km²); *cap.* Gaborone.
Bot·ti·cel·li (bot·i·CHEL·ee), **Sandro.** 1444?–1510, an Italian painter.
bot·tle *n.* **1** a usu. narrow-necked container for liquids: *~ of wine.* **2 the bottle** alcoholic drink; **hit the bottle** *Slang.* drink to excess. **3** an infant's nursing bottle. **—*v.* bot·tles, bot·tled, bot·tling** put in a bottle: *~d beer;* **bottle up** confine or repress: *Don't ~ up your anger.* **—bot·tle·neck** *n.* anything hindering progress or causing a slowdown, as a narrow spot in a busy road.
bot·tom (BOT·um) *n.* **1** the part which is underneath, supporting, or lowest: *the ~ of the sea; the ~ of a ship; a new recruit starting at the ~.* **2** *Informal.* buttocks: *spank a child's ~.* **3** the basis, essence, or true cause: **At bottom** (i.e.

basically) *he is a good man; Let's get to the ~ of this.* **4** Also **bot·tom·land,** rich alluvial soil along a river. ***—adj.*** lowest; last: *That's my ~ offer; You can* **bet your bottom dollar** (*Informal.* bet everything you have). ***—v.*** **bottom (out)** of prices, etc., reach the lowest level before rising. **—bottoms up!** a drinking toast. **—from the bottom of one's heart** most sincerely. **—bot·tom·less** *adj.: a ~ pit.* **—bottom line** *Informal.* the result that counts, as the final figure in a financial statement.

bot·u·lism (BOCH·uh–) *n.* a kind of food poisoning caused by a bacterial toxin, esp. in improperly canned foods.

bou·doir (BOOD·wahr) *n.* a woman's private bedroom or sitting room.

bouf·fant (boo·FAHNT) *adj.* full; puffed out: *a ~ hairdo; ~ sleeves.*

bough (BOW) *n.* a limb of a tree.

bought *pt.* & *pp.* of BUY.

bouil·la·baisse (bool·yuh·BACE) *n.* a chowder containing many kinds of fish and shellfish. **—bouil·lon** (BOOL·yon) *n.* a clear broth.

boul·der (BOLE·dur) *n.* a large, usu. rounded stone.

boule (BOOL) *n.* a pear-shaped synthetic gem.

boul·e·vard (BOOL·uh·vard) *n.* a broad street, often tree-lined.

bounce *v.* **bounc·es, bounced, bounc·ing** **1** spring or spring back; move up and down elastically: *The ball ~d off the backboard; a ball ~ing down the road; a child ~ing a ball.* **2** *Informal.* of a check, be sent back because of insufficient funds. **3** *Slang.* eject for rowdy behavior. ***—n.*** **1** a bouncing or the capacity for it. **2** vigor and enthusiasm; **bounc·ing** *adj.: a ~ baby boy.* **3 the bounce** *Slang.* a dismissal. **—bounce back** *Informal.* start again with new vigor. **—bounc·er** *n.* **—bounc·y** *adj.: a ~ mattress.*

[1]bound *v.* leap, spring, jump, etc.: *kangaroos ~ing across the plains.* ***—n.*** **by leaps and bounds** very rapidly.

[2]bound *n.* usu. **bounds,** a limit, border, or boundary: *within the ~s of reason.* ***—v.*** be, mark, or have a limit. **—out of bounds** outside the permitted area or limits: *Pool halls and drinking are out of ~s for children.* **—bound·less** adj.: *~ enthusiasm;* **bound·less·ly** *adv.;* **bound·less·ness** *n.*

[3]bound *pt.* & *pp.* of BIND. ***—adj.*** **1** tied; obligated: *~ by his promise; ~ to obey the law.* **2** certain; determined: *We are ~ to see him; They're ~ on seeing him.* **3** going to: *~ for home.* **—bound up in** (or **with**) deeply involved or connected with.

bound·a·ry *n.* **-ries** a limit or border. **—bound·en** *adj.* obligatory; required: *Helping the aged is our ~ duty.*

boun·te·ous (BOWN·tee·us) or **boun·ti·ful** *adj.* generous; plentiful: *~ gifts.* **—boun·te·ous·ly** or **boun·ti·ful·ly** *adv.* **—boun·te·ous·ness** or **boun·ti·ful·ness** *n.* **—boun·ty** *n.* **-ties** **1** a generous gift; also, liberality: *Thank the Lord for His ~.* **2** a reward: *The hunter collected a ~ on wolves.*

bou·quet *n.* **1** (boh·KAY) a bunch of cut flowers; hence, a compliment: *brickbats and ~s.* **2** (boo·KAY) an aroma, as of wine, brandy, etc.

bour·bon (BUR·bun) *n.* a whiskey distilled from a mash of corn, malt, and rye.

bour·geois (boor·ZHWA) *n. sing.* & *pl.* **1** a member of the middle class, esp. a property owner, shopkeeper, etc.; a capitalist. **2** one who is conventionally or selfishly middle-class or capitalistic in outlook. ***—adj.:*** *~ attitudes undermining the arts.* **—bour·geoi·sie** (boor·zhwah·ZEE) *n.* the bourgeois or capitalist class. **—bour·geois·i·fy** (–ZHWAH–) *v.* **-fies, -fied, -fy·ing:** *a ~d revolutionary;* **bour·geois·i·fi·ca·tion** (–CAY–) *n.*

bourse (BOORS) *n.* a money market or stock exchange, esp. in Europe.

bout (BOWT) *n.* a spell of some activity, fit of illness, etc.: *a boxing ~; a ~ of flu; a drinking ~.*

bou·tique (boo·TEEK) *n.* a small fashionable shop, owned by a **bou·ti·quier** (boo·tee·KYAY) *n.*

bou·ton·niere (boo·tn·EER) *n.* a flower to be worn in a buttonhole.

bo·vine (BOH–) *adj.* of or like an ox or cow; also, stupid: *a ~ laziness.* ***—n.:*** *contented ~s grazing in the fields.*

[1]bow *n.* the front part of a ship; opposed to STERN; ***adj.:*** *the ~ lines.* ***—v.*** bend the head or body, esp. as a sign of respect, submission, etc.: *~ down in worship; ~ed with age.* Also ***n.*** **—bow and scrape** be slavishly polite.

[2]bow (BOH) *n.* **1** a weapon for shooting arrows, made of a shaft curved by a string stretched from end to end; also, a light stick strung with horsehair for playing a violin, viola, etc. **2** a knot with loops: *Tie a ~ in her hair.* **3** something curved, esp. a rainbow. ***—v.*** **1** bend or curve. **2** play with a bow: *~ed his fiddle.*

bowd·ler·ize *v.* **-iz·es, -ized, -iz·ing** expurgate: *a ~d edition of Shakespeare.* **—bowd·ler·ism** *n.* **—bowd·ler·i·za·tion** (–ZAY–) *n.*

bow·el *n.* **1** an intestine: *He had a pain in his ~s.* **2 bowels** *pl.* deep interior: *down in the ~s of the coal mine.* **—bowel movement** an evacuation of the bowels.

bow·er *n.* a recess shaded by trees or vines.

[1]bowl (BOLE) *n.* a deep, rounded dish; hence, a bowl-shaped part *(the ~ of a smoking pipe)* or structure, as an amphitheatre.**—bowl·ful** *n.*

[2]bowl (BOLE) *n.* a heavy ball used in bowls, bowling, etc.; also, a throw of such a ball. ***—v.*** **1** play at bowls or bowling. **2** roll a ball. **—bowl along** move quickly along. **—bowl over** knock over, esp. with something rolled; hence, overwhelm, as with surprise.

bowl·der (BOLE–) *n.* same as BOULDER.

bow·legs (BOH–) *n.pl.* legs curved outward. **—bow·leg·ged** *adj.*

bowl·er (BOH·lur) *n.* **1** one who bowls. **2** *Brit.* a derby hat.
bow·line (BOH–) *n.* a knot used to prevent a loop from slipping.
bowl·ing (BOH–) *n.* any of several games in which a ball is rolled down a wooden lane **(bowling alley)** to knock over wooden pins. **—bowls** *n.* **1** bowling. **2** *Brit.* a game in which balls are rolled across a smooth lawn **(bowling green)** as close as possible to a target ball.
bow·man (BOH·mun) *n.* **-men** an archer. **—bow·sprit** *n.* a spar projecting from a sailing ship's bow. **—bow·string** (BOH–) *n.* a cord for an archer's bow. **—bow tie** a necktie that is worn knotted into a bow.
¹box *n.* any of several evergreen shrubs or trees with a close-grained wood; **box·wood** *n.*
²box *n.* **1** a usu. rectangular receptacle or container, often with a lid. **2** a marked-off or enclosed area, as for a witness or jury; also, a separate compartment of seats in a theater. **3** a booth or small shelter: *a sentry ~.* **4** a predicament. **—*v.*** put in a box; block or confine as if in a box.
³box *n.* a blow with the hand. **—*v.*** **1** strike with the hand. **2** engage in boxing.
box·car *n.* an enclosed freight car.
box·er *n.* **1** one who boxes; pugilist. **2** a sturdy, deep-chested dog with a short coat. **3 Boxer** a member of a Chinese secret society that started the anti-foreign **Boxer Rebellion** in 1900. **—boxer shorts** undershorts like a prizefighter's shorts.**—box·ing** *n.* the sport of fighting with one's fists.
box office a ticket office at a theater; hence, the proceeds from ticket sales.
boy *n.* **1** a male child. **2** *Informal.* a man, esp. one of a team: *out drinking with the ~s.* **3** a male servant. **—*interj.:*** *Oh ~! a new game!* **—boy·hood** *n.* **—boy·ish** *adj.:* **boy·ish·ly** *adv.*
boy·cott *v.* refuse to deal with as a sign of protest, to punish, or to persuade. ***n.:*** *a ~ of non-union products.*
boy·friend *n. Informal.* a male friend, esp. a girl's steady escort. **—boy scout** a member of the **Boy Scouts,** a club stressing outdoor life and helpfulness to others.
boy·sen·ber·ry *n.* **-ber·ries** a blackish-red berry, a cross between the loganberry, blackberry, and raspberry.
bp. bishop. **—b.p.** bills payable; boiling point.
bpl. birthplace.
B.P.O.E. Benevolent and Protective Order of Elks.
br. branch; brother; brown. **—Br** bromine. **—Br.** Britain; British. **—b.r.** bills receivable.
bra (BRAH) *n.* a brassiere. **—bra·less** *adj.: a ~ feminist.*
brace *n.* **1** something used to support, clamp, hold things in place, etc.: *He wore a ~ to support his weak leg; a ~ supporting the east wall.* **2 braces** *pl.* a wire device for straightening the teeth; also, *Brit.* suspenders. **3** either of the signs { } used to link words, numbers, etc. **4** a crank-shaped handle for holding and turning a drilling bit, i.e. **brace and bit.** **5** *pl.* **brace** a pair: *a ~ of pistols.* **—*v.* brac·es, braced, brac·ing** **1** strengthen or support, esp. with a brace. **2** fortify or prepare: *~ yourself for some bad news.* **3** invigorate: *~ing mountain air.* **—brace up** take heart. **—brace·let** *n.* an ornament worn around the arm or wrist: *a charm ~.*
bra·ce·ro (bruh·SAIR·oh) *n.* a Mexican allowed to work temporarily in the U.S.
brack·en *n.* a large common fern with a tough stem.
brack·et *n.* **1** any of several devices, usually L-shaped, used to support a shelf or balcony, wall lamp, etc.; also, a shelf so supported. **2** either of the signs [ ] used to enclose words, numbers, etc.; also, a brace or parenthesis. **3** a range within a graded scale: *a higher tax ~; the 12–18 age ~.* **—*v.*** **1** support with a bracket. **2** enclose, link, or set aside with or as if with brackets.
brack·ish *adj.* somewhat salty.
bract *n.* a modified leaf on the stalk or at the base of a flower.
brad *n.* a thin, small-headed nail: *flooring ~s.*
brae (BRAY) *n. Scot.* a sloping bank or hillside.
brag *v.* **brags, bragged, brag·ging** boast. Also ***n.*** **—brag·ger** or **brag·gart** *n.* **—brag·ga·do·ci·o** (brag·uh·DOH·shee·oh) *n.* a braggart; also, boasting or cockiness: *political ~ of the ruling party.*
Brah·man (–mun) *n.* **1** Also **Brah·ma,** the chief of the Hindu trinity and creator of the world. **2** Also **Brah·min,** a member of the highest Hindu caste. **3** usu. **Brahmin,** an upper-class member of the Establishment: *the Boston ~s.* **4** Also **Brah·ma,** a hump-backed breed of cattle related to the Indian zebu. **—Brah·man·ism** *n.* the Hindu religion and its social system; **Brah·man·ic** (–MAN·ic) *adj.* **—Brah·ma·pu·tra** (–POO·truh) a long river entering the Bay of Bengal at the Ganges delta. **—Brahmin** See BRAHMAN, *n.* 2, 3.
Brahms, Johannes. 1833–1897, a German composer.
braid *n.* an interwoven or plaited cord of three or more strands; hence, ornamental trim: *gold ~.* **—*v.:*** *to wear one's hair ~ed.*
Braille (BRAIL) *n.* a writing system for the blind that uses raised dots representing characters which are read by touching; also **braille.**
brain *n.* **1** the center of a vertebrate's nervous system, located in the cranium. **2** often **brains** *pl.* intelligence; **brain·y** *adj.;* **brain·less** *adj.* **3** an electronic computing or guidance device; also, *Slang.* an intelligent person. **—*v.*** hit over the head. **—have on the brain** think about constantly. **—rack** (or **cudgel**) **one's brains** think hard. **—brain·child** *n.*

Informal. a new idea or invention. —**brain death** death as determined by the permanent cessation of brain activity. —**brain drain** the emigration of scientists, professionals, etc. from a country; **brain-drain** *v.* of professionals, emigrate from one's country. —**brain·storm** *n.* a sudden inspired idea; **brain·storm·ing** *n.* pooling of such ideas by a problem-solving group. —**brain·wash** *v.* coercively indoctrinate (a person) into a radically new set of beliefs. —**brain wave** a rhythmic electric impulse in the brain; also, brainstorm.

braise *v.* **brais·es, braised, brais·ing** brown and simmer slowly: *~d beef.*

[1]**brake** *n.* **1** bracken. **2** a thicket, as of cane plants.

[2]**brake** *n.* a device for checking motion, esp. of a vehicle: *Put on the ~s.* —**brake·less** *adj.* —**brake fluid** the liquid used in a hydraulic brake. —**brake·man** *n.* **-men** an assistant to a train conductor or engineer. —**brake shoe** a curved block that presses against and slows down a wheel.

bram·ble *n.* a prickly shrub or vine of the rose family, as the blackberry or loganberry.

bran *n.* the coarse seed covering of cereals separated by sifting.

branch *n.* a part, division, or extension separate from the main body, as a limb of a tree, a tributary of a river, a part of a family with a common ancestor, or a local office or division of a company: *the various ~es of biology.* —***v.*** put out or separate into branches. —**branch off** leave the main path or part. —**branch out** undertake new activities: *a newspaper ~ing out into magazines.*

brand *n.* **1** a piece of burning or burnt wood; hence, an iron (**branding iron**) used red-hot to mark cattle, criminals, etc.; also, the mark so made. **2** a label or mark identifying a particular product; also, the product so marked, known by a **brand name.** **3** a characteristic kind; also, a stigma: *the ~ of Cain* (i.e. murderer). —***v.*** mark, esp. with a brand; also, stigmatize: *an experience forever ~ed on his memory; was ~ed a traitor.* —**bran·dish** *v.* wave around; display: *~ a sword.* —**brand-new** *adj.* absolutely new and unused.

bran·dy *n.* **-dies** a liquor distilled from wine or fermented fruit juices: *peach ~.* —***v.*** **-dies, -died, -dy·ing** treat or preserve with brandy: *~d cherries.*

brash *adj.* **1** hasty; rash. **2** impudently self-assertive: *a ~ young man.* —**brash·ly** *adv.* —**brash·ness** *n.*

Bra·sí·lia (bruh·ZEEL·yuh) capital of Brazil.

brass *n.* **1** an alloy of copper and either zinc or tin. **2** something made of brass, esp. a musical instrument (as a trumpet). **3** *Informal.* brazen impudence. **4** *Slang.* high-ranking officers, executives, etc. as a group, each of whom is a **brass hat.** —***adj.:*** *a ~ doorknob.*

bras·se·rie (–suh·REE) *n.* a restaurant serving food and beer.

brass hat See BRASS, *n.* 4.

bras·siere (bruh·ZEER) *n.* a woman's undergarment to support the breasts.

brass tacks *Informal.* essentials; basic facts. —**brass·y** *adj.* **1** of or like brass. **2** harsh and blaring; gaudy: *a ~ voice; a ~ hairdo.*

brat *n.* a child, esp. one who misbehaves. —**brat·ty** *adj.*

bra·va·do (bruh·VAH·doh) *n.* a false and swaggering courage. —**brave** *adj.* **1** courageous. **2** splendid: *~ banners.* —***n.*** an American Indian warrior. —***v.*** **braves, braved, brav·ing** challenge or endure with courage. —**brave·ly** *adv.* —**brav·er·y** or **brave·ness** *n.* —**bra·vo** (BRAH·voh) *interj.* & *n.* a shout of approval. —**bra·vu·ra** (bruh·VYOOR·uh) *n.* a display of bravery or brilliance, esp. outstanding musical technique.

brawl *n.* a noisy, disorderly fight or quarrel. —***v.:*** *~ing in barrooms.* —**brawl·er** *n.*

brawn *n.* big, powerful muscles; great strength: *The bully was all ~ and no brains.* —**brawn·y** *adj.* **brawn·i·er, -i·est.**

bray *n.* the noisy, harsh call of a donkey. —***v.:*** *Stop ~ing like an ass.*

braze *v.* **braz·es, brazed, braz·ing** solder with a hard metal, such as brass. —**braz·er** *n.*

bra·zen (BRAY–) *adj.* **1** of or like brass: *~ candlesticks.* **2** of sounds, blaring; brassy. **3** shameless; gaudy; impudent: *~ lies.* —**bra·zen·ly** *adv.* —**bra·zen·ness** *n.*

bra·zier (BRAY·zhur) *n.* **1** a brass-worker. **2** a metal container holding live coals, as for grilling meat.

Bra·zil (bruh·ZIL) the largest country in South America; 3,286,488 sq.mi. (8,511,965 km²); *cap.* Brasília. —**Bra·zil·ian** (–ZIL·yun) *adj.* & *n.* —**Brazil nut** the edible nut of a tropical South American tree.

Braz·za·ville (BRAH·zuh·vil) capital of the People's Republic of the Congo.

breach (BREECH) *n.* **1** a violation; breaking: *a* **breach of contract; breach of the peace** (i.e. public disturbance); **breach of promise** (esp. to marry someone). **2** a cessation of friendship. **3** a break, gap, or rift: *a ~ in the castle wall.* —***v.*** break; make a breach in.

bread (BRED) *n.* a food produced by baking a usu. leavened dough of flour mixed with milk or water; hence, food, one's livelihood, etc.: *worked hard for his daily ~.* —***v.*** coat with bread crumbs: *~ed veal cutlets.* —**break bread** eat; share a meal. —**bread and butter** one's livelihood. —**bread·bas·ket** *n.* **1** a grain-growing area. **2** *Slang.* stomach. —**bread·board** *n.* a board to knead or cut bread on; also, one for laying out experimental electric circuits. —**bread·fruit** *n.* the round, starchy fruit of a tropical tree, which resembles bread when baked. —**bread·stuff** *n.* grain, flour, etc. for making bread.

breadth (BREDTH) *n.* **1** width: *a* ~ *of 7″.* **2** scope; range: ~ *of interest.* **3** liberality: *He has a great* ~ *of mind about religion.*

bread•win•ner *n.* one whose earnings support a family.

break (BRAKE) *v.* **breaks, broke, bro•ken, break•ing** **1** separate into two or more pieces, esp. by force; burst; also, make or become inoperative; detach: *The baseball broke the window; a blister* ~*s; the radio is broken;* ~ *off a piece for me.* **2** disturb the order, continuity, etc. of: *soldiers* ~*ing step; a scrape that* ~*s the skin.* **3** pause; interrupt: *Let's* ~ *for lunch.* **4** reduce the force of: *The haystack broke his fall.* **5** make submissive or tame; ruin; collapse: ~ *a wild horse; Grief* ~*s his spirit; tortured until he broke.* **6** surpass; violate: *Don't* ~ *the speed limit;* ~ *a law;* ~ *a promise.* **7** appear, become, begin, change, etc. suddenly: *Dawn broke; a news story* ~*s; The teen-ager's voice broke.* **8** enter or pass by force: *The vault was broken into.* **—*n.*** **1** a breaking; something broken. **2** a pause or interruption. **3** a usu. sudden change, dash, etc.: *a* ~ *in the weather; make a* ~ *for it.* **4** *Informal.* a piece of luck, esp. an opportunity: *Give the kid a fair* ~. **—break•a•ble** *adj.* & *n.* **—break down** **1** become inoperative. **2** collapse, esp. into tears. **3** separate, usu. into simpler parts, esp. for analysis. **4** overcome. **—break in** **1** enter by force; **break-in** *n.* **2** prepare (a person or thing) for new duties, use, etc. **3** interrupt. **—break off** stop or discontinue (esp. a relationship) abruptly: *The speaker broke off in mid-sentence.* **—break out** **1** occur suddenly. **2** develop a rash. **3** escape. Hence **break•out** *n.* **—break up** **1** disperse; take to pieces. **2** end, esp. a relationship; **break•up** *n.* **3** *Informal.* erupt or make erupt into laughter; also, upset; lose composure. **—break•age** *n.* **1** a breaking; also, the amount broken. **2** the cost of loss by breaking. **—break•down** *n.* **1** failure: ~ *of machinery.* **2** collapse: *a nervous* ~. **3** analysis: *a* ~ *of population figures.* **—break•er** *n.* **1** one that breaks. **2** a wave that breaks into foam on a beach, reef, etc. **—break•fast** *n.* the morning meal; also ***v.*** **—break•front** *adj.* having a front with a projecting center portion: *a* ~ *cabinet;* also ***n.*** **—break•neck** *adj.* dangerous: *at* ~ *speed.* **—break•through** *n.* a sudden advance, as through obstacles or in knowledge or technology: *medical* ~*s.* **—break•wa•ter** *n.* a structure shielding a harbor, shore, etc. from heavy waves.

bream (BREEM, BRIM) *n.* **1** any of several carplike European fishes. **2** any of several freshwater sunfishes.

breast (BREST) *n.* **1** a mammary gland, esp. in a human: *a child at its mother's* ~. **2** the front of an upper human torso or the analogous part in animals: *a* ~ *of chicken.* **3** the seat of emotions: *Anger rose in his* ~*;* **make a clean breast of** make a complete confession of. **—breast•bone** *n.* the sternum. **—breast-feed** *v.* **-feeds, -fed, -feed•ing** feed (a baby) at the breast, not from a bottle. **—breast•plate** *n.* a piece of armor covering the breast. **—breast•stroke** *n.* a swimming stroke done prone in the water, with both arms sweeping to the sides and back to the breast. **—breast•work** *n.* a low temporary wall for defense.

breath (BRETH) *n.* **1** the act or power of breathing; also, the air inhaled and exhaled: *Take a deep* ~. **2** a slight breeze, esp. a fragrant one: *a* ~ *of summer.* **3** a whisper; also, a trace. **—out of breath** breathing quickly, as from exertion. **—take one's breath away** thrill; overawe. **—breath•less** *adj.:* ~ *with anticipation;* **breath•less•ly** *adv.* **—breathe** (BREEDH) *v.* **breathes, breathed, breath•ing** **1** take in and expel air: *a runner* ~*ing heavily.* **2** live: *while I yet* ~. **3** utter: *Don't* ~ *a word of this.* **4** rest. **—breath•er** *n.* **1** one that breathes. **2** *Informal.* a short rest. **—Breath•a•lyz•er** (BRETH·uh–) *Trademark.* a device that uses a breath sample to measure alcohol in the blood; also **breath•a•lyz•er** *n.* **—breath•tak•ing** *adj.* thrilling.

brec•ci•a (BRECH·ee·uh) *n.* a rock made up of sharp fragments bound together in a matrix.

bred *pt.* & *pp.* of BREED.

breech *n.* **1** the buttocks; **breech•cloth** *n.* a loincloth. **2** the part of a gun behind the bore or barrel. **3 breech•es** (BRICH–) *pl.* trousers, esp. knee-length ones: *riding* ~*es.*

breed *v.* **breeds, bred, breed•ing** **1** produce offspring; hence, cause; originate: *Poverty* ~*s crime; Disease* ~*s in unsanitary conditions.* **2** raise; rear: *born and bred in this county.* **3** mate, esp. to improve or change the stock: *Williams* ~*s fine hunting dogs.* **4** produce more fissionable material than is used, as in a **breed•er reactor.** **—*n.*** a kind, sort, etc.; hence, a type of animal, plant, etc. produced by controlled breeding: *a new* ~ *of horse.* **—breed•ing** *n.* **1** reproduction; also, ancestry. **2** upbringing; also, good manners, politeness, etc.

breeze *n.* **1** a light wind: *a cool* ~. **2** *Informal.* a simple task. **—*v.* breez•es, breezed, breez•ing** go quickly and easily: ~*d into the room.* **—breeze•way** *n.* a covered, usu. open-sided connecting passage, as between a house and garage. **—breez•y** *adj.* with breezes blowing: *a* ~ *day; a gossip columnist's* ~ (i.e. light and easy) *style;* **breez•i•ly** *adv.;* **breez•i•ness** *n.*

Bre•men (BREM·un) a West German port.

breth•ren *Archaic* & *Formal pl.* of BROTHER.

Bre•ton (BRETN) *n.* an inhabitant or native of Brittany; also, its Celtic language. **—*adj.:*** *fine* ~ *cuisine.*

bre•vet (bri·VET) *n.* a commission to a higher rank without an increase in pay. **—*v.* -vets, -vet•(t)ed, -vet•(t)ing. —bre•vet•cy** *n.* **-cies.**

bre•vi•ar•y (BREE·vee·er·ee) *n.* **-ar•ies** a book containing the required daily prayers, hymns, etc. for some clerics.

brev·i·ty *n.* shortness of time or expression: "*~ is the soul of wit.*"

brew *v.* **1** prepare (tea, beer, etc.) by steeping, boiling, etc. **2** be forming: *Trouble is ~ing.* ***—n.*** something brewed, esp. beer. **—brew·er** *n.* one who brews beer, ale, etc.; **brew·er·y** *n.* **-er·ies** a place where beer or ale is brewed.

Brezh·nev (BREZH·nef), **Leonid.** born 1906, general secretary of the Soviet Communist Party and president of the U.S.S.R.

bri·ar (BRY·ur) *n.* **1** same as BRIER. **2** a pipe made of brier root.

bribe *v.* **bribes, bribed, brib·ing** corrupt, influence, or suborn with a bribe: *a lawyer caught ~ing the jury.* ***—n.*** a gift, esp. of money, given to influence someone's conduct improperly. **—brib·er·y** (BRY·buh·ree) *n.*

bric-a-brac *n.* small ornamental knickknacks.

brick *n.* a rectangular building block of baked clay; something of this shape: *a ~ of ice cream.* **—v.** pave or construct with bricks: *~ed up the old doorway.* **—brick·bat** *n.* a piece of brick thrown as a weapon; hence, an insult: *The speech received both bouquets and ~s.* **—brick·lay·er** *n.* one who builds with bricks; **brick·lay·ing** *n.*

brid·al (BRY·dl) *n.* & *adj.* (of) a wedding: *a ~ bouquet;* **bridal suite** a suite of hotel rooms for newlyweds. **—bride** *n.* a woman recently or about to be married; *masc.* **bride·groom.** **—brides·maid** *n.* a bride's female attendant.

[1]**bridge** (BRIJ) *n.* **1** a structure that spans and provides passage across an obstructing depression, esp. a waterway; also, something resembling this in form (as the upper, bony part of the nose or a piece of wood that raises the strings on a violin, cello, etc.) or in function: *Faith is the ~ from despair to salvation;* **burn one's bridges (behind one)** leave oneself no way back. **2** a raised platform on a ship, from which one commands. **3** a partial denture attached to one's natural teeth. ***—v.*** **bridg·es, bridged, bridg·ing** join with, be, or build a bridge: *~ the gap;* **bridge·a·ble** *adj.*

[2]**bridge** *n.* a four-handed card game with two common forms, CONTRACT BRIDGE and AUCTION BRIDGE.

bridge·head *n.* a fortified advance position to protect troops as they cross, land, or invade. **—Bridge·port** a city in Connecticut. **—Bridge·town** capital of Barbados. **—bridge·work** *n.* one or more dental bridges.

bri·dle (BRY·dl) *n.* the harness for a horse's head; hence, a control, curb, etc. ***—v.*** **-dles, -dled, -dling** **1** : *a ~d pony; ~ your enthusiasm.* **2** raise the head with the chin tucked in, as a sign of scorn, anger, etc. **—bridle path** a path for horseback riding.

brief (BREEF) *adj.* **1** short in length or duration: *a ~ letter.* **2** concise; curt: *a ~ reply.* — ***n.*** a condensed summary, esp. of a legal case. ***—v.*** summarize; give essential information or instructions to, as at a **brief·ing** *n.* a meeting for this purpose. **—brief·ly** *adv.* **—brief·ness** *n.* **—brief·case** *n.* a rectangular case, often of leather, for books, papers, etc. **—briefs** *pl.* men's short, closefitting underpants.

bri·er (BRY·ur) *n.* **1** a kind of heath whose roots are used for tobacco pipes. **2** any plant with a thorny, woody stem, as the blackberry and the wild rose. **—bri·er·y** *adj.*

brig *n.* **1** a square-rigged ship with two masts. **2** a ship's prison.

bri·gade (bri·GADE) *n.* **1** a military unit of two or more battalions or regiments. **2** a group with special tasks or duties: *Call the fire ~.* **—brig·a·dier** (brig·uh·DEER) **general** an officer ranking just above a colonel.

brig·and (BRIG·und) *n.* a member of a band of outlaws or robbers; **brig·and·age** *n.* **—brig·an·tine** (BRIG·un·teen) *n.* a ship with square-rigged foremast and fore-and-aft-rigged mainmast.

bright (BRITE) *adj.* **1** shining with much light: *a ~ star.* **2** vividly colored: *a ~ green hat.* **3** famous; cheerful; auspicious; intelligent: *a ~ prospect; a ~ young girl.* Also ***adv.*** **—bright·ly** *adv.;* **bright·ness** *n.* **—bright·en** *v.: Her face ~ed at the news; The sun ~ed the landscape;* **bright·en·er** *n.*

Brigh·ton (BRY·tun) a resort city in S.E. England.

bril·liant (BRIL·yunt) *adj.* exceptionally bright, vivid, splendid, intelligent, talented, famous, etc.: *~ sunshine; ~ fall colors; a ~ maneuver; a ~ young composer.* **—bril·liant·ly** *adv.* **—bril·liance** or **bril·lian·cy** *n.* **—bril·lian·tine** (BRIL·yun·teen) *n.* an oily hair dressing.

brim *n.* **1** the edge or rim of a cup, bowl, etc. **2** the projecting rim of a hat. ***—v.*** **brims, brimmed, brim·ming** be full to the brim. **—brim·ful** *adj.* completely full. **—brim·less** *adj.: a ~ hat.*

brim·stone *n.* sulfur: *The preacher called down fire and ~.*

brin·dle(d) (-dl, -dld) *adj.* tawny or gray with darker markings: *a ~d lion.*

brine *n.* salt-saturated water; the ocean. **—brin·y** *adj.: the ~ deep.*

bring *v.* **brings, brought** (BRAWT), **bring·ing** **1** carry or cause to come along (with): *~ your gun with you; Don't ~ a friend.* **2** cause; cause to appear, come to a certain place or condition, etc.: *The sun ~s warmth; brought to grief by fate; He ~s a charge* (before the court). **3** persuade: *couldn't ~ himself to leave.* **4** sell for: *What will it ~ on the open market?* **—bring about** cause. **—bring forth** produce; give birth to. **—bring off** do successfully. **—bring out** cause to appear. **—bring to** (or **around**) revive from unconsciousness. **—bring up** **1** raise; rear. **2** vomit. **3** introduce (a fact, topic, etc.).

brink *n.* the edge of a steep drop; hence, verge: *on the ~ of financial collapse.* **—brink·man·ship** *n.* the strategy of pushing a risky situation to the crisis point.

bri·o (BREE·oh) *n.* vigor; liveliness.

bri·oche (bree·OHSH) *n.* a rich, round, yeast-leavened roll.

bri·quet(te) (bri·KET) *n.* a small block of compressed coal dust, sawdust, etc. used as fuel, kindling, etc.: *charcoal ~s.*

Bris·bane (BRIZ·bain, –bun) seaport and capital of Queensland state, Australia.

brisk *adj.* **1** quick; active: *a ~ walk; a ~ sale.* **2** sharp; invigorating: *a ~ breeze.* —**brisk·ly** *adv.;* **brisk·ness** *n.*

bris·ket (BRIS·kit) *n.* the meat from an animal's breast.

bris·ling *n.* a sprat, esp. canned as a sardine.

bris·tle (BRISL) *n.* a short stiff hair, as on an animal, a brush, etc. —***v.*** **-tles, -tled, -tling** **1** of hair, stand on end. **2** show fear, anger, hostility, etc.: *~ing with indignation.* **3** be thick with: *a plan ~ing with objections.*

Bris·tol ((BRIS·tl) a seaport in S.W. England.

Brit. Britain; British. —**Brit·ain** (BRITN) same as GREAT BRITAIN.—**Bri·tan·nia** (–TAN–) a female figure symbolizing Britain. —**britannia (metal)** a pewterlike alloy of tin, copper, and antimony. —**Bri·tan·nic** *adj.* British.

britch·es *n.pl. Informal.* breeches.

Brit·i·cism *n.* a characteristically British word or idiom. —**Brit·ish** *adj.* of Britain, its people, or the Commonwealth. —***n.*** **1 the British** the people of Britain. **2** the English language as spoken in Britain; also called **British English.** —**British Columbia** the westernmost Canadian province; 366,255 sq.mi. (948,596 km^2); *cap.* Victoria. —**British Commonwealth (of Nations)** former name of the COMMONWEALTH OF NATIONS. —**British Honduras** former name of BELIZE. —**British Isles** Great Britain, Ireland, and nearby islands. —**British thermal unit** the amount of heat required to raise 1 lb. of water through 1°F; about 252 cal. or 1,054 joules. —**Brit·on** (BRITN) *n.* one of the pre-Anglo-Saxon people of Great Britain; also, a native of Britain.

brit·tle (BRITL) *adj.* hard but very easily broken, as thin glass, ice, bones, etc. —***n.*** a brittle candy with nuts: *peanut ~.* —**brit·tle·ness** *n.*

bro. *pl.* **bros.** brother.

broach (BROHCH) *n.* a tool for tapping a cask; also, a tool for finishing a drilled hole. —***v.*** **1** tap (a cask); enlarge and finish (a hole). **2** bring up (a subject): *a good time to ~ the topic.*

broad (BRAWD) *adj.* **1** laterally wide; of wide scope: *a ~ selection.* **2** expansive; clear: *the ~ ocean; in ~ daylight.* **3** obvious: *a ~ accent; a ~ hint.* **4** ribald: *~ humor.* **5** liberal, tolerant, etc.: *has ~ views on religion.* **6** general: *the ~ outline.* —***n.*** *Slang.* a woman, esp. one disliked. —**broad·ly** *adv.* —**broad·ness** *n.* —**broad·band** *adj.* having a wide range of frequencies; hence, general: *~ radio systems; ~ objectives.* —**broad·brush** *adj.* rough; general: *~ estimates.* —**broad·cast** *v.* **-casts,** *pt.* & *pp.* **-cast(·ed), -cast·ing** **1** transmit widely, esp. by radio or television. **2** scatter (seed) widely. —***n.*** an act of broadcasting; a broadcast program: *We interrupt this ~. . . .;* ***adj.:*** *~ journalism; ~ sowing;* ***adv.:*** *seed sown ~;* **broad·cast·ing** *n.* & *adj.;* **broad·cast·er** *n.* —**broad·cloth** *n.* a smooth, closely woven cloth, usu. of cotton or wool, originally in double width, used for shirts, pajamas, etc. —**broad·en** *v.* make or become broad(er): *Reading ~s the mind; The river ~s here.* —**broad jump** same as LONG JUMP. —**broad·loom** *adj.* woven on a wide loom: *~ carpet;* ***n.:*** *wall-to-wall ~.* —**broad-mind·ed** *adj.* tolerant; unprejudiced; **broad-mind·ed·ly** *adv.;* **broad·mind·ed·ness** *n.* —**broad·side** *n.* **1** the side of a ship above the water; also, a salvo of all the guns on one side; hence, a barrage of criticism or abuse. **2** a large, usu. folded sheet of paper printed, esp. if across the fold, as for political tracts, advertising, etc.; also **broad·sheet·** —**broad-spec·trum** *adj.* effective against many things: *a ~ pesticide.* —**broad·sword** *n.* a wide-bladed slashing sword. —**broad·tail** *n.* the shiny, rippled pelt of a kind of Asian lamb, esp. of one prematurely born. —**Broad·way** a New York street, center of the city's theater and entertainment district.

bro·cade (broh·CADE) *n.* a rich fabric with a raised design, of gold, silver, etc.

broc·co·li (BROC·uh·lee) *n.* a vegetable related to the cauliflower, having many small flower heads.

bro·chette (broh·SHET) *n.* a skewer for roasting or broiling.

bro·chure (broh·SHOOR) *n.* a pamphlet.

brogue (BROHG) *n.* **1** a rough, sturdy, ankle-high work shoe; also **bro·gan** (BROH·gun). **2** a stout oxford shoe. **3** a regional pronunciation, esp. an Irish accent.

broi·der *v.* embroider. —**broi·der·y** *n.*

broil *v.* cook by direct exposure to flame or great heat. —**broil·er** *n.* **1** a pan or grill for broiling. **2** a young chicken suitable for broiling.

broke *pt.* of BREAK; ***adj.*** *Informal.* penniless. —**bro·ken** (BROH·kun) *pp. of* BREAK; ***adj.*** **1** uneven: *~ ground.* **2** crushed; beaten: *His pride was ~.* **3** disturbed, esp. by divorce: *a ~ marriage; a ~ home.* **4** incorrectly spoken: *answered in ~ French.* —**bro·ken·ly** *adv.* —**bro·ken·ness** *n.* —**bro·ken-down** *adj.* worn out; useless: *a ~ car.* —**bro·ken-heart·ed** *adj.: a jilted lover, sad and ~.*

bro·ker (BROH–) *n.* an agent for buying, selling, making contracts, etc. —**bro·ker·age** (–ij) *n.* a broker's fee or business.

bro·mide (BROH–) *n.* **1** a salt of bromine, esp. **potassium bromide,** a sedative. **2** a dull, obvious remark or idea; also, its author; **bro·mid·ic** (–MID–) *adj.* trite. —**bro·mine** (BROH·meen) *n.* a foul-smelling, nonmetallic liquid element used esp. in antiknock gasoline.

bronch(o)- *comb.form.* having to do with the bronchi.—**bron•chi•tis** (–KYE–) *n.* inflammation of the bronchi; **bron•chit•ic** (–KIT–) *adj.* —**bron•chus** (–kus) *n., pl.* **-chi** (–kye) either of the two branches of the trachea that lead to the lungs; **bron•chi•al** (–kee·ul) *adj.:* ~ *pneumonia;* **bron•chi•al•ly** *adv.*

bron•co (BRONG·koh) *n.* in the West, a half-tamed or wild horse. —**bron•co•bust•er** *n.* a cowboy who tames broncos.

bron•to•saur (–tuh·sor) or **bron•to•sau•rus** (–SOR·us) *n.* **-saurs, -sau•rus•es** or **-sau•ri** (–rye) an herbivorous dinosaur up to 80 ft. (24.384 m) long.

Bronx, the a borough of New York City. —**Bronx cheer** *Slang.* a noise of disapproval; raspberry.

bronze (BRONZ) *n.* **1** an alloy of copper and tin; also, something, esp. a work of art, made of this. **2** a yellowish- or reddish-brown. —***adj.*** of or like bronze. —***v.*** **bron•zes, bronzed, bronz•ing:** *a sun-* ~*d beachcomber.* —**Bronze Age** a stage of human culture marked by the use of bronze weapons and tools.

brooch (BROHCH, BROOCH) *n.* an ornamental pin worn on a woman's dress.

brood (BRUDE) *n.* the offspring in one family, esp. baby birds hatched at one time: *seven children in the Jones's noisy* ~. —***v.*** **1** hatch (eggs) by sitting on them; hover protectively over, as a mother hen. **2** ponder or worry (about). —***adj.*** kept for breeding: *a* ~ *mare.* —**brood•er** *n.* **1** one that broods. **2** a heated enclosure for raising chicks without a hen. —**brood•y** *adj.* ready or inclined to brood: *a* ~ *hen; a* ~ *poetic soul.*

¹brook *v.* put up with: *The teacher* ~*ed no disobedience.*

²brook *n.* a small stream: *babbling* ~*s.* —**brook•let** *n.* a small brook. —**brook trout** a speckled trout of E. North America prized as a game fish.

Brook•lyn (–lin) a borough of New York City.

broom *n.* **1** a brushlike tool with a long handle **(broom•stick),** used for sweeping: *"A new* ~ *sweeps clean"* (i.e. A new administration is ruthless). **2** a long-stemmed bush of the pea family.

bros. brothers.

broth *n.* a clear stock left after boiling meat or vegetables in water: *beef* ~.

broth•el (BROTH·ul) *n.* a prostitute's place of business; whorehouse.

broth•er (BRUDH·ur) *n.* **1** a son of the same parents (as another person). **2** a fellow man; also, a fellow member of any group; esp., a fellow black. **3** a lay member of a religious group: ~*John.* —**broth•er-in-law** *n.* **brothers-in-law** **1** one's spouse's brother; the husband of one's spouse's sister. **2** one's sister's husband. —**broth•er•hood** *n.* **1** a brotherly bond or feeling. **2** an organization of people who share a belief, occupation, etc.: *an Indian* ~. —**broth•er•ly** *adj.* of or like a brother; kindly: ~ *love;* **broth•er•li•ness** *n.*

brougham (BROOM, BROO·um) *n.* a closed carriage or early type of limousine with an open driver's seat.

brought *pt.* & *pp.* of BRING.

brou•ha•ha (broo·HAH·hah) *n.* an uproar.

brow *n.* **1** the ridge over the eyes; an eyebrow; the forehead: *with wrinkled* ~. **2** the edge of a cliff, esp. if overhanging. —**brow•beat** *v.* **-beats, -beat, -beat•en, -beat•ing** intimidate, esp. by harsh looks or speech: *a* ~*en clerk.*

brown *n.* the color of chocolate. —***adj.*** of the color brown; tanned. —***v.*** make or become brown, esp. by cooking. —**Brown, John.** 1800–1859, an American abolitionist executed for treason. —**brown•ish** *adj.* —**brown-bag** *v.* **-bags, -bagged, -bag•ging** *Informal.* carry one's own food or liquor to a restaurant, club, etc. or carry a lunch to work or school, esp. in a brown-paper bag; **brown-bag•ging** *n.;* **brown-bag•ger** *n.* —**brown•ie** (–ee) *n.* **1** a helpful little elf. **2** **Brownie** a junior member of the Girl Scouts, aged 7 to 9. **3** a flat, rich, usu. chocolate cake with nuts. —**Brown•ing, Elizabeth Barrett.** 1806–61, wife of **Robert Browning,** 1812–89, both English poets. —**brown•out** *n.* a partial reduction of lighting during a power shortage. —**Brown Power** a movement for greater rights for Mexican Americans. —**brown•stone** *n.* a reddish-brown sandstone; also, a building faced with this.

browse (BROWZ) *v.* **brows•es, browsed, brows•ing** examine or peruse (books, merchandise, etc.) in a casual way: *Come in and* ~. —***n.:*** *Tender shoots, shrubs, and twigs are* ~ *for cattle; a book good for only a* ~.

Brue•ghel (BROOG·ul), **Pieter.** 1520?–69, Dutch painter.

bru•in (BROO·in) *n.* a bear.

bruise (BROOZ) *n.* an injury that discolors the skin but does not break it. —***v.*** **bruis•es, bruised, bruis•ing** **1** inflict or suffer a bruise; also, dent; damage the surface of: *a* ~*d apple.* **2** crush, as in a mortar. **3** hurt the feelings of: *a* ~*d ego.* —**bruis•er** *n. Informal.* a big, strong, pugnacious man.

bruit (BROOT) *v.* spread or circulate (a rumor, story, etc.): *news* ~*ed about.*

brunch *n.* a late-morning meal combining breakfast and lunch; also ***v.***

Bru•nei (broo·NYE) a sultanate in N.W. Borneo; 2,226 sq.mi. (5,765 km²); *cap.* Bandar Seri Begawan.

bru•net (broo·NET) *adj.* dark in color; having dark hair and complexion; also ***n;*** *fem.* **bru•nette** *adj.* & *n.*

brunt *n.* the hardest or greatest part: *receive the* ~ *of an attack.*

brush *n.* **1** an area covered with low, rough shrubs and small trees; also, broken or cut branches; brushwood: *a ~ fence; a ~ fire.* **2** any of several utensils consisting of bristles fastened in a handle, used for applying shaving cream, paint, etc. or for cleaning teeth, clothing, hair, floors, etc. **3** an animal's bushy tail. **4** a light touch, encounter, or skirmish: *His heart attack was a ~ with death.* **5** an electrical contact for a revolving part, as in a motor or generator. **—v. 1** clean, arrange (hair), or spread with a brush; wipe away. **2** graze; touch lightly. **—brush·off** *n. Slang.* an abrupt, cold rejection: *Betty always gave him the ~;* **v. brush off. —brush up on** refresh one's knowledge of. **—brush·wood** *n.* a thicket; also, cut or broken branches of trees.

brusque (BRUSK) *adj.* impolitely curt and abrupt: *a ~ manner.* **—brusque·ly** *adv.* **—brusque·ness** *n.*

Brus·sels (BRUSLZ) capital of Belgium. **—Brussels sprouts** the small, cabbagelike heads that grow on the erect stalk of a vegetable of the mustard family.

bru·tal (BROO·tl) *adj.* cruel; savage; also, coarse; unrefined: *~ murders;* **bru·tal·ly** *adv.;* **bru·tal·i·ty** (–TAL–) *n.* **-ties. —bru·tal·ism** *n.* a style of architecture using massive, crude shapes to suggest brute strength; **bru·tal·ist** *n.* & *adj.* **—bru·tal·ize** (BROO–) *v.* **-iz·es, -ized, -iz·ing** make brutal; treat brutally: *~d by hard work and poverty.* **—brute** (BROOT) *n.* an unreasoning animal; hence, a coarse, cruel, or unthinking person. **—adj. 1** unthinking; not rational: *~ force; a ~ beast; the* **brute** (i.e. harsh, true, but unexplained) **fact. 2** beastlike; cruel; stupid. **—brut·ish** *adj.* savage: *the primitive's ~ condition;* **brut·ish·ly** *adv.*

b.s. balance sheet; bill of sale. **—B.S.** or **B.Sc.** Bachelor of Science.

B.S.A. Boy Scouts of America.

bskt. basket.

btry. battery.

B.t.u. or **B.T.U.** British thermal unit.

bu. bureau; bushel.

bub·ble (BUBL) *n.* **1** a roundish, enclosed, usu. hollow object, as a body of gas in a liquid or solid or air surrounded by a thin film. **2** an unrealistic idea or plan. **3** something bubble-shaped, as a kind of woman's hairdo or a car with a **bub·ble·top,** a transparent dome top. **4** bubbletop. **—v. bub·bles, bub·bled, bub·bling** make or sound like bubbles. **—bubble gum** chewing gum that can be blown into bubbles. **—bub·bly** (BUB·lee) *adj.: ~ champagne; ~ good spirits.*

bu·bo (BEW·boh) *n.* **-boes** a swollen lymph gland, esp. in the groin or armpit, a symptom of the acute contagious disease **bu·bon·ic** (bew·BON·ic) **plague.**

buc·ca·neer (buck·uh·NEER) *n.* a freebooter; pirate.

Bu·chan·an (bew·CAN·un), **James.** 1791–1868, 15th U.S. President (1857–61).

Bu·char·est (boo·cuh·REST) capital of Romania.

buck *n.* **1** a full-grown male animal, esp. a deer. **2** a vigorous young man. **3** *Slang.* a dollar. **4** an act of bucking. **—adj.** male: *a ~ rabbit.* **—v. 1** of a horse, leap and plunge to throw the rider off. **2** resist: *You can't ~ the system.* **3** charge with the head lowered. **—buck for** *Informal.* strive hard for. **—buck up** cheer up. **—pass the buck** *Informal.* pass on responsibility. **—buck·board** *n.* a four-wheeled buggy on a light plank body.

buck·et *n.* **1** a pail; hence, the amount it holds, also called a **buck·et·ful. 2** the scoop of a dredge, steam shovel, etc. **—kick the bucket** *Slang.* die. **—bucket seat** a seat with a rounded back, for one passenger.

buck·eye *n.* a kind of horse chestnut. **—buck fever** *Informal.* the nervousness of a new hunter seeing game for the first time.

buck·le *n.* **1** a device for fastening a strap or belt. **2** a wrinkle, bend, etc. **—v. -les, -led, -ling 1** secure with a buckle: *~ up your seat belt.* **2** fold, warp, wrinkle, etc., esp. under heat or pressure. **—buckle down** start working very hard. **—buckle under** yield to pressure. **—buck·ler** *n.* a small round shield.

buck-pass·er *n.* one who passes the buck.

buck·ram (–rum) *n.* a heavy, sometimes two-ply fabric, stiffened with starch or glue, used in clothing and bookbinding.

buck·saw *n.* a two-handed wood saw set in a frame. **—buck·shot** *n.* a large size of lead shot. **—buck·skin** *n.* a soft, strong, yellowish-gray leather; **adj.:** *~ leggings.* **—buck·thorn** *n.* any of several related small trees or shrubs. **—buck·tooth** *n.* a projecting front tooth; **buck·toothed** *adj.* **—buck·wheat** *n.* a plant with heart-shaped leaves, grown for its three-sided seeds which are used as grain.

bu·col·ic (bew·COL·ic) *adj.* of or having to do with shepherds or rural life: *~ poetry; ~ pleasures.*

bud *n.* **1** a sprouting plant part containing immature leaves, flowers, etc. **2** a partly opened flower: *rose ~s.* **3** something incipient and immature. **—v. buds, bud·ded, bud·ding** put out buds; hence, begin to develop: *a ~ing scholar.* **—nip in the bud** stop (something) at an early stage.

Bu·da·pest (BOO·duh–) capital of Hungary.

Bud·dha (BOOD·uh) the title of Siddhartha Gautama (563?–483? B.C.), an Indian sage who founded **Bud·dhism,** a religion that teaches the way to NIRVANA. **—Bud·dhist** *adj.* & *n.: a ~ monk.*

bud·dy (BUD·ee) *n.* **bud·dies** *Informal.* a companion or friend.

budge *v.* **budg·es, budged, budg·ing** move the slightest bit: *Stay here and don't ~! The stubborn mule couldn't be ~d.*

budg·er·i·gar (BUJ·uh·ree·gahr) *n.* an Australian parakeet with green, yellow, and blue feathers; also **budg·ie** *Informal.*

budg·et *n.* **1** a statement of expected expenditure and income: *a government's annual ~.* **2** an allocated sum. **3** a limited amount of spending money: *I can't afford luxuries; I'm on a ~;* ***adj.*** cheap: *~ meals; a ~ store.* **—*v.*** make a budget; plan or allot as if by a budget: *~ed $6 for transportation; A busy man must ~ his time.*

budg·ie (BUJ·ee) *n. Informal.* budgerigar.

Bue·nos Ai·res (bway·nus·AIR·eez) capital of Argentina.

buff *n.* **1** a block or wheel for polishing covered with soft leather, velvet, etc. **2** a brownish yellow. **3** *Informal.* bare skin: *in the ~.* **4** *Informal.* a devotee or enthusiast: *a jazz ~.* **—*adj.*** of the color buff. **—*v.*** polish, esp. with a buff.

buf·fa·lo (BUF·uh·loh) *n.* any of several wild oxen, as the domesticated **water buffalo** of Asia, the **Cape buffalo** of Africa, and the North American bison. **—Buf·fa·lo** (BUF·uh·loh) a city on E. Lake Erie in New York.

buff·er *n.* **1** one that buffs. **2** something that lessens impact, shock, acidity, etc.; **buffer state** a neutral country between two large rivals.

¹buf·fet (BUF·it) *v.* strike, drive, or toss about: *an airplane ~ed by heavy winds; a man ~ed by fate.* **—*n.*** a blow, esp. with the hand.

²buf·fet (buh·FAY) *n.* **1** a sideboard. **2** a meal with food set out on a table or sideboard for guests to serve themselves.

buf·foon (buh·FOON) *n.* a clown; an habitual joker. **—buf·foon·er·y** *n.* **—buf·foon·ish** *adj.: coarse, ~ humor.*

bug *n.* **1** any insect or insectlike animal, esp. a pest of the order Hemiptera: *bed~s; June ~s.* **2** *Informal.* a disease-causing germ or virus: *There is a flu ~ going around.* **3** *Informal.* an enthusiast: *a ham radio ~.* **4** *Informal.* a fault or problem in a machine or process: *working the ~s out of his invention.* **5** a hidden microphone for monitoring conversations. **—*v.*** **bugs, bugged, bug·ging** **1** *Slang.* pester; annoy. **2** of eyes, stick out; **bug-eyed** *adj.* **3** conceal a microphone in; overhear with a bug. **—bug·bear** *n.* **1** a bogey; also **bug·a·boo.** **2** a persistent annoyance.

bug·gy (BUG·ee) *n.* **bug·gies** a light, usu. four-wheeled carriage.

bu·gle (BEW·gl) *n.* a small, trumpetlike, usu. valveless brass instrument; also ***v.*** **-gles, -gled, -gling.** **—bu·gler** *n.*

build (BILD) *v.* **builds, built, build·ing** **1** construct (dwellings, barns, shops, etc.): *Army engineers ~ing bridges.* **2** base; accept as a basis. **3** develop; begin and expand: *~ing for the future.* **—*n.*** physical makeup: *a heavy ~.* **—build·er** *n.* **—build·ing** *n.* **1** the act or trade of building. **2** a house, barn, factory, etc.; a structure that has walls and a roof. **—build up** **1** expand; increase, accumulate; develop with buildings: *~ing up a supply of cash; a heavily* **built-up** *part of the city.* **2** cause to seem better: *~ing up a new product.* Hence **build·up** *n.* **—built-in** *adj.* included as an integral part: *rooms with ~ bookshelves; a ~ drive for profits.*

Bu·jum·bu·ra (BOO·joom·boor·uh) capital of Burundi.

bulb *n.* **1** a roundish underground bud from which a plant, as a tulip, onion, etc. grows; also, any of these plants. **2** something with a rounded, bulging end, as the glass shell of an incandescent lamp *(light ~): the ~ of a syringe.* **—bul·bous** (–bus) *adj.* having bulbs or shaped like a bulb: *a ~ nose.*

Bul·gar·i·a (–GAIR·ee·uh) a country on the Black Sea in S.E. Europe; 42,823 sq.mi. (110,-912 km²); *cap.* Sofia. **—Bul·gar·i·an** *adj.* & *n.*

bulge (BULJ) *n.* a protruding or swollen part: *~s of fat.* **—*v.*** **bulg·es, bulged, bulg·ing:** *a sack ~ing with toys.*

bulk *n.* **1** volume, quantity, mass, etc., esp. if great; **in bulk** in large, often unpackaged lots. **2** Also **bulk·age** (–ij), indigestible matter in the intenstines that stimulates elimination. **3 the bulk of** the greater part of. **—*v.*** be large or important. **—bulk·head** *n.* a vertical partition, esp. one dividing a ship or airplane into compartments: *a fireproof ~.* **—bulk·y** *adj.* **bulk·i·er, -i·est** having bulk; also, large and clumsy: *a ~* (i.e. relatively heavy) *sweater.*

bull. bulletin.

bull (BOOL) *n.* **1** an adult male bovine; also, the adult male of the elephant, walrus, etc. **2** an investor who buys stocks, bonds, etc. expecting price rises. **3** a papal decree. **4** *Slang.* nonsense; **shoot the bull** talk idly. **—*adj.*** **1** male: *a ~ calf.* **2** bull-like. **3** characterized by rising prices: *a ~ market.* **—a bull in a china shop** a clumsy or tactless person. **—take the bull by the horns** grapple boldly with a difficult situation. **—bull·dog** *n.* a short-haired dog with a pug nose and strong jaws; ***v.*** wrestle (a steer) to the ground by the horns. **—bull·doze** *v.* **-doz·es, -dozed, -doz·ing** push, clear, gouge, etc. with a bulldozer; hence, force or intimidate: *~d into signing a petition.* **—bull·doz·er** *n.* a heavy tractor having a wide frontal blade for digging, pushing earth, grading, etc.

bul·let (BULL·it) *n.* a small metal projectile fired from a gun. **—bul·let·proof** *adj.: a ~ vest for protection.*

bul·le·tin (BULL·uh·tn) *n.* **1** an announcement, esp. of news, public interest, etc.: *a late news ~.* **2** a periodical report, esp. for a society, group, etc. **—bulletin board** a board to post notices on.

bull·fight *n.* a spectacle in which men, or **bull·fight·ers,** provoke and then kill a fierce bull; **bull·fight·ing** *n.* **—bull·finch** *n.* an Old World songbird with a heavy bill and a black head. **—bull·frog** *n.* a large frog whose male has a deep croak. **—bull·head** *n.* **1** any of several North American catfishes. **2** one who is unthinkingly stubborn; **bull·head·ed** *adj.: ~ opposition.*

bul·lion (BULL·yun) *n.* gold or silver, esp. in ingots.

bull·ish *adj.* **1** bull-like. **2** expecting, having, or causing a price rise: *~ speculators;* **bull·ish·ness** *n.* **—bull·ock** (BULL·uk) *n.* a castrated bull. **—bull pen** an area where relief pitchers practice during a baseball game. **—bull session** an informal, unstructured discussion. **—bull's-eye** *n.* a circle marking the center of a target; a shot hitting this.

bul·ly (BULL·ee) *n.* **bul·lies** one who threatens or is cruel to a weaker person. **—*v.* bul·lies, bul·lied, bul·ly·ing** intimidate; be a bully. **—*adj.* & *interj.*** first-rate.

bul·rush (BULL–) *n.* any of several tall sedges or reeds that grow in marshes.

bul·wark (BULL·wurk) *n.* **1** a defensive wall or rampart. **2** a protection or defense: *the ~ of the free world.*

bum *n.* a loafer, vagrant, or hobo. **—*v.* bums, bummed, bum·ming** *Informal.* **1** live by begging; loaf: *~ing around.* **2** beg; cadge: *Can I ~ $5?* **—*adj.*** *Informal.* false; worthless; not working properly: *~ advice; ~ steer* (i.e. bad direction or tip). **—on the bum** *Informal.* living as a bum; malfunctioning. **—bum·mer** *n.* *Slang.* a disappointing or unpleasant experience, esp. a frightening reaction to an hallucinogen.

bum·ble·bee *n.* a large, hairy, black-and-yellow bee.

bump *v.* **1** knock or collide (with) forcibly. **2** *Informal.* displace. **—*n.*** **1** a blow or collision. **2** a projecting bulge or hump: *a ~ on his head; ~s in the road.* **—bump into** *Informal.* meet by chance. **—bump off** *Slang.* murder. **—bump·er** *n.* **1** an impact-absorbing device, esp. a metal bar protecting either end of an automobile. **2** a brimful cup of drink; hence, something exceptionally large; ***adj.:*** *a ~ crop.* **—bumper sticker** a slogan-bearing sign to stick on a bumper.

bump·kin *n.* an awkward, naive rustic: *a country ~.*

bump·tious (BUMP·shus) *adj.* arrogantly self-assertive; **bump·tious·ly** *adv.* **—bump·y** *adj.* **bump·i·er, -i·est** having or marked by bumps: *a ~ road; a ~ ride.*

bun *n.* **1** a usu. sweetened roll: *a cinnamon ~.* **2** a coil of hair at the back of the head.

bunch *n.* **1** a number of similar things growing or fastened together: *a ~ of bananas.* **2** *Informal.* a group: *a ~ of fellow workers.* **—*v.*** cluster into a bunch; also, form into a mass. **—bunch·y** *adj.*

bun·co (BUNG·coh) *n.* *Informal.* a confidence scheme. **—*v.* -cos, -coed, -co·ing** swindle.

bun·dle *n.* **1** a number or group of things tied together or wrapped up; a package: *a ~ of sticks; a ~ of clothes for the cleaners.* **2** a group. **3** *Slang.* a great amount of money: *made a ~ at the races.* **—*v.*** **1** tie or pack into a bundle; **bundle up** dress in warm clothes. **2** dispatch quickly: *~d the children off to school.*

bung *n.* a stopper used to plug a bunghole.

bun·ga·low (BUNG·guh·loh) *n.* a house of one or one-and-one-half stories: *a back-split ~.*

bung·hole *n.* a hole in the side of a barrel or cask through which it is filled or emptied.

bun·gle *v.* **-gles, -gled, -gling** do or work clumsily or improperly; botch; ***n.:*** *a technological ~.* **—bun·gler** *n.*

bun·ion (BUN·yun) *n.* a swollen, painful deformity of the ball of the big toe.

bunk *n.* **1** *Slang.* meaningless talk. **2** a sleeping place, esp. a narrow bed or berth. **—*v.*** sleep in or provide with a bed, often a makeshift one: *We ~ed in the old cabin.* **—bunk beds** a pair of beds set one above the other. **—bunk·er** *n.* **1** a storage area for fuel oil, coal, etc. on a ship. **2** a fortified, often underground, shelter. **3** in golf, a hazard, as a sandy hollow or mound of earth.

bunko same as BUNCO.

bun·kum *n.* *Slang.* nonsense; bunk.

bun·ny *n.* **bun·nies** **1** *Informal.* a rabbit. **2** an attractive, scantily clad nightclub waitress; hence, *Slang.* a woman attractive as a sexual playmate.

Bun·sen (BUN·sn) **burner** a laboratory gas burner producing a very hot flame.

bunt *v.* *Baseball.* hit (the ball) a short distance with a half swing; ***n.:*** *The batter reached first base on a ~.*

bun·ting *n.* **1** a light cloth for flags, streamers, etc. **2** a hooded, baglike outdoor garment for an infant. **3** any of several short-billed birds of the finch family.

buoy (BOO·ee, BOY) *n.* **1** a floating marker anchored to indicate a channel, hidden hazard, etc. **2** a ring-shaped device for keeping a person afloat; life buoy. **—*v.*** (BOY) **1** mark with buoys. **2** keep afloat; sustain; also, encourage: *a barrel ~ed up by air; spirits ~ed up by the good news.* **—buoy·ant** (BOY·unt) *adj.* **1** able to float or keep something afloat: *a ~ cork.* **2** resilient; cheerful; hopeful: *~ good spirits.* **—buoy·ant·ly** *adv.;* **buoy·an·cy** *n.*

buq·sha (BOOK·shuh) *n.* the 40th part of a Yemeni riyal.

bur or **burr** *n.* **1** the prickly seedcase or fruit of some plants; also, a plant bearing burs. **2** a person or thing that sticks to one like a bur. **—bur·ry** *adj.*

bur. bureau.

bur·den *n.* **1** something carried; esp., a ship's cargo: *The camel is a beast of ~.* **2** an onerous responsibility, worry, task, etc.: *She bore the ~ of caring for her father;* **the burden of proof** the obligation to prove one's point. **3** the central idea; also, a chorus or refrain: *the ~ of the argument.* **—v.:** *a heavily ~ed horse; Don't ~ me with your problems.* **—bur·den·some** *adj.*

bur·dock *n.* a coarse, hairy weed with large leaves and prickly flower heads.

bu·reau (BYOOR·oh) *n.* **-reaus** or **-reaux** (–oze) **1** a chest of drawers for storing clothes; dresser. **2** an office: *a news ~; a tourist ~.* **3** a governmental department or subdepartment. **—bu·reau·cra·cy** (–ROC–) *n.* **-cies** **1** a hierarchy of nonelected public officials. **2** an administrative system that is unimaginatively and inefficiently bound by fixed rules and red tape; **bu·reau·crat** *n.;* **bu·reau·crat·ic** (–CRAT–) *adj.;* **bu·reau·cra·tize** (–ROC·ruh–) *v.* **-tiz·es, -tized, -tiz·ing.**

bu·ret(te) (byoo·RET) *n.* a graduated glass cylinder with a tap near the bottom, for measuring a gas or liquid.

burg *n. Informal.* a city or town.

bur·gee (BUR·jee) *n.* a triangular or swallow-tailed naval identification flag.

bur·geon (BUR·jun) *v.* sprout leaves or buds; hence, expand or develop rapidly: *~ing high-rise developments.*

bur·ger (BUR·gur) *n. Informal.* a hamburger; ***comb. form.*** a patty (as specified) in a bun: as in *soyaburger* (hamburger with soya protein); *eggburger.*

bur·gess (BUR·jis) *n.* a citizen of a borough.**—burgh** (BURG) *n.* an incorporated Scottish town; borough. **—burgh·er** *n.* a solid citizen, esp. of a city or town; a bourgeois.

bur·glar (BUR·glur) *n.* one who commits **bur·gla·ry** *n.* **-ries** the breaking and entering of a building to commit a crime, esp. robbery. **—bur·glar·ize** *v.* **-iz·es, -ized, -iz·ing** *Informal.* commit burglary on. **—bur·glar·i·ous** (–GLAIR·ee·us) *adj.* **—bur·glar·proof** *adj.: a ~ vault.* **—bur·gle** *v.* **-gles, -gled, -gling** burglarize.

bur·go·mas·ter (BUR·guh–) *n.* a mayorlike magistrate of some countries of Europe.

Bur·gun·dy (BUR·gun·dee) *n.* **-dies** a usu. red table wine, esp. one made in the Burgundy region of France.

bur·i·al (BER·ee·ul) *n.* the act of burying a body: *~ at sea.*

burl *n.* a roundish outgrowth on a tree.

bur·lap *n.* a coarse, open-weave fiber cloth used esp. for bags.

bur·lesque (bur·LESK) *n.* **1** a travesty or parody. **2** a vaudeville entertainment having low humor, striptease acts, etc. **—v. -lesques, -lesqued, -lesqu·ing** imitate satirically or humorously.

bur·ly (BUR·lee) *adj.* **-li·er, -li·est** husky; big and strong: *a ~ policeman.*

Bur·ma (BUR·muh) a country in S.E.Asia; 261,790 sq.mi. (678,033 km²); *cap.* Rangoon. **—Bur·mese** (bur·MEEZ) *adj.* & *n.*

burn *v.* **burns,** *pt.* & *pp.* **burned** or **burnt, burn·ing** **1** be or set on fire; give off intense heat; also, destroy, damage, be destroyed or damaged by heat, fire, acid, radiation, or electricity. **2** consume as fuel; of rocket engines, fire to provide thrust. **3** feel or make feel hot; sunburn. **4** feel something, as anger, very intensely: *~ing with desire.* **5** *Slang.* cheat, esp. by selling inferior drugs to. **—n.** **1** an injury or mark made by burning: *A first-degree ~ reddens the skin.* **2** a firing of a rocket engine. **—burn·er** *n.* something that burns, heats, or emits flame, esp. a heating element or a stove: *a gas ~.*

bur·nish *v.* polish: *~ed steel.* **—n.** luster; gloss. **—bur·nish·er** *n.*

bur·noose (bur·NOOS) *n.* a loose, hooded cloak worn esp. by Arabs.

burn·out *n.* the cessation of firing of a rocket or jet engine.

Burns, Robert. 1759–1796, Scottish poet.

burp *n.* a belch. **—v.** belch or cause to belch: *~ the baby after feeding.* **—burp gun** an automatic pistol or light machine gun.

burr *n.* **1** a rough edge left by cutting, drilling, etc. **2** a roughly trilled "r"; also, a style of pronunciation marked by this: *the Scottish ~.* **3** a whirring sound. **4** same as BUR. **—bur·ry** *adj.*

bur·ro (BUR·oh) *n.* a small donkey.

bur·row (BUR·oh) *n.* a tunnel or hole dug by a rabbit, mole, etc. **—v.** dig a burrow; hence, search, move, or progress as if digging a burrow: *~ing through books and papers.*

bur·ry *adj.* **bur·ri·er, bur·ri·est** See BUR, BURR.

bur·sa (BUR·suh) *n.* **-sas** or **-sae** (–see) a fluid-filled sac easing friction at a joint. **—bur·sa·ry** (BUR·suh·ree) *n.* **-ries** **1** the treasury of a college or university; its treasurer is a **bur·sar** (BUR·sur). **2** *Brit.* a grant of money to a student.**—bur·si·tis** (bur·SYE–) *n.* the swollen inflammation of a bursa.

burst *v.* **bursts, burst, burst·ing** **1** break or explode, esp. from internal pressure; be very full: *The creek ~ its banks; The police ~ into the house; ~ing* (i.e. very eager) *to tell their story; a room* **bursting at the seams** *with people.* **2** begin, emerge, or do suddenly: *~ into tears; Gasoline ~s into flames; Don't* **burst in upon** (i.e. interrupt) *our meeting.* **—n.** a bursting; also, a sudden outbreak, spurt, or effort: *a ~ of speed; a ~ of applause; a ~ of machine-gun fire.*

Bu·run·di (boo·ROON·dee) a landlocked E. African country; 10,747 sq. mi. (27,834 km²); *cap.* Bujumbura. **—Bu·run·di·an** *adj.* & *n.*

bur·y (BER·ee) *v.* **bur·ies, bur·ied, bur·y·ing** **1** hide in the ground: *~d treasure.* **2** put (a corpse) in the ground, underwater, etc., usu. with funeral rites. **3** hide; engross: *~ one's face in a pillow; ~d in a novel all day.* **—bury the hatchet** make peace.

bus *n.* **bus·(s)es** **1** a large public conveyance usu. having a fixed route and stopping points,

or **bus stops.** **2** *Informal.* an automobile. —*v.* **bus·(s)es, bus(s)ed, bus·(s)ing** **1** transport or travel by bus. **2** act as a busboy. —**miss the bus** lose an opportunity.
bus. business.
bus·boy *n.* a waiter's helper who sets and clears tables; *fem.* **bus·girl.**
bus·by (BUZ·bee) *n.* **-bies** a formal military fur hat.
busgirl See BUSBOY.
bush (BOOSH) *n.* **1** a small woody plant with many branches; shrub. **2** wild, uninhabited land, esp. if forested. —*v.* be thick like a bush. —**beat around the bush** approach or discuss a topic indirectly. —**bushed** *adj. Informal.* very tired. —**bush·y** *adj.* **bush·i·er, -i·est:** *a fox's ~ tail.*
bush·el *n.* a dry measure equal to 4 pecks.
bush·ing *n.* a cylindrical metal sleeve used to guide a shaft or reduce friction.
bush league *Slang.* a minor league, considered second-rate. —**Bush·man** *n.* **-men** a member of a nomadic people in S.W. Africa. —**bush·mas·ter** *n.* a large poisonous viper of Central and South America. —**bush·whack** *v.* ambush; **bush·whack·er** *n.*
busi·ness (BIZ·nis) *n.* **1** one's work or occupation; also, one's rightful concern: *~ before pleasure; None of your ~!* **2** activity, matter, etc.: *Waiting in line is a tiresome ~.* **3** a commercial undertaking; a store, factory, etc.; hence, commercial activity: *~ is booming.* —**mean business** be in earnest. —**busi·ness·like** *adj.* efficient; systematic. —**busi·ness·man** *n.* **-men** or **busi·ness·wom·an, -wom·en** one engaged in business, esp. as an owner or boss.
bus·kin *n.* a thick-soled, high-laced boot, as worn by ancient actors.
bus·man's holiday a vacation spent in activity like one's usual work.
buss *n.* & *v. Informal.* kiss.
bus stop See BUS.
[1]**bust** *n.* a sculpture of someone's head and upper chest; also, a woman's bosom.
[2]**bust** *v. Slang.* **1** burst, break, punch, tame, etc.: *He ~ed my toy! bronco-~ing cowboys.* **2** arrest; of police, raid: *~ed for peddling drugs.* **3** demote: *~ed to private.* **4** make or become penniless: *~ed until payday.* —*n. Slang.* **1** an arrest or police raid. **2** a failure or financial collapse: *California or ~! boom and ~.* **3** a punch. —**bust·er** *n.*
bus·tle (BUSL) *n.* **1** a pad worn under a woman's skirt to extend it at the back. **2** brisk, busy activity: *The office was all in a ~.* —*v.* **-tles, -tled, -tling** move or work busily and fussily: *a ~ing stock exchange.*
bust·y *adj. Informal.* big-breasted.
bus·y (BIZ·ee) *adj.* **bus·i·er, -i·est** working; active; occupied; in use: *as ~ as a bee; a very ~ businessman; a ~ marketplace; a ~ day; ~ with his homework; The phone is ~.* —*v.* **bus·ies, bus·ied, bus·y·ing:** *~d themselves with hobbies.* —**bus·i·ly** *adv.* —**bus·y·ness** (BIZ·ee·nis) *n.* —**bus·y·bod·y** *n.* **-bod·ies** a meddlesome, nosy person. —**bus·y·work** *n.* useless work to keep one occupied.
but *conj.* **1** yet; however; on the contrary: *tall ~ thin; She visited, ~ could not stay long.* **2** if not; except; other than: *He would have come ~ that he was too busy.* **3** that: *I don't doubt ~ it will rain.* —*prep.* except: *Everyone ~ Jim had fled the scene; wouldn't be alive today* **but for** *his doctor.* —*adv.* only: *There was ~ one survivor; You need ~ move and he will shoot.* —*n.* an exception, condition, etc.: *no ~s about it.*
bu·tane (BYOO–) *n.* a colorless, flammable gas used as a fuel and in synthetic rubber.
butch (BOOCH) *n.* **1** *Slang.* a lesbian in the male role. **2** a haircut shorter than a crew cut.
butch·er (BOOCH·ur) *n.* **1** one who kills or dresses meat for sale or consumption. **2** a brutal mass killer. **3** a bungler. —*v.* [corresponding to the *n.* senses] **1:** *~ed a steer.* **2:** *Millions were ~ed in the war.* **3:** *They ~ed the job despite the instructions.* —**butch·er·y** *n.* **-er·ies.**
but·ler *n.* a chief male houseservant.
butt *n.* **1** a large cask. **2** the larger or handle end; a remaining or broken end: *the ~ of a pistol; a cigarette ~.* **3** *Slang.* a cigarette. **4** *Informal.* the buttocks. **5** a target; an object of ridicule: *the ~ of a joke.* **6** a butting action. —*v.* **1** abut. **2** strike or push with the head or horns; **butt in** *Informal.* interfere.
butte (BYOOT) *n.* an isolated, flat-topped hill with steep sides.
but·ter *n.* **1** a thick, rich food product made by churning milk. **2** a similar product: *cocoa ~.* —*v.* spread butter on. —**butter up** flatter. —**but·ter·y** *adj.* —**but·ter-and-eggs** *n.* a weed with clusters of orange and yellow, snapdragonlike flowers. —**but·ter·cup** *n.* a shiny yellow wildflower. —**but·ter·fat** *n.* the fatty part of milk that is churned into butter. —**but·ter·fin·gers** *n. sing.* & *pl.* one who clumsily drops things; **but·ter·fin·gered** *adj.* —**but·ter·fly** *n.* **-flies** any of various slender, often colorful, four-winged insects that fly by day. —**but·ter·milk** *n.* the milky liquid that is left after milk is churned for butter, made commercially by fermenting skim milk. —**but·ter·nut** *n.* the oblong, edible, oily nut of a North American walnut tree. —**but·ter·scotch** *n.* a syrup, candy, or flavoring made with butter and brown sugar.
but·tock (BUT·uk) *n.* either of the two fleshy rounded parts at the back of the hips.
but·ton (BUTN) *n.* **1** a disk or knob used to fasten or ornament clothing. **2** a similar object, esp. an electric switch: *push the ~.* —*v.* fasten with a button: *~ your shirt.* —**button up one's lip** *Slang.* be quiet. —**but·ton·hole** *n.* a slit or loop through which a button is

passed; ***v.*** **-holes, -holed, -hol·ing** stop and force (someone) to listen. **—but·ton·hook** *n.* a device for drawing buttons through buttonholes.

but·tress (BUT·ris) *n.* an external support built against a wall; hence, any support; ***—v.:*** *faith ~ed by miracles.*

bu·tut (boo·TOOT) *n.* 1/100 of a dalasi.

bux·om (BUX·um) *adj.* plump and attractive; full-bosomed.

buy (BYE) *v.* **buys, bought** (BAWT), **buy·ing** **1** acquire by payment or sacrifice; also, bribe: *~ing groceries; ~ freedom with our lives; The jury was bought by the prosecution.* **2** *Slang.* believe: *Don't ~ that nonsense.* ***—n.*** *Informal.* a purchase; esp., a bargain: *a great ~ at $9.95.* **—buy in(to)** purchase shares in (a company). **—buy out** buy someone's shares in or control of (a business). **—buy up** buy as much as one can of. **—buy·er** *n.: a* **buyer's market** *with abundant supply and low prices.*

buzz *v.* make a vibrating, prolonged, z-like sound: *bees ~ing in the field; a stock exchange ~ing with excitement.* **2** fly an airplane low over: *~ed the airfield.* ***—n.*** **1** a buzzing sound; also, the sound of much activity, talk, etc.: *a ~ of rumor in the hall.* **2** the sound made by a buzzer.

buz·zard (BUZ·urd) *n.* any of several Old World hawks or New World vultures and condors.

buz·zer *n.* an electric signaling device that makes a buzzing sound. **—buzz saw** a circular power saw. **—buzz word** a technical-sounding term that is part of the jargon of a professional group.

B.V. Blessed Virgin.

bwa·na (BWAH·nuh) *n.* in Africa, a master; also, sir.

bx. box.

by (BYE) *prep.* **1** beside; near; at: *over ~ the door; stopping ~ a friend's home to visit.* **2** through the means, agency, medium, direction, etc. of: *trapped ~ a landslide; a book (written) ~ Dickens; "One if ~ land, two if ~ sea"; ~ way of New York.* **3** during; no later than: *work ~ night; bills due ~ the end of the month.* **4** according or in relation to: *Play ~ the rules; I swear ~ my faith! a lawyer ~ profession.* **5** past: *He ran ~ us at full speed.* **6** to the extent of: *missed the target ~ a mile.* **7** in the amount, lot, or unit of: *apples ~ the bushel; paid ~ the hour.* **8** [used to indicate multiplication, division, linking of dimensions, etc.]: *Multiply 17 ~ 43; Divide 14 ~ 2 to get 7; a room 10′ ~ 12′.* ***—adv.:*** *Keep close ~* (i.e. near) *in case of trouble; Don't lay it ~* (i.e. aside) *just yet; Stop ~* (i.e. visit) *on your way home; passed ~ and went down the street.* **—by and by** eventually. **—by and large** on the whole. **—by oneself** without others. **—by the by** or **by the way** incidentally.

bye *n.* an advance to the next round of a tournament because there is no other contestant with whom one can be paired: *Smith had a ~ to the semi-finals.*

by-e·lec·tion *n.* a special election to fill a vacant seat between regular elections.

Bye·lo·rus·sian (byel·uh·RUSH·un) **Soviet Socialist Republic** a W. European republic of the U.S.S.R.; *cap.* Minsk. Also **Bye·lo·rus·sia. —Bye·lo·rus·sian** *adj.* & *n.*

by·gone (BYE·gon) *adj.* past: *the ~ glories of yesteryear.* ***—n.:*** *"Let ~s be ~s"* (i.e. forgive and forget). **—by·law** *n.* a subsidiary rule or regulation passed by a company, city, etc. to regulate its own affairs. **—by-line** *n.* the writer's name printed at the head of a newspaper story. **—by·pass** *n.* a road or passage around something; ***v.:*** *The canal ~es the rapids.* **—by·path** *n.* a secondary or rarely used path or road. **—by-prod·uct** *n.* something produced incidentally to the chief product, as molasses and syrup in sugar manufacture.

By·ron (BY·run), **George Gordon.** 1788–1824, English poet. **—By·ron·ic** (–RON–) *adj.: ~ melancholy.*

by·stand·er *n.* a non-participating onlooker: *An innocent ~ was wounded.*

byte (BITE) *n.* in computers, a unit of information, often 8 bits in length.

by·way *n.* **1** a bypath: *highways and ~s.* **2** a less known or subsidiary topic or area: *the ~s of history.* **—by·word** *n.* a common saying; hence, a person or thing that is typical or notorious, as "Watergate" for political corruption.

By·zan·ti·um (bi·ZAN·shee·um) the ancient name of Istanbul and capital of the **By·zan·tine** (BIZ·un·teen) **Empire** (A.D. 330–1453).

C

C or **c** (SEE) *n.* **C's** or **c's** the third letter of the English alphabet; hence, third in a series; third highest: *a grade of C.* **—c.** or **C.** cape; carat; cent; center; centigrade or Celsius; centimeter; century; circa; copyright; cubic. **—C 1** the Roman numeral for 100. **2** carbon; centigrade or Celsius. **3** *Music.* the first tone of the C major scale. **—C.** Catholic; Church; Congress; Court.

ca. circa. **—Ca** calcium. **—CA** California. **—C.A.** Central America; chartered accountant.

C.A.B. Civil Aeronautics Board.

cab *n.* **1** a taxicab. **2** the driver's compartment of a locomotive, truck, crane, etc.

ca·bal (cuh·BAL) n. a group of conspirators or plotters; a conspiracy. ***—v.*** **-bals, -balled, -bal·ling** join or form a cabal.

cab·a·la (CAB·uh·luh) *n.* **1** a mystic Jewish theosophy of the Middle Ages. **2** any esoteric system of beliefs; also **cab·a·lism. —cab·a·list** *n.* **—cab·a·lis·tic** *adj.*

ca·ba·na (cuh·BAN·uh) *n.* a shelter used as a bathhouse near a beach or swimming pool.

cab·a·ret (cab·uh·RAY) *n.* a restaurant providing liquor and light entertainment; also, the entertainment itself.

cab·bage (CAB·ij) *n.* a vegetable with a dense round head of thick leaves.

cab·driv·er (CAB·dry–) *n.* one who drives a taxicab; also **cab·by** or **cab·bie** *n.* **cab·bies** *Informal.*

cab·in (CAB–) *n.* **1** a small, rough dwelling of one story. **2** a room on a ship or boat; an enclosed space in an airplane for crew, cargo, or passengers; **cabin boy** a servant boy on a ship; **cabin class** passenger ship accommodation intermediate between tourist class and first class; **(cabin) cruiser** a small powered craft with living facilities built in.

cab·i·net (CAB–) *n.* **1** a cupboardlike structure for housing or displaying objects or equipment: *a china* ~ ; *A console TV comes in a* ~ ; **cab·i·net·mak·er** *n.* a maker of woodwork and furniture, i.e. **cab·i·net·work** *n.* **2** the advisory council of a head of state or chief executive of a government.

ca·ble (CAY·bl) *n.* **1** a rope of large diameter, usu. of steel or fiber. **2** the anchor cable of a ship: *The ~ broke and our ship began to drift.* **3** a unit of length equal to 100 or 120 fathoms; also **cable length. 4** a bundle of insulated electrical conductors. **5** a cablegram. ***—v.*** **ca·bles, ca·bled, ca·bling** transmit a message to (someone) by electrical cable. **—cable car** one drawn by a moving cable, as on a hill or across a canyon. **—ca·ble·gram** *n.* a telegram transmitted by submarine cable. **—cable TV** television reception by cable from a central antenna serving many customers.

cab·man *n.* a cabdriver.

ca·bo·chon (CAB·uh·shon) *n.* a precious stone cut and polished with a rounded face but no facets.

ca·boo·dle (cuh·BOO·dl) *n.* *Informal.* **the whole (kit and) caboodle** the whole lot.

ca·boose (cuh·BOOS) *n.* the car at the end of a freight train with sleeping and kitchen facilities for the train crew.

cab·ri·o·let (cab·ree·uh·LAY) *n.* **1** a horse-drawn, two-wheeled, covered carriage. **2** a kind of convertible coupe.

cab·stand *n.* a parking place for taxicabs waiting for passengers.

ca·ca·o (cuh·COW) *n.* **-os** a small tropical American tree that yields seeds, called **cacao (beans),** from which cocoa and chocolate are made.

cac·ci·a·to·re (cah·chuh·TOR·ee) *adj.* cooked with tomatoes, onions, and herbs: *veal ~; chicken ~.*

cache (CASH) *n.* **1** a hiding place, originally for food and supplies for future use. **2** goods hidden in a cache. ***—v.*** **cach·es, cached, cach·ing:** *The explorers ~d their provisions in a cave.*

ca·chet (–SHAY) *n.* **1** a mark or seal as an indication of official approval on a letter or document. **2** a mark of excellence or authenticity. **3** a design or advertisement stamped or printed on mail.

cack·le *v.* **-les, -led, -ling** **1** make the shrill cry of a hen. **2** laugh in such a way: *The old man ~d with glee.* **—*n.*** a hen's cry or laughter like it. **—cack·ler** *n.*

caco- *comb. form.* bad; incorrect: as in **ca·coph·ony** (cuh·COF·uh·nee) *n.* **-nies** unpleasant or discordant sound. **—ca·coph·o·nous** *adj.*

cac·tus (CAC·tus) *n., pl.* **-ti** (–tye) or **-tus·es** any of a large group of leafless, often spiny desert plants with fleshy stems.

cad *n.* an ill-mannered, ungentlemanly person. **—cad·dish** *adj.* **—cad·dish·ly** *adv.* **—cad·dish·ness** *n.*

ca·dav·er (cuh·DAV·ur) *n.* a dead body, esp. a corpse for dissection. **—ca·dav·er·ous** *adj.* corpselike; pale and gaunt; also **ca·dav·er·ic.**

caddice See CADDIS, CADDIS FLY.

cad·die (CAD·ee) or **cad·dy** *n.* **cad·dies** one hired to assist a golfer, esp. to carry his clubs. **—*v.* cad·dies, cad·died, cad·dy·ing** act as a caddie.

cad·dis (CAD·is) *n.* a kind of coarse fabric; also **cad·dice.** **—cad·dis fly** a four-winged insect resembling a moth, whose larva, **caddis worm,** lives in water and is used for bait by anglers. Also **cad·dice.**

cad·dy (CAD·ee) *n.* **cad·dies** a small container or chest, esp. one for tea.

-cade *comb. form.* procession; parade: as in *motorcade, cavalcade.*

ca·dence (CAY–) *n.* **1** a rhythm or flow of sound. **2** a timed measure, as for a march or dance. **3** modulation of pitch and volume of the voice; hence, the general character of the voice: *the pleasant ~ of her voice.* **4** a musical progression toward an harmonic conclusion. **—ca·denced** *adj.*

ca·den·za (cuh·DEN·zuh) *n.* a parenthetic or-namental flourish, either vocal or instrumental, just before the end of a work of music.

ca·det (cuh·DET) *n.* **1** a younger son or brother. **2** any student in a military academy. **3** a trainee: *a ~ teacher.* **—ca·det·ship** *n.* **—Ca·dette scout** a girl scout of age 12 to 14 years.

cadge *v.* **cadg·es, cadged, cadg·ing** get by begging; sponge or beg. **—cadg·er** *n.*

cad·mi·um (CAD·mee·um) *n.* a metallic element used in alloys, esp. for plating metals. **—cad·mic** *adj.*

cad·re (CAD·ree) *n.* **1** framework; structure. **2** a trained force, usu. military, around which a larger organization can be built: *A ~ of revolutionaries operated in each village.*

ca·du·ce·us (cuh·DEW·see·us) *n., pl.* **-ce·i** (–see·eye) the winged staff of Mercury, now used as the emblem of the medical profession. **—ca·du·ce·an** *adj.*

cae·cal, cae·cum same as CECAL, CECUM.

Cae·sar (SEE·zur) *n.* **1 Gaius Julius.** ca. 100–44 B.C., general and dictator at Rome. **2** a title for Roman emperors after and including **Augustus** (63 B.C.–A.D. 14): *"Render unto ~ what is ~'s."* **3** often **caesar** *n.* an absolute ruler; **Cae·sar·ism** *n.* autocracy. **—Cae·sar·e·an** (si·ZAIR·ee·un) *adj.* of or having to do with Caesar. **—Caesarean (section)** delivery of a fetus by surgical incision into the uterus through the abdominal wall.

cae·si·um (SEE·zee–) same as CESIUM.

cae·su·ra (si·ZHOOR·uh) *n.* **-ras** or **-rae** (–ree) in poetry, a slight pause or break in the middle of a line of verse. **—cae·su·ral** or **cae·su·ric** *adj.*

C.A.F. cost and freight.

ca·fé (–FAY) *n.* a small restaurant or bar; also **cafe.** **—ca·fé au lait** (–oh·LAY) *n.* **1** hot milk and coffee in equal proportions. **2** a light brown color. **—caf·e·te·ri·a** (–uh·TEER·ee·uh) *n.* a restaurant where customers serve themselves at a counter and carry food to the tables. **—caf·fein(e)** (–FEEN) *n.* an alkaloid found in tea, coffee, and cola extract that acts as a stimulant and diuretic.

caf·tan (–TAN) *n.* a long-sleeved garment reaching to the ankles and worn with a sash.

cage *n.* **1** an enclosure for animals, consisting of an open structure of metal or wooden bars or wire. **2** a similar structure or enclosure: *an elevator ~.* **—*v.* cag·es, caged, cag·ing** put or keep in a cage. **—cage·ling** *n.* a caged bird. **—cage·y** *adj. Informal.* **ca·gi·er, -gi·est** **1** cautious; wary. **2** cunning; sly. Also **cag·y.** **—cag·i·ly** *adv.* **—cag·i·ness** *n.*

ca·hoots (cuh·HOOTS) *n. Slang.* **in cahoots** *(with)* in partnership, usu. of an improper nature.

cai·man (CAY–) *n.* any of a group of tropical American reptiles closely related to the crocodile.

Cain the eldest son of Adam and Eve. **—raise Cain** cause an uproar.

cairn *n.* a pile of stones set up as a monument.

Cai·ro (KYE·roh) capital of Egypt.

cais·son (CAY·sahn) *n.* **1** a usu. two-wheeled ammunition wagon. **2** a watertight chamber filled with air under high pressure, used for underwater construction. **—caisson disease** same as DECOMPRESSION SICKNESS.

cai·tiff *n. Archaic.* a base and cowardly person. **—*adj.:*** *a ~ knight.*

ca·jole (cuh–) *v.* **-joles, -joled, -jol·ing** persuade or coax, esp. with flattery; wheedle: *The child was ~d into the dentist's chair.* **—ca·jol·er** *n.* **—ca·jol·er·y** *n.* **—ca·jole·ment** *n.*

Ca·jun (CAY·jun) *n.* a Louisianian descended from French immigrants exiled from Acadia.

cake *n.* **1** a mass of dough fried or baked, usu. small, flat, and round: *a barley ~.* **2** a leavened sweet loaf, baked and often iced. **3** a solid, shaped mass: *a ~ of soap.* **—*v.* cakes, caked, cak•ing** harden into a solid mass; encrust: *Hands ~d with mud.* **—take the cake** *Informal.* win or merit first prize. **—cake•walk** *n.* a show dance characterized by an elaborate walk with a high prance; **cake•walk•er** *n.*

cal. calendar; caliber; calorie. **—Cal.** California.

ca•la•bash (CAL·uh–) *n.* a tropical American tree bearing a fruit gourd; also, the gourd of this tree; hence, a bottle, bowl, pipe, etc. made from this gourd.

cal•a•boose (CAL·uh–) *n. Slang.* a jail.

ca•la•di•um (cuh·LAY·dee·um) *n.* any of various large-leaved plants of the arum family found in tropical America.

cal•a•mine (CAL·uh–) *n.* a pinkish mixture of zinc and iron oxides used in skin lotions, ointments, etc.

ca•lam•i•ty (cuh·LAM·i·tee) *n.* **-ties** a disastrous event; a great affliction. **—ca•lam•i•tous** *adj.* **—ca•lam•i•tous•ly** *adv.* **—ca•lam•i•tous•ness** *n.*

calc. calculate(d).

cal•car•e•ous (–CARE·ee·us) *adj.* resembling, containing, or composed of calcium, calcium carbonate, or lime; chalky. **—cal•ced•o•ny** (cal·SED–) *n.* **-nies** same as CHALCEDONY. **—calci-** *comb.form.* calcium; lime. **—cal•cic** (CAL·sic) *adj.* of, containing, or having to do with calcium or lime. **—cal•cif•er•ous** (–SIF·uh·rus) *adj.* yielding or containing calcium or calcium carbonate. **—cal•ci•fy** (CAL·si·fye) *v.* **-fies, -fied, -fy•ing** harden by accumulation of calcium or calcium carbonate; **cal•ci•fi•ca•tion** (–CAY–) *n.* **—cal•ci•mine** (CAL–) *n.* a white or pale-colored wash or paint for plaster surfaces; ***v.* -mines, -mined, -min•ing** paint with calcimine. **—cal•cine** *v.* **-cines, -cined, -cin•ing** reduce to quicklime or similar dry powder by heating but not melting; **cal•ci•na•tion** (–NAY–) *n.* **—cal•cite** *n.* any of the common, natural, crystalline forms of calcium carbonate; **cal•cit•ic** (–SIT–) *adj.* **—cal•ci•um** (CAL·see·um) *n.* a soft, whitish, metallic element found in combination in limestone, chalk, marble, bone, etc. **—calcium carbonate** a common, natural compound of calcium found in limestone, chalk, shells, plant ash, etc.

cal•cu•late (CAL·kyuh–) *v.* **-lates, -lat•ed, -lat•ing 1** compute mathematically or scientifically. **2** evaluate or predict by common sense: *a ~d risk.* **3** design with a purpose; plan; **cal•cu•lat•ed** *adj.: a ~ insult; a plan ~ to succeed.* **—cal•cu•la•ble** *adj.;* **cal•cu•la•bly** *adv.* **—cal•cu•lat•ing** *adj.* shrewd, clever, etc. in a selfish way: *a cold and ~ villain.* **—cal•cu•la•tion** (–LAY–) *n.* **1** the process or result of calculating. **2** shrewd deliberation. **—cal•cu•la•tor** *n.* one that calculates, esp. an electronic machine that does arithmetic computations. **—cal•cu•lus** (CAL·kyuh·lus) *n., pl.* **-li** (–lye) or **lus•es 1** an abnormal stonelike growth in the body. **2** a system of computing using algebraic symbols: *differential ~; integral ~.*

Cal•cut•ta (cal·CUT·uh) a city and seaport of N.E. India.

cal•de•ra (cal·DARE·uh) *n.* a large basin-shaped volcanic crater.

cal•dron (CAWL·drun) *n.* a large vat or pot for boiling: *a witches' ~.*

cal•en•dar (CAL·un·dur) *n.* **1** a system for determining the days, weeks, and months of a year; also, a table or chart showing this. **2** an ordered list; schedule: *the court ~.* **—*v.*** record on a calendar or schedule.

cal•en•der *n.* a roller machine that gives a smooth or glossy finish to cloth, paper, etc. **—*v.*** process with a calender.

cal•ends (CAL·endz) *n. sing. & pl.* the first day of a month in the ancient Roman calendar. **—ca•len•du•la** (cuh·LEN·juh·luh) *n.* a plant such as the pot marigold, with composite yellow or orange flowers.

calf (CAF) *n.* **calves** (CAVZ) **1** the thick, fleshy back part of the lower leg in humans. **2** the young of cattle and other large mammals such as the elephant; moose, and whale. **—calf** or **calf•skin** *n.* leather made from calf hides.

Cal•ga•ry (CAL·guh·ree) a city in S. Alberta, Canada.

cal•i•ber or **cal•i•bre** (CAL·i·bur) *n.* **1** the diameter of a bullet or other projectile; also, the inside diameter of the barrel of a gun. **2** quality or excellence: *a man of high ~.* **—cal•i•brate** *v.* **-brates, -brat•ed, -brat•ing 1** find the caliber of (a tube). **2** fix or adjust the graduations of a measuring instrument: *a well ~d thermometer.* **—cal•i•bra•tor** *n.* **—cal•i•bra•tion** (–BRAY–) *n.*

cal•i•co (CAL·i·coh) *n.* **-co(e)s** a rough cotton cloth with a printed pattern. **—*adj.*** spotted: *a ~ cat.*

ca•lif (CAY·lif) *n.* same as CALIPH.

Calif. *Abbrev.* for **Cal•i•for•ni•a** (–FOR·nee·uh) a W. state of the U.S.; 158,693 sq. mi. (411,013 km²); *cap.* Sacramento. **—Cal•i•for•ni•an** *n.* & *adj.* **—California poppy** an herb with yellow to red flowers and finely divided leaves; also, its flower, the state flower of California. **—cal•i•for•ni•um** *n.* a man-made, metallic, radioactive element.

cal•i•per (CAL–) *n.* usu. **calipers** *pl.* an instrument with two curved legs, for measuring thicknesses or the diameters of tubes. **—*v.*** measure with calipers.

ca•liph (CAY·lif) *n.* the head of Islam; the title of Mohammed's successors. **—ca•liph•ate** *n.*

cal•is•then•ics (–THEN–) *n.* simple physical exercises designed to develop grace and strength. **—cal•is•then•ic** *adj.*

calk (CAWK) *v.* same as CAULK.

call (CAWL) *v.* **1** to shout. **2** of an animal, to cry. **3** summon; command to come. **4** name; deem or consider: *Let's ~ it even and go home.* **5** talk with on the telephone. **6** demand payment, to see cards in a game, etc. **7** end: *The game was ~ed because of rain.* **—*n.*** [corresponding to the *v.* senses] **1:** *a ~ for help; a roll ~ by a teacher.* **2:** *a bird's mating ~.* **3:** *a divine ~ to the ministry; a ~ to battle; a strike ~.* **4:** *a bad ~ by an umpire in baseball.* **5:** *a three-minute telephone ~.* **6:** *too many ~s on my time; a loan to be repaid on ~.* **7** in card games, a bid. **8** a visit: *a service ~ by a repairman.* **—call•er** *n.* **—call down** reprimand. **—call in 1** summon as help. **2** withdraw from circulation. **—call off 1** cancel. **2** read out aloud. **—call (on)** pay a short visit (to). **—call one's bluff** challenge a pretentious claim. **—call up 1** recollect; cause to recollect. **2** telephone. **3** summon to military service; **call-up** *n.* **—on call** available: *doctors on ~ in an emergency; Please stay* **within call** (i.e. close enough to hear a call).

cal•la (lily) (CAL·uh) a decorative plant of the arum family.

call•back *n.* a notice to consumers to return a defective product; recall. **—call-board** *n.* a bulletin board for notices or schedules, as for theater rehearsals or train times. **—call girl** a prostitute who can be summoned by telephone.

calli- *comb. form.* beautiful: as in *callisthenics.* **—cal•lig•ra•phy** (kuh·LIG·ruh·fee) *n.* penmanship; fine handwriting; **cal•lig•ra•pher** *n.;* **cal•li•graph•ic** (–GRAPH–) *adj.*

call-in *n.* same as PHONE-IN. **—call•ing** *n.* a vocation, esp. to a religious occupation; any occupation or profession.

cal•li•o•pe (cuh·LYE·uh·pee) *n.* a musical instrument operated by a set of steam whistles.

cal•li•per same as CALIPER. **—cal•lis•then•ics** same as CALISTHENICS.

Cal•lis•to (cuh·LIS·toe) **1** in Greek mythology, a nymph changed into a bear, which became the constellation Ursa Major. **2** one of the moons of Jupiter.

call number a set of letters and numbers by which a library book is identified.

cal•los•i•ty (cal·OS–) *n.* **-ties** callousness; also, a callus. **—cal•lous** (CAL·us) *adj.* toughened; insensitive: *~ skin; a ~ disregard for suffering.* **—*v.*** become or make callous. **—cal•lous•ly** *adv.* **—cal•lous•ness** *n.*

cal•low (CAL·oh) *adj.* youthful; inexperienced; *a ~ lad.* **—cal•low•ness** *n.*

call-up *n.* a summons to military service.

cal•lus (CAL–) *n.* **cal•lus•es** a tough, thick area of skin or bark. **—*v.*** form or produce a callus.

calm (CAHM) *n.* **1** state of peacefulness; serenity. **2** at sea, a time or state of no wind; doldrums. **—*adj.:*** *a cool and ~ reaction.* **—*v.*** become calm; quiet or soothe; also **calm down. —calm•ly** *adv.* **—calm•ness** *n.*

cal•o•mel (CAL·uh–) *n.* mercurous chloride, a tasteless, white powder used as a purgative.

cal•o•rie (CAL·uh·ree) *n.* **-ries 1** the amount of heat needed to raise by 1°C the temperature of one gram of water *(small calorie)* or of one kilogram of water *(large calorie).* **2** the large calorie used as a measure of the energy in food. Also **cal•o•ry, -ries. —ca•lor•ic** (kuh·LOR–) *adj.* **—cal•o•rif•ic** (cal·uh·RIF–) *adj.* productive of heat: *the ~ value of a fuel.* **—cal•o•rim•e•ter** (cal·uh·RIM·uh–) *n.* a device for measuring heat; **cal•o•rim•e•try** (–tree) *n.* the measuring of heat; **ca•lor•i•met•ric** (–MET–) *adj.;* **ca•lor•i•met•ri•cal•ly** *adv.*

cal•u•met (CAL·yuh–) *n.* an ornamented, ceremonial pipe of the American Indians.

cal•um•ny (CAL·um·nee) *n.* **-nies** a malicious lie; false accusation. **—ca•lum•ni•ate** (cuh·LUM·nee–) *v.* **-ates, -at•ed, -at•ing** slander; malign; **ca•lum•ni•a•tor** *n.* **—ca•lum•ni•a•tion** (–AY–) *n.* **—ca•lum•ni•ous** (–LUM·nee·us) *adj.;* **ca•lum•ni•ous•ly** *adv.*

Cal•va•ry (CAL·vuh·ree) a hill near ancient Jerusalem, the site of Christ's crucifixion.

calve (CAV, CAHV) *v.* **calves, calved, calv•ing** bear a calf. **—calves** *pl.* of CALF.

Cal•vin (CAL–), **John.** 1509–1564, a French theologian whose doctrine **Cal•vin•ism** asserts predestination and salvation by grace. **—Cal•vin•ist** *n.* & *adj.* **—Cal•vin•is•tic** (–NIS–) *adj.*

calyces a *pl.* of CALYX.

ca•lyp•so (cuh·LIP·soh) *n.* **-sos** a type of folk song originating in the West Indies, characterized by improvised lyrics of topical interest. —***adj.:*** *They danced to a ~ rhythm.*

ca•lyx (CAY–, CAL–) *n.* **-lyx•es** or **-ly•ces** (–li·seez) the outer ring of usu. green, leaflike sepals of a flower.

cam *n.* a noncircular wheel used to give an up-and-down or eccentric motion to a connected part.

ca•ma•ra•de•rie (cam·uh·RAD·uh·ree) *n.* fellowship and loyalty among friends or comrades.

cam•ber (CAM–) *n.* a slight curvature, as of a road surface; also, the adjustment of automobile wheels to make them closer together at the bottom. **—*v.*** to arch; curve; bend.

cam•bi•um (CAM·bee–) *n.* **-bi•ums** or **-bi•a** the layer of growing cells between the wood and bark of woody plants.

Cam•bo•di•a (–BOH·dee·uh) a S.E. Asian country; 69,898 sq. mi. (181,035 km²); *cap.* Phnom Penh; also called **Kampuchea. —Cam•bo•di•an** *n.* & *adj.*

Cam•bri•an (CAM·bree·un) *n.* the earliest period of the Paleozoic era of the earth beginning about 600 million years ago. **—*adj.:*** *~ rocks and fossils.*

cam·bric (CAME–) *n.* a delicate white linen or cotton fabric.

Cam·bridge (CAME–) **1** a city of S.E. England; also, the university situated there. **2** a city of E. Massachusetts.

Cam·den (CAM–) a city in S.W. New Jersey.

came *pt.* of COME.

cam·el (CAM–) *n.* a domestic, cud-chewing beast of burden with a humped back and long neck, used in the desert areas of W. Asia and N. Africa. —**cam·el·back** *n.* **1** *They crossed the desert on ~;* ***adj.*** humpbacked. **2** a rubber compound used in retreading tires.

ca·mel·li·a (cuh·MEEL·yuh) *n.* any of a group of shrubs of the tea family from Asia, esp. japonica; also, its roselike flower.

ca·mel·o·pard (cuh·MEL·uh–) *n. Archaic.* the giraffe.

camel's hair a fabric made with camel's hair or a substitute: *the artist's* **camel's-hair brush** *made of squirrel's-tail hair.*

Cam·em·bert (CAM·um·bare) *n.* a creamy, rich cheese, originally from France.

cam·e·o (CAM·ee·oh) *n.* **-os** **1** a small carving raised above its background, as on a layered gem, shell, medallion, etc. **2** in drama, television, or films, a brief appearance by a famous person: *a ~ role.* —***v.*** **-os, -oed, -o·ing** portray or present in cameo.

cam·er·a (CAM·uh·ruh) *n.* an apparatus for taking photographs or motion pictures; in television, a device that changes light images into electrical signals; **in camera** in a judge's chambers; in private. —**cam·er·a·man** *n.* **-men** the operator of a TV or movie camera.

Cam·er·oon or **Cam·er·oun** (cam·uh·ROON) a republic in C. Africa; 183,569 sq. mi. (475,442 km²); *cap.* Yaoundé. —**Cam·er·oon·i·an** or **Cam·er·oun·i·an** *n.* & *adj.*

cam·i·sole (CAM–) *n.* a woman's sleeveless undergarment covering the torso.

cam·o·mile (CAM–) same as CHAMOMILE.

cam·ou·flage (CAM·uh·flahzh) *n.* a disguise, effected by imitating the surroundings; also, the materials that help this; hence, any deceptive concealment. —***v.*** **-flag·es, -flaged, -flag·ing:** *They ~d the tanks with saplings.*

¹camp *n.* **1** a place for, or a group of rough and temporary shelters, usu. in the country, esp. military or recreational; also, the people in a camp: *an army ~; a fishing ~; a mining ~.* **2** a side in a debate or fight: *the opposing ~.* **3** break camp pack up and leave after camping. —***v.*** make, shelter in, or live in a camp; also **camp out.**

²camp *n.* something so exaggerated, unnatural, or outlandish as to be considered amusing. —***adj.:*** *~ art;* also **camp·y** *adj.* **camp·i·er, -i·est.:** *~ acting.* —**camp·i·ly** *adv.* —**camp·i·ness** *n.*

cam·paign (–PAIN) *n.* **1** an organized activity aimed at a specific goal: *a fund-raising ~; a presidential ~.* **2** a particular phase of a war: *the Italian ~.* —***v.:*** *The candidate ~ed from door to door.* —**cam·paign·er** *n.*

cam·pa·ni·le (cam·puh·NEE·lee) *n.* **-les** or **-li** (–lee) a bell tower, usu. one built as a separate structure. —**cam·pa·nol·o·gy** (–NOL·uh·jee) *n.* the science and art of casting and ringing bells; **cam·pa·nol·o·gist** *n.*

camp·er *n.* **1** one who lives in a camp, esp. a recreational camp. **2** a vehicle designed or adapted for camping. —**camp·fire** *n.* an open fire at a camp; also, a gathering around it. —**campfire girl** a member of the **Camp Fire Girls,** a U.S. national organization founded in 1910. —**camp follower** an unofficial adherent of a party; a hanger-on, esp. of an army; hence, a prostitute or peddler. —**camp·ground** *n.* **1** an area for camping, often public, with facilities provided. **2** the site of a camp meeting.

cam·phor (CAM·fur) *n.* an aromatic, medicinal gummy substance obtained from an Asiatic evergreen of the laurel family, the **camphor tree.** —**cam·phor·at·ed** *adj.* treated with camphor: *~ oil.*

camp meeting an evangelical meeting held outdoors and lasting several days. —**camp·o·ree** (cam·puh·REE) *n.* a regional assembly or outing of boy or girl scouts; cf. JAMBOREE. —**camp·site** *n.* a place fit or prepared for a camp. —**camp·stool** *n.* a portable, folding stool. —**cam·pus** (CAM·pus) *n.* **-pus·es** the land and buildings of an educational institution. —**campy** See ²CAMP.

cam·shaft *n.* the shaft on which a cam is mounted.

¹can *auxiliary v., pt.* **could** (COOD, like *hood*) [indicating] **1** ability: *He ~ ride a horse.* **2** likelihood: *What ~ have happened here?* **3** capacity: *He ~ be nasty at times.* **4** permission: *I ~ not accept that check.*

²can *n.* **1** a metal container: *milk ~; garbage ~.* **2** a can that is sealed airtight to preserve the contents. **3** *Slang* a jail. —***v.*** **cans, canned, can·ning** **1:** *We ~ tomatoes; a jar of ~d preserve.* **2** record on tape or film: *~d laughter.* **3** *Slang.* fire from a job. **4** *Slang.* stop: *~ that chatter!* —**can·ner** *n.*

Can. Canada; Canadian.

Ca·naan (CAY·nun) biblical Palestine, the promised land of the Israelites; hence, a promised land. —**Ca·naan·ite** *n.*

Can·a·da (CAN·uh·duh) the Commonwealth country in the N. half of North America; 3,851,809 sq.mi. (9,976,139 km²); *cap.* Ottawa. —**Ca·na·di·an** (cuh·NAY·dee·un) *n.* & *adj.* —**Canada (goose)** a large wild goose with a white bar across cheeks and neck, native to North America.

ca·naille (cuh·NAIL) *n.* riff-raff; rabble: *the dirty ~ of the streets.*

ca·nal (cuh·NAL) *n.* **1** a man-made waterway: *a shipping ~ ; an irrigation ~.* **2** a duct or passage in the body: *the alimentary ~.* —**ca·nal·boat** *n.* a barge for use on canals. —**ca·nal·ize** (cuh·NAL–, CAN·ul–) *v.* **-iz·es, -ized, -iz·ing** build a canal; direct into or provide with a channel or outlet; **ca·nal·i·za·tion** (–ZAY–) *n.* —**Canal Zone** the territory around the Panama Canal.

ca·na·pé (CAN·uh·pee) *n.* a cracker or piece of toast, with a tasty topping, forming an appetizer: *anchovy ~s.*

ca·nard (cuh·NARD) *n.* a false rumor spread purposely; hoax.

ca·nar·y (cuh·NAIR·ee) *n.* **-nar·ies** a type of small, bright yellow songbird of the finch family that is native to the Canary Islands. —**canary (yellow)** *n.* & *adj.*

Canary Islands a group of Spanish islands off N.W. Africa; also called "the Canaries."

ca·nas·ta (kuh·NAS·tuh) *n.* a card game developed from rummy that uses two decks of cards.

Can·ber·ra (CAN·buh·ruh) the capital of Australia.

canc. canceled.

can·can *n.* a lively French show dance characterized by high kicking.

can·cel *v.* **-cels, -cel(l)ed, -cel·(l)ing** **1** cross out; draw a line through; hence, in printing, to delete or omit. **2** mark to prevent reuse: *a ~d stamp.* **3** withdraw; invalidate: *a ~d order.* **4** in arithmetic, to remove a common element from both sides of an equation or the numerator and denominator of a fraction. **5** neutralize; counterbalance; also **cancel out:** *The two arguments ~ each other out.* —***n.*** **1** a cancellation. **2** in printing, a deletion; also, the part deleted. —**can·cel·la·tion** *n.: The ~ made the check nonnegotiable.* —**can·cel·(l)a·ble** *adj.* —**can·cel·(l)er** *n.*

can·cer *n.* a malignant uncontrolled growth of cells in some part of the body; also, the disease, often fatal, caused by such a growth; hence, any growing evil: *Electoral corruption is a ~ in the body politic;* **can·cer·ous** *adj.;* **can·cer·ous·ly** *adv.* —**Can·cer** a N. constellation and the fourth sign of the zodiac.

can·de·la (–DEE–) *n.* unit of luminous intensity. —**can·de·la·brum** (–LAH·brum) *n.* **-brums** or **-bra** (–bruh) a many-branched, usu. ornamental candlestick; also **can·de·la·bra, -bras.** —**can·des·cent** (–DES–) *adj.* glowing with extreme heat; incandescent. —**can·des·cence** *n.* —**can·did** *adj.* **1** unbiased; impartial. **2** honest; sincere; forthright: *~ criticism can endanger friendships.* **3** informal; unposed. —**can·did·ly** *adv.* —**can·did·ness** *n.* —**can·di·date** *n.* one who competes for or is eligible for an office, degree, etc.: *a ~ for mayor; a Ph.D. ~.* —**can·di·da·cy** (–duh·see) *n.* **-cies:** *an unopposed ~;* also **can·di·da·ture** *Brit.* —**candid camera** a camera used for quick informal pictures.

candied *pp.* & *adj.* See CANDY.

can·dle *n.* a usu. cylindrical mass of tallow, wax, etc. with a wick of cotton fiber through it, which is burned to produce light. —***v.*** **-dles, -dled, -dling** inspect eggs, esp. for freshness, by holding them before a strong light; **can·dler** *n.* —**can·dle·light** *n.* **1** light shed by a candle: *dining by ~.* **2** dusk; early evening. —**Can·dle·mas** (CAN·dl·mus) *n.* February 2, a church festival in honor of the Virgin Mary. —**can·dle·pin** *n.* a slim, well-tapered pin used in a bowling game called **can·dle·pins.** —**can·dle·pow·er** *n.* light intensity, measured by a unit called a candle. —**can·dle·stick** *n.* a holder for a single candle. —**can·dle·wick** *n.* cotton yarn used for wicks and for embroidery: *a ~ dressing gown.* —**can·dor** (–dur) *n.* candidness; impartiality; forthrightness; sincerity; also **can·dour** *Brit.*

C and W country and western (music).

can·dy (–dee) *n.* **-dies** (–deez) a sugar-based confection made with flavoring, fruit, nuts, etc. —***v.*** **-dies, -died, -dy·ing** turn into sugar crystals; cook in sugar or syrup; saturate or encrust with sugar. —**can·died** (CAN·deed) *adj. ~ apples; ~ dates; ~* (i.e. sweet or flattering) *words.* —**can·dy-striped** *adj.* with thin, bright-colored stripes on a plain, usu. white background. —**candy striper** a young volunteer nursing assistant.

cane *n.* **1** a thin, woody, usu. flexible stem, of a grass, as sugar cane and bamboo, of a palm, as rattan, or other plant such as the raspberry; also, the plants themselves. **2** material, esp. rattan, woven into chairs, baskets, etc. **3** a walking stick; also, a rod for flogging. —***v.*** **canes, caned, can·ing** make or repair with cane; flog. —**can·er** *n.* —**cane·brake** *n.* a dense growth of cane plants. —**cane sugar** sugar made from sugar cane.

ca·nine (CAY–) *adj.* pertaining to the group of animals that includes dogs, jackals, wolves, and foxes: *~ devotion.* —***n.*** **1** a dog. **2** one of the four sharp cuspid teeth between the incisors and pre-molars; also **canine tooth.** —**Ca·nis Ma·jor** (CAY·nis·MAY·jur) a constellation of the S. Hemisphere near Orion. —**Canis Mi·nor** (–MYE·nur) an equatorial constellation near Orion.

can·is·ter (CAN–) *n.* **1** a light box of metal, plastic, etc. with a lid, used for storing tea, flour, crackers, etc. **2** a cylindrical projectile containing shot, tear gas, etc.

can·ker (CANG·kur) *n.* **1** a disease that eats away tissue, as a rot or rust in plants; an ulcerous sore, esp. in the mouth. **2** a plant-eating insect larva; also called **can·ker·worm.** —**can·ker·ous** *adj.*

can·na (CAN·uh) *n.* a genus of tropical plants grown for their large leaves and bright, irregular flowers.

can·na·bis (CAN·uh–) *n.* dried flowering tops of the female hemp plant, the source of marijuana and hashish; hence, marijuana; also, the plant.

canned *pt.* & *pp.* of ²CAN. —***adj.*** recorded for reproduction: ~ *music, applause.*

can·nel (coal) (CAN·ul) *n.* a dense, volatile coal with a bright flame, a source of gas and oil.

can·ner·y *n.* **can·ner·ies** a canning factory.

can·ni·bal (CAN·uh·bl) n. one who eats human flesh; also, an animal that feeds on its own kind; hence, a brutal savage; ***adj.:*** ~ *tribes;* **can·ni·bal·ism** *n.* —**can·ni·bal·is·tic** (–IS–) *adj.* —**can·ni·bal·ize** *v.* **-iz·es, -ized, -iz·ing** tear up (old equipment, machines, etc.) for parts to repair other equipment with; **can·ni·bal·i·za·tion** (–ZAY–) *n.*

can·non (CAN·un) *n.* **-nons** or **-non** **1** a large, heavy gun mounted on a platform or carriage; a large-bore, automatic gun on an aircraft. **2** *Brit.* a carom shot in billiards. —**can·non·ade** (–uh·NADE) *n.* an attack with, or prolonged volley of cannon fire; ***v.*** **-ades, -ad·ed, -ad·ing.** —**can·non·ball** *n.* a heavy metal ball used as cannon shot; ***v.*** *Informal.* to move quickly and with great force. —**can·non·eer** (–uh·NEER) *n.* one who tends and fires cannon. —**cannon fodder** men considered merely as expendable war materiel.

can·not (CAN·ot, cuh·NOT) can not. —**cannot but** can only; must: *One ~ but praise his daring.*

can·nu·la (CAN·yuh·luh) *n.* **-las** or **-lae** (–lee) a narrow, surgical drainage tube inserted into a cavity, tumor, duct, etc. in the body.

can·ny (CAN·ee) *adj.* **can·ni·er, can·ni·est** capable; shrewd; wily; prudent: *a ~ businessman.* —**can·ni·ly** *adv.* —**can·ni·ness** *n.*

ca·noe (cuh·NOO) *n.* **-noes** a slender boat of shallow draught with pointed ends, usu. moved by paddles. —***v.*** **-noes, -noed, -noe·ing** travel or . ansport in a canoe: *He ~d the load across the bay.* —**ca·noe·ist** *n.*

can·on (CAN·un) *n.* **1** a basic principle; criterion for judgment. **2** a law or rule of the church, collectively called **canon law.** **3** a list of things accepted as genuine and essential, as the books of the Bible, the list of Roman Catholic saints, etc.: *the ~ of Shakespeare's works.* **4** a cleric living under a special rule, esp. one serving in a cathedral; his office or endowment is a **can·on·ry** (CAN·un·ree) *n.* **-ries.** **5** in music, a round. —**ca·non·i·cal** (kuh·NON–) *adj.* **1** accepted; orthodox. **2** of or having to do with a clergyman canon; **ca·non·i·cal·ly** *adv.;* **ca·non·i·cals** *n. pl.* the vestments prescribed for an officiating priest; **canonical hour** one of seven prescribed daily times for prayer. —**can·on·ize** *v.* **-iz·es, -ized, -iz·ing** **1** recognize officially; accept into a canon, esp. of a saint. **2** revere. —**can·on·iz·a·tion** *n.*

ca·ñon (CAN·yun) *n.* same as CANYON.

canon law See CANON, *n.* 2. —**canonry** See CANON, *n.* 4.

can·o·py (CAN·uh·pee) *n.* **-pies** (–peez) an overhanging cover, esp. for ornament or protection: *the ~ over a four-poster bed; a ~ of trees; the ~* (i.e. cockpit cover) *of an airplane.* —***v.*** **-pies, -pied, -py·ing:** *a ~d entrance.*

canst *Archaic.* the form of CAN used with *thou.*

¹cant *n.* a sloping or angled surface, edge, or position; slant; hence, a blow causing an upset or tilt. —***adj.:*** *a ~ buttress.* —***v.*** tilt; angle; bevel.

²cant *n.* **1** argot; jargon: *thieves' ~; lawyers' ~.* **2** empty, hypocritical, conventional speech: *all this ~ about virtue.* —***v.:*** *They will ~ about charity but won't give a penny.* —**cant·ing·ly** *adv.*

can't cannot. —**Cant.** Cantonese.

can·ta·bi·le (cahn·TAH·bi·lay) *adj.* & *adv. Music.* in a fluid, songlike style.

can·ta·loup(e) (CANT·uh·lope) *n.* a small, orange-fleshed muskmelon with a hard, ribbed rind.

can·tan·ker·ous (–TANG·kuh·rus) *adj.* argumentative; bad-tempered. —**can·tan·ker·ous·ly** *adv.* —**can·tan·ker·ous·ness** *n.*

can·ta·ta (cun·TAH·tah) *n.* a piece of choral music with solos and accompaniment, usu. dramatic, though not acted.

can·teen (–TEEN) *n.* **1** a place that sells refreshments and small provisions: *a factory ~.* **2** a recreation center, esp. at a military base. **3** a small metal flask for liquids.

can·ter *n.* a gentle gallop: *He rode at a ~.* —***v.:*** *His horse ~ed along.* —**Can·ter·bur·y** (CAN·tur·ber·ee) a city in Kent, S.E. England. —**Canterbury bell(s)** a cultivated plant that bears attractive bell-shaped flowers.

can·thar·i·des (–THAIR·i·deez) *n. pl.* a medicine prepared from the **can·thar·is** (CAN·thur–), a blister beetle, and used as a skin irritant.

can·ti·cle (CAN–) *n.* a song or chant, usu. from the Bible, used in a church service.

can·ti·le·ver (CAN·tl·ee·vur) *n.* a projecting structure or support fastened only at one end. —***v.*** build as or support with a cantilever. —**cantilever bridge** one built of two cantilevers meeting but not supporting each other. —**can·tle** *n.* the projecting rear support on a saddle.

can·to (CAN·toh) *n.* **-tos** a major division of a long poem.

can·ton (CAN·tun) *n.* an administrative or territorial division, esp. a state in Switzerland; **can·ton·al** *adj.* —***v.*** **1** divide; apportion. **2** quarter (troops) in lodgings.

Can·ton **1** (CAN·tun) a city in N.E. Ohio. **2** (can·TAHN) a city in S.E. China; **Can·ton·ese** (–tuh·NEEZ) *n. sing.* & *pl.* a native of Canton, China; also, its regional language; ***adj.:*** *the ~ dialect.*

can·ton·ment (–TONE–, –TON–) *n.* the billeting of troops; also, temporary housing for troops.
can·tor (CAN·tur) *n.* a solo or lead singer in a church or synagogue; precentor.
can·vas (CAN·vus) *n.* **1** a strong, coarsely woven cloth used for sails, tents, etc. **2** something made using canvas, as an oil painting on canvas. **3** sails or tents collectively. **—under canvas** **1** with sails spread. **2** in tents. ***—adj.:*** *~ deck shoes.* ***—v.*** **-vas·es, -vased, -vas·ing** cover with canvas. **—can·vas·back** *n.* a North American wild duck with a gray back and reddish head and neck.
can·vass (CAN·vus) *v.* **1** discuss; examine thoroughly: *to ~ ballots.* **2** go about asking opinions, votes, orders, donations, etc.: *~ing for the Heart Fund.* ***—n.*** [corresponding to the *v.* senses] **1:** *a complete ~ of the proposal.* **2:** *a door-to-door ~ for the Republican candidate.* **—can·vass·er** *n.*
can·yon (CAN·yun) *n.* a narrow valley with high, sheer walls; a gorge.
caou·tchouc (COW·chook) *n.* rubber in crude form.
cap *n.* **1** a soft, light head-covering: *nurse's ~; baseball ~.* **2** any covering, lid, or topmost part: *bottle ~; mushroom ~.* **3** percussion cap; esp., a small explosive charge in a paper capsule, for use in a toy gun called a **cap pistol** or **cap gun.** ***—v.*** **caps, capped, cap·ping** **1** cover; place a cap on. **2** equal; outdo: *He can ~ that trick.* **—cap in hand** humbly.
cap. capacity; capital city; capital letter. —**C.A.P.** Civil Air Patrol.
ca·pa·ble (CAY·puh·bl) *adj.* competent: *a ~ manager; He did a ~ job;* **capable of** with the potential for: *a man ~ of murder; a problem ~ of solution;* **ca·pa·bly** *adv.* **—ca·pa·bil·i·ty** (–BIL–) *n.* **-ties.** **—ca·pa·cious** (kuh·PAY·shus) *adj.* able to hold a great deal; expansive: *a ~ dining room;* **ca·pa·cious·ly** *adv.;* **ca·pa·cious·ness** *n.*—**ca·pac·i·tance** (kuh·PAS·i·tunce) *n.* an electric nonconductor's ability to store energy, measured as the ratio of charge on either of two opposite surfaces of the nonconductor to the potential between them. **—ca·pac·i·tive** *adj.* **—ca·pac·i·tive·ly** *adv.* **—ca·pac·i·tate** (–PAS–) *v.* **-tates, -tat·ed, -tat·ing** make fit, able, or ready.—**ca·pac·i·tor** (–tur) *n.* an electrical device for holding a stored charge in a circuit; formerly called *condenser.*—**ca·pac·i·ty** (–PAS·i·tee) *n.* **-ties** **1** the ability to receive, hold, absorb, etc.: *a ~ for learning.* **2** the volume or amount held: *a storage ~ of 30 tons; a theater with a large seating ~;* ***adj.:*** *A ~ crowd packed the arena.* **3** power; productive capability: *a man working at his full ~.* **4** position; role: *He acted in his official ~.*
cap-a-pie (cap·uh·PEE) *adv.* from head to foot; completely: *armed ~.*
ca·par·i·son (cuh·PAIR·i·sun) *n.* decorative covering for a horse and its harness; rich finery. ***—v.:*** *trees ~ed in autumn gold.*
cape *n.* **1** a full, sleeveless outer garment hanging from the shoulders. **2** a point of land projecting into a sea, lake, river, etc.: *Cape Cod; Cape of Good Hope.* **—Cape buffalo** See BUFFALO. **—Cape Cod cottage** a compact bungalow of one or one-and-one-half stories with a central chimney and gabled roof.
ca·per (CAY–) *n.* **1** a flower bud or young berry of a Mediterranean shrub pickled for use as a seasoning; also, the shrub itself. **2** a light, playful jump; a bold trick. **3** *Slang.* a crime. **—cut a caper** (or **capers**) to frolic about; play a foolish prank. ***—v.:*** *a lamb ~ing lightly across the meadow.*
cape·skin *n.* a soft sheepskin leather. **—Cape Town** the legislative capital of South Africa.—**Cape Verde** (–VURD) an African country consisting of 15 islands off the W. coast; 1,557 sq.mi. (4,033 km²); *cap.* Praia.
cap·ful *n.* the amount that a cap can hold. **—cap gun** See CAP, *n.* 3.
cap·il·lar·i·ty (–LAIR·i·tee) *n.* **-ties** the interaction of a solid and liquid surface that results in attraction or repulsion of the liquid; the attraction, esp. in tubes, is called **capillary action** (or **attraction**).—**cap·il·lar·y** (CAP·i·ler·ee) *adj.* **1** hairlike; slender; with a small bore: *a ~ tube.* **2** of or having to do with capillarity. ***—n.,*** *pl.* **-il·lar·ies** a capillary tube, esp. any of the tiny blood vessels linking the arteries to the veins.
cap·i·tal (CAP·i·tl) *adj.* **1** most important; most serious: *an act of ~ folly.* **2** subject to the death penalty: *a ~ offense.* **3** excellent: *a ~ meal.* Hence **cap·i·tal·ly** *adv.* ***—n.*** **1** capital city. **2** capital letter. **3** the often ornate top of a pilaster or column. **4** material or financial assets engaged in or available for the production of goods and profit; the total monetary value of a person or corporation; also, capitalists or investors collectively.—**capital (city)** the chief city, esp. governmental center. **—capital goods** goods such as machinery and equipment used in the production of other goods. **—cap·i·tal·ism** *n.* an economic system with free markets and private ownership of capital; **cap·i·tal·ist** *n.* a person who owns invested capital or supports capitalism; **cap·i·tal·is·tic** (–IS–) *adj.;* **cap·i·tal·is·tic·al·ly** *adv.* **—cap·i·tal·ize** (CAP·i·tl·ize) *v.* **-iz·es, -ized, -iz·ing** **1** write with or as a capital letter. **2** take advantage of; profit from: *~ on someone else's bad luck.* **3** supply capital for: *~ a business venture.* **4** convert to capital. **5** calculate the value of. **—capital (letter)** a large letter, as A, B, C. **—capital punishment** punishment by death. **—capital ship** a warship of the highest rank. **—capital stock** the total amount of capital invested in a corporation, issued as shares.—**cap·i·ta·tion** (–TAY–)

n. a standard per-capita tax or levy.—**cap·i·tol** (CAP·i·tul) *n.* **1** a state legislature building. **2 Capitol** the U.S. Congress building in Washington, D.C.—**ca·pit·u·late** (–PICH·uh–) *v.* **-lates, -lat·ed, -lat·ing** surrender on stated terms; yield; cease resistance; **ca·pit·u·la·tion** (–LAY–) *n.*

ca·pon (CAY·pahn) *n.* a rooster, gelded and fattened for eating.

cap·o·ral (CAP·uh·rul) *n.* a kind of tobacco.

ca·pote (cuh·POTE) *n.* a hooded cloak or cape.—**cap pistol** See CAP, *n.* 3.

cap·pric·cio (cuh·PREE·chee·oh) *n.* **-pric·cios** or **-pric·ci** (–chee) *Music.* an imaginative instrumental piece with a spirited tempo and free form. —**ca·price** (cuh·PREECE) *n.* **1** a whim; unmotivated desire or change; fickleness; capriciousness. **2** *Music.* a cappriccio. —**ca·pri·cious** *adj.: a ~ lover.* —**ca·pri·cious·ly** *adv.* —**ca·pri·cious·ness** *n.*

Cap·ri·corn (CAP–) *n.* **1** a S. constellation, also called **Cap·ri·cor·nus,** and the tenth sign of the zodiac.—**cap·ri·ole** (CAP·ree–) *n.* a nimble jump, esp. a stationary leap by a horse with all four feet off the ground; also ***v.* -oles, -oled, -ol·ing.**

caps· capital letters; capsule.

cap·si·cum (CAP·si–) *n.* any of a group of shrubby plants, including hot and sweet peppers; also, their spicy seeds and pods used in seasonings.

cap·size (CAP–) *v.* **-siz·es, -sized, -siz·ing** overturn; upset: *The canoe ~d in the storm.*

cap·stan (CAP·stun) *n.* **1** esp. on ships, an upright cylinder which is rotated to wind in a cable, lift loads, etc. **2** in a tape recorder, a rotating spindle which moves the tape at a constant speed.

cap·su·lar (CAP·suh·lur) *adj.* in, of, or like a capsule.—**cap·sul·ate(d)** *adj.* made or put into a capsule. —**cap·sule** (CAP·sl, –sule) *n.* **1** an enclosed protective covering, as for bodily organs, seeds, spores, oral doses of medicine, etc. **2** a separable enclosure for people, instruments, etc. in an airplane or rocket: *The space ~ almost burned on re-entry.* —***v.* -sules, -suled, -sul·ing** capsulize. —***adj.*** brief and concise: *a ~ news report.*—**cap·sul·ize** *v.* **-iz·es, -ized, -iz·ing 1** put into a capsule. **2** condense; express concisely: *~d news.*

Capt. captain.—**cap·tain** (–tin) *n.* **1** a leader; outstanding figure: *~ of the baseball team; ~s of industry.* **2** a military officer ranking just below a major; a naval officer ranking just below a commodore or rear admiral. **3** the commander of a ship, fortress, garrison, etc.; the chief pilot of an airplane, usu. civil. —***v.:*** *He ~ed the squad all season.* —**cap·tain·cy** *n.* **-cies; cap·tain·ship** n.

cap·tion *n.* **1** a brief legend for a picture or cartoon; a subtitle in a movie. **2** a heading; title. —***v.:*** *The artist ~s his own cartoons.* —**cap·tious** (–shus) *adj.* **1** overly critical; carping. **2** designed to trap; sophistical: *~ questions.* —**cap·tious·ly** *adv.* —**cap·tious·ness** *n.* —**cap·ti·vate** *v.* **-vates, -vat·ed, -vat·ing** enthrall; charm: *~d by her beauty;* **cap·ti·va·tor** *n.* —**cap·ti·va·tion** (–VAY–) *n.* —**cap·tive** (–tiv) *n.* **1** a prisoner, esp. in war; one who is confined against his will. **2** one who is captivated. —***adj.:*** *~ birds; The prisoner hated his ~ state.* —**captive audience** a group, as in a classroom, forced by circumstances to pay attention.—**cap·tiv·i·ty** (–TIV–) *n.* —**cap·tor** *n.* one who captures. —**cap·ture** (–chur) *v.* **-tures, -tured, -tur·ing 1** seize by force or guile: *~d men; the ~d city.* **2** record permanently: *~ his face on film.* —***n.*** **1** the act of capturing. **2** one that has been captured.

Cap·u·chin (CAP·yoo–) *n.* **1** a friar of a Franciscan order whose habit is distinguished by a special hood. **2 capuchin** a type of South American monkey that has black hair on its crown as if wearing a monk's hood.

car *n.* **1** an automobile. **2** a wheeled vehicle on rails: *a cattle ~; dining ~.* **3** a compartment for passengers, freight, etc. in an elevator, dirigible, cable car, etc.

car. carat(s).—**C.A.R.** Civil Air Regulations.

ca·ra·bao (cah·ruh·BOW) *n.* **-bao(s).** a water buffalo.

car·a·bi·neer or **car·a·bi·nier** (cair·uh·bi·NEER) *n.* a soldier equipped with a carbine.

Ca·ra·cas (cuh·RAH·cus) capital of Venezuela.

car·a·cole (CAIR·uh–) *n.* in riding, a horse's half turn to either side. —***v.* -coles, -coled, -col·ing.**

caracul same as KARAKUL.

ca·rafe (cuh·RAF) *n.* a metal or glass bottle for serving wine, water, coffee, etc.

car·a·mel (CAIR·uh·mul) *n.* **1** burnt sugar that is dark and bitter, used for coloring and flavoring. **2** a rich, chewy candy.

car·a·pace (CAIR·uh–) *n.* a bony protective shell, as of a turtle, lobster, etc.

car·at (CAIR·ut) *n.* **1** same as KARAT. **2** a unit of weight for gems, equal to 200 milligrams.

car·a·van (CAIR·uh–) *n.* **1** a party of traders, pilgrims, etc. traveling together for safety; hence, a line of vehicles: *a circus ~.* **2** a van. —**car·a·van·sa·ry** (–VAN·suh·ree) *n.* **-ries** an inn for caravans; also **car·a·van·se·rai** (–rye, –ray), **-rais.**

car·a·vel (CAIR·uh–) *n.* a small sailing ship of the 15th and 16th c. with a high stern and broad bow.

car·a·way (CAIR·uh–) **seeds** *n. pl.* the aromatic seeds of a parsleylike herb, called **caraway,** used for seasoning.

car·bide (CAHR–) *n.* a compound of carbon and one other element: *calcium ~.*

car·bine (–been, –bine) *n.* a light rifle with a short barrel. —**car·bi·neer** same as CARABINEER.

carbo- *comb. form.* carbon. **—car·bo·hy·drate** *n.* a compound of carbon, oxygen, and hydrogen, as cellulose, starch, sugar, etc. **—car·bo·lat·ed** (CAHR·buh–) *adj.* treated or mixed with **car·bol·ic acid,** a caustic compound with antiseptic and anaesthetic properties, used in making aspirin, plastics, etc. **—car·bon** (–bun) *n.* **1** a common element found in all organic compounds, in coal, petroleum, and other fuels, and isolated in diamonds and graphite. **2** a carbon paper; a carbon copy. **—car·bo·na·ceous** (–NAY·shus) *adj.* yielding, made of, or pertaining to carbon. **—car·bon·ate** *v.* **-ates, -at·ed, -at·ing** mix with carbon dioxide: *Soda water is ~d;* **n.** (*also* -nit) a salt or ester of carbonic acid; **car·bon·a·tion** (–NAY–) *n.* **—carbon black** a fine powdered carbon used as a pigment in ink; lampblack. **—carbon copy 1** a duplicate document made with carbon paper. **2** an exact copy; **car·bon-cop·y** *v.* **—carbon dating** a technique for dating carboniferous artifacts, which measures their content of **carbon 14,** a radioactive isotope of carbon; **car·bon-date** *v.* **—carbon dioxide** a heavy, odorless, colorless, incombustible gas produced by fermentation, combustion, and respiration. It forms a weak acid, **car·bon·ic acid,** when mixed with water. **—car·bon·i·fer·ous** (–NIF·uh·rus) *adj.* **1** containing or yielding a form of carbon. **2 Carboniferous** of or from a period of the Paleozoic era of the earth beginning about 345 million years ago when much coal was formed; ***n.*** the period itself. **—carbon monoxide** a light, odorless, colorless, combustible, very poisonous gas, produced by the incomplete burning of carbon. **—carbon paper** a thin sheet coated on one side with a usu. carbon-based pigment and inserted between two sheets of paper for copying what is being written or typed. **—carbon tet·ra·chlo·ride** (–tet·ruh·CLOR·ide) a colorless, noncombustible, poisonous liquid used as a cleaning solvent.**—Car·bo·run·dum** (cahr·buh·RUN·dum) *Trademark.* any of various abrasives made of silicon carbide.

car·boy *n.* a large bottle, usu. for dangerous liquids, protected by a wicker basket or a box.

car·bun·cle (CAHR·bung·cl) *n.* **1** a painful inflammation under the skin which produces pus. **2** a red garnet. **—car·bun·cu·lar** (–BUNG·kyuh·lur) *adj.*

car·bu·ret·or (CAHR·buh·ray·tur) *n.* in internal combustion engines, the device which combines air and fuel for proper burning. **—car·bu·re·tion** (–RAY–) *n.* the process of mixing air and a vaporized hydrocarbon (as gasoline) for exploding in an engine.

car·bu·rize (CAHR·buh–) *v.* **-riz·es, -rized, -riz·ing** compound or impregnate (esp. a metal) with carbon. **—car·bu·ri·za·tion** (–ZAY–) *n.*

car·cass (CAHR·cus) *n.* **1** an animal corpse, esp. one dressed for meat. **2** *Informal.* the human body. **3** useless remains: *the ~ of a wrecked car.*

carcin(o)- *comb.form.* tumor or cancer. **—car·cin·o·gen** (–SIN·uh·jun) *n.* a substance which causes cancer; **car·ci·no·gen·ic** (–noh·JEN·ic) *adj.;* **car·ci·no·ge·nic·i·ty** (–NIS–) *n.* **—car·ci·no·ma** (–NOH·muh) *n.* **-mas** or **-ma·ta** (–muh·tuh) an epithelial cancer; **car·ci·nom·a·tous** (–NOM·uh·tus) *adj.*

card. cardinal.

[1]**card** *n.* a wire brush for combing and cleaning unspun wool; a brush for raising the nap on fabric. ***—v.:*** *~ed wool.* **—card·er** *n.*

[2]**card** *n.* **1** a small, stiff rectangular piece of paper, used for many purposes, as a *playing ~, postcard,* etc.; for identification, as a *membership ~, business ~, calling ~;* for mailed greetings, as a *Christmas ~;* for information, as an *index ~.* **2** a program at an event, esp. sports. **3** *Informal.* a witty or eccentric person. **—cards** *n. pl.* any game using playing cards. **—card·board** *n.* & *adj.* a thick board made of several layers of paper pulp. **—card-car·ry·ing** *adj.* **1** officially registered: *a ~ Communist.* **2** *Informal.* authentic; veritable: *a ~ neurotic.* **—card catalog** a catalog made on index cards, esp. one for books.

car·di·ac (CAHR·dee·ac) *adj.* of or having to do with the heart or heart disease. ***—n.*** a heart patient.

Car·diff (CAHR·dif) the chief city of Wales.

car·di·gan (CAHR·di·gun) *n.* a sweater or knitted jacket that opens down the front.

car·di·nal (CARDN·ul) *n.* **1** a dignitary of the Roman Catholic Church ranking next below the pope; **car·di·nal·ate** (–it, –ate) *n.* **2** a crested red finch of North America. **3** a bright red. ***—adj.*** principal; main: *the ~ virtues;* **car·din·al·ly** *adv.* **—cardinal flower** the scarlet lobelia, a North American plant with bright red flowers. **—cardinal number** a simple counting number, 1, 2, etc. as opposed to *first, second,* etc.; cf. ORDINAL.**—cardinal points** the four main compass directions of North, South, East, and West.

cardi(o)- *comb.form.* the heart: as in **car·di·o·gram** (CARD·ee·uh·gram), **-graph** same as ELECTROCARDIOGRAM, -GRAPH; **car·di·o·graph·ic** (–GRAPH·ic) *adj.;* **car·di·og·ra·phy** (–OG·ruh·fee) *n.* **—car·di·ol·o·gy** (–OL·uh·jee) *n.* the study of the heart, its diseases, and their treatment; **car·di·ol·o·gist** *n.* **—car·di·o·vas·cu·lar** (–VAS·kyuh·lur) *adj.* pertaining to the blood vessels and the heart.

card·sharp(·er) or **card shark** *Informal.* one skilled in winning card games by cheating.

care *n.* **1** worry; anxiety: *free from ~.* **2** supervision: *under a doctor's ~.* **3** attention; caution: *handle with ~!* **4** an object of anxiety or responsibility: *free from ~s and worries.*—***v.*** **cares, cared, car·ing 1** feel anxiety, interest, or liking: *Who ~s?* **2** object; be concerned: *I couldn't ~ less!* **—care for 1** take care of. **2** desire: *~ for coffee?* **3** like:

I don't ~ for his kind at all!—**(in) care of** at the address of. —**take care of** provide for; see to.

CARE (CAIR) Cooperative for American Relief to Everywhere, Inc.

ca·reen (cuh·REEN) *v.* **1** tip (a ship) to one side, esp. for cleaning; tilt or lean. **2** rush headlong unsteadily: *~ed downhill and hit a curb.*

ca·reer (cuh·REER) *n.* **1** a progression through life, business, etc.; vocation or life work: *a brilliant ~; a civil service ~.* **2** activity; progress; speed: *collapsed in full ~.* —***adj.:*** *a ~ diplomat.* —***v.*** move swiftly; hurtle.

care·free *adj.* without care or worry; also, not requiring care. —**care·ful** *adj.* **1** characterized by or using attention, vigilance, or caution: *~ not to offend; Be ~ near the highway.* **2** painstaking; thorough: *A ~ job takes time;* **care·ful·ly** *adv.;* **care·ful·ness** *n.* —**care·less** *adj.* **1** unconsidered; ill-considered; negligent: *a ~ error; a ~ observation; a ~ workman.* **2** indifferent: *He was bold, and ~ of the consequences.* **3** carefree; effortless: *an easy, ~ grace;* **care·less·ly** *adv.;* **care·less·ness** *n.*

ca·ress (cuh·RES) *n.* **1** a kind or loving touch; a kiss, hug, etc. **2** a light touch. —***v.:*** *Lovers ~ing; A warm breeze ~es my cheek.* —**ca·ress·er** *n.* —**ca·ress·ing·ly** *adv.*

car·et (CAIR·ut) *n.* the mark (‸) used to show where something is to be inserted in written or printed matter.

care·tak·er (CAIR·tay·kur) *n.* one hired to oversee and maintain property, buildings, etc., often in the owner's absence. —***adj.*** performing routine functions while awaiting a replacement: *a ~ government.*—**care·worn** (CAIR–) *adj.* marked by grief or anxiety: *a haggard, ~ face.*

car·fare *n.* the price of a bus or streetcar ride.

car·go *n.* **-go(e)s** the goods loaded in a ship, airplane, truck, etc. —**car·goed** *adj.* loaded: *ships ~d with gold.*

car·hop *n.* one who waits on cars at a drive-in restaurant.

Car·ib (CAIR·ib) *n.* a member of an Amerindian people of South America, coastal Central America, and the Lesser Antilles; also, their language. —***adj.:*** *a ~ dialect.* Also **Car·i·ban** *n.* & *adj.* —**Car·ib·be·an (Sea)** (cair·i·BEE·un) a part of the Atlantic Ocean bounded by the Yucatan Peninsula, the West Indies, South America, and Central America. —**Car·ib·be·an** *adj.*

car·i·bou (CAIR·i·boo) *n.* a large North American deer similar to the reindeer.

car·i·ca·ture (CAIR·i·cuh·choor) *n.* an exaggerated or distorted picture or writing that satirizes one's peculiarities; hence, any distortion: *Don Quixote is a ~ of the romantic hero.* —***v.*** **-tures, -tured, -tur·ing:** *a man ~d as a bear.* —**car·i·ca·tur·ist** (CAIR·i·kuh·choor·ist) *n.*

car·ies (CAIR·eez) *n.* tooth decay; bone decay.

car·il·lon (CAIR·i·lon) *n.* a set of tuned bells played by means of a keyboard; also, the music played. —**car·il·lon·er** (–lun·er) or **car·il·lon·neur** (–luh·NUR) *n.*

Ca·ri·na (cuh·RYE·nuh) *n.* a constellation visible in the S. Hemisphere.

car·i·ous (CAIR·ee·us) *adj.* having caries.

car·load (–lode) *n.* the amount that a freight car can hold; hence, a standard weight unit for shipping.

car·min·a·tive (cahr·MIN·uh·tiv) *n.* a medicine used for purging gas from the digestive tract. —***adj.:*** *~ action.*

car·mine (CAHR·mun, –mine) *n.* a deep red pigment produced from the cochineal insect; also, the color; also ***adj.***

car·nage (CAHR·nij) *n.* massive killing. —**car·nal** (CAHR·nul) *adj.* **1** sensual; fleshly: *Lust is ~.* **2** worldly: *the ~ pursuits of a sin city.* —**car·nal·ly** *adv.* —**car·nal·i·ty** (–NAL–) *n.* —**car·na·tion** (–NAY–) *n.* **1** a cultivated herb with red, white, or pink many-petaled flowers; also, the flower. **2** a medium-red color.

car·nau·ba (cahr·NAU·buh) *n.* a Brazilian palm, whose leaves yield a hard wax used in polishes, candles, lipsticks, etc.; also, the wax.

car·nel·ian (cahr·NEEL·yun) *n.* a clear reddish chalcedony, used as a gemstone.

carney or **carnie** same as CARNY.

car·ni·val (CAHR·ni·vul) *n.* **1** a traveling amusement show with rides, games, etc.; hence, any set of planned amusements: *a winter ~.* **2** the pre-Lent season of riotous merrymaking; hence, any festival, revelry, etc. —**car·ni·vore** (CAHR·ni–) *n.* **1** a member of the order of flesh-eating mammals, or **Car·niv·o·ra** (cahr·NIV·uh·ruh), which includes the cats, dogs, bears, seals, etc. **2** a plant that feeds on insects. —**car·niv·o·rous** (cahr·NIV·uh·rus) *adj.* flesh- or insect-eating; **car·niv·o·rous·ly** *adv.;* **car·niv·o·rous·ness** *n.* —**car·ny, car·nie** or **car·ney** (CAHR·nee) *n.* **-nies** or **-neys** *Informal.* **1** a carnival. **2** a carnival worker; also, his argot: *talking ~.* —***adj.:*** *popcorn, candied apples, and other ~ food.*

car·ol (CAIR·ul) *n.* a joyous song, often devotional or laudatory: *a Christmas ~.* —***v.*** **car·ols, car·ol(l)ed, car·ol·(l)ing:** *robins ~ing to the spring.*

car·om (CAIR·um) *n.* a hit and rebound; esp. in billiards, a shot where the cue ball rebounds from one ball to strike another. —***v.:*** *The truck ~ed off the wall.*

car·o·tene (CAIR·uh·teen) *n.* a hydrocarbon, orangish-yellow to red, found in many plants, esp. carrots, and a source of Vitamin A for animals; also **car·o·tin.**

ca·rot·id (cuh·ROT·id) *adj.* pertaining to one or both of the **carotid arteries** that carry blood via the neck to the head.

ca·rouse (cuh·ROWZ) *v.* **-rous·es, -roused, -rous·ing** revel and drink heavily. **—*n.*** a drinking party or spree; also **ca·rous·al** (cuh·ROW·zul). **—car·ou·sel** (cair·uh·SEL) *n.* a merry-go-round.

¹carp *v.* find fault pettily or captiously: *a ~ing critic.*

²carp *n.* an edible, large-scaled fish found in quiet, fresh waters.

car·pal (CAHR·pul) *adj.* of or having to do with the wrist. **—*n.*** a wrist bone.

Car·pa·thi·an (cahr·PAY·thee·un) **Mountains** or **Carpathians** *n.pl.* a C. European mountain range extending from Czechoslovakia to Romania.

car·pe di·em (cahr·pee·DEE·em) *Latin.* the philosophy of making the most of present circumstances.

car·pel (CAHR·pel) *n.* a leaflike, seed-producing part of a flower.

car·pen·ter (CAHR–) *n.* a workman who builds and repairs wooden objects, as houses, ships, etc. **—*v.*:** *a well-~ed house.* **—car·pen·try** (–tree) *n.*

car·pet (CAHR·pit) *n.* a thick, heavy covering for floors and stairs. **—*v.*:** *a room ~ed with broadloom.* **—on the carpet** being or called to be reprimanded. **—car·pet·bag** *n.* a 19th c. cloth traveling bag; **car·pet·bag·ger** *n.* a Northerner exploiting unsettled conditions in the South during Reconstruction; **car·pet·bag·ger·y** *n.* **—car·pet·ing** *n.* carpet material; carpets collectively.

car pool a cooperative of automobile commuters who rotate the task of driving others in their own cars.**—car·port** *n.* an automobile shelter, usu. under an extension of a house's roof.

car·ra·geen (moss) (CAIR·uh·geen) *n.* an edible, dark red, branching seaweed used for jellies, fodder, and an extract called **car·ra·geen·an** or **car·ra·geen·in** used in foods and medicine.

car·rel (CAIR·ul) *n.* an individual study space in a library, usu. enclosed.

car·riage (CAIR·ij) *n.* **1** a wheeled passenger vehicle: *horse and ~; baby ~.* **2** the transport of goods. **3** posture; bearing. **4** a movable support: *gun ~; typewriter ~.* **—carriage trade** the wealthy, esp. their patronage.**—car·ri·er** *n.* **1** one who carries: *letter ~; paper ~.* **2** a commercial transporter. **3** a box or basket on a vehicle, esp. a bicycle. **4** one who passes on a disease or genetic trait while remaining unaffected. **5** an aircraft carrier. **—carrier pigeon** a message-carrying pigeon. **—carrier (wave)** an electromagnetic wave carrying a signal, as sound or a picture.

car·ri·on (CAIR–) *n.* dead, rotting flesh. **—*adj.*** carrion-eating: *~ crow; ~ beetle.*

car·rot (CAIR·ut) *n.* **1** the edible, orange root of a vegetable. **2** an inducement: *the ~ and the stick.* **—car·rot·y** *adj.* red.

car·rou·sel (cair·uh·SEL) same as CAROUSEL.

car·ry (CAIR·ee) *v.* **car·ries, car·ried, car·ry·ing** **1** hold and convey; bear. **2** transport: *a pipe ~ing water.* **3** travel: *Voices ~ over the water.* **4** hold: *~ your head high.* **5** take: *~ a joke too far.* **6** win: *Independents ~d the day; The motion ~d.* **7** entail: *Murder ~s the death penalty.* **8** support (a debtor, an enterprise, etc.): *He ~d the firm through hard times.* **9** have for sale. **10** publish; broadcast. **—*n.*, *pl.*** **car·ries** **1** the act or manner of carrying: *a fireman's ~.* **2** the range of a projectile. **3** a portage. **—carry away** sway beyond control: *~d away by anger.* **—carry on** **1** manage. **2** persevere. **3** act foolishly, excessively, immorally, etc. **—carry out** enact; accomplish. **—carry over** transfer; postpone; **car·ry·o·ver** *n.: a ~ of 3 days' unfinished business.* **—car·ry·all** *n.* any very capacious carriage, automobile, shopping bag, etc. **—carrying charge** the charge or interest for paying in installments. **—car·ry·ing-on** *n.* **car·ry·ings-on** improper behavior.

car·sick *adj.* nauseated, esp. while traveling in a car, train, etc. **—car·sick·ness** *n.*

Car·son (CAHR·sun) **City** capital of Nevada.

cart *n.* **1** a sturdy, two-wheeled utility vehicle usu. drawn by horses, oxen, etc. **2** any light, wheeled vehicle: *grocery ~; golf ~.* **—*v.*** transport; convey: *to ~ produce to market.* **—cart·age** (–ij) *n.* transport by cart or truck; also, carting charge. **—cart·er** *n.* one engaged in cartage.

carte blanche (CART·blahnsh), *pl.* **cartes blanches** (CART·blahnsh) a free hand; full discretionary power.

car·tel (–TEL) *n.* a monopolistic group of commercial interests: *The oil ~ forces prices up.*

Car·ter, James Earl, Jr. born 1924, 39th U.S. President (1977-1981).

Car·te·sian (cahr·TEE·zhun) *adj.* of or having to do with Descartes or his philosophical system, **Car·te·sian·ism.** **—*n.*** a Cartesian philosopher. **—Cartesian coordinate system** a basic system for the graphic representation, in 2 or 3 dimensions, of an algebraic equation.

Car·thage (CAHR·thij) an ancient Phoenician city in N. Africa. **—Car·tha·gin·i·an** (–uh·JIN–) *adj.* & *n.*

car·ti·lage (CAHR·tl·ij) *n.* a flexible, tough tissue related to bone; gristle. **—car·ti·lag·i·nous** (–LAJ·i·nus) *adj.*

car·tog·ra·phy (cahr·TOG·ruh·fee) *n.* the making of charts or maps; **car·tog·ra·pher** *n.* **—car·to·graph·ic** (–tuh·GRAPH·ic) *adj.* **—car·ton** (CAHR·tn) *n.* a cardboard box; container for milk, cigarettes, etc. **—car·toon** (cahr·TOON) *n.* **1** a humorous or satirical drawing. **2** a comic strip. **3** an animated cartoon. Also ***v.*** **—car·toon·ist** *n.***—car·tridge** (CAHR·trij) *n.* **1** a case or capsule of material, as film, ink, and tape, for use in an apparatus. **2** the phonograph unit holding the stylus and pickup. **3** a usu. cylindrical case containing the explosive charge and primer for a gun. —**cart·wheel** *n.* **1** a sideways handspring. **2** *Slang.* a large coin, esp. a dollar.

carve *v.* **carves, carved, carv·ing** **1** cut out or form artistically; sculpture: *~d woodwork; a figure ~d out of stone.* **2** divide; slice and serve: *to ~ a turkey.* —**carv·er** *n.* —**carv·ing** *n.: a wood ~ing.*

car·wash *n.* a place equipped for washing automobiles.

car·y·at·id (cair·ee·AT·id) *n.* **-ids** or **-id·es** (–uh·deez) a sculptured female figure used for a column.

ca·sa·ba (cuh·SAH·buh) *n.* a sweet, white-fleshed winter melon with a thick, yellow rind.

Cas·a·blan·ca (cas·uh·BLANG·cuh) an Atlantic seaport in Morocco.

Cas·a·no·va (cas·uh·NOH·vuh) *n.* a philanderous lover.

cas·cade (–CADE) *n.* a steep waterfall or series of waterfalls or something resembling it: *adorned by ~s of lace.* —**v. -cades, -cad·ed, -cad·ing:** *The stream ~d over the cliff.*—**Cascade Range** a mountain range in N. California, Oregon, and Washington, forming part of the Sierra Nevada Mts.

cas·car·a (sa·gra·da) (cas·CAIR·uh·suh·GRAY·duh) *n.* the bark of the California buckthorn used as a laxative; also, the laxative or the tree itself.

¹case *n.* **1** a situation; also, an instance or subject of it: *a ~ of cheating; 7 ~s of measles; If that's the ~, you're in trouble!* **2** a situation as a matter of litigation; cause: *The lawyer stated his ~ simply.* **3** a grammatical variation of a noun, pronoun, or adjective, as *them* is the objective case of *they.* —**in any case** anyhow. —**in case** in the event: *In ~ of death inform relatives;* **just in case** [used elliptically]: *Take your umbrella just in ~* (it rains). —**v. cas·es, cased, cas·ing** *Informal.* inspect as a prelude to theft: *burglars ~ing a bank.*

²case *n.* **1** a container; box: *a ~ of beer; a glass display ~.* **2** a cover: *a watch ~.* **3** the frame for a door or window. —**v.** put in a case.

ca·se·in (cay·SEEN) *n.* a protein obtained from milk, used in foods, plastics, paints, and cheese.

case·ment *n.* a window sash opening on hinges; also, the window itself, or **casement window.**

case·work *n.* social work involving individual cases; **case·work·er** *n.*

cash *n.* ready money or its equivalent; also, immediate payment. —**v.** exchange for cash: *~ a check.* —**cash in** **1** turn into cash, as bonds or gambling chips. **2** *Slang.* die. **3** exploit fully; profit from: *~ in on a favorable market.* —**cash-and-carry** *n.* a purchasing system of paying cash and taking delivery of goods. —**cash crop** one for sale, not for consumption on the farm.

cash·ew (CASH·oo) *n.* the edible kidney-shaped nut of a tropical tree; also, the tree itself.

cash·ier (ca·SHEER) *n.* **1** one who receives customers' payments: *a supermarket ~.* **2** a financial officer of a bank or company. —**v.** dismiss, usu. in disgrace: *an employee ~ed for theft.* —**cashier's check** a check issued by a bank through its cashier.

cash·mere (CAZH·meer) *n.* a soft fabric originally made from the wool of Tibetan and N. Indian goats; also, the wool itself or a garment of cashmere.

cash register a machine, with a drawer for cash, that records sales, totals bills, etc.

cas·ing *n.* an outer covering, as of sausages, tires, doors, and windows.

ca·si·no (cuh·SEE·noh) *n.* **-nos** a gambling house, usu. providing additional entertainment.

cask *n.* a barrel for liquids; also, the amount it holds.—**cas·ket** *n.* **1** a coffin. **2** a small box for valuables.

Cas·pi·an (CAS·pee·un) **Sea** the world's largest inland sea, in S.W. Asia.

casque (cask) *n.* a military helmet.

Cas·san·dra (cuh·SAN·druh) *n.* a prophet of doom whose warnings, though true, are disregarded.

cas·sa·va (cuh·SAH·vuh) *n.* the starchy root of a tropical plant used for tapioca, bread, etc.; also, the plant itself.

cas·se·role (CAS·uh–) *n.* a deep, usu. covered dish for baking and serving food; also, the food thus cooked.

cas·sette (cuh·SET) *n.* a cartridge for photographic film or magnetic tape.

cas·sia (CASH·uh) *n.* **1** the bark of a S.E. Asian tree, used for cinnamon; also, the tree. **2** any of a group of E. Indian plants that yield senna.

cas·si·no (cuh·SEE–) *n.* a card game.

Cas·si·o·pe·ia (cas·ee·uh·PEE·uh) a constellation visible in the N. Hemisphere.

cas·sit·er·ite (cuh·SIT–) *n.* a dark, heavy, tin-bearing ore.

cas·sock (CAS·uk) *n.* a usu. black, ankle-length garment worn by clergymen, choir singers, etc.

cas·so·war·y (CAS·uh·wer·ee) *n.* **-war·ies** any of a group of flightless birds of Australia and New Guinea, related to the emu.

cast *v.* **casts, cast, cast·ing** **1** throw; place; discard: *an angler ~ing his line; ~ing a net; ~ your ballot; A snake ~s its skin.* **2** form in a mold: *~ a bronze statue.* **3** assign (an actor) to a role. **4** calculate: *~ a horoscope.* **5** search: *a hound ~ing about for scent.* **6** **cast off** free (a ship) from a dock. —**n.** **1** a throw: *a ~ of the dice.* **2** something thrown or discarded: *a worm ~* (i.e. excrement). **3** something molded, esp. a rigid plaster-of-Paris dressing for a broken bone. **4** the actors in a play. **5** hue; quality: *a ruddy ~; a noble ~ of mind.*

cas·ta·nets (cas·tuh·NETS) *n.pl.* a pair of small, hollowed-out pieces of wood, ivory, etc. held in the hand and clicked together for rhythm, used esp. in Spanish dancing.

cast·a·way (CAST–) *adj.* thrown away; set adrift or marooned as a survivor: *a ~ sailor.* ***—n.:*** *~s landing on the beach.*

caste (CAST) *n.* **1** a usu. hereditary social class defined by rigid barriers, as traditional in Hinduism. **2** status; prestige: *afraid of losing ~.*

cas·tel·lat·ed (CAS·tuh·lay·tid) *adj.* like a castle, with turrets and battlements.

cast·er or **cas·tor** (CAS·tur) *n.* **1** a ball or swiveling wheel fitted to furniture, machines, etc. to make moving easier. **2** a small container for salt, relish, etc. for use at the table.

cas·ti·gate (CAS–) *v.* **-gates, -gat·ed, -gat·ing** reprove strongly; punish; **cas·ti·ga·tor** *n.*—**cas·ti·ga·tion** (–GAY–) *n.*

Cas·tile (cas·TEEL) a region of N. and C. Spain, once a kingdom. —**Cas·til·ian** (cas·TIL·yun) *n.* **1** a citizen or native of Castile. **2** its dialect, now the dominant form of European Spanish; ***adj.:*** *the ~ accent.*

cast·ing *n.* **1** something molded or cast: *a brass ~.* **2** the excrement of earthworms. **3** a snake's discarded skin. —**casting vote** a chairman's vote used to break a tie.—**cast iron** a hard, non-malleable iron-carbon alloy, made by casting.

cas·tle (CASL) *n.* **1** a large fortified dwelling or group of buildings, esp. one built in the Middle Ages; stronghold: *"A man's home is his ~."* **2** in chess, a rook. —**castles in the air** (or **in Spain**) impractical plans; daydreams. —**cas·tled** same as CASTELLATED.

cast-off *adj.* discarded: *~ clothes.* —**cast·off** *n.* someone or something discarded: *dressed in his brother's ~s.*

Cas·tor See POLLUX.

cas·tor (CAS·tur) *n.* **1** same as CASTER. **2** a beaver hat. —**castor oil** a thick yellow oil derived from the beans of the tropical **cas·tor-oil plant** and used as a cathartic, lubricant, etc.

cas·trate (CAS·trate) *v.* **-trates, -trat·ed, -trat·ing** remove the sex glands of; geld or spay; **cas·trat·er** *n.* —**cas·tra·tion** (–TRAY–) *n.*

cas·u·al (CAZH·oo·ul) *adj.* **1** accidental; chance: *a ~ meeting.* **2** easy-going; nonchalant; informal: *a ~ attitude to work; ~ clothing.* **3** occasional: *~ labor.* —**cas·u·al·ly** *adv.* —**cas·u·al·ness** *n.*—**cas·u·al·ty** (CAZH·ul·tee) *n.* **-ties 1** a victim, wounded, missing, or killed, of an accident or military action: *a traffic ~; heavy ~s suffered by the enemy.* **2** a serious accident.—**cas·u·ist·ry** (CAZH·oo·is·tree) *n.* **1** subtle reasoning about right and wrong. **2** clever but false rationalization; sophistry. —**cas·u·ist** *n.;* **cas·u·is·tic** (–IS–) *adj.;* **cas·u·is·tic·al·ly** *adv.*

ca·sus bel·li (CAIS·us·BEL·eye) *Latin.* a cause of or pretext for a war.

cat *n.* **1** a mammal of the family that includes the lion, lynx, leopard, panther, etc.; esp., a small domesticated species kept as a pet or to catch mice; **let the cat out of the bag** reveal a secret. **2** *Slang.* a jazz musician; a guy. **3** *Slang.* a caterpillar tractor. **4** a malicious, gossipy woman; **cat·ty** *adj.* **cat·ti·er, cat·ti·est; cat·ti·ly** *adv.;* **cat·ti·ness** *n.*

cat. catalog.—**cat(a)-** or **cath-** *comb.form* [indicating] down; against; thoroughly; according to: as in *catabolism, catalog, catechism, category.* —**ca·tab·o·lism** (kuh·TAB·uh·lizm) *n.* the breakdown of living tissue in plants and animals into simpler substances or waste products; destructive metabolism; **cat·a·bol·ic** (cat·uh·BOL·ic) *adj.;* **cat·a·bol·ic·al·ly** *adv.*—**cat·a·clysm** (CAT·uh·clizm) *n.* a sudden, destructive change, as a great flood, war, etc.; **cat·a·clys·mic** (–CLIZ·mic) *adj.*—**cat·a·combs** (CAT·uh·cohmz) *n.pl.* underground burial places connected by tunnels and chambers.—**cat·a·falque** (CAT·uh·falc) *n.* a decorated platform for a coffin at a funeral.

Cat·a·lan (CATL·an) *n.* a citizen or native of Catalonia; also, its Romance language, related closely to Provençal; ***adj.:*** *a ~ custom.*

cat·a·lep·sy *n.* an abnormal state of rigid physical immobility and unconsciousness; **cat·a·lep·tic** (–LEP–) *adj.* & *n.*—**cat·a·log(ue)** (CATL·og) *n.* a complete, organized, often descriptive list, as of merchandise, library books, art exhibits, etc. —***v.*** **-log(ue)s, -log(u)ed, -log(u)·ing:** *I have my butterflies all ~d.* —**cat·a·log(u)·er** *n.*

Cat·a·lo·ni·a (catl·OH·nee·uh) a region of N.E. Spain, once a republic.

ca·tal·pa (cuh·TAL·puh) *n.* any of a group of North American and Asiatic trees with broad leaves and long, thin pods.

ca·tal·y·sis (cuh·TAL·uh–) *n., pl.* **-ses** (–seez) the speeding up or other change induced in a chemical reaction by the presence of an agent called a **cat·a·lyst** or **cat·a·lyz·er** (CAT·uh–) which itself undergoes no change: *Enzymes act as catalysts in digestion.* —**cat·a·lyt·ic** (–LIT·ic) *adj.;* **catalytic converter** an antipollution device that uses a chemical catalyst to render exhaust gases such as carbon monoxide harmless; **cat·a·lyt·i·cal·ly** *adv.* —**cat·a·lyze** *v.* **-lyz·es, -lyzed, -lyz·ing** act on or change, as a catalyst does: *The discovery of America ~d world exploration.*

cat·a·mar·an (cat·uh·muh·RAN) *n.* **1** a slender raft of logs, usu. propelled by a paddle. **2** a twin-hulled sailboat.

cat·a·mount (CAT·uh–) *n.* any of the wildcats, as the puma, cougar, or lynx.

cat·a·pult (CAT·uh–) *n.* a device for launching or hurling objects, as airplanes from a ship, pilots from an airplane, or missiles and stones in ancient warfare; slingshot. **—v.:** *~ed to wealth by a lottery win; He ~s out of bed at 5 each morning.* **—cat·a·ract** (CAT·uh–) *n.* **1** a great rush or flood of water; esp., a steep waterfall. **2** an opacity on the lens of the eye.**—ca·tarrh** (cuh·TAR) *n.* inflammation of and discharge from a mucous membrane. **—ca·tas·tro·phe** (cuh·TAS·truh·fee) *n.* a great calamity; disaster; total failure; **cat·a·stroph·ic** (cat·uh·STROF–) *adj.;* **cat·a·stroph·i·cal·ly** *adv.*

cat·bird *n.* a gray, North American songbird with a mewing call.**—cat·boat** *n.* a boat with a single mast and sail set well forward. **—cat·call** *n.* a loud, rude noise expressing disapproval of a performer, speaker, etc. **—v.:** *a singer booed and ~ed off the stage.*

catch *v.* **catch·es, caught** (CAWT), **catch·ing** **1** take and hold: *~ a ball; a barrel to ~ rain in.* **2** get; grasp: *~ sight of; ~ hell; ~ one's meaning.* **3** overtake; intercept; manage to hear, see, etc.: *~ him in time; ~ a train; ~ a movie.* **4** apprehend: *~ him sleeping at work.* **5** get or be tangled, stuck, etc.: *a finger caught in a door.* **6** be affected by: *~ the mumps; ~ fire.* **7** take hold: *flames ~ing on wood.* **8** act as a catcher. ***—n.*** **1** the act of catching; also, a simple ball game. **2** what is caught; hence, a desirable acquisition: *a small ~ of fish; Her husband was a real ~.* **3** a latch; fastener. **4** a small fragment; piece; snatch: *~es of songs.* **5** a break in the voice. **6** an unforeseen complication, problem, etc.: *What's the ~?* **—catch at** reach out to grasp; seize on: *"A drowning man will ~ at a straw."* **—catch on** **1** come to comprehend. **2** become well-known or popular. **—catch one's breath:** *After running a mile I stopped to ~ my breath.* **—catch up:** *The police cruiser ~es up with a speeding car; to ~ up on lost sleep; caught up in the latest fad.* **—catch·all** *n.* something to hold or apply to many different things; ***adj.:*** *"Flu" is a ~ term for many maladies.* **—catch-as-catch-can** *adv.* in any way possible; ***adj.:*** *~ wrestling; a hurried, ~ news report.* **—catch·er** *n.* in baseball, one who receives the pitcher's throw behind homeplate. **—catch·ing** *adj.* **1** contagious. **2** catchy. **—catch·ment area** (or **basin**) the region from which a river collects its water. **—catch·pen·ny** *adj.* & *n.* **-pen·nies** (an article) making cheap money; cheap and trashy (article): *a store packed with ~ goods.* **—Catch-22** a paradoxical situation in which one is victimized either way, as an applicant refused a job because he lacks job experience. **—catch·up** same as KETCHUP. **—catch·word** *n.* **1** a slogan. **2** a guide word, as at the top of a page. **—catch·y** *adj.* **catch·i·er, -i·est** **1** memorable; attractive: *a ~ song.* **2** tricky.

cat·e·chism (CAT·uh·kizm) *n.* **1** a set of questions and answers used for instruction, esp. in religion. **2** oral instruction or examination by question and answer; **cat·e·chist** *n.* **—cat·e·chize** (–KIZE) *v.* **-chiz·es, -chized, -chiz·ing:** *The teacher ~d* (i.e. examined) *him on geography.***—cat·e·chu·men** (–CUE·mun) *n.* one being instructed in religion prior to baptism. **—cat·e·gor·i·cal** (–GOR·i·kl) *adj.* absolute; unconditional: *a ~ denial;* **cat·e·gor·i·cal·ly** *adv.* **—cat·e·go·rize** (CAT·uh–) *v.* **-riz·es, -rized, -riz·ing:** *a ~d shopping list;* **cat·e·go·ri·za·tion** (–ZAY–) *n.* **—cat·e·go·ry** (CAT·uh·gor·ee) *n.* **-go·ries** a basic division or class, esp. in logic or philosophy: *two ~s of chemical compounds, organic and inorganic.*

ca·ter (CAY–) *v.* **1** furnish (a reception, party, etc.) with food, entertainment, or other service. **2** gratify: *~ing to every whim.* **—ca·ter·er** *n.*

cat·er-cor·ner(ed) *adj.* diagonal. ***—adv.:*** *a sofa set ~ across the room.*

cat·er·pil·lar (CAT·ur–) *n.* **1** a usu. hairy, wormlike larva of a butterfly, moth, etc. **2 Caterpillar** *Trademark.* a vehicle moved by two endless metal tracks instead of wheels; ***adj.:*** *a ~ tractor.***—cat·er·waul** (CAT·ur·wall) *v.* howl or screech like a cat. Also ***n.*****—cat·fish** *n.* any of a group of scaleless fish with a big head and catlike whiskers around the mouth.**—cat·gut** *n.* a tough string, made of the intestines of sheep, horses, etc., used for sutures, stringing rackets, etc.

ca·thar·sis (cuh·THAR–) *n., pl.* **-ses** (–seez) a purification or release, esp. of the emotions by witnessing tragic drama or by some other outlet or expression. **—ca·thar·tic** *adj.* purifying or purging; ***n.*** a strong laxative.**—ca·thed·ral** (cuh·THEE·drul) *n.* the principal church of a diocese.**—cath·e·ter** (CATH·i–) *n.* a long, flexible tube inserted into a canal or cavity in the body, usu. to remove fluid, as urine from the bladder.**—cath·ode** (CATH–) *n.* the negatively charged electrode of an electrolytic cell or electron tube or the positive terminal of a primary cell; opposed to ANODE; **ca·thod·ic** (cuh·THOD·ic) *adj.* **—cathode rays** the beam of electrons emitted from the cathode of a vacuum tube, i.e. **cath·ode-ray tube,** as used in producing radar and TV images.**—cath·o·lic** (CATH·uh·lic) *adj.* **1** universal; comprehensive; liberal: *a person of ~ tastes.* **2 Catholic** pertaining to Catholics, esp. Roman Catholics, or their church; ***n.*** a member of one of the historically undivided Christian churches, esp. the Roman Catholic Church, whose system, theology, and rites are called **Ca·thol·i·cism** (kuh·THOL·i·sizm). **—cath·o·lic·i·ty** or **Catholicity** (–LIS–) *n.* **—cat·i·on** (CAT·eye·un) *n.* a positively charged ion; cf. ANION; **cat·i·on·ic** (–ON–) *adj.*

cat•kin *n.* a long, drooping cluster of flowers, as on the birch or willow. —**cat•like** *adj.* like a cat; silent: ~ *footsteps.* —**cat•nap** *n.* a brief, light sleep. Also ***v.*** **-naps, -napped, -nap•ping.**—**cat•nip** *n.* a fragrant mint much liked by cats. —**cat-o'-nine-tails** *n.sing. & pl.* a whip with usu. nine knotted lashes fastened to a handle. —**cat's cradle** a game in which a string, looped through one's fingers in intricate but symmetrical designs, is transferred from player to player. —**cat's-eye** *n.* **-eyes** a gem, marble, etc. that reflects light with a distinctive gleam.

CAT scanner an X-ray machine used in "computerized axial tomography." See TOMOGRAPHY.

Cats•kills or **Cats•kill Mountains** a mountain range in S.E. New York, part of the Appalachians.

cat's-paw *n.* one used by another to do something risky or disreputable.

cat•sup same as KETCHUP.

cat•tail *n.* a marsh plant with a cylindrical, brown, furry flower spike on a tall stem.

cat•tle *n.* cows, bulls, and other domestic bovines collectively.—**cat•tle•man** *n.* **-men** a rancher, cowboy.

catty See CAT.—**cat•ty-cor•ner(ed)** *adj. & adv.* same as CATER-CORNER(ED).

CATV community antenna television.

cat•walk *n.* a narrow, usu. elevated walkway.

Cau•ca•sia (caw·CAY·zhuh) same as CAUCASUS, def.1. —**Cau•ca•sian** (–CAY–) *adj.* **1** of or having to do with the Caucasus or its peoples. **2** of or having to do with the ethnic division that includes peoples of Europe, N. Africa, and S.W. Asia. —***n.*** a Caucasian person. —**Cau•ca•soid** (CAW·cuh–) *adj. & n.* Caucasian.—**Cau•ca•sus** (CAW·cuh–) **1** a region between the Black and Caspian seas. **2** a mountain range in this region.

cau•cus (CAW·cus) *n.* a party's political meeting to debate policy, select candidates, etc. —***v.*** **-cus•(s)es, -cus(s)ed, -cus•(s)ing:** *They ~d all night.*

cau•dal (CAWDL) *adj.* of or having to do with the tail or hind parts: *the ~ fin.* —**cau•dal•ly** *adv.*

cau•dil•lo (cow·DHEEL·yoh) *n.* **-dil•los** a military dictator, esp. in a Spanish-speaking country.

caught *pt. & pp.* of CATCH.

caul (CAWL) *n.* a membrane sometimes covering a baby's head at birth.

caul•dron (CAWL·drun) *n.* same as CALDRON.

cau•li•flow•er (CAW·li–) *n.* the large, white, flower head of a kind of cabbage; also, the plant itself. —**cauliflower ear** an ear misshapen and scarred by blows received in boxing.

caulk (CAWK) *v.* seal or make tight, usu. with a filler, seams in a boat, pipe joints, cracks, etc. —**caulk•er** *n.*

caus•al (CAW·zul) *adj.* of, pertaining to, or expressing a cause: ~ *connection;* **caus•al•ly** *adv.;* **cau•sal•i•ty** (–ZAL–) *n.* —**cau•sa•tion** (–ZAY–) *n.* the act of causing; a cause-and-effect relation; a cause. —**cause** (CAWZ) *n.* **1** that which produces or is responsible for an effect, change, etc.: *the ~ of a fire.* **2** grounds; reason: *fired from his job for good ~.* **3** a goal actively pursued or strongly supported: *the ~ of justice.* **4** legal case; issue. —***v.*** **caus•es, caused, caus•ing** bring about; effect; make happen. —**cause cé•lè•bre** (suh·LEB·ruh) *n., pl.* **causes cé•lè•bres** (CAWZ·suh·LEB·ruh) a famous legal case or controversy, as the "Dreyfus Affair." —**cau•se•rie** (COH·zuh·ree) *n.* a light, informal bit of writing or discussion.

cause•way (CAWZ–) *n.* a raised road or path across water or marshy ground.

caus•tic (CAW·stic) *adj.* **1** able to destroy or eat into (esp. flesh) chemically. **2** sharp; biting: ~ *wit.* —***n.:*** *Lye is a potent ~.* —**caus•ti•cal•ly** *adv.* —**caus•tic•i•ty** (–TIS–) *n.*—**cau•ter•ize** (CAW·tuh·rize) *v.* **-iz•es, -ized, -iz•ing** burn (tissue) with a hot iron or a caustic to kill infection, remove tissues, etc.; **cau•ter•i•za•tion** (–ZAY–) *n.*

cau•tion (CAW·shun) *n.* **1** prudence; wariness. **2** a warning. **3** *Informal.* an extraordinary person or thing: *She's a ~!* —***v.*** warn; admonish: *~ed against driving too fast.* —**cau•tion•ar•y** *adj.: ~ advice.* —**cau•tious** *adj.* careful; prudent; **cau•tious•ly** *adv.;* **cau•tious•ness** *n.*

cav. cavalry.—**cav•al•cade** (CAV·ul–) *n.* a parade or procession, esp. of horses; hence, any series or advance: *the ~ of history.* —**cav•a•lier** (cav·uh·LEER) *n.* **1** an armed rider. **2** a gallant; lady's escort. **3 Cavalier** a partisan of Charles I of England. —***adj.*** **1** casual; offhand: *a ~ indifference to others' rights.* **2** arrogant. —**cav•a•lier•ly** *adv.;* **cav•a•lier•ness** *n.*—**cav•al•ry** (CAV·ul·ree) *n.* **-ries** **1** mobile troops riding horses or in motor vehicles. **2** horses and riders collectively. —**cav•al•ry•man** *n.* **-men.**

cave *n.* an underground cavity with an opening, usu. on a cliff or hillside. —***v.*** **caves, caved, cav•ing;** esp. **cave in** **1** collapse: *The old tunnel ~d in.* **2** give in: *Don't ~ in to pressure.*

ca•ve•at (CAY·vee–) *n.* a warning. —**caveat emp•tor** *Latin.* "Let the buyer beware," i.e. assure himself of a product's quality before buying.

cave-in *n.* the site or action of a collapse. —**cave•man** *n.* **1** a Stone Age cave dweller. **2** *Informal.* a rough, strong man, esp. one brutal to women.—**cav•ern** (CAV·urn) *n.* a large cave, as Carlsbad Caverns; **cav•ern•ous** *adj.* deep and hollow; huge.

cav•i•ar(e) (CAV·ee·ar) *n.* the salted eggs of the sturgeon, salmon, etc. eaten as an appetizer.

cav•il *v.* **-ils, -il(l)ed, -il•(l)ing** needlessly criticize or object to: *This is no time to ~ over trivialities;* also ***n.*** **—cav•il•(l)er** *n.*
cav•i•ty *n.* **-ties** a hollow place in a solid body: *A dentist fills ~s.*
ca•vort (cuh·VORT) *v.* prance; caper: *young bucks ~ing on the dance floor.*
ca•vy (CAY·vee) *n.* **-vies** any of a group of South American rodents, such as the guinea pig.
caw *n.* the harsh call of a crow, raven, etc.; ***v.:*** *Rooks ~ed from the treetops.*
cay (CAY, KEE) *n.* a sandy or coral reef off a coast; key.
cay•enne (pepper) (kye·EN) *n.* a spicy, red pepper made from a kind of capsicum.
cay•man (–men) *n.* **-mans** same as CAIMAN.
Ca•yu•ga (cai·YOO·guh) *n.* (a member of) a native Iroquoian Indian tribe, formerly living in central New York state; also, the language of this tribe.
cay•use (KYE·yoose) *n.* **-us•es** a small Western range horse, originally bred by the **Cayuse** Indians of Oregon.
Cb columbium. **—CB** citizens band (radio).
CBC Canadian Broadcasting Corporation.
C.B.D. cash before delivery.
CB•er *n. Informal.* one who uses a CB radio.
CBS Columbia Broadcasting System.
CBW chemical and biological warfare; chemical and biological weapons.
cc. chapters; cubic centimeter (also **c.c.**). **—c.c.** or **C.C.** carbon copy.
CCC Civilian Conservation Corps; Community Credit Corporation.
CCTV closed-circuit television.
ccw counterclockwise.
cd. cord. **—cd** candela.**—c.d.** cash discount. **—Cd** cadmium.**—C.D.** Civil Defense; **CD** certificate of deposit.
Cdr. or **CDR** Commander.
Ce cerium.**—C.E.** chemical engineer; civil engineer.
cease (SEECE) *v.* **ceas•es, ceased, ceas•ing** stop; discontinue: *The music faded and ~d;* also ***n.;*** **without cease** without end or pause. **—cease-fire** *n.* a pause in open warfare: *The U.N. demanded a ~.* **—cease•less** *adj.* endless; continual; **cease•less•ly** *adv.;* **cease•less•ness** *n.*
ce•cum (SEE·cum) *n., pl.* **ce•ca** (–cuh) a pouchlike formation at the beginning of the large intestine; **ce•cal** *adj.*
ce•dar (SEE·dur) *n.* any of a group of evergreen trees having usu. reddish, hardy, fragrant wood; also, this wood. ***—adj.:*** *a ~ chest.*
cede (SEED) *v.* **cedes, ced•ed, ced•ing 1** surrender ownership of; grant; give over: *land ~d to the state.* **2** yield. **—ced•er** *n.*
ce•di (SAY·dee) *n.* the basic unit of currency in Ghana, equal to 100 pesewas.
ce•dil•la (si·DIL·uh) *n.* a mark put below a c, as "ç:" to indicate an "s" sound.
ceil•ing (SEE·ling) *n.* **1** the interior, overhead covering of a room. **2** an upper limit, as of visibility, operable altitude for an airplane, prices and wages, etc. **—hit the ceiling** *Slang.* get excited and angry.
cel•an•dine (SEL·un·dine) *n.* a biennial herb with yellow flowers, related to the poppy; also, a perennial European plant called "lesser celandine" related to the buttercup.
cel•e•brant (SEL·uh·brunt) *n.* **1** a priest officiating at a religious ceremony. **2** a celebrator: *New Year's Eve ~s.***—cel•e•brate** (SEL·uh–) *v.* **-brates, -brat•ed, -brat•ing 1** hold festivities, rites, etc. in honor of: *He ~d his victory with a drink; ~ing the Passover.* **2** extol publicly; make known: *~ one's virtues.* **3** perform solemnly, as a marriage, Mass, etc. **—cel•e•brat•ed** *adj.* famous: *France is ~ for its wines.* **—cel•e•bra•tor** *n.* **—cel•e•bra•tion** (–BRAY–) *n.* **—ce•leb•ra•to•ry** (–LEB–) *adj.* **—ce•leb•ri•ty** (suh·LEB·ri·tee) *n.* **-ties 1** renown. **2** a famous person.
ce•ler•i•ty (suh·LER·i·tee) *n.* rapidity.
cel•e•ry (SEL·uh·ree) *n.* a plant of the parsley family, grown for its crisp, edible stem, eaten raw or cooked.
ce•les•ta (suh·LES·tuh) *n.* a keyboard instrument producing light, bell-like tones; also **ce•les•te.—ce•les•tial** (suh·LES·chul) *adj.* **1** pertaining to the sky or the heavens. **2** divine; heavenly; hence, perfect: *~ beauty.* **—ce•les•tial•ly** *adv.* **—celestial navigation** the determination of one's position and course by observing heavenly bodies. **—celestial sphere** the sphere centered around the earth, on which stars, planets, etc. seem to turn.
ce•li•ac (SEE·lee·ac) *adj.* abdominal.
cel•i•bate (SEL·uh·bit) *n.* one who stays unmarried, esp. because of a religious vow. — ***adj.:*** *a ~ priest.* **—cel•i•ba•cy** (–buh·see) *n.*
cell *n.* **1** a small, separate space, as in a honeycomb; hence, a similar room to accommodate a monk, prisoner, etc. **2** a basic unit of a larger structure, as the smallest independent unit of living tissue *(a blood ~),* the basic component of an electric battery *(a dry ~),* the smallest unit of a usu. revolutionary party, movement, etc. **-celled** *comb.form.: a single-~ animal.* **—cel•lar** (SEL·ur) *n.* **1** a usu. underground storage room; also, its contents, esp. a store of wine. **2** a basement. **—in the cellar** *Informal.* in last place in a league. **—cel•lar•age** (–ij) *n.* **1** a fee for storage in a cellar. **2** cellars collectively; storage room. **—cel•lar•et** (–RET) *n.* a cabinet for liquor, wine, glasses, etc.; also **cel•lar•ette. —cel•lo** (CHEL·oh) *n.* **cel•los** a large bass instrument of the violin family; violoncello; also **'cello; cel•list** *n.***—cel•lo•phane** (SEL·uh·fane) *n.* a thin, transparent moistureproof wrapping material used to keep foods, cigarettes, etc. fresh.**—cel•lu•lar** (SEL·yuh·lur)

adj. of or having to do with cells; cell-like; porous: ~ *rubber.*—**Cel·lu·loid** (SEL·yuh–) *Trademark.* a flammable, colorless material, used for toys, combs, photographic film, etc.; **celluloid** *n.* this material; also, motion-picture film; hence, a movie or the movies; ***adj.:*** *an unreal* ~ *world.*—**cel·lu·lose** (SEL·yuh·lohs) *n.* the basic substance of plant tissues, found esp. in wood pulp, cotton, etc. and used in making paper, artificial textiles, etc.; **cellulose acetate** a cellulose compound used in varnishes, rayon, nonflammable films, etc.—**cel·lu·los·ic** (–LOH·sic) *adj.* & *n.*

Cel·si·us (SEL·see·us) *adj.* pertaining to the temperature scale having 0° and 100° as the respective freezing and boiling points of water.

Celt (SELT, KELT) *n.* a member of a group of ancient European peoples, including the Britons and Gauls; also, a speaker of a Celtic language or a descendant of one.—**Cel·tic** *n.* & *adj.* (of) a group of Indo-European languages including Irish and Scottish Gaelic, Welsh, Breton, Cornish, etc.

cem·ba·lo (CHEM·buh·loh) *n., pl.* **-li** (–lee) or **-los** a harpsichord; **cem·ba·list** *n.*

ce·ment (si·MENT) *n.* **1** a substance, esp. a powder of clay and lime, pastelike when mixed with water but hardening to a stony mass and used to bind building materials, make concrete, etc.: *Paper* ~ *is an adhesive.* **2** concrete; mortar. **3** a hard crust covering the roots of a tooth.—***v.*** bind or cover with cement; join firmly: *He* ~*ed over the crack in the wall;* ~ *a union;* **ce·men·ter** *n.* —**ce·men·ta·tion** (–TAY–) *n.* the bonding of two substances under great heat, without melting, as iron and carbon to make steel. —**ce·men·tum** (–MEN–) *n.* same as CEMENT, *n.* 3.

cem·e·ter·y (SEM·uh·ter·ee) *n.* **-ter·ies** a burial ground.

cen. central; century.

cen·o·bite (SEN·uh–) *n.* a member of a monastic community, as distinguished from a hermit. —**cen·o·bit·ic** (–BIT·ic) or **-i·cal** *adj.*

cen·o·taph (SEN·uh–) *n.* a monument to a person buried elsewhere: *a* ~ *of the Unknown Soldier.* —**cen·o·taph·ic** (–TAF–) *adj.*

Ce·no·zo·ic (see·nuh·ZOH·ic) *n.* the most recent era of geological time, beginning about 65 million years ago, when mammals, birds, etc. evolved. —***adj.:*** ~ *rock formations.*

cen·ser (SEN·sur) *n.* a vessel for burning incense, esp. in religious ceremonies; thurible.

cen·sor (SEN·sur) *n.* **1** one authorized to prohibit or edit movies, news, books, etc. to make them conform to standards of morality, military or political security, etc.: *The* ~ *cut 10 minutes from the film.* **2** one of two officials of ancient Rome who conducted the census and supervised public morals. —***v.:*** *Mail from the troops was* ~*ed.* —**cen·sor·ship** *n.* —**cen·so·ri·al** (–SOR–) *adj.:* ~ *power.* —**cen·so·ri·ous** *adj.* fault-finding. **cen·so·ri·ous·ly** *adv.;* **cen·so·ri·ous·ness** *n.* —**cen·sure** (–shur) *n.* **1** harsh criticism; disapproval, esp. official. **2** censorship. Also ***v.*** **-sures, -sured, -sur·ing; cen·sur·a·ble** *adj.;* **cen·sur·er** *n.* —**cen·sus** (SEN–) *n.* an official count of the population, usu. including a record of age, sex, occupation, etc.

cent (SENT) *n.* a unit or piece of money equal to 1/100th of the dollar, guilder, etc.; a penny.—**cent.** centigrade; central; century. —**cen·tare** (SEN–) same as CENTIARE.—**cen·taur** (SEN·tor) *n.* **1** in Greek myths, a monster that is half man and half horse. **2 Centaur** or **Cen·tau·rus** (–TOR–) a constellation visible in the S. Hemisphere.—**cen·ta·vo** (sen·TAH·voh) *n.* **-vos** a unit or piece of money equal to 1/100th of the Cuban or Mexican peso, the Brazilian cruzeiro, the Portuguese escudo, etc. —**cen·te·nar·i·an** (–tuh·NAIR·ee·un) *n.* one who is at least 100 years old.—**cen·te·nar·y** (–TEN·uh·ree) *adj.* & *n.* **-nar·ies** or **cen·ten·ni·al** (–TEN·ee·ul) (of) a 100th anniversary or its celebration.

cen·ter (SEN·tur) *n.* **1** the point equidistant from a figure's outermost edges, said esp. of a circle: *He hit the target right in the* ~. **2** a focus or source of ideas, activity, etc., as a nerve center, shopping center, etc.: *Paris is a* ~ *for fashion; An active person is always at the* ~ *of things.* **3** in sports, a player who is stationed or plays in the middle: *The* ~ *passes the ball to the quarterback.* **4** political moderates or their position; also **Center.** —***v.*** **1** have, place at, or send to a center: *The story* ~*s on a murder;* ~ *a typewriter carriage.* **2** concentrate; focus: *The student's efforts were* ~*ed on his examinations.* —**cen·ter·board** *n.* a keel that can be raised and lowered, for a small sailboat. —**center of gravity** the point at or on which a body will balance. —**cen·ter·piece** *n.* a decorative object that is placed in a central position.

cen·tes·i·mal (sen·TES·i·mul) *adj.* divided into or relating to 100ths. —**cen·tes·i·mo** (sen·TES·i·moh) *n.* a unit or piece of money equal to 1/100th of the Italian lira (*pl.* **-mi**), Uruguayan peso, Chilean escudo, etc. (*pl.* **-mos**). —**centi-** *comb. form.* hundredth. —**cen·ti·are** (–air) *n.* in land measure, one square meter, 1/100th of an are. —**cen·ti·grade** former term for CELSIUS. —**cen·ti·gram** *n.* 1/100th of a gram; also **centigramme** *Brit.* —**cen·ti·li·ter** (–lee·tur) *n.* 1/100th of a liter; also **cen·ti·li·tre** *Brit.* —**cen·time** (SAHN·teem) *n.* a unit or piece of money equal to 1/100th of a franc, Algerian dinar, etc. —**cen·ti·me·ter** *n.* 1/100th of a meter; also **cen·ti·me·tre** *Brit.* —**cen·ti·me·ter-gram-sec·ond** *adj.* having the centimeter, gram, and second as the basic units of length, mass, and time: *a* ~ *system of measure.* —**cen·ti·**

mo *n.* **-mos** a unit or piece of money equal to 1/100th of the Spanish peseta, Paraguayan bolívar, etc. **—cen·ti·pede** (SEN–) *n.* a worm-shaped, insectlike creature with a pair of legs on each of its many body segments.

cen·tral (SEN·trul) *adj.* **1** at or near the center; easily accessible: *a ~ location for a new store.* **2** main; essential; dominant: *the ~ government in Washington; Freedom is ~ to our way of life.* **3** operated from one main location: *a house with ~ heating.* **—*n.*** a main telephone exchange; hence, one of its operators. **—cen·tral·ly** *adv.* **—cen·tral·i·ty** (–TRAL–) *n.* **—Central African Republic** a country in C. Africa; 240,535 sq. mi. (622,984 km²); *cap.* Bangui. **—Central America** the countries S. of Mexico and N. of South America; **Central American** *adj.* **—cen·tral·ize** (SEN–) *v.* **-iz·es, -ized, -iz·ing** **1** bring to a center. **2** put (government, offices, etc.) under one main control; **cen·tral·ism** *n.;* **cen·tral·ist** *n.* & *adj.;* **cen·tral·is·tic** (–LIS–) *adj.* **—central nervous system** in vertebrates, the brain and spinal cord. **—cen·tre** *chiefly Brit.* center. **—centri-** *comb.form.* center. **—cen·trif·u·gal** (–TRIF·yoo·gul) *adj.* tending to move away from the center using **centrifugal force** which pulls a rotating object outward from the center; **cen·trif·u·gal·ly** *adv.* **—cen·tri·fuge** (SEN·truh·fyooj) a centrifugal machine, usu. used to separate substances of differing densities, as cream from milk. **—cen·trip·e·tal** (–TRIP·uh·tul) *adj.* tending to move toward the center using **centripetal force** which holds a rotating object toward the center, as gravity holds the moon in orbit; **cen·trip·e·tal·ly** *adv.* **—cen·trist** (SEN–) *n.* a member of a moderate political party. **—*adj.:*** *a ~ position between right and left.* **—centro-** *comb.form.* center. **—cen·tro·some** (SEN·truh·sohm) *n.* a protoplasmic body that is the dividing center in a cell.

cen·tu·ry (SEN·chuh·ree) *n.* **-ries** **1** a period of 100 years: *The 19th ~ runs from 1801 to 1900.* **2** a body of troops in the Roman army, commanded by a **cen·tu·rion** (–TOOR·ee·un, –TYOOR–). **—century plant** an American agave that blooms once after a long life, then dies.

ceph·a·lo·pod (SEF·uh·luh–) *n.* any of a group of highly developed mollusks, such as the squid, octopus, etc., with tentacles and a beaked mouth.

ce·ram·al (suh·RAM·ul) *n.* same as CERMET. **—ce·ram·ic** (–RAM–) *n.* a product of ceramics; ***adj.:*** *~ industries, tiles.* **—ce·ram·ics** *n. sing.* the art of making earthenware, porcelain, etc. by firing clay or a similar material. **—ce·ram·ist** or **ce·ram·i·cist** *n.*

ce·re·al (SEER·ee·ul) *n.* a grass producing an edible grain, as wheat, oats, rice, etc.; also, such a grain; hence, a food made from any of these grains, as oatmeal or cornflakes. **—*adj.:*** *~ grasses.*

cer·e·bel·lum (ser·uh·BEL·um) *n.* **-bel·lums** or **-bel·la** the part of the brain that controls muscular coordination; **cer·e·bel·lar** *adj.* **—cer·e·brum** (SER·uh–, suh·REE–) *n.* **-brums** or **-bra** (–bruh) the most important and, in man, largest part of the brain, which is surrounded by the **cerebral cortex,** the gray matter that controls the most complex nervous activities. **—cer·e·bral** *adj.* **1** pertaining to the cerebrum or brain: *~ hemorrhage.* **2** intellectual: *a hard, ~ style of verse.* **—cer·e·bral·ly** *adv.* **—cerebral palsy** a nervous disorder manifested in a lack of muscular coordination. **—cer·e·brate** *v.* **-brates, -brat·ed, -brat·ing** think; **cer·e·bra·tion** (–BRAY–) *n.*

cere·cloth (SEER–) *n.* a wax-coated cloth formerly used to shroud the dead. **—cere·ment** *n.* a shroud for the dead, esp. a cerecloth.

cer·e·mony (SER·uh·moh·nee) *n.* **-nies** **1** a set of prescribed formal acts appropriate to a wedding, religious rite, or other function; also, the function itself. **2** courteous behavior; formality: *Let's not* **stand on ceremony** *among friends.* **—cer·e·mo·ni·al** (–MOH·nee·ul) *adj.*: *~ robes;* ***n.*** a ceremony; ritual; **cer·e·mo·ni·al·ly** *adv.* **—cer·e·mo·ni·ous** (–MOH–) *adj.* **1** given to great formality. **2** ceremonial. **—cer·e·mo·ni·ous·ly** *adv.;* **cer·e·mo·ni·ous·ness** *n.*

ce·re·us (SEER·ee·us) *n.* any of a group of tall, often night-blooming American cacti.

ce·rise (suh·REES) *n.* & *adj.* clear, bright red.

ce·ri·um (SEER·ee·um) *n.* a soft, iron-gray metallic element.

cer·met (SIR·met) *n.* a strong, highly heat-resistant material, made of a ceramic bonded with a metal; ceramal.

cert. certificate; certification; certified.

cer·tain (SIRTN) *adj.* **1** specified; limited: *He received a ~ portion of the profits; to a ~ extent.* **2** particular but not specified: *I met a ~ man; The play has a ~ appeal.* **3** convinced; confident: *~ of his own strength; Are you ~ he is coming?* **4** definite; sure; proven; indubitable: *We are ~ to win; It is ~ that 2 + 2 is 4.* **—*pron.*** some: *~ of his friends deserted him.* **—for certain** without doubt; for sure. **—cer·tain·ly** *adv.* **—cer·tain·ty** *n.* **-ties** **1** sureness of mind. **2** a definite or proven fact or belief. **—for a certainty** without a doubt. **—cer·tif·i·cate** (sir·TIF·i·kit) *n.* a usu. official document testifying to a qualification, fact, etc.: *a teaching ~; a ~ of ownership.* **—*v.*** (–cate) **-cates, -cates, -cat·ed, -cat·ing** grant a certificate to. **—cer·ti·fi·ca·tion** (–CAY–) *n.* **—cer·ti·fy** (SIR·ti·fye) *v.* **-fies, -fied, -fy·ing** **1** to certificate. **2** declare, endorse, guarantee, etc., usu. by a certificate; esp., declare to be insane: *A ~d mental case is hospitalized;* **cer·ti·fi·a·ble** (–FYE·uh·bl) *adj.*: *a ~ lunatic;* **cer·ti·fi·a·bly** *adv.;* **cer·ti·fi·er** *n.* **—certified check** a check for which payment is guaranteed by the bank. **—certified milk**

dairy milk that conforms to certain medical regulations. —**certified public accountant** an accountant qualified to practice under state law. —**cer·ti·tude** (SIR·ti–) *n.* sureness; certainty.

ce·ru·le·an (suh·ROO·lee·un) *adj.* sky-blue.

ce·ru·men (suh·ROO·mun) *n.* earwax.

Cer·van·tes (sir·VAN·teez) **Saavedra, Miguel de.** 1547–1616, Spanish author, best known for *Don Quixote.*

cer·vix (SIR–) *n., pl.* **-vic·es** (–vi·seez) or **-vix·es** the neck; also, the neck-shaped lower end of the uterus. —**cer·vi·cal** *adj.*

Ce·sar·e·an or **Ce·sar·i·an** (si·ZAIR·ee·un) *n.* & *adj.* same as CAESAREAN.

ce·si·um (SEE·zee·um) *n.* a soft, silver-white metallic element used in photoelectric cells.

ces·sa·tion (se·SAY–) *n.* a ceasing: *a brief ~ of pain.* —**ces·sion** (SESH·un) *n.* a ceding to someone else, as of land or rights.

cess·pool *n.* a covered pit or buried tank for sewage.

ce·ta·ce·an (si·TAY·shun) *n.* an aquatic mammal of a group that includes whales, dolphins, and porpoises. —***adj.*** also **ce·ta·ceous** (–shus).

Ce·tus (SEE·tus) *n.* a constellation visible in the S. Hemisphere.

Cey·lon (suh·LON) former name of SRI LANKA; **Cey·lon·ese** (sel·uh·NEEZ) *n.* & *adj.*

cf. compare. —**Cf** californium. —**c.f.** or **C.F.** cost and freight. —**c/f** or **C/F** carried forward.

CFA franc a money unit worth 1/50 of a French franc, used in the "African Financial Community" including Cameroon, Chad, Congo, and other former French colonies.

c.f.i. or **C.F.I.** cost, freight, and insurance.

cg. or **cgm.** centigram. —**C.G.** coast guard; commanding general; consul general.

c.g.s. or **C.G.S.** centimeter-gram-second.

ch. chain; champion; chaplain; church. —**c.h.** or **C.H.** clearinghouse; courthouse; customhouse.

Cha·blis (SHAB·lee) *n.* a dry, white wine.

cha-cha (CHAH·chah) *n.* a ballroom dance of Latin American origin; also, the music for it. —***v.*** **-chas, -chaed, -cha·ing.** Also **cha-cha-cha.**

Chad a country in N.C. Africa; 495,755 sq.mi. (1,284,000 km²); *cap.* N'Djamena (Fort-Lamy). —**Chad·i·an** *adj.* & *n.*

cha·dor (CHUD·or) *n.* a long, usu. black garment traditionally worn by Iranian women draped around the body from head to foot.

chafe *v.* **chafes, chafed, chaf·ing** **1** annoy; vex; be irritated or impatient: *workmen ~ing under heavy loads.* **2** rub so as to warm (hands, etc.); also, wear away by rubbing action: *a sore made by a ~ing harness.*

chaf·er (CHAY·fur) *n.* any of a large group of beetles, e.g. the cockchafer and june beetle.

chaff *n.* **1** the husks of grain and other matter discarded in threshing; hence, anything trivial or worthless: *separate the wheat from the ~.* **2** light teasing; banter. —***v.*** tease jovially: *to ~ a guy about his girls;* **chaff·er** *n.* —**chaff·y** *adj.* **chaff·i·er, -i.est.**

chaf·fer *v.* bargain for; haggle about: —**chaf·fer·er** *n.*

chaf·finch *n.* a small European songbird.

chaf·ing (CHAY–) dish a dish with a heating device for cooking or warming food at the table.

cha·grin (shuh·GRIN) *n.* distress or irritation at failure, embarrassment, etc.: *Another man got the job, much to his ~.* —***v.*** **-grins, -grined, -grin·ing** cause chagrin to.

chain *n.* **1** a series of connected metal links used for binding, transmitting power, etc. **2 chains** *pl.* fetters; bonds: *the ~s of love.* **3** a unit of measure equal to 66 ft./20.12 m *(surveyor's chain)* or 100 ft./30.48 m *(engineer's chain).* **4** a series of usu. similar, connected things: *a coast-to-coast supermarket ~; a ~ of events; a ~ of atoms.* —***v.*** bind, connect, or confine by or as if by chains: *a dog ~ed to a post.* —**chain gang** a group of prisoners chained together for outdoor labor. —**chain letter** a letter asking the recipient to send copies of it to others, who are to do the same. —**chain mail** flexible body armor made of meshed metal links. —**chain reaction** a usu. self-sustaining series of events, esp. chemical or nuclear reactions, each of which causes the next one in the series; **chain-re·act** *v.* —**chain saw** a portable power saw with the teeth driven on an endless chain. —**chain-smoke** *v.* **-smokes, -smoked, -smok·ing** smoke a continuous series of cigarettes; **chain smoker.** —**chain (store)** one of a chain of retail stores.

chair *n.* **1** a seat having a back support for one person. **2** a position of dignity, authority, etc., as a professorship or chairmanship; hence, a chairman: *Address all questions to the ~.* **3** *Slang.* the electric chair. —***v.*** preside over; also **take the chair.** —**chair car** a parlor car. —**chair lift** a ski lift with chairs to ride in. —**chair·man** *n.* **-men** the person presiding at a meeting; head of a board, committee, etc.; **chair·man·ship** *n.; fem.* **chair·wom·an, -wom·en; chair·per·son** *n.*

chaise (SHAYZ) *n.* a light, two- or four-wheeled pleasure carriage. —**chaise longue** (–long), *pl.* **chaise longues** (–longz) or **chaises** (SHAYZ) **longues** a chair with the seat extended to support the legs; also **chaise lounge** (–lownj).

chal·ced·o·ny (cal·SEDN·ee) *n.* **-nies** a pale, waxy, translucent quartz, including carnelian, onyx, etc. —**chal·ce·don·ic** (cal·suh·DON–) *adj.*

chal·co·py·rite (cal·cuh·PYE–) *n.* a yellow ore of copper; copper pyrites.

cha·let (sha·LAY) *n.* **1** a Swiss dwelling with balconies and large projecting eaves; a house, cottage, etc. in similar style. **2** an Alpine herdsman's hut.

chal·ice (–is) *n.* a goblet, esp. a cup for Eucharistic wine.

chalk (CHAWK) *n.* a soft, white limestone; hence, prepared chalk or a substitute used to write on blackboards. ***—v.*** rub, treat, write, etc. with chalk; **chalk up** record; score; attribute: *He ~ed up his error to youth and inexperience.* **—chalk·y** *adj.* **chalk·i·er, -i·est; chalk·i·ness** *n.* **—chalk·board** *n.* a blackboard.

chal·lenge (–unj) *v.* **chal·leng·es, chal·lenged, chal·leng·ing** **1** demand identification: *When ~d by the sentry, he gave the password.* **2** dare; invite to take part in a duel, game, etc. **3** excite to effort, courage, etc. **4** dispute; question the truth of; object to (a prospective juror. **—chal·leng·er** *n.* **—chal·lenge·a·ble** *adj.* ***—n.*** [corresponding to the *v.* senses] **1:** *"Who goes there?" is the sentry's ~.* **2:** *The boxer issued a ~ to all comers.* **3:** *Journalism offers many ~s to a resourceful writer.* **4:** *The ~ was upheld and the juror dropped.*

chal·lis or **chal·lie** (SHAL·ee) *n.* a light, fine clothing fabric of cotton, wool, etc.

cham·ber (CHAIM–) *n.* **1** a room, esp. a bedroom; a hall for assemblies, receptions, etc.; hence, a council, board, legislative body, etc. **2 chambers** *pl.* a judge's office. **3** a place for the charge or cartridge in a gun; any enclosed space: *a pump ~.* **—cham·bered** *adj.* having chambers; also, enclosed in a chamber. **—cham·ber·lain** (CHAIM–) *n.* a high official at court; a treasurer; the steward for a lord or monarch. **—cham·ber·maid** *n.* a maid who makes beds and cleans rooms. **—chamber music** music written for small ensembles, such as a string quartet. **—chamber of commerce** an association of local businessmen promoting a community's commercial interests. **—chamber pot** a vessel used as a toilet in a bedroom.

cham·bray (SHAM–) *n.* a light, usu. cotton fabric for clothing, woven with white threads across a colored warp.

cha·me·le·on (cuh·MEEL·yun) *n.* any of a group of lizards able to change color to match the surroundings; hence, a changeable person.

cham·fer *n.* a beveled edge or corner; groove or flute. ***—v.*** cut or shape a chamfer in (wood, stone, etc.).

cham·ois (SHAM·ee) *n. sing.* & *pl.* **1** a goatlike mountain antelope of Europe and W. Asia. **2** a soft leather used esp. as a polishing cloth; also **cham·my, cham·mies.**

cham·o·mile (CAM·uh–) *n.* a daisylike, fragrant herb whose bitter dried flowers are used in a medicinal tea.

champ *v.* chew or bite vigorously; gnash the teeth; **champ (at) the bit** show impatience or restlessness (to begin something). ***—n.*** *Informal.* a champion.

cham·pagne (sham·PAIN) *n.* a sparkling white wine, esp. one made in Champagne, France.

cham·paign (sham·PAIN) *n.* an expanse of level, open land.

cham·pi·on (–pee·un) *v.* defend; fight for (a cause, person, etc.). ***—n.*** **1** a valiant defender: *a ~ of liberty.* **2** one holding first place or winning first prize, esp. in sports; ***adj.:*** *a ~ boxer; a ~ poodle.* **—cham·pi·on·ship** *n.*

Chan. or **Chanc.** chancellor; chancery.

chance *n.* **1** an apparently uncaused event; luck: *It was by ~ that we met in Moscow.* **2** a risk or reliance on chance; a gamble: *Take a ~!* **3** possibility; opportunity: *only a small ~ he'll come; You haven't got a ~.* ***—v.*** **chanc·es, chanced, chanc·ing** **1** meet, come, happen, etc. accidentally: *to ~ on a discovery.* **2** hazard; risk: *It's too dangerous; don't ~ it!* — ***adj.:*** *a ~ meeting of old friends.*

chan·cel *n.* the altar area of a church, used by the choir and clergy. **—chan·cel·ler·y** (–suh·luh·ree) *n.* **-cel·ler·ies** the rank or office of a chancellor; also, the offices of a consulate or embassy; also **chan·cel·lor·y** (–luh·ree) **—chan·cel·lor** (–suh·lur) *n.* **1** any of several high officials, including the heads of some European governments, the titular heads of some universities, and church officials. **2** in some U.S. states, a judge in a court of equity. **—chan·cel·lor·ship** *n.* **—chan·cer·y** *n.* **-cer·ies** **1** a chancellery. **2** an office of public archives. **3** a court of equity.

chan·cre (SHANG·cur) *n.* a hard, red sore which is the first symptom of syphilis; **chan·crous** (–crus) *adj.* **—chan·croid** *n.* a soft venereal ulcer, nonsyphilitic and caused by a bacterium; **chan·croi·dal** (–CROY–) *adj.*

chanc·y (CHAN·see) *adj.* **chanc·i·er, -i·est** *Informal.* risky.

chan·de·lier (shan·duh·LEER) *n.* a many-branched hanging light fixture. **—chan·dler** *n.* **1** a retailer of provisions: *a ship's ~.* **2** a candle maker or seller. **—chan·dler·y** *n.*

change (CHAINJ) *v.* **chang·es, changed, chang·ing** **1** make or become different: *Smith ~d his name; leaves ~ing color; Can you ~ a dollar* (for quarters, dimes, etc.)? **2** exchange: *We had to ~ seats.* **3** enter, put, take, etc. something in place of something else: *~ your clothes; All passengers ~ trains!* ***—n.*** **1** an alteration or difference; variety: *a refreshing ~ in the weather; Let's eat out for a ~.* **2** something to be substituted: *I brought one ~ of clothes.* **3** money returned from an overpayment; money in smaller units, esp. coins: *a jingling pocketful of ~.* **4** a pattern or sequence for ringing bells; **ring the changes** go through all possible variations. **—change hands** pass from one owner to another. **—change one's tune** alter one's story or attitude. **—change·a·ble** *adj.*: *~ weather; a ~ temperament.* **—chang·er** *n.* **—change·less** *adj.* **—change·ful** *adj.* **—change·ling** *n.* a child substituted for one that is stolen. **—change of life** menopause. **—change·o·

ver *n.* a complete conversion from one system, activity, etc. to another.

chan·nel (CHANL) *n.* **1** a long, narrow, usu. deep way for something to pass in, as a stream bed, the navigable part of a waterway *(a shipping ~),* a large strait (as the *English Channel*), a groove, trench, or duct. **2** any path of transmission, communication, or activity, as a frequency range for one radio or TV signal; **channels** *pl.* official lines of communication: *a petition sent through proper ~s.* **—v. -nels, -nel(l)ed, -nel·(l)ing** make a channel for or in; send through a channel: *~ing his finances to worthy causes;* also **chan·nel·ize** *v.* **-iz·es, -ized, -iz·ing; chan·nel·i·za·tion** (–ZAY–) *n.* **—Channel Islands** a British island group in the English Channel off Normandy.

chan·son (SHAN·sun) *n.* a song. **—chant** *n.* a melody in which many words are sung to one note, esp. a religious song; hence, a rhythmic and repetitive utterance. **—v. 1** sing or speak in a chant. **2** sing of: *a poet ~ing his love's virtue.* **—chant·er** *n.* **—chan·teuse** (shan·TOOZ) *n.* a female singer, esp. in a nightclub. **—chan·tey** (SHAN·tee) *n.* **-teys** or **-ties** a sailor's work song. **—chan·ti·cleer** *n.* a rooster. **—chan·try** (CHAN·tree) *n.* **-tries** an endowment for the singing of Masses for a deceased; also, a chapel endowed for this purpose. **—chan·ty** *n.* **-ties** same as CHANTEY.

Cha·nu·kah (KHA·noo–) same as HANUKKAH.

cha·os (KAY·os) *n.* total disorganization: *bring order out of ~;* **cha·ot·ic** (kay·OT·ic) *adj.;* **cha·ot·i·cal·ly** *adv.*

chap *v.* **chaps, chapped, chap·ping** to dry, roughen, or crack because of cold or wind: *~d lips.* **—n.** *Informal.* a fellow; a guy. **—chap.** chapter.

chap·ar·ral (shap·uh·RAL) *n.* in S.W. United States, an area of thick shrubs.

chap·book *n.* a popular pamphlet containing tracts, ballads, romances, etc., as once sold by chapmen.

cha·peau (sha·POH) *n.* **-peaus** or **-peaux** (–OZE) a hat. **—chap·el** *n.* a small church; a place of worship in a home, school, prison, etc. **—chap·er·on(e)** (SHAP·uh·rone) *n.* a mature person who escorts or supervises a social gathering of young people or a single young woman. **—v. -ones, -oned, -on·ing:** *Teachers will ~ all school dances.* **—chap·er·on·age** *n.*

chap·fall·en *adj.* downcast; crestfallen.

chap·lain (–lin) *n.* a clergyman serving in a chapel, or in the military, a club, prison, etc. **—chap·lain·cy** *n.* **-cies.**

chap·let (–lit) *n.* **1** a garland of flowers, jewels, etc. for the head. **2** a string of beads, esp. one used in reciting prayers. **—chap·let·ed** *adj.*

Chap·lin, Sir Charles (Charlie). 1889–1977, British movie actor and pantomime comedian. **—Chap·lin·esque** *adj.*

chap·man *n.* **-men** *Brit.* formerly, a traveling salesman; peddler.

chaps (CHAPS, SHAPS) *n.pl.* protective leather leggings worn by cowboys.

chap·ter *n.* **1** a major division in a book; hence, something similar: *School was an exciting ~ of my boyhood.* **2** a local branch of a society; also, a meeting of canons, monks, etc. **—chapter and verse** exact authority (for a statement).

char *n.* **1** one of several trouts including the brook trout. **2** *Brit.* a charwoman. **3** charcoal. **—v. chars, charred, char·ring 1** work as a charwoman. **2** burn to charcoal; scorch and blacken.

char·a·banc (SHAIR·uh·bang, –bank) *n. Brit.* a sightseeing bus.

char·ac·ter (CAIR·uc–) *n.* **1** the distinctive personality of a person, group, etc.; hence, reputation; moral strength: *Suffering builds ~.* **2** a person in a story, drama, etc.; an odd person; an individual. **3** a distinguishing property; nature. **4** a symbol, as a letter or ideogram; also, its style: *italic ~s.* **—in** (or **out of**) **character** true (or false) to one's nature or role. **—char·ac·ter·is·tic** (–IS–) *n.* an identifying or distinctive property; also ***adj.:*** *the ~ odor of chlorine gas;* **char·ac·ter·is·ti·cal·ly** *adv.* **—char·ac·ter·ize** *v.* **-iz·es, -ized, -iz·ing 1** portray or describe as being a certain thing or a certain way. **2** be a characteristic of; give a characteristic to: *Snow is ~d by whiteness;* **char·ac·ter·i·za·tion** (–ZAY–) *n.*

cha·rades (shuh·RAIDZ) *n.pl.* [takes *sing. v.*] **1** a game in which each participant acts out words and phrases that have to be guessed by his team. **2 charade** *sing.* a pretense or false show.

char·broiled *adj.* broiled over a charcoal fire. **—char·coal** *n.* **1** a dark gray, light, porous, carbonaceous material made by partially burning wood, bone, etc. and used as fuel, in filters, etc. **2** a crayon or pencil made of this substance; also, a sketch done with it.

chard *n.* the greens of a kind of beet used as a vegetable.

charge *v.* **charg·es, charged, charg·ing 1** fill, load, or saturate: *air ~d with excitement; We have to have our battery ~d.* **2** impose on, as a task, responsibility, instruction, etc.: *~d me with the task of reorganizing the office.* **3** ask (so much) in payment; mark as a debit: *I can't ~ less than $5.* **4** accuse, esp. officially. **5** rush forward in attack. **6** buy on credit: *went shopping and ~d a lot of clothes.* **—n. 1** a load, as a quantity of explosive, electricity, etc.: *a positive or negative ~.* **2** duty, custody, command, etc.; responsibility; also, a subject of such responsibility: *the judge's ~ to the jury; a babysitter's little ~s;* **in charge (of)** having authority, responsibility, etc. **3** a price; a debit on account: *Will that be cash or ~?* **4** accusation: *The ~ is first degree murder.* **5** an attack:

the ~ of the Light Brigade; a fierce cavalry ~. **6** *Informal.* a thrill: *He got a real ~ out of it.* —**charge·a·ble** (CHAHR·juh·bl) *adj.* —**charge account** an arrangement for buying on credit. —**charge card** (or **plate**) same as CREDIT CARD. —**char·gé d'af·faires** (shahr·ZHAY·duh·FAIR), *pl.* **char·gés** (–ZHAY, –ZHAYZ) **d'af·faires** (–FAIR) a subordinate diplomatic official in charge of an embassy, delegation, etc. —**charg·er** *n.* **1** a large platter. **2** a war horse. **3** a person or thing that charges.

Cha·ri-Nile (SHAH·ree·NILE) *n.* a language group in C. and E. Africa.

char·i·ot (CHAIR·ee·ut) *n.* a light, horse-drawn, two-wheeled cart, used formerly in racing, war, parades, etc. —**char·i·o·teer** (–TEER) *n.*

cha·ris·ma (kuh·RIZ·muh) *n.* **1** a gift of divine grace. **2** a magical quality of arousing the devotion of one's followers. —**char·is·mat·ic** (–MAT–) *adj.*

char·i·ty (CHAIR–) *n.* **1** a usu. Christian love for one's fellow man: *St. Paul urged faith, hope and ~.* **2** a fair or forgiving attitude in judging others. **3** *pl.* **-ties** aid to the poor and needy; almsgiving; also, an institution for this purpose: *Give money to ~s.* —**char·i·ta·ble** *adj.*

char·la·tan (SHAHR·luh·tun) *n.* one claiming skills or knowledge he does not have; a phony. —**char·la·tan·ism** *n.;* **char·la·tan·ry** *n.* **-ries.**

Char·le·magne (SHAHR·luh·main) A.D. 742–814, king of the Franks and founder of the Holy Roman Empire.

Charles·ton (CHARL·stun) **1** capital of West Virginia. **2** a seaport city in South Carolina. —***n.*** a lively dance in 4/4 time, popular in the 1920's.

char·ley (CHAR·lee) **horse** a muscular soreness or stiffness caused by strain or a blow.

Char·lotte (SHAHR·lut) a city in North Carolina.

Char·lotte·town (SHAHR·lut–) capital of Prince Edward Island.

charm *n.* **1** an attractive or pleasing quality or attribute: *Ah, the ~s of youth!* **2** a magic formula, ritual, object, etc.; hence, a trinket worn usu. on a bracelet; **work like a charm** function perfectly; succeed. —***v.*** **1** attract, please, win over, etc. by charm: *We were ~ed by the view.* **2** influence, protect, etc. by or as if by magic: *He led a ~ed life.* —**charm·er** *n.* —**charm·ing** *adj.* —**charm·ing·ly** *adv.*

char·nel (house) a building or vault for bones and corpses. —**char·nel** *adj.* sepulchral.

Char·on (CAIR·un) in Greek myths, the ferryman who takes the dead across the Styx to Hades.

chart *n.* **1** a map, esp. one for sea navigation. **2** a sheet or display showing special information with graphs, tables, etc. —***v.*** **1** map out; plan: *~ a course.* **2** put onto a chart. —**chart·less** *adj.* —**char·ter** *n.* **1** a written authorization founding or giving rights to a corporation, university, etc. **2** a constitution or manifesto of political principles. **3** the hiring of a bus, ship, airplane, etc. —***v.*** **1** give a charter to. **2** hire or lease: *a ~ed bus.* —**charter member** a member since the founding of the group.

char·treuse (shahr·TROOZ) *n.* bright greenish yellow.

char·wom·an *n.* **-wom·en** a hired cleaning woman.

char·y (CHAIR·ee) *adj.* **char·i·er, -i·est** cautious; sparing: *an old curmudgeon, ~ of kind words.* —**char·i·ly** *adv.* —**char·i·ness** *n.*

[1]chase (CHACE) *v.* **chas·es, chased, chas·ing** **1** pursue; hunt; fetch quickly. **2** drive away. **3** *Informal.* rush: *The boys went ~ing down the street.* —***n.*** **1** pursuit: *the thrill of* **the chase** (i.e. hunting). **2** that which is hunted. —**chas·er** *n.* **1** *Informal.* a light drink following hard liquor. **2** a person or thing that chases. —**give chase** pursue.

[2]chase (CHACE) *n.* a groove, slot, etc. —***v.*** **chas·es, chased, chas·ing** engrave or emboss metal: *~d silver.* —**chas·er** *n.*

chasm (CAZM) *n.* **1** an abyss. **2** a rift, as between former friends. —**chas·mal** *adj.*

chas·sis (SHAS·ee) *n., pl.* **chas·sis** (–eez) a supporting framework, as of a car, truck, radio, or TV set; also, the landing-gear assembly of an airplane.

chaste *adj.* **1** pure; free from improper sexual relations. **2** of simple, restrained style. —**chaste·ly** *adv.* —**chaste·ness** *n.* —**chas·ten** (CHAY·sn) *v.* correct by punishing; temper; purify: *One must ~ a too bold wit;* **chas·ten·er** *n.* —**chas·tise** (–TIZE) *v.* **-tis·es, -tised, -tis·ing** punish by beating or severe reprimand; **chas·tise·ment** *n.* —**chas·ti·ty** (CHAS·ti·tee) *n.* chasteness.

chas·u·ble (CHAZ·yoo·bl) *n.* the sleeveless outer vestment worn by a priest at Mass.

chat *v.* **chats, chat·ted, chat·ting** talk in a light, easy manner. —***n.:*** *a ~ about old times; Roosevelt's fireside ~s on radio.*

cha·teau or **châ·teau** (sha·TOH) *n.* **-teaus** or **-teaux** (–TOZE) **1** a French castle; a manor house. **2** a wine-producing estate in France. —**chat·e·laine** (SHATL·ain) *n.* **1** the mistress of a chateau or large household. **2** a decorative clasp or chain for a watch, purse, etc. worn at the waist.

Chat·ta·noo·ga (chat·uh·NOO·guh) a city in S.E. Tennessee.

chat·tel (CHATL) *n.* a piece of personal property, not real estate, such as may be used to secure a **chattel mortgage.**

chat·ter *n.* **1** a rapid series of brief, meaningless sounds, as of a squirrel, some birds, or teeth rattling with cold. **2** fast, idle conversation. —***v.:*** *No ~ing in class, please!* —**chat·ter·er** *n.* —**chat·ter·box** *n.* a constant talker.

—chat·ty *adj.* **chat·ti·er, chat·ti·est** inclined to chat; hence, informal: *a ~ news report.* **—chat·ti·ly** *adv.* **—chat·ti·ness** *n.*

Chau·cer (CHAW·sur), **Geoffrey.** 1340?–1400, English poet best known for *The Canterbury Tales.*

chauf·feur (SHOH·fur) *n.* one employed as the driver of another's car. **—*v.*:** *He ~ed his boss around town.*

chau·vin·ism (SHOH·vuh·nizm) *n.* a blind, often aggressive loyalty to one's nation, race, sex, etc. **—chau·vin·ist** *n.*: *a male ~;* **chau·vin·is·tic** (–NIS–) *adj.;* **chau·vin·is·ti·cal·ly** *adv.*

cheap (CHEEP) *adj.* **1** available for little cost, effort, etc. relative to the value; selling goods at a low price: *~ at the price.* **2** low in value; of low quality: *~ shoes won't last; a ~ trick.* **3** *Informal.* ashamed: *to feel ~.* **4** *Informal.* stingy. **—*adv.*:** *to sell a house ~.* **—cheap·ly** *adv.;* **cheap·ness** *n.* **—cheap·en** *v.* become or make cheap: *goods ~ed by a shrinking market.* **—cheap·skate** *n. Slang.* a stingy person.

cheat (CHEET) *v.* **1** get, deprive of, etc. by dishonesty or deceit; act or play dishonestly: *~ing at cards; An impostor ~ed me out of $20.* **2 cheat on** (someone), be sexually unfaithful to: *Jim was ~ing on his wife.* **3** disappoint; deprive of: *An illness ~ed him of his hopes.* **—*n.*** **1** the act of cheating; a trick or deception. **2** one who cheats. **—cheat·er** *n.*

check *n.* **1** control; stoppage; the position of a threatened king in chess: *Keep your horse in ~.* **2** an examination or verification; hence, a mark (✓) showing that a check has been made. **3** a token for reclaiming one's hat, baggage, etc. **4** a small square or a regular pattern of squares: *red and white ~s on the tablecloth.* **5** a bill in a restaurant, bar, etc. **6** a signed authorization for a bank to pay money from one's account. **—*v.*** **1** stop: *He ~ed his first impulse.* **2** in chess, to threaten the king. **3** control; examine, inspect for accuracy, proper condition, etc.; also, tick with a check mark: *Please ~ my addition.* **4** refer or correspond to a list, original copy, authority, etc.: *His version ~ed with mine; I'll have to ~ with* (i.e. consult) *the boss on this.* **5** receive or turn over baggage, clothing, etc. for storage or shipment. **6** have a pattern of squares: *a ~ed shirt.* **—check·er** *n.* **—check in (at)** or **check into** formally enter a hotel, factory, etc.; sign in. **—check out (of)** formally leave (an establishment) after paying dues, etc. **—check·book** *n.* a book of forms for writing checks on an account.

check·er *n.* a piece used in the game of checkers. **—*v.*** **1** mark with a pattern of regular squares. **2** vary: *That was a bright spot in his ~ed career.* **—check·ers** *n.* a game played by two with 12 pieces each on a **check·er·board** which has 64 squares in two alternate colors. **—check·er·ber·ry** *n.* **-ber·ries** the red, edible fruit of the wintergreen; the plant itself.

checking account a bank account on which checks may be written. **—check·list** n. a list of items to be referred to and verified. **—check·mate** *n.* in chess, a position of check which cannot be escaped; hence, total defeat; ***v.*** **-mates, -mat·ed, -mat·ing** **—check·off** *n.* the automatic deduction of union dues from a paycheck.**—check·out** *n.* a checking out or a place for it: *a supermarket ~; a ~ counter.* **—check·point** *n.* a place where vehicles are stopped and inspected, as at a national border. **—check·room** *n.* a place for leaving parcels, hats, etc. in temporary safekeeping. **—check·up** *n.* an inspection; hence, a medical examination.

ched·dar (CHED·ur) or **Cheddar (cheese)** *n.* a firm, smooth, white-to-yellow cheese, ranging from sharp to mild in flavor.

cheek *n.* **1** the part of a face below either eye; something like a cheek, esp. one buttock; **cheeked** *adj.* **2** *Informal.* impudence; **cheek·y** *adj.* **cheek·i·er, -i·est; cheek·i·ly** *adv.;* **cheek·i·ness** *n.* **—cheek by jowl** close together. **—tongue in cheek** ironically. **—cheek·bone** *n.* the bone just under the eye.

cheep *n.* a weak, high-pitched cry, as the chirp of a young bird. Also ***v.***

cheer *n.* **1** a shout of enthusiasm or encouragement. **2** joyous mood; hopeful state of mind: *Be of good ~; What ~?* **3** hospitality; hence, food and drink: *Christmas ~;* **cheers** *interj.* used as a drinking toast. **—*v.*** **1** hearten; become or make glad: *~ up; things will improve.* **2** shout a cheer; support: *Let's all ~ for the home team; ~ them on.* **—cheer·ful** *adj.* **1** having or causing cheer. **2** willing. Hence **cheer·ful·ly** *adv.;* **cheer·ful·ness** *n.* **—cheer·y** *adj.* **cheer·i·er, -i·est; cheer·i·ly** *adv.;* **cheer·i·ness** *n.;* **cheer·less** *adj.;* **cheer·less·ly** *adv.;* **cheer·less·ness** *n.* **—cheer·lead·er** *n.* the leader of a group cheering, esp. at a game or rally.

cheese (CHEEZ) *n.* a protein-rich food made from pressed milk curd. **—cheese·bur·ger** *n.* a hamburger with a layer of cheese over the meat. **—cheese·cake** *n.* **1** a cake made of cottage cheese in a crust of sweet crumbs. **2** *Informal.* a photograph of an attractive, scantily clad woman; ***adj.*:** *~ magazines.* **—cheese·cloth** *n.* a light, porous cotton gauze. **—cheese·par·ing** (–pair–) *n.* **1** stinginess. **2** a trifle saved by a miser. Hence ***adj.*:** *petty, ~ economies.* **—chees·y** *adj.* **chees·i·er, -i·est** **1** like cheese. **2** *Slang.* inferior; tawdry; **chees·i·ness** *n.*

chee·tah (CHEE·tuh) *n.* a swift wild cat of Africa and S. Asia with a tawny, black-spotted coat, sometimes trained to hunt.

chef *n.* a cook, esp. a head cook.**—chef d'oeuvre** (shay·DURV), *pl.* **chefs d'oeuvre** (shay–) a masterpiece.

Che·khov (CHEK·awf), **Anton.** 1860–1904, Russian author of short stories and plays.

che·la (KEEL·uh) *n.* **-lae** (–lee) the grabbing claw of a crab, scorpion, etc.

chem. chemical; chemist; chemistry. **—chem·i·cal** (KEM–) *adj.* of or having to do with chemistry or chemicals; ***n.*** a chemical substance; **chem·i·cal·ly** *adv.* **—chemical engineering** the technology of chemical processes and their use in industries, such as the petroleum industry; **chemical engineer. —chemical warfare** warfare using nonexplosive chemicals, as various gases, poisons, etc.

che·mise (shuh·MEEZ) *n.* a woman's shirtlike undergarment; hence, a loose, waistless dress; shift.

chem·ist (KEM–) *n.* **1** a chemistry specialist. **2** *Brit.* a pharmacist. **—chem·is·try** (KEM·is·tree) *n.* **-tries** **1** the science of the composition, combination, and reactions of substances and their elements. **2** the composition or properties: *the ~ of copper; the odd ~ of mob hysteria.* **—chemo-** *comb.form.* chemistry; chemical. **—chem·o·sphere** *n.* an atmospheric stratum with heavy photochemical activity, beginning about 20 miles high. **—chem·o·ster·i·lant** (–STER·i·lunt) *n.* a chemical sterilizing agent, used to stop insects, rodents, and such pests from breeding. **—chem·o·ther·a·py** (–THER·uh·pee) *n.* the use of chemicals to treat disease; **chem·o·ther·a·peu·tic** (–PYOO·tic) or **-peu·ti·cal** *adj.* **—chem·ur·gy** (KEM·ur·jee) *n.* the utilization of organic materials, esp. farm products or by-products, in chemical industries; **chem·ur·gic** (–UR–) *adj.;* **chem·ur·gist** *n.*

che·nille (shi·NEEL) *n.* a cord having a fuzzy pile, used in trim and embroidery; also, a cloth made with this cord.

cheque (CHEK) *Chiefly Brit.* bank check.

cher·ish *v.* **1** hold dear; show love for. **2** keep in the mind with attachment or affection: *a ~ed memory; We all ~ed hopes of his return.*

Cher·o·kee (CHER·uh·kee) *n.* (a member of) a tribe of American Indians now concentrated in Tennessee and Oklahoma; also, their Iroquoian language. ***—adj.:*** *the ~ alphabet.*

che·root (shuh·ROOT) *n.* a cigar with both ends cut square.

cher·ry *n.* **cher·ries** **1** a firm, small, fleshy fruit, having a small hard pit, of a tree of the rose family; also, the tree itself or its wood. **2** bright red color.

chert *n.* a kind of quartz that resembles flint.

cher·ub *n.* **1** *pl.* **-ub·im** an angel of the second highest rank. **2** *pl.* **-ubs** a chubby, rosy-faced child. **—che·rub·ic** (–ROO·bic) *adj.: a ~ face.*

Ches·a·peake (CHES·uh·peek) **Bay** an inlet of the Atlantic Ocean extending into Virginia and Maryland.

chess *n.* a game played on a checkerboard, or **chess·board,** by two people, each using 16 pieces called **chess·men,** *sing.* **-man.**

chest *n.* **1** a large storage or shipping box with a lid; also, a treasury or fund: *the community ~.* **2** a piece of furniture with drawers for clothes; also called **chest of drawers.** **3** the front of the body, from the bottom of the ribs to the neck; **-chested** *comb.form.:* as in *big-chested, flat-chested.*

ches·ter·field *n.* **1** a semi-fitted, fly-front overcoat, often velvet-collared. **2** a sofa with well-padded back and upright armrests.

chest·nut *n.* **1** the edible nut, enclosed in a prickly case, of a tree of the beech family; also, the tree itself, or its wood; a reddish brown. **2** a stale joke, tale, etc.

che·val (shuh·VAL) **glass** a full-length mirror mounted between supports so as to be tilted. **—chev·a·lier** (shev·uh·LEER) *n.* a member of an order of merit, as the French Legion of Honor.

chev·i·ot (SHEV·ee·ut) *n.* a sturdy, wool cloth for coats and suits; also, a soft, strong cotton shirting.

chev·ron (SHEV·run) *n.* a badge of V-shaped stripes on a uniform sleeve, showing military rank.

chew (CHOO) *v.* grind or mash with the teeth; masticate. ***—n.*** an act of chewing; something chewed, esp. a quid of tobacco. **—chew out** *Slang.* severely upbraid. **—chew over** ponder. **—chew the rag** (or **fat**) *Slang.* talk casually; chat. **—chew·er** *n.* **—chew·a·ble** *adj.* **—chew·y** *adj.* **chew·i·er, -i·est** thick and requiring much chewing. **—chewing gum** an insoluble substance, usu. chicle, sweetened and flavored for chewing.

Chey·enne (shy·AN, –EN) capital of Wyoming. ***—n.*** (a member of) a tribe of American Indians now living in Montana, South Dakota, and Oklahoma; also, their Algonquian language; ***adj.:*** *a ~ saddle.*

chg. charge.

Chiang Kai-shek (chang·kye·SHEK) 1887–1975, Chinese general and former president of the Republic of China on Taiwan.

Chi·an·ti (kee·AHN·tee) *n.* a dry, red wine, esp. one made in the Monti Chianti region of Tuscany, Italy.

chiao (TYOW) *n. sing. & pl.* a unit of money equal to 1/10th of the yuan of the People's Republic of China.

chi·a·ro·scu·ro (kee·ahr·uh·SKYOOR·oh) *n.* **-ros** a style or technique of painting using light-and-shade effects; hence, a painting in this style; also, the treatment of light and shade in a painting.

chic (SHEEK) *adj.* elegant and fasionable; stylishly dressed. ***—n.*** sophistication; stylishness. **—chic·ly** *adv.*

Chi·ca·go (shuh·CAH·go) a city in N.E. Illinois, America's second largest. **—Chi·ca·go·an** *n.*

chi·cane (shi·CANE) *n.* & *v.* **-canes, -caned, -can·ing** (use or get by) chicanery. —**chi·can·er·y** (–CAY·nuh–) *n.* **-er·ies** trickery; also, a deception; trick.

Chi·ca·no (–CAH–) *n.* **-nos** an American of Mexican origin. —***adj.:*** *the ~ community.*

chi·chi (SHEE·shee) *adj.* over-refined; affectedly elegant. —***n.*** a person, thing, or quality that is chichi.

chick *n.* **1** a young domestic fowl. **2** *Slang.* a young woman. —**chick·a·dee** (–uh–) *n.* a small, gray, black-capped North American bird.

Chick·a·saw (–uh·saw) *n.* (a member of) an American Indian tribe now concentrated in Oklahoma; also, their language; also ***adj.***

chick·en *n.* **1** the common barnyard fowl, raised for its flesh and eggs; also, its edible flesh: *fried ~.* **2** *Slang.* a coward. —***adj.*** *Slang.* **1** cowardly; also **chick·en-heart·ed** and **chick·en-liv·ered.** **2** adhering to petty details or rules. —**chicken (out)** withdraw because of fear. —**chicken feed** *Slang.* a paltry sum of money; pittance. —**chicken pox** a contagious, usu. childhood disease, causing fever and a blistering rash. —**chicken wire** a light wire mesh, usu. six-sided, used for fencing.

chick·pea (–pee) *n.* a leguminous plant of S. Europe and Asia bearing edible seeds; also, the seeds.

chick·weed *n.* a low, spreading plant with white flowers.

chic·le *n.* the tasteless, gumlike, solidified latex of the sapodilla, and the basic ingredient in chewing gum.

chic·o·ry (CHIC·uh·ree) *n.* **-ries** a perennial herb with blue, daisylike flowers, whose leaves are used in salads and whose roasted roots are often added to ground coffee. —**chic·o·ried** (–reed) *adj.: a cup of ~ coffee.*

chide *v.* **chides,** *pt.* **chid** or **chid·ed,** *pp.* **chid, chid·ed** or **chid·den, chi·ding** reprove mildly; scold.

chief *n.* the leader of a group, organization, etc.; the one highest in rank: *Geronimo was an Indian ~.* —***adj.*** most important; highest ranking: *the ~ of police; my ~ worry.* —**in chief** of the highest authority; head: *editor in ~; commander in ~.* —**chief·ly** *adv.* —**Chief Executive** the President of the U.S. —**Chief Justice** the judge who presides over the Supreme Court. —**chief of state** the formal but not political head of a nation, as the British Queen. —**chief·tain** (–tin) *n.* a chief, esp. of a tribe, clan, band, etc.; **chief·tain·cy** *n.* **-cies.**

chif·fon (shi·FON) *n.* a light, diaphanous fabric of silk, nylon, etc. —***adj.*** light and fluffy: *pineapple ~ pie.* —**chif·fon·y** (SHIF·uh·nee) *adj.: a ~ silk scarf.* —**chif·fon·ier** (shif·uh·NEER) *n.* a tall chest of drawers.

chig·ger *n.* **1** a blood-sucking mite larva that causes severe irritation. **2** a tropical flea; also **chig·oe,** *pl.* **-oes.**

chi·gnon (SHEEN·yon) *n.* a coil of hair worn at the nape of the neck or back of the head.

Chi·hua·hua (chi·WAH·wuh) *n.* a small, short-haired Mexican dog with large ears.

chil·blain *n.* an itchy, red swelling of the toes, ears, nose, etc. caused by exposure to cold: *to catch ~s.*

child (CHILED) *n., pl.* **chil·dren** (CHILL·drun) **1** baby; infant; **with child** pregnant. **2** a pre-pubescent person. **3** offspring; hence, descendant: *the ~ren of Israel.* **4** one deeply influenced by: *a ~ of his times;* **child·hood** *n.* —**child·bear·ing** *n.* childbirth; ***adj.:*** *a woman of ~ age.* —**child·bed** *n.* the state of a woman in **child·birth** *n.* the act of giving birth. —**child·ish** *adj.* foolish and immature; **child·ish·ly** *adv.;* **child·ish·ness** *n.* —**child·less** *adj.;* **child·less·ly** *adv.;* **child·less·ness** *n.* —**child·like** *adj.* like a child, esp. innocent, naive, etc.: *~ candor.* —**child's play** an easy or trivial job.

Chil·e (CHIL·ee) a coastal country in S.W. South America; 292,258 sq.mi. (756,945 km²); *cap.* Santiago; —**Chil·e·an** *n.* & *adj.*

chil·i (CHIL·ee) *n.* **chil·ies** **1** the pod of a tropical American capsicum, dried to make a pungent pepper, often ground to make **chili powder;** also, the plant. **2** same as **chili con car·ne** (CHIL·ee·kun·CAR·nee), a hot dish with chili, meat, beans, etc. Also **chil·e,** *pl.* **chil·es** and **chil·li,** *pl.* **chil·lies.** —**chili sauce** a sauce made with chilies or sweet peppers and tomatoes.

chill *n.* **1** a feeling of coldness, often causing shivers; also, cool weather: *~s running down my spine; the ~ of a fall day.* **2** a discouragement; unfriendliness. —***adj.*** **chill·er, chill·est** **1** : *a ~ December wind; He was silenced by a ~ stare.* —***v.*** **1** make or get cold: *The skiers were ~ed to the bone.* **2** discourage; dampen (spirits, friendliness, etc.). —**chill factor** same as WINDCHILL. —**chilli(es)** See CHILI. —**chill·y** *adj.* **chill·i·er, -i·est:** *a ~ reception;* **chill·i·ly** *adv.;* **chill·i·ness** *n.*

chi·m(a)e·ra (kye·MEER·uh) *n.* **1** in Greek myths, a monster with a lion's head, goat's body, and a serpent's tail. **2** a terrible or bizarre fantasy; an unrealistic plan. —**chi·mer·i·cal** (kye·MER·i·kul) *adj.* given to fanciful plans; fantastic and impractical: *a ~ plan for reform.*

chime *n.* **1** a bell. **2** often **chimes,** a set of bells rung in melody: *~s ringing on a Sunday morning; We have ~s instead of a doorbell.* **3** harmony. —***v.*** **chimes, chimed, chim·ing** **1** ring or sound, esp. in harmony: *The clock ~d three.* **2** agree: *Your idea ~s with my own.* —**chime in** join in (a conversation, song, etc.) with agreement or harmony.

chimera same as CHIMAERA.

chim·ney (CHIM·nee) *n.* **-neys** **1** a vertical vent for the smoke and gases from a fireplace, furnace, etc. **2** a glass tube shielding a lamp flame.

chimp *n. Informal* for **chim·pan·zee** (–ZEE, –PAN·zee) an intelligent, middle-sized African ape.

chin *n.* the part of the lower jaw below the lower lip; **chin·less** *adj.* —***v.* chins, chinned, chin·ning** pull (oneself) up while hanging by the hands until the chin is level with or above the hands.

Chin. China; Chinese. —**chi·na** (CHYE·nuh) *n.* porcelain; esp. tableware of porcelain: *a ~ doll; Set the best ~ for our company.*—**Chi·na** (CHYE·nuh) **1** the People's Republic of China on the Asian mainland; 3,691,523 sq.mi. (9,561,000 km²); *cap.* Peking. **2** the Republic of China on TAIWAN and other coastal islands; *cap.* Taipei. —**China Sea** the Pacific Ocean off the S. and E. coasts of China. —**Chi·na·town** *n.* the Chinese quarter of a large city outside China. —**China watcher** an observer of mainland China and its government.

chinch (bug) a white-winged insect that attacks grain crops.

chin·chil·la (–CHIL·uh) *n.* **1** a small South American rodent with a prized soft gray fur; also, its fur. **2** a deep-napped heavy wool cloth used for coats.

Chin·ese (chye·NEEZ) *n. sing. & pl.* **1** a native of China or a descendant of one. **2** one of a group of related languages of China, esp. Mandarin. —***adj.*** pertaining to the nation, people, culture, or language of China: *the ~ Empire.* —**Chinese checkers** a game somewhat like checkers, played with marbles on a star-shaped board. —**Chinese lantern** a brightly-colored, collapsible paper lantern.

chink *n.* **1** a small crack; ***v.*** fill in cracks: *The pioneers ~ed their log cabins before winter.* **2** a sharp, metallic click; ***v.:*** *coins ~ing in my pocket.*

chi·no (CHEE·no) *n.* a usu. khaki-colored cotton cloth; **chinos** *pl.* casual trousers made of this cloth.

Chi·nook (shuh·NOOK) *n.* (a member of) any of a group of American Indian tribes of Oregon; also, the language of a Chinook tribe; **chinook** *n.* a warm onshore wind in the Pacific Northwest. —**Chi·nook·an** *n.* a language group composed of Upper and Lower Chinook; also ***adj.***

chintz (CHINTS) *n.* a brightly patterned cotton cloth, usu. with a glossy finish. —**chintz·y** *adj.* **chintz·i·er, -i·est** of or decorated with chintz; hence, cheap and tacky; stingy.

chin-up *n.* the exercise of chinning oneself.

chip *n.* **1** a small cut or broken piece: *Wood ~s littered the carpenter's shop.* **2** a flaw showing where a chip has been made: *a ~ in the glass.* **3** a gambling token: *when the ~s are down* (i.e. when the situation is crucial); *let the ~s fall where they may.* **4** a thin, crispy snack: *corn ~s.* **5** a small strip of something edible: *fish and ~s.* **6** an integrated circuit: *a silicon ~.* —***v.* chips, chipped, chip·ping** cut or shape by chipping; also, knock a chip from: *I ~d my tooth when I fell.* —**chip in** contribute. —**chip off the old block** one just like his father.

chip·munk *n.* a small striped ground-dwelling North American rodent of the squirrel family.

chipped beef thin slices of smoked or dried beef.

chip·per *n.* a person or machine that chips. —***adj.*** *Informal.* cheerful; vigorous; lively: *as ~ as a sparrow.* —***v.* chipper up** cheer up.

Chip·pe·wa (CHIP·uh·waw) *n.* same as OJIBWA; also **Chip·pe·way** (–way).

chip·py *n.* **chip·pies** *Slang.* a prostitute; also, a promiscuous young woman.

chip shot in golf, a short lobbed shot onto the green.

chiro- *comb.form.* hand. —**chi·rog·ra·phy** (kye·ROG·ruh·fee) *n.* handwriting; also, calligraphy; **chi·rog·ra·pher** *n.;* **chi·ro·graph·ic** (kye·ruh·GRAPH·ic) or **-i·cal** *adj.* —**chi·ro·man·cy** (KYE·ruh·man·see) *n.* palmistry. —**chi·rop·o·dy** (kuh·ROP·uh·dee) *n.* podiatry; **chi·rop·o·dist** *n.* —**chi·ro·prac·tic** (kye·ruh·PRAC·tic) *n.* the treatment of disease by the manipulation of the spine or other parts of the body; ***adj.:*** *a ~ doctor,* or **chi·ro·prac·tor** *n.*

chirp *v.* utter a high, short sound, as small birds and insects such as crickets and grasshoppers do. —***n.*** a tweet; peep. —**chir·rup** (CHUR·up) *v.* chirp repeatedly; also, make a similar noise, esp. by sucking, as in urging a horse forward; ***n.:*** *the ~ of bullets whizzing by.*

chis·el (CHIZL) *n.* a metal tool with a beveled cutting edge used to shape or cut wood, stone, or metal. —***v.* -els, -el(l)ed, -el·(l)ing 1** shape or work with a chisel: *~ a groove in the plank.* **2** *Informal.* cheat or get by cheating: *The crook ~d me out of $30.* —**chis·el·er** *n.*

chit *n.* **1** a short note; hence, a voucher for food, drink, merchandise, etc.: *meal ~s.* **2** a child. **3** a forward young woman: *a mere ~ of a girl.*

chit·chat *n.* small talk; chat; gossip.

chi·tin (KYE·tn) *n.* a hard, colorless, horny substance forming the outer covering of insects, crabs, etc. —**chi·tin·ous** *adj.*

chit·ter·lings (CHIT·linz) *n.pl.* the small intestines of hogs cooked, usu. fried, for food; also **chit·lins, chit·lings.**

chiv·al·ry (SHIV·ul·ree) *n.* **1** the qualities of a perfect knight, such as courage, courtesy, and honor: *Is ~ dead?* **2** the system of medieval knighthood; knights collectively: *the Age of ~;* **chi·val·ric** (–VAL–) *adj.* —**chiv·al·rous** (SHIV·ul·rus) *adj.:* *a ~ gentleman of the old school;* **chiv·al·rous·ly** *adv.;* **chiv·al·rous·ness** *n.*

chives *n.pl.* [often takes *sing. v.*] a seasoning for soups, salads, etc. made from the long, narrow leaves of the **chive,** a plant related to the onion, leek, etc.

chlor(o)- *comb.form.* green; hence, chlorine. **—chlo·ral** (CLOR·ul) *n.* **1** a thin, colorless liquid made from alcohol and chlorine, used to make DDT and **chloral hydrate,** a strong sedative. **2** chloral hydrate. **—chlor·dan(e)** *n.* a poisonous, chlorinated oil used as insecticide. **—chlor·ide** *n.* a compound of chlorine and another element or radical: *Sodium ~ is table salt.* **—chlo·ri·nate** *v.* **-nates, -nat·ed, -nat·ing** treat with chlorine or a compound of it, usu. to purify (esp. water); **chlo·ri·na·tor** *n.;* **chlo·ri·na·tion** (–NAY–) *n.* **—chlo·rine** (CLOR·een) *n.* a greenish-yellow, poisonous, foul-smelling, gaseous element used to disinfect, bleach, and in various manufacturing processes. **—chlo·ro·form** *n.* a volatile, pleasant-smelling liquid, used as an anesthetic, in refrigerants, etc.; ***v.*** anesthetize or kill with chloroform. **—chlo·ro·phyl(l)** (CLOR·uh·fil) *n.* the green coloring in plant cells which is necessary for photosynthesis, and is contained in minute bodies called **chlo·ro·plasts.**

chm. or **chmn.** chairman.

chock *n.* a block or wedge used to support or keep a barrel, wheel, boat hull, etc. from moving. **—*v.:*** *We ~ed the back wheels and jacked up the car.* **—*adv.*** as close, tight, etc. as possible. **—chock-a-block** *adj.* & *adv.: families crammed ~ into tenements.* **—chock-full** *adj.* as full as possible: *a mouth stuffed ~ o' words.*

choc·o·late (CHOC·lit, CHAWK–) *n.* **1** a powder, syrup, solid, etc. made from roasted and processed cacao seeds; hence, a drink or confection made with chocolate. **2** a deep reddish-brown. **—*adj.:*** *a ~ bar.* **—choc·o·lat·(e)y** *adj.: sweet and ~.*

Choc·taw *n.* (a member of) an American Indian tribe now concentrated in Oklahoma; also, their Muskhogean language. Also ***adj.***

choice *n.* **1** selection; the act of choosing: *I can't make a ~!* **2** alternative; the power of choosing: *The draftee had no ~.* **3** the thing chosen; hence, the best one or portion: *the people's ~.* **4** a variety to choose from: *a big ~ of jackets.* **—*adj.*** **choic·er, choic·est** of high quality; well chosen: *~ cuts of beef.*

choir (KWIRE) *n.* **1** a group of singers, esp. in a church; also, a section of an orchestra: *the Vienna Boy's ~; the reed ~.* **2** the part of the church used by the choir. **—choir·boy** *n.* a boy in a choir. **—choir·mas·ter** *n.* the conductor of a choir.

choke *v.* **chokes, choked, chok·ing** **1** have difficulty in breathing; strangle: *to ~ on a piece of bread.* **2** clog; limit the flow of air, water, etc. in the windpipe, a stream, etc.; also, reduce the airflow in the carburetor; hence, suppress as if by choking: *a child ~d with bare hands; a pipe ~d with mud; a flower bed ~d with weeds; ~ back one's tears.* **3** grip (a bat, golf club, etc.) closer to the hitting end: *The batter ~d up for an infield hit.* **—choke up** *Informal.* **1** fail to perform under pressure. **2** be or make speechless due to emotion: *He was all ~d up by their kindness.* **—*n.*** **1** the action or sound of choking. **2** the air valve in a carburetor. **3** a narrowing of the bore of a gun near the muzzle; also called **choke·bore.** **—chok·er** *n.* a short, close-fitting necklace.

chol·er (COLL·ur) *n.* anger; grouchiness; **chol·er·ic** *adj.: a rough, ~ temper.* **—chol·er·a** (COLL·uh·ruh) *n.* a severe contagious disease of the digestive system, often fatal.**—cho·les·ter·ol** (cuh·LES·tuh·rawl) *n.* a fat-soluble substance found in the brain, blood, other body tissues and some foods, which is linked to hardening of the arteries.

chomp *v.* bite; chew.

chon (CHON) *n. sing.* & *pl.* a unit of money equal to 1/100th of a South Korean won.

choose *v.* **choos·es, chose** (CHOZE), **cho·sen** (CHOH·zun), **choos·ing** **1** pick according to one's judgment; select: *You must ~ your friends wisely.* **2** prefer; resolve: *I chose to stay here.* **—choos·(e)y** *adj.* **choos·i·er, -i·est** *Informal.* cautious in choosing; fussy: *Don't be so ~; they're all alike;* **choos·i·ness** *n.*

chop *v.* **chops, chopped, chop·ping** **1** cut with a heavy blade, as an ax, cleaver, etc.: *~ wood for a fire.* **2** hit with a short, sharp stroke. **3** cut into small pieces: *~d liver.* **—*n.*** **1** a chopping blow: *He cut the cable with the first ~; a karate ~.* **2** a piece chopped off; esp., a small cut of meat with a bone: *pork ~s.* **3** an official permit or stamp of quality: *first-~* (*Informal.* first-grade or top quality) *goods.* **4** a short, jerky motion, as of waves.

chop·house *n.* a restaurant, esp. a steak house.

Cho·pin (SHOW·pan), **Frédéric.** 1810–1849, a Polish composer.

chop·per *n.* **1** a person or thing that chops. **2** *Informal.* a helicopter. **—chop·py** *adj.* **chop·pi·er, chop·pi·est** irregular or changeable: *a ~ wind, sea;* **chop·pi·ly** *adv.;* **chop·pi·ness** *n.*

chops *n.pl.* the jaws and surrounding flesh: *a dog licking his ~s after a meal.*

chop·stick *n.* one of a pair of slender sticks held in one hand and used as a fork in China, Japan, etc.

chop su·ey (–SOO·ee) a Chinese-American dish of meat, bean sprouts, and other assorted vegetables in a sauce, with rice.

cho·ral (COR·ul) *adj.* pertaining to or performed by a choir or chorus; **cho·ral·ly** *adv.* **—cho·ral(e)** (cuh·RAL) *n.* **1** a simple choral hymn in the Protestant church; hence, its melody as set in harmony for voices or instruments: *a Bach ~.* **2** a choir.

chord (CORD) *n.* **1** a set of three or more musical notes sounded together in harmony; ***v.*** harmonize; also, play or sing chords: *~ his guitar.* **2** a line linking two points on a curve or circle. **3** *Archaic.* the string of a musical instrument; hence, a feeling or emotional reaction: *Her sad story struck a sympathetic ~.*

chore *n.* a task or tiresome job, esp. a routine one: *John did his ~s before breakfast.*

cho·re·a (cuh·REE·uh) *n.* a nervous disorder causing irregular and uncontrolled muscular twitching, as St. Vitus's dance. —**chor·e·o·graph** (COR·ee·uh–) *v.* create the choreography for: *a well ~ed show song;* **chor·e·og·ra·pher** (cor·ee·OG·ruh·fur) *n.;* **chor·e·o·graph·ic** (cor·ee·uh·GRAPH·ic) *adj.;* **chor·e·o·graph·i·cal·ly** *adv.* —**chor·e·og·ra·phy** (cor·ee·OG·ruh·fee) *n.* **1** dancing. **2** the art of designing dances or ballets. —**cho·rine** (COR·een) *n. Informal.* a chorus girl.—**chor·is·ter** (COR·is·tur) *n.* a member of a choir, esp. a choirboy; also, the leader of a choir.

chor·tle *v.* **-tles, -tled, -tling** give a gleeful, throaty chuckle: *She ~d in triumph.* —***n.:*** *a ~ of delight.*

cho·rus (COR·us) *n.* **1** a choir; also, any group of people who sing, dance, recite, etc. together, esp. the supporting players in a musical drama. **2** the part performed by a chorus; also, a piece of harmonic music written for a chorus; hence, something said or sung in unison: *a ~ of praise.* **3** a repeated part of a song or tune; refrain; **in chorus** in unison; all together. —***v.*** **-rus·es, -rus(s)ed, -rus·(s)ing** utter in unison. —**chorus girl** (or **boy**) a young woman (or man) who sings and dances in the chorus of a musical show or revue.

chose(n) See CHOOSE.—**cho·sen** *adj.* selected; preferred; elect: *God's ~ people.*

chow *n.* **1** *Informal.* food; ***v.*** **chow down** eat. **2** a heavy-set dog of Chinese origin, with a thick dark coat and black tongue; also **chow chow.** —**chow·chow** *n.* a relish made of pickled chopped vegetables.

chow·der *n.* a thick stewlike soup usu. of seafood with a milk base; a similar dish: *clam ~; corn ~.*

chow mein (–MANE) a Chinese-American dish of fried noodles served with a thick stew of chopped meat and vegetables.

Chr. Christ; Christian. —**chrism** (CRIZM) *n.* consecrated oil used in church sacraments. —**Christ** (CRY–) *n.* a title and name of Jesus of Nazareth. —**chris·ten** (CRIS·un) *v.* **1** baptize; also, name at baptism: *I ~ thee Margaret.* **2** name and dedicate formally, as a ship; **chris·ten·ing** *n.;* **Chris·ten·dom** *n.* Christians collectively; also, the Christian world. —**Chris·tian** *adj.* of or having to do with Christ, his teachings, the religion based on them, or its followers: *~ charity; ~ piety;* ***n.*** a believer in Christ; a member of a Christian church; **Christian Era** the era starting from the birth of Christ, with dates marked A.D. —**Chris·ti·an·i·ty** (–chee·AN·i·tee) *n.* a religion based on Christ's teachings; also, the state of being Christian: *His ~ made him forswear hatred.* —**Chris·tian·ize** (CRIS·chuh·nize) *v.* **-iz·es, -ized, -iz·ing** make Christian in belief or character. —**Christian name** first name; a name given at baptism. —**Christian Scientist** a believer in **Christian Science,** a religion teaching spiritual healing, founded by Mary Baker Eddy about 1866. —**chris·tie** or **chris·ty** (CRIS·tee) *n.* **-ties** a turn in downhill skiing, also used to slow down or stop, made with a sideways skid. —**Christ·like** *adj.* like Christ; exhibiting patience, purity, and other virtues. —**Christ·mas** (CRIS·mus) *n.* December 25, a Christian and legal holiday celebrating the birth of Christ. —**Christ·mas·tide** *n.* the Christmas season, December 24 to January 6. —**Christmas tree** a usu. evergreen tree decorated and set up at Christmas. —**christy** same as CHRISTIE.

chro·mat·ic (croh·MAT·ic) *adj.* **1** of or having to do with color. **2** *Music.* of or having to do with the chromatic scale which proceeds by half-tones: *a ~ harmonica.* —**chro·mat·i·cal·ly** *adv.* —**chro·mat·i·cism** *n.* —**chro·ma·tic·i·ty** (croh·muh·TIS·i·tee) *n.* the quality of a color with respect to hue and purity. —**chro·ma·tid** (CROH·muh–) *n.* either strand of a chromosome before cell division; **chro·ma·tin** *n.* the DNA-containing substance in the nucleus of a cell. —**chro·ma·tog·ra·phy** (croh·muh·TOG·ruh·fee) *n.* the separation, purification, and recording of the substances in liquid or gaseous solution by means of differential rates of adsorption, separation, etc. in a device called a **chro·mat·o·graph** (–MAT–), the result of which is a **chro·mat·o·gram,** a graph line or a series of usu. colored bands or spots. —**chro·mat·o·graph·ic** (–GRAF–) *adj.;* **chro·mat·o·graph·i·cal·ly** *adv.* —**chrome** *n.* **1** chromium; hence, an alloy or pigment made with it: *~ steel; ~ yellow; ~ green.* **2** chromium-plated trim, as of an automobile's bumper. —**chro·mic** (CROH–) *adj.: ~ acid.* —**chro·mi·um** *n.* (CROH·mee·um) a hard, gray, metallic element used in alloys, pigments, and corrosion-resistant plating. —**chromo-** *comb.form.* color. —**chro·mo·lith·o·graph** (croh·muh·LITH·uh·graf) *n.* a many-colored lithograph; also called **chro·mo,** *pl.* **-mos.** —**chro·mo·some** (CROH·muh·sohm) *n.* any of the gene-bearing bodies in the nucleus of a cell; **chro·mo·so·mal** (–SOH·mul) *adj.* —**chro·mo·sphere** (CROH·mus·feer) *n.* a gaseous layer around a star, between the photosphere and the corona; **chro·mo·spher·ic** (–FER·ic) *adj.*

chron. chronicle; chronological; chronology. —**Chron.** Chronicles. —**chron·ic** (CRON·ic) *adj.* persistent; recurrent; long-affected; ceaseless: *a ~ head cold; a ~ sufferer; a ~ complainer;* **chron·i·cal·ly** *adv.* —**chron·i·cle** *n.* **1** a bare historical record of events; an account. **2 Chronicles** the name of two books of the Old Testament, I and II Chronicles. —***v.*** **-cles, -cled, -cling** narrate or record, as in a chronicle: *He ~d the history of the Roman Empire.* —**chron·i·cler** *n.* —**chrono-** *comb. form.* time. —**chron·o·graph** (CRON·uh·graf) *n.* any device for precisely measuring time, as a stopwatch; **chron·o·graph·ic** (–GRAF–) *adj.* —**chron·o·log·i·cal** (cron·uh·LOJ·i·cul) *adj.* **1** according to chronology: *in ~ order.* **2** measured by time: *~ age as opposed to mental age;* **chron·o·log·i·cal·ly** *adv.* —**chro·nol·o·gist** (cruh·NOL·uh·jist) *n.* —**chro·nol·o·gy** (cruh·NOL·uh·jee) *n.* **-gies** the determination or arrangement of the dates and temporal sequence of events; hence, a list or table showing this: *The ~ of prehistory is still uncertain.* —**chro·nom·e·ter** (cruh·NOM·i·tur) *n.* a very precise watch, clock, etc.

chrys·a·lis (CRIS·uh–) *n.* **chrys·a·lis·es** or **chry·sal·i·des** (cri·SAL·i·deez) **1** the pupa of an insect; also, its firm cocoon. **2** something immature but developing; also, a surrounding protection: *youth emerging from the ~ of naivety.* —**chry·san·the·mum** (cri·SANTH·uh–) *n.* any of a genus of colorful, fall-blooming perennial, composite flowers. —**chrys·o·lite** (CRIS·uh–) *n.* same as OLIVINE.

chub *n.* any of several carplike freshwater fishes. —**chub·by** (CHUB·ee) *adj.* **chub·bi·er, chub·bi·est** plump; fleshy: *a ~ face.* —**chub·bi·ness** *n.*

[1]chuck *v.* **1** tap or pinch lightly, esp. under the chin. **2** toss easily; throw. **3** *Informal.* throw away; dismiss: *to ~ out old shoes; ~ it, it's hopeless now.* —***n.*** [corresponding to the *v.* senses] **1:** *a loving ~.* **2:** *a quick ~ to the outfield.*

[2]chuck *n.* **1** a device for holding a tool, bit, or piece of work in a drill, lathe, etc. **2** a cut of beef from the neck and shoulder blade: *ground ~; a ~ steak.* **3** food: *a ~ wagon.* —**chuck·hole** *n.* a rough hole in a road.

chuck·le *v.* **-les, -led, -ling** laugh gently or to oneself; ***n.:*** *a satisfied ~.*

chuck wagon a wagon carrying food and kitchen equipment for feeding loggers, cowboys, etc.

chug *n.* a short, heavy, dull sound, as of a laboring engine. —***v.*** **chugs, chugged, chug·ging** make this sound or move while doing so: *an old car ~ing up the hill.*

chuk·ka (CHUCK·uh), **chuk·kar** (–ur), or **chuk·ker** *n.* a playing period in polo. —**chukka (boot)** an ankle-length boot.

chum *n.* a close friend: *a reunion of old school ~s.* —***v.*** **chums, chummed, chum·ming:** *He ~d around with Pete all summer.* —**chum·my** *adj.* **chum·mi·er, chum·mi·est** *Informal.* friendly: *He was too ~ for a total stranger;* **chum·mi·ly** *adv.;* **chum·mi·ness** *n.*

chump *n.* a dupe; a fool.

Chung·king (CHOONG–) a city in S.C. China.

chunk *n.* a thick, heavy piece; hence, a large amount: *a ~ of wood; a big ~ of time.* —**chunk·y** *adj.* **chunk·i·er, -i·est** **1** stocky; thickset: *a ~ build.* **2** having chunks in it: *a thick, ~ soup;* **chunk·i·ly** *adv.;* **chunk·i·ness** *n.*

church *n.* **1** a building for public, usu. Christian worship; also, a religious service. **2** **Church** Christians as a body; also, some organized sect within this body: *the universal ~; the Church of England.* **3** religious as opposed to secular power: *~ and state.* **4** a congregation. **5** the clergy. —**church·go·er** *n.* a regular attender of church; **church·go·ing** *n.* & *adj.* —**church·man** *n.* **-men** a regular church member. —**Church of Christ, Scientist** the official name of the Christian Science organization. —**Church of England** the official and established church in England. —**church·war·den** *n.* an elected lay official of an Anglican or Episcopal Church. —**church·wom·an** *n.* **-wom·en** an active woman member of a church. —**church·yard** *n.* the grounds of a church, esp. as a burial place.

Church·ill **1** **Sir Winston.** 1874–1965, a British statesman and wartime prime minister. **2** a river in C. Canada, flowing into Hudson Bay.

churl *n.* an ill-bred, bad-tempered person; boor; **churl·ish** *adj.:* *~ manners;* **churl·ish·ly** *adv.;* **churl·ish·ness** *n.*

churn *n.* a container for agitating milk or cream to make butter. —***v.*** make butter in a churn; hence, to produce or suffer violent agitation; also, move with a churning effect: *The car ~ed through a snowbank.* —**churn out** produce rapidly and mechanically: *He ~ed out one trashy novel after another.*

chute (SHOOT) *n.* **1** a waterfall or rapids; also, a steep passage, through, etc. to slide things down: *a mail ~.* **2** *Informal.* a parachute.

chut·ney (CHUT·nee) *n.* **-neys** a spicy, hot relish of fruits, herbs, chilies, etc.

chutz·pa(h) (HOOT·spuh, *like* FOOT–) *n.* *Slang.* boldness; effrontery; nerve.

Ci. curie. —**C.I.** cost and insurance.

Cia. *Spanish.* company. —**C.I.A.** Central Intelligence Agency.

ciao (CHOW) *interj. Informal.* greetings; goodbye.

ci·ca·da (si·CAY·duh) *n.* any of a group of large insects with transparent wings, the males of which produce a high, droning sound.

cic·a·trix (SIC·uh–) *n., pl.* **-tri·ces** (–TRY·seez) scar tissue on an animal or plant.

Cic·e·ro (SIS·uh·roh), **Marcus Tullius.** 106–43 B.C., a Roman orator and statesman. —**ci·ce·ro·ne** (sis·uh·ROH·nee) *n.* **-nes** or **-ni** (–nee) a sightseeing guide.

C.I.D. Criminal Investigation Department.

-cide *comb.form.* **1** killer of: as in *herbicide.* **2** the killing of: as in *homicide.*

ci·der (SYE·dur) *n.* the pressed juice of apples, used as a beverage, either unfermented

(sweet cider) or fermented **(hard cider),** and to make vinegar, applejack, etc.

Cie. *French.* company.

c.i.f. or **C.I.F.** cost, insurance, and freight.

ci·gar (si·GAHR) *n.* a cylindrical roll of tobacco for smoking. **—cig·a·ret(te)** (sig·uh·RET) *n.* a roll of finely cut tobacco covered with thin paper. **—cig·a·ril·lo** (sig·uh·RIL·oh) *n.* **-ril·los** a small slender cigar.

cil·i·a (SIL·ee·uh) *n.pl.* hairlike projections forming a fringe, esp. on a cell; also, eyelashes. **—cil·i·ate** *adj.* having cilia; ***n.*** any of several protozoans having many cilia. **—cil·i·um** *sing.* of CILIA.

C. in C. Commander in Chief.

cinch *n.* **1** the belt used to fasten a saddle or pack on a horse. **2** *Slang.* a firm grip; hence, a certainty; something easy to do or guaranteed: *He'll win, that's a ~; The job's a ~; a ~ to win.* **—*v.*** **1** tighten a belt or cinch. **2** *Slang.* make sure of : *~ed the game.*

cin·cho·na (sing·COH·nuh) *n.* a South American evergreen tree whose bark yields quinine and related alkaloids; also, the bark.

Cin·cin·nat·i (sin·suh·NAT·ee) a city in S.W. Ohio.

cinc·ture (SINK·chur) *n.* the act of encircling; hence, girdle; belt; also ***v.*** **-tures, -tured, -tur·ing**

cin·der *n.* **1** a piece of hard, solid residue of burning; also, embers; glowing coals. **2 cinders** *pl.* ashes. **—cinder block** a construction block of coal cinders and cement. **—cin·der·y** *adj.*

Cin·der·el·la (–EL·uh) *n.* a person or thing of merit suffering neglect for a time.

cin·e·ma (SIN·uh·muh) *n.* **1** usu. **the cinema,** the art, industry, or medium of motion-picture films; also, these films collectively: *the influence of the ~ on American life.* **2** *Brit.* a motion-picture theater; also, a motion picture. **—cin·e·mat·ic** (sin·uh·MAT·ic) *adj.;* **cin·e·mat·i·cal·ly** *adv.* **—cin·e·ma·theque** (sin·uh·muh·TEK) *n.* a small theater for innovative and experimental films. **—cin·e·ma·tog·ra·phy** (–TOG·ruh·fee) *n.* the art of making motion pictures; **cin·e·mat·o·graph·ic** (–mat·uh·GRAF–) *adj.* **—cinema ve·ri·té** (–ver·i·TAY) a film or filmmaking in a style suggesting documentary realism.

cin·e·rar·i·um (sin·uh·RAIR·ee·um) *n. pl.* **-i·a** (–ee·uh) a depository for the ashes of cremated bodies.

cin·na·bar (SIN·ub–) *n.* the principal ore of mercury; also, its bright red color.

cin·na·mon (SIN·uh·mun) *n.* **1** a spice produced from the fragrant bark of a group of E. Asian trees of the laurel family; also, the bark or the tree. **2** a yellowish brown.

cinque·foil (SINK–) *n.* any of several plants of the rose family having five-lobed leaves.

C.I.O. Congress of Industrial Organizations.

ci·on (SYE·un) *n.* same as SCION, *n.* 1.

ci·pher (SYE·fur) *n.* **1** zero (0) as indicating no quantity; hence, a nonentity. **2** any Arabic numeral. **3** a coding system; also, a coded message. **—*v.*** solve or calculate arithmetically.

cir. or **circ.** circular; circulation. **—cir·ca** (SIR·cuh) *prep.* about: *My people immigrated here ~ 1900.* **—cir·ca·di·an** (sir·CAY·dee·un) *adj.* in biology, acting or occurring in roughly 24-hour cycles: *a ~ rhythm;* **cir·ca·di·an·ly** *adv.* **—cir·can·ni·an** (sir·CAN·ee·un) or **cir·can·nu·al** (–CAN·yoo·ul) *adj.* in biology, acting or occurring in one-year cycles: *~ hibernation habits.* **—cir·cle** (SIR·cl) *n.* **1** a plane figure every point of which is equidistant from the center; also, the area bounded by this figure; hence, something like this in shape: *the ~ of Stonehenge.* **2** something which repeats or comes back on itself; a cycle: *the ~ of the seasons;* **come full circle** complete something and return to the starting point. **3** a group of people with similar interests: *a sewing ~; financial ~s.* **—*v.*** **-cles, -cled, -cling** enclose or move in a circle: *The teacher ~d six errors; The jet ~d above the airport.* **—cir·clet** (SIR·clit) *n.* a small circle, esp. as an ornament: *with a gold ~ around her brows.* **—cir·cuit** (SIR·kit) *n.* **1** the path or distance around something; hence, the traveling of that path: *The ~ of the estate is marked by a fence; the ~ of the moon around the earth.* **2** a regular course traveled by a salesman, preacher **(circuit rider),** judge **(circuit judge),** entertainer, athletic competitor, etc.: *a band playing on the nightclub ~; the professional golf ~.* **3** a path for electric current, with its wiring and other equipment. **—circuit breaker** a device for stopping the flow of electricity under special conditions, such as overload. **—circuit court** a court which sits in more than one place within a jurisdiction. **—cir·cu·i·tous** (sir·CUE·i·tus) *adj.* lengthy and indirect: *a ~ route through hilly country;* **cir·cu·i·ty** *n.* **-ties; cir·cu·i·tous·ly** *adv.* **—cir·cuit·ry** (SIR·cuh·tree) *n.* **-ries** the design or components of an electrical circuit; also, these circuits collectively. **—cir·cu·lar** (SIR·kyuh·lur) *adj.* **1** of or having to do with a circle; also, shaped like or moving in a circle: *a ~ haystack; a ~ saw.* **2** repeating itself; also, circuitous: *~ reasoning.* **3** distributed to many people: *a ~ notice.* **—*n.*** an advertisement, leaflet, etc. for mass distribution. **—cir·cu·lar·i·ty** (sir·cue·LAIR·i·tee) *n.* **-ties** **—cir·cu·lar·ize** (SIR·cue–) *v.* **-iz·es, -ized, -iz·ing** publicize or poll with circulars; **cir·cu·lar·i·za·tion** (–ZAY–) *n.* **—cir·cu·late** *v.* **-lates, -lat·ed, -lat·ing** move, often in a circuit, from place to place, person to person, etc.: *A fan ~s air in a room; the host ~ing at a party; This paper ~s widely.* **—cir·cu·la·tion** (–LAY–) *n.* **1** the act of circulating, esp. of blood in the body. **2** the distribution or total sales of a newspaper, magazine, etc. —**cir·cu·la·to·ry** (SIR·kyuh·luh·tor·ee) *adj.: The* **circulatory system** *contains the heart, blood vessels, and lymphatic vessels.* —**circum-** *comb.form.* around; surrounding. —**cir·cum·am·bu·late** (–AM·byoo·late) *v.* **-lates, -lat·ed, -lat·ing** walk around. —**cir·cum·cise** (–size) *v.* **-cis·es, -cised, -cis·ing** cut off the foreskin of (a male) or clitoris of (a female); **cir·cum·ci·sion** (–SIZH·un) *n.* —**cir·cum·fer·ence** (sir·CUM–) *n.* the perimeter of a circle or other figure; hence, outer boundary. —**cir·cum·flex** *n.* a mark (ˆ , ⁀ , ˜) written above a vowel to show quality, pitch, etc. —**cir·cum·lo·cu·tion** (–loh·CUE–) *n.* an indirect, lengthy, or evasive expression. —**cir·cum·lu·nar** (–LOO·nur) *adj.* around the moon. —**cir·cum·nav·i·gate** (–NAV–) *v.* **-gates, -gat·ed, -gat·ing** sail all the way around, esp. the world; **cir·cum·nav·i·ga·tion** (–GAY–) *n.: Drake's ~ of the earth.* —**cir·cum·po·lar** (–POH·lur) *adj.* around or near the N. or S. Pole; of stars, always above the horizon. —**cir·cum·scribe** *v.* **-scribes, -scribed, -scrib·ing** draw a line around; hence, restrict, limit in scope, etc.: *a narrowly ~d field of specialization;* **cir·cum·scrip·tion** (–SCRIP–) *n.* —**cir·cum·so·lar** (–SOH·lur) *adj.* around the sun. —**cir·cum·spect** *adj.* prudent; wary of the consequences; **cir·cum·spec·tion** (–SPEC–) *n.* —**cir·cum·stance** (SIR–) *n.* **1** a relevant or determining fact or event, accompanying another; hence, any event or occurrence. **2** determining factors beyond one's control; chance: *a victim of ~.* **3** financial condition: *in straitened ~s.* **4** ceremony: *pomp and ~.* **5** situation; condition: *under no ~; in the ~s.* —**cir·cum·stan·tial** (–STAN·shul) *adj.* **1** pertaining to or determined by circumstances: *purely ~ evidence.* **2** detailed. **3** incidental. —**cir·cum·stan·tial·ly** *adv.* —**cir·cum·vent** (–VENT) *v.* **1** overcome by craft; thwart: *a plan ~ed by the enemy.* **2** get around; avoid: *~ing the rules.* **3** encircle: *~ed by perils.* —**cir·cus** (SIR·cus) *n.* **-cus·es** **1** a usu. traveling entertainment consisting of trained animals, acrobats, clowns, etc. performing in a tent. **2** *Slang.* an uproarious display or entertainment. —**cir·cus·(s)y** *adj.* —**cirque** (SIRK) *n.* a semicircular, steepwalled hollow in a mountain, often at the head of a valley.

cir·rho·sis (suh·ROH–) *n., pl.* **-ses** (–seez) a severe, chronic disease of the liver. —**cir·rho·tic** (–ROT–) *adj.*

cir·rus (SEER·us) *n., pl.* **cir·ri** (SEER·eye) a usu. white, high, thin, cloud. —**cir·ro·cu·mu·lus** (–CUE·myuh·lus) *n.* a regular formation of small, puffy clouds at a great height. —**cir·ro·stra·tus** (–STRAY–, –STRAT–) *n.* a layer of high, thin, hazy clouds.

cis- *comb.form.* on this side of. —**cis·at·lan·tic** (sis·ut·LAN·tic) *adj.* on this (i.e. speaker's) side of the Atlantic. —**cis·lu·nar** (sis·LOO·nur) *adj.* between the earth and the moon's orbit.

cis·tern (SIS–) *n.* a storage tank for water, esp. rainwater.

cit. citation; cited; citizen.

cit·a·del (SIT·uh·dl) *n.* a fortress; hence, a stronghold, refuge, etc.

cite *v.* **cites, cit·ed, cit·ing** **1** quote; also, list, refer to, or bring forward as proof, example, etc. **2** commend for bravery, dedication, etc. **3** call to appear in court. —**ci·ta·tion** (–TAY–) *n.* [corresponding to the *v.* senses] **1:** *He has ~s to prove it.* **2:** *The corporal received a ~ for heroism.* **3:** *a ~ for contempt of court.*

cit·i·fy (SIT·i·fye) *v.* **-fies, -fied, -fy·ing** urbanize; make refined: *a high-class, ~d air about him.* —**cit·i·zen** (SIT·i·zun) *n.* **1** a member of a state, owing allegiance to it and having full rights in it. **2** one who lives in or was born in a (specified) city: *the ~s of New York.* **3** a civilian. —**cit·i·zen·ess** *n. fem.* —**cit·i·zen·ry** *n.* citizens collectively: *the ~ of Switzerland.* —**cit·i·zen·ship** *n.* —**citizens band** either of two short-wave radio frequencies used for private transmissions.

cit·ric acid an acid usu. derived from lime or lemon juice, used in flavorings and in making **cit·rates** which are salts or esters of this acid. —**cit·ron** (SIT·run) *n.* **1** a fragrant, lemon-like fruit with a thick rind; also, the tree it grows on, native to Asia. **2** a melon having a thick, hard rind. **3** the preserved or candied rind of either citron. —**cit·ron·el·la** (–EL·uh) *n.* a pale yellow, fragrant oil used in perfumes and insect repellents; also, the Asiatic grass it is made from. —**cit·rus** (SIT·rus) *n.* any of a group of thorny, evergreen trees bearing acid fruit, as the orange, grapefruit, lemon, lime, and kumquat; also, one of their fruits. —***adj.:*** *~ fruit;* also **cit·rous** (–rus).

cit·y (SIT·ee) *n.* **cit·ies** a large or important town, esp. one given a charter by a state or otherwise incorporated. —**city hall** a municipal government building; hence, a bureaucratic administration: *"You can't fight ~ hall"* (i.e. it is futile). —**city manager** an unelected chief administrator of a city. —**cit·y-state** *n.* a city and its surrounding territory forming a sovereign state: *the ~s of ancient Greece.*

civ. civil; civilian.

civ·et (SIV·it) *n.* **1** a strong-smelling, yellowish-brown substance used in perfumes and obtained from the **civet (cat),** a catlike, carnivorous mammal of Africa. **2** the fur of this animal.

civ·ic *adj.* of or having to do with a city, citizenship, etc.: *one's ~ duties.* —**civ·ics** *n.pl.* [takes *sing. v.*] the study of the rights and duties of citizenship in relation to government. —**civies** same as CIVVIES. —**civ·il** (SIV·il) *adj.* **1** pertaining to the citizen or the state as a political body. **2** pertaining to the people in general, not the military or religious. **3** civilized; polite: *Keep a ~ tongue in your head.* **—civ·il·ly** *adv.* **—civil defense** a system of warning, defense, and emergency aid for the people in case of war, natural disasters, etc. **—civil disobedience** nonviolent resistance to governmental authority as a protest or a matter of conscience. **—civil engineering** a branch of engineering dealing with roads, tunnels, and other public works; **civil engineer.** **—ci·vil·i·an** (–VIL·yun) *n.* one who is not a member of a military or paramilitary organization; ***adj.:*** *a soldier's return to ~ life.* **—ci·vil·i·ty** (–VIL–) *n.* **-ties** politeness; acceptable behavior; a polite act. **—civ·i·lize** (SIV–) *v.* **-liz·es, -lized, -liz·ing** bring to a higher degree of civilization; also, refine: *~d manners;* **civ·i·liz·er** *n.;* **civ·i·li·za·tion** (–ZAY–) *n.* **1** the act of civilizing. **2** the culture of a time, place, people, etc.: *the ancient Aztec ~.* **3** a high degree of cultural, social, and technological development; hence, a country or countries so developed: *The castaways returned to ~.* **—civil law** the body of law governing private rights within a state; cf. CRIMINAL LAW, INTERNATIONAL LAW. **—civil liberties** a person's freedom of speech, thought, action, etc. consistent with the public good. **—civil rights** a person's rights as a citizen, esp. the right to equal treatment regardless of sex, race, religion, etc. **—civil servant** a member of the **civil service,** the administrative branch of a government. **—civil war** a war waged by factions within a nation; **Civil War** the war between the N. and S. states of the Union (1861–65). **—civ·(v)ies** (SIV·eez) *n.pl.* *Informal.* civilian clothing as distinguished from a uniform.

C.J. Chief Justice.

ck. cask; check; cook.

cl. class; clause; clearance; clergyman; **cl** centiliter(s). **—c.l.** carload; center line; civil law; common law. **—Cl** chlorine.

clack *v.* **1** make a short, hard sound: *Typewriters ~ed in the office.* **2** chatter: *~ing tongues.* Also ***n.*** **—clack·er** *n.*

clad *adj.* [old *pp.* of CLOTHE] clothed or covered: *a warmly ~ hunter.* **—clad·ding** *n.* a covering or coating, as of metal on metal.

claim *v.* **1** assert one's right to; also, maintain as a fact: *He ~ed the crown; ~s to get 30 miles to the gallon with his new car.* **2** take; ask for: *Fire ~ed three lives; Go and ~ our bags.* **—*n.*** **1** a demand, request, or assertion; also, a right to something: **lay claim to** *an inheritance; too many ~s on my time; a ~ to fame.* **2** something claimed, esp. land: *The prospector staked his ~.* **—claim·ant** *n.* one who claims.

clair·voy·ance (–VOY–) *n.* the ability to perceive what is beyond the senses; also, sharp intuition. **—clair·voy·ant** *n.* & *adj.* **—clair·voy·ant·ly** *adv.*

clam *n.* **1** any of several bivalve mollusks often used for food. **2** *Informal.* a taciturn person; **clam up** stop talking. **—*v.* clams, clammed, clam·ming** dig for clams. **—clam·bake** *n.* an outdoor party at which clams are steamed or baked; hence, any large, lively gathering.

clam·ber *v.* climb awkwardly, usu. with both hands and feet: *~ing over a fence.*

clam·my *adj.* **clam·mi·er, clam·mi·est** unpleasantly moist, cool, and sticky: *~ skin;* **clam·mi·ly** *adv.;* **clam·mi·ness** *n.*

clam·or (–ur) *n.* a loud noise or shouting; a violent protest, demand, etc. **—*v.:*** *children ~ing for attention.* Also **clam·our** *Brit.* **—clam·or·ous** *adj.* **—clam·or·ous·ly** *adv.*

clamp *n.* **1** a band, vise, etc. for holding objects together. **2** a firm grip. **—*v.*** fasten or hold firmly, as in a clamp; **clamp down** *Informal.* become severe or repressive; impose restrictions; **clamp·down** *n.: a harsh ~ on tax evaders.* **—clam·shell** *n.* the shell of a clam; hence, a dredging bucket hinged like such a shell.

clan *n.* a group of families, as in the Scottish Highlands, claiming descent from a common ancestor; hence, a group of associates, relatives, etc.; clique: *a Mafia ~.*

clan·des·tine (–DES·tin) *adj.* kept secret; underhand: *a ~ love affair.* **—clan·des·tine·ly** *adv.*

clang *n.* a loud, ringing, metallic sound; ***v.:*** *The dinner bell ~ed at 6:00.* **—clan·gor** (CLANG·ur, CLANG·gur) *n.* a prolonged clang; a clanging din; **clan·gour** *Brit.*

clank (CLANGK) *n.* an abrupt, loud, metallic sound; ***v.:*** *chains ~ing in the dungeon.*

clan·nish *adj.* forming a group that excludes outsiders. **—clan·nish·ly** *adv.* **—clan·nish·ness** *n.* **—clans·man** *n.* **-men.**

clap *n.* **1** a loud, flat noise, as of the palms of two hands struck sharply together; applause; also, a loud explosive noise, as of thunder. **2** a blow or slap. **3 the clap** *Slang.* gonorrhea. **—*v.* claps, clapped, clap·ping 1** strike the palms together; applaud; make any clapping act or noise. **2** slap: *~d his friend on the back.* **3** put, move, do, etc. suddenly and roughly: *~d him in irons.* **—clap·board** (CLAB·urd, CLAP·bord) *n.* a long, narrow board with one edge thicker than the other, used as siding on houses; ***v.*** cover with clapboards. **—clap·per** *n.* the tongue of a bell. **—clap·trap** *n.* cheap rhetoric used in a speech, writing, etc. merely to win applause; ***adj.:*** *cant and ~ sentiment.*

claque (CLAK) *n.* a group hired to applaud in a theater.

clar·et (CLAIR·ut) *n.* a dry red table wine; also, its purplish red color. **—clar·i·fy** *v.* **-fies, -fied, -fy·ing** make or become clear or pure: *~ your meaning; ~d butter;* **clar·i·fi·ca·tion** (–CAY–) *n.* **—clar·i·net** (clair·i·NET) *n.* a single-reed woodwind instrument with finger holes and keys; **clar·i·net·(t)ist** (–NET–) *n.* —**clar·i·on** (CLAIR·ee·un) *adj.* clear and ringing: *the bugle's ~ call.* —**clar·i·ty** *n.* clearness.

clash *n.* **1** a conflict; disagreement: *the ~ of opposing interests.* **2** a loud, confused, usu. metallic sound of colliding: *the ~ of cymbals.* —**v.** [corresponding to the *n.* senses] **1:** *These colors ~; troops ~ing with the enemy.* **2:** *oildrums ~ing together.*

clasp *n.* **1** a fastener, as a pin, hook, buckle, etc. **2** a firm grip or embrace. —**v.** **1** fasten with or as with a clasp: *a sweater ~ed at the neck.* **2** grip with the hand; embrace: *~ed it to his breast.*

class *n.* **1** a distinctive group with a common characteristic and name; hence, a social division based on status, economic function, etc.: *the upper ~; the working ~.* **2** a group defined by quality, level, condition, etc.: *first-~ honors; second-~ citizen.* **3** a group of students, or **class·mates,** instructed together, usu. in the same room, or **class·room;** also, a group of students in the same course or graduating in the same year: *a biology ~; the ~ of 1958.* **4** *Slang.* style, high quality, etc.: *a man with ~;* **class·y** *adj.* **class·i·er, -i·est:** *a very ~y car.* —**v.** put in a class; classify. —**class·less** *adj.: a ~ society.* —**class action** a law suit brought on behalf of all parties affected by an alleged injustice. —**clas·sic** (CLAS·ic) *adj.* **1** of the highest quality; of traditionally recognized importance, value, excellence, etc.; hence, standard, typical: *the ~ style of Milton; the ~ book on slavery; the ~ symptoms of smallpox.* **2** pertaining to Greek and Roman culture; hence, simple and refined in style; enduring: *the smooth, ~ lines of a car; the ~ fall jacket.* —**n.** **1** person, thing, or event considered as classic: *Homer is a ~; This salad is a culinary ~.* **2** **classics** *pl.* Greek and Roman literature. —**clas·si·cal** *adj.* **1** of or pertaining to ancient Greek and Roman culture or its qualities of simplicity, form, purity, etc.: *~ literature; a ~ scholar; ~ excellence in art.* **2** a system or style established by tradition: *~ economics; the ~ music of Beethoven and Mozart.* **3** classic. —**clas·si·cal·ly** *adv.* —**clas·si·cism** (CLAS·i·sizm) *n.* **1** adherence to the stylistic standards of ancient Greece and Rome, as clarity, form, restraint, and grace. **2** classical scholarship. —**clas·si·cist** *n.* —**clas·si·fied** *adj.* **1** designated as secret: *a ~ report on nuclear weapons.* **2** arranged by topic: *~ advertising.* —**clas·si·fi·a·ble** *adj.* —**clas·si·fi·ca·tion** (–CAY–) *n.* —**clas·si·fy** *v.* **-fies, -fied, -fy·ing** put in groups according to type, topic, etc. —**classmate, classroom, classy** See CLASS.

clas·tic *adj.* **1** formed from pieces of earlier rock: *a ~ sandstone.* **2** that can be taken apart: *a ~ anatomical model.*

clat·ter *v.* make or move with a loud rattling sound; **n.:** *the ~ of pots and pans.*

clause (CLAWZ) *n.* **1** a part of a sentence having its own subject and verb. **2** a section of a document.

claus·tro·pho·bi·a (–truh·FOH·bee·uh) *n.* an abnormal fear of closed spaces. —**claus·tro·pho·bic** *adj.: to feel ~ in elevators.*

clav·i·chord (CLAV·i·cord) *n.* a keyboard instrument used before the piano was invented. —**clav·i·cle** (CLAV·i·cl) *n.* the collarbone, connecting the shoulder blade and the breastbone. —**cla·vier** (cluh·VEER) *n.* **1** any stringed keyboard instrument. **2** a keyboard.

claw *n.* **1** a usu. sharp, curving nail on the foot of a bird, lizard, cat, etc.; also, the pincer of a lobster, some insects, etc. **2** anything shaped like a claw, as the curved, split head of a **claw hammer** used for pulling nails. —**v.** grasp, scratch, dig, or move using or as if using claws: *a dog ~ing at a locked door.*

clay *n.* **1** a fine-grained kind of earth, plastic when wet, used for molding, brick-making, and ceramics; also, wet ground or mud. **2** the human body: *this mortal ~.* —**clay·ey** *adj.* **clay·i·er, -i·est.** —**Clay, Henry.** 1777–1852, American politician. —**clay·more** *n.* a large Highland broadsword; also, a kind of land mine. —**clay pigeon** a disk tossed as a target in trapshooting.

cld. called; cleared.

clean (CLEEN) *adj.* **1** free from dirt, clutter, or disease; hence, free from any thing undesirable, as obscenity *(a ~ joke),* radioactivity *(a ~ blast),* dishonesty *(a ~ game),* complications *(~ lines),* illegal drugs, sin, etc.; **come clean** *Slang.* confess. **2** complete; thorough: *a ~ sweep.* —**adv.** [corresponding to the *adj.* senses] **1:** *play it ~.* **2:** *~ out of sight.* —**v.** **1** make or become clean: *He won't ~ up after his sister.* **2** **clean up** *Informal.* make a large profit. —**clean·ly** *adv.* —**clean·ness** *n.* —**clean·er** *n.* —**clean-cut** *adj.* with distinct outlines; hence, neat and wholesome: *a ~ young man.* —**clean·ly** (CLEN·lee) *adj.* **-li·er, -li·est** habitually clean and tidy. —**clean·li·ness** *n.: "~ is next to godliness."* —**clean room** an area free of dust, germs, etc. used for assembling precision equipment, laboratory experiments, etc. —**cleanse** (CLENZ) *v.* **cleans·es, cleansed, cleans·ing** clean; purify: *~ your heart of sin.* —**cleans·er** *n.* a solvent or detergent for cleaning: *a kitchen ~.* —**clean·up** *n.* **1** a thorough cleaning. **2** a large profit. —**adj.** in baseball, fourth in the batting order.

clear (CLEER) *adj.* **1** free from dimness or darkness, as a cloudless sky; hence, free from anything unwanted or obscuring, as impurity *(~ tones),* debt or deduction *(a ~ title; a ~ profit),* obstruction *(~ sailing ahead),* contents *(a ship ~ of cargo),* flaws or blemishes *(a ~*

complexion), guilt *(a ~ conscience),* contact *(Stand ~!),* or roughness *(~ lumber).* **2** transparent; obvious: *~ glass; It's as ~ as day.* **3** perceptive; keen: *a ~ head for thinking.* ***—adv.*** **1** in a clear manner: *I hear you loud and ~.* **2** completely: *It flew ~ across the lake.* ***—v.*** **1** make or become clear: *The sky is ~ing; ~ up a difficulty; They ~ed the land of trees; ~ed of a murder charge.* **2** make a net profit of: *We ~ed $40 a day.* **3** free from or pass through encumbrances or checking procedures; get approval: *~ing a check; A motion ~ed the committee.* **4** go over, under, past, etc. without touching: *The horse ~ed the fence.* **—clear·ly** *adv.* **—clear·ness** *n.* **—clear the air** resolve differences or tensions. **—clear out** *Informal.* go away; leave. **—in the clear** *Informal.* free of suspicion, danger, or obstructions. **—clear·ance** (CLEER·unce) *n.* **1** the distance at which something passes by another; clearing space: *a bridge with a ~ of 16 ft.* **2** a permission to proceed: *~ papers.* **3** a clearing: *a warehouse ~; a ~ sale.* **—clear-cut** *adj.* plain; distinctly outlined: *a ~ case of fraud.* **—clear-head·ed** *adj.* sensible; mentally clear. **—clear·ing** (CLEER–) *n.* **1** an area in the woods that is free of trees. **2** the process of balancing checks and bills between various banks, which is performed in a **clear·ing·house.** **—clearstory** same as CLERESTORY.

cleat (CLEET) *n.* **1** a wooden or metal plate, wedge, or projection, used to support, protect, prevent slipping, etc.; esp., a projection on the sole of a shoe to get a grip; **cleats** *pl.* a pair of shoes, as for baseball, fitted with cleats. **2** on boats, a usu. two-horned projection around which a rope may be wound.

cleav·age (CLEE·vij) *n.* the act of splitting; also, a division, split, etc. **—¹cleave** (CLEEV) *v.* **cleaves,** *pt.* **cleft, cleaved** or **clove** (CLOHV), *pp.* **cleft, cleaved** or **clo·ven, cleav·ing** split; divide; pass through. **—cleav·er** *n.* a butcher's heavy, broad-bladed chopping tool.

²cleave (CLEEV) *v.* **cleaves, cleaved, cleav·ing** cling *(to);* remain faithful *(to).*

clef *n.* a symbol on a musical staff indicating the pitch of the notes.

cleft *pt.* & *pp.* of ¹CLEAVE. ***—adj.*** split: *a ~ palate.* ***—n.*** a fissure; split; rift: *a ~ in the rock.*

clem·a·tis (CLEM·uh–) *n.* any of a genus of colorfully flowering vines of the buttercup family.

clem·en·cy *n.* mercy, as of a judge toward an offender: *a plea for ~.* **—Clem·ens** (CLEM·unz), **Samuel L.** 1835–1910, American humorist who wrote under the pen name "Mark Twain." **—clem·ent** (CLEM·unt) *adj.* lenient or forgiving; also, mild, as weather. **—clem·ent·ly** *adv.*

clench *v.* close, grip, or fasten tightly: *~ one's teeth; a ~ed fist.* ***—n.*** a tight grip.

Cle·o·pat·ra (clee·uh·PAT·ruh) 69–30 B.C., queen of Egypt.

clere·sto·ry (CLEER·stor·ee) *n.* **-ries** in buildings, a windowed wall rising above the roof of an adjoining part; hence, a similar structure, as for ventilation in railroad cars.

cler·gy (CLUR·jee) *n.* **-gies** [usu. takes *pl. verb*] the body of people ordained for religious service, as monks, priests, rabbis, etc.; opposed to LAITY. **—cler·gy·man** *n.* **-men** or **cler·gy·wom·an** *n.* **-wom·en** a member of the clergy; also **cler·ic** (CLER·ic) *n.* **—cler·i·cal** *adj.* **1** pertaining to the clergy: *a ~ collar.* **2** pertaining to clerks, office work, etc.: *Typing is a ~ skill; a ~ error.* **—cler·i·cal·ism** *n.* support for clerical influence in secular affairs; also, this influence. **—clerk** (CLURK) *n.* **1** an office worker, as one who types, keeps accounts, etc.; also, an official in charge of records: *the county ~.* **2** one who sells in a store or gives service at a counter: *a sales ~; a hotel ~.* **3** a cleric: *a ~ in holy orders.* ***—v.:*** *Karen ~ed in her father's store.* **—clerk·ship** *n.*

Cleve·land (CLEEV·lund) a port city in N.E. Ohio. **—Cleveland, (Stephen) Grover.** 1837–1908, 22nd and 24th U.S. President (1885–89, 1893–97).

clev·er *adj.* **1** mentally agile; intelligent; witty; also, displaying these qualities: *a ~ trick.* **2** manually dexterous. **—clev·er·ly** *adv.* **—clev·er·ness** *n.*

clew (CLOO) same as CLUE.

cli·ché (clee·SHAY) *n.* a trite or overworked expression, sentiment, etc.; e.g. "Last but not least." **—cli·chéd** (clee·SHADE) *adj.* hackneyed: *a ~d phrase.*

click *n.* a short, sharp metallic sound, as of cocking a gun. ***—v.*** **1:** *A soldier ~s his heels coming to attention; to ~ one's tongue in delight.* **2** *Informal.* be a success; also, work or get along well together.

cli·ent (CLYE·unt) *n.* one who receives the services of a professional such as a lawyer, accountant, or agent; hence, one receiving a service in a dependent relationship: *a welfare ~; a prostitute's ~s;* **client (state)** a dependent nation. **—cli·en·tele** (cly·en·TEL) *n.* clients collectively.

cliff *n.* a high, steep-faced rocky prominence. **—cliff·han·ger** *n.* a serialized adventure story or movie whose episodes end in suspense; hence, any suspenseful situation.

cli·mac·ter·ic (cly·MAC–) *n.* a period of major change; esp., the menopause. **—cli·mac·tic** *adj.* forming a climax: *the final, ~ assault on Berlin.* **—cli·mate** (CLYE·mit) *n.* **1** the average weather of a region, including rainfall, temperature, wind, etc.; also, the region so considered: *He moved to a drier ~.* **2** the temper or condition of a place or time: *the political ~ of Portugal.* **—cli·ma·tic** (cly·MAT·ic) *adj.:* *~ variations;* **cli·mat·i·cal·ly** *adv.* **—cli·ma·**

tol·o·gy (cly·muh·TOL·uh·jee) *n.* the science that studies climate; **cli·ma·tol·o·gist** *n.;* **cli·ma·to·log·i·cal** (–tuh·LOJ·i·cl) *adj.* —**cli·max** (CLYE–) *n.* **1** the most important or significant, often final, part or event; culmination: *The story had a thrilling ~.* **2** orgasm. —***v.*** **-max·es, -maxed, -max·ing** attain or bring to a climax.

climb (CLIME) *v.* **1** ascend; go up: *The moon ~ed the night sky; Our stock ~ed slowly.* **2** go up (something) esp. using the hands and feet; move in a similar fashion: *Jack fell while ~ing the tree; ~ up on my knee; It was easier to ~ down the mountain.* —***n.*** a place for or act of climbing: *The pilot put the plane into a steep ~.* —**climb·a·ble** *adj.* —**climb·er** *n.*

clime *n. Poetic.* climate; region.

clinch *v.* **1** fasten firmly; hence, make certain or final: *The salesman ~ed the deal; The team ~ed the victory.* **2** in boxing, hold tight; also, *Slang.* embrace passionately. —***n.*** an act or the result of clinching: *The boxers went into a ~.* —**clinch·er** *n.* a decisive argument, event, etc.

cling *v.* **clings, clung, cling·ing** hold on (to); adhere (to); remain with. —**clinging vine** *Informal.* a woman who is too dependent on a man. —**cling(·stone)** *n.* a kind of peach whose flesh adheres to the pit; ***adj.:*** *a ~ peach.*

clin·ic *n.* **1** a medical treatment facility for outpatients; also such a facility run cooperatively by a group of specialists: *a dental ~.* **2** medical instruction by the examination and treatment of patients before the students. **3** any instruction session or counseling center: *a writer's ~.* —**clin·i·cal** *adj.* **1** of or having to do with treatment of illness: *a ~ thermometer; a doctor's ~ experience.* **2** impersonal; efficient; scientific: *a cold, ~ evaluation.* —**clin·i·cal·ly** *adv.* —**cli·ni·cian** (cli·NISH·un) *n.* one who practices clinical medicine, psychiatry, etc.

clink *v.* make a short, sharp, ringing sound: *They ~ed glasses in a toast.* —***n.*** **1** this sound. **2** *Slang.* a jail: *tossed into the ~.* —**clin·ker** *n.* **1** a piece of fused, incombustible residue left when coal is burned; slag. **2** *Slang.* a mistake, esp. in music.

¹clip *v.* **clips, clipped, clip·ping** **1** hold tightly; esp. fasten with a clip. **2** *Football.* block an opponent from behind. —***n.*** **1** a device for fastening or holding things together: *a paper ~; a tie ~.* **2** a device for holding the cartridges for a rapid-fire gun.

²clip *v.* **clips, clipped, clip·ping** **1** cut off, out, or short, esp. with shears, scissors, etc.: *~ing an article from the magazine; terse, ~d speech.* **2** *Informal.* hit with a short, quick blow. **3** *Slang.* cheat, esp. by overcharging. —***n.*** a fast pace: *moving along at a pretty good ~.*

clip·board *n.* a small writing board having a clip to hold paper with. —**clip joint** an establishment, esp. a nightclub, that cheats customers. —**clip·per** *n.* **1** often **clippers** *pl.* a tool for clipping, esp. shears for hair, wool, etc. **2** a long, narrow sailing ship; hence, any fast means of travel, as a sled. —**clip·ping** *n.* something clipped off or out, esp. a piece from a newspaper.

clique (CLEEK) *n.* a small exclusive group, usu. social or political. —**cli·qu(e)y** (CLEE·kee) or **cli·quish** *adj.: narrow, ~ interests.*

cli·to·ris (CLIT·uh·ris) *n.* a sensitive erectile structure at the upper end of the vulva. —**cli·to·ral** *adj.*

clk. clerk.

clo. clothing.

cloak (CLOKE) *n.* a loose, usu. sleeveless outer garment; hence, a concealment; pretense: *under the ~ of darkness;* ***v.*** cover with a cloak; conceal. —**cloak-and-dag·ger** *adj.* pertaining to spies: *James Bond's ~ adventures.* —**cloak·room** *n.* a room where coats, hats, etc. may be left for a time.

clob·ber *v. Slang.* strike hard and repeatedly; defeat; trounce.

cloche (CLOHSH) *n.* a woman's close, bell-shaped hat.

clock *n.* **1** an ornament either embroidered or woven on the ankle of hosiery. **2** a timepiece that is not a watch; hence, a measuring device, as a speedometer; **around the clock** continuously; day and night. —***v.*** check with a clock or stopwatch: *The police ~ed him at 80 m.p.h.* —**clock·wise** *adv.* & *adj.* in the same direction a clock's hands move in. —**clock·work** *n.* the mechanism of a clock; hence, any similar machinery; **like clockwork** smoothly and precisely.

clod *n.* a lump of earth, mud, etc.; hence, a dolt, lout, or boor. —**clod·dish** *adj.: ~ manners.* —**clod·hop·per** *n.* **1** a rustic, clumsy, or stupid person. **2** a heavy, thick-soled shoe or boot.

clog *n.* **1** a heavy wooden or wooden-soled shoe. **2** a block of wood; hence, an encumbrance. —***v.*** **clogs, clogged, clog·ging** **1** hinder; encumber. **2** fill up and block, as a pipe or stream bed; *a drain ~d with grease.* —**clog·gy** *adj.*

cloi·son·né (cloy·zuh·NAY) *n.* a kind of enamelwork decoration separated into compartments by metal strips; also ***adj.*** —**clois·ter** (CLOY·stur) *n.* **1** a covered walk with an open colonnade facing usu. on a quadrangle. **2** a place secluded for religious life; monastery or convent. —***v.*** seclude from the world, in or as if in a monastery. —**clois·tral** *adj.*

clone *n.* an asexually produced individual that is genetically an exact copy of its parent, as a plant variety multiplied from rooted cuttings; ***v.*** **clones, cloned, clon·ing** produce as a clone.

clop *v.* **clops, clopped, clop·ping** make the sharp, hollow sound of a horse's hoof on pavement. —***n.*** this sound.

close *adj.* **clos·er, clos·est 1** densely packed; with small or no interstices; detailed: *a ~ weave; soldiers in ~ ranks; precise, ~ reasoning.* **2** near; with little between; intimate; next to the skin; thorough; accurate: *an attack at ~ range; 6–5 is a ~ score; two ~ friends; a ~ cap; a ~ shave; kept under ~ observation; a ~ copy.* **3** closed in; cramped; strict; stifling or poorly ventilated; restricted: *a prisoner in ~ confinement; Open the window, it's ~ in here; a period of ~ credit.* **4** of vowels, pronounced with the tongue near the palate: *"Pin" has a ~ vowel.* **5** concealed; secretive; stingy: *as ~ as an oyster; ~ with his money.* **—adv.:** *Keep ~ by; The bullet hit ~ to the mark.* **—v.** (CLOZE) **clos·es, closed, clos·ing 1** stop up an opening or passage; also, shut: *~ off access; ~ the door.* **2** end; make final: *We shall ~ our discussion; ~ a deal.* **3** make or become close; join: *The troops ~d with the enemy; The order was given to ~ ranks; ~ your hand into a fist.* **—n.** (CLOZE) a conclusion: *Evening marks the ~ of a day.* **—close·ly** *adv.* **—close·ness** *n.* **—close down** stop entirely: *a factory ~d down by the strike.* **—close in** encircle and advance upon: *The hunters ~d in on the fox.* **—close out** sell all of a store's goods; sell (a business). **—close call** (or **shave**) *Informal.* a narrow escape. **—closed circuit** an unbroken circuit; hence, radio or TV transmission by wire, not broadcasting. **—closed shop** an establishment where all workers must join the union. **—close·fis·ted** *adj.* stingy. **—close-knit** *adj.* strongly united. **—close·mouthed** *adj.* taciturn. **—clos·et** (CLOZ·it) *n.* **1** a small room or cabinet for storage of clothes, household goods, etc.: *a broom ~.* **2** a room for private meetings, study, prayer, etc. **—v.** shut up or withdraw: *a scholar ~ed with his books.* **—close-up** *n.* a picture taken at close range; hence, a detailed examination: *a revealing ~ of the president.* **—clo·sure** (CLOH·zhur) *n.* **1** an act of or a device for closing. **2** cloture.

clot *n.* a mass of thickened or coagulated liquid, esp. blood. **—v. clots, clot·ted, clot·ting** coagulate.

cloth *n.* **1** a woven, knitted, or felted fabric of natural or synthetic fibers; also, a piece of this for a specific purpose, as a tablecloth. **2** often **the cloth,** the clergy or its distinctive dress. **—clothe** (CLOHDH) *v.* **clothes,** *pt.* & *pp.* **clothed** or **clad, cloth·ing** put clothes on; dress; hence, cover: *villainies ~d in fine words.* **—clothes** (*also* CLOZE) *n.pl.* or **cloth·ing** *n.* garments; coverings; **clothes·horse** *n.* a frame to hang clothes on; hence, an affectedly fine dresser; **clothes·pin** *n.* a clip for holding clothes on a line; **clothes·press** *n.* a clothes closet; wardrobe. **—cloth·ier** (CLOH·dhee·ur) *n.* one who makes or sells clothing; also, a cloth dealer.

clo·ture (CLOH·chur) *n.* the ending of a legislative debate by taking a vote on the issue.

cloud *n.* **1** a distinct, visible mass of water vapor hanging high in the air; hence, any light or puffy visible mass in the air: *storm ~s on the horizon; a ~ of dust.* **2** swarm: *a ~ of horsemen.* **3** anything that threatens, causes gloom, or bodes ill. **—v. 1** cover or become covered with or as if with clouds: *~ed vision; Anger ~ed his face.* **2** make or become gloomy, sad, etc.; also, taint: *a ~ed reputation.* **—in the clouds** in a fanciful dream; also, impractical. **—on cloud nine** *Slang.* joyfully elated. **—under a cloud 1** depressed. **2** under suspicion. **—cloud·less** *adj.* **—cloud·burst** *n.* a sudden downpour. **—cloud·let** *n.* a small cloud. **—cloud seeding** the scattering of chemicals in clouds to cause rainfall. **—cloud·y** *adj.* **cloud·i·er, -i·est** covered with clouds; hence, not clear: *a ~ sky, day, notion;* **cloud·i·ly** *adv.;* **cloud·i·ness** *n.*

clout (CLOWT) *v. Informal.* hit hard with the hand; in baseball, hit (the ball) far. **—n.** *Informal.* **1** a heavy blow. **2** influence, esp. political: *a senator with lots of ~ in Washington.*

clove (CLOHV) *n.* **1** the dried flower bud of an Asian evergreen tree used, either whole or ground, as a spice called **cloves. 2** one of the segments of a compound bulb: *a ~ of garlic.* **—v.** a *pt.* of [1]CLEAVE. **—clo·ven** (CLOH·vn) a *pp.* of [1]CLEAVE; ***adj.*** split. **—cloven foot** (or **hoof**) the sign of Satan, usu. pictured with cloven hoofs. **—clo·ven-hoofed** or **clo·ven-foot·ed** *adj.* **1** having split hoofs, as cattle and sheep. **2** satanic.

clo·ver (CLOH–) *n.* a trefoil with thick purple, pink, or white flower heads, used for pasturage. **—in (the) clover** in ease or prosperity. **—clo·ver·leaf** *n.* **-leafs** or **-leaves** a highway interchange having ramps forming the shape of a four-leaf clover.

clown *n.* **1** a professional jester or buffoon, esp. in a circus or parade. **2** an awkward, ill-mannered person; also, one who constantly jokes or acts silly. **—v.** act as or like a clown; play jokes or act silly: *Don't ~ around; this is serious.* **—clown·ish** *adj.;* **clown·ish·ly** *adv;* **clown·ish·ness** *n.*

cloy *v.* satiate, esp. with something sweet or rich; sate; surfeit: *~ed with too much candy.* **—cloy·ing·ly** *adv.*

C.L.U. Chartered Life Underwriter.

club *n.* **1** a thick, heavy, usu. tapered piece of wood used as a weapon; hence, a stick for striking the ball in various sports: *a golf ~.* **2** a playing card marked with a stylized black clover leaf; also, the marking; **clubs** the suit so marked: *~s is* (or *are*) *trump.* **3** a group of people united for a common purpose, as social, sporting, charitable, etc.; also, their meeting place. **—v. clubs, clubbed, club·bing 1** beat with or as with a club: *He was ~d to death with an ax handle.* **2** join together. **—club·ba·ble** *adj.* sociable; fit for a club. **—club·foot**

n. a usu. congenital malformation of the foot; also, a foot so malformed. —**club·house** *n.* a building occupied by a club. —**club sandwich** a sandwich of three slices of toast, various meats, dressing, lettuce, etc. —**club soda** carbonated water, used as a mix for other drinks. —**club steak** a small beefsteak cut from the end of the loin.

cluck *v.* make the clicking sound of a hen calling her chicks; hence, make a similar sound, as to coax a horse, express interest or concern, etc. —***n.*** **1** a clucking sound: *a ~ of approval.* **2** *Slang.* a dull or incompetent person.

clue (CLOO) *n.* a fact, word, object, or idea that suggests the solution to a puzzle, mystery, crime, etc. —***v.*** **clues, clued, clu(e)·ing** give a clue to; inform: *~ me in.* —**not have a clue** *Informal.* be ignorant.

clump *n.* **1** a mass or lump; also, a group of trees, plants, etc. standing or growing together. **2** the sound of tramping feet. —***v.*** walk heavily.

clum·sy (CLUM·zee) *adj.* **-si·er, -si·est 1** uncoordinated; awkward; unwieldy: *a ~ amateur; a ~ weapon.* **2** inept: *a ~ apology.* —**clum·si·ly** *adv.* —**clum·si·ness** *n.*

clung *pt.* & *pp.* of CLING.

clunk *n.* the heavy, flat sound of metal being struck. —**clunk·er** *n. Slang.* a noisy old machine in poor repair.

clus·ter *n.* a group of similar objects situated together: *a ~ of grapes; "Stray" begins with a consonant ~.* —***v.*** be, gather, or place in a cluster: *people ~ed on streetcorners.*

1clutch *n.* a nest of eggs; also, the chicks hatched from them.

2clutch *v.* **1** grasp or hold suddenly or tightly, esp. with hands or claws; make a grab: *A drowning man will ~ at a straw.* **2** operate a clutch. —***n.*** **1** a tight hold; the act of clutching; usu. **clutches** *pl.* hands; hence, control: *in the ~es of the devil.* **2** a device for engaging and disengaging a drive mechanism from the motor, as in an automobile. **3** *Informal.* a critical or dangerous situation: *He always comes through* **in the clutch.**

clut·ter *n.* a disordered state; a number of objects in disorganized array; jumble. —***v.*** litter with a disorganized mass of objects: *a ~ed-up room.*

cm. centimeter. —**Cm** curium.

cmdg. commanding.

Cmdr. commander.

cml. commercial.

C/N or **CN** credit note.

C.N.S. central nervous system.

co- *prefix.* together; jointly; with: as in *cooperate, coheir.* —**c/o** or **C/O** care of. —**co.** or **Co.** company; county. —**c.o.** care of; carried over; cash order. —**Co** cobalt. —**CO** Colorado. —**C.O.** commanding officer; conscientious objector.

coach *n.* **1** an enclosed passenger vehicle, as a four-wheeled carriage *(a stage ~),* a bus, or a railroad car; also, a cheaper class of airline travel. **2** one who trains or instructs others, esp. athletes *(a baseball ~),* students (i.e. a private tutor), and singers *(a voice ~).* —***v.*** train; instruct; tutor: *Bill had to be ~ed for his French examination.* —**coach·man** *n.* **-men** the driver of a carriage or coach.

co·ad·ju·tor (–uh·JOO·tur) *n.* an assistant, esp. one designated to help and succeed a bishop.

co·ag·u·late (–AG·yuh–) *v.* **-lates, -lat·ed, -lat·ing** change (a liquid) to a thick solid or semisolid state; clot; set; **co·ag·u·la·tion** (–LAY–) *n.* —**co·ag·u·lant** (–AG·yuh·lunt) *n.* a substance causing coagulation; **co·ag·u·la·tive** (–luh·tiv) *adj.;* **co·ag·u·la·tor** (–lay–) *n.;* **co·ag·u·lum** *n.* **-lums** or **-la** a coagulated mass; clot.

coal (COLE) *n.* an organic, black or brown, combustible rock used as a fuel; also, a piece of this for burning; hence, a piece of glowing wood, coal, etc.; an ember. —***v.*** provide with or take on a supply of coal. —**carry coals to Newcastle** engage in superfluous labor, like watering a rain-soaked lawn. —**rake** (or **haul**) **over the coals** reprimand severely.

co·a·lesce (–uh·LES) *v.* **-les·ces, -lesced, -les·cing** grow together; unite into one group, mass, etc. —**co·a·les·cent** *adj.* —**co·a·les·cence** *n.*

coal field a region rich in coal. —**coal gas** a gas made from coal, used for heating, lighting, etc.

co·a·li·tion (–uh·LISH·un) *n.* a combination into one; esp., a usu. temporary union of people, political parties, states, etc. for a common purpose. —**co·a·li·tion·ist** *n.*

coal oil kerosene. —**coal tar** a thick, black liquid by-product of the destructive distillation of coal, used to make creosote, pitch, and many synthetic chemicals.

coarse (CORCE) *adj.* **coars·er, coars·est 1** ordinary; inferior; hence, vulgar, unrefined, offensive: *~ food; ~ manners.* **2** consisting of large, rough particles; having a rough, harsh texture or appearance: *~ sand; ~-grained wood.* —**coarse·ly** *adv.* —**coarse·ness** *n.* —**coars·en** *v.* make or become coarse.

coast (COHST) *n.* **1** the land along the sea: *campaigned ~ to ~* (i.e. from Atlantic to Pacific). **2** *U.S.* the Pacific seaboard, as in "Coast (mountain) Ranges" and "coast rhododendron." **3** a slope for sledding or tobogganing. **4** the act of coasting. —***v.*** **1** sail along a seacoast. **2** move without acceleration or effort, as sledding down a hill, gliding on a bicycle without pedaling, etc. —**coast·al** *adj.: ~ shipping.* —**coast·er** *n.* a pad or disk placed under a glass to protect the surface it rests on. —**coaster brake** a bicycle brake in the rear hub applied by pedaling backwards —**coast guard** or **Coast Guard**

the military and police force which patrols a nation's seacoast and territorial waters; **coast·guards·man** *n.* **-men.** **—coast·line** *n.* the outline or boundary of a coast.

coat *n.* **1** a sleeved outer garment reaching at least to the waist; hence, a natural outer covering as an animal's fur or feathers. **2** a thin layer covering something, as paint on a wall; also **coat·ing.** **—*v.*** apply or be a coat on something: *~ed the floor with wax; Frost ~ed the window;* **coat·ed** *adj.: smooth, ~ paper.* **—coat of arms** the heraldic insignia of a person, family, institution, etc. **—coat of mail** a garment of chain mail worn as armor. **—coat·tails** *pl.* the back flaps of a coat; hence, a politician's popularity that is strong enough to carry a follower to victory.

co·au·thor (coh·AW·thur) *n.* a collaborating author. **—*v.:*** *The husband-and-wife team ~ed the report.*

coax (COHX) *v.* use persistent kindness, flattery, or effort to persuade or to produce a desired effect: *He ~ed his mother into agreeing; had to ~ the old car up the hill.* **—coax·ing·ly** *adv.*

co·ax·i·al (coh·AK·see·ul) *adj.* having a common axis; **coaxial cable** (or **line**) a line for transmitting television, telephone, and telegraph signals, made of a conducting core insulated from an outer conducting tube. **—co·ax·i·al·ly** *adv.*

cob *n.* **1** the central core of an ear of corn: *corn on the ~.* **2** a male swan. **3** a thickset horse with short legs.

co·balt (COH·bawlt) *n.* a hard, gray metallic element used in alloys, pigments, etc. **—cobalt blue** a deep-to-greenish blue.

cob·ble *v.* **cob·bles, cob·bled, cob·bling** **1** make or repair, esp. footwear. **2** make roughly and quickly. **—*n.*** cobblestone. **—cob·bler** *n.* **1** one who repairs shoes. **2** a deep fruit pie with a thick crust only on top: *cherry ~; peach ~.* **—cob·ble·stone** *n.* a rounded stone of medium size, as used for paving.

CO·BOL (COH·ball) *n.* a standard computer language for business purposes.

co·bra (COH·bruh) *n.* a poisonous snake of Asia and Africa that can spread its neck skin into a hood.

cob·web *n.* a web or a fine thread spun by a spider; hence, something flimsy but ensnaring: *~s of suspicion.*

co·cain(e) (coh·CAIN) *n.* an alkaloid drug made from the dried leaves of the South American **co·ca** (COH·cuh) shrub, and used as a local anesthetic, a stimulant, and an addictive narcotic.

coc·cus (COC·us) *n., pl.* **coc·ci** (COC·sye) a spherical bacterium; **-coccus** *comb.form.* as in *streptococcus, gonococcus.*

coc·cyx (COC·six) *n., pl.* **-cy·ges** (–SYE·jeez) the triangular bone at the base of the spine.

coch·i·neal (COCH·uh·neel) **insect** a North American insect, the dried body of which is used to make **cochineal,** a deep red pigment.

coch·le·a (COC·lee·uh) *n., pl.* **-le·ae** (–lee·ee) or **-le·as** the spiral tube of the inner ear, which is essential for hearing. **—coch·le·ar** *adj.*

cock *n.* **1** the adult male of the common barnyard fowl; also, any male bird. **2** a leader or dominant person: *the ~ of the walk.* **3** a valve for controlling liquid or gas flow; faucet. **4** the hammer of a gun; also, its raised position, when ready for firing. **5** a small, cone-shaped pile, usu. of hay. **—*v.*** **1** turn up or to one side: *~ed a quizzical eye.* **2** put in a position of readiness to fire (as a gun) or to hit (as a fist or arm). **—cock·ade** (co·CADE) *n.* a knot of ribbon worn as a badge on the hat. **—cock·a·ma·mie** or **cock·a·ma·my** (coc·uh·MAY·mee) *adj. Slang.* nonsensical; silly. **—cock·a·tiel** (coc·uh·TEEL) *n.* a small crested parrot with gray and yellow feathers. **—cock·a·too** (COC·uh·too) *n.* **-toos** a large crested parrot with feathers of white, red, orange, etc. **—cock·a·trice** (COC·uh·tris) *n.* a mythical serpent able to kill with its glance. **—cock·cha·fer** (COC·chay·fur) *n.* a large European beetle destructive to plants. **—cock·crow** *n.* sunrise. **—cocked hat** a hat with its brim turned up so as to form three corners. **—cock·er·el** (COK·uh·rul) *n.* a rooster less than a year old. **—cock·er spaniel** a small breed of spaniel with long ears, silky coat, and a square muzzle. **—cock·eye** *n.* a squinting eye. **—cock·eyed** *adj.* **1** cross-eyed; askew. **2** *Slang.* absurd; also, drunk: *a wild ~ notion.* **—cock·fight** *n.* a fight between gamecocks often fitted with sharp metal spurs. **—cock·le** *n.* **1** any of several weeds that grow in grainfields. **2** an edible shellfish; **cockles of one's heart** one's deepest feelings; **cock·le·shell** *n.* the heart-shaped shell of a cockle; also, a light boat. **—cock·ney** (COC·nee) *n.* often **Cock·ney,** a native of London's East End; also, the distinctive dialect of this district; ***adj.:*** *a ~ accent.* **—cock of the walk** a leader, esp. one who is too self-assured. **—cock·pit** *n.* **1** an enclosed area for cockfights. **2** the room in an airplane for the pilot and sometimes the crew and passengers. **—cock·roach** (–rohch) *n.* any of several nocturnal insect pests found esp. in houses. **—cocks·comb** *n.* **1** the red, fleshy, comblike crest on a rooster's head. **2** coxcomb. **—cock·sure** *adj.* totally certain, esp. arrogantly self-confident. **—cock·tail** *n.* **1** a mixed, usu. iced alcoholic drink, as a martini or manhattan. **2** a kind of appetizer: *fruit ~; shrimp ~.* **—cock·y** *adj.* **cock·i·er, -i·est** jauntily conceited; cocksure; **cock·i·ly** *adv.;* **cock·i·ness** *n.*

co·co (COH·coh) *n.* **-cos** the coconut palm or a coconut. **—co·coa** (COH·coh) *n.* **1** a chocolate powder made from cacao seeds; also, a beverage made from cocoa, sugar, and water or milk. **2** a light reddish brown. —**cocoa butter** a whitish-yellow fat obtained from cacao seeds and used in cosmetics, soap, etc. —**co•coa•nut** same as COCONUT. —**co•co•nut** (COH·cuh·nut) *n.* the large fruit of the tropical **coconut palm,** which is a husk-covered, hard-shelled seed containing a milky fluid, or **coconut milk,** and lined with an edible white meat that yields **coconut oil** used in soaps, foods, etc.

co•coon (cuh·COON) *n.* the fibrous covering spun by some insect larvae as a case for the pupa; also, the egg case spun by spiders and other insects.

cod *n.* any of several fishes of northern waters valuable for food and **cod-liv•er oil,** rich in vitamins A and D.

c.o.d. or **C.O.D.** cash (or collect) on delivery.

co•da (COH·duh) *n.* a formally separate, concluding passage of a piece of music.

cod•dle *v.* **cod•dles, cod•dled, cod•dling** **1** pamper. **2** cook in water just below the boiling point: *~d eggs.*

code *n.* **1** a systematic collection of laws or regulations; hence, a set of ethical obligations: *the Napoleonic ~; the building ~; a ~ of honor.* **2** a set of usu. arbitrary symbols that carry meaning, as one for communication, one for expressing information for a computer, or one designed to conceal the meaning of a text: *Morse ~; a spy breaking the enemy's ~.* —***v.*** **codes, cod•ed, cod•ing** put into a code: *a ~d message.*

co•dein(e) (COH·deen) *n.* a mild narcotic derived from opium, used esp. as a sedative and a cough depressant.

code name a name used to disguise the identity of a secret agent or operation.

code word a word with a disguised meaning: *"Hegemony" is a Chinese ~ for Soviet expansionism.*

co•dex (COH·dex) *n.* *pl.* **-di•ces** (–di·seez) a manuscript volume, esp. of an ancient text.

cod•fish *n.* same as COD.

codg•er (COJ·ur) *n.* *Informal.* an odd old fellow: *a decent old ~.*

codices *pl.* of CODEX. —**cod•i•cil** (COD·i–) *n.* a supplement to a will, usu. modifying it. —**cod•i•fy** (COD·i·fye) *v.* **-fies, -fied, -fy•ing** arrange; systematize; **cod•i•fi•er** *n.* —**cod•i•fi•ca•tion** (–CAY–) *n.*: *the ~ of traditional custom into law.*

cod•ling *n.* **1** a young cod; also, a hake. **2** a kind of green cooking apple. —**cod-liver oil** See COD.

co•ed (COH·ed) *n.* *Informal.* a female student at a coeducational school; ***adj.*** *Informal.* coeducational; pertaining to coeds: *a ~ school; new ~ fashions.* —**co•ed•u•ca•tion** (coh·ej·uh·CAY–) *n.* the education of males and females together, in the same school or class; **co•ed•u•ca•tion•al** *adj.*

co•ef•fi•cient (coh·uh·FISH·unt) *n.* **1** a letter or number multiplying an algebraic expression: *7 is the numerical ~ of 7xy.* **2** a constant number as the measure of a property or characteristic: *Each material has a different ~ of expansion; a ~* (i.e. measure) *of culture.*

coe•len•ter•ate (si·LENT·uh·rate) *n.* any of a phylum of simple aquatic animals having a single body cavity, including corals, jellyfishes, etc.

co•e•qual (coh·EEK·wul) *adj.* mutually equal, esp. in age or rank; also ***n.*** —**co•e•qual•i•ty** (–KWOL–) *n.* —**co•e•qual•ly** (–EEK–) *adv.*

co•erce (–ERCE) *v.* **-erc•es, -erced, -erc•ing** compel or restrain by fear, violence, etc.; also, gain or effect by force: *a pacifist ~d into joining the army;* **co•erc•er** *n.;* **co•er•ci•ble** *adj.;* **co•er•cion** (–shun) *n.;* **co•er•cive** (–siv) *adj.*

co•e•val (–EE·vul) *adj.* of the same time period: *~ developments in France and England.* —**co•e•val•ly** *adv.*

co•ex•ist (–ig·ZIST) *v.* exist at the same place and time (with); get along side by side (with); **co•ex•is•tence** *n.*: *the peaceful ~ of U.S.A. and Russia.*

co•ex•ten•sive (coh·ik·STEN·siv) *adj.* having the same temporal or spatial extent. —**co•ex•ten•sive•ly** *adv.*

C. of C. Chamber of Commerce.

cof•fee (CAW·fee) *n.* a caffeine-containing beverage made from the roasted and ground seeds **(coffee beans)** of a small tropical tree; also, the tree or its seeds. —**coffee break** a short refreshment break in the working day, usu. at mid-morning or mid-afternoon. —**coffee cake** a sweet cake often with nuts, raisins, icing, etc. —**cof•fee•house** *n.* a restaurant serving coffee and light refreshments, often acting as a social gathering place. —**coffee klatch** same as KAFFEE-KLATSCH. —**coffee pot** a pot for making and serving coffee. —**coffee shop** a small restaurant; café. —**coffee table** a low table usu. placed in front of a couch; **cof•fee-ta•ble book** a large lavishly illustrated book designed for display, esp. on a coffee table.

cof•fer (CAW·fur) *n.* a strongbox or vault for storing valuables; hence, often **coffers** *pl.* fund, treasury: *the municipal ~s.* —**cof•fer•dam** *n.* a temporary, watertight enclosure used to keep a submerged area dry for construction of piers, bridges, etc. —**cof•fin** *n.* a usu. oblong box used to bury the dead in.

C. of S. Chief of Staff.

cog *n.* **1** a tooth or projection, usu. on a gear or wheel **(cog•wheel)** used to transmit motion; also, a cogwheel. **2** a person or thing seen as a necessary but unimportant part of a large, impersonal operation.

cog. cognate.

co•gent (COH·junt) *adj.* powerfully convincing, as by its logicality and rigor: ~ *arguments.* —**co•gen•cy** (COH·jun·see) *n.* —**co•gent•ly** *adv.*

cogged *adj.* fitted with cogs.

cog•i•tate (COJi–) *v.* **-tates, -tat•ed, -tat•ing** think intently (about); ponder. —**cog•i•ta•tion** (–TAY–) *n.* —**cog•i•ta•tive** (–tay·tiv) *adj.*

cog•nac (CONE·yak) *n.* a fine brandy, esp. one from around Cognac, France.

cog•nate *adj.* related through a common origin, esp. of words or languages; also, similar in nature. —***n.:*** *French and Italian are ~s.*

cog•ni•tion (cog·NISH·un) *n.* the process of knowing, including perception and thought, but not emotion; the result of this, a perception or thought; **cog•ni•tive** (COG·ni·tiv) *adj.* —**cog•ni•zance** (COG·ni·zunce) *n.* **1** conscious knowledge of something; awareness. **2** *Law.* the right of a court to hear a case; also, the hearing of the case. —**take cognizance of** recognize; be aware of. —**cog•ni•za•ble** *adj.* —**cog•ni•zant** (–zunt) *adj.*

cog•no•men (cog·NOH·mun) *n.* **-no•mens** or **-nom•i•na** (–NOM·i·nuh) a surname, esp. an ancient Roman family name, as "Caesar"; also, any name, esp. a nickname.

co•gno•scen•te (cone·yoh·SHEN·tay) *n., pl.* **-ti** (–tee) one with special knowledge; a connoisseur: *a new literary style in vogue with the cognoscenti.*

cog railway a railway on which a locomotive pulls itself up a steep incline by means of a cogwheel meshing with a cogged rail. —**cogwheel** See COG.

co•hab•it (–HAB·it) *v.* live together as man and wife, esp. when not married. —**co•hab•i•ta•tion** (–TAY–) *n.*

co•heir (–AIR) *n.* a joint heir: *Three brothers were ~s to the estate.*

co•here (coh·HERE) *v.* **-heres, -hered, -her•ing** **1** hold together; stick (to). **2** be united, logically consistent, etc. —**co•her•ence** *n.: Logical ~ makes for clarity.* —**co•her•ent** *adj.* **1** holding together. **2** orderly; consistent; intelligible: *a ~ argument; ~ speech.* —**co•her•ent•ly** *adv.* —**co•he•sion** (coh·HEE·zhun) *n.* the act or state of cohering; hence, a tendency to stick together; in physics, the molecular attraction binding a substance together. —**co•he•sive** (–HEE·siv) *adj.* —**co•he•sive•ly** *adv.* —**co•he•sive•ness** *n.*

co•ho (COE·ho) *n.* a small salmon of the N. Pacific.

co•hort (COE·hort) *n.* **1** a group. **2** a companion; follower: *The burglar and his ~s were caught red-handed.*

coif *n.* **1** a tight-fitting cap. **2** also **coif•fure** (cwah·FYOOR), a hair style. —**coif•feur** (cwah·FUR) *n.* a male hairdresser; *fem.* **coif•feuse** (cwah·FURZ).

coil *v.* wind or move in a spiral or circular shape; loop: ~ *the rope and hang it up; a snake ~ing around its prey.* —***n.*** **1** a series of connected loops or circles; spiral; also one loop of this: *a radiator ~; a ~ of hair.* **2** a length of conducting wire wound spirally around a nonconducting core; also, an electrical device consisting essentially of this: *an induction ~.*

coin *n.* a piece of metal money; also, coins collectively; hence, *Slang.* money. —***v.*** mint coins from metal; hence, create a new word, phrase, etc.: *Did Churchill ~ "iron curtain?"* —**coin money** make a big profit. —**coin•er** *n.* —**coin•age** (–ij) *n.* **1** the act of minting coins; also, the coins minted. **2** an invented word or phrase.

co•in•cide (–in·SIDE) *v.* **-cides, -cid•ed, -cid•ing** occupy or occur at the same point in space or time; also, be identical; agree: *Our tastes in music ~.* —**co•in•ci•dence** (–IN–) *n.* a coinciding; esp., a remarkable and seemingly accidental instance of events happening together: *What a ~ that you both came today!* **co•in•ci•dent** *adj.* —**co•in•ci•den•tal** (–in·suh·DEN·tl) *adj.;* **co•in•ci•den•tal•ly** *adv.*

co•i•tus (COH·i–) *n.* sexual intercourse; also **co•i•tion** (–ISH·un). —**co•i•tal** *adj.: post-~ pill.*

coke *n.* **1** a clean, hot-burning fuel used esp. in metal industries, made by removing gases from a bituminous coal, or **coking coal.** **2** *Slang.* cocaine. **3 Coke** *Trademark.* "Coca-Cola," a soft drink.

col. collect; college; colony; color; column. —**Col.** colonel; Colorado. —**COL** cost of living; **COLA** cost-of-living adjustment.

co•la (COH·luh) *n.* **1** any of several African trees that bear caffeine-containing nuts, or **cola nuts,** used as a flavoring and in medicines; also, the extract of this nut. **2** a carbonated soft drink flavored with cola extract. **3** a *pl.* of ¹COLON.

col•an•der (CULL·un–) *n.* a bowllike perforated utensil for draining foods.

cold *adj.* **1** of a low temperature as compared to a norm, esp. body temperature: *a ~ day; to feel ~; ~ hands; The supper is ~ now.* **2** lacking in sympathy, encouragement, emotion, etc.; objective; sexually frigid: *a ~ personality; ~ comfort; His appeals left them ~; ~ logic.* **3** *Informal.* unprepared: *go into an examination ~.* **4** *Informal.* unconscious: *out ~ on the floor; knock someone ~.* —***adv.*** *Informal.* totally; absolutely: *I asked for a raise and he turned me down ~.* —***n.*** **1** a condition of cold, esp. cold weather. **2** a viral infection of the upper respiratory system, causing a stuffed or runny nose and malaise: *Put on a coat; you'll catch (a) ~.* —**in cold blood** without emotion: *murdered in ~ blood.* —**cold•ly** *adv.* —**cold•ness** *n.* —**cold-blood•ed** *adj.* **1** without feeling; ruthless: *a ~-blooded killer.* **2** having a body temperature that varies with the environment, as fishes and reptiles. —**cold cream** a cleansing and softening emulsion for the skin. —**cold cuts** slices of assorted cold meats. —**cold feet** a lack of courage or confidence. —**the cold shoulder** *Informal.* a snub; deliberate indifference; **cold-shoul·der** *v.: Don't ~ an old friend.* —**cold snap** a sudden period of cold weather. —**cold sore** a blister on the lips, usu. accompanying a cold or fever. —**cold storage** refrigerated storage for preserving food, fur coats, etc.; hence, temporary suspension of an idea, plan, etc. until needed. —**cold turkey** *Slang.* **1** abrupt and total withdrawal from an addictive drug. **2** in a blunt or matter-of-fact manner. —**cold war** a state of suppressed, nonmilitary hostility between nations.

cole *n.* any of a genus of plants related to the cabbage, as rape and Brussels sprouts.

Cole·ridge (COLE·rij), **Samuel T.** 1772–1834, English poet and critic.

cole·slaw *n.* finely shredded raw cabbage as a salad; also **cole slaw.**

col·ic *n.* severe abdominal pain. —**col·ick·y** *adj.: a ~ child.*

col·i·se·um (–SEE·um) *n.* a large stadium for sports or other public entertainment.

co·li·tis (cuh·LYE·tis) *n.* an inflammation or dysfunction of the colon.

coll. collect; collection; college.

col·lab·o·rate (cuh·LAB·uh–) *v.* **-rates, -rat·ed, -rat·ing** work together with others, esp. on a book or article; also, cooperate with an invading or occupying enemy force; **col·lab·o·ra·tive** *adj.;* **col·lab·o·ra·tor** *n.: a ~ convicted of treason.* —**col·lab·o·ra·tion** (–RAY–) *n.*

col·lage (cuh·LAHZH) *n.* an artistic composition using diverse items, as bits of paper, wood, cloth, etc. glued onto a board: *That essay is a ~ of quotations.*

col·lapse (cuh·LAPS) *v.* **-laps·es, -lapsed, -laps·ing** **1** fall down or fold in; cave in; fail totally; lose energy, health, etc.: *The barn ~d in the storm; He ~d from fatigue.* **2** fold up or make more compact, as for packing. —***n.:*** *the ~ of a business venture.* —**col·laps·i·ble** *adj.: a ~ boat.*

col·lar (COLL·ur) *n.* something that encircles the neck, esp. the part of a garment that does so, the leather band so worn by a dog, or that part of a harness; also, something resembling a collar, as on a pipe. —***v.*** **1** put a collar on (something). **2** take hold of; detain; arrest. —**col·lar·less** *adj.* —**col·lar·bone** *n.* the clavicle.

col·lard (COLL·urd) *n.* usu. **collards** *pl.* the coarse edible leaves of a kind of cabbage that does not form a head.

col·late (cuh·LATE) *v.* **-lates, -lat·ed, -lat·ing** **1** compare closely and note variants: *a scholar ~ing ancient texts.* **2** assemble (pages) in proper order. —**col·la·tor** (cuh·LAY·tur) *n.* —**col·lat·er·al** (cuh·LAT·uh·rul) *adj.* **1** from the same ancestors by a different line of descent: *a ~ branch of the family.* **2** parallel; also, subordinate; supporting: *~ evidence.* **3** pertaining to or secured by **collateral** *n.* property pledged as security for a loan or obligation. —**col·la·tion** (cuh·LAY–) *n.* **1** an act or the result of collating. **2** a light meal, as in monasteries. —**col·league** (COLL·eeg) *n.* an associate, esp. a fellow member of a profession: *a doctor's medical ~s.*

col·lect *v.* (cuh·LECT) **1** bring or come together into a group or mass; accumulate: *people ~ing on street corners; ~ baseball cards for a hobby.* **2** get control of (oneself, one's thoughts, etc.); **col·lect·ed** *adj.* self-controlled; calm. **3** ask for and receive (payment, taxes, etc.): *~ing one's debts.* —***n.*** (COLL·ect) a short prayer used in a church service. —***adj.*** & ***adv.*** (cuh·LECT) paid for by the receiver: *telephone me ~.* —**col·lect·i·ble** or **-a·ble** *adj.* & *n.* —**col·lec·tion** *n.: a stamp ~.* —**col·lec·tive** (cuh·LEC·tiv) *adj.* pertaining to a group acting as or being a unit: **collective bargaining** *between a trade union and management; a* **collective farm** *worked and managed by a group.* —***n.*** a collective organization such as a collective farm: *an editorial ~;* **col·lec·tive·ly** *adv.* —**collective noun** a singular noun denoting a group, as *flock.* —**col·lec·tiv·ism** *n.* a system of collective ownership and control of the economy; **col·lec·tiv·ist** *n.* & *adj.;* **col·lec·tiv·ize** *v.* **-iz·es, -ized, -iz·ing** organize according to collectivist principles. —**col·lec·tor** *n.*

col·leen (COLL·een) *n.* an Irish girl.

col·lege (COLL·ij) *n.* **1** an institution of higher education granting the bachelor's degree; one of the undergraduate divisions of a university; also, an institution for specialized or professional training: *Bryn Mawr ~; Balliol ~; a business ~; ~ of education.* **2** a group of people with common duties: *~ of cardinals; electoral ~.* —**col·le·giate** (cuh·LEE·jut) *adj.* —**col·le·gi·al·i·ty** (–jee·AL·i·tee) *n.* the sharing of power between the Pope and bishops. —**col·le·gian** (cuh·LEE·jun) *n.* a college student. —**col·le·gi·um** (–LEE·jee·um) *n., pl.* **-gi·a** or **-gi·ums** an executive body whose members have equal power, esp. in Russia.

col·lide (cuh·LIDE) *v.* **col·lides, col·lid·ed, col·lid·ing** **1** come into violent contact; hit. **2** clash; be at odds.

col·lie (COLL·ee) *n.* a large long-haired dog bred in Scotland to herd sheep.

col·lier (COLL·yur) *n. Brit.* a coal miner; also, a coal ship. —**col·lier·y** (–yuh·ree) *n.* **col·lier·ies** *Brit.* a coal mine.

col·li·mate (COLL·uh–) *v.* **-mates, -mat·ed, -mat·ing** make (light rays) parallel; adjust the line of sight of a telescope, surveyor's level, etc.

col·li·sion (cuh·LIZH·un) *n.* a colliding: *a head-on ~.*

col•lo•cate (COLL·uh–) *v.* **-cates, -cat•ed, -cat•ing** place side by side or close together. —**col•lo•ca•tion** *n.: a ~ of "open" and "door" forming a phrase.*

col•lo•di•on (cuh·LOH·dee·un) *n.* a pale, flammable, viscous, quick-drying solution used in photographic plates, to protect wounds, etc. —**col•loid** (COLL·oid) *n.* a suspension of very fine, insoluble particles in a gaseous, liquid, or solid medium, as gelatin, foam rubber, or fog; ***adj.:*** *Silica gel is in ~ form.* —**col•loid•al** (cuh·LOY·dul) *adj.*

colloq. colloquial. —**col•lo•qui•al** (cuh·LOH·kwee·ul) *adj.* characteristic of informal conversation. —**col•lo•qui•al•ism** *n.* a colloquial word or phrase, as "fly off the handle" for "lose one's temper." —**col•lo•qui•al•ly** *adv.* —**col•lo•qui•um** (cuh·LOH·kwee·um) *n., pl.* **-qui•a** (–uh) or **-qui•ums** a conference or seminar. —**col•lo•quy** (COLL·uh·kwee) *n.* **-quies** a usu. formal conversation; also, a work written in this form.

col•lu•sion (cuh·LOO·zhun) *n.* secret agreement for an improper or fraudulent purpose: *in ~ with the enemy.* —**col•lu•sive** (–siv) *adj.: ~ trickery.*

col•lu•vi•um (cuh·LOO·vee·um) *n., pl.* **-vi•a** or **-vi•ums** rubble and rock debris at the foot of a slope or cliff.

Colo. Colorado.

co•logne (cuh·LONE) *n.* a perfumed liquid made of fragrant oils in an alcohol base; **co•logned** *adj.* —**Co•logne** a manufacturing city of W. West Germany.

Co•lom•bi•a (cuh·LUM·bee·uh) a republic of N.W. South America; 439,737 sq.mi. (1,138,-914 km²); *cap.* Bogotá. —**Co•lom•bi•an** *adj.* & *n.*

Co•lom•bo (cuh·LUM·boh) capital of Sri Lanka.

[1]**co•lon** (COH·lun) *n.* **-lons** or **-la** **1** a punctuation mark (:) used before an example, list, quotation, etc. **2** the lower part of the large intestine from the cecum to the rectum; **co•lon•ic** (kuh·LON·ic) *adj.*

[2]**co•lon** (cuh·LONE) *n.* **-lons** or **-lon•es** (–LOH·nes) the basic unit of currency in Costa Rica and El Salvador.

colo•nel (CUR·nul) *n.* a military officer ranking above a lieutenant colonel and below a brigadier general.

co•lo•ni•al (cuh·LOH·nee·ul) *adj.* of or having to do with a colony or colonies: *~ possessions; Britain was a ~ power.* **2 Colonial** pertaining to the period in U.S. history before independence: *~ architecture.* Also ***n.*** one who lives in a colony; **co•lo•ni•al•ly** *adv.;* **co•lo•ni•al•ism** *n.* the policy and practice of acquiring and maintaining foreign colonies; **co•lo•ni•al•ist** *n.* —**col•o•nist** (COL·uh–) *n.* one who lives in a colony, esp. a first settler. —**col•o•nize** *v.* **-niz•es, -nized, -niz•ing** settle in or establish a colony: *New York was ~d by the Dutch;* **col•o•niz•er** *n.;* **col•o•ni•za•tion** (–ZAY–) *n.*

col•on•nade (coll·uh·NADE) *n.* a row of evenly spaced columns.

col•o•ny (COLL·uh·nee) *n.* **-nies** **1** a dependency in a distant land controlled by and often settled with emigrants from the mother country; also, the emigrants who settle there; **the Colonies** the 13 former British colonies that first made up the U.S. **2** a group of people of the same nation or calling living in one area; also, a group of organisms living together as a unit: *an artists' ~; a ~ of ants.*

col•o•phon (COLL·uh·fon) *n.* an inscription in a book giving particulars of its publisher, date, type, paper used, etc.; also, a publisher's trademark.

col•or (CULL·ur) *n.* **1** the quality of things as they appear in reflected light, esp. red, blue, green, etc. as distinguished from black, white, or gray: *a movie in living ~!* **2** skin color, esp. as indicating health or embarrassment: *The patient had lost ~; He changed ~ when the subject was mentioned.* **3 the colors** flag, emblem, etc. used to signify a nation, military unit, etc.: *serving with the ~s;* **nail one's colors to the mast** declare one's stand and refuse to change; **with flying colors** victoriously: *She came out of the exam with flying ~s.* **4** a lively or interesting quality; also, appearance; nature: *add local ~ to a story; greed under the ~ of frugality; see him in his true* **colors.** —***v.*** **1** change the color of; give color to; also, alter or misrepresent: *a story ~ed by the reporter's prejudices.* **2** blush.

Col•o•ra•do (col·uh·RAD·oh) a state in western U.S.; 104,247 sq.mi. (269,998 km²); *cap.* Denver. —**Col•o•ra•dan** *adj.* & *n.* —**Colorado beetle** a black-and-yellow striped beetle that destroys potato leaves; potato beetle. —**Colorado River** a river of western U.S. flowing into the Gulf of California.

col•or•ant (CULL·uh·runt) *n.* a coloring agent. —**col•or•a•tion** (–RAY–) *n.* the state or manner of being colored. —**col•or•a•tu•ra** (–ruh·TOOR·uh) *n.* elaborate trills, runs, etc. in music; also, a soprano specializing in such music. —**color bar** same as COLOR LINE. —**col•or•blind** *adj.* unable to perceive or distinguish certain colors; **col•or•blind•ness** *n.* —**col•or•cast** *v.* telecast in color; ***n.:*** *a ~ of a Christmas parade.* —**col•ored** *adj.* **1** having color. **2** distorted; biased: *a highly ~ed account.* **3** non-Caucasian, esp. Negro; ***n.,*** *pl.* **colored** or **coloreds:** *the ~s* (i.e. racially mixed people) *of South Africa.* —**col•or•fast** *adj.* with colors that will not fade or run: *~ cotton.* —**col•or•ful** *adj.* **1** having strong or attractive colors: *~ clothing.* **2** lively; interesting: *a ~ character.* —**col•or•ful•ly** *adv.;* **col•or•less** *adj.;* **col•or•less•ly** *adv.* —**color line** (or **bar**) restrictions imposed on non-whites, as in voting rights, eating in restaurants, and use of beaches.

co•los•sus (cuh·LOSS·us) *n., pl.* **-los•si** (–sye) or **-los•sus•es** something, like a statue of Apollo in ancient Rhodes, of huge size, power, or importance: *General Motors, a ~ of American industry.* **—co·los·sal** (–ul) *adj.: a ~ dam on the Nile; ~ pride;* **co·los·sal·ly** adv.

col·our *n.* & *v. Brit.* color.

col·por·teur (COLL·por·tur) *n.* a peddler or distributor of religious books.

colt *n.* a young horse, donkey, etc., esp. a male; hence, an inexperienced youth. **—colt·ish** *adj.* frisky; lively: *~ escapades.* **—colt·ish·ly** *adv.*

Co·lum·bi·a (cuh·LUM·bee·uh) capital of South Carolina. **—Columbia River** a river in N.W. United States and S.W. Canada. **—col·um·bine** (COLL·um–) *n.* any of several plants of the buttercup family with spurred, five-petaled flowers of various colors. **—co·lum·bi·um** (cuh·LUM·bee–) *n.* same as NIOBIUM. **—Co·lum·bus** (cuh·LUM–) capital of Ohio. **—Columbus, Christopher.** 1451–1506, Italian explorer in the employ of Spain; **Columbus Day** the second Monday in October, a U.S. holiday commemorating the discovery of America.

col·umn (COLL·um) *n.* **1** a pillar, with its base and capital, usu. supporting a roof or upper story; also, something resembling this: *the spinal ~.* **2** a vertical section of print on a page; also, a regular feature in a newspaper or magazine, written by a **col·um·nist:** *This page has two ~s; a Hollywood gossip ~; a political ~ist.* **3** a long row, as of troops. **—col·um·nar** (cuh·LUM·nur), **col·umned** *adj.*

com- *prefix.* together: as in *commensurate, compatriot, compress.* **—com.** comedy; comma; commentary; commerce; commission; committee; common.

co·ma (COH·muh) *n.* a prolonged period of deep unconsciousness, esp. as caused by injury, poison, or disease.

Co·man·che (cuh·MAN·chee) *n.* (a member of) an American Indian tribe now living in Oklahoma; also, their language. ***—adj.:*** *a ~ pony.*

co·ma·tose (COH·muh–) *adj.* of, like, or affected with coma.

comb (COHM) *n.* **1** a toothed instrument for untangling, arranging, and sometimes holding in place the hair; also, a similar instrument for untangling wool, a horse's coat, etc.: *a tortoise-shell ~; a fine-tooth ~.* **2** the fleshy, usu. red crest on a rooster's head; also, the crest of a wave. ***—v.*** **1** arrange, clean, etc. with a comb. **2** search thoroughly: *The police ~ed the house for clues.*

comb. combination; combining.

com·bat (cum·BAT) *v.* **-bats, -bat·(t)ed, -bat·(t)ing** fight; oppose: *Help ~ heart disease.* ***—n.*** (COM–) a fight, esp. active warfare as opposed to military support: *~ boots; hand-to-hand ~; ~ zone;* **combat fatigue** a nervous condition caused by prolonged military combat. **—com·bat·ant** (cum·BAT·unt) *n.* **—com·bat·ive** (cum·BAT·iv) *adj.* **—comb·er** (COH·mur) *n.* same as BREAKER, *n.* 2.

com·bi·na·tion (–NAY–) *n.* **1** the act or state of combining or being combined. **2** a united entity or group, esp. of business interests. **3** the series of letters and numbers that, when turned on a dial, will open a **combination lock,** as on a bank vault. **—com·bine** (cum·BINE) *v.* **-bines, -bined, -bin·ing** come or bring together; unite: *~ our efforts; ~ business with pleasure.* ***—n.*** (COM–) **1** a mobile machine that both cuts and threshes grain. **2** a combination, esp. of business interests. **—combining form** a form in which a word combines with other words or word elements to make new compounds and derivatives, as *auto-, demo-, -crat, -pede, multi-.*

comb·ings (COH·mingz) *n.pl.* loose hair, wool, etc. removed by combing.

com·bo (COM·boh) *n. Informal.* a small group of musicians: *a jazz ~.*

com·bus·tion (cum·BUS·chun) *n.* a burning; chemical reaction in a gaseous medium with release of heat: *spontaneous ~ of rags soaked with oil; the internal ~ engine of an auto.* **—com·bus·tive** (–BUS·tiv) *adj.* **—com·bus·ti·ble** *adj.* & *n.;* **com·bus·ti·bly** *adv.;* **com·bus·ti·bil·i·ty** (–BIL–) *n.*

comd. or **comdg.** commanding.

Comdr. commander.

Comdt. commandant.

come (CUM) *v.* **comes, came, come, com·ing** **1** move towards a position, condition, or state; arrive at this; also, be next: *~ to my house; ~ing down the street; The water came to a boil; the ~ing attraction.* **2** occur; happen; also, be available: *Christmas ~s once a year; F ~s before G.* **3** originate: *a man who ~s from Brooklyn; He ~s of good stock.* **4** *Informal.* have an orgasm. **—come across (**or **upon**) find or meet unexpectedly. **—come around** **1** recover. **2** change one's opinion or stand. **—come back** return, esp. to power, status, etc.; **come·back** *n.* **—come between** separate; cause trouble between. **—come by** acquire. **—come down (in the world)** descend in status; **come·down** *n.* **—come down (with)** become afflicted (with a disease): *Bill came down with measles.* **—come into** receive, esp. by inheritance: *She will ~ into $500 on her aunt's death.* **—come off** **1** become detached. **2** happen; succeed; fare. **—come out** **1** make a public debut: *Young women used to ~ out at 18.* **2** turn out. **—come through** *Informal.* give or do what is required. **—come to** **1** amount to: *That ~s to $5.65.* **2** (–TOO) regain consciousness: *The boxer came to an hour later.* **—come to pass** happen: *It came to pass that. . . .* **—come up with** *Informal.* find: *trying to ~ up with a better idea.* **—come what may** no matter what. **—how come?** *Informal.* Why?

co·me·di·an (cuh·MEE·dee·un) *n.* **1** one who writes or acts in a comedy. **2** an amusing person, esp. a professional entertainer: *a nightclub ~.* **—co·me·di·enne** (cuh·mee·dee·EN) *n. fem.* **—com·e·dy** (COM·uh·dee) *n.* **-dies** (–deez) **1** a play with a light, amusing tone; also, a work of literature with a happy ending; hence, this genre. **2** an amusing aspect, event, etc. —**co•me•dic** (kuh·MEE·dic) *adj.*

come•ly (CUM·lee) *adj.* **-li•er, -li•est** attractive; good-looking; **come•li•ness** *n.*

come-on *n. Slang.* an allurement; inducement. —**com•er** (CUM·ur) *n. Informal.* a promising or rapidly progressing person.

co•mes•ti•ble (cuh·MES·ti·bl) *adj.* edible. —**n.:** *a basket of ~s.*

com•et (COM·it) *n.* a celestial body, usu. orbiting the sun, with a small, bright center, a glowing "head" around it, and often a long glowing tail.

come•up•pance (–UP·unce) *n. Informal.* just retribution: *You'll get your ~.*

com•fit (CUM–) *n.* a confection, esp. a candied nut, fruit, etc.

com•fort (CUM·furt) *v.* soothe; console; ease: *~ them in their hour of sorrow.* —***n.*** **1** consolation; also, a person or thing that gives consolation: *Your letter was a great ~.* **2** ease; contentment; well-being; also, something that causes this: *all the ~s of home.* —**com•fort•a•ble** *adj.* being in a state of or giving comfort: *~ in his new home; a ~ chair; a ~ income;* **com•fort•a•ble•ness** *n.;* **com•fort•a•bly** *adv.* —**com•fort•er** *n.* a warm quilt. —**com•fort•less** *adj.* —**comfort station** a public toilet. —**com•fy** *adj.* **-fi•er, -fi•est** *Informal.* comfortable: *a nice ~ pillow.*

com•ic *adj.* **1** of or having to do with comedy or comic strips: *a ~ actor.* **2** humorous; also **com•i•cal.** —***n.*** **1** a humorous person, esp. a professional comedian. **2** *Informal.* a comic book; also **comics** *pl.* a section of comic strips, as in a newspaper; funnies: *full-color ~s.* —**com•i•cal•ly** *adv.* —**comic book** a booklet of comic strips telling adventurous or humorous stories. —**comic strip** a usu. humorous series of drawings telling a story.

com•ing *adj.* approaching; also, *Informal.* showing promise of success: *the ~ thing in neckwear.*

Com•in•tern (COM–) *n.* the Communist International or Third International, from 1919 to 1943 a Moscow-based organization of Communist parties.

com•i•ty *n.* **-ties** civility; courtesy; community: *our place in the ~ of nations.*

coml. commercial.

comm. commerce; commission; commonwealth.

com•ma (COM·uh) *n.* a punctuation mark (,) showing a slight separation or pause within a sentence or clause.

com•mand (cuh·MAND) *v.* **1** order with or be in authority; hence, receive as one's due: *I ~ you to stop; the ~ing officer; Strength ~s respect.* **2** have in one's control; also, overlook so as to control: *a fort built on ~ing heights.* —***n.*** **1** an order or the giving of it; also, authority or ability to give commands: *Who is in ~?* **2** the area or forces under one officer's control. **3** control: *a good ~ of Spanish.* —**com•man•dant** (COM·un·dant) *n.* a commanding officer. —**com•man•deer** (com·un·DEER) *v.* seize by force, esp. by military order. —**com•mand•er** (–MAND–) *n.* one who commands, esp. a commanding officer; also, a naval officer ranking just below a captain. —**commander in chief,** *pl.* **commanders in chief** the supreme commander of all of the armed forces of a nation. —**com•mand•ment** (–MAND–) *n.* a command or precept; esp. **Commandment,** one of the ten laws given by God to Moses. —**command module** a spacecraft containing astronauts and main controls and designed for reentry. —**com•man•do** (cuh·MAN·doh) *n.* **-do(e)s** (–doze) a member of a small military force trained for quick raids into enemy territory; also, the force itself. —**command performance** an entertainment given at the command of a ruler. —**command post** the field headquarters of a fighting unit.

com•mem•o•rate (–MEM–) *v.* **-rates, -rat•ed, -rat•ing** honor or keep the memory of; also, be a memorial to: *a plaque ~ing war dead.* —**com•mem•o•ra•tion** (–RAY–) *n.* —**com•mem•o•ra•tive** (–ruh·tiv) *adj.: a ~ stamp.*

com•mence (cuh·MENCE) *v.* **-men•ces, -menced, -menc•ing** begin; start. —**com•mence•ment** *n.* **1** a beginning. **2** a ceremony for the granting of degrees or diplomas.

com•mend (cuh·MEND) *v.* **1** praise; recommend. **2** entrust to another's care: *~ the souls of the departed to God.* —**com•mend•a•ble** *adj.* praiseworthy: *~ bravery;* **com•mend•a•bly** *adv.;* **com•men•da•to•ry** *adj.* —**com•men•da•tion** (–DAY–) *n.*

com•men•su•ra•ble (cuh·MEN·shur·ruh·bl) *adj.* measurable by the same standard, esp. of numbers evenly divisible by the same whole number. —**com•men•su•ra•bly** *adv.* —**com•men•su•ra•bil•i•ty** (–BIL–) *n.* —**com•men•su•rate** (–rit) *adj.* **1** proportionate: *a salary ~ to his worth; ~ with work done.* **2** coextensive; equal.

com•ment (COM·ent) *n.* an explanatory or critical note or remark; also, a statement of reaction or opinion: *"No ~," replied the politician; His odd behavior excited a lot of ~.* —***v.:*** *refused to ~ on the assassination attempt.* —**com•men•tar•y** *n.* **-tar•ies** **1** usu. **commentaries,** memoirs or a simple narrative. **2** a systematic series of comments, as on a text *(a Biblical ~)* or a sports event *(a running ~ on the game).* **3** something that illustrates or reflects on something: *Pollution is a sad ~ on civilization.* —**com•men•tate** *v.* **-tates, -tat•ed, -tat•ing** write a commentary; also, act as a **com•men•ta•tor,** one who reports and comments on news and politics on radio or TV.

com·merce (COM–) *n.* **1** intercourse; dealings. **2** the buying and selling of commodities; trade: *Chamber of ~.* —**com·mer·cial** (cuh·MUR·shul) *adj.* **1** of, pertaining to, or suitable for commerce: *New York is the ~ capital of the U.S.* **2** oriented to profit-making: *~ television relies on advertising; ~ drama.* —***n.*** a radio or TV advertisement. —**com·mer·cial·ly** *adv.* —**com·mer·cial·ism** *n.* excessive emphasis on the making of a profit. —**com·mer·cial·ize** *v.* **-iz·es, -ized, -iz·ing** make commercial; put on a business basis: *~d religion.*

Com·mie (COM·ee) *n.* & *adj. Informal.* Communist; also **Com·my, com·mie,** *pl.* **Com·mies, com·mies.**

com·mi·na·tion (–NAY–) *n.* threat; denunciation. —**com·min·a·to·ry** (COM·i·nuh–) *adj.*

com·min·gle (cuh·MING·gl) *v.* **-gles, -gled, -gling** mingle or mix together.

com·mis·er·ate (–MIZ·uh–) *v.* **-ates, -at·ed, -at·ing** sympathize; feel or show pity for. —**com·mis·er·a·tion** (–RAY–) *n.* —**com·mis·er·a·tive** (–MIZ·uh·ray·tiv) *adj.*

com·mis·sar·i·at (com·i·SAIR·ee·ut) *n.* **1** a military body that supplies and transports an army's provisions. **2** until 1946, a ministry in the Soviet government, presided over by a **com·mis·sar** (COM·i·sar). —**com·mis·sar·y** (COM·i·ser·ee) *n.* **-sar·ies 1** a store of food and other provisions. **2** a lunchroom, esp. in a movie studio. —**com·mis·sion** (cuh·MISH·un) *n.* **1** the act of committing: *the ~ of a crime.* **2** a task or job entrusted to someone else, esp. an order to administer something, produce a work of art, etc.; also, the granting of certain military ranks or the rank itself; **in** (or **out of**) **commission** in (or out of) working order or active service. **3** a group entrusted with a task, often as a government agency: *~ on the status of women.* **4** a salesman's fee, usu. a percentage of the sale price: *a 2% ~ on all sales.* —***v.*** give a commission to or for: *A lieutenant is a ~ed officer; The king ~ed him to explore the West; a painting ~ed by the city.* —**com·mis·sion·er** *n.* a member of a commission; also, the head of a usu. governmental agency: *the ~ of education;* **com·mis·sion·er·ship** *n.* —**com·mit** (cuh·MIT) *v.* **-mits, -mit·ted, -mit·ting 1** do (something wrong, as an error, crime, sin, etc.); perpetrate. **2** entrust; give into someone's care or custody; esp., put into a prison or mental hospital: *~ a man to prison; ~ a poem to memory, paper, writing.* **3** pledge or promise (oneself or resources) to an action or use; declare one's mind: *I won't ~ myself on that issue.* —**com·mit·ment** *n.: He gave a firm ~ to invest in our firm; heavy financial ~s.* —**com·mit·tal** *n.* a committing. —**com·mit·tee** (–MIT–) *n.* a usu. chosen group that considers, acts on, promotes, or reports on particular matters: *a finance ~; ~ for economic development.* —**com·mit·tee·man** *n.* **-men;** *fem.* **com·mit·tee·wom·an, -wom·en.**

com·mode (cuh·MODE) *n.* **1** a chest of drawers. **2** a portable washstand in a cupboard. **3** a low chair containing a chamber pot. —**com·mod·i·ous** (–MOH–) *adj.* suitably spacious: *a ~ closet.* —**com·mod·i·ty** (–MOD–) *n.* **-ties** an article of use, esp. one transported and traded, as farm and mining products, textiles, and lumber. —**commodity exchange** (or **market**) a market for buying and selling supply contracts for sugar, grains, butter, coffee, wool, etc.

com·mo·dore (COM·uh–) *n.* a wartime navy officer ranking just below a rear admiral; also, the head of a yacht club, fleet, etc.

com·mon (COM·un) *adj.* **1** belonging to, affecting, or pertaining to more than one, esp. a group or community; shared; public: *the ~ good; two apartments with a ~ wall; This park is ~ property; a ~ criminal.* **2** frequent; usual; general; also, most widely known: *Cows are a ~ rural sight; a ~ occurrence; the ~ cat.* **3** ordinary; without distinction of quality or rank: *a ~ sailor, soldier; a* **common or garden variety** (of any article). **4** coarse, vulgar, or below average: *~ decency; the ~ people; ~ manners.* —***n.*** **1** a piece of land owned by and open to the public. **2** commons *pl.* the common people; **the Commons** House of Commons, the lower house of a parliament, as in Britain or Canada. —**in common** jointly; shared. —**com·mon·ly** *adv.* —**com·mon·ness** *n.* —**com·mon·al·ty** *n.* **-ties** the common people. —**common carrier** a commercial concern for carrying goods, people, and messages nationwide. —**common denominator** a number evenly divisible by the denominator of two or more fractions, as 14 for 3/7 and ½. —**com·mon·er** *n.* one without noble rank. —**common factor** (or **divisor**) a number that evenly divides into two or more other numbers, as 8 for 16 and 24. —**common fraction** a fraction expressed by an integral numerator separated by a horizontal or vertical line from an integral denominator. —**common ground** shared opinions or interests. —**common law** the uncodified body of law based on custom and court decisions: *a common-law marriage* (i.e. one based on cohabitation and valid by the common law). —**common logarithm** a logarithm with a base of 10. —**common market** an economic union of nations, usu. lowering mutual trade barriers; esp. **the Common Market,** the European Economic Community. —**common multiple** a multiple of two or more numbers, as 18 for 2, 3, 6, and 9. —**com·mon·place** *n.* a frequent thing; also, a trite or obvious remark or topic; platitude; ***adj.:*** *a movie with a ~ theme.* —**common sense** sound practical judgment; also, the opinion of the ordinary man; **com·mon-sense, com·mon-sen·si·ble**

or **com·mon-sen·si·cal** *adj.* **—com·mon·weal** (–weel) *n.* the public good. **—com·mon·wealth** (–welth) *n.* **1** the body of citizens in a state; also, a nation or state: *the ~ of Massachusetts; ~ of Australia.* **2** an association of sovereign states, esp. the **Commonwealth of Nations** made up of Britain and former British colonies.

com·mo·tion (cuh·MOH–) *n.* violent disturbance; tumult; noisy confusion: *a mob making a ~ in the streets.*

com·mu·nal (cuh·MYOO·nl, COM·yoo·nl) *adj.* **1** of or having to do with a commune or a system of common property; shared: *~ living; a ~ farm.* **2** of or pertaining to a community or ethnic group; public: *~ strife; ~ elections;* **com·mu·nal·ly** *adv.;* **com·mu·nal·ize** *v.* **-iz·es, -ized, -iz·ing:** *the ~ing of natural resources.* **—com·mu·nard** or **Com·mu·nard** (com·yoo·NARD) *n.* a member of a commune or of the Commune (1871). **—com·mune** (cuh·MYOON) *v.* **-munes, -muned, -mun·ing** converse, esp. mentally: *~ing with Nature.* **—*n.*** (COM·yoon) **1** a group of people living and working together: *a hippie ~.* **2** the smallest division of government in some European countries, esp. France, resembling a township. **3 the Commune (of Paris)** the revolutionary government of Paris, 1789–94, or in 1871. **—com·mu·ni·ca·ble** (–MEW–) *adj.* that can be easily communicated: *mumps is a ~ disease;* **com·mu·ni·ca·bil·i·ty** (–BIL–) *n.* **—com·mu·ni·cant** *n.* one who does or may receive Communion. **—com·mu·ni·cate** *v.* **-cates, -cat·ed, -cat·ing** **1** pass on to or share with another, as a disease, information, feelings, etc; make known: *~ing by letter or telephone.* **2** administer or receive Holy Communion. **3** be adjoined or connected: *~ing rooms.* **—com·mu·ni·ca·tion** (–CAY–) *n.* **1** the act or means of communicating; also, a message: *The outpost received a ~ from headquarters.* **2 communications** *pl.* system of moving messages or troops, supplies, etc.; **communications satellite** a man-made earth satellite that relays or sends radio, TV, and other signals, **—com·mu·ni·ca·tive** (cuh·MYOO·ni·cay·tiv) *adj.* talkative: *a child with a ~ disposition;* **com·mu·ni·ca·tor** *n.* **—com·mun·ion** (cuh·MYOO·nyun) *n.* **1** a sharing: *a ~ of interests.* **2** fellowship; a group of people connected by religion. **3** intimate communication: *hold ~ with oneself.* **4 Communion** Holy Communion or the Lord's Supper. **—com·mu·ni·qué** (cuh·MYOO·ni·cay) *n.* an official announcement, esp. to the press; bulletin. **—com·mu·nism** (COM·yuh·nizm) *n.* **1** a social system based on the collective ownership of wealth and the absence of social class. **2** Communism the revolutionary communist system as practices esp. in the U.S.S.R., based on the theories of Marx and Lenin and controlled by the **Communist Party. —com·mu·nist** or **Com·mu·nist** *n. & adj.* **—com·mu·nis·tic** (–NIS–) *adj.* **—com·mu·ni·ty** (cuh·MYOO·ni·tee) *n.* **-ties** **1** a group of people, as living in one place, sharing the same government, background, interests, etc., esp. the whole population of a town, region, etc.: *a leader with the support of the whole ~; a religious ~; the Jewish ~.* **2** a sharing: *a ~ of interests.* **—community antenna television** cable TV. **—community chest** a fund established by a community for charitable purposes. **—community college** a junior college serving and supported by one community. **—community property** jointly held property of husband and wife.

com·mu·ta·tion (–TAY–) *n.* a commuting or commutating. **—commutation ticket** a transportation ticket at a reduced rate for commuters. **—com·mu·ta·tive** (COM·yuh–, cum·YOO–) *adj. Math.* giving the same result regardless of the order in which the steps are taken: *Simple addition is ~;* **com·mu·ta·tor** *n.* a device for reversing the direction of electric current flow, used in direct current generators and electric motors; hence **com·mu·tate** *v.* **-tates, -tat·ed, -tat·ing. —com·mute** (cuh·MUTE) *v.* **-mutes, -mut·ed, mut·ing** **1** change; substitute; convert; esp., reduce the severity of (a penalty): *a death sentence ~d to life imprisonment.* **2** travel regularly between one's home and place of work that is some distance away; ***n.*** trip; distance: *It's a two-hour ~ to work.*

Commy same as COMMIE.

Com·o·ros (COM·uh·rose) a republic consisting of several islands between E. Africa and Madagascar; 838 sq. mi. (2,171 km²); *cap.* Moroni.

comp. comparative; compilation; composition; compound.

com·pact (–PACT) *adj.* **1** densely packed; solid: *a ~ mass.* **2** terse or condensed: *a ~ style of writing.* **3** occupying a small space. **—*n.*** (COM–) **1** a small case for face powder, rouge, etc. **2** a small car. **3** an agreement: *a trade ~.* **—*v.*** (cum·PACT) pack tightly together; assemble. **—com·pact·ly** *adv.* **—com·pact·ness** *n.* **—com·pac·tor** (cum·PAC·tur) *n.* any of various machines for compacting, esp. earth to a firm density or trash into small bundles.

com·pan·ion (cum·PAN·yun) *n.* **1** a comrade; close associate; hence, one who lives or travels with another, often paid to do so: *a faithful ~.* **2** one of a pair or group; ***adj.:*** *the ~ volume.* **—com·pan·ion·a·ble** *adj.* friendly: *a ~ smile;* **com·pan·ion·a·bly** *adv.* **—com·pan·ion·less** *adj.* **—com·pan·ion·ship** *n.: close ~.* **—com·pan·ion·way** (cum·PAN·yun–) *n.* a staircase leading below deck on a ship. **—com·pa·ny** (CUM·puh·nee) *n.* **-nies** **1** a group of people; esp. a musical or theatrical troupe, a business organization, the officers and men of a ship, or a military unit smaller than a battalion. **2** guest(s): *We're having ~*

for supper. **3** one's associates or companions: *"A man is known by the ~ he keeps."* **4** companionship; fellowship: *the pleasure of your ~.* **—in company with** together with. **—keep company** **1** associate (with): *an engaged couple keeping ~.* **2** accompany: *Keep him ~.* **—part company** end an association (with).

com·pa·ra·ble (COM·puh·ruh·bl) *adj.* able or worthy to be compared: *Apples and pears are not ~;* **com·pa·ra·bly** *adv.* **—com·par·a·tive** (cum·PAIR·uh·tiv) *adj.* **1** pertaining to or using comparison: *~ linguistics.* **2** compared to something else; relative: *a ~ stranger.* **3** indicating the second of the three **degrees of comparison** which indicate relative degree in adjectives and adverbs, as "more" in "much–more–most"; cf. POSITIVE and SUPERLATIVE; ***n.:*** *"Better" is the ~ of "good."* **—com·par·a·tive·ly** *adv.* **—com·pare** (cum·PAIR) *v.* **-pares, -pared, -par·ing** **1** examine to note differences and similarities: *~ "King Lear" with "Macbeth."* **2** liken (to); hold similar: *"Shall I ~ thee to a summer's day?"* **3** be similar enough to merit comparison: *Restaurants can't ~ with home cooking.* **—beyond** (or **without**) **compare** unequaled; superlatively: *delicious beyond ~.* **—com·par·i·son** (cum·PAIR·i·sun) *n.* **1** a comparing: *~s are odious.* **2** similarity: *two points of ~.* **—in comparison** when or if compared (with): *a bargain, in ~ with the regular price.*

com·part·ment (cum·PART–) *n.* a division of a space, structure, etc; a separate room or area: *the glove ~.* **—com·part·men·tal·ize** (–MEN–) *v.* **-iz·es, -ized, -iz·ing:** *Science has become more ~d.*

com·pass (CUM·pus) *n.* **1** a device for indicating direction, esp. one with a magnetic needle that points north: *the 32 points* (i.e. directions) *of the ~.* **2** usu. **compasses** *pl.* a V-shaped device with two hinged legs for drawing circles, measuring distances, etc. **3** extent; boundary: *beyond the ~ of your experience.* **—*v.*** **1** surround; go all the way around. **2** achieve; also, comprehend: *what the mind cannot ~.* **3** plot; contrive.

com·pas·sion (cum·PASH·un) *n.* sorrow or sympathy for another's sufferings, with desire to help; **com·pas·sion·ate** (–it) *adj.: a tender, ~ heart;* **com·pas·sion·ate·ly** *adv.* **—com·pat·i·ble** (cum·PAT–) *adj.* able to live, function, or get along together: *a ~ couple; a ~ color telecast may be viewed on a black and white set;* **com·pat·i·bly** *adv.;* **com·pat·i·bil·i·ty** (–BIL–) *n.*

com·pa·tri·ot (cum·PAY·tree·ut) *n.* **1** a fellow countryman. **2** a colleague. **—com·pa·tri·ot·ic** (–OT–) *adj.: ~ friends.*

com·peer (COM·peer) *n.* a peer; person of equal rank; also, a comrade: *~s at a military training camp.*

com·pel (cum·PEL) *v.* **-pels, -pelled, -pel·ling** **1** force: *He was ~d to beg by hunger.* **2** get by force, pressure, etc.: *The troops ~d submission.* **—com·pel·ling** *adj.* forceful; causing respect, interest, belief, etc.: *a ~ line of argument; a ~ tale.* **—com·pel·ling·ly** *adv.*

com·pen·di·um (cum·PEN·dee·um) *n., pl.* **-di·a** (–uh) or **-di·ums** a short but comprehensive summary. **—com·pen·di·ous** *adj.: a ~ world history; a ~ dictionary.*

com·pen·sate (COM–) *v.* **-sates, -sat·ed, -sat·ing** pay (for); make up (for); counterbalance (a defect or variation): *A worker is ~d for his injury; His boldness only ~s for an inner timidity.* **—com·pen·sa·tion** (–SAY–) *n.* **—com·pen·sa·to·ry** (cum·PEN·suh–) *adv.: ~ damages of $500.*

com·pete (cum·PEET) *v.* **-petes, -pet·ed, -pet·ing** **1** strive (with); vie for or as if for a prize: *~ing with the best runners in the state; two lads ~ing for a girl's love.* **2** strive successfully; rival: *The corner store cannot ~ with the supermarket.* **—com·pe·tence** (COM·puh–) *n.* **1** ability or fitness: *The court questioned the ~ of the witness.* **2** sufficient means for livelihood: *living on a tidy ~.* Also **com·pe·ten·cy, -cies.** **—com·pe·tent** (COM·pi·tunt) *adj.* sufficiently able, qualified, etc.; adequate: *a ~ judge of character; ~ to handle the task; He did a ~ job;* **com·pe·tent·ly** *adv.* **—com·pe·ti·tion** (–TISH–) *n.* the act of competing; also, a contest or match; also, one's rivals. **—com·pet·i·tive** (cum·PET·i·tiv) *adj.* liking or ready to compete: *a ~ spirit.;* **com·pet·i·tor** *n.* one who competes.

com·pile (cum–) *v.* **-piles, -piled, -piling** collect (information, literature, etc.) from different sources (into a list, book, etc.): *~ a list of grievances; ~ a volume of ballads.* **—com·pi·la·tion** (com·puh·LAY–) *n.* **—com·pil·er** (–PYE–) *n.*

com·pla·cent (cum·PLAY·sunt) *adj.* self-satisfied; unconcerned; content: *an air of ~ superiority.* **—com·pla·cent·ly** *adv.* **—com·pla·cence** or **com·pla·cen·cy** *n.: smug ~.*

com·plain (cum–) *v.* **1** express or describe one's dissatisfaction, discomfort, annoyance, etc.: *~ of a sore back; He ~ed about the neighbor's dog.* **2** state a grievance or accusation formally; one who complains thus is a **com·plain·ant.** **—com·plaint** *n.* **1** a complaining; also, an accusation or grievance: *a noisy ~; File a ~ with the police.* **2** a cause for complaining, esp. an illness: *a stomach ~.*

com·plai·sant (cum·PLAY·zunt, –sunt) *adj.* eager to please; obliging; courteous. **—com·plai·sance** *n.*

com·pleat (cum·PLEET) *adj.* having all necessary skills and attributes; complete: *"The ~ Angler"; the ~ showman.*

com·plect·ed (cum–) *adj.* *Regional.* same as COMPLEXIONED.

com·ple·ment (COM·pluh·munt) *n.* **1** something that completes: *Fine wine is a ~ to a good meal.* **2** *Grammar.* a word or words completing a predicate, as "sad" in "I feel sad." **3** a complete set or number: *a ship with its ~*

of men; a full ~ of 32 teeth. **—v.** (com·pluh·MENT) be or give the complement to: *A flower ~ed her good looks.* **—com·ple·men·ta·ry** (–MEN–) *adj.: ~ colors, as red and green, combine to form white.* **—complementary angle** one of a pair of angles that add up to 90°. **—com·plete** (cum·PLEET) *adj.* **1** having all of its parts; entire: *a ~ deck of cards.* **2** perfect; thorough: *~ happiness; a ~ fool; a ~ and total stranger.* **3** concluded; finished: *The job is ~; a ~ day.* **—v. -pletes, -plet·ed, -plet·ing** make complete; also, conclude: *~ the exercise before you stop.* **—com·plete·ly** *adv.: He is ~ confused.* **—com·plete·ness** *n.* **—com·ple·tion** *n.: payment on ~ of the work.*

com·plex *adj.* (cum·PLEX, COM–) **1** composed of distinct but connected parts: *a* **complex sentence** *with main and subordinate clauses;* opposed to SIMPLE. **2** intricate; complicated: *a problem too ~ for me to solve.* **—n.** (COM–) **1** a combination of related things, as buildings, socio-political elements, etc.: *an apartment ~; vitamin B ~.* **2** a set of repressed psychological impulses; hence, any obsessive fear, belief, etc.: *an inferiority ~.* **—com·plex·i·ty** (–PLEX–) *n.* **-ties.** **—complex fraction** a fraction with a fraction in its numerator or denominator or both, as 1½/4 or 2/3¼. **—com·plex·ion** (cum·PLEK·shun) *n.* **1** the natural color and texture of the skin, esp. of the face: *a pale ~.* **2** character; appearance: *The new weapon has altered the ~ of modern warfare.* **—com·plex·ioned** *adj.: a dark-~ed man.* **—complex number** a number of the pattern $3+5\sqrt{-1}$.

com·pli·ant (cum·PLY·unt) *adj.* tending to comply, give in, or yield. **—com·pli·ant·ly** *adv.* **—com·pli·ance** or **com·pli·an·cy** *n.;* **in compliance with:** *a delivery made in ~ with a customer's wish.*

com·pli·cate (COM·pli–) *v.* **-cates, -cat·ed, -cat·ing** make complex, involved, or difficult. **—com·pli·cat·ed** *adj.* hard to analyze, solve, or understand: *a ~ math problem.* **—com·pli·ca·tion** (–CAY–) *n.*

com·plic·i·ty (cum·PLIS–) *n.* association in guilt: *suspected of ~ in the plot.*

com·pli·ment (COM·pli–) *n.* **1** an expression of praise, admiration, or politeness. **2 compliments** *pl.* usu. formal greetings; regards: *He paid his ~s to the guest of honor; My ~s to the chef.* **—v.** pay a compliment to: *He was ~ed on his new job.* **—com·pli·men·ta·ry** (–MEN–) *adj.* **1** expressing a compliment: *a ~ remark.* **2** gratis: *a ~ copy of a new book.*

com·ply (cum–) *v.* **-plies, -plied, -ply·ing** act in accordance (with); yield: *to ~ with a kidnapper's demands.*

com·po·nent (cum·POH–) *n.* an element in a complex object or group: *He added new ~s to his stereo system.* **—adj.:** *Hydrogen and oxygen are ~ elements in water.*

com·port (cum–) *v.* **1** behave: *He ~ed himself well;* **com·port·ment** *n.* **2** *Formal.* be in agreement with or suitable to: *Low manners do not ~ with high ideals.*

com·pose (cum–) *v.* **-pos·es, -posed, -pos·ing** **1** make up or constitute, as out of parts or elements: *Air is mainly ~d of oxygen and nitrogen.* **2** create, esp. a work of music or literature: *~ing a symphony;* **com·pos·er** *n.* **3** set (type), as a compositor. **4** settle (a quarrel, differences, etc.); also, calm, gain control of (one's feelings, thoughts, or features); **com·posed** *adj.* in control of oneself: *Throughout the argument she remained ~;* **com·pos·ed·ly** *adv.;* **com·po·sure** (–zhur) *n.* **—com·pos·ite** (cum·POZ·it) *adj.* **1** made up of distinct separate parts. **2** of or pertaining to the *Compositae,* a large family of plants having compound flower heads, as the daisy, chrysanthemum, and dandelion: *a ~ flower.* **—n.** something composite: *His character was a ~ of instinct and education.* **—com·po·si·tion** (–puh·ZISH·un) *n.* **1** the act, art or result of composing: *an English ~; ~ by linotype.* **2** the arrangement of parts or elements; hence, constitution; makeup: *a photographer's sense of ~.* **—com·pos·i·tor** (–POZ–) *n.* a typesetter. **—com·post** (COM–) *n.* a combination of decayed plant matter, garbage, and manure, used as a fertilizer: *a ~ heap.* **—com·pote** *n.* **1** fruit stewed or preserved in syrup. **2** a shallow, stemmed serving dish.

[1]**com·pound** *n.* the area enclosing a group of buildings, as of a factory, prison, or residences.

[2]**com·pound** *n.* something made by the union of two or more parts or elements, esp. a word such as "spaceship," or a chemical substance, as common salt or water; also ***adj.*** **—v.** (cum·POUND) **1** mix together or produce by combining: *A pharmacist ~s drugs as prescribed.* **2** calculate (compound interest): *interest ~ed quarterly.* **3** make greater: *The "solution" only ~ed our problems.* **—compound eye** one made up of many simple, visually functioning eyes, as in insects and some crustaceans. **—compound fracture** a broken bone causing an open wound in the skin. **—compound interest** interest charged on the principal of the debt and the accumulated interest. **—compound sentence** one made up of independent clauses.

com·pre·hend (com·pri·HEND) *v.* **1** grasp mentally; understand: *Do you ~ the endlessness of time?* **com·pre·hen·sion** (–HEN–) *n.;* **com·pre·hen·si·ble** *adj.;* **com·pre·hen·si·bly** *adv.;* **com·pre·hen·si·bil·i·ty** (–BIL–) *n.* **2** include; take in as part of a whole; **com·pre·hen·sive** *adj.: ~ examinations; ~ insurance coverage;* **com·pre·hen·sive·ly** *adv.;* **com·pre·hen·sive·ness** *n.*

com·press (cum·PRES) *v.* **-press·es, -pressed, -press·ing** pack or squeeze into a smaller space; condense. **—n.** (COM·pres) a pad of gauze or cloth used to apply moisture, heat, cold, or pressure to the body, as to stop bleeding or relieve pain. —**com•pressed** (cum·PREST) *adj.:* ~ *air* (i.e. under more than atmospheric pressure). —**com•pres•sion** (cum·PRESH–) *n.: the extreme* ~ *of his style; the* ~ *chamber of an auto engine;* **com•press•i•ble** (–PRES–) *adj.;* **com•press•i•bil•i•ty** (–BIL–) *n.;* **com•press•ive** (–PRESS–) *adj.;* **com•press•or** (–PRES·ur) *n.* a machine for compressing, usu. air or another gas.

com•prise (cum·PRIZE) *v.* **-pris•es, -prised, -pris•ing** **1** contain; be composed of: *a team* ~*ing 18 players.* **2** *Informal.* make up; constitute: *18 players* ~ *the team.*

com•pro•mise (COM·pruh·mize) *n.* **1** the settlement of a difference or disagreement by concessions on both sides. **2** something between extremes. —***v.*** **-mis•es, -mised, -mis•ing** **1** settle by or make a compromise. **2** damage or risk someone's good name: *Dick and Jane were caught in a* ~*ing situation.*

comp•trol•ler (cun·TROH–) same as CONTROLLER.

com•pul•sion (cum·PUL–) *n.* **1** an act of compelling or the state of being compelled: *He only obeyed under* ~. **2** an obsessive urge. —**com•pul•sive** (–siv) *adj.: a* ~ *smoker;* **com•pul•sive•ly** *adv.;* **com•pul•sive•ness** *n.* —**com•pul•so•ry** (–suh·ree) *adj.* **1** exerting compulsion: ~ *measures.* **2** required or forced esp. by law or regulation: ~ *school attendance.*

com•punc•tion (cum·PUNK–) *n.* a feeling of guilt, regret, or remorse: *He had no* ~*s about cheating on his income tax.*

com•pute (cum·PYOOT) *v.* **-putes, -put•ed, -put•ing** calculate mathematically or with a computer; **com•put•a•ble** *adj.* —**com•pu•ta•tion** (com·pyoo·TAY–) *n.* —**com•put•er** (cum·PYOOT·ur) *n.* an electronic machine that stores, manipulates, and analyzes information and performs mathematical calculations. —**com•put•er•ize** *v.* **-iz•es, -ized, -iz•ing:** ~*d traffic signals;* **com•put•er•iz•a•ble** *adj.;* **com•put•er•i•za•tion** (–ZAY–) *n.*

comr. commissioner.

com•rade (COM·rad) *n.* **1** a close friend; associate: ~ *in arms* (fellow soldier). **2 Comrade** a member of a left-wing group, esp. a communist. —**com•rade•ly** *adj.* —**com•rade•ship** *n.*

COM•SAT (COM·sat) Communications Satellite Corporation.

con *adv.* against; in opposition; ***n.*** **1** a vote, person, argument, etc., against something: *the pros and* ~*s of capital punishment.* **2** *Slang.* a convict. —***v.*** **cons, conned, con•ning** **1** study or peruse carefully; learn by heart: ~*ing his lessons.* **2** *Slang.* swindle; cheat; ***adj.:*** *a* ~ *artist; a* ~ *game.* —**con-** same as COM-. —**con.** consort; concerto; consul.

Con•a•kry (CON·uh·kree) capital of the Republic of Guinea.

con bri•o (–BREE·oh) *adv. Music.* with vigor or liveliness.

conc. concentrate.

con•cat•e•na•tion (–uh·NAY–) *n.* a connected group of events or things: *a* ~ *of misfortunes.* —**con•cat•e•nate** (–CAT·uh–) *adj.*

con•cave (–CAVE) *adj.* curved inward like the inside surface of a ball. —**con•cav•i•ty** (–CAV–) *n.* **-ties.**

con•ceal (cun·SEEL) *v.* keep secret or out of sight; hide: *The guerrilla leader always carried a* ~*ed weapon.* —**con•ceal•ment** *n.*

con•cede (cun·SEED) *v.* **-cedes, -ced•ed, -ced•ing** **1** admit (as true or valid); acknowledge: *I* ~ *your point.* **2** grant; yield; give up: *They* ~*d the game after 5 innings.*

con•ceit (cun·SEET) *n.* **1** a too high estimation of one's own worth: *a pompous chap, full of* ~*;* **con•ceit•ed** *adj.* **2** a contrived, whimsical metaphor or notion, as calling laburnums "dropping-wells of fire." —**con•ceive** (cun·SEEV) *v.* **-ceives, -ceived, -ceiv•ing** **1** become pregnant with (a child); become pregnant. **2** understand; imagine; form an idea or notion: *Who could* ~ *of such a thing? They have* ~*d a great dislike for him;* **con•ceiv•a•ble** (–uh·bl) *adj.;* **con•ceiv•a•bly** (–uh·blee) *adv.;* **con•ceiv•a•bil•i•ty** (–BIL–) *n.*

con•cel•e•brant (–SEL·uh·brunt) *n.* one of two or more priests who concelebrate; **con•cel•e•brate** *v.* **-brates, -brat•ed, -brat•ing** celebrate Communion or a mass jointly. —**con•cel•e•bra•tion** (–BRAY–) *n.*

con•cen•trate *v.* **-trates, -trat•ed, -trat•ing** **1** focus or fix one's attentions, efforts, etc. *(on):* ~ *on the task in hand.* **2** bring or come close together; focus. **3** make (a solution) stronger: ~*d milk* (with water removed); ***n.:*** *dilute the* ~ *to make soup; Vitamin C* ~. —**con•cen•tra•tion** (–TRAY–) *n.: troop* ~*s along a hostile border;* **concentration camp** a prison camp for prisoners of war, political prisoners, and other internees. —**con•cen•tric** (–SEN–) *adj.* having a common center or axis: ~ *annual rings in a tree trunk; a target's* ~ *circles.* —**con•cen•tric•al•ly** *adv.* —**con•cen•tric•i•ty** (–TRIS–) *n.*

con•cept (–sept) *n.* a usu. general idea or notion of a class or thing: *the* ~ *of the atom.* —**con•cep•tion** (–SEP–) *n.* **1** the act or process of conceiving: *the* ~ *of a child;* ~ *of new ideas.* **2** concept; idea: *You've no* ~ *of what I'm talking about.* —**con•cep•tu•al** (–SEP·choo·ul) *adj.;* **con•cep•tu•al•ly** *adv.: two* ~ *distinct notions;* **con•cep•tu•al•ize** *v.* **-iz•es, -ized, -iz•ing:** *It is hard to* ~ *the infinity of space.*

con•cern (cun·SURN) *v.* **1** relate to; be of importance to; hence, cause worry or anxiety to: *a recommendation addressed "To whom it may* ~*"; a mother* ~*ed about her child's safety; That does not* ~ *you!* **2** engage or busy *(with);* involve *(with): They* ~ *themselves with politics.* —***n.*** **1** something which involves or concerns: *It's your* ~*, not mine.* **2** regard; anxiety: *Her illness is a cause of deep* ~. **3** a business firm: *a big mining*

~. —**con·cerned** *adj.* involved; anxious: *a ~ citizen; a parent ~ for her child.* —**con·cern·ing** *prep.* about; with regard to. —**con·cern·ment** *n.*

con·cert *n.* **1** a program of public musical entertainment. **2** unity in action, opinion, etc.: *working* **in concert** *with others; the ~ of Europe against Napoleonic France;* **con·cert·ed** (cun·SUR·tid) *adj.* mutually planned or accomplished; combined: *made ~ efforts to topple the government;* **con·cert·ed·ly** *adv.* —**con·cer·ti·na** (–sir·TEE·nuh) *n.* a small, accordionlike musical instrument. —**con·cert·mas·ter** *n.* the first violinist and usu. assistant conductor of an orchestra. —**con·cer·to** (cun·CHER·toh) *n.* **-tos** or **-ti** (–tee) a piece of music for one or more solo instruments and orchestra: *a piano ~.*

con·ces·sion (cun·SESH·un) *n.* **1** the act of conceding; also, the thing conceded: *a ~ to public demand.* **2** a piece of land or a privilege granted, to a **con·ces·sion·naire** (–NAIR), by a government or business, esp. to operate an industry or other business: *a mining ~; a food ~ at a fair.* —**con·ces·sive** (cun·SES·iv) *adj.* pertaining to a concession: *"Although he left" is a ~ clause.*

conch (CONK, CONCH) *n.* **conchs** (CONKS) or **conch·es** (CON·chiz) any of several large sea mollusks; also, their spiral shell.

con·ci·erge (–si·AIRZH) *n.* the doorkeeper and usu. custodian of a building, esp. an apartment building.

con·cil·i·ate (–SIL·ee–) *v.* **-ates, -at·ed, -at·ing** win the goodwill of; placate; **con·cil·i·a·tor** *n.;* **con·cil·i·a·to·ry** *adj.* —**con·cil·i·a·tion** (–AY–) *n.* the act or state of conciliating, esp. the settlement of a dispute by compromise with the help of a third party.

con·cise (–SICE) *adj.* brief but expressing much; terse: *a ~ style; a ~ report.* —**con·cise·ly** *adv.* —**con·cise·ness** or **con·ci·sion** (–SIZH·un) *n.*

con·clave *n.* a private or secret assembly, esp. of cardinals to elect a new pope.

con·clude (cun·CLOOD) *v.* **-cludes, -clud·ed, -clud·ing** **1** end; finish: *~ a meeting; The fair ~d on Friday.* **2** resolve; also, decide on the basis of inference. **3** agree on; settle: *~ a business deal.* —**con·clu·sion** (–CLOO·zhun) *n.: came to the ~ that . . . ; a foregone ~* (that is predetermined or inevitable). —**con·clu·sive** (—CLOO·siv) *adj.* decisive; final: *~ proof;* **con·clu·sive·ly** *adv.*

con·coct (cun–) *v.* prepare (usu. a food or drink) by mixing; hence, invent: *a ~ed excuse;* **con·coc·tion** *n.: a new banana-strawberry ~.*

con·com·i·tant (–COM·i·tunt) *adj.* happening along with something else; accompanying: *circumstances ~ with an event.* —***n.:*** *Disease is a ~ of poverty.*

con·cord (CON–) *n.* harmony or agreement, as in music, grammar (i.e. of case, number, gender, or person), or between people: *an era of peace and ~ between England and France.* —**Concord** a town in Massachusetts, the site of Revolutionary War battles; **Concord** (CONK·urd) **grape** a dark-blue, sweet grape. —**con·cor·dant** (cun·COR·dunt) *adj. agreeing: ~ musical notes; actions ~ with principles.* —**con·cor·dance** (–COR·dunce) *n.* **1** the state of being concordant. **2** an alphabetical list of a book's important words given with their contexts: *a Bible ~.* —**con·cor·dat** (–COR–) *n.* an official agreement, esp. one between a pope and a state.

con·course (CON–) *n.* **1** a coming together; hence, a great crowd. **2** a large space milling with people, as the main hall of a railroad terminal or a broad thoroughfare.

con·cres·cence (–CRES·unce) *n.* a growing together, as of cells or flower petals. —**con·crete** *adj.* **1** existing in real experience of the senses, not abstract; also, specific, not general; definite: *~ plans for development; ~ facts.* **2** made of **concrete** *n.* a hard, conglomerate building material made of sand, small stones, and cement: *~ building blocks; a ~ road surface.* —***v.*** **-cretes, -cret·ed, -cret·ing** **1** (*also* –CREET) form or harden into a solid mass. **2** pave or coat with concrete: *~d sidewalks.* —**con·cre·tion** (–CREE–) *n.* a hardening or solidifying; also, something solidified, as minerals in rock or stones in the kidney.

con·cu·bine (–kyuh–) *n.* a wife of secondary status in polygamous societies; hence, any woman cohabiting with a man who is not her husband. —**con·cu·bi·nage** (–KEW·buh·nij) *n.*

con·cu·pis·cence (–KYOO·pi·sunce) *n.* a strong, usu. sensual desire; esp., lust; **con·cu·pis·cent** *adj.*

con·cur (–CUR) *v.* **-curs, -curred, -cur·ring** act or happen together; also, agree: *I ~ with your judgment.* —**con·cur·rent** *adj.* **1** concurring; taking place at the same time: *~ three-year sentences.* **2** parallel; also, tending to meet: *~ lines.* —**con·cur·rent·ly** *adv.* —**con·cur·rence** *n.* —**concurrent resolution** one passed by both houses of a legislature.

con·cus·sion (–KUSH·un) *n.* a severe shock; hence, injury to the brain by a blow or a jarring shock.

con·demn (–DEM) *v.* **1** utter strong criticism of; declare guilty; also, sentence or doom (*to* prison, execution, or any unpleasant fate): *atrocities ~ed by humanity.* **2** judge or declare unfit for use: *the old wooden bridge was ~ed.* **3** *U.S.* appropriate for public use: *farmland ~ed to make a park.* —**con·dem·na·tion** (–NAY–) *n.* —**con·dem·na·to·ry** (–DEM·nuh·tor·ee) *adj.*

con·dense (–DENCE) *v.* **-dens·es, -densed, -dens·ing** **1** make or become more dense or concentrated: *Dew is ~d water vapor; ~ light rays with a lens.* **2** express in fewer words: *a*

~d book. —**con·den·sa·ble** *adj.* —**con·den·sa·tion** (–SAY–) *n.* —**condensed milk** evaporated and sweetened milk. —**con·dens·er** *n.* **1** same as CAPACITOR. **2** any device for condensing, esp. light rays or vapors.

con·de·scend (–di·SEND) *v.* perform actions beneath one's dignity; esp., act patronizingly (to): *"His Lordship" ~ed to smile at me! his* **condescending** *manner.* —**con·de·scen·sion** *n.* —**con·de·scend·ing·ly** *adv.*

con·dign (cun·DINE) *adj.* merited, though harsh: *~ punishment.*

con·di·ment *n.* a food seasoning, as relish, mustard, or spices.

con·di·tion (cun·DISH·un) *n.* **1** what something else depends on: *allowed to go* **on condition that** *she return by noon;* **con·di·tion·al** *adj.: "If" and "unless" start ~ clauses;* **con·di·tion·al·ly** adv.: *an offer made ~, i.e. if I sell my house.* **2** a state of being, fitness, or health: *a motor in excellent ~.* **3** a disease: *a skin ~ such as acne.* **4** conditions circumstances: *dangerous working ~s.* **5** position in society: *people of all ranks and ~s.* —***v.*** **1** control; make conditional: *a life ~ed by his father's whims.* **2** put into good condition; **con·di·tion·er** *n.: an air ~; a ~ for your hair.* **3** train, esp. to give a **conditioned response,** an automatic reaction to an artificial stimulus, as a dog's salivation upon hearing a bell; also, accustom *(to).* —**in** (or **out of**) **condition** physically fit (or unfit).

con·do (–doh) *n.* **-dos** *Informal.* condominium (*n.* 2).

con·dole (cun–) *v.* **-doles, -doled, -dol·ing** feel or express sympathy *(with).* —**con·do·lence** (–DOH–) *n.: my ~s to the widow.*

con·dom (–dum) *n.* a thin rubber sheath for the penis in sexual intercourse, used to prevent venereal disease or conception.

con·do·min·i·um (–duh·MIN·ee·um) *n.* **1** a territory controlled by two or more states: *the former Anglo-Egyptian ~ in the Sudan.* **2** a residential building or complex in which single units are owned individually and the common property is jointly owned; hence, a unit in this.

con·done (cun·DOHN) *v.* **-dones, -doned, -don·ing** overlook or implicitly forgive (misbehavior): *She ~d his drunkenness but not his infidelity.* —**con·do·na·tion** (–duh·NAY–) *n.*

con·dor (–dur) *n.* a large vulture of the Andes Mountains; also, a similar, nearly extinct vulture of S. California.

con·duce (cun–) *v.* **-duc·es, -duced, -duc·ing** tend to lead (to); contribute (to); **con·du·cive** (–siv) *adj.: an atmosphere ~ to study.* —**con·duct** *n.* (CON–) **1** behavior; deportment: *early parole for good ~.* **2** management; handling: *the ~ of foreign affairs.* —***v.*** (cun·DUCT) **1** lead; guide; also, manage or handle; direct (esp. an orchestra): *A guide ~s a tour; ~ing the financial affairs of a corporation.* **2** behave: *~ yourself like a lady.* **3** transmit, esp. heat or electricity; hence **con·duc·tion** *n.;* **con·duc·tive** (–tiv) *adj.;* **con·duc·tiv·i·ty** (–TIV–) *n.* —**con·duc·tance** (–DUC·tunce) *n.* the ability of something to conduct electricity. —**con·duc·tor** (–tur) *n.* **1** the leader or director of an orchestra; also, the person in charge of a bus, passenger train, etc. **2** something that conducts electricity or heat, as copper or water.

con·duit (–dit, –doo·it) *n.* a pipe, channel, or tubing for carrying liquids, enclosing electric wires, etc.

con·dyle (–dile) *n.* a rounded projection at the end of a bone which forms part of a joint. —**con·dy·lar** (–duh·lur) *adj.*

cone *n.* **1** a three-dimensional surface or solid with a usu. circular base, tapering to a point. **2** anything in this shape, as an ice-cream cone, the cone of a volcano, the dry, scaly, rounded fruit of trees of the pine family, and color-sensitive cells on the retina.

Con·es·to·ga (wagon) (–uh·STOH·guh) a sturdy covered wagon used esp. by prairie pioneers.

co·ney (COH·nee) *n.* **-neys** or **-nies** same as CONY. —**Coney** (COH·nee) **Island** a seaside resort and amusement park in Brooklyn, N.Y.

conf. conference.

con·fab·u·late (cun·FAB·yuh–) *v.* **-lates, -lat·ed, -lat·ing** talk together informally; confer; chat; **con·fab·u·la·tion** (–LAY–) n. —**con·fab** *v.* **-fabs, -fabbed, -fab·bing** *Informal.* confabulate; ***n.*** confabulation.

con·fec·tion (cun·FEC–) *n.* a delicacy; a sweet treat, as candy, comfit, or ice cream. —**con·fec·tion·er·y** *n.* **-er·ies** **1** confections collectively. **2** the shop of a **con·fec·tion·er,** one who makes or sells confections.

confed. confederation; **Confed.** Confederate. —**con·fed·er·ate** (cun·FED–) *v.* **-ates, -at·ed, -at·ing** join or form into an alliance of people, organizations, states, etc. —***n.*** (–uh·rit) an ally; associate; ***adj.:*** *~ government.* —**Confederate** *n.* & *adj.* a supporter of or pertaining to the **Confederate States of America** (also called **the Confederacy**), the league of 11 southern states that seceded in 1860 and 1861: *a ~ dollar; the ~ army.* —**con·fed·er·a·tion** (–RAY–) *n.* **1** the act of confederating. **2** an alliance or union, usu. of states or countries; also **con·fed·er·a·cy** (–FED–), **-cies.** —**Confederation** **1** the 13 original United States, 1781 to 1789. **2** the federal union of the Canadian provinces.

con·fer (cun·FUR) *v.* **-fers, -ferred, -fer·ring** **1** consult *(with);* exchange views. **2** grant; bestow: *~ an honorary degree on the president.* —**con·fer·ment** *n.* —**con·fer·ee** (con·fuh·REE) *n.* one on whom something is conferred; also, one taking part in a conference. —**con·fer·ence** (CON·fuh·runce) *n.* **1** a conferring: *have a ~ with her son's teacher.* **2** a formal meeting for discussion and debate: *the U.N. ~ on crime.* **3** a league of sports teams, schools, etc.

con·fess (cun·FES) *v.* **1** acknowledge or admit, usu. a crime or fault; esp., tell one's sins to a priest: *~ (to) a murder; ~ to (having) suspicions about him.* **2** of a priest, hear and absolve someone's sins. **—con·fes·sed·ly** *adv.* **—con·fes·sion** (–FESH·un) *n.* **1** the act or result of confessing, esp. a written statement *(a prisoner forced to sign a ~)* or the telling of one's sins. **2** a declaration of religious beliefs; hence, a Christian denomination. **—con·fes·sion·al** *n.* an enclosure for private confession. **—con·fes·sor** (–FES·ur) *n.* one who confesses; also, a priest who hears confessions.

con·fet·ti (cun·FET·ee) *n.pl.* [takes *sing. v.*] little pieces of colored paper thrown at weddings and other celebrations.

con·fi·dant *n.* a friend trusted with personal secrets; *fem.* **con·fi·dante** (–DANT, –dant). **—con·fide** (cun–) *v.* **-fides, -fid·ed, -fid·ing** **1** tell or give to another in secrecy or trust: *It is unwise to ~ state secrets to anyone; ~ children to a neighbor's care.* **2** trust *(in): ~ in the Lord.* **—con·fi·dence** (CON–) *n.* **1** trust; reliance: *I put no ~ in his promises.* **2** a feeling of assurance in oneself: *facing the future with ~.* **3** a trusting secrecy: *This news was told in strictest ~; She took her brother into her ~.* **4** a secret: *Never betray a ~.* ***—adj.*** exploiting someone's trust in order to swindle; hence **confidence game; confidence man. —con·fi·dent** *adj. sure of oneself; certain: a ~ and self-assertive salesman; an accused man ~ of the outcome of a trial;* **con·fi·dent·ly** *adv.* **—con·fi·den·tial** (–DEN·shul) *adj.* **1** secret or secretive: *~ information.* **2** trusted with private affairs: *a ~ servant;* **con·fi·den·tial·ly** *adv.* **—con·fi·den·ti·al·i·ty** (–shee·AL–) *n.*

con·fig·u·ra·tion (cun·fig·yuh·RAY–) *n.* an arrangement of parts; structure; outline or shape: *the ~ of a constellation; a personality ~; the ~ of the ocean floor.*

con·fine (cun–) *v.* **-fines, -fined, -fin·ing** keep within limits or barriers; restrict; shut in: *His social life was ~d to weekends; a soldier ~d to quarters.* **—con·fine·ment** (–FINE–) *n.* a being confined, esp. in bed to give birth: *She had a long ~.* **—con·fin·er** *n.* **—con·fines** (CON–) *n.pl.* limits: *within the ~ of your home.*

con·firm (cun–) *v.* **1** strengthen; esp. show the truth of: *Adversity only ~s his determination; a rumor ~ed by later reports.* **2** make more certain, binding, or definite; esp. to admit as a full member of a congregation: *~ airline reservations; His appointment was ~ed by Senate; His son was ~ed at 13.* **—con·firm·a·to·ry** (cun·FIRM·uh–) *adj.* **—con·fir·ma·tion** (–MAY–) *n.* **—con·firmed** (cun–) *adj.* inveterate: *a ~ alcoholic.*

con·fis·cate (CON–) *v.* **-cates, -cat·ed, -cat·ing** seize (property) by public authority: *The heroin was ~d by the police;* **con·fis·ca·tor** *n.* **—con·fis·ca·tion** (–CAY–) *n.* **—con·fis·ca·to·ry** (–FIS·cuh–) *adj.*

con·fla·gra·tion (–fluh·GRAY–) *n.* a big fire, esp. one very destructive.

con·flict *n.* (CON–) a fight; struggle; also, a clash of opposing forces, viewpoints, etc.: *His story of the accident is in ~ with yours.* ***—v.*** (cun·FLICT): *a man torn by ~ing desires.* **—conflict of interest** a clash between an official's public duty and his private interest.

con·flu·ence (–floo·unce) *n.* a flowing together (as of two rivers); also, a coming together (as of a crowd); also **con·flux. —con·flu·ent** *adj.: ~ streams.*

con·form (cun·FORM) *v.* **1** correspond to or be like (a pattern): *a building that ~s to specifications.* **2** comply with (a law, rules, or customs); be obedient: *She would not ~ to school dress regulations.* **—con·form·er** *n.* **—con·form·ism** *n.* **—con·form·ist** *n.* **—con·form·a·ble** *adj. agreeable: Her demands were ~ to reason.* **—con·for·ma·tion** (–fur·MAY–) *n.* formation or structure. **—con·form·i·ty** (–FORM–) *n.* agreement: *acting in ~ with his wishes;* also **con·for·mance.**

con·found (cun–) *v.* **1** perplex. **2** defeat; refute: *an attempt to ~ the critics.* **3** mix up: *"confusion worse ~ed"; We had ~ed fact and fancy.* **—con·found·ed** *adj.* [euphemism for] damned: *You ~ idiot!*

con·fra·ter·ni·ty (–fruh·TUR–) *n.* **-ties** **1** a brotherhood or association of colleagues, or **con·freres** (CON·frairz), *sing.* **-frere** (–frair). **2** a religious or charitable group.

con·front (cun·FRUNT) *v.* **1** come face to face with; meet and challenge: *two armies ~ing each other.* **2** bring into direct contact *(with): He was ~ed with the facts.* **—con·fron·ta·tion** (–frun·TAY–) *n.: the civil rights ~s of the 1960's.*

Con·fu·cian·ism (cun·FYOO·shun–) *n.* the system of ethics of **Con·fu·cius,** c. 551–479 B.C., Chinese moral philosopher. **—Con·fu·cian** *adj.* & *n.: ~ teachings; a dedicated ~.*

con·fuse (cun–) *v.* **-fus·es, -fused, -fus·ing** **1** bewilder; perplex. **2** fail to distinguish; blur the distinction between: *I always ~ Peter and his twin brother; Don't ~ the issues!* **—con·fus·ed·ly** *adv.* **—con·fus·ing·ly** *adv.* **—con·fu·sion** *n.* **1:** *the ~ of tongues at the tower of Babel.* **2** disorder; bewilderment: *carefully laid plans suddenly* **thrown into confusion.**

con·fute (cun–) *v.* **-futes, -fut·ed, -fut·ing** prove (a person, statement, etc.) wrong. **—con·fu·ta·tion** (–few·TAY–) *n.*

Cong. Congress; Congressional.

con·ga (CONG·guh) *n.* **1** an Afro-Cuban dance performed by several dancers moving in single file. **2** a tall, thin, hand-beaten drum.

con·geal (cun·JEEL) *v.* thicken or solidify, as by freezing: *~ed blood.* **—con·geal·ment** *n.* **—con·ge·la·tion** (–juh·LAY–) *n.*

con·ge·ner (CON·juh–) *n.* a person or thing of the same class or genus, as butter and margarine, lion and other cats, etc. **—con·gen·ial** (cun·JEEN·yul) *adj.* of similar tastes and character; hence agreeable; pleasant: *~ friends; ~ work;* **con·gen·ial·ly** *adv.;* **con·ge·ni·al·i·ty** (–AL–) *n.* **—con·gen·i·tal** (cun·JEN·i·tl) *adj.* from birth: *~ brain damage; a ~ thief;* **con·gen·i·tal·ly** *adv.*

con·ger (eel) (CONG·gur) a marine eel with coarse edible flesh.

con·ge·ries (CON·juh·reez) *n. sing. & pl.* a collection; pile: *an ill-assorted ~ of buildings.*

con·gest (cun·JEST) *v.* clog; be or make too full, esp. (parts of the body) with blood. **—con·ges·tive** (–tiv) *adj.* **—con·ges·tion** (–chun) *n.: nasal ~; traffic ~ during rush hours.*

con·glom·er·ate (cun·GLOM–) *v.* **-ates, -at·ed, -at·ing** form into a usu. round mass. **—*adj.*** (–uh·rit) cemented together from diverse elements: *a ~ rock;* ***n.*** **1** mixture: *New York is a ~ of ethnic cultures.* **2** a corporation with widely diversified enterprises and interests. **—con·glom·er·a·tion** (–RAY–) *n.*

Con·go (CONG·goh) a C. African river. **—People's Republic of the Congo** a republic in W.C. Africa; 132,047 sq. mi. (342,000 km²); *cap.* Brazzaville; formerly **Congo (Brazzaville). —Democratic Republic of the Congo** former name of ZAIRE. **—Con·go·lese** *adj.* & *n.*

con·grat·u·late (cun·GRACH·uh–) *v.* **-lates, -lat·ed, -lat·ing** express pleasure at another's success or good luck. **—con·grat·u·la·tion** (–LAY–) *n.: ~s on your promotion!* **—con·grat·u·la·to·ry** (–GRACH–) *adj.*

con·gre·gate (CONG·gruh–) *v.* **-gates, -gat·ed, -gat·ing** gather together. **—con·gre·ga·tion** (–GAY–) *n.* **1** a gathering. **2** people attending a place of worship, esp. those present at a service; **con·gre·ga·tion·al** *adj.* **—Con·gre·ga·tion·al** *adj.* pertaining to the union of Protestant churches that practice **Con·gre·ga·tion·al·ism,** the self-government of local congregations; **Con·gre·ga·tion·al·ist** *n.*

con·gress (CONG·grus) *n.* **1** a meeting; conference. **2** a national legislature. **3** **Congress** the Senate and the House of Representatives of the U.S.; a member of the House is a **con·gress·man, -men** or **con·gress·wom·an, -wom·en.** **—Con·gres·sion·al** (–GRESH·uh·nl) *adj.: a Congressional hearing;* **Congressional district** (each electing a representative); **Congressional Record** (i.e. official report of proceedings). **—con·gres·sion·al·ly** *adv.*

con·gru·ent (CONG·groo·unt, cong·GROO–) *adj.* corresponding; coincident: *~ triangles;* **con·gru·ent·ly** *adv.* **—con·gru·ence** or **con·gru·en·cy** *n.* **—con·gru·ous** (CONG·groo·us) *adj.* congruent; appropriate; coherent; **con·gru·ous·ly** *adv.* **—con·gru·i·ty** (cong·GROO–) *n.*

con·i·cal (CON·i·cl) or **con·ic** *adj.* shaped like or pertaining to a cone: *a conical cap; The parabola and ellipse are* **conic sections; coni·c(al) projection** a map with radiating meridians and concentric parallels. **—con·i·fer** (CON·i·fur) *n.* a cone-bearing, usu. evergreen tree or bush, as larch, hemlock, pine, spruce, and fir; **co·ni·fer·ous** (cuh·NIF·uh·rus) *adj.: ~ trees make ~ forests.*

conj. conjugation; conjunction.

con·jec·ture (cun·JEK·chur) *v.* **-tures, -tured, -tur·ing** speculate; guess. **—*n.:*** *a report based on mere ~.* **—con·jec·tur·al** (–chuh·rul) *adj.* **—con·jec·tur·al·ly** *adv.*

con·join (cun–) *v.* join together. **—con·join·er** *n.* **—con·joint** *adj.* **—con·joint·ly** *adv.: citizens acting ~ with the police.* **—con·ju·gal** (CON·juh·gul) *adj.* of or having to do with marriage: *a spouse's ~ rights to sex; ~ bliss of honeymooners.* **—con·ju·gal·ly** *adv.* **—con·ju·gate** (–juh–) *v.* **-gates, -gat·ed, -gat·ing** **1** give the inflected forms of (a verb, as *conjugates,* etc. above). **2** join together. **—*adj.*** (–git) joined together, esp. paired. **—con·ju·ga·tion** (–GAY–) *n.: "Take–took–taken" is a* **strong conjugation;** *"kill," "move," "add," etc. belong to* **weak conjugations.** **—con·ju·ga·tion·al** *adj.* **—con·junct** (cun–) *adj.* joined; associated. **—con·junc·tion** *n.* **1** a joining together, association, or union: *Heat exists in ~ with fire.* **2** a word that connects other words or groups of words, as *but, and, or.* **—con·junc·ti·va** (–TYE·vuh) *n.* **-vas** or **-vae** (–vee) the mucous membrane that covers the eyeball and lines the inside of the eyelids. **—con·junc·tive** (–JUNK·tiv) *adj.* **1** conjoining; also, conjoined. **2** serving as a conjunction: *"But" is a ~ word;* ***n.:*** *"And," "also," "moreover," etc. are ~s.* **—con·junc·ti·vi·tis** (cun·junc·ti·VYE·tis) *n.* the inflammation of the conjunctiva. **—con·junc·ture** (cun·JUNK·chur) *n.* a union of circumstances, esp. a critical situation.

con·jure *v.* **-jures, -jured, -jur·ing** **1** (cun·JOOR) *Formal.* appeal to, esp. by an oath. **2** (CON·jur) summon (spirits, the devil, etc.) by a spell or magic; hence, perform magic; **conjure up** call or bring to mind; contrive: *The music ~d up visions of the Orient.*

conk *v.* hit over the head. **—conk out** *Informal.* stop functioning; collapse with fatigue or lose consciousness: *Our motor ~ed out; Father just ~ed out after a hard day.*

Conn. Connecticut.

con·nect (cuh·NECT) *v.* **1** link, join, be joined (to or with), etc.; esp., wire into an electric circuit; also, make a communications link; link mentally; **con·nect·ed** *adj.* joined, esp. by blood or marriage. **2** enable (passengers) to continue a journey: *Catch a ~ing flight out of Boston.* **3** *Sports.* make solid contact, usu. with a ball: *~ed for a line drive.* **—con·nect·ed·ly** *adv.* **—con·nec·tor** or **con·nect·er** *n.* **—con·nec·tion** *n.* **1:** *No ~ exists between hanging and the murder rate; a loose ~ in my toaster; Speak louder, we have a bad ~; I missed my ~ in Boston.* **2** a group or a person one is associated with, esp. a relative or an influential friend: *~s on her mother's side; He got his job through ~s.* **—in this** (or **that, what,** etc.) **connection** in relation to this (or that, what, etc.). **—con·nec·tive** (–tiv) *adj.* connecting: *~ tissue;* ***n.*** a word that connects, as a relative pronoun or conjunction.

Con·nect·i·cut (cuh·NET–) a state in northeastern U.S.; 5,009 sq.mi. (12,973 km²); *cap.* Hartford.

con·nip·tion (fit) (cuh·NIP–) *n. Informal.* a fit of violent rage, alarm, excitement, etc.; tantrum: *Grandma would have a ~ if she knew.*

con·nive (cuh·NIVE) *v.* **con·nives, con·nived, con·niv·ing** **1** intentionally ignore wrongdoing: *~ing at liquor violations.* **2** secretly cooperate or conspire: *~ing with underworld figures.* **—con·niv·ance** *n.* **—con·niv·er** *n.*

con·nois·seur (con·uh·SIR) *n.* a discriminating expert: *a ~ of French brandies.*

con·note (cuh·NOTE) *v.* **con·notes, con·not·ed, con·not·ing** of words, convey as a meaning secondary to the strict meaning or denotation. **—con·no·ta·tion** (con·uh·TAY–) *n.: the unpleasant ~s of "capitalist";* **con·no·ta·tion·al** *adj.* **—con·no·ta·tive** (CON·uh·tay·tiv) *adj.*

con·nu·bial (cuh·NEW·bee·ul) *adj.* of marriage; conjugal: *~ bliss.*

con·quer (CONG·cur) *v.* **1** defeat, esp. by fighting: *~ing his fears of the unknown.* **2** gain by usu. military victory: *~ed territories.* **—con·quer·or** *n.* **—con·quest** (CONG·kwest) *n.: the ~ of Mt. Everest; Mexico was a Spanish ~.* **—con·quis·ta·dor** (cong·KEE·stuh–) *n.* **-dors** or **-dor·es** a 16th-century Spanish conqueror in Central or South America.

Con·rail Consolidated Rail Corporation.

cons. consonant; constitution(al). **—Cons.** constable; consul.

con·san·guin·e·ous (–GWIN·ee·us) *adj.* related by blood; **con·san·guin·i·ty** *n.: the ~ of different Christian faiths.*

con·science (CON·shunce) *n.* an awareness of right and wrong, with a drive to avoid wrongdoing: *Billy stole an apple and had it* **on his conscience** *all week.* **—in (all) conscience** in truth; also, in fairness. **—con·sci·en·tious** (con·shee·EN·shus) *adj.* **1** ruled by or according to one's moral convictions: *A* **conscientious objector** *refuses to go to war.* **2** careful; meticulous: *a ~ workman.* Hence **con·sci·en·tious·ly** *adv.;* **con·sci·en·tious·ness** *n.* **—con·scious** (CON·shus) *adj.* **1** aware of or alert to: *~ of the risks involved.* **2** awake and mentally active: *~ after a long sleep.* **3** aware of oneself, one's thoughts, and one's actions: *a ~ artist.* **4** deliberate: *made a ~ effort to improve.* **—con·scious·ly** *adv.* **—con·scious·ness** *n.;* **con·scious·ness-rais·ing** *n.* the increasing of personal awareness as a means of greater self-fulfillment.

con·script (cun·SCRIPT) *v.* draft for military service. **—*n.*** (CON–) one conscripted; draftee; ***adj.*** drafted. **—con·scrip·tion** (–SCRIP–) *n.*

con·se·crate (CON·suh–) *v.* **-crates, -crat·ed, -crat·ing** make or set aside as sacred, hallowed, or for religious use; also, dedicate. **—con·se·cra·tion** (–CRAY–) *n.: the ~ of a new chapel.*

con·sec·u·tive (–SEK·yuh·tiv) *adj.* following in unbroken succession or logical order: *He missed three ~ days of school.* **—con·sec·u·tive·ly** *adv.*

con·sen·sus (–SEN–) *n.* the majority opinion; general agreement: *There is no ~ on capital punishment.* **—con·sent** (cun·SENT) *v.* agree *(to);* give approval *(to);* ***n.:*** *power legitimized by the ~ of the people; a plan adopted by common ~.* **—con·sent·er** *n.*

con·se·quence (CON·suh·kwence) *n.* **1** a result or effect: *His theft was discovered and* **in consequence** *he was fired;* **con·se·quent** *adj.: a major fire, with a ~ loss of life.* **2** importance: *a woman of some ~.* **—con·se·quent·ly** *adv.* **—con·se·quen·tial** (–KWEN·shul) *adj.* **1** resulting, esp. secondarily: *~ damages.* **2** of importance; hence, self-important: *a ~ manner.*

con·serve (cun·SURV) *v.* **-serves, -served, -serv·ing** **1** keep in sound or unchanged condition; preserve from waste or destruction. **2** preserve (fruits) by stewing with sugar; ***n.:*** *a jar of ~s.* **—con·ser·va·tion** (–VAY–) *n.* **1** the action of conserving: *the ~ of the patient's strength.* **2** the protection or careful and controlled use of natural resources, wildlife, etc.; also **con·ser·van·cy** (cun·SUR·vun·see). **—con·ser·va·tion·ist** (–VAY–) *n.* one who believes in protecting the natural environment. **—con·ser·va·tive** (cun·SUR·vuh·tiv) *adj.* **1** preservative. **2** conforming to moderate or traditional tastes, views, etc.: *a ~ investment portfolio; a ~ estimate; a ~ tie.* **3** given to **con·ser·va·tism,** a tendency to resist usu. social or political change; ***n.:*** *Churchill was a Conservative;* **con·ser·va·tive·ly** *adv.* **—con·ser·va·tor** (CON–) *n.* a protector or guardian, esp. for one legally incompetent. **—con·ser·va·to·ry** (–SUR–) *n.* **-ries** **1** a school of music, drama, etc. **2** a glass-covered building or room for growing plants and flowers.

con·sid·er (cun·SID·ur) *v.* think (about): *After much thought, he gave his* **considered opinion;** *It is a good job, all things ~ed; Try to ~ my point* *of view; I* ~ (i.e. regard) *it an honor; does well* **considering** (i.e. taking into account) *his age.* —**con·sid·er·a·ble** *adj.* important enough to consider; large; numerous; **con·sid·er·a·bly** *adv.* —**con·sid·er·ate** (–it) *adj.* thoughtful (of others): *a polite,* ~ *young man.* —**con·sid·er·a·tion** (–AY–) *n.* **1** thought: *They voted after lengthy* ~*; Cost was an important* ~ (i.e. something to be thought about) *in the purchase; Have some* ~ *for her feelings; His* ~*s on religion were too bold.* **2** a payment: *He will assign you a better seat, for a* ~.

con·sign (cun·SINE) *v.* **1** give over, esp. to someone's care; deliver: *an orphan* ~*ed to the state's custody;* ~ *papers to the fire.* **2** send (merchandise), esp to an agent for sale. —**con·sign·or** or **-sign·er** *n.;* **con·sign·ee** (cun·sye·NEE) *n.* —**con·sign·ment** *n.* a consigning; a shipment of goods; **on consignment** to be paid for as and when sold.

con·sist (cun·SIST) *v.* **1** be made up: *a team* ~*ing of 6 players.* **2** have as basis: *Loyalty* ~*s in devotion.* —**con·sis·ten·cy** *n.* **-cies** **1** degree of thickness or solidity: *mud of a gummy* ~. **2** agreement; conformity to previous actions, principles, etc.; **con·sis·tent** *adj.: a* ~ *policy throughout his career; a story not* ~ *with facts; a* ~ *loser;* **con·sis·tent·ly** *adv.* —**con·sis·to·ry** *n.* **-ries** a solemn council, as of a church.

consol. consolidated.

¹con·sole (cun·SOLE) *v.* **-soles, -soled, -sol·ing** comfort; lessen the unhappiness of; **con·so·la·to·ry** (–SOH·luh–) *adj.* —**con·so·la·tion** (con·suh·LAY–) *n.*

²con·sole (CON–) *n.* **1** a cabinet for a TV, radio, etc. that sits on the floor. **2** that part of an organ having the stops, keys, pedals, etc.; also, an electrical control panel, as of a washer.

con·sol·i·date (cun·SOL–) *v.* **-dates, -dat·ed, -dat·ing** **1** form or combine into one mass or organization: *a* ~*d school district.* **2** make secure or firm; strengthen: ~*ing the gains of last year.* —**con·sol·i·da·tor** *n.* —**con·sol·i·da·tion** (–DAY–) *n.*

con·som·mé (con·suh·MAY) *n.* a clear soup of meat or vegetable broth.

con·so·nance (CON·suh·nunce) *n.* **1** agreement; harmony, esp. of musical notes. **2** a rhymelike agreement of similar consonants but not vowels, as in *pull* and *will.* —**con·so·nant** *adj.* in agreement: *a statement not* ~ *with his previous remarks;* ***n.*** a sound or letter other than *a, e, i, o, u;* **con·so·nan·tal** (–NAN·tl) *adj.: p, t, k, etc. are* ~ *sounds.*

con·sort (CON–) *n.* a ruling monarch's spouse: *Philip is Queen Elizabeth's prince* ~. —***v.*** (cun·SORT) **1** agree *(with).* **2** associate: ~*ing with bad characters.* —**con·sor·ti·um** (cun·SOR·shee·um) *n., pl.* **-ti·a** a combination of banks, large companies, etc. for a large-scale investment: *an oil-pipeline* ~.

con·spec·tus (cun·SPEC–) *n.* an overall view; summary. —**con·spic·u·ous** (cun·SPIC·yoo·us) *adj.* easily observed; outstanding; attention-getting: *the* **conspicuous consumption** *of luxuries by the newly rich.* —**con·spic·u·ous·ly** *adv.: a notice displayed* ~. —**con·spic·u·ous·ness** *n.*

con·spir·a·cy (cun·SPEER·uh·see) *n.* **-cies** a working together, esp. of a group planning and acting jointly and secretly to do something wrong; also, the group or their plot. —**con·spire** (–SPIRE) *v.* **-spires, -spired, -spir·ing** **1** plot together. **2** work together: *Events* ~*d to thwart his aim.* —**con·spir·a·tor** (–SPEER·uh–) *n.;* **con·spir·a·to·ri·al** (–TOR–) *adj.* —**con·spir·er** *n.*

const. or **Const.** constable; constitution(al). —**con·sta·ble** (–stuh·bl) *n.* **1** a minor peace officer, as the policeman in a rural area. **2** *Brit.* a policeman. —**con·stab·u·lar·y** (–STAB–) *n.* **-lar·ies** **1** a body of constables. **2** an armed paramilitary police force; ***adj.:*** ~ *powers.*

con·stant (CON·stunt) *adj.* **1** continual; unchanging; repeated: *a* ~ *flow of water; the* ~ *round of parties.* **2** faithful: *a* ~ *lover.* —***n.*** an unchanging factor or quantity; of. VARIABLE. —**con·stan·cy** *n.* —**con·stant·ly** *adv.* —**Con·stan·tine** (CON·stun·teen) **(the Great).** A.D. 275?–337, first Christian emperor of Rome. —**Con·stan·ti·no·ple** (–NOH·pl) former name of ISTANBUL.

con·stel·la·tion (–LAY–) *n.* a group of stars thought to resemble something (as a person or animal) and named after it, as the Great Bear, Gemini, or Libra.

con·ster·na·tion (–NAY–) *n.* stunned shock or amazement; dismay.

con·sti·pa·tion (–PAY–) *n.* difficult, painful, and infrequent evacuation of the bowels. —**con·sti·pate** (CON–) *v.* **-pates, -pat·ed, -pat·ing** affect with constipation.

con·stit·u·en·cy (cun·STICH·oo·un·see) *n.* **-cies** an electoral district; also, a body of voters. —**con·stit·u·ent** *n.* **1** a member of a constituency: *A Congressman addresses his* ~*s.* **2** a part; component. —***adj.*** **1** electoral: *a* ~ *body.* **2** component: *Fat is a* ~ *part of milk.* **3** empowered to write or amend a constitution: *a* ~ *assembly.* —**con·sti·tute** (CON–) *v.* **-tutes, -tut·ed, -tut·ing** **1** be the parts of; form; make up: *12 people* ~ *a jury; Such acts* ~ *fraud.* **2** set up; appoint: ~ *an assembly; a duly* ~*d representative.* —**con·sti·tu·tive** (CON·sti·tue·tiv) *adj.* essential: *Fairness is a* ~ *part of justice.* —**con·sti·tu·tion** (–TUE–) *n.* **1** the makeup of anything; esp., a person's physical condition: *a weak* ~. **2** the basic rules or laws of a state, nation, corporation, club, etc.: **the Constitution** *of the U.S. enacted in 1789.* —**con·sti·tu·tion·al** *adj.* [corresponding to the *n.* senses] **1:** *a* ~ *inability to tell a lie;* ***n.*** a regular walk for the sake of one's health. **2:** *Is this law* ~ (i.e. permitted by the constitution)? *a* ~ *convention; a* ~ *amendment;* **con·sti·**

tu·tion·al·ly *adv.* **con·sti·tu·tion·al·i·ty** (–NAL–) *n.*

constr. construction.

con·strain (cun·STRAIN) *v.* **1** compel; force. **2** restrain; confine: *~ed in iron chains.* —**con·strained** *adj.: a ~* (i.e. artificial) *smile;* **con·strain·ed·ly** *adv.* —**con·straint** *n.* **1** force: *The prisoner only obeyed* **under constraint.** **2** restraint: *the ~s of military discipline.* **3** a usu. awkward repression of one's feelings. —**con·strict** (cun·STRICT) *v.* make smaller; cramp; inhibit; **con·stric·tion** *n.;* **con·stric·tive** (–tiv) *adj.* **con·stric·tor** *n.* **1** a muscle that compresses, as those of the pharynx used in swallowing. **2** a snake that kills its prey by squeezing, as a boa or anaconda.

con·struct (cun·STRUCT) *v.* make; put together; draw (a geometrical figure): *~ a bridge; ~ an argument;* **con·struc·tor** *n.* —**con·struc·tion** (–STRUC–) *n.* **1** a constructing; the business of building; hence, the way something is built; also, a building: *a ~ site.* **2** an interpretation; also, the arrangement of words in a phrase or sentence. —**con·struc·tive** *adj.* useful: *~ criticism;* **con·struc·tive·ly** *adv.* —**con·struc·tion·ist** *n.* one who interprets laws, the Constitution, etc. in a certain way: *a strict ~.* —**con·strue** (cun·STROO) *v.* **-strues, -strued, -stru·ing** **1** interpret. **2** analyze grammatically. —**con·stru·a·ble** *adj.*

con·sub·stan·ti·a·tion (–stan·shee·AY–) *n.* the coexistence of Christ's body and blood with the Eucharistic bread and wine; cf. TRANSUBSTANTIATION.

con·sul (CON·sl) *n.* **1** one of the chief magistrates of ancient Rome or of Napoleon, the First Consul. **2** an official appointed to protect a country's citizens and business interests in a foreign city. —**con·su·lar** (–lur) *adj.* —**con·sul·ship** n. —**con·sul·ate** (–it) *n.* the position, residence, or premises of a consul; also, a consular government, as in France, 1799–1804. —**con·sult** (cun·SULT) *v.* **1** ask or refer to for advice or information; consider. **2** confer *(with).* —**con·sult·ant** (–unt) *n.* one consulted for an expert opinion. —**con·sul·ta·tion** (con·sl·TAY–) *n.* —**con·sul·ta·tive** (–SUL·tuh·tiv) *adj.*

con·sume (cun·SOOM) *v.* **-sumes, -sumed, -sum·ing** **1** destroy. **2** use up; eat or drink; purchase and use for oneself. **3** engross: *Physics was her ~ing interest.* —**con·sum·a·ble** *adj.* & *n.: food, fuel, and other ~s.* —**con·sum·er** *n.* purchaser: **consumer goods** *such as food, appliances, and cars that supply human needs;* cf. PRODUCER GOODS. —**con·sum·er·ism** *n.* a movement for protecting consumers from false advertising, unsafe products, etc.; Naderism; **con·sum·er·ist** *n.*

con·sum·mate (cun·SUM·it) *adj.* perfect; complete: *a ~ artist.* —**v.** (CON·suh·mate) **-sum·mates, -sum·mat·ed, -sum·mat·ing** to complete; conclude; fulfill (a marriage) with an act of sexual intercourse. —**con·sum·ma·tion** (–MAY–) *n.*

con·sump·tion (cun·SUM–) *n.* **1** a consuming or being consumed: *the ~ of surplus food.* **2** tuberculosis of the lungs. —**con·sump·tive** (–tiv) *adj.: the ~ needs of society; a ~ cough;* **n.** one afflicted with consumption.

cont. containing; continent; continue(d); control.

con·tact *n.* **1** the touching of two objects; also the state of being in touch or having a communications link. **2** an electrical connection. **3** an association; also, a useful person. —**v.** place or come or get in contact with. —**adj.:** *~ transmission of a disease.* —**contact flying** flying by observing land marks; cf. INSTRUMENT FLYING. —**contact lens** a light corrective lens placed on the eye's surface. —**contact sports** sports such as football and basketball that involve body contact and hindering. —**con·ta·gion** (cun·TAY·jun) *n.* **1** the passing of a disease from one person to another by contact; also, a disease so passed on or its cause. **2** the general spread of an idea, emotion, etc. —**con·ta·gious** *adj.: Malaria is infectious, not ~; a still ~ smallpox victim; Laughter is ~.* —**con·ta·gious·ly** *adv.* —**con·ta·gious·ness** *n.*

con·tain (cun·TAIN) *v.* **1** hold within (oneself or itself); have a capacity of: *can't ~ his enthusiasm; The bottle ~s 6 liters.* **2** hold in check; hold back: *~ the enemy on the left flank;* **con·tain·ment** *n.: a policy of ~ of the Communist menace.* —**con·tain·er** *n.* one that contains; also, a large shipping receptacle of usu. standard size that can be carried easily on a **container ship,** or on a specially designed railroad car, or **container car.** —**con·tain·er·i·za·tion** (–ZAY–) *n.* the packing and shipping of freight in containers; hence **con·tain·er·ize** *v.* **-iz·es, -ized, -iz·ing.**

con·tam·i·nate (cun·TAM–) *v.* **-nates, -nat·ed, -nat·ing** dirty, infect, or taint by contact. —**con·tam·i·nant** (–nunt) *n.: radioactive ~s in the water.* —**con·tam·i·na·tive** (–nuh·tiv) *adj.* —**con·tam·i·na·tion** (–NAY–) *n.*

contd. continued.

con·temn (cun·TEM) *v.* treat or regard with contempt.

contemp. contemporary.

con·tem·plate (CON·tum–) *v.* **-plates, -plat·ed, -plat·ing** **1** consider or regard thoughtfully. **2** consider as likely; intend: *~ing suicide.* —**con·tem·pla·tion** (–PLAY–) *n.: ~ of God's goodness.* —**con·tem·pla·tive** (cun·TEM·pluh·tiv) *adj.: a ~ monk;* also **n.** —**con·tem·pla·tor** (CON·tum·play·tur) *n.*

con·tem·po·rar·y (cun·TEM·puh·rer·ee) *adj.* **1** of the same time; also **con·tem·po·ra·ne·ous** (–RAY·nee·us): *~ events.* **2** present-day; modern: *~ trends in art.* —**n.,** *pl.* **-ries** a person of the same period as another: *Hitler and Stalin were ~s.* —**con·tem·po·ra·ne·i·ty**

(–NEE–) or **con·tem·po·ra·ne·ous·ness** (–RAY–) *n.* **—con·tem·po·ra·neus·ly** (–RAY–) *adv.*

con·tempt (cun·TEMT) *n.* **1** scorn; a regarding or being regarded as base, negligible, worthless, etc.: *Cowards deserve ~.* **2** disrespectful disobedience: *~ of court; ~ of Congress.* **—con·tempt·i·ble** *adj.* deserving contempt: *a ~ scoundrel;* **con·tempt·i·bly** *adv.* **—con·temp·tu·ous** (cun·TEM·choo·us) *adj.* full of or showing contempt: *~ of weaklings; a ~ sneer;* **con·temp·tu·ous·ly** *adv.*

con·tend (cun·TEND) *v.* **1** compete, esp. in combat or debate (*for* a prize, etc.). **2** argue; claim: *He ~s that you lied.* **—con·tend·er** *n.*

con·tent *n.* (CON–) **1** also **contents** *pl.* what is contained; subject matter: *the ~s of the box; a book's table of ~s.* **2** substance: *a book with no intellectual ~.* **3** amount contained: *the fat ~ of milk.* ***—v.*** (cun·TENT) satisfy; please; ***adj.:*** *resting ~ with his lot in life;* ***n.:*** *drank to his heart's ~;* **con·tent·ed** *adj.: "~ with little, though wishing for more";* **con·tent·ed·ly** *adv.;* **con·tent·ed·ness** *n.*

con·ten·tion (cun·TEN–) *n.* **1** strife; rivalry; **con·ten·tious** (–shus) *adj.: a ~ claim, hard to settle; a ~ and argumentative man;* **con·ten·tious·ly** *adv.;* **con·ten·tious·ness** *n.* **2** a disputed assertion.

con·tent·ment *n.* contented state: *a life of peace and ~.*

con·ter·mi·nous (cun·TUR·muh·nus) *adj.* having the same or a common boundary. **—conterminous United States** the continental U.S. minus Alaska.

con·test *n.* **1** a competition: *a beauty ~.* **2** a struggle, dispute, or fight. ***—v.*** (cun·TEST) **1** compete for: *to ~ a seat in an election.* **2** challenge; fight or argue over: *His wife will ~ the divorce;* **con·test·a·ble** *adj.;* **con·test·ant** *n.*

con·text *n.* the surrounding words that determine a word's meaning; hence, circumstances; background: *was unfairly quoted out of ~; a dangerous admission in the ~ of the trial.* **—con·tex·tu·al** (cun·TEX·choo·ul) *adj.*

contg. containing.

con·tig·u·ous (cun·TIG·yoo·us) *adj.* in contact; next in space or time: *Canada is ~ with the U.S.: ~ pictures make a movie;* **con·tig·u·ous·ly** *adv.* **—con·ti·gu·i·ty** (con·tig·YOO–) *n.*

con·ti·nence *n.* self-restraint, esp. the ability to control a bodily need, as sex. **—con·ti·nent** *adj.* having to do with or showing continence; ***n.*** **1** one of the seven large continuous land masses, viz. Europe, Asia, Africa, North and South America, Australia, and Antarctica. **2 the Continent** mainland Europe. **—con·ti·nen·tal** (–NEN·tl) *adj.* **1** pertaining to a continent; **Continental Divide** the watershed separating rivers flowing to the Atlantic from those flowing to the Pacific; **continental shelf** the gradually sloping sea bed between a continent and the **continental slope** where the bottom drops more steeply to the depths. **2 Continental** European; **Continental breakfast** usu. coffee and rolls with butter. **3 Continental** of or pertaining to the American Revolution and the Continental Congress: *~ money; ~ army;* ***n.*** a Continental soldier or supporter; also, a Continental dollar, eventually valueless; **not care** (or **give**) **a continental** not care at all. **—con·ti·nen·tal·ly** *adv.*

con·tin·gen·cy (cun·TIN·jun·see) *n.* **-cies** a possibility that depends on chance or uncertain conditions: *prepared for all ~s;* ***adj.:*** *a ~ plan; a lawyer's* **contingency fee** *chargeable only if he wins the case.* **—con·tin·gent** *adj.* possible but uncertain; dependent (*on* or *upon*): *His arrival is ~ on good weather;* ***n.*** a number of things or group of people forming part of a larger group: *a ~ of troops, cavalry, ships; The Michigan ~ joined last night.* **—con·tin·gent·ly** *adv.*

con·tin·u·al (cun·TIN·yoo·ul) *adj.* unceasing; repeated frequently: *the ~ passage of time; ~ coughing;* **con·tin·u·al·ly** *adv.* **—con·tin·u·ance** (–unce) *n.* **1** a continuing; the period something lasts: *his ~ in office; the ~ of a crisis.* **2** an adjournment of court proceedings. **—con·tin·u·a·tion** (–AY–) *n.* a continuing (part): *Chapter 6 is a ~ of the story.* **—con·tin·ue** *v.* **-ues, -ued, -u·ing** **1** go on (being or doing something); carry on (*at* or *in* a place, condition, etc.): *The strike ~s; ~s to be late.* **2** resume after stopping: *We shall ~ after lunch.* **3** extend; retain: *The mandate was ~d for another year.* **4** adjourn; delay: *The hearing was ~d for a week.* **—con·tin·u·ous** (cun·TIN·yoo·us) *adj.* going on without break or interruption; **con·tin·u·ous·ly** *adv.* **—con·tin·u·um** (cun·TIN·yoo·um) *n.* **-u·ums** or **-u·a** a continuous thing: *Time is a ~.* **—con·tin·nu·i·ty** (–NEW–) *n.* **-ties** **1** a continuous quality. **2** a TV, radio, or movie script; also, linking material for a radio or TV program.

con·tort (cun·TORT) *v.* twist out of shape; deform: *a face ~ed by rage.* **—con·tor·tion** *n.* **—con·tor·tion·ist** *n.* a performer who can put his body in strange postures.

con·tour (CON·toor) *n.* outline; shape or surface. ***—adj.*** following the contours (as of the land): **contour lines** *connecting points of equal elevation, as shown on a* **contour map; contour plowing** *across slopes instead of up and down helps prevent erosion on a hillside.*

contr. contract(ion); contralto.**—contra-** *comb. form.* against; opposite to. **—con·tra·band** *n.* illegal or smuggled goods; ***adj.:*** *~ whiskey.* **—con·tra·cep·tion** (–SEP–) *n.* the prevention of conception; **con·tra·cep·tive** (–tiv) *adj.* & *n.: ~ techniques; oral ~s;* **con·tra·cept** *v.: ~ing and aborting babies.*

con·tract *n.* **1** an agreement, esp. if legally binding. **2** the final bid in a hand of **contract bridge** in which one scores toward the game only the points one has bid. **—con·trac·tu·al** (cun·TRAC·choo·ul) *adj.;* **con·**

trac·tu·al·ly *adv.* —**v.** **1** agree in a contract: *They ~ed to supply steel for the railroad.* **2** (cun·TRACT) get; acquire: *~ a heavy debt; ~ measles.* **3** (cun·TRACT) make or become smaller, as by drawing in; shorten by omitting letters: ~ (i.e. wrinkle) *one's brow; Cold ~s metals; "I'm" is a ~ed form of "I am"*; **con·trac·tile** (–tl) *adj.* able to contract or compress; **con·trac·til·i·ty** (–TIL–) *n.* —**con·trac·tion** (–TRAC–) *n.;* **con·trac·tor** *n.*

con·tra·dict (–truh·DICT) *v.* state the opposite of; deny the truth or correctness of: *~ the facts; ~ his claim; Don't ~ me!* **con·tra·dic·tion** *n.: full of mistakes and internal ~s;* **con·tra·dic·to·ry** *adj.: ~ accounts of the robbery.* —**con·tra·dis·tinc·tion** (–TINK–) *n.* a contrasting distinction: *Humans, in ~ to animals, can talk;* **con·tra·dis·tinc·tive** (–TINK·tiv) *adj.*

con·trail *n.* the visible trail of condensed water or ice particles behind a high-flying aircraft; condensation trail; vapor trail.

con·tra·in·di·cate (–IN–) *v.* **-cates, -cat·ed, -cat·ing** of symptoms, make (a treatment) undesirable or unsafe; **con·tra·in·di·cant** *n.* —**con·tra·in·di·ca·tion** (–CAY–) *n.* —**con·tral·to** (cun·TRAL·toh) *n.* **-tos** the lowest female singing voice.

con·trap·tion (cun·TRAP–) *n. Informal.* a gadget: *a new-fangled ~ for polishing shoes.*

con·tra·pun·tal (–PUN·tl) *adj.* of or having counterpoint: *a ~ style.* —**con·tra·ry** (CON·trer·ee) *adj.* **1** opposed; incompatible; also, adverse: *~ winds; two ~ statements.* **2** (*also* cun·TRAIR·ee) perversely stubborn: *a ~ child.* —**n.,** *pl.* **-ries** something opposite: **on the contrary,** *he was very kind; despite all indications* **to the contrary.** —**con·trar·i·ly** *adv.* —**con·tra·ri·wise** *adv.* —**con·tra·ri·ness** or **-ri·e·ty** (–RYE·uh·tee) *n.* **-ties.** —**con·trast** (cun·TRAST) *v.* **1** set in opposition to show differences: *Compare and ~ two poems.* **2** exhibit differences when placed, seen, etc. together: *Her behavior ~s sharply with his.* —**n.** (CON–) a contrasting; also, a difference, esp. between light and dark tones on a picture: *New York was* (or *displayed*) *a sharp ~ to the Midwest; not enough ~ in this photograph.* —**con·tras·tive** (–TRAS·tiv) *adj.* —**con·tra·vene** (con·truh·VEEN) *v.* **-venes, -vened, -ven·ing** go, stand, act, or speak in opposition to: *~ zoning regulations; I will ~ your claim.* —**con·tra·ven·tion** (–VEN–) *n.: acts in ~ of state law.* —**con·tre·temps** (con·truh·TAHNG) *n. sing.* & *pl.* an unfortunate or awkward occurrence.

contrib. contribution; contributor. —**con·trib·ute** (cun·TRIB·yoot) *v.* **-utes, -ut·ed, -ut·ing** **1** give, donate, or cause together with others: *~ to the United Appeal; His actions will* **contribute to** *his own downfall.* **2** submit (articles, stories, etc.) to a magazine: *a ~ing editor.* —**con·tri·bu·tion** (–BYOO–) *n.* —**con·trib·u·tor** (–TRIB–) *n.;* **con·trib·u·to·ry** *adj.: an accident victim's ~ negligence in not watching the traffic;* **n.,** *pl.* **-ries:** *a ~ to a pension plan.*

con·trite *adj.* remorseful (for wrongdoing); **con·trite·ly** *adv.;* **con·trite·ness** *n.: a penitent's ~ of heart.* —**con·tri·tion** (–TRISH–) *n.: tears of ~.*

con·trive (cun·TRIVE) *v.* **-trives, -trived, -triv·ing** plan; devise; scheme; also, accomplish, as by scheming: *~d to break in by an air vent; escaped by a rope ladder ~d out of bedsheets.* —**con·trived** *adj.: an obviously ~ alibi.* —**con·triv·ance** (–unce) *n.: a ~ for peeling potatoes.* —**con·triv·er** *n.*

con·trol (cun·TROLE) *v.* **-trols, -trolled, -trol·ling** **1** direct; regulate; restrain: *a ~d economy; ~ your temper.* **2** verify by comparing with a standard: *a ~d experiment.* —**n.** **1:** *exercising ~ over new buildings; a pitcher with good ~ of the ball; gun-~ legislation.* **2** something used as a standard for comparison: *They grew 6% faster than the ~.* **3** a device, regulation, etc. for controlling: *a pilot at the ~s.* —**con·trol·la·ble** *adj.* —**con·trol·ler** *n.* **1** one who supervises finances and spending; comptroller. **2** one who regulates: *an air-traffic ~.* —**con·tro·ver·sy** *n.* **-sies** a conflict of opinion; dispute: *public ~ over abortion.* —**con·tro·ver·sial** (–VUR·shul) *adj.: ~ issues; a ~ author;* **con·tro·ver·sial·ly** *adv.* —**con·tro·vert** (CON·truh–) *v.* deny; argue against or about: *a much ~ed topic.* —**con·tro·vert·i·ble** (–VUR–) *adj.*

con·tu·ma·cy (CON–, –TUE–) *n.* **-cies** headstrong resistance to authority. —**con·tu·ma·cious** (–MAY–) *adj.;* **con·tu·ma·cious·ly** *adv.* —**con·tu·me·ly** (cun·TUE–, CON–) *n.* **-lies** overbearing and humiliating words or action; insult; **con·tu·me·li·ous** (–MEE·lee·us) *adj.: ~ treatment;* **con·tu·me·li·ous·ly** *adv.*

con·tuse (–TUSE) *v.* **-tus·es, -tused, -tus·ing** bruise. —**con·tu·sion** *n.*

co·nun·drum (cuh·NUN–) *n.* a riddle involving a pun, e.g. "When is a dress like a chair? When it's sat-in."

con·ur·ba·tion (–BAY–) *n.* a group of continuous urban areas: *There are 7 million people in the Greater London ~.*

con·va·lesce (–LES) *v.* **-lesc·es, -lesced, -lesc·ing** recover after an illness or injury; get better. —**con·va·les·cence** *n.* —**con·va·les·cent** *adj.* & *n.: a home for ~s.*

con·vec·tion (cun·VEC–) *n.* internal movement in a liquid or gas, caused esp. by uneven heating; also, transfer of heat by this: *A space heater sets up ~ currents.* —**con·vec·tion·al** *adj.: Equatorial forests thrive on ~ rains.* —**con·vec·tive** *adj.: a ~ discharge of electricity by the motion of charged particles.* —**con·vec·tor** *n.* a room heating unit, as in a steam or hot-water system.

con•vene (cun·VEEN) *v.* **-venes, -vened, -ven•ing** meet; convoke: *The meeting ~s at 3:00; The mayor ~d the town council;* **con•ven•er** *n.* —**con•ven•ience** *n.* **1** the quality of being convenient: *the ~ of shopping by telephone.* **2** ease or personal comfort; also, an appliance, product, etc. that serves this: *We will see you* **at your convenience;** *pop-up toaster, electric kettle, and such ~s of our time.* —**convenience food** prepackaged, easy-to-prepare food, as a TV dinner. —**con•ven•ient** (cun·VEEN·yunt) *adj.* handy; labor-saving; adapted for one's ease or comfort: *5 ~ locations to shop; a ~ illness during exam week;* **con•ven•ient•ly** *adv.* —**con•vent** *n.* a community of nuns; also, a nunnery; **con•ven•tu•al** (–VEN–) *adj.: monks and nuns in their ~ garb;* ***n.*** a member of a convent or monastery; **Conventual** a Franciscan of the Order of Friars Minor Conventual. —**con•ven•ti•cle** (–VEN–) *n.* a meeting, esp. a secret religious assembly. —**con•ven•tion** (–VEN–) *n.* **1** a meeting, esp. of delegates: *the Democratic national ~; a sales ~.* **2** an international agreement: *the Geneva ~.* **3** accepted custom or usage; also, a practice so sanctioned; **con•ven•tion•al** *adj.* customary; ordinary; **conventional wisdom** accepted belief(s); **con•ven•tion•al•ly** *adv.;* **con•ven•tion•al•i•ty** (–AL–) *n.;* **con•ven•tion•al•ize** (–VEN–) *v.* **-iz•es, -iz•ed, -iz•ing:** *a ~d flower pattern.* —**con•ven•tion•eer** (–NEER) *n.* one attending a convention. —**conventual** See CONVENT.

con•verge (cun·VURJ) *v.* **-verg•es, -verged, -verg•ing** move toward a common point or goal: *~ing lines.* —**con•ver•gence** or **-gen•cy** *n.* —**con•ver•gent** *adj.*

con•ver•sant (cun·VUR·snt) *adj.* familiar; acquainted: *a lawyer ~ with contract law.* —**con•ver•sa•tion** (–SAY–) *n.* a talk between two or more people: *a ~ over drinks with an old friend; the fine art of ~;* **conversation piece** a novel object; something of curiosity value; **con•ver•sa•tion•al** *adj.;* **con•ver•sa•tion•al•ly** *adv.;* **con•ver•sa•tion•al•ist** *n.: a skilled and witty ~.* —[1]**con•verse** (cun·VERSE) *v.* **-vers•es, -versed, -vers•ing** talk *(with)* informally. —[2]**con•verse** (CON–) *adj.* contrary; opposite; ***n.:*** *His generosity is the ~ of her stinginess.* —**con•verse•ly** (cun·VERS·lee) *adv.: Our summer is New Zealand's winter, and ~.* —**con•vert** (cun·VURT) *v.* **1** change or adapt to a different form, use, etc.: *Alchemists wanted to ~ iron to gold; ~ dollars to pounds for a British vacation; a barn ~ed into a restaurant.* **2** convince (someone) to adopt new principles, esp. as a religion: *a ~ed Catholic;* ***n.*** (CON–) one converted: *a new ~ to Christianity.* **3** illegally take, dispose of, or use another's property. —**con•ver•sion** *n.* —**con•vert•er** or **con•ver•tor** *n.* —**con•vert•i•ble** *adj.: a bond ~ to stock;* ***n.*** a car with a roof that can be lowered or taken off.

con•vex *adj.* rounded outward, as the outer surface of a ball: *a ~ lens.* —**con•vex•i•ty** (cun·VEX–) *n.* **-ties.**

con•vey (cun·VAY) *v.* **1** move from place to place; conduct: *a pipe to ~ water.* **2** pass on; communicate: *I ~ed my sympathies to the bereaved.* **3** transfer ownership of: *~ land to the church.* —**con•vey•ance** *n.* **1** : *the ~ of freight; the ~ of an estate; a deed of ~.* **2** a means for conveying; a vehicle. —**con•vey•a•ble** *adj.* —**con•vey•or** or **con•vey•er** *n.* —**conveyor (belt)** an endless belt, chain, etc. for moving objects, as on an assembly line.

con•vict (cun·VICT) *v.* declare or prove guilty. —***n.*** (CON–) one serving a prison term. —**con•vic•tion** *n.* **1** a convicting: *two ~s for petty theft.* **2** firm belief: *have the courage of one's ~s.* —**con•vince** (cun·VINCE) *v.* **-vinc•es, -vinced, -vinc•ing** persuade; bring to a firm belief: *I was ~d of his innocence; ~ the judge that you were elsewhere at the time.* —**con•vinc•er** *n.* —**con•vinc•ing** *adj.* —**con•vinc•ing•ly** *adv.: a ~ argued case.*

con•viv•i•al (cun·VIV·ee·ul) *adj.* fond of, suited to, or having good company, good food, and good drink: *a ~ host; a ~ time at a party.* —**con•viv•i•al•y** *adv.* —**con•viv•i•al•i•ty** (–AL–) *n.*

con•voke (cun·VOKE) *v.* **-vokes, -voked, -vok•ing** summon to a meeting or assembly. —**con•vo•ca•tion** (–CAY–) *n.* **1** a convoking. **2** an assembly of churchmen, members of a university, etc.

con•vo•lut•ed (CON·vuh·loo·tid) *adj.* coiled, esp. intricately; hence, complicated: *long, ~ sentences.* —**con•vo•lu•tion** (–LOO–) *n.* something folded, twisted, or coiled together, esp. intricately; complication: *the ~s of the surface of the brain.*

con•voy *v.* accompany to protect on a journey. —***n.*** an armed escort, as for ships; also, a group traveling together for safe or orderly transport: *a ~ of merchant ships.*

con•vulse (cun·VULSE) *v.* **-vuls•es, -vulsed, -vuls•ing** shake violently; throw into a convulsion or spasm. —**con•vul•sion** (–VUL–) *n.* **1** an unnatural, violent muscular contraction; a fit; seizure: *epileptic ~s; ~s of laughter.* **2** a violent upheaval, as a revolution, earthquake, etc. —**con•vul•sive** (–siv) *adj.* —**con•vul•sive•ly** *adv.*

co•ny (COH·nee) *n.* **-nies** **1** a rabbit; also, any of several rabbitlike mammals. **2** rabbit fur.

coo *n.* the low, gentle murmuring of doves; also, any similar sound. —***v.*** **coos, cooed, coo•ing:** *Lovers billing and ~ing on park benches.*

cook *v.* **1** prepare for eating by boiling, baking, frying, etc.; undergo this: *Who will ~ supper? The eggs are ~ing now.* **2** treat with heat. **3** *Informal.* happen: *What's ~ing?* **4** *Slang.* falsify; also, botch: *The embezzler ~ed the ac-*

counts. **5** *Slang.* also **cook with gas,** perform well; do or feel the right thing: *Now you're ~ing!* **—n.** one who cooks. **—cook one's goose** ruin (one) completely. **—cook up** *Informal.* invent; concoct. **—cook·book** *n.* a book of recipes. **—cook·er** *n.: preparing potatoes in a pressure ~.* **—cook·er·y** *n. Brit.* cooking. **—cook·ie** or **cook·y** *n.* **cook·ies** a small, usu. flat cake made from a stiff, sweet dough. **—cook·out** *n.* a meal prepared and eaten outdoors, as on an outing. **—Cook's tour** a rapid guided tour of points of interest.

cool *adj.* **1** somewhat cold; also, protecting or relieving from heat; *a ~ summer jacket.* **2** unemotional: **a** unexcited; composed; steady: *~ as a cucumber;* **b** restrained; understated: *~ jazz; TV is a ~ medium;* **c** unfriendly; unenthusiastic: *~ to the new idea;* **d** calmly impudent. **3** *Slang.* excellent. **—n.:** *the ~ of a summer night; He lost his ~ and tried to hit me.* **—v.** make or become cool: *Leave him to* **cool off** (or **cool down**); *he'll come back; an air-~ed engine.* **—cool one's heels** *Informal.* be forced to wait. **—cool·ly** *adv.* **—cool·ness** *n.* **—cool·ant** *n.* a fluid used, as in an engine, to remove excess heat. **—cool·er** *n.* one that cools or a cooling container; also, an iced drink; *Slang.* jail.

Coo·lidge (COO·lij), **Calvin.** 1872–1933, 30th U.S. President (1923–29).

coo·lie (COO·lee) *n.* an unskilled, often exploited Oriental laborer.

coon *n. Informal.* raccoon. **—coon's age** *Informal.* a very long time: *haven't seen him in a ~'s age.* **—coon·hound** *n.* a dog bred and trained to hunt raccoons. **—coon·skin** *adj. & n.: Daniel Boone wore a ~ (cap).*

coop *n.* a cage, pen, etc., esp. for poultry; *Slang.* a jail: *The convict* **flew** (i.e. escaped from) **the coop.** **—v.:** *The jury was ~ed up in a hotel during the trial.*

co-op (COH·op) *n.* cooperative: *We do all our shopping at the ~.*

coop·er *n.* one who makes or mends barrels, tubs, casks, etc.; also **v.** **—coop·er·age** (–ij) *n.* **—Coop·er, James F.** 1789–1851, American author.

co·op·er·ate (–OP·uh–) *v.* **-ates, -at·ed, -at·ing** work with others, esp. for a common goal; also **co-operate, coöperate.** **—co·op·er·a·tor** *n.* **—co·op·er·a·tion** (–RAY–) *n.* **—co·op·er·a·tive** (–OP·uh·ruh·tiv) *adj.* **1** inclined to cooperate. **2** of or being an enterprise owned and usu. operated by members for their own benefit: *a ~ apartment house;* **n.** a cooperative enterprise, esp. a store: *a farmer's ~.* **—co·op·er·a·tive·ly** *adv.*

co-opt (–OPT) *v.* **1** choose as a partner or colleague. **2** absorb into a culture, organization, etc.; also, take over; *a revolutionary ~ed by the system.* **—co-op·ta·tion** (–TAY–) or **co-op·tion** *n.* **—co-op·ta·tive** (–OP·tuh·tiv) or **co-op·tive** *adj.*

co·or·di·nate (–OR·dn·it) *adj.* **1** of equal importance or rank: *~ clauses of a sentence.* **2** linking two parallel grammatical structures: *a ~ conjunction.* **—n.** **1** something coordinate; **coordinates** *pl.* matching clothes: *shirt-pant-sweater coordinates in navy blue.* **2** a letter or number used as a reference in precisely locating something: *the x-~ on a graph.* **—v.** (–dn·ate) **-ates, -at·ed, -at·ing** **1** make or become coordinate. **2** work or cause to work harmoniously together: *a ~d assault on the beach.* Also **co-ordinate, coördinate.** **—co·or·di·nate·ly** *adv.* **—co·or·di·na·tor** *n.* **—co·or·di·na·tion** (–NAY–) *n.* **1** a coordinating. **2** the harmonious functioning of various muscles in a complex action.

coot *n.* **1** any of several ducklike water birds: *bald as a ~; silly* (or *stupid*) *as a ~.* **2** *Informal.* a silly, usu. old man. **—coot·ie** (COO·tee) *n. Slang.* a louse.

cop *v.* **cops, copped, cop·ping** take, seize, or steal; **cop out** *Slang.* withdraw from or avoid commitment; back out. **—n.** *Slang.* a policeman.

cop. copyright.

co·part·ner *n.* a partner, esp. in a business.

[1]cope *n.* an outer, enveloping cloak worn by clergy ceremonially; hence, anything that covers like a canopy; **cop·ing** *n.* the rooflike topping of a stone or brick wall.

[2]cope *v.* **copes, coped, cop·ing** contend, usu. successfully; come to grips: *teenagers trying to ~ (with life).*

Co·pen·ha·gen (coh·pun·HAY·gun, –HAH–) capital of Denmark.

Co·per·ni·cus (–PUR–), **Nicolaus.** 1473–1543, Polish astronomer. **—Co·per·ni·can** (–PUR·ni·cun) *adj.: The ~ system presents the earth as going around the sun.*

cope·stone *n.* topping or capping stone.

cop·i·er *n.* one that copies, esp. a duplicating machine.

co·pi·lot (COH·pye·lut) *n.* an assistant pilot.

cop·ing *n.* See [1]COPE.

co·pi·ous (COH·pee·us) *adj.* plentiful in quantity or in words, speech, etc.: *~ supplies of water; ~ notes.* **—co·pi·ous·ly** *adv.* **—co·pi·ous·ness** *n.*

cop-out *n.* an act of or excuse for copping out; also, one who cops out.

cop·per *n.* **1** a softish, highly conductive metallic element. **2** its reddish-brown color. **3** Brit. a penny. **4** *Slang.* a policeman. **—adj:** *~ wire, tan.* **—cop·per·y** *adj.* **—cop·per·as** (COP·uh·rus) *n.* a greenish iron compound used in making ink and fertilizers. **—cop·per·head** *n.* a poisonous North American viper.

coppice same as COPSE.

co·pra (COH–, COP–) *n.* dried coconut meat from which oil is extracted.

copse or **cop·pice** (–is) *n.* a thicket of shrubs or small trees.

Copt *n.* one of a people descended from the ancient Egyptians; also, a member of the Christian **Coptic Church** of Egypt and Ethiopia. —**Cop·tic** *n.* the Afro-Asiatic liturgical language of the Coptic Church; also ***adj.***

cop·ter *n. Informal.* a helicopter.

cop·u·la (COP·yuh–) *n.* a linking verb connecting subject and predicate, as in "Man *is* mortal," "Jane *will be* here," "He *seems* happy."—**cop·u·late** *v.* **-lates, -lat·ed, -lat·ing** engage in coitus; **cop·u·la·tion** (–LAY–) *n.* **cop·u·la·tive** (COP·yuh·luh·tiv) *adj.* linking: *a ~ verb; ~ conjunctions such as "and."* —**cop·u·la·to·ry** *adj.*

cop·y *n.* **cop·ies** **1** a reproduction; transcription; imitation. **2** a single specimen of a printed text, photograph, etc. **3** material to be typeset; hence, the words of an advertisement, written by a **cop·y·writ·er** *n.* **4** subject matter for a story: *The election upset was good ~.* —***v.*** **cop·ies, cop·ied, cop·y·ing** reproduce; transcribe; imitate; **cop·y·ist** *n.* —**cop·y·book** *n.* a book containing samples of proper handwriting. —**copy boy** a helper in a newspaper office who does errands, delivers copy, etc. —**cop·y·cat** *n.* [child's word] an imitator of others. —**copy desk** the desk where newspaper copy is edited before typesetting; **cop·y-ed·it** *v.* edit (a manuscript) for publication. —**cop·y·read·er** *n.* one who reads and corrects copy and (for a newspaper) also writes headlines. —**cop·y·right** *n.* an author's legal right to reproduce, sell, publish, etc. a work of music, literature, etc.; ***v.:*** *a ~ed play:* ***adj.*** copyrighted: *a ~ news story.* —**copy-writer** See COPY, *n.* 3.

co·quet (coh·KET) *v.* **-quets, -quet·ted, -quet·ting** flirt *(with).* —**co·quette** (coh·KET) *n.* a woman who frivolously seeks men's attentions. —**co·quet·ry** (COH·kuh–) *n.* **-ries.** —**co·quet·tish** (–KET–) *adj.*

cor. corner; corpus; correct; correspondence. —**Cor.** Corinthians (book of the Bible).

cor·a·cle (COR·uh·cl) *n.* a light, roundish boat made of waterproof material stretched over a frame of wood, wicker, etc.

cor·al (COR·ul) *n.* **1** a stonelike substance formed from the skeletons of marine polyps; also, one of these polyps. **2** a deep or yellowish pink or red. —***adj.:*** *a ~ reef; ~ atolls.* —**Coral Sea** the Pacific Ocean N. E. of Australia, S. E. of New Guinea, and W. of the New Hebrides. —**coral snake** any of a group of brightly banded poisonous snakes of tropical America and southern U.S.

cor·bel (COR·bul) *n.* a usu. wooden or stone projection from a wall that supports a weight above it.

cord *n.* **1** a thin rope of several strands or fibers; hence, something similar, as **a** a thin electrical cable; **b** a cordlike body part: *vocal ~s; umbilical ~;* **c** a rib on cloth; **cords** *pl.* corduroy pants. **2** a measure of cut wood piled 4 ft. × 4 ft. × 8 ft.; 128 cu. ft.; 3.625 cu. m. —***v.*** **1** tie or provide with a cord or cords. **2** pile in a cord. —**cord·age** *n.* **1** cords and ropes collectively, esp. the ropes of a ship's rigging. **2** an amount of wood measured in cords.

cor·dial (COR·jul) *adj.* heartfelt; warm; friendly. —***n.*** a liqueur; also, a stimulant. —**cor·dial·ly** *adv.* —**cor·di·al·i·ty** (–jee·AL–) *n.* **-ties.**

cor·dil·le·ra (–YAIR·uh, –DIL·uh·ruh) *n.* a chain or system of mountain ranges; **cor·dil·le·ran** *adj.* —**cord·ite** *n.* a smokeless explosive produced in cord form. —**cord·less** *adj.* operating without cord, i.e. by battery power: *a ~ electric shaver.*

Cór·do·ba (COR·duh·buh) a C. Spanish city; also, a city in Argentina. —**cor·do·ba** *n.* the basic Nicaraguan unit of money, equal to 100 centavos.

cor·don (COR·dn) *n.* **1** a line of police, soldiers, or forts guarding or isolating an area. **2** a decorative cord worn as a sign of honor: *The* **cordon bleu** (cor·dohn·BLUR, –BLOO) *is a great honor; a ~ bleu chef.* —***v.:*** *The bombed building was* **cordoned off** *by troops.*

cor·do·van (COR·duh·vun) *n.* a fine, colored leather, used esp. for shoes.

cor·du·roy (COR·duh–) *n.* a stout-ribbed fabric; **corduroys** *pl.* trousers made of this.

core *n.* the central part of something, as the hard, seed-containing part in fruits; also, the essence: *an apple ~; the ~ of a mold; the ~ of the argument; a scheme that is rotten* **to the core** (i.e. through and through). —***v.*** **cores, cored, cor·ing** remove the core of; **cor·er** *n.*

CORE Congress of Racial Equality.

core city the center of a large urban area; inner city; also called "central city."

co·re·spon·dent (coh·ri·SPON·dunt) *n.* a person charged in a divorce action with having committed adultery with the sued spouse.

Cor·fam *Trademark.* an artificial leather material; also ***n.***

co·ri·an·der (COR·ee–) *n.* a Mediterranean herb whose seeds are used as flavoring.

cork *n.* **1** the thick outer bark of the Mediterranean **cork oak,** used for bottle stoppers, insulation, floats, etc. **2** a stopper for a bottle, esp. one made of cork; ***v.*** seal or provide with a cork. —**corked** *adj.* fouled because of a defective cork: *~ wine.* —**cork·er** *n. Slang.* an astounding thing or person. —**cork·screw** *n.* a pointed metal spiral with a handle used for pulling corks from bottles.

corm *n.* a bulblike, scaleless underground stem that can produce new plants.

cor·mo·rant (–runt) *n.* a large, hook-billed diving bird that catches fish; hence, a glutton.

corn *n.* **1** a cultivated cereal grass bearing kernels on large ears; maize; also, the kernels or ears of this. **2** *Brit.* any cereal grass or its seeds, esp. the dominant grain of an area. **3** *Slang.* something outdated or oversentimental. **4** a thickening of the skin at a point of friction or pressure. **—v.** preserve (meat) with salt or brine: *~ed beef.* **—corn borer** a moth larva that feeds on the stalks and ears of corn. **—corn bread** a bread made with corn meal. **—corn·cob** *n.* the woody core of an ear of corn: *a ~ pipe* (i.e. one with a bowl made from this). **—corn·crib** *n.* a ventilated drying bin for corn.

cor·ne·a (COR·nee·uh) *n.* the transparent covering over the pupil and iris of the eye. **—cor·ne·al** *adj.: a ~ transplant.*

corn ear·worm a moth larva that feeds esp. on corn ears.

cor·ner *n.* **1** the intersection of two lines, planes, or streets: *the ~ of the room; a figure with 4 square ~s; meet me at the ~.* **2** an area or region, esp. a quiet or remote place: *the (four) ~s* (i.e. distant parts) *of the earth.* **3** a difficult position to escape from: *a tight ~.* **4** sufficient control of a commodity to force a price rise: *a ~ on wheat.* **—v. 1** turn a corner. **2** drive into a corner: *a fugitive ~ed by the police.* **3** gain control of: *~ the market on wheat.* **—around the corner** nearby; in the near future. **—cut corners** economize. **—cor·ner·stone** *n.* **1** a stone joining walls at a corner, often one ceremonially laid in a building's foundation. **2** basic foundation: *Free elections are the ~ of democracy.*

cor·net (–NET) *n.* a trumpetlike instrument having three valves. **—cor·net·(t)ist** *n.*

corn flour *Brit.* corn starch. **—corn·flow·er** *n.* a garden plant with showy composite flowers of blue, pink, or white.

cor·nice (–nis) *n.* a usu. projecting decorative molding along the top of a wall, room, or building.

corn·meal *n.* meal ground from maize corn. **—corn pone** same as PONE. **—corn snow** coarse-grained snow resulting from melting and refreezing. **—corn·stalk** *n.* a stem of a maize plant. **—corn·starch** *n.* a refined corn flour used to thicken sauces and in making **corn sugar,** a dextrose, and **corn syrup** containing glucose.

cor·nu·co·pi·a (–nuh·COH·pee·uh) *n.* **1** a horn of plenty, shown overflowing with fruits. **2** an abundance.

Corn·wall a county in the S.W. tip of England.

corn·y *adj.* **corn·i·er, -i·est** *Informal.* hackneyed; oversentimental: *a ~ joke; ~ old love songs.*

co·rol·la (–ROL·uh) *n.* the petals around a flower. **—cor·o·lar·y** (COR·uh·ler·ee) *n.* **-ol·lar·ies** a logical consequence; result; accompanying fact. **—*adj.*:** *good diet and the ~ good health.* **—co·ro·na** (cuh·ROH·nuh) *n.* **-nas** or **-nae** (–nee) something crownlike, as a glowing ring around the sun (a gaseous ring outside the chromosphere), moon, etc. or the upper part of a tooth or skull.

cor·o·nach (COR·uh·nukh) *n.* a Scottish or Irish funeral lament; dirge.

Co·ro·na·do (–NAH·doh), **Francisco Vásquez de.** 1510–1554, Spanish explorer.

cor·o·nal (COR·uh·nl) *adj.* of or pertaining to a corona; ***n.*** a crown or garland. **—cor·o·nar·y** (COR·uh·ner·ee) *adj.* **1** of or like a crown. **2** encircling; pertaining to the arteries that conduct blood to the heart muscle; ***n.,*** *pl.* **-nar·ies** same as **coronary thrombosis** or **coronary occlusion,** a blockage in a coronary artery. **—cor·o·na·tion** (–NAY–) *n.* the crowning of a king, queen, pope, etc. **—cor·o·ner** (COR·uh–) *n.* a public official who investigates deaths that may not be natural. **—cor·o·net** (–uh·NET) *n.* **1** a jeweled headband; ornamental garland. **2** a smaller crown worn by nonsovereign nobility or royalty.

corp. corporation. **—corpora** *pl.* of CORPUS. **—cor·po·ral** (COR·puh·rul) **1** *n.* a noncommissioned officer below sergeant in the Army or Marines. **2** *adj.* physical: *~ punishment.* **—cor·po·rate** (–rit) *adj.* **1** of, like, or shared by a united group: *~ endeavors.* **2** being or of a **cor·po·ra·tion** (–RAY–), a group authorized to act as one legal entity, as a business firm or municipality. **—cor·po·re·al** (–POR·ee·ul) *adj.* of the body; also, tangible; material; **cor·po·re·al·ly** *adv.;* **cor·po·re·al·i·ty** (–AL–) *n.* **—corps** (COR) *n. sing. & pl.* an organized group of people under one leadership: also, a subdivision of the armed forces or of the Army: *the Marine ~; the Tank ~;* **corps de ballet** (–duh·bal·AY) a ballet troupe exclusive of soloists. **—corpse** (CORPS) *n.* a dead, usu. human body. **—corps·man** (COR·mun) *n.* **-men** same as AIDMAN. **—cor·pu·lent** (COR·pyuh·lunt) *adj.* obese; with a fat body; **cor·pu·lence** (–lunce) or **-len·cy** *n.* **—cor·pus** *n., pl.* **-por·a** (–puh·ruh) a body, esp. if dead; hence, a body of writings, legal texts, etc.: *the Shakespearean ~.* **—Cor·pus Christ·i** (–CRIS·tee) **1** a Roman Catholic festival honoring the Eucharist. **2** a city in S. Texas. **—cor·pus·cle** (COR·puh·sl) *n.* a tiny particle; also, a small, free-floating blood or lymph cell: *red and white ~s;* **cor·pus·cu·lar** (–PUS·kyuh·lur) *adj.: the ~ theory of light.* **—cor·pus de·lic·ti** (–di·LIC·tye) the factual evidence of a crime; hence, loosely, the body of a murder victim.

corr. correct(ion); correspond(ence).

cor·ral (cuh·RAL) *n.* **1** a pen for horses or cattle. **2** a defensive circle of vehicles, as wagons. **—v. cor·rals, cor·ralled, cor·ral·ling:** *~d wild horses.*

cor·rect (cuh·RECT) *v.* **1** set right the errors or excesses of: *~ your addition; lenses to ~ astigmatism.* **2** discipline; point out the errors of: *~ing exam papers.* **—*adj.* 1** conforming to the truth or to a standard: *the ~ information; a ~ translation.* **2** proper: *~ manners; a ~ young man.* **—cor·rect·a·ble** *adj.* **—cor·rec·

tion *n.* **1** a correcting. **2** that which is used to make, mark, or effect a correction: *The clock needed a ~ of two minutes.* **—cor·rec·tion·al** *adj.: A prison should be a ~ institution.* **—cor·rec·tive** (–tiv) *adj.* & *n.* **—cor·rect·ly** *adv.* **—cor·rect·ness** *n.*

cor·re·late *v.* **-lates, -lat·ed, -lat·ing** stand in or bring into a mutual or systematic relationship: *Can we ~ lower speed limits with greater safety?* **—n.:** *The diameter of a circle is a ~ of its circumference;* **adj.:** *several ~ factors.* **—cor·re·la·tion** (–LAY–) *n.* **—cor·rel·a·tive** (cuh·REL·uh·tiv) *adj.* **1:** *strikes and the ~ loss of productivity.* **2** used (together) to express a mutual relation: *~ conjunctions such as "both" . . . "and";* **n.:** *"Either" and "or" are ~s.*

cor·re·spond (cor·uh·SPOND) *v.* **1** agree *(with): costs not ~ing with budget estimates.* **2** be parallel or similar *(to): The Senate ~s to the British House of Lords.* **3** communicate by mail: *a ~ing member of a society.* **—cor·re·spond·ing·ly** *adv.: Inflation causes a ~ high increase in wages.* **—cor·re·spond·ence** *n.* [corresponding to the *v.* senses] **1:** *There is no ~ with last year's costs.* **2:** *a strict ~ between their jobs.* **3:** *A* **correspondence course** *is conducted by mail; the unpublished ~* (i.e. letters, etc.) *of great men.* **—cor·re·spond·ent** *adj.: ~ wage increases;* **n.** someone who communicates by mail; esp., a reporter or commentator who sends reports from a distance: *our Peking ~; a war ~.*

cor·ri·dor *n.* **1** a long passageway or hall. **2** a narrow path for access or transportation: *a high-speed rail ~ to downtown; air ~s to West Berlin through East Germany.*

cor·ri·gen·dum (–JEN–) *n., pl.* **-da** something to be corrected in a printed text, often listed on a separate sheet: *Always check the ~da before reading a book.* **—cor·ri·gi·ble** (COR·i·juh·bl) *adj.* able to be corrected.

cor·rob·o·rate (kuh·ROB·uh–) *v.* **-rates, -rat·ed, -rat·ing** support (other evidence, a theory, etc.): *The witness ~d my story;* **cor·rob·o·ra·tive** (–ROB·uh·ray·tiv, –ruh–) *adj.;* **cor·rob·o·ra·tor** *n.;* **cor·rob·o·ra·tor·y** *adj.* **—cor·rob·o·ra·tion** (–RAY–) *n.*

cor·rode (cuh·RODE) *v.* **cor·rodes, cor·rod·ed, cor·rod·ing** eat away, destroy, or deteriorate slowly, as by chemical action: *a badly ~d stove pipe.* **—cor·ro·sion** *n.* **—cor·ro·sive** (–siv) *adj.: the ~ action of salt water.*

cor·ru·gate *v.* **-gates, -gat·ed, -gat·ing** form into parallel ridges and furrows: *a ~d* (i.e. wrinkled) *brow; ~d iron roofing.* **—cor·ru·ga·tion** (–GAY–) *n.*

cor·rupt (cuh·RUPT) *adj.* **1** no longer pure; made evil, tainted, or immoral. **2** venal: *~ politicians.* **—v.:** *Power ~s.* **—cor·rupt·i·ble** *adj.* **—cor·rup·tion** *n.: bribery and ~.* **—cor·rupt·ly** *adv.* **—cor·rupt·er** or **cor·rup·tor** *n.*

cor·sage (–SAHZH) *n.* a small bouquet worn by a woman on the shoulder, waist, or wrist. **—cor·sair** *n.* a pirate; a pirate ship: *Barbary ~s.* **—cor·set** *n.* a tight, often laced, woman's undergarment for shaping the figure.

Cor·si·ca a French island in the Mediterranean. **—Cor·si·can** *adj.* & *n.*

cor·tege or **cor·tège** (cor·TEZH) *n.* a following of attendants; also, a procession: *a funeral ~.*

Cor·tes (cor·TEZ), **Hernando.** 1485–1547, Spanish explorer.

cor·tex *n., pl.* **-ti·ces** (–ti·seez) or **-tex·es** an outer layer of covering tissue on an organ or plant part: *cerebral ~; adrenal ~.* **—cor·ti·cal** *adj.* of a cortex, esp. the brain cortex. **—cor·ti·sone** *n.* a hormone from the adrenal cortex used to treat various disorders.

co·run·dum (cuh·RUN–) *n.* the second-hardest mineral (aluminum oxide), used for cutting, polishing, and (in its transparent forms) as a gem.

cor·us·cate *v.* **-cates, -cat·ed, -cat·ing** flash; glitter: *a ~ing light; ~ing wit.* **—cor·us·ca·tion** (–CAY–) *n.*

cor·vette (–VET) *n.* a light, fast warship.

co·ry·za (cuh·RYE·zuh) *n.* a head cold; the common cold.

C.O.S. cash on shipment; chief of staff.

cos lettuce same as ROMAINE.

Co·sa Nos·tra (COH·zuh·NOHS·truh) the U.S. Mafia.

co·sign *v.* sign (a document) along with another. **—co·sig·na·to·ry** (–SIG·nuh–) *n.* **-ries:** *~s of a peace treaty;* also **adj.** **—co·sign·er** *n.* one who cosigns, esp. a promissory note, so as to be responsible for it in case of default.

cos·met·ic (–MET–) *n.* **1** a substance, as lipstick, face powder, or eye shadow, for beautifying the skin or hair. **2** anything that superficially covers up defects. **—adj.:** *~ preparations; a merely ~ antipoverty program;* **cos·met·i·cal·ly** *adv.* **—cos·me·ti·cian** (–TISH·un) *n.* one trained in the use of cosmetics. **—cos·me·tol·o·gist** (–TOL·uh·jist) *n.* a beautician; **cos·me·tol·o·gy** *n.*

cosm(o)- *comb. form.* **1** of the world or universe. **2** of outer space. **—cos·mic** *adj.* **1** of or relating to the cosmos: *~ harmony;* **cosmic rays** high-speed charged particles entering the earth's atmosphere from outer space. **2** huge; endless; **cos·mi·cal·ly** *adv.* **—cos·mo·chem·is·try** *n.* the science of the chemical makeup of the universe. **—cos·mo·gen·ic** (–JEN–) *adj.* caused by cosmic rays. **—cos·mog·o·ny** (–MOG–) *n.* **-nies** the origin of the universe; also, an account of this: *mythical ~s;* **cos·mo·gon·ic** (–GON–) *adj.* **—cos·mol·o·gy** (–MOL·uh·jee) *n.* **-gies** the philosophy or science of the universe as an ordered physical entity; **cos·mol·o·gist** *n.* **—cos·mo·log·i·cal** (–LOJ–) *adj.* **—cos·mo·naut** *n.* a Soviet astronaut; **cos·mo·nau·tics** (–NAW–) *n.pl.* [takes *sing. v.*] astronautics. **—cos·mop·o·lis** (–MOP–) *n.* a large city with a cosmopolitan population. —**cos·mo·pol·i·tan** (–POL·i·tun) *adj.* **1** representing or common to the whole world. **2** not narrow or regional in outlook: *the ~ world of art.* Also ***n.:*** *a ~ and a famous world traveler;* also **cos·mop·o·lite** (–MOP–) *n.* —**cos·mos** *n.* **1** the universe as an ordered whole; hence, any complex, harmonious system. **2** *pl.* **cosmos** any of a genus of colorful, composite tropical flowers.

Cos·sack *n.* one of a S. Russian people known as mounted warriors; ***adj.:*** *~ horsemen.*

cost *n.* **1** a price paid for something; **costs** *pl.* the expenses of a court case: *fined $50 and ~s.* **2** loss; expense: *We will win* **at all costs** (or **at any cost**); *He rushed to enlist without stopping to* **count the cost.** —***v.*** **1 costs, cost, cost·ing** require or entail as a payment or loss: *Bread ~s too much; His mistake ~ him his life.* **2 costs, cost·ed, cost·ing** determine the cost of.

co·star *n.* a star of equal rank.—***v.*** **-stars, -starred, -star·ring:** *a show ~ing John Wayne; John Wayne ~s in it.*

Cos·ta Ri·ca (cos·tuh·REE·cuh) a country in S. Central America; 19,575 sq.mi. (50,700 km^2); *cap.* San José. —**Cos·ta Ri·can** (–cun) *adj.* & *n.*

cost·ly *adj.* **-li·er, -li·est** costing a great deal: *~ furs and jewels; a ~ production delay.* —**cost·li·ness** *n.* —**cost of living** the average cost of food, shelter, clothing, and other necessities.

cos·tume *n.* a set of clothes, esp. one: **a** representing a period, place, or class; **b** worn on stage; **c** suited to an occasion. —***v.*** **-tumes, -tumed, -tum·ing:** *an actress ~d in Elizabethan style.* —**costume jewelry** inexpensive artificial ornaments made of glass, plastics, wood, leather, etc. —**cos·tum·er** or **cos·tum·ier** (–TUE–) *n.*

co·sy (COH·zee) *adj.* **co·si·er, co·si·est** same as COZY.

cot *n.* **1** a narrow bed of canvas over a usu. collapsible frame. **2** also **cote** (COHT), a shelter or shed, esp. for animals: *dove ~.* —**co·te·rie** (COH·tuh·ree) *n.* a usu. exclusive circle of people with a shared interest: *a literary ~.*

co·ter·mi·nous (–TUR·muh·nus) *adj.* same as CONTERMINOUS.

co·til·lion (–TIL·yun) *n.* **1** a lively dance with complex steps. **2** a formal ball.

cot·tage (–tij) *n.* a small, usu. rural house; also, a summer house; **cot·tag·er** *n.* —**cottage cheese** a soft, mild cheese made from soured skim milk. —**cot·ter, cot·tar** or **cot·ti·er** *n.* **1** a peasant farmer under any of several land-tenure systems. **2 cotter (pin)** a split pin, used to hold parts in place, inserted through a hole and fastened by spreading the tips.

cot·ton (COTN) *n.* thread or cloth made from the white, fluffy seed hairs of a bushy plant; also, the seed hairs or the plant itself. —**cotton (on) to** *Informal.* understand; catch on. —**cotton to** *Informal.* get along with; become friendly with. —**cot·ton·y** *adj.* —**Cotton Belt** the region of southern U.S. where cotton is grown. —**cotton gin** a machine for cleaning seeds from cotton fibers. —**cot·ton·mouth** same as WATER MOCCASIN. —**cot·ton·seed** *n.* the seed of the cotton plant, which yields **cottonseed oil** used in margarine, soap, linoleum, etc. and **cottonseed meal** used in feed and fertilizer. —**cot·ton·tail** *n.* a small, white-tailed North American rabbit. —**cot·ton·wood** *n.* any of a group of poplars having fluff around the seeds.

cot·y·le·don (cotl·EEDN) *n.* the first leaf sprouting from a seed.

couch *n.* a piece of furniture for sitting or lying down; sofa. —***v.*** **1** lay or lie on or as on a couch: *Ambushers ~ed in the bushes.* **2** to phrase: *a request ~ed in formal prose.* —**couch·ant** (–unt) *adj.* lying, but with the head raised. —**cou·chette** (coo·SHET) *n.* a train compartment that converts to provide sleeping berths.

cou·gar (COO·gur) *n.* a large, light-brown wildcat.

cough (CAWF) *v.* emit air forcefully and noisily from the lungs; also, utter or expel by coughing: *He ~ed up the fishbone that was choking him.* —***n.:*** *a cold with a bad ~.*

could (COOD) *pt.* of CAN [also used to express possibility, conditionality, permission, etc.]: *~ I see you for a minute? It ~ happen here; It ~ be serious, if the doctor is late.* —**could·n't** (COOD·nt) could not.

cou·lee (COO·lee) *n.* **1** a stream bed or gully that is dry in summer. **2** a stream of lava.

cou·lomb (COO–, –LOMB) *n.* the amount of electricity transferred by one ampere in one second.

coun·cil *n.* a body or assembly chosen to discuss, advise, administer, or legislate; esp., a municipal government: *city ~.* —**coun·cil(l)·lor, coun·cil·man, -men** or **coun·cil·wom·an, -wom·en** *n.* —**coun·sel** (–sul) *v.* **-sels, -sel(l)ed, -sel·(l)ing** give advice to; urge; consult: *The priest ~d patience in adversity;* ***n.*** **1** a deliberation; advice; consultation: *Let us* **take counsel** *together; You give me good ~; I will* **keep my own counsel** (i.e. not reveal my plans). **2** *pl.* **counsel** a legal adviser; lawyer(s): *~ for the defense.* —**coun·se(l)·lor** *n.* **1:** *a career ~ at our high school.* **2** a lawyer. **3** a children's supervisor at a summer camp.

[1]**count** *n.* a European noble whose rank is analogous to that of an earl.

[2]**count** *v.* **1** recite numbers in ascending order; match (a series of objects) to such a series of numbers; total up: *I will ~ to ten: one, two . . . ; Let's* **count heads** *to see how many are here; ~ your money.* **2** consider; take into consideration; **count in** include; **count out** exclude: *~ yourself fortunate; If we ~ Billy, there are*

6; ~ me in for the party; If it's illegal, ~ me out. **3** depend: *You can ~ on rain tomorrow.* **4** be of significance or value: *Family ties ~ for less these days.* **—n.** **1** a counting: *He got it right on the third ~; What's the ~ (i.e. total) now?* **2** a charge in an indictment: *five ~s of robbery.* **3** account; reckoning. **—count down** count in reverse order; **count•down** *n.: The ~ continued "3, 2, 1 . . . blast off!"* **—count•a•ble** *adj.*

coun•te•nance (COWN·tn·unce) *n.* **1** a person's face, esp. as expressing his feelings; also, a look of approval. **2** composure; self-control: *His icy stare put him* **out of countenance;** *The joke was so funny she could not* **keep her countenance.** **—v. -nanc•es, -nanced, -nanc•ing** approve; tolerate.

[1]**count•er** *n.* **1** someone or something that counts: *a calorie ~'s guide to dieting.* **2** a token, chip, etc. used for counting or in games. **3** a long table, board, or other flat surface for displaying wares, conducting business, serving or preparing food, etc.: *the jewelry ~; a lunch ~; a kitchen ~.*

[2]**coun•ter** *adv.* & *adj.* contrary; in the opposite direction: *Your ideas are ~ to all common sense; thoughts that run ~ to our ideas.* **—v.** act or speak in opposition to; strike or answer back; offset: *efforts to ~ inflationary losses; The boxer ~ed with a left hook.* **—n.** the opposite; a checking action: *an effective ~ to the attack.* **—counter-** *comb. form.* **1** contrariety or opposition to: retaliation against. **2** correspondence to: as in *counterpart, countersign.* **—coun•ter•act** *v.* oppose; offset; check: *an antidote to ~ a poison;* **coun•ter•ac•tion** *n.;* **coun•ter•ac•tive** *adj.* **—coun•ter•at•ack** *v.: We lost one battle, but ~ed the next day;* also **n.** **—coun•ter•bal•ance** *v.* **-anc•es, -anced, -anc•ing** offset; oppose with equal weight; also **n.** **—coun•ter•claim** *n.* an opposing claim, as in law against a plaintiff; also **v.** **—coun•ter•clock•wise** *adj.* & *adv.* opposite in direction to the turning of a clock's hands. **—coun•ter•cul•ture** *n.* a culture with values opposed to the rest of society, esp. among the young; **coun•ter•cul•tur•al** *adj.;* **coun•ter•cul•tur•ist** *n.* **—coun•ter•es•pi•on•age** (–ES·pee·uh·nazh) *n.* secret activity to thwart enemy spying. **—coun•ter•feit** (–fit) *v.* make an imitation of (esp. money) so as to deceive or cheat: *He only ~ed grief when she died;* **n.** & **adj.:** *This $10 bill is a ~; a ~ twenty;* **coun•ter•feit•er** *n.* **—coun•ter•in•sur•gen•cy** *n.* action to suppress insurgent rebels, esp. guerrillas; **coun•ter•in•sur•gent** *adj.* & *n.* **—coun•ter•in•tel•li•gence** *n.* action to thwart or mislead enemy spies or saboteurs.

count•er•man *n.* **-men** one who serves customers at a counter.

coun•ter•mand (COWN–) *v.* revoke or call back (an order) with an opposite order. **—coun•ter•mea•sure** *n.: France took ~s against the new tariff.* **—coun•ter•of•fen•sive** *n.: a ~ against the invaders.* **—coun•ter•pane** (COWN–) *n.* a bedspread. **—coun•ter•part** (COWN–) *n.* something similar or analogous; also, a complement: *The Secretary of State met his Russian ~.* **—coun•ter•point** *n.* **1** a melody in contrasting harmony to the main melody; also, music having this. **2** a foil or contrast for something: *The funeral was a sad ~ to springtime.* **—coun•ter•poise** *n.* counterbalance; equilibrium; **v. -pois•es, -poised, -pois•ing** **—coun•ter•pro•duc•tive** *adj.* having results counter to those desired: *a ~ censorship law.* **—coun•ter•rev•o•lu•tion** *n.* a movement to reverse the result of an earlier revolution; **coun•ter•rev•o•lu•tion•ar•y** *adj.* & *n.* **-ar•ies** **—coun•ter•sign** *v.* sign (an already signed document) to authenticate (it); **n.** **1** such a signature; also **coun•ter•sig•na•ture.** **2** a secret password. **—coun•ter•sink** *v.* **-sinks, -sunk, -sink•ing** widen (a drilled hole) near a surface so that a screw or bolt head will sit flush; **n.** such a widening or a tool for making it. **—coun•ter•spy** *n.* **-spies** one doing counterespionage. **—coun•ter•ten•or** *n.* the highest male singing voice, above a tenor.**—coun•ter•vail** *v.* offset; act against successfully; also, compensate: *a ~ing tendency.* **—coun•ter•weight** *n.* a counterbalance.

count•ess (–tis) *n.* an earl's or count's wife or widow.

count•less (–lis) *adj.* too numerous to be counted: *~ hordes of insects.*

coun•tri•fied (CUN–) *adj.* rustic; also, rural. **—coun•try** (CUN·tree) *n.* **-tries** **1** a nation; also, its territory. **2** a district or region: *mountainous ~.* **3** a rural area: *living out in the ~.* **—adj.** **1** rural; also, rustic: *~ roads, manners; a ~ bumpkin.* **2** pertaining to **country and western** music, a modernization of the rural folk music of the S. and W. United States: *a country singer.* **—country club** a suburban social club, usu. having a golf course. **—coun•try-dance** *n.* a native English folk dance in which dancers are arranged in two facing lines, a square, or a circle. **—coun•try•man** *n.* **-men** a person from one's own country; also, a rustic; *fem.* **coun•try•wom•an, -wom•en.** **—country music** or **country and western** See COUNTRY, *adj.* 2. **—coun•try•side** *n.* a rural area.

coun•ty (–tee) *n.* **-ties** the major administrative division of a state, province, or of a country, as in Britain.

coup (COO) *n.* **coups** (COOZ) **1** a sudden, strikingly successful action: *The promotion was a big ~ for Smith.* **2** a sudden, usu. violent change in government: *a bloodless ~ by the army;* also **coup d'état** (–day·TAH). **—coup de grâce** (–duh·GRAHS) a merciful deathblow to a sufferer.

coupe (COOP) *n.* a closed, two-door car smaller than a sedan; also **cou•pé** (coo·PAY).

cou•ple (CUPL) *v.* **-ples, -pled, -pling** join or link together; unite; also, copulate. **—n.** **1** two similar things: *a ~ of old boots;* hence loosely, a few: *a ~ (of) days ago.* **2** two people, esp. a man and a woman considered as partners or mates: *a married ~; ~s swirling on the dance floor.* **3** a link or fastener. —**cou·pler** *n.* —**cou·plet** (CUP·lit) *n.* two consecutive, usu. rhyming lines of verse in the same meter. —**cou·pling** *n.* **1** a joining. **2** a device for linking parts, esp. for connecting two railroad cars.

cou·pon (COO–, CUE–) *n.* **1** a ticket, part of a package or advertisement, etc. entitling the bearer to a discount, refund, etc. or for use in ordering by mail. **2** a detachable interest certificate on a bond.

cour·age (CUR·ij) *n.* the ability to persevere in the face of danger or hardship; bravery: *Do you have the* **courage of your convictions** (to do what you feel is right)? —**cou·ra·geous** (cuh·RAY·jus) *adj.* —**cou·ra·geous·ly** *adv.*

cou·ri·er (COOR·ee·ur, CUR–) *n.* one who carries messages, official papers, goods, etc.: *a diplomatic ~; a ~ bringing heroin into New York.* —**course** (CORS) *n.* **1** a progression in space or time: *the ~ of events;* also, normal order, development, or duration: *the ~ of true love; The disease has run its ~* (i.e. is over): *Old age comes to all* **in due course** (i.e. at the proper time). **2** route; direction; line of action: *Our plane is* **on** (or **off**) **course** *for Chicago; What ~ are we sailing? Your only ~ is to flee!* **3** an ordered series of: **a** lectures or study programs; **b** parts of a meal *(a six-~ dinner);* **c** medical treatments. **4** a layer of bricks, building stones, etc. —*v.* **cours·es, coursed, cours·ing** **1** move, run, or flow swiftly; **cours·er** *n. Poetic.* a fast horse. **2** hunt (esp. deer or rabbits) with hounds. —**in the course of** during: *lost $6,000 in the ~ of a month.* —**of course** **1** certainly. **2** as one would expect: *He left early, of ~;* **matter of course** something usual or natural.

court (CORT) *n.* **1** a king, queen, etc. with his or her family, retinue, advisers, and ministers; an assembly of this; also, a royal palace. **2** a judge or judges who try legal cases; also, the place where this is done: *Order in the ~.* **3** an open area with one or more buildings around it; courtyard; also, an open area for playing tennis, basketball, etc. —*v.* try to gain the favor or love of; woo; also, tempt: *Don't ~ disaster by driving fast!* —**out of court** without a trial: *a case settled out of ~.* —**pay court to** *Formal.* woo. —**cour·te·ous** (CUR·tee·us) *adj.* gracious and considerate in behavior; **cour·te·ous·ly** *adv.* —**cour·te·san** (COR·ti·zun) *n.* a prostitute with a wealthy or high-ranking clientele; also **cour·te·zan.** —**cour·te·sy** (CUR·tuh·see) *n.* **-sies** (an instance of) polite, considerate, well-mannered behavior. —**court·house** *n.* a building housing law courts. —**cour·ti·er** (COR·tee·ur) *n.* a member of a royal court. —**court·ly** (CORT–) *adj.* **-li·er, -li·est** polite and dignified; refined: *~ love, manners;* **court·li·ness** *n.* —**court-mar·tial** *n.* **courts-mar·tial** or **court-mar·tials** a military court that tries offenders against military law; also, such a trial; *v.* **-tials, -tial(l)ed, -tial·(l)ing:** *~d for disobeying orders.* —**court·room** *n.* a room in which a law court sits. —**court·ship** *n.* a wooing. —**court·yard** *n.* an open area surrounded by buildings or one inside a large building.

cous·in (CUZN) *n.* a child of one's aunt or uncle; also called "first cousin."

cou·ture (coo·TOOR) *n.* the work of a **cou·tu·ri·er** (coo·TOOR·ee·ur) *n.* one who designs and makes high-fashion clothes for women; *fem.* **cou·tu·rière** or **cou·tu·ri·ere** (–ee·ur).

co·va·lence (coh·VAY·lunce) *n.* the number of pairs of electrons an atom can share with another, as in a chemical bond called a **co·va·lent bond.**

cove (COHV) *n.* a smallish, usu. sheltered bay.

cov·en (CUV·un, COH·vun) *n.* a group of assembled witches.

cov·e·nant (CUV·uh·nunt) *n.* a solemn agreement or mutual promise. —*v.*: *~ed to deliver the steel on Aug. 18; to ~ for a sum of $75.*

Cov·en·try (CUV·un·tree) an industrial city in S.C. England.

cov·er (CUV·ur) *v.* **1** place something or be in front of, on top of, etc., esp. so as to conceal or protect; hence, lie or extend over: *a snow-~ed mountain; ~ your tracks; She* **covered** (i.e. substituted) **for** *me during my vacation; a war hero ~ed with glory;* **cover up** conceal errors or crimes; **cov·er-up** *n.* **2** deal with; apply to; report on; travel over: *This book ~s the whole subject; a reporter ~ing an event; can't ~ more than 40 miles a day.* **3** have, get, or be enough to deal with; also, protect; insure: *a fund to ~ all expenses; Bill ~ed my bet; The shortstop shifted to ~ third base.* **4** protect by shooting to keep the enemy away; also, keep a gun aimed at: *~ me while I run for help; Keep him ~ed so he won't escape.* —*n.* **1** something that covers: *Put the ~ on the box; a sniper firing from ~; The ~ of this book is torn;* **Take cover** (i.e. get in a protected spot), *they are shooting at you;* **under cover** protected; also, in secrecy; disguised. **2** a mailing envelope or wrapper: *our brochure sent under separate ~.* **3** a single place setting. —**cov·er·ing** *n.* —**cov·er·age** (–ij) *n.* a covering; *a newspaper's ~ of an election; insurance ~.* —**cov·er·alls** *n.pl.* a one-piece suit of protective work clothes. —**cover charge** a fixed additional charge in a restaurant, night club, etc. —**cover crop** clover, vetch, rye, etc. grown to enrich soil and prevent erosion. —**covered wagon** a pioneer wagon with an arched roof of canvas. —**cov·er·let** (–lit) *n.* a bedspread. —**cov·ert** (COH·vurt, CUV–) *adj.* hidden or disguised; *n.* a hiding place, esp. for game; **cov·ert·ly** *adv.;* **covert (cloth)** a strong, lightweight twill used esp. for suits and coats.

cov·et (CUV·it) *v.* desire greatly (what is another's). —**cov·et·ous** (–us) *adj.;* **cov·et·ous·ly** *adv.;* **cov·et·ous·ness** *n.*

cov·ey (CUV·ee) *n.* **-eys** a brood or small group of birds such as quail.

cow *n.* **1** an adult female bovine; also an adult female walrus, elephant, moose, etc. **2 cows** [in cowboy use] cattle. —*v.* intimidate. —**till the cows come home** forever.

cow·ard (–urd) *n.* one shamefully lacking in courage; also ***adj.;*** **cow·ard·ice** (–is) *n.* —**cow·ard·ly** *adj. & adv.: a ~ excuse; a ~ lion;* **cow·ard·li·ness** *n.*

cow·bird *n.* a kind of blackbird that lays eggs in other birds' nests. —**cow·boy, cow·girl** or **cow·hand** *n.* one who tends or herds cattle on a ranch. —**cow·catch·er** *n.* a projecting metal device on the front of a train to push obstacles off the tracks.

cow·er *v.* huddle or cringe in fear.

cowgirl, cowhand See COWBOY. —**cow·hide** *n.* leather made from a cow's hide; hence, a whip of braided rawhide or leather.

cowl *n.* **1** a hood on a monk's habit. **2** a hood-shaped metal chimney cap. **3** the part of an auto body before and supporting the windshield and dashboard. **4** a removable metal cover over an airplane engine; also **cowl·ing.**

cow·lick *n.* a tuft of hair that stubbornly sticks up. —**cow·man** *n.* **-men** a cattle rancher.

co-work·er *n.* one who works with some one else.

cow-poke or **cow·punch·er** *n. Informal.* a cowboy. —**cow pony** a horse ridden while tending cattle. —**cow·pox** *n.* a mild, smallpoxlike disease caused by a virus that provides humans with a temporary immunity to smallpox.—**cow·slip** *n.* any of four flowering plants, esp. the marsh marigold.

cox *n. Informal.* coxswain. —**cox·comb** *n.* a foolish, conceited fop. —**cox·swain** *n.* one who commands a ship's boat or a racing shell.

coy *adj.* bashful; also, pretending to be shy. —**coy·ly** *adv.* —**coy·ness** *n.*

coy·o·te (kye·OH·tee, KYE·ote) *n.* a small W. North American wolf.

coy·pu (–poo) *n.* a beaverlike South American animal valued for its fur; nutria.

coz·en (CUZN) *v.* deceive; cheat with a petty trick. —**coz·en·age** (–ij) *n.*

co·zy (COH·zee) *adj.* **-zi·er, -zi·est 1** snug; warm and comfortable. **2** *Informal.* beneficial as a result of collusion: *a ~ little deal.* —***n.,*** *pl.* **-zies** a covering for a teapot to keep it warm. —**co·zi·ly** *adv.* —**co·zi·ness** *n.*

cp. compare. —**c.p.** chemically pure. —**C.P.** command post; Communist Party.

C.P.A. certified public accountant.

cpd. compound.

Cpl. corporal.

C.P.O. chief petty officer. —**C.P.O.M.** master chief petty officer.—**C.P.O.S.** senior chief petty officer.

c.p.s. cycles per second.

CQ charge of quarters.

cr. credit(or); crown. —**Cr** chromium.

crab *n.* **1** any of various 10-legged, broad-shelled crustaceans. **2 Crab** the constellation Cancer. **3** a louse that infests the pubic area in humans. **4** an ill-tempered grumbler; **crab·by** *adj.* **crab·bi·er, crab·bi·est; crab·bi·ly** *adv.;* **crab·bi·ness** *n.* **5** a crab apple. —*v. Informal.* **1** criticize sourly. **2** ruin by meddling: *Don't ~ my act.* —**crab apple** a small, tart apple or the tree it grows on. —**crab·bed** (–id) *adj.* **1** crabby. **2** barely legible because cramped: *~ handwriting.* —**crab·grass** *n.* any of several grasses regarded as a weed in lawns. —**crab louse** same as CRAB, *n.* 3.

crack *v.* **1** make or cause to make a short, sharp noise: *~ the whip.* **2.** break without separating into pieces: *a ~ed egg.* **3** change suddenly to a higher or a hoarse sound: *His voice ~ed.* **4** distil (petroleum) into its component chemicals. **5** solve: *Detective Brown ~ed the case.* **6** hit sharply. **7** *Informal.* open: **a** to read: *~ a book;* **b** by force: *~ the safe;* **c** to consume: *~ed a bottle of champagne.* **8** *Informal.* tell: *Stop ~ing jokes!* —***n.*** **1** a short, sharp noise. **2** a narrow split or gap. **3** a cracking: *a ~ in his voice.* **4** break: *at the ~ of dawn.* **5** a sharp blow; hence, an attempt: *I'll have a ~ at it.* **6** a smart remark; quip. —***adj.*** first-rate: *a ~ shot* (i.e. good marksman). —**crack down** become more strict or punitive; **crack·down** *n.: a ~ on smugglers.* —**crack up** **1** crash, esp. in a car or plane; also, break down laughing; hence, *Informal.* break down mentally; **crack-up** *n.* **2** praise: *School isn't all it's ~ed up to be.* —**get cracking** move or work quickly. —**crack·er** *n.* **1** a thin, dry biscuit. **2** a firecracker. **3** a party favor that opens with a snapping noise. —**crack·er·jack** *n. & adj. Slang.* first-rate (person or thing). ***n.*** —**crack·le** *v.* **-les, -led, -ling** make small cracking noises: *the ~ing fire;* also ***n.*** **1:** *the ~ of small-arms fire.* **2** many small cracks on china or porcelain; hence **crack·le·ware** *n.* —**crack·pot** *n. Informal.* an unbalanced or eccentric person; ***adj.:*** *some ~ notion.*

-cracy *comb. form.* government by: as in *plutocracy, democracy.*

cra·dle (CRAY·dl) *n.* **1** a baby's bed on rockers. **2** a frame to support something, esp. a telephone handset; also, a frame or a scythe that lays cut grain down evenly. **3** birthplace: *the ~ of civilization.* —*v.* **-dles, -dled, -dling** rock or place in or as if in a cradle: *~ing the child in her arms.* —**rob the cradle** have a much younger spouse or sweetheart. —**from cradle to grave** all one's life. —**cra·dle·song** *n.* a lullaby.

craft *n.* **1** *pl.* **craft** a vessel or aircraft: *Small ~ were swamped in the storm.* **2** *pl.* **crafts** a skill or skilled trade: *arts and ~s; the people in a ~;* ***adj.:*** *a ~ union;* **crafts•man** *n.* **-men** a skilled worker; artisan; **crafts•man•ship** *n.: This cabinet is a work of fine ~.* **3** sly cunning; skill in deceiving; **craft•y** *adj.* **craft•i•er, craft•i•est:** *a ~ fox;* **craft•i•ly** *adv.;* **craft•i•ness** *n.*

crag *n.* a rugged, steeply projecting mass of rock; **crag•gy** *adj.* **crag•gi•er, crag•gi•est, —crag•gi•ness** *n.*

cram *v.* **crams, crammed, cram•ming** **1** fill too full or too fast; jam: *~ his books into the locker; a bag ~d full of dirty clothes.* **2** feed or eat too much or too fast. **3** study hard at the last minute: *~ing for a physics test;* ***n.:*** *saved by a desperate ~.* **—cram•mer** *n.*

cramp *n.* **1** a sharp and painful muscle contraction; **cramps** *pl.* sharp abdominal pains. **2** a paralyzing stiffness of overused muscles: *writer's ~* (in the hand). ***—v.*** **1:** *My leg ~ed while I was asleep.* **2** restrict to or place in a small space; **cramp one's style** *Slang.* hinder one's usual ability or performance. **3** turn (a vehicle's wheels) sharply.

cran•ber•ry *n.* **-ber•ries** a small red berry, used esp. for jelly and juice; also, the bush it grows on.

crane *n.* **1** any of several long-legged, long-necked wading birds; hence loosely, a heron or stork. **2** a hoisting machine having a projecting arm or a horizontal track.***—v.*** **cranes, craned, cran•ing** stretch (one's neck) for a better view. **—crane fly** a long-legged mosquitolike fly.

cra•ni•um (CRAY·nee·um) *n.* **-ni•ums** or **-ni•a** the skull, esp. the part enclosing the brain. **—cra•ni•al** *adj.: ~ nerves connect the sense organs of the head with the brain.*

crank *n.* **1** a handle or rod bent at right angles to a rotating shaft. **2** *Informal.* an eccentric; also, a grouch. ***—v.*** start or operate with a crank; **crank out** churn out: *an author ~ing out three romances a year.* **—crank up** *Informal.* start up; prepare. **—crank•shaft** *n.* a shaft turned by or having a crank: *A* **crank•case** *houses the ~ of an auto engine.* **—crank•y** *adj.* **crank•i•er, -i•est** **1** irritable; eccentric. **2** working badly or fitfully.

cran•ny *n.* **cran•nies** a crevice; small corner: *searched in every nook and ~.*

crap *n.* *Vulgar.* excrement; hence, something phony or worthless. **—crap•py** *adj.* **crap•pi•er, crap•pi•est.**

crape *n.* black crepe used to indicate mourning.

crap•pie (CRAP·ee) *n.* any of several North American freshwater gamefishes related to the bass.

craps *n. pl.* [takes *sing.v.*] a gambling game played with two dice; also, a losing roll of 2, 3, or 12 and sometimes 7. **—crap•shoot•er** *n.* a craps player.

crash *v.* **1** collide, break, fall, land, etc. with a great noise or damage. **2** collapse: *the day the stockmarket ~ed.* **3** *Informal.* enter without permission or invitation: *~ the party.* **4** *Slang.* sleep, esp. for free or in a crash pad or place for nonpaying, temporary guests: *~ing with friends when he was broke.* ***—n.*** **1** a crashing sound: *the ~ of cymbals.* **2** a crashing, esp. a collision or a **crash landing,** a forced landing with damage to the aircraft; **crash-land** *v.* **2** a financial collapse. ***—adj.*** *Informal.* done with all possible effort and speed: *a ~ diet;* **crash pad** *Slang.* a temporary sleeping place.

crass *adj.* coarse; grossly stupid: *~ hedonism;* **crass•ly** *adv.;* **crass•ness** *n.*

-crat *comb. form.* one who belongs to or supports a kind of government: as in *democrat, bureaucrat, autocrat.*

crate *n.* a storage or shipping case, esp. one made of wooden slats. ***—v.*** **crates, crat•ed, crat•ing:** *Movers ~d the piano.*

cra•ter *n.* a funnel- or bowl-shaped hollow, as the mouth of a volcano: *the ~s on the moon; a soldier hiding in a bomb ~.*

cra•vat (cruh·VAT) *n.* a scarflike cloth worn loosely as a necktie; also, a necktie.

crave *v.* **craves, craved, crav•ing** **1** ask for; beg. **2** desire strongly; **crav•ing** *n.: the occasional ~ for a smoke even after quitting.*

cra•ven (CRAY·vun) *adj.* cowardly; ***n.:*** *a base ~.* **—cra•ven•ly** *adv.* **—cra•ven•ness** *n.*

craw *n.* a bird's crop; an animal's stomach. **—stick in the** (or **one's**) **craw** be unacceptable to one. **—craw•fish** *n.* same as CRAYFISH.

crawl *v.* **1** move by pulling the body along the ground; creep on hands and knees; hence, move slowly. **2** swim a crawl stroke. **3** be covered with crawling things; hence, of the skin, feel as if so covered: *The kitchen floor was ~ing with ants; a scary movie that makes one's flesh ~.* ***—n.*** **1** a crawling movement; slow pace: *rush-hour traffic slowed to a ~.* **2** a fast, overarm stroke done prone in the water: *the Australian ~.* **—crawl•er** *n.* **—crawl•y** *adj.* creepy.

cray•fish *n.* a small, freshwater crustacean resembling the lobster.

cray•on (CRAY·on, –un) *n.* a drawing stick of charcoal, colored wax, or chalk; also, a drawing made with this. ***—v.:*** *a ~ed sketch.* **—cray•on•ist** *n.*

craze *v.* **craz•es, crazed, craz•ing** make or become crazy. ***—n.*** a short-lived fad or mania. **—cra•zy** *adj.* **-zi•er, -zi•est** **1** insane. **2** *Informal.* absurdly fond: *She's ~ about him.* **3** *Informal.* impractical or eccentric: *a ~ scheme.* Also ***n.,*** *pl.* **-zies** a crazy person. **—crazy quilt** a quilt of multi-colored, irregular pieces.**—cra•zi•ly** *adv.* **—cra•zi•ness** *n.*

C.R.C. Civil Rights Commission.

creak (CREEK) *v.* make a harsh, squeaking sound like that of unoiled door hinges. ***—n.:*** *a terrible ~ in the bedroom floor.* **—creak•y** *adj.* **creak•i•er, -i•est** **1** full of creaks: *~ old stairs.* **2** rundown. **—creak•i•ly** *adv.* **—creak•i•ness** *n.*

cream (CREEM) *n.* **1** the yellowish, fatty content of milk. **2** something with a thick, smooth consistency, as a cosmetic, a liqueur, etc.: *facial ~; cold ~.* **3** a light yellowish white. **4** the best part: *the ~ of the crop.* —***v.*** **1** work to a creamy consistency; also, add cream to. **2** remove the best of. **3** *Slang.* beat or destroy thoroughly. —**cream·y** *adj.* **cream·i·er, -i·est; cream·i·ly** *adv.;* **cream·i·ness** *n.* —**cream cheese** a soft, smooth cheese made with cream. —**cream·er** *n.* a pitcher for cream. —**cream·er·y** *n.* **-er·ies** a place for the processing or sale of dairy products.

crease *n.* **1** a line or wrinkle made usu. by folding or pressing. **2** a special zone marked by lines, as in hockey or cricket.—***v.*** **creas·es, creased, creas·ing** : *Don't ~ my new tie; trousers that ~ easily.* **2** graze with a bullet.

cre·ate (cree·ATE) *v.* **-ates, -at·ed, -at·ing** **1** cause to exist; make: *God ~d heaven and earth; Laurence Olivier* **created the part** (i.e. was first to act the role). **2** cause; also, give a rank or title to. —**cre·a·tion** *n.* **1** a creating; something created: *God's ~ of heaven and earth.* **2** the world: *I've looked all over ~ for the fountain of youth.* —**cre·a·tive** (–tiv) *adj.* **1:** *~ powers.* **2** inventive; imaginative: *~ dance; ~ writing.* —**cre·a·tiv·i·ty** (–TIV–) *n.* —**cre·a·tor** *n.* one who creates; **Creator** God. —**crea·ture** (CREE·chur) *n.* an animal or person; esp., a person dependent on and subservient to another; **creature comforts** physical comforts, as good food and shelter.

crèche (CRESH, CRAISH) *n.* a stable scene representing Christ's Nativity.

cre·dence (CREED·nce) *n.* belief: *to give no ~ to slanderous rumors.* —**cre·den·tial** (cri·DEN·shul) *n.* something that justifies confidence in or credit to someone; esp. **credentials** *pl.* documents stating one's right or ability to fill an office, do a job, etc. —**cre·den·za** (cri·DEN·zuh) *n.* a usu. legless sideboard. —**cred·i·ble** *adj.* believable; **cred·i·bly** *adv.;* **cred·i·bil·i·ty** (–BIL–) *n.;* **credibility gap** a reluctance to accept esp. official statements at face value. —**cred·it** *v.* **1** believe (in): *a difficult story to ~.* **2** attribute to: *I* **credit** *him* **with** *some intelligence.* **3** mark down as a payment into an account: *$50 has been ~ed to your account.* —***n.*** **1** belief. **2** good reputation; hence, financial reliability; also, the amount of money loaned or the time allowed for repayment; **on credit** to be paid for later. **3** the money remaining in an account. **4** acknowledgement; praise; also, a source of this: *Give ~ where ~ is due; Bill's fund-raising* **does credit** (i.e. brings honor) *to the community; The* **credits** *at the beginning or end of a literary or artistic production acknowledge the contributions of writers, producers, actors, technicians, etc.;* **cred·it·a·ble** *adj.: a ~* (i.e. respectable) *performance in the playoffs;* **cred·it·a·bly** (–uh·blee) *adv.* —**credit card** a card allowing one to buy on credit up to a maximum amount, i.e. the **credit line,** or line of credit. —**cred·i·tor** (–tur) *n.* a person to whom money is owed. —**credit union** a cooperative savings and loan institution. —**cre·do** (CREE·doh, CRAY–) *n.* **-dos** a declaration of belief. —**cred·u·lous** (CREJ·uh·lus) *adj.* too willing to believe: *~ buyers are often cheated;* **cred·u·lous·ly** *adv.;* **cre·du·li·ty** (cruh·DEW–) *n.*

Cree *n.* (a member of) an Amerindian tribe of Canada, now spread from Quebec to Alberta; also, their Algonquian language.

creed *n.* a statement of belief, esp. of religious convictions: *the Nicene ~.*

creek (CREEK, CRIK) *n.* a small stream. —**up the creek (without a paddle)** *Informal.* out of luck; in trouble.

Creek *n.* an Amerindian confederacy whose members are now concentrated in Oklahoma; also, their Muskhogean language.

creel *n.* a wicker basket used to carry a fisherman's catch.

creep *v.* **creeps, crept, creep·ing** **1** move close to the ground; also, move stealthily, gradually, etc.: *a child ~ing on all fours; Old age ~s up on you.* **2** of plants, grow along the ground, a tree, a wall, etc. **3** move slowly out of position or shape. **4** feel the uneasy sensation of things crawling over one: *The noise made my flesh ~.* —***n.*** **1 the creeps,** *Informal.* creepy feeling: *a spooky old house that gives me the ~s.* **2** *Slang.* a petty or worthless person. —**creep·y** *adj.* **creep·i·er, -i·est** feeling or causing fear or disgust; **creep·i·ly** *adv.;* **creep·i·ness** *n.* —**creep·er** *n.*

cre·mate (CREE–) *v.* **-mates, -mat·ed, -mat·ing** burn up (a dead body); the resulting ashes are **cre·mains** (–MAINZ) *n.pl.* —**cre·ma·tion** (–MAY–) *n.* —**cre·ma·to·ry** (CREE–) *n.* **-ries** a furnace or building for cremating; also **cre·ma·to·ri·um** (–TOR–) *n.* **-ri·ums** or **-ri·a.** Also ***adj.***

crème (CREM, CREEM) *n.* a sweet liqueur, as chocolate-flavored **crème de ca·ca·o** (–duh·COH·coh, –duh·cuh·CAH·oh) or mint-flavored **crème de menthe** (–MAHNT, –MENTH).

cren·el·(l)ate (CRENL·ate) *v.* **-el·(l)ates, -el·(l)at·ed, -el·(l)at·ing** provide with battlements. —**cren·el·(l)a·tion** (–AY–) *n.*

Cre·ole (CREE–) *n.* **1** anyone of European descent born in Spanish America or the West Indies. **2** one who is descended from the original French settlers in Louisiana; also, their French patois. **3** someone of European and Negro ancestry who speaks a French or Spanish dialect. Also ***adj.*** —**cre·ole** *adj.* served or cooked with tomatoes, onions, peppers, and spices: *~ sauce.*

cre·o·sote (CREE·uh–) *n.* a pungent liquid used to preserve wood, distilled from wood or coal tar.

crepe or **crêpe** (CRAPE) *n.* **1** a thin fabric with a crinkled surface. **2** a thin, crepelike paper; also **crepe paper.** **3** crinkly crude rubber in sheets used esp. for shoe soles; also **crepe rubber.** **3** a thin pancake; **crêpe su·zette** (–soo·ZET) *n.* **crêpe(s) su·zettes** a pancake rolled in an orange sauce and served in flaming brandy.

crept *pt.* & *pp.* of CREEP.

cre·pus·cu·lar (cri·PUS·kyuh·lur) *adj.* of, like, or active in twilight: ~ *insects;* ~ *light.*

cresc. *Abbrev.* for **cre·scen·do** (–SHEN–) *adj.* & *adv.* gradually growing in volume; ***n.:*** *The chairman heard a ~ of complaints; The symphony ended with a great ~.* **—cres·cent** (CRES·nt) *n.* **1** the shape of the moon when less than half of it is visible, having one convex and one concave edge. **2** something in this shape: *a ~ roll; lives on Chalice Crescent.* **3** **Crescent** the symbol of Islam: *the Cross and the ~.*

cress *n.* a plant with pungent leaves that are used in salads or as a garnish: *garden ~.*

crest *n.* **1** a tuft, comb, etc. on top of an animal's head; hence, the top or peak: *the ~ of a hill; the ~ of a wave.* **2** a coat of arms or other heraldic device. **—*v.*** come to or form a crest; **crest·ed** *adj.: the ~ flycatcher.* **—crest·fal·len** *adj.* dejected; disappointed.

cre·ta·ceous (cri·TAY·shus) *adj.* containing or made up of chalk. **—the Cretaceous (Period)** a geological period beginning about 130 million years ago, marked by the dying out of dinosaurs and the thriving of mammals.

Crete (CREET) a Greek Island in the Mediterranean; **Cre·tan** *n.* & *adj.*

cre·tin (CREE·tn) *n.* **1** one afflicted with **cre·tin·ism,** deformity and mental deficiency caused by a congenital thyroid deficiency. **2** a very stupid person.

cre·tonne (CREE·tahn) *n.* a heavy, printed cotton fabric used for drapery and upholstery.

cre·vasse (cri·VAS) *n.* a deep crack in a glacier; also, a crack in a levee.

crev·ice (–is) *n.* a narrow opening; fissure.

¹crew *pt.* of CROW.

²crew *n.* a group that works together, as the men on a ship or airplane, in a racing shell, etc.: *The plane was repaired by the ground ~;* **crew·man** *n.* **-men.** **—crew cut** a man's very short haircut.

crew·el (CREW·ul) *n.* a loosely twisted, two-stranded yarn used in embroidery. **—crew·el·work** *n.*

crew neck a neckline that fits closely at the base of the throat, as of some sweaters.

crib *n.* **1** a manger; hence, a high-sided baby's bed. **2** a bin or small building for grain storage; also, a supporting framework, as in a mine tunnel. **3** *Informal.* a translation or other aid used dishonestly by a student; pony. **4** an extra hand for the dealer in cribbage.**—*v.*** **cribs, cribbed, crib·bing** **1** shut up or confine. **2** *Informal.* cheat on an exam; use a crib. **—crib·ber** *n.* **—crib·bage** (–ij) *n.* a card game in which scores are kept using pegs on a **cribbage board.**

crick *n.* a painful muscular cramp, esp, in the neck.

crick·et *n.* **1** a grasshopperlike insect whose male chirps by rubbing his wings together. **2** a British game played between teams of 11 using a ball, bat, and two wickets. **3** fair or sportsmanlike behavior. **—crick·et·er** *n.*

cried *pt.* & *pp.* of CRY. **—cri·er** (CRY·ur) *n.* one who cries out, shouts announcements, a sales pitch, etc.: *the town ~.*

crime *n.* **1** a major illegal act or omission; a felony or misdemeanor. **2** a disgraceful or regrettable condition or act.

Cri·me·a (cry·MEE·uh) a Russian peninsula in the Black Sea. **—Cri·me·an** *adj.: the ~ peninsula; the* **Crimean War** (1853–56) in which Russia lost to Britain, France, Turkey, and Sardinia.

crim·i·nal *adj.* of, being, or guilty of a crime: *a ~ record; ~ negligence; ~ offenders; a lawyer specialized in* **criminal law** (as opposed to *civil law*); ***n.*** one guilty of a crime. **—crim·i·nal·i·ty** (–NAL–) *n.* **—crim·i·nal·ly** *adv.* **—crim·i·nol·o·gy** (–NOL–) *n.* the study of crime, criminals, and punishment; **crim·i·nol·o·gist.** *n.*

crimp *v.* make wavy, corrugated, bent, etc.; pinch (as the edges of a pie crust) to seal together. **—*n.*** something crimped; esp. **crimps** *pl.* hair waved or curled, as with a curling iron. **—crimp·er** *n.* **—put a crimp in** *Informal.* inhibit; hinder.

crim·son (–zun) *n.* a purplish red; ***adj.:*** *~ clover* (a variety); ***v.*** make crimson.

cringe (CRINJ) *v.* **cring·es, cringed, cring·ing** crouch, draw back, or cower in fear; hence, fawn servilely: *a ~ing coward.* **—cring·er** *n.*

crin·kle *v.* **-kles, -kled, -kling** **1** wrinkle; crease; ripple: *~d up the piece of paper.* **2** rustle. **—*n.:*** *~s around his eyes.* **—crin·kly** *adj.* **-kli·er, -kli·est:** *a ~ silk* (that makes a rustling sound).

crin·o·line (–uh·lin) *n.* a stiff fabric used to line garments; hence, a petticoat of this.

crip·ple *n.* a physically disabled person or animal. **—*v.*** **crip·ples, crip·pled, crip·pling** make a cripple; hence, weaken; damage: *Storms ~d rescue efforts; ~ing diseases.* **—crip·pler** *n.*

cri·sis (CRY–) *n., pl.* **-ses** (–seez) **1** a turning point; crucial situation. **2** a dangerous or unsettled condition: *the energy ~; an international monetary ~.*

crisp *adj.* **1** firm and easy to break: *a ~ cracker; ~ carrots.* **2** well-defined; neat; clear and precise: *a ~ speech; ~ architectural design.* **3** bracing: *~ morning air.* **—*v.:*** *well-~ed bacon.* **—*n.:*** *toast burned* **to a crisp.** **—crisp·ly** *adv.* **—crisp·ness** *n.* **—crisp·y** *adj.*

criss·cross *v.* **1** make crossing lines on. **2** move back and forth over: *searchlights ~ing* *the night sky.* **—*n.*** a set of crossing lines; hence, tick-tack-toe.**—*adj.:*** *a ~ design.* **—*adv.*** **1:** *sticks lying ~ on the floor.* **2** awry: *plans that went ~.*

crit. critic(al); criticism. **—cri·ter·i·on** (cry·TEER·ee·un) *n., pl.* **-i·a** or **-i·ons** a standard of judgment: *Wealth is no ~ of worth.* **—crit·ic** *n.* **1** one who criticizes: *The congressman replied to his ~s.* **2** one who discusses and judges esp. works of art: *an art ~ for the newspaper.* **—crit·i·cal** *adj.* **1** of or being a crisis; decisive; crucial. **2** faultfinding: *a highly ~ account.* **3** of critics or criticism; evaluative: *a ~ review of the book.* **crit·i·cal·ly** *adv.* **—crit·i·cism** *n.* **1** the judgment of art, literature, etc. by a critic: *the principles of literary ~.* **2** disapproval; faultfinding; an expression of this. **—crit·i·cize** *v.* **-ciz·es, -cized, -ciz·ing** **1** find fault with: *You're always ~ing my clothes!* **2** evaluate critically. **—cri·tique** (cri·TEEK) *n.* a critical review, discussion, or analysis.

crit·ter *n. Informal.* creature; animal.

croak (CROKE) *n.* the low, rough sound made by a frog. **—*v.*** **1** make a croak; utter with such a sound; grumble: *an old woman ~ing her last words.* **2** *Slang.* kill or die. **—croak·er** *n.*

Cro·a·tia (croh·AY·shuh) a constituent republic of Yugoslavia; *cap.* Zagreb; **Cro·a·tian** *n.* & *adj.*

cro·chet (croh·SHAY) *n.* a heavy lace made with one hooked needle. **—*v.*** **-chets, -cheted, -chet·ing:** *a ~ed sweater.* **—cro·chet·er** (–SHAY·ur) *n.*

crock *n.* a pot, jar, etc. of earthenware; **crock·er·y** *n.* earthenware or crocks collectively. **—crocked** *adj. Slang.* intoxicated. **—Crock Pot** *Trademark.* an electrical ceramic pot for slow cooking.

croc·o·dile *n.* a large, swimming reptile with a long tail and strong jaws coming to a sharper point than an alligator's.

cro·cus (CROH–) *n.* **-cus·es** or **-ci** (–sye) a flower related to the iris having yellow, purple, or white blooms.

Croe·sus (CREE–) a Lydian king of the 6th cent. B.C., known for his great wealth.

crois·sant (cruh·SAHNT) *n.* a crescent-shaped roll of rich pastry.

Cro-Mag·non (croh·MAG·nun) *n.* a Caucasoid prehistoric man of Europe, Asia, and North Africa.

Crom·well, Oliver. 1599–1658, English politician and head of the Commonwealth.

crone *n.* a witchlike, scrawny old woman.

cro·ny (CROH·nee) *n.* **-nies** a close friend; long-time friend.

crook *n.* **1** a hooked stick, tool, or part; esp. a shepherd's staff. **2** *Informal.* a thief or swindler. **—*v.*** bend: *He comes whenever she ~s her little finger* (to summon him). **—by hook or by crook** by any means. **—crook·ed** (–id) *adj.* bent or curving; also, dishonest. **—crook·ed·ly** *adv.* **—crook·ed·ness** *n.*

croon *v.* sing, hum, etc. softly; hence, sing (a song) in a soft voice: *~ a lullaby.* **—croon·er** *n.* a professional singer of popular songs who uses a soft, smooth voice.

crop *n.* **1** a pouchlike part in a bird's gullet for the partial breakdown of food. **2** a whip handle; also, a short riding whip. **3** a close haircut. **4** an agricultural product; also, a specific amount of this: *a good ~ of corn; planting a ~ of wheat.* **5** a group or batch: *a new ~ of trainees.* **—*v.*** **crops, cropped, crop·ping** **1** cut off short; trim; cut the ends off: *a closely ~d head.* **2** plant a crop on. **3** harvest. **—crop up** (or **out**) turn up without warning. **—crop-dust·ing** *n.* the spraying of pesticides on crops from an aircraft; **crop-dust** *v.* **—crop·land** *n.* land used for planting crops. **—crop·per** *n.* one that crops; sharecropper; **come a cropper** fail completely; come to grief.

cro·quet (croh·CAY) *n.* a lawn game in which wooden balls are knocked through hoops with wooden mallets. **—cro·quette** (croh·KET) *n.* a small mass of minced food coated with bread crumbs, then deep-fried.

cro·sier (CROH·zhur) *n.* a staff with a hooked end, carried by a bishop or abbot. **—cross** *n.* **1** a vertical post or beam with a horizontal piece near the top; hence **Cross,** a representation of the cross Christ was crucified on and a symbol of Christianity. **2** a burden or affliction: *We all have our ~es to bear.* **3** a mark or design made by two intersecting lines: *He couldn't write, so he marked his ~ on the deed.* **4** a hybrid: *a ~ between a horse and an ass.* **—*v.*** **1** go or reach from one side to the other: *~ing the wide prairies.* **2** draw a line or cross through to cancel: *~ed out the error.* **3** meet and pass by; intersect; **cross one's path** meet; **cross one's mind** occur to one. **4** place or be crosswise; place across one another: *~ your fingers* (for luck). **5** make the sign of the cross on or over: *~ing oneself in church.* **6** oppose; thwart. **7** cause to breed with a different species or variety. **—*adj.*** **1** situated crosswise or across; intersecting; **cross·bar** *n.;* **cross·beam** *n.* **2** contrary; opposing. **3** angry; bad-tempered. **4** hybrid. Hence **cross·ly** *adv.;* **cross·ness** *n.* **—cross·bones** *n.pl.* two thighbones laid across one another: *skull and ~s.* **—cross·bow** *n.* a powerful bow mounted on a stock grooved to guide the arrow. **—cross·breed** *v.* **-breeds, -bred, -breed·ing** breed or cause to breed with a different species, variety, etc.; also ***n.*** a crossbred plant or animal; **cross·bred** *adj.:* *~ sheep.* **—cross-coun·try** *adj.* **1** across open country: *~ skiing.* **2** across a nation. Also ***adv.*** **—cross·cur·rent** *n.* a current or tendency running counter to another. **—cross·cut** *v.* **-cuts, -cut, -cut·ting** cut across (a wood grain, course, etc.). ***—adj.*** **1** for crosscutting: *a ~ saw.* **2** sawed or cut across the grain; also ***n.*** shortcut: *a ~ through the schoolyard.* **—cross-ex·am·ine** (–ZAM–) *v.* **-ines, -ined, -in·ing** question closely to check someone's previous answers; **cross-ex·am·in·a·tion** (–NAY–) *n.* **—cross-eye** *n.* an eye turned inward toward the nose; **cross-eyed** *adj.* **—cross-file** *v.* **-files, -filed, -fil·ing** file candidate's papers in the primaries of more than one party. **—cross·fire** *n.* intersecting lines of gunfire; hence, convergence of several things from different sources: *a ~ of questioning.* **—cross hairs** fine lines on an optical eyepiece to assist sight or alignment. **—cross·hatch** *v.* mark with obliquely intersecting parallel lines. **—cross·ing** *n.* **1** an intersection **2** a place for crossing a street, river, etc. **—cross·o·ver** *n.* a crossing; esp. a short track for switching a train to another line. **—cross·piece** *n.* a transverse piece. **—cross-pol·li·nate** *v.* **-nates, -nat·ed, -nat·ing** fertilize (a plant or flower) with pollen from another; **cross-pol·li·na·tion** (–NAY–) *n.* **—at cross-pur·pos·es** without understanding each other's purpose. **—cross-ques·tion** *v.* same as CROSS-EXAMINE. **—cross-ref·er·ence** *n.* a reference to another part of the same book, list, etc.; **cross-re·fer** *v.* **—cross·road** *n.* an intersecting or connecting road; **crossroads** [takes *sing.* or *pl.* verb] a meeting point for roads, cultures, etc.; also, a point where one must choose or decide. **—cross section** **1** a place or piece cut at right angles to the axis of something. **2** a sample representation of the whole; **cross-sec·tion·al** *adj.: ~ area.* **—cross talk** garbled sounds intruding from another telephone, radio, or tape channel. **—cross·walk** *n.* a pedestrian crossing marked on a street. **—cross·wind** *n.* a wind at 90° to one's course. **—cross·wise** *adv.* & *adj.* across; so as to intersect; crossing; also **cross·ways** *adv.: lying ~ on the bed.* **—cross·word puzzle** a game in which clues are given for words to be written in interlocking patterns of numbered squares.

crotch *n.* the point where two tree branches fork, or where the legs diverge at the human pelvis.

crotch·et *n.* a stubborn or eccentric whim. **—crotch·et·y** *adj.: a ~ old man.*

crouch *v.* lower the body with legs bent and limbs tucked in, as in cringing or preparing to run or leap. Also ***n.***

croup (CROOP) *n.* laryngeal obstruction, as by infection, causing a deep, barking cough and wheezing.

crou·pi·er (CROO·pee·ur) *n.* one in charge of a gaming table, as at roulette.

crou·ton (CROO·tahn) *n.* a cube of toasted bread served in salads, soups, etc.

crow (CROH) *n.* **1** any of a group of common black birds with a harsh call. **2** a crowing: *arising at cock's ~.* ***—v.*** **1** *pt.* also **crew,** utter a rooster's shrill cry. **2** exult; feel or express triumph: *a track star ~ing over his new record.* **3** make happy sounds as a baby does. **—as the crow flies** in a straight line. **—crow·bar** *n.* a steel or iron prying bar with a bent end flattening to a chisellike, notched tip.

Crow (CROH) *n.* (a member of) a tribe of N. Plains Indians now settled in S.E. Montana; also, their Siouan language.

crowd *n.* **1** a large number of people in a mass; throng; people in general. **2** a group with a shared interest: *got mixed up with the theater ~.* ***—v.*** **1** gather in a crowd. **2** move or make move in a crowd; force ahead. **3** fill or cram to excess. **4** press, shove, stand close to, etc.; hence, *Informal.* pressure: *a batter ~ing the plate; Don't ~ me.* **—crowd (on) sail** spread more sail to increase speed.

crow·foot (CROH–) *n.* **-foots** a buttercup, or any other plant having leaves or flowers shaped like a bird's foot.

crown *n.* **1** a garland or wreath for the head; also, a jeweled headdress, diadem, etc. indicating sovereignty; **the Crown** a monarch; monarchical power; also, the government of a constitutional monarchy: *a Crown* (i.e. government) *attorney.* **2** the top or a crownlike part of something, esp. of a tree, tooth, or a head. ***—v.*** **1** put a crown on; also honor as: *~ed King of England; ~ed man of the year.* **2** be or be at the top or best point: *the ~ing glory.* **3** cap (a tooth) with an artificial crown. **4** *Informal.* hit over the head: *She ~ed him with a rolling pin.* **—crown colony** a colony controlled by the British government. **—crown prince(ss)** an heir apparent to a throne.

crow's-foot *n., pl.* **-feet** a fine wrinkle at the outside corner of the eye. **—crow's-nest** *n.* an elevated, partly enclosed lookout platform, as on a ship's mast.

cro·zier (CROH·zhur) *n.* same as CROSIER. **—cru·ces** (CROO·seez) a *pl.* of CRUX. **—cru·cial** (CROO·shul) *adj.* decisive; supremely important: *a ~ decision; a ~ test of courage.* **—cru·cial·ly** *adv.* **—cru·ci·ble** (CROO·suh·bl) *n.* a heat-resistant pot or container for heating esp. metals to a very high temperature. **—cru·ci·fix** (CROO–) *n.* a representation of Christ on the Cross; a cross. **—cru·ci·fix·ion** (–FIK·shun) *n.* the crucifying of Christ; also **Crucifixion. —cru·ci·form** *adj.* cross-shaped. **—cru·ci·fy** *v.* **-fies, -fied, -fy·ing** execute by nailing or tying to a cross; hence, torment.

crud *n. Slang.* **1** a deposit of dirt or filth; hence, something worthless or disgusting; **crud·dy** *adj.* **2** **the crud** a poorly identified illness.

crude *adj.* **1** raw or unprocessed: *~ rubber, ~ oil;* ***n.*** crude petroleum. **2** boorish; unrefined; ill-mannered: *a ~ habit.* **—crude·ly** *adv.* **—crude·ness** or **cru·di·ty** *n.*

cru·el (CROO·ul) *adj.* causing grief or pain; inhumane; harsh: *a ~ taskmaster; a ~ north wind.* **—cru·el·ly** *adv.* **—cru·el·ty** *n.* **-ties.**
cru·et (CROO·ut) *n.* a small glass bottle for serving vinegar, oil, etc.
cruise (CROOZ) *v.* **cruis·es, cruised, cruis·ing** **1** sail or drive about with no particular goal, as for pleasure, to patrol, or waiting for developments: *a taxi ~ing for a fare.* **2** operate at efficient, long-distance speed. ***—n.:*** *tourists on a Caribbean ~* (i.e. pleasure voyage). **—cruise missile** a small, pilotless, long-range jet-powered missile that flies low to elude enemy radar and strikes with deadly accuracy. **—cruis·er** *n.* **1** a cabin cruiser. **2** a police patrol car. **3** a light, fast warship smaller than a battleship.
crul·ler *n.* a deep-fried sweet cake shaped like a stretched and twisted doughnut.
crumb (CRUM) *n.* **1** a scrap or small fragment, as of bread. **2** *Slang.* a contemptible person. ***—v.*** break into or cover with crumbs. **—crum·ble** *v.* **-bles, -bled, -bling** break into small pieces. **—crum·bly** *adj.: ~ lumps of dry clay.* **—crum·my** *adj.* **crum·mi·er, crum·mi·est** *Slang.* worthless, cheap; wretched. Also **crumb·y; crum·mi·ness** *n.* **—crum·pet** *n.* a small, round, unsweetened griddle cake similar to a muffin. **—crum·ple** *v.* **-ples, -pled, -pling** **1** crush or become crushed into wrinkles. **2** collapse; break down.
crunch *v.* chew, grind, crush, etc. with a loud noise; hence, make such a noise: *~ing potato chips; snow ~ing underfoot.* ***—n.*** **1** a crunching. **2** a difficult situation; a critical moment; pinch: *Our friends deserted us in the ~.* **—crunch·y** *adj.: ~ corn chips, snow.*
cru·sade (croo·SADE) *n.* **1 Crusade** one of the European military expeditions against Moslems in the Holy Land (11th to 13th cent.). **2** a zealous battle for a cause. ***—v.*** **-sades, -sad·ed, -sad·ing:** *~ing knights.* **—cru·sad·er** *n.: an equal-rights ~.*
cruse (CROOZ, CROOS) *n.* a small earthen vessel for liquids.
crush *v.* **1** press or squeeze so as to break or damage; crowd; crumple so as to wrinkle: *~ed into the corner by the mob; You ~ed my new suit.* **2** grind or break into small pieces: *~ed ice.* **3** overcome, destroy: *a ~ing defeat.* ***—n.*** **1** a crushing; also, a dense crowd of people: *A little boy was trampled in the ~.* **2** *Informal.* an infatuation: *a ~ on her teacher.* **3** a fruit juice drink: *lemon ~.* **—crush·er** *n.*
crust *n.* **1** the hard surface of a loaf of bread; also, a piece made mostly of this. **2** a pastry shell: *pie ~.* **3** any hard outer layer, as of the earth. **—crust·y** *adj.: ~ French bread.* **—crus·tal** (CRUS·tl) *adj.: ~ rocks of the moon's surface.* **—crus·ta·cean** (–TAY·shun) *n.* any of a group of usu. aquatic arthropods having a hard shell; e.g. clams, lobsters, shrimp; ***adj.:*** *~ life;* also **crus·ta·ceous** (–shus). **—crustal, crusty** See CRUST.
crutch *n.* a prop or aid; esp. a stick with a padded crosspiece that rests in the armpit used as a support for walking: *The injured skier was on ~es for 6 weeks.*
crux *n.* **crux·es** or **cru·ces** (CROO·seez) **1** the essential or crucial point; *the ~ of the matter.* **2** a difficult problem.**—cru·zei·ro** (croo·ZAY·roh) *n.* **-ros** the basic unit of money in Brazil, equal to 100 centavos.
cry *v.* **cries, cried, cry·ing** **1** sob and weep; shed tears. **2** shout; call out; also, utter a characteristic sound: *the boy who ~d "wolf."* **3** announce or proclaim: *a peddler ~ing his wares.* ***—n.,*** *pl.* **cries** **1** a bout of weeping: *Have a good ~.* **2** a shout or characteristic utterance: *the ~ of the wolf; a ~ for help.* **—a far cry** something quite different. **—cry·ba·by** *n.* **-bies** one who cries or complains too much. **—cry·ing** *adj.* demanding attention: *a ~ shame, need.*
cryo- *comb.form.* very cold. **—cry·o·bi·ol·o·gy** (–OL·uh·jee) *n.* the study of plant and animal life at very low temperatures. **—cry·o·gen·ics** (–JEN–) *n.pl.* [takes *sing.v.*] the study of very low temperatures and of processes using them; **cry·o·gen·ic** *adj.;* **cry·o·gen·i·cal·ly** *adv.* **—cry·o·lite** *n.* a white mineral used in aluminum refining. **—cry·on·ics** (–ON–) *n.pl.* [takes *sing.v.*] the preservation of bodies by freezing. **—cry·o·probe** *n.* a surgical tool for freezing body tissue in order to destroy them; **cry·o·sur·ger·y** (–SUR–) *n.*
crypt (CRIPT) *n.* an underground burial vault. **—crypt·a·nal·y·sis** (–NAL–) *n.* the solving or breaking of secret codes. **—cryp·tic** *adj.* **1** secret; mystifying: *a ~ comment.* **2** using a secret code. **—cryp·ti·cal·ly** *adv.* **—crypto-** *comb.form.* coded; secret; covert or hidden. **—cryp·to** *n.* a secret member of any group. **—cryp·to·com·mu·nist** *n.* a covert or undeclared communist. **—cryp·to·gram** *n.* a message in code; **cryp·tog·ra·phy** (–TOG–) *n.* the art of using or breaking codes; **cryp·tog·ra·pher** *n.* **—cryp·to·nym** (–tuh·nim) *n.* a secret name.
crys·tal (CRIS·tl) *n.* **1** colorless transparent quartz; also, a high-quality glass used for tableware: *Why, it's ~ clear! fine ~ goblets.* **2** a clear cover over a watch face. **3** a regular three-dimensional structure of atoms, ions, or molecules: *ice ~s.* **—crys·tal·line** (–lin) *adj.: the ~ structure of some gems; ~ salt; ~ clarity.* **—crys·tal·lize** *v.* **-tal·liz·es, -tal·lized, -tal·liz·ing** **1** form into crystals; take on a crystalline structure. **2** take on a fixed, definite form: *vague notions that ~d into a theory.* Hence **crys·tal·li·za·tion** (–ZAY–) *n.* **—crys·tal·log·ra·phy** (–OG·ruh·fee) *n.* the the scientific study of crystals; **crys·tal·lo·graph·er** *n.;* **crys·tal·lo·graph·ic** (–GRAF–) or **-i·cal.** *adj.*
cs. case. **—Cs** cesium. **—CS** a kind of tear gas. **—C.S.** chief of staff; Christian Science; civil service. **—C/S** cycles per second.

C.S.A. Confederate States of America.
C.S.M. command sergeant major.
C.S.T. Central Standard Time.
ct. cent; county; court.—**Ct.** or **CT** Connecticut. —**C.T.** Central Time.
ctg(e). cartage.
ctn. carton.
ctr. center.
cu. cubic. —**Cu** copper.
cub *n.* **1** a young bear, lion, fox, etc. **2** a novice: *~ reporter for the Post.*
Cu·ba (CUE·buh) a republic and island in the Caribbean; 44,218 sq.mi. (114,524 km^2); *cap.* Havana. —**Cu·ban** (–bun) *adj.* & *n.*
cub·by(·hole) *n.* a small space, compartment, or room.
cube *n.* **1** a solid shape bounded by 6 equal squares: *sugar ~s.* **2** the product of a number multiplied by itself twice; *8 is the ~ of 2 (= 2 × 2 × 2); 2 is the* **cube root** *of 8.* —***v.*** **cubes, cubed, cub·ing** **1** multiply by itself twice; *2 ~d is 8.* **2** shape or cut into cubes. —**cu·bic** *adj.* **1** cube-shaped; also **cu·bi·cal. 2** extended in three dimensions: *1 ~ yard is 1 yard long, wide, and deep;* **cubic measure** a measure of volume, as the cu. ft., cu. centimeter, etc. **3** raised to or relating to the third degree: *a ~ equation.* —**cu·bi·cle** (CUE·bi·cl) *n.* a small room or compartment: *a dormitory ~.* —**cub·ism** (CUE·bizm) *n.* a style of art employing abstract geometrical forms. —**cub·ist** *n.* & *adj.* —**cu·bis·tic** (–BIS–) *adj.* —**cu·bit** (CUE–) *n.* an old-fashioned measure of length; 18–22 inches; 45–56 cm.
Cub (Scout) a member of the junior branch (ages 8–10) of the Boy Scouts.
cuck·old (–uld) *n.* a man with an unfaithful wife; ***v.:*** *a ~ed husband;* **cuck·old·ry** *n.*
cuck·oo (COO·coo) *n.* **1** an Old World bird with a distinctive call that lays its eggs in other birds' nests; also, a related New World bird. **2** *Informal.* a foolish or silly person; ***adj.*** crazy; silly: *nearly ~ with fear; a head full of ~ ideas.*
cu·cum·ber (CUE·cum–) *n.* a long, thin, green vegetable with a white flesh, used raw or pickled; also, the vine it grows on: *stays* **cool as a cucumber** *under provocation.*
cud *n.* a mouthful of food that animals such as cattle, deer, and camels bring up from their stomachs for rechewing. —**chew the cud** ponder; ruminate.
cud·dle *v.* **cud·dles, cud·dled, cud·dling** hold or nestle close; hug: *~ing up on cold winter nights.* —**cud·dly** or **cud·dle·some** *adj.: a ~ kitten.*
cudg·el (CUJ·ul) *n.* a stout club: *the only one around to* **take up the cudgels for** *the underdog.* —***v.*** **-els, -el(l)ed, -el·(l)ing:** *~d to death; couldn't solve the problem, hard as I* **cudgeled my brains** (i.e. thought hard).
cue *n.* **1** a signal indicating when the next speech, action, etc. should occur in a play; hence, a hint or indication. **2** a long tapered stick used to strike the **cue ball** in billiards and similar games. —***v.*** **cues, cued, cu·ing** **1** hit with a cue. **2** give (an actor, singer, etc.) a cue; also, insert: *music* **cued into** *a script.* —**cue card** a large piece of cardboard with writing on it, held by a stagehand to prompt a television performer.
cues·ta (KWES·tuh) *n.* a hill or ridge with a cliff on one side and a slope on the other.
cuff *n.* **1** a band or folded piece of cloth on the end of a shirt sleeve or pant leg. **2** strike, usu. lightly with an open hand; ***v.:*** *a bear cub ~ed into line by its mother.* —**on the cuff** on credit. —**off the cuff** impromptu: *an off-the-cuff remark.* —**cuff link** a removable ornamental button for shirt cuffs.
cui·sine (kwi·ZEEN) *n.* a style of cooking; also, food so cooked: *the best Breton ~.*
cuke *n. Informal.* a cucumber.
cul-de-sac (–SAC) *n.* a dead-end street; blind alley.
cu·li·nar·y (CUE·li·ner·ee, CULL·i–) *adj.* of kitchens or cookery: *~ expertise.*
cull *v.* select; gather; pick over. —***n.*** something rejected.
cul·len·der *n.* same as COLANDER.
cul·mi·nate *v.* **-nates, -nat·ed, -nat·ing** reach its climax or best point: *Years of hard work ~d in a big promotion.* —**cul·mi·na·tion** (–NAY–) *n.*
cu·lotte (–LOT) *n.* usu. **culottes** *pl.* a trouser-like divided skirt; ***adj.:*** *a culotte dress.*
cul·pa·ble (–puh·bl) *adj.* blameworthy: *~ negligence.* —**cul·prit** *n.* an accused or guilty person. —**cul·pa·bly** *adv.;* **cul·pa·bil·i·ty** (–BIL–) *n.*
cult *n.* **1** a system of religious worship: *a ~ of Zeus.* **2** a strong or faddish devotion to a person, or **cult-fig·ure,** thing, or idea: *the ~ of old movies.* —**cult·ism** *n.* **cult·ist** *n.* —**cul·ti·var** *n.* a cultivated, not naturally growing variety of a plant. —**cul·ti·vate** *v.* **-vates, -vat·ed, -vat·ing** **1** prepare (soil) for growing plants; also, grow; foster: *~ an interest in music.* **2** refine; improve; hence **cul·ti·vat·ed** *adj.: a man of ~d tastes.* **3** get to know; seek the goodwill of: *~ing powerful politicians.* Hence **cul·ti·va(t·a)·ble** *adj.: ~ soil;* **cul·ti·va·tion** *n.;* **cul·ti·va·tor** *n.* —**cul·tur·al** *adj.* having to do with culture: *In a changing society, we often suffer from* **cultural lag** *in one area or another;* **cul·tur·al·ly** *adv.* —**cultural revolution** a fundamental change in a society's values and culture; **cultural revolutionary.** —**cul·tu·ra·ti** (–chuh·RAH·tee) *n.pl.* cultured people. —**cul·ture** (–chur) *n.* **1** a growing or cultivating; also, something so grown: *a bacterial ~* (i.e. colony or growth); *the ~ of the mind; physical ~.* **2** the characteristic behavior, arts, beliefs, etc. of a society: *primitive ~s in Africa; Greek ~; the* **culture shock** *of being thrust suddenly into a new society.* **3** intellectual and emotional refinement; artistic, literary,

etc. activity.—**cul·tured** *adj.* **1** refined: *a ~ gentleman.* **2** artificially cultivated: *a ~ pearl; a ~ variety of rose.* —**cul·ture-vul·ture** *n. Slang.* one who is very fond of or eager for culture, esp. the arts.

cul·vert *n.* a drainage passage under a railroad, highway, etc.

cum. cumulative. —**cum** *prep.* plus: *an apartment- ~ -workshop.*

cum·ber *v.* obstruct; burden. —**cum·ber·some** or **cum·brous** *adj.*

cum·in *n.* a seedlike, aromatic fruit of an herb used as a flavoring.

cum lau·de (–LOUD·uh, –dee) *Latin.* with honors.

cum·mer·bund *n.* a wide sash or waistband in men's formal dress.

cu·mu·la·tive (CUE·myuh·luh·tiv) *adj.* increasing by accumulation or continued addition: *the ~ effect of long hardship; ~ interest* (added to the principal sum and earning more interest). —**cu·mu·la·tive·ly** *adv.* —**cu·mu·lo·nim·bus** *n.* a very high cumulus cloud with a spreading top, often linked with thunderstorms; thunderhead or thundercloud. —**cu·mu·lus** (CUE·myuh·lus) *n.,pl.* **-li** (–lye) a cloud with a flat bottom and high rounded peaks on top.

cu·ne·i·form (cue·NEE·uh–) *adj.* wedge-shaped: *~ characters used in Sumerian, Assyrian, and Persian writing.* —***n.*** this system of writing.

cun·ner *n.* a small N. Atlantic food fish.

cun·ning *adj.* **1** shrewd; cleverly deceptive. **2** skillfully made or done. **3** cute: *a ~ red dress.* —***n.*** **1** craftiness; skill in deception. **2** skill; dexterity. —**cun·ning·ly** *adv.*

cup *n.* **1** a small, bowllike drinking container, usu. with a handle: *~ and saucer; a ~ of tea.* **2** a cupful; an 8 oz. measure of capacity; 236.59 ml. **3** something shaped like a cup, esp. a small bowl. —***v.*** **cups, cupped, cup·ping** shaped or put into a cup: *~ one's hand.* —**in one's cups** intoxicated. —**cup·bear·er** *n.* one who serves wine: *~ to the King of Persia.* —**cup·board** (CUB·urd) *n.* a small cabinet or closet: *The plates are in the ~ over the stove.* —**cup·cake** *n.* an individual cake baked in a cup-shaped container. —**cup·ful** *n.*

cu·pid (CUE–) *n.* a small, winged boy representing **Cupid,** the Roman love god. —**cu·pid·i·ty** (cue·PID–) *n.* **-ties** lust for wealth.

cup of tea *Informal.* what suits or appeals (to one): *Coin-collecting is not my ~.* —**cu·po·la** (CUE·puh·luh) *n.* a small dome on a roof.

cu·prite (CUE–) *n.* an ore of copper. —**cu·pro·nick·el** (cue·proh·NIK·ul) *n.* a copper-nickel alloy used in coins.

cur *n.* a mongrel; a worthless dog.

cur. currency; current.

cu·ra·çao (kyoor·uh·SOH) *n.* a sweet liqueur flavored with orange peel.

cu·rate (KYOOR·it) *n.* a clergyman assistant to a parish priest; **cu·ra·cy** *n.* **-cies.** —**cur·a·tive** (KYOOR·uh·tiv) *adj.* able to cure: *~ powers;* ***n.:*** *a ~ for fever.* —**cu·ra·tor** (cue·RAY·tur, KYOOR·uh·tur) *n.* one who administers a museum, art gallery, etc.; **cu·ra·to·ri·al** (–TOR·ee·ul) *adj.*

curb *n.* **1** a check or restraint; also a strap or chain used with a bit to check a horse. **2** a raised border for a street forming part of the gutter; also **curb·ing** *n.; Some drive-in restaurants offer* **curb service. 3** a market for unlisted securities; hence **curb broker, curb exchange.** —***v.*** control; also, make (one's dog) defecate in the gutter: *~ your tongue; ~ your dog.* —**curb·stone** *n.* edging of stones or cement forming a curb.

curd *n.* the coagulated solid part of milk. —**cur·dle** *v.* **-dles, -dled, -dling** **1** thicken (milk) into curd. **2** seem to coagulate: *The scream in the night ~d their blood with fear.*

cure *n.* **1** a healing. **2** a drug or therapy that heals: *a ~ for the common cold.* —***v.*** **cures, cured, cur·ing** **1** heal; make better: *a plan to ~ the world's problems.* **2** preserve (bacon, fish, etc.) by salting, smoking, etc.: *hickory-~d bacon; ~ tobacco by drying.* —**cur·a·ble** *adj.* —**cur·er** *n.* —**cu·ré** (cue·RAY, KYOOR·ay) *n.* a French parish priest. —**cure-all** *n.* a panacea; a supposedly universal cure.

cu·ret·tage (kyoor·uh·TAHZH) *n.* the medical scraping of a body cavity with a usu. spoon-shaped **cu·ret(te)** (cue·RET).

cur·few *n.* an evening hour at which one must be off the streets: *a soldier disciplined for violating ~; a ~ of 8:00 p.m. for children under 15.*

Cu·ri·a (KYOOR·ee·uh) *n.,pl.* **-ae** (–ee) the judicial and administrative organization through which the Pope rules the Church.

Cu·rie (cue·REE, KYOOR·ee), **Marie.** 1867–1934, French chemist born in Poland, co-discoverer with husband **Pierre Curie,** 1859–1906, of radioactivity of thorium; **cu·rie** *n.* a basic unit of radioactivity; 3.7×10^{10} disintegrations per second.

cu·ri·os·i·ty (–OS–) *n.* **-ties** **1** a being curious: "*~ killed the cat.*" **2** a novel or unusual object; also **cu·ri·o** *n.* **-os:** *the village ~ shop.* —**cu·ri·ous** (KYOOR·ee·us) *adj.* **1** eager to learn; hence, nosy; meddlesome: *a ~ little boy pestering his mom; ~ questions are rude.* **2** peculiar; interestingly odd: *What a ~ thing to say!* —**cu·ri·ous·ly** *adv.*

cu·ri·um (KYOOR·ee·um) *n.* a highly radioactive artificial element.

curl *n.* something with a coiled or incurved shape, esp. a ringlet of hair. —***v.*** give a curl or curved shape to; have this shape. *Smoke ~s from his pipe; Betty helped Mary ~ her hair.* —**curl·y** *adj.* **curl·i·er, -i·est:** *naturally ~ hair.* —**curl·er** *n.* a device for curling hair.

cur·lew *n.* a wading bird with a long narrow bill that curves downward.

curl·i·cue *n.* an ornate curl, as a flourish on a letter.

curl·ing *n.* a game in which round stones are slid toward a target across ice by two teams of four each.

cur·mudg·eon (–MUJ·un) *n.* an ill-tempered person; grouch.

cur·rant (CUR·unt) *n.* **1** any of several sour berries related to the gooseberry: *red ~s; black ~ jelly.* **2** a small, seedless dried grape used esp. in baking: *~ wine.*

cur·ren·cy (–un·see) *n.* **-cies 1** the state or duration of being current: *a rumor that had wide ~; a coin not in ~.* **2** money circulating, esp. as legal tender: *~ exchange rates; paper ~.* **—cur·rent** (CUR·unt) *adj.* **1** circulating: *~ coin.* **2** now occurring; of the present: *Read a newspaper for ~ events;* **current assets** *are readily available as cash.* **3** prevalent; generally accepted: *the ~ usage of a phrase.* ***—n.* 1** something flowing in a path, as air, water, or electricity: *The Gulf Stream is a warm ~; The ampere is a measure of ~ flow.* **2** a course or tendency: *the ~ of 20th-century liberalism; the ~ of unrest that swept campuses.* **—cur·rent·ly** *adv.* at present: *legislation ~ under review.* **—cur·ric·u·lum** (cuh·RIC·yuh·lum) *n.,pl.* **-la** or **-lums** a school's program of studies; also, a course: *Is music on your school's ~?* **cur·ric·u·lar** *adj.* **—curriculum vi·tae** (–VYE·tee) a résumé; vita.

[1]**cur·ry** *v.* **cur·ries, cur·ried, cur·ry·ing** brush or rub down (a horse) with a **cur·ry·comb. —curry favor (with)** flatter to gain favor.

[2]**cur·ry** *n.* **cur·ries** a sauce or dish seasoned with **curry (powder),** a spicy mixture of turmeric and other spices. ***—v.* cur·ries, cur·ried, cur·ry·ing:** *~d chicken.*

curse *n.* **1** a calling down of evil on someone or something; hence, an oath, esp. one using a sacred name. **2** a bane or scourge: *Scurvy was the ~ of old-time sailors.* ***—v.* curs·es,** *pt.* & *pp.* **cursed** or **curst, curs·ing 1** utter a curse against; swear at. **2** afflict: *~d with poverty in old age.* **—cur·sed** (CUR·sid, CURST) *adj.* hateful.

cur·sive (–siv) *adj.* of printing or writing, with letters connected to each other: *~ script.* **—cur·so·ry** *adj.* hurried; quick: *a ~ reading of a book;* **cur·so·ri·ly** (–suh·ri·lee) *adv.*

curt *adj.* short, brusque; nearly rude: *a ~ response to a complaint;* **curt·ly** *adv.;* **curt·ness** *n.* **—cur·tail** (–TAIL) *v.* cut short; reduce; **cur·tail·ment** *n.: protesting the ~ of military expenditure.*

cur·tain (CUR·tn) *n.* a piece of fabric hung before a stage, window, etc. to veil or shut off view. ***—v.*** furnish or conceal with a curtain: *One end of the cabin was* **curtained off** *for the ladies.* **—curtain call** a performer's return to the stage in answer to prolonged applause.

curt·sey (–see) *n.* & *v.* **-seys, -seyed, -sey·ing** curtsy. **—curt·sy** (–see) *n.* **-sies** a bow of respect by women made by bending the knees: *The girl dropped a graceful ~.* ***—v.* -sies, -sied, -sy·ing:** *~ to the Queen.*

cur·va·ceous (–VAY·shus) *adj.* having a full and rounded figure: *a ~ blonde.* **—cur·va·ture** (–vuh·chur) *n.* a curving or curved part: *~ of the spine; the ~ of space, of the earth.* **—curve** *n.* **1** a line, shape, or outline that bends with no straight portion. **2** a baseball pitched so as to swerve near the batter. ***—v.* curves, curved, curv·ing:** *The road ~s quite sharply.* **—cur·vet** *n.* a leap by a horse in which the back legs leave the ground just before the front legs touch down. ***—v.* -vets, -vet·(t)ed, -vet·(t)ing. —curv·y** *adj.* **curv·i·er, -i·est** having a curve or curves: *a top hat with a ~ brim.*

cush·ion (COOSH·un) *n.* something that absorbs shock or protects from a blow or hardness, as a pillow or pad; also, the bouncy rim of a billiard table: *a Hovercraft riding on a ~ of air.* ***—v.*** pad; protect from or absorb the shock of: *a youth ~ed from the realities of life.* **—cush·ion·y** *adj.*

Cush·it·ic (–IT–) *n.* an Afro-Asiatic language group of N.E. Africa, including Somali. ***—adj.:*** *the ~ language group.*

cush·y (COOSH·ee) *adj.* **cush·i·er, -i·est** easy or comfortable: *a ~ job.*

cusp *n.* a pointed peak or end, as of a leaf or tooth. **—cus·pid** *n.* a single-pointed (i.e. canine) tooth.

cus·pi·dor *n.* a spittoon.

cuss *n.* & *v.* *Informal.* same as CURSE.

cus·tard (–turd) *n.* a dessert made with a milk-and-egg mixture, sweetened and often flavored, that is baked or boiled until set.

cus·to·di·an (–TOH–) *n.* one who has custody; a caretaker or janitor; **cus·to·di·al** *adj.: ~ duties.* **—cus·to·dy** (–tuh·dee) *n.* **-dies 1** safekeeping; guardianship: *The divorced couple fought for ~ of the child.* **2** legal detention; imprisonment: *a suspect* **taken into custody** (or *put* **in custody**).

cus·tom (–tum) *n.* **1** an habitual act or practice; conventional usage; **cus·tom·ar·y** *adj.;* **cus·tom·ar·i·ly** *adv.* **2 customs** *pl.* tax on imported goods. ***—adj.* & *comb. form.*** made to order or specializing in made-to-order goods: *a ~ tailor; a* **cus·tom-built** *house; a* **cus·tom-made** *suit; a life of* **cus·tom-tai·lored** *comfort.* **—cus·tom·er** *n.* one who purchases something, esp. regularly; also, *Informal.* a fellow; *a tough ~.* **—cus·tom·house** *n.* an office at which customs are paid. **—cus·tom·ize** *v.* **-iz·es, -ized, -iz·ing** build or alter to specifications.

cut *v.* **cuts, cut, cut·ting 1** separate, pierce the surface of, make a narrow gap in, shorten, etc. with a sharp edge or object; also, strike a sharp blow: *~ the apple in two; a farmer ~ing* (i.e. harvesting) *wheat; I ~ my leg on the barbed wire; He got his hair ~; ~ a horse on the flank with a whip.* **2** have (a new tooth) pierce the gum. **3** reduce, shorten: *~ the work week to 30 hours.* **4** intersect; also, move directly or change direction quickly. **5** divide (a deck of cards). **6** make or shape by cutting, digging, grinding, etc.: ~ *glass;* ~ *a road through the hills.* **7** yield to cutting. **8** dilute; dissolve. ***—n.:*** *a* ~ *on his chin from shaving; Sirloin is a choice* ~ *of beef; The road ran through a* ~ *in the rock; a* ~ *in pay during a recession; a stylish* ~ (of hair or clothes); *a 40%* ~ *(Slang.* share) *in the profits; Cadillacs are* **a cut** (*Informal.* somewhat) **above** *other cars; a write-up illustrated with* ~*s* (i.e. pictures). **—cut and run** run away quickly. **—cut back** reduce; prune; **cut·back** *n.: a budgetary* ~. **—cut both ways** have good and bad effects. **—cut ice (with)** have influence; make an impression. **—cut in** intrude, as in front of a moving car; interrupt (a conversation or to dance with one of a dancing couple). **—cut off** separate; interrupt; discontinue; deprive of something. **—cut out** **1** *Informal.* stop; leave suddenly: ~ *out that noise; Time to* ~ *out.* **2** suited: *not* ~ *out for medical school.* **—cut up** *Informal.* **1** criticize harshly. **2** play pranks, clown around, etc.; **cut·up** *n.* one who does so. **—cut-and-dried** (or **-dry**) *adj.* already prepared, as by formula; routine.

cu·ta·ne·ous (cue·TAY·nee·us) *adj.* on or of the skin: ~ *ulcers.*

cut·a·way (CUT·uh–) *n.* a tailcoat.

cute *adj.* **cut·er, cut·est** **1** pretty; dainty: *a* ~ *little hat.* **2** affectedly pleasing; artificial: *a* ~ *act.* **—cute·ly** *adv.;* **cute·ness** *n.* **—cute·sy** or **cute·sie** *adj.* cute in a mannered or deliberate way.

cut·i·cle (CUE·ti·cl) *n.* **1** the tough skin at the edge of a nail. **2** the surface layer of skin. **—cu·tic·u·lar** (–TIC–) *adj.*

cut·lass (–lus) *n.* a short, curved slashing sword. **—cut·ler** *n.* one who sells or makes knives and other cutting tools. **—cut·ler·y** *n.* knives, scissors, etc.; also, tableware such as spoons, forks, and knives.

cut·let (–lit) *n.* a small leg or rib cut of meat: *veal* ~*s.*

cut·off *n.* a cutting off or what results from it; hence, a shortcut: *wears* ~*s* (i.e. jeans cut short) *in the summer;* **adj.**: *a* ~ *point; valve; the* ~ *date* (of an agreement). **—cut·out** *n.* a pattern, picture, etc. designed to be or that has been cut out. **—cut-rate** *adj.* offered or sold at a reduced price. **—cut·ter** *n.* **1** one that cuts. **2** a small, fast boat or sleigh. **—cut·throat** *n.* a murderer; also ***adj.*** merciless; bloodthirsty: ~ *competition;* **cutthroat trout** a western trout with a red splotch on its lower jaw. **—cut·ting** *n.* a short slip for propagation; ***adj.*** hurting the feelings: ~ *remarks.*

cut·tle·bone *n.* the chalky internal shell of the cuttlefish, used to supplement feed for cage birds. **—cut·tle·fish** *n.* a squidlike mollusk that secretes an inky fluid from which sepia is made.

cut·up See CUT. **—cut·worm** *n.* a very destructive, night-feeding moth larva.

cw clockwise.

c.w.o. cash with order. **—CWO** chief warrant officer.

cwt. hundredweight.

-cy *suffix.* **1** state; action: as in *accuracy, bankruptcy.* **2** rank or position: as in *chaplaincy.*

cy·an (blue) (SYE·un) a greenish blue. **—cy·a·nid(e)** (SYE·uh–) *n.* any of a group of compounds, esp. the poisonous sodium and potassium cyanides. **—cy·an·o·gen** (–AN·uh–) *n.* a colorless, poisonous gas containing carbon and nitrogen. **—cy·a·no·sis** (–NOH–) *n.* an unhealthy blue color of the skin caused by lack of oxygen in the blood; **cy·a·not·ic** (–NOT–) *adj.*

cy·ber·na·tion (sye·bur·NAY–) *n.* the use of computers to control machines; **cy·ber·nate** (SYE–) *v.* **-nates, -nat·ed, -nat·ing** **—cy·ber·net·ics** (–NET–) *n.pl.* [takes *sing. v.*] the study of information flow and control processes in men and machines;**cy·ber·net·ic** *adj.;* **cy·ber·net·(i·c)ist** or **cy·ber·ne·ti·cian** (–TISH·un) *n.*

cyc(l). cyclopedia. **—cycl(o)-** *comb. form.* circular or cyclic. **—cy·cla·mate** (SYE·cluh–) *n.* an artificial salt of sodium or calcium used as a sugar substitute. **—cy·cla·men** (SYE·cluh–) *n.* a plant related to the primrose, having white, pink, or purple flowers. **—cy·cle** *n.* **1** the time in which a usu. periodically recurring event occurs; also, one complete occurrence of a periodic action or event: *the life* ~*; alternating current which reverses direction at 60* ~*s per second.* **2** a long time. **3** a set of songs or poems on one theme: *the Homeric* ~. **4** a bicycle, tricycle, or motorcycle; ***v.*** **-cles, -cled, -cling** ride a cycle; **cy·clist** *n.* **—cy·clic** or **cy·cli·cal** *adj.* of, like, or occurring in a cycle; **cy·cli·cal·ly** *adv.* **—cy·clom·e·ter** (–CLOM·i–) *n.* an instrument for measuring the distance traveled by a rotating wheel. **—cy·clone** *n.* a weather phenomenon of a central low-pressure area surrounded by winds spiralling toward the center, including storm conditions like hurricanes and tornados; esp. a tornado; **cy·clon·ic** (–CLON–) *adj.* **—cy·clo·p(a)e·di·a** (–PEE·dee·uh) *n.* an encyclopedia. **—cy·clo·tron** *n.* a high-speed particle accelerator using alternating electric fields.

cyg·net (SIG·nut) *n.* a young swan.

cyl. *Abbrev.* for **cyl·in·der** (SIL–) *n.* a solid shape bounded by two parallel circles of the same size and the lines connecting corresponding points on their edges; also, a cylindrical object, as a tin can or a piston chamber of an engine. **—cy·lin·dri·cal** (–LIN–) *adj.:* ~ *oil drums.*

cym·bal (SIM·bl) *n.* a slightly concave brass disk used as a percussion instrument. **—cym·bal·ist** *n.*

cyme (SIME) *n.* a usu. flat-topped flower cluster that blooms from the center outward. **—cy·mose** *adj.* cymelike or bearing cymes: *Crab apples and certain dogwoods have* ~ *flowers.*

cyn·ic (SIN–) *n.* a usu. sarcastic person who believes all people act from self-interest; **cyn·i·**

cal *adj.: a ~ rejection of high ideals;* **cyn·i·cal·ly** *adv.* —**cyn·i·cism** *n.: a deep ~ about political morality.* —**cy·no·sure** (SYE·nuh–) *n.* something that attracts attention, admiration, etc.: *The returning war hero was the ~ of all eyes.*

C.Y.O. Catholic Youth Organization.

cy·press (SYE–) *n.* any of several evergreen trees of the pine family with scalelike leaves: *the ~ swamps of Louisiana.*

Cy·prus (SYE–) an island and republic in the E. Mediterranean; 3,572 sq. mi. (9,251 km^2); *cap.* Nicosia. —**Cyp·ri·ot** (SIP·ree·ut) *adj.* & *n.: Greek and Turkish ~s.*

cyst (SIST) *n.* an abnormal sac in the body containing fluid; **cyst·ic** *adj.;* **cystic fibrosis** a hereditary disease affecting the pancreas, mucous membranes, and respiratory system.

-cyte or **cyto-** *comb.form.* cell: as in *leukocyte.* —**cy·tol·o·gy** (sye·TOL–) *n.* the scientific study of cells; **cy·to·log·ic** (–LOJ–) or **-i·cal** *adj.;* **cy·tol·o·gist** (–TOL–) *n.* —**cy·to·plasm** (SYE·tuh–) *n.* the protoplasm of a cell outside the nucleus; **cy·to·plas·mic** (–PLAZ–) *adj.* —**cy·to·sine** (SYE·tuh·seen) *n.* one of the basic coding chemicals in DNA and RNA.

C.Z. Canal Zone.

czar (ZAR) *n.* **1** a Russian emperor (until 1917); *fem.* **cza·ri·na.** (zah·REE·nuh). **2** a powerful leader; also, autocrat: *energy ~ in the Republican cabinet.* —**czar·ist** *n.* & *adj.*

Czech (CHEK) *n.* a Czechoslovakian, esp. from Bohemia or Moravia; also, the Slavic language of the Czechs; also ***adj.*** —**Czech·o·slo·va·ki·a** (chek·uh·sloh·VAH·kee·uh) a country in C. Europe; 49,371 sq. mi. (127,869 km^2); *cap.* Prague. —**Czech·o·slo·vak** (–SLOH–) or **-va·ki·an** (–VAH·kee·un) *adj.* & *n.*

D or **d** (DEE) *n.* **D's** or **d's** the fourth letter of the English alphabet. **—D** **1** fourth in a series; the lowest grade above a failure: *a D on his algebra test.* **2** the Roman numeral for 500. **3** deuterium. **—'d** did; had; would. **—d'** do. **—d.** date; day(s); degree; diameter; died; penny or pence *(Brit.).* **—D.** December; Democrat(ic); doctor; duchess; duke; Dutch.

da. daughter; day(s). **—D.A.** District Attorney.

dab *v.* **dabs, dabbed, dab·bing** put on, touch, or strike with a light, quick, usu. soft stroke: *a child ~ing paste on paper; ~d his eyes with his handkerchief.* **—n.:** *A quick ~ removed the smudge; Put a little ~ of butter on the toast.*

dab·ble *v.* **dab·bles, dab·bled, dab·bling** **1** spatter with water; splash. **2** play splashing in the water; hence, work or do amateurishly: *~ in science; a banker who likes to ~ at gardening.* **—dab·bler** *n.*

Dac·ca (DAC·uh) capital of Bangladesh.

dace *n.* a small, minnowlike, freshwater fish related to the carp.

da·cha (DAH·chuh) *n.* a country house in the U.S.S.R.

dachs·hund (DAHKS·hoond) *n.* a breed of dog with a long, low body, a pointed snout, and drooping ears.

Da·cron (DAY·cron) *Trademark.* a synthetic fiber or a wrinkle-free cloth made from it; also **da·cron** *n.*

dac·tyl (–tl) *n.* a metrical foot having a long or stressed syllable followed by two short or unstressed syllables. **—dac·tyl·ic** (–TIL–) *adj.* & *n.*: *~ hexameter.*

dad *n. Informal.* father.

Da·da or **da·da** (DAH·dah) *n.* an artistic and literary movement started in 1916 as a violent break with tradition. **—Da·da·ism** *n.* **—Da·da·ist** *adj.* & *n.*

dad·dy (DAD·ee) *n.* **dad·dies** [child's word] father. **—daddy long·legs** *sing.* & *pl.* **1** a spiderlike arachnid with long, thin legs. **2** *Brit.* a crane fly.

dae·mon (DEE·mun) *n.* same as DEMON.

daf·fo·dil (DAF·uh·dil) *n.* a yellow flower, a kind of narcissus, that blooms in early spring.

daf·fy (DAF·ee) *adj.* **daf·fi·er, daf·fi·est** *Informal.* daft; **daf·fi·ness** *n.* **—daft** *adj.* insane; also, foolish; zany; **daft·ness** *n.*

dag·ger (DAG·ur) *n.* **1** a pointed, two-edged knife used for stabbing; **at daggers drawn** in open hostility; **look daggers at** stare at with hate or fury. **2** a mark (†) used as a reference.

da·guerre·o·type (duh·GAIR·uh–) *n.* an early process for making photographs involving long exposure of a sensitized plate; also, such a photograph.

dahl·ia (DAL·yuh) *n.* a perennial plant with tuberous roots and showy composite flowers.

Da·ho·mey (duh·HO·mee) former name of BENIN.

dai·ly (–lee) *adj.* of, for, done, or occurring every day: *our ~ bread; a ~ rate of $12.* ***—adv:*** *Take 2 pills twice ~.* **—n.,** *pl.* **-lies** a newspaper put out every weekday. **—daily double** a bet on the winners in two races. **—daily dozen** a set of routine daily exercises.

dain·ty (–tee) *adj.* **-ti·er, -ti·est** **1** delicate and pleasing: *a ~ centerpiece for the table; a ~ dance step.* **2** fussy; fastidious: *a ~ eater.* **—n.,** *pl.* **-ties** a delicacy. **—dain·ti·ly** *adv.* **—dain·ti·ness** *n.*

dai·qui·ri (DYE·kuh·ree, DAK–) *n.* a cocktail of rum, sugar, and lime or lemon juice.

dair·y *n.* **dair·ies** a farm specializing in milk production; also, a place where milk and milk products are processed or sold; **dair·y·ing** *n.* **—dair·y·man** *n.* **-men; dair·y·maid** *n.* a female helper in a dairy.

da·is (DAY·is) *n.* an elevated platform for a speaker, special guest, etc.

dai·sy (–zee) *n.* **-sies** a composite flower with white rays and a yellow center; also, any similar flower. **—push up daisies** be in one's grave.

Da·kar (dah·CAR) capital of Senegal.

Da·ko·ta (duh·COH·tuh) *n.* (a member of) any of several Amerindian tribes now settled in North and South Dakota, Montana, and Minnesota; also, their Siouan language. **—Da·ko·tan** *adj.* & *n.*

Da·lai (DAH·lye) **Lama** the head of Lamaism.
da·la·si (dah·LAH·see) *n.* the basic unit of money in Gambia, equal to 100 bututs.
dale *n.* a valley: *hill and ~.*
Dal·las (DAL·us) a city in N. Texas.
dal·ly (–lee) *v.* **dal·lies, dal·lied, dal·ly·ing** **1** waste time: *a child ~ing over supper.* **2** trifle or play: *~d with the idea of buying a new car.* **3** flirt; **dal·li·ance** *n.: a brief ~ with a young actress.* —**dal·li·er** *n.*
Dal·ma·tian (–MAY·shun) *n.* a breed of white dog with black spots and a short, thick coat.
dam *n.* **1** an obstacle built across a watercourse; ***v.* dams, dammed, dam·ming:** *~d the creek to make a duck pond; It is unhealthy to* **dam up** *your anger.* **2** a mother, esp. of four-legged animals: *a thoroughbred horse with registered sire and ~.*
dam·age (–ij) *n.* **1** injury or hurt, esp. resulting in loss: *$1,500 ~ to his car in an accident.* **2 damages** *pl.* money as a recompense for loss or impairment: *~s for defamation of character.* —***v.* -ag·es, -aged, -ag·ing** cause or suffer damage: *She ~d her toy; Smaller cars ~ more easily; a badly ~d building.* —**dam·age·a·ble** *adj.*
Dam·a·scene (–uh·seen) *adj.* & *n.* —**dam·a·scene** *v.* **-scenes, -scened, -scen·ing** decorate (esp. steel) with wavy lines or inlaid gold and silver, as is done to **Damascus steel,** a strong steel for sword blades. —**Da·mas·cus** (duh·MAS–) capital of Syria. —**dam·ask** (DAM·usk) *n.* **1** a rich fabric with a woven-in pattern, used esp. for table linen. **2** Damascus steel. Also ***adj.;*** **damask rose** an Asiatic rose that is the source of attar of roses.
dame *n.* **1** lady: *Dame Fortune.* **2** *Brit.* **Dame** a title for women corresponding to knight. **3** *Slang.* a woman.
damn (DAM) *v.* **1** criticize severely; condemn; also, condemn to hell: *a play ~ed by the critics; the ~ed and the saved;* **damn with faint praise** praise so slightly as to imply fault. **2** curse or swear saying "damn": *~ it all!* —***n.*** a damning; **not care** (or **give) a damn** not care at all; **not worth a damn** worthless. —**dam·na·ble** (DAM·nuh·bl) *adj.;* **dam·na·bly** *adv.* —**dam·na·tion** (–NAY–) *n.* a damning or being damned: *sent to eternal ~.* —**damned** (DAMD) *adj. Informal.* absolute; utter: *a ~fool;* ***adv.*** very: *A ~ fine mess we're in now.* —**damn(e)d·est** *adj. superl.* utmost.
Damocles See SWORD OF DAMOCLES.
Da·mon (DAY·mun) **and Pyth·i·as** (PITH·ee·us) two proverbially devoted friends, as in classical legend.
damp *n.* **1** harmful gas, as in a coal mine. **2** a moderate wetness; ***adj.:*** *shoes ~ from the rain;* ***v.*** make damp; also, reduce the enthusiasm, force, or power of: *a defeat that didn't ~ his spirit;* also **damp·en.** —**damp·ness** *n.* —**damp·ish** *adj.* —**damp·er** *n.* something that depresses or damps, as a plate for checking the draft in a flue, or a felt pad for stopping a piano string's vibration: *His father's presence put a ~ on the party.*
dam·sel (–zl) *n. Archaic.* a maiden: *Knights rescued ~s in distress.* —**dam·sel·fly** *n.* **-flies** a small, slender kind of dragonfly.
dam·son (–zn) *n.* a small, dark plum.
Dan. Daniel; Danish.
dan *n.* a level of proficiency in Japanese sports or games: *a second-~ judo expert.*
dance *v.* **danc·es, danced, danc·ing** **1** move the body and feet rhythmically, usu. to music; also, perform (a particular dance step): *~ing the cha-cha.* **2** move lightly, esp. up and down: *a boxer ~ing around the ring.* —***n.*** **1** a set of dancing movements, as the tango or waltz; also, music for a dance. **2** a party given for dancing. **3** dancing: *a school of ~.* —**danc·er** *n.*
dan·de·li·on (DAN·duh·lye·un) *n.* a bright-yellow composite flower having edible, jagged leaves.
dan·der *n. Informal.* **get one's dander up** make or become angry.
dandify See DANDY.
dan·dle *v.* **-dles, -dled, -dling** bounce (a child) up and down, as on one's knee or in one's arms.
dan·druff *n.* whitish flakes of dead skin from the scalp.
dan·dy (–dee) *n.* **-dies** **1** a man who is overly stylish and careful in dress; fop; **dan·di·fy** *v.* **-fies, -fied, -fy·ing** **2** *Informal.* something excellent of its type; ***adj.*** **-di·er, -di·est:** *That's fine and ~ by me!*
Dane *n.* a person from or living in Denmark.
dan·ger (DAIN·jur) *n.* exposure to or risk of harm; also, a source of this: *The sick boy was in ~ of (losing) his life.* —**dan·ger·ous** (–juh·rus) *adj.: Firefighting is a ~ occupation.* —**dan·ger·ous·ly** *adv.: a ~ sharp corner.*
dan·gle (DANG·gl) *v.* **-gles, -gled, -gling** hang loosely and swing; also, make to do so; **dangling participle** one without a proper relation to what it modifies, e.g. "*Standing* on the porch, the moon looked beautiful."
Dan·iel (DAN·yul) **1** an Old Testament prophet: *~ in the lion's den.* **2** a wise judge, esp. if youthful: *"a ~ come to judgment."*
Dan·ish (DAY·nish) *adj.* pertaining to Danes or Denmark: *~ cheese.* —***n.*** **1** the Danish language. **2** also **Danish pastry,** a rich pastry, usu. with filling and icing.
dank *adj.* injuriously or unpleasantly damp: *a ~ dungeon.* —**dank·ly** *adv.* —**dank·ness** *n.*
dan·seur (dahn·SUR) *n.* a male ballet dancer; *fem.* **dan·seuse** (–SOOZ).
Dan·te (DAHN·tay) **Alighieri.** 1265–1321, Italian poet. —**Dan·te·an** *n.* & *adj.*
Dan·ube (–yoob) a European river flowing into the Black Sea. —**Da·nu·bi·an** (–YOO·bee·un) *adj.*

dap·per *adj.* **1** spruce and trim; smartly dressed. **2** small and nimble.

dap·ple *v.* **dap·ples, dap·pled, dap·pling** mark with spots. **—dap·ple(d)** *adj.: a horse with a ~d rump.*

D.A.R. Daughters of the American Revolution.

dare *v.* **dares** [or **dare** if followed by the infinitive without *to*], **dared, dar·ing** **1** challenge: *I ~ you to hit me;* ***n.:*** *I did it on a ~.* **2** have the boldness (to); face boldly: *How ~ he insult her? I* **dare say** (i.e. think it likely) *it is cold outside; ~ing great dangers; "~ to be a Daniel."* **—dar·er** *n.* **—dare·dev·il** *n.* one who acts with reckless courage; ***adj.:*** *~ stunt-flying.* **—dar·ing** *n.* & *adj.: a man of great ~; a ~ hero;* **dar·ing·ly** *adv.*

Dar es Sa·laam (–suh·LAHM) capital of Tanzania.

dark *adj.* **1** lacking in light; not bright or light; hence, obscure; hidden; mysterious; unenlightened: *a ~ day* (i.e. overcast); *~ blue; ~ hair; a deep, ~ secret;* **Dark Ages** *of Europe* (i.e. early Middle Ages); *Africa, once the* **Dark Continent.** **2** gloomy; also, evil; angry: *a ~ look.* ***—n.*** darkness; hence, ignorance: *They agreed to keep her* **in the dark** *about the plan.* **—dark·ly** *adv.* **—dark·ness** *n.* **—dark adaptation** the eye's adjustment to light. **—dark·en** *v.* dim: *Clouds ~ed the sky; Her face ~ed with rage;* **darken someone's door** be an unwelcome visitor. **—dark horse** a contestant whose strength is still unknown. **—dark·ling** *adv.* & *adj. Poetic.* in the dark. **—dark·room** *n.* a room made dark for photographic developing. **—dark·some** *adj. Poetic.* somewhat dark.

dar·ling *n.* a person or thing much loved or preferred. ***—adj.*** **1:** *my ~ Clementine.* **2** *Informal.* charming: *What a ~ purse!*

darn **1** *n.* & *v. Informal* [euphemism] damn; **darn(ed)** *adj.* & *adv.* **2** *v.* repair (a hole, garment, etc.) by interlacing yarn or thread: *to ~ old socks;* ***n.*** a hole thus repaired; **darn·er** *n.*

dar·nel (–nl) *n.* any of a group of weed grasses.

darning needle a large needle for darning; also, a dragonfly.

dart *n.* **1** a pointed missile that is thrown, blown by a blowgun, etc.; **darts** *pl.* [takes *sing. v.*] a game in which darts are thrown at a target for scores. **2** a sudden, fast movement. **3** a seam joining the edges of a fold or cut to improve a garment's fit. ***—v.:*** *The frog ~ed out his tongue to catch the fly; a rabbit ~ing across the road.* **—dart·er** *n.* any of several small freshwater fishes of the perch family.

Dar·win, Charles. 1809–82, English naturalist whose theory **Dar·win·ism** holds that evolution took place by natural selection. **—Dar·win·i·an** (–WIN–) *adj.* & *n.* **—Dar·win·ist** *n.* & *adj.*

dash *v.* **1** move, throw, or strike with violent speed; hence, destroy: *The winner ~ed* (i.e. ran) *across the finish line; ~ed the cup to the ground; Her hopes were ~ed; I* **dashed off** (i.e. wrote hastily) *a letter to my family.* **2** splash. **3** mix with a bit of another substance: *water ~ed with vinegar.* ***—n.*** [corresponding to the *v.* senses] **1:** *a quick ~ for safety; set a record in the 100-meter~.* **2:** *a ~ of ice water in the face.* **3:** *add a ~ of vanilla extract.* **4** vigorous, spirited action. **5** a punctuation mark (—). **—dash·board** *n.* an instrument panel below a vehicle's windshield. **—dash·er** *n.* a plunger with paddles for agitating cream in a churn.

da·shi·ki (dah·SHEE·kee) *n.* a loose, brightly colored shirt or tunic.

dash·ing *adj.* spirited; also, stylish: *a ~ young lieutenant.*

das·tard (–turd) *n.* a cowardly villain. **das·tard·ly** *adj.*

dat· dative.

da·ta (DAY·tuh, DAT–) *n.pl.* [used also with *sing. v.*] basic information; facts as a basis for analysis. **—data bank** a file of information stored in a computer; also, the place housing it. **—da·ta·ma·tion** (–MAY–) *n.* electronic data processing. **—data processing** operations to convert, store, analyse, etc. data; **data processor.**

[1]date *n.* a sweet oblong fruit of the **date palm** tree.

[2]date *n.* **1** the time at which something exists, happens, is made, etc.; esp., the day of the month and the year: *one's ~ of birth; Today's ~ is the 19th.* **2** *Informal.* a social meeting, esp. between a male and female; also, a person with whom one has a date: *make a ~ for coffee; a ~* (i.e. appointment) *with destiny.* ***—v.*** **dates, dat·ed, dat·ing** **1** record or mark the date on: *a postcard ~d March 3.* **2** determine or show the date or age of: *Carbon 14 is used to ~ artifacts; That expression ~s you, Father.* **3** have or make a date (with): *Is your sister old enough to ~ boys?* **—date from** or **date back to** be in existence since. **—out of date** old-fashioned; obsolete. **—to date** until now. **—up to date** modern; using or knowing current ideas or methods. **—dat(e)·a·ble** *adj.: a ~ piece of pottery.* **—dat·ed** *adj.* old-fashioned. **—date·less** *adj.* **1** undated. **2** timeless; also, too old to date. **3** undying: *~ fame.* **—date·line** *n.* the place and date of origin of a document or story, as "Washington, July 8." **—dating bar** a bar for single people to find dates in. **—da·tive** (DAY·tiv) *n.* a grammatical case indicating esp. the indirect object, as "him" in "Give him the book"; ***adj.:*** *the ~ case.* **—da·tum** (DAY–, DAT–) *n., pl.* **-ta** or **-tums** a fact, known or conceded. See also DATA.

daub *v.* **1** smear or coat, as with grease, clay, plaster, etc.; also, to soil or dirty: *hands all ~ed with ink.* **2** paint crudely or rapidly. ***—n.*** **1** material for daubing: *a hut made of wattle and ~* (i.e. mud or clay). **2** a daubing; a smear or stain; also, a crude painting. **—daub·er** *n.*

daugh·ter (DAW·tur) *n.* a female offspring; also, a descendant thought of as female: *Italian, French, and Spanish are ~s of Latin.* —**daugh·ter-in-law** *n.* **-ters-in-law** the wife of one's son. —**daugh·ter·ly** *adj.: ~ respect for her parents.*

daunt *v.* dishearten; frighten. —**daunt·less** *adj.: a ~ hero.* —**daunt·less·ly** *adv.* —**daunt·less·ness** *n.*

dau·phin *n.* the eldest son of a king of France.

dav·en·port (DAV–) *n.* a large couch, often a daybed.

Da·vid (DAY–) the second king of Israel: *a son of ~'s line.*

Da·vis (DAY–), **Jefferson.** 1808–1889, president of the Confederate States of America.

dav·it *n.* one of a pair of cranes for holding or raising and lowering a ship's small boat from the side.

Da·vy Jones's Locker the sea bottom, considered the grave of the drowned.

daw·dle *v.* **-dles, -dled, -dling** waste time; idle; loiter. —**daw·dler** *n.*

dawn *n.* the first light of day; daybreak; hence, beginning: *the ~ of a new age.* —***v.*** become light at sunrise; hence, begin to develop, be clear, etc.: *Day ~ed; A bright idea* **dawned upon** *him; It ~ed on me that I was free.*

day *n.* **1** the period from sunrise to sunset; **day and night** continually. **2** the 24-hour period from midnight to midnight; **day after day** or **day in, (and) day out** every day; always. **3** a part of the day for working: *a 12-hour ~; It's* **all in a day's work** (i.e. a normal thing); *I'm exhausted, let's* **call it a day** (i.e. stop working); *insisted on having a* **day in court** (i.e. opportunity to present their side in the dispute) **4** a period of success, power, etc.: *a politician who has had his ~* (i.e. is no longer important). **5** an era or age: *in Chaucer's ~; in ~s of yore.* **6** contest: *Our greater strength* **carried the day.** —**day·bed** *n.* a couch convertible to a bed. —**day·book** *n.* a book for daily records; diary. —**day·break** *n.* dawn. —**day care** care of pre-school children, usu. while the mother works, as at a **day-care center** or **day nursery.** —**day·dream** *n.* a reverie; an unrealistic, pleasant thought; ***v.:*** *~ed about inheriting money.* —**day·light** *n.* **1** sunlight; daytime: *working by ~.* **2** understanding; also, an end to something hard or unpleasant: *We may never* **see daylight** *on this problem.* **3 daylights** *Slang.* wits: *I scared the ~s out of you with the toy gun.* —**day·light-sav·ing time** plan used in the summer by which clocks are advanced one hour to lengthen the working day. —**day nursery** same as DAY-CARE CENTER. —**Day of Atonement** Yom Kippur. —**day school** a private school without facilities to board students. —**day student** a college student living off campus. —**day·time** *n.* same as DAY, *n.* 1.

Day·ton (–tn) a manufacturing city in S. W. Ohio.

daze *v.* **daz·es, dazed, daz·ing** stun; confuse. —***n.:*** *He was in a ~ for hours after he was hit on the head.*

daz·zle (DAZL) *v.* **daz·zles, daz·zled, daz·zling** dim the vision of, overpower, or impress, as by bright light or brilliance: *~ing light reflected from the water; a ~ing beauty.* Also ***n.*** —**daz·zler** *n.*

db or **dB** decibel.

dbl. double.

d.c. or **D.C.** direct current. —**D.C.** District of Columbia; Doctor of Chiropractic.

D.D. demand draft; Doctor of Divinity.

D-day *n.* the starting date for a military operation; esp., June 6, 1944, when the Allies invaded Europe.

D.D.S. Doctor of Dental Science; Doctor of Dental Surgery.

DDT a powerful insecticide.

DE Delaware. —**de-** *comb.form* [indicating] **1** removal; motion away from: as in *depilatory, detrain.* **2** reversal; opposite of: as in *de-escalate.* **3** down; reduction: as in *devalue, decline.*

dea·con (DEE·cn) *n.* **1** a lay assistant to a minister. **2** in some churches, a clergyman ranking below a priest. —**dea·con·ess** *n. fem.*

de·ac·ti·vate (–AC–) *v.* **-vates, -vat·ed, -vat·ing** make inactive or non-functional: *The army expert ~d the time bomb.* —**de·ac·ti·va·tion** (–VAY–) *n.*

dead (DED) *aj.* **1** no longer alive; also, inanimate: *Old Jones is ~ and buried; ~ as a doornail.* **2** like dead: *~ with fatigue; lay ~* (i.e. insensible) *to the world.* **3** lacking: **a** feeling: *ears ~ with the cold;* **b** warmth or interest: *a ~ party;* **c** sensitivity: *~ to all shame;* **d** brightness or resilience: *a ~ tennis ball.* **4** not in use; unusable; not active: *The referee ruled it a ~ ball* (i.e. out of play); *a ~ battery* (i.e. with no charge); *The telephone has gone ~; ~ soil* (i.e. infertile). **5** exact; unerring; complete: *I hit it ~ center; a ~ shot with a rifle; The ship fell into a ~ calm;* ***adv.:*** *stopped ~ in his tracks; Are you ~ certain?* —***n.*** **1:** *the quick and the ~* (i.e. dead people). **2** darkest or coldest part: *the ~ of night; the ~ of winter.* —**dead·beat** *n. Slang.* one who does not pay his debts or his fair share. —**dead duck** *Slang.* one sure to fail, to be killed, etc. —**dead·en** *v.* **1** reduce the force, brightness, or vigor of; deprive of sensation: *a soul ~ed by the blows of fate.* **2** to soundproof. —**dead end** **1** a street, hall, alley, etc. open at only one end. **2** something with no chance for progress. Hence **dead-end** *adj.: a ~ street; a bright young man stuck in a ~ job.* —**dead heat** a race or contest ending in a tie. —**dead letter** **1** a letter that cannot be delivered or returned, as because of an illegible address. **2** a rule or law no longer enforced but not yet repealed. —**dead·line** *n.* the time by which something must be done. —**dead·lock** *n.* a standstill resulting from two unrelenting forces; ***v.:*** *union and management* ~*ed over wage increases.* —**dead·ly** *adj.* **-li·er, -li·est** **1** causing death; to the death; very harmful: ~ *machine-gun fire; a* ~ *duel; the seven* **deadly sins** *that cause spiritual death.* **2** deathlike: *a* ~ *silence.* **3** extreme; absolute: *in* ~ *earnest.* **4** unerring: *a* ~ *aim.* —***adv.*** like death; also, very: *a* ~ *dull speech.* —**dead·pan** *adj.* & *adv.* without expression or emotion: *a* ~ *comedian; a* ~ *face.* —**dead reckoning** the determination of a ship's location by using a compass and logbook, but no astronomical observations. —**dead ringer** See [2]RING. —**Dead Sea** a salt lake on the Jordan-Israel border; the lowest spot below sea level on the earth's surface. —**dead weight** the weight of anything that is heavy and motionless; hence, a heavy burden. —**dead·wood** *n.* **1** wood dead on a tree. **2** a useless burden, as unproductive personnel.

deaf *adj.* unable to hear; hence, unwilling to pay heed: *Poor man, he's* ~ *as a post;* ~ *to her entreaties.* —**deaf·ness** *n.* —**deaf·en** *v.: a* ~*ing roar from the machinery.* —**deaf-mute** *n.* & *adj.* (one) who is deaf and dumb.

deal (DEEL) *v.* **deals, dealt** (DELT), **deal·ing** **1** give out; distribute, esp. cards to players: *to* ~ *someone four aces; The dictator* ~*t a blow to free speech.* **2** do business: *Realtors* ~ *in real estate;* **deal with** manage; behave with; also, be about: ~ *fairly with your partners; how to* ~ *with emotional problems; a book* ~*ing with economics.* —***n.*** **1** a turn to deal: *Is it my* ~ *now?* **2** a considerable amount or degree: *a great (or good)* ~ *of money; a good* ~ *richer than before.* **3** a business arrangement; hence, *Informal.* any treatment or arrangement; also, a bargain: *Our salesman closed the* ~*; All he wants is a square* (i.e. fair) ~*; a great* ~ *on carpets; The reforms promised a new* ~ *for the poor* (i.e. greater social justice); *big* ~*!* **4** fir or pine wood cut into planks; also, a plank of this. —**deal·er** *n.: The* ~ *also shuffles the cards; a used-car* ~. —**deal·er·ship** *n.* a franchised sales agency: *a* ~ *covering upstate New York.* —**deal·ing** *n.: I have no* ~*s with liars; Watch out for his crooked* ~ (i.e. behavior).

dean *n.* **1** the head of a body of canons, as in a cathedral. **2** the head of a faculty or other division in a university: ~ *of Humanities;* ~ *of Men; The* **dean's list** *recognizes students with very high marks.* **3** a senior or most respected member: *the* ~ *of American historians.* —**dean·er·y** *n.* **-er·ies,** —**dean·ship** *n.*

dear (DEER) *adj.* **1** beloved: *my* ~*est friend;* ***n.:*** *Come, my* ~. **2** warmly regarded: *a* ~ *old buddy;* ~ *Mr. Smith* [in letters]. **3** expensive. **4** sincere: *His* ~*est hope was for peace.* —***interj.:*** ~, ~, *what is wrong?* ~ *me!* —**dear·ly** *adv.* —**dear·ness** *n.*

Dear·born a city near Detroit, Michigan.

Dear John (letter) a letter from a wife or girl friend, esp. to a soldier away from home, breaking off a relationship.

dearth (DIRTH) *n.* a scarcity, esp. of food: *in time of* ~ *and famine; a crippling* ~ *of raw materials.*

death (DETH) *n.* **1** the act of dying or state of being dead; also, a cause of this: *The murderer was* **put to death** (i.e. executed). **2** destruction; also, killing: ~ *to fascism! Arms sellers are called "merchants of* ~*."* —**at the point of death** or **at death's door** near death, as from illness. —**catch** (or **take**) **one's death of** become seriously ill with. —**death on** devastating to: *a collection agency that is* ~ *on defaulters.* —**to death** extremely: *bored to* ~. —**death·bed** *n.* the bed one is dying on; hence, one's last hours of life. —**death·blow** *n.* a blow that kills; anything destructive. —**death·less** *adj.* immortal: ~ *prose.* —**death·like** *adj.: a* ~ *pallor.* —**death·ly** *adj.* resembling or causing death: *a* ~ *silence; a* ~ *wound;* ***adv.:*** ~ *quiet.* —**death mask** See MASK. —**death rattle** a gurgle in the throat made by a dying person. —**death row** a section of prison housing those awaiting execution. —**death's-head** *n.* a skull symbolizing death. —**Death Valley** a deep, dry valley in E.C. California and S. Nevada. —**death·watch** *n.* a vigil kept over the dying or dead.

deb *n. Informal.* a debutante.

de·ba·cle (di·BAH·cl) *n.* a sudden rout, disaster, or collapse.

de·bar (di–) *v.* **-bars, -barred, -bar·ring** shut out (as from a right); prevent: ~*d from the practice of medicine.* —**de·bar·ment** *n.*

de·bark (di–) *v.* unload; disembark. —**de·bar·ka·tion** (–CAY–) *n.*

de·base (di–) *v.* **-bas·es, -based, -bas·ing** lower in character or worth: ~*d coinage;* ~*d morals.* —**de·base·ment** *n.*

de·bate (di–) *v.* **-bates, -bat·ed, -bat·ing** **1** discuss or consider an issue from both sides: *I* ~*d whether to go or stay.* **2** participate in a formal contest of argument: *a good* ~*ing style; the* ~*ing club.* —***n.:*** *a* ~ *in the Senate.* —**de·bat·a·ble** *adj.* —**de·bat·er** *n.*

de·bauch (di–) *v.* deprave; also, engage in sensual dissipation. —**deb·au·chee** (di·baw·CHEE) *n.* one who debauches. —**de·bauch·er·y** *n.* **-er·ies:** *drunken* ~*s.*

de·ben·ture (di·BEN·chur) *n.* a bond guaranteed only by the general credit of the issuer.

de·bil·i·tate (di·BIL–) *v.* **-tates, -tat·ed, -tat·ing** make weak or feeble: *a* ~*ing sickness.* —**de·bil·i·ty** *n.* **-ties** a weakness, esp. of body.

deb·it *n.* **1** a sum owed, as recorded in an account; ***v.:*** ~ *my account for the purchase.* **2** a drawback or disadvantage.

deb·o·nair(e) (–uh·NAIR) *adj.* jauntily cheerful; gracious. —**deb·o·nair·ly** *adv.*

de·bouch (di·BOOSH) *v.* emerge or make emerge into an open area: *infantry* ~*ing onto the plain.*

de·brief (dee·BREEF) *v.* question (a diplomat, astronaut, etc.) at the end of a mission to obtain information. —**de·brief·ing** *n.*

de•bris or **dé•bris** (duh·BREE, DAY·bree) *n.* broken remains; rubble: *the ~ of an earthquake.*

debt (DET) *n.* something one owes; also, the state of owing: *owe a ~ of gratitude; deeply in ~ because of gambling.* **—debt•or** (DET·ur) *n.*

de•bug (dee–) *v.* **-bugs, -bugged, -bug•ging** remove the bugs (*n.* 1, 4, or 5) from.

de•bunk (dee–) *v. Informal.* reveal the falseness of: *~ing the myth of male superiority.*

De•bus•sy (deb·yoo·SEE), **Claude.** 1862–1918, French composer.

de•but (di·BYOO, DAY–) *n.* **1** a first performance or appearance. **2** the formal introduction of a young woman, called a **deb•u•tante** (DEB·yoo·tahnt), to society. Also **dé•but.**

Dec. December.

deca- *comb. form.* ten: as in *decagon, Decalog.* **—dec•ade** *n.* a 10-year period; also, any group of 10.

dec•a•dence (DEC·uh–) *n.* a decline or decay, esp. in art or morals: *the ~ of Byzantine art; our current educational ~;* **dec•a•dent** *adj.* & *n.;* **dec•a•dent•ly** *adv.*

dec•a•gon (DEC·uh–) *n.* a closed plane figure having ten sides.

de•cal (di·CAL, DEE·cal) *n.* a design transferred onto a surface from specially prepared paper; **de•cal•co•ma•ni•a** (di·cal·kuh·MAY·nee·uh) *n.* the process of doing this; also, a decal.

Dec•a•log(ue) (DEC·uh·log) *n.* the Ten Commandments.

de•camp (di–) *v.* **1** break camp and leave. **2** run away, usu. secretly: *an embezzler ~ing with $100,000.*

de•cant (di·CANT) *v.* pour (a liquid) gently, so as not to stir up the sediment: *~ wine into smaller bottles.* **—de•cant•er** *n.* an ornamental bottle for serving wine, sherry, etc.

de•cap•i•tate (di·CAP–) *v.* **-tates, -tat•ed, -tat•ing** behead. **—de•cap•i•ta•tion** (–TAY–) *n.: ~ by guillotine in France.*

dec•a•syl•la•ble (DEC·uh–) *n.* a 10-syllable line of verse. **—dec•a•syl•lab•ic** (–LAB–) *adj.* & *n.* **—de•cath•lon** (di·CATH·lon) *n.* a contest consisting of 10 track-and-field events, part of the Olympics since 1912; **de•cath•lete** (–leet) *n.* one who competes in this.

de•cay (di–) *v.* **1** lose power, health, beauty, etc. **2** decompose; rot; undergo radioactive disintegration: *~ing meat.* **—*n.*** [corresponding to the *v.* senses] **1:** *the ~ of the patient's mental faculties; a town fallen into ~.* **2:** *Prevent tooth ~; the slow ~ of radium.*

de•cease (di·SEECE) *n.* death. **—*v.* -ceas•es, -ceased, -ceas•ing** die; **deceased** *adj.* & *n.: pay our respects to the ~.* **—de•ced•ent** (di·SEED·nt) *n. Law.* a dead person.

de•ceit (–SEET) *n.* **1** dishonesty: *a sales pitch full of ~.* **2** a trick: *the con man's various ~s.* **3** deceitfulness: *a villain of great ~.* **—de•ceit•ful** *adj.: a ~ politician; ~ statistics;* **de•ceit•ful•ly** *adv.;* **de•ceit•ful•ness** *n.* **—de•ceive** (di·SEEV) *v.* **-ceives, -ceived, -ceiv•ing** mislead deliberately, as by lying, tricking, or cheating; act deceitfully. **—de•ceiv•er** *n.*

de•cel•er•ate (dee·SEL–) *v.* **-ates, -at•ed, -at•ing** go or cause to go more slowly. **—de•cel•er•a•tion** (–RAY–) *n.*

De•cem•ber (di·SEM–) *n.* the 12th month of the year. It has 31 days.

de•cen•cy (DEE·sn·see) *n.* **1** decentness; propriety. **2 decencies** *pl.* social proprieties: *Observe the ~s when in good company.*

de•cen•ni•al (di·SEN·ee·ul) *adj.* **1** of or lasting 10 years. **2** occurring every 10 years: *the ~ census.* **—*n.*** a tenth anniversary.

de•cent (DEE·snt) *adj.* **1** fitting; conforming to social convention, or modesty: *~ and respectable people.* **2** acceptable: *a ~ student; a ~ job.* **3** kind: *a ~ man.* **4** adequately dressed: *Don't come in; I'm not ~!* **—de•cent•ly** *adv.;* **de•cent•ness** *n.*

de•cen•tral•ize (dee·SEN·trul–) *v.* **-iz•es, -ized, -iz•ing** distribute something concentrated (as power, population, industry) over a wider area: *~ing Federal bureaucracy.* **—de•cen•tral•i•za•tion** (–ZAY–) *n.*

de•cep•tion (di·SEP–) *n.* **1** a deceiving or being deceived. **2** a trick, lie, etc.: *a skillful magician's ~s.* **—de•cep•tive** (–tiv) *adj.* **—de•cep•tive•ly** *adj.: a ~ simple question.*

deci- *comb.form.* one tenth. **—dec•i•bel** (DES–) *n.* the unit of intensity of sound: *A whisper measures 20 ~s, an automobile horn up to 90.*

de•cide (di–) *v.* **-cides, -cid•ed, -cid•ing 1** settle; resolve: *The issue was ~d by flipping a coin; The court case was ~d in favor of Mr. Smith.* **2** make up one's mind: *I can't ~ whether I like it or not.* **3** cause to decide: *A sense of fair play ~d me on the question.* **—de•cid•ed** *adj.* definite; also, determined: *a ~d advantage; a very ~d young man;* **de•cid•ed•ly** *adv.* **—de•cid•a•ble** *adj.*

de•cid•u•ous (di·SIJ·oo·us) *adj.* **1** of leaves, antlers, etc., falling off or out at a certain time: *Baby teeth are ~.* **2** having deciduous leaves: *a ~ tree; a ~ forest.*

dec•i•gram (DES–) *n.* 1/10 of a gram; also, *Brit.* **dec•i•gramme. —dec•i•li•ter** *n.* 1/10 of a liter; also, *Brit.* **dec•i•li•tre. —dec•i•mal** (DES·i·ml) *adj.* of or based on units of ten or tenths: *~ currency; the ~ system for weights and measures.* **—*n.*** a fraction **(decimal fraction)** with any power of ten as a denominator, expressed by a dot, or **decimal point,** followed by the numerator; thus .05 = 5/100. **—dec•i•mal•ize** *v.* **-iz•es, -ized, -iz•ing** convert to a decimal system. **—dec•i•mate** *v.* **-mates, -mated, -mat•ing** destroy a large portion (originally, one tenth) of: *cities ~d by plague.* **—dec•i•me•ter** *n.* 1/10 of a meter; also, *Brit.* **dec•i•me•tre.**

de·ci·pher (di·SYE·fur) *v.* interpret (something written) despite illegibility or a code; decode: *The teacher ~ed his scrawled notes.* —**de·ci·pher·a·ble** *adj.*

de·ci·sion (di·SIZH·un) *n.* **1** a deciding or resolution; also, a statement of this: *The judge's ~ was appealed to a higher court.* **2** the ability to decide; also, determined firmness. —**de·ci·sive** (di·SYE·siv) *adj.* **1** determining or deciding; crucial: *the ~ moment of the war.* **2** definite. **3** determined; firm: *a man of ~ judgment.* —**de·ci·sive·ly** *adj.* —**de·ci·sive·ness** *n.*

dec·i·stere (DES·i·steer) *n.* 1/10 of a stere.

deck *n.* **1** a floor of a ship, esp. the main one; **clear the decks** make ready: *The next batter is* **on deck** (i.e. ready). **2** a platform or other surface similar to a ship's deck. **3** a pack of cards. —***v.*** **1** provide or cover with a deck. **2** adorn; ornament: *~ the halls.* **3** *Slang.* knock to the floor. —**deck hand** a common sailor who works on deck.

deck·le (edge) *n.* a ragged untrimmed edge on paper. —**deck·le-edged** *adj.*

de·claim (di–) *v.* **1** recite or speak dramatically. **2** inveigh: *~ against higher taxes.* —**dec·la·ma·tion** (dec·luh·MAY–) *n.* —**de·clam·a·to·ry** (di·CLAM·uh–) *adj.*

dec·la·ra·tion (dec·luh·RAY–) *n.* an announcement or statement: *his ~ of innocence; a false ~ made to customs; the* **Declaration of Independence** (of the American colonies, 1776). —**de·clar·a·to·ry** (–CLAIR–) or **de·clar·a·tive** (–tiv) *adj.* making a statement. —**de·clare** (di–) *v.* **-clares, -clared, -clar·ing** **1** state or make known formally; announce: *The judges ~d the winner.* **2** state definitely: *Well, I ~!* [an exclamation of surprise]. **3** *Bridge.* name a trump suit or "no-trump." —**dec·lar·er** *n.*

de·clas·si·fy (dee–) *v.* **-fies, -fied, -fy·ing** make (secret papers) public or no longer classified. —**de·cline** (di–) *v.* **-clines, -clined, -clin·ing** **1** slope or move downwards; deteriorate; lessen: *land ~ing to the valley floor; rapidly ~ing health.* **2** refuse; say no (to): *He ~d our kind invitation.* **3** give the cases of: *~ the pronoun "I";* **de·clin·a·ble** *adj.* —***n.:*** *a ~ in prices; a shallow ~ to the beach; The tuberculosis patient went into a slow ~.*

de·cliv·i·ty (–CLIV–) *n.* **-ties** a downhill slope. —**de·cliv·i·tous** (–tus) *adj.*

de·code (dee–) *v.* **-codes, -cod·ed, -cod·ing** translate out of code; **de·cod·er** *n.*

dé·col·le·tage (–TAZH) *n.* the exposing of neck and shoulders by a low neckline; also, such a dress or neckline: *the allure of deep ~.* —**dé·col·le·té** (day·col·uh·TAY) *adj.* of dresses, having a low, revealing neckline; also, wearing such a dress.

de·col·o·nize (dee·COL·uh–) *v.* **-niz·es, -nized, -niz·ing** make (a colony) independent. —**de·col·o·ni·za·tion** (–ZAY–) *n.*

de·col·or·ize (dee·CUL–) *v.* **-iz·es, -ized, -iz·ing** remove color from —**de·col·or·iz·er** *n.*

de·com·mis·sion (dee·cuh·MISH·un) *v.* take out of service: *a ~ed aircraft carrier.*

de·com·pen·sa·tion (–SAY–) *n.* failure of the heart to maintain circulation.

de·com·pose (dee·cum·POZE) *v.* **-pos·es, -posed, -pos·ing** break down into its component parts; also, rot. —**de·com·po·si·tion** (–ZISH·un) *n.*

de·com·press (dee·cum–) *v.* reduce the pressure on. —**de·com·pres·sion** (–PRESH·un) *n.* as in **decompression sickness,** a painful paralysis of the joints and abdomen caused by a too rapid release from pressure, as when deep-sea divers or caisson workers surface too quickly.

de·con·ges·tant (dee·cun·JES·tunt) *n.* something that relieves congestion: *nasal ~s.*

de·con·tam·i·nate (dee·cun·TAM–) *v.* **-nates, -nat·ed, -nat·ing** free from contaminants, esp. radioactivity or poison gas. —**de·con·tam·i·na·tion** (–NAY–) *n.*

de·con·trol (dee·cun·TROLE) *v.* **-trols, -trolled, -trol·ling** remove the controls from: *~ing the economy.*

dé·cor or **de·cor** (day·COR) *n.* a style of decoration: *a new Scandinavian home ~.* —**dec·or·ate** (DEC·uh–) *v.* **-ates, -at·ed, -at·ing** **1** ornament; embellish: *~ing the basement for the party; an idea for ~ing* (i.e. painting, wallpapering, etc.) *the bedroom;* **dec·o·ra·tive** (–ruh·tiv) *adj.;* **dec·o·ra·tive·ly** *adv.* **2** honor with an award, medal, etc.: *a Marine ~d for heroism.* —**dec·or·a·tion** (–uh·RAY–) *n.: Christmas ~s;* **Decoration Day** same as MEMORIAL DAY; **dec·o·ra·tor** *n.: an interior ~.* —**dec·o·rous** (DEC·uh·rus, di·COR·us) *adj.* displaying decorum; **dec·o·rous·ly** *adv.* —**de·co·rum** (di·COR·um) *n.* seemliness or propriety in speech, action, appearance, etc.

de·cou·page or **dé·cou·page** (day·coo·PAZH) *n.* the decoration of surfaces with usu. paper cutouts covered by layers of varnish or lacquer.

de·coy (di–) *n.* something used to draw others into danger, as a wooden bird to lure others within range of a hunter. —***v.*** trick or lure into a trap.

de·crease (di·CREECE) *v.* **-creas·es, -creased, -creas·ing** grow or cause to grow smaller, less, etc.: *a ~d defense capability.* —***n.*** (DEE–): *a 40% ~ in the budget; Traffic deaths are* **on the decrease.** —**de·creas·ing·ly** *adv.*

de·cree (di·CREE) *n.* an official order or judgment, as of a king or court. —***v.*** **-crees, -creed, -cree·ing:** *The general had public honors ~d to him.*

dec·re·ment (DEC·ruh–) *n.* a decrease, esp. if gradual; also, the amount of it.

de·crep·it (di·CREP–) *adj.* worn-out or broken-down, esp. by long use. **—de·crep·i·tude** *n.*

de·cre·scen·do (day·cruh·SHEN·doh) *adj.* & *adv. Music.* decreasing in loudness. ***—n.,*** *pl.* **-dos:** *a symphony closing with a gentle ~.*

de·cry (di–) *v.* **-cries, -cried, -cry·ing** criticize openly and strongly: *~ing feeble efforts at legislative reform.*

ded·i·cate v. **-cates, -cat·ed, -cat·ing** **1** devote or commit, as to a sacred use, to a cause, etc.: *institutions ~d to the preservation of freedom; ~ a chapel; a humanitarian ~d to helping others.* **2** address (a book, song, etc.) to someone as a mark of honor: *~d to those who died in Vietnam;* **ded·i·ca·to·ry** *adj.: ~ verses.* **—ded·i·ca·tion** (–CAY–) *n.*

de·duce (di–) *v.* **-duc·es, -duced, -duc·ing** **1** infer by reasoning. **2** trace, as from the origin: *to ~ one's lineage.* Hence **de·duc·i·ble** *adj.* **—de·duct** (–DUCT) *v.* subtract; take away; **de·duct·i·ble** *adj.: a tax-~ expense.* **—de·duc·tion** *n.* a deducing or deducting: *a clever ~ by Sherlock Holmes; Allowable ~s from income tax include some medical bills.* **—de·duc·tive** (–tiv) *adj.* of or characterized by inference from premises to conclusions: *~ logic;* cf. INDUCTION; **de·duc·tive·ly** *adv.*

deed *n.* **1** something done; action: *brave ~s of heroes; chaste both in word and ~.* **2** a signed legal document, esp. conferring ownership of property; ***v.*** convey by deed.

dee·jay *n. Informal.* a disc jockey.

deem *v. Formal.* believe; consider: *The scout ~ed it unwise to proceed.*

de-em·pha·size *v.* **-siz·es, -sized, -siz·ing** reduce the emphasis on.

deep *adj.* **1** being or extending far down, in, or back: *the ~ blue sea; a field 200 ft. ~.* **2** from a depth: *take a ~ breath.* **3** of sound, low in pitch; of color, rich or dark. **4** powerful; also, profound; wise: *~ emotions; a ~ sleep; a ~ silence; a ~, scholarly study.* **5** very involved: *a man ~ in debt.* **6** mysterious: *a ~ secret.* **7** very serious or grave: *in ~ trouble for skipping school.* ***—adv.:*** *dig ~ in the earth; lost ~ in the woods; work ~ into the night; "Still waters run ~."* ***—n.:*** *denizens of* **the deep** (i.e. ocean); *in the ~* (i.e. dead) *of night.* **—go off the deep end** *Informal.* yield to anger or excitement. **—deep·ly** *adv.* **—deep·ness** *n.* **—deep·en** *v.* become or make deeper: *the ~ing gloom.* **—deep·freeze** *n.* **1** a freezer for quickly freezing food; **Deep·freeze** *Trademark.* **2** a suspension of action or vital functions; ***v.*** **-freez·es,** *pt.* **-froze** or **-freezed,** *pp.* **-froz·en** or **-freezed, -freez·ing.** **—deep-fry** *v.* **-fries, -fried, -fry·ing** fry (potatoes, onions, etc.) immersed in fat. **—deep-root·ed** *adj.* firmly implanted, as a plant with deep roots: *~ prejudice.* **—deep-sea** *adj.* of the deep parts of the sea: *~ diving; ~ exploration.* **—deep-seat·ed** *adj.* **1** well below the surface. **2** deep-rooted. **—deep-set** *adj.* deeply set. **—Deep South** the states of Alabama, Georgia, Louisiana, and Mississippi. **—deep space** space beyond the moon or the solar system.

deer *n. sing.* & *pl.* any of a group of ruminant mammals having cloven hooves, including moose, elk, white-tailed deer, caribou, etc. **—deer·fly** *n.* **-flies** any of several bloodsucking flies smaller than horseflies. **—deer·skin** *n.* & *adj.* (a leather or garment) made of deer hide.

de-es·ca·late (dee·ES·cuh–) *v.* **-lates, -lat·ed, -lat·ing** decrease the scope or intensity of: *~d the war.* **—de-es·ca·la·tion** (–LAY–) *n.*

def. defense; definite; definition.

de·face (di–) *v.* **-fac·es, -faced, -fac·ing** disfigure the surface or lettering of: *arrested for ~ing the War Memorial.* **—de·face·ment** *n.*

de fac·to (di·FAC·toh) in actual fact; actual(ly); not DE JURE.

de·fal·cate (di·FAL–) *v.* **-cates, -cat·ed, -cat·ing** misappropriate money entrusted to one. **—de·fal·ca·tion** (–CAY–) *n.*

de·fame (di–) *v.* **-fames, -famed, -fam·ing** injure (someone's) reputation by libel or slander. **—def·a·ma·tion** (def·uh·MAY–) *n.* **—de·fam·a·to·ry** (di·FAM·uh–) *adj.* **—de·fam·er** (di·FAY·mur) *n.*

de·fault (di–) *v.* fail to do something, as appear in court, repay a loan, or enter a contest. ***—n.:*** *The plaintiff lost his case by ~;* **in default of** because of the lack or absence of.

de·feat (di·FEET) *v.* **1** thwart; frustrate: *~ your own purpose.* **2** beat: *The Yankees were ~ed 2–1.* ***—n.:*** *the ~ of Napoleon.* **—de·feat·ism** *n.* a too ready acceptance or expectation of defeat; **de·feat·ist** *adj.* & *n.: a ~ attitude.*

def·e·cate (DEF·uh–) *v.* **-cates, -cat·ed, -cat·ing** **1** empty the bowels of excrement. **2** free or become free from impurities. **—def·e·ca·tion** (–CAY–) *n.*

de·fect (di–) *n.* a lack, fault, or imperfection: *a speech ~.* ***—v.*** desert to another cause, party, etc.: *a spy ~ing to the Soviets;* **de·fec·tor** *n.;* **de·fec·tion** *n.* **—de·fec·tive** (–tiv) *adj.* having a defect: *sent the ~ clock back to the factory; A ~ verb lacks some of the usual forms* e.g. "ought"; ***n.*** a subnormal person: *a mental ~.*

de·fend (di–) *v.* **1** protect; fight for; also, argue on behalf of: *~ yourself! I ~ your right to speak; ~ing a thesis.* **2** *Law.* speak for someone accused or sued (called a **de·fend·ant**); also, contest (a claim or action). **—de·fend·er** *n.: "Defender of the Faith"* (a title of English monarchs). **—de·fense** (–FENCE) *n.* **1** an act or means of defending: *The best ~ is a good offense; civil ~; a ~ of his theory against critics.* **2** a defendant and his lawyer(s); their case: *counsel for the ~.* Also **de·fence** *Brit.* **—defense mechanism** an unconscious psychological protection against unpleasant truths or feelings. —**de·fense·less** *adj.;* **de·fen·si·ble** *adj.;* **de·fen·sive** (–siv) *adj.* & *n.: Their strong attack kept us* **on the defensive.**

de·fer (di·FUR) *v.* **-fers, -ferred, -fer·ring** **1** put off until later; esp., delay induction into the military; **de·fer·ment** *n.: a draft ~ for a college student.* **2** yield to someone's request or opinion, esp, as a courtesy: *I ~ to your superior judgment;* **def·er·ence** (DEF·uh·runce) *n.* courteous respect: *in ~ to the feelings of others;* **def·er·en·tial** (–REN·shul) *adj.*

de·fi·ance (di·FYE·unce) *n.* **1** a challenge: *explorers bidding ~ to nature.* **2** bold refusal to obey authority. —**in defiance of** despite; defying. —**de·fi·ant** (–unt) *adj.: a ~ young hoodlum;* **de·fi·ant·ly** *adv.*

de·fi·cien·cy (–FISH·un·see) *n.* a being deficient or its amount: *a severe mental ~; a ~ of $19; A* **deficiency disease** *is caused by a lack of vitamins or minerals.* —**de·fi·cient** (–unt) *adj.* lacking something necessary; also, insufficient: *a diet ~ in vitamin C.* —**def·i·cit** (DEF–) *n.* the amount by which a sum is too small; a deficiency in money: *huge budgetary ~s;* **deficit spending** (or **financing**) the use of borrowed money to make expenditures.

[1]de·file (di–) *v.* **-files, -filed, -fil·ing** make dirty or impure; desecrate; dishonor: *a murderer's hands ~d with blood; Adultery ~s the marriage bed.* —**de·file·ment** *n.*

[2]de·file (di–, DEE–) *n.* a narrow pass or valley. —***v.*** **-files, -filed, -fil·ing** go in single file.

de·fine (di–) *v.* **-fines, -fined, -fin·ing** **1** state the meaning of: *Please ~ your terms.* **2** state or show the limits of; specify; describe precisely: *a clearly ~d picture of the moon; a law ~ing the court's powers.* Hence **de·fin·a·ble** (di·FYE·nuh–) *adj.;* **de·fin·er** *n.* —**def·i·nite** (DEF·uh·nit) *adj.* **1** well defined; exact; distinct: *working toward a ~ goal; a ~ advantage over others.* **2** certain: *I want a ~ answer;* **definite article** See ARTICLE; **def·i·nite·ly** *adv.;* **def·i·nite·ness** *n.* —**def·i·ni·tion** (–NISH·un) *n.* **1** a defining or determining; esp., a statement of a word's meaning. **2** distinctness; clarity: *a photo with good ~.* —**de·fin·i·tive** (di·FIN·uh·tiv) *adj.* **1** conclusive; also, the most complete and reliable to date: *a ~ answer; the ~ text of Homer.* **2** defining; explicit: *a ~ statement of the conservative viewpoint.* —**de·fin·i·tive·ly** *adv.*

def·la·grate (DEF·luh–) *v.* **-grates, -grat·ed, -grat·ing** burn rapidly at a great heat. —**def·la·gra·tion** (–GRAY–) *n.: the ~ of niter.*

de·flate (di–) *v.* **-flates, -flat·ed, -flat·ing** **1** let air or gas out of (something inflated); also, reduce the self-esteem or conceit of: *~ a bicycle tire; a ~d ego.* **2** reduce prices or available money. —**de·fla·tion** (–FLAY–) *n.* **1** a deflating. **2** a decrease in prices and production caused by a shrinking money supply or a lower demand. —**de·fla·tor** *n.*

de·flect (di–) *v.* turn aside or from a straight course: *light rays ~ed by a prism.* —**de·flec·tion** n.: *the ~ from zero of an ammeter needle.*

de·flow·er (di–) *v.* take away the virginity of (a woman); spoil. —**def·lo·ra·tion** (def·luh·RAY–) *n.*

De·foe (di·FOH), **Daniel.** 1660–1731, English novelist and pamphleteer.

de·fog (di–) *v.* **-fogs, -fogged, -fog·ging** remove fog or condensation from. —**de·fog·ger** *n.: an auto's rear-window ~.*

de·fo·li·ant (–FOH·lee·unt) *n.* a chemical defoliating agent. —**de·fo·li·ate** *v.* **-ates, -at·ed, -at·ing** cause the leaves to fall from: *jungles ~d in Vietnam;* **de·fo·li·a·tion** (–AY–) *n.*

de·for·est (dee·FOR·ist) *v.* clear of trees: *~ed hillsides;* **de·for·est·a·tion** (–TAY–) *n.*

de·form (di–) *v.* destroy the natural form of; disfigure; mar; also, become deformed. —**de·formed** *adj.* misshapen: *a poor ~ beggar.* —**de·for·ma·tion** (dee·for·MAY–) *n.* —**de·form·i·ty** *n.* **-ties** a physical or moral flaw; blemish; disfigurement: *a severe ~ in his spine.*

de·fraud (di–) *v.* deprive of something by fraud; swindle: *a widow ~ed of her life savings.* —**de·fraud·er** *n.*

de·fray (di–) *v.* pay for: *a collection to ~ the costs of the convention.* —**de·fray·al** (–FRAY·ul) *n.*

de·frost (di–) *v.* **1** thaw: *~ing frozen meat.* **2** free or make free of ice: *time to ~ the refrigerator.* —**de·frost·er** *n.*

defs. definitions.

deft *adj.* skillful and quick: *a ~ woodcarver.* —**deft·ly** *adv.* —**deft·ness** *n.*

de·funct (di–) *adj.* no longer existing; dead: *a ~ committee.*

de·fuse (dee·FYOOZ) *v.* **-fus·es, -fus·ed, -fus·ing** remove the fuse of (an explosive); hence, make less dangerous or tense: *~ing the confrontation with demonstrators.*

de·fy (di–) *v.* **-fies, -fied, -fy·ing** **1** challenge, esp. to do the impossible: *a death-~ing leap; I ~ you to swear your innocence!* **2** resist; defeat: *the courage to ~ government regulations; a mystery that ~s solution.*

deg. degree.

de·gas (dee–) *v.* **-gas·(s)es, -gassed, -gas·sing** free of gas: *~d wood.*

De Gaulle (duh·GAWL), **Charles.** 1890–1970, French general and president.

de·gauss (dee·GOUSE) *v.* neutralize the magnetic properties of: *~ a ship to protect it from mines.*

de·gen·er·ate (di·JEN–) *v.* **-ates, -at·ed, -at·ing** decline from a previous, stronger, or better condition. —***adj.*** (–uh·rit) degraded, as from normality; esp., sexually perverted; also ***n.*** —**de·gen·er·a·cy** *n.;* **de·gen·er·a·tion** (RAY–) *n.* —**de·gen·er·a·tive** (–ruh·tiv) *adj.*

de·grade (di–) *v.* **-grades, -grad·ed, -grad·ing** **1** decrease in rank, quality, or moral character; corrupt; disgrace: *Theft is a ~ing act.* **2** break down chemically. **—deg·ra·da·tion** (deg·ruh·DAY–) *n.* **—de·grad·a·ble** (di·GRAY–) *adj.: ~ plastics to fight pollution;* **de·grad·a·bil·i·ty** (–BIL–) *n.*

de·gree (di–) *n.* **1** a level or stage in a progression or series; also, a relative amount or manner: *art students at all ~s of proficiency; third-~ burns* (i.e. of the worst kind); *first-~ murder* (of the most serious nature); *The economy improved* **by degrees** (i.e. step by step) *all last year; Each contributes in its own ~; a man wealthy to the highest* (or last) *~; people of all ~s and stations in life; "Less" is the comparative ~ of "little."* **2** a unit of measurement, as for temperatures or angles: *a Celsius ~; a 90-~* (i.e. right) *angle.* **3** a rank or title conferred by a college or university: *working on a ~ in economics.*

de·hire (dee–) *v.* **-hires, -hired, -hir·ing** dismiss (an employee).

de·horn (dee–) *v.* remove the horns of: *~ed cattle.*

de·hu·man·ize (dee–) *v.* **-iz·es, -ized, -iz·ing** make machinelike or inhuman: *a ~d assembly-line job.* **—de·hu·man·i·za·tion** (–ZAY–) *n.*

de·hu·mid·i·fy (dee·hew·MID–) *v.* **-fies, -fied, -fy·ing** reduce the moisture content of (esp. air); **de·hu·mid·i·fi·er** *n.* **—de·hu·mid·i·fi·ca·tion** (–CAY–) *n.*

de·hy·drate (dee·HYE–) *v.* **-drates, -drat·ed, -drat·ing** dry, esp. foods to preserve them: *~d coffee* (i.e. instant coffee). **—de·hy·dra·tion** (–DRAY–) *n.: High fever, heavy perspiration, etc. may cause ~.*

de·hy·dro·gen·ate (dee·hye·DROJ–) *v.* **-ates, -at·ed, -at·ing** take the hydrogen from: *~d alcohol.* **—de·hy·dro·gen·a·tion** (–NAY–) *n.*

de·ice (dee–) *v.* **-ic·es, -iced, -ic·ing** make or keep free of ice. **—de·ic·er** *n.: an electric windshield ~.*

de·i·fy (DEE–) *v.* **-fies, -fied, -fy·ing** make into a god; also, regard or worship as a god. **—de·i·fi·ca·tion** (–CAY–) *n.*

deign (DAIN) *v.* condescend: *The king ~ed to visit us.*

de·i·on·ize (dee·EYE·uh–) *v.* **-iz·es, -ized, -iz·ing** deprive of ions. **—de·i·on·i·za·tion** (–ZAY–) *n.: water purified by ~.*

de·ism (DEE–) *n.* a belief in God founded on reason, usu. holding that God created the world but does not control or affect it. **—de·ist** *n.* **—de·is·tic** (dee·IS–) or **-ti·cal** *adj.* **—de·i·ty** (DEE–) *n.* **-ties** **1** a divine being; **the Deity** God. **2** divinity.

dé·jà vu (day·zhah·VEW) a feeling of having previously experienced a novel situation.

de·ject·ed (di–) *adj.* sad; downcast. **—de·jec·tion** *n.: the gloomy ~ of a disappointed lover.*

de ju·re (dee·JOOR·ee) by right; legal: *A ~ government may not have de facto power.*

deka- *comb.form.* same as DECA-.

del. delegate; delete.

Del. *Abbrev.* for **Del·a·ware** (DEL·uh–) **1** a state in eastern U.S.; 2,057 sq.mi. (5,328 km²); *cap.* Dover; **Del·a·war·e·an** (–WAIR–) *adj.* & *n.* **2** *n.* (a member of) an Amerindian tribe formerly of the Delaware River Valley, now living in Oklahoma; also, their Algonquian language: *The* **Delaware River** *runs from S. New York, between Pennsylvania and New Jersey, into* **Delaware Bay,** *an inlet of the Atlantic.*

de·lay (di–) *v.* **1** put off until a later time; make late: *a ~ed-action bomb defused by the army; a snowstorm that ~ed our train.* **2** linger; be late. ***—n.:*** *Fix the leak without ~; a two-hour ~.*

de·le (DEE·lee) *v.* **-les, -led, -le·ing** delete (something printed). ***—n.*** a symbol to give this instruction.

de·lec·ta·ble (di·LEC·tuh·bl) *adj.* very pleasing; delicious; also ***n.*** **—de·lec·ta·tion** (dee·lec·TAY–) *n.* delight; entertainment: *a juggling act presented for your ~.*

del·e·gate (DEL·i–) *v.* **-gates, -gat·ed, -gat·ing** **1** select as a representative; ***n.*** (–git) one so selected: *a convention ~.* **2** entrust to someone as an agent: *A leader must know how to ~ authority.* **—del·e·ga·tion** (–GAY–) *n.* **1** a delegating. **2** a group of delegates.

de·lete (di·LEET) *v.* **-letes, -let·ed, -let·ing** omit; strike out: *~ my name from the list.* **—de·le·tion** (–LEE–) *n.*

del·e·te·ri·ous (del·i·TEER–) *adj.* harmful: *the ~ effects of drunkenness.* **—del·e·te·ri·ous·ly** *adv.*

delft(·ware) *n.* a pottery having a blue design painted on a white glaze.

Del·hi (DEL·ee) a city in N. India, adjacent to New Delhi, India's capital; also called "Old Delhi."

del·i (DEL·ee) *n.* **-is** *Informal.* a delicatessen.

de·lib·er·ate (di·LIB–) *v.* **-ates, -at·ed, -at·ing** consider carefully; take counsel. ***—adj.*** (–rit) **1** intentional; well thought out: *a ~ act of violence; a ~ plan.* **2** slow and careful: *a ~ stride.* Hence **de·lib·er·ate·ly** *adj.;* **de·lib·er·ate·ness** *n.* **—de·lib·er·a·tion** (–RAY–) *n.* **1** careful pondering: *the judge's lengthy ~s.* **2** deliberateness: *the ~ of the murderer's manner.* **—de·lib·er·a·tive** (–tiv) *adj.: The legislature is a ~ body.*

del·i·cate (–kit) *adj.* **1** pleasing; fine, as by lightness, softness, intricacy, subtlety, etc.: *a ~ fabric; a ~ shade of pink; a ~ weave.* **2** easily damaged; in precarious health; needing care and tact or great skill and sensitivity: *a ~ young lady; the ~ question of your divorce; a ~ surgical operation.* **3** having refined sensitivity, skill, tact, sensory discrimination, etc.: *a ~ ear for music.* Hence **del·i·cate·ly** *adv.;* **del·i·cate·ness** *n.* **—del·i·ca·cy** (–kuh·see) *n.* **-cies**

1 delicateness. 2 a choice or dainty food. —**del·i·ca·tes·sen** (–TESN) *n.* a shop selling ready-to-eat food such as smoked meats, cheeses, salads, etc.; also, such food.

de·li·cious (di·LISH·us) *adj.* very pleasing, esp. to the taste or smell: *a ~ loaf of bread;* **Delicious** *n.* a sweet variety of red apple. —**de·li·cious·ly** *adv.* —**de·li·cious·ness** *n.*

de·light (di–) *v.* be very pleased; cause great pleasure to: *a hunter ~ing in the chase; The new toy ~ed Billy; He was ~ed with his new toy; ~ed to meet you, sir.* —***n.:*** *His daughter took ~ in new fashions; all the ~s of a well-furnished table.* —**de·light·ful** *adj.: a ~ new movie;* **de·light·ful·ly** *adv.*

De·li·lah (di·LYE·luh) the treacherous mistress of Samson; ***n.*** a temptress.

de·lim·it (di·LIM–) *v.* set out the limits or bounds of: *a committee to ~ the territory.* —**de·lim·i·ta·tion** (–TAY–) *n.*

de·lin·e·ate (di·LIN·ee–) *v.* **-ates, -at·ed, -at·ing** sketch; portray; hence, outline in words. —**de·lin·e·a·tion** (–AY–) *n.*

de·lin·quent (di·LINK·wunt) *adj.* 1 overdue: *a ~ account.* 2 guilty by acting against or neglect of duty or rules; ***n.:*** *a juvenile ~.* —**de·lin·quent·ly** *adv.* —**de·lin·quen·cy** (–see) *n.* **-cies.**

del·i·quesce (–KWES) *v.* **-quesc·es, -quesced, -quesc·ing** liquefy by taking moisture from the air; also, melt away. —**del·i·ques·cent** *adj.: Calcium chloride is ~.* —**del·i·ques·cence** *n.*

de·lir·i·um (di·LEER·ee·um) *n.* **-i·ums** or **-i·a** a short mental disturbance characterized by excited activity, hallucinations, and incoherence; hence, a frenzied excitement: **delirium tre·mens** (–TREE·munz), *which involves trembling, occurs in chronic alcoholics.* —**de·lir·i·ous** (–us) *adj.: ~ with fever, joy.* —**de·lir·i·ous·ly** *adv.*

de·liv·er (di·LIV–) *v.* 1 rescue; set free: *~ us from evil;* **de·liv·er·ance** (–unce) *n.* 2 hand over or convey; hence, send to a target or audience: *~ the package to the customer; ~ing the song with gusto; a boxer ~ing a hard punch;* **deliver (the goods)** perform as expected or required. 3 help to give birth (to): *a woman ~ed by a doctor; a midwife ~ing a baby.* —**de·liv·er·er** *n.* —**de·liv·er·y** *n.* **-er·ies** 1 a delivering; the manner of delivering: *a parcel marked "Cash on ~"; an orator with effective ~; the* **delivery room** *for childbirth in a hospital.* 2 something delivered.

dell *n.* a small, usu. wooded glen: *the farmer in the ~.*

de·louse (dee–) *v.* **-lous·es, -loused, -lous·ing** clean the lice from.

del·phin·i·um (–FIN·ee–) *n.* any of a genus of plants bearing spikes of colorful flowers on tall stalks.

del·ta (–tuh) *n.* 1 the fourth letter of the Greek alphabet (**Δ, δ**). 2 a usu. triangular, alluvial piece of land at a river mouth: *the Nile ~.* —**delta ray** the track of a delta particle, an electron released from matter by alpha or other cosmic rays passing through it. —**delta waves** the slow brain waves of deepest sleep.

de·lude (di·LOOD) *v.* **-ludes, -lud·ed, -lud·ing** mislead into believing what is false.

del·uge (DEL·yooj) *n.* a flood, downpour, etc. —***v.*** **-ug·es, -uged, -ug·ing** flood: *a movie star ~d with fan mail.*

de·lu·sion (di·LOO·zhun) *n.* a deluding, esp. a persistent false belief in something unreal: *His offer is a snare and a ~; suffering from ~s of grandeur* (e.g. thinking one is Jesus Christ); **de·lu·sion·al** *adj.;* **de·lu·sive** (–siv) *adj.*

de·luxe (di·LUX, di·LOOKS) *adj.* of outstanding luxury or comfort: *a ~ sedan.*

delve *v.* **delves, delved, delv·ing** dig deeply, as in study: *~ing into old land deeds.*

Dem. Democrat(ic).

de·mag·net·ize (dee·MAG·ni–) *v.* **-iz·es, -ized, -iz·ing** take away the magnetic properties of: *a ~d iron bar.* —**de·mag·net·i·za·tion** (–tuh·ZAY–) *n.*

dem·a·gog(ue) (–uh·gog) *n.* a leader who manipulates the people's passions. —**dem·a·gog·ic** (–GOJ–) *adj.* —**dem·a·gog·y** (–goh·jee) or **dem·a·gog·uer·y** (–gog·uh·ree) *n.*

de·mand (di–) *v.* 1 ask for vehemently or as a right: *I ~ justice.* 2 require: *a crisis that ~s tact;* **de·mand·ing** *adj.* making too many demands; also, requiring much care, patience, etc.: *a ~ child, job.* —***n.*** 1 a demanding or being demanded: *a loan repayable* **on demand** (i.e. when asked for); *Bibles are always* **in demand;** *Congress did not yield to their ~s.* 2 the readiness and ability to buy a product: *supply and ~; scarcity caused by greater ~.*

de·mar·cate (di·MAR–) *v.* **-cates, -cat·ed, -cat·ing** mark the boundaries of or separating: *~ing Spanish possessions from Portuguese.* —**de·mar·ca·tion** (–CAY–) *n.: a line of ~.*

dé·marche (day·MARSH) *n.* a maneuver or initiative, esp. in diplomacy.

de·mean (di–) *v.* 1 behave; conduct (oneself); **de·mean·or** *n.* 2 degrade; humble; debase: *Manual labor is not ~ing.*

de·ment·ed (di·MEN–) *adj.* insane. —**de·men·ti·a** (–MEN·shuh) *n.* serious mental deterioration.

de·mer·it (–MER–) *n.* a fault or offense; also, a score against one for this: *a schoolboy with 3 ~s for being late.*

de·mesne (di·MAIN) *n.* 1 *Law.* possession and use of land by the owner: *hold an estate in ~.* 2 the land attached to a mansion; also, a region, domain, etc.: *the royal ~.*

De·me·ter (di·MEE·tur) Greek goddess of grain and farming.

demi- *comb.form.* half; part(ly): as in **dem·i·god** *n.* a hero born of a god and a mortal; also, any godlike person.
dem·i·john *n.* a large bottle with a narrow neck, enclosed in wickerwork.
de·mil·i·ta·rize (dee·MIL–) *v.* **-riz·es, -riz·ed, -riz·ing** keep free of military equipment and troops: *the ~d zone* (between hostile nations).
dem·i·mon·daine (–DAIN) *n.* a woman on the borderline of respectability, as a rich man's mistress; **dem·i·monde** (–mond) *n.* such women as a class.
de·min·er·al·ize (dee·MIN–) *v.* **-iz·es, -ized, -iz·ing** remove salts from: *~d sea water.*
de·mise (di·MIZE) *n. Law.* death; also, the passing on of a sovereign's rights.
dem·i·tasse (–tas) *n.* a small cup of (or for serving) strong black coffee.
dem·o (DEM·oh) *n. Informal.* **1** a demonstration; esp., a record or tape as a sample of someone's talent. **2** a demonstrator (automobile, etc.).
de·mo·bi·lize (di·MOH–) *v.* **-liz·es, -lized, -liz·ing** free from military service: *a division ~d in 1947.* **—de·mo·bi·li·za·tion** (–ZAY–) *n.*
de·moc·ra·cy (di·MOC·ruh·see) *n.* **-cies** government by the people; also, a political system so governed, either directly or through representatives: *the foundations of our ~.* **—dem·o·crat** (–uh·crat) *n.* **—dem·o·crat·ic** (–CRAT·ic) *adj.* **1:** *~ institutions, rights.* **2** of or having social equality; of or for all the people: *a ~ form of literature.* Hence **dem·o·crat·i·cal·ly** *adv.* **—Democratic Party** the older of the two main parties in the U.S.; **Democrat** *n.;* **Democratic** *adj.* **—de·moc·ra·tize** (di·MOC·ruh–) *v.* **-tiz·es, -tized, -tiz·ing:** *~ing politics in ex-colonies.*
dé·mo·dé (day·moh·DAY) *adj.* out-of-fashion.
de·mog·ra·phy (di·MOG·ruh·fee) *n.* the study of population using statistics; **de·mog·ra·pher** *n.* **—de·mo·graph·ic** (dee·muh·GRAF·ic) *adj.;* **de·mo·graph·i·cal·ly** *adv.*
dem·oi·selle (dem·wuh·ZEL) *n.* a young woman.
de·mol·ish (di–) *v.* wreck totally; tear down: *~ing the old hotel; evidence that ~ed his argument.* **—dem·o·li·tion** (–uh·LISH·un) *n.*
de·mon (DEE·mun) *n.* **1** a devil or evil spirit; hence, an evil person or thing: *Don't touch ~ rum; a spelling ~* (i.e. hard-to-spell word). **2** one who acts with great zeal or skill: *a ~ for work.* **—de·mon·ic** (di·MON·ic) *adj.*
de·mon·e·tize (dee·MON·i–) *v.* **-tiz·es, -tized, -tiz·ing** stop using (a metal) as money. **—de·mon·e·ti·za·tion** (–ZAY–) *n.*
de·mo·ni·ac (di·MOH·nee·ac) or **-ni·a·cal** (dee·muh·NYE·uh·cl) *adj.* of or like a demon; also, possessed by a devil; **de·mo·ni·a·cal·ly** *adv.* **—de·mon·ol·o·gy** (dee·muh·NOL·uh·jee) *n.* a work about or study of demons.
dem·on·strate (DEM·un–) *v.* **-strates, -strat·ed, -strat·ing** **1** show or prove, as by examples or reasoning; also, display the operation of (a product): *~ the fallacy of his argument;* **de·mon·stra·ble** (di·MON·struh·bl) *adj.;* **de·mon·stra·bly** *adv.* **2** display (one's views, feelings, etc. by parading, shouting, or other overt acts): *crowds ~ing against the war; Children ~ their affection.* **—dem·on·stra·tion** (–STRAY–) *n.* **—dem·on·stra·tor** (DEM–) *n.* **—de·mon·stra·tive** (–MON·struh·tiv) *adj.* **1** demonstrating; subject to demonstration: *a ~ truth.* **2** displaying one's feelings openly. **3** indicating the one(s) referred to: *a ~ pronoun, as "this," "that," or "those"; a ~ adjective;* also ***n.*** Hence **de·mon·stra·tive·ly** *adv.;* **de·mon·stra·tive·ness** *n.*
de·mor·al·ize (–MOR–) *v.* **-iz·es, -ized, -iz·ing** weaken the morals, morale, or discipline of: *a young girl ~d by a bad upbringing; The platoon was ~d by defeat.* **—de·mor·al·i·za·tion** (–ZAY–) *n.*
De·mos·the·nes (di·MOS·thuh·neez) 384?–322 B.C., Athenian orator and politician.
de·mote (di–) *v.* **-motes, -mot·ed, -mot·ing** lower in rank or station: *The foreman was ~d because he was lazy.* **—de·mo·tion** (–MOH–) *n.*
de·mot·ic (–MOT–) *adj.* of the common people: *writing Egyptian in the ~ script; ~ Greek.*
de·mul·cent (–MUL–) *adj.* soothing; relieving irritation. ***—n.*** an oily or sticky medicine for soothing esp. mucous membranes.
de·mur (di–) *v.* **-murs, -murred, -mur·ring** **1** *Formal.* object or take exception; scruple; ***n.:*** *an offer accepted without ~.* **2** *Law.* put in a demurrer.
de·mure (di·MYOOR) *adj.* **-mur·er, -mur·est** reserved and modest; also, affectedly so; **de·mure·ly** *adv.;* **de·mure·ness** *n.* **—de·mur·rage** (di·MUR·ij) *n.* the delay of a cargo conveyance beyond the time for loading or unloading; also, a compensation for this. **—de·mur·rer** (–MUR–) *n.* an objector or objection, esp. a plea for dismissal of a claim on the contention that the supporting facts are not relevant.
den *n.* **1** a wild animal's lair: *Daniel in the lion's ~.* **2** a squalid or hidden dwelling: *a ~ of iniquity; ~ of thieves.* **3** a quiet, cozy room, as a study.
Den· Denmark.
de·na·ture (dee·NAY–) *v.* **-tures, -tured, -tur·ing** alter the natural qualities of; esp., of alcohol, tea, etc., make unfit for consumption; of fissionable matter, make unusable in nuclear weapons.
den·drite *n.* a branching extension of a nerve cell that receives impulses. **—den·dro·chron·ol·o·gy** (–cruh·NOL·uh·jee) *n.* the study of tree rings to date climatic events of the past. **—den·drol·o·gy** (–DROL–) *n.* the science of trees; **den·dro·log·ic** (–LOJ·ic) or **-i·cal** *adj.;* **den·drol·o·gist** (–DROL–) *n.*

den·gue (DENG·gee) *n.* a mosquito-transmitted fever causing great weakness, pain, esp. in the joints, and skin eruptions.

de·ni·al (–NYE·ul) *n.* a denying or a statement of it: *the ~ of a charge, of justice, of one's child;* **de·ni·er** *n.*

de·nier (DEN·yur) *n.* a unit of weight indicating the fineness of yarns: *20-~ nylon stockings.*

den·i·grate *v.* **-grates, -grat·ed, -grat·ing** blacken (the name of); belittle: *~ing the governor's motives and character.* **—den·i·gra·tion** (–GRAY–) *n.*

den·im *n.* a heavy, twilled cotton cloth: *jeans of blue ~;* **denims** *pl.* clothes made of this.

den·i·zen *n.* one who lives in a place: *the finny ~s* (i.e. fishes) *of the deep.*

Den·mark a constitutional monarchy in N. Europe; 16,629 sq.mi. (43,069 km²); *cap.* Copenhagen.

de·nom·i·nate (di·NOM–) *v.* **-nates, -nat·ed, -nat·ing** to name; indicate: *Democracy ~s a form of government;* also ***adj.*** (-nit); **denominate number** one linked to a unit of measure, as in "10 miles" or "5 dollars." **—de·nom·i·na·tion** (–NAY–) *n.* **1** a naming; **de·nom·i·na·tive** (–NOM–) *adj.* **2** a name, esp. of a class, group, etc.: *coins of small ~s* (e.g. nickels and dimes); *⅝ and ⅜ are fractions of one ~, i.e. having the same* **de·nom·i·na·tor** (i.e. divisor). **3** a particular sect or church; **de·nom·i·na·tion·al** (–NAY–) *adj.: ~ schools.*

de·no·ta·tion (dee·noh·TAY–) *n.* the strict meaning or the thing indicated: *A logician considers a word's ~, but a writer its connotations.* **—de·no·ta·tive** (DEE·noh·tay·tiv, di·NOH·tuh·tiv) *adj.* **—de·note** (di–) *v.* **-notes, -not·ed, -not·ing** indicate; also, be the symbol for: mean: *A skull and crossbones ~s danger.*

de·noue·ment (day·noo·MAHNG) *n.* the conclusion or untangling of a complicated plot.

de·nounce (di–) *v.* **-nounc·es, -nounced, -nounc·ing** **1** revile in public; also, accuse or inform against: *Mr. Smith ~d his neighbor as a Communist.* **2** repudiate: *~ing an international trade agreement.* **—de·nounce·ment** *n.*

de no·vo (dee·NOH·voh) *Latin.* once more; anew.

dense (DENCE) *adj.* **dens·er, dens·est** **1** having a great deal in a small space; compact; thick: *~ African jungles; a ~ cloud of smoke.* **2** stupid; thick-headed; **dense·ly** *adv.;* **dense·ness** *n.: She found the student's ~ frustrating.* **—den·si·ty** *n.* **-ties** **1** denseness: *a high-~ population area; the ~ of the forest.* **2** compactness of substance; relative weight: *Ice has a lower ~ than water.* **3** the relative opaqueness of a photographic negative, measured by a **den·si·tom·e·ter** (–TOM·i·tur) *n.*

dent *n.* an impression made by hitting or pressing in: *a ~ in the fender; After two days he had hardly made a ~ in his work* (i.e. an appreciable start on it). **—*v.:*** *A tin can is easily ~ed.*

den·tal (–tl) *adj.* of the teeth or dentistry: *A ~ consonant is made with the tongue touching the back of the upper teeth* (e.g. "th"); **dental floss** a sturdy thread for cleaning between teeth; **dental hygienist** one who assists a dentist, esp. by cleaning teeth; **dental plate** a denture. **—den·tate** *adj.* having teeth or toothlike projections: *~ leaves.* **—den·ti·frice** (–fris) *n.* a powder, paste, etc. for cleaning teeth. **—den·tin** also **den·tine** (–teen); *n.* the hard, dense body of a tooth, under the enamel; **den·ti·nal** *adj.* **—den·tist** *n.* one professionally trained to care for teeth; **den·tis·try** *n.* **—den·ti·tion** (–TISH·un) *n.* the number, arrangement, and kind of teeth: *the characteristic ~ of ruminants.* **—den·ture** (–chur) *n.* a set of false teeth.

de·nu·cle·ar·ize (dee·NEW·clee·uh–) *v.* **-iz·es, -ized, -iz·ing** make or keep free of nuclear weapons: *~ing Europe will be difficult.*

de·nude (di·NEWD) *v.* **-nudes, -nud·ed, -nud·ing** make bare: *a hillside ~d by excessive lumbering.* **—de·nu·da·tion** (dee·new·DAY–) *n.*

de·nun·ci·a·tion (di·nun·see·AY–) *n.* a denouncing.

Den·ver capital of Colorado.

de·ny (di·NYE) *v.* **-nies, -nied, -ny·ing** **1** claim to be false; reject; also, refuse to accept, recognize, etc.: *It is hard to ~ that he is guilty; ~s all charges; Will you ~ your own son?* **2** refuse to give; say no to: *All appeals were ~d; Was she ~d her civil rights?* **deny oneself** forgo gratification or pleasure.

de·o·dar (DEE·uh–) *n.* a Himalayan cedar grown ornamentally and for timber.

de·o·dor·ant (–OH·duh·runt) *n.* a deodorizer for the body; ***adj.:*** *a ~ spray.* **—de·o·dor·ize** *v.* **-iz·es, -ized, -iz·ing** remove or mask the unpleasant odor of; **de·o·dor·iz·er** *n.*

de·ox·i·dize (dee·OX–) *v.* **-diz·es, -dized, -diz·ing** take oxygen from, esp. out of a compound. **—de·ox·y·ri·bo·nu·cle·ic** (–rye·boh·new·CLEE·ic) **acid** a nucleic acid found in all living cells that transmits genetic information.

dep· department; departure; deposit; depot; deputy.

de·part (di–) *v.* **1** leave; also, deviate (from): *All trains ~ from track 3.* **2** die; **departed** *n.* & *adj.: the dear ~; our ~ brethren.*

de·part·ment *n.* **1** an element in a larger organization: *the U.S. Dept. of Labor; France is divided into ~s instead of provinces or states; A* **department store** *sells many kinds of goods in different sections of the store.* **2** an area of interest or knowledge. **—de·part·ment·al** (–MEN·tl) *adj.: the ~ budget committee.* **—de·part·ment·al·ize** *v.* **-iz·es, -ized, -iz·ing** divide into departments: *a ~d school.*

de·par·ture (–chur) *n.* a departing: *a ~ from routine.*

de·pend (di–) *v.* **1** rely *(on);* trust: *You can ~ on him to get things done;* **de·pend·a·ble** *adj.*

trustworthy: *a ~ worker;* **de·pend·a·bil·i·ty** (–BIL–) *n.* **2** be contingent on or determined by: *Whether we'll have a picnic ~s on the weather.* —**de·pend·ence** *n.* a depending: *a youth having a ~ on drugs;* also **de·pend·ance.** —**de·pend·en·cy** *n.* **-cies** dependence; also, something dependent, as a region ruled by but not forming part of another country: *The Channel Islands are British ~s.* —**de·pend·ent** (–PEN–) *adj.* **1** relying on another, esp. for food, shelter, etc.: *a tax deduction for each ~ child;* also ***n.*** **2** determined or controlled by another; subordinate: *a ~ clause; a ~ variable.* Also **de·pend·ant.**

de·pict (di–) *v.* portray in a picture or words: *a rural landscape ~ed in watercolors.* —**de·pic·tion** *n.*

dep·il·ate *v.* **-ates, -at·ed, -at·ing** remove hair from. —**de·pil·a·to·ry** (di·PIL·uh–) *adj.;* also ***n.,*** *pl.* **-ries:** *a ~ for the legs.*

de·plane (di–) *v.* **-planes, -planed, -plan·ing** get off an airplane: *Our group ~d at Kennedy Airport.*

de·plete (di–) *v.* **-pletes, -plet,ed, -plet·ing** use up: *Overspending ~d our budget.* —**de·ple·tion** (di·PLEE–) *n.: the rapid ~ of oil reserves.* —**de·ple·ta·ble** (di·PLEE·tuh·bl) *adj.: Coal is a ~ resource.*

de·plore (di–) *v.* **-plores, -plored, -plor·ing** feel deep regret about; also, disapprove strongly: *The people ~ corruption in high places.* —**de·plor·a·ble** *adj.: a ~ lack of cleanliness.* —**de·plor·a·bly** *adv.*

de·ploy (di–) *v.* arrange strategically: *~ed the National Guard near the demonstrators.* —**de·ploy·ment** *n.*

de·po·lar·ize (dee·POH·luh–) *v.* **-iz·es, -iz·ed, -iz·ing** make unpolarized: *~d light.* —**de·po·lar·iz·er** *n.: A ~ is added to some batteries to ensure a steady current.* —**de·po·lar·i·za·tion** (–ZAY–) *n.*

de·po·lit·i·cize (dee·puh·LIT–) *v.* **-ciz·es, -cized, -ciz·ing** remove from the realm of politics: *an attempt to ~ the busing debate.*

de·pon·ent (di·POH·nunt) *n.* one who gives a deposition for use in court.

de·pop·u·late (dee·POP·yoo–) *v.* **-lates, -lat·ed, -lat·ing** reduce greatly or totally the population of: *The Black Death once ~d Europe.* —**de·pop·u·la·tion** (–LAY–) *n.*

de·port (di–) *v.* **1** conduct (oneself): *~ yourself with dignity;* **de·port·ment** *n.* **2** expel (an alien or a criminal) from the country; **de·por·ta·tion** (–TAY–) *n.: subject to ~ for illegal entry.* —**de·por·tee** (–TEE) *n.* a deported person.

de·pose (di·POZE) *v.* **-pos·es, -pos·ed, -pos·ing** **1** remove from power or office: *an emperor ~d by the army.* **2** testify under oath, usu. in writing.

de·pos·it (di·POZ–) *v.* **1** put (money or valuables) for safekeeping, as a security, etc.: *~ed $25 a week in a savings account.* **2** leave or lay down: *gravel ~ed by receding glaciers.* —***n.:*** *keep $100 on ~ in a checking account; You must pay a ~ on the soda bottle; newly discovered ~s of iron and oil.* —**dep·o·si·tion** (dep·uh·ZISH·un) *n.* **1** the act of deposing. **2** a depositing: *a heavy ~ of silt;* **dep·o·si·tion·al** *adj.* **3** written testimony taken under oath. —**de·pos·i·tor** *n.;* **de·pos·i·to·ry** (di·POZ–) *n.* **-ries** a place for depositing things: *a ~ for secret government documents; a* **depository library** *to receive all government publications.* —**de·pot** (DEE·poh) *n.* **1** a place for storing and distributing things, esp. military supplies. **2** a bus or railroad station.

de·prave (di–) *v.* **-praves, -praved, -prav·ing** corrupt; make wicked or perverted. —**de·praved** *adj.* —**de·prav·i·ty** (–PRAV–) *n.* **-ties.**

dep·re·cate (DEP·ruh–) *v.* **-cates, -cat·ed, -cat·ing** **1** disapprove of; plead against: *a banker ~ing plans for monetary reform.* **2** loosely, belittle: *The mayor ~d his influence on city politics.* —**dep·re·ca·tion** (–CAY–) *n.: a shy self-~ among scholars.* —**dep·re·ca·to·ry** *adj.*

de·pre·ci·ate (di·PREE·shee–) *v.* **-ates, -at·ed, -at·ing** **1** lessen the value of; fall in value: *Once out of the showroom, a car ~s fast.* **2** disparage. —**de·pre·ci·a·tion** (–AY–) *n.* —**de·pre·ci·a·to·ry** (–PREE·shuh–) *adj.*

dep·re·da·tion (–ri·DAY–) *n.* a plundering or laying waste: *the harsh ~s of estate taxes.*

de·press (di–) *v.* **1** press or push down: *~ the lever.* **2** lower the level of bodily or other activity; make sad or impoverished: *Bill was* **depressed** *when his wife left him; The economy is ~ed; a* **depressed area** *with poverty and high unemployment;* **de·pres·sant** (–sunt) *adj.* & *n.: a ~ drug for a heart condition; a ~ to calm the nerves.* —**de·pres·sion** (–PRESH·un) *n.* **1** a depressing or being depressed, as a state of extreme sadness or a period of severe reduction in economic activity: *the Great Depression of the 1930's.* **2** an area lower than its surroundings. —**de·pres·sive** (–PRES·iv) *adj.* —**de·pres·sor** *n.: a physician's tongue ~;* ***adj.:*** *a ~ muscle, nerve* (that lowers arterial blood pressure).

de·prive (di–) *v.* **-prives, -prived, -priv·ing** take or keep something away from: *a prisoner ~d of his civil rights.* —**dep·ri·va·tion** (dep·ruh·VAY–) *n.: a child raised in hunger and ~.*

de·pro·gram (–PROH–) *v.* **-grams, -gram(m)ed, -gram·(m)ing** bring (a religious convert) back to his former way of life by attacking his beliefs in closed-door sessions; **de·pro·gram·(m)er** *n.*

dept. department.

depth *n.* **1** the quality or degree of deepness: *a submarine cruising at a ~ of 400 ft.; She has great ~ of learning.* **2** a deep thing or place: *in the ~s of outer space; lurking in the ocean ~s; from the ~s of my heart.* —**in depth** thorough(ly) and with penetration: *an in-~ news report.* —**out of one's depth** beyond one's competence: *"I* *have ventured far beyond my* ~." —**depth charge** an explosive set to explode at a certain depth under water, used against submarines.

de·pute (di–) *v.* **-putes, -put·ed, -put·ing** delegate. —**dep·u·ta·tion** (–TAY–) *n.* a person or group appointed to represent others; delegation. —**dep·u·ty** (DEP·yuh·tee) *n.* **-ties** one appointed to act officially for another: *My* ~ (i.e. assistant) *will run things while I'm gone; the Italian Chamber of Deputies* (i.e. people's representatives); *a* ~ *of the French legislature;* **adj.:** ~ *sheriff;* **dep·u·tize** *v.* **-tiz·es, -tized, -tiz·ing.**

der. derivation; derivative.

de·rail (di–) *v.* run or cause to run off the rails: *a* ~*ed train.* —**de·rail·ment** *n.*

de·rail·leur (di·RAY·lur) *n.* a device for shifting a bicycle chain from one gear to another.

de·range (di·RAINJ) *v.* **-rang·es, -ranged, -rang·ing** make disturbed, disordered, or insane: *a* ~*d killer.* —**de·range·ment** *n.*

der·by (DUR·bee, *Brit.* DAR–) *n.* **-bies** **1** a hat with a rounded crown and a thin, rolled brim. **2** **Derby** any of several annual horse races: *Epsom's* ~ *at Surrey, England; the Kentucky* ~. **3** an open race or contest.

der·e·lict (DER·uh–) *adj.* **1** neglectful: ~ *in one's duty.* **2** abandoned: *a* ~ *car rusting in a field;* **n.** something abandoned, as a ship at sea or an indigent or vagrant social outcast. —**der·e·lic·tion** (–LIC–) *n.* an abandoning or neglecting, as of duty.

de·ride (di–) *v.* **-rides, -rid·ed, -rid·ing** ridicule; laugh at with contempt.

de ri·gueur (duh·ree·GUR) required by fashion or social convention: *Black tie is* ~ *at this function.*

de·ri·sion (di·RIZH–) *n.* a deriding or ridiculing; **de·ri·sive** (–RYE·siv) or **de·ri·so·ry** (–RYE·suh·ree) *adj.:* ~ *jeers.* —**de·ri·sive·ly** *adv.*

deriv. derivation; derivative; derived. —**de·riv·a·tive** (di·RIV·uh·tiv) *adj.* derived from another source: *His poetry is very* ~ (i.e. borrowed from others' work); **n.:** *"Classify" is a* ~ *of "class"; plastics made from petroleum* ~*s.* —**de·rive** (di–) *v.* **-rives, -rived, -riv·ing** **1** receive or come from (a source): *He* ~*s great satisfaction from his work; problems* ~*ing from social change.* **2** trace the origin of; also, infer: *Etymologists* ~ *words; a conclusion* ~*d from flimsy evidence.* —**der·i·va·tion** (–VAY–) *n.*

der·ma (–muh) or **der·mis** *n.* the inner layer of skin containing blood vessels; **der·mal** or **der·mic** *adj.* —**der·ma·ti·tis** (–TYE·tis) *n.* a skin inflammation. —**der·ma·tol·o·gy** (–TOL·uh·jee) *n.* the branch of medicine specializing in the disorders of the skin; **der·ma·tol·o·gist** *n.*

der·o·gate (DER·uh–) *v.* **-gates, -gat·ed, -gat·ing** **1** take away: *not wanting to* ~ *from the colonel's authority.* **2** disparage. —**der·o·ga·tion** (–GAY–) *n.* —**de·rog·a·to·ry** (di·ROG·uh–) *adj.: A* ~ *clause takes away the right to alter a will; a* ~ (i.e. insulting) *remark.*

der·rick (DER·ic) *n.* a usu. stationary hoisting apparatus; also, a framework built to support equipment over a drill hole: *an oil* ~.

der·ri·ère (der·ee·AIR) *n.* the buttocks.

der·ring-do (der·ing·DOO) *n.* bold deeds; reckless bravery: *"Desperate deeds of* ~*."*

der·rin·ger (DER·in·jur) *n.* a large-caliber, short-barreled pistol.

der·vish (DUR–) *n.* a member in any of the ascetic Islamic religious orders, some of which do a whirling dance.

DES "diethylstilbestrol," a synthetic estrogen.

de·salt (dee·SAWLT) *v.* remove salts from. Also **de·sal·i·nate** (dee·SAL–) *v.* **-nates, -nat·ed, -nat·ing** and **de·sal·i·nize** *v.* **-niz·es, -nized, -niz·ing.** —**de·sal·i·na·tion** (–NAY–) *n.: the* ~ *of sea water for irrigation.*

des·cant *n.* a sung or played harmony to a simple melody; any song: *the nightingale's amorous* ~. —**v.** (–CANT) sing; also, comment *(on)* at length: ~*ing on the theme of solar energy.*

Des·cartes (day·CART), **René.** 1596–1650, French mathematician and philosopher.

de·scend (di·SEND) *v.* **1** move or extend down(ward); go down on or along: *a hillside* ~*ing to the sea;* ~ *a staircase to reach the basement.* **2** sink or stoop (to): ~*ed to name-calling in public.* **3** come from ancestors; pass by inheritance: ~*ed from kings; an heirloom that has* ~*ed in the family;* **de·scend·ant** *n.: children, grandchildren, and later* ~*s.* **4** attack suddenly; swoop or pounce: *The police* ~*ed on the thieves hideout.* —**de·scend·ent** *adj.* descending. —**de·scent** *n.* **1** a descending: *a rapid* ~ *from 20,000 ft.; the* ~ *of pirates on the coast.* **2** a downward slope. **3** ancestry; lineage; *Hispanics of Mexican* ~.

de·scribe (di–) *v.* **-scribes, -scribed, -scrib·ing** **1** outline: *a set of compasses used to* ~ *an arc.* **2** write or tell about, esp. with graphic detail: ~ *the house you live in.* —**de·scrib·er** *n.* —**de·scrib·a·ble** (–SCRYE·buh·bl) *adj.* —**de·scrip·tion** (–SCRIP–) *n.* a describing, esp. a picture of something in words: *a detailed* ~ *of the scene; a suspect who fits the* ~*; merchandise of every* ~ (i.e. kind). —**de·scrip·tive** (–tiv) *adj.:* ~ *linguistics* (describes language structure).

de·scry (di–) *v.* **-scries, -scried, -scry·ing** detect; catch sight of: *The lookout* ~*d an approaching ship.*

des·e·crate (DES·uh–) *v.* **-crates, -crat·ed, -crat·ing** treat sacrilegiously. —**des·e·cra·tion** (–CRAY–) *n.*

de·seg·re·gate (dee·SEG·ri–) *v.* **-gates, -gat·ed, -gat·ing** eliminate racial segregation in: *busing to* ~ *schools.* —**de·seg·re·ga·tion** (–GAY–) *n.*

de·se·lect (dee·si·LECT) *v.* dismiss while still in training: *a* ~*ed Peace Corps volunteer.*

de·sen·si·tize (dee·SEN–) *v.* **-tiz·es, -tized, -tiz·ing** make insensitive or less sensitive.

—de·sen·si·ti·za·tion (–ZAY–) *n.: treating hay fever by ~ to pollen.*

¹des·ert (DEZ–) *n.* a region barren because of limited rainfall: *the Sahara Desert;* ***adj.:*** *a ~ island.* **—de·sert** (di·ZURT) *v.* abandon; leave (one's post, military service) without permission: *The cad ~ed his wife and children;* **de·sert·er** *n.: ~s are subject to courtmartial;* **de·ser·tion** *n.*

²de·sert (di·ZURT) *n.* something deserved: *a villain who got his just ~s.* **—de·serve** (di·ZURV) *v.* **-serves, -served, -serv·ing** be worthy of: *He ~d better* (treatment) *than that; an allowance given to* **deserving** *candidates.* **—de·served** *adj.: ~ punishment.* **—de·serv·ed·ly** (–ZUR·vid·lee) *adv.*

des·ic·cate (DES·i–) *v.* **-ic·cates, -ic·cat·ed, -ic·cat·ing** dry, esp. to preserve: *~d vegetables.* **—des·ic·cant** (–kunt) *adj.* & *n.* (something) that dries. **—des·ic·ca·tor** *n.: a chemical ~.* **—des·ic·ca·tion** (–CAY–) *n.*

de·sid·er·a·tum (di·sid·uh·RAY–) *n., pl.* **-ta** a thing needed and longed for.

de·sign (di·ZINE) *n.* **1** plan; intention: *evil ~s on his nephew's inheritance; His answer was vague* **by design. 2** a plan, blueprint, outline, etc.: *a ~ engineer; ~s for a new garage.* **3** the combination of color, shape, parts, etc. in something; also, a pattern in decoration: *a mural with good ~ for the room; a pretty ~ on the towels; a school of fashion ~.* ***—v.*** **1** intend; devise; plan: *a job ~ed to lead to promotion.* **2** make a design for: *~ airplanes for the Air Force.* **—de·sign·er** *n.: a Paris fashion ~.* **—des·ig·nate** (DEZ·ig–) *v.* **-nates, -nat·ed, -nat·ing 1** specify; indicate; name: *powers ~d as being under state jurisdiction.* **2** select for an office, task, etc.: *The* **designated hitter** *bats for the pitcher during the game;* ***adj.*** picked out but not yet holding office: *The president ~ takes office on Jan. 1.* **—des·ig·na·tion** (–NAY–) *n.* **—de·sign·ing** (–ZYE–) *n.* the art or work of creating designs; ***adj.*** that designs; also, cunningly scheming.

de·sire (di·ZIRE) *v.* **-sires, -sired, -sir·ing 1** wish for; long for. **2** request: *The queen ~s an audience with the pope.* ***—n.*** a desiring or something desired: *looked at her with great ~.* **—de·sir·a·ble** *adj.;* **de·sir·a·bly** *adv.* **—de·sir·a·bil·i·ty** (–BIL–) *n.* **—de·sir·ous** (–ZYE·rus) *adj.* desiring; wishing.

de·sist (de·ZIST) *v.* stop: *a court order to cease and ~* (from an action).

desk *n.* **1** a flat-topped piece of furniture for writing. **2** a counter, stand, etc. for doing business: *check into the hotel at the front ~; ~ clerk.* **3** a department: *a newspaper's city ~.*

Des Moines (duh·MOIN) capital of Iowa.

des·o·late (–uh·lit) *adj.* **1** not fit for habitation; esp., barren, deserted, ravaged, etc.: *a ~ Arctic plain.* **2** cheerless; lonely; abandoned. ***—v.*** (–lait) **-lates, -lat·ed, -lat·ing:** *farmlands ~d by a tornado.* **—des·o·la·tion** (–LAY–) *n.: the ~ of a lonely old man.*

de·spair (di–) *v.* lose all hope: *Columbus never ~ed of reaching India.* ***—n.:*** *the depths of ~.*

des·patch *v.* & *n.* same as DISPATCH.

des·per·ate (–puh·rit) *adj.* **1** ready to do anything because of despair; of deeds, so performed: *a ~ murder; a ~ criminal,* or **des·per·a·do** (–puh·RAH·doh), *pl.* **-do(e)s. 2** in great need, want, etc. **3** very grave or intense: *~ poverty.* **—des·per·ate·ly** *adv.* **—des·per·ate·ness** or **des·per·a·tion** (–AY–) *n.: acting out of ~; "lives of quiet desperation."*

de·spise (di·SPIZE) *v.* **-spis·es, -spised, -spis·ing** have contempt or disdain for: *a beggar "~d and rejected of men."* **—des·pi·ca·ble** (di·SPIC·uh·bl, DES·pic–) *adj.;* **des·pi·ca·bly** *adv.* **—de·spite** (di–) *prep.* in spite of: *escaped ~ a heavy guard;* ***n.:*** *She stayed out late* **in despite of** *her father's warning.*

de·spoil (di–) *v.* rob; plunder: *was thrown in jail and soon ~ed of his innocence.* **—de·spoil·er** *n.* **—de·spoil·ment** or **de·spo·li·a·tion** (di·spoh·lee·AY–) *n.: ~ of the region by bandits.*

de·spond (di–) *v.* lose hope and lose heart. ***—n.:*** *the slough of ~.* **—de·spond·ent** *adj.* sad and hopeless: *a ~ rejected lover.* **—de·spond·en·cy** *n.* a feeling of utter hopelessness and discouragement: *suicide from sheer ~.*

des·pot *n.* a ruler with unlimited power; also, a tyrant: *the enlightened ~s of late 18th-century Europe.* **—des·pot·ic** (–POT–) *adj.;* **des·pot·i·cal·ly** *adv.* **—des·pot·ism** *n.: a middle course between anarchy and ~.*

des·sert (di·ZURT) *n.* a course of fruit, pie, sweet foods, etc. at the end of a meal. **—des·sert·spoon** *n.* a spoon smaller than a tablespoon and larger than a teaspoon.

de·sta·bi·lize (dee·STAY–) *v.* **-liz·es, -lized, -liz·ing** make less or not stable: *~ing foreign governments.*

des·ti·na·tion (–NAY–) *n.* the place something or someone is going to; also, the purpose or ultimate use. **—des·tine** (–tin) *v.* **-tines, -tined, -tin·ing 1** direct or aim at, reserve for, etc. a goal or purpose: *a man ~d to rule; travelers* **destined** (i.e. bound) **for** *the Caribbean.* **2** predetermine; **des·tin·y** *n.* **-tin·ies** fate.

des·ti·tute *adj.* **1** devoid: *a boulevard ~ of trees.* **2** needy; penniless: *died leaving his family ~.* **—des·ti·tu·tion** (–TUE–) *n.* extreme poverty.

de·stroy (di–) *v.* demolish; ruin; undo; kill: *a hotel ~ed by fire; a king ~ed by pride; His reform efforts were ~ed by the depression.* **—de·stroy·er** *n.* **1** one that destroys. **2** a small, fast warship: *A* **destroyer escort** *is smaller, slower, and is used to protect convoys.* **—destroying angel** a pale-colored, very poisonous mushroom. **—de·struct** (di–) *n.* the deliberate destroying of a missile in flight; also ***v.;*** **de·struc·tor** *n.* **—de·struct·i·ble** *adj.* able to be destroyed; **de·struct·i·bil·i·ty** (–BIL–) *n.* **—de·struc·**

tion *n.* a destroying; also, a means for destroying: *The Lord will rain death and ~ on sinners.* —**de·struc·tive** (–tiv) *adj.: the ~ distillation of wood to produce wood alcohol and wood gas;* **de·struc·tive·ly** *adv.;* **de·struc·tive·ness** *n.*

des·ue·tude (DES·wi–) *n.* disuse: *Legislatures should repeal laws that* **fall into desuetude.**

des·ul·to·ry *adj.* not thorough or well organized; disconnected; random: *poor scholarship marked by ~ research.*

det. detached; detail. —**DET** "diethyltryptamine," a hallucinogen.

de·tach (di–) *v.* separate; disengage: *~ a coupon from the book; troops ~ed to scout ahead.* —**de·tached** *adj.* **1** not connected: *A ~ house does not share a wall with any other house.* **2** impartial; with detachment. —**de·tach·ment** *n.* **1** impartiality; lack of prejudice. **2** a body of men, ships, etc. detached for special service.

de·tail (di–, DEE–) *n.* **1** a particular or small item or part; also, details in general or the treatment of them: *I won't bore you with the ~s of my plan; a painter devoting great attention to ~; a report of their activities* **in detail.** **2** a group separated for a specific task; also, the task: *a platoon on guard ~.* —***v.*** **1** list or tell (of) in detail; **de·tailed** *adj.: a ~ list of complaints.* **2** detach for a specific task: *two corporals ~ed to guard the prisoner.*

de·tain (di–) *v.* **1** hold back; delay: *~ed at customs for two hours.* **2** keep in custody.

de·tect (di–) *v.* discover; find out: *a machine to ~ the presence of radioactive matter; ~ed three arithmetic errors in the bill.* —**de·tec·tor** *n.: a suspect taking the lie-~ test.* —**de·tect·a·ble** or **-i·ble** *adj.* —**de·tec·tion** *n.* —**de·tec·tive** (–tiv) *n.* one who investigates crimes, finds criminals, etc.: *private ~s; a police ~;* ***adj.:*** *~ novels.*

dé·tente or **de·tente** (day·TAHNT) *n.* a lessening of strain or hostility, as between nations.

de·ten·tion (–TEN–) *n.* a detaining: *a house of ~* (i.e. jail): *a* **detention home** (for young offenders).

de·ter (di–) *v.* **-ters, -terred, -ter·ring** hinder or discourage: *The threat of counter-attack will ~ the enemy from nuclear warfare.* —**de·ter·ment** *n.* —**de·ter·rence** (di·TUR·unce) *n.* the act or a means of deterring; **de·ter·rent** *adj.* & *n.: The Bomb is the great ~ to another world war.*

de·ter·gent (di·TUR·junt) *n.* a cleaning agent; esp., a synthetic soap substitute; ***adj.:*** *a strong ~ action.*

de·te·ri·o·rate (di·TEER·ee·uh–) *v.* **-rates, -rat·ed, -rat·ing** make or become weaker, worse, etc.: *Polio causes muscles to ~;* **de·te·ri·o·ra·tion** (–RAY–) *n.*

de·ter·mi·nate (–nit) *adj.* having definite limits: *a ~ number, as "3," not a variable, as "x";* **de·ter·mi·na·cy** *n.;* **de·ter·mi·nant** *n.* & *adj.* —**de·ter·mi·na·tion** (–NAY–) *n.* a determining or being determined: *the ~ of the speed of light; a ~ to act properly.* —**de·ter·mine** (di·TUR·min) *v.* **-mines, -mined, -min·ing** **1** resolve or decide; also, cause to decide: *The incident made me ~ to change my life;* **determined** *adj.* firm; resolute: *a very ~ salesman;* **de·ter·mined·ly** *adv.;* **de·ter·mined·ness** *n.* **2** fix beforehand; cause: *Is intelligence ~d solely by heredity?* **3** settle; fix; resolve; also, find out: *The courts ~ questions of guilt; a ship ~ing its position by radar; a committee to ~ next year's budget needs.* —**de·ter·min·ism** *n.* the doctrine that all actions are controlled by prior causes not subject to man's will; **de·ter·min·ist** *n.* & *adj.*

deterrence, deterrent See DETER.

de·test (di–) *v.* abhor; hate intensely. —**de·test·a·ble** *adj.* —**de·tes·ta·tion** (dee·tes·TAY–) *n.*

de·throne (di–) *v.* **-thrones, -throned, -thron·ing** remove from a throne or other position of power: *a ~d king.* —**de·throne·ment** *n.*

det·o·nate *v.* **-nates, -nat·ed, -nat·ing** explode. —**det·o·na·tor** *n.* something used to set off an explosive charge. —**det·o·na·tion** (–NAY–) *n.*

de·tour (DEE·toor) *n.* a roundabout or secondary route used when the main road is closed; also, any circuitous path. —***v.:*** *forced to ~ around bureaucratic obstacles.*

de·tox·i·fy (dee·TOX–) *v.* **-fies, -fied, -fy·ing** remove a poison or its effect from. —**de·tox·i·fi·ca·tion** (–CAY–) *n.: Police often send drunks to ~ centers to sober up.*

de·tract (di–) *v.* take away; diminish: *a scar that ~s from his good looks;* **de·trac·tor** (di–) *n.: Should an author respond publicly to his ~s?* —**de·trac·tion** *n.*

de·train (dee–) *v.* get or put off a train: *troops ~ing in Dover for the Channel crossing.* —**de·train·ment** *n.*

det·ri·ment *n.* harm; damage: *He pursued the high-pressure job to the ~ of his health.* —**det·ri·men·tal** (–MEN·tl) *adj.: the ~ effects of smoking.* —**det·ri·men·tal·ly** *adv.*

de·tri·tus (di·TRY–) *n.* material remaining after disintegration and breakdown, esp. of rocks: *~ buildups clogging the channel.*

De·troit (di–) port and manufacturing city in Michigan, on the **Detroit River** (linking Lake St. Clair and Lake Erie).

deuce (DEWCE) *n.* **1** a two in dice-playing or cards. **2** a tie score in tennis. **3** devil: *What the ~ are you doing here?* **deuc·ed** (DEW·sid, DEWST) *adj.: a ~ nuisance!*

Deut. Deuteronomy.

deu·te·ri·um (dew·TEER·ee·um) *n.* a heavy isotope of hydrogen, used in atomic reactors and bombs: *A* **deu·ter·on** (DEW·tuh·ron) *is its nucleus, composed of a proton and a neutron.*

Deu·ter·on·o·my (dew·tuh·RON·uh·mee) the fifth book of the Old Testament.

deut·sche (DOY·chuh) **mark** the basic unit of money in West Germany, equal to 100 pfennigs.

dev. deviation.

de·val·ue (dee·VAL·yoo) *v.* **-ues, -ued, -u·ing** or **de·val·u·ate, -ates, -at·ed, -at·ing** reduce the value of; esp., reduce the value of (a currency) in international trade. —**de·val·u·a·tion** (–AY–) *n.: the ~ of the British pound;* **de·val·u·a·tion·ist** *n.*

dev·as·tate (DEV·uh–) *v.* **-tates, -tat·ed, -tat·ing** **1** destroy totally; lay waste. **2** overwhelm: *a ~ing beauty.* —**dev·as·ta·tion** (–STAY–) *n.: ~ by earthquake and flood.* —**dev·as·tat·ing·ly** *adv.*

de·vel·op (di·VEL·up) *v.* **1** grow or cause to grow larger, better, more mature, more complex, etc.: *a child's ~ing body; foreign aid to* **developing** *nations* (i.e. poor countries just becoming industrialized); *Reading ~s the mind; a fully ~ed plan of attack.* **2** make or become visible, active, usable, clear, etc.: *film ~ed by treating it with chemicals* (so that the picture can be seen); *Farmland is being ~ed* (i.e. built on) *for new housing and industry; Pneumonia has ~ed from the flu.* **3** come to have gradually: *She ~ed an interest in politics.* —**de·vel·op·a·ble** *adj.* —**de·vel·op·er** *n.: Real-estate ~s buy land to build on and sell.* —**de·vel·op·ment** *n.* a developing; something developed; esp., an occurrence or new state of affairs: *recent ~s in international trade.* —**de·vel·op·men·tal** (–MEN·tl) *adj.: ~ psychology deals with how people grow and mature.*

de·vi·ate (DEE·vee–) *v.* **-ates, -at·ed, -at·ing** turn away (esp. from a standard or norm): *a refusal to ~ from his plan.* —***adj.*** (*also* –vee·it) deviating; ***n.*** one who deviates, esp. from social or moral standards; also, a sexual pervert. Also **de·vi·ant** *adj.* & *n.* —**de·vi·ance** *n.* —**de·vi·a·tor** *n.* —**devi·a·tion** (–AY–) *n.*

de·vice (di–) *n.* **1** something devised, as: **a** a scheme or clever plan; **b** a usu. mechanical contrivance: *a ~ to fool the competition; a new ~ for polishing floors.* **2** a design or emblem, as on a coat of arms. —**leave to one's own devices** allow to do what one will or can.

dev·il *n.* **1** a demon; **the Devil** the supreme evil spirit. **2** a wicked or reckless person. **3** an unfortunate person. **4** a printer's helper. —***v.*** **-ils, -il(l)ed, -il·(l)ing** **1** badger; torment. **2** prepare (esp. ham or eggs) with hot seasonings. —**between the devil and the deep (blue) sea** in an unpleasant dilemma. —**the devil to pay** much trouble. —**a devil of a:** *a ~* (i.e. extreme instance) *of a job to fix that car.* —**give the devil his due** be fair to or honest about a bad or disliked person. —**go to the devil** **1** go to hell! **2** be ruined, esp. morally. —**play the devil with** upset; ruin. —**speak of the devil (and he appears)** [said when one who is being discussed comes along]. —**dev·il·ish** *adj.* **1** like a devil; esp., mischievous. **2** *Informal.* extreme. —**dev·il·ish·ly** *adv.;* **dev·il·ish·ness** *n.* —**dev·il·ment** or **dev·il·(t)ry** *n.* **-(t)ries** mischief: *young lads up to some ~ or other.* —**dev·il-may-care** *adj.* reckless; not caring: *a ~ flying ace.* —**devil's advocate** one who argues a side in a case for argument's sake. —**devil's-food cake** a dark chocolate cake.

de·vi·ous (DEE·vee·us) *adj.* **1** not straight; erring. **2** underhand; not straightforward: *~ trickery.* —**de·vi·ous·ly** *adv.* —**de·vi·ous·ness** *n.*

de·vise (di·VIZE) *v.* **-vis·es, -vised, -vis·ing** **1** contrive; plot: *~ a pipe to bring water to the house; ~ing the murder of the king.* **2** leave (real estate) to someone by will; it is left by a **de·vi·sor** to a **de·vi·see;** hence **devise** *n.* a bequest or a document, clause, etc. doing this.

de·vi·tal·ize (dee·VYE·tl–) *v.* **-iz·es, -ized, -iz·ing** lessen or destroy the vitality of.

de·void (di–) *adj.* having none (of); totally without: *a tyrant ~ of human feelings.*

de·voirs (duv·WAHRZ) *n.pl.* respects or courtesies: *pay ~ to one's lord.*

dev·o·lu·tion (–LOO–) *n.* a devolving: *for ~ of power from London to a Scottish parliament.* —**de·volve** (di·VOLV) *v.* **-volves, -volved, -volv·ing** pass on (to someone else): *The job has ~d upon his eldest son.*

De·vo·ni·an (–VOH–) *n.* & *adj.* (of) a geological period of the Paleozoic era, beginning about 405 million years ago.

de·vote (di–) *v.* **-votes, -vot·ed, -vot·ing** set apart or dedicate for a special purpose: *~ one's life to politics.* —**de·vot·ed** *adj.* very dedicated, faithful, or loving: *Your ~ servant;* **de·vot·ed·ly** *adv.* —**dev·o·tee** (dev·uh·TEE) *n.* a devoted worshiper, follower, supporter, etc.: *~s of Isis; a ~ of the ballet.* —**de·vo·tion** (–VOH–) *n.* **1** a devoting or being devoted; esp., great love or loyalty: *a soldier's ~ to duty.* **2** religious dedication; **devotions** *pl.* prayers; worship; **de·vo·tion·al** *adj.: ~ music.*

de·vour (di·VOUR) *v.* **1** eat greedily. **2** consume: *~ed with curiosity; a house ~ed by fire.* **3** read, look at, listen to, etc. greedily: *He ~s whodunits at one a week.* —**de·vour·er** *n.*

de·vout (di–) *adj.* very pious; also, earnest; heart-felt. —**de·vout·ly** *adv.: "a consummation ~ to be wish'd."* —**de·vout·ness** *n.*

dew *n.* moisture that condenses on cool bodies at night. —**dew·ber·ry** *n.* **-ber·ries** a ground-trailing blackberry. —**dew·claw** *n.* a toe or hoof, as in deer, dogs, pigs, etc., which does not touch the ground. —**dew·drop** *n.* a drop of dew. —**dew·lap** *n.* a flap of loose skin hanging from an animal's throat.

DEW line the Distant Early Warning line of radar stations along the 70th parallel in North America.

dew point the air temperature at which dew forms. —**dew·worm** same as ANGLEWORM. —**dew·y** *adj.* **dew·i·er, -i·est** wet (as) with dew: *~-eyed innocence.*

dex·ter·ous *adj.* **1** skillful with one's hands; also, clever; mentally quick. **2** done with dexterity. Also **dex·trous.** **—dex·ter·ous·ly** *adv.* **—dex·ter·i·ty** (–TER–) *n.: Threading a needle demands manual ~.*

dex·trin(e) (–trin) *n.* a sticky substance made from starch and used in glues, for sizing, and in syrups. **—dex·trose** *n.* a form of pure sugar found in grapes, honey, and animal body fluids and used in jams, canning fruits, and in candy.

D.F. Defender of the Faith; direction finder.

D.F.C. Distinguished Flying Cross.

D.F.M. Distinguished Flying Medal.

dg. decigram(s). **—D.G.** Dei gratia (by God's grace); director general.

dhar·ma (DAR·muh, DUR–) *n.* in Eastern religions, moral or religious law; also, truth; nature.

dhow (DOW) *n.* a single-masted, lateen-rigged Arabian ship.

di- *prefix.* **1** two; twofold: as in *dichotomy.* **2** also **dia-** through; across; apart; opposite: as in *diagonal, diagnose, diamagnetic.*

Di didymium.

dia. diameter.

di·a·be·tes (dye·uh·BEE·teez, –tus) *n.* any of several diseases marked by excessive urination, esp. **diabetes mel·li·tus** (–muh·LYE·tus), or sugar diabetes, in which a deficiency of natural insulin causes excess sugar in the blood and urine. **—di·a·bet·ic** (–BET·ic) *adj.* & *n.*

di·a·bol·ic (dye·uh·BOL–) or **-i·cal** *adj.* devilish; evil or cruel: *a ~ plan to kidnap a child.* **—di·a·bol·i·cal·ly** *adv.*

di·a·crit·ic (dye·uh·CRIT–) or **-i·cal** *adj.* indicating a distinction; **diacritical mark** or **diacritic** *n.* a mark used with a letter, as in ā, ă, â, ä, or ç, to show a modification of its sound.

di·a·dem (DYE·uh–) *n.* a crown, wreath, etc. worn by a sovereign.

di·aer·e·sis same as DIERESIS.

diag. diagonal; diagram.

di·ag·nose (dye·ig·NOHSS) *v.* **-nos·es, -nosed, -nos·ing** identify, esp. a disease, from symptoms: *The mechanic ~d the problem as a clogged carburetor.* **—di·ag·no·sis** (–NOH–) *n., pl.* **-ses** (–seez): *The doctor's ~ was "measles."* **—di·ag·nos·tic** (–NOS–) *adj.* having to do with diagnosis: *~ tests.* **—di·ag·nos·ti·cian** (–TISH·un) *n.*

di·ag·o·nal (dye·AG·uh·nl) *adj.* running from one corner to the opposite in an at least four-sided figure; hence, on a slant; oblique. **—*n.*** a diagonal line, as a virgule; also, a cloth with a slanting weave; twill. **—di·ag·o·nal·ly** *adv.*

di·a·gram (DYE·uh–) *n.* a sketch or line drawing used to show the structure, functioning, etc. of something. **—*v.* -grams, -gram(m)ed, -gram·(m)ing:** *The statistician ~d the results of his search.* **—di·a·gram·mat·ic** (–MAT·ic) or **-i·cal** *adj.* **—di·a·gram·mat·i·cal·ly** *adv.*

di·al (DYE·ul) *n.* **1** a circular surface used to indicate measures of time, temperature, etc.: *the ~ of a wrist watch; a barometer ~.* **2** a disk that can be turned to select, adjust, etc. an apparatus: *Tune in to a radio station or television channel by using a knoblike ~; telephones with buttons instead of a ~ for making connections.* **—*v.* -als, -al(l)ed, -al·(l)ing:** *~ 411* (a telephone number) *for information.* **—di·al-a-** *comb.form* [used to indicate a service available by telephone]: *~bus; ~prayer.*

dial. *Abbrev.* for **di·a·lect** (DYE·uh–) *n.* a regionally or socially distinct form of a language, esp. if nonstandard. **—di·a·lec·tal** (–LEC–) *adj.*

di·a·lec·tic (dye·uh·LEC–) *n.* **1** reasoned discussion; logic. **2** also **dialectics** [takes *sing.* or *pl. v.*] the Hegelian process of thesis, antithesis, and synthesis; hence, a set of contradictory ideas, their discussion, or resolution. **—*adj.*** also **di·a·lec·ti·cal:** *~ materialism.*

di·a·log(ue) (DYE·uh·log) *n.* **1** a conversation; hence, a literary work representing a conversation or the conversational element in a literary work: *the Socratic ~s of Plato; a play with fast-paced ~.* **2** constructive discussion: *the ~ between Protestants and Catholics.*

dial tone the buzzing sound indicating that a telephone line is open for use.

di·al·y·sis (dye·AL·i–) *n., pl.* **-ses** (–seez) the separation of different substances in a solution by passing it across a semipermeable membrane, as is done to cleanse the blood in an artificial-kidney machine, or "dialysis machine."

di·a·mag·net·ic (–NET–) *adj.* repelled by a magnetic field: *Glass is a ~ (substance).* **—di·a·mag·net·ism** (–MAG–) *n.*

di·am·e·ter (dye·AM·i–) *n.* the greatest width of a figure; esp., a line through the center of a circle, sphere, cylinder, etc.: *a ball 3 in. in ~.* **—di·a·met·ri·cal** (dye·uh·MET–) *adj.* **1** of or on a diameter. **2** totally opposite: *~ viewpoints.* **—di·a·met·ri·cal·ly** *adv.: philosophies ~ opposed to each other.*

di·a·mond (DYE·uh·mund) *n.* **1** a crystalline form of nearly pure carbon and the hardest naturally occurring mineral, used as a gem and as an industrial abrasive; **diamond in the rough** a good person with unpolished manners. **2** a figure having four equal sides and two pairs of equal angles, one of which is acute; also, something shaped like this, as a card marked with this shape in red or a baseball field, esp. the infield. **—diamond anniversary** (or **jubilee**) a 60th or 75th year. **—di·a·mond·back** *n.* a large, poisonous rattlesnake of the southern U.S.

Di·an·a (dye·AN·uh) the Roman goddess of hunting and of the moon.

di·an·thus (dye·AN·thus) *n.* a genus of flowers including the pinks, carnations, and sweet William.

di·a·pa·son (dye·uh·PAIZ·un) *n.* the full range of a musical instrument; hence, an organ stop producing its whole range: *love, sorrow, anger, and the whole ~ of human emotion.*

di·a·per (DYE·pur, DYE·uh–) *n.* an absorbent cloth folded around a baby like underpants. —*v.* put a diaper on.

di·aph·a·nous (dye·AF·uh·nus) *adj.* of fabrics, fine and able to be seen through: *a ~ blouse.*

di·a·pho·ret·ic (dye·uh·fuh·RET·ic) *n.* a medicine that increases perspiration; *adj.: a ~ treatment.*

di·a·phragm (DYE·uh·fram) *n.* **1** a dome-shaped muscle separating the abdominal and chest cavities. **2** a thin disk or cone that vibrates to produce sound. **3** a disk with an opening used to regulate light entering a camera. **4** a cap placed as a contraceptive over the opening to the uterus. —**di·a·phrag·mat·ic** (–frag·MAT·ic) *adj.*

di·ar·rh(o)e·a (dye·uh·REE·uh) *n.* too frequent and watery bowel movement.

di·ar·y (DYE·uh·ree) *n.* **-ar·ies** a day-by-day record of one's thoughts, experiences, etc.: *He wrote in his ~ every night at bedtime.* —**di·a·rist** *n.*

Di·as·po·ra (dye·AS·puh·ruh) *n.* a scattering of a people, esp. the Jews; hence, the Jews living outside Israel.

di·as·tol·e (dye·AS·tuh·lee) *n.* the regularly recurring expansion of the heart following a systole. —**di·a·stol·ic** (dye·uh·STOL·ic) *adj.: ~ blood pressure* (i.e. the lower of the two numbers expressing blood pressure, as 80 in 120/80).

di·a·ther·my (DYE·uh–) *n.* the heating of body tissues with high-frequency electricity as a medical treatment.

di·a·tom (DYE·uh–) *n.* a single-celled alga with a cell wall of mostly silica.

di·a·tom·ic (dye·uh·TOM–) *adj.* of a molecule, having two atoms.

di·at·o·mite (dye·AT·uh–) *n.* a light earth composed of diatoms and used as a filter, abrasive, etc.

di·a·ton·ic (dye·uh·TON–) *adj. Music.* of or in a standard, 8-tone major or minor scale.

di·a·tribe (DYE·uh–) *n.* a violent criticism; bitter invective.

di·az·e·pam (dye·AZ·uh–) *n.* a tranquilizer.

dib·ble *n.* a pointed gardener's tool for making holes, as for bulbs, seeds, and slips.

dice *n.pl., sing.* **dice** or **die** **1** small cube(s) having 1 to 6 spots on its respective sides, used in games and gambling; **no dice** no luck; "no." **2** [takes *sing. v.*] a game played with dice. —*v.* **dic·es, -diced, -dic·ing** **1** play with dice. **2** chop into small cubes: *~d carrots.* —**dic·ey** (DYE·see) *adj.* **dic·i·er, -i·est** *Informal.* risky; uncertain.

di·chot·o·my (dye·COT·uh·mee) *n.* **-mies** a division into two, usu. opposed parts: *the ~ of right and wrong.* —**di·chot·o·mous** (–uh·mus) *adj.*

dick *n. Slang.* a detective.

dick·ens (–nz) *n.* deuce; devil: as in **play the dickens with, what the dickens?**

Dick·ens, Charles. 1812–1870, English novelist.

dick·er *v.* haggle: *~ing with the salesman over prices.*

dick·ey *n.* **-eys** **1** a detachable false shirt or blouse front. **2** a little bird; also **dick·ey·bird.** Also **dick·y,** *pl.* **dick·ies.**

di·cot·y·le·don (dye·cotl·EE·dn) *n.* a plant having two cotyledons. —**di·cot·y·le·don·ous** (–us) *adj.*

dict. dictator; dictionary. —**Dic·ta·phone** *Trademark.* a machine that records speech for later transcription. —**dic·tate** *v.* **-tates, -tat·ed, -tat·ing** **1** read or say (something) for someone else to write down: *an executive ~ing a letter to his secretary.* **2** command with authority; give orders: *Don't let your brother ~ to you; ~ing the terms of surrender.* —*n.* order; command: *the ~s of conscience; in obedience to God's ~s.* —**dic·ta·tion** (–TAY–) *n.* —**dic·ta·tor** (DIC–) *n.* one who dictates; esp., an absolute, usu. unconstitutional ruler; tryant; **dic·ta·tor·ship** *n.: the ~ of the proletariat* (in Marxist ideology); **dic·ta·to·ri·al** (–TOR·ee·ul) *adj.*

dic·tion *n.* **1** choice of words for expressing ideas. **2** the way one pronounces words: *a singer with poor ~.* —**dic·tion·ar·y** *n.* **-ar·ies** a book listing words in alphabetical order, with pronunciation, meaning, and other information on them; also, a book that translates words of one language into another: *a Russian-English ~.*

dic·tum *n.* **-tums** or **-ta** a formal pronouncement of one's opinion.

did *pt.* of DO.

di·dac·tic (dye·DAC–) *adj.* intended to teach; moralizing: *~ poetry; a ~ manner.* —**di·dac·ti·cism** *n.*

did·dle *v.* **did·dles, did·dled, did·dling** *Informal.* **1** cheat. **2** waste (time) with trivialities: *~d away a month on useless research.* **3** juggle. —**did·dler** *n.*

did·n't (DIDNT) did not.

di·do (DYE·doh) *n.* **-do(e)s** *Informal.* mischievous trick; caper.

di·dym·i·um (dye·DIM–) *n.* a mixture of two rare-earth elements, neodymium and praseodymium, used to color glass for filters.

[1]die (DYE) *n.* **1** *sing.* of DICE. **2** *pl.* **dies** a hard metal device used to shape material, as by stamping (coins or medals), by cutting (threads on a screw), or by extrusion (as wire).

[2]die (DYE) *v.* **dies, died, dy·ing** **1** stop living, existing, or functioning: *The "right to bear arms" is a tradition that* **dies hard;** *The passenger pigeon* **died out** (i.e. became extinct) *years ago; people* **dying off** *one by one with the plague; Pete never retired because he wanted to* **die in harness**

(i.e. while still actively working); *a gunfighter who* **died with his boots on** (i.e. while still active). **2** lose power, vigor, or force; **die down** or **die away:** *waiting for the wind to ~ down.* **3** *Informal.* desire very much: *~ing to go to the dance; ~ing for a cigarette.* **—die·hard** *n.* one who stubbornly refuses to give in or change; ***adj.:*** *a ~ conservative.*

diel·drin (DEEL–) *n.* a powerful insecticide, used esp. to kill chinch bugs in grain fields.

di·e·lec·tric (dye·i·LEC–) *n.* an electrical nonconductor, e.g. glass; also ***adj.***

di·er·e·sis (dye·ER·uh–) *n., pl.* **-ses** (–seez) two dots over a vowel to show that it is in a separate syllable, as in *naïve* (nah·EEV).

die·sel (DEE·zl) *n.* **1** a **diesel engine,** an internal-combustion engine without spark plugs that burns oil by the heat of air compression. **2** a truck, locomotive, etc. driven by such an engine.

¹di·et (DYE·ut) *n.* an assembly or parliament, as the legislature of Japan: *The Diet of Worms, Germany, declared Luther a heretic in 1521.*

²di·et *n.* **1** one's regular food and drink: *an unhealthy ~ of popcorn and other snacks; Bill's reading is a steady ~ of cheap westerns.* **2** a special regimen of food and drink: *went on a low-fat ~ to lose weight; a salt-free ~.* **—*v.:*** *He lost 10 lbs. by ~ing for three months;* **di·et·er** *n.* **—di·e·ta·ry** (DYE·uh·ter·ee) *adj.: Jewish ~ laws.* **—di·e·tet·ic** (dye·uh·TET·ic) *adj.* of or for a diet, esp. a restricted one: *~ soft drinks;* **di·e·tet·ics** *is the study of healthy diets; A* **di·e·ti·tian** (–TISH·un) or **-ti·cian** *may plan meals for a hospital, a restaurant, a school cafeteria, etc.*

dif(f). difference; different. **—dif·fer** (DIF·ur) *v.* be different; also, disagree; *After much useless arguing, we had to* **agree to differ** *over politics; regions with widely ~ing climates.* **—dif·fer·ence** *n.* **1** a being different; also, a factor that distinguishes: *no ~ between our viewpoints; a ~ of opinion; The only ~ between the cars is the color.* **2** the amount by which things differ: *12 is the ~ between 6 and 18;* **make a difference** matter; be important; **split the difference** divide it equally; hence, compromise: *The negotiations split the ~ for a 7% raise* (i.e. halfway between 5% and 9%). **3** a disagreement: *Don't settle your ~s by fighting.* **—dif·fer·ent** *adj.* **1** not the same; dissimilar; hence, peculiar; unusual: *Her opinions are very ~ from his; How do you like my new tie? Well, it's ~.* **2** other; distinct: *I called seven ~ times; Order a ~ meal if they're out of fish.* Hence **dif·fer·ent·ly** *adv.* **—dif·fer·en·tial** (–REN·shul) *adj.* of or expressing a difference or distinction: *a ~ treatment of minorities;* **differential calculus** *is used esp. to determine the rate of change of a continuously varying quantity.* ***—n.*** **1** same as **differential gear,** a gear arrangement that allows a vehicle's drive wheels to turn at different speeds when cornering. **2** an absolute or percentage difference: *the standard 15% wage ~ between two job classifications.* **—dif·fer·en·ti·ate** (–REN·shee·ate) *v.* **-ates, -at·ed, -at·ing** be, make, have, or recognize a difference (between): *He is color-blind and can't ~ red and green; species ~d by the length of fur; Color ~s the two hybrid roses;* **dif·fer·en·ti·a·tion** (–AY–) *n.*

dif·fi·cult *adj.* **1** requiring effort, strength, skill, patience, etc.; not easy: *It is ~ to get through medical school; a ~ problem for homework.* **2** hard to please, manage, get along with, etc.: *a ~ child spoiled by his grandparents.* **—dif·fi·cul·ty** *n.* **-ties:** *a task of extraordinary ~; reads French with some ~; overcoming all ~s; a businessman in financial ~s.*

dif·fi·dent *adj.* not self-confident; timid: *He demurred with a ~ smile.* **—dif·fi·dence** *n.* **—dif·fi·dent·ly** *adv.*

dif·fract (di·FRACT) *v.* break up (light rays) into bands of light and dark or of different colors, as when passing around the edge of an object or through a small slit, hole, or a **diffraction grating,** a glass plate with many parallel lines close together. **—dif·frac·tion** *n.* **—dif·frac·tive** *adj.*

dif·fuse (di·FYOOZ) *v.* **dif·fus·es, dif·fused, dif·fus·ing** spread out widely: *the smell of perfume ~d throughout the room.* ***—adj.*** (di·FYOOS) diffused; also, verbose: *~ light produces no glare; a ~, rambling report.* **—dif·fu·sion** (–FEW–) *n.: the ~ of gases in the air; the ~ of knowledge.* **—dif·fuse·ness** *n.* **—dif·fuse·ly** *adv.* **—dif·fu·sive** (–siv) *adj.: the ~ power of gases.*

dig *v.* **digs, dug, dig·ging** **1** break up or scoop out earth, esp. for making or getting things: *~ing in the garden* (to prepare it for planting); *~ing a hole; ~ potatoes.* **2** poke: *He dug me in the ribs with his umbrella.* **3** *Slang.* notice; like; understand: *~ that car! doesn't ~ abstract art.* ***—n.*** **1** a poke; hence, a cutting remark aimed (at someone). **2** an archeological excavation site. **—dig in** **1** *Informal.* begin to eat or work. **2** take a firm position; dig oneself a trench. **—dig out** or **dig up** find (out) by much looking or research: *a reporter trying to ~ up some information.* **—dig·ger** *n.*

dig. *Abbrev.* for **di·gest** (DYE·jest) *n.* a short compilation or summary, esp. from diverse sources: *a legal ~; a weekly news ~.* ***—v.*** (di·JEST) **1** summarize and arrange. **2** break down (food) for absorption into the blood stream, as in the digestive system; hence, assimilate mentally: *having read the report, but not ~ed its implications;* **di·gest·i·ble** *adj.;* **di·gest·i·bil·i·ty** (–BIL–) *n.;* **di·ges·tion** (–JES·chun) *n.* the system for digesting or the ability to digest food: *a man with a delicate ~;* **di·ges·tive** (–JES·tiv) *adj.: Saliva and bile are ~ juices; food canal and accessory glands making up the* **digestive system.**

dig·it (DIJ·it) *n.* **1** a finger, thumb, or toe. **2** an Arabic numeral: *five-~ figures* (i.e. from 10,000 to 99,999). **—dig·it·al** *adj.: A* **digital**

clock *shows the time with numbers, not hands;* **digital computer** one that calculates using numbers, usually binary; **dig·it·al·ly** *adv.* —**dig·i·tal·is** (dij·i·TAL·is) *n.* a strong drug for heart ailments, derived from the purple foxglove.

dig·ni·fied *adj.* having dignity: *an aloof, ~ demeanor.* —**dig·ni·fy** *v.* **-fies, -fied, -fy·ing** give dignity to: *to ~ cowardice with the name of "prudence."* —**dig·ni·ty** *n.* **-ties** **1** intrinsic worth or value; also, respect owed to something: *the ~ of human suffering; the ~ of the Presidency; treated them with great ~.* **2** a calm, stately manner: *Don't lose your ~ by giggling in church.* **3** a high rank or office, held by a **dig·ni·tar·y** *n.* **-tar·ies.**

di·graph (DYE·graf) *n.* a pair of letters standing for one sound, as *ph* (= f) or *ea* in *head.*

di·gress (dye–) *v.* stray from the main subject. —**di·gres·sion** (–GRESH·un) *n.: The historian included a ~ on tribal customs.* —**di·gres·sive** (–siv) *adj.: a loose, ~ style of storytelling.*

dike *n.* **1** a bank or levee to prevent flooding of low ground. **2** same as DYKE.

dil. dilute.

Di·lan·tin (dye·LAN–) *Trademark.* a drug used to control epilepsy.

di·lap·i·dat·ed (di·LAP·i·day·tid) *adj.* falling to pieces; shabby; broken-down: *a ~ truck.* —**di·lap·i·da·tion** (–DAY–) *n.*

dil·a·ta·tion (–TAY–) *n.* an enlarging or stretching: *~ and curettage of the uterus.* —**di·late** (dye–) *v.* **-lates, -lat·ed, -lat·ing** **1** make wider or bigger: *eye drops to ~ the pupils.* **2** write or speak at length: *~ing on a subject.* —**di·la·tion** (–LAY–) *n.*

dil·a·to·ry (DIL·uh·tor·ee) *adj.* causing or inclined to delay; slow: *filibuster as a ~ tactic; ~ proceedings in committee.*

di·lem·ma (–LEM·uh) *n.* a choice between equally bad alternatives: *Isolationism or imperialism—we are* **on the horns of a dilemma.**

dil·et·tante (dil·uh·TAHNT, –TAHN·tee) *n.* **-tantes** or **-tan·ti** (–tee) one who merely dabbles in the arts. —**dil·et·tant·ish** *adj.*

dil·i·gent (–junt) *adj.* careful; assiduous; painstaking. —**dil·i·gence** *n.* —**dil·i·gent·ly** *adv.*

dill *n.* an herb used in pickling; **dill pickle** a cucumber pickled with dill.

dil·ly *n.* **dil·lies** *Slang.* something remarkable: *The storm was a ~.*

dil·ly·dal·ly *v.* **-dal·lies, -dal·lied, -dal·ly·ing** waste time, esp. by hesitating or loitering.

dil·u·ent (DIL·yoo·unt) *n.* a diluting agent; also ***adj.*** —**di·lute** (dye·LOOT, di–) *v.* **-lutes, -lut·ed, -lut·ing** weaken by adding something else: *wine ~d with water;* ***adj.:*** *~ sulphuric acid.* —**di·lu·tion** (–LOO–) *n.*

dim. dimension; diminuendo; diminutive.

dim *adj.* **dim·mer, dim·mest** **1** not bright or clear; also, not clearly perceived: *Do not read in ~ light; a ~ recollection; hills ~ in the distance.* **2** not perceiving clearly: *"My eyes are ~, I cannot see";* **take a dim view of** regard with disapproval or skepticism. —***v.*** **dims, dimmed, dim·ming** make or become dim. —**dim·ly** *adv.* —**dim·ness** *n.* —**dim·mer** *n.* —**dims** *n.pl.* an automobile's parking lights.

dime *n.* a ten-cent coin; **a dime a dozen** cheap or easy to get.

di·men·sion (di·MEN–) *n.* **1** a measurable magnitude, as length, width, and depth: *Time is often thought of as a fourth ~.* **2** size; also, importance or range: *a disaster of great ~s.* —**di·men·sion·al** *adj.: We live in a three-~ world.*

di·min·ish (di·MIN–) *v.* make or become smaller, less strong, etc.: *an enterprise affected by the law of* **diminishing returns** (i.e. proportionately less profit for increased effort); **dim·i·nu·tion** (–NEW–) *n.* —**di·min·u·en·do** (–yoo·EN·doh) *adj.* & *adv. Music.* with gradually decreasing loudness; also ***n.*** —**di·min·u·tive** (–MIN·yuh·tiv) *adj.* very small; ***n.*** a suffix denoting smallness, as *-ie, -let,* or *-kin* or a word formed with one, as *birdie, bracelet,* or *catkin.*

dim·i·ty *n.* **-ties** a light, strong cotton fabric.

dimmer See DIM.

di·mor·phic (dye–) *adj.* having or occurring in two distinct forms: *The primrose has ~ flowers.* —**di·mor·phism** *n.*

dim·ple *n.* a small depression, esp. in a body part, as on the chin. —***v.*** **-ples, -pled, -pling:** *Her cheeks ~d when she laughed.* —**dim·ply** *adj.*

dim·wit *n. Informal.* a simpleton; **dim·wit·ted** *adj.*

din *n.* a continuous, confused loud noise. —***v.*** **dins, dinned, din·ning:** *firebells ~ing in his ears; Industriousness was* **dinned into** *him as a child.*

di·nar (di·NAR) *n.* the basic unit of money in several Arab countries and in Yugoslavia; also, 1/100 of a rial (Iran).

dine *v.* **dines, dined, din·ing** eat dinner; also, provide with dinner: *Betty and Jim usually* **dine out** (as at a restaurant) *once a week; going all out to wine and ~ influential patrons.* —**din·er** (DYE–) *n.* **1:** *A busboy should not speak to the ~s.* **2** a restaurant car on a train; also, a restaurant built like one: *ham and eggs at Pete's ~.* —**din·ette** (dye·NET) *n.* a nook or alcove for eating in: *buying a ~ set* (i.e. table and chairs) *for their new apartment.*

ding(·dong) *n.* the sound of a bell; **ding-a-ling** *n. Slang.* a crazy person.

din·ghy (DING·ee, –ghee) *n.* **-ghies** a small rowboat; also, a life raft.

din·gle *n.* a small wooded valley.

din·go (DING·go) *n.* **-goes** an often tawny, medium-sized wild dog of Australia.

ding·us *n. Informal.* a gadget; a thing whose name does not come to mind.

din·gy (–jee) *adj.* **-gi·er, -gi·est** dark and dirty; shabby: *a ~ coal-mining town;* **din·gi·ly** *adv.;* **din·gi·ness** *n.*

din·ky *adj. Informal.* **-ki·er, -ki·est** small and insignificant.

din·ner *n.* **1** the main meal of the day, at noon or in the evening. **2** a formal banquet; **dinner jacket** a tuxedo. **—din·ner·ware** *n.* plates, bowls, cups, etc. for serving dinner.

di·no·flag·el·late (dye·nuh·FLAJ·uh·lit) *n.* any of numerous tiny algae in plankton, some of which help cause red tides.

di·no·saur (DYE–) *n.* any of the often large, now extinct lizards of the Mesozoic era, found in fossils.

dint *n.* a dent. **—by dint of** by the effort or means of: *He got rich by ~ of long, hard hours of work.*

di·o·cese (DYE·uh·sis, –seece) *n.* the area under a bishop's care. **—di·oc·e·san** (dye·OS·i·sn) *adj.: discussions at the ~ synod.*

di·ode (DYE–) *n.* a two-electrode vacuum tube or semiconductor, esp. a rectifier.

Di·og·e·nes (dye·OJ·uh·neez) 412?–323 B.C., Greek philosopher and ascetic.

Di·o·ny·sus (dye·uh·NYE·sus) Greek god of wine and revels; Bacchus. **—Di·o·ny·sian** (–NISH·un) *adj.: ~ orgies.*

di·o·ram·a (dye·oh·RAM·uh) *n.* a three-dimensional exhibit of a scene with modeled figures arranged in front of a painted background.

di·ox·ide (–OX–) *n.* a compound having two atoms of oxygen in the molecule.

dip *v.* **dips, dipped, dip·ping 1** immerse, briefly in a liquid: *sheep ~d in disinfectant; ~ fabric into a vat of dye.* **2** ladle or scoop out; hence, reach down into to take out: *~ water from the bucket with a cup; Hard times forced them to ~ into life savings to pay the rent.* **3** go down: *The moon ~d behind the trees.* **4** go down and up again; make to do so: *~ the flag; prices ~d at the end of the year.* **5** read or study superficially: *~d into Russian history.* **—*n.*** **1** a dipping; esp., a brief swim: *a quick ~ in the pool.* **2** something to dip in: *sheep ~; onion-and-garlic ~ for potato chips.* **3** a downward sloping, depression, or course: *an airplane's ~ in salute; a ~ in the road.*

diph·the·ri·a (dif·THEER·ee·uh, dip–) *n.* a dangerous contagious disease spread by a bacillus and characterized by a membrane clogging the throat. **—diph·the·ri·al** *adj.*

diph·thong (DIF–, DIP–) *n.* a sound composed of two vowel sounds uttered together, as in *boil, pain,* and *cold.*

dipl. diplomat(ic).

dip·loid *adj.* having twice the number of chromosomes found in a normal reproductive cell: *a ~ cell;* also ***n.***

di·plo·ma (–PLOH·muh) *n.* a certificate of educational accomplishment: *a doctor's ~.* **—di·plo·ma·cy** (–PLOH–) *n.* **1** the art of a diplomat; skill in conducting relations between countries: *the elaborate etiquette of international ~.* **2** skill in dealing with people; tact. **—dip·lo·mat** (DIP·luh–) *n.* **1** one empowered to represent his government in dealing with another government. **2** one who is tactful and skillful in dealing with people. Also **di·plo·ma·tist** (–PLOH·muh–). **—dip·lo·mat·ic** (–MAT–) *adj.: a ~ bartender good at settling disputes; An ambassador enjoys* **diplomatic immunity** (i.e. freedom from arrest, taxes, etc.) *abroad;* **diplomatic corps** the staff of one country's diplomatic service at the capital of another.

di·pole (antenna) (DYE–) a radio or TV antenna consisting of a metal rod or wire split and separated in the center.

dip·per *n.* **1** something that dips, as a diving bird. **2** a long-handled cup or scoop; also BIG DIPPER or LITTLE DIPPER.

dip·so·ma·ni·a (–MAY·nee·uh) *n.* an uncontrollable craving for liquor.

dip·stick *n.* a stick dipped in a liquid (as engine oil) to measure its depth.

dip·ter·ous *adj.* two-winged, as mosquitoes and other insects; also **dip·ter·an** *adj. & n.*

dir. director.

dire *adj.* **dir·er, dir·est** terrible; disastrous; also, extreme: *~ threats; in ~ poverty.*

di·rect (di·RECT, dye–) *v.* **1** point or send; also, addressed: *remarks ~ed to his employees; ~ your reply to me, c/o my brother; Can you ~ me to the library* (i.e. tell me how to get there)? **2** give orders or guidance to; control; regulate: *~ed an industrial firm; to ~ a film.* **—*adj.*** **1** straight; unswerving; not stopping, interrupted, etc.: *in a ~ line from A to B; a ~* (i.e. undeflected) *hit on target.* **2** with nothing intervening or mediating: *~ sunlight; a ~* (i.e. unbroken) *line of descent; dialogue reported in ~ discourse* (See DISCOURSE); *a ~ tax* (as income tax) *paid by the person it is levied on.* **3** blunt; straightforward; candid: *~ answers.* **4** total; diametrical: *the ~ antithesis of love.* **—*adv.:*** *We flew New York to Los Angeles ~; appealing ~ to the voters.* **—direct current** electricity flowing in one direction only. **—di·rect·ness** *n.* **—di·rec·tion** *n.* **1:** *working under the ~ of experts.* **2** often **directions,** *pl.* instructions on how to use or do something, get somewhere, etc.: *detailed ~s for using the lawn mower.* **3** spatial orientation; where something is facing or going, as North, South, left, up, etc.: *Which ~ did he run? Bill has a poor sense of ~* (i.e. is always getting lost); *new ~s in literary criticism.* **—di·rec·tion·al** *adj.: a ~ radio antenna* (for signals from a particular direction). **—di·rec·tive** (–tiv) *n.* an order or rule: *~s on hiring minority citizens.* **—di·rect·ly** *adv.* **1** in a direct or straightforward manner: *smiling ~ at us.* **2** immediately: *leave ~ after work;* ***conj.***

Brit. as soon as: ~ *I had done it, I regretted it.* —**direct mail** advertising matter mailed to people on a list, as by a mail-order house. —**direct object** a word that receives the action of a verb, as *book* in "Give me the book." —**di·rec·tor** *n.* one who directs: *a ~ of TV shows; a ~ of General Motors* (i.e. a member of the *Board of ~s*); **di·rec·tor·ate** *n.;* **di·rec·tor·ship** *n.* —**di·rec·to·ry** *n.* **-ries** an alphabetical list of names along with addresses, phone numbers, etc.

dirge (DIRJ) *n.* a song or poem lamenting someone's death.

dir·ham (duh·RAM) *n.* the basic money unit in Morocco, equal to 100 francs; also, 1/20 of an Iraqi dinar and 1/1000 of a Libyan dinar.

dir·i·gi·ble (DEER–, duh·RIJ–) *n.* an airship; ***adj.*** steerable.

dirk *n.* a straight-bladed dagger.

dirn·dl *n.* a full skirt gathered at the waist; also, a dress having this and a tight bodice.

dirt *n.* **1** soil or earth. **2** grime; filth; **eat dirt** accept humiliating treatment; retract a statement. **3** corruption or obscenity; pornography; also, slanderous gossip. —**dirt-cheap** *adj. Informal.* very cheap. —**dirt farmer** one who works his land alone, without hired help or tenant farmers. —**dirt road** an unpaved road. —**dirt·y** *adj.* **dirt·i·er, -i·est** **1** soiled; unclean: ~ *hands;* **2** unfair; low; base: *a ~ trick.* **3** immoral; taboo; smutty: ~ *books;* ~ *words.* **4** stormy; also, hostile: ~ *weather; gave us a ~ look.* —***v.*** **dirt·ies, dirt·ied, dirt·y·ing:** *children taught not to* **dirty their hands** (i.e. shame themselves) *by stealing and lying.* —**dirt·i·ness** *n.* —**dirty linen** private affairs of an embarrassing nature. —**dirty pool** *Slang.* unfair play.

dis- *prefix* [indicating] **1** negation, reversal, or removal: as in *displease, disunite, disbar.* **2** apart; abroad: as in *disrupt, disseminate.*

dis·a·ble (–AY·bl) *v.* **-bles, -bled, -bling** make unable, unfit, unqualified, etc., as by wounding: *~d veterans; a tank ~d by a land mine; Marriage ~d her from inheriting.* —**dis·a·bil·i·ty** (–BIL–) *n.* **-ties:** *a ~ pension for the crippled.*

dis·a·buse (–BYOOZ) *v.* **-bus·es, -bused, -bus·ing** free of mistaken ideas.

di·sac·cha·ride (dye·SAC·uh–) *n.* any of several sugars, as sucrose and lactose.

dis·ad·van·tage (–VAN·tij) *n.* something that harms, works against, hinders, etc.; a drawback: *at a great ~ in the contest; events that turned out to our ~.* —**dis·ad·van·taged** (–tijd) *adj.* lacking an acceptable basic standard of living. —**dis·ad·van·ta·geous** (–TAY·jus) *adj.*

dis·af·fect (dis·uh·FECT) *v.* cause to be unfriendly, disloyal, or rebellious: *the ~ed masses of the unemployed.* —**dis·af·fec·tion** *n.*

dis·a·gree (–uh·GREE) *v.* **-grees, -greed, -gree·ing** **1** fail to agree; differ; hence, quarrel. **2** cause distress or upset, as foods *with* particular people. —**dis·a·gree·a·ble** (–uh·bl) *adj.* unpleasant; also, ill-tempered: *a ~ day; a ~ old grouch;* **dis·a·gree·a·bly** *adv.;* **dis·a·gree·a·ble·ness** *n.* —**dis·a·gree·ment** *n.*

dis·al·low (dis·uh·LOU) *v.* refuse to allow or accept: *The review board ~ed his claim.* —**dis·al·low·ance** *n.*

dis·ap·pear (–PEER) *v.* cease to be seen or to exist: *The magician made the rabbit ~; whales ~ing because of excessive hunting.* —**dis·ap·pear·ance** *n.: sudden ~ of spring snow.*

dis·ap·point (–POINT) *v.* fail to fulfill the hopes or wishes of; let down; also, frustrate: *We felt* **disappointed** *by his poor performance;* a **disappointing** *turnout at the meeting.* —**dis·ap·point·ment** *n.: His performance was a bit of a ~.*

dis·ap·pro·ba·tion (–ap·ruh·BAY–) *n.* disapproval. —**dis·ap·prove** (–PROOV) *v.* **-ap·proves, -ap·proved, -ap·prov·ing** not accept or approve; have or express a bad opinion: *Father ~d of long hair.* —**dis·ap·prov·al** (–PROO·vul)

dis·arm *v.* **1** make less hostile; make favorably inclined; also, allay: *a confession to ~ their suspicions; won over the audience with a* **dis·arm·ing** *smile.* **2** take weapons away from; also, reduce or do away with military strength: *a robber ~ed by the police;* **dis·ar·ma·ment** *n.: a nuclear ~ treaty.*

dis·ar·range *v.* **-rang·es, -ranged, -rang·ing** disturb the order or arrangement of: *clothes ~d by being slept in.* —**dis·ar·range·ment** *n.*

dis·ar·ray *n.* disorder; disorganized dress: *As the rain fell, the procession broke up in ~.* —***v.:*** *papers ~ed by the wind.*

dis·as·sem·ble *v.* **-bles, -bled, -bling** take to pieces: *a bicycle ~d for shipping.* —**dis·as·sem·bly** *n.*

dis·as·so·ci·ate *v.* **-ates, -at·ed, -at·ing** end or break off an association of: *~d himself from the movement.*

dis·as·ter (–ZAS–) *n.* a great misfortune causing much death or damage; calamity: *The hurricane-stricken town was declared a* **disaster area** *by the governor.* —**dis·as·trous** (–trus) *adj.: a ~ drought in Kansas;* **dis·as·trous·ly** *adv.: a tide running ~ high.*

dis·a·vow (–uh·VOW) *v. Formal.* claim that one does not know about, approve of, or is associated with: *The President ~ed the incriminating evidence.* —**dis·a·vow·al** *n.*

dis·band (–BAND) *v.* break up (an organization): *a ~ed regiment.*

dis·bar (–BAR) *v.* **-bars, -barred, -bar·ring** expel as a lawyer. —**dis·bar·ment** *n.*

dis·be·lieve (–LEEV) *v.* **-lieves, -lieved, -liev·ing** refuse or fail to believe. —**dis·be·lief** *n.: a story arousing widespread ~ and suspicion.* —**dis·be·liev·er** *n.*

dis·bur·den (–BUR–) *v.* rid of or eliminate a burden: *Confession helps to ~ one's conscience.*

dis·burse (–BURCE) *v.* **-burs·es, -bursed, -burs·ing** pay out; distribute: *The treasurer ~d the authorized amount.* **—dis·burse·ment** or **dis·burs·al** *n.: ~s of large research grants.*

disc *n.* **1** same as DISK. **2** a phonograph record.

dis·card (dis·CARD) *v.* get rid of; throw away, as a useless playing card. ***—n.*** something, as a card or cards, discarded: *old values thrown* **into the discard** *since World War II.*

disc brake an automobile brake operated by the pressure applied to the sides of a disc locked on to the moving wheel.

dis·cern *v.* perceive; distinguish: *able to ~ mountains in the distance; an astute and* **discerning** *judge of character.* **—dis·cern·i·ble** *adj.* **—dis·cern·ing·ly** *adv.* **—dis·cern·ment** *n.*

dis·charge *v.* **-charg·es, -charged, -charg·ing** unload; send forth (contents of something); be free of (an obligation); let go of (someone): *The bus ~d its passengers; ~ing the ship of its cargo; ~ the cargo; a river ~ing into Lake Erie; a battery ~ing electricity; ~ your rifle in the air; The pistol ~d accidentally; ~ing a capacitor; Jim ~d his debts* (by paying); *~ one's duty* (by doing it); *a prisoner ~d early on parole; a clerk ~d* (i.e. fired) *for theft; ~d from the navy.* ***—n.:*** *the ~ of the cargo; the ~ of his legal responsibilities as husband; a dishonorable ~ from the Marines; His ~ came in the mail; electrical ~* (as a spark across a gap); *a ~ of pus and blood.*

dis·ci·ple (di·SYE·pl) *n.* a student or follower; esp., one of Christ's 12 apostles; also, a member of the **Disciples of Christ,** a Protestant denomination stressing Biblical authority and practicing baptism by immersion. **—dis·ci·pline** (DIS·uh·plin) *n.* **1** an area of learning. **2** training to produce self-control, obedience, proper conduct, etc.; also, the results of this: *a child subjected to strict ~; Military ~ means automatic obedience; monastic ~.* **3** corrective punishment. ***—v.*** **-plines, -plined, -plin·ing** subject to discipline (defs. 2 and 3): *well ~d troops; a ~d writer; Do you ~ your child by spanking?* **—dis·ci·plin·er** *n.* **—dis·ci·pli·nar·y** *adj.: ~ action.* **—dis·ci·pli·nar·i·an** (–NAIR–) *n.: a strict ~ but a poor teacher.*

disc jockey the announcer on a radio program of recorded music.

dis·claim (–CLAIM) *v.* **1** claim that one has no knowledge of, connection with, etc.: *~ed complicity in the plot.* **2** renounce one's claim (to). **—dis·cla·ma·tion** (–MAY–) *n.* **—dis·claim·er** (–CLAY–) *n.* a statement of disclamation.

dis·close (–CLOZE) *v.* **-clos·es, -closed, -clos·ing** make visible or known; reveal: *The convict ~d the names of his accomplices.* **—dis·clo·sure** (–CLOH·zhur) *n.: ~s that shocked the nation.*

dis·co *n. Informal.* a discotheque; ***adj.:*** *~ dancing, music;* ***v.*** **-coes, -coed, -co·ing.**

dis·col·or *v.* change or spoil in color, as by stains or running. **—dis·col·or·a·tion** (–RAY–) *n.*

dis·com·bob·u·late (–BOB·yuh–) *v.* **-lates, -lat·ed, -lat·ing** *Informal.* upset; disorder; confuse: *~d by the news.*

dis·com·fit (–CUM–) *v.* frustrate; confuse; disconcert. **—dis·com·fi·ture** (–CUM·fi·chur) *n.*

dis·com·fort (–CUM·furt) *n.* lack of comfort, bodily or mental; unease; also, an instance or a cause of this: *suffering severe ~s.* ***—v.:*** *~ed by tight shoes.*

dis·com·mode (–cuh·MODE) *v.* **-com·modes, -com·mod·ed, -com·mod·ing** *Formal.* cause inconvenience or trouble to.

dis·com·pose (–cum·POZE) *v.* **-pos·es, -posed, -pos·ing** upset the composure, poise, or order of: *~d by the sudden bad news.* **—dis·com·po·sure** (–POH·zhur) *n.*

dis·con·cert (–cun·SURT) *v.* perturb; ruin the calm self-control of; also, frustrate (a plan, scheme, etc.).

dis·con·nect (–cuh·NECT) *v.* break the connection of or between: *~ one freight car from the next; ~ the toaster from the power source* (i.e. unplug it). **—dis·con·nec·tion** *n.* **—dis·con·nect·ed** *adj.* not or badly linked together: *a ~ narrative; ~ thoughts;* **dis·con·nect·ed·ly** *adv.*

dis·con·so·late (–CON·suh·lit) *adj.* sad; downcast; inconsolable. **—dis·con·so·late·ly** *adv.*

dis·con·tent (–cun·TENT) *n.* a lack of contentment or satisfaction. **—dis·con·tent·ed** *adj.: ~ with one's progress.*

dis·con·tin·ue (–cun·TIN·yoo) *v.* **-ues, -ued, -u·ing** cease or cause to cease; break off: *~ payments until the defects are repaired;* **dis·con·tin·u·ance** (–unce) or **dis·con·tin·u·a·tion** (–AY–) *n.* **—dis·con·ti·nu·i·ty** (–NEW–) *n.* **-ties** a gap or break **—dis·con·tin·u·ous** (–TIN–) *adj.* not continuous; having breaks and interruptions; **dis·con·tin·u·ous·ly** *adv.*

dis·cord *n.* **1** disagreement; dispute; quarreling: *the apple of ~* (i.e. a cause of rivalry and contention). **2** disharmony in music; a harsh dissonance; din. **—dis·cord·ant** (–COR·dunt) *adj.*

dis·co·theque (DIS·cuh·tek) *n.* a place for dancing to recorded music.

dis·count *n.* an amount deducted for early payment, buying in bulk, etc.: *a 5% ~ on cash orders; soiled goods sold* **at a discount. *—v.*** **1** reduce the price of; deduct (an amount) from the price of something: *We ~ all goods in the warehouse; ~ 2% from the regular price.* **2** allow for or anticipate bias, exaggeration, etc.; also, disregard as unreliable: *~ing much of what you read in the papers.* **—dis·count·a·ble** *adj.: ~ merchandise.* **—dis·count·er** *n.*

dis·coun·te·nance *v.* **-nanc·es, -nanced, -nanc·ing** **1** abash. **2** disapprove of.

discount house (or **store**) a store that sells goods at reduced prices.

dis·cour·age (–CUR·ij) *v.* **-ag·es, -aged, -ag·ing** **1** dishearten; make less confident, hopeful, or courageous: *The troops were ~d by early defeats.* **2** try to dissuade; deter: *Heavy seas ~d rescue efforts.* **—dis·cour·age·ment** *n.* **—dis·cour·ag·ing** *adj.*; **dis·cour·ag·ing·ly** *adv.*

dis·course *n.* **1** a formal speech; treatise: *Descartes' ~ on Method.* **2** verbal communication; **direct discourse** a quotation using someone's own words, as *He said "I will come"*; **indirect discourse** rephrasing of what someone said, as *He said he would come.* **—*v.*** **-cours·es, -coursed, -cours·ing** **1** speak or write at length: *~ing on Roman history.* **2** converse.

dis·cour·te·ous (–CUR·tee·us) *adj.* rude and ill-mannered. **—dis·cour·te·ous·ly** *adv.* **—dis·cour·te·sy** *n.* **-sies:** *apologize for one's ~s.*

dis·cov·er (–CUV·ur) *v.* **1** find (out); realize; get knowledge of: *Police ~ed several clues to the mystery.* **2** be first to learn of, see, etc.: *Columbus ~ed America.* **—dis·cov·er·er** *n.* **—dis·cov·er·y** (–CUV·uh·ree) *n.* **-er·ies:** *the ~ of insulin by Banting; new ~s in science.*

dis·cred·it (–CRED–) *v.* **1** disbelieve. **2** damage the credibility or reputation of: *~ed by the revelation.* **—*n.*:** *Lying does ~ to anyone; an error that stands to his ~.* **—dis·cred·i·ta·ble** (–tuh·bl) *adj.*: *~ behavior.*

dis·creet (–CREET) *adj.* having good judgment; judiciously silent; also, tastefully modest: *keeping a ~ silence; known for her ~ charm.* **—dis·creet·ly** *adv.*

dis·crep·an·cy (–CREP·un·see) *n.* **-cies** a disagreement; conflict: *serious ~s between the two witnesses' stories.* **—dis·crep·ant** *adj.*: *They gave ~ versions of the incident.*

dis·crete (–CREET) *adj.* distinct and individual; not continuous; separate: *a stereo set made up of 4 ~ component units;* **dis·crete·ly** *adv.*; **dis·crete·ness** *n.* **—dis·cre·tion** (–CRESH·un) *n.* **1** discreetness; prudence: *He excused himself saying "~ is the better part of valor"; You can't marry before the age of ~.* **2** freedom to choose or act as one wishes: *I leave this to your ~; authorized to incur expenses* **at his discretion.** **—dis·cre·tion·ar·y** *adj.*: *the ~ power of the court; ~ income* (supplying more than life's necessities).

dis·crim·i·nate (–CRIM–) *v.* **-nates, -nat·ed, -nat·ing** **1** make or see a distinction (between), esp. intelligently: *a man of* **discriminating** *good taste in clothes; ~ between good and bad poetry.* **2** act differently towards something or someone, esp. as a result of prejudice: *a club that ~s against new immigrants* (by excluding them). **—dis·crim·i·nat·ing** *adj.* having or showing knowledge and thoughtful judgment; judicious. **—dis·crim·i·na·tion** (–NAY–) *n.* ability to discriminate; also, prejudice: *~ against minorities in housing.* **—dis·crim·i·na·to·ry** (–CRIM–) *adj.*: *~ tariffs promote trade with some nations and discourage it with others.*

dis·cur·sive (–CUR·siv) *adj.* **1** moving from topic to topic freely: *a ~ letter.* **2** logical, not intuitive: *~ reasoning.* **—dis·cur·sive·ly** *adv.* **—dis·cur·sive·ness** *n.*

dis·cus *n.* **-cus·es** a heavy, round, flattish missile hurled for distance in a contest called the **discus (throw).**

dis·cuss (–CUS) *v.* talk about; consider (a topic) in speech or writing. **—dis·cus·sion** *n.* **—dis·cus·sant** (–CUS·unt) *n.* one who discusses or comments, as at a seminar, panel discussion, etc.

dis·dain (–DAIN) *v.* contemn; consider or reject as unworthy: *~ed to save himself by informing on others.* **—*n.*** haughty contempt: *a look of proud ~.* **—dis·dain·ful** *adj.*: *a ~ silence.* **—dis·dain·ful·ly** *adv.*

dis·ease (di·ZEEZ) *n.* illness; a harmful disturbance of a living organism's function: *heart ~; contagious ~s; Air pollution is a ~ of industrial societies.* **—dis·eased** (–EEZD) *adj.*: *a ~ liver; ~ crops.*

dis·em·bark (–BARK) *v.* go or put ashore (from a ship). **—dis·em·bar·ka·tion** (–CAY–) *n.*

dis·em·bod·y (–BOD·ee) *v.* **-bod·ies, -bod·ied, -bod·y·ing** release from a body: *a ~d spirit.* **—dis·em·bod·i·ment** *n.*

dis·em·bow·el (–BOW·ul) *v.* **-els, -eled, -el·ing** remove the bowels of: *Criminals were sometimes ~d after hanging.* **—dis·em·bow·el·ment** *n.*

dis·en·chant (–CHANT) *v.* set free from mistaken belief or enchantment: *~ed with life as an actor.* **—dis·en·chant·ment** *n.*

dis·en·cum·ber (–CUM–) *v.* *Formal.* release from a burden or hindrance: *~ed of his responsibilities as mayor.*

dis·en·fran·chise (–FRAN–) *v.* **-chis·es, -chised, -chis·ing** same as DISFRANCHISE.

dis·en·gage (–GAIJ) *v.* **-gag·es, -gaged, -gag·ing** free from an entanglement, involvement, or commitment: *Troops were ~d from the border confrontation.* **—dis·en·gage·ment** *n.*

dis·en·tan·gle (–TANG·gl) *v.* **-gles, -gled, -gling** **1** free from something that tangles or ties up: *~ing his hair from the comb.* **2** untangle: *to ~ a snarled ball of wool.* **—dis·en·tan·gle·ment** *n.*

dis·e·qui·lib·ri·um (–LIB·ree·um) *n.* a removal or absence of equilibrium.

dis·es·tab·lish *v.* end the established state of, esp. a state church: *The Catholic Church was ~ed during the French Revolution.* **—dis·es·tab·lish·ment** *n.*

dis·es·teem (–uh·STEEM) *n.* the condition of being little esteemed. Also ***v.***

dis·fa·vor (–FAY·vur) *n.* a being disapproved of or out of favor: *fell into ~ at the court.* **—*v.*:** *a plan ~ed by the board of directors.*

dis·fig·ure (–FIG·yur) *v.* **-ures, -ured, -ur·ing** mar the appearance of: *~d by a burn on her face.* **—dis·fig·ure·ment** *n.*

dis·fran·chise (–FRAN–) *v.* **-chis·es, -chised, -chis·ing** deprive of a right, esp. citizenship rights or the right to vote. **—dis·fran·chise·ment** *n.*

dis·gorge (–GORJ) *v.* **-gorg·es, -gorged, -gorg·ing** spew forth, esp. something swallowed; hence, give up (as something stolen); discharge: *a dragon ~ing smoke and flame; a river ~ing into the ocean.*

dis·grace (–GRACE) *n.* a loss of favor, good name, or honor; also, a cause of this: *Soldier, you're a ~ to the uniform.* **—*v.* -grac·es, -graced, -grac·ing:** *~d his family by being sent to jail.* **—dis·grace·ful** *adj.* shameful: *~ behavior.* **—dis·grace·ful·ly** *adv.*

dis·grun·tle (–GRUN–) *v.* **-tles, -tled, -tling** make ill-humored by displeasing: *a fisherman ~d at the rainy weather.*

dis·guise (–GUYZ) *v.* **-guis·es, -guised, -guis·ing** change the appearance of so as to conceal identify; also, cover up; hide: *a warship ~d to look like a merchant vessel; a robber ~d as a policeman; a false smile ~ing hostility.* **—*n.* 1** a means of disguising, as a wig, mask, or clothes: *put on your ~s.* **2** *went to the party in ~; A calamity may be a blessing in ~; He made no ~ of his anger.*

dis·gust (–GUST) *n.* a feeling of sickened distaste, repugnance, or offense. **—*v.*:** *~ed by his poor performance.* **—dis·gust·ed** *adj.* feeling disgust; **dis·gust·ed·ly** *adv.* **—dis·gust·ing** *adj.* causing disgust; **dis·gust·ing·ly** *adv.*

dish *n.* **1** a shallow, concave container for food; **dishes** *pl.* dishes, bowls, plates, cups, etc. collectively: *wash the ~es.* **2** a serving of food; also, food prepared in some way. **3** *Slang.* a good-looking woman; also, one's preference. **4** same as EARTH STATION. **—*v.*** put in a dish; **dish out** (or **up**) put (food) into a dish; hence, *Informal.* give out, esp. freely: *~ing out homework to the weaker students.*

dis·ha·bille (dis·uh·BEEL) *n.* a being partly or carelessly dressed: *came to the door in ~.*

dis·har·mo·ny (–HAR–) *n.* absence of harmony or agreement. **—dis·har·mo·ni·ous** (–MOH·nee·us) *adj.*

dish·cloth *n.* a cloth to wash dishes with.

dis·heart·en (–HAR·tn) *v.* discourage; dismay: *The defeat ~ed us all.* **—dis·heart·en·ing** *adj.*

dished (DISHT) *adj.* concave like a dish.

di·shev·el (–SHEV·ul) *v.* **-els, -el(l)ed, -el·(l)ing** disorder, muss, or rumple (hair or clothing); do so to (a person): *still ~d two hours after rising.* **—di·shev·el·ment** *n.*

dis·hon·est (–ON–) *adj.* not truthful or honest: *~ profits* (as from smuggled goods). **—dis·hon·es·ty** *n.* **-ties:** *petty ~s.*

dis·hon·or (dis·ON·ur) *n.* a lack or loss of respect, honor, etc.; shame; also, a cause of this: *"Death before ~."* **—*v.* 1** disgrace. **2** show disrespect to: *Don't ~ your grandparents.* **3** refuse to pay or cash (a bill, check, etc.). **—dis·hon·or·a·ble** *adj.: a ~ discharge from the Air Force.* **—dis·hon·or·a·bly** *adv.*

dish·rag *n.* a dishcloth. **—dish·tow·el** *n.* a towel for drying dishes. **—dish·ware** *n.* tableware. **—dish·wash·er** *n.* a person or machine that washes dishes. **—dish·wa·ter** *n.* water to wash dishes and cooking utensils in; also, water that has been so used.

dis·il·lu·sion (–LOO·zhun) *v.* free of illusions or misconceptions; hence, disappoint or embitter by so doing; **dis·il·lu·sioned** *adj.: a very ~ young man.*

dis·in·cline (–CLINE) *v.* **-clines, -clined, -clin·ing** be or make unwilling or reluctant. **—dis·in·cli·na·tion** (–NAY–) *n.*

dis·in·fect (–FECT) *v.* make free of disease germs: *drinking water ~ed with chlorine.* **—dis·in·fect·ant** *adj.* & *n.* (something) that disinfects: *Formaldehyde is used as a ~ for clothing.* **—dis·in·fec·tion** *n.*

dis·in·gen·u·ous (–JEN·yoo·us) *adj.* not honest, open, sincere: *a ~ reply to the lawyer's question.*

dis·in·her·it (–HER·it) *v.* bar from inheriting: *She was ~ed for marrying against her father's will.*

dis·in·te·grate (–IN–) *v.* **-grates, -grat·ed, -grat·ing** break up into smaller or component parts; hence, of nuclei, emit a subatomic particle or ray: *The meteorite ~d in the atmosphere.* **—dis·in·te·gra·tion** (–GRAY–) *n.: the radioactive ~ of uranium.*

dis·in·ter (–TUR) *v.* **-ters, -terred, -ter·ring** dig up from the earth or a grave; exhume. **—dis·in·ter·ment** *n.*

dis·in·ter·est·ed (–IN–) *adj.* unbiased, impartial: *a ~ observer.*

dis·in·tox·i·cate (–TOX–) *v.* **-cates, -cat·ed, -cat·ing** free from intoxicants. **—dis·in·tox·i·ca·tion** (–CAY–) *n.: the ~ of alcoholics.*

dis·join (–JOIN) *v.* separate; keep from joining. **—dis·joint** *v.* break at the joints; also, dislocate; put out of joint: *a ~ed turkey; What a ~ed society we live in; a ~ed* (i.e. incoherent and badly connected) *speech.*

disk *n.* a round, flat part or plate; esp., a cartilage pad between vertebrae: *Bill slipped* (i.e. dislocated) *a ~ while playing football.* Also **disc.**

dis·like (–LIKE) *v.* **-likes, -liked, -lik·ing** not like: *I rather ~ cauliflower; Jane ~s playing with dolls.* **—*n.*:** *a feeling of ~; a ~ for* (or *of*) *dogs; The newlyweds didn't know each other's likes and ~s yet.*

dis·lo·cate (DIS·loh–, –LOH–) *v.* **-cates, -cat·ed, -cat·ing** move (esp. a bone of the body) from its proper position; hence, disturb: *a*

~d shoulder; retail sales ~d by a recession. —**dis·lo·ca·tion** (–CAY–) *n.*

dis·lodge *v.* **-lodg·es, -lodged, -lodg·ing** move forcibly from a position: *Artillery fire ~d the enemy's infantry; a blow ~ing the filling from a tooth.*

dis·loy·al (–LOY·ul) *adj.* not loyal; unfaithful: *~ troops attacked the palace.* —**dis·loy·al·ty** *n.* **-ties** a being disloyal or a disloyal act. —**dis·loy·al·ly** *adv.*

dis·mal (DIZ·mul) *adj.* gloomy; depressing; sad: *a ~ lack of skill; ~ weather;* **Dismal Swamp** a wild marshland in N.E. North Carolina and S.E. Virginia.

dis·man·tle (–MAN–) *v.* **-tles, -tled, -tling** strip of covering, equipment, weapons, etc.; also, take apart: *the ~d hulk of an abandoned bus; a large desk ~d for shipping.* —**dis·man·tle·ment** *n.*

dis·may (–MAY) *v.* dishearten, make afraid, or daunt, esp. about the future: *workers ~ed at possible layoffs.* —***n.:*** *Final exams filled me with ~.* —**dis·may·ing·ly** *adv.*

dis·mem·ber (–MEM–) *v.* cut or tear the limbs from; hence, divide or tear into pieces: *a ~ed corpse; The Church was ~ed by the Reformation.* —**dis·mem·ber·ment** *n.: the ~ of Austria-Hungary after World War I.*

dis·miss (–MIS) *v.* **1** allow or cause to leave; send away; also, release from a job, service, etc.: *Class ~ed! He ~ed his chauffeur for reckless driving.* **2** put out of one's mind; also, reject in court: *~ the rumors as nonsense.* —**dis·miss·al** *n.: early ~ on Fridays.*

dis·mount (–MOUNT) *v.* **1** get down from a horse, vehicle, etc.; also, cause to get off: *We ~ed from our bicycles and walked; a knight ~ed by his opponent in a joust.* **2** remove (something) from its mounting; hence, take apart: *~ a cannon from its carriage; a lock ~ed for cleaning.*

Dis·ney (DIZ·nee), **Walter E.** 1901–1966, American producer of animated cartoons and movies. —**Dis·ney·esque** (–ESK) *adj.: a charming ~ fantasy.*

dis·o·bey (–BAY) *v.* refuse or fail to obey. —**dis·o·be·di·ent** (–BEE·dee·unt) *adj.: a ~ child.* —**dis·o·be·di·ence** *n.: a soldier court-martialed for ~.*

dis·o·blige (–BLIGE) *v.* **-blig·es, -bliged, -blig·ing** fail or refuse to oblige (someone), as by not granting a request; hence, offend; inconvenience.

dis·or·der (–OR–) *n.* **1** a lack of orderly arrangement. **2** a disturbance in functioning; mild disease: *pulmonary ~s.* **3** an upset to the public peace; also, a riot. —***v.:*** *a ~ed mind; lost a book on the badly ~ed desk.* —**dis·or·der·ly** *adj.: a ~ pile of junk; arrested for being drunk and ~; ~ conduct* (such as fighting in public). —**dis·or·der·li·ness** *n.*

dis·or·gan·ize (–OR–) *v.* **-iz·es, -ized, -iz·ing** break up the orderly or systematic organization of. —**dis·or·gan·i·za·tion** (–ZAY–) *n.* —**dis·or·gan·ized** *adj.* lacking coherence or a system.

dis·o·ri·ent (–OR–) *v.* cause to be lost, alienated, confused, etc. by deprivation of one's bearings or cultural frame of reference: *became ~ed in the dark forest; the ~ed youth of post-War Germany.* Also **dis·o·ri·en·tate, -tates, -tat·ed, -tat·ing.** —**dis·o·ri·en·ta·tion** (–TAY–) *n.*

dis·own (–OHN) *v.* deny that one owns, knows, or is connected with; reject: *children ~ed by their parents.*

dis·par·age (–PAIR·ij) *v.* **-ag·es, -aged, -ag·ing** cause to be less esteemed; also, treat or talk about slightingly; **dis·par·age·ment** *n.* —**dis·par·ag·ing** *adj.: ~ remarks;* **dis·par·ag·ing·ly** *adv.: whisper ~ about the new teacher.*

dis·pa·rate (DIS·puh·rit, –PAIR·it) *adj.* fundamentally unlike; also, unequal. —**dis·par·i·ty** (–PAIR·i·tee) *n.* **-ties.**

dis·pas·sion (–PASH·un) *n.* calm objectivity. —**dis·pas·sion·ate** (–it) *adj.* unemotional; calmly impartial: *a cool ~ examination of the problem.* —**dis·pas·sion·ate·ly** *adv.*

dis·patch (–PACH) *v.* **1** send with directness or great speed: *Police cars were ~ed to the scene of the crime; radio-~ed delivery vehicles.* **2** deal with or finish quickly; also, kill quickly: *~ed the morning's business; The bull was ~ed at the end of the bullfight.* —***n.*** **1** a dispatching. **2** fast efficiency: *working with ~.* **3** a message, report, etc., as for a government, a news service, or the military. —**dis·patch·er** *n.* one who sends out trains, buses, taxies, etc. on schedule or as needed.

dis·pel (–PEL) *v.* **-pels, -pelled, -pel·ling** get rid of by scattering or driving off: *The sun ~d the early morning fog; reason ~ing the mists of ignorance.*

dis·pen·sa·ry (–PEN–) *n.* **-ries** a place where medicines are given out, as in a school or factory. —**dis·pen·sa·tion** (–SAY–) *n.* **1** a dispensing: *the ~ of the laws.* **2** an exemption from a rule or law: *a papal ~ allowing the remarriage.* **3** an ordering of events; also, a resulting system or rule: *Capitalists fled from the new ~ in Russia after the Revolution; living under the Christian ~.* —**dis·pense** (–PENCE) *v.* **-pens·es, -pensed, -pens·ing** distribute; give out; hence, prepare and give out (medicines): *a rich man ~ing largesse to the poor; A judge ~s* (i.e. administers) *justice;* **dispense with** get along without; also, get rid of: *Shall we ~ with the formalities?* —**dis·pen·sa·ble** *adj.* —**dis·pen·ser** *n.* one that dispenses, esp. a device for the convenient dispensing of a commodity: *an automatic towel ~.*

dis·perse (–PURCE) *v.* **-pers·es, -persed, -pers·ing** **1** break up and scatter: *The crowd ~d when the riot police appeared; new chemicals to*

~ oil slicks in the harbor. **2** spread widely. **—dis·per·sal** or **dis·per·sion** *n.: the natural dispersal of seeds; the dispersion of light waves.*

dis·pir·it (di·SPEER–) *v.* make sad, downcast, or discouraged: *players ~ed by successive failures.*

dis·place (–PLACE) *v.* **-plac·es, -placed, -plac·ing** move from its proper place: *After World War II many* **displaced persons** (i.e. those uprooted by war and political strife) *came to the U.S.; a ship that ~s 12,000 tons* (of water). **—dis·place·ment** *n.* a displacing; also, the amount displaced or by which something is displaced: *the ~ of John as treasurer of the club; the ~ of the star by optical parallax; Ships are rated according to their ~* (of water which is equal to their weight).

dis·play (–PLAY) *v.* exhibit; expose clearly to view; show: *~ merchandise in the store window; liked to ~ her learning.* ***—n.:*** *a ~ of new fashions; Select the one you like from the ~; a ~ of courage.*

dis·please (–PLEEZ) *v.* **-pleas·es, -pleased, -pleas·ing** be unpleasing to; annoy. **—dis·pleas·ure** (–PLEZH·ur) *n.* the feeling one has when displeased.

dis·port (–PORT) *v.* esp. **disport oneself** *Formal.* frolic; play.

dis·pos·a·ble (–POH·zuh–) *adj.* **1** available to be used: *a ~ income of $2,000 a year* (for spending, saving, etc. after meeting taxes and other obligations). **2** to be used and then thrown away: *~ pop bottles;* ***n.:*** *~s add to the garbage.* **—dis·pos·al** *n.* **1** a disposing: *proper ~ of chessmen on the board; a sewage ~ system;* **at one's disposal** to be used as one desires. **2** a device for shredding garbage that is flushed down a drain, usu. fitted in the kitchen sink. **—dis·pose** (–POZE) *v.* **-pos·es, -posed, -pos·ing** **1** make willing, likely, or susceptible: *not ~d to go out today; The government's well (or ill)* **disposed** *to your request* (i.e. favors or disfavors it). **2** set in order; arrange: *troops ~d in battle line; "Man proposes, God ~s."* **3 dispose of** deal with, esp. settle: *trying to ~ of her uncle's debts; ~ing of land by signing it over to his wife; the dangers involved in ~ing* (i.e. getting rid) *of nuclear wastes.* **—dis·pos·er** *n.* **—dis·po·si·tion** (–ZISH·un) *n.* **1** a disposing of something; also, the power to dispose or use: *the ~ of waste; ~ of property by sale or gift; His heirs have ~ of the land.* **2** an arrangement; the way something is disposed; also, one's general tendency; temperament: *an elegant ~ of furniture; a strong ~ to laze in the sun; a pleasant ~.*

dis·pos·sess (–puh·ZES) *v.* deprive of possession, esp. of land; evict: *~ed dirt farmers.* **—dis·pos·ses·sion** *n.*

dis·praise (–PRAYZ) *v.* **-prais·es, -praised, -prais·ing** speak in disapproval of; disparage. Also ***n.***

dis·proof (–PROOF) *n.* a disproving.

dis·pro·por·tion (–POR–) *n.* an absence of proportion. **—dis·pro·por·tion·ate** (–POR·shuh·nit) *adj.: A ~ number of rich people send their children to university.*

dis·prove (–PROOV) *v.* **-proves, -proved, -prov·ing** prove wrong or false: *attempts to ~ the theory of evolution.*

dis·pu·ta·tion (–TAY–) *n.* a debate or dispute; esp., the oral defense of an academic thesis; **dis·pu·ta·tious** *adj.* given to arguing: *a ~ committee.* **—dis·pute** (–PYOOT) *v.* **-putes, -put·ed, -put·ing** **1** argue or debate (about): *The speaker offered to ~ (the issue) with all comers.* **2** argue against the rightness or validity of: *a ~d election.* **3** quarrel; also, oppose; fight for. ***—n.:*** *Her claim to first prize is* **beyond dispute;** *a contract settlement that is still* **in dispute. —dis·put·er** *n.;* also **dis·pu·tant. —dis·pu·ta·ble** *adj.*

dis·qual·i·fy (–KWOL–) *v.* **-fies, -fied, -fy·ing** make or declare unfit, ineligible, or unentitled: *~d from football by low grades; a racehorse ~d because it was drugged.* **—dis·qual·i·fi·ca·tion** (–CAY–) *n.*

dis·qui·et (–KWYE–) *v.* disturb; upset the peace of mind of: *~ing news about rising unemployment.* ***—n.*** worry; anxiety; also **dis·qui·e·tude** *n.: a feeling of ~ about the risk of war.*

dis·qui·si·tion (–ZISH·un) *n.* a lengthy discussion or inquiry; treatise.

Dis·rae·li (diz·RAY·lee), **Benjamin.** 1804–1881, British statesman and Prime Minister.

dis·re·gard *v.* pay no attention to; also, pay no respect to. ***—n.:*** *~ of the law against speeding; show ~ for one's teachers.* **—dis·re·gard·ful** *adj.*

dis·re·pair *n.* the state of being neglected and needing repairs.

dis·rep·u·ta·ble (–REP–) *adj.* not respectable or in good repute: *a ~ businessman; a ~ cocktail bar.* **—dis·re·pute** (–PYOOT) *n.* a state of ill repute; disgrace.

dis·re·spect (–SPECT) *n.* absence of respect; rudeness: *without ~ to one's elders.* **—dis·re·spect·ful** *adj.: a ~ remark.*

dis·robe *v.* **-robes, -robed, -rob·ing** take off clothing, esp. outer robes: *~d and dived into the pool.*

dis·rupt (–RUPT) *v.* break apart; hence, disturb; disorder: *attempts to ~ debate in the Senate.* **—dis·rup·tion** *n.: temporary ~s in TV broadcasting.* **—dis·rup·tive** (–tiv) *adj.: There were two ~ students in the class.*

dis·sat·is·fy (–SAT–) *v.* **-fies, -fied, -fy·ing** fall short of satisfying; cause discontent in: *~d workers out on strike.* **—dis·sat·is·fac·tion** (–FAC–) *n.*

dis·sect (–SECT) *v.* cut into pieces for anatomical study; hence, analyze very finely. **—dis·sec·tion** *n.: a ~ of the causes of the revolution.*

dis·sem·ble (–SEM–) *v.* **-bles, -bled, -bling** **1** hide under a false guise: *~d his emotions.* **2** feign: *~ing sympathy.* **—dis·sem·blance** (–blunce) *n.* **—dis·sem·bler** *n.*

dis·sem·i·nate (–SEM–) *v.* **-nates, -nat·ed, -nat·ing** spread widely or to many people. **—dis·sem·i·na·tion** (–NAY–) *n.: Radio and TV permit the wide ~ of knowledge.*

dis·sen·sion (–SEN–) *n.* disagreement, esp. one causing hostility; quarrel. **—dis·sent** (–SENT) *v.* not agree; hold a different opinion (from): *One of the justices gave a ~ing opinion.* **—*n.*** disagreement; esp., nonacceptance of the doctrines of the Church of England. **—dis·sent·er** (–SEN·tur) *n.;* **Dissenter** a religious nonconformist in Great Britain. **—dis·sen·tient** (–SEN·shunt) *adj.* dissenting; ***n.*** one who dissents.

dis·ser·ta·tion (–TAY–) *n.* a long treatise; esp., a doctoral thesis.

dis·ser·vice (–SER·vis) *n.* a harmful or injurious action: *McCarthyism did a great ~ to the cause of democracy.*

dis·sev·er (–SEV–) *v.* separate; divide into parts.

dis·si·dence (–dunce) *n.* disagreement; difference. **—dis·si·dent** *adj.: the expulsion of ~ trade unionists;* ***n.:*** *political ~s.*

dis·sim·i·lar (–SIM–) *adj.* not similar; unlike; **dis·sim·i·lar·i·ty** (–LAIR–) *n.* **-ties. —dis·si·mil·i·tude** (–MIL–) *n.* lack of resemblance.

dis·sim·u·late (–SIM–) *v.* **-lates, -lat·ed, -lat·ing** hide one's true feelings; dissemble. **—dis·sim·u·la·tor** *n.* **—dis·sim·u·la·tion** (–LAY–) *n.*

dis·si·pate *v.* **-pates, -pat·ed, -pat·ing** **1** disperse: *morning fog ~d by the sun.* **2** vanish or fade away; cause to do so; hence, waste foolishly; engage in wasteful, excessive pleasures: *a fortune ~d by bad investments; a prodigal ~ing his wealth in casinos.* **—dis·si·pa·tion** (–PAY–) *n.: a life of drunken ~.*

dis·so·ci·ate (–SOH·shee–) *v.* **-ates, -at·ed, -at·ing** separate from association; cut off; **dis·so·ci·a·tion** (–AY–) *n.*

dis·sol·u·ble (–SOL·yoo–) *adj.* that can be dissolved. **—dis·so·lute** *adj.* profligate, immoral, and dissipated. **—dis·so·lute·ly** *adv.* **—dis·so·lute·ness** *n.* **—dis·so·lu·tion** (–LOO–) *n.* a dissolving. **—dis·solve** (–ZOLV) *v.* **-solves, -solved, -solv·ing** **1** (make) go into solution; also, disappear as into a liquid: *One scene ~d into the next;* ***n.:*** *scenes changing in a series of ~s.* **2** break up; bring to an end; destroy. **3** melt: *~d in tears at the news.*

dis·so·nance (DIS·uh·nunce) *n.* lack of harmony or agreement; discord: *a poet seeking harmony "from life's ~."* **—dis·so·nant** *adj.*

dis·suade (–SWADE) *v.* **dis·suades, dis·suad·ed, dis·suad·ing** advise or persuade not to do something. **—dis·sua·sion** *n.* **—dis·sua·sive** (–siv) *adj.*

dist. distance; distinguish(ed); distinct.

dis·taff *n.* a stick for holding wool or flax for use in spinning; hence, womanly occupations; women: *related to the Jones family on the* **distaff side** (i.e. female side).

dis·tal (–tl) *adj.* far from a point of origin or attachment: *the ~* (i.e. outer) *end of a leaf;* **dis·tal·ly** *adv.*

dis·tance (–tunce) *n.* a measure of farness in space or time or of remoteness in similarity or relation: *the ~ between Houston and Phoenix; traveling quite a ~* (i.e. a long way); *We saw the sea in the ~; in the remote ~s of history;* **go** (or **last**) **the distance** complete an entire activity. **—keep one's distance** remain aloof or detached; **keep someone at a distance** prevent someone from becoming friendly. **—*v.* -tanc·es, -tanced, -tanc·ing** outrun; outstrip; outdo; also, place or keep at a distance. **—dis·tant** *adj.* not close; far; away: *on the ~ horizon; in the not-too-~ future; a ~ relation; 40 miles ~ from the lake; He acknowledged it with a rather ~* (i.e. cold and aloof) *smile;* **dis·tant·ly** *adv.;* **dis·tant·ness** *n.*

dis·taste (–TAIST) *n.* dislike; aversion. **—dis·taste·ful** *adj.*

dis·tem·per (–TEM–) *n.* a disease or disorder; esp., an infectious viral disease of young dogs and cats, often fatal.

dis·tend (–TEND) *v.* **1** swell, esp. from internal pressure: *starving children with ~ed stomachs.* **2** stretch out. **—dis·ten·si·ble** *adj.* **—dis·ten·tion** or **dis·ten·sion** *n.*

dis·tich (–tik) *n.* a couplet.

dis·til(l) (–TIL) *v.* **-til(l)s, -tilled, -till·ing** **1** fall or cause to fall in drops; also, extract or emerge as an essential element: *a book that is the ~d wisdom of the ages.* **2** produce or purify by subjecting to distillation. **—dis·til·late** (DIS·tuh–) *n.* a liquid resulting from distillation, as gasoline or whiskey. **—dis·til·la·tion** (–LAY–) *n.* the controlled vaporization of a liquid mixture such as crude oil or grain mash, followed by a condensation of the vapor. **—dis·till·er** *n.* one that distills, esp. a producer of distilled alcoholic beverages; **dis·till·er·y** *n.* **-er·ies** a place where alcoholic liquor is made.

dis·tinct (–TINCT) *adj.* **1** different; individual; clearly specified: *four ~ species of animals.* **2** clearly perceived or perceivable; marked; well-defined; definite: *the ~ outline of her silhouette; a ~ hint of fall in the air.* **—dis·tinct·ly** *adv.;* **dis·tinct·ness** *n.* **—dis·tinc·tion** *n.* **1** a distinguishing or making a difference, as in treatment: *employees paid without ~ of sex.* **2** a difference; also, a trait, characteristic etc. that makes a difference. **3** excellence; special honor; superiority; also, something in recognition of this: *a statesman of ~; earned several military ~s.* **—dis·tinc·tive** (–tiv) *adj.* characteristic; marking the distinctness of: *the ~ aroma of good coffee;* **dis·tinc·tive·ly** *adv.;* **dis·tinc·tive·ness** *n.* **—dis·tin·guish** (–TING·gwish) *v.* **1** mark as different: *Speech ~es people from animals.* **2** perceive a difference; discriminate: *~ between good and bad art.* **3** perceive; make out: *barely able to ~ the hills in the distance.* **4** make famous, respected, etc.: *~ oneself by gallantry in battle;* **distinguished** *adj.* famous; eminent; also, having a dignified and superior manner: *a ~ author; the Distinguished Service Medal; a ~ gentleman.* **—dis·tin·guish·a·ble** *adj.*

distn. distillation.

dis·tort (–TORT) *v.* twist out of its normal shape or condition; also, alter or twist (the truth, a story, etc.). **—dis·tor·tion** *n.: a newspaper that published gross ~s of the truth.*

distr. distribution; distributor.

dis·tract (–TRACT) *v.* **1** draw (one's attention) to something else: *Don't ~ me while I'm working.* **2** bewilder; throw into confusion; upset emotionally. **—dis·trac·tion** *n.* [corresponding to the *v.* senses of DISTRACT] **1:** *welcomed any ~s from his work; the ~s* (i.e. amusements) *available in the big city.* **2:** *driven to ~ by grief.* **—dis·trait** (–STRAY) *adj.* absent-minded; inattentive. **—dis·traught** (–TRAWT) *adj.* mentally agitated; upset; also, mad: *~ with fear and pain.*

dis·tress (–TRESS) *n.* **1** suffering; deep sorrow; worry. **2** trouble; danger: *a ship in ~ sends a* **distress signal.** **—*v.*:** *We were ~ed by the news of your illness; a* **distressing** *report on the economy; a* **distressed area** (with high unemployment, poverty, etc.) **—dis·tress·ful** *adj.*

dis·trib·ute (–TRIB·yoot) *v.* **-utes, -ut·ed, -ut·ing** **1** divide or pass out among many, esp. in shares: *a magazine ~d nationwide* (for sale); *Tips were ~d equally among the staff.* **2** put into classes or kinds. **3** spread. **—dis·tri·bu·tion** (–BYOO–) *n.: the ~ network of a marketing firm.* **—dis·trib·u·tive** (–TRIB·yuh·tiv) *adj.: a ~ adjective, which refers to all members of a set, e.g. "all," "none"; Multiplication is ~ over addition, i.e.* $x(y+z) = xy + xz$; **dis·trib·u·tive·ly** *adv.* **—dis·trib·u·tor** (–TRIB·yuh·tur) *n.* one that distributes; esp., a device that sends electricity to an engine's spark plugs in the correct order.

dis·trict *n.* an area or region; esp., region separated off for a legal or administrative purpose: *the farming ~; an electoral ~;* **district attorney** the public prosecutor for a judicial district; **district heating** a way of supplying the heating and hot-water needs of an area or neighborhood from a central source; **District of Columbia** the U.S. federal capital region, i.e. the city of Washington.

dis·trust (–TRUST) *n.* an absence of faith, confidence, trust, etc. **—*v.*:** *Every one ~s flatterers.* **—dis·trust·ful** *adj.* **—dis·trust·ful·ly** *adv.: stared ~ at the stranger.*

dis·turb (–TURB) *v.* **1** interrupt; upset the peace, quiet, etc. of: *Don't ~ me while I'm working; A gunshot ~ed the quiet of the night; I'm even more* **disturbed** *about it today; found it very* **disturbing** *news.* **2** disorder; throw into confusion. **3** upset mentally: *a ward for* **disturbed** *patients.* **4** trouble: *Don't ~ yourself for me.* **—dis·turb·ance** *n.: widespread political ~s and riots.* **—dis·turb·er** *n.: arrested as a ~ of the peace.*

dis·u·nite (–yoo·NITE) *v.* **-nites, -nit·ed, -nit·ing** undo the union of; cause dissension among; separate: *a family ~d by quarrels over the inheritance.* **—dis·u·ni·ty** (–YOO–) *n.*

dis·use (–YOOSE) *n.* the condition of not being used: *a parking bylaw that fell into ~.* **—dis·used** *adj.: a ~ mine shaft.*

ditch *n.* a trench dug in the earth, often containing water: *drainage ~es on the roadside; an irrigation ~; ready to fight* **to the last ditch** (i.e. to the end). **—*v.*** **1** dig a ditch around or in. **2** drive a car into a ditch; also, land a plane on water and escape. **3** *Slang.* get rid of; avoid: *was ~ed after the first date.*

dith·er *n.* a state of nervous excitement or confusion: *all in a ~ over losing his hat.* **—*v.*** act indecisively: *He ~s when he should be studying.*

dit·to *n.* the same as above; also, a mark (") indicating this; also **ditto mark.**

dit·ty (DIT·ee) *n.* **dit·ties** a simple little song.

di·u·ret·ic (dye·yoo·RET·ic) *adj.* increasing the secretion of urine; ***n.:*** *Digitalis, caffeine, and even water in large quantities are ~s.*

di·ur·nal (dye·URN·ul) *adj.* **1** daily: *the ~ rotation of the earth.* **2** of or active in the daytime: *~ animals; ~ flowers that close up at night.* **—di·ur·nal·ly** *adv.*

div. divided; dividend; division; divorced.

di·va (DEE·vuh) *n.* **-vas** or **-ve** (–vay) a leading female opera singer; prima donna.

di·va·gate (DYE·vuh–) *v.* **-gates, -gat·ed, -gat·ing** *Formal.* wander: *~ from the topic; ~ing from his proper goal.* **—di·va·ga·tion** (–GAY–) *n.*

di·van (DYE–, di·VAN) *n.* a couch, esp. one with neither back nor arms.

dive *v.* **dives,** *pt.* **dived** or **dove,** *pp.* **dived, div·ing** **1** plunge head-first into water, as a swimmer; hence, submerge, as a submarine, descend deeply, as an aircraft, or leap from an aircraft, as a parachutist. **2** enter vigorously (*into* an activity): *~d into his studies.* **3** rush, dart, or plunge *(into).* **—*n.*** **1** a diving: *The pilot put his plane into a ~.* **2** *Informal.* a cheap, squalid bar, gambling house, etc. **—div·er** *n.*

di·verge (di·VURJ, dye–) *v.* **-verg·es, -verged, -verg·ing** draw apart; differ; move away from: *Our opinions ~d from the consensus; rays that ~ from a central point;* **di·ver·gence** *n.: a ~ of viewpoints;* **di·ver·gent** *adj.: widely ~ interests.* **—di·vers** (DYE·vurz) *adj.* several and various: *~ sorts of card games.* **—di·verse** (dye–) *adj.* different in kind; of various kinds: *people of ~ backgrounds;* **di·verse·ly** *adv.* **—di·ver·si·fy** (–VUR–) *v.* **-fies, -fied, -fy·**

ing make various or diverse; esp., to extend business activities into different areas: *a well-∼d investment portfolio; a company ∼ing to protect itself from market changes;* **di·ver·si·fi·ca·tion** (–CAY–) *n.* —**di·ver·si·ty** (–VUR–) *n.* difference; variety. —**di·vert** (di–, dye·VURT) *v.* **1** turn aside: *∼ a stream into a new channel.* **2** distract the attention of; hence, amuse: *a false attack to ∼ the enemy.* Hence **di·ver·sion** *n.: golf, bridge, and other ∼s;* **di·ver·sion·ar·y** *adj.: a ∼ maneuver.*

di·vest (dye–, di·VEST) *v.* **1** strip; deprive of clothes, property, rights, etc.: *a boxer ∼ed of his title.* **2 divest oneself of** get rid of: *a company forced to ∼ itself of some of its holdings.*

di·vide (di–) *v.* **-vides, -vid·ed, -vid·ing 1** separate, esp. into parts or groups; distribute: *∼ the books into fiction and nonfiction; ∼ the pie among all six; We ∼ the expenses and each pays a share; The path ∼s here into two branches.* **2** cause disagreement among: *The caucus was ∼d on the issue; ∼ and rule a far-flung empire.* **3** determine how many times (one number) is contained in (another): *∼ 7 into 21; 36 ∼d by 9 is 4; 4 ∼s into 36 nine times.* —***n.*** a dividing; esp., a watershed: *the Great Divide* (i.e. the Rocky Mountains). —**div·i·dend** *n.* **1** a number to be divided. **2** a stockholder's share of profits; also, the total of all of these; hence, a bonus. —**di·vid·er** *n.* one that divides; esp., a partition; also **dividers** *pl.* an instrument with two steel points used for measuring.

di·vine (di–) *v.* **-vines, -vined, -vin·ing** foretell or predict by magic or special insight; hence, conjecture; guess; **di·vi·ner** *n.;* **div·i·na·tion** (–NAY–) *n.* —***adj.*** **-vin·er, -vin·est 1** of or like a god; relating to or derived from God; theological: *Plato thought the planets were ∼ beings; James I upheld the ∼ right of kings* (to rule). **2** extremely good; superb; hence, *Informal.* delightful: *a positively ∼ dress.* —***n.*** a scholar or student of theology. —**di·vine·ly** *adv.* —**divining rod** a forked stick that shows where water or a mineral deposit is by dipping downward when passed over it by a diviner. —**di·vin·i·ty** (–VIN–) *n.* **-ties 1** the state of being divine; also, deity; **the Divinity** God. **2** theology: *students of ∼.*

di·vis·i·ble (di·VIZ·uh·bl) *adj.* able to be divided, esp. evenly: *7 is not evenly ∼ by 3;* **di·vis·i·bil·i·ty** (–BIL–) *n.* —**di·vi·sion** (–VIZH·un) *n.* **1** the act of dividing: *cell ∼; long ∼* (e.g. 37,428 ÷ 6,959); *Adam Smith advocated* **division of labor** (i.e. each employee doing a part of the complete process). **2** a being divided: *∼s in the party between Right and Left.* **3** a line, boundary, etc. that divides. **4** the result of dividing; a part, portion, section, class, etc.; esp., a large unit in the armed forces or a part of a league in sports: *the Western ∼.* Hence **di·vi·sion·al** *adj.* —**di·vi·sive** (–VYE·siv) *adj.* tending to divide: *Busing is a very ∼ issue;* **di·vi·sive·ly** *adv.;* **di·vi·sive·ness** *n.* —**di·vi·sor** (–VYE·zur) *n.* a number to be divided into another: *In "10 ÷ 2" 10 is the dividend, 2 the ∼.*

di·vorce (di–) *n.* the complete legal termination of a marriage; hence, a deep separation. —***v.*** **-vorc·es, -vorced, -vorc·ing:** *a ∼d couple; a dreamer ∼d from daily realities.* —**di·vorce·ment** *n.: a bill of ∼* (in Jewish law). —**di·vor·cee** or **di·vor·cée** (–SEE, –SAY) *n.* a divorced woman.

div·ot (–ut) *n.* a piece of ground torn out by the stroke of a golf club.

di·vulge (di·VULJ) *v.* **-vulg·es, -vulged, -vulg·ing** make known (something secret): *refused to ∼ details of campaign expenses.* —**di·vulg·ence** (–junce) *n.*

div·vy (DIV·ee) *v.* **div·vies, div·vied, div·vy·ing** *Slang.* divide: *bank robbers ∼ing up the loot.*

Dix·ie (–see) the Southern states of the U.S. —**Dix·ie·land** *n.* a jazz in duple time marked by improvisations; ***adj.:*** *a ∼ beat.*

diz·zy *adj.* **diz·zi·er, diz·zi·est 1** having a whirling unsteady feeling in the head; giddy and prone to fall; also, causing this feeling: *Looking down from the bridge made me ∼.* **2** *Informal.* silly or lightheaded: *a ∼ blonde.* —***v.*** **diz·zies, diz·zied, diz·zy·ing:** *∼ing heights.* —**diz·zi·ly** *adv.* —**diz·zi·ness** *n.*

DJ disc jockey.

Dja·kar·ta (juh·CAR·tuh) same as JAKARTA.

Dji·bou·ti (jih·BOOT·ee) a republic of E. Africa between Ethiopia and Somalia on the Gulf of Aden; formerly called "French Somaliland" and "Territory of Afars and Issas"; 8,494 sq.mi. (21,999 km²); *cap.* **Djibouti.**

dk. dark; deck; dock.

dlv. delivery.

D.Lit(t). Doctor of Letters.

DLO dead-letter office.

dlvy. delivery.

DM deutsche mark.

D.M.D. Doctor of Dental Medicine.

DMT "dimethyltryptamine," a hallucinogen.

DMZ demilitarized zone.

DNA deoxyribonucleic acid.

Dne·pro·pe·trovsk (nep·roh·puh·TRAWFSK) a city in the Ukraine, on the river **Dnei·per** (NEE·pur) which flows from N.W. Soviet Union S. to the Black Sea.

¹do (DOO) *v.* **does** (DUZ), *pt.* **did,** *pp.* **done** (DUN), **do·ing 1** perform; fulfill; complete; also, work at; deal successfully with: *∼ your duty; ∼ a job; ∼ your best to help; He did 5 years in the Marines; What's done is done* (i.e. can't be changed); *What do you ∼* (i.e. work at) *for a living? I can't ∼ this problem!* **2** make; also, render; grant: *∼ a painting; ∼ me a favor;* **do justice to** handle or treat as one deserves or requires. **3** cause; effect: *Kindness ∼s wonders; Crying ∼s no good.* **4** deal with, work on, etc.; esp., clean, arrange, etc.: *∼ the dishes; Who ∼s* *your hair?* **5** fasten; also do up: *~ your shirt.* **6** present or perform; play: *Our class is ~ing "Hamlet."* **7** behave: *~ unto others; as I say, not as I ~.* **8** consider proper; approve: *It's just not done!* **done** *adj.: not the ~ thing.* **9** suffice; serve: *This hat will ~ nicely;* **do duty for:** *a knapsack ~ing duty for a pillow;* **do the trick** have the desired result: *We had to* **make** *the old carpet* **do** *for another year; When times are hard, you* **make do with** *what you have;* **do without** *get along without.* **10** fare; get on: *How do you do? How're you ~ing on the new job?* **11 do for** attend to; care for: *They ~ for you in the rest home;* **do oneself well** (or **proud**) succeed so as to justify pride. **12** travel; move at; also, tour: *a car ~ing 20 m.p.h.; How to ~ Europe on $15 a day.* **13** cook: *How do you like your steak done?* **done** *adj.* cooked; **done·ness** *n.: a microwave oven with a dial for degrees of ~.* **14** cheat: *a widow done out of her life savings.* **15** [as an auxiliary verb in questions, negations, inversions; for emphasis; to refer to an earlier verb]: *~ you know what I know? I ~ not; Never did I see the like! I ~ declare! run as fast as I ~.* —***n.,*** *pl.* **dos** or **do's** **1** something to be done: *too many* **do's and don'ts** (i.e. rules and customs). **2** *Informal.* party; social event: *a big ~ at the country club.* —**do by** deal with or treat: *Do as you would be done by.* —**do in** *Slang.* **1** kill. **2** tire out: *all done in after a hard day.* —**have to do with** be related or connected to.

[2]do (DOH) *n. Music.* the first or last tone of the diatonic scale.

do. ditto.

D.O.A. dead on arrival.

DOB date of birth.

dob·bin *n.* a patient, plodding farm horse.

Do·ber·man (DOH–) **pin·scher** (PIN·shur) a large, short-haired dog with a pointed snout.

dob·son·fly *n.* **-flies** a four-winged insect with a large water-dwelling larva.

doc. document.

doc *n. Slang.* doctor. —**do·cent** (DOH–) *n.* a university teacher not on the regular faculty. —**doc·ile** (DOSS·ul) *adj.* easy to teach, control, etc.; submissive; **doc·ile·ly** *adv.;* **do·cil·i·ty** (–SIL–) *n.*

[1]dock *n.* **1** the place for the accused in a courtroom. **2** any of several weeds related to buckwheat. —***v.*** cut off the end of; hence, make a deduction from: *~ a horse's tail; wages ~ed for being late.*

[2]dock *n.* **1** an area of water beside a pier or between piers. **2** a pier or wharf; hence, a loading platform. —***v.*** move or come into a dock; hence, link (two spacecraft) together in space; become so linked: *~ing maneuvers.* —**dock·age** (–ij) *n.* the use of a dock; a charge for this.

dock·et *n.* a list, as of court cases tried or to be tried, things to be done, contents of a package, etc. —***v.*** put (a summary of a case) on a docket; list (a case) for action before a court.

dock·hand, dock·er or **dock·work·er** *n.* a longshoreman: *The harbor was closed by a ~s' strike.* —**dock·yard** *n.* a shipyard.

doc·tor (–tur) *n.* **1** one who holds a **doc·tor·ate** (–it), a university degree of the highest level: *Who can be sure, when* **doctors disagree** *about something?* **2** a physician; an M.D. —***v.*** **1** treat medically; hence, repair. **2** alter or adulterate, esp. to decive: *an accountant accused of ~ing the books; ~ed dice* (i.e. loaded); *a ~ed* (i.e. castrated) *cat.* —**doc·tor·al** *adj.: a ~ candidate, degree.* —**doc·tri·naire** (–NAIR) *adj.* applying a preconceived doctrine regardless of the facts; also ***n.*** —**doc·trine** (–trin) *n.* something taught, as a set of theories, dogmas, basic beliefs, etc.: *the ~s of the Church of England; the Monroe Doctrine;* **doc·tri·nal** (–truh·nul) *adj.*

doc·u·ment (DOK·yuh·munt) *n.* an official paper, as a deed or birth certificate, forming the proof or basis of something: *submitting ~s to the court.* —***v.*** (–yuh·ment): *a well ~ed claim.* —**doc·u·men·ta·ry** (–MEN–) *adj.* **1** concerning or being documents: *~ proof of his bigamy* (e.g. both marriage certificates). **2** wholly factual and unbiased; ***n.,*** *pl.* **-ries** a film or TV show of this nature: *a ~ on the war in Vietnam.* —**doc·u·men·ta·tion** (–TAY–) *n.* (the providing of) documents or references.

dod·der *n.* a parasitic vine of the morning-glory family that grows on other plants by means of suckers. —***v.*** tremble or move shakily because of old age; **dod·der·er** *n.*

dodge (DOJ) *v.* **dodg·es, dodged, dodg·ing** avoid by a sudden movement or by a trick; move quickly or trickily: *went to Canada to ~ the draft; ~ a blow; ~d behind a rock.* —***n.*** **1** a dodging; means of evasion: *using investments as a tax ~.* **2** a clever scheme, expedient, or plan. —**dodg·er** *n.*

do·do *n.* **1** a long-extinct, flightless bird: *"dead as a ~."* **2** a stupid or old-fashioned person.

doe (DOH) *n.* a full-grown female deer, rabbit, antelope, etc.

do·er (DOO–) *n.* one who does; esp., a person of vigorous action. —**does** See DO.

doe·skin *n.* a soft leather of doe's, or often lamb's, skin.

does·n't (DUZNT) does not.

doff *v.* take off; also, lift (one's hat): *~ed his heavy coat at the door.*

dog *n.* **1** a domesticated canine that is related to the wolf. **2** *Informal.* a fellow; also, a low, worthless person. **3** *Slang.* a very bad, unattractive, etc. person or thing. **4** an andiron; also, any of several devices for holding or gripping. —***v.*** **dogs, dogged, dog·ging** track, pursue, etc. like a dog; hence, beset: *an expedition ~d by mishaps and problems.* —**a dog's age** *Informal.* a very long time. —**dog in the man-**

ger one who denies to others what he cannot use himself. **—go to the dogs** be ruined, morally or otherwise. **—let sleeping dogs lie** do not change a situation and cause unnecessary trouble. **—put on the dog** show off as though wealthy and refined. **—dog·bane** *n.* any of several poisonous plants. **—dog·cart** *n.* a light two-wheeled carriage with a pair of seats back to back. **—dog·catcher** *n.* one paid to capture and deal with stray dogs.

doge (DOHJ) *n.* formerly, the chief magistrate of Genoa or Venice.

dog-ear *n.* a turned-down corner of a page; **dog-eared** *adj.* **—dog-eat-dog** *n.* ruthless competition; ***adj.:*** *the ~ world of business.* **—dog·fight** *n.* a rough fight, as between dogs; hence, an aerial combat between two or more fighter planes. **—dog·fish** *n.* any of several small sharks. **—dog·ged** (–gid) *adj.* persistent; stubborn; **dog·ged·ly** *adv.;* **dog·ged·ness** *n.* **—dog·ger·el** *n.* badly written, often humorous verse; also ***adj.*** **—dog·gie** (DOG·ee) **bag** a bag for taking leftovers from a restaurant, as if for one's dog. **—dog·gone** (–GAWN, –GON) *adj. Informal.* damned. **—dog·gy** *n.* **dog·gies** [child's word] dog; also ***adj.*** **dog·gi·er, dog·gi·est** of or like a dog: *~ behavior.* **—dog·house** *n.* a shelter for a dog; **in the doghouse** in a state of disfavor.

do·gie or **do·gy** (DOH·gee) *n.* **-gies** a motherless calf.

dog·leg *n.* a sharp bend; something, as a fairway, so shaped.

dog·ma (–muh) *n.* a belief or set of beliefs held strongly and often on the basis of authority, esp. that of a church. **—dog·mat·ic** (–MAT–) *adj.* **1** of dogma: *~ theology* (concerning the content of the Christian faith). **2** asserted by authority alone: *a ~ statement; A scientist should not be ~* (i.e. oversure of himself). Hence **dog·mat·i·cal·ly** *adv.;* **dog·ma·tism** (DOG·muh–) *n.*

do-good·er (DOO–) *n. Informal.* a well-meaning but impractical and naive social reformer.

dog·tooth *n.* a canine tooth. **—dogtooth violet** an early spring wildflower of the lily family. **—dog·trot** *n.* a gentle, slow trot; ***v.*** **-trots, -trot·ted, -trot·ting.** **—dog·wood** *n.* any of many small trees or shrubs, the most common of which have attractive four-leaved flowers.

dogy same as DOGIE.

Do·ha (DOH·huh) capital of Qatar.

doi·ly *n.* **-lies** a small, decorative lace or linen mat.

do·ings *n. pl.* things that are done or that occur. **—do-it-your·self** *adj.* of or meant for use by an amateur rather than a paid professional: *a book on ~ plumbing repairs; a ~ backyard barbecue;* **do-it-your·self·er** *n.*

dol. dollar.

dol·ce vi·ta (dole·chay·VEE·tah) a life of sweet self-indulgent luxury.

dol·drums (DOLE–, DOLL–) *n.pl.* a region near the equator where there are light, changeable winds and many calms; hence, a period or mood of depression, listlessness, inactivity, etc.: *in the ~ after he lost his job.*

dole *n.* a grant of assistance, as food, clothes, or money, to the needy; esp., a payment by government to the unemployed. **—*v.* doles, doled, dol·ing** give out as charity, or sparingly bit by bit: *a social worker who ~d out sympathy to all and sundry.*

dole·ful *adj.* causing, having, or expressing sorrow: *~ news.* **—dole·ful·ly** *adv.*

doll *n.* **1** a small figure in the form of a human, esp. used as a child's toy. **2** an attractive but unintelligent woman. **—doll up** *Informal.* dress finely, as for a special occasion: *all ~ed up for the graduation dance.*

dol·lar (DOLL·ur) *n.* the basic money unit in the U.S., Canada, Australia, and other countries. **—dollar diplomacy** the use of a government's power to further its overseas economic or financial interests; also, diplomacy helped by financial resources.

dollies See DOLLY.

dol·lop (DOLL·up) *n.* an amount or serving: *a ~ of ice cream; a ~ of rye in a glass.*

dol·ly *n.* **dol·lies** **1** [child's word] a doll. **2** a low, wheeled platform, as used for moving heavy objects, for getting under an automobile, for moving a TV or movie camera around on, etc.

dol·men (DOLE·mun, DOLL–) *n.* a prehistoric monument formed by a large flat stone laid across upright stones.

do·lo·mite (DOH·luh–, DOL·uh–) *n.* a somewhat soft mineral or rock made up of calcium and magnesium carbonates, as in the *dolomite Alps* or *Dolomites* in N.E. Italy.

do·lor (DOH·lur) *n. Poetic.* sorrow, mental distress. **—do·lor·ous** (DOH·luh·rus, DOL–) *adj.: ~ lamentations; a ~ misfortune;* **do·lor·ous·ly** *adv.;* **do·lor·ous·ness** *n.*

dol·phin *n.* **1** any of several small, whalelike sea mammals. **2** a warm-water marine fish with colors that change when it is taken from the water.

dolt *n.* a stupid person. **—dolt·ish** *adj.*

dom. domestic; dominion. — **-dom** *suffix.* **1** a rank or domain: as in *kingdom, dukedom.* **2** the condition or state of: as in *boredom, saintdom.* **3** the totality of: as in *Christendom.*

do·main (doh–) *n.* an area under one's rule or control; hence, a range or field of activity or concern: *Medicine is in the general ~ of science.*

dome *n.* a hemispherical roof, vault, etc.

do·mes·tic (duh·MES–) *adj.* **1** of or concerning the household, home life, etc.: *a ~ quarrel between husband and wife; a ~ sort of woman* (who enjoys home life and working at home); ***n.*** a servant in someone's home; **do·mes·tic·i·ty** (–TIS–) *n.* 2 not foreign; from or concerning one's own country: *~ politics; ~ wine.* 3 tame: *~ animals.* —**do·mes·ti·cal·ly** *adv.* —**do·mes·ti·cate** *v.* **-cates, -cat·ed, -cat·ing** tame; make accustomed to living with humans: *~d cattle;* **do·mes·ti·ca·tion** (–CAY–) *n.* —**domestic science** same as HOME ECONOMICS. —**dom·i·cile** (–sile, –sil) *n.* one's home or residence; ***v.*** **-ciles, -ciled, -cil·ing:** *a Cuban now ~d in the state of Georgia;* **dom·i·cil·i·ar·y** (–SIL·ee·er·ee) *adj.*

dom·i·nant *adj.* prevailing; dominating; esp. in genetics, overpowering another gene or trait parallel to it: *brown eyes ~ over blue when genes for both are present;* **dom·i·nance** *n.;* **dom·i·nant·ly** *adv.* —**dom·i·nate** *v.* **-nates, -nat·ed, -nat·ing** control; overpower; exercise sway over: *cliffs that ~ the city.* —**dom·i·na·tion** (–NAY–) *n.* —**dom·i·neer** *v.* rule (over); behave tyrannically: *a big* **domineering** *bully.*

Do·min·i·can (–MIN·i·cun) **Republic** the country on the E. two-thirds of Hispaniola in the West Indies; 18,816 sq.mi. (48,734 km²); *cap.* Santo Domingo. —**Dominican** *adj.* & *n.*

dom·i·nie (–nee) *n.* 1 *Scot.* a schoolteacher. 2 *Informal.* a clergyman.

do·min·ion *n.* 1 sovereignty; control; rule; also, the field or territory over which it is exercised; domain: *the Lord's ~ over land and sea.* 2 **Dominion** one of the independent, co-equal overseas nations loyal to the British Crown, as Canada, Australia, or New Zealand.

dom·i·no *n.* **-no(e)s** 1 a costume consisting of a loose cloak and mask worn at masquerades; such a mask, covering the upper face. 2 an oblong piece of black wood, plastic, etc. with from 1 to 6 white spots on either half, used in a game called **domino(e)s** [takes *sing. v.*] —**domino effect** the fall of one thing causing the collapse of the next, which is leaning on the first, and so on down the line; chain reaction; **domino theory** the belief that a Communist takeover in one nation will lead to its neighbors' also falling to the Communists.

don *n.* 1 **Don** a respectful term of address for men in Spanish: *Don Carlos.* 2 at Oxford and Cambridge universities, a fellow, tutor, or head.

don *v.* **dons, donned, don·ning** put on (clothing).

Do·ña (DOH·nyuh) *n.* a title used with a Spanish lady's first name.

do·nate (DOH–, –NATE) *v.* **-nates, -nat·ed, -nat·ing** give, esp. to a worthy cause: *~ old clothes to the Salvation Army.* —**do·na·tion** (–NAY–) *n.: political ~s of corporations.*

done *pp.* of ¹DO. —***adj.*** See ¹DO, *v.* 8 & 13.

Do·netsk (duh·NETSK) a city in the Ukraine in Russia.

dong *n.* the basic unit of money in Vietnam.

Don Ju·an (–WAHN) in Spanish legend, a notorious seducer of women; hence, a rake.

don·key (DONG·kee) *n.* **-keys** an ass; hence, a headstrong or stupid person. —**a donkey's years** *Slang.* a long time.

don·ny·brook *n.* a wild brawl.

do·nor (DOH·nur) *n.* one who donates: *a blood ~.*

Don Qui·xo·te (–kee·HOH·tee) an idealistic, impractical fighter of evil, the hero of a satiric novel of the same name, by Cervantes.

don't do not. —***n.*** a prohibition or order not to do something: *do's and ~s.*

do·nut (DOH–) *n.* *Informal.* doughnut.

doo·dad *n.* a small object or ornament, esp. one whose name has been temporarily forgotten: *a clutter of ~s on the coffee table.*

doo·dle *v.* **-dles, -dled, -dling** draw idly and aimlessly, esp. while preoccupied. —***n.*** a drawing so made. —**doo·dler** *n.* —**doo·dle·bug** *n.* the larva of the ant lion.

doom *n.* 1 a judgment, esp. an adverse one: *pronounced his ~.* 2 fate; hence, death; ruin: *young soldiers sent to their ~.* —***v.*** condemn; consign to a bad fate: *~ed to die young.* —**dooms·day** *n.* the day of God's final judgment on the world.

door (DORE) *n.* 1 a hinged, swinging, or sliding panel that covers an entrance, esp. to a house, room, etc. 2 a doorway; hence, a means or path of access: *training that opens the ~ to new careers.* —**at one's door:** *The boss laid the blame at the secretary's ~.* —**darken (someone's) door** visit (someone). —**door·jamb** *n.* one of the upright pieces framing a doorway. —**door·keep·er** *n.* a guardian at a door. —**door·knob** *n.* handle for opening and shutting a door. —**door·man** *n.* **-men** an attendant who opens a building's door for people, calls taxis for them, etc. —**door·mat** *n.* a mat for wiping the feet at an entranceway; hence, *Informal.* one who passively suffers indignities from others. —**door·plate** *n.* a plate mounted on a door bearing the occupant's name. —**door·sill** *n.* threshold. —**door·step** *n.* a step or steps in front of an outside door. —**door·way** *n.* the opening or entranceway fitted with a door. —**door·yard** *n.* a yard about the door to a house.

do·pa (DOH·puh) *n.* an amino acid that produces a neural chemical **do·pa·mine** (–meen), essential to normal nerve-functioning in the brain.

dop·ant (DOH·punt) *n.* an impurity added to an electrical semiconductor to affect its properties. —**dope** *n.* 1 a liquid, esp. a viscous one, used to give desired properties to a surface; hence, any adulterant or additive such as an antiknock in gasoline, a preservative in foods, and a stimulant for race horses. 2 *Informal.* a narcotic or other intoxicating drug;

thus, *Slang.* a dull or half-witted person. **3** *Slang.* special information. **—v. dopes, doped, dop·ing** apply or give dope to. **—dope fiend** a drug addict. **—dop·(e)y** (DOH·pee) *adj.* **dop·i·er, -i·est** dazed, as if drugged: *feeling ~ after the drink; You ~* (i.e. stupid) *fool!*

Dor·ic *adj.* of a style of architecture, having restrained simplicity, fluted columns, and plain capitals.

dorm *n. Informal.* short for DORMITORY. **—dor·mant** (–munt) *adj.* asleep; inactive,; torpid: *animals and plants ~ in winter; arousing our ~ interest in art;* **dor·man·cy** *n.* **—dor·mer (window)** a window set upright in and projecting from a sloping roof. **—dor·mi·to·ry** *n.* **-ries** a room or building with sleeping accommodations for a large group.

dor·mouse *n., pl.* **-mice** a nocturnal, squirrel-like, Old World rodent that hibernates in winter.

dor·sal (–sul) *adj.* of or on the back: *a ~ fin.* **—dor·sal·ly** *adv.*

Dort·mund an industrial city in W. West Germany.

do·ry *n.* **-ries** a flat-bottomed, high-sided fishing boat.

dos·age (DOH·sij) *n.* the amount of a dose. **—dose** *n.* **1** an amount of medicine or treatment given at one time. **2** *Slang.* an infection of a venereal disease. **—v. dos·es, dosed, dos·ing** treat: *Mother ~d us with vitamin pills in winter.* **—do·sim·e·ter** (doh·SIM·i–) *n.* a machine for measuring the dosage of radiation received; **do·sim·e·try** (–tree) *n.*

dos·si·er (DOSS·yay) *n.* a file of papers about someone or something.

dost (DUST) *Archaic.* the form of DO used with *thou.*

Dos·to·(y)ev·sky (daws·taw·YEF·skee), **Fyodor.** 1821–1881, Russian novelist.

DOT Department of Transportation.

dot *n.* a small point, speck, etc., esp. over an "i" or "j"; **on the dot** precisely on time. **—v. dots, dot·ted, dot·ting** **1** mark or make with a dot: *a ~d line;* **dot one's i's and cross one's t's** be precise, minutely correct, etc. **2:** *fishing boats ~ing the bay; cattle ~ing the green pasture.*

dote *v.* **dotes, dot·ed, dot·ing** **1** be feeble-minded with old age; **dot·age** (DOH·tij) *n.: Poor Grandma is in her ~;* **dot·ard** (DOH·turd) *n.* a doting person. **2** be excessively fond of: *just ~s on her son; a ~ing grandfather.*

doth (DUTH) *Archaic.* does.

dot·tle *n.* a plug of unsmoked tobacco left in a pipe.

dot·ty *adj.* **dot·ti·er, dot·ti·est** **1** full of dots. **2** *Informal.* feeble-minded; eccentric.

Dou·ay (doo·AY) **Version** (or **Bible**) an English translation of the Bible for Roman Catholics.

dou·ble (DUBL) *adj.* **1** twice as much, many, strong, etc.; two instead of one: *a ~ thickness of paper; an egg with a ~ yolk.* **2** twofold; in a pair: *~ doors; a ~ boiler.* **3** for two: *a ~ harness; a ~ bed.* **4** having two senses, characters, etc.; hence, deceitful: *Jones led a ~ life; a ~ meaning; a ~ agent.* **5** having more petals than normal: *a ~ rose.* **6** an octave below normal: *a ~ bassoon.* **—adv.** two together; two instead of one; twofold: *rides ~ on his bike; hit on the head and seeing ~; fold it ~.* **—n.** **1** a double quantity, strength, etc.: *12 is the ~ of 6; Scotch, and make it a ~* (i.e. twice the usual serving). **2** one that is just like another; hence, substitute, as for an actor. **3** a hit that allows the batter to get to second base. **4** a sharp turn or evasion while running. **5 doubles,** *pl.* a game with two players on each side. **—v. -bles, -bled, -bling** **1** make or become double: *~ your money; The population ~d in ten years.* **2** fold in two; also, close up: *~d his fists in anger.* **3** go around (a cape, headland, etc.). **4** serve or stand in for another; serve two purposes; play two roles: *The cook* **doubled in brass** (*Slang.* played a second role, like a musician playing two brass instruments) *as a dishwasher; The table ~d as a writing desk.* **5** turn sharply or back on one's path: *The dogs* **doubled back** *to find the scent again.* **—double up** **1** bend (esp. one's body) or fold double: *Hit in the stomach, he ~d up in* pain. **2** share (esp. accommodations) in pairs: *~ up to make room for everybody.* **—on the double** at an extra quick pace; very fast. **—double agent** a spy working for both sides. **—double bass** the largest and the deepest-toned of the violin family of stringed instruments. **—double boiler** an upper saucepan for food set over a lower one holding boiling water. **—dou·ble-breast·ed** *adj.* overlapping in front with two rows of buttons: *a ~ blazer.* **—dou·ble-cross** *v. Informal.* betray by doing the opposite of what was agreed to; also ***n.;*** **dou·ble-cross·er** *n.* **—double date** a date involving two couples; **dou·ble-date** *v.* **-dates, -dat·ed, -dat·ing.** **—dou·ble-deal** *v.* act with duplicity; deceive or cheat; **dou·ble-deal·ing** *n. & adj.;* **dou·ble-deal·er** *n.* **—dou·ble-deck·er** *n.* something that has two tiers or layers, as a bus, bunk beds, a sandwich, etc. **—dou·ble en·ten·dre** (doo·blahn·TAHN·druh) a word or phrase with two meanings, one of them usu. risqué. **—dou·ble-head·er** *n.* two ball games between the same teams on the same day. **—dou·ble-joint·ed** *adj.* having a joint that permits a limb, digit, etc. to move with exceptional freedom. **—double play** in baseball, a play in which two runners are put out. **—dou·ble-space** *v.* **-spac·es, -spaced, -spac·ing** type leaving alternate lines blank. **—dou·blet** *n.* **1** one of a pair, esp. of words such as "ward" and "guard," with the same source but different lines of development.

2 a man's tightly fitted jacket once worn in Europe. **—double take** delayed reaction to something unusual, as by a second glance, often used as a comic device. **—double talk** ambiguous or nonsensical talk that appears to make sense. **—dou·bloon** (dub·LOON) *n.* formerly, a Spanish coin. **—dou·bly** (DUB·lee) *adv.* to twice the degree or amount; also, in a double manner: *to be ~ sure.*

doubt (DOWT) *n.* **1** a lack of certainty, conviction, or trust: *the benefit of the ~; He will* **beyond** (or **without**) **doubt** (i.e. certainly) *win the race.* **2** state of being uncertain: *Are you in ~ about the future?* **no doubt** certainly; also, probably. **—*v.*** be uncertain or distrustful about; also, think unlikely: *not that I ~ your sincerity; We ~ that he will come;* **doubt·er** *n.* **—doubt·ful** *adj.: feel ~ about tomorrow's weather; The outcome is still ~; a man of ~ character;* **doubt·ful·ly** *adv.* **—doubting Thomas** a persistent or habitual doubter. **—doubt·less** *adj.* & *adv.: He will ~ be here by suppertime;* **doubt·less·ly** *adv.*

douche (DOOSH) *n.* a stream of water sent against a part or cavity of the body; also, a device for doing so: *a vaginal ~.* **—*v.*** **douch·es, douched, douch·ing** apply or use a douche.

dough (DOH) *n.* **1** a soft, elastic mixture of flour, liquid, etc. prepared for baking. **2** *Slang.* money. **—dough·boy** *n.* a U.S. infantryman in World War I. **—dough·nut** *n.* a ring of leavened dough fried in fat.

dough·ty (DOW·tee) *adj.* **-ti·er, -ti·est** brave; valiant.

dough·y (DOH·ee) *adj.* like dough: *~ bread* (i.e. not baked long enough); *a ~* (i.e. soft and pale) *complexion.*

Doug·las (DUG·lus) **fir** a large coniferous tree of W. North America cut for lumber.

Doug·lass (DUG·lus), **Frederick** 1817?–1895, American Negro writer and abolitionist.

dour (DOO·ur, DOW·ur) *adj.* stern; obstinate; also, gloomy; silent and ill-tempered. **—dour·ly** *adv.* **—dour·ness** *n.*

douse *v.* **dous·es, doused, dous·ing** **1** drench; plunge into a liquid. **2** *Informal.* put out (a light).

¹dove a *pt.* of DIVE.

²dove (DUV) *n.* **1** a pigeon, esp. a small, wild one. **2** a gentle or peaceful person; esp., one opposed to war or military threats. **—dov·ish** *adj.* **—dove-cote** (–coht, –cot) *n.* a nesting home for doves or pigeons; also **dove·cot.**

Do·ver (DOH·vur) **1** capital of Delaware. **2** a port in S.E. England on the **Strait of Dover** separating England and France.

dove·tail *n.* a wedge-shaped projection fit into a groove in another piece to make a joint firm and solid; ***v.*** fit together thus: *a cabinet with ~ed corners; Our plans ~ed perfectly.*

dow·a·ger (–uh·jur) *n.* a widow having a title or property from her dead husband; hence, an old woman of social standing; ***adj.:*** *the ~ duchess.*

dow·dy *adj.* **-di·er, -di·est** shabby or plain in clothing or appearance. **—dow·di·ly** *adv.* **—dow·di·ness** *n.*

dow·el *n.* a peg fitting into a hole to join pieces or parts together. **—*v.* -els, -el(l)ed, -el·(l)ing** join with dowels.

dow·er *n.* **1** a dowry. **2** a widow's share of her husband's property for her lifetime. **—*v.*** provide with a dowry or dower.

dow·itch·er *n.* a long-billed shore bird related to the snipes and the sandpiper.

Dow-Jones average an average of selected stocks on the New York exchange, used as an economic indicator.

¹down *n.* very fine, fluffy feathers or hair.

²down *adv.* **1** at or towards a lower position, quieter or worse state, smaller volume, etc.: *Sit ~! came ~ with the flu; quieting ~ the children; cut ~ the essay to 2,000 words.* **2** southwards; also, away from the speaker: *gone ~ to Florida.* **3** as partial payment, usu. in cash: *paid $10,000 ~ on the house.* **4** in writing: *Put it ~ in your book.* **5** in subjection: *trying to hold us ~.* **6** toward a later time: *~ through the ages.* **—*adj.*** **1** in or at a low position. **2** out of play: *The ball is ~ on the 10-yard line.* **3** behind; trailing: *~ 6–0 in the 6th inning.* **4** completed: *one ~, two to go.* **5** less active; ill; despondent: *~ with a cold; feeling ~.* **6** **down on** hostile to. **—*prep.*** **1** down along, through, etc.: *run ~ the hill; ~ the eons of time.* **2** to or at a lower or later point: *sailing ~ the Hudson; That's 2 miles ~ the road.* **3** along: *walking ~ 45th Street.* **—*n.*** **1** **downs** *pl.* grassy uplands. **2** a decline: *ups and ~s.* **3** in football, a play to advance the ball. **—*v.*** cause to go or be down; defeat: *~ed the ball on the 25-yard line; ~ed the Dodgers* 5–2. **—down and out** destitute, friendless, etc. **—down in the dumps** (or **mouth**) *Informal.* sad; depressed. **—down on one's luck** *Informal.* unfortunate. **—down the drain** *Informal.* gone; lost. **—down to the ground** completely: *The promotion suits him ~ to the ground.* **—down-at-the-heels** *adj.* shabby; run-down. **—down·beat** *n.* a descending stroke of a conductor's baton showing the principal accent in a measure; ***adj.*** gloomy; realistic and grim; also, relaxed. **—down·cast** *adj.* pointed down; dejected: *with ~ eyes.* **—down(·er)** *n. Slang.* a depressant drug. **—down·fall** *n.* **1** a heavy fall of snow or rain. **2** a sudden fall from power, wealth, etc.; cause of this: *Drink was his ~;* **down·fall·en** *adj.* **—down·grade** *n.* a downward slope; hence, any path of decline: *an aging leader* **on the downgrade; *v.* -grades, -grad·ed, -grad·ing** lower the status, pay, importance, etc. of: *~d the report to mere rumor.* **—down·heart·ed** *adj.* depressed. **—down·hill** *adj.* & *adv.* downward along a hill or to a lower status, condition, etc.; ***n.*** a downhill skiing race; **down·hill·er** *n.* a contestant in this. —**down-home** *adj. Informal.* characteristically Southern (U.S.); also, rustic or folksy.

Down·ing Street a London street having British government offices and (No. 10) the Prime Minister's residence.

down payment a first payment, made at the time of purchase. —**down·pour** *n.* a very heavy rain. —**down·range** *adv.* & *adj.* (further) along a missile's intended path. —**down·right** *adj.* **1** plainspoken; candid. **2** thoroughgoing; absolute: *a ~ lie;* also ***adv.*** absolutely: *He was ~ antagonistic.* —**down·shift** *v.* shift to a lower gear. —**down·siz·ing** *n.* the scaling down in size and weight of American automobiles to make them more fuel-efficient.

Down's syndrome a chromosomal, congenital defect causing physical and mental retardation and slightly mongoloid appearance; mongolism.

down·stage *adv.* & *adj.* of, at, or toward the front of the stage; ***n.:*** *move to ~.* —**down·stairs** *adv.* down a set of stairs; on or to a lower floor; ***adj.:*** *a ~ apartment; She is ~;* ***n.:*** *The ~ has been painted.* —**down·stream** *adj.* & *adv.* (further) in the direction that water is flowing. —**down·stroke** *n.* a downward stroke. —**down·swing** *n.* **1** a downward swing. **2** a decline, esp. in business. —**down-to-earth** *adj.* practical. —**down·town** *n.* the lower, central, or business district of a city or town; ***adj.*** & ***adv.*** (being) in or to downtown: *~ businesses; went ~.* —**down·trod·den** *adj.* oppressed; trampled, as by tyranny. —**down·turn** *n.* same as DOWNSWING. —**down under** *Informal.* (in or to) Australia or New Zealand. —**down·ward** *adj.* & *adv.* (being or moving) toward a lower, inferior, or later place, condition, etc.; also **down·wards** *adv.* —**down·wind** *adj.* & *adv.* (further) in the direction the wind is blowing.

down·y *adj.* **down·i·er, -i·est** of, like, or covered with down; **downy mildew** a fungus parasitic on the leaves of many plants that was responsible for the Irish potato famine of 1845–46; **downy woodpecker** a small North American woodpecker with dark wings and white back and belly.

dow·ry *n.* **-ries** the property a woman brings to her husband at marriage; hence, a natural talent or gift.

dowse (DOWZ) *v.* **dows·es, dowsed, dows·ing** use a **dowsing rod,** same as DIVINING ROD. —**dows·er** *n.*

dox·ol·o·gy (–OL·uh·jee) *n.* **-gies** a formula expressing praise of God.

doy·en (–un) *n.* the senior member of a group; *fem.* **doy·enne** (–en).

doz. dozen.

doze *n.* a short nap; light sleep. —***v.*** **doz·es, dozed, doz·ing:** *~ing in the sun; tends to* **doze off** *watching TV late.*

doz·en (DUZN) *n.* a group of 12: *three ~ eggs; sold in ~s;* **dozens of** very many. —**doz·enth** *adj.*

doz·er *n. Informal.* bulldozer.

doz·y *adj.* **doz·i·er, -i·est** drowsy; sleepy.

D.P. displaced person.

dpt. department.

dr. debit; debtor; dram. —**Dr.** Doctor; Drive (street name). —**D.R.** dead reckoning; deposit receipt.

drab *adj.* **drab·ber, drab·best** **1** grayish- or yellowish-brown; ***n.*** this color or a cloth of drab. **2** dull; faded; monotonous: *~ gray walls; the ~ routine of an assembly-line job.* —**drab·ly** *adv.* —**drab·ness** *n.*

drach·ma (DRAK·muh) *n., pl.* **-mas, -mae** (–mee), or **-mai** (–mye) the basic unit of money in Greece.

Dra·co (DRAY·coh) **1** a constellation near the North Star. **2** a lawgiver of ancient Greece; **Dra·co·ni·an** (–COH–) *adj.* harsh or strict like Draco.

draft *n.* **1** an act of pulling or drawing; the weight pulled or amount of fish caught in one draw of the net; a draft animal is used to pull heavy loads: *a ~* (i.e. drink) *of water; beer* **on draft** (i.e. to be drawn from a cask or keg); *sitting in a ~* (i.e. current of air) *by the window;* **draft·y** *adj.* **draft·i·er, -i·est; draft·i·ness** *n.* **2** a device for controlling air flow. **3** the depth of water drawn by a ship: *a shallow-~ vessel.* **4** a paper directing a bank to pay a specified amount to the person in whose favor it is drawn. **5** a sketch or plan of work to be done, made usu. by a **drafts·man, -men; drafts·man·ship** *n.* **6** a preliminary version of something written. **7** a selection, as of new players by sports teams; also, of men for military service by a **draft board; draft·ee** *n.* one thus chosen. —***adj.*** **1** on draft: *~ beer.* **2** preliminary or rough: *a ~ version of the bill.* **3** used for pulling loads: *~ animals.* —***v.*** **1** select by a draft. **2** compose, sketch, or draw up, esp. in rough form: *~ a proposal.*

drag *n.* **1** something dragged, as a net, harrow, grapnel, sledge, etc.; also, a dragging; something that slows or hinders, esp. the resistance of air or fluid to a moving body. **2** *Slang.* **a** female attire worn by a man; **b** something boring; **c** a puff on a cigar, cigarette, etc. **d** a street: *the main ~.* **3** a drag race. —***v.*** **drags, dragged, drag·ging** **1** pull or draw with difficulty, esp. along the ground; trail; hence, move or cause to move slowly, tediously, against one's will, etc.: *had to ~ the tree behind the cart; The meeting* **dragged on** *with his terrible speeches; Don't ~ me into your problems; ~d his son off to see the ball game; Time ~s near lunch hour; Don't* **drag out** *the meeting with useless questions;* **drag one's feet** (or **heels**) move or act reluctantly. **2** search or fish with a net, hook, etc.: *~d the river for the drowned man.*

3 *Slang.* puff (on a cigarette, cigar, etc.). —**drag·ger** *n.* —**drag·gy** *adj.* **drag·gi·er, -drag·gi·est** slow-moving; dull. —**drag·net** *n.* **1** a fishing net pulled across the bottom of a body of water. **2** a set of coordinated procedures for finding men wanted by police.

drag·o·man (–uh·mun) *n.* **-mans** or **-men** in the Near East, an interpreter.

drag·on (–un) *n.* in myths, a large lizard or snake, winged and usu. fire-breathing: *modern science slaying the ~ of superstition.* —**drag·on·fly** *n.* **-flies** any of an order of flying insects with four large, gauzy wings; they feed on insects caught in flight. **dragon lizard** a flesh-eating Indonesian lizard up to 11 ft. (3.353 m) long.

dra·goon (druh·GOON) *n.* a heavily armed cavalryman. —***v.*** harass; coerce: *~ed into making a contribution.*

drag parachute See PARACHUTE. —**drag (race)** an acceleration race over a short, straight course **(drag strip),** often between specially built cars **(drag·sters).**

drain *v.* **1** draw or flow out of; hence, exhaust; make empty: *~ gasoline from the can; John felt ~ed after his exams.* **2** dry by drawing liquid from; discharge or receive water: *~ing farmland; a creek that ~s the region; The region ~s into the creek.* **3** become emptied or exhausted: *Her enthusiasm ~ed away.* —***n.*** **1** a means of draining, as a **drain·pipe** *n.* **2** a draining, a burden, depletion, etc.: *a ~ on his financial resources; a brain ~.* —**drain·age** (–ij) *n.* **1** a draining; also, a system of ditches, pipes, etc. for draining. **2** that which is drained off. **3** an area drained; also **drainage basin.**

drake *n.* a male duck.

Drake, Sir Francis. 1540?–1596, English sailor and buccaneer who circumnavigated the globe.

dram *n.* **1** 1/8 ounce (Apothecaries' weight); 1/16 ounce (Avoirdupois weight). **2** a fluid dram. **3** a small drink, esp. of alcohol.

dra·ma (DRAH·muh, DRAM–) *n.* **1** a play for stage, TV, or radio; the art or institution of the theater or plays: *a student of Japanese ~.* **2** a unified series of exciting events; a being dramatic: *a hostage ~ at the embassy.*

Dram·a·mine (–meen) *Trademark.* a drug used against motion sickness.

dra·mat·ic (druh·MAT–) *adj.* **1** of or for drama: *~ irony; ~ unity.* **2** vivid, striking, exciting, etc.: *a rather ~ entrance;* **dra·mat·i·cal·ly** *adv.* —**dramatics** *n.pl.* [takes *sing. v.*] dramatic behavior; also, theatrical performance or production. —**dram·a·tist** (DRAM·uh–) *n.* a playwright. —**dram·a·tize** *v.* **-tiz·es, -tized, -tiz·ing** adapt for dramatic presentation; hence, present or regard dramatically: *always ~s his problems;* **dram·a·ti·za·tion** (–ZAY–) *n.*

drank *pt.* of DRINK.

drape *v.* **drapes, draped, drap·ing** **1** cover or hang with cloth in loose folds; hang (cloth) thus: *a coffin ~d with black cloth; a towel ~d over his head.* **2** hang or rest casually or loosely: *his arm ~d over her shoulders.* —***n.*** draped cloth; esp. **drapes,** curtains. —**drap·er** (DRAY–) *n. Brit.* one who sells cloth, dry goods, etc. —**dra·per·y** *n.* **-per·ies** **1** *Brit.* dry goods; also, a draper's establishment. **2** draped cloth; also, the draping or arranging of material; **draperies** curtains.

dras·tic *adj.* forceful; harsh; extreme: *~ measures to put down the revolt.* —**dras·ti·cal·ly** *adv.*

draught (DRAFT) *n., adj.* & *v. Brit.* same as DRAFT. —**draughts** *n.pl.* checkers. —**draughts·man, draught·y** same as DRAFTSMAN, DRAFTY.

Dra·vid·i·an (druh·VID·ee·un) *n.* a non-Indo-European family of languages or peoples of S. India; ***adj.:*** *Malayalam is a ~ language.*

draw *v.* **draws,** *pt.* **drew,** *pp.* **drawn, draw·ing** **1** pull with effort; drag; hence, lead; move gradually or slowly: *an engine ~ing a long train; a horse-~n carriage; I* **drew** *him* **aside** *for a private word; The racer drew ahead; A small boat ~s alongside (of) a ship.* **2** attract; hence, elicit; cause: *Sugar ~s ants; The hotel's* **drawing card** *is a good sand beach; a threat that ~s no reply.* **3** pull in; inhale; also, let or cause (air) to flow: *I'll defy this law while I ~ breath* (i.e. as long as I live); *~ing courage from her example; The cat drew in his claws; a chimney that ~s well.* **4** pull out; extract; pick randomly; hence, take out the entrails of (esp. a bird); also, receive or withdraw: *~ a sword from a scabbard; The gunfighter drew and fired; having a tooth ~n; ~ lots; a bank account ~ing 8% interest; ~ money from the bank.* **5** shape, make larger or longer, as by stretching or pulling. **6** portray with lines or words; sketch; write out: *hire a lawyer to ~ his will; ~ a picture;* **draw the line** set a limit not to be gone past. **7** infer; make: *~ a conclusion; ~ analogies between things.* **8** need (a depth of water) to float in. **9** bend (a bow). **10** tie (a contest). **11** steep: *Let the tea ~.* —***n.*** **1** a drawing: *a fast-~ gunfighter.* **2** something drawn, esp. a tied contest. **3** an attraction. **4** a gully. —**draw a bead on** aim at. —**draw down** deplete; consume: *a war ~ing down military supplies.* —**draw on** **1** approach; cause to go on. **2** take from; use; exploit: ~ing on years of experience; a check ~n on this bank. —**draw out** **1** prolong. **2** induce to talk. —**draw up** **1** set in order; also, straighten stiffly: *~ herself up in the chair.* **2** draft: *~ up a treaty.* **3** come to a stop: *drew up in front of the corral.* —**draw·back** *n.* **1** a disadvantage; detriment; hindrance. **2** withdrawal: *a ~ of troops from the front.* —**draw·bridge** *n.* a bridge able to be raised or swung aside, as to let ships pass. —**draw·down** *n.* a reduction; depletion. —**draw·er** *n.* **1** one that draws. **2** a container in a desk, bureau, etc. that slides in and out. **3 drawers,** *pl.* underpants. **—draw·ing** *n.* **1** an act or instance of drawing. **2** the act or skill of portraying by drawn lines; a representation so made: *pencil ~s on display at the gallery.* **—drawing board** a board used for drawing up plans: *Back to the old ~ing board!* (i.e. Let's start again by replanning.) **—drawing room** a room for receiving guests; parlor.

drawl *n.* a way of speaking that lengthens the vowel sounds: *a Texas ~.* Also ***v.***

drawn *adj.* **1** strained and haggard. **2** eviscerated: *a ~ chicken.* **—drawn butter** melted and often seasoned butter, used as a sauce. **—draw·string** *n.* a cord that is pulled to close a bag or to tighten clothing, curtains, etc.

dray *n.* a low cart or sled for heavy loads.

dread (DRED) *v.* fear greatly (to): *He ~ed the sight of his father; ~s a letter from the draft board; ~ to go into battle.* ***—n.:*** *lived in ~ of being found out.* ***—adj.*** dreaded; also, held in awe: *the ~ majesty of the Lord.* **—dread·ful** *adj.* **1** causing dread. **2** very unpleasant or severe: *~ news; a ~ storm.* **—dread·ful·ly** *adv.* **—dread·nought** (–nawt) *n.* a large battleship with heavy armor and big guns.

dream (DREEM) *n.* **1** a group of subjective images, thoughts, etc. in a sleeper's mind; also, a reverie or daydream. **2** a vision or ideal, esp. if unreal; also, something very excellent, desirable, etc.: *Our vacation was a ~.* ***—v.* dreams,** *pt. & pp.* **dreamed** or **dreamt** (DREMT), **dream·ing** **1** have a dream. **2** be in a reverie; daydream. **3** suppose; imagine: *I wouldn't* **dream of** *having you pay the bill; a planner* **dreaming up** (i.e. inventing) *a new transit system.* **—dream·er** *n.* **—dream·like** *adj.: a ~ vision.* **—dream world** sleep; also, a lovely but unreal place or state; a world of illusion; also **dream·land. —dream·y** *adj.* **dream·i·er, -i·est** given to daydreaming; also, like a dream; hence, *Informal.* perfect; lovely; **dream·i·ly** *adv.;* **dream·i·ness** *n.*

drear·y (DREER·ee) *adj.* **drear·i·er, -i·est** gloomy; causing boredom, low spirits, etc.; also **drear** *Poetic.* **—drear·i·ly** *adv.* **—drear·i·ness** *n.*

dredge *n.* a scoop, bucket, net, etc. for dragging along the bottom of a body of water; also, a ship fitted with this. ***—v.* dredg·es, dredged, dredg·ing** **1** clean or deepen a channel or harbor with a dredge. **2** gather or search for with a dredge: *~ing oysters in the shallows; trying to* **dredge up** *news about the scandal.* **3** sprinkle: *~ meat cubes with flour; ~ spices over something.*

dregs *n. pl.* the sediment from a liquid, esp. a drink; hence, the most worthless part: *the ~ of society.*

Drei·ser (DRY·sur), **Theodore.** 1871–1945, American novelist.

drench *v.* soak; wet thoroughly: *~ed by a sudden downpour.*

Dres·den (DREZ·dun) a city in East Germany; **Dresden china** a white-glazed porcelain with decoration in relief and bright colors.

dress *v.* **1** put clothes on; also, put formal clothes on: *a mother ~ing her child; Don't come in, I'm ~ing; to ~ for dinner;* **dressed (up) to kill** (i.e. very finely). **2** decorate: *~ing the store's display window.* **3** comb and arrange (hair); groom (an animal). **4** put or get (troops) in straight lines. **5** prepare for cooking or use; finish: *a pre-~ed chicken; ~ed lumber; ~ed leather.* **6** apply dressing to (a wound). ***—n.*** **1** clothing, esp. external; also, formal clothing: *neglect of one's ~; a full-~ affair.* **2** a woman's or girl's one-piece outer garment; **dress·mak·er** *n.;* **dress·mak·ing** *n.* ***—adj.*** of clothes, formal; requiring such clothes: *a ~ shirt.* **—dress down** scold vigorously. **—dress up** dress specially or formally. **—dres·sage** (druh·SAHZH) *n.* a kind of show riding in which a horse's maneuvers are controlled by barely visible motions of the rider. **—dress circle** the first tier of seats in a theater, where formal dress was once required. **—dress·er** *n.* **1** one who dresses: *a very fine ~.* **2** a bureau or chest of drawers, usu. with a mirror. **—dress·ing** *n.* **1** a bandage, medication, etc. applied to a wound. **2** a sauce for salads, etc. **3** a bread-and-seasoning stuffing, as for poultry. **—dressing gown** an informal robe worn while lounging, preparing to dress, etc. **—dressing room** a room, as in a theater to change costumes, makeup, etc. in. **—dress rehearsal** a rehearsal in full costume. **—dress·y** *adj.* **dress·i·er, -i·est** **1** given to fancy dressing. **2** stylish; formal: *a rather ~ suit.*

drew *pt.* of DRAW.

drib·ble *v.* **drib·bles, drib·bled, drib·bling** **1** flow or fall in a small, unsteady stream; allow or cause to do so; also, slobber. **2** in sports, move the ball or puck by a series of bounces, taps, or kicks. ***—n.:*** *A ~ of saliva fell from his lips; a little ~ of funds to the committee; a rapid ~ at center court.* **—drib·let** *n.* a drop; also, a small amount. **—dribs and drabs** *Informal.* tiny amounts.

dried, drier, dries, driest See DRY.

drift *n.* **1** a drifting; also, one's course while drifting. **2** a movement; tendency; also, tenor, gist, etc.: *the ~ of the political situation; the ~ of their conversation.* **3** a pile of sand, snow, etc. deposited by wind; sand, stones, etc. deposited by a glacier or its waters. ***—v.*** **1** move aimlessly, esp. with a current, breeze, etc.; stray idly; cause to drift: *a ship ~ing north along the coast; Children just ~ing through school.* **2** pile or be piled up in a drift: *~ing sand.* **—drift·er** *n.* one that drifts, esp. a homeless wanderer. **—drift·wood** *n.* wood drifting in or cast on shore by the water.

drill *n.* **1** a tool for making a hole in something hard: *a dentist's ~; a hand ~* (usu. brace and bit). **2** a repeated series of physical or mental exercises used in teaching; esp., a military procedure for training in marching and use of weapons; **drill·mas·ter** *n.* **3** a furrow to plant seeds in; also, a machine that plants seeds in rows of holes or furrows: *a seed ~.* **4** a heavy, strong cotton cloth used esp. for work clothes. **5** a kind of W. African baboon. **—*v.*** **1** make a hole (in) with a drill; hence, *Informal.* throw hard and fast; shoot. **2** train with or undergo a drill: *The teacher ~ed his class in the multiplication tables; had German* **drilled into** *him at school.* **—drill·er** *n.* **—drill press** an upright power drill in which the drilling bit is lowered onto the work by a lever; **drill·ship** *n.* a ship equipped for drilling on the sea bed, as for oil.

dri·ly (DRY·lee) *adv.* same as DRYLY.

drink *v.* **drinks, drank, drunk, drink·ing** **1** swallow (a liquid); hence, absorb; also, take in mentally or with the senses: *~ing in the sights of New York.* **2** consume alcoholic beverages; also, make or take part in a toast: *He ~s like a fish; Let's* **drink to** *the bride and groom; ~ing a toast to them.* **—*n.*** **1** a beverage; also, an amount drunk: *Have a ~; ~s for everyone.* **2** alcoholic beverages; also, their excessive use: *driven to ~ by loneliness.* **—drink someone under the table** remain sober while one's drinking partner gets drunk. **—drink·a·ble** *adj.* & *n.* **—drink·er** *n.*

drip *v.* **drips, dripped, drip·ping** **1** fall or let (liquid) fall in drops: *water ~ing off the roof; a ~ing faucet.* **2** be overflowing or soaked: *a voice ~ing with irony.* **—*n.*** **1** a dripping; the noise of it. **2** *Slang.* an unlikable or boring person. **—drip coffee** coffee made by pouring hot water over finely ground coffee **(drip grind)** in a pot (as a **Drip·o·la·tor** *Trademark*), the coffee dripping into a lower section of the pot. **—drip-dry** *adj.* of clothes, made to dry while hung dripping wet. **—drip·pings** *n. pl.* juices that drip from cooking meat: *make gravy from the ~.*

drive *v.* **drives, drove** (DROHV), **driv·en, driv·ing** (DRY·ving) **1** make to move in some direction: *~ing cattle to market.* **2** force to move fast or violently; force to work: *A south wind drove us on; The boss drove his men very hard.* **3** make something move to a goal or target; hit hard and fast: *The golfer drove the ball from the tee; The lecturer drove his point home with an example; ~ a nail* (i.e. hit it with a hammer). **4** bore; drill; dig: *~ a tunnel under the canal; ~ a well.* **5** compel; impel; put into a state: *~n to despair; ~n mad by pain.* **6** give power or motion to: *a steam-~n engine.* **7** operate, ride in, or convey in a vehicle: *~ a car; ~ down the street; ~ me home.* **8** carry on; conduct: *~ a bargain.* **9** move, esp. hard or fast: *a ~ing rain.* **—*n.*** **1** a driving, esp. a trip in a car; also, a herding together or movement of animals: *Let's go for a ~; a cattle ~.* **2** a driving of a ball: *a line ~ to center field.* **3** a road; also, driveway. **4** a campaign: *a fund-raising ~.* **5** energy; dynamism: *a salesman with lots of ~.* **6** a strong urge: *a powerful sex ~.* **7** the mechanism that transmits motion: *a motorcycle with a chain ~.* **—drive at** intend; mean: *What are you ~ing at?* **—drive-in** *adj.* providing service to patrons who remain in cars: *a ~ bank; ~ movies;* also ***n.***

driv·el *v.* **-els, -el(l)ed, -el·(l)ing** drool; let saliva dribble from the mouth; hence, speak foolish nonsense. **—*n.*** meaningless or silly talk. **—driv·el·(l)er** *n.*

driv·er (DRY·vur) *n.* **1** one who drives: *the ~'s seat; a truck ~.* **2** a golf club with a wooden head for driving the ball from the tee. **—drive shaft** a shaft that transmits motion, as to the rear axle of an automobile. **—drive-up** *adj.* drive-in: *a ~ window.* **—drive·way** *n.* a usu. short private road to one's garage, parking lot, etc.

driz·zle *v.* **driz·zles, driz·zled, driz·zling** rain or sprinkle in fine droplets: *a misty ~ing rain;* also ***n.*** **—driz·zly** *adj.: a cold, ~ day.*

drogue (DROHG) *n.* **1** a sea anchor. **2** a cone-shaped device towed behind an aircraft as a target, for midair refueling of an aircraft, etc.; also, a parachute used to slow and steady a returning space capsule.

droll (DROLE) *adj.* quaintly amusing. **—drol·ly** *adv.* **—droll·er·y** *n.* **-er·ies** drollness; also, something droll.

drom·e·da·ry (DROM·uh–) *n.* **-ries** a one-humped domesticated camel.

drone *n.* **1** a non-working male honeybee serving only for reproductive purposes; hence, a parasitic idler. **2** a pilotless aircraft guided by remote control: *sending up ~s for target practice.* **3** a low humming or monotonous wound or voice; also, a pipe of a bagpipe that makes such a sound steadily; ***v.*** **drones, droned, dron·ing** utter such a sound: *The chairman ~d on with the financial report.*

drool *v.* **1** run or let (saliva) run from the mouth: *~ing infants.* **2** *Informal.* show excessive pleasure at or in anticipation of something: *~ing over the chance to go to Europe.* Also ***n.***

droop *v.* sag or hang down; also, be weak, dispirited, etc.; allow to do so: *spirits ~ing at the bad news.* Also ***n.*** **—droop·y** *adj.: rather ~ flowers.*

drop *n.* **1** a tiny, usu. globular mass of liquid; hence, a small drink (as of alcohol); any minute amount; **a drop in the bucket** (or **ocean**) a tiny or trivial portion. **2** a drop-shaped pendant, candy, etc.: *gum ~s.* **3** a falling, descent, or decrease: *a ~ in the price of milk.* **4** a dropping; a deposit or a place for it: *a parachute ~ of supplies; The spy left papers at the ~;* **at the drop of a hat** immediately; without hesitation. **5** the distance from a higher to a lower level; a steep cliff or slope. **6** something to be lowered, as a stage curtain, or **drop curtain,** or a trap door. **7 the drop** *Slang.* an advantage, esp. of having a gun pointed at someone. **—*v.*** **drops, dropped, drop·ping**

1 fall or let fall, esp. in drops; lower; decrease; descend: *troops ~d by parachute; ~ a bomb; Prices ~.* **2** fall or cause to fall as from weakness, a blow, wounds, etc.: *~ from exhaustion; The hunter ~d the moose with one shot.* **3** move to a position that is inferior, less active, or further back: *a runner* **dropping back** *in the race;* **dropping behind** *in the race.* **4** say or write casually: *~ names; ~ a hint; ~ us a letter when you can.* **5** cease a connection with; also, omit: *~d his old friends; ~ing g's at the ends of words.* **6** put down; deposit: *~ off this book at the library; Can you ~ me at 5th St.?* **7** visit informally: *Do* **drop in;** *~ by our place; I'll ~ around on Monday.* **8** *Slang.* swallow: *~ing acid.* —**drop off** to decrease. —**drop out** withdraw from a contest, school (before graduating), conventional society, etc. —**drop·in** *n.* **1** a casual visitor. **2** a place for informal visits; ***adj.:*** *a ~ center for teenagers.* —**drop kick** a kick made just as a dropped ball bounces from the ground; **drop-kick** *v.* —**drop·let** *n.* a small drop. —**drop·off** *n.* **1** a dropping off; decline. **2** *Informal.* delivery. —**drop·out** *n.* one who drops out. —**drop·per** *n.* **1** one who drops: *a name-~.* **2** a glass tube with a rubber bulb on one end and a small opening at the other, used to measure out drops. —**drop·pings** *n.pl.* animal excrement.

drop·sy *n.* a swelling caused by abnormal water retention in tissues; edema. —**drop·si·cal** *adj.*

dross *n.* a scum of waste formed on molten metals; hence, worthless impurities; rubbish. —**dross·y** *adj.*

drought (DROWT) *n.* an extended period of unusually dry weather; also **drouth.**

drove *pt.* of DRIVE. —***n.*** a herd or large group, as of animals, moving or driven: *~s of cattle on the road to market; ~s of flies.* —**dro·ver** *n.* one who herds animals, esp. to market.

drown *v.* **1** kill or die by submersion in liquid, esp. water. **2** flood; overwhelm: *his voice ~ed out by the traffic; tried to ~* (i.e. get rid of) *his sorrows in drink.* —**drown·proof·ing** *n.* a technique for avoiding drowning by relaxing and using one's natural buoyancy.

drowse (DROWZ) *v.* **drows·es, drowsed, drows·ing** sleep lightly; doze; also ***n.*** —**drow·sy** *adj.* **-si·er, -si·est:** *feeling ~ sitting in the sun; a ~ day.* —**drow·si·ly** *adv.* —**drow·si·ness** *n.*

drub *v.* **drubs, drubbed, drub·bing** thrash or defeat soundly.

drudge *n.* one who does menial, boring, or plodding work. —***v.*** **drudg·es, drudged, drudg·ing** —**drudg·er·y** *n.* **-er·ies:** *escape from the ~ of housework.*

drug *n.* a substance administered in medicines to affect the body; also, a narcotic, hallucinogen, barbiturate, etc., esp. if addictive or abused. —***v.*** **drugs, drugged, drug·ging** **1** give a drug to; esp., affect with a narcotic. **2** mix a drug with. —**drug on the market** something hard to sell because of lack of demand. —**drug·gist** *n.* one who sells drugs, esp. a retail pharmacist. —**drug·store** *n.* a retail pharmacy that sells prescription drugs and other articles.

dru·id or **Dru·id** (DROO·id) *n.* a member of a pagan priestly order among the ancient Celts in Britain, Ireland, and Gaul; *fem.* **dru·id·ess.** —**dru·id·ic** (–ID·ic) or **-i·cal** *adj.* —**dru·id·ism** *n.*

drum *n.* **1** a hollow cylinder (or other shape) with a membrane stretched over an open end, beaten as a percussion instrument; also, an eardrum. **2** a drumlike cylinder, as a barrel or a cartridge holder for a machine gun. **3** the sound of a beaten drum; also **drum·beat.** —***v.*** **drums, drummed, drum·ming** **1** play (a drum); make a similar noise, as by tapping one's fingers or by beating the wings, as a bird does. **2** force by repetition: *~d the names of the Presidents into his head.* —**drum out of** expel from in disgrace. —**drum up** get (customers, business, interest, etc.) by persistent canvassing or effort.

drum·lin *n.* an elongated hill of glacial earth and rock.

drum major a leader of a marching band; **drum ma·jor·ette** (–may·juh·RET) a female drum major or baton twirler with a band. —**drum·mer** *n.* **1** one who play a drum. **2** a traveling salesman. —**drum·stick** *n.* **1** a stick used to beat a drum. **2** the lower part of a leg of chicken, turkey, etc.

drunk *pp.* of DRINK.—***adj.*** intoxicated; also, pertaining to or caused by drunkenness: *~ and disorderly conduct.* —***n.*** **1** a bout of drunkenness. **2** same as **drunk·ard** *n.* one who is drunk, esp. habitually. —**drunk·en** *adj.* drunk: *a ~ driver; ~ driving;* **drunk·en·ly** *adv.;* **drunk·en·ness** *n.* —**drunk tank** a cell for people arrested for drunkenness.

drupe *n.* a fleshy, unsegmented fruit with a stone in the middle; e.g. peach, olive, cherry.

dry *adj.* **dri·er, dri·est** **1** not wet; having or yielding no water or moisture; not under water: *~ as a bone; ~ as dust; not a ~* (i.e. not crying) *eye at the funeral; a ~ well; ~ land; a ~ cow* (not yielding milk). **2** having or providing little rain: *a ~ season; ~ weather; ~ areas.* **3** of or relating to solids, not liquids: **dry goods** *are cloth, clothing, and related items;* **dry measure** *uses pints, quarts, pecks, and bushels to measure grain, vegetables, etc.* **4** dehydrated; also, without butter or jam: *~ toast.* **5** without moisture or lubrication: *a ~ cough.* **6** prohibiting alcoholic drink; also, supporting prohibition: *a ~ county;* ***n.,*** *pl.* **drys** *Informal.* prohibitionist. **7** not sweet: *a ~ wine.* **8** plain; unadorned; hence, **a** dull: *a ~ recitation of facts;* **b** subtly witty or ironic: *~ humor;* **c** unproductive. —***v.*** **dries, dried, dry·ing** make or become dry; **dry out** detoxify from the effects of alcohol; **dry up** *Slang.* stop talking. —**dry·ly** *adv.* —**dry·ness** *n.*

dry·ad (–ud, –ad) *n.* in myths, a nymph of the forest.

dry cell a battery cell having the electrolyte in paste form; also **dry battery.** **—dry-clean** *v.* clean with a solvent other than water; **dry-clean·er** *n.;* **dry-clean·ing** *n.* **—dry dock** a watertight dock that may be emptied to hold a ship under repair or one being built; **dry-dock** *v.* put in a dry dock. **—dry·er** *n.* **1** usu. **dri·er,** a substance added to paint, varnish, etc. to speed its drying. **2** a machine, appliance, or person that dries: *clothes ~.* **—dry farming** a method of cultivation adapted to dry areas, as in W. Texas; **dry-farm** *v.;* **dry-farm·er** *n.* **—dry goods** See DRY, *adj.* 3. **—dry ice** solid carbon dioxide used as a cooling agent: *~ passes from solid to gas at −78.5° C;* **Dry Ice** *Trademark.* **—dry measure** See DRY, *adj.* 3. **—dry run** a rehearsal or trial. **—dry·wall** *n.* a panel of wallboard or plasterboard.

d.s. days after sight; **d.s.** or **D.S.** *Music.* (repeat) from this sign.

D.Sc. Doctor of Science.

D.S.C. Distinguished Service Cross. **—D.S.M.** Distinguished Service Medal. **—D.S.O.** Distinguished Service Order.

d.s.p. died without issue.

D.S.T. Daylight Saving Time.

d.t. delirium tremens.

D.Th. Doctor of Theology.

D.T.'s (DEE·teez) *Informal.* delirium tremens.

Du. Dutch.

du·al (DEW·ul) *adj.* of or for two; twofold; double: *~ tires on a truck trailer; ~ controls on a training aircraft;* **du·al·i·ty** (–AL–) *n.* **—du·al·ism** *n.* a belief that the world is composed of two basic substances or forces; **du·al·ist** *n.* & *adj.*

dub *v.* **dubs, dubbed, dub·bing** **1** add new voices or sounds to a movie or sound track: *~ in English dialogue for a French film.* **2** dress leather by rubbing usu. **dub·bin** (a greasy paste) into it. **3** tap with a sword to make a knight: *I ~ thee Sir Francis.* **4** give a new name, title, or nickname to: *~d him "The King of Hearts."* **—n.** **1** *Slang.* a bungler. **2** what is dubbed in a sound track.

du·bi·ous (DEW·bee·us) *adj.* **1** doubting: *~ about your claim.* **2** causing doubt; questionable: *a ~ claim; rather ~ business practices.* **—du·bi·ous·ly** *adv.* **—du·bi·ous·ness** *n.* **—du·bi·e·ty** (dew·BYE·uh–) *n.* **-ties.**

Dub·lin capital of the Republic of Ireland.

du·cal (DEW·cl) *adj.* of a duke or duchy: *families of ~ rank.* **—duc·at** (DUCK·ut) *n.* a former gold coin in Europe; hence, *Slang.* an admission ticket. **—duch·ess** *n.* a duke's wife; also, a woman who rules a duchy. **—duch·y** *n.* **duch·ies** a dukedom; land ruled by a duke or duchess, as Luxembourg.

¹duck *n.* a strong, usu. cotton cloth; ducks clothes, esp. pants, made of this.

²duck *n.* any of several species of web-footed water birds smaller than geese: *John took to auto mechanics like a ~ to water* (i.e. readily); **like water off a duck's back** producing no effect. **—v.** **1** submerge in water for a short time. **2** lower (oneself, one's head, body, etc.) to avoid being seen or hurt: *~, they're shooting!* **3** evade or dodge: *tried to ~ washing the dishes; He ~ed out of the room.* **—duck·bill** *n.* a platypus. **—duck·board** *n.* a slatted board used as flooring or a walkway on wet or muddy areas. **—duck·ling** *n.* a young duck. **—duck·pin** *n.* a short, thick bowling pin; **duckpins** *pl.* [takes *sing. v.*] a game played with these. **—duck soup** *Slang.* a very easy thing to do. **—duck·y** *adj.* **duck·i·er, -i·est** *Informal.* pleasing; excellent.

duct *n.* a tube, pipe, channel, etc. for conducting air, liquids, etc, or electrical wires and cables: *tear ~s; hot air ~s for heating.* **—duc·tile** (–tl) *adj.* **1** of solids, able to be stretched or drawn into shape without breaking; e.g. copper, aluminum, silver, etc.; **2** docile; tractable. **—ductless gland** an endocrine gland, releasing its hormones into the blood or lymph system directly.

dud *n.* **1** *Informal.* a bomb or shell that fails to explode; hence, a failure, something worthless or with no effect; also ***adj.*** **2** **duds** *pl. Informal.* clothes; also, one's belongings.

dude *n.* **1** *Informal.* a dandy or fop; hence, a city dweller or Easterner in the West; **dude ranch** one run as a vacation spot for guests. **2** *Slang.* a guy; fellow.

dudg·eon (DUJ·un) *n.* angry indignation: *in high ~.*

due *adj.* **1** owed; to be paid or submitted; esp., payable immediately: *an assignment ~ on Friday; a bill ~ at the end of March.* **2** proper; suitable; adequate: *with all ~ respect; in ~ time; the right to* **due process (of law)** (i.e. fair treatment according to the laws) *as guaranteed by the Constitution.* **3** expected or scheduled: *a volcano ~ to erupt any day now; Our bus is ~ at 4:30.* **—adv.** directly: *~ south.* **—n.** **1** something owed to or deserved by someone; **give the devil his due** give deserved credit even to one's enemy. **2** **dues** *pl.* a fee, esp. for membership; **pay one's dues** *Slang.* earn privileges, acceptance, etc. by hard work, suffering, or experience. **—due to** **1** attributable to: *a crisis that was ~ to lack of foresight.* **2** *Informal.* because of: *game cancelled ~ to rain.*

du·el (DEW·ul) *n.* **1** a formal combat between two people, as to settle a point of honor. **2** a contest between two: *a ~ of wits.* Also ***v.*** **du·els, du·el(l)ed, du·el·(l)ing.** **—du·el(l)ist** *n.*

du·en·de (doo·EN·day) *n.* a magical and inspiring personal magnetism: *a flamenco dancer gifted with great ~.* **—du·en·na** (dew·EN·uh) *n.* a female chaperone, esp. for a young woman in a Spanish household.

du·et (dew·ET) *n.* a piece of music for two singers or players; also, the performing pair.

duf·fel (DUF·ul) **bag** a long cloth bag for one's personal effects. **—duffel coat** a knee-length coat of heavy wool, often hooded. Also **duf·fle.**

duf·fer *n. Informal.* one who is bumbling and incompetent; esp., such a golfer.

dug *pt.* & *pp.* of DIG. **—dug·out** *n.* **1** a canoe made of a hollowed-out tree trunk. **2** a rough shelter dug at least partly into the ground; also, a roofed and sunken shelter for baseball players.

Duis·burg (DOOS·boork) a city near the junction of the Rhine and Ruhr rivers in West Germany.

duke *n.* **1** a nobleman of rank next below prince; also, a ruler of a duchy or **duke·dom** (often a small state in Europe). **2 dukes** *Slang.* fists.

dul·cet (-sit) *adj.* sweet or soothing, esp. to the ear. **—dul·ci·mer** *n.* either of two instruments with steel strings; the ancient one is trapezoidal and played with two hand-held hammers; the violin-shaped American one, also called **dul·ci·more,** is played like a guitar.

dull *adj.* **1** mentally slow; insensitive; not perceiving sharply: *a ~-witted student; ~ hearing.* **2** sluggish; not active: *a week of ~ trading in New York.* **3** not sharp, bright, or clear: *a ~ sword; ~ gray walls; ~ sounds.* **4** boring; repetitive; tedious: *a ~ speech.* **5** overcast: *a ~ day.* **—*v.*:** *a mind ~ed by drugs; to ~ a knife, the appetite.* **—dul(l)·ness** *n.* **—dul·ly** *adv.* **—dull·ard** *n.* a stupid person.

Du·luth (duh·LOOTH) a port city on Lake Superior in Minnesota.

du·ly (DEW·lee) *adv.* in a due and proper way, time, etc.: *~ elected officials.*

Du·ma (DOO·muh) *n.* a legislative assembly in czarist Russia.

Du·mas (DOO·mah), **Alexandre.** "Dumas père" (1802–1870), French author of the *Three Musketeers,* or his son "Dumas fils" (1824–1895), also an author.

dumb *adj.* **1** unable to speak, either permanently or temporarily: *struck ~ with shock.* **2** silent: *a ~ show.* **3** *Informal.* stupid. **—dumb·ly** *adv.* **—dumb·ness** *n.* **—dumb·bell** *n.* **1** a short bar with often rounded weights on either end, lifted for exercise. **2** *Slang.* a stupid person. **—dumb·found** *v.* strike speechless, as with amazement. **—dumb·wait·er** *n.* a small elevator for bringing usu. food to a different floor.

dum·dum (bullet) a bullet that expands on impact, causing a jagged wound.

dum·found same as DUMBFOUND.

dum·my *n.* **dum·mies** **1** a model of a human figure: *a tackling ~* (for practice); *a ventriloquist's ~.* **2** an imitation or substitute for something, as one acting secretly for another person; ***adj.:*** *a ~ corporation; a ~ gun* (i.e. not a working one). **3** *Slang.* a mute person; also, a stupid person; ***v.*** **dum·mies, dum·mied, dum·my·ing** usu. **dummy up,** refuse to answer questions. **4** the exposed hand of the declarer's partner in bridge.

dump *v.* **1** unload, empty, or drop in a large mass; hence, get rid of abruptly: *~ the garbage onto the pile; was ~ed by his girl friend.* **2** sell in large quantities abroad at a low price: *~ed surplus radios to keep the domestic price up.* **—*n.*** **1** a place for dumping something, esp. garbage; also, a storage depot: *an ammunition ~.* **2** *Slang.* a rundown, dirty place: *This apartment is a real ~!* **3 the dumps** a depressed state of mind. **—dump on** (someone) *Slang.* criticize harshly; harass verbally.

dump·ling *n.* a ball of dough boiled or steamed, unstuffed for serving with meats, or stuffed with fruit as a dessert.

dump truck a truck with a body that can be tilted up to unload through a tailgate.

dump·y *adj.* **dump·i·er, -i·est** short, squat, and plump.

[1]**dun** *adj.* dull grayish-brown. **—*n.*** this color; also, a dun horse.

[2]**dun** *v.* **duns, dunned, dun·ning** ask (a debtor) repeatedly for payment. **—*n.*** **1** a dunning. **2** one who duns.

dunce *n.* a slow-witted person.

dun·der·head *n.* a stupid person.

dune *n.* a hill of sand made by the wind. **—dune buggy** a light automobile adapted, as by fitting with wide tires, for driving on soft sand.

dung *n.* excrement, esp. from animals. **—*v.*** spread dung on, esp. as manure.

dun·ga·ree (dung·guh·REE) *n.* a coarse cotton cloth; esp., blue denim; **dungarees** *pl.* work clothes, esp. pants or overalls made of dungaree.

dun·geon (-jun) *n.* a dark, usu. underground jail or cell.

dunk *v.* submerge or dip into a liquid: *likes to ~ his toast* (in coffee); *~ed in the lake by his brother.* **—dunk·er** *n.*

Dun·kirk a port city in N. France.

du·o (DEW·oh) *n.* **-os** a duet; hence, any pair.

du·o·dec·i·mal (dew·uh·DES·uh·mul) *adj.* of 12 or 12ths: *a ~ system of measuring* (e.g. 12 in. to the foot, 60 min. in an hour, 24 hrs. a day).

du·o·de·num (dew·uh·DEE·num) *n.* **-nums** or **-na** the portion of the small intestine where it joins the stomach. **—du·o·de·nal** (–DEE·nl) *adj.: ~ ulcers.*

dup. duplicate.

dupe *v.* **dupes, duped, dup·ing** trick; cheat by fooling. **—*n.*** one easily deceived.

du·ple (DEW–) *adj.* double: *~ time* (having two beats to the bar). **—du·plex** *adj.* double: *~* (i.e. two-ply) *paperboard;* also ***n.*** **1** a **duplex house** having two separate dwelling units. **2** a **duplex apartment** having rooms on two floors. **—du·pli·cate** *v.* **-cates, -cat·ed, -cat·ing** **1** make or become double; also, do or cause to occur again: *~ one's earlier perform-*

ance. **2** copy exactly, as with a **duplicating machine** or **du·pli·ca·tor.** ***—adj.*** (–kit) double; being an exact copy: *In* **duplicate bridge** *each hand is replayed by different players.* ***—n.*** (–kit) an exact copy; a double of something: *an application prepared* **in duplicate** (with an exact copy of the original). **—du·pli·ca·tion** (–CAY–) *n.* **—du·plic·i·ty** (–PLIS–) *n.* **-ties** deception by acting so as to conceal one's real intent or feelings; **du·plic·i·tous** (–tus) *adj.* double-dealing; **du·pli·ci·tous·ly** *adv.*

du·ra·ble (DYOOR·uh–, DOOR–) *adj.* long-lasting, esp. despite use and wear: **durable goods** or **durables** *are things like cars, appliances, and furniture.* **—durable press** a chemical process for fixing the shape, creases, etc. of a garment and making it wrinkle-resistant; **du·ra·ble-press** *adj.* **—du·ra·bil·i·ty** (–BIL–) *n.*

dur·ance (DYOOR·unce, DOOR–) *n.* imprisonment: *in ~ vile.* **—du·ra·tion** (–RAY–) *n.* the time during which something lasts or continues to exist: *closed for the ~* (of the war). **—du·ress** (dew·RESS) *n.* coercion by force or threats; also, imprisonment: *not obliged to keep a promise made* **under duress. —dur·ing** *prep.* **1** throughout the course of time of: *It's hot ~ the summer.* **2** at one point in the course of: *wounded ~ the battle.*

durst *Archaic pt.* of DARE.

du·rum (DYOOR–, DOOR–) *n.* a hardy wheat whose flour is used in macaroni, spaghetti, etc.

dusk *n.* the partial darkness of twilight. **—dusk·y** *adj.* **dusk·i·er, -i·est** **1** dim; darkish; gloomy. **2** dark-skinned; swarthy. **—dusk·i·ly** *adv.* **—dusk·i·ness** *n.*

Düs·sel·dorf (DOO·sul–) city on the Rhine in West Germany.

dust *n.* **1** fine particles of solid matter; earth: *~ all over the end table;* **bite the dust** die in battle; be defeated; **shake the dust from one's feet** leave in anger or contempt; **throw dust in someone's eyes** mislead; confuse. **2** a worthless thing; a humiliated state. ***—v.*** **1** remove the dust from; **dust off** *Informal.* to ready for use again. **2** sprinkle (with) dust or any powder: *~ the fingerprints with white powder; ~ sugar over the cakes.* **—dust·less** *adj.* **—dust bowl** an area of dry blowing soil, no longer fertile. **—dust devil** a small whirlwind of dust, litter, etc. **—dust·er** *n.* **1** a person or implement that dusts: *a crop ~; feather ~.* **2** a light housecoat. **—dust jacket** the printed protective wrapper of a hardcover book. **—dust·pan** *n.* a flat pan for collecting sweepings. **—dust storm** a windstorm or whirlwind bearing clouds of dust. **—dust·y** *adj.* **dust·i·er, -i·est** filled with or like dust.

Dutch *adj.* **1** of the Netherlands or its people. **2** of the Pennsylvania Dutch. ***—n.*** **1** the language of the Netherlands, related to German and English. **2 the Dutch** [takes *pl. v.*] the people of the Netherlands; also, the Pennsylvania Dutch; **Dutch·man** *n.* **-men** a Hollander. ***—adv.*** **go Dutch** *Informal.* have each pay his own share, as on a date. **—Dutch courage** *Informal.* bravery inspired by alcohol. **—Dutch door** one whose top and bottom halves may be opened and shut independently. **—Dutch elm disease** a destructive fungus disease of elm trees, carried by a bark beetle. **—Dutch oven** a heavy, lidded pot for slow cooking. **—Dutch treat** *Informal.* an entertainment for which each person pays his own share. **—Dutch uncle** *Informal.* one given to making harsh and forthright criticisms: *scolded him like a ~ uncle.*

du·ti·ful or **du·te·ous** (DEW–) *adj.* doing one's duty; obedient: *a ~ child;* **du·ti·ful·ly** *adv.* **—du·ty** *n.* **-ties** **1** something that one ought to do; a feeling of obligation; hence, what one is required to do by a job, trade, or profession: *felt it his patriotic ~ to vote; Do your ~; The foreman's ~s include supervision; A doctor is* **(in) duty bound** *to save the lives of people.* **2** service, esp. military; **on** (or **off**) **duty** actively doing one's job or work (or not doing so for the present). **3** the service, work, or function esp. of equipment: *heavy-~ pots and pans;* **do duty for** serve as. **4** a tax, esp. one on imported or exported goods; **du·ti·a·ble** *adj.: goods ~ at 10%;* **du·ty-free** *adj.: ~ cigarettes.*

D.V. Douay Version; Deo volente (i.e. God willing).

D.V.M. Doctor of Veterinary Medicine.

Dvo·řak (DVOR·zhak), **Anton.** 1841–1904, Czech composer.

dwarf *n.* **dwarfs** or **dwarves** **1** an abnormally small person, plant, animal, etc.; ***adj.:*** *~ trees* (e.g. bonsai); *~ marigolds;* **dwarf·ism** *n.* **2** in folk tales, a deformed or ugly dwarf with magic powers. ***—v.*** cause to be or remain too small; also, make look small by contrast: *The carrier ~ed the destroyer beside it.* **—dwarf (star)** a relatively small star with average or lower brightness. **—dwarf·ish** *adj.*

dwell *v., pt. & pp.* **dwelled** or **dwelt** reside; stay or remain for a long time; **dwell·ing** *n.* a residence; **dwell·er** *n.: cave ~s; city ~s.* **—dwell (up)on** think, speak, write, etc. about at length.

dwin·dle *v.* **-dles, -dled, -dling** make or become less by steady degrees: *our ~ing oil resources.*

dwt. pennyweight.

Dy dysprosium.

dy·ad *n.* a pair.

dyb·buk (DIB·uk) *n.* **dyb·buks** or **dyb·buk·im** (dib·oo·KEEM) in Jewish folklore, a dead person's spirit that takes over a living person's body.

dye *n.* **1** a substance used to color or stain something, esp. fabrics, leather, hair, etc. **2** the resultant color. ***—v.*** **dyes, dyed, dye·ing** color or be colored in this way: *~d her hair black;* **dyed-in-the-wool** *adj.* complete; thorough: *a ~ conservative.* **—of the deepest dye** of the most extreme kind. **—dy•er** *n.* **—dye•stuff** *n.* same as DYE, *n.* 1.

dying See DIE.

dyke *n. Slang.* a lesbian, esp. a masculine type; also **dike. —dyk•ey** *adj.: ~ mannerisms.*

dy•nam•ic (dye·NAM·ic) *adj.* **1** of or relating to physical force causing motion; **dynamics** *n.pl.* [with *sing. v.*] the physical study of forces and motions. **2** active; tending to produce change or action; energetic: *a ~ sales campaign;* **dy•na•mism** (DY·nuh–) *n.: the ~ of her personality.* **—*n.*** a force producing change or action: *a reformer driven by an inner dynamic.* **—dy•na•mite** *n.* an explosive made of nitroglycerin or ammonium nitrate mixed with an absorbing material; hence, *Informal.* something that has a dangerous or explosive force. Also ***v.*** **-mites, -mit•ed, -mit•ing** blow up with dynamite: *guerrillas ~ing the bridge;* **dy•na•mit•er** *n.* **—dy•na•mo** *n.* **-mos** an electrical generator; hence, a forceful and energetic person. **—dy•na•mom•e•ter** (–MOM–) *n.* a device used to measure mechanical force or power, esp. of an engine.

dy•nas•ty (DYE·nuh·stee) *n.* **-ties** a series of rulers or powerful leaders of one family; also, their rule. **—dy•nas•tic** (–NAS–) *adj.*

dys- *comb. form.* diseased; difficult; impaired; bad. **—dys•en•ter•y** (DIS·n–) *n.* **-ter•ies** an infection of the large intestine marked by painful, often bloody diarrhea. **—dys•func•tion** *n.* an impairment of normal functioning. **—dys•lex•i•a** (–LEX·ee·uh) *n.* an inability to read; abnormal difficulty in reading, often caused by brain damage; **dys•lex•ic** *adj.* **—dys•pep•si•a** *n.* disturbed or difficult digestion; indigestion; **dys•pep•tic** *adj.* & *n.* **—dys•pro•si•um** (–PROH·zee·um) *n.* a rare-earth metallic element. **—dys•to•pi•a** (–TOH·pee·uh) *n.* a place where life is utterly bad; the opposite of a utopia; **dys•to•pi•an** *adj.* **—dys•tro•phy** (DIS·truh·fee) *n.* **-phies** **1** a disorder characterized by neural or muscular degeneration: *muscular ~.* **2** faulty nutrition.

dz. dozen.

E

E or **e** (EE) *n.* **E's** or **e's** the fifth letter of the English alphabet; hence, the fifth in a series. **—E** **1** *Music.* the third tone of the C major scale. **2** energy. **3** einsteinium. **—E.** or **e.** east(ern); engineer(ing). **—E.** English; Easter; Earl. **—e-** *prefix.* See EX-.

each (EECH) *pron.* every one of two or more (taken separately): *He spoke to ~ of us; They glared at* **each other;** ***adj.:*** *a gift for ~ child;* ***adv.*** to or for each: *tickets costing $15 ~.*

ea·ger (EE·gur) *adj.* full of desire; keenly wanting: *a sales clerk ~ to please customers; Jim is an* **eager beaver** *—he never rests;* **ea·ger·ly** *adv.;* **ea·ger·ness** *n.*

ea·gle (EE·gl) *n.* **1** a large, powerful bird of prey having keen vision; **ea·gle-eyed** *adj.: The ~ forest ranger spotted distant smoke.* **2** a former $10 U.S. gold coin. **3** in golf, a score of two under par on a hole. **—ea·glet** *n.* a young eagle.

E. & O.E. errors and omissions excepted.

ear (EER) *n.* **1** the organ of hearing, esp. its visible, outer part; hence, the sense of hearing; also, anything resembling an ear, as a pitcher's handle: *the abalone's* **ear shell;** *a good ~ for music; You have my ~* (i.e. attention); *Tell me, I'm* **all ears** (i.e. listening); *He's* **up to the ears** (i.e. deeply) *in debt; Friends and comrades,* **lend me your ears** (i.e. pay attention)! *I can* **play** *that song* **by ear** (i.e. extemporaneously); *I forgot my lines, so I* **played it by ear** (i.e. improvised); *John* **turned a deaf ear** *to* (i.e. refused) *her pleas for more money.* **2** the grain-bearing spike of a cereal such as corn or wheat. **—ear·ache** (–ake) *n.* a pain or ache in the ear. **—ear·drop** *n.* a hanging ornament for the ear; also, an earring. **—ear·drum** *n.* a vibrating membrane in the ear. **—eared** *adj.: a sharp-~ listener; golden-~ wheat; The sea lion is an* **eared seal.** **—ear·ful** *n.* something startling or unpleasant: *You said an ~!*

earl (URL) *n.* a British peer ranking below a marquis but above a viscount. **—earl·dom** *n.*

ear lobe the lower part of the outer ear.

ear·ly (UR·lee) **-li·er, -li·est** **1** *adj.* & *adv.* near the beginning (of a period); before (in time); not late; soon: *I went to bed ~ and rose ~; In ~ spring, trees are in bud; "The* **early bird** *catches the worm"* (i.e. gets the prize); *at your ~est convenience;* **early on** at or during an early stage (*in* a period or activity). **2** *adj.* of a historical period or epoch; primitive: *~ man chipped tools from stone;* **Early American** (i.e. Colonial) *furniture.*

ear·mark (EER–) *n.* a mark to identify, designate, etc.; ***v.:*** *funds ~ed for emergencies.* **—ear·muffs** *n.pl.* coverings for the ears against cold, noise, etc.

earn (URN) *v.* deserve or gain as reward, wages, profit, etc.: *to ~ a living; two weeks' ~ed vacation; Savings deposits ~ interest;* **earn·ings** *n. pl.* money one earns. **—earn·er** *n.*

ear·nest (UR·nist) *adj.* serious and eager: *an ~ attempt to succeed; an ~ worker;* **ear·nest·ly** *adv.;* **ear·nest·ness** *n.* **—in earnest** serious(ly): *She started studying in ~ only on the eve of the exam; Surely you can't be in ~!* ***—n.*** a pledge or surety: *His first poem was an ~ of greater works to come.*

ear·phone (EER–) *n.* a sound receiver worn in or on the ear. **—ear·plug** *n.* a plug for keeping sound or water out of the ear. **—ear·ring** *n.* a ring worn as an ear ornmanent. **—ear·shot** *n.* hearing range: *Try to stay within ~ in case I need you.* **—ear·split·ting** *adj.* painfully loud or high-pitched.

earth (URTH) *n.* **1** the planet we live on, often **Earth;** also, the world and its peoples: *from the ~ to the moon; The ~ rejoices;* **down to earth** sensible and realistic; **on earth** [as an intensive] of all things; ever: *How* (or *Where, When, Why,* etc.) *on ~ did this happen?* **2** dry land; ground; also, soil; dirt: *cultivation of the ~;* **run to earth** hunt down. **—earth·born** *adj.* mortal. **—earth·bound** *adj.* tied to earthly things; also, worldly; unimaginative. **—earth·day** *n.* the 24-hour day used in measuring time on other celestial bodies. **—Earth Day** an April day set aside to publicize environmental concerns. —**earth·en** *adj.* of earth or baked clay; **earth·en·ware** *n.* pottery made of coarse, porous clay. —**earth·light** *n.* light reflected by the earth on the dark side of the moon. —**earth·ling** *n.* human being; also, a worldling. —**earth·ly** *adj.* **-li·er, -li·est 1** of the earth; also, worldly; temporal: *our ~ existence.* **2** possible: *What ~ good is that piece of junk?* —**earth·li·ness** *n.* —**Earth Mother** the earth viewed as a divine, life-giving female; hence, a sensuous, maternal woman. —**earth·mov·er** *n.* a bulldozer. —**earth·quake** *n.* a shaking of the earth. —**earth science** any science such as geology, meteorology, or geography that studies the earth. —**earth·shak·ing** *adj.* of profound significance. —**earth·shine** *n.* same as EARTHLIGHT. —**earth station** a dish-shaped rooftop antenna for receiving television signals directly from orbiting satellites. —**earth·work** *n.* piled up earth used for defense. —**earth·worm** *n.* a smooth, reddish-brown, segmented worm that burrows in moist soil. —**earth·y** *adj.* **earth·i·er, earth·i·est** of or like earth; hence, crude; vulgar: *~ humor.* —**earth·i·ness** *n.*

ear·wax (EER–) *n.* the yellowish secretion from the ear; cerumen. —**ear·wig** *n.* a tiny insect having a pincerlike rear part.

ease (EEZ) *n.* **1** comfort; relaxation: *Stand* **at ease!** *a millionaire's life of ~;* **take one's ease** relax. **2** naturalness; poise: *the reassuring ~ of her manner.* **3** facility: *She passed the exam with ~.* —***v.*** **eas·es, eased, eas·ing** make less painful or difficult: *The windfall check ~d his money troubles; an injection to ~ the pain;* **ease up** (or **off**) (i.e. relax) *a little on a holiday.* —**ease·ful** *adj.* —**ease·ful·ly** *adv.*

ea·sel (EE·zl) *n.* a frame or tripod to support an artist's canvas, a blackboard, etc.

ease·ment (EEZ·munt) *n. Law.* a limited right (as of passage) on land owned by another.

eas·i·ly (EE·zl·ee) *adv.* in an easy way; without doubt: *She won ~; She is ~ the winner;* **eas·i·ness** *n.*

east (EEST) *n.* **1** where the sun rises; the direction opposite west. **2 East** the eastern part of the world, of a country, region, town, etc.: *In the U.S., East is N. of the Mason-Dixon line, from the Alleghenies (sometimes the Mississippi) to the Atlantic seaboard: the three wise men from the East* (i.e. Orient). —***adj.*** or ***adv.:*** *an ~* (i.e. from the east) *wind; a ship sailing ~* (i.e. to the east) *is* **east·bound** *adj.* —**East Asia** the region comprising E. China, Japan, North and South Korea, Taiwan, and other islands. —**East Berlin** See BERLIN. —**East China Sea** the sea off the Chinese coast, extending north from Taiwan to Japan. —**East·er** *n.* a Christian spring festival commemorating Christ's resurrection celebrated on **Easter Sunday.** —**east·er·ly** *adj.* & *adv.* toward or from the east: *an ~ wind, or an* **easterly** *n.* **-lies.** —**east·ern** *adj.: the ~ U.S.;* **Eastern** of the East: *the* **Eastern shore** *of Chesapeake Bay;* **Eastern Standard Time** *used in the Eastern States;* **east·ern·er** or **East·ern·er** *n.* —**Eastern (Orthodox) Church** a federation of Christian churches, including Greek and Russian Orthodox. —**Eastern Hemisphere** the half of the earth composed of Europe, Africa, Asia, and Australia. —**East Germany** See GERMANY. —**East Indian** *adj.* of India or of the East Indies; ***n.*** a person from India or the East Indies. —**East Indies** S.E. Asia, particularly, the Malay Archipelago. —**east·ward** (–wurd) *n., adj.* & *adv.;* **east·ward·ly** *adj.* & *adv.;* **east·ward(s)** *adv.*

eas·y (EE·zee) *adj.* **eas·i·er, eas·i·est** involving little effort; without constraints; not hard; smooth: *an ~ life; an ~ victory; ~ as ABC; affable, ~ manners; an ~ pace; a loan on ~ terms.* —***adv.*** *Informal: "Easier said than done";* **easy come, easy go** easy to get and to spend; **easy does it** do it in a relaxed manner; **go easy** use moderation; **take it easy** relax. —**eas·y·go·ing** (–GO–) *adj.* having a relaxed attitude. —**easy mark** *Informal.* one easy to impose upon. —**on easy street** without financial worries.

eat (EET) *v.* **eats, ate, eat·en, eat·ing** take in as food; consume; also, corrode: *We ~ to live; ~ a meal; metal ~n away by rust; moths ~ing* (i.e. making) *holes in cloth; What's ~ing* (*Informal.* bothering) *you?* **eat·er** *n.* —***n.*** esp. **eats** *pl. Slang.* food. —**eat·a·ble** *adj.* & *n.: Any ~s in that bag?* —**eat·er·y** *n.* **-ries** *Informal.* restaurant.

eau de Co·logne (oh·duh·cuh·LONE) same as COLOGNE.

eaves (EEVZ) *n.pl.* the lower edges of a roof projecting beyond the walls of the house. —**eaves·drop** *v.* **-drops, -dropped, -drop·ping** listen secretly: *electronic ~ing;* **eaves·drop·per** *n.*

ebb *n.* the flowing back of the tide; hence, a decline: *the* **ebb and flow** *of fortune; fortunes at a low ~.* —***v.:*** *life ~ing away fast.*

eb·on·ite (EB·uh–) *n.* vulcanite. —**eb·on·y** (EB·uh·nee) *n.* **-on·ies** the hard, dark wood of a tree related to the persimmon; ***adj.:*** *an ~ statue; ~* (i.e. black) *complexion.*

e·bul·lient (i·BOOL·yunt, –BUL–) *adj.* bubbling, as with excitement; **e·bul·lience** (–yunce) *n.* exuberance. —**e·bul·li·tion** (eb·uh·LISH·un) *n.* outburst: *an ~ of joy.*

ec·cen·tric (ic·SEN–) *adj.* not concentric; off-center; hence, odd; peculiar: *Pluto's ~ orbit; an ~ wheel for up-and-down movement; his ~ behavior;* ***n.*** an eccentric person. —**ec·cen·tri·cal·ly** *adv.* —**ec·cen·tric·i·ty** (–TRIS–) *n.* **-ties:** *the ~s of old age.*

eccl. ecclesiastic(al); **Eccl.** or **Eccles.** *Abbrev.* for **Ec·cle·si·as·tes** (i·clee·zee·AS·teez) a book of the Bible. —**ec·cle·si·as·tic** (–AS–) *n.* a clergyman; ***adj.*** also **ec·cle·si·as·ti·cal,**

relating to a church as an institution; ~ *reform;* **ec·cle·si·as·ti·cal·ly** *adv.* —**Ecclus.** *Abbrev.* for **Ec·cle·si·as·ti·cus** a book of the Apocrypha.

ECG electrocardiogram.

ech·e·lon (ESH·uh·lon) *n.* **1** a steplike formation: *aircraft flying in ~.* **2** a level of authority or responsibility: *in the higher ~s of the company.*

e·chid·na (i·KID·nuh) *n.* a small, egg-laying, ant-eating mammal of Australia and New Guinea, also called "spiny anteater."

ech·o (EK·oh) *n.* **-oes** a reflected or repeated sound. —***v.*** **-oes, -oed, -o·ing** make an echo; also, reverberate or repeat: *a child ~ing her mother's words.* —**e·cho·ic** (–COH–) *adj.* imitative in sound, as *ding-dong.* —**ech·o·lo·cate** (–LOH–) *v.* **-cates, -cat·ed, -cat·ing** locate (objects) by reflected sound, as bats do; **ech·o·lo·ca·tion** (–CAY–) *n.;* **echo sounding** determination of underwater distances by means of a sound-reflecting device called **echo sounder.**

ECHO virus or **ech·o·vi·rus** (EK–) *n.* a group of viruses found in the gastrointestinal tract causing symptoms of meningitis and respiratory ailments.

é·clair (ay·CLAIR) *n.* an oblong piece of pastry with cream or custard filling.

é·clat (ay·CLAH) *n.* a brilliant or striking success or applause: *performed with great ~.*

ec·lec·tic (i·CLEC–) *adj.* drawing or drawn from various sources; ***n.*** a philosopher, artist, etc. who uses eclectic methods. —**ec·lec·ti·cism** *n.*

e·clipse (i·CLIPS) *n.* the darkening of the sun *(solar eclipse)* by the moon's shadow or that of the moon *(lunar eclipse)* by the earth's shadow; ***v.*** **e·clips·es, e·clipsed, e·clips·ing** overshadow: *a movie star ~d by her more famous daughter.* —**e·clip·tic** (–CLIP–) *n.* the sun's apparent annual path through the celestial sphere.

ec·logue (EC·log) *n.* a short pastoral poem.

ECM European Common Market.

eco- *comb. form.* environment: as in **e·co·cide** (EE·cuh–, EC·uh–) *n.* environmental destruction, esp. by pollutants.

E. co·li (EE·COH·lye) an intestinal bacterium, *Escherichia coli,* used in genetic research, insulin-making, etc.

e·col·o·gy (ee·COL·uh·jee) *n.* the study of the relationship between organisms and their environment; also, this relationship; hence, an environmental system: *the linguistic ~ of words in their grammatical and semantic relationships;* **e·col·o·gist** *n.;* **e·co·log·i·cal** (–LOJ–) or **-log·ic** *adj.;* **e·co·log·i·cal·ly** *adv.*

econ. economic(s); economist; economy. —**e·co·nom·ic** (ee·cuh·NOM–, ec·uh–) *adj.* having to do with economics or economy; also, economical; **e·co·nom·i·cal** *adj.* not wasteful of resources: *Spending money on a freezer is ~;* **e·co·nom·i·cal·ly** *adv.* —**e·co·nom·ics** *n.pl.* [takes *sing. v.*] the science of the production, distribution, and consumption of goods and services. —**e·con·o·mist**(–CON–) *n.* a specialist in economics. —**e·con·o·mize** (–CON–) *v.* **-miz·es, -mized, -miz·ing** be economical; **e·con·o·miz·er** *n.* —**e·con·o·my** (–CON–) *n.* **-mies** **1** management and use of resources; also, thrift or an instance of it. **2** a system of managing resources: *A major strike could cripple a capitalist ~; a rural ~.* —***adj.*** designed to save money: *A subcompact is an ~ car.*

ECOSOC U.N. Economic and Social Council.

e·co·sys·tem (EE·coh–, EC·uh–) *n.* the system of harmonious relationships between the living and nonliving things of nature and their environment.

ec·ru (EC·roo) *n.* & *adj.* light tan or beige.

ec·sta·sy (EC·stuh·see) *n.* **-sies** rapture, esp. of delight. —**ec·stat·ic** (ic·STAT–) *adj.* —**ec·stat·i·cal·ly** adv.

ecto- *comb. form.* external: as in **ec·to·plasm** (EC·tuh·plazm) *n.* **1** the outer portion of a cell's cytoplasm. **2** the supposed vaporous emanation of a spiritualistic medium that may materialize as an apparition at a séance.

-ectomy *comb.form.* surgical removal: as in *appendectomy, vasectomy.*

Ec·ua·dor (EC·wuh·dor) a country in N.W. South America; 109,484 sq. mi. (283,561 km²); *cap.* Quito.

ec·u·men·i·cal (ek·yoo·MEN–) *adj.* of the Christian Church as a whole; promoting Church unity; **ec·u·men·i·cal·ly** *adv.* —**ec·u·men·ism** *n.* a movement for Church unity.

ec·ze·ma (EC·suh·muh, eg·ZEE–) *n.* a skin inflammation with redness, itching, and lesions. —**ec·zem·a·tous** (eg·ZEM·uh·tus) *adj.*

-ed *suffix.* **1** [past tense or past participle]: as in *edited, sprayed.* **2** [forming *adj.* from *n.*]: as in *whiskered.* —**ed.** edited; edition; editor.

E·dam (cheese) (EE·dum) a mild yellow cheese that comes in a round shape with a red rind.

ed·dy (ED·ee) *n.* **ed·dies** a circular current (of water, wind, fog, dust, etc.); ***v.*** **ed·dies, ed·died, ed·dy·ing** to whirl: *Convention crowds ~d about in the hotel lobby.*

e·del·weiss (AY·dl·vice) *n.* an Alpine plant with white woolly flowers.

e·de·ma (i·DEE·muh) *n.* swelling, as of the ankles and feet, produced by accumulation of fluid in the tissues; dropsy.

E·den (EE·dn) *n.* in the Bible, the garden where Adam and Eve first lived; hence, a paradise.

edge (EJ) *n.* **1** the cutting side of a blade; hence, sharpness; keenness: *That cookie* **took the edge off** (i.e. dulled) *my appetite; Oil producers* **have an edge** (i.e. advantage) **on** *the world market;* **2** a border or brink; boundary: *trim the ~s of a lawn;* **on edge** edgy. —***v.*** **edg·**

es, edged, edg·ing **1** form a border or trimming on. **2** move gradually, esp sideways: *~d out the door.* **—edg·er** *n.* **—edge·ways** or **edge·wise** *adv.* with the edge forward; sideways. **—edg·y** *adj.* **edg·i·er, -i·est** tense or anxious; **edg·i·ness** *n.*

edh *n.* an Old Germanic letter for the "th" sound, used as a phonetic symbol for the "th" of "them."

ed·i·ble (ED·i·bl) *adj.* fit to eat; eatable; ***n.*** usu. **edibles** *pl.* food. **—ed·i·bil·i·ty** (–BIL–) *n.*

e·dict (EE–) *n.* an order of the highest authority; decree.

ed·i·fice (–fis) *n.* an imposing building. **—ed·i·fy** (–fye) *v.* **-fies, -fied, -fy·ing** improve morally; uplift: *an ~ing example;* **ed·i·fi·ca·tion** (–CAY–) *n.;* **ed·i·fi·er** *n.*

Ed·in·burgh (–bur·uh, –bur·oh) capital of Scotland.

Ed·i·son, Thomas A. 1847–1931, American inventor.

edit. edited; edition; editor. **—ed·it** *v.* prepare (a manuscript, newspaper, film, tape, etc.) for publication or presentation. **—e·di·tion** (i·DISH·un) *n.* **1** the form in which a book, newspaper, or other publication is issued; also, the copies of it printed at that time: *a popular ~ of Shakespeare's works; The entire late city ~ was seized by the police.* **2** a form in which something is presented or appears: *a younger ~ of her mother.* **—ed·i·tor** (–tur) *n.* one who edits; also, a viewing device for editing film or videotape. **—ed·i·to·ri·al** (–TOR·ee·ul) *adj.* of or by an editor; ***n.*** an article containing an editor's opinion; **ed·i·to·ri·al·ly** *adv.;* **ed·i·to·ri·al·ize** *v.* **-iz·es, -ized, -iz·ing; -i·za·tion** (–ZAY–) *n.* **—editor in chief,** *pl.* **editors in chief** chief editor; **ed·i·tor·ship** *n.*

Ed·mon·ton (–mun·tun) capital of Alberta.

EDP electronic data processing.

eds. editions; editors.

E.D.T. Eastern Daylight Time.

educ. education(al). **—ed·u·ca·ble** (EJ·oo·cuh·bl) *adj.* capable of being educated or trained: *special classes for ~ mentally handicapped children;* **ed·u·ca·bil·i·ty** (–BIL–) *n.* **—ed·u·cate** *v.* **-cates, -cat·ed, -cat·ing** instruct in order to develop the knowledge or skills of; send to school or pay for (someone's schooling); **ed·u·ca·tor** *n.* **—ed·u·ca·tion** (–CAY–) *n.* **1** schooling; also, mental development. **2** teaching; also, the study of teaching methods, principles, etc.; **ed·u·ca·tion·al** *adj.;* **ed·u·ca·tion·al·ly** *adv.* **—e·duce** (i·DUCE) *v.* **-duc·es, -duced, -duc·ing** *Formal.* draw out; develop; also, deduce.

-ee *n. suffix.* **1** the recipient or subject of an action: as in *absentee, appointee, mortgagee, escapee, standee.* **2** one suggestive of another, esp. one of small size: as in *bootee, goatee.*

EE electrical engineer.

E.E.C. European Economic Community.

EEG electroencephalogram.

eel *n.* a snakelike fish.

e'er (AIR) *adv. Poetical.* ever.

-eer *n. suffix.* a person or action having to do with: as in *charioteer, electioneer, mountaineer.*

ee·rie or **ee·ry** (EER·ee) *adj.* **-ri·er, -ri·est** weird or mysterious in a frightening manner: *~ shadows dancing on a wall; an ~ cry from the swamp.* **—ee·ri·ly** *adv.*

eff. efficiency.

ef·face (i·FACE) *v.* **ef·fac·es, ef·faced, ef·fac·ing** remove or blot out (something) as if by rubbing away. **—ef·face·a·ble** *adj.* **—ef·face·ment** *n.*

ef·fect (i·FECT) *n.* **1** what is produced by a cause; also, power to produce a result; hence, a resulting impression: *The medicine had some ~; it* **took effect** *quickly; Advice has no ~ on him; a former custom no more* **in effect;** *a proclamation to* **give effect** *to a bill; raised his voice merely* **for effect;** *special sound ~s used in a movie.* **2** meaning or intent: *I'll furnish you a letter* **to that effect.** **3 effects** *pl.* goods: *household ~s; personal ~s, as clothing, jewelry, etc.* **—*v.*** bring about; realize: *a treaty ~ing a settlement; a medicine to ~ a cure;* **ef·fect·er** *n.* **—ef·fec·tive** (–tiv) *adj.: a new timetable ~ on Monday; a forceful and ~ speaker; antibiotics ~ against bacteria;* **ef·fec·tive·ly** *adv.;* **ef·fec·tive·ness** *n.* **—ef·fec·tor** *n.* a muscle, gland, etc. that can respond to a nerve impulse. **—ef·fec·tu·al** (–FEC·choo·ul) *adj.* adequate to achieve a desired effect: *an ~ demand that brought prompt supplies;* **ef·fec·tu·al·ly** *adv.* **—ef·fec·tu·ate** *v.* **-ates, -at·ed, -at·ing** bring about; make happen.

ef·fem·i·nate (i·FEM·uh·nit) *adj.* womanish; soft or delicate. **—ef·fem·i·na·cy** (–nuh·see) *n.*

ef·fen·di (i·FEN·dee) *n.* **-dis** a landowner or white-collar worker in an Arab country; formerly used as a Turkish title meaning "Master" or "Sir."

ef·fer·ent (EF·uh·runt) *adj.* carrying (impulses) from a central point (as the brain) outward (to the muscles), as nerves; cf. AFFERENT.

ef·fer·vesce (ef·ur·VES) *v.* **-vesc·es, -vesced, -vesc·ing** of liquids, bubble and hiss as gas is let off; hence, be ebullient or excited. **—ef·fer·ves·cence** *n.* **—ef·fer·ves·cent** *adj.;* **ef·fer·ves·cent·ly** *adv.*

ef·fete (e·FEET) *adj.* worn out or decadent: *an ~ civilization.* **—ef·fete·ly** *adv.* **—ef·fete·ness** *n.*

ef·fi·ca·cious (–CAY·shus) *adj.* esp of medicines, sure to have the desired effect; **ef·fi·ca·cious·ly** *adv.* **—ef·fi·ca·cy** (EF·i·cuh·see) *n.: a drug of proven ~.* **—ef·fi·cient** (i·FISH·unt) *adj.* producing the desired result or product with the least waste of resources; capable: *an ~ executive;* **ef·fi·cient·ly** *adv.;* **ef·fi·cien·cy** *n.: an ~ expert; an* **efficiency apartment** *consisting of a room and kitchenette.*

ef·fi·gy (EF·uh·jee) *n.* **-gies** a crude image or representation, esp. of a hated person: *a dictator burned in ~.*

ef·flo·resce (–RES) *v.* **-resc·es, -resced, -resc·ing** blossom out; also, become powdery or form a deposit. —**ef·flo·res·cent** *adj.* —**ef·flo·res·cence** *n.*

ef·flu·ence (EF·loo·unce) *n.* an outflow; emanation. —**ef·flu·ent** (–unt) *adj.* flowing out, as a stream from a lake or reservoir; ***n.*** esp., chemically treated sewage or factory waste. —**ef·flu·vi·um** (–FLOO·vee·um) *n.* **-vi·ums** or **-vi·a** an unpleasant vapor or odor.

ef·fort (EF·urt) *n.* energy required to do something; hence, a strong attempt or its result: *Power steering takes little ~; His ~s were greatly appreciated.* —**ef·fort·less** *adj.;* **ef·fort·less·ly** *adv.;* **ef·fort·less·ness** *n.*

ef·fron·ter·y (i·FRUN·tuh·ree) *n.* **-ter·ies** boldness in defying norms of courtesy or propriety; impudence: *What ~ to speak to the Queen before being spoken to!*

ef·ful·gence (i·FUL·junce) *n.* splendor; brilliance. —**ef·ful·gent** *adj.*

ef·fuse (i·FYOOZ) *v.* **ef·fus·es, ef·fused, ef·fus·ing** pour forth. —**ef·fu·sion** (–FEW·zhun) *n.* an act of pouring out or something poured out, as feelings, body fluids such as lymph or blood escaping into surrounding tissues or cavities, etc. —**ef·fu·sive** (–siv) *adj.: an ~ speech; ~ rocks formed from solidified lava;* **ef·fu·sive·ly** *adv.;* **ef·fu·sive·ness** *n.*

eft *n.* a newt, esp. during the two to three years it lives on land before returning to water.

E.F.T. electronic funds transfer.

e.g. for example. —**Eg.** Egypt(ian).

e·gad (i·GAD) *interj.* a mild oath: *Egad! He actually gave to charity?*

e·gal·i·tar·i·an (–TAIR–) *n.* & *adj.* (one) supporting equality for all. —**e·gal·i·tar·i·an·ism** *n.*

egg *n.* **1** the oval or round body laid by birds, reptiles, fishes, etc. that hatches into a living young; also, an egg cell; **egg on one's face** *Informal.* embarrassment from having blundered. **2** *Slang.* a person: *She's a good ~.* —***v.*** **egg one on** incite or urge. —**egg·beat·er** *n.* **1** a rotary device for beating eggs. **2** *Slang.* helicopter. —**egg (cell)** an ovum; female germ cell. —**egg foo yo(u)ng** (–YUNG) a Chinese-American dish of egg, meat, and vegetables. —**egg·head** *n. Slang.* an intellectual. —**egg·nog** *n.* a beverage made of eggs beaten up with milk and sugar, sometimes also containing liquor. —**egg·plant** *n.* a large, egg-shaped purplish fruit of a vegetable of the same name. —**egg·roll** *n.* a preparation of minced vegetables and meat rolled in an egg-dough casing and deep-fried. —**egg·shell** *n.* & *adj.* (fragile like) the covering of an egg.

e·gis (EE·jis) *n.* same as AEGIS.

eg·lan·tine (–lun–) *n.* a wild rose with sweetly scented leaves and flowers and bright red or orange fruits; sweetbrier.

e·go (EE·goh) *n.* **e·gos** **1** the thinking, feeling, and acting being as perceived by oneself. **2** self-esteem: *Being ignored hurt his ~.* —**e·go·ism** *n.* self-centeredness; conceit; cf. ALTRUISM. —**e·go·tism** (–guh–) *n.* a more overt and annoying kind of egoism, expressed in speech and behavior; **e·go·(t)ist** *n.* **e·go·(t)is·tic** (–IS–) or **-ti·cal** *adj.;* **e·go·(t)is·ti·cal·ly** *adv.* —**e·go·cen·tric** (–SEN–) *n.* & *adj.* (one who is) self-centered. —**ego trip** a self-centered or self-realizing activity; **e·go-trip** *v.* **-trips, -tripped, -trip·ping; e·go-trip·per** *n.*

e·gre·gious (i·GREE·jus) *adj.* outrageous; blatant: *an ~ blunder.* —**e·gre·gious·ly** *adv.;* **e·gre·gious·ness** *n.*

e·gress (EE·gres) *n.* an exit.

e·gret (EE·grit, EG·rit) *n.* any of various wading birds of the heron family that grow long plumes during their breeding season.

E·gypt (EE·jipt) a republic in N.E. Africa; 386,-662 sq. mi. (1,001,449 km²); *cap.* Cairo. —**E·gyp·tian** (–JIP·shun) *n.* & *adj.* (having to do with Egypt or) a person from Egypt or the extinct Hamitic language of ancient Egypt.

eh (AY) *interj.* [used at the end of an utterance in a doubtful or questioning way]: *from Canada, eh?*

EHF extremely high frequency.

EHV extra high voltage.

ei·der (EYE·dur) *n.* a large sea duck of northern regions, whose soft down **(ei·der·down)** is used as stuffing in pillows, quilts, etc.

ei·det·ic (eye·DET–) *adj.* extremely vivid: *A person gifted with ~ imagery has a photographic memory.*

eight (ATE) *n., adj.* & *pron.* one more than 7; the number 8 or VIII: *There are ~ of them; ~ girls; That's an ~* (card); **eighth** *n.* & *adj.* —**eight ball** in pool, a black ball numbered 8; **behind the eight ball** *Slang.* in a hazardous position. —**eight·een** (–TEEN) *n., adj.,* & *pron.* 18 or XVIII; **eight·eenth** (–TEENTH) *n.* & *adj.* —**eight·y** *n., adj.* & *pron., n.pl.* **eight·ies** 80 or LXXX; **the eighties** numbers, years, etc. from 80 through 89; **eignt·i·eth** (–ith) *n.* & *adj.*

Ein·stein (INE·stine), **Albert.** 1879–1955, German-born American physicist, formulator of the theory of relativity. —**ein·stein·i·um** (–STY·nee·um) *n.* an artificially produced radioactive element.

Eir·e (AIR·uh) Gaelic name of the Republic of Ireland.

Ei·sen·how·er (EYE·zun–), **Dwight D.** 1890–1969, American general and 34th U.S. President (1953–61).

ei·stedd·fod (eye·STEDH·vawd) *n.* an annual Welsh festival of the arts.

ei·ther (EE·dhur, EYE–) *pron.* (the) one or the other: *~ of the twins can wear this;* ***adj.:*** *Sit on ~ stool; can write with ~ hand* (i.e. both hands); ***conj.:*** *Say ~ yes or no.* —***adv.*** also: *If you don't go, I won't ~.*

e·jac·u·late (i·JAK·yuh–) *v.* **-lates, -lat·ed, -lat·ing** **1** discharge, esp. semen; **2** utter (something) suddenly. —**e·jac·u·la·tion** (–LAY–) *n.;* **e·jac·u·la·to·ry** (–luh·tor·ee) *adj.: ~ prayers; an ~ duct.* —**e•ject** (i·JECT) *v.* throw out; **e•jec•tion** *n.: bailed out of the disabled aircraft in an* **ejection seat.**

eke (EEK) *v.* **ekes, eked, ek•ing** add to; supplement: *managed to* **eke out** *her livelihood by begging.*

EKG electrocardiogram; electrocardiograph.

e•kis•tics (i·KIS–) *n.pl.* the study of human settlements and their planning. —**e•kis•tic** or **-ti•cal** *adj.*

ek•pwe•le (ek·pwuh·LAY) *n.* the basic money unit of Equatorial Guinea, equal to 100 centimos.

el. elevation. —**el** **1** *Informal.* elevated (railroad). **2** same as ELL.

e•lab•o•rate (i·LAB·uh·rit) *adj.* prepared in great detail; hence, ornate. —***v.*** (-uh·rate) **-rates, -rat•ed, -rat•ing:** *He only hinted at the rumor and would not ~ (on it).* —**e•lab•o•rate•ly** *adv.;* **e•lab•o•rate•ness** *n.* —**e•lab•o•ra•tion** (–RAY–) *n.*

e•lan (ay·LAHN) *n.* spirit; enthusiasm; dash.

e•land (EE·lund) *n.* either of two species of African antelopes with spiraled horns.

e•lapse (i·LAPS) *v.* **e•laps•es, e•lapsed, e•laps•ing** of time, to pass; go by.

e•las•tic (i·LAS–) *adj.* rubberlike; hence, springy; buoyant: *A steel spring is ~; an ~ temperament.* —***n.*** a fabric interwoven with rubber strands; also, a garter or band made of this. —**e•las•tic•i•ty** (–TIS–) *n.: All substances have some ~; words in common use with much ~ of meaning.* —**e•las•ti•cize** (–LAS–) *v.* **-ciz•es, -cized, -ciz•ing:** *an ~d waistband.* —**e•las•to•mer** (–LAS·tuh–) *n.* a rubberlike synthetic polymer, as polyurethane foam rubber; **e•las•to•mer•ic** (–MER–) *adj.*

e•late (i·LATE) *v.* **e•lates, e•lat•ed, e•lat•ing** fill with high spirits, as by joy, pride, etc. —**e•la•tion** (–LAY–) *n.*

el•bow (EL·boh) *n.* the outer part of the joint between the upper and lower arm, esp. bent, as when jostling, working, etc.; also, this shape: *an ~ pipe joint; ~ macaroni.* —***v.:*** *to ~ (one's way) through a crowd.* —**at one's elbow** close by. —**out at (the) elbows** in worn-out clothes; hence, poverty-stricken. —**elbow grease** *Informal.* hard work. —**elbow room** space to work in comfortably.

El•brus (EL·broos), **Mount.** the highest mountain peak in Europe, in the Soviet Caucusus.

¹eld•er *adj.* older; senior: *your ~ brother; an ~ statesman.* —***n.*** a respected older member of a tribe, community, church, etc.: *Listen to your ~s.*

²el•der *n.* a small tree or shrub of the honeysuckle family bearing clusters of purple berries called **el•der•ber•ry** *n.* **-ber•ries** used in preserves, wines, etc.

el•der•ly *adj.* [deferential use] old: *homes for the ~.* —**elder statesman** a senior retired politician. —**el•dest** (–dist) *adj.* oldest, esp. of surviving family members.

El Do•ra•do or **El•do•ra•do** (el·duh·RAH·doh) *n.* **-dos** a legendary place that is rich in gold.

elec(t). electric(al); electricity.

e•lect (i·LECT) *v.* choose, esp. in a formal way, as by voting: *She ~ed law rather than teaching for a career;* ***adj.*** chosen: *the President-~* (i.e. not yet installed); *the ~ few;* **the elect** *n.pl.* a specially chosen group: *the ~ of God* (i.e. chosen for salvation). —**e•lec•tion** (–LEC–) *n.* the act or process of electing; **e•lec•tion•eer** (–NEER) *v.* work for the success of a candidate or party in an election. —**e•lec•tive** (–tiv) *adj.* based on or having to do with an election: *the ~ office of President; an ~ government; ~* (i.e. nonessential) *surgery;* ***n.*** an optional subject in a program of studies. —**e•lec•tor** (–tur) *n.* one having the right to elect; **e•lec•tor•al** (–tuh·rul) *adj.;* **electoral college** a body of electors chosen by the people to elect the U.S. President and Vice-President; **electoral vote** the votes cast by the electoral college. —**e•lec•tor•ate** (–rit) *n.* people qualified to vote, collectively.

E•lec•tra (i·LEC·truh) in Greek myth, a daughter of Agamemnon who plotted with her brother to murder their mother.

e•lec•tric (i·LEC–) or **e•lec•tri•cal** *adj.* **1** of, run by, or charged with electricity: *an electric battery.* **2** exciting; thrilling. —**e•lec•tri•cal•ly** *adv.* —**electric chair** (sentence of) death by electrocution; also, the chair used in this; **electric eye** same as PHOTOELECTRIC CELL; **electric(al) storm** thunderstorm. —**e•lec•tri•cian** (–TRISH·un) *n.* one who installs, operates, or repairs electrical equipment. —**e•lec•tric•i•ty** (–TRIS–) *n.* a form of energy generated by friction, induction, or chemical changes, and capable of producing heat, light, etc., as observed in natural phenomena such as lightning and in certain fishes and eels; also, electric current, esp. as a public utility. —**e•lec•tri•fy** (–LEC–) *v.* **-fies, -fied, -fy•ing** **1** charge with electricity; hence, excite; thrill: *The whole town was ~d by the news.* **2** provide or equip with electricity: *an ~d railroad;* **e•lec•tri•fi•ca•tion** (–CAY–) *n.;* **e•lec•tri•fi•er** *n.* —**electro-** *comb. form.* electrical(ly): as in **e•lec•tro•car•di•o•gram** (–CAR·dee·oh–) *n.* a tracing made by an **e•lec•tro•car•di•o•graph** *n.* an instrument that detects and records the electrical impulses produced by heartbeats; **e•lec•tro•car•di•o•graph•ic** (–GRAF–) *adj.;* **e•lec•tro•car•di•og•ra•phy** (–OG·ruh·fee) *n.* —**e•lec•tro•chem•i•cal** (–KEM–) *adj.* having to do with **e•lec•tro•chem•is•try** (–tree) *n.* the science dealing with chemical action and electrical energy. —**e•lec•tro•cute** *v.* **-cutes, -cut•ed, -cut•ing** kill by the action of electricity; **e•lec•tro•cu•tion** (–CUE–) *n.* —**e•lec•trode** (–LEC–) *n.* a conductor of outgoing or incoming current in an electrical circuit, as the anode or cathode of an electric cell. —**e•lec•**

tro·de·pos·it (–POZ–) *v.* to deposit (usu. a metal) by electrolysis, as in electroplating; **e·lec·tro·dep·o·si·tion** (–ZISH–) *n.* **—e·lec·tro·dy·nam·ics** (–NAM–) *n.pl.* a branch of physics dealing with the interactions of electric currents and magnetic forces. **—e·lec·tro·en·ceph·a·lo·gram** (–SEF·u·luh–) *n.* a tracing made by an **e·lec·tro·en·ceph·a·lo·graph** *n.* an instrument that measures the electrical activity of the brain. **—e·lec·trol·o·gist** (–TROL–) *n.* one trained to destroy hair roots, tumors, etc. with an electrified needle. **—e·lec·trol·y·sis** (–TROL–) *n.* **1** the decomposition into its parts of an electrolyte. **2** the destruction of hair roots, tumors, etc. using an electrified needle. **—e·lec·tro·lyte** (–LEC·truh–) *n.* a chemical solution that will conduct an electric current; **e·lec·tro·lyt·ic** (–LIT–) *adj.;* **e·lec·tro·lyt·i·cal·ly** *adv.* **—e·lec·tro·mag·net** (–MAG·nit) *n.* a magnet that has a coil of wire around it through which a current is passed to magnetize it; **e·lec·tro·mag·net·ic** (–NET–) *adj.: Radio waves, light, X rays, gamma rays, etc. are forms of ~ radiation.* **—e·lec·tro·mo·tive** (–MOH·tiv) **force** electric pressure that causes the flow of electricity through a circuit, usu. measured in volts. **—e·lec·tron** (–LEC–) *n.* any of the negatively charged particles in an atom. **—e·lec·tron·ic** (–TRON–) *adj.* of or having to do with electrons or electronic devices or equipment; **electronic data processing** *using computers;* **electronic surveillance** *by bugging, wiretaps, etc.* **e·lec·tron·i·cal·ly** *adv.;* **electronic music** music composed of sounds produced with electronic devices, assembled on magnetic tape, and played through loudspeakers. **—e·lec·tron·ics** *n.pl.* the science of the behavior and control of electrons through vacuums, semiconductors, and gases for use in devices such as the electron tube, photoelectric cell, and transistor; **—electron microscope** a microscope that uses a beam of electrons instead of light to project enlarged images on a fluorescent surface or photographic plate. **—electron tube** a sealed glass or metal tube, either gas-filled or evacuated, for the controlled flow of electrons. **—e·lec·tro·plate** (–LEC–) *v.* **-plates, -plat·ed, -plat·ing** coat (something) with metal by electrolysis. **—e·lec·tro·scope** (–LEC–) *n.* a device for detecting minute electrical charges and identifying them as positive or negative. **—e·lec·tro·shock therapy** shock therapy using electric current. **—e·lec·tro·stat·ics** (–STAT–) *n.pl.* the physics of static electricity; **e·lec·tro·stat·ic** *adj.: ~ printing, as xerography, reproduces originals without ink or pressure, using an electrically charged black powder.* **—e·lec·tro·ther·a·py** (–THER–) *n.* therapy using electricity, as in diathermy. **—e·lec·tro·type** (–LEC–) *n.* a printing plate duplicated by electrolysis from a wax or plastic impression of the original type or engraving.

el·ee·mos·y·nar·y (el·i·MOS·uh·ner·ee) *adj.* of, for, or supported by charity.

el·e·gant (EL·i·gunt) *adj.* graceful; tasteful; polished; also, rich and luxurious in style: *an ~ diction; a life of ~ ease;* **el·e·gant·ly** *adv.* **—el·e·gance** (–gunce) *n.*

el·e·gi·ac (el·i·JYE·uc, i·LEE·jee·ac) *adj.* in the form or style of an elegy; also, sad; mournful; also **el·e·gi·a·cal** (–JYE·uh·cul). **—el·e·gy** (EL·i·jee) *n.* **-gies** a melancholy poem, usu. one mourning a dead person, as Milton's *Lycidas.*

elem. elementary. **—el·e·ment** (EL·i·munt) *n.* **1** something basic, esp. a basic or constituent part: *the* **elements** *of algebra; the French ~ in English; criminal ~s of society; All matter is composed of 100-odd ~s, from actinium to zirconium;* **element 104** *and* **element 105** *are man-made radioactive ~s; There is an ~* (i.e. atom) *of truth in what he says.* **2** the environment, esp. as made up of the forces of nature; hence, rough weather; *a storm-tossed vessel at the mercy of the* **elements;** *Out of water, a fish is* **out of its element;** *She's* **in her element** *as a social worker.* **—el·e·men·tal** (–MEN·tl) *adj.* having to do with natural forces; also, basic: *the ~ fury of a volcano in action; sex, hunger, and such ~ urges; the ~ gods of the pagans.* **—el·e·men·ta·ry** (–MEN·tuh·ree) *adj.* basic or fundamental; primary; simple: *~ arithmetic; ~, my dear Watson! electron, proton, and, such supposedly indivisible* **elementary particles** *of matter; The first six (or sometimes eight) grades constitute* **elementary school.**

el·e·phant (EL·uh·funt) *n.* a huge, herbivorous mammal of Africa or Asia with a long snout, or trunk, and ivory tusks growing from either side of its upper jaw. **—el·e·phan·ti·a·sis** (–TYE·uh–) *n.* a tropical skin disease caused by a wormlike parasite and resulting in swelling and hardening of parts of the body. **—el·e·phan·tine** (–FAN·tine, –teen) *adj.* of or like elephants; huge, clumsy, etc.

elev. elevation. **—el·e·vate** (EL·uh–) *v.* **-vates, -vat·ed, -vat·ing** lift or raise, esp. to a higher rank, plane, or quality; also, elate or exhilarate: *a commoner ~d to the peerage; an ~ing religious experience; sagging spirits ~d by success; an* **elevated (railroad)** *with other traffic passing underneath.* **—el·e·va·tion** (–VAY–) *n.: the ~ of bishops to the cardinalate; flying at an ~ of 30,-000 ft.; You get a good view of the countryside from this ~; at an ~* (i.e. angular distance) *of 30° above the horizon.* **—el·e·va·tor** (EL·uh·vay·tur) *n.* **1** a cage or platform for traveling up and down in a building or mine. **2** a tall structure in which grain is stored. **3** a movable horizontal flap on the tail section of an aircraft for making it go up or down.

e·lev·en (i·LEV·un) *n., adj. & pron.* one more than 10; the number 11 or XI: *~ of them; ~*

boys; a football ~ (i.e. team); **e·lev·enth** *n.* & *adj.;* **eleventh hour** just before it is too late: *eleventh-hour preparation for an exam.*

elf *n.* **elves** (ELVZ) a mischievous little fairy. —**elf·in** or **elf·ish** *adj.* —**elf·ish·ly** *adv.* —**elf·ish·ness** *n.*

El Grec·o (–GREC·oh), 1541?–1614? Spanish painter.

el·hi (EL·hye) *adj.* of or having to do with elementary and high-school grades: *an* ~ *publishing division.*

e·lic·it (i·LIS·it) *v.* draw out: ~ *a response.* —**e·lic·i·ta·tion** (–TAY–) *n.*

e·lide (i·LIDE) *v.* **e·lides, e·lid·ed, e·lid·ing** drop or leave out a sound or syllable for euphony or rhythm, as *send'st* for *sendest.*

el·i·gi·ble (EL·i·juh·bl) *n.* & *adj.* (one) qualified or fit to be chosen. —**el·i·gi·bil·i·ty** (–BIL–) *n.*

E·li·jah (i·LYE·juh) in the Bible, a prophet of Israel in the 9th c. B.C.

e·lim·i·nate (i·LIM–) *v.* **-nates, -nat·ed, -nat·ing** get rid of; reject from within: *Body wastes are* ~*d; The primaries* ~ *the weaker candidates from the race; tighten a budget by* ~*ing unnecessary expenses.* —**e·lim·i·na·tion** (–NAY–) *n.: the* ~ *of poverty and hunger.*

e·lis·ion (i·LIZH·un) *n.* an eliding.

e·lite (i·LEET, ay–) *n.* **1** [takes *pl. v.*] a group considered to be superior: *a private school for the* ~. **2** a size of typewriter type that gives 12 characters to the linear inch. —**e·lit·ism** *n.* rule by an elite; **e·lit·ist** *n.* & *adj.*

e·lix·ir (i·LIK·sur) *n.* a fragrant alcoholic syrup containing medicine: *The alchemists sought the* **elixir of life,** *a mythical substance that would prolong life indefinitely.*

E·liz·a·beth (i·LIZ·uh–) **I** queen of England, 1558–1603; **Elizabeth II** born 1926, queen of Britain since 1952. —**E·liz·a·be·than** (–BEETH·un) *n.* & *adj.* (a person) of the time of Elizabeth I.

elk *n.* a large mooselike deer of N. Europe; also, the smaller North American wapiti.

ell *n.* **1** something L-shaped, as a joint of tubing or an annex to a building. **2** a former measure of cloth length, equal to 45 in. (112 cm): *"Give him an inch and he'll take an* ~*"* (i.e. take too much).

el·lipse (i·LIPS) *n.* **el·lip·ses** (–siz) an oval-shaped symmetrical closed curve. —**el·lip·sis** (–LIP–) *n., pl.* **-ses** (–seez) an omission of a word or words from a grammatically complete sentence, as in "I can and I will"; also, marks indicating this, as "A stitch in time. . . ." —**el·lip·soid** *n.* a slightly flattened sphere, as of the earth; whose plane sections are circles or ellipses; also ***adj.;*** **el·lip·soid·al** (–SOID–) *adj.* —**el·lip·ti·cal** or **-tic** *adj.: an elliptic* (i.e. ellipselike) *arch; elliptical geometry; elliptical* (i.e. marked by ellipsis) *language.* —**el·lip·ti·cal·ly** *adv.: The earth moves* ~ *around the sun.*

elm *n.* a family of large, hardy trees valued for lumber and shade.

el·o·cu·tion (–uh·CUE–) *n.* the art of public speaking. —**el·o·cu·tion·ist** *n.*

e·lon·gate (i·LONG·gate) *v.* **-gates, -gat·ed, -gat·ing** make or become longer, esp. out of proportion; **e·lon·gate** or **-gat·ed** *adj.: an elongate leaf; an elongated figure.* —**e·lon·ga·tion** (–GAY–) *n.*

e·lope (i·LOPE) *v.* **e·lopes, e·loped, e·lop·ing** run away together (to get married). —**e·lope·ment** *n.* —**e·lop·er** *n.*

el·o·quent (EL·uh–) *adj.* forceful or fluent in expression: *an* ~ *speech;* ~ *gestures;* **el·o·quent·ly** *adv.* —**el·o·quence** *n.*

El Pas·o (el·PAS·oh) a city in W. Texas.

El Sal·va·dor (el·SAL·vuh·dor) a country in Central America; 8,260 sq.mi. (21,393 km²); *cap.* San Salvador.

else (ELS) *adj.* [following modified pronoun] other: *Anyone* ~*? someone* ~*'s book.* —***adv.*** **1** in a different manner; at a different place or time: *How* ~*? Where* ~ *shall we go?* **2** otherwise: *Finish the job, (or)* ~ *you won't be paid; Finish it in time* **or else,** *she was warned.* —**else·where** *adv.* somewhere else.

e·lu·ci·date (i·LOO·suh–) **-dates, -dat·ed, -dat·ing** make (something) clear by illustrating or explaining. —**e·lu·ci·da·tion** (–DAY–) *n.*

e·lude (i·LOOD) *v.* **e·ludes, e·lud·ed, e·lud·ing** escape the mental or physical grasp of by some cunning quality: *The answer to this riddle* ~*s me; arrested after* ~*ing the police for a year;* **e·lud·er** *n.;* **e·lu·sion** (–LOO·zhun) *n.* —**e·lu·sive** (–LOO·siv) *adj.* hard to get, catch, or grasp: *an* ~ *concept;* ~ *like a will-o'-the-wisp;* **e·lu·sive·ly** *adv.;* **e·lu·sive·ness** *n.*

el·ver *n.* a young eel.

elves *pl.* of ELF.

E·ly·si·um (i·LIZH·ee·um, –LIZ–) in Greek myth, the abode of the virtuous after death; also **Elysian Fields; Elysium** *n.* paradise. —**E·ly·si·an** (i·LIZH·un) *adj.*

em *n.* the square of any type size; also, a unit of type measure, or "em pica," equal to about 1/16 in. (0.16 cm) —**'em** [short form] them. —**em-** *v. prefix.* as in *embalm, embattle, emboss.* —**EM** enlisted men.

e·ma·ci·ate (i·MAY·shee–, –see–) *v.* **-ates, -at·ed, -at·ing** make lean, as by hunger or illness. —**e·ma·ci·a·tion** (–AY–) *n.*

em·a·nate (EM·uh–) *v.* **-nates, -nat·ed, -nat·ing** originate, as from a source; also, emit: *From where do these rumors* ~*? the authority she* ~*s!* —**em·a·na·tion** (–NAY–) *n.*

e·man·ci·pate (i·MAN–) *v.* **-pates, -pat·ed, -pat·ing** to free from slavery or restraint; **e·man·ci·pa·tor** *n.* —**e·man·ci·pa·tion** (–PAY–) *n.: the* ~ *of women; President Lincoln's* **Emancipation Proclamation** *of 1863; Catholic* ~ *in Britain.*

e·mas·cu·late (i·MAS·kyuh–) *v.* **-lates, -lat·ed, -lat·ing** castrate; hence, weaken: *freedom of speech ~d by censorship;* **e·mas·cu·la·tor** *n.* —**e·mas·cu·la·tion** (–LAY–) *n.*

em·balm (im·BAHM) *v.* preserve (a dead body) from decay using spices, chemicals, etc.; hence, preserve; also, perfume. —**em·balm·er** *n.*

em·bank (im·BANK) *v.* protect or support with an **em·bank·ment** *n.* a bank of earth, stone, etc. raised to hold back water or support a roadway.

em·bar·go (im·BAR–) *n.* **-goes** a temporary government order prohibiting commerce with a foreign country, esp. the movement of ships or goods: *to lift the economic ~ against Cuba;* ***v.*** **-goes, -goed, -go·ing** prohibit or hold up: *mail to Canada ~d in U.S. during a strike; a press release ~d till 6 p.m.*

em·bark (im·BARK) *v.* **1** put (passengers or cargo) on board (ship, airplane, etc.). **2** get on board; hence, set out: *This is where you ~ for Europe; She is ~ing on a new career.* —**em·bar·ka·tion** (–KAY–) *n.*

em·bar·rass (im·BAIR·us) *v.* **1** make or become uneasy or nervous: *parents ~ed by a child's behavior; a sensitive child who ~es easily.* **2** hinder ease of movement; burden: *students ~ed by heavy workloads; pensioners much ~ed for life's necessities in inflationary times.* —**em·bar·rass·ing** *adj.* —**em·bar·rass·ment** *n.: social ~s of the underprivileged; a wealthy man's ~ of riches.*

em·bas·sy (EM·buh·see) *n.* **-bas·sies** a mission from one head of state to another; also, an ambassador and his staff, his position, residence, or offices abroad.

em·bat·tle (im·BAT–) *v.* usu. **em·bat·tled** *adj.* ready for battle.

em·bed (im·BED) *v.* **-beds, -bed·ded, -bed·ding** fix firmly; also, plant: *bricks ~d in mortar; an embryo ~d in the uterus wall.*

em·bel·lish (im·BEL–) *v.* decorate with added ornamentation; enhance: *a slightly ~ed truth, though not a falsehood.* —**em·bel·lish·ment** *n.*

em·ber *n.* a glowing piece of wood or coal in the remains of a fire; usu. **embers** *pl.*

em·bez·zle (–BEZL) *v.* **-bez·zles, -bez·zled, -bez·zling** steal (money, securities, etc. entrusted to one's care). —**em·bez·zle·ment** *n.* —**em·bez·zler** *n.*

em·bit·ter (–BIT–) *v.* make bitter or resentful. —**em·bit·ter·ment** *n.*

em·bla·zon (–BLAY·zn) *v.* **1** decorate with a coat of arms or other insignia. **2** extol. —**em·bla·zon·ment** *n.*

em·blem *n.* a representative object or identifying mark or design: *the hammer-and-sickle ~ of communism.* —**em·blem·at·ic** (–MAT–) *adj.: The cross is ~ of Christianity.*

em·bod·y (im·BOD·ee) *v.* **-bod·ies, -bod·ied, -bod·y·ing** **1** give form to (an ideal, thought, feelings, etc.); personify: *democratic ideals ~d in the U.S. constitution.* **2** incorporate; *The new models ~ many gas-saving features.* —**em·bod·i·ment** *n.: Solomon was the ~ of wisdom.*

em·bold·en (–BOLE·dun) *v.* give the courage (to do something).

em·bo·lism (EM·buh–) *n.* the blocking of an artery by an embolus. —**em·bo·lus** *n., pl.* **-li** (–lye) an object such as a blood clot, gas bubble, or globule of fat floating in the blood. —**em·bol·ic** (–BOL–) *adj.*

em·boss (–BOSS) *v.* make (a design, lettering, etc.) stand out on a surface; also, decorate in relief: *an ~ed letterhead.* —**em·boss·ment** *n.*

em·bou·chure (ahm·boo·SHOOR) *n.* the method of applying the lips to the mouthpiece of a wind instrument; "lipping."

em·bow·er (–BOW–) *v.* enclose in a bower.

em·brace (im·BRACE) *v.* **-brac·es, -braced, -brac·ing** **1** clasp with the arms to show love or friendship; hug: *He ~d her; Father and son ~d.* **2** contain; include: *an education ~ing all the arts and sciences.* **3** accept; take up: *left home to ~ the monastic life.* —***n.:*** *lovers' passionate ~s.*

em·bra·sure (–BRAY·zhur) *n.* a beveled opening in a wall with one side wider than the other, as for castle windows or in a parapet wall for firing guns through.

em·bro·cate (EM·bruh–) *v.* **-cates, -cat·ed, -cat·ing** rub (a body part) with a liniment. —**em·bro·ca·tion** (–CAY–) *n.* a liniment.

em·broi·der (im·BROY–) *v.* embellish, esp. with embroidery; hence, exaggerate. —**em·broi·der·y** *n.* **-der·ies** ornamenting of fabrics with needlework; hence, something so ornamented; also, an embellishment or exaggeration.

em·broil (–BROIL) *v.* involve (a person or country) in trouble, esp. in a quarrel. —**em·broil·ment** *n.*

em·bry·o (–bree·oh) *n.* **-os** an undeveloped plant (in its seed) or animal, as in a mother's womb, esp. during the first two months of pregnancy; **in embryo** in an undeveloped stage; **em·bry·on·ic** (–ON–) *adj.* —**em·bry·ol·o·gy** (–OL·uh·jee) *n.* the biology of the formation and development of embryos; **em·bry·ol·o·gist** *n.* —**em·bry·o·log·ic** (–LOJ–) or **-i·cal** *adj.*

em·cee *n. Informal* [short form] master of ceremonies; ***v.*** **-cees, -ceed, -cee·ing:** *a beauty pageant ~d by a TV star.*

e·mend (i·MEND) *v.* make scholarly corrections in (a text). —**e·men·da·tion** (–DAY–) *n.*

emer. emeritus.

em·er·ald (–uld) *n.* & *adj.* bright green (precious stone).

e·merge (i·MURJ) *v.* **e·merg·es, e·merged, e·merg·ing** come forth, as if from hiding; come out into view: *Venus ~d from the sea; New viruses have ~d* (i.e. evolved as new forms) *recently;* **e·mer·gent** *adj.: the ~ nations of*

Africa; **e·mer·gence** *n.* —**e·mer·gen·cy** *n.* **-cies** a suddenly arising situation requiring quick action, as a flood or heart attack: *the Emergency Broadcast System to warn by AM radio against an enemy attack.*

e·mer·i·tus (–MER–) *adj.* of a professor, retired from active service; ***n.,*** *pl.* **-ti** (–tye); *fem.* **-ta,** *pl.* **-tae** (–tee).

Em·er·son (–sun), **Ralph Waldo.** 1803–82; U.S. writer.

em·er·y *n.* **-er·ies** a hard, coarse corundum used for grinding and polishing, coated in powdered form on **emery board, emery cloth,** etc.

e·met·ic (i·MET–) *n.* & *adj.* (a substance) that induces vomiting.

E.M.F. or **e.m.f.** electromotive force.

-emia *n. suffix.* (specified) condition of the blood: as in *anemia, leukemia.*

em·i·grate *v.* **-grates, -grat·ed, -grat·ing** go (*from* one country or region) to settle in another; **em·i·grant** *n.* & *adj.;* **em·i·gra·tion** (–GRAY–) *n.* —**é·mi·gré** (EM·uh·gray) *n.* a political fugitive, as the Royalists who fled the French Revolution or Hungarians in 1956.

em·i·nence *n.* prominent or distinguished position: *his ~ as a scientist; Your Eminence* [form of addressing a cardinal]; *an ~* (i.e. elevated spot) *overlooking the sea;* **em·i·nent** *adj.* —**eminent domain** a government's right to appropriate private property for public use. —**em·i·nent·ly** *adv.*

e·mir (i·MEER) *n.* in Moslem countries, a ruler or chieftain; **e·mir·ate** (–it, –ate) *n.* an emir's territory.

em·is·sar·y (EM·i·ser·ee) *n.* **-is·sar·ies** one sent on a mission, often secret; also, a spy. —**e·mit** (i·MIT) *v.* **e·mits, e·mit·ted, e·mit·ting** send out or discharge (heat, fumes, odors, sounds, etc.) **e·mit·ter** *n.;* **e·mis·sion** *n.:* EPA standards for automobile ~ control.

Em·my (EM·ee) *n.* **Em·mys** an annual award for outstanding TV producers, performers, etc.

e·mol·li·ent (i·MOL·yunt) *n.* & *adj.* softening or soothing (agent, medicine, etc.).

e·mol·u·ment (i·MOL·yuh–) *n.* usu. **emoluments** *pl.* reward for work, usu. other than wages.

e·mote (i·MOTE) *v. Informal.* **e·motes, e·mot·ed, e·mot·ing** act emotionally. —**e·mo·tion** (–MOH–) *n.* an intense feeling, as joy, anger, love, or fear; **e·mo·tion·al** *adj.: an ~ speech; ~ character; ~ disorders;* **e·mo·tion·al·ly** *adv.;* **e·mo·tion·al·ism** *n.;* **e·mo·tion·al·ize** *v.* **-iz·es, -ized, -iz·ing** make emotional; express emotionally. —**e·mo·tive** (–tiv) *adj.*

emp. emperor; empress.

em·path·ic (–PATH–) *adj.* of or showing **em·pa·thy** (–puh·thee) *n.* identification with another's feelings or ideas; **em·pa·thize** *v.* **-thiz·es, -thized, -thiz·ing:** *to ~ with someone.*

em·pen·nage (–NAHZH) *n.* an aircraft's tail assembly.

em·per·or (–ur) *n.* the male ruler of an empire.

em·pha·sis (–fuh–) *n., pl.* **-ses** (–seez) special stress put on syllables, words, thoughts, actions, etc. because of their relative importance. —**em·pha·size** *v.* **-siz·es, -sized, -siz·ing:** *The speaker ~d each point by pounding the table.* —**em·phat·ic** (–FAT–) *adj.: "She does drive" is an ~ form; an ~ denial; an ~ "yes";* **em·phat·i·cal·ly** *adv.*

em·phy·se·ma (–fuh·SEE·muh) *n.* a lung disease in which the air sacs become enlarged, lose elasticity, and are unable to function efficiently.

em·pire *n.* a group of territories under a sovereign ruler, usu. an emperor; also, sovereign rule; hence, an extensive business or other organization with unified control: *financial ~.*

em·pir·ic (–PEER–) *n.* one who relies on practical experience. —**em·pir·i·cal** *adj.* **1** based on experiment and observation: *the ~ method of scientific research.* **2** based merely on practical experience: *an amateur doctor's ~ remedies;* —**em·pir·i·cal·ly** *adv.* —**em·pir·i·cism** *n.;* —**em·pir·i·cist** *n.* & *adj.*

em·place·ment (–PLACE–) *n.* a positioning; also, a platform on which heavy guns are placed for firing.

em·ploy (–PLOY) *v.* make use of or put to work on a regular basis: *I could use some help but couldn't afford to ~ you; a housewife not gainfully ~ed; methods ~ed to get votes; Skills not ~ed may atrophy; how to ~ your spare time.* —***n.*** service: *200 people in their ~.* —**em·ploy·a·ble** *adj.: an ~ alien; ~ skills.* —**em·ploy·e(e)** (em·PLOY·ee, –EE) *n.* one who is employed; **em·ploy·er** (–PLOY–) *n.* —**em·ploy·ment** *n.* an employing or being employed, esp. a job: *a housewife who has no problem finding (outside) ~; An* **employment agency** *places workers and bills employers for the service.*

em·po·ri·um (–POR·ee–) *n.* **-ri·ums** or **-ri·a** (–ee·uh) a large retail store with a variety of goods.

em·pow·er (–POW–) *v.* give (someone) power, authority, or ability (to do something).

em·press (–pris) *n.* an emperor's wife or the woman ruler of an empire.

emp·ty (–tee) *adj.* **-ti·er, -ti·est** containing nothing; also, meaningless: *"~ vessels make the most sound"; The house is ~ but not vacant; an ~ promise.* —***n.,*** *pl.* **-ties:** *Return the ~s* (i.e. containers) *for refund or refill.* —***v.*** **-ties, -tied, -ty·ing** make or become empty, often by pouring; also, discharge: *to ~ a pitcher; The hall ~d at the sound of the siren; The Volga ~s into the Caspian Sea.* —**emp·ty-hand·ed** *adj.* —**emp·ti·ly** *adv.* —**emp·ti·ness** *n.* —**empty set** *Math.* one without members; null set.

em·py·re·an (–pye·REE·un, –PEER·ee·un) *n.* the highest heaven; also, the sky. —***adj.*** heavenly; sublime; also **em·py·re·al.**

e·mu (EE·mew) *n.* a large flightless bird of Australia, related to but smaller than an ostrich.

e.m.u. or **E.M.U.** electromagnetic unit.

em·u·late (EM·yuh–) *v.* **-lates, -lat·ed, -lat·ing** try to equal or excel (an admired person or his qualities). **—em·u·la·tion** (–LAY–) *n.* **—em·u·la·tive** (EM·yuh·lay·tiv) *adj.* **—em·u·la·tor** (EM–) *n.* **—em·u·lous** (–lus) *adj.*

e·mul·si·fy (i·MUL–) *v.* **-fies, -fied, -fy·ing** make an emulsion of; **e·mul·si·fi·ca·tion** (–CAY–) *n.;* **e·mul·si·fi·a·ble** (–MUL·si·fye·uh·bl) *adj.;* **e·mul·si·fi·er** *n.* **—e·mul·sion** (i·MUL–) *n.* **1** a dispersion in the form of fine droplets of one liquid in another in which it does not dissolve, as oil in water or pigments in latex to make "emulsion paints." **2** a light-sensitive coating used on camera film, plates, or paper; **e·mul·si·ble** or **e·mul·sive** (–siv) *adj.*

en- *v. prefix.* as in *enable, enlighten, enliven.* — **-en** *suffix.* **1** [forming verbs] as in *darken, widen, broaden.* **2** [forming adjectives] as in *earthen, golden, wooden.*

en·a·ble (–AY·bl) *v.* **-bles, -bled, -bling** give ability or power, esp. legally: *Education ~s one to qualify for jobs; Congress has to pass an* **enabling act** *for a territory to become a state.*

en·act (in–) *v.* **1** pass (a bill or law); **en·act·ment** *n.* **2** act out (a role) on stage. **—en·ac·tor** *n.*

en·am·el (i·NAM·ul) *n.* **1** a hard, glasslike substance used to decorate and protect the surface of metal, glass, or pottery; also, a kind of glossy paint: *Kitchen appliances and bathroom fixtures are often* **en·am·el·ware** *metal products.* **2** the hard outer covering of a tooth. —***v.*** **-els, -el(l)ed, -el·(l)ing:** *an ~d brick; a Chinese ~d plate;* **en·am·el·(l)er** *n.*

en·am·or (i·NAM·ur) *v.* esp. **enamored of** very fond of: *He's quite ~d of her;* also **en·am·our** *Brit.*

en bloc as a whole; all together: *voted ~ to kill the legislation.*

enc(l). enclosure.

en·camp (–CAMP) *v.* camp; also, put (as soldiers) in a camp; **en·camp·ment** *n.*

en·cap·su·late (–CAP·suh–) *v.* **-lates, -lat·ed, -lat·ing** encase in or as if in a capsule; also **en·cap·sule** (–CAP·sl, –syool) **-sules, -suled, -sul·ing; en·cap·su·la·tion** (–LAY–) *n.* **—en·case** (in–) *v.* **-cas·es, -cased, -cas·ing** put in or as if in a case.

-ence See -ANCE.

encephal(o)- *comb. form.* brain: as in **en·ce·phal·ic** (en·suh·FAL–) *adj.* of or near the brain; **en·ceph·a·li·tis** (–sef·uh·LYE–) *n.* inflammation of the brain; **en·ceph·a·lit·ic** (–LIT–) *adj.* **—en·ceph·a·lo·gram** (–SEF·uh–) [short form] electroencephalogram.

en·chain (in–) *v.* chain; also, captivate; hold fast.

en·chant (in–) *v.* charm, as if with magic; bewitch; **en·chant·ing** *adj.;* **en·chant·ing·ly** *adv.* **—en·chant·er** *n.; fem.* **en·chant·ress** (–tris). **—en·chant·ment** *n.*

en·chi·la·da (–chuh·LAH·duh) *n.* a rolled tortilla with a filling of meat or cheese, peppers, etc.

en·ci·pher (–SYE·fur) *v.* put (a message) into cipher; **en·ci·pher·ment** *n.*

en·cir·cle (–SUR·cl) *v.* circle; **en·cir·cle·ment** *n.*

en·clave (EN–, AHN–) *n.* a territory of one country lying inside the boundaries of another: *Goa was a Portuguese ~ in India; Goa was Portugal's Indian* **ex·clave.**

en·close (in·CLOZE) *v.* **-clos·es, -closed, -clos·ing** **1** shut up, as with a fence: *an ~d convent* (i.e. of cloistered nuns). **2** include, as in an envelope or parcel: *an ~d check.* **—en·clo·sure** (–zhur) *n.* **1** something that shuts up, as surrounding walls; also, an enclosed space, as a corral. **2** something included, as a check with a covering letter.

en·code (in–) *v.* **-codes, -cod·ed, -cod·ing** put (a message) into code: *In a color telecast, three primary color signals are combined in an* **en·cod·er** *for transmission.*

en·co·mi·um (–COH·mee–) *n.* **-ums** or **-mi·a** (–uh) *Formal.* high praise; eulogy.

en·com·pass (–CUM·pus) *v.* **1** contain, as if encircled: *a mind that could ~ vast knowledge.* **2** accomplish: *a plot that ~ed his ruin.*

en·core (AHNG·core) *interj.* once more! repeat! —***n.*** a popular call to repeat a stage performance or act; also, a repetition made in response to such a call; ***v.:*** *The audience ~d the violinist three times.*

en·coun·ter (in·COWN–) *v.* come up against; confront: *to ~ difficulties;* ***n.*** an unexpected meeting; also, a confrontation; ***adj.:*** *Members of an* **encounter group** *meet in sensitivity-training sessions to talk about and act out hostile feelings and reactions to help them get along with others more effectively.*

en·cour·age (in·CUR·ij) *v.* **-ag·es, -aged, -ag·ing** give courage, hope, confidence, support, etc., esp. to do something; also, stimulate; foster: *The news was quite* **encouraging.** **—en·cour·age·ment** *n.* **—en·cour·ag·ing·ly** *adv.*

en·croach (in·CROHCH) *v.* trespass or intrude (*on* or *upon* someone's land, time, or other property) gradually: *The sea ~es on land by erosion.* **—en·croach·ment** *n.*

en·crust (in–) *v.* cover with, form, or form into a crust: *shoes ~ed with mud.* **—en·crus·ta·tion** (–TAY–) *n.*

en·cul·tu·rate (–CUL·chuh–) *v.* **-ates, -at·ed, -at·ing** adapt to the habits, ideas, attitudes, etc. of the society one lives in; **en·cul·tu·ra·tion** (–RAY–) *n.*

en·cum·ber (in·CUM–) *v.* burden, obstruct, or crowd, as with a large family, debts, junk, etc. so as to hinder freedom of movement or action: *a page ~ed with footnotes.* **—en·cum·brance** (–brunce) *n.*

ency(c). encyclopedia.
-ency See -ENCE.
en·cyc·li·cal (in·SIC–) *n.* a letter from the Pope to bishops worldwide. —**en·cy·clo·p(a)e·di·a** (in·sye·cluh·PEE·dee·uh) *n.* a book or set of books providing wide information on every field of knowledge or on a specific area if a specialized work. —**en·cy·clo·p(a)e·dic** (–PEE·dic) *adj.: a man of ~ knowledge.*
en·cyst (–SIST) *v.* enclose or become enclosed in a cyst. —**en·cyst·ment** *n.*
end *n.* **1** an extremity or limit, as of a line or of anything extended in space or time: *Tie a knot at each ~ of the rope; The meeting came to an ~ at midnight; the front ~ and the rear ~ of a car; ~s play at each ~ of the line in football; an old man nearing his ~* (i.e. death); *The gruesome sight made his hair* **stand on end** (i.e. straight up or out); *raining for days* **on end** (i.e. continuously); *He gave us* **no end** (i.e. a great deal) *of trouble; The unemployed find it hard to* **make (both) ends meet** (i.e. make income equal expenditures). **2** a fragment or piece of something having extension: *Gather all the candle ~s from the cake;* ODDS AND ENDS. **3** goal; purpose: *Have your ~ clearly in view; Does the ~ justify the means?* —***v.:*** *The school year ~s with graduation; The gunman* **ended up** *in jail.*
en·dan·ger (–DAIN·jur) *v.* put in danger, as of death: *With few of them left, whooping cranes are an* **endangered species.**
en·dear (–DEER) *v.* make dear or lovable: *the* **endearing** *ways of children;* **en·dear·ing·ly** *adv.* —**en·dear·ment** *n.* something that expresses affection, as a word or caress: *"Honey" is a term of ~.*
en·deav·or (in·DEV·ur) *v.* try or attempt, esp. in an earnest and sustained manner: *~ to do good;* ***n.:*** *a lifetime of honest ~ to succeed.*
en·dem·ic (–DEM–) *adj.* belonging to a particular region because of favorable conditions, as certain plants and diseases: *Is complacency ~ to academic groups?* —***n.:*** *Epidemics come and go but an ~ tends to remain in a region or community.*
end·ing *n.* the last part: *a story with a happy ~; "-es" is a plural ~* (i.e. suffix).
en·dive *n.* either of two varieties of a salad vegetable that is related to chicory, one with curled leaves and the other *(escarole)* with broad, smooth leaves.
end·less *adj.* **1** eternal or boundless, or seeming so: *an ~ nuisance, stretch of sea.* **2** with the ends joined together: *the ~ chain of a block and tackle;* **end·less·ly** *adv.;* **end·less·ness** *n.* —**end man** either of the two men at the ends of a line of performers in a minstrel show who carry on a comic conversation with the interlocutor or "straight man." —**end·most** *adj.* farthest.
endo- *comb.form.* within; inner: as in **en·do·car·di·um** (–CAR–) *n.* the membrane lining the inside of the heart. —**en·do·crine** (–crin, –crine) *adj.* having to do with an **endocrine (gland),** as the thyroid, adrenal, and pituitary, that secretes hormones directly into the bloodstream; also, hormonal; **en·do·cri·nol·o·gy** (–cri·NOL·uh·jee) *n.;* **en·do·cri·nol·o·gist** *n.* —**en·dog·a·my** (–DOG·uh·mee) *n.* the custom of marrying within one's own tribe; **en·dog·a·mous** (–mus) *adj.* —**en·dog·e·nous** (–DOJ·uh·nus) *adj.* growing or developing from within, as spores within a cell or a disease from inside the body; **en·dog·e·nous·ly** *adv.* —**en·do·plasm** *n.* the inner part of a cell's cytoplasm; cf. ECTOPLASM.
end organ a terminal structure, as the retina (end organ of vision) and other nerve endings in the body.
en·dorse (in·DORCE) *v.* **-dors·es, -dorsed, -dors·ing** **1** sign (a check, money order, or a document), usu. on the back, as indication of approval. **2** approve of or support (a candidate, product, service, etc.) —**en·dorse·ment** *n.* —**en·dors·er** *n.*
en·do·scope (–duh–) *n.* an instrument for examining the inside of a hollow organ such as the bladder or rectum; **en·do·scop·ic** (–SCOP–) *adj.* —**en·do·ther·mic** (–THUR–) *adj.* having to do with absorption of heat: *Ice and salt form an ~ mixture;* also **en·do·ther·mal.**
en·dow (en·DOW) *v.* provide (someone) with money, property, talents, or other asset: *well ~ed by nature with beauty and wit;* **en·dow·ment** *n.: a million-dollar ~* (i.e. fund) *for a college; an ~ (insurance) policy.*
end product the final result of a series of processes or activities. —**end run** a football play in which the ball carrier tries to run around one end of the opponent's line; hence, an evasive tactic. —**end table** a small low table used beside a sofa or other larger piece of furniture.
en·due (en–) *v.* **-dues, -dued, -du·ing** usu. **endued with,** provided with (a quality).
en·dure (en–) *v.* **-dures, -dured, -dur·ing** **1** tolerate; bear (something or someone), esp. for a long time; **en·dur·ance** *n.* **2** last; continue in existence, esp. in spite of opposite influences; **enduring** *adj.: an ~ peace.* —**en·dur·a·ble** *adj.* —**en·dur·o** (en·DURE·oh) *n.* an endurance race.
end use the final use to which a product is put; **end-us·er** or **end-con·sum·er** *n.* —**end·ways** or **end·wise** *adj. & adv.* with the end forward; lengthwise; on end. —**end zone** in a football field, the 10 yds. behind either goal line.
-ene *n. suffix.* hydrocarbon: as in *benzene, naphthalene.* —**E.N.E.** east-northeast.
en·e·ma (EN·i·muh) *n. Med.* the sending up of a liquid (as a purgative) into the rectum.
en·e·my (–mee) *n.* **-mies** one who wishes to harm or hates another; also, anything harmful or injurious: *Indifference is the ~ of progress.*

en·er·get·ic (–JET–) *adj.* vigorous; forceful; **en·er·get·i·cal·ly** *adv.* —**en·er·gize** (–jize) *v.* **-giz·es, -gized, -giz·ing** give energy to; **en·er·giz·er** (–jye·zur) *n.* —**en·er·gy** (EN·ur·jee) *n.* **-gies** capacity for action; ability to do work: *a youngster full of ~; All her* **energies** *are applied to winning a gold medal; Solar ~, chemical ~, electrical ~, mechanical ~, and atomic ~ are different kinds; potential and kinetic ~ are forms of ~.*

en·er·vate *v.* **-vates, -vat·ed, -vat·ing** lessen the physical, mental, or moral vigor of, as by a hot, damp climate, indulgence in luxury, etc. —**en·er·va·tion** (–VAY–) *n.*

en·fee·ble (in·FEE·bl) *v.* **-bles, -bled, -bling** make feeble; debilitate. —**en·fee·ble·ment** *n.*

en·fi·lade (EN·fuh·lade, –fuh·lahd) *n.* gunfire along the length of a line of enemy troops.

en·fold (in–) *v.* wrap up; also, embrace.

en·force (in–) *v.* **forc·es, forced, forc·ing** force (esp. obedience to, understanding of, etc.): *Police ~ the law; ~d idleness due to hospitalization; facts and figures to ~ an argument.* —**en·force·a·ble** *adj.* —**en·force·ment** *n.*

en·fran·chise (in·FRAN·chize) *v.* **-chis·es, -chised, -chis·ing** give voting rights to; also, set free (slaves). —**en·fran·chise·ment** (–chiz·munt, –chize–) *n.*

eng. engine; engineer(ing). —**Eng.** England; English.

en·gage (in·GAJE) *v.* **1** be busy, occupied, or involved: *scientists ~d in research; ~d in conversation.* **2** promise or bind (oneself): *She's ~d to (marry) my brother; He ~d himself as an apprentice for 3 years.* **3** hold; lock together; also, meet in combat: *Trinkets ~ a child's attention; The gears won't ~; He ~d the foe in hand-to-hand combat.* **4** hire: *to ~ a lawyer.* —**en·gaged** *adj.* —**en·gage·ment** *n.: a day crowded with outside ~s; an ~ ring for my beloved; territory recaptured after a brief ~ with the enemy.* —**en·gag·ing** *adj.* pleasing; charming; **en·gag·ing·ly** *adv.*

En·gels (ENG·gulz), **Friedrich.** 1820–1895, German socialist and associate of Karl Marx.

en·gen·der (in·JEN–) *v.* give rise to; produce: *Poverty ~s crime.*

en·gine (EN·jun) *n.* a mechanism, esp. one that uses fuel energy to produce work: *medieval ~s of warfare; a steam ~; an internal-combustion ~.* —**en·gi·neer** (–NEER) *n.* one who designs, manages, or operates machinery and systems to utilize power and materials: *an electrical ~; mining ~; sanitary ~.* —***v.*** plan and manage: *a demonstration ~ed by students.* —**en·gi·neer·ing** *n.* the profession of an engineer; the scientific use of energy and materials for practical purposes.

Eng·land (ING·glund) the United Kingdom exclusive of Northern Ireland, Scotland, and Wales; *cap.* London. —**Eng·lish** (ING·glish) *n.* **1** the Germanic language of England, used also in the British Commonwealth, the U.S., and other countries. **2 the English** *pl.* the people of England. —***adj.*** having to do with England, its people, or its language. —**English Channel** the strait separating England from the European continent. —**English horn** a woodwind instrument similar to the oboe but larger and with a lower tone. —**Eng·lish·man** (–mun) *n.* **-men** a person, esp. a man, born or living in England; *fem.* **Eng·lish·wom·an, -wom·en.**

engr. engineer; engraved.

en·graft (in–) *v.* graft (a shoot) from one plant to another; hence, implant.

en·gram *n.* the supposed change in the nerve tissue of the brain that explains memory, learning, etc.

en·grave (in–) *v.* **-graves, -graved, -grav·ing** cut, carve, or etch (letters, designs, etc.) in (wood, stone, metal, etc.) esp. for printing from; hence, impress: *childhood experiences ~d in his memory.* —**en·grav·ing** *n.* —**en·grav·er** *n.*

en·gross (in·GROSE) *v.* **1** absorb the entire attention of: *~ed in homework; an* **engrossing** *thriller.* **2** copy (a text, as of a document) in large handwriting. —**en·gross·ment** *n.*

en·gulf (in–) *v.* swallow up, as by waves: *~ed by fear.*

en·hance (in–) *v.* **-hanc·es, -hanced, -hanc·ing** raise or increase (the value, beauty, or other desirable quality): *prestige ~d by victories.* —**en·hance·ment** *n.*

e·nig·ma (uh·NIG·muh) *n.* a perplexing person (because of a mixture of conflicting qualities) or a thing of ambiguous or cryptic nature. —**e·nig·mat·ic** (–MAT–) or **-i·cal** *adj.: the Mona Lisa's enigmatic smile;* **e·nig·mat·i·cal·ly** *adv.*

en·jamb(e)·ment (in·JAM·munt) *n.* the running on of a sentence from one verse to the next, as in blank verse: "Nor tackle, sail, nor mast; the very rats/Instinctively had quit it."

en·join (in–) *v.* **1** command: *Secrecy had been ~ed on them.* **2** prohibit by an injunction.

en·joy (in–) *v.* have, esp. take pleasure in: *to ~ good health;* **enjoy oneself** have a good time. —**en·joy·a·ble** (–JOY·uh–) *adj.* —**en·joy·ment** *n.*

enl. enlarged; enlisted.

en·large (in·LARJ) *v.* **-larg·es, -larged, -larg·ing** make or become larger; **enlarge (up)on** discuss at length; expatiate on. —**en·large·ment** *n.*

en·light·en (in·LITE·n) *v.* inform, esp. so as to remove misunderstanding, error, etc.: *an instructive and* **enlightening** *talk; Can you ~ me on your interest rates?* —**en·light·en·ment** *n.*

en·list (in–) *v.* join or get (someone) to join the military or a cause or undertaking; **enlisted man** in the armed forces, one who is not an officer, from recruit to sergeant major and corresponding grades. **—en·list·ee** (–TEE) *n.* **—en·list·ment** *n.*

en·liv·en (in·LYE·vun) *v.* put life into (a party, surroundings, or something dull).

en masse (en·MAS) all together; in one body: *The staff resigned ~.*

en·mesh (in–) *v.* take in or as if in a net; entangle.

en·mi·ty (–muh·tee) *n.* **-ties** hostility or hatred, as between enemies.

en·no·ble (in·NOH·bl) *v.* **-bles, -bled, -bling** raise to noble rank; also, make noble: *a character purified and ~d by suffering.* **—en·no·ble·ment** *n.*

en·nui (ahn·WEE) *n.* boredom; weariness.

e·nor·mi·ty *n.* **-ties** **1** outrageous or monstrous quality, as of a crime, wickedness, offense, etc.; also, such an offense itself. **2** *Informal.* vastness or immensity, as of a task, problem, etc.; also **e·nor·mous·ness. —e·nor·mous** (i·NOR·mus) *adj.* very much exceeding the normal size, amount, or degree: *an ~ appetite; ~ expense;* **e·nor·mous·ly** *adv.*

e·nough (i·NUF) *adj.* sufficient: *was man ~ to apologize to her; There are blankets ~* (i.e. a sufficient number) *for everyone; There is ~ food* (i.e. a sufficient quantity); *food ~ for everyone.* ***—n.*** & ***pron.*** a sufficient number or amount: *I've had ~ of this; That will be ~.* ***—adv.:*** *Sure ~ he was late* (i.e. as usual); *well ~ to sit up in bed; glad ~* (i.e. quite glad) *to get out.* **—e·now** (i–) *Archaic.* enough.

en·plane (en–) *v.* **-planes, -planed, -plan·ing** board an aircraft.

enquire, enquiry same as INQUIRE, INQUIRY.

en·rage (in–) *v.* **-rag·es, -raged, -rag·ing** put in a rage; infuriate.

en·rap·ture (in·RAP–) *v.* **-tures, -tured, -tur·ing** transport with joy.

en·rich (in–) *v.* make rich; improve in quality: *vitamin-~ed cereal.* **—en·rich·ment** *n.*

en·rol(l) (in·ROLE) *v.* **-rolls, -rolled, -roll·ing** enter on a roll or list, as a member of a body (of students, electors, or a club). **—en·rol(l)·ment** *n.*

en route (ahn·ROOT) on the way (to or from a place).

ENS or **Ens.** Ensign.

en·sconce (in–) *v.* **-sconc·es, -sconced, -sconc·ing** establish (oneself) securely or snugly.

en·sem·ble (ahn·SAHM·bl) *n.* an integrated set or whole whose parts together produce a single effect, as a matching costume and accessories, music of several parts, a group of singers or actors performing cooperatively, etc.: **ensemble playing** (or **acting**) *does not promote the star system.*

en·shrine (in–) *v.* **-shrines, -shrined, -shrin·ing** enclose in or as in a shrine; hence, keep or cherish as sacred: *civil rights ~d in the constitution.*

en·shroud (in–) shroud or veil.

en·sign (EN·sn) *n.* **1** (*also* EN·sine) a flag or emblem. **2** the lowest rank of commissioned officer in the U.S. Navy.

en·si·lage (EN·suh·lij) *n.* ensiled green fodder. **—en·sile** (en·SILE) *v.* **-siles, -siled, -sil·ing** preserve (fodder) in a silo.

en·slave (in–) *v.* **-slaves, -slaved, -slav·ing** make a slave of. **—en·slave·ment** *n.*

en·snare (in–) *v.* **-snares, -snared, -snar·ing** snare; also, catch as in a net.

en·sue (in–) *v.* **-sues, -sued, -su·ing** follow, esp. as a consequence; result: *a drought and then a famine in the ~ing year; After the heavy rains a flood ~d.*

en·sure (in·SHOOR) *v.* **-sures, -sured, -sur·ing** make certain or secure: *Registration ~s delivery of mail.*

-ent same as -ANT.

en·tail (in–) *v.* **1** make (something) necessary (as a requirement): *Success ~s hard work.* **2** *Law.* limit (property) to a specified inheritor or line of heirs. **—en·tail·ment** *n.*

en·tan·gle (in·TANG·gl) *v.* **-gles, -gled, -gling** make or be tangled in a difficult or perplexing situation: *got ~d in a family feud.* **—en·tan·gle·ment** *n.*

en·tente (ahn·TAHNT) *n.* a friendly understanding, esp. between governments; also, the parties to this.

en·ter *v.* **1** go or come in (to); also, join: *~ed the house through the window; knock before ~ing; ~ the practice of law; ~ the army; Don't* **enter into** *an argument with him.* **2** enroll or get into (a group, list, or record): *time to ~your child in school; words ~ed in a dictionary; ~ a plea of guilty; ready to* **enter (up)on** *a new career.*

enter(o)- *comb.form.* intestine: as in **en·ter·ic** (–TER–) *adj.* intestinal; **en·ter·i·tis** (–RYE–) *n.* inflammation of the intestines; **en·ter·o·vi·rus** (–VYE–) *n.* any of a group of RNA viruses that infect the alimentary canal.

en·ter·prise (–prize) *n.* a project or undertaking that requires initiative and daring; also, these qualities; **en·ter·pris·ing** *adj.: an ~ businessman.*

en·ter·tain (–TAIN) *v.* **1** receive as a guest: *The Smiths ~ed the Joneses; They ~ a lot on weekends.* **2** please or amuse: *children ~ed by a clown; The show was very* **en·ter·tain·ing** *adj.;* **en·ter·tain·er** *n.;* **en·ter·tain·ment** *n.* **3** consider; hold in the mind: *to ~ doubts.*

en·thral(l) *v.* **-thral(l)s, -thralled, -thrall·ing** captivate by fascinating. **—en·thral(l)·ment** *n.*

en·throne (–THRONE) *v.* **-thrones, -throned, -thron·ing** put on a throne; hence, exalt. **—en·throne·ment** *n.*

en·thuse (in·THEWZ) *v.* **-thus·es, -thused, -thus·ing** *Informal.* show or fill with **en·thu·si·asm** (–zee·azm) *n.* intense interest or admiration approaching zeal; **en·thu·si·ast** *n.* one who is keenly interested in something.

—**en·thu·si·as·tic** (–AS–) *adj.;* **en·thu·si·as·ti·cal·ly** *adv.*

en·tice (in–) *v.* **-tic·es, -ticed, -tic·ing** lure or tempt by skillful or crafty means. —**en·tice·ment** *n.*

en·tire (in–) *adj.* whole; unbroken as a unit: *The ~ audience broke into cheers.* —**en·tire·ly** *adv.* quite; completely: *I ~ agree with you.* —**en·tire·ty** *n.: a proposal rejected* **in its entirety.**

en·ti·tle (in·TYE–) *v.* **-tles, -tled, -tl·ing** **1** give a claim or right (*to* something): *You're ~d to your opinions.* **2** title: *a book ~d "Roots."* —**en·ti·tle·ment** *n.*

en·ti·ty *n.* **-ties** existence; also, a person or thing that has independent existence.

entom(ol). entomological; entomology.

en·tomb (in·TOOM) *v.* place in a tomb; bury. —**en·tomb·ment** *n.*

en·to·mol·o·gy (–tuh·MOL·uh·jee) *n.* a branch of zoology concerned with the study of insects; **en·to·mol·o·gist** *n.* —**en·to·mo·log·i·cal** (–LOJ–) *adj.*

en·tou·rage (ahn·too·RAHZH) *n.* a group of attendants; retinue.

en·tr'acte (ahn·TRACT) *n.* the interval between two acts of a stage performance; also, a show put on during this period.

en·trails *n.pl.* the inner parts, esp. intestines, from a body; guts.

en·train (in–) *v.* put or go on board a train.

[1]**en·trance** (in–) *v.* **-tranc·es, -tranced, -tranc·ing** transport with joy, as in a dream or trance; **en·tranc·ing** *adj.: an ~ beauty;* **en·tranc·ing·ly** *adv.*

[2]**en·trance** (EN·trunce) *n.* **1** the act of entering. **2** a door or other passageway; also **en·trance·way.** **3** permission or right to enter; admission. —**en·trant** *n.* one who enters.

en·trap (in–) *v.* **-traps, -trapped, -trap·ping** catch (as) in a trap. —**en·trap·ment** *n.*

en·treat (in·TREET) *v.* ask earnestly and persuasively. —**en·treat·y** *n.* **-treat·ies** an earnest request.

en·trée or **en·tree** (AHN·tray) *n.* **1** the right or freedom to enter. **2** the main dish of a meal.

en·trench (in–) *v.* put trenches around; hence, fortify or make secure. —**en·trench·ment** *n.*

en·tre·pre·neur (ahn·truh·pruh·NOOR) *n.* one who organizes and manages a business, assuming risks and seeking profits. —**en·tre·pre·neur·i·al** *adj.*

en·tro·py (EN·truh·pee) *n.* **-pies** a property of matter by which the heat generated in doing work results in a lessening of available energy in a system and its gradual winding down; the tendency to inertness.

en·trust (in–) *v.* trust (someone) with a responsibility; also, trust (a responsibility) to (someone): *I ~ these valuables to your care; ~ him with my money.*

en·try (–tree) *n.* **-tries** **1** the act, right, or a place of entering, as a door or gate. **2** the act of placing in a record or listing, as of words entered alphabetically in a dictionary; also, a thing or person so entered, as an **entry word** or a competitor in a contest.

en·twine (in–) *v.* **-twines, -twined, -twin·ing** twine together or around.

e·nu·mer·ate (i·NEW–) *v.* **-ates, -at·ed, -at·ing** count; also, list or name one by one; **e·nu·mer·a·tor** *n.* —**e·nu·mer·a·tion** (–AY–) *n.*

e·nun·ci·ate (i·NUN·see–) *v.* **-ates, -at·ed, -at·ing** pronounce, esp. clearly; also, set forth systematically, as a theory or doctrine. —**e·nun·ci·a·tion** (–AY–) *n.: an announcer with good ~* (i.e. manner of pronunciation).

en·u·re·sis (en·yoo·REE–) *n.* *Med.* habitual bed-wetting.

env. envelope. —**en·vel·op** (in·VEL·up) *v.* **-ops, -oped, op·ing** cover completely: *mountain tops ~d in mist;* **en·vel·op·ment** *n.* —**en·ve·lope** (EN·vuh·lope, AHN–) *n.* a cover, esp. a flat paper container for mailing letters in.

en·ven·om (in·VEN·um) *v.* taint with venom or poison; also, embitter.

en·vi·a·ble (EN·vee·uh–) *adj.* worthy of being envied: *my former aide now in an ~ position;* **en·vi·a·bly** *adv.* —**en·vi·ous** (–us) *adj.* feeling or showing envy: *Cinderella's sisters were ~ of her beauty and jealous of her success with the prince;* **en·vi·ous·ly** *adv.;* **en·vi·ous·ness.** *n.*

en·vi·ron·ment (in·VYE·run·munt) *n.* surroundings, esp. as affecting the development of an individual or community. —**en·vi·ron·men·tal** (–MEN–) *adj.: Pesticides, exhaust fumes, and industrial wastes cause ~ pollution; ~ art, sculpture, and theater involve or engage the viewer as well as artist; The Environmental Protection Agency deals with pollution problems;* **en·vi·ron·men·tal·ist** *n.* —**en·vi·rons** (–VYE–) *n.pl.* surroundings; also, suburbs.

en·vis·age (–VIZ·ij) *v.* **-ag·es, -aged, -ag·ing** form a detailed mental picture of, esp. under some particular aspect such as the future; picture; also **en·vi·sion** (–VIZH·un).

en·voy (EN–, AHN–) *n.* **1** a messenger. **2** a diplomat ranking next below ambassador. **3** a short farewell message in the form of a literary postscript or concluding stanza; also **en·voi.**

en·vy (–vee) *n.* **-vies** ill feeling because of a rival's accomplishment; also, the object of the feeling: *"green with ~"; our sports car, the ~ of the neighborhood; racked by petty jealousies and ~s.* —***v.*** **-vies, -vied, -vy·ing:** *John ~s Tim's blond hair; Some girls ~ him;* **en·vy·ing·ly** *adv.*

en·zyme (–zime) *n.* a mostly protein, complex catalytic substance secreted by living cells that is found in yeast and digestive juices and that helps in the breakdown of fats, carbohydrates, etc.: *Body irritants may be released by ~ detergents while helping to dissolve stains.* —**en·zy·mat·ic** (–MAT–) *adj.*

E·o·cene (EE·uh·seen) *n.* & *adj.* (of) the second epoch of the Cenozoic era of the earth beginning about 55 million years ago, marked by the rise of mammals: ~ *rocks.*

eolian same as AEOLIAN.

e·o·lith·ic (ee·uh·LITH–) *adj.* of the early Stone Age, characterized by crude stone tools, or **e·o·liths** (EE–).

e.o.m. end of month.

e·on (EE·un, –on) *n.* a long and indefinite period of time; an age.

-eous *adj. suffix.* having the nature of: as in *aqueous, erroneous, vitreous.*

EPA Environmental Protection Agency.

ep·au·let(te) (EP·uh·let) *n.* an ornamental shoulder pad on a military uniform.

e·pee or **é·pée** (EP·ay, ay·PAY) *n.* a sharp-pointed, rigid sword with a circular guard used in fencing.

e·pergne (i·PURN) *n.* a tiered ornamental dish or stand for fruit, candy, etc., used on a dining table as a centerpiece.

e·phed·rine (i·FED·rin) *n.* a drug that shrinks mucous membranes, used in treating asthma, hay fever, etc.

Eph(es). Ephesians (New Testament book).

e·phem·er·al (i·FEM·uh·rul) *adj.* short-lived, as glory or pleasures; originally, lasting no more than a few days, as certain plants, insects such as the mayfly, or **e·phem·er·ids,** and a fever of cattle.

epi- *prefix.* on; among: as in *epicenter, epidemic.*

ep·ic *n.* & *adj.* (a long poem) in a majestic style or heroic in nature: *the* ~ *deeds of Ulysses; Homer's* ~*s; an action-packed western movie* ~.

ep·i·cen·ter *n.* the point on the earth's surface directly above the focus of an earthquake. **—ep·i·cen·tral** (–SEN–) *adj.*

ep·i·cure *n.* a person with a highly refined taste for food and wine. **—ep·i·cu·re·an** (–kew·REE·un) *n.* same as EPICURE; ***adj.*** given to sensuous pleasure, esp. of eating and drinking.

ep·i·dem·ic (–DEM–) *adj.* spreading rapidly, as contagious diseases. ***—n.*** an epidemic disease; also, any rapid development, as of a fad; cf. ENDEMIC. **—ep·i·dem·i·cal·ly** *adv.* **—ep·i·de·mi·ol·o·gy** (–dee·mee·OL·uh·jee) *n.* the branch of medicine concerned with epidemics.

ep·i·der·mis (–DUR–) *n.* the outer layer of the skin. **—ep·i·der·mal** *adj.*

ep·i·glot·tis (–GLOT–) *n.* a lidlike piece of elastic cartilage that closes the windpipe during swallowing.

ep·i·gram *n.* a terse witty saying, esp. one with a paradox in it, e.g. "Revenge is a kind of wild justice." **—ep·i·gram·mat·ic** (–MAT–) *adj.* **—e·pig·ra·phy** (i·PIG·ruh·fee) *n.* the study of ancient inscriptions.

ep·i·lep·sy *n.* **-sies** a chronic nervous disorder marked by convulsions and unconsciousness. **—ep·i·lep·tic** (–LEP–) *n.* one who has epilepsy; ***adj.:*** *an* ~ *fit.*

ep·i·log(ue) (–log) *n.* a concluding act or piece, as at the end of a play, poem, etc.; cf. PROLOG.

ep·i·neph·rin(e) (–NEF·rin) *n.* an adrenal hormone used therapeutically to stimulate the heart, relax muscles, etc.

E·piph·a·ny (i·PIF·uh·nee) *n.* a Christian festival held on January 6 in commemoration of the visit of the Magi to Jesus at Bethlehem.

ep·i·phyte (EP·uh·fite) *n.* same as AIR PLANT.

e·pis·co·pa·cy (i·PIS·cuh·puh·see) *n.* **-cies 1** episcopal government. **2** episcopate. **—e·pis·co·pal** (i·PIS·cuh·pl) *adj.* of bishops; also **E·pis·co·pal:** *the* **(Protestant) Episcopal Church** *of the U.S.;* **E·pis·co·pa·li·an** (–PAIL·yun) *n.* & *adj.* (a member) of this church. **—e·pis·co·pate** (i·PIS·cuh·pit) *n.* a bishop's rank, term of office, or see; also, bishops collectively.

ep·i·sode *n.* an incident in a continuous course of events that is complete in itself, as in a literary or artistic work; hence, such a musical passage; also, any occurrence or event: *an* ~ *of his childhood; a coronary* ~. **—ep·i·sod·ic** (–SOD–) *adj.;* **ep·i·sod·i·cal·ly** *adv.*

e·pis·tle (i·PISL) *n. Formal.* a letter; **Epistle** one of the apostolic letters of the New Testament. **—e·pis·to·lar·y** (i·PIS·tuh·ler·ee) *adj.*

ep·i·taph (–taf) *n.* a short inscription, as on a tombstone or tablet, in memory of a dead person.

ep·i·tha·la·mi·um (–thuh·LAY·mee·um) *n.* a wedding song.

ep·i·the·li·um (–THEE·lee·um) *n., pl.* **-li·a** (–lee·uh) a kind of tissue that covers body surfaces, as the skin and mucous membrane. **—ep·i·the·li·al** (–lee·ul) *adj.*

ep·i·thet *n.* a word or phrase to characterize someone, usu. descriptive, as "doubting Thomas," often disparaging, as "bloody fool."

e·pit·o·me (i·PIT·uh·mee) *n.* a summary or abstract giving essential features; hence, a representative or type: *Satan, the* ~ *of evil.* **—e·pit·o·mize** *v.* **-miz·es, -mized, -miz·ing** make a summary of; also, typify.

e plu·ri·bus u·num (ee·PLOOR·i·bus·YOO·num) *Latin.* "out of many, one," a U.S. motto.

ep·och (EP·uk, EE·pok) *n.* a period of time, esp. with reference to some memorable event; era: *Man's moon-landing was an* **ep·och-mak·ing** *event.* **—ep·och·al** (EP·uh·kul) *adj.*

ep·ox·y (EP·ox·ee, ep·OX·ee) *n.* **-ox·ies** a durable synthetic resin used for adhesives, protective coatings, etc.; ***v.*** **-ox·ies, -ox·ied, -ox·y·ing** to glue with epoxy resin.

ep·si·lon *n.* the fifth letter of the Greek alphabet (E, ϵ).

Ep·som (–sum) **salt(s)** a white crystalline magnesium salt used as a laxative.

eq. equal; equation. **—eq·ua·ble** (EK·wuh·bl) *adj.* not liable to change suddenly; steady: *an* ~ *temper;* **eq·ua·bly** (–blee) *adv.;* **eq·ua·bil·i·**

ty (–BIL–) *n.* —**e·qual** (EE·kwul) *adj.* of the same amount, number, size, value, degree, spread, advantage, etc.; even; uniform: *A dollar divides into 4 ~ parts of 25¢ each; The right to* **equal time** *on radio or TV to air an opposing view; ~ employment opportunity for minorities; I don't feel* **equal to** (i.e. fit enough for) *the usual walk today;* ***n.:*** *David and Goliath were not ~s;* ***v.*** **e·quals, e·qual(l)ed, e·qual·(l)ing:** *4 + 5 equals 3 × 3; a record that has not been ~d, let alone broken.* —**e·qual·ly** *adv.* —**e·qual·i·ty** (–KWOL–) *n.* **-ties** the state or an instance of being equal: *~ of opportunity.* —**e·qual·ize** (EE·kwul–) *v.* **-iz·es, -ized, -iz·ing** make equal, even, or uniform; **e·qual·iz·er** *n.;* **e·qual·i·za·tion** (ee·kwuh·li·ZAY–) *n.* —**equal time** See EQUAL, *adj.* —**e·qua·nim·i·ty** (–NIM–) *n.* evenness of mind or temper. —**e·quate** (–KWAIT) *v.* **e·quates, e·quat·ed, e·quat·ing** treat (one thing) as equal (to another): *Do not ~ happiness with wealth;* **e·quat·a·ble** *adj.* —**e·qua·tion** *n.* **1** a statement in which two quantities are balanced with an equal sign (=). **2** a variable element in a complex whole; also, a correction or allowance for this; factor: *the human ~; the personal ~.* —**e·qua·tor** (–KWAY·tur) *n.* an imaginary circle around a sphere, esp. the earth or a heavenly body, to divide it equally into N. and S. hemispheres; also, the corresponding circle in the celestial sphere; **e·qua·to·ri·al** (–TOR·ee·ul, EK·wuh–) *adj.* having to do with the earth's equator: *an ~ current;* **Equatorial Guinea** a republic on the African west coast; 10,830 sq. mi. (28,051 km²); *cap.* Malabo (Santa Isabel).

eq·uer·ry (EK·wuh·ree, i·KWER·ee) *n.* **eq·uer·ries** an officer attending on a member of the British royal family; formerly, one in charge of horses. —**e·ques·tri·an** *n.* & *adj.* (a rider) on horseback: *a circus performer's ~ skills; ~ events at the Olympics; The Roman ~ order served in the cavalry;* **e·ques·tri·enne** (–tree·EN) *n. fem.*

equi- *comb. form.* equal(ly): as in **e·qui·an·gu·lar** (–ANG·gyuh–) *adj.* having all angles equal, as a square. —**e·qui·dis·tant** (–DIS·tunt) *adj.* equally distant. —**e·qui·lat·er·al** (–LAT–) *n.* & *adj.* (a figure) having all sides equal. —**e·qui·lib·ri·um** (–LIB·ree–) *n.* state of balance; also, poise.

e·quine (EE–, EK·wine) *n.* & *adj.* (of or like) a horse.

e·qui·nox (EE·kwuh–) *n.* either of two times, about March 21 and September 22, when the sun crosses the equator and day and night are of equal length all over the globe. —**e·qui·noc·tial** (–NOK·shul) *adj.:* *~ gales produced by the fast change in the sun's position.*

equip. equipment. —**e·quip** (i·KWIP) *v.* **e·quips, e·quipped, e·quip·ping** supply or provide with what is needed to make an occupation or function more efficient: *a car ~d with power steering; a party well ~d for camping out;* **e·quip·ment** *n.* —**e·quip·age** (EK·wi·pij) *n.* a carriage with horses, driver, and attendants.

e·qui·poise (EK·wuh·poiz) *n.* even balance; also, a force or weight that restores balance; counterbalance. —**eq·ui·ta·ble** (EK·wi·tuh–) *adj.* characterized by equity; *preferential hiring of minority candidates considered ~ by some and unjust by others;* **eq·ui·ta·bly** *adv.*

eq·ui·ta·tion (–TAY–) *n.* horsemanship.

eq·ui·ty (EK·wit·ee) *n.* **-ties** **1** fairness; justice; hence, law that goes beyond common law and statutes, based on reason and the spirit of the law: *a court of ~.* **2** what a property is worth beyond what is owed on it.

equiv. *Abbrev.* for **e·quiv·a·lent** (i·KWIV·uh–) *n.* & *adj.* (something) having equal force, value, effect, etc.: *Today's dollar is the ~ of a quarter some years back; Few words have exact ~s in different languages;* **e·quiv·a·lence** *n.* —**e·quiv·o·cal** (i·KWIV·uh·cl) *adj.* capable of more than one interpretation; hence, doubtful; suspicious: *an ~ reply;* **e·quiv·o·cal·ly** *adv.* —**e·quiv·o·cate** (–KWIV·uh–) *v.* **-cates, -cat·ed, -cat·ing** use words of double meaning in order to deceive; **e·quiv·o·ca·tion** (–CAY–) *n.:* *"~ is halfway to lying";* **e·quiv·o·ca·tor** (–KWIV·uh–) *n.*

-er **1** *n. suffix.* agent or other person or thing related to thing specified: as in *gardener, singer, six-footer.* **2** *comp. suffix:* as in *harder, taller.* —**Er** erbium.

e·ra (EER·uh, AIR·uh) *n.* a period of time, esp. one starting from a particular event or one with distinctive characteristics: *the Christian ~; the Victorian ~.* —**ERA** Equal Rights Amendment.

e·rad·i·cate (i·RAD–) *v.* **-cates, -cat·ed, -cat·ing** uproot; hence, get rid of completely; eliminate: *reforms to ~ social injustices;* **e·rad·i·ca·tor** *n.* —**e·rad·i·ca·tion** (–CAY–) *n.*

e·rase (i·RACE) *v.* **e·ras·es, e·rased, e·ras·ing** wipe out, esp. by rubbing or scraping, as by a rubber **e·ras·er,** or magnetically, as by a tape recorder's **erase head; e·ras·a·ble** (–RAY·suh–) *adj.* —**e·ras·ure** (–shur) *n.*

E·ras·mus (i·RAZ·mus), **Desiderius.** 1466?–1536, Dutch humanist.

er·bi·um (UR·bee·um) *n.* a rare-earth metallic element.

ere (AIR) *prep.* & *conj. Archaic.* before.

e·rect (i·RECT) *adj.* upright, esp. straight, not bent or lying down: *~ posture.* —***v.*** make erect; put up (a building, statue, etc.); hence, establish: *a monument ~ed in memory of war heroes;* **e·rec·tion** *n.;* **e·rect·ly** *adv.;* **e·rect·ness** *n.;* **e·rec·tor** *n.* —**e·rec·tile** (–REC·tl) *adj.* capable of erection, as the penis or clitoris.

ere·long (air·LONG) *adv.* before long.

er·e·mite (ER·uh–) *n.* hermit.

erg (URG) *n.* the unit of energy in the metric system.

er•go (UR–) *adv.* therefore; hence.

er•go•nom•ics (–NOM–) *n.pl.* the science of human work and efficient working conditions.

er•gos•ter•ol (–GOS·tuh·role) *n.* a steroid alcohol, prepared from yeast or ergot that produces vitamin D when exposed to ultraviolet light and is used in preventing and curing rickets. **—er•got** (UR·gut) *n.* a parasitic fungus of cereal plants, esp. rye.

Er•ie (EER·ee) **1 Lake.** one of the five Great Lakes. **2** a city in N.W. Pennsylvania.

Er•in *Poetic.* Ireland.

er•mine (UR·min) *n.* the white winter fur of a weasel, esp. the stoat, that is valuable as trimming and is traditionally used on the robes of European judges and peers as a symbol of rank; **er•mined** *adj.*

e•rode (i·RODE) *v.* **e•rodes, e•rod•ed, e•rod•ing** wear away by gradual action, esp. of water, wind, acid, etc.: *Canyons are the result of* **e•ro•sion** (–zhun) *n.;* **e•ro•sion•al** *adj.* **—e•ro•sive** (–siv) *adj.;* **e•ro•sive•ness** *n.*

e•rog•e•nous (i·ROJ·uh·nus) or **er•o•gen•ic** (air·uh·JEN–) *adj.* sexually sensitive, as the genital, oral, and such zones of the body; also, arousing sexual desire. **—E•ros** (AIR·os, EER–) the Greek god of love.

erosion, erosive See ERODE.

e•rot•ic (i·ROT–) *adj.* of or having to do with sexual love; **e•rot•i•cal•ly** *adv.* **—e•rot•i•ca** (–i·cuh) *n.pl.* erotic literature or art.

err (UR, AIR) *v.* do or be wrong.

er•rand (ER·und) *n.* a trip to carry out something (as to deliver a message) for someone else; also, the object of the trip: *hired to run ~s for the boss; Florence Nightingale's ~ of mercy.*

er•rant (ER·unt) *adj.* **1** roving: *an ~ knight.* **2** straying: *~ sheep.* **—er•rat•a** (–RAH·tuh) *n.pl.* errors made (in a book or other publication). **—er•rat•ic** (–RAT–) *adj.* irregular or eccentric: *~ behavior; an ~ clock;* **er•rat•i•cal•ly** *adv.* **—er•ro•ne•ous** (uh·ROH·nee·us, er·OH–) *adj.* mistaken; incorrect; **er•ro•ne•ous•ly** *adv.* **—er•ror** (AIR·ur) *n.* something mistaken, a wrong or incorrect action, a misplay or failure in a game, etc.; mistake: *She's in ~ about my birth date; an ~ of judgment.*

er•satz (UR·zahts, ER–) *adj.* a substitute or imitation product, usu. inferior: *the ~ culture of the newly rich.*

Erse (URCE) *n.* & *adj.* same as GAELIC.

erst(•while) *adv. Archaic.* formerly. **—erst•while** *adj.* former: *her ~ admirer.*

ERTS *n.* Earth Resources Technology Satellite.

e•ruct (i·RUCT) *v.* belch. **—e•ruc•ta•tion** (–TAY–) *n.*

er•u•dite (ER·yuh–, ER·uh–) *adj.* learned; scholarly; **er•u•dite•ly** *adv.* **—er•u•di•tion** (–DISH–) *n.*

e•rupt (i·RUPT) *v.* break out or burst forth: *Volcanoes ~ (lava); hot water and steam ~ing from a geyser; A riot ~s; Milk teeth ~ during a baby's first year.* **—e•rup•tion** *n.: rashes and other skin ~s.* **—e•rup•tive** (–tiv) *adj.*

-ery *n. suffix.* place, occupation, condition, quality, etc.: as in *archery, bakery, savagery.*

er•y•sip•e•las (–SIP·uh·lus) *n.* a painful infectious skin disease appearing on the scalp or face as a dark red, patchy inflammation; also called "St. Anthony's fire."

er•y•the•ma (–THEE·muh) *n.* reddening of the skin due to infection, allergy, etc. **—erythro-** *comb. form.* red: as in **e•ryth•ro•cyte** (–RITH–) *n.* red blood cell; **e•ryth•ro•my•cin** (–MY·sin) *n.* an antibiotic similar in action to penicillin.

Es einsteinium. **-es** *suffix.* **1** plural noun: as in *ashes, glasses, ladies, leaves.* **2** third pers. sing. pres. tense of verb: as in *defies, goes, washes.*

E•sau (EE·saw) in the Bible, the older son of Isaac and brother of Jacob.

es•ca•late (ES·cuh–) *v.* **-lates, -lat•ed, -lat•ing** rise as on an escalator; hence, increase, expand, intensify, develop, etc.; **es•ca•la•tion** (–LAY–) *n.* **—es•ca•la•tor** (ES·cuh·lay·tor) *n.* a moving staircase on an endless belt; **escalator clause** a provision for adjusting wages, prices, etc. usu. upward under specified conditions; **es•ca•la•tor•y** (–luh·tor·ee) *adj.: a settlement considered too ~.*

es•cal•(l)op (–SCAL–, –SCAH–) same as SCALLOP.

es•ca•pade (ES·cuh–) *n.* an adventurous act, esp. one involving freedom from restraint. **—es•cape** (–CAPE) *v.* **-capes, -caped, -cap•ing 1** get away (from): *convicts ~ing from prison; Air has ~d from the tire; A cry of pain ~d her lips; Her name ~s* (i.e. eludes) *me.* **2** stay free of: *Many criminals ~ being caught; ~d death by sheer luck.* **—*n.*** an escaping or a means of escaping: *a narrow ~ from death; Romances are her favorite ~* (i.e. from reality): *He clambered down the fire ~.* **—*adj.:*** *an ~ hatch; ~ valves, velocity.* **—es•cap•ee** (–PEE) *n.* one that has escaped, esp. from confinement. **—es•cape•ment** *n.* a device, as in a timepiece or a typewriter, that regulates movement by means of a ratchet mechanism.**—escape velocity** the minimum velocity required to be free of a gravitational field and move into outer space. **—es•cap•ism** *n.* flight from unpleasant realities, responsibilities, etc. by means of diversions; **es•cap•ist** *n.* & *adj.: an ~ attitude.*

es•ca•role (ES·cuh–) *n.* See ENDIVE.

es•carp•ment (is·CARP–) *n.* a steep slope or embankment.

-escence *n. suffix.* corresponding to **-escent** *adj. suffix.* **1** beginning to be: as in *luminescent, obsolescent.* **2** displaying light: as in *incandescent, iridescent.*

es•chew (es·CHOO) *v.* shun; avoid: *~ vice.*

es•cort *n.* (ES–) a person or group accompanying another to give protection or as courtesy: *a police ~; came to the dance without an ~* (i.e. male companion); **—v.:** (–CORT) *The receptionist ~ed the visitor to the door; 50 aircraft ~ed the royal yacht.*

es·crow (ES·croh) *n. Law.* esp. **in escrow,** of a *grantor's* money, deeds, bonds, etc., held by a third party, or *escrow agent,* to be given to the *grantee* when terms stated in a contract are met.

es·cu·do (–COO·doh) *n.* **-dos** the basic monetary unit of Chile and Portugal, equal to 100 centesimos (Chile) or centavos (Portugal).

es·cutch·eon (is·CUTCH·un) *n.* a shield or similar plate on which a coat of arms is displayed.

E.S.E. east-southeast.

-ese *n. & adj. suffix.* (of a) country or dialect: as in *Portuguese, Chinese, legalese.*

Es·ki·mo (–cuh·moh) *n.* **-mos** one of a native people of the Arctic, properly called "the Inuit"; also, their language; **Es·ki·mo(·an)** (–MOH·un) *adj.* **—Eskimo dog** any of several breeds of powerful dogs used to pull sleds in the Arctic, including the Siberian husky and the Alaskan malamute.

e·soph·a·gus (i·SOF·uh–) *n., pl.* **-gi** (–jye) the tube that carries food down to the stomach; gullet.

es·o·ter·ic (–TER–) *adj.* of a system, ideas, doctrine, literature, etc., unintelligible except to those initiated; abstruse.

esp. especially. **—ESP** extrasensory perception.

es·pa·drille (ES·puh·dril) *n.* a light canvas shoe with plaited or rubber sole.

es·pal·ier (–PAL·yur) *n.* a shrub or tree trained to grow flat on a framework; also, the lattice or other framework used.

es·pe·cial (–PESH·ul) *adj.* special in a preeminent manner; exceptional: *a special consideration given in her ~ case.* **—es·pe·cial·ly** *adv.*: *an ~ severe winter.*

Es·pe·ran·to (–puh·RAHN·toh) *n.* an artificial international language based on common elements of European languages, e.g. "Esperanto meritas vian konsideron" (Esperanto deserves your consideration).

es·pi·o·nage (ES·pee·uh·nahzh, –nij) *n.* spying for political, military, or industrial purposes.

es·pla·nade (–pluh·NAHD, –NADE) *n.* a place designated as a public walk or drive, usu. along a shore.

es·pous·al (i·SPOW·zl) *n.* an espousing of a cause or idea; **espousals** *n.pl.* formerly, betrothal or wedding ceremonies; **es·pouse** (–SPOWZ) *v.* **-pous·es, -poused, -pous·ing** advocate; adopt; take up.

es·pres·so (–PRES–) *n.* **-pres·sos** coffee brewed under steam pressure.

es·prit (–PREE) *n.* lively wit. **—es·prit de corps** (es·pree·duh·COR) group spirit; comradeship.

es·py (es·PYE) *v.* **-pies, -pied, -py·ing** catch sight of, esp. something small or partly hidden.

-esque *adj. suffix.* like: as in *arabesque, picturesque, statuesque.*

Esq(r). *Abbrev.* for **es·quire** (ES·kwire) *n.* an Anglo-Saxon title used formally after a man's surname to show courtesy instead of "Mr." or other prefixed title: *John Smith, Esq.*

-ess *n. suffix.* female: as in *empress, lioness, mistress;* [considered discriminatory in] *Jewess, negress, poetess,* etc.

es·say (ES·ay) *n.* **1** a literary composition, usu. short and in prose, less formal than a treatise; **es·say·ist** *n.* **2** (*also,* es·AY) a trial; attempt. **—v.** (*usu.* es·AY) attempt: *Before leaping in, she ~ed to find out how deep the water was;* **es·say·er** *n.*

es·sence (ES·nce) *n.* **1** the basic or most important nature or quality, as "greenness" of *grass: The ~ of good manners is thoughtfulness; Time is* **of the essence** (i.e. a most important consideration) *in an emergency.* **2** something abstracted, extracted, or distilled, as the gist of a speech, a meat extract, a perfume, etc. **—es·sen·tial** (i·SEN·shul) *adj.*: *Attar of roses is an* **essential oil** *extracted from rose petals; Shelter is necessary for survival, but food is ~ to life;* **n.** *The three R's are the ~s of a good education;* **es·sen·tial·ly** *adv.*

est. established; estimate(d). **—E.S.T.** Eastern Standard Time. — **-est** *suffix.* **1** *adj. & adv.* superlative degree: as in *greatest; soonest.* **2** *v. Archaic.* second pers. sing. pres. tense: as in *singest, walkest;* also **-st** as in *canst, didst.* **—est** Erhard Seminars Training.

es·tab·lish (uh·STAB–) *v.* set up on a firm foundation; hence, make accepted: *a company ~ed in 1827; A dentist ~es himself in a neighborhood; It takes time for a practice to get ~ed as a custom; Words get ~ed by usage; evidence needed to ~ a motive; the state-~ed Church of England.* **—es·tab·lish·ment** *n.* an establishing or thing established, as a household or business with all its members or employees; also **the Establishment,** the socially dominant group; the elite: *The ~ prefers Scotch to marijuana and pinstripes to jeans; the literary ~.*

es·tate (is·TATE) *n.* **1** a large property, including a house: *an industrial ~.* **2** what one owns, esp. as left by a deceased person: *real ~; an ~ tax.* **3** condition or stage in life: *The boy reached man's ~* (i.e. adulthood); *The nobles, clergy, and common people were the* **three estates;** See FOURTH ESTATE.

es·teem (is·TEEM) *n.* high regard. **—v.** regard highly; also, consider: *Your ~ed journal; I ~ it an honor.*

es·ter *n.* an organic compound resulting from the reaction of an acid with an alcohol, as fats and oils.

Esth. Esther (Old Testament book). **—Es·ther** (ES·tur) in the Bible, the Jewish wife of a

Persian king who saved her people from massacre.

esthete, esthetic, etc. same as AESTHETE, AESTHETIC, etc.

es·ti·ma·ble (ES·tuh·muh·bl) *adj.* worthy of esteem. **—es·ti·mate** *v.* **-mates, -mat·ed, -mat·ing** judge or give an approximate calculation of the worth, size, etc. of: *I ~ the project will cost $100,000;* ***n.*** (–mit) an opinion, esp. an approximate calculation: *What is your ~ for producing this book?* **—es·ti·ma·tor** *n.* **—es·ti·ma·tion** (–MAY–) *n.* an opinion or judgment; also, esteem.

Es·to·ni·a (–TOE–) a constituent republic of the U.S.S.R. in N.E. Europe; *cap.* Tallinn. **—Es·to·ni·an** *n.* & *adj.* (a person from or the Finno-Ugric language) of Estonia.

es·trange (is·TRAINJ) *v.* **-trang·es, -tranged, -trang·ing** make (a friend or relative) indifferent or unfriendly: *living alone, ~d from family and friends.* **—es·trange·ment** *n.*

es·tro·gen (ES·truh·jun) *n.* a group of sex hormones (including "estrone," "estriol," and "estradiol") that are responsible for a woman's secondary female characteristics; **es·tro·gen·ic** (–JEN–) *adj.* **—es·trus** *n.* the period of heat in female mammals excepting primates; **es·trous** (–trus) *adj.*

es·tu·ar·y (ES·choo·er·ee) *n.* **-ar·ies** the mouth of a large river into which the tide flows from the sea.

-et *n. suffix.* little: as in *baronet, sonnet, tablet, turret.*

e·ta (AY·tuh, EE–) *n.* the seventh letter of the Greek alphabet (H, η).

E.T.A. estimated time of arrival.

et al. (et·AL) *Abbrev.* and others. **—etc.** *Abbrev.* for **et cet·er·a** (et·SET·uh·ruh, –SET·ruh) and other things; and so forth.

etch (ECH) *v.* produce (a drawing or other design) on (a metal or glass plate) by the action of acid; hence, engrave deeply: *a tragic event ~ed in her memory;* **etch·er** *n.* **—etch·ing** *n.* the art or the process used in making etched designs; also, such a design or its engraved plate.

E.T.D. estimated time of departure.

e·ter·nal (i·TUR·nl) *adj.* timeless; also, everlasting; perpetual: *the "~ triangle" of a third party involved with a married couple; Rome, the "~ city," because of its long history; the ~ flame at John Kennedy's grave; God* **the Eternal. —e·ter·nal·ly** *adv.* **—e·ter·ni·ty** *n.* **-ties** endlessness of time; also, an infinite or seemingly endless period; *an ~ of anxious waiting.*

-(e)th *v. suffix. Archaic.* third person sing. pres. tense: as in *doth, walketh.* See also -TH.

eth·ane (ETH–) *n.* a refrigerant or fuel gas got from natural gas and coal gas. **—eth·a·nol** (ETH·uh–) *n.* ethyl alcohol. **—e·ther** (EE·thur) *n.* **1** a colorless, volatile, sweet-smelling liquid got by the action of sulphuric acid on ethyl alcohol and used as an anesthetic. **2** the invisible substance once thought to fill all space; **e·the·re·al** (i·THEER·ee·ul) *adj.* heavenly; also, airy; light: *her ~ beauty; ~ music;* **e·the·re·al·ly** *adv.*

eth·ic (ETH–) *n.* a rule of conduct; also, a system of such rules: *the Protestant work ~;* **ethics** *n.pl.* **1** [takes *sing. v.*] moral philosophy; also, the moral quality of an action. **2** [takes *pl. v.*] rules of conduct: *His professional ~ are atrocious.* **—eth·i·cal** *adj.*: *The firing was quite legal though not ~* (i.e. not morally right); *very ~ as a lawyer though a man of poor morals; An "ethical drug" is a prescription drug;* **eth·i·cal·ly** *adv.*

E·thi·o·pi·a (ee·thee·OH·pee·uh) an E. African country; 471,778 sq. mi. (1,221,900 km²); *cap.* Addis Ababa. **—E·thi·o·pi·an** *n.* & *adj.*

eth·nic (ETH–) *adj.* of or having to do with people, esp. of minorities, grouped according to linguistic, national, religious, or racial characteristics; ethno-cultural: *The French are an ~ group in the U.S. but one of Canada's two founding nations; an ~ restaurant;* ***n.*** a member of an ethnic group; **eth·ni·cal·ly** *adv.*: *The Scots and the Irish are ~ quite close.* **—eth·nic·i·ty** (–NIS–) *n.*: *immigration quotas based on ~.* **—ethno-** (ETH·noh–) *comb.form.* ethnic: as in **eth·no·cen·trism** *n.* ethnic chauvinism; **eth·no·cul·tur·al** *adj.* ethnic. **—ethnol.** *Abbrev.* for **eth·nol·o·gy** (–NOL·uh·jee) *n.* the anthropology of racial and cultural groups, their origins, distribution, and characteristics; **eth·nol·o·gist** *n.*; **eth·no·log·ic** (–LOJ–) or **-i·cal** *adj.*; **eth·no·log·i·cal·ly** *adv.*

e·thol·o·gy (–THOL·uh·jee) *n.* the biology of animal behavior; **eth·o·log·i·cal** (–LOJ–) *adj.* **—e·thos** (EE–) *n.* the distinctive moral and ethical attitude of a person or group; code of values.

eth·yl (ETH·ul) *n.* the hydrocarbon base of common alcohol, ether, etc.; **Ethyl** *Trademark.* an antiknock lead and ethyl compound for mixing with gasoline; **eth·yl·ic** (–THIL–) *adj.* **—eth·yl·ene** (–uh·LEEN) *n.* a gaseous hydrocarbon with an unpleasant odor used as an anesthetic, to make polyethylene, and in **ethylene glycol,** automobile antifreeze.

e·ti·ol·o·gy (ee·tee·OL·uh·jee) *n.* **-gies** the study of origins or causes, esp. of diseases, as a branch of medicine. **—e·ti·o·log·ic** (–LOJ–) or **-i·cal** *adj.*

et·i·quette (ET·i·kut, –ket) *n.* conventional rules of behavior, as in polite society, a particular profession, etc.: *Social ~ includes table manners.*

E·trus·can (i·TRUS·cun) *n.* & *adj.* (of or having to do with) the extinct language of or a tribe of people that lived in ancient **E·tru·ri·a** (–TROOR–) in W.C. Italy.

et seq. and the following (ones).

-ette *n. suffix.* **1** female: as in *majorette, usherette.* **2** small; also, imitation or substitute: as in *cigarette, leatherette, flannelette.*

é·tude (AY·tude) *n.* a piece of instrumental music written esp. for students to practice various techniques.

ETV educational television.

ety(m). *Abbrev.* for **et·y·mol·o·gy** (et·i·MOL·uh·jee) *n.* **-gies** the study of the origin and development of words; also, the history of a particular word; **et·y·mol·o·gist** *n.* —**et·y·mo·log·i·cal** (–LOJ–) *adj.*

Eu europium. —**eu-** *n.* & *adj. suffix.* good; well; true: as in *euphony, euphonious, euphoria.*

eu·ca·lyp·tus (yoo·cuh·LIP–) *n.* a tall evergreen tree of the myrtle family, valued for its medicinal oil and timber.

Eu·cha·rist (YOO·cuh–) *n.* Communion or the consecreted bread and wine used in it. —**Eu·cha·ris·tic** (–RIS–) or **-ti·cal** *adj.*

eu·chre (YOO·cur) *n.* a card game played with the 32 highest cards of the pack.

Eu·clid (YOO–) Greek mathematician of the 3rd cent. B.C. —**Eu·clid·e·an** (–CLID·ee·un) or **Eu·clid·i·an** *adj.: ~ geometry.*

eu·gen·ics (yoo·JEN–) *n.pl.* [takes *sing. v.*] the science of improving the human race by selective control of reproduction and thereby heredity. —**eu·gen·ic** *adj.;* **eu·gen·i·cal·ly** *adv.;* **eu·gen·i·cist** *n.*

eu·lo·gy (YOO·luh·jee) *n.* **-gies** a formal speech or a piece of writing in high praise of a person or event; **eu·lo·gist** *n.;* **eu·lo·gis·tic** (–JIS–) *adj.* —**eu·lo·gize** (YOO·luh–) *v.* **-giz·es, -gized, -giz·ing** praise highly **eu·lo·giz·er** *n.*

eu·nuch (YOO·nuk) *n.* a castrated man.

eu·phe·mism (YOO·fuh–) *n.* an inoffensive term used in place of another considered offensive, e.g., "funeral director" for *undertaker.* —**eu·phe·mis·tic** (–MIS–) *adj.;* **eu·phe·mis·ti·cal·ly** *adv.*

eu·phe·nics (yoo·FEN·ix) *n.* the science of improving human beings by genetic engineering and by surgical means.

eu·pho·ny (YOO·fuh·nee) *n.* **-nies** pleasantness or smoothness of sounds, esp. spoken. —**eu·pho·ni·ous** (–FOH·nee·us) *adj.: "Syllabication" is more ~ than "syllabification"; ~ music.*

eu·pho·ri·a (yoo·FOR·ee·uh) *n.* a feeling of well-being or high spirits (*Slang:* "highs"), esp. as produced by drugs such as amphetamines or cocaine. —**eu·phor·ic** *adj.;* **eu·phor·i·cal·ly** *adv.*

Eu·phra·tes (yoo·FRAY·teez) a river in S.W. Asia that joins the Tigris in Iraq and flows into the Persian Gulf.

Eur. Europe(an). —**Eu·rail·pass** (YOOR–) *n.* a discount ticket for tourist travel on European railroads. —**Eur·a·sia** (yoo·RAY·zhuh) Europe and Asia as one land mass; **Eur·a·sian** *adj.* of or having to do with Eurasia; ***n.*** a person of mixed European and Asian descent.

eu·re·ka (yoo·REE·kuh) *interj.* indicating triumph at a discovery; Greek for "I have found it," as Archimedes exclaimed on solving a problem.

Eu·rip·i·des (yoo·RIP·i·deez), 480?–406? B.C.; Greek dramatist.

Eur(o)- *comb. form.* Europe: as in *Eurasia, Eurobond.* —**Eu·ro·bond** *n.* a bond issued by a non-European, esp. U.S. corporation, for sale in Europe and paid for in the currency of the country of issue, as **Eu·ro·dol·lars,** U.S. dollars deposited in European banks, or **Eu·ro·banks,** handling such funds. —**Eu·rope** (YOOR·up) the continent west of Asia and north of Africa; **Eu·ro·pe·an** (–uh·PEE·un) *n.* & *adj.;* **European Economic Community** the common market formed by Belgium, Netherlands, Luxembourg, France, West Germany, and Italy, later joined by Denmark, Ireland, and the U.K.; **European plan** a hotel charging rate that covers room but not meals; cf. AMERICAN PLAN. —**eu·ro·pi·um** (yoo·ROH·pee·um) *n.* a rare-earth chemical element. —**Eu·ro·po·cen·tric** (–SEN–) *adj.* considering Europe as the center of the world.

eu·r(h)yth·mic (yoo·RITH–) *adj.* having to do with **eur(h)ythmics** *n.pl.* a system of musical training through expressive bodily movements.

Eu·sta·chi·an (yoo·STAY·shun, –kee·un) **tube** a tube that connects the middle ear with the throat and helps equalize pressure on both sides of the eardrum by taking in air, as when swallowing.

eu·tha·na·si·a (yoo·thun·NAY·zhuh) *n.* the causing of death in order to end prolonged suffering in terminal cases; mercy killing.

eu·then·ics (yoo·THEN–) *n.pl.* [takes *sing. v.*] improvement of the human race by control of environmental factors.

eu·troph·i·cate (yoo·TROF–) *v.* **-cates, -cat·ed, -cat·ing** of bodies of water, to become **eu·troph·ic** *adj.* polluted by excess of nutrients such as nitrates and phosphates from human wastes; **eu·troph·i·ca·tion** (–CAY–) or **eu·troph·y** (YOO·truh·fee) *n.*

E.V.A. extravehicular activity.

e·vac·u·ate (i·VAC·yoo–) *v.* **-ates, -at·ed, -at·ing** **1** empty (bowels, stomach, etc.); hence, discharge (bodily wastes). **2** remove (people) or withdraw from (a building or area); **e·vac·u·ee** (–yoo·EE) *n.* an evacuated person. —**e·vac·u·a·tion** (–AY–) *n.*

e·vade (i·VADE) *v.* **e·vades, e·vad·ed, e·vad·ing** use trickery to escape or dodge (enemies, responsibilities, and other unwelcome things): *She successfully ~d the reporters' question: Taxes may be avoided but not ~d; a draft* **e·vad·er** *n.*

e·val·u·ate (i·VAL·yoo–) *v.* **-ates, -at·ed, -at·ing** determine the amount, quality, or value of (nonmaterial things such as evidence, someone's performance, career, etc.). —**e·val·u·a·tion** (–AY–) *n.*

ev·a·nes·cent (–NES–) *adj.* tending to fade away from sight; vanishing: *an ~ dream;* **ev·a·nes·cence** *n.*

e·van·gel·i·cal (i·van·JEL–) *adj.* **1** relating to the four Gospels. **2** of Protestant churches such as the Methodist and Baptist, stressing faith and the preaching of the Gospels rather than ritual and good works for salvation; ***n.*** a member of such a church. Also **e•van•gel•ic.** —**e•van•gel•i•cal•ism** (–JEL–) or **e•van•gel•ism** (–VAN–) *n.* —**e•van•gel•ist** (–VAN–) *n.* **1 Evangelist** one of the four who wrote the Gospels: Matthew, Mark, Luke, or John. **2** a preacher of the Gospel, esp. a revivalist; **e•van•gel•is•tic** (–IS–) *adj.;* **e•van•gel•is•ti•cal•ly** *adv.* —**e•van•gel•ize** (–VAN–) *v.* **-iz•es, -ized, -iz•ing** preach the Gospel (to): *St. Thomas ~d India.*

Ev•ans•ville (EV·unz·vil) a city in S.W. Indiana.

e•vap•o•rate (i·VAP·uh–) *v.* **-rates, -rat•ed, -rat•ing** change (a liquid or solid) into vapor; also, become vapor; hence, disappear: *Heat ~s water; Water ~s into vapor or steam; Hopes ~;* **evaporated milk** whole milk thickened by evaporating to about half its weight for canning; **e•vap•o•ra•tion** (–RAY–) *n.;* **e•vap•o•ra•tor** *n.* —**e•vap•o•rite** *n.* a mineral deposit formed by the evaporation of sea water; ***adj.:*** *Gypsum, rock salt, and phosphate rocks are of* **e•vap•o•rit•ic** (–RIT–) *formation.* —**e•vap•o•trans•pi•ra•tion** (–RAY–) *n.* the total loss of moisture from the soil by evaporation and transpiration.

e•va•sion (i·VAY·zhun) *n.* an act of evading: *charged with tax ~.* —**e•va•sive** (–siv) *adj.: an ~ answer; a midair collision avoided by a pilot's ~ action;* **e•va•sive•ly** *adv.;* **e•va•sive•ness** *n.*

Eve (EEV) in the Bible, the first woman and the wife of Adam.

eve (EEV) *n.* the evening or day before; hence, a period before (an event or occasion): *New Year's ~; on the ~ of her wedding.*

e•ven (EE·vn) *adj.* **1** of equal level; flat; smooth: *an ~ surface.* **2** having equal intervals; uniform; regular: *the ~ hum of an engine.* **3** that divide equally, leaving no remainder; exact: *property divided in ~ shares; ~ numbers, 2, 4, 6, 8, etc.; Give me an ~ dozen.* **4** equal: *Give the girls an ~ break with the boys; a judge meting out* **even-hand•ed** (i.e. impartial) *justice; an* **even-tem•pered** (i.e. equable) *woman; He vowed to* **get even** *with* (i.e. get revenge on) *her for jilting him; The business is beginning to* **break even** (i.e. have gains equaling losses) *after 10 years.* —***adv.*** [to emphasize a comparison]: *He can't ~ walk, let alone run; John is as tall as his mother, his sister is ~ taller; The patient died* **even as** (i.e. just as) *the doctor arrived; She won't go* **even if** *she is invited; He is still sore,* **even so** (i.e. still) *he should forgive her; refuses to eat* **even though** (i.e. although) *she is hungry.* —***v.*** make or become even: *Use the trimmer to ~ the edges; Little inequalities ~ out in the long run.* —**e•ven•ly** *adv.;* **e•ven•ness** *n.*

eve•ning (EEV·ning) *n.* the final part of day and the early part of night; **evening primrose** any of a group of tall herbs with saucer-shaped white, yellow, or pink flowers that open in the evening; **evening star** either of the two planets, Venus or Mercury, seen as bright stars in the evening sky; **e•ven•song** *n.* vespers.

e•vent (i·VENT) *n.* **1** a happening, esp. one of relative importance; also, an item in a program of sports: *The first day of school is an ~ in a child's life; swimming ~s.* **2** result; consequence. —**in any event** or **at all events** whatever happens. —**in the event of** (or **that**) in case (of). —**e•vent•ful** *adj.* full of noteworthy events; **e•vent•ful•ly** *adv.;* **e•vent•ful•ness** *n.*

e•ven•tide (EE·vn–) *n. Archaic.* evening.

e•ven•tu•al (–choo·ul) *adj.* ultimate; **e•ven•tu•al•ly** *adv.* —**e•ven•tu•al•i•ty** (–AL–) *n.* **-ties** a possible outcome. —**e•ven•tu•ate** (–VEN–) *v.* **-ates, -at•ed, -at•ing** turn out; result.

ev•er *adv.* **1** at any time; by any chance: *Does she ~ complain?* **2** at all times; forever: *~ and anon; lived happily ~ after; yours ~.* **3 ever so** *Informal.* very: *~ so many instances; ~ so often.* **4** [following a *superl.*]: *the greatest boxer ~!* (i.e. that ever lived).

Ev•er•est (–ist), **Mount.** a Himalayan mountain, the highest in the world.

ev•er•glade *n.* swampland, as in the **Everglades** of Florida. —**ev•er•green** *n.* & *adj.* (a plant or tree) that has green leaves all year round, as pine, spruce, etc.: *Most tropical plants are ~s.* —**ev•er•last•ing** (–LAST–) *n.* & *adj.* (lasting) an eternity; **ev•er•last•ing•ly** *adv.* —**ev•er•more** (–MOR) *adv.* forever.

ev•er•y (EV·ree) *adj.* **1** each of a group [including all, or one after another if indefinite]: *Trains leave here ~ hour.* **2** all possible [with abstract *n.*]: *You have ~ reason to be proud of her.* —**every now and then** (or **again**) occasionally; also **every so often.** —**ev•er•y•bod•y** (EV·ree·bod·ee, –bud·ee) *pron.* everyone: *~ and his brother walks over Jim's lawn.* —**ev•er•y•day** *adj.* daily; hence, ordinary: *words in ~use; An ~ occurrence is one that happens almost every day; clothes for ~ wear.* —**ev•er•y•one** (–wun) *pron.* every person. —**ev•er•y•thing** *n.* & *pron.* every thing; all; hence, something very important: *children are ~ to her.* —**ev•er•y•where** *adv.* in or to every place: *Look ~;* also **ev•er•y•place.**

e•vict (i·VICT) *v.* eject a tenant (from a house or land) by legal process. —**e•vic•tion** (–VIC–) *n.;* **e•vic•tor** *n.*

ev•i•dence *n.* something that supports an assertion: *Stolen property is ~ of theft; The testimony of witnesses proved strong ~; mere hearsay ~; a signed receipt produced in ~ against a defaulter; The hit-and-run car was nowhere* **in evidence** (i.e. to be seen). —***v.*** **-denc•es, -denced, -denc•ing** be a sign of: *Spontaneous tears ~d his sorrow.* —**ev•i•dent** *adj.* clear and plain to the understanding: *Her language showed her ~ displeasure;* **ev•i•dent•ly** *adv.*

e•vil (EE·vl) *n.* & *adj.* (anything) very bad, harmful, or unlucky: *an amulet worn to ward off the* **evil eye;** *deliver us, O Lord, from ~; the* **Evil**

One (i.e. the Devil); *idleness, the root of all ~; an* **evil-mind·ed** (i.e. malicious) *gossip.* **—e·vil·do·er** (–doo·ur) *n.* **—e·vil·ly** *adv.*

e·vince (i·VINCE) *v.* **e·vinc·es, e·vinced, e·vinc·ing** *Formal.* reveal or manifest (one's feeling, quality, interest, etc.)

e·vis·cer·ate (i·VIS·uh–) *v.* **-ates, -at·ed, -at·ing** disembowel; hence, deprive of something vital. **—e·vis·cer·a·tion** (–RAY–) *n.*

e·voke (i·VOKE) *v.* **e·vokes, e·voked, e·vok·ing** call forth; elicit, esp. a response from the mind or emotions. **e·voc·a·tive** (–VOC·uh·tiv) *adj.: an incident ~ of old memories.* **—ev·o·ca·tion** (ev·uh·CAY–) *n.*

ev·o·lu·tion (–LOO–) *n.* an evolving; development; also, a result of this: *The ~ of the horseless carriage into the automobile; the organic ~ of man from lower forms of life; Darwin's theory of ~ by natural selection;* **ev·o·lu·tion·ar·y** *adj.;* **ev·o·lu·tion·ism** *n.;* **ev·o·lu·tion·ist** *n.* **—e·volve** (i·VOLV) *v.* **e·volves, e·volved, e·volv·ing** develop gradually; unfold, esp. in an orderly way; come about by a natural process of development.

ewe (YOO) *n.* a female sheep.

ew·er (YOO·ur) *n.* a wide-mouthed water pitcher.

ex. example; except(ed); express; extra. **—Ex.** Exodus. **—ex-** *prefix. & prep.* **1** from; out of: as in *ex officio, ex warehouse; excursion, express.* **2** former: as in *ex-president, ex-wife;* hence **ex** *n.* **ex·es** *Informal.* one's divorced spouse.

ex·ac·er·bate (ig·ZAS·ur–) *v.* **-bates, -bat·ed, -bat·ing** irritate; also, aggravate or make (difficulties, pain, disease, etc.) worse. **—ex·ac·er·ba·tion** (–BAY–) *n.*

ex·act (ig·ZACT) *adj.* **1** agreeing in every detail; correct: *an ~ copy; the ~ size of a room.* **2** characterized by or capable of precision: *Psychology is not an* **exact science** *like physics or chemistry; an ~ memory;* **ex·act·ly** *adv.;* **ex·act·ness** *n.* **—*v.*** demand *(from)* or require *(of): penalties ~ed of defaulters;* **ex·ac·tion** *n.* **—ex·act·ing** *adj.: an ~ work schedule; a child who is very ~ in his demands;* **ex·act·ing·ly** *adv.;* **ex·act·ing·ness** *n.* **—ex·ac·ti·tude** *n.* the quality or an instance of exactness: *a woman of great ~.*

ex·ag·ger·ate (ig·ZAJ·uh–) *v.* **-ates, -at·ed, —at·ing** magnify or overstate (something): *Cartoonists ~ features out of proportion; She always ~s; an ~d account of events;* **ex·ag·ger·a·tive** (–ray·tiv) *adj.;* **ex·ag·ger·a·tor** *n.* **—ex·ag·ger·a·tion** (–RAY–) *n.*

ex·alt (ig·ZAWLT) *v.* raise in rank, power, dignity, glory, etc.; elevate; glorify: *saints ~ed to the honors of the altar; ~ a commonplace thing to the skies; has an ~ed opinion of himself.* **—ex·al·ta·tion** (–TAY–) *n.: great joy and ~.*

ex·am (ig·ZAM) *n. Informal.* an examination or a set of examination questions; **ex·am·ine** (–in) *v.* **-ines, -ined, -in·ing 1** study or closely observe (a patient, situation, etc.). **2** interview or question (an applicant, witness, etc.); also, test (a student); **ex·am·in·er** *n.;* **ex·am·i·nee** (–NEE) *n.* a person examined. **—ex·am·i·na·tion** (–NAY–) *n.: the ~ of a new theory; medical ~ by a doctor; found to be a fake on close ~.*

ex·am·ple (ig·ZAM–) *n.* a person or thing that is typical of the rest of a group, esp. one likely to be followed or copied: *canines* — **for example,** *a dog; Your conduct should* **set an example** *for your children; He was punished as an ~ for the whole class; Christ taught by precept and ~; the worst ~ of a polluted stream.*

ex·as·per·ate (ig·ZAS–) *v.* **-ates, -at·ed, -at·ing** irritate or annoy intensely. **—ex·as·per·a·tion** (–RAY–) *n.: gave up in sheer ~.*

exc. excellent; except.

ex·ca·vate (EX·cuh–) *v.* **-vates, -vat·ed, -vat·ing** make a hollow in; hence, dig or dig out: *an ~ing machine to dig a building foundation; Archaeologists ~ ancient ruins; Pompeii was ~d* (i.e. uncovered by digging); **ex·ca·va·tor** *n.* **—ex·ca·va·tion** (–VAY–) *n.*

ex·ceed (ic·SEED) *v.* go beyond; hence, surpass: *to ~ the speed limit.* **—ex·ceed·ing** *adj.* extreme; great: *met with ~ good fortune;* **ex·ceed·ing·ly** *adv.: an ~ beautiful day.*

ex·cel (ic·SEL) *v.* **-cels, -celled, -cel·ling** surpass others: *He ~s at tennis and in basket-weaving.* **—ex·cel·lence** (EK·sl·unce) *n.: a girl noted for ~ in drawing; just one of her many ~s;* also **ex·cel·len·cy, -cies;** (His, Her, or Your) **Excellency** a title of honor [used in addressing a foreign ambassador, archbishop, and others]; **ex·cel·lent** *adj.* of outstanding merit; **ex·cel·lent·ly** *adv.* **—ex·cel·si·or** (ec·SEL·see·or) *adj. & interj.* "ever upward" (New York State's motto); ***n.*** (–ur) soft fine wood shavings used for packing fragile things.

ex·cept (ic·SEPT) *v.* leave out; exclude. **—ex·cept(·ing)** *prep. & conj.* but: *Everyone ~ him was here; I'm OK* **except for** *a headache; Informal: I'm OK except I have a headache.* **—ex·cep·tion** (–SEP–) *n.* **1** an excepting; also, a person or thing excepted: *an ~ to the rule.* **2** an objection: *She* **takes exception** (i.e. objects) *to his language;* **ex·cep·tion·a·ble** *adj.* objectionable. **—ex·cep·tion·al** *adj.* unusual; rarely, handicapped; **ex·cep·tion·al·ly** *adv.*

ex·cerpt (ic·SURPT) *v.* take out (passages) from a book; ***n.*** (EK·surpt) an extract; passage (from a book).

ex·cess (ic·SES) *n.* what is greater than or exceeds a limit; surplus: *an ~ of expenditure over income; given to gambling, drinking, and such ~es; assets* **in excess of** (i.e. more than) *$3 billion; broken-hearted because she had loved him* **to excess** (i.e. too much); ***adj.*** (EK·ses): *an ~ profits tax; a higher rate for ~ baggage;* **ex·ces·sive** *adj.;* **ex·ces·sive·ly** *adv.*

exch. exchange(d). **—ex·change** (ics·CHAINJ) *v.* **-chang·es, -changed, -chang·ing** give (a thing) in return for something else; give and receive: *a customer ~ing her birthday gift* *at the store; We ~ greetings at Christmas.* ***—n.*** **1** a trade or swapping: *an ~ of prisoners after a war; a watch given in ~ for stamps; an overseas ~ student under a Fulbright ~ program.* **2** a place for exchanging things or services: *a commodity ~; telephone ~* (where lines are connected); *the stock ~.* **3** money or a document for setting or adjusting payments, currency differences, etc.: *a bill of ~; the* **exchange rate** *on the Canadian dollar; foreign ~ earned by exports.* **—ex·change·a·ble** *adj.*

ex·cheq·uer (ics·CHEK·ur, ECS·chek·ur) *n.* **1** the national treasury: *Britain's Chancellor of the Exchequer is the finance minister.* **2** *Informal.* finances.

ex·cise (EC·size, –sice) *n.* a tax or duty levied within a country on the manufacture and sale of commodities such as liquor and tobacco, on purchases in the form of sales tax, and services in the form of business licenses, entertainment tax, etc.; ***adj.:*** *an* **ex·cis·a·ble** *commodity.* **—ex·cise** (ik·SIZE) *v.* **-cis·es, -cised, -cis·ing** remove by cutting; **ex·ci·sion** (–SIZH·un) *n: surgical ~ of diseased tissue.*

ex·cite (ic·SITE) *v.* **-cites, -cit·ed, -cit·ing** **1** arouse the thoughts or feelings of; provoke; also, thrill: *The story ~d the kids; Rumors ~ curiosity;* **ex·cit·ed** *adj.* stirred up; **ex·cit·ed·ly** *adv.: came running up and spoke to us ~;* **ex·cite·ment** *n.: a trip full of ~s; forgot her hat in her ~;* **ex·cit·ing** *adj.: The news was very ~; an ~ adventure.* **2** stir up or make active: *a hive of ~d bees in hot pursuit; The* **ex·cit·er** *of an A-C generator supplies current to produce a magnetic field; electrons in an* **excited state** *of higher energy.* **—ex·cit·a·ble** *adj.;* **ex·cit·a·bil·i·ty** (–BIL–) *n.* **—ex·ci·ta·tion** (–TAY–) *n.* **—ex·ci·ton·ics** (–suh·TON–) *n.pl.* the physics of excited electrons in a crystal structure.

ex·claim (ics·CLAIM) *v.* utter suddenly and vehemently: *"Ouch," she ~ed in pain;* **ex·cla·ma·tion** (–MAY–) *n.: An* **ex·clam·a·to·ry** (–CLAM·uh–) *word or sentence is ended with an* **exclamation mark** (or **point**), *as "Alas!"*

exclave See ENCLAVE.

ex·clude (ics·CLOOD) *v.* **-cludes, -clud·ed, -clud·ing** keep out or prohibit (from): *no one ~d on the basis of color, age, or sex;* **ex·clu·sion** (–CLOO·zhun) *n.: gifts, benefits, and other nontaxable ~s;* **to the exclusion of** so as to exclude. **—ex·clu·sive** (–siv) *adj.: used to be a very ~ neighborhood; costing $5,000* **exclusive of** (i.e. not including) *taxes; Patents confer ~ rights on inventors; an ~ news story;* ***n.*** a story or article granted to or obtained by only one journal; **ex·clu·sive·ly** *adj.;* **ex·clu·sive·ness** *n.*

ex·cog·i·tate (–COJ–) *v.* **-tates, -tat·ed, -tat·ing** think out (a plan, device, etc.)

ex·com·mu·ni·cate (–cuh·MEW–) *v.* **-cates, -cat·ed, -cat·ing** cut off from membership, esp. of a church by a formal act of **ex·com·mu·ni·ca·tion** (–CAY–) *n.*

ex·co·ri·ate (ic·SCOR·ee–) *v.* **-ates, -at·ed, -at·ing** strip off the skin of; hence, denounce harshly. **—ex·co·ri·a·tion** (–AY–) *n.*

ex·cre·ment (EX·cruh·munt) *n.* waste from the bowels; **ex·cre·men·tal** (–MEN·tl) *adj.*

ex·cres·cence (ics·CRES·unce) *n.* an outgrowth from a plant or animal body, esp. an abnormal one such as a wart or bunion; **ex·cres·cent** *adj.*

ex·cre·ta (–CREE·tuh) *n.pl.* body wastes; excretions. **—ex·crete** (–CREET) *v.* **-cretes, -cret·ed, -cret·ing** eliminate from the body; **ex·cre·tion** (–CREE–) *n.: Sweat, carbon dioxide, urine, etc. are bodily ~s;* **ex·cre·to·ry** (EX·cruh·tor·ee) *adj.: the body's ~ functions.*

ex·cru·ci·at·ing (ics·CROO·shee·ay–) *adj.* of mental or bodily pain, acute; hence, extreme; **ex·cru·ci·at·ing·ly** *adv.: an ~ detailed analysis.*

ex·cul·pate (EX·cul–) *v.* **-pates, -at·ed, -pat·ing** clear (someone) of alleged fault or blame; **ex·cul·pa·tion** (–PAY–) *n.*

ex·cur·sion (ic·SCUR·zhun) *n.* **1** an outward movement; hence, a pleasure trip by air, train, ship, etc.; also, the people on it; ***adj.:*** *a round-trip economy ~ ticket;* **ex·cur·sion·ist** *n.* **2** a digression; **ex·cur·sive** (–siv) *adj.* digressive; **ex·cur·sive·ly** *adv.* **ex·cur·sive·ness** *n.* **—ex·cur·sus** *n.* a scholarly or literary digression.

ex·cuse (ic·SKYOOZ) *v.* **-cus·es, -cused, -cus·ing** overlook an offending person or an offense; also, free one(self) from a blame, duty, obligation, etc.: *We ~ you this time; We won't ~ your rudeness a second time; You are ~d from punishment; I will* **excuse myself** *for the rest of this session; You are ~d* (i.e. You can leave). ***—n.*** (ic·SKYOOS) an act or instance of excusing: *There's no ~* (i.e. justification) *for being late; A faulty watch is a lame ~; a poor ~ for* (i.e. example of) *a watch.* **—ex·cus·a·ble** *adj.: an ~ offense;* **ex·cus·a·ble·ness** *n.*

ex·e·cra·ble (EC·si·cruh–) *adj.* detestable: *an ~ crime.* **—ex·e·crate** *v.* **-crates, -crat·ed, -crat·ing** curse with much loathing; also, loathe; **ex·e·cra·tion** (–CRAY–) *n.*

ex·e·cute (EX·uh–) *v.* **-cutes, -cut·ed, -cut·ing** **1** carry out to completion; put into effect (a plan, order, will, law, etc.): *The President generally ~s what the Congress legislates; Nurses ~ doctors' orders; Each step has to be ~d gracefully in performing this dance; The testator named no one to ~ his will.* **2** put (a condemned person) to death. **—ex·ec·u·tive** (ig·ZEK·yuh·tiv) *adj.* having to do with the carrying out of a business or governmental function: *an ~ committee, director, secretary; an ~* (i.e. managerial) *chef; The F.B.I. is an ~ arm of government; secrecy is the guise of ~ privilege of confidentiality;* **Executive Mansion** (i.e. White House). ***—n.*** the executive branch of government; also, a business manager. **—ex·e·cu·tion** (ex·uh·CUE–) *n.* **1** an executing or the manner of it. **2** the putting to death of a condemned person; **ex·e·cu·tion·er** *n.* —**ex·ec·u·tor** (–ZEK–) *n.* one who is to carry out the provisions of a will; *fem.* **ex·ec·u·trix.**

ex·e·ge·sis (–JEE·sis) *n., pl.* **-ses** (–seez) the critical interpretation of a word or passage, esp. from the Bible, as by an **ex·e·gete** (EX·uh·jeet) *n.*

ex·em·plar (ig·ZEM·plar, –plur) *n.* an ideal pattern or a model worthy of imitation. —**ex·em·pla·ry** (–pluh·ree) *adj.: praised for ~ conduct; awarded* **exemplary damages** (i.e. as a warning to others) *besides compensation for loss suffered.* —**ex·em·pli·fy** (–ZEM–) *v.* **-fies, -fied, -fy·ing** serve as an example of: *Martha's life ~s service;* **ex·em·pli·fi·ca·tion** (–CAY–) *n.*

ex·empt (ig·ZEMPT) *v.* release or free from a general obligation or requirement; ***adj.:*** *The infirm are ~ from the draft;* **ex·emp·tion** *n.: granted ~ from jury duty; dependents as tax ~s.*

ex·er·cise (–size) *v.* **-cis·es, -cised, -cis·ing** put to active use or work; also, exert: *I walk my dog to ~ him; to ~ restraint in our use of energy; The judge was ~ing his powers in sending them to jail; advised to ~* (the body) *daily for 30 minutes; He was quite ~d* (i.e. troubled) *over her remarks.* — ***n.:*** *Take a little ~, said the doctor; a lesson followed by translation ~s; a poem that shows much ~ of the imagination; Teaching requires the ~ of care and patience; graduation* **exercises** (i.e. ceremonies); **ex·er·cis·er** *n.*

ex·ert (ig·ZURT) *v.* put or bring into action; exercise; wield: *to ~ authority; You must* **exert yourself** (i.e. try hard) *to achieve anything;* **ex·er·tion** *n.: the ~ of undue influence; the diplomat's ~s in the cause of peace.*

ex·hale (–HALE) *v.* **-hales, -haled, -hal·ing** breathe out; also give out (vapor, smoke, odors, etc.) or rise as they do: *We inhale oxygen and ~ carbon dioxide; odors ~ing from the sewage plant;* **ex·ha·la·tion** (ex·huh·LAY–) *n.*

ex·haust (ig·ZAWST) *v.* to empty out, drain off, or use up (strength, supplies, or other contents): *an ~ed oil well; Overspending ~ed our resources; a very* **exhausting** *climb; He ~ed the subject* (i.e. discussed it thoroughly) *within the hour.* —***n.:*** *noisy car ~s; The ~ fumes are mostly carbon monoxide; Use the fan as an air ~.* —**ex·haust·i·ble** *adj.;* **ex·haus·tion** (–ZAWS·chun) *n.* great fatigue; **ex·haus·tive** (–tiv) *adj.* thorough; **ex·haust·less** *adj.* inexhaustible.

ex·hib·it (ig·ZIB–) *v.* to display for public notice: *Artists ~ their work; evidence ~ed in court; listened to the verdict without ~ing* (i.e. manifesting) *any emotion.* —***n.*** a thing exhibited, as an art object or collection or a piece of legal evidence. —**ex·hi·bi·tion** (ex·uh·BISH·un) *n.* a public showing, esp. an organized display. —**ex·hi·bi·tion·ism** *n.* a tendency to attract attention to oneself excessively, as by indecent exposure; **ex·hi·bi·tion·ist** *n.;* **ex·hi·bi·tion·is·tic** (–IS–) *adj.* —**ex·hib·i·tor** or **ex·hib·it·er** *n.*

ex·hil·a·rate (ig·ZIL·uh–) *v.* **-rates, -rat·ed, -rat·ing** fill with high spirits: *Riding the roller coaster is very* **exhilarating; ex·hil·a·ra·tive** (–ray·tiv) *adj.* —**ex·hil·a·ra·tion** (–RAY–) *n.*

ex·hort (ig·ZORT) *v.* urge earnestly, as a preacher does; **ex·hor·ta·tion** (–TAY–) *n.*

ex·hume (igz·YOOM, ix·HUME) *v.* **-humes, -humed, -huming** dig (a corpse) out of its grave; hence, bring to light from a buried state; **ex·hu·ma·tion** (ex·hyuh·MAY–) *n.*

ex·i·gen·cy (EX·uh·jun·see) *n.* **-cies** a situation of need requiring urgent action; also, the need or urgency of it: *the ~s of life in a war zone;* **ex·i·gent** *adj.*

ex·ig·u·ous (eg·ZIG·yoo·us) *adj.* sparing or scanty; meager: *an ~ diet.*

ex·ile (EG·zile, EK·sile) *v.* force (someone or oneself) to leave his home or country for a period. —***n.*** an exiled person, his banishment, or its period.

Ex·im·bank Export-Import Bank of the U.S.

ex·ist (ig·ZIST) *v.* to be; have being or life: *Does God ~? We can't ~ without food;* **ex·ist·ence** (–unce) *n.: the ~ of ghosts; Will the universe go out of ~? a fugitive's precarious ~;* **ex·ist·ent** *adj.* —**ex·is·ten·tial** (eg·zis·TEN–) *adj.* of or having to do with **ex·is·ten·tial·ism** *n.* the philosophy of Søren Kierkegaard, Frederich Nietzsche, Jean-Paul Sartre, and others that stresses living as the only reality and man as responsible to himself and for his own existence; **ex·is·ten·tial·ist** *n.* & *adj.*

ex·it (EG·zit, EK·sit) *n.* a way out, as from a stage, building, or highway; hence, a going out, departure, or death; ***v.*** **1** : *Some ~ed by the fire escape, others through windows.* **2** [as a stage direction] (he, she, it) goes out: *"(Antigonus) exit, pursued by a bear."*

exo- *prefix.* outside or outer: as in **ex·o·bi·ol·o·gy** (–OL–) *n.* the biology of possible life in the universe outside the earth; **ex·o·crine** (EX·uh·crin, –crine, –creen) **gland** one, such as the salivary and tear glands, that empties its secretion through a duct into the intestines or outside the body; cf. ENDOCRINE. —**Exod.** *Abbrev.* for **Ex·o·dus** (EX·uh–), a book of the Bible describing the departure of the Israelites from Egypt; **exodus** *n.* a mass departure.

ex of·fi·ci·o (ex·uh·FISH·ee·oh) by virtue of one's official position.

ex·og·a·mous (–OG·uh·mus) *adj.* marrying only outside of one's tribe; the custom is **ex·og·a·my** (–OG–) *n.* —**ex·og·e·nous** (ek·SOJ·uh·nus) *adj.* growing by additions on the outside, as tree stems; **ex·og·e·nous·ly** *adv.*

ex·on·er·ate (ig·ZON–) *v.* **-ates, -at·ed, -at·ing** clear or free (someone) of guilt or responsibility for an action; **ex·on·er·a·tion** (–AY–) *n.*

ex·or·bi·tant (ig·ZOR·bi·tunt) *adj.* execessive or unreasonable: ~ *prices,* ~ *demands;* **ex·or·bi·tant·ly** *adv.* —**ex·or·bi·tance** *n.*

ex·or·cise (–size– *v.* **-cis·es, -cised, -cis·ing** solemnly adjure (an evil spirit) to leave a possessed person; hence, to free (such a person or haunted place) of an evil spirit; also **ex·or·cise; ex·or·cism** *n.;* **ex·or·cist** *n.*

ex·o·sphere (EX·uh–) *n.* the outermost part of the atmosphere; **ex·o·spher·ic** (–SFER–) *adj.* —**ex·o·ther·mal** (–THUR·mul) or **ex·o·ther·mic** *adj.* of a chemical change, attended by liberation of heat, as in combustion.

ex·ot·ic (ig·ZOT–) *adj.* of plants, fish, foods, fashions, words, etc., introduced from abroad; hence, strangely fascinating or enticing: ~ *dancing;* ***n.*** a belly dancer or stripper; **ex·ot·i·ca** *n.pl.* exotic things collectively.

exp. expense(s); export(ed); exporter; express.

ex·pand (ic·SPAND) *v.* make or become larger, esp. in extent, by unfolding, opening, spreading, etc.: *Heat* ~*s metals; a flooded river* ~*ing into a lake;* $(a + b)^2$ *is* ~*ed into* $a^2 + b^2 + 2ab$*; A professor* **expands (up)on** *a theme during a lecture;* **ex·pand·a·ble** or **ex·pan·si·ble** *adj.* that may be expanded. —**ex·panse** (–SPANCE) *n.: the vast* ~*s of outer space; the broad* ~ *of his chest;* **ex·pan·sion** *n.;* **ex·pan·sion·ist** *n.* & *adj.* (a nation) that tends to expand its territory at the expense of other nations. —**ex·pan·sive** (–siv) *adj.* expanding; extensive; capable of or causing expansion: *A couple of drinks will make him* ~ (i.e. open and demonstrative); **ex·pan·sive·ly** *adv.;* **ex·pan·sive·ness** *n.*

ex par·te (ex·PAR·tee) **1** *Law.* without benefit to the other party. **2** partisan.

ex·pa·ti·ate (ic·SPAY·shee–) *v.* **-ates, -at·ed, -at·ing** write or talk at length (*on* or *upon* a subject); **ex·pa·ti·a·tion** (–AY–) *n.*

ex·pa·tri·ate (–PAY·tree–) *v.* **-ates, -at·ed, -at·ing** withdraw (oneself) from one's native country and settle abroad; exile; also, deprive of acquired citizenship. —***n.*** one who has left his native country. —**ex·pa·tri·a·tion** (–AY–) *n.*

ex·pect (ic·SPECT) *v.* look forward to, usu. with certainty, often with hope or confidence: *I'm* ~*ing company; He'll be here by noon,* **I expect** (i.e. I suppose); *His wife* **is expecting** (i.e. pregnant); **ex·pect·a·ble** *adj.* —**ex·pect·an·cy** (–un·see) *n.* **-cies** the state of expecting or something expected: *Americans born between 1970 and 1975 had a* **life expectancy** *of 70.6 years;* **ex·pect·ant** *adj.: an* ~ *but unwed mother;* **ex·pect·ant·ly** *adv.* —**ex·pec·ta·tion** (–TAY–) *n.* the act of expecting or the thing expected or hoped for: *Contrary to* **expectations,** *she quit school.*

ex·pec·to·rant (ic·SPEC·tuh·runt) *n.* & *adj.* (a medicine) that helps to expectorate; **ex·pec·to·rate** *v.* **-rates, -rat·ed, -rat·ing** cough up phlegm; discharge sputum; also, spit; **ex·pec·to·ra·tion** (–RAY–) *n.*

ex·pe·di·ence (–PEE·dee·unce) *n.* same as **ex·pe·di·en·cy** (–see) *n.* **-cies 1** suitability for a specific, usu. selfish purpose, without regard for principles. **2** expedient. —**ex·pe·di·ent** *n.* a political step or move; also, a convenient device: *a phone call as an* ~ *for leaving a meeting;* ***adj.:*** *The legislators thought it* ~ *to vote themselves a raise now rather than after reelection;* **ex·pe·di·ent·ly** *adv.* —**ex·pe·dite** (EC·spuh–) *v.* **-dites, -dit·ed, -dit·ing** speed up or facilitate: *a small gift to* ~ *service; a stamped envelope to* ~ *a reply;* **ex·pe·dit·er** or **-di·tor** *n.* —**ex·pe·di·tion** (–DISH·un) *n.* **1** efficient speed; **ex·pe·di·tious** (–DISH·us) *adj.;* **ex·pe·di·tious·ly** *adv.* **2** a journey (of people, ships, etc.) organized for a definite purpose: *a whaling* ~*;* **ex·pe·di·tion·ar·y** *adj.: the British* ~ *force sent to France in 1939; Cuban* ~ *forces in Africa.*

ex·pel (ic·SPEL) *v.* **-pels, -pelled, -pel·ling** drive out; also, dismiss: *Air is* ~*d from the lungs; Students* ~*d from school;* **ex·pel·lee** (–LEE) *n.* one expelled from his country; **ex·pel·la·ble** *adj.*

ex·pend (ic·SPEND) *v.* use up (large sums, resources, etc.); spend: *the energies* ~*ed in tracking down Nessie;* **ex·pend·a·ble** *adj.:* ~ *supplies; an* ~ *regiment; paper, pencil, ink, and such* **expendables** *n.pl.,* —**ex·pend·i·ture** (–SPEN·di·chur) *n.:* a spending or what is spent: *Every project requires the* ~ *of time, money, and other resources; capital* ~*s on building, equipment, and such assets.* —**ex·pense** (ic·SPENCE) *n.* cost plus incidental expenditure: *Children educated at their parents'* ~*; speeding up production* **at the expense of** *quality; a salesman who gets salary, car, and* **expenses** (i.e. money for incidental expenditure); *enjoys a generous commission and* **expense account** (i.e. reimbursement of business expenditures); *A gas guzzler is a great* ~*;* **ex·pen·sive** (–siv) *adj.* high-priced; **ex·pen·sive·ly** *adv.*

ex·pe·ri·ence (ic·SPEER·ee·unce) *n.* what one lives through, i.e. sees, feels, does, etc.; what happens to one; also, the knowledge gained: *Everyone learns by* ~*; childhood* ~*s;* ***v.*** **-enc·es, -enced, -enc·ing:** *She'd never* ~*d starvation; a qualified and* **experienced** *teacher.* —**ex·per·i·ment** (ic·SPER–) *n.* a controlled action or process to discover something unknown or to test or demonstrate a known fact. —***v.:*** *The Wright brothers* ~*ed with different types of airplanes;* **ex·per·i·ment·er** *n.;* **ex·per·i·men·ta·tion** (–TAY–) *n.;* **ex·per·i·men·tal** (–MEN–) *adj.;* **ex·per·i·men·tal·ly** *adv.* —**ex·pert** (EC·spurt, *adj. also* ic·SPURT) *n.* & *adj.* skillful and knowledgeable (person); specialist: *his* ~ *opinion; an* ~ *cook; a cooking* ~*;* **ex·pert·ly** *adv.;* **ex·pert·ness** *n.;* **ex·pert·ise** (–TEEZ) *n.* an expert's skill or knowledge.

ex·pi·ate (EC·spee–) *v.* **-ates, -at·ed, -at·ing** pay the penalty for; atone for: *to* ~ *a crime;* **ex·pi·a·tor** *n.;* **ex·pi·a·tor·y** *adj.:* ~ *sacrifices;* **ex·pi·a·tion** (–AY–) *n.*

ex·pi·ra·tion (–RAY–) *n.* a breathing out or expiring: *inspiration and ~ through the lungs;* **ex·pi·ra·to·ry** (–SPY–) *adj.* —**ex·pire** (ic·SPIRE) *v.* **-pires, -pired, -pir·ing** breathe out; hence, die; come to an end: *Your license has ~d; When did she ~?* —**ex·pi·ry** (ic·SPY–, EK·spuh·ree) *n.* **-ries:** *lease will not be renewed on ~.*

ex·plain (ic·SPLAIN) *v.* make (something) clear and understandable: *Your language is vague—please ~; He couldn't ~ his absence last night; tried to* **explain** *it* **away; explain oneself** make one's meaning clear; also, justify one's conduct; **ex·plain·a·ble** *adj.;* **ex·plan·a·to·ry** (–SPLAN–) *adj.* —**ex·pla·na·tion** (ex·pluh·NAY–) *n.: A full ~ is called for; in ~ of his conduct.*

ex·ple·tive (EC·spluh·tiv) *n.* & *adj.* (a syllable, interjection, etc.) that merely fills out an utterance or a line of verse, as "there" or "it" *(It is easy to say so),* "Ahem," and "Goodness," often an oath or obscenity: *an edited transcript with ~s deleted.*

ex·pli·ca·ble (EX·plic·uh–) *adj.* explainable: *puzzling but ~ behavior;* **ex·pli·cate** *v.* **-cates, -cat·ed, -cat·ing** analyze or expose (a passage, theory, etc.); **ex·pli·ca·tion** (–CAY–) *n.*

ex·plic·it (–PLIS–) *adj.* clearly stated, explained, or pictured; not vague: *~ sex dealing with intercourse;* **ex·plic·it·ly** *adv.;* **ex·plic·it·ness** *n.*

ex·plode (ic·SPLODE) *v.* **-plodes, -plod·ed, -plod·ing** burst with a loud noise; also, blow up (a theory or idea) or erupt; hence, expand suddenly: *A bomb ~s or is ~d; A boiler ~s under pressure; Pent-up discontent ~s into a riot; superstitions and myths ~d by science; an ~ing population;* **exploded** *adj.* of a drawing, model, or view of a mechanism, showing components separated but in their relative positions: *an ~ view of a carburetor.*

ex·ploit (EX–) *n.* a daring deed; feat. —***v.*** *(usu.* ic·SPLOIT) make use of, often in an unfair and selfish manner: *People should ~ natural resources, not other people;* **ex·ploit·er** *n.;* **ex·ploit·a·tive** (–tiv) *adj.: ~actions; an ~ wage offer;* also **ex·ploi·tive.** —**ex·ploi·ta·tion** (–TAY–) *n.: industry built by the ~ of the Third World; a publicity campaign for the ~* (i.e. promotion) *of a product.*

ex·plore (ic·SPLOR) *v.* **-plores, -plored, -plor·ing** search (a new region) so as to learn about it: *a lunar rover to ~ the moon's surface; A surgeon ~s a wound;* **ex·plor·a·to·ry** *adj.: an ~ voyage; ~ surgery;* **ex·plor·er** *n.* —**ex·plo·ra·tion** (–RAY–) *n.: Columbus's ~ of the world resulted in the discovery of America.*

ex·plo·sion (–SPLOH·zhun) *n.* an exploding or its noise; also, a sudden expansion or increase: *knowledge ~;* **ex·plo·sive** (–siv) *n.* & *adj.* (a substance such as gunpowder) that tends to explode or cause an explosion: *her ~ temper;* **ex·plo·sive·ly** *adv.;* **ex·plo·sive·ness** *n.*

ex·po (EC·spoh) *n.* **-pos** an international exhibition or world's fair: *Expo 67 in Montreal.*

ex·po·nent (ic·SPOH·nunt) *n.* **1** one that expounds; hence, an advocate (of a policy, method, theory, etc.) or its exemplifier: *an ~ of free trade.* **2** in algebra, a symbol indicating an operation, as 3 in a^3; **ex·po·nen·tial** (–NEN–) *adj.;* **ex·po·nen·tial·ly** *adv.*

ex·port (ec·SPORT) *v.* send or carry away to a foreign country, esp. goods for sale. —***n.*** (EX·port) an exporting or thing exported; also **ex·por·ta·tion** (–TAY–) *n.* —**ex·port·er** *n.*

ex·pose (ic·SPOZE) *v.* **-pos·es, -posed, -pos·ing** **1** lay open; hence, display; reveal: *Bikinis ~ much of the body.* **2** leave unprotected from the elements: *the Spartan custom of ~ing unwanted babies.* **3** uncover (sensitized film or plate for photochemical action). —**ex·po·sé** (–ZAY) *n.* an exposition; esp., an exposure of a crime or a scandal. —**ex·po·si·tion** (–ZISH·un) *n.* **1** an explanation in spoken or written form; hence, the first part of a dramatic plot or of a sonata which states the main theme. **2** a large exhibition. —**ex·pos·i·tor** (–POZ–) *n.;* **ex·pos·i·tor·y** *adj.* explanatory: *~ writing.*

ex post fac·to (–FAC·toh) after the fact: *An ~ law has retroactive force.*

ex·pos·tu·late (ic·SPOS·chuh–) *v.* **-lates, -lat·ed, -lat·ing** plead or argue earnestly (*with* someone to dissuade him from some action, or *about* something requiring attention); **ex·pos·tu·la·tion** (–LAY–) *n.*

ex·po·sure (ic·SPOH·zhur) *n.* **1** an exposing or being exposed: *charged with indecent ~ at a beach; a corrupt politician afraid of public ~ in the press; The child died of ~.* **2** aspect; facing: *a house with an eastern ~.* **3** *Photog.: An ~ meter measures light intensity to determine the correct ~ (time) for a subject; 20 ~s per roll of film.*

ex·pound (ic·SPOUND) *v.* set forth or explain systematically, as by an authority in the subject.

ex·press (ic·SPRESS) *v.* **1** squeeze out (juice, oil, milk from the breast, etc.). **2** put (thoughts or feelings) into words, music, signs, or symbols: *Can't* **express himself** *in correct English; a sign (÷) ~ing division; a nod to ~ assent.* **3** send by express. —***adj.*** **1** clearly and directly stated: *his ~ wish; with the ~ purpose of talking to you; She's the ~* (i.e. exact) *image of her mother.* **2** fast and direct: *an ~ train; an ~ parcel; an ~ highway;* ***adv.*** by express. —***n.*** an express bus, train, or other service for transporting people or things; also, such a system or the things transported. —**ex·pres·sion** (–PRESH·un) *n.* **1** the expressing of meaning or beauty: *She sings with ~.* **2** something expressed or that expresses thoughts and feelings, as a word, phrase, gesture, look, sigh, or tone: *a slang ~; the ~ of sadness on his face.* **3** a mathematical representation in symbols, as $x + y = 13$. —**ex·**

pres·sion·less *adj.* —**ex·pres·sion·ism** *n.* an artistic style developed as a reaction to impressionism that gives form to the artist's strong inner feelings and is exemplified by Van Gogh, Gauguin, O'Neill, and Kafka; **ex·pres·sion·ist** *n.* & *adj.;* **ex·pres·sion·is·tic** (–IS–) *adj.* —**ex·pres·sive** *adj.* full of meaning; eloquent; **ex·pres·sive·ly** *adv.;* **ex·pres·sive·ness** *n.;* **ex·press·ly** *adv.* clearly; explicitly; *The rules ~ permit it.* —**ex·press·man** *n.* **-men** one who collects and delivers express letters, packages, etc. —**ex·press·way** *n.* a limited-access divided highway for high-speed traffic.

ex·pro·pri·ate (–PROH·pree–) *v.* **-ates, -at·ed, -at·ing** take (land) from the owner for public use, as for schools, parks, etc.; **ex·pro·pri·a·tor** *n.;* **ex·pro·pri·a·tion** (–AY–) *n.*

expt. experiment.

ex·pul·sion (ic·SPUL–) *n.* an expelling or being expelled or forced out.

ex·punge (ic·SPUNJ) *v.* **-pung·es, -punged, -pung·ing** remove completely: *a remark ordered ~d from the records.*

ex·pur·gate *v.* **-gates, -gat·ed, -gat·ing** purify (a book or other writing) of objectionable matter: *an ~d edition;* **ex·pur·ga·tion** (–GAY–) *n.*

ex·qui·site (–zit, –QUIZ·it) *adj.* of great excellence because of elaborateness in workmanship, delicacy of texture, keenness of taste, etc.: *~ lace; ~ joy; ~ taste; ~* (i.e. acute) *pain.*

ext. extension; exterior; external; extinct; extra; extract.

ex·tant (EC·stunt, –STANT) *adj.* of documents, etc., still existing; also, not extinct.

ex·tem·po·re (ic·STEM·puh·ree) *adj.* & *adv.* (spoken or done) without the use of notes or memory; offhand; also **ex·tem·po·rar·y** or **ex·tem·po·ra·ne·ous** (–RAY–) *adj.;* **ex·tem·po·rar·i·ly** or **ex·tem·po·ra·ne·ous·ly** (–RAY–) *adv.* —**ex·tem·po·rize** (–TEM–) *v.* **-riz·es, -rized, -riz·ing** improvise; also, devise as a temporary expedient: *an ~d shelter.*

ex·tend (ic·STEND) *v.* **1** stretch out in length, area, scope, etc.: *hands ~ed in welcome; to ~ a vacation by another week; convalescents and disabled given* **extended care** *in a nursing home; an* **extended family** *of relatives under the same roof with the nuclear family.* **2** offer: *to ~ a loan to someone;* **ex·tend·er** *n.;* **ex·tend·i·ble** *adj.* —**ex·ten·sion** (–TEN–) *n.* an extending or something extended as a continuation or addition; also, range or extent: *an ~ cord; listening on an ~ (phone); a university ~ service for evening classes or home study.* —**ex·ten·sive** (–siv) *adj.* having great extent of area, scope, influence, etc.: *~ knowledge of many subjects; plentiful lands put to* **extensive farming** *though without intensive cultivation;* **ex·ten·sive·ly** *adv.;* **ex·ten·sive·ness** *n.* —**ex·ten·sor** (–TEN·sur) *n.* See FLEXOR. —**ex·tent** (ic·STENT) *n.* the degree, scope, or area of extension; also, extended space: *the ~ of one's influence; trust him to a certain ~ and no farther; to the ~ of $2,000.*

ex·ten·u·ate (ic·STEN·yoo–) *v.* **-ates, -at·ed, -at·ing** make (an offense or guilt) seem less serious: *pardoned because of ~ing circumstances;* **ex·ten·u·a·tion** (–AY–) *n.: excuses offered in ~ of his misdeed.*

ex·te·ri·or (ic·STEER·ee·ur) *n.* & *adj.* (on) the immediate outside: *the brick ~ of a house; an oil-based ~ paint; shooting the ~s for a movie;* **ex·te·ri·or·ly** *adv.*

ex·ter·mi·nate (ic·STUR·muh–) *v.* **-nates, -nat·ed, -nat·ing** destroy by killing: *a poison to ~ rats; Smallpox was ~d;* **ex·ter·mi·na·tor** *n.* —**ex·ter·mi·na·tion** (–NAY–) *n.: the ~ of vice; Nazi ~ camps for Jews.*

ex·tern (EC·sturn) *n.* one who is professionally connected with an institution, but does not live in it; cf. INTERN. —**ex·ter·nal** (ic·STUR·nl) *adj.* on or from the outside, esp. as not related to the subject: *rubbing alcohol for ~ application only; an ~ influence; the minister for* **external** (i.e. foreign) **affairs; externals** *n.pl.* outward aspects or features such as one's clothing, manners, etc.: *the ~s of religious practice;* **ex·ter·nal·ly** *adv.*

ex·tinct (ex–, ix–) *adj.* no longer active or existing: *an ~ volcano; ~ animals such as the dodo and dinosaurs.* —**ex·tinc·tion** (ik·STINK–) *n.* an extinguishing or a being or becoming extinct: *the ~ of one's hopes; the ~ of the "passenger pigeon."* —**ex·tin·guish** (ic·STING–) *v.* put out (as a fire); hence, put an end to (hopes, passions, debts, rights, etc.); **ex·tin·guish·a·ble** *adj.;* **ex·tin·guish·er** *n.*

ex·tir·pate (EC·stur–) *v.* **-pates, -pat·ed, -pat·ing** root out (a race, family, species, evil, etc.); **ex·tir·pa·tion** (–PAY–) *n.*

ex·tol(l) (ic·STOLE) *v.* **-tol(l)s, -tolled, -toll·ing** praise highly; exalt.

ex·tort (ic·STORT) *v.* get (money, promises, confessions, etc. from someone) by force or intimidation; **ex·tort·er** *n.* —**ex·tor·tion** *n.;* **ex·tor·tion·ate** (–it) *adj.: ~ prices; ~ demands; ~ fees; ~ taxes;* **ex·tor·tion·ate·ly** *adv.;* **ex·tor·tion·er** or **-tion·ist** *n.*

ex·tra (EX·truh) *adj.* more or larger than normal: *at no ~ charge; more work for ~ pay;* ***adv.:*** *an ~ special quality;* ***n.*** something or someone extra, as a special edition of a newspaper, an additional favor, or an actor for a minor role. —**extra-** *prefix.* outside; beyond; besides: as in *extracurricular, extrasensory.*

ex·tract (ic·STRACT) *v.* draw out *(from)* by physical or mental effort, as by pulling (a tooth), mechanically separating (metal from ore), pressing (juice from fruit), deducing or deriving (a principle or mathematical root), taking out (a passage from a book), etc. —***n.*** (EX–) something extracted: *meat ~; an ~ from*

Shakespeare; a cosmetic ~ like musk. —**ex·trac·tion** (–TRAC–) *n.* something extracted; also, a person's lineage: *a man of noble ~.* —**ex·trac·tive** (–tiv) *adj.: ~ metallurgy; Lumbering, fishing, and mining are ~ industries.* —**ex·trac·tor** *n.*

ex·tra·cur·ric·u·lar (–cuh·RIC·yuh·lur) *adj.* outside the regular curriculum, as sports, dramatics, hobbies, and such noncredit school activities.

ex·tra·dite *v.* **-dites, -dit·ed, -dit·ing** deliver (a prisoner) to another state or country where he is wanted for a crime; **ex·tra·di·tion** (–DISH·un) *n.*

ex·tra·dos (EX–, –STRAY–) *n. Archit.* the outside curve of an arch. —**ex·tra·ga·lac·tic** (–guh·LAC–) *adj.* outside the Galaxy or Milky Way: *~ nebulae.* —**ex·tra·mar·i·tal** (–MAIR·uh·tl) *adj.* outside marriage; adulterous. —**ex·tra·mu·ral** (–MYOOR·ul) *adj.* outside a college; between colleges; *~ sports.* —**ex·tra·ne·ous** (–STRAY·nee·us) *adj.* from outside; also, irrelevant: *polluted by ~ substances; an ~ remark;* **ex·tra·ne·ous·ly** *adv.* —**ex·traor·di·nar·y** (–STROR·dn·er·ee) *adj.* not ordinary; unusual; **ex·traor·di·nar·i·ly** *adv.* —**ex·trap·o·late** (–STRAP·uh–) *v.* **-lates, -lat·ed, -lat·ing** *Math.* follow a trend beyond the established range, as by extending a graph or curve: *The population of A.D. 2000 may be ~d* (i.e. obtained by extrapolating) *from the present figures;* **ex·trap·o·la·tion** (–LAY–) *n.* —**ex·tra·sen·so·ry** (–SEN·suh·ree) *adj.* outside normal sense-perception. —**ex·tra·ter·res·tri·al** (–RES·tree·ul) *adj.* outside the earth. —**ex·tra·ter·ri·to·ri·al** (–TOR·ee·ul) *adj.* outside one's territory; **ex·tra·ter·ri·to·ri·al·i·ty** (–AL–) *n.* the principle that diplomats should be under the jurisdiction of their own countries when sent abroad; hence, diplomatic immunity. —**ex·trav·a·gant** (–STRAV·uh·gunt) *adj.* excessive; hence, wasteful: *~ praise; an ~ spender;* **ex·trav·a·gant·ly** *adv.;* **ex·trav·a·gance** *n.* **ex·trav·a·gan·za** (–GAN·zuh) *n.* a spectacular stage or screen production. —**ex·tra·ve·hic·u·lar** (–vee·HIC·yoo·lur) *adj.* outside a vehicle, esp. a spacecraft. —**ex·tra·ver·sion** or **ex·tro·ver·sion** (–VUR–) *n.* the attitude of an extravert; **ex·tra·vert** or **ex·tro·vert** *n.* one whose interests are more in other people and in his environment than in himself; **ex·tra·vert(·ed)** or **ex·tro·vert(·ed)** *adj.*

ex·treme (ic·STREEM) *adj.* farthest away, esp. from a middle; hence, excessive; drastic: *~ cold; ~ heat; the ~ right; ~ joy; ~ measures.* —***n.:*** *the ~s of joy and despair; disappointing* **in the extreme** (i.e. extremely); *She went* **to extremes** *in order to please him.* —**ex·treme·ly** *adv.;* **ex·treme·ness** *n.;* **ex·trem·ism** *n.* a stance, philosophy, or activity that is not moderate, esp. the far left or far right in politics; **ex·trem·ist** *n.* & *adj.* —**ex·trem·i·ty** (ic·STREM–) *n.* **-ties** an extreme part, condition, or degree: *no one else to turn to in her ~; the ~ of despair;* **extremities** *pl.* hands and feet.

ex·tri·cate *v.* **-cates, -cat·ed, -cat·ing** free (someone or oneself) from a difficult situation; **ex·tri·ca·ble** *adj.* —**ex·tri·ca·tion** (–CAY–) *n.*

ex·trin·sic (–TRIN–) *adj.* not belonging or inherent (*to* a subject); external; **ex·trin·si·cal·ly** *adv.*

extrovert(ed) same as EXTRAVERT(ED).

ex·trude (ic·STROOD) *v.* **-trudes, -trud·ed, -trud·ing** stick out; also, force out (a ductile material such as a metal, plastic, or rubber) as through a die; **ex·tru·sion** (–STROO·zhun) *n.;* **ex·tru·sive** (–siv) *adj.: Basalts, obsidian, and pumice are ~ rocks of hardened lava.*

ex·u·ber·ant (ig·ZOO·buh·runt) *adj.* overflowing (with cheer); profuse (in growth): *an ~ youth; ~ vegetation;* **ex·u·ber·ance** (–unce) *n.;* **ex·u·ber·ant·ly** *adv.*

ex·ude (ig·ZOOD, ZYOOD) *v.* **-udes, -ud·ed, -ud·ing** come out or send out, as sweat through pores; ooze: *a hostess ~ing charm;* **ex·u·da·tion** (–DAY–) *n.*

ex·ult (ig·ZULT) *v.* rejoice in triumph; be jubilant; **ex·ult·ant** (–unt) *adj.;* **ex·ult·ant·ly** *adv.;* **ex·ul·ta·tion** (–TAY–) *n.*

ex·urb (–URB) *n.* a region beyond a city's suburbs, usu. inhabited by the well-to-do; **ex·ur·ban** *adj.;* **ex·ur·ban·ite** *n.* & *adj.;* **ex·ur·bi·a** (–bee·uh) *n.* exurbs and the exurban way of life.

eye *n.* **1** the organ of sight or any of its parts: *blond hair and blue ~s; a black ~* (i.e. bruise around the eye). **2** often **eyes** *pl.* vision; hence, observation; judgment: *guilty in the ~s of the law; She has* **an eye for** *detail;* **lay** (or **set**) **eyes on** look at; see; **make eyes at** ogle; look amorously at; **see eye to eye (with)** have identical views (with); **with an eye to** hoping for. **3** anything resembling an eye, as a needle's hole, buds on potatoes, the calm center of a developing hurricane, etc. —***v.*** **eyes, eyed, ey(e)·ing** look at; observe; watch. —**eyed** *adj.* having eyes or eyelike markings: *"~ like a peacock";* ***comb.form.*** as in *one-eyed, almond-eyed.* —**eye·ball** *n.* the ball-shaped part of an eye; **eyeball to eyeball** face to face. —**eye·bank** *n.* an agency for distributing eyes donated for corneal transplants. —**eye·brow** *n.* the arch of bone and growth of hair over each eye. —**eye-catch·ing** *adj. Informal.* striking; also, conspicuous: *an ~ design;* **eye-catch·er** *n.* —**eye·ful** *n.* a sight, view, or person likely to please one: *He got an ~* (i.e. more than he expected to see). —**eye·glass** *n.* a lens to aid vision, usu. **eye·glass·es** *pl.* —**eye·lash** *n.* a hair or fringe of hairs on the edge of an **eye·lid,** upper or lower, that covers the eyeball. —**eye·let** (–lit) *n.* a small hole, usu. rimmed with metal, as for a shoelace to pass through, or edged with stitches, as in embroidered designs. —**eye·lin·er** *n.* a cosmetic preparation applied to the base of the eyelashes. —**eye-o·pen·er** *n.* something that surprises and enlightens, as a piece of news; also, *Informal.* an early-morning drink. —**eye·piece** *n.* the viewing lens of a microscope, telescope, etc. —**eye shadow** a cosmetic preparation applied on the upper eyelids. —**eye·sight** *n.* vision. —**eye·sore** *n.* an unpleasant sight. —**eye·strain** *n.* weariness of the eye(s). —**eye·tooth** *n., pl.* **-teeth** an upper canine tooth. —**eye·wash** *n.* **1** an eye lotion. **2** *Informal.* something said or done to impress or flatter. —**eye·wit·ness** *n.* one who can testify about a happening because he has seen it in person.

ey·rie or **ey·ry** (AIR·ee, EYE·ree) *n.* **-ries** same as AERIE.

ey·rir (AY·reer) *n., pl.* **au·rar** (AU·rar) an Icelandic money unit equal to 1/100 of a krona.

Ezek. Ezekiel (Old Testament book).

F

F or **f** (EF) *n.* **F's** or **f's** the sixth letter of the English alphabet; hence, sixth in a series. **—f 1** *Math.* function. **2** *Optics.* focal length; relative aperture of a lens; also **f/. 3** farad. **—f.** or **F.** farad; feminine; folio(s); following; forte *(Music);* franc(s); frequency. **—F 1** a failing grade in examinations or schoolwork. **2** Fahrenheit; fluorine. **3** the fourth tone in the musical scale of C major. **4** farad. **—F.** Fahrenheit; February; French; Friday.

fa (FAH) *Music.* the fourth tone of the diatonic scale.

F.A.A. Federal Aviation Administration (since 1967) or Agency (1958–67).

Fa·bi·an (FAY·bee·un) *n.* & *adj.* (a member) of the **Fabian Society,** a British socialist organization. **—Fa·bi·an·ism** *n.*

fa·ble (FAY·bl) *n.* a story with a moral and animals as characters; hence, a myth; invention. **—fa·bled** *adj.* famous in legends or stories: *the ~ monster of Loch Ness.*

fab·ric *n.* **1** a material, as flannel or other cloth, that is put together by weaving, knitting, or felting: *a fine textile ~ of linen fibers.* **2** any structure of different elements: *the ~ of society weakened by civil wars.* **—fab·ri·cate** *v.* **-cates, -cat·ed, -cat·ing** create; assemble; manufacture; also, make up in order to deceive: *separately ~d parts of a house;* **fabricated food** *supplements made from vegetable or synthetic substances;* **fab·ri·ca·tor** *n.* **—fab·ri·ca·tion** (–CAY–) *n.: That report was pure ~.*

fab·u·list (FAB·yoo–) *n.* a teller or writer of fables, as Aesop. **—fab·u·lous** (–yoo·lus) *adj.* like a fable; hence, incredible; also, wonderful: *the ~ treasures of sunken ships;* **fab·u·lous·ly** *adv.: a ~ wealthy man.*

fac. facsimile; faculty.

fa·çade or **fa·cade** (fuh·SAHD) *n.* the front of a building; hence, a false or put-on appearance: *His cordiality is only a ~.*

face *n.* **1** the front of the human head; also, a countenance or expression: *a child* **making faces** *in the mirror; They finally met* **face to face;** *called him a liar* **to his face;** *married him* **in the face of** (i.e. despite) *opposition from her family; seems a good plan* **on the face of it** (i.e. from all appearances). **2** the front, main, or outer surface; also, appearance: *the ~ of a clock; the ~s of a crystal; Industry has changed the ~ of the land.* **3** prestige, dignity: *He* **lost face** *by refusing the challenge; She* **saved face** *by giving a new interpretation of her words;* **face-sav·ing** *adj.: a ~ solution to a problem.* **—*v.* fac·es, faced, fac·ing 1** look or be turned toward; hence, meet (a person); also, meet in a bold or hostile way; confront: *a window ~ing east; time to* **face up** *to the unpleasant situation;* **face down** face boldly. **2** provide a surface or trimming to: *a house ~d with brownstone;* **fac·ing** *n.: a walnut veneer ~; a military coat's* **facings** (i.e. cuffs, collar, and trimmings). **—face·down** *n.* a confronting. **—face fly** a fly similar to the housefly, which pesters cattle by settling on their faces. **—face·less** *adj.: the ~ crowds of large cities.* **—face·lift(·ing)** *n.* cosmetic surgery for getting rid of face wrinkles and such signs of age; hence, treatment to improve the appearance: *The city hall got a ~ for the centennial;* **face-lift** *v.* **—face off** start or resume play in hockey or lacrosse; hence, confront; **face-off** *n.: a big-power ~ that brought the world to the brink of war.* **—face-saving** See FACE, *n.* 3. **—fac·et** (FAS·it) *n.* one of many sides, aspects, or phases, as a surface of a cut gem: *An insect's compound eye has six-sided lensed ~s; to study the many ~s of a problem;* also ***v.* -ets, -et·(t)ed, -et·(t)ing; fac·et·ed** *adj.* & *comb.form.: a ~ rock crystal; a multi-~ personality.*

fa·ce·tious (fuh·SEE·shus) *adj.* aiming to be humorous, esp. by witty remarks: *Stop being ~!* **fa·ce·tious·ly** *adv.* **—fa·ce·tious·ness** *n.*

face value the stated value, as on a bond or bill; hence, apparent value or meaning: *A lady's word may be taken at ~.* **—fa·cial** (FAY·shul) *adj.* of the face: *a ~ expression;* **facial tissue** *for use as a handkerchief; a ~ massage;* ***n.*** a treatment for the face, as given in a beauty parlor. **—fa·cial·ly** *adv.*

fac·ile (FAS·il, –ile) *adj.* easily done; fluent; also, glib; superficial; pliant: *a ~ task; a ~ writer; a salesman's ~ pitch;* **fac·ile·ly** *adv.* —**fa·cil·i·tate** (–SIL–) *v.* **-tates, -tat·ed, -tat·ing** make easier: *Good tools will ~ the job;* **fa·cil·i·ta·tion** (–AY–) *n.* —**fa·cil·i·ty** (–SIL–) *n.* **-ties** ease; aptitude; also, something that helps a particular purpose: *a dog's natural ~ in swimming; an indoor swimming ~; library and sports ~s.*

fac·sim·i·le (–SIM·i·lee) *n.* an exact copy, esp. of something graphic; also, an electronic device for transmitting documents and pictures; ***adj.:*** *printed in Tokyo from ~ pages sent by microwave.*

fact *n.* **1** something that is real, actual, or true: *Is the UFO report ~ or fiction? Give me ~s and figures* (i.e. precise information); *Pollution is a ~ of life;* **the facts of life** the basics of sex and reproduction; **as a matter of fact** or **in (point of) fact** actually; really. **2** *Law.* a crime: *aided the accused as an accessory before the ~.* —**fact finder** an investigator, esp. one of a **fact-find·ing** committee, as in a labor dispute.

fac·tion (–shun) *n.* **1** a minority group within an organization, working against its larger interests; clique: *a party torn by warring ~s.* **2** party strife. —**fac·tion·al; fac·tious** *adj.: a factional leader with a factious spirit.* —**fac·tion·al·ism** *n.*

fac·ti·tious (–TISH·us) *adj.* contrived; sham: *a ~ smile.*

fac·tor (–tur) *n.* **1** a circumstance or element contributing to a result: *Strength of materials is a* **safety factor** *in construction; 2 and 3 are ~s of 6;* ***v.:*** *6 is ~ed into 2 and 3.* **2** trading agent: *a fur company ~.* —**fac·to·ri·al** (–TOR·ee·ul) *n.* & *adj.: ~ mathematics; The ~ of 5 is 5×4×3×2×1.* —**fac·to·ry** (–tuh·ree) *n.* **-ries** a building in which products are manufactured; industrial plant: *a car ~; a ~ hand* (i.e. worker).

fac·to·tum (–TOH–) *n.* a servant with various duties.

fac·tu·al (FAC·choo·ul) *adj.* containing facts; like fact: *a ~ report;* **fac·tu·al·ly** *adv.*

fac·u·la (FAK·yuh·luh) *n., pl.* **-lae** (–lee) a patch of light seen near the sun's edge or near sunspots.

fac·ul·ty *n.* **-ties** **1** an ability or power: *the ~ of speech; a will made while in full possession of his ~s.* **2** the membership of a profession, esp. a teaching staff; hence, an academic division: *the medical ~; the ~ of Arts.*

fad *n.* a temporary fashion or craze, as "streaking" in the early 70's; **fad·dish** *adj.* —**fad·dist** *n.*

fade *v.* **fades, fad·ed, fad·ing** become faint; gradually lose color, brilliance, freshness, strength, etc.: *The music ~d in the distance; well-worn, ~d jeans; Childhood memories ~ with age; worn brakes that ~* (i.e. lose stopping power). —**fade in** (or **out**) of motion pictures, (make) appear (or disappear) gradually; of sounds, make or become more (or less) distinct. —**fade·less** *adj.* —**fad·ing** *n.* variation of intensity in radio reception.

faecal, faeces same as FECAL, FECES.

faer·ie or **faer·y** (FAIR·ee) *n.* **faer·ies** *Archaic.* fairyland; also, a fairy.

fag *n. Slang.* **1** short for **fag·got** (–gut) *n.* a male homosexual; **fag·got·y** *adj.* **2** a cigarette. **3** *Brit.* a schoolboy in servitude to another; a menial; ***v.*** **fags, fagged, fag·ging:** *too* **fagged out** *for more work; still* **fagging away** *at his task.* —**fag end** a frayed or worn-out end or edge; remnant: *the ~end of the day.* —**fag·(g)ot** *n.* a bundle of sticks or of iron rods; ***v.*** ornament with **fag·(g)ot·ing,** a zigzag stitch across two finished edges.

Fah(r). *Abbrev.* for **Fahr·en·heit** (FAIR·un·hite) *n.* a thermometer scale with 32° as the freezing point and 212° the boiling point of water; ***adj.*** *the ~ scale.*

fa·ience or **fa·ïence** (fye·AHNCE,fay–) *n.* an opaquely glazed earthenware with colorful decorations.

fail *v.* be wanting, lacking, or negligent; also, not succeed: *He ~ed the test; her ~ing health; Don't ~ me when I need you most.* —***n.:*** *I'll be there tomorrow* **without fail** (i.e. for sure). —**failing** *n.: Laziness is one of his ~s;* ***prep.*** in the absence of.

faille (FILE, FAIL) *n.* a ribbed silk or rayon fabric.

fail-safe *adj.* providing safety against failure: *a ~ device to open doors in an emergency.* —**fail·ure** (–yur) *n.: a business ~; The party was a ~.*

fain *adv.* & *adj. Archaic.* glad(ly): *"I would ~ die a dry death."*

faint *adj.* weak or feeble: *a ~ voice; not the ~est idea where he is; I feel ~.* —***v.:*** *He ~ed* (i.e. became unconscious) *on hearing the bad news.* —***n.:*** *came out of the ~ in no time.* —**faint-heart·ed** *adj.* lacking courage; timid; **faint·ly** *adv.;* **faint·ness** *n.*

[1]**fair** *adj.* **1** just; according to the rules: *a ~ and impartial judge; ~ play;* **fair and square** in a just and open way. **2** [in the general senses of "good" or "pleasing"]: *a ~* (i.e. attractive) *maiden; a ~* (i.e. favorable) *wind; ~* (i.e. clear) *weather; ~* (i.e. light-colored) *hair; a ~* (i.e. moderately good) *guess.* —**fair·ly** *adv.: We treat our employees ~* (i.e. justly); *He looks ~* (i.e. reasonably) *happy.* —**fair·ness** *n.*

[2]**fair** *n.* an exhibition of agricultural or industrial goods; *a state ~; a world's ~.*

fair ball in baseball, a ball that is not foul. —**fair·ground(s)** *n.* a place to hold fairs, carnivals, and other outdoor events. —**fair-haired boy** *Informal.* a favorite. —**fair shake** *Informal.* an even chance. —**fair-trade agreement** one to abide by minimum prices. —**fair·way** *n.* the mowed area of a golf course between tee and green.

fair·y *n.* **fair·ies 1** a supernatural being resembling humans but usually much smaller, often mischievous and endowed with magical powers: *a* **fairy godfather** (i.e. a powerful benefactor); *Cinderella's* **fairy godmother.** —**fair·y·land** *n.* the mythical land of fairies; hence, any beautiful or enchanting place. **2** *Slang.* a male homosexual. —**fairy tale** a story about fairies; also, made-up information.

fait ac·com·pli (FATE·ah·cohm·PLEE), *pl.* **faits ac·com·plis** (FATE·ah·cohm·PLEE) an accomplished fact; hence, something that cannot be helped or changed.

faith *n.* trust; belief; also, a particular belief or religion: *their ~ in God; non-Christian ~s;* **in good faith** (i.e. sincerely). —**faith·ful** *adj.* loyal; dedicated: *a ~ servant;* ***n.*** [takes *pl. v.*] practicing believers: *The ~ march to the temple;* **faith·ful·ly** *adv.* —**faith·less** *adj.* without faith; also, disloyal; **faith·less·ly** *adv.*

fake *v.* **fakes, faked, fak·ing** pretend; counterfeit: *A good Rembrandt is hard to ~; to ~ an accident;* —***adj.*** false; sham: *a ~ masterpiece;* ***n.:*** *Her French accent is only a ~.* —**fake book** an unauthorized edition of the melodies of popular songs. —**fak·er** *n.* a person who pretends or counterfeits; **fak·er·y** *n.*

fa·kir (fuh·KEER) *n.* a Moslem or Hindu holy beggar known for feats of magic and endurance.

fa·la·fel (fuh·LAH·fl) *n.* a Middle-Eastern sandwich, usu. containing fresh vegetables, beans, and spices.

fal·chion (FAL·chun, –shun) *n.* a broad-bladed, curved medieval sword.

fal·con (FAL·cun) *n.* a hawk used in the sport of **fal·con·ry** to hunt smaller birds; **fal·con·er** *n.* one who trains falcons or hunts with them.

fal·de·ral (FOL·duh·rol) *n.* a useless trifle; nonsense.

fall (FAWL) *v.* **falls, fell, fall·en, fall·ing 1** drop freely; move down; collapse; hence, decline in value, power, health, etc.: *The leaves ~ in the autumn; We tripped and fell; The roof fell in; bad teeth that fell out; the men who will ~ in battle; a government about to ~; Prices will soon ~; The temperature fell sharply; to ~ ill.* **2** occur or be allotted or divided naturally or by chance: *My birthday ~s on a Thursday; problems that ~ into several classes; sad duties that ~ upon us.* —***n.*** **1** drop; collapse; also, the act or result of falling: *a bad ~ from the roof; the ~ of prices; the ~ of the government; Niagara Falls is not a high fall(s);* **the Fall** the expulsion of Adam and Eve from paradise; man's fall from grace. **2** autumn. —**fall back** give way; retreat: *The enemy will ~ back soon.* —**fall back on** rely on; turn to for help: *a friend to ~ back on.* —**fall behind** fail to keep up with: *Some marchers soon fell behind; to ~ behind in one's payments.* —**fall flat** fail completely: *My plans and her jokes always ~ flat.* —**fall for** *Informal.* fall in love with: *He fell for her right away; We won't ~ for* (i.e. be deceived by) *the trick.* —**fall foul of** quarrel, clash, or lose favor with: *to ~ foul of the boss.* —**fall in:** *The troops were ordered to ~ in* (i.e. get in formation). —**fall in with** meet; join: *Why did he ~ in with criminal elements?* —**fall into line** comply; obey: *The dissidents won't ~ into line.* —**fall out:** *The sergeant told them to ~ out* (i.e. leave their place in formation). —**fall out (with)** quarrel (with); *the partners had a* **falling out.** —**fall over backward(s)** or **fall (all) over oneself** try very hard; be very eager: *These waiters fall over backward to give good service; He fell (all) over himself trying to help me.* —**fall short** fail to reach a goal: *results that ~ short of one's expectations.* —**fall through** fail: *wild schemes that often ~ through.* —**fal·la·cy** (FAL·luh·see) *n.* **-cies** false or erroneous reasoning; an incorrect or deceptive idea: *prejudices based on old ~s;* **fal·la·cious** (fuh·LAY·shus) *adj.* —**fall guy** *Slang.* a scapegoat. —**fal·li·ble** *adj.* subject to error; **fal·li·bly** *adv.* **fal·li·bil·i·ty** (–BIL–) *n.* —**falling star** a meteor. —**fall line 1** where the mountains meet the plain. **2** in skiing, the fastest path down a slope.

Fal·lo·pi·an (fuh·LOH·pee·un) **tube** either of a pair of tubes that carry the egg cells from the ovary to the uterus; also **fallopian tube.**

fall·out *n.* radioactive particles from a nuclear explosion in the air; hence, an unforeseen result; side effect.

fal·low (FAL·oh) *adj.* **1** unseeded or unused: *fields that* **lie fallow; fal·low·ness** *n.* **2** light brownish yellow; **fallow deer** a small Eurasian deer with fallow, spotted coat.

false (FAWLCE) *adj.* **fals·er, fals·est** not true; unreal; misleading; unfaithful: *~ arguments convincing no one; a set of ~ teeth; The noise was just a ~ alarm;* **false·ly** *adv.;* **false·ness** *n.* —**false·hood** *n.* a lie; lack of sincerity or truth: *an obvious ~.* —**fal·set·to** (fawl·SET·oh) *n.* **-set·tos** an artificially high singing voice, esp. of a tenor. —**fal·sies** (FAWL·seez) *n. Informal* [takes *pl.v.*] pads inside a brassiere. —**fal·si·fy** (FAWL–) *v.* **-fies, -fied, -fy·ing** make or prove false: *a clerk fired for ~ing the records; Facts ~ your theory;* **fal·si·fi·a·ble** *adj.;* **fal·si·fi·er** *n.* **fal·si·fi·ca·tion** (–CAY–) *n.* —**fal·si·ty** *n.* **-ties** a lie; falseness: *the ~ of his testimony.*

fal·ter (FAWL–) *v.* **-ters, -tered, -ter·ing** waver or hesitate; stumble; stammer: *Our courage began to ~; a* **faltering** *motor;* **fal·ter·ing·ly** *adv.*

fame *n.* renown; reputation; esteem: *eager for ~ and fortune.* —**famed** *adj.:* famous: *a region ~ for its lakes.*

fa·mil·ial (fuh·MIL·yul) *adj.* having to do with a family: *Most ~ diseases, such as hemophilia, are inherited; The Basque language seems without ~ relationships.* —**fa·mil·iar** (–MIL–) *adj.* having to do with close association: *a ~* (i.e. well-known) *voice; good friends on ~* (i.e. intimate or informal) *terms; Don't get ~ with strangers; experts*

~ (i.e. acquainted) *with the problem;* ***n.*** a companion or friend; hence, an evil spirit: *A black cat was believed to be a witch's ~.* **—fa·mil·i·ar·i·ty** (–AIR–) *n.* **-ties:** *The lawyer showed poor ~ with* (i.e. knowledge of) *the case; She resented such ~s* (i.e. liberties) *as necking and petting on her first date; moving about with easy ~* (i.e. informality) *among her guests.* **—fa·mil·i·ar·ize** (–MIL–) *v.* **-iz·es, -ized, -iz·ing:** *He ~d himself with the facts of the case.* **—fa·mil·i·ar·ly** *adv.*

—fam·i·ly *n.* **-lies** the social unit of parents and children; also, the children alone; hence, any group or set with a common origin or with similar characteristics, often living under the same roof or with a common head: *A cougar belongs to the cat ~; Both English and Hindi belong to the Indo-European ~ of languages; a notorious Mafia ~.* ***—adj.:*** *Birth control devices aid* **family planning;** *All our recreation is taken in the* **family room; family tree** a chart showing the ancestors and descendants of a family.

fam·ine (FAM·in) *n.* a widespread and serious shortage, esp. of food. **—fam·ish** *v.* **-ish·es, -ished, -ish·ing** (cause to) suffer from hunger: *a lean and ~d look.*

fa·mous (FAY·mus) *adj.* well-known; esteemed; **fa·mous·ly** *adv. Informal.* very well: *We got along ~.*

¹fan *n.* a semicircular, often folding device for blowing air for ventilation or cooling; also, a similar rotary device equipped with blades or vanes, as an electric room-fan or the fan behind a car radiator driven by a **fan belt:** *An alluvial ~ is a river's fan-shaped deposit.* ***—v.*** **fans, fanned, fan·ning 1:** *a room packed with people ~ing themselves; The wind helped to ~ the flames; anger ~d into fury by insults. The policemen* **fanned out** (i.e. spread out) *over the neighborhood in search of the murderer.* **2** *Baseball.* strike out.

²fan *n.* an enthusiastic follower or admirer: *a football ~; a ~ of the Beatles.*

fa·nat·ic (fuh·NAT–) *n.* & *adj.* (one who is) overzealous or unreasonably enthusiastic: *a religious ~; a ~ for cleanliness;* also **fa·nat·i·cal** *adj.: ~ sect; ~ ideas.* **—fa·nat·i·cal·ly** *adv.* **—fa·nat·i·cism** *n.*

fan belt See ¹FAN, *n.* 1.

fan·ci·er *n.* one with a special interest in animals, plants, etc.: *an orchid ~; a ~ of fine wines.* **—fan·ci·ful** *adj.* imaginative: *a ~ poet; ~ stories;* **fan·ci·ful·ly** *adv.;* **fan·ci·ful·ness** *n.* **—fan·cy** *n.* imagination; whim; taste: *words and pictures meant to tickle your ~; doing whatever strikes her ~; a ~ for heart-shaped cookies.* ***—adj.*** **-ci·er, -ci·est** extravagant; expensive: *$10,000 is a ~ price for a used car; She never wore ~ shoes to school.* ***—v.*** **-cies, -cied, -cy·ing** imagine: *She ~s herself as a doctor in five years; He doesn't ~* (i.e. like) *lazy students.* **—fancy dress** imaginative costume, as for a masquerade; **fan·cy-free** *adj.* free from romantic attachments; **fan·cy·work** *n.* crochet, embroidery, and other decorative needlework.

fan·dan·go (–DANG·goh) *n.* a lively Spanish dance; also, its music.

fan·dom (–dum) *n.* a particular group of fans, as of a star.

fane *n.* a temple or church.

fan·fare *n.* a sounding of trumpets; hence, a flourish; also, publicity: *a narrow win announced with much ~.*

fang *n.* one of the sharp and pointed teeth of carnivorous mammals; canine tooth; also, a venomous tooth of a reptile.

fan-jet *n.* a jet engine with a rotating fan for extra thrust; turbofan engine. **—fan·light** *n.* a semicircular window, usu. over a door.

fan·ny *n.* **fan·nies** *Slang.* the buttocks.

fan·tail *n.* a pigeon or goldfish with a fanlike tail or fin.

fan·ta·si·a (–TAY·zhuh, –tuh·ZEE·uh) *n.* a free-form, fanciful musical piece, as some of Bach's organ pieces or modern swing music. **—fan·ta·size** *v.* **-siz·es, -sized, -siz·ing** indulge the imagination; daydream (about); also **fan·ta·sy, -sies, -sied, -sy·ing. —fan·tas·tic** (–TAS–) *adj.* **1** unreal; strange: *a ~ theory that no one will believe.* **2** *Informal.* incredible; wonderful: *~ prices; a ~ movie.* Also **fan·tas·ti·cal. —fan·tas·ti·cal·ly** *adv.* **—fan·tas·ti·cal·ness** or **-cal·i·ty** (–CAL–) *n.* **—fan·ta·sy** (FAN·tuh·see) *n.* **-sies** imagination; daydream; highly imaginative fiction: *Space travel is no longer a ~;* **fan·ta·sist** *n.*

fan·zine (–zeen) *n.* a magazine for fans, esp. of science fiction.

F.A.O. (United Nations) Food and Agriculture Organization.

far *adj.* **far·ther** (–dhur), **far·thest** (–dhist) distant; remote: *a ~ country; in the ~ future; the ~ end of the field; the farthest of all the houses.* — ***adv.*** at, to, or from a distance in time or position: *We like to travel ~; He lives farther down the road; She will* **go far** (i.e. succeed) *in her career; a job ~* (i.e. much) *easier than the old one;* **As** (or **so**) **far as** *I can tell, it won't rain today; This is the best deal* **by far** (i.e. without doubt); **far and away** (i.e. beyond doubt) *my best friend; carrying his message* **far and wide** (i.e. everywhere); **Far be it from me** *to* (i.e. I would never) *question his sincerity; His success* **so far** (i.e. till now) *has been because of his parents.* **—far·a·way** *adj.* **1** distant: *~ voices.* **2** dreamy: *a ~ expression.*

far·ad (FAIR·ud) *n.* the unit of electrical capacitance.

farce *n.* a humorous play full of funny situations and ridiculous happenings; hence, a mockery: *The new censorship laws make a ~ of freedom of speech.* **—far·ci·cal** (–si·cul) *adj.: ~ humor; ~ attempts at impressing the audience.*

fare *v.* **fares, fared, far·ing 1** get on; do: *How did he ~ in his new job? He ~d well at the exam; She couldn't have ~d any better.* **2** *Archaic.* go or travel. ***—n.*** **1** fee paid for transportation: *The ~ to the airport is $5;* hence, a paying passenger. *The cabbie took his ~ downtown.* **2** food; diet: *plain but wholesome ~.* **—fare·well**

(–WEL) *interj.* good-bye; ***n.*** an expression of good wishes at parting: *to bid someone ~;* ***adj.:*** *a ~ speech.*

Far East E. Asia, esp. China, Japan, Korea, and nearby islands; rarely, S.E. Asia. —**far·fetched** *adj.* contrived; unlikely: *a story too ~ to be true.* —**far-flung** *adj.* widely scattered; also, distant: *the ~ oases of the Sahara.*

fa·ri·na (fuh·REE·nuh) *n.* finely ground meal or flour used as a breakfast cereal and in puddings. —**far·i·na·ceous** (fair·uh·NAY·shus) *adj.* starchy; mealy.

farm *n.* **1** a tract of land on which crops are grown and livestock raised. **2 farm (club)** a minor-league baseball or hockey team associated with or owned by a major league club. —***v.:*** *They ~ many acres in the East;* **farm·ing** *n.* & *adj.: wheat ~ on the plains; the ~ business;* **farm out** send (work) out to be done by others. —**farm·er** *n.: a sheep ~ from Montana.* —**farm·hand** *n.* one who works on a farm. —**farm·house** *n.* the dwelling house on a farm. —**farm·land** *n.* land that is or can be used for agriculture. —**farm·stead** *n.* the land and buildings of a farm. —**farm·yard** *n.* the area next to or surrounded by the buildings of a farm.

far-off *adj.* remote: *the ~ times and places of his childhood.*

fa·rouche (fuh·ROOSH) *adj.* shy; also, uncouth; unsociable.

far-out *adj.* **1** very distant: *the ~ stars of our galaxy.* **2** *Informal.* far from the ordinary; unconventional: *~ music.*

far·ra·go (fuh·RAY–, –RAH–) *n.* **-goes** a jumble or mixture.

far-reach·ing *adj.* having wide-ranging effects or importance: *the ~ tax reforms proposed by Congress.*

far·ri·er *n. Brit.* someone, as a blacksmith, who shoes horses; also, a horse veterinarian.

far·row *v.* & *n.* (give birth to) a litter of pigs.

far·see·ing *adj.* able to see far; esp. showing foresight; farsighted. —**far·sight·ed** *adj.* **1:** *a ~ leader.* **2** not able to see near objects as clearly as distant ones: *Convex glasses are worn to correct* **far·sight·ed·ness** *n.* —**farther** *a comp.* of FAR. —**far·ther·most** *adj.* remotest. —**farthest** *a superl.* of FAR.

far·thing (–dhing) *n.* an old British coin worth one fourth of a penny; hence, something small or of little value; a small sum.

far·thin·gale *n.* a device, usu. consisting of hoops, worn in the 16th and 17th c. to support wide skirts; also, such a skirt or petticoat.

f.a.s. or **F.A.S.** free alongside ship.

fas·ci·cle (FAS·i·cl) *n.* a small cluster or bunch, as of fibers or flowers; hence, one of the parts of a volume published in installments. —**fas·ci·cled** *adj.*

fas·ci·nate (FAS·uh–) *v.* **-nates, -nat·ed, -nat·ing** captivate, esp. in an irresistible or compelling way: *Poetry ~s him; a* **fas·ci·nat·ing** *personality;* **fas·ci·nat·ing·ly** *adv.* —**fas·ci·na·tion** (–NAY–) *n.*

fas·cism (FASH·izm) *n.* a political system or philosophy based on absolute loyalty to a one-party dictatorship, militarism, and usu. racism and nationalism; **fas·cist** *n.* & *adj.*

fash·ion (FASH·un) *n.* **1** the manner of doing something; the way something is: *walks in a peculiar ~; men of all ~s; can speak Chinese* **after** (or **in**) **a fashion** (i.e. moderately well). **2** what is current in styles of dress, speech, conduct, etc. in a particular place or time: *when hoop skirts were in ~.* —***v.*** make in a creative way: *idols ~ed out of clay.* —**fash·ion·a·ble** *adj.* stylish; **fash·ion·a·bly** *adv.*

fast *adj.* **1** firm; secure; hence, steadfast; also, non-fading: *a ~ hold on a rope; They've been ~ friends since boyhood; dyed in ~ colors.* **2** swift; rapid: *a ~ runner; a ~ highway; a ~ watch* (running ahead of the actual time). **3** *Informal.* wild in the pursuit of pleasure: *a ~ crowd; a ~ life.* **4** dishonest or deceptive: *out to make a ~ buck; They pulled* **a fast one** (*Slang.* clever trick) *on me.* —***adv.:*** *He is ~* (i.e. deeply) *asleep; driving too ~; one who* **plays fast and loose** (i.e. acts dishonestly or dishonorably) *with his girls.* —***v.*** abstain from food as penance or in protest: *She used to ~ during Lent.* —***n.*** **1:** *just broke his ~ since his demands have been met.* **2** one that fastens: *a door ~; A stern ~ is a rope or cable.* —**fast·back** *n.* (an automobile with) a roof that is styled in an unbroken curve down the back. —**fast-breed·er reactor** a breeder reactor using high-energy neutrons to produce nuclear fuel. —**fas·ten** (FASN) *v.* make fast, as by tying or gluing; fix: *drives with eyes ~ed on the road in front;* **fas·ten·er** or **fas·ten·ing** *n.* a device that fastens, as a zipper, hook, clip, etc. —**fast-food** *adj.* having to do with food such as hamburgers and hot dogs that may be prepared and served fast: *the ~ industry.*

fas·tid·i·ous (–TID·ee·us) *adj.* hard to please because disdainfully critical (of quality of food, clothes, etc.): *a ~ dresser;* **fas·tid·i·ous·ly** *adv.;* **fas·tid·i·ous·ness** *n.*

fast·ness *n.* **1** a secure place; stronghold: *hiding in the ~es of the jungle.* **2** the quality of being fast or firm. —**fast-talk** *v. Informal.* persuade by fast and often deceitful talking. —**fast time** same as DAYLIGHT SAVING TIME.

fat *n.* an oily substance of animal tissue, considered a sign of luxury on one hand and excess on the other, used as a cooking medium; hence, anything rich or superfluous: *trim the ~ off a heavy budget;* **the fat is in the fire** the damage is done; there will be trouble; **the fat of the land** the best of everything; luxury. —***adj.*** **fat·ter, fat·test** filled out with fat; hence, rich, abundant; fertile; also, heavy, dull: *a ~ man, pocketbook; ~ cattle, lands.*

fa·tal (FAY·tl) *adj.* inevitable; also, causing death: *the ~ hour; a ~ accident; ~ injuries;* **fa·tal·ly** *adv.* —**fa·tal·ism** *n.* the belief or attitude that events, esp. unlucky ones, are predetermined and inevitable; **fa·tal·ist** *n.;* **fa·tal·is·tic** (–IS–) *adj.;* **fa·tal·is·ti·cal·ly** *adv.* —**fa·tal·i·ty** (fuh·TAL–) *n.* **-ties** deadliness; also, death or other calamity: *the reduced* ~ *of cancer; traffic* ~*s during a weekend; The* ~ *rate increases with highway speeds.*

fat·back *n.* dried and salted fat from a hog's back. —**fat cat** a wealthy benefactor; also, a wealthy or lazy person. —**fat chance, fat lot** (of good, etc.) *Slang.* very little (chance, good, etc.). —**fat·ly** *adv.* —**fat·ness** *n.*

fate *n.* **1** the inevitable outcome of events, often unfavorable; also, the divine agency supposed to be directing earthly events, esp. the **Fates,** three goddesses of Greek and Roman myths. **2** death; doom: *"as sure as* ~*."* —**fat·ed** (FAY·tid) *adj.: the "death row" of prisoners* ~ *to die; the ill-*~ *voyage of the Titanic;* **fate·ful** *adj.* decisive for the future; momentous: *The* ~ *hour of a jury's* ~ *verdict;* **fate·ful·ly** *adv.*

fath. fathom.

fat·head *n.* a dull-witted person; **fat·head·ed** *adj.*

fa·ther (FAH·dhur) *n.* a male parent; hence, originator: *the "Founding Fathers" who wrote the U.S. Constitution; "Satan," the father of lies;* **Father** God; also, a Christian priest, esp. as a prefixed title; ***v.*** be the father or begetter of; hence, have the responsibility for; also, impose; foist: *Jim had* ~*ed the child; wrongly* ~*ed on John;* **fa·ther·hood** *n.;* **fa·ther·less** *adj.* —**fa·ther-in-law** *n.* **fa·thers-in-law** the father of one's spouse. —**fa·ther·land** *n.* one's native or ancestral country. —**fa·ther·ly** *adj.;* **fa·ther·li·ness** *n.*

fath·om (FADH·um) *n.* a measure of depth equal to 6 ft. (1.8 m); ***v.*** to sound (a depth); hence, get to the bottom of; figure out; **fath·om·a·ble** *adj.* —**fa·thom·e·ter** (–DHOM·i–) *n.* a sonar echo-sounding device; **Fathometer** *Trademark.* —**fath·om·less** *adj.* not fathomable or comprehensible.

fa·tigue (fuh·TEEG) *n.* weariness from exertion resulting in reduced capacity for work; ***v.*** **-tigues, -tigued, -tigu·ing:** *too* ~*d to walk; A* ~*d axle cracks and breaks under continued strain.* —**fatigue duty** military duty of a menial nature, carried out in "fatigue clothes" or **fatigues** *pl.* work clothing.

fat lot See FAT CHANCE.

Fats(o) *n.* *Slang* [nickname] a fat person. —**fat·ten** *v.* make or become fat. —**fat·ty** *adj.* **fat·ti·er, fat·ti·est** containing fat; also, very plump: *stearic acid and such* ~ *acids containing many carbon atoms; a* ~ (i.e. greasy) *food; a* ~ *person.* —***n.,*** *pl.* **fat·ties** *Informal.* a fat person.

fat·u·ous (FACH·oo·us) *adj.* stupid and self-satisfied; **fat·u·ous·ly** *adv.;* **fat·u·ous·ness** *n.* —**fa·tu·i·ty** (fuh·TUE·i·tee) *n.* **-ties.**

fau·bourg (foh·BOOR) *n.* a suburb of a French city; also, a suburb become a city district.

fau·cal *adj.* of the fauces; pharyngeal: *The "t" of "button" is a* ~ *plosive sound.* —**fau·ces** (FOH·seez) *n.* the entrance to the pharynx where the tonsils are located.

fau·cet (FAW·sit) *n.* a fixture with a valve-device for drawing liquid from a pipe or cask; tap; spigot.

Faulk·ner (FAWK·nur), **William.** 1897–1962, U.S. novelist.

fault *n.* an imperfection, flaw, or error; also, the blame for it: *Everyone has* ~*s; a service* ~ *in tennis; The San Andreas Fault is a visible break in the rock stratum; Who was* **at fault** (i.e. to blame) *in the accident? She's generous* **to a fault** (i.e. excessively); *always trying to* **find fault (with** *someone*); *a constant* **fault·find·er** *n.;* **fault·find·ing** *n.* & *adj.;* **fault·less** *adj.;* **fault·less·ly** *adv.;* **fault·less·ness** *n.* —***v.*** blame: *You can't* ~ *her driving for the flat tire.* —**fault·y** *adj.* **fault·i·er, -i·est** defective: *a fire from a* ~ *electrical connection;* **fault·i·ly** *adv.;* **fault·i·ness** *n.*

faun (FAWN) *n.* a half-human, half-goat Roman deity of fields and herds. —**fau·na** (FAW·nuh) *n.* the animal life or animals of a particular period or region: *the flora and* ~ *of North America.*

Faust (FOWST) a dramatic character from German legends who sells his soul to the devil in return for magical powers.

fau·vism (FOH·vizm) *n.* a French movement in art between 1903 and 1907 marked by bright colors and bold designs: *Henri Matisse was the leading* **fau·vist** *n.*

faux pas (FOH·PAH) *sing., pl.* **faux pas** (–PAHZ) a social blunder or embarrassing mistake.

fa·vel·a (fah·VEL·uh) *n.* a Portuguese slum.

fa·vor (FAY·vur) *n.* friendly regard or approval; also, a token of this, as a gift or an act of kindness: *Do me a small* ~*; justice without fear or* ~*; noisemakers and such party* ~*s; a woman's sexual* **favors** (i.e. intimacies); *a check made out* **in favor of** *a company.* —***v.:*** *He* ~*ed his nephew with a job; Which candidate do you* ~*? She* ~*s* (i.e. resembles) *her father;* **fa·vor·er** *n.* —**fa·vor·a·ble** *adj.: weather* ~ *for a picnic;* **fa·vor·a·bly** *adv.* —**fa·vor·ite** (–it) *n.* one specially liked; ***adj.:*** *a child's* ~ *toy; a teacher's* ~ *pupil;* **favorite son** a candidate for national office favored by people of his own region; **fa·vor·it·ism** *n.* partiality towards particular people. —**fa·vour** *Brit.* favor.

¹fawn *v.* show friendliness in the manner of a dog, esp. by cringing or flattery; **fawn·er** *n.*

²fawn *n.* a young deer less than a year old; also, the pale yellowish brown of its coat; also ***adj.***

fax *n.* same as FACSIMILE.

fay *n.* a fairy; elf.

faze *v.* **faz·es, fazed, faz·ing** *Informal.* upset: *Nothing could ever* ~ *him.*

F.B.I. Federal Bureau of Investigation.

F.C.C. Federal Communications Commission.

F.D. Fire Department.

F.D.A. Food and Drug Administration.

F.D.I.C. Federal Deposit Insurance Corporation.

Fe Iron.

fe·al·ty (FEE·ul·tee) *n.* **-ties** allegiance, as of a vassal to his lord.

fear (FEER) *n.* an emotion felt in the presence of danger or some threat to one's well-being: *the ~ of darkness; a ~ of heights; the salutary ~* (i.e. reverence) *of God; tiptoeing* **for fear of** *waking the baby.* —***v.:*** *We ~ed for his life; She ~s to fly.* —**fear·ful** *adj.;* **fear·ful·ly** *adv.;* **fear·ful·ness** *n.* —**fear·less** *adj.;* **fear·less·ly** *adv.;* **fear·less·ness** *n.* —**fear·some** (–sum) *adj.* frightful; also, timid.

fea·si·ble (FEE·zuh–) *adj.* possible to carry out or do, esp. conveniently: *It's possible to drive 1,000 miles nonstop but hardly ~; a ~* (i.e. plausible) *story considering the circumstances;* **fea·si·bil·i·ty** (–BIL–) *n.: a ~ study for a bridge across the river;* **fea·si·bly** *adv.*

feast (FEEST) *n.* an elaborate or sumptuous meal; also, a festival: *a wedding ~; Hanukkah, the ~ of lights.* —***v.:*** *He ~s his friends each Christmas; ~ your eyes on beauty.*

feat (FEET) *n.* a remarkable deed or exploit: *herculean ~s of strength.*

feath·er (FEDH·ur) *n.* **1** one of the light, soft, thin outgrowths covering a bird's body; **feather in one's cap** an accomplishment. **2** kind: *"Birds of a ~* (i.e. of the same kind) *flock together."* —***v.*** **1** supply or furnish with feathers; **feather one's nest** enrich oneself by taking advantage of a position. **2** turn (the blade of an oar or those of an airplane propeller or helicopter rotor) so as to avoid water or air resistance. —**feath·er·bed·ding** *n.* the practice of forcing an employer to hire unnecessary labor or to pay for idle labor. —**feath·ered** *adj.: our ~ friends, the birds.* —**feath·er·edge** *n.* a thin and easily damaged edge. —**feath·er·weight** *n.* a boxer weighing between 119 and 126 lb. (54 and 57 kg for Olympics). —**feath·er·y** *adj.* feathered; also, light or soft like feathers.

fea·ture (FEE·chur) *n.* **1** an outstanding detail or quality: *has handsome ~s* (i.e. cast of face) *though not an Apollo; the physical ~s of a region.* **2** an outstanding or special item offered for sale, a story or article of special interest, a full-length movie, etc.: *a ~ writer; a ~-length movie.* —***v.*** **-tures, -tured, -tur·ing:** *a store that ~s discounts; Who was ~d in that Broadway hit?* —**fea·ture·less** *adj.: the ~ wastes of the Sahara.*

Feb. February.

feb·ri·fuge (FEB·ruh·fyooj) *n.* & *adj.* (a substance) that reduces fever. —**fe·brile** (FEE·brul, FEB–) *adj.* feverish; of fever.

Feb·ru·ar·y (FEB·roo·er·ee, FEB·yoo–) *n.* **-ar·ies** the second month of the year, with 28 days or, in leap years, 29 days.

fe·ces (FEE·seez) *n.pl.* waste from the intestines; **fe·cal** (FEE·kul) *adj.*

feck·less (FEK·lis) *adj.* ineffective; futile; also, irresponsible; **feck·less·ly** *adv.;* **feck·less·ness** *n.*

fe·cund (FEC·und, FEE–) *adj.* fruitful; fertile: *da Vinci's ~ genius; the ~ earth;* **fe·cun·di·ty** (fi·CUN–) *n.* —**fe·cun·date** (FEE–) *v.* **-dates, -dat·ed, -dat·ing** make fecund; fertilize; **fe·cun·da·tion** (–DAY–) *n.*

fed *pt.* & *pp.* of FEED; **fed up** *Informal.* tired and disgusted. —***n.*** *Informal.* **1** same as FEDERAL, *n.* 1. **2 the Fed** Federal Reserve Bank; Federal Reserve Board; Federal Reserve System. —**fed.** federal; federated; federation.

fed·a·yeen (fed·ah·YEEN) *n.pl.* Arab guerrillas.

fed·er·al (–ul) *adj.* having to do with federalism; hence, of a central government: *The Supreme Court of the U.S. is the highest ~ court; D.C. is a ~ district;* **fed·er·al·ist** *n.* & *adj.* —**Federal** *n.* **1** an agent or officer of the U.S. government. **2** a supporter or soldier of the U.S. government in the Civil War; also, a member of the Federalist Party. —**fed·er·al·ism** *n.* a system in which a central government has the authority in matters of national concern and states or provinces have the powers given them by the country's constitution, as in the U.S. and Switzerland. —**Fed·er·al·ist** *n.* & *adj.;* **Federal(ist) Party** a U.S. political party between 1789 and 1816. —**fed·er·al·ly** *adv.* —**fed·er·al·ize** *v.* **-iz·es, -ized, -iz·ing,** unite into a federal union or put under federal control; **fed·er·al·i·za·tion** (–ZAY–) *n.* —**fed·er·ate** *v.* —**ates, -at·ed, -at·ing** unite into a **fed·er·a·tion** (–AY–) *n.* a union of many member nations, states, or organizations; league: *The American Federation of Labor.* —**fedn.** federation.

fe·do·ra (fi·DOR·uh) *n.* a man's soft felt hat with the crown creased lengthwise.

fee *n.* **1** a charge or payment for professional services: *a lawyer's ~; college tuition ~s.* **2** *Law.* ownership of land: *"hold in fee"* (i.e. own); *"fee simple"* (i.e. complete ownership).

fee·ble *adj.* **-bler, -blest** weak from sickness or age; hence, ineffective: *a ~ voice; a ~ attempt;* **fee·ble·ness** *n.;* **fee·bly** *adv.* —**fee·ble·mind·ed** *adj.* mentally retarded; **fee·ble·mind·ed·ly** *adv.;* **fee·ble·mind·ed·ness** *n.*

feed *v.* **feeds, fed, feed·ing** **1** give food to; hence, supply; provide: *Mother ~s the baby; ~ this to the cat; information fed into a computer; news to ~* (i.e. satisfy) *your curiosity.* **2** eat; **feed (up)on** prey on; also, be supplied or satisfied with: *Cattle ~ on carefully selected feed in* **feed lots.** —***n.*** food for animals; hence, material to feed into a machine or furnace; also, the feeding mechanism. —**feed·back** *n.* in automatic systems, the return of part of the output as input, as in the on-and-off switching in a home heating system; hence, any similar process: *a course modified with the help of ~ from students.* —**feed·bag** *n.* a feed-filled bag fastened to a horse's head. —**feed·er** *n.* one that feeds: *Feed lots fatten up ~ cattle; local ~ airlines connecting with a major one.* —**feed lot** See FEED, *v.* 2.

feel *v.* **feels, felt, feel·ing** **1** be aware of; perceive; experience (something or one's own state of being): *You will ~ better after resting; A nail or hair cannot ~; I ~ for you in your misery; Do you* **feel like** *taking a walk? No, I don't* **feel up to** *it today.* **2** test, perceive, seem, or be aware of by touching: *The doctor felt my pulse; She felt in her pockets for the key; He* **feels his way** *about in the dark; The room ~s warm; Let's* **feel out** (i.e. find out the thinking of) *the membership on this issue.* —***n.*** **1** the sense of touch; also, an act of feeling or touching. **2** how something feels when touched. —**feel·er** *n.* one that feels another out, as an insect's antenna or an observation or suggestion to find out what a person thinks. —**feel·ing** *n.* the sense of touch; also, any experience of sensation or emotion, esp. as tending to influence one's thought: *a numb ~; a ~ of joy; sounded as if his* **feelings** (i.e. sensitivities) *had been hurt; What are your ~s on the abortion issue?* Also ***adj.*** sensitive; sympathetic: *a ~ remark.* —**feel·ing·ly** *adv.*

feet *pl.* of FOOT.

feign (FAIN) *v.* pretend: *He's only ~ing sickness; She wants to ~* (i.e. make up) *an excuse for being absent.* —**feint** *n.* pretense: *a surprise attack after a ~ of retreating;* ***v.:*** *He dribbled the ball after ~ing a pass.*

feist·y (FYE·stee) *adj.* **feist·i·er, -i·est** spirited; esp., quarrelsome.

feld·spar *n.* a mineral found in crystalline rock and containing aluminum, silica, and other elements.

fe·lic·i·tate (fuh·LIS–) *v.* **-tates, -tat·ed, -tat·ing** *Formal.* congratulate (someone on something, as a promotion, wedding, etc.); **fe·lic·i·ta·tion** (–TAY–) *n.* —**fe·lic·i·ta·tor** (–LIS–) *n.* —**fe·lic·i·tous** (–tus) *adj.* delightful; also, delightfully expressed; appropriate: *a ~ occasion; a most ~ way of expressing herself;* **fe·lic·i·tous·ly** *adv.* —**fe·lic·i·ty** *n.* **-ties** **1** happiness; good fortune. **2** gracefulness of expression; also, a graceful or apt expression.

fe·line (FEE–) *n.* & *adj.* (an animal) of the cat family; also, catlike: *Lions and tigers are ~s; crept forward with ~ stealth.*

fell **1** *pt.* of FALL. **2** *v.* strike down or cut down: *a tree ~ed with one blow of the ax.* **3** *adj.* fierce or deadly; **at one fell swoop** suddenly and all at once: *took care of everything at one ~ swoop.* **4** *n.* an animal's hide; pelt.

fel·lah (FEL·uh) *n.* **fel·lahs, fel·la·hin** (–HEEN) or **-heen** in Arab countries, a peasant or laborer.

fel·la·ti·o (fuh·LAY·shee·oh, fuh·LAH·tee·oh) *n.* oral stimulation of the penis.

fel·loe (FEL·oh) *n.* same as FELLY.

fel·low (FEL·oh) *n.* **1** *Informal.* a male person. **2** a comrade; companion; mate; also, peer: *They were ~s at school; The ~ to this glove is missing; The world has not produced a ~ to Shakespeare's genius.* **3** a member of a learned society; also, a student on a fellowship. —***adj.*** of the same rank or condition: *our ~ citizens;* **fel·low·man** *n.* a fellow human being; **fellow traveler** a sympathizer or supporter of a party, esp. Communist, without being a member. —**fel·low·ship** *n.* **1** companionship; community of interest; also, membership. **2** a group or society. **3** at a university, a position or award given to a graduate student to help him study further.

fel·ly (FEL·ee) *n.* **fel·lies** the rim of a wheel, or a section of it, that is supported by the spokes.

fel·on (FEL·un) *n.* **1** one who has committed a **fel·o·ny** *n.* **-nies,** a crime such as rape, arson, robbery, or kidnapping, that is more serious than a misdemeanor; **fe·lo·ni·ous** (fuh·LOH·nee·us) *adj.* **2** same as WHITLOW.

felt **1** *pt.* & *pp.* of FEEL. **2** *n.* a fabric made with wool mixed with fur, hair, etc. matted together by steam and pressure instead of being woven or knitted; ***v.*** make into felt; **felt·ing** *n.* felt cloth.

fe·luc·ca (fuh·LUC·uh, –LOO–) *n.* a small, lateen-rigged ship of the Mediterranean.

fem. feminine. —**fe·male** (FEE–) *adj.* **1** of the sex that produces eggs or bears young. **2** forming a receptacle for a corresponding male part: *The vagina is a ~ structure; A pistillate flower has only the ~ organ of pollination; a ~ electric socket; A bolt turns in the ~ groove inside a nut.* —***n.*** a female person, animal, flower, etc. —**fem·i·nine** (FEM·uh·nin) *adj.* having to do with women or their characteristics; also, effeminate: *a ~ fashion; "-ess" is a ~ suffix; the ~ gender;* ***n.*** the feminine gender or a word or a form in this, as *she* or *actress;* **fem·i·nin·i·ty** (–NIN–) *n.* —**fem·i·nism** *n.* the women's rights movement or its principles; **fem·i·nist** *n.* & *adj.* —**fem lib** women's liberation. —**femme fa·tale** (fem·fuh·TAL), *pl.* **femmes fatales** (fem·fuh·TALZ) a seductress.

femto- *comb.form.* one quadrillionth: as in *femtoampere, femtosecond.*

fe·mur (FEE–) *n.* **fe·murs** or **fem·o·ra** (FEM·uh·ruh) the thighbone; **fem·o·ral** (FEM·uh–) *adj.: a ~ artery.*

fen *n.* **1** esp. in England, a marsh or swamp. **2** a money unit equal to 1/100 of a Chinese yuan.

fence *n.* **1** a barrier of stakes, stones, or wire put around property for protection or privacy; **on the fence** hesitating about which side of a dispute to join. **2** a receiver of stolen goods; also, a place where such are bought and sold. —***v.*** **fenc·es, fenced, fenc·ing** **1** enclose or keep out with a fence. **2** practice the sport of fencing; also, parry questions; **fenc·er** *n.*

—**fence-mend·ing** *n.* the improving of a neglected relationship. —**fenc·ing** *n.* **1** swordplay using a foil, epee, or saber. **2** material for putting up a fence.

fend *v.* defend: *had to* **fend for himself** (i.e. provide for himself) *after his parents died; She used judo to* **fend off** *her attacker.* —**fend·er** *n.* a protective or shielding device, as the metal covers over an automobile's tires, the screen in front of a fireplace, or a buffer for protecting a ship's side when docking.

fen·es·tra·tion (–TRAY–) *n.* **1** the arrangement of windows in a building. **2** the cutting of a tiny window in the inner ear to treat deafness.

fen·nel (FENL) *n.* an herb of the parsley family yielding fragrant leaves and aromatic seeds used in flavoring.

F.E.P.C. Fair Employment Practices Committee.

fe·ral (FEER·ul) *adj.* untamed; wild; savage: *fell into a ~ rage.*

fer-de-lance (fair·duh·LAHNCE) *n. sing. & pl.* a large poisonous tropical American pit viper related to the rattlesnakes.

fer·ment *n.* (FUR·ment) a substance or organism, as yeast and bacteria, that causes fermentation; hence, a state of agitation or unrest: *the ~ that swept over U.S. campuses in the 60's.* —***v.*** (fur·MENT) to be in fermentation or cause fermentation in: *Yeast ~s the starch in bread dough; Cheese is a ~ed food.* —**fer·men·ta·tion** (–TAY–) *n.* a change such as the souring of milk, ripening of cheese, or curing of silage brought about by the action of enzymes, bacteria, and such agents.

fer·mi·um (FUR·mee·um) *n.* an artificial radioactive metallic chemical element.

fern *n.* one of a large group of flowerless, seedless plants that have stems and fronds and that reproduce by means of spores; **fern·er·y** *n.* **-er·ies** a collection of ferns or the place where they are grown.

fe·ro·cious (fuh·ROH·shus) *adj.* fierce; bloodthirsty; hence, excessive; extreme: *pangs of ~ hunger;* **fe·ro·cious·ly** *adv.;* **fe·ro·cious·ness** or **fe·roc·i·ty** (fuh·ROS–) *n.* **-ties** fierce cruelty; also, a ferocious act.

-ferous *adj. suffix.* bearing: as in *coniferous, metalliferous.*

fer·ret (FER·it) *n.* a weasellike animal trained for use by hunters and rat-catchers. —***v.*** **ferret out** force out of hiding; search out (facts, secrets, the truth, etc.).

fer·ric (FER·ic) *adj.* of or derived from iron; **ferric oxide** iron oxide, used as a pigment, in abrasives, etc.

Fer·ris (FER·is) **wheel** an amusement device consisting of a large upright wheel with a fixed axis and seats swinging from its rim.

ferro- *comb.form.* iron: as in **fer·ro·con·crete** *n.* reinforced concrete; **fer·ro·mag·net·ic** (–NET–) *adj.* easily magnetized, as iron, steel, cobalt, or nickel. —**fer·rous** (FER·us) *adj.* of or derived from iron: *Steel is a ~ alloy;* **ferrous oxide** monoxide of iron.

fer·rule (FER·ul, –ool) *n.* a metal ring or cap put at the end of a cane, tube, tool handle, etc. for added strength.

fer·ry (FER·ee) *n.* **fer·ries** a conveyance, as a boat, hydrofoil, or aircraft, for people and goods, esp. across water; also, a ferry system or the place where a ferry is boarded; ***v.*** **fer·ries, fer·ried, fer·ry·ing** cross or convey by ferry: *Airplanes are ~d* (i.e. flown) *from factory to delivery points.* —**fer·ry·boat** *n.* —**fer·ry·man** *n.* **-men.**

fer·tile (FUR·tl) *adj.* of persons, land, plants, one's mind, etc., productive (of young, crops, seeds, ideas, etc.): *~ soil; ~ eggs; a storyteller's ~ imagination;* **fer·til·i·ty** (–TIL–) *n.: multiple births caused by ~ drugs.* —**fer·til·ize** (FUR·tl–) *v.* **-iz·es, -ized, -iz·ing** make fertile, as by use of fertilizer (on land) or by impregnating (an egg cell); **fer·til·iz·er** *n.* a substance such as manure or chemical nutrients put in the soil to enrich it; **fer·til·i·za·tion** (–ZAY–) *n.*

fer·ule (FER·ul, –ool) *n.* a ruler used for punishing schoolchildren.

fer·vent (FUR·vunt) *adj.* showing earnestness or devotion; impassioned: *a ~ prayer; a ~ plea for mercy;* **fer·vent·ly** *adv.;* **fer·ven·cy** *n.* —**fer·vid** *adj.* fervent in a too eager manner: *a ~ preacher;* **fer·vid·ly** *adv.* —**fer·vor** (–vur) *n.* earnestness or enthusiasm; zeal: *religious ~.*

-fest *comb.form.* festival: as in *funfest, Octoberfest.* —**fes·tal** (FES·tl) *adj.* festive.

fes·ter *n.* a small ulcer or sore filled with pus; ***v.*** to form pus; also, rankle or cause to rankle; embitter: *Hatred ~ed in his mind.*

fes·ti·val (FES·ti·vul) *n.* a celebration or an occasion of feasting and fun: *a music ~; a Christmas ~.* —**fes·tive** (–tiv) *adj.* having to do with a feast or festival; hence, joyous; gay: *New Year's is a ~ occasion; in a ~ mood;* **fes·tive·ly** *adv.;* **fes·tive·ness** *n.* —**fes·tiv·i·ty** (–TIV–) *n.* **-ties** merrymaking; also, a festive activity: *Christmas ~s ending with fireworks.* —**fes·toon** (fes·TOON) *n.* a garland of flowers or other decorative material for hanging in a loop. ***v.:*** *an altar ~ed with garlands and streamers.*

F.E.T. field-effect transistor; federal excise tax.

fet·a (cheese) (FET·uh) *n.* a firm white cheese made in Greece from goat's milk.

fe·tal (FEE·tl) *adj.* of a fetus; **fetal position** the curled-up position characteristic of a fetus in the womb.

fetch *v.* **1** bring; get: *Go to the pump and ~ water for your bath; The car will ~ $2,000 if you sell it now; skidded off the road and* **fetched up** (i.e. stopped) *against a tree.* **2** draw forth (a sigh, groan, tears, etc.). **3** *Informal.* deal: *She ~ed* *him one on the jaw.* —**fetch·ing** *adj.* attractive; **fetch·ing·ly** *adv.*

fete or **fête** (FAIT) *n.* a lavish entertainment or party, often one held outdoors; ***v.*** **fetes** or **fêtes, fet·ed** or **fêt·ed, fet·ing** or **fêt·ing:** *The Olympic hero was ~d everywhere he went.*

fetich same as FETISH.

fet·id (FET–, FEET–) *adj. Formal.* offensive-smelling; stinking; **fet·id·ness** *n.*

fet·ish (FET–, FEET–) *n.* **1** an idol, image, or other object of superstitious devotion: *He makes a ~ of brushing his teeth thrice a day.* **2** a nonsexual object or an obsessive attachment to it for its erotic value; also **fet·ich** (–ish); **fet·ish·ism** or **fet·ich·ism** *n.;* **fet·ish·ist** *n.*

fet·lock *n.* the projection at the back just above a horse's or donkey's hoof with a tuft of hair on it.

fet·ter *n.* a shackle for the feet; hence, a restraint: *the ~s of superstition;* ***v.*** hamper; also, restrain.

fet·tle *n.* **in fine fettle** in good physical condition.

fe·tus (FEE·tus) *n.* a developing animal embryo, esp. an unborn infant after the first two months of conception; **fe·tol·o·gy** (–TOL–) *n.;* **fe·tol·o·gist** *n.*

feud (FEWD) *n.* a long-lasting quarrel, esp. between families or clans, often vengeful and bitter; ***v.:*** *the ~ing Hatfields and McCoys of Kentucky;* **feu·dal** *adj.*

feu·dal (FEW·dl) *adj.* of or like **feu·dal·ism** *n.* the economic, social, and political system of medieval Europe binding vassals to the military service of their lords from whom they received fiefs of land, buildings, and the serfs or peasants working the land; **feu·dal·is·tic** (–IS–) *adj.* —**feu·da·to·ry** (FEW–) *n.* **-ries** a feudal vassal or his fief.

fe·ver (FEE–) *n.* abnormally high body temperature; hence, a restless or excited state: *emotions stirred to a* **fever pitch** *before a riot;* **fe·ver·ish** *adj.;* **fe·ver·ish·ly** *adv.;* **fe·ver·ish·ness** *n.* —**fever blister** (or **sore**) cold sore. —**fe·ver·few** *n.* a species of chrysanthemum.

few *n., pron. & adj.* not many: *~ books are missing; 10 or fewer;* **a few** some; **quite a few** *Informal.* a good many; **the few** the minority.

fey *adj.* formerly, doomed; now, fairylike, strange, or unusual: *a ~ character.*

fez *n.* **fez·zes** a red, brimless felt cap with a tassel hanging from the crown, worn by Arab men.

ff. folios; following (pages); fortissimo.

FHA Federal Housing Administration.

fi·an·cé (fee·ahn·SAY) *n.* a man engaged to be married; *fem.* **fi·an·cée** (–SAY).

fi·as·co (fee·AS·coh) *n.* **-co(e)s** an utter failure.

fi·at (FEE·at, –ut) *n.* an executive, usu. arbitrary order; decree: **fiat money** *has no silver reserves backing it up.*

fib *n.* a trivial little lie; ***v.*** **fibs, fibbed, fib·bing; fib·ber** *n.*

fi·ber or **fi·bre** (FYE·bur) *n.* a threadlike strand of an animal, vegetable, or mineral substance such as muscle tissue, wool, cotton, or asbestos; also, this spun or woven into materials with strength and toughness; hence, strength or character: *Rayon, fiberglass, and nylon are synthetic ~s; a man of strong moral ~.* —**fi·ber·board** *n.* a building material pressed from wood and other fibers. —**fi·ber·fill** *n.* a fluffy padding material made of synthetic fiber. —**fi·ber·glass** *n.* finespun glass woven into cloth, made into plastic material for boards, or in woolly form as insulation; **Fi·ber·glas** *Trademark.* —**fiber optics** *n.pl.* transmission of light around bends and curves through a bundle of flexible filaments of glass or plastic; **fi·ber-op·tic** *adj.;* **fi·ber·scope** *n.* a flexible fiber-optic instrument for examining internal organs such as the stomach. —**fi·bril** (FYE–) *n.* a small fiber; **fi·bril·late** *v.* **-lates, -lat·ed, -lat·ing** split up into fibrils; esp. of the heart muscles, undergo **fi·bril·la·tion** (–LAY–) *n.* uncoordinated twitching or tremors of muscle fibers. —**fi·brin** (FYE–) *n.* a white, fibrous substance formed in blood clots from **fi·brin·o·gen** (–BRIN·uh·jun) *n.* a protein present in blood serum; **fi·brin·ous** (FYE–) *adj.* —**fi·broid** (FYE–) *n. & adj.* (of or having to do with) a benign tumor that grows in the muscle fibers of the walls of the uterus. —**fi·bro·sis** (–BROH–) *n.* excessive growth of fibrous tissue. —**fi·brous** (FYE·brus) *adj.* having fibers; also, like fiber.

fib·u·la (FIB·yuh·luh) *n.,pl.* **-lae** (–lee) or **-las** the smaller of the two bones between the knee and the ankle; **fib·u·lar** *adj.*

-fic *suffix.* making: as in *prolific, scientific.*

FICA Federal Insurance Contributions Act.

fiche (FEESH, FISH) *n.* short form of MICROFICHE.

fich·u (FISH·oo) *n.* a light triangular scarf worn by women draped over the shoulders and tied loosely at the breast.

fick·le *adj.* inconstant or changeable like the weather: *a ~ lover;* **fick·le·ness** *n.*

fic·tion *n.* something made up in the mind; hence, literature of the imagination including novels, short stories, and plays; **fic·tion·al** *adj.;* **fic·tion·al·ize** *v.* **-iz·es, -ized, -iz·ing:** *a highly ~d story of Jesus;* **fic·tion·al·ly** *adv.* —**fic·ti·tious** (–TISH·us) *adj.* imaginary; not real; assumed: *a ~ character like Oliver Twist; "John Doe" is a ~ name; checked in under a ~* (i.e. false) *name.* —**fic·tive** (–tiv) *adj.* not genuine; also, fictional: *seeking solace in the ~ world of TV;* **fic·tive·ly** *adv.*

fid·dle (FIDL) *Informal. n.* **1** a violin. **2** a falsification of accounts: *a tax ~.* —***v.*** **fid·dles, fid·dled, fid·dling 1** play on a violin; **fiddle away** (or **around**) waste time. **2** tamper with, esp. accounts: *good at ~ing tax returns;* **fid·**

dler *n.* —**fiddler crab** a small burrowing crab, the male of which has one claw much larger than the other. —**fid·dle·sticks** *interj.* nonsense!

fi·del·i·ty (fuh·DEL–, fye–) *n.* **-ties** **1** loyalty, esp. faithfulness to a duty or trust: *an employer protected by ~ bonds issued to employees against losses due to dishonesty or negligence.* **2** the degree of accuracy of electronic sound or picture reproduction: *a high-~ radio receiver.*

fidg·et (FIJ·it) *v.* move or act nervously or restlessly; ***n.*** this condition or a person who fidgets; **the fidgets** *n.pl.* a fit of nervousness; **fidg·et·y** *adj.*

fi·do (FYE·doh) *n.* **-dos** a coin with a minting error.

fi·du·ci·ar·y (fi·DEW·shee·er·ee) *adj.* held or holding in trust; of a trustee: *Executors act in a ~ capacity;* ***n., pl.*** **-aries** a trustee.

fie (FYE) *interj.* shame: *~ on you!*

fief (FEEF) *n.* an estate granted by a feudal lord to a vassal.

field (FEELD) *n.* **1** a piece of open land, esp. one put to a specific use, as for crops, pasture, or aircraft landing; also, a wide expanse: *a ~ of ice; a football ~.* **2** an area seen through a telescope, covered by one scanning of a TV camera's beam, etc. **3** an area of interest, influence, or activity: *Geography is outside my ~; The moon is within the earth's gravitational ~; He doesn't go steady, but* **plays the field** (i.e. dates many girls). —***v.*** **1** in baseball, cricket, etc., catch or stop a batted ball; act as a **field·er:** *a skilled diplomat ~ing reporters' questions with ease.* **2** put (people) on a field: *The party ~ed 200 candidates in the last election.* —**field day** a day for outdoor sports or activities; hence, an occasion of unrestricted freedom or enjoyment. —**field glass(es)** binoculars for outdoor use. —**field goal** **1** in football, a goal kicked from the field. **2** in basketball, a basket scored while the ball is in play. —**field gun** same as FIELD PIECE. —**field hand** a farm laborer. —**field hockey** hockey played on a field of grass. —**field marshal** in some countries, an army officer ranking next below a commander in chief. —**field piece** a cannon mounted on a carriage. —**field-test** *v.* test (a product) under actual conditions of use.

fiend (FEEND) *n.* **1** the devil; hence, an evil spirit or a wicked person. **2** *Informal.* one devoted or addicted to something: *a fresh-air ~; a bridge ~;* **fiend·ish** *adj.;* **fiend·ish·ly** *adv.;* **fiend·ish·ness** *n.*

fierce (FEERCE) *adj.* **fierc·er, fierc·est** **1** extremely violent in temper or manner: *a ~ battle, dog, loyalty; the ~ heat of summer.* **2** *Slang.* very bad: *It was ~ of me to lose my temper;* **fierce·ly** *adv.;* **fierce·ness** *n.*

fi·er·y (FYE·uh·ree) *adj.* **fi·er·i·er, -i·est** burning; like fire; full of fire: *the Ku Klux Klan's ~ crosses; a ~ speech; a ~* (i.e. inflamed) *sore;* **fi·er·i·ness** *n.*

fi·es·ta (fee·ES·tuh) *n.* esp. in Spanish-speaking countries, a religious or secular festival.

FIFA International (Soccer) Football Federation.

fife *n.* a flutelike musical instrument, used with drums.

FIFO (FYE·foh) *n.* first-in first-out (method of inventory valuation).

fif·teen (–TEEN) *n., adj. & pron.* five more than 10; 15 or XV; **fif·teenth** *n. & adj.* —**fifth** *n. & adj.* (the one) following the fourth; 1/5; esp., a fifth of a U.S. gallon: *The* **Fifth Amendment** *to the U.S. Constitution guarantees that a person cannot be forced to testify against himself in criminal cases;* **fifth column** a group working secretly for a foreign enemy; **fifth wheel** a superfluous or burdensome person or thing. —**fif·ty** (–tee) *n. & adj.* **-ties** 50 or L; **the fifties** numbers, years, etc. ending in 50 through 59; **fif·ti·eth** (–ith) *n. & adj.;* **fif·ty-fif·ty** *adj. & adv. Informal.* equal(ly): *a ~ chance of winning; divided ~.*

fig *n.* a tree of the mulberry family bearing edible pear-shaped fruit hidden among deeply lobed leaves.

fig. figurative(ly); figure(s).

fight (FITE) *v.* **fights, fought** (FAWT), **fight·ing** struggle or contend against; also, get by fighting: *We ~ for survival; ~ your way through life; a battle well fought; He couldn't* **fight back** *his tears; She* **fought off** *sleep by pinching herself; determined to* **fight it out** (or *~ to a finish*); *Never* **fight shy of** (i.e. avoid) *facing the truth;* —***n.:*** *Who won the ~? still full of ~* (i.e. fighting spirit) *though thrice beaten.* —**fight·er** *n.* —**fighting chance** a chance to win after a hard struggle.

fig-leaf *n.* a leaf used traditionally in sculpture to hide the genitals of nude figures.

fig·ment *n.* something made up: *a mere ~ of the imagination.*

fig·u·ra·tion (–yuh·RAY–) *n.* a forming; also, a form or appearance. —**fig·u·ra·tive** (FIG·yuh·ruh·tiv) *adj.* using figures of speech; not literal; **fig·u·ra·tive·ly** *adv.* —**fig·ure** (FIG·yur) *n.* **1** number or amount; also, a numeral: *The President gets a six-~ salary; Did the saleslady mention a ~? Accountants are good at* **figures** (i.e. math); *The plane did a* **figure eight.** **2** a shape or pattern: *A parabola is a geometric ~; the 69 "school ~s" of* **figure skating.** **3** a shape of one's body: *She diets to keep her ~; He's a handsome ~; an artist good at ~ drawing; Napoleon is a historical ~* (i.e. personage). **4** a similarity or likeness; image: *Clowns cut funny ~s; She was a ~ of misery; similes, metaphors, and such* **figures of speech.** —***v.*** **-ures, -ured, -ur·ing** **1** calculate: *That's too much to* **figure up** (i.e. add) *without a calculator; difficult to* **figure out** (i.e. understand) *what this poem means.* **2** appear prominently: *Galahad ~s in Arthurian legends.* **3** imagine; also, picture: *I had* **figured** (i.e. relied) **(up)on** *your helping us;* **figured** (i.e. patterned) *wallpaper.* —**fig·ure·**

head *n.* an ornamental carved figure on the bow of a ship; hence, a person in a high position but without real power. **—fig·u·rine** (–REEN) *n.* a statuette.

fig·wort (–wurt) *n.* a family of about 3,000 herbs, trees, and shrubs, some of which have medicinal value, as the foxglove.

Fi·ji (FEE·jee) a country made up of two main and 500 smaller islands in the S.W. Pacific; 7,055 sq. mi. (18,272 km²); *cap.* Suva.

fil·a·ment *n.* a thread or a threadlike part, as the wire that glows in an electric bulb or the cathode of an electron tube, the stalk of a flower's stamen, etc.; **fil·a·men·tous** (–MEN–) *adj.* **—fi·lar** (FYE·lur) *adj.* threadlike; **fi·lar·i·a** (fi·LAIR–) *n.* a threadlike parasite that causes **fil·a·ri·a·sis** (–RYE–) *n.* same as ELEPHANTIASIS.

fil·bert (FIL–) *n.* same as HAZELNUT; also, the tree.

filch *v.* steal casually (something of small value, as candy from a counter); **filch·er** *n.*

file *n.* **1** a smoothing or grinding metal tool with a ridged surface. **2** a container such as a folder, drawer, or cabinet for keeping papers in order, usu. threaded with a wire, rod, or other device; also, such an arrangement or the set of papers: *"Your application is* **on file** *for future reference," said the* **file clerk. 3** a row of persons, animals, or things, one behind the other: *to march* **in file. —*v.* files, filed, fil·ing** [corresponding to the *n.* senses] **1:** *The rough edge will hurt unless* **filed away;** *a carpentry floor sprinkled with iron* **filings** (i.e. particles). **2:** *A lawsuit is ~d* (i.e. officially begun); *Correspondents ~* (i.e. transmit) *stories to their papers; Please ~ away these letters;* **file·a·ble** *adj.;* **fil·er** *n.* **3:** *Shoppers kept* **filing in** *through the turnstiles when the doors opened.*

fi·let (fi·LAY, FIL·ay) *n.* same as FILLET, *n.* 2; **filet mi·gnon** (fi·LAY·min·YONE), *pl.* **fi·lets mi·gnons** (fi·LAY·min·YONES) a choice tenderloin cut of beef.

fil·i·al (FIL·ee·ul, FIL·yul) *adj.* of a son or daughter, as to a parent: *~ love.*

fil·i·bus·ter *n.* the use of delaying tactics to obstruct the passage of a bill in a legislature, esp. by prolonged speechmaking; ***v.:*** *In 1964 U.S. senators tried for 75 days to ~ a civil rights bill; Huey Long once ~ed 15½ hours in 1935;* **fil·i·bus·ter·er** *n.*

fil·i·gree *n.* ornamental lacelike openwork of gold or silver wire; ***v.* -grees, -greed, -gree·ing:** *Our picture window was ~d with frost.*

Fil·i·pi·no (–PEE–) *adj.* & *n.* **-nos** (of or having to do with) a person from the Philippines.

fill *v.* **1** put something into so as to occupy (a space) fully: *~ a glass; a ~ing meal; Dentists ~ cavities; Please* **fill up** *my gas tank; sails* **filled out** *by the wind; Will you ~ out this form?* **2** supply what is called for (in an order, prescription, etc.). **3** put (someone or oneself) into (a position or office): *An employment agency helps ~ vacancies; Ms. Smith has ~ed the principalship; She had the qualifications and experience to* **fill the bill** (i.e. answer a need); *The vice-principal* **fills in** (i.e. substitutes) *for the principal when the latter is away and later* **fills her in** (i.e. brings her up to date) *on what happened during her absence; He is her* **fill-in** (i.e. substitute). **—*n.:*** *He ate his ~ from the smorgasbord; Earth, gravel, and garbage are used as ~s.* **—fill·er** *n.* person or thing that fills, such as ground wood added to synthetic resin for hardness and strength, the hose of a gas pump, a short item used to fill a newspaper column, etc.

fil·lér (FEEL·ur) *n.* a Hungarian money unit equal to 1/100 of a forint.

fil·let (FIL·it) *n.* **1** a ribbonlike strip or band. **2** (*also* fi·LAY, FIL·ay) a slice of boneless, lean meat or fish, esp. a FILET MIGNON. **—*v.*** **1** (FIL·it) bind: *hair ~ed with a headband.* **2** (*also* fi·LAY, FIL·ay) bone and slice (fish or meat) into fillets.

fill-in See FILL, *v.* 3. **—fill·ing** *n.* something used to fill something else: *The dentist used a plastic ~; a cheese ~ for a sandwich.* **—filling station** same as GAS STATION.

fil·lip (FIL·up) *n.* an outward flip of a finger from the thumb, as in flicking a crumb off a sleeve; hence, something that goads or stimulates: *The tax was abolished as a ~ to industry;* ***v.:*** *a cocktail to ~ your appetite.*

Fill·more, Millard. 1800–1874, 13th U.S. President (1850–1853).

fil·ly (FIL·ee) *n.* **fil·lies** a young female horse.

film *n.* a membrane or similar layer, as of oil on water; hence, thin, flexible material coated with a light-sensitive substance and made into sheets or rolls for taking photographs; also, a motion picture; ***v.:*** *a movie ~ed* (i.e. photographed) *on location in Spain; tabletops ~ed* (i.e. coated) *with dust.* **—film·y** *adj.* **film·i·er, -i·est:** *a ~* (i.e. thin) *curtain; "the ~-dome spider"; ~* (i.e. hazy) *windowpanes.* **—film·dom** (–dum) *n.* the motion-picture industry or its personnel. **—film·og·ra·phy** (–OG·ruh–) *n.* **-phies** a list of motion pictures according to actor, director, topic, etc. **—film·set** *n.* a motion-picture set; ***v.*** set type photographically on film rather than in metal. **—film·strip** *n.* a length of film containing still pictures, diagrams, illustrations, etc. for use as a teaching aid.

fils (FILCE) *n. sing.* & *pl.* in Bahrain, Iraq, Jordan, Kuwait, and Yemen (Aden), 1/1,000 of a dinar.

fil·ter *n.* **1** a porous device for straining out dust, smoke, germs, or impurities from a liquid or gas medium in which they are suspended; also, the porous material used such as felt, paper, sand, or charcoal. **2** a device or substance for absorbing certain light rays and frequencies, as the color filter of a camera lens. **—*v.:*** *Air conditioners ~ out dust and pollen of the outside air; Use ~ed water; Most viruses are* **fil·ter·**

a•ble (i.e. capable of being passed) *through porcelain filters that bacteria cannot pass through.* **—filter tip** a cigar(ette) with a tip that filters the smoke before it is inhaled.

filth *n.* foul dirt; obscenity; moral corruption; **filth•i•ness** *n.;* **filth•y** *adj.* **filth•i•er, -i•est** disgustingly dirty; **filthy lucre** *Informal.* money.

fil•tra•ble (FIL·truh–) *adj.* that can be filtered; same as FILTERABLE. **—fil•trate** *v.* **-trates, -trat•ed, -trat•ing** to filter; ***n.*** a filtered fluid; **fil•tra•tion** (–TRAY–) *n.:* *~ air cleaners use wool felt, cotton batting, etc.; a city's water ~ plant.*

fin *n.* a winglike or fanlike organ of a fish used for swimming, turning, and balancing its body in water; also, any similar structure: *an aircraft's tail ~; a radiator's cooling ~s.*

fin. finance; financial; finish. **—Fin.** Finland; Finnish.

fi•na•gle (fuh·NAY·gl) *v.* **-gles, -gled, -gling** *Informal.* get (something) by devious or tricky means; wangle; **fi•na•gler** *n.*

fi•nal (FYE·nl) *adj.* last; decisive; definitive: *our ~ offer; a ~ decision.* **—*n.*** something final, as a deciding game, the last examination in a course, etc.; often **finals** *pl.* **—fi•na•le** (fuh·NAH·lee, –NAL–) *n.* the conclusion or last part, as of a play or piece of music. **—fi•nal•ist** (FYE·nuh–) *n.* one who takes part in the finals of a competition. **—fi•nal•i•ty** (fye·NAL–) *n.* **-ties** conclusiveness. **—fi•nal•ize** (FYE·nl–) *v.* **-iz•es, -ized, -iz•ing** make final; complete; **fi•nal•i•za•tion** (–ZAY–) *n.* **—fi•nal•ly** (FYE–) *adv.* at last: *They ~ got there.*

fi•nance (–NANCE, FYE–) *n.* **1** (the science of) the management of money, esp. public revenue: *an expert in ~; the Minister of Finance.* **2 finances** *pl.* money resources; funds. **—*v.*** **-nanc•es, -nanced, -nanc•ing** provide or get money for: *Couldn't get a bank loan to ~ his new car, so he went to a* **finance company** *offering a lien on his salary.* **—fi•nan•cial** (–NAN–) *adj.;* **fi•nan•cial•ly** *adv.* **—fin•an•cier** (–SEER) *n.* an investor; also, one skilled in finance.

finch *n.* a bird of the family of seedeaters including goldfinches, buntings, and grosbeaks, all with sharp, cone-shaped bills for crushing seeds.

find (FINED) *v.* **finds, found, find•ing 1** come upon by accident or by searching; also, reach or obtain: *The child found a dime on the lawn and shouted, "Finders keepers, losers weepers"; Please ~ me a cab; Rivers ~ their way to the sea;* **find out** (i.e. learn or ascertain) *when the flight arrives; The jury found* (i.e. decided and declared) *against the accused and for the defendant.* **2** experience; perceive: *She ~s people forgetting her in her old age.* **3** provide; supply: *to ~ funds for a project; This broker charges a* **finder's fee** *to arrange a mortgage on your house.* **—find•er** *n.* **—find fault:** *He ~s fault with* (i.e. complains about) *everything and everybody.* **—find oneself:** *After trying several jobs, he finally found himself as a social worker.* **—*n.*** a finding or something found; also **find•ing:** *the findings* (i.e. discoveries) *of modern science; A notions department supplies a dressmaker's* **findings** (i.e. things other than basic materials) *such as buttons, threads, and zippers.*

fin-de-siè•cle (fan·duh·see·EC·luh) *adj.* of or having to do with the close of the 19th cent.; also, decadent: *the ~ Versailles of Louis XIV.*

fine *adj.* **fin•er, fin•est 1** excellent: *a ~ young man; I feel ~; ~* (i.e. bright or clear) *weather; Gold alloy that is 18 carats ~ is 75% pure gold.* **2** thin; sharp; delicate; subtle: *the ~ cutting edge of a knife; the ~ point of a pen; a ~ distinction; ~ lace; Sand is ~r than gravel.* **—*adv.:*** *Friday will suit me ~* (Informal); *a ~-drawn distinction; fiberglass made of ~-spun glass;* also **fine•ly; fine•ness** *n.* **—*n.*** a sum of money paid as a penalty or punishment; ***v.*** **fines, fined, fin•ing:** *The judge ~d him $25 for speeding.* **—fine arts** arts concerned with the expression of visual beauty, i.e. painting, sculpture, and architecture, often taken to include also poetry, music, drama, and dancing. **—fin•er•y** (FYE·nuh·ree) *n.* **-er•ies** showy clothes, jewelry, etc. **—fine print** the less favorable parts of a contract or agreement, which are usu. printed in small type. **—fi•nesse** (fi·NES) *n.* skillfulness; also, cunning or diplomacy; ***v.*** **-ness•es, -nessed, -ness•ing** use finesse; bring or accomplish by finesse: *~d my queen with his jack.* **—fine-tune** *v.* regulate by making small adjustments.

fin•fish *n.* a true fish, not a shellfish.

fin•ger (FING·gur) *n.* one of the five divisions of the hand, esp. any of the four exclusive of the thumb; hence, anything corresponding to or resembling a finger: *the ~ of a glove; a ~ of light;* **fingered** *adj.: giant trees with ~ roots; the light-~ pickpocket; the ~ limpet.* **—*v.*** **-gers, -gered, -ger•ing 1** touch with or use the fingers on (a musical instrument in playing). **2** *Slang.* point out (a victim, potential loot, etc.). **—keep** (or **have**) **one's fingers crossed** be waiting in hope. **—put one's finger on** point out exactly. **—fin•ger•board** *n.* the part of the neck of a violin or guitar against which the strings are pressed by the player's fingers to produce the desired tones. **—finger bowl** a small bowl for rinsing the fingers at a meal. **—fin•ger•ing** *n.* the act, process, or method of using the fingers in playing a musical instrument. **—finger painting** painting by using the fingers, hand, or arm to spread paint on moistened paper; **fin•ger-paint** *v.* **—fin•ger•print** *n.* an impression of the lines that form arches, loops, and whorls on the fingertips, used as a positive means of identification; ***v.:*** *arrested, photographed, and ~ed.* **—fin•ger•tip** *n.* **at one's fingertips** within easy reach or control: *has several languages at his ~s.*

fin•i•al (FIN·ee·ul) *n.* an ornament forming the topmost part or apex of a peaked or arched structure, as the screw on top of a lampshade.

fin·i·cal *adj.* same as **fin·ick·y** *adj.* fussy; also **fin·ick·ing.**

fi·nis (FIN·is, FYE·nis) *n.* **-nis·es** the conclusion; end. **—fin·ish** *v.* **1** bring to completion; also, reach the end of: *Out of 10 who started the race only 4 ~ed; Let me ~ this chapter.* **2** make complete; hence, polish: *a roughed-in storeroom that needs ~ing; Give the table top a ~ing touch with this paint; a* **finishing school** *to prepare young women for social life.* **—*n.*** the last part of something; hence, something used in finishing; also, a finished quality or effect: *The "Charge of the Light Brigade" was a fight to the ~; paints, varnishes, waxes, and such ~es; the glossy ~ of supercalendered paper; His manner lacks ~.* **—fin·ished** *adj.* **—fin·ish·er** *n.*

fi·nite (FYE–) *adj.* **1** having limits; neither infinite nor infinitesimal: *mortal man's ~ existence;* **fi·nite·ly** *adv.;* **fi·nite·ness** *n.* **2 finite verb** one with a definite person, number, and tense, as "goes," distinguished from "to go" (infinitive) or "going" (participle or gerund).

fink *Slang. n.* a strikebreaker, informer, or other undesirable person. **—fink out** back out; **fink-out** *n.* a retreat or cop-out.

Fin·land (–lund) a N. European republic; 130,-120 sq. mi. (337,009 km²); *cap.* Helsinki. **—Finn** *n.* a person of or from Finland; **Finn.** *Abbrev.* for **Finn·ish** *n.* & *adj.* (having to do with Finland, Finns, or) the language of the Finns: *Hungarian and ~ belong to the* **Fin·no-U·gric** (fin·oh·OO·gric) *sub-family of the Uralic group of languages.*

fin·nan had·die (FIN·un·HAD·ee) smoked haddock produced by a Scottish method.

fin·ny (FIN·ee) *adj.* **fin·ni·er, fin·ni·est** of or having to do with fins or fish.

fiord (FYORD) *n.* an inlet of the sea with steep cliffs on both sides, as in Norway.

fir *n.* a pyramid-shaped evergreen tree of the pine family.

fire *n.* **1** a burning or its flame, fuel for burning, the destruction caused by a blaze, etc.: *Light the ~; Your bed may* **catch fire** *if you smoke in bed; a house* **on fire;** *~ insurance.* **2** something resembling a fire, as strong feeling, zeal, or enthusiasm: *eyes full of ~.* **3** a discharge of firearms or an action resembling it: *a decision still* **hanging fire** (i.e. delayed); *We will* **open fire** (i.e. start shooting) *as soon as the enemy is sighted; The politician was* **under fire** (i.e. under attack) *from the media.* **—*v.* fires, fired, fir·ing** [corresponding to the *n.* senses] **1:** *Pottery is ~d in a kiln; adventure stories that ~ the imagination.* **2:** *She left the meeting all* **fired up** *at the imagined insult.* **3:** *The press* **fired away** *with questions throughout the interview; He prefers to* **fire off** (i.e. write and send) *memos instead of phoning.* **4** discharge from a job: *He was told to resign or be ~d;* **fir·er** *n.* **—fire ant** an ant with a burning sting that is a serious pest in the southern U.S. **—fire·arm** *n.* a hand weapon such as a rifle or pistol that fires a bullet or shell using gunpowder. **—fire·ball** *n.* a ball of fire such as the great luminous cloud resulting from a nuclear explosion, or something resembling a ball of fire such as lightning or a brilliant meteor; also, a very energetic person. **—fire·base** *n.* a military base delivering heavy gunfire. **—fire·boat** *n.* a boat with fire-fighting equipment. **—fire·bomb** *n.* a bomb designed to start a fire; ***v.:*** *an opposition leader ~ed and killed in his home.* **—fire·box** *n.* **1** the fire-containing chamber of a furnace or boiler. **2** a box with a signalling device for alerting a fire station. **—fire·brand** *n.* a piece of burning wood; hence, an agitator. **—fire·break** *n.* a strip of plowed or cleared land meant to stop a spreading fire. **—fire·brick** *n.* a brick made of refractory **fire·clay** to withstand high temperatures and used to line furnaces and kilns. **—fire·bug** *n. Informal.* a pyromaniac. **—fire·crack·er** *n.* a firework consisting of a paper roll of explosive and a fuse. **—fire·damp** *n.* the explosive methane-air mixture formed in coal mines. **—fire·dog** *n.* an andiron. **—fire drill** an exercise to teach the proper procedure in case of a fire. **—fire engine** an automotive truck for transporting firefighters and firefighting equipment. **—fire escape** a fire-proof stairway outside a building; also, a ladder or other means of escaping a fire. **—fire extinguisher** a portable apparatus for spraying chemicals to put out fires. **—fire·fight·er** *n.* one trained in **fire·fight·ing** *n.* **—fire·fly** *n.* **-flies** any of various night beetles that give off flashes of light; lightning bug. **—fire·house** *n.* a fire station. **—fire hydrant** a fireplug. **—fire irons** utensils such as poker, shovel, and tongs for use at a fireplace. **—fire·man** *n.* **-men** a firefighter; also, a stoker. **—fire·place** *n.* a place for an open fire, esp. a framed one built in a room at the base of a chimney. **—fire·plug** *n.* a street outlet to draw water from in case of a fire. **—fire·pow·er** *n.* the capacity and effectiveness of a military unit or weapon to deliver fire. **—fire·proof** *adj.* that resists burning; ***v.***cover or chemically treat (materials) with fire-retardants or fire-resistants: *Ammonium phosphate, borax, and zinc chloride are* **fire-re·tard·ant** *n.* & *adj.; Stone, brick, gypsum blocks, etc. are* **fire-re·sist·ant** *n.* & *adj.* **—fire·screen** *n.* a screen for use at a fireplace as protection against flying sparks. **—fire·side** *n.* & *adj.* (having to do with) a hearth or home: *an intimate ~ chat instead of a formal press conference.* **—fire station** a building in which fire engines and fire fighters are housed. **—fire·storm** *n.* a huge fire, as from a nuclear explosion or bombing raid, that generates inrushing winds fanning it; hence, a similar phenomenon: *A ~ of telegrams and phone calls hit the White House.* **—fire tower** a tower used as a lookout by forest rangers. **—fire·trap** *n.* a place from which escape in case of fire would be practically impossible. **—fire truck** a fire engine.

—**fire·wa·ter** *n.* [American Indian's term] alcoholic liquor. —**fire·wood** *n.* wood for fuel. —**fire·work** *n.* a noise- or light-producing device such as a firecracker or rocket for signaling or for displays; **fire·works** *n., sing. & pl.* a spectacular display using firecrackers, rockets, etc. —**firing line** the front line of an activity, controversy, campaign, etc. —**firing pin** the mechanism of a firearm that sets off the primer. —**firing squad** a group of soldiers that carries out a death sentence by firing; also, one that fires a volley of shots as a tribute at a military funeral.

firm *adj.* **1** not affected by pressure, movements, or change: *healthy, ~ muscles; as ~ as a rock; an infant that is ~ on its feet; a ~ price.* **2** fixed or resolute: *a ~ voice; a teacher who is ~ with pranksters; a practicing Catholic very ~ in her beliefs.* —***adv.*** firmly: *Stand ~ and do not surrender; certain beliefs that we all hold ~ to.* —**firm·ly** *adv.* **firm·ness** *n.* —***v.:*** *prices ~ing up after going down; Let's ~ up the contract and close the deal.* —***n.*** a business enterprise or partnership. —**fir·ma·ment** *n.* the sky considered as a vault with stars fixed in it.

first *adj.* coming before all others in time, position, rank, etc. —***adv.*** before all others; for the first time. —***n.*** a person, thing, place, or position that is first; **at first** in the beginning; initially. —**first aid** emergency care given to a sick or injured person; **first-aid** *adj.: ~ treatment.* —**first·born** *n. & adj.* the oldest (child). —**first class** the first group in a classification, as of passengers, mail, etc.; **first-class** *adj. & adv.: sealed letters and such ~ mail; She always flies ~.* —**first floor** the ground floor; in the U.K. and Europe, the floor above ground floor. —**first-hand** *adj. & adv.* (got) from the original source: *I learned it (at) ~; ~ information.* —**first lady** or **First Lady** the wife of a chief of state, esp. of the U.S. President. —**first lieutenant** a U.S. military officer ranking below captain and above second lieutenant. —**first·ling** *n.* the first of its kind, as produce or offspring. —**first·ly** *adv.* first. —**first name** Christian name; given name. —**first person** a verb or pronoun such as *am, we,* or *our* that refers to the speaker or writer; hence, use of such forms: *a ~ account; a narrative in the ~.* —**first-rate** *adj. & adv.* excellent(ly). —**first sergeant** in the U.S. Army and Marine Corps, a master sergeant serving as assistant to the commander of a company or battery; also, a rank next below sergeant major. —**first strike** a nuclear attack in anticipation of one by the enemy; **first-strike** *adj.: second-strike deterrents against an enemy's ~ capability.* —**first string** the best group of players, not alternates or substitutes; **first-string** *adj.* first-rate.

firth *n.* esp. in Scotland, a narrow arm of the sea; estuary.

fis·cal (FIS·cul) *adj.* having to do with public revenue or corporate finance: *The U.S.* **fiscal year** *ends June 30; the budget for ~ 1978;* **fis·cal·ly** *adv.*

fish *n., pl.* **fish;** also **fish·es** (fish species). any of a large group of water animals with fins, gills, and scales; also, its flesh used as food. —***v.*** (try) to catch fish; hence, search for, catch, or pull out: *Children ~ for compliments; ~ed out his will from a cabinet.* —**fish-and-chips** *n.pl.* a dish of fried fish and French fries. —**fish·bowl** *n.* a glass bowl for keeping live fish, open to view from all sides. —**fish·er** *n.* **1** one who catches fish; also **fish·er·man.** **2** a rare species of marten with brown fur. —**fish·er·y.** *n.* **-er·ies** fishing as a business; also, a fishing establishment. —**fish-eye lens** a camera lens with a 180°-wide field of vision. —**fish·hook** *n.* a hook for catching fish. —**fish-lad·der** *n.* a waterway built as an ascending series of connected pools that enables fish to pass over a dam or falls on their way to spawning grounds upstream. —**fish·wife** *n.* **-wives** a woman who sells fish, considered as foul-mouthed. —**fish·y** *adj.* **fish·i·er, -i·est** dull-looking like a fish's eye; also, like fish in taste, smell, or touch; slippery; hence, doubtful: *a ~ story;* **fish·i·ness** *n.*

fis·sile (FISL) *adj.* fissionable. —**fis·sion** *n.* a splitting apart: *Nuclear ~ releases energy, as in atomic bombs; Simple plants such as algae and organisms such as amoebas multiply by cellular ~;* **fis·sion·a·ble** *adj.* capable of fission: *Uranium and plutonium are ~.* —**fis·sion·al** *adj.* —**fis·sure** (FISH·ur) *n.* a cleft or crack, as in rocks.

fist *n.* a tightly closed or clenched hand, as in hitting; **fist·fight** *n.* a fight with bare fists. —**fist·ful** *n.* handful. —**fis·ti·cuffs** *n.pl.* a fight using fists; also, boxing.

fis·tu·la (FIS·chuh·luh) *n.* **-las** or **-lae** (–lee) a wound or ulcer forming an abnormal body passage between two hollow organs, as the bladder and rectum, or connecting a hollow organ such as the stomach with the outside; **fis·tu·lous** (–lus) or **fis·tu·lar** *adj.* of a fistula; also, tubelike.

¹fit *adj.* **fit·ter, fit·test** suited to a certain purpose, occasion, or use: *food ~ for a king; news that is ~ to be printed; the struggle for existence resulting in the survival of the ~est; She keeps "fit as a fiddle" by regular exercise;* ***adv.:*** *He* **thought fit** (or **saw fit**) *to invite some and leave out others.* —***v.*** **fits, fit·ted, fit·ting** to be right or the right size for: *"If the cap ~s wear it"; a punishment that ~s the crime; all* **fitted out** (i.e. equipped or prepared) *for a costume party; a room* **fitted up** *as a study.* —***n.:*** *The cut of his coat is fashionable but the ~ is poor; a tight ~.* —**fit·ly** *adv.* —**fit·ness** *n.* —**fit·ter** *n.* —**fit·ting** *adj.* suitable or appropriate: *a ~ occasion for a speech; a ~ answer to an impertinent question.* —***n.*** **1** an adjustment of clothes to make them fit properly: *a customer who insists on several ~s before his suit is finished.* **2** a small, detachable machine part: *elbows, nipples, clamps, and such pipe ~s;* **fit·ting·ly** *adv.*

²fit *n.* a sudden attack or convulsion; seizure; also, an outburst or spell: *an epileptic ~; a ~ of fury; She studies by* **fits and starts,** *not regularly.* —**fit·ful** *adj.* irregular; restless; **fit·ful·ly** *adv.;* **fit·ful·ness** *n.*

five *n., adj. & pron.* one more than four; the number 5 or V; hence, a group of 5 or something numbered 5 or having 5 units, as a basketball team, playing card, domino, or five-dollar bill; **five-and-ten (-cent store)** a variety store, usu. selling inexpensive items.

fix *v.* **fix·es, fixed, fix·ing** **1** make firm or steady; fasten; hence, repair: *an appointment ~d for 2 p.m.; On whom shall we ~ the blame?* **fix** *your eyes* **on** *the picture; a house that needs some* **fixing up** *before we move in.* **2** arrange; prepare; set up: *The hairdresser will ~ your hair; I could ~ dinner for you; She* **fixed** *me* **up** *in a new job.* **3** influence dishonestly: *The race was ~d; tried to ~ the jury.* **4** punish: *He threatened to ~ me.* —***n.*** **1** position: *A navigator gets the ~ of his ship from the stars; The executive with two appointments for the same hour was in a ~* (i.e. awkward situation). **2** *Slang.* a dishonest influencing or a contest or situation so influenced. **3** *Slang.* a shot of a narcotic. —**fix·a·ble** *adj.* —**fix·a·tion** (–SAY–) *n.* a fixing, esp. of one's sexual interest on some object or person; hence **fix·ate** *v.* **-ates, -at·ed, -at·ing.** —**fix·a·tive** (–uh·tiv) *n. & adj.* (a chemical or other substance) that fixes a drawing, living tissue, perfume, etc. to prevent changes happening to it. —**fixed** (FIXT) *adj.: pensioners on ~ incomes; the ~ gaze of a dead person; a race suspected of being ~; A* **fixed star** *is so far away its position never seems to change;* **fix·ed·ly** (–id–) *adv.;* **fix·ed·ness** *n.* —**fix·er** *n.* —**fix·ings** *n.pl. Informal.* accessories: *a turkey served with all the ~s.* —**fix·i·ty** *n.* **-ties** fixedness; also, something fixed. —**fix·ture** *n.* a person or thing that is part of a situation or place: *A chandelier is a lighting ~; so long on the job, she seems a ~ in the office.*

fizz *n. & v.* (make the sound of) an effervescing drink: *Gulp it down while it ~es.* —**fiz·zle** *v.* **fiz·zles, fiz·zled, fiz·zling** end feebly after a lively start; fail: *The party ~d out when the drinks didn't arrive;* ***n.*** a fiasco.

fjord (FYORD) *n.* same as FIORD.

fl. floor; (he or she) flourished; fluid.

FL or **Fla.** Florida.

flab *n. Informal.* excess of flabby flesh. —**flab·ber·gast** *v.* dumbfound. —**flab·by** *adj.* **flab·bi·er, flab·bi·est** lacking firmness or strength: *~ muscles;* **flab·bi·ly** *adv.;* **flab·bi·ness** *n.* —**flac·cid** (FLAC·sid, FLAS–) *adj.* flabby; also, limp; feeble.

flack *n. Slang.* press agent; ***v.:*** *~ing for a movie star;* **flack·er·y** *n.* propaganda.

flac·on (FLAC·un) *n.* a small stoppered bottle for perfumes.

flag *n.* **1** a piece of fabric, usu. with a distinctive colored design, used as an emblem or banner, often hoisted on a **flag·pole** or **flag·staff:** *June 14 is* **Flag Day** *in the U.S. in memory of the adoption of the Stars and Stripes in 1777; A* **flag·ship** *carries a* **flag officer,** *of one of the top five ranks of the navy, commanding a fleet or squadron.* **2** the wild iris or *blue flag,* the reedlike *sweet flag,* or the cattail plant or flower. **3** a slab of **flag·stone** for paving. —***v.*** **flags, flag·ged, flag·ging** **1** to signal: *We* **flagged down** *the first cab that came along.* **2** droop; slacken: *As time wore on interest seemed to ~; a pep talk to cheer up* **flagging** *spirits;* **flag·ging·ly** *adv.*

flag·el·late (FLAJ·uh–) *v.* **-lates, -lat·ed, -lat·ing** to whip; **flag·el·la·tion** (–LAY–) *n.* —**flag·el·late** *n. & adj.* (a protozoan) having a **fla·gel·lum** (fluh·JEL–) *n.,pl.* **-gel·la** or **-gel·lums** a whip or whiplike organ that helps bacteria, sponges, etc. to move about.

flag·eo·let (flaj·uh·LET) *n.* a flutelike instrument, but blown like a recorder.

fla·gi·tious (–JISH·us) *adj.* infamous; villainous.

flag officer See FLAG, *n.* 1.

flag·on (–un) *n.* a vessel, usu. large, with a spout and handle, for wine or other liquids; also, its contents of about two quarts.

flagpole See FLAG, *n.* 1.

fla·grant (FLAY·grunt) *adj.* of violations, errors, etc., notoriously bad; **(in) fla·gran·te de·lic·to** (fluh·GRAN·tee·duh·LIC·toh) red-handed; **fla·grant·ly** *adv.*

flagship, flagstaff, flagstone See FLAG, *n.* 1 & 3. —**flag-wav·ing** *n.* a chauvinistic appeal to the emotions.

flail *n.* a farm tool for threshing grain; ***v.*** strike with or wave (arms) about as with a flail.

flair *n.* a keen sense; also, aptitude or taste: *a ~ for fashionable clothes.*

flak *n.* antiaircraft gunfire; hence, criticism: *A* **flak jacket** *protects one from flying shell fragments.*

flake *n.* **1** a small, thin piece or mass: *a ~ of snow; ~s of rust.* **2** *Slang.* one who is unconventional; nut. —***v.*** **flakes, flaked, flak·ing:** *Old paint tends to ~ off;* **flake off** *Slang.* beat it; **flake out** *Slang.* collapse or lie down exhausted; hence, fail or flop. —**flak·y** (FLAY·kee) *adj.* **flak·i·er, -i·est** **1** of flakes: *a crisp and ~ pie crust.* **2** *Slang.* eccentric: *the oddball's ~ behavior.* —**flak·i·ly** *adv.* —**flak·i·ness** *n.*

flam·bé (flahm·BAY) *n. & adj.* (a dessert or other dish) served flaming. —**flam·beau** (–BOH) *n.,pl.* **-beaux** (–BOZE) or **-beaus** a flaming torch. —**flam·boy·ant** (–BOY·unt) *adj.* flamelike in form or color; hence, ornate or showy; **flam·boy·ance** (–uns) or **flam·boy·an·cy** *n.;* **flam·boy·ant·ly** *adv.* —**flame** *n.* a brightly burning fire; hence, a strong passion; *Informal.* a sweetheart; ***v.*** **flames, flamed, flam·ing** blaze, grow hot, glow, or burst out like a flame: *the ~ing fall colors; cheeks ~ing with emotion; Her eyes ~d with fury;* **flam·ing** *adj.;* **flam·ing·ly** *adv.*

fla·men·co (fluh·MENG·coh) *n.* a kind of Spanish dance characterized by vigorous stamping, clapping, and singing to the rhythm of castanets and guitar music.

flame·out *n.* a failure of a jet engine due to faulty combustion of fuel. —**flame thrower** a military weapon for shooting burning fuel under pressure like water from a fire hose. —**fla·min·go** (fluh·MING–) *n.* **-go(e)s** a water bird with long legs, curved bill, and neck like a swan's with feathers colored bright red to pink. —**flam·ma·ble** (FLAM·uh·bl) *adj.* that catches fire easily, as gasoline; **flam·ma·bil·i·ty** (–BIL–) *n.: a ~ test for clothing fabrics.*

Flan·ders formerly, a separate political unit, now a region divided among Belgium, France, and the Netherlands, mostly inhabited by **Flem·ings** speaking **Flem·ish,** a Germanic language allied to Dutch: **Flanders Field** *is a U.S. cemetery in Belgium for 368 dead of World War I.* —**Flemish** *adj.* having to do with Flanders, the Flemings, or Flemish.

flange (FLANJ) *n.* a projecting rim of a wheel, rail, girder, etc.; ***v.*** **flang·es, flanged, flang·ing:** *pipe ends ~d and bolted together.*

flank *n.* **1** the fleshy side above the hips; hence, a cut of beef corresponding to this part. **2** the side of anything, as of a mountain or military formation. —***v.:*** *appeared in public ~ed by bodyguards; a body of troops ~ed and overpowered in a surprise attack.* —**flank·er** *n.* a person protecting a flank, as on a football team.

flan·nel (FLANL) *n.* a soft, warm woolen cloth with a napped surface; **flannels** *n.pl.* flannel trousers or woolen underwear; **flan·nel·et(te)** (flan·uh·LET) *n.* a soft light napped cotton cloth.

flap *n.* **1** a broad, flat piece of material attached on one side, as the cover of a pocket, the gummed end of an envelope, and the hinged back sections of a plane's wings. **2** the sound made by a flap, as of wings beating the air or oars on water. **3** a stir or commotion. —***v.*** **flaps, flapped, flap·ping:** *a sail ~ing in the wind; a young bird trying to ~ away from its nest; Mr. Macmillan was considered not easily* **flap·pa·ble** (–puh·bl) *adj.* excitable. —**flap·jack** *n.* pancake. —**flap·per** *n.* a person or thing that flaps, as a broad fin or a bird learning to fly; also, a girl of the 1920's who was aggressively unconventional in dress and manners.

flare *n.* an outburst of flame or short-lived, unsteady blaze of light, as a rocket signal shot into the air or a solar eruption. —***v.*** **flares, flared, flar·ing:** *The candle sputtered, ~d, and went out; tends to* **flare up** (i.e. get excited) *at the least provocation; Only skirts used to be* **flared** (i.e. cut widened towards the bottom), *then everyone was sporting* **flares** (i.e. bell-bottom pants). —**flare-up** *n.* an outburst, sudden increase, or intensification.

flash *n.* **1** a sudden, brief brilliance, as of lightning or that made by the flashbulb of a camera; hence, any similar feeling or display, as of inspiration, wit, or a **flash in the pan,** a brilliant but short-lived effort or attempt. **2** a brief period; also, something coming or passing in an instant: *I remembered the whole episode in a ~; First came a teletype ~, then the long obituary; the ~ of her smile.* —***v.*** give out a sudden bright light; also, come or send forth suddenly like a flash: *a lighthouse signal ~ing every few seconds; headlights ~ing by on the highway; A train ~ed into view; AP ~ed the news of the assassination across the nation; The policeman walked in after ~ing his badge;* **flash·er** *n.* —***adj.*** sudden or instantaneous: *a* **flash burn** *caused by exposure to radiation; a* **flash flood** *following heavy rainfall.* —**flash·back** *n.* a narration or portrayal, as in a play or movie, of an episode from the past; a similar portrayal of the future is a **flash-for·ward.** —**flash·bulb** or **flash·lamp** *n.* a lighting device that works with a camera shutter and is triggered by a **flash gun.** —**flash burn** See FLASH, *adj.* —**flash·card** *n.* any of a series of cards bearing words, pictures, etc. displayed before students to get quick responses in drilling them in math, reading, etc. —**flash-forward** See FLASHBACK. —**flash gun** See FLASHBULB. —**flash·ing** *n.* sheet metal used to cover roof joints and angles. —**flashlamp** same as FLASHBULB. —**flash·light** *n.* a portable electric lamp. —**flash point** the lowest temperature at which a flammable substance will ignite in the presence of a flame. —**flash tube** a gas-filled spiral tube used in lasers to amplify light or one used in a stroboscope to produce flashes. —**flash·y** *adj.* **flash·i·er, -i·est** brilliant; also, gaudy or showy in a cheap way: *a ~ dress;* **flash·i·ly** *adv.;* **flash·i·ness** *n.*

flask *n.* a container for liquids, usu. with a narrow, closable outlet, often a flat bottle, as for carrying liquor in the pocket, or a round vessel, as used in laboratories.

flat *adj.* **flat·ter, flat·test** **1** horizontal and plane; not round, high, or thick: *the ~ top of a table; a ~ tire* (i.e. deflated). **2** not changeable; absolute: *a ~ refusal; a ~ rate of interest.* **3** of colors, tastes, sounds, and other perceptions, not distinctive: *a ~, not glossy paint; a ~ musical note* (i.e. a half note below the normal pitch); *soda pop that is stale and ~; the ~ "a" of "cat."* —***adv.:*** *placed ~ last in class; denied* **flat out** (i.e. outright) *that he had received bribes; drove* **flat out** (i.e. at full speed) *to the hospital on hearing the news; Commuters may cross the Atlantic in nothing ~* (i.e. in no time at all); *All his enterprises having* **fallen flat,** *he is quite broke;* **flat·ly** *adv.;* **flat·ness** *n.* —***n.*** **1** something flat, as a deflated tire, swamp land, the palm of the hand, a flat musical note or its symbol (b), etc. **2** an apartment. —***v.*** **flats, flat·ted, flat·ting** make or become flat. —**flat·bed** *n.* a truck or trailer whose body is a platform without sides. —**flat·boat** *n.* a flat-bottomed boat, usu. with square ends, for freight and passengers. —**flat·car** *n.* a railroad car without sides or roof, used for freight. —**flat·fish** *n.* a fish such as the flounder and sole that has a flat body with both eyes on the upper surface. —**flat·foot** *n.,pl.* **-feet** a condition in which the arch of the instep has flattened. —**flat·foot·ed** *adj.* & *adv. Informal.* direct(ly); firm(ly). —**Flat·head** *n.* a member of a Salish Indian tribe of Montana. —**flat·i·ron** *n.* an iron for pressing clothes. —**flat·ten** *v.* make or become flat: **flat·worms** *such as tapeworms and flukes have flattened bodies.*

flat·ter *v.* please (a person) by praising or otherwise making (him) feel elated: *I was* ~*ed to receive the award; He* **flatters himself** *on his musical talent; The portrait* ~*s her;* **flat·ter·er** *n.;* **flat·ter·ing·ly** *adv.* —**flat·ter·y** *n.* **flat·ter·ies.**

flat·top *n. Informal.* an aircraft carrier.

flat·u·lence (FLACH·uh·lunce) *n.* accumulation of gas in the stomach or intestines; also **fla·tus** (FLAY–) *n.* —**flat·u·lent** *adj.* full of gas; also, windy or pompous.

flat·ware *n.* flat tableware such as plates, platters, knives, or spoons. —**flatworm** See FLATTEN.

flaunt (FLAWNT) *v.* display or parade (oneself, one's wealth, or other possessions); also, flutter or wave proudly, as flags or banners; **flaun·ting·ly** *adv.*

flau·tist (FLAW–, FLOU–) *n.* flutist.

fla·vor (FLAY·vur) *n.* & *v.* (give) the smell and taste that are distinctive of a substance: *Spices, fruit, etc. have natural* ~*s; Vanilla beans yield an extract used to* ~ *ice cream; "Vanillin" is an artificial* **fla·vor·ing;** *romances with an exotic flavor* (i.e. air or quality). —**fla·vored** *adj.* —**fla·vor·ful** or **fla·vor·some** *adj.* —**fla·vor·less** *adj.* —**fla·vour** *Brit.* flavor.

flaw *n.* an imperfection such as a crack or blemish that mars something, esp. structurally; **flawed** *adj.: a* ~ *diamond; a character* ~ *by a weakness for drink;* **flaw·less** *adj.;* **flaw·less·ly** *adv.;* **flaw·less·ness** *n.*

flax *n.* any of various herbs and shrubs, usu. bearing blue or white flowers, raised for their fiber to make linen and coarse yarns and their seed, **flax·seed,** for making linseed oil; **flax·en** *adj.* (made) of flax; also, pale-yellow; also **flax·y.**

flay *v.* strip off the skin of; hence, criticize or scold harshly.

flea (FLEE) *v.* a tiny, wingless jumping insect that sucks the blood of animals. —**flea·bane** *n.* any of many plants of the composite family with violet or orange-colored flowers, once believed to drive away fleas. —**flea collar** an animal collar containing insecticide. —**flea market** an open-air bazaar dealing in cheap, usu. secondhand goods.

fleck *n.* & *v.* (mark with) a spot or patch: *skin* ~*ed with freckles; floating* ~*s of snow* (i.e. flakes).

fled *pt.* & *pp.* of FLEE.

fledge (FLEJ) *v.* **fledg·es, fledged, fledg·ing** grow or equip (as if) with feathers: *to* ~ *an arrow; a full-*~*d acrobat; a mere* **fledg·ling** (i.e. young bird) *of a poet.*

flee *v.* **flees, fled, flee·ing** run away, as from danger or evil; vanish: *refugees* ~*ing an earthquake; All but one guard had fled.*

fleece *n.* a sheep's or similar animal's woolly covering; ***v.*** **fleec·es, fleeced, fleec·ing** shear or strip (someone): *a poor widow* ~*d of her savings by con men;* **fleec·er** *n.* —**fleec·y** *adj.* **fleec·i·er, -i·est** like, covered with, or made of fleece: ~ *clouds;* **fleec·i·ly** *adv.;* **fleec·i·ness** *n.*

fleer *n.* & *v.* grimace; jeer; gibe.

fleet *n.* a unified group, as of ships, airplanes, or automobiles; **fleet admiral** the highest rank of U.S. naval officer with a five-star insignia. —***adj.*** swift: *Antelopes are* ~ *of foot;* **fleet·ly** *adv.;* **fleet·ness** *n.* —***v.*** pass swiftly; **fleet·ing** *adj.: Worldly joys are* ~*; the* ~ *glimpse of one's beloved;* **fleet·ing·ly** *adv.: thought she spoke to him* ~ *in a dream.*

Flem. Flemish; **Fleming, Flemish** See FLANDERS.

flesh *n.* **1** the soft tissue beneath the skin, esp. the muscle and fat of animals: *Animal* ~ *is regarded as meat; stories that make your* ~ *creep* (i.e. horrify); ~*-colored* (i.e. yellowish-pink) *tights; the* ~*-eating Venus' flytrap; decaying* ~ *full of maggots of* **flesh flies;** *hankering for the* **flesh·pots** (i.e. luxuries) *of one's native land.* **2** the body; also, bodily nature: *dreamed she saw her dead child* **in the flesh;** *"The spirit is willing but the* ~ *is weak"; pimps, prostitutes, and such* **flesh-ped·dlers;** *Your* **own flesh and blood** (i.e. blood relatives) *are more important than in-laws.* —***v.*** feed, grow, or fill out with flesh: *An artist* ~*es out his sketch with live characters; a well* **-fleshed** *steer.* —**flesh fly** See FLESH, *n.* 1. —**flesh·ly** *adj.* **-li·er, -li·est** bodily; sensual; also, worldly: *a* ~ *school of poetry;* **flesh·li·ness** *n.* —**flesh-peddler** See FLESH, *n.* 2. —**flesh-pot** See FLESH, *n.* 1. —**flesh·y** *adj.* **flesh·i·er, -i·est** fat; also, like flesh; pulpy: *apples, oranges, grapes, and such* ~ *fruits.*

fleur-de-lis (flur·duh·LEE) *n.* **fleurs-de-lis** (flur·duh·LEEZ) the lilylike design originally used on early French flags, seen also in the Boy Scout emblem.

flew *pt.* of FLY.

flex *v.* bend (a limb); also, contract (a muscle); **flex·i·ble** *adj.* that can be bent without breaking, as wire or leather; hence, adaptable: *a* ~ *mind; a* ~ *schedule;* ~ *working hours in a* **flex-time** *system;* **flex·or** *muscles bend a limb, extensors straighten;* **flex·i·bil·i·ty** (–BIL–) *n.;* **flex·i·bly** *adv.* —**flex·ure** (–shur) *n.* a bending, curving, or folding.

flib·ber·ti·gib·bet (–tee·JIB·it) *n.* a flighty or gossipy person.

flick *n.* **1** a light, quick stroke or movement, as of a whip; also, the snapping sound made by it. **2** *Slang.* a movie: *a porn shop showing skin* ~*s.* —***v.:*** *a pocket knife (Brit.* **flick knife**) *that can* *be ~ed open or shut; ~ on* (i.e. switch on) *a light; She ~ed a crumb off her sleeve.* —**flick·er** *v.* waver or flutter: *a ~ing fire about to die; shadows ~ing on a wall;* ***n.*** **1:** *Is there a ~ of hope left? pure vodka without a ~ of color or scent.* **2** a woodpecker with a call sounding like "flicker."

flied a *pt.* of FLY (baseball sense). —**fli·er** (FLY·ur) *n.* **1** one that flies, as an aviator, or that moves with great speed, as a fast bus or train. **2** a handbill. **3** *Informal.* a reckless enterprise. —**flight** (FLITE) *n.* **1** a fleeing: *Jesus' ~ into Egypt; defeated forces* **put to flight;** *fugitives who* **take to flight** *across the border.* **2** a flying or its manner, distance, etc.: *the ~ of time; ~s of fancy; seasonal ~s of birds to warmer climes; the touchdown of Flight 202 from London; a* **flight attendant** *such as a steward or air hostess; a* **flight bag** *to fit under the seat in front of you; planes landing on an aircraft carrier's* **flight deck;** *the ostrich, emu, penguin, and such* **flightless** *birds; the* **flight path** *of an I.C.B.M.; The* **flight recorder** *was expected to yield vital clues to the cause of the crash; an astronaut in top* **flight·worth·y** *condition.* **3** a set of stairs. —**flight·y** *adj.* **flight·i·er, -i·est** frivolous or silly; **flight·i·ness** *n.*

flim·flam *v.* **-flams, -flam·med, -flam·ming** *Informal.* cheat or trick; hence ***n.*** deception; nonsense.

flim·sy (–zee) *adj.* **-si·er, -si·est** thin or frail: *a ~ excuse; ~ evidence;* ***n.*** a sheet of thin paper or copy prepared on such paper; **flim·si·ly** *adv.;* **flim·si·ness** *n.*

flinch *v.* draw back or wince in the face of something painful or requiring courage; ***n.*** a flinching.

fling *v.* **flings, flung, fling·ing** **1** throw sharply and with force: *She flung her books on the table and strode out; flung into jail without being charged; danced in the nude ~ing all modesty to the winds.* **2** dash; rush: *He flung out of the room in a huff.* —***n.*** **1** a casual attempt; also, a spree of self-indulgence: *She* **had a fling at** *journalism before joining the convent.* **2** a Scottish dance.

Flint a city of S.E. Michigan. —**flint** *n.* a hard quartz that gives off sparks when struck with steel, formerly used in **flint·lock** guns; also, an alloy with this quality, used in cigarette lighters; **flint·y** *adj.* **flint·i·er, -i·est.** —**flint glass** a type of heavy glass used in optical instruments.

flip *v.* **flips, flipped, flip·ping** **1** toss or move something jerkily so that it turns on its side: *A coin is ~d to settle a dispute; She ~d through the book for pictures.* **2** flick or strike: *to ~ at a fly; to ~ marbles out of a ring; a ~-down seat in a theater; That was the last straw, and he* **flipped (his lid)** (*Slang.* lost self-control). —***n.*** a flipping. —***adj.*** **flip·per, flip·pest** *Informal.* flippant; **flip·pant** (–unt) *adj.* of attitudes and expressions, not respectful: *a ~ answer to a serious question;* **flip·pant·ly** *adv.;* **flip·pan·cy** *n.* —**flip-flop** *n.* a backward somersault or a change, as of opinion, resembling one; also ***v.*** **-flops, -flopped, -flop·ping.** —**flip·per** *n.* the finlike swimming organ of seals, whales, etc.; also, the paddlelike shoe of a skin diver. —**flip side** *Informal.* the back or the less important side, esp. of a phonograph record.

flirt *v.* **1** play at love: *to ~ with waitresses; You're ~ing with danger.* **2** flutter; flick. —***n.:*** *She is a coquette and he's a ~.* —**flir·ta·tion** (–TAY–) *n.;* **flir·ta·tious** *adj.* fond of flirting.

flit *v.* **flits, flit·ted, flit·ting** flutter or fly about like a bird: *thoughts ~ing across a troubled mind; Time ~s by.*

flitch *n.* a side of bacon.

float (FLOTE) *n.* something that stays on the surface of a medium or moves along lightly as if suspended, as a cork, air bladder, raft, or a vehicle forming an exhibit in a parade; also, a beverage with a lump of ice cream in it. —***v.:*** *can't swim, can't even ~; efforts to ~ a sunken ship; a resort town with a ~ing* (i.e. moving and changing) *population; the two bottom* **floating ribs** *not attached in front; A bond issue is ~ed* (i.e. placed for sale) *on the market; the ~ing* (i.e. varying) *exchange value of a currency; an electronic calculator's ~ing decimal point; a ~ing* (i.e. undecided) *voter.* —**float·a·tion** (–AY–) *n.* flotation. —**float·er** *n.*

flock *n.* **1** a group of animals of the same kind such as birds or sheep; also, people of the same following: *A pastor tends his ~;* ***v.:*** *children ~ing around their mother.* **2** a woolly or fibrous tuft or mass used in stuffing or decoration.

floe *n.* a sheet or broken-off piece of floating ice.

flog *v.* **flogs, flogged, flog·ging** whip or beat with a stick; **flog·ger** *n.*

flood (FLUD) *n.* a great flow or overflow of water, as of rivers after heavy rains, when the tide rises in a **flood·tide,** or when a **flood·gate,** or sluice, is opened in a dam; also, anything similar: *a ~ of tears;* **the Flood** in the Bible, the great deluge of Noah's time. —***v.:*** *a basement ~ed by a spring thaw.* —**flood·light** *n.: Niagara Falls lit by ~s;* ***v.*** **-lights,** *pt.* & *pp.* **-light·ed** or **-lit, -light·ing.** —**flood·plain** *n.* a plain bordering a river and made fertile by the sediments left by its flood waters.

floor (FLORE) *n.* **1** the inside, supporting or bottom surface, esp. of a room: *the ~ of the ocean; the top ~* (i.e. story) *of a building.* **2** where a legislature or other body meets; hence, the right to be heard: *Mr. Chairman, may I have the ~?* **3** a lower limit. —***v.*** **1** provide with a floor or **floor·ing,** as of tiles or wood. **2** knock down or defeat (someone): *felt utterly ~ed* (i.e. confused) *by the question.* —**floor·board** *n.* a board or one of the strips forming a floor. —**floor exercise** a gymnastic exercise performed without an apparatus. —**floor leader** a member of a legislature who leads his party's activity in it. —**floor manager**

a department-store employee or sales manager who supervises clerks and looks after customers; formerly **floor·walk·er.** —**floor show** the entertainment presented at a nightclub or restaurant.

floo·zy or **floo·zie** *n.* **-zies** *Slang.* a woman of low morals.

flop *v.* **flops, flopped, flop·ping** move about or drop down in a loose or clumsy way; hence, fail: *could hear the fish ~ing on the deck; The diver ~d in the pool on her belly; The play ~d.* —***n.:*** *a* **flop-eared** *basset hound; The party was a total ~* (i.e. failure). —**flop·house** *n.* a cheap hotel. —**flop·py** *adj.* **flop·pi·er, flop·pi·est** soft and flexible, like a hound's ear.

Flo·ra (FLOR·uh) *n.* the Roman goddess of flowers; **flora** *n.* the plants of a specified region or period; **flo·ral** *adj.* of flowers: *a ~ wreath; a ~ emblem.*

Flor·ence (–unce) a city of C. Italy; **Flor·en·tine** (–teen) *n.* & *adj.*

flo·res·cence (–RES·unce) *n.* a blossoming state or period; **flo·res·cent** *adj.* —**flor·id** *adj.* **1** of a complexion, flushed, as with emotion. **2** ornate or showy: *a ~ style.*

Flor·i·da a S.E. state of the U.S.; 58,560 sq.mi. (151,670 km²); *cap.* Tallahassee.

flor·in *n.* any of various silver or gold coins of European countries, as the Dutch guilder. —**flor·ist** *n.* one who grows or deals in flowers.

floss *n.* soft silky fluff or fiber, as spun by silkworms, found on milkweed seeds, or candy spun from sugar; also, silk yarn or thread, as used in embroidery or as dental floss to clean between teeth; ***v.:*** *Brush and ~ your teeth.* —**floss·y** *adj.* **floss·i·er, -i·est** like floss, esp. showy or stylish.

flo·ta·tion (–TAY–) *n.* an act or process of floating; floatation: *the ~ process of extracting minerals from ores.* —**flo·til·la** (–TIL·uh) *n.* a small fleet; also, a fleet of small ships. —**flot·sam** (–sum) *n.* floating debris, esp. from a shipwreck: *the* **flotsam and jetsam** (i.e. discards and derelicts) *of a nation destroyed by war.*

flounce *v.* **flounc·es, flounced, flounc·ing** move (*off, out,* etc.) with an abrupt or jerky motion as if in impatience or disdain; ***n.*** **1** such a movement. **2** a wide, rufflelike strip of cloth gathered and sewed at the upper edge around a skirt; **flounc·y** *adj.*

floun·der *v.* struggle or stumble about as if in deep snow: *to ~ through a speech;* —***n.*** **1** a floundering. **2** any of a group of saltwater fishes with flattened bodies and both eyes on the same side of the head.

flour *n.* the powdered and sifted meal of a cereal such as wheat for baking bread, biscuits, etc.; ***v.*** coat or cover with flour or a similar product. —**flour·y** *adj.*

flour·ish (FLUR–) *v.* **1** flower forth and thrive; be at the peak or prime: *The Aztec civilization ~ed in Mexico before the Spanish conquest.* **2** wave about; brandish: *to ~ a sword.* —***n.*** a waving or showy movement, writing, or musical passage: *a ~* (i.e. fanfare) *of trumpets.*

flout *v.* treat (advice, order, law, etc.) with scorn; ***n.*** a scornful act or speech; **flout·er** *n.*

flow (FLOH) *v.* move or seem to move smoothly and steadily, as a stream of water: *eyes ~ing with tears; hair that ~s in the wind; The ~ing* (i.e. rising) *tide swells a river; wealth ~ing out of an exploited nation.* —***n.:*** *the ~ of words from a fluent talker; the ebb and ~ of tides; the ~ of electricity from the negative to the positive pole of a battery; a* **flow chart** (i.e. diagram) *to show the movement of materials and personnel in operating a plant.*

flow·er *n.* the seed-producing part of a plant, usu. having colorful petals, scent, and honey; also, a plant cultivated for its flowers; hence, a blossoming or flourishing part or period: *Bamboos are rarely seen* **in flower;** *plucked from life in the ~* (i.e. best part) *of her youth; Sulfur vapor condenses into powdery "flowers of sulfur";* —***v.*** bloom or develop: *Some plants ~ once and wither away; the early ~ing of his genius; The "rose window" has a* **flowered** *design.* —**flower child** a hippie. —**flower girl** a young girl attending a bride with flowers. —**flower head** a composite flower such as the chrysanthemum or the sunflower that is made up of many little flowers. —**flower people** hippies. —**flow·er·pot** *n.* a container for growing flowers. —**flow·er·y** *adj.* **-er·i·er, -er·i·est** full of or like flowers; hence, ornate; **flow·er·i·ness** *n.*

flown *pp.* of FLY.

fl. oz. fluid ounce(s).

flu (FLOO) *n.* influenza; also, a virus infection such as "intestinal flu."

flub *n.* & *v.* **flubs, flubbed, flub·bing** *Informal.* bungle.

fluc·tu·ate (FLUK·choo–) *v.* **-ates, -at·ed, -at·ing** go up and down in a wavelike motion; vary irregularly: *~ing temperatures;* **fluc·tu·a·tion** (–AY–) *n.*

flue (FLOO) *n.* a passage such as a pipe or tube for conveying smoke, air, etc., as in a chimney or pipe organ. —**flu·ent** (FLOO·unt) *adj.* esp. of writing or speech, flowing smoothly; **flu·ent·ly** *adv.;* **flu·en·cy** *n.* —**flu·er·ic(s)** (floo·ER–) same as FLUIDIC(s).

fluff *n.* **1** soft fur or feathers as inside a pillow; also, nap, as on a woolen blanket. **2** something woolly or light. **3** a blunder, esp. in saying one's lines on the stage. —***v.:*** *A pillow is ~ed up when making a bed; No one ~ed a line in yesterday's TV premiere.* —**fluff·y** *adj.* **fluff·i·er, -i·est:** *a ~ angel cake; a ~ ball of a chick.*

flu·id (FLOO–) *n.* a liquid or gaseous substance such as water, mercury, or air; ***adj.*** having to do with fluids; also, flowing or changeable: *a ~ diet* (of nonsolid foods); *Pending a settlement, the situation remains ~; cash, savings, and such ~ assets; A* **fluid dram** *equals 1/8* **fluid ounce** (29.57 ml); *An automobile's* **fluid drive** (or

clutch) *transmits motion by the spinning force of oil.* —**flu·id·ic** (floo·ID–) *adj.* using the force of fluids instead of mechanical or electrical power in amplifying and controlling devices, as for timing, counting, etc.; **flu·id·ics** *n.pl.* the technology of fluidic devices. —**flu·id·ly** *adv.*; **flu·id·i·ty** (–ID–) *n.*

fluke (FLOOK) *n.* **1** a flatfish; also, a flatworm or trematode. **2** the flat, triangular, pointed tip of each arm of an anchor or a similarly shaped head of an arrow, a lobe of a whale's tail, etc. **3** a stroke of luck; **fluk·y** *adj.* **fluk·i·er, -i·est** *Informal.* lucky; also, uncertain.

flume (FLOOM) *n.* a narrow, deep valley or channel; hence, a flowing channel or chute used in irrigation, logging, mining, etc.

flung *pt.* of FLING.

flunk *v. Informal.* fail (in schoolwork): *Teachers ~ poor students; Some students ~ed their math test; to* **flunk out** *of school* (i.e. be dismissed).

flun·ky (FLUNG·kee) *n.* **-kies** [contemptuous term] a menial servant; lackey; also **flun·key, -keys.**

flu·or (FLOO·ur) *n.* same as FLUORITE. —**flu·o·resce** (floo·uh·RES) *v.* **-resc·es, -resced, -resc·ing** become **flu·o·res·cent** *adj.* giving off light by **flu·o·res·cence** *n.* the property of transforming radiations such as ultraviolet rays and X rays into a different wavelength or color; also, light thus emitted: *A* **fluorescent lamp** (or **tube**) *contains mercury vapor that is acted on by electricity to produce* **fluorescent light.** —**fluor·i·date** (FLOR·uh–) *v.* **-dates, -dat·ed, -dat·ing** add fluorides to (drinking water); **fluor·i·da·tion** (–DAY–) *n.* —**flu·o·ride** (FLOOR–, FLOR–) *n.* a fluorine compound such as "calcium fluoride." —**flu·o·rine** (FLOOR·een, FLOR–) *n.* a poisonous, gaseous chemical element; **flu·o·rite** *n.* a mineral that is the chief source of fluorine. —**flu·o·ro·car·bon** (–CAR·bun) *n.* any of various fluorine-carbon compounds used as lubricants, refrigerants, and aerosol propellants. —**fluor·o·scope** *n.* an instrument consisting of an X-ray machine and a fluorescent screen for viewing internal organs in operation. —**flu·or·spar** *n.* same as FLUORITE.

flur·ry (FLUR·ee) *n.* **flur·ries** a sudden gust of wind, snow, or rain; hence, a brief commotion or spurt of activity: *a ~ of trading on the stock exchange;* ***v.*** **flur·ries, flur·ried, flur·ry·ing:** *got all ~d* (i.e. agitated) *when they heard who was coming to dinner.*

flush *v.* **1** make or become red or glowing: *cheeks ~ed with joy.* **2** (make) flow or rush out: *to ~ a toilet; guerrillas ~ed from their hideouts with gas.* **3** make flush or even. —***n.*** **1** an excited condition; glow: *in the first ~ of victory.* **2** a rapid flow or outgrowth: *the first ~ of spring grass.* **3** a hand of the same suit of cards. —***adj.*** **1** glowing with vigor; lusty: *the ~ faces of healthy youth.* **2** abundant; prosperous: *oil-rich Arabs ~ with money.* **3** even; level: *lines of type ~ with the margin; a ~ door without panels;* ***adv.:*** *lines printed ~ on the left; was hit ~* (i.e. squarely) *on the chin.*

flus·ter *v.* upset or make nervous; ***n.:*** *The office was thrown into a ~ by the visit from headquarters.*

flute (FLOOT) *n.* **1** a high-pitched wind instrument consisting of a slender tube with holes along its stem which are fingered by the **flut·ist** (or **flau·tist**) while blowing over a hole near one end. **2** one of the ornamental grooves or furrows running parallel along a column; also, a similar decorative groove in a **flut·ed** garment, furniture leg, or armor; **flut·ing** *n.* such grooves or the decoration.

flut·ter *v.* (cause to) beat or flap (wings) rapidly and irregularly; also, move about or act in this way: *The chick ~ed its wings as if to fly; flags ~ing in the wind; waiters ~ing about taking orders during a rush hour; The patient's pulse ~ed awhile before regaining its rhythm.* —***n.*** a nervous or agitated state; flurry: *bad acoustics causing ~* (i.e. fluctuation of sound); **flut·ter·y** *adj.*

flux *n.* **1** a flow or flowing, as of the tides, magnetic energy, etc.; hence, change: *Languages are in a continual state of ~.* **2** in soldering, smelting, etc., a substance that helps fusion, as limestone in the extraction of iron from ore.

fly *v.* **flies, flew, flown** (FLONE), **fly·ing** move or cause to move swiftly and lightly, as a bird through the air: *has never flown in a plane; He ~s kites for fun; tried to ~ (across) the Atlantic in a balloon; a pilot who flew refugees out of Vietnam; a ship ~ing before the wind; windows ~ing open in a storm; The batter* **flied** *the ball high in the air; a testimony that* **flies in the face of** (i.e. contradicts) *all available evidence; a man who* **flies off the handle** (i.e. gets angry) *at the least provocation; In her fury she* **let fly** (i.e. burst out) *with some four-letter words; came out of the ordeal* **with flying colors** (i.e. victoriously). —***n.,*** *pl.* **flies** **1** a flying; **on the fly** while flying; also, hurriedly. **2** a flying part, as the flapping edge of a flag; also, a flap, as in a garment to conceal buttons, zipper, etc. or one serving as the door of a tent. **3** a baseball batted high in the air. **4** a winged insect; also, something resembling it, used on a fishing hook as a lure; **fly in the ointment** something that lessens the value or usefulness of what it affects, as an unwelcome guest at a party. —**fly·a·ble** (–uh·bl) *adj.* —**fly·blown** *adj.* infested with blowfly larvae; contaminated; hence, bad. —**fly·by** *n.* **-bys** a flight of a craft that flies close to or past an object under observation, esp. one in space such as Mars or the moon. —**fly-by-night** *n.* & *adj.* (one) that quits without paying debts. —**fly-by-wire** *adj.* having to do with craft that are remotely controlled, as from a computer. —**fly-cast** *v.* to fish by use of flylike lures attached to the hook. —**fly·catch·er** *n.* any of various birds that prey on insects in flight.

—fly·er *n.* same as FLIER. **—flying boat** a seaplane with a boatlike hull. **—flying buttress** in Gothic architecture, an arched prop or brace that supports a wall from the outside, its other end being set in a pier. **—flying fish** any of various fishes of warm seas that have fins that can be spread like wings for gliding over distances of up to 1,000 ft. (300 m) after a leap. **—flying saucer** a mysterious flying object, esp. one disk-shaped, reported seen in the skies. **—flying squad** a highly mobile unit for special tasks. **—flying squirrel** any of various squirrels that can glide through the air using winglike folds of skin stretching between the forelegs and hindlegs. **—fly·leaf** *n.* **-leaves** a blank leaf at the beginning or end of a book. **—fly·pa·per** *n.* a strip of sticky paper for catching flies. **—fly·speck** *n.* a speck of dirt left by a fly; hence, a tiny spot or flaw. **—fly·way** *n.* the regular flight path of a migratory bird. **—fly·weight** *n.* a boxer weighing not more than 112 lb., or 51 kg for Olympics. **—fly·wheel** *n.* a heavy wheel attached to the shaft of an engine to regulate its speed.

fm. fathom. **—Fm** fermium. **—FM** frequency modulation.

fn. footnote.

f-number *Photog.* the ratio of the focal length of a lens to its diameter: *The lower the ~ the shorter the required exposure time.*

fo. folio. **—F.O.** field officer; foreign office; forward observer.

foal (FOLE) *n.* the young of an animal of the horse family; colt or filly; ***v.*** give birth to (a colt or filly).

foam (FOME) *n.* a mass of fine bubbles, as formed in or on a liquid by fermentation, agitation, etc.; also, a rigid or spongy material made by the dispersal of bubbles in liquid rubber, plastic, etc.; ***v.:*** *boiling, ~ing water; like a furious giant* **foaming at the mouth; foam·y** *adj.*

fob *n.* a short ribbon, chain, etc., often with an ornament, attached to a pocket watch or key ring: *his and hers key ~s.* **—*v.* fobs, fobbed, fob·bing; fob off** trick (someone) or pass (something) off by trickery.

F.O.B. or **f.o.b.** free on board.

fo·cal (FOH·cl) *adj.* of or at a focus; **focal length** the distance from a lens or mirror to the point where rays passing through or reflected by it converge; focus.

fo'c'sle (FOKE·sl) *n.* same as FORECASTLE.

fo·cus (FOH–) *n.* **-cus·es** or **-ci** (–sye) **1** the meeting point of rays of light, heat, or sound; also, focal length; hence, an adjustment of this to get a sharp image; **in** (or **out of**) **focus** clear (or blurred). **2** center of attention. **—*v.* -cus·es, -cus(s)ed, -cus·(s)ing** adjust (a lens, the eyes, etc.) so as to get a sharp image; hence, concentrate.

fod·der (FOD·ur) *n.* coarse or dried food for farm animals, as alfalfa, corn, hay, etc.

foe *n.* an enemy, esp. an actively hostile one.

foehn (FANE, FURN) *n.* a warm, dry wind blowing down mountainsides in the Alps.

foe·man (FOH·mun) *n.* a foe.

foe·tal, foe·tus (fee–) same as FETAL, FETUS.

fog *n.* a thick mist or cloud that is close to the ground and cuts visibility, called a **fog·bank** when seen as a dense mass: *rash of accidents on a* **fog·bound** *expressway.* **—*v.* fogs, fogged, fog·ging** cover with fog; also, be or become obscured or bewildered: *a ~d car window; Liquor ~s the mind.* **—fogey** See FOGY. **—fog·gy** *adj.* **fog·gi·er, fog·gi·est** full of fog; cloudy: *~ weather; not the ~est notion what she meant.* **—fog·gi·ly** *adv.;* **fog·gi·ness** *n.* **—fog·horn** *n.* a warning siren used on lighthouses and ships in foggy weather.

fo·gy (FOH·gee) *n.* **-gies** one who is old-fashioned in thinking and behavior: *an old ~;* also **fo·gey, -geys.**

foi·ble *n.* a minor personal weakness, esp. one easy to overlook.

foil *n.* **1** a thin-rolled sheet of a metal such as tin, aluminum, or lead, as used for wrapping. **2** a person or thing that acts as a mirror setting another off, as a "straight man" for a comedian. **3** a blunted sword used in fencing. **4** a hydrofoil: *a ~-borne craft; a boat with submerged ~s.* **—*v.*** thwart or frustrate, as by throwing pursuers off a scent.

foist *v.* palm off: *secondhand stuff ~ed on unwary buyers.*

fol. folio; following.

fold *v.* **1** bend or double over, as to wrap or enclose: *A letter is ~ed to put in an envelope; candy ~ed* (i.e. wrapped) *in foil; standing with ~ed arms; a child ~ed in her mother's embrace.* **2** *Informal.* fail: *A business ~s (up) when broke.* **—*n*** **1** a folding or bend: *hidden in the ~s of a drape; anticlines, synclines, and such ~s in rock; an easy-to-store* **fold·a·way** *cot; a* **fold·out** *picture on an oversize page in a magazine.* **2** a sheep pen; also, a flock, esp. a church congregation: *the prodigal's return to the ~.* **— -fold** *comb.form.* (specified) number of parts or times: as in *threefold, manifold, twofold.* **—fold·er** *n.* something that folds or is folded, as a file for papers or an advertising leaflet.

fol·de·rol or **fol·de·ral** same as FALDERAL.

foldout See FOLD, *n.* 1.

fo·li·age (FOE·lee·ij) *n.* leaves of a plant or tree. **—fo·li·ate** *v.* **-ates, -at·ed, -at·ing** make into or like leaves; hence, make into foil; also, separate into layers; ***adj. & comb.form.:*** *a trifoliate cloverleaf; a graphite's foliate(d) structure;* **fo·li·a·tion** (–AY–) *n.: the ~ of mica schist into layers.* **—fo·li·o** (FOE·lee·oh) *n.* **-os** **1** a leaf of a book; also, a page number. **2** the largest book size resulting from sheets of paper folded once; also, a once-folded sheet of any size.

folk (FOKE) *n.* **1** the common people, esp. as a social or cultural group: *city ~.* **2 folks** *pl.*

Informal. people: *old ~s; How are your ~s* (i.e. family)? —***adj.*** being traditional with the common people: *~ dancing.* —**folk·lore** *n.* the traditional customs, beliefs, sayings, etc. of a people; **folk·lor·ist** *n.* —**folk music** music of the common people, including dance songs and folk songs, handed down from generation to generation. —**folk rock** folk songs sung to a rock rhythm. —**folk song** a traditional song of popular origin, as Negro spirituals, ballads, etc.; **folk·sing·er** *n.;* **folk·sing·ing** *n.* —**folk·sy** (-see) *adj.* **-si·er, -si·est** *Informal.* friendly or sociable in style. —**folk·way** *n.* a habit or custom common within a social group.

foll. following.

fol·li·cle (FOL·i·cl) *n.* a body cavity or sac: *hair ~s in the skin; Graafian ~s contain egg cells in the ovary;* **follicle-stimulating hormone** a sex hormone released by the pituitary.

fol·low (FOL·oh) *v.* **1** go or come after; hence, pursue: *Thanksgiving ~ed by Christmas; Your shadow ~s you; The reasons are* **as follows;** *a salesman who* **follows up** *his letters with phone calls; a* **fol·low-up** *visit; The man emigrated first and his family* **followed suit** (i.e. did the same thing); *service offered as a* **fol·low-through** *after sales.* **2** result; ensue: *wars ~ing from enmities.* **3** obey: *Christians ~ Christ's doctrines.* **4** understand: *a lecturer difficult to ~.* —**fol·low·er** *n.* —**fol·low·ing** **1** *adj.: for the ~ reasons.* **2** *n.: a party with a large ~ in the South; People and things found on the premises were* **the following.** **3** *prep.: a dance ~ dinner.*

fol·ly (FOL·ee) *n.* **fol·lies** (–eez) the quality or an instance of lack of good sense, propriety, or foresight; foolishness: *the ~ of accepting free rides; the ~s and excesses of youth;* **follies** *n.pl.* a revue: *ice ~s.*

fo·ment (foh·MENT) *v.* stir up or incite (trouble, rebellion, etc.). —**fo·men·ta·tion** (–TAY–) *n.* **1** a lotion, poultice, or compress applied for heat and moisture. **2** incitement.

fond *adj.* loving, often excessively; also, cherished: *a ~ parent; ~ and foolish hopes; a child* **fond of** *ice cream;* **fond·ly** *adv.;* **fond·ness** *n.* —**fon·dle** (FON·dl) *v.* **-dles, -dled, -dling** pet; caress.

fon·du(e) *n.* a preparation of wine-flavored melted cheese eaten by dipping bread in it.

font *n.* **1** a source or spring; also, a bowl or basin for holy water, esp. one used at baptism. **2** a complete set of printing type of the same size and style.

food *n.* anything for consumption, esp. to sustain life or nourish growth: *died for lack of ~ and water; ~ and drink; Fertilizers are plant ~s; the Bible as ~ for the soul.* —**food chain** the system of producer-consumer-decomposer that food energy goes through, as when green plants are nourished by sunlight, animals nourished by green plants, man by animals, bacteria by dead bodies, and so on, many such chains making the **food cycle** of an ecological community, as in the sea. —**food poisoning** poisoning caused by eating food contaminated by bacteria, as in botulism, or chemicals such as zinc, lead, and copper. —**food processor** a multi-purpose kitchen appliance with attachments for chopping, slicing, mixing, shredding, etc. —**food stamp** a stamp issued to people on low incomes to exchange for food. —**food·stuff** *n.* a material such as grain, meat, vegetables, etc. that has food value. —**food web** same as FOOD CYCLE.

fool *n.* a silly or idiotic person; also, a jester, as in the Middle Ages. —***v.*** **1** trick or deceive: *Many get ~ed on April 1.* **2** *Informal.* act like a fool: *Stop* **fooling around** *and start studying; She* **fooled away** *her time till the eve of exams; It's dangerous to* **fool with** *explosives.* —**fool·er·y** *n.* **-er·ies** a foolish action or foolish behavior. —**fool·har·dy** *adj.* **-di·er, -di·est** foolishly daring; **fool·har·di·ness** *n.* —**fool·ish** *adj.* showing lack of good sense and judgment: *a ~ action; a ~ young man;* **fool·ish·ly** *adv.;* **fool·ish·ness** *n.* —**fool·proof** *adj.* so safe or simple as not to be mishandled, misunderstood, etc. even by a fool. —**fools·cap** *n.* a size of writing paper measuring about 13 in. (33 cm) by 17 in. (43 cm). —**fool's paradise** state of happiness based on false hopes or illusions.

foot *n., pl.* **feet** **1** the part of the leg that touches the ground when one is standing or walking; also, something corresponding to this, as the foot of a chair or stocking: *Those living nearby came* **on foot** (i.e. walked); *She* **put** *her* **foot down** (i.e. was firm) *in not admitting latecomers; children getting* **under foot** (i.e. in the way). **2** a part opposed to the head or top part, as the foot of a page, hill, bed, sail, etc. **3** *Brit.* soldiers on foot; infantry. **4** a measure of length based on the human foot, equal to 12 in. (0.3048 m); also, a unit of verse based on the syllable: *"Five and twenty sailors" has three trochaic feet.* —***v.*** **1** find the sum of (a column of figures). **2** pay (costs, a bill, etc.): *Don't* **set foot** (i.e. take a single step) *in this room; They* **footed it** (i.e. walked) *home after missing the bus.* —**foot·age** *n.* length measured in feet; also, a length of motion-picture film. —**foot·ball** *n.* **1** a game played between two teams defending a goal at either end of a field and using an inflated ball; also, rugby or soccer. **2** the oval ball used in football and rugby or the spherical ball of soccer. —**foot·board** *n.* an upright board forming the foot of a bed; also, any board or plank used to rest the feet on. —**foot·bridge** *n.* a bridge for walking across. —**foot-can·dle** *n.* a unit of illumination equal to the light thrown by one candle at a distance of one foot. —**foot·ed** *adj. & comb. form.: a satyr ~ like a goat; a child's ~ pajamas; man and other two-~ animals.* — **-footer** *comb. form.* one measuring (specified) feet: as in *seven-footer.* —**foot·fall** *n.* the sound of a footstep. —**foot·hill** *n.* a hill at the foot of higher mountains. —**foot·hold** *n.* a place to hold on to with a foot; hence, a secure or advantageous position. —**foot·ing** *n.* a placing of the feet; also, a foothold or something forming a foot, as the lowest part of a building foundation; hence, basis: *two people on a friendly ~.* —**foot·less** *adj.* having no feet or foundation; also, clumsy or inept; **foot·less·ness** *n.* —**foot·lights** *n.pl.* a row of stage lights at foot level. —**foot·ling** *adj. Informal.* trifling or silly. —**foot·lock·er** *n.* a chest kept at the foot of one's bed, as in barracks. —**foot·loose** *adj.* free to move about or do as one pleases. —**foot·man** *n.* **-men** a male servant doing odd jobs; doorman. —**foot·note** *n.* a note placed at the foot of a page or end of a chapter or book explaining or amplifying the text; ***v.:*** *a heavily ~d thesis.* —**foot·pad** *n.* a padded foot of a soft-landing spacecraft. —**foot·path** *n.* a path used by those on foot. —**foot·print** *n.* an impression or mark made by a foot. —**foot·race** *n.* a running race. —**foot·rest** *n.* a support on which to rest the feet. —**foot soldier** an infantryman. —**foot·sore** *adj.* having feet that are sore, esp. from walking. —**foot·step** *n.* the sound or impression made by feet: *pupils* **following in** *their master's* **footsteps** (i.e. example). —**foot·stool** *n.* a low stool to rest the feet on. —**foot·wear** *n.* things to wear on the feet; shoes, boots, slippers, etc. —**foot·work** *n.* the manner of using the feet, as in dancing or fencing.

fop *n.* a dandy; **fop·per·y** *n.* **fop·per·ies; fop·pish** *adj.*

for (FOR, fur) *prep.* [indicating purpose, goal, object, fitness, exchange, duration, etc.]: *to go ~ a walk; catch the plane ~ Las Vegas; a letter ~ you; She has no ear ~ music; translated it word ~ word; slept ~ 10 hours; The eggs are ~ hatching; famous ~ fine cooking; a lawyer acting ~ his client; a good guy ~ all I know; ~ my part, I did nothing; a child named ~ her mother.* —***conj.*** because: *I smoke it, ~ I like it.*

for- *prefix.* away; apart: as in *forgo, forswear;* cf. FORE-. —**for.** foreign; forestry. —**F.O.R.** free on rail.

fora a *pl.* of FORUM.

for·age (–ij) *n.* a search or what is searched out for food, esp. grass and winter fodder for farm animals, as hay, straw, and silage. —***v.*** **-ag·es, -ag·ed, -ag·ing:** *Primitive man lived by ~ing;* **for·ag·er** *n.*

fo·ra·men (–RAY·mun) *n., pl.* **-ram·i·na** (–RAM·i·nuh) or **-ra·mens** a small opening, as the one in the skull for the spinal cord to pass through.

for·ay *v.* pillage; also, to invade (into). —***n.*** a raid; also, an excursion.

forbad(e) *pt.* of FORBID.

for·bear (–BARE) *v.* **-bears, -bore, -borne** (–BORN), **-bear·ing** **1** keep from doing or saying; also, be patient and control oneself; **for·bear·ance** (–unce) *n.: forgiveness of injuries and ~ under provocation.* **2** same as FOREBEAR.

for·bid (–BID) *v.* **-bids,** *pt.* **-bad** or **-bade** (–BAD), *pp.* **-bid·den, -bid·ding** order not to do something: *forbade his children to smoke; "Forbidden fruit is sweet"; outsiders ~en (use of) the cottage; God ~ (the predicted earthquake)!* —**for·bid·ding** *adj.* that causes fear or dislike: *The pool looked cold and ~; a man of ~ appearance;* **for·bid·ding·ly** *adj.*

forbore, forborne See FORBEAR.

force *n.* **1** physical, mental, or moral power or strength, esp. its active use; also, its cause, intensity, or effect: *He used ~ to open the door; can move objects by sheer ~ of will; goes on making the same mistakes by ~ of habit; Idioms have greater ~ than other phrases; A gyroscope illustrates the ~ of inertia; Lower speed limits are now* **in force.** **2** a body of people or anything having force: *a task ~ to study reform; a police ~; the armed* **forces** (i.e. army, navy, etc.); *storms, earthquakes, and such ~s of nature.* —***v.*** **forc·es, forced, forc·ing** get something done by overcoming resistance: *He ~d the door (open); a confession ~d from the prisoner; promises ~d out of someone; a bribe ~d (up)on an honest official; She ~d her way through the crowd.* —**forced** (FORST) *adj.: the plane's ~ landing; ~ labor in a work camp; smiles that look ~; a ~-air heating system.* —**force·ful** *adj.: a ~ speaker, personality, style, presentation;* **force·ful·ly** *adv.;* **force·ful·ness** *n.*

for·ceps *n. sing. & pl.* a pair of pincers or tongs used by surgeons, dentists, et al. for grasping, pulling, compressing, etc.: *Obstetrical ~ grasp the baby's head.*

for·ci·ble *adj.* **1** got or done by the use of force: *a burglar's ~ entry; liable to ~ ejection from the hall.* **2** showing force: *a rather ~ argument;* **for·ci·bly** *adv.*

ford *n.* a place in a stream that is shallow enough to cross by wading or driving through. —***v.:*** *Oxen used to ~ the Thames at Oxford;* **ford·a·ble** *adj.*

Ford **1 Gerald R.** born 1913, 39th U.S. President (1974–1977). **2 Henry.** 1863–1947, American automobile manufacturer.

fore *adj.* in the front or forward, not back or aft: *the ~ end of a firearm; a page's ~ edge* (i.e. opposite the back or stitched edge); *the ~ hatch of a ship.* —***adv.*** toward the bow of a ship; **fore and aft** at, to, or from bow and stern; **fore-and-aft** *adj.* lengthwise: *a ~ rigged ship; British-army style ~* (i.e. placed lengthwise) *cap.* —***n.*** front: *a candidate* **come to the fore** *only recently.* —***interj.*** [used as a warning]: *The golfer shouted ~ and swung his club.* —***comb. form.*** before or front: as in *fore-loader, forefather, foreplay.* —**fore·arm** *n.* the part of the arm between elbow and wrist; ***v.*** (–ARM) arm beforehand: *"Forewarned is ~ed"; came to the debate ~ed with facts and figures.* —**for(e)·bear** *n.* ancestor.

—**fore·bode** (–BODE) *v.* **-bodes, -bod·ed, -bod·ing** esp. of things, predict; warn of (usu. something unfavorable): *a dream ~ing a fatal crash;* **fore·bod·ing** *n.* presentiment: *dark ~s of disaster.* —**fore·cast** *n.* prediction; ***v.*** **-casts, -cast(·ed), -cast·ing:** *Snow is ~ for Christmas; economic indicators ~ing a recession;* **fore·cast·er** *n.* —**fore·cas·tle** (FOKE·sl) *n.* the raised deck near a ship's bow; also, crew's quarters in the forward part, as in a cargo ship. —**fore·close** *v.* (–CLOSE) *v.* **-clos·es, -closed, -clos·ing** close in advance; also, preclude: *an embargo ~ing trade; A mortgage is ~d and the property sold if payments to the lender are not kept up;* **fore·clo·sure** *n.* —**fore·doom** (–DOOM) *v.: a plot that was ~ed to failure because not kept secret.* —**fore·fa·ther** *n.* an ancestor. —**fore·fend** (–FEND) *v.* same as FORFEND. —**fore·fin·ger** (FOR·fing·gur) *n.* the finger next to the thumb. —**fore·foot** *n.* **-feet** one of the front feet of an animal or insect with four feet or more. —**fore·front** (–frunt) *n.* the extreme front; the position of the greatest activity or importance. —**fore·gath·er** (–GADH·ur) *v.* same as FORGATHER. —**fore·go** (–GO) *v.* **-goes, -went, -gone, -go·ing** **1** go before; precede: *From the ~ing facts I deduce the earth is round; The jury was packed and the verdict a* **foregone conclusion** (i.e. known or predictable in advance). **2** same as FORGO. —**fore·ground** *n.* the part of a picture that looks the closest: *The children were in the ~ of the picture with the mountains in the background.* —**fore·hand** *n.* in tennis and such racket games, a stroke with the palm of the hand turned forward; also, a similar shot or pass in ice hockey; ***adj.:*** *a ~ drive, grip, stroke;* **fore·hand·ed** *adj.* mindful of future needs; thrifty; hence, well-to-do. —**fore·head** (FOR·id, –hed) *n.* the part of the face above the eyebrows.

for·eign (FOR·in) *adj.* situated in, belonging to, or dealing with an outside country or place: *a ~ accent; English as a ~ language; our ~ policy; Laziness is ~ to her nature; sued for leaving a ~ object inside a patient; American children of ~-born immigrants;* **for·eign·er** *n.;* **foreign minister** one in charge of a government's foreign affairs, heading a department often called the **Foreign Office.**

fore·know (–NOH) *v.* **-knows, -knew, -known, -know·ing** have prior knowledge, or **fore·knowl·edge** by use of divine or psychic power. —**forelady** See FOREMAN, def. 2. —**fore·leg** *n.* one of the front legs of an animal; **fore·limb** *n.* a foreleg or a corresponding arm, fin, or wing. —**fore·lock** *n.* a lock of hair, as of a horse, growing just above the forehead. —**fore·man** (–mun) *n.,pl.* **-men** **1** the leader of a jury. **2** one in charge of workmen or a section of a plant; *fem.* **fore·la·dy, -dies** or **fore·wom·an, -wom·en.** —**fore·mast** *n.* the mast near a ship's bow. —**fore·most** (–mohst) *adj.* & *adv.* first in position or importance: *He fell head ~; the ~ champion of civil rights.* —**fore·name** *n.* first name; **fore·named** *adj.* before-mentioned; aforesaid. —**fore·noon** *n.* & *adj.* (of or having to do with) the part of the day before noon; morning: *a ~ session.*

fo·ren·sic (fuh·REN–) *adj.* pertaining to courts of law or argumentation: *a lawyer's ~ abilities;* **forensic medicine** medical science applied to legal problems; **forensics** *n.pl.* the art of debating; **fo·ren·si·cal·ly** *adv.*

fore·or·dain (–DAIN) *v.* determine in advance; predestine; **fore·or·di·na·tion** (–NAY–) *n.* —**fore·part** *n.* the front or earlier part. —**fore·play** *n.* sexual stimulation before intercourse. —**fore·quar·ter** *n.* the front half of a side of beef, lamb, pork, etc. —**fore·run·ner** *n.* one who goes before another preparing the way; precursor; harbinger; also, warning sign. —**fore·sail** *n.* the principal sail on the foremast of a ship. —**fore·see** (–SEE) *v.* **-sees, -saw, -seen, -see·ing** see or realize in advance; **fore·see·a·ble** *adj.: no rain expected in the ~ future.* —**fore·shad·ow** (–SHAD–) *v.* indicate something to follow; give advance warning of. —**fore·sheet** *n.* one of the sheets of a foresail; **foresheets** *pl.* the forward part of an open boat. —**fore·shore** *n.* the part of a shore covered during high tide. —**fore·short·en** (–SHOR·tn) *v.* portray (an object) shortened in front for proper perspective effect; make compact. —**fore·sight** *n.* the act or power of foreseeing; also, provision for the future; **fore·sight·ed** *adj.: His ~ planning averted a famine;* **fore·sight·ed·ness** *n.* —**fore·skin** *n.* the fold of skin covering the end of the penis.

for·est (–ist) *n.* a large wooded area; also, the trees and underbrush in it: *a ~ of antennas;* ***v.*** cover with a forest; **for·est·a·tion** (–AY–) *n.*

fore·stall *v.* take advance action to prevent or get ahead of: *early negotiations to ~ a strike; the ~ing of trading by large-scale advance buying.*

for·est·ed *adj.* wooded; **for·est·er** *n.* one trained in **for·est·ry** *n.* the science of forest cultivation and management of timber resources.

fore·taste *n.* an advance taste; first experience; ***v.*** (–TASTE) **-tastes, -tast·ed, -tast·ing.** —**fore·tell** (–TEL) *v.* **-tells, -told, -tell·ing** indicate beforehand; predict. —**fore·thought** *n.* previous consideration; hence, foresight. —**fore·to·ken** (–TOH·kun) *v.* indicate beforehand. —**fore·top** *n.* the platform at the top of a foremast.

for·ev·er (fur·EV·ur) *adv.* endlessly; always; also **for·ev·er·more** (–MOR).

fore·warn *v.* warn in advance. —**fore·wing** *n.* a front wing. —**forewoman** See FOREMAN, *n.*

2. —**fore·word** *n.* a short preface. —**for·feit** (–fit) *v.* lose or be deprived of (something) as a punishment: *You ~ your license by drunk driving.* —***n.*** a forfeiting; also, a fine or penalty imposed: *murder punished by ~ of life;* also **for·fei·ture** (–fich·ur). —***adj.*** lost by forfeiture. —**for·fend** (–FEND) *v. Archaic.* forbid; also, prevent: *Heaven ~!* —**for·gath·er** (–GADH–) *v.* assemble; come together. —**forgave** *pt.* of FORGIVE.

forge (FORJ) *n.* a furnace in which metal is heated or wrought; also, a smithy. —***v.*** **forg·es, forged, forg·ing 1** form or shape, as metal in a forge: *to ~ bonds of friendship.* **2** make or imitate falsely, as a passport, check, or signature; counterfeit. **3 forge ahead** move forward steadily. —**forg·er** *n.* one who forges or commits **for·ger·y** *n.* **-ger·ies,** counterfeiting of documents, art objects, signatures, etc.; also, something forged: *the Vermeer ~s.*

for·get (fur·GET) *v.* **-gets, -got, -got·ten, -get·ting** fail to remember; also, neglect or disregard; **forget oneself 1** say or do something improper. **2** be unselfish: *She ~s herself in the service of others.* —**for·get·ta·ble** *adj.* —**for·get·ful** *adj.* apt to forget; also, negligent; **for·get·ful·ly** *adv.;* **for·get·ful·ness** *n.* —**for·get-me-not** *n.* a tiny, yellow-centered, usu. sky-blue flower that grows in clusters, considered a symbol of true love.

for·give (–GIV) *v.* **-gives, -gave, -giv·en, -giv·ing** pardon, esp. give up the wish to punish: *to ~ and forget wrongs; ~ an enemy; all debts ~n* (i.e. cancelled); **for·giv·a·ble** *adj.;* **for·give·ness** *n.;* **for·giv·er** *n.* —**for·giv·ing** *adj.;* **for·giv·ing·ly** *adv.*

for·go (–GO) *v.* **-goes, -went, -gone, -go·ing** do without (something) in a self-denying way, usu. from expediency: *She worked nights, often ~ing sleep.*

forgot, forgotten See FORGET.

for·int *n.* the basic money unit of Hungary, equal to 100 fillér.

fork *n.* **1** an implement with a handle and two or more prongs or tines for eating, pitching hay, etc.; hence, something resembling it, as a tuning fork. **2** where branches of a tree, stream, or road meet; also, one of the branches. —***v.*** use a fork to lift, throw, dig, etc.; also, divide into forks; **fork over** (or **out, up**) *Informal.* hand over (money). —**forked** *adj.: ~* (i.e. zigzag) *lightning; ~ stick;* **forked tongue** deceitful speech. —**fork·ful** *n.* **-fuls.** —**fork·lift (truck)** a vehicle with a pronged device in front that is slid under heavy objects for moving them, as in a warehouse.

for·lorn (–LORN) *adj.* wretched and forsaken: *the deserted and ~ look of hungry children;* **forlorn hope** a nearly hopeless enterprise; **for·lorn·ly** *adv.*

form *n.* **1** shape or structure; hence, kind: *water in the ~ of rain and snow; Proteus could assume any ~; the ~ and content of a poem; the plural ~ of a noun; light, heat, and other ~s of energy.* **2** a way, method, or manner of doing something: *"Good morning" is the accepted ~ of greeting before noon; considered bad ~ to smoke in church; mere ~s and ceremonies.* **3** a frame or mold: *Concrete is poured into ~s for setting; Type is set and locked into ~s for printing.* **4** a document to be filled out: *a tax ~; an application ~.* —***v.*** to shape, take shape, put into shape, etc.: *Ice is ~ing on the window; a party ~ed of neighbors; habits ~ed in childhood; ~ yourselves into circles.* — **-form** *comb.form.* having (specified) form: as in *cruciform, uniform, vermiform.* —**form·al** (–ul) *adj.* in accordance with a form, rule, custom, or convention: *A tuxedo is a ~ costume; A contract is a ~ agreement; a ~ invitation; a ~ garden laid out in geometrical designs;* **for·mal·ly** *adv.;* **for·mal·ism** *n.*

for·mal·de·hyde (–MAL–) *n.* a colorless, pungent, water-soluble gas used as a disinfectant and preservative.

for·mal·i·ty (–MAL–) *n.* **-ties** attention to forms and ceremonies; hence, stiffness; also, a rule, custom, or convention. —**for·mal·ize** (FOR·muh–) *v.* **-iz·es, -ized, -iz·ing** make formal or give a form to: *The fleur-de-lis is a ~d iris; language ~d as grammar;* **for·mal·i·za·tion** (–ZAY–) *n.* —**for·mat** *n.* shape, design, or arrangement: *The Bible has been printed in many ~s; a meeting in the ~ of a panel discussion;* ***v.*** **-mats, -mat·ted, -mat·ting:** *computerized book ~ing; data ~d into character form.* —**for·ma·tion** (–MAY–) *n.* a forming or the manner of forming; also, something formed: *the ~ of ice on a lake; planes flying in ~; rock ~s.* —**form·a·tive** (–tiv) *adj.* of or having to do with form and growth: *the ~ influences of home, school, and society; the ~ years of childhood.*

for·mer *adj.* **1** previous: *stories of ~ times.* **2** first-mentioned of two: *Of Leslie and John, the ~ (one) is a girl.* —**for·mer·ly** *adv.* in the past.

form·fit·ting *adj.* close-fitting on the wearer's body.

for·mic *adj.* having to do with ants or an acidic fluid emitted by ants, spiders, and such insects.

For·mi·ca (for·MY·cuh) *Trademark.* heat-resistant plastic covering material for counters and tabletops.

for·mi·da·ble (–duh·bl) *adj.* causing awe, admiration, and alarm: *a ~ opponent, threat, task, list of qualifications.*

form·less *adj.* shapeless: *Fluids are ~; the voices of ~* (i.e. immaterial) *beings.* —**form letter** a letter so written or printed that it may be dated and addressed to many people.

For·mo·sa (–MOH·suh) former name of TAIWAN.

for·mu·la (–myuh·luh) *n.* **-las** or **-lae** (–lee) **1** a set expression for social or religious use; also, a set of symbols expressing a mathematical truth or chemical composition, as "You are welcome," "I baptize thee . . . ," $2\pi r$, H_2SO_4, etc. **2** a set of specifications; also, a recipe, plan, preparation, etc. in which one is used: *a soap-making ~; The baby's ~ needs warming up; a ~ for success; a* **Formula One** *Grand Prix racing car* (built to specifications of size, weight, engine capacity, etc.); **formula investing** investing opportunely in selected securities according to a plan. **—for·mu·late** *v.* **-lates, -lat·ed, -lat·ing** express in a formula or systematically; also, prepare using a formula: *Einstein ~d relativity; A pharmacist ~s prescriptions;* **for·mu·la·tion** (–LAY–) *n.: different ~s of rubber for various uses;* **for·mu·la·tor** (FOR–) *n.*

for·ni·cate *v.* **-cates, -cat·ed, -cat·ing** commit **for·ni·ca·tion** (–CAY–) *n.* sexual intercourse other than between husband and wife; **for·ni·ca·tor** *n.*

for·sake (fur–) *v.* **-sakes, -sook, -sak·en, -sak·ing** give up (a person or thing to which one is attached): *Friends forsook him when he was in jail; a recluse who has ~n his kith and kin; bad habits that he forsook on marriage.*

for·sooth (–SOOTH) *adv. Archaic.* in truth; no doubt.

for·swear (–SWARE) *v.* **-swears, -swore, -sworn, -swear·ing** **1** swear solemnly to avoid (something considered evil, as a bad habit). **2** deny what one is sworn to; **forswear oneself** perjure oneself.

for·syth·i·a. (–SITH–) *n.* a shrub of the olive family bearing clusters of yellow, bell-shaped blossoms in early spring; also called "golden bell."

fort *n.* a fortified place; also, a permanent army post; hence, *Informal: The parents went out shopping leaving the children to* **hold the fort** (i.e. take care of things). **—forte** (FORT) *n.* one's strong point: *I'm a plumber, carpentry is not my ~.* **—for·te** (FOR·tay, –tee) *adj. & adv. Music.* loud(ly) and strong(ly).

Forth, Firth of. estuary of the river Forth in S.E. Scotland.

forth *adv.* forward; on(ward); out into view: *Christ went ~ to meet them; From that day ~ they let him alone;* **and so forth** et cetera; **back and forth** to and fro. **—forth·com·ing** *adj.* approaching; coming forward or out: *our ~ movie attractions; No help seemed ~.* **—forth·right** *adj. & adv.* straightforward: *was very ~ in her answers; told us ~ the pay was too low;* **forth·right·ly** *adv.;* **forth·right·ness** *n.* **—forth·with** *adv.* at once.

for·ti·fy *v.* **-fies, -fied, -fy·ing** strengthen (a place *with* a fort, a person *with* courage, nourishment, etc.); hence, enrich: *milk ~d with vitamins and minerals; ~d wines with up to 21% alcohol;* **for·ti·fi·er** (–fye·ur) *n.;* **for·ti·fi·ca·tion** (–CAY–) *n.* **—for·tis·si·mo** (–TIS·uh·moh) *adj. & adv. Music.* very loud(ly). **—for·ti·tude** *n.* strength of mind that enables one to endure pain, misfortune, etc. patiently.

Fort Knox (–NOX) in Kentucky, site of U.S. Army Armor Center and gold depository. **—Fort-La·my** (for·lah·MEE) capital of Chad. **—Fort Lau·der·dale** (–LAW–) city in S.E. Florida.

fort·night *n.* two weeks; **fort·night·ly** *adj. & n.* (a periodical) appearing every two weeks; also ***adv.***

FOR·TRAN (FOR·tran) *n.* a computer programming language using algebraic and English expressions.

for·tress (–tris) *n.* a fortified place.

for·tu·i·tous (–TUE·i·tus) *adj.* esp. of fortunate events, happening by chance; accidental; **for·tu·i·tous·ly** *adv.* **—for·tu·nate** (–chuh·nit) *adj.* of people and circumstances, lucky: *saved from fire by a ~ change of wind;* **for·tu·nate·ly** *adv.* **—for·tune** (–chun) *n.* **1** one's lot or luck, good or bad; hence, success; *my good ~ to be born in this country; a Gypsy who lives by* **for·tune·tell·ing** *n. & adj.;* **for·tune·tel·ler** *n.* **2** wealth; hence, a large amount of money: *That sofa will cost you a ~;* **fortune hunter** one who seeks wealth, esp. by marriage.

Fort Wayne (–WAIN) a city in N.E. Indiana. **—Fort Worth** a city in N. Texas.

for·ty (FOR·tee) *n., adj. & pron.* four times 10; the number 40 or XL: *scored a ~; ~ acres; some ~ of them;* **for·ties** *n.pl.* numbers, years, etc. (ending in) 40 through 49; **for·ti·eth** (–tee·ith) *adj. & n.* **—for·ty-five** *n., adj. & pron.* 45 or XLV; also, a forty-five caliber (.45) pistol, a phonograph record that plays 45 r.p.m., etc. **—for·ty-nin·er** (–NYE·nur) *n.* one who went to California in the 1849 gold rush. **—forty winks** *Informal.* a short nap.

fo·rum (FOR·um) *n.* **-rums** or **-ra** (–ruh) the public square of an ancient Roman city; hence, a place for public discussion; also, a tribunal: *TV as a ~ of public affairs.*

for·ward (–wurd) *adj.* toward the front, not backward; hence, advanced; prompt; eager; also, bold or pushy in manners: *a ~ movement; a ~ young man; ~ buying of grain* (for later delivery); **for·ward·ness** *n.* ***—adv.:*** *ideas brought ~; I* **look forward to** (i.e. anticipate with pleasure) *our meeting;* also **for·wards.** ***—n.*** a front-line player in team games such as hockey and basketball. ***—v.:*** *mail ~ed to a new address; to ~* (i.e. promote) *a plan;* **for·ward·er** *n.* an agent for forwarding goods.

forwent *pt.* of FORGO.

fos·sil *n.* a hardened remnant of an animal or plant dating from a previous geological period, preserved in rock or in coal deposits; hence, an antiquated person: *an old ~ of a professor;* ***adj.:*** *a ~ fern; depletion of the earth's* **fossil fuels** (i.e. coal, oil, and natural gas). **—fos·sil·ize** *v.* **-iz·es, -ized, -iz·ing** change into a fossil; also, become set or rigid in one's ways; **fos·sil·i·za·tion** (–ZAY–) *n.*

fos·ter *v.* **1** help to grow or develop, as a **foster parent,** someone other than a natural parent, does to a **foster child.** **2** encourage or cultivate: *to ~ good habits in youth; hopes ~ed by promises.* —**foster brother** (or **sister**) another child raised by the same foster parent(s), sometimes in a **foster home** for many orphans or neglected children.

fought *pt.* & *pp.* of FIGHT.

foul (FOWL) *adj.* **1** rotten or filthy; hence, disagreeable: *the ~ air around a garbage dump; medicine with a ~ taste; warned of ~* (i.e. stormy) *weather; a ~* (i.e. violent) *crime.* **2** not fair; against rules: *a struggle for power by fair means or ~; a* **foul ball** *that lands outside the* **foul lines** *in* **foul territory. 3** tangled; clogged up; *~ ropes; The fire won't burn because of a ~ chimney.* —***adv.:*** *to play ~; penalties for those who* **run** (or **go, fall**) **foul of** (i.e. get in trouble with) *the law.* —***v.:*** *Auto exhausts ~ the air; Their last-minute change of mind* **fouled up** *our plans; Lives were lost when a tanker ~ed* (i.e. hit) *a ferry.* —***n.*** anything foul, such as an infraction of a rule, a collision or entangling, or a foul ball. —**foul·ly** *adv.;* **foul·ness** *n.*

fou·lard (foo·LARD) *n.* a soft, lightweight silk or other fabric, usu. decorated with a printed pattern, used for ties, scarves, handkerchiefs, etc.

foul ball See FOUL, *adj.* 2. —**foul·ing** *n.* a messy deposit, as in a sewage pipe or in the barrel of a gun after firing. —**foul line** See FOUL, *adj.* 2. —**foul-mouthed** *adj.* abusive: *a ~ fishwife.* —**foul play** unfair play; also, treacherous violence: *The coroner suspected ~.* —**foul territory** See FOUL, *adj.* 2. —**foul-up** *n. Informal.* a mix-up or mess.

found *v.* **1** *pt.* & *pp.* of FIND: *the lost-and-~ column of a newspaper.* **2** to base; hence, establish: *an argument ~ed on facts, not hearsay; America's* **founding fathers** *such as Franklin, Hamilton, Madison, and Washington.* **3** cast (metal), as in a foundry. —***n.*** free board and lodging: *$90 a week and ~.* —**found art** art based on objects that are not fashioned by the artist (as a carving) but on **found objects,** i.e. natural objects or discards such as driftwood, shells, and junk having aesthetic value: *publish an old grocery list as a* **found poem.** —**foun·da·tion** (–DAY–) *n.: a house with a concrete ~; a woman's* **foundation garment** *such as a corset or girdle with bra; a cosmetic ~ for applying makeup; a ~* (i.e. institution) *for research, cultural promotion, or humanitarian work.* —**found·er** *n.* one who founds an institution or casts metals; ***v.*** collapse or fail: *A ship ~s in a storm* (to the bottom of the sea); *A horse ~s from overwork and limps; a business that ~ed during the recession.* —**founding father** See FOUND, *v.* 2. —**found·ling** *n.* an infant found abandoned. —**found object, found poem** See FOUND ART. —**found·ry** *n.* **-ries** a shop where metal is molded into products such as engine blocks, dies, or printing type.

fount *n.* a source; font; same as **foun·tain** (–tn) *n.* a spring of water, esp. an artificial jet or flow supplied by pipes and having a basin-like receptacle: *a ~ of knowledge; in quest of the ~ of youth; a girl he met at the office (drinking) ~; a soda ~ selling sodas, milkshakes, etc.* —**foun·tain·head** *n.* the original source, as of a stream: *God as the ~ of all wisdom.* —**fountain pen** a pen containing a reservoir of ink.

four (FOR) *n., pron.* & *adj.* one more than three; the number 4 or IV. —**four-flush** *v. Informal.* to make a false claim or bluff; **four-flush·er** *n.* —**four·fold** *adj.* & *adv.* with four parts; also, four times or 400%. —**4-H (club)** a usu. government-sponsored youth organization pledged to the improvement of skills ("head, heart, hands, and health") for social service, esp. in rural areas; **4-H·er** *n.* —**Four Hundred** or **the 400** the exclusive social set of a community. —**four-in-hand** *n.* the simplest necktie with a slipknot and two hanging ends overlapping in front. —**four-letter word** any of the most offensive words of the language such as *cock, fuck,* or *shit.* —**four-o'clock** *n.* any of a family of perennials bearing fragrant white, pink, red, or yellow flowers that open late in the afternoon and close in the morning. —**four-post·er** *n.* a bed with four posts to support a canopy. —**four·score** *n.* eighty. —**four·some** *n.* a group of four, as for a game of golf. —**four·square** *adj.* & *adv.* square-shaped; hence, solidly based, unyielding, or forthright. —**four·teen** (FOR·TEEN) *n., adj.* & *pron.* four more than 10; 14 or XIV; **four·teenth** *n.* & *adj.* —**fourth** (FORTH) *n., adj.* & *adv.* **1** next after third: *the ~ gear of a car; placed ~ in the examination.* **2** one of four equal parts. —**fourth-class** *adj.* & *adv.* next below third class, esp. parcel post. —**fourth dimension** See DIMENSION. —**fourth estate** the public press or journalism. —**four-wheel** *adj.* of or affecting four wheels: *a ~ drive.*

fowl *n.* a bird, esp. any of the larger domestic birds such as chicken, duck, goose, or turkey; also, their flesh used as food. —***v.*** hunt or catch wild fowl, as with a **fowl·ing piece** (or **gun**), a lightweight shotgun; **fow·ler** *n.*

fox *n.* a small, wild, flesh-eating, bushy-tailed canine animal, usu. considered crafty and sly; hence, such a person. —***v.*** to trick by craftiness; **foxed** *adj.* discolored or stained. —**fox·glove** (–gluv) *n.* any of a group of plants of the figwort family with bell-shaped flowers growing in long clusters that yield the drug digitalis. —**fox·hole** *n.* a hole dug as a shelter against gunfire for one or two soldiers. —**fox·hound** *n.* a breed of keen-scented hounds used in fox-hunting. —**fox terrier** a smooth-coated or wire-haired kind of small, lively, black-and-white pet dog formerly used to drive out foxes from hiding. —**fox trot** **1** a gait, as of a horse, that seems to combine a trot and a pace. **2** a ballroom dance in 4/4 time combining short rapid steps with slow ones; **fox-trot** *v.* **-trots, -trot·ted, -trot·ting.**

—**fox·y** *adj.* **fox·i·er, -i·est:** *a* ~ (i.e. wily) *old trader; a* ~ (*Slang.* attractive) *woman; the* ~ (i.e. soured or grapey) *flavor of certain wines.*

foy·er (FOY·ur, –ay) *n.* an entrance hall or lobby, esp. one used as a lounge, as in a theater, apartment house, or hotel.

fp. foolscap; freezing point.

FPC Federal Power Commission; fish protein concentrate.

f.p.m. or **FPM** feet per minute.

f.p.s. or **FPS** feet per second.

fr. fragment; franc(s); from. —**Fr** Francium. —**Fr.** Father; France; French; Friday.

fra·cas (FRAY·cus) *n.* a noisy fight or brawl.

frac·tion *n.* **1** a breaking; hence, a broken part of a whole, esp. a fragment or insignificant portion: *a candidate who got only a* ~ *of the vote.* **2** *Math.* a quantity expressed with a numerator and denominator, as 2/5, 2a/b + 3, or 0.4 (a decimal fraction); **frac·tion·al** *adj.: Dimes, nickles, etc. are* ~ *currency, not basic units such as the dollar and franc; A mixture such as petroleum may be separated into its constituents, naphtha, benzene, gasoline, etc. because of their different boiling points, using* ~ *distillation, in* **frac·tion·at·ing** *chambers;* **frac·tion·a·tion** (–AY–) *n.;* **frac·tion·al·ly** *adv.* —**frac·tious** (–shus) *adj.* rebellious; also, irritable or peevish. —**frac·ture** (–chur) *n.* a breaking, esp. a break or crack, as in bones, rocks, or gems; ***v.*** **-tures, -tured, -tur·ing:** *Bones* ~ *in various ways.*

frag *n. Slang.* short form of FRAGMENTATION GRENADE; ***v.*** **frags, fragged, frag·ging** kill or injure with a fragmentation grenade. —**frag·ile** (FRAJ·ul, –ile) *adj.* easily broken; hence, tenuous; short-lived: *a* ~ *toy; a* ~ *truce;* **fra·gil·i·ty** (fruh·JIL–) *n.* —**frag·ment** (–munt) *n.* a broken-off part; also, an incomplete part, as of a conversation, or an unfinished work such as Coleridge's "Kubla Khan"; **frag·men·ta·tion** (–TAY–) *n.;* **fragmentation grenade** one that explodes into jagged pieces of metal; **frag·men·tar·y** (FRAG–) *adj.*

fra·grant (FRAY·grunt) *adj.* pleasant-smelling; **fra·grance** *n.*

frail *adj.* fragile; delicate; weak: *in* ~ *health; her* ~ *beauty.* —**frail·ty** *n.* **-ties** weakness or fault, esp. moral: *human* ~.

frame *n.* **1** a structure, esp. a basic or skeletal system that gives something its shape or form, as of a **frame house** built mostly or partly of wood with walls covered by brick, stucco, boards, etc.; also, the borders of a picture or of a pair of glasses: *a man of slender* ~*; Bright weather puts her in a cheerful* **frame of mind** (i.e. mood); *a graph drawn with a time-temperature* **frame of reference;** *a judgment made without a clear* ~ *of reference* (i.e. standards). **2** something having a frame, as an individual picture on a strip of motion-picture film, one of the series of question-and-answer steps into which a topic is divided in programmed instruction, one of the 10 sequences in which scores are recorded at bowling, etc. —***v.*** **frames, framed, fram·ing 1:** *standing there* ~*d in the doorway; the Constitution as originally* ~*d by the Founding Fathers.* **2** *Slang.* implicate falsely: *She was* ~*d by agents who had planted the drugs in her room;* hence **frame-up** *n.* —**fram·er** *n.* —**frame house, frame of mind, frame of reference** See FRAME, *n.* 1. —**frame·work** *n.* frame: *free elections within the* ~ *of a democratic society.*

franc *n.* the basic money unit of France, Belgium, Switzerland, and about 20 other European and African countries; also, a coin or note worth one franc or 100 centimes. —**France** (FRAN–, FRAH–) a country of W. Europe; 211,208 sq. mi. (547,026 km²); *cap.* Paris. —**fran·chise** (–chize) *n.* the privilege or right granted to a **fran·chis·ee** (–chye·ZEE) by a government to vote, operate a public utility, etc. or by a company or other **fran·chis·er** to market a product or service. —**fran·ci·um** (–see·um) *n.* a radioactive, metallic chemical element. —**Franco-** *comb. form.* France; French: as in **Fran·co-A·mer·i·can** *adj.* of or having to do with France and America; ***n.*** a person of Franco-American descent; **Fran·co·phone** *n.* & *adj.* French-speaking (person).

fran·gi·ble (–juh·bl) *adj.* liable to break; **fran·gi·bil·i·ty** (–BIL–) *n.*

Frank *n.* a member of the group of Germanic tribes that established the **Frank·ish** empire which, after Charlemagne's time, broke up into France, Italy, and Germany. —[1]**frank 1** *adj.* freely expressing what one feels or thinks; **frank·ly** *adv.;* **frank·ness** *n.* **2** *v.* send or mark (mail) for postage-free transmission, as by prepaying or using sender's authorized signature instead of stamps. **3** *n.* the franking privilege of members of Congress and certain U.S. officials or a mark put on mail to indicate this. —[2]**frank** *n. Informal.* frankfurter. —**Frank·en·stein** (–stine) *n.* a monster that endangers its own creator. —**Frank·fort** (–furt) capital of Kentucky. —**Frank·furt** a city of West Germany. —**frank·furt·er** *n.* a smoked sausage of beef or beef and pork. —**frank·in·cense** *n.* a gum resin of certain trees of Africa and Asia, burned as an incense since ancient times.

Frank·lin, Benjamin. 1706–1790, American statesman, philosopher, and scientist.

fran·tic *adj.* wildly excited; frenzied; **fran·ti·cal·ly** *adv.*

frap·pé (–PAY) *n.* a partly frozen drink or a dessert similar to sherbet; ***adj.*** partly frozen or chilled; **frappe** (FRAP) *n.* a thick milkshake; rarely, a frappé.

frat *n. Informal.* a fraternity. —**fra·ter·nal** (fruh·TUR·nl) *adj.* **1** brotherly. **2** of twins, whether of the same or different sexes, developed from different egg cells, not *identical twins.* **3** having to do with a **fraternal soci-**

ety (or **order**) such as Freemasons or Elks, professing mutual help and fellowship. —**fra·ter·nal·ly** *adv.* —**fra·ter·ni·ty** (–TUR–) *n.* **-ties** **1** brotherliness. **2** a group of people of the same profession or interests: *the medical ~; the Greek-letter ~s such as Phi Beta Sigma.* —**frat·er·nize** (FRAT–) *v.* **-niz·es, -nized, -niz·ing** associate in a friendly manner; —**frat·er·ni·za·tion** (–ZAY–) *n.* —**frat·ri·cide** *n.* one who kills his brother or sister; also, such an act; **frat·ri·ci·dal** (–SYE·dl) *adj.*

Frau (FROW) *n., pl.* **Frau·en** the German for "Mrs."; hence, a wife.

fraud *n.* a trick, trickster, or trickery. —**fraud·u·lent** (FRAW·juh·lunt) *adj.* dishonest; deceptive; **fraud·u·lent·ly** *adv.;* **fraud·u·lence** *n.*

fraught (FRAWT) *adj.* loaded or filled: *an undertaking ~ with danger.*

Fräu·lein (FROY·line) *n.* the German for "Miss"; hence, an unmarried, esp. young woman.

fray *n.* a noisy quarrel or dispute; battle; melee. —***v.*** wear through or become worn by rubbing; hence, strain: *a ~ed cuff; ~ed nerves, tempers.*

fra·zil (ice) (FRAY–, FRAZ–) ice formed in fine crystals in turbulent water.

fraz·zle (FRAZ·ul) *v.* **fraz·zles, fraz·zled, fraz·zling** make or become exhausted or frayed; ***n.*** this state: *worn to a ~.*

F.R.B. Federal Reserve Board.

freak (FREEK) *n.* **1** a person or thing that is unusual, odd, or queer: *Saved from ruin by a ~ of fortune; a double-headed ~ of nature;* ***adj.:*** *A ~ snowstorm hit us in July;* **freak·ish** *adj.* **2** *Slang.* a user of an illicit drug; hence, an addict or devotee: *a drug-addict turned into a Jesus ~; an acid ~; a baseball ~;* ***v.*** **freak out** have an extreme mental reaction, as by use of a drug or by some emotional experience; **freak-out** *n. Slang.* the act of freaking out or one who has freaked out; **freak·y** *adj.*

freck·le *n.* a small, brown spot on the skin. —***v.*** **freck·les, freck·led, freck·ling:** *the tendency to ~ under exposure to sunlight;* **freck·led** or **freck·ly** *adj.*

Fred·er·ick the Great king of Prussia, 1740–1786. —**Fred·er·icks·burg** (FRED·ricks–) city of N.E. Virginia. —**Fred·er·ic·ton** (FRED·ric·tun) capital of New Brunswick.

free *adj.* **free·er, free·est** not bound or hampered; having liberty; without restraints or controls: *a prisoner ~ on parole; a people enjoying ~ speech; Please feel ~ to browse around; won two ~* (i.e. gratis) *tickets to the show; fired for being too ~ with company funds; an engaging,* **free and easy** (i.e. relaxed and uninhibited) *manner; led a ~ and easy life in New York; an analyst using* **free association** *to help his patients relax and talk about their past; the* **free enterprise** *system of a capitalist economy with a minimum of government control; the* **free flight** *of a rocket after its fuel is burned up; goods delivered* **free on board** *a customer's train or ship at a specified place.* —***adv.:*** *Children admitted ~* (i.e. gratis); **free·ly** *adv.* —***v.*** **frees, freed, free·ing:** *slaves ~d from bondage; to ~ a room of dust.* —**free association** See FREE, *adj.* —**free·bie** or **free·bee** *n. Informal.* something free of charge, as complimentary tickets. **free·boot·er** *n.* a plunderer. **free·born** *adj.* not born in slavery; **freed·man** *n.* **-men** one freed from slavery. —**free·dom** (–dum) *n.* a state of being free; also, a right or privilege: *a foreign dignitary granted the ~ of the city.* —**free enterprise, free flight** See FREE, *adj.* —**free-for-all** *n.* a contest in which anyone may take part; hence, a brawl. —**free·hand** *adj.* without mechanical aids: *a ~ drawing.* —**free·hold** *n.* & *adj.* (an estate) held with some degree of ownership, not as a LEASEHOLD; **free·hold·er** *n.* —**free lance** one whose services are not committed to any one employer; also **free-lanc·er.** —***adj.:*** *a* **free-lance** *editor;* ***v.*** **-lanc·es, -lanced, -lanc·ing:** *Since resigning she has been ~ing as a consultant.* —**free·load** *v. Informal.* get things or make a living at another's expense; sponge; **free·load·er** *n.* —**free love** sexual love without marriage or other social restrictions. —**free·man** (–mun) *n.* **-men** one who is not a slave or serf; citizen. —**Free·ma·son** (FREE·may·sun) *n.* a member of the fraternal society called "Ancient Free and Accepted Masons," originally of the building trades, but now open to all professing belief in one God; **Free·ma·son·ry** *n.* —**free port** a port without customs or duties within its limits. —**free-stand·ing** *adj.* without external supports: *the world's tallest ~ structure.* —**free·stone** *n.* a peach, cherry, or other such fruit whose pit does not cling to its flesh. —**free·style** *n.* a competition such as swimming or figure skating in which no style is specified. —**free·think·er** *n.* a rationalist who shuns established religious beliefs based on the authority of a church or bible; **free·think·ing** *adj.*

Free·town capital of Sierra Leone.

free university a student-run university devoted to subjects of their choice and without grades, credits, and such restrictions. —**free verse** a form of verse without the structure imposed by a meter or rhythm. —**free·way** *n.* a main highway allowing free flow of traffic because of fully controlled accesses and grade-separated interchanges. —**free·wheel** (–HWEEL, –WEEL) *n.* a device that allows a bicycle or automobile to coast freely; **free·wheel·ing** *adj.* unrestrained or uninhibited. —**free will** the power of free choice, esp. in regard to one's salvation; cf. DETERMINISM; **free-will** *adj.: a ~ offering.* —**free world** countries not under totalitarian, esp. Communist rule.

freeze *v.* **freez·es, froze, fro·zen, freez·ing** harden or solidify with cold, making affected objects fixed or stuck fast, often injuring or killing life: *It is ~ing weather below 32°F or 0°C, the* **freezing point** *of water; so cold even the pipes are frozen; The car skidded off the frozen bridge; As the ghost appeared, the audience sat frozen to their chairs; The sight of the corpse made us ~ in our tracks; A dentist ~s the jaw* (with anesthetic) *before pulling a tooth; The lake* **froze over** *during the windy night.* **—n.:** *The last ships to leave the harbor were caught in the ~; a ~ on prices and wages to halt inflation.* **—freez·a·ble** *adj.* **—freeze-dry** *v.* **-dries, -dried, -dry·ing** dehydrate (food, medicines, etc. for preservation) by freezing and evaporating the moisture content in a vacuum: *~d coffee.* **—freez·er** *n.* one that freezes, esp. a chest or room in which perishable foods may be kept.

freight (FRATE) *n.* **1** goods carried by water, land, or air transportation. **2** the payment for such transportation; also **freight·age** (–ij). **3** a **freight train** made up of **freight cars.** **—v.** to send by or load with freight. **—freight·er** *n.* a ship or plane carrying freight; also, a person who handles freight.

Fre·mont (FREE–) a city of W. California.

French *n.* the language of France; **the French** the people of France. **—adj.** of France or its language, people, culture, etc.; **French·man** (–mun) *n.* **-men;** *fem.* **French·wom·an, -wom·en.** **—French door** a door that opens in the middle and has glass panes from top to bottom. **—French dressing** a salad dressing of oil, vinegar, and seasonings. **—French fries** deep-fried strips of potato; **French-fry** *v.* **-fries, -fried, -fry·ing** fry (potatoes, shrimps, onion rings, etc.) in deep fat; also, **french-fry.** **—French Gui·an·a** (–gee·AN·uh) a French overseas department (province) in N.E. South America; *cap.* Cayenne. **—French horn** a brass wind instrument with a coiled tube that flares out as a wide bell. **—French leave** a departure made secretly or in a hurry. **—French toast** a slice of bread dipped in an egg-and-milk mixture and sautéed.

fre·net·ic (fri·NET–) *adj.* frantic or frenzied; **fre·net·i·cal·ly** *adv.* **—fren·zy** (–zee) *n.* **-zies** emotional agitation tending to violent activity: *in a ~ of despair;* **fren·zied** (–zeed) *adj.: shaking his fists in ~ rage.*

Fre·on (FREE–) *Trademark.* any of various commercially produced fluorocarbon fluids, used esp. as refrigerants and in aerosol spray cans.

freq. frequency; frequent(ly). **—fre·quen·cy** (FREE–) *n.* **-cies** the number of times that cycles, oscillations, vibrations, or other repeated events occur in a given period; also, occurrences in a given sample: *"The" has the highest ~ among English words;* **frequency modulation** radio transmission by varying the frequency of waves, instead of amplitude, to correspond to fluctuations in the audio or video signals; FM. **—fre·quent** (FREE–) *adj.* occurring often; constant: *a ~ visitor to the zoo;* **v.** (-KWENT) go habitually to: *an alcoholic ~ing bars and taverns;* **fre·quent·er** *n.* **—fre·quent·ly** *adv.*

fres·co (–coh) *n.* **-co(e)s** water-color painting on fresh plaster, as done on church ceilings; **v. -co(e)s, -coed, -co·ing:** *"The Creation of Adam" was ~d by Michelangelo.*

fresh *adj.* **1** new or pure, not stale, used, preserved, etc.: *She's ~ as a daisy; the ~ morning air; not salted, canned, or frozen but ~ meat; a ~start in life after failures; a tragedy still ~ in our memories; a* **fresh breeze** *blowing 19–24 m.p.h.* (29–38 km/h). **2** inexperienced. **3** *Informal.* bold or impudent. **—fresh·ly** *adv.;* **fresh·ness** *n.* **—fresh·en** *v.: a cream to ~ your complexion; Use the powder room to* **freshen up** *before dinner.* **—fresh·et** (–it) *n.* a rush of fresh water, as from a thaw or heavy rain. **—fresh·man** (–mun) *n.* **-men** a beginner, esp. a first-year student; **adj.:** *a ~ senator* (in his first year); *~ English.* **—fresh·wa·ter** *adj.* **1** of or living in lakes and streams, not in salty water: *a ~ fish.* **2** inexperienced: *a ~ sailor.* **3** out-of-the-way; obscure: *a ~ college.*

Fres·no (FREZ–) a city of C. California.

fret *v.* **frets, fret·ted, fret·ting** **1** to worry or be vexed: *tends to ~ and fume over trifles; a child ~ing against parental control.* **2** eat away; corrode: *river banks ~d by the force of water.* **—n.** **1** irritation; **fret·ful** *adj.;* **fret·ful·ly** *adv.;* **fret·ful·ness** *n.* **2** erosion. **3** one of the ridges across the fingerboard of a guitar, banjo, etc. as guides for fingering. **4** a right-angled ornamental design or pattern, seen carved or in relief as **fret·work; fret·saw** *n.* a saw with a long and narrow blade for cutting curved outlines.

Freud (FROID), **Sigmund.** 1856–1939, Austrian physician who founded psychoanalysis; **Freud·i·an** (–ee·un) *n.* & *adj.*

Fri. Friday.

fri·a·ble (FRY·uh·bl) *adj.* crumbly, as sandstone or dry soil.

fri·ar (FRY·ur) *n.* a member of one of the traditionally noncloistered mendicant orders of Roman Catholic religious, i.e. Augustinians, Carmelites ("white friars"), Dominicans ("black friars"), and Franciscans ("gray friars"); **fri·ar·y** *n.* **-ar·ies** a monastery of friars.

fric·as·see (FRIC·uh–, –uh·SEE) *n.* a dish of meat, esp. chicken, cut into pieces, stewed, and served with a thick gravy; **v. -as·sees, -as·seed, -as·see·ing:** *~d veal.*

fric·tion (–shun) *n.* resistance from rubbing of one thing against another: *Oil and grease reduce ~; office ~s due to personality differences;* **fric·tion·al** *adj.*

Fri·day (FRY·day, –dee) *n.* **1** the sixth day of the week. **2** a faithful helper: *my man ~; a girl ~; wanted, a clerk ~.*

fridge short form of REFRIGERATOR.

fried *pt.* & *pp.* of FRY. **—fried·cake** *n.* a doughnut or cruller.

friend (FREND) *n.* one who is not an enemy; also, a supporter, esp. a liked person: *~ or foe? a ~ of the poor; my girl ~; "man's best friend"* (i.e. dog); **be** (or **make**) **friends with** be (or become) a friend of; **Friend** a member of the Society of Friends; Quaker. —**friend·less** *adj.* —**friend·ly** *adj.* **-li·er, -li·est** of or like a friend; favorable; rarely ***adv.:*** *"Drive friendly"*; **friend·li·ness** *n.* —**friend·ship** *n.*

frier same as FRYER.

frieze (FREEZ) *n.* a decorative horizontal band, as the one containing carved figures on a classical building above the columns or one of wallpaper or similar design around the walls of a room below the ceiling.

frig·ate (–it) *n.* formerly, a medium-sized sailing warship, as "Old Ironsides"; now, a warship of 2,000 tons (2,032 metric tons) or more, often larger than a destroyer.

fright (FRITE) *n.* fear, esp. when sudden and passing: *Your Halloween costume gave me quite a ~; Her hat was a real ~* (*Informal.* fearsome thing). —**fright·en** *v.* cause to feel sudden fear or become afraid: *a child ~ed into obeying; Her screams ~ed off her attacker;* **fright·en·ing** *adj.: the ~ experience of being kidnapped;* **fright·en·ing·ly** *adv.: the ~ high numbers of rape victims.* —**fright·ful** *adj.* **1:** *a ~* (i.e. terrible) *tragedy.* **2** [as intensifier, *Informal*] *:What a ~ snob! She left in a ~ haste.* —**fright·ful·ly** *adv.* alarmingly; also, *Informal.* very: *I'm ~ sorry;* **fright·ful·ness** *n.*

frig·id (FRIJ–) *adj.* **1** extremely cold, as in the **Frigid Zone,** either of the two regions within the Arctic and Antarctic circles. **2** cold or aloof in manner; also, esp. of a woman, without normal sexual desire. —**frig·id·ly** *adv.;* **fri·gid·i·ty** (–JID–) *n.*

frill *n.* a ruffle or similar edging or trimming; hence, something serving as an ornament: *trading stamps, games, and other ~s to attract shoppers;* **frill·y** *adj.*

fringe (FRINJ) *n.* a border ornament or trimming of loose threads or cords, as on a shawl or rug, often tied in bunches; hence, something peripheral or minor: *a clipped ~ of hair over the forehead; the cant and jargon spoken on the ~s of society;* ***v.*** **fring·es, fringed, fring·ing:** *trees ~ing a lawn; the ~d petals of the gentians; a ~ing coral reef growing outward from the shoreline;* ***adj.:*** *the poor TV reception experienced in* **fringe** (i.e. outer) **areas;** *pension, health insurance, and such* **fringe benefits** *for employees; the drooping, white flowers of the* **fringe tree,** *also called "old man's beard."*

frip·per·y *n.* **frip·per·ies** cheap finery; hence, affected elegance: *the ~s of speech and behavior.*

Fris·bee *Trademark.* a saucer-shaped plastic disk for tossing back and forth in games; also **fris·bee** *n.*

Fri·sian (FRIZH·un, FREE–) *n.* & *adj.* (of or having to do with) the Germanic language or people of the Friesland province of the Netherlands and of the **Frisian Islands** along the N. European coast from the Netherlands to Denmark.

frisk *v.* **1** move in a lively, playful manner: *lambs ~ing about in the sun.* **2** search (a person) for concealed weapons or goods, as police do after an arrest. —**frisk·y** *adj.* **frisk·i·er, -i·est** frolicsome: *a ~ little pup;* **frisk·i·ly** *adv.;* **frisk·i·ness** *n.*

frit·ter *n.* a small cake of fried batter containing corn, sliced fruit, fish, or other filling; ***v.*** waste little by little: *to ~ away one's time and energies in worthless pursuits.*

friv·o·lous (–uh·lus) *adj.* trivial; also, light-minded; giddy: *a ~ remark; ~ behavior;* **friv·o·lous·ly** *adv.* —**fri·vol·i·ty** (–VOL–) *n.* **-ties:** *the ~s of a flighty woman.*

friz(z) *v.* form (hair) into tight little curls; ***n.*** such hair. —**friz·zle** *v.* **friz·zles, friz·zled, friz·zling** to frizz or curl; also, to sizzle, fry, or broil. —**friz·zly** or **friz·zy** *adj.* curly.

fro (FROH) *adv.* **to and fro** to (somewhere) and back; back and forth.

frock *n.* **1** formerly, an outer garment or robe worn by friars and monks; also, a man's double-breasted **frock-coat** in the 19th c. **2** a woman's or child's dress.

frog *n.* **1** a small, tailless, amphibious jumping animal with long hind legs and webbed feet. **2** a corded loop with a button passing through it used as an ornamental fastener. **3** hoarseness; also **frog in the throat.** —**frog·man** *n.* **-men** a diver equipped with air supply, face mask, and flippers for long periods of exploration or demolition work under water.

frol·ic *n.* play or fun, esp. of a light-hearted, carefree nature; ***v.*** **-ics, -icked, -ick·ing** make merry; gambol about; **frol·ick·er** *n.* —**frol·ic·some** (–sum) *adj.*

from (FRUM, FROM) *prep.* **1** [indicating a starting point or source]: *It's 10 miles ~ home to school; I know him ~ way back in the old country; knows about rockets* **from the ground up;** *looks great ~ my point of view; cars priced ~ $4,000 up; Tell her ~ me to get lost; lifelike because painted ~ life.* **2** [indicating a cause or motive]: *shivering ~ cold; sounds fine ~ what I was told; speaking ~ envy.* **3** [indicating a difference or distinction]: *Men are different ~ animals; Can you tell a frog ~ a toad?*

frond *n.* a large leaf, as of ferns or palms; also, a leaflike shoot, as of lichens and seaweeds.

front (FRUNT) *n.* **1** the forward or most important part or side: *The driver is seated in ~; a shirt ~ covered by a tie; Top marks place you in ~; parked* **in front of** *a house; a cold ~* (i.e. of air) *moving in from the Arctic.* **2** a scene of activity: *No news from the western ~* (of battle); *trouble brewing on the labor ~.* **3** a face or cover: *His geniality is a mere ~; put on a bold ~; a club used as a ~ for loansharking.* —***adj.:*** *a ~ seat; news that made the ~ page; fighting in the*

~ *lines.* —**v.:** *The cottage ~s on a lake; windows ~ing the street.* —**front·age** (–ij) *n.* (extent of) land between a building and a street, river, or lake that it faces; also, a building's exposure: *a 60-foot ~; a church with a southern ~; an expressway with a parallel* **frontage road** (i.e. service road) *for access to properties along it.* —**front·al** *adj.: a direct, ~ attack; the ~ lobe of the brain; from toplessness to ~ nudity.* —**fron·tier** (frun·TEER) *n.* **1** the border between two countries: *a shooting incident on the Sino-Russian ~.* **2** a region whose borders are being extended into newly explored territory: *the ~s opened up by space exploration;* **adj.:** *a ~ town; in the ~ days when the pioneers were moving West;* **fron·tiers·man** *n.* **-men** a man living on the frontier. —**fron·tis·piece** *n.* an illustrated page facing a book's title page. —**front money** advance payment. —**front office** headquarters; hence, administrative authority. —**front-run·ner** *n.* the leading contender.

frosh *n. sing.* & *pl. Informal.* freshman.

Frost, Robert L. 1874–1963, American poet. —**frost** *n.* a freezing, the state of being frozen, or frozen dew, vapor, or hoarfrost; **v.** cover with or like frost; **frost·ed** *adj.: a ~ car window; ~ glass for window panes, electric bulbs, etc.; crunchy ~ flakes* (covered with sugar); *a ~ cake* (covered with frosting). —**frost·bite** *n.* injury to skin and body tissue from exposure to cold; **v. -bites, -bit, -bit·ten, -bit·ing:** *a ~n foot.* —**frost heave** a heaving of the ground caused by moisture freezing underneath. —**frost·ing** *n.* icing. —**frost·y** *adj.* **frost·i·er, -i·est** freezing or covered with frost; also, cold or unfriendly: *a ~ welcome.*

froth *n.* foam, esp. as spume or scum; hence, something worthless: *a discussion that was all ~ and no substance.* —**v.:** *an overworked horse ~ing at the mouth; the ~ing waves whipped by a wind.* —**froth·y** *adj.* **froth·i·er, -i·est:** *a ~ discussion.*

frou·frou (FROO·froo) *n.* rustling, as of a woman's skirts; also, frilly trimming or ruffles that rustle or swish.

fro·ward (FROH·urd) *adj.* of people, difficult to manage; willful; **fro·ward·ness** *n.*

frown *v.* wrinkle the forehead, as in disapproval; hence, show displeasure: *Our teacher ~s (up)on latecomers;* **n.** such an expression or face.

frow·zy *adj.* **-zi·er, -zi·est** untidy or unkempt; also **frow·sy.**

froze See FREEZE. —**fro·zen** (FROH·zun) *adj.* **1** hardened by cold, as for preservation: *~ food.* **2** made motionless, stiff, or fixed: *~ with fear; rents ~ for two years; foreign assets ~* (i.e. no more liquid) *while the war was on.*

FRS Federal Reserve System.

frt. freight.

fruc·ti·fy (–tuh·fye) *v.* **-fies, -fied, -fy·ing** bear fruit; make productive: *plans that didn't ~.* —**fruc·tose** *n.* fruit sugar, found combined with glucose (as sucrose) in sweet fruits and honey. —**fru·gal** (FROO·gl) *adj.* sparing, not wasteful; simple in regard to food, clothing, etc.: *a ~ meal; a ~ people;* **fru·gal·ly** *adv.;* **fru·gal·i·ty** (–GAL–) *n.* —**fruit** (FROOT) *n.* **1** the edible, often sweet, fleshy, and juicy part of a plant or tree, as apples, bananas, or grapes; also, any seed-bearing or useful plant product, as pea pods, cereal grains, green peppers, and such vegetables: *thanksgiving for the ~s of the earth.* **2** product or result; outcome: *the ~ of our labors; work that did not* **bear fruit;** also **v.** be productive; **fruit·ful** *adj.;* **fruit·ful·ly** *adv.;* **fruit·ful·ness** *n.;* **fruit·less** *adj.;* **fruit·less·ly** *adv.;* **fruit·less·ness** *n.* —**fruit·cake** *n.* a rich cake containing raisins, nuts, spices, etc. —**fruit fly** any of several kinds of flies whose larvae eat their way through fruits. —**fru·i·tion** (–ISH·un) *n.* fulfillment; realization: *the ~ of our hopes.* —**fruit·y** *adj.* **fruit·i·er, -i·est** rich or mellow in flavor, tone of voice, interest, etc.

frump *n.* a woman who is **frump·ish** *adj.* shabby; dowdy; also **frump·y, frump·i·er, -i·est.**

frus·trate *v.* **-trates, -trat·ed, -trat·ing** prevent (as an opponent) from accomplishing something or getting something done; make (someone) ineffective: *felt ~d in her attempts to educate her child;* **frus·tra·tion** (–TRAY–) *n.: a life of loneliness and ~; took to drinking to forget his ~s.*

frus·tum *n.* **-tums** or **-ta** the base section of a pyramid or cone left after the top is cut off in a plane parallel to the base.

frwy. freeway.

fry *v.* **fries, fried, fry·ing** cook in a pan or on a griddle, esp. using fat; hence **fry(ing) pan:** *"Out of the ~ into the fire"* (i.e. from something bad to something worse). —**n.** **1** *pl.* **fries,** something fried, as FRENCH FRIES; also, an outdoor social gathering at which fried food is served. **2** *pl.* **fry** young fish: *small ~.* —**fry·er** *n.* a utensil for deep-frying; also, a chicken suitable for frying, usu. larger than a BROILER.

FSH follicle-stimulating hormone.

FSLIC Federal Savings and Loan Insurance Corporation.

ft. feet; foot; fort.

FTC Federal Trade Commission.

fuch·sia (FEW·shuh) *n.* any of numerous plants bearing funnel-shaped red, white, or pink flowers that droop from long stalks; also, the purplish red of its flowers.

fuck *v. Vulgar slang.* copulate; **n.** an act of copulation.

fud·dle *v.* **fud·dles, fud·dled, fud·dling** confuse or stupefy, as with drink; **n.** a fuddled condition.

fud·dy-dud·dy *n.* **-dud·dies** *Informal.* a fussy or obscure, usu. elderly person.

fudge (FUJ) *n.* **1** a rich, soft, often chocolate-flavored candy. **2** nonsense. —**v. fudg·es,**

fudged, fudg·ing fake; falsify; hedge or cheat: *likes to ~ on his income tax.*

fu·el (FEW·ul) *n.* a substance such as coal, gasoline, ethane, or chemicals, which when burned produces heat or power: *Uranium and hydrogen are atomic ~s liberating energy by fusion or fission.* **—*v.* -els, -el(l)ed, -el·(l)ing** supply with or get fuel: *a plane ~ing up before a flight.* **—fuel cell** a device, as used in spacecraft, for producing electricity from the chemical energy of the reaction of a fuel such as hydrogen with an oxidizer.

fu·gi·tive (FEW·ji·tiv) *n.* one who flees; also, something fleeting or transitory. **—*adj.:*** *the ~ slaves; trying to finish a job during the ~ hours of daylight.* **—fugue** (FYOOG) *n.* **1** a musical composition in the manner of a flight or chase interweaving several melodic strands or voices introduced in succession. **2** an amnesia patient's wandering away to a new place or life forgetting his real identity.

füh·rer or **fueh·rer** (FYOOR·ur) *n.* a fascist leader; the title of Adolf Hitler.

-ful *suffix.* **1** *n.* [*pl.* sometimes as *cupsful*] amount for filling: as in *cupful, spoonful, handful.* **2** *adj.* full of (a quality): as in *sorrowful, soulful, tuneful.*

ful·crum (FULL–, FUL–) *n.* **-crums** or **-cra** the point of leverage or support, as of a crowbar; hence, the means of exerting pressure or influence.

ful·fil(l) (full·FIL) *v.* **-fil(l)s, -filled, -fill·ing** perform, carry out, realize, complete, etc. something that is expected or required, as a promise, prophecy, duty, order, etc.: *Customer orders to be ~d; in search of a ~ing* (i.e. satisfying) *job; She* **fulfilled herself** *as an actress after trying nursing and teaching;* **ful·fil(l)·ment** *n.* **—full** *adj.* complete in number, amount, extent, etc.; having everything needed to fill or satisfy: *The glass is ~ to the brim; It is* **full of** *water; "~ speed ahead!" shouted the captain; I'll cooperate to the ~est extent; a ~ skirt generous with material; a garden in ~ bloom; a popular movie playing to ~ houses; an associate professor promoted to ~ professor.* **—*adv.:*** *The ball hit her ~* (i.e. squarely) *in the face; knows ~* (i.e. quite) *well he is wrong.* **—*n.:*** *was paid* **in full** (i.e. completely) *on termination; "apt" in ~ is "apartment"; exploits his employees* **to the full** (i.e. as much as possible). **—*v.* 1** make full: *a dress ~ed with wide folds.* **2** shrink and thicken (wool and other cloths), as a **ful·ler** does, formerly with **fuller's earth,** a bleaching clay used also in the refining of oils. **—ful(l)·ness** *n.* **—ful·ly** *adv.* **—full·back** *n.* in football, an offensive back playing from a position directly behind the quarterback; also, a defensive player in soccer and such games. **—full-blood·ed** *adj.* purebred; hence, vigorous; also, genuine or authentic. **—full-blown** *adj.* of flowers, fully grown; mature. **—full-bod·ied** *adj.* having much flavor or strength, as wines. **—full-dress** *adj.* observing all formalities: *a ~ rehearsal; a ~ debut.* **—fuller's earth** See FULL, *v.* 2. **—full-fledged** *adj.* fully developed; of full rank. **—full-length** *adj.: standing before a ~ mirror; a ~ movie.* **—full moon** the moon in its fully illuminated phase. **—full-scale** *adj.* not reduced in size; complete: *a ~ investigation.* **—full-time** *adj.* & *adv.* not part-time; **full time:** *"Full time" normally should not exceed 8 hours a day or 48 hours a week.*

ful·mar (FULL·mur) *n.* a sea bird of northern regions; a petrel.

ful·mi·nate (FUL·muh–) *v.* **-nates, -nat·ed, -nat·ing** thunder forth (threats, denunciations, etc.); also, protest vehemently: *the media ~ing against police brutality;* **ful·mi·na·tion** (–NAY–) *n.*

ful·some (FULL·sum) *adj.* of praise, flattery, etc., excessive or insincere; **ful·some·ly** *adv.;* **ful·some·ness** *n.*

fu·ma·role (FEW·muh–) *n.* a volcanic vent or hole in the ground emitting steam, carbon dioxide, etc., as in Yellowstone National Park; **fu·ma·rol·ic** (–ROL–) *adj.*

fum·ble *v.* **-bles, -bled, -bling** fail to catch (a ball); also, grope clumsily; hence, bungle: *a ~d job;* **fum·bler** *n.*

fume *n.* a choking or offensive gas, smoke, or vapor, as from an exhaust. **—*v.* fumes, fumed, fum·ing:** *Oak ~d* (i.e. treated) *with ammonia gas for a darker color; The boss is ~ing* (i.e. angry) *about slow mail delivery.* **—fu·mi·gate** (FEW–) *v.* **-gates, -gat·ed, -gat·ing** treat (a room, tree, etc.) with fumes to disinfect or kill pests; **fu·mi·ga·tor** *n. Hydrogen cyanide and ethylene oxide are* **fu·mi·gants. —fu·mi·ga·tion** (–GAY–) *n.* **—fum·y** (FEW·mee) *adj.* **fum·i·er, -i·est** full of fumes; vaporous.

fun *n.* amusement or what provides amusement; sport: *Life is not all* **fun and games;** *throwing snowballs* **for fun** (or **in fun**); *likes to* **poke fun at** (or **make fun of**) *her cooking; Snowmobiling is ~.* **—*adj.:*** *had a ~ time at the party.*

func·tion (FUNK·shun) *n.* **1** what a person or thing is supposed to do or perform; hence, office or duty: *The heart's ~ is to pump blood; the ~s of a bank.* **2** a formal occasion such as a wedding or an opening ceremony. **3** *Math.* a variable quantity or something that is related to another: *A circle's radius is a ~ of its area.* **—*v.*** perform; operate: *a transmission that is not ~ing well; someone to ~ as chairman of the meeting.* **—func·tion·al** *adj.* having to do with operation rather than structure or decoration: *~ architecture; In a* **functional disorder** *there are no organic causes for the mind's not working properly; A* **functional illiterate** *is unable to perform minimally as a literate in spite of some schooling;* **func·tion·al·ly** *adv.* **—func·tion·ar·y** (–er·ee) *n.* **-ar·ies** an official with routine duties. **—function word** a preposition, auxiliary verb, or conjunction that has little meaning of its own but has a grammatical function, as to connect subject and predicate in "She *is* good."

fund *n.* a stock or supply, esp. of money: *a man with a ~ of ancedotes; Give to the heart ~; a check not honored because of insufficient ~s in the account; Welfare payments come out of public ~s.* —**v.:** *a federally ~ed program; A short-term debt is ~ed* (i.e. converted) *into a long-term one at a fixed interest rate.* —**fun·da·men·tal** (–MEN–) *adj.* essential or basic: *a citizen's ~ rights as in the first 8 amendments to the U.S. Constitution;* **n.** a fundamental principle or fact: *the ~s of algebra;* **fun·da·men·tal·ly** *adv.* —**fun·da·men·tal·ism** *n.* belief in or following of a literal interpretation of the Bible; **fun·da·men·tal·ist** *n.* & *adj.*

fu·ner·al (FEW·nuh·rul) *n.* a ceremony honoring a dead person before cremation or burial; **funeral home** (or **parlor**) an establishment where dead bodies are embalmed and prepared for the funeral, managed by a **funeral director** i.e. undertaker or mortician. —**fu·ner·ar·y** *adj.: a ~ urn;* **fu·ne·re·al** (few·NEER·ee·ul) *adj.* gloomy or dismal: *a ~ expression;* **fu·ne·re·al·ly** *adv.*

fun·gi·cide (FUN·juh–) *n.* a fungus-destroying chemical. —**fun·gus** (FUNG–) *n., pl.* **-gi** (–jye) or **-gus·es** any of the lowest members of the plant kingdom, having no stems, leaves, flowers, or chlorophyll, including mushrooms, molds, and mildews; **fun·gal** or **fun·gous** (–gus) *adj.*

fu·nic·u·lar (few·NIC·yuh·lur) *n.* & *adj.* (a mountain railway) worked by a rope or cable, as in the Alps.

funk *n. Informal.* **1** panic; lack of courage; also, a state of depression: *blue ~.* **2** an art form using strange or bizarre objects; also, funky music. —**funk·y** *adj.* **funk·i·er, -i·est** *Slang.* smelly or earthy; hence, down-to-earth; having the qualities of jazz and similar music, fashionable clothes, etc.; excellent: *in ~ platform shoes.* —**funk·i·ness** *n.*

fun·nel (FUNL) *n.* **1** a wide-mouthed, tapering utensil for pouring liquids, grain, etc. into a narrow-mouthed container; hence, anything of similar shape: *the ~ of a tornado.* **2** a smokestack or flue. —**v. fun·nels, fun·nel(l)ed, fun·nel·(l)ing:** *the ~ing of aid to poor countries; state secrets ~d out through the embassies.*

fun·nies *n.pl.* comic strips or a section of a newspaper containing these. —**fun·ny** *adj.* **fun·ni·er, fun·ni·est** **1** amusing. **2** *Informal.* tricky or queer: *a ~ feeling.* —**fun·ni·ly** *adv.;* **fun·ni·ness** *n.* —**funny bone** a sensitive spot at the back of the elbow that produces a painful tingling sensation when struck; hence, one's sense of humor.

fur *n.* **1** the soft, thick hair of mink, ermine, sable, fox, etc.; also, this processed and made into a garment. **2** a furlike coating, as on a sick person's tongue or lime deposit on a surface. —**v. furs, furred, fur·ring** cover or become covered with fur: *a ~d kettle.*

fur. furlong.

fur·be·low (FUR·buh·loh) *n.* a flounce or ruffle; hence, something showy or superfluous: *frills and ~s.*

fur·bish *v.* burnish; also, renovate.

Fu·ries (FYOOR·eez) *n.pl.* three snake-haired female avengers of Greek and Roman myths. —**fu·ri·ous** (FYOOR·ee·us) *adj.* filled or done with fury; wild or violent: *a ~ storm, attack; working at a ~ pace;* **fu·ri·ous·ly** *adv.*

furl *v.* roll up (a flag, umbrella, sail, etc.).

fur·long *n.* a unit of distance equal to 1/8 mile (0.2 km).

fur·lough (–loh) *n.* leave of absence from duty, esp. in the military. —**v.** give furlough to.

fur·nace (–nis) *n.* a chamber in which fuel is burned to heat buildings, melt metals, etc.

fur·nish *v.* supply, provide, or equip with what is useful or needed: *a library well ~ed with books; a loan to ~ an apartment* (i.e. with furniture); *music ~ed by a band; Can you ~ one good reason why you're late?* —**fur·nish·ings** *n.pl.* furniture, carpets, cushions, etc. and dress accessories, esp. men's. —**fur·ni·ture** *n.* the usu. movable equipment such as chairs, tables, and beds for living or working, as for a home, office, or ship.

fu·ror (FYOOR·or) *n.* a noisy outburst of approval, fury, etc. from a crowd; uproar; also **fu·rore** *Brit.*

fur·ri·er (FUR·ee·ur) *n.* one who processes or deals in furs; **fur·ri·er·y** *n.* **-er·ies** the furrier's business or craft. —**fur·ring** *n.* (the applying of) thin strips of wood or metal to level a floor or wall before covering it with boards or plaster.

fur·row (FUR·oh) *n.* a track cut in the ground by a plough; also, anything similar, as a rut made by a wheel or a deep wrinkle on one's brow. —**v.:** *a face ~ed with age.*

fur·ry *adj.* **fur·ri·er, fur·ri·est** of, covered with, or soft like fur; **fur·ri·ness** *n.*

fur·ther *adj.* & *adv.* a *comp.* of FAR; farther; more distant; also, additional(ly): *Go no ~; No ~ action is necessary; until ~ notice; refused to discuss it any ~.* —**v.** bring closer; promote; advance: *to ~ the aims of justice;* **fur·ther·ance** (–unce) *n.* —**fur·ther·more** *adv.* moreover. —**fur·ther·most** *adj.* furthest. —**fur·thest** *adj.* & *adv. superl.* of FAR. farthest.

fur·tive (–tiv) *adj.* stealthy or sneaky: *took a few ~ steps and stole a glance into the room;* **fur·tive·ly** *adv.;* **fur·tive·ness** *n.*

fu·ry (FYOOR·ee) *n.* **-ries** rage or frenzy tending to violence: *the ~ of the elements* (i.e. stormy weather); *the proverbial ~ of a scorned woman; He flew into a ~ when told he'd been swindled;* **Fury** any of the FURIES or one like them.

furze (FURZ) *n.* a spiny, evergreen shrub of the pea family with fragrant yellow flowers; gorse.

fuse (FEWZ) *n.* **1** a slow-burning wick ("safety fuse") as in blasting or a mechanical or electrical device, usu. **fuze,** for setting off an explosive charge, as in guns and shells. **2** a cartridge or plug containing a wire or metal strip that melts and breaks an electrical circuit as a safety device; **blow a fuse** *Informal.* lose one's temper. **—v. fus·es, fused, fus·ing** **1** melt, esp. unite or blend by melting together: *furnaces to ~ zinc and copper into brass; a party ~d out of many factions.* **2** furnish with a fuse; also **fuze.** **—fu·see** (few·ZEE) *n.* **1** a large-headed friction match. **2** a signal flare used on railroads and highways.

fu·se·lage (FEW·suh·lahzh) *n.* the body of an airplane housing the controls, crew, passengers, and cargo.

fu·si·ble (FEW·zuh–) *adj.* that can be fused: *Alloys are more ~ than pure metals;* **fu·si·bil·i·ty** (–BIL–) *n.* **—fu·si·form** *adj.* spindle-shaped.

fu·sil·ier or **fu·sil·eer** (–EER) *n.* a soldier armed with a **fu·sil,** a flintlock musket. **—fu·sil·lade** (FEW·suh·lade, –lahd) *n.* rapid gunfire: *a ~ of questions from the press.*

fu·sion (FEW·zhun) *n.* a fusing, fused mass, or a union: *the anti-labor ~ party of Australia; the ~ of deuterium and tritium atoms in the hydrogen bomb.*

fuss *n.* unnecessary bother, esp. about trivial things: *He kicked up a ~* (i.e. row) *because I spilled some soup; What a ~ she makes of her picture in the paper!* **—v.:** *She ~ed about all morning but achieved little; He ~es a lot over his wife and kids.* **—fuss·budg·et** (–buj·it) or **fuss·pot** *n. Informal.* one who fusses over trifles. **—fuss·y** *adj.* **fuss·i·er, -i·est:** *very ~* (i.e. particular) *about his steaks; a dress too ~* (i.e. fancy) *to be worn to school; a ~ baby; a job too ~* (i.e. full of details requiring much attention) *to finish in one day;* **fuss·i·ly** *adv.;* **fuss·i·ness** *n.*

fus·tian (–chun) *n.* a coarse twilled cloth with a velvety pile; hence, inflated talk or writing; bombast; claptrap.

fus·ty *adj.* **-ti·er, -ti·est** stale-smelling or musty; hence, old-fashioned; out-of-date; **fus·ti·ly** *adv.;* **fus·ti·ness** *n.*

fut. future (tense).

fu·tile (FEW·tl, –tile) *adj.* **1** of no use; ineffectual: *All his attempts proved ~.* **2** vain or frivolous. **—fu·tile·ly** *adv.;* **fu·til·i·ty** (–TIL–) *n.*

fu·ture (FEW·chur) *n.* **1** time to come after the present; also, events to come: *She faces an uncertain ~; a career with a ~* (i.e. bright prospects); *He'll be more careful* **in future;** *savings to provide* **for the future.** **2** an English verb form constructed with "shall" or "will," as "will die." **3 futures** *pl.* commodities and stocks bought for future acceptance or delivery. ***—adj.:*** *the ~ tense of a verb; our ~ life* (i.e. after death); *the* **future shock** *or distress of coping with the rapidly changing values of modern society.* **—fu·tur·ism** (FEW–) *n.* an Italian art movement, lasting from about 1909 to 1916, that glorified the energy and speed of the machine age; **fu·tur·ist** *n.* & *adj.;* **fu·tur·is·tic** (–RIS–) *adj.* **—fu·tu·ri·ty** (few·TURE·i·tee, –CHOOR–) *n.* **-ties** a future condition or event, esp. **futurity race,** a horse race in which the contestants are nominated at birth. **—fu·tur·ol·o·gy** (–OL·uh·jee) *n.* a study of future trends based on the science and technology of the present; **fu·tur·ol·o·gist** *n.*

futz (FUTS) *v. Slang.* **futz around** loaf or fool around.

fuze See FUSE *n. 1, v. 2.* **—fuzee** same as FUSEE.

fuzz (FUZ) *n. sing.* & *pl.* **1** loose, fluffy fibers, particles, or hairs, as of down or wool, on a peach or a caterpillar's back, etc. **2 the fuzz** *Slang.* the police; policeman. **—v.** make or become fuzzy; **fuz·zy** *adj.* **fuz·zi·er, fuz·zi·est** of or like fuzz; hence, blurred or indistinct: *a politician whose speeches are ~ on the issues; a ~ photograph;* **fuz·zi·ly** *adv.;* **fuz·zi·ness** *n.*

fwd. *forward.* **—FWD** front-wheel drive.

-fy *v. suffix.* make or become: as in *liquefy, glorify, simplify.*

FYI for your information.

G

G or **g** (JEE) *n.* **G's** or **g's** **1** the seventh letter of the English alphabet; hence, the seventh in a series. **2** *Slang.* $1,000. —**G** or **G.** **1** the fifth tone of the C major scale. **2** German. **3** general (a movie rating). —**g.** or **G.** game; gauge; good; gram(s); (acceleration of) gravity; gulf. —**g** gram(s).

Ga gallium. —**Ga.** or **GA** Georgia. —**G.A.** General Assembly.

gab *v.* **gabs, gabbed, gab·bing** *Informal.* talk rapidly, excessively, or thoughtlessly; chatter; also ***n.*** esp. **the gift of gab,** fluency of speech; **gab·ber** *n.*

gab·ar·dine (–deen) *n.* **1** fabric of cotton, wool, or rayon with raised, diagonal ribs; also, a garment made of this cloth. **2** long, coarse cloak or smock worn in the Middle Ages, esp. by Jews. Also **gab·er·dine.**

gab·ble *v.* **gab·bles, gab·bled, gab·bling** **1** talk quickly or incoherently; jabber; babble. **2** cackle. —***n.:*** *the ~ at a bazaar.*

gab·bro *n.* **gab·bros** granular igneous rock rich in feldspar and pyroxene. —**gab·bro·ic** (–BROH–) *adj.;* **gab·broid** (GAB–) *adj.*

gab·by *adj.* **gab·bi·er, gab·bi·est** *Informal.* talkative; **gab·bi·ness** *n.*

gaberdine same as GABARDINE.

Ga·be·ro·nes (gab·uh·ROH·nis) former name of GABORONE.

gab·fest *n. Informal.* a gathering; also, a prolonged chat or gossiping.

ga·ble *n.* the triangular part of a wall at the end of a ridged roof; **ga·bled** *adj.*

Ga·bon (gah·BOHN) a republic on the W.C. coast of Africa; 103,347 sq.mi. (267,667 km^2); *cap.* Libreville. —**Gab·on·ese** (–NEEZ) *n.* & *adj., sing.* & *pl.*

Ga·bo·ro·ne (gah·buh·ROH·nay) capital of Botswana.

Ga·bri·el (GAY·bree·ul) in the Bible, an archangel.

[1]**gad** or **Gad** *interj.* a mild oath.

[2]**gad** *v.* **gads, gad·ded, gad·ding** roam; wander about; **gad·a·bout** *n. Informal.* rambler seeking pleasure.

gad·fly *n.* **-flies** a horsefly; also, a persistently annoying person.

gadg·et (GAJ·it) *n.* a small mechanical device; also, any trivial object. —**gadg·e·teer** (–TEER) *n.* —**gadg·et·ry** *n.*

gad·o·lin·i·um (–LIN·ee–) *n.* a metallic rare-earth element.

Gael. Gaelic. —**Gael** (GAIL) *n.* a speaker of Irish or Scottish Gaelic; **Gael·ic** *n.* & *adj.* (of) the Celtic language of Scotland or Ireland.

gaff *n.* **1** a pole with an iron hook used to land fish. **2** a pole that supports the top edge of a fore-and-aft sail. **3** *Slang.* abuse; **stand the gaff** endure harsh treatment. —***v.*** land a fish with a gaff.

gaffe (GAF) *n.* a clumsy social blunder.

gaf·fer *n.* an old man.

gag *v.* **gags, gagged, gag·ging** **1** prevent speech by stopping up the mouth; hence, restrain free speech. **2** block off or obstruct; hence, choke or retch: *~ a valve; ~d on his first puff of tobacco.* **3** make or tell jokes. —***n.:*** *A ~ kept the kidnapped heiress from speaking; the dictator's ~ on the free press; They laughed at his ~s; The flying saucer story turned out to be a ~.*

ga·ga·ku (gah·GAH·koo) *n.* ancient Japanese court or ceremonial music.

gage *n.* **1** a pledge or challenge to fight; formerly, a glove, hat, or similar object thrown down as a gesture of defiance. **2** same as GAUGE; ***v.*** **gag·es, gaged, gag·ing.**

gag·gle *n.* a flock of geese; also, a geeselike group or cluster of people.

gag·man *n.* **-men** a writer of jokes or comic routines.

gai·e·ty (GAY–) *n.* **-ties** **1** a being gay; cheerfulness; also gay or festive entertainment: *join in the ~s of the season.* **2** bright, showy appearance: *~ of dress.* —**gaily** See GAY.

gain *v.* get, obtain, or acquire, esp. as an achievement, addition, advantage, or profit: *He ~ed recognition by his memoirs; Our firm ~ed $10,000 in the deal; You ~ weight by overeating; The climbers soon ~ed the summit; This clock ~s* (i.e. is faster by) *a few seconds each day; slowly*

~ing strength after an illness; A faster runner was **gaining on** (i.e. drawing nearer to) *the champion; an ally* **gained over** *to our side by influence;* **gain·er** *n.* **—*n.:*** *a ~ in efficiency; losses and ~s; ill-gotten ~s; a capital ~s tax.* **—gain·ful** *adj.* profitable; **gain·ful·ly** *adv.: ~ employed.* **—gain·say** *v.* **-says, -said, -say·ing** deny; also, contradict; **gain·say·er** *n.*

gait *n.* manner or style of moving on foot; also, a horse's trot, pace, canter, or gallop. **—gait·ed** *adj.: a smooth-~ animal.*

gai·ter *n.* **1** an outer covering for the leg reaching from the instep to ankle, mid-calf, or knee; legging; spat. **2** an ankle-high, elastic-sided shoe; also, a cloth-topped overshoe.

gal *n. Informal.* girl. **—gal.** gallon(s). **—Gal.** Galatians (New Testament book).

ga·la (GAY·luh, GAL·uh) *n.* a celebration or festival. **—*adj.*** festive: *The party was a ~ event.*

ga·lac·tic (guh·LAC–) *adj.* **1** of or from milk. **2** having to do with a galaxy: *~ noise from the Milky Way.* **—ga·lac·tose** *n.* a simple sugar found in milk together with glucose.

Gal·a·had a knight of King Arthur's Round Table, noted for his purity and chivalry; ***n.*** a model of purity or nobility.

gal·ax·y (GAL·uk·see) *n.* **-ax·ies** **1** one of the many systems of stars, gas, and cosmic dust that form the universe; esp., the **Galaxy,** or the Milky Way. **2** a collection of illustrious people or things.

gale *n.* a strong wind; hence, an outburst: *~-force winds* (32 to 63 m.p.h. or 50 to 102 km/h); *~s of laughter.*

ga·le·na (guh·LEE·nuh) *n.* a mineral that is the chief ore of lead.

Gal·i·lee (GAL–) **1** a region of N. Israel. **2 Sea of.** a lake in N.E. Israel.

Gal·i·le·o (gal·i·LEE·oh) 1564–1642, Italian astronomer.

¹gall (GAWL) *n.* **1** a bitter secretion of the liver stored in the **gall·blad·der;** bile; hence, anything bitter to endure; rancor; resentment. **2** *Informal.* impudence: *had the ~ to phone me collect.*

²gall (GAWL) *v.* rub a sore spot on the skin; hence, annoy. **—*n.*** **1** sore caused by chafing. **2** a growth on plant tissue caused by parasites.

gal·lant (GAL·unt *for adj.* 1,2; guh·LANT, –LAHNT *for adj.* 3 & *n.*) *adj.* **1** showy or dashing. **2** stately or noble; brave; high-spirited: *as ~ a ship as ever sailed; The losers put up a ~ fight.* **3** courteous, esp. polite to women. **—*n.*** a stylish young man; man attentive to women. **—gal·lant·ly** (GAL–) *adv.* **—gal·lant·ry** (GAL–) *n.* **-ries** brave, spirited, or courteous behavior or action: *a soldier's ~ in battle; courted her with little ~s.*

gallbladder See ¹GALL.

gal·le·on (GAL·ee·un) *n.* a type of large sailing ship used esp. by the Spanish in the 15th and 16th centuries.

gal·ler·y *n.* **gal·ler·ies** **1** a long, narrow outdoor balcony; porch. **2** a balcony in a theater or public place, esp. the topmost balcony; also, the people seated in this area; hence, any group of spectators: *a performance applauded by the ~.* **3** a long, narrow room or passageway; underground tunnel or passage. **4** an institution for displaying or selling works of art: *the National Art ~.* **—gal·ler·ied** *adj.: a ~ house.*

gal·ley (GAL·ee) *n.* **1** a ship of former times propelled by oars and sails. **2** the kitchen of an airplane or ship. **3** in printing, a tray holding type that has been set; hence **galley (proof).**

Gal·lic (GAL·ic) *adj.* having to do with Gaul or France: *Caesar's ~ wars; a ~ accent.* **—Gal·li·cism** *n.* a French custom or characteristic.

gal·li·mau·fry (–MAW·free) *n.* **-fries** jumble; mixture.

gal·li·nule (GAL–) *n.* a swimming and wading bird of the rail family.

gal·li·um (GAL–) *n.* a rare metallic chemical element used like mercury in thermometers.

gal·li·vant (GAL–) *v.* roam about seeking fun.

gal·lon (GAL·un) *n.* a liquid measure equal to 4 quarts or 8 pints: *A U.S. ~ is 3785.411 cc; the imperial ~ is 4546.087 cc.*

gal·lop (GAL·up) *n.* the fastest pace of a horse or other four-legged animal. **—*v.:*** *a mare ~ing across a field;* **gal·lop·er** *n.*

gal·lows (GAL·oze) n. **-lows(·es)** a structure of usu. two upright posts and a crossbeam used for hanging condemned criminals.

gall·stone *n.* a small mass like a pebble formed in the gallbladder or bile duct.

Gal·lup poll a survey of public opinion on a certain issue.

gal·lus·es *n. pl. Regional.* suspenders.

ga·lore (guh·LORE) *adj.* in great numbers; plentiful: *a big sale with bargains ~.*

ga·losh (guh–) *n.* high rainproof overshoe.

galv. galvanized. **—gal·van·ic** (–VAN–) *adj.* producing electric current; electrical in effect: *a ~ battery; The sudden call produced a ~* (i.e. nervous) *reaction.* **—gal·va·nism** (GAL·vuh–) *n.* chemically produced electricity. **—gal·va·nize** *v.* **-niz·es, -nized, -niz·ing** **1** stimulate with electric current; hence, excite or startle: *~d into activity by the good news.* **2** to coat metal with rustproof zinc; **gal·va·niz·er** *n.;* **gal·va·ni·za·tion** (–ZAY–) *n.* **—gal·va·nom·e·ter** (–NOM–) *n.* a device for measuring small electric currents. **—gal·va·no·met·ric** (–MET–) *adj.*

gam *n. Slang.* a leg, esp. of a woman.

Ga·ma (GAH·muh, GAM–), **Vasco da.** 1469?–1524, Portuguese explorer.

Gam·bi·a a republic on Africa's W. coast; 4,361 sq.mi. (11,295 km²); *cap.* Banjul. **—Gam·bi·an** *n.* & *adj.*

gam·bit *n.* a way of beginning a chess game by sacrificing a minor piece to gain an advantage; hence, an opening move, esp. a strategic one.

gam·ble *v.* **-bles, -bled, -bling** **1** bet or play games of chance; risk or lose something by gambling: *He* **gambled away** *the money he had won.* **2** speculate; take a risk: ~ *on the stock market;* ~ *on having good weather.* **—*n.*** a risky act: *take a* ~ *on a new product.* **—gam·bler** *n.*

gam·bol (–bl) *v.* **-bols, -bol(l)ed, -bol·(l)ing** frolic or caper about, as a lamb does; also ***n.***

gam·brel (roof) a roof, as of barns, that has two slopes on each side, the lower slope being steeper.

game *n.* **1** a form of playing; a diversion; pastime; also, a competitive activity: *a football* ~; *a* ~ *of chess.* **2** a single contest in a competition; also, the number of points needed to win it: *win 3 out of 4* ~*s; 21 points is a* ~ *in casino.* **3** any activity similar to sports in risk-taking, planning, competitiveness, etc.: *the* ~ *of diplomacy; the advertising* ~*; We saw through his* ~*;* **the game is up** the plan has failed. **4** animals hunted for food or sport; also, their flesh: *hunt for* ~*; eat deer and other* ~. **—*v.* games, gamed, gam·ing** gamble; **game·ster** *n.* **—*adj.* gam·er, gam·est** **1** plucky or brave; also, ready: ~ *for a ride;* **game·ly** *adv.;* **game·ness** *n.* **2** lame: *a* ~ *leg.* **—game·cock** *n.* a rooster bred for cockfighting. **—game fish** a fish that is sought for sport with a hook and line. **—game·keeper** *n.* a person taking care of wildlife on a private preserve. **—game plan** planned strategy: *a politician's campaign* ~. **—game point** the point before the end of a game; also, the winning point. **—games·man·ship** *n.* skill in winning games, esp. by stratagems. **—game·some** *adj.* playful; frolicsome.

gam·ete (GAM·eet, guh·MEET) *n.* a plant or animal reproductive cell capable of uniting with another to form a new individual. **—ga·met·ic** (guh·MET–) *adj.*

game theory a mathematical method of determining the best strategy in games, business, war, etc. **—gamey** same as GAMY.

gam·in *n.* a street urchin; waif; **ga·mine** (–MEEN) *n.* a roguish but charming girl.

gam·ma *n.* the third letter of the Greek alphabet. **—gamma globulin** a protein group in blood plasma, containing antibodies that fight infections. **—gamma ray** an electromagnetic radiation emitted by a radioactive substance.

gam·mer *n. Archaic.* old woman.

gam·mon *n.* **1** a smoked ham or side of bacon. **2** nonsensical or deceptive talk.

gam·ut *n.* a complete musical scale; hence, the full range of anything: *the whole* ~ *of emotions from joy to despair.*

gam·(e)y (GAY·mee) *adj.* **gam·i·er, -i·est** **1** having the flavor of game, esp. when spoiled; hence, racy; salacious. **2** plucky. **—gam·i·ness** *n.*

gan·der *n.* **1** a male goose. **2** *Slang.* a look, esp. a close one, as if craning one's neck.

Gan·dhi (GAHN·dee, GAN–), **Mohandas K.** 1869–1948, Hindu religious leader and Indian nationalist, called "Mahatma."

gang *n.* **1** a group of people associating or working together, esp. a band of criminals or delinquents: *a road* ~ *repairing streets; a* ~ *of young toughs.* **2** a set of similar implements designed to work together, as a **gang·plow** or a **gang·saw.** **—*v.*** form into groups: *Boys* ~*ed (up) together at the corner; children* **ganging up on** (*Informal.* attacking) *a bully.* **—gang bang** *Slang.* the copulation of several men one after another with the same person; **gang-bang** *v.*

Gan·ges (GAN·jeez) a river in N. India and Bangladesh.

gang·land *n.* the gangster world.

gan·gle *v.* **-gles, -gled, -gling** move awkwardly or loosely. **—gan·gling** *adj.* **-gli·er, -gli·est** tall, thin, and awkward; loosely built. Also **gan·gly.**

gan·gli·on (GANG·glee·un) *n.* **-gli·a** or **-gli·ons** a group of nerve cells forming a center for transmitting impulses. **—gan·gli·on·ic** (–ON·ic) *adj.*

gangly same as GANGLING.

gang·plank *n.* a removable ramp for boarding or leaving a ship. **—gangplow, gangsaw** See GANG, *n.* 2.

gan·grene (GANG·green, –GREEN) *n.* the dying of body tissue due to interruption of the blood supply; ***v.* -grenes, -grened, -gren·ing:** *amputated the foot* ~*d by frostbite.* **—gan·gre·nous** (–gruh·nus) *adj.*

gang·ster *n.* a criminal or racketeer.

Gang·tok (GUNG–) capital of Sikkim.

gang·way *n.* a passageway; also, a gangplank; ***interj.*** make way!

gan·net (GAN·it) *n.* a large black-and-white sea bird.

gantlet same as GAUNTLET.

gan·try (–tree) *n.* **-tries** a fixed or movable framework for supporting a crane, railroad signals, etc.; also, a structure for servicing rockets.

GAO General Accounting Office.

gaol (jail) *n. Brit.* jail; **gaol·er** *n.*

gap *n.* an opening or break; also, an obvious difference; disparity: *A missing tooth leaves a* ~*; crossed the Rockies through a mountain* ~*; a* ~ *of 10 years in your narrative; Lying builds up a credibility* ~*; the generation* ~*; a missile* ~ *with the Russians?*

gape *v.* **gapes, gaped, gap·ing** open widely, esp. open the mouth to yawn; hence, to stare with the mouth open: *The abandoned quarry* ~*d before us; a* ~*ing wound; natives* ~*ing at foreign tourists.* **—*n.:*** *stifling a bored* ~*; mouth opened in a* ~ *of surprise.*

gar(·fish) *n.* a fierce freshwater fish with elongated body and snout.

GAR, G.A.R. Grand Army of the Republic.

ga·rage (guh·RAHZH, –RAHJ) *n.* a shelter for cars; also, a car repair shop. **—*v.* -rag·es, -raged, -rag·ing** put or keep in a garage. **—garage sale** a sale of used household articles held at the seller's home.

garb *n.* clothing or style of dress; hence, outward appearance: *a nun's ~; in formal ~; give confusion the ~ of order.* **—v.:** *~ed in her new outfit.*

gar·bage (–bij) *n.* discarded food; hence, anything useless or worthless.

gar·ban·zo (–BAN·zoh) *n.* **-zos** same as CHICKPEA.

gar·ble *v.* **-bles, -bled, -bling** distort, misrepresent, or intentionally scramble.

gar·çon (gar·SOHN) *n.* a waiter in a restaurant. **—gar·çon·niere** (gar·saw·NYAIR) *n.* a bachelor's room or apartment.

gar·den (GAR·dn) *n.* **1** a plot of land for growing flowers, fruit, or vegetables; hence, any fertile area: *a lush resort in the* **garden spot** *of our state.* **2** an area for public recreation: *zoological ~(s).* **—v.** work in a garden; **gar·den·er** *n.* **—adj.:** *water the lawn with a ~ hose; tomatoes and other ~ vegetables; an unexciting* **garden variety** (i.e. ordinary) *restaurant.*

Garden Grove a city of S.W. California.

gar·de·ni·a (–DEEN·yuh) *n.* a shrub with fragrant white or yellow flowers. **—garden spot, garden variety** See GARDEN, *n.* 1.

Gar·field, James A. 1831–81, 20th U.S. President (1880–81).

gar·gan·tu·an or **Gar·gan·tu·an** (–GAN·choo·un) *adj.* enormous; huge; *a ~ appetite.*

gar·gle *v.* **-gles, -gled, -gling** rinse the throat with liquid kept in motion by exhaled breath. **—n.:** *a salt-water ~ for a sore throat.*

gar·goyle (–goil) *n.* a grotesquely shaped waterspout projecting from the gutter of a building.

Gar·i·bal·di (gair·uh·BAWL·dee), **Giuseppe.** 1807–82, Italian patriot and general.

gar·ish (GAIR–) *adj.* gaudy; showy; glaring; **gar·ish·ly** *adv.;* **gar·ish·ness** *n.*

gar·land (–lund) *n.* a wreath of leaves or flowers. **—v.:** *Roses ~ed the bride.*

gar·lic *n.* a plant related to the onion; also, its strong-smelling bulb, used in cooking; **gar·lick·y** *adj.*

gar·ment (–munt) *n.* an article of clothing.

gar·ner *v.* gather and store; acquire; collect.

gar·net (–nit) *n.* a glossy mineral whose deep-red variety is used as a gem.

gar·nish *v.* decorate or adorn, esp. food: *~ a platter with parsley.* **—n.:** *a ~ of mushrooms with the steak.*

gar·nish·ee (–ni·SHEE) *v.* **-ees, -eed, -ee·ing** legally withhold a debtor's money to pay his debts: *wages ~d by the loan company;* **gar·nish·ment** *n.* a notice to garnishee.

gar·ni·ture (–chur) *n.* an embellishment.

gar·ret (GAIR·it) *n.* an attic.

gar·ri·son (GAIR·i·sun) *n.* the troops stationed in a fortified place; also, the fort itself. **—v.:** *troops ~ed in Europe during the War.* **—garrison state** a country dominated by military personnel.

gar·rote or **ga·rotte** (guh·ROT, –ROTE) *n.* strangulation by an iron collar, cord, wire, etc.; also, the device used. **—v. gar·rotes, gar·rot·ed, gar·rot·ing** or **ga·rottes, ga·rot·ted, ga·rot·ting:** *The robber ~ed his victim with a wire.*

gar·ru·lous (GAIR·uh·lus) *adj.* talkative; wordy. **—gar·ru·lous·ly** *adv.* **—gar·ru·lous·ness** *n.;* also **gar·ru·li·ty** (–ROO–) *n.*

gar·ter *n.* a band or strap to hold up a stocking. **—v.** to support with a garter. **—garter snake** a harmless, longitudinally striped, North American snake.

Gar·y (GAIR·ee) a city of N.W. Indiana.

gas *n.* **gas·(s)es 1** a shapeless fluid such as air which can expand indefinitely; **gas·e·ous** (–ee·us) *adj.:* *Steam is water in a ~ state.* **2** any gas or volatile liquid that is used as a fuel, anesthetic, poison, irritant, or illuminant; esp., gasoline: *The stalled taxi was out of ~; Step on the ~* (i.e. accelerator pedal) *to go faster; natural ~ for home heating; a criminal executed in a* **gas chamber** (with poison gas). **3** *Slang.* a source of great pleasure or excitement. **—v. gas·(s)es, gassed, gas·sing: Gas up** *the car before a trip; a murderer sentenced to be ~d.*

gash *n.* a long, deep wound. **—v.:** *legs ~ed by barbed wire.*

gas·house *n.* a gas-manufacturing plant.

gas·ket (–kit) *n.* a leakage-preventing seal around a joint or closure.

gas·light *n.* (the light of) a lamp, or **gas lamp,** that burns an illuminating gas, as used by campers. **—gas mask** a mask worn to prevent the breathing in of poisonous fumes or smoke. **—gas·o·hol** *n.* an automotive fuel that is a blend of 90% unleaded gasoline and 10% ethyl alcohol. **—gas·o·line** or **gas·o·lene** (GAS–, –LEEN) *n.* a flammable liquid distilled from petroleum and used as a motor fuel; gas.

gasp *v.* breathe in sharply as from shock; also, pant: *an asthmatic ~ing for breath; The winded messenger ~ed his report.* **—n.** a gasping; **at the last gasp** on the point of death.

gas·sy *adj.* **gas·si·er, gas·si·est** full of or producing stomach gas; flatulent. **—gas station** where gasoline, oil, etc. for motor vehicles are sold.

gas·tric *adj.* having to do with the stomach; **gastric juice** the acidic digestive fluid produced by stomach glands. **—gas·tri·tis** (–TRY–) *n.* inflammation of the stomach lining. **—gastro-** *comb. form.* of the stomach: as in **gas·tro·en·ter·ol·o·gy** (–ROL–) *n.* branch of medicine dealing with the digestive system; **gas·tro·in·tes·ti·nal** (–TES–) *adj.* of the stomach and intestines. **—gas·tron·o·my** (–TRON–) *n.* the art of good eating; **gas·tro·nom·ic** or **-i·cal** (–NOM–) *adj.* **—gas·tro·pod** (–truh·pod) *n.* a single-shelled, soft-bodied mollusk such as snails and slugs.

gas·works *n.* [takes *sing. v.*] a gas-manufacturing plant.

gate *n.* **1** a movable barrier controlling passage through an entrance in a fence, wall, castle, etc. which is hung on a **gate·post;** hence, a door or valve controlling water flow in a canal, dam, lock, etc.; also, a gateway. **2** the total amount of money taken or the number of spectators at an event. **3** a computer circuit having one output activated by a combination of signals to the inputs. **—give (someone) the gate** *Slang.* dismiss or reject (someone). **—gate-crash·er** *n. Informal.* one who enters without an invitation or without paying. **—gate·keep·er** *n.* one who tends a gate. **—gatepost** GATE, *n.* 1. **—gate·way** *n.* an opening for a gate; hence, a means of entrance: *St. Louis is the ~ to the West.*

gath·er *v.* **1** bring together; collect; assemble; also, accumulate; increase: *He ~ed his friends for the reunion; The detective ~ed evidence; A farmer ~s his crop; old books ~ing dust; a car ~ing speed as it rolls downhill.* **2** draw: *~ed a shawl around herself; ~ing his brows in a frown; a skirt ~ed at the waist* (into pleats or folds); ***n.*** pleat: *remove the* **gathers** *to remodel a dress.* **3** guess; infer; conclude: *I ~ you're not coming.* **—gath·er·er** *n.* **—gath·er·ing** *n.*: *Thanksgiving and other family ~s; a ~ of clouds before a storm.*

GATT General Agreement on Tariffs and Trade.

gauche (GOHSH) *adj.* awkward, esp. socially; **gau·che·rie** (goh·shuh·REE) *n.* a clumsy or tactless action.

gau·cho (GOW·choh) *n.* **-chos** a cowboy of the South American plains.

gaud (GAWD) *n.* a cheap ornament or trinket. **—gaud·y** *adj.* **gaud·i·er, -i·est** tastelessly colorful; flashily ornamented; **gaud·i·ly** *adv.;* **gaud·i·ness** *n.*

gauge (GAYJ) *n.* **1** a standard measurement, as for the thickness of wire, widths of railroad tracks, sizes of bores, etc.: *a 12-~ shotgun.* **2** a measuring instrument: *a pressure ~; a water-level ~; rain ~.* **3** a means of estimating or judging: *Looks are no sure ~ of character.* —***v.*** **gaug·es, gauged, gaug·ing:** to measure; also, judge: *a director ~ing an actress's performance.*

Gau·guin (goh·GAN), **Paul.** 1848–1903, French painter.

Gaul (GAWL) the N.W. European part of the ancient Roman Empire; also, a native of Gaul or a modern Frenchman; **Gaul·ish** *n.* the Celtic language of Gaul.

gaunt *adj.* haggard and thin; also, desolate or grim-looking; **gaunt·ness** *n.*

gaunt·let (GAWNT–, GAHNT–) *n.* **1** a protective glove, esp. from a suit of armor; **throw down the gauntlet** challenge (to fight). **2** two rows of armed men who strike a person forced to run between them; hence, any ordeal: *His work* **ran the gauntlet** *of criticism before being accepted.*

gauss (GOWCE) *n.* **gauss(·es)** a unit for measuring the strength of a magnetic field.

gauze *n.* a thin, transparent, loosely-woven fabric; **gauz·y** *adj.* **gauz·i·er, -i·est; gauz·i·ness** *n.*

gave *pt.* of GIVE.

gav·el (GAV·ul) *n.* a small mallet used by an auctioneer or chairperson.

ga·votte (guh·VOT) *n.* an old French dance like a lively minuet.

G.A.W. guaranteed annual wage.

gawk *v.* to stare stupidly; ***n.*** an awkward or clumsy person; **gawk·y** *adj.* **gawk·i·er, -i·est:** *a growing boy's ~ limbs;* **gawk·i·ness** *n.* **—gawk·ish** *adj.*

gay *adj.* **gay·er, -est** **1** joyous; lively; merry; given to (social) pleasure; also, licentious or immoral. **2** brightly colored: *a ~Mardi Gras costume.* **3** homosexual: *a ~ bar;* **Gay Liberation** a movement championing homosexual rights. **—gai·ly** *adv.: ~ trimmed in red, white, and blue;* also **gay·ly. —gay·e·ty** same as GAIETY.

gaz. gazette; gazetteer.

Ga·za (GAH·zuh) a port on the S.E. Mediterranean Sea, capital of the **Gaza Strip,** a coastal area occupied by Israel in 1967.

gaze *v.* **gaz·es, gazed, gaz·ing** to look steadily and with fascination. **—*n.:*** *Their eyes met in a bewildered ~.* **—gaz·er** *n.* **—ga·ze·bo** (guh·ZEE–, –ZAY–) *n.* **-bo(e)s** belvedere.

ga·zelle (guh·ZEL) *n.* **-zelle(s)** a small, swift, graceful antelope of Asia and Africa.

ga·zette (guh·ZET) *n.* an official government journal; also, in titles, a newspaper: *"The Phoenix Gazette."* —***v.*** **-zettes, -zet·ted, -zet·ting** publish or list in a gazette. **—gaz·et·teer** (gaz·uh·TEER) *n.* a dictionary of names of places, seas, mountains, etc.

gaz·pa·cho (gahz·PAH–) *n.* a cold Spanish vegetable soup.

ga·zump (guh·ZUMP) *v. Brit. Slang.* cheat or swindle, esp. by raising the agreed-on price of a house at the last moment.

GB **1** Great Britain; also **G.B.** **2** code name of SARIN.

GCA ground-controlled approach (of aircraft).

G.C.T. Greenwich civil time.

gd(s) good(s).

Gd gadolinium.

GDP gross domestic product.

Ge germanium.

ge·an·ti·cline (jee·AN–) *n.* an upward fold of the earth's crust. **—ge·an·ti·cli·nal** (–CLYE–) *adj.* & *n.*

gear *n.* **1** equipment, esp. tools or clothing for a special purpose: *packed camping ~ for the trip; The soldier left his ~ in the barracks; dressed up in the latest ~.* **2** a toothed wheel that meshes with another toothed element to transmit motion, often in a system of such gears; **in** (or **out of**) **gear** (not) connected to the motor or (not) working properly; **in high gear** in the highest speed range; also, at high efficiency. —***v.*** provide with or connect by gears; put into gear; adjust; equip: *A car's rear wheels are ~ed to the motor; a factory ~ing production to demand; hikers ~ed for an outing; a team ~ing up for a game.* **—gear·box** *n.* an automobile transmission. **—gear·shift** *n.* a device for changing from one gear to another. —**gear·wheel** *n.* cogwheel.

gee (JEE) *interj.* expressing surprise.

geese *pl.* of GOOSE.

gee whiz *interj.* gee; **gee-whiz** *adj. Informal.* admirable; spectacular; exciting: *a ~ kid.*

gee·zer *n. Slang.* an eccentric old man.

Gei·ger(-Müller) counter (GUY·gur–) an electronic device for detecting and measuring radioactivity.

gei·sha (GAY·shuh, GEE–) *n.* **-sha(s)** a Japanese girl trained as a social entertainer and companion for men.

gel (JEL) *n.* a jellylike substance formed by the thickening of a colloidal solution. —***v.* gels, gelled, gel·ling:** *Egg white ~s when heated.* —**gel·a·tin(e)** (–tin) *n.* a substance like glue formed by boiling animal bones, hoofs, etc., and used in food, drugs, and photographic film. —**ge·lat·i·nous** (–LAT·uh·nus) *adj.*

geld *v.* castrate. —**geld·ing** *n.* a castrated animal, esp. a horse.

gel·id (JEL–) *adj.* ice-cold; frozen.

gel·ig·nite (JEL–) *n.* an explosive with a nitrate base.

gem (JEM) *n.* a precious or semiprecious stone cut and polished as a jewel; hence, anything highly valued: *A Picasso was the ~ of his collection.*

gem·i·nate (JEM–) *v.* **-ates, -at·ed, -at·ing** make or become double or paired. —**Gem·i·ni** (JEM·i·nye, –nee) *n.* **1** a N. constellation and the third sign of the zodiac; also called "The Twins."

gem·(m)ol·o·gy (–OL·uh·jee) *n.* the study of gems; **gem·(m)ol·o·gist** *n.;* **gem·(m)o·log·i·cal** (–LOJ–) *adj.* —**gem·stone** *n.* a stone that may be cut and polished as a gem.

-gen *n. suffix.* something that produces or is produced: as in *allergen, antigen, hydrogen, nitrogen.*

gen. general; genitive. —**Gen.** (rank of) general; Genesis.

gen·darme (ZHAHN·darm) *n.* a soldier serving as a policeman, esp. in France; **gen·dar·me·rie** or **-mer·y** (–DAR–) *n.* a body of gendarmes.

gen·der *n.* **1** sex: *the female ~; had his ~ changed.* **2** *Gram.* one of the categories (masculine, feminine, or neuter) into which words are grouped.

gene (JEEN) *n.* a unit of a chromosome that determines the inheritance of a certain characteristic. —**ge·ne·al·o·gy** (jee·nee·AH·luh·jee) *n.* **-gies** a record or study of family history; lineage or pedigree; **ge·ne·al·o·gist** *n.;* **ge·ne·a·log·i·cal** (–LOJ–) *adj.* —**gene pool** all the genes of a species. —**genera** a *pl.* of GENUS.

gen·er·al *adj.* **1** applicable to or true of the whole; common, prevalent, or widespread; not limited, specialized, precise, or detailed: *a constitution promoting the ~ welfare; a ~ feeling of unrest in the cities; All bears have the same ~ features, but differ in color and size; She quickly sketched the ~ outline of the scheme.* **2** having the highest rank: *a store's ~ manager; postmaster-~.* —***n.* 1:** *His report concentrates on the ~ and ignores the particular; The weather,* **in general,** *is rainy throughout May.* **2** a U.S. military officer of the second highest rank, next below **General of the Air Force** or **General of the Army,** or an officer of the highest rank in the Marine Corps; **gen·er·al·ship** *n.* —**general assembly** a legislature, as of South Carolina; **General Assembly** the supreme deliberative body of the United Nations. —**gen·er·al·is·si·mo** (–LIS–) *n.* **-mos** the supreme commander of all armed forces in some countries. —**gen·er·al·i·ty** (–AL–) *n.* **-ties:** *The lecturer spoke in vague ~s; The ~ of people pay their taxes.* —**gen·er·al·ize** *v.* **-iz·es, -ized, -iz·ing:** *He frequently ~d without revealing specific plans: The scientist ~d a law from several experiments;* **gen·er·al·i·za·tion** (–ZAY–) *n.* —**gen·er·al·ly** *adv.:* *~ speaking, it's a friendly town; an obscure fact not ~ known.* —**general paresis** See PARESIS. —**general practitioner** a physician who is not a specialist. —**general staff** a group of military officers who aid a high commander in planning and supervising operations. —**general store** a store selling a wide variety of merchandise but not in separate departments.

gen·er·ate (JEN–) *v.* **-ates, -a·ted, -a·ting** bring into being; originate; produce, esp. by a chemical process: *heat ~d by burning coal; a diplomat ~ing good will; Insects ~ countless offspring;* **gen·er·a·tive** (–tiv) *adj.* —**gen·er·a·tion** (–AY–) *n.* **1:** *the ~ of electricity by Niagara Falls.* **2** all people of about the same age range considered as one step in the line of descent; also, the average time period between generations: *the postwar ~; four ~s of Smiths at the family reunion; Parents talking to their teenagers help bridge the* **generation gap.** —**gen·er·a·tor** (–ay·tur) *n.* one that generates, esp. a machine turning mechanical energy into electrical energy.

ge·ner·ic (juh·NER–) *adj.* having to do with an entire group, class, or genus; hence, general, not specific; also, without a trademark: *Thorns are a ~ feature in roses; the ~ name for Coke, Pepsi, etc. is "cola."* **ge·ner·i·cal·ly** *adv.* —**gen·er·ous** (JEN–) *adj.* giving freely; noble or magnanimous; ample; abundant: *gave up his seat in a ~ act; served a ~ portion of pie;* **gen·er·ous·ly** *adv.;* **gen·er·ous·ness** *n.;* **gen·er·os·i·ty** (–OS–) *n.* **-ties.**

gen·e·sis *n., pl.* **-ses** (–seez) the coming into being of something; origin: **Genesis,** *the first book of the Bible, is about the creation of the universe.*

gene-splic·ing *n. Informal.* genetic engineering; recombinant-DNA technology. —**genetic code** the organization of chemical elements in the chromosome determining the characteristics passed on from generation to generation. —**genetic engineering** scientific manipulation of genes or gene processes to create or eliminate traits. —**ge·net·ics** (juh·NET–) *n.* [takes *sing. v.*] the study of heredity and variations; **ge·net·ic** *adj.;* **ge·net·i·cal·ly** *adv.;* **ge·net·i·cist** *n.*

Ge·ne·va (juh·NEE·vuh) a city of S.W. Switzerland.

Gen·ghis (JEN·giz) **Khan** 1162?–1227, Mongolian conqueror.

ge·nial (JEEN·yul) *adj.* favorable to life or growth; cheerful and amiable; kindly: *Oranges thrive in Spain's ~ climate; made welcome by his ~ host;* **ge·nial·ly** *adv.;* **ge·ni·al·i·ty** (–AL–) *n.*

-genic *adj. suffix.* producing, produced by, or suitable for production or reproduction by: as in *carcinogenic, photogenic.*

ge·nie (JEE·nee) *n.* **-nies** or **-ni·i** (–nee·eye) a supernatural being, often serving humans; a jinni; See also GENIUS, *n.* 2.

gen·i·ta·li·a (jen·i·TAIL·yuh) or **gen·i·tals** (JEN–) *n.pl.* the external sex organs; **gen·i·tal** *adj.* of reproduction or reproductive organs; **gen·i·tal·ly** *adv.* —**gen·i·to·u·ri·nar·y** (–YOOR·i·ner·ee) *adj.* of the genital and urinary organs.

gen·i·tive (–tiv) *adj.* having to do with the grammatical case that expresses possession or source; ***n.:*** *"His" is in the ~.*

gen·ius (JEEN·yus) *n.* **1** *pl.* **-ius·es** exceptional natural ability or inclination, esp. great intellectual capacity or creativity; also, a person with such ability: *He has a ~ for learning languages; An I.Q. of 140 or more makes you a "genius."* **2** *pl.* **ge·ni·i** (–nee·eye) the distinctive spirit of an age, nation, place, or group; also, one who strongly influences another: *Fitzgerald captured the ~ of the "Lost Generation"; driven to murder by his evil ~.*

genl. general.

Gen·o·a (JEN·oh·uh) seaport of N.W. Italy.

gen·o·cide (JEN·uh–) *n.* the systematic destruction of a racial, political, or cultural group; **gen·o·ci·dal** (–SYE·dl) *adj.*

-gen·ous (–us) *adj. suffix.* producing, generating, or produced by: as in *endogenous, erogenous, nitrogenous.* —**gen·re** (ZHON·ruh) *n.* a type or kind, esp. **genre painting,** a style that treats everyday subjects realistically; also, any class of literary composition: *Science fiction as a 20th c. ~.*

gens (JENZ) *n., pl.* **gen·tes** (–teez) a Roman clan consisting of families with a common ancestor and name.

gent (JENT) *n. Informal.* a man. —**genteel** *adj.* polite; stylish; esp., affectedly or prudishly elegant: *learned the ~ arts in finishing school; an aging belle living in ~ poverty.*

gen·tian (JEN·shun) *n.* one of many species of plants with brilliant, usu. blue flowers and fringed in the *fringed gentian.*

gen·tile or **Gen·tile** *n.* a non-Jew or a Christian; also, formerly, a heathen or pagan; ***adj.:*** *A Jew married to a ~ girl.*

gen·til·i·ty (–TIL–) *n.* **-ties** **1** the condition of being of gentle birth; also, such people: *The family lost its ~ with its fortune; balanced a teacup on his knee in perfect ~.* —**gen·tle** *adj.* **-tler, -tlest** **1** kind; considerate; mild; soft; tame; moderate: *a mother's ~ touch; a ~ detergent for dry skin; soothed by her ~ voice; barely heard the ~ knock; a wild horse now ~ as a lamb; nearly flat terrain with only a ~ incline;* ***v.*** **-tles, -tled, -tling:** *a wild cat he couldn't ~; Soft music ~d her nerves;* **gen·tly** *adv.;* **gen·tle·ness** *n.* **2** of the upper classes; refined; well-bred: *Good manners go with ~ birth.* —**gen·tle·folk(s)** *n.pl.* people of good upbringing. —**gen·tle·man** *n.* **-men** a polite or well-bred man; **gen·tle·man·ly** *adv.* —**gen·tle·wom·an** *n.* **-wom·en** a lady; also, a female attendant of a woman of rank. —**gen·try** (–tree) *n.* **-tries** people of gentle birth; also, people of a specified class: *The new governor entertained the local ~; the teaching ~.*

gen·u·flect *v.* bend the knee, esp. in worship; **gen·u·flec·tion** (–FLEC–) *n.*

gen·u·ine (JEN·yoo·in) *adj.* real and not fake; true; also, sincere: *a ~ antique; ~ sorrow;* **gen·u·ine·ly** *adv.;* **gen·u·ine·ness** *n.*

ge·nus (JEE–) *n., pl.* **gen·er·a** (JEN·uh·ruh) or **ge·nus·es** a kind or sort; class; esp., a plant or animal classification under *family,* comprising many *species,* as genus *Rosa* with hundreds of rose species.

geo- *comb.form.* of the earth; geographical: as in **ge·o·cen·tric** (–SEN–) or **-tri·cal** *adj.* with the earth as center: *the ~ theory of the universe;* **ge·o·cen·tri·cal·ly** *adv.* —**ge·o·chem·is·try** (–KEM–) *n.* the chemistry of the earth's crust. —**ge·o·chro·nol·o·gy** (–NOL–) *n.* the study of the chronology of the formation of the earth and of its plant and animal life from geologic data. —**ge·ode** (JEE–) *n.* a stonelike formation with a cavity lined with crystals. —**ge·o·des·ic** (–DES–) **dome** a strong though unsupported hemispherical framework of triangle-shaped blocks made up of short, straight bars in tension; **geodesic line** the shortest line between two points, as an arc with the smallest curvature if the points are on a sphere. —**ge·od·e·sy** (–OD–) *n.* applied mathematics, used esp. in surveying, dealing with measurements on the curved surface of the earth; **ge·od·e·sist** *n.;* **ge·o·des·ic** (–DES–) or **ge·o·det·ic** (–DET–) *adj.* —**geodetic surveying** surveying that takes into account the earth's curvature; **ge·o·det·i·cal·ly** *adv.* —**geog.** geography; geographic(al); **ge·og·ra·phy** (–OG–) *n.* **-phies** the science of the earth's natural features, climate, inhabitants, resources, etc.; **ge·og·ra·pher** *n.;* **ge·o·graph·ic** (–GRAF–) or **-i·cal** *adj.;* **ge·o·graph·i·cal·ly** *adv.* —**geol.** geology; geologic(al); **ge·ol·o·gy** (–OL–) *n.* **-gies** the science of the structure and history of the earth's crust; **ge·ol·o·gist** *n.;* **ge·o·log·ic** (–LOJ–) or **-i·cal** *adj.;* **ge·o·log·i·cal·ly** *adv.* —**geom.**

geometry; geometrical. **—ge·o·mag·net·ism** (–MAG–) *n.* the science of the magnetic properties of the earth; **ge·o·mag·net·ic** (–NET–) *adj.* **—ge·om·e·ter** (–OM–) or **ge·om·e·tri·cian** (–TRISH–) *n.* a specialist in **ge·om·e·try** (–OM–) *n.* the mathematics of points, lines, angles, surfaces, and solid figures; **ge·o·met·ric** (–MET–) or **-ri·cal** *adj.;* **geometric progression** a sequence of terms with a fixed ratio between any two successive terms, as 3, 9, 27, 81, and 243; **ge·o·met·ri·cal·ly** *adv.* **—ge·o·mor·phol·o·gy** (–FOL–) *n.* the geology of the nature, origin, and evolution of the surface features of the earth. **—ge·o·phys·ics** (–FIZ–) *n.pl.* the science of the earth's physical forces, including geology, meteorology, seismology, etc.; **ge·o·phys·i·cal** *adj.;* **ge·o·phys·i·cist** *n.* **—ge·o·pol·i·tics** (–POL–) *n.pl.* the study of politics in relation to geography, esp. as affecting foreign policies.

George III 1738–1820, king of Great Britain, 1760–1820. **—George·town** capital and chief port of Guyana. **—Geor·gia** (JOR·juh) a S.E. state of the U.S.; 58,876 sq.mi. (152,488 km²); *cap.* Atlanta; **Geor·gian** *adj.* & *n.* **—Georgian Soviet Socialist Republic** a republic of the U.S.S.R. east of the Black Sea; *cap.* Tbilisi.

ge·o·sci·ence *n.* any earth science; **ge·o·sci·en·tist** *n.* **—ge·o·sta·tion·a·ry** (–STAY–) or **ge·o·syn·chro·nous** (–SING·cruh·nus) *adj.* of an artificial communications satellite, orbiting at the same speed and in the same direction as the earth so that it acts as a fixed relay station. **—ge·o·syn·cline** (–SIN–) *n.* a long furrow in the earth's crust filled with sediment; **ge·o·syn·cli·nal** (–CLY·nul) *adj.* & *n.* **—ge·o·ther·mal** or **-mic** (–THUR–) *adj.* of the earth's internal heat. **—ge·ot·ro·pism** (–OT·ruh–) *n.* the tendency, as of a plant's roots, to grow downward because of the earth's gravity

ger. gerund. **—Ger.** German(y).

ge·ra·ni·um (juh·RAY·nee·um) *n.* a garden plant or wildflower with showy scarlet, pink, white, or purple blossoms.

ger·bil(le) (JUR·bil) *n.* a mouselike desert rodent with long hind legs.

ger·i·at·rics (–AT–) *n.* a branch of medicine dealing with aging and the diseases of the aged; **ger·i·at·ric** *adj.: a ~ ward.*

germ (JURM) *n.* **1** the seed, bud, or earliest form of a living thing; hence, source or origin: *the oil-rich wheat ~; Inspiration is the ~ of poetry.* **2** a microscopic creature, as a bacterium; microbe; **-ger·man** (JUR·mun) *comb.form.* having the same parents; also, closely related: *brothers-german; a cousin-german* (i.e. first cousin).

Ger·man (JUR·mun) *n.* a person of or from Germany; also, the language of the Germans; ***adj.*** of Germany, its people, or their language.

ger·mane (jur·MAIN) *adj.* closely related: *points that are interesting but not ~ to our discussion;* **ger·mane·ly** *adv.;* **ger·mane·ness** *n.*

Ger·man·ic (–MAN–) *adj.* German in origin: *Germans, Dutch, and Flemings are ~ peoples speaking ~ languages.* **—ger·ma·ni·um** (–MAY·nee–) *n.* a brittle, gray-white, metallic chemical element used in transistors. **—German measles** same as RUBELLA. **—German shepherd** an intelligent, wolflike dog trained for police work or for guiding the blind. **—Ger·ma·ny** (–muh·nee) a former country of C. Europe, divided since 1945 into East Germany (**German Democratic Republic;** 41,767 sq.mi./108,176 km²; *cap.* East Berlin) and West Germany (**Federal Republic of Germany;** 95,934 sq.mi./248,468 km²; *cap.* Bonn).

germ cell a reproductive cell, as a sperm (male) or egg (female), whose hereditary substance is **germ plasm** consisting of chromosomes; *the* **germ theory** *of the spread of infectious diseases;* **germ warfare** *using disease bacteria;* **ger·mi·cide** (JUR·muh–) *n.* a germ-destroyer, as an antiseptic; **ger·mi·ci·dal** (–SYE·dl) *adj.* **—ger·mi·nal** (–muh·nl) *adj.* of germs; also, embryonic. **—ger·mi·nate** *v.* **-nates, -nat·ed, -nat·ing** sprout; begin to grow; also, cause to sprout; **ger·mi·na·tion** (–NAY–) *n.*

Ge·ron·i·mo (juh·RON·uh·moh) 1829–1909, Apache Indian chief.

ger·on·tol·o·gy (jer·on·TOL·uh·jee) *n.* the scientific study of aging and the problems of the elderly; cf. GERIATRICS. **—ge·ron·to·log·ic** (–LOJ–) or **-i·cal** *adj.* **—ger·on·tol·o·gist** (–TOL–) *n.*

ger·ry·man·der (jer·ee·MAN–) *v.* **-ders, -dered, -der·ing** divide into voting areas that give one political party an unfair advantage; ***n.*** the practice of gerrymandering.

Gersh·win, George. 1898–1937, an American composer.

ger·und (JER–) *n.* the "-ing" form of a verb used as a noun, as in "enjoy *eating*" or "good *eating.*"

Ge·samt·kunst·werk (guh·ZAHMT·koonst·vairk) *n.* an art work created by a combination of different forms such as music, drama, and dance.

ges·so (JES·oh) *n.* a plasterlike coating used on wooden surfaces to cover the grain before painting or gilding them for picture frames, furniture, etc.

ge·stalt (guh·SHTAHLT) *n.* a totality of form or structure that cannot be divided into parts or analyzed: *the* **Gestalt psychology** *of human perception and behavior.*

Ge·sta·po (guh·STAH·poh) *n.* **-pos** the Nazi German secret police.

ges·ta·tion (jes·TAY–) *n.* (period of) pregnancy; hence, development. **—ges·tate** (JES–) *v.* **-tates, -tat·ed, -tat·ing.**

ges·tic·u·late (jes·TIK·yuh–) *v.* **-lates, -lat·ed, -lat·ing** make vigorous gestures, esp. instead of words: *Too shocked to speak, he ~d helplessly;* **ges·tic·u·la·tion** (–LAY–) *n.* **—ges·ture** (JES·chur) *n.* a motion of the body expressing or emphasizing an idea or feeling; hence, any act or remark indicating attitude, frequently made only for effect: *stamping his foot merely as an angry ~; gave up her seat as a noble ~ to the old lady.* **—v. -tures, -tured, -tur·ing:** *~d to the waiter for the bill.* **—ges·tur·al** *adj.*

Ge·sund·heit (guh·ZOONT·hite) *interj.* [used when someone sneezes] Your health!

get *v.* **gets,** *pt.* **got,** *pp.* **got** or **got·ten** (GOTN), **get·ting** **1** obtain; earn; gain; buy; receive; fetch; catch (a disease): *He got a better job; You must ~ some rest; ~ing a bad reputation; She got herself new shoes; Go and ~ me a drink; Add 2 + 1 to ~ 3; The children got colds.* **2** reach; become; cause to come, go, do, or be in a certain condition: *We got home early; planning to ~ married; can you ~ your wife to listen?* **3** *Informal.* overcome physically or emotionally, esp. irritate or puzzle; strike, take vengeance on, or kill: *The mounties got their man; Her pleas finally got him; Nothing ~s me more than rudeness.* **4** *Informal.* understand; hear: *I didn't ~ your point.* **5** have, esp. as an obligation: *Our team has got to win!* **6** manage or contrive: *~ to see the previews.* **7** communicate with: *~ him on the phone.* **8** beget; ***n.*** (animal) offspring. **—get along** manage fairly well; also, be on friendly terms. **—get around** **1** circulate. **2** evade: *How to ~ around the law.* **3** trick, esp. by flattery. **—get at** to reach, esp. with a bribe: *No one got at the honest jury; what are you getting at* (i.e. implying)? **—get away** leave; escape; **get away with** accomplish without punishment: *students ~ing away with cheating.* **—get by:** *Can you ~ by without a loan?* **—get it** *Informal.* be punished: *He got it for being late.* **—get off** come out of; leave; escape or help escape: *A smart lawyer got him off.* **—get off on** get pleasure or excitement from: *~ off on drugs.* **—get on:** *~ on the bus! She ~s on* (i.e. is friendly) *with everyone; old people ~ing on in years; Hot weather ~s on his nerves.* **—get out:** *quickly got out of town; The secret may ~ out.* **—get over:** *He can't ~ over* (i.e. forget) *her death.* **—get through** **1** finish. **2** survive. **3** establish communication: *couldn't ~ through to the operator.* **—get together** assemble; also, agree. **—get up** arise, esp. from bed. **—get·a·way** *n.* *Informal.* escape. **—get-to·geth·er** *n.* an informal social gathering.

Get·tys·burg a town in S. Pennsylvania, the site of a chief Civil War battle.

get-up *n.* costume: *wearing a bizarre ~;* **get-up-and-go** *Informal n.* ambition.

gew-gaw (GYOO–) *n.* a bauble or trinket.

gey·ser (GUY·zur) *n.* a spring that periodically ejects columns of hot water and steam.

G-force *n.* the force of gravity: *Astronauts encounter high ~s during blastoff and re-entry.*

Gha·na (GAH·nuh) a republic of W. Africa; 92,100 sq.mi. (238,537 km²); *cap.* Accra. **—Gha·na·ian** (gah·NAY·un) or **Gha·ni·an** (GAH·nee·un) *adj.* & *n.*

ghast·ly *adj.* **-li·er, -li·est** **1** terrifying, horrible; very unpleasant. **2** ghostlike; deathly; pale. **—ghast·li·ness** *n.*

gha(u)t (GAWT, GAHT) *n.* in India, a flight of steps leading down to a river landing.

gher·kin (GUR·kin) *n.* a variety of, or any small cucumber used for pickling.

ghet·to (GET·oh) *n.* **-to(e)s** a section of a city inhabited by a minority group prevented from living elsewhere by economic, legal, or social pressure. **—ghet·to·ize** *v.* **-iz·es, -ized, -iz·ing** restrict in or cause to become a ghetto.

ghost *n.* the spirit of a dead person, supposed to appear to the living as a pale, shadowy form; hence, a faint trance, suggestion, or shadow, as a secondary television or photographic image: *a candidate without a ~ of a chance; a deserted* **ghost town** *of the days of the gold rush;* **give up the ghost** die. **—v.** *Informal.* write (another person's autobiography, speech, etc.) for payment; also **ghost·write, -writes, -wrote, -writ·ten, -writ·ing; ghost·writ·er** *n.* **—ghost·ly** *adj.*

ghoul (GOOL) *n.* a legendary evil spirit that robs graves and feeds on the dead; **ghoul·ish** *adj.;* **ghoul·ish·ly** *adv.*

G.H.Q. General Headquarters.

g.i. or **G.I.** gastrointestinal; general issue; **gi.** gills (measure). **—GI** government issue (clothing, equipment, etc.); ***adj.*** of or issued by the U.S. military; conforming to military regulations: *a ~ haircut.* **—n.,** *pl.* **GI's** or **GIs** a U.S. serviceman, esp. an enlisted soldier.

gi·ant (JYE·unt) *n.* a huge, imaginary manlike being of enormous strength; hence, a person or thing of great size or powers: *General Motors is a corporate ~; the "San Francisco Giants."* — ***adj.:*** *California's ~ redwood trees; the long, zigzag ~ slalom in skiing.* **—gi·ant·ess** *n. fem.* **—gian·tism** same as GIGANTISM.

gib·ber (JIB·ur, GIB–) *v.* speak rapidly and unintelligibly; chatter. **—gib·ber·ish** (JIB–, GIB–) *n.* incoherent or meaningless talk.

gib·bet (JIB·it) *n.* a gallows. **—v.** **1** hang on a gibbet. **2** hold up to public ridicule.

gib·bon (GIB·un) *n.* a small, long-armed ape of S.E. Asia and the East Indies.

gib·bous (GIB·us) *adj.* **1** curved outward, protuberant; hence, humped or humpbacked. **2** of the moon or a planet, more than half full but less than a circle. **—gib·bous·ly** *adv.;* **gib·bous·ness** *adj.*

gibe (JIBE) *v.* **gibes, gibed, gib·ing** make jeering remarks; taunt; sneer; ***n.:*** *siblings trading ~s.* Also **jibe.**

gib·lets (JIB·lits) *n.pl.* the edible viscera of a fowl, as the heart, liver, or gizzard.

Gi·bral·tar (ji·BRAWL·tur) a British colony and fortress occupying 2.3 sq.mi. (6 km²) on a peninsula in S. Spain, consisting mostly of the **Rock of Gibraltar,** a limestone hill: *Gibraltar dominates the* **Strait of Gibraltar,** *a narrow waterway linking the Mediterranean with the Atlantic Ocean.*

Gib·son (GIB·sun) *n.* a dry martini garnished with a small onion.

gid·dy (GID·ee) *adj.* **gid·di·er, gid·di·est** having or causing dizziness; hence, frivolous or fickle: *climb to ~ heights; a ~ young flirt.* **—gid·di·ness** *n.*

gift *n.* **1** something given; a present; hence, natural ability or talent: *a million dollar ~ to charity; a ~ for drawing; advanced courses for* **gifted** (i.e. talented) *children.* **2** the act or power of giving: *a job within the mayor's ~.*

gig (GIG) *n.* **1** an open, two-wheeled, horse-drawn carriage. **2** a long, light ship's boat. **3** a fishing spear. **4** *Slang.* a job, esp. a one-time engagement for a jazz or rock musician. Also ***v.*** **gigs, gigged, gig·ging.**

giga- *comb.form.* one billion: as in **gi·ga·bit** (JIG·uh–) *n.* in computer processing, an informational unit of one billion bits. **—gi·gan·tic** (jye·GAN–) *adj.* giantlike; huge; immense; **gi·gan·tism** *n.* excessive growth of the body or of plants.

gig·gle (GIG·ul) *v.* **gig·gles, gig·gled, gig·gling** laugh in a silly or nervous way; ***n.:*** *gave a shrill ~ at the joke.* **—gig·gly** *adj.* **gig·gli·er, gig·gli·est.**

GI·GO (GUY–, GEE–) in computer language, "garbage in, garbage out"; worthless input results in worthless output.

gig·o·lo (JIG·uh·loh) *n.* **-los** a man paid as a woman's escort or lover.

Gi·la (HEE·luh) **monster** a large, black-and-orange poisonous lizard of S.W. United States.

gild *v.* **gilds,** *pt.* & *pp.* **gild·ed** or **gilt, gild·ing** cover with gold leaf or gold-colored material; hence, make deceptively attractive in appearance; **gild the lily** unnecessarily adorn something beautiful. ***—n.*** same as GUILD. **—gild·er** *n.* **—gild·ing** *n.*: *the ~ on a bracelet; a mere ~ of politeness.*

gill *n.* **1** an organ in fish, etc. for breathing in water. **2** (JIL) a ¼ pint liquid measure (0.-1183 L).

gilt a *pt.* & *pp.* of GILD; also ***adj. —n.*** same as GILDING. **—gilt-edge(d)** *adj.* of the highest quality: *~ securities are safe investments.*

gim·bals (GIM·bulz, JIM–) *n.pl.* a device for keeping a ship's compass, etc. horizontal by counteracting motion.

gim·crack (JIM–) *n.* a showy, worthless object; also ***adj.*** **—gim·crack·er·y** *n.*

gim·let *n.* **1** a small hole-boring hand tool with a screw point. **2** a cocktail of gin or vodka with lime juice, sugar, and carbonated water.

gim·mick *n.* an ingenious device, scheme, deception, or concealed condition: *a sports car equipped with the latest ~s.; pens given out as an advertising ~.* **—gim·mick·ry** *n.* **-ries. —gim·mick·y** *adj.*

gimp *n.* a lame person or walk; **gimp·y** *adj.*

gin (JIN) *n.* **1** a trap or snare; also a COTTON GIN; ***v.*** **gins, ginned, gin·ning** remove seeds from cotton. **2** an alcoholic liquor distilled from grain, flavored usu. with juniper berries.

gin·ger (JIN·jur) *n.* a tropical plant with a pungent rootstock used as a spice; also, the spice itself; hence, *Informal.* liveliness or spirit; **gin·ger·y** *adj.* **—ginger ale** a ginger-flavored carbonated soft drink. **—gin·ger·bread** *n.* **1** a ginger-flavored molasses cake. **2** gaudy or elaborate ornamentation. **—gin·ger·ly** *adv.* very carefully or cautiously; ***adj.:*** *in a ~ way.* **—gin·ger·snap** *n.* a crisp ginger-flavored molasses cookie.

ging·ham (GING·um) *n.* a yarn-dyed cotton fabric often designed in checks, stripes, or plaids.

gin·gi·vi·tis (jin·juh·VYE·tis) *n.* inflammation of the gums.

gink·go (GING·koh) *n.* **-goes** an Asian ornamental tree with fan-shaped leaves; also **ging·ko.**

gin·seng (JIN–) *n.* an herb of Asia and North America with an aromatic root used in medicine.

gip, Gipsy same as GYP, GYPSY.

gi·raffe (juh·RAF) *n.* a cud-chewing African animal with a very long neck and legs and a tawny, spotted coat.

gird *v.* **girds,** *pt.* & *pp.* **gird·ed** or **girt, gird·ing** **1** encircle with a belt; hence, surround: *~d with besiegers.* **2** fasten; equip; invest with; prepare: *His sword was ~d on; trousers ~d up with rope; ~ing himself for the blow.* **—gird (up) one's loins** prepare for action. **—gird·er** *n.* a main horizontal supporting beam. **—gir·dle** *n.* an encircling or confining band, esp. a woman's elasticized undergarment worn about the hips and waist; ***v.*** **-dles, -dled, -dling:** *a park ~d by trees.*

girl *n.* **1** a female child or a young unmarried woman. **2** a female servant. **3** a sweetheart or female companion; also, a girlfriend. **—girl·hood** *n.* **—girl·ish** *adj.* **—girl Friday** an efficient female (office) assistant with a variety of duties. **—girl·friend** *n. Informal.* a girl who is one's friend or sweetheart. **—gir·lie** (–lee) *adj. Slang.* of a magazine or show, displaying nude women. **—girl scout** a member of the **Girl Scouts** of America, a character-building youth organization.

girt **1** a *pt.* & *pp.* of GIRD. **2** *v.* put a girdle around; gird. **—girth** *n.* **1** the measurement around something; circumference. **2** a band around an animal's body to hold a saddle or pack on its back.

gis·mo (GIZ–) *n.* same as GIZMO.

gist (JIST) *n.* the essential or main point: *the ~ of an argument.*

give (GIV) *v.* **gives, gave, giv·en, giv·ing** **1** hand over: *I gave her a book; ~s often to charity; How much can he ~* (i.e. as price) *for the car?* **2** let have: *gave him the benefit of the doubt; ~ the devil his due.* **3** present; provide: *~ing a party; Concerts are ~n here.* **4** devote: *has ~n his life* *to the cause.* **5** produce: *Cows ~ milk.* **6** yield: *The lock gave under pressure.* **7** afford a view; open: *The windows ~ onto the yard.* ***—n.*** a yielding under pressure; elasticity: *a concrete walk has no ~.* **—giv·er** *n.* **—give away** **1** give as a gift. **2** present a bride to the groom. **3** reveal: *Don't ~ away the secret.* **—give in** yield: *forced to ~ in to her demands.* **—give it to** *Informal.* scold or beat. **—give out** **1** distribute or make known. **2** wear out; break down; become exhausted. **—give to understand** cause to understand; assure. **—give up** **1** surrender; devote. **2** stop doing, trying, or hoping: *~ up smoking.* **—give way** See WAY. **—give-and-take** *n.* a fair exchange, esp. of ideas or remarks; banter. **—give·a·way** *n.* **1** an unintentional revelation. **2** something given away without charge. **—giv·en** *adj.* **1** specified: *on a ~ date.* **2** assumed. **3** habitually disposed: *~ to staying up late.* **—given name** first name; name given to a person, as at baptism, besides his surname or family name. **—give-up** *n.* a stock-market practice in which a financial institution orders a broker to yield part of his commission to another broker.

giz·mo *n.* **-mos** *Slang.* a device or gadget.

giz·zard (GIZ·urd) *n.* the food-grinding second stomach of a bird.

Gk. Greek.

gla·brous (GLAY·brus) *adj.* hairless; smooth.

gla·cé (gla·SAY) *adj.* candied or frozen; also, glossy; glazed.

gla·cial (GLAY·shul) *adj.* **1** relating to glaciers or to a **glacial epoch,** a period, as the Ice Age, when much of the earth was covered by glaciers. **2** very cold; **gla·cial·ly** *adv.* **—gla·ci·ate** (GLAY·shee–) *v.* **-ates, -at·ed, -at·ing** act on or cover with ice or glaciers; **gla·ci·a·tion** (–AY–) *n.* **—gla·ci·ol·o·gy** (–OL–) *n.* the scientific study of glaciers; **gla·ci·ol·o·gist** *n.* **—gla·cier** (–shur) *n.* a huge body of ice slowly moving downhill or spreading across land.

¹glad *n. Informal.* gladiolus.

²glad *adj.* **glad·der, glad·dest** causing or feeling joy or pleasure; pleased: *a ~ occasion; ~ to hear the good news; I'm ~ to help;* **glad·ly** *adv.;* **glad·ness** *n.* **—glad·den** (GLADN) *v.* make or become glad.

glade *n.* an open space in a forest.

glad hand a jovial, often insincere greeting; **glad-hand** *v.*

glad·i·a·tor (GLAD·ee·ay·tur) *n.* a man trained to fight for public entertainment in ancient Rome; **glad·i·a·to·ri·al** (–TOR–) *adj.* **—glad·i·o·lus** (–OH–) *n., pl.* **-li** (–lye) or **-lus·es** a plant of the Iris family with sword-shaped leaves and spikes of brightly colored flowers. Also **glad·i·o·la** (–OH·luh).

glad·some *adj.* joyful; cheerful; delightful; **glad·some·ly** *adv.*

Glad·stone (bag) a small hinged suitcase that opens into two equal compartments.

glam·o(u)r (GLAM·ur) *n.* alluring charm, romance, or excitement. **—glam·o(u)r·ous** (–uh·rus) *adj.* **—glam·o(u)r·ize** *v.* **-iz·es, -ized, -iz·ing** make glamorous; idealize; **glam·o(u)r·i·za·tion** (–ZAY–) *n.*

glance *v.* **glanc·es, glanced, glanc·ing** strike and be deflected obliquely; hence, look quickly; flash or gleam with light: *a ~ing blow; She ~d at us as we passed by.* ***—n.:*** *Saw what was going on with a ~ through the window; the ~ of swords in the sun.*

gland *n.* an organ such as the liver or pancreas that produces a fluid, as bile, milk, or sweat, for use in or elimination from the body. **—glandes** *pl.* of GLANS. **—glan·du·lar** (GLAN·juh·lur) *adj.*: *Mononucleosis is "~ fever."*

glans (–z) *n., pl.* **glan·des** (–deez) the tip of the penis or of the clitoris.

glare *v.* **glares, glared, glar·ing** **1** shine with a harsh, painfully bright light. **2** stare angrily or fiercely. ***—n.:*** *the ~ of a headlight in his eyes; shot a ~ of hatred at him.* **—glar·ing** *adj.: ~ neon lights; immediately noticed the ~* (i.e. conspicuous) *error;* **glar·ing·ly** *adv.*

Glas·gow (GLAS·goh, –coh) the largest city and a port of S.W. Scotland.

glas·phalt (–fawlt) *n.* a road-paving material of asphalt combined with crushed glass. **—glass** *n.* **1** a hard, brittle, usu. transparent substance made by melting sand with lime, potash, etc. **2** an object made of glass: *milk served in a ~; The ~* (i.e. mirror) *reflected his face; saw the moon through a ~* (i.e. telescope); **glasses** *n.pl.* eyeglasses or binoculars. **3** the amount contained in a drinking glass: *Have a ~ of milk;* also **glass·ful** *n.* **glass·fuls.** ***—adj.*** made of glass. **—glass blowing** the art of forming molten glass into an object by blowing air into it through a tube; **glass blower. —glass·ware** *n.* glass objects. **—glass wool** glass spun into fibers like wool and used for filtering and insulation. **—glass·y** *adj.* **glass·i·er, -i·est** **1** like glass; smooth. **2** lifeless; expressionless: *an idiot's ~ stare;* **glass·i·ly** *adv.*

glau·coma (glaw·COH·muh) *n.* an eye disease in which pressure within the eyeball results in retinal damage and gradual loss of vision.

glaze *v.* **glaz·es, glazed, glaz·ing** **1** provide a window frame, etc. with glass. **2** cover pottery or food with a smooth, glossy surface. ***—n.:*** *a ~ of ice on the pond; Hot water dulled the china's ~.* **—gla·zier** (GLAY·zhur) *n.* one who fits windows, etc. with glass.

gleam (GLEEM) *n.* a brief flash or dim glow of light; hence, a brief or faint show: *a mere ~ of hope.* ***—v.:*** *A fire ~ed in the dark; eyes momentarily ~ing with humor.* **—gleam·y** *adj.*

glean (GLEEN) *v.* pick up the grain left by reapers; hence, gather (facts or news) bit by bit; **glean·er** *n.;* **glean·ings** *n.pl.* things collected by gleaning.

glebe (GLEEB) *n.* a piece of land forming part of a clerical benefice.

glee *n.* **1** merriment; lively delight. **2** an unaccompanied song for three or more different singing voices; **glee club** a group organized for singing choral songs or part-songs. —**glee·ful** *adj.* —**glee·man** *n.* **-men** *Archaic.* minstrel.

glen *n.* a narrow valley. —**Glen·dale** a city of S.W. California, near Los Angeles. —**glen·gar·ry** (-gair·ee) *n.* **-gar·ries** a woolen bonnet or cap, originally from Glengarry, Scotland, typical of Highlanders.

glib *adj.* **glib·ber, glib·best** smooth and fluent, often in an insincere way: *unconvinced by her ~ excuses;* **glib·ly** *adv.;* **glib·ness** *n.*

glide *v.* **glides, glid·ed, glid·ing** **1** move along smoothly and with ease. **2** descend (in a plane) without using the engine. —***n.:*** *the prone ~ and back ~ in swimming; saw the plane's long ~.* —**glid·er** *n.* a person or thing that glides, esp. an engineless aircraft kept aloft by air currents; also, a swinging porch seat suspended in a frame.

glim·mer *v.* give a weak, flickering light; hence, appear dimly. —***n.:*** *a ~ of distant candlelight; story without even a ~ of truth.*

glimpse (GLIMPS) *v.* **glimps·es, glimpsed, glimps·ing** see or look at briefly and hastily. —***n.:*** *caught a ~ of the speeding car.*

glint *n.* a flash or gleam of light; hence, a brief appearance. —***v.:*** *Light ~ed from the crystal glasses.*

glis·san·do (gli·SAHN·doh) *adj.* & *adv.* performed musically by gliding quickly up or down the scale. —***n.,*** *pl.* **-di** (-dee) or **-dos** a part played in this way.

glis·ten (GLIS·un) *v.* shine brightly by reflecting light; sparkle: *Dew ~ed on the grass;* also ***n.*** —**glis·ter** *v. Archaic.* glisten.

glitch *n.* an unwanted surge of electricity or a false electronic signal; hence, *Slang.* a minor mishap or malfunction.

glit·ter *v.* shine brightly with a flashing light; sparkle; hence, be showy or attractive. —***n.:*** *the ~ of diamonds; a circus parade's ~; decorate costumes with ~* (i.e. small, shiny objects). —**glit·ter·y** *adj.*

gloam·ing (GLOH·ming) *n.* twilight.

gloat (GLOTE) *v.* take pleasure in a greedy, selfish, or sadistic manner: *thieves ~ing over their loot; to ~ over a rival's misfortune.*

glob *n.* a drop or globule; also, a rounded lump. —**glob·al** (GLOH·bl) *adj.* of the whole earth; worldwide; hence, all-inclusive; **glob·al·ism** *n.* internationalism, esp. in plans or outlook; **glo·bal·ly** *adv.* —**globe** *n.* anything spherical, esp. the earth or a model of it; also, a nearly round glass object, as a fishbowl; **globe·trot** *v.* **-trots, trot·ted, -trot·ting** travel all over the world; **globe·trot·ter** *n.* —**glob·u·lar** (GLOB·yuh·lur) *adj.* **1** spherical. **2** composed of globules. —**glob·ule** *n.* a tiny ball or drop. —**glob·u·lin** *n.* a protein in plant seeds, blood plasma, etc. that is soluble in dilute salt solutions but not in pure water.

glock·en·spiel (-speel) *n.* a percussion instrument of tuned metal bars played with light hammers and sounding like bells.

gloom *n.* darkness or dimness; hence, a dejected or depressed state of mind or atmosphere: *a melancholy feeling of ~; the ~ of the old graveyard.* —**gloom·y** *adj.* **gloom·i·er, -i·est; gloom·i·ly** *adv.;* **gloom·i·ness** *n.*

glop *n. Slang.* a liquid or viscous mixture, esp. unappetizing food; hence, anything tasteless, worthless, or corny.

glo·ri·fy *v.* **-fies, -fied, -fy·ing** **1** give praise, honor, worship, or glory to; also, exalt to heaven: *a martyr ~d after death.* **2** make something seem more splendid than it actually is. —**glo·ri·fi·ca·tion** (-CAY-) *n.* —**glo·ri·fi·er** *n.* —**glo·ri·ous** *adj.* **1** having, giving, or deserving glory: *the ~ Fourth of July.* **2** magnificent; delightful: *~ fall weather; had a ~ time at the party;* **glo·ri·ous·ly** *adv.* —**glo·ry** *n.* **-ries** **1** great honor, fame, or praise, esp. of God. **2** the source of renown; splendor; magnificence; prosperity: *Long hair was her ~; the ~ of ancient Greece.* **3** heavenly bliss: *a painting of saints in ~;* **in one's glory** in a state of great joy, gratification, etc. —***v.*** **-ries, -ried, -ry·ing** rejoice proudly; exalt.

¹gloss *n.* a commentary on, a brief note within, or a translation of a text; ***v.*** explain or annotate. —**glos·sa·ry** (-uh·ree) *n.* **-ries** a short dictionary of difficult or technical words; **glos·sar·i·al** (-SAIR·ee·ul) *adj.* —**glos·so·la·li·a** (-LAY·lee·uh) *n.* unintelligible, meaningless speech occurring in religious ecstasy and schizophrenia.

²gloss *n.* a shiny surface; luster; hence, a deceptive appearance; ***v.*** **gloss over** try to ignore or hide: *The report ~es over his faults.* —**gloss·y** *adj.* **gloss·i·er, -i·est** having a lustrous surface; ***n.,*** *pl.* **gloss·ies** a magazine or photograph printed on smooth, shiny paper; **gloss·i·ly** *adv.;* **gloss·i·ness** *n.*

glot·tis *n.* **glot·tis·es** or **glot·ti·des** the narrow space in the larynx between the vocal cords. —**glot·tal** *adj.: "Button" has a ~ "t" sound.*

glove (GLUV) *n.* a fitted hand covering with separated fingers; also, a large, padded leather covering used on the hand in baseball, boxing, etc. —***v.*** **gloves, gloved, glov·ing:** *warmly ~d for the winter.*

glow (GLOH) *v.* **1** shine brightly and steadily because or as though intensely heated. **2** have a bright, reddish color; flush or blush. **3** show warm emotion: *~ing with pride for his son.* —***n.:*** *the ~ of burning coal; a ruddy ~ of health on her cheeks; felt a ~ of love.*

glow·er (GLOU·ur) *v.* stare angrily or sullenly; ***n.*** a scowl.

glow•worm (GLOH–) *n.* an insect or insect larva that emits light, esp. a firefly.

glox•in•i•a (glok·SIN·ee·uh) *n.* a tropical American plant with velvety leaves and bell-shaped red, white, or purple flowers.

gloze *v.* **gloz•es, glozed, gloz•ing** gloss over or extenuate.

glu•cose (GLOO–) *n.* a sugar occurring naturally in animals and plants, esp. fruits, used by cells for energy; also, a syrup made from starch and used to sweeten food.

glue (GLOO) *n.* a sticky substance used to join things, esp. one made from animal gelatin; ***v.*** **glues, glued, glu•ing:** *a broken cup ~d together.* **—glue•y** *adj.* **glu•i•er, -i•est.**

glum *adj.* **glum•mer, glum•mest** gloomy; sullen; morose; **glum•ly** *adv.;* **glum•ness** *n.*

glut *v.* **gluts, glut•ted, glut•ting** fill or feed to excess; satiate; hence, oversupply (a market): *a long trip to ~ his appetite for travel.* ***—n.:*** *There seems a ~ of cookbooks on the market.*

glu•ten (GLOO·tn) *n.* a sticky, elastic mixture of proteins found in grain; **glu•ten•ous** *adj.* **—glu•ti•nous** *adj.* sticky; gluey.

glut•ton *n.* a person who overeats or one who has an inordinate capacity for something: *a ~ for work;* **glut•ton•ous** *adj.;* **glut•ton•ous•ly** *adv.* **—glut•ton•y** *n.* **glut•ton•ies.**

gly•cer•in(e) (GLIS·uh·rin) *n.* a thick, sweet, clear liquid made from fats and oils and used in lubricants, foods, and explosives; also **gly•cer•ol** (GLIS·uh·rol). **—gly•co•gen** (GLYE·cuh·jun) *n.* a carbohydrate made and stored chiefly in the liver and converted into glucose when needed. **—gly•col** (GLYE–) *n.* same as ETHYLENE GLYCOL. **—gly•co•side** (GLYE·cuh–) *n.* any compound yielding sugar on hydrolysis; **gly•co•sid•ic** (–SID–) *adj.*

gm. gram(s); **G.M.** general manager; grand master.

Gmc. Germanic.

G-man *n., pl.* **G-men** an F.B.I. agent.

G.M.T. Greenwich mean time.

gnarl (NARL) *n.* a twisted, protruding knot on a tree. **—gnarled** (NARLD) or **gnarl•y** *adj.* knotty; misshapen.

gnash (NASH) *v.* grind together: *~ing his teeth in rage.*

gnat (NAT) *n.* any tiny, winged, usu. biting insect.

gnaw (NAW) *v.* consume, corrode, or produce by biting; hence, torment: *a dog ~ing a bone; Mice ~ holes; Remorse ~ed at his heart.* **—gnaw•er** *n.*

gneiss (NICE) *n.* a coarse-grained rock made of layers of minerals, usu. quartz, feldspar, and mica.

gnome (NOME) *n.* a dwarf of folklore who lives underground and guards treasures of precious ores. **—gnom•ish** *adj.*

gno•to•bi•ol•o•gy (noh·toh·bye·OL–) or **gno•to•bi•ot•ics** (–OT–) *n.* [takes *sing. v.*] the study of animals raised in a gnotobiotic environment; **gno•to•bi•ot•ic** (–OT–) *adj.* free of germs or containing only known germs. **—gno•to•bi•ol•o•gist** (–OL–) *n.*

GNP gross national product.

gnu (NEW) *n.* a large, horned African antelope with high, massive shoulders.

go *v.* **goes** (GOZE), **went, gone** (GAWN, GON), **go•i•ng** **1** move or pass (away from the speaker); also, move or pass on; be active: *You can ~ now; The machine ~s when you switch it on; a rumor ~ing through town; another year to ~ before I retire; My eyesight is ~ing* (i.e. weakening). **2** move or tend (*to* someone or something): *You shouldn't have gone to such trouble for me; $5 will not ~ far* (i.e. purchase much at today's prices); *evidence that ~s to prove he was wrong; She had to ~ to court to establish her claim.* **3** be, become, or be put (in a certain way or condition): *Where will this sofa ~? She will ~ mad when she hears this; Many ~ hungry all over the world; How did the interview ~? The cork went pop.* —Fans are **going ape** (*Slang.* crazy) *over that star; She* **goes at** *everything she takes up with energy; He would never* **go back on** (i.e. break) *a promise; The project* **went by the board** (i.e. was abandoned) *when the director died; The governor said if he pardoned too many criminals, the people wouldn't* **go for it;** *What's* **going on** (i.e. happening) *in there? She decided to* **go it** (i.e. act) **alone** *when no help could be got; The competition tried to* **go one better** (i.e. excel) *by cutting prices; Many businesses* **go under** (i.e. fail) *during each recession; The child wouldn't* **let go** (i.e. release) *of her mother's hand; A very reserved man at work, he* **lets himself go** *during office parties.* — ***n.*** *Informal: He will have another ~* (i.e. attempt) *at the top prize next year; It was* **no go** (i.e. failure) *each time he applied for membership; vitamins for people* **on the go** (i.e. active) *from 9 to 5.* ***—adj.*** *Informal: All systems are ~* (i.e. in perfect order) *for the blastoff.*

GO general order.

goad (GODE) *n.* a pointed rod used to urge animals forward; hence, a driving impulse. — ***v.:*** *students ~ed to activity by approaching examinations.*

go-a•head (–uh·hed) *n.* *Informal.* permission; signal: *waiting for the leader's ~.*

goal (GOLE) *n.* a desired aim, attained after some effort; hence, in a race or in games such as football and hockey, the place to be reached for winning or scoring; also, such a score: *the ~ of one's ambition; scored two ~s in one minute.* **—goal•ie** (–ee), **goal•keep•er** or **goal•tend•er** *n.* a player who defends the goal against the opposing team. **—goal post** one of a pair of posts marking the goal in hockey, soccer, lacrosse, etc.

goat (GOTE) *n.* **1** a cud-chewing, horned, and usu. bearded animal related to but stronger than sheep; **get one's goat** *Informal.* annoy or irritate one. **2** *Informal.* a scapegoat. **—goat•ee** (–TEE) *n.* a small, pointed beard on a man's chin. —**goat·herd** *n.* one who tends goats. —**goat·skin** *n.* (a container of) leather made from a goat's skin.

gob *n.* **1** *Slang.* a sailor in the U.S. Navy. **2** *Informal.* a lump or mass; also **gob·bet** (–bit). —**gob·ble** *v.* **gob·bles, gob·bled, gob·bling 1** swallow greedily: *food ~d up in a hurry.* **2** make the throaty sound of a male turkey, or **gob·bler.** —**gob·ble·dy·gook** (–dee·GOOK) *n. Informal.* speech or writing that is in comprehensible or meaningless because of its pompous or involved style; also **gob·ble·de·gook.**

go-be·tween (GO·bi–) *n.* an intermediary or messenger between two parties.

Go·bi (GOH·bee) an Asian desert, lying mostly in Mongolia; 500,000 sq. mi. (1.3 million km^2).

gob·let (–lit) *n.* a bowl-shaped drinking cup with a stem and foot but no handles.

gob·lin *n.* a mischievous elf or sprite of folklore.

go-cart *n.* a small, low-slung toy wagon; also, a kart.

god *n.* **1** a supreme being considered as supernatural and immortal; also, a male deity or idol; **God** the creator and ruler of the universe for those who believe in one supreme being. **2** a deified person or thing. —**god·child** *n.* **-chil·dren** one sponsored by a godparent, as at baptism; a **god·daugh·ter** or **god·son.** —**god·dam(n)** *n., adj. & v.,* **god·damned** or **god·dam(n)** *adj. & adv.* stronger forms of DAMN. —**god·dess** (–is) *n.* a female god. —**god·fa·ther** (–fah–) *n.* a man who sponsors a person at baptism. —**god·for·sak·en** (–SAY·cun) *adj.* desolate; dismal; miserable. —**god·head** (–hed) *n.* divinity; also **god·hood; Godhead** God.

Go·di·va (–DYE·vuh) a legendary woman of Coventry, England, who rode naked through the streets on a horse to get a tax abolished.

god·less *adj.* not religious; also, wicked; **god·less·ness** *n.* —**god·ly** (–lee) *adj.* **-li·er, -li·est** of or from God; also, pious or devoted to God; **god·li·ness** *n.* —**god·moth·er** *n.* a woman sponsoring a person at baptism. —**god·par·ent** *n.* a godfather or godmother. —**god·send** *n.* something much-needed or desired that one gets as if sent by God. —**god·son** See GODCHILD. —**God·speed** (–SPEED) *n.* success: *to bid* (or *wish*) *one ~.*

Goe·the (GUR·tuh), **Johann Wolfgang von.** 1749–1832, German poet.

go·fer (GOH·fur) *n. Slang.* one who fetches things for another. —**go-get·ter** *n. Informal.* one who is aggressively ambitious.

gog·gle *v.* **gog·gles, gog·gled, gog·gling** stare with bulging or surprised eyes (at something); **gog·gle-eyed** *adj.: The ~ audience never took their eyes off her; a ~ fish.* —**gog·gles** *n.pl.* large protective eyeglasses as worn by motorcyclists and divers.

go-go *n.* a discotheque; also, discotheque dancing. —***adj.:*** *a topless ~ dancer cavorting on the stage; the ~* (i.e. unrestrained) *pace of 20th c. life; a ~* (i.e. speculative) *investment fund; a very ~* (i.e. stylish) *jacket and slacks.*

go·ing *n.: the coming and ~ of winter; It was hard ~ driving up that hill.* —***adj.:*** *a ~ concern* (i.e. smoothly running business); *The best candidate ~* (i.e. available) *is employed with the competition; The ~* (i.e. prevailing) *rate for this job is $20 an hour; a lucky young man who has many things* **going for** (i.e. in favor of) *him; It's* **going to** *get colder as the days go by.* —**go·ing-o·ver** *n.* a thorough examination; also, a scolding or beating. —**go·ings-on** *n.pl. Informal. The ~ in that house were the talk of the town.*

goi·ter or **goi·tre** (GOY·tur) *n.* a thyroid disorder resulting in an abnormal swelling in the front of the neck; **goi·trous** (–trus) *adj.*

gold *n.* a bright-yellow precious metallic element used for jewelry and as an international monetary standard; hence, money; also, bright yellow color. —**gold·beat·er** *n.* one who beats gold into gold leaf. —**gold·brick(·er)** *n. Milit. Slang.* one who shirks work; loafer. —**gold digger** *Slang.* a woman who uses her charms to get money from men. —**gold·en** *adj.* **1** very valuable; also, bright yellow. **2** excellent; also, prosperous; flourishing: *the ~ age of poetry; a ~* (i.e. 50th year) *jubilee;* **golden ag·er** (–AY·jur) *Informal.* a person over 65 years old. —**golden calf** in the Bible, an idol worshiped by the Israelites; hence, wealth as an object of worship. —**Golden Fleece** in Greek myth, a fleece of gold recovered by Jason and the Argonauts from a dragon guarding it. —**Golden Gate** the strait through which you enter San Francisco Bay from the Pacific. —**gold·en·rod** *n.* a common wildflower of the composite family with slender stems like wands, blooming in late summer with golden yellow flowers. —**golden rule** a basic rule of conduct, esp. the one that says, "Treat others as you would like them to treat you." —**gold·field** *n.* a district in which gold is mined. —**gold·filled** *adj.* esp. of jewelry, with a gold layer over base metal. —**gold·finch** *n.* a common songbird whose male is bright yellow with a black patch on its head. —**gold·fish** *n.* any of scores of fancy varieties of a type of carp with bright colors ranging from gold to red, kept in glass bowls as ornamental fish. —**gold·smith** *n.* a worker skilled in making articles of gold; also, a dealer in them. —**gold standard** a system by which a country's basic money unit is made equal to and exchangeable for a specified amount of gold.

golf (GOLF, GAWLF) *n.* a game played with a small, hard ball and long-handled **golf clubs** on an outdoor **golf course** (or **links**) having a series of 9 or 18 holes, each with a tee, fairway, putting green, and one or more hazards, the players trying to hit the ball into the holes with as few strokes as possible. —*v.* play golf; **golf•er** *n.*

Go•li•ath (guh·LYE·uth) in the Bible, a Philistine giant killed by David.

gol•ly (GOL·ee) *interj.* expressing surprise, pleasure, etc.

-gon *comb.form.* a figure with (so many) angles: as in *pentagon, octagon, polygon.*

go•nad (GOH–) *n.* a male or female sex gland; an ovary or a testis; **go•na•do•trop(h)•in** (–nad·uh·TROH·pin, –fin) *n.* a hormone that regulates the gonads; **go•na•do•trop(h)•ic** (–TROP·ic, –TROF·ic) *adj.*

gon•do•la (–duh·luh) *n.* a long, narrow boat with peaked prow and stern, used on the canals of Venice, rowed or poled by a **gon•do•lier** (–LEER); hence, something resembling a gondola such as an enclosed suspended car used as a ski lift, a car suspended from under an airship, a low-sided open-topped railroad car, or **gondola car,** for bulk freight such as coal, the whirling compartment of a centrifuge machine used for astronaut training, etc.

gone *pp.* of GO. **1:** *I'll be* ~ (i.e. away) *for three days in Chicago; something too* **far gone** (i.e. in too poor a condition) *to be put right.* **2** *Informal: He wore a* ~ (i.e. removed from reality) *expression; He's quite* **gone on** (i.e. in love with) *her.* —**gon•er** *n. Informal.* a person or thing beyond help: *One glance from her and you're a* ~*!*

gon•fa•lon (–fuh·lon, –lun) *n.* a flag or standard suspended from a crosspiece, as some church banners.

gong *n.* a large metal disk that is struck for use as a bell or as a musical instrument.

gon•o•coc•cus (–COC·us) *n., pl.* **-coc•ci** (–COC·sye) the germ that causes gonorrhea; **gon•o•coc•cal** *adj.* —**gon•or•rh(o)ea** (–uh·REE·uh) *n.* a veneral disease usu. transmitted during sexual intercourse; **gon•or•rh(o)e•al** (–REE·ul) *adj.*

goo *n. Slang.* anything thick and sticky, as glue; hence, sentimentality; **goo•ey** *adj.*

goo•ber *n. Informal. Southern.* a peanut.

good *adj., comp.* **bet•ter,** *superl.* **best** having a desirable quality: *Rain is* ~ *for crops, not for a game of football;* $2 + 2 = 4$ **holds good** (i.e. is valid) *under all conditions; She's been away a* ~ (i.e. considerable) *while; so tired I'm* **as good as** (i.e. almost) *dead; a round-trip ticket* **good for** *a year; This pen is* **no good** (i.e. useless). —***n.:*** *The laws work for the common* ~*; What* ~ *is food you can't eat?* **goods** *n.pl.* movable personal property; also, merchandise; things for sale; **have the goods on** *Slang.* know something incriminating about; *freed on condition he would leave the country* **for good (and all)** (i.e. forever); *Good advice, well taken, works* **to our good.** —***adv.*** *Informal: can't see* ~ (i.e. well) *through the fog; It's raining* **good and** (i.e. really) *heavy; Unsuccessful throughout life, he* **made good** (i.e. succeeded) *only by marrying a wealthy widow.* —**good-by(e)** or **good•by(e)** *interj.* farewell; also ***n.,*** *pl.* **-bys** or **-byes.** —**good-for-noth•ing** *n.* & *adj.* (one who is) worthless or disreputable. —**Good Friday** the Friday before Easter, commemorating Christ's crucifixion. —**good-heart•ed** *adj.* kind and generous. —**Good Hope, Cape of.** the cape at the S. tip of Africa; also, a province of South Africa. —**good•ish** *adj.* fairly good, great, or large. —**good-look•ing** *adj.* handsome or pretty. —**good•ly** (–lee) *adj.* **-li•er, -li•est** excellent; good-looking; considerable: *a* ~ *sum of money.* —**good•man** (–mun) *n. Archaic.* the master of a household; "Mister." —**good-na•tured** (–nay·churd) *adj.* likable or friendly; **good-na•tured•ly** *adv.* —**good•ness** *n.* the condition or quality of being good, esp. morally: *For goodness' sake stop complaining.* —**Good Sa•mar•i•tan** (-suh·MAIR·i·tn) one who takes pity on another in misery and aids him unselfishly. —**good-tem•pered** *adj.* not easily annoyed; good-humored. —**good turn** a good deed or favor. —**good•wife** *n.* **-wives** *Archaic.* the mistress of a household; "Mrs." —**good will** friendly feeling; also, the reputation enjoyed by a business that is valued with its assets; also **good•will; goodwill industries** organizations working for the handicapped, helped by Goodwill Industries of America, Inc. —**good•y** *n.* **good•ies** *Informal.* something good, esp. to eat; ***adj.*** affectedly pious or moral; ***interj.*** a child's exclamation indicating delight; **good•y-good•y** *n.* & *adj.* (one who is) affectedly or abjectly good.

goof *Slang. n.* **1** blunder. **2** a stupid person. —***v.:*** *Somebody* ~*ed and the invitations never got mailed; comes home late after* **goofing around** (i.e. wasting time) *all evening; fired for* **goofing off** (i.e. loafing) *on the job;* **goof-off** *n.* shirker. —**goof•ball** *n. Slang.* a barbiturate, stimulant, tranquilizer, etc. used nonmedically. —**goof•y** *adj.* **goof•i•er, -i•est** silly or crazy.

goo•gol *n.* 1 followed by 100 zeroes; **goo•gol•plex** *n.* 10 multiplied by itself googol times.

gook *n. Slang.* **1** something sticky or slimy. **2** [disparaging term] a native, esp. of an Oriental country.

goon *n. Slang.* a ruffian, esp. one hired to break up strikes, help prison guards, etc.; also, a stupid person.

goop *n. Slang.* something sticky and semiliquid.

goose *n.* **1** *pl.* **geese** a web-footed bird that is larger than a duck and smaller than a swan, to which it is related; the female of the gander and a supposedly stupid bird. **2** *pl.* **goos•es** a tailor's smoothing iron with a curved **goose•neck** handle; **cook one's goose** See COOK. —**goose•ber•ry** *n.* **-ber•ries** the small, oval, tart fruit of a thorny shrub related to the currant, commonly used in preserves and pies. **—goose·flesh** *n.* a skin condition resembling a plucked goose's skin caused by cold, fear, etc.; also **goose·bumps, goose pimples.**

G.O.P. "Grand Old Party" (the U.S. Republican Party).

go·pher (GOH·fur) *n.* any of a group of burrowing rodents with large cheek pouches; "pocket gopher"; also, a ground squirrel of the prairies related to the chipmunk.

Gor·di·an (–dee·un) **knot** something intricate like the knot tied by the legendary Gordius, king of Phrygia, and cut by Alexander the Great; **cut the Gordian knot** end a perplexity with a quick, bold stroke.

gore *n.* **1** clotted blood. **2** a long, triangular or wedge-shaped piece of cloth inserted in a garment, sail, etc. to adjust width or shape. —***v.*** **gores, gored, gor·ing** pierce or wound with a horn or tusk.

gorge (GORJ) *n.* **1** a narrow canyon with steep walls. **2** what has been swallowed: *a murder so gruesome it* **makes one's gorge** *rise.* **3** a mass, as of ice, choking a passage. —***v.*** **gorg·es, gorged, gorg·ing** stuff with food: *children at a party ~ing themselves with cake.* **—gor·geous** (GOR·jus) *adj.* splendid, esp. in a colorful way; **gor·geous·ly** *adv.;* **gor·geous·ness** *n.*

Gor·gon·zo·la (–ZOH·luh) *n.* a white Italian cheese with a strong flavor.

go·ril·la (guh·RIL·uh) *n.* an African ape, the largest of the anthropoids; hence, *Slang.* a man resembling a gorilla in strength or size.

Gor·ki (GOR·kee) a large industrial city on the Volga, named after **Maxim Gorki,** 1868–1936, Russian novelist and playwright.

gor·mand·ize (–mun·dize) *v.* **-iz·es, -ized, -iz·ing** eat like a glutton; **gor·mand·iz·er** *n.*

gorse same as FURZE.

gor·y *adj.* **gor·i·er, -i·est** bloody; hence, horrible; **gor·i·ly** *adv.;* **gor·i·ness** *n.*

gosh *interj.* an exclamation of surprise: *by ~ !* (by God).

gos·hawk *n.* the largest of a group of swift-flying hawks once used in falconry. **—gos·ling** (–GOZ–) *n.* a young goose.

gos·pel (–pl) *n.* truth accepted without question, esp. **gospel truth,** as from the Christian **Gospels,** the first four books of the New Testament; also, Christianity: *to preach the Gospel to the Indians;* **gos·pel·(l)er** *n.* a gospel preacher.

gos·sa·mer (GOS·uh·mur) *n.* & *adj.* light and filmy (substance as of cobwebs seen floating in the air or sheer fabric resembling it).

gos·sip *n.* idle talk about people and their usu. private affairs; also, a person who indulges in this; ***v.:*** *People start ~ing when an unwed girl becomes pregnant.* **—gos·sip·y** *adj.*

got *pt.* & *pp.* of GET; **have got** *Informal: Have you got* (i.e. do you have) *a match? I* **have (got) to** (i.e. must) *go home now.*

Goth *n.* a member of a Germanic people that overran the Roman Empire in the 3rd, 4th, and 5th c. A.D.; hence, a barbarian. **—Goth·ic** *n.* & *adj.* **1** (the E. Germanic language) of the Goths. **2** (having to do with) a style of architecture developed in Europe in the Middle Ages. **3** (having to do with a style of) fiction dealing with the supernatural and the grotesque.

got·ta (GOT·uh) *Informal.* "have got to." See GOT. **—got·ten** a *pp.* of GET, except in **has** (or **have) got** See GOT.

Gou·da (cheese) (GOW·duh, GOO–) a flat, round cheese similar to Edam but with more fat.

gouge (GOWJ) *n.* a chisel with a concave blade for cutting grooves and holes; also, a channel or hole made with a gouge. —***v.*** **goug·es, gouged, goug·ing** **1** dig or scoop out, as with a gouge: *Torturers ~d out his eyes.* **2** *Informal.* extort money from: *a retailer charged with (price) ~ing;* **goug·er** *n.*

gou·lash (GOO–) *n.* a highly seasoned stew of meat and vegetables.

gourd (GORD, GOORD) *n.* the fruit of a vine such as the cucumber, pumpkin, or squash; also, a related but inedible, hard-shelled fruit such as the calabash that is dried for use as a container.

gourde (GOORD) *n.* the basic money unit and a coin of Haiti worth 100 centimes.

gour·mand (GOOR·mund, –mahnd) *n.* a lover of good food and wine. **—gour·met** (GOOR·may) *n.* a discriminating expert of food and drink: *an expensive ~ restaurant featuring specialties.*

gout (GOWT) *n.* a metabolic disease caused by excess of uric acid and characterized by swelling of the joints, esp. that of the big toe; **gout·y** *adj.* **gout·i·er, -i·est:** *~ arthritis;* **gout·i·ness** *n.*

gov. or **Gov.** government; governor.

gov·ern (GUV·urn) *v.* control or regulate: *a college's ~ing body; learn to ~ your temper; conduct ~ed by Christian principles; the British Sovereign merely reigns and does not ~; supply and demand ~ing prices; "to" ~s "him," not "he";* **gov·ern·a·ble** *adj.;* **gov·ern·ance** (–unce) *n.* **—gov·ern·ess** (–is) *n.* a woman who teaches and supervises children in their home. **—gov·ern·ment** *n.* a rule or governing, a system of governing such as democracy or dictatorship, a governing body of people such as the U.S. President and his cabinet, or a country that is governed; **gov·ern·men·tal** (–MEN·tl) *adj.* **—gov·er·nor** *n.* **1** the head of a state or colony; also, a member of a governing body or "board of governors"; **gov·er·nor·ship** *n.* **2** a mechanical device to control machine speed, as by operating a rheostat on an electric motor. **—governor general,** *pl.* **governors general** or **governor generals** a chief governor, as of Canada.

gown *n.* a long, loose outer garment or robe, as worn by judges and academics or a woman's formal dress, as worn at a wedding; also, a *dressing gown* or *nightgown.* **—*v.*:** *capped and ~ed for a graduation ceremony.*

G.P. general practitioner. **—gp.** group.

GPA grade-point average.

G.P.O. General Post Office; Government Printing Office.

G.Q. General Quarters.

Gr. Greece; Greek. **—gr.** grade; grain(s); gram(s); gravity; gross.

Graaf·i·an (GRAH·fee·un) See FOLLICLE.

grab *v.* **grabs, grabbed, grab·bing** **1** snatch suddenly, esp. in an eager or greedy manner: *A dog ~s at a bone; She* **grabbed hold** *of the* **grab bar** *when she slipped in the bath.* **2** *Informal.* make an impression on: *Elton John's music ~s me while Sinatra leaves me cold.* **—*n.*** a snatch; grasp: *an elected office* **up for grabs** *every four years; articles wrapped in* **grab bags** *to be sold unseen at a fixed price; The candidate offered a* **grab bag** (i.e. miscellaneous assortment) *of promises.* **—grab·ber** *n.* **—grab·by** *adj.* **grab·bi·er, grab·bi·est** avaricious.

grace *n.* **1** a pleasing quality such as charm, beauty, or elegance: *A defeated candidate concedes an election with* **good** (or **bad**) **grace;** *Jane puts on little* **airs and graces** *to impress the boys;* **Your** (or **His, Her**) **Grace** [title used in addressing or referring to an archbishop, duke, or duchess]. **2** divine favor; also, good will: *Adam's disobedience and fall from ~; to say ~* (i.e. short prayer for divine favor) *before a meal; three days of ~ to pay up after a debt falls due;* **in one's good** (or **bad**) **graces** favored (or disliked) by. **—*v.* grac·es, graced, grac·ing** bring charm or elegance to (an occasion, as by someone's presence); honor (someone), as with a title. **—grace·ful** *adj.* attractive in form, movement, or behavior; **grace·ful·ly** *adv.;* **grace·ful·ness** *n.;* **grace·less** *adj.* **—grace note** *Music.* an extra note added for ornament. **—gra·cious** (GRAY·shus) *adj.* having or showing qualities befitting a high station in life, as courtesy, indulgence, and elegance: *the Queen's ~ smile; a ~ speech; a suburban mansion fit for ~ living;* ***interj.*** indicating surprise; **gra·cious·ly** *adv.;* **gra·cious·ness** *n.*

grack·le (GRAKL) *n.* any of several kinds of North American blackbirds.

grad. graduate(d). **—grad** *n. Informal.* a graduate. **—gra·da·tion** (gray·DAY–) *n.* a step or degree in something showing progressive change; also, such change: *the ~s from violet to red in the rainbow; no ~ between "married" and "unmarried."* **—grade** *n.* **1** one of a series of steps or degrees, as of schools (Grade One to 12 or 13) and military ranks (*recruit* or *seaman* through *general* or *admiral*). **2** a classification according to quality, as of beef (*prime, choice,* etc.), eggs, coal, or lumber. **3** an achievement rating such as A, B, C, D, E, S ("satisfactory"), etc.: *Those receiving F ("fail") do not* **make the grade.** **4** a road level or ground level: *~ crossing; ~ separation.* **—*v.* grades, grad·ed, grad·ing:** *Only steer and heifer can be ~d prime beef; a term paper ~d "A"; to clear a right of way and ~* (i.e. level or slope) *it for a highway;* **-grade** *comb. form.* stepping or walking: as in *plantigrade* (i.e. walking on the sole of the foot), *retrograde.* **—grade crossing** railroad crossing on the same level. **—grade-point average** average obtained by dividing total points by number of credits earned. **—grad·er** *n.* **1** an earth-leveling machine. **2** a school pupil: *a first ~.* **—grade school** *U.S.* elementary school; also **the grades.** **—grade separation** a crossing that uses an overpass or underpass. **—gra·di·ent** (GRAY·dee·unt) *n.* a slope or its inclination. **—grad·u·al** (GRAJ·oo·ul) *adj.* by steps or degrees; little by little; **grad·u·al·ly** *adv.* **—grad·u·al·ism** *n.* the theory or policy of seeking social or political change gradually, not suddenly; **grad·u·al·ist** *n.* **—grad·u·ate** *v.* **-ates, -at·ed, -at·ing** **1** finish a course of study; also, give a diploma to: *He ~d from Harvard; (was) ~d with honors.* **2** mark or divide into gradations: *a thermometer ~d in degrees Celsius; a tax rate so ~d that rich people pay comparatively more than the less rich.* Also ***n.*** & ***adj.*** (GRAJ·oo·it): *a Yale ~; a ~ student working on his M.A.; a ~ nurse;* **grad·u·a·tor** *n.;* **grad·u·a·tion** (–AY–) *n.*

graf·fi·to (gruh·FEE·toh) *n., pl.* **-ti** (-tee) a crude drawing or writing done on a public wall, rock, etc.

graft *v.* **1** join (a shoot or bud, called "scion") from one plant or tree (called "stock") to another and make it grow; hence, produce (a new or improved fruit, flower, etc.); also, transplant skin or bone in this manner. **2** of politicians, public officials, etc., make money by illegal means. **—*n.*:** *different types of ~ such as cleft, splice, and saddle; a skin ~ or transplant; ~ in the form of protection money.* **—graft·er** *n.*

gra·ham (GRAY·um) *adj.* whole-wheat: *~ flour, crackers.*

Grail *n.* the cup used by Jesus at the Last Supper, sought by knights of medieval legend.

grain *n.* **1** a small, hard seed, esp. cereal or its plant; also, cereal seeds collectively: *per capita consumption of food ~;* **grain alcohol** *made chiefly from grain.* **2** a tiny, hard bit or particle, as of sugar, salt, pollen, etc.: *Take tall tales with a* **grain of salt;** *the fuel-oxidizer ~* (i.e. material) *in a solid-propellant rocket.* **3** a unit of weight equal to ¼ carat. **4** fiber pattern of wood, layer arrangement of stone, etc.; hence, natural inclination: *Punctuality goes against the ~ for a slow person.* **—grained** *adj.* marked like wood, marble, etc. **—grain elevator** tall structure in which grain is loaded, cleaned, and stored for shipment. **—grain·y** *adj.* **grain·i·er, -i·est** having a grain or texture; also, consisting of particles: *the speckled, ~ appearance of a photographic enlargement;* **grain·i·ness** *n.*

gram *n.* the basic unit of weight in the metric system, equal to about 1/28 oz.; *Brit.* **gramme; -gram** *comb. form.* **1** record or drawing: as in *cablegram, monogram, diagram.* **2** number of grams: as in *kilogram, milligram.*

gram·i·ci·din (–SYE·dn) *n.* an antibiotic locally applied to treat skin ailments, pleurisy, and sinus infections caused by bacteria that are **Gram-pos·i·tive,** that stain when tested by Hans Gram's method.

gram·mar (GRAM·ur) *n.* the rules governing the formation of words and sentences; hence, correctness of spoken or written expression; **grammar school** a nontechnical, academic secondary school (in the U.K.) or an elementary school (in the U.S.); **gram·mar·i·an** (gruh·MAIR·ee·un) *n.* an expert in grammar. **—gram·mat·i·cal** (–MAT–) *adj.* having to do with (correct) grammar: *a ~ error; good ~ English;* **gram·mat·i·cal·ly** *adv.*

Gram·my (–mee) *n.* **Gram·mys** or **Gram·mies** an annual award for achievement in the recording industry. **—gram·o·phone** *n. Brit.* phonograph.

Gram-positive See GRAMICIDIN.

gran·a·ry (GRAN·uh·ree, GRAY–) *n.* **-ries** storehouse for threshed grain.

grand *adj.* **1** imposing in size *(~ piano);* high in rank or dignity *(~ rabbi, ~ old man);* important or main *(~ staircase, ~ total).* **2** *Informal.* very satisfying: *had a ~ time at the party.* **—*n.*** *sing. & pl. Slang.* $1,000: *50 ~* (i.e. $50,000). **—grand·ly** *adv.;* **grand·ness** *n.* **—gran·dam(e)** *n. Archaic.* an old woman, esp. a grandmother. **—grand·child** *n.* **-chil·dren** a child of one's son or daughter; a **grand·son** or **grand·daugh·ter. —grande dame** (grahn·DAHM), *pl.* **grandes dames** (grahn·DAHM) *French.* an elderly woman of prestige. **—gran·dee** (–DEE) *n.* a Spanish or Portuguese nobleman of the highest rank; hence, an important personage. **—grand·daugh·ter** See GRANDCHILD. **—gran·deur** (GRAN·jur) *n.* greatness or magnificence of appearance, style, quality, nobility, etc. **—grand·fa·ther** *n.* See GRANDPARENT; **grandfather clause** a legal provision in several S. states of the U.S. to give the vote to unqualified descendants of white voters, declared unconstitutional in 1915; **grandfather('s) clock** a large clock that stands on the floor in a tall, upright case. **—gran·dil·o·quent** (–DIL·uh–) *adj.* pompous in diction and tone; **gran·dil·o·quence** *n.* **—gran·di·ose** (–dee·ose) *adj.* imposing or magnificent; also, showy or pompous; **gran·di·ose·ly** *adv.* **—grand jury** a jury of usu. more than 12 persons that hears evidence and decides whether to indict an accused person for trial by a petit jury. **—grand·ma** (–mah, –muh) *n. Informal.* grandmother. **—grand mal** (grahn·MAL) the severest form of epileptic seizure. **—grand·mas·ter** *n.* an unusually skilled player, esp. an international winner in chess. **—grand·moth·er** *n.* See GRANDPARENT. **—grand opera** a musical drama with a serious theme and spectacular stage effects that is completely sung or recited. **—grand·pa** *n. Informal.* grandfather. **—grand·par·ent** (–pair·unt) *n.* a parent of one's father or mother; a grandfather or grandmother. **—grand piano** a large piano with horizontal frame and strings. **—grand prix** (grahn·PREE), *pl.* **grand prix** (–PREEZ) an international contest, esp. one of a series of races for Formula One cars. **—Grand Rapids** a city of S.W. Michigan. **—grand slam** a winning of all the tricks in a hand of bridge or all the four major golf or tennis championships in one year; in baseball, a home run hit with a runner on each base. **—grandson** See GRANDCHILD. **—grand·stand** *n.* the main seating place for the spectators at a sporting event; ***v.*** *Informal.* make an attention-getting display, or **grandstand play,** as in baseball.

grange (GRAINJ) *n.* a farm or farmhouse with its barn and other buildings; **Grange** a national U.S. association of farmers, organized in 1867.

gran·ite (GRAN·it) *n.* a hard, igneous rock with grains of quartz, feldspar, and other minerals in it; **gran·ite·ware** *n.* household ironware with a granitelike mottled gray enamel; **gra·nit·ic** (–NIT–) *adj.* like granite in firmness and endurance.

gran·ny or **gran·nie** (–nee) *n.* **gran·nies** *Informal.* a grandmother or elderly woman; also, a fussy person.

gra·no·la (gruh·NOH·luh) *n.* a prepared breakfast cereal of rolled oats and other ingredients that is used as a health food.

grant *v.* allow (a request, permission, claim, etc.); also, confer (property or other right or benefit): *leave of absence ~ed to an employee; I ~ that my words were misleading; Don't* **take** *it* **for granted** (i.e. assume) *that you will get a raise every year.* **—*n.*** something granted, as money, land, etc.

Grant, Ulysses S. 1822–85, a Union general in the Civil War and 18th U.S. President (1869–77).

gran·tee *n.* one to whom a grant is made; **grant·or** or **grant·er** *n.* **—grant-in-aid** *n.* **grants-in-aid** a money grant or subsidy given to a person or institution for an educational or public-service project; **grants·man·ship** *n.* the art of obtaining grants.

gran·u·lar (–lur) *adj.* grainy: *"Corn snow" is ~; the ~ white cells in the bloodstream;* **gran·u·lar·i·ty** (–LAIR–) *n.* **—gran·u·late** *v.* **-lates, -lat·ed, -lat·ing** form granules; become granular or roughen: *A wound surface ~s in healing; ~d honey;* **gran·u·la·tion** (–LAY–) *n.* **—gran·ule** (–yool) *n.* a grain or small crystal, as of sugar or snow pellets; also, one of the small, short-lived patches of gas in the sun's photosphere.

grape *n.* the small, round, juicy berry that grows in clusters on various woody vines; also, such a vine or the usu. dark, purplish-red color of the fruit. —**grape·fruit** *n.* a large, round, yellowish citrus fruit of a tree of the rue family. —**grape hyacinth** an herb of the lily family with spikes of bell-shaped blue or white flowers. —**grape·shot** *n.* small iron balls formerly used as cannon shot. —**grape·vine** *n.* **1** a grape-bearing vine. **2** *Informal.* word-of-mouth spreading of news, gossip, etc.

graph (GRAF) *n.* a chart or drawing using lines, curves, bars, or circles ("pie chart") to present in picture form relationships between quantities, e.g. how temperature changes with time of day; ***v.:*** *Attendance of pupils may be ~ed against corresponding school days along a pair of axes.*— **-graph** *comb. form.* a recording instrument or something recorded: as in *telegraph, monograph, autograph.* —**graph·ic** *adj.* **1** vivid or realistic: *a ~ description of the accident.* **2** having to do with graphs; also **graph·i·cal.** **3** of or about drawing, painting, printing, engraving, etc., i.e. the **graphic arts; graph·ic** *n.* a work of graphic art; also, a graphic display by computer on a cathode-ray-tube terminal. — **graphics** *n.pl.* [takes *sing. v.*] **1** mathematical drawing, as in engineering and architecture; also, calculations based on it. **2** design, including type, using graphic arts; also, graphic arts. **3** production of graphic displays by computer, as on a cathode-ray tube. —**graph·i·cal·ly** *adv.* —**graph·ite** *n.* a soft, black carbon mineral used in "lead" pencils and for electrodes, crucibles, etc. —**graph·ol·o·gist** *n.* a handwriting expert. —**graph·ol·o·gy** (–OL·uh·jee) *n.* the study of handwriting as indicative of character. — **-graphy** *comb. form.* writing; science of; treatise about (as specified): as in *cryptography, calligraphy, geography.*

grap·nel *n.* **1** a small anchor for boats and balloons, with several flukes or hooks. **2** an instrument with several claws at the end for seizing and holding, as an enemy ship. —**grap·ple** *v.* **grap·ples, grap·pled, grap·pling** grip and hold; hence, struggle or wrestle: *more problems than she could* **grapple with** *in one day.* —***n.*** a struggle; also, a grapnel or **grappling iron** (or **hook**).

GRAS (food additive) "Generally Recognized As Safe."

grasp *v.* seize and hold firmly, as with the hand: *The swimmer ~ed the rope thrown to him; an idea difficult to ~* (i.e. with the mind); *ready to ~ at any available opportunity.* —***n.*** hold: *Success seemed within her ~; a good ~ of Russian grammar.* —**grasp·ing** *adj.* greedy; avaricious.

grass *n.* **1** any of various plants with jointed stems and long, narrow leaves eaten by grazing animals and cultivated on lawns; hence, lawn; also, any cereal grass such as wheat, barley, or corn. **2** *Slang.* marijuana. —**grass·y** *adj.* **grass·i·er, -i·est.** —**grass·hop·per** *n.* any of two families (short-horned and long-horned) of leaping insects such as locusts and katydids that often damage crops. —**grass·land** *n.* pasture land. —**grass roots** *Informal.* the common people who form the basic strength of any popular movement; the rank and file; **grass-root(s)** *adj.: a candidate with ~ support.* —**grass widow** *Informal.* a woman separated from her husband.

grate *v.* **grates, grat·ed, grat·ing** **1** grind by scraping or rubbing, as cabbage with a **grat·er:** *grated cheese.* **2** scrape or scratch or make a rasping sound, as an iron gate on its hinges; hence, irritate or have an unpleasant effect: *raucous voices that ~ on our ears;* **grat·ing·ly** *adv.* —***n.*** **1** a framework of bars forming a protective screen, as in a window; grill; also **grat·ing.** **2** a horizontal framework of bars for holding burning fuel, as in a fireplace.

grate·ful *adj.* thankful; also, pleasing: *a ~ task;* **grate·ful·ly** *adv.;* **grate·ful·ness** *n.* —**grat·i·fy** *v.* **-fies, -fied, -fy·ing** give pleasure to; also, satisfy; indulge: *fancies that ~ one's desires;* **grat·i·fi·ca·tion** (–CAY–) *n.* —**grat·is** (GRAT–, GRAY–) *adj.* & *adv.* free of charge: *tickets mailed ~; ~ copies of a new book.* —**grat·i·tude** (GRAT–) *n.* thankfulness. —**gra·tu·i·tous** (gruh·TUE·i·tus) *adj.* unjustified; uncalled-for; *a ~ insult;* **gra·tu·i·tous·ly** *adv.;* **gra·tu·i·tous·ness** *n.* —**gra·tu·i·ty** (–TUE–) *n.* **-ties** a small money gift; tip.

grau·pel (GROU·pul) *n.* snowfall in pellets; "soft hail."

gra·va·men (gruh·VAY–) *n.* **-va·mens** or **-vam·i·na** (–VAM·uh·nuh) the essential part of a complaint.

¹grave *adj.* **grav·er, grav·est** weighty; hence, serious; solemn: *~ doubts; a mourner's ~ expression;* **grave·ly** *adv.;* **grave·ness** *n.* —**gra·ve** (GRAH·vay) *adj.* & *adv. Music.* slow(ly).

²grave *n.* a hole dug in the ground to bury a corpse; also, a mound of earth or tomb; hence, death: *from the cradle to the ~; has one foot in the ~* (i.e. is near death); *enough to make him turn over in his ~* (i.e. so shocking). —***v.*** **graves,** *pt.* **graved,** *pp.* **grav·en** or **graved, grav·ing** **1** carve; hence, impress deeply: *idols and such* **graven images** *of stone and wood.* **2** clean and tar (a ship's bottom): *the ~ing docks of shipyards.*

grave (accent) a mark originally indicating a vowel of low pitch, used also to mark prominence of syllable, as in "an agèd genius."

grav·el *n.* rock fragments, pebbles, etc. that are coarser than sand: *Streams and melting glaciers formed ~ pits; the ~ culture method of hydroponics; ~ in the urine* (i.e. particles of kidney stones). —**grav·el·ly** *adj.* like gravel; harsh-sounding.

grave·stone *n.* inscribed stone or monument marking a grave; **grave·yard** *n.* a cemetery: *an* *auto ~; Diamond Shoals, the "~ of the Atlantic"; a* **graveyard shift** (of workers) *starting near midnight.*

grav•id *adj.* pregnant.

gra•vim•e•ter (gruh·VIM·i–) *n.* a gravity-measuring device, used in determining the shape and depth of rock layers; **grav•i•met•ric** (–MET–) *adj.* —**grav•i•tate** *v.* **-tates, -tat•ed, -tat•ing** move or tend to(ward), by or as if by gravity: *two kindred souls ~ing towards each other;* **grav•i•ta•tive** *adj.* —**grav•i•ta•tion** (–TAY–) *n.;* **grav•i•ta•tion•al** *adj.: No ~ force at the center of the earth; energy-carrying ~ waves radiated by accelerating masses;* **grav•i•ta•tion•al•ly** *adv.* —**grav•i•ty** (GRAV–) *n.* **-ties** **1** the force of gravitation, esp. the earth's pull on objects: *~ causes weight; The lower an object's center of ~* (i.e. weight), *the more stable it is.* **2** weightiness; seriousness: *the ~ of the situation.*

gra•vure (gruh·VYOOR) *n.* (a plate or print made by) an intaglio process such as photogravure or rotogravure.

gra•vy (GRAY·vee) *n.* **-vies** **1** sauce made by thickening with flour, seasoning, etc. the juice given off by meat in cooking. **2** *Slang.* a surplus beyond what is expected or needed; **gravy train** source of easy money; sinecure; also **gravy boat,** a gravy dish, originally boat-shaped.

gray *adj.* of the dull color that is a blend of black and white or the color of aging hair; hence, dismal; dreary; also, vague or intermediate: *a ~ area;* **gray•ness** *n.* —***n.*** a gray color, animal such as a gray horse, or gray cloth: *"Gray Friars" used to dress in ~.* —***v.*** make or become gray: *hair ~ed by age.* —**gray•beard** *n.* an old man. —**gray birch** a North American birch with a hard grayish-white bark. —**gray•hound** same as GREYHOUND. —**gray•ish** *adj.* somewhat gray. —**gray•ling** *n.* a troutlike freshwater game fish of cool or arctic regions. —**gray matter** the grayish tissue of the brain and spinal cord; hence, intelligence.

graze *v.* **graz•es, grazed, graz•ing** **1** (put to) feed on grass, as sheep and cattle do; **gra•zier** (GRAY·zhur) *n.* **2** touch, scrape, or scratch in passing; ***n.*** a grazing or abrasion.

Gr. Br(it). Great Britain.

grease *n.* (GREECE) a thick oily substance such as melted animal fat; lubricant; **grease•paint** *n.* stage makeup. —***v.*** (GREECE, GREEZ) **greas•es, greased, greas•ing** **1** smear with grease; lubricate. **2** *Slang.* to bribe, esp. **grease the hand** (or **palm**) **of.** —**greas•y** *adj.* **greas•i•er, -i•est** containing grease; also, soiled with grease; **greasy spoon** *Slang.* a cheap, unsanitary restaurant.

great (GRATE) *adj.* **1** imposing in size or degree: *a ~ man; a ~ reader; for a ~ while; the four ~ powers* (i.e. nations). **2** remarkable or surprising: *a ~ rascal; showed ~ ignorance.* **3** *Informal.* very good: *The party was ~ fun; You're ~!* —**great•ly** *adv.* —**great•ness** *n.* —**great anteater** same as ANT BEAR. —**great auk** See AUK. —**Great Britain** England, Scotland, and Wales, sometimes including also Northern Ireland. —**great circle** a circle, esp. on the earth's surface, whose plane passes through the center of the sphere, as the equator: *A great-circle route is the shortest between two points.* —**great•coat** *n.* a heavy overcoat. —**Great Dane** a large, graceful, strong, short-coated breed of mastiff. —**Greater Antilles** See ANTILLES. —**great-grand•child** (–GRAN–) *n.* **-chil•dren** a child of one's grandchild; **great-grand•parent** *n.* —**great•heart•ed** (–HAR·tid) *adj.* noble or generous; also, fearless. —**Great Lakes** a series of five lakes on the U.S.-Ontario border, viz. Lakes Ontario, Erie, Huron, Michigan, and Superior. —**Great Salt Lake** a saltwater lake in N.W. Utah.

grebe (GREEB) *n.* any of a family of lobe-footed wading and diving birds related to the loon.

Gre•cian (GREE·shun) *n.* & *adj.* Greek. —**Greco-** *comb.form.* Greek (and): as in *Greco-Roman, Greco-Russian.* —**Greece** a country of S.E. Europe; 50,944 sq.mi. (131,944 km²); *cap.* Athens.

greed *n.* excessive desire for money, food, power, etc. —**greed•y** *adj.* **-i•er, -i•est** avaricious; gluttonous: *looked at her with ~ eyes; a child ~ for candy;* **greed•i•ly** *adv.;* **greed•i•ness** *n.*

Greek *n.* a person of or from Greece; also, his language: *It's* **Greek** (i.e. unintelligible) **to** *me;* ***adj.:*** *the established* **Greek Orthodox Church** *of Greece; chemical warfare using* **Greek fire** *which water could not put out; Phi Beta Kappa, Phi Mu, and such* **Greek-let•ter** *fraternities and sororities.*

green *n.* & *adj.* **1** (of) the color of greenery; hence, a grassy plot of land: *a suburban* **green belt** *of trees and parks around a heavily built-up area;* **greens** *pl.* green leaves and branches; also, a golf course or its putting green. **2** (of) the color of unripe fruit; hence, immature; inexperienced. **3** (of) the color of a sickly complexion; hence, pale-looking: *~ with envy; "the ~-eyed monster"* (i.e. jealousy). **4** (of) the color symbolizing hope, promise, safety, etc. as used on U.S. paper money, for uniforms, etc. —**green•ish** *adj.;* **green•ish•ness** *n.;* **green•ness** *n.* —***v.*** make or become green. —**green•back** *n.* a piece of U.S. paper money. —**green•bean** *n.* a pod of the kidney bean. —**green belt** See GREEN, def. 1. —**Green Beret** a member of the Special Forces of the U.S. Army. —**green card** a visa or permit to live in the U.S. and qualify for citizenship after a few years. —**green•er•y** *n.* **-er•ies** grass and growing vegetation. —**green•groc•er** (–groh·sur) *n.* *Brit.* a seller of fruits and vegetables. —**green•horn** *n.* *Informal.* a new arrival or recruit, esp. one who is easily duped. —**green•house** *n.* a glass-covered building for climate-controlled cultivation of plants. —**Green•land**

(–lund) an arctic island, the world's largest, belonging to Denmark; *cap.* Godthaab. —**green manure** growing plants such as alfalfa, grasses, and legumes plowed into the soil to fertilize it. —**green onion** a scallion. —**green pepper** same as SWEET PEPPER. —**green power** power based on money. —**green revolution** increased production of food grains in developing countries, aided by fertilizers and pesticides. —**green·room** *n.* offstage waiting room for performers. —**Greens·bor·o** (–buh·ruh) a city of N. North Carolina. —**green·sward** *n.* grassy turf. —**green thumb** skill in gardening. —**green turtle** a sea turtle with a greenish shell. —**Green·wich** (GREN·ich, *Brit.* GRIN·ij) a borough of London, England, located on the prime meridian, whose local time, **Greenwich (mean) time,** is the basis for time zones throughout the world. —**green·wood** *n.* a forest in full leaf; woodlands.

greet *v.* meet (someone), esp. to welcome: *guests ~ed at the door; She ~s everyone with a smile; an order ~ed with a hail of bullets;* **greet·er** *n.* —**greet·ing** *n.* welcome; also, a wish such as "Good morning" or a season's **greetings,** often conveyed by a **greeting card.**

gre·gar·i·ous (gruh·GAIR·ee·us) *adj.* tending to herd or flock together; also, growing in clusters; social, as ants; hence, sociable, not solitary; **gre·gar·i·ous·ly** *adv.;* **gre·gar·i·ous·ness** *n.*

Gre·go·ri·an (–GOR·ee·un) *adj.* **1** of Pope **Gregory I** (St. Gregory or "Gregory the Great"), 540?–604, who introduced **Gregorian chant** or plainsong. **2** of Pope **Gregory XIII,** 1502–85, who introduced the now widely used **Gregorian calendar,** adjusting the Julian Calendar and decreeing a leap year every fourth year.

grem·lin *n.* a goblin usu. blamed for mechanical mishaps. —**grem·mie** or **grem·my** *n.* **grem·mies** *Slang.* a poor surfer.

Gre·na·da (gruh·NAY·duh) a Commonwealth country of the West Indies; 133 sq.mi. (344 km²); *cap.* St. George's.

gre·nade (gruh·NADE) *n.* a small bomb thrown by hand or fired from a rifle. —**gren·a·dier** (–uh·DEER) *n.* a soldier trained to throw hand grenades. —**gren·a·dine** (–uh·deen) *n.* **1** a cordial syrup made from pomegranates. **2** a dress fabric of silk, wool, or cotton.

grew *pt.* of GROW.

grey *usu. Brit.* gray. —**grey·hound** *n.* a swift-footed dog with long, powerful legs and keen sight, trained to hunt hares and in **greyhound racing** using a mechanical rabbit on an electric rail around a track.

grid *n.* a framework resembling a grate or grill; gridiron; hence, the lead plate in a storage battery, a football field, a system of horizontal and vertical lines as coordinates for locating points on a map, a mesh or screen controlling the intensity of the electron beam from a cathode, an interconnecting network of electronic transmission systems or radio or television stations, etc. —**grid·dle** *n.* a heavy, flat metal plate for cooking bacon, pancakes (**griddle cake**), etc. —**grid·i·ron** (GRID·eye·urn) *n.* a grill for broiling; hence, anything resembling this, as a football field, the structure above a stage for manipulating scenery, or a clock pendulum with rods of different metals.

grief (GREEF) *n.* acute sorrow, esp. one of short duration caused by some misfortune: *Hopes of a lifetime* **came to grief** *when the bank crashed.* —**griev·ance** (GREE·vunce) *n.* a complaint or its real or imagined cause: *the ~ procedure to settle a dispute.* —**grieve** (GREEV) *v.* **grieves, grieved, griev·ing** feel or cause grief; **griev·er** *n.;* **griev·ous** (GREE·vus) *adj.* causing suffering; hence, severe or grave: *a ~ wound, wrong, crime, pain, loss;* **griev·ous·ly** *adv.;* **griev·ous·ness** *n.*

grif·fin or **grif·fon** (GRIF·un) *n.* a mythical eagle with the hind legs and tail of a lion; also **gryph·on.**

grill *n.* **1** a gridiron; hence, a dish of broiled meat, fish, etc.; also, a **grill·room** or small restaurant. **2** usu. **grille,** a protective metal screen or grating, as in front of an automobile radiator; also, a vent or window covered with a grating. —**v.** broil; hence, torture with questions: *~ed cheese; a lawyer ~ing a witness.* —**grill·work** *n.* a pattern of grilles.

grim *adj.* **grim·mer, grim·mest** fierce; not relenting; horrible or ghastly: *a battle fought with ~ resolve; the ~ prospect of unemployment; a joke too ~ to laugh at;* **grim·ly** *adv.;* **grim·ness** *n.*

grim·ace (–is, –MACE) *n.* a twisted or distorted face, as of one in pain or trying to amuse. —**v. -ac·es, -aced, -ac·ing:** *~d in disgust at the burned steak.* —**grime** *n.* dirt, esp. soot, rubbed into a surface, as the skin; **grim·y** *adj.* **grim·i·er, -i·est:** *the ~ faces of miners.*

Grimm, Jakob (1785–1863) and **Wilhelm** (1786–1859), German brothers who collected fairy tales.

grin *n.* a broad smile showing the teeth; also, a baring of the teeth in anger, pain, or scorn; **v. grins, grinned, grin·ning:** *nodded and ~d her approval; pain so bad he had to* **grin and bear it.**

grind (GRINED) *v.* **grinds, ground, grind·ing** **1** reduce to powder by friction, as grain in a mill; also, rub or press together, as teeth by an angry person, or when a crank turns: *to ~ out music on a hand organ; a train ~ing to a halt at a station.* **2** work hard or long: *the diligent worker ~ing away at her tasks.* —**n.:** *the dull ~ of a routine job; coffee of a coarse ~* (i.e. particle size); *become a ~* (i.e. hard worker) *so as to graduate with honors.* —**grind·er** *n.* —**grind·stone** *n.* a millstone; also, a sharpening or polishing instrument with a revolving stone.

gri·ot (GREE·oh) *n.* a roving musician-entertainer and storyteller of W. Africa.

grip *n.* a firm hold or tight grasp; also, a way of holding a racket or golf club, something to hold with, as a handle, or a handbag or small suitcase: *a country in the ~ of a famine; a youngster who* **comes to grips with** (i.e. tries to handle) *a problem.* **—v. grips, gripped, grip·ping:** *a frightened child ~ing its mother's hand; a novel that ~s your interest;* **grip·ping·ly** *adv.* **—gripe** *v.* **gripes, griped, grip·ing** *Informal.* complain. **—gripes** *n.pl.* pain in the intestines. **—grippe** (GRIP) *n.* influenza.

gris-gris (GREE·gree) *n. sing. & pl.* a charm, amulet, or fetish, as in voodoo cults.

gris·ly (GRIS·lee) *adj.* **gris·li·er, -li·est** horrible; ghastly.

grist *n.* ground grain such as meal or flour; also, grain to be ground, as in a **grist·mill; grist to** (or **for**) **one's mill** matter for profit or advantage to one. **—gris·tle** (GRISL) *n.* cartilage, esp. in table meats; **gris·tly** *adj.* **-tli·er, -tli·est** cartilaginous. **—grit** *n.* **1** fine gravel, sand, or coarse-grained sandstone; **grits** *n.pl.* coarsely ground corn, oats, wheat, etc.; esp. in southern U.S., ground hominy, eaten boiled or fried. **2** pluck; obstinate courage; **v. grits, grit·ted, grit·ting** clench or grind the teeth in determination: *She ~d her teeth and bore the pain.* **—grit·ty** *adj.* **grit·ti·er, grit·ti·est:** *a ~ salad; a ~* (i.e. brave) *little girl.*

griz·zled (GRIZ·ld) *adj.* gray-haired; streaked with gray; **griz·zly** (–lee) *adj.* **griz·zli·er, griz·zli·est** grayish, as a massive, ferocious animal of W. North America called **grizzly (bear),** *pl.* **griz·zlies** or **grizzly bears.**

groan (GRONE) *n.* a deep sound made from the throat to express pain, disapproval, grief, etc.: *the ~s of the wounded on a battlefield.* **—v.:** *The report card made the parent ~ in dismay; a dining table ~ing under its load.*

groat (GROTE) *n.* a former British coin worth four pennies; hence, a trifling sum.

gro·cer (GROH·sur) *n.* a dealer in food and other household supplies; **gro·cer·y** *n.* **-cer·ies** a grocer's store or the food products sold by one.

grog *n.* an alcoholic drink, esp. rum diluted with water. **—grog·gy** *adj.* **grog·gi·er, grog·gi·est** *Informal.* drunk or feeling like it; shaky, dazed; **grog·gi·ly** *adv.;* **grog·gi·ness** *n.*

groin *n.* **1** the fold or depression between belly and thigh; hence, in architecture, the curved edge formed by two intersecting vaults; **groin(ed) vault. 2** a jettylike structure of asphalt and sand to protect a coast from erosion.

grom·met (–mit) *n.* a ring or loop used as a fastening or reinforcement or to protect an opening or the thing passing through it.

groom *n.* **1** a bridegroom. **2** a man or boy who takes care of horses. **—v. 1** take care of (a horse, dog, etc.) by cleaning and currying. **2** make neat and tidy in appearance: *a well-~ed man.* **3** prepare (someone) for an office. **—grooms·man** *n.* **-men** a bridegroom's attendant.

groove *n.* **1** a channel, furrow, or rut; hence, a routine; **in the groove** *Slang.* in top form; working smoothly, like a needle playing in the groove of a phonograph record; groovy. **2** *Slang.* something enjoyable. **—v. grooves, grooved, groov·ing** *Slang.* react with empathy: *to ~ to swing music; ~ with someone; everyone ~ing* (i.e. enjoying himself) *in his own way.* **—groov·y** *adj. Slang.* **groov·i·er, -i·est** swinging; excellent: *a ~ hairstyle.*

grope *v.* **gropes, grop·ed, grop·ing** feel one's way about as if blind or in the dark or uncertain: *always ~ing for a better expression.* **—n.** *Slang.* a sexual exploration: *from group ~ to orgy.*

gros·beak (GROHS·beek) *n.* a bird of the finch family with a strong beak for cracking seeds.

gro·schen (GROH·shun) *n. sing. & pl.* a money unit of Austria and a bronze coin worth 1/100 of a schilling.

gros·grain (GROH–) *n.* a corded fabric of silk or rayon used for ribbons, etc.

gross (GROSE) *adj.* **1** thick; dense; coarse; flagrant: *a ~ injustice; fired for ~ misconduct; ~ eating habits.* **2** whole or entire, with nothing deducted: *a physician's ~ income including overhead, salaries, etc.; a company's ~ sales.* **—n. 1** *pl.* **gross·es** the total amount. **2** *sing. & pl.* 12 dozen; 144. **—v.:** *How much did you ~* (i.e. earn before deductions) *last year?* **—gross·ly** *adv.;* **gross·ness** *n.* **—gross national product** the value of all goods and services produced, usu. in a year. **—gross ton** 2,240 lb. (1,016 kg); long ton.

grosz (GRAWSH) *n., pl.* **gro·szy** (–shee) a money unit of Poland, equal to 1/100 of a zloty.

gro·tesque (groh·TESK) *adj.* unnatural or fantastic in appearance, shape, or manner; bizarre and ludicrous: *A gargoyle is a ~ form of caricature.* **—n.** a painting or sculpture containing medallions, sphinxes, foliage, etc. in grotesque style. **—gro·tesque·ly** *adv.;* **gro·tesque·ness** *n.* **—grot·to** (–toh) *n.* **-to(e)s** a cave or a cavelike place or garden shelter. **—grot·ty** *adj. Brit. Slang.* grotesque; miserable: *feeling dead ~!*

grouch *Informal. n.* a grumbler; a grumbling or sulky mood; also, a complaint. **—v.** complain in a surly, ill-tempered manner. **—grouch·y** *adj.;* **grouch·i·ly** *adv.;* **grouch·i·ness** *n.*

¹ground *pt.* of GRIND; **ground glass** nontransparent glass with a roughened surface; also, glass in powder form.

²ground *n.* **1** bottom; foundation; also, what is at the bottom; sediment: *coffee ~s* (i.e. particles) *in a cup.* **2** the earth's surface or a piece of it; land; hence, an area or region: *fighter planes directed by ~-controlled radar; an airline's* **ground crew** *of mechanics and such nonflying personnel; the ~s of* (i.e. around) *a school, mansion,* *estate; fishing ~s; picnic ~s; a gold crescent on a green ~* (i.e. background); *the ~* (i.e. connection) *of an appliance to conduct leaking electricity to earth; Research theses are supposed to* **break new ground,** *not rehash old discoveries.* **3** basis; reason: *On what* **grounds** *did he resign?* **4** a fighting position: *Don't* **shift your ground** *in the middle of an argument; Continue fighting and don't* **give ground; Hold** (or **stand**) **your ground!** *The idea is* **gaining** (or **losing**) **ground** *that mercy killing is all right.* **—v.:** *a pilot ~ed by illness; aircraft ~ed by fog; arguments ~ed on facts; a graduate student well ~ed in the basic arts and sciences; an appliance ~ed by its own metal frame.* **—ground ball** same as GROUNDER. **—ground cloth** a protective sheet put on the ground, as under a sleeping bag. **—ground cover** low plants or shrubbery to decorate the ground and protect the topsoil against erosion. **—ground crew** See GROUND, *n.* 2. **—ground-effect machine** same as AIR CUSHION VEHICLE. **—ground·er** *n.* a baseball hit along the ground. **—ground floor** the floor nearest to the ground; hence, a position of advantage, as at the outset of a venture: *The man who owns the business* **got in on the ground floor. —ground glass** See [1]GROUND. **—ground·hog** *n.* woodchuck. **—ground·less** *adj.* baseless. **—ground·ling** *n.* a plant or animal whose habitat is close to the ground; also, a person of inferior artistic taste. **—ground·mass** *n.* the main body of a rock in which crystals or pebbles are set. **—ground rule** a basic rule, as of a game. **—ground·sheet** *n.* same as GROUND CLOTH. **—ground speed** speed of an aircraft relative to the ground. **—ground·swell** *n.* a growing wave of popular concern, support, etc. **—ground water** the water that supplies wells and springs. **—ground·work** *n.* foundation; basis: *the three R's as the ~ of a good education.* **—ground zero** point on the ground directly above or beneath an exploding atomic bomb.

group (GROOP) *n.* a number of persons, animals, or things belonging, classed, or associated together: *a ~ of people; English and Dutch belong to the Germanic ~ of languages; Battalions and squadrons form military ~s or units; a low* **group insurance** *rate for club employees and members; psychodrama used as a* **group (psycho)therapy** *method; physicians in* **group practice** *practicing* **group medicine. —v.** form or arrange into a group; **group·er** *n.* any of various large food fishes of the sea bass family, found in warm waters, as the "Nassau grouper." **—group·ie** (–ee) *n. Informal.* a young female fan of a pop group, esp. one who follows them for sexual relations.

grouse *n. sing. & pl.* any of a family of game birds resembling domestic fowl, as the *ruffed grouse* and the *Canada spruce grouse* or "fool hen." **—v. grous·es, groused, grous·ing** *Informal.* grumble; **n.** complaint; **grous·er** *n.*

grout *n.* a thin mortar or plaster; **v.** fill up (a space), finish (a wall, ceiling, etc.), or fix with grout.

grove (GROHV) *n.* a small wood without underbrush; group of trees.

grov·el (GRUVL, GROVL) *v.* **-els, -el(l)ed, -el·(l)ing** crawl or cringe (at the feet of or before someone feared): *to ~ in the dust.*

grow (GROH) *v.* **grows, grew** (GROO), **grown** (GRONE), **grow·ing** develop, as animals and plants from seed, becoming bigger; *Children* **grow up** *to be adults; the* **growing pains** (i.e. stresses and strains) *of childhood and youth; seems fashionable to ~ one's hair; Days ~* (i.e. become) *shorter in the fall; Habits seem to* **grow on** *people like vines on walls;* **grow·er** *n.*

growl *n. & v.* (make) a low, throaty sound, as a dog warning an approaching stranger, thunder in the distance, or the stomach of a hungry person; rumble; also, grumble; **growl·er** *n.*

grown *pp.* of GROW; **adj.** mature: *a ~ man.* **—grown-up** *n. & adj.* adult. **—growth** (GROHTH) *n.* a growing, what has grown, or amount grown: *the ~ of grass in the spring; tumors and such cancerous ~s; a* **growth company** *or* **growth industry** *with greater than average ~; The anterior lobe of the pituitary secretes a* **growth hormone;** *a* **growth ring,** *or annual ring, showing a year's ~ of wood.*

groyne (GROIN) same as GROIN, *n.* 2.

grub *v.* **grubs, grubbed, grub·bing** dig (up); toil; also, rummage about: *A farmer ~s up roots to prepare the soil; ~ing for potatoes.* **—n. 1** an insect larva, as of a beetle; also, a toiler; drudge. **2** *Slang.* food. **—grub·by** *adj.* **grub·bi·er, grub·bi·est** grimy; also, infested, as cattle or sheep, with fly maggots. **—grub·stake** *n. & v.* **-stakes, -staked, -stak·ing** *Informal.* (supply with) food and equipment in return for a share of the proceeds, as merchants used to supply prospectors for gold.

grudge (GRUJ) *n.* ill will borne against another; also, a reason for such feeling: *a* **grudge fight** *to avenge a defeat.* **—v. grudg·es, grudged, grudg·ing** begrudge; **grudg·er** *n.;* **grudg·ing** *adj.* reluctant; unwilling; **grudg·ing·ly** *adv.*

gru·el (GROO·ul) *n.* liquid food, as for invalids, made by boiling meal in water or milk; a thin porridge. **—gru·el·(l)ing** *adj.* exhausting; tiring: *a ~ race, training, contest;* **n.** a grueling experience.

grue·some (GROO·sum) *adj.* causing fear and loathing because of something frightful or hideous: *a ~ scene of massacre; ~ details;* **grue·some·ly** *adv.;* **grue·some·ness** *n.*

gruff *adj.* rough in speech and manner; also, having a deep and harsh voice: *a ~ reply, voice, sergeant;* **gruff·ly** *adv.;* **gruff·ness** *n.*

grum·ble *v.* **grum·bles, grum·bled, grum·bling** growl, mutter, or rumble in a surly or peevish manner: *He ~d his thanks;* **n.** complaint; rumble; **grum·bler** *n.*

grump·y *adj.* **grump·i·er, -i·est** grouchy; ill-humored; **grump·i·ly** *adv.;* **grump·i·ness** *n.*

grun·gy (GRUN·jee) *adj.* **-gi·er, -gi·est** *Slang.* ugly; unpleasant: *the squalor of a ~ movie house and strip joint.*

grun·ion (GRUN·yun) *n.* a small silvery fish of the California coast that comes up the beaches to spawn and may be caught by hand.

grunt *n.* **1** the short, deep guttural sound made by a hog; hence, an expression of boredom, disapproval, effort, etc. **2** a family of ocean fishes of the Atlantic coast, such as the "pigfish" or "sailor's-choice" that grunt when taken out of water. ***—v.:*** *He merely ~ed his approval.*

Gru·yère (gri·YAIR) *n.* a variety of firm, light-yellow, whole-milk cheese.

gr. wt. gross weight.

gryphon same as GRIFFIN.

G.S.A. General Services Administration.

G-string *n.* **1** the string on a musical instrument that sounds the G note. **2** a loincloth to cover the genitals, as worn by strippers.

G-suit (JEE·soot) *n.* a garment worn by astronauts, pilots, etc. to withstand G-forces.

gt. great; drop (Latin "gutta"). **—GT** grand touring (car); gross ton. **—Gt. Brit.** Great Britain.

gtd. guaranteed.

GU *Abbrev.* for **Guam** (GWAHM) a U.S. island territory and air and naval base, about 1,500 mi. (2,410 km) E. of the Philippines; *cap.* Agana.

gua·na·co (gwuh·NAH·coh) *n.* a wild wool-bearing, 4-foot-high (about 122 cm) animal related to the camel and the llama.

gua·nine (GWAH·neen) *n.* a crystalline substance, one of the four nitrogenous purine bases of DNA and RNA. **—gua·no** (GWAH·noh) *n.* **-nos** the waste matter of sea birds used as a fertilizer; also, any similar manure.

gua·ra·ní (gwah·rah·NEE) *n.* **1** *pl.* **-ni(e)s** the basic money unit of Paraguay, equal to 100 centimos. **2 Guarani,** *pl.* **-nis** (a member of) a group of South American Indian tribes or their language of the "Tupi-Guarani" family.

guar·an·tee (gair·un·TEE) *n.* **1** a promise or pledge to carry out a service as represented or to replace, repair, or refund the price of a product if it proves unsatisfactory within a stipulated period: *a TV set with a year's ~ of service and five years on parts.* **2** a guaranty or something having its force: *no sure ~ of happiness.* ***—v.*** **-tees, -teed, -tee·ing** stand behind; also, promise or pledge: *an automobile ~d for 12,000 miles or one year. "Satisfaction ~d or your money back";* **guar·an·tor** *n.* one who gives a guarantee or guaranty. **—guar·an·ty** (GAIR·un·tee) *n.* **-ties** *Law.* a usu. written agreement by which a guarantor promises to pay another's debt if the latter fails to pay; hence, something given or taken as security for this promise; ***v.*** **-ties, -tied, -ty·ing:** *collateral to ~ a loan.*

guard (GARD) *v.* protect or defend, esp. by watching over (someone or something) against potential harm or danger or to prevent escape, as the Coast Guard or a sentry does: *a vaccination to ~ against disease; "We will see" was his* **guarded** (i.e. cautious) *reply.* ***—n.*** a person, group, or contrivance that guards: *a prison ~; A watchdog keeps ~ over a house; A sentry stands ~ at a gate;* **on** (or **off**) **one's guard** (un)prepared; **guard·house** *n.* where a military guard is housed; also, a military jail. **—guard·i·an** (–ee·un) *n.* a custodian, esp one in charge of a minor or a person unable to take care of himself or of his property: *Parents are their own children's "guardians by nature";* ***adj.:*** *a ~ angel;* **guard·i·an·ship** *n.* **—guard·rail** *n.* a protective rail(ing), as at the side of a staircase or highway. **—guard·room** *n.* a room for the use of guards; also, a room for keeping prisoners. **—guards·man** *n.* **-men** a member of the U.S. National Guard.

Gua·te·ma·la (gwah·tuh·MAH·luh) a country of N.W. Central America; 42,042 sq.mi. (108,889 km²); *cap.* **Guatemala City. —Gua·te·ma·lan** *n.* & *adj.*

gua·va (GWAH·vuh) *n.* the yellow or red, round or pear-shaped fruit containing hard seeds surrounded by grainy flesh of a tropical tree of the myrtle family.

gu·ber·na·to·ri·al (goo·bur·nuh·TOR·ee·ul) *adj.* of a governor or his office.

guck *n. Slang.* a gooey or mucky substance; **guck·y** *adj.*

Guern·sey (GURN·zee) *n.* **-seys** a breed of dairy cattle of fawn color with white markings.

guer·ril·la (guh·RIL·uh) *n.* a member of a volunteer force of irregulars fighting in small bands, usu. behind enemy lines, using hit-and-run tactics, sabotage, kidnappings, and such terrorist actions: *the ~ warfare of the Irish Republican Army; The Symbionese Liberation Army was an urban ~ group;* also **guer·il·la —guerrilla theater** drama performed on the streets or in parks dealing with controversial issues; street theater.

guess (GESS) *n.* & *v.* (form) a usu. correct estimate or judgment without sufficient evidence; conjecture; surmise: *Can you ~ her age? Your ~ is as good as mine; I ~* (*Informal.* suppose) *I was wrong.* **—guess·ti·mate** *n.* & *v. Informal.* (form) an estimate based on guessing. **—guess·work** *n.* guessing.

guest (GEST) *n.* a person receiving hospitality or being entertained at a home, club, etc. or a patron of a hotel or restaurant; also, a performer invited to take part in a show or program; ***adj.:*** *a ~ appearance; a ~ worker in West Germany.*

guff *n. Slang.* nonsense; empty talk.

guf·faw (guh·FAW) *n.* a coarse or loud laugh; ***v.:*** *to ~ at an off-color joke.*

Gui·a·na (gee·AN·uh, –AH·nuh) a region of N.E. South America divided into Guyana, Surinam, and French Guiana.

guid·ance (–unce) *n.* leadership or direction such as given to students on what courses to take ("educational guidance"), in choosing a career ("vocational guidance"), or to a missile in flight by means of radar, computers, etc. —**guide** (GUYED) *n.* a person or thing that shows the way, as on a tour; also, guidebook or guidepost; ***v.* guides, guid·ed, guid·ing** act as a guide; **guided missile** one that is guided to its target by signals from the ground or by devices inside it. —**guide·book** *n.* a book of information for tourists or travelers. —**guide·line** *n.* usu. **guidelines** *pl.* advice on policy by a controlling authority: *new ~s on energy conservation.* —**guide word** a word placed at the head of a page showing the first or last entry on it. —**gui·don** (GUY·dn, –don) *n.* an identifying flag, streamer, or pennant; also, a soldier who carries it.

guild (GILD) *n.* an association of people with a common interest, as of merchants or craftsmen of the same trade; hence, a labor union. —**guil·der** (GIL–) *n.* the basic money unit of the Netherlands and a silver coin worth 100 cents. —**guild·hall** *n.* a guild's meeting place; **guilds·man** *n.* **-men** a guild member.

guile (GUYLE) *n.* slyness and cunning; deceit: *a man full of ~;* **guile·ful** *adj.* —**guile·less** *adj.;* **guile·less·ness** *n.*

guil·le·mot (GIL·uh–) *n.* a Northern sea bird of the auk family with a slender, pointed bill.

guil·lo·tine (GIL·uh·teen) *n.* a heavy blade slid down grooves in an upright frame, used as a beheading machine; ***v.*** (gil·uh·TEEN) **-tines, -tined, -tin·ing:** *Many were ~d during the French Revolution.*

guilt (GILT) *n.* the fact or feeling of having done wrong; also, responsibility for blame: *a lawyer trying to establish ~; a ~-ridden conscience;* **guilt·less** *adj.;* **guilt·y** *adj.* **guilt·i·er, -i·est:** *a ~ look;* **guilt·i·ly** *adv.;* **guilt·i·ness** *n.*

guimpe (GIMP, GAMP) *n.* a blouse worn under a low-necked dress or jumper.

Guin·ea (GIN·ee), **Republic of.** a country on the W. coast of Africa; 94,926 sq.mi. (245,857 km^2); *cap.* Conakry; **Guin·e·an** *n.* & *adj.;* See also EQUATORIAL GUINEA. —**Guin·ea-Bis·sau** (–bi·SOW) a country on the W. coast of Africa; formerly "Portuguese Guinea"; 13,948 sq.mi. (36,125 km^2); *cap.* Bissau. —**guin·ea** *n.* a former British gold coin worth 21 shillings. —**guinea fowl** a W. African bird related to the pheasant and raised for its flesh and the eggs of the **guinea hen.** —**guinea pig** any of a group of furry rodents of South America much used in scientific testing and as pets.

guise (GUYZ) *n.* a garb or outward aspect, esp. a deceptive one: *under the ~ of friendship.*

gui·tar (guh·TAR) *n.* a musical instrument with six strings that are strummed or plucked; **gui·tar·ist** (–TAR–) *n.*

gulch *n.* a deep, narrow ravine.

gulden same as GUILDER.

gulf *n.* a large arm of an ocean extending into the land, as the Gulf of Mexico or Gulf of Aden; hence, a chasm or wide gap: *the ever-widening ~ between Russia and China.* —**Gulf States** Texas, Louisiana, Mississippi, Alabama, and Florida which border the Gulf of Mexico. —**Gulf Stream** a warm current flowing from the Gulf of Mexico and across the Atlantic toward N.W. Europe.

gull *n.* **1** any of a family of long-winged, gray-and-white ocean birds related to the terns, useful as scavengers around shore waters and destroyers of insects inland. **2** an easy victim of cheating, dupe; ***v.:*** *Con men ~ed her out of her savings;* **gull·i·ble** *adj.;* **gull·i·bil·i·ty** (–BIL–) *n.*

gul·let (–lit) *n.* the throat, including the esophagus and pharynx.

Gul·li·ver's Travels a novel by Jonathan Swift of four imaginary voyages.

gul·ly (GULL·ee) *n.* **gul·lies** a small ravine, esp. one worn by running water. —**gulp** *v.* swallow hastily or nervously: *He ~ed it down and hurried to the door; bravely ~ing back* (i.e. suppressing) *her tears;* ***n.:*** *He drained the bitter cup at one ~;* **gulp·er** n.

¹gum *n.* usu. **gums** *n.pl.* the firm, pink supporting tissue around the base of the teeth.

²gum *v.* **gums, gummed, gum·ming** smear or treat with something gummy; also, *Slang.* clog or mess up: *Keep the plans secret and don't let anyone* **gum up** *the works.* —***n.*** a sticky, water-soluble sap of certain trees such as the sapodilla, plum, peach, and eucalyptus, used for mucilage, drugs, candy, etc., esp. **gum arabic** obtained from an African acacia tree, used also in perfumes and textile manufacture.

gum·bo (–boh) *n.* **-bos** **1** the okra plant or its sticky pods; also, a chicken-and-rice soup thickened with this. **2** fine, silty prairie soil that is sticky when wet. **3** a Black French dialect of Louisiana.

gum·boil *n.* an abscess on the gums.

gum·drop *n.* a sweet and jellylike but stiff candy made with gum arabic.

gum·my (GUM·ee) *adj.* **gum·mi·er, gum·mi·est** sticky; covered with or giving off gum.

gump·tion *n. Informal.* enterprise and initiative.

gum resin a natural strong-smelling mixture of gum and resin, as asafetida, frankincense, and myrrh. —**gum·shoe** *n.* **1** a rubber overshoe; **gumshoes** *pl.* sneakers. **2** *Slang.* detective; ***v.* -shoes, -shoed, -shoe·ing.**

gun *n.* **1** a weapon using an explosive, usu. **gun·pow·der** made of saltpeter, sulfur, and charcoal, to shoot a bullet, shell, or other missile through a metal tube, esp. a cannon or machine gun; also, a rifle, pistol, or revolver. **2** something resembling a gun, as an *air gun* or an engine's throttle; also, *Slang.* a large surfboard. **3** a gunman; also, *Informal.* someone important, or "big gun"; *Slang* [jocular use] "*You son of a gun* (i.e. bastard)!" —***v.* guns, gunned, gun·ning** shoot (at) with a gun; also, speed: *motorcyclists ~ing their motors.* **—great guns** *Informal.* fast and furiously; vigorously: *going great ~s; blowing great ~s.* **—jump the gun** start too soon; also, get a head start. **—spike one's guns** frustrate one's efforts. **—stick to one's guns** be firm; refuse to retreat. **—gun·boat** *n.* a small, armed patrol boat; **gunboat diplomacy** military threats used to enforce treaties. **—gun·cot·ton** *n.* an explosive of cotton or other fiber soaked in a mixture of nitric and sulfuric acids, dried, and pressed into blocks. **—gun·fight** *n.* a fight using guns; **gun·fight·er** *n.* **—gun·fire** *n.* the firing of a gun or guns.

gung-ho *adj. Informal.* eager and enthusiastic.

gunk *n. Slang.* something thick and messy. **—gunk hole** a small cove or fishing harbor.

gun·lock *n.* a mechanism that sets off the charge in a gun. **—gun·man** *n.* **-men** an armed gangster. **—gun·met·al** *n.* formerly, a bronze used for making cannon; now, a dark-gray alloy with a bluish tinge.

gun·nel (GUNL) *n.* **1** a kind of eel-shaped fish of the N. Atlantic. **2** same as GUNWALE.

gun·ner *n.* a military man trained to use artillery or who has charge of a ship's guns; **gun·ner·y** *n.* heavy guns collectively or the science of making and using them.

gun·ny *n.* a burlap of jute or hemp; **gun·ny·bag** *n.*; **gun·ny·sack** *n.*

gun·play *n.* exchange of gunshots. **—at gun·point** under threat of being shot. **—gunpowder** See GUN, *n.* 1. **—gun·run·ning** *n.* smuggling of guns and ammunition. **—guns and butter** diplomacy using military and economic power. **—gun·ship** *n.* a heavily armed helicopter. **—gun·shot** *n.* shot, shooting, or range of a gun. **—gun-shy** *adj.* frightened by the sound of a gun, as some hunting dogs. **—gun·sling·er** *n.* gunman or gunfighter. **—gun·smith** *n.* one who makes or repairs small guns. **—gun·wale** (GUNL) *n.* the upper edge of a ship's or boat's side.

gup·py (GUP·ee) *n.* **gup·pies** a colorful tropical aquarium fish, also called "rainbow fish" or "peacock fish," whose grayish-green female bears living young.

gur·gle *n.* & *v.* **-gles, -gled, -gling** (flow with or make) the bubbling sound of water from a narrow-neck bottle.

Gur·kha (GOOR·kuh, GUR–) *n.* any of a warlike people of Nepal.

gu·ru (GOOR·oo) *n.* a Hindu religious teacher or guide; hence, a leader in any field: *McLuhan, the communications ~.*

gush *v.* pour out copiously, as water from a spring or blood from a wound; hence, express oneself effusively; ***n.*** a copious flow. **—gush·er** *n.* one who gushes; also, an oil well that flows without pumping. **—gush·y** *adj.* **gush·i·er, -i·est** *Informal.* effusive or sentimental.

gus·set *n.* a triangular or diamond-shaped piece of cloth, metal, etc. used to strengthen or enlarge, as over a seam in a garment or at a truss joint.

gus·sie or **gus·sy** (GUS·ee) *v.* **gus·sies, gus·sied, gus·sy·ing** *Slang.* smarten or dress up: *get ~d up for the party.*

gust *n.* a sudden burst or rush of wind; also, of rain, smoke, fire, sounds, or feelings. **—*v.*** blow in gusts: *winds ~ing to 30 mi. an hour.*

gus·ta·to·ry (–tuh·tor·ee) *adj.* of the sense of taste: *Your cooking is a ~ delight!* **—gus·to** (GUS·toh) *n.* **-tos** zest or relish.

gust·y *adj.* **gust·i·er, -i·est** marked by gusts: *a ~ day;* **gust·i·ly** *adv.*; **gust·i·ness** *n.*

gut *n.* the alimentary canal or a part of it, esp. intestines. **—guts** *n.pl.* **1** bowels; entrails; hence, *Informal.* the essential or working parts. **2** *Informal.* pluck or courage; also, impudence; **hate someone's guts** dislike someone intensely. **—*v.* guts, gut·ted, gut·ting** disembowel; hence, destroy the inside of: *a building ~d by a fire.* **—*adj.*** *Informal.* vital or basic; also, from one's inner self: *a ~ feeling of what is right; the ~ issues of the campaign;* **gut course** *Informal.* an easy-to-pass course. **—gut·less** *adj. Informal.* cowardly. **—guts·y** *adj.* **guts·i·er, -i·est** *Slang.* bold or lusty.

gut·ter *n.* a channel such as the ditch along the side of a street or the trough at the edge of a roof for carrying away rainwater or the grooves on either side of a bowling alley; hence, a low or wretched place: *the language of the ~.* **—*v.:*** *rainwater ~ing downhill; wax running down the sides of a ~ing candle.* **—gut·ter·snipe** *n.* a street urchin.

gut·tur·al (GUT·uh·rul) *adj.* of the throat; hence, rasping: *The hard "g" of "go" is a ~ sound; German sounds very ~ to the English;* ***n.:*** *~s are better known as velar sounds.*

gut·ty *adj.* **gut·ti·er, gut·ti·est** *Slang.* gutsy; also, basic or strongly evocative; having gut quality.

[1]guy *n.* a steadying or guiding rope, chain, or wire attached to a tent or tower; ***v.:*** *a free-standing, not ~ed structure.*

[2]guy *n. Informal.* a fellow: *a regular ~* (i.e. a good sport); *a wise ~* (i.e. a conceited fellow); *You* **guys** (i.e. boys and/or girls; fellows). **—*v.*** tease or ridicule.

Guy·a·na (guy·AN·uh) a republic on South America's N.E. coast; 83,000 sq. mi. (214,969 km^2); *cap.* Georgetown. **—Guy·a·nese** (–NEEZ) *n.* & *adj., sing.* & *pl.* (of or having to do with Guyana) or a person of or from Guyana.

guy·ot (gee·OH) *n.* a flat-topped submarine mountain.

guz·zle *v.* **guz·zles, guz·zled, guz·zling** eat or drink (something) greedily; **guz·zler** *n.*

gym (JIM) *n.* [short form] gymnasium; also, physical education. **—gym·kha·na** (–KAH–) *n.* a place for athletic contests; also, a contest or meet for horseriders or automobile drivers. **—gym·na·si·um** (–NAY·zee·um) *n.* **-si·ums**

or **-si·a** a room or building equipped for physical training and indoor athletics. —**gym·nast** (JIM–) *n.* a gymnastic expert; **gym·nas·tic** (–NAS–) *adj.* having to do with **gym·nas·tics** *n.pl.* exercises for physical fitness; **gym·nas·ti·cal·ly** *adv.* —**gym·no·sperm** (JIM·nuh–) *n.* a plant or tree whose fruit is not in an ovary as in angiosperms but exposed, as in conifers such as pines and firs.

gy·ne·col·o·gist (guy·nuh·COL·uh·jist, jye–) *n.* a medical specialist in **gy·ne·col·o·gy** *n.* a branch of medicine that, together with obstetrics, deals with specifically female functions and diseases; **gy·ne·co·log·ic** (–LOJ–) or **-i·cal** *adj.: a gynecological examination before getting married.*

gyp (JIP) *n.* & *v.* **gyps, gypped, gyp·ping** *Slang.* cheat(er); swindle(r); *adj.: ~ artist, ~ joint.* —**gyp·lure** *n.* a synthetic pheromone sex attractant used to trap gypsy moths. —**gyp·per** or **gyp·ster** *n.* swindler.

gyp·sum (JIP–) *n.* a hydrate of calcium sulfate, occurring in mineral form as alabaster and selenite, and used to make plaster of Paris, fertilizers, and **gypsum board,** a plasterboard.

Gyp·sy (JIP·see) *n.* **-sies** **1** a member of a wandering people, originally from India, with a Sanskrit-based language of their own; also called "Romany," "Zingaro," etc.; also **gyp·sy.** **2** the Indic language of the Gypsies; Romany. —**gyp·sy** *n.* one that is like a gypsy; ***adj.:*** *~ music; a ~ trucker* (i.e. an independent operator); **gypsy cab** one with no license to cruise for fares; **gypsy moth** a brownish moth, originally from Europe, whose larvae are destructive to trees.

gy·rate (JYE–) *v.* **-rates, -rat·ed, -rat·ing** turn with a swinging motion in a circular or spiral course, as a tornado, a figure skater, or a spinning top: *the ~ing hips of a rock singer.* **gy·ra·tion** (–RAY–) *n.;* **gy·ra·tor** (JYE–) *n.*

gyr·fal·con (JUR·fal·cun, –fawl–) *n.* an arctic falcon, the largest of the family.

gy·ro (JYE·roh) *n. Informal.* gyrocompass or gyroscope; **gyro-** *comb.form.* gyrating: as in *gyrocompass, gyropilot.* —**gy·ro·com·pass** (–cum·pus) *n.* a compass with a motor-driven gyroscope. —**gy·ro·pi·lot** *n.* a gyroscopic device to keep a ship or aircraft on course automatically; autopilot. —**gy·ro·scope** *n.* a heavy wheel or disk mounted in a movable frame to spin on an axis that resists change by gravity or by any other force, used in a **gy·ro·sta·bi·liz·er** (–STAY–) to counteract the rolling motion of a ship or aircraft; **gy·ro·scop·ic** (–SCOP–) *adj.*

gyve (JIVE) *n.* & *v.* **gyves, gyved, gyv·ing** *Archaic.* fetter.

H

H or **h** (AICH) *n.* **H's** or **h's** **1** the eighth letter of the English alphabet; hence, the eighth in a series. **2** anything H-shaped. **—H** henry; hydrogen. **—H.** or **h.** hard(ness); height; heroin; high; hit(s); hour(s); husband.

ha. hectare. **—ha** (HAH) *interj.* indicating surprise, joy, anger, etc.

Hab. Habakkuk (Old Testament book).

ha·be·as cor·pus (HAY·bee·us·COR·pus) *Law.* a writ requiring a prisoner to be produced in court to determine if he is being held legally.

hab·er·dash·er *n.* a dealer in haberdashery. **—hab·er·dash·er·y** *n.* **-er·ies** hats, ties, shirts, socks, etc. for men; also, a store that sells such items.

ha·bil·i·ment (huh·BIL·uh·munt) *n.* dress or attire; **habiliments** *pl.* garments.

hab·it *n.* **1** a settled tendency or disposition, acquired by practice, to perform an action almost automatically: *got into the ~ of taking drugs; makes a ~ of smoking in bed; a bad ~ that is difficult to break.* **2** a costume, as of nuns or priests. **3** a characteristic mode or appearance: *the prismatic or pyramidal ~ of a crystal; the twining ~ of a vine.* **—hab·it·a·ble** *adj.* able to be inhabited: *this ~ globe;* **hab·it·a·ble·ness** or **hab·it·a·bil·i·ty** (–BIL–) *n.;* **hab·it·a·bly** *adv.* **—hab·it·ant** (–unt) *n.* an inhabitant or settler, esp. a farmer, as in French Canada and Louisiana. **—hab·i·tat** *n.* natural habitation, esp. of a plant or animal; also, an underwater laboratory; Sealab. **—hab·i·ta·tion** (–TAY–) *n.* occupancy; hence, a home or settlement. **—hab·it-form·ing** *adj.* addictive: *Marijuana may not be ~, but narcotics are.* **—ha·bit·u·al** (huh·BICH·oo·ul) *adj.* done by habit; steady; also, customary: *his ~ drunkeness; her ~ place at the table;* **ha·bit·u·al·ly** *adv.;* **ha·bit·ual·ness** *n.* **—ha·bit·u·ate** (–BICH·oo·ate) *v.* **-ates, -at·ed, -at·ing** make used to: *a dog ~d to being let out at night; She ~d herself to the harsh climate;* **ha·bit·u·a·tion** (–AY–) *n.* **—ha·bit·u·é** (–BICH·oo·ay) *n.* a frequenter.

ha·ci·en·da (hah·see·EN·duh) in Spanish America, a large country estate, farm, ranch, or plantation; also, the main dwelling on it.

hack *v.* **1** cut or chop crudely: *He ~ed at the plowed field with a hoe.* **2** *Slang.* manage successfully: *just couldn't ~ it.* ***—n.*** **1** a common horse that may be hired for riding; also, an old or worn-out horse; hence, a drudge or plodding worker: *a literary ~.* **2** *Informal.* a taxicab.

hack·a·more *n.* a halter for breaking horses.

hack·ber·ry *n.* **-ber·ries** any of a group of trees related to the elms with cherrylike fruit; also called "nettle tree" and "netleaf hackberry."

hack hammer a tool for dressing stone. **—hack·ie** *n. Informal.* same as HACKMAN. **—hacking cough** a dry cough without discharge of phlegm. **—hacking jacket** one for use when riding, with **hacking** (i.e. slanted and flapped) **pockets.**

hack·le *n.* a neck feather of a fowl; **hackles** *pl.* hairs on a dog's neck that bristle when it is angry; **raise the hackles of** or **get one's hackles up** *Informal.* become or make (someone) angry or ready to fight.

hack·man *n.* **-men** a cabdriver. **—hack·ney** (–nee) *n.* **-neys** a common horse or a carriage or coach for hire; ***v.*** use too often; **hack·neyed** (–need) *adj.* clichéd. **—hack·saw** *n.* a saw for cutting metal. **—hack·work** *n.* the work of a hack, as done for hire.

had *pt.* & *pp.* of HAVE.

had·dock (–uck) *n.* a N. Atlantic food fish related to but smaller than cod.

Ha·des (HAY·deez) in Greek myth, the underworld; **hades** *n. Informal.* hell.

hadj same as HAJJ.

had·n't had not. **—hadst** *Archaic.* the form of *had* used with THOU.

had·ron (HAD·ron) *n.* any of a class of strongly interacting subatomic particles, including protons, neutrons, and most mesons; **had·ron·ic** (–RON–) *adj.*

haemo- same as HEMO-.
haf·ni·um (HAF·nee·um) *n.* a silvery metallic chemical element.
haft *n.* a hilt or handle.
hag *n.* an ugly old woman, esp. a witch.
Hag·ga·da(h) (huh·GAH·duh) *n., pl.* **-doth** (–dohth) *n.* **1** the illustrative, nonlegal part of the Talmud. **2** a narrative from the Exodus read at the Seder feast.
hag·gard (–urd) *adj.* careworn or emaciated; **hag·gard·ly** *adv.*
hag·gis *n.* a Scottish dish of minced heart, liver, lungs, etc. of a sheep or calf boiled in the animal's stomach with suet, oatmeal, and seasonings.
hag·gle *v.* **hag·gles, hag·gled, hag·gling** argue about (or over) a price or bargain; ***n.*** such a bargaining; **hag·gler** *n.*
hag·i·og·ra·phy (hag·ee·OG·ruh·fee) *n.* literature or a book dealing with lives of saints; **hag·i·og·ra·pher** *n.*
Hague (HAIG), **The.** political capital of the Netherlands.
hah *interj.* same as HA.
hahn·i·um *n.* an artificial radioactive chemical element; element 105.
hai·ku (HYE·koo) *n. sing.* & *pl.* a Japanese poem of three lines of a total of 17 syllables.
[1]**hail** *v.* greet; also, call (to): *They ~ed us as we drove by* **within hail(ing distance)**; *Jesus was ~ed (as) king of the Jews; Stand at the curb and ~ a cab; Most Chinese* **hail from** *China.* **—*n.*** a shout or cheer. **—*interj.:*** *All ~! "~ to the chief!"*
[2]**hail** *n.* (a shower of) frozen raindrops falling during a thunderstorm; hence, a shower of stones, bullets, blows, or other affliction. **—*v.:*** *It was ~ing all night; The mob ~ed insults at them.*
hail·er *n.* a bullhorn. **—Hail Mary** same as AVE MARIA.
hail·stone *n.* a pellet of hail. **—hail·storm** *n.* a storm with hail.
hair *n.* any of the fine, threadlike outgrowths from the skin of mammals, esp. from the human head; also, such hairs collectively; **get in one's hair** *Slang.* annoy one; **let one's hair down** act in an uninhibited manner; be unrestrained; **not turn a hair** show no reaction; **split hairs** make too fine distinctions; **to a hair** exactly; **hair·less** *adj.*; **hair·like** *adj.* **—hair·ball** *n.* a small mass of hair found in the stomach of a cow, cat, and such animals that lick their coats. **—hair(s)·breadth** *n.* & *adj.* very narrow (space): *He had a ~ escape in the accident.* **—hair·brush** *n.* a stiff brush for grooming the hair. **—hair·cloth** *n.* a fabric of cotton and horse's or camel's hair for use in upholstery and stiffening garments. **—hair·cut** *n.* the process or style of cutting the hair of the head. **—hair·do** (–doo) *n.* **-dos** (–dooz) way of arranging a woman's hair; coiffure. **—hair·dress·er** *n.* one who cuts and styles hair, esp. women's. **—hair·line** *n.* a very thin line; also, the outline of the hair above the forehead: *the receding ~ of a balding man;* ***adj.:*** *a questionable ~ decision; a ~ crack or fracture; a ~ space, printing stroke.* **—hair·piece** *n.* a toupee or a small wig as a hair accessory. **—hair·pin** *n.* a U-shaped metal or plastic pin used by women to keep their hair in place; ***adj.:*** *a ~ bend in the road.* **—hair-rais·er** *n.* something terrifying, esp. a story; **hair-rais·ing** *adj.* terrifying. **—hairs·breadth** *n.* & *adj.* same as HAIRBREADTH. **—hair·split·ting** *n.* & *adj.* (a) making too fine distinctions. **—hair·spray** *n.* a spray to keep the hair in place. **—hair·spring** *n.* a fine spring used to regulate the balance wheel of a watch. **—hair·style** *n.* coiffure; **hair·styl·ing** *n.* the work of a hairstylist; **hair·styl·ist** *n.* hairdresser. **—hair trigger** a delicately adjusted trigger that operates by the slightest pressure; **hair-trig·ger** *adj.: ~ laughter, nerves.* **—hair·y** *adj.* **hair·i·er, -i·est** covered with hair; also, of or like hair: *the ~ vetch; ~ woodpecker; a ~* (*Slang.* difficult or unpleasant) *situation;* **hair·y-chest·ed** *adj.* virile or robust; **hair·i·ness** *n.*
Hai·ti (HAY·tee) a West Indian republic, in the W. part of Hispaniola; 10,714 sq. mi. (27,750 km^2); *cap.* Port-au-Prince; **Hai·tian** (–shun, –tee·un) *n.* & *adj.* (of or having to do with Haiti), a person of or from Haiti, or the creole French spoken there.
hajj or **hadj** (HAJ) *n.* a pilgrimage to Mecca; **haj·ji** or **had·ji** (HAJ·ee) *n.* one who has made this pilgrimage.
hake *n.* a marine food fish related to the cod.
ha·la·la (huh·LAH·luh) *n.* a fractional money unit of Saudi Arabia equal to 5 qursh.
hal·berd or **hal·bert** (HAL–, HAWL–) *n.* a medieval weapon that is a battle-ax and spear in one.
hal·cy·on (HAL·see·un) *adj.* tranquil; prosperous: *in the ~ days of one's youth.*
hale *adj.* **hal·er, hal·est** healthy: *a ~ and hearty golden ager.*
hale *v.* **hales, haled, hal·ing** haul (a person): *was ~d into court.*
ha·ler (HAH·lur) *n.* a money unit of Czechoslovakia, equal to 1/100 of a koruna.
half (HAF) *n., pl.* **halves** (HAVZ) one of two equal parts making up something; also, one of a pair: *"~ a loaf is better than no bread"; one's better ~;* **in half** in two. **—*adj.:*** *a ~ hour; a ~ quart.* **—*adv.:*** *A ~ full glass is ~ empty: a potato that is ~ cooked;* **not half bad** *Informal.* not at all bad; good. **—half-and-half** *n., adj.* & *adv.* (a mixture, as of milk and cream) consisting of or in two equal parts. **—half·back** *n.* one of a pair of football players positioned with the fullback and quarterback behind the line of scrimmage. **—half-baked** *adj. Informal.* poor in planning or judgment: *a ~ idea, scheme, youth, visionary.* **—half-blood** *n.* an offspring that is **half-blood·ed** *adj.* born of parents of

different stocks or races; also, related through only one common parent. —**half-breed** *n.* & *adj.* [usu. offensive] (one) born of parents of differently colored races. —**half boot** a boot reaching halfway to the knee. —**half brother** (or **sister**) a brother (or sister) related through only one common parent. —**half-caste** *n.* & *adj.* [sometimes offensive] (one) of mixed European and Asian ancestry. —**half-cocked** *adj.* without full thought or consideration, like a firearm whose hammer is pulled back only halfway before firing. —**half dollar** a 50-cent coin of the U.S. or Canada. —**half-heart·ed(·ly)** *adj.* & *adv.* unwilling(ly) or uninterested(ly). —**half-life** *n.* the time taken for half the atoms of a radioactive sample to break down in a steady proportion of decreasing amounts. —**half-mast** *n.* the position of flying a flag halfway from the top of its mast as a sign of respect to a dead person or as a distress signal. —**half·pen·ny** (HAY·puh·nee) *n.* & *adj.* (worth) half a (British) penny; *pl.* **half·pence** (sum of money) or **half·pen·nies** (separate coins). —**half pint** *Slang.* a small person; **half-pint** *adj.: a ~ hero.* —**half sister** See HALF BROTHER. —**half sole** the front half of a sole; **half-sole** *v.* **-soles, -soled, -sol·ing:** *a repaired and ~d shoe, boot, etc.* —**half-staff** same as HALF-MAST. —**half step** a short military marching step; also, a musical half tone. —**half·tone** *n.* a picture-printing method by which shades intermediate between black and white are engraved as dots of varying size by photographing the picture through a fine screen. —**half-track** *n.* an army vehicle with tractor treads at the rear and wheels in front. —**half-truth** *n.* a deceptive statement giving only some of the facts. —**half·way** *adj.* & *adv.* midway; also, incomplete(ly); **meet** (or **go**) **halfway** be ready to make a helpful compromise; **halfway house** a rehabilitation center for former drug addicts, convicts, mental patients, etc. —**half-wit** *n.* fool; dolt; **half-wit·ted** *adj.* very stupid.

hal·i·but (HAL–, HOL–) *n.* any of a family of flatfishes of the flounder group caught in northern seas and widely used as food.

Hal·i·fax a seaport and capital of Nova Scotia.

hal·ite *n.* rock salt.

hal·i·to·sis (–TOH–) *n.* bad breath caused by a disorder of the stomach or mouth.

hall *n.* **1** a common passageway such as a corridor; hallway; also, a foyer or lobby. **2** a room, esp. a large one, such as a townhall, for meetings, parties, and such common uses. **3** an educational or residential building containing offices, housing a dormitory, etc.

hal·le·lu·jah or **hal·le·lu·iah** (hal·uh·LOO·yuh) *interj.* "Praise the Lord"; ***n.*** a hymn with this theme.

hall·mark *n.* & *v.* (put) an official mark guaranteeing quality, as Goldsmith's Hall in London used to stamp on gold and silver objects; hence, a distinguishing characteristic: *the ~s of a gentleman.*

hal·lo (huh·LOH) *n., v.* & *interj.* call or shout to greet or attract attention; also **hal·loa** (–LOH). —**hal·loo** (–LOO) *n., v.* & *interj.* **-loos, -looed, -loo·ing** hallo, esp. as used to urge (hounds) on in hunting.

hall of fame a memorial building in honor of celebrated people.

hal·low (HAL·oh) *v.* consecrate; also, consider holy. —**hal·lowed** (*also* -oh·wid *in "Hallowed be thy name"*) *adj.* blessed. —**Hal·low·een** or **Hal·low·e'en** (hal·oh·EEN, hol–) *n.* Allhallow's eve; October 31, esp. the evening.

hal·lu·ci·nate (huh·LOO·suh–) *v.* **-nates, -nat·ed, -nat·ing** (cause) to have a **hal·lu·ci·na·tion** (–NAY–) *n.* a seeing or experiencing things that are unreal or dreamlike, as when delirious or under the influence of a **hal·lu·ci·no·gen** (–LOO·sin·uh·jun) or a **hal·lu·ci·no·gen·ic** (–JEN–) drug such as LSD, STP, DMT, mescaline, etc. —**hal·lu·ci·na·tive** (–LOO·suh·nay·tiv) *adj.* —**hal·lu·ci·na·to·ry** *adj.*

hall·way *n.* a passageway; corridor.

ha·lo (HAY·loh) *n.* **-lo(e)s** a circle of light, as sometimes seen around the sun, moon, or other heavenly body and symbolically pictured around the heads of saints and such personages as a mark of glory.

hal·o·gen (–uh·jun) *n.* any of the five chemical elements astatine, flourine, chlorine, bromine, and iodine that combine with metals to form salts.

halt *n.* a usu. brief stop: *The strike brought operations* **to a halt;** *effective steps to* **call a halt** *to wasteful spending.* —***v.*** **1** (cause) to stop: *Halt! Who goes there? The marchers ~ed for refreshments.* **2** hesitate or waver. —***adj.*** *Archaic.* lame: *curing the ~ and the sick.*

hal·ter (HAWL·tur) *n.* **1** a rope or strap around the neck, as for leading a horse, esp. one connected to a headstall, a noose for hanging, etc.; hence, death by hanging; ***v.*** tie with or put a halter on; hence, restrain. **2** a woman's backless bodice, often **halters** or **halter top,** held by a strap around the back of the neck.

halt·ing *adj.* faltering; also, lame or limping: *his ~ gait; testified in a ~ voice;* **halt·ing·ly** *adv.*

hal·va(h) (HAHL·vah) *n.* a sweet, pasty Turkish confection of ground sesame seeds and honey.

halve (HAV) *v.* **halves, halved, halv·ing** divide or share equally; also, reduce to half. —**halves** (HAVZ) *n.pl.* of HALF; **by halves** incompletely; **go halves** share equally; rarely **halv·ers,** half shares: as in "go halvers (with)," "do by halvers."

hal·yard (HAL·yurd) *n.* a rope or tackle for hauling a sail, flag, etc. up or down.

ham *n.* **1** the back of a thigh and buttock, as of a pig, esp. as salted and dried or smoked meat: *squatted on his* **hams;** *a breakfast of ~ and eggs; a ~ sandwich.* **2** *Informal.* an inexpert or clumsy performer; amateur: *a radio ~* (i.e. operator); ***adj.:*** *a ~ actor;* ***v.*** **hams, hammed, ham·ming:** *spoiled his act by* **hamming it up** (i.e. overacting).

Ham·burg a city-state and port of N. West Germany. **—ham·burg(·er)** *n.* ground beef, a patty of such meat, or one cooked and sandwiched in a split bun: *~ with the works* (i.e. ketchup, mustard, tomato slice, onion, and pickle).

Ham·il·ton (–tun) a city and port of S.E. Ontario.

Ham·ite *n.* a Caucasoid people of N. and E. Africa including ancient Egyptians, Somalis, and Berbers; **Ha·mit·ic** (–MIT–) *adj.: Cushitic is a ~ language group.*

Ham·let (–lit), prince of Denmark, the hero of Shakespeare's play of that name. **—ham·let** *n.* a small village.

ham·mer (HAM·ur) *n.* a pounding tool, usu. with a metal head set crosswise at the end of a wooden handle; also, anything similar, as one of the wooden mallets inside a piano, an auctioneer's gavel, the striking mechanism of a firing pin, or a bone of the middle ear: *a* **ham·mer-and-tongs** (i.e. vigorous) *approach to a problem; Unclaimed articles go* **under the hammer** (i.e. the auctioneer's gavel, for auction sale). **—*v.*** work with or as if with a hammer; strike with repeated blows; hence, work hard: **hammering away** *at her dissertation; to* **hammer out** *a solution to a vexing problem.* **—hammer and sickle** a Communist emblem symbolizing the laborer and the farmer. **—ham·mer·head** *n.* any of various sharks with a mallet-shaped head and eyes on each end. **—ham·mer·lock** *n.* a wrestling hold in which the opponent's arm is held twisted behind his back. **—hammer throw** an athletic contest using a metal ball attached to a steel wire, thrown for distance. **—ham·mer·toe** *n.* a bent and deformed toe.

ham·mock (–uk) *n.* a cradlelike swinging couch, as one of netted cord slung by its ends between supports.

ham·per (HAM·pur) *v.* impede the movement or hinder the freedom of: *A heavy snowfall ~ed our progress.* **—*n.*** a large covered basket or container, as for food, wine, laundry, or mail.

ham·ster *n.* a small rodent of the mouse family with large cheek pouches and a short tail.

ham·string *n.* either of the two tendons at the back of the knee connecting the three **hamstring muscles** of the thigh; in quadrupeds such as the horse, a large tendon at the back of the hock. **—*v.*** **-strings,** *pt. & pp.* **-strung** or **-stringed, -string·ing** cripple or disable, (as if) by cutting the hamstring: *press freedom hamstrung by restrictions.*

hand *n.* **1** the end part of the forearm that is below the wrist, used for grasping and holding; hence, a limb or other part similar to the human hand in appearance or use, as the foot of a clawed bird or the hands of a clock. **2** a person or his action, skill, or power: *All ~s on deck; Give me a ~ to move this desk; Pilate would have no ~ in the crucifixion; a great ~ at basket-weaving; writes a legible ~; fell into the* **hands** *of the enemy.* **3** what is given with the hand: *The audience gave him a big ~* (i.e. round of applause) *as he entered; dared not ask her ~ in marriage; the warm ~ of friendship.* **4** the cards dealt to or held by a player in a game; also, a round of play. **—at hand** close by; **hand in** (or **and**) **glove** in close cooperation; **hand in hand** together; **hands down** easily; **on hand** within reach; also, present; **on the one** (or **other**) **hand** from one (or the opposite) point of view; **out of hand** out of control; also, forthwith: *a petition rejected out of ~.* **—*v.*** give or do with the hand or as if with the hand: *She ~ed him his drink; courteously ~ed her into the car; a legend* **handed down** *from generation to generation; an opinion ~ed down by a court; so successful everyone* **hands it** (i.e. gives credit) *to her.* **—hand·bag** *n.* a small bag to hold in the hand, esp. a woman's purse. **—hand·ball** *n.* a game played by striking a rubber ball with the hand against a wall or board. **—hand·bill** *n.* a notice that is passed out or distributed by hand. **—hand·book** *n.* a short manual or guidebook; also, a book for recording bets. **—hand·car** *n.* a small, open, four-wheeled railroad car used by workmen, formerly operated by pumping a handle. **—hand·cart** *n.* a cart that is pulled or pushed by hand. **—hand·clasp** *n.* a handshake. **—hand·craft** *n.* handicraft; ***v.:*** *not machine-made but ~ed parts.* **—hand·cuff** *n.* one of a pair of metal rings joined by a short chain, used in restraining prisoners; ***v.*** manacle; also, check or hinder. **—hand·ed** *adj.* or *comb.form.* having hands or a certain kind or number of hands: *a two-~ stroke; a left-~ writer;* **hand·ed·ness** *n.*

Han·del (HAN·dl), **George F.** 1685–1759, English composer, born in Germany.

hand·ful *n.* **-fuls** **1** what the hand can hold; hence, a small number or amount. **2** *Informal.* a person or thing that is hard to manage. **—hand·gun** *n.* a firearm such as a pistol that is held and fired with one hand. **—hand·i·cap** (HAN·dee–) *n.* **1** a disadvantage or hindrance: *poverty as a ~ to progress.* **2** a disadvantage or advantage, as allowances of time, distance, or weight, given to competitors in a contest or game to give everyone an equal chance to win; also, a game or race in which such handicaps are used; ***v.*** **-caps, -capped, -cap·ping:** *~d by a speech defect; the* **handicapped** *such as the deaf, blind, crippled, retarded, and the mentally ill; trapshooting competitors ~d up to 9 meters.* **—hand·i·cap·per** *n.* **—hand·i·craft** *n.* the skillful making of articles by hand; also, a trade or art using such skill, as macrame, ceramics, or basket-weaving; also, a handicraft product or artifact; **hand·i·craft·er** or **hand·i·crafts·man** *n.* **-men** —**hand·i·work** *n.* handwork; also, work done personally; an individual achievement: *the universe as the ~ of God.* —**hand·ker·chief** (HANG·kur·chif) *n.* **-chiefs** or **-chieves** (–cheevz) a usu. square piece of cloth carried on one's person for wiping the face, hands, etc.; also, a kerchief. —**han·dle** (HAN·dl) *n.* the part of a tool, door, cup, etc. for holding, grasping, or manipulating it; **fly off the handle** *Informal.* lose one's temper; ***v.*** **han·dles, han·dled, han·dling** take, operate, manage, or control (as if) with one's hand(s); also, respond to control: *A crowd has to be tactfully ~d; a car that ~s well;* **hand·ler** *n.* —**han·dle·bar** *n.* a bar with a handle at each end for steering a bicycle or motorcycle; also, a **handlebar moustache** that resembles a handlebar. —**hand·made** *adj.* made by hand, not by machine. —**hand·maid(·en)** *n.* formerly, a female personal attendant; hence, auxiliary: *logic as the ~ of philosophy.* —**hand-me-down** *n.* something, as a garment, handed down from an older person; ***adj.*** secondhand or cheap: *an ill-fitting ~ suit.* —**hand·out** *n. Informal.* something handed out as charity, free gift, promotional literature, or an official version, as of a news story. —**hand·pick** *v.* pick (fruits or vegetables) or choose (as one's supporters or aides); **hand·picked** *adj.* personally selected, often unfairly. —**hand·rail** *n.* a rail for holding as support, as along a stairway. —**hand·set** *n.* a modern one-piece telephone receiver and mouthpiece. —**hand·shake** *n.* a friendly clasping and shaking of each other's hands; also, a money gift: *a golden ~* (i.e. generous payment on parting). —**hands-off** *adj.* noninterfering. —**hand·some** (–sum) *adj.* **-som·er, -som·est** good-looking, usu. in a manly way; also, generous; considerable: *a ~ horse, treatment, gift, amount;* **hand·some·ly** *adv.;* **hand·some·ness** *n.* —**hands-on** *adj.* involving active participation. —**hand·spring** *n.* a tumbling forward or backward on the hands, making a full circle in midair before landing on the feet. —**hand·stand** *n.* a standing on one's hands with the legs up. —**hand-to-hand** *adj.* & *adv.* close together; involving physical contact: *fought ~; a ~ combat.* —**hand-to-mouth** *adj.* spending or consuming with no provision for the future; precarious: *a ~ existence.* —**hand·work** *n.* work done with one's hands; **hand·work·er** *n.* —**hand·writ·ing** (–RITE–) *n.* writing by hand or its style; **hand·writ·ten** (–RITN) *adj.* —**hand·y** (–ee) *adj.* **hand·i·er, -i·est** **1** convenient; also, readily available: *Keep your pencils ~; An eraser will* **come in handy** *for corrections.* **2** skilled, usu. without training, for odd jobs: *a husband ~ around the house;* **hand·i·ly** *adv.;* **hand·i·ness** *n.* —**hand·y·man** *n.* **-men** one who does odd jobs.

hang *v.* **hangs,** *pt.* & *pp.* **hanged** (in "kill" senses) or **hung, hang·ing** **1** attach, fasten, or suspend so as to swing or turn freely; also, be suspended: *A coat is hung on a hook; pictures ~ing on a wall; laundry hung out to dry; hung her head in shame; condemned to be ~ed by the neck; Judas ~ed himself;* **Hang it!** (i.e. Damn it!). **2** cover or furnish with something suspended, as a wall with tapestry or a window with drapes. **3** be or seem suspended, as when undecided, idle, etc.: *A* **hung jury** *is one that cannot agree on a verdict; His career ~s* (i.e. depends) *on your recommendation; Time is ~ing on his hands since he quit his job.* —***n.*** **1** the way something hangs; also, *Informal.* how something is done or what something means: *I like the ~ of that curtain; I couldn't get the ~ of his poem.* **2** a trifle: *don't care a ~ for him.* —**hang around** (or **about**) *Informal.* loiter or stand by idly. —**hang back** be reluctant: *so shy he ~s back from group activities.* —**hang in there** *Informal.* keep on; persevere; don't give up. —**hang loose** *Informal.* be relaxed. —**hang on** keep one's hold or grip. —**hang out** *Informal.* live or stay; also, frequent; **let it all hang out** *Informal.* let one's hair down; be uninhibited. —**hang up** put back on a hanger or hook, as the receiver at the end of a phone call: *She* **hung up on** *the harassing caller.*

hang·ar (–ur) *n.* a shed or shelter, as for aircraft.

hang·dog *adj.* sneaking or shamefaced. —**hang·er-on** *n.* **-ers-on** [contemptuous use] dependent or follower. —**hang gliding** the sport of gliding or soaring using a kitelike device that carries the glider harnessed underneath it. —**hang·ing** *n.* death by hanging; ***adj.*** that hangs; also, deserving death by hanging; **hangings** *n.pl.* things hung, as draperies or curtains. —**hang-loose** *adj.* relaxed; uninhibited. —**hang·man** *n.* **-men** executioner. —**hang·nail** *n.* a shred of dead or loose skin near a fingernail. —**hang·out** *n. Slang.* a place where one hangs out; frequent resort. —**hang·o·ver** (HANG·oh–) *n. Informal.* aftereffects such as headache, dizziness, and depression following a drinking bout. —**hang-up** *n. Slang.* a mental or emotional problem.

hank *n.* a coil or loop, as of hair or thread.

han·ker (HANG·kur) *v.* yearn; long or crave (*for* or *after* wealth, renown, etc.); **han·ker·ing** *n.* longing.

han·kie or **han·ky** *n.* **-kies** *Informal.* handkerchief.

han·ky-pan·ky (hang·kee·PANG·kee) *n. Informal.* underhand dealings or affairs.

Ha·noi (hah·NOY) capital of Vietnam.

han·som (–sum) *n.* a two-wheeled one-horse-drawn carriage with the driver's seat high up behind the cab; also **hansom cab.**

Ha·nuk·kah (HAH·nuh·kuh) *n.* a Jewish festival in December to commemorate the rededication of the Temple of Jerusalem in 165 B.C.

hao·le (HOW·lay, –lee) *n.* in Hawaii, a non-Polynesian, esp. a white.

hap *n. Archaic.* happening; also, a chance or lot; ***v.* haps, happed, hap·ping** happen; occur by chance. **—hap·haz·ard** (–HAZ·urd) *adj.* careless or chancy: *a ~ filing of papers;* ***adv.*** *books left ~ over the desk;* ***n.*** *gifts selected* **at haphazard; hap·haz·ard·ly** *adv.;* **hap·haz·ard·ness** *n.;* **hap·haz·ard·ry** *n.* **—hap·less** *adj.* unlucky; **hap·less·ly** *adv.;* **hap·less·ness** *n.*

hap·loid *n.* & *adj.* (cell or gamete) with a single set of unpaired chromosomes in each nucleus.

hap·ly *adv.* by chance.

hap·pen *v.* take place, esp. by chance; occur: *The accident ~ed on the highway; You're late, what ~ed?* **—happen (up)on** meet or find by chance. **—happen to** be done to or experienced by: *What could have ~ed to our child?* **—hap·pen·ing** *n.* an occurrence; also, an event, activity, or performance of a spontaneous or vital nature with many participants, as action painting and "Living Theater." **—hap·pen·stance** *n.* a chance circumstance or happening.

hap·pi (HAP·ee) **coat** a loose Japanese outer coat.

hap·py (HAP·ee) *adj.* **hap·pi·er, hap·pi·est** **1** glad or pleased; also, fortunate: *a ~ family; a ~ chance.* **2** felicitous or apt: *a ~ expression.* **—hap·pi·ly** *adv.;* **hap·pi·ness** *n.* **-happy** *comb.form.* light-headed or dazed: as in *bomb-happy, trigger-happy, gold-happy.* **—hap·py-go-luck·y** *adj.* easygoing; light-hearted.

ha·ra-ki·ri (HAH·ruh·KEER·ee) *n.* suicide by disembowelment, as once practiced by the samurai.

ha·rangue (huh·RANG) *n.* & *v.* **-rangues, -rangued, -rangu·ing** (address in or deliver) a long and loud, esp. scolding speech; tirade.

har·ass (HAIR·us, huh·RAS) *v.* bother or torment unceasingly, as by repeated raids, demands, cares, worries, etc.; **har·ass·ment** *n.*

Har·bin a city of Manchuria, China.

har·bin·ger (–jur) *n.* & *v.* (one that goes before to) announce what is to come: *the early-blooming "harbinger-of-spring."*

har·bor (HAR·bur) *n.* a protected area of deep water on the coast of a sea or lake where ships may dock; hence, shelter; place of safety or refuge. **—*v.*** come to anchor; hence, be or give a hiding place to an undesirable person, thing, or feeling: *hair that ~s fleas; ~ing grudges;* **har·bor·age** (–ij) *n.* **—har·bour** *Brit.* harbor.

hard *adj.* **1** too firm to penetrate, cut, or crush, as rock, nuts, strong muscles, etc.; hence, of liquor, high in alcohol content; of water, difficult to form lather with soap; of money and currency, made of metal, not paper, or backed by gold. **2** not soft, weak, tentative, or visionary: *a ~ and unyielding character; faced with ~ evidence, decisions, facts; take a good ~ look.* **3** tough to endure; distressing; harsh; severe; rough: *work that is too ~ for me; the ~ times of the Depression; left with ~ feelings; The baby gave us a ~ time; said ~ things to her lover; ~ winter weather; Everyone dislikes* **hard and fast** (i.e. strict) *rules; was* **hard put** (i.e. barely able) *to find a night's lodging in that strange city; a big spender* **hard up** *for* (*Informal.* in great need of) *funds at the end of each month; the ~ "c" and "g" of "cat" and "gut," etc., not soft as in "city" and "gem."* **4** demanding great physical or mental effort; not easy: *a habit ~ to break; a list of ~ words; an earphone for the* **hard of hearing** (i.e. those who don't hear well); *a knot ~ to undo; the long, ~ march to freedom.* **—hard·ness** *n.* **—*adv.*:** *The lake is frozen ~ enough to skate on; boys working ~ to finish an exercise; Running makes you breathe ~; Inflation hits everyone ~; It will go ~ with you if you don't pay up; took that defeat very ~; a church ~* (i.e. close) *by the school.* **—hard·back** *n.* a book with hard covers. **—hard-bit·ten** (–BITN) *adj.* tough or stubborn. **—hard·board** *n.* board of pressed wood-chip fibers. **—hard-boiled** *adj.* of an egg, boiled with its shell until firm inside; hence, *Informal.* of persons, callous or tough. **—hard·bound** *adj.* hard-cover. **—hard cider** See CIDER. **—hard-core** *adj.* chronic or extreme: *the ~ unemployed and unemployables of a community; explicit, ~ pornography.* **—hard-cov·er** *adj.* of books, bound in cloth, board, or other stiff cover, not paperback. **—hard drug** heroine, cocaine, morphine, or other addictive drug. **—hard·en** *v.* make hard or become solidified; hence, make or become able to endure; also, make or become unfeeling or pitiless: *~ed by training; ~ed criminals;* **hard·en·er** *n.* **—hard·hack** *n.* a species of spirea with flowers growing in narrow, crowded clusters. **—hard hat** a protective helmet worn by miners, construction workers, etc.; hence, an outspoken reactionary. **—hard·head·ed** *adj.* **1** stubborn. **2** practical; realistic: *a ~ businessman.* **—hard·heart·ed** *adj.* cruel; unfeeling. **—har·di·hood** (–dee–) *n.* daring or sturdiness; also, audacity or boldness.

Har·ding, Warren G. 1865–1923, 29th U.S. President (1921–23).

hard-line *adj.* unyielding in policy, esp. political; **hard-lin·er** *n.* **—hard·ly** *adv.* **1** barely; almost not; probably not: *I can ~ walk; ~ anyone turned up at the meeting; You can ~ expect to be paid for such poor work.* **2** in a hard manner: *was dealt with ~ and severely.* **—hard-nosed** *adj. Informal.* shrewd and tough: *a ~ politician.* **—hard palate** See PALATE. **—hard·pan** *n.* subsoil too cemented and compacted for roots to penetrate. **—hard rock** the original rock'n'roll with a loud and steady beat. **—hard·scrab·ble** *adj.* earning a bare subsistence; also, of land, barren. **—hard sell** *Informal.* high-pressure salesmanship; **hard-sell** *adj.:* *~ tactics.* **—hard·shell(ed)** *adj. Informal.* uncompromising or rigid, esp. in religious matters. **—hard·ship** *n.* a hard-to-bear condition such as hunger, sickness, or pain. —**hard·stand** *n.* a hard-surfaced parking area, as for aircraft. —**hard·tack** *n.* a hard, dry biscuit or unleavened bread, as once used by sailors and soldiers. —**hard·top** *n.* a convertible-style automobile with a rigid roof but no posts between front and rear windows. —**hard·ware** *n.* **1** metal articles, tools, utensils, etc. **2** weaponry, equipment, and apparatuses such as the physical units of a computer system, not programs or software. —**hard·wood** *n.* tough, compact wood, as of broad-leaved trees such as the oak, teak, ebony, and mahogany; ***adj.:*** *a ~ floor.* —**har·dy** (–dee) *adj.* **hard·i·er, -i·est** strong and robust: *our ~ pioneers; ~ annuals that can endure the frost;* **hard·i·ly** *adv.;* **hard·i·ness** *n.*

hare *n.* a rabbitlike furry animal but longer and with longer ears, a split upper lip, and powerful hind legs; jack rabbit: *~s do not burrow but are very active in the spring; "mad as a March ~."* —**hare·bell** *n.* bluebell. —**hare·brained** *adj.* giddy or flighty. —**hare·lip** *n.* cleft lip; **hare·lipped** *adj.*

har·em (HAIR·um) *n.* women's section of a traditional Moslem household; also, the women living there, esp. those associated with one man; hence, an animal's mates collectively.

hark *v.* listen! —**hark back** recall or refer back (*to* an earlier subject or occasion). —**hark·en** same as HEARKEN.

har·le·quin (HAR·luh–) *n.* a comic character wearing a tight-fitting costume in diamond-shaped patches of color, originally from Italian pantomime.

har·lot (–lut) *n.* a prostitute; **har·lot·ry** *n.*

harm *n.* & *v.* (cause) hurt with pain or distress; **harm·ful** *adj.;* **harm·ful·ly** *adv.* —**harm·less** *adj.;* **harm·less·ly** *adv.;* **harm·less·ness** *n.*

har·mon·ic (–MON–) *adj.* having to do with musical harmony. —***n.*** a musical overtone; **har·mon·i·cal·ly** *adv.* —**har·mon·i·ca** (–MON–) *n.* a small wind instrument with metal reeds that is played with the mouth; mouth organ. —**harmonic motion** vibrating motion like that of a pendulum. —**harmonics** *n.pl.* [takes *sing. v.*] the science of musical sounds. —**har·mo·ni·ous** (–MOH·nee·us) *adj.* arranged so that the parts agree; also, agreeing in feelings, actions, etc.; concordant: *a ~* (i.e. sweet-sounding) *melody; the ~ relationships in a multiracial community;* **har·mo·ni·ous·ly** *adv.;* **har·mo·ni·ous·ness** *n.* —**har·mo·ni·um** *n.* a small type of reed organ. —**har·mo·nize** (HAR–) *v.* **-niz·es, -nized, -niz·ing** be in or make harmony: *Complementary colors ~ well; music ~d in chords;* **har·mo·niz·er** *n.;* **har·mo·ni·za·tion** (–ZAY–) *n.* —**har·mo·ny** (–muh·nee) *n.* **-nies** musical agreement of sounds, esp. of various tones and chords; hence, agreement in thoughts, feelings, words, actions, etc.; accord; also, any orderly arrangement: *the ~ of color and form in a painting; the peace and ~ of a happy family; people living in ~ with the environment; racial ~.*

har·ness (–nis) *n.* a combination of straps, bands, etc. for hitching an animal to what it pulls, as a horse to a carriage or plow; also, similar trappings to tie a person to a parachute, restrain an automobile driver for safety, or have a child or dog in one's control; **in harness** at one's regular occupation. —***v.*** put a harness on; also, utilize the power of (water, wind, atomic energy, etc.).

harp *n.* the oldest of stringed musical instruments, played by a **harp·ist** by plucking its strings with the fingers. —***v.*** play on a harp; **harp (up)on** refer continually to (a tiresome subject).

har·poon (–POON) *n.* a spear with a long coiled line attached, thrown or shot to catch whales and such sea animals; ***v.*** strike or catch with a harpoon; **har·poon·er** *n.*

harp·si·chord (–cord) *n.* the medieval forerunner of the piano, whose strings are plucked by tabs connected to the keyboard.

har·py *n.* **-pies** **1** a cruel and greedy person like the **Harpies** (*sing.* **Har·py**) of Greek myth, winged monsters with a woman's head and bird's body. **2** a tropical American eagle.

har·ri·dan (HAIR·i·dn) *n.* a shrewish old woman.

har·ri·er (HAIR·ee·ur) *n.* **1** a breed of dog smaller than the English foxhound, used to hunt hares. **2** a cross-country runner. **3** one who harries; also, a kind of hawk that preys on rodents, reptiles, and poultry, also called "marsh hawk."

Har·ris·burg (HAIR–) capital of Pennsylvania.

Har·ri·son (HAIR–) **1 Benjamin.** 1833–1901, 23rd U.S. President (1889–93). **2 William H.** 1773–1841, 9th U.S. President (1841).

har·row (HAIR·oh) *v.* **1** break up and level plowed ground, as with a harrow. **2** lacerate, wound, or distress: *a* **harrowing** (i.e. painful) *experience.* —***n.*** an implement with a set of revolving disks *(disk harrow),* or one with spikes or teeth for breaking and smoothing the soil.

har·ry (HAIR·ee) *v.* **har·ries, har·ried, har·ry·ing** harass or torment; also, raid or pillage.

harsh *adj.* **1** disagreeably rough to the senses: *~ flavor, portrait, sounds, colors, climate.* **2** cruel or unfeeling: *a ~ parent.* —**harsh·ly** *adv.;* **harsh·ness** *n.*

hart *n.* an antlered male of the European red deer. —**har·te·beest** (–tuh·beest) *n.* a large, now scarce African antelope.

Hart·ford (–furd) capital of Connecticut.

har·um-scar·um (HAIR·um·SCAIR–) *adj.* & *adv.* (in a) reckless and irresponsible (way).

har·vest *n.* the season for gathering in crops of grain, fruit, vegetables, etc.; also, the gathering in or the crop itself; hence, the fruit or reward of one's labors. —***v.*** reap; **har·vest·er** *n.* a person or machine that harvests crops.

has third person *sing.* of HAVE. **—has-been** (HAZ·bin) *n. Informal.* a person or thing whose heyday is past.

hash *v.* **1** chop into small pieces for cooking; hence, make a mess of. **2** *Informal.* discuss; **hash out** settle by discussing; **hash over** talk over. **—*n.*** **1** cooked food hashed and fried or baked; hence, a mixture or hodgepodge; **make a hash of** make a mess of; **settle one's hash** *Informal.* subdue, silence, or make an end of one. **2** *Slang.* short for **hash·ish** (–eesh, –ish) *n.* a narcotic prepared from the resin yielded by the flowering tops of the hemp plant; also **hash·eesh.**

Has·id *n., pl.* **-id·im** a member of the **Ha·sid·ic** (–SID–) Jewish sect founded in Poland in the 1700's; **Has·i·dism** (HAS–) *n.*

has·n't (HAZ·nt) has not.

hasp *n.* a fastening device for a door or lid consisting of a hinged metal clasp fitting over a staple through which a peg or padlock is put to secure it.

has·sle *n. Informal.* a wrangle, argument, or tussle; ***v.*** **has·sles, has·sled, has·sling** have a hassle; also, harass or pester.

has·sock (–uk) *n.* a cushioned seat or footstool.

hast *Archaic.* the form of *have* used with THOU.

haste *n.* hurry, esp. in a careless manner: *"~ makes waste"*; **make haste** same as **has·ten** (HAY·sn) *v.* hurry or speed up; also, be quick: *Let me ~ to add no offense was meant.* **—hast·y** (HAY·stee) *adj.* **hast·i·er, -i·est** quick; also, too quick or quick-tempered; rash; **hast·i·ly** *adv.;* **hast·i·ness** *n.* **—hasty pudding** mush of cornmeal or, in Britain, of flour or oatmeal.

hat *n.* a head covering with a brim and crown for formal or outdoor wear: *You* **pass the hat** *round to take up a collection;* **take off one's hat to** *someone as a sign of respect;* **throw one's hat into the ring** *to enter a contest;* **(keep) under one's hat** *Informal.* (keep) private or confidential.

hatch *n.* **1** an opening, as in a ship's deck for loading cargo; also, a trapdoor covering it. **2** an opening or door in a spacecraft or aircraft. **3** a set of hatched lines; also **hatch·ing.** **—*v.*** **1** draw or engrave fine parallel lines for shading effect. **2** keep (eggs) warm so as to bring out the young; also, come out or bring forth (young) from eggs; hence, to plot or scheme: *prisoners ~ing an escape plot;* **hatch·er** *n.* **—hatch·back** *n.* an automobile with a trunk whose hinged door lifts all the way to the roof.

hat·check *adj.* having to do with the checking of coats and hats: *a ~ girl; a ~ stand.*

hatch·er·y *n.* **-er·ies** a place where eggs are hatched.

hatch·et *n.* a small, short-handled ax, as used to kill; tomahawk; **bury** (or **dig up**) **the hatchet** make peace (or war); **hatchet job** *Informal.* a malicious attack; **hatchet man** *Informal.* one hired to deal viciously with opponents.

hatch·way *n.* a hatch or entrance.

hate *v.* **hates, hat·ed, hat·ing** dislike intensely, usu. with malice and a tendency to hurt; hence, shrink from: *I ~ getting soaked; ~ ice cream; ~ to disturb you;* **hat·er** *n.* **—*n.*** hostility or an object of it; ***adj.:*** *flooded by ~ mail; a ~ campaign.* **—hate·ful** *adj.;* **hate·ful·ly** *adv.;* **hate·ful·ness** *n.*

hath *Archaic.* has.

ha·tred (HAY–) *n.* ill will; strong dislike.

hat·ter *n.* one who makes or deals in hats.

hau·berk (HAW–) *n.* a long tunic of chain mail.

haugh·ty (HAW·tee) *adj.* **-ti·er, -ti·est** proud in bearing or manner, esp. scornful of others; **haugh·ti·ly** *adv.;* **haugh·ti·ness** *n.*

haul *v.* **1** pull or tug with sustained force; hence, transport: *the ~ing of freight by truck or train;* **haul off and** *Informal.* move suddenly to (do something, as to hit); *so I ~ed off and kissed her.* **2** shift or change, as a wind or a sailing ship's course. **—*n.*** a load, amount, or distance hauled: *fled with a million-dollar ~; a short-~ flight;* **in** (or **over**) **the long haul** over a long period. **—haul·age** (–ij) *n.* a hauling (charge).

haunch *n.* hindquarter, including hip, buttock, and top of thigh: *A dog sits on its ~es; a ~* (i.e. loin and leg) *of venison.*

haunt *v.* visit continually or seem to stay in a place, as a spirit inhabiting a house; hence, plague or obsess: *Memories from her past ~ her in her dreams.* **—*n.*** a frequently visited place: *revisiting the ~s of one's youth; a favorite ~ of criminals.* **—haunt·ed** *adj.: That house is ~* (by ghosts). **—haunt·ing** *adj.: a ~ melody;* **haunt·ing·ly** *adv.*

haut·boy (HOH–) *n.* an early version of the modern oboe; also **haut·bois** *sing. & pl.*

haute (OTE) *adj. French.* high-class or upper; **haute cou·ture** (ote·coo·TOOR) leading fashion designers or their products; **haute cui·sine** (ote·kwee·ZEEN) the art of master chefs or their specialties.

hau·teur (hoh·TUR) *n.* haughtiness.

Ha·van·a (huh·VAN·uh) **1** capital of Cuba. **2** a cigar made of Cuban tobacco.

have (HAV, huv, uv) *v.* **has** (HAZ, huz, uz), **had** (HAD, hud, ud), **hav·ing** **1** hold or possess; also, get, take, keep, etc.: *We ~ a home; Please ~ a chair; She's ~ing* (i.e. bearing or begetting) *a baby; Always ~ my advice in mind; won't ~ any pranks in school.* **2** [indicating necessity or obligation]: *It's midnight, I ~ (got) to go.* **3** [indicating completed action]: *Everyone has come; She'll ~ left by 10 p.m.* **—*n.*** a rich person or nation: *the* **haves** *and the have-nots.* **—have at** go at (someone); attack. **—have coming** deserve: *She had the raise coming to her after what she achieved for the firm.* **—have done with** cease or stop: *One last time and we shall ~ done with gambling.* **—have had it** *Informal.*

reach an end with something: *No more drinking, I ~ had it.* **—have it out** settle (*with* someone) by fighting or arguing. **—have on** be wearing. **—have to do with** be related to; also, associate with: *Geology has to do with the earth; She won't ~ anything to do with him.*

ha·ven (HAY·vun) *n.* a harbor or refuge.

have-not *n.* one with little material resources. **—haven't** have not.

hav·er·sack (HAV–) *n.* a bag for supplies or equipment, usu. worn by soldiers, hikers, etc. with a strap over one shoulder.

hav·oc (–uc) *n.* widespread harm or destruction, as caused by an earthquake or tornado: *a scandal that* **played havoc with** (i.e. greatly damaged) *many reputations.*

haw *n.* the hawthorn or its berry. **—*v.*** See HEM AND HAW.

Ha·wai·i (huh·WYE·ee) or **Hawaiian Islands** a group of islands in the N. Pacific, forming a U.S. state; 6,450 sq. mi. (16,705 km²); *cap.* Honolulu. **—Ha·wai·ian** (–WYE·un) *n.* & *adj.* (of or having to do with Hawaii or) a person or the Polynesian language of Hawaii.

hawk *n.* **1** a family of birds of prey with sharp eyesight, similar to eagles but smaller, including harriers, goshawks, and buzzards. **2** one who favors war; cf. DOVE; **hawk·ish** *adj.* **—*v.*** **1** hunt with or like hawks. **2** peddle wares by shouting, as a **hawk·er** *n.* huckster. **3** clear the throat noisily. **—hawk-eyed** *adj.* sharp-eyed.

hawse (HAWZ) *n.* the part of a ship's bow containing the **hawse·holes** through which a rope or cable, or **haw·ser** (–zur), for towing the ship is passed.

haw·thorn *n.* any of a large group of thorny shrubs and small trees of the rose family with fragrant white, pink, or red flowers and fruits like little apples: *The English ~ is favored for hedges.* **—Haw·thorne, Nathaniel.** 1804–64, a major U.S. writer of fiction.

hay *n.* cut and dried grass, alfalfa, clover, etc. for use as fodder; **hit the hay** *Slang.* go to bed; **make hay while the sun shines** make the most of an opportunity. **—*v.*** mow grass, etc. and prepare hay. **—hay·cock** *n.* hay piled in a heap to dry in the field.

Hay·dn (HYE–), **Franz J.** 1732–1809, Austrian composer.

Hayes (HAYZ), **Rutherford B.** 1822–93, 19th U.S. President (1877–81).

hay fever an allergic reaction with running nose, itchy eyes, sneezing, etc. caused by the pollen of trees and grasses. **—hay·fork** *n.* a pitchfork; also, a mechanical device for loading hay. **—hay·loft** *n.* a loft in a barn or stable for storing hay. **—hay·mak·er** *n. Slang.* a knockout blow. **—hay·mow** *n.* a pile of hay in a barn; also, the mow or loft where it is stored. **—hay·rick** or **hay·stack** *n.* an outdoor stack of hay. **—hay·seed** *n.* **1** grass, seed, chaff, etc. from hay. **2** *Slang.* a rustic or bumpkin. **—hay·wire** *n.* wire for tying up bales of hay; **go haywire** *Slang.* of a person or operation, go crazy or get upset.

haz·ard (–urd) *n.* a risk or chance; also, an obstacle in golf: *A stunt man's life is full of ~s; Smoking is a health ~;* ***v.*** venture or expose to risk: *to ~* (i.e. make) *a guess.* **—haz·ard·ous** (–ur·dus) *adj.* risky; also, dangerous.

haze *n.* mist, smoke, dust, etc. thinly spread in the air, reducing visibility; hence, vagueness; **ha·zy** *adj.* **-zi·er, -zi·est; ha·zi·ly** *adv.;* **ha·zi·ness** *n.* **—*v.* haz·es, hazed, haz·ing** force (newcomers to a group, as among students) to do humiliating things; **haz·er** *n.*

haz·el (HAY·zl) *n.* any of various shrubs and trees of the birch family bearing small, edible, light-brown nuts; ***adj.*** light or yellowish brown. **—ha·zel·nut** *n.* (the nut of) the hazel.

Hb hemoglobin. **—HB** hard black (pencil).

H.B.M. His (or Her) Britannic Majesty.

H-bomb *n.* a hydrogen bomb.

h.c. for the sake of honor. **—H.C.** Holy Communion; House of Commons.

H.C.F. highest common factor.

hd. head. **—HD** heavy duty.

hdbk. handbook.

hdqrs. headquarters.

he (HEE) *n.* & *pron., objective* HIM, *possessive* HIS; *pl.* THEY, *objective* THEM, *possessive* THEIR(s) the male animal or human being (referred to); also, anyone: *"Terry" could be a ~ or a she; ~ that is without sin, let him . . . ; Everyone gets what ~* (or she) *deserves.*

He helium. **—H.E.** His Eminence; His (or Her) Excellency; high explosive.

head (HED) *n.* **1** the part of the body containing the brain, eyes, ears, nose, and mouth; the top part in humans and front part in quadrupeds; hence, the chief, top, upper, or leading part of anything, as of a ship (i.e. the bow, etc.), pin, bed, procession, government, etc.: *A boil* **comes to a head** *before festering; the ~* (i.e. source) *of a river; a movement gathering ~* (i.e. strength). **2** an individual: *500 ~ of cattle; catering to a party at $5 a ~;* **-head** *comb. form. Slang.* addict: as in *acidhead, pothead, teahead.* **3** the cutting or hitting part of a hammer, golf club, ends of a drum, etc. **4** mind or brains: *has a good ~ for figures.* **5** short form of *headland, heading, headword,* etc. **—*adj.:*** *a ~ clerk; a ~ cold; a ~ gate.* **—*v.:*** *A president ~s a corporation; children ~ing home after school; to ~* (i.e. turn) *a boat toward shore; a letter ~ed with a place and date; to* **head off** *trouble by preventive measures.* **—give one his head** let one do as he likes. **—go to one's head** affect one's mind, as to intoxicate or make conceited. **—head over heels** completely or recklessly. **—keep** (or **lose**) **one's head** keep (or lose) one's self-control. **—make head or tail of** understand even a little of. **—out of** (or **off**) **one's head** *Informal.* crazy. **—over one's head** beyond one's grasp; also, without regard for one's claims or authority. —**turn one's head** make one giddy or conceited. —**head·less** *adj.* —**head·ache** (–ake) *n.* **1** pain in the head; **head·ach·y** *adj.* **2** *Informal.* source of annoyance. —**head·board** *n.* a board or frame at the head of something, as of a bed. —**head cold** a common cold affecting the nasal passages. —**head·dress** *n.* a usu. elaborate covering for the head. **-headed** *comb.form.* having a specified kind or number of heads: as in *double-headed, muddle-headed.* —**head-first** *adj.* & *adv.* (done or going) with the head first. —**head·gear** (–geer) *n.* headdress; also, the harness for an animal's head. —**head·hunt·er** *n.* a primitive who kills his enemies and collects their heads; also, an aggressive personnel recruiter; **head·hunt·ing** *n.* —**head·ing** *n.* **1** a topic or title placed at the beginning of a piece of writing. **2** the traveling direction of a ship or plane. —**head·land** *n.* a point of land projecting into water; cape. —**head·light** *n.* a bright light of a locomotive or automobile. —**head·line** *n.* a printed line at the top of a page or at the head of a news story: *a bank robbery making* **headlines** (i.e. important news) *all over the country;* **v. -lines, -lined, -lin·ing** make or be the main attraction or news event. —**head·long** *adj.* & *adv.* with the head first; hence, with uncontrolled speed or force; reckless(ly): *a ~ plunge; ran ~ into oncoming traffic.* —**head·mas·ter** *n.* principal (of some schools); *fem.* **head·mis·tress.** —**head-on** *adj.* & *adv.* frontal(ly); direct(ly): *coming ~ against each other; a ~ collision.* —**head·phone** *n.* an earphone with a band to put over the user's head. —**head·quar·ters** *n.pl.* [takes *sing.* or *pl. v.*] administrative center; also, place from where orders are issued for a police force, army, etc. —**head·rest** *n.* a support for the head, as in a barber's chair; also, a head-restraint; **head-re·straint** *n.* a support at the top of an automobile seat's back to protect the occupant, esp. in a rear-end collision. —**head·room** *n.* overhead space or clearance. —**head·set** *n.* a pair of headphones or earphones, often with an attached transmitter. —**head·ship** *n.* the office or position of a head. —**head·stall** *n.* the part of a bridle or halter that fits on the head. —**head start** the advantage of a start ahead of one's peers or competitors; also, a program to help the poor or handicapped of a community. —**head·stone** *n.* a stone or tablet placed at the head of a grave. —**head·strong** *adj.* rash or foolish in having one's own way. —**head·wait·er** *n.* the chief waiter in a restaurant. —**head·wa·ters** *n.pl.* the streams that form the source of a river. —**head·way** *n.* **1** progress or advance. **2** headroom. **3** the interval between two successive buses, trains, etc. on the same route. —**head wind** a wind blowing directly opposite the direction something is traveling in. —**head·word** *n.* a word that forms the heading of a paragraph, dictionary entry, etc., as **head** in this dictionary. —**head·y** *adj.* **head·i·er, -i·est** apt to affect the head, as an intoxicant; also, rash or impetuous.

heal (HEEL) *v.* **1** make or get well, as a wound, sore, burn, etc.; cure (a disease or sick person); hence, end (breached relations). **2** free from or get rid of (anything bad): *Time ~s all sorrows.* —**heal·er** *n.* —**health** (HELTH) *n.* sound condition of body or mind; also, a toast drunk to wish someone well; also ***adj.;*** **health food** food that is naturally health-giving; **health·ful** *adj.* good for the health; **health·ful·ly** *adv.;* **health·ful·ness** *n.* —**health resort** a place having a spa. —**health·y** *adj.* **health·i·er, -i·est** having good health; also, showing or giving health: *a ~ child, appearance, climate, appetite;* **health·i·ly** *adv.;* **health·i·ness** *n.*

heap (HEEP) *n.* a mass or pile of things; hence, *Informal.* a large amount: *a ~ of sand; a ~ of trouble.* —**v.** form in to a heap; amass; also, load; hence, bestow: *to ~ riches; ~ a plate with food; insults ~ed upon the vanquished.*

hear (HEER) *v.* **hears, heard** (HURD), **hear·ing** **1** perceive by the ear; hence, listen. **2** receive information: *heard from home yesterday.* —**hear·er** *n.* —**hear·ing** *n.* **1** sense by which sounds are perceived; also, the range of this perception; earshot: *said in the ~ of strangers.* **2** a listening or receiving of information: *was given a patient ~ by the committee.* —**hear·ing-aid** *n.* a small sound-amplifying device worn in the ear. —**heark·en** (HAR·kun) *v. Archaic.* listen (*to* prayer, etc.); heed. —**hear·say** (HEER–) *n.* & *adj.* (based on) something one has heard but not verified, as a rumor or gossip: *merely ~; ~ evidence.*

hearse (HURSE) *n.* a vehicle for taking the dead to the grave.

heart (HART) *n.* **1** the hollow, muscular organ that pumps blood throughout the body, traditionally considered as the seat of one's feelings, esp. love, sympathy, courage, etc., and the center or most vital part of one's being: *a kind ~; He broke her ~; the very ~ of things.* **2** a heart-shaped figure, as on a playing card; also, a card so marked: *the queen of ~s.* —**after one's own heart** as one likes or desires it. —**at heart** in one's innermost nature. —**by heart** by or from memory: *recite it by ~.* —**set one's heart on** desire eagerly. —**take to heart** be much moved by. —**with all one's heart** with all sincerity and good will. —**heart·ache** (–ake) *n.* great sorrow or anguish. —**heart attack** same as CORONARY THROMBOSIS. —**heart·beat** *n.* one contraction and dilation of the heart. —**heart·break** (–brake) *n.* extreme sorrow or disappointment; **heart·break·ing** *adj.: ~ news;* **heart·bro·ken** (–broh·kn) *adj.* —**heart·burn** *n.* a burning feeling as if from near the heart, caused by the rising up of stomach acid; **heart·**

burn·ing *n.* intense jealousy or resentment. **-heart·ed** *comb.form.* with a specified kind of heart: as in *hard-hearted, stout-hearted.* **—heart·en** *v.* cheer up. **—heart·felt** *adj.* sincere; genuine.

hearth (HARTH) *n.* fireside; floor near a fireplace; hence, home or family life; **hearth·side** *n.* fireside; **hearth·stone** *n.* the stone forming a hearth; also, home.

heart·land *n.* a central, key region of a nation. **—heart·less** *adj.* without kindness, sympathy, or courage; **heart·less·ly** *adv.;* **heart·less·ness** *n.* **—heart-rend·ing** *adj.* distressing. **—heart·sick** or **heart·sore** *adj.* sick at heart. **—heart·strings** *n.pl.* one's deepest feelings. **—heart·throb** *n.* a heartbeat. **—heart-to-heart** *adj.* frank and sincere. **—heart·warm·ing** *adj.* kindling feelings of warmth and geniality. **—heart·wood** *n.* the wood forming the core of a tree trunk. **—heart·y** *adj.* **heart·i·er, -i·est** **1** full of vigor and enthusiasm: *a ~ welcome.* **2** showing or promoting good health: *a ~ appetite, meal, eater.* **—heart·i·ly** *adv.;* **heart·i·ness** *n.* **—heart·y** *n.* **heart·ies** *Archaic.* a fellow sailor; comrade.

heat (HEET) *n.* **1** the quality of being hot to the touch; also, pungency of taste; high temperature; the form of energy that causes expansion, melting, etc.: *the ~ of summer.* **2** great feeling or excitement: *a female mammal* **in heat** (i.e. recurring period or condition of sexual excitement); *He said it in the ~ of the argument.* **3** a single effort; hence, a preliminary round, as in a race, that qualifies candidates for the finals: *a dead ~* (i.e. a tie). **4** *Informal.* pressure: *Police apply the ~ to force a confession.* **—*v.*** make or become hot or warm; also, excite or become excited; **heat·ed** *adj.: a ~ wire, argument;* **heat·ed·ly** *adv.;* **heat·less** *adj.* **—heat engine** an engine for getting mechanical energy from heat, as a gasoline engine. **—heat·er** *n.* an appliance that provides heat: *a space ~.* **—heat exchanger** a device of the type of an automobile radiator for changing heat from one medium to another for elimination or for use, as in a nuclear reactor. **—heat exhaustion** a mild form of heatstroke.

heath (HEETH) *n.* **1** open wasteland covered by shrubs such as heather. **2** any of a family of shrubs and plants, esp. European heather, including also the American blueberry, cranberry, azalea, and trailing arbutus. **—heath·y** *adj.* **—heath·en** *n.* **-then(s)** a person of no religion or culture; formerly, one who was not a Christian, Jew, or Moslem; ***adj.:*** *~ customs;* also **heath·en·ish; heath·en·dom** *n.* paganism; also **heath·en·ism. —heath·er** (HEDH·ur) *n.* a shrub of the heath family with scalelike leaves and purplish, bell-shaped flowers, common on moors in the British Isles; **heath·er·y** *adj.*

heating pad an electrically heated pad to apply warmth to the body. **—heat lightning** lightning seen near the horizon, esp. on hot days, whose thunder is too distant to be heard. **—heat pipe** an enclosed heat-transferring device using a continuous cycle of evaporation and condensation from one end to the other. **—heat pump** a refrigerating apparatus for extracting heat from the air, ground, water, etc. so as to cool the place heat is taken from or heat what it is delivered to. **—heat sink** a device that gets rid of unwanted heat from a system. **—heat·stroke** *n.* illness from exposure to excessive heat.

heave (HEEV) *v.* **heaves,** *pt. & pp.* **heaved** or **hove** (HOHV), **heav·ing** **1** raise or lift (something heavy); also, rise, swell, or utter in a heavy manner: *to ~ anchor and sail away; She ~d a sigh of relief; A ship* **heaves in(to) sight** *on the horizon; The ground ~s from an earthquake; sailors ~ing at* (or *on*) (i.e. pulling) *a rope.* **2** rise and fall; lift and throw; hence, retch or vomit: *the ~ing waves; They ~d the stone through the window; stomach ~s at the lurid crime;* **heave to** stop, as a sailing ship. **—*n.:*** *the ~ of the sea; with a mighty ~* (i.e. pull or throw); **heaves** *pl.* a lung disease of horses, marked by difficult breathing and heaving sides. **—heave ho!** cry of sailors pulling in the anchor; **heave-ho** *n.* *Informal.* dismissal.

heav·en (HEVN) *n.* a place of great happiness; **Heaven** God's dwelling place; where the blessed go after death; **move heaven and earth** do one's utmost; **the heavens** *pl.* the firmament; **heavens! for heaven's sake!** exclamations of surprise, protest, etc. **—heav·en·ly** *adv.* **—heav·en·ward** (–wurd) *adj.* & *adv.;* also **heav·en·wards.**

heav·y (HEV·ee) *adj.* **heav·i·er, -i·est** **1** of great weight; hence, much or large in quantity, intensity, degree, etc.; hard to endure or manage: *a ~ load, rain, vote, smoker, odor; ~ news, taxes, traffic.* **2** looking heavy or thick, somber or slow, ponderous, etc.: *~ features, reading; a ~ lecture, heart* (i.e. sorrowful). **—*adv.:*** *a deed that lies ~ on his conscience; Time* **hangs heavy** *on her hands* (i.e. drags). **—*n., pl.*** **heav·ies** something heavy, as a large wave; also, a heavy person, one of consequence, or an actor in a nonheroic or villainous role. **—heav·i·ly** *adv.;* **heav·i·ness** *n.* **—heav·y-du·ty** *adj.* designed for hard use; durable: *a ~ shock absorber; ~ shoes.* **—heav·y-hand·ed** *adj.* awkward; also, oppressive. **—heav·y-heart·ed** *adj.* sad or gloomy. **—heavy hydrogen** same as DEUTERIUM. **—heavy industry** industry that supplies other industries with basic products such as steel, oil, machinery, etc. **—heav·y·set** *adj.* having a stocky build. **—heavy water** water compounded with heavy hydrogen, used in nuclear reactors. **—heav·y·weight** *n.* a boxer weighing over 175 lb. (81 kg for Olympics); *Informal.* a person of much intelligence or consequence.

Heb. Hebrew; Hebrews (New Testament book) **—He·bra·ic** (hi·BRAY–) *adj.* of the Hebrews or their language, culture, etc. **—He·brew**

(HEE–) *n.* an Israelite or Jew; also, the ancient or modern Semitic language of the Hebrews; ***adj.*** Jewish; Hebraic.

Heb·ri·des (HEB·ruh·deez) a group of islands, **Inner** and **Outer Hebrides,** off N.W. Scotland; also called "Western Isles"; **Heb·ri·de·an** (–DEE·un) *n.* & *adj.*

hec·a·tomb (–tome, –toom) *n.* a large-scale slaughter for sacrifice, as of 100 cattle in ancient Greece.

heck *n.* & *interj. Informal.* hell: *a ~ of a job; What the ~!*

heck·le *v.* **-les, -led, -ling** taunt or harass (a speaker); **heck·ler** *n.*

hec·tare *n.* a metric unit of area equal to 100 ares or 10,000 sq. meters.

hec·tic *adj.* of life or activity, feverish; excited or exciting; **hec·ti·cal·ly** *adv.*

hecto- *comb.form.* 100: as in **hec·to·gram** *n.* unit of 100 grams; **hec·to·li·ter** (–lee·tur) *n.* unit of 100 liters; **hec·to·me·ter** *n.* unit of 100 meters.

hec·tor (–tur) *n.* & *v.* bully; bluster(er), like **Hec·tor,** Trojan hero, portrayed as a bully in early drama.

he'd (HEED) he had; he would.

hedge (HEJ) *n.* row of bushes planted as a fence; hence, a boundary, barrier, or means of protection, as against financial loss: *a ~ fund; an investment as a ~ against inflation.* —***v.*** **hedg·es, hedged, hedg·ing** enclose or protect: *~d in* (or *about*) *by restrictions; to ~ a bet by making one also on the opposite side; ~ing against commodity price changes by selling futures; a politician accused of ~ing on the issues* (i.e. of being evasive); **hedg·er** *n.* —**hedge fund** an investment group or partnership for speculative buying and selling of stocks. —**hedge·hog** *n.* any of a family of Old World animals similar to the American porcupine. —**hedge·hop** *v.* **-hops, -hopped, -hop·ping** fly a plane, as for crop-dusting, close to the ground. —**hedge·row** (–roh) *n.* a hedge of bushes.

he·don·ism (HEE·dn·izm) *n.* (the philosophy of) living only for pleasure; **he·don·ist** *n.* —**he·do·nis·tic** (–NIS–) *adj.*

-hedron *comb.form.* a crystal or figure with a specified number of sides: as in *hexahedron, polyhedron;* **-hedral** *adj.*

heed *v.* pay attention to; ***n.*** attention or notice: *pay* (or *give*) *~ to advice; took (no) ~ of warnings.* —**heed·ful** *adj.;* **heed·ful·ly** *adv.;* **heed·ful·ness** *n.* —**heed·less** *adj.;* **heed·less·ly** *adv.;* **heed·less·ness** *n.*

hee·haw *n.* & *v.* bray; also, guffaw.

heel *n.* **1** the hindmost part of a foot, below the ankle; hence, anything resembling a human heel in shape, function, or position, as the hock of an animal or hind toe of a bird, the hind part of a shoe or sock, an end crust of bread, or any bottom part or portion; **heel·less** *adj.* **2** *Informal.* a despicable person. —***v.*** **1** furnish with a heel; also, follow closely behind, as a dog in pursuit; **heel·er** *n.* **2** lean to one side; also, make (a ship) list. —**at heel, (up)on one's heels** or **on the heels of** close behind. —**down at the heel(s)** shabby or poor, as with worn-out shoe heels. —**kick up one's heels** be lively or have fun. —**heeled** *adj. Informal.* having money: *a well-~ backer.*

heft *Informal. n.* weight; bulk; ***v.*** lift; heave; **heft·y** *adj.* **heft·i·er, -i·est** heavy; bulky; well-built; **heft·i·ly** *adv.;* **heft·i·ness** *n.*

he·gem·o·ny (hi·JEM·uh·nee, HEJ·uh·moh–) *n.* **-nies** dominance, esp. of one nation over the others of a group.

he·gi·ra (hi·JYE·ruh) *n.* a journey of safety or escape; **Hegira** Mohammed's flight from Mecca to Medina, A.D. 622, the beginning of the Moslem era.

Hei·del·berg (HYE·dl–) a city of S.W. West Germany.

heif·er (HEF·ur) *n.* a young cow that has not yet had a calf.

heigh-ho (HYE–, HAY–) *interj.* expressing joy, surprise, boredom, etc.

height (HITE) *n.* **1** how high or tall a person or thing is; also, elevation or altitude. **2** the topmost point. —**height·en** *v.* bring to a height or become high(er); hence, make or become greater; increase. —**heights** *n.pl.* an eminence or hill.

hei·nous (HAY·nus) *adj.* hatefully bad; **hei·nous·ly** *adv.;* **hei·nous·ness** *n.*

heir (AIR) *n.* one who is in line to inherit another's property, as **heir apparent** if no stronger claimant is possible, **heir presumptive** if on condition that no nearer relative is born; *pl.* **heirs apparent** (or **presumptive**). —**heir·ess** (–is) *n.* female heir, esp. one inheriting great wealth. —**heir·loom** *n.* a personal possession handed down from generation to generation.

heist (HIGHST) *n.* & *v. Slang.* (commit) armed robbery.

held *pt.* & *pp.* of HOLD.

Hel·e·na (–i·nuh) capital of Montana. —**Hel·en of Troy** in Greek myth, the beautiful queen of King Menelaus, whose kidnaping caused the Trojan War.

hel·i·cal *adj.* like a helix or screw; spiral: *~ gears.* —**helices** a *pl.* of HELIX. —**hel·i·coid** (HEL·i–) or **-coi·dal** (–COY·dl) *adj.* shaped like a spiral. —**hel·i·con** *n.* a coiled, shoulder-borne brass tuba. —**hel·i·cop·ter** *n.* an aircraft that lifts off vertically, flies, and hovers with the aid of large rotor blades mounted horizontally on its top.

helio- *comb.form.* sun: as in *heliocentric, heliotrope.* —**he·li·o·cen·tric** (hee·lee·uh·SEN–) *adj.* with the sun as center. —**he·li·o·graph** (HEE–) *n.* a signaling device using flashes of reflected sunlight. —**he·li·o·trope** *n.* a plant with lance-shaped, heavily veined leaves and huge clusters of tiny, fragrant flowers colored lilac to dark-blue that always face the sun; ***adj.*** reddish-purple; **he·li·o·trop·ic** (–TROP–) *adj.* of plants, turning toward the sun. —**he·li·**

um (–lee·um) *n.* a lightweight gas and chemical element, first spotted through the sun's light.
hel·i·pad *n.* a helicopter-landing surface; **hel·i·port** *n.* a helicopter airport.
he·lix (HEE–) *n.* **-lix·es** or **-li·ces** (–luh·seez) a spiral.
he'll (HEEL) he will; he shall.
hell *n.* **1** a place of eternal torment as punishment for damned souls. **2** *Slang* [used to emphasize anything good or bad]: *Who the ~ is he? a* **hell of a** (i.e. very bad) *nuisance; one ~ of a* (i.e. very) *nice girl.* —**hell·ish** *adj.;* **hell·ish·ly** *adv.;* **hell·ish·ness** *n.* —**hell-bent** *adj.* & *adv. Informal.* firmly determined; at full speed; reckless(ly). —**hell·cat** *n.* a witch or shrew.
hel·le·bore (–uh·bor) *n.* any of various plants of the crowfoot family with poisonous roots; also, a white hellebore of the lily family.
Hel·lene (–een) *n.* a Greek. —**Hel·len·ic** (–LEN–) *adj.* Greek, esp. of ancient Greek history, language, or culture; **Hel·len·ism** (HEL–) *n.;* **Hel·len·ist** *n.;* **Hel·len·is·tic** (–IS–) *adj.*
hell-for-leath·er *adj.* & *adv. Informal.* hell-bent.
hell·gram·mite (–gruh–) *n.* the larva of the dobson fly, used as fish bait.
hell·hole *n. Informal.* a detestable place.
hel·lion (HEL·yun) *n. Informal.* a rascal or troublemaker.
hel·lo (huh·LOH) *n.* & *interj.* an exclamation of greeting or response.
hel·lu·va [a respelling of the slang phrase "hell of a"] very (good, bad, etc., as implied or expressed): *a ~ job; You're one ~ guy.*
helm *n.* a ship's steering wheel or gear; hence, a position of control: *at the ~ of the nation.*
hel·met *n.* a protective covering for the head; **hel·met·ed** *adj.*
helms·man (HELMZ·mun) *n.* **-men** one who steers a ship.
hel·ot (–ut) *n.* a slave or serf, like the **Helots** of ancient Sparta.
help *v.* **1** provide (someone) with a useful thing or needed service: *Please ~ me set the table; someone to* **help out** *in the kitchen; Do* **help yourself** *to the drinks; another* **helping** (i.e. portion) *of cake.* **2** improve; make better: *a medicine to ~ your cough.* **3** avoid: *couldn't ~ falling asleep in church;* **cannot help but** (i.e. is obliged to) *admire her patience.* —***n.*** aid or assistance; also, a person or other source of aid: *~ wanted; kitchen ~ at $10 an hour.* —**help·ful** *adj.;* **help·ful·ly** *adv.;* **help·ful·ness** *n.* —**help·less** *adj.;* **help·less·ly** *adv.;* **help·less·ness** *n.* —**help·mate** *n.* helpful partner, as wife; also **help·meet** *Archaic.*
Hel·sin·ki (HEL·sing·kee) capital of Finland.
hel·ter-skel·ter *adv.* in confusion or disorderly haste; ***adj.:*** *a ~ condition, attitude, retreat;* ***n.*** anything helter-skelter.
helve (HELV) *n.* a handle, as of a hatchet.
Hel·ve·tian (–VEE·shun) *n.* & *adj.* Swiss.
¹hem *n.* the usu. folded and sewn-down border or edge of a garment; ***v.*** **hems, hemmed, hem·ming** put a hem on; hence, enclose or confine: *a lake ~d in* (or *about, around*) *by hills; ~d in by one's enemies.*
²hem *interj., n.* & *v.* **hems, hemmed, hem·ming** (make) the sound of clearing the throat; **hem and haw** hesitate in speech; also, stall or put off.
he-man *n.* **-men** *Informal.* an obviously virile man.
hemat(o)- same as HEMO-. —**hem·a·tite** *n.* the iron ore *ferric oxide* occurring as a reddish-brown mineral. —**he·ma·tol·o·gy** (hee·muh·TOL–) *n.* the physiology of the blood; **he·ma·tol·o·gist** *n.* a physician specialized in blood disorders. —**heme** (HEEM) *n.* the red-colored nonprotein part of hemoglobin.
hemi- *prefix.* half: as in *hemiplegia, hemisphere.*
Hem·ing·way, Ernest. 1899–1961, major American novelist.
hem·i·ple·gi·a (–PLEE–) *n.* paralysis of one side of the body. —**hem·i·sphere** *n.* half of a sphere, esp. the northern, southern, western, or eastern half of the earth; **hem·i·spher·i·cal** (–SFER–) *adj.*
hem·line *n.* a hem, esp. the bottom edge of a skirt as determining its length.
hem·lock *n.* a parsleylike poisonous herb; also, an evergreen tree of the pine family.
hemo- *comb.form.* blood: as in **he·mo·glo·bin** (HEE–) *n.* the iron-protein coloring matter of the red blood cells. —**he·mo·phil·i·a** (–FIL–) *n.* a hereditary blood disorder affecting males that makes bleeding difficult to control because the blood does not clot normally; **he·mo·phil·ic** *adj.;* **he·mo·phil·i·ac** *n.* a hemophilic patient. —**hem·or·rhage** (HEM·uh·rij) *n.* & *v.* **-rhag·es, -rhaged, -rhag·ing** (have) a heavy bleeding; **hem·or·rhag·ic** (–RAJ–) *adj.* —**hem·or·rhoids** (–roidz) *n.pl.* swellings about the anus, often with bleeding; piles.
hemp *n.* a tall Asiatic plant of the mulberry family, kinds of which are the source of fiber for rope and cordage, marijuana, hashish, and oil; **hemp·en** *adj.*
hem·stitch *n.* & *v.* (stitch) an ornamental openwork pattern on fabric.
hen *n.* a female bird, esp. of the domestic fowl.
hence *adv.* from this (place, time, source, or origin); consequently: *many years ~; "Grapes are sour," ~ the sour-grapes philosophy.* —**hence·forth** or **hence·for·ward** *adv.* from this time on.
hench·man *n.* **-men** a right-hand man, often a self-serving political follower.
hen·na *n.* an Egyptian privet whose orange-red dye is used widely, esp. to color nails and hair; ***v.*** **hen·nas, hen·naed, hen·na·ing:** *an Eastern beauty with ~d nails.*
hen·peck *v.* domineer over (one's husband).
hen·ry (–ree) *n.* **-ries** or **-rys** the MKS unit of inductance.

hep *adj. Slang.* an earlier form of ²HIP.
hep·ar·in *n.* an anticoagulant drug derived from the liver and used in thrombosis and embolism against blood clots. —**he·pat·ic** (hi·PAT–) *adj.* of the liver; **he·pat·i·ca** *n.* liverwort. —**hep·a·ti·tis** (–TYE–) *n.* inflammation of the liver, usu. due to a virus, as in *infectious hepatitis.*
hep·cat *n.* one who is hip. —**hepped** same as HIPPED. —**hep·ster** *n.* same as HIPSTER.
hepta- *comb.form.* seven: as in *heptagon* (i.e. seven-sided figure), *heptameter* (i.e. a seven-footed verse), *heptarchy* (i.e. rule by seven).
her (HUR, ur) objective or possessive case of SHE; ***pron.:*** *I know* ~; *Informal: I'm older than* ~; *That's* ~ (i.e. she); ***adj.:*** ~ *voice.* —**hers** (HURZ) *pron.: The purse is* ~; *his books and* ~; ~ *are neater.*
He·ra (HEER·uh) in Greek myth, the wife of Zeus.
her·ald (HER·uld) *n.* formerly, a public official in charge of announcements, ceremonies, coats-of-arms, etc.; hence, an announcer or harbinger; ***v.:*** *birds* ~*ing the dawn.* —**he·ral·dic** (huh·RAL–) *adj.* of heraldry or heralds. —**her·ald·ry** (HER·ul·dree) *n.* **-ries** coats of arms or their science and art; also, heraldic pomp.
herb (URB, HURB) *n.* any seed plant with fleshy stems that is used for food and in medicines and perfumes; **her·ba·ceous** (–BAY–) *adj.* green and fleshy, not woody like a tree or shrub: *a* ~ *border of perennials;* **herb·age** (–ij) *n.* green foliage; also, grass or pasturage. —**her·bal** *n.* & *adj.* (a book) of herbs; **her·bal·ist** *n.* —**her·bar·i·um** (–BAIR–) *n.* **-i·ums** or **-i·a** a botanical collection of dried plants. —**her·bi·cide** *n.* a weed-killer; **her·bi·ci·dal** (–SYE–) *adj.* —**her·bi·vore** *n.* an animal that is **her·bi·vor·ous** (–BIV·uh·rus) *adj.* plant-eating.
her·cu·le·an (–kyuh·LEE·un) *adj.* having or requiring great strength like that of Hercules; **Her·cu·les** (HUR·kyuh·leez) a hero of Greek and Roman myths, famous for 12 feats of strength; also a N. constellation.
herd *n.* a group of large animals such as cattle, horses, or elephants that are kept or live together; hence, a crowd of common people or children. —***v.*** form (into) or take care of as a herd or flock, as a **herds·man** *n.* **-men.**
here (HEER) *n.* & *adv.* (at, in, to, or into) this place; also, at this point or time: *Come* ~; ~ *let us pause;* **here below** on earth; **neither here nor there** not relevant. —**here·a·bout(s)** *adv.* about or near here. —**here·af·ter** (–AF–) *n.* & *adv.* (in) the future or life after the present: *what may happen in the* ~. —**here·by** (–BY) *adv. Formal.* by this means, as by a document; in this way.
he·red·i·tar·y (huh·RED–) *adj.* by inheritance, as titles, or by heredity, as parental characteristics; also, traditional, as customs, friendships, etc. —**he·red·i·ty** (–RED–) *n.* **-ties** the passing on of parental characteristics to offspring through genes; also, such qualities, traits, etc. or the tendency to inherit them.
Her·e·ford (HUR·furd, HER·uh–) *n.* a reddish-brown breed of beef cattle with white faces, developed in Herefordshire, England; also, a similarly marked American breed of swine.
here·in (–IN) *adv. Formal.* in this (document, matter, etc.). —**here·of** (–OV) *adv. Formal.* of or about this. —**here·on** (–ON) *adv. Formal.* on this. —**here's** (HEERZ) here is.
her·e·sy (HER·uh·see) *n.* **-sies** an opinion or belief, esp. religious, that is opposed to the orthodox or established position. —**her·e·tic** (HER·uh–) *n.* & *adj.* —**he·ret·i·cal** (huh·RET–) *adj.;* **he·ret·i·cal·ly** *adv.*
here·to (–TOO) *adv. Formal.* to this (document); **here·to·fore** *adv. Formal.* up to this time. —**here·un·to** (–UN–) *adv. Formal.* to this. —**here·up·on** (–PON) *adv. Formal.* upon this; also, immediately after. —**here·with** (–WIDH) *adv.* with this; also, by this.
her·it·a·ble (HER–) *adj.* that can be inherited; **her·it·age** (–ij) *n.* what is inherited, as a title, property, traditions, etc.
her·maph·ro·dite (–MAF·ruh–) *n.* a person, animal, or organism with male and female organs, like the son of Hermes and Aphrodite; **her·maph·ro·dit·ic** (–DIT–) *adj.* bisexual. —**Her·mes** (–meez) in Greek myth, a messenger of the gods. —**her·met·ic** (–MET–) *adj.* airtight; **her·met·i·cal·ly** *adv.*
her·mit *n.* a religious recluse; **her·mit·age** (–ij) *n.* a hermit's secluded dwelling place.
her·ni·a (–nee·uh) *n.* **-as** or **-ae** (–ee) a bulging of an organ through weakened tissue surrounding it, as a loop of the intestine pushing out through the lower abdomen; rupture; **her·ni·al** *adj.* —**her·ni·ate** *v.* **-ates, -at·ed, -at·ing** protrude so as to form a hernia: *a* ~*d* (i.e. slipped) *disk;* **her·ni·a·tion** (–AY–) *n.*
he·ro (HEER·oh) *n.* **-roes** **1** a man admired for his noble qualities or exploits, as the central characters in novels, plays, etc. **2** *pl.* also **-ros,** a hero sandwich.
He·rod·o·tus (huh·ROD·uh–) 485?–425? B.C., a Greek historian.
he·ro·ic (–ROH–) *adj.* **1** of, about, or like heroes: *Courage and nobility are* ~ *qualities; The "Iliad" is a* ~ *poem.* **2** daring and bold: ~ *measures;* **heroics** *n. pl.* extravagant or showy behavior. Also **he·ro·i·cal** *adj.* —**he·ro·i·cal·ly** *adv.* —**heroic verse** iambic pentameter.
her·o·in (HER·oh–) *n.* a pain-relieving, habit-forming narcotic derived from morphine.
her·o·ine (–in) *n.* a woman hero. —**her·o·ism** *n.* great courage or bravery; also, the qualities and actions of a hero or heroine.
her·on (HER·un) *n.* one of a family of cranelike wading birds having long necks, bills, and legs; **her·on·ry** *n.* **-ries** a nesting place of herons.

hero sandwich a large sandwich with a roll sliced lengthwise and filled with cold cuts and vegetables.

her·pes (HUR·peez) *n.* a blister-forming viral disease, **herpes simplex** forming "cold sores" or "fever sores" around the mouth and **herpes zos·ter,** or shingles, affecting nerves on one side of the chest and abdomen. **—her·pe·tol·o·gy** (–TOL–) *n.* the zoology of reptiles and amphibians.

Herr (HAIR) *n., pl.* **Her·ren** *German.* a man; [as title] "Mr." or "Sir."

her·ring (HER–) *n.* a family of small, widely used food fishes of the N.Atlantic including the shad, sardine, and alewife. **—her·ring·bone** *n.* a pattern of rows of slanted lines arranged like the ribs on a herring's spine, as in twilled fabrics, bricklaying, or a climbing step in skiing.

hers See HER. **—her·self** (–SELF) *pron.* reflexive or emphatic of SHE: *proud of ~; sitting all by ~; She ~ said it; not quite ~ when unwell.*

hertz (HURTS) *n. sing.* & *pl.* the unit of frequency equal to one cycle per second. **—Hertz·i·an waves** electromagnetic radiation, as in radio.

he's (HEEZ) he is; he has.

hes·i·tant (HEZ·i·tunt) *adj.* hesitating; undecided; doubtful; **hes·i·tant·ly** *adv.;* **hes·i·tan·cy** *n.* **-cies. —hes·i·tate** *v.* **-tates, -tat·ed, -tat·ing** be doubtful or undecided; also, talk or act doubtfully or undecidedly: *She ~d before saying "yes"; ~d about jumping down; "He who ~s is lost";* **hes·i·tat·ing·ly** *adv.* **—hes·i·ta·tion** (–TAY–) *n.*

hetero- *comb.form.* other or different: as in **het·er·o·dox** *adj.* not orthodox. **—het·er·o·ge·ne·ous** (–JEE·nee·us) *adj.* composed of different kinds of things; mixed: *a ~ group, population;* **het·er·o·ge·ne·ous·ly** *adv.* **—het·er·o·sex·u·al** (–SEX·shoo·ul) *adj.* attracted to the opposite sex; also, of different sexes: *~ twins;* ***n.*** a heterosexual individual.

heu·ris·tic (hew·RIS–) *adj.* based on or involving trial and error: *a ~ approach, teaching method, computer program.*

hew *v.* **hews,** *pt.* **hewed,** *pp.* **hewed** or **hewn, hew·ing** **1** cut or form by cutting or chopping, as with an ax or chisel: *~n timber; the enemy ~d down in battle; to ~ one's way through a jungle;* **hew·er** *n.* **2** hold fast; adhere: *~ to rules and regulations.*

HEW Health, Education, and Welfare (U.S. Dept.).

hex *n.* & *v.* (cast) a spell; jinx.

hex. hexagon. **—hexa-** *comb.form.* six: as in *hexagon, hexapod.* **—hex·a·chlo·ro·phene** (–CLOR·uh·feen) *n.* an antiseptic powerful against skin bacteria. **—hex·a·gon** (–uh·gon) *n.* a polygon of six angles and sides; **hex·ag·o·nal** (–SAG·uh·nl) *adj.* **—hex·am·e·ter** (–SAM·i·tur) *n.* six-footed verse. **—hex·a·pod** *n.* & *adj.* (an insect) having six legs.

hey (HAY) *interj.* used to ask a question, attract attention, or express surprise.

hey·day *n.* the time of greatest strength, prosperity, etc.; acme; prime.

hf. half. **—Hf** hafnium. **—H.F.** or **h.f.** high frequency.

hg. hectogram(s). **—Hg** mercury.

HGH human growth hormone.

hgt. height.

hgwy. highway.

H.H. Her (or His) Highness; His Holiness.

hhd. hogshead.

hi (HYE) *interj.* hello: *~ there!* **—HI** Hawaii.

hi·a·tus (hye·AY–) *n.* **-tus·es** a break or gap in the continuity of something uttered, composed, etc., as between the two a's running together in "Cuba and China": *Some speakers fill this ~ with an intrusive "r."*

hi·ba·chi (hi·BAH·chee) *n.* **-chis** a charcoal-burning brazier and grill: *a Japanese restaurant with ~ cuisine.*

hi·ber·nate (HYE–) *v.* **-nates, -nat·ed, -nat·ing** pass the winter in an inactive condition: *bats, bears, chipmunks, and such ~ing animals;* **hi·ber·na·tor** *n.* **—hi·ber·na·tion** (–NAY–) *n.*

hi·bis·cus (–BIS–) *n.* a mallow-family group of plants, shrubs, and trees with colorful, usu. bell-shaped flowers.

hic·cup *n.* the sharp, clicking noise of a breathing spasm, or **hiccups** *pl.;* ***v.*** **-cups, -cup(p)ed, -cup·(p)ing:** *how to stop ~ing.* Also **hic·cough** (–cup).

hick *n.* & *adj.* [often contemptuous] rustic: *whether ~ or city slicker; Plains was a mere ~ town.*

hick·ey *n.* **-eys** *Informal.* a gadget or device.

hick·o·ry *n.* **-ries** any of a group of hardwood trees of the walnut family, some bearing edible nuts, as the pignut and pecan; ***adj.:*** *a ~ switch, chair, walking stick.*

hi·dal·go (hi·DAL–) *n.* **-gos** a Spanish noble ranking below a grandee.

hidden tax an indirect tax such as an excise or customs duty.

[1]hide *n.* a raw or tanned skin of a large animal. **—*v.*** **hides, hid·ed, hid·ing** *Informal.* flog or thrash: *a good ~ing.*

[2]hide *v.* **hides,** *pt.* **hid,** *pp.* **hid·den** or **hid, hid·ing** keep or remain secret or out of sight: *the sun ~n by clouds; gone into ~ing to escape arrest; words with a ~n meaning; a children's game of* **hide-and-seek. —hide·a·way** *n.* a place of seclusion, refuge, or retreat, as a quiet restaurant; ***adj.:*** *a ~ bed in a sofa.*

hide·bound *adj.* **1** of cattle, with the skin sticking close to the body. **2** narrow-minded and obstinate.

hid·e·ous (–ee·us) *adj.* extremely ugly or revolting; **hid·e·ous·ly** *adv.;* **hid·e·ous·ness** *n.*

hide-out *n.* a place of hiding, as of guerrillas.

hie (HYE) *v.* **hies, hied, hy·ing** or **hie·ing** *Archaic or Poetic.* hasten: *~ hither; ~d him(self) to the chase.*

hi·er·ar·chy (HIGH·uh·rar·kee) *n.* **-chies** a graded or ranked organization, as of authority in the church, in a civil service, etc.; also, the body of people in such authority; hence, a graded series: *a ~ of values governing conduct; the ~ of the animal kingdom;* **hi·er·ar·chic** (–RAR–) or **-chi·cal** (–AR–) *adj.* —**hi·er·o·glyph** (HIGH·uh·ruh·glif) *n.* a hieroglyphic. —**hi·er·o·glyph·ic** (–GLIF–) *n.* a picture or symbol expressing an idea, as in ancient Egyptian and Aztec writing; ***adj.*** of or like hieroglyphics; hence, hard to read; **hieroglyphics** *n.pl.* a system of writing using pictures and symbols instead of an alphabet. —**hi·er·o·phant** (HIGH·uh·ruh·fant) *n.* a priest of ancient Greece; hence, a spokesman or advocate.

hi·fa·lu·tin *adj.* same as HIGHFALUTING.

hi-fi (HYE·fye) *n.* & *adj.* high fidelity (equipment).

hig·gle·dy-pig·gle·dy (HIG·ul·dee–) *adj.* & *adv.* in disorder; jumbled.

high *adj.* **1** of things, tall; esp., taller than ordinary; at a great height: *a ~ mountain; 10,000 ft. ~; a ~ dive* (i.e. from a great height). **2** great or advanced in quality or extent, importance, seriousness, etc.: *a ~ priest; at ~ speed; ~ crimes; the ~er apes; a ~ voice* (i.e. in pitch); *~ manner* (i.e. conceit); *~ noon* (i.e. at its peak); *in ~ spirits after a couple of drinks.* **3** *Informal.* intoxicated, esp. under the influence of a drug. —***adv.:*** *birds that fly ~; tempers running ~ during a debate; stars ~ up in the sky.* —***n.:*** *a record that hits a new ~; the ~s and lows of atmospheric pressure; ~s induced by narcotics, yoga, etc.; commands issued from* **on high** (i.e. as if from heaven).—**high and dry** stranded; all alone; **high and low** everywhere. —**high·ball** *n.* a mixed alcoholic drink served in a tall glass. —**high beam** beam of headlight switched to illuminate the way far ahead. —**high·born** *adj.* of noble birth. —**high·boy** *n.* a high chest of drawers mounted on relatively tall legs. —**high·brow** *n.* & *adj. Informal.* (one) of supposedly great knowledge or culture. —**high·er-up** *n. Informal.* one in a higher rank or position. —**high·fa·lu·tin(g)** (–fuh·LOO·tn) *adj. Informal.* high-sounding or bombastic. —**high fidelity** sound reproduction with high accuracy and low distortion; **high-fi·del·i·ty** (–DEL–) *adj.: ~ amplifier, reception.* —**high-flown** (–flone) *adj.* excessively high or bombastic. —**high frequency** a radio frequency of 3 to 30 megahertz. —**High German** the official and literary form of German. —**high-hand·ed** *adj.* overbearing in manner; also, without consideration for others' feelings; **high-hand·ed·ly** *adv.;* **high-hand·ed·ness** *n.* —**high-hat** *adj. Slang.* snobbish; ***v.*** **-hats, -hat·ted, -hat·ting** treat snobbishly. —**high·land** *n.* & *adj.* (of or in) a region that is higher than its surroundings, as the **High·lands** of N. and W. Scotland; **high·land·er** or **High·land·er** *n.* —**high-lev·el** *adj.* involving persons of high rank: *a ~ meeting of Soviet leaders.* —**high·light** *n.* the most prominent part, as a light-reflecting spot on a shiny object; hence, an important or interesting aspect or feature of something; ***v.*** **-lights, -light·ed, -light·ing** give prominence to; be a highlight of: *a year ~d by achievements in science.* —**high·ly** *adv.: a ~* (i.e. very) *entertaining act; speaks ~* (i.e. well) *of her; a ~ placed official.* —**high-mind·ed** *adj.* marked by high principles or feelings; **high-mind·ed·ness** *n.* —**high·ness** *n.* high state; **Her (His, Your) Highness** [style of addressing or referring to royalty]. —**high-pres·sure** *adj.* using aggressive methods, esp. in selling; also, involving much worry and tension; ***v.*** **-pres·sures, -pres·sured, -pres·sur·ing:** *was ~d into buying that lemon of a car.* —**high-rise** *n.* & *adj.* (a building) having many stories; **high-ris·er** *n.* a high-rise; also, a bicycle with high handlebars. —**high·road** *n.* a main road; also, a direct or easy route (*to* something). —**high school** secondary school consisting of grades 9 through 12, if four-year, or 10 through 12 if *senior high school.* —**high seas** the open ocean outside of national jurisdictions. —**high-spir·it·ed** *adj.* proud; brave; fiery: *a ~* (i.e. frisky) *horse.* —**high-strung** *adj.* easily excited. —**high-ten·sion** (–TEN–) *adj.* high-voltage. —**high-test** *adj.* of gasoline, vaporizing easily. —**high tide** (the time of) the highest level of the tide; hence, climax. —**high time** a time allowing no more delay. —**high·way** *n.* a public road; also, highroad; **high·way·man** *n.* **-men** a highway robber. —**high wire** rope or cable stretched high for aerialists to perform on; tightrope.

hi·jack (HYE–) *v.* seize control of (a bus, truck, airplane, etc. for purposes of extortion); ***n.*** a hijacking; **hi·jack·er** *n.*

hike *v.* **hikes, hiked, hik·ing** **1** take a long walk; tramp or march. **2** *Informal.* pull up and hitch; hence, raise or increase: *waded the stream with skirts ~d up; prices ~d to keep up with wages.* —***n.*** **1** a walk or march. **2** a raising or increase. —**hik·er** *n.*

hi·lar·i·ous (huh·LAIR·ee·us) *adj.* noisily merry; **hi·lar·i·ous·ly** *adv.;* **hi·lar·i·ty** *n.*

hill *n.* an elevation on the earth's surface, smaller than a mountain; a pile, heap, or mound. —**hill·bil·ly** *n.* **-bil·lies** a person from a backwoods region, esp. of the southern U.S. —**hill·ock** *n.* a small hill. —**hill·side** *n.* the slope of a hill. —**hill·top** *n.* the top of a hill. —**hill·y** *adj.* **hill·i·er, -i·est** full of hills; also, steep; **hill·i·ness** *n.*

hilt *n.* the handle of a sword, dagger, or similar weapon or tool; **(up) to the hilt** to the very limit: *dressed to the ~; in debt up to the ~.*

him *pron.* objective case of HE: *She knows ~; Informal: She's older than ~; It's ~* (i.e. he) *all right.*

Hi·ma·la·yas (him·uh·LAY·uz, –MAHL·yuz) *n.pl.* world's highest mountain system, located along India's northern borders, separating it from Tibet; **Hi·ma·la·yan** *adj.*

him·self (–SELF) *pron.* reflexive or emphatic form of HE: *not quite ~ today; works by ~; He ~ did it.*

hind (HINED) *n.* **1** the adult female of the red deer. **2** a British farm hand. ***—adj.*** *comp.* **hind·er,** *superl.* **hind·most** or **hind·er·most** rear; back. **—Hind.** Hindi; Hindu.

¹hin·der *v.* keep back or restrain; hence, prevent the progress of: *Thick underbrush ~ed our progress; parked cars ~ing snow removal.* **—²hind·er** (HINE·dur) *adj.* See HIND.

Hin·di (–dee) India's official language, spoken mainly in N. India.

hindmost See HIND. **—hind·quar·ter** (HINED·kwor·tur) *n.* the back half of a side of beef, lamb, etc.; **hindquarters** *pl.* a quadruped's hind pair of legs; haunches.

hin·drance (–drunce) *n.* a hindering; also, obstacle.

hind·sight (HINED–) *n.* a being wise after the event; understanding of what should have been done; cf. FORESIGHT.

Hin·du (–doo) *n.* a follower of Hinduism; ***adj.*** of or having to do with **Hin·du·ism** *n.* the ancient religion of India, with worship of many gods, the caste system, and belief in reincarnation. **—Hin·du·stan** (–STAN) the Hindi-speaking northern part of India; **Hin·du·stan·i** (–STAN·ee) *n.* a dialect of Hindi influenced by Persian, and spoken also in Pakistan.

hinge (HINJ) *n.* a natural or artificial joint on which a door, gate, lid, knees, clamshells, etc. move, turn, or depend; hence, a pivotal or determining factor; ***v.*** **hing·es, hinged, hing·ing:** *a cover ~d to move up and down; Everything ~s* (i.e. depends) *on her decision.*

hint *n.* an indirect or slight indication; also, trace: *Her winking at me was a ~; There's a ~ of frost in the air;* ***v.*** *She didn't suggest leaving, only* **hinted at** *the lateness of the hour.*

hin·ter·land *n.* the inland region behind a coast, as one served by a port; also, a region far from any urban center.

¹hip *n.* **1** the seed-containing fruit of the wild rose. **2** the joint of the thighbone with the ear-shaped **hip·bone** of the pelvis; also **hip·joint.** **3** the fleshy side below the waist covering a hipjoint; **hip-hug·ger** *pants,* or **hip·hug·gers.** **—hipped** *adj.* & *comb. form:* as in *broad-hipped; a ~ roof with sloped instead of vertical ends.*

²hip *adj.* **hip·per, hip·pest** *Slang.* alert or informed; wise to what is new and modish; not square; ***n.*** this condition; also **hip·ness.** ***—v.*** **hips, hipped, hip·ping** keep up-to-date; wise up; also, render hip; **hipped** *adj.* obsessed: *~ on golf.* **—hip·pie** or **hip·py** *n.* **hip·pies** *Slang.* a dropout from conventional society who lives a carefree life in communes, with long hair, free love, drugs, mysticism, etc.; **hip·pie·dom** *n.;* **hip·pie·ness** *n.*

hip·po (–poh) *n.* **hip·pos** *Informal.* hippopotamus.

Hip·poc·ra·tes (hi·POC·ruh·teez) 460?–370? B.C., Greek physician; **Hip·po·crat·ic** (–CRAT–) **oath** oath setting forth a physician's code of ethics.

hip·po·drome (HIP·uh–) *n.* an arena or indoor facility for horse racing, circuses, rodeos, etc. **—hip·po·pot·a·mus** (–POT·uh–) *n.* **-mus·es** or **-mi** (–mye) one of a family of large-headed, short-legged, thick-skinned herbivorous African animals related to hogs: *~s live in rivers, lakes, and marshy ponds.*

hip·ster *n. Slang.* one who is hip, esp. to jazz; **hip·ster·ism** *n.*

hire *v.* **hires, hired, hir·ing** engage for pay, esp. on a temporary basis; also, get or give the use of (a thing) or the work or services of (a person) in return for payment: *to* **hire out** *a laborer or tool.* ***—n.*** a hiring or payment for it: *cabs* **for hire;** *a good worker worth every penny of his ~.* **—hire·ling** *n.* & *adj.* (one) who will do anything for pay; mercenary.

Hi·ro·shi·ma (heer·uh·SHEE·muh) a seaport of Japan, rebuilt after destruction by the first U.S. atomic bomb.

hir·sute (HUR–) *adj.* hairy.

his (HIZ) *adj.* & *pron.* of or to him: *Those are ~; ~ neckties; a friend of ~.*

His·pan·ic (–PAN–) *adj.* of Spanish origin; also, Latin-American; **His·pan·ics** *n.pl.* Spanish-speaking Americans. **—His·pan·io·la** (–puh·NYOH·luh) a West Indian island divided between Haiti and the Dominican Republic. **—His·pa·no** (–PAN·oh) *n.* **-nos** a Spanish-speaking American.

hiss *v.* make a sharp sound as of air escaping from a tire or of geese and snakes when excited; hence, show disapproval by hissing: *so bad he was* **hissed off** *the stage;* ***n.:*** *amid ~es and hoots from spectators.*

hist. historian; historical; history. **—hist** *interj.* used to attract attention.

his·ta·mine (–meen, –min) *n.* a substance of body tissues that is released in reaction to irritating substances from outside, causing symptoms of allergy. **—his·to·gram** (–tuh–) *n.* a statistical graph of a frequency distribution using rectangles. **—his·tol·o·gy** (–TOL–) *n.* the biology of tissue structure; **his·tol·o·gist** *n.*

his·to·ry (–tuh·ree) *n.* **-ries** a branch of knowledge dealing with the recording and study of past events: *Europe's ancient ~; cavemen of an era before the dawn of ~* (i.e. human records); *Man's moon landing* **made history** (i.e. was so important); *a patient with a ~* (i.e. past) *of heart trouble; Watergate is no more news, but ~* (i.e. a past event); **his·to·ri·an** (–TOR·ee·un) *n.* a history scholar or writer of history.**—his·tor·ic** (–TOR–) *adj.* famous or important in history; also, historical; **his·tor·i·cal** *adj.* of or having to do with history or having reference to the past; also, factual, not fictitious; **his·tor·i·cal·ly** *adv.* —**his·to·ric·i·ty** (–RIS–) *n.* authenticity; genuineness as a historical fact. —**his·to·ri·og·ra·pher** (–OG·ruh·fur) *n.* an official history writer; also, a specialist in **his·to·ri·og·ra·phy** (–fee) *n.* the study of history writing and research.

his·tri·on·ics (–ON–) *n.* [takes *sing.* or *pl. v.*] **1** dramatic representation; dramatics. **2** affected display of emotion; artificial manner. —**his·tri·on·ic** *adj.*

hit *v.* **hits, hit, hit·ting** **1** come against with force; strike; not miss: *The car ~ (against) a tree; The dart ~ the bull's-eye; a nation hard ~* (i.e. severely affected) *by famine; He* **hit out** *against his attackers; a good fielder who couldn't ~.* **2** reach or find: *Drive on till you ~ the highway; an event that ~ the headlines; She* **hit (up)on** (i.e. found by chance) *a clever plan; The two* **hit it off** (i.e. got along well) *from the beginning;* **hit·ter** *n.* —***n.:*** *an unfair ~ below the belt; The player chalked up more misses than ~s; a play that is a box-office ~* (i.e. success); *a ~* (*Slang.* dose or measure) *of cocaine;* **hit-and-run:** *a ~ military tactic; a ~ baseball play; a warrant for a ~ driver; a* **hit-or-miss** (i.e. aimless) *effort.*

hitch (HICH) *v.* **1** pull or move jerkily; yank: *~ed up his trousers carefully before sitting down.* **2** fasten; hence, harness: *a sleeve that ~es on to doorknobs; a horse ~ed to a wagon.* **3** *Informal.* hitchhike: *I ~ed a ride home instead of walking.* —***n.:*** *a ~ to a sock that won't stay up; tied it to the* **hitching post** *with a ~* (i.e. knot) *of the rope; Everything went off without a ~* (i.e. obstacle); *a two-year ~* (i.e. service) *in the navy.* —**hitch·hike** *v.* **-hikes, -hiked, -hik·ing** travel by getting rides along the way; **hitch·hik·er** *n.*

hith·er (HIDH·ur) *adj.* & *adv.* to or on this side; **hither and thither** here and there; also **hither and yon.** —**hith·er·to** (–TOO) *adv.* until now.

Hit·ler, Adolf. 1889–1945, Nazi leader and dictator of Germany, 1933–1945.

hit man a hired murderer.

hive *n.* a beehive; hence, a place of busy activity; ***v.*** **hives, hived, hiv·ing** put (bees) or settle in a hive; also, lay up for future use: *Bees ~ honey.* —**hives** *n.* [takes *sing.* or *pl. v.*] an itching and burning skin rash caused by allergies.

H.J. [on epitaphs] *Latin.* "Here lies."

H.L. House of Lords.

H.M. Her (or His) Majesty. —**H.M.S.** Her (or His) Majesty's Ship (or Service).

Ho holmium.

hoa·gy or **hoa·gie** (HOH·gee) *n.* **-gies** a hero sandwich.

hoard *v.* get and store away (money, goods, etc.) for future use or sale; ***n.:*** *a squirrel's ~ of nuts for the winter; a miser's ~ of wealth; the profiteer's ~ of scarce commodities.* —**hoard·er** *n.* —**hoard·ing** *n.* a temporary fence of boards put up around a work site; hence, *Brit.* billboard.

hoar·frost *n.* white frost; frozen dew; ice crystals.

hoarse *adj.* **hoars·er, hoars·est** of sounds or voice, rough and husky; **hoarse·ness** *n.* —**hoars·en** *v.* make or become hoarse.

hoar·y *adj.* **hoar·i·er, -i·est** white or gray; also, white-haired with age; hence, ancient: *shook his ~ head; a ~ legend;* **hoar·i·ness** *n.*

hoax (HOKES) *n.* a fraud or practical joke; ***v.:*** *a publisher ~ed into buying a fabricated autobiography;* **hoax·er** *n.*

hob *n.* **1** elf; hobgoblin; **play** (or **raise**) **hob** *Informal.* make mischief (with). **2** shelf or ledge at the back or side of a fireplace. **3** the target peg in quoits. **4** a gear-cutting metal device.—**hob·ble** *n.* & *v.* **hob·bles, hob·bled, hob·bling** (move in) an awkward walk, as of a horse whose front legs are tied: *an injured skier ~ing around on crutches;* **hob·ble·de·hoy** *n.* a clumsy or gawky, esp. adolescent boy; **hobble skirt** a long skirt of the early 1900's, having a restrictive band above the ankles. —**hob·by** *n.* **hob·bies** a leisure-time activity or pursuit outside of one's main occupation, indulged in for fun and profit; **hob·by·ist** *n.;* **hob·by·horse** *n.* a child's rocking horse or a stick with a horse's head; hence, one's favorite topic or pet theory. —**hob·gob·lin** *n.* a goblin; also, a bogy. —**hob·nail** *n.* a large-headed nail for boot soles: *a* **hobnailed** *boot.* —**hob·nob** *v.* **-nobs, -nobbed, -nob·bing** associate familiarly *(with).*

ho·bo (HOH·boh) *n.* **-bo(e)s** a tramp.

Hob·son's choice a choice with no alternative.

Ho Chi Minh (HOH·chee·min) 1890?–1969, Vietnamese leader; **Ho Chi Minh City** a seaport and the largest city of Vietnam, formerly called Saigon.

hock *n.* **1** the backward-bending hind-leg joint of a horse, cat, etc.; also, the corresponding joint in a fowl's leg. **2** *Slang.* pawn; also ***v.;*** **in hock** indebted.

hock·ey (–ee) *n.* same as ICE HOCKEY; also FIELD HOCKEY.

hock·shop *n.* pawnshop.

ho·cus-po·cus (HOH·cus·POH–) *n.* meaningless formula; deceptive talk; also, trickery; sleight of hand.

hod *n.* an open trough or box fixed to the top of a staff, used for carrying bricks, mortar, etc. up ladders, etc.; also, a coal scuttle.

ho-dad *n.* *Slang.* a nonsurfing frequenter of beaches; hence, a square; also **ho-dad·dy.**

hod carrier a helper in construction work.

hodge·podge *n.* a jumble or mixture.

Hodg·kin's (HOJ–) **disease** a cancerous, sometimes fatal disease of the lymph nodes, spleen, etc.

hoe *n.* a farm tool consisting of a thin blade set across the end of a long handle; ***v.*** **hoes, hoed,**

hoe·ing cut, weed, or loosen (soil) with a hoe. —**hoe·cake** *n.* a thin cornmeal bread. —**hoe·down** *n.* a rollicking, rural kind of square dance of southern U.S. origin; also, the music for this.

hog *n.* a pig, esp. one raised for meat, weighing above 120 lb. (54.43 kg); hence, a coarse, filthy, or selfish person; one who is hoggish: *a road hog.* —***v.*** **hogs, hogged, hog·ging** grab or use selfishly: *~ing both lanes of the freeway.* —**go the whole hog** *Informal.* go all the way; do thoroughly.

ho·gan (HOE·gahn) *n.* an earth-covered Navaho dwelling.

hog·back *n. Geol.* a long, narrow steep-sided ridge. —**hog·gish** *adj.* filthy, greedy, or selfish. —**hog·nose (snake)** any of a family of North American snakes that hiss and flatten their snouts when disturbed; also called "blowing adder." —**hogs·head** *n.* a large cask; also, a liquid measure, varying from 63 to 140 gals. (238 to 530 L). —**hog-tie** *v.* **-ties, -tied, -ty·ing** or **tie·ing** make helpless, as by tying the feet. —**hog·wash** *n.* swill; also, baloney; nonsense. —**hog-wild** (–wiled) *adj. Informal.* wild with excitement: *to go ~.*

ho-hum *interj.* expression of boredom.

hoi pol·loi (–puh·LOY) *n.pl.* the common people.

hoist *v.* raise or lift, as a flag or sail, usu. with some mechanical means; ***n.*** a hoisting or a hoisting machine, as derricks and cranes. —**hoist with one's own petard** See PETARD.

hoke *v.* **hokes, hoked, hok·ing** *Slang.* esp. **hoke up** overplay (a stage or screen part) in a cheap or sensational manner; **hok·ey** *adj.* —**ho·kum** *n. Slang.* bunk; humbug.

hold (HOLED) *v.* **holds, held, hold·ing** have or take in one's possession, as by the hand or in one's physical or mental power: *a mother ~ing a child; ~ yourself erect; When the wind blows ~ on to your hat; a package being held for you at the post office; to ~ a fort against invaders; borrowers held responsible for books; a staff meeting to be held at 4 p.m.; a rule that ~s good in all cases; a man held in great esteem by all; cannot* **hold down** (i.e. stay in) *a job long enough to pay his debts; The preacher* **held forth** (i.e. talked) *too long from the pulpit;* **hold·er** *n.* —***n.*** **1** a holding, manner of holding, thing to hold by or with, a holding influence, or an order to hold; **catch** (or **lay, take**) **hold of** seize or get possession of. **2** a cargo compartment in a ship or airplane. —**hold out** continue resisting: *a labor union* **holding out for** *more concessions.* —**hold over** postpone or retain; also, keep or stay (in an office) for a longer period. —**hold up** maintain; continue; also, stop, esp. by force. —**hold·ing** *n.* land or other property; **holdings** *pl.* stocks and bonds; **holding pattern** an oval flight course at a specified height for an aircraft awaiting clearance to land. —**hold·out** *n.* refusal to agree or submit; also, a person or group resisting thus. —**hold·o·ver** *n.* a person or thing remaining from a previous time. —**hold·up** *n.* a stoppage, esp. a forcible one for robbery.

hole *n.* **1** an opening in or through something; **pick holes in** pick out errors or flaws in. **2** a pit, cave, burrow, etc.; hence, a dingy or dirty place; an awkward position; **in the hole** in difficulties. **3** in golf, one of the usu. 18 hollows on the green; also, a unit of play from tee to hole. —***v.*** **holes, holed, hol·ing** make a hole in (something); also, drive into a hole; **hole up** hide oneself.

hol·i·day *n.* a day of freedom from work, usu. for a religious or other celebration; **holidays** *pl.* vacation. —***adj.:*** *a ~ mood; a ~ weekend* (of three days). —***v.*** spend a holiday or vacation.

holier-than-thou, holiness See HOLY.

Hol·land (–und) same as NETHERLANDS. —**hol·lan·daise** (–daiz) **sauce** a creamy sauce of egg yolks, butter, etc. —**Hol·land·er** *n.* a Dutch person or ship.

hol·ler *n.* & *v. Informal.* shout; yell. —**hol·lo** (huh·LOH) or **hol·loa** (huh·LOH) *n., interj.* & *v.* **hol·los, hol·loed, hol·lo·ing** [used esp. to attract attention] hello.

hol·low (HOL·oh) *adj.* **1** empty, not solid inside; hence, concave; also, looking sunken or sounding empty: *a ~ ball, tube, dish, voice, laughter, cheeks, eyes.* **2** not real or genuine; false: *~ hopes, promises, sentiments.* —**hol·low·ness** *n.* —***n.*** a cavity; depression; valley. —***v.*** make hollow: *river banks ~ed by erosion; a container* **hollowed out** *of a gourd.* —***adv.:*** *a heavyweight champion who can* **beat** *anyone* **hollow** (i.e. completely) *in 10 minutes flat.* —**hol·low·(w)are** (HOL·uh·wair) *n.* tableware such as bowls, cups, etc.; cf. FLATWARE.

hol·ly *n.* **hol·lies** (–leez) an evergreen tree with glossy green leaves and bright red berries. —**hol·ly·hock** *n.* a tall, hardy, mallow-family plant with large stalks of colorful flowers. —**Hol·ly·wood** **1** a district of Los Angeles, Calif., home of the American motion picture industry. **2** a city of S.E. Florida.

Holmes (HOMES), **Oliver W.** 1841–1935, associate justice of the U.S. Supreme Court, 1902–32.

hol·mi·um (HOLE·mee–) *n.* a metallic chemical element.

hol·o·caust (HOL·uh–) *n.* a large-scale destruction, esp. of lives, as by fire: *a nuclear ~;* **the Holocaust** the Nazi massacre of Jews. —**Hol·o·cene** (–seen) *n.* & *adj.* (of) the present geologic epoch beginning about 10,000 years ago. —**hol·o·gram** *n.* a three-dimensional picture made on photographic film using laser light instead of a lens; **ho·log·ra·phy** (–LOG–) *n.* —**hol·o·graph** *v.* make a hologram of; produce by holography; ***n.*** & ***adj.*** (a manuscript, letter, will, etc.) wholly written in the hand of the person whose name it bears. **—hol·o·graph·ic** (–GRAF–) *adj.;* **hol·o·graph·i·cal·ly** *adv.*

Hol·stein (HOLE·steen, –stine) *n.* a breed of large black-and-white dairy cattle; also **Hol·stein-Frie·sian** (–FREE·zhun).

hol·ster (HOLE–) *n.* a leather case for a pistol, usu. attached to a belt.

ho·ly (HOH–) *adj.* **-li·er, -li·est** worthy of worship or reverence, esp. because of spiritual perfection; also, belonging to or devoted to God; **ho·li·er-than-thou** *adj.* implying superior goodness: *a ~ attitude, manner, smugness;* **ho·li·ness** *n.;* **Your** (or **His**) **Holiness** title used in addressing (or referring to) the Pope. **—Holy Communion** the Christian sacrament of receiving consecrated bread and wine as Christ's body and blood; Eucharist. **—Holy Land** Palestine. **—Holy Roman Empire** a union of Italy and Germany under German kings from A.D. 962 to 1806. **—Holy Spirit** (or **Ghost**) the third person of the Trinity; also, the spirit of God. **—ho·ly·stone** *n.* & *v.* **-stones, -stoned, -ston·ing** (scrub the decks of ships with) a piece of soft sandstone. **—holy water** water blessed for religious use.

hom·age (HOM·ij) *n.* an act or show of reverence.

hom·burg *n.* a man's soft felt hat with a curved brim and the crown dented lengthwise.

home *n.* **1** one's dwelling place, where one belongs, often including family and surroundings: *"~, sweet ~"; comes from a broken ~; to feel quite* **at home** (i.e. ease); *She won't be (at) ~ after 8* (i.e. not receiving calls). **2** a native place or habitat: *Alaska is the ~ of the kodiak bear.* **3** in games, a goal or home plate. **—adj.:** *~ office, front, comfort.* **—adv.** at or to one's home; hence, to where one belongs; to the point aimed at: *I'm going ~; Drive the nail ~; The point was* **brought home to** (i.e. impressed on) *him.* **—v. homes, homed, hom·ing** go, return, or send home: *the ~ing pigeon: An aircraft landing in fog will* **home onto** *a radar signal for guidance; the infrared ~ing system of the "Sidewinder" missile.* **—home·less** *adj.* **—home·base** same as HOME PLATE. **—home·bod·y** *n.* **-bod·ies** a person who prefers home and family to outside attractions. **—home·com·ing** *n.* a coming or returning to one's home or school, esp. an annual campus celebration. **—home economics** the management of a household as a course of study, including housekeeping, cooking, child care, etc.; domestic science. **—home-grown** *adj.* grown or produced at home; local: *~ vegetables, fruit, politicians.* **—home·land** *n.* **1** one's native land. **2** an independent region established for a black tribe within South Africa. **—home·ly** *adj.* **-li·er, -li·est** suited to home life; hence, plain; also, plain-looking: *~ pleasures, wife, virtues;* **home·li·ness** *n.* **—home·made** *adj.* made at home: *a ~ cake; furniture that looks ~* (i.e. lacking finish). **—home·mak·er** *n.* a manager of a household, esp. a housewife; **home·mak·ing** *n.*

homeo- *comb.form.* similar: as in *homeopathy, homeostasis.* **—ho·me·o·path** *n.* a practitioner of **ho·me·op·a·thy** (–OP·uh·thee) *n.* medical system in which a disease is treated by giving minute doses of a drug which would produce symptoms of the disease in a healthy person; **ho·me·o·path·ic** (–PATH–) *adj.* **—ho·me·o·sta·sis** (–STAY–) *n.* an organism's tendency or ability to maintain stability independently of its environment by regulation of its internal processes and systems such as respiration, circulation, hormones, etc.

home plate the slab beside which a baseball batter stands while batting.

Ho·mer (HOH–) the Greek epic poet, reputed author of the *Iliad* and the *Odyssey;* **Ho·mer·ic** (–MER–) *adj.*

hom·er (HOH·mur) *n.* & *v.* *Informal.* (hit) a home run in baseball. **—home·room** *n.* a room where all members of a class report. **—home run** a baseball hit that enables the batter to touch all bases and return to home plate. **—home·sick** *adj.* sad because away from home; **home·sick·ness** *n.* **—home·spun** *n.* & *adj.* (cloth) spun or made at home; hence, plain: *~ wit, manners.* **—home·stead** (–sted) *n.* a place, including land and buildings, where a family has made its home; **home·stead·er** *n.* one who has a homestead, esp. one who has acquired it by U.S. laws since 1862. **—home·stretch** *n.* the last stretch of a race track before the finish line; hence, a concluding part. **—home·ward** (–wurd) *adj.* & *adv.;* **home·wards** (–wurdz) *adv.* toward home: *a homeward trek; traveling homeward(s).* **—home·work** (–wurk) *n.* work done at home, esp. schoolwork outside the classroom: *Both debaters had apparently done their ~* (i.e. prepared themselves). **—home·y** *adj.* **hom·i·er, -i·est** having the atmosphere of a home; **home·y·ness** *n.*

hom·i·cide *n.* one who kills another; also, the crime: *justifiable ~ committed in self-defense;* **hom·i·ci·dal** (–SYE·dl) *adj.*

hom·i·let·ics (–LET–) *n.pl.* [takes *sing. v.*] the art of composing and delivering sermons. **—hom·i·ly** *n.* **-lies** (–leez) a sermon; also, a moralizing speech.

homing pigeon a breed of pigeon trained to carry home written messages over long distances.

hom·i·ny *n.* hulled corn, often coarsely ground, as "hominy grits."

homo- *comb.form.* same: as in *homograph, homosexual.* **—ho·mo** *n.* **1** *pl.* **-mi·nes** *Latin.* man, as in *Homo Sapiens.* **2** *pl.* **-mos** [short form] homosexual. **—ho·mo·ge·ne·ous** (–JEE·nee·us) *adj.* of the same kind or of uniform composition; not heterogeneous; **ho·mo·ge·ne·ous·ly** *adv.;* **ho·mo·ge·ne·i·ty** (–NEE–) *n.* —**ho·mog·e·nize** (huh·MOJ·uh–) *v.* **-niz·es, -nized, -niz·ing** make homogeneous, as in **homogenized milk** which has its fat particles evenly distributed so that cream does not form; **ho·mog·e·niz·er** *n.* —**hom·o·graph** *n.* a word that is the same as another in spelling, as "lead" *n.* and "lead" *v.* —**ho·mol·o·gous** (–MOL·uh·gus) *adj.* corresponding in origin, structure, etc., as the flipper of a seal and the foreleg of a horse, ethanol and glycerol (both alcohols), etc.; **hom·o·log(ue)** (–log) *n.* a homologous thing or part; **ho·mol·o·gy** (–MOL–) *n.* —**hom·o·nym** (–nim) *n.* a word that is the same as another in pronunciation and spelling, as "bear" *v.* and "bear" *n.;* often, also, a homophone. —**hom·o·phile** *n.* & *adj.* homosexual. —**hom·o·phone** *n.* a word that is pronounced like another, as "bear" and "bare," or "shoe" and "shoo."

Ho·mo sa·pi·ens (HOH·moh SAY·pee·enz, –SAP·ee–) "intelligent man," i.e. human beings as a species, from about 300,000 B.C.: *Modern man is a subspecies, "Homo sapiens sapiens."*

ho·mo·sex·u·al (–SEK·shoo·ul) *n.* & *adj.* (a person) sexually attracted to those of the same sex; **ho·mo·sex·u·al·i·ty** (–AL–) *n.* such a tendency or activity.

hon. honor; also **Hon.** honorable; honorary.

Hon(d). *Abbrev.* for **Hon·du·ras** (–DURE·us) a Central American republic; 43,277 sq. mi. (112,088 km²); *cap.* Tegucigalpa. —**Hon·du·ran** *n.* & *adj.*

hone *n.* & *v.* **hones, honed, hon·ing** (sharpen a razor, knife, or other cutting tool using) a fine-grained stone; **hon·er** *n.*

hon·est (ON·ist) *adj.* **1** of people, honorable and truthful; not lying, cheating, or stealing: *an ~ politician; an* **honest broker** (i.e. neutral mediator). **2** of things, genuine; pure; having to do with an honest person: *an ~ face, opinion, piece of work; ~ profits, goods;* **hon·est·ly** *adv.* —**hon·es·ty** *n.*

hon·ey (HUN·ee) *n.* **-eys** **1** the sweet, thick, golden liquid made by **hon·ey·bees** from the nectar of flowers and stored in honeycombs. **2** anything sweet like honey; also, a darling; ***adj.*** sweet or dear. —***v.*** **hon·eys** or **hon·ies, hon·eyed** or **hon·ied, hon·ey·ing** sweeten; also, talk sweetly (to): *staved off eviction by ~ing up the landlady.* —**hon·ey·comb** (–kome) *n.* a wax structure made of six-sided cells; also, anything resembling this; ***v.:*** *a landscape ~d with apartments.* —**hon·ey·dew** *n.* a sweet and sticky substance found on leaves and stems of plants, as secreted by aphids, leafhoppers, and such insects: *The* **honeydew melon** *has a whitish rind and sweet, green flesh.* —**honey locust** a tree of the pea family with a slender trunk and featherlike foliage, whose pods contain a sweetish pulp. —**hon·ey·moon** *n.* the vacation taken by a newly married couple; hence, an initial period of harmonious relations, as between a new President and Congress; also ***v.;*** **hon·ey·moon·er** *n.* —**hon·ey·suck·le** *n.* any of a family of shrubs and vines such as the woodbine, having trumpet-shaped, nectar-filled flowers.

Hong Kong a British crown colony on China's S.E. coast; 1,126 sq. mi. (2,916 km²); *cap.* Victoria.

honk n. a wild goose's cry or a sound resembling it, as of a foghorn or automobile horn; ***v.:*** *parked outside and ~ed for his date to come out.* —**hon·ky** or **hon·kie** (HONG·kee) *n. Slang.* [contemptuous use] a white person. —**hon·ky-tonk** *n. Slang.* a cheap nightclub or dancehall; ***adj.:*** *~ music.*

Hon·o·lu·lu (–uh·LOO·loo) capital of Hawaii.

hon·or (ON·ur) *n.* **1** keen personal sense of right and wrong; integrity: *a man of ~; to take a pledge* **on one's honor;** *a code of ~; an ~ system.* **2** respect felt or shown because of a person's integrity; high regard: *Lincoln is held in high ~; in ~ of the war heroes; Olympic gold medalists* **do honor to** *their countries;* **Your** (or **Her, His**) **Honor** [title of respect for judges and certain officials]. **3** an act of respect or a thing bestowed on a respected person; credit; distinction: *a pass with* **honors; do the honors** act as a host or hostess. —***v.:*** *felt ~ed by the invitation; All credit cards ~ed* (i.e. accepted) *here;* **hon·or·er** *n.* —**hon·or·a·ble** *adj.: an ~ discharge for faithful service; an ~ deed;* **the Honorable** [title of various government officials]; **hon·or·a·ble·ness** *n.;* **hon·or·a·bly** *adv.* —**hon·o·rar·i·um** (–RAIR·ee–) *n.* **-i·ums** or **-i·a** a voluntary fee offered for a professional service; **hon·o·rar·y** (ON·uh·rer·ee) *adj.* given or done as an honor: *an ~ degree; an ~ position;* **hon·o·rar·i·ly** *adv.* —**hon·or·i·fic** (–RIF–) *n.* & *adj.* (a word or title) conferring or showing respect, as "Pundit." —**hon·our** *Brit.* honor.

hooch *n. Slang.* inferior or illicitly made alcoholic liquor.

-hood *n. suffix.* **1** state or quality: as in *childhood, falsehood.* **2** group: as in *brotherhood, neighborhood.* —**hood** **1** *n.* & *v.* (provide with) a covering for the head and neck or something looking like one, as the fold of cloth over the back of an academic gown, an automobile engine's metal cover, a canopy over a window, the expanded neck of a cobra, the crests of certain birds, etc.; **hood·ed** *adj.: a ~ crow, seal, pitcher plant.* **2** short for **hood·lum** *n.* a young ruffian, esp. a member of a gang.

hoo·doo *n.* **-doos** (a person or thing bringing) bad luck; also, voodoo; ***v.*** make unlucky.

hood·wink *v.* mislead or dupe, as if by blindfolding.

hoo·ey *n.* & *interj. Slang.* nonsense; bunk.

hoof *n.* **hoofs** or **hooves** the hard, horny covering on the feet of animals called "ungulates," such as horses, pigs, and cattle; **on the hoof** alive. **—*v.*** *Informal.* walk or dance; **hoofed** *adj.* having hoofs.

hook *n.* **1** a curved or bent piece of stiff material, as metal or wood, for catching, as a *fish hook,* to hang things on, as a *coat hook,* or as **hook and eye** (i.e. loop), a fastening device. **2** a strike or blow, as in boxing, given with a curving motion. **—by hook or by crook** by any means, fair or foul. **—off the hook** *Informal.* out of trouble; free of responsibility. **—*v.*** catch (as fish) or by a trick; also, in games, throw or hit a hook: *~ed herself a husband;* **hook up** connect or set up (a radio, telephone, etc.).

hook·a(h) *n.* an Arabian smoking pipe connected by a long tube to a vase of water through which the smoke is drawn to cool it.

hooked *adj.* **1** bent like a hook, having hooks, or made by hooking: *a ~ rug.* **2** *Informal.* addicted: *She is ~ on heroin.* **—hook·er** *n. Slang.* a prostitute. **—hook·up** *n.* a radio or telephone setup, esp. a network of radio and television stations. **—hook·worm** *n.* a small round worm that enters the body through the skin and attaches itself to the intestinal wall, living as a parasite and causing "hookworm disease." **—hook·y** *n.* **play hooky** *Informal.* stay out of school without permission.

hoo·li·gan (–gun) *n.* a hoodlum.

hoop *n.* a large ring, as one of the flat bands holding the staves of a barrel together, any of the flexible rings forming a frame to hold out a **hoop skirt,** or a ring used as a *hula hoop;* ***v.*** bind or fasten with a hoop. **—hoop·la** *n. Informal.* ballyhoo; hullabaloo.

hoo·poe (–poo) *n.* an Old World bird related to hornbills, having an erectile crest of feathers.

hoop skirt See HOOP.

hooray same as HURRAH.

hoose·gow *n. Slang.* jail.

Hoo·sier (–zhur) *n.* [nickname] a native or resident of Indiana.

hoot *n.* & *v.* (utter) the cry of an owl; shout in disapproval or scorn: *an actor ~ed off the stage; doesn't care a ~* (*Informal.* the least bit); **hoot·er** *n.* **—hoot·en·an·ny** (HOO·tn·an·ee) *n.* **-an·nies** an informal folk-singing session.

Hoo·ver, Herbert C. 1874–1964, 31st U.S. President (1929–33).

hooves a *pl.* of HOOF.

[1]**hop** *n.* **1** a short leap on one foot, as in hopscotch, or on both feet, as birds do, or on all fours, as frogs. **2** *Informal.* a short trip or plane flight; also, a dance. **3** *Slang.* dope, esp. opium. **—*v.* hops, hopped, hop·ping:** *rabbits ~ing across a field; had to ~ about with one foot in a cast; ~* (i.e. board) *a train; a fence low enough to ~* (i.e. leap over); *to* **hop up** (*Informal.* supercharge) *an engine;* **hopped up** *Slang.* under the influence of narcotics.

[2]**hop** *n.* a vine of the mulberry family whose dried flower clusters, or **hops,** are used to flavor beer, ale, etc.

hope *n.* a confident belief that something will be realized as desired; also, the thing hoped for, reason for hoping, or a person one has hopes in: *Any ~ of success? She's the ~ of the family.* **—*v.* hopes, hoped, hop·ing:** *Let's ~ for the best; didn't ~ to recover; still kept* **hoping against hope. —HOPE** (Project) Health Opportunity for People Everywhere. **—hope·ful** *n.* & *adj.* (a person) feeling or giving hope: *~ of victory; a ~ sign; young medical-school ~s;* **hope·ful·ly** *adv.: waited ~ for the results; ~* (*Informal.* It is hoped) *everyone will pass;* **hope·ful·ness** *n.* **—hope·less** *adj.;* **hope·less·ly** *adv.;* **hope·less·ness** *n.*

hop·head *n. Slang.* a drug addict.

Ho·pi (–pee) *n.* (one of) a Pueblo Indian tribe; also, their Shoshonean language.

hop·per *n.* **1** one that hops, esp. an insect such as the locust or leafhopper. **2** a container that can be emptied from the bottom, as a railroad car for bulk freight such as coal, a seeding machine or drill, etc. **—hop·sack(·ing)** *n.* fabric with a coarse, loose weave. **—hop·scotch** *n.* a children's game played by hopping through the squares of a figure drawn on the ground to pick up a stone tossed into it.

hor. horizontal.

Hor·ace (–is) 65–8 B.C., Roman poet; **Ho·ra·tian** (–RAY–) adj.

horde *n.* a crowd or throng, esp. one considered to be invading or rapacious: *the Tartar ~s; ~s of immigrants, shoppers, children.*

hore·hound *n.* an herb of the mint family whose bitter-tasting leaves and stems are used in cough medicines and candy.

ho·ri·zon (huh·RYE·zn) *n.* where earth and sky seem to meet; hence, the limit of one's experience or perception: *travel for broadening one's ~s.* **—hor·i·zon·tal** (–ZON·tl) *n.* & *adj.* (a line, surface, direction, etc.) that is level, not vertical; flat or even: *a gymnast performing on the ~ bars;* **hor·i·zon·tal·ly** *adv.*

hor·mone *n.* a chemical substance produced in a particular part of an organism, as adrenalin or auxin, to regulate functions such as growth, sex, and metabolism; **hor·mo·nal** (–MOH·nl) *adj.*

horn *n.* **1** either of a pair of hard, bony projections on the head of a hoofed animal; also, a similar protrusion, as on the head of a snail or insect. **2** the substance that horns, birds' beaks, hoofs, fingernails, etc. are made of. **3** a container hollowed out of horn, a brass-wind instrument, or other sounding device, as a *hunting horn, French horn, automobile horn,* etc. **—*adj.*** made of horn. **—*v.* horn in (on)** *Infor-*

mal. intrude; butt in. —**Horn, Cape.** the S. tip of South America. —**horn•bill** *n.* a tropical bird with an immense horny bill. —**horn•blende** (–blend) *n.* a lustrous green, brown, or black mineral containing aluminum silicate, occurring in granitic rocks. —**horn•book** *n.* a flat board with a handle, containing the alphabet, numbers, or similar elementary teaching material, protected by a sheet of clear horn, used in the days when paper was scarce. —**horned** *adj.* having horns; **horned owl** an owl with hornlike tufts on its head; **horned toad** a toadlike lizard with horny spines on its head and body; **horn•less** *adj.* —**hor•net** (–nit) *n.* any of several large social wasps that give painful stings. —**horn of plenty** same as CORNUCOPIA. —**horn•pipe** *n.* a lively dance, once popular among sailors, or the music for it, played on a wind instrument made partly of horn. —**horn•y** *adj.* **horn•i•er, -i•est** **1** made of horn or horned; also, hard or calloused. **2** *Slang.* aroused sexually.

ho•rol•o•gy (–ROL–) *n.* the science of measuring time; also, the art of making timepieces; **ho•rol•o•gist** *n.;* **hor•o•log•i•cal** (–LOJ–) *adj.* —**hor•o•scope** (HOR·uh–) *n.* an astrological forecast based on the positions of the planets and the signs of the zodiac at a given time, as at one's birth; also, a chart showing such positions.

hor•ren•dous (–REN·dus) *adj.* liable to instill horror: *~ red tape.* —**hor•ri•ble** *adj.* dreadful; also, *Informal.* extremely unpleasant: *a ~ torture chamber; a ~ odor;* **hor•rib•ly** *adv.* —**hor•rid** *adj.* frightful: *such ~ manners!* **hor•rid•ly** *adv.* —**hor•ri•fy** *v.* **-fies, -fied, -fy•ing** cause to feel horror; shock: *felt ~d by the atrocities; a ~ing scene.* —**hor•ror** (HOR·ur) *n.* fear mixed with revulsion; also, something that causes such feeling: *the ~ of a child witnessing a crime; the ~s of wasteful government spending; a ~ movie.*

hors de com•bat (or·duh·cawm·BAH) *French.* put out of action; disabled. —**hors d'oeu•vre** (or·DURV), *pl.* **-vres** (–DURVZ) an appetizer such as anchovies, canapes, or olives.

horse *n.* **1** a strong, four-legged, solid-hoofed animal with a mane and a long tail of hair, used for riding and for pulling or carrying loads. **2** a piece of gymnasium equipment used for vaulting; also, a supporting frame, as a clotheshorse or sawhorse. —**v.** **hors•es, horsed, hors•ing** provide with a horse; **horse around** *Informal.* fool around. —**adj.** of a horse or horses: *a ~ doctor; ~ louse.* —**from the horse's mouth** *Informal.* authoritatively; **horse of another color** a different matter. —**horse•back** *n.* & *adv.* (on) a horse's back. —**horse chestnut** any of a family of shade trees and shrubs bearing spikes of tiny white flowers and large brown poisonous seeds resembling chestnuts. —**horse•feath•ers** *n.* & *interj. Slang.* nonsense. —**horse•flesh** *n.* the flesh of a horse; also, horses collectively. —**horse•fly** *n.* **-flies** a large insect that sucks the blood of cattle and horses. —**horse•hair** *n.* a stiff fabric made of hairs from a horse's tail or mane; ***adj.:*** *~ stuffing for a sofa.* —**horse•hide** *n.* leather from horse's hide. —**horse latitudes** regions of calm air around the earth at about 30° N. and S. latitudes. —**horse•laugh** *n.* a boisterous laugh. —**horse•man** *n.* **-men** a cavalryman; also, one who rides or manages horses; **horse•man•ship** *n.* —**horse opera** *Slang.* a cheap western. —**horse•play** *n.* boisterous play. —**horse•pow•er** *n.* a unit of engine power, i.e. 550 foot-pounds of work per second or 746 watts. —**horse•rad•ish** *n.* a pungent relish made of the grated root of a mustard-family herb; also, this plant. —**horse sense** *Informal.* common sense. —**horse•shoe** (–shoo) *n.* & *v.* **-shoes, -shoed, -shoe•ing** (fit a horse with) a U-shaped metal plate nailed to the hoof for protection; **horse•sho•er** *n.;* **horse•shoes** *n.pl.* a game of pitching horseshoes so as to get them around a stake 40 ft. (12.192 m) away. —***adj.:*** horseshoe-shaped: *a ~ magnet, table;* **horseshoe crab** a crablike sea animal with a horseshoe-shaped shell and long, spiny tail; king crab. —**horse•tail** *n.* a rushlike plant with a hollow, jointed stem, used as "scouring rush" because it contains the abrasive silica. —**horse•whip** *n.* & *v.* **-whips, -whipped, -whip•ping** (beat with) a whip for driving horses. —**horse•wom•an** *n.* **-wom•en** *fem.* of HORSEMAN. —**hors•(e)y** *adj.* **hors•i•er, -i•est** fond of or having to do with horses or horse racing: *the ~ set frequenting racetracks;* **hors•i•ness** *n.*

hort. horticultural; horticulture.

hor•ta•tive (–tiv) or **hor•ta•to•ry** *adj.* exhorting; giving advice.

hor•ti•cul•ture *n.* the science and art of gardening, esp. of fruit trees, vegetables, and flowers; **hor•ti•cul•tur•al** (–CUL–) *adj.;* **hor•ti•cul•tur•ist** *n.*

Hos. Hosea (Old Testament book).

ho•san•na (–ZAN·uh) *n.* & *interj.* praise to God.

hose (HOZE) *n.* **1** *pl.* **hos•es** a tube of flexible material for watering, putting out fires, etc. **2** *pl.* same as **ho•sier•y** (–zhur·ee) *n.* socks and stockings; also, tight breeches formerly worn by men. —**v.** **hos•es, hosed, hos•ing:** *~ a lawn; ~ down a stone-throwing mob.*

hosp. hospital. —**hos•pice** (–pis) *n.* a lodging for travelers; also, a home for the sick or poor. —**hos•pi•ta•ble** (–tuh·bl, –PIT·uh·bl) *adj.* kind and courteous to guests and others seeking hospitality; also, receptive to new ideas. —**hos•pi•tal** (–pi·tl) *n.* an institution where sick and injured are treated. —**hos•pi•tal•i•ty** (–TAL–) *n.* **-ties** friendly and generous treatment of guests and strangers. —**hos•pi•tal•ize** *v.* **-iz•es, -ized, -iz•ing** put (a patient) into a hospital for medical, surgical, or related care; **hos•pi•tal•i•za•tion** (–ZAY–) *n.* —**host** (HOHST) *n.* **1** one who receives and accommodates or entertains a guest; hence, an innkeeper; also, an organism such as a plant or animal on which a parasite feeds, or an embryo into which a graft is transplanted; ***v.*** act as a host or emcee (for a TV show or other event). **2** a large number, originally an army: *~s of relatives; a ~ of objections.* **3** a wafer used in Holy Communion; **Host** a consecrated wafer. —**hos•tage** (HOS·tij) *n.* a person handed over or seized and held as a pledge or guarantee. —**hos•tel** (–tl) *n.* a lodging place, esp. a supervised "youth hostel"; **hos•tel•er** *n.* a hostel guest; **hos•tel•ry** *n.* **-ries** an inn or hotel. —**host•ess** (HOH·stis) *n.* a woman who entertains a guest; also, one who works in or is hired for entertaining or service roles, as in managing a hotel, in a restaurant or dance hall, as an airline stewardess, etc. —**hos•tile** (–tl, –tile) *adj.* of an enemy; hence, unfriendly; unsuitable: *a ~ reviewer; a climate ~ to polar bears; received with ~ looks;* **hos•tile•ly** *adv.;* **hos•til•i•ty** (–TIL–) *n.* **-ties:** *Pearl Harbor and ensuing ~s* (i.e. warfare); *the barbarian's ~ to civilization.* —**hos•tler** *n.* one who takes care of horses at an inn; also, one who services a locomotive or truck between runs.

hot *adj.* **hot•ter, hot•test** **1** having a high temperature; also, sharp or pungent to the taste: *Fire is ~; ~ peppers.* **2** having the feeling of high heat: *Running makes you ~; a ~* (i.e. fiery) *temper; a ~* (i.e. fresh) *scent; police in ~* (i.e. very close) *pursuit of a getaway car; a place getting too ~* (i.e. dangerous) *for lawbreakers; a ~* (i.e. live) *wire.* **3** *Slang.* causing heat; excited; passionate; fashionable or successful: *a ~* (i.e. wanted) *criminal; ~ jazz; successful but* **not so hot** *as we thought;* **hots** *n.pl.* strong sexual desire. —**make it hot for** *Informal.* make things uncomfortable for. —**hot•ly** *adv.* —**hot•ness** *n.* —**hot air** *Slang.* empty talk or writing. —**hot•bed** *n.* a place of rapid growth, as a glass-covered bed of earth heated by fermenting manure: *slums as the ~ of vice and crime.* —**hot-blood•ed** *adj.* easily excited; reckless. —**hot•box** *n.* a bearing overheated by friction, as at the end of an axle of a railroad car. —**hot•cake** *n.* pancake; **sell like hotcakes** *Informal.* sell rapidly. —**hot dog** *Informal.* a sandwich made with a hot frankfurter in a split roll; ***interj.*** *Slang.* an exclamation of approval or enthusiasm.

ho•tel (–TEL) *n.* a commercial establishment providing food and lodging, esp. for travelers; **ho•tel•ier** (–tel·YAY) *n.* hotel-keeper.

hot flash sensation of heat passing over the body, often experienced by women during menopause. —**hot•foot** *n.* **-foots** prank of lighting a match in the welt of an unsuspecting person's shoe; ***adv.*** *Informal.* in haste; ***v.*** **hotfoot it** *Informal.* go hastily. —**hot•head** *n.* a rash or fiery-tempered person; **hot•head•ed** *adj.* —**hot•house** *n.* & *adj.* (of or from) a greenhouse. —**hot line** a telephone or other communication line for use in a crisis. —**hot pants** women's short shorts. —**hot plate** a small portable electric stove. —**hot potato** *Informal.* a troublesome question or subject that no one wants to handle. —**hot rod** *Slang.* an automobile modified for fast acceleration and speeds; **hot rod•der** *Slang.* one who drives a hot rod. —**hot seat** *Slang.* a situation or position in which one is subject to harassment or criticism. —**hot•shot** *n.* & *adj. Slang.* (one who is) flashily skillful.

Hot•ten•tot *n.* (a member of) a nomadic people of S.W. Africa or their language; also ***adj.***

hot water *Informal.* trouble: *found himself in ~.*

hound *n.* **1** a short-haired, long-eared hunting dog that tracks its prey by scent. **2** *Informal.* an enthusiastic pursuer: *a party ~; publicity ~; autograph ~.* —***v.*** keep chasing; also, urge on: *a debtor ~ed by creditors.* —**hounds•tooth (check)** a small woven broken-check pattern with hook.

hour *n.* one of the 24 periods of 60 minutes each into which a day is divided; hence, any fixed period: *closed during the lunch ~; office* **hours** *from 9 to 5;* **after hours** after the regular school or business hours. —**hour•ly** *adj.* & *adv.: an ~ rate of pay; paid ~.* —**hour•glass** *n.* a time-measuring device consisting of two glass bulbs containing enough sand or liquid to run for an hour through the narrow neck connecting the top bulb to the bottom one.

hou•ri (HOOR·ee, HOW–) *n.* **-ris** one of the beautiful nymphs of the Moslem Paradise.

house *n.* **hous•es** (HOW·ziz) **1** a living place, esp. as an establishment, often including a **house•hold** of family and servants, headed by the **house•hold•er** and managed by a **house•keep•er,** usu. the "lady of the house," or housewife: *Father* **keeps house** (i.e. does the housework) *while unemployed; a swallow's hanging ~; a snail with its ~ on its back; the royal House* (i.e. family including ancestors and descendants) *of Windsor; the ~ of David; a fraternity ~; visitors versus ~* (i.e. school or dormitory); *the ~s of heaven* (i.e. 12 portions of the zodiac). **2** an organization or institution; also, an assembly or audience: *a publishing ~; The drinks are* **on the house** (i.e. free); *the House of Representatives; playing to a full ~; Her singing* **brings down the house** (*Informal.* is loudly applauded). —***v.*** (HOWZ) **hous•es, housed, hous•ing:** *The refugees were ~d in tents; old furniture ~d in the attic.* —**house•ful** *adj.* —**house•less** *adj.* —**house arrest** an arrested person's confinement in his own house. —**house•boat** *n.* a barge fixed up as a dwelling. —**house•boy** *n.* a male servant of a household. —**house•break•ing** *n.* the act of breaking into a house to commit a crime. —**house•bro•ken** *adj.* of a domestic pet, trained to live in a house, esp. knowing where to defecate and urinate. —**house·clean·ing** *n.* getting rid of bad conditions, as in cleaning a house and its furnishings. —**house·coat** *n.* a woman's long-skirted garment for casual indoor wear. —**house·fly** *n.* **-flies** the common two-winged fly. —**household** See HOUSE, *n.* 1; ***adj.*** domestic: ~ *expenses;* **household word** a familiar name or saying. —**housekeeper** See HOUSE, *n.* 1; **house·keep·ing** *n.* housework; also, bookkeeping, paperwork, and such domestic details of business management; ***adj.*** having kitchen facilities: *a large ~ suite at $100 a day.* —**house·lights** *n. pl.* lights in a theater auditorium. —**house·maid** *n.* a female servant doing housework. —**house·moth·er** *n.* a woman in charge of young people living together, as in a dormitory. —**House of Commons** the lower house of a parliament. —**house of ill fame** a brothel. —**House of Lords** the upper, nonelective house of the British Parliament. —**House of Representatives** the lower house of the U.S. Congress or of certain state legislatures. —**house·top** *n.* roof: *This is private, don't shout it* **from the housetops.** —**house·wares** *n.pl.* dishes, small appliances, and such kitchen equipment and household articles. —**house·warm·ing** *n.* a party to celebrate the moving into a new home. —**house·wife** *n.* **-wives** **1** woman head of a household; **house·wife·ly** *adj.;* **house·wif·er·y** *n.* housekeeping. **2** (*usu.* HUZ·if) *esp. Brit.* a sewing box. —**house·work** *n.* washing, cooking, and other housekeeping work. —**hous·ing** *n.* **1** the providing of shelter; also, lodging or houses collectively: *open ~ without racial discrimination; overpopulation and ~ problems.* **2** frame, box, plate, etc. for holding a mechanical part in place. **3** an ornamental saddle cover.

Hous·ton (HEW·stun) a city and port of S. Texas.

hove (HOHV) a *pt.* & *pp.* of HEAVE.

hov·el (HUVL) *n.* a miserable dwelling; hut.

hov·er (HUV·ur) *v.* be in a fluttering, suspended, or lingering state: *a bird ~ing over its nest; The patient ~ed between life and death;* **hover-** *comb.form. esp. Brit.* having to do with an air cushion vehicle: as in *hoverferry, hovertrain, hoverport* (i.e. hovercraft terminal); **Hov·er·craft** *Trademark.* an air cushion vehicle; also **hovercraft** *n.*

how *adv.* & *conj.* **1** in what way, state, condition, etc.: *Hello, ~ are you? Show me ~ to swim; don't know ~ this happened;* **And how!** *Informal.* very much so! **How do you do?** [used formally on being introduced] hello. **2** to what degree, extent, effect, etc.: *~ old are you? ~ do you mean? Tell us ~ much you're asking;* **How about** (i.e. What do you say to) *buying me a drink?* **3** *Informal.* why: *~ is that?* **How come?** Why?: *~ come* (i.e. why is it that) *you're late?* **4** by what name: *~ are you known around here? ~* (i.e. at what price) *do you sell these goods?* —***n.:*** *the hows and whys of the situation.* —**how·be·it** *adv. Archaic.* nevertheless.

how·dah *n.* a canopied seat for riding on an elephant or camel.

how·dy (–dee) *interj. Informal.* hello. —**how·e'er** (–AIR) *Poet. form* of **how·ev·er** (–EV·ur) *conj.* & *adv.* **1** in whatever way or to whatever extent: *couldn't succeed ~ hard he tried; ~ did you manage that?* **2** nevertheless; but: *I'm busy; ~, I will come.*

how·itz·er (HOW·it·sur) *n.* a short gun for firing shells and such projectiles at a high angle and low velocity.

howl *n.* & *v.* (give) a long, loud, and mournful cry, as dogs and wolves; also, yell or shout from amusement or scorn: *a speaker mercilessly ~ed down; was ~ed off the stage.* —**howl·er** *n.* one that howls; also, *Informal.* a ridiculous blunder. —**howl·ing** *adj.: a ~* (i.e. desolate) *wilderness; a ~* (*Informal.* great) *success.*

how·so·ev·er (–EV·ur) *adv.* HOWEVER, def. 1.

how-to *adj.* giving practical instructions on how to do something: *a ~ book.*

hoy·den (–dn) *n.* a saucy or boisterous girl; tomboy; **hoy·den·ish** *adj.*

Hoyle, E. 1672–1769, an authority on card games; **according to Hoyle** according to the rules; exact(ly).

H.P., h.p. or **hp.** high pressure; horsepower.

H.Q. or **h.q.** headquarters.

hr(s). hour(s).

H.R. House of Representatives.

H.R.H. Her (or His) Royal Highness.

H.S. or **h.s.** high school.

H.T. high tension. —**ht.** heat; height; **hts** heights.

hua·ra·che (huh·RAH·chee) *n.* a flat, leather-thonged sandal worn in Latin American countries.

hub *n.* the central part around which a wheel turns; hence, a center of activity.

hub·bub *n.* confused noise, as of a milling crowd; also, uproar.

hub·by *n.* **hub·bies** *Informal.* husband.

hub·cap *n.* a metal cap covering the end of an axle.

hu·bris (HEW–) *n.* extreme arrogance.

huck·le·ber·ry *n.* **-ber·ries** a shrub of the heath family with blueberrylike fruit.

huck·ster *n.* a peddler of small articles; also, a loud or petty salesman; hence, *Slang.* an adman, esp. a producer of commercials; ***v.*** peddle; haggle; promote.

HUD Housing and Urban Development (U.S. Dept.).

hud·dle *n.* & *v.* **hud·dles, hud·dled, hud·dling** (crowd together or confer in) a closely packed group, as of football players between plays; **hud·dler** *n.*

Hud·son (–sn) a river in E. New York. —**Hudson Bay** a landlocked sea in N.E. Canada connected to the Atlantic and Arctic oceans.

hue (HEW) *n.* color, esp. as the modification of a basic color; **hued** *adj.: a reddish-~ orange.* —**hue and cry** a shouting of alarm; outcry.

huff *n.* & *v.* (get into) a fit of peevish anger. —**huff·y** *adj.* **huff·i·er, -i·est** in a huff; easily offended; **huff·i·ness** *n.*

hug *v.* **hugs, hugged, hug·ging** clasp closely in an embrace; hence, cling or stay close to: *a low-slung car that ~s the road; The bus moved forward, ~ing the right side of the highway;* ***n.*** a close embrace. —**hug·ger** *n.*

huge (HYOOJ) *adj.* **hug·er, hug·est** very large in mass or bulk: *a ~ belly, deficit; a ~* (i.e. great in scope) *undertaking;* **huge·ly** *adv.;* **huge·ness** *n.*

hug·ger-mug·ger *n.* & *adj.* (in) a confused condition; disorder(ly).

Hu·go (HEW·go), **Victor M.** 1802–85, French poet and novelist.

Hu·gue·not (HEW·guh–) *n.* any French Protestant of the 16th and 17th centuries.

huh *interj.* expressing contempt, surprise, question, etc.

hu·la (HOO·luh) *n.* a Hawaiian dance marked by swaying of hips and graceful gestures. —**hula hoop** a light hoop for twirling around the hips for exercise or as a toy; **Hu·la-Hoop** *Trademark.*

hulk *n.* a heavy, unwieldy, or clumsy person or thing, esp. an old ship that is out of service; **hulk·ing** *adj.: a big ~ heavyweight of a man.*

hull n. the outer covering of a fruit or seed; also, the calyx of some fruits such as the strawberry; hence, the outer frame on which a ship or similar vessel floats: *A submarine has a double ~.* —***v.*** remove the hulls or shells of (grains, peas, nuts, oysters, strawberries, etc.); **hull·er** *n.*

hul·la·ba·loo (HUL·uh·buh·loo) *n.* **-loos** clamor; disturbance.

hum *v.* **hums, hummed, hum·ming** make a low, continuous sound with lips closed, as in sounding out a melody without words: *an office ~ing with activity.* —***n.:*** *the ~ of bees, machines, a busy concourse.* —**hum·mer** *n.*

hu·man (HEW·mun, YOO–) *adj.* of, having to do with, or having the form or characteristics of people: *"To err is ~";* ***n.*** a person, or **human being; hu·man·ly** *adv.: everything that was ~ possible;* **hu·man·ness** *n.* —**hu·mane** (–MANE) *adj.* kind and sympathetic: *~ treatment of prisoners; a ~ society for the protection of children and animals;* **hu·mane·ly** *adv.;* **hu·mane·ness** *n.* —**hu·man·ism** (HEW·muh–, YOO–) *n.* a movement or philosophy emphasizing human worth and values, as opposed to a supernatural or ascetic view of life, and leading to a better appreciation of the humanities; **hu·man·ist** *n.* & *adj.;* **hu·man·is·tic** (–IS–) *adj.;* **hu·man·is·ti·cal·ly** *adv.* —**hu·man·i·tar·i·an** (–TAIR–) *n.* & *adj.* (a person such as a philanthropist) promoting human welfare; **hu·man·i·tar·i·an·ism** *n.* —**hu·man·i·ty** (–MAN–) *n.* **-ties** **1** mankind. **2** a human or humane quality. **3 the humanities** *pl.* branches of learning concerned with culture, not science, as religion, philosophy, languages and literature, history, and fine arts. —**hu·man·ize** (HEW–, YOO–) *v.* **-iz·es, -ized, -iz·ing** make or become human or humane; **hu·man·iz·er** *n.;* **hu·man·i·za·tion** (–ZAY–) *n.* —**hu·man·kind** (–kined) *n.* people; mankind. —**hu·man·oid** *n.* & *adj.* nearly human (being or creature), as prehistoric types such as the Neanderthal man and the androids of science fiction. —**human rights** fundamental civil, economic, political, and social rights, as of a free human being.

hum·ble *adj.* **-bler, -blest** modest and unpretentious; also, abject and lacking in self-respect: *a man of ~ birth.* —***v.*** **-bles, -bled, -bling:** *a proud man ~d in defeat; A king ~s himself in penance.* —**hum·ble·ness** *n.* —**hum·bly** (–blee) *adv.*

hum·bug *n.* a person or thing that is a fraud. —***v.*** **-bugs, -bugged, -bug·ging** deceive; trick. —***interj.*** nonsense!

hum·ding·er (–DING–) *n. Slang.* someone or something that is extraordinary or striking.

hum·drum *n.* & *adj.* commonplace (person or thing).

hu·mer·us (HEW·mur–) *n.,pl.* **-mer·i** (–eye) the bone of the upper arm or forelimb; **hu·mer·al** *adj.*

hu·mid (HEW–) *adj.* of the air, moist or damp; **hu·mid·ly** *adv.* —**hu·mid·i·fy** (–MID–) *v.* **-fies, -fied, -fy·ing** make humid, as with a **hu·mid·i·fi·er** *n.* —**hu·mid·i·ty** *n.* dampness; also, the amount of it in the air. —**hu·mi·dor** (HEW–) *n.* a container or apparatus for keeping tobacco moist.

hu·mil·i·ate (–MIL·ee–) *v.* **-ates, -at·ed, -at·ing** to humble or disgrace (someone); hurt the self-esteem of; **hu·mil·i·at·ing** *adj.: a ~ defeat;* **hu·mil·i·at·ing·ly** *adv.;* **hu·mil·i·a·tion** (–AY–) *n.* —**hu·mil·i·ty** (–MIL–) *n.* the quality of being genuinely humble; lack of false pride.

hum·ming·bird *n.* any of a family of tiny American birds that make a humming sound by the extremely rapid vibration of their wings when hovering.

hum·mock (–muk) *n.* a small, rounded hill; knoll.

hu·mor (HEW·mur) *n.* **1** an amusing quality, as of a funny or ludicrous situation; also, the capacity to appreciate this; hence, an expression of it in speech or writing: *a good sense of ~; a ~ magazine.* **2** state of mind; also, fancy or whim; **out of humor** in a bad mood. —***v.*** indulge: *Children, the sick, and the aged have to be ~ed now and then.* —**hu·mor·ist** *n.* —**hu·mor·less** *adj.;* **hu·mor·less·ly** *adv.;* **hu·mor·less·ness** *n.* —**hu·mor·ous** (–us) *adj.* amusing or funny; **hu·mor·ous·ly** *adv.;* **hu·mor·ous·ness** *n.* —**hu·mour** *Brit.* humor.

hump *n.* a lumpy formation, as on the back of a camel or as a deformity, as of a **hump·back,** or hunchback; **hump·backed** *adj.: the ~ salmon* ("pink salmon"); **over the hump** *Informal.* past a difficult period or phase. —***v.:*** *A cat ~s* (i.e. arches) *its back when enraged.*

humph *n.* & *interj.* (a snorting sound) expressing doubt, dissatisfaction, etc.

hu·mus (HEW–) *n.* the dark part of soil that is rich in decaying matter.

Hun *n.* one of a warlike Asiatic people who invaded Europe in the 4th and 5th centuries A.D. under Attila; **hun** *n.* a vandal.

hunch *n.* **1** *Informal.* premonition: *I had a ~ it was going to snow.* **2** hump; ***v.:*** *pupils ~ed in concentration over their books; sitting ~ed up in a sulky mood.* —**hunch·back** *n.* a person with a curvature of the spine; humpback.

hun·dred (–drid) *n.* & *adj.* ten times ten; 100 or C: *three ~ boys; ~s of* (i.e. a large number of) *boys;* **hun·dredth** *n.* & *adj.* 100th (part). —**hun·dred·fold** *n., adj.* & *adv.* (being) a hundred times as much or as many. —**hun·dred·weight** *n.* a unit of weight equal to 100 lb. (45.36 kg) in the U.S. and Canada, 112 lb. (50.8 kg) in the U.K., or 50 kg **(metric hundredweight).**

hung *pt.* & *pp.* of HANG; **hung up** *Slang.* having a hang-up or mental fixation: *is* **hung up on** (i.e. infatuated by) *every girl he meets; a kid who is really hung up on sports.*

Hung. Hungarian; Hungary. —**Hun·gar·i·an** (hung·GAIR·ee·un) *n.* & *adj.* (of or having to do with Hungary or) an inhabitant or the language of Hungary. —**Hun·ga·ry** (HUNG·gur·ee) a country of C. Europe; 35,919 sq. mi. (93,030 km^2); *cap.* Budapest.

hun·ger (HUNG·gur) *n.* pain or discomfort of the stomach because of the body's need for food; hence, starvation; also, any strong desire or craving: *Prisoners go on a* **hunger strike** *to enforce demands or in protest;* ***v.:*** *A child ~s for affection.* —**hung jury** See HANG, *v.* 3. —**hun·gry** (–gree) *adj.* **-gri·er, -gri·est:** *a ~ stomach; the ~ eyes of starving people; souls ~ for salvation;* **hun·gri·ly** *adv.*

hunk (HUNGK) *n. Informal.* a large chunk or slice (of bread, meat, cheese, etc.): *an earth-shaking five-minute ~ of history in the making.*

hun·ker *v.* squat (down) on one's haunches; **hun·kers** *n. pl.* haunches.

hun·ky-do·ry (hung·kee·DOR·ee) *adj. Slang.* satisfactory; fine.

Hun·nish or **hun·nish** *adj.* like a Hun; savage.

hunt *v.* to chase, harry, kill, or catch (game) for food or sport; also, search: *to ~ down an escaped convict; researchers ~ing in the library; police ~ing up evidence.* —***n.*** a hunting, search, or a group hunting party. —**hunt·er; hunts·man** *n.* **-men;** *fem.* **hunt·ress** (–tris).

hur·dle *n.* an obstacle or barrier to jump over, as in a race called **hurdles** *pl.* —***v.*** **-dles, -dled, -dling** jump over or overcome (an obstacle); **hur·dler** *n.*

hur·dy-gur·dy *n.* **-dies** a hand organ, or "barrel organ," played by turning a handle.

hurl *v.* throw with force or violence, as a javelin or spear: *The two warriors ~ed themselves at each other; The mob started ~ing insults at the speaker;* ***n.*** a forcible throw: *a ~ of the discus.* —**hurl·er** *n.* —**hurl·y-burl·y** *n.* **-burl·ies** turmoil; uproar.

Hu·ron (HYOOR·un) *n.* (one of) an Iroquois Indian tribe of Oklahoma and Quebec, formerly living near **Lake Huron,** one of the Great Lakes.

hur·rah (huh·RAH) *n., v.* & *interj.* shout of joy or approval; cheer; also **hur·ray** (–RAY).

hur·ri·cane *n.* a whirling tropical storm with winds of 74 mi. (117 km) per hour or more; **hurricane lamp** (or **lantern**) an oil lamp with a tall glass chimney to protect its flame from winds.

hur·ry (–ree) *v.* **hur·ries, hur·ried, hur·ry·ing** make haste, often with some excitement and confusion: *~ up if you want to be on time;* ***n.:*** *In the ~ she forgot her purse;* **hur·ried** *adj.: a ~ departure to catch the train;* **hur·ried·ly** *adv.*

hurt *v.* **hurts, hurt, hurt·ing** feel or cause pain physically or mentally: *hit a stone and ~ her foot; She ~ herself; He ~ her feelings; The injured foot ~s;* ***n.:*** *The ~ was forgotten but scars remained;* **hurt·ful** *adj.* harmful. —**hur·tle** *v.* **-tles, -tled, -tling** rush or move with a clattering or rattling sound: *A train ~s past at a crossing; The truck skidded and ~d across the street into a shop window.*

hus·band (HUZ·bund) *n.* a male spouse; also, any married man; ***v.*** manage (resources, strength, etc.) economically. —**hus·band·man** *n.* **-men** *Archaic.* farmer. —**hus·band·ry** *n.* farming; also, careful management: *animal ~* (i.e. care of farm animals).

hush *n., v.* & *interj.* quiet; silence: *to* **hush up** *a secret by paying* **hush money** *to the person likely to tell;* **hush-hush** *adj. Informal.* secret.

hush puppy a cornmeal fritter.

husk *n.* & *v.* (remove) the outer covering of (cereals, esp. corn); **husk·er** *n.;* **husking bee** corn-husking as a party during pioneer days. —**husk·y** *adj.* **husk·i·er, -i·est** **1** hoarse: *a ~ voice.* **2** big and strong; ***n., pl.*** **husk·ies** such a person; **husk·i·ly** *adv.;* **husk·i·ness** *n.* —**hus·ky** *n.* **-kies** a hardy sled dog of the Arctic; also called "Siberian husky"; also **Hus·ky.**

hus·sar (huh·ZAR) *n.* a light cavalryman, originally of Hungary.

hus·sy (HUZ·ee, HUS·ee) *n.* **hus·sies** **1** a mischievous girl. **2** a lewd woman.

hus·tings *n. sing.* & *pl.* in a political campaign, the speaking platform or stage; also, the proceedings leading up to the election.

hus·tle (HUSL) *v.* **-tles, -tled, -tling** **1** rush or push (someone) along: *a child ~d to bed while watching TV; a gate-crasher ~d out the door.*

2 sell (esp. goods of dubious value) aggressively: *caught ~ing stolen goods; a woman charged with ~ing* (*Slang.* soliciting). **—*n.*:** *a used-car salesman who lacks ~* (i.e. drive); *the ~ and bustle of a big city; makes a living by some ~* (*Informal.* racket) *or other.* **—hus·tler** *n.*

hut *n.* a plain or crudely made little dwelling or cabin.

hutch *n.* **1** a cupboard with shelves for dishes, etc.: *a combined buffet and ~.* **2** a pen or coop, as a rabbit cage; also, a shack: *a hatchback model of an automobile equipped with a ~* (i.e. a foldable tent).

hut·ment *n.* a hut or group of huts.

Hut·ter·ite *n.* a member of an Anabaptist sect living communally in South Dakota, Montana, and Alberta.

hutz·pa(h) (HOOT·spuh) same as CHUTZPAH.

huz·za(h) (huh·ZAH) same as HURRAH.

H.V. or **h.v.** high velocity; high voltage.

hwy. highway.

hy·a·cinth (HYE·uh–) *n.* a garden plant of the lily family with spikes of fragrant bell-shaped flowers.

hy·ae·na (hye·EE·nuh) same as HYENA.

hy·brid (HYE–) *n.* & *adj.* (anything) of mixed origin or structure, as the mule (from a jackass and a mare), "oramon" (from orange and lemon): *"Talkative" is a ~ word composed of English and Latin elements; a ~ computer system combining analog and digital devices;* **hy·brid·ism** *n.* **—hy·brid·ize** *v.* **-iz·es, -ized, -iz·ing** crossbreed: *a ~d variety of corn;* **hy·brid·i·za·tion** (–ZAY–) *n.;* **hy·brid·i·zer** *n.*

hydr(o)- *comb.form.* water or containing hydrogen. **—hy·dra** (HYE·druh) *n.* a tiny freshwater polyp with stinging tentacles like the snakelike heads of **Hydra,** a monster of Greek myth. **—hy·dran·ge·a** (–DRAIN·jee·uh) *n.* a shrub related to the currants, bearing large, showy clusters of white, pink, or bluish flowers. **—hy·drant** (–drunt) *n.* a discharge pipe with a nozzle, connected to a water main and serving as a street outlet for water to put out fires. **—hy·drate** *n.* a chemical compound of a substance with a definite amount of water, usu. a salt containing "water of crystallization," as *blue vitriol,* which is hydrated copper sulfate; ***v.*** **-drates, -drat·ed, -drat·ing** combine with water. **—hy·draul·ic** *adj.* of hydraulics; also, working with water or by liquid pressure: *~ engineering; a ~ brake; ~ cement hardens under water;* **hy·draul·i·cal·ly** *adv.;* **hy·draul·ics** (–DRAW–) *n.pl.* the physics of the behavior of liquids at rest, or **hy·dro·stat·ics,** and of liquids in motion, or **hy·dro·dy·nam·ics.** **—hy·dro** *adj.* hydroelectric. **—hy·dro·car·bon** (–CAR·bun) *n.* a compound such as benzene or naphthalene containing only hydrogen and carbon. **—hy·dro·ceph·a·lus** (–SEF·uh–) *n.* abnormal enlargement of the head from excess of fluids in the brain. **—hy·dro·chlo·ric acid** (–CLOR·ic) a highly corrosive acid with a strong odor, widely used in industry. **—hy·dro·dy·nam·ic** (–NAM–) *adj.* of hydrodynamics; See HYDRAULICS. **—hy·dro·e·lec·tric** (–LEC–) *adj.* having to do with the generation of electricity by water power. **—hy·dro·flu·or·ic** (–FLOR–) **acid** a corrosive and poisonous acid used in etching glass. **—hy·dro·foil** *n.* a vessel that skims over water at high speeds using winglike structures attached to its hull; also, such a structure. **—hy·dro·gen** (–druh·jun) *n.* a colorless, odorless gaseous element that combines with oxygen to form water; **hy·dro·gen·ate** (HYE·druh·juh–, hye·DROJ·uh–) *v.* **-ates, -at·ed, -at·ing** combine or treat with hydrogen: *Oils are ~d to improve their quality;* **hy·dro·gen·a·tion** (–AY–) *n.* **—hydrogen bomb** an extremely powerful nuclear weapon whose energy is derived from the fusion of hydrogen atoms. **—hydrogen peroxide** a colorless compound of hydrogen and oxygen, used as an antiseptic and bleach; also called "oxygenated water." **—hy·drog·ra·phy** (–DROG·ruh·fee) *n.* a branch of geography that studies the surface waters of the earth such as oceans, rivers, and lakes; **hy·drog·ra·pher** *n.* **—hy·drol·y·sis** (–DROL–) *n.,pl.* **-ses** (–seez) decomposition by chemical reaction with water, as in the making of soap, sugar, alcohols, etc. **—hy·drom·e·ter** (–DROM–) *n.* an instrument for testing the specific gravity of liquids. **—hy·dro·pho·bi·a** (–FOH·bee·uh) *n.* abnormal fear of water, as in rabies; hence, rabies. **—hy·dro·phone** *n.* an instrument for detecting sounds transmitted through water, as from a submarine. **—hy·dro·plane** *n.* a motorboat whose hull is so shaped as to enable it to skim over water at high speeds; **hy·dro·plan·ing** *n.* the dangerous gliding of a rubber-tired vehicle on a wet pavement when it reaches a critical high speed. **—hy·dro·pon·ics** (–PON–) *n.pl.* [takes *sing. v.*] the growing of plants in water instead of soil, with the necessary nutrients added; soilless agriculture; **hy·dro·pon·ic** *adj.;* **hy·dro·pon·i·cal·ly** *adv.* **—hy·dro·sphere** *n.* the water covering the earth's surface, as oceans, lakes, and rivers, distinguished from the land surface, or lithosphere. **—hy·dro·stat·ic** (–STAT–) *adj.* having to do with hydrostatics; See HYDRAULICS. **—hy·dro·ther·a·py** (–THER·uh·pee) *n.* medical treatment using water, as whirlpool baths, showers, sprays, etc. **—hy·dro·ther·mal** (–THUR–) *adj.* having to do with igneous activity involving heated water. **—hy·drous** (–drus) *adj.* containing water in chemical combination. **—hy·drox·ide** (–DROX–) *n.* a compound containing the **hy·drox·yl** (–il) group of one hydrogen and one oxygen atom.

hy·e·na (hye·EE·nuh) *n.* a carrion-eating wolf-like animal of Africa and Asia, considered cowardly, with a weird cry like a hysterical laugh.

hy·giene (HYE·jeen) *n.* the observation and practice of health standards: *dental, mental, public, personal* ~; **hy·gi·en·ic** (–jee·EN·ic, –JEEN·ic) *adj.* sanitary; healthful; **hy·gi·en·i·cal·ly** *adv.*; **hy·gi·en·ist** (HYE–, –JEE–) *n.*

hy·grom·e·ter (hye·GROM·uh·tur) *n.* an instrument for measuring humidity; **hy·grom·e·try** (–tree) *n.*

hying a *pres. part.* of HIE.

hy·men (HYE·mun) *n.* a membrane partially closing the entrance to the vagina in virgins. —**hy·me·ne·al** (–muh·NEE·ul) *n.* & *adj.* (a song) of marriage.

hymn (HIM) *n.* & *v.* (sing) a song of praise, esp. in honor of God. —**hym·nal** (HIM·nul) *n.* a collection of hymns; also **hymn·book.** —**hym·no·dy** (–nuh·dee) *n.* **-dies** hymns or their singing and composition.

hyp. hypothesis; hypothetical.

hype *Slang. n.* **1** same as HYPODERMIC; hence, a drug addict. **2** exaggerated promotion; hence, deception: *the ~ about "redeeming social value" of erotica;* ***v.*** **hypes, hyped, hyp·ing** stimulate or excite, as by a drug injection; hence, promote in a sensational manner: *the business of ~ing sex to juveniles; a* **hyped-up** *sales pitch.*

hyper- *prefix.* more than normal(ly): as in *hyperactive, hypersensitive;* **hy·per** *adj. Informal.* overactive. —**hy·per·a·cid·i·ty** (–uh·SID–) *n.* acid indigestion, as if from excess of stomach acid; **hy·per·ac·id** (–AS–) *adj.* —**hy·per·ac·tive** (–AC·tiv) *adj.* overactive; **hy·per·ac·tiv·i·ty** (–TIV–) *n.* —**hy·per·bar·ic** (–BAIR–) *adj.* of greater-than-normal pressure: *~ chamber; ~ oxygen treatment.* —**hy·per·bo·la** (hye·PUR·buh·luh) *n.* a curve made by cutting a right circular cone in a plane at a greater angle with the base than that made by a side of the cone; **hy·per·bo·le** (–buh·lee) *n.* a figure of speech using exaggeration for effect, as in "to look daggers"; **hy·per·bol·ic** (–BOL–) *adj.* exaggerated or exaggerating; also, of or having to do with a hyperbola; **hy·per·bol·i·cal·ly** *adv.* —**hy·per·bo·re·an** (–BOR·ee·un) *n.* & *adj.* (a person) of a far northern region; hence, arctic or frozen. —**hy·per·crit·i·cal** (–CRIT–) *adj.* too critical. —**hy·per·sen·si·tive** (–SEN–) *adj.* too sensitive; **hy·per·sen·si·tiv·i·ty** (–TIV–) *n.* —**hy·per·ten·sion** (–TEN–) *n.* high blood pressure; **hy·per·ten·sive** *adj.* —**hy·per·thy·roid** (–THYE–) *n.* & *adj.* (having to do with) an overactive thyroid gland or a person suffering from it; **hy·per·thy·roid·ism** (–ROID–) *n.* this condition, as in goiter. —**hy·per·tro·phy** (–PUR·truh·fee) *n.* & *v.* **-phies, -phied, -phy·ing** (undergo) abnormal enlargement of an organ, as of the prostate; **hy·per·troph·ic** (–TROF–) *adj.* —**hy·per·ve·loc·i·ty** (–LOS–) *n.* a relatively high velocity, as of supersonic craft and nuclear particles.

hy·phen (HYE·fn) *n.* a mark (-) used to show word division, as in compound words, or syllable division, as at the end of a line. —**hy·phen·ate** *v.* **-ates, -at·ed, -at·ing** use a hyphen in (a word); **hyphenated** *adj.* of supposedly divided allegiance, as an Irish-American or Franco-German; **hy·phen·a·tion** (–AY–) *n.*

hyp·no·sis (hip·NO–) *n.,pl.* **-ses** (–seez) a trancelike condition in which a subject will act according to the suggestions of the person who induces the condition, or **hyp·no·tist** (–nuh–). —**hyp·not·ic** (–NOT–) *n.* & *adj.* (something) producing sleep or hypnotism; **hyp·not·i·cal·ly** *adv.* —**hyp·no·tism** (HIP·nuh–) *n.* the science or an act of hypnotizing. —**hyp·no·tize** (HIP·nuh–) *v.* **-tiz·es, -tized, -tiz·ing** induce hypnosis in.

hy·po (HYE–) *n.* **1** same as HYPE. **2** *Informal.* hypodermic. **3** sodium thiosulfate (formerly "hyposulfite") as a photographic fixing agent that prevents fading. —**hypo-** *prefix.* beneath or less than: as in *hypodermic, hypothyroid.* —**hy·po·cen·ter** *n.* the focus of an earthquake; also, the point on the ground directly under a nuclear bomb blast. —**hy·po·chon·dri·a** (–CON–) *n.* abnormal anxiety over one's health; **hy·po·chon·dri·ac** *n.* & *adj.* —**hy·poc·ri·sy** (–POC–) *n.* **-sies** a pretending to be what one is not, esp. very good or religious; **hyp·o·crite** (HIP·uh·crit) *n.* one who pretends thus; **hyp·o·crit·i·cal** (–CRIT–) *adj.*; **hyp·o·crit·i·cal·ly** *adv.* —**hy·po·der·mic** (hye·puh·DUR–) *adj.* beneath the skin: *a ~ syringe with a ~ needle for giving a ~ injection;* ***n.*** a hypodermic syringe or injection. —**hy·po·gly·ce·mi·a** (–SEE·mee·uh) *n.* deficiency of glucose in the blood; **hy·po·gly·cem·ic** *adj.* —**hy·pot·e·nuse** (hye·POTN·uce) *n.* the side of a right triangle opposite the right angle. —**hy·poth·e·cate** (–POTH–) *v.* **-cates, -cat·ed, -cat·ing** hypothesize. —**hy·poth·e·sis** (–POTH·i·sis) *n.,pl.* **-ses** (–seez) an assumed or likely explanation of a set of facts for further study or verification; **hy·poth·e·size** *v.* **-siz·es, -sized, -siz·ing** make a hypothesis; assume; **hy·po·thet·i·cal** (–THET–) *adj.* conjectural; also, conditional: *Which nation will survive a nuclear war is ~;* **hy·po·thet·i·cal·ly** *adv.* —**hy·po·thy·roid·ism** (–THYE–) *n.* underactivity of the thyroid gland, as in cretinism; **hy·po·thy·roid** *n.* & *adj.*

hys·sop (HIS·up) *n.* an evergreen shrub of the mint family used in salads and soups and formerly in medicine.

hys·ter·ec·to·my (his·tuh·REC·tuh·mee) *n.* **-mies** surgical removal of the uterus. —**hys·te·ri·a** (–STEER–, –STER–) *n.* uncontrollable excitement, as in a neurotic condition brought on by an unbearable situation and sometimes resulting in paralysis of a limb or other physical problem; **hys•ter•ic** (–STER–) *n.* & *adj.* (a person) suffering from hysteria; **hys•ter•i•cal** *adj.* wildly excited; also, *Informal.* wildly funny; —**hys•ter•i•cal•ly** *adv.;* **hys•ter•ics** *n.pl.* a fit of uncontrollable laughter or crying. —**hys•ter•ot•o•my** (–OT·uh·mee) *n.* **-mies** incision into the uterus, as in a Caesarean section or for an abortion.

Hz or **hz** hertz.

I

I or **i** (EYE) *n.* **I's** or **i's** **1** the ninth letter of the English alphabet. **2** the Roman numeral for "1." —**I** **1** iodine; interstate highway. **2** *pron., objective* ME, *possessive* MY or MINE; *pl.* WE, *objective* US, *possessive* OUR(S) the person who is speaking or writing. —**I.** or **i.** island(s); isle(s). —**i.** interest; intransitive; island. —**I** Island; Isle.

IA or **Ia.** Iowa.

-ial same as -AL: as in *cordial, jovial.*

i·amb (EYE·am) *n.* a metrical foot of one unstressed syllable followed by one stressed, as in "the knell of parting day" (3 feet). —**i·am·bic** (eye·AM–) *n.* an iamb or a verse of iambs; ***adj.:*** ~ *verse.* —**i·am·bus** (eye·AM–) *n.* same as IAMB.

-ian same as -AN.

I.A.T.A. International Air Transport Association.

-iatric(al) *comb.form.* medical; medicinal: as in *geriatric, psychiatric.* —**iatrics** *comb.form.* treatment of disease: as in *pediatrics.* **-iatry** *comb. form.* medical treatment: as in *podiatry, psychiatry.*

ib. ibidem.

I·be·ri·a (eye·BEER·ee·uh) the European peninsula containing Spain and Portugal; also called "Iberian Peninsula"; **I·be·ri·an** *n.* & *adj.*

i·bex (EYE–) *n.* **i·bex·es** any of several types of wild goats found in the Alps and the Himalayas.

ibid. *Abbrev.* for **ib·i·dem** *Latin.* in the same place (of book or page).

i·bis (EYE–) *n.* any of a family of wading birds related to the herons.

-ible same as -ABLE; **-ibly** same as -ABLY.

Ib·sen (IB·sn), **Henrik.** 1828–1906, Norwegian playwright.

IC integrated circuit. — **-ic** *suffix.* **1** *adj.* of, having to do with, related to, etc.: as in *poetic, scenic;* also **-ical.** **2** *n.* a person or thing: as in *arithmetic, emetic, lunatic;* **-ically** *adv. suffix.*

I.C.B.M. intercontinental ballistic missile.

I.C.C. Interstate Commerce Commission.

Ice. Iceland(ic). —**ice** *n.* **1** water frozen solid or as a layer. **2** a frozen dessert of sweetened fruit juice without milk or cream. **3** *Slang.* diamonds. —***v.*** **ic·es, iced, ic·ing** cover with, turn to, or make cool with ice; **iced** *adj.* containing ice: ~ *coffee.* —**break the ice** make a start, esp. by overcoming some initial difficulty. —**cut no ice** *Informal.* have no effect. —**on ice** *Informal.* in reserve; also, safely assured. —**on thin ice** in a dangerous position. —**ice age** glacial epoch; **Ice Age** Pleistocene. —**ice bag** a bag of crushed ice applied to the body to relieve pain or inflammation. —**ice·berg** *n.* a huge piece of ice broken off from a glacier and floating in the sea with only its tip showing above water. —**ice·boat** *n.* a craft resembling a sailboat but equipped with runners for running on ice; also, an icebreaker. —**ice·bound** *adj.* frozen in (as ships) or obstructed by ice. —**ice·box** *n.* a cabinet with ice in it for keeping foods cold; also, a refrigerator. —**ice·break·er** *n.* a ship that can plow or smash a way through ice. —**ice·cap** *n.* a large ice-covered area in the polar regions. —**ice cream** a frozen dessert of sweetened and flavored cream. —**ice floe** an unbroken sheet of floating sea ice. —**ice hockey** a game played on ice by opposing teams of six each wearing skates and equipped with sticks having curved ends to drive a disk, or puck, into the opposite side's goal. —**ice·house** *n.* a building in which ice is made or stored. —**Icel.** Iceland(ic). —**Ice·land** (–lund) an island republic between Greenland and Norway; 39,769 sq. mi. (103,000 km²); *cap.* Reykjavik. **Ice·land·er** *n.;* **Ice·land·ic** (–LAND–) *n.* & *adj.* (of Iceland, its people, or) the N.Germanic language of Iceland. —**ice·man** *n.* **-men** one who sells or delivers ice. —**ice milk** a dessert like ice cream but made with skim milk. —**ice pack** **1** an ice bag or similar application. **2** an expanse of masses of broken, piled-up ice. —**ice pick** a sharp-pointed tool for chipping or breaking ice. —**ice skate** a boot or shoe fitted with a metal runner or blade for skating on ice; **ice-skate** *v.* **-skates, -skat·ed, -skat·ing; ice-skat·er** *n.* —**ice storm** a storm in which rain freezes as it falls, coating everything with a glaze of ice. —**ice water** water from melting ice; also, water chilled for drinking.

i·chor (EYE·cor) *n.* in Greek myth, a fluid running in the veins of the gods instead of blood.

ich·thy·ol·o·gy (ic·thee·OL–) *n.* the scientific study of fishes; **ich·thy·ol·o·gist** *n.*

i·ci·cle (EYE·sicl) *n.* a hanging piece of ice formed by the freezing of dripping water. —**ic·ing** (EYE·sing) *n.* a sweet, creamy mixture for coating cakes and such baked goods; frosting; **icing on the cake** pleasure or benefit beyond proper expectation.

I.C.J. International Court of Justice.

ick·y *adj.* **ick·i·er, -i·est** *Slang.* disgusting and distasteful.

i·con (EYE·con) *n.* an image or figure; esp. in the Eastern Church, a sacred painting or mosaic. —**i·con·o·clast** (–CON·uh–) *n.* one who attacks an established belief or institution; **i·con·o·clas·tic** (–CLAS–) *adj.*

-ics *suffix.* a subject of study; also, the characteristics of something: as in *acoustics, aesthetics, mechanics.*

ic·tus *n.* stress or accent in verse.

I.C.U. intensive care unit.

i·cy (EYE·see) *adj.* **i·ci·er, i·ci·est** of, covered with, or like ice; cold: *an ~ road, reception, wind;* **i·ci·ly** *adv.;* **i·ci·ness** *n.*

id *n.* the unconscious part of the psyche responsible for one's instinctual drives seeking pleasure and gratification. —**id.** idem. —**I'd** (IDE) I had; I should; I would. —**ID** or **Id(a).** Idaho. —**I.D.** identification.

I·da·ho (EYE·duh–) a N.W. state of the U.S.; 83,557 sq.mi. (216,412 km²); *cap.* Boise.

ID card identification (or identity) card.

i·de·a (eye·DEE·uh) *n.* **1** a mental image, thought, or meaning; concept: *Words express ~s; This was not my ~ of a picnic.* **2** plan; scheme: *What's the big ~? a man of ~s* (i.e. resourcefulness). —**i·de·al** (–ul) *n.* a perfect type; hence, a goal to achieve: *a woman of high ~s;* **adj.:** *This is ~ weather for a picnic; A geometrical point is a purely ~* (i.e. imaginary) *concept;* —**i·de·al·ism** (eye·DEE·ul·izm) *n.* thought or behavior based on how things ought to be rather than how they are in reality; hence, the neglecting of practical matters; also, in art, literature, etc., representation of imagined types rather than of exact likenesses; **i·de·al·ist** *n.;* **i·de·al·is·tic** (–IS–) *adj.;* **i·de·al·is·ti·cal·ly** *adv.* —**i·de·al·ize** (eye·DEE–) *v.* **-iz·es, -ized, -iz·ing** form an ideal; think of as ideal: *womanhood ~d in the Virgin Mary;* **i·de·al·i·za·tion** (–ZAY–) *n.;* **i·de·al·ly** *adv.* —**i·de·ate** (eye·DEE–) *v.* **-ates, -at·ed, -at·ing** form ideas; form the idea of; **i·de·a·tion** (–AY–) *n.;* **i·de·a·tion·al** *adj.*

i·dem (EYE–, EE–) *pron.* the same as mentioned already. —**i·den·ti·cal** (eye·DEN–) *adj.* same; also, exactly alike: *the ~ voice I heard yesterday; ~ signatures; ~ twins* (i.e. not fraternal). —**i·den·ti·fy** (–DEN–) *v.* **-fies, -fied, -fy·ing** **1** recognize; know or establish the identity of. **2** associate: *a dramatic character with whom an audience ~s* (i.e. sympathizes); *reluctant to ~ himself with the radicals.* —**i·den·ti·fi·a·ble** *adj.* —**i·den·ti·fi·ca·tion** (–CAY–) *n.* —**I·den·ti·kit** (–DEN–) *Trademark.* a set of separately drawn facial features used to make a composite picture of a described person. —**i·den·ti·ty** (–DEN–) *n.* **-ties** **1** sameness; also, individuality or personality: *working together because of ~ of interests.* **2** who somebody is, or what something is; also, the name of somebody or something: *Show your* **identity card** *for admission; an adolescent suffering an* **identity crisis** *because of internal changes and social pressures.*

id·e·o·gram or **id·e·o·graph** (ID·ee·uh–, EYE–) *n.* a symbol such as a Chinese character or a picture that anyone can understand, as in pictographs, that stands for a whole idea instead of the words for it. —**i·de·ol·o·gy** (eye·dee·OL–, id·ee·OL–) *n.* **-gies** a set of doctrines characteristic of a person, group, or class: *Communist and capitalist ~s;* **i·de·o·log·i·cal** (–LOJ–) *adj.*

ides *n. sing.* & *pl.* in the ancient Roman calendar, the 15th of March, May, July, or October or the 13th of any other month.

id·i·o·cy (ID·ee·uh·see) *n.* **-cies** great stupidity, as of an idiot; also, a stupid expression or action. —**id·i·om** (ID·ee·um) *n.* **1** a particular language or dialect with its distinctive characteristics: *the Bible in the ~ of the Elizabethans.* **2** an expression that is peculiar to a particular language; also, an individualistic style: *"get one's goat" is an ~ hard to translate into another language; the Shakespearian ~.* —**id·i·o·mat·ic** (–MAT–) *adj.: "Go slowly" is grammatical but "Go slow" is ~;* **id·i·o·mat·i·cal·ly** *adv.* —**id·i·o·path·ic** (–PATH–) *adj.* of diseases, having an unknown origin, or peculiar to the individual: *~ epilepsy.* —**id·i·o·syn·cra·sy** (–SING·cruh·see) *n.* **-sies** a peculiarity of style or behavior, as a mannerism, a writer's style, or one's reaction to a drug; **id·i·o·syn·crat·ic** (–CRAT–) *adj.* —**id·i·ot** (–ut) *n.* a very stupid person; **idiot box** *Slang.* a television set; **idiot card** (or **board**) *Slang.* a cue card for prompting a performer; **id·i·ot·ic** (–OT–) *adj.;* **id·i·ot·i·cal·ly** *adv.*

i·dle (EYE·dl) *adj.* **i·dler, i·dlest** **1** not active: *factories lying ~; an ~ but not lazy worker; an ~ mind.* **2** lazy; hence, useless; worthless: *"~ folks have the most labor"; ~ pleasures, gossip, curiosity.* —**v. i·dles, i·dled, i·dling:** *to ~ away* (i.e. waste) *a summer; workers ~d by layoffs; An automobile left ~ing* (i.e. with the engine running but not engaged) *wastes gas;* **i·dler** *n.* —**i·dle·ness** *n.;* **i·dly** *adv.*

i·dol (EYE·dl) *n.* an object of worship, esp. a statue; hence, a false god; also, an object of ardent admiration: *a movie ~.* —**i·dol·a·try** (–DOL·uh·tree) *n.* **-tries** idol worship; **i·dol·a·ter** *n.;* **i·dol·a·trous** (–trus) *adj.* —**i·dol·ize** *v.* **-iz·es, -ized, -iz·ing** regard or treat as an idol: *Mammon is wealth ~d.*
i·dyl(l) (EYE·dl) *n.* a simple, charming, and picturesque, hence, usu. rural scene or description: *the ~s of Theocritus; Tennyson's "Idylls of the King" are Arthurian stories;* **i·dyl·lic** (eye·DIL–) *adj.* full of beauty and peace: *an ~ existence on sabbatical leave; in the ~ surroundings of a village retreat.*
-ie or **-y** *suffix.* indicating littleness, familiarity, etc.: as in *birdie, auntie, hankie.* —**i.e.** namely; that is. —**I.E.** Indo-European.
-ier *n. suffix.* person (in a specified occupation or activity): as in *clothier, financier.*
I.F., i.f. or **i-f** intermediate frequency.
if *conj.* **1** in case that: *You'll get wet ~ it rains.* **2** granting; allowing; although: *It will cost only $5, ~ that! a welcome, ~ uninvited guest.* **3** whether: *Ask ~ she will come.* —***n.*** condition: *Your money refunded with no ~s, ands, or buts.* —**if·fy** *adj.* **if·fi·er, if·fi·est** *Informal.* uncertain; chancy: *The outcome is rather ~.*
-ify same as -FY.
ig·loo *n.* **-loos** a dome-shaped Eskimo dwelling made of blocks of compact snow; also **ig·lu.**
ig·ne·ous (IG·nee·us) *adj.* fiery; also, formed by the cooling of melted, usu. volcanic material: *Pumice and granite are ~ rocks.* —**ig·nite** (–NITE) *v.* **-nites, -nit·ed, -nit·ing** catch or set on fire; **ig·nit·a·ble** *adj.* —**ig·ni·tion** (–NISH·un) *n.* an igniting, esp. an apparatus or device for igniting the fuel in an engine: *a rocket's ~ system.*
ig·no·ble (–NO–) *adj.* not noble; shameful; **ig·no·bly** *adv.*
ig·no·min·y (IG·nuh–) *n.* **-min·ies** disgrace; humiliation; also, a disgraceful action, quality, or outcome: *the ~ of defeat;* **ig·no·min·i·ous** (–MIN·ee·us) *adj.;* **ig·no·min·i·ous·ly** *adv.*
ig·no·ra·mus (–RAY–) *n.* **-mus·es** an ignorant person. —**ig·no·rance** (IG·nuh·runce) *n.* the state of being **ig·no·rant** (–runt) *adj.* lacking knowledge or education; also, unaware: *an ~ rustic, answer; ~ of what went on behind his back;* **ig·no·rant·ly** *adv.* —**ig·nore** (–NOR) *v.* **-nores, -nored, -nor·ing** pay no attention to; refuse to notice: *to ~ an insult; felt ~d by others.*
i·gua·na (i·GWAH·nuh) *n.* any of a family of tropical New World lizards.
IGY International Geophysical Year.
IHS Jesus (Christ).
i·ke·ba·na (ee·kay·BAH·nah) *n.* the Japanese art of arranging flowers.
i·kon (EYE·con) same as ICON.
IL Illinois. —**il-** same as IN- before "l": as in *illumine, illegible, illiterate.*
il·e·i·tis (il·ee·EYE–) *n.* inflammation of the **il·e·um** (IL·ee–) *n.,pl.* **il·e·a** the lower portion of the small intestine; **ileo-** *comb.form.;* **il·e·al** *adj.* —**il·i·ac** or **il·i·al** *adj.* having to do with the **il·i·um** *n.* the winglike portion of the hip bones; **ilio-** *comb.form.*
Il·i·ad (IL·ee·ud) Homer's epic poem about the Trojan War.
ilk *n.* kind; class: **of that** (or **her, his**) **ilk.**
Ill. Illinois. —**I'll** I will; I shall. —**ill.** illustrated; illustration.
ill *adj.* & *adv.* **worse** (WURSE), **worst** (WURST) —***adj.*** bad: *He bore no one ~ will; ~* (i.e. sick) *with the flu; fell into ~ repute; nervous and* **ill at ease** *in company.* —***adv.*** badly: *speaks ~ of his neighbors; fared ~ at the finals; was generous when he could ~* (i.e. scarcely) *afford to pay.* —***n.*** something bad, esp. sickness or evil: *the ~s of our mortal existence.* —**ill-ad·vised** *adj.* acting or done without good advice or proper consideration; **ill-ad·vis·ed·ly** *adv.* —**ill-bred** *adj.* badly brought up; rude.
il·le·gal (i·LEE·gul) *adj.* against the law or rules; **il·le·gal·ly** *adv.* —**il·le·gal·i·ty** (–GAL–) *n.* **-ties** unlawfulness; also, an illegal act.
il·leg·i·ble (–LEJ–) *adj.* impossible to read; **il·leg·i·bly** *adv.;* **il·leg·i·bil·i·ty** (–BIL–) *n.*
il·le·git·i·mate (–luh·JIT·uh·mit) *adj.* born of parents not married to each other; also, contrary to law, custom, or logic: *an ~ conclusion, use of funds, expression, claim to property;* **il·le·git·i·mate·ly** *adv.;* **il·le·git·i·ma·cy** *n.*
ill-fat·ed *adj.* with an evil fate; unlucky: *the ~ voyage of the Titanic.* —**ill-fa·vored** *adj.* ugly; also, unpleasant. —**ill-got·ten** *adj.* obtained by evil means: *~ gains, goods, wealth.* —**ill-hu·mored** *adj.* irritable; sullen. —**il·lib·er·al** *adj.* narrow-minded; also, stingy. —**il·lic·it** (–LIS–) *adj.* not allowed by law or by the rules; **il·lic·it·ly** *adv.;* **il·lic·it·ness** *n.* —**il·lim·it·a·ble** (–LIM–) *adj.* without limit; measureless; **il·lim·it·a·bly** *adv.*
Il·li·nois (–NOY) **1** a Midwestern state of the U.S.; 56,400 sq. mi. (146,075 km^2); *cap.* Springfield; **Il·li·nois·an** *n.* & *adj.* **2** a member of an Indian people, or "Illiniwek" Indians, formerly living between the Mississippi and Wabash rivers.
il·lit·er·ate (–LIT·uh·rit) *n.* & *adj.* (one who is) uneducated, esp. not knowing how to read or write; also, lacking basic knowledge in one's field of study; **il·lit·er·a·cy** (–uh·see) *n.* **-cies** —**ill-man·nered** *adj.* having bad manners; rude. —**ill-na·tured** *adj.* of a mean disposition; disagreeable; **ill-na·tured·ly** *adv.* —**ill·ness** *n.* sickness. —**il·log·i·cal** *adj.* not logical or sensible; **il·log·i·cal·ly** *adv.;* **il·log·i·cal·i·ty** (–CAL–) *n.* —**ill-starred** *adj.* ill-fated; unlucky. —**ill-suit·ed** *adj.* badly suited; unsuitable. —**ill-tem·pered** *adj.* having a bad temper; irritable. —**ill-timed** *adj.* coming at the wrong time; inopportune. —**ill-treat** *v.* treat cruelly or unfairly; **ill-treat·ment** *n.*
il·lume (–LOOM) *v.* **il·lumes, il·lumed, il·lum·ing** same as **il·lu·mi·nate** (–LOO–) *v.* **-nates, -nat·ed, -nat·ing** **1** supply with light: *Gas*

lamps ~ the streets; an ~ing grenade; society of ~ing engineers; to ~ (i.e. make clear) *an obscure passage.* **2** decorate (initial letters, borders, etc. of a manuscript) with colors and designs, as in the Middle Ages. Also **il·lu·mine** (–min), **-mines, -mined, -min·ing. —il·lu·mi·nat·ing** *adj.* that clears up or explains: *a very ~ talk;* **il·lu·mi·nat·ing·ly** *adv.;* **il·lu·mi·na·tor** *n.* **—il·lu·mi·na·tion** (–NAY–) *n.* **—illus.** illustration.

ill-us·age (ILL·YOO·sij, –zij) *n.* ill-treatment; **ill-use** *n.* (ILL·yoos) & *v.* (ill·YOOZ) **-us·es, -used, -us·ing** (subject to) bad treatment.

il·lu·sion (i·LOO·zhun) *n.* **1** a misleading effect produced on the eye or mind: *the ~ of movement produced by a series of still pictures; an optical ~; under the ~* (i.e. false belief) *that wealth would make him happy.* **2** a kind of tulle used for veils. **—il·lu·sion·ism** *n.* use of illusions in art or sculpture; **il·lu·sion·ist** *n.* **—il·lu·sive** (–siv) or **il·lu·so·ry** (–suh·ree) *adj.* due to or based on an illusion; deceptive: *an ~ peace; ~ hopes.*

illust. illustrated; illustration. **—il·lus·trate** (IL·us–) *v.* **-trates, -trat·ed, -trat·ing** make clear or lucid; also, provide with pictures, diagrams, etc.; hence, serve to explain: *The falling apple ~s gravitation; a well-~d book, lecture;* **il·lus·tra·tor** *n.* **—il·lus·tra·tion** (–TRAY–) *n.: meanings better explained by ~ than by definition; ~s in color.* **—il·lus·tra·tive** (–LUS·truh·tiv, IL·us·tray·tiv) *adj.* serving to illustrate: *sentences ~ of word meanings; an ~ example;* **il·lus·tra·tive·ly** *adv.* **—il·lus·tri·ous** (–LUS·tree·us) *adj.* brilliantly eminent or distinguished: *our ~ founding fathers; an ~ family;* **il·lus·tri·ous·ly** *adv.;* **il·lus·tri·ous·ness** *n.*

ill will dislike; hostility.

I.L.O. International Labor Organization.

ILS instrument landing system.

I'm (IME) I am. **—im-** same as IN- before *b, m, p:* as in *imbalance, immerse, implement.*

im·age (–ij) *n.* **1** a visual, optical, or electronic representation of a scene or object, as in a mirror, on a camera or TV screen, etc.; hence, a likeness or picture: *the very ~ of her father; An* **image converter** *tube is used to get a visible ~ of an infra-red source.* **2** a physical representation, as a statue or idol. **3** a mental picture or concept; hence, its expression, esp. a simile or metaphor: *drama as the ~ of life; the ivory-tower ~ of bankers; hired a PR expert to polish up their public ~.* **—*v.*** **-ag·es, -aged, -ag·ing** form an image (of); also, imagine: *a scene hard to ~ in one's waking hours; ~d in solid bronze; a slide that ~s sharply.* **—im·age·ry** (–ij·ree) mental images or their figurative expression, as in poetry. **—i·mag·i·na·ble** (–MAJ·uh·nuh·bl) *adj.* conceivable; **i·mag·i·na·bly** *adv.* **—i·mag·i·nal** (–MAJ·uh·nl) *adj.* of images; also, of an imago. **—i·mag·i·nar·y** (–MAJ·uh–) *adj.* not real but imagined; also, imaginable: *The square root of a negative quantity is ~; U.F.O.'s may not be entirely ~;* **i·mag·i·na·tion** (–NAY–) *n.* the use, esp. when effective, of the power to imagine: *the fertile ~ of storytellers; Your ghost story sounds mere ~; resourceful executives gifted with ~ and judgment;* **i·mag·i·na·tive** (–nuh·tiv) *adj.: She is more ~ than practical; ~ literature;* **i·mag·i·na·tive·ly** *adv.* **—i·mag·ine** (–MAJ·in) *v.* **-ines, -ined, -in·ing** form an image of; also, think or conceive of: *~ yourself flying like a bird; cannot ~ our living like Victorians; I ~* (i.e. suppose) *that's what she meant.* **—im·ag·ism** (IM·uh·jizm) *n.* a school of poetry of the early 1900's stressing the use of clear images, free rhythms, and exact words from common speech: *Ezra Pound was the chief* **im·ag·ist** *n.* **—i·ma·go** (–MAY–) *n.* **i·ma·gos** or **i·mag·i·nes** (–MAJ·uh·neez) an adult insect as it comes out of the pupa stage.

im·bal·ance (–BAL–) *n.* lack of balance or proportion.

im·be·cile (–buh·sl) *n.* & *adj.* (one who is) very foolish or stupid; **im·be·cil·ic** (–SIL–); **im·be·cil·i·ty** (–SIL–) *n.*

im·bed (–BED) same as EMBED.

im·bibe (–BIBE) *v.* **-bibes, -bibed, -bib·ing** drink (esp. alcoholic liquor); inhale; assimilate; absorb (moisture; hence, ideas or principles); **im·bib·er** *n.* **—im·bi·bi·tion** (–BISH·un) *n.* the imbibing of moisture by a colloidal system, as in plants, resulting in swelling of tissues; **im·bi·bi·tion·al** *adj.*

im·bri·cate *v.* **-cates, -cat·ed, -cat·ing** overlap, as fish scales, tiles, shingles, etc. ***—adj.*** (–kit) overlapping; also, ornamented with such a pattern. **—im·bri·ca·tion** (–CAY–) *n.* an overlapping (pattern).

im·bro·glio (–BROLE·yoh) *n.* **-glios** a complicated and confusing situation, as in drama or politics.

im·brue (–BROO) *v.* **-brues, -brued, -bru·ing** soak or stain (*with* blood of slaughter).

im·bue (–BEW) *v.* **-bues, -bued, -bu·ing** soak; permeate; hence, inspire (*with* principles, ideas, etc.).

I.M.F. International Monetary Fund.

imit. imitation; imitative. **—im·i·ta·ble** (–tuh·bl) *adj.* that can be imitated. **—im·i·tate** *v.* **-tates, -tat·ed, -tat·ing** be, look, or act like (another person or thing): *a successful novelist as a model for aspiring writers to ~* (i.e. copy); *Do not ~* (i.e. mimic) *people like an ape or parrot; can ~* (i.e. reproduce) *any bird call; wallpaper ~ing* (i.e. resembling) *wood paneling;* **im·i·ta·tor** *n.* **—im·i·ta·tion** (–TAY–) *n.: art as the ~ of life; "~ is the sincerest form of flattery"; composed* **in imitation** *of Keats's style;* ***adj.:*** *a mere ~ diamond; ~ leather.* **—im·i·ta·tive** (–tay·tiv) *adj.;* **im·i·ta·tive·ly** *adv.*

im·mac·u·late (–MAC·yuh·lit) *adj.* without stain or blemish; hence, without blame or sin; also, spotlessly clean: *a house in ~ condition;* **im·mac·u·late·ly** *adv.;* **im·mac·u·late·ness** *n.*

im·ma·nent (IM·uh·nunt) *adj.* indwelling or inherent; also, subjective; of God, pervading (the universe), not transcendent; **im·ma·nence** or **im·ma·nen·cy** *n.;* **im·ma·nent·ly** *adv.*

im·ma·te·ri·al (–TEER·ee·ul) *adj.* not important; also, spiritual, not material.

im·ma·ture (–TURE, –CHOOR) *adj.* undeveloped; not mature; **im·ma·tu·ri·ty** *n.*

im·meas·ur·a·ble (–MEZH·uh·ruh·bl *adj.* vast; boundless; **im·meas·ur·a·bly** *adv.*

im·me·di·a·cy (–MEE·dee·uh·see) *n.* **-cies** (something that has) direct relevance to the present time, place, etc.: *a question that lacks ~; the ~s* (i.e. urgent needs) *of life.* —**im·me·di·ate** (–MEE·dee·ut) *adj.* with nothing coming between: *an ~ reply; our ~ neighbor on the right; the ~, not remote cause of the accident; One's ~ family comes first;* **im·me·di·ate·ly** *adv.*

im·me·mo·ri·al (–MOR·ee·ul) *adj.* going back beyond memory; ancient: *from* **time immemorial; im·me·mo·ri·al·ly** *adv.*

im·mense (–MENCE) *adj.* so large as to seem difficult to measure: *~ rocks, waste, amount of food; an ~ difference; an ~* (*Informal.* splendid) *poem;* **im·mense·ly** *adv.;* **im·men·si·ty** *n.*

im·merse (–MURSE) *v.* **im·mers·es, im·mersed, im·mers·ing** lower into a liquid so as to be covered by it; hence, involve deeply: *Keep it ~d in the liquid; sat ~d in thought;* **im·mer·sion:** *baptism by ~; an ~ program of language teaching; the electric coil of an* **immersion heater** *for liquids; the painful* **immersion foot** *disease resulting from long exposure to moist cold.*

im·mi·grant (IM·uh·grunt) *n.* a nonnative admitted to a country to settle in it; hence, a plant or animal observed in a new area; ***adj.:*** *children of ~ parents; ~ birds.* —**im·mi·grate** *v.* **-grates, -grat·ed, -grat·ing:** *Joseph Pulitzer ~d to America from Hungary;* **im·mi·gra·tion** (–GRAY–) *n.*

im·mi·nent *adj.* likely or about to happen soon without further warning: *A storm is ~ when black clouds gather;* **im·mi·nence** *n.;* **im·mi·nent·ly** *adv.*

im·mis·ci·ble (–MIS·uh·bl) *adj.* that cannot be mixed or blended, as oil and water; **im·mis·ci·bil·i·ty** (–BIL–) *n.*

im·mit·i·ga·ble (–MIT·i·guh–) *adj.* that cannot be mitigated.

im·mo·bile (–MOH·bl) *adj.* firmly fixed; also, motionless; **im·mo·bil·i·ty** (–BIL–) *n.* —**im·mo·bi·lize** *v.* **-liz·es, -lized, -liz·ing** make immobile or unable to move; **im·mo·bi·li·za·tion** (–ZAY–) *n.*

im·mod·er·ate (–MOD·uh·rit) *adj.* not moderate; excessive; **im·mod·er·ate·ly** *adv.;* **im·mod·er·ate·ness** *n.*

im·mod·est (–MOD·ist) *adj.* not modest; also, indecent; **im·mod·est·ly** *adv.;* **im·mod·es·ty** *n.*

im·mo·late *v.* **-lates, -lat·ed, -lat·ing** (kill as a) sacrifice; **im·mo·la·tion** (–LAY–) *n.*

im·mor·al (–MOR–) *adj.* morally wrong, esp. in sexual matters; lewd; **im·mor·al·ly** *adv.* —**im·mo·ral·i·ty** (–RAL–) *n.* **-ties** vice; also, an immoral act or practice.

im·mor·tal (–MOR·tl) *n.* & *adj.* everlasting, divine, or very famous (being or person): *man's ~ soul; her ~ fame; the ~s of the Greek and Roman pantheon; the 40 ~s* (i.e. members) *of the French Academy, the ~s* (i.e. great personages) *of the International College of Surgeons;* **im·mor·tal·ly** *adv.* —**im·mor·tal·i·ty** (–TAL–) *n.* —**im·mor·tal·ize** (–MOR–) *v.* **-iz·es, -ized, -iz·ing** make immortal: *Shakespeare was ~d by his plays.*

im·mo·tile (–MOH·tl) *adj.* not motile.

im·mov·a·ble (–MOO·vuh–) *adj.* that cannot be moved; hence, unyielding: *steadfast and ~ in purpose; land, trees, buildings, and such* **immovables** *n.pl.;* **im·mov·a·bly** *adv.* —**im·mov·a·bil·i·ty** (–BIL–) *n.*

im·mune (IM·yoon) *adj.* free or protected (from something disagreeable to which one is normally liable); also, having to do with immunity: *No one is ~ from error; a world made ~ from smallpox; ~ against attacks; ~ to polio, measles; The* **immune response** (or **reaction**) *causes rejection of foreign tissue;* **im·mu·ni·ty** (–MYOO–) *n.: babies born with passive ~ against certain diseases; diplomatic ~;* **im·mu·nize** (IM·yuh–) *v.* **-niz·es, -nized, -niz·ing; im·mu·ni·za·tion** (–ZAY–) *n.: Vaccination is active ~.* —**im·mu·nol·o·gy** (–NOL–) *n.* a branch of medicine dealing with resistance to disease and reactions to foreign bodies, as in allergies; **im·mu·no·log·ic** or **-i·cal** (–LOJ–) *adj.* **im·mu·nol·o·gist** (–NOL–) *n.* —**immuno-** *comb.form.* immune; immunity; immunology: as in **im·mu·no·as·say** (–AS·ay) *n.* analysis of a body substance through its antibody-producing reactions; **im·mu·no·gen·ic** (–JEN–) *adj.* immunity-producing; **im·mu·no·glob·u·lin** (–GLOB·yuh–) *n.* the immunity-producing globulin (protein) component of serum; **im·mu·no·sup·pres·sive** (–PRES·iv) *adj.* suppressing natural immune reactions, as to organ transplants: *an ~ drug;* **im·mu·no·sup·pres·sant** *n.* & *adj.*

im·mure (–MYOOR) *v.* **im·mures, im·mured, im·mur·ing** shut up within walls; also, entomb in a wall.

im·mu·ta·ble (–MYOO·tuh–) *adj.* unchangeable; **im·mu·ta·bly** *adv.;* **im·mu·ta·bil·i·ty** (–BIL–) *n.*

imp. imperative; imperfect; imperial; import(ed). —**imp** *n.* a young demon; also, a mischievous child; **imp·ish** *adj.*

im·pact *n.* a striking together; collision; hence, influence for change; effect: *designed to collapse on ~; ~ craters made by meteorites; the ~ of TV on our culture.* —***v.*** pack in: *refugees ~ed into tenements in nontaxable federally* **impacted areas;** *An* **impacted** (wisdom) **tooth** *cannot break through the gum.*

im·pair (–PAIR) *v.* lessen in quality, value, strength, etc.: *health ~ed by drugs;* **im·pair·ment** *n.*

im·pa·la (–PAH·luh) *n.* an African antelope.
im·pale (–PALE) *v.* **-pales, -paled, -pal·ing** pierce through with or fix upon something pointed, as a stake; **im·pale·ment** *n.*
im·pal·pa·ble (–PAL·puh–) *adj.* that cannot be felt or perceived: *a too fine, ~ distinction;* **im·pal·pa·bly** *adv.*
im·pan·el (–PAN–) *v.* **-els, -el(l)ed, -el·(l)ing** put (a person) on a list for jury duty; also, select (a jury); **im·pan·el·ment** *n.*
im·part (–PART) *v.* give a part of; hence, share; communicate: *the ~ing of knowledge or information to pupils; lighting designed to ~ an air of mystery to the scene.* **—im·par·tial** (–PAR·shul) *adj.* not partial to any side; unbiased; fair: *an ~ judge;* **im·par·tial·ly** *adv.* **—im·par·ti·al·i·ty** (–AL–) *n.* **-ties.**
im·pass·a·ble (–PASS·uh–) *adj.* that cannot be traveled over or through: *an ~ road; a pass made ~ by snow and ice.* **—im·passe** (IM·pas) *n.* **-pass·es** a passage closed at one end; hence, a deadlock.
im·pas·si·ble (–PAS–) *adj.* unable to suffer pain; hence, impassive; **im·pas·si·bil·i·ty** (–BIL–) *n.* **—im·pas·sioned** (–PASH·und) *adj.* full of feeling: *an ~ appeal, plea, speech.* **—im·pass·ive** (–PAS·iv) *adj.* not showing emotion: *a face ~ in suffering;* **im·pass·ive·ly;** **im·pas·siv·i·ty** (–SIV–) *n.*
im·pas·to (–PAS·toh) *n.* **-tos** the technique or style of applying paint thickly to canvas, ceramics, etc.
im·pa·tience (–PAY·shunce) *n.* lack of patience; also, eager restlessness; **im·pa·tient** *a sales clerk ~ with customers; pupils growing ~ for the class to be dismissed; a man in a hurry, always ~ of the least delay;* **im·pa·tient·ly** *adv.* **—im·pa·ti·ens** (–PAY·shee·enz) *n.* a genus of plants of the balsam family that burst their seed capsules with elastic force when ripe; touch-me-not.
im·peach (–PEECH) *v.* charge (a public official such as a judge, senator, or president) with misbehavior: *In the U.S., the House of Representatives ~es by a majority vote and the Senate tries those ~ed; to ~* (i.e. question) *a person's honor or motives;* **im·peach·a·ble** *adj.;* **im·peach·ment** *n.*
im·pearl (–PURL) *v.* form into or adorn with pearls.
im·pec·ca·ble (–PECK·uh–) *adj.* without error or flaw; **im·pec·ca·bly** *adv.* **—im·pec·ca·bil·i·ty** (–BIL–) *n.*
im·pe·cu·ni·ous (–pi·KYOO·nee·us) *adj.* having no money because of spending habits; penniless; **im·pe·cu·ni·ous·ness** *n.*
im·ped·ance (–PEED·nce) *n.* the total effective resistance of an electric circuit to an alternating current, composed of reactance and ohmic resistance. **—im·pede** (–PEED) *v.* **-pedes, -ped·ed, -ped·ing** slow up movement or progress of by getting in the way. **—im·ped·i·ment** (–PED–) *n.* a hindrance; also, a physical defect, esp. in speech; **im·ped·i·men·ta** (–MEN·tuh) *n.pl.* baggage, supplies, and such encumbrances, as of an army on the march.
im·pel (–PEL) *v.* **-pels, -pelled, -pel·ling** urge or drive forward, as by a strong desire: *~d by a sense of duty.* **—im·pel·ler** *n.* a rotor, propeller, or similar device.
im·pend (–PEND) *v.* be about to happen, as if dropping from a suspended state; threaten: *the ~ing crisis.*
im·pen·e·tra·ble (–PEN·i·truh–) *adj.* that cannot be penetrated or understood; also, not receptive to influences: *an ~ jungle, metal, mystery, mind;* **im·pen·e·tra·bly** *adv.* **—im·pen·e·tra·bil·i·ty** (–BIL–) *n.*
im·pen·i·tent (–PEN–) *n.* & *adj.* (one who is) not sorry for having done wrong; **im·pen·i·tence** *n.*
imper. *Abbrev.* for **im·per·a·tive** (–PER·uh·tiv) *adj.* having the nature of a command; hence, that must be done: *It is ~ that we set out at once; "Stop!" is a verb in the* **imperative mood;** ***n.:*** *Food and fresh air are physiological ~s; English ~s* (i.e. sentences) *usually have no expressed subject.*
im·per·cep·ti·ble (–SEP–) *adj.* not easily perceived; very slight or gradual; **im·per·cep·ti·bly** *adv.* **—im·per·cep·tive** (–SEP·tiv) or **im·per·cip·i·ent** (–SIP·ee·unt) *adj.* not perceiving; lacking perception or understanding.
imperf. *Abbrev.* for **im·per·fect** (–PUR·fict) *adj.* not perfect; defective; also, of the verb tense expressing incomplete action; e.g. "was taking" or "used to take"; ***n.*** the imperfect tense or a verb form (as above); **im·per·fect·ly** *adv.***—im·per·fec·tion** (–FEC–) *n.* lack of perfection; deficiency; fault.
im·per·for·ate (–PUR·fuh·rit, –rate) *adj.* not perforated (with a hole or holes) in the normal way: *~ stamps* (without rouletting); *an ~ hymen.*
im·pe·ri·al (–PEER·ee·ul) *adj.* of an empire, emperor, or empress; hence, having or showing authority, majesty, or superior quality: *Her Imperial Majesty; an ~ guard;* **imperial gallon** about 1 1/5 of the U.S. gallon. ***—n.*** a small pointed beard below the lower lip. **—im·pe·ri·al·ism** (–PEER·ee·ul–) *n.* the policy of ruling over smaller or weaker countries and exploiting them as colonies; **im·pe·ri·al·ist** *n.* & *adj.;* **im·pe·ri·al·is·tic** (–IS–) *adj.* **—im·pe·ri·al·ly** *adv.*
im·per·il (–PER–) *v.* **-ils, -il(l)ed, -il·(l)ing** endanger; jeopardize.
im·pe·ri·ous (–PEER–) *adj.* overbearing; domineering; also, imperative or urgent; **im·pe·ri·ous·ly** *adv.;* **im·pe·ri·ous·ness** *n.*
im·per·ish·a·ble (–PER–) *adj.* enduring; indestructible; **im·per·ish·a·bly** *adv.*
im·per·ma·nent (–PUR–) *adj.* not permanent or lasting; **im·per·ma·nence** *n.*
im·per·me·a·ble (–PUR·mee·uh–) *adj.* not permitting fluids to pass through, as clay, membranes, etc.

im·per·son·al (–PUR·sn·ul) *adj.* without reference to a person; hence, having no personal feeling: *an ~ directive, suggestion, force* (as of the elements), *verb* (as in "It rains"); **im·per·son·al·ly** *adv.* —**im·per·son·ate** (–PUR·suh–) *v.* **-ates, -at·ed, -at·ing** play the part of or pretend to be: *an actor ~ing a lunatic; charged with ~ing a police officer;* **im·per·son·a·tor** *n.;* **im·per·son·a·tion** (–AY–) *n.*

im·per·ti·nent (–PUR–) *adj.* not relevant; also, not showing due respect; **im·per·ti·nent·ly** *adv.;* **im·per·ti·nence** *n.*

im·per·turb·a·ble (–TUR–) *adj.* that cannot be disturbed; calm: *an ~ temper.*

im·per·vi·ous (–PUR–) *adj.* not capable of being passed through; also, not affected by: *cloth ~ to moisture; a person ~ to reason, pity, criticism.*

im·pe·ti·go (–puh·TYE–) *n.* **-gos** a contagious skin infection of the face, hands, and limbs, characterized by yellow, crusty sores. —**im·pet·u·ous** (–PECH·oo·us) *adj.* marked by impulsive force; hence, rash, not thoughtful: *~ speed, torrents, outburst; an ~ nature;* **im·pet·u·ous·ly** *adv.* —**im·pet·u·os·i·ty** (–OS–) *n.* —**im·pe·tus** (IM·puh–) *n.* a driving force or impulse: *rolling downhill under the ~ acquired from gravity; a new agreement to give a fresh ~ to trade.*

im·pi·e·ty (–PYE·uh–) *n.* **-ties** lack of reverence; also, an impious act.

im·pinge (–PINJ) *v.* **-ping·es, -pinged, -ping·ing** make an impact *(on);* hence, encroach *(upon): billiard balls ~ing on one another; where a ray of light ~s on a surface; measures that ~ on individual rights;* **im·pinge·ment** *n.*

im·pi·ous (IM·pee·us) *adj.* irreverent or profane; **im·pi·ous·ly** *adv.*

imp·ish *adj.* of an imp; mischievous: *an ~ grin;* **imp·ish·ly** *adv.;* **imp·ish·ness** *n.*

im·plac·a·ble (–PLAC·uh–, –PLAY–) *adj.* that cannot be appeased: *an ~ foe; ~ hatred;* **im·plac·a·bly** *adv.* —**im·plac·a·bil·i·ty** (–BIL–) *n.*

im·plant (–PLANT) *v.* plant or fix firmly, as in the mind: *high ideals ~ed in children;* ***n.*** something implanted in living tissue: *an ~ of a tendon from another part of the body.*

im·plau·si·ble (–PLAW·zuh–) *adj.* not plausible; **im·plau·si·bly** *adv.;* **im·plau·si·bil·i·ty** (–BIL–) *n.*

im·ple·ment (–pluh–) *n.* a tool or device used in some activity, as in agriculture (plow, shovel, etc.) or war (sword, gun, etc.). —***v.*** (–ment) to effect or carry out (an order, reform, plans, decisions, etc.); **im·ple·men·ta·tion** (–TAY–) *n.*

im·pli·cate *v.* **-cates, -cat·ed, -cat·ing** show (someone) to have a role, usu. in something disgraceful: *a confession ~ing others in the robbery; ~d but not involved in the fraud;* **im·pli·ca·tive** (–pluh·cay·tiv) *adj.* —**im·pli·ca·tion** (–CAY–) *n.* an implicating; also, something implied or inferred: *the ~s of being fired rather than resigning.* —**im·plic·it** (–PLIS–) *adj.* **1** implied or suggested, not expressed: *an ~ permission; obligations ~ in the contract.* **2** unhesitating; absolute: *~ obedience expected from children.* —**im·plic·it·ly** *adv.*

im·plode (–PLODE) *v.* **-plodes, -plod·ed, -plod·ing** burst inward, as when a vacuum tube breaks: *"the ~ing or contracting energies" of the modern world; stars that ~;* **im·plo·sion** *n.: the post-war baby boom and the student ~;* **im·plo·sive** (–siv) *adj.*

im·plore (–PLOR) *v.* **-plores, -plored, -plor·ing** beg (someone) earnestly, as if in distress (*to* do or avoid something); **im·plor·ing·ly** *adv.*

im·ply (–PLY) *v.* **-plies, -plied, -ply·ing** hint at or suggest without saying; also, signify or suggest as a logical consequence: *a smile ~ing consent; Rights ~ duties.*

im·po·lite (–puh–) *adj.* not polite or courteous; **im·po·lite·ly** *adv.;* **im·po·lite·ness** *n.*

im·pol·i·tic (–POL–) *adj.* not politic or expedient; unwise; **im·pol·i·tic·ly** *adv.*

im·pon·der·a·ble (–PON·duh·ruh–) *n.* & *adj.* (something) that cannot be weighed or measured exactly: *the many ~s* (i.e. factors and circumstances) *of the human condition.*

im·port (–PORT) *v.* **1** bring in, as merchandise, from a foreign country; **im·port·er** *n.* **2** mean or signify: *What does this remark ~?* —***n.*** (IM–) **1** something brought in from an external source: *Balance of trade depends on ~s and exports.* **2** signification; also, significance or importance: *the full ~ of his words; matters of great ~.* —**im·por·tance** (–POR·tunce) *n.* the quality of being important; significance; **im·por·tant** (–POR·tunt) *adj.* meaning much; of significant quality or value; also, pretentious: *an ~ announcement; VIP's are very ~ people; looking very ~;* **im·port·ant·ly** *adv.* —**im·por·ta·tion** (–TAY–) *n.* an importing or a thing imported.

im·por·tu·nate (–POR·chuh·nit) *adj.* persistent in asking; troublesome; **im·por·tu·nate·ly** *adv.* —**im·por·tune** (–TUNE) *v.* **-tunes, -tuned, -tun·ing** ask repeatedly and annoyingly; **im·por·tu·ni·ty** (–TUE–) *n.* **-ties.**

im·pose (–POZE) *v.* **-pos·es, -posed, -pos·ing** to place as a burden (*on* or *upon* someone): *A fine is ~d on delinquents;* **impose (up)on:** *uninvited guests ~ing themselves on* (i.e. taking advantage of) *a family; sorry to ~ upon your generosity;* **im·po·si·tion** (–ZISH·un) *n.* —**im·pos·ing** *adj.* impressive because of size, excellence, or appearance: *an ~ building, personality, display;* **im·pos·ing·ly** *adv.*

im·pos·si·ble (–POS–) *adj.* that cannot be; not possible (to be done, to be true, to tolerate, etc.): *It's ~ to please everyone; an ~ situation, person;* **im·pos·si·bly** *adv.;* **im·pos·si·bil·i·ty** (–BIL–) *n.* **-ties.**

im·post (IM·pohst) *n.* **1** a duty or tax. **2** the top part of a column, pier, or wall on which the end of an arch rests. —**im·pos·tor** (–POS·tur) *n.* one who deceives or cheats others by pretending to be what he is not; also **im·pos·ter; im·pos·ture** (–POS·chur) *n.* a fraud or deception.

im·po·tent (IM·puh·tunt) *adj.* lacking power or strength; esp. of males, unable to copulate; **im·po·tent·ly** *adv.* —**im·po·tence** or **im·po·ten·cy** *n.*

im·pound (–POUND) *v.* **1** put (a stray animal) in a pound; also, seize and hold (evidence) in legal custody. **2** collect and confine in a reservoir: *water ~ed in dams.* —**im·pound·ment** *n.*

im·pov·er·ish (–POV–) *v.* make poor; deprive of resources; **im·pov·er·ish·ment** *n.*

im·prac·ti·ca·ble (–PRAC–) *adj.* not practicable; **im·prac·ti·cal** *adj.* not practical; **im·prac·ti·cal·i·ty** (–CAL–) *n.*

im·pre·cate (IM·pruh–) *v.* **-cates, -cat·ed, -cat·ing** call down (evil *on* someone); hence, curse; **im·pre·ca·tor** *n.;* **im·pre·ca·tion** (–CAY–) *n.*

im·pre·cise (–SICE) *adj.* not precise; **im·pre·cise·ly** *adv.* —**im·pre·cis·ion** (–SIZH·un) *n.*

im·preg·na·ble (–PREG·nuh–) *adj.* **1** that cannot be overcome by force: *an ~ fortress, argument, belief.* **2** that can be impregnated. —**im·preg·na·bly** *adv.* —**im·preg·nate** *v.* **-nates, -nat·ed, -nat·ing** make pregnant; fertilize (ovum); also, charge or fill; **im·preg·na·tion** (–NAY–) *n.: ~ of wood with a preservative.*

im·pre·sa·ri·o (–SAH·ree·oh) *n.* **-os** an organizer or manager of an opera, concert company, or other musical entertainment.

im·press (–PRESS) *v.* **1** force (someone) to serve in the armed forces: *people ~ed into the military;* **im·press·ment** *n.: ~ of seamen during the War of 1812.* **2** to stamp or imprint; hence, fix strongly in the mind; have a strong impact on the mind or feelings of: *He ~ed us with his learning; She ~es on everyone the urgency of her mission;* **im·press·i·ble** *adj.;* **im·press·i·bil·i·ty** (–BIL–) *n.* —**im·pres·sion** (–PRESH·un) *n.* act of impressing or a result of it: *a thumb ~; a favorable ~ made by a successful candidate; a 20,000-copy ~ of a book; a comic* ("impressionist") *good at doing ~s* (i.e. imitations) *of celebrities;* **im·pres·sion·a·ble** *adj.* sensitive to influences: *the ~ mind of children;* also **im·press·i·ble.** —**im·pres·sion·ism** *n.* a style of painting, literature, etc. striving for suggestive impressions rather than execution of realistic detail; **im·pres·sion·ist** *n.* & *adj.;* **im·pres·sion·is·tic** (–IS–) *adj.* —**im·pres·sive** (–PRES·iv) *adj.* making a strong, esp. favorable impression on the mind or feelings: *an ~ speaker, sight, ceremony;* **im·pres·sive·ly** *adv.;* **im·pres·sive·ness** *n.*

im·pri·ma·tur (–pruh·MAH·tur) *n.* official approval to publish, as in the Roman Catholic Church. —**im·print** (–PRINT) *v.* mark by pressure; impress: *A newborn animal may become permanently ~ed* (i.e. attached) *to* (or *on, by*) *the parent, handler, etc. whom it first recognizes;* ***n.*** (IM·print) something imprinted, esp. the publisher's name and the place and date of publication in a book, usu. at the foot of the title page; also, a lasting impression or effect: *the ~ of years of suffering on her face.*

im·pris·on (–PRIZN) *v.* put in prison; hence, confine; **im·pris·on·ment** *n.*

im·prob·a·ble (–PROB–) *adj.* not probable; unlikely; **im·prob·a·bly** *adv.;* **im·prob·a·bil·i·ty** (–BIL–) *n.*

im·promp·tu (–PROMP·tue) *adj.* & *adv.* offhand; (done) on the spur of the moment; spontaneous(ly); ***n.*** an impromptu speech, song, performance, etc.

im·prop·er (–PROP–) *adj.* not suitable, correct, in good taste, etc.; **im·prop·er·ly** *adv.* —**im·pro·pri·e·ty** (–PRY·uh–) *n.* **-ties** lack of propriety; also, an improper act, remark, language use, etc.

im·prove (–PROOV) *v.* **-proves, -proved, -prov·ing** make or become better: *The patient is ~ing; how to ~ your chances; land ~d* (i.e. made more valuable) *by cultivation; can't do much to* **improve (up)on** *nature;* **im·prov·a·ble** *adj.* —**im·prove·ment** *n.: much room for ~ in your work; A "B" grade is an ~ on a "C"; home ~ loans.*

im·prov·i·dent (–PROV–) *adj.* not providing for the future; **im·prov·i·dence** *n.;* **im·prov·i·dent·ly** *adv.* —**im·pro·vise** (IM–) *v.* **-vis·es, -vised, -vis·ing** make or do something without preparation or prepared material: *spent the night in an ~d shelter; a minstrel who ~s as he sings;* **im·pro·vis·er** or **im·pro·vi·sor** *n.;* **im·pro·vi·sa·tion** (–ZAY–) *n.*

im·pru·dent (–PROOD·nt) *adj.* not prudent; rash or indiscreet; **im·pru·dence** *n.*

im·pu·dent (IM·pyuh–) *adj.* shamelessly rude or impertinent; **im·pu·dent·ly** *adv.;* **im·pu·dence** *n.*

im·pugn (–PYOON) *v.* attack (a person's motives, character, action, or statement) as false or worthless.

im·pulse (IM–) *n.* a sudden driving force or impetus; also, its effect: *acted on an ~ without thinking; an electrical ~; the ~ of a wave, curiosity, hunger; nerve ~s traveling from receptor organs to effectors;* ***adj.:*** *~ buying by shoppers* (who decide to buy on the spur of the moment). —**im·pul·sion** (–PUL–) *n.* an impelling (force); a sudden inclination; impetus. —**im·pul·sive** (–PUL·siv) *adj.* **1** impelling: *an ~ force.* **2** done or acting on impulse: *an ~ child, retort, demand.* —**im·pul·sive·ly** *adv.;* **im·pul·sive·ness** *n.*

im·pu·ni·ty (–PYOO–) *n.* freedom from punishment, injury, or other consequence: *One seldom breaks the law with ~.*

im·pure (–PYOOR) *adj.* not pure, clean, or chaste; **im·pur·i·ty** *n.* **-ties** contamination; also, foreign matter, as in food, water, air, etc.

im·pute (–PYOOT) *v.* **-putes, -put·ed, -put·ing** charge or attribute: *not guilty of the crimes ~d to her; examine actions without ~ing motives;* **im·put·a·ble** *adj.;* **im·pu·ta·tion** (–TAY–) *n.*

in. inch(es). —**In** Indium. —**IN** Indiana.

in *prep.* **1** enclosed by limits of (space, time, etc.): *She's ~ the house; happened ~ a minute; rolling ~ the snow; Go ~* (i.e. into) *the house.* **2** [indicating various relationships]: *green ~ color; girl ~ a million; a degree ~ science; a party ~ his honor; went ~ search of help.* **—*adv.:*** *Come ~, please; She isn't ~ today; All late comers are* **in for** *trouble today; Don't let everyone* **in on** *the secret; tell only those who are* **in with** (i.e. friends with) *us.* **—*adj.:*** *The votes are ~ and counted; a train on the ~ track; "It is ~* (*Informal.* fashionable) *to eat out"; an ~ joke, group, word.* **—*n.:*** *has been there so long she knows all the* **ins and outs** *of the place; the* **ins** *of a society fighting outs such as immigrants; She could get you an ~ with* (*Informal.* introduction to) *her boss.* **—*comb.form.:*** as in *in-depth study, in-service training, an in-crowd* (i.e. clique), *drive-in, sit-in, teach-in, wader-in,* **—*prefix.*** **1:** as in *incoming, indoors, insight.* **2** not; lack of: as in *inability, inaccessible.* [The more common of such compounds, whose basic meaning and pronunciation are the same as in the base word in each case, are placed at the foot of this and the following pages.]

in ab·sen·ti·a (–ub·SEN·shuh) *Latin.* in (his, her, or their) absence: *a degree conferred ~.*

in·ac·ti·vate (–AC·tuh–) *v.* **-vates, -vat·ed, -vat·ing** make no longer active; **in·ac·ti·va·tion** (–VAY–) *n.*

in·ad·e·quate (–AD·uh·kwit) *adj.* not adequate; unable to cope with a situation: *feeling very ~ in her job;* **in·ad·e·quate·ly** *adv.* —**in·ad·e·qua·cy** (–kwuh·see) *n.* **-cies.**

in·ad·vert·ent (–VUR·tunt) *adj.* inattentive; also, unintentional; **in·ad·vert·ent·ly** *adv.* —**in·ad·vert·ence** *n.*

in·al·ien·a·ble (–AIL·yuh·nuh–) *adj.* that cannot be taken away, as basic or fundamental rights; **in·al·ien·a·bly** *adv.* —**in·al·ien·a·bil·i·ty** (–BIL–) *n.*

in·am·o·ra·ta (–uh·RAH·tuh) *n.* one's sweetheart or female lover.

in·ane (–ANE) *adj.* **-an·er, -an·est** empty; also, silly; **in·an·i·ty** (–AN–) *n.* **-ties.** —**in·a·ni·tion** (–NISH·un) *n.* starved condition; hence, lack of vigor or vitality.

in·ap·pre·ci·a·ble (–uh·PREE·shuh–) *adj.* not appreciable; negligible; **in·ap·pre·ci·a·bly** *adv.*

in·ap·ti·tude (–AP·tuh–) *n.* lack of aptitude or skill.

in·ar·tic·u·late (–TIK·yuh·lit) *adj.* unable to speak fluently and readily; also, incoherent or irrational: *burst into an ~ rage;* **in·ar·tic·u·late·ly** *adv.*

in·as·much (in·uz·MUCH) **as** to the extent that; since.

in·au·gu·ral (–AW·gyuh·rul) *n.* & *adj.* (a ceremony or speech) that inaugurates. —**in·au·gu·rate** (–AW·gyuh–) *v.* **-rates, -rat·ed, -rat·ing** make a formal beginning of (a new era, policy, institution, etc.); hence, install (a new president) in office; **in·au·gu·ra·tion** (–RAY–) *n.: Jan. 20 is* (presidential) **Inauguration Day** *in the U.S.*

in·board *adj.* & *adv.* in the hull or toward the middle of (a ship, boat, or other craft); ***n.*** an inboard engine of a motorboat.

in·born *adj.* of qualities, existing at birth; innate: *an ~ talent.*

in·bound *adj.* inward bound: *~ traffic; an ~ flight.*

in·bred *adj.* resulting from inbreeding; also, inborn. —**in·breed** *v.* **-breeds, -bred, -breed·ing** breed from closely related plants, animals, or persons, esp. in order to preserve purity of stock or strain: *inbred corn fertilized with its own pollen; hereditary illnesses due to ~ing within the faith, as by marriage between first cousins; Travel broadens the mind, ~ing* (i.e. narrow social or cultural life) *does not.*

inc. increase; incorporated (also **Inc.**).

In·ca (ING·cuh) *n.* a member of a highly civilized Indian people of South America who ruled in Peru and other countries before the Spanish conquest in the 1500's; **In·can** (–cun) *n.* & *adj.*

in·cal·cu·la·ble (–CAL–) *adj.* too great or too many to be counted; hence, unpredictable:

---

inability
inaccessible
inaccuracy
inaccurate
inaction
inactive
inactivity
inadmissible
inadvisability
inadvisable
inanimate
inapplicable
inapposite
inappreciative
inapproachable
inappropriate
inapt
inartistic
inattention
inattentive
inaudible
inaudibly
inauspicious

~ *harm; an ~ mood, temper;* **in·cal·cu·la·bly** *adv.*

in·can·des·cent (–DES·nt) *adj.* glowing red-hot or white-hot, as the filament of an **incandescent lamp,** electric bulb; **in·can·des·cence** *n.*

in·can·ta·tion (–TAY–) *n.* (the use of) words chanted as a magical formula or spell.

in·ca·pa·ble (–CAY·puh–) *adj.* not capable; **in·ca·pa·bil·i·ty** (–BIL–) *n.* —**in·ca·pac·i·tate** (–cuh·PAS–) *v.* **-tates, -tat·ed, -tat·ing** disqualify; disable; make incapable; **in·ca·pac·i·ta·tion** (–TAY–) *n.* —**in·ca·pac·i·ty** (–PAS–) *n.* **-ties** lack of capacity; also, a legal disqualification.

in·car·cer·ate (–CAR·suh–) *v.* **-ates, -at·ed, -at·ing** imprison; —**in·car·cer·a·tor** *n.* —**in·car·cer·a·tion** (–RAY–) *n.*

in·car·na·dine (–CAR·nuh–) *v.* **-dines, -dined, -din·ing** make red like blood.

in·car·nate (–CAR·nit) *adj.* having bodily form; hence, personified: *a moneylender who is greed ~;* ***v.*** (–nate) **-nates, -nat·ed, -nat·ing** make or be incarnate; hence, be the embodiment of; realize: *She ~s all wifely virtues;* **in·car·na·tion** (–NAY–) *n.: Jesus Christ as the* **Incarnation** *of the second person of the Trinity; the very ~ of vice.*

in·case (–CASE) *v.* same as ENCASE.

in·cen·di·ar·y (–SEN·dee–) *adj.* & *n.* **-ar·ies** (a person or thing) that sets fire: *an ~ bomb, crime, speech* (i.e. one that stirs up violence); *arrested as an ~;* **in·cen·di·a·rism** *n.* —**in·cense** *n.* (IN–) the perfume or smoke from a gum or spice burned for fragrance, usu. as part of a ritual; ***v.*** (–SENCE) **-cens·es, -censed, -cens·ing** make (someone) very angry (*at, by, with,* or *against* someone or something); **in·cense·ment** *n.*

in·cen·tive (–SEN·tiv) *n.* & *adj.* (something such as an award, bonus, loan, pay, etc.) tending or designed to stimulate or encourage (*to* greater effort or output).

in·cep·tion (–SEP–) *n.* beginning or commencement (of a plan, undertaking, organization, business, program, etc.); **in·cep·tive** (–tiv) *adj.*

in·cer·ti·tude (–SUR·tuh–) *n.* uncertainty; also, insecurity.

in·ces·sant (–SES·nt) *adj.* ceaseless or uninterrupted, as noises, rain, annoying phone calls, complaining, etc.; **in·ces·sant·ly** *adv.*

in·cest *n.* sexual relations between those closely related by blood, as brother and sister or uncle and niece. —**in·ces·tu·ous** (–SES·choo·us) *adj.;* **in·ces·tu·ous·ly** *adv.;* **in·ces·tu·ous·ness** *n.*

inch *n.* a unit of length that is 12th of a foot, and equal to 2.54 cm; also, a unit of rainfall, snow, or pressure, based on height of the liquid in a specified container, as of mercury in the barometer measuring pressure; hence, smallest amount or least bit. —**by inches** gradually, or **inch by inch;** also, only just: *missed the shot by ~s; came* **within an inch of** *losing the election; She's* **every inch** (i.e. completely) *a lady.* —***v.*** move little by little, or inch by inch; edge one's way (*along, back, forward,* etc.): *The shy child ~ed away and tripped out of sight.*

in·cho·ate (–COH·it) *adj.* just begun; undeveloped; also **in·cho·a·tive** (–tiv): *"Begin to," "get going," etc. are ~ or inceptive verb forms.*

inch·worm *n.* a looper; also called "measuring worm."

in·ci·dence (IN·suh–) *n.* the falling or striking of a projectile, ray, or beam on a surface; also, the rate or frequency with which something occurs: *angle of ~ of light rays; the ~ of an indirect tax on manufacturer or consumer; a high ~ of vandalism.* —**in·ci·dent** *n.* an occurrence, esp. one of minor significance, usu. related to something major: *a border ~ leading to war;* ***adj.*** **1** falling or striking: *light ~ (up)on a photographic subject.* **2** incidental *(to).* —**in·ci·den·tal** (–DEN·tl) *n.* & *adj.* (something) that happens or is likely to happen along with something else that is more important; also, nonessential; casual: *problems ~ to setting up in business; ~ expenses,* or **incidentals** *n.pl.;* **incidental music** accompaniment or background music; **in·ci·den·tal·ly** *adv.* by the way.

in·cin·er·ate (–SIN·uh–) *v.* **-ates, -at·ed, -at·ing** burn to ashes, as in an **in·cin·er·a·tor** *n.;* **in·cin·er·a·tion** (–RAY–) *n.*

in·cip·i·ent (–SIP·ee·unt) *adj.* just beginning to be(come) apparent: *an ~ growth of facial hair; ~ pneumonia;* **in·cip·i·ence** *n.*

in·cise (–SIZE) *v.* **-cis·es, -cised, -cis·ing** cut into with a sharp tool, as to carve or engrave; **in·ci·sion** (–SIZH·un) *n.* a gash or cut, as in a surgical operation; **in·ci·sive** (–SYE·siv) *adj.* keen or cutting: *~ criticism, mind, wit;* **in·ci·sive·ly** *adv.;* **in·ci·sive·ness** *n.* —**in·ci·sor** (–zur) *n.* any of the sharp-edged cutting teeth in the front of a mammal's upper and lower jaws.

in·cite (–CITE) *v.* **-cites, -cit·ed, -cit·ing** stir up (hatred, riot, etc.) or urge (a person *to* action); **in·cite·ment** *n.*

incl. including; inclusive.

in·clem·ent (–CLEM–) *adj.* severe; also, rough or stormy; **in·clem·en·cy** *n.* **-cies:** *the ~s of the weather.*

in·clin·a·ble (–CLYE·nuh–) *adj.* disposed, esp. favorably. —**in·cli·na·tion** (–NAY–) *n.* an inclining: *the ~* (i.e. angle) *of an orbit from the equator; led a life of ease following every ~* (i.e. liking) *of body and mind; an unwelcome visitor with no ~ to leave.* —**in·cline** (–CLINE) *v.* **-clines, -clined, -clin·ing** (cause to) slope, lean, or bend; hence, dispose or be disposed; be or make favorable or willing: *with head ~d in prayer; an* **inclined plane** *such as a plank or ramp for raising heavy loads by pushing instead of lifting; She's ~d to think her son is innocent.* —***n.*** (IN–) a slope.

inclose, inclosure same as ENCLOSE, ENCLOSURE.

in·clude (–CLOOD) *v.* **-cludes, -clud·ed, -clud·ing** take in as part of something: *batteries not ~d in the price; Does "he" ~ "she" in general statements?* —**in·clu·sion** (–CLOO·zhun) *n.* an including or something included, as chloroplasts in cells; **in·clu·sive** (–siv) *adj.: February 1st to 10th ~* (i.e. including both days); *an ~* (i.e. including much or all) *list; a hotel's moderate ~ rates; costs only $25* **inclusive of** (i.e. counting) *taxes;* **in·clu·sive·ly** *adv.;* **in·clu·sive·ness** *n.*

incog. *Abbrev.* for **in·cog·ni·to** (–COG·nuh·toh, –cog·NEE–) *adj., adv.* & *n.* **-tos** (with) a concealed or disguised identity: *a king traveling ~; an ~ hard to penetrate.*

in·co·her·ent (–HEER·unt) *adj.* not coherent; **in·co·her·ent·ly** *adv.;* **in·co·her·ence** *n.*

in·com·bus·ti·ble (–cum·BUS–) *n.* & *adj.* (something) that is not combustible.

in·come (–cum) *n.* money that comes in, or other benefit or gain received on account of services or capital, esp. in a given period; **income tax** a government tax on net income. —**in·com·ing** *n.* & *adj.* coming in: *the ~ of a tide; the ~ year, chairman, mail.*

in·com·mode (–cuh·MODE) *v.* **-com·modes, -com·mod·ed, -com·mod·ing** inconvenience; annoy.

in·com·mu·ni·ca·do (–CAH·doh) *adj.* & *adv.* (held) without means of communication, as prisoners.

in·com·pa·ra·ble (–COM·puh·ruh·bl) *adj.* that cannot be compared, esp. because unequaled: *~ skill, beauty, wit.*

in·com·pat·i·ble (–cum·PAT–) *adj.* not compatible (*with* one another), as different drugs, blood types, temperaments, etc.; **in·com·pat·i·bil·i·ty** (–BIL–) *n.*

in·com·pe·tent (–COM·puh·tunt) *n.* & *adj.* (one) that is not competent; **in·com·pe·tent·ly** *adv.;* **in·com·pe·tence** or **-ten·cy** *n.*

in·com·plete (–cum·PLEET) *adj.* not complete; **in·com·plete·ly** *adv.;* **in·com·plete·ness** *n.*

in·con·gru·ous (–CONG·groo·us) *adj.* lacking agreement of parts or harmony with surroundings; not suitable or appropriate; **in·con·gru·ous·ly** *adv.* —**in·con·gru·ous·ness** or **in·con·gru·i·ty** (–GROO–) *n.* **-ties.**

in·con·se·quen·tial (–KWEN·shul) *adj.* of no consequence; unimportant; also, irrelevant; **in·con·se·quen·tial·ly** *adv.* —**in·con·se·quence** (–CON–) *n.*

in·con·sid·er·a·ble (–SID–) *adj.* not worth considering because trivial or small; negligible. —**in·con·sid·er·ate** (–it) *adj.* without consideration for others; **in·con·sid·er·ate·ly** *adv.;* **in·con·sid·er·ate·ness** *n.*

in·con·sol·a·ble (–cun·SOH·luh–) *adj.* of persons, grief, etc., that cannot be consoled; **in·con·sol·a·bly** *adv.*

in·con·spic·u·ous (–SPIC–) *adj.* not conspicuous or attracting any attention; **in·con·spic·u·ous·ly** *adv.*

in·con·stant (–CON·stunt) *adj.* not constant; changeable; **in·con·stant·ly** *adv.;* **in·con·stan·cy** *n.*

in·con·test·a·ble (–TES·tuh–) *adj.* not contestable; indisputable; **in·con·test·a·bly** *adv.* —**in·con·test·a·bil·i·ty** (–BIL–) *n.*

in·con·ti·nent (–CON–) *adj.* not continent, esp. in regard to sex or other natural urges such as to urinate; **in·con·ti·nence** *n.* —**in·con·ti·nent·ly** *adv.*

in·con·tro·vert·i·ble (–VUR–) *adj.* that cannot be controverted; **in·con·tro·vert·i·bly** *adv.*

in·con·ven·ience (–VEEN·yunce) *n.* lack of comfort or ease; also, something that is inconvenient. —***v.*** **-ienc·es, -ienced, -ienc·ing** cause trouble or bother to. —**in·con·ven·ient** (–VEEN–) *adj.* not convenient or opportune; **in·con·ven·ient·ly** *adv.*

in·cor·po·rate (–COR–) *v.* **-rates, -rat·ed, -rat·ing** **1** unite into or combine with so as to form one body: *a plan ~ing many suggestions.* **2** make into a legal body or corporation: *A business is ~d for limiting the liability of investors;* **incorporated** *adj.: an ~ town;* **in·cor·po·ra·tor** *n.;* **in·cor·po·ra·tion** (–RAY–) *n.* —**in·cor·po·re·al** (–POR·ee·ul) *adj.* not having material form, as angels and spirits; spiritual; **in·cor·po·re·al·ly** *adv.*

in·cor·ri·gi·ble (–COR·i·juh–) *adj.* that cannot be changed or reformed: *an ~ habit, person;* **in·cor·ri·gi·bly** *adv.* —**in·cor·ri·gi·bil·i·ty** (–BIL–) *n.*

in·cor·rupt·i·ble (–RUP·tuh–) *adj.* not subject to corruption; esp., morally upright; **in·cor·rupt·i·bly** *adv.* —**in·cor·rupt·i·bil·i·ty** (–BIL–) *n.*

incr. increase(d). —**in·crease** (–CREECE) *v.* **-creas·es, -creased, -creas·ing** make or be-

---

incommensurate
incommunicable
incomprehensible
incomprehension
incompressible
inconceivable
inconclusive
incongruent
inconsistency
inconsistent
incoordination
incorrect

come greater in size, degree, number, etc.: *World population is ~ing every minute; Demands ~ while supplies dwindle;* **in·creas·ing·ly** *adv.* more and more. —**in·crease** (IN·creece) *n.* growth or its result: *an ~ of 10° from the normal; Prices seem always* **on the increase** *in our economy.*

in·cred·i·ble (–CRED–) *adj.* too unusual or improbable to believe: *an ~ feat of endurance;* **in·cred·i·bly** *adv.;* **in·cred·i·bil·i·ty** (–BIL–) *n.* —**in·cred·u·lous** (–CREJ·oo·lus) *adj.* unwilling to believe; showing disbelief: *an ~ shaking of the head;* **in·cred·u·lous·ly** *adv.;* **in·cre·du·li·ty** (–DEW–) *n.* disbelief.

in·cre·ment (ING·cruh·munt, IN–) *n.* amount or quantity of increase: *the annual ~s in a wage scale;* **in·cre·men·tal** (–MEN–) *adj.*

in·crim·i·nate (–CRIM–) *v.* **-nates, -nat·ed, -nat·ing** accuse of or involve in wrongdoing: *suspected of the crime because of ~ing circumstances;* **in·crim·i·na·to·ry** *adj.* —**in·crim·i·na·tion** (–NAY–) *n.*

incrust(ation) same as ENCRUST(ATION).

in·cu·bate (ING·kyuh–) *v.* **-bates, -bat·ed, -bat·ing** sit on (eggs) or brood as a female bird does; hence, artificially develop (eggs, cultures of microorganisms, premature babies, etc.) in an **in·cu·ba·tor** (–bay·tur); also, of germs, develop in a body before symptoms of the infection appear; **in·cu·ba·tion** (–BAY–) *n.: Measles have an* **incubation period** *of 10 to 14 days.* —**in·cu·bus** (ING·kyuh–) *n.* an evil spirit supposed to lie on and oppress a sleeping person, as in a nightmare or "incubus attack"; hence, anything oppressive or burdensome.

in·cul·cate (–CUL–, IN·cul–) *v.* **-cates, -cat·ed, -cat·ing** impress (ideas, habits, facts, etc.) into the minds of others, esp. by strong repetition: *prejudice ~d in children by parents;* **in·cul·ca·tion** (–CAY–) *n.*

in·cul·pate (–CUL–, IN·cul–) *v.* **-pates, -pat·ed, -pat·ing** same as INCRIMINATE.

in·cum·ben·cy (–CUM·bun·see) *n.* **-cies** (term of) office of an incumbent; also, a duty or obligation. —**in·cum·bent** *n.* & *adj.* (a person) holding an office or position: *candidates challenging the ~ mayor; Mr. Jones, the present ~; felt it* **incumbent (up)on** *him* (i.e. to be an obligation) *to impose a penalty.*

incumber, incumbrance same as ENCUMBER, ENCUMBRANCE.

in·cu·nab·u·la (–kyoo·NAB·yuh·luh) *n.pl.* **1** beginnings; first traces or earliest stages. **2** books printed before 1501; *sing.* **-u·lum.**

in·cur (–CUR) *v.* **-curs, -curred, -cur·ring** meet with or bring down on oneself (an inconvenience or something unpleasant such as displeasure, debts, or expenses). —**in·cur·sion** (–CUR·zhun) *n.* an invasion or raid.

in·cus (ING–) *n., pl.* **-cu·des** (–CUE·deez) the small, anvil-shaped middle bone of the middle ear.

ind. independent; index; industrial; industry. —**Ind.** India(n); Indiana.

in·debt·ed (–DET·id) *adj.* owing money, gratitude, etc.; **in·debt·ed·ness** *n.*

in·de·cen·cy *n.* **-cies** lack of decency; also, an obscene act or expression. —**in·de·cent** (–DEE·snt) *adj.* **1** not decent or becoming. **2** morally bad or obscene: **Indecent assault** *is a lesser crime than rape;* **indecent exposure** (of genitals); **in·de·cent·ly** *adv.*

in·de·ci·pher·a·ble (–SYE·fuh·ruh–) *adj.* that cannot be deciphered.

in·de·ci·sion (–SIZH·un) *n.* tendency to hesitate; irresolution. —**in·de·ci·sive** (–SYE·siv) *adj.* not decisive or conclusive; also, vacillating; **in·de·ci·sive·ly** *adv.;* **in·de·ci·sive·ness** *n.*

in·deed (–DEED) *adv.* certainly; really; ***interj.*** expressing surprise, doubt, irony, etc.

indef. indefinite.

in·de·fat·i·ga·ble (–FAT·i·guh–) *adj.* untiring; tireless; **in·de·fat·i·ga·bly** *adv.*

in·de·fea·si·ble (–FEE·zuh–) *adj.* that cannot be done away with or annulled, as certain rights and claims; **in·de·fea·si·bly** *adv.*

in·def·i·nite (–DEF·uh·nit) *adj.* not definite; not defining, precise, or certain: *an ~ answer* (such as "Maybe"), *period of time, pronoun* (such as "some," "few," and "many"), *article* ("a" or "an"); **in·def·i·nite·ly** *adv.* **in·def·i·nite·ness** *n.*

in·del·i·ble (–DEL–) *adj.* that cannot be erased or blotted out: *an ~ ink, impression, memory;* **in·del·i·bly** *adv.*

in·del·i·cate (–DEL·i·kit) *adj.* lacking delicacy or propriety; coarse or tactless. —**in·del·i·ca·cy** *n.* **-cies.**

in·dem·ni·fy (–DEM–) *v.* **-fies, -fied, -fy·ing** insure against or make compensation for (hurt, loss, damage, etc.); **in·dem·ni·fi·ca·tion** (–CAY–) *n.* —**in·dem·ni·ty** (–DEM–) *n.* **-ties** security or insurance; also, compensation such as war reparations exacted from a defeated nation.

in·dent (–DENT) *v.* **1** make a dent, notch, or recess on an edge or border: *a paragraph ~ed five spaces from the left margin; coves and capes that ~ a coastline;* ***n.*** such a notch, indentation, or indention. **2** make a dent or depression, as of a pattern on metal; hence, stamp: *an asphalt that ~s easily.* —**in·den·ta·tion** (–TAY–) *n.* an indenting or its result: *an ~ test for hardness using an* **in·dent·er** or **in·den·tor; in·den·**

---

inculpable
incurable
incurious
indecorous
indefensible
indefinable
indemonstrable

tion (–DEN–) *n.* an indenting or the blank space left by indenting a line or paragraph. —**in·den·ture** (–DEN·chur) *n.* & *v.* **-tures, -tured, -tur·ing** (bind by) a written contract, usu. **indentures** *pl.,* esp. one binding a person to someone's service: *Plantation workers used to be slaves or ~d servants or immigrants; was apprenticed to a carpenter by ~s.*

In·de·pend·ence (–PEN–) a city of W. Missouri. —**in·de·pend·ence** *n.* freedom; the quality of being independent: **Independence Day** *in the U.S. is July 4, on which day in 1776 the Declaration of Independence was adopted.* —**in·de·pend·ent** *n.* & *adj.* (one who is) free from the rule, control, or influence of others: *an ~ businessman, country, thinker, income; Republicans, Democrats, and ~s; has nothing* **independent of** (i.e. apart from) *his pension;* **in·de·pend·ent·ly** *adv.*

in-depth *adj.* profound or thorough: *an ~ study, interview, report.*

in·de·scrib·a·ble (–SCRYE·buh–) *adj.* that cannot be described or is beyond description; **in·de·scrib·a·bly** *adv.*

in·de·ter·mi·nate (–TUR·mi·nit) *adj.* not determined; vague; inconclusive; **in·de·ter·mi·nate·ly** *adv.;* **in·de·ter·mi·na·cy** (–nuh·see) *n.*

in·dex *n.* **-dex·es** or **-di·ces** (–duh·seez) something that points or indicates, as the forefinger, or **index finger,** a fist sign beside a note or paragraph, a THUMB INDEX, the percentage variation from a normal, as in prices, wages, cost of living, etc., a listing of authors or subjects, as at the end of a book or in a library catalog, a figure (as 3 in ab^3) showing the power to which a mathematical quantity is raised, the amount that a light ray bends in passing into a different medium, or **index of refraction,** etc.: *"The face is the ~ of the mind"; The lower a gem's refractive ~ the less its luster; the former Roman Catholic Index of books prohibited because harmful to faith or morals.* —**v.:** *a well-~ed book; the ~ing of wages, interest, etc. to adjust them up or down according to cost of living;* **in·dex·a·tion** (–SAY–) *n.*

In·di·a (–dee·uh) **1** a republic of S. Asia; 1,266,602 sq. mi. (3,280,483 km^2); *cap.* New Delhi. **2** a region and country S. of the Himalayas, formerly under British rule, comprising the present India, Pakistan, and Bangladesh. —**India ink** a drawing and lettering ink prepared from a pigment of lampblack with glue or gum; **In·di·a·man** (–mun) *n.* **-men** a large merchant ship formerly plying between India and England. —**In·di·an** (–un) *n.* **1** a person of American Indian origin; also, an American Indian language: *just one of the ~s* (i.e. not a chief). **2** a person from India —***adj.*** of or having to do with Indians, their languages, or with the East Indies. —**In·di·an·a** (–dee·AN·uh) a Middle Western U.S. state; 36,291 sq. mi. (93,993 km^2); *cap.* **In·di·an·ap·o·lis** (–NAP·uh–). —**Indian corn** same as CORN, *n.* 1; **Indian file** single file; **Indian meal** cornmeal. —**Indian Ocean** the ocean S. of India extending from Africa to Australia. —**Indian paintbrush** a wild flower of the figwort family bearing small, green flowers surrounded by showy, petallike bracts colored crimson, yellow, or pink. —**Indian pipe** a heath-family herb of North America and E. Asia that resembles a group of clay pipes because of its long stems having a white or pink bell-shaped flower at the end. —**Indian summer** a brief period of mild weather sometimes occurring late in the fall. —**India paper** a very thin tough paper used for Bibles, air editions of newspapers, etc. —**In·dic** *adj.* of or having to do with the Indo-European languages of India such as Sanskrit, Hindi, and Bengali.

indic. indicative. —**in·di·cate** *v.* **-cates, -cat·ed, -cat·ing** point to, point out, signify, or state briefly: *A clock's hands ~ time; A nod ~s assent; She ~d it was their last date; language so poor remedial English seems ~d;* **in·di·ca·tion** (–CAY–) *n.* —**in·dic·a·tive** (–DIC·uh·tiv) *adj.: symptoms ~ of a disease; In "She is gone; Are you coming?" the verbs are in the* **indicative mood,** *not the imperative or subjunctive;* **n.:** *"is gone" and "are coming" are ~s;* **in·dic·a·tive·ly** *adv.* —**in·di·ca·tor** (–cay·tur) *n.* —**indices** a *pl.* of INDEX. —**in·di·ci·a** (–DISH·ee·uh) *n.pl.* characteristic or distinctive marks; also, postal markings put on mail.

in·dict (–DITE) *v.* charge with a crime; **in·dict·a·ble** *adj.;* **in·dict·ment** *n.: A grand jury hands up an ~ to a judge.*

in·dif·fer·ence (–DIF·uh·runce) *n.* lack of interest; also, lack of concern, esp. as to the importance of something: *~ shown in careless work; Her religion is a matter of ~ to me;* **in·dif·fer·ent** *adj.: couldn't remain ~ in a family dispute; apathetic and ~ to the sufferings of the poor; a novel of ~* (i.e. mediocre) *quality;* **in·dif·fer·ent·ly** *adv.*

in·di·gence *n.* privation or need.

in·dig·e·nous (–DIJ·uh·nus) *adj.* of races, species, etc., belonging or proper (*to* a particular region, country, soil, or climate as native to it), not exotic or imported; also, inborn or innate: *an ~ tribe; Koalas are ~ to Australia.*

in·di·gent (–junt) *n.* & *adj.* needy (person).

in·di·gest·i·ble (–JES–) *adj.* of foods, difficult to digest; **in·di·ges·tion** (–chun) *n.* poor digestion.

in·dig·nant (–DIG·nunt) *adj.* righteously angry or scornful (*at* or *about* an injustice or *with* someone); **in·dig·nant·ly** *adv.* —**in·dig·na·tion** (–NAY–) *n.* righteous anger. —**in·dig·ni·ty** (–DIG–) *n.* **-ties** something done or said that hurts one's dignity or self-respect.

---

indestructible

indeterminable

in·di·go (–di·goh) *n.* **-go(e)s** a deep blue dye, or **in·dig·o·tin** (–DIG·uh–) once got from the Indian "indigo plant" but now made from aniline; **indigo bunting** a small finch; **indigo snake** a dark-blue snake of southern U.S.

in·di·rect (–RECT) *adj.* not straight or straightforward; also, secondary: *an ~ route, cause; an ~* (i.e. devious or dishonest) *dealing, method; ~* DISCOURSE; **indirect object** *such as "me" in "Give it to me".* —**indirect tax** one paid indirectly, unlike income tax, as on cigarettes when included in the price; **in·di·rec·tion** *n.;* **in·di·rect·ly** *adv.;* **in·di·rect·ness** *n.*

in·dis·creet (–CREET) *adj.* not discreet; **in·dis·creet·ly** *adv.* —**in·dis·cre·tion** (–CRESH·un) *n.* imprudence; also, an indiscreet act or remark.

in·dis·crim·i·nate (–CRIM·uh·nit) *adj.* without care in making choices or decisions; also, haphazard: *an ~ pile, reader; ~ in her attacks, compliments, friendships;* **in·dis·crim·i·nate·ly** *adv.*

in·dis·pen·sa·ble (–PEN·suh–) *n.* & *adj.* (something) absolutely essential; **in·dis·pen·sa·bly** *adv.* —**in·dis·pen·sa·bil·i·ty** (–BIL–) *n.*

in·dis·posed (–POZED) *adj.* not well disposed; also, slightly ill; **in·dis·po·si·tion** (–ZISH–) *n.*

in·dis·sol·u·ble (–SOL·yoo–) *adj.* that cannot be undone; lasting.

in·dite (–DITE) *v.* **-dites, -dit·ed, -dit·ing** compose (a poem, speech, letter, etc.).

in·di·um (–dee–) *n.* a silver-white metallic chemical element.

in·di·vid·u·al (–VIJ·oo·ul) *n.* & *adj.* (of or having to do with) a separate person, animal, or thing: *standing room besides ~ seating for 200; lectures followed by ~ coaching; rights of the ~ as opposed to those of society as a whole; treat children as ~s; each ~ of a species; an ~* (i.e. distinctive) *style; an obnoxious ~* (i.e. person); **in·di·vid·u·al·ly** *adv.* as individuals; singly. —**in·di·vid·u·al·ism** *n.* any of various doctrines stressing individual existence, freedom, importance, self-interest, etc.; also, individuality; **in·di·vid·u·al·ist** *n.* & *adj.;* **in·di·vid·u·al·is·tic** (–LIS–) *adj.* —**in·di·vid·u·al·i·ty** (–AL–) *n.* **-ties** the sum of a person's distinctive characteristics; one's individual condition or existence; also, an individual characteristic or trait. —**in·di·vid·u·al·ize** (–VIJ·oo·uh–) *v.* **-iz·es, -ized, -iz·ing** make individual; also, treat as individuals: *~d instruction of students; a style that ~s her performance;* **in·di·vid·u·al·i·za·tion** (–ZAY–) *n.* —**in·di·vid·u·ate** (–VIJ·oo–) *v.* **-ates, -at·ed -at·ing** make or become individual: *the psychological process of* **in·di·vid·u·a·tion** (–AY–) *n.*

In·do·chi·na (–CHYE·nuh) the S.E. Asian peninsula S. of China, esp. Vietnam, Laos, and Cambodia comprising the former "French Indochina."

in·doc·tri·nate (–DOC·truh–) *v.* **-nates, -nat·ed, -nat·ing** teach (a specific doctrine), esp. fill a subject's mind (*with* the beliefs of a particular party or sect); **in·doc·tri·na·tion** (–NAY–) *n.*

In·do-Eu·ro·pe·an (–yoor·uh·PEE·un) *n.* & *adj.* (of or having to do with) a family of languages originally spoken in India, Iran, and Europe, to which English belongs.

in·do·lent (IN·duh·lunt) *adj.* idle or lazy: *an ~ worker; an ~* (i.e. inactive) *ulcer; ~* (i.e. painless) *cyst or tumor;* **in·do·lence** *n.*

in·dom·i·ta·ble (–DOM·i·tuh–) *adj.* unconquerable; unyielding: *~ courage, will, spirit;* **in·dom·i·ta·bly** *adv.*

In·do·ne·si·a (–duh·NEE·zhuh) a S.E. Asian republic consisting of many thousand islands, the chief of which is Java; 735,272 sq. mi. (1,904,345 km²); *cap.* Jakarta; **In·do·ne·sian** *n.* & *adj.*

in·door (IN·dore) *adj.* done, used, situated, etc. within a building: *an ~ game; ~ photography.* —**in·doors** (IN·DORZ) *adv.: go, stay, keep ~.*

indorse same as ENDORSE.

in·du·bi·ta·ble (–DEW·bi·tuh–) *adj.* that cannot be doubted; **in·du·bi·ta·bly** *adv.*

in·duce (–DEWSS) *v.* **-duc·es, -duced, -duc·ing** lead on (to); bring about; hence, influence or persuade: *a carrot to ~ a donkey to proceed; drugs to ~ sleep; ~d abortion, labor; ~d current* (i.e. by electrical induction); *radioactivity ~d by bombardment or irradiation;* **in·duce·ment** *n.* external influence or attempt to entice or tempt one to action: *scholarships as ~s to study;* **in·duc·er** *n.* —**in·duct** (–DUCT) *v.* install, enroll, or introduce (*into* an office or position, the military, *to* a benefice, etc.); **in·duct·ee** (–TEE) *n.;* **in·duc·tor** *n.* —**in·duct·ance** (–unce) *n.* electrical property of inducing electromotive forces, measured in henrys. —**in·duc·tion** (–DUC–) *n.* **1** process of inducing electrical or magnetic properties: *~coils, heating.* **2** an inducting, as into military service or an office: *~ ceremonies, papers.* **3** process of reasoning from particular facts to general principles; opposite of DEDUCTION; also, a conclusion so reached. —**in·duc·tive** (–DUC·tiv) *adj.: ~ logic, reactance;* **in·duc·tive·ly** *adv.*

indue same as ENDUE.

in·dulge (–DULJ) *v.* **-dulg·es, -dulged, -dulg·ing** yield or give in to (one's pleasures, wants, wishes, or whims): *~ a fondness or craving for candy; a sick child who needs some ~ing; She rarely* **indulges in** *abusive language.* —**in·dul·gence**

---

indiscernible
indisputable
indistinct
indistinguishable
indivisible

n. an indulging or something one indulges in; also, in the Roman Catholic Church, remission of punishment due for sins: *craved the* ~ (i.e. forbearance) *of a tired audience;* **in·dul·gent** *adj.;* **in·dul·gent·ly** *adv.*

in·du·rate (IN·dew–) *v.* **-rates, -rat·ed, -rat·ing** harden (a substance, a tissue, a person in a habit, etc.); inure; ***adj.*** (-rit) hardened or callous: ~ *to public opinion:* **in·du·ra·tion** (–RAY–) *n.:* ~ *of tissue around a wound;* **in·du·ra·tive** (–tiv) *adj.* hardening.

in·dus·tri·al (–DUS·tree·ul) *adj.* of industries: **industrial arts** *teaching mechanical and technical skills; an* ~ (i.e. man-made) *diamond; a suburban area zoned as an* **industrial park** *for businesses and industries; factory production speeded up by machines during England's* **Industrial Revolution** *from about 1750; modern* ~ *nations of the West;* **in·dus·tri·al·ly** *adv.* **in·dus·tri·al·ism** *n.* social and economic organization dominated by industries; **in·dus·tri·al·ist** *n.* owner or controller of an industrial enterprise. —**in·dus·tri·al·ize** *v.* **-iz·es, -ized, -iz·ing** make or become industrial: *Material progress lies in ~ing; Japan is highly ~d;* **in·dus·tri·al·i·za·tion** (–ZAY–) *n.* —**in·dus·try** (–tree) *n.* **-tries** **1** a business activity or enterprise: *Primary or extractive ~s such as fishing and mining, secondary or manufacturing ~s, and distributive ~s that serve the consumer; American* ~ (i.e. collectively). **2** habitually hard-working quality; also, systematic effort: *Diligence and* ~ *got her to the top;* **in·dus·tri·ous** (–DUS·tree·us) *adj.: an* ~ *clerk, housewife;* ~ *like ants and bees;* **in·dus·tri·ous·ly** *adv.:* **in·dus·tri·ous·ness** *n.*

in·dwell *v.* **-dwells, -dwelt, -dwell·ing** dwell in or animate: *an ~ing force, spirit, principle.*

In·dy car a racing car with a powerful rear-mounted engine; "Indianapolis car."

-ine *suffix.* **1** *adj.* like: as in *Alpine, crystalline.* **2** *n.* derivative: as in *caffeine, flourine, nectarine.*

in·e·bri·ate (–I E·bree–) *v.* **-ates, -at·ed, -at·ing** intoxicate; ***n.*** & ***adj.*** (–it) drunk(ard); **in·e·bri·a·tion** (–AY–) *n.*

in·ed·it·ed (–ED–) *adj.* unpublished.

in·ef·fa·ble (–EF·uh–) *adj.* not capable of being expressed in words: *that old* ~ *charm; the* ~ *happiness of heaven;* ~ *beauty; the* ~ *name of Jehovah* (too sacred to be uttered); **in·ef·fa·bly** *adv.*

in·ef·fi·cient (–uh·FISH·unt) *adj.* not efficient; also, incapable; **in·ef·fi·cient·ly** *adv.* **in·ef·fi·cien·cy** *n.*

in·el·e·gant (–EL·i·gunt) *adj.* not elegant; coarse or crude; **in·el·e·gant·ly** *adv.;* **in·el·e·gance** *n.*

in·el·i·gi·ble (–EL·i·juh·bl) *n.* & *adj.* (one who is) not eligible or suitable. —**in·el·i·gi·bil·i·ty** (–BIL–) *n.*

in·e·luc·ta·ble (–i·LUC·tuh–) *adj.* not to be struggled with or avoided, as fate; **in·e·luc·ta·bly** *adv.*

in·ept (–EPT) *adj.* inappropriate or tactless: *an* ~ *comparison;* ~ *remarks; a brave but* ~ (i.e. bungling) *military officer;* **in·ept·ly** *adv.* —**in·ept·i·tude** or **in·ept·ness** *n.*

in·er·rant (–ER·unt) *adj.* not erring; **in·er·ran·cy** *n.: the* ~ *of the word of God.*

in·ert (–URT) *adj.* lacking inherent power or quality, as to act or move: *argon, neon, and other* ~ *gases used as filters because noncombining with other elements; an* ~ *electorate;* **in·ert·ly** *adv.;* **in·ert·ness** *n.* —**in·er·tia** (–shuh) *n.* tendency of matter to remain in its state of rest or motion unless acted on by an outside force; hence, inertness or sluggishness: *the self-adjusting* ~ *reel of a safety belt; an aircraft engine with an* **inertia starter** *that has a flywheel spun by hand;* **in·er·tial** *adj.: a missile kept on course by means of an* **inertial guidance** *system using a gyroscope.*

in·es·cap·a·ble (–SCAY·puh–) *adj.* that cannot be escaped; inevitable, as a logical conclusion, moral necessity, etc.; **in·es·cap·a·bly** *adv.*

in·es·ti·ma·ble (–ES·tuh·muh–) *adj.* too great or precious to be calculated; invaluable; **in·es·ti·ma·bly** *adv.*

in·ev·i·ta·ble (–EV·i·tuh–) *adj.* unavoidable, as a natural occurrence or phenomenon: *Death is ~; an* ~ *result, delay, war; a tourist with his* ~ *camera;* **in·ev·i·ta·bly** *adv.* —**in·ev·i·ta·bil·i·ty** (–BIL–) *n.*

in·ex·haust·i·ble (–ig·ZAWST–) *adj.* that cannot be exhausted; also, tireless: *the ocean's* ~ *riches; a man of* ~ *energy;* **in·ex·haust·i·bly** *adv.*

in·ex·o·ra·ble (–EX·uh·ruh–) *adj.* that cannot be altered by begging or entreaty; relentless: *a dictator's* ~ *demands; awaiting his* ~ *doom; the* ~ *logic of her reasoning;* **in·ex·o·ra·bly** *adv.*

in·ex·pe·ri·ence (–SPEER·ee·unce) *n.* lack of experience or consequent lack of skill, wisdom, etc.; **in·ex·pe·ri·enced** *adj.* —**in·ex·pert** (–EX–, –ik·SPURT) *adj.* inexperienced; also, unskilled.

---

inedible
ineducable
ineffaceable
ineffective
ineffectual
inefficacious
inefficacy
inelastic
inelasticity
inequality
inequitable
inequity
ineradicable
inexact
inexcusable
inexpedient
inexpensive
inexpressive

in·ex·pi·a·ble (–EX·pee·uh–) *adj.* that cannot be expiated or atoned for.

in·ex·pli·ca·ble (–EX·pli·cuh–, –ex·PLIC–) *adj.* that cannot be explained or accounted for; mysterious; **in·ex·pli·ca·bly** *adv.*

in·ex·press·i·ble (–PRESS–) *adj.* that cannot be expressed or described; **in·ex·press·i·bly** *adv.*

in ex·tre·mis (in·ik·STREE–, –STRAY–) *Latin.* at the point of death.

in·ex·tri·ca·ble (–EX·tri·cuh–, –ik·STRIC–) *adj.* that one cannot extricate oneself from; also, that cannot be disentangled: *~ difficulties; an ~ problem;* **in·ex·tri·ca·bly** *adv.*

inf. infantry; infinitive.

in·fal·li·ble (–FAL·uh–) *adj.* not capable of failing or being wrong: *an ~ authority, remedy, test, method;* **in·fal·li·bly** *adv.* **—in·fal·li·bil·i·ty** (–BIL–) *n.*

in·fa·mous (IN·fuh·mus) *adj.* having or giving a scandalous reputation: *an ~ crime, plot, traitor.* **—in·fa·my** (–fuh·mee) *n.* **-mies** a disgraceful or wicked act; also, disgrace or wickedness: *the ~ of Pearl Harbor.*

in·fan·cy (IN·fun–) *n.* **-cies** the state or period of being an infant; hence, any initial period: *in Caxton's days when printing was in its ~.* **—in·fant** (–funt) *n.* a baby; also, a legal minor: *no extra charge for ~s;* **adj.:** *the ~ Jesus; an ~ prodigy; ~ mortality* (i.e. death before age 1); *an ~* (i.e. young) *nation.* **—in·fan·ti·cide** (–FAN–) *n.* the killing of an infant; also, the killer. **—in·fan·tile** (IN·fun·tile, –til) *adj.* of or like an infant; having to do with infancy; **infantile paralysis** poliomyelitis. **—in·fan·ti·lism** (–FAN–) *n.* immature or undeveloped condition in an adult. **—in·fan·try** (–fun·tree) *n.* **-tries** (branch of an army consisting of) troops, or **in·fan·try·men** (*sing.* **-man**) trained and equipped to fight on foot.

in·farct (–FARCT) *n.* an area of tissue killed by the blockage of an artery leading to it by a clot or embolus; **in·farc·tion** *n.* death of tissue in an **in·farct·ed** area.

in·fat·u·ate (–FACH·oo–) *v.* **-ates, -at·ed, -at·ing** affect (a person) with a foolish, usu. short-lived passion; **in·fat·u·a·tion** (–AY–) *n.*

in·fect (–FECT) *v.* cause an unhealthy condition in; become diseased, as with a germ or virus; hence, to influence, as if in a bad way: *an open wound may become ~ed; She ~ed the whole class with her enthusiasm.* **—in·fec·tion** *n.* disease caused by a spreading virus or bacterium; also, the spreading: *airborne ~; a secondary ~ such as sinusitis resulting from a virus cold.* **—in·fec·tious** (–shus) *adj.: ~ hepatitis, mononucleosis; ~* (i.e. spreading) *laughter;* **in·fec·tious·ly** *adv.;* **in·fec·tious·ness** *n.* **—in·fec·tive** (–tive) *adj.* infectious. **—in·fec·tor** *n.*

in·fe·lic·i·tous (–fuh·LIS·i·tus) *adj.* not felicitous; inappropriate; **in·fe·lic·i·ty** *n.* **-ties.**

in·fer (–FUR) *v.* **-fers, -ferred, -fer·ring** conclude (from facts or evidence); also, loosely, imply; **in·fer·ence** (IN·fuh–) *n.* **—in·fer·en·tial** (–REN·shul) *adj.* relating to or deducible by inference: *an ~ judgment; ~ evidence.*

in·fe·ri·or (–FEER·ee·ur) *n.* & *adj.* (one) that is lower in position, merit, or quality. **—in·fe·ri·or·i·ty** (–OR–) *n.* a being inferior.

in·fer·nal (–FUR·nl) *adj.* hellish; also, damned: *an ~ scheme, region;* **in·fer·nal·ly** *adv.* **—in·fer·no** *n.* **-nos** a hell-like place or condition.

in·fest (–FEST) *v.* overrun in large numbers, as with pests or parasites: *hair ~ed with lice;* **in·fest·er** *n.* **—in·fes·ta·tion** (–TAY–) *n.*

in·fi·del (IN·fuh·dl) *n.* an unbeliever. **—in·fi·del·i·ty** (–DEL–) *n.* **-ties** (act of) disloyalty between spouses; unfaithfulness; also, lack of religious faith.

in·field *n.* an inner area such as is enclosed by a racetrack or bounded by the bases in a baseball field; also, the defensive players, or **in·field·ers,** who cover first, second, and third base and shortstop.

in·fight·ing *n.* fighting within a group, as between associates, or at close quarters, as in boxing or fencing; **in·fight·er** *n.*

in·fil·trate (–FIL–, IN·fil–) *v.* **-trates, -trat·ed, -trat·ing** pass gradually through or into; penetrate (a region or organization) secretly with hostile intent; **in·fil·tra·tor** *n.* **—in·fil·tra·tion** (–TRAY–) *n.*

in·fi·nite (IN·fuh·nit) *n.* & *adj.* (something) that is endlessly great or vast: *her ~ patience; God's ~ goodness; God* **the Infinite; in·fi·nite·ly** *adv.* **—in·fin·i·tes·i·mal** (–TES·uh·mul) *n.* & *adj.* (something) that is extremely minute; **in·fin·i·tes·i·mal·ly** *adv.* **—in·fin·i·tive** (–FIN·uh·tiv) *n.* a verb form that is not limited to any person, number, or tense, as "to go" in "I (or *we, they,* etc.) want (or *wanted*) to go." **—in·fin·i·tude** (–FIN–) *n.* infinite condition; also, something that is infinite in extent; **in·fin·i·ty** (–FIN–) *n.* **-ties** infinitude; also, an indefinite number: *10/3 equals 3.333* **to infinity.**

in·firm (–FURM) *adj.* not firm or strong; esp., weak because of age; **in·firm·ly** *adv.;* **in·firm·ness** *n.* **—in·fir·ma·ry** (–muh·ree) *n.* **-ries** a small hospital; also, a dispensary. **—in·fir·mi·ty** (–FUR–) *n.* **-ties** weakness; illness; flaw of character.

in·flame (–FLAME) *v.* **-flames, -flamed, -flam·ing 1** set on or catch fire; make or become excited: *words apt to ~ a mob to fury.* **2** make or become sore or swollen: *an ~d wound.* **—in·flam·ma·tion** (–MAY–) *n.* **—in·flam·ma·ble** (–FLAM·uh–) *adj.: an ~ temper; a highly ~ gas;* **in·flam·ma·bil·i·ty** (–BIL–)

---

inextinguishable
infeasible
infertile

n. **in·flam·ma·to·ry** (–muh·tor·ee) *adj.: an ~ speech; an ~ lung condition.*
in·flate (–FLATE) *v.* **-flates, -flat·ed, -flat·ing** expand, as with air, or increase abnormally: *to ~ a tire; an ego ~d with pride; prices ~ing at a 30% annual rate;* **in·flat·a·ble** (–FLAY–) *adj.: an ~ toy, vest, mattress.* **—in·fla·tion** (–FLAY–) *n.* rise of prices and fall in the buying power of money; **in·fla·tion·ar·y** *adj.: an ~ wage settlement; wages and prices rising in an ~ spiral; unemployment during an ~ recession;* **in·fla·tion·ism** *n.;* **in·fla·tion·ist** *n. & adj.*
in·flect (–FLECT) *v.* change or vary (tone or pitch of voice, form of a word to show number, gender, tense, etc.); **in·flec·tion** *n.: the rising ~ of an interrogative sentence; grammatical ~s of "go" such as "goes" and "gone"; "-ed," "-ing," "-est," and other ~s;* **in·flec·tion·al** *adj.: Latin and Greek are more ~ than English; Suffixes are either derivational or ~.* **—in·flex·i·ble** (–FLEX–) *adj.* rigid or unyielding in thought or will; **in·flex·i·bly** *adv.;* **in·flex·i·bil·i·ty** (–BIL–) *n.* **—in·flex·ion** (–shun) *n. Brit.* inflection.
in·flict (–FLICT) *v.* give or impose (suffering, punishment, or anything painful *on* or *upon* someone); **in·flic·tion** *n.;* **in·flic·tive** (–tiv) *adj.*
in-flight *adj.* during flight: *an ~ movie, refueling.*
in·flo·res·cence (–RES·nce) *n.* a growing flower cluster or its arrangement as a spike, panicle, etc.; also, a blossoming or flowering.
in·flow (–floh) *n.* a flowing in. **—in·flu·ence** (IN·floo–) *n.* indirect power or its effect; also, its agent or cause: *a man of much ~ though of no formal authority; accused of ~ peddling; the moon's ~ on tides; caught driving under the ~* (of liquor); *She's a good ~ on him;* ***v.*** **-enc·es, -enced, -enc·ing** have or use influence: *a jury ~d by news stories; Do stars ~ our fate?* **—in·flu·en·tial** (–EN·shul) *adj.* having or using much influence; **in·flu·en·tial·ly** *adv.* **—in·flu·en·za** (–EN·zuh) *n.* a contagious virus disease; flu; grippe. **—in·flux** *n.* inflow.
in·fo (–foh) *n. Informal.* information.
infold same as ENFOLD.
in·form (–FORM) *v.* give facts or news to (about a subject); tell: *a letter to ~ you of our decision; Do keep us ~ed of your progress; neighbors ~ing (up)on* (or *against*) *each other to the police;* **in·form·er** *n.*
in·for·mal (–FOR·mul) *adj.* not formal in style, esp. of speech or writing; colloquial; **in·for·mal·ly** *adv.* **—in·for·mal·i·ty** (–MAL–) *n.* **-ties** lack of formality or ceremony; also, an informal act.
in·for·mant (–FOR·munt) *n.* one who supplies information, usu. for scientific use, as in anthropology or linguistics. **—in·for·ma·tion** (–MAY–) *n.* facts, data, news, etc.; also, their communication: *an ~ officer; a mind full of ~ but with little wisdom; computerized ~ storage and retrieval;* **information science** the science of the storage, retrieval, and dissemination of information; **information theory** the science of the transmission and use of information by means of telephone, radar, and other communication devices; **in·for·ma·tion·al** (–MAY–) *adj.* **—in·for·ma·tive** (–FOR·muh·tiv) *adj.* instructive; **in·for·ma·tive·ly** *adv.* **—in·formed** *adj.* knowing the facts: *a well-~ journalist; Sterilization requires ~ consent.*
infra- *prefix.* beneath; under: as in *infrared, infrasonic.*
in·frac·tion (–FRAC–) *n.* infringement or violation: *a minor ~ of a rule.*
in·fra dig (IN·fruh–) beneath one's dignity.
in·fran·gi·ble (–FRAN–) *adj.* inviolable or unbreakable.
in·fra·red *n. & adj.* (beyond) the red end of the visible spectrum: *~ rays or "heat rays" are used in heat treatments* (DIATHERMY), *to detect heat from weather satellites, photograph without light, etc.* **—in·fra·son·ic** (–SON–) *adj.* below audible range; **in·fra·sound** *n.* low-frequency sound. **—in·fra·struc·ture** (–STRUC–) *n.* installations, facilities, or resources backing up an operation.
in·fre·quent (–FREE–) *adj.* not frequent; rare: *an ~ visitor;* **in·fre·quent·ly** *adv.* **—in·fre·quence** or **-quen·cy** *n.*
in·fringe (–FRINJ) *v.* **-fring·es, -fringed, -fring·ing** break or violate: *a publication ~ing a copyright; a structure that* **infringes (up)on** *a private right or territory;* **in·fringe·ment** *n.*
in·fu·ri·ate (–FYOOR·ee–) *v.* **-ates, -at·ed, -at·ing** make furious; enrage; **in·fu·ri·at·ing** *adj.;* **in·fu·ri·at·ing·ly** *adv.*
in·fuse (–FYOOZ) *v.* **-fus·es, -fused, -fus·ing** **1** pour (liquid) over; hence, steep or let soak, as tea, herbs, etc. **2** instill (a quality *into* people or minds); inspire (people or minds *with* a quality): *flagging spirits ~d with fresh courage.* **—in·fu·sion** (–FEW·zhun) *n.* **—in·fu·si·ble** *adj.* hard to fuse or melt.
-ing *suffix. n. & pres. part.* as in *loving, happening, painting.*
in·gath·er·ing (–GADH–) *n.* a gathering in; harvest.
in·gen·ious (–JEEN·yus) *adj.* inventive and skillful in thought or action: *an ~ device, theory, explanation; ~ at finding excuses;* **in·gen·i·ous·ly** *adv.;* **in·gen·i·ous·ness** or **in·ge·nu·i·ty** (–NEW–) *n.*
in·ge·nue (AN·juh·noo) *n.* an artless and innocent young woman as a dramatic character; also, one in such a role. **—in·gen·u·ous** (–JEN·yoo·us) *adj.* simple and artless; hence, frank or candid: *a child's ~ answer, smile, explanation;* **in·gen·u·ous·ly** *adv.;* **in·gen·u·ous·ness** *n.*
in·gest (–JEST) *v.* take into the body like food; absorb; **in·ges·tion** (–chun) *n.;* **in·ges·tive** (–tiv) *adj.*
in·gle *n.* a fire or fireplace. **—in·gle·nook** *n.* a fireplace.

in·glo·ri·ous (–GLOR–) *adj.* disgraceful; also, obscure; **in·glo·ri·ous·ly** *adv.*

in·got (ING·gut) *n.* metal cast into a bar or similar convenient shape.

ingraft same as ENGRAFT.

in·grain *n.* & *adj.* (IN–) (yarn, carpeting, etc.) dyed before manufacture. —***v.*** (–GRAIN) work into the grain or fiber: *habits ~ed in us from childhood; ~ed prejudices; an ~ed* (i.e. out-and-out) *liar.*

in·grate *n.* an ungrateful person. —**in·gra·ti·ate** (–GRAY·shee–) *v.* **-ates, -at·ed, -at·ing** try to bring (oneself) into favor (*with* someone); **in·gra·ti·at·ing** *adj.: an ~ smile;* **in·gra·ti·a·tion** (–AY–) *n.* —**in·grat·i·tude** (–GRAT–) *n.* ungratefulness.

in·gre·di·ent (–GREE–) *n.* something that goes into the making of a mixture, esp. a food or medicinal preparation: *the ~s of a cocktail; the essential ~s of chivalry.* —**in·gress** *n.* entrance.

in·grow·ing or **in·grown** *adj.* growing or grown in, esp. embedded in the flesh: *an ~ toenail.*

in·gui·nal (ING·gwuh·nl) *adj.* of or near the groin: *~ hernia.*

in·hab·it (–HAB–) *v.* live or dwell in; **in·hab·i·ta·ble** (–tuh·bl) *adj.;* **in·hab·it·ant** (–unt) *n.* one inhabiting a place: *America's original ~s; a city of two million ~s.*

in·hal·ant (–HAY·lunt) *n.* & *adj.* (medicine or drug) that is inhaled. —**in·ha·la·tor** (IN·huh·lay·tur) *n.* an apparatus for administering medicinal vapors or oxygen in first aid. —**in·hale** (–HALE) *v.* **-hales, -haled, -hal·ing** breathe in (air, vapor, smoke, etc.); **in·ha·la·tion** (–LAY–) *n.;* **in·hal·er** (–HAY–) *n.* one who inhales; also, an inhaling device or inhalator.

in·here (–HEER) *v.* **-heres, -hered, -her·ing** belong or be inherent. —**in·her·ent** (–HEER·unt, –HAIR–) *adj.* existing in as an inborn or inseparable quality: *the ~ goodness of human nature; basic rights ~ in citizenship;* **in·her·ent·ly** *adv.*

in·her·it (–HER–) *v.* receive as a bequest in a will, as a hereditary trait, or as something passed along: *a chair she ~ed from her predecessor;* **in·her·it·a·ble** *adj.;* **in·her·it·ance** (–unce) *n.;* **in·her·i·tor** *n.*

in·hib·it (–HIB–) *v.* forbid (a person from doing something); hinder (an action or process). **in·hib·i·tor** *n.* —**in·hi·bi·tion** (–BISH·un) *n.* a check, esp. a mental blocking of one's own thinking or behavior.

in-house *adj.* & *adv.* inside a group or institution: *artwork done ~ rather than farmed out.*

in·hu·man (–HEW·mun) *adj.* not human: *Cannibalism is cruel and ~; ~ poverty and misery; His stamina seems ~;* **in·hu·man·ly** *adv.* —**in·hu·man·i·ty** (–MAN–) *n.* **-ties** cruelty.

in·hume (–HUME) *v.* **-humes, -humed, -hum·ing** bury; inter; **in·hu·ma·tion** (–MAY–) *n.*

in·im·i·cal (–IM–) *adj.* hostile; also, harmful; **in·im·i·cal·ly** *adv.*

in·im·i·ta·ble (–IM·it·uh–) *adj.* that cannot be imitated; matchless; **in·im·i·ta·bly** *adv.*

in·iq·ui·ty (–IK·wuh–) *n.* **-ties** wickedness; also, a wicked act; **in·iq·ui·tous** (–tus) *adj.* wicked; **in·iq·ui·tous·ly** *adv.*

in·i·tial (i·NISH·ul) *n.* & *adj.* first (letter of a name): *My ~ reaction was to refuse; John Smith's ~s* (i.e. J.S.); ***v.*** **-tials, -tial(l)ed, -tial(l)ing** mark with initials; **in·i·tial·ly** *adv.* at first. —**in·i·ti·ate** (i·NISH·ee–) *v.* **-ates, -at·ed, -at·ing** **1** begin; get going: *~ a project, plan, talks.* **2** admit (person *into* a special group or to a field of knowledge or activity): *a day for ~ing new members; ~ed into the cult of Apollo;* **in·i·ti·a·tor** *n.* —**in·i·ti·a·to·ry** (–uh·tor·ee) *adj.* —**in·i·ti·a·tion** (–AY–) *n.* —**in·i·ti·a·tive** (–NISH·ee·uh·tiv) *n.* the action of taking a first step; also, the ability required for this; hence, enterprise: *a man of great ~; The stronger nation should take the ~ for peace talks; Voters may propose a law through an ~* (i.e. a process of petitioning the lawmaking body).

in·ject (–JECT) *v.* introduce or force into, as serum into the bloodstream or fuel into the cylinders of an internal-combustion engine: *funds to ~ new life into an ailing business;* **in·jec·tion** *n.;* **in·jec·tor** *n.*

in·junc·tion (–JUNK–) *n.* an order, esp. one issued by a court prohibiting a proposed action or to stop something such as a labor strike.

in·jure (IN·jur) *v.* **-jures, -jured, -jur·ing** hurt or do harm or damage: *the dead and ~d in battle; a put-on look of* **injured** *innocence;* **in·jur·y** *n.* **-jur·ies:** *forgiveness of ~s; ~s suffered in an accident.* —**in·ju·ri·ous** (–JOOR·ee·us) *adj.* harmful; also, offensive: *bad publicity ~ to a business.*

in·jus·tice (–JUS·tis) *n.* an unjust act; also, lack of justice.

ink (INGK) *n.* & *v.* (cover, mark, or stain with) a colored liquid for writing, printing, or drawing. —**ink·blot** *n.* a blot of ink; also, one of a set of irregular, inkblotlike figures used in a psychological test called "Rorschach test" or **inkblot test.** —**ink·horn** *n.* a container of horn formerly used to hold ink. —**ink·ling** *n.* a hint or vague notion. —**ink·stand** *n.* a stand to hold pens, having also an **ink·well** *n.* a small pot of ink. —**ink·y** *adj.* **ink·i·er, -i·est** dark or black like ink; also, stained with ink; **ink·i·ness** *n.*

in·laid (IN–, –LAID) *adj.* (decorated with a design, material, etc.) set in the surface as an inlay: *an ~ table top.*

in·land (IN·lund) *adj.* **1** situated in or toward the interior of a country: *an ~ town; ~ water-*

inharmonious
inhospitable
inhumane
injudicious

ways such as canals, rivers, and lakes. **2** domestic; internal: *sources of ~ revenue such as income, excise, estate, and gift taxes.* **—adv.:** *to travel ~ by boat.* **—n.** an inland area; interior.

in-law *n. Informal.* a relative by marriage.

in·lay *v.* **-lays, -laid, -lay·ing** set in or insert (a piece of wood or metal, pattern, or illustration) into a surface; also, decorate thus. **—n.** something inlaid, as a mosaic, bone graft, or dental filling.

in·let *n.* a narrow strip of water extending or running from a sea, lake, or river, into the land, as a small bay or creek; hence, way of entry.

in·mate *n.* a person living with others, esp. one confined in a prison or institution.

in me·di·as res (–MAY·dee·ahs·RACE) *Latin.* in(to) the midst of it, esp. of a dramatic action.

in me·mo·ri·am (–muh·MOR·ee·um) *Latin.* in memory (of).

in·most *adj.* most inward; secret: *one's ~ thoughts.*

inn *n.* a hotel; also, in names, a restaurant or tavern.

in·nards (IN·urdz) *n.pl. Informal.* internal organs, parts, or workings.

in·nate (IN–, –NATE) *adj.* existing from birth or by nature in a person or thing; inborn: *an ~ vigor or strength, defect, instinct;* **in·nate·ly** *adv.*

in·ner *adj.* situated farther in, esp. deep inside: *an ~ organ of the body; the earth's ~ core; ~* (i.e. mental or spiritual) *peace; an influential* **inner circle** *of friends; the overcrowded, poverty-stricken, and crime-ridden* **inner city** *being abandoned in favor of the suburbs; a nonconformist* **in·ner-di·rect·ed** *personality; one's* **in·ner·most** *thoughts and desires.* **—Inner Hebrides** See HEBRIDES. **—in·ner·sole** *n.* insole. **—in·ner·spring mattress** one with a padded casing and coil springs inside. **—inner tube** the inflatable rubber tube inside some makes of tires.

in·ner·vate (i·NUR–, IN·ur–) *v.* **-vates, -vat·ed, -vat·ing** supply (an organ or muscle) with nerves; **in·ner·va·tion** (–VAY–) *n.*

in·ning *n.* in baseball, a play period in which both teams have a turn at bat; also, such a turn. **—innings** *pl.* **1** an inning in cricket. **2** opportunity for action.

inn·keep·er *n.* the owner or manager of a hotel.

in·no·cence (IN·uh·sunce) *n.* the quality or state of being innocent. **—in·no·cent** *adj.* **1** doing or having done no harm or wrong; hence, without sin or guilt; not deserving punishment (for an offense): *declared ~ of the charge of theft; an ~* (i.e. harmless) *pastime.* **2** without guile; hence, naive or simple: *an ~ infant; too ~ to be suspicious of anyone.* **—n.** a child or a simple-minded adult. **—in·no·cent·ly** *adv.*

—in·noc·u·ous (–NOK·yoo·us) *adj.* harmless; inoffensive; hence, unexciting: *an ~ drug, speech;* **in·noc·u·ous·ly** *adv.;* **in·noc·u·ous·ness** *n.*

in·nom·i·nate (–NOM·uh·nit) **bone** hipbone.

in·no·vate (IN·uh–) *v.* **-vates, -vat·ed, -vat·ing** make changes; also, bring in (something new) as a change; **in·no·va·tive** (–tiv) *adj.;* **in·no·va·tor** *n.* **—in·no·va·tion** (–VAY–) *n.* introduction of changes; also, a new method, device, or other change.

in·nu·en·do (–new·EN·doh) *n.* **-does** an indirect derogatory remark or reflection; insinuation.

in·nu·mer·a·ble (–NEW·muh·ruh–) *adj.* too numerous to be counted.

in·oc·u·late (i·NOC·yoo–) *v.* **-lates, -lat·ed, -lat·ing** introduce a serum or vaccine into the body, usu. by injection, to give immunity against infectious diseases such as smallpox and measles; **in·oc·u·la·tion** (–LAY–) *n.*

in·op·er·a·tive (–OP·uh·ruh·tiv) *adj.* not working; without effect.

in·or·di·nate (–OR·dn·it) *adj.* disorderly; immoderate; **in·or·di·nate·ly** *adv.*

in·or·gan·ic (–GAN–) *adj.* not organic or of vegetable or animal origin; mineral.

in·pa·tient (–pay·shunt) *n.* a patient who lives in the hospital while receiving treatment.

in·put *n.* & *v.* **-puts,** *pt.* & *pp.* **-put·ted** or **-put, -put·ting** (what is) put into (a machine or system) as raw materials for manufacturing, data for processing, etc.

in·quest *n.* a coroner's inquiry to find out the cause of a suspicious death; also, the jury holding it or their finding.

in·qui·e·tude (–KWYE·uh–) *n.* uneasiness of mind or body.

in·quire (–KWIRE) *v.* **-quires, -quired, -quir·ing** ask (*about* or *into* a subject); **in·quir·er** *n.;* **in·quir·ing** *adj.* curious and alert: *She has a very ~ mind;* **in·quir·ing·ly** *adv.* **—in·quir·y** (–kwuh·ree, –KWIRE–) *n.* **-quir·ies** a request for information; also, a formal investigation. **—in·qui·si·tion** (–ZISH·un) *n.* an intensive or ruthless questioning in the style of the **Inquisition,** a former Roman Catholic Church tribunal for the suppression of heresy; **in·quis·i·tor** (–KWIZ–) *n.;* **in·quis·i·to·ri·al** (–TOR–) *adj.* **—in·quis·i·tive** (–KWIZ·i·tiv) *adj.* questioning or curious in a prying manner; **in·quis·i·tive·ly** *adv.;* **in·quis·i·tive·ness** *n.*

in re (–RAY, –REE) *Latin.* in the matter of.

in-res·i·dence (–REZ–) *adj.* of an artist or professional, having duties as a teacher, consultant, etc.

I.N.R.I. "Jesus of Nazareth, King of the Jews."

in·road *n.* invasion; also, encroachment: *to make ~s on one's time, health, savings.*

---

inoffensive
inoperable
inopportune

in•rush *n.* a rushing in; influx; **in•rush•ing** *n.* & *adj.*
ins. inches; insurance.
in•sa•lu•bri•ous (–LOO·bree·us) *adj.* not healthful.
in•sane *adj.* (of or for the) mentally ill; also, very foolish; **in•sane•ly** *adv.* —**in•san•i•ty** (–SAN–) *n.: judged not guilty by reason of ~.*
in•sa•ti•a•ble (–SAY·shuh–) *adj.* that cannot be satisfied: *an ~ appetite, greed;* **in•sa•ti•ate** (–it) *adj.* that is never satisfied; **in•sa•ti•a•bly** *adv.;* **in•sa•ti•ate•ly** *adv.*
in•scribe *v.* **-scribes, -scribed, -scrib•ing** write in or engrave in a lasting manner: *a tombstone ~d with one's name; works indelibly ~d in her memory; to ~ a book* (i.e. autograph or dedicate it). —**in•scrip•tion** (–SCRIP–) *n.*
in•scru•ta•ble (–SCROO·tuh–) *adj.* too mysterious to be understood by human scrutiny; **in•scru•ta•bly** *adv.;* **in•scru•ta•bil•i•ty** (–BIL–) *n.*
in•seam (–seem) *n.* the inner seam of a trouser leg, shoe, etc.
in•sect *n.* a small, six-legged arthropod such as a fly, mosquito, or beetle, that has a body divided into head, thorax, and abdomen; also, a spider, centipede, tick, or such wingless or crawling creature. —**in•sect•i•cide** (–SEC–) *n.* an insect-killing substance; **in•sect•i•cid•al** (–SYE–) adj. —**in•sec•ti•vore** *n.* an insectivorous plant or animal; **in•sec•tiv•o•rous** (–TIV·uh·rus) *adj.* insect-eating.
in•se•cure (–si·CURE) *adj.* not secure or feeling safe; involving fear or anxiety: *an ~ child, job, lock;* **in•se•cure•ly** *adv.* —**in•se•cu•ri•ty** (–KYOOR–) *n.* **-ties.**
in•sem•i•nate (–SEM–) *v.* **-nates, -nat•ed, -nat•ing** put semen into; also, spread as if by sowing seeds; implant (ideas in a group, in minds, etc.); **in•sem•i•na•tor** *n.;* **in•sem•i•na•tion** (–NAY–) *n.: artificial ~ by husband or donor.*
in•sen•sate (–SEN–) *adj.* without sensation; also, stupid or unfeeling. —**in•sen•si•ble** (–SEN–) *adj.* **1** not sensitive. **2** unconscious or numb: *lay there ~ and bleeding.* **3** not easy to sense or perceive: *It grew cold by ~ degrees.* —**in•sen•si•bly** *adv.* —**in•sen•si•bil•i•ty** (–BIL–) *n.* —**in•sen•ti•ent** (–SEN–) *adj.* not sentient; lacking life or feeling; **in•sen•tience** *n.*
in•sep•a•ra•ble (–SEP·uh·ruh–) *n.pl.* & *adj.* (persons or things) that cannot be parted or separated; **in•sep•a•ra•bly** *adv.* —**in•sep•a•ra•bil•i•ty** (–BIL–) *n.*
in•sert *v.* (–SURT) put something into (a place designed for it, as a key into a lock). —***n.*** (IN–) something inserted: *an 8-page advertising ~ in a newspaper.* —**in•ser•tion** *n.: ornamental lace ~s in cloth.*
in•set *v.* (–SET) **-sets, -set, -set•ting** set in: *a picture ~ with the text;* ***n.*** (IN–) something inset or inserted.
in•shore *adj.* & *adv.* close to the shore: *driven ~ by currents; ~ winds, fishing.*
in•side *n.* an inner side, position, part, etc.: *the ~ of a room; the insides* (*Informal.* internal organs) *of the body;* ***adj.:*** *an ~ page; ~ information, talk;* **inside track** advantageous position, as in a race; ***prep.:*** *will be here* **inside of** (i.e. within) *an hour; ~ the house;* ***adv.:*** *stays ~ all morning; an umbrella turned* **inside out** *by the wind.* —**in•sid•er** (–SYE·dur) *n.* one who belongs to a group or place, and is often specially privileged.
in•sid•i•ous (–SID·ee·us) *adj.* treacherous; working secretly: *an ~ plot, disease;* **in•sid•i•ous•ly** *adv.;* **in•sid•i•ous•ness** *n.*
in•sight *n.* power to see into and understand a situation; **in•sight•ful** *adj.*
in•sig•ni•a (–SIG·nee·uh) *n.* **-ni•a(s)** a distinguishing mark of position or rank, as on a military uniform; emblem; also **in•sig•ne** (–SIG·nee), *pl.* **-ni•a.**
in•sin•cere (–SEER) *adj.* not sincere; **in•sin•cer•i•ty** (–SER–) *n.* **-ties.**
in•sin•u•ate (–SIN·yoo–) *v.* **-ates, -at•ed, -at•ing** hint or imply something dishonorable about a person in a cowardly way; also, introduce (oneself) into a place artfully or slyly; **in•sin•u•a•tor** *n.* —**in•sin•u•a•tion** (–AY–) *n.*
in•sip•id (–SIP–) *adj.* without flavor; dull; tasteless; **in•sip•id•ly** *adv.;* **in•si•pid•i•ty** (–PID–) *n.* **-ties.**
in•sist (–SIST) *v.* be firm about a request, statement, or demand: *He ~ed on accompanying her; She ~ed and he agreed;* **in•sist•ing•ly** *adv.* —**in•sist•ence** *n.;* **in•sist•ent** *adj.;* **in•sist•ent•ly** *adv.*
in si•tu (–SYE·too) *Latin.* in its original place or position.
in•so•far (–FAR) *adv.* to such a degree or extent *(as).*
insol. insoluble.
in•so•la•tion (–LAY–) *n.* solar radiation; also, exposure to sun's rays.
in•sole *n.* an inside sole of a shoe.
in•so•lent (–suh–) *adj.* openly defiant or insulting; **in•so•lent•ly** *adv.;* **in•so•lence** *n.*
in•sol•u•ble (–SOL·yoo–) *n.* & *adj.* (something) that cannot be dissolved; also, insolvable; **in•sol•u•bly** *adv.;* **in•sol•u•bil•i•ty** (–BIL–) *n.* —**in•sol•va•ble** (–SOL·vuh–) *adj.* not solvable; **in•sol•vent** *n.* & *adj.* (one) unable to pay one's debts: *an ~ debtor, estate, inheritance;* **in•sol•ven•cy** *n.*
in•som•ni•a (–SOM·nee·uh) *n.* sleeplessness; **in•som•ni•ac** *n.* & *adj.*

---

insanitary
insensitive
insignificance
insignificant
insolvable

in·so·much (–MUCH) *adv.* to such a degree (*as* or *that*).

in·sou·ci·ant (–SOO·see·unt) *adj.* carefree or unconcerned: *an ~ manner, person;* **in·sou·ci·ance** *n.*

insp. inspector. —**in·spect** (–SPECT) *v.* examine carefully or critically; **in·spec·tion** *n.;* **in·spec·tor** *n.*

in·spire (–SPIRE) *v.* **-spires, -spired, -spir·ing** breathe in; hence, be the cause of life, vigor, new thought or feeling, or anything infused *in(to)* a person: *words to ~ followers with confidence; Her warning ~d fear and respect in their hearts; rumors ~d by malice; the ~d word of God;* **in·spir·er** *n.* —**in·spir·ing** *adj.* that inspires: *a very ~ speech;* **in·spir·ing·ly** *adv.* —**in·spi·ra·tion** (–RAY–) *n.: The chest expands during ~; started composing on a sudden ~; lifelong companions who were a source of mutual ~; the ~ of Scripture;* **in·spi·ra·tion·al** *adj.: ~ literature; an ~ speaker.* —**in·spir·it** (–SPEER–) *v.* put spirit into; hearten.

inst. instant; institute; institution.

in·sta·bil·i·ty (–BIL–) *n.* lack of stability, firmness, or determination.

in·stal(l) (–STAWL) *v.* **-stal(l)s, -stalled, -stall·ing** put or establish (a person, thing, or oneself) in a place or position: *a ceremony to ~ a new president; She ~s herself in front of the TV at 6 p.m. daily; fixtures ~d by a plumber;* **in·stall·er** *n.;* **in·stal·la·tion** (–LAY–) *n.* —**in·stal(l)·ment** *n.* any of several parts (as of a large amount, long story or article, etc.) due at regular intervals: *a freezer purchased on an* **installment plan.**

in·stance (–stunce) *n.* **1** occasion or event; also, a person or thing considered as a case or example: *could cite many ~s of his misconduct; He wasn't invited* **in the first instance,** *then he stayed too long; Children at half fare, Tony* **for instance.** **2** request or urging: *She was invited at my ~.* —***v.*** **-stanc·es, -stanced, -stanc·ing** illustrate or cite: *a weakness of character ~d by his conduct.* —**in·stant** (–stunt) *n.* & *adj.* (of or in) a moment, esp. the present: *Come here this ~! TV with an ~-on button; an* **instant replay** *of the videotape of a striking segment of a live telecast; an ~-start fluorescent tube; ~ coffee* (ready in an instant); *your letter of the 14th ~* (i.e. present month); **in·stant·ly** *adv.* —**in·stan·ta·ne·ous** (–TAY·nee·us) *adj.* coming or happening in an instant: *~ death by electrocution, ~ reaction;* **in·stan·ta·ne·ous·ly** *adv.* —**in·stan·ter** (–STAN–) *adv.* at once; instantly; **in·stan·ti·ate** (–STAN·shee–) *v.* **-ates, -at·ed, -at·ing** represent by an instance; **in·stan·ti·a·tion** (–AY–) *n.*

in·state (–STATE) *v.* **-states, -stat·ed, -stat·ing** install (a person in office).

in·stead (–STED) *adv.* in place (of): *I'll have tea ~ (of coffee).*

in·step *n.* the upper surface of the arch of the foot: *an ~ kick in soccer.*

in·sti·gate (IN·sti–) *v.* **-gates, -gat·ed, -gat·ing** incite or provoke (a person) to something considered bad: *~ a rebellion, quarrel, assassination; ~ workers to strike;* **in·sti·ga·tor** *n.;* **in·sti·ga·tion** (–GAY–) *n.*

in·stil(l) *v.* **-stil(l)s, -stilled, -still·ing** impart gradually; put in (as if) drop by drop, over a period: *good manners ~ed in(to) youth; to ~ knowledge, principles, love of work;* **in·stil(l)·ment** *n.*

in·stinct *n.* an unlearned, inborn tendency to behave in a certain way: *the mating ~; the ~ for self-preservation; an ~* (i.e. knack or gift) *for the right word;* ***adj.*** **instinct with** filled or charged with (life, beauty, pity, force. etc.); **in·stinc·tive** (–STINC·tiv) *adj.* not thought out; spontaneous; **in·stinc·tive·ly** *adv.* —**in·stinc·tu·al** (–choo·ul) *adj.* relating to instincts.

in·sti·tute (IN·stuh–) *v.* **-tutes, -tut·ed, -tut·ing** establish or initiate, as a legal action, an inquiry, etc. —***n.*** **1** something established, as legal principles. **2** an organization for art, science, or education, esp. an advanced or specialized school, as one in technical subjects; also, a short teaching program: *a summer ~.* —**in·sti·tut·er** or **-tu·tor** *n.* —**in·sti·tu·tion** (–TUE–) *n.* **1** an organization for educational, religious, or social work; also, a building used by one: *a charitable ~.* **2** an establishing or thing established, as a law or custom: *slavery abolished as an ~; She's quite an ~ around here.* —**in·sti·tu·tion·al** *adj.: Apartheid is ~ racism; ~ care for the infirm; ~ advertising for sales promotion;* **in·sti·tu·tion·al·ize** *v.* **-iz·es, -ized, -iz·ing** make institutional or make into or put in an institution; **in·sti·tu·tion·al·i·za·tion** (–ZAY–) *n.* —**in·sti·tu·tion·al·ly** *adv.*

instr. instructor; instrument. —**in·struct** (–STRUCT) *v.* impart information to with explicit details: *teachers ~ing pupils in a subject; A client ~s his solicitor; A judge ~s a jury;* **in·struc·tion** *n.;* **instructions** *pl.* directions; orders; **in·struc·tion·al** *adj.;* **in·struc·tive** (–tiv) *adj.* serving to teach; **in·struc·tor** *n.;* **in·struc·tor·ship** *n.* —**in·stru·ment** (IN·struh–) *n.* a person or thing used as a means, esp. an implement for delicate scientific or artistic use: *a stringed musical ~; navigational ~s such as a compass and sextant; A deed of conveyance is a legal ~; refused to be used as an ~ of subversion; Only ~s are used in* **instrument flying** *and landing, as in fog.* —***v.*** (–ment) equip with instruments: *a system fully ~ed for safety; an ~ed landing on Mars.* —**in·stru·men·tal** (–MEN·tl) *adj.* serving as a means; also, having to do with instruments: *an editor ~ in the publication of many books; ~ music;* **in·stru·men·tal·ist** *n.;* **in·stru·men·tal·i·ty** (–TAL–) *n.* **-ties** a serving as a means; agency. —**in·stru·men·ta·tion** (–TAY–) *n.* use of instruments; also, arrangement or composition of music for instruments.

in·sub·or·di·nate (–BOR·dn·it) *adj.* not submitting to authority; disobedient; **in·sub·or·di·na·tion** (–NAY–) *n.*

in·sub·stan·tial (–STAN–) *adj.* flimsy, as a cobweb; also, imaginary, as dreams.

in·suf·fer·a·ble (–SUF·uh·ruh–) *adj.* unbearable: *an ~ bore; ~ insolence;* **in·suf·fer·a·bly** *adv.*

in·su·lar (IN·suh·lur) *adj.* of or like an island in being isolated from the surroundings; also, as an islander is supposed to be, i.e. narrow-minded; **in·su·lar·i·ty** (–LAIR–) *n.* —**in·su·late** (IN·suh–) *v.* **-lates, -lat·ed, -lat·ing** isolate or separate (a conductor or source of energy such as heat, sound, or electricity) with a nonconducting material so as to keep from losing or transferring energy; **in·su·la·tor** *n.;* **in·su·la·tion** (–LAY–) *n.: Clothing gives* (or *is*) *~ against heat and cold.* —**in·su·lin** *n.* a sugar-regulating hormone produced in a part of the pancreas called "the islands of Langerhans": *Too much ~ reduces blood sugar causing* **insulin shock.**

in·sult *n.* (IN–) & *v.* (–SULT) (do or say) something that humiliates another by being insolent, rude, or contemptuous; **in·sult·ing** *adj.: a very ~ remark;* **in·sult·ing·ly** (–SUL–) *adv.*

in·su·per·a·ble (–SOO–) *adj.* that cannot be overcome or passed over, as barriers, difficulties, etc.; **in·su·per·a·bly** *adv.*

in·sup·port·a·ble (–POR–) *adj.* not supportable, i.e. that cannot be put up with or justified.

in·sur·a·ble (–SHOOR–) *adj.* capable of being or fit to be insured. —**in·sur·ance** (–SHOOR·unce) *n.* **1** an undertaking to compensate or protect against specified losses in return for a fee; also, such a fee or premium. **2** action, process, means, or business of insuring; also, the state of being insured. —**in·sure** (–SHOOR) *v.* **-sures, -sured, -sur·ing** **1** give, take, or get insurance on (property, person, life, etc.) for an **in·sured,** i.e. an insured person, as an **in·sur·er,** i.e. an insuring company, does. **2** same as ENSURE.

in·sur·gen·cy (–SUR–) *n.* **-cies** a minor revolt. —**in·sur·gent** *n.* & *adj.* (a rebel or one) rising up or acting against an established government; **in·sur·gence** *n.*

in·sur·mount·a·ble (–MOWN–) *adj.* that cannot be surmounted; insuperable; **in·sur·mount·a·bly** *adv.*

in·sur·rec·tion (–REC–) *n.* an uprising or outbreak against established authority; **in·sur·rec·tion·ist** *n.*

int. interest; interior; internal; international.

in·tact (–TACT) *adj.* untouched or whole (after something that might have impaired or damaged it).

in·tagl·io (–TAL·yoh) *n.* **-ios** a design engraved into a hard surface, as seen on gems and used as a printing method.

in·take *n.* **1** an opening where a fluid enters a container: *the* **intake manifold** *of a carburetor connecting it with the engine cylinders.* **2** a taking in, esp. of a fluid through a narrow opening; also, the amount of liquid or gas taken in.

in·tan·gi·ble (–TAN–) *n.* & *adj.* (something) that cannot be touched, felt, or grasped by the mind: *Goodwill is an ~ business asset; the ~ charisma of leadership; stocks, bonds, patents, and such ~s;* **in·tan·gi·bly** *adv.*

in·te·ger (IN·tij–) *n.* something that is whole, not a fraction, as a number or zero. —**in·te·gral** (–grul) *adj.* **1** essential as part of a whole; also, formed of such parts: *Limbs are ~ parts of our bodies; an ~ design.* **2** whole; unified; unbroken: *an ~ personality, structure;* **n.** a whole (number); **integral calculus** the mathematics of integrals of functions, as the speed of a projectile based on rate of change. —**in·te·grate** (IN·tuh–) *v.* **-grates, -grat·ed, -grat·ing** make (into) or become whole; bring parts together into one, as different racial groups in society: *an ~d school system; transistors, resistors, and capacitors in one* **integrated circuit** *instead of being wired together;* **in·te·gra·tion** (–GRAY–) *n.;* **in·te·gra·tive** (IN·tuh·gray·tiv) *adj.* —**in·teg·ri·ty** (–TEG–) *n.* trustworthy moral character; also, soundness or completeness of anything; entirety: *a man of ~; a dramatization that lacks ~; a treaty guaranteeing territorial ~; a manuscript preserved in its ~.*

in·teg·u·ment (–TEG·yuh–) *n.* an organism's natural outer covering such as a skin, shell, or husk.

in·tel·lect (IN·tl–) *n.* mind or intelligence: *one of the greatest ~s of our time.* —**in·tel·lec·tu·al** (–LEC·choo·ul) *adj.* having to do with or interested in things of the mind rather than of the emotions: *Chess is an ~ game; reasoning, judgment, and such ~ processes; a woman of ~ tastes;* **n.:** *Academics are ~s;* **in·tel·lec·tu·al·ly** *adv.;* **in·tel·lec·tu·al·ism** *n.;* **in·tel·lec·tu·al·ize** *v.* **-iz·es, -ized, -iz·ing** make intellectual or treat intellectually, esp. without considering emotional aspects; also, philosophize. —**in·tel·li·gence** (–TEL–) *n.* **1** ability to learn, understand, remember, and respond to situations requiring use of the mind: *an ~ test; A person's mental age divided by chronological age and multiplied by 100 gives the* **intelligence quotient.** **2** news or information of a vital nature: *The Central Intelligence Agency;* **in·tel·li·gent** *adj.: an ~ dog; an ~ but ill-advised remark;* **in·tel·li·gent·ly** *adv.* —**in·tel·li·gent·si·a** (–JENT·see·uh) *n. sing.* or *pl.* the intellectual class (of a society). —**in·tel·li·gi·ble** (–TEL–) *adj.* that

---

insufficient
insuppressible
insusceptible

can be understood by the mind: *an ~ but not reasonable explanation;* **in·tel·li·gi·bly** *adv.;* **in·tel·li·gi·bil·i·ty** (–BIL–) *n.*

in·tem·per·ate (–TEM·puh·rit) *adj.* not moderate or showing self-control: *an ~ outburst; a man of ~ habits* (esp. in regard to drinking); **in·tem·per·ance** *n.;* **in·tem·per·ate·ness** *n.*

in·tend (–TEND) *v.* have as an aim or purpose; hence, to mean: *I ~ to go home after work; an offense that was not ~ed; a gift ~ed for the bride;* **in·tend·ant** (–unt) *n.* a government official supervising a district in South American countries; **in·tend·ed** *n.* & *adj.* prospective (husband or wife): *a note from your ~.* —**in·tense** (–TENCE) *adj.* of high degree; sharply focused; very keen: *~ light, heat, pain, happiness; an ~ personality* (i.e. strong in head and heart); **in·tense·ly** *adv.;* **in·ten·si·ty** *n.* **-ties; in·ten·si·fy** *v.* **-fies, -fied, -fy·ing** make or become (more) intense; strengthen; **in·ten·si·fi·ca·tion** (–CAY–) *n.;* **in·ten·sive** (–TEN·siv) *adj.: an ~ study;* **intensive farming** *to produce several crops each year with heavy use of labor, fertilizer, etc.; a hospital's well-equipped* **intensive care unit** *for critically ill patients; an ~ pronoun such as "herself";* ***n.*** an intensive word such as *very, bloody,* or *goddamn;* also **in·ten·si·fi·er; in·ten·sive·ly** *adv.;* **in·ten·sive·ness** *n.* —**in·tent** (–TENT) *n.* what is deliberately intended or meant: *with malicious ~; assault with ~ to kill;* **to all intents and purposes** in every way; practically; ***adj.*** attentive or earnest: *an ~ look; a student* **intent on** *passing her exams;* **in·tent·ly** *adv.;* **in·tent·ness** *n.* —**in·ten·tion** (–TEN–) *n.* what is intended; plan or aim; also, meaning or significance: *What are his ~s in regard to* (i.e. marrying) *her?* **in·ten·tion·al** *adj.* with an intended aim or purpose; deliberate: *an ~ snub;* **in·ten·tion·al·ly** *adv.*

in·ter (–TUR) *v.* **-ters, -terred, -ter·ring** bury (a corpse).

inter- *comb.form.* between or among; each other: as in *interact, interface.* —**in·ter·act** (–ACT) *v.* act on or influence each other; **in·ter·ac·tion** *n.;* **in·ter·ac·tive** *adj.* —**in·ter a·li·a** (IN·tur·ay·lee·uh) *Latin.* among other things. —**in·ter·a·tom·ic** (–TOM–) *adj.* between atoms. —**in·ter·breed** *v.* **-breeds, -bred, -breed·ing** same as HYBRIDIZE. —**in·ter·ca·lar·y** (–TUR·kuh·ler·ee) *adj.* intercalated, as February 29; **in·ter·ca·late** *v.* **-lates, -lat·ed, -lat·ing** insert between or among; interpolate; **in·ter·ca·la·tion** (–LAY–) *n.*

in·ter·cede (–SEED) *v.* **-cedes, -ced·ed, -ced·ing** plead (*with* someone in authority *for* a favor); also, mediate. —**in·ter·cept** (–SEPT) *v.* **1** cut off, stop, or seize (a flowing or moving person or thing before reaching target or destination): *~ a letter, an enemy bomber using an* **in·ter·cep·tor** *plane or missile; to ~ a fleeing convict, a forward pass in football, a flow of oil;* **in·ter·cep·tion** *n.* **2** *Math.* cut off a part of (a line, arc, solid, etc.); ***n.*** an intercepted part (of a line, etc.). —**in·ter·ces·sion** (–SESH·un) *n.* an interceding, as by prayer or mediation by an **in·ter·ces·sor** *n.;* **in·ter·ces·so·ry** *adj.* —**in·ter·change** *v.* (–CHANGE) exchange; also, cause (two things) to change places or to happen by turns; ***n.*** (IN–) an interchanging; esp., a junction in the shape of a *cloverleaf, diamond,* etc. designed for unchecked flow of traffic between a highway or freeway and a secondary road or another freeway; **in·ter·change·a·ble** *adj.* —**in·ter·col·le·gi·ate** (–cuh·LEE·jit, –jee·it) *adj.* between or among colleges or universities. —**in·ter·com** *n.* short for **in·ter·com·mu·ni·ca·tion system,** a radio or telephone setup of amplifiers and loudspeakers for communicating between different parts of an office, factory, apartment building, etc.; **in·ter·com·mu·ni·cate** (–MEW–) *v.* **-cates, -cat·ed, -cat·ing** communicate with each other. —**in·ter·con·nect** (–NECT) *v.* connect with one another; **in·ter·con·nec·tion** *n.* —**in·ter·con·ti·nen·tal** (–NEN·tl) *adj.* between or across continents: *an ~ railroad, ballistic missile, migration.* —**in·ter·cos·tal** (–COS·tl) *n.* & *adj.* (a part) situated between the ribs: *an ~ muscle.* —**in·ter·course** *n.* dealings between people; also, sexual union or coitus: *social ~; ~ with the Deity.* —**in·ter·de·nom·i·na·tion·al** (–NAY–) *adj.* between religious denominations. —**in·ter·de·part·men·tal** (–MEN·tl) *adj.* between different departments. —**in·ter·de·pend·ent** (–PEN–) *adj.* dependent upon one another; **in·ter·de·pend·ence** *n.* —**in·ter·dict** (–DICT) *v.* prohibit or forbid by decree; also, cut off (as churches in the territory of a feudal lord) by an interdict of the Roman Catholic Church; ***n.*** (IN–) a prohibition; **in·ter·dic·tion** (–DIC–) *n.* —**in·ter·dis·ci·pli·nar·y** (–DIS–) *adj.* involving more than one academic discipline.

in·ter·est (IN·trist, –tuh·rist) *n.* **1** condition or feeling of wanting to know or learn about and share or take part in: *takes ~ in politics; his only ~* (i.e. subject of interest) *in life; a dull story without much ~* (i.e. interesting quality). **2** business or activity that one has a share in; also, such a share; hence, benefit or advantage: *sold his ~ in the farm; supported by the business ~s of the town; working* **in the interest(s)** (i.e. for the good) *of humanity; a 5% ~ paid on savings; He returned the insult* **with interest** (i.e. something added). —***v.:*** *Nothing ~s him more than partying; Could I ~ you in a new car?* **in·ter·est·ed** *adj.: not ~ in a new car at this time; as an ~ party to the deal;* **in·ter·est·ing** *adj.;* **in·ter·est·ing·ly** *adv.*

in·ter·face *n.* a common surface or boundary through which two bodies, regions, or systems interact or communicate: *the air, water, and ground transportation ~s around Manhattan.*

in·ter·faith (–FAITH) *adj.* of or involving different faiths or religions: *an ~ conference.*

in·ter·fere (–FEER) *v.* **-feres, -fered, -fer·ing** get in the way (of each other, *in, with,* or *between* people or affairs): *to ~ in a family dispute; The catcher ~d by hampering the batter's swing;* **in·ter·fer·ence** *n.: foreign ~ in a country's internal affairs; sound distortion due to ~ of radio signals.* —**in·ter·fer·ing** *adj.* officious and nosy; meddlesome: *a very ~ mother-in-law.* —**in·ter·fer·om·e·ter** (–ROM–) *n.* a precision device using interference of light rays to measure distances, angles, etc.; **in·ter·fer·om·e·try** (–tree) *n.* —**in·ter·fer·on** (–FEER–) *n.* a protein molecule produced by cells to fight a viral infection.

in·ter·fuse (–FEWZ) *v.* **-fus·es, -fused, -fus·ing** be diffused through; also, fuse together; blend; mix.

in·ter·ga·lac·tic (–guh·LAC–) *adj.* between or among galaxies; *unending ~ space.*

in·ter·gla·cial (–GLAY·shul) *n.* & *adj.* (a period) between glacial epochs: *a warm ~ (period).*

in·ter·im *n.* & *adj.* (for) the meantime: *an ~ report; without a job in the ~ while management changed hands.*

in·te·ri·or (–TEER·ee·ur) *adj.* inside or inner, not exterior; also, inland: *a house's ~ walls; Style, color, pattern, etc. are elements of* **interior design** *used in* **interior decoration** *of houses, offices, automobiles, etc. to make them pleasant and comfortable;* ***n.:*** *the ~s of a building; The U.S. Department of the Interior looks after the nation's natural resources.*

interj. interjection. —**in·ter·ject** (–JECT) *v.* throw in or interpose (a remark, question, etc.); **in·ter·jec·tion** (–JEC–) *n.* something interjected, esp. an exclamatory word considered as a part of speech, as *alas, ouch,* etc.; **in·ter·jec·tion·al** *adj.* —**in·ter·jec·tor** *n.*

in·ter·lace (–LACE) *v.* **-lac·es, -laced, -lac·ing** pass over and under each other; also, arrange this way, as reeds or fibers in basket-weaving: *an ~ing pattern; roads ~ing with streams.*

in·ter·lard *v.* mix or intersperse: *a speech ~ed with anecdotes.*

in·ter·leaf *n.* **-leaves** a usu. blank leaf inserted between the leaves of a book. —**in·ter·leave** *v.* **-leaves, -leaved, -leav·ing:** *illustrated pages ~d with print.*

in·ter·line (–LINE) *v.* **-lines, -lined, -lin·ing** insert between the lines (of): *a text ~d with notes.* —**in·ter·lin·e·ar** (–LIN·ee·ur) *adj.* inserted between lines or in alternate lines: *an ~ translation.* —**in·ter·lin·ing** (IN·tur·lye–) *n.* an extra lining inserted in a garment; also, a middle layer, as of a quilt.

in·ter·link (–LINK) *v.* link together.

in·ter·lock (–LOK) *v.* lock or fit tightly together, as the pieces of a jigsaw puzzle; also, operate together, as railroad signals. —***n.*** an interlocking condition, device, or arrangement.

in·ter·loc·u·tor (–LOC–) *n.* one who takes part in a dialogue, as the center man who questioned the end men in a minstrel show; **in·ter·loc·u·to·ry** *adj.* happening or done during the course of something, as a decree pronounced during a legal action.

in·ter·lope (–LOPE) *v.* **-lopes, -loped, -lop·ing** encroach, esp. into another's territory for trade or profit-making; **in·ter·lop·er** *n.*

in·ter·lude (–lood) *n.* an interval of musical or dramatic entertainment.

in·ter·mar·ry (–MAIR–) *v.* **-mar·ries, -mar·ried, -mar·ry·ing** marry or become connected by marriage across racial, religious, or familial boundaries: *Jews ~ing with gentiles;* **in·ter·mar·riage** (–rij) *n.*

in·ter·me·di·ar·y (–MEE·dee–) *n.* **-ar·ies** a go-between or mediator; ***adj.:*** *an ~ role, stage of development.* —**in·ter·me·di·ate** (–MEE·dee·it) *n.* & *adj.* (a person or thing) in between: *an ~ shade of green; an ~ automobile between standard and compact size; an ~ range* (i.e. about 1,500 mi./2,414 km) *ballistic missile;* **intermediate school** one linking primary and high school, often comprising grades 4 through 8 or 9.

in·ter·ment (–TUR–) *n.* an interring or burial.

in·ter·mez·zo (–MET·soh) *n.* **-mez·zos** or **-mez·zi** (–see) a short musical or other composition for playing between the acts of an opera or play.

in·ter·mi·na·ble (–TUR·muh·nuh–) *adj.* endless-seeming; long and tiring; **in·ter·mi·na·bly** *adv.*

in·ter·min·gle (–MING–) *v.* **-gles, -gled, -gling** mingle or mix together.

in·ter·mis·sion (–MISH–) *n.* a temporary halt or break in an activity or performance, as between a play's acts. —**in·ter·mit** (–MIT) *v.* **-mits, -mit·ted, -mit·ting** stop for a time; **in·ter·mit·tent** (–MIT·nt) *adj.* stopping and starting again: *an ~ fever; an ~ volcano erupting in cycles;* **in·ter·mit·tent·ly** *adv.*

in·ter·mix (–MIX) *v.* intermingle.

in·ter·mod·al (–MOH·dl) *adj.* of several modes: *an ~ container that can be shipped by plane, rail, truck, or ship.*

in·ter·mo·lec·u·lar (–muh·LEK·yuh–) *adj.* existing or acting between molecules.

in·tern(e) *n.* a medical or other professional receiving in-service training; **in·tern·ship** *n.* —***v.*** (–TURN) **1** be an intern. **2** confine, esp. aliens, in a certain place, as during wartime; **in·ter·nee** (–NEE) *n.* one so confined; **in·tern·ment** *n.* —**in·ter·nal** (–TUR·nl) *adj.* inside or inner, not external: *an historical reference as* **internal evidence** *of the date of a publication; Hormones are ~ secretions; the* **internal combustion** *within an engine's cylinders; an* **in·ter·nal-com·bus·tion engine; internal medicine** *dealing with the nonsurgical treatment of diseases of* *the heart, lungs, stomach, and such ~ organs; a government's* **internal revenue** *derived from taxing domestic goods and services, not from export and import duties;* **in·ter·nal·ly** *adv.*

in·ter·na·tion·al (–NASH–) *adj.* having to do with relationships between nations: *the Canada-U.S. ~ border; the high seas or ~ waters 200 mi. from a country's shore;* **international law** *comprises laws of war, peace, and neutrality;* ***n.*** esp. **International,** an international socialist organization; **in·ter·na·tion·al·ism** *n.;* **in·ter·na·tion·al·ly** *adv.* —**in·ter·na·tion·al·ize** (–NASH–) *v.* **-iz·es, -ized, -iz·ing** bring under international control.

interne same as INTERN.

in·ter·ne·cine (–NEE·sn, –sine) *adj.* of wars, struggles, feuds, etc., destructive to both sides.

internee See INTERN. —**in·tern·ist** (–TURN–) *n.* a specialist in internal medicine.

in·ter·nun·ci·o (–NUN·see–) *n.* **-os** (–oze) a papal envoy ranking below a nuncio.

in·ter·of·fice (–OF·is) *adj.* between or within the offices of an organization.

in·ter·per·son·al (–PUR·suh·nl) *adj.* between persons: *~ relationships, attraction.*

in·ter·plan·e·tar·y (–PLAN–) *adj.* between planets or in their region: *~ travel; an ~ probe into ~ space.*

in·ter·play *n.* interaction.

In·ter·pol (–pole) *n.* a Paris-based organization of the police forces of over 100 countries.

in·ter·po·late (–TUR·puh–) *v.* **-lates, -lat·ed, -lat·ing** insert (new or spurious matter) into a passage or text; also, alter it thus; **in·ter·po·la·tion** (–LAY–) *n.* —**in·ter·po·la·tor** *n.*

in·ter·pose (–POZE) *v.* **-pos·es, -posed, -pos·ing** put forward (between); also, place between: *a remark ~d at the wrong moment; got hurt when he ~d himself between the fighters;* **in·ter·po·si·tion** (–ZISH·un) *n.*

in·ter·pret (–TUR·prit) *v.* explain or bring out a meaning that is not apparent; *to ~ a dream, Scripture, a dramatic role* (by one's acting); *to ~* (i.e. translate) *for foreign tourists;* **in·ter·pre·ta·tion** (–TAY–) *n.;* **in·ter·pret·er** *n.* —**in·ter·pre·tive** (–tiv) or **in·ter·pre·ta·tive** (–tay·tiv) *adj.* explanatory; **in·ter·pre·ta·tive·ly** *adv.*

in·ter·ra·cial (–RAY–) *adj.* having to do with different races: *an ~ incident, marriage.*

in·ter·reg·num (–REG–) *n.* an interval between two regimes; hence, a pause or break in a continuous activity.

in·ter·re·late (–LATE) *v.* **-lates, -lat·ed, -lat·ing** have or bring into a mutual relationship; **in·ter·re·lat·ed** *adj.;* **in·ter·re·lat·ed·ness** *n.* —**in·ter·re·la·tion** *n.;* **in·ter·re·la·tion·ship** *n.*

interrog. interrogative. —**in·ter·ro·gate** (–TAIR·uh–) *v.* **-gates, -gat·ed, -gat·ing** question (a prisoner, witness, etc.) formally and systematically in a search for facts; **in·ter·ro·ga·tor** *n.;* **in·ter·ro·ga·tion** (–GAY–) *n.* —**in·ter·rog·a·tive** (–ROG·uh·tiv) *n.* & *adj.* (a word used in) asking a question: *an ~ adverb such as "when," "where," or "why"; ~ pronouns such as "who" and "what" are ~s;* **in·ter·rog·a·to·ry** *adj.* interrogative.

in·ter·rupt (–RUPT) *v.* make a break in; also, break in upon (a person, his speech, etc.): *Sorry to ~ you; an* **in·ter·rupt·er** *used to open and close an electrical circuit;* **in·ter·rup·tion** (–RUP–) *n.;* **in·ter·rup·tive** (–tiv) *adj.*

in·ter·scho·las·tic (–scuh·LAS–) *adj.* between schools: *an ~ debate;* also **in·ter·school** (–SCOOL).

in·ter·sect (–SECT) *v.* cut or cross (each other); **in·ter·sec·tion** *n.* a crossing or the place of crossing, as of lines, streets, etc.: *traffic accidents at a busy ~.*

in·ter·sperse (–SPURCE) *v.* **-spers·es, -spersed, -spers·ing** put here and there among other things; hence, vary (something): *greenery ~d with flowers;* **in·ter·sper·sion** *n.*

in·ter·state (–STATE) *adj.* between states, as of the U.S.: *an ~ highway; Interstate Commerce Commission.*

in·ter·stel·lar (–STEL·ur) *adj.* between stars or in their region: *~ space, travel, cloud.*

in·ter·stice (–TUR·stis) *n.* **-stic·es** a narrow opening, crack, or similar intervening space, as in network; **in·ter·sti·tial** (–STISH·ul) *adj.: the ~ fluid seeping out of the blood-vessel network.*

in·ter·tid·al (–TYE·dl) *adj.* between high-tide and low-tide levels: *fauna of the ~ zone.*

in·ter·twine (–TWINE) *v.* **-twines, -twined, -twin·ing** twine together; interlace; also **in·ter·twist** (–TWIST).

in·ter·ur·ban (–UR·bun) *adj.* between cities: *an ~ transportation system.*

in·ter·val (–vul) *n.* a break or gap of space, time, pitch, or other factor: *labor pains at 10-minute ~s; trees planted at ~s of 10 meters;* **at intervals** here and there; also, now and then.

in·ter·vene (–VEEN) *v.* **-venes, -vened, -ven·ing** be, come, or go between (events, persons, etc.): *to ~ in a dispute; the ~ing period before their reunion.* —**in·ter·ven·tion** (–VEN–) *n.;* **in·ter·ven·tion·ism** *n.* interference of one nation in another's affairs; **in·ter·ven·tion·ist** *n.* & *adj.*

in·ter·view (–vyoo) *n.* & *v.* (have) a personal conversation (with), as between an employer and job applicant or a journalist and his subject, or **in·ter·view·ee** (–EE); also, the news story or article setting forth the conversation: *The foreign minister agreed to be ~ed via satellite;* **in·ter·view·er** *n.*

in·ter·weave (–WEEV) *v.* **-weaves,** *pt.* **-wove** or **-weaved,** *pp.* **-wov·en** (–WOH·vun) or **-weaved, -weav·ing** weave together; interlace.

in·tes·tate (–TES–, –tit) *n.* & *adj.* (one who has died) without making a will.

in·tes·tin·al (–TES–) *adj.* of the intestines: *an ~ bypass operation;* **intestinal fortitude** pluck or guts. —**in·tes·tine** (–TES·tin) *n.* the alimentary tube from the end of the stomach to the anus, divided into the narrow *small intestine* and the wider *large intestine;* bowel; ***adj.*** within a country: *~ strife.*

in·ti·ma·cy (–muh·see) *n.* **-cies** personal closeness; also, an intimate act, esp. sexual. —**in·ti·mate** (–mit) *n.* & *adj.* (one who is) personally close or familiar: *two people on ~ terms; the ~ atmosphere of a nightclub; an ~ knowledge of the subject;* ***v.*** (–mate) **-mates, -mat·ed, -mat·ing** announce or notify; also, suggest delicately or indirectly; **in·ti·ma·tion** (–MAY–) *n.* notification; also, hint: *~s of immortality.* —**in·ti·mate·ly** *adv.*

in·tim·i·date (–TIM–) *v.* **-dates, -dat·ed, -dat·ing** frighten by display of superior strength, power, learning, etc.: *a witness ~d into silence;* **in·tim·i·da·tion** (–DAY–) *n.*

intl. international.

in·to (–too) *prep.* [indicating movement toward or to the inside of]: *went ~ the room; bumped ~ him by accident; translate from French ~ English; quit school a month ~ Grade 11; She's now ~* (*Informal.* involved in) *art; 4 ~ 20* (i.e. 20 divided by 4) *is 5.*

in·tol·er·a·ble (–TOL·uh·ruh–) *adj.* unbearable; too much to endure: *shouted in ~ pain; the ~ Acts of 1774;* **in·tol·er·a·bly** *adv.* —**in·tol·er·ance** (–TOL–) *n.* the quality of being intolerant; also, allergy or sensitivity to something. —**in·tol·er·ant** *adj.* not tolerant, esp. of other's opinions or beliefs; bigoted: *too* **intolerant of** *opposition to be a democrat.*

in·to·na·tion (–toh·NAY–) *n.* the act or style of intoning or chanting; also, the rise and fall of the voice in speech: *Questions have a rising ~.* —**in·tone** (–TONE) *v.* **-tones, -toned, -ton·ing** recite (as a prayer or psalm) in a singing voice or in a monotone.

in to·to (–TOH·toh) *Latin.* totally; as a whole.

in·tox·i·cant (–TOX·i·kunt) *n.* & *adj.* (anything) that intoxicates, as an alcoholic liquor. —**in·tox·i·cate** (–TOX–) *v.* **-cates, -cat·ed, -cat·ing** make drunk or as if drunk: *Power ~s; ~d by the idea;* **in·tox·i·ca·tion** (–CAY–) *n.*

intra- *comb.form.* within; inside of: as in *intramural, intrauterine;* **in·tra·cit·y** (–SIT–) *adj.* within the city.

in·trac·ta·ble (–TRAC·tuh–) *adj.* hard to manage; resisting control or direction.

in·tra·dos (IN·truh–, –TRAY–) *n.* the inner curve of an arch or vault.

in·tra·mo·lec·u·lar (–LEC·yuh–) *adj.* within a molecule or molecules.

in·tra·mu·ral (–MYOOR–) *adj.* between members of the same school: *~ sports.*

in·tra·mus·cu·lar (–MUS·kyuh–) *adj.* within a muscle: *an ~ injection.*

intrans. intransitive.

in·tran·si·gent (–TRAN–) *n.* & *adj.* (one who is) uncompromising, esp. in politics; **in·tran·si·gence** *n.*

in·tran·si·tive (–TRAN·suh·tiv) *n.* & *adj.* (a verb such as "arrive," "seem," or "lie") that does not have a direct object; **in·tran·si·tive·ly** *adv.*

in·tra·state (–STATE) *adj.* within a state: *~ commerce.*

in·tra·u·ter·ine (–YOO·tuh·rin, –rine) **device** a birth control device such as a spiral or loop of plastic fitted in the uterus.

in·tra·ve·nous (–VEE·nus) *adj.* within or into a vein or veins: *an ~ injection;* **in·tra·ve·nous·ly** *adv.*

intrench same as ENTRENCH.

in·trep·id (–TREP–) *adj.* brave or fearless, esp. against new or unknown dangers: *an ~ fireman, explorer;* **in·trep·id·ly** *adv.* —**in·tre·pid·i·ty** (–PID–) *n.*

in·tri·cate (–tri·kit) *adj.* hard to follow or understand because complicated like a maze or elaborate like filigree work: *an ~ plot, problem, pattern;* **in·tri·cate·ly** *adv.* —**in·tri·ca·cy** (–cuh·see) *n.* **-cies.** —**in·trigue** (–treeg) *n.* a secret, often underhanded plot or scheme, as for overthrow of someone or an illicit love affair. —***v.*** **-trigues, -trigued, -trigu·ing:** *a story opening likely to ~ the reader; gets ahead by ~ing against his rivals; found the revelation very* **in·trigu·ing** *adj.;* **in·trigu·ing·ly** *adv.*

in·trin·sic (–TRIN–) *adj.* existing within, as something essential or inherent, not extrinsic: *The ~ value of a coin is what its metal is worth; the ~ merit of an action besides its usefulness;* **in·trin·si·cal·ly** *adv.*

intro(d). introduction; introductory. —**in·tro·duce** (–DUCE) *v.* **-duc·es, -duced, -duc·ing** bring in or put in; also, bring forward for use, knowledge, etc.: *A new fashion is ~d (into the market); The chairman ~s a speaker (to the audience); a party to ~* (i.e. begin or open) *the New Year;* **in·tro·duc·to·ry** (–DUC–) *adj.*

in·tro·it (–TROH–, IN·troh–) *n.* a psalm or hymn recited at the beginning of Mass or similar Christian service.

in·tro·mit (–MIT) *v.* **-mits, -mit·ted, -mit·ting** insert; put in; **in·tro·mis·sion** *n.*

in·tro·spec·tion (–SPEC–) *n.* an examining of one's own thoughts and feelings; **in·tro·spec·tive** (–tiv) *adj.;* **in·tro·spec·tive·ly** *adv.* —**in·tro·vert** (IN·truh–) *n.* one who is more concerned with his own thoughts and feelings than in the world around him, as an extrovert is; **in·tro·vert·ed** *adj.;* **in·tro·ver·sion** (–VUR–) *n.*

in·trude (–TROOD) *v.* **-trudes, -trud·ed, -trud·ing** thrust or push in where not invited or expected: *to ~ on a person's privacy; a bore who ~s his views on everyone;* **in·trud·er** *n.;* **in·tru·sion** (–TROO–) *n.* —**in·tru·sive** (–siv) *adj.* forcing in: *Molten magma forms ~ rocks by pushing up from below the surface; Some use an ~ "r" sound* *in "India and China";* **in·tru·sive·ly** *adv.;* **in·tru·sive·ness** *n.*

intrust same as ENTRUST.

in·tu·i·tion (–tue·ISH–) *n.* (something known or learned by) direct insight without conscious reasoning; **in·tu·i·tive** (–TUE·it–) *adj.;* **in·tu·i·tive·ly** *adv.*

in·tu·mesce (–MES) *v.* **-mesc·es, -mesced, -mesc·ing** swell or enlarge, as a tumor or boil; **in·tu·mes·cence** *n.*

In·u·it (IN·oo–) *n. sing. & pl.* Eskimo (people or language).

in·un·date (IN·un–) *v.* **-dates, -dat·ed, -dat·ing** overflow, as in a flood; deluge: *advertisers ~d with job applications;* **in·un·da·tion** (–DAY–) *n.*

in·ure (–YOOR) *v.* **-ures, -ured, -ur·ing 1** accustom oneself (*to* something hard to bear). **2** take effect; accrue.

inv. invoice.

in va·cu·o (–VAC·yoo·oh) *Latin.* (as if) in a vacuum.

in·vade (–VADE) *v.* **-vades, -vad·ed, -vad·ing** enter (another's territory) to conquer or as if to take possession; hence, violate: *a household ~d by unexpected guests; army worms ~ing fields;* **in·vad·er** *n.*

[1]in·va·lid (IN·vuh–) *n. & adj.* (a person who is) weak or sickly; **v.** disable or render weak.

[2]in·val·id (–VAL–) *adj.* not valid: *an ~ claim, check, marriage;* **in·val·i·date** *v.* **-dates, -dat·ed, -dat·ing** deprive of legal force or effect; **in·val·i·da·tion** (–DAY–) *n.* —**in·val·id·ly** *adv.*

in·val·u·a·ble (–VAL·yoo·uh–) *adj.* of value that cannot be estimated; priceless; **in·val·u·a·bly** *adv.*

in·var·i·a·ble (–VAIR·ee·uh–) *n. & adj.* (something) constant and unchanging; **in·var·i·a·bly** *adv.: ~ late on Monday mornings.*

in·va·sion (–VAY–) *n.* an invading, as by an attacking force, disease germs, etc.: *~ of privacy by electronic snooping.*

in·vec·tive (–VEC·tiv) *n.* a violent attack in words, spoken or written. —**in·veigh** (–VAY) *v.* make a verbal attack *(against).*

in·vei·gle (–VAY–, –VEE–) *v.* **-gles, -gled, -gling** mislead (someone) or obtain (something) by trickery: *~d into buying worthless stock;* **in·vei·gler** *n.*

in·vent (–VENT) *v.* make up or think up (something new); originate: *Who ~ed the wheel? good at ~ing excuses;* **in·ven·tor** *n.* —**in·ven·tion** *n.* an inventing or something invented: *Modern ~s make living comfortable; a report that is pure ~; "Necessity is the mother of ~"* (i.e. power of inventing). —**in·ven·tive** (–tiv) *adj.: an ~ mind; man's ~ capacity, powers;* **in·ven·tive·ly** *adv.;* **in·ven·tive·ness** *n.* —**in·ven·to·ry** (IN·vun–) *n.* **-ries** an itemized list of goods in stock, property, etc., as for valuation; also, the things so listed: *fast ~ turnover; annual marking down of ~;* **v. -ries, -ried, -ry·ing:** *stock ~d monthly.*

in·ver·ness (–NES) *n.* a man's loose coat with removable cape; also, the cape itself.

in·verse *adj.* inverted or reversed, esp. mathematically: *an ~ function; Addition and subtraction are ~ operations;* **n.:** *a/b is the ~ of b/a;* **in·verse·ly** *adv.: Light intensity is ~ related to distance.* —**in·vert** (–VURT) *v.* turn in an opposite direction, esp. upside down: *A mirror reverses its image, a lens ~s it; Quotation marks are ~ed commas;* **in·ver·sion** *n.: the ~ of subject and verb in "Did I?"; temperature ~ trapping smoke and noxious gases in the air.*

in·ver·te·brate (–VUR–, –brit) *n. & adj.* backboneless (animal such as a worm or mollusk).

in·vest (–VEST) **1** spend or put out (money, time, energy, and such resources) with the expectation of later benefit; **in·vest·ment** *n.: Education is a good ~ for life; an ~ of three million;* **in·ves·tor** *n.* **2** clothe or endow (a person *with* an office, dignity, authority, right, etc.); **in·ves·ti·ture** *n.* a formal investing, as of a king.

in·ves·ti·gate (–VES–) *v.* **-gates, -gat·ed, -gat·ing** search into (a situation or incident) systematically so as to learn the facts; **in·ves·ti·ga·tive** (–gay·tiv) *adj.;* **in·ves·ti·ga·tor** *n.;* **in·ves·ti·ga·tion** (–GAY–) *n.*

investiture, investment See INVEST.

in·vet·er·ate (–VET·uh·rit) *adj.* of a habit, custom, practice, feeling, etc., long-established; also, of persons, habitual: *an ~ prejudice, liar, smoker;* **in·vet·er·a·cy** *n.*

in·vi·a·ble (–VYE·uh–) *adj.* not viable or capable of surviving.

in·vid·i·ous (–VID·ee·us) *adj.* tending to cause envy or animosity: *an ~ comparison, discrimination, rule;* **in·vid·i·ous·ly** *adv.;* **in·vid·i·ous·ness** *n.*

in·vig·o·rate (–VIG·uh–) *v.* **-rates, -rat·ed, -rat·ing** fill with vigor; **in·vig·o·rat·ing** *adj.: The swim was very ~; an ~ climate, tonic;* **in·vig·o·ra·tion** (–RAY–) *n.*

in·vin·ci·ble (–VIN–) *adj.* that cannot be overcome or subdued: *~ courage, ignorance;* **in·vin·ci·bly** *adv.* —**in·vin·ci·bil·i·ty** (–BIL–) *n.*

in·vi·o·la·ble (–VYE·uh·luh–) *adj.* that must not or cannot be violated: *an ~ sanctuary, promise; the ~ gods;* **in·vi·o·la·bly** *adv.;* **in·vi·o·la·bil·i·ty** (–BIL–) *n.* —**in·vi·o·late** (–lit) *adj.* not violated; sacred or pure: *keep an oath ~; the shrine's ~ sanctity.*

in·vis·i·ble (–VIZ–) *adj.* not visible; out of sight or hidden; **in·vis·i·bly** *adv.* —**in·vis·i·bil·i·ty** (–BIL–) *n.*

in·vite (–VITE) *v.* **-vites, -vit·ed, -vit·ing** ask politely to be present somewhere or do something, as a guest: *was ~d to the wedding; Your dress may ~* (i.e. provoke) *comment; an* **inviting** (i.e. attractive and alluring) *sight;* **in·vit·ing·ly**

adv. —**in·vi·ta·tion** (–TAY–) *n.: admission by ~ only; printed ~s;* **in·vi·ta·tion·al** *adj.: an ~ lecture not open to the public; an ~ tournament.*

in vi·tro (–VEE·troh) in an artificially maintained condition, as an embryo in a test tube, not **in vi·vo** (–VEE·voh) , in the living body.

in·vo·ca·tion (–vuh·CAY–) *n.* an invoking or appeal to God or similar higher power; also, the words or formula used.

in·voice *n.* a list of goods or services provided showing payment due for them. —***v.*** **-voic·es, -voiced, -voic·ing** enter on an invoice; also, bill.

in·voke (–VOKE) *v.* **-vokes, -voked, -vok·ing** appeal to a higher power such as God or spirits or to an authority (as of a law, ruling, etc.) for help or protection: *a prayer ~ing God's blessing; penalties ~d only in times of national crises; the ~ing of aid, mercy, a special privilege.*

in·vo·lu·cre (–LOO·cur) *n.* a circle or ring of small leaves or bracts at the base of a flower.

in·vol·un·tar·y (–VOL–) *adj.* not willed or controlled by the will, as reflex actions: *the ~ muscles of the intestines;* **in·vol·un·tar·i·ly** *adv.;* **in·vol·un·tar·i·ness** *n.*

in·vo·lute (IN·vuh–) *adj.* rolled inward, as the scrolls of an Ionic column; also, curled in a spiral, as some shells; hence, intricate or involved; **in·vo·lu·tion** (–LOO–) *n.* an involving or entanglement; also, an involute part. —**in·volve** (–VOLV) *v.* **-volves, -volved, -volv·ing** **1** enfold or include; hence, take up: *a job that ~s manual work; Rights ~ duties.* **2** entangle: *didn't like to get ~d in the dispute;* **in·volved** *adj.* complicated. —**in·volve·ment** *n.*

in·vul·ner·a·ble (–VUL·nuh·ruh–) *adj.* that cannot be attacked or hurt: *an ~ fortress, argument, position;* **in·vul·ner·a·bly** *adv.* —**in·vul·ner·a·bil·i·ty** (–BIL–) *n.*

in·ward (–wurd) *adj.* (directed toward the) inside; inner: *an ~ curve, slant; one's ~ nature.* —***adv.*** toward the inside; into one's mind or soul; also **in·wards.** —**in·ward·ly** *adv.: was ~ happy at her discomfort.*

in·wrought (–RAWT) *adj.* of a pattern or decoration, woven or worked in.

I/O input/output.

i·o·dide (EYE·uh–) *n.* a compound of iodine and another element. —**i·o·din(e)** (EYE·uh–) *n.* a nonmetallic chemical element used in photography and as an antiseptic. —**i·o·dize** (EYE·uh–) *v.* **-diz·es, -dized, -diz·ing** treat with iodine or an iodide, as **iodized** (table) **salt.**

i·on (EYE·un, –on) *n.* an electrically charged atom or group of atoms; ANION or CATION; **i·on·ic** (–ON–) *adj.*

I·on·ic (eye·ON–) *adj.* having to do with **I·o·ni·a** (–OH·nee–) , an ancient Greek colony of Asia Minor, or of a style of architecture of Asiatic Greeks characterized by scrolls in the capitals of the columns.

i·on·ize (EYE·un–) *v.* **-iz·es, -ized, -iz·ing** (cause to) separate into ions, as acids, bases, and salts in solutions; **i·on·i·za·tion** (–ZAY–) *n.;* **i·on·iz·er** *n.* —**i·on·o·sphere** (–ON·uh–) *n.* the outer atmosphere of the earth that is ionized by solar radiation and cosmic rays; **i·on·o·spher·ic** (–SFER–) *adj.*

I.O.O.F. Independent Order of Odd Fellows.

i·o·ta (eye·OH·tuh) *n.* the ninth letter of the Greek alphabet, corresponding to "i"; hence, the least bit or amount; jot.

I.O.U *n.* **I.O.U.'s** a signed note bearing these letters meaning "I owe you" to acknowledge a debt.

I·o·wa (EYE·uh·wuh) a Midwestern U.S. state; 56,290 sq. mi. (145,790 km²); *cap.* Des Moines; **I·o·wan** *n.* & *adj.*

I.P.A. International Phonetic Alphabet.

ip·e·cac (IP·uh–) or **ip·e·cac·u·an·ha** (–yoo·AN·uh) *n.* an expectorant made from the dried roots of a South American shrub of the same name.

ip·so fac·to (IP·soh·FAC·toh) *Latin.* by the very fact.

I.Q. intelligence quotient.

Ir. Ire; Ireland; Irish. —**Ir** iridium. —**I.R.** internal revenue; information retrieval.

I.R.A. Irish Republican Army.

I·ran (–RAN) a country of S.W. Asia, the former "Persia"; 636,296 sq. mi. (1,648,000 km²); *cap.* Teheran. —**I·ra·ni·an** (–RAY·nee·un) *n.* & *adj.* (of or having to do with) a person of Iran or a language such as Persian, Kurdish, or Pashto belonging to a subbranch of the Indo-European family. —**I·raq** (–RAK) a republic W. of Iran in the ancient region of "Mesopotamia"; 167,925 sq. mi. (434,924 km²); *cap.* Baghdad; **I·ra·qi** *n.* & *adj.* (of or having to do with) a person from Iraq or the Arabic language spoken there.

i·ras·ci·ble (–RAS·uh–) *adj.* easily angered; hot-tempered; **i·ras·ci·bil·i·ty** (–BIL–) *n.* —**i·rate** (eye·RATE) *adj.* angry; **i·rate·ly** *adv.;* **i·rate·ness** *n.*

IRBM intermediate range ballistic missile.

ire *n.* anger; wrath, as shown in looks, words, actions, etc.; **ire·ful** *adj.*

Ire. *Abbrev.* for **Ire·land** (–lund) one of the British Isles, divided into the Republic of Ireland and Northern Ireland. —**Republic of Ireland** or **Eire;** 27,136 sq. mi. (70,283 km²); *cap.* Dublin.

i·ren·ic (–REN–) *adj.* promoting peace, esp. in religious disputes.

ir·i·des·cent (eer·i·DES·nt) *adj.* displaying rainbowlike colors when seen from different angles, as mother-of-pearl; **ir·i·des·cence** *n.* —**i·rid·i·um** (–RID–) *n.* a white, heavy metallic chemical element. —**i·ris** (EYE–) *n.* **1** any of a family of plants with sword-shaped leaves bearing three-petalled flowers of varying color, stylized as the fleur-de-lis. **2** the colored part around the pupil of the eye. **3 Iris** the Greek goddess of the rainbow.

I·rish *n.* & *adj.* (of or having to do with) the people of Ireland or the Celtic language or the English dialect spoken there; **get one's Irish up** *Informal.* arouse one's temper; **I·rish·man** *n.* **-men; I·rish·wom·an** *n.* **-wom·en.** —**Irish coffee** coffee containing whiskey and topped with cream.

irk *v.* cause a feeling of weariness or annoyance in; **irk·some** (–sum) *adj.: an ~ task, delay; ~ restrictions.*

i·ron (EYE·urn) *n.* a hard, strongly magnetic, heavy metallic element used for tools and machinery, esp. as steel; hence, any tool or weapon of iron, a flatiron, a golf club, branding iron, etc.; **irons** *pl.* handcuffs or shackles. —***v.*** press and smooth (cloth) with a heated flatiron; **i·ron·ing** *n.* clothes ironed or for ironing; **iron out** smooth out (differences, difficulties, etc.) —***adj.*** made of or like iron in hardness: *an ~ constitution.* —**Iron Age** in human culture, the period when man began to work and use iron. —**i·ron·clad** *adj.* difficult to get out of, as if armored with iron plates: *an ~ guarantee;* ***n.*** an ironclad warship. —**Iron Curtain** the barrier of censorship and secrecy separating Communist E. Europe from noncommunist countries. —**ironic(al)** See IRONY. —**iron lung** an artificial respiratory chamber in which a paralyzed person can be kept alive for treatment. —**i·ron·stone** *n.* iron ore; also, a type of hard white English pottery. —**i·ron·ware** *n.* pots, tools, etc. of iron; hardware. —**i·ron·work·er** *n.* a person whose work is the erecting and connecting of the structural steel framework of buildings; **i·ron·works** *n. sing & pl.* a place where iron and steel products are made.

i·ro·ny (EYE·ruh·nee) *n.* **-nies** a saying, happening, or situation that is apparently contrary to what is intended or desirable, as when one says "Wonderful!" about something infuriating: *By an* **irony of fate,** *he received his inheritance the day he died.* —**i·ron·ic** (–RON–) or **-i·cal** *adj.;* **i·ron·i·cal·ly** *adv.*

Ir·o·quois (EER·uh·kwoy) *n., pl.* **-quois** (–kwoy, –kwoiz) (a member of) any of six tribes of Indians of upper New York State; also, any of their languages. —**Ir·o·quoi·an** (–KWOY·un) *n.* & *adj.*

ir·ra·di·ate (–RAY·dee–) *v.* **-ates, -at·ed, -at·ing** expose to rays of light or other radiation: *a countenance ~d with joy; food preserved by being ~d with gamma rays or electrons;* **ir·ra·di·a·tion** (–AY–) *n.*

ir·ra·tion·al (–RASH–) *adj.* **1** not endowed with reason: *Animals are ~ creatures; became ~ with rage.* **2** contrary to reason: *Superstitions are ~.* **3 irrational number** a real number that cannot be expressed in integers, as the square root of 2. —**ir·ra·tion·al·ly** *adv.* —**ir·ra·tion·al·i·ty** (–NAL–) *n.* **-ties.**

ir·re·claim·a·ble (–CLAIM–) *adj.* that cannot be reclaimed; **ir·re·claim·a·bly** *adv.*

ir·rec·on·cil·a·ble (–SYE·luh–) *adj.* that cannot be reconciled or brought into harmony: *an ~ enemy; ~ differences of attitude;* **ir·rec·on·cil·a·bly** *adv.* —**ir·rec·on·cil·a·bil·i·ty** (–BIL–) *n.*

ir·re·cov·er·a·ble (–CUV·uh·ruh–) *adj.* that cannot be recovered or remedied; **ir·re·cov·er·a·bly** *adv.*

ir·re·deem·a·ble (–DEE·muh–) *adj.* that cannot be brought back or exchanged; also, beyond remedy.

ir·re·den·tist (–DEN–) *n.* a nationalist working for emancipation of fellow countrymen or territories under foreign rule, as the **Irredentists** of Italy, active from 1878 to 1881.

ir·re·duc·i·ble (–DEW·suh–) *adj.* that cannot be reduced or brought to a desired or simpler condition.

ir·ref·ra·ga·ble (–REF·ruh·guh–) *adj.* that cannot be refuted or denied; also **ir·ref·u·ta·ble** (–REF·yoo·tuh–, ref·YOO·tuh–).

ir·re·gard·less (–GARD–) *adj. Nonstandard.* regardless.

ir·reg·u·lar (–REG·yuh–) *adj.* not obeying the usual rules, as in conduct, organization, or features: *an ~ marriage, coastline; ~ troops, behavior; "go-went-gone" are parts of an ~ verb.* —***n.*** a soldier not of a regular army. —**ir·reg·u·lar·ly** *adv.* —**ir·reg·u·lar·i·ty** (–LAIR–) *n.* **-ties.**

ir·rel·e·vant (–REL·uh·vunt) *adj.* not pertinent or to the point; **ir·rel·e·vant·ly** *adv.* **ir·rel·e·vance** *n.*

ir·re·li·gious (–LIJ·us) *adj.* not religious; also, impious.

ir·re·me·di·a·ble (–MEE·dee·uh–) *adj.* that cannot be remedied or corrected; **ir·re·me·di·a·bly** *adv.*

ir·rep·a·ra·ble (–REP·uh·ruh–) *adj.* that cannot be repaired or put right.

ir·re·place·a·ble (–PLAIS·uh–) *adj.* that cannot be replaced.

ir·re·press·i·ble (–PRES–) *adj.* that cannot be repressed or controlled.

ir·re·proach·a·ble (–PROH·chuh–) *adj.* blameless; **ir·re·proach·a·bly** *adv.*

ir·re·sist·i·ble (–ZIS·tuh–) *adj.* that cannot be resisted because too strong or fascinating; **ir·re·sist·i·bly** *adv.*

ir·res·o·lute (–REZ·uh–) *adj.* not resolute; indecisive; **ir·res·o·lute·ly** *adv.* —**ir·res·o·lu·tion** (–LOO–) *n.*

ir·re·spec·tive (–SPEC·tiv) *adj.* regardless *(of).*

ir·re·spon·si·ble (–SPON–) *adj.* not responsible; **ir·re·spon·si·bly** *adv.* —**ir·re·spon·si·bil·i·ty** (–BIL–) *n.*

ir·re·triev·a·ble (–TREE·vuh–) *adj.* that cannot be retrieved or recovered.

ir·rev·er·ent (–REV–) *adj.* not reverent or respectful; **ir·rev·er·ence** *n.*
ir·re·vers·i·ble (–VUR·suh–) *adj.* that cannot be reversed or changed.
ir·rev·o·ca·ble (–REV·uh·cuh–) *adj.* that cannot be revoked or altered; **ir·rev·o·ca·bly** *adv.*
ir·ri·ga·ble (EER·i·guh·bl) *adj.* that can be irrigated. —**ir·ri·gate** *v.* **-gates, -gat·ed, -gat·ing** supply with flowing water or other liquid, as land for cultivation or a body part to cleanse it; **ir·ri·ga·tor** *n.;* **ir·ri·ga·tion** (–GAY–) *n.*
ir·ri·ta·ble (EER·i·tuh–) *adj.* easily irritated; also, highly sensitive, as skin or other plant or animal tissue to an **ir·ri·tant** (–tunt) *n.* & *adj.* (something) causing irritation; **ir·ri·ta·bil·i·ty** (–BIL–) *n.* —**ir·ri·tate** (EER·i–) *v.* **-tates, -tat·ed, -tat·ing** **1** annoy: *His comments ~d the speaker.* **2** stimulate biologically, as by light, heat, pressure, or touch; also, make sore or sensitive, as mucous membranes by irritant poisons such as arsenic and lead. —**ir·ri·ta·tion** (–TAY–) *n.*
ir·rupt (–RUPT) *v.* rush in or burst in; hence, of a species, to increase suddenly in numbers; **ir·rup·tion** *n.;* **ir·rup·tive** (–tiv) *adj.*
I.R.S. Internal Revenue Service.
Ir·ving (UR–), **Washington.** 1783–1859, U.S. author.
is (IZ) See BE. —**is.** or **Is.** island(s); isle(s). —**Is(a).** Isaiah.
I·saac (EYE·zuk) in the Bible, one of the patriarchs, the father of Jacob and Esau.
I·sa·iah (–ZAY·uh) an 8th c. B.C. Hebrew prophet; also, a book of the Old Testament containing his teachings.
I.S.B.N. international standard book number.
-ish *adj. suffix.* of or like, esp. somewhat or inclined to be, often with derogatory force: as in *girlish, selfish, uppish, reddish, sixish* (*Informal.* about 6).
Ish·tar same as ASTARTE.
i·sin·glass (EYE·zn–) *n.* **1** a form of gelatin got from the air bladders of fishes such as the sturgeon. **2** thin sheets of mica used as an insulator against heat and electricity.
I·sis (EYE–) the mother goddess of the ancient Egyptians, sister and wife of Osiris.
isl(s). island(s); isle(s).
Is·lam (IS·lahm) the Moslem religion, Moslems collectively, or Moslem countries. —**Is·lam·a·bad** (–LAH·muh–) capital of Pakistan. —**Is·lam·ic** (–LAH·mic) *adj.* Moslem.
is·land (EYE·lund) *n.* a usu. small land mass surrounded by water; hence, any isolated place such as a "traffic island" for the safety of pedestrians or the pancreatic "islands (i.e. groups of cells) of Langerhans" in which insulin is formed; **is·land·er** *n.* —**isle** (ILE) *n.* a small island; **is·let** (EYE·lit) *n.* a tiny island.
ism (IZM) *n. Informal.* a doctrine or cause, as *communism, fascism, jingoism,* etc. **-ism** *n. suffix.* conduct, condition, or quality; also, an instance of it: as in *archaism, liberalism, heroism.*
is·n't (IZ·nt) is not.
iso- *comb.form.* equal or similar: as in **i·so·bar** (EYE·suh–) *n.* a line on a weather map connecting places of equal atmospheric pressure; **i·so·bar·ic** (–BAIR–) *adj.*
i·so·late (EYE·suh–) *v.* **-lates, -lat·ed, -lat·ing** separate from others; also, obtain (a substance) in a free or uncombined state; **i·so·la·tion** (–LAY–) *n.* physical separation imposed by circumstances: *Robinson Crusoe's life of ~; a hospital's ~ ward for contagious diseases;* **i·so·la·tor** (–lay·tur) *n.* —**i·so·la·tion·ist** (–LAY–) *n.* & *adj.* (of or having to do with) an advocate of a policy of noninvolvement of one's country in international relations; **i·so·la·tion·ism** *n.* such a policy.
i·so·mer (EYE·suh–) *n.* a chemical compound that is isomeric with another; **i·so·mer·ic** (–MER–) *adj.* composed of the same elements in the same proportion but in a different arrangement: *"Normal butane" and "isobutane" are ~ forms of butane* (C_4H_{10}); **i·som·er·ism** (–SOM–) *n.*
i·so·met·ric (–MET–) *adj.* having equality of measure: *~ exercises, or* **isometrics,** *involve tensing (with little movement) of muscles against each other or against a fixed object; An ~ crystal has three equal axes, e.g. cube-shaped;* **i·so·met·ri·cal·ly** *adv.*
i·so·prene (EYE·suh·preen) *n.* a hydrocarbon used in making synthetic rubber.
i·sos·ce·les (–SOS·uh·leez) *adj.* of a triangle, with two equal sides.
i·sos·ta·sy (eye·SOS·tuh·see) *n.* stability, as of the earth's crust, caused by equality of pressure; **i·so·stat·ic** (–STAT–) *adj.;* **i·so·stat·i·cal·ly** *adv.*
i·so·therm (EYE·suh–) *n.* a line on a map connecting places of the same average temperature; **i·so·ther·mal** (–THUR·mul) *adj.*
i·so·ton·ic (eye·suh·TON–) *adj.* **1** of solutions, having the same osmotic pressure. **2** involving shortening of a muscle, not ISOMETRIC: *an ~ exercise, contraction.*
i·so·tope (EYE·suh–) *n.* any of several forms of a chemical element with the same chemical properties but different atomic weights: *Deuterium and tritium are ~s of hydrogen;* **i·so·top·ic** (–TOP–) *adj.;* **i·so·top·i·cal·ly** *adv.*
Isr. *Abbrev.* for ISRAEL(1). —**Is·ra·el** (IZ·ree·ul, –ray–) **1** a country on the E. shore of the Mediterranean, established by the U.N. in 1948 as a homeland for Jews; 7,992 sq. mi. (20,700 km^2); *cap.* Jerusalem; **Is·rae·li** (–RAY·lee) *n.* & *adj.* **2** the ancient land of the Jews, or Palestine, esp. the N. part inhabited by 10 of the 12 tribes descended from Jacob; hence, the Jewish people or Hebrews; **Is·ra·el·ite** (IZ·ree–, –ray–) *adj.* of or having to do with the Jews of ancient Israel; ***n.*** an Israelite Jew.

is·su·ance (ISH·oo·unce) *n.* an official issuing, as of a decree. —**is·sue** (ISH·oo) *v.* **is·sues, is·sued, is·su·ing** put forth or put out; also, come out: *to ~ a proclamation, stamps and coins, a publication; clothing ~d to G.I.'s; smoke ~ing from a chimney.* —***n.*** **1** what is issued or comes out: *a new ~ of an old book consisting of 2,000 copies; a pair of government-~ boots; died without ~* (i.e. offspring). **2** result or outcome: *awaiting the ~ of an election.* **3** subject of a dispute or controversy: *The point* **at issue** *is not how but where; hesitated to* **take issue** (i.e. disagree) *with his boss.* —**is·su·er** *n.*

-ist *n. suffix.* (a person) of (specified) occupation, following, belief, etc.: as in *botanist, humorist, specialist.*

Is·tan·bul (–BOOL) a city and seaport of N. W. Turkey, formerly "Constantinople."

isth·mi·an (IS·mee·un) *n.* & *adj.* (a native or inhabitant) of an isthmus: *the Isthmian games of ancient Greece.* —**isth·mus** (IS·mus) *n.* a narrow strip of land connecting two large areas across water, as of Panama or Corinth.

it *pron., possessive* ITS; *pl.* THEY, *objective* THEM, *possessive* THEIR(s) the one spoken about; also, an indefinite or impersonal subject or object: *Who is ~? The baby, it's crying; "~ never rains but ~ pours"; It's nice to see you; She's quite* **with it** (*Slang.* up-to-date). —***n.*** in children's games such as tag, the player who initiates the action, as catching, finding, etc.

It. Italian; Italy.

I.T.A. Initial Teaching Alphabet.

ital. italic(ized). —**Ital.** Italian. —**I·tal·ian** (–TAL·yun) *n.* & *adj.* (of or having to do with Italy), a person of or from Italy, or the Romance language spoken there. —**i·tal·ic** (–TAL–, eye–) **1** *n.* & *adj.* (a type or letter) that slants to the right; **italics** *n.pl.* italic type. **2 Italic** *adj.* of or having to do with ancient Italy, its people, or their dialects; ***n.*** a branch of Indo-European comprising Latin and Italic dialects. —**i·tal·i·cize** (–TAL–) *v.* **-ciz·es, -cized, -ciz·ing** print in italics or underline to indicate italics. —**It·a·ly** (IT·uh·lee) a country of S. Europe; 116,304 sq. mi. (301,225 km²); *cap.* Rome.

itch *n.* skin irritation that makes one want to scratch; hence, a restless, uneasy longing or desire: *Mites cause* **the itch** *or scabies; an ~ for gold;* ***v.:*** *I'm ~ing to get at his throat; the ~ing palm of an avaricious man.* —**itch·y** *adj.* **itch·i·er, itch·i·est; itch·i·ness** *n.*

-ite *n. suffix.* person or thing derived from or connected with: as in *ebonite, sulfite, Trotskyite.*

i·tem (EYE–) *n.* a separate unit or article in an enumeration, list, or group: *a news ~;* **i·tem·ize** *v.* **-iz·es, -ized, -iz·ing** list in detail: *an ~d bill instead of a vague statement;* **i·tem·i·za·tion** (–ZAY–) *n.*

it·er·ate (IT·uh–) *v.* **-ates, -at·ed, -at·ing** repeat; do or say again; **it·er·a·tion** (–RAY–) *n.*

i·tin·er·ant (eye·TIN–) *n.* & *adj.* (one) traveling from place to place: *an ~ preacher, musician, judge.* —**i·tin·er·ar·y** (–TIN–) *n.* **-ar·ies** a plan, route, or record of a journey; also, a traveler's guidebook.

-itis *n. suffix.* a disease or diseaselike condition: as in *appendicitis, bronchitis, electionitis* (i.e. election fever).

it'll it will; it shall. —**it's** it is; it has. —**its** *adj.* & *pron.* possessive of IT: *all of ~ legs; They are ~;* **it·self** (–SELF) *pron.* emphatic or reflexive form of IT: *the very thing ~; a child able to walk* **by itself;** *Alcohol is not bad* **in itself.**

it·ty-bit·ty or **it·sy-bit·sy** *adj. Informal.* tiny or small.

ITV instructional television.

-(i)ty *n. suffix.* quality or state: as in *ability, profanities* (i.e. instances of profanity).

I.U.D. intrauterine device.

i.v. or **I.V.** intravenous(ly).

I've I have. — **-ive** *adj. suffix.* tending to or having the nature of: as in *evasive, fugitive, talkative.*

i·vied (EYE·veed) *adj.* covered with ivy.

i·vo·ry (EYE·vuh–) *n.* the hard, creamy-white substance of the tusks of elephants, walruses, etc.; ***adj.*** of or like ivory; creamy-white; **i·vo·ries** *n.pl. Slang.* things made of ivory, as piano keys, teeth, billiard balls, or dice. —**Ivory Coast** a republic on the W. coast of Africa; 124,504 sq. mi. (322,463 km²); *cap.* Abidjan. —**ivory tower** a place or condition of existence away from the harsh realities of life.

i·vy (EYE·vee) *n.* **i·vies** any of various creeping and climbing evergreen vines with smooth and shiny leaves, five-pointed in the common, or English ivy. —**Ivy League** group of eight famous schools of N.E. United States, i.e. Harvard, Yale, Princeton, Pennsylvania, Columbia, Cornell, Brown, and Dartmouth.

I.W.W. Industrial Workers of the World.

-ize *v. suffix.* cause to be, become, or treat (like): as in *alphabetize, finalize, legalize.*

J

J or **j** (JAY) *n.* **J's** or **j's** the 10th letter of the English alphabet. —**J** joule; also **j.** —**J.** Journal; Judge; Justice.

Ja. January. —**J.A.** Judge Advocate.

jab *n.* & *v.* **jabs, jabbed, jab·bing** (give) a quick poke (with something pointed) or blow (as in boxing).

jab·ber *n.* & *v.* chatter. —**jab·ber·wock·y** *n.* gibberish; meaningless syllables.

ja·bot (zha·BOH, JAB·oh) *n.* a ruffle or frill on the front of a shirt or blouse.

jac·a·ran·da (–RAN–) *n.* any of a kind of beautiful tropical trees and shrubs, esp. one species with clusters of tiny, fernlike leaves and bluish-white flowers.

ja·cinth (JAY–) *n.* same as HYACINTH.

jack *n.* **1** a male, esp. a young fellow or helper: *They fired* **every man jack;** *"A ~ of all trades and master of none"; A ~* (i.e. playing card) *ranks below king and queen.* **2** a simple mechanism or device; something handy, as a pebble or piece used in the children's game of **jacks,** a small ball or flag, a machine to lift the wheel of an automobile, or an outlet or receptable for plugging in a telephone, etc.; ***v.* jack up** raise; also, raise (prices, wages, etc.).

jack·al (–awl, –ul) *n.* a foxlike wild dog that hunts by night in packs and feeds on carrion.

jack·a·napes (JAK·uh–) *n.* a pert or forward fellow or child. —**jack·ass** *n.* a male donkey; also, a stupid person. —**jack·boot** *n.* a heavy military boot; hence, oppression or bullying behavior: *~ tactics;* **jack·boot·ed** *adj.* ruthless: *~ force.* —**jack·daw** *n.* the dusky-black common crow of Europe and N. Africa.

jack·et (–it) *n.* a short coat; also, an outer covering, as a book's *dust jacket,* the skin of a potato, etc.

Jack Frost frost personified; freezing weather. —**jack·ham·mer** *n.* a pneumatic hammer for drilling rocks and concrete. —**jack-in-the-box** *n.* **-box·es** a toy consisting of a small box from which a figure springs when the lid is opened. —**jack-in-the-pul·pit** *n.* **-pits** a North American wild plant of the arum family having a club-shaped spike of flowers ("jack") arched over by a hoodlike flap ("the pulpit"). —**jack·knife** *n.* **-knives** a large pocketknife; also, a dive in which the body is doubled up in midair before straightening up to hit the water; ***v.* -knifes, -knifed, -knif·ing** double up like a jackknife, as two railroad cars in an accident. —**jack·leg** *adj.* amateur or unprofessional; also, makeshift. —**jack-of-all-trades** *n.* **jacks-** one who can do different kinds of work satisfactorily. —**jack-o'-lan·tern** *n.* a lantern made of a hollowed-out pumpkin cut to look like a face. —**jack·pot** *n.* the accumulated stakes of a poker game or a similar big prize or windfall. —**jack rabbit** a long-eared North American hare with strong hind legs: *the jack-rabbit starts of a hot rodder.* —**jack·screw** *n.* a combination lever-and-screw for raising houses and other such heavy loads.

Jack·son (–sn) capital of Mississippi. —**Jack·son** (–sn), **Andrew.** 1767–1845, 7th U.S. President (1829–1837). —**Jack·son·ville** (–sn·vil) a port of N.E. Florida.

jack·stones *n.pl.* same as JACKS. —**jack·straw** *n.* a thin strip of wood or plastic used in the children's game of **jackstraws** in which such strips are thrown down in a pile to be picked up one at a time without disturbing the rest. —**jack-tar** *n.* a sailor. —**jack-up** *n.* an increase.

Ja·cob (JAY·cub) in the Bible, a son of Isaac and twin brother and rival of Esau. —**Jacob's ladder** any of various herbs of the phlox family with ladderlike leaves and large blue or white flowers.

jac·quard (juh·CARD) *n.* an elaborately figured weave done automatically on the **Jacquard loom** and used in table damask, brocades, tapestry, etc.; also, such fabric.

jade *n.* **1** a hard, tough, green or white gemstone occurring as nephrite and **jade·ite** and used for carvings and jewelry; ***adj.*** light-green. **2** a worn-out horse; also, a disreputable woman; ***v.* jades, jad·ed, jad·ing** dull or wear out, as with hard work or overindulgence in something: *a ~d look, appetite;* **jad·ed·ly** *adv.;* **jad·ed·ness** *n.*

jag *v.* **jags, jagged, jag·ging** cut or tear unevenly: *a ~d edge.* **—n. 1** a pointed projection, as of rock. **2** *Slang.* a drinking bout or spree; also, a fit: *a crying ~.*

jag·uar (JAG·wahr) *n.* a leopardlike but more heavily built ferocious cat of the W. hemisphere.

jai a·lai (HYE·lye, –uh·lye) a fast Spanish game resembling handball but played with a basketlike container called "cesta" strapped to the player's forearm.

jail *n.* a prison, esp. one for temporary confinement or for minor offenses; ***v.*** confine (as if) in jail. **—jail·bird** *n. Informal.* a prisoner; also, a habitual lawbreaker. **—jail·break** *n.* an escape from prison. **—jail·er** or **jail·or** *n.* one in charge of a jail or prisoners.

Ja·kar·ta (juh·KAR·tuh) capital of Indonesia.

jal·ap (JAL·ap) *n.* a Mexican vine of the morning-glory family or a purgative drug made from its roots.

ja·lop·y (–LOP–) *n.* **-lop·ies** an old automobile or aircraft in poor condition.

jal·ou·sie (JAL·uh·see) *n.* a window or shutter made of horizontal slats or louvers that may be tilted, like Venetian blinds, to let in air and light but keep out rain.

jam *v.* **jams, jammed, jam·ming** press, squeeze, or wedge in (between two surfaces); hence, block or get blocked, get caught in, bruise, etc.: *logs ~ing a river; a bus ~d with passengers; The car skidded when the driver ~d on the brakes; A ~d lock or window is hard to open; enemies ~ing* (i.e. interfering with) *each other's radio messages.* **—n. 1:** *a traffic ~ at a busy intersection; If you're* **in a jam** (*Informal.* tight spot) *give me a call.* **2** a fruit preserve.

Jam. *Abbrev.* for **Ja·mai·ca** (juh·MAY·cuh) a Caribbean island country; 4,232 sq. mi. (10,962 km²); *cap.* Kingston. **—Ja·mai·can** (–cun) *n.* & *adj.*

jamb(e) (JAM) *n.* a leglike upright piece forming part of a frame, as of a door.

jam·bo·ree (–buh·REE) *n.* a large gathering for revelry or festivities; also, a Boy Scout rally.

James·town a village of S.E. Virginia, where the first English settlement in America was made in 1607.

jam·packed *adj.* tightly packed, as a stadium with spectators. **—jam session** *Informal.* a lively gathering of musicians playing improvisations.

Jan. January.

jan·gle (JANG·gl) *n.* & *v.* **-gles, -gled, -gling** (make) a harsh, usu. metallic clashing noise, as of pots and pans: *Screaming children ~* (i.e. upset) *one's nerves.*

jan·i·tor (JAN·i·tur) *n.* one in charge of the cleaning, heating, and maintenance of a building; custodian; **jan·i·tor·i·al** (–TOR–) *adj.* **—jan·i·tress** *n.*

Jan·u·ar·y (JAN·yoo·er·ee) *n.* **-ar·ies** the first month of the year, with 31 days, the month of **Ja·nus** (JAY–), a Roman god with two faces to look backward and forward; **Ja·nus-faced** *adj.* two-faced or deceiving.

Jap. Japan(ese); **Jap** *n.* [derogatory] Japanese. **—Ja·pan** (juh·PAN) an island country off the E. coast of Asia, separated from it by the **Sea of Japan;** 143,751 sq. mi. (372,313 km²); *cap.* Tokyo. **—ja·pan** *n.* & *v.* **-pans, -panned, -pan·ning** (give a glossy finish with) a hard varnish as on Japanese lacquer ware. **—Jap·a·nese** (–uh·NEEZ) *n. sing.* & *pl.* (of or having to do with Japan), a person or the people of Japan or their language; **Japanese beetle** a voracious garden pest that entered America around 1916.

jape *n.* & *v.* **japes, japed, jap·ing** jest or gibe; **jap·er** *n.;* **jap·er·y** *n.*

ja·pon·i·ca (–PON–) *n.* a species of camellia; also, Japanese quince.

jar[1] *n.* & *v.* **jars, jarred, jar·ring** (cause) a harsh, esp. grating shock or sound: *nerves ~d by the shaking and rattling of the long ride; ~ing* (i.e. discordant) *sounds, colors, opinions.* **2** *n.* a wide-mouthed container, usu. round, for holding liquids, cosmetics, canned fruit, etc.

jar·di·niere (–dn·EER) *n.* an ornamental pot or stand for plants and flowers.

jar·ful *n.* **-fuls** the amount a jar will hold.

jar·gon (–gun, –gon) *n.* language that is unintelligible because meaningless or obscure, as of a particular occupational group or profession: *academic ~.*

Jas. James.

jas·mine (JAZ·min) *n.* a fragrant white or reddish flower of a vine or shrub of the olive family, originally from the Orient.

jas·per *n.* an opaque, usu. red, yellow, or brown granular quartz.

ja·to (JAY·toh) *n.* the "jet-assisted takeoff" system of an aircraft, using small rockets attached to its body; also **JATO.**

jaun·dice (JAWN·dis) *n.* & *v.* **-dic·es, -diced, -dic·ing** (be affected with) a liver ailment resulting in a yellow discoloration of the skin and eyes: *a* **jaundiced** (i.e. jealous or prejudiced) *view, eye.*

jaunt *n.* & *v.* (take) a short pleasure trip or excursion.

jaun·ty *adj.* **-ti·er, -ti·est** stylish: *a hat set at a ~ angle; ~* (i.e. lively and carefree) *steps;* **jaun·ti·ly** *adv.;* **jaun·ti·ness** *n.*

Ja·va (JAH·vuh) the most populous island of Indonesia, where fossils of the prehistoric **Java man** were discovered in 1891, also noted for its coffee; **java** *n. Slang.* coffee. **—Jav·a·nese** (–NEEZ) *adj.* & *n., sing.* & *pl.*

jav·e·lin (JAV·lin, –uh·lin) *n.* a light wooden or metal spear, esp. one over 8½ ft. (260 cm) long, thrown for distance as a field sport.

jaw *n.* either of the two sets of bones containing teeth and forming the mouth; **jaws** *pl.* a mouth or narrow entrance (to a valley, channel, etc.); also, a gripping or holding part, as of a vise. —***n.*** & ***v.*** *Informal.* (indulge in) talk at great length or in a scolding or boring manner. —**jaw·bone** *n.* a bone of a jaw, esp. a lower jaw; ***v.*** **-bones, -boned, -bon·ing** *Informal.* pressure or persuade from a position of power or influence. —**jaw·break·er** (–bray·kur) *n. Informal.* something that is hard on the jaws, as a kind of candy or a hard-to-pronounce word.

jay *n.* any of various crowlike but smaller and more colorful birds such as the *blue jay;* also **jay·bird.**

Jay·cee *n.* a member of a junior chamber of commerce, a worldwide organization for leadership training and community work. —**jay·vee** *n. Informal.* (member of) a junior varsity team.

jay·walk *v.* of pedestrians, cross a street without regard to traffic regulations; **jay·walk·er** *n.*

jazz *n.* **1** native American music, developed by blacks, characterized by emotional appeal, fast rhythms, and improvisation. **2** *Slang.* empty talk; nonsense: . . . *and all that* ~ (i.e. and the rest of it). —***adj.:*** *a* ~ *band;* ~ *music, fans.* —***v.*** play (music) as jazz; **jazz up** *Slang.* add life, color, or appeal to (something): *a news report too much* ~*ed up to sound factual.* —**jazz·man** *n.* **-men** a jazz musician. —**jazz·y** *adj.* **jazz·i·er, -i·est** like jazz; hence, *Slang.* lively or showy: *a* ~ *new suit;* **jazz·i·ly** *adv.;* **jazz·i·ness** *n.*

J.C.C. Junior Chamber of Commerce.

J.C.S. Joint Chiefs of Staff.

jct. junction.

J.D. Doctor of Laws.

jeal·ous (JEL·us) *adj.* fearful or suspicious about losing what is one's own to a rival, as a loved one or one's rights; also, envious: *a* ~ *husband; rivals* ~ *of each other; a* ~ (i.e. watchful) *guardian of religious freedom; walked out in a* ~ *rage;* **jeal·ous·ly** *adv.* —**jeal·ous·y** *n.* **-ous·ies** resentfulness against rivals; also, envy.

jeans (JEENZ) *n.pl.* pants made of denim or similar cloth.

jeep *n.* a small, sturdy, usu. open automobile with four-wheel drive for use on rough terrain and in demanding jobs; **Jeep** *Trademark.*

jeer *n.* & *v.* (make) a scoffing cry or remark; ridicule; **jeer·ing·ly** *adv.*

Jef·fer·son (JEF·ur·sn), **Thomas.** 1743–1826, 3rd U.S. President (1801–09). —**Jefferson City** capital of Missouri. —**Jef·fer·so·ni·an** (–SOH–) *n.* & *adj.*

Je·ho·vah (ji·HO·vuh) God, as in the Old Testament. —**Jehovah's Witnesses** a U.S. Christian sect started in the 1870's.

je·hu (JEE·hew) *n. Informal.* a fast or furious driver, as **Jehu** in the Bible.

je·june (ji·JOON) *adj.* empty or barren; without substance; not interesting or satisfying to the mind; also, immature. —**je·ju·num** (–JOO–) *n.* portion of the small intestine between the duodenum and the ileum; **je·ju·nal** *adj.*

jell *v.* become like jelly; set; hence, of ideas, plans, etc., take definite form; ***n.*** jelly; **jel·li·fy** *v.* **-fies, -fied, -fy·ing** change into jelly. —**jel·ly** *n.* & *v.* **jel·lies, jel·lied, jel·ly·ing** (congeal as) a semisolid, partly transparent food made from fruit juices, starch, etc. by the thickening action of gelatin or pectin; also, any **jel·ly·like** substance such as the tissue of jellyfish. —**jel·ly·bean** *n.* a candy made of jellied sugar. —**jel·ly·fish** *n.* an umbrella-shaped sea animal trailing stinging tentacles; also, a spineless person. —**jel·ly·roll** *n.* a sheet of sponge cake spread with jelly and rolled up.

jen·net (–it) *n.* a female ass; also, jenny. —**jen·ny** *n.* **jen·nies** the female of certain animals and birds; also, a SPINNING JENNY.

jeop·ard·ize (JEP·ur–) *v.* **-iz·es, -ized, -iz·ing** put in jeopardy; imperil. —**jeop·ard·y** *n.* **-ard·ies** danger or peril: *Your life may be in* ~ *if you return to that country.*

Jer. *Abbrev.* for **Jer·e·mi·ah** (–MYE·uh) Hebrew prophet of the 7th and 6th cent. B.C. whose "Lamentations" form an Old Testament book; **jer·e·mi·ad** (–MYE–) *n.* a mournful complaint.

Jer·i·cho (–coh) city of W. Jordan and site of the biblical town whose walls fell down when the Israelites marched around it blowing their trumpets.

jerk *n.* **1** a quick, sharp pull, push, or twist; also, a muscular contraction or twitch, as when the knee is tapped by a physician. **2** *Slang.* one considered as stupid or dull. —***v.*** **1:** *She* ~*ed her arm away from her captor; a train* ~*ing along its usual route.* **2** cut (beef, etc.) into strips for drying and preserving: *Reindeer meat may be* ~*ed, smoked, or canned.* —**jerk·y** *adj.;* **jerk·i·ly** *adv.;* **jerk·i·ness** *n.*

jer·kin *n.* a short, sleeveless, close-fitting jacket, esp. one common in the 16th cent.

jerk·wa·ter *n.* a rural train; ***adj.*** out-of-the way or unimportant: *a* ~ *town.*

jer·ry-built *adj.* shoddily or cheaply constructed.

jer·sey *n.* **-seys** **1** a close-fitting pullover made of a plain-stitch knitted fabric; also, the fabric. **2** **Jersey** a breed of small dairy cattle, originally from Jersey, Channel Islands. —**Jersey City** major seaport and industrial city of New Jersey.

Je·ru·sa·lem (juh·ROO·suh–) capital of Israel and holy city of Jews, Christians, and Moslems.

jess *n.* a short strap around a falcon's leg for attaching a leash.

jes·sa·mine (JES·uh·min) same as JASMINE.

jest *n.* something said for fun, often to tease or mock: *She said it only* **in jest** (i.e. not seriously). —***v.:*** *She doesn't* ~ *about holy things;* **jest·er** *n.*

a clown or fool, as in a medieval court; **jest·ing·ly** *adv.*

Jes·u·it (JEZH·yoo–, JEZ–) *n.* a member of the Society of Jesus, a religious order founded in 1534. —**Je·sus** (JEE·zuz) **Christ,** 4? B.C.–A.D. 29, founder of Christianity.

[1]**jet** *n.* & *adj.* (lignite coal) that is a deep glossy black; **jet-black** *adj.* very black.

[2]**jet** *n.* **1** stream of water, steam, flame, etc. sent out under pressure, as through a narrow nozzle or spout; also, such an opening or vent. **2** a jet-propelled aircraft. —*v.* **jets, jet·ted, jet·ting 1** spout; gush: *water ~ing from a fountain.* **2** travel by jet: *~ over to London.* —**jet lag** the exhaustion felt after jetting fast through several time zones because of the disruption of the body's 24-hour biological rhythms; also **jet fatigue, jet syndrome.** —**jet·lin·er** (–lye·nur) *n.* a commercial jet airliner. —**jet·port** *n.* an airport for jet airplanes. —**jet·pro·pelled** *adj.* driven by **jet propulsion,** the forward reaction of burned gases from an engine shooting backward through exhausts. —**jet·sam** (–sum) *n.* jettisoned cargo washed ashore; hence, discarded stuff. —**jet set** fashionable people who make frequent air journeys, esp. in the pursuit of pleasure. —**jet stream** any of several wide bands of strong winds blowing at high altitudes from west to east; also, a jet engine exhaust. —**jet·ti·son** *v.* throw (goods) overboard in an emergency so as to lighten a ship or aircraft; *n.* such goods. —**jet·ty** *n.* & *v.* **jet·ties, jet·tied, jet·ty·ing** (a wall or other structure built) to jut out into the water, as a landing pier or breakwater.

jeu d'es·prit (zhuh·des·PREE), *pl.* **jeux d'es·prit** (zhuhz–) *French.* play of wit or a witticism.

Jew *n.* a follower of Judaism; Hebrew; **Jew·ish** *adj.;* **Jew·ish·ness** *n.*

jew·el 1 *n.* & *v.* **-els, -el(l)ed, -el·(l)ing** (adorn or set with) a precious stone or gem: *a ~d ring.* **2** *n.* a jeweled ornament; hence, something or someone very precious: *a ~ of a wife.* —**jew·el·(l)er** *n.* —**jew·el·ry** *n.* jewels collectively. —**jew·el·weed** *n.* a species of impatiens.

Jew·ry *n.* Jewish people; formerly, ghetto. —**jew's-harp** (JOOZ–) *n.* a small musical instrument that is played by holding it between the teeth and twanging a piece projecting from its metal frame.

jez·e·bel (JEZ·uh–) *n.* a shameless or wicked woman like **Jezebel,** the wife of an Israelite king.

j.g. junior grade.

jib *n.* a triangular sail set ahead of the foremast. —**jib** *v.* **jibs, jibbed, jib·bing** refuse to move forward, as a shying horse; *n.* such an animal. —**jibe 1** *v.* **jibes, jibed, jib·ing** agree: *Your story doesn't ~ with his.* **2** *n.* & *v.* same as GIBE.

jif·fy *n.* **jif·fies** *Informal.* moment: *will be back in a ~.*

jig *n.* **1** a lively folk dance, often in triple time, or the music for it. **2 the jig is up** it's finished. **3** any of various devices that work with an up-and-down motion, as a spoon-shaped fishing lure or a mechanical coal cleaner. **4** device for holding machine work and guiding a tool to the proper spot. —*v.* **jigs, jigged, jig·ging** dance a jig; also, jerk or move up and down. —**jig·ger** *n.* a measure for serving liquor, usu. 1½ oz. —**jig·gle** *n.* & *v.* **jig·gles, jig·gled, jig·gling** (give) a slight shake or jerk; **jig·gly** *adj.* —**jig·saw** *n.* a narrow blade that cuts along irregular lines with a rapid up-and-down motion; **jigsaw puzzle** a picture sawed into small irregular pieces for fitting back together.

ji·had (–HAHD) *n.* a Moslem holy war or crusade for reform.

jilt *v.* cast off (a lover) faithlessly or unfeelingly; *n.* a woman who jilts; **jilt·er** *n.*

Jim Crow or **jim crow** discrimination against American Negroes; **Jim Crow·ism.**

jim-dan·dy (–DAN–) *adj.* & *n.* **-dies** (a person or thing) that is excellent or first-rate.

jim·my *n.* & *v.* **jim·mies, jim·mied, jim·my·ing** (pry open with) a short crowbar used esp. by burglars.

jim·son·weed *n.* a large bushy plant of the nightshade family with poisonous leaves and seeds; also called "Jamestown weed."

jin·gle *n.* a clinking sound like that of little bells, coins, or keys striking together; also, a verse or music that is catchy because of the sound repetitions in it: *an advertising ~.* —*v.* **-gles, -gled, -gling:** *keys ~ing in his pocket.* —**jin·gly** *adj.*

jin·go (JING·goh) *n.* **-goes** one who is jingoistic. —**jin·go·ism** *n.* the attitude or policy of chauvinistic aggressiveness towards other countries; **jin·go·ist** *n.;* **jin·go·is·tic** (–IS–) *adj.*

jin·ni (–nee) *n., pl.* **jinn** in Moslem legend, a guardian spirit such as the good jinni that helped Aladdin.

jin·rik·i·sha or **jin·rick·sha** (–RIK·shaw) *n.* a light, two-wheeled, hooded, man-drawn cart formerly used in Oriental countries as a taxicab.

jinx *n.* & *v.* (person or thing thought) to bring bad luck to (someone).

jit·ney (–nee) *n.* **-neys** a cab or bus that travels a regular route serving a small community, as in some resort areas.

jit·ter·bug *n.* a lively ballroom dance of the 1940's featuring acrobatic swings and lifts; *v.* **-bugs, -bugged, -bug·ging:** *~ing to swing music.* —**jit·ters** *n.pl. Informal.* the fidgets; a fit of nervousness; **jit·ter·y** *adj.* nervous.

jive *Slang. n.* swing music or dancing; jazz; hence, talk that is insincere or tiring. —*v.* **jives, jived, jiv·ing 1** tease; kid. **2** dance to or play jive music. —*adj.* pretentious; insincere; phoney.

Joan (JONE) **of Arc, St.** 1412–31, French heroine, burned at the stake as a witch, but declared a saint in 1920.

Job (JOBE) a man who suffered much but kept his faith in God, as told in the Old Testament book of the same name.

job *n.* a piece of work, esp. one done for pay; hence, employment: *does a good ~ in his present position; summer ~s for students; a handyman hired to do* **odd jobs** *around the house; fired for drinking* **on the job;** *employees resorting to* **job actions** *such as slowdowns, sick-outs, and demonstrations instead of striking.* **—v. jobs, jobbed, job·bing** handle (retail goods purchased wholesale or a large-scale operation) in small quantities or piece by piece. **—job action** See JOB, *n.* **—job bank** a computerized system that matches job vacancies with unemployed workers. **—job·ber** *n.* **1** one who does piecework or one who jobs as a middleman. **2** one who uses a position of trust for private ends. **—job·hold·er** *n.* one with a steady job. **—job·hop·ping** *n.* frequent changing of jobs for financial gain. **—job lot** an assortment of goods, including inferior stuff, bought or sold in one lot.

jock *n. Informal* [short form] **1** disc jockey; jockey. **2** jockstrap. **3** *Slang.* athlete. **—jock·ey** (JOK·ee) *n.* one who rides horses in races. **—v. -eys, -eyed, -ey·ing** **1** ride (a horse) in a race. **2** try to gain an advantage by skillful maneuvering; also, trick or cheat. **—jock·strap** *n.* a pouched belt to protect the genitals of male athletes; hence, *Slang.* an athlete.

jo·cose (–COSE) *adj.* given to joking or jesting; **jo·cose·ly** *adv.* **—jo·cos·i·ty** (–COS–) *n.* **-ties; jo·cose·ness** *n.* **—joc·u·lar** (JOC·yuh·lur) *adj.* **1** fond of joking: *a ~ fellow.* **2** meant to be funny: *in a ~ vein;* **joc·u·lar·i·ty** (–LAIR–) *n.* **—joc·und** *adj.* merry or cheerful; **joc·und·ly** *adv.* **—jo·cun·di·ty** (–CUN–) *n.*

jodh·purs (JOD–) *n.pl.* breeches for riding that are loose and full above the knees and close-fitting below.

¹jog *n.* a little shove or nudge. **—v. jogs, jogged, jog·ging** give a jog to; hence, move (along) with a shaking motion; also, run slowly: *People ~ for exercise;* **jog·ger** *n.* **—¹jog·gle** *n.* a slight shake or jerk; **v. jog·gles, jog·gled, jog·gling** shake slightly.

²jog *n.* **1** a notch or a projecting part; also, unevenness. **2** a sharp and brief change of direction, as in a road. **—²jog·gle** *n.* a joint made with jogs in the surfaces to be joined; **v. jog·gles, jog·gled, jog·gling** join using a joggle or joggles.

Jo·han·nes·burg (–HAN·is–) a city of N.E. South Africa.

john (JON) *n. Slang.* **1** a toilet. **2** a prostitute's client. **—John** the Apostle of Christ who wrote the fourth Gospel; also, this Gospel. **—John Birch Society** See BIRCHER. **—John Bull** the English (nation). **—John Doe** a person whose true name is unknown. **—john·ny** *n.* **john·nies** a short gown worn by hospital patients; **John·ny-jump-up** (–JUMP–) *n.* a violet or pansy. **—John Paul II** born 1920, Pope since 1978. **—John·son** (JON·sn) **1 Andrew,** 1808–75, 17th U.S. President (1865–69). **2 Lyndon B.** 1908–73, 36th U.S. President (1963–69). **3 Samuel,** 1709–84, English lexicographer and author; **John·so·ni·an** (–SOH·nee·un) *n.* & *adj.* **—John the Baptist** the forerunner of Jesus and his baptizer.

joie de vi·vre (zhwah·duh·VEEV·ruh) *French.* joy of living.

join *v.* bring or come together (with); hence, associate with or come into the company of: *broken pieces ~ed together; a junction where one street ~s another; to ~ the Navy; She will ~ us in a minute.* **—join·er** *n.* **1** a person or thing that joins, esp. a carpenter or woodworker specializing in intricate joining work. **2** *Informal.* one who likes to join groups. **—joint** *n.* **1** a joining or place of joining: *a pipe ~; a dovetail ~; the ball-and-socket ~ at the shoulder;* **out of joint** dislocated; hence, in bad condition. **2** a jointed part or division: *the middle ~ of a finger; a butcher's ~* (i.e. section) *of meat for roasting.* **3** *Slang.* a cheap establishment such as a hotel, restaurant, or other place where people meet. **4** *Slang.* a marijuana cigarette. **—v.** fit together for joining; also, divide or cut up at the joints, as a butcher does: *an insect's ~ed legs; a perfectly ~ed space suit.* **—adj.** shared or sharing: *a ~ bank account; the Joint Chiefs of Staff* (forming the U.S. President's military advisory board); **joint·ly** *adv.*

joist *n.* one of the parallel beams supporting a floor or ceiling from wall to wall.

joke *n.* something that arouses laughter, as a funny story, remark, or prank; also, a person or thing to laugh at; **v. jokes, joked, jok·ing** jest or tease; **jok·ing·ly** *adv.* **—jok·er** *n.* **1** one who jokes. **2** in some games, an extra card useful as a wild card or highest trump. **3** a tricky clause, phrase, or word inserted in a document to nullify its effect.

jol·lies (–eez) *n.pl. Slang.* fun; pleasure. **—jol·li·fi·ca·tion** (–CAY–) *n.* merrymaking. **—jol·lity** *n.* **-ties** merriment; exuberant mirth. **—jol·ly** (JOL·ee) *adj.* **jol·li·er, jol·li·est** full of fun; merry. **—v. jol·lies, jol·lied, jol·ly·ing** humor (someone); also, make fun of good-naturedly. **—jol·li·ly** *adv.;* **jol·li·ness** *n.*

jolt *n.* & *v.* (give or experience) a sudden jerk, knock, or surprise: *The news of death came as a ~ to his loved ones.* **—jolt·y** *adj.*

Jo·nah (JOH·nuh) in the Bible, a prophet who was thrown overboard during a storm and spent three days in the belly of a big fish.

Jones, John Paul. 1747–92, American naval officer in the Revolutionary War.

jon·gleur (JONG·glur) *n.* a wandering minstrel of the Middle Ages.

jon·quil (JONG–) *n.* any of several yellow narcissuses of the amaryllis family.

Jon·son, Ben. 1572?–1637, English dramatist and poet.

Jor·dan (–dn) **1** a river flowing into the Dead Sea through Israel and Jordan. **2** a Near Eastern country east of Israel; 37,738 sq. mi. (97,740 km²); *cap.* Amman. —**Jor·da·ni·an** (–DAY–) *n.* & *adj.*

Jo·seph (JOH·zuf) **1** the husband of Mary, mother of Jesus. **2** in the Bible, Jacob's favorite son, who became governor of Egypt.

josh *v. Informal.* tease playfully; **josh·er** *n.*

Josh. *Abbrev.* for **Josh·u·a** (–oo·uh) a book of the Bible telling about Joshua, Moses' successor, who led the Israelites into the promised land. —**Joshua tree** a small yucca tree of the deserts of S.W. United States.

joss *n.* a Chinese god or idol.

jos·tle (JOSL) *v.* **-tles, -tled, -tling** push or shove, as in a crowd; ***n.*** a jostling.

jot n. a very small amount; iota: *don't care one ~; not a ~ of truth in the story.* —***v.*** **jots, jot·ted, jot·ting** write (down) hastily and briefly; **jot·ter** *n.;* **jotting** *n.* a brief note.

joule (JOWL, JOOL) *n.* a unit of energy equal to 10 million ergs.

jounce *n.* & *v.* **jounc·es, jounced, jounc·ing** jolt or bounce; **jounc·y** *adj.: a ~ ride in a jeep.*

jour. *Abbrev.* for **jour·nal** (JUR·nl) *n.* **1** a daily account or record such as a diary or log, a daily publication such as a newspaper, or a daily bookkeeping record. **2** the part of an axle or shaft turning in a bearing, or **journal box.** —**jour·nal·ese** (jur·nl·EEZ) *n.* language and style that is typical of newspapers and magazines. —**jour·nal·ism** (JUR·nl–) *n.* **1** the gathering and publishing of news through the mass media. **2** journalistic writing. **3** newspapers and magazines collectively; **jour·nal·ist** *n.;* **jour·nal·is·tic** (–LIS–) *adj.* —**jour·ney** (JUR·nee) *v.* **-neys, -neyed, -ney·ing** go on a journey; ***n.*** a travel, usu. of some duration, to a definite place; also, the distance covered. —**jour·ney·man** *n.* **-men** a qualified and experienced though not master workman: *a ~ carpenter.*

joust *v.* engage in a joust; ***n.*** combat using lances between two knights on horseback, esp. as part of a medieval tournament, or **jousts** *pl.*

Jove (JOHV) same as JUPITER.—**jo·vi·al** (JOH·vee·ul) *adj.* full of good humor and fun: *a ~ mood;* **jo·vi·al·ly** *adv.* —**jo·vi·al·i·ty** (–AL–) *n.*

jowl *n.* jaw; also, the lower, hanging part of a face or head, as the dewlap of cattle, the wattle of a fowl, the head and shoulders of salmon, etc.; **jow·ly** *adj.*

joy *n.* great delight or happiness; also, a cause or an expression of it: *She leaped for ~ on hearing the news; the ~s and sorrows of life; There's ~ in heaven.*

Joyce, James. 1882–1941, Irish poet and novelist.

joy·ful *adj.* full of or causing joy: *That was ~ news;* **joy·ful·ly** *adv.;* **joy·ful·ness** *n.;* **joy·less** *adj.* —**joy·ous** (–us) *adj.* full of or endowed with joy: *a ~ mood, heart, family.* —**joy ride** a ride taken for the fun of it, esp. in a stolen automobile; **joy rider; joy riding.**

J.P. Justice of the Peace.

jr. or **Jr.** Junior.

jt. joint.

ju·bi·lant (JOO·buh·lunt) *adj.* showing great joy; exultant; **ju·bi·lant·ly** *adv.* —**ju·bi·la·tion** (–LAY–) *n.* rejoicing; also, a joyful occasion. —**ju·bi·lee** (JOO·buh–) *n.* rejoicing; also, a time of rejoicing or celebration, esp. an anniversary such as "DIAMOND jubilee," "golden jubilee" (50th anniversary), or "silver jubilee" (25th anniversary).

Ju·dah (JOO·duh) the ancient kingdom of S. Palestine inhabited by the tribes of Benjamin and Judah, sons of Jacob; **Ju·da·ic** (–DAY–) *adj.* of the Jews or Judaism; **Ju·da·ism** (JOO·duh·izm) *n.* the Jewish religion or way of life. —**Ju·das (Is·car·i·ot)** (JOO·dus·is·CAIR·ee·ut) the disciple who betrayed Jesus; **judas** *n.* a traitor; **Judas tree** same as REDBUD, a tree of the type on which Judas is believed to have hanged himself. —**Ju·de·a** (–DEE–) S. Palestine, or Judah, under Persian, Greek, and Roman rule.

Judg. *Abbrev.* for **Judges,** an Old Testament book. —**judge** (JUJ) *n.* one who decides, esp. a public official in a court of law who hears and decides cases; justice; also, one who decides questions of merit, taste, etc.; referee: *a Supreme Court ~; I'm no ~ of wines;* ***v.*** **judg·es, judged, judg·ing:** *the court's power to ~ cases; motives that are hard to ~* (i.e. criticize); *I ~d it better to remain silent; Who's ~ing (at) the beauty contest?* **judge·ship** *n.* —**judg·ment** *n.* a judging, its result such as an opinion or a sentence, or the ability to judge: *an error of ~; to pass ~ without hearing both sides; an accident that seemed a ~ on* (i.e. punishment for) *his driving habits;* also **judge·ment; judg·men·tal** (–MEN·tl) *adj.;* **Judgment Day** same as DOOMSDAY. —**ju·di·ca·to·ry** (JOO·dic·uh–) *n.* & *adj.* (having to do with) a court of law or its administrative system. —**ju·di·ca·ture** (–chur) *n.* a court of law or its administration of justice; also, a judge's position or jurisdiction. —**ju·di·cial** (–DISH·ul) *adj.* of a judge: *a ~ decision, process, mind, review;* **ju·di·cial·ly** *adv.* —**ju·di·ci·ar·y** (–DISH·ee–) *adj.* of the administration of justice: *~ proceedings;* ***n.,*** *pl.* **-ar·ies** a court system; also, judges collectively. —**ju·di·cious** (–DISH·us) *adj.* wise in deciding; sound in judgment: *a ~ parent, selection, use, decision;* **ju·di·cious·ly** *adv.*

ju·do (JOO·doh) *n.* a Japanese sport or weaponless method of self-defense in which balance, timing, leverage, etc. are used to throw an opponent. —**ju·do·ka** *n. sing. & pl.* a judo player.

jug. 1 *n.* a large, narrow-mouthed container, usu. with a handle, for liquids: *a milk* ~. **2** *n. & v.* **jugs, jugged, jug·ging** *Slang.* (put in) jail.

jug·ger·naut *n.* something massive and overpowering that crushes anything in its path.

jug·gle *v.* **jug·gles, jug·gled, jug·gling** manipulate or play tricks with (figures, facts, words, etc.) as a **jug·gler** does with balls, plates, etc. by tossing them up and catching them as a feat of dexterity; **jug·gler·y** *n.* **jug·gler·ies** sleight of hand; trickery; fraud.

jug·u·lar (JUG·yoo·lur) *adj.* of the neck or throat, esp. of the two large **jugular veins** that take down blood from the head and neck to the heart. —***n.*** a jugular vein.

juice (JOOSE) *n.* **1** the liquid part or essence of plant or animal tissue: *orange* ~; *the natural* ~ *or gravy of meat; gastric* ~*s of the stomach.* **2** *Slang.* a medium such as electricity or gasoline that supplies power; also, alcoholic liquor; ***v.*** **juic·es, juiced, juic·ing:** *music to* **juice up** (i.e. enliven) *a party.* —**juice·head** *n. Slang.* an alcoholic. —**juic·er** *n.* a kitchen appliance for extracting juice from fruit. —**juic·y** *adj.* **juic·i·er, -i·est** full of juice; also, *Informal.* exciting because scandalous or racy; **juic·i·ly** *adv.;* **juic·i·ness** *n.*

ju·jit·su or **ju·jut·su** (joo·JIT·soo) *n.* the Japanese system of wrestling from which judo developed.

ju·jube (JOO·joob, –joo·bee) *n.* a lozenge of gummy, fruit-flavored candy.

juke·box *n.* a coin-operated record player, as used in restaurants, bars, etc.

Jul. July.

ju·lep (JOO·lup) *n.* an iced and sweetened drink of whiskey or brandy flavored with mint; also **mint julep.**

ju·li·enne (joo·lee·EN) *n. & adj.* (a clear soup made with vegetables) cut into long thin strips: ~ *potatoes.*

Ju·ly (joo·LYE) *n.* the seventh month of the year, having 31 days.

jum·ble *n. & v.* **-bles, -bled, -bling** (mix up in) a disorderly mass or confusion.

jum·bo *adj. & n.* **-bos** (something) very large of its kind, esp. a **jumbo jet** airliner.

jump *v.* move with sudden muscular effort using the feet and legs: *She* ~*s out of bed at 5 a.m.; He* ~*ed in and drove off; escaped by* ~*ing* (i.e. into) *a passing train; Let us not* ~ *to conclusions before all the facts are in; Prices* ~ *as supplies dwindle; This is where the derailed cars* ~*ed the tracks; She* ~*ed at the long-awaited opportunity; He* ~*ed* (i.e. started ahead of) *the green signal;* ~*s on* (i.e. berates) *his students at the slightest mistakes; The bondsman lost his money when the prisoner* **jumped bail** (i.e. disappeared). —***n.:*** *the "high* ~*" as a track-and-field event; Oil prices took a* ~ *yesterday;* **have** (or **get**) **the jump on** have an advantage over. —**jump·er** *n.* **1** a person or thing that jumps: **jump(er) cables** *close an electrical circuit by jumping or bypassing a break in it.* **2** a loose jacket or sleeveless dress worn to protect one's clothes; **jumpers** *pl.* rompers. —**jumping bean** the seed of a Mexican spurge which jumps and rolls because of the caterpillar growing inside it. —**jump·ing-off point** (or **place**) point of departure. —**jump suit** a parachutist's one-piece suit or a woman's similar suit of jacket and trousers belted in the middle. —**jump the gun** See GUN. —**jump·y** *adj.* **jump·i·er, -i·est** jittery; nervous; **jump·i·ly** *adv.;* **jump·i·ness** *n.*

jun *n. sing. & pl.* a money unit of North Korea, equal to 1/100 of a won. —**jun.** junior. —**Jun.** June; Junior.

junc. or **Junc.** junction.

jun·co (JUNG·coh) *n.* **-co(e)s** a small bird of the finch family, often seen in the winter; also called "snowbird."

junc·tion *n.* a joining; also, a place of joining, as of roads. —**junc·ture** (–chur) *n.* a joining, esp. a critical moment in the coming together of events: *At that* ~ *he was lost for words.*

June (JOON) *n.* the sixth month of the year, with 30 days.

Ju·neau (JOO·noh) capital of Alaska.

jun·gle (JUNG·gl) *n.* a wildly overgrown tropical forest; also, a place hard to survive in: ASPHALT JUNGLE *the* ~ *of city slums.*

jun·ior (JOON·yur) *n. & adj.* (a person) younger or lower in rank than another, or SENIOR: *John Smith, Junior* (i.e. son of John Smith); *a college or high school* ~ (in his next-to-last year); *a* ~ *partner.* —**junior college** one offering two-year programs, either as the first two years for a bachelor's degree or as technical training for semiprofessional jobs. —**junior high school** grades 7, 8, and 9 of school. —**junior varsity** a school or college team composed of those less qualified and experienced than the varsity.

ju·ni·per (JOO·nuh–) *n.* any of a group of evergreen shrubs and trees of the cypress family having fragrant, berrylike cones.

[1]junk *n.* a Chinese flat-bottomed ship with four-cornered sails and a high poop.

[2]junk *n.* **1** old or worthless material; rubbish. **2** *Slang.* a narcotic, esp. heroin. —***v.*** discard as junk; **junk·er** *n. Slang.* a discarded automobile.

Junk·er (YOONG·kur) *n.* a member of the landed aristocracy of Prussia.

junk·et *n.* **1** a rennet pudding. **2** an excursion or trip, esp. one taken by an official at public expense. —***v.*** go on a junket.

junk food food such as candy, potato chips, cake, and soda that have little nutritive value.

—**junk·ie** or **junk·y** *n., pl.* **junk·ies** *Informal.* a drug addict. —**junk mail** unsolicited third-class mail such as advertising circulars.
Ju·no wife of Jupiter and queen of the gods.
jun·ta (HOON·tuh, JUN–) *n.* a group of military men ruling a country after a coup d'état. —**jun·to** (JUN·toh) *n.* **-tos** a clique or faction.
Ju·pi·ter (JOO·puh·tur) **1** in Roman myth, the supreme god or ruler of gods and men; Jove; Zeus. **2** the largest planet of the solar system, fifth closest to the sun.
Ju·ras·sic (–RAS–) *n.* & *adj.* (of) the second period of the Mesozoic era of the earth beginning about 180 million years ago when flying reptiles and birds appeared.
ju·rid·i·cal (–RID–) *adj.* having to do with the administration of justice; **ju·rid·i·cal·ly** *adv.* —**ju·ris·dic·tion** (–DIC–) *n.* legal authority in regard to its extent or territory: *outside a court's* ~; **ju·ris·dic·tion·al** *adj.* —**ju·ris·pru·dence** (–PROO–) *n.* the science or philosophy of law; also, legal knowledge or skill. —**ju·rist** *n.* a legal scholar such as a judge or lawyer; **ju·ris·tic** (–RIS–) *adj.* —**ju·ror** (JOOR·ur) *n.* one who takes an oath as a member of a jury. —**ju·ry** **1** *n., pl.* **-ries** a select group of people who hear evidence and give a verdict, as in a court trial, who determine the cause of a death at an inquest, or who decide the winner in a contest; **ju·ry·man** *n.* **-men.** **2** *adj.* of a mast, rig, etc., for temporary use.
just *adj.* due or appropriate according to a moral, social, esthetic, or other standard; also, of people, observing such a standard: *a ~ and upright man; got his ~ reward; a ~ and impartial decision; a ~ price, praise, measure;* **just·ly** *adv.;* **just·ness** *n.* —***adv.*** **1** exactly or nearly (as stated or at a certain time or place): *Saw her* **just now;** *not sleepy ~ now; I'll do ~ as you say; That's ~ what I need; ~* (i.e. barely) *missed her bus.* **2** *Informal.* simply; truly; really: *I'm ~ fine; looks ~ perfect.* —**just the same** even so; nevertheless. —**jus·tice** (–tis) *n.* **1** a being just; fairness; also, just treatment, esp. by process of law: *"~ delayed is ~ denied"; a picture that does not* **do justice** *to* (i.e. treat fairly) *the subject.* **2** a judge; also, a **justice of the peace,** a local magistrate. —**jus·ti·fy** *v.* **-fies, -fied, -fy·ing** make or show to be just or right: *conduct that is difficult to ~; printed lines ~d* (i.e. made right length) *by spacing out the words.* —**jus·ti·fi·a·ble** (–FYE·uh–) *adj.;* **jus·ti·fi·a·bly** *adv.* —**jus·ti·fi·ca·tion** (–CAY–) *n.*
jut *n.* & *v.* **juts, jut·ted, jut·ting** (a projection, part, etc. made or formed so as to) stick out or stand out, as a balcony or jetty.
jute *n.* a strong, shiny fiber made from a plant of the basswood family and used to make gunnysacks, cordage, rope, etc.
juv. *Abbrev.* for **ju·ve·nile** (JOO·vuh·nl, –nile) *n.* a young and immature person; also, a young plant or animal such as a two-year-old race horse; ***adj.:*** *a ~ acting role, phase of development; a* **juvenile court** *dealing with* **juvenile delinquents** (i.e. offenders below legal age, usu. 18); *the* **juvenile hormone** *controlling larva development.*
jux·ta·pose (JUX·tuh–) *v.* **-pos·es, -posed, -pos·ing** put close together or side by side; **jux·ta·po·si·tion** (–ZISH–) n.
J.V. or **j.v.** junior varsity.

K

K or **k** (KAY) *n.* **K's** or **k's** the 11th letter of the English alphabet. —**K** potassium; kilo (thousand); Kelvin (temperature scale). —**k.** karat; kilo(s); kopek(s); krona; krone. —**k** kilo(s).

Kaa·ba (KAH·buh) *n.* the holiest spot at Mecca, housing a sacred stone.

kabob same as KEBAB.

Ka·bu·ki (–BOO·kee) *n.* a form of Japanese drama using pantomime, song, and dance.

Ka·bul (KAH–) capital of Afghanistan.

kad·dish (KAH–) *n.* a Jewish hymn of praise used also as a mourner's prayer.

kaf·fee·klatsch (COF·ee·clach) *n.* an informal social gathering at which coffee is served.

kaftan same as CAFTAN.

kail same as KALE.

kai·ser (KYE·zur) *n.* an emperor, esp. one of the **Kaisers** of Germany and Austria up to 1918.

kale *n.* a cabbagelike vegetable with loose, curly leaves instead of a head.

ka·lei·do·scope (kuh·LYE·duh–) *n.* a tube fitted with mirrors that reflect colored beads and pieces of glass at one end in an endless variety of patterns as the tube is rotated and viewed; **ka·lei·do·scop·ic** (–SCOP–) *adj.*

kalends, kalsomine same as CALENDS, CALCIMINE.

ka·ma·a·i·na (kah·mah·ah·EE·nah) *n. Hawaiian.* a longtime resident of Hawaii.

Ka·ma (KAH·muh) the Hindu god of love; **Ka·ma·su·tra** (kah·muh·SOO·truh) an ancient Sanskrit love manual.

Kam·chat·ka (–CHAT·kuh) the peninsula extending southward from E. Siberia.

ka·mi·ka·ze (kah·mi·KAH·zee) *n.* (a plane or pilot making) a suicide attack, as the Japanese in World War II; ***adj.*** suicidal; self-destructive: *a ~ taxi driver.*

Kam·pa·la (–PAH–) capital of Uganda.

Kam·pu·che·a (–CHEE·uh) same as CAMBODIA.

kan·ga·roo (kang·guh·ROO) *n.* **-roos** any of a family of Australian marsupial mammals with powerful hind legs on which they hop about using the heavy tail for balance and support. —**kangaroo court** an unauthorized court, often a mock one, as set up by prison inmates.

Kan(s). *Abbrev.* for **Kan·sas** (–zus), a Midwestern U.S. state; 82,264 sq. mi. (213, 063 km^2); *cap.* Topeka. —**Kansas City** either of two cities on the Kansas-Missouri border, one in Missouri and the other in Kansas.

Kant, Immanuel. 1724–1804, German philosopher. —**Kant·i·an** *n.* & *adj.*

ka·o·lin(e) (KAY·uh·lin) *n.* a pure white clay of feldspar used in making high-grade pottery.

ka·on (KAY–) *n.* the heaviest meson, weighing about 967 times as much as an electron; also **K-mes·on.**

ka·pok (KAY–) *n.* a lightweight fiber got from the seedpods of an East Indian tree for use in mattresses, life jackets, etc.

kap·pa (CAP·uh) *n.* the 10th letter of the Greek alphabet (Κ, κ).

ka·put (kuh·POOT) *adj. Informal.* **be** (or **go**) **kaput** fail; be unsuccessful; be finished.

Ka·ra·chi (kuh·RAH·chee) Pakistan's main seaport and largest city.

kar·a·kul or **car·a·cul** (KAIR·uh·kul) *n.* the curly, silky, usu. black fleece of young lambs of a broad-tailed sheep of C. Asia; also, the sheep.

kar·at (KAIR·ut) *n.* 1/24 part (i.e. proportion of pure gold in an alloy): *Only 10/24 of 14 ~ gold is alloy.*

ka·ra·te (kuh·RAH·tee) *n.* an Oriental form of unarmed combat using kicks, punches, and "chops" aimed at the most vulnerable parts of the opponent's body.

kar·ma (KAR·muh) *n.* in Buddhism and Hinduism, life and actions as determining one's fate; hence, fate or destiny; **kar·mic** *adj.*

karst *n.* a limestone region with a dry and barren surface, characterized by deep fissures and underground streams.

kart *n.* a small, low, four-wheeled, one-seater automobile used for racing, or **kart·ing.**

Kat(h)·man·du (kaht·mahn·DOO) capital of Nepal.

ka·ty·did (KAY·tee–) *n.* any of a family of large grasshopperlike long-horned green insects.

kay·ak (KYE–) *n.* a light Eskimo canoe having a deck top covered with seal skin and a cockpit in the middle for the paddler.

kay·o (KAY·OH) *Slang. n.* a knockout in boxing; ***v.* -os, -oed, -o·ing** knock out.

ka·zoo (kuh·ZOO) *n.* **-zoos** a toy musical instrument like an oboe consisting of a short tube stopped at one end with a membrane or paper that vibrates when the tube is hummed into.

kc kilocycle(s); **kc/s** kilocycles per second. **—K.C.** Knights of Columbus; King's Counsel.

kcal kilocalorie(s).

K.D. or **k.d.** knocked down (i.e. not assembled).

Keats, John. 1795–1821, English poet.

ke·bab or **ke·bob** (kuh·BOB) *n.* a dish of pieces of marinated meat cooked with vegetables stuck on a skewer.

kedge *v.* **kedg·es, kedged, kedg·ing** move (a boat) by hauling on a rope attached to a small anchor thrown some distance in the water; ***n.*** such an anchor.

keel *n.* the main timber or steel piece laid lengthwise along the hull of a boat to support its framework; hence, a ridgelike part; **on an even keel** in a level position; hence, stable or steady. ***—v.*** esp. **keel over,** turn over; also, *Informal.* collapse or faint. **—keel·boat** *n.* a freight boat with a keel and pointed prow. **—keel·haul** *v.* rebuke severely, like hauling one under a ship's keel. **—keel·son** (KEL·sn, KEEL–) *n.* a reinforcing structure running above the keel of a boat.

[1]keen *adj.* **1** having a fine edge; hence, sharp or biting: *a ~ blade, eyesight, pain.* **2** very eager; full of enthusiasm: *~ competition; ~ on winning; ~ about flying.* **3** *Slang.* wonderful. **—keen·ly** *adv.* **—keen·ness** *n.*

[2]keen *n.* & *v.* (make a sound suggesting) a wailing or lamentation.

keep *v.* **keeps, kept, keep·ing** **1** continue to have and hold in one's possession, control, or care: *You may not ~ library books too long; The wedding was kept a secret* (i.e. not revealed); *What ~s* (i.e. prevents) *you from going? They ~* (i.e. raise) *hogs on the farm;* **keeps** *very much* **to himself** *since his wife died.* **2** maintain or preserve without change of condition: *Salt ~s meat without spoiling; to ~ children amused; a well-kept lawn; trying to* **keep up** *payments on the loan.* **3** be faithful to: *Does he ~ appointments?* ***—n.*** care or charge; also, support or livelihood; **for keeps** for the winner to keep; also, *Informal.* forever. **—keep·er** *n.* **—keep·ing** *n.* care; also, observance: *a practice that is* **in keeping with** (i.e. according to) *custom.* **—keep·sake** *n.* something to keep in memory of someone; memento.

keg *n.* a small cask or barrel.

keg·ler *n. Informal.* one who bowls.

kelp *n.* an iodine-rich seaweed or its ashes.

Kelt(ic) same as CELT(IC).

Kel·vin *adj.* of a temperature-measuring scale with 273° as the freezing point of water and 373° as its boiling point.

ken *v.* **kens, kenned, ken·ning** *Scottish.* know or have knowledge. ***—n.*** range of knowledge. **—Ken.** Kentucky.

Ken·ne·dy (KEN·uh·dee), **John F.** 1917–63; 35th U.S. President (1961–63).

ken·nel (KENL) *n.* & *v.* **ken·nels, ken·nel(l)ed, ken·nel·(l)ing** (keep in) a doghouse; **kennels** *pl.* a boarding establishment for dogs.

ke·no (KEE–) *n.* a gambling game similar to bingo or lotto.

Ken·tuck·y (–TUCK–) an E. C. state of the U.S.; 40,395 sq. mi. (104,623 km²); *cap.* Frankfort; **Ken·tuck·i·an** *n.* & *adj.*

Ken·ya (KEN·yuh, KEEN–) an E. C. African country; 224,961 sq. mi. (582,645 km²); *cap.* Nairobi. **—Ken·yan** *n.* & *adj.*

ke·pi (KEP·ee) *n.* a French military cap with a flat top and a visor.

Ke·pone (KEE–) *Trademark.* a highly toxic chemical once used in pesticides.

kept *pt.* & *pp.* of KEEP; ***adj.*** maintained for sexual relations: *a ~ woman, boy.*

ker·a·tin (KAIR·uh·tn) *n.* the protein substance of horn, nails, hair, and feathers. **—ke·rat·i·nous** (–RATN·nus) *adj.* horny.

kerb *Brit.* curb (*n.* 2).

ker·chief (KUR·chif) *n.* **-chiefs** or **-chieves** (–cheevz) a usu. square piece of cloth used by women as a head covering or scarf; also, a handkerchief.

kerf *n.* a cut or a channel carved by an ax or saw.

ker·nel (CUR·nl) *n.* **1** a seed of the corn plant or a grain of wheat or other cereal. **2** the inner, edible part of a nut, fruit pit, etc.; hence, the core or essence.

ker·o·sene or **ker·o·sine** (KAIR·uh·seen) *n.* a thin oil distilled from petroleum and used as a fuel, esp. in aircraft engines, and as a solvent.

kes·trel *n.* a small European falcon; also called "windhover."

ketch *n.* a two-masted fore-and-aft-rigged ship.

ketch·up *n.* a seasoned sauce, esp. a thick one made with tomatoes.

ket·tle *n.* a metal container for boiling liquids. **—ket·tle·drum** *n.* a drum made of parchment stretched over the flat top of a hollow copper or brass hemisphere. **—kettle of fish** a matter or affair, esp. of an awkward kind.

[1]key (KEE) *n.* **keys** a low island or reef: as in *Florida Keys, Key West.*

[2]key (KEE) *n.* **keys** **1** a small metal device with one end cut in a particular design for fitting into the **key·hole** of a door, padlock, etc. to lock or unlock it; also, something shaped or used like a key: *the ~ of a tin can.* **2** something that provides access or entry, as the solution to a problem or the explanation of a set of symbols: *a dictionary's pronunciation*

~; *Gibraltar was the ~ to the Mediterranean.* **3** one of a set of disks or buttons forming a **key·board** operated with the fingers, as in playing certain musical instruments, operating a typewriter, or a **key punch** machine for punching cards or tapes for data processing; ***v.:*** *to* **keyboard, key·punch,** *or* **key·stroke** *a text or data for processing; input charged at $10 per 1,000* **keystrokes** (i.e. taps of keys). **4** a musical scale or system based on a basic tone or keynote, as "C major"; hence, a tone or style of expression: *spoke in a low ~.* **—*adj.*** important or controlling: *~ personnel, industries, issues; a "key grip"* (i.e. head of a stage crew). **—*v.*** **keys, keyed, key·ing:** *a properly ~ed violin; The speech was ~ed to the mood of the audience; crazy fans* **keyed up** (i.e. excited) *to a fever pitch.* **—keyboard** See ²KEY, *n.* 3. **—key club** a private club whose members usu. have keys to the premises. **—keyhole** See ²KEY, *n.* 1. **—key·note** *v.* **-notes, -not·ed, -not·ing** give the keynote or keynote address of; ***n.*** the basic note of a musical scale; hence, the basic idea or policy theme, as set forth in a **keynote speech** (or **address**) given at a convention; **key·not·er** *n.* **—keypunch** See ²KEY, *n.* 3. **—key·stone** *n.* the central, topmost stone of an arch; hence, central principle. **—keystroke** See ²KEY, *n.* 3. **—key word** a word that forms the key or guide to other words, as a guide word in a dictionary. **—Key West** the westernmost of the chain of islands S. of Florida.

kg or **kg.** kilogram(s).

K.G.B. the Soviet secret police.

kha·ki (KAK·ee, KAH–) *n.* a strong, twilled, yellowish-brown cloth for uniforms, esp. military; hence, the color or a uniform made of khaki, usu. **kha·kis** *pl.* **—*adj.*** dull yellowish-brown; also, made of khaki cloth.

khan (KAHN, KAN) *n.* a Turkish title, now used for "Mister" in some C. Asian countries.

Khar·kov (KAR·kawf) an industrial city of the Ukraine.

Khar·toum (kar·TOOM) capital of Sudan.

khe·dive (kuh·DEEV) *n.* the title of the Turkish viceroys of Egypt between 1867 and 1914.

Khmer (KMAIR) *n.* a member of the dominant cultural group or the language of Cambodia.

kHz kilohertz.

kib·ble *v.* **kib·bles, kib·bled, kib·bling** grind coarsely; ***n.*** coarsely ground meal.

kib·butz (ki·BOOTS) *n., pl.* **kib·but·zim** (–boot·SEEM) an Israeli collective farm.

kibe *n. Archaic.* a chilblain, esp. on the heel.

kib·itz (KIB·its) *v. Informal.* look on at a card game and offer unwanted advice; **kib·itz·er** *n.* one who kibitzes; hence, a meddler.

ki·bosh (KYE–) *n. Slang.* **put the kibosh on** put an end to; squelch.

kick *v.* **1** strike (out) with a foot, esp. forward; also, force or move by a kick: *A soccer ball is ~ed; a horse that ~s; slip-on shoes easy to ~ off.* **2** *Informal.* complain or grumble. **3** *Slang.* get rid of (a habit). **—*n.:*** *a football ~; the ~* (i.e. recoil) *of a gun when fired; smokes pot* **for kicks** (*Slang.* for the pleasure). **—kick·back** *n. Informal.* money illegally paid back to a patron in return for a benefit such as a job, business, contract, etc. **—kick·er** *n.* **1** one that kicks. **2** *Slang.* something that gives a kick or jolt. **—kick in** *Slang.* contribute one's share. **—kick off** *Informal.* begin (a campaign, proceedings, etc.), as by putting a ball in play with a **kick·off** *n.* in football or soccer, a PLACE KICK. **—kick over** start operating, as an automobile engine beginning to fire. **—kick·stand** *n.* on a bicycle or motorcycle, a short metal bar that is kicked into position to stand the vehicle up when not in use. **—kick·y** *adj.* **kick·i·er, -i·est** *Slang.* exciting; providing kicks.

kick·shaw *n.* a trifle such as a delicacy or bauble.

kid *n.* **1** *Informal.* a child; also, a young man or woman; ***adj.:*** *my ~* (i.e. younger) *brother; mere ~ stuff* (i.e. suitable for kids); **kid·dish** *adj.* **2** a young goat, its flesh for food, or its skin or leather, i.e. **kid·skin,** for shoes and gloves, i.e. **kid gloves:** *handle a temperamental person with ~ gloves* (i.e. with special consideration). **—*v.*** **kids, kid·ded, kid·ding** tease; also, fool; **kid·der** *n.* **kid·ding·ly** *adv.* **—kid·dy** or **kid·die** *n.* **kid·dies** a small child. **—kid·nap** *v.* **-naps, -nap(p)ed, -nap·(p)ing** abduct (someone, esp. a child) usu. for ransom or as a hostage; **kid·nap·(p)er** *n.*

kid·ney (–nee) *n.* **-neys** **1** either of a pair of bean-shaped organs situated at the back above the waist that separate waste matter from the blood and pass it as urine into the bladder: *A* **kidney machine** *is used for artificial dialysis; A calculus or* **kidney stone** *is a hard mineral deposit in a kidney.* **2** nature or sort: *a man of a different ~.* **—kidney bean** a kidney-shaped bean such as the mottled "pinto bean" and the white "navy bean."

kidskin See KID. **—kid·vid** *n. Slang.* children's television.

kiel·ba·sa (kyel·BAH·suh) *n., pl.* **-si** (–see) or **-sas** a smoked Polish sausage.

Ki·ev (KEE·ef) capital of the Ukrainian S.S.R.

kie·sel·gu(h)r (KEE·zl·goor) *n.* a diatomite.

Ki·ga·li (kee·GAH·lee) capital of Rwanda.

kill *v.* cause (the) death (of); hence, do away with: *Cain ~ed Abel; "Thou shalt not ~"; played cards to ~ time till dinner; Journalists ~ stories* (i.e. by discarding type) *they cannot use; a ~ing* (i.e. exhausting) *job; You're* **killing** (*Slang.* very funny). **—*n.*** a killing or something killed, as by a hunter or beast, an aircraft or missile shot down, etc. **—kill·deer** *n.* a small North American plover with a cry like "kill dee"; also **kill·dee.** **—kil·ler (whale)** a large voracious porpoise that can kill a whale. **—kill·ing** *n.* slaughter; also, *Informal.* a profit or windfall, as from a sale, stocks, etc. **—kill-joy** *n.* one who spoils others' fun.

kiln (KIL, KILN) *n.* & *v.* (burn, bake, or dry in) a high-temperature furnace or oven for making lime, bricks, ceramics, etc.

ki·lo (KEE–, KIL–) *n.* **-los** short for KILOGRAM, KILOMETER. **—kilo-** *prefix.* one thousand: as in **kil·o·cy·cle** (KIL·uh·sye·cl) *n.* former name for KILOHERTZ. **—kil·o·gram** *n.* unit of weight equal to 1,000 grams; *Brit.* **kil·o·gramme. —kil·o·hertz** (–hurts) *n. sing.* & *pl.* 1,000 hertz. **—kil·o·li·ter** (KIL·uh·lee–) *n.* unit of volume equal to 1,000 liters; *Brit.* **kil·o·li·tre. —ki·lo·me·ter** (–LOM·uh–, KIL·uh–) *n.* unit of length equal to 1,000 meters; *Brit.* **ki·lo·me·tre. —kil·o·ton** (–uh·tun) *n.* unit of weight equal to 1,000 tons; also, the explosive force of 1,000 tons of TNT. **—kil·o·volt** (–uh–) *n.* unit of electromotive force equal to 1,000 volts. **—kil·o·watt** (–uh·wot) *n.* unit of electrical power equal to 1,000 watts; **kil·o·watt-hour** *n.* unit of electrical energy equal to the work done by one kilowatt acting for one hour.

kilt *n.* a knee-length pleated skirt, usu. of tartan, worn by men in the Scottish Highlands; **kilt·ed** *adj.* kilt-wearing: ~ *regiments.* **—out of kilt·er** *Informal.* not in proper working order.

ki·mo·no (kuh·MOH·nuh) *n.* **-nos** the traditional Japanese outer garment of men and women, a long, loose robe with a wide sash around the waist; also, a woman's dressing gown, sometimes spelled "kimona."

kin *n.* a relative or kinsman; also, relatives or kindred: *He's no ~ of mine; The victim has to be identified and* **next of kin** (i.e. the nearest relative) *informed first;* ***adj.*** related: *He's ~ to me.* **—kin** *suffix.* little: as in *catkin, lambkin.* **—kind** (KINED) *adj.* sincerely sympathetic and considerate: *Be ~ to animals; had a ~ word for everyone.* ***—n.*** a natural group of people, animals, or things; hence, nature: *He's one of our own ~; a difference of degree not of ~* (i.e. nature or character); *an insult that was paid back* **in kind** (i.e. with insult); *payment in cash or in ~* (i.e. goods or produce); *said nothing of the ~* (i.e. nothing at all like that); **kind of** *Informal.* sort of; **of a kind** of the same kind; also, of a poor quality.

kin·der·gar·ten (KIN·dur·gar·tn) *n.* a class or school preparing young children for first grade by games and other pleasant occupations; **kin·der·gar·t(e)n·er** *n.* a child or teacher in a kindergarten.

kind·heart·ed (KINED·HAR·tid) *adj.* kind by nature; sympathetic.

kin·dle (KIN·dl) *v.* **-dles, -dled, -dling** set on fire; also, light up or arouse like fire: *~ a fire, tinder, anger, interest; a face ~d with joy; the ~ing temperatures of various substances.* **—kind·ling** *n.* material such as dry wood: *tinder, ~, and firewood to build a campfire.*

kind·ly (KINED–) *adj.* **kind·li·er, -li·est** disposed to be kind; friendly; also, agreeable: *the ~ old gentleman; a ~ climate; ~ attentions;* ***adv.:*** *words ~ meant; thank you ~; Few dogs* **take kindly to** (i.e. like) *cats;* **kind·li·ness** *n.* **—kind·ness** *n.* kind nature, treatment, or act: *the many ~es shown to me.*

kin·dred (–drid) *adj.* naturally related or similar: *~ tribes, languages, facts, phenomena, natures; a ~ soul.* ***—n.*** relatives or family.

kine *n.pl. Archaic.* cows; also, cattle.

kin·e·scope (KIN·uh–) *n.* a television picture tube. **—ki·ne·sics** (–NEE–) *n.pl.* the study of bodily movements and gestures as part of language. **—kin·es·the·si·a** (–is·THEA·zhuh) *n.* the sensation of muscle movements. **—ki·net·ic** (–NET–) *adj.* of or by motion: *the* **kinetic energy** *of a falling object.*

kin·folk(s) *n.pl.* family or relatives.

King, Martin Luther, Jr. 1929–68, American civil-rights leader. **—King James Bible** same as AUTHORIZED VERSION. **—king** *n.* a male sovereign; hence, a male person supreme in a certain sphere or class; also, a chess piece or playing card designated as king: *the ~ of Denmark; the ~ of the beasts; when comedy was ~; an oil ~* (i.e. tycoon); ***adj.*** chief in size or importance; **king·ly** *adj.;* **king·ship** *n.* **—king·bolt** *n.* a vertical bolt or tie rod. **—king crab** same as HORSESHOE CRAB. **—king·dom** *n.* a king's domain or territory; also, a division, as of the natural world into animal, vegetable, and mineral kingdoms. **—king·fish·er** *n.* any of a family of bright-colored crested birds with long, heavy bills with which they spear fish. **—king·pin** *n.* in bowling games, the chief or front pin; hence, *Informal.* the most important person or thing: *the ~ of the underworld.* **—king·size(d)** *adj. Informal.* large: *a ~ cigarette, meal, bed* (approx. 78 × 80 in. / 1.98 × 2.03 m).

Kings·ton (–tun) seaport and capital of Jamaica.

King Tut See TUTANKHAMEN.

kink *n.* a twist or tight curl, as in a wire or rope; hence, something that obstructs or prevents smooth operation; also, a muscle spasm: *the only ~* (i.e. quirk) *in his personality; a few ~s to be ironed out in our plan;* ***v.:*** *Railroad tracks may expand and ~ upward.*

kin·ka·jou (KING·kuh·joo) *n.* a raccoonlike animal of South and Central America that lives in trees.

kink·y *adj.* having kinks: *~ hair; ~ goods* (*Slang.* got by crooked means); ~ (i.e. far-out, offbeat) *clothes;* ~ (i.e. perverted) *sex.*

kins·folk (KINZ–) *n.pl.* same as KINFOLK.

Kin·sha·sa (keen·SHAH·sah) capital of Zaire.

kin·ship *n.* family relationship. **—kins·man** (KINZ·mun) *n.* **-men** relative, esp. a male; *fem.* **kins·wom·an, -wom·en.**

ki·osk (KEE–) *n.* a lightly built, open-sided structure, as a bandstand, newsstand, etc.

Ki·o·wa (KYE·uh·wah) *n.* a member of an American Indian people of Oklahoma.

kip *n.* **1** the untanned hide of a young or small animal. **2** the basic money unit of Laos, equal to 100 ats.
Kip·ling, Rudyard. 1865–1936, English author.
kip·per *v.* cure (fish) by salting and drying or smoking; ***n.*** a kippered herring or salmon.
kirk *n.* in Scotland, a church; **Kirk** the Scottish Presbyterian Church.
kir·tle *n.* in the Middle Ages, a woman's gown or dress; also, a man's tunic or coat.
kis·met (KIZ–) *n.* fate or destiny.
kiss *n.* a caress with the lips; hence, a gentle touch; also, a small candy or cake; ***v.:*** *She ~ed them "good night"; gentle winds ~ing the treetops;* **kiss·a·ble** *adj.;* **kiss·er** *n.* one who kisses; also, *Slang.* mouth. —**kissing disease** See MONONUCLEOSIS.
kit *n.* a set of tools, supplies, parts, etc. for a specific use: *a shaving ~; model airplane ~; first-aid ~;* **the whole kit and caboodle** *Informal.* the whole lot.
kitch·en *n.* a room or place for cooking food. —**kitch·en·et(te)** (–NET) *n.* a small kitchen or cooking facility. —**kitchen midden** same as MIDDEN. —**kitchen police** military personnel detailed to help in an army kitchen; also, such a detail. —**kitch·en·ware** *n.* kitchen utensils or small appliances.
kite *n.* **1** a bird of prey of the hawk family noted for its long, narrow wings and graceful gliding. **2** a device for flying in the air at the end of a long string, made of a light, usu. geometrical framework covered with paper or plastic.
kith *n.* **kith and kin** friends and relatives.
kitsch *n.* trashy art or its pretentious quality; **kitsch·y** *adj.*
kit·ten (KITN) *n.* a young cat; **kit·ten·ish** *adj.* playful like a cat; coquettish. —**kit·ty** *n.* **kit·ties** **1** [pet name] cat; also, kitten. **2** a fund of money, esp. one pooled for a common purpose. —**kit·ty-cor·ner(ed)** *adj.* same as CATER-CORNER(ED).
ki·wi (KEE·wee) *n.* a flightless, shaggy, long-billed bird of New Zealand.
K.J.V. King James Version (of the Bible).
K.K.K. or **KKK** Ku Klux Klan.
kl kiloliter(s).
Klan *n.* (a chapter of) the Ku Klux Klan; **Klans·man** *n.* **-men.**
klatsch (CLACH) *n.* an informal social gathering.
Klee·nex *Trademark.* tissue-paper handkerchief.
kleig light same as KLIEG LIGHT.
klep·to·ma·ni·a (–tuh·MAY·nee·uh) *n.* an obsessive impulse to steal, esp. things that the stealer, or **klep·to·ma·ni·ac,** has no use for.
klieg (KLEEG) **light** a high-intensity carbon-arc light used on motion picture sets.
klutz *n. Slang.* a clumsy person.
km kilometer(s); **km²** square kilometers.
km/h kilometers per hour.
K-mes·on (KAY·mes–, –mee–) same as KAON.
knack (NAK) *n.* ability to do something with cleverness and skill: *easy once you get the ~ of it; a ~ for cooking.*
knack·wurst (NAHK–) *n.* a thick, spicy frankfurter.
knap·sack (NAP–) *n.* a soldier's or hiker's bag for supplies, carried strapped to the back.
knave (NAVE) *n.* a rogue or dishonest person; also, a jack (playing card); **knav·ish** *adj.;* **knav·ish·ly** *adv.* —**knav·er·y** *n.* **-er·ies** rascality.
knead (NEED) *v.* work by pressing and squeezing (dough, clay, muscles, etc.); **knead·er** *n.*
knee (NEE) *n.* the leg joint between thigh and lower leg, protected in front by a movable bone called **knee·cap.** —***v.*** **knees, kneed, knee·ing** touch or hit with the knee. —**knee-deep** *adj.* sunk to the knees: *~ water; found himself ~ in trouble;* **knee-high** *adj.* reaching the knees. —**knee·hole** *n.* a space, as in a desk, for the user's knees. —**knee-jerk** *adj.* of behavior, predictable because automatic like a reflex action. —**kneel** (NEEL) *v.* **kneels,** *pt.* & *pp.* **knelt** or **kneeled, kneel·ing** go down on one's knee(s), as in prayer.
knell (NEL) *v.* ring (a bell) solemnly, as at someone's death; ***n.*** such a ringing or its sound; hence, the indication of an end.
knelt a *pt.* & *pp.* of KNEEL.
knew *pt.* of KNOW.
knick·ers (NIK–) *n.pl.* loose breeches gathered at the knee; also **knick·er·bock·ers.**
knick·knack (NIK·nak) *n.* a small trivial or dainty article or trinket.
knife (NIFE) *n.* **knives** (NIVES) a cutting tool with a blade and a handle, as used with a fork for eating; also, a cutting blade, as of a lawnmower; **under the knife** undergoing surgery. —***v.*** **knifes, knifed, knif·ing** stab or cut through (as if) with a knife.
knight (NITE) *n.* **1** in the Middle Ages, a military man honored as a loyal servant of the king; hence, a British rank just below baronet with the title "Sir." **2** a man of chivalry; also, a member of an order or society of "Knights" such as the **Knights of Columbus,** a Roman Catholic fraternal society. —***v.:*** *Charlie Chaplin was ~ed by Queen Elizabeth II in 1975.* —**knight·hood** *n.* the rank of a knight or knights collectively; also, chivalry. —**knight·ly** *adj.* chivalrous or brave.
knish (kuh·NISH) *n.* a pastry of dough with a filling of meat, cheese, fruit, etc.
knit (NIT) *v.* **knits,** *pt.* & *pp.* **knit** or **knit·ted, knit·ting** **1** make (a fabric or article of clothing) by looping, instead of weaving, thread or yarn closely together with long needles: *to ~ a sweater; A fractured bone ~s* (i.e. joins together) *in the course of time; a close-~ group of researchers; brows ~ed* (i.e. drawn together) *in a*

frown; **knit·ter** *n.* —**knit·wear** *n.* knitted clothing.

knives *pl.* of KNIFE.

knob (NOB) *n.* a rounded bulge made for ornament or as a handle fixed to a door, drawer, etc.; also, a small rounded hill; **knobbed** (NOBD) *adj.;* **knob·bly** or **knob·by** *adj.* **knob·bi·er, knob·bi·est.**

knock (NOK) *n.* a sharp blow with something hard or solid, as a fist, knuckles, gavel, etc.: *a ~ on the door.* —*v.* strike; pound; collide: *was ~ed down in the first round; The ball ~ed the vase off the table; likes to ~* (*Slang.* attack or criticize) *people in authority; An engine that ~s* (i.e. makes a rattling or ringing noise) *needs antiknock in the fuel.* —**knock·er** *n.* —**knock about** (or **around**) roam; also, treat roughly. —**knock down** 1 fell; also, indicate (an auctioned item) as sold, with a knock of the gavel. 2 disassemble. —**knock off** *Informal.* 1 deduct: *We'll ~ 10% off the price.* 2 stop (work or other activity): *We ~ off (work) at 5 p.m.; Will you please ~ it* (i.e. the nuisance) *off?* 3 finish routinely: *a prolific writer ~ing off one romance after another.* 4 overcome; also, kill. —**knock out** to defeat, as in boxing, or put (a pitcher) out of a game of baseball; make inoperative: *power lines ~ed out by a storm; Two drinks are enough to ~ him out;* **knock·out** *n.* & *adj.: won it on a technical ~; a ~ blow; stupefied by ~ drops in his drink; a ~* (*Slang.* outstanding) *performance.* —**knock together** put together or compose hastily. —**knock-kneed** *adj.* with the legs bent inward at the knees so that they touch in walking; **knock-knees** *n.pl.* such knees. —**knock·wurst** (NOK–) same as KNACKWURST.

knoll (NOLE) *n.* a small rounded hill; mound.

knot (NOT) 1 a tie or fastening made with one or more cords, ropes, etc.; hence, something that resembles a knot in closeness, intricacy, or lumpiness of form: *a figure-eight ~; Why tie yourself* **in knots** (i.e. get nervous) *over nothing? ~s of people standing around chatting;* **tie the knot** *Informal.* get married. 2 one nautical mile (per hour). —*v.* **knots, knot·ted, knot·ting** tie in a knot; tangle in knots; also, unite closely or form into a hard lump. —**knot·grass** *n.* a weed of the buckwheat family with jointed stems. —**knot·hole** *n.* a hole left by a knot that has fallen out of a board or tree trunk. —**knot·ty** *adj.* **knot·ti·er, knot·ti·est:** *~ pine wood; a ~* (i.e. complex) *problem.*

knout (NOWT) *n.* & *v.* (flog with) a whip of a kind formerly used in Russia.

know (NO) *v.* **knows, knew** (NEW), **known** (NOHN), **know·ing** be well-acquainted with (a person or thing), having the subject firmly in the mind or memory: *Do I ~ you? He ~s how to type; Infants don't ~* (i.e. distinguish) *right from wrong; He should* **know better** *than to make promises he can't keep; I will* **let you know** (i.e. inform you) *when the parcel arrives; Mother* **knows best** (i.e. is the best guide); **in the know** *Informal.* having inside information. —**know·a·ble** (NO·uh–) *adj.* —**know-how** *n.* *Informal.* expertise or practical knowledge. —**know·ing** *adj.* having knowledge in a special way: *a ~* (i.e. shrewd) *smile; a ~ wink;* **know·ing·ly** *adv.: wouldn't ~ hurt a fly.* —**know(-it)-all** *n.* & *adj.* (one) pretending to know everything. —**knowl·edge** (NOL·ij) *n.* 1 act or fact of knowing; also, what is known: *a book of ~.* 2 understanding or awareness: *things beyond our ~;* **to (the best of) one's knowledge** as far as one knows. —**knowl·edge·a·ble** (–uh·bl) *adj.* well-informed; intelligent; **knowl·edge·a·bly** *adv.*

Knox·ville (NOX·vil) a city of E. Tennessee.

knuck·le *n.* a finger joint, esp. one joining a finger to the rest of the hand; also, the knee or hock joint of an animal such as a pig used as food. —*v.* **-les, -led, -ling; knuckle down** apply oneself earnestly (*to* a task); **knuckle under** submit or yield (*to* a person or thing). —**knuck·le·bone** *n.* one of the bones forming a knuckle. —**knuck·le·head** *n.* *Informal.* stupid person.

knurl (NURL) *n.* a small projection or knob; also, a ridge formed of such, as the milling on the edge of a coin; **knurled** *adj.* milled; also, gnarled.

KO (KAY·OH) *v.* **KO's, KO'd, KO'ing** *Slang.* in boxing, to knock out; *n.* a knockout. Also **K.O., k.o.**

ko·a·la (–AH–) *n.* a small Australian marsupial resembling a sloth or a teddy bear that lives in eucalyptus trees, feeding on their leaves and buds.

kob·o (KOB·oh) *n. sing.* & *pl.* a money unit of Nigeria equal to 1/100 of a naira.

ko·bold (KOH·bawld) *n.* a goblin of German folklore.

ko·di·ak (KOH·dee·ak) **bear** a large brown bear native to Kodiak Island, Alaska.

K. of C. Knight(s) of Columbus.

kohl·ra·bi (–RAH·bee, KOHL–) *n.* **-bies** a vegetable related to the cabbage with leafstalks growing from its edible, bulb-shaped stem.

kola same as COLA.

ko·lin·sky (–LIN·skee) *n.* **-skies** the golden-brown fur of an Asiatic mink, also called "China mink" or "Tartar sable."

kook *n.* *Slang.* one considered crazy or eccentric; **kook·y** or **kook·ie** *adj.;* **kook·i·ness** *n.*

kook·a·bur·ra (COOK·uh·bur·uh) *n.* an Australian kingfisher, also called "laughing jackass" because of its cry.

ko·pe(c)k (KOH·pek) *n.* a Russian money unit and coin equal to 1/100 of a ruble.

Ko·ran (koh·RAN) the sacred book of the Moslems.

Ko·re·a (–REE·uh) an Asian peninsula and former country opposite Japan, since World War II divided into **North Korea,** 46,540 sq. mi. (120,538 km^2), *cap.* Pyongyang, and **South**

Korea, 38,022 sq. mi. (98,477 km^2), *cap.* Seoul. **—Ko•re•an** (–REE·un) *n.* a person from or the language of Korea; ***adj.*** of Korea, its people, or their language.

ko•ru•na (COR·uh·nah) *n.* **-nas** or **-ny** (-nee) the basic money unit of Czechoslovakia, equal to 100 halers.

ko•sher (COH·shur) *adj.* of a food or establishment, meeting the requirements of Jewish dietary law; hence, legitimate or proper.

kow•tow *v.* show slavish respect (to); ***n.*** an act of kowtowing.

K.P. kitchen police.

K.P.H. or **k.p.h.** kilometers per hour.

Kr krypton.

kraal (KRAHL) *n.* & *v.* (shut up in) an enclosed village for South African natives; also, a pen or enclosure for animals in S. Africa.

kraut same as SAUERKRAUT.

Krem•lin the citadel of Moscow; hence, the Soviet government, formerly housed in the Kremlin. **—Krem•lin•ol•o•gy** (–NOL·uh·jee) *n.* the study of the Soviet government and its policies; **Krem•lin•ol•o•gist** *n.*

Krish•na (–nuh) a Hindu god, an incarnation of Vishnu.

kro•na (CROH·nuh) *n.* **1** *pl.* **-nor** the basic money unit and a coin of Sweden. **2** *pl.* **-nur** the basic money unit and a coin of Iceland. **—kro•ne** (–nuh) *n., pl.* **-ner** the basic money unit and a coin of Norway or Denmark.

Kru•ger (CROO·gur) **rand** a South African gold coin worth 31 rand.

kryp•ton (CRIP·tahn) *n.* a rare inert gaseous chemical element.

KS Kansas.

kt. karat; knight.

ku•chen (COO·cun) *n.* a German coffee cake.

ku•dos (CUE–) *n. Informal.* credit for an achievement; glory; fame.

kud•zu (COOD·zoo) *n.* an Oriental vine of the pea family, grown to prevent soil erosion, for forage, and for its fiber.

Ku Klux Klan (KOO–, KEW–) a secret terrorist U.S. organization that is anti-Black, anti-Semitic, anti-Catholic, etc.

ku•lak (coo·LAHK) *n.* a well-to-do Russian farmer of a class that opposed collectivization of the land in the 1930's.

kum•quat (CUM·kwaht) *n.* a Chinese citrus fruit that looks like a miniature orange and has a sweet, edible skin.

kung fu (COONG·FOO) the Chinese form of karate.

Kurd *n.* a member of a nomadic Moslem people of **Kur•di•stan,** a mountainous region of S.W. Asia lying in Turkey, Iran, and Iraq. **—Kurd•ish** *n.* & *adj.* (the Iranian language) of the Kurds.

ku•rus (koo·ROOSH) *n. sing.* & *pl.* a money unit equal to 1/100 of the Turkish lira.

Ku•wait (koo·WAIT, –WITE) an Arab emirate on the Persian Gulf; 7,768 sq. mi. (20,118 km^2); *cap.* **Kuwait.**

kv kilovolt(s). **—kw** kilowatt(s).

kvetch *v.* complain in a nagging or whining manner; ***n.*** one who does this.

kwa•cha (KWAH·chah) *n. sing.* & *pl.* the basic money unit of Malawi and Zambia.

Kwang•chow (KWAHNG·CHOH) same as CANTON.

kwa•shi•or•kor (kwah·shee·OR–) *n.* a protein-deficiency disease affecting esp. children on a mainly starchy diet and characterized by stunted growth and potbelly.

KWIC (KWIC) *n.* "key-word-in-context," a computer-generated index for retrieving a portion of material together with its keyword.

KY or **Ky.** Kentucky.

kyat (CHAHT) *n.* the basic money unit of Burma, equal to 100 pyas.

ky•mo•graph (KYE·muh–) *n.* an instrument for graphically recording on a drum wavelike motions such as muscular contractions or the pulse.

Kyo•to (kee·OH·toh) a cultural center and former capital of Japan.

L

L or **l** (EL) *n.* **L's** or **l's** **1** the 12th letter of the English alphabet. **2** the Roman numeral for 50. —**L** *n.* **L's** something L-shaped, as an extension forming a right angle with the main building or a pipe-joint. —**L.** or **l.** lake; latitude; left; length; line (*pl.* **LL.** or **ll.**); lira(s); lire; liter(s); pound(s). —**L.** Latin. —**L** Lebanese; Libra; liter(s); longitude. —**l** liter(s).

La lanthanum. —**la** (LAH) *n. Music.* the sixth tone of the diatonic scale. —**La.** or **LA** Louisiana. —**L.A.** Los Angeles.

Lab. Labrador. —**lab** *n. Informal.* laboratory.

la·bel (LAY·bl) *n.* a slip attached to something to identify or describe it, its ownership, or its destination. —*v.* **-bels, -bel(l)ed, -bel·(l)ing** assign (a person or thing) to a particular class: *All luggage should be ∼d; was ∼d a Communist because of his leftist leanings;* **la·bel·(l)er** *n.*

la·bi·al (LAY·bee·ul) *n.* & *adj.* (a speech sound) made with the lips, as "b," "m," and "p." —**la·bi·um** *n., pl.* **-bi·a** (-bee·uh) a lip or liplike part such as the **labia ma·jo·ra** (–muh·JOR·uh) and **labia mi·no·ra** (–mi·NOR·uh), the outer and inner folds respectively of the vulva.

la·bile (LAY·bl, –bile) *adj.* apt to change; unstable or fluctuating, as blood pressure.

la·bor (LAY·bur) *n.* **1** hard work or exertion, esp. physical; hence, the pains of childbirth; also, a piece of work: *sentenced to two years' hard ∼; a* **labor of love,** *not done for pay; the ∼s of Hercules; An electric toothbrush is a* **la·bor-sav·ing** *device.* **2** workers as distinguished from management; also, labor unions collectively. —*v.* work, esp. with much effort: *a truck ∼ing uphill with a heavy load; a practical-minded woman who* **labors under** *no delusions; Why ∼ a point that is so obvious? the* **la·bored** *breathing of an asthmatic;* **lab·or·er** *n.* —**lab·o·ra·to·ry** (LAB·ruh·tor·ee) *n.* **-ries** a place for scientific research or manufacture, esp. of drugs and chemicals. —**Labor Day** the first Monday of September, a legal holiday in the U.S. and Canada in honor of workers: *Service industries tend to be* **la·bor-in·ten·sive** (i.e. investing much on labor) *rather than capital-intensive.* —**la·bo·ri·ous** (luh·BOR·ee·us) *adj.* **1** requiring much labor or hard work; also, labored. **2** industrious or hard-working. —**la·bo·ri·ous·ly** *adv.* —**labor of love, labor-saving** See LABOR, *n.* 1. —**labor union** a workers' organization for the protection of their rights as wage-earners, esp. by collective bargaining. —**la·bour** *Brit.* labor.

Lab·ra·dor (LAB·ruh–) a large peninsula of N.E. Canada.

la·bur·num (luh·BUR–) *n.* a small tree or shrub of the pea family having bright yellow blossoms hanging in clusters.

lab·y·rinth (LAB·uh–) *n.* a building with a confusing network of passageways; maze; hence, the inner ear with its intricate chambers and channels; **lab·y·rin·thine** (–RIN·thin) *adj.* like a labyrinth; complicated.

lac *n.* a resinous substance deposited by scale insects on the soapberry and acacia trees of Asia, used in making shellac.

lace *n.* **1** open fabric woven in patterns with threads of linen or similar soft material. **2** an ornamental braid used for trimming uniforms. **3** a string or cord pulled through eyelets to tie a shoe, tighten a corset, etc. —*v.* **lac·es, laced, lac·ing:** *to ∼ up a shoe; a uniform ∼d with gold; He likes his coffee ∼d with rum;* **lace into** attack physically; also criticize severely.

lac·er·ate (LAS·uh–) *v.* **-ates, -at·ed, -at·ing** tear (flesh or tissues) irregularly; **lac·er·a·tion** (–RAY–) *n.: a ∼ caused by a fishhook;* **lac·er·a·tive** *adj.*

lace·work *n.* lace; also, any lacelike decoration.

lach·ry·mal or **lac·ri·mal** (LAC·ruh·mul) *adj.* tear-producing, as either of the **lachrymal glands** one above each eye, or **lachrymals** *n.pl.* —**lach·ry·mose** *adj.* given to shedding tears; also, mournful.

lack *v.* be without; also, have not enough of: *A novice ∼s experience; She's not ∼ing in enthusiasm.* —*n.* absence or shortage; also, the thing lacked. —**lack·a·dai·si·cal** (–uh·DAY·zi·cl) *adj.* lacking enthusiasm or interest.

lack·ey (LAK·ee) *n.* **-eys** a footman; hence, a servile follower; toady.

lack·lus·ter *adj.* dull or drab; *Brit.* **lack·lus·tre.**

la·con·ic (luh·CON–) *adj.* brief in expression; terse; **la·con·i·cal·ly** *adv.*

lac·quer (LAK·ur) *n.* & *v.* (coat metal, wood, etc. with) a resinous varnish made from the sap of trees such as the Asiatic sumac, or "lacquer tree" or "varnish tree," and from compounds of cellulose, resin, or lac in an evaporating solution: *a ~ed vase;* **lac·quer·er** *n.;* **lac·quer·work** or **lac·quer·ware** *n.*

lacrimal same as LACHRYMAL.

la·crosse (luh·CROS) *n.* a field game played between teams using rackets having a net at one end to throw a small rubber ball into the opposing team's goal.

lact(o)- *comb.form.* (derived from) milk: as in **lac·tase** *n.* an enzyme that helps in the digestion of milk sugar. —**lac·tate** *v.* **-tates, -tat·ed, -tat·ing** of mammary glands, produce milk; **lac·ta·tion** (–TAY–) *n.: Cows have a ~ period of about 10 months.* —**lac·te·al** (–tee·ul) *adj.* of milk; also, lymphatic; ***n.*** a lymph vessel. —**lac·tic** *adj.* of or from (sour) milk; **lactic acid** acid of sour milk. —**lac·tose** *n.* the sugar of milk.

la·cu·na (luh·CUE·nuh) *n.* **-nas** or **-nae** (–nee) a gap, esp. a missing part of a text or manuscript; also, a cavity in a bone or cartilage.

lac·y (LAY·see) *adj.* **lac·i·er, -i·est** of or like lace; **lac·i·ness** *n.*

lad *n.* a youth; also, a fellow.

lad·der *n.* a climbing device, usu. a framework of two long sidepieces connected by rungs.

lad·die (LAD·ee) *n. Scottish.* lad.

lade *v.* **lades,** *pt.* & *pp.* **lad·ed** or **lad·en, lad·ing** **1** load, as cargo on a ship: *a bill of lading.* **2** take up (liquids), as with a ladle. —**lad·en** (LAY·dn) adj. burdened *(with): a tree ~ with fruit.*

la-di-da or **la-de-da** (lah·dee·DAH) *adj. Informal.* affectedly polished or refined; excessively genteel.

la·dle (LAY·dl) *n.* & *v.* **-dles, -dled, -dling** (dip out with) a long handled spoon with cup-shaped bowl; **la·dler** *n.*

la·dy (LAY·dee) *n.* **-dies** **1** a woman of refinement or high social position; also, a British title: *Lady Chatterly.* **2** [as a term of courtesy]: *~s and gentlemen; the ~* (i.e. mistress) *of the house.* —**lady beetle** or **la·dy·bug** *n.* a small round beetle with a bright red or yellow spotted back, useful against plant lice; also **la·dy·bird.** —**la·dy·fin·ger** (LAY·dee·fing·gur) *n.* a finger-shaped spongecake. —**la·dy-in-wait·ing** *n.* **la·dies-** a queen's or princess's attendant. —**la·dy·like** *adj.* like a lady; also, suitable for a lady. —**la·dy·love** *n.* sweetheart. —**la·dy·ship** *n.* a lady's rank or position; **Ladyship** [preceded by "Her" or "Your," used in referring to or addressing a woman with the title "Lady"]. —**la·dy-slip·per** *n.* any of several kinds of orchids whose flowers have slipper-shaped lips; also **la·dy's-slip·per** and "moccasin flower."

La·e·trile (LAY·uh·tril) *Trademark.* a drug prepared from apricot or peach kernels, bitter almonds, etc. for use in cancer therapy.

La·fa·yette (lah·fi·YET), **Marquis de.** 1757–1834, French general who served in the American Revolutionary army.

lag *v.* **lags, lagged, lag·ging** fall behind (instead of keeping up): *to ~ behind in studies; As the speaker droned on interest ~d; players' turns decided by ~ing* (i.e. tossing marbles toward a "lag line"). —***n.*** interval or amount by which a person or thing lags: *a time ~.*

la·ger (beer) (LAH·gur) *n.* a light, mellow beer that has been stored up to six months.

lag·gard (LAG·urd) *n.* & *adj.* (one) that falls behind; slow: *a ~ at homework; a ~ pace;* **lag·gard·ly** *adj.* & *adv.*

la·gn(i)appe (lan·YAP) *n.* a small gift given to a customer with his purchase.

la·goon (luh·GOON) *n.* a shallow body of water near or connected with a larger one.

La·gos (LAY–) capital of Nigeria.

La·hore (luh·HOR) a city of N.E. Pakistan.

laid *pt.* & *pp.* of [1]LAY; **laid-back** *adj. Slang.* relaxed in style; easy-going. —**lain** *pp.* of LIE.

lair *n.* the den of a wild animal.

laird *n.* in Scotland, a landowner.

lais·sez faire (les·ay·FAIR) the principle of noninterference by government in private enterprise; **lais·sez-faire** *adj.*

la·i·ty (LAY·uh·tee) *n.* **-ties** lay people as distinguished from clergy.

lake *n.* a body of water surrounded by land; also, a pool (of oil, tar, lava, etc.)

lal·ly·gag (LAH·lee–) *n.* same as LOLLYGAG.

lam *v.* **lams, lammed, lam·ming** *Slang.* flee; ***n.*** **on the lam** in flight or hiding.

la·ma (LAH·muh) *n.* a Lamaist monk. —**La·ma·ism** *n.* Buddhism as practiced in Tibet and Mongolia; **La·ma·ist** *n.* & *adj.* —**la·ma·ser·y** *n.* **-ser·ies** a Lamaist monastery.

lamb (LAM) *n.* the young of a sheep; hence, a person thought of as young and innocent; also, lamb's meat or skin. —***v.*** bring forth a lamb.

lam·bast(e) (–BAIST, –BAST) *v.* **-bastes, -bast·ed, -bast·ing** *Informal.* thrash or scold severely.

lamb·da (LAM·duh) *n.* the 11th letter of the Greek alphabet (Λ, λ).

lam·bent *adj.* of a flame, playing lightly or gently (over a surface): *~ light, wit* (i.e. gently brilliant); **lam·bent·ly** *adv.* **lam·ben·cy** *n.*

lamb·kin *n.* a little lamb. —**lamb·skin** *n.* (leather from) a lamb's skin.

lame *adj.* **lam·er, -est** **1** crippled or limping: *a ~ man, back* (i.e. painful), *excuse* (i.e. weak). **2** *Slang.* square; not up-to-date. —***v.*** **lames,**

lamed, lam·ing make lame. —**lame·ly** *adv.;* **lame·ness** *n.*

la·mé (–MAY) *n.* a brocaded fabric of silk, wool, etc. interwoven with gold or silver.

lame·brain *n. Informal.* a slow-witted person. —**lame duck** **1** someone disabled or helpless. **2** a public official such as a Congressman serving the last part of his term after being defeated in a reelection.

la·mel·la (luh·MEL·uh) *n., pl.* **-mel·lae** (–lee) or **-mel·las** a thin, platelike structure, as of a bivalve mollusk or one of the gills on the underside of a mushroom cap.

la·ment (luh·MENT) *n.* an expression of grief, as by wailing or in a poem or song; hence, an elegy or dirge. —***v.*** grieve; mourn: *~ing the death of her beloved; our late* **la·ment·ed** *friend;* **lam·en·ta·ble** (LAM·un·tuh–, luh·MEN–) *adj.: a ~ tragedy; the ~* (i.e. regrettable) *condition of our slums;* **lam·en·ta·bly** *adv.* —**lam·en·ta·tion** (–TAY–) *n.*

lam·i·na (LAM·uh·nuh) *n.,pl.* **-nae** (-nee) or **-nas** a thin plate or layer; hence, the blade of a leaf; **lam·i·nar** *adj.: the smooth* **laminar flow** *of air over an airplane wing;* **lam·i·nal** *adj.* —**lam·i·nate** *v.* **-nates, -nat·ed, -nat·ing** split, beat, or roll, as metal, into layers; also, make in layers bonded together as plywood, safety glass, plastics, etc.; ***adj.*** (-nit) laminated: *a ~ tabletop.* —**lam·i·na·tion** (–NAY) *n.*

lamp *n.* a device that gives light or heat using electricity, gas, oil, kerosene, etc., as a *sunlamp, hurricane lamp,* or "floor lamp." —**lamp·black** *n.* fine black soot used as a pigment; carbon black.

lam·poon *n.* & *v.* (attack by use of) a satirical piece of writing ridiculing a person; **lam·poon·er·y** *n.*

lamp·post *n.* a post supporting a street lamp.

lam·prey (LAM·pree) *n.* **-preys** an eellike fish which, instead of jaws, has a mouth that it uses to suck blood from other fish.

la·nai (–NYE) *n.* in Hawaii, a verandah or open-sided living room.

lance *v.* **lanc·es, lanced, lanc·ing** pierce or cut open with a lance or lancet: *to ~ a boil.* —***n.*** **1** any of various sharp-pointed implements such as the large, steel-tipped wooden spear used by medieval knights or a small, two-edged, surgical knife, or **lan·cet.** **2** also **lanc·er,** a cavalryman armed with a lance; **lance corporal** a U.S. marine ranking above a private first class and below a corporal. —**Lan·ce·lot** (LAN·suh–) in Arthurian legends, the most outstanding of the Knights of the Round Table and the lover of Guinevere.

land *n.* the solid surface of the earth: *Columbus sighted ~; cultivable ~* (i.e. soil); *a house price inclusive of ~* (i.e. plot); *this ~* (i.e. country) *of ours; back in the ~* (i.e. realm) *of the living.* —***v.*** come or bring to land: *A pilot ~s his plane; Passengers ~ after docking; to ~ a fish; ~* (i.e. get) *a job, contract; Thefts could ~ you in jail.* —**land·less** *adj.*

lan·dau (LAN·dow, –daw) *n.* a four-wheeled carriage with two facing seats and two folding hoods meeting at the top from either end.

land·ed *adj.: ~ gentry* (i.e. owning land); *~ property* (i.e. real estate). —**land·er** *n.* a space vehicle designed to land, as on a planet. —**land·fall** *n.* land sighted after a voyage; also, the sighting or landing. —**land·fill** *n.* garbage or rubbish disposal by burying it layer by layer under earth: *a sanitary ~ site.* —**land·form** *n.* a physical feature of the earth's surface, as a hill, plateau, or cirque. —**land grant** gift of land by the government for agricultural colleges, railroads, etc. —**land·holder** *n.* an owner or occupant of land; **land·hold·ing** *n.* & *adj.* —**land·ing** *n.* **1** a landing or place for landing. **2** the level part at the end of a flight of stairs; ***adj.:*** **landing craft** *for bringing men and equipment close to shore; the undercarriage or* **landing gear** *of an aircraft consisting of wheels or floats;* **landing strip** air strip. —**land·la·dy** *n.* **-dies** *fem.* of LANDLORD. —**land·locked** *adj.* **1** surrounded by land, as a country, bay, or harbor. **2** confined to fresh water, as salmon. —**land·lord** *n.* one who rents property to others; also, the keeper of an inn or rooming house. —**land·lub·ber** *n.* [sailor's term] one who is not used to the sea; **land·lub·ber·ly** *adj.* —**land·mark** *n.* something that stands out on a landscape, serving to identify a locality; also, a memorable event: *a ~ in the history of space travel.* —**land·mass** *n.* a continent or similar large unbroken area of land. —**land office** a government office recording sales and transfers of public lands; **land-of·fice business** *Informal.* a thriving business. —**land·scape** *n.* (picture of) land scenery; ***v.*** **-scapes, -scaped, -scap·ing** redesign land and what is on it so as to please the eye, as a **landscape architect** (or **gardener**); **landscape architecture** (or **gardening**). —**land·slide** *n.* **1** the sliding of a mass of earth or rocks down a slope; also, such a displaced mass. **2** in an election, a large majority of votes: *a ~ defeat, victory.* —**lands·man** *n.* **-men** one who lives on land, not a seaman. —**land·ward** (–wurd) *adj.* & *adv.* toward the land; also **land·wards** *adv.*

lane *n.* a narrow way, path, or strip, esp. one marked out or designated for runners, aircraft, ships, automobiles, etc. going in the same direction.

Lang·er·hans (LAHNG·ur·hahnz) See ISLAND.

lan·guage (LANG·gwij) *n.* **1** a system of communication, esp. human speech or the speech of one group of people: *written ~; African ~s; the ~ of the blind; computer ~.* **2** a style of verbal expression: *strong ~.*

lan·guid (LANG·gwid) *adj.:* tired or bored, as on a hot and humid day; not disposed to exert oneself; **lan·guid·ly** *adv.;* **lan·guid·ness** *n.* —**lan·guish** (LANG–) *v.* suffer from languidness; pine or droop; hence, lose energy or vigor: *a promising genius now ~ing in prison; the*

~ing looks of a forlorn lover. —**lan·guor** (LANG·gur) *n.* weakness, sluggishness, or indifference caused by enervating conditions; also, effeteness or softness: *the ~ of a tropical existence;* **lan·guor·ous** *adj.: a life of ~ ease;* **lan·guor·ous·ly** *adv.*

lank *adj.* **1** straight, with tendency to bend (as tall grass) or to lie limp (as hair); **lank·ly** *adv.;* **lank·ness** *n.* **2** awkwardly lean and tall; **lank·y** *adj.* **lank·i·er, -i·est:** *a lanky-legged colt;* **lank·i·ly** *adv.;* **lank·i·ness** *n.*

lan·o·lin (LANL·in) *n.* a waxlike substance made from a greasy coating on the wool of sheep, and used in ointments, cosmetics, as a dressing for fur, etc.; also called "wool wax."

Lan·sing capital of Michigan.

lan·tan·a (–TAH·nuh) *n.* a tropical shrub of the verbena family.

lan·tern *n.* a chamber or case to hold a light, as a *hurricane lantern,* or to regulate light, as the top part of a lighthouse or a small windowed turret crowning a dome; also, an early projector called "magic lantern." —**lan·tern-jawed** *adj.* having a long, thin jaw.

lan·tha·num (LAN·thuh–) *n.* a metallic element, the first of the **lan·tha·nide series** of rare-earth elements.

lan·yard (–yurd) *n.* a short rope or cord for holding or fastening something, as attached to a whistle, knife, or pistol and worn around the neck.

La·os (LAH·ose) a S.E. Asian republic; 91,429 sq. mi. (236,800 km²); *cap.* Vientiane. —**La·o·tian** (–OH·shun) *n.* & *adj.*

lap *n.* **1** the knees and upper legs of a sitting person forming a place where something may be held; also, the loose front part of a garment when held up to hold or catch something: *a child in her mother's ~: in the ~ of the gods* (i.e. beyond human help); *in the ~ of luxury.* **2** an overlapping part; also, one circuit of a race course: *the last ~ of a journey.* **3** a splashing or lapping sound. —***v.*** **laps, lapped, lap·ping** **1** lay partly over another, as shingles on a roof: *a ~d seam.* **2** wrap or enfold, as with a canvas or in a blanket. **3** drink, as cats and dogs do; hence, beat gently with a lapping sound: *waves ~ing a shore; wary of ~ing up* (i.e. consuming eagerly) *advice from strangers.*

lap·a·ro·scope (LAP–) *n.* an optical instrument inserted through the abdominal wall or the vagina; **lap·a·ros·co·py** (–ROS–) *n.* examination of the inside of the abdomen using a laparoscope.

La Paz (lah·PAHZ) governmental and business cap. of Bolivia.

lap belt a safety belt across the lap, as in an automobile. —**lap·board** *n.* a board placed over the lap for use as a table or desk. —**lap·dog** *n.* a small pet dog.

la·pel (luh·PEL) *n.* the folded-back part of a coat coming down from the collar.

lap·i·dar·y (–der·ee) *adj.* having to do with the making of precious stones: *the ~ art; a ~ wheel;* ***n., pl.*** **-dar·ies** a craftsman of gems; also, their cutting and polishing.

lap·in *n.* rabbit fur.

lap·is laz·u·li (LAP·is·LAZ·yoo·lye, –lee) an azure-blue semiprecious stone or mineral.

Lapp *n.* a member of a Mongoloid people of the **Lap·land** region of Norway, Sweden, Finland, and Russia, that lies above the Arctic Circle; **Lap·land·er** *n.*

lap·pet *n.* a loose-hanging flap or fold of a garment or of flesh, as the lobe of the ear or a bird's wattle. —**lap robe** a blanket or other covering for the lap.

lapse (LAPS) *n.* a slip (of the tongue, memory, or pen); a slipping back (into sin, savagery, etc.); a passage (into silence); the ending (of a privilege through neglect or of a custom through disuse). —***v.*** **laps·es, lapsed, lap·sing:** *Your lease ~s unless renewed in three days; a once splendid palace now ~d into ruin; a ~d Catholic.*

lap·wing *n.* the crested European plover.

lar·board (–burd) *n.* & *adj.* port or left (side of a ship).

lar·ce·ny (–suh·nee) *n.* **-nies** *Law.* theft; **lar·ce·nous** (–nus) *adj.;* **lar·ce·nist** *n.*

larch *n.* a tall, slender, deciduous tree of the pine family valued for its durable wood.

lard *n.* the melted and clarified fat of hogs; ***v.*** put bacon on or into (slits in meat) to improve its flavor: *a poor speech though ~ed with biblical quotations.* —**lard·er** *n.* pantry; hence, food supply. —**lard·y** *adj.*

la·res and pe·na·tes (LAIR·eez·un·puh·NAY·teez) the household gods of the ancient Romans; hence, one's most cherished household effects.

large *adj.* **larg·er, larg·est** [a more formal term for] big; big in dimensions or quantity: *a ~ household, fortune; ~ powers; pictured (as) ~ as (in) life; a* **larg·er-than-life** (i.e. great) *personality; the ~ calorie, intestine.* —***adv.:*** *looming ~ on the horizon; disappointment writ ~ on his face.* —***n.*** **at large:** *The rapist is at ~* (i.e. free); *a* **Con·gress·man-at-large** *representing an entire state; appealed to the people at ~* (i.e. as a whole). —**large·ly** *adv.* **1** for the most part: *He is ~ to blame for what happened.* **2** generously: *contributed ~ to the campaign;* **large·ness** *n.* —**large-heart·ed** *adj.* generous. —**large-scale** *adj.: a ~ map; ~ waste.* —**lar·gess(e)** (LAR·jis) *n.* a generous or showily large bestowal or gift(s). —**larg·ish** *adj.* somewhat large. —**lar·go** *adj.* & *adv. Music.* (in a) stately or slow tempo; ***n.*** such a musical piece.

lar·i·at (LAIR·ee·it) *n.* a lasso; also, a rope for tethering a grazing animal.

lark *n.* **1** any of a family of small songbirds, esp. the skylark; also, a meadow lark. **2** *Informal.* a frolic or prank; ***v.:*** *was ~ing all night in the park.* —**lark·spur** *n.* same as DELPHINIUM.

lar·va (–vuh) *n., pl.* **-vae** (–vee) or **-vas** the immature, usu. wormlike stage of an insect, as a caterpillar, grub, or maggot; also, a tadpole; **lar·val** *adj.*

lar·yn·gi·tis (lair·un·JYE–) *n.* (hoarseness from) inflammation of the larynx. —**lar·ynx** (LAIR–) *n.* **lar·ynx·es** or **la·ryn·ges** (–RIN·jeez) the sound-producing organ or "voice box" containing the vocal cords, situated above the windpipe; **la·ryn·ge·al** (–RIN·jee–) *adj.*

la·sa·gna (luh·ZAHN·yuh) *n.* a dish of noodles in ribbon form baked with layers of chopped meat, cheese, and tomato sauce; also **la·sa·gne.**

las·car (–cur) *n.* an East Indian sailor.

las·civ·i·ous (luh·SIV·ee·us) *adj.* lewd or lustful; **las·civ·i·ous·ness** *n.*

lase (LAZE) *v.* **las·es, lased, las·ing** emit or subject to laser light. —**la·ser** (LAY·zur) *n.* a device producing an intense, penetrating beam of light ("light amplification by stimulated emission of radiation"); optical maser.

lash *n.* **1** the flexible striking part of a whip. **2** eyelash. **3** a stroke or blow, as with a whip; also, something that hurts like a lash. —***v.*** **1:** *a tiger* ~*ing its tail; sails* ~*ed by a wind; could hear the rain* ~*ing against the window; The editorial* **lashed out** *at police brutality; a tongue-lashing he'll never forget.* **2** tie or bind with a rope, cord, chain, etc.; **lash·ing** *n.* such tying material. —**LASH** the system of loading huge freighters with preloaded barges of cargo: *LASH ships carry "Lighters Aboard SHip."*

lass *n.* young girl; also, a sweetheart, esp. **las·sie** (LAS·ee) *Scot.*

Las·sa (LAH·suh) **fever** a highly contagious, usu. fatal African virus disease.

las·si·tude (LAS·uh–) *n.* weariness or languor resulting from dejection, overexertion, etc.

las·so (LAS·oh, la·SOO) *n.* **-so(e)s** a cowboy's rope with a noose at one end for catching livestock; ***v.*** **las·soes, las·soed, las·so·ing** rope or catch with a lasso; **las·so·er** *n.*

last *adj.* a *superl.* of LATE. **1** coming at the end of a series; hence, lowest in importance: *the* ~ *boy in his class; the* ~ *man I want to see;* **on one's last legs** at the end of one's resources. **2** coming after all others in time; hence, latest or most recent: *your* ~ *letter; her* ~ *will and testament.* —***adv.:*** *Z comes* ~ *in the alphabet; She was fine when I* ~ *saw her.* —***v.*** to continue to exist and be useful: *Well-made goods* ~ *a long time; provisions to* ~ *a winter; The funds* ~*ed* (i.e. were enough for) *us a year; a just and* **lasting** *peace.* —***n.*** **1:** *the* ~ *of the series;* **at (long) last** after a long time; **breathe one's last** die. **2** a foot-shaped block on which to form or repair a shoe, used by cobblers; **stick to one's last** mind one's own business. —**last-ditch** *adj.* having to do with a final effort: *a* ~ *attempt; our* ~ *supporters.* —**last hurrah** final attempt before quitting. —**Last Judgment** God's judgment on mankind at the end of the world. —**last·ly** *adv.* at the end. —**last offices** See OFFICE. —**last resort** refuge: *took to drinking as a* (or *the*) ~ *resort.* —**last straw** the last of many intolerable things, like the straw that broke the camel's back in the fable. —**last word** **1** the final authority, as in a subject of dispute. **2** *Informal.* the latest or most fashionable thing.

lat. latitude. —**Lat.** Latin.

la·ta·ki·a (lat·uh·KEE·uh) *n.* a Turkish smoking tobacco exported chiefly from **Latakia,** Syria's main seaport.

latch *n.* a fastening device inside a door, window, etc. consisting of a small lever falling into a notch which may be opened from the outside by a **latch·key** or a **latch·string** passed outside through a hole in the door. —***v.:*** *a cabin door* ~*ed shut; a lonesome girl looking for someone to* **latch on to** (*Informal.* attach herself to). —**latch·et** (–it) *n. Archaic.* strap or thong for fastening a shoe or sandal.

late *adj.* **lat·er** or **lat·ter, lat·est** or **last** **1** coming or happening after an expected time; hence, at an advanced time: *She's never* ~ *for work; the* ~ *city edition of a newspaper.* **2** recent (in regard to death, retirement, occurrence, etc.): *her* ~ *husband; a* ~ *model car; our* ~ *mayor; the* ~ *floods.* —***adv.*** **lat·er, lat·est** or **last** **1** after the usual or expected time: *They arrived* ~. **2** at an advanced point in time: *It happened* ~ *at night.* **3** recently: *our* ~ *lamented friend; as* ~ *as last week;* **of late** lately; recently. —**late·com·er** (–cum–) *n.* one who has come late or recently. —**late·ly** *adv.* recently; **late·ness** *n.*

la·tent (LAIT·nt) *adj.* lying hidden though in existence: *one's* ~ *abilities, the* ~ *undeveloped image photographed on film;* **la·tent·ly** *adv.;* **la·ten·cy** *n.*: *the pre-pubertal* ~ *period of sexual development.*

lat·er·al (LAT·uh·rul) *adj.* sideways: *a* ~ *movement; a* ~, *not terminal bud; a* **lateral pass** (thrown toward the sidelines or away from the opposite goal) *in football.* —***n.*** something lateral, as a pass in football. —**lat·er·al·ly** *adv.*

la·tex (LAY–) *n.* the milky juice from the barks of plants and trees such as milkweed and rubber; also, a rubber or plastic emulsion, as used in paints and adhesives.

lath (LATH, –DH) *n.* one of the thin, narrow strips of wood or metal forming a lattice or a framework for plastering, as for the walls of a frame house; ***v.*** cover or line with laths. —**lathe** (LAIDH) *n.* a machine for shaping pieces of wood, metal, etc. by turning them against a cutting tool; ***v.*** **lathes, lathed, lath·ing** shape on a lathe; **lath·er** *n.* —**lath·ing** or **lath·work** *n.* laths or their installation.

lath·er (LADH·ur) *n.* & *v.* (cover with or form) froth or foam, as produced by soap and water or by a sweating horse: *Soap does not* ~ *in hard water; to* ~ *before shaving; Why work yourself into a* ~ (*Slang.* state of excitement) *over a trifle?* —**lath·er·y** *adj.*

Lat·in *n.* the language of ancient Rome, a person who spoke Latin, or one who speaks a language such as French, Italian, Spanish, or Portuguese that is descended from Latin; ***adj.:*** *the ~ temperament.* —**Latin America** that part of the W. Hemisphere S. of the U.S., including the West Indies, where Spanish, Portuguese, and French are the official languages; **Latin American; Lat·in-A·mer·i·can** *adj.* —**La·ti·no** (–TEE–) *n.* **-nos** a Latin American.

lat·ish (LAY–) *adj.* & *adv.* somewhat late.

lat·i·tude *n.* **1** the distance N. or S. of a point on the globe from the equator, measured in degrees; also, a place or region with reference to its latitude: *cold, high, low ~s.* **2** degree of freedom of thought or action: *Adults are allowed greater ~ than minors.* —**lat·i·tu·di·nal** (–TUE–) *adj.* —**lat·i·tu·di·nar·i·an** (–tue·dn·AIR·ee·un) *n.* & *adj.* (one who is) liberal in his views, esp. in religious matters.

la·trine (luh·TREEN) *n.* a toilet for the use of many, as in a camp or factory.

lat·ter (LAT·ur) *adj.* a *compar.* of LATE. later or more recent; also, the last-mentioned, usu. the second of two: *the ~ half of the century* (i.e. from 1950 to 1999); *Of Tom, (Dick,) and Harry, the ~* (i.e. Harry) *is the baby;* **lat·ter·ly** *adv.* recently. —**lat·ter-day** *adj.* of recent times: *a ~ problem;* **Latter-day Saint** a Mormon.

lat·tice (LAT·is) *n.* (a window, door, or gate with) a framework of crossed wooden or metal strips; **lat·ticed** *adj.;* **lat·tice·work** *n.* a lattice or lattices collectively.

Lat·vi·a (LAT·vee·uh) a Soviet republic on the Baltic Sea; **Lat·vi·an** *n.* & *adj.*

laud *n.* & *v.* praise or acclaim; **laud·a·ble** *adj.;* **laud·a·bly** *adv.*

laud·a·num (LAWD·num) *n.* a solution of opium in alcohol.

laud·a·to·ry (LAW·duh–) *adj.* expressing praise: *a ~ speech.*

laugh (LAF) *v.* make the sounds and bodily movements of one who is amused, joyous, scornful, etc.; **laugh at** ridicule. —***n.*** act of laughing; also, something that causes laughter, or is **laugh·a·ble** *adj.;* **laugh·a·bly** *adv.: The story is ~ absurd.* —**laughing gas** nitrous oxide which sometimes causes laughter when inhaled. —**laughing jackass** same as kookaburra. —**laugh·ing·ly** *adv.* in a laughing manner. —**laugh·ing·stock** *n.* object of ridicule. —**laugh·ter** *n.* the sound or action of laughing.

launch **1** *n.* an open motorboat used for short trips; also, a large boat carried by a warship. **2** *v.* set in motion, as a ship slid into water or a missile shot into the air: *money to ~ her in business; ~ an attack, threats;* ***n.*** a launching; **launch(ing) pad** platform from which a missile or spacecraft is launched, usu. at a **launching site** such as Cape Canaveral, Florida, by means of a **launch vehicle,** a rocket system to boost the craft into orbit; **launch window** a limited period suitable for launching a spacecraft because of the changing positions of the planets.

laun·der *v.* wash and iron (clothes, linens, etc.); hence, make (illegal funds) clean by channeling through a third party such as a foreign bank to hide their source; **laun·der·er** *n., fem.* **laun·dress** (–dris). —**laun·dro·mat** (–druh–) *n.* a self-service laundry; **Laundromat** *Trademark.* —**laun·dry** (–dree) *n.* **-dries** a place for laundering clothes, etc.; also, a batch of such items before or after laundering; **laundry list** a long list of items.

lau·re·ate (LOR·ee·it) *n.* & *adj.* (a person) honored for accomplishment in arts or science: *a poet ~; a Nobel ~;* **lau·re·ate·ship** *n.* —**lau·rel** (LOR·ul) *n.* any of a family of tropical trees and shrubs with aromatic leaves used by the ancient Greeks to crown athletes; **laurels** *pl.* fame or victory.

la·va (LAH·vuh, LAV·uh) *n.* melted rock from a volcano; also, this solidified.

la·vage (luh·VAHZH) *n.* the medicinal washing out of an organ such as the stomach.

lav·a·lier(e) (lav·uh·LEER) *n.* an ornament worn on a chain around the neck; also, a microphone used that way.

lav·a·to·ry (LAV·uh–) *n.* **-ries** a toilet, a washbowl with running water, or a washroom equipped with either or both. —**lave** *v.* **laves, laved, lav·ing** *Poet.* wash; bathe. —**lav·en·der** *n.* & *adj.* (pale-purple) flowers and leaves of a fragrant European mint: *He's all ~ and old lace* (i.e. gentle-mannered). —**lav·ish** *adj.* spending or spent very generously and freely: *~ praise, expenditure, gifts; ~ with other people's money;* ***v.*** bestow or spend liberally; hence, squander: *love and care ~ed on an ingrate;* **lav·ish·ly** *adv.;* **lav·ish·ness** *n.*

law *n.* **1** a written or unwritten rule or regulation governing conduct, recognized by a society; also, a codified set of such regulations, this as a subject of study or as a profession, etc.: *tax ~s; maintenance of ~* (i.e. control imposed by laws) *and order; went to ~* (i.e. a court) *to establish his claim; You* **read law** (i.e. study law) *for several years before entering the ~* (i.e. legal profession); *got into trouble with the ~* (i.e. police). **2** any rule or principle: *Newton's ~s of motion; a ~ of nature such as gravitation; ~s of hospitality; observe* **the Law** (i.e. God's commands in the Old Testament) *and the prophets.* —**law-a·bid·ing** *adj.* obedient to the law: *a ~ citizen.* —**law·break·er** *n.* one who goes against the law; **law·break·ing** *n.* & *adj.* —**law·ful** *adj.* according to the law: *a ~ claim, arrest, heir;* **law·ful·ly** *adv.;* **law·ful·ness** *n.* —**law·giv·er** *n.* one who makes laws; lawmaker; **law·giv·ing** *n.* & *adj.* —**law·less** *adj.* without laws; also, breaking the law; disorderly: *a ~ tribe, life; ~ behavior;* **law·less·ness** *n.* —**law·mak·er** *n.* one who helps make laws, as a legislator; **law·mak·ing** *n.* legislation; ***adj.***

legislative. —**law·man** (–mun) *n.* **-men** a law officer such as a sheriff or marshal.

lawn *n.* **1** a usu. thin, plain-weave cotton or linen cloth used for handkerchiefs, lingerie, curtains, etc. **2** (a plot of) close-cropped, grass-covered land for recreation or as part of landscaping; **lawn mower** a machine for mowing lawns. —**lawn·y** *adj.*

law·ren·ci·um (–REN·see–) *n.* a short-lived radioactive element.

law·suit (–soot) *n.* a case in a law court. —**law·yer** *n.* one qualified to practice law, advising and representing clients in legal matters.

lax *adj.* loose or relaxed, not tight or strict: ~ *discipline, morals, tissue* or *soil* (i.e. in texture), *vowels* (pronounced with relaxed muscles, not tense); **lax·i·ty** or **lax·ness** *n.;* **lax·ly** *adv.* —**lax·a·tive** *n.* & *adj.* (a medicine) that helps to make the bowels loose.

lay *v.* **1** *pt.* of LIE[2]. **2 lays, laid, lay·ing** cause to lie; hence, set or put down, esp. in a particular way: *to ~ chairs around a room; A bricklayer ~s bricks; She laid it aside for later reading; started to ~* (i.e. arrange) *the table for dinner; I'll ~* (i.e. make) *a bet the baby will be a girl; a teacher who ~s* (i.e. puts) *much emphasis on neatness; a well-laid* (i.e. well-devised) *plan; Birds ~* (i.e. produce) *eggs; nothing like a rain to ~* (i.e. settle) *the dust; a body* **laid to rest** (in a grave); *She ~s claim* (i.e. claims) *to her uncle's estate; lost his cool and started to* **lay about him** (i.e. hit out) *with his stick; a committee to* **lay down** *rules and regulations; They managed to* **lay hold of** (i.e. grab) *the burglar; It's wise to* **lay in** (i.e. store up) *provisions for winter; The factory was shut down and workers* **laid off** (i.e. dismissed from work) *for months; The paint has been* **laid on** *rather thick; Please* **lay out** *these pages in proper order; You* **lay over** (i.e. stop and wait) *in Rome and catch a flight next day for Bombay; All the children were* **laid up** (i.e. sick in bed) *with the flu.* —***n.*** **1** the way something is laid or lies: *the ~ of the land as seen from the air.* **2** *Slang.* partner to get for sexual intercourse: *She's not an easy ~.* **3** a narrative poem for singing; also, a song or tune. —***adj.*** nonprofessional, esp. not of the clergy: *~ people; too technical for ~ readers.* —**lay·a·way** (LAY·uh–) *n.* an article reserved for a customer on payment of a deposit to be claimed later after the full price is paid: *Use our* **layaway plan** *for Christmas.* —**lay·er** *n.* **1** one that lays. **2** one thickness or stratum, esp. one of several, as in a **layer cake** that has a filling between the layers. —**lay·er·ing** *n.* method of growing roots for new plants from a twig or shoot while attached to its parent. —**lay·ette** (–ET) *n.* the outfit of clothes, blankets, etc. for a newborn infant. —**lay figure** an unreal or unimportant character like the puppets used by artists instead of living models. —**lay·man** (–mun) *n.* **-men** one who is an outsider in relation to a particular profession, esp. one who is not a clergyman. —**lay·off** *n.* a temporary dismissal of an employee; also, the period of it. —**lay·out** *n.* the arrangement or design of something that has been planned, as of a camp, a newspaper page, or an advertisement. —**lay·o·ver** *n.* a break or delay in the course of a journey.

la·zar (LAZ·ur) *n.* a leper. —**Laz·a·rus** (LAZ·uh–) a leper in one of Jesus' parables; also, a man whom Jesus raised from the dead.

laze *v.* **laz·es, lazed, laz·ing** be lazy or idle; **la·zy** (LAY·zee) *adj.* **-zi·er, -zi·est** not willing to work or exert oneself; also, slow-moving or sluggish: *a ~ youth, habit, stream;* **la·zi·ly** *adv.;* **la·zi·ness** *n.* —**la·zy·bones** *n. Informal.* a lazy person. —**Lazy Su·san** (SOO·zun) a revolving tray used on the table to place small items of food within easy reach of everyone.

lb. pound(s). —**lbs.** pounds.

l.c. lower case; in the place cited. —**L.C.** Library of Congress.

l.c.d. or **L.C.D.** least (or lowest) common denominator. —**LCD** liquid-crystal diode.

l.c.m. or **L.C.M.** least (or lowest) common multiple.

L-do·pa (el·DOH·puh) *n.* an isomer of dopa used to treat Parkinson's disease.

lea *n.* a meadow or pasture.

leach (LEECH) *v.* (be) subject to washing action; also, remove by such action: *the ~ing method of separating metal from ore; the health hazard of silver-plated cups that ~ too much lead; Heavy rainfall can ~ out minerals from fertile soil; the ~ing field of a sewage system.*

[1]lead (LEED) *v.* **leads, led, lead·ing** **1** show the way by going in front; hence, guide or direct: *I ~, you follow; "~ us not into temptation"; a mob led by a demagogue; the events that* **led up** *to the war.* **2** be first (in): *She ~s* (the class) *in all subjects; the float ~ing the parade; the batter who* **leads off** *in an inning.* **3** pass (life, time, etc. in a particular way): *She ~s a lonely life.* —***n.*** **1** one that leads, as the principal part in a play, the opening paragraph of a news report, an insulated electrical conductor, a clue, a leash, etc. **2** a leading, a being first, or the margin by which one leads, as in a race. —***adj.*** leading: *the ~ car.* —**lead·er** *n.;* **lead·er·ship** *n.*

[2]lead (LED) *n.* **1** a soft, heavy, bluish-gray metallic element that is poisonous in compounds such as "lead acetate" and "lead arsenate." **2** something made of lead, as bullets, a plumb bob, or a strip of metal to space out lines of type; **lead·ing** *n.* such strips. **3** the graphite used in pencils. —***v.*** to cover, weight, fix (glass in position), treat, or mix with lead. —***adj.*** made of or with lead: *a ~ pencil, pipe;* **lead poisoning,** *or plumbism, is caused by ingesting lead or lead salts.* —**lead·ed** *adj.* containing tetraethyl lead: *~ gasoline.* —**lead·en** *adj.* made of or like lead in weight, color, dullness, etc.: *~ limbs, skies, thoughts, spirits.* —**[1]lead·ing** See [2]LEAD, *n.* 2.

²lead·ing (LEE–) *adj.* that leads; hence, chief: *a ~* (i.e. influential) *citizen; the* **leading** (i.e. front) **edge** *of an airfoil; a* **leading question** (so worded as to suggest a desired answer). **—lead time** time required for a plan or design to be executed, as in the manufacture of a new product.

leaf (LEEF) *n.* **leaves** (LEEVZ) **1** one of the thin, flat, green parts of a tree or plant; **leaf·less** *adj.* **2** something similar to a leaf such as a flower petal, a sheet of paper or metal, a movable part of a table's top, door, or gate, etc. **—*v.*** **1** bear leaves, as a tree or plant. **2** turn through the pages of a book. **—leaf·age** (–ij) *n.* foliage. **—leafed** *adj.* same as LEAVED. **—leaf·hop·per** *n.* an insect that feeds on plant juices; **leaf insect** an insect that resembles a leaf. **—leaf·let** (–lit) *n.* a printed, often folded sheet, as for direct-mail advertising; also, a small leaf or a part of a compound leaf. **—leaf mold** decayed leaves forming a top layer of soil; also, a mold affecting foliage. **—leaf·stalk** (–stawk) *n.* the narrow part of the leaf connecting the blade to the stem of the plant or tree; petiole. **—leaf·y** *adj.* **leaf·i·er, -i·est** having many leaves; also, resembling a leaf.

league (LEEG) *n.* **1** a measure of distance, usu. equal to 3 nautical miles (5.556 km). **2** an alliance of organizations with common interests, as in sports or politics: **League of Nations** (1920–46); **League of Women Voters** (1920); *major ~* (i.e. class or category) *baseball;* **out of one's league** *Informal.* out of one's own class; **in league** allied; **—*v.*** **leagues, leagued, leagu·ing** form into a league; **leagu·er** *n.* a league member.

leak (LEEK) *v.* (allow something to) go in or out, as through a hole or crack: *a ~ing boat; Spies ~ into a country; accused of ~ing state secrets; Truth will ~ out.* **—*n.:*** *a ~ in the dike; plugging a security ~; a politically inspired news ~.* **—leak·age** (–ij) *n.* a leaking, leaked thing, or its amount. **—leak·y** *adj.* **leak·i·er, -i·est:** *a ~ roof.*

leal (LEEL) *adj. Scot.* loyal.

¹lean (LEEN) *v.* **leans,** *pt.* & *pp.* **leaned** or **leant, lean·ing** bend or incline from a normal position (*toward, against, on,* or *upon* something, as for support): *the Leaning Tower of Pisa; ~ the ladder against the wall; a doctrine ~ing toward heresy;* **lean over backwards** same as BEND OVER BACKWARDS. **—*n.*** inclination; also **leaning. —lean-to** (–too) *adj.* of a roof, having a single slope, usu. set against a larger structure. **—*n., pl.*** **-tos** a shelter, shed, or extension with a lean-to roof.

²lean (LEEN) *adj.* **1** without too much fat: *~ meat, a ~ and wiry build.* **2** meager or scanty: *a fuel mixture that is too ~* (i.e. not rich enough) *for proper combustion.* **—lean·ness** *n.*

leap (LEEP) *n.* a jump or spring, esp. one suggesting lightness; **by leaps and bounds** swiftly; ***v.*** **leaps,** *pt.* & *pp.* **leaped** or **leapt** (LEEPT, LEPT) **leap·ing** (cause) to jump (over): *horses ~ing a fence; "Look before you ~"; An idea ~d to her mind; to ~ at an opportunity.* **—leap·frog** *n.* & *v.* **-frogs, -frogged, -frog·ging** (leap over as in) a game in which players jump, with legs spread wide, over the bent back of each of the other players. **—leap year** a year of 366 days, with February 29 as the extra day, occurring every fourth year.

learn (LURN) *v.* **learns,** *pt.* & *pp.* **learned** or **learnt, learn·ing** **1** acquire a skill or knowledge, as by study, experience, etc.: *to ~ a poem by heart; Children ~ to walk; to ~ dancing; a* **learn·ed** (–id) *scholar, society, profession; a* **learned** *skill, response, habit;* **learn·er** *n.* **2** come to know: *I ~d about the accident; ~d that he is in the hospital.* **—learn·ing** *n.* knowledge: *a man of great ~.*

lease (LEECE) *n.* a contract by which a **lessor** lets a **lessee** have the use of property such as land, buildings, or automobiles for a certain period on payment of a rent; hence, the right thus acquired, its period, or the property itself: *surgery to give you a* **new lease on life. —*v.*** **leas·es, leased, leas·ing** give or take a lease on; **leas·er** *n.* **—lease·hold** *n.* property held by a lease; **lease·hold·er** *n.*

leash (LEESH) *v.* check or hold (an animal) on a leash. **—*n.*** a line, chain, or strap.

least (LEEST) *adj.* a *superl.* of LITTLE; smallest, slightest, or lowest: *12 is the* **least** (or **lowest**) **common denominator** *of ½, ⅓, and ¼, same as the* **least common multiple** *of 2, 3, and 4.* **—*n.:*** *The ~ I ask is pity; If you can't pay for it,* **at least** *say "thank you";* **not in the least** not at all. **—*adv.*** a *superl.* of LITTLE: *I like Mondays ~.* **—least·wise** *Informal.* at any rate; also **least·ways** *Regional.*

leath·er (LEDH·ur) *n.* animal skin prepared for making shoes, coats, gloves, etc.; also, such an article. **—*adj.*** made of leather; also **leath·ern. —leath·er·neck** *n. Slang.* a U.S. marine. **—leath·er·y** *adj.* tough and flexible like leather; **leath·er·i·ness** *n.*

¹leave (LEEV) *v.* **leaves, leaved, leav·ing** put forth leaves; **leaved** *adj.* & *comb. form.* having (such or so many) leaves: *a lovely tree when fully ~; a four-~ clover.*

²leave (LEEV) *v.* **leaves, left, leav·ing** **1** go or depart (from a place): *a flight ~ing (New York) for London; She just left (here);* **leav·er** *n.* **2** let (a person or thing) be; let remain: *Don't ~ your baby alone; left the door open; no food left on the table;* **leave off** stop or cease; **leave out** omit or ignore. **—*n.*** permission: *asked ~ to speak; It was time to* **take leave of** (i.e. leave) *his family; granted* **leave of absence** (i.e. permission to be absent) *from duty; back home* **on leave;** *a year's ~* (i.e. free time away from duty).

leav·en (LEVN) *n.* a substance such as yeast or baking powder, also called **leav·en·ing,** that causes fermentation in batter or dough by releasing carbon dioxide which lightens and raises it; hence, a spreading influence bringing about change. —***v.*** make batter or dough rise; hence, lighten, temper, or enliven: *poetry ~ed with wit.*

leaves *pl.* of LEAF.

leave-tak·ing *n.* parting; farewell. —**leav·ings** *n. pl.* what is left; leftovers or remnants.

Leb·a·non (–uh·nun) an Asian country at the E. end of the Mediterranean; 4,015 sq. mi. (10,400 km^2); *cap.* Beirut; **Leb·a·nese** (–NEEZ) *adj.* & *n., sing.* & *pl.*

lech *n.* & *v. Slang.* lust. —**lech·er** *n.* a man who indulges in **lech·er·y** *n.* lust; lewdness; debauchery; **lech·er·ous** (–us) *adj.;* **lech·er·ous·ness** *n.*

lec·i·thin (LES·uh–) *n.* a fatty substance of plant and animal tissues, found esp. in egg yolk, soybeans, corn, etc.

lec·tern *n.* a tall reading stand, as used by a **lec·tor** (–tur) reading at a church service. —**lec·ture** (–chur) *n.* an instructive talk, given by a **lec·tur·er** usu. to a class; also, a scolding; ***v.*** **-tures, -tured, -tur·ing** give a lecture (to); also, scold. —**lec·ture·ship** *n.*

led *pt.* & *pp.* of LEAD. —**LED** light-emitting diode, as used in electronic display panels.

le·der·ho·sen (LAY·dur·hoh·zun) *n.pl.* short leather pants worn by men and boys in Bavaria.

ledge (LEJ) *n.* a narrow shelf or ridge standing out from an upright surface: *a window ~; a ~ of rock near a shore.* —**ledg·er** *n.* a book in which money transactions are recorded.

lee *n.* a side that is sheltered from wind, as of a ship or an island; also, shelter; ***adj.*** sheltered or away from the wind; leeward, not windward: *a ~ side, shore, tide.*

Lee, Robert E. 1807–70, Confederate general in the American Civil War.

leech *n.* a small worm, also called "bloodsucker," once used in medicine to remove blood from patients; hence, a hanger-on; ***v.*** drain or exhaust: *work that ~es the life out of one.*

leek *n.* an onionlike but mild-flavored vegetable.

leer *n.* & *v.* (look with) a sly, suggestive, or evil glance. —**leer·y** *adj.* **leer·i·er, -i·est** *Informal.* suspicious; wary.

lees (LEEZ) *n.pl.* dregs or sediment, as of wine during fermentation.

lee·ward (LEE·wurd, LOO–) *adj.* & *adv.* away from the wind; toward the lee; ***n.*** the lee side. —**Leeward Islands** a group of about 15 islands forming part of the Lesser ANTILLES. —**lee·way** *n.* leeward drift of ship or aircraft from course; also, the degree of such deviation; hence, a margin of safety or tolerance; latitude or elbow room.

left *n.* the side of the body or the hand to the north when one is facing east; usu. **Left** or **left·ist** *n.* in politics, a liberal or radical position, party, or person, esp. one advocating social and economic reform. —**left** *adj.* & *adv.* on or toward the left: *turn ~ at the lights;* **left·ist** *adj.: a ~view, position.* —**left** *pt.* & *pp.* of ²LEAVE. —**left-hand** *adj.: a ~blow, turn, screw thread.* —**left-hand·ed** *adj.* habitually using the left hand instead of the right; also, done with the left hand: *a ~* (i.e. insincere) *compliment;* ***adv.:*** *pitches ~;* **left-hand·ed·ly** *adv.* —**left·o·ver** (LEFT·oh–) *n.* & *adj.* (thing) that is left, as scraps of food. —**left wing** the more leftist section of a political party; **left-wing** *adj.;* **left-wing·er** *n.* —**left·y** *n.* **left·ies** *Slang.* a left-handed person.

leg *n.* **1** one of the limbs in humans and animals used for support and for moving about; also, any part suggesting a leg, as of trousers, of a table, chair, etc.; **pull one's leg** *Informal.* tease or kid. **2** one of the stages of a course, as in a relay race, a journey, etc. —***v.*** **legs, legged, leg·ging** *Informal.* go on foot: *The car broke down and we had to* **leg it** *the rest of the way.*

leg. legal; legislative; legislature. —**leg·a·cy** (LEG·uh·see) *n.* **-cies** an inheritance or bequest; hence, anything handed down by a predecessor or from the past. —**le·gal** (LEE·gul) *adj.* of or having to do with law, esp. not against the law: *Gambling is lawful where it is ~; ~ capacity, control, ownership;* **le·gal·ly** *adv.* —**legal age** majority. —**le·gal·ese** (–EEZ) *n.* the specialized language of legal forms and documents. —**legal holiday** a holiday set by statute, as New Year's Day or Thanksgiving. —**le·gal·ism** *n.* strict adherence to the letter of the law; also, a legal expression or rule; **le·gal·is·tic** (–LIS–) *adj.* —**le·gal·i·ty** (–GAL–) *n.* **-ties** legal quality or aspect. —**le·gal·ize** (LEE·guh–) *v.* **-iz·es, -ized, -iz·ing** make legal: *~d prostitution;* **le·gal·i·za·tion** (–ZAY–) *n.* —**legal tender** the type of money legally acceptable in payment of a debt: *1,000 pennies may not be ~ for $10.* —**leg·ate** (–it) *n.* a special envoy of the pope. —**leg·a·tee** (–TEE) *n.* one to whom a legacy is bequeathed. —**le·ga·tion** (–GAY–) *n.* **1** a legate's mission. **2** a diplomatic mission headed by a minister and ranking below an embassy.

le·ga·to (li·GAH·toh) *adj.* & *adv. Music.* (performed) in a smooth and connected manner.

leg·end (LEJ·und) *n.* **1** a story or tradition connected with the history of a people, as the Arthurian legend, St. George and the Dragon, etc. **2** an inscription, as on a medal, or an explanation, as of an illustration or of symbols used on a map. —**leg·end·ar·y** (LEJ·un·der·ee) *adj.: the ~ stories about Charlemagne; became a ~ figure even during his life.*

leg·er·de·main (lej·ur·duh·MAIN) *n.* sleight of hand, as when a magician takes rabbits out of a hat; hence, trickery or deception.

leg·ged (LEG·id, LEGD) *adj.* & *comb.form.* having (so many or such) legs: as in *three-~ race; long-~.* —**leg·ging** *n.* a leg-covering: *children's woolen ~s.* —**leg·gy** (LEG·ee) *adj.* **leg·gi·er,**

leg·gi·est having long legs: *a ~ chorus girl; ~ colts look awkward.*

leg·horn (LEG·horn, –urn) *n.* often **Leghorn,** a breed of small chicken, developed in Italy, the best in egg-laying.

leg·i·ble (LEJ–) *adj.* clear enough to read; **leg·i·bly** *adv.* —**leg·i·bil·i·ty** (–BIL–) *n.*

le·gion (LEE·jun) *n.* **1** an army, esp. a 3,000-to-6,000-man unit of soldiers in ancient Rome; hence, a large number: *tax evaders—their name is ~;* **le·gion·ar·y** *adj.* & *n.* **-ar·ies.** **2** usu. **Legion,** a society, as of ex-servicemen; **le·gion·naire** (–NAIR) *n.* a member of a Legion; **legionnaire's disease** an infectious disease with symptoms of pneumonia, caused by a bacteria-like organism, which resulted in many deaths during an American Legion convention in 1976.

legis. legislative; legislature. —**leg·is·late** (LEJ–) *v.* **-lates, -lat·ed, -lat·ing** make laws; also, bring about (reforms, morals, etc.) by legislating; **leg·is·la·tor** *n.* —**leg·is·la·tion** (–LAY–) *n.* (the making of) laws. —**leg·is·la·tive** (LEJ–) *adj.: a ~ body, decree; ~ reforms;* **leg·is·la·tive·ly** *adv.* —**leg·is·la·ture** (–chur) n. a lawmaking body such as the U.S. Congress. —**le·git** (luh·JIT) *adj. Slang,* legitimate: *from nightclub circuits to ~ theater;* ***n.:*** *strictly on the ~.* (i.e. within the law). —**le·git·i·ma·cy** (luh·JIT·uh·muh·see) *n.* a being lawful or legitimate; **le·git·i·mate** (–mit) *adj.* rightful according to law or other standard: *a ~ heir, claim, conclusion, purpose;* **legitimate theater** drama of literary merit, excluding musical comedies, motion pictures, etc.; **le·git·i·mate·ly** *adv.* —**le·git·i·mize** *v.* **-miz·es, -mized, -miz·ing** make or declare to be legitimate; also **le·git·i·ma·tize.**

leg·man *n.* **-men** one engaged in work that involves much moving about, or **leg·work,** esp. an on-the-scene reporter or an assistant on routine duties outside the office. —**leg·room** *n.* room for the legs while seated, as in a car.

leg·ume (–yoom, lig·YOOM) *n.* (the pod or seed of) a plant of the pea family, as the bean, peanut, alfalfa, or clover. —**le·gu·mi·nous** (–GYOO·mi·nus) *adj.*

legwork See LEGMAN.

lei (LAY, LAY·ee) *n.* **1** *pl.* **leis** a Hawaiian garland or wreath of flowers. **2** *pl.* of LEU.

Leip·zig (LIPE·sig) a city of S. C. East Germany.

lei·sure (LEE·zhur, LEZH–) *n.* time that one may spend for rest and recreation; ***adj.:*** *~ hour, time; the ~ class* (of people not working for a living); **lei·sured** (LEZH·urd) *adj.* having much leisure; leisurely. —**lei·sure·ly** *adj.* & *adv.* unhurried(ly): *working at a ~ pace; a ~ meal; Let's drive ~ but without slowing down.*

leit·mo·tif or **leit·mo·tive** (LITE·moh·teef) *n.* leading or dominant theme.

lek *n.* the basic money unit of Albania, equal to 100 qintar.

LEM (LEM) *n.* a lunar excursion module.

lem·ming *n.* a mouselike arctic animal noted for periodic migrations in large numbers.

lem·on (–un) *n.* a pale-yellow oval-shaped citrus fruit; hence, *Slang.* a person or thing that turns sour or disagreeable, esp. a bad buy such as a defective car; ***adj.*** pale-yellow; **lem·on·y** *adj.* —**lem·on·ade** (–NADE) *n.* a drink made of lemon juice, sugar, and water.

lem·pi·ra (–PEER·uh) *n.* the basic money unit of Honduras, equal to 100 centavos.

le·mur (LEE–) *n.* a fluffy-furred, long-tailed primate of Malagasy.

lend *v.* **lends, lent, lend·ing** **1** give (money, goods, or services) temporarily: *~ me $50 at 10% interest, your car for an hour, an ear* (i.e. listen to me), *a hand* (i.e. help me); *a subject that* **lends itself to** (i.e. is capable of) *dramatic treatment.* **2** give or impart: *Her presence ~s distinction to the proceedings.* —**lend·er** *n.* —**lend-lease** *n.* U.S. aid given under the Lend-Lease Act, 1941, to nations fighting the Axis powers.

length *n.* **1** how long or extended an object or period is; **at length** finally; also, fully. **2** a unit of measure or any specific distance: *Our horse won the race by a ~* (i.e. horse's length); *a ~ of rope.* —**length·en** *v.* make or become longer. —**length·wise** *adj.* & *adv.* in the direction of the length; also **length·ways.** —**length·y** *adj.* **length·i·er, -i·est** very long; also, too long: *a ~ speaker, speech, essay;* **length·i·ly** *adv.*

le·ni·ent (LEE·nee·unt, LEEN·yunt) *adj.* mild; hence, merciful: *~ climate, judge;* **le·ni·ence** or **le·ni·en·cy** *n.*

Len·in, Vladimir Ilyich. 1870–1924, founder of Russian communism, or **Len·in·ism** *n.* —**Len·in·grad** the U.S.S.R.'s second largest city and a seaport on the Gulf of Finland.

len·i·tive (–tiv) *n.* & *adj.* (something) that soothes or lessens; palliative. —**len·i·ty** *n.* leniency.

lens *n.* a piece of glass or other transparent body that focuses or spreads light rays, as in the eye and in cameras, microscopes, telescopes, etc.; also, any focusing device for sound waves, electrons, etc.

Lent *n.* a 40-day (excluding Sundays) period of penitence in Christian churches lasting from Ash Wednesday to Easter Sunday; **Lent·en** *adj.* —**lent** *pt.* & *pp.* of LEND.

len·til *n.* an ancient food plant of the pea family, valued for its nutritious, lens-shaped seeds; also, the seed.

Le·o (LEE·oh) *n.* a N. constellation and the fifth sign of the zodiac. —**le·one** (lee·OHN) *n.* the basic money unit of Sierra Leone, equal to 100 cents. —**le·o·nine** (LEE·uh–) *adj.* of or like a lion. —**leop·ard** (LEP·urd) *n.* a large fierce cat of Asia and Africa valued for its black-spotted skin; also, the related jaguar or a panther.

le·o·tard (LEE·uh–) *n.* usu. **leotards** *pl.* a tight-fitting, one-piece garment, as worn by acrobats; also, tights.

lep·er *n.* one who has leprosy; also, an outcast.

lep·re·chaun (LEP·ruh·cawn) *n.* a fairy of Irish folklore.

lep·ro·sy (–ruh·see) *n.* a chronic infectious and ulcerous disease of the skin and nerves that causes disfigurement; **lep·rous** (–rus) *adj.*

lep·ton (–tahn) *n., pl.* **-ta** a money unit of Greece, equal to 1/100 drachma.

les·bi·an (LEZ·bee·un) *n.* & *adj.* (a woman) homosexual; **les·bi·an·ism.** *n.*

lese majesty (leez–) an offense against the sovereign, esp. treason. **—le·sion** (LEE·zhun) *n.* injury to tissue, as an ulcer, tumor, or abscess.

Le·so·tho (luh·SOH·toh) a mountainous kingdom bordered on all sides by South Africa; 11,720 sq.mi. (30,355 km²); *cap.* Maseru.

less *adj.* a *compar.* of LITTLE; not as much or as many; smaller, fewer, or lower in rank, importance, quantity, etc.: *~ sugar; 10 items or ~ (Informal.* fewer). ***—adv.*** not as much or as often. ***—prep.*** minus: *$10,000 ~ deductions.* ***—n.*** a smaller amount: *a little ~ of it.* **— -less** *adj. suffix.* not having or involving: as in *useless, endless, painless.*

les·see (–SEE) *n.* See LEASE.

less·en (LESN) *v.* make or become less. **—less·er** *adj.* a *compar.* of LITTLE; smaller or less important: *acquitted on a ~ charge; the Lesser* ANTILLES, *the ~ panda.*

les·son (LESN) *n.* a learning exercise or something learned: *driving ~s* (i.e. instruction); *a ~ in French grammar; Let her tragedy be a ~* (i.e. warning) *for us.*

les·sor (–or) *n.* See LEASE.

lest *conj.* (for fear) that: was cautious *~ he be misunderstood; afraid ~ he should miss the bus.*

-let *n. suffix.* small (object or article of attire): as in *bracelet, leaflet, wristlet.*

let *v.* **lets, let, let·ting** allow (to go, have, pass, etc.): *Who ~ the cat out? We can't ~ him (come) in; Let us* (i.e. I propose that we) *pray; Surgeons used to ~ blood (run out) as a cure; a house to ~* (i.e. for rent); *doesn't have the training,* **let alone** (i.e. not to mention) *experience for the job; felt badly* **let down** *by his friends; Only friends were* **let in on** (i.e. told) *the secret; a first offender* **let off** *with a light sentence; likes to* **let on** (Informal. pretend) *that she is of wealthy stock;* **let out** **1** release or make known. **2** rent. **3** make larger: *~out the sail;* **let up** *Informal.* stop or pause. ***—n.*** in a racket game, an interference with play; **without let or hindrance** without obstacles. **—let·down** *n.* a slowing up; also, a disappointment.

le·thal (LEE·thul) *adj.* (capable of) causing death: *a ~ dose, weapon, gas chamber;* **le·thal·ly** *adv.*

leth·ar·gy (–ur·jee) *n.* a dull, sluggish, or tired state. **—le·thar·gic** (–THAR–) *adj.;* **le·thar·gi·cal·ly** *adv.*

let's let us.

Lett *n.* Latvian.

let·ter (LET·ur) *n.* **1** a character of the alphabet, as A, B, C, etc.: *a capital ~; follow orders* **to the letter** (i.e. precisely); *observing* **the letter of the law** (i.e. literal meaning) *without its spirit.* **2** a written communication: *the art of ~ writing.* **3** **letters** [takes *sing.* or *pl. v.*] literature; also, learning: *a man of ~.* ***—v.*** mark with or inscribe in letters: *a well-~ed poster;* **let·tered** *adj.* literate; also, learned; **let·ter·er** *n.* **—letter bomb** a bomb in the form of a postal envelope that explodes when opened. **—letter box** mailbox; **letter carrier** mail carrier. **—let·ter·head** *n.* (writing paper printed at the top with) one's name and address. **—let·ter·ing** *n.* (the art of making) drawn, printed, or stamped letters. **—let·ter-per·fect** *adj.* correct in every detail. **—let·ter·press** *n.* printing from raised type; also, text as distinguished from pictures. **—letters patent** *pl.* an official document granting a person some right or authority, as a title to land.

let·tuce (–is) *n.* (the large, crisp, green leaves of) a plant much used in salads.

let·up *n. Informal.* pause; slackening.

le·u (LEH·oo) *n., pl.* **lei** (LAY) the basic money unit of Romania, equal to 100 bani.

leu·co·cyte or **leu·ko·cyte** (LOO·cuh·cite) *n.* a white blood cell. **—leu·ke·mi·a** (loo·KEE·mee·uh) *n.* a cancerous, often fatal, uncontrolled growth of leucocytes; **leu·ke·mic** *adj.*

lev (LEF) *n., pl.* **le·va** (LEV·uh) the basic money unit of Bulgaria, equal to 100 stotinki.

Lev. Leviticus.

lev·ee (LEV–) *n.* **1** a wall of banked-up earth and sandbags put up along a river's bank to contain floods. **2** a formal reception, as by a sovereign or by the U.S. President.

lev·el (–ul) *adj.* horizontal; equal in height everywhere: *Adjust the legs to make the table ~; flood waters ~ with the second floor; a ~* (i.e. not heaped) *teaspoonful; always keeps a ~* (i.e. sensible) *head;* **lev·el-head·ed** *adj.* ***—n.*** **1** something that is level; also, a height or depth; relative position or elevation: *a lake above sea ~; rose to a ~ of 15 ft.; a high ~ of achievement; Water seeks its own ~* (i.e. horizontal condition, with the surface everywhere at the same altitude). **2** an instrument used to determine if a plane is horizontal. ***—v.*** **-els, -el(l)ed, -el·(l)ing** make horizontal or on the same level: *a town ~d by an earthquake; words ~d* (i.e. directed) *at his critics; Prices are expected to rise and then* **level off** (i.e. stay the same); *Come on now,* **level** (i.e. be honest) **with** *me;* **lev·el·(l)er** *n.*

lev·er (LEV–, LEE–) *n.* a device such as a crowbar for exerting force; hence, a means of exerting power or moral force: *used his position as a*

~ *to get some votes;* **lev·er·age** (–ij) *n.* means of applying force; hence, advantage or effectiveness.

le·vi·a·than (luh·VYE·uh·thun) *n.* a huge and monstrous thing or animal.

Le·vi's (LEE·vize) *Trademark.* close-fitting heavy blue-denim trousers; also **le·vis** *n.pl.*

lev·i·tate *v.* **-tates, -tat·ed, -tat·ing** (cause) to rise and float in the air: *a magnetically ~d transportation system.* **—lev·i·ta·tion** (–TAY–) *n.* the lifting or rising of a body, esp. by spiritualistic power.

Le·vit·i·cus (luh·VIT–) a book of the Old Testament.

lev·i·ty *n.* **-ties** lack of proper seriousness; frivolity.

lev·u·lose (–yoo·lohs) *n.* same as FRUCTOSE.

lev·y *v.* **lev·ies, lev·ied, lev·y·ing** **1** raise (taxes, armies, etc.) by legal authority. **2** seize (property in satisfaction of a claim). **3** wage: *to* **levy war on** (or **against**) *them.* —*n., pl.* **lev·ies** a tax or fine collected; also, enlistment for military service or the men enlisted.

lewd (LOOD) *adj.* indecent; obscene; **lewd·ly** *adv.;* **lewd·ness** *n.*

lex·i·cal *adj.* having to do with vocabulary rather than grammar; **lex·i·cal·ly** *adv.* **—lex·i·cog·ra·phy** (–COG·ruh·fee) *n.* the work or art of compiling a dictionary; **lex·i·cog·ra·pher** *n.* **—lex·i·co·graph·ic** (–GRAF–) or **-i·cal** *adj.* **—lex·i·con** (–cun) *n.* the vocabulary of a language; also, a dictionary, esp. of a classical language.

Lex·ing·ton (–tun) a city of Kentucky.

L.F. or **l.f.** low frequency; **lf.** lightface (type).

L.H. or **l.h.** left hand.

L.H.D. Doctor of Humane Letters.

Lha·sa (LAH·suh) capital of Tibet.

Li lithium. **—L.I.** Long Island.

li·a·bil·i·ty (–BIL–) *n.* **-ties** a being liable; disadvantage or obligation: *No one would admit ~ for the accident; a spouse who is a ~* (i.e. burden) *rather than an asset; heavy ~s* (i.e. debts) *leading to bankruptcy.* **—li·a·ble** (LYE·uh–) *adj.* subject to (a responsibility or risk): *If you play with fire, you are ~ to get burned; carrier not ~ for damage to luggage; Everyone is ~ to make mistakes now and then.*

li·ai·son (LEE·uh·zon, lee·AY–) *n.* communication between different parts of an army, civilian bodies, etc. for cooperation; also, illicit sexual relationship.

li·ar (LYE·ur) *n.* one who tells lies.

lib *n.* [short form] liberation. **—lib·ber** *n. Informal.* a liberationist, esp. a feminist.

li·ba·tion (lye·BAY–) *n.* a ceremonial pouring out (of wine, oil, etc.) as an offering to a god; also, the liquid poured out; hence, *Informal.* a drink(ing).

li·bel (LYE·bl) *n.* the hurting of someone's good name by publishing something (written, printed, drawn, etc.) unjustly; also, material that libels. **—*v.*** **-bels, -bel(l)ed, -bel·(l)ing** defame by a libel; **li·bel·(l)er** *n.* **—li·bel·(l)ous** *adj.*

lib·er·al (–uh·rul) *adj.* free, generous, or broad-minded; not narrow, strict, or prejudiced: *a ~ giver of tips; a ~ supply of provisions; very ~ in his interpretation of the Bible.* **—*n.*** one who is in favor of progress and reform; **Liberal** a member of a Liberal Party, as in Britain and Canada. **—lib·er·al·ism** *n.* **—liberal education** education in the **liberal arts** i.e. languages, literature, philosophy, history, etc. for their cultural value instead of a scientific, technical, or professional education. **—lib·er·al·i·ty** (–RAL–) *n.* **—lib·er·al·ize** *v.* **-iz·es, -ized, -iz·ing** make or become liberal: *~d abortion laws;* **lib·er·al·i·za·tion** (–ZAY–) *n.* **—lib·er·al·ly** *adv.* generously. **—lib·er·ate** *v.* **-ates, -at·ed, -at·ing** set free, as from slavery, confinement, enemy occupation, male dominance, etc.; **lib·er·a·tor** *n.;* **lib·er·a·tion** (–RAY–) *n.;* **lib·er·a·tion·ist** *n.* **—Li·ber·i·a** (lye·BEER·ee·uh) a republic on Africa's W. coast founded by freed American slaves; 43,000 sq. mi. (111,369 km^2); *cap.* Monrovia; **Li·ber·i·an** *n.* & *adj.* **—lib·er·tar·i·an** (–TAIR–) *n.* & *adj.* (of or having to do with) liberty in thought and action or one who believes in freedom of the will: *a right-wing civil ~;* **lib·er·tar·i·an·ism** *n.* **—lib·er·tine** (–teen) *n.* & *adj.* (one) without moral restraints; licentious (person). **—lib·er·ty** *n.* **-ties** freedom from restraints such as slavery: *prisoners set* **at liberty** (i.e. free); *~ of thought, action, etc.; doesn't let boys* **take liberties** (i.e. to be too familiar) *with her on dates.* **—Liberty Bell** a traditional symbol of American independence, commissioned in 1751 to hang in the Pennsylvania State House.

li·bi·do (li·BEE·doh, –BYE–) *n.* energy derived from the instincts, esp. the sexual urge. **—li·bid·i·nal** (–BID·n·ul) *adj.* having to do with the libido; **li·bid·i·nous** *adj.* lustful; lewd; lascivious.

Li·bra (LYE·bruh, LEE–) a S. constellation and the seventh sign of the zodiac.

li·brar·i·an (lye·BRAIR·ee·un) *n.* one in charge of a library; also, one trained in library science. **—li·brar·y** (LYE·brer·ee) *n.* **-brar·ies** a collection of books, manuscripts, tapes, etc.; also, a place where such a collection is housed. **—li·bret·to** (li·BRET·oh) *n.* **-bret·tos** or **-bret·ti** (–tee) (a book containing) the words of an opera or similar long musical composition, written by a **li·bret·tist** *n.*

Li·bre·ville (lee·br·VEEL) capital of Gabon.

Lib·ya (LIB·ee·uh) a N. African republic on the Mediterranean; 679,362 sq. mi. (1,759,540 km^2); *caps.* Tripoli and Benghasi; **Lib·y·an** *n.* & *adj.*

lice *pl.* of LOUSE.

li·cense (LYE·snce) *n.* **1** a formal or legal permission to do something as a member of society, as driving, marrying, or practicing a profession. **2** irresponsible use of freedom. Also **li·cence.** —***v.*** **-cens·es, -censed, -cens·ing:** *a ~d medical practitioner.* —**li·cen·see** (–SEE) *n.* one granted a license. —**li·cen·ti·ate** (–SEN·shee·it) *n.* one licensed to practice an art or profession; also, a university degree between a bachelor's and a doctor's. —**li·cen·tious** (–shus) *adj.* lawless, hence, immoral or lewd; **li·cen·tious·ly** *adv.;* **li·cen·tious·ness** *n.*

li·chi or **li·chee** (LEE·chee) *n.* same as LITCHI.

li·chen (LYE·cun) *n.* a flowerless plant resembling moss that grows on bare rocks, tree stumps, etc.

lic·it (LIS–) *adj.* permitted by law; not forbidden; **lic·it·ly** *adv.*

lick *v.* **1** pass the tongue over; also, play over like a tongue: *She ~ed her fingers; flames ~ing the walls.* **2** *Informal.* beat or thrash; also, conquer: *a good* **licking;** *has every problem ~ed* (i.e. under control); *a thesis* **licked into shape** (*Informal.* put in proper form) *by year's end.* —***n.:*** *a ~ of your ice-cream cone; a salt ~;* **lick and a promise** *Informal.* a hasty performance, as of washing or cleaning. —**lick·e·ty-split** *adv. Informal.* at full speed. —**lick·spit·tle** *n. Informal.* a toady.

lic·o·rice (LIC·uh·ris, –rish) *n.* (black-colored candy flavored with) an extract of the sweet roots of an herb of the pea family.

lid n. **1** a movable cover, as of a pot or box; also, eyelid. **2** a curb or check: *tighter measures to put the ~ on smuggling.* **3** *Slang.* a one-ounce package of marijuana. —**lid·ded** *adj.*

li·dar (LYE–) *n.* radar using a pulsed laser beam.

li·do (LEE·doh) *n.* **-dos** a beach resort or bathing facility.

¹lie (LYE) *n.* & *v.* **lies, lied, ly·ing** (utter) a deliberate falsehood, esp. a cowardly one: *The "candid camera" that never ~s; His entire life seemed a ~; Facts* **give the lie to** *his claim of innocence* (i.e. show it to be untrue).

²lie (LYE) v. **lies, lay, lain, ly·ing** **1** of a person or a heavy body, place oneself or be in a horizontal position, as when tired: *Bathers ~ on the beach; Let me ~ down for a while; The books lay on the floor.* **2** stay or exist (as specified): *Who ~s buried here? Mexico ~s (to the) south of us; Her future ~s in medicine, not law.* —***n.*** the way in which something lies; lay: *the ~ of the land.*

Liech·ten·stein (LIK·tun·shtine) an independent principality between Switzerland and Austria; 61 sq.mi. (157 km²); *cap.* Vaduz.

lied (LEED) *n., pl.* **lied·er** a German song of the Romantic era.

lie detector a device for measuring changes in blood pressure, pulse, breathing, etc. as reflecting the mind of a subject under questioning.

lief (LEEF) *adv. Archaic.* **would** (or **had**) **as lief** would (or had) as willingly (do something).

liege (LEEJ) *adj.* of a feudal lord (or vassal), having a right to (or obliged to give) homage and loyal service: *~ lord, sovereign;* ***n.*** lord: *My ~!* **liege·man** *n.* **-men** vassal.

lien (LEEN, LEE·un) *n. Law.* a claim on another's property because of a debt incurred on it, as when a contractor is not paid for work done on a house.

lieu (LOO) *n.* **in lieu of** instead of. —**lieut.** *Abbrev.* for **lieu·ten·ant** (loo·TEN·unt) *n.* an officer who acts in place of one above him, esp. a commissioned officer ranking just below captain, as in the U.S. Army, Air Force, and Marine Corps; **lieutenant general** a rank below general, **lieutenant colonel** a rank below colonel, **first lieutenant** and **second lieutenant** ranks below captain; in the U.S. Navy: **lieutenant commander, lieutenant** and **lieutenant junior grade,** successive ranks below commander. —**lieutenant governor** a public official next in rank to governor, as in a U.S. state, or the governor of a Canadian province appointed by the governor general. —**lieu·ten·an·cy** *n.* **-cies.**

life *n.* **lives** **1** a being alive or active, as people, animals, and plants, distinguished from minerals; also, human life or a living being: *lives lost in an accident; Is there ~ after death?* **2** the length of an individual's life; also, the period of existence of anything thought of as having a beginning and end: *our ~ expectancy; the ~ of a lease.* **3** a way of living; also, a biography: *a ~ of Napoleon; He led a dog's ~.* **4** liveliness or spirit; also, its source: *She's the ~ of the party.* —**life·belt** *n.* a beltlike life preserver. —**life·blood** *n.* something life-giving, as blood to the body. —**life·boat** *n.* a boat built for rescue work or one carried on a ship for use if the ship is to be abandoned. —**life·buoy** *n.* a ring-shaped float thrown to drowning people. —**life expectancy** See EXPECTANCY. —**life·guard** *n.* a person trained in lifesaving, esp. in water. —**life insurance** (insurance to pay) a sum of money to one's heirs in case of death. —**life jacket** a life preserver made like a sleeveless jacket. —**life·less** *adj.: Minerals are ~; a ~ corpse; a quite ~ performance.* —**life·like** *adj.* exactly like the subject in real life: *a ~ statute.* —**life·line** *n.* a rope or line thrown to save a person in water; hence, the only means or route for sending help to one in distress. —**life·long** *adj.* involving a lifetime. —**life net** a large sheet or net of canvas held on the ground for people from a burning building to jump into. —**life preserver** a device in the shape of a belt, jacket, or ring, usu. filled with air, cork, or kapok, to keep a person afloat. —**lif·er** *n. Informal.* one sentenced to life imprisonment; also, a career member of the military. —**life raft** an inflatable boat or raft for use in case of a shipwreck or an airplane crash at sea. —**life·sav·er** *n.* one trained in lifesaving; also, *Informal.* a person or thing helpful to someone in distress; **life·sav·ing** *n.* & *adj.* (designed or used for) the saving of lives: *a ~ apparatus.* —**life science** a science dealing with life and living things, as biology, biochemistry, medicine, or sociology. —**life-size(d)** *adj.* of a painting, statue, etc., of the same size as the subject. —**life style** a way of life characteristic of a person or group. —**life-sup·port system** a system designed to provide oxygen, food, water, and such essentials of life to people in space, on a planet, under water, etc. —**life·time** *n.* & *adj.* (lasting) the entire life of a person or thing: *a ~ occupation; the chance of a ~* (i.e. a rare chance). —**life vest** same as LIFE JACKET. —**life·work** *n.* the main work of one's life.

LIFO (LYE·foh) *n.* the "last-in-first-out" method of inventory valuation.

lift *v.* **1** raise or rise to a higher level or position: *Can you ~ this weight? a drink to ~* (i.e. elevate) *your spirits; refused to ~ a finger to help us.* **2** remove or withdraw: *A blockade is ~ed; The fog will ~ at dawn; when the rain ~s* (i.e. stops for a time). **3** *Informal.* steal: *caught ~ing things from shops; a passage ~ed from a copyrighted work.* —***n.*** **1** a lifting or its result or extent: *An airfoil creates a ~ in reaction to gravity; The victory gave his spirits quite a ~; A ~ of 200 lbs. is beyond me; the haughty ~ of her chin; Let's give her a ~* (i.e. ride) *home.* **2** anything that lifts or elevates, as a *chair lift,* one of the layers forming the heel of a shoe, a promotion, or *(Brit.)* an elevator. —**lift·off** *n.* the vertical blastoff of a space vehicle or missile. —**lift pump** a pump that lifts a liquid to the desired level. —**lift truck** same as FORKLIFT TRUCK.

lig·a·ment (LIG·uh–) *n.* a strong fibrous band of tissue fastening bones together or holding organs in place. —**li·gate** (LYE–) *v.* **-ates, -at·ed, -at·ing** bind with a ligature; **li·ga·tion** (–GAY–) *n.* —**lig·a·ture** (LIG·uh·chur) *n.* a binding, something used in tying, as a thread used by a surgeon to tie off a blood vessel, or something tied together, as the characters *ffl* and *æ.*

li·ger (LYE·gur) *n.* the hybrid offspring of a lion and a tigress.

¹light (LITE) *n.* **1** that by which we see, including ultraviolet and infrared radiation; also, a source or supply of light, as the sun, a lamp, a match or cigarette lighter, a lighthouse or a traffic light, a window, a famous person or "luminary," etc. **2** the quality or condition of being lit or illumined; also, a bright object or anything shining: *the contrasts of ~ and shade in a picture; the ~* (i.e. gleam) *in her eyes.* —***adj.*** bright or lit: *a ~ complexion; as ~ as dawn; a ~ hallway.* —***v.*** **lights,** *pt.* & *pp.* **light·ed** or **lit, light·ing:** *Let's ~ a candle; streets lit by electricity; 6 o'clock is ~ing-up time; a face lit by joy.* —**in (the) light of** considering; **see the light (of day)** come to be or be made public; **shed** (or **throw) light on** make clear; clarify.

²light (LITE) *adj.* **1** not heavy; of little or less-than-usual weight, amount, force, severity, etc.: *~ as a feather; a ~ jacket, snowfall, punishment;* ***adv.:*** *Let us travel ~* (i.e. without too much baggage). **2** having qualities suggesting little weight; delicate, nimble, cheerful, etc.: *a ~ body frame, step, spirits; a ~ wine* (i.e. table wine, with less alcohol). **3** lacking due weight or seriousness: *~ of purpose; a bit* **light in the head** (i.e. foolish or crazy; also, dizzy); **makes light of** (i.e. considers not serious) *her child's thievery.* —***v.*** **lights,** *pt.* & *pp.* **light·ed** or **lit, light·ing** come down (from an animal's back, from flight, etc.): *a bird ~ing on a tree; The blow ~d on the wrong head; Her eyes ~d* (i.e. by chance) *on a face in the crowd;* **light into** *Slang.* attack or scold.

light bulb an incandescent lamp. —**light·en** *v.* make or become lighter or more cheerful: *The confession ~ed her heart.* —**light·er** *n.* **1** a person or thing that lights: *a cigarette ~.* **2** a boat or barge for carrying cargo between ships and shore; **light·er·age** (–ij) *n.* (charge for) transportation using lighters. —**light·face** *n.* light printing type, not boldface. —**light-fin·ger·ed** *adj.* having light fingers; also, thievish. —**light-foot·ed** *adj.* stepping gracefully. —**light-head·ed** *adj.* silly or frivolous; also, dizzy. —**light-heart·ed** *adj.* without cares and worries; happy and gay. —**light heavyweight** a boxer weighing between 160 and 175 lbs. (75 and 81 kg for Olympics). —**light·house** *n.* **-hous·es** (–how·ziz) a tower with a flashing light at the top to warn or guide ships. —**light industry** industry producing consumer goods, not heavy industry. —**light·ing** *n.* the arrangement of lights, as in a room; also, the act of supplying or kindling a light. —**light·ly** *adv.* [corresponding to *adj.* senses of ²LIGHT] **1:** *Snow fell ~ outside; dressed ~ because of heat.* **2:** *She stepped ~ aside; took the bad news ~.* **3:** *a matter too serious to be treated ~; speaks ~ of his elders.* —**light meter** a light-measuring instrument; exposure meter. —**light·ness** *n.* light color, brightness, or the amount of light. —**light·ning** *n.* & *adj.* (quick as) a flash of light in the sky caused by electrical discharges from clouds: *a ~ raid; with ~ speed;* **lightning bug** same as FIREFLY; **lightning rod** a rod of metal fixed to a roof for grounding electricity from lightnings. —**light opera** same as OPERETTA. —**light pen** (or **pencil**) a pen-shaped photoelectric device for using on a cathrode-ray-tube screen to activate a computer to change or modify images, as in editing a text. —**lights** *n.pl.* the lungs of sheeps, pigs, etc. used as food. —**light·ship** *n.* a ship designed and built for use as a floating lighthouse. —**light show**

a kaleidoscopic display of lights and colors accompanied by rock music. —**light·some** (–sum) *adj.* light and elegant; light-hearted; nimble. —**light·weight** *n.* a boxer weighing between 126 and 135 lbs. (57 and 60 kg for Olympics); ***adj.*** light in weight; hence, unimportant. —**light-year** *n.* a unit of astronomical distance equal to the distance that light travels in one year; approx. 6 trillion miles (9.5 trillion km).

lig·ne·ous (LIG·nee·us) *adj.* woody or hard: *a ~ tumor.* —**lig·ni·fy** *v.* **-fies, -fied, -fy·ing** make into or become like wood by deposits of a celluloselike substance called **lig·nin.** —**lig·nite** *n.* a low-quality, brownish-black coal with a woody texture; also called "brown coal."

lik·a·ble (LYE·kuh–) *adj.* easy to like; **lik·a·ble·ness** *n.* —**like** *prep.* [indicating similarity]: *She swims ~ a fish; She is ~ her brother; It's just ~* (i.e. characteristic of) *her to be generous; I don't feel ~ working; looks ~* (it is going to) *rain; citrus fruits ~* (i.e. such as) *oranges and lemons.* —***adj.*** similar: *as ~ as two peas; The firm contributed $1,000 and the workers chipped in with a ~ amount;* ***comb. form.*** similar to; characteristic of: as in *catlike, milklike, bell-like.* —***adv.*** *Informal.* probably: *~ enough it'll rain.* —***conj.*** *Informal.* as (if): *tastes good ~ a cigarette should; looks ~ it is going to rain.* —***n.*** **1** a similar person or thing: *When shall we see her ~ again? prefers cats, dogs,* **and the like** *to humans; Society has no place for* **the likes of** *him.* **2** something one likes: *All have their* **likes** *and dislikes.* —**like crazy** (or **the devil, hell, mad,** etc.) furiously: *works ~ the devil;* **like hell!** certainly not. —***v.*** **likes, liked, lik·ing** feel well towards: *I ~ company; She'd ~* (i.e. wishes to have) *a drink; Do as you ~* (i.e. wish); **like·a·ble** *adj.* same as LIKABLE. —**like·ly** *adj.* **-li·er, -li·est:** *There's a ~* (i.e. probable) *chance of rain tonight; It's ~ to* (i.e. probable that it will) *rain; a ~ night for rain;* ***adv.:*** *It'll most ~ rain tonight;* **like·li·hood** *n.* —**like-mind·ed** *adj.* of the same way of thinking; **like-mind·ed·ness** *n.* —**lik·en** (LYE·kun) *v.* consider as similar; compare. —**like·ness** *n.* similarity; resemblance: *She bears a ~ to her mother; This statue is a good ~ of her;* **in the likeness of** in the form or appearance of: *made in the image and ~ of God.* —**like·wise** *adv.* in the same way (as another); also, moreover; besides. —**lik·ing** (LYE–) *n.: Everything was not to her ~; showed a ~ for French wines.*

li·ku·ta (lee·KOO·tah) *n., pl.* **ma·ku·ta** a monetary unit of Zaire equal to 1/100 of a zaire.

li·lac (LYE·luc, –lac, –loc) *n.* a shrub bearing clustered blossoms that are usu. light purple; also, this color; ***adj.:*** *a ~ gown, dress.*

Lil·li·pu·tian (–PYOO·shun) *n.* & *adj.* (tiny like) an inhabitant of Lilliput in Swift's *Gulliver's Travels;* also, a narrow-minded person.

Li·long·we (–LONG·way) capital of Malawi.

lilt *n.* & *v.* (sing, play, or move in) a lively rhythm.

lil·y *n.* **lil·ies** any of a family of plants with stemless leaves that grow from bulbs and bear bell-shaped flowers with six parts, typically white, as in the **lily of the valley.** —**lil·y-liv·ered** (–LIV·urd) *adj.* cowardly. —**lil·y-white** *adj.* pure white: *not so ~* (i.e. innocent) *as she claims; a ~* (i.e. whites-only) *neighborhood.*

Li·ma (LEE·muh) capital of Peru. —**li·ma** (LYE·muh) **bean** a common tropical bean that bears broad pods.

limb (LIM) *n.* a leg, arm, or wing; also, a similar appendage, as the branch of a tree; **out on a limb** *Informal.* in a dangerous or precarious position. —**limb·less** *adj.*

lim·ber *adj.* & *v.* (make or become) supple or nimble: *some exercises to help you* **limber up.** —**lim·ber·ly** *adv.*

lim·bo *n.* **-bos** **1** a place for forgotten or unwanted persons and things, like the **Limbo** of Christian theologies, a region of confinement for those barred from heaven because unbaptized. **2** a West Indian acrobatic dance that involves bending over backwards and passing under a horizontal pole.

Lim·bur·ger (**cheese**) a semisoft ripened cheese with a strong odor.

[1]**lime** *n.* & *v.* **limes, limed, lim·ing** (treat with) a white substance used in making mortar and cement, got by heating **lime·stone** and such materials containing calcium carbonate in a **lime·kiln** (–kil, –kiln).

[2]**lime** *n.* a citrus fruit like lemon but greener, smaller, and more acid. —**lime·ade** (lye·MADE) *n.* a sweet beverage made with lime juice.

limekiln See [1]LIME. —**lime·light** *n.* & *v.* spotlight, formerly produced by incandescent lime.

lim·er·ick *n.* a five-line humorous verse rhymed in the pattern AABBA.

limestone See [1]LIME. —**lim·ey** (LYE·mee) *n.* **-eys** *Slang.* an Englishman, esp. a sailor.

lim·it *n.* a boundary; hence, a maximum or minimum: *within the ~s of decency; a speed ~ for drivers; about lowering the age ~ for voting;* **the limit** *Slang.* as much as one can take: *She is the ~!* **lim·it·less** *adj.* —***v.*** set a limit to or restrict: *~ your cable to 21 words;* **lim·i·ta·tion** (–TAY–) *n.* **lim·it·ed** *adj.: a ~ company* (with limited liability of members); *a 200-copy* **limited edition** *of a book; a ~-stop bus or train service; a* **limited** (not all-out) **war; lim·it·er** *n.*

limn (LIM) *v.* **limns, limned, limn·ing** (LIM·ing, –ning) paint or draw; hence, portray; describe; **lim·ner** (LIM·ur, LIM·nur) *n.*

lim·o (LIM·oh) *n.* **-os** [short form] limousine.

li·mo·nite (LYE·muh–) *n.* a yellowish or brownish mineral that is a source of iron and ocher; **li·mo·nit·ic** (–NIT–) *adj.*

lim·ou·sine (LIM·uh·zeen) *n.* a chauffeured luxury automobile.

limp *n.* & *v.* (walk or proceed with or as if with) a lameness or halt. —***adj.*** droopy or weak: *a* *body ~ with exhaustion; a ~ leaf; a ~* (i.e. weak) *argument;* **limp·ly** *adv.;* **limp·ness** *n.*

limp·et (–it) *n.* a mollusk that clings to rocks, moving about at high tide.

lim·pid *adj.* softly clear or transparent: *a ~ stream; ~ eyes, prose style;* **lim·pid·ly** *adv.* —**lim·pid·ness** or **lim·pid·i·ty** (–PID–) *n.*

lim·y (LYE·mee) *adj.* **lim·i·er, -i·est** of or containing lime; also, covered with birdlime; sticky.

lin. lineal; linear. —**lin·age** (LYE·nij) *n.* number of lines of print or writing; also, a rate or charge per line.

linch·pin *n.* a pin that keeps a wheel in place on its axle; hence, a key person or element.

Lin·coln (LING·cun), **Abraham.** 1809–65; 16th U.S. President (1861–65). —**Lincoln** capital of Nebraska.

lin·den *n.* any of a family of soft-wooded shade trees with heart-shaped leaves, bearing white or yellow clusters of flowers full of nectar.

line *n.* **1** a piece of thread or wire considered in its length but not width or thickness; hence, anything resembling it: *a clothes ~ for drying laundry; an angler's hook and ~; a plumb ~; a straight or curved ~ drawn on paper; the ~s on an aged man's face; a stanza of four ~s of verse; The young actress forgot her* **lines** (i.e. words to speak) *in the middle of the play; Please drop me a ~* (i.e. brief letter) *when you arrive there.* **2** something thought of as forming a line: *the Mason-Dixon ~* (i.e. border) *between Pennsylvania and Maryland; the ~* (i.e. circle) *of the equator; a ~* (i.e. row) *of trees along a road; a noble ~* (i.e. family) *of kings; an artillery's* **line of fire;** *the front* **line of battle;** *communication ~s between two cities; the gas ~ leading from tank to engine.* **3** something organized or laid down, as a plan, policy, business, occupation, etc.: *members of a party working along the same ~s; Stamp collecting is not (in) my ~; A store cannot carry every ~* (i.e. brand) *of goods; the* **line of credit** (i.e. maximum amount) *extended by a bank to a borrower; There seemed little truth in the official ~* (i.e. statement) *handed out to the press.* —**bring into line** cause to agree or conform. —**draw the** (or **a**) **line** set a limit. —**on the line** *Informal.* in a position of high risk. —**out of line** in disagreement; also, disorderly or rude. —**toe the line** conform. —***v.*** **lines, lined, lin·ing** **1** mark with lines; arrange or form a line: *~d writing paper; a forehead ~d with age; People ~d the route of the parade; Athletes* **line up** *for a race.* **2** put or serve as a lining in: *a coat ~d with silk; bookshelves ~ing a library's walls.* —**lin·e·age** (LIN·ee·ij) *n.* line of descent from an ancestor; also, such descendants or family. —**lin·e·al** (LIN·ee·ul) *adj.* in a line of descent; also, hereditary: *a ~ descendant, heir; ~ relatives.* —**lin·e·a·ment** (LIN·ee·uh–) *n.* usu. **lineaments** *pl.* distinctive features (of a face). —**lin·e·ar.** (LIN·ee·ur) *adj.* proceeding in a straight line; also, long or having to do with length: *A meter is a unit of ~ measure; an air cushion vehicle propelled by the magnetic waves of a* **linear motor.** —**line·back·er** *n.* a football player positioned behind the defensive line. —**line drive** a baseball hit in almost a straight line close to the ground. —**line·man** *n.* **-men** **1** one who works on a telegraph, telephone, electric, or railroad line. **2** a football player positioned on the line of scrimmage. —**lin·en** *n.* a tough yarn or cloth woven of fibers of flax; hence, sheets, tablecloths, napkins, etc. of linen. —**line of credit** See LINE, *n.* 3. —**line of scrimmage** in football, an imaginary line parallel to the goal lines at the most forward point of the ball when it is on the ground. —**line printer** a usu. computer-operated device that prints an entire line at a time. —**lin·er** (LYE·nur) *n.* **1** an airplane or ship belonging to a transportation line. **2** material serving as a lining. —**lines·man** *n.* **-men** a sports official who watches the lines during play to assist the referee or umpire, as in football and tennis; also, a lineman. —**line·up** *n.* an arrangement or listing of persons, as of suspects for identification or players taking part in a game. —**lin·ey** (LYE·nee) *adj.* same as LINY.

ling *n.* a North American marine food fish of the cod family. — **-ling** *n. suffix.* small or dependent: as in *hireling, princeling, sapling, underling.*

lin·ger (LING·gur) *v.* take time to leave, as if reluctant: *guests who ~ at the door when leaving;* **lin·ger·er** *n.* —**lin·ger·ing** *adj.: ~ doubts; a ~ look.*

lin·ge·rie (lan·zhuh·REE, lahn·zhuh·RAY) *n.* women's underclothing and night clothes.

lin·go (LING–) *n.* **-goes** *Informal.* speech that sounds foreign or is unintelligible to one; also, jargon. —**lin·gua fran·ca** (LING·gwuh·FRANG·cuh) a hybrid mixture of languages, as pidgin, for easy communication between speakers of different languages. —**lin·gual** (LING·gwul) *n. & adj.* (a sound) made with the tongue, as "l" or "d." —**lin·guist** (LING–) *n.* a specialist in linguistics; also, a polyglot person. —**lin·guis·tics** (–GWIS–) *n.pl.* [takes *sing. v.*] the science of language, including the study of pronunciation, syntax, meaning, derivation, etc.; **lin·guis·tic** *adj.;* **lin·guis·ti·cal·ly** *adv.*

lin·i·ment (LIN·uh·munt) *n.* a soothing medication for rubbing on the skin.

lin·ing (LYE·ning) *n.* the inner layer or covering of a surface, as of a coat, wall, etc.

link (LINGK) *n.* anything that connects, as a *cuff link* or one of the loops of a chain; also, a connected part, as of sausage: *The present forms a ~ with the past and the future.* —***v.*** join; connect: *persons ~ed with a crime.* —**link·age** (–ij) *n.* a linking or a system of links. —**linking verb** same as COPULA. —**links** *n.pl.* golf course. —**link-up** *n.* a linking together;

also, a rendezvous: *a ~ of space vehicles, military forces.*

Lin·nae·us (li·NEE–), **Carolus.** 1707–78, Swedish botanist.

lin·net (LIN·ut) *n.* a small Old World finch, usu. brown, with dark streaks on its back. —**li·no·le·um** (li·NOH·lee·um) *n.* a hard, canvas-backed floor covering made from linseed oil.

Lin·o·type (LYE·nuh–) *Trademark.* a keyboard-operated machine that sets type in entire lines; also **linotype** *n.* & *v.*

lin·seed *n.* flaxseed, which yields **linseed oil** used in paints, varnishes, and in making linoleum. —**lin·sey-wool·sey** (LIN·zee·WOOL·zee) *n.* a coarse cloth of linen and wool. —**lint** *n.* soft fleecy material scraped from linen, formerly used as a dressing for wounds; also, bits of fluff or fuzz of any material; **lint·y** *adj.* **lint·i·er, -i·est.**

lin·tel (–tl) *n.* the horizontal beam or bar over a window or door.

lin·y (LYE·nee) *adj.* like a line; also, marked with or full of lines.

li·on (LYE·un) *n.* a large, strong animal of the cat family from Africa and S. Asia whose male has a distinctive flowing mane and is considered the king of beasts; hence, a person distinguished by bravery, strength, or fame; —**lion's share** biggest portion. —**li·on·ess** *n.* a female lion. —**li·on·heart·ed** *adj.* courageous; brave. —**li·on·ize** (LYE·un–) *v.* **-iz·es, -ized, -iz·ing** treat (a person) as a hero or celebrity; **li·on·i·za·tion** (–ZAY–) *n.*

lip *n.* **1** either of the two fleshy folds, upper and lower, forming the mouth; hence, a lip-shaped edge of an opening, as of a pitcher, bell, crater, etc.; also, a liplike part. **2** *Slang.* insolent talk. —***adj.*** formed or done with the lips: *a ~ consonant, or labial; ~* (i.e. insincere) *worship.* —**lipped** *adj.* & *comb.form.* having a (specified kind of) lip: *a ~ pitcher; the two-~ snapdragon.* —**lip·py** *adj.* **lip·pi·er, lip·pi·est** insolent; **lip·pi·ness** *n.* —**lip reading** understanding of speech by watching the speaker's lip movements, as practiced by the deaf; **lip-read** *v.;* **lip reader.** —**lip service** merely verbal or insincere show of devotion or good will. —**lip·stick** *n.* a small stick of cosmetic paste for coloring the lips. —**lip-sync(h)** (LIP·SINK) *v.* synchronize lip movements with previously recorded sound, or speech sounds with lip movements, as in dubbing a motion picture in a different language; ***n.*** a lip-synching.

liq. liquid; liquor. —**liq·ue·fy** (LIK·wuh·fye) *v.* **-fies, -fied, -fy·ing** change to a liquid state; **liq·ue·fac·tion** (–FAC–) *n.* —**li·queur** (li·CUR) *n.* a sweetened and flavored syrupy alcoholic liquor. —**liq·uid** (LIK·wid) *n.* a substance that flows readily, as water; ***adj.:*** *~ food; ~ fire from a flame thrower; ~ eyes, sky, blue* (i.e. clear and bright); *a bird's ~ notes; ~ verse* (i.e. smooth-flowing); *~ assets such as cash and bank deposits, bills receivable, etc. that can be quickly converted into cash;* **liq·uid·i·ty** (–WID–) *n.* —**liq·ui·date** (LIK·wuh–) *v.* **-dates, -dat·ed, -dat·ing** **1** clear off (a debt, accounts, mortgages, etc.) by paying what is owed; also, settle the affairs of (a bankrupt business) by dividing up its assets among creditors. **2** get rid of, often by violent means: *rivals ~d by a dictator.* —**liq·ui·da·tor** *n.* —**liq·ui·da·tion** (–DAY–) n. —**liq·uid·ize** *v.* **-iz·es, -ized, -iz·ing** make liquid, as fruit or vegetables, using a **liq·uid·iz·er** *n.* —**liquid measure** (system of) measurement of liquid volume using units such as the quart and the liter. —**liq·uor** (LIK·ur) *n.* a distilled alcoholic drink such as whiskey or gin; also, any liquid.

li·ra (LEER·uh) *n., pl.* **li·re** (–ray) or **li·ras** the basic money unit of Italy equal to 100 centesimi.

Lis·bon (LIZ·bun) capital of Portugal.

lisle (LILE) *n.* a fine, tightly twisted thread, originally from Lille, France, used to make knitted garments and hosiery.

lisp *v.* speak like a child or imperfectly, esp. to substitute "th" and "dh" for "s" and "z," as in "kithing cudhindh" (kissing cousins). —***n.*** a lisping or lisping sound.

lis·som(e) (LIS·um) *adj.* lithe or nimble in a delicate or feminine way.

¹list *n.* & *v.* (set forth in) a series (of names, words, figures, etc.). —**list·ing** *n.* a setting forth or entering (in a list); also, an entry. —**list price** the marked-up retail price of a product, as entered in a list or catalog, from which discounts are figured. —**lists** *n.pl.* narrow lanes of an arena in which medieval knights used to charge at each other on horseback in the sport called "tilts"; also, the tournament; **enter the lists** enter a struggle or contest.

²list *n.* & *v.* tip or tilt to one side, as a ship that is leaking.

³list *v. Archaic.* please: *"The wind bloweth where it ~eth."*

lis·ten (LISN) *v.* try to hear, understand, or follow: *~ to a speech, the radio, advice, one's parents;* **listen in** *to a radio program, conversation;* **lis·ten·er** *n.*

list·less *adj.* having no energy or enthusiasm; **list·less·ly** *adv.;* **list·less·ness** *n.*

Liszt (LIST), **Franz.** 1811–86, Hungarian pianist and composer.

lit a *pt.* & *pp.* of LIGHT —**lit.** liter(s); literal(ly); literature.

lit·a·ny (LITN·ee) *n.* **-nies** a form of prayer consisting of a series of supplications.

li·tchi (LEE·chee) *n.* an evergreen Chinese tree bearing clusters of bright-red raisinlike fruits, called **lichi nuts** when dried.

Lit.D. Doctor of Letters.

li·ter (LEE·tur) *n.* a metric unit of capacity equal to 1,000 cc and 1.057 liquid quarts or 0.908 dry quart.

lit·er·a·cy (LIT·uh·ruh·see) *n.* ability to read and write. —**lit·er·al** (–ul) *adj.* following the exact words; hence, matter-of-fact: *a ~ translation, meaning* (i.e. not figurative), *interpretation, account* (i.e. not exaggerated); **lit·er·al·ly** *adv.* —**lit·er·al·ism** *n.* adherence to the literal meaning; also, realism in artistic representation; **lit·er·al·ist** *n.* —**lit·er·ar·y** *adj.* having to do with literature or the formal language of literature: *a ~ style; the ~ profession; a ~ agent* (i.e. authors' representative). —**lit·er·ate** (–it) *n.* & *adj.* (one) who can read and write; also, well-read or educated (person); **lit·er·ate·ly** *adv.* —**lit·e·ra·ti** (–RAH·tee) *n.pl.* the educated class; **lit·e·ra·tim** *adv.* letter for letter; literally. —**lit·er·a·ture** (–uh·chur) *n.* **1** writings of a period, country, or language having lasting appeal because of subject, style, etc.; also, writings on a particular subject: *classical ~; porn ~.* **2** any printed material such as pamphlets or notices.

lith(o). lithography.

lithe (LYDHE) *adj.* **lith·er, lith·est** having a supple, slender, or nimble grace; **lithe·ly** *adv.* **lithe·ness** *n.* —**lithe·some** (–sum) *adj.* having agile vigor; lissome.

lith·i·um (LITH·ee–) *n.* a soft, silver-white chemical element, the lightest of metals.

lith·o·graph (LITH·uh–) *n.* & *v.* (make) a print or copy by **li·thog·ra·phy** (–THOG·ruh–) *n.* printing process using a flat plate so treated that only the portions to be printed are ink-receptive; **li·thog·ra·pher** *n.* —**lith·o·graph·ic** (–GRAF–) *adj.*; **lith·o·graph·i·cal·ly** *adv.* —**li·thol·o·gy** (–THOL–) *n.* the study of rocks. —**lith·o·sphere** (LITH·uh–) *n.* the earth's solid part, excluding the hydrosphere.

Lith·u·a·ni·a (lith·oo·AY·nee·uh) a N.E. European republic of the U.S.S.R.; *cap.* Vilnius. —**Lith·u·a·ni·an** (–un) *n.* & *adj.* (a person from or the language) of Lithuania.

lit·i·gant (–gunt) *n.* a party to a lawsuit. —**lit·i·gate** *v.* **-gates, -gat·ed, -gat·ing** engage in a lawsuit; **lit·i·ga·tor** *n.*; **lit·i·ga·tion** (–GAY–) *n.* —**li·ti·gious** (–TIJ·us) *adj.* disputable at law; also, given to litigation; quarrelsome; **li·ti·gious·ness** *n.*

lit·mus *n.* a dye that turns red when put into acid and blue in alkalis, used as a chemical indicator on **litmus paper:** *a decisive* **litmus test.**

li·tre (LEE·tur) *n. Brit.* same as LITER.

Litt.D. Doctor of Letters.

lit·ter *n.* **1** scattered rubbish; hence, untidiness or disorder. **2** the young borne at one birth by an animal. **3** a single-passenger vehicle consisting of a couch, often curtained, borne on the shoulders of four men; also, a stretcherlike device for transporting a sick or injured person. **4** straw, hay, leaves, etc. forming a bedding for animals; also, a layer formed on a forest floor by decaying leaves. —***v.:*** *hallways ~ed with paper; Wood shavings ~ed the floor.*

lit·ter·a·teur (–uh·TUR) *n.* a literary man.

lit·ter·bug *n.* a person who litters parks, highways, etc.; ***v.*** **-bugs, -bugged, -bug·ging:** *fined $50 for ~ing.*

lit·tle (LITL) *adj. comp.* **lit·tler, less** or **less·er,** *superl.* **lit·tlest** or **least** **1** small, esp. in an endearing way: *the ~ finger; a poor ~ girl; a dear ~ man.* **2** not much or long; short: *stay a ~ while; not the least bit worried.* **3** small-minded or petty: *the ~ thoughts of ~ minds.* —***adv.*** *comp.* **less,** *superl.* **least** **1** slightly; somewhat: *a ~ tired; is ~ known around here.* **2** not at all: *It matters ~; thinks ~ of the prices of things.* —***n.*** a small amount, short time or distance, etc.: *Wait a ~; It evaporated* **little by little;** *He exaggerated things, but she* **made little of** *the incident.* —**lit·tle·ness** *n.* —**Little Dipper** a group of seven stars, smaller than the BIG DIPPER, with the North Star at the end of the "handle," in the constellation Ursa Minor. —**Little Rock** capital of Arkansas. —**little slam** in bridge, the winning of 12 tricks. —**little theater** amateur or experimental drama.

lit·to·ral (LIT·uh·rul) *n.* & *adj.* (region) of or near a seashore: *~ land rights, currents.*

lit·ur·gy *n.* **-gies** ritual for public worship, as in a Christian church; **lit·ur·gist** *n.* —**li·tur·gi·cal** (–TUR–) *adj.*; **li·tur·gi·cal·ly** *adv.*

liv·a·ble (LIV·uh–) *adj.* that can be lived, lived in, or lived with: *a ~* (i.e. endurable) *existence, climate; a ~* (i.e. habitable) *room, house; a ~* (i.e. easy to live with) *person;* **liv·a·ble·ness** or **liv·a·bil·i·ty** (–BIL–) *n.* —**live** (LIV) *v.* **lives, lived, liv·ing** have, continue in, maintain, or pass a life: *You will ~ long; He ~s on bread and water; a family ~ing in harmony; She ~s* (i.e. resides) *in a suburb; A martyr's memory ~s on; a scandalous past difficult to* **live down** (i.e. so that it will be forgotten); *He* **lived it up** (*Informal.* spent freely) *and was broke in no time; ideals too high to* **live up to** (i.e. live in accordance with). —***adj.*** (LYVE) having life or its qualities such as movement, growth, heat, energy, light, etc.: *~ coals; a ~* (i.e. not dead) *lobster, wire, cigar, topic* or *issue, audience* (of actual people), *telecast* (i.e. as it happens). —***adv.:*** *was broadcast ~* (i.e. not from tape or film). —**live·a·ble** (LIV·uh–) *adj.* same as LIVABLE. —**-lived** (LIVED, LIVD) *comb.form.* as in *short-~.* —**live-in** *adj.* (LIV–) (involving) living where working: *a ~ job, maid.* —**live·li·hood** (LYVE–) *n.* means of living; subsistence. —**live·long** (LIV–) *adj.* the whole wearisome length of: *the ~ day, night, summer.* —**live·ly** (LYVE–) *adj.* **-li·er, -li·est** full of life: *a ~ conversation, time, imagination; ~ colors;* ***adv.*** in a lively manner; **live·li·ness** *n.* —**live oak** a beautiful evergreen oak of S.E. United States with wide-spreading branches and dark, glossy, oblong leaves. **—liv·en** (LYE·vun) *v.* make or become lively: *Let's ~ things up a bit.* **—¹liv·er** (LIV–) *n.: a loose ~; a clean ~.*

²liv·er *n.* the glandular organ that secretes bile, and that was once considered the seat of emotion; also, an animal's liver used as food.

liveried See LIVERY.

liv·er·ish *adj. Informal.* bilious or sour-tempered.

Liv·er·pool a seaport of N.W. England; **Liv·er·pud·li·an** (–PUD–) *n. & adj.*

liver spot a patchy discoloration of the skin, or "chloasma," often seen during pregnancy. **—liv·er·wort** (–wurt) *n.* a class of liver-shaped, mosslike, little plants that grow on rocks, tree trunks, etc. in damp and shady places. **—liv·er·wurst** *n.* a sausage made of ground liver.

liv·er·y *n.* **-er·ies** a characteristic uniform or garb, as formerly issued to servants, esp. retainers in charge of horses; hence, the keeping and hiring out of horses, carriages, cars, boats, etc.; **liv·er·ied** *adj.* uniformed, as a chauffeur. **—liv·er·y·man** *n.* **-men** a liveried servant; hence, a person keeping a **livery stable** of horses for hire.

lives *pl.* of LIFE.**—live·stock** *n.* farm animals such as cattle, pigs, sheep, poultry, geese, and rabbits. **—live wire** a wire carrying electric current; hence, *Informal.* an energetic and enterprising person.

liv·id *adj.* blue-gray; black-and-blue; also, very pale, as with rage or cold.

liv·ing *adj.* having life or to do with life: *a ~ being, monument, memory; ~ languages, conditions.* **—*n.*** a being alive, manner of life, or livelihood: *"plain ~ and high thinking"; our high standard of ~; to beg for a ~; the* **living** (persons) *and the dead.* **—living room** a room for lounging, entertaining, etc. in a home. **—living wage** a wage sufficient for maintaining a reasonable standard of living.

liz·ard (–urd) *n.* any of a large suborder of reptiles such as the chameleon and the iguana with four legs and tail and a long body with dry, scaly skin.

LL. Late Latin. **—ll.** lines. **—'ll** will.

lla·ma (LAH·muh) *n.* a smaller and humpless camel of South America, related to the alpaca.

lla·no (LAH·noh) *n.* **-nos** any of the vast, treeless plains of Spanish America that are rich with grass in the wet season.

LL.B. Bachelor of Laws. **—LL.D.** Doctor of Laws.

LM lunar module. **—lm** lumen.

LNG liquefied natural gas.

lo (LOH) *interj.* look: *~ and behold!*

load (LODE) *n.* something carried, as in a cart or on an animal's back; pack; hence, a definite quantity, also considered as a unit of weight: *two truck ~s of gravel; a man with* **loads** (*Informal.* plenty) *of experience; That's a ~* (i.e. burden) *off my mind.* **—*v.*** **1** put a load (on a carrier or into a receptacle): *a ship ~ed with grain; grain ~ed into a ship; A gun or camera has to be ~ed before shooting.* **2** to burden or weight: *a mind ~ed with anxiety; Cheaters use ~ed dice to make them fall as desired.* **—load·ed** *adj.* **1** carrying a load or charge. **2** *Slang.* having a lot of money. **3** *Slang.* drunk. **—load·er** *n.* **—load·ing** *n.* **—load·star, load·stone** same as LODESTAR, LODESTONE.

¹loaf (LOHF) *n.* **loaves** a mass of baked bread in a handy shape or other food such as meat or fish molded like bread.

²loaf (LOHF) *v.* spend time idly; idle away) a period of time; **loaf·er** *n.*

loam (LOME) *n.* a fertile, easy-to-work soil that is a mixture of sand, clay, and silt; **loam·y** *adj.*

loan (LONE) *v.* lend; ***n.*** a lending or something lent, esp. money; **loan shark** *Informal.* one who lends money at illegal interest rates; **loan-shark·ing** *n.* **—loan·word** *n.* a word borrowed from a foreign language, as *beef, mutton, veal,* and *pork* from French.

loath (LOHTH) *adj.* strongly unwilling (*to* do something). **—loathe** (LOHDH) *v.* **loathes, loathed, loath·ing** abhor or hate with disgust; **loath·ing** *n.* intense disgust or hatred. **—loath·ly** *Rare. adj.* loathssome; ***adv.*** unwillingly. **—loath·some** *adj.* disgusting; **loath·some·ly** *adv.*

loaves (LOHVZ) *pl.* of ¹LOAF.

lob *v.* **lobs, lobbed, lob·bing** in games such as tennis, baseball, and soccer, to hit, throw, or kick a ball in a high arc but without much force; ***n.*** such a stroke, throw, or kick; **lob·ber** *n.*

lobate same as LOBED.

lob·by (LOB·ee) *n.* **lob·bies** **1** a vestibule or entrance hall of a hotel, theater, apartment building, etc. **2** a group that lobbies. **—*v.*** **lob·bies, lob·bied, lob·by·ing** attempt to influence the decisions of lawmakers, officials, etc., as by talking to legislators outside the room where they deliberate; **lob·by·ist** *n.*

lobe *n.* a rounded, projecting, usu. fleshy part, as a division of the lung, brain, or liver, the lower ear, etc.; **lobed** or **lo·bate** (LOH–) *adj.: a coot's ~ foot; a ~ leaf.* **—lo·bot·o·my** (–BOT·uh·mee) *n.* **-mies** a surgical operation on the front lobe of the brain.

lob·ster *n.* a crustacean with two large pincerlike claws and a fanlike tail, relished as a sea food.

lob·ule *n.* a small lobe or part of a lobe; **lob·u·lar** *adj.*

lo·cal (LOH·cl) *adj.* of or having to do with a particular place or body part: *national and ~ news; a ~ anesthetic for pulling a tooth; a feeder or ~-service airline; Regional dialects, customs, etc. lend* **local color** *to writing; a municipality's* **local option** (i.e. legal right) *to prohibit liquor.* **—*n.***

something local, as a bus service, a branch of a national body, etc. —**lo·cal·ly** *adv.* —**lo·cale** (–CAL) *n.* the setting of a story or scene of an event. —**lo·cal·i·ty** (–CAL–) *n.* **-ties** **1** a neighborhood or region. **2** awareness or recognition of where one is: *a good sense of* ~. —**lo·cal·ize** (LOH·cuh–) *v.* **-iz·es, -ized, -iz·ing** make local: *a ~d disease, outbreak; a legend difficult to ~;* **lo·cal·i·za·tion** (–ZAY–) *n.* —**lo·cate** (LOH–) *v.* **-cates, -cat·ed, -cat·ing** find out the position of; also, establish (oneself) in a place: *to ~ a story in a newspaper; a suitable place to ~ one's business; a correspondent ~d in London;* **lo·ca·tion** (–CAY–) *n.* **1** where something is: *a good ~ for a factory.* **2** a locating: *a Hollywood movie shot* **on location** (i.e. away from the studio) *in Spain;* **lo·ca·tor** *n.* —**loc·cit.** in the place cited.

loch (LOK, LOKH) *n.* in Scotland, a lake; also, a partially landlocked narrow bay, or "sea loch."

lock *n.* **1** something that closes, fastens, or fixes so as to stop movement or action: *money kept under ~ and key; A series of ~s* (i.e. watertight chambers) *helps ships to move from one water level to another through a canal; an air ~; a wrestler's arm ~; took over the department* **lock, stock and barrel** (i.e. in its entirety). **2** a bunch or tuft, as of hair, wool, cotton, etc. —***v.:*** *Brakes should not ~* (i.e. jam); *funds* **locked in** (i.e. committed) *to a retirement plan; striking workers* **locked out** *of a factory till the employer's demands are met; convicts* **locked up** *in jail; cattle ~ing horns in a fight; A missile* **locks on to** *its target by radar.* —**lock·er** *n.* a chest, closet, or compartment for storage that can be locked; **locker room** a room with lockers for athletes to change clothes: *a* **lock·er-room** (i.e. coarse) *joke.* —**lock·et** *n.* a small ornamental case containing a keepsake, usu. attached to a necklace. —**lock·jaw** *n.* a severe tetanus attack preventing opening of the jaws. —**lock·nut** *n.* a nut that locks in place or keeps another nut in place. —**lock·out** *n.* the closing of a plant by an employer to force settlement of a strike. —**lock·smith** *n.* a maker or repairer of locks. —**lock step** a marching one behind another as closely as possible. —**lock-up** *n.* a jail, esp. one for temporary custody.

lo·co (LOH–) *adj. Slang.* crazy, as cattle become by eating the narcotic **lo·co·weed** of W. North America.

lo·co·mo·tion (–MOH·shun) *n.* (the power of) motion from place to place; **lo·co·mo·tive** (–tiv) *n.* & *adj.* (having or causing locomotion, as) an engine that moves a train: *Plants have no ~ faculty; an electric ~; a ~ engineer.* —**lo·co·mo·tor a·tax·i·a** (–MOH·tur·uh·TAX–) inability to coordinate muscle movements because of damage to the central nervous system, usu. caused by syphilis. —**locoweed** See LOCO. —**lo·cus** (LOH–) *n., pl.* **-ci** (–sye) a place, position, or point, esp. one of many forming a set or system.

lo·cust (LOH–) *n.* **1** a short-horned grasshopper that usu. moves about in swarms destroying crops; also, a cicada. **2** a shrub or shade tree of the pea family, esp. the spiny *black locust* tree with fragrant white flowers.

lo·cu·tion (–CUE–) *n.* a peculiar phrase or other form of expression; also, a manner of expression.

lode *n.* a vein or stratum of metal ore, formerly one with magnetic properties, as magnetite, or **lode·stone.** —**lode·star** *n.* a guiding star, esp. the North Star, which shows the way like a lodestone used as a compass.

lodge (LOJ) *n.* **1** a place to reside, esp. temporarily, as an inn, a summer cottage, or a room rented by a **lodg·er;** also, an Indian dwelling such as a wigwam or tepee. **2** a den or lair of a beaver or otter. **3** a branch of a fraternal society. —***v.*** **lodg·es, lodged, lodg·ing** **1:** *a house that ~s students; is ~ing at a motel; a bullet ~d* (i.e. stuck) *in a bone.* **2** put or lay formally: *to ~ a protest, complaint with the police.* —**lodg·ing** *n.: a ~ for the night;* **lodgings** *pl.* rooms; **lodging house** rooming house. —**lodg(e)·ment** *n.* a military position gained; also, a depositing or accumulation.

lo·ess (LOH·is, LES) *n.* a wind-borne, silt-size dust forming a fertile topsoil, as in C. and S.W. United States. —**lo·ess·i·al** (–ES·ee·ul) *adj.*

loft *n.* **1** an upper room or place, as an attic, where hay is stored in a barn, the gallery of a church where the organ is kept, a pigeon's house, etc. **2** in golf, the slope of the hitting face of a club; also, a high stroke or the height given to a lofted ball. —***v.*** in golf, bowling, and marbles, shoot or throw relatively high into the air. —**loft·y** *adj.* **loft·i·er, -i·est** high in an imposing or conspicuous way: *a ~ spire, mountain; a ~* (i.e. grand) *style, ~ ideals; a ~* (i.e. haughty) *manner, sneer;* **loft·i·ly** *adv.;* **loft·i·ness** *n.*

log *n.* **1** a felled trunk or branch of a tree: *a raft of ~s; ~s of firewood; a ~ cabin.* **2** a block of wood, or "log chip," at the end of a line thrown into water from a ship to determine its speed; hence, a ship's daily record of progress, or **log·book;** also, a similar record of an operation or performance, as of an airplane or computer. —***v.*** **logs, logged, log·ging:** *a forest destroyed by ~ing; The speed was ~d at 10 knots; a pilot who has ~d a million miles.*

log [short form] logarithm. — **-log** same as -LOGUE.

lo·gan·ber·ry (LOH·gun–) *n.* **-ber·ries** a blackberrylike purplish-red fruit that grows in clusters on a trailing vine.

log·a·rithm (LOG·uh–) *n.* in algebra, an exponent: *In* 3^5 $(= 3 \times 3 \times 3 \times 3 \times 3 = 243)$, *the ~ of 243 to the base 3 is 5;* **log·a·rith·mic** (–RIDH–) *adj.*

logbook See LOG, *n.* 2.
loge (LOHZH) *n.* a booth, stall, or box (in a theater or opera house); also, the forward part of a theater mezzanine.
log·ger *n.* lumberjack. **—log·ger·head** *n.* blockhead; **at loggerheads** disputing. **—log·ging** *n.* the harvesting and transportation of trees from the forest to the sawmill.
log·gi·a (LOJ·ee·uh) *n.* a gallery or arcade protected from the sun but open to the air.
log·ic (LOJ–) *n.* the science of reasoning and inference; also, its principles, a particular system of logic, reasoning itself, or a logical result or outcome: *There's little ~ in your argument;* **log·i·cal** *adj.;* **log·i·cal·ly** *adv.;* **lo·gi·cian** (–JISH·un) *n.* **—lo·gis·tic** (–JIS–) *adj.* of or having to do with **lo·gis·tics** *n.pl.* [takes *sing. v.*] the science of planning and carrying out operations, esp. military, involving transport of men, equipment, and supplies: *the ~s manager of an election campaign;* **lo·gis·ti·cal** *adj.;* **lo·gis·ti·cal·ly** *adv.;* **lo·gis·ti·cian** (–STISH–) *n.*
log·jam *n.* obstruction caused by logs jamming a watercourse; hence, piled-up work, a deadlock, or similar obstacle to progress.
log·o (LOH·goh) *n.* **-os** short form of **log·o·type** *n.* an identifying symbol of an organization, for use in advertising and promotion of its image.
log·roll·ing *n.* in politics, cooperation between parties, as in a legislature by voting for each other's bills, like pioneers helping to roll logs off each other's clearings.
-logue *comb. form.* something spoken or written (as specified): as in *epilogue, monologue, ideologue* (i.e. ideologist). — **-logy** *comb. form.* a way of speaking or writing; also, a subject: as in *tautology, geology, zoology.*
lo·gy (LOH·gee) *adj.* **-gi·er, -gi·est** *Informal.* sluggish, as from overeating; also, groggy.
loin *n.* **1** the back of the body between the hips and the ribs, i.e. the lumbar region, considered as the seat of strength and generative power; **gird up one's loins** prepare for action. **2** corresponding part of an animal's body: *a ~ of pork.* **—loin·cloth** *n.* a piece of cloth worn by men in warm countries, wrapped around the hips and between the thighs.
loi·ter *v.* move around aimlessly and slowly; hence, spend (time) idly: *~ing around downtown; likes to ~ away his leisure hours.* **—loi·ter·er** *n.*
loll *v.* move about in a relaxed or lazy manner; also, droop or hang loosely, as a dog's tongue in hot weather. **—lol·li·pop** or **lol·ly·pop** *n.* a piece of hard candy stuck on a short stick or handle. **—lol·ly·gag** *v.* **-gags, -gagged, -gag·ging** *Informal.* dawdle; loaf.
Lo·mé (–MAY) capital of Togo.
Lond. *Abbrev.* for **Lon·don** (LUN·dun) **1** the capital of the United Kingdom, in S.E. England. **2** a city of S.E. Ontario.
lone *adj.* [literary use, attributive only] solitary; isolated; lonesome: *the ~ traveler; the ~ nights; An outlaw is a ~ wolf; Texas, the "Lone Star State."* **—lone·ly** *adj.* **-li·er, -li·est** being alone and gloomy; also, alone and isolated: *a ~ widow; the ~ hearts column of a paper; a ~ village, house, tree;* **lone·li·ness** *n.* **—lon·er** (LOH·nur) *n. Informal.* one who prefers to live or work alone. **—lone·some** *adj.* feeling lonely; also, causing one to feel lonely; solitary: *a ~ bachelor, orphan, road, existence;* **lone·some·ly** *adv.;* **lone·some·ness** *n.*
long *adj.* **long·er** (LONG·gur), **long·est** (LONG·gist) **1** extending (much) from end to end: *a ~ rope; 10 ft. ~ and 3 ft. wide; a book 250 pages ~; a ~* (i.e. longer than it is broad) *skull, board.* **2** lasting much in time: *It's been a ~ stretch without a holiday; a ~ memory; the ~ vowels of "food," "feed," and "foe."* **3** risky; little likely to succeed: *a ~ chance; the ~ odds of 10 to 1.* **4** having plenty of: *~ on excuses, kindness, anecdotes, brains.* ***—adv.*** (for) a long time past or to come: *~ ago; ~ before Columbus; You won't have to wait ~; sat up all night ~* (i.e. throughout); **as** (or **so**) **long as** provided that. ***—n.*** a long time or something lasting long: *The next bus will be here before ~; Is the "o" of "dog" a ~ or a short* (sound)? **the long and short of it** the substance or gist (of something that may be condensed). ***—v.*** have a strong desire (for); yearn: *a ~ing, lingering look; ~s to be free.* — **long.** longitude. **—Long Beach** a seaport and tourist resort in S. California. **—long·boat** *n.* the largest boat carried by a sailing ship. — **long·bow** (–boh) *n.* a bow drawn by hand to shoot a feathered arrow; cf. CROSSBOW. **—long-dis·tance** (–DIS·tunce) *adj.* of or having to do with a great distance: *a ~ phone call, mover, runner;* ***adv.:*** *called London ~;* **long distance** long-distance telephone, exchange, or operator. **—lon·gev·i·ty** (–JEV–) *n.* long life. **—long-faced** *adj.* looking glum or sad. **—Long·fel·low** (LONG·fel·oh), **H. W.** 1807–1882, American poet. **—long-hair** *n.* & *adj. Informal.* **1** (an intellectual) with preference for classical rather than popular music. **2** a hippie. **—long·hand** *n.* ordinary handwriting, not shorthand. **—long·horn** *n.* a breed of cattle with long horns. **—long hundredweight** the British hundredweight, equal to 112 lb. (50.8 kg). **—long·ing** *n.* a desire for something hard to attain; **long·ing·ly** *adv.* **—Long Island** an island of New York State lying S. of Connecticut. **—lon·gi·tude** (LON·juh–) *n.* distance E. or W. of the prime meridian, measured in degrees from 0 to 180 in either direction; **lon·gi·tu·di·nal** (–TUE·dn·ul) *adj.* of longitude or length; also, lengthwise: *~ lines run N. to S. from pole to pole; a ~ measurement; ~* (i.e. not transverse) *stripes, waves;* **lon·gi·tu·di·nal·ly** *adv.* **—long jump** an athletic jump in which distance is the aim. **—long-lived** (–livd, –lived) *adj.* having a long life or exis-

tence. —**long play** a long-playing record; **long-play·ing** *adj.* of a 12-inch phonograph record, playing up to half an hour at 33⅓ r.p.m. —**long-range** *adj.* having a long range of time or distance: *a ~ forecast, plan, trend, missile.* —**long·shore·man** (-mun) *n.* **-men** one who loads and unloads ships on a waterfront. —**long shot** *Informal.* something difficult to achieve, esp. one carrying great rewards for the achiever, as a bet at long odds; **not by a long shot** not at all. —**long·stand·ing** *adj.* that has existed for a long time: *a ~ complaint, invitation, feud.* —**long·suf·fer·ing** *n.* & *adj.* (the quality of) enduring insults, pain, injury, etc. for a long time. —**long-term** *adj.* of a loan, capital gain, loss, assets, etc., based on a rather long period. —**long ton** the British ton of 2,240 lb. (1,016 kg). —**lon·gueur** (long·GUR) *n.* a long and dull passage in a book or a similar period in a performance. —**long-wind·ed** (-WIN·did) *adj.* **1** of a speech or a written piece, tiresomely long. **2** not getting out of breath easily, as some horses and runners.

look *v.* **1** direct the eyes in order to see: *If you want to see, ~ ! "~ before you leap"; She ~ed me in the face before asking; was ~ing* (i.e. searching) *through some papers.* **2** face or be turned: *The window ~s south; a church ~ing on a highway.* **3** appear to be: *She doesn't ~ her age; He's 70 and ~s it.* **4** turn one's mind, memory, hopes, etc.: *Parents* **look after** (i.e. take care of) *their children; He* **looks down on** (i.e. regards with some contempt) *old people; I* **look forward to** (i.e. anticipate with pleasure) *your birthday party; The child* **looks up to** (i.e. admires) *her teacher; to* **look up** *words in a dictionary; Business is* **looking up** (i.e. improving); *Do* **look** *us* **up** (i.e. visit us) *when you're in town.* —***n.:*** *a cold ~; I don't like the ~* (i.e. appearance) *of that lawn; judging merely from the ~s of things; His good ~s got him the job.* —**look·er** *n.;* **look·er-on** (-ON) *n.* **look·ers-on** an observer; onlooker. —**looking glass** mirror. —**look·out** *n.* **1** a person keeping watch. **2** a watching or an esp. high place from which to watch; also, *Informal.* a thing to watch or worry about: *police* **on the lookout** *for the escapees; That's your ~!* —**look-see** *n. Slang.* a quick visual inspection.

loom *n.* a machine for weaving thread or yarn into cloth. —***v.*** **1** weave using a loom. **2** come into view dimly, often threateningly; as in mirages over the horizon: *war ~ing on the horizon; Unemployment ~s large in our view of the future.*

loon *n.* **1** any of a family of birds that look like large ducks and that dive under the water for fish. **2** a stupid or crazy person. —**loon·(e)y** *n.* & *adj. Slang.* **loon·i·er, -i·est** lunatic; crazy (person); **loony bin** insane asylum.

loop *n.* the shape of a curve that crosses itself, as in a written "l," hence, anything in this shape: *the ~ knot of a lasso; a ~ antenna attached to a TV set; A belt is passed through ~s; the elevated railroad ~ in downtown Chicago; a plastic ~ as an intrauterine device.* —***v.:*** *ridges that ~ on the tip of a finger; An aerialist* **loops the loop** (i.e. turns in vertical loops). —**loop·er** *n.* a caterpillar such as the cankerworm or the inch worm that crawls by looping its body. —**loop·hole** *n.* an opening in a fortress wall for shooting through or for observation; hence, a means of escape: *a ~ in the wording of a statute; tax ~s.*

loose *adj.* **loos·er, loos·est** not tight, compact, or firm; hence, untied, relaxed, or slack: *a ~ jacket, tooth, soil, weave; a cat that is ~* (i.e. not penned up) *at night; a man of ~ morals; a reputation ruined by the ~ tongue of a ~ woman; a mad dog* **on the loose** (i.e. roaming free). —***v.*** **loos·es, loosed, loos·ing** make loose: *to ~ a grip, knot; ~* (i.e. shoot) *a volley or blast.* —***adv.*** loosely. —**loose·ly** *adv.* —**loose·ness** *n.* —**loose-leaf** *adj.* allowing the leaves to be rearranged or replaced: *a ~ binder, file, notebook.* —**loos·en** *v.* make or become loose(r): *Liquor ~s his tongue; Laxatives ~ bowels.* —**loose end** an unfinished thing or condition, as the strands at a rope's end: *found himself* **at loose ends** (i.e. uncertain what to do) *when laid off.* —**loose·strife** *n.* any of various plants of the primrose family with spikes of purple or yellow flowers.

loot *n.* goods of value taken away, as during a riot or following a natural disaster; plunder; also, *Slang.* money or gifts received; ***v.*** sack: *stores ~ed and burned by insurgents;* **loot·er** *n.*

lop *v.* **lops, lopped, lop·ping** **1** cut off a limb or branch; ***n.*** cut-away or discarded parts, as of trees; **lop·per** *n.* **2** hang limply; droop; ***adj.*** & ***comb.form.:*** *born with lop ears; a lop-eared rabbit.* —**lop-sid·ed** (-SYE·did) *adj.* leaning to one side; unsymmetrical; uneven: *a ~ pumpkin, attitude;* **lop-sid·ed·ly** *adv.;* **lop-sid·ed·ness** *n.*

lope *n.* & *v.* **lopes, loped, lop·ing** move at an easy, bounding gait or stride.

lo·qua·cious (-KWAY·shus) *adj.* inclined to talk at length with fluency or ease; talkative. —**lo·quac·i·ty** (-KWAS-) *n.*

lor·an *n.* a radio navigation system used by ships and aircraft that is based on the time interval between signals received from transmitting stations.

lord *n.* **1** one who has power over others, as a feudal "lord of the manor": *the ~ of the jungle.* **2 Lord** [as a title of respect]: *the ~ God; the ~ Jesus Christ; The House of ~s* (i.e. British nobles), *or* **the Lords,** *presided over by the* **Lord (High) Chancellor,** *Britain's highest judicial official; pl.* **Lords (High) Chancellor.** —***v.*** **lord it (over)** act in an authoritarian way (toward). —**lord·ly** *adj.* **-li·er, -li·est** noble; also, haughty; ***adv.*** in a lordly manner. —**Lord's Day** Sunday. —**lord·ship** *n.* the rank of a lord: [as a title] *Your* (or *His*) *Lordship.* —**Lord's Prayer** the Christian prayer beginning with

"Our Father"; **Lord's Supper** Holy Communion.

lore *n.* traditional knowledge on a particular subject, as "Irish lore," "folklore," etc.

lor·gnette (lor·NYET) *n.* eyeglasses fixed to the end of a handle.

lorn *adj. Archaic.* forsaken; desolate.

lor·ry (LOR·ee) *n.* **lor·ries** *Brit.* a motor truck.

Los An·gel·es (laus·AN·juh·lus, –leez) a seaport of S.W. California.

lose (LOOZ) *v.* **los·es, lost** (LAUST, LOST), **los·ing** **1** cease to have; fail to keep, get, exist, etc.: *lost his life in an accident; ~ one's wallet, patience, balance.* **2** cause the loss of: *A bad error lost him his job.* **—lose oneself** become bewildered or engrossed. **—be lost (up)on** of counsel, advice, etc., be wasted upon (someone). **—lost in** absorbed in (thought, contemplation, etc.). **—lost to** insensible to (shame, decency, etc.). **—los·er** *n.* **—loss** (LAUCE, LOSS) *n.* a losing, being lost, or a person, thing, etc. lost: *a crash with a great ~ of lives; ~es and gains in business;* **at a loss** *for words* (i.e. not knowing what to say). **—loss leader** article put on sale at a loss to attract customers by its low price. **—lost cause** a failed or hopeless cause.

lot *n.* **1** the deciding of something by chance, as in a lottery by picking one out of many bits of paper, wood, etc.: *They* **cast** (or **drew) lots** *to determine who would keep Christ's seamless tunic; decided to* **throw** (or **cast) in** *his lot* (i.e. join) *with whoever would pay him; his unhappy ~* (i.e. fate). **2** a plot of land: *a parking ~.* **3** a set of persons or things: *goods for auction divided into ~s; They're not a bad ~* (of people). **4** *Informal.* a great deal; great many; *I have* **lots of** *time on holidays; quite* **a lot of** *time; had to pay* **a lot** (of money) *for the car; had* **lots** *to eat and drink at the party.*

loth (LOHTH) same as LOATH.

Lo·thar·i·o (–THAIR–) *n.* **-os** a philanderer.

lo·tion (LOH–) *n.* a liquid medicinal or cosmetic preparation to apply to the skin or a body part.

lot·ter·y (LOT·uh·ree) *n.* **lot·ter·ies** a gambling game in which prizes are awarded to ticket holders by the drawing of lots. **—lot·to** (LOT·oh) *n.* a game of chance similar to bingo.

lo·tus (LOH–) *n.* **1** any of various plants related to the waterlily and a flower sacred to Egyptians, Hindus, and Chinese. **2** in Greek myth, a fruit inducing a state of dreamy languor if eaten, as in the **lo·tus-eat·ers** of the *Odyssey.* **—lotus position** a sitting posture in yoga with legs folded and the arms resting on the knees.

loud *adj.* **1** having great intensity of sound; not quiet; also, noisy: *a ~ and clear voice; a* **loud·mouthed** *politician.* **2** offensive in manner or taste: *a ~ dress; ~ colors, people.* —***adv.*** loudly. **—loud·ly** *adv.* **—loud·ness** *n.* **—loud·speak·er** *n.* an electrical sound-amplifying device.

Lou·is (LOO·ee) the name of three French kings: **Louis XIV** (1643–1715), **XV** (1715–74), **XVI** (1774–92) who was guillotined during the Revolution. **—Lou·i·si·an·a** (–ee·zee·AN·uh) a southern U.S. state; 48,523 sq.mi. (125,674 km^2); *cap.* Baton Rouge; **Lou·i·si·an·(i·)an** *n.* & *adj.* **—Lou·is·ville** (LOO·ee·vil) a city of N. Kentucky.

lounge (LOWNJ) *v.* **loung·es, lounged, loung·ing** stand, sit, or move about in a relaxed or lazy manner; hence, pass (time) thus: *He ~s away his leisure hours on the beach.* —***n.*** a room for lounging; also, a couch or sofa.

lour *n.* & *v.* same as [2]LOWER.

louse (LOUS) *n.* **1** *pl.* **lice** a small wingless parasitic insect or pest that lives on the sap of plants, as aphids, or on the blood of animals, as crab lice and body lice. **2** *pl.* **lous·es** *Slang.* someone considered as mean and contemptible. —***v.*** **louse up** *Slang.* spoil or mess (something) up. **—lous·y** (LOU·zee) *adj.* **lous·i·er, -i·est** **1** infested with lice. **2** *Slang.* contemptible or disgusting; also, oversupplied: *~ with riches.*

lout *n.* a clumsy or ill-mannered man; **lout·ish** *adj.;* **lout·ish·ness** *n.*

lou·ver (LOO–) *n.* an arrangement of sloping slats or boards over an opening to regulate light and air; also, one of these slats or boards; **lou·vered** *adj.: a ~ door.* Also **lou·vre(d).**

love (LUV) **1** *n.* & *v.* **loves, loved, lov·ing** (feel) a strong liking or affection for a thing or person, often sexual; also, the object of such affection. **2** *n.* a zero score in tennis. **—in love** affected by love: *Jack is in ~ (with Jill).* **—make love** **1** show one's love (*to* another person), as by embracing or kissing. **2** have sexual intercourse *(with);* **love·mak·ing** *n.* **—lov(e)·a·ble** *adj.* **—love·bird** *n.* any of several kinds of small parrots, often kept as cage birds, remarkable for their affectionate manner toward mates. **—love·lorn** *adj.* suffering because of unreturned love. **—love·ly** *adj.* **-li·er, -li·est** beautiful; also, *Informal.* delightful; **love·li·ness** *n.* **—lov·er** *n.* one who loves, as a sweetheart, paramour, or a devotee: *a ~ of wine.* **—love seat** a sofa for two persons. **—love·sick** *adj.* suffering with love; also, expressing such suffering: *a ~ poem;* **love·sick·ness** *n.* **—lov·ing** *adj.* affectionate; **lov·ing·ly** *adv.;* **loving cup** a large, two-handled ornamental vessel, often with cover, used formerly for ceremonial drinking at weddings and banquets, now as athletic trophies.

[1]**low** (LOH) *adj.* **1** near the ground or bottom; hence, short, not high or tall: *a ~ wall, level, position, bow, neckline, temperature.* **2** inferior; base; depressed; not elevated or noble: *a ~ price, opinion, grade, thought, deed, company.*

—adv.: *aim, fly, speak* ~; **lay low** knock down; also, conquer or kill; **lie low** remain hidden. —***n.*** something low, as a gear, pressure, region, etc. —**low·ness** *n.*

²low (LOH) *n.* & *v.* (make) the characteristic sound of a cow.

low beam beam of headlight switched to show the way in front of the vehicle. —**low·born** *adj.* of low or humble birth. —**low·boy** *n.* a low chest of drawers. —**low·brow** (–brow) *n.* & *adj. Informal.* (one) having little interest in intellectual or cultural matters. —**low-cal** *adj. Informal.* low-calorie. —**Low Countries** Belgium, Netherlands, and Luxembourg. —**low·down** *n. Slang.* true facts; **low-down** *adj. Informal.* mean or contemptible.

Low·ell (LOH·ul), **James R.** 1819–91, American poet and essayist.

¹low·er **1** *adj.* & *adv.* compar. of LOW: *the* ~ (i.e. more representative) *house of a legislature; the* ~ *lip; Lower California, a peninsula in N.W. Mexico; the* ~ (i.e. down the river) *Mississippi; Lower* (i.e. earlier) *Carboniferous Period; aim, fly* ~. **2** *v.* make or become lower: *to* ~ *a flag; Do not* ~ *yourself; to* ~ *expenses, the tone of voice.*

²low·er (LOU·ur) *v.* look dark and threatening, as skies, clouds, faces, etc. —**low·er·ing** *adj.* threatening or frowning; also **low·er·y; low·er·ing·ly** *adv.*

lower case in printing, small, not capital letters; **low·er-case** *adj.: upper and* ~ *letters;* ***v.*** **-cas·es, -cased, -cas·ing** make lower case. —**lower class** class of society including farm laborers, the unskilled, unemployed, etc. —**low·er·most** *adj.* lowest. —**lowest common denominator, lowest common multiple** See LEAST. —**low frequency** a radio frequency between 30 and 300 kilohertz. —**Low German** Dutch, Flemish, Frisian, and such Germanic languages, esp. of the Low Countries; also, the dialect of the lowlands of N. Germany: *English is of* ~ *origin.* —**low-grade** *adj.* of inferior grade or quality; also, low in range: *a* ~ *fever.* —**low-key(ed)** *adj.* of low intensity; hence, subdued or restrained in style: *a* ~ *approach.* —**low·land** (–lund) *n.* a low or flat region, as in the **Lowlands** of Scotland. —**low·ly** (–lee) *adj.* **-li·er, -li·est** humble and meek; also, low in rank or position: *a man of* ~ *origin; a* ~ *occupation, opinion;* ***adv.*** humbly; also, in a low manner or voice; **low·li·ness** *n.* —**low·mind·ed** (–MINED–) *adj.* low or mean. —**low profile** a style or behavior that is inconspicuous or unobtrusive. —**low-rise** *adj.* only a few stories high. —**low-spir·it·ed** (–SPEER–) *adj.* dejected. —**low-ten·sion** *adj.* low-voltage. —**low tide** (or **water**) the level or time when the tide is lowest; hence, the lowest point reached by anything; also **low-wa·ter mark.**

¹lox or **LOX** *n.* liquid oxygen, as used in rockets.

²lox *n.* a kind of smoked salmon.

loy·al (–ul) *adj.* staunchly faithful to one's king, country, friends, etc.; **loy·al·ly** *adv.* —**loy·al·ist** *n.* one who does not join a popular revolt but supports the government, as the **Loyalists** during the American Revolution and the Spanish Civil War. —**loy·al·ty** *n.* **-ties** faithfulness; also, attachment: *conflicting* ~*s.*

loz·enge (LOZ·nj) *n.* a candy, cough drop, etc., originally diamond-shaped or rhomboidal.

LP *Trademark.* long-playing record; also ***n.,*** *pl.* **LPs** or **LP's.**

LPG liquefied petroleum gas; also **LP-gas.**

L.P.N. Licensed Practical Nurse.

Lr lawrencium.

LSD a powerful hallucinogenic drug; "lysergic acid diethylamide."

LSS life-support system.

Lt. Lieutenant.

Ltd. or **ltd.** limited.

Lu lutetium.

Lu·an·da (loo·AHN·duh) capital of Angola.

lu·au (LOO·ou) *n.* a Hawaiian feast.

lub·ber *n.* a big or clumsy sailor; also, a landlubber; **lub·ber·ly** *adj.* & *adv.*

Lub·bock (–uk) a city of N.W. Texas.

lube (LOOB) *n.* lubricating oil; also, *Informal.* a lubrication: *a* ~ *job.* —**lu·bri·cant** (–kunt) *n.* & *adj.* (an oil, grease, etc.) that reduces friction between moving parts, as of a machine. —**lu·bri·cate** (LOO–) *v.* **-cates, -cat·ed, -cat·ing** apply a lubricant to (machinery); hence, make smooth or slippery; **lu·bri·ca·tor** *n.;* **lu·bri·ca·tion** (–CAY–) *n.* —**lu·bri·cious** (–BRISH·us) or **lu·bri·cous** (LOO·bri·cus) *adj.* slippery; also, lewd; **lu·bric·i·ty** (–BRIS–) *n.* **-ties.**

lu·cent (LOO·snt) *adj.* giving off light; also, clear; **lu·cent·ly** *adv.*

lu·cerne (loo·SURN) *n. Brit.* alfalfa.

luces a *pl.* of LUX.

lu·cid (LOO–) *adj.* shining; clear; easy to understand: *a* ~ *style; a will made by a mental patient during a* ~ *interval;* **lu·cid·ly** *adv.* —**lu·cid·i·ty** (–SID–) *n.* —**Lu·ci·fer** (LOO·suh–) *n.* "light-bearer," Satan's name before his fall from heaven; hence, the Devil. —**Lu·cite** *Trademark.* a tough acrylic resin or plastic, often used instead of glass.

luck *n.* chance; fortune, esp. good fortune or prosperity: *As* ~ *would have it, . . .; good* ~ *!* —***v.*** esp. **luck out** *Informal.* to be lucky. —**luck·less** *adj.* —**luck·y** *adj.* **luck·i·er, -i·est** fortunate, esp. by mere chance: *a* ~ *winner, escape, star;* **luck·i·ly** *adv.;* **luck·i·ness** *n.*

lu·cra·tive (LOO·cruh·tiv) *adj.* producing wealth; profitable: *a* ~ *business, career;* **lu·cra·tive·ly** *adv.;* **lu·cra·tive·ness** *n.* —**lu·cre** (LOO·cur) *n.* riches: *the worship of filthy* ~.

lu·cu·bra·tion (loo·cue·BRAY–) *n.* a laborious or elaborate work or composition.

lu·di·crous (LOO·di·crus) *adj.* laughably incongruous or ridiculous; **lu·di·crous·ly** *adv.;* **lu·di·crous·ness** *n.*

luff *v.* sail into the wind; ***n.*** act of turning a ship's bow toward the wind.

lug *v.* **lugs, lugged, lug·ging** pull or tug; carry (something heavy). —***n.*** **1** a projection by which an object may be held or carried, as a pitcher's handle. **2** [short form] lugsail. —**lug·gage** (LUG·ij) *n.* suitcases and such traveler's baggage. —**lug·ger** *n.* a lugsail-rigged boat. —**lug·sail** *n.* a four-cornered sail held by a yard slanting across the mast.

lu·gu·bri·ous (loo·GOO·bree·us) *adj.* sad or mournful in an exaggerated way; **lu·gu·bri·ous·ly** *adv.;* **lu·gu·bri·ous·ness** *n.*

Luke in the Bible, the third Gospel or its reputed author, St. Luke.

luke·warm *adj.* tepid or barely warm; hence, lacking warmth or enthusiasm; **luke·warm·ly** *adv.;* **luke·warm·ness** *n.*

lull *v.* (become) calm: *to ~ a person's fears or suspicions; a child ~ed to sleep;* ***n.*** a period of calm or lessened activity: *a ~ in a storm, conversation; a ~ in trade.* —**lull·a·by** (LUL·uh·bye) *n.* **-bies** a song to lull a baby to sleep.

lu·lu (LOO·loo) *n. Slang.* a person or thing that is remarkable or outstanding.

lum·ba·go (–BAY–) *n.* pain in the lower back, or **lum·bar** region.

lum·ber *n.* logs sawn and dressed into boards, planks, etc.; also, useless furniture and household articles taking up room; ***v.*** **1** cut down and saw logs into lumber; **lum·ber·ing** *n.* **2** move along heavily and noisily; **lum·ber·ing** *adj.* ponderous or bulky. —**lum·ber·jack** *n.* logger; **lum·ber·man** *n.* a logger or one who deals in lumber; **lum·ber·yard** *n.* a place where lumber is kept for sale.

lu·men (LOO–) *n., pl.* **-mi·na** or **-mens** a unit of light measurement. —**lu·mi·nar·y** (LOO·muh·ner·ee) *n.* **-nar·ies** a light-giving body such as the sun or moon; also, a famous person. —**lu·mi·nes·cence** (–NES–) *n.* light without burning or heat, as given off by fireflies, phosphorus, etc. and by fluorescence; cold light; **lu·mi·nes·cent** *adj.* —**lu·mi·nous** (–nus) *adj.* giving off light: *a ~ celestial body; a watch's ~ dial; ~ paints; a ~* (i.e. clear or enlightening) *performance;* **lu·mi·nous·ly** *adv.;* **lu·mi·nos·i·ty** (–NOS–) *n.*

lum·mox (LUM·ux) *n. Informal.* a stupid or clumsy person.

lump *v.* heap together or make into a lump or lumps; **lump it** *Informal.* endure it. —***n.*** a shapeless solid mass; also, a swelling or bump: *a ~ of coal, sugar; a painful ~ on the head;* **in the lump** in one mass; *a* **lump in the throat** *felt by one overcome by emotion.* —***adj.:*** *~ sugar.* —**lump·ish** *adj.* —**lump·ec·to·my** (–PEC·tuh·mee) *n.* **-mies** surgical removal of a breast cancer. —**lumps** *pl. Informal.* hard blows or punishments. —**lump sum** an amount paid in one complete payment. —**lump·y** *adj.* **lump·i·er, -i·est** full of lumps; also, heavy and clumsy, as a "lumpfish" or "lumpsucker" of N. waters; **lump·i·ness** *n.*

lu·na·cy (LOO·nuh–) *n.* **-cies** great folly; also, insanity. —**lu·nar** (LOO·nur) *adj.* of the moon: *A* **lunar (excursion) module** *takes astronauts to the moon's surface and back from a command module that stays in orbit.* —**lu·na·tic** (LOO·nuh–) *n.* one who is insane or utterly foolish; ***adj.:*** *a ~ idea, asylum* (i.e. for the insane); **lunatic fringe** an extremist or fanatical section (of a movement, society, etc.)

lunch *n.* & *v.* (have) a light meal at midday: *He ~es at the cafeteria;* **lunch·eon** (–chun) *n. Formal.* lunch: *a ~ appointment;* **luncheon meat** ready-to-eat, packaged meat. —**lunch·eon·ette** (–uh·NET) *n.* a small restaurant serving light meals. —**lunch·room** *n.* a room, as in a school or place of work, in which to eat lunch; also, a luncheonette.

lu·nette (loo·NET) *n.* a crescent-shaped figure or opening.

lung *n.* either of a pair of baglike breathing organs in humans and other vertebrates; also, a device such as an *iron lung.*

lunge (LUNJ) *n.* & *v.* **lung·es, lunged, lung·ing** (make) a sudden thrust, as with a sword, or a forward leap.

lung·fish *n.* a fish that has an air bladder besides gills to enable it to breathe in the air and in water.

lunk(·head) *n. Informal.* a dolt.

lu·pine (LOO–) *adj.* of a wolf or wolves; also, wolflike. —**lu·pin(e)** (–pin) *n.* any of a group of plants of the pea family with star-shaped compound leaves and long clusters of usu. yellow or bright-blue flowers as in the bluebonnet.

lurch *v.* stagger or lean suddenly to one side. —***n.*** **1** a lurching movement. **2 leave in the lurch** desert (someone) in need of help.

lure *n.* & *v.* **lures, lured, lur·ing** (a device such as a bait or decoy used) to tempt or entice; also, an attraction or the power of such attraction: *the ~s of Las Vegas; ~d away by false hopes.*

lu·rid (LOOR·id) *adj.* shining with a red or fiery light; hence, gruesome or sensational: *a ~ sunset; a ~ tale of murder; ~ details, crimes;* **lu·rid·ly** *adv.;* **lu·rid·ness** *n.*

lurk *v.* lie in wait or move about stealthily: *an intruder ~ing in the shadows; Doubts still ~ed in his mind.*

Lu·sa·ka (loo·SAH·kah) capital of Zambia.

lus·cious (LUSH·us) *adj.* sweet and delicious; also, appealing to the senses: *a ~ pear, apple pie; ~ lips, poetry, scenery;* **lus·cious·ly** *adv.;* **lus·cious·ness** *n.*

lush **1** *adj.* excessively luxuriant in growth: *~ vegetation, jungles.* **2** *n. Slang.* an excessive drinker.

lust *n.* & *v.* (have) an intense longing or desire, esp. sexual: *the ~ for gold; the ~s of the flesh; to ~ after a woman;* **lust·ful** *adj.;* **lust·ful·ly** *adv.*

lus·ter *n.* brightness or brilliance of polish, beauty, reputation, etc.; **lus·ter·ware** *n.* pottery glazed with metallic oxides. Also **lus·tre, lus·tre·ware.** —**lus·trous** (–trus) *adj.* glossy; brilliant. —**lus·trum** *n.* a ceremonial purification held in ancient Rome every five years; **lus·tral** *adj.*

lust·y *adj.* **lust·i·er, -i·est** full of vigor; robust: *a ~ lass, eater; ~ cheers;* **lust·i·ly** *adv.;* **lust·i·ness** *n.*

lute *n.* an ancient stringed musical instrument with a flat-topped, pear-shaped body and a distinctive bent-back head. —**lu·ta·nist** or **lu·te·nist** *n.* a lute player.

lu·te·ti·um (loo·TEE·shee·um) *n.* a rare-earth metallic element.

Lu·ther (LOO–), **Martin.** 1483–1546, German theologian and leader of the Reformation; **Lu·ther·an** *n.* & *adj.* (a member) of the church originated by Luther; **Lu·ther·an·ism** *n.*

lut·ist (LOO–) *n.* a lute player.

lux *n.* **lux·es** or **lu·ces** (LOO·seez) a unit of illumination equal to one lumen per square meter.

Lux·em·bourg (LUX·um·burg) a duchy between Belgium and West Germany; 998 sq. mi. (2,586 km^2); *cap.* **Luxembourg.**

lux·u·ri·ant (lug·ZHOOR·ee·unt) *adj.* rich or abundant in growth, as jungle vegetation; also, rich in ornament; florid; **lux·u·ri·ant·ly** *adv.;* **lux·u·ri·ance** *n.* —**lux·u·ri·ate** *v.* **-ates, -at·ed, -at·ing** indulge oneself; revel: *bathers ~ing in the summer sun;* **lux·u·ri·a·tion** (–AY–) *n.* —**lux·u·ri·ous** (–ZHOOR–) *adj.* fond of or contributing to luxury: *a ~ existence; hotel; ~ surroundings, food;* **lux·u·ri·ous·ly** *adv.* —**lux·u·ry** (LUK·shuh·ree, LUG·zhuh–) *n.* **-ries** ease and comfort provided by expensive food, clothes, amusements, and such superfluities rather than life's necessities; also, their use or the things themselves: *Cake would be a ~ for people who can't buy bread; lived in ~ all her life;* ***adj.:*** *a ~ apartment, hotel; ~ goods.*

Lu·zon (loo·ZON) the largest of the Philippine islands.

Lw lawrencium.

lx lux.

-ly *adj. suffix.* **1** like: as in *manly, queenly.* **2** occurring every (specified period): as in *daily, hourly.* —***adv.*** in a (specified) manner: as in *happily, icily, musically.*

ly·ce·um (lye·SEE–, LYE·see–) *n.* an adult-education organization providing lectures, concerts, etc.; also, a lecture hall.

lye *n.* a strong alkaline solution or solid, usu. of sodium hydroxide or potassium hydroxide, used in making soap and for household cleaning.

ly·ing (LYE–) pres. part. of LIE. —***n.*** & ***adj.*** (the habit of) telling lies: *a ~ tongue.* —**ly·ing-in** *n.* (confinement in) childbirth; ***adj.:*** *a ~ hospital, period.*

lymph (LIMF) *n.* a plasmalike transparent yellowish fluid of body tissue that seeps out of capillaries, flows through a system of **lym·phat·ic** (–FAT–) vessels, and is returned to the blood near the heart; **lymph node** (or **gland**) a knotlike formation along a lymphatic vessel that occurs in clusters in the groin, neck, armpits, etc. and helps fight infections and filter out foreign matter; **lymph·oid** *adj.* of or having to do with lymph or the tissue of lymph nodes.

lynch (LINCH) *v.* of a mob, to kill (an accused person) without trial, often by hanging. —**lynch·er** *n.*

lynx *n.* a short-tailed wild cat related to the bobcat, with pointed and tufted ears, valued for its coat; **lynx-eyed** *adj.* sharp-eyed.

Lyon (lee·AWN) French name of **Ly·ons** (LYE·unz), France's third largest city. —**ly·on·naise** (lye·uh·NAZE) *adj.* prepared with finely sliced fried onions: *~ potatoes, sauce.*

lyre *n.* an ancient stringed musical instrument like a small harp, used by the Greeks for accompanying songs and recitations. —**lyr·ic** (LEER–) *n.* a short poem with a songlike quality, expressing the poet's deeply felt personal reactions to things, as an elegy, ode, or sonnet; **lyrics** *pl.* the words of a song as distinguished from the music. —***adj.:*** *a ~* (i.e. melodic) *quality, poet, tenor* (with a higher and lighter voice); **lyr·i·cal** *adj.* expressive of emotion; enthusiastic: *a humdrum affair, nothing to be ~ about;* **lyr·i·cal·ly** *adv.* —**lyr·i·cist** (LEER–) *n.* writer of verses for songs; also, a lyric poet; **lyr·i·cism** *n.* —**lyr·ist** *n.* **1** (LYE–) a lyre player. **2** (LEER–) a lyricist.

ly·ser·gic (–SUR–) **acid** See LSD.

-lysis *comb.form.* disintegration or decomposition: as in *electrolysis, hydrolysis.* — **-lyte** *comb. form.* subject of decomposition: as in *electrolyte, hydrolyte.*

L.Z. landing zone.

M

M or **m** (EM) *n.* **M's** or **m's** **1** the 13th letter of the English alphabet. **2** Roman numeral for 1,000; mass; male. **—M.** or **m.** male; married; masculine; mile(s); minute(s); month; moon. **—M.** Medieval; Monday; Monsieur (*pl.* **MM.**). **—m.** or **m** meter(s).

ma (MAH) *n. Informal.* mother.

MA Massachusetts. **—M.A.** Master of Arts; mental age.

ma'am (MAM) *n. Informal* [in direct address] madam.

ma·ca·bre (muh·CAH·bruh, –bur) *adj.* dealing with death, esp. its gruesome aspects: *a ~ story;* **ma·ca·bre·ly** *adv.*

mac·ad·am (muh·CAD·um) *n.* (a road surface or pavement made of) crushed stone or gravel packed firmly in layers, often with tar or asphalt as binding material; **mac·ad·am·ize** *v.* **-iz·es, -ized, -iz·ing:** *a ~d road.*

Ma·cao (muh·COW) a Portuguese province consisting of a seaport on the S. coast of China and three islands.

ma·caque (muh·CAHK, –CAK) *n.* any of several species of large, short-tailed monkeys of S. Asia, including the barbary ape and the rhesus.

mac·a·ro·ni (–ROH·nee) *n.* dried flour paste, usu. in the form of short tubes, that is boiled or baked for food. **—mac·a·roon** (–ROON) *n.* a small, sweet cookie made of egg white and crushed almonds or coconut.

ma·caw (muh·CAW) *n,* a gaudily plumed, long-tailed parrot of tropical America with a screeching cry.

Mac·beth (–BETH) the principal character of one of Shakespeare's tragedies.

Mac·ca·bees (MAC·uh–) either of two books of the Old Testament Apocrypha dealing with a Jewish dynasty that ruled Palestine for over 100 years from about 140 B.C.

mace *n.* **1** a medieval hand weapon or club with a spiked metal head; hence, a ceremonial, club-shaped staff used, esp. in legislatures, as a symbol of authority. **2** a spice made from the dried outer covering of nutmeg seeds.

Mace a liquid tear-gas spray; *Trademark:* "Chemical Mace."

Mac·e·do·ni·a (mas·uh·DOH·nee·uh) an ancient kingdom of S.E. Europe, now a region of Greece, Yugoslavia, and Bulgaria; **Mac·e·do·ni·an** (–DOH–) *n.* & *adj.*

mac·er·ate (MAS–) *v.* **-ates, -at·ed, -at·ing** soften by soaking, as gum to make mucilage or flowers to extract perfume: *~d skin;* **mac·er·a·tion** (–RAY–) *n.*

mach. machine; machinery; machinist.

Mach (MAHK) *n.* the ratio of the speed of an object to the speed of sound: *Mach 2 is twice the speed of sound;* also **mach.**

ma·che·te (muh·SHET·ee) *n.* a large, heavy knife of Latin America, used for cutting sugar cane and as a weapon.

Mach·i·a·vel·li·an (mak·ee·uh·VEL·ee·un) *adj.* crafty or deceitful, as counseled by **Niccolo Machiavelli,** 1469–1527, Italian writer on statecraft.

ma·chic·o·lat·ed (muh·CHIK·uh·lay–) *adj.* having machicolations; **ma·chic·o·la·tion** (–LAY–) *n.* in medieval fortifications, an opening, either in the roof of a passageway or in the floor of a projecting gallery, for throwing missiles at attacking enemies.

mach·i·na·tion (mak·i·NAY–) *n.* a cunning plot or scheme to harm someone; **mach·i·nate** (MAK–) *v.* **—ma·chine** (–SHEEN) *n.* **1** a mechanical device or appliance, esp. one with coordinated moving parts to transmit power for a desired end: *A lever is a simple ~; a printing ~; a ~-made, not handmade product; a calculating ~.* **2** a person or group that works like a machine, without thought or will: *a propaganda ~; the war ~.* **—v. -chines, -chined, -chin·ing** process or finish with a machine; **ma·chin·a·ble** (–SHEEN·uh–) *adj.* **—machine gun** an automatic weapon that fires ammunition fed into it from a belt or a magazine continuously and rapidly; **ma·chine-gun** *v.* **-guns, -gunned, -gun·ning; machine gunner. —machine language** a system of signs, characters, or symbols readable by a computer, as one consisting of binary digits. **—ma·chin·er·y** *n.* **-er·ies** machines or machine parts collectively: *well-oiled ~* (i.e. mechanism); *different ~s for the sales and service functions.* **—ma·chin·ist** (–SHEEN–) n. one skilled in the making and operation of machines or machine tools.

ma·chis·mo (mah·CHEEZ–) *n.* strong or aggressive masculinity, as displayed in swearing, fighting, copulating, and such aspects of a macho.

Mach number same as MACH.

ma·cho (MAH–) *adj.* & *n.* **-chos** virile (man).

macintosh same as MACKINTOSH.

mack·er·el *n.* a valuable food fish of the N. Atlantic, colored silvery white below and blue or green with wavy black stripes on its back; hence **mackerel clouds; mackerel sky** a sky dappled like a mackerel's back.

mack·i·naw (coat) short heavy winter coat, usu. in a plaid pattern.

mac(k)·in·tosh *n.* a waterproof raincoat.

Ma·con (MAY·cun) a city in Georgia.

mac·ra·me (MAC·ruh·may) *n.* the art of knotting cord, rope, or string into articles such as purses, belts, and other accessories.

mac·ro *adj.* & *comb.form.* large or large-scale: as in *macrocosm, macroscopic; a ~ unit, lens.* **—mac·ro·bi·ot·ics** (–bye·OT–) *n.pl.* [takes *sing. v.*] the science of prolonging life, esp. by a diet of unprocessed natural foods; **mac·ro·bi·ot·ic** *adj.: a Zen ~ diet; a ~ food cult.* **—mac·ro·cosm** *n.* a large and complex whole, as the universe; **mac·ro·cos·mic** (–COS–) *adj.* **—ma·cron** (MAY·crun) *n.* a mark placed over a vowel (e.g. ā, ē) to indicate length or stress. **—mac·ro·scop·ic** (–SCOP–) *adj.* large enough to be seen by the naked eye; also, large-scale: *a ~ issue;* **mac·ro·scop·i·cal** *adj.*

mad *adj.* **mad·der, mad·dest** excited; showing anger, enthusiasm, etc., esp. in an insane or foolish manner; hence, crazy; insane: *She's ~ about learning to fly; was ~ at me because I was late; It's ~ to quit school when you're doing so well; That dog may be ~* (i.e. having rabies); *works* **like mad** (*Informal.* furiously) *on the eve of a test;* **mad·ly** *adv.;* **mad·ness** *n.*

Mad·a·gas·car (–GAS·cur) a country off the E. coast of Africa, consisting of the island of Madagascar and nearby smaller islands; 226,-658 sq.mi. (587,041 km²); *cap.* Tananarive (Antananarivo).

mad·am (MAD·um) *n.* **1** *pl.* **-ams** a woman who keeps a brothel. **2** *pl.* **mes·dames** (may·DAHM) [used in addressing] a lady. **—mad·ame** (MAD·um, muh·DAM) *n. French* [used in addressing a French-speaking married woman, as "Dear Madame," or prefixed like "Mrs."] *pl.* **mesdames.**

mad·cap *n.* & *adj.* reckless or impulsive (person): *a ~ scheme to raise money.*

mad·den (MADN) *v.* make or become mad, esp. irritate; **mad·den·ing** *adj.;* **mad·ding** *adj.* frenzied; also, maddening.

mad·der **1** *comp.* of MAD. **2** *n.* a red dye, esp. "Turkey red," made from the roots of a plant of the same name grown in Europe and Asia.

made *pt.* of MAKE.

Ma·deir·a (–DEER–) **Islands** a group of Portuguese islands off the N.W. coast of Africa, noted for the fortified **Madeira** or **madeira** wine made there.

ma·de·moi·selle (mad·uh·muh·ZEL) *n. French, pl.* **mes·de·moi·selles** (made·mwah·ZEL) an unmarried, usu. young French-speaking woman. [also used like "Miss" as a title]

made-to-meas·ure *adj.* made to the customer's measurements; custom-tailored. **—made-to-or·der** *adj.* made according to the customer's requirements. **—made-up** *adj.* not real; also, finished with makeup: *a ~ word, excuse; a ~ beauty, nose.*

mad·house *n.* a scene of uproar and confusion; also, an insane asylum.

Mad·i·son (–sn) capital of Wisconsin; **James Madison,** 1751–1836, 4th U.S. President (1809–17).

mad·man *n.* **-men** a lunatic; *fem.* **mad·wom·an, -wom·en.**

Ma·don·na (muh·DON·uh) Mary as the mother of Jesus; also, a picture or statue of her.

Ma·dras (muh·DRAS, –DRAHS) a city on the S.E. coast of India. **—mad·ras** (MAD·rus) *n.* a plain-weave fabric, originally from Madras, noted for its bleeding colors.

Ma·drid (muh·DRID) capital of Spain.

Mad·ri·gal (–ri·gul) *n.* a part-song or short love poem popular in the 16th century.

mael·strom (MAIL·strum) *n.* a violently confused or turbulent condition or situation, like **Maelstrom,** a dangerous whirlpool off the Norwegian coast.

mae·nad (MEE–) *n.* a frenzied woman, like a **Maenad,** one of the female attendants of Bacchus.

ma·es·tro (MICE·troh, mah·ES–) *n.* **-tros** or **-tri** (–tree) a great musical composer, teacher, or performer; hence, a masterly performer in any art.

Ma(f)·fi·a (MAH·fee·uh) *n.* an underworld organization of criminals, Sicilian in origin, a member of which is a **ma·fi·o·so** or **Mafioso** (–OH–) *n., pl.* **-si** (–see).

mag. magazine; magnetism; magneto; magnitude. **—mag** **1** *n. Slang.* magazine. **2** *adj.* made of magnesium alloy: *~ wheels.* **—mag·a·zine** (–uh·ZEEN) *n.* **1** an often illustrated periodical of popular interest carrying a variety of articles. **2** a place where a supply is stored, as of type in a typesetting machine, film in a camera, cartridges inside a machine gun, or a place for storing military supplies and gunpowder.

mag·da·len (–duh·lun) or **mag·da·lene** (–leen) *n.* a reformed prostitute, as Mary Magdalene in the Bible.

Ma·gel·lan (muh·JEL·un), **Ferdinand.** 1480?–1521, a Portuguese navigator.

ma·gen·ta (muh·JEN·tuh) *n.* & *adj.* purplish red (dye).

mag·got (–ut) n. *the* wormlike larva of a two-winged fly; **mag·got·y** *adj.*

Ma·gi (MAY·jye) *n.pl.* of **Ma·gus,** in the Bible, any of the "Three Wise Men" from the East who visited Jesus in his crib. **—mag·ic** (MAJ–) *n.* **1** the art of creating illusions by sleight of hand and such tricks. **2** supposed supernatural power of influencing natural events or of controlling human actions by ritual use of incantations, spells, rites, fetishes, talismans, etc.; hence, any inexplicable or mysterious power: *Witchcraft and sorcery are kinds of ~; the ~ of love;* **adj.:** *a ~ potion; Midas's ~ touch.* **—mag·i·cal** *adj.;* **mag·i·cal·ly** *adv.* **—ma·gi·cian** (muh·JISH·un) *n.* a person who practices magic; sorcerer.

mag·is·te·ri·al (maj·is·TEER·ee·ul) *adj.* **1** having to do with authority; also, authoritative or overbearing. **2** of a magistrate. **—mag·is·trate** (MAJ–) *n.* a government official administering the law, esp. a judge of a minor court, as a justice of the peace; **mag·is·tra·cy** (–truh·see) *n.* **-cies.**

mag·ma *n.* molten rock, the source of igneous rock: *~ is extruded as lava;* **mag·mat·ic** (–MAT–) *adj.*

Mag·na C(h)ar·ta (MAG·nuh·CAR·tuh) the charter of civil and political liberties granted by King John in 1215 to the English people. **—mag·nan·i·mous** (–NAN·uh·mus) *adj.* noble or generous-spirited, as in forgiving injuries, not being petty, etc.; **mag·nan·i·mous·ly** *adv.* **—mag·na·nim·i·ty** (–nuh·NIM–) *n.* **—mag·nate** *n.* a person of wealth or position, as in business or industry.

mag·ne·sia (–NEE·zhuh) *n.* magnesium oxide, a white, alkaline powder used as a laxative and in industry. **—mag·ne·si·um** *n.* a light, silver-white, metallic element. **—mag·net** (–nit) *n.* an object that attracts, because of the force of a **magnetic field** around it: *A piece of lodestone is a natural ~; An electrically charged coil of wire is an induced ~;* **mag·net·ic** (–NET–) *adj.: Iron and nickel are ~ elements; A* **magnetic needle** *points to the earth's* **magnetic poles** *lying near the geographic poles; a leader with a ~ personality;* **mag·net·i·cal·ly** *adv.* **—magnetic recording** the recording of sounds, video material, computer data, etc. by variations in the magnetized area on a tape, wire, disc, or other medium. **—mag·net·ism** (MAG–) *n.* magnetic force or the power of attraction: *a singer who has lost her ~.* **—mag·net·ite** *n.* a black mineral that is an important source of iron. **—mag·net·ize** *v.* **-iz·es, -ized, -iz·ing** make or become magnetic so as to attract; hence, charm or hypnotize: *an audience ~d by a singer's voice;* **mag·net·iz·a·ble** *adj.;* **mag·net·iz·er** *n.;* **mag·net·i·za·tion** (–ZAY–) *n.* **—mag·ne·to** (–NEE·toh) *n.* **-tos** a small generator in which electricity is produced in a coil of wire moving through a magnetic field. **—mag·ne·tom·e·ter** (–nuh·TOM–) *n.* an instrument for measuring the strength of a magnetic field. **—mag·ne·to·sphere** (–NEE·tuh–) *n.* the upper atmospheric region dominated by the earth's magnetism; **mag·ne·to·spher·ic** (–SFEER–) *adj.* **—magnet school** an integrated public school with superior facilities, designed to attract students of all races.

mag·nif·i·cent (–NIF–) *adj.* impressive because of beauty, richness, or splendor: *a ~ palace, tribute, voice; Chicago's "Magnificent Mile" lined with elegant hotels, stores, and offices;* **mag·nif·i·cent·ly** *adv.* **—mag·nif·i·cence** *n.* **—mag·nif·i·co** (–NIF–) *n.* **-co(e)s** a person of high rank; grandee. **—mag·ni·fy** (MAG–) *v.* **-fies, -fied, -fy·ing** make (seem) larger, as with a lens, or **magnifying glass;** hence, exaggerate; **mag·ni·fi·er** *n.;* **mag·ni·fi·ca·tion** (–CAY–) *n.* **—mag·nil·o·quent** (–NIL·uh–) *adj.* grandiloquent; **mag·nil·o·quence** *n.* **—mag·ni·tude** (MAG–) *n.* greatness of size or strength; degree of importance: *the direction and ~ of a force; an earthquake of ~ 7.6 on the Richter scale; The faintest stars are of the sixth ~; a problem* **of the first magnitude. —mag·no·li·a** (–NO–) *n.* any of a group of trees and shrubs with large, dark-green leaves, sweet-smelling, usu. snowy-white flowers, and cone-like fruits. **—mag·num** *n.* (a bottle of wine or liquor containing) two quarts. **—magnum o·pus** (–OH·pus) masterpiece; one's greatest work.

mag·pie *n.* a noisy bird of the crow family, related to the jays, usu. black-and-white with a long tail.

Magus See MAGI.

Mag·yar (MAG·yar, MOJ·ar) *n.* & *adj.* (a member or the Finno-Ugric language) of the chief people of Hungary; Hungarian.

ma·ha·ra·ja(h) (mah·huh·RAH·juh) *n.* a former ruler of an Indian state; *fem.* **ma·ha·ra·ni** or **-nee** (–nee). **—ma·ha·ri·shi** (–RISH·ee) *n.* a Hindu sage or spiritual leader. **—ma·hat·ma** (–HAHT–, –HAT–) *n.* in India, a great and holy man, as "Mahatma Gandhi."

Mahican See MOHICAN.

mah-jong(g) (–JONG, –ZHONG) *n.* a game of Chinese origin, played by four people using 144 engraved oblong tiles.

ma·hog·a·ny (–HOG·uh–) *n.* **-nies** the dark reddish-brown wood of a large tropical American tree of the same name; also, the color; ***adj.:*** *~ furniture.*

Ma·hom·et (–HOM·it) same as MOHAMMED.

ma·hout (muh·HOUT) *n.* an elephant-driver or keeper.

maid *n.* a female servant; also, a maiden. **—maid·en** *n.* a young unmarried woman; ***adj.*** of a maiden; untried; first-time: *a ~* (i.e. unmarried) *aunt; a ship's ~ voyage; a member's ~ speech in the legislature.* **—maid·en·hair** *n.* a species of fern with finely divided fronds; **maidenhair tree** same as GINKGO. **—maid·en·head** *n.* the hymen. **—maid·en·hood** *n.* period of life before a woman's marriage; also, virginity. **—maid·en·ly** *adj.* of or like a maiden: *~ reserve.* **—maiden name** a woman's surname before marriage. **—maid-in-wait·ing** *n.* **maids-** a queen's or princess's female attendant. **—maid of honor** an unmarried young woman as a chief bridesmaid; also, a maid-in-waiting. **—maid·serv·ant** (–unt) *n.* a woman servant; housemaid.

¹mail *n.* body armor of metal plates, rings, etc.; **mailed** *adj.* protected with mail.

²mail *n.* a postal system or what is sent through it, as letters, parcels, etc.; also, bags of mail: *No ~ on holidays; reading my morning ~; the origin of the* **mails** (i.e. postal system) *in Europe;* ***adj.:*** *a ~ carrier, clerk, chute.* **—*v.*** send by mail. **—mail·box** *n.* a box into which outgoing mail is dropped by the public; also, a private box for receiving mail. **—mail·er** *n.* a person or machine that addresses, stamps, or mails; also, a small container for mailing things, or an advertising leaflet. **—mail·man** *n.* **-men** a man who carries or delivers mail. **—mail order** an order for goods by mail; **mail-or·der** *adj.: a ~ catalog, business, house* (i.e. firm that sells by mail).

maim *v.* cripple or mutilate.

main *adj.* chief or principal, esp. of a system or connected whole: *the ~ street* (*Slang:* **main drag, main stem**) *of a town; the ~ course of a meal; a sentence's ~ and subordinate clauses; a hustler, with his eye ever on the* **main chance** (i.e. the most advantageous opportunity). **—*n.* 1** a principal channel, as of water, gas, sewage, or electricity: *The water ~ burst;* **in the main** for the most part. **2** with might and main with all one's strength. **3** *Archaic.* the ocean: *the western ~;* **Spanish main** South American mainland. **—main·ly** *adv.*

Maine (MAIN) the largest of the New England states; 33,215 sq.mi. (86,026 km²); *cap.* Augusta.

main·frame *n.* a computer's central processing unit, not a PERIPHERAL. **—main·land** (–land, –lund) *n.* the main landmass, as distinguished from outlying islands: *the Chinese ~;* **main·land·er** *n.* **—main·line** *n.* the principal road, route, etc.; *Slang.* a large vein; ***v.*** **-lines, -lined, -lin·ing** inject (heroin or other narcotic) into a large vein. **—main·mast** *n.* the principal mast of a vessel; **main·sail** *n.* the largest sail on the mainmast. **—main·spring** *n.* the principal spring of a watch or clock; hence, chief incentive. **—main·stay** *n.* a mainmast's supporting wire or rope; hence, chief support. **—main·stream** *n.* the principal current; the main direction of flow; the prevailing trend. **—Main Street** a small town's principal street; hence, provincialism, mediocrity, etc.; ***adj.:*** *a politican who has lost touch with the masses and ~ America;* **main·street** *v.* campaign for election along main streets; **main·street·er** *n.*

main·tain (–TAIN) *v.* keep in existence; keep active or unimpaired; defend: *Police ~ law and order; An automobile has to be ~ed in running condition; income to ~ a family; couldn't ~ his innocence in the face of overwhelming evidence;* **main·tain·a·ble** (–TAIN–) *adj.;* **main·tain·a·bil·i·ty** (–BIL–) *n.* **—main·te·nance** (MAIN·tn·unce) *n.* a maintaining; support; means of living.

main·top *n.* the platform at the head of a mainmast.

ma·iol·i·ca (muh·YOL–) same as MAJOLICA.

mai·son·ette (may·zuh·NET) *n.* a duplex apartment or small house.

mai·tre d' (may·tur·DEE) *n., pl.* **-d's** (–DEEZ) short form of **maî·tre d'hôtel** (may·truh·doh·TEL) *n., pl.* **maî·tres-** (may·truh–) a headwaiter or chief steward.

maize (MAIZ) *n.* same as CORN, *n.* 1.

Maj. Major.

ma·jes·tic (muh·JES–) *adj.* having majesty or grandeur; stately and lofty in appearance; also **ma·jes·ti·cal; ma·jes·ti·cal·ly** *adv.* **—maj·es·ty** (MAJ·is·tee) *n.* **1** lofty grandeur. **2** (Your, His, Her) **Majesty, -ties** [title used in speaking to or of a king, queen, emperor, etc.].

ma·jol·i·ca (muh·JOL–) *n.* Italian white-glazed pottery; faience; delft.

ma·jor (MAY·jur) *adj.* relatively greater in size, importance, etc., not minor: *a ~ disagreement, improvement, poet, portion, subject of study; a ~ chord based on a ~ scale.* **—*v.*** of a student, specialize: *She's ~ing in history.* **—*n.* 1:** *She's a history ~* (i.e. student with history as main subject); *His ~* (i.e. main subject) *is music.* **2** in the U.S. Army, Air Force, and Marine Corps, a commissioned officer ranking above a captain and below a lieutenant colonel. **—ma·jor·do·mo** (MAY·jur·DOH·moh) *n.* **-mos** a chief steward or butler. **—majorette** short form of DRUM MAJORETTE. **—major general,** *pl.* **major generals** in the U.S. Army, Air Force, and Marine Corps, a commissioned officer ranking above a brigadier general and below a lieutenant general. **—ma·jor·i·ty** (muh·JOR–) *n.* **-ties 1** more than half the total number (of votes, people, etc); also, the excess of votes on one side over the total of the rest. **2** the legal age of responsibility or adulthood, usu. 18 or 21. **3** the military rank of a major. **—major scale** a musical scale having half steps after the third and seventh notes. **—ma·jus·cule** (muh·JUS–, MAJ·us–) *n.* large or capital letter, as in medieval manuscripts.

make *v.* **makes, made, mak·ing 1** bring (something) into being; hence, form, shape, or put together: *She ~s dresses; ~s his living as a plumber; died without ~ing a will; Everyone ~s mistakes; Poets are born, not made; John can't ~* (i.e. arrange) *a bed; "Haste ~s waste"; They ~ peace after each fight; What do you ~ of* (i.e.

how do you interpret) *this telegram?* **2** cause to; also cause (oneself) to be or become: *children made to do their homework; ~ sure it is locked; They'll ~* (i.e. become) *good teachers.* **3** attain; reach; achieve: *tried hard but couldn't ~ it; had to run to ~* (i.e. catch) *the 5:30 (train); a story sensational enough to ~ the front page; a challenge that could either ~ you* (i.e. get you success) *or break you.* **—n.:** *the year and ~* (i.e. brand) *of a car;* **on the make** seeking profit, adventure, etc.; **mak·er** *n.* **—make away with 1** get rid of or kill. **2** steal. **—make believe** pretend or imagine; **make-be·lieve** *n.* & *adj.: His exploits are mere ~; a ~ moon-landing.* **—make do** *with margarine when butter is scarce.* **—make for** *the exits when the alarm sounds.* **—make out 1** see or understand: *It's too faint for me to ~ out.* **2** (try to) prove: *not the cure-all it is made out to be.* **3** write or fill out: *Please ~ this out in duplicate.* **4** *Informal.* succeed: *How are you ~ing out in your new job? She wasn't easy to ~ out with* (*Slang.* succeed in having sex with). **—make off** run away; **make off with** steal. **—make over 1** change or alter. **2** transfer the ownership of. **—make up 1** put together; compose: *an audience made up of students; She's good at ~ing up excuses; time to ~ up your mind* (i.e. decide). **2** restore or compensate for (something lost): *drive faster to* **make up for** *lost time; I'll* **make it up to** *you for breaking your china; friends ~ing up* (i.e. becoming reconciled) *after a fight.* **3** put on (cosmetics, stage costumes, etc.) **—make·shift** *n.* & *adj.* (something) temporary or substitute: *a ~ bed of hay.* **—make·up** or **make-up** *n.* & *adj.* [corresponding to the *v.* senses] **1:** *the page ~ and design of a newspaper; a ~ editor.* **2** *Informal: a ~ examination for students who were ill.* **3:** *an actor wearing too much ~.* **—make-work** *n.* & *adj.* (work) devised mainly to keep people employed: *a ~ government project.* **—mak·ing** *n.*: *His marriage to the rich widow was the ~* (i.e. cause of success) *of him; a youngster with the* **makings of** (i.e. potential for becoming) *a soldier; Publicity spoiled our plans while they were still* **in the making.**

makuta *pl.* of LIKUTA.

Mal. Malachi (Old Testament book); Malayan.

mal- *prefix.* bad(ly); poor(ly): as in *maladjusted, maladroit.*

Ma·la·bo (muh·LAH–) capital of Equatorial Guinea.

mal·a·chite (MAL·uh·kite) *n.* a green copper ore used for ornaments.

mal·ad·just·ed (–uh·JUST–) *adj.* not well adjusted to one's environment; **mal·ad·just·ment** *n.* **—mal·a·droit** (mal·uh–) *adj.* not adroit; clumsy or awkward; **mal·a·droit·ly** *adv.;* **mal·a·droit·ness** *n.* **—mal·a·dy** (MAL·uh·dee) *n.* **-dies** a bodily disorder, often one that is deep-seated or that may prove fatal.

Mal·a·gas·y (–uh·GAS·ee) **Republic** same as MADAGASCAR.

ma·laise (ma·LAZE) *n.* a disordered condition; also, a vague feeling of discomfort.

mal·a·mute (MAL·uh–) *n.* a strong, heavy-coated sled dog of Alaskan origin.

mal·a·pert *n.* & *adj. Archaic.* (one who is) saucy or impudent.

mal·a·prop·ism (MAL·uh–) *n.* a ludicrous mixing up of similar words, e.g. "a nice derangement of epitaphs," as Mrs. Malaprop says in Sheridan's *The Rivals.*

ma·lar·i·a (muh·LAIR·ee·uh) *n.* a mosquito-borne parasitic disease characterized by periodic chills and fever; **ma·lar·i·al** *adj.*

ma·lar·k(e)y *n. Slang.* bunkum; nonsense.

mal·a·thi·on (–uh·THYE–) *n.* a general-purpose phosphate insecticide of low toxicity.

Ma·la·wi (muh·LAH·wee) a republic of S. E. Africa, formerly "Nyasaland"; 45,747 sq.mi. (118,484 km²); *cap.* Lilongwe.

Ma·lay (MAY–, muh·LAY) *n.* a brown-skinned Mongoloid people of Malaysia, the Philippines, and Indonesia; also, any of their languages; also ***adj.*** **—Ma·lay·a** (muh·LAY·uh) same as MALAY PENINSULA. **—Mal·a·ya·lam** (–uh·YAH·lum) *n.* a language of S.W. India. **—Ma·lay·an** (–LAY·un) *n.* & *adj.* Malay. **—Malay Archipelago** the group of islands between S.E. Asia and Australia, chiefly Indonesia and the Philippines. **—Malay Peninsula** the S.E. Asian peninsula extending from Singapore to the Isthmus of Kra, Thailand. **—Ma·lay·sia** (–LAY–) a S.E. Asian federation of 13 states including most of the Malay Peninsula ("West Malaysia") and "East Malaysia" (Sabah and Sarawak); 127,316 sq. mi. (329,749 km²); *cap.* Kuala Lumpur; **Ma·lay·sian** *n.* & *adj.*

mal·con·tent (MAL·cun–) *n.* & *adj.* (one) who is dissatisfied or rebellious.

mal de mer (–duh·MAIR) *French.* seasickness.

Mal·dive Islands or **Mal·dives** a republic consisting of about 2,000 coral islands in the Indian Ocean, W. of Sri Lanka; 115 sq.mi. (298 km²); *cap.* **Ma·le** (MAH·lay).

male *n.* & *adj.* (a person, animal, plant, or flower) of the kind that fertilizes the female for begetting offspring: *The penis and the stamen are ~ reproductive organs; A ~ plant has only flowers with stamens; A ~ flower has no pistils; a ~* (i.e. projecting) *electrical plug to fit into a female; Feminists fight* **male chauvinism.**

mal·e·dic·tion (–uh·DIC–) *n.* a curse; **mal·e·dic·tor·y** *adj.* **—mal·e·fac·tor** (MAL·uh–) *n.* an evildoer or criminal; *fem.* **mal·e·fac·tress; mal·e·fac·tion** (–FAC–) *n.* **—ma·lef·ic** (–LEF–) *adj.* baleful or malicious; **ma·lef·i·cent** (–snt) *adj.* doing evil; harmful; **ma·lef·i·cence** *n.* **—ma·lev·o·lent** (–LEV·uh–) *adj.* wishing others evil; malicious; **ma·lev·o·lence** *n.* **—mal·fea·sance** (–FEE·zns) *n. Law.* misconduct by a public official. **—mal·for·ma·tion** (–MAY–) *n.* an abnormal or faulty formation of a body (part), as a hunched back; **mal·formed** *adj.* **—mal·func·tion** (–FUNK–) *v.* fail to function properly; ***n.*** a malfunctioning.

Ma·li (MAH·lee) a republic of W. Africa; 478,-767 sq.mi. (1,240,000 km²); *cap.* Bamako. —**Ma·li·an** *n.* & *adj.*

mal·ice (–is) *n.* desire to harm another; **ma·li·cious** (muh·LISH·us) *adj.* spiteful; **ma·li·cious·ly** *adv.* —**ma·lign** (muh·LINE) *v.* speak evil of; slander; ***adj.*** **1** injurious; also, malicious: *a ~ doctrine, influence.* **2** cancerous: *a ~ tumor.* —**ma·lig·nant** (–LIG·nunt) *adj.* **1** malign: *a ~ look, fairy.* **2** likely to spread and prove fatal if not checked; not benign: *a ~ growth, lump in the breast; ~ hypertension, cholera.* —**ma·lig·nan·cy** (–nun·see) *n.;* **ma·lig·ni·ty** *n.*

ma·lin·ger (muh·LING·gur) *v.* pretend illness in order to escape duty; **ma·lin·ger·er** *n.*

mal·i·son *n. Archaic.* malediction.

mall (MAWL) *n.* **1** a broad, parklike walk or promenade, as stretches from the Capitol to the Lincoln Memorial in Washington, D.C. **2** a pedestrians-only street lined with shops; also, such a shopping center but fully covered and air-conditioned.

mal·lard (–urd) *n.* a common wild duck.

mal·le·a·ble (MAL·ee·uh–) *adj.* of metals, that can be hammered or pressed into thin sheets, as gold, silver, copper, etc., not stiff like cast iron; hence, of a character, that can be trained; adaptable; **mal·le·a·bly** *adv.* **mal·le·a·bil·i·ty** (–BIL–) *n.* —**mal·let** (–it) *n.* a hammer with a wooden head, short-handled for driving a chisel or long-handled for use in polo or croquet; **mal·le·us** (MAL·ee–) *n., pl.* **mal·le·i** (–eye) the hammer-shaped outermost bone of the middle ear.

mal·low (MAL·oh) *n.* any of a large family of herbs, shrubs, and trees such as the hibiscus, hollyhock, marshmallow, cotton plant, and okra.

mal·nour·ished (–NUR·isht) *adj.* poorly nourished. —**mal·nu·tri·tion** (–TRISH·un) *n.* a malnourished condition resulting from improper diet. —**mal·oc·clu·sion** (–uh·CLOO–) *n.* improper meeting of teeth because of receding or protruding lower jaw. —**mal·o·dor·ous** (–OH·duh·rus) *adj.* having a bad odor; stinking. —**mal·prac·tice** (–PRAC·tis) *n.* improper conduct or treatment by a professional, esp. neglect of a patient by a physician.

malt (MAWLT) *n.* barley or other grain that is first soaked and allowed to sprout, then kiln-dried and aged for use in beer-making and distilling; ***v.*** change into malt or treat with malt: **malted milk** *is made with dried milk and malt extract powder mixed in milk.*

Mal·ta (MAWL·tuh) an island republic S. of Sicily; 122 sq.mi. (316 km²); *cap.* Valetta. —**Mal·tese** (–TEEZ) *n.* & *adj.*

Mal·thu·sian (–THOO–) *n.* & *adj.* (a believer in the theory) of **Malthus, Thomas R.** 1766–1834, that population increases would result in world food shortages. —**Mal·thu·sian·ism** *n.*

malt liquor beer, ale, etc. made from malt by fermentation. —**malt·ose** (MAWL–) *n.* malt sugar formed from starch by the action of an enzyme.

mal·treat (–TREET) *v.* treat brutally; abuse; **mal·treat·ment** *n.*

mama See MAMMA.

mam·bo (MAHM–) *n.* **-bos** a musical form or dance of Cuban Negro origin.

ma(m)·ma (MAH·muh) *n. Informal.* mother. —**mam·mal** (–ul) *n.* a class of vertebrates such as human beings, dogs, bats, and whales whose females nourish their young with milk from the breast, or **mam·mar·y** (MAM·uh·ree) **gland;** **mam·ma·li·an** (–MAY·lee·un) *n.* & *adj.* —**mam·mog·ra·phy** (–MOG·ruh·fee) *n.* X-ray examination of the breast to detect abnormalities; **mam·mo·gram** *n.*

mam·mon (–mun) *n.* the greedy pursuit of wealth, personified as **Mammon.**

mam·moth (–muth) *n.* a huge prehistoric hairy kind of elephant with large curved tusks; ***adj.*** gigantic; colossal: *a ~ enterprise, undertaking.*

man. manual. —**Man.** Manitoba.

man *n., pl.* **men** **1** an adult human male, in roles such as suitor, husband, servant, follower, or a person with virile qualities: *lived together as ~ and wife; all the king's men; was ~ enough to apologize.* **2** (a member of) the human race; hence, a person or individual: *~ is mortal; a chess ~; The ~ in the street* (i.e. the average person) *doesn't bother about God; Is ~ descended from the apes? fought the invaders* **as one** (or **a**) **man** (i.e. everybody fought); *were wiped out* **to a man** (i.e. all were lost). —***v.*** **mans, manned, man·ning** **1** supply with people, usu. men, for defense or hard work: *Sailors ~ a ship.* **2** put courage into (oneself): *They ~d themselves to face the ordeal.* —***comb. form.*** **1** man: as in *mailman, salesman, countryman.* **2** person: as in *man-eater, manhandle, manpower.* —**man-a·bout-town** *n., pl.* **men-** a man of society who spends much time in clubs, theaters, etc.

Man, Isle of. an island in the Irish Sea, between England and Ireland.

man·a·cle *n.* & *v.* **-cles, -cled, -cling** (restrain with or as if with) handcuffs or fetters, usu. **manacles:** *prisoner in ~s; a ~d press.*

man·age (–ij) *v.* **-ag·es, -aged, -ag·ing** handle or make use of (people, resources, etc.) efficiently: *someone to ~ the sales department; a ~ing editor; a horse difficult to ~* (i.e. control); *seems to ~ well on such a low income;* **man·age·a·ble** *adj.;* **man·age·a·bly** *adv.;* **man·age·a·bil·i·ty** (–BIL–) *n.* —**man·age·ment** *n.* a managing, being managed, or a group of managers: *labor and ~;* **man·age·men·tal** (–MEN·tl) *adj.* —**man·ag·er** *n.;* **man·a·ge·ri·al** (–uh·JEER–) *adj.: a ~ position, responsibility.*

Ma·na·gua (mah·NAH·gwah) capital of Nicaragua.

Ma·na·ma (muh·NAM·uh) capital of Bahrain.

ma·ña·na (muh·NYAH·nuh)*n.* & *adv.* [implying procrastination] tomorrow.

man-at-arms *n., pl.* **men-** a soldier, esp. one heavily armed and mounted.

man·a·tee *n.* a large plant-eating mammal of warm coastal waters and rivers with flippers in front and a flat, rounded tail; also called "sea cow."

Man·ches·ter a seaport of N.W. England.

Man·chu (–choo) *n.* & *adj.* (a member) of a Mongoloid people of Manchuria who ruled China from 1644 to 1912. —**Man·chur·i·a** (–CHOOR·ee·uh) a region of N. E. China; **Man·chur·i·an** *n.* & *adj.*

man·ci·ple *n.* a buyer of provisions for a college or monastery.

man·da·mus (–DAY–) *n.* a writ from a higher court to a lower one or to a public institution or official ordering an action as a matter of duty.

man·da·rin (MAN·duh–) *n.* **1 Mandarin** the most widely spoken form of Chinese, the dialect of N. China. **2** a high military or civil official of the former Chinese empire. **3** a tangerine orange.

man·date *n.* an order or command; hence, authority or commission: *claimed to rule under a ~ from heaven; Britain had a ~ from the League of Nations to administer Iraq, a* **man·dat·ed** *territory; An elected representative gets his ~ from the people.* —**man·da·to·ry** (MAN·duh–) *adj.* having the nature of a mandate; hence, obligatory: *a ~ sentence for manslaughter;* **man·da·to·ri·ly** *adv.*

Man·de (MAHN·day) *n.* & *adj.* (of or having to do with) an ancient Negroid group of peoples of W. Africa or their languages.

man·di·ble *n.* a movable mouth part used for chewing or biting, as the lower jaw in humans, the upper or lower part of a bird's beak, an insect's jawlike appendages, etc. —**man·dib·u·lar** (–DIB·y o–) *adj.*

Man·din·go (–DING–) *n.* one of the Mande group.

man·do·lin (MAN·duh–, –LIN) *n.* a musical instrument with a pear-shaped body like a lute's and four to six pairs of strings; **man·do·lin·ist** (–LIN–) *n.*

man·drake *n.* **1** any of several plants of the nightshade family with a forked root; also **man·drag·o·ra** (–DRAG–) **2** a May apple.

man·drel or **man·dril** (–drul) *n.* a tool-carrying shaft or spindle of a lathe; also, a bar or rod around which metal or glass tubing is shaped.

man·drill *n.* a large W. African baboon whose male has a blue and scarlet face and rump.

mane *n.* the long and heavy hair around the neck of a lion, horse, etc.; **maned** *adj.*

man-eat·er *n.* a cannibal or an animal that eats human flesh, as the tiger or a shark; **man-eat·ing** *adj.*

ma·nege (muh·NEZH) *n.* horsemanship or a trained horse's movements; also, a riding school.

ma·nes (MAY·neez) *n.* the revered spirit of a dead person, like the **Manes,** or dead ancestors, of ancient Romans.

ma·neu·ver (muh·NEW–) *n.* a tactical movement, as of the military or of warships; hence, a skillful use of people, situations, etc. for private ends, as to achieve or escape something; manipulation; stratagem: *political ~s; NATO* **maneuvers** (i.e. military exercises) *in the Atlantic;* **v.:** *~ing for position in a power struggle; managed to ~ the vice-president out of his job; a small car easy to ~ into any parking space;* **ma·neu·ver·a·ble** *adj.*

man Friday See FRIDAY. —**man·ful** *adj.* courageous; resolute; **man·ful·ly** *adv.*

man·ga·nese (MANG·guh–) *n.* a grayish-white metallic chemical element used in alloys such as bronze and steel.

mange (MAINJ) *n.* an itchy skin disease of domestic animals caused by mites.

man·gel(-wur·zel) (MANG·gl·wur–) *n.* a European beet used for livestock feed.

man·ger (MAIN·jur) *n.* a long box or trough for livestock to eat from, as in a stable.

¹man·gle (MANG–) *v.* **-gles, -gled, -gling** tear, hack, or crush so as to mutilate; hence, botch or ruin (something).

²man·gle *n.* & *v.* **-gles, -gled, -gling** (press or smooth linens using) an ironing machine equipped with rollers.

man·go (MANG–) *n.* **-go(e)s** the delicious and sometimes acid, pulpy, kidney-shaped fruit of a tropical tree of the same name.

man·grove (MANG–) *n.* a tropical tree of salty coastal waters that grows in thickets formed by roots sent down from its own branches.

man·gy (MAIN·jee) *adj.* **-gi·er, -gi·est** having the mange; hence, shabby or contemptible; **man·gi·ness** *n.*

man·han·dle *v.* **-dles, -dled, -dling** handle or treat roughly.

Man·hat·tan (–HATN) the smallest borough and the heart of New York City, formed by **Manhattan Island.** —**manhattan** *n.* a cocktail of whiskey and sweet vermouth.

man·hole *n.* a covered hole for access to a sewer, ship's tank, etc. —**man·hood** *n.* the condition of being a man; also, manly character or men collectively (of a country). —**man-hour** *n.* a cost-accounting unit of one hour's work by one person. —**man·hunt** *n.* an organized hunt for a criminal or fugitive.

ma·ni·a (MAY·nee·uh) *n.* a mental disorder characterized by uncontrolled excitement; hence, excessive enthusiasm or a craze; **comb. form.** mania for (a specified thing): as in *dipsomania, kleptomania, megalomania.* —**ma·ni·ac** (MAY·nee–) *n.* & *adj.* wildly insane (person); **ma·ni·a·cal** (muh·NYE·uh·cl) *adj.* —**man·ic** *adj.* like or suffering from mania. —**man·ic-de·pres·sive** (–PRES·iv) *adj.* having to do with a psychosis involving alternating periods of mania and depression; ***n.*** a manic-depressive patient.

man·i·cure *v.* **-cures, -cured, -cur·ing** trim, clean, and polish (fingernails): *a well-~d hand, lawn.* (kept like one's hand). *—n.* the care of the hands; also, a treatment, as given by a **man·i·cur·ist** (–cure–) *n.*

man·i·fest *adj.* plain and clear: *lying ~ to the view; a ~ error, truth; Some thought territorial expansion America's* **manifest destiny** *in the 19th century;* **man·i·fest·ly** *adv.* —**n.** an itemized cargo or passenger list. —***v.*** display; reveal; also, prove: *She ~ed little interest in the proceedings; Her true feelings began to ~ themselves later; the facts as well ~ed by documents;* **man·i·fes·ta·tion** (–TAY–) *n.: wagging its tail in ~ of joy; a strike as a ~ of political support.* —**man·i·fes·to** (–FES·toh) *n.* **-to(e)s** a public declaration of plans or policies, as by a party or government.

man·i·fold *adj.* **1** many and various: *the ~ duties and responsibilities of a job.* **2** having many parts or facets: *his ~ wisdom; a ~ plan, villain.* —***n.*** a pipe fitting with many lateral connections: *an automobile engine's intake ~.* —***v.*** make manifold; also, duplicate, as in making carbon copies.

man·i·kin (MAN·uh·kin) same as MANNEQUIN.

Ma·ni·la (muh·NIL·uh) the leading port and capital of the Philippines. —**Manila hemp** a strong fiber from the leaves of the "Abaca" banana plant, esp. useful for making ropes, formerly also used in **Manila paper,** a tough, buff-colored wrapping paper.

man in the street the average person.

man·i·oc *n.* same as CASSAVA.

ma·nip·u·late (muh·NIP–) *v.* **-lates, -lat·ed, -lat·ing** handle with skill, dexterity, or craftiness: *good at ~ing marionettes; ~d the electorate to get himself elected; accounts ~d in anticipation of the audit;* **ma·nip·u·la·tive** (–l·tiv) *adj.;* **ma·nip·u·la·tor** *n.* —**ma·nip·u·la·tion** (–LAY–) *n.*

Man·i·to·ba (–TOH·buh) a Prairie Province of Canada; 251,000 sq.mi. (650,087 km²); *cap.* Winnipeg.

man·kind (–kined) *n.* the human race; human beings; also, men, as distinguished from women or womankind. —**man·ly** *adj.* **-li·er, -li·est** befitting a man; also, as a man should be; courageous, honorable, etc.: *~ sports; a very ~ youngster;* ***adv.*** in a manly way; **man·li·ness** *n.* —**man-made** *adj.: ~ laws; a ~* (i.e. synthetic) *fiber.*

Mann (MAHN), **Thomas.** 1875–1955, German novelist, moved to the U.S. in 1938.

man·na (MAN·uh) *n.* food dropped from heaven to aid the Israelites in the wilderness; hence, a miraculous supply; also, spiritual nourishment.

manned (MAND) *adj.* controlled by or carrying human beings: *a ~ spacecraft, satellite.*

man·ne·quin (MAN·uh·kin) *n.* a model of the human body, as used to display clothes in shop windows or by artists, tailors, etc.; also, a woman who models clothes for buyers.

man·ner *n.* **1** a way of behaving, esp. one characteristic of a person or conventional within a group: *Children have to learn (good)* **manners;** *bad ~s; his aristocratic ~; Hold your fork in this ~* (i.e. way). **2** kind or sort: *All ~ of* (i.e. every kind of) *people were there.* —**man·nered** *adj.* **1** having a certain way of behaving: *a well-~ child.* **2** artificial; showing a mannerism: *a ~ style, writer.* —**man·ner·ism** *n.* a manner or style that is excessive or peculiar: *"The Madonna of the Long Neck" shows 16th century ~s; French ~s are different from American.* —**man·ner·ly** *adj.* & *adv.* polite(ly); **man·ner·li·ness** *n.*

man·ni·kin (MAN·uh·kin) same as MANNEQUIN.

man·nish *adj.* suggestive of a man's traits or manners; masculine: *her ~ bearing; a ~ way, style;* **man·nish·ly** *adv.;* **man·nish·ness** *n.*

man·noeu·vre *n.* & *v. Brit.* same as MANEUVER.

man of letters an author or literary scholar. —**man-of-war** *n., pl.* **men-** formerly, a warship.

ma·nom·e·ter (muh·NOM–) *n.* an instrument for measuring the pressure exerted by a gas or liquid, as the sphygmomanometer used to take blood pressure.

man·or (MAN·ur) *n.* (the mansion on) a large estate; formerly, the house of a feudal lord, or "lord of the manor"; also **man·or-house; ma·no·ri·al** (–NOR–) *adj.*

man·pow·er *n.* the power of human strength; also, the supply of people for work, including the unemployed and the retired seeking work: *a nation's ~ policies.*

man·qué (mahng·KAY) *adj.* [follows its noun] unfulfilled or frustrated: *a poet ~.*

man·sard *n.* a gambrel roof with ridges on four sides instead of two; also, the story immediately below it.

manse *n.* a parsonage, esp. a Scottish Presbyterian one.

man·ser·vant (–vunt) *n.* **men·ser·vants** a male servant.

man·sion *n.* a stately or imposing residence.

man-size(d) *adj.* full-size or large: *a ~ dinner, job.*

man·slaugh·ter (MAN·slaw–) *n. Law.* the unlawful killing of one human being by another but not with malice as in murder. —**man·slay·er** *n.* one who commits murder or manslaughter.

man·sue·tude (MAN·swi–) *n. Archaic.* gentleness or meekness.

man·ta (–tuh) *n.* **1** a square-shaped scarf worn as a cape by Latin American women. **2** the wide-finned **manta ray** or "devil fish." —**man·teau** (–TOH) *n.* a woman's mantle or cloak. —**man·tel** (–tl) *n.* the framework, often with stone or marble facing, around a fireplace; also, the shelf on top, or **man·tel·piece** *n.* —**man·tel·et** *n.* a woman's short mantle or cape. —**man·til·la** (–TIL·uh) *n.* a light scarf worn on the head by Spanish and Latin American women.

man·tis *n.* **-tis·es** or **-tes** (–teez) any of a family of insects with long forelegs for catching their prey, often seen lifted as if in prayer, hence "praying mantis"; also **man·tid.**

man·tis·sa (–TIS·uh) *n.* the decimal part of a common logarithm.

man·tle *n.* anything that covers or envelops, as a loose outer garment, the burning hood of meshwork covering the flame in a gas lamp, the outer body wall of mollusks that secretes the shell material and forms oyster pearls, the part of the earth between crust and core, etc.: *a ~ of snow on the mountain; ~ of darkness.* **—*v.* -tles, -tled, -tling** cover or be covered, as a pond with scum; also, flush or blush.

man·tra (–truh) *n.* a Hindu or Buddhist sacred utterance or chant.

man·u·al (–yoo·ul) *adj.* involving use of the hands or requiring physical skill; not automatic: *a ~-shift transmission; the* **manual alphabet** *used by deaf-mutes; ~ labor;* **manual training** *in arts and crafts,* **—*n.*** **1** a handbook: *a car owner's ~.* **2** the formal handling routine of a rifle or other weapon; also **manual of arms.** **3** the manual keyboard of an organ. **—man·u·al·ly** *adv.* —**manuf.** manufacture(r); manufacturing. **—man·u·fac·to·ry** *n.* a factory. **—man·u·fac·ture** (–FAC–) *v.* **-tures, -tured, -tur·ing** make from raw materials, esp. by use of machines and on a large scale: *hand-made and ~d goods; Extractive industries supply ~ing industries; natural and ~d gases; a ~d* (i.e. invented) *excuse.* **—*n.*** a product or the act or process of making it: *goods of foreign ~;* **man·u·fac·tur·er** *n.* **—man·u·mit** (–MIT) *v.* **-mits, -mit·ted, -mit·ting** free from slavery; **man·u·mis·sion** (–MISH·un) *n.* **—ma·nure** (–NURE) *n.* & *v.* **-nures, -nured, -nur·ing** (fertilize with) animal excrement such as dung. **—man·u·script** (–yuh–) *adj.* written by hand; ***n.*** something written, not printed: *the typed ~ of a book; an illuminated medieval ~; learned theses lying in ~* (i.e. unpublished).

Manx *n.* & *adj.* (of) the Isle of Man, its inhabitants, or their Celtic language.

man·y (MEN·ee) *adj., comp.* **more,** *superl.* **most** (MOHST) consisting of a large number; numerous: *~ men, things.* **—*n.* & *pron.*** a large number (of persons or things): *A* **good many** *(people) were killed and a* **great many** (i.e. larger number) *were wounded.* **—man·y·fold** *adv.* many times. **—man·y-sid·ed** *adj.* having many sides, aspects, possibilities, etc.

Ma·o·ri (MOU·ree) *n.* a Polynesian native of New Zealand; also, the language of the Maoris; ***adj.:*** *a ~ chief.*

mao tai (MOU·tye) a vodkalike Chinese liquor.

Mao Tse-tung (MOU·dzuh·DOONG) 1893–1976, Chinese communist leader; **Mao·ism** *n.;* **Mao·ist** *n.* & *adj.*

map *n.* a representation of a part of the earth on a plane surface showing the more important places, rivers, mountains, seas, etc.; also, a similar chart of the heavens to show positions of the stars; **on the map** well known; ***v.* maps, mapped, map·ping** make a map of; hence, plan: *to ~ out* (a project, one's time, etc.); **map·per** *n.*

ma·ple (MAY–) *n.* **1** any of over 100 species of shady trees of temperate regions, bearing double-winged seeds, or "keys," and having leaves that grow opposite each other: **maple sugar** *is made from* **maple syrup** *prepared by boiling the sap, esp. of the "sugar maple."* **2** the hard, light-colored wood of the maple; also, the flavor of maple syrup or sugar.

Ma·pu·to (muh·POO·toh) capital of Mozambique.

mar *v.* **mars, marred, mar·ring** spoil the beauty of; damage slightly: *furniture ~d by scratches; Nothing could ~ her happiness.*

mar. maritime. **—Mar.** March.

mar·a·bou (MAIR·uh·boo) *n.* the adjutant stork.

ma·ra·ca (muh·RAH–) *n.* a rattle made of a gourd with seeds or lead inside, used in pairs as a percussion instrument in Latin American countries.

mar·a·schi·no (mair·uh·SKEE·noh, –SHEE–) **cherry** an artificially colored cherry used in desserts and beverages for flavor, originally preserved in **maraschino,** a liqueur made from a black Dalmatian cherry.

mar·a·thon (MAIR·uh–) *n.* **1** an activity requiring great endurance: *a ~ session.* **2** a long-distance (42.2km) foot race, as at the Olympics, like that of the runner who brought the news of victory at **Marathon** in ancient Greece to the Athenians.

ma·raud (muh·RAUD) *v.* raid and plunder; pillage; **ma·raud·er** *n.*

mar·ble *n.* a hard limestone rock, cut for use in architecture and carved into sculptures; also, a small ball of marble, glass, or stone used in the children's game of **marbles** *pl.* **—*adj.*** of or like marble, esp. hard, white, and cold. **—*v.* -bles, -bled, -bling** to color or make like the variegated pattern of marble: *a book's ~d edges; meat with a* **marbling** *of fat;* also **mar·ble·ize, -iz·es, -ized, -iz·ing:** *a ~d candle.*

mar·cel (–SEL) *n.* & *v.* **-cels, -celled, -cel·ling** (set the hair in) a flat wave, as was once popular in France.

March *n.* the third month of the year, with 31 days.

[1]march *v.* walk in military style; hence, progress steadily: *could hear the troops ~ing outside; She ~ed out of the room as if displeased; At the alarm, ~ the children out in single file; History ~es on;* **marching orders** dismissal. **—*n.:*** *We'll be* **on the march** (i.e. moving along) *after breakfast; It's a day's ~ to the camp; A slow ~ suits a funeral procession; "The Stars and Stripes Forever" is a ~;* **stole a march on** *us by camping out near the box office to buy the first ticket; a* **march-past** *of troops in review.*

²march *n.* a border or frontier (district), as the **Marches** of Wales or Scotland separating it from England. —**marchioness** See MARQUIS.

Mar·co·ni (–COH·nee), **Guglielmo.** 1874–1937, Italian inventor of radio.

Mar·di Gras (MAR·dee·GRAH) carnival celebration of Shrove Tuesday in the French tradition, as in New Orleans.

¹mare *n.* a mature female horse, donkey, etc.; **mare's nest** a "discovery" that turns out to be deceptive; also, a mess.

²ma·re (MAIR·ee) *n., pl.* **-ri·a** one of the dark, flat areas of the moon or Mars, once thought to be seas.

mar·ga·rine (MAR·juh·rin, –reen) *n.* a butter substitute made from animal fats and vegetable oils; oleo.

marge or **mar·gent** (–junt) *n. Archaic.* margin or border. —**mar·gin** (–jin) *n.* an edge or border, as the blank space around the written or printed matter on a page: *won the election by a narrow* ~ (i.e. small majority or plurality); *within the allowed* ~ *of error; a price markup with a large* ~ *of profit;* **mar·gin·al** *adj.:* ~ *differences, land* (whose yield will barely cover costs); **mar·gin·al·ly** *adv.* —**mar·gi·na·li·a** (–NAY–) *n.pl.* notes in the margins.

mar·grave *n.* formerly, a German title for the governor of a border province.

mar·gue·rite (–guh·REET) *n.* a species of daisy.

ma·ri·a·chi (mar·ee·AH·chee) *n.* **-chis** an itinerant Mexican band of musicians and singers; also, their music or a member of the group.

Mar·i·an (MAIR–) *adj.* of the Virgin Mary.

Ma·rie An·toi·nette (muh·REE·an·twuh·NET) 1755–93, Louis XVI's queen, guillotined during the French Revolution.

mar·i·gold (MAIR–) *n.* a garden plant related to chrysanthemums with usu. orange or yellow flower heads.

mar·i·jua·na or **mar·i·hua·na** (mair·uh·WAH·nuh) *n.* a drug prepared from the hemp plant, less strong than hashish, smoked as a narcotic.

ma·rim·ba (muh·RIM·buh) *n.* an African type of xylophone, having resonating tubes or gourds underneath the wooden bars for a richer tone.

ma·ri·na (muh·REE·nuh) *n.* a small harbor for pleasure craft with service and restaurant facilities. —**mar·i·nade** (–NADE) *n.* a spicy solution or sauce to tenderize meat or add flavor to foods; ***v.*** **-nades, -nad·ed, -nad·ing** or **mar·i·nate** (MAIR–) **-nates, -nat·ed, -nat·ing:** *marinated leg of lamb;* **mar·i·na·tion** (–NAY–) *n.* —**ma·rine** (muh·REEN) *adj.* of the sea; nautical; naval: *a* ~ *fish, propeller;* ~ *biology, engineering, insurance;* ***n.*** **1** a soldier specially trained for assault operations by sea and land; **Marine** a member of the U.S. Navy's **Marine Corps. 2** the ships of a country collectively: *the merchant* ~. —**mar·i·ner** (MAIR–) *n.* a sailor.

mar·i·o·nette (–ee·uh·NET) *n.* a puppet controlled by strings or wires held by the puppeteer hidden above the stage.

mar·i·tal (MAIR·i·tl) *adj.* of marriage; conjugal: ~ *vows, bliss, tax deduction;* **mar·i·tal·ly** *adv.*

mar·i·time (MAIR–) *adj.* near the sea; seafaring: *a* ~ *nation; Canada's* ~ *provinces;* ~ *laws* (of shipping and navigation).

mar·jo·ram (MAR·juh·rum) *n.* an aromatic herb of the mint family used for flavoring foods.

Mark in the Bible, the second Gospel or its reputed author, St. Mark.

¹mark a German money unit, either the ostmark of East Germany or the deutsche mark of West Germany, both equal to 100 pfennigs.

²mark *n.* **1** a scratch, spot, trace, etc. made on an object: *an "X"* ~*; a punctuation* ~*; "On your* ~*, get set, go!" He* **made his mark** (i.e. gained recognition) *as an inventor.* **2** a target or goal; standard; person or thing aimed at: *I don't feel up to the* ~ *on Monday mornings; Her replies to questions were all off the* ~*; Drunks are easy* ~*s* (i.e. victims) *for pickpockets.* **3** indication of some quality; also, a rating or grade: *the* ~ *of a gentleman; high* ~*s in history.* —***v.:*** *a face* ~*ed by scars; Fireworks* ~*ed the end of the celebrations;* ~ (i.e. note) *my words well; items* **marked down** *for quick sale; She's* **marking time** (i.e. waiting) *for the right moment to spring the surprise;* **mark·er** *n.* —**mark·down** *n.* a price reduction; also, its amount. —**marked** *adj.* easily distinguished: ~ *differences of color; a* ~ *man with no chance of escape* (from attack, suspicion, etc.); **mark·ed·ly** *adv.* noticeably; plainly.

mar·ket (–kit) *n.* a place for buying and selling goods, or **mar·ket·place;** also, the people in it, trade activity, demand for or supply of goods, etc.: *farmers driving to* ~*; a lively* ~*; priced right out of the* ~*; no* ~ *for air conditioners in the winter; I'm* **in the market** *for* (i.e. interested in buying) *a new car every few years; Excess supply creates a buyer's* ~ *with low prices.* —***v.:*** *the art of* ~*ing used cars; a talent that is difficult to* ~*;* **mar·ket·a·ble** *adj.* —**mar·ket·et** *n.*

mark·ing *n.* a mark, marks, or their arrangement, as on a bird or animal.

mark·ka (–kah) *n., pl.* **-kaa** (–kah) the basic money unit of Finland, equal to 100 pennia.

marks·man (–mun) *n.* **-men** one who shoots, esp. a skilled one; **marks·man·ship** *n.;* **marks·wom·an** *n.* **-wom·en.**—**mark·up** *n.* (amount of) increase in price of an article; also, (the percentage) amount added to the cost of a product in determining its selling price.

marl *n.* a soil mixture of clay, sand, and calcium carbonate, as "shell marl" or "greensand marl," used for fertilizer.

mar·lin *n.* a kind of large marine game fish with a spear like a swordfish's; also called "spearfish." —**mar·lin(e)·spike** (MAR·lin–)

n. a pointed iron tool used by sailors to separate strands of rope.

mar·ma·lade (MAR·muh–) *n.* a clear jelly made of a fruit such as orange and pieces of its rind.

mar·mo·re·al (–MOR·ee·ul) *adj.* of or like marble; smooth, white, cold, etc.; also **mar·mo·re·an.**

mar·mo·set (MAR·muh·zet) *n.* a small, thick-furred, long-tailed monkey of S. and C. America.

mar·mot (–mut) *n.* any of a large group of rodents of the squirrel family including woodchucks; a ground squirrel.

[1]ma·roon (muh·ROON) *n.* & *adj.* (of) a very dark brownish red.

[2]ma·roon *v.* be left stranded and helpless: *people ~ed on rooftops by a flood.* **—n.** one left marooned like fleeing black slaves on West Indian islands in the 18th century; also, such a slave: *The British and the Jamaican Maroons signed a peace treaty in 1738.*

mar·plot *n.* one that mars or spoils a plan by blundering or interfering.

marque (MARK) *n.* make of automobile: *the Mercedes ~.* **—mar·quee** (–KEE) *n.* a canopy over an entrance, as of a theater or hotel; also, a large tent. **—mar·quess** (–kwis) *n. Brit.* marquis. **—mar·que·try** (MAR·kuh·tree) *n.* decorative inlaid work on furniture with patterns of wood, metal, shell, mother-of-pearl, etc. **—mar·quis** *n.* a nobleman ranking below a duke and above an earl or count; *fem.* **mar·quise** (–KEEZ) or **mar·chio·ness** (MAR·shuh·nis), *Brit.* **—mar·qui·sette** (–ki·ZET, –kwuh–) *n.* a sheer, meshed fabric used for mosquito nets, curtains, etc.

mar·riage (MAIR·ij) *n.* **1** a marrying or similar close union. **2** a wedding. **3** wedlock; married life: *a long and happy ~.* **—mar·riage·a·ble** *adj.* **—mar·ried** (MAIR·eed) *n.* & *adj.* (of) a married person: *~ bliss, life, woman, couples; newly ~s* (i.e. married couples); *young ~s.*

mar·row (MAIR·oh) *n.* the soft fatty substance filling the cavities of bones; hence, the best or inmost part: *felt chilled to the ~; a* **mar·row·bone** *soup.*

mar·ry (MAIR·ee) *v.* **mar·ries, mar·ried, mar·ry·ing** take as husband or wife; also, unite, as a minister does at a wedding: *Parents used to* **marry off** *their girls; a much-~d celebrity.*

Mars *n.* the planet nearest the earth and fourth from the sun, named after the Roman god of war.

Mar·seil·laise (–suh·LAIZ) *n.* France's national anthem. **—Mar·seille** (mar·SAY) French name of **Mar·seilles** (–SAY, –SAILS), France's greatest seaport, on the Mediterranean.

marsh *n.* a tract of low, hence often wet, soft land; swamp; bog; **marsh·y** *adj.* **marsh·i·er, -i·est.**

mar·shal (–shul) *n.* **1** in the U.S., an officer of a federal court assigned to a district; also, a chief police officer or an official of the fire department. **2** an army officer of the highest rank; also, a field marshal. **3** an official in charge of parades, processions, etc. **—v. -shals, -shal(l)ed, -shal·(l)ing** usher or present in an orderly fashion: *to ~ forces, facts, arguments, people* (as into a royal presence).

Mar·shall (–shul) **1 George C.** 1880–1959, American General who proposed the **Marshall Plan** for Europe's economic recovery after World War II. **2 John.** 1755–1835, U.S. Supreme Court Chief Justice.

marsh gas methane. **—marsh·mal·low** (–mel·oh, –mal·oh) *n.* a soft, white, spongy candy made from corn syrup, sugar, albumen, and gelatin, originally made from the root of the marsh mallow plant. **—marsh marigold** a marsh plant of the buttercup family with bright yellow flowers.

mar·su·pi·al (–SOO·pee·ul) *n.* & *adj.* (a mammal such as the kangaroo, koala, or opossum) that carries its young in a pouch outside the mother's body.

mart *n.* marketplace or center of trade.

mar·ten *n.* (the soft, thick fur of) a weasellike animal.

mar·tial (–shul) *adj.* of war; warlike: *~ spirit, bearing, music, arts such as karate and judo;* **martial law** military rule imposed on civilians in a crisis. **—mar·tial·ly** *adv.* **—Mar·tian** *n.* & *adj.* (a supposed inhabitant) of Mars.

mar·tin (–tn) *n.* any of several birds of the swallow family, esp. the "purple martin" with long, pointed wings and forked tail.

mar·ti·net (–tn·ET) *n.* a very rigid disciplinarian: *a ~ of an editor.*

mar·tin·gale *n.* a strap of a horse's harness fastening the nose-band to the girth for preventing rearing.

mar·ti·ni (–TEE·nee) *n.* **-nis** a cocktail made of gin or vodka and dry vermouth.

mar·tyr (–tur) *n.* one who suffers much because of his beliefs or principles, as the early Christians put to death for their faith: *a ~ to the cause of freedom.* **—v.** cause to suffer or be killed as a martyr. **—mar·tyr·dom** (–dum) *n.*

mar·vel (–vl) *n.* & *v.* **-vels, -vel(l)ed, -vel·(l)ing** (something that causes one) to be filled with astonishment; wonder; also, express wonder at: *a ~ of architectural achievement; Everyone ~s at her patience.* **—mar·vel·ous** (–us) *adj.* wonderful; incredible; splendid; also, *esp. Brit.* **mar·vel·lous; mar·vel·lous·ly** *adv.;* **mar·vel·ous·ness** *n.*

Marx, Karl. 1818–83, German political philosopher and founder of modern socialism. **—Marx·ism** *n.* a theory of class struggles leading to inevitable communism, as developed by Marx and Engels; **Marx·ist** or **Marx·i·an** *n.* & *adj.*

Mar·y (MAIR·ee) the mother of Jesus. —**Mary Jane** *Slang.* marijuana. —**Mar·y·land** (–lund) a S.E. state of the U.S.; 10,577 sq.mi. (27,394 km²); *cap.* Annapolis. —**Mary Magdalene** the woman out of whom Jesus cast seven demons, identified with the penitent woman pardoned by Jesus.

mar·zi·pan *n.* an almond-flavored candy shaped into fruits, meats, and toys.

mas. or **masc.** masculine.

mas·ca·ra (–CAIR·uh) *n.* cosmetic coloring for the eyelashes, eyebrows, etc. —***v.* -ras, -raed, -ra·ing.**

mas·con (MAS–) *n.* "mass concentration" of dense material in places on the moon's surface, posited to explain differences in gravity.

mas·cot *n.* a person, animal, or thing kept as a source of good luck.

mas·cu·line (MAS·kyuh·lin) *n.* & *adj.* (a gender, word, or form) that refers to or is considered distinctive of the male: *~ courage, aggressiveness; a ~ voice; the ~ gender of "moon" in German; "He," "his," "him" are ~s;* **mas·cu·lin·i·ty** (–LIN–) *n.*

ma·ser (MAY·zur) *n.* an electronic device that emits and amplifies microwaves.

Mas·e·ru (MAZ·uh·roo) capital of Lesotho.

mash *n.* & *v.* (reduce to) a soft, pulpy mass, as of crushed malt or grain in hot water in making beer, whiskey, etc. or of bran or meal in water for feeding horses: *a dish of ~ed potatoes; a finger ~ed* (i.e. crushed) *by a door.*

M.A.S.H. or **MASH** mobile army surgical hospital.

mash·er *n.* **1** one that mashes. **2** *Slang.* a man who frequently makes passes at women.

mask *n.* & *v.* (cover or conceal as with) an artificial likeness of a person's face or a piece of material worn over part of the face: *a Halloween ~; a* **death mask** (i.e. wax or plaster cast of a dead person's face); *a gas ~; Surgeons, fencers, and baseball catchers wear ~s; a* **masked** *gunman; ~ed dancers at a* **masked ball;** *A painter protects certain areas using* **masking tape;** *a hypocrite wearing the ~ of friendship; tried to ~ her true feelings by smiling; a* **mask·er** *taking part in a masquerade.*

mas·och·ism (–uh·kizm) *n.* the pleasure or sexual satisfaction derived from one's own pain and suffering. —**mas·och·ist** *n.;* **mas·och·is·tic** (–KIS–) *adj.;* **mas·och·is·ti·cal·ly** *adv.*

ma·son (MAY·sn) *n.* one who builds with stone, clay, brick, or concrete; **Mason** same as FREEMASON; **Ma·son·ic** or **ma·son·ic** (–SON–) *adj.* —**Ma·son-Dix·on line** the S. boundary of Pennsylvania, once the dividing line between N. states and the slave states of the South. —**mason jar** a tight-closing glass jar used in home canning; also **Mason jar.** —**ma·son·ry** (–sn·ree) *n.* **-ries** **1** a structure built by a mason, as stonework or brickwork. **2** a mason's trade or skill; **Masonry** same as FREEMASONRY.

masque (MASK) *n.* a theater entertainment of the 1600's having an allegorical theme, with actors wearing masks, and characterized by singing, dancing, and pageantry; also, a masked ball or masquerade: *a Twelfth Night court ~.* —**mas·quer·ade** (–kuh·RAID) *n.* a party at which masks and fancy costumes are worn; hence, a disguise or false pretense; ***v.* -ades, -ad·ed, -ad·ing:** *Princes used to ~ as paupers; charlatans ~ing* (i.e. posing) *as physicians;* **mas·quer·ad·er** *n.*

¹Mass or **mass** *n.* a Roman Catholic celebration of the Eucharist: *one of Palestrina's ~es* (i.e. musical settings of the Mass).

²mass *n.* **1** bulk or quantity of matter, esp. large; large size or number; also, the greater part or majority: *An elephant's body has ~; The ~ of an iceberg is under water; Individuals showed interest, but* **in the mass** (i.e. as a whole) *people didn't care.* **2** an amount or lump; expanse: *a small ~ of dough; a chimney spewing ~es of smoke; The flower beds were ~es of color; a politician's appeal to* **the masses** (i.e. common people). —***adj.:*** *a ~ meeting of citizens; a crowd seized with ~ hysteria; ~* (i.e. large-scale) *buying.* —***v.*** form or gather into a mass: *troops ~ed along a border.*

Mass. *Abbrev.* for **Mas·sa·chu·setts** (mas·uh·CHOO·sits) a New England state; 8,257 sq.mi. (21,385 km²); *cap.* Boston.

mas·sa·cre (MAS·uh·cur) *n.* a large-scale, esp. merciless slaughter of people or animals. —***v.* -cres, -cred, -cring:** *innocent infants ~d by Herod.*

mas·sage (muh·SAHZH, –SAHJ) *n.* a rubdown of the body or a part by kneading, stroking, etc. for relaxing muscles or stimulating activity in an organ: *a cardiac ~; a body rub in a* **massage parlor** *featuring nudes.* —***v.* mas·sag·es, mas·saged, mas·sag·ing** give a massage to; **mas·sag·er** or **mas·sag·ist** *n.* Also **mas·seur** (–SUR) *n., fem.* **mas·seuse** (–SOOZ).

mass-cult *n. Informal.* popular culture as spread through television and other mass media.

mas·sif (MAS·if, ma·SEEF) *n.* a compact group of mountains and peaks. —**mas·sive** (–iv) *adj.* having a large mass; large in quantity, scope, or degree: *a man of ~ build; ~ rocks; a ~ assault, hemorrhage; threat of ~ retaliation using atomic weapons; a ~* (i.e. impressive) *structure;* **mas·sive·ly** *adv.;* **mas·sive·ness** *n.;* **mass·less** *adj.: the ~ neutrino particle.* —**mass-mar·ket paperback** a paperback edition in the size 4 × 7 in. (10.16 × 17.78 cm) for sale through newsstands, supermarkets, etc. —**mass medium** a medium of communication with the masses, as motion pictures, newspapers, magazines, radio, or television, collectively **(mass) media** [usu. with *pl.v.*] —**mass-pro·duce** (–DUCE) *n.* **-duc·es, -duced, -duc·**

ing produce on a large scale, esp. by use of machinery; **mass production.**

¹mast *n.* fallen nuts of forest trees serving as food for swine.

²mast *n.* a long vertical pole or spar supporting a ship's sails, yards, rigging, etc.; also, any supporting post, as of a flagpole, crane, derrick, aerial, or antenna.

mas·tec·to·my (–TEC–) *n.* **-mies** surgical removal of a breast.

mas·ter *n.* **1** a person with power or authority, as the male head of a household, the captain of a merchant ship, a male teacher or tutor esp. in Britain, the owner of a slave, etc.; **Master** [courtesy title for a boy not old enough for "Mister"]. **2** a great artist, musician, or author; also, one who has reached a high level of learning or skill: *the old ~s* (i.e. great painters before 1700); *apprentices, journeymen, and ~s; a golf ~; a bachelor working on her ~'s* (i.e. university degree). **3** a controlling source or original, as the matrix of a phonograph record or a duplicating stencil or plate. ***—adj.:*** *a ~ plumber; a ~ bedroom, switch* (i.e. main); *the ~ tape* (of a motion picture). ***—v.*** become master of or expert in: *She has ~ed her subject; learning to ~ her temper; Can man ~ the elements?* **—mas·ter·ful** *adj.* domineering, esp. by force of personality; also, masterly: *the ~ Sherlock Holmes; a ~ performance;* **mas·ter·ful·ly** *adv.* **—master key** a key that opens many locks. **—mas·ter·ly** *adj.* & *adv.* expert(ly); skillful(ly): *a ~ command of the language; a ~ executed work.* **—mas·ter·mind** *n.* one who plans and directs an operation or enterprise; ***v.:*** *a plot ~ed by the Kremlin.* **—master of ceremonies** **1** one in charge of the formalities of a ceremonial function, as at a church service. **2** one who hosts an entertainment program or banquet, introducing guests, performers, etc. **—mas·ter·piece** *n.* a masterly piece of workmanship; one's greatest work. **—master plan** an overall or general plan, as of a city. **—master sergeant** a high-ranking noncommissioned officer of the U.S. Army, Air Force, or Marine Corps. **—mas·ter·ship** *n.* the position or function of a master; also, expert knowledge or authority. **—mas·ter·stroke** *n.* a masterly action or its effect: *a ~ of genius.* **—mas·ter·work** *n.* a masterpiece. **—mas·ter·y** *n.* **-ter·ies** command or control: *her ~ of Latin; an election giving one party ~* (i.e. the upper hand) *over another.*

mast·head (–hed) *n.* **1** the top of a ship's mast. **2** in a newspaper or magazine, the title, address, etc. usu. carried at the top of the editorial page; also, the "flag" or name plate at the top of the front page.

mas·tic *n.* the pale yellowish resin of a Mediterranean tree used for caulking and in varnishes, plasters, etc. **—mas·ti·cate** *v.* **-cates, -cat·ed, -cat·ing** chew (food) or crush (rubber) to a pulp; **mas·ti·ca·tion** (–CAY–) *n.*

mas·tiff *n.* an ancient breed of dog with a broad head, drooping ears, and short muzzle.

mas·to·don (MAS·tuh–) *n.* a huge extinct type of elephant with distinctive nipplelike projections on its molars. **—mas·toid** *n.* & *adj.* (having to do with) a bony projection behind the ear: *a ~ infection.*

mas·tur·bate *v.* **-bates, -bat·ed, -bat·ing** stimulate the genitals (of) for sexual pleasure; **mas·tur·ba·tor** *n.;* **mas·tur·ba·tion** (–BAY–) *n.*

¹mat *n.* **1** a plaited, woven, or felted piece of coarse material or small rug for use on the floor as covering, protective padding, for wiping shoes upon, etc.: *a door ~; bath ~; a place ~* (for table settings). **2** a thick tangle or knotted condition: *a ~ of messy hair.* ***—v.*** **mats, mat·ted, mat·ting:** *~d hair; a wall ~d with ivy.*

²mat *n.* & *v.* **mats, mat·ted, mat·ting** **1** (put) a border or background, as for a picture in framing it. **2** (give) a dull surface or finish (to metals, glass, colors, etc.); ***adj.*** of a surface, without gloss or luster; rough.

³mat *n. Informal.* matrix (printer's mold).

mat·a·dor (MAT·uh–) *n.* a bullfighter.

¹match *n.* **1** a person or thing that is like another, hence considered in an equal or opposite role: *A flyweight is no ~ for a heavyweight; a good ~ as husband and wife.* **2** a matching or mating, as a contest or a marriage: *a football ~.* ***—v.:*** *Red and green contrast, they don't ~; Her beauty is ~ed by her wit;* **matching funds** *to induce the recipient to come up with half the project's costs.* **—match·less** *adj.* without equal; peerless.

²match *n.* **1** a splinter of wood or a cardboard strip tipped with a substance that will catch fire under friction, as when struck on the specially prepared surface of a "safety match." **2** in muskets and such **match·lock** guns, a wick or cord lighted to set off the powder charge. **—match·book** *n.* a folder of safety matches.

match·mak·er *n.* **1** one who makes matches for burning. **2** one who arranges marriages or boxing matches. **—match·mak·ing** *n.*

match·wood *n.* pine, aspen, and such wood splintered for making "match sticks."

mate *v.* **mates, mat·ed, mat·ing** join as a pair or couple, esp. in sexual union: *a frog's ~ing call; Some animals don't ~ in captivity; A queen bee ~s with a drone.* ***—n.*** **1** either individual of a matched pair or couple; also, a companion: *Where is the ~ to this sock?* **2** an assistant or helper; also, a deck officer of a merchant ship or a naval petty officer.

ma·té or **ma·te** (MAH·tay, MAT·ay) *n.* an aromatic tea made from the leaves of a South American holly and drunk from a gourd container.

ma·te·ri·al (muh·TEER·ee·ul) *n.* basic matter or resource from which other things may be made: *raw ~(s); writing ~s such as paper and pencil; gathered enough ~ for a book; She's promota-*

ble because she's executive ~. —***adj.*** **1** physical and tangible, not spiritual or ideal; hence, worldly or tending to corrupt: *the ~ world; ~ well-being, possessions, comforts, greed.* **2** having substance or importance: *evidence, facts, testimony ~ to a case or argument.* —**ma·te·ri·al·ism** *n.* a theory, doctrine, or tendency that stresses matter and material aspects to the prejudice of the intellectual and the spiritual; **ma·te·ri·al·ist** *n.* & *adj.;* **ma·te·ri·al·is·tic** (–IS–) *adj.;* **ma·te·ri·al·is·ti·cal·ly** *adv.* —**ma·te·ri·al·ize** (–TEER–) *v.* **-iz·es, -ized, -iz·ing** take material form or give material form to; also, be realized: *impractical plans that don't ~; A spirit may ~ at a séance;* **ma·te·ri·al·i·za·tion** (–ZAY–) *n.* —**ma·te·ri·al·ly** *adv.* —**ma·te·ri·el** or **ma·té·ri·el** (–teer·ee·EL) *n.* military or industrial equipment, supplies, etc. as distinguished from manpower.

ma·ter·nal (–TUR·nl) *adj.* **1** motherly: *the ~ instinct.* **2** on or from the mother's side of the family: *a ~ aunt, grandfather, inheritance.* —**ma·ter·nal·ly** *adv.* —**ma·ter·ni·ty** *n.* & *adj.* (having to do with) motherhood: *a hospital's ~ ward; ~ benefits, wear* (for the pregnant).

math. mathematical; mathematician; mathematics. —**math** *n.* short for **math·e·mat·ics** (–uh·MAT–) *n.pl.* [takes *sing.v.*] a science dealing with quantities and their relationships using numbers, as in arithmetic, symbols, as in algebra, and figures, as in geometry; **math·e·mat·i·cal** *adj.;* **math·e·mat·i·cal·ly** *adv.* —**math·e·ma·ti·cian** (–TISH·un) *n.*

mat·i·nee or **mat·i·née** (mat·n·AY) *n.* an afternoon performance of a play, opera, motion picture, etc. —**mat·ins** (MAT·nz) *n.pl.* a morning prayer service.

Ma·tisse (mah·TEES), **Henri.** 1869–1954, French painter.

matri- *comb.form.* mother: as in **ma·tri·arch** (MAY·tree·arc) *n.* a mother who is the head of a family, tribe, etc.; **ma·tri·ar·chy** *n.* **-chies.** —**ma·tri·ar·chal** (–AR·cul) *adj.* —**ma·tri·cide** (MAT·ruh–, MAY–) *n.* one who kills his mother; also, the crime; **ma·tri·ci·dal** (–SYE·dl) *adj.* —**ma·tric·u·late** (–TRIC·yoo–) *v.* **-lates, -lat·ed, -lat·ing** enroll in or be admitted to a college as a student; **ma·tric·u·la·tion** (–LAY–) *n.* —**mat·ri·mo·ny** (MAT·ruh·moh·nee) *n.* **-nies** marriage, esp. as a sacrament; also, the married state; **mat·ri·mo·ni·al** (–MOH–) *adj.* —**ma·trix** (MAY–) *n., pl.* **-tri·ces** (–seez) or **-trix·es** a mold by which something is formed or shaped, as the skin at the base of a fingernail, the rock or groundmass in which crystals are found embedded, a female die for casting types, or a papier-mâché impression for making printing plates. —**ma·tron** (MAY·trun) *n.* a mature woman in a supervisory role, as in a hospital, dormitory, jail, or school; **ma·tron·ly** *adv.* —**matron of honor** a married woman as chief bridesmaid.

Matt. Matthew.

matte (MAT) *n.* **1** unrefined metal, as copper, that sinks to the bottom of a smelter. **2** dull surface of finish; mat; ***adj.:*** *a ~ photographic print, projection screen;* also **matt:** *a semimatt print; v.* **mats, mat·ted, mat·ting.**

mat·ter (MAT·ur) *n.* **1** material or substance that makes up something, esp. physical: *Solid, liquid, and gas are states in which ~ exists; the mind's sway over ~; foreign ~* (i.e. material). **2** a subject of thought, speech, activity, etc.: *business ~s; a ~ of common knowledge; a ~ of life and death; What's the ~?* (i.e. What's wrong?). **3** material or things: *printed ~; reading ~; postal ~ classified as second-class.* —**as a matter of fact** actually. —**no matter** regardless of: *No ~ who asks you, refuse; I forget who said it, but it's no ~* (i.e. not important); ***v.*** have importance; count: *Does it ~ who said it? It ~s little.* —**mat·ter-of-fact** *adj.* factual; also, prosaic: *a ~ tone of voice;* **mat·ter-of-fact·ly** *adv.;* **mat·ter-of-fact·ness** *n.*

Mat·thew (MATH·yoo) in the Bible, the first Gospel or its reputed author, St. Matthew, an apostle of Christ.

mat·tock (–uk) *n.* a digging and cutting implement resembling a pickax but with a flat blade.

mat·tress *n.* a padding of straw, foam rubber, etc. to sleep on, usu. on a bed; also, an air mattress.

mat·u·ra·tion (mach·oo·RAY–) *n.* maturing process; **mat·u·ra·tion·al** *adj.;* **mat·u·ra·tive** *adj.* —**ma·ture** (muh·TURE, –CHOOR) *adj.* **-tur·er, -tur·est** fully developed or grown; ripe: *~ fruits; a ~ youth; her ~ wisdom; a ~ wine; a bond that will be ~* (i.e. due for payment) *in 10 years.* —***v.*** **-tures, -tured, -tur·ing:** *Some ~ faster than others; A wine has to ~ to have body.* —**ma·ture·ly** *adv.* —**ma·tu·ri·ty** (–TURE–, –CHOOR–) *n.* matured condition.

ma·tu·ti·nal (–TUE–) *adj.* of the morning; early in the day.

mat·zo (MAHT·suh, –soh) *n., pl.* **-zoth** (–sote) or **-zos** (a piece of) unleavened bread eaten at the Passover.

maud·lin *adj.* sentimental in a tearful or silly way: *a ~ soap opera; gets ~ when drunk.*

maul *n.* a heavy mallet or hammer for driving stakes, wedges, etc. —***v.*** bruise or mangle; also, handle roughly: *~ed by a tiger, critics;* **maul·er** *n.*

maun·der *v.* talk or act in a rambling or confused manner; **maun·der·er** *n.*

Mau·pas·sant (MOH·puh·sahnt), **Guy de.** 1850–93, French novelist.

Mau·re·ta·ni·a (–ruh·TAY–) ancient region of Africa N. of the Atlas Mountains. —**Mau·ri·ta·ni·a** (–ruh·TAY–) a republic of W. Africa; 397,956 sq.mi. (1,030,700 km^2); *cap.* Nouakchott.

Mau·ri·ti·us (–RISH·us) island country E. of Madagascar in the Indian Ocean; 720 sq.mi. (1,865 km^2); *cap.* Port Louis.

mau·so·le·um (–suh·LEE–, –zuh–) *n.* **-le·ums** or **-le·a** a magnificent tomb built above ground, as the Taj Mahal or the original Mausoleum of Halicarnassus, Turkey, one of the "seven wonders" of the ancient world.

mauve (MOHV, MAUV) *n.* & *adj.* (dye) of a delicate shade of purple or violet.

mav·er·ick (MAV·uh–) *n.* & *adj. Informal.* nonconformist, esp. in politics; originally, an unbranded calf from the herd of Samuel Maverick of Texas.

ma·vin or **ma·ven** (MAY–) *n. Informal.* expert; connoisseur.

ma·vis (MAY–) *n.* the European "song thrush."

maw *n.* the oral cavity through which a bird, animal, machine, etc. devours something.

mawk·ish *adj.* sentimental in an excessive or insincere style: *a ~ scene from Dickens;* **mawk·ish·ly** *adv.;* **mawk·ish·ness** *n.*

max. maximum. —**max·i** (MAK·see) *n., adj.* & *comb.form, pl.* **max·is** maximum; very long: *a miniskirt under a maxicoat; A dress of ~ length is a ~; a* (very large) *~-taxi.*

max·il·la (–SIL·uh) *n., pl.* **-il·lae** (–lee) the upper jaw bone; also, either of a pair of insect mouth-parts used for handling food. —**max·il·lar·y** (MAX–) *adj.* & *n.* **-il·lar·ies:** *the ~ bone; The mandible is the inferior ~.*

max·im *n.* a proverb or precept, esp. a practical rule of conduct, as "A stitch in time saves nine." —**max·i·ma** a *pl.* of MAXIMUM. —**max·i·mize** *v.* **-miz·es, -mized, -miz·ing** magnify or increase to the utmost; intensify highly: *to ~ profits with minimum output; stayed long enough on the job to ~ his pension before retiring.* —**max·i·mum** *n.* & *adj.* (of) the greatest possible or attained (quantity, number, value, etc.): *the ~ (speed limit) on a highway; yesterday's ~ temperature; a ~-security prison;* **max·i·mal** *adj.;* **max·i·mal·ly** *adv.*

May *n.* the fifth month of the year, having 31 days.

may auxiliary *v., pt.* **might** (MITE) **1** [expressing possibility]: *I ~ be late; You might have asked yesterday; It ~ rain tonight; then again it might not.* **2** [expressing permission]: *You ~ eat; ~ I have an apple?* **3** [expressing hope, contingency, etc.]: *I work so that you ~ be happy; ~ you be happy!*

Ma·ya (MAH·yuh) *n.* one of a highly civilized tribe of Central American Indians or their language; **Ma·yan** *n.* & *adj.*

May apple a North American perennial herb of the barberry family that grows in shady areas, has dark-green, umbrellalike leaves with five to seven lobes and a white flower, and whose roots are often used as a purgative.

may·be (–bee) *adv.* perhaps.

May Day May 1, a spring festival in some countries; also, labor day in socialist countries. —**May·day** *n.* a distress signal used by ships and aircraft to radio for help. —**may·flow·er** *n.* a plant that flowers in early spring, esp. the trailing arbutus or an anemone; **Mayflower** the ship that brought the Pilgrims to America in 1620. —**may·fly** *n.* **-flies** a short-lived, four-winged fly of ponds and streams, common in early spring, serving as food for fish; also called "day fly." Also **May fly.**

may·hem (MAY·hem, –um) *n.* **1** *Law.* crime of violence that maims a person. **2** violent or willful damage.

may·n't (MAINT) may not.

may·o (MAY·oh) short for **may·on·naise** (MAY·uh·naze) *n.* a thick salad dressing made of egg yolks.

may·or (–ur) *n.* the elected head of a city or borough; *fem.* **may·or·ess; may·or·al** *adj.* —**may·or·al·ty** (–ul·tee) *n.* **-ties** a mayor's term of office or position. —**may·or·ship** *n.*

May·pole *n.* a decorated pole around which merrymakers dance on May Day; **May queen** a girl chosen as queen of May Day festivities.

maze *n.* a labyrinth; also, anything intricate or confusing; **maz·y** *adj.*

ma·zur·ka (–ZUR·kuh) *n.* a lively Polish folk dance or the music for it.

M.B.A. Master of Business Administration.

M·ba·ba·ne ('m·bah·BAH·nay, –BAHN) capital of Swaziland.

mc. megacycle(s). —**M.C.** master of ceremonies; Member of Congress.

Mc·Coy (muh·COY) *n.* **the real McCoy** *Slang.* the real or genuine person or thing.

Mc·Kin·ley (muh·KIN·lee) **1 Mount.** North America's highest mountain, in Alaska; 20,320 ft. (6,194 m). **2 William.** 1843–1901, 25th U.S. President (1897–1901).

Md. or **MD** Maryland. —**Md** mendelevium. —**M.D.** Doctor of Medicine.

mdse. merchandise.

me (MEE) *pron.* objective case of I: *Give it to ~; She likes you and ~.* —**Me.** or **ME** Maine. —**M.E.** Master of Education; Mechanical Engineer; Middle English.

¹mead (MEED) *n.* an alcoholic drink made from honey.

²mead (MEED) *n. Archaic.* meadow. —**mead·ow** (MED·oh) *n.* (a tract of) moist, low-lying, level grassland; also **mead·ow·land; mead·ow·y** *adj.* —**mead·ow·lark** *n.* either of two species of North American songbirds, "eastern meadowlark" and "western meadowlark," having yellow breasts marked with a black "V." —**mead·ow·sweet** *n.* a species of spiraea.

mea·ger or **mea·gre** (MEE·gur) *adj.* poor or scanty; also, thin, not fleshy or rich: *a ~ diet, attendance; a ~ face, soil.* —**mea·ger·ly** or **mea·gre·ly** *adv.;* **mea·ger·ness** or **mea·gre·ness** *n.*

meal (MEEL) *n.* **1** coarsely ground and unbolted grain, esp. corn; also, any substance ground to powder: *bone ~.* **2** food for eating at any one time, usu. a **meal·time** such as morning, noon, and evening; breakfast, lunch, dinner, etc. —**meal·y** *adj.* **meal·i·er, -i·est** of, like, or covered with meal; hence, mealy-mouthed. —**meal·y·bug** *n.* a sap-sucking scale insect covered with a white sticky powder. —**meal·y-mouthed** *adj.* not speaking plainly; given to mincing matters.

¹mean (MEEN) *v.* **means, meant** (MENT), **mean·ing** have in mind, as thought, intention, or purpose; hence, signify or refer to: *What does "lark" ~? "Smoke" ~s a cigar to him, to her it ~s fire; I didn't ~ to hurt you; I* **mean well** (i.e. have good intentions); *Your friendship ~s much* (i.e. is of great importance) *to us.*

²mean (MEEN) *adj.* **1** bad by nature or disposition; petty, selfish, hard to manage, etc.: *Backbiting is ~; always generous to the poor, never ~; I feel ~ after saying that.* **2** *Informal.* skillful: *an excellent pitcher who throws a ~ curve; plays a ~ banjo.* **3** low; humble; poor; common: *the ~est flower of the field; a ~ cottage;* **no mean** (i.e. a fine) *tribute to a budding poet.* —**mean·ly** *adv.* —**mean·ness** *n.*

³mean (MEEN) *n.* & *adj.* (something) in the middle or halfway between (greater and lesser things, opposites, or extremes); average: *7 is the ~ of 3, 5, 9, and 11; the ~ annual temperature; the "golden mean" between too much and too little of anything.* —**means** *n.pl.* [takes *sing.* or *pl.v.*] agency or resource by which a purpose is achieved: *people of moderate ~* (i.e. wealth); *a* **means test** *to check how poor you are; the* **ways and means** *of avoiding a tax; got through* **by means of** *cheating;* **By all means** (i.e. certainly) *let's help her if we can;* **by no means** not at all.

me·an·der (mee·AN–) *n.* & *v.* (follow) a winding course, as of a stream with a series of U-bends; hence, wander aimlessly; **me·an·der·er** *n.*

mean·ie or **mean·y** (MEE·nee) *n.* **mean·ies** *Informal.* one who is mean or petty.

mean·ing (MEEN–) *n.* what is meant, as by a word, action, gesture, or other expression. —**mean·ing·ful** *adj.;* **mean·ing·ful·ly** *adv.* —**mean·ing·less** *adj.*

meant *pt.* & *pp.* of ¹MEAN.

mean·time *n.* & *adv.* (in the) time interval; also **mean·while.**

meany same as MEANIE.

mea·sles (MEE·zulz) *n.pl.* [takes *sing.v.*] **1** a contagious virus disease characterized by inflammation of the mucous membranes, high fever, and a rash; rubeola; also called "seven-day measles." **2** a milder disease than rubeola, characterized by a pink rash; rubella; German measles; also called "three-day measles." —**mea·sly** (MEEZ·lee) *adj.* **-sli·er, -sli·est** having measles; also, *Informal.* worthless or contemptible.

meas·ure (MEZH·ur) *n.* **1** the length, weight, area, capacity, etc. of something according to some standard; also, a measuring standard, instrument, or thing measured: *A hectare is a ~ of area; Use a tape ~; was given six ~s of grain;* **beyond measure** exceedingly; **for good measure** as extra; **in a measure** to some degree. **2** something measured rhythmically, as a foot of verse, a bar of music, or a dance. **3** a course of action; also, an act of a legislature; statute: *~s against crime; a ~ awaiting a vote.* —**v. -ures, -ured, -ur·ing:** *a tailor ~ing a customer; a room ~ing 10 × 12; rejected because it didn't* **measure up** (**to** *expectations*); *a ~d portion, beat* (of a drum), *mile* (for checking speed); *the ~d tread (of a walk); ~d* (i.e. careful and precise) *speech.* —**meas·ur·a·ble** *adj.;* **meas·ur·a·bly** *adv.* —**meas·ure·less** *adj.* immeasurable; also, very great. —**meas·ure·ment** *n.* way, act, result, or system of measuring: *the ~s of a room, of a female figure* (i.e. bust, waist, and hips).

meat (MEET) *n.* animal flesh used as food, esp. the "red meat" of cattle, hogs, and sheep; hence, food; also, edible part, substance, or essence: *Romances are* **meat and drink** *to her; Scoop out the ~ of a coconut; the ~ of his argument; "One man's ~ is another man's poison."* —**meat·ball** *n.* a ball of ground or chopped meat: *spaghetti and ~s.* —**meat·head** *n. Slang.* a dunce or blockhead. —**meat·man** *n.* **-men** butcher. —**meat·pack·ing** *n.* the industry of slaughtering animals and preparing their meat for sale. —**meat·y** *adj.* **meat·i·er, -i·est:** *a ~ morsel, texture, essay;* **meat·i·ness** *n.*

mec·ca (MEC·uh) *n.* a place one longs to visit, as **Mecca** in Saudi Arabia, chief holy city of Moslems.

mech. mechanical; mechanics. —**me·chan·ic** (muh·CAN–) *n.* a workman skilled in the use of tools and machinery; machinist. —**me·chan·i·cal** (–CAN–) *adj.* of or having to do with machines or mechanics: *a girl with ~ aptitude; a puppet's ~* (i.e. machinelike) *movements; The longer a crowbar, the greater its* **mechanical advantage;** *A draftsman's* **mechanical drawing** *made with instruments shows the exact shape and size of the object to be made;* **mechanical engineering** *deals with ~ power and machinery;* **me·chan·i·cal·ly** *adv.* —**me·chan·ics** (–CAN–) *n.pl.* **1** [takes *sing.v.*] the physics of forces acting on bodies when at rest and in motion. **2** [takes *pl.v.*] practical or functional details: *the ~ of playing on an instrument; ~ of punctuation.* —**mech·a·nism** (MEC·uh–) *n.* mechanical part, system, or machinery: *the ~ of a watch, of the universe; a defense ~;* **mech·a·nis·tic** (–NIS–) *adj.;* **mech·a·nis·ti·cal·ly** *adv.* —**mech·a·nize** (MEC·uh–) *v.* **-niz·es, -nized, -niz·ing** do (work) using machinery rather than by hand; also, equip with machinery, as an army with armored vehicles, tanks, etc.; **mech·a·niz·er** *n.;* **mech·a·ni·za·tion** (–ZAY–) *n.*

med. medical; medicine; medieval; medium.

M.Ed. Master of Education.

med·al (MEDL) *n.* a metal disk resembling a coin, to commemorate a person or event, given as an award for achievement, bearing a religious emblem or picture; **med·al·(l)ist** *n.* one awarded a medal; also, a medal designer. **—me·dal·lion** (muh·DAL·yun) *n.* a large medal; also, medal design, as of a tablet or architectural panel or one on a carpet.

med·dle *v.* **med·dles, med·dled, med·dling** interfere or busy oneself with (other people's affairs); **med·dler** *n.;* **med·dle·some** (–sum) *adj.: a ~ busybody.*

me·di·a (MEE·dee·uh) *n.pl.* [often used as *sing.*] See MEDIUM: *a* **media event** *that has been stage-managed for its publicity value.* **—me·di·ae·val** (mee·dee·EE·vul) same as MEDIEVAL. **—me·di·al** (–ul) *adj.* mean or average; also, median. **—me·di·an** (MEE·dee·un) *n.* & *adj.* middle or intermediate (number, line, etc.): *The ~ of 1, 3, 5, 7, and 11 is 5; of 1, 3, 5, and 7, it is 4* (i.e. the average of the middle figures); *the* **median (strip)** *separating the opposite lanes of a highway.* **—me·di·ate** (MEE·dee–) *v.* **-ates, -at·ed, -at·ing** act as a go-between (in a dispute); hence, bring about (a settlement or peace) or settle (a strike) by mediating; ***adj.*** (–dee·it) with something intervening or in the middle; not direct or immediate: *a ~ logical inference;* **me·di·ate·ly** *adv.* **—me·di·a·tion** (–AY–) *n.;* **me·di·a·tor** (MEE–) *n., fem.* **me·di·a·trix** (–AY–).

med·ic *n. Informal.* a medical student, practitioner, or a member of a medical corps. — **med·i·ca·ble** *adj.* curable; also, medically usable; **med·i·ca·bly** *adv.* **—Med·i·caid** or **med·i·caid** *n.* a medical program to help the needy, established by the U.S. Congress in 1965. **—med·i·cal** *adj.* of or having to do with medicine; **med·i·cal·ly** *adv.* **—medical examiner** a coroner or similar public officer. **—med·i·ca·ment** (MED·i–, muh·DIC–) *n.* a medicine. **—Med·i·care** or **med·i·care** *n.* a program of medical and hospital services for people of 65 years and over, as established in the U.S. in 1965. **—med·i·cate** *v.* **-cates, -cat·ed, -cat·ing** treat with medicine; **med·i·ca·tive** *adj.* **med·i·ca·tion** (–CAY–) *n.* **—me·dic·i·nal** (muh·DISN·ul) *adj.* of or having to do with the curing of diseases; **me·dic·i·nal·ly** *adv.* **—med·i·cine** (–sin) *n.* **1** a substance or preparation used in preventing or treating disease. **2** the science or art of treating and preventing diseases. **—medicine ball** a heavy leather ball tossed from person to person in a group for exercise. **—medicine man** a physician who relies on supernatural power, as a shaman or witch doctor. **—med·i·co** *n.* **-cos** *Informal.* a medical student or practitioner.

me·di·e·val (mee·dee·EE·vul, med·ee–) *adj.* of the Middle Ages; **me·di·e·val·ism** *n.;* **me·di·e·val·ist** *n.*

me·di·o·cre (mee·dee·OH·cur) *adj.* of average or ordinary quality; relatively inferior; **me·di·oc·ri·ty** (–OC–) *n.* **-ties.**

med·i·tate *v.* **-tates, -tat·ed, -tat·ing** think (on a topic); hence, consider or contemplate (revenge or similar action); **med·i·ta·tive** (–tiv) *adj.;* **med·i·ta·tive·ly** *adv.;* **med·i·ta·tion** (–TAY–) *n.*

Med·i·ter·ra·ne·an (Sea) (–tuh·RAY·nee·un) the sea enclosed by Europe, Africa, and Asia; **Mediterranean** *adj.: the ~ origin of Western civilization; a ~ route.*

me·di·um (MEE·dee–) *n.* **-di·ums** or **-di·a** **1** a means of conveying or communicating: *Speech is a ~ of communication; Money is a ~ of exchange for goods; spiritualistic ~s; the press as an advertising ~; The media find* (rarely *finds*) *bad news makes good headlines; newer media* (rarely **medias**) *such as radio and television.* **2** a substance or environment in which something exists or operates: *a culture ~ for bacteria; ether as the ~ through which light is transmitted; an artist who paints in the oil ~* (i.e. pigment with oil as vehicle). **3** a middle condition or quality: *the happy ~ or "golden mean" between extremes;* ***adj.:*** *a man of ~ height; a ~ income group; a ~ frequency range.* **—me·di·um·is·tic** (–MIS–) *adj.* of or like a spiritualistic medium.

med·lar (–lur) *n.* a tree of the rose family bearing fruit resembling crab apples.

Med·lars (–lurz) *n.* the computerized "Medical Literature Analysis and Retrieval System" of the National Library of Medicine in Bethesda, Md.

med·ley (–lee) *n.* **-leys** **1** mixture of various elements, or parts: *butterfly, backstroke, breaststroke, and ~ races; a musical ~ of marches.* **2** a hodgepodge or jumble.

me·dul·la (–DUL·uh) *n.* **-dul·las** or **-dul·lae** (–lee) a core or cavity, as of a bone, hair, or kidney. **—medulla ob·lon·ga·ta** (–long·GAH·tuh), *pl.* **medulla oblongatas** or **medullae ob·lon·ga·tae** (–tee) an extension of the spinal cord into the back of the brain containing nerve centers of the body's vital functions.

meed *n. Poetic.* deserved portion, as of praise.

meek *adj.* patient and submissive, not self-assertive: *the ~ and gentle Christ; too ~* (i.e. spiritless) *and spineless;* **meek·ly** *adv.;* **meek·ness** *n.*

meer·schaum (MEER·shum, –shawm) *n.* (a tobacco pipe with a bowl made of) a soft, white, clayey mineral.

meet *v.* **meets, met, meet·ing** **1** come into contact or communication: *We were at the party but didn't ~; Parallel lines never ~; where 42nd Street ~s 6th Avenue.* **2** come into contact or communication by design: *I'd like you to ~ my family; I have to ~ the flight landing at 8:30; I ~ with my students after each lecture.* **3** **meet with** meet by chance; come across; come upon: *Cabbies ~ with all sorts of people; She met* *with* (i.e. experienced) *failure; Her idea met with* (i.e. received) *approval.* **4** deal with as required; satisfy: *to ~ a debt, deadline, challenge, threat, an enemy.* ***—n.*** a coming together; also, the place of meeting or the people at it. ***—adj.*** *Archaic.* becoming or proper: *It is ~ and just.* **—meet·ing** *n.* a gathering or assembly, esp. to discuss or decide on something; **meet·ing·house** *n.* a building used for public worship, as by Quakers.

meg. megohm(s). **—meg(a)-** *comb.form.* large; one million: as in *megalith, megaton.* **—meg·a·cy·cle** (MEG·uh·sye–) *n.* former term for MEGAHERTZ. **—meg·a·death** *n.* in atomic warfare, a unit of one million deaths. **—meg·a·hertz** (MEG·uh·hurts) *n. sing.* & *pl.* one million hertz. **—meg·a·lith** *n.* a stone of great size used in a prehistoric monument such as a dolmen; **meg·a·lith·ic** (–LITH–) *adj.* **—meg·a·lo·ma·ni·a** (–uh·loh·MAY–) *n.* a mental disorder marked by delusions of personal grandeur, power, wealth, etc.; **meg·a·lo·ma·ni·ac** *n.* & *adj.* **—meg·a·lop·o·lis** (–LOP–) *n.* a continuous region of several metropolitan areas, as of New York, Boston, Washington, Philadelphia, and Baltimore; conurbation. **—meg·a·phone** *n.* a funnel-shaped, hand-held device for making a voice louder, as used by cheerleaders. **—meg·a·ton** (–tun) *n.* the explosive power of one million tons of TNT.

me·gil·lah (muh·GIL·uh) *n. Slang.* a boringly detailed account.

meg·ohm *n.* one million ohms.

mei·o·sis (mye·OH–) *n., pl.* **-ses** (–seez) in sexually reproducing organisms, a two-stage division to halve the number of chromosomes in a sex cell; **mei·ot·ic** (–OT–) *adj.*

Me·kong (may·KONG) the greatest river in S.E. Asia, rising in Tibet and emptying into the China Sea.

mel·a·mine (–uh·meen) *n.* a thermosetting plastic used for dinnerware, tabletops, electrical parts, etc.

mel·an·cho·li·a (–un·COH–) *n.* a mental illness marked by extreme depression; **mel·an·cho·li·ac** *n.* & *adj.* **—mel·an·chol·ic** (–COL–) *adj.* suffering from melancholia; also, melancholy. **—mel·an·chol·y** (–col·ee) *adj.* & *n.* **-chol·ies** gloomy, depressing, or pensive (condition or mood): *a ~ person, thought, scene, smile, song; afflicted with ~.*

Mel·a·ne·sia (mel·uh·NEE–) the part of Oceania N.E. of Australia, including Fiji, New Guinea, and the Solomon Islands; **Mel·a·ne·sian** *n.* & *adj.*

mé·lange (may·LAHNZH, –LAHNJ) *n. French.* an incongruous mixture; hodgepodge.

me·lan·ic (–LAN–) *n.* & *adj.* (one) having melanism or melanosis. **—mel·a·nin** (MEL·uh–) *n.* the dark pigment of the skin, hair, iris, feathers, etc. whose abnormal development is **mel·a·nism,** opposite of ALBINISM. **—mel·a·no·ma** (–NOH–) *n.* **-mas** or **-ma·ta** (–muh·tuh) a blackish tumor such as a malignant mole; **mel·a·no·sis** *n.* a melanin abnormality, as seen after a sunburn.

Mel·ba (MEL·buh) **toast** a very thin, crisp toast; also **melba toast.**

Mel·bourne (–burn) a S.E. Australian seaport.

meld *n.* & *v.* **1** in games such as pinochle and rummy, (announce or show) a scoring card or combination. **2** blend.

me·lee (MAY·lay, may·LAY) *n.* a confused hand-to-hand fight among a number of people.

mel·io·rate (MEEL·yuh–) *v.* **-rates, -rat·ed, -rat·ing** make or become better; **mel·io·ra·tive** (–tiv) *adj.* **—mel·io·ra·tion** (–RAY–) *n.*

mel·lif·lu·ous (muh·LIF·loo·us) *adj.* flowing like honey: *~ voice, speech, words;* **mel·lif·lu·ous·ly** *adv.*

mel·low (MEL·oh) *adj.* & *v.* (make or become) soft, sweet, genial, etc., as fruit when it ripens; not sharp, harsh, or strident: *~ apples, wines, tones* (as of a violin), *soil* (that is rich and loamy), *colors, wisdom; People tend to ~ with age;* **mel·low·ness** *n.*

me·lo·de·on (muh·LOH·dee·un) *n.* a suction-operated reed organ or harmonium; **me·lod·ic** (–LOD–) *adj.* of or like melody; also, melodious; **me·lod·i·cal·ly** *adv.* **—me·lo·di·ous** (–LOH·dee·us) *adj.* tuneful; pleasant-sounding; **me·lo·di·ous·ly** *adv.;* **me·lo·di·ous·ness** *n.*

mel·o·dra·ma (MEL·uh·drah·muh) *n.* drama of a sensational kind with much action and play of emotion. **—mel·o·dra·mat·ic** (–MAT–) *adj.;* **mel·o·dra·mat·i·cal·ly** *adv.;* **mel·o·dra·mat·ics** *n.pl.* exaggerated or emotional behavior.

mel·o·dy (–uh·dee) *n.* **-dies** sweet music; also, a song or tune; **mel·o·dist** *n.*

mel·on (–un) *n.* the usu. large, juicy fruit of any of several trailing plants of the gourd family, as the watermelon, muskmelon, canteloupe, etc.

melt *v.* change or pass from solid to liquid state; also, dissolve, as sugar in coffee; hence, disappear gradually, as clouds or mist in the sun; blend or merge: *Wax has a low* **melting point** (i.e. melting temperature); *Immigration has made America the* **melting pot** (or crucible) *of many cultures.* ***—n.*** melted metal, esp. a quantity melted at one time.

mel·ton (MEL·tn) *n.* a short-napped, heavy, smooth, woolen cloth used for overcoats.

melt·wat·er *n.* water from melted snow and ice.

Mel·ville (–vil), **Herman.** 1819–91, American novelist.

mem. member; memoir; memo(s); memorial. **—mem·ber** *n.* a limb or similar organ of a plant or animal; hence, a distinct part or unit of a whole: *a ~ of a family, Congress, a mathematical set;* **mem·ber·ship** *n.* —**mem·brane** *n.* a soft, thin, pliable sheet or layer of tissue covering a body surface or separating spaces, as the eardrum; **mem·bra·nous** (–bruh·nus) *adj.*

me·men·to (mi·MEN·toh) *n.* **-to(e)s** a souvenir. —**mem·o** *n.* **-os** [short form] memorandum. —**mem·oir** (–wahr, –wor) *n.* **1** a biographical notice or a report based on personal knowledge of a person or subject. **2 memoirs** *pl.* a wide-ranging first-hand record of events, as of a war, or of recollections, as of one's life; also, the proceedings of a learned society. —**mem·o·ra·bil·i·a** (–ruh·BIL–) *n.pl.* (account of) things and events worth remembering about a subject; **mem·o·ra·ble** (–ruh·bl) *adj.* worth remembering; notable; **mem·o·ra·bly** *adv.* —**mem·o·ran·dum** (–RAN–) *n.* **-dums** or **-da** a short or informal note, as to help one to remember something; also, an internal business communication. —**me·mo·ri·al** (muh·MOR·ee·ul) *n.* & *adj.* (a statue, publication, holiday, etc.) that commemorates an event or person; **Memorial Day** a holiday in honor of American servicemen, usu. the last Monday in May. —**mem·o·rize** (MEM·uh–) *v.* **-riz·es, -rized, -riz·ing** learn by heart; **mem·o·riz·er** *n.;* **mem·o·ri·za·tion** (–ZAY–) *n.* —**mem·o·ry** (–uh·ree) *n.* **-ries** the capacity to keep something in mind and recall it afterwards; also, a person, thing, or event that is remembered, the store of such things, or the length of time during which they are remembered: *to commit a formula to ~; recite it from ~; the coldest winter in living ~; a monument erected* **in memory of** *war heroes; a calculator with ~* (i.e. storing and recall system); *a computer's* **memory bank** (i.e. data bank).

Mem·phis (–fis) a city of S.W. Tennessee.

men *pl.* of MAN.

men·ace (–is) *n.* & *v.* **-ac·es, -aced, -ac·ing** (be) a threat or danger: *hoodlums ~ing people in elevators; a ~ to society;* **men·ac·ing** *adj.: a very ~ look;* **men·ac·ing·ly** *adv.*

mé·nage or **me·nage** (may·NAHZH, muh–) *n.* household. —**me·nag·er·ie** (–NAJ·uh·ree) *n.* collection of wild animals, as for a zoo or a circus.

mend *v.* of things damaged or needing improvement, make or become as good as before or as they should be: *glue to ~ a broken toy; a loafer told to ~ his ways or be fired;* **n.:** *The ~ in his coat was showing;* **on the mend** of health, improving; **mend·er** *n.*

men·da·cious (–DAY·shus) *adj.* lying; not truthful; **men·da·cious·ly** *adv.* —**men·dac·i·ty** (–DAS–) *n.* **-ties 1** untruthfulness; also **men·da·cious·ness. 2** a lie.

Men·del, Gregor. 1822–84, Austrian botanist who formulated **Men·del·ism,** his theory of heredity.

men·de·le·vi·um (–duh·LEE·vee·um) *n.* a radioactive chemical element.

Men·dels·sohn (MEN·dl·sun), **Felix.** 1809–47, German composer.

men·di·cant (–kunt) *n.* & *adj.* begging (friar). —**mend·di·can·cy** *n.*

men·folk(s) *n.pl. Informal.* men, esp. of a family or other group.

men·ha·den (–HAY·dn) *n.* a species of herring of Atlantic coastal waters, used for feed, oil, and fertilizer.

me·ni·al (MEE·nee·ul) *n.* & *adj.* domestic (servant); also, servile (person); **me·ni·al·ly** *adv.*

men·in·gi·tis (–JYE–) *n.* a dangerous brain disease caused by viruses or bacteria.

me·nis·cus (mi·NIS–) *n.* **-cus·es** or **-ci** (–sye, –skye) the concave or convex top surface of a liquid in a tube; also, anything crescent-shaped, as a lens that is concave on one side and convex on the other; **me·nis·coid** (–NIS–) *adj.*

Men·non·ite (MEN·uh–) *n.* a member of a Christian sect noted for their simple living and worship and opposition to military service, taking oaths, etc.

men·o·pause (MEN·uh–) *n.* the normal cessation of menstruation, occurring in most women between the ages of 45 and 50; also, hormonal changes accompanying this; climacteric; **men·o·paus·al** (–PAW·zul) *adj.*

men·o·rah (muh·NOR·uh) *n.* the seven- or nine-branched candelabrum used in Jewish rites.

men·ses (–seez) *n.pl.* the usu. monthly flow of blood from the uterus. —**men·stru·al** (–stroo·ul) *adj.* having to do with **men·stru·a·tion** (–AY–) *n.* discharge of the menses; **men·stru·ate** *v.* **-ates, -at·ed, -at·ing.**

men·sur·a·ble (MEN·shu–) *adj.* measurable; **men·sur·a·bil·i·ty** (–BIL–) *n.* —**men·sur·a·tion** (–RAY–) *n.* the geometrical measurement of lengths, areas, and volumes.

mens·wear *n.* clothing for men.

-ment *n. suffix.* indicating act, state, result, etc. of a verbal action: as in *abutment, government, statement; merriment* (from *adj.*).

men·tal (MEN·tl) *adj.* **1** of the mind: *~ development.* **2** of mental disease: *a ~ case, hospital.* —**mental age** level of intelligence as the average chronological age of others of that level, as determined by tests: *man with a ~ age of 12 years.* —**men·tal·ly** *adv.* —**men·tal·i·ty** (–TAL–) *n.* **-ties** mental capacity or attitude. —**mental reservation** a qualification of a statement that is not expressed by the speaker. —**mental retardation** condition of below-normal mental development; formerly **mental deficiency.**

men·thol (–thawl, –thole) *n.* a soft white substance with the pleasant odor and cooling properties of peppermint; **men·tho·lat·ed** (–lay·tid) *adj.* containing or treated with menthol.

men·tion *v.* refer to or cite: *No one even ~ed it; $100 a night,* **not to mention** (i.e. not counting) *tips.* —***n.*** a reference or citation: *received an honorable ~ though no award;* **make mention of** refer to.

men·tor (–tur) *n.* a trusted adviser or teacher, like **Mentor,** Ulysses' trusted friend.

men·u (–yoo) *n.* **-us** a list of food dishes or the food served, as at a restaurant.

me·ow (mee·OW) *n.* & *v.* (make) the cry of a cat; also **me·ou.**

me·phit·ic (muh·FIT–) *adj.* bad-smelling; hence, noxious.

mer. meridian.

mer·can·tile (MUR·cun·til, –tile, –teel) *adj.* having to do with merchants or trade: *a ~ economy, firm; ~ law.* —**mer·ce·nar·y** (MUR·suh·ner·ee) *adj.* & *n.* **-nar·ies** (a soldier or other hired person) working mainly for money; hireling: *a ~motive;* **mer·ce·nar·i·ly** *adv.;* **mer·ce·nar·i·ness** *n.* —**mer·cer** *n. esp. Brit.* a dealer in textiles. —**mer·cer·ize** *v.* **-iz·es, -ized, -iz·ing** treat (fine cotton) chemically for added luster, strength, and deeper dye. —**mer·chan·dise** (MUR·chun–) *v.* **-dis·es, -dised, -dis·ing** trade in (goods or commodities), esp. by use of market research, packaging, and promotion methods; ***n.*** goods; commodities; **mer·chan·dis·er** *n.* Also **mer·chan·dize** *v.,* **mer·chan·diz·er** *n.* —**mer·chant** (–chunt) *n.* & *adj.* mercantile (businessman such as a wholesaler, retailer, or shopkeeper); **mer·chant·a·ble** *adj.* fit for marketing; marketable. —**mer·chant·man** (–mun) *n.* **-men** a cargo ship; also **merchant ship.** —**merchant marine** a nation's cargo and passenger ships collectively; also, their personnel.

mer·ci (–SEE) *interj. French.* thanks.

mer·cu·ri·al (–KYOOR·ee·ul) *adj.* **1** changeable in mood: *a ~ temperament.* **2** of or containing mercury; also **mer·cur·ic, mer·cur·ous.** —***n.*** a mercurial drug such as the antiseptic **Mer·cu·ro·chrome** (–KYOOR·uh–) *Trademark.* —**mer·cu·ri·al·ly** *n.* —**mer·cu·ry** (MUR·kyuh·ree) *n.* **1** a heavy, silver-white, normally liquid metallic element used in thermometers, barometers, etc.; hence, a column of mercury. **2 Mercury** in Roman myths, the swift-footed messenger of the gods; also, the planet nearest to the sun and the smallest in the solar system.

mer·cy (MUR·see) *n.* **-cies** kindness or compassion shown to someone out of generosity: *justice tempered with ~; have ~ on a poor beggar; It's a ~* (i.e. blessing) *he wasn't killed in the fire;* **at the mercy of** in the power of; **mercy killing** same as EUTHANASIA. —**mer·ci·ful** *adj.;* **mer·ci·ful·ly** *adv.* —**mer·ci·less** *adj.;* **mer·ci·less·ly** *adv.*

mere (MEER) *adj., superl.* **mer·est** nothing more or better than: *a ~ child; the ~est folly;* **mere·ly** *adv.* simply; only.

mer·e·tri·cious (mer·uh·TRISH·us) *adj.* alluring or attractive in a deceptive way: *a hooker's ~ charms;* **mer·e·tri·cious·ly** *adv.;* **mer·e·tri·cious·ness** *n.*

mer·gan·ser (–GAN–) *n.* any of a group of fish-eating ducks equipped with bills notched at the edges, hence called "sawbill," having a crested head, esp. the *hooded merganser.*

merge (MURJ) *v.* **merg·es, merged, merg·ing** become swallowed up so as to lose one's own identity, as smaller companies (into a large corporation); hence, combine or consolidate; **merg·er** *n.* a merging; absorption.

me·rid·i·an (muh·RID·ee·un) *n.* **1** an imaginary line drawn from pole to pole passing through a particular point on the globe for measuring its longitude. **2** the highest point; culmination; prime: *in the ~ of his glory.*

me·ringue (muh·RANG) *n.* a dessert topping for pies, puddings, etc., made with egg whites and sugar beaten stiff and baked: *a lemon ~ pie.*

me·ri·no (muh·REE–) *n.* **-nos** a fine-wooled Spanish breed of sheep, its soft heavy fleece, or the wool, cloth, etc. made from it.

mer·it *n.* real worth; what one has earned: *a mere copy without any ~; a question decided on its* **merits;** *an Order of Merit;* ***adj.:*** *the* **merit system** *of appointing and promoting people in jobs; ~ pay; a scout wearing a ~ badge.* —***v.*** earn; deserve: *well-~ed praise.* —**mer·i·toc·ra·cy** (–TOC·ruh·see) *n.* **-cies** rule by the talented; also, a system that promotes it. —**mer·i·to·ri·ous** (–TOR·ee·us) *adj.* full or worth or merit: *a ~ action, conduct, service;* **mer·i·to·ri·ous·ly** *adv.;* **mer·i·to·ri·ous·ness** *n.*

Mer·lin a magician and seer who helped King Arthur; **merlin** *n.* a small falcon, or "pigeon hawk."

mer·maid *n.* an imaginary sea creature in the shape of a woman with a fish's body from the waist down; *masc.* **mer·man, -men.**

mer·ri·ment *n.* hilarious fun; gaiety. —**mer·ry** *adj.* **mer·ri·er, mer·ri·est** full of fun, laughter, enjoyment, etc.: *a ~ laugh, tune, Christmas;* **make merry** have fun; **mer·ri·ly** *adv.;* **mer·ri·ness** *n.* —**mer·ry-go-round** *n.* an amusement ride with wooden horses and other animals going up and down in a whirl on a revolving platform; hence, a busy whirl of activities. —**mer·ry·mak·ing** *n.* & *adj.* (having or full of) fun or merry entertainment; **mer·ry·mak·er** *n.*

me·sa (MAY·suh) *n.* a steep-sided hill with a flat top.

mé·sal·li·ance (may·zuh·LYE·unce, –zal·YAHNCE) *n. French.* a marriage with a person of lower social position.

mes·cal (–CAL) *n.* **1** an alcoholic drink made by Mexicans from the sap of certain agaves; also, such a cactus plant. **2** same as PEYOTE also **mes·ca·line** (–leen, –lin).

mesdames *pl.* of MADAM(E). —**mesdemoiselles** *pl.* of MADEMOISELLE.

mesh *n.* one of the openings between the cords or wires of a net, sieve, screen, etc.; also, a woven netlike material: *a 60-mesh screen has 60 ~es to the inch; fine or coarse ~; caught in the* **meshes** (i.e. threads or network) *of a spider's web;* **in mesh** interlocked. —**v.** entangle; also, engage or interlock, as gears or zippers; hence, integrate; coordinate. —**mesh·work** *n.* network; meshes. —**mesh·y** *adj.*

mes·mer·ism (MEZ–) *n.* [the former term for] hypnotism, believed to be "animal magnetism" by Franz Mesmer (1734–1815) and others; **mes·mer·ic** (–MER–) *adj.;* **mes·mer·ist** (MEZ–) *n.* —**mes·mer·ize** *v.* **-iz·es, -ized, -iz·ing** hypnotize.

meso- *comb.form.* middle; midway: as in **mes·on** (MESS–) *n.* an elementary nuclear particle such as a kaon, pion, or muon with a mass intermediate between that of an electron and a proton. —**Mes·o·po·ta·mi·a** (–uh·puh·TAY·mee·uh) an ancient region of S.W. Asia between the rivers Tigris and Euphrates; **Mes·o·po·ta·mi·an** *n.* & *adj.* —**mes·o·sphere** *n.* the layer of the atmosphere between stratosphere and thermosphere; **mes·o·spher·ic** (–SFAIR–) *adj.* —**Mes·o·zo·ic** (–ZOH–) *n.* & *adj.* (of) the era of geologic time intermediate between Paleozoic and Cenozoic eras, beginning about 220 million years ago.

mes·quit(e) (–KEET) *n.* a thorny tree or shrub of the pea family that grows in hot, dry climates, common in S.W. United States and Mexico.

mess *n.* **1** a state of things that is untidy, unpleasant, or confused: *What a ~! made a ~ of the work he was given.* **2** a group of people, as in the army, who regularly eat together; hence, such eating together as **mess·mates** or their eating place, or **mess hall. 3** a portion of food, esp. a dish of something, as of meal or cereal: *a ~ of collard greens.* —**v.** [corresponding to the *n.* senses] **1:** *an office ~ed up by a Christmas party; salesmen* **messing about** (or **around**) *in the office instead of being out in the field.* **2:** *invited to ~ with the officers.* —**mess·y** *adj.* untidy or unpleasant; **mess·i·ly** *adv.;* **mess·i·ness** *n.*

mes·sage (MES·ij) *n.* a communication: *a ~* (i.e. a commercial) *from our sponsor; the President's ~ to Congress; a poem with a ~* (i.e. theme or idea); **get the message** *Informal.* take the hint or understand what is implied; **v.:** *The captain had ~d "fire on board" before crash-landing.*

Messeigneurs *pl.* of MONSEIGNEUR.

mes·sen·ger (MESN·jur) *n.* one who carries a message or goes on a mission or errand; **messenger RNA** a ribonucleic acid that carries the message or code for the formation of a particular protein.

Mes·si·ah (muh·SYE·uh) *n.* the "deliverer" promised to Israel by the prophets, identified with Jesus by Christians; **messiah** *n.* the leader of a cause. —**Mes·si·an·ic** (mes·ee·AN·ic) *adj.* of or having to do with a Messiah: *the ~ prophecy, times, age of peace and freedom.*

messieurs *pl.* of MONSIEUR. —**Messrs.** *pl.* of MR: *Messrs. T. Jones & Co.; Messrs. Jones, Smith, and McGrath.*

messmate See MESS.

mes·ti·zo (–TEE·zoh) *n.* **-zo(e)s** a Latin American of mixed parentage, esp. of white and American Indian descent; *fem.* **mes·ti·za.**

met *pt.* & *pp.* of MEET. —**met.** metropolitan.

met(a)- *prefix.* beyond; over; after: as in *metabolism, metaphysics, metempsychosis.* —**me·tab·o·lism** (muh·TAB·uh–) *n.* the process by which a living being transforms food into energy (destructive metabolism or "catabolism") and into living tissue (constructive metabolism or "anabolism"): *the basal ~ of a body at rest;* **met·a·bol·ic** (–BOL–) *adj.* —**me·tab·o·lite** (–TAB–) *n.* a substance that is essential to or that is produced by metabolism. —**me·tab·o·lize** (–TAB–) *v.* **-liz·es, -lized, -liz·ing** subject to or undergo metabolism. —**met·a·car·pus** (–uh·CAR–) *n., pl.* **-pi** (–pye) the part of the hand, including five **met·a·car·pal** bones, between wrist and fingers. —**met·a·gal·ax·y** (–GAL·ux·ee) *n.* **-ax·ies** the universe of galaxies outside the Milky Way.

met·al (METL) *n.* **1** a mineral substance such as iron, lead, or copper that has a shiny surface, conducts heat and electricity, can be melted, etc.; also, an alloy or anything made out of metal. **2** basic material; also, mettle. —**me·tal·lic** (muh·TAL–) *adj.: a ~ luster, gray, sound, voice;* **me·tal·li·cal·ly** *adv.* —**met·al·lif·er·ous** (–LIF·uh·rus) *adj.* yielding metal: *~ rocks, deposits, compounds.* —**met·al·loid** *n.* & *adj.* (an element such as silicon or arsenic) having metallic properties. —**met·al·lur·gy** (METL·ur·jee) *n.* the extraction of metals from their ores and their modification for use; **met·al·lur·gic** (–UR–) or **-gi·cal** *adj.;* **met·al·lur·gi·cal·ly** *adv.;* **met·al·lur·gist** *n.* —**met·al·ware** *n.* —**met·al·work** *n.* artistic work using metal; also, artistic things made of metal; **met·al·work·er** *n.;* **met·al·work·ing** *n.*

met·a·mor·phic (–MOR·fic) *adj.* having to do with metamorphosis or metamorphism: *Gneiss, marble, quartzite, slate, etc. are ~ rocks.* —**met·a·mor·phism** (–MOR·fizm) *n.* change in the form and composition of rocks by heat, pressure, etc. —**met·a·mor·pho·sis** (–MOR·fuh–) *n., pl.* **-ses** (–seez) a complete change of form, character, etc. as if by magic: *the ~ of a frog or butterfly;* **met·a·mor·phose** (–MORE–) *v.* **-phos·es, -phosed, -phos·ing:** *Tadpoles, caterpillars, etc. are ~d into frogs, butterflies, etc.; Slate is ~d shale;* **met·a·mor·phous** (–fus) *adj.* —**met·a·phor** (MET·uh–) *n.* a figure of speech using words in a meaning different from their literal sense, implying a comparison, as in "dawn of civilization"; **met·a·phor·ic** (–FOR–) or **-i·cal** *adj.;* **met·a·phor·i·cal·ly** *adj.;* **met·a·phor·i·cal·ly** *adv.* —**met·a·phys·ics** (–FIZ–) *n.pl.* [with *sing.v.*]

a division of philosophy that studies fundamental problems of knowledge and reality beyond those of the physical world, as existence, essence, causality, etc.; speculative philosophy; **met·a·phys·i·cal** *adj.;* **met·a·phys·i·cal·ly** *adv.;* **met·a·phy·si·cian** (–ZISH·un) *n.* —**me·tas·ta·sis** (–TAS·tuh–) *n.,pl.* **-ses** (–seez) the transfer of a disease, esp. cancer, from one part of the body to another; also, the secondary tumor caused in the process; **me·tas·ta·size** *v.* **-siz·es, -sized, -siz·ing.** —**met·a·tar·sus** (–TAR–) *n., pl.* **-si** (–sye) the part of the foot between ankle and toes; **met·a·tar·sal** *n.* & *adj.* (a bone) of the metatarsus: *the ~ arch.* —**me·tath·e·sis** (–TATH·uh–) *n., pl.* **-ses** (–seez) transposition of letters or sounds in a word, as "perty" for "pretty."

mete (MEET) *v.* **metes, met·ed, met·ing** usu. **mete out,** measure out; apportion or allot: *~ out punishment, rewards, justice.*

met·em·psy·cho·sis (–sye·COH–) *n., pl.* **-ses** (–seez) reincarnation of a soul in a different body, as in Buddhist belief.

me·te·or (MEE·tee·ur) *n.* the streak of light seen as a "shooting star" or "falling star" in the sky when a meteoroid glows on entering the atmosphere, reaching the earth as a **me·te·or·ite** if it does not burn up; **me·te·or·ic** (–OR–) *adj.* of or like a meteor in swiftness, brilliancy, etc.: *a movie star's ~ rise to fame;* **me·te·or·i·cal·ly** adv. —**me·te·or·it·ic** (–RIT–) *adj.* —**me·te·or·oid** (MEE·tee–) *n.* a chunk of metal or rock falling through space. —**me·te·or·ol·o·gy** (–ROL·uh·jee) *n.* the study of the atmosphere, esp. weather; **me·te·or·ol·o·gist** *n.;* **me·te·or·o·log·i·cal** (–LOJ–) *adj.*

me·ter (MEE–) *n.* **1** rhythm in music or verse, based on units such as beats, length or stress of syllables, etc.: 4/4 *~; the 4-line ballad ~; iambic ~.* **2** the basic unit of length in the metric system, equal to 39.37 in. **3** a measuring and often recording instrument, as for gas, electricity, distances, times, etc.; ***v.:*** *a seeder with a ~ing device for proper spacing; ~ed postage, mail* (stamped with a postage meter). — **-meter** *comb. form.* **1** measuring device: as in *odometer, thermometer.* **2** meter(s): as in *centimeter, kilometer.* —**me·ter-kil·o·gram-sec·ond** *adj.* of a system of measurement, having meter, kilogram, and second as units of length, mass, and time respectively; MKS system: *"Newton" is the unit of force in the ~ system.* —**meter maid** a female police employee who issues tickets for parking violations.

meth *Slang.* short form of METHEDRINE. —**meth·a·done** (METH·uh·dohn) or **meth·a·don** *n.* a substitute narcotic drug used in the treatment of addiction to heroin, morphine, and opium. —**meth·am·phet·a·mine** (–FET·uh·meen) *n.* a stimulant amphetamine, also used in weight control; also known as "speed." —**meth·ane** *n.* a flammable gaseous hydrocarbon formed in marshes, mines, etc. by the decomposition of vegetable matter. —**meth·a·nol** *n.* same as WOOD ALCOHOL. —**Meth·e·drine** (–dreen) *Trademark.* methamphetamine.

me·thinks (–THINKS) *v.* **-thought** *Archaic.* it seems to me.

meth·od (–ud) *n.* an orderly way or procedure for doing something: *new teaching ~s; the proper ~ of brushing teeth; There's* **method in his madness** (i.e. his behavior is not so crazy as it seems). —**me·thod·i·cal** (–THOD–) *adj.* orderly; systematic; **me·thod·i·cal·ly** *adv.* —**Meth·od·ist** *n.* & *adj.* (a member) of a protestant denomination based on the teachings of John Wesley; Wesleyan; **Meth·od·ism** *n.* —**meth·od·ize** *v.* **-iz·es, -ized, -iz·ing** make methodical. —**meth·od·ol·o·gy** (–DOL·uh·jee) *n.* **-gies** the science of method; also, a particular system: *the ~ of structural linguistics.*

Me·thu·se·lah (muh·THOO·zuh·luh) in the Bible, a patriarch who lived 969 years.

meth·yl (METH·ul) *n.* a hydrocarbon radical found in **methyl alcohol,** or wood alcohol, and other organic compounds.

me·tic·u·lous (muh·TIC·yoo·lus) *adj.* careful, often finicky about minute details: *a ~ dresser;* **me·tic·u·lous·ly** *adv.;* **me·tic·u·lous·ness** *n.*

mé·tier (may·TYAY) n. a field of work in which one is specially skilled; forte.

mé·tis (may·TEES) *n. sing.* & *pl.* a person of mixed French and American Indian descent.

me·tre (MEE·tur) *n. Brit.* METER, *n.* 1 & 2. —**met·ric** or **met·ri·cal** *adj.* of or having to do with meter: *The decimal* **metric system** *of measurement has meter, gram, and liter as basic units; a* **metric ton** *of 1,000 kilograms or 1.1 short tons;* **metrical** *rhythm; a* **metrical** *translation;* **met·ri·cal·ly** *adv.* —**met·ri·cate** *v.* **-cates, -cat·ed, -cat·ing;** also **met·ri·cize, -ciz·es, -cized, -ciz·ing** change into the metric system. —**met·ri·ca·tion** (–CAY–) *n.* (process of) conversion to the metric system.

met·ro or **Met·ro** (–roh) *n.* **-ros** **1** an underground railway. **2** a metropolitan regional government; **metro** *adj.* metropolitan. —**Met·ro·lin·er** *n.* a high-speed Amtrak train.

me·trol·o·gy (–TROL·uh·jee) *n.* the science or a system of measurement. —**met·ro·nome** (MET·ruh–) *n.* a device that ticks to mark time at an adjustable speed, used by musicians; **met·ro·nom·ic** (–NOM–) *adj.*

me·trop·o·lis (muh·TROP·uh–) *n.* a large, important, or capital city; a center of some (specified) activity: *crime ~ of the U.S.* —**met·ro·pol·i·tan** (–POL–) *adj.: a ~ area including city and suburbs.*

met·tle (METL) *n.* quality of character or temperament; also, spirit; courage; **on one's mettle** ready to do one's best; **met·tle·some** (–sum) *adj.* high-spirited: *a ~ horse.*

mev or **Mev.** million electric volts.
[1]**mew** *n.* &*v.* same as MEOW. —**mewl** *n.* & *v.* (make) a feeble or whining cry, as a baby.
[2]**mew** *v.* confine; **mews** *n.pl.* [with *sing v.*] *Brit.* originally, coach houses around a court or alley, later converted into dwellings or "mews flats"; hence, such an alley or street.
Mex. Mexican; Mexico. —**Mex·i·co** a republic lying just S. of the U.S.; 761,605 sq.mi. (1,-972,547 km²); *cap.* **Mexico City; Mex·i·can** (–cun) *n.* & *adj.*
mez·za·nine (MEZ·uh·neen) *n.* a middle story between a building's ground floor and second floor; also, a balcony over the main floor, as of a theater, esp. its forward part. —**mez·zo-so·pra·no** (MET·soh–, MEZ·oh–) *n.* **-nos** (a singer with) a voice between contralto and soprano.
MF medium frequency.
M.F.A. Master of Fine Arts.
mfd manufactured. —**mfg.** manufacturing. —**mfr(s).** manufacturer(s).
mg. milligram. —**Mg** magnesium.
mgr. or **Mgr.** manager; monseigneur; monsignor.
mgt. management.
Mhz or **MHz** megahertz.
mi. mile(s); mill(s). —**mi** (MEE) *n.Music.* the third tone of the diatonic scale. —**MI** Michigan; military intelligence.
MIA missing in action.
Mi·am·i (my·AM·ee) a city of S.E. Florida; **Miami Beach** a resort center on an island off Miami.
mi·oaw or **mi·aow** (mee·OW) *n.* & *v.* same as MEOW.
mi·as·ma (my·AZ·muh) *n.* an evil-smelling vapor, considered infectious, as of swamps; **mi·as·mic** or **mi·as·mal** *adj.*
mi·ca (MY·cuh) *n.* a mineral that is formed of very thin transparent layers; **mica schist** a rock composed of mica and quartz.
mice *pl.* of MOUSE.
Mich. Michigan.
Mi·chel·an·ge·lo (my·cl·AN·juh·loh), 1475–1564, Italian artist and poet.
Mich·i·gan (MISH·i·gun) a Midwestern U. S. state; 58,216 sq. mi. (150,779 km²); *cap.* Lansing. —**Lake Michigan** one of the Great Lakes, bordered by Michigan, Wisconsin, Illinois, and Indiana.
Mick·ey Mouse *n.* & *adj. Slang.* (something) trivial, petty, or second-rate.
Mic·mac *n.* & *adj.* (a member) of an Algonquian Indian tribe of E. Canada.
MICR "magnetic ink character recognition" for computer-processing of checks, records, etc.
micro- *comb. form.* very small: as in *microcosm, microfilm, microorganism.* —**mi·crobe** (MY–) *n.* a disease-causing microorganism; also, an alga, mold, protozoan, or yeast; **mi·cro·bi·al** (–CROH–) or **mi·cro·bic** *adj.;* **mi·cro·bi·ol·ogy** (–OL–) *n.;* **mi·cro·bi·ol·o·gist** *n.* —**mi·cro·bus** *n.* a small bus, a variation of the station wagon. —**mi·cro·com·put·er** (-PYOOT–) *n.* a computer system built around one or more microprocessors. —**mi·cro·cosm** (–cozm) *n.* a little world; miniature universe; **mi·cro·cos·mic** (–COZ–) *adj.* —**mi·cro·dot** *n.* printed matter photographically reduced to the size of a dot. —**mi·cro·e·lec·tron·ics** (–TRON–) *n.pl.* [with *sing. v.*] the electronics of microminiaturized circuits. —**mi·cro·fiche** (–feesh) *n. sing.* & *pl.,* rarely **-fich·es** *pl.* card-size sheet of microfilm containing many pages. —**mi·cro·film** *n.* & *v.* (make) a film copy (of a document, book, etc.) in highly reduced size. —**mi·cro·form** *n.* microfiche, microfilm, or other such method of information storage. —**mi·cro·gram** *n.* one millionth of a gram. —**mi·cro·graph** *n.* & *v.* (take) a photograph using a microscope; also, write or print in minute characters. —**mi·crom·e·ter** (–CROM–) *n.* an instrument for measuring very small dimensions, used in microscopes, surveyor's instruments, and the **micrometer caliper** which can measure accurately to 0.0025 mm (0.0001 in.). —**mi·cro·min·i·a·ture** (–MIN–) *adj.* of extremely small electronic parts or circuits: *a ~ component;* also **mi·cro·min·i·a·tur·ized.** —**mi·cron** *n.* one millionth of a meter. —**Mi·cro·ne·sia** (–NEE·zhuh) the part of Oceania E. of the Philippines, including Guam in the Mariana group and the Caroline, Gilbert, and Marshall Islands; **Mi·cro·ne·sian** *n.* & *adj.* —**mi·cro·or·gan·ism** (–OR·guh–) *n.* a microscopic animal or vegetable organism such as a bacterium, fungus, or virus.—**mi·cro·phone** *n.* an instrument for changing sound into electrical signals, for transmission as in a telephone or for magnification as in a public-address system. —**mi·cro·proc·es·sor** (–PROS–) *n.* a data processing unit built on a tiny silicon chip. —**mi·cro·pub·lish·ing** *n.* publishing in microform. —**mi·cro·scope** *n.* an optical instrument for viewing very minute objects; **mi·cros·co·py** (–CROS·cuh·pee) *n.;* **mi·cro·scop·ic** (–SCOP–) *adj.;* **mi·cro·scop·i·cal·ly** *adv.* —**mi·cro·sec·ond** (–SEC·und) *n.* one millionth of a second. —**mi·cro·sur·ger·y** (–SUR–) *n.* operation on microscopic structures such as blood cells. —**mi·cro·text** *n.* a microform text. —**mi·cro·wave** *n.* a radio wave varying between 1mm and 30 cm in length, as used in radar, television, and **microwave ovens** for cooking food electronically.
mid. middle. —**mid** 1 *prep. Archaic.* amid; also **'mid.** 2 *adj.* & *comb. form.* middle: *in ~ ocean, career, winter; mid-morning, mid-Fifties;* **mid·air** *n.* & *adj.* (a point) in the air well above the ground: *left suspended in ~; a ~ collision of aircraft.*

Mi·das (MY·dus) in Greek myth, a king who had the power to change whatever he touched into gold.

mid·cult *n.* middle-class culture, only moderately intellectual; middlebrow culture. —**mid·day** *n.* & *adj.* noon.

mid·den (MIDN) *n.* a refuse heap, esp. an archeological find containing tools, pottery, etc. left by prehistoric people.

mid·dle (MIDL) *adj.* intermediate or in between two extremes of length, duration, size, attitude, etc.: *a ~ position between Right and Left;* ***n.*** a middle point, part, etc.: *the ~ of a room, night, street; measures 25 inches round the ~* (i.e. waist). —**middle age** the time of life between youth and old age, usu. 40 to 65 years; **mid·dle-aged** *adj.* **Middle Ages** the period of European history between A.D. 500 and 1500. —**Middle America** the American middle class with moderate political views; also, the Middle West; **Middle American.** —**mid·dle·brow** *n.* & *adj. Informal.* moderately intellectual (person), neither highbrow nor lowbrow. —**middle class** the social class between the upper class and the lower working class, with an above-average education and standard of living; **mid·dle-class** *adj.* —**middle ear** the part of the ear between the external ear and the inner ear, including the eardrum and three small bones in humans. —**Middle East** a large region of N.E. Africa and S.W. Asia, including Iran, Iraq, the Arabian peninsula, Turkey, Egypt, and Sudan; **Middle Eastern.** —**Middle English** the English language between about 1100 and 1500. —**mid·dle·man** *n.* **-men** a go-between or intermediary; also, a trader such as a packer, wholesaler, or retailer who stands between producer and consumer. —**mid·dle·most** *adj.* same as MIDMOST. —**mid·dle-of-the-road** *adj.* of moderate views, esp. in politics, avoiding extremes; **mid·dle-of-the-road·er** *n.* —**middle school** one linking elementary and high school, usu. formed by grades 5 to 8. —**mid·dle·weight** *n.* a person of average weight, esp. a boxer weighing between 147 and 160 lbs. (67 and 75 kg for Olympics). —**Middle West(ern)** same as MIDWEST(ern). —**mid·dling** *adj.* of average size, degree, or quality, often mediocre. —**mid·dy** *n.* **mid·dies** *Informal* **1** midshipman. **2** a loose blouse with a sailor collar; also **middy blouse.** —**Mid·east** same as MIDDLE EAST.

midge (MIJ) *n.* a small fly or insect such as a gnat. —**mid·get** (MIJ·it) *n.* & *adj.* (a person or thing) proportionately small of its kind: *a circus featuring ~s; ~ golf* (played indoors), *submarine, car racing.*

mid·i (MID·ee) *n.* & *comb. form.* (a coat, dress, or skirt) reaching to the middle of the calf. —**mid·land** (–lund) *n.* & *adj.* (in) the middle or interior region of a country. —**mid·most** (–mohst) *n., adj.* & *adv.* (the part or area) nearest the middle. —**mid·night** (–nite) *n.* & *adj.* (of or at) the middle of the night; 12 o'clock at night; **midnight sun** the sun seen above the horizon continuously for six months of the year in the polar regions, as in parts of Norway, the "land of the midnight sun." —**mid·point** *n.* the middle part or stage of anything having duration or extension. —**mid·riff** *n.* the middle portion of the human body, as bared by a two-piece bathing suit; also, diaphragm (*n.* 1). —**mid·ship·man** (–mun) *n.* **-men** a student naval officer; **mid·ships** *adv.* same as AMIDSHIPS. —**midst** *n.* a middle or surrounded position: *a refugee who has landed in our ~; couldn't help him* **in the midst of** *my other preoccupations;* ***prep.*** *Archaic* or *Poetic.* amidst; also **'midst.** —**mid·stream** *n.* the middle of a stream. —**mid·sum·mer** n. the middle of summer, esp. the summer solstice. —**mid·term** *n.* & *adj.* (in) the middle of a term of office, school, etc. —**mid·town** *n.* & *adj.* (in) the middle section of a town between downtown and uptown. —**mid·way** *n.* at a fair or carnival, an avenue containing amusements, side shows, and concessions; ***adj.*** & ***adv.*** in the middle: *a ~ point; collapsed ~ between home and school.* —**mid·week** *n.* & *adj.* (in) the middle of the week; —**mid·week·ly** *adj.* & *adv.* —**Mid·west** the N. central region of the U.S. forming the American heartland, bounded by the Rockies, the S. boundaries of Kansas and Missouri, the Ohio River, and the Appalachians; **Mid·west·ern** *adj.;* **Mid·west·ern·er** *n.* —**mid·wife** *n.* **-wives** a woman who helps mothers in childbirth; **mid·wife·ry** (MID–, –WIFE·uh·ree) *n.* the work of a midwife. —**mid·win·ter** *n.* the middle of winter, esp. the winter solstice. —**mid·year** *n.* & *adj.* (in) the middle of the year.

mien (MEEN) *n.* one's appearance, bearing, or demeanor as expressive of character or mood: *a man of sorrowful ~.*

miff *n.* & *v. Informal.* (put into) a peevish fit: *was ~ed by his remarks;* **miff·y** *adj.* touchy.

MIG or **Mig** (MIG) *n.* a Soviet jet fighter.

might *pt.* of MAY. —***n.*** overwhelming strength, power, or authority: *a dictator who thinks ~ is right; attacked the problem with all her ~; fought with might and* MAIN. —**might·y** *adj.* **might·i·er, -i·est** extremely strong or great: *the ~ warrior; a ~ blow;* ***adv.*** *Informal.* extremely; very: *That's ~ nice of you; I care ~ little;* **might·i·ly** *adv.;* **might·i·ness** *n.*

mi·gnon·ette (min·yuh·NET) *n.* a hardy garden plant with soft-green leaves and tall spikes of fragrant, tiny, yellowish-green flowers; also, the yellowish-green color.

mi·graine (MY·grain) *n.* a severe kind of repeatedly occurring headache, usu. on one side, sometimes accompanied by nausea and vomiting.

mi·grant (MY·grunt) *n.* & *adj.* migrating (farm laborer or worker). —**mi·grate** (MYE–) *v.* **-grates, -grat·ed, -grat·ing** move to another region or country periodically, as birds and animals to warmer climates in the winter, or permanently, as emigrants and immigrants; **mi·gra·tion** (–GRAY–) *n.;* **mi·gra·tion·al** *adj.;* **mi·gra·to·ry** (MY·gruh·tor·ee) *adj.: a ~ bird, pattern, habit.*

mi·ka·do (mi·KAH·doh) *n.* **-does** the ancient title of Japanese emperors, given up in 1945.

mike *n. Informal.* microphone; microgram.

mil *n.* a 1/1000 unit, as of an inch (25.4 microns) in measuring the diameter of a wire, of a liter (i.e. milliliter), or of the Cyprus pound. —**mil.** military.

mi·la·dy or **mi·la·di** (mi·LAY·dee) *n.* an English-speaking noblewoman; also, a woman of fashion.

Mi·lan (mi·LAN) a city of N.W. Italy; **Mil·a·nese** (–NEEZ) *n.* & *adj.*

milch (MILK, MILCH) *adj.* of cows and such domestic animals, kept for milking, not for meat, draft, etc.

mild (MILED) *adj.* moderate or agreeable, not severe or harsh: *a ~ winter, cheese, cigarette, rebuke;* **mild·ly** *adv.;* **mild·ness** *n.*

mil·dew (MILL–) *n.* & *v.* (affect or be covered with) a minute whitish fungus that attacks plants and materials such as paper, leather, cloth, etc. in damp weather; **mil·dew·y** *adj.*

mile *n.* a unit of length equal to 5,280 ft. (1.609 km); also, a nautical mile. —**mile·age** (–ij) *n.* a per-mile traveling allowance, car-rental rate, etc.; also, the number of miles traveled, covered, etc.: *an EPA ~ test of fuel consumption; the ~ on an odometer; New York to Moscow is 4,683 miles on the air ~ chart; not much ~ left on those tires; political ~ from dirty tricks.* —**mile·post** (–pohst) *n.* a signpost indicating distance from a given point in miles. —**mil·er** (MY·lur) *n.* one who competes in a mile race. —**mile·stone** *n.* a stone put up as a milepost; hence, a significant stage or event, as during a journey or career.

mi·lieu (meel·YUR, –YOO) *n.* the immediate environment, esp. social.

mil·i·tant (–tunt) *n.* & *adj.* (one who is) aggressive or warlike, esp. in fighting for a cause or movement: *a ~ attitude, churchman, conservationist; ~ trade unionism;* **mil·i·tant·ly** *adv.;* **mil·i·tan·cy** *n.* —**mil·i·ta·rism** (–tuh·rizm) *n.* the spirit, policy, or condition of being aggressively prepared for war; **mil·i·ta·rist** *n.* **mil·i·ta·ris·tic** (–RIS–) *adj.* —**mil·i·ta·rize** (–tuh–) *v.* **-riz·es, -rized, -riz·ing** prepare and equip (an army, nation, etc.) for war; also, give a military character to (a government). —**mil·i·tar·y** (–ter·ee) *adj.* of or having to do with soldiers or an army, or the **military** *n. sing.* & *pl.,* also **-tar·ies** *pl.: the ~s of various countries; a ~ uniform, government; ~ spirit, personnel;* **military police** soldiers who carry out police duties in an army or on military posts; **mil·i·tar·i·ly** (–TER–) *adv.* —**mil·i·tate** *v.* **-tates, -tat·ed, -tat·ing** of facts, evidence, etc., have force or weight (against, rarely for something or someone). —**mi·li·tia** (muh·LISH·uh) *n.* an organization of civilians drafted to help their country in an emergency; also, a section of the army on standby, as a state National Guard or Reserve force in the U.S., **mi·li·tia·man** *n.* **-men.**

milk *n.* the white liquid from the mammary glands of a cow or other female mammal; also, a similar liquid, as found in a coconut, the latex of trees and plants, or milk of magnesia. —*v.* draw milk from (a domestic animal); also, extract (a resource such as money or ideas) from, often illicitly: *an estate ~ed dry by litigation;* **milk·er** *n.* one that milks; also, an animal that yields milk. —**milk glass** a whitish glass resembling porcelain. —**milk·maid** *n.* a dairymaid or a woman who milks cows; **milk·man** *n.* **-men** a man who sells or delivers milk. —**milk of magnesia** a milklike suspension of magnesium hydroxide in water used as an antacid and laxative. —**milk·shake** *n.* a frothy drink of milk shaken with flavoring and ice cream. —**milk·sop** *n.* a sissy. —**milk tooth** any of the first 20 teeth a baby gets that later fall out. —**milk·weed** *n.* any of a family of plants with stems containing a milky juice and pods of seeds with tufts of silky hair on them. —**milk·y** *adj.* **milk·i·er, -i·est** white like or containing or yielding milk; **milk·i·ness** *n.* —**Milky Way** the galaxy to which the sun belongs, seen in the sky as a whitish band of starlight.

[1]**mill** *n.* **1** a machine that grinds grain, traditionally between two huge, flat **mill·stones,** one turning against the other, powered by a **mill·wheel** driven by a current of water or a canal called a **mill·race,** or **mill·stream,** often flowing from a **mill·pond,** or **mill·dam. 2** any of various machines that grind pepper, stones, etc., that press the juice of sugar cane, apples, etc., or that stamp coins. **3** a factory or establishment with a routine or repetitive operation: *a cotton ~; paper ~; steel ~; photocopying ~; diploma ~* (i.e. school granting degrees of dubious value); **through the mill** *Informal.* through hard practical training or experience. —*v.: grain ~ed into flour or meal; a ~ed* (i.e. ridged) *edge,* or **mill·ing,** *given to a coin; impatient crowds ~ing about* (i.e. in circles or in confusion).

[2]**mill** *n.* a thousandth part of a dollar; **mill·age** (–ij) *n.* taxation rate in mills per dollar; mill rate.

milldam See [1]MILL.

mil·len·ni·um (mil·EN·ee·um) *n.* **mil·len·ni·ums** or **mil·len·ni·a** a thousand-year period, esp. **the millennium** prophesied in the Bible

(Revelation), one of peace and happiness; **mil·len·ni·al** *adj.* —**millepede** same as MILLIPEDE.

mil·ler *n.* the owner or operator of a grain mill.

mil·let (–it) *n.* a widely used food cereal bearing creamy white seeds on long stalks; also, similar grasses used as forage.

milli- *comb.form.* thousandth part: as in **mil·li·am·pere** (–AM·peer) *n.* 1/1,000 ampere. —**mil·liard** (–yurd, –yard) *n. Brit.* 1,000 millions. —**mil·li·bar** *n.* unit of atmospheric pressure. —**mil·lieme** (meel·YEM) *n.* 1/1,000 pound (Egypt, Sudan). —**mil·li·gram** *n.* 1/1,000 gram; *Brit.* **mil·li·gramme.** —**mil·lime** (–im, –eem) *n.* 1/1,000 dinar (Tunisia). —**mil·li·me·ter** (–mee·tur) *n.* 1/1,000 meter; *Brit.* **mil·li·me·tre.**

mil·li·ner (MIL·uh–) *n.* one who makes or deals in millinery; **mil·li·ner·y** *n.* **-ner·ies** women's hats; also, the hat business.

milling machine one with toothed cutters for shaping metal into slots, gears, etc.

mil·lion (MIL·yun) *n.* 1,000,000: *valued at 10 ~ dollars; ~s* (i.e. many millions) *of dollars;* **mil·lion·th** *n.* & *adj.* (being) the last of a million or one of a million equal parts. —**mil·lion·aire** (–NAIR) *n.* a very wealthy person, esp. one who has a million or more dollars, pounds, francs, etc. —**mil·li·pede** (–peed) *n.* a many-legged, wormlike arthropod that feeds on decaying plant matter. —**mil·li·sec·ond** *n.* 1/1,000 second. —**mil·li·volt** *n.* 1/1,000 volt.

millpond, millrace, millstone, millstream, mill wheel See ¹MILL. —**mill·wright** (–rite) *n.* one who sets up or repairs machinery in a mill or factory.

milque·toast or **Milque·toast** (MILK·tohst) *n.* & *adj.* very timid (person).

milt *n.* the sperm or sperm-filled reproductive glands of a male fish, or **milt·er** *n.*

Mil·ton (–tn), **John.** 1608–74, English poet, author of *Paradise Lost.*

Mil·wau·kee (–WAW–) a city of S.E. Wisconsin.

mime *n.* acting by bodily movements and gestures; also, a mimic or his performance; ***v.*** **mimes, mimed, mim·ing** act without speech, as in a pantomine. —**mim·e·o** (MIM·ee·oh) short form of **mim·e·o·graph** *n.* & *v.* (make copies of graphic matter with) a stencil duplicating machine. —**mi·me·sis** (mi·MEE–) *n.* artistic imitation; also, mimicry; **mi·met·ic** (–MET–) *adj.* imitative. —**mim·ic** *adj.* of actions and gestures, pretended or imitative; ***n.*** one skilled in mimicking; ***v.*** **-icks, -icked, -ick·ing** resemble or imitate, as a leaf insect or parrot; also, ape, esp. for fun; **mim·ick·er** *n.;* **mim·ic·ry** (–ree) *n.* **-ries:** *Animals use ~ as protective coloration; humor by ~.* —**mi·mo·sa** (–MOH·suh) *n.* a pea-family or acacia-related tree, shrub, or herb of warm climates whose featherlike leaves respond to stimuli by closing and drooping.

min. minimum; minister; minor; minute(s).

min·a·ret (–uh·RET) *n.* a slender tower, usu. attached to a mosque, with a surrounding balcony at the top from which the muezzin calls people to prayer.

min·a·to·ry (MIN·uh·tor·ee) *adj.* menacing or threatening.

mince *v.* **minc·es, minced, minc·ing** chop up into very small pieces; hence, affect a daintiness of speech or delicacy of manner, as by restraining one's words or walking with shortened or **minc·ing** steps; **not to mince (matters** or) **words** be plain or outspoken; **mince·pie** *n.* a pie filled with **mince·meat,** a mixture of minced meat, beef suet, apples, raisins, currants, spices, etc.

mind (MINED) *n.* the faculty by which a person remembers, thinks, understands, reasons, wills, etc.: *What's on your ~ ? Keep that in ~; She has* (or *is*) *an analytical ~;* **blow one's mind** *Slang.* experience hallucinations, as by use of LSD; also, be overwhelming, as to surprise or baffle; **change one's mind** change one's intention or opinion; **make up one's mind** decide; **out of one's mind** mentally ill; crazy; **put in mind** remind. —***v.*** pay attention (to): *~ the step* (ahead of you); *Who's ~ing* (i.e. in charge of) *the store? ~ your own business* (i.e. don't meddle in others'); *Do you ~* (i.e. object to) *closing the door?* **never mind** it does not matter. —**mind-bend·ing, mind-blow·ing** or **mind-ex·pand·ing** *adj.* psychedelic; hallucinogenic. —**mind·ed** *adj.* & *comb.form.* having a (specified) kind of mind: *high-~; if you're so ~* (i.e. inclined). —**mind·ful** *adj.* aware or careful; **mind·ful·ly** *adv.;* **mind·ful·ness** *n.* —**mind·less** *adj.* stupid or careless; **mind·less·ly** *adv.;* **mind·less·ness** *n.* —**mind reader** one who seems to guess others' thoughts; also, one gifted with ESP. —**mind's eye** imagination.

¹mine *pron.* possessive case of I: *your children and ~; a friend* **of mine** (i.e. belonging to me). —***adj.*** *Archaic* [used before a vowel or "h" or after the qualified noun] *~ eyes; sister ~.*

²mine *n.* **1** an excavation for extracting a mineral from the earth; also, a deposit of such a mineral; hence, an abundant source or supply: *a book as a gold ~ of information.* **2** an explosive charge laid under water or ground to blow up an enemy's fortifications, vehicles, or ships. —***v.*** **mines, mined, min·ing** [corresponding to the *n.* senses] **1:** *Gold used to be ~d here; We're ~ing for coal;* **min·er** *n.* **2:** *a highway ~d by the enemy; The ship sank after being ~d.* —**mine·lay·er** *n.* a ship or submarine used to lay mines under water. —**min·er·al** (MIN·uhr·ul) *n.* & *adj.* (of or containing) a substance other than animal or vegetable, which occurs naturally in the earth and is mined or quarried for use, as metals, precious stones, salt, etc.;

also, coal, petroleum, natural gas, calcium, and such substances taken from the earth: *Is it animal, vegetable, or ~? diseases due to ~ deficiencies.* —**min·er·al·ize** *v.* **-iz·es, -ized, -iz·ing:** *~d water* (impregnated with minerals); *metal ~d as* (i.e. converted into) *ore;* **min·er·al·i·za·tion** (–ZAY–) *n.* —**mineral jelly** same as PETROLATUM. —**min·er·al·o·gy** (–ROL–, –RAL–) *n.* the science of minerals; **min·er·al·o·gist** *n.* —**min·er·a·log·i·cal** (–LOJ–) *adj.;* **min·er·a·log·i·cal·ly** *adv.* —**mineral oil** an oily liquid with no color, taste, or odor that is obtained from petroleum and used as a laxative and in cosmetics; also, any oil of mineral origin. —**mineral spring** a spring whose water contains dissolved minerals. —**mineral water** water containing mineral salts or gases.

Mi·ner·va (–NUR–) the Roman goddess of wisdom and warfare.

mi·ne·stro·ne (min·uh·STROH·nee) *n.* a thick vegetable soup, originally Italian.

mine·sweep·er *n.* a ship equipped to remove enemy mines laid under water.

min·gle *v.* **-gles, -gled, -gling** mix or blend, esp. without losing identity; associate: *~d feelings of joy and sorrow; boys ~ing with girls.*

ming tree a bonsai.

min·gy (MIN·jee) *adj.* **-gi·er, -gi·est** *Informal.* mean and stingy.

min·i (MIN·ee) *adj.* & *comb.form.* miniature; very small: as in *miniskirt, minibus; a ~ tour;* ***n.,*** *pl.* **min·is** a mini dress, skirt, coat, etc. —**min·i·a·ture** (MIN·ee·uh·chur) *n.* a copy or representation on a much smaller scale than its original, as a painting on ivory or vellum: *a ~ of whisky* (i.e. tiny bottle); *the Taj Mahal carved* **in miniature;** ***adj.:*** *a ~ doll house; ~ golf;* **min·i·a·tur·ist** *n.;* **min·i·a·tur·ize** *v.* **-iz·es, -ized, -iz·ing:** *~d electronic components; the ~d computer;* **min·i·a·tur·i·za·tion** (–ZAY–) *n.* —**min·i·bike** *n.* a small motorcycle for use on country roads and trails. —**min·i·bus** *n.* a very small bus. —**min·i·com·put·er** (–cum·PYOO–) *n.* a small computer designed to do many jobs. —**min·i·cy·cle** *n.* a sturdier version of the minibike. —**min·im** *n.* & *adj.* (smallest) amount or portion, as a half note in music, 1/60 of a fluid dram, or a downward stroke in writing; **min·i·mal** *adj.* the smallest or least possible: *a ~ charge; ~ terms, standards;* **min·i·mal·ly** *adv.* —**minimal art** abstract painting or sculpture in simple shapes and minimum colors. —**min·i·mize** *v.* **-miz·es, -mized, -miz·ing** reduce to a minimum; also, belittle. —**min·i·mum** *adj.* & *n.* **-mums** or **-ma** least or lowest (amount): *a low ~ wage; Yesterday's ~ temperature; expenses reduced to a ~; a ~-security prison.*

min·ion (MIN·yun) *n.* a servile follower; favorite servant.

miniscule rare spelling of MINUSCULE. —**min·i·se·ries** *n.* a television drama presented in a series of parts spread over many days: *"Roots" was a 12-hour, 8-part ~.* —**min·i·skirt** *n.* a short skirt with the hemline well above the knee: *a* **min·i·skirt·ed** *drum majorette.* —**min·i·state** *n.* one of the smaller, newly independent states.

min·is·ter *n.* an agent or public official, as a member of a government cabinet, a diplomat ranking below ambassador, or a "minister of religion," as a protestant clergyman. —***v.*** serve: *to ~ to the (needs of the) sick;* **min·is·tra·tion** (–TRAY–) *n.* —**min·is·te·ri·al** (–TEER–) *adj.* —**min·is·trant** (–trunt) *n.* & *adj.* —**min·is·try** (–tree) *n.* **-tries** a minister's office, term, or duties: *a Tory ~* (i.e. government or cabinet); *the foreign ~* (i.e. government department); *called to the ~* (i.e. clergy).

mink *n.* a small weasel or its lustrous, deep-brown fur made into a coat, cape, or stole.

Minn. Minnesota. —**Min·ne·ap·o·lis** (min·ee·AP·uh·lis) a city of S.E. Minnesota.

min·ne·sing·er (MIN·uh–) *n.* a German love poet and singer of the Middle Ages.

Min·ne·so·ta (–uh·SOH·tuh) a Midwestern state of the U.S.; 84,068 sq.mi. (217,735 km²); *cap.* St. Paul; **Min·ne·so·tan** *n.* & *adj.*

min·now (–oh) *n.* a fish of the carp family, often used as bait, as the "common shiner."

Mi·no·an (–NOH·un) *n.* & *adj.* (an inhabitant) of Crete at the time of its Bronze Age civilization, 3000 to 1100 B.C.

mi·nor (MY·nur) *adj.* lesser in importance, rank, size, extent, etc.: *a ~ repair, baseball league, musical scale* (with half steps after the second and fifth notes); *~ subject* (of a program of studies). —***n.*** **1** a person under the age of adulthood, usu. 18. **2** a minor subject of study; ***v.:*** *a history major ~ing in German.* —**mi·nor·i·ty** (–NOR–) *n.* **-ties** **1** a part, group, or number that is less than half, not a majority: *the Catholic ~; blacks, Jews, Orientals and such ~ groups.* **2** the state of being a minor.

Min·o·taur (MIN·uh·tor) a human monster with a bull's head, fathered by the legendary king **Mi·nos** (MYE–) of Crete and later confined in the Labyrinth and fed with human beings until slain by Theseus.

Minsk capital of the Byelorussian S.S.R.

min·ster *n.* a church attached to a monastery; also, a great cathedral such as Westminster or York in England.

min·strel (–strul) *n.* **1** a traveling poet-musician of the Middle Ages; **min·strel·sy** *n.* **-sies** minstrels collectively, their occupation, or a collection of their songs. **2** a member of a **minstrel show,** an American variety show featuring comics with blackened faces.

[1]**mint** *n.* a place where money is coined. —***v.*** coin (money or anything similar); also, invent or fabricate; **mint·er** *n.;* **mint·age** (–ij) *n.* —**a mint of money** a vast sum of money; **in mint condition** of books, stamps, coins, and such products, as good as new.

²mint *n.* any of a large family of square-stemmed plants such as peppermint, lavender, and rosemary, whose fragrant leaves or oil is used in perfumes, flavoring, medicine, etc.; **mint·y** *adj.*—**mint julep** See JULEP.

min·u·end (–yoo·end) *n.* a number from which another is to be subtracted. —**min·u·et** (–yoo·ET) *n.* a slow, stately 17th century dance for couples; also, the music for it. —**mi·nus** (MY–) *prep.* [indicating subtraction or negative] *3 ~ 2 is 1; a temperature of ~ 5 degrees* (i.e. 5 below zero); *returned home ~* (*Informal.* without) *his hat;* ***n.*** the **minus sign** (–) indicating subtraction or negative; ***adj.:*** *a B ~ grade; a ~ temperature; a ~ quantity such as "–2ab."* —**mi·nus·cule** (mi·NUS–, MIN·us–) *n.* a small or lowercase letter; ***adj.*** minute: *a ~ script, increment, percentage.* —**¹mi·nute** (my·NEWT) *adj.* **-nut·er, -nut·est** very small or insignificant; requiring close scrutiny; hence, detailed: *~ insects, details, instructions;* **mi·nute·ly** *adv.;* **mi·nute·ness** *n.* —**²min·ute** (MIN·it) *n.* **1** a 60th part of an hour or of an angular degree; hence, a moment: *Wait a ~;* **The minute (that)** (i.e. as soon as) *the teacher turns her back, the children start talking.* **2 minutes** *pl.* the official record of the proceedings at a meeting. —***adj.:*** *quick-cooking ~ rice, steak; a clock's ~ hand.* —**min·ute·man** *n.* **-men** **1** a volunteer of the American Revolutionary War trained to fight "at a minute's notice." **2 Minuteman** a solid-propellant intercontinental ballistic missile that can be launched quickly. —**minute steak** a thin beefsteak for fast frying. —**mi·nu·ti·ae** (–NEW·shee·ee) *n.pl.* minute details; *sing.* **mi·nu·ti·a** (–shee·uh).

minx *n.* a pert or saucy girl; **minx·ish** *adj.*

Mi·o·cene (MY·uh·seen) *n.* & *adj.* (of) the fourth epoch of the Cenozoic era of the earth, beginning about 26 million years ago.

mir·a·cle (MEER·uh–) *n.* an action or event that is beyond human power or understanding, as raising the dead to life; also a marvelous person or thing: *She's a ~ of patience.* —**mi·rac·u·lous** (–RAC·yoo·lus) *adj.: a ~ recovery from cancer; his ~ good fortune;* **mi·rac·u·lous·ly** *adv.* —**mi·rage** (–RAHZH) *n.* an optical illusion of water or phantom images caused by refraction of light in hot air, as over the ocean when a ship may be seen in the sky; hence, something unattainable or illusory.

mire *n.* a marsh; also, slush or deep mud; ***v.*** **mires, mired, mir·ing** (cause to) get stuck or sink in mud; also, soil with mud. —**mir·y** *adj.* **mir·i·er, -i·est** muddy; swampy; dirty.

mir·ror (MEER·ur) *n.* & *v.* (reflect, as in) a glass with its back coated with silver; also, a similar shiny surface: *a building ~ed in a reflecting pool; the face as a ~ of character.*

mirth *n.* gaiety and fun, esp. with laughter. —**mirth·ful** *adj.;* **mirth·ful·ly** *adv.*

MIRV (MURV) *n.* **MIRV's** a long-range missile with multiple warheads for different targets; "Multiple Independently-targeted Re-entry Vehicle."

mis- *prefix* [with negative sense]: as in *mislead, misshapen.* —**mis·ad·ven·ture** (–VEN·chur) *n.* mishap; misfortune: *not homicide but death by ~* (i.e. accident). —**mis·al·li·ance** (–uh·LYE·unce) *n.* unsuitable alliance, esp. in marriage. —**mis·al·lo·ca·tion** (–CAY–) *n.* improper allocation (of funds, resources, etc.) —**mis·an·thrope** (MIS·un–) *n.* one who distrusts or hates everyone; **mis·an·throp·ic** (–THROP–) *adj.;* **mis·an·thro·py** (–AN·thruh·pee) *n.;* **mis·an·thro·pist** *n.* —**mis·ap·ply** (–uh·PLY) *v.* **-ap·plies, -ap·plied, -ap·ply·ing** apply (funds or resources) illegally or wastefully; **mis·ap·pli·ca·tion** (–CAY–) *n.* —**mis·ap·pre·hend** (–ri·HEND) *v.* misunderstand; **mis·ap·pre·hen·sion** (–HEN–) *n.* —**mis·ap·pro·pri·ate** (–PROH–) *v.* **-ates, -at·ed, -at·ing** take (funds, etc.) wrongly or dishonestly; **mis·ap·pro·pri·a·tion** (–AY–) *n.* —**mis·be·got·ten** (–bi·GOTN) *adj.* illegitimate; bastard. —**mis·behave** (–HAIV) *v.* **-haves, -haved, -hav·ing** behave badly: *got drunk and ~ed (himself);* **mis·be·hav·ior** *n.* —**mis·be·liev·er** (–LEE·vur) *n.* *Archaic.* heretic or unbeliever. —**mis·brand** *v.* brand or label misleadingly.

misc. miscellaneous; miscellany.

mis·cal·cu·late (–CAL·kyuh–) *v.* **-lates, -lat·ed, -lat·ing** calculate or estimate (a result or outcome) wrongly; **mis·cal·cu·la·tion** (–LAY–) *n.* —**mis·call** (–CAWL) *v.* misname. —**mis·car·riage** (–CAIR·ij) *n.* failure of intended or proper result: *A "spontaneous abortion" or expulsion of an embryo or fetus from the uterus is a ~; a bad trial resulting in a ~ of justice; freight not delivered because of ~.* —**mis·car·ry** (–CAIR·ee) *v.* **-car·ries, -car·ried, -car·ry·ing** have a miscarriage. —**mis·cast** (–CAST) *v.* **-casts, -cast, -cast·ing** cast in an unsuitable role.

mis·ce·ge·na·tion (mis·i·juh·NAY–) *n.* marriage between a white and a member of another race. —**mis·cel·la·ne·ous** (–uh·LAY·nee·us) *adj.* of a collection, of varied or mixed items through similar; also, many-sided: *a ~ talent;* **mis·cel·la·ne·ous·ly** *adv.;* **mis·cel·la·ne·ous·ness** *n.* —**mis·cel·la·ny** (MIS·uh·lay·nee) *n.* **-nies** a miscellaneous literary collection.

mis·chance *n.* (a piece of) bad luck. —**mis·chief** (–chif) *n.* harm or injury caused by irresponsible behavior; also the cause or doer of the harm, or the annoyance caused: *a prankster charged with public ~; boys full of ~; eyes full of ~* (i.e. playful teasing). —**mis·chie·vous** (MIS·chi·vus) *adj.: ~ children, looks, rumors;* **mis·chie·vous·ly** *adv.;* **mis·chie·vous·ness** *n.*

mis·ci·ble (MIS·uh–) *adj.* of a liquid, capable of being mixed (with another).

mis·com·mu·ni·ca·tion (–cuh·mew·nuh·CAY–) *n.* defective or erroneous communication. —**mis·con·ceive** (–cun·SEEV) *v.* **-ceives, -ceived, -ceiv·ing** misunderstand; **mis·con·cep·tion** (–SEP–) *n.* —**mis·con·duct** (–CON–) *n.* improper behavior, esp. adultery; also, mismanagement, esp. in public office. —**mis·con·strue** (–cun·STROO) *v.* **-strues, -strued, -stru·ing** misinterpret; **mis·con·struc·tion** (–STRUC–) *n.* —**mis·count** *v.* count incorrectly; ***n.*** such a count. —**mis·cre·ant** (MIS·cree·unt) *n.* & *adj.* (one who is) villainous or depraved. —**mis·cue** (–CUE) *v.* **-cues, -cued, -cu·ing** miss one's cue or cue ball; ***n.*** an error. —**mis·deal** (–DEEL) *v.* **-deals, -dealt** (–DELT), **-deal·ing** deal (playing cards) wrongly; ***n.*** such a deal. —**mis·deed** (–DEED) *n.* a wrong or wicked deed; crime. —**mis·de·mean·or** (–di·MEE·nur) *n.* a violation such as a traffic offense or assault and battery that is less serious than a felony; also, a misdeed. —**mis·di·rect** (–RECT) *v.* direct wrongly; **mis·di·rec·tion** (–REC–) *n.* —**mis·do·ing** (–DOO–) *n.* wrongdoing; **mis·do·er** *n.* —**mise en scène** (mee·zahn·SEN) *French.* a stage setting; hence, surroundings or milieu.

mi·ser (MY·zur) *n.* a stingy person who hoards money, loving it for its own sake; **mi·ser·ly** *adj.;* **mi·ser·li·ness** *n.* —**mis·er·a·ble** (MIZ·uh·ruh·bl) *n.* & *adj.* wretched, poor, or unhappy (person): ~ *life, slums, weather;* **mis·er·a·bly** *adv.* —**mis·er·y** (MIZ·uh·ree) *n.* **-er·ies** a cause or condition of being miserable: *a life of ~; the ~s of war.*

mis·fea·sance (–FEE·zunce) *n.* *Law.* illegal performance of a lawful action. —**mis·file** *v.* **-files, -filed, -fil·ing** file (a paper, etc.) in the wrong place. —**mis·fire** *v.* **-fires, -fired, -fir·ing** fail to fire or to achieve intended effect, as a plan; ***n.:*** *the ~ in a badly tuned engine.* —**mis·fit** *n.* one not well-adjusted socially or in a job; also, a badly fitted garment; ***v.*** **fits, fit·ted, fit·ting:** *~d in his brother's clothes.* —**mis·for·tune** (–FOR·chun) *n.* (a piece of) bad luck. —**mis·giv·ing** (–GIV–) *n.* usu. **misgivings** *pl.* feelings of doubt or lack of confidence. —**mis·gov·ern** (–GUV–) *v.* govern badly; **mis·gov·ern·ment** *n.* —**mis·guide** *v.* **-guides, -guid·ed, -guid·ing** mislead, esp. into wrongdoing; **mis·guid·ance** (–GUY·dunce) *n.* —**mis·guid·ed** *adj.* mistaken; in error: *He's well-meaning but very ~;* **mis·guid·ed·ly** *adv.* —**mis·han·dle** (–HAN–) *v.* **-dles, -dled, -dling** treat or manage badly. —**mis·hap** *n.* an unlucky, usu. minor accident. —**mis·hear** (–HEER) *v.* **-hears, -heard** (–HURD), **-hear·ing** hear wrongly.

mish·mash *n.* a hodgepodge.

mis·in·form (–FORM) *v.* give (someone) false or misleading information; **mis·in·for·ma·tion** (–MAY–) *n.* —**mis·in·ter·pret** (–TUR–) *v.* understand or interpret incorrectly; **mis·in·ter·pre·ta·tion** (–TAY–) *n.* —**mis·judge** (–JUJ) *v.* **-judg·es, -judged, -judg·ing** judge wrongly or unjustly; **mis·judg·ment** *n.* —**mis·la·bel** (–LAY–) *v.* **-bels, -bel(l)ed, -bel·(l)ing** label incorrectly or falsely. —**mis·lay** (–LAY) *v.* **-lays, -laid, -lay·ing** misplace (something); hence, lose. —**mis·lead** (–LEED) *v.* **-leads, -led, -lead·ing** to lead (someone) to go, think, or act in error or badly: *misled by illegible writing, bad companions, his guilty look;* **mis·lead·ing** *adj.:* *~ advertising;* **mis·lead·ing·ly** *adv.* —**mis·man·age** (–MAN·ij) *v.* **-ag·es, -aged, -ag·ing** manage badly or dishonestly; **mis·man·age·ment** *n.* —**mis·match** *v.* match badly, as incompatible marriage partners; ***n.:*** *The boxers were an obvious ~.* —**mis·name** *v.* **-names, -named, -nam·ing** name incorrectly or inappropriately; **mis·no·mer** (–NOH–) *n.* (use of) a wrongly given name: *It's (using) a ~ to call a whale a fish.*

mis(o)- *comb.form.* hatred or hating: as in **mi·sog·a·mist** (–SOG–) *n.* one who hates marriage; **mi·sog·a·my** *n.* hatred of marriage. —**mi·sog·y·nist** (–SOJ–) *n.* one who hates women; **mi·sog·y·ny** *n.* hatred of women; **mi·sog·y·nous** (–nus) *adj.*

mis·place (–PLACE) *v.* **-plac·es, -placed, -plac·ing** put in a wrong place: *A ~d key is often lost; realized only when jilted that his affections had been ~d* (i.e. bestowed on the wrong person). —**mis·play** (–PLAY) *v.* play (a game) wrongly; ***n.*** a wrong play. —**mis·print** *n.* a printing error; ***v.*** (–PRINT) print incorrectly. —**mis·pri·sion** (–PRIZH·un) *n.* *Law.* criminal neglect of duty, actively or passively: *~ of felony* (i.e. concealment of another's felony). —**mis·pro·nounce** (–NOUNCE) *v.* **-nounc·es, -nounced, -nounc·ing** pronounce incorrectly; **mis·pro·nun·ci·a·tion** (–see·AY–) *n.* —**mis·quote** (–KWOTE) *v.* **-quotes, -quot·ed, -quot·ing** quote incorrectly; **mis·quo·ta·tion** (–TAY–) *n.* —**mis·read** (–REED) *n.* **-reads, -read** (–RED), **-read·ing** read wrongly; hence, misunderstand. —**mis·rep·re·sent** (–ri·ZENT) *v.* represent incorrectly or falsely; **mis·rep·re·sen·ta·tion** (–TAY–) *n.* —**mis·rule** (–ROOL) *n.* bad government; also, disorder or anarchy; ***v.*** **-rules, -ruled, -rul·ing** govern badly.

¹miss *v.* **1** fail to attain a desired end, reach or hit something, achieve a purpose, etc.: *a ~ed shot; She ~ed the target; to ~an opportunity, a bus, joke, someone in a crowd; a ~ing* (i.e. misfiring) *engine; just ~ed* (i.e. escaped) *being hit.* **2** feel the absence of a liked person: *I'll ~ you when you're gone.* —***n.:*** *a hit or a ~; strikes, spares, and ~es in bowling.* —**miss·ing** *adj.* lost or absent: *The child is ~; the theory of the evolutionary* **missing link** *between apes and man.*

²miss *n.* **miss·es 1** a young unmarried woman or girl. **2 Miss** [title used before an unmarried girl's or woman's name]: *Miss (Mary) Jones; Miss M. Jones; Miss America* (personified); rarely: *Miss Mary.*

Miss. Mississippi.

mis·sal (MISL) n. a book used by the celebrant at a Mass, containing prayers, readings, etc.
mis·shape (–SHAPE) *v.* **-shapes,** *pt.* & *pp.* **-shaped** or **-shap·en, -shap·ing** form in a bad shape; **mis·shap·en** *adj.* deformed: *a ~ limb.*
mis·sile (MISL) *n.* something directed at a target, esp. a weapon such as a stone, spear, bullet, rocket, *guided missile,* etc. **—mis·sil(e)·ry** (–ree) *n.* military missiles collectively; also, their design and operation, the work of a **mis·sile·man** *n.* **-men. —mis·sion** (MISH·un) *n.* the sending of people on an assignment; also, the people thus sent or their assigned task: *a ~* (to preach the Gospel) *to the Indies; collecting money for the ~s; a diplomatic ~ to China; a rescue ~; a pilot who has flown numerous* (bombing) *~s over Vietnam; a message of ~ accomplished; an Apollo space ~* (of exploration); *her lifelong ~* (i.e. calling) *of caring for the sick.* **—mis·sion·ar·y** (–ner·ee) *n.* **-ar·ies** a person on a religious mission; ***adj.:*** *a ~ priest, society, zeal.* **—mis·sion·er** *n.* missionary.
mis·sis (MIS·uz) *n. Informal.* one's wife; also, the mistress of a household.
Mis·sis·sip·pi (mis·uh·SIP·ee) **1** the largest North American river, which rises in N. Minnesota and empties into the Gulf of Mexico. **2** a S. state of the U.S.; 47,716 sq.mi. (123,584 km²); *cap.* Jackson; **Mis·sis·sip·pi·an** (–SIP–) *n.* & *adj.;* **Mississippian period** the earlier half of the Carboniferous.
mis·sive (MIS·iv) *n.* an epistle or long letter (sent to someone).
Mis·sour·i (mi·ZOOR·ee) **1** a river of W. central U.S., flowing from S.W. Montana into the Mississippi. **2** a Midwestern state of the U.S.; 69,686 sq.mi. (180,486 km²); *cap.* Jefferson City; **Mis·sour·i·an** *n.* & *adj.*
mis·spell (–SPEL) *v.* **-spells,** *pt.* & *pp.* **-spelled** or **-spelt, -spell·ing** spell incorrectly; **mis·spell·ing** *n.* **—mis·spend** (–SPEND) *v.* **-spends, -spent, -spend·ing** spend improperly; also, waste or squander: *a ~t youth.* **—mis·state** (–STATE) *v.* **-states, -stat·ed, -stat·ing** state incorrectly or falsely; **mis·state·ment** *n.* **—mis·step** *n.* a wrong step; also, a mistake.
mis·sus same as MISSIS.
mist *n.* a fog that is not too thick to see through nor so thin as a haze; hence, something that dims or blurs vision: *a ~* (i.e. fine spray) *of perfume; lost in the ~s of antiquity;* ***v.*** make or become misty, as eyes with tears.
mis·take (–STAKE) *n.* an error of observation, judgment, expression, action, etc.; misunderstanding: *Our ~, Sir!; opened by ~;* **make no mistake (about it)** you may be sure. **—*v.* -takes, -took, -tak·en, -tak·ing:** *I mistook her words; twins often ~n for each other;* **mis·tak·a·ble** *adj.* **—mis·tak·en** (–TAY·cun) *adj.: I may be ~* (i.e. wrong); *a ~ notion;* **mis·ta·ken·ly** *adv.*
mis·ter *n.* **1** the full form of MR. **2** *Informal.* sir: *Hey, ~!*
mis·time (–TIME) *v.* **-times, -timed, -tim·ing** say or do at the wrong time.
mis·tle·toe (MISL·toh) *n.* a parasitic evergreen plant associated with Christmastime, bearing thickly clustered leaves, tiny yellow flowers, and white shiny berries.
mistook *pt.* of MISTAKE.
mis·tral (MIS·trul, mi·STRAHL) *n.* a cold northerly wind from the W. Alps blowing over S. France and causing frost damage to crops.
mis·treat (–TREET) *v.* ill-treat; **mis·treat·ment** *n.*
mis·tress (MIS·tris) *n.* **1** a woman in a ruling or controlling position, as the female head of a household or a teacher or expert, esp. in a special subject such as dancing: *Britain used to be the ~ of the seas.* **2** a woman who regularly has sex with a man she is not married to. **3 Mistress** *Archaic.* Mrs.; Miss.
mis·tri·al (MIS·try·ul) *n.* a judgment that a trial is of no legal effect: *Since the jurors could not agree on a verdict, the judge declared a ~.* **—mis·trust** (–TRUST) *n.* & *v.* (feel) a lack of trust or confidence; **mis·trust·ful** *adj.;* **mis·trust·ful·ly** *adv.*
mist·y *adj.* **mist·i·er, -i·est** covered with mist; blurred; **mist·i·ly** *adv.;* **mist·i·ness** *n.*
mis·un·der·stand (–STAND) *v.* **-stands, -stood, -stand·ing** fail to understand (a message, person, etc.) correctly; **mis·un·der·stand·ing** *n.* failure to understand properly; hence, a quarrel or falling out. **—mis·use** (–YOOZ) *v.* **-us·es, -used, -us·ing** use (a thing) or treat (a person) improperly; ***n.*** (–YOOS): *a ~ of words, authority.*
mite *n.* **1** a tiny, insectlike, usu. parasitic creature, as a chigger, that sucks the blood of animals, juice of plants, or torments human beings, as the "grain mite" and the "itch mite." **2** a tiny amount, small coin, or very small creature.
mi·ter or **mi·tre** (MY·tur) *n.* **1** the tall, pointed ceremonial headdress of ecclesiastics of the rank of bishop and higher, that is joined in two folding halves facing front and back. **2** a corner joint of two beveled or rabbeted pieces fitting together in a right angle; also **miter joint. —*v.* -ters** or **-tres, -tered** or **-tred, -ter·ing** or **-tring:** *two boards ~d together.*
mit·i·gate *v.* **-gates, -gat·ed, -gat·ing** make or become mild or less harsh; moderate; mollify; alleviate: *~ anger, pain, a disaster, the cold;* **mit·i·ga·tion** (–GAY–) *n.* **—mit·i·ga·tive** (–gay·tiv) *adj.;* **mit·i·ga·tor** *n.;* **mit·i·ga·to·ry** (–guh·tor·ee) *adj.*
mi·to·sis (–TOH–) *n.* cell division that leaves the new cells with their own nuclei and the same number of chromosomes as the original cell; **mi·tot·ic** (–TOT–) *adj.*
mi·tral (MY·trul) *adj.* like a miter: *the ~ valve of the heart;* **mi·tre** same as MITER.
mitt *n.* a protective covering for the hand but without fingers: *a (baseball) catcher's ~; an oven ~; babies' ~s.* **—mit·ten** *n.* a glove that covers

the four fingers together and the thumb separately.

mix *v.* **mix·es,** *pt.* & *pp.* **mixed** or **mixt, mix·ing** combine so as to associate together: *to* ~ *ingredients for a cake; a visit* ~*ing business with pleasure; a sociable woman who* ~*es well with all classes of people; Oil and water do not* ~. —***n.:*** *a cake* ~*; gin with your favorite* ~ (such as tonic). —**mix·a·ble** *adj.* —**mixed** *adj.: a* ~ *group* (of men and women); *a* ~ *bag* (of assorted items); *a* ~ *marriage* (between people of different religions or races); *a* ~ *metaphor* (with clashing comparisons); *something of doubtful value received with* ~ *feelings* (e.g. joy and regret). —**mixed number** a number with an integer and a fraction, as 2⅓. —**mixed-up** *adj.* confused. —**mix·er** *n.* one that mixes: *an electric food* ~*; too shy to be a good* ~ (i.e. in society). —**mixt.** *Abbrev.* for **mix·ture** (–chur) *n.* a mixing, being mixed, or something mixed: *a freezing* ~ *of salt and crushed ice.* —**mix-up** *n.* a confusion or a confused state.

miz·(z)en *n.* & *adj.* (a fore-and-aft sail) on the mizzenmast; **miz·zen·mast** *n.* in a ship with two or three masts, the one nearest the stern.

mk(s). mark(s); markka(s). —**MKS** meter-kilogram-second.

mktg. marketing.

ml. milliliter. —**ML** Middle Latin.

MLD or **m.l.d.** minimum lethal dose.

Mlle(s). Mademoiselle(s).

mm. millimeter(s). —**MM.** Messieurs.

Mme(s). Madame(s).

Mn manganese. —**MN** Minnesota.

mne·mon·ic (ni·MON–) *adj.* of or meant to help the memory: *jingles, rhymes, and such* ~ *devices.*

mo(s). month(s). —**Mo.** or **MO** Missouri. —**Mo** molybdenum. —**M.O.** mail order; medical officer; money order.

moan (MONE) *n.* & *v.* (say with or utter) a low and mournful sound: *"I wish I were dead," she* ~*ed.*

moat (MOTE) *n.* & *v.* (surround with) a deep and wide ditch, usu. water-filled, as around a fortress wall or zoo display area.

mob *n.* **1** a disorderly or riotous crowd; also, the common people or masses. **2** *Informal.* a criminal group; gang. —***v.*** **mobs, mobbed, mob·bing** crowd around or into, as a mob: *a movie star* ~*d by autograph hunters; shoppers* ~*ing stores.*

Mo·bile (moh·BEEL, MOH–) a seaport of S.W. Alabama.

mo·bile (MOH·bl, –beel) *adj.* moving or movable: *a* ~ *library; a* ~ (i.e. changeable in expression) *face; an upwardly* ~ *social class;* **mo·bil·i·ty** (–BIL–) *n.* —***n.*** (–beel) a delicately balanced, usu. suspended decoration or art object made of pieces of metal or plastic attached to wires and rods so as to move in currents of air. —**mobile home** a large trailer used as a home. —**mo·bi·lize** (MOH·buh–) *v.* **-liz·es, -lized, -liz·ing** put into motion or active use; also, organize or get ready, as troops for war; **mo·bi·liz·er** *n.* —**mo·bi·li·za·tion** (–ZAY–) *n.*

MOBS "Multiple Orbit Bombardment System" of satellites carrying nuclear warheads.

mob·ster *n.* member of a criminal group or mob; gangster.

moc·ca·sin (MOC·uh–) *n.* a heelless sandal or slipper of soft leather, originally used by North American Indians; also, a water moccasin.

mo·cha (MOH·cuh) *n.* a fine variety of coffee, originally shipped from Mocha, Yemen. —***adj.*** flavored with coffee or coffee and chocolate: ~ *cakes, puddings.*

mock *v.* make fun of; ridicule, esp. by imitating or caricaturing: *a* ~*ing gesture; They* ~*ed and jeered at him;* ***adj.*** pseudo; imitation: ~ *turtle soup; staged a* ~ *battle;* **mock·er** *n.;* **mock·er·y** *n.* —**mock·he·ro·ic** (–hi·ROH–) *adj.* imitative of heroic style or character, as *Don Quixote* or *The Rape of the Lock.* —**mock·ing·bird** *n.* a songbird of southern U.S. that imitates the calls of other birds. —**mock-up** *n.* an accurately built model, usu. full-size, for studying, testing, or display, as of an airplane.

mod. moderate; moderato; modern. —**mod** *n.* & *adj.* (of or like) one who is bold and unconventional in dress and behavior.

mod·al (MOH·dul) *adj.* of or having to do with a mode; **modal auxiliary** an auxiliary verb such as "can," "might," or "shall" that expresses a grammatical mood when used with another verb; **mo·dal·i·ty** (–DAL–) *n.* —**mode** *n.* a method, manner, or style, esp. one that is usual, customary, or current: *the* ~ *of life of Eskimos; the major and minor* ~*s in music; dressed in the latest* ~. —**mod·el** (MODL) *n.* a person or figure that imitates or is to be imitated or copied: *a wax* ~ *for a marble statute; a* ~ *who poses nude; She's a* ~ *of decorum; the make and* ~ (i.e. particular design) *of your automobile;* ***adj.:*** *a* ~ *pupil, house* (on display); *his* ~ *behavior.* —***v.*** **-els, -el(l)ed, -el·(l)ing:** *She* ~*s herself on her mother; trained in* ~*ing clothes at fashion shows;* ~*s at $100 an hour.* —**mod·er·ate** (–it) *adj.* within proper bounds, esp. not excessive: *She is* ~ *in her expenses; a man of* ~ *habits; a* ~ *drinker;* ***n.:*** *a political* ~*, more liberal than conservative;* **mod·er·ate·ly** *adv.;* **mod·er·ate·ness** *n.* —***v.*** (–rate) **-ates, -at·ed, -at·ing:** *She exercised a* ~*ing influence on him; Who's* ~*ing* (i.e. acting as moderator) *(on) the panel discussion?* —**mod·er·a·tion** (–RAY–) *n.* —**mod·er·a·tor** (MOD–) *n.* one who presides.

mod·ern *adj.* recent or current; also, up-to-date: *The New World was settled in* ~ *times;* ~ *architecture, fashions, views;* ***n.:*** *ancients and* ~*s.* —**Modern English** the English language since about 1500. —**mod·ern·ism** *n.* modern views or methods; also, a modern idiom or usage; **mod·ern·ist** *n.* & *adj.;* **mod·ern·is·tic** (–NIS–) *adj.* —**mod·ern·ly** *adv.;* **mod·ern·**

ness or **mod·er·ni·ty** (–DUR–) *n.* —**mod·ern·ize** *v.* **-iz·es, -ized, -iz·ing** make or become modern; **mod·ern·iz·er** *n.;* **mod·ern·i·za·tion** (–ZAY–) *n.*

mod·est (–ist) *adj.* proper in one's behavior or appearance, being unassuming, shy, decent, etc.: *a ~ sales pitch, not loud or vulgar; a ~ little cottage; a ~ demand; not ~ enough to wear to church;* **mod·est·ly** *adv.* —**mod·es·ty** *n.* the quality of being properly humble, shy, decent, etc. —**mod·i·cum** *n.* a small amount: *a ~ of wine, truth, taste, manners.*

modif. modification. —**mod·i·fy** *v.* **-fies, -fied, -fy·ing** change or alter, esp. to limit or moderate: *to ~ a method, demand, one's tone of voice; In "too little" "too" ~s "little";* **mod·i·fi·er** *n.;* **mod·i·fi·ca·tion** (–CAY–) *n.* —**mod·ish** (MOH·dish) *adj.* overly fashionable or stylish: *too ~ for my tastes;* **mod·ish·ly** *adv.;* **mod·ish·ness** *n.* —**mod·u·lar** (MOJ·uh·lur) *adj.* constructed with modules; hence, capable of adaptation or expansion: *a ~ system; ~ equipment, house construction;* **mod·u·lar·i·ty** (–LAIR–) *n.* —**mod·u·lar·ize** (MOJ·uh–) *v.* **-iz·es, -ized, -iz·ing** make modular; **mod·u·lar·i·za·tion** (–ZAY–) *n.* —**mod·u·late** (MOJ–) *v.* **-lates, -lat·ed, -lat·ing** regulate or adjust, as the tone or pitch of one's voice is speaking, from one key to another in a musical composition, the frequency or amplitude of video and audio signals in broadcasting, etc.; **mod·u·la·tor** *n.;* **mod·u·la·tion** (–LAY–) *n.* —**mod·ule** (MOJ·ool) *n.* **1** a standard size or measure: *toothpaste in six metric ~s.* **2** a structural unit or component with a specific function in a larger unit or system: *building ~s; a lunar excursion ~; a learning ~.* —**mo·dus o·pe·ran·di** (MOH·dus·op·uh·RAN·dye) *Latin.* mode of operation or procedure; **modus vi·ven·di** (–VEN·dye) *Latin.* mode of living or coexisting.

Mo·ga·di·shu (–DEE·shoo) capital of Somalia.

mo·gul (MOH–) *n.* **1** magnate: *a movie ~.* **2** a bump on a ski run.

mo·hair (MOH–) *n.* a fabric made of the hair of the Angora goat, usu. blended with wool.

Mo·ham·med (–HAM·id) A.D. 570?–632, founder of the Moslem religion, or **Mo·ham·med·an·ism; Mo·ham·med·an** *n.* & *adj.* Moslem. Also **Mu·ham·mad, Mu·ham·mad·an, Mu·ham·mad·an·ism.**

Mohave same as MOJAVE.

Mo·hawk (MOH–) *n.* (a member of) an Iroquois Indian people who originally lived in the region of the **Mohawk River,** a tributary of the Hudson. Also ***adj.***

Mo·he·gan (–HEE·gun) *n.* (a member of) an Algonquian Indian people formerly living in W. Connecticut; also ***adj.*** —**Mo·hi·can** (–HEE·cun) *n.* (a member of) a tribe of Algonquian Indians, including the Mohegans, formerly living along the Hudson River; also ***adj.***

Mohs' (MOZE) **scale** scale for hardness of minerals ranging from 1 (talc) to 10 (diamond).

moi·e·ty (–uh·tee) *n.* **-ties** a portion, esp. half (*of* something).

moire (MWAR) or **moi·ré** (mwah·RAY, maw–) *n.* & *adj.* (a silk or rayon) having a wavelike pattern or clouded appearance.

moist *adj.* moderately wet: *skin ~ with perspiration;* **moist·ly** *adv.;* **moist·ness** *n.* —**mois·ten** (MOISN) *v.* make or become moist. —**moist·ture** (–chur) *n.* liquid that causes moistness, esp. water vapor, as in the air; **mois·tur·ize** *v.* **-iz·es, -ized, -iz·ing** make (skin, air, etc.) moist, as a cosmetic cream.

Mo·ja·ve (–HAH·vee) **Desert** a desert of S.E. California.

mol. molecular; molecule. —**mol** (MOLE) *n.* same as [3]MOLE, *n.* 2; **mo·lal** *adj.*

mo·lar (MOH·lur) *n.* & *adj.* (a tooth) adapted for grinding.

mo·las·ses (–LAS·iz) *n.* a thick, sticky, brown syrup obtained as a by-product during the refining of cane sugar.

[1]**mold** *n.* crumbly rich soil.

[2]**mold** *n.* & *v.* (become covered with) a greenish or whitish fungous growth, as seen on bread, cheese, etc.

[3]**mold** *n.* a frame, matrix, hollow, etc. that gives form or shape to what is put in it; also, the shape or form or what is formed in a mold, as a jelly or pudding: *monotonous characters cast in the same ~.* —***v.*** form or shape: *a figure ~ed out of clay; a character ~ed by experience.*

Mol·da·vi·a (–DAY–) a historic region of S.C. Europe now lying in E. Romania and the **Moldavian Soviet Socialist Republic; Mol·da·vi·an** *n.* & *adj.*

mold·board *n.* a type of plow that lifts and turns the soil as it tills. —**mold·er** **1** *n.* one that molds or shapes something. **2** *v.* crumble or decay, esp. by turning into dust: *the ~ing ruins of an ancient temple.* —**mold·ing** *n.* the act or process of molding; also, a continuous contoured surface or strip for decoration or finish, as on a cornice, the side of an automobile's body, etc. —**mold·y** *adj.* **mold·i·er, -i·est** mold-covered; also, stale or musty; **mold·i·ness** *n.*

[1]**mole** *n.* a congenital, usu. dark protuberance on the skin.

[2]**mole** *n.* a small furry burrowing animal that lives underground.

[3]**mole** *n.* **1** a breakwater, esp. one formed of large stones, earth, or masonry. **2** quantity of a substance with mass in grams equal to its molecular weight; also called "gram molecule." —**mol·e·cule** (MOL·uh–) *n.* a small particle, esp. the smallest particle of a chemical element or compound, composed of atoms; **mo·lec·u·lar** (–LEK·yuh–) *adj.*

mole·hill *n.* a small mound of earth thrown up by a mole; **mole·skin** *n.* the skin of the mole used as fur; also, a cotton fabric used for work-clothes.

mo·lest (–LEST) *v.* annoy (a weaker person), esp. bother (a female or child) indecently; **mo·lest·er** *n.: a child ~er.* —**mo·les·ta·tion** (moh·les·TAY–) *n.*

Mo·lière (mole·YAIR), 1622–73, French playwright.

moll (MOL) *n. Slang.* a gangster's mistress or girl friend.

mol·li·fy *v.* **-fies, -fied, -fy·ing** calm or soothe (a person or his feelings). —**mol·lusk** or **mol·lusc** *n.* a soft-bodied, shell-enclosed creature such as a snail, oyster, or octopus. —**mol·ly·cod·dle** *v.* **-cod·dles, -cod·dled, -cod·dling** to pamper or fuss over; ***n.*** a boy used to being pampered.

Mo·lo·tov (MOH·luh·tof) **cocktail** a crude hand grenade made of a bottle of gasoline and a wick.

molt *v.* of a bird, insect, snake, etc., shed its feathers, skin, shell, or similar worn-out body covering; ***n.*** this act or process.

mol·ten (MOLE·tn) *adj.* melted: ~ *lava, metal;* **mol·ten·ly** *adv.*

mo·ly (MOH·lee) *n.* in Greek myth, a magical herb; also, the European wild garlic.

mo·lyb·de·num (muh·LIB·duh–) *n.* a hard, heat-resistant element used in alloys such as steel.

mom *n. Informal.* mother. —**mom-and-pop** *adj. Informal.* family-operated: *a ~ store.*

mo·ment (MOH·munt) *n.* **1** a short space of time; instant; *I'll be with you in a ~; the ~ of truth* (i.e. critical point). **2** weight or importance: *a matter of great ~;* **mo·men·tous** (–MEN·tus) *adj.* —**mo·men·tar·i·ly** (–ter–) *adv.* for or in a moment; also, soon; **mo·men·tar·i·ness** *n.* —**mo·men·tar·y** (MOH–) *adj.* lasting only a moment. —**mo·men·to** (–MEN–) *n.* **-toes** same as MEMENTO; souvenir. —**mo·men·tum** (–MEN–) *n.* **-tums** or **-ta** the force of a moving body; impetus: *a campaign gaining ~ as it progresses.*

mom·my (MOM·ee) *n.* **mom·mies** [child's word] mother.

Mon. Monday.

Mon·a·co (MON·uh–) a principality lying on the French Mediterranean coast; 0.73 sq.mi. (1.89 km²); *cap.* **Monaco.**

mon·arch (–urk) *n.* **1** a supreme ruler such as a king, queen, emperor, or sultan; **mo·nar·chic** (–NAR·kic) or **-chi·cal** *adj.* **2** an orange-and-black migratory butterfly that feeds on milkweed. —**mon·arch·y** *n.* **-arch·ies** a country ruled by a monarch, usu. with limited power, as in Britain; **mon·arch·ism** *n.;* **mon·arch·ist** *n.*

mon·as·ter·y (MON·uh·ster·ee) *n.* **-ter·ies** a place where a community of monks or nuns lives an ascetic, or **mo·nas·tic** (–NAS–) life; also **mo·nas·ti·cal** *adj.* —**mo·nas·ti·cism** (–NAS–) *n.* the condition or system of living a monastic life.

mon·au·ral (–OR·ul) *adj.* same as MONOPHONIC; **mon·au·ral·ly** *adv.*

Mon·day (MUN·dee, –day) *n.* the usu. first working day of the week, following Sunday.

mon·e·tar·y (MON·uh–) *adj.* having to do with money, esp. coinage or currency: *a ~ policy, system, unit, value.* —**mon·ey** (MUN·ee) *n.* **mon·eys** or **mon·ies** an authorized medium of exchange, esp. coins or paper notes; hence, wealth or property: *a man of ~; ~s* (i.e. sums of money) *owed by you;* **in the money** *Slang.* rich or prosperous; also, among the top prize-winners of a race or contest. —**mon·ey·bags** *n.pl. Informal.* a rich and avaricious person. —**mon·eyed** (–eed) *adj.* rich; wealthy. —**mon·ey·lend·er** *n.* one who lends money at interest. —**mon·ey·mak·er** *n.* one skilled in acquiring wealth; also, a profit-making scheme or product; **mon·ey·mak·ing** *n.* & *adj.* —**money of account** a monetary denomination such as the mill used only in reckoning, not issued as a coin or note. —**money order** a document issued at a post office or bank ordering payment of a specified amount on the purchaser's behalf to another person.

-monger *comb.form* [derogatory] dealer in: as in *rumormonger, scandalmonger.*

mon·go (MONG–) *n.* **-gos** a money unit of Outer Mongolia, equal to 1/100 of a tugrik. —**Mon·gol** (–gul, –gole) *n.* & *adj.* same as MONGOLIAN. —**Mon·go·li·a** (–GO–) a E.C. region of Asia divided into Inner Mongolia (N. region of the People's Republic of China) and Outer Mongolia, or **Mongolian People's Republic,** 604,250 sq.mi. (1,565,000 km²); *cap.* Ulan Bator; **Mon·go·li·an** *n.* & *adj.* (a native) of Mongolia. —**Mon·gol·ic** (–GOL–) *n.* & *adj.* (having to do with) a subfamily of languages in Mongolia. —**Mon·gol·ism** (MONG·guh–) *n.* same as DOWN'S SYNDROME. —**Mon·gol·oid** (MONG·guh–) *n.* & *adj.* (a member) of a race of peoples characterized by stocky build, yellowish skin, and slanted eyes, including the Inuit and the peoples of China, Japan, Indonesia, etc.

mon·goose (MONG–) *n.* **-goos·es** a small carnivorous mammal of S. Asia and Africa, related to the civet cat and noted as a destroyer of rats and poisonous snakes such as the cobra.

mon·grel (MUNG·grul, MONG–) *n.* & *adj.* (mixed in origin or character as) a dog of no recognizable breed: *a ~ dialect.*

monied same as MONEYED; **monies** a *pl.* of MONEY.

mon·i·ker or **mon·ick·er** (MON·uh–) *n. Slang.* nickname.

mo·nism (MOH–, MON–) *n.* the metaphysical doctrine of the oneness of reality, as opposed to dualism, pluralism, etc.; **mo·nist** *n.;* **mo·nis·tic** (–NIS–) *adj.*

mo·ni·tion (–NISH·un) *n.* admonition; also, an intimation or warning of danger. —**mon·i·tor** (–tur) *v.* watch or check on the performance of (a person or thing): *a ~ing station listening to broadcasts.* —***n.*** **1** a student helping a teacher in class. **2** a television receiver used in a studio showing a picture as being photographed or broadcast. —**mon·i·tor·y** *adj.*

monk (MUNGK) *n.* a male religious living in a monastery; **monk·ish** *adj.;* **monk·ish·ly** *adv.;* **monk·ish·ness** *n.*

mon·key (MUNG·kee) *n.* **-keys** any of the smaller long-tailed apes or primates. —***v.*** *Informal.* fool or tamper *(with).* —**monkey business** *Informal.* tricky or mischievous behavior; **mon·key·shines** *n.pl. Slang.* clownish jokes or pranks. —**monkey wrench** a wrench with a jaw that is adjustable to various sizes of nuts; **throw a monkey wrench into** disrupt or obstruct the functioning of (something going smoothly).

monk's cloth a heavy basket-weave cloth of cotton or linen used for draperies. —**monks·hood** *n.* same as ACONITE.

mon·o (MON·oh) *n.* short form of MONONUCLEOSIS or MONOPHONIC. —**mon(o)-** *comb.form.* one; single: as in *monomania, monorail.* —**mon·o·chro·mat·ic** (–croh·MAT–) *adj.* of one color; consisting of a single wavelength; **mon·o·chro·mat·i·cal·ly** *adv.;* **mon·o·chrome** (MON·uh·crohm) *n.* & *adj.* (a painting, print, etc.) in a single color or shades of one color: *a ~* (i.e. black and white) *television signal.* —**mon·o·cle** (MON·uh–) *n.* an eyeglass for one eye. —**mon·o·cot·y·le·don** (–cotl·EE·dn) *n.* a flowering plant such as grasses, palms, and lilies that has a single cotyledon in its seed embryo; **mon·o·cot·y·le·don·ous** *adj.* —**mon·o·dy** *n.* **-dies** a mourning or dirge, esp. as sung by a single person; also, a musical composition for a single voice; **mon·o·dist** *n.;* **mo·nod·ic** (–NOD–) *adj.* —**mo·nog·a·my** (–NOG·uh·mee) *n.* marriage with one person at a time; **mo·nog·a·mist** *n.;* **mo·nog·a·mous** *adj.* —**mon·o·gram** *n.* a design combining the initials of a name; ***v.*** **-grams, -grammed, -gram·ming:** *~d jewelry, linen, stationery.* —**mon·o·graph** *n.* a scholarly work treating a single subject exhaustively. —**mon·o·lin·gual** (–LING·gwul) *adj.* limited to one language. —**mon·o·lith** *n.* a single massive block of stone, as a monument or column; hence, a person or thing that is massive and unyielding; **mon·o·lith·ic** (–LITH–) *adj.: a ~* (i.e. single-crystal) *silicon chip.* —**mon·o·log(ue)** (–log) *n.* a long speech; also, a soliloquy or other dramatic piece involving one actor; **mon·o·log(u)·ist** *n.* —**mon·o·ma·ni·a** (–MAY–) *n.* a mental disorder involving one fixed idea; **mon·o·ma·ni·ac** *n.* & *adj.* —**mon·o·mer** *n.* a combining molecule of a polymer. —**mon·o·nu·cle·o·sis** (–clee·OH–) *n.* a blood disease of young people caused by an abnormality of single-nucleus blood cells; also called "glandular fever" and "kissing disease." —**mon·o·phon·ic** (–FON–) *adj.* having to do with sound reproduction using a single channel. —**mo·nop·o·list** (–NOP–) *n.* one who has a monopoly or favors monopoly; **mo·nop·o·lis·tic** (–LIS–) *adj.* —**mo·nop·o·lize** (–NOP–) *v.* **-liz·es, -lized, -liz·ing** have, get, or keep (something) exclusively: *to ~ a conversation.* —**mo·nop·o·ly** *n.* **-lies** exclusive marketing control of a commodity or service, as most public utilities; also, a company enjoying such absence of competition. —**mon·o·rail** *n.* (a vehicle traveling on) a single rail, with the cars either suspended from the rail or balanced on top of it. —**mon·o·syl·la·ble** (MON·uh·sil·uh·bl) *n.* a word of one syllable; **mon·o·syl·lab·ic** (–LAB–) *adj.* —**mon·o·the·ism** (–THEE–) *n.* belief or doctrine that there is only one God; **mon·o·the·ist** *n.;* **mon·o·the·is·tic** (–IS–) *adj.* —**mon·o·tone** *n.* sameness of tone of utterance, style of writing, etc.; **mo·not·o·nous** (–NOT·uh·nus) *adj.* tiresome because unvarying in tone or style; **mo·not·o·ny** *n.* —**mon·ox·ide** (–OX–) *n.* an oxide with one atom of oxygen per molecule.

Mon·roe (mun·ROH), **James.** 1758–1831, 5th U.S. President (1817–25). —**Mon·ro·vi·a** (–ROH·vee·uh) capital of Liberia.

Mon·sei·gneur (–sen·YUR) *n., pl.* **Mes·sei·gneurs** (–YUR) a French title of honor given to persons of high rank. —**mon·sieur** (muh·SYUR) *n.* **mes·sieurs** (MES·urz) a gentleman; **Monsieur** French title equivalent to "Mr." or "Sir." —**Mon·si·gnor** (–SEEN·yur) *n.* **-gnors** or **-gno·ri** (–NYOR·ee) a title given to certain dignitaries of the Roman Catholic Church.

mon·soon (–SOON) *n.* a seasonal wind blowing over the Indian Ocean, esp. in the summer, accompanied by heavy rains.

mon·ster (–stur) *n.* a huge, ugly, or wicked creature such as a dragon; also, a grossly malformed birth; ***adj.*** huge: *a ~ rally.*

mon·strance (–strunce) *n.* in the Roman Catholic Church, a vessel for displaying the consecrated host for adoration.

mon·strous (–strus) *adj.* like a monster; also, wicked: *a ~ crime;* **mon·strous·ly** *adv.;* **mon·strous·ness** *n.;* **mon·stros·i·ty** (–STROS–) *n.* **-ties.**

Mont. Montana. —**mon·tage** (–TAHZH) *n.* in photography, motion pictures, etc., a combining or blending of many distinct pictures for a special effect. —**Mon·tan·a** (–TAN·uh) a N.W. state of the U.S.; 147,138 sq.mi. (381,-086 km^2); *cap.* Helena; **Mon·tan·an** *n.* & *adj.* —**Mont Blanc** (mawng·BLAHNG) the highest mountain in the Alps; 15,771 ft. (4,807 m). —**Mon·te Car·lo** (mon·tee·CAR·loh) a gambling resort in Monaco. —**Mon·tes·so·ri** (mon·tuh·SOR·ee) **method** a method of teaching children from three to six years old by helping them to develop their abilities through guided play, devised by Dr. Maria Montessori, 1870–1952, Italian educator.

—Mon·te·vid·e·o (mon·tuh·vi·DAY·oh) capital of Uruguay. **—Mont·gom·er·y** (–GUM–) capital of Alabama.

month (MUNTH) *n.* one of the 12 divisions of the year, from 28 to 31 days long, January through December: *The lunar ~ of about 29½ days is the period of one revolution of the moon around the earth.* **—month·ly** *adj.* & *adv.* every month; once a month; ***n.,*** *pl.* **-lies** a monthly publication.

Mont·pel·ier (–PEEL·yur) capital of Vermont.

Mont·re·al (–tree·AWL) largest city of Quebec, a seaport on the St. Lawrence River.

mon·u·ment (MON·yuh–) *n.* a tablet, statue, pillar, building, etc. put up in commemoration of a person or event: *a place of historic or scenic interest set apart as a "national ~" for public use.* **—mon·u·men·tal** (–MEN·tl) *adj.* of or like a monument: *of ~ significance; his ~* (i.e. colossal) *ignorance;* **mon·u·men·tal·ly** *adv.*

moo *n.* & *v.* **moos, mooed, moo·ing** (make) the sound or call of a cow.

mooch *Slang. v.* get (money, food, etc.) by begging; sponge; **mooch·er** *n.* beggar; cadger.

mood *n.* **1** a grammatical aspect indicating whether the action of a verb is thought of as a fact ("indicative mood": *I am going*), a wish or supposition ("subjunctive mood": *if I were to go*), or a command ("imperative mood": *Please go*). **2** a state of mind; a feeling or attitude: *approachable when she is in a good ~; a man of ~s* (i.e. of uncertain temper); **mood·y** *adj.* **mood·i·er, -i·est** gloomy; sullen; **mood·i·ly** *adv.;* **mood·i·ness** *n.*

moon *n.* a heavenly body that is the earth's natural satellite, taking about 29½ days for a full circle, from one new moon to the next, during which period it waxes from "crescent" to "full" moon and then wanes; also, any satellite of a planet: *the ~s of Jupiter.* ***—v.*** spend time or wander *(about* or *around)* idly. **—moon·beam** *n.* a ray of moonlight. **—moon·light** (–lite) *n.* the light of the moon; ***v.*** *Informal.* work at a job, as at night, in addition to a regular one; **moon·light·er** *n.* **—moon·lit** *adj.* lighted by the moon: *~ night.* **—moon·scape** *n.* a view of the moon's surface. **—moon·shine** *n.* **1** moonlight. **2** foolish notions; empty talk. **3** *Informal.* illegally made alcoholic liquor. **—moon·shot** *n.* the launching of a spacecraft to(ward) the moon. **—moon·stone** *n.* a whitish variety of feldspar cut and used as a gem. **—moon·struck** *adj.* dazed, dreamy, or mentally unbalanced. **—moon·walk** (–wauk) *n.* an astronaut's walk on the moon. **—Moon·ie** *n.* **Moon·ies** a member of the Unification Church, a cult founded by the Rev. Sun Myung Moon, a Korean millionaire.

Moor *n.* a N.W. African, originally of Mauretania, esp. a member of the people that conquered Spain in the 8th cent. A.D.; **Moor·ish** *adj.*

moor *n.* a tract of marshy wasteland, usu. heather-covered; heath; also **moor·land. —*v.*** secure (a ship, boat, etc.) in place by fastening it by rope or chain to shore or by anchors; **moor·ing** *n.* also **moor·ings** *n.pl.* the place to which a craft is moored; also, anchors or chains by which something is secured in place; hence, a person's ties or attachments, as of religion or society, that give him security.

moose *n.* a North American elk with flattened antlers, the largest member of the deer family.

moot *adj.* debatable: *a ~ point, question; an impeachment made ~* (i.e. of no consequence) *by resignation;* ***v.*** raise for discussion. **—moot court** a mock court for law students to practice in.

mop *n.* an implement for wiping floors, usu. a handle with a bundle of rags or a sponge at the end; also, a thick head of unruly hair. ***—v.*** **mops, mopped, mop·ping:** *a handkerchief to ~ your brow;* **mop up** clear out (an occupied battle area of stragglers, etc.); **mop-up** *n.*

mope *v.* **mopes, moped, mop·ing** be gloomy or in low spirits; ***n.*** a gloomy person; **mopes** *n.pl.* low spirits; **mop·ish, mop·(e)y** (MOH–) *adj.;* **mop·i·ness** *n.*

mo·ped (MOH–) *n.* a light motorcycle that can be pedaled.

mop·pet (–it) *n. Informal.* a little child.

mo·raine (muh·RAIN) *n.* rock, dirt, sand, etc. deposited by a moving glacier.

mor·al (–ul) *adj.* **1** right according to accepted standards of good conduct; also, having to do with right and wrong: *led a ~ life; Infants are not ~; a ~* (i.e. sexually well-behaved) *woman; a ~ book, question, responsibility.* **2** inspiring confidence; morale-raising: *a ~ victory, certainty; with my ~ support.* ***—n.*** a moral lesson: *a story with a ~;* **morals** *n.pl.* moral principles: *a question of ~s; a woman of good ~s.* **—mo·rale** (–RAL) *n.* mental or moral condition in regard to discipline and confidence: *the ~ of an army, team; Alcohol didn't boost his ~.* **—mor·al·ist** (MOR–) *n.* an expert in morals; also, an improver of morals; **mor·al·is·tic** (–LIS–) *adj.;* **mor·al·is·ti·cal·ly** *adv.* **—mo·ral·i·ty** (–RAL–) *n.* **-ties** moral quality, system, instruction, etc.; also, virtue, esp. sexual. **—mor·al·ize** *v.* **-iz·es, -ized, -iz·ing** think, talk, or write about morals; also, improve the morals of; **mor·al·i·za·tion** (–ZAY–) *n.* **—mor·al·ly** *adv.*

mo·rass (–RAS) *n.* a swamp or marsh; hence, a messy situation.

mor·a·to·ri·um (–TOR–) *n.* **-ri·ums** or **-ri·a** an official delay or suspension, as on legal action to collect a debt, testing of nuclear weapons, etc.

Mo·ra·vi·an (–RAY–) *adj.* of **Mo·ra·vi·a,** a region of Czechoslovakia, or of a Protestant sect founded there; ***n.*** a person from or the dialect of Moravia.

mo·ray (MOR·ay, muh·RAY) *n.* a large, thick-bodied, fierce eel of tropical seas.
mor·bid *adj.* diseased or sickly; unwholesome; gruesome: *a ~ growth, curiosity, interest in death; ~ details of a crime;* **mor·bid·ly** *adv.* **—mor·bid·i·ty** (–BID–) *or* **mor·bid·ness** *n.*
mor·dant (–dnt) *adj.* incisive; caustic; pungent: *~ wit, criticism;* ***n.*** a chemical that fixes colors; also, an etching agent; **mor·dan·cy** *n.;* **mor·dant·ly** *adv.*
more comp. of MANY or MUCH; ***adj.:*** *We need ~ help;* ***adv.:*** *I couldn't agree ~ with you; People are eating out* **more and more;** *The baby is* **more or less** *asleep; more or less six months old;* ***n.*** *the ~ the merrier; asked for ~ (of it);* ***pron.:*** *Many were killed, ~ were wounded.* **—more·o·ver** (–OH·vur) *adv.* besides; in addition.
mo·rel (muh·REL) *n.* an edible mushroom.
mo·res (MOR·ayz, –eez) *n.pl.* the traditional, morally binding rules and customs of a society: *"One wife at a time" is part of our sexual ~.*
Mor·gan (–gun) *n.* an American breed of horse.
morgue (MORG) *n.* **1** a place where unidentified bodies are kept temporarily, as of victims of accidents or violent deaths. **2** a newspaper reference library stocking obituaries, news clippings, etc.
mor·i·bund *adj.* in the process of dying out: *a ~ custom, civilization.*
Mor·mon (–mun) *n.* a member of the Church of Jesus Christ of Latter-day Saints; **Mor·mon·ism** *n.*
morn *n. Poetic.* same as **morn·ing** *n.* the beginning of day, the period from dawn to noon. **—morning glory** any of a family of climbing plants, esp. one with trumpet-shaped flowers that stay open only in the morning. **—morning sickness** the sickness felt in the morning during the first few months of pregnancy. **—morning star** a planet, esp. Venus, seen in the morning sky.
Mo·roc·co (muh·ROC·oh) **1** a mountainous country in N.W. Africa; 172,414 sq.mi. (446,550 km^2); *cap.* Rabat; **Mo·roc·can** *n.* & *adj.* **2** *n.* a kind of fine leather made from goat skins.
mo·ron (MOR·on) *n.* a foolish or stupid person; formerly, a classification of a mentally retarded person with an I.Q. between 50 and 75; **mo·ron·ic** (–RON–) *adj.;* **mo·ron·i·cal·ly** *adv.*
Mo·ro·ni (–ROH–) capital of Comoros.
mo·rose (muh·ROSE) *adj.* glum and unsociable; gloomy; **mo·rose·ly** *adv.;* **mo·rose·ness** *n.*
mor·pheme (–feem) *n.* any of the smallest word units of a language, as affixes, inflections, roots, etc. that are studied in morphology; **mor·phem·ic** *adj.* **—mor·phine** (–feen) *n.* a narcotic drug made from opium and used medically to relieve pain. **—mor·phol·o·gy** (–FOL–) *n.* (study of) form and structure, as of animals and plants, of words and inflections, etc.; **mor·phol·o·gist** *n.;* **mor·pho·log·i·cal** (–fuh·LOJ–) *adj.*
mor·ris *n.* a vigorous folk dance of rural England performed by trained men.
mor·row (MOR·oh) *n. Poetic.* morning; also, the next day.
Morse code an alphabet of dots and dashes invented by **Samuel Morse,** 1791–1872, for use in telegraphy.
mor·sel (–sl) *n.* a small portion (of food), piece, or amount: *a choice ~* (i.e. something tasty or pleasing).
mor·tal (–tl) *adj.* of or having to do with death: *Man is ~* (i.e. subject to death); *one's ~ enemy; in ~ fear; ~* (i.e. human) *limitations; ~ sin* (leading to spiritual death); *in a ~* (i.e. great) *hurry;* ***n.*** a human being; **mor·tal·ly** *adv.* **—mor·tal·i·ty** (–TAL–) *n.* death, esp. its rate in proportion to population: *a ~ table showing life expectancy.*
mor·tar (–tur) *n.* **1** a bowl of porcelain or other hard material for pounding substances to a powder using a pestle. **2** a short-range cannon that fires shells (dropped down its muzzle) in a high arc, as over a hill or fortification. **3** a hardening mixture of lime, cement, etc. for use between bricks or stones in building. **—mor·tar·board** *n.* **1** a square board used by masons to hold and work mortar. **2** an academic cap with a square board on top from which a tassel hangs.
mort·gage (MOR·gij) *n.* a pledging of property as security for the payment of a loan or debt to the lender, or **mort·ga·gee** (–JEE) *n.;* also, the deed by which this is conveyed by the owner of the property, or **mort·ga·ger** or **-gor** (–jur) *n.* **—*v.* -gag·es, -gaged, -gag·ing** transfer one's rights by or as if by a mortgage: *to ~ one's house, future, happiness.*
mor·ti·cian (–TISH·un) *n.* an undertaker. **—mor·ti·fy** *v.* **-fies, -fied, -fy·ing** **1** punish one's body; also, be punished: *Saints ~ their bodies, desires, etc. by fasting and penance; felt ~d* (i.e. humiliated) *by her son's poor manners.* **2** become gangrenous. **—mor·ti·fi·ca·tion** (–CAY–) *n.*
mor·tise (–tis) *n.* & *v.* **-tis·es, -tised, -tis·ing** (cut) a hole or notch in one part of a joint into which the tenon of the other part fits: *beams ~d, not nailed together.* Also **mor·tice.**
mor·tu·ar·y (MOR·choo–) *n.* **-ar·ies** a place where dead bodies are kept before burial or cremation; funeral home; ***adj.:*** *a ~ chapel, service.*
mo·sa·ic (moh·ZAY–) *n.* a picture or design made with small colored pieces of stone, glass, etc. inlaid on a surface such as a floor, ceiling, or wall: *the nation as a ~ of many cultures;* ***adj.:*** *a ~ design, pavement; the* **mosaic disease** *of plants such as corn and tobacco resulting in spotted leaves.*
Mo·sa·ic (moh·ZAY–) *adj.* having to do with Moses: *the ~ law of the Pentateuch.*

Mos·cow (–cow, –coh) capital of the U.S.S.R.

Mo·ses (MOH·ziz) the lawgiver of the Israelites who led them out of slavery in Egypt.

mo·sey (MOH·zee) *v.* **-seys, -seyed, -sey·ing** *Slang.* move *(along)* at a leisurely pace.

Mos·lem (MOZ·lum) *n.* & *adj.* (an adherent) of the religion founded by Mohammed. —**mosque** (MOSK) *n.* a Moslem place of public worship.

mos·qui·to (muh·SKEE·toh) *n.* **-to(e)s** a two-winged, blood-sucking insect that is often a carrier of disease germs, as of malaria and yellow fever; **mosquito net** a net hung over a bed, chair, etc. to keep out mosquitoes.

moss *n.* a tiny green plant that grows in cushionlike clusters on damp banks, rocks, and trees; **moss·y** *adj.* —**moss·back** *n.* an old turtle with algae growing on its back; hence, an old fogy; a very conservative person.

most (MOHST) *adj.* & *adv.* superl. of MANY & MUCH: *a ~ interesting subject; ~ people like dogs; She loves children ~; remarks that were irrelevant* **for the most part;** *as ~* (*Informal.* almost) *anyone will tell you;* ***suffix.:*** as in *foremost, uppermost, utmost.* —***n.*** & ***pron.:*** *Boys are ~ of the group; a group that is noisier than ~; an engine that gives only 20 m.p.g.* **at (the) most.** —**most·ly** *adv.* mainly; usually.

mot (MOH) *n.* **mots** (MOZE) a witty saying.

mote *n.* a speck of dust.

mo·tel (moh·TEL) *n.* a roadside establishment providing furnished rooms and parking spaces for travelers.

mo·tet (moh·TET) *n.* a polyphonic vocal composition, usu. of a religious nature.

moth *n.* an insect that resembles a butterfly but is less brightly colored, that flies mostly at night, and whose larvae eat wool, fur, etc.; **moth·ball** *n.* a small ball of camphor or naphthalene used to keep moths away from clothing; **in mothballs** in storage.

moth·er (MUDH·ur) *n.* a female parent; hence, source or origin of anything; ***adj.:*** *the ~ church; ~ country, tongue* (i.e. one's first language); ***v.*** produce or protect, as a mother does. —**moth·er·hood** *n.;* **moth·er·less** *adj.;* **moth·er·ly** *adj.;* **moth·er·li·ness** *n.* —**moth·er-in-law** *n.* **moth·ers-in-law** the mother of one's spouse. —**moth·er·land** *n.* one's native or ancestral country. —**moth·er-of-pearl** *n.* the glossy inner lining of the shells of the pearl oyster and other mollusks, used in making buttons, beads, etc.

mo·tif (–TEEF) *n.* in art, literature, and music, a dominant theme, main feature, or recurring pattern: *the love ~ of romances.* —**mo·tile** (MOH·tl) *adj.* of organisms, capable of motion; **mo·til·i·ty** (–TIL–) *n.* —**mo·tion** (MOH·shun) *n.* **1** a moving: *Newton's laws of ~; when a train is* **in motion. 2** a gesture; also, a formal proposal made in a legislature or court of law: *a ~ for adjournment;* **go through the motions** (*of* doing something), do (it) routinely or half-heartedly. —***v.:*** *The chairman ~ed* (i.e. gestured to) *us to be seated.* —**mo·tion·less** *adj.* without moving. —**motion picture** a series of contiguous pictures giving the impression of movement when projected; also, a story in this form. —**motion sickness** nausea felt by passengers on a ship, plane, etc. —**mo·ti·vate** (MOH–) *v.* **-vates, -vat·ed, -vat·ing** provide with or influence as a motive; impel; **mo·ti·va·tion** (–VAY–) *n.;* **mo·ti·va·tion·al** *adj.: ~ analysis, drives, research.* —**mo·tive** (–tiv) **1** *n.* & *adj.* (having as) cause of an action or motion: *Revenge was the ~ for the murder; the ~ power of steam;* ***suffix.*** moving: as in *automotive, electromotive.* **2** *n.* a basic melody or motif, as the first four notes of Beethoven's "Fifth Symphony."

mot·ley (–lee) *adj.* many-colored, as a clown's garment; also, varied in character: *a ~ dress, crowd, collection.*

mo·to·cross (MOH·tuh–) *n.* & *adj.* cross-country (motorcycle race). —**mo·tor** (MOH·tur) *n.* one that gives motion, usu. by electric power; also, an internal combustion engine; hence, an automobile; ***adj.:*** *a rubber-tired ~ vehicle; the brain's ~ area controlling ~ neurons that impart ~ impulses to muscles;* ***v.*** go or convey by automobile; **mo·tor·a·ble** *adj.: a ~ road.* —**mo·tor·bike** *n.* *Informal.* motorcycle. —**mo·tor·boat** *n.* a boat propelled by a motor. —**mo·tor·cade** *n.* a procession of motor vehicles. —**mo·tor·car** *n.* automobile. —**motor court** a motel. —**mo·tor·cy·cle** *n.* & *v.* **-cles, -cled, -cling** (travel by) a heavier and larger type of bicycle powered by an internal-combustion engine; **mo·tor·cy·clist** *n.* —**motor home** an automotive recreational vehicle built on a truck chassis and having living facilities. —**motor hotel** (or **inn**) a hotel with parking facilities for guests. —**mo·tor·ist** *n.* a traveler by automobile. —**mo·tor·ize** *v.* **-iz·es, -ized, -iz·ing** equip with a motor or motor vehicles: *a ~d regiment;* **mo·tor·i·za·tion** (–ZAY–) *n.* —**mo·tor·man** (–mun) *n.* **-men** a driver of an electric train or streetcar. —**motor scooter** a scooterlike vehicle with an engine mounted over the rear wheel and the driver seated with feet on a floorboard. —**motor truck** an automotive truck for carrying freight. —**motor vehicle** an automotive vehicle such as an automobile, bus, truck, etc. for use on roadways.

mot·tle (MOTL) *v.* **mot·tles, mot·tled, mot·tling** mark with blotches or streaks of different colors; **mot·tled** *adj.: a ~ skin, finish, leaf.*

mot·to (–toh) *n.* **-to(e)s** a rule of conduct, usu. a brief expression such as "Be prepared," put on a coat of arms or badge.

moue (MOO) *n.* a pout or grimace.

mould (MOLD), **moult** (MOLT), etc. *Brit.* spelling of MOLD, MOLT, etc.

mound *n.* & *v.* (heap up as) a bank of earth or stones; also, a knoll. —**mount** *v.* **1** climb on or toward the top of; also, rise or ascend: *to ~ a ladder, horse, platform; the ~ing cost of living; Police came ~ed* (on horseback). **2** place or fix in proper position: *to ~ a specimen* (on a slide), *stamps* (in an album), *gems* (in gold), *guns* (on a gun-carriage). **—n. 1** mountain: *Mount Everest; Mt. McKinley.* **2** an animal or machine on which one is mounted. **3** a place to mount something on, as a backing or support: *a cardboard ~ for a picture.* **—mount·a·ble** *adj.* **—mount·er** *n.* **—moun·tain** (–tn) *n.* a very high hill or mass of land, often rising to a peak; also, a group of such formations: *Everest, the world's highest ~ is in the Himalayan ~s; ~s* (i.e. huge heaps) *of garbage; a ~ of work awaiting a vacationer; They are apt to "make a ~ out of a molehill"* (i.e. magnify small difficulties). **—mountain ash** a rose-family tree that grows in high places and has pinnate compound leaves, clusters of white flowers, and red, berrylike fruits. **—moun·tain·eer** (–NEER) *n.* one who lives in the mountains; also, a skilled climber of mountains; **v.** climb mountains as a sport. **—mountain goat** same as ROCKY MOUNTAIN GOAT. **—mountain laurel** an evergreen shrub or tree of the heath family, found in E. North America, with dark, glossy leaves and pink, white, or purple flowers. **—mountain lion** a wildcate of W. North America, smaller than a jaguar. **—moun·tain·ous** (–us) *adj.* full of mountains; also, huge like a mountain. **—moun·te·bank** (MOUN·tuh–) *n.* a charlatan or quack. **—Mount·ie** or **Mount·y** (MOUN·tee) *n.* **Mount·ies** a member of the Canadian Mounted Police. **—mount·ing** *n.* same as MOUNT, *n.* 3.

mourn (MORN) *v.* feel or express sorrow or grief (for): *to ~ a death, loss; ~ing for a dear one;* **mourn·er** *n.;* **mourn·ing** *n.* the expression of grief at someone's death, the usu. black clothes worn as a sign of it, or the period of such expression: *The nation goes into ~ for 30 days when a president dies.* **—mourn·ful** *adj.* sorrowful; **mourn·ful·ly** *adv.;* **mourn·ful·ness** *n.*

mouse (MOUS) *n., pl.* **mice 1** a small gnawing animal with soft fur and pointed snout, esp. the *house mouse* found worldwide and used in laboratories; also, a timid person. **2** *Slang.* a black eye. **—v.** (MOUZ) **mous·es, moused, mous·ing** hunt for mice, as a **mous·er** such as a cat does. **—mouse·trap** *n.* a trap for catching mice. **—mousey** same as MOUSY.

mousse (MOOSE) *n.* a light, molded, chilled dessert made with gelatin and whipped cream: *coffee, maple, banana ~.*

mous·tache (mus·TASH, MUSS·tash) same as MUSTACHE.

mous·(e)y (MOU·see, –zee) *adj.* **mous·i·er, -i·est** like a mouse; timid; stealthy; **mous·i·ness** *n.*

mouth *n.* an opening through which food is taken into the body, and in which speech sounds are made; also, any opening or entrance resembling a mouth, as of a cave, jar, or river (where it empties into a larger body of water); **down in** (or **at**) **the mouth** *Informal.* in low spirits. **—v.** (MOUDH) declaim; utter (words) in an affected manner; also, form (words) with the mouth silently. **—mouthed** *adj. & comb.form.:* as in *openmouthed, loudmouthed; a ~ shell.* **—mouth·ful** *n.* **-fuls 1** a small quantity, as will fill a mouth. **2** *Informal.* a hard-to-pronounce word or string of words. **3** *Informal.* an appropriate or significant remark: *You said a ~.* **—mouth organ** same as HARMONICA. **—mouth·piece** *n.* **1** a part or structure that serves as a mouth, as of a water pipe, or that is placed at or near a person's mouth, as of a musical instrument that is blown into, a tobacco pipe, a telephone, etc. **2** person or periodical acting as spokesman for another. **—mouth·wash** *n.* a liquid preparation for rinsing the mouth. **—mouth·wa·ter·ing** *adj.* very appetizing or tasty. **—mouth·y** *adj.* **mouth·i·er, -i·est** loudmouthed; very talkative.

mou·ton (MOO·tahn) *n.* fur made from a sheepskin, dyed to look like beaver or seal.

mov(e)·a·ble (MOO·vuh–) *adj.* that can be moved from place to place, as furniture; **mov·(e)ables** *n.pl.* personal property. **—move** (MOOV) *v.* **moves, moved, mov·ing 1** change place or position (of): *Stand still without ~ing; Who ~d this desk? People ~ from inner cities to suburbs.* **2** (cause to) act or operate; be active: *A door ~s on hinges; Professors ~ in academic circles; a story that ~s people to tears; Purgatives ~* (i.e. evacuate) *bowels.* **3** go or come; proceed: *a train ~ing fast; police trying to keep the crowds ~ing; Let's ~ on; New neighbors ~ in on Monday; luxury goods difficult to ~* (i.e. sell) *in hard times.* **4** apply formally *(for)* or propose *(that)*: *The lawyer ~d for a new trial.* **—n.:** *dared not make a ~ for fear of being shot; the ~s of a chess game; a warning as a first ~* (i.e. action) *before firing someone; Orders keep three waitresses constantly* **on the move** (i.e. moving); **—move·ment** *n.* the motion of a person or thing in a particular manner or direction: *the ~ of the earth around the sun; troop ~s along a border; a 17-jewel watch ~* (i.e. mechanism); *a reform ~; a sonata in three ~s* (i.e. parts); *bowel ~* (i.e. emptying or stool). **—mov·er** *n.* one that moves, esp. in the business of moving furniture and equipment belonging to residences, offices, homes, etc. from one place to another. **—mov·ie** (MOO·vee) *n.* **1** same as MOTION PICTURE; also **moving picture. 2** a motion-picture theater; **the movies** *pl.* a movie showing; also, the motion-picture industry.

mow (MOH) *v.* **mows,** *pt.* **mowed,** *pp.* **mowed** or **mown** (MONE), **mow·ing** cut down (grass, grain, an army, etc.): *to ~ a lawn;* **mow down:** *troops mercilessly ~d down;* **mow·er** *n.* **—n.** (MOU) a haymow; hayloft.

mox·ie (MOX·ee) *n. Slang.* pluck; guts.

Mo·zam·bique (moh·zam·BEEK) a country on the coast of S.E. Africa; 302, 330 sq.mi. (783,-030 km²); *cap.* Maputo.

moz·za·rel·la (mot·suh·REL·uh) *n.* a soft, white, mild-flavored Italian cheese.

Mo·zart (MOH·tsart), **Wolfgang A.** 1756–91, Austrian composer.

M.P. melting point; member of parliament; metropolitan police; military police; mounted police.

m.p.g. miles per gallon. —**m.p.h.** miles per hour. —**m.p.m.** meters per minute.

mRNA messenger RNA.

Mr. (MIS·tur), *pl.* **Messrs.** (MES·urz) [prefixed title used with man's surname or title]: *Mr. T. Jones; Mr. Jones; Mr. Chairman.* —**Mrs.** (MIS·iz), *pl.* **Mmes.** [prefixed title for married woman]: *Mrs. (Mary) Jones.*

¹Ms. (MIZ), *pl.* **Mses** (MIZ·eez) [prefixed title used with a woman's surname]: *Ms. (Mary) Jones.*

MS., ²Ms. or **ms.** *pl.* **MSS., Mss.** or **mss.** manuscript. —**M.S.** or **M.Sc.** Master of Science. —**MS** Mississippi; multiple sclerosis.

Msgr. Monsignor.

MSgt or **M/Sgt** Master Sergeant.

MSS., Mss. or **mss.** manuscripts.

M.S.T. Mountain Standard Time.

MT Montana.

mtg(e). mortgage.

Mt(n). or mt(n). mountain; **Mts.** or **mts.** mountains.

mu (MEW) *n.* the 12th letter of the Greek alphabet (M, μ).

much *n.* & *adj., comp.* **more,** *superl.* **most** (in) a great amount, degree, quantity, etc.: *He spent ~ time on the project; His donations amounted to ~; She tends to* **make much** *of the little she gave; two hours a week is* **not much of** *a contribution;* **How much** *money did she give?* —**adv.:** *Prices are ~ higher than two years ago; Wages are ~* (i.e. nearly) *the same as last year;* **How much** *will you pay?*

mu·ci·lage (MEW·sl·ij) *n.* a sticky vegetable substance used as an adhesive, usu. made by dissolving gum arabic in water: *The glue on a postage stamp is a ~ made with dextrin.* —**mu·ci·lag·i·nous** (–LAJ·uh·nus) *adj.: Seaweeds, flaxes, etc. are ~; a ~ plant cell.*

muck *n.* **1** farmyard manure; hence, dirt or filth. **2** dark soil rich in decaying matter. —**muck·y** *adj.* —**muck·rak·er** (–ray–) *n.* a journalist who searches for and writes sensationally about corruption in government, big business, etc.; **muck·rake** *v.* **-rakes, -raked, -rak·ing.**

mu·cous (MEW·cus) *adj.* secreting mucus, as the **mucous membrane** lining body cavities; hence, slimy. —**mu·cus** (MEW–) *n.* a thick, slimy fluid produced by the inner lining of the nose, sinuses, windpipe, vagina, etc. for lubrication and protection.

mud *n.* **1** soft, sticky, wet earth. **2** an abusive, malicious attack. —**mud·dle** *n.* & *v.* **mud·dles, mud·dled, mud·dling** (bring into) a mess or disorder: *found herself in a ~ difficult to get out of; to ~ a task, issue, plan; managed to* **muddle through** *the mission; Liquor tends to ~ your thinking;* **mud·dle·head·ed** (–HED–) *adj.* confused; bungling; inept. —**mud·dler** *n.* —**mud·dy** *adj.* **mud·di·er, mud·di·est:** *~ shoes, water, thinking;* **v. mud·dies, mud·died, mud·dy·ing** make or become covered with mud; also, make cloudy or confused: *~d clothes; ~d reasoning;* **mud·di·ness** *n.* —**mud·guard** (–gard) *n.* **1** a covering over a vehicle's wheel for protection from mud thrown up by it; fender. **2** same as SPLASHGUARD. —**mud·sling·ing** *n.* slanderous attack against an opponent; **mud·sling·er** *n.*

mu·ez·zin (mew·EZ–) *n.* at a mosque, an official who calls the people to prayer.

muff *n.* **1** a short, tubelike covering of fur or other warm material into which the hands are inserted to keep them warm. **2** a bungling or awkward handling; **v.** bungle or miss (a catch), esp. in baseball.

muf·fin *n.* a small round cake of wheat flour or corn meal.

muf·fle *v.* **muf·fles, muf·fled, muf·fling** cover closely so as to keep warm or to deaden a sound: *She was ~d in a scarf; ~d voices.* —**muf·fler** *n.* something that muffles, as a scarf or the silencing device attached to an automobile engine.

muf·ti (–tee) *n.* civilian costume, not a uniform.

mug *n.* **1** a cylindrical metal or earthenware drinking cup with a handle, formerly often decorated with a grotesque face. **2** *Slang.* face or mouth. —**v. mugs, mugged, mug·ging** *Slang.* **1** make faces, as a ham actor. **2** make a mug shot of (a person's face). **3** attack (a person) to rob, as a **mug·ger** does.

mug·gy (MUG·ee) *adj.* **mug·gi·er, mug·gi·est** hot and humid: *a ~ day; ~ weather;* **mug·gi·ness** *n.*

mug shot a police photograph of a criminal's face.

mug·wump *n.* one who withdraws support from his political party, esp. in an aloof or self-important manner.

Mu·ham·mad (moo·HAM·ud), **Mu·ham·mad·an, Mu·ham·mad·an·ism** See MOHAMMED.

Muk·den (MOOK–) former name of SHENYANG.

muk·luk (MUK–) *n.* (a boot in the style of) a usu. knee-high Eskimo boot made of the skin of seal or reindeer.

mu·lat·to (–LAT·oh) *n.* **-toes** a person of mixed white and black descent, esp. one born of a white and a black parent.

mul·ber·ry *n.* **-ber·ries** any of a family of trees that bear small edible purplish or reddish fruits resembling blackberries and whose leaves, esp. of the "white mulberry," have been used as food for the silkworm since ancient times.

mulch *n.* loose vegetable material such as straw, leaves, and wood chips spread around plants to reduce evaporation, enrich the soil, etc.; ***v.:*** *to ~ a tree, an orchard, the ground.*

mulct *n.* a fine or penalty; ***v.*** get by fraud or extortion: *poor clients ~ed of their savings.*

mule *n.* **1** the usu. sterile hybrid offspring of a jackass and a horse; also, *Informal.* one who is stubborn; **mul·ish** *adj.;* **mul·ish·ly** *adv.;* **mul·ish·ness** *n.* **2** a spinning machine introduced in 1779 combining the principles of two earlier machines. **3** a backless slipper for women. **—mule deer** a North American deer with a black-tipped tail and ears like a mule's. **—mu·le·teer** (–TEER) *n.* a mule driver; also **mule skinner** *Informal.*

mull *v.* **1** ponder (*over* a problem, etc.); dawdle. **2** make a warm, sweetened spiced drink of (wine, cider, or other beverage): *~ed ale.*

mul·le(i)n (MULL·in) *n.* any of over 100 kinds of plants of the figwort family, esp. the "common mullein" with thick, velvety leaves and clusters of yellow flowers on tall spikes.

mul·let (MUL·it) *n.* either of two families of edible fishes of warm waters, esp. the "gray" and the "red" mullets.

mul·li·gan (–gn) **stew** *Slang.* a stew of odds and ends of meat, fish, etc.

mul·li·ga·taw·ny (–guh·TAW·nee) *n.* a highly seasoned soup, usu. of chicken stock, originally from India.

mul·lion (MUL·yun) *n.* a slim, vertical bar dividing window panes.

multi- *comb.form.* many: as in **mul·ti·col·ored** *adj.* having many colors. **—mul·ti·far·i·ous** (–FAIR·ee·us) *adj.* diverse. **—mul·ti·lin·gual** (–LING·gwul) *n.* & *adj.* (one) that uses many languages. **—mul·ti·me·di·a** (–MEE–) *adj.* using several communications media: *a ~ kit, presentation.* **—mul·ti·mil·lion·aire** (–NAIR) *n.* one whose wealth is estimated at many millions of dollars, pounds, etc. **—mul·ti·na·tion·al** (–NASH–) *adj.* with branches in more than two countries: *a ~ corporation.* **—mul·ti·ple** *n.* a number got by multiplying a whole number by itself two or more times; ***adj.*** manifold; having many parts: *a* **mul·ti·ple-choice** *question with several answers to choose from.* **—multiple sclerosis** a disease of the nervous system characterized by hardening of tissues and eventual paralysis of the legs, hands, eyesight, speech, etc. **—mul·ti·plex** *adj.* having to do with the transmission of many signals at once on the same carrier wave: *~ radio transmission, channel.* **—mul·ti·pli·cand** (–CAND) *n.* a number that is to be multiplied by another, or **multiplier.** **—mul·ti·pli·ca·tion** (–CAY–) *n.* **1** a multiplying or increase. **2** a short method of adding equal numbers many times, in an operation indicated by a **multiplication sign** (X). **—mul·ti·plic·i·ty** (–PLIS–) *n.* a great number or variety: *a ~ of interests.* **—mul·ti·pli·er** (–ply·ur) *n.* See MULTIPLICAND. **—mul·ti·ply** *v.* **-plies, -plied, -ply·ing** increase in number; also, find the mathematical product of: *2 ~d by 3 is 6.* **—mul·ti·pur·pose** *adj.* serving several purposes: *a ~ fabric, kit.* **—mul·ti·ra·cial** (–RAY–) *adj.* of several races: *a ~ society.* **—mul·ti·stage** *adj.* having several stages: *a ~ rocket, pump.* **—mul·ti·tude** *n.* a large number, esp. of people; **mul·ti·tu·di·nous** (–TUE·dn·us) *adj.* very numerous. **—mul·ti·ver·si·ty** (–VUR–) *n.* **-ties** a vast and complex university system, as of California. **—mul·ti·vi·ta·min** (–VYE·tuh–) *adj.* containing all the vitamins essential to health: *a ~ tablet.*

mum *n.* short form of CHRYSANTHEMUM. ***—adj.*** & ***interj.*** silent: *Let's keep ~ about this; Mum's the word!* (i.e. Keep silent about this!). **—mum·ble** *n.* & *v.* **-bles, -bled, -bling** (speak in) a low, indistinct mutter, as because of embarrassment; **mum·bler** *n.* **—mum·ble·ty-peg** *n.* a game of throwing a knife so as to make it stick in the ground. **—mum·bo jum·bo** (–JUM–) meaningless or ritualistic talk; also, a fetish or idol.

mu·mes·on (MEW·mes–) *n.* same as MUON.

mum·mer *n.* a person who wears a fancy costume or a mask, as at a festival or in a pantomime; **mum·mer·y** *n.* **mum·mer·ies** a dumb show or other performance by mummers.

mum·my (MUM·ee) *n.* **mum·mies** a dead body embalmed for burial and preservation, as in ancient Egypt; **mum·mi·fy** *v.* **-fies, -fied, -fy·ing** make into or like a mummy: *~d customs;* **mum·mi·fi·ca·tion** (–CAY–) *n.*

mumps *n. sing.* & *pl.* a contagious virus disease of the salivary glands characterized by painful swelling of the sides of the face and neck.

mun. municipal.

munch *v.* chew vigorously or with a crunching sound.

mun·dane *adj.* commonplace or everyday: *~ affairs, activities; our ~* (i.e. worldly) *existence;* **mun·dane·ly** *adv.*

Mu·nich (MEW·nic) a city of S.E. West Germany.

mu·nic·i·pal (mew·NIS·uh·pl) *adj.* of a municipality: *~ government, council, police, library;* **—mu·nic·i·pal·i·ty** (–PAL–) *n.* **-ties** a locally self-governing, usu. incorporated city, town, or borough.

mu·nif·i·cent (mew·NIF–) *adj.* generous or lavish in a princely way: *a ~ gift, person;* **mu·nif·i·cent·ly** *adv.;* **mu·nif·i·cence** *n.*

mu·ni·tions (mew·NISH·unz) *n.pl.* military supplies such as guns, bombs, and equipment; **munition** *adj.*: *a ~ plant.*

mu·on (MEW–) *n.* a meson with a mass of about 207 times that of an electron.

mu·ral (MYOOR·ul) *n.* & *adj.* (a large-size painting or decoration) done on a wall: *a ~ painting;* **mu·ral·ist** *n.*

mur·der *n.* **1** the crime of killing a person, esp. on purpose. **2** *Informal.* something hard or unpleasant, as a job, the weather, etc. ***—v.:*** *brutally ~ed in cold blood; to ~* (i.e. botch or mangle) *a song, the English language;* **mur·der·er** *n.; fem.* **mur·der·ess.** **—mur·der·ous**

(–us) *adj.: with ~ intent; a ~ blow, hate, heat wave;* **mur·der·ous·ly** *adv.*

mur·i·at·ic (mew·ree·AT–) **acid** same as HYDROCHLORIC ACID.

murk *n.* darkness and gloom, as because of a vapor or mist. —**murk·y** *adj.* **murk·i·er, -i·est:** *the ~ smoke-filled air; ~ logic;* **murk·i·ly** *adv.;* **murk·i·ness** *n.*

mur·mur *n.* a soft, low, continuous but indistinct sound or voice, as of a grumbling person, the flow of a stream, distant voices, or a diseased heart valve. —***v.:*** *to ~ a prayer; ~ one's thanks; ~ about poor wages;* **mur·mur·er** *n.*

mur·rain (MUR·un) *n.* **1** an infectious disease of cattle, as anthrax. **2** *Archaic.* plague.

mus. museum; music.

Mus·cat capital of Oman; **Muscat and Oman** former name of OMAN.

mus·ca·tel (–cuh·TEL) *n.* a sweet dessert wine made from **mus·cat** grapes having the odor of musk.

mus·cle (MUSL) *n.* a fibrous body tissue distributed in bands and bundles, esp. as organs that help in work and movement, as of the biceps, the stomach, and the heart; hence, physical strength or power: *Develop your ~s; a he-man with more ~ than brains; those ~ cars with animal names;* ***v.*** **-cles, -cled, -cling:** *He jumped the queue and ~d his way in;* **-muscled** *comb.form.* as in *well-~, hard-~.* —**mus·cle-bound** *adj.* rigid or stiff, as muscles from too much exercise. —**mus·cu·lar** (MUS·kyuh·lur) *adj.* of muscles: *~ strength; a ~* (i.e. having good muscles) *build;* **mus·cu·lar·i·ty** (–LAIR–) *n.* —**muscular dystrophy** an inherited disease that causes muscles to weaken and waste away. —**mus·cu·la·ture** (MUS·kyuh·luh·chur) *n.* system or arrangement of muscles.

muse (MYOOZ) *n.* the source of inspiration, esp. of a poet; **the Muses** in Greek and Roman myths, nine goddesses of the arts and sciences. —***v.*** **mus·es, mused, mus·ing** ponder or reflect meditatively *(on, over, upon): a poet ~ing over his past.* —**mu·sette** (mew·ZET) *n. Milit.* a small canvas or leather knapsack; also **musette bag.** —**mu·se·um** (mew·ZEE–) *n.* a place where objects of cultural and scientific value are stored and exhibited.

[1]**mush** *n.* & *v.* travel over snow with a dog sled; ***interj.*** a shout urging sled dogs forward.

[2]**mush** *n.* (a soft, thick, pulpy mass like) corn meal boiled in water; hence, *Informal.* weak sentimentality; **mush·y** *adj.* **mush·i·er, -i·est.**

mush·room *n.* a usu. umbrellalike, rapidly-sprouting, fleshy fungus; ***adj.:*** *the ~* (i.e. umbrella-shaped) *cloud following a nuclear blast; the ~* (i.e. fast) *growth of a boom town;* ***v.:*** *the ~ing of fast-food outlets.*

mu·sic (MEW·zic) *n.* **1** a rhythmic sound or sequence of sounds that is pleasing to the ear. **2** the art of making such sounds systematically, using the voice or instruments. **3** written music. —**face the music** *Informal.* face the consequences, as of one's actions. —**mu·si·cal** *adj.: a ~ voice, family, instrument, ear;* ***n.*** a play or motion picture having a sentimental or humorous theme worked out with much singing and dancing, as *My Fair Lady* and *Hair;* also called **musical comedy; mu·si·cal·ly** *adv.* —**mu·si·cale** (–CAL) *n.* a party featuring a musical program. —**mu·sic·ian** (–ZISH·un) *n.* one skilled in music, esp. as a composer or performer; **mu·sic·ian·ly** *adj.* —**mu·si·col·o·gy** (–zi·COL·uh·jee) *n.* the study of the principles, history, etc. of music; **mu·si·col·o·gist** *n.*

musk *n.* a strong-smelling substance from a gland of the **musk deer** and other animals that is used in making perfume; **musk·y** *adj.;* **musk·i·ness** *n.*

mus·keg *n.* a mossy bog or swamp of the far N. regions of North America.

mus·kel·lunge (MUS·kuh·lunj) *n. sing.* & *pl.* a prized North American game and food fish, the largest of the pike family; also **mus·kie** (–kee).

mus·ket (–kit) *n.* a heavy muzzle-loading shoulder firearm of former times; **mus·ket·eer** (–TEER) *n.* —**mus·ket·ry** *n.* muskets collectively; also, small-arms fire.

Mus·k(h)o·ge·an (mus·COH·gee·un) *n.* & *adj.* (of) a family of American Indian languages of S.E. North America.

musk·mel·on (–mel·un) *n.* any of a group of gourd-family vines including the honey dew and the cantaloupe that bear sweet fruit with a distinctive musklike flavor. —**musk ox** a shaggy-haired wild ox of the Arctic that gives off a musky smell. —**musk·rat** *n.* a ratlike rodent with a musky odor that lives in burrows near streams and rivers and is valued for its coat of long, shiny hair.

Mus·lim (MUZ–) same as MOSLEM.

mus·lin (MUZ–) *n.* a closely woven cotton cloth used for sheets; in Britain, a sheer cotton fabric, originally made in Iraq and India.

muss *n.* & *v.* (put into) a rumpled or disordered condition: *lightweight, wrinkle-free, hard-to-muss clothes;* **muss·y** *adj.* **muss·i·er, -i·est; muss·i·ly** *adv.*

mus·sel (MUSL) *n.* a clamlike bivalve mollusk, valued as food and for mother-of-pearl.

Mus·sul·man *n.* a Moslem.

[1]**must** *auxiliary v. pres.* & *past* **1** [expressing obligation]: *I ~ go now; You ~ not be late.* **2** [expressing possibility, certainty, etc.] *You ~ be tired; This book ~ be John's.* —***n.*** *Informal.* necessity: *A black tie is a ~;* ***adj.*** *Informal: a ~ book, item of clothing.*

[2]**must** *n.* the fermenting juice of grapes; new wine.

mus·tache (mus·TASH, MUSS·tash) *n.* hair growing on a man's upper lip.

mus·tang *n.* a small, hardy horse of S.W. United States.

mus·tard (–tird) *n.* a pungent condiment in paste or powder form prepared from the seeds of a plant, "black" or "white" mustard, whose leaves are used as greens. —**mustard gas** an oily liquid with a mustardlike odor that vaporizes into a poison gas, used in chemical warfare.

mus·ter *v.* **1** of troops, assemble. **2** collect (soldiers, resources, one's courage, etc.). **3 muster in** (or **out**) enlist in (or discharge from) the military. —***n.*** an assembly; **pass muster** be up to the required standard.

must·n't (MUS·nt) must not.

mus·ty (–tee) *adj.* **-ti·er, -ti·est** stale or moldy, as from dampness or lack of fresh air: *a ~ odor, taste, air; ~* (i.e. antiquated) *ideas, customs;* **mus·ti·ly** *adv.;* **mus·ti·ness** *n.*

mu·ta·ble (MEW·tuh–) *adj.* changeable by nature; also, fickle; **mu·ta·bil·i·ty** (–BIL–) *n.;* **mu·ta·bly** (–blee) *adv.* —**mu·tant** (–tnt–) *n.* & *adj.* (an animal such as the white turkey or a plant such as the pink grapefruit) produced by mutation. —**mu·tate** (MEW–) *v.* **-tates, -tat·ed, -tat·ing** (cause) to undergo mutation. —**mu·ta·tion** (–TAY–) *n.* gene change caused by radiations, chemicals, etc. resulting in the appearance of new characteristics that are transmitted to offspring; **mu·ta·tion·al** *adj.* —**mu·ta·tive** (MEW·tuh·tiv) *adj.* marked by change.

mute *adj.* dumb or silent: *deaf and ~; ~ with astonishment; the ~ "b" of dumb;* ***n.*** a dumb person; also, a silencing device, as on a musical instrument; ***v.*** **mutes, mut·ed, mut·ing** muffle or soften the sound of (a voice, violin string, etc.). —**mute·ly** *adv.;* **mute·ness** *n.*

mu·ti·late (MEW·tl·ate) *v.* **-lates, -lat·ed, -lat·ing** deprive (a person, literary work, song, etc.) of an essential part, as by maiming or crippling; **mu·ti·la·tor** *n.* —**mu·ti·la·tion** (–LAY–) *n.*

mu·ti·ny (MEW·tn·ee) *n.* **-nies** a rebellion, esp. by soldiers or sailors against their officers; ***v.*** **-nies, -nied, -ny·ing** rebel. —**mu·ti·nous** (–nus) *adj.* —**mu·ti·neer** (–NEER) *n.*

mutt *n. Slang.* a mongrel dog; also, a despised person.

mut·ter *v.* speak (words, curses, etc.) in a low and indistinct voice, as if angry or dissatisfied; ***n.*** what is muttered; grumble.

mut·ton (MUTN) *n.* the flesh of mature sheep used as food; **mut·ton·y** *adj.* —**mut·ton·chops** *n.pl.* sideburns that are narrow at the top and broad and rounded at the bottom.

mu·tu·al (MEW·choo·ul) *adj.* relating to or shared by each other: *the ~ affection between spouses; Jim and John are ~ enemies; Jack is their ~ friend* (i.e. friend of both); **mu·tu·al·ly** *adv.* —**mutual fund** an investment company whose members pool their capital to invest in stocks and other securities.

muu·muu (MOO·moo) *n.* a long, loose-fitting dress for informal wear, originally from Hawaii.

Mu·zak (MEW–) *Trademark.* recorded background music transmitted by telephone line or FM radio.

muz·zle (MUZL) *n.* **1** the mouth of an animal such as the dog, horse, or cow that is at the end of a projecting part of the head; hence, the mouth of the barrel of a gun or pistol: *a ~-loading firearm.* **2** a cover made of straps or wires put around an animal's muzzle; ***v.*** **muz·zles, muz·zled, muz·zling** put a muzzle on; restrain (a person, newspaper, etc.) from speaking out; gag.

Mv mendelevium. —**MV** motor vessel.

my *adj.* possessive case of I: *This is ~ book; ~ dear boys;* ***interj.:*** *Oh, ~!*

my·col·o·gy (–COL–) *n.* the branch of botany dealing with fungi; **my·col·o·gist** *n.* —**my·co·log·i·cal** (–LOJ–) *adj.*

my·e·li·tis (my·uh·LYE–) *n.* inflammation of the spinal cord or of the bone marrow.

My·lar *Trademark.* polyester film used for electrical insulation, magnetic tape, etc.; also **mylar** *n.*

my·na(h) (MY–) *n.* a bird of the starling family, native to India, esp. a "talking" species often kept as a pet.

my·o·pi·a (–OH·pee·uh) *n.* nearsightedness; shortsightedness; **my·op·ic** (–OP–) *adj.*

myr·i·ad (MEER·ee·ud) *n.* & *adj.* (consisting of) an indefinitely large number. —**myr·i·a·me·ter** (MEER·ee·uh·mee–) *n.* a unit of 10,000 meters.

myr·mi·don (MUR·muh–) *n.* an unquestioning, esp. unscrupulous follower; **Myrmidons** *pl.* in Greek myth, a warlike people who followed Achilles to the Trojan War.

myrrh (MUR) *n.* a fragrant gum resin used in making incense and perfume since ancient times; **myrrh·ic** *adj.*

myr·tle (MUR·tl) *n.* an evergreen Mediterranean shrub with fragrant flowers, leaves, and berries; also, the common periwinkle.

my·self (–SELF) *pron.* reflexive or emphatic of I or ME: *I speak only for ~; hurt ~ in the dark; I'm not ~* (i.e. well as usual) *today.*

mys·ter·y (MIS·tuh·ree) *n.* **-ter·ies** **1** something hidden from human knowledge because hard to understand or explain: *the ~ of the Holy Trinity; the ~s of the universe; Her disappearance has remained a ~; a ~ (novel)* (i.e. detective story). **2** something secret; also, secrecy: *an air of ~; the ~s* (i.e. rites) *of the Christian religion.* —**mys·te·ri·ous** (–TEER·ee·us) *adj.;* **mys·te·ri·ous·ly** *adv.;* **mys·te·ri·ous·ness** *n.* —**mys·tic** (MIS–) *n.* one who seeks to learn about God and supernatural things through intuition rather than by use of reason; ***adj.*** of mystics or mysticism; also, mysterious or occult; also **mys·ti·cal; mys·ti·cal·ly** *adv.;* **mys·ti·cism** *n.* the philosophy or doctrines of mystics, esp. in regard to the knowledge of God through meditation and spiritual insight. —**mys·ti·fy** *v.* **-fies, -fied, -fy·ing** puzzle or perplex; also, make (something) mysterious; **mys·ti·fi·ca·tion** (–CAY–) *n.* —**mys·tique** (–TEEK) *n.* the air of mystery about a person or thing; *the feminine ~ of the Mona Lisa; the*

~ (i.e. impressive professionalism) *of bullfighting.*

myth (MITH) *n.* a primitive, often supernatural story current among a people that seeks to explain something in nature, as stories of creation of the universe; also, such stories collectively; mythology: *Greek ~.* **2** any person or thing considered an invention. **—myth·i·cal** *adj.* **—my·thol·o·gy** (mi·THOL·uh·jee) *n.* **-gies** the study of myths; also, a group of myths; **my·thol·o·gist** *n.* **—myth·o·log·i·cal** (–LOJ–) *adj.*

N

N or **n** (EN) *n.* **N's** or **n's** the 14th letter of the English alphabet. —**N** nitrogen. —**n** an indefinite number; nano-. —**N.** or **n.** name; navy; neuter; new; nomination; noun. —**N.** noon; Norse; north(ern); November. —**n.** net; north(ern); noun; number. —**'n'** and: as in *show 'n' tell, rock 'n' roll.*

Na sodium. —**N.A.** North America; not applicable; not available.

N.A.A.C.P. National Association for the Advancement of Colored People.

nab *v.* **nabs, nabbed, nab·bing** *Informal.* snatch; seize quickly, esp. arrest (a person).

na·bob (NAY–) *n.* a wealthy or important man.

na·celle (nuh·SEL) *n.* the metal casing enclosing an engine on or in the wing of an airplane.

na·cre (NAY·cur) *n.* mother-of-pearl.

Na·der (NAY·dur) **Ralph.** born 1934, American consumer advocate; **Na·der·ism** *n.*

na·dir (NAY–) *n.* the lowest point; opposite of ZENITH: *the ~ of one's career, decadence, hopes.*

nae (NAY) *adj.* & *adv. Scottish.* no.

nag *v.* **nags, nagged, nag·ging** find fault with continually; hence, annoy or vex: *Stop ~ing me; ~d by doubts; a ~ing backache.* —***n.*** **1** one who nags; scold. **2** an old or worn-out horse.

Na·ga·sa·ki (NAH·guh·SAH·kee) a Japanese city rebuilt after destruction by U.S. atomic bomb. —**Na·go·ya** (nah·GO·yah) a Japanese manufacturing center.

Na·ha (NAH·hah) capital of Okinawa.

nai·ad (NAY–, NYE–) *n.* **1** in Greek and Roman myths, the guardian nymph of a river or stream. **2** the incomplete adult stage of insects such as dragonflies and damselflies when they are wingless and live in water.

na·ïf (nah·EEF) *adj.* same as NAIVE.

nail *n.* **1** the horny growth at the ends of fingers and toes. **2** a pointed metal spike with a broadened head that is hit with a hammer to drive it into pieces of wood or other material for fastening them; ***v.*** fasten or secure, as with a nail: *Let's* **nail down** *the offer with a small deposit.*

nain·sook (NAIN–) *n.* a soft, light muslin.

nai·ra (NYE·ruh) *n.* the basic money unit of Nigeria, equal to 100 kobo.

Nai·ro·bi (nye·ROH·bee) capital of Kenya.

na·ive or **na·ïve** (nah·EEV) *adj.* simple or unsophisticated; also, foolishly simple; **na·ive·ly** or **na·ïve·ly** *adv.* —**na·ive·té** or **na·ïve·té** (–TAY, –EEV–) *n.* artlessness; also, a naive action or remark; also **na·ive·ty** (–EEV–) *n.* **-ties.**

na·ked (NAY·kid) *adj.* unclothed; hence, uncovered or plain; bare: *a body lying ~; the ~ sword* (out of its sheath); *the ~ truth;* **naked eye** eye unaided by a magnifying glass, esp. a microscope or telescope; **na·ked·ly** *adv.;* **na·ked·ness** *n.*

N.A.M. National Association of Manufacturers.

nam·by-pam·by (NAM·bee·PAM·bee) *adj.* & *n.* **-bies** (a person or talk that is) silly or sentimental.

name *n.* **1** word(s) by which a person, animal, place, or thing is called or known: *your ~ and address; She called him* **names** (i.e. bad names); **name-call·ing** *n.;* **in name only** not in reality; without power or influence; **in the name of** by the authority of (God, the king, etc.). **2** reputation; fame: *earned a bad ~ in society; the greatest ~* (i.e. person) *in boxing;* ***adj.:*** *a ~ brand* (i.e. well-known) *detergent.* —***v.*** **names, named, nam·ing:** *a baby ~d for his father; a general accusation without ~ing any offenders; ~ the days of the week; ~d to the chairmanship; You ~* (i.e. mention) *it;* **name·a·ble** *adj.* —**name-drop·ping** *n.* the mentioning of important persons in a familiar way in order to impress others; **name-drop·per** *n.* —**name·less** *adj.* without a name because not given one, cannot be described, not famous, etc.; **name·less·ly** *adv.* —**name·ly** *adv.* that is to say; viz. —**the name of the game** *Informal.* the essential thing; a goal or the means of attaining it. —**name·plate** *n.* a plate, plaque, etc. bearing a person's name. —**name·sake** *n.* one with the same name as another, esp. if named after that other person.

Na·mib·i·a (nuh·MIB·ee·uh) a country of S. Africa; 318, 261 sq. mi. (824, 292 km²); *cap.* Windhoek.

nan·keen (–KEEN) *n.* a firm-textured cloth finished without size or bleach, originally made in China from a yellowish kind of cotton; also **nan·kin.** —**Nan·king** a city of E. China.

nan·ny (NAN·ee) *n.* **nan·nies** *Brit.* a child's domestic nurse. —**nanny goat** a female goat.

nano- (NAN·ch–) *comb.form.* billionth: as in **na·no·me·ter, na·no·sec·ond.**

nap **1** *n.* & *v.* **naps, napped, nap·ping** (take) a brief, light sleep; **catch (one) napping** catch (one) off his guard. **2** *n.* soft or downy surface, as of fur, velvet, etc.; **napped** *adj.;* **nap·py** *adj.*

na·palm (NAY·pahm) *n.* highly flammable jellied gasoline, used in bombs and flame throwers, because it clings to everything it touches causing death and destruction by fire; ***v.:*** *the ~ing of enemy territory.*

nape *n.* the back of the neck.

na·per·y *n. Rare.* table linen.

naph·tha (NAF·thuh, NAP–) *n.* a flammable petroleum product used as a cleaning agent and solvent. —**naph·tha·lene** (–leen) *n.* a white crystalline hydrocarbon got from coal tar for use in mothballs, dyes, etc.

nap·kin *n.* a small towel or piece of cloth or paper used for wiping the lips, etc. while eating; also, a SANITARY NAPKIN.

Na·ples (NAY·plz) a seaport of S. Italy.

Na·po·le·on (nuh·POH·lee·un) **I** or Napoleon Bonaparte, 1769–1821, French general and conqueror of Europe; **Na·po·le·on·ic** (–ON–) *adj.*: *the ~ civil code, wars.* —**napoleon** *n.* **1** a former French gold coin worth 20 francs. **2** a pastry with a custardlike filling.

narc or **nark** *n. Slang.* a police agent enforcing narcotics laws. —**nar·cis·sism** (NAR·suh·sizm) *n.* preoccupation with one's own beauty; **nar·cis·sist** *n.* & *adj.;* **nar·cis·sis·tic** (–SIS·tic) *adj.* —**Nar·cis·sus** (–SIS–) in Greek myth, a youth who fell in love with his reflection in a pond, was drowned, and then changed into a **nar·cis·sus** *n.* **-cis·sus(·es)** or **-cis·si** (–sye) a plant of the amaryllis family, as the daffodil and the jonquil, with sword-shaped leaves and tall shoots of fragrant, six-petaled white or yellow flowers. —**nar·co·lep·sy** (NAR·cuh–) *n.* an illness characterized by irresistible attacks of sleep. —**nar·co·sis** (–COH–) *n.* a state of stupor induced by a narcotic; **nar·cot·ic** (–COT–) *n.* & *adj.* (of) a drug such as opium, morphine, codeine, or heroin that deadens pain and causes stupor: *a ~ addict, effect;* **nar·co·tism** *n.* —**nar·co·tize** (NAR·cuh–) *v.* **-tiz·es, -tized, -tiz·ing** subject to a narcotic; dull or deaden; **nar·co·ti·za·tion** (–ZAY–) *n.*

nard same as SPIKENARD.

nar·es (NAIR·eez) *n.pl.* nostrils; *sing.* **nar·is.**

nark **1** *n.* & *v. Brit. Slang.* (turn) spy or informer for police. **2** same as NARC.

Nar·ra·gan·sett (nair·uh·GAN·sit) *n.* (an American Indian of) a tribe that lived in the region of **Narragansett Bay,** an inlet of the Atlantic extending into Rhode Island.

nar·rate (NAIR–) *v.* **-rates, -rat·ed, -rat·ing** relate or tell (a story, adventures, etc.); **nar·ra·tor** (–RAY·tur, NAIR·ay–) *n.;* **nar·ra·tion** (–RAY–) *n.* —**nar·ra·tive** (NAIR·uh·tiv) *n.* & *adj.* (in the form of) a story or tale that recounts events: *a long ~; a ~ poem; ~ prose style.*

nar·row (NAIR·oh) *adj.* limited or small in width: *a ~ street, margin; a ~* (i.e. not liberal) *viewpoint; a ~* (i.e. restricted) *circle of friends; a ~* (i.e. close) *escape, majority; "Meat" means animal flesh in the ~est sense;* ***v.*** make or become narrower. —***n.*** something narrow; usu. **narrows** *pl.* a narrow passage, as a strait or a mountain pass. —**nar·row·ly** *adv.;* **nar·row·ness** *n.* —**nar·row-mind·ed** *adj.* limited in outlook, not broad-minded; **nar·row-mind·ed·ness** *n.*

nar·thex *n.* a transverse vestibule or porch of a basilica, as in Byzantine churches.

nar·whal (–wul) *n.* an arctic whale whose male has a long spiral tusk like the fabled unicorn's.

nar·y (NAIR·ee) *adj.* **nary a(n)** not one: *with ~ a cent in his pocket.*

N.A.S. National Academy of Sciences.

NASA (NAS·uh) National Aeronautics and Space Administration.

na·sal (NAY·zl) *adj.* of or through the nose: *a ~ bone, sound, voice;* ***n.:*** *"M," "n," and "ng" are ~s* (i.e. nasal letters and sounds); *the ~s* (i.e. bones) *forming the bridge of the nose;* **na·sal·ly** *adv.* —**na·sal·ize** *v.* **-iz·es, -ized, -iz·ing** utter or speak nasally: *the ~d vowels of the French "bon" and "vin";* **na·sal·i·za·tion** (–ZAY–) *n.*

nas·cent (NAS·nt, NAY·snt) *adj.* being born or formed; beginning to develop: *hydrogen in a ~ state during a chemical reaction;* **nas·cence** *n.*

Nash·ville (–vil) capital of Tennessee.

Nas·sau (NAS·aw) capital of the Bahamas.

na·stur·tium (nuh·STUR·shum) *n.* any of a group of trailing or climbing garden plants having brightly-colored, spurred flowers with five sepals and petals and long-stalked umbrella-shaped leaves that are sometimes used in salads.

nas·ty (NAS·tee) *adj.* **-ti·er, -ti·est** disgusting or offensive to good taste; very unpleasant: *a ~ remark, smell, temper, job; ~ weather;* **nas·ti·ly** *adv.;* **nas·ti·ness** *n.*

nat. national; native; natural;

na·tal (NAY·tl) *adj.* of or from birth: *~ day, hour, death rate.* —**na·tal·i·ty** (–TAL–) *n.* **-ties** birthrate.

na·tes (NAY·teez) *n.pl.* buttocks.

na·ta·to·ri·um (nay·tuh·TOR·ee·um) *n.* an indoor swimming facility.

na·tion (NAY–) *n.* a people with a common history and culture, usu. living under one government in a country of their own and using the same language: *a newly independent African ~; the Jewish ~; the United Nations Organization; the Six Nations* (i.e. tribes) *federation of Iroquois;* **na·tion·hood** *n.* —**na·tion·al** (NASH·uh·nl) *adj.: a ~ anthem, academy, monument;* ***n.*** a citizen or subject: *foreign ~s granted American citizenship; an Israeli who was a U.S. ~;* **na·tion·al·ly** *adv.* —**National Guard** as volunteer reserve group organized in each state as part of the U.S. Army and Air Force. —**na·tion·al·ism** (NASH–) *n.* devotion to one's country, esp. in protecting its independence; **na·tion·al·ist** *n.* & *adj.;* **na·tion·al·is·tic** (–LIS–) *adj.* —**na·tion·al·i·ty** (nash·uh·NAL–) *n.* **-ties:** *Gypsies of many ~s* (i.e. nations); *a Soviet citizen of Estonian ~* (i.e. ethnic origin). —**na·tion·al·ize** (NASH–) *v.* **-iz·es, -ized, -iz·ing** make national, esp. take (an industry, institution, land, etc.) under national control; **na·tion·al·i·za·tion** (–ZAY–) *n.* —**national park** a park, monument, historic site, or recreational area set aside by a national government for public use. —**na·tion·wide** *adj.* existing throughout the nation; national: *~ television.* —**na·tive** (NAY·tiv) *adj.* **1** inborn, not acquired: *~ instincts, abilities; one's ~ land* (i.e. of birth), *language.* **2** born or originating in a certain place: *~ African customs; a* **na·tive-born** *American of German descent.* —**na·tive** *n.* a person, animal, or plant belonging to a certain place, esp. by origin: *tourists and other foreigners meeting ~s; The koala is an Australian ~;* **native American** an American Indian. —**na·tiv·ism** *n.* a self-protective attitude or policy typical of natives towards immigrants and foreigners; **na·tiv·i·ty** (nuh·TIV–) *n.* **-ties** birth; **the Nativity** the birth of Christ; also, Christmas. —**natl.** national.

NATO (NAY·toh) North Atlantic Treaty Organization.

nat·ty (NAT·ee) *adj.* **nat·ti·er, nat·ti·est** neat and trim in dress or appearance: *a ~ dresser;* **nat·ti·ly** *adv.*

nat·u·ral (NACH·uh·rul) *adj.* **1** of or having to do with nature: *the ~ beauty of the countryside; storms, earthquakes, and such ~ phenomena; water, minerals, land, forests, and such* **natural resources;** *a ~* (i.e. illegitimate) *son.* **2** of or having to do with the innate character or nature of a person or thing; not artificial or formal: *looks more ~ without a wig; her ~ gifts, voice; a ~ note* (i.e. not sharp or flat musically); **nat·u·ral·ness** *n.* —***n.*** one naturally suited for a job, role, etc. —**natural childbirth** delivery by a mother emotionally and physically trained to bear the pain without the help of an anesthetic. —**natural gas** a hydrocarbon gas formed in the earth from organic matter, much used as fuel. —**natural history** the nontechnical, popular study of the animals, plants, minerals, and other things in nature; **nat·u·ral·ist** *n.* one who studies natural history; also, an advocate of **nat·u·ral·ism** *n.* the use of what is natural and realistic, instead of the unscientific and the supernatural, in art, fiction, drama, etc.; **nat·u·ral·is·tic** (–LIS–) *adj.* —**nat·u·ral·ize** *v.* **-ze·es, -ized, -iz·ing** make or become (like a) native, as aliens by taking up citizenship: *"Spaghetti" is a ~d Italian word; The African violet was ~d long ago;* **nat·ur·al·i·za·tion** (–ZAY–) *n.* —**nat·u·ral·ly** *adv.: He likes girls, ~; can't talk ~ when on stage; the ~ unsuspecting child.* —**natural science** a science dealing with nature, as biology, physics, chemistry, or geology, as distinguished from the humanities and social sciences; **natural scientist.** —**natural selection** the process by which only the fittest or best-adapted of a species survive in the struggle for food, shelter, and other necessities of life. —**na·ture** (NAY·chur) *n.* **1** the world of animals, plants, minerals, forces such as instincts, and phenomena such as wind and rain that are not made by man: *Everyone loves ~; Nudists socialize in a state of ~; the calls of ~* (to urinate and defecate). **2** innate character; real quality: *It is the dog's ~ to bark; lazy* **by nature;** *a pursuit of a scholarly ~* (i.e. kind). —**nature study** the study of the life and phenomena in nature at the elementary level. —**na·tur·ist** *n.* nudist.

Nau·ga·hyde (NAW·guh–) *Trademark.* a leatherlike vinyl fabric.

naught (NAWT) *n.* nothing; zero. —**naugh·ty** (NAW·tee) *adj.* **-ti·er, -ti·est** **1** disobedient; mischievous: *a ~ child.* **2** off-color: *a ~ joke.* —**naugh·ti·ly** *adv.;* **naugh·ti·ness** *n.*

Nau·ru (nah·OO·roo, NAH·roo) an island country in the C. Pacific Ocean; 8 sq. mi. (21 km²); *cap.* Yaren.

nau·sea (NAW·zhuh, –zee·uh) *n.* sickness of the stomach that makes one want to vomit; hence, loathing or disgust; **nau·se·ate** (NAW·shee–, –zhee–, –zee–, –see–) *v.* **-ates, -at·ed, -at·ing:** *The very mention of certain foods ~s her;* **nau·se·at·ing** *adj.: a very ~ experience;* **nau·se·a·tion** (–AY–) *n.* —**nau·seous** (NAW·shus, –zee·us) *adj.* feeling or causing nausea; hence, disgusting or loathesome: *She feels ~ in the morning; foods that are ~ to some.*

naut. *Abbrev.* for **nau·ti·cal** (NAW–) *adj.* of sailors, ships, or navigation: *"amidships," "fo'c'sle," and such ~ terms;* **nautical mile** distance unit of 6,076 ft. (1,852 m) used in air and sea navigation, equal to 1/60 of a degree of the earth's circumference; sea mile; **nau·ti·cal·ly** *adv.* —**nau·ti·lus** *n.* **-lus·es** or **-li** (–lye) a mollusk with a spiral shell divided into many chambers lined with mother-of-pearl. —**nav.** naval; navigable; navigation.

Nav·a·ho (NAV·uh·hoh) *n., pl.* **-ho** or **-ho(e)s** a member or the language of an American Indian people of New Mexico, Arizona, and Utah; also **Nav·a·jo** (–hoh), **-jo(e)s.**

na·val (NAY·vl) *adj.* of or having to do with a navy; **naval stores** products such as pitch and tar used in building and repairing wooden sailing ships, now including also rosin, turpentine, and other products from resinous trees. **—nave** *n.* the central or main part of a church where the congregation is seated.

na·vel (NAY·vl) *n.* a depression in the center of the belly where the umbilical cord was attached at birth. **—navel orange** a seedless orange with a navellike formation at its apex.

nav·i·ga·ble (NAV·i·guh·bl) *adj.* that can be navigated: *a* ~ *river* (wide and deep enough for craft); *a* ~ (i.e. steerable) *balloon;* **nav·i·ga·bly** *adv.;* **nav·i·ga·bil·i·ty** (–BIL–) *n.* **—nav·i·gate** *v.* **-gates, -gat·ed, -gat·ing** **1** steer, guide, or manage (a ship, plane, etc.) through (the sea, air, etc.); also, negotiate one's way (past or through). **2** get through (a river, sea, etc.) in a craft. **3** *Informal.* move or walk steadily. **—nav·i·ga·tion** (–GAY–) *n.* the science of guiding a craft on its course through water, air, or space; also, a navigating. **—nav·i·ga·tor** (NAV–) *n.* one who navigates; also, an explorer of the seas. **—na·vy** (NAY·vee) *n.* **-vies** **1** a nation's warships collectively or the naval establishment including yards, offices, and personnel. **2** [short form] navy blue. **—navy bean** a white variety of bean, as used for "Boston baked beans." **—navy blue** a dark purplish blue. **—navy yard** a shipyard for naval vessels.

nay *adv.* **1** not only that but also: *poor, nay, destitute!* **2** *Archaic.* no; opposite of AYE. ***—n.*** a negative vote(r).

Na·zi (NAHT·see) *n.* & *adj.* (a member) of the German fascist party that ruled from 1933 to 1945 under Hitler; **Na·zi·sm** or **Na·zi·ism** (–see·izm) *n.*

N.B. New Brunswick; nota bene. **—Nb** niobium.

NBC National Broadcasting Company.

N-bomb *n.* same as NEUTRON BOMB.

NBS National Bureau of Standards.

N.C. or **NC** North Carolina; no charge.

N.C.O. noncommissioned officer.

Nd neodymium. **—N.D., ND** or **N.Dak.** North Dakota.

N'Djamena same as FORT LAMY.

N.E. or **n.e.** northeast(ern). **—N.E.** New England. **—NE** Nebraska. —Ne neon.

N.E.A. National Education Association.

Ne·an·der·thal (nee·AN·dur·thawl) *n.* & *adj.* (a primitive man) of the Stone Age; also **neanderthal** *adj.* backward or primitive: *his* ~ *views on white supremacy; a* ~ *male chauvinist.*

Ne·a·pol·i·tan (nee·uh·POL·uh·tn) *n.* & *adj.* (a native or inhabitant) of Naples; **Neapolitan ice cream** a brick of ice cream with several layers of different flavors.

neap tide either of the two lowest high tides of a month; cf. SPRINGTIDE.

near (NEER) *adj.* close (in distance, relationship, feelings, time, etc.): *Her house is* ~, *not far from here; a* ~ *relative, friend;* **near miss** (i.e. almost a hit); *Holidays are* ~; ~ *silk;* **near beer** (with less than ½ percent alcohol); *the* ~*est* (i.e. most direct) *route;* ***adv.:*** *Holidays are drawing* ~; *Peace seemed* **near at hand;** ~ (*Informal.* nearly) *frozen;* ***prep.*** close to: *a house* ~ *school;* ***v.*** approach. **—near·ness** *n.* **—near·by** (NEER–, –BYE) *adj.* & *adv.: lives* ~; *a* ~ *place.* **—Near East** the countries of S.W. Asia and N.E. Africa; also, Middle East; **Near Eastern.** **—near·ly** *adv.: It's* ~ (i.e. almost) *10 p.m.; We're* ~ (i.e. closely) *related.* **—near·sight·ed** *adj.* not able to see far because of defective eyesight; **near·sight·ed·ly** *adv.;* **near·sight·ed·ness** *n.*

¹neat (NEET) *adj.* clean and orderly; hence, pleasing: *a* ~ *kitchen; writes a* ~ *hand; a* ~ *mind looking for nice distinctions; a* ~ *profit of $100,000;* ~ (i.e. undiluted) *brandy.* **—neat·ly** *adv.;* **neat·ness** *n.*

²neat *n. Rare.* an ox or cow: as in *neat's-foot oil.*

'neath (NEETH) *Poet.* beneath.

neat's-foot oil an oil made from the bones of cattle, used for softening leather.

neb *n. Scottish.* a tip, esp. a beak; nib; also, a snout or a person's mouth.

neb·bish *n. Slang.* a pitifully inept or dull person.

Neb(r). *Abbrev.* for **Ne·bras·ka** (nuh·BRAS·kuh) a Midwestern state of the U.S.; 77,227 sq.mi. (200,017 km²); *cap.* Lincoln. **—Ne·bras·kan** *n.* & *adj.*

neb·u·la (NEB·yuh·luh) *n.* **-las** or **-lae** (-lee) any of the cloudlike, hazy patches seen in the sky at night which are either interstellar clouds of gas and dust or distant galaxies; **neb·u·lar** *adj.: the* ~ *hypothesis of the origins of the solar system;* **neb·u·lous** (–lus) *adj.* cloudlike or hazy; also, confused or vague. **—neb·u·los·i·ty** (–LOS–) *n.* **-ties** nebulous matter or condition.

nec·es·sar·y (NES·uh·ser·ee) *adj.* & *n.* **-es·sar·ies**(something) that is needed or required in a pressing manner: *Food, shelter, and clothing are* ~*s of life; the* ~ *repairs after a car accident; a* ~ (i.e. logical) *consequence of an action; the* ~ (i.e. unavoidable) *evils of our existence;* **nec·es·sar·i·ly** (–SAIR–) *adv.* **—ne·ces·si·tate** *n.* **-tates, -tat·ed, -tat·ing** make necessary: *Crime* ~*s punishment;* **ne·ces·si·tous** (–tus) *adj.* in great need or poverty; **ne·ces·si·tous·ly** *adv.* **—ne·ces·si·ty** (–SES–) *n.* **-ties** an urgent or pressing need or thing needed: *Food is a* ~ *for life; driven to beg by family* ~ (i.e. poverty); "~ *is the mother of invention*"; **of necessity** necessarily.

neck *n.* the narrow, slender part connecting the head to the rest of the body; hence, anything resembling it, as a narrow strip of land, the narrowest part of a bottle, violin, tooth, etc.: **risks his neck** (i.e. risks breaking it) *in rock-*

climbing; After several warnings he **got it in the neck** (*Slang.* was severely dealt with); *I'm* **up to my neck** (i.e. terribly busy) *in work.* —**neck and neck** running equal, as two horses in a race. —**stick one's neck out** act too boldly or foolishly. —***v.*** *Slang.* kiss and caress. —**neck·er·chief** (–chuf, –cheef) *n.* **-chiefs** or **-chieves** (–cheevz) a handkerchieflike piece of cloth worn about the neck. —**neck·lace** (–lis) *n.* an ornamental chain or string of jewels, beads, etc. worn around the neck. —**neck·line** *n.* the line formed by the edge of a garment around, esp. at the front of the neck: *a square ~; a plunging ~.* —**neck·tie** *n.* a strip of cloth worn around the neck under a collar, tied at the front of the neck with its loose ends hanging down; **neck·wear** *n.* neckties, scarfs, etc. collectively.

ne·crol·o·gy (–CROL·uh·jee) *n.* **-gies** an obituary (list or record, as kept by a church). —**nec·ro·man·cy** (NEC·ruh·man·see) *n.* sorcery or fortunetelling by communicating with the dead; **nec·ro·man·cer** *n.* —**ne·crop·o·lis** (–CROP–) *n.* a cemetery, as found on the site of an ancient city. —**ne·cro·sis** (–CROH–) *n.* death of body tissues, as after a severe burn or in gangrene; **ne·crot·ic** (–CROT–) *adj.*

nec·tar (–tur) *n.* a sweet or delicious drink, as the liquid that bees gather from flowers; originally, the drink of the gods of Greek myth. —**nec·tar·ine** (–REEN) *n.* a variety of peach with a smooth skin.

née or **nee** (NAY, NEE) *adj.* [used before a married woman's maiden name] born: *Mary Jones, ~ Smith.*

need *n.* **1** a lack of something useful or desired; also, the thing lacking: *She's in ~ of vitamins; men's daily ~s; Our ~s come before our wants; Sewers are a crying ~ here; "A friend in ~* (i.e. an exigency) *is a friend indeed."* **2** a requirement: *no ~ to apologize; prepared to sacrifice my life* **if need be.** —***v.*** [corresponding to the *n.* senses] **1:** *Everyone ~s love and understanding.* **2:** *You ~ not hurry.* —**need·ful** *n.* & *adj.* (what is) required or necessary.

nee·dle *n.* **1** a slender, pointed piece of steel with a hole at the thicker end through which a thread is passed for sewing; also, a similar instrument carrying a thread for knitting, crocheting, hooking, etc. **2** anything resembling a needle, as the pointer of a gauge or meter, the vibrating pin in the pickup mechanism of a phonograph, the pointed leaf of a pine, or the injecting end of a surgical syringe; *Informal.* an injection of a drug. —***v.*** **-dles, -dled, -dling** tease or annoy with gibes, provocative comments, etc. —**nee·dle·point** *n.* & *adj.* (of or having to do with) embroidery made on an open-mesh canvas background: *a ~ design;* **needlepoint (lace)** lace made with a needle instead of a bobbin.

need·less *adj.* unnecessary; **need·less·ly** *adv.;* **need·less·ness** *n.*

nee·dle·wom·an (NEE·dl·woom·un) *n.* **-wom·en** a woman who does **nee·dle·work** (–wurk) *n.* embroidery, needlepoint, knitting, and such work done with a needle.

need·n't (NEED·nt) need not. —**needs** *adv.* [used with *must*] necessarily. —**need·y** *adj.* **need·i·er, -i·est** in need; poor or destitute; **need·i·ness** *n.*

ne'er (NAIR) *Poetic.* never. —**ne'er-do-well** *n.* & *adj.* (one who is) worthless or irresponsible.

ne·far·i·ous (ni·FAIR·ee·us) *adj.* extremely wicked or villainous: *a ~ scheme; ~ activities, deeds;* **ne·far·i·ous·ly** *adv.;* **ne·far·i·ous·ness** *n.*

neg. negative. —**ne·gate** (ni·GATE) *v.* **-gates, -gat·ed, -gat·ing** nullify; also, deny the existence of; **ne·ga·tion** (–GAY–) *n.* —**neg·a·tive** (NEG·uh·tiv) *adj.* saying "no"; opposite; against or on the other side of something considered positive: *the ~ side of a debate; ~ film* (with reversed image); *a ~ TB test; −3 has a ~ sign; The anode is the ~ electrode in a battery.* —***n.*** something negative, as a word, vote, or reply, a minus sign or quantity, a film or photographic image, a battery terminal to which current flows, etc.; **in the negative** saying "no"; in denial. —***v.*** **-tives, -tived, -tiv·ing** deny; vote against; also, disprove. —**neg·a·tive·ly** *adv.* —**negative income tax** a subsidy paid by government to the poor to guarantee a minimum income. —**neg·a·tiv·ism** *n.* a negative attitude or tendency.

neg·lect (nig·LECT) *n.* give too little attention or care to: *Do not ~ your health, your duties, or* (i.e. omit) *to write home;* ***n.:*** *parental ~ of children; fired for ~ of duty;* **neg·lect·ful** *adj.* —**neg·li·gee** (–ZHAY) *n.* a woman's light and loose-fitting dressing gown; hence, careless or informal attire. —**neg·li·gent** (–junt) *adj.* habitually or extremely careless; **neg·li·gent·ly** *adv.;* **neg·li·gence** *n.* —**neg·li·gi·ble** *adj.* that can be neglected; trifling or unimportant: *a ~ amount, error.*

ne·go·ti·ate (ni·GOH·shee–) *v.* **-ates, -at·ed, -at·ing** **1** discuss (and arrange) (a treaty, settlement, sale, loan, etc.): *While both sides ~d, the strike continued; to ~ a peace settlement.* **2** sell, transfer, or assign (something negotiable, as a check, funds, etc.). **3** successfully go past (a turn), over (a fence), etc.; **ne·go·ti·a·ble** (–shee·uh–, –shuh–) *adj.;* **ne·go·ti·a·tor** (–ay·tur) *n.* —**ne·go·ti·a·tion** (–AY–) *n.*

ne·gri·tude (NEG·ruh–, NEE·gruh–) *n.* the fact of being a Negro, esp. the value of black or African culture; also **Ne·gro·ness** (NEE·groh–) *n.* —**Ne·gro** (NEE·groh) *adj.* & *n.* **-groes** [less favored than "black" or "African"] (of) a member of the Negroid group or black race of mankind; **Ne·groid** (NEE–) *n.* & *adj.* (a member) of a race of mankind native to Africa, distinguished by dark skin, kinky hair, and broad lips and nose.

ne·gus (NEE–) *n.* hot, sweetened wine flavored with lemon juice and nutmeg.

Neh·ru (NAY·roo), **Jawaharlal.** 1889–1964; first prime minister of India (1947–64).

neigh (NAY) *n.* & *v.* (utter) the characteristic cry of a horse; whinny.

neigh·bor (NAY·bur) *n.* one living near another; *our next-door ~; Love thy ~* (i.e. fellowman); ***v.*** live or be situated nearby: *Mexico ~s the U.S.;* **neigh·bor·ing** *adj.* Also **neigh·bour** *Brit.* —**neigh·bor·hood** *n.* a particular region, place, or district with the people living there: *a high-income ~;* **in the neighborhood of** *Informal.* near (a place); also approximately: *in the ~ of $50,000.* —**neigh·bor·ly** *adj.* like good neighbors; friendly; **neigh·bor·li·ness** *n.*

nei·ther (NEE·dhur, NYE–) *adj.* & *pron.* not the one or the other: *a shoe that fits ~ foot; ~ of the feet;* **conj.:** *It's ~ here nor there.*

nel·son (–sun) *n.* a wrestling hold in which leverage is applied with one arm ("half nelson") or both ("full nelson") passed from behind and under the opponent's arm(s) against his neck and head.

nem·a·tode (NEM·uh–) *n.* any of a group of worms including hookworms and pinworms having unsegmented bodies pointed at both ends and living in soil, water, or as parasites in animals and plants.

nem·e·sis (NEM·uh–) *n., pl.* **-ses** a fate which the victim has deserved; retribution; also, the punishing agent; **Nemesis** the Greek goddess of vengeance.

neo- *comb.form.* new or recent: as in **ne·o·clas·si·cism** (nee·oh·CLAS–) *n.* the revival of classical principles or practices in literature and the arts; **ne·o·clas·sic** or **-si·cal** *adj.* —**ne·o·co·lo·ni·al·ism** (–LOH–) *n.* domination by the great powers of smaller countries through economic, political, and military influence; **ne·o·co·lo·nial** *adj.;* **ne·o·co·lo·nial·ist** *n.* & *adj.* —**ne·o·dym·i·um** (–DIM–) *n.* a rare-earth metallic element used in alloys and to color glass. —**ne·o·im·pres·sion·ism** (–PRESH–) *n.* a French movement of the late 1800's based on pointillism as a reaction against impressionism. —**ne·ol·o·gism** (–OL·uh·jizm) *n.* a new word or phrase, or a new meaning for an established word; also **ne·ol·o·gy** *n.* **-gies.** —**ne·on** (NEE–) *n.* an inert gaseous element found in the air, used in lamps and advertising signs for the bright glow it gives when an electric current is passed through it. —**ne·o·na·tal** (–NAY·tl) *adj.* of the newborn, esp. less than a month old: *~ diseases, mortality;* **ne·o·nate** (NEE·uh–) *n.* a newborn infant. —**neon lamp** (or **light**) one formed by a neon-filled glass tube. —**ne·o·phyte** (NEE·uh·fite) *n.* a new convert; hence, a novice or beginner. —**ne·o·plasm** (NEE·uh–) *n.* a new or abnormal growth such as a tumor; **ne·o·plas·tic** (–PLAS–) *adj.* —**ne·o·prene** (NEE·uh·preen) *n.* a synthetic rubber resistant to heat, oil, weather, gasoline, etc., used for making hose, insulation, shoe soles, etc.

Ne·pal (ni·PAWL) a Himalayan kingdom on India's N. border; 54,362 sq.mi. (140,797 km²); *cap.* Kathmandu. —**Nep·a·lese** (–LEEZ) *n.* & *adj., sing.* & *pl.* —**Ne·pa·li** (–PAH·lee) *n.* & *adj.* (of) the official language of Nepal.

ne·pen·the (nuh·PEN·thee) *n.* in Greek myth, a drug or drink capable of banishing sorrow; **ne·pen·thes** (–theez) *n.* a pitcher plant.

neph·ew (NEF·yoo) *n.* son of one's brother, sister, brother-in-law, or sister-in-law.

neph·rite (NEF–) *n.* a variety of jade. —**ne·phri·tis** (–FRYE–) *n.* inflammation of the kidneys; **ne·phrit·ic** (–FRIT–) *adj.*

ne plus ul·tra (nee·plus·UL·truh) the acme or culmination (of some achievement).

nep·o·tism (NEP·uh–) *n.* favoritism shown to relatives, as in giving jobs.

Nep·tune the fourth largest planet of the solar system, named for the Roman god of the sea. —**nep·tu·ni·um** (–TUE–) *n.* a radioactive metallic element.

Ne·re·id (NEER·ee–) in Greek myth, one of 50 sea nymphs, daughters of a sea god, **Ne·re·us.**

Ne·ro (NEER·oh) a cruel and depraved Roman emperor (A.D. 54–68).

nerve (NURV) *n.* **1** a strand or fiber that carries impulses of sensation and motion between the sense organs and the brain; also, a vein of a leaf or rib of an insect's wing. **2** mental or bodily strength; courage; vigor; ***v.*** **nerves, nerved, nerv·ing** give strength or courage to: *She ~d herself to receive the tragic news.* **3** *Informal.* boldness or impudence. —**get on one's nerves** *Informal.* annoy or irritate one. —**nerve cell** a neuron; **nerve center** a group of nerve cells controlling a specific function such as respiration or vision; hence, a headquarters or center of activity. —**nerve gas** a poisonous gas used in warfare whose principal effect is on the nervous system. —**nerve·less** *adj.* without strength or vigor; also, without nervousness; **nerve·less·ly** *adv.;* **nerve·less·ness** *n.* —**nerve-(w)rack·ing** *adj.* very trying on one's nerves: *a ~ job, ordeal.* —**nerv·ous** (–us) *adj.* **1** jumpy or restless: *feeling somewhat ~ at the fag end of a day; She's ~ by nature.* **2** animated or vigorous: *the ~ energy that drives him forward.* **3** of the nerves; **nervous breakdown** a sudden emotional illness accompanied by depression, fatigue, lack of appetite, feelings of inadequacy, etc.; **nervous system** the bodily system consisting of the brain, spinal cord, nerves, and nerve endings; **ner·vous·ly** *adv.;* **ner·vous·ness** *n.* —**nerv·y** *adj.* **nerv·i·er, -i·est** **1** *Informal.* brash or impudent. **2** showing or requiring courage; bold or courageous. **3** *Brit.* nervous or excitable. —**nerv·i·ly** *adv.;* **nerv·i·ness** *n.*

-ness *n.suffix.* as in *fastness, forgiveness, goodness.*
nest *n.* **1** a cozy place for retiring into, esp. a structure built of twigs or straw in which birds lay and hatch eggs; also, a place similarly used by insects, fishes, and other animals; hence, a place swarming with (something bad); hangout: *a ~ of vice, criminals, thieves.* **2** a group of articles (often of gradually varying size) fitting into one another: *a ~ of tables, drinking cups.* —**v.:** *A stork ~s on roofs and chimneys; stacking chairs and* **nesting** *tables.* —**nest egg** money put aside as a reserve or to start a fund. —**nes·tle** (NESL) *v.* **-tles, -tled, -tling** shelter or settle cozily: *a village ~d in a valley; She ~d down into the chair by the fire; ~d* (i.e. pressed) *the frightened child in her arms.* —**nest·ling** (NEST–) *n.* a bird too young to leave its nest.
¹net *n.* **1** a fabric knotted or woven of string, thread, hair, etc. with regularly spaced meshes, esp. something made of such fabric, as for catching fish, butterflies, etc., for dividing a court in games such as tennis and volleyball, for protection against mosquitoes, to keep hair in place, etc. **2** a trap or snare. —**v. nets, net·ted, net·ting** catch (as if) in a net or enclose (as if) with a net: *to ~ fish.*
²net *n.* & *adj.* (an amount, profit, price, or weight) left over after deductions from gross: *a person's ~ income;* **net worth** (i.e. assets minus liabilities). —**v. nets, net·ted, net·ting** clear or yield as profit: *~d $10,000 from the sale.*
Neth. Netherlands. —**neth·er** (NEDH·ur) *adj.* lower or under: *the ~ regions* (under the earth). —**Neth·er·lands** (NEDH·ur·landz) a kingdom of N.W. Europe on the North Sea; 15,892 sq.mi. (41,160 km²); *caps.* Amsterdam & The Hague. —**Netherlands Antilles** two groups of six islands in the Lesser Antilles; also called "Dutch West Indies." —**neth·er·most** *adj.* lowest. —**nether world** Hades or hell.
net·ting *n.* the making a net or fishing with a net; also, net material.
net·tle (NETL) *n.* a weed with stinging bristles; **v. net·tles, net·tled, net·tling** irritate; vex; annoy; **net·tle·some** (–sum) *adj.* irritating; annoying.
net·work (–wurk) *n.* mesh or something resembling it, as a system or roads, veins, etc. that cross each other, or a group of radio or television stations that may broadcast the same programs simultaneously; **adj.:** *~ television, operations.*
neu·ral (NEW·rul) *adj.* of a nerve or the nervous system; **neu·ral·ly** *adv.* —**neu·ral·gia** (–RAL–) *n.* sharp pain along the route of a nerve; **neu·ral·gic** *adj.* —**neu·ras·the·ni·a** (–THEE·nee·uh) *n.* a neurotic condition; **neu·ras·then·ic** (–THEN–) *adj.* —**neu·ri·tis** (–RYE–) *n.* an inflammation of a nerve or nerves, as in shingles or sciatica; **neu·rit·ic** (–RIT–) *adj.* —**neuro-** *comb.form.* nerve: as in *neurology, neurosis.* —**neurol.** *Abbrev.* for **neu·rol·o·gy** (–ROL–) *n.* a branch of medicine dealing with the nervous system and its diseases; **neu·rol·o·gist** *n.;* **neu·ro·log·i·cal** (–LOJ–) *adj.* —**neu·ron** (NEW·ron) *n.* a nerve-cell body and its processes such as dendrites; also **neu·rone** (–rohn). —**neu·ro·sci·ence** (newr·oh·SYE·unce) *n.* a science dealing with the nervous system or mental phenomena, as psychology; **neu·ro·sci·en·tist** *n.* —**neu·ro·sis** (new·ROH–) *n., pl.* **-ses** (–seez) a mental disorder characterized by anxiety, phobias, insecurity, and depression; **neu·rot·ic** (–ROT–) *n.* & *adj.;* **neu·rot·i·cal·ly** *adv.*
neut. *Abbrev.* for **neu·ter** (NEW·tur) *n.* & *adj.* (a grammatical form or word, an animal, plant, or insect) that is neither masculine nor feminine; sexless, as "It," "das Kind" (*German.* child), a worker bee, or a spayed animal; **v.** spay or castrate (an animal). —**neu·tral** (NEW·trul) *n.* & *adj.* (one) of or belonging to neither side, as a nation not joining in a war; indifferent: *Gray is a ~ color; Water is chemically ~* (i.e. neither acid nor alkaline); *a car in ~* (gear); **neu·tral·ly** *adv.* —**neu·tral·ism** *n.* the policy or practice of keeping neutral, esp. in international relations; nonalignment; **neu·tral·ist** *n.* & *adj.;* **neu·tral·i·ty** (–TRAL–) *n.* —**neu·tral·ize** *v.* **-iz·es, -ized, -iz·ing** make neutral (chemically, politically, in artistic effect, etc.); **neu·tral·i·za·tion** (–ZAY–) *n.* —**neutral spirits** ethyl alcohol of 190 proof or over. —**neu·tri·no** (–TREE–) *n.* **-nos** an elementary particle with no electric charge and a mass near zero. —**neu·tron** (NEW·tron) *n.* a chargeless subatomic particle that combines with protons to form the nucleus of all atoms except of hydrogen; **neutron bomb** an atomic bomb that would release radioactive neutrons taking lives but without the blast destructive to property.
Nev. *Abbrev.* for **Ne·vad·a** (–VAD–, –VAH–) a W. state of the U.S.; 110,540 sq.mi. (286,297 km²); *cap.* Carson City; **Ne·vad·an** *n.* & *adj.*
nev·er *adv.* not ever; at no time; also, not at all: *~ mind.* —**nev·er·more** *adv.* never again. —**nev·er-nev·er land** a never-attainable, imaginary condition or unreal place. —**nev·er·the·less** (–dhuh·LES) *adv.* however.
ne·vus (NEE–) *n., pl.* **-vi** (–vye) a birthmark or mole.
new *adj.* **1** now or recently come into being, use, possession, etc.: *a ~ car; Our ~ house is only 10 years old; a ~ look, arrival, fashion, idea.* **2** seen or known for the first time: *the discovery of the New World; ~ evidence on an old murder; Greece is ~ to her; She is ~* (i.e. not yet accustomed) *to Greece.* —**adv.** recently; newly: *a ~-found friend.* —**New·ark** (–urk) a city of New Jersey. —**New Bed·ford** (–furd) a seaport of S.E. Massachusetts. —**new blood** new people for bringing fresh ideas or vigor into an organization. —**new·born** *adj.* just born; also, born anew; **n.** *sing.* & *pl.* a newborn child.

—**New Bruns·wick** (BRUNZ–) a province of S.E. Canada; 28,354 sq.mi. (73,437 km²); *cap.* Fredericton. —**new·com·er** (–cum–) *n.* a new or recent arrival, often a beginner. —**New Deal** President Franklin D. Roosevelt's program for economic recovery and social welfare during the Depression; **New Dealer.** —**New Delhi** capital of India.

new·el (–ul) *n.* a post or pillar supporting the handrails of a staircase, esp. at either end of it; also, the central pillar of a winding staircase.

New England the N.E. section of the U.S., made up of Maine, Vermont, New Hampshire, Massachusetts, Rhode Island, and Connecticut; **New Eng·land·er.** —**new·fan·gled** (NEW·FANG·gld) *adj.* [disparaging] newly put together: ~ *ideas.* —**new-fash·ioned** *adj.* of a new fashion. —**new-found** *adj.* newly found; **New·found·land** (NEW·fund·land) a large island off the E. coast of Canada, forming a province together with the adjoining part of Labrador; 156,185 sq.mi. (404,517 km²); *cap.* St. John's. —**New Guinea** the world's second largest island, situated N. of Australia, divided into Irian Jaya (Indonesia) and Papua New Guinea. —**New Hamp·shire** (–shur, –sheer) a New England state; 9,304 sq.mi. (24,097 km²); *cap.* Concord. —**New Ha·ven** (–HAY·vun) a city of S. Connecticut. —**New Jersey** an E. state of the U.S.; 7,835 sq.mi. (20,295 km²); *cap.* Trenton. —**New Left** the radical social and political movement of the 1960's among American youth. —**new·ly** *adv.* recently or freshly: *a ~ married couple; a ~ paved driveway;* **new·ly·wed** *n.* one recently married; **new·ness** *n.* —**new math(ematics)** school mathematics that is based on set theory, symbolic logic, number systems, etc. —**New Mexico** a S.W. state of the U.S.; 121,666 sq.mi. (315,113 km²); *cap.* Santa Fe. —**new moon** the beginning of the first phase of the moon when it appears totally dark before waxing from a thin crescent to a half moon. —**New Or·le·ans** (–OR·lee·unz, –or·LEENZ) a seaport of S.E. Louisiana. —**New·port News** a seaport of S.E. Virginia. —**news** *n.pl.* [takes *sing.v.*] new or recent events, esp. as reported in a newspaper or broadcast on radio or television: *Yesterday's ~ is today's history;* **news·boy** *n.* a boy who distributes newspapers; **news·cast** *n.* a radio or television broadcast of news; **news·cast·er** *n.;* **news·deal·er** *n.* a retailer of newspapers and magazines; **news·let·ter** *n.* a bulletin or report periodically issued to a group to keep them informed of happenings in their field of interest; **news·mag·a·zine** (–zeen) *n.* a magazine that summarizes and comments on current events. —**news·man** *n.* **-men** a news reporter; also, a newsdealer; **news·pa·per** *n.* a periodical, esp. a daily publication, containing news and comments, features, and advertising; **news·pa·per·man** *n.* **-men** a newspaper publisher, editor, reporter, etc.; *fem.* **news·pa·per·wom·an, -wom·en.** —**new·speak** *n.* (style of) official language meant to deceive the public. —**news·print** *n.* paper used for printing newspapers, esp. cheap, unsized paper made from wood pulp. —**news·reel** *n.* a short motion picture of news events, as shown in a movie theater. —**news·stand** *n.* a stand at which newspapers, etc. are sold. —**news·wor·thy** (–wur·dhee) *adj.* having interest or importance as news. —**news·y** *adj.* **news·i·er, -i·est** *Informal.* containing much news.

newt *n.* a small amphibious salamander.

New Testament the latter half of the Bible containing the life and teachings of Christ. —**New·ton** (–tn), **Sir Isaac.** 1642–1727, English physicist; **newton** *n.* unit of force in the MKS system; 100,000 dynes. —**new town** a city planned and built as a small self-contained community away from a large urban area to reduce overcrowding. —**New World** the Western Hemisphere. —**New Year('s)** the first day(s) of a new year; **New Year's Day** January 1; **New Year's Eve** the evening of December 31. —**New York** a N.E. state of the U.S.; 49,576 sq.mi. (128,401 km²) *cap.* Albany; **New York (City)** in New York State, the largest city of the U.S., consisting of the boroughs of Manhattan (Island), the Bronx, Queens, Brooklyn, and Richmond (Staten Island); **New York·er** a person of or from New York City or New York State. —**New Zea·land** (–ZEE·lund) a British Commonwealth country in the S. Pacific consisting mainly of two islands; 103,736 sq. mi. (268,675 km²); *cap.* Wellington; **New Zea·land·er.**

next *adj.* nearest, esp. after: ~ *Sunday, house, train* (i.e. after this or closest to a specified one); ***prep.:*** nearest to: *Our house is ~ yours; the church ~ the school;* **adv.:** *4 comes ~ after 3; What did she do ~?* —**next door** very close, esp. in the next house: *They live next door; our next-door neighbors.* —**next of kin** See KIN.

nex·us *n.* a link or connection.

Nez Percé (NEZ·purce, nay·pur·SAY) *n.* (one of) an American Indian people now confined to a small reservation in Idaho.

Nfld. Newfoundland.

N.G. National Guard; no good (also **n.g.**).

ngwee ('ng·GWEE) *n. sing.* & *pl.* a money unit of Zambia, equal to 1/100 of a kwacha.

N.H. or **NH** New Hampshire.

Ni nickel.

ni·a·cin (NYE·uh–) *n.* nicotinic acid.

Ni·ag·a·ra (nye·AG·ruh) *n.* a cataract or torrent, like **Niagara Falls,** a waterfall on the **Niagara River** flowing from Lake Erie into Lake Ontario.

Nia·mey (nyah·MAY) capital of Niger.

nib *n.* a point or tip, esp. of a fountain pen. **—his nibs** *Informal* [used like "His lordship"] an important person.

nib·ble *n.* & *v.* **nib·bles, nib·bled, nib·bling** (take) a small, gentle, or cautious bite, as fish at bait; **nib·bler** *n.*

Nic·a·ra·gua (nik·uh·RAH·gwuh) a Central American country; 50,193 sq.mi. (130,000 km²); *cap.* Managua; **Nic·a·ra·guan** *n.* & *adj.*

nice *adj.* **nic·er, nic·est** **1** agreeable; good; proper: *a ~ girl, party, time; ~ weather.* **2** subtle; refined; requiring care or exactness: *a ~ legal distinction, shade of meaning, ear for music.* **—nice·ly** *adv.;* **nice·ness** *n.* **—nice Nel·ly** (or **Nel·lie**)(-lee), *pl.* **nice Nel·lies** one who is overly prudish in speech or behavior; **nice-Nel·ly** or **-Nel·lie** *adj.;* **nice-Nel·ly·ism** *n.* **—ni·ce·ty** (NYE·suh·tee) *n.* **-ties** daintiness; exactness; also, something dainty or refined; *~s of courteous behavior; does everything she touches* **to a nicety** (i.e. with exactness).

niche (NICH) *n.* & *v.* **nich·es, niched, nich·ing** **1** (to place in) a recess in a wall, as a statue or vase. **2** a suitable position: *earned himself a ~ in the organization.*

nick *n.* & *v.* (make) a small or superficial cut or chip: *a table top with ~s and scratches; ~ed himself while shaving; a collision avoided by braking* **in the nick of time** (i.e. just in time).

nick·el *n.* & *v.* **-els, -el(l)ed, -el·(l)ing** (plate with) a hard silver-white metallic element used in alloys, as in the U.S. and Canadian 5-cent coins; hence, a 5-cent piece. **—nick·el·o·de·on** (–uh·LOH·dee·un) *n.* an early type of jukebox operated with a nickel; also, an early movie theater that charged a nickel for admission. **—nickel silver** an alloy of copper, zinc, and silver.

nick·er *n.* & *v.* neigh.

nick·name *n.* a familiar name given to a person or place, either a descriptive term, as "Fatty," "the Empire State," etc., or a pet name, as "Lizzie"; **v. -names, -named, -nam·ing:** *a President ~d "Old Hickory."*

Nic·o·si·a (–uh·SEE–) capital of Cyprus.

nic·o·tine (–uh·teen) *n.* a poisonous alkaloid found in tobacco. **—nic·o·tin·ic** (–TIN–) **acid** a vitamin of the B group, used against pellagra.

niece (NEECE) *n.* the daughter of one's brother, sister, brother-in-law, or sister-in-law.

Niel·sen (NEEL·sun) **rating** an estimate of how many people watch a television program, based on nationwide samplings by the A.C. Nielsen Company.

Nie·tzsche (NEE·chuh), **Friedrich.** 1844–1900, German philosopher.

nif·ty (–tee) *adj.* **-ti·er, -ti·est** *Informal.* smart or stylish.

Ni·ger (NYE·jur) a republic of W.C. Africa; 489, 191 sq. mi. (1,267,000 km²); *cap.* Niamey. **—Ni·ger·i·a** (nye·JEER·ee·uh) a republic of W. Africa; 356,669 sq.mi. (923,768 km²); *cap.* Lagos; **Ni·ge·ri·an** *n.* & *adj.*

nig·gard (–urd) *n.* & *adj.* stingy (person); **nig·gard·ly** *adj.* & *adv.;* **nig·gard·li·ness** *n.*

nig·ger (NIG·ur) *n.* **1** [offensive except in black use] a Negro. **2** a member of an underprivileged group of society.

nig·gle *v.* **nig·gles, nig·gled, nig·gling** work fussily; be finicky; **nig·gling** *n.* & *adj.* trifling or petty (work or activity).

nigh *adj., adv.* & *prep. Archaic.* near(ly): *the ~ horse; time drawing ~; well ~ finished; ~ unto death.*

night (NITE) *n.* the period from dusk to dawn when it is dark; hence, darkness; also, a period of gloom or unhappiness. **—night blindness** inability of the eye to adjust to faint light. **—night·cap** *n.* a cap worn with nightclothes; also, *Informal.* an alcoholic drink taken at bedtime; **night clothes** clothes such as pajamas for wearing while in bed. **—night·club** *n.* a place of nighttime entertainment that serves food and liquor with music and dancing. **—night crawler** a large earthworm. **—night·dress** *n.* nightgown. **—night·fall** (–fawl) *n.* the coming of night; dusk. **—night·gown** *n.* a loose, light garment that a woman or girl wears in bed. **—night·hawk** *n.* a bird related to the whippoorwill that feeds on flying insects at dusk and dawn. **—night·ie** (–ee) *n. Informal.* a nightgown or nightshirt. **—night·in·gale** *n.* a European thrush famed for its song; **Florence Nightingale,** 1820–1910, pioneer English nurse. **—night letter** a telegram sent at reduced rates during the night. **—night life** pleasure-seeking activity at night, esp. in nightclubs. **—night·ly** *adj.* & *adv.* at night; also, every night. **—night·mare** *n.* a distressing dream; also, a frightening experience; **night·mar·ish** *adj.* **—night owl** *Informal.* one who stays up and works at night. **—night·rid·er** (–rye·dur) *n.* a member of a mounted gang committing acts of violence and intimidation by night. **—night·shade** *n.* a large botanical family including poisonous tropical plants such as Jimson weed, belladonna, and bittersweet as well as useful ones such as potato, tomato, tobacco, and eggplant. **—night·shirt** *n.* a long, loose shirt that gave way to pajamas early in the 20th century. **—night·soil** *n.* human waste used as fertilizer. **—night·spot** *n. Informal.* nightclub. **—night·stand** *n.* a small bedside table; also **night table.** **—night·stick** *n.* a policeman's club. **—night·time** *n.* the period of darkness from dusk to dawn. **—night·walk·er** *n.* one who goes out at night as a thief, prostitute, etc. **—night·wear** (–ware) *n.* nightclothes.

nig·ri·tude *n.* darkness; blackness.

ni·hil·ism (NYE·uh·lizm) *n.* in politics, philosophy, etc., the rejection of all traditional and existing beliefs, practices, institutions, etc.;

ni·hil·ist *n.* & *adj.;* **ni·hil·is·tic** (–LIS–) *adj.* —**nil** *n.* nothing.

Nile a river of N.E. Africa flowing through Egypt into the Mediterranean.

nim·ble *adj.* light and quick: *a young dancer's ~ feet; the ~ fingers of a piano player; a ~ mind, wit;* **nim·ble·ness** *n.;* **nim·bly** *adv.*

nim·bus *n., pl.* **-bi** (–bye) or **-bus·es** **1** a dark-gray rain cloud. **2** a disk-shaped halo; circle of radiant light.

nim·rod *n.* hunter; **Nimrod** in the Bible, a mighty hunter.

nin·com·poop (NIN·cum–) *n.* a foolish or silly person.

nine *n., adj.* & *pron.* one more than eight; the number 9 or IX; **ninth** (NINETH) *n.* & *adj.* —**nine·pins** *n.pl.* a bowling game using nine instead of 10 pins. —**nine·teen** *n., adj.* & *pron.* one more than 18; the number 19 or XIX; **nine·teenth** *n.* & *adj.* —**nine·ty** *n., adj.* & *pron.* **-ties** nine times 10; **nine·ti·eth** (–tee·uth) *n.* & *adj.*

nin·ny *n.* **nin·nies** fool.

ninth See NINE.

ni·o·bi·um (nye·OH·bee–) *n.* a soft, gray, metallic element used in alloys.

nip *n.* & *v.* **nips, nipped, nip·ping** **1** to pinch or bite, as a crab with its claws; *A gardener ~s off shoots to check growth.* **2** blight or destroy, as by frost: *a wonderful scheme* **nipped in the bud.** **3** drink (liquor) in nips (*n.* 3). —***n.*** **1** a pinch or bite; also, a bit. **2** a biting cold; also, pungent flavor. **3** a sip of liquor. —**nip and tuck** neck and neck; closely matched. —**nip·per** *n.* one that nips, as the claw of a crab; **nippers** *n.pl.* pliers, pincers, etc. —**nip·ple** *n.* a small projection on a breast or udder through which milk is drawn; teat; also, a teatlike part.

Nip·pon [Japanese name] Japan; **Nip·pon·ese** (–EEZ) *n.* & *adj., sing.* & *pl.*

nip·py *adj.* **nip·pi·er, nip·pi·est** sharp or biting: *~ fall weather.*

nir·va·na (–VAH·nuh, –VAN·uh) *n.* in Buddhism, (a state of) supreme bliss.

Ni·sei (NEE·say) *n. sing.* & *pl.* one born in North America of Japanese immigrant parents.

ni·si (NYE·sye) *adj. Law.* of a decree or order, not absolute or final.

nit *n.* the egg or young of a louse or similar insect.

ni·ter (NYE–) *n.* a nitrate used in making gunpowder or as fertilizer.

nit-pick·ing *n.* & *adj.* fault-finding in a petty manner; **nit-pick·er** *n.*

ni·trate (NYE–) *n.* a salt or ester of nitric acid; ***v.*** **-trates, -trat·ed, -trat·ing** treat with nitric acid or a nitrate; **ni·tra·tion** (–TRAY–) *n.* —**ni·tre** *Brit.* niter. —**ni·tric acid** a strong, nitrogen-containing acid used in making explosives, fertilizers, and drugs. —**ni·tri·fy** (NYE–) *v.* **-fies, -fied, -fy·ing** **1** treat with nitrogen or a nitrogen compound. **2** produce (nitrates, nitrites, etc.) by bacterial action. —**ni·tri·fi·ca·tion** (–CAY–) *n.* —**ni·trite** *n.* a salt or ester of nitrous acid. —**ni·tro** (NYE·troh) *n. Informal.* nitroglycerine; ***comb.form.*** nitrogen-containing: as in **ni·tro·cel·lu·lose** (–SEL·yoo·lohs) *n.* a highly flammable ester of cellulose; guncotton; **ni·tro·cel·lu·los·ic** (–LOH–) *adj.* —**ni·tro·gen** (NYE·truh·jun) *n.* a colorless, odorless gas that makes up four fifths of the atmosphere; **ni·trog·e·nous** (–TROJ·uh·nus) *adj.* —**ni·tro·glyc·er·in(e)** (–GLIS·uh·rin) *n.* a heavy, oily, explosive liquid used in dynamite, rocket propellants, and to dilate blood vessels for easing cardiac pain. —**ni·trous** (–trus) **acid** an unstable nitrogen-containing acid; **nitrous oxide** a gas that is sweetish in odor, used as an anesthetic; laughing gas.

nit·ty-grit·ty *n. Slang.* the basic facts (of a situation, problem, etc.).

nit-wit *n.* an idiot.

nix *v. Slang.* disapprove of; forbid; say "no" to; ***adv.*** & ***interj.*** no; stop!

Nix·on (NIX·un) ,**Richard M.** born 1913, 37th U.S. President (1969–1974, resigned).

N.J. or **NJ** New Jersey.

N.L.R.B. National Labor Relations Board.

N.M., NM or **N.Mex.** New Mexico.

N.N.E. north-northeast.

N.N.W. north-northwest.

no (NOH) *adv.* [used to deny, refuse, etc.]: *Do you want it, yes or ~? ~, I don't! That is ~ small job;* ***adj.:*** *That's ~* (i.e. not any) *job for me; works for ~ pay.* —***n.,*** *pl.* **no(e)s** a refusal, denial, or a negative vote(r): *a flat ~; The ~s* (i.e. not ayes) *have it.*

No. **1** north(ern). **2** also **no.,** *pl.* **Nos.** or **nos.** number.

No **1** nobelium. **2** *n. sing.* & *pl.* the oldest type of Japanese classical drama, performed by masked actors using music and dancing, accompanied by a chorus; also **Noh.**

No·ah (NOH–) in the Bible, the patriarch who was saved from the great Flood in the ark he built at God's bidding.

No·bel (–BEL) **prize** any of the six annual international awards in the fields of physics, chemistry, physiology or medicine, literature, peace, and economics, the first five founded by **Alfred B. Nobel** (1833–96), a Swedish chemist. —**No·bel·ist** *n.* a Nobel-prize winner. —**no·be·li·um** (–BEE·lee–) *n.* a man-made radioactive chemical element.

no·bil·i·ty (–BIL–) *n.* **-ties** a being noble, high social rank, or nobles as a class. —**no·ble** *adj.* **-bler, -blest** **1** famous; excellent; high by birth; *a ~ family, deed, sentiment, edifice* (i.e. lofty). **2** chemically stable; unaffected by oxygen: *~ gases such as helium and neon; Gold and silver are ~ metals.* —***n.*** a person of noble birth or rank; **no·ble·man** *n.* **-men** a peer. —**no·ble·ness** *n.;* **no·bly** *adv.* —**no·blesse o·blige** (–BLES·oh·BLEEZH) "Noble birth obliges one to be noble in conduct and behavior." —**no·ble·wom·an** *n.* **-wom·en** a peeress.

no·bod·y (NOH·bud·ee, –bod–) *pron.* no one; ***n., pl.*** **-bod·ies** a person of no importance.

noc·tur·nal (–TUR·nl) *adj.* of or during the night: *~ animals are active at night; a ~ emission* (i.e. "wet dream"); **noc·tur·nal·ly** *adv.* —**noc·turne** (NOC·turn) *n.* a form of dreamy or romantic musical composition, esp. for the piano.

noc·u·ous (NOK·yoo·us) *adj.* harmful; damaging; **noc·u·ous·ly** *adv.*

nod *v.* **nods, nod·ded, nod·ding** bend the head downward briefly, as in greeting an acquaintance, to indicate agreement, or when sleepy: *He ~d assent; flowers ~ing in the wind; "(Even) Homer sometimes ~s"* (i.e. makes mistakes). —***n.*** a nodding of the head: *A project is given the ~* (to go ahead). —**nod·dy** *n.* **nod·dies** a tropical tern with a rounded tail.

node *n.* a knot or joint, as the part of a stem from which leaves grow or the small knots along a lymphatic vessel; **nod·al** (NOH–) *adj.* —**nod·ule** (NOJ·ool) *n.* a small knob, lump, or swelling, as the nitrogenous growths on the roots of legumes, a rounded mineral concretion, etc.; **nod·u·lar** (–lur) *adj.*

No·el or **No·ël** (noh·EL) *n.* Christmas; **noel** or **noël** *n.* a Christmas song or carol.

no-fault *adj.* of automobile insurance, divorce, etc., involving no fixing of blame: *a ~ medical malpractice insurance.* —**no-frills** *adj.* of a service or product, without nonessential features that add to cost: *a ~ air fare, grocery.*

nog *n.* an alcoholic eggnog. —**nog·gin** (NOG·in) *n.* **1** a small cup or mug (of liquor), originally ¼ pint. **2** *Informal.* the head.

no-good *n.* & *adj. Informal.* worthless (person or thing).

Noh same as NO, def. 2.

no-hit·ter *n.* a baseball game in which a pitcher allows the opposing team no base hits.

no·how (NOH–) *adv. Informal.* in no way.

noise *n.* a harsh, disagreeable, or unwanted sound: *the ~ of a city street; static ~ in radio reception; "snow" caused by ~* (i.e. unwanted signals) *in television equipment;* **noise pollution** *of the environment from airports, automobiles, industry, etc.* —***v.*** **nois·es, noised, nois·ing** spread (*about* or *abroad,* as a story or report) by rumor. —**noise·less** *adj.;* **noise·less·ly** *adv.* —**noise·mak·er** (–may–) *n.* a horn or similar device used to make noise at a party. —**noi·some** (–sum) *adj.* foul-smelling or harmful: *a ~ odor.* —**nois·y** (–zee) *adj.* **nois·i·er, -i·est:** *Rock music is loud to some, ~ to others; ~ neighbors; a ~ quarrel;* **nois·i·ly** *adv.;* **nois·i·ness** *n.*

nol·le pros·e·qui (NOL·ee·PROS·uh·kwye) *Law.* a prosecutor's notice of "not proceeding further with the suit."

no-load *n.* a mutual fund that charges no commission on sales.

no·lo con·ten·de·re (NOH·loh·cun·TEN·duh·ree) *Law.* declaration of no defense but without admitting guilt; "no contest." —**nol-pros** *v.* **-pros·ses, -prossed, -pros·sing** drop (a case) by entering a nolle prosequi.

nom. nominative.

no·mad *n.* & *adj.* (one) of a people such as Bedouins and Gypsies with no settled home but wandering about from place to place; **no·mad·ic** (–MAD–) *adj.*

no man's land **1** an area or scope of activity that is indefinite or ambiguous. **2** land separating opposing armies.

nom de guerre (–GAIR) *French, pl.* **noms de guerre** pseudonym. —**nom de plume** (–duh·PLOOM), **noms de plume** pen name. —**no·men·cla·ture** (NOH·mun·clay·chur) *n.* a system of naming: *the binomial ~ used in biology; musical ~.* —**nom·i·nal** (NOM·i·nl) *adj.* in name only; hence, slight or negligible: *a ~ leader; a ~ amount;* **nom·i·nal·ly** *adv.* —**nom·i·nate** *v.* **-nates, -nat·ed, -nat·ing** name, often appoint, to an office or position: *~d but not elected; ~d as executor of an estate;* **nom·i·na·tor** *n.* —**nom·i·na·tion** (–NAY–) *n.* —**nom·i·na·tive** (NOM·uh·nuh·tiv) *n.* & *adj.* (a word or the grammatical case of a word) naming the subject of a verb: *"She" is in the ~ (case).* —**nom·i·nee** (–NEE) *n.* a nominated person.

non- [A prefix freely added, usu. without a hyphen except before capitalized words, to adjectives and adverbs to mean "not" and to nouns to mean "not a," "opposite of," or "lack of." The more common of such compounds, whose basic meaning and pronunciation can be inferred from the constituent elements, are placed at the bottom of this and the following pages.]

non·age (–ij, NOH·nij) *n.* period of being legally a minor; also, period before maturity; immaturity.

---

nonabsorbent
nonadministrative
nonattendance
nonbeliever
nonbelligerent
nonbreakable
nonchargeable
nonclerical
noncombustible
noncommercial
noncommunicable
non-Communist
noncompeting
noncompetitive
nonconforming
noncontagious
noncrystalline
nondeductible
nondiscrimination
nondistinctive

non·a·ge·nar·i·an (–uh·juh·NAIR·ee·un) *n.* & *adj.* (one) in his nineties. —**non·a·gon** *n.* a plane figure with nine sides and angles.

non·a·ligned (–uh·LINED) *adj.* in international politics, neutral; **non·a·lign·ment** *n.* —**non·book** *n.* a book in form only, otherwise a mere compilation or anthology.

nonce usu. **for the nonce** for the time being; **nonce word** a word made up for the occasion: *Many ~ words gain currency, as "O.K." and "nowhereness."*

non·cha·lant (–shuh·lunt, –shuh·LAHNT) *adj.* coolly indifferent; unconcerned; **non·cha·lant·ly** *adv.* —**non·cha·lance** (–lunce, –LAHNCE) *n.*

non·com *n.* [short form] noncommissioned officer. —**non·com·bat·ant** (–com·BAT·nt, –COM·buh·tunt) *n.* & *adj.* (a nurse, chaplain, or civilian) not taking part in actual combat. —**non·com·mis·sioned** (–MISH·und) **officer** in the armed forces, an enlisted man with the rank of corporal through sergeant major. —**non·com·mit·tal** (–kuh·MITL) *adj.* not committing oneself: *"We will see" is his usual ~ reply.* —**non com·pos men·tis** (–COM·pus–) *Latin.* not of sound mind. —**non·con·duc·tor** (–DUC·tur) *n.* a substance that does not conduct heat, electricity, or sound; insulator. —**non·con·form·ist** (–FORM–) *n.* one who does not conform to prevailing attitudes or behavior, as a **Nonconformist** of the 1600's who refused to conform to the Church of England; **non·con·form·i·ty** *n.* —**non·co·op·er·a·tion** (–RAY–) *n.* refusal to cooperate, esp. as civil disobedience. —**non·cred·it** *adj.* not having academic credit, as toward a degree. —**non·dair·y** *adj.* not made with milk or milk products. —**non·de·script** (–dis·CRIPT) *n.* & *adj.* (a person or thing) not easily described because not distinctive. —**non·drink·er** *n.* one who does not use alcoholic beverages. —**none** (NUN) *pron.* no one; not any: *~ of them is* (or *are*) *here; wants ~ but the best; ~ other than John;* **adv.** not at all: *I'm ~ the richer for the raise; "~ so deaf as those who will not hear."* —**non·en·ti·ty** (–EN–) *n.* **-ties** one, esp. a person, of little importance; also, something that has no real existence.

nones (NOHNZ) *n. sing.* & *pl.* the ninth day before the ides of a month in the ancient Roman calendar.

none·such (NUN–) *n.* & *adj.* (person or thing) that is unequaled or unique. —**none·the·less** (–LES) *adv.* nevertheless; however. —**non-Eu·clid·e·an** (–yoo·CLID·ee·un) *adj.* of geometry, not according to Euclid, esp. in regard to the postulate about parallel lines. —**non·e·vent** (–i·VENT) *n.* an event that is made too much of, esp. when it does not take place as predicted. —**non·fat** *adj.* of foods, not fatty. —**non·fer·rous** (–FAIR·us) *adj.* (containing or made) of metals other than iron. —**non·fic·tion** *n.* writings such as history, biography, and essays. —**non·he·ro** (–HEER·oh) *n.* same as ANTIHERO. —**non·in·ter·ven·tion** (–VEN–) *n.* avoidance of intervention, esp. in the affairs of another nation or in another jurisdiction. —**non·met·al** (–MET–) *n.* an element such as a gas, bromine, sulphur, etc. that does not have metallic qualities; **non·me·tal·lic** (–TAL–) *adj.*: *the ~ luster of quartz.* —**no-no** *n. Slang.* something forbidden as not good for one. —**non·pa·reil** (–puh·REL) *n.* & *adj.* (person or thing) that is unequaled or peerless. —**non·par·ti·san** (–PAR–) *adj.* not partisan, esp. in regard to political parties. —**non·per·son.** *n.* one who is considered as not existing or as rejected. —**non·plus** *v.* **-plus·(s)es, -plus(s)ed, -plus·(s)ing** perplex or puzzle utterly or hopelessly. —**non·pre·scrip·tion** (–SCRIP–) *adj.* of drugs, etc., available without a doctor's prescription. —**non·prof·it** (–PROF–) *adj.* of organizations, etc., not run for profit, as cultural foundations, the Red Cross, etc. —**non·pro·lif·er·a·tion** (–RAY–) *n.* the stoppage of the spread of nuclear weapons. —**non·res·i·dent** (–REZ–) *n.* & *adj.* (a person) living elsewhere, not where he goes to work, to school, etc.; **non·res·i·dence** *n.* —**non·re·sist·ant** (–ZIS–) *n.* & *adj.* (a person) who submits passively to unjust authority or force; **non·re·sist·ance** *n.* —**non·re·stric·tive** (–STRIC–) *adj.* not RESTRICTIVE grammatically. —**non·rig·id** (–RIJ–) *adj.* not rigid, esp. of airships that remain in shape by gas pressure; **non·ri·gid·i·ty** (–JID–) *n.* —**non·sched·uled** (–SKEJ·oold) *adj.* of a flight or airline, not serving a particular route or following a regular timetable, as charters. —**non·sec·tar·i·an** (–TAIR–) *adj.* not restricted to a particular religion. —**non·sense** *n.* & *adj.* (something) that makes no sense or is worthless or stupid: *What ~ to say I stole your purse; a ~ syllable* (without sense associations); *~ verses;* **non·sen·si·cal** (–SEN–) *adj.*; **non·sen·si·cal·ly**

---

noneducational
nonelastic
nonemotional
nonexchangeable
nonexplosive
nonflowering
nonfreezing
nonfunctional
nonhereditary
nonhuman
nonidentical
nonimportation
nonindustrial
nonintoxicating
nonirritating
nonlegal
nonliterary
nonmigratory

adv. —**non seq.** *Abbrev.* for **non se·qui·tur** (–SEK·wi·tur) an inference or observation that does not logically follow from what was said before it. —**non-sked** *n.* & *adj. Informal.* nonscheduled. —**non·stick** *adj.* of a cooking utensil or its surface, not allowing food to stick. —**non·stop** *adj.* & *adv.* (that goes) without stopping. —**non·sup·port** *n.* failure to provide for one's legal dependent. —**non·trop·po** (–TRAW·poh) *Music.* as specified but moderately. —**non-U** *adj. Informal.* not upper-class. —**non·un·ion** (–YOON·yun) *adj.* not made by, belonging to, or recognizing a labor union: *a ~ worker, job, company.* —**non·vi·o·lence** (–VYE·uh–) *n.* avoidance of the use of force, as in civil rights movements; **non·vi·o·lent** *adj.*

noo·dle *n.* **1** a flour paste, usu. made with egg, in ribbon form. **2** a simpleton; also, *Slang.* the head.

nook *n.* a secluded corner or spot.

noon *n.* & *adj.* (of or at) 12 o'clock in the daytime; midday; also **noon·day, noon·time, noon·tide** (Archaic).

no one no person; not anybody.

noose *n.* & *v.* **noos·es, noosed, noos·ing** (catch or share in) a loop made in a rope with a slipknot that tightens as the free end is pulled.

no-par (-value) *adj.* of stocks, having no nominal or par value, only a market value.

nope *adv. Informal.* no.

nor *conj.* [used after a negative, esp. *neither* or *not*] and not (either): *Neither John ~ Mary was there; will not eat ~ drink anything.*

Nor. North; Norway; Norwegian.

NORAD (NOR·ad) North American Air Defense Command.

Nor·dic *n.* & *adj.* (a person, esp. a Scandinavian) of the N. Germanic racial type characterized by tall stature, long head, and light hair.

no-re·turn *adj.* of bottles, not to be returned for refund of deposit.

Nor·folk (–fuk) a seaport of S.E. Virginia.

norm *n.* a standard or model for a group to follow; also, a group's average performance as a measuring standard. —**nor·mal** (–ml) *n.* & *adj.* (a condition, level, amount, etc.) that is standard or usual: *"Loves her he" is not the ~ word order in English; a temperature above (the) ~; Frost is ~ at this time of year; a man of ~ I.Q.;* **nor·mal·cy** (–see) *n.: the return to ~ after a war;* **nor·mal·ly** *adv.* **nor·mal·i·ty** (–MAL–) *n.* —**nor·mal·ize** (NOR·muh–) *v.* **-iz·es, -ized, -iz·ing** make normal; **nor·mal·i·za·tion** (–ZAY–) *n.* —**normal school** a two-year training school for elementary-school teachers.

Nor·man (–mun) *n.* a member of an originally Viking group from Normandy which conquered England in 1066; also, a person of or from **Nor·man·dy,** a region of N.W. France. —***adj.*** of Normandy, the Normans, or their French dialect.

norm·a·tive (–uh·tiv) *adj.* setting a norm or standard: *a ~ influence, grammar, principles.*

Norse *n.* & *adj.* (the people or the language) of Norway or of ancient Scandinavia; Norwegian; **Norse·man** *n.* **-men** a Scandinavian of ancient times. —**north** *n.* the direction to the left of one facing the rising sun, to which a compass needle points; also **North,** a region in this direction; **the North** northern U.S. comprising the states N. of Maryland, the Ohio River, and Missouri; ***adj.*** & ***adv.*** from, in, or toward the north: *A north(erly) wind blows from the ~.* —**North America** the N. continent of the Western Hemisphere, from Greenland to Panama, including also the West Indies; **North American.** —**North Car·o·li·na** (cair·uh·LYE·nuh) a S. state of the U.S.; 52,586 sq.mi. (136,197 km²); *cap.* Raleigh; **North Car·o·lin·i·an** (–LIN·ee·un). —**North Dakota** a Midwestern U.S. state; 70,665 sq.mi. (183,022 km²); *cap.* Bismarck; **North Dakotan.** —**north·east** (–EEST) *n.* (a region in or toward) the direction midway between N. and E.; ***adj.*** & ***adv.*** from, in, or toward the northeast; **north·east·er** *n.* a wind or storm from the N.E.; **north·east·er·ly** *adj.* & *adv.;* **north·east·ern** *adj.;* **north·east·ward** (–wurd) *adj.* & *adv.;* also **north·east·wards** *adv.* —**north·er** *n.* a strong north wind or storm, esp. a winter wind over Texas and the Gulf of Mexico; **north·er·ly** *adj.* & *adv.* from or toward the north; ***n.*** a norther. —**north·ern** *adj.* of, from, in, or toward the north; **Northern** *adj.* of the North; **north·ern·most** *adj.;* **north·ern·er** *n.* a person of or from the North, esp. of the U.S.; **Northern Ireland** the former Ulster province of Ireland, remaining part of the U.K.; 5,462 sq.mi. (14,146 km²); *cap.* Belfast; **northern lights** aurora borealis. —**North Korea** See KOREA. —**North·man** *n.* **-men** Norseman. —**North Pole** the earth's northern-

nonnegotiable
nonobservance
nonpaying
nonpoisonous
nonpolitical
nonporous
nonprofessional
nonrefillable
nonreligious
nonresidential
nonreturnable
nonscientific
nonsocial
nonsustaining
nontaxable
nontechnical
nontoxic
nontransferable
nonvoting
nonwhite

most point. —**North Sea** the sea between Great Britain and the European mainland. —**North Star** the bright star almost directly above the North Pole and hence appearing fixed in the firmament with other stars rotating around it; lodestar; polestar. —**North Vietnam** See VIETNAM. —**north·ward** (–wurd) *adj.* & *adv.* toward the north; also **north·wards** *adv.* —**north·west** (–WEST) *n.* (a region in or toward) the direction midway between N. and W.; **the Northwest** the region of the U.S. consisting of Washington, Oregon, and Idaho; ***adj.*** & ***adv.*** from, in, or toward the northwest; **north·west·er·ly** *adj.* & *adv.;* **north·west·ern** *adj.;* **north·west·ward** *adj.* & *adv.;* also **north·west·wards** *adv.;* **Northwest Territories** the northernmost part of Canada comprising the districts of Mackenzie, Keewatin, and Franklin; 1,304,903 sq.mi. (3,379,683 km^2); *cap.* Yellowknife. —**Norw.** Norway; Norwegian. —**Nor·way** a country of N. Europe; 125,182 sq.mi. (324,219 km^2); *cap.* Oslo. —**Nor·we·gian** (–WEE·jun) *n.* & *adj.* (of or having to do with Norway or) a person of or from Norway or the Scandinavian language spoken there.

Nos or **nos.** numbers.

nose (NOZE) *n.* **1** the breathing and smelling organ with two openings forming part of the face just above the mouth; hence, the sense of smell: *Dogs have good ~s; a reporter's ~ for news.* **2** the projecting front part of a ship, plane, etc. —***v.*** **nos·es, nosed, nos·ing** **1** smell (out). **2** nuzzle. **3** push (something off, one's way into, etc.) with a forward part, as a bulldozer. **4** search or pry (into someone's affairs). —**nose out** defeat (one's opponent) by a narrow margin; **on the nose** *Slang.* precisely; **pay through the nose** pay too much (for a product or service); **under one's nose** in plain view. —**nose·bleed** *n.* a bleeding from the nose. —**nose cone** the cone-shaped front section of a rocket or missile. —**nose dive** a swift downward plunge of an airplane, kite, etc.; hence, a sudden drop (in price); **nose-dive** *v.* **-dives, -dived, -div·ing.** —**nose·drops** *n.pl.* medication for dropping into the nose. —**nose·gay** *n.* a bouquet. —**nose·piece** *n.* something that goes over the nose or that is like a nose in position, as the rotating piece holding the objective lenses of a microscope. —**nosey** same as NOSY.

no-show *n.* a person who neither cancels nor shows up to claim his passenger reservation.

nos·ing (NOH·zing) *n.* a projecting part or edge.

nos·tal·gia (–TAL·juh) *n.* a sentimental yearning for a period or condition that is past; **nos·tal·gic** *adj.*

nos·tril *n.* either of the openings of the nose.

nos·trum *n.* a cure-all offered by a quack.

nos·(e)y (NOH·zee) *adj.* **nos·i·er, -i·est** *Informal.* prying or inquisitive; **nos·i·ly** *adv.;* **nos·i·ness** *n.*

not *adv.* [negative in function]: *Black is ~ white; Tell him ~ to worry; It may ~ rain—I hope ~; She's* **not at all** (i.e. certainly not) *my kind of woman.*

no·ta be·ne (NOH·tuh·BEE·nee) *Latin.* note well. —**no·ta·ble** (NOH·tuh–) *n.* & *adj.* noteworthy or distinguished (person): *a ~ event, contribution to science, figure;* **no·ta·bly** *adv.;* **no·ta·bil·i·ty** (–BIL–) *n.* —**no·ta·rize** (NOH·tuh–) *v.* **-riz·es, -rized, -riz·ing** certify (a document), as a lawyer or notary. —**no·ta·ry** *n.* **-ries** a person legally authorized to certify documents, take oaths, etc.; also **notary public.** —**no·ta·tion** (–TAY–) *n.* **1** a noting down or what is noted down; annotation. **2** a method or system of representing words, quantities, and such technical data using signs and symbols, as in mathematics and music; **no·ta·tion·al** *adj.*

notch *n.* & *v.* (make) a V-shaped cut on an edge or surface, as on a stick to keep a tally; also, anything resembling it, as a narrow mountain defile or the angle formed by a coat's collar with the lapel ("notched lapel"); **notch·back** *n.* (an automobile with) a back that has the rear window meeting the top of the trunk at an angle, not as on a fastback.

note *n.* **1** what is jotted down, esp. a short letter or memorandum; also, a *promissory note, bank note,* or piece of paper money; **compare notes** exchange views. **2** a musical tone or sound; hence, an expression with a certain signification: *the ~s of a trumpet; the ~ of triumph in her voice.* **3** observation or notice; hence, distinction: *men of ~; a woman of ~ in public life.* —***v.*** **notes, not·ed, not·ing:** *Please ~ down what I say; Did you ~ the color of her hair? a* **noted** *surgeon, ~d* (i.e. widely known) *for heart transplants.* —**note·book** *n.* a book to make notes in. —**note·wor·thy** (–wur·dhee) *adj.* remarkable; impressive.

noth·ing (NUTH–) *n.* no thing; not anything; zero: *There's ~ in his pocket; lovers whispering sweet ~s to each other; Something is better than ~;* ***adv.*** not at all: *That is ~ remarkable; went ahead ~ daunted by reverses.* —**nothing doing** *Informal.* definitely not! **in nothing flat** *Informal.* in no time at all; very fast; **think nothing of** consider as easy to achieve or unimportant. —**noth·ing·ness** *n.* nonexistence; also, worthlessness.

no·tice (NOH·tis) *n.* **1** warning: *was fired with a month's ~ in writing; She* **served notice** (i.e. stated) *that she was quitting.* **2** attention; also, a posted sign or published account for drawing attention: *facts that escaped his ~; newspaper ~s of births and deaths;* ***v.*** **-tic·es, -ticed, -tic·ing:** *Did you ~* (i.e. perceive with the mind) *his accent? a play favorably ~d* (i.e. reviewed) *in the press.* —**no·tice·a·ble** (–ti·suh·bl) *adj.* easily noticed or worth noticing; **no·tice·a·bly** *adv.* —**no·ti·fy** (NOH·tuh·fye) *v.* **-fies, -fied, -fy·ing** inform officially or formally; **no·ti·fi·ca·tion** (–CAY–) *n.* —**no·tion** (NOH–) *n.* **1** a vague idea, intention, or belief; also, a whim or fancy: *no ~ of what's in his mind;* **no·tion·al** *adj.* **2 notions** *n.pl.* miscellaneous small articles such as sewing things. —**no·to·ri·e·ty** (noh·tuh·RYE·uh·tee) *n.* a being notorious; ill fame; **no·to·ri·ous** (–TOR·ee·us) *adj.* famous in a bad way: *a ~ lawyer, ~ for cheating;* **no·to·ri·ous·ly** *adv.*

not·with·stand·ing (–STAND–) *prep., conj.* & *adv.* in spite of: *~ the lateness of the hour; the lateness of the hour ~; ~* (i.e. although) *it is late.*

Nouak·chott (nwahk·SHOT) capital of Mauritania.

nou·gat (NOO·gut) *n.* a candy made of sugar paste with nuts and sometimes fruit in it.

nought (NAWT) same as NAUGHT.

noun *n.* a word that is the name of a person, thing, place, action, etc.

nour·ish (NUR–) *v.* feed and thus help to grow; foster; **nour·ish·ing** *adj.* nutritious: *Milk is ~;* **nour·ish·ment** *n.: Plants draw ~ from the soil.*

nou·veau riche (noo·voh·REESH), *pl.* **nou·veaux riches** (–voh·REESH) *French.* a newly rich person; parvenu.

Nov. November.

no·va (NOH·vuh) *n.* **-vas** or **-vae** (–vee) a star that "explodes" into sudden brilliance and then fades away. —**No·va Sco·tia** (NOH·vuh·SCOH·shuh) a province of S.E. Canada; 21,425 sq.mi. (55,490 km²); *cap.* Halifax; **Nova Scotian.** —**nov·el** (NOV·ul) *adj.* new in an unusual or strange way. —***n.*** a book-length work of prose fiction dealing with human life and experiences; **nov·el·ette** (–LET) *n.* a short novel; also **no·vel·la** (–VEL·uh); **nov·el·ist** *n.* the author of a novel; **nov·el·ize** *v.* **-iz·es, -ized, -iz·ing** make a novel of (a play, biography, etc.); **nov·el·i·za·tion** (–ZAY–) *n.* —**nov·el·ty** *n.* **-ties** novel quality; also, something novel, esp. a small decorative or useful article.

No·vem·ber (–VEM–) *n.* the 11th month of the year, having 30 days. —**no·ve·na** (–VEE–) *n.* in the Roman Catholic Church, a series of prayers or services spread over nine days or occasions.

nov·ice (–is) *n.* a beginner, or new recruit, esp. in a religious order. —**no·vi·ti·ate** (–VISH·ee·it) *n.* a novice's training period or quarters. —**No·vo·cain** *Trademark.* procaine; also **novocain(e)** *n.*

NOW (NOW) National Organization for Women.

now *adv.* **1** at this instant, time, juncture, etc.: *I want my dinner ~; She'll be here just ~* (i.e. very soon); **now and then** (or **again**) once in a while. **2** [used more as an interjection than as an adverb of time]: *~ hear this; Well, ~, what do you think? ~, ~, don't do that!* —***conj.*** since: *~ (that) you're 18, you can vote.* —***n.*** & ***adj.*** (of) the present time, hour, age, etc.: *From ~ on we are friends; By ~ she must be home; up-to-date fashions for the ~ generation.* —**now·a·days** (NOW·uh–) *adv.* in these days; at the present time.

no·way(s) *adv.* in no way. —**no·where** *adv.* not anywhere: *She was ~ to be seen;* ***n.:*** *It came (from) out of ~;* **nowhere near** not nearly. —**no·wise** *adv.* not at all.

nox·ious (NOK·shus) *adj.* harmful or injurious to health: *~ fumes, weeds, influences* (i.e. corrupting).

noz·zle (NOZL) *n.* a vent or spout shaped for controlling the flow of a gas or liquid, as of a bellows or garden hose.

Np neptunium. —**N.P.** Notary Public; No Protest; New Paragraph.

N.R.C. National Research Council.

N.S. Nova Scotia.

N.S.C. National Security Council.

N.S.F. National Science Foundation; not sufficient funds (also **n.s.f.**).

N.S.W. New South Wales.

N.T. New Testament; Northern Territory (Australia).

nth (ENTH) *adj.* multiplied an indefinite (or "n") number of times; **to the nth degree** to the utmost.

NTP normal temperature and pressure.

nt. wt. net weight.

nu (NEW) *n.* the 13th letter of the Greek alphabet (N,ν).

nu·ance (NOO·ahnce) *n.* a subtle variation (of meaning, tone, or color); **nu·anced** *adj.*

nub *n.* knob or lump; hence, *Informal.* point or gist; also **nub·bin.** —**nub·ble** *n.* a knob or lump. —**nub·b(l)y** *adj.* **nub·b(l)i·er, nub·b(l)i·est** of a surface, knotted or lumpy.

nu·bile (NEW·bl, –bile) *adj.* of a girl, ready for marriage; marriageable.

nu·cle·ar (NEW·clee·ur) *adj.* **1** of or forming a nucleus or core: *Parents and children form the* **nuclear family.** **2** of or having to do with the atomic nucleus: *~ energy, physics, fission, fusion, weapon;* **nuclear reactor** (for controlled production of atomic energy). —**nu·cle·ate** (–it) *adj.* having a nucleus; ***v.*** (–ate) **-ates, -at·ed, -at·ing** form as or into a nucleus; **nu·cle·a·tion** (–AY–) *n.* —**nu·cle·ic** (–CLEE–) **acid** a complex organic acid such as DNA or RNA found in the nuclei of cells. —**nu·cle·on** (NEW·clee–) *n.* a neutron or proton; **nu·cle·on·ic** (–ON–) *adj.;* **nu·cle·on·ics** *n.pl.* the branch of physics dealing with atomic nuclei and nucleons. —**nu·cle·us** *n., pl.* **-cle·i** (–clee·eye) or **-cle·us·es** core or center of activity, esp. the central part of a plant or animal cell containing genetic material and the positively charged particle at the center of an atom in which matter and energy are concentrated. —**nu·clide** *n.* a particular constitution of an atomic nucleus: *The chlorine 37 ~ has a nucleus of 17 protons and 20 neutrons;* **nu·clid·ic** (–CLID–) *adj.*

nude *n.* & *adj.* (the undraped human figure or the condition of being) unclothed or naked, esp. as in art: *a ~ model; a revue featuring ~s; on* *stage* **in the nude** (i.e. naked); ~ (i.e. flesh-colored) *stockings;* **nu·di·ty** *n.*

nudge (NUJ) *n.* & *v.* **nudg·es, nudged, nudg·ing** (give) a gentle push or jog (as with the elbow); **nudg·er** *n.*

nu·die (NEW·dee) *n. Slang.* a show, magazine, etc. featuring nudes. —**nud·ism** (NEW·dizm) *n.* principle or practice of social nudity; **nud·ist** *n.*

nu·ga·to·ry (NEW·guh–) *adj. Formal.* trifling; hence, invalid or futile in effect.

nug·get (NUG·it) *n.* a lump of something precious from the earth: *gold ~s.*

nui·sance (NEW·snce) *n.* a troublesome or annoying person, thing, or situation.

nuke *n. Slang.* a nuclear weapon or power-generating station.

null *adj.* **1** of no effect, esp. legal; invalid: *a law declared* **null and void** *by a court.* **2** zero; empty; amounting to nothing: *The set of all square circles is a* **null set** (i.e. empty set). —**null·i·ty** *n.* —**nul·li·fy** *v.* **-fies, -fied, -fy·ing** make valueless; declare null and void; annul; **nul·li·fi·ca·tion** (–CAY–) *n.*

Num(b). Numbers (Old Testament book).

numb (NUM) *v.* & *adj.* (make) insensible or benumbed, as with cold, shock, etc. **numb·ly** *adv.;* **numb·ness** *n.*

num·ber *n.* **1** a numeral figure that tells how many, as 1978 or LXX: *cardinal ~s such as 1, 2, 3, etc. and ordinal ~s such as 1st, 2nd, 3rd, etc.; Accountants are good at* **numbers** (i.e. arithmetic). **2** amount; quantity; collection; group: *total ~ of 100; A good ~ are going hungry; Their ~ is large;* **A number of** *others are homeless;* **beyond** (or **without**) **number** too many to be counted. **3** one of a series: *What ~ did you dial? the license ~ of your car; a very popular ~* (i.e. item, as of a program). **4** in grammar: *"Fish" could be (in the) singular or plural ~; "Goes" is the singular ~ of "go."* —**v. 1** count or give a number to: *a ~ing machine; ~ed among the chosen few.* **2** limit (the number of): *A terminally ill patient's days are ~ed.* **3** amount to; add up to: total: *The dead ~ed 100.* —**Numbers** a book of the Old Testament containing a census of the Israelites. —**numbers game** game of betting on the appearance of specific numbers in daily published statistics such as bank financial balances; also **numbers (pool), numbers racket.** —**num·ber·less** *adj.* countless. —**numbskull** same as NUMSKULL. **nu·mer·al** (NEW·muh·rul) *n.* & *adj.* (a symbol or expression such as 35, XXXV, or thirty-five) denoting a number or numbers. —**nu·mer·ate** (NEW–) *v.* **-ates, -at·ed, -at·ing** count or list; enumerate; **nu·mer·a·tor** *n.* in a fraction, the number above the line; **nu·mer·a·tion** (–RAY–) *n.* —**nu·mer·ic** (–MER–) *adj.* numerical; using figures, not letters: *a ~ code, computer readout;* **nu·mer·i·cal** *adj.* of or having to do with numbers: *~ analysis, control, order, quantity, value;* **nu·mer·i·cal·ly** *adv.* —**nu·mer·ol·o·gy** (new·muh·ROL·uh·jee) *n.* fortunetelling using numbers such as birthdates; **nu·mer·ol·o·gist** (–ROL–) *n.* —**nu·me·ro u·no** (NOO·muh·roh·OO·noh) *Informal.* the "number one" or most important member of a group, often oneself. —**nu·mer·ous** (NEW·muh·rus) *adj.* consisting of or being many: *~ gifts, books, complaints; a ~* (i.e. large) *clientele, progeny;* **nu·mer·ous·ly** *adv.;* **nu·mer·ous·ness** *n.*

nu·mis·mat·ics (new·miz·MAT–) *n.pl.* [with *sing. v.*] the study or collecting of coins, paper money, medals, tokens, credit cards, and such items of monetary interest; **nu·mis·mat·ic** *adj.;* **nu·mis·ma·tist** (–MIZ·muh–) *n.*

num(b)·skull *n.* a blockhead; dunce.

nun *n.* a woman living in a convent under religious vows.

nun·ci·o (NUN·shee·oh, –see–) *n.* **-os** a papal ambassador.

nun·ner·y *n.* **nun·ner·ies** [former term] a convent.

nup·tial (NUP·shul) *adj.* of a wedding; **nup·tials** *n.pl.* wedding ceremony; **nup·tial·ly** *adv.*

nurse *n.* **1** a person trained to take care of the sick. **2** a woman hired to care for another's children; also **nurse·maid.** —**v. nurs·es, nursed, nurs·ing 1** suckle: *special diet for ~ing mothers.* **2** take care of, esp. in a protective manner: *dedicated to ~ing the sick; He's staying home ~ing a cold; seems healthier to forgive than ~ a grudge; has been at the bar ~ing the same drink all evening.* —**nurse practitioner** a nurse trained to carry out the more routine functions of a physician. —**nurs·er·y** *n.* **-er·ies 1** a children's room. **2** a nursery school or day-care center. **3** a place where plants are grown for transplanting, experimentation, etc.; **nurs·er·y·man** *n.* **-men.** —**nursery rhyme** a simple poem such as "Little Jack Horner" or "Sing a song of sixpence." —**nursery school** a pre-kindergarten school. —**nursing home** a private institution that takes care of the aged, sick, and disabled. —**nurs·ling** *n.* a suckling child. —**nur·ture** *n.* & *v.* **-tures, -tured, -tur·ing** (give) nourishment or training (to): *A greenhouse ~s plants; a well-~d child; ~ builds on nature; a friendship ~d from childhood.*

nut *n.* **1** (a dry, hard fruit with) a seed or kernel enclosed in a shell of woody fiber, as the walnut, peanut, or coconut. **2** a small metal block with a threaded hole to screw on to and lock a bolt in place: *~s and bolts.* **3** *Slang.* an eccentric or crazy person; also, a devotee or enthusiast: *No use talking to that ~; an ecological ~.* —**nuts** *adj.: He's not just misinformed, he's ~!* (i.e. crazy); *He's ~ about skateboarding; John is ~ about* (i.e. very fond of) *Mary;* ***interj.*** expressing scorn: *If you won't listen to me, ~ to you!* —**nut·crack·er** *n.* **1** an implement for cracking nuts open. **2** a bird of the crow family with sharp claws for holding nuts, esp. pine cones, while opening them. —**nut·hatch** *n.* any of a family of climbing birds that have a habit of wedging nuts in the bark of a tree to hack them open with their bills. —**nut·meg** *n.* (the spice got from) the aromatic seed of an East Indian tree. —**nut·pick** *n.* a table implement for digging out the kernels of cracked nuts.

nu·tri·a (NEW·tree·uh) *n.* the short blue-brown fur of the coypu; also, a coypu.

nu·tri·ent (NEW·tree·unt) *n. & adj.* nourishing (substance or ingredient); **nu·tri·ment** *n.* a nutrient substance. —**nu·tri·tion** (–TRISH·un) *n.* (the study of) the process by which food is assimilated by an organism; also, nourishment; **nu·tri·tion·al** *adj.;* **nu·tri·tion·al·ly** *adv.;* **nu·tri·tion·ist** *n.;* **nu·tri·tious** *adj.* nourishing; having food-value; **nu·tri·tive** (NEW·truh·tiv) *adj.* nutritious; also, nutritional: ~ *functions, process, plasma.*

nuts and bolts basic or essential working features. —**nut·shell** *n.* the shell enclosing a nut; **in a nutshell** concisely; in a few words. —**nut·ty** *adj.* **nut·ti·er, nut·ti·est** **1** nutlike or containing nuts: *a ~flavor, cookie.* **2** *Slang.* nuts or crazy; also, enthusiastic. —**nut·ti·ness** *n.*

nuz·zle (NUZL) *v.* **nuz·zles, nuz·zled, nuz·zling** rub or push against (as if) with the nose or snout; also snuggle or nestle; **nuz·zler** *n.*

NV Nevada.

N.W. or **n.w.** northwest(ern).

N.Y. or **NY** New York; **N.Y.C.** New York City.

ny·lon (NYE–) *n.* a strong, elastic synthetic product widely used as fibers, sheets, tubes, etc.; **nylons** *pl.* nylon stockings.

nymph (NIMF) *n.* **1** in Greek and Roman myths, a goddess of nature inhabiting the water (naiads), woods (dryads), hills (oreads), etc. **2** the wingless but adultlike larva stage in the metamorphosis of insects such as grasshoppers and chinch bugs. —**nym·pho·ma·ni·a** (–MAY–) *n.* excessive sexual desire in a woman; **nym·pho·ma·ni·ac** *n. & adj.*

N.Z. New Zealand.

O

O or **o** (OH) *n.* **O's** or **o's** **1** the 15th letter of the English alphabet. **2** zero. **3** ohm. **—O** **1** (OH) *interj. Archaic.* same as OH. **2** old; oxygen. **—O.** Ocean; October; Ohio.

oaf (OHF) *n.* a stupid or awkward fellow; **oaf·ish** *adj.*

oak (OHK) *n.* any of hundreds of species of strong and sturdy trees of the beech family that bear nuts called acorns; ***adj.*** also **oak·en,** made of oak wood. **—Oak·land** (–lund) a seaport of California.

oa·kum (OH–) *n.* a caulking material used in the seams of wooden ships, for packing joints in pipes, etc.

oar *n.* a broad-bladed implement used in rowing a boat; **rest on one's oars** rest after doing some work; **oars·man** *n.* **-men.** **—oar·lock** *n.* a U-shaped support or notch in one side of a boat for holding the oar in place.

O.A.S. Organization of American States.

o·a·sis (oh·AY–) *n., pl.* **-ses** (–seez) in a desert, a fertile spot with water and some vegetation.

oat (OHT) *n.* a cereal grass bearing grain used as livestock feed and in making oatmeal, etc.; also **oats** *sing.* & *pl.;* **oat·en** *adj.* **—oat·cake** *n.* a thin flat oatmeal cake or bread.

oath (OHTH) *n.* **1** a solemn promise, often calling on God as witness: *the President's ~ of office; a witness testifying* **under oath** (i.e. to tell the truth). **2** a swearing or a swearword; curse.

oat·meal (OHT·meel) *n.* meal or flakes made from oats; also, this cooked as porridge.

OAU Organization of African Unity.

ob- *prefix.* toward or against: as in *obverse, obnoxious, obdurate.* **—ob.** (he or she) died. **—Ob(ad).** Obadiah (Old Testament book).

ob·bli·ga·to (ob·luh·GAH·toh) *n.* **-tos** or **-ti** (–tee) *n.* & *adj.* (an instrumental part) accompanying a solo: *an aria with trumpet ~.*

ob·du·rate (OB·dyuh·rut, –duh–) *adj.* obstinate or hardhearted: *an ~ refusal, sinner;* **ob·du·rate·ly** *adv.* **—ob·du·ra·cy** (–ruh·see) *n.*

o·be·di·ent (–BEE·dee·unt) *adj.* obeying; submissive: *an ~ child;* **o·be·di·ent·ly** *adv.;* **o·be·di·ence** *n.* **—o·bei·sance** (–BAY·snce, –BEE–) *n.* (a gesture of) homage or deference; **o·bei·sant** *adj.*

ob·e·lisk (OB·uh–, OH·buh–) *n.* a four-sided tapering pillar of stone with a pyramidal top, originally erected near ancient Egyptian temples.

o·bese (–BEECE) *adj.* excessively fat; **o·be·si·ty** (–BEE–) *n.*

o·bey (–BAY) *v.* carry out (an order); be guided by (the authorities, one's conscience, etc.).

ob·fus·cate (OB–, –FUS–) *v.* **-cates, -cat·ed, -cat·ing** confuse or obscure: *drugs that ~ the mind; arguments ~ing the issues;* **ob·fus·ca·tion** (–CAY–) *n.*

o·bi (OH·bee) *n.* a broad sash worn with a kimono.

o·bit (OH–, OB–) *n. Informal.* obituary.

ob·i·ter (OB–, OH–) **dic·tum** *pl.* **ob·i·ter dic·ta** an incidental observation; a judgment made in passing.

o·bit·u·ar·y (oh·BICH·oo·er·ee) *n.* **-ar·ies** notice announcing a death; also, a short biography accompanying the notice.

obj. object(ive). **—ob·ject** (OB·jikt) *n.* a person or thing that a feeling, thought, or action is directed toward: *the ~ of his attentions; an unidentified flying ~; In "John loves Mary," "Mary" is the grammatical ~ of the verb; What is the ~* (i.e. goal or purpose) *of your research?* **—*v.*** (ub·JECT) oppose or disapprove strongly; be opposed (*to* something); **ob·jec·tor** *n.;* **ob·jec·ti·fy** *v.* **-fies, -fied, -fy·ing** make objective; **ob·jec·ti·fi·ca·tion** (–CAY–) *n.* **—ob·jec·tion** (–JEC–) *n.* an expression of or the reason for objecting; **ob·jec·tion·a·ble** *adj.* open to objection; also, unpleasant or offensive: *an ~ report; ~ language.* **—ob·jec·tive** (–JEC·tiv) *n.* something in the position of object, esp. an intended object or a definite goal: *a great achiever who always aims at clear ~s; The ~ of a microscope or telescope is the part closest to the object being viewed;* ***adj.:*** *an ~* (i.e. not subjective) *look, analysis, report; an ~ test with facts to be merely checked and no room for essay-*

type answers; "Me," "them," "whom," etc. are in the ~ case; **ob·jec·tive·ly** *adv.;* **ob·jec·tive·ness** or **ob·jec·tiv·i·ty** (–TIV–) *n.* —**object lesson** a practical illustration of a principle, esp. one that teaches a lesson. —**ob·jet d'art** (ob·zhay·DAR), *pl.* **ob·jets** (ob·zhay) **d'art** *French.* a small object of artistic value. —**objet trou·vé** (–troo·VAY) *French.* a FOUND ART object.

ob·jur·gate *v.* **-gates, -gat·ed, -gat·ing** *Formal.* scold or rebuke harshly; **ob·jur·ga·tion** (–GAY–) *n.*

obl. oblique, oblong.

ob·late *adj. Geom.* flattened at the poles: *an ~ spheroid;* ***n.*** a lay person dedicated to religious life and work: *"Oblates of Mary Immaculate."* —**ob·la·tion** (–LAY–) *n.* an offering to God; sacrifice.

ob·li·gate (OB·luh–) *v.* **-gates, -gat·ed, -gat·ing** bind morally or legally: *did not feel ~d to shop there in spite of gifts received;* **ob·li·ga·tion** (–GAY–) *n.* what one is obliged to do because of an agreement or by one's position, occupation, relationships, etc.: *no ~ to tip our staff; some ~ to pay for a damage; the duties and ~s of a job;* **ob·lig·a·to·ry** (–LIG·uh–) *adj.* —**o·blige** (uh·BLIJE) *v.* **o·blig·es, o·bliged, o·blig·ing** bind (people) by force of law, custom, conscience, etc.: *The law ~s us to drive on the right; much ~d by* (i.e. grateful for) *your kindness; ready to ~* (i.e. do a favor) *whenever she can;* **o·blig·ing** *adj.* willing to do favors; **o·blig·ing·ly** *adv.*

ob·lique (uh·BLEEK, *rarely* –BLIKE) *adj.* **1** slanting, not perpendicular or parallel: *Acute and obtuse angles are ~ angles.* **2** indirect, often underhand: *an ~ reference, glance, accusation;* **oblique case** the case of an indirect object, as "me" in "Give it to me." —**ob·lique·ly** *adv.* —**ob·lique·ness** or **ob·liq·ui·ty** (–LIK–) *n.*

ob·lit·er·ate (–LIT–) *v.* **-ates, -at·ed, -at·ing** destroy all traces of; wipe out (signs, marks, etc.) completely; **ob·lit·er·a·tor** *n.;* **ob·lit·e·ra·tion** (–RAY–) *n.*

ob·liv·i·on (–LIV·ee·un) *n.* the condition of being forgotten; also, forgetfulness: *People pass into ~ by death, neglect, etc.;* **ob·liv·i·ous** *adj.* forgetful or unaware: *~ of the passage of time;* **ob·liv·i·ous·ly** *adv.;* **ob·liv·i·ous·ness** *n.*

ob·long *n.* & *adj.* (an object or figure that is) rectangular or longer than broad.

ob·lo·quy (OB·luh·kwee) *n.* **-quies** abusive condemnatory language; hence, disgrace: *The deposed president lived in ~ till death.*

ob·nox·ious (–NOK·shus) *adj.* unbearably offensive or objectionable: *an ~ person; ~ manners; became ~ to everyone;* **ob·nox·ious·ly** *adv.;* **ob·nox·ious·ness** *n.*

o·boe (OH·boh) *n.* a double-reed woodwind instrument with a high-pitched tone; **o·bo·ist** *n.*

obs. obsolete.

ob·scene (–SEEN) *adj.* immoral or indecent: *~ dancing, gestures, language, literature, phone calls;* **ob·scene·ly** *adv.* —**ob·scen·i·ty** (–SEN–) *n.*

ob·scure (–SKYOOR) *adj.* **1** not clear or distinct; hard to follow: *an ~ passage in a book; an ~ meaning, corner;* ***v.*** **-scures, -scured, -scur·ing:** *the sun ~d by clouds.* **2** little known: *an ~ village, genius.* —**ob·scure·ly** *adv.;* **ob·scur·i·ty** *n.* —**ob·scu·rant·ism** (–SKYOOR·un·tizm) *n.* opposition to progress and enlightenment; **ob·scu·rant·ist** *n.* & *adj.*

ob·se·quies (OB·suh·kweez) *n.pl.* funeral rites. —**ob·se·qui·ous** (–SEE·kwee·us) *adj.* obedient in a servile or fawning manner; **ob·se·qui·ous·ly** *adv.;* **ob·se·qui·ous·ness** *n.*

ob·serv·ant (–ZUR·vunt) *adj.* mindful (of rules, customs, etc.); also, watchful: *alert and ~ while driving.* —**ob·ser·va·tion** (–VAY–) *n.* **1** act or process of perceiving: *an error of ~.* **2** a remark or comment. —**ob·serv·a·to·ry** (–ZUR·vuh–) *n.* **-ries** a building equipped with a telescope, etc. for astronomical research. —**ob·serve** (–ZURV) *v.* **-serves, -served, -serv·ing** **1** abide by or keep (a law, custom, religious holiday, etc.); **ob·serv·ance** *n.* **2** to notice; also, examine or study: *changes ~d at puberty; Astronomers ~ the stars;* **ob·serv·a·ble** *adj.;* **ob·serv·er** *n.* **3** to comment or remark: *"Pride goeth before a fall," he ~d wisely.*

ob·sess (–SES) *v.* of ideas, feelings, and impulses, occupy one's mind in an unreasonable or unhealthy manner: *so ~ed about cleanliness he washes every hour;* **ob·sess·ion** *n.;* **ob·ses·sion·al** *adj.;* **ob·ses·sive** (–iv) *adj.;* **ob·ses·sive·ly** *adv.*

ob·sid·i·an (–SID·ee·un) *n.* a natural black-colored glass formed by the cooling of lava.

ob·so·lesce (–LES) *v.* **-lesc·es, -lesced, -lesc·ing** be obsolescent; **ob·so·les·cent** (–LES·nt) *adj.* becoming obsolete or out-of-date: *an ~ custom, mode of travel;* **ob·so·les·cence** *n.* —**ob·so·lete** (OB·suh–, –LEET) *adj.* fallen into disuse; outmoded: *an ~ word, implement;* **ob·so·lete·ly** *adv.;* **ob·so·lete·ness** *n.*

ob·sta·cle (OB·stuh–) *n.* something that stands in the way of one's progress: *an ~ to success; the fences, ditches, hurdles, etc. of an* **obstacle course.**

ob·stet·rics (–STET–) *n.pl.* [takes *sing. v.*] branch of medicine concerned with childbirth; **ob·stet·ric** or **-ri·cal** *adj.: ~ nurse, ward, forceps;* **ob·ste·tri·cian** (–TRISH·un) *n.*

ob·sti·nate (OB·stuh·nit) *adj.* not yielding to reason or remedies: *remained ~ in his belief till death; an ~ habit, fever;* **ob·sti·nate·ly** *adv.;* **ob·sti·na·cy** *n.*

ob·strep·er·ous (–STREP–) *adj.* noisy or disorderly in an unruly way: *~ behavior;* **ob·strep·er·ous·ly** *adv.;* **ob·strep·er·ous·ness** *n.*

ob·struct (–STRUCT) *v.* block movement or activity by placing obstacles in the way: *a pile-up ~ing traffic; Tall buildings ~ our view;* **ob·struc·tion** *n.: an ~ in the windpipe; charged with*

~ *of justice.* —**ob·struc·tion·ist** *n. & adj.* (one) that obstructs: *an ~ policy, tactic; A filibusterer is an ~.* —**ob·struc·tion·ism** *n.*

ob·tain (ub·TAIN) *v.* **1** secure or get through effort, planning, etc.: *evidence ~ed by the police; how to ~ a license; to ~ knowledge, credit.* **2** of customs, rules, etc., be prevalent or in use: *superstitious practices still ~ing in primitive societies.* —**ob·tain·a·ble** *adj.;* **ob·tain·ment** *n.*

ob·trude (ub·TROOD) *v.* **-trudes, -trud·ed, -trud·ing** push out; also, thrust (oneself or one's concerns) forward where not wanted: *~d its head and looked out; never ~s his ideas on others;* **ob·stru·sion** (–TROO–) *n.* —**ob·tru·sive** (–siv) *adj.* pushing or showy: *an ~ color;* **ob·tru·sive·ly** *adv.;* **ob·tru·sive·ness** *n.*

ob·tuse (–TUE–) *adj.* not acute or sharp: *an* **obtuse angle** (of more than 90°); *too ~* (i.e. dull-witted) *to get the point;* **ob·tuse·ly** *adv.;* **ob·tuse·ness** *n.*

obv. *Abbrev.* for **ob·verse** (–VURCE) *adj.* **1** the front, as the side of a coin with the head or other main design. **2** *Logic.* being a counterpart. —***n.*** **1** the principal side or front. **2** *Logic.* a counterpart: *"No man is immortal" is the ~ of "Man is mortal."* —**ob·verse·ly** *adv.*

ob·vi·ate (OB·vee–) *v.* **-ates, -at·ed, -at·ing** remove (a difficulty, need, etc.) by anticipating; **ob·vi·a·tion** (–AY–) *n.* —**ob·vi·ous** (OB·vee–) *adj.* plain (to the view): *an ~ truth; It is ~ they cannot get along;* **ob·vi·ous·ly** *adv.;* **ob·vi·ous·ness** *n.*

oc·a·ri·na (oc·uh·REE·nuh) *n.* an egg-shaped molded wind instrument that produces a soft whistling sound when blown into.

occas. occasional(ly). —**oc·ca·sion** (uh·CAY·zhun) *n.* a particular time, esp. one favorable to an event's taking place: *great ~s such as weddings; on the rare ~ of an earthquake; a football game as the ~ of a fight;* **on occasion** now and then. —***v.*** cause: *Their enmity is well-known, but what ~ed the fight?* —**oc·ca·sion·al** *adj.* happening now and then, not regularly: *a forecast of ~ showers; ~ references, music* (for special occasions), *chairs* (for auxiliary use); **oc·ca·sion·al·ly** *adv.*

oc·ci·dent (OC·suh·dunt) *n.* the west, esp. **Occident,** Europe and the Americas, as distinguished from the Orient. —**oc·ci·den·tal** or **Oc·ci·den·tal** (–DEN–) *n. & adj.* (a native) of the West; **Oc·ci·den·tal·ize** *v.* **-iz·es, -ized, -iz·ing** make Western in character or culture.

oc·clude (uh·CLOOD) *v.* **oc·cludes, oc·clud·ed, oc·clud·ing** block in, shut out, or obstruct to prevent passage: *clots ~ing blood supply in a coronary artery; the* **occluded front** *formed by cold air overtaking and forcing up a warm air mass; Upper and lower teeth should ~* (i.e. meet properly); **oc·clu·sion** *n.;* **oc·clu·sive** *adj.*

oc·cult (uh·CULT, OC·ult) *adj.* of sciences, practices, etc., hidden or concealed from ordinary human knowledge, as astrology, alchemy, and magic: *Fortunetellers claim to know* **the occult** (i.e. occult matters). —**oc·cult·ism** *n.;* **oc·cul·tist** *n.*

oc·cu·pa·tion (–PAY–) *n.* **1** an occupying by an enemy. **2** work which one is trained to do or does habitually: *a teacher by ~, though unemployed;* **oc·cu·pa·tion·al** *adj.: The bends is an ~ disease of divers;* **occupational therapy** *helps overcome handicaps by participation in selected activities;* **oc·cu·pa·tion·al·ly** *adv.* —**oc·cu·py** (OK·yuh·pye) *v.* **-pies, -pied, -py·ing** **1** take up or engage (attention, time, space, etc.): *hobbies to ~ your spare time; keep children ~d and out of trouble.* **2** have possession of: *moved in and ~d their house; an ~d seat; an ~d position soon to fall vacant;* **oc·cu·pan·cy** (–pun·see) *n.* **-cies; oc·cu·pant** (–punt) *n.* **3** take possession of by force: *when France was ~d by the Germans.* —**oc·cu·pi·er** *n.*

oc·cur (uh·CUR) *v.* **oc·curs, oc·curred, oc·cur·ring** of an event, thing, etc., happen (to be found) or be met with: *When did his death ~? "The" ~s more frequently than any other word; Did that ever ~ to you?* (i.e. come to your mind?); **oc·cur·rence** (–CUR–) *n.*

o·cean (OH·shun) *n.* one of the great expanses of water around the globe, esp. the Atlantic, Pacific, Indian, Arctic, or Antarctic ocean; hence, a great number or quantity: *~s of trouble, funds, time.* —**O·ce·an·i·a** (oh·shee·AY·nee·uh) a group of Pacific islands divided into MICRONESIA, MELANESIA, and POLYNESIA. —**o·ce·an·ic** (–shee·AN–) *adj.* —**o·cean·ar·i·um** (–NAIR·ee–) *n.* **-i·ums** or **-i·a** an aquarium with large tanks in which fishes are placed together without separation. —**o·cean·go·ing** *adj.: an ~ vessel; ~* (i.e. maritime) *commerce, world.* —**o·cean·og·ra·phy** (–NOG·ruh·fee) *n.* the study of oceans and marine life; **o·cean·og·ra·pher** *n.;* **o·cean·o·graph·ic** (–GRAF–) *adj.*

o·cel·lus (–SEL–) *n., pl.* **o·cel·li** (–eye) the single-lens light-sensitive eye of some insects such as ants.

o·ce·lot (OS·uh–, OH·suh–) *n.* the medium-sized spotted wild cat found from Texas to Paraguay.

o·cher or **o·chre** (OH·cur) *n.* earth containing iron oxide, used as a pigment; also, its yellow to brownish-red color.

o'·clock (uh·CLOK) *adv.* according to the clock: *8 ~ in the morning, or 8 a.m.*

OCR optical character recognition.

oct. octavo. —**Oct.** October. —**oct(a)-** or **octo-** *comb.form.* eight: as in **oc·ta·gon** (OC·tuh–) *n.* an eight-sided plane figure; **oc·tag·o·nal** (–TAG–) *adj.* —**oc·tane** *n.* a petroleum hydrocarbon that gives quality to gasoline: *The higher the* **octane number** (or **rating**) *of a gasoline the less the engine knocks.* —**oc·tave** (OC·tiv, –tave) *n.* **1** an interval of eight full musical tones; also, the series of tones making up such an interval or the eighth full tone from any given tone. **2** a group of eight (verses, festival days, etc.). —**oc·ta·vo** (–TAH–) *n.* **-vos** (a book having) the page size of 6 by 9 in. (15.24 by 22.86 cm), each leaf being one eighth of a large sheet. —**oc·tet(te)** (oc·TET) *n.* a musical composition or group of singers or players with eight voices or instruments; also, a set of eight. —**Oc·to·ber** (ok·TOH–) *n.* the tenth month of the year (eighth in the old calendar), having 31 days. —**oc·to·ge·nar·i·an** (–ji·NAIR·ee·un) *n.* & *adj.* (one) in his eighties. —**oc·to·pus** (OC·tuh–) *n.* **-pus·es** or **-pi** (–pye) a soft-bodied sea mollusk with eight arms or tentacles. —**oc·to·syl·lab·ic** (–LAB–) *n.* & *adj.* (a verse) of eight syllables.

oc·u·lar (OK·yuh·lur) *adj.* of the eye or by eyesight; visual; ***n.*** the eyepiece lens(es) of a microscope or telescope. —**oc·u·list** *n.* [former term] ophthalmologist.

OD (OH·dee) *n.* **OD's** *Slang.* (one who has taken) an overdose of a narcotic; ***v.*** **OD's, OD'd** or **ODed, OD'ing** or **ODing** take sick or die from an OD. —**O.D.** Doctor of Optometry; Officer of the Day; overdraft; overdrawn.

o·da·lisque or **o·da·lisk** (OH·dl·isk) *n.* (painting of) a concubine in a harem.

odd *adj.* **1** remaining as extra: *an ~ stocking without a mate; the* **odd man out** *after others have paired off; Keep the ~ change after payments; hundred-~* (i.e. 100 plus a few); *working at ~* (i.e. casual or occasional) *jobs.* **2** not even: *1, 3, 5, 7, etc. are the ~ numbers.* **3** strange; unusual; peculiar: *an ~ hairstyle; an ~-looking creature;* **odd·ball** *n.* & *adj. Slang.* eccentric; **odd·i·ty** *n.* **-ties** peculiar person or thing; **odd·ly** *adv.;* **odd·ness** *n.* —**odd·ment** *n.* an odd bit or remnant. —**odds** *n. sing.* & *pl.* the difference in one's favor; advantage: *betting ~ of five to one* (paying five for every one staked if successful); **The odds** (i.e. chances) **are** *we will win; died fighting against heavy ~;* **at odds** in disagreement; **odds and ends** miscellaneous things; **odds-on** *adj.* sure (to win): *the ~ favorite.*

ode *n.* a ceremonious lyric poem in an exalted style.

O·des·sa (–DES–) a seaport of S.W. Ukraine.

O·din (OH–) the chief god of Norse mythology.

o·di·ous (OH·dee·us) *adj.* hateful in an offensive or disagreeable way: *an ~ epithet; ~ cruelty;* **o·di·ous·ly** *adv.;* **o·di·ous·ness** *n.* —**o·di·um** (OH·dee–) *n.* widespread hatred of the kind that results in disgrace.

o·dom·e·ter (oh·DOM·uh–) *n.* an instrument that records the distance traveled by a vehicle.

o·dor (OH·dur) *n.* what makes anything smell good or bad: *the detection of ~s; natural and synthetic ~s; the ~ of scandal; a company* **in bad odor** (i.e. having a bad name) *with the law;* **o·dor·less** *adj.* —**o·dor·ous** or **o·dor·if·er·ous** (–RIF–) *adj.* giving forth an odor; fragrant. —**o·dour** *Brit.* odor.

od·ys·sey (OD·uh·see) *n.* **od·ys·seys** a long wandering or journey, as of the Greek hero **O·dys·se·us** (oh·DIS·yoos, –ee·us) in the ancient epic poem **Od·ys·sey.**

O.E. Old English.

O.E.C.D. Organization for Economic Cooperation and Development.

O.E.D. Oxford English Dictionary.

oed·i·pal or **Oed·i·pal** (ED·uh·pul, EE–) *adj.* relating to the Oedipus complex. —**Oed·i·pus** in Greek myth, a king who unwittingly married his mother after killing his father; **Oedipus complex** in psychoanalysis, an unconscious childhood attachment to one's parent of the opposite sex, as explaining personality disorders in adult life.

oe·no·phile (EE·nuh·file) *n.* a lover or connoisseur of wine.

O.E.O. Office of Economic Opportunity.

o'er (OR, OHR) *Poet.* over.

oe·soph·a·gus (ee·SOF·uh–) same as ESOPHAGUS. —**oes·tro·gen** (EES·truh·jun) same as ESTROGEN.

of (ov, uv) *prep.* **1** [indicating origin or cause]: *born ~ noble blood; died ~ hunger; a house ~ cards; north ~* (i.e. from) *New York.* **2** [indicating a relationship]: *children ~ God; the works ~ man; love ~* (i.e. for) *truth.* **3** being; having (to do with): *words ~ advice; the State ~ Ohio; a house ~ prayer.* **4** before: *10 minutes ~ 8.* **5** during: *~ late* (i.e. recently); *~ an evening.*

off (AWF, OF) *adv.* away: *took his hat ~; went ~ without a word; turn ~ the tap; pay ~ a loan; saw me ~ at the airport;* **off and on** now and then. —***prep.*** away from: *The hat is ~ his head; anchored ~ the coast; an ~-the-rack* (i.e. ready-to-wear, not custom-made) *suit; when you get ~ work.* —***adj.*** away: *I'll be ~ soon; The lights are ~* (i.e. not on); *an ~* (i.e. unlikely) *chance.* —***interj.*** away: *~ with you!*

off. office(r); official.

of·fal (AWF·ul, OF–) *n.* garbage; also, waste (animal parts such as viscera, industrial by-products, etc.). —**off-beat** *n. Music.* a weakly accented beat; ***adj.*** off the regular rhythm; hence, of an unusual kind: *~ theater.* —**off-col·or** (AWF·CUL·ur) *adj.* not the right color; also, improper; risqué.

of·fend (uh·FEND) *v.* do wrong; displease; hurt (one's sense of right and wrong): *Teacher will be ~ed; It ~s against good manners; ~s good taste;* **of·fend·er** *n.* —**of·fense** (–FENCE, AWF–) *n.: Speeding is a traffic ~; strong language likely to* **give offense;** *too meek to* **take offense;** *The ~ was not intended; weapons of ~ and defense;* also **of·fence** *Brit.* —**of·fen·sive** (–FEN·siv) *adj.* **1** unpleasant or insulting: *an ~ smell; ~ language.* **2** attacking; aggressive: *an ~ army, weapon;* ***n.*** attack: *an army on the ~; a new ~; a peace ~* (i.e. aggressive move for peace); **of·fen·sive·ly** *adv.;* **of·fen·sive·ness** *n.*

of·fer (AWF·ur, OF–) *v.* **1** hold out for acceptance: *Many ~ed (to) help; Some ~ed suggestions.* **2** present: *prayers and sacrifices ~ed to*

God; The enemy ~ed little resistance; didn't even ~ (i.e. attempt) *to defend themselves; if the opportunity ~s* (i.e. presents itself). ***—n.:*** *refused all ~s of help; $200 was a good ~;* **of·fer·ing** *n.: the ~ of prayers; a plate to collect church ~s; course ~s at a school.* **—of·fer·to·ry** *n.* **-ries** **1** the offering of bread and wine at a church service, esp. the Mass; also, the prayers accompanying this. **2** the taking up of the offerings of the congregation at public worship.

off·hand *adj.* & *adv.* (said or done) without preparation: *~ remarks; a speech delivered ~.* **—off-hour** *n.* a period outside of business hours or rush hours.

of·fice (AWF·is, OF–) *n.* **1** a place from which a service is carried out: *Our ~ is closed on Sundays; the post ~.* **2** a position of responsibility, esp. public: *the highest ~ of the nation.* **3** service: *through the good* **offices** *of a friend; reciting the divine ~* (i.e. prayers); *the last ~s* (i.e. rites for the dead). **—of·fice·hold·er** *n.* a government official. **—office hours** hours of business. **—of·fi·cer** *n.* anyone holding a position of authority: *chief executive ~; a police ~; commissioned and warrant ~s of the armed forces.* **—of·fi·cial** (uh·FISH·ul) *adj.* having to do with an office; hence, authorized; also, formal: *an ~ uniform, announcement, record; Is the appointment ~?* ***n.*** a person holding office; officer; **of·fi·cial·dom** (–dum) *n.;* **of·fi·cial·ism** *n.;* **of·fi·cial·ly** *adv.* **—of·fi·ci·ant** (–ee·unt) *n.* an officiating clergyman. **—of·fi·ci·ate** *v.* **-ates, -at·ed, -at·ing** perform official duties (*as* chairman, *at* a ceremony, etc.). **—of·fi·cious** (–shus) *adj.* meddlesome, esp. from a position of authority; **of·fi·cious·ly** *adv.;* **of·fi·cious·ness** *n.*

off·ing (AWF–) *n.* the distant sea as seen from the shore; hence, the immediate future: *Many reforms are* **in the offing** (i.e. impending). **—off·ish** *adj. Informal.* aloof or reserved in manner. **—off-key** *adj.* not on the right (musical) note; not harmonious. **—off-lim·its** *adj.* out of bounds. **—off-line** *adj.* & *adv.* not ON-LINE. **—off·print** *n.* & *v.* (make) a separate print or small edition from a larger publication, as of a magazine article. **—off-sea·son** (–see·zun) *n.* & *adj.* (the period) outside the regular season: *an ~ fare to Florida.* **—off·set** *n.* **1** a transferring, as printing from an impression made by type on a rubber cylinder instead of directly on paper. **2** a bend in a screwdriver to enable it to reach a hidden screwhead. ***—v.*** (–SET) **-sets, -set, -set·ting** balance; compensate for: *higher wages to ~ inflationary price hikes.* **—off·shoot** *n.* something proceeding from a main part, as a branch growing from a main stem; derivative. **—off·shore** *adj.* & *adv.* away from the shore: *winds blowing ~; an ~ oil well.* **—off·side** *adj.* & *adv.* in hockey, soccer, etc., illegally ahead of the puck, ball, etc. **—off·spring** *n., pl.* **-spring(s)** descendant or progeny; also, outcome. **—off·stage** *n.* part of the stage not visible to the audience; ***adj.*** & ***adv.*** private(ly); behind the scenes. **—off-the-cuff** *adj.* & *adv. Informal.* offhand. **—off-the-re·cord** *adj.* confidential. **—off-track** *adj.* away from the race track: *~ betting.* **—off-white** *n.* & *adj.* (of) a grayish or yellowish white. **—off-year** *n.* year of reduced activity or production; also, a year outside of a regular presidential election year.

O.F.M. Order of Friars Minor (Franciscans).

oft (AWFT) *adv. Poet.* often. **—of·ten** (AWFN, –tn) *adv.* frequently; also **of·ten·times.**

o·gle (OH·gl) *v.* **o·gles, o·gled, o·gling** glance with amorous desire at; ***n.*** an amorous glance; **o·gler** *n.*

o·gre (OH·gur) *n.* a man-eating monster of folklore; *fem.* **o·gress** (–gris); **o·gre·ish** *adj.*

oh *interj.* calling someone's attention, expressing surprise, etc.: *Oh John! Oh boy! Oh yes? Oh no! Oh-oh!*

OH Ohio **—O·hi·o** (oh·HYE·oh) a Midwestern U.S. state; 41,222 sq.mi. (106,764 km^2); *cap.* Columbus; **O·hi·o·an** *n.* & *adj.*

ohm *n.* a unit of electrical resistance; **ohm·ic** *adj.*

o·ho (oh·HOH) *interj.* expressing surprise, taunting, etc.

oil *n.* **1** a greasy or fatty liquid that is lighter than water, obtained from mineral, animal, or vegetable matter. **2** petroleum. **3** oil color or oil painting. ***—v.*** treat, supply, or lubricate with oil. ***—adj.*** of or having to do with oil; **oil·cloth** *n.* heavy waterproof cloth treated with oil or paint and used as covering for tables, walls, etc. **—oil color** paint in which oil is the vehicle. **—oil-shale** shale containing oil. **—oil·skin** *n.* oilcloth; usu. **oilskins** *n.pl.* clothes made of oilskin. **—oil well** a well drilled for obtaining petroleum. **—oil·y** *adj.* **oil·i·er, -i·est** **1** of or like oil; greasy: *~ cloth, hands.* **2** too smooth; unctuous; fawning: *his ~ tongue; her ~ smile.*

oink *n.* & *v.* (make) the noise of a hog.

oint·ment *n.* a fatty medicinal or cosmetic preparation to put on the skin.

O·jib·wa (oh·JIB·way, –wah) *n.* (a member of) an Algonkian-speaking Indian people who formerly lived around Lake Superior; also **O·jib·way.**

OK or **o·kay** (–KAY, OH–) *adj., adv.* & *interj.* all right; ***n., pl.*** **OK's** or **o·kays** approval; ***v.*** **OK's** or **o·kays, OK'd** or **o·kayed, OK'ing** or **o·kay·ing** approve. **—o·key-doke** (OH·kee·DOKE) *adj.* & *interj. Slang.* same as OK; also **o·key-do·key.**

OK or **Okla.** Oklahoma. **—O·kie** (OH·kee) *n.* a migrant agricultural worker from Oklahoma in the 1930's.

O·ki·na·wa (oh·kuh·NAH·wuh) an island prefecture of Japan, off its S. tip; 922 sq.mi. (2,389 km^2); *cap.* Naha.

O·kla·ho·ma (oh·cluh·HOH·muh) a S.C. state of the U.S.; 69,919 sq.mi. (181,089 km^2); *cap.* **Oklahoma City; O·kla·ho·man** *n.* & *adj.*

o·kra (OH·kruh) *n.* an African plant bearing sticky green pods used in stews, to thicken soup, etc.

old *adj.* **old·er** or **eld·er, old·est** or **eld·est** **1** grown in years; not young: *an ~ lady.* **2** having existed, been in use, etc. for some time: *~ clothes; a good ~ friend.* **3** (advanced) in age: *How ~ is the baby? She's a year ~.* **4** former: *a teacher's ~ students; ~ school ties.* —***n.*** the past time: *days* **of old; the old** old persons or things; **old·ish** *adj.* somewhat old; **old·ness** *n.* —**old country** immigrant's original country. —**old·en** *adj. Poet.* old: *in ~ days.* —**old-fash·ioned** (–und) *adj.* old in fashion, ways, tastes, etc.; also out-of-fashion: *an ~ dress.* —**old fog(e)y** See FOGY. —**Old Glory** the U.S. flag. —**old hand** an experienced person. —**old hat** *Slang.* commonplace; passé. —**old·ie** or **old·y** *n.* **-old·ies** *Informal.* something old, as a once-popular song or movie. —**old lady** *Slang.* one's mother or wife. —**old-line** *adj.* established; conservative. —**old maid** a woman who has never married; also, a prim or fussy person; **old-maid·ish** *adj.* —**old man** *Slang.* one's father or husband. —**old master** a distinguished European painter before 1700; also, a work by an old master. —**old school** the conservative or old-fashioned group of society; **old-school** *adj.* —**old·ster** *n. Informal.* an old person. —**Old Testament** the earlier part of the Bible containing the history of the Jews; "the Hebrew Bible." —**old-time** *adj.* of the past; of long standing; **old-tim·er** *n. Informal.* a veteran; oldster. —**Old World** Europe, Asia, and Africa; the Eastern Hemisphere; **Old-World** *adj.*

o·lé (oh·LAY) *interj. & n. Spanish.* a shout of approval.

o·le·ag·i·nous (oh·lee·AJ·i·nus) *adj.* producing oil; also, oily.

o·le·an·der (OH·lee–) *n.* a poisonous shrub with lance-shaped leaves and roselike flowers.

o·le·ic (–LEE–) **acid** an unsaturated fatty acid used in soaps. —**ole(o)-** *comb. form.* oil: as in *oleaginous, oleomargarine.* —**o·le·o** (OH·lee·oh) *n.* short form of **o·le·o·mar·ga·rine** (–MAR·juh·rin) *n.* same as MARGARINE.

ol·fac·to·ry (–FAC·tuh–) *adj.* of the sense of smell: *~ organ, nerves.*

ol·i·gar·chy (OL·uh·gar·kee) *n.* **-chies** a state or corporation ruled by a small group; also, the group or their government; **ol·i·gar·chic** (–GAR·kic) or **-chi·cal** *adj.* —**Ol·i·go·cene** (OL·uh·go·seen) *n. & adj.* (of) the third epoch of the Cenozoic era of the earth, beginning about 40 million years ago.

o·li·o (OH·lee·oh) *n.* **-os** a stew of meats and vegetables; hence, a medley; also, a hodgepodge.

ol·ive (OL·iv) *n.* a Mediterranean evergreen tree with soft gray-green leaves, bearing small, oval fruit that is purple to black when ripe and contains much oil; ***adj.*** yellow to yellow-green; **olive branch** the branch of the olive as a peace emblem; **olive drab** a dark olive cloth, formerly used for army uniforms; **olive green** the color of the unripe olive; yellowish green. —**ol·i·vine** (–veen) *n.* a greenish silicate of magnesium or iron.

O·lym·pi·a (–LIM·pee·uh) **1** capital of Washington. **2** a plain in ancient Greece where **O·lym·pic games,** or **Olympics,** were held every four years: *The modern international Olympics started in 1876.* —**O·lym·pi·an** (–pee·un) *adj.* of or from Olympia or Olympus; hence, celestial or exalted like a god; ***n.*** **1** an Olympic athlete. **2** a god. —**O·lym·pus** a mountain in N. Greece, the supposed home of the gods.

om (OHM) *n.* a Hindu mantra or sacred syllable.

O·ma·ha (OH·muh·haw) a city of E. Nebraska; ***n.*** (a member of) an American Indian people who lived in the Omaha area.

O·man (oh·MAHN) an independent sultanate on the S.E. coast of the Arabian Peninsula; 82,000 sq.mi. (212,400 km²); *cap.* Muscat.

om·buds·man (OM·budz·mun, –BUDZ–) *n.* **-men** an independent government official investigating citizens' complaints against the government.

o·me·ga (–MEE·guh, –MAY–) *n.* the last letter of the Greek alphabet. (Ω,ω).

om·e·let(te) (OM·lit, –uh·lit) *n.* eggs beaten and cooked in a pan without stirring.

o·men (OH·mun) *n.* something considered as foretelling a future event, as a howling dog supposed to mean death. —**om·i·nous** (OM·uh·nus) *adj.* (as if) threatening evil; **om·i·nous·ly** *adv.*

o·mis·sion (–MISH·un) *n.* an omitting or thing omitted. —**o·mit** (–MIT) *v.* **o·mits, o·mit·ted, o·mit·ting** fail to include; also, fail to do; *to ~ a name from a list; Do not ~ to look down from the top of the tower.*

omni- *comb.form.* all: as in *omnibus, omnipotent.* —**om·ni·bus** (OM·nuh–) *n.* **-bus·es** original form of BUS; ***adj.*** dealing with many items at once: *an ~ bill.* —**om·nip·o·tent** (–NIP·uh·tunt) *adj.* all-powerful, as God; **the Omnipotent** God; **om·nip·o·tence** *n.* —**om·ni·pres·ent** (–PREZ·nt) *adj.* present everywhere at all times, as God: **om·ni·pres·ence** *n.* —**om·nis·cient** (–NISH·unt) *adj.* knowing all things, as God; **om·nis·cience** *n.* —**om·ni·um-gath·er·um** (OM·nee–) *n.* a miscellaneous collection or assemblage. —**om·niv·o·rous** (–NIV·uh·rus) *adj.* eating any sort of food indiscriminately, as a bear: *an ~ reader;* **om·niv·o·rous·ly** *adv.;* **om·niv·o·rous·ness** *n.*

on (AWN,ON) *prep.* **1** [indicating position implying contact from above or imposition]: *the food ~ the table; shoes ~ your feet; pictures ~ the wall; sitting ~ a committee* (i.e. as a member); *a tax ~ profits; heaped insult ~ insult; was ~ the phone all morning.* **2** toward: *a march ~ Washington.* **3** by means of: *talking ~ the* *phone.* **4** [indicating an engaged condition or process]: *a house ~ fire; cars ~ sale; men ~ business.* **5** [indicating time]: *~ a clear day; ~ our departure; ~ your birthday.* **6** concerning: *a lecture ~ poetry; books ~ Milton; bent ~ mischief.* —**adv.** **1** [corresponding to *prep.* 1]: *Put your coat ~;* **on and off** now and then; **on to** *Informal.* aware of. **2** [indicating the beginning of an activity]: *Turn the lights ~.* **3** [indicating continuation of an activity]: *Let's move ~; Hold ~ to the ropes; Go ~ with your speech! The story went* **on and on** (i.e. without stopping); **and so on** et cetera; and so forth. —**adj.** in progress or operation: *The movie is ~; The switch was ~; Press the ~ button.*

on·a·ger (ON·uh·jur) *n.* **1** a wild ass of W.C. Asia. **2** a catapult used in ancient and medieval warfare.

once (WUNCE) *adv.* (at) one time; on one occasion: *visits us ~ a year; a ~* (i.e. formerly) *wealthy man; never ~* (i.e. ever) *was late;* **once (and) for all** finally and conclusively; **once in a while** now and then; **once upon a time** long ago. —**conj.** as soon as: *You can ask him ~ he is here.* —**n.** one time: *Lend me the car just this ~;* **adj.** former: *the ~ and future king.* —**at once 1** immediately. **2** simultaneously. —**once-o·ver** *n. Informal.* a quick, evaluating look or action.

on·com·ing (ON·cum–) *n.* & *adj.* approach(ing): *the ~ (of) winter; ran into ~ traffic.*

one (WUN) *n.* a single person or thing; also, the cardinal number 1: *Are you the ~ who phoned? 1 is the smallest whole number;* **at one** in agreement. —**adj.:** *~ boy; two people of ~* (i.e. same) *mind; a call from ~* (i.e. a certain) *John Smith;* **one·ness** *n.* —**pron.:** *We have room for only ~; ~* (i.e. any person) *should be kind to animals; ~ for you and ~ for me; family members who love* **one another.**

O·nei·da (oh·NYE·duh) *n.* (a member of) an Iroquois Indian people formerly living in C. New York state.

O'Neill (oh·NEEL), **Eugene.** 1888–1953, U.S. playwright.

one-lin·er *n.* a joke or wisecrack in one sentence.

on·er·ous (ON·uh·rus) *adj.* burdensome or laborious: *an ~ task; ~ duties.*

one·self (wun·SELF) *pron.* one's own self: *a job difficult to do all* **by oneself** (i.e. without help); **be oneself** act naturally; also, feel well or normal. —**one-sid·ed** (WUN·SYE·did) *adj.* having one side more prominent or more developed; hence, unequal; uneven; also, prejudiced: *a ~ leaf, game, decision, umpire.* —**one-time** *adj.* former. —**one-to-one** *adj.* of two sets, matching every element in one with one and only one in the other: *no ~ correspondence between vowel sounds and letters.* —**one-track** *adj. Informal.* thinking about just one thing: *a ~ mind.* —**one-up** (–UP) *adj. Informal.* in a position of advantage (over another); **one-up·man·ship** *n.* the art or practice of keeping one step ahead of one's competitor. —**one-way** *adj.* in one direction only: *~ traffic, ticket* (i.e. not round-trip), *mirror* (to hide behind and look through).

on·go·ing *adj.* progressing; moving forward.

on·ion (UN·yun) *n.* a plant of the lily family with a pungent edible bulb; also, the bulb. —**on·ion·skin** *n.* a tough, thin, translucent paper.

on-line *adj.* & *adv.* directly connected to a computer: *an ~ typewriter; a sorter operating ~.* —**on·look·er** *n.* a spectator.

on·ly (OHN·lee) *adj.* alone of its kind; sole: *an ~ son; the ~ boy for my girl.* —**adv.** solely: *~ one pair of feet; He's ~* (i.e. just) *a child; I can ~ walk or run; I would fly* **if only** *I could; I would be* **only too** *glad to fly.* —**conj.** but: *I would fly, ~ I have no wings.*

on·o·mat·o·poe·ia (on·uh·mat·uh·PEE·uh) *n.* imitation of sounds, as in word-formation (e.g. "meow," "crash"), or the use of words suggestive of sense, as in Dryden's "The double double double beat of the thundering drum"; **on·o·mat·o·poe·ic** or **on·o·mat·o·po·et·ic** (–poh·ET·ic) *adj.*

On·on·da·ga (on·un·DAW·guh, –DAH–) *n.* a member of an Iroquois Indian people formerly living in C. New York state.

on·rush *n.* a rushing forward; **on·rush·ing** *adj.* —**on·set** *n.* a vigorous start or attack: *the ~ of a disease, winter, of an enemy.* —**on·shore** *adj.* & *adv.* on or toward the shore; not offshore: *~ oil; winds blowing ~.* —**on·slaught** (ON·slawt) *n.* a violent attack.

Ont. *Abbrev.* for **On·tar·i·o** (–TAIR·ee·oh) **1** a S.E. Canadian province; 412,582 sq. mi. (1,068,582 km²); *cap.* Toronto; **On·tar·i·an** *n.* & *adj.* **2 Lake Ontario** the smallest of the Great Lakes.

on·to (ON·too) *prep.* **1** to and upon: *thrown ~ the ground.* **2** *Informal.* on to; aware of: *Don't let the other guy get ~ our plans.*

on·tog·e·ny (–TOJ·uh·nee) *n.* (the history of) the development of an individual organism from egg to birth and growth. —**on·tol·o·gy** (–TOL–) *n.* the metaphysics of being and reality.

o·nus (OH–) *n.* burden or responsibility: *the ~ of proving a theory.*

on·ward (–wurd) *adv.* forward; also **on·wards.** —**adj.:** *the ~ march of events; an ~ journey.*

on·yx (ON·ix) *n.* a banded variety of marble or agate used as a gem, esp. for carving cameos.

oo·dles (OO·dlz) *n.pl. Informal.* a great amount (*of* something).

o·o·lite (OH·uh–) *n.* a limestone rock or deposit with a concentric or radial crystalline structure; **o·o·lit·ic** (–LIT–) *adj.:* *~ limestone, chert.*

oomph *n. Slang.* sexual attractiveness; also, vigor.

oops same as WHOOPS.

ooze (OOZ) *v.* **ooz·es, oozed, ooz·ing** leak out or seep gradually, as through small holes: *blood ~ing from a wound; a broken pot ~ing water.* —***n.*** **1** something that oozes. **2** mud or slime, esp. the deposit at the bottom of a body of water. **3** a bog or marsh. —**oo·zy** *adj.* **-zi·er, -zi·est** oozing; also, slimy; **oo·zi·ness** *n.*

op (art) abstract painting in geometric patterns creating optical illusions of flickering movement; optical art.

op. opus. —**O.P.** observation post; Order of Preachers; out of print.

o·pac·i·ty (–PAS–) *n.* **-ties** a being opaque; also, something opaque.

o·pal (OH·pl) *n.* a gemstone remarkable for reflecting light in a rainbowlike play of colors. —**o·pal·es·cent** (–LES·nt) *adj.;* **o·pal·es·cence** *n.*

o·paque (oh·PAKE) *adj.* impenetrable by light, sound, heat, etc., esp. not transparent or translucent; hence, mentally obtuse or stupid; **o·paque·ly** *adv.;* **o·paque·ness** *n.*

op art same as OP.

op. cit. in the work cited.

ope *v.* **opes, oped, op·ing** *Archaic.* open.

OPEC (OH·pec) Organization of Petroleum Exporting Countries.

Op-Ed (page) a newspaper page, usu. facing the editorial page, containing special features.

o·pen (OH·pn) *adj.* **1** not closed, covered, confined, clogged, etc.: *Walk in through the ~ door; an ~ box, wound, view; ~ waters* (i.e. not frozen). **2** having holes: *Netting is an ~ fabric.* **3** public, not secret: *an ~ violation, challenge, letter.* **4** undecided: *an ~ question.* **5** receptive; not prejudiced: *an ~ mind; a mind* **open to** *suggestions.* **6** generous: *gives to charity with an ~ hand; quite ~* (i.e. straightforward) *with everyone.* —***v.*** make or become open: *to ~ a carton; the door ~ing on the left; Schools ~ after holidays.* —***n.*** **the open** **1** open land or water; the outdoors; public knowledge. **2** a tournament open to amateurs and professionals: *the U.S. Open* (i.e. golf tournament). —**o·pen·er** *n.* —**o·pen·ly** *adv.;* **o·pen·ness** *n.* —**open air** the outdoors; **o·pen-air** *adj.: an ~ theater.* —**o·pen-and-shut case** *Informal.* something that is straightforward or obvious. —**o·pen-end·ed** *adj.* unlimited. —**o·pen-faced** *adj.* **1** candid-looking. **2** of a sandwich, without a top slice of bread. —**o·pen-hand·ed** *adj.* liberal in giving. —**o·pen-heart surgery** surgery done on a heart while its functions are carried on by mechanical means. —**o·pen-hearth** *adj.* of a steel-melting furnace, that is open directly to the furnace. —**open house** hospitality that is open to everyone, esp. a social event at an institution for a promotional purpose; **open housing** housing without discrimination against race, religion, etc. —**o·pen·ing** *n.* **1** a gap or hole; also, a clearing. **2** a beginning of operations. **3** a vacant position or job. —**o·pen-mind·ed** *adj.* free from prejudices; receptive to new ideas. —**open shop** a business employing union and nonunion workers, not a CLOSED SHOP. —**o·pen·work** *n.* ornamental work with openings in it.

op·er·a (OP·uh·ruh) *n.* **1** a *pl.* of OPUS. **2** a dramatic composition in which the text is set to music, usu. with orchestral accompaniment; **op·er·at·ic** (–RAT–) *adj.;* **opera glasses** small binoculars for use in a theater. —**op·er·a·ble** (OP·uh·ruh·bl) *adj.* **1** practicable; feasible. **2** that can be surgically operated on. —**op·er·ate** *v.* **-ates, -at·ed, -at·ing** **1** work; run: *He ~s an elevator; elevators ~ing night and day; unfavorable factors ~ing against us.* **2** perform surgery. —**op·er·a·tion** (–RAY–) *n.* **1** an action or procedure: *the smooth ~ of a machine; the ~ of a law, plan, factory; a surgical ~ to remove a tumor; addition, subtraction, and other arithmetical ~s.* **2** a planned and executed mission or project: *military ~s; Operation Breadbasket;* **op·er·a·tion·al** *adj.* having to do with operation; also, functioning. —**op·er·a·tive** (OP·uh·ruh·tiv) *adj.* effective: *an ~ clause; ~ treatment;* ***n.*** an operator, esp. a spy or detective. —**op·er·a·tor** *n.* **1** a skilled worker: *a telephone ~.* **2** *Informal.* a skillful user of men and materials for his own ends: *a smooth ~.* —**op·er·et·ta** (–RET·uh) *n.* a light, short opera such as Gilbert and Sullivan's *The Mikado.*

oph·thal·mic (of·THAL–) *adj.* of the eye(s); **oph·thal·mol·o·gist** (–MOL–) *n.* an eye specialist; **oph·thal·mol·o·gy** *n.* the branch of medicine dealing with the eyes and eye diseases. —**oph·thal·mo·scope** (–THAL–) *n.* an optical instrument for viewing the interior of the eye.

o·pi·ate (OH·pee·it) *n.* & *adj.* **1** (a narcotic drug) containing opium. **2** (anything) that soothes or dulls pain.

o·pine (oh·PINE) *v.* **o·pines, o·pined, o·pin·ing** express the opinion *(that).* —**o·pin·ion** (uh·PIN·yun) *n.* a conclusion or judgment that seems true or probable though open to dispute: *a matter of ~, not a certainty; has a good ~ of the applicant; a doctor's professional ~; an ~* (i.e. legal statement) *handed down by a court;* **o·pin·ion·at·ed** *adj.* obstinate in one's opinions.

o·pi·um (OH·pee–) *n.* a powerful narcotic obtained from the seeds of an Asiatic poppy.

o·pos·sum (uh·POS–) *n.* a furry, tree-dwelling North American marsupial that will pretend to be dead if surprised on the ground.

op·po·nent (uh·POH·nunt) *n.* one who opposes, esp. in a formal contest such as a game or election.

op·por·tune (OP·ur–) *adj.* done or happening at a favorable time; timely: *an ~ arrival, moment;* **op·por·tune·ly** *adv.* —**op·por·tun·ism** (–TUE–) *n.* the taking selfish advantage of opportunities regardless of principles; **op·por·tun·ist** *n.;* **op·por·tu·nis·tic** (–NIS–) *adj.* —**op·por·tu·ni·ty** (–TUE–) *n.* **-ties** a favorable occasion; also, a good chance or prospect: *an ~ for mischief; a job ~.*

op·pose (uh·POZE) *v.* **op·pos·es, op·posed, op·pos·ing** be or place in the way of, against, or in contrast: *We ~ war; Truth is ~d to falsehood; Man, as ~d to beasts, can talk; You pick up objects by ~ing thumb to fingers; the* **op·pos·a·ble** *thumb of man and the great apes.* —**op·po·site** (OP·uh·zit) *n.* & *adj.* (anything) set against or contrary (*to* something): *Truth is the ~ of lying; They have ~ meanings; diametrically ~, as north and south; the house ~ to ours* (across the street); ***prep.*** & ***adv.:*** *the house ~ ours; the tree standing ~; Liz Taylor playing ~* (i.e. in a complementary role with) *Burton;* **op·po·site·ly** *adv.* —**opposite number** a person or thing corresponding to another in a different system or organization; counterpart. —**op·po·si·tion** (–ZISH·un) *n.* act of opposing or state of being opposed; contrast; also, one that opposes: *the leader of the Opposition* (party) *in parliament; A "full moon" is in ~ to* (i.e. directly facing) *the sun.*

op·press (uh·PRES) *v.* **1** keep down in a cruel way: *an ~ed minority; poor people ~ed by heavy taxes.* **2** weigh down; burden: *minds ~ed with anxiety.* —**op·pres·sion** *n.* —**op·pres·sor** *n.* —**op·pres·sive** (–siv) *adj.: the ~ heat of summer; ~ laws, taxation;* **op·pres·sive·ly** *adv.;* **op·pres·sive·ness** *n.*

op·pro·bri·ous (uh·PROH·bree·us) *adj.* scornful or abusive: *~ epithets;* **op·pro·bri·ous·ly** *adv.* —**op·pro·bri·um** *n.* scornful condemnation; infamy: *a term of ~.*

opt. optical; optician; optional.

opt *v.* choose (*to* do something, *for* a course of action, *out of* a group, etc.): *Half the membership* **opted** (i.e. dropped) **out.** —**op·ta·tive** (OP·tuh·tiv) *n.* & *adj.* (a verb mood) expressing wish or desire, as "Would (that) I were wealthy!"

op·tic *adj.* of the eye or eyesight: *the ~ nerve;* **op·ti·cal** *adj.* having to do with light and vision: *an ~ instrument, illusion, defect such as myopia; ~ scanning of print for computer processing using a photoelectric* **optical scanner; op·ti·cal·ly** *adv.* —**optical art** same as OP ART. —**optical maser** same as LASER. —**op·ti·cian** (–TISH·un) *n.* one who makes or sells eyeglasses. —**op·tics** *n.pl.* [takes *sing. v.*] the branch of physics dealing with light and its properties and phenomena.

op·ti·mism (OP·tuh–) *n.* the philosophy of looking at the bright side of things or of taking the most hopeful view; **op·ti·mist** *n.;* **op·ti·mis·tic** (–MIS–) *adj.* —**op·ti·mum** *n.* & *adj.* (amount, degree, condition, etc.) that is the best or most favorable to some end: *the ~ temperature for eggs to hatch;* **op·ti·mal** *adj.;* **op·ti·mal·ly** *adv.*

op·tion (OP·shun) *n.* the right or privilege of choosing; also, a choice: *the ~ of paying a fine or going to jail; a stock ~ to buy or sell stocks at a given price within a specified period; a publisher buying an ~ on an author's future work;* **op·tion·al** *adj.* not required: *an ~ course of study;* **op·tion·al·ly** *adv.*

op·tom·e·try (–TOM·uh·tree) *n.* the testing of eyes for vision and prescribing of glasses to correct defects; **op·tom·e·trist** *n.*

op·u·lent (OP·yuh·lunt) *adj.* suggestive of great wealth and luxury: *the ~ court of a prince; an ~* (i.e. abundant) *growth of hair;* **op·u·lence** *n.*

o·pus (OH–) *n.,pl.* **op·er·a** or **o·pus·es** a work, esp. a musical composition, its number indicating the order of publication: *Symphony No. 6 in B minor, ~ 74.*

or *conj.* introducing an alternative ("black or white") or equivalent ("opus, or work").

-or *n. suffix.* **1** one that does (as specified): as in *actor, creator, objector.* **2** an abstract quality or condition: as in *horror, pallor, terror.*

OR operating room; Oregon; owner's risk (also **o.r.**).

or·a·cle (OR·uh·cl) *n.* **1** a very wise person or his prophetic utterance. **2** in ancient Greece and Rome, an answer, often cryptically worded, given by a god to a crucial question put through a priest concerning the future; also, such a priest(ess) or a place such as Delphi where oracles were delivered. —**o·rac·u·lar** (–RAK–) *adj.* like an oracle; mystifying; **o·rac·u·lar·ly** *adv.*

o·ral (OR·ul) *adj.* of or having to do with the mouth: *Does a mouthwash help ~ hygiene? ~ contraceptive* (i.e. the Pill); *~* (i.e. spoken) *and written language; an* **oral history** *in the form of tape-recorded interviews with people of the time.* —***n.:*** *failed his ~s* (i.e. oral tests); **o·ral·ly** *adv.*

or·ange (OR·inj) *n.* a round, reddish-yellow, citrus fruit (tree); also, reddish yellow; ***adj.*** of the color orange. —**or·ange·ade** (–JADE) *n.* a drink made with orange juice, sugar, and water. —**orange pekoe** a larger size or grade of PEKOE. —**or·ange·ry** *n.* **-ries** a hothouse for growing oranges in a cold climate.

o·rang·u·tan (o·RANG·oo·tan) *n.* a large arboreal ape of Borneo and Sumatra; also **o·rang·ou·tang.**

o·rate (o·RATE) *v.* **o·rates, o·rat·ed, o·rat·ing** speak in a pompous manner; **o·ra·tion** (–RAY–) *n.* a rhetorical or ceremonial speech; **or·a·tor** (OR·uh–) *n.* an eloquent public speaker; **or·a·tor·i·cal** (–TOR–) *adj.;* **or·a·tor·i·cal·ly** *adv.* —**or·a·tor·i·o** (–TOR–) *n.* **-os** a musical composition, originally on a biblical theme, as in Handel's *Messiah,* sung to orchestral accompaniment by soloists and a chorus. —**or·a·to·ry** (OR·uh–) *n.* **-ries** **1** skill in or the art of public speaking. **2** a small chapel.

orb *n.* globe, esp. the sun, moon, or other heavenly sphere. —**or·bit** *n.* & *v.* (move in or put into) a circular path, as of a planet or artificial satellite: *an ~ing observatory; a service module in a parking ~ around the moon; the ~* (i.e. range) *of one's ambitions;* **or·bit·al** *adj.* —**or·bit·er** *n.* one that orbits, as a space shuttle.

or·chard (OR·churd) *n.* a plot containing fruit trees or nut trees; also, the trees collectively; **or·chard·ist** or **or·chard·man** *n.*

or·ches·tra (OR·ki·struh) *n.* **1** a group of musicians playing together on various stringed, wind, and percussion instruments; also, the instruments collectively. **2** the space, or **orchestra pit,** between the audience and the stage in a theater; also, the whole main floor of a theater. —**or·ches·tral** (–KES·trul) *adj.* —**or·ches·trate** (OR·ki–) *v.* **-trates, -trat·ed, -trat·ing** compose or arrange (music), as for an orchestra; hence, organize harmoniously: *a well-~d effort;* **or·ches·tra·tion** (–STRAY–) *n.*

or·chid (OR·kid) *n.* **1** a beautiful flower with three petals, including a specially shaped "lip," as in the lady-slipper; also, a pale purple. **2** an orchid plant.

ord. ordained; order; ordinal.

or·dain (–DAIN) *v.* decree or establish, as by a supreme power; hence, invest (a priest, minister, or rabbi) with his office: *as God had ~ed from eternity; was ~ed priest by his bishop.*

or·deal (–DEEL, OR–) *n.* a severe test or experience.

or·der *n.* **1** arrangement according to a system; harmony with what is considered good: *words in alphabetical ~; a room left in good ~; Police maintain law and ~* (in society). **2** an authoritative telling of what one wants; command or requisition: *"Go home" is an ~, not a request; a money ~ purchased at a bank; a customer's ~; delivery of an ~* (i.e. what is ordered). **3** rank; grade; class: *The squirrel, beaver, and rat families belong to the rodent ~ of the mammal class; Barons are the lowest ~ of nobles; an intellect of a high ~; Ministers and priests are said to* **take (holy) orders.** **4** an organized social or religious group: *the Carmelite Order; the Loyal Order of Moose.* **5** a form or style: *the Doric, Ionic, and Corinthian ~s of Greek architecture.* —**v.** [corresponding to the *n.* senses] **1:** *to ~* (i.e. arrange) *one's life, affairs.* **2:** *Doctors ~ patients to bed; She ~ed* (dinner) *for the family.* —**order about** (or **around**) tell to do this and that in a domineering way. —**call to order** order (a group or a member) to be quiet; **in order that** so that; **in order to** as a means to; so as to; **in** (or **out of**) **order** (not) working properly; also, (not) according to rules; **on order** ordered but not yet received; **to order** as required by buyer. —**or·der·ly** *adj.* well-behaved; also, well-organized; ***adv.*** in a well-organized manner; ***n.,*** *pl.* **-lies** a male attendant, as in a hospital or in the service of an army officer; **or·der·li·ness** *n.* —**or·di·nal** *n.* & *adj.* (a number such as 1st, 2nd, 3rd, etc.) expressing order in a series. —**or·di·nance** (OR·dn·unce) *n.* a law or regulation, esp. one made by a local authority such as a municipality. —**or·di·nar·y** (OR·dn·er·ee) *adj.* **1** usual or normal: *an ~ experience; Snow in summer is something* **out of the ordinary.** **2** common; hence, inferior: *an ~ dress; a very ~ girl, wine, poet.* —**or·di·nar·i·ly** (–NAIR–) *adv.* —**or·di·nate** *n.* the distance of a point on a graph along its vertical axis. —**or·di·na·tion** (–NAY–) *n.* an ordaining or being ordained as priest, minister, or rabbi. —**ord·nance** (ORD·nunce) *n.* military weapons and ammunition; also, the tools used in their manufacture and maintenance. —**or·do** (OR·doh) *n.* **-dos** or **-di·nes** (–neez) an annual Roman Catholic calendar containing detailed directions for each day's Mass and breviary.

Or·do·vi·cian (–VISH·un) *n.* & *adj.* (of) the second period of the Paleozoic era of the earth, beginning about 400 million years ago.

or·dure (OR·jur) *n.* dung or filth.

ore *n.* rock or mineral from which gold, silver, iron, sulfur, fluorides, and such metals and other deposits may be extracted.

öre (UR·uh) *n. sing.* & *pl.* a money unit and coin of Denmark, Norway, and Sweden, equal to 1/100 of a krona or krone.

o·re·ad (OR·ee–) *n.* in Greek myth, a mountain nymph.

Ore(g). Oregon.

o·reg·a·no (–REG·uh–) *n.* the Mediterranean marjoram.

Or·e·gon (OR·i·gun, –gon) a N.W. state of the U.S.; 96,981 sq.mi. (251,180 km²); *cap.* Salem; **Or·e·go·ni·an** (–GOH–) *n.* & *adj.*

org. organic; organization; organized.

or·gan (–gun) *n.* **1** a keyboard musical instrument used esp. in churches for the solemnity and grandeur of its sound effects which are produced by air forced through pipes, as in a *pipe organ,* or electrically, as in an *electronic organ;* also, any similar instrument such as a hand organ or mouth organ. **2** a body part with a specific function: *the ~ of speech, locomotion, digestion; the reproductive ~s of plants and animals.* **3** means of action or communication: *the army as an ~ of government; the official ~* (i.e. publication) *of a party.*

or·gan·dy or **or·gan·die** (OR·gun·dee) *n.* **-dies** a thin, stiff, transparent cotton fabric used for evening dresses, trimmings, etc.

or·gan·ic (–GAN–) *adj.* **1** of or having to do with a bodily organ: *an ~* (i.e. not functional) *disorder.* **2** relating to organization as a unit or whole, like that of a living organism: *the ~ unity of a literary work; ~ architecture that seems to grow out of its surroundings.* **3** of or having to do with living things; animal or vegetable: *~ evolution, fertilizers, matter* (such as peat), *chemistry* (of carbon compounds that make up living tissues). —**or·gan·i·cal·ly** *adv.* —**or·gan·ism** (OR·guh–) *n.* a living thing; **or·gan·**

is·mic (–NIZ–) *adj.* —**or·gan·ist** (OR·guh–) *n.* an organ player. —**or·gan·i·za·tion** (–guh·ni·ZAY–) *n.* an organizing, a being organized, or an organized thing: *the United Nations Organization; a business ~; an ~ man* (dedicated to his company); **or·gan·i·za·tion·al** *adj.* —**or·gan·ize** (OR·guh–) *v.* **-iz·es, -ized, -iz·ing** **1** make or form into a working unit or whole: *to ~ a campaign, one's thoughts, an essay; earthworms and such less ~d forms of life.* **2** form (into) a union or organization: *~d labor.* —**or·gan·iz·er** *n.* —**organo-** *comb.form.* organ or organic; **or·ga·no·phos·phate** (–FOS–) *n.* an organophosphorus pesticide such as malathion or parathion; **or·ga·no·phos·pho·r(o)us** (–fuh·rus) *adj.* containing phosphorus and carbon.

or·gan·za (–GAN–) *n.* a dress fabric like organdy made of silk or a synthetic.

or·gasm (OR·gazm) *n.* the climax of sexual excitement; **or·gas·mic** (–GAZ–) or **or·gas·tic** (–GAS–) *adj.*

or·gi·as·tic (–jee·AS–) *adj.* of or having to do with orgies. —**or·gy** (–jee) *n.* **-gies** (a party for) unrestrained indulgence in eating, drinking, sex, etc.

o·ri·el (OR·ee·ul) *n.* an upper-story bay window projecting outward from the wall face.

o·ri·ent (OR·ee·unt) *Poet. n.* the east; ***adj.*** rising: *the ~ sun.* —***v.*** (–ent) adjust (oneself) to a new situation; **o·ri·en·tate** (OR·ee–) *v.* **-tates, -tat·ed, -tat·ing** orient; also, place facing east; **o·ri·en·ta·tion** (–TAY–) *n.* —**Orient** E. Asia, as distinguished from Europe and America; **O·ri·en·tal** (–EN·tl) *n.* & *adj.* (a native) of the Orient: *Chinese are ~s; an ~ language.* —**or·i·en·teer·ing** (–ee·un·TEER–) *n.* the sport of navigating through the woods with map and compass.

or·i·fice (OR·uh·fis) *n.* a mouthlike opening or aperture, as of a tube.

o·ri·flamme (OR·uh·flam) *n.* a brightly colored banner, once carried to battle as an emblem; hence, a rallying point.

orig. origin; original(ly).

o·ri·ga·mi (or·uh·GAH·mee) *n.* the Japanese art of folding paper to make decorative objects.

or·i·gin (OR·uh·jin) *n.* a coming into being; beginning; hence, ancestry: *one's land of ~; "orgy" is of Greek ~; a man of humble ~; the ~s of civilization.* —**o·rig·i·nal** (–RIJ·uh·nl) *adj.* **1** initial or earliest: *the ~ inhabitants of the New World; translated from the ~ Latin* (text). **2** new; hence, inventive; also, not copied: *a very ~ idea; his ~ mind; an ~ work.* Also ***n.:*** *the ~ of the Mona Lisa; a translation close to the ~;* **o·rig·i·nal·ly** *adv.* **o·rig·i·nal·i·ty** (–NAL–) *n.* a being original, fresh, or creative.—**o·rig·i·nate** (–RIJ–) *v.* **-nates, -nat·ed, -nat·ing** come or bring into being, esp. as new: *Where did the rumor ~? Who ~d it?* **o·rig·i·na·tor** *n.;* **o·rig·i·na·tion** (–NAY–) *n.*

o·ri·ole (OR·ee–) *n.* an insect-eating songbird with beautiful feathers that weaves a hanging nest.

O·ri·on (aw·RYE·un) a bright constellation near the equator; also called "the Great Hunter."

or·i·son (–sun) *n. Archaic.* prayer.

Or·lon *Trademark.* an acrylic fiber used esp. for fabrics.

or·mo·lu (OR·muh·loo) *n.* brass or bronze resembling gold, used to decorate furniture.

or·na·ment (OR·nuh·munt) *n.* something added for greater beauty, as rings, bracelets, Christmas-tree decorations, etc.: *loveliness that needs no ~; a woman who is an ~ to her home;* ***v.*** (–ment) beautify; embellish: *lace to ~ a dress;* **or·na·men·ta·tion** (–TAY–) *n.* —**or·na·men·tal** (–MEN·tl) *adj.* —**or·nate** (–NATE) *adj.* much ornamented: *an ~ vase; ~* (i.e. flowery) *prose;* **or·nate·ly** *adv.;* **or·nate·ness** *n.*

or·ner·y (OR·nuh·ree) *adj. Informal.* mean or irritable: *an ~ beast, remark.*

ornith. *Abbrev.* for **or·ni·thol·o·gy** (–THOL–) *n.* the scientific study of birds; **or·ni·thol·o·gist** *n.* —**or·ni·tho·log·i·cal** (–thuh·LOJ–) *adj.*

oro- *comb.form.* mountain: as in **o·rog·e·ny** (–ROJ·uh–) *n.* formation of mountains; **o·rog·ra·phy** (–ROG·ruh–) *n.* geography of mountains.

o·ro·tund (OR·uh–) *adj.* of utterance, full-voiced or resonant; also, bombastic or pompous.

or·phan (OR·fun) *n.* a child deprived of a parent, often both, by death; ***adj.:*** *an ~ child, home* (i.e. for orphans); ***v.:*** *~ed by war, death, fire.* —**or·phan·age** (–ij) *n.* an institution that takes care of orphans. —**or·phan·hood** *n.*

Or·phe·us (OR·fee–) in Greek myth, a musician who could charm birds and beasts by playing on his lyre; **Or·phic** *adj.*

or·ris *n.* a species of iris whose underground stem, or **or·ris·root,** yields a fragrant oil used in perfumes.

ortho- *comb.form.* straight or correct: as in **or·tho·don·tia** (–DON·shuh) *n.* orthodontics; **or·tho·don·tics** *n.pl.* [takes *sing.v.*] the branch of dentistry dealing with the correction of tooth irregularities, as by use of braces; **or·tho·don·tic** *adj.;* **or·tho·don·tist** *n.* —**or·tho·dox** (OR·thuh–) *adj.* generally accepted or traditional, esp. in religious doctrine, practices, etc.: *an ~ Jew; the Eastern Orthodox Church;* **or·tho·dox·y** *n.* —**or·thog·ra·phy** (–THOG–) *n.* **-phies** (study or system of) spelling; **or·tho·graph·ic** (–GRAF–) *adj.* —**or·tho·pe·dics** (–PEE–) *n.pl.* [takes *sing.v.*] surgical correction and treatment of bone and joint deformities, diseases, fractures, etc.; **or·tho·pe·dic** *adj.;* **or·tho·pe·dist** *n.*

or·to·lan (OR·tl·un) *n.* a European bunting prized for its meat.

Or·well·i·an (–WEL–) *adj.* of society, dehumanized and regimented, as in the novel *1984* by **George Or·well** (–OR–), 1903–50, English writer.
Os osmium. —**O.S.** ordinary seaman. —**o.s.** or **o/s** out of stock.
O·sage (oh·SAJE) *n.* a member of a Siouan Indian people now living in Oklahoma.
O·sa·ka (–SAH–) a seaport of S. Japan.
O.S.B. Order of St. Benedict.
Os·car (–cur) *n.* a statuette awarded annually by the Academy of Motion Picture Arts and Science to the best stars, directors, producers, etc.
os·cil·late (OS·uh–) *v.* **-lates, -lat·ed, -lat·ing** swing like a pendulum; vary, as an electric current; hence, vacillate; **os·cil·la·tor** *n.;* **os·cil·la·tion** (–LAY–) *n.* —**os·cil·lo·scope** (–SIL·uh–) *n.* an instrument that shows variations of electrical current on a fluorescent screen; **os·cil·lo·scop·ic** (–SCOP–) *adj.;* **os·cil·lo·scop·i·cal·ly** *adv.*
os·cu·late (OS·kyuh–) *v.* **-lates, -lat·ed, -lat·ing** kiss; **os·cu·la·tion** (–LAY–) *n.*
-ose *suffix.* **1** *n.* carbohydrate: as in *cellulose, fructose.* **2** *adj.* full of or fond of: *bellicose, jocose, verbose.*
O.S.F. Order of St. Francis.
o·sier (OH·zhur) *n.* a willow whose pliable twigs are used in making baskets and furniture.
O·si·ris (oh·SYE–) in ancient Egypt, the chief god of the underworld.
-osis *suffix.* process or condition: as in *acidosis, metamorphosis, neurosis.*
Os·lo (OS–, OZ–) capital of Norway.
os·mi·um (OZ·mee–) *n.* a hard, brittle, metallic chemical element used in alloys.
os·mo·sis (–MOH–) *n.* the tendency of liquids and gases to pass through a semipermeable membrane or other porous material in order to equalize concentration on both sides: *Plant roots absorb minerals and oxygen enters the blood by ~;* **os·mot·ic** (–MOT–) *adj.*
os·prey (OS·pree) *n.* a bird of prey of the hawk family that catches fish with its sharp talons by diving into water feet first.
os·si·fy (OS·uh–) *v.* **-fies, -fied, -fy·ing** change into bone, as cartilage in old people; hence, make or become hardened, as in practices, attitudes, etc.; **os·si·fi·ca·tion** (–CAY–) *n.* —**os·su·ar·y** (OS·yoo·er·ee) *n.* **-ar·ies** a cave, vault, or urn containing bones of the dead.
os·ten·si·ble (–TEN–) *adj.* professed or seeming: *an ~ reason, not the real one;* **os·ten·si·bly** *adv.* —**os·ten·ta·tion** (–TAY–) *n.* a showy or pretentious display of wealth;
os·ten·ta·tious (–TAY·shus) *adj.;* **os·ten·ta·tious·ly** *adv.*
os·te·op·a·thy (os·tee·OP·uh·thee) *n.* a system of medicine that emphasizes the relationship of bones and muscles to the functioning of body organs; **os·te·o·path** (OS·tee·uh–) *n.;* **os·te·o·path·ic** (–PATH–) *adj.*
os·tler (OS·lur) *n. Rare.* hostler.
ost·mark *n.* See [1]MARK.
os·tra·cize (OS·truh–) *v.* **-ciz·es, -cized, -ciz·ing** banish (someone) from society, as in ancient Greece; **os·tra·cism** *n.*
os·trich *n.* a large, heavy, long-legged, flightless but swift-footed African bird, fabled to hide its head in the sand when frightened.
Os·we·go (–WEE–) **tea** a North American mint or the tea brewed from its leaves.
O.T. Old Testament.
O·thel·lo (–THEL·oh) one of Shakespeare's tragic characters, the Moorish hero of the play of that name.
oth·er (UDH·ur) *pron.* & *adj.* (different) person or thing from one already mentioned or implied: *my ~ parent; any ~ question; ~ than that; some ~ time, not now; One is David, who is the ~? Tom, Dick, and ~s;* **every other** every second (person or thing); **the other day** (or **night**) recently. —***adv.*** otherwise: *~ than to say "no."* —**oth·er·wise** (–wize) *adv.* **1** differently: *should be alive today but God willed ~;* ***adj.:*** *How could it be ~?* **2** in other respects: *an ~ eligible candidate* (but for his age). —**oth·er·world·ly** (–WURLD–) *adj.* of or having to do with a world to come, as after death; also, mental or imaginative: *a man of ~* (i.e. spiritual) *concerns;* **oth·er·world·li·ness** *n.*
o·ti·ose (OH·shee–) *adj.* purposeless or useless: *~ remarks, criticism.*
o·ti·tis (–TYE–) *n.* inflammation of the ear;
oto- *comb.form.* ear: as in **o·to·lar·yn·gol·o·gy** (–lair·ing·GOL–) *n.* medical specialty dealing with ailments of the ear, nose, and throat; **o·tol·o·gy** (–TOL–) *n.* branch of medicine dealing with the ear; **o·to·scope** (OH·tuh–) *n.* ear-examining instrument.
OTS Officer Training School.
Ot·ta·wa (OT·uh·wuh) **1** *n.* a member of an Indian people of S. Ontario and Michigan. **2** the capital of Canada, in S.E. Ontario, on the **Ottawa River,** a branch of the St. Lawrence.
ot·ter (OT·ur) *n.* an animal of the weasel family that lives close to water and feeds on fish.
ot·to·man (OT·uh–) *n.* a low, cushioned seat or footstool; **Ot·to·man** *n.* & *adj.* Turk(ish).
Oua·ga·dou·gou (wah·guh·DOO·goo) capital of Upper Volta.
ou·bli·ette (oo·blee·ET) *n.* a dungeon that can be opened only from the top.
ouch *interj.* expressing sudden pain.
ought (AWT) *auxiliary v.* [expressing what is right, desirable, due, etc.]: *You ~ to* (i.e. should) *know better; She ~ not be kept waiting.* —**ought·n't** ought not.
oui (WEE) *adv. French.* yes.
Oui·ja (WEE·juh) **board** *Trademark.* an oblong board with letters and numbers printed on it and a pointer that is supposed to be guided by

spirits when it indicates answers to questions, as at a séance.

ounce *n.* a unit of weight equal to 1/16 pound avoirdupois (28.3495 g) or 1/12 pound troy (31.1035 g); also, a *fluid ounce* or 1/16 pint (29.5735 ml).

our (OWR, AHR) *adj.* possessive case of WE: *~ family, books, dog.* **—ours** (OWRZ, AHRZ) *pron.* possessive of WE: *None of these is ~; ~ is a poodle;* **our·self** (–SELF) *pron.* [used by a court, editor, and others using "we" instead of "I"] myself; **our·selves** (–SELVZ) *pron.* reflexive or emphatic of WE or US: *We ~ did it; We speak only for ~.*

-ous *adj. suffix.* having: as in *ambitious, glorious, porous.*

oust *v.* drive or force out; expel: *an unruly player ~ed from a game.* **—oust·er** *n.* expulsion; eviction.

out *adv.* **1** away from the usual place, condition, etc., esp. away from the center or inside of something; hence, into the open: *She is gone ~; dropped ~ of school; when the moon comes ~; a coming-~* (i.e. into society) *party.* **2** forth; beyond: *stuck ~ her tongue; let the dog ~; to farm ~ work.* **3** to completion or exhaustion: *cried her heart ~; fought it ~ with him; The lights are going ~; The batsman flied ~* (i.e. was retired). **4** lacking; short: *I was ~ $5 after paying the bills; She was a few feet ~* (i.e. in error) *in her estimate;* **out of:** *We're ~ of coffee; bilked ~ of her savings; cried ~ of* (i.e. because of) *pain; carved ~ of* (i.e. from) *wood.* **—adj.:** *an ~ tray for papers going out; fashions that are in now and ~ later; He is* **out to** (i.e. intends to) *make money;* **out for** in search of. **—v.:** *Murder will ~* (i.e. be discovered). **—prep.** out through or along: *went ~ the door; driving ~ Lakeshore.* **—n.:** *people considered ~s in an exclusive society; without an ~* (*Informal.* excuse) *or alibi; knows all the ins and ~s;* **on the outs** *Informal.* quarreling; at odds. **—out-** *comb.form.* as in *outpatient, outlying, outshout.* **—out·age** (–ij) *n.* an interruption or suspension, as a power failure. **—out-and-out** *adj.* utter; complete: *an ~ falsehood.* **—out·back** *n.* back country; hinterland. **—out·bal·ance** (–BAL–) *v.* **-anc·es, -anced, -anc·ing** outweigh. **—out·bid** (–BID) *v.* **-bids,** *pt.* & *pp.* **-bid** or **-bid·den, -bid·ding** make a higher bid than. **—out·board** *adj.* outside the hull or body of a boat or other craft: *An* **outboard motor** *is fitted to a boat's stern;* **n.** an outboard motor or a boat equipped with one. **—out·bound** *adj.* traveling outward. **—out·break** *n.* a sudden occurrence or development, as of a war, disease, etc. **—out·build·ing** *n.* a building separate from the main building. **—out·burst** *n.* a bursting out, as of fury, laughter, joy, etc. **—out·cast** *n.* & *adj.* (a person or animal) that is cast out from home or society. **—out·class** (–CLAS) *v.* surpass. **—out·come** *n.* result; consequence. **—out·crop** *n.* the coming to the surface or an exposed surface of a rock or stratum; **v.** project or appear on the surface. **—out·cry** *n.* **-cries** an uproar; also, a crying out or scream. **—out·dat·ed** (–DAY–) *adj.* out-of-date. **—out·dis·tance** (–DIS–) *v.* **-tanc·es, -tanced, -tanc·ing** outstrip. **—out·do** (–DOO) *v.* **-does, -did, -done, -do·ing** do better than (others, previously, etc.). **—out·door** *adj.* of the outdoors; open-air: *an ~ game, life, theater.* **—out·doors** *adv.: sleeps ~; gone ~;* **n.** open air: *a lover of the great ~.* **—out·draw** (–DRAW) *v.* **-draws, -drew, -drawn, -draw·ing** attract a larger crowd than. **—out·er** *adj.* farther out; also, external: *an ~ circle, ear, garment.*

Outer Hebrides See HEBRIDES. **—Outer Mongolia** See MONGOLIA.

out·er·most *adj.* farthest from the center. **—outer space** space beyond the atmosphere; also, interstellar space; **out·er·wear** *n.* clothes worn over other clothes, as sweaters, jackets, coats, etc. **—out·face** *v.* **-fac·es, -faced, -fac·ing** face boldly. **—out·field** *n.* in baseball, the playing area or players beyond the infield; **out·field·er** *n.* **—out·fit** *n.* **1** equipment for an activity; also, a set of clothes; **v. -fits, -fit·ted, -fit·ting:** *~d for a camping trip; to ~ an expedition;* **out·fit·ter** *n.* **2** a group such as a business organization or military unit. **—out·flank** (–FLANK) *v.* outmaneuver or outwit, as by getting around the flank of enemy troops. **—out·flow** *n.* a flowing out or what flows out. **—out·fox** *v.* outwit; outsmart. **—out·gen·er·al** (–JEN–) *v.* surpass in leadership. **—out·go** *n.* **-goes** expenditure; **out·go·ing** *adj.* **1** sociable. **2** going out: *the ~ tide; the ~* (i.e. retiring or defeated) *president.* **—out·grow** (–GROH) *v.* **-grows, -grew, -grown, -grow·ing** grow faster than (someone), too large for (clothes), or out of (early habits, friendships, etc.); **out·growth** *n.* a growing out or offshoot; hence, a result or development. **—out·guess** (–GES) *v.* outwit. **—out·house** *n.* a small outbuilding, esp. one used as a toilet. **—out·ing** *n.* a short pleasure trip, ride, walk, etc. **—out·land·ish** (–LAN–) *adj.* very strange or bizarre. **—out·last** (–LAST) *v.* last longer than; outlive. **—out·law** *n.* & *v.* (declare to be) a person deprived of his legal rights, or a notorious criminal; **out·law·ry** *n.* **—out·lay** *n.* spending of money or other resources; also, what is spent; **v. -lays, -laid, -lay·ing** expend. **—out·let** *n.* a means of letting something out, as from a container: *an ~ for one's energies, emotions; an ~ from a lake; plug into an electrical ~; a retail ~* (i.e. market or store). **—out·line** *n.* (a drawing, plan, or summary giving) the shape or main features of a subject: *the ~ of a novel; to draw a map* **in outline; v. -lines, -lined, -lin·ing:** *a skyscraper ~d against the sky; He ~d his proposals for a settlement.* **—out·live** (–LIV) *v.* **-lives, -lived, -liv·ing** live longer than; survive: *Cannons have ~d their usefulness.* **—out·look** *n.* **1** what one sees with the mind, esp. about the future; prospect or point of view: *a cheerful ~ on life.* **2** what one sees on looking out; view; also, a place to look out from; lookout. **—out·ly·ing** *adj.* lying outside the limits or away from the center: *an ~ district.* **—out·ma·neu·ver** (–muh·NEW·vur) *v.* **-vers, -vered, -ver·ing** defeat by maneuvering; also, esp. *Brit.* **out·ma·noeu·vre, -vres, -vred, -vring.** **—out·mod·ed** (–MOH–) *adj.* out of fashion or out-of-date. **—out·num·ber** (–NUM–) *v.* exceed in number. **—out-of-bounds** *adj.* & *adv.* outside one's limits, as in a game or when straying. **—out-of-date** *adj.* old-fashioned or obsolete. **—out-of-door** *adj.* outdoor; **out-of-doors** *adv.* outdoors. **—out-of-the-way** *adj.* not commonly known; also, remote or unfrequented. **—out-of-town·er** *n. Informal.* someone from out of town. **—out·pa·tient** *n.* a patient not living in the hospital where he is treated. **—out·per·form** (–FORM) *v.* achieve better results than. **—out·play** (–PLAY) *v.* play better than. **—out·point** (–POINT) *v.* win more points than. **—out·post** *n.* **1** a base or camp, esp. military, away from the main camp; also, the personnel assigned to it: *the last ~s of a vanishing empire.* **2** a frontier settlement. **—out·pour·ing** *n.* a pouring out, esp. an uncontrolled expression: *the ~s of a tortured soul.* **—out·pull** (–PULL) *v.* outdraw. **—out·put** *n.* **1** (the amount of) work done, esp. over a period, as of a machine. **2** processed information from a computer: *printout, visual display, and other ~ devices.* Also ***v.*** **-puts, -put·ted, -put·ting** produce as output. **—out·rage** *n.* (extreme offense felt or anger aroused by) a gross violation of the rights or feelings of others; ***v.:*** **-rag·es, -raged, -rag·ing:** *a massacre that ~d humanity; felt ~d by the false report;* **out·ra·geous** (–RAY·jus) *adj.* extremely offensive or shocking: *an ~ insult, crime, demand; ~ prices;* **out·ra·geous·ly** *adv.* **—out·rank** *v.* rank higher than. **—out·ré** (oo·TRAY) *adj.* exaggerated; also, outlandish. **—out·reach** (–REECH) *v.* reach out; also, overreach; ***n.*** the act of reaching out or its extent. **—out·rid·er** (OUT·rye–) *n.* an attendant on horseback accompanying a carriage or wagon; hence, any mounted attendant; also, a harbinger. **—out·rig·ger** *n.* (a boat or canoe equipped with) a projecting bracket or framework on either side for supporting the oars or for steadying the craft. **—out·right** *adj.* & *adv.* complete(ly); utter(ly): *an ~ denial; an ~ and unconditional offer; was run over and killed ~* (i.e. then and there). **—out·run** (–RUN) *v.* **-runs, -ran, -run·ning** run faster than; also, exceed. **—out·sell** (–SEL) *v.* **-sells, -sold, -sell·ing** sell more than. **—out·set** *n.* a setting out; start. **—out·shine** (–SHINE) *v.* **-shines,** *pt.* & *pp.* **-shone,** or **-shined, -shin·ing** shine more brightly than; hence, surpass. **—out·side** *n.* & *adj.* (on) an outer side or location; exterior: *house in need of inside and ~ repairs; to wash the ~ of a car; a favorable impression from the ~; an ~* (i.e. remote) *possibility;* ***adv.*** & ***prep.*** on or to the outside (of): *She's waiting ~* (the door); **at the outside** at the most; **outside of** *Informal.* outside; **out·sid·er** *n.* one from outside a group or region. **—out·size** *n.* (a garment of) an unusually large size; **out·size(d)** *adj.* **—out·skirts** *n.pl.* districts away the center, as of a city; borders. **—out·smart** (–SMART) *v.* outdo in smartness of by cunning. **—out·spend** (–SPEND) *v.* **-spends, -spent, -spend·ing** spend more than (a limit, another person, etc.). **—out·spo·ken** (–SPOH–) *adj.* open and blunt in speech: *an ~ critic; was ~ in his comments;* **out·spo·ken·ly** *adv.;* **out·spo·ken·ness** *n.* **—out·spread** (–SPRED) *adj.* extended: *with ~ arms; with wings ~.* **—out·stand·ing** (–STAN–) *adj.* **1** projecting; hence, prominent: *an ~ leader.* **2** unsettled: *claims still ~;* **out·stand·ing·ly** *adv.* **—out·sta·tion** (OUT·stay–) *n.* an outpost in an unsettled area. **—out·stay** (–STAY) *v.* **1** stay longer than. **2** have greater power of endurance than. **—out·stretched** (–STRECHT) *adj.* outspread; stretched out. **—out·strip** (–STRIP) *v.* **-strips, -stripped, -strip·ping** go faster than; hence, surpass. **—out·vote** (–VOHT) *v.* **-votes, -vot·ed, -vot·ing** defeat in voting. **—out·ward** (–wurd) *adj.* **1** external: *the ~ man; ~ beauty, behavior.* **2** moving or turned toward the outside: *an ~ journey;* ***adv.*** also **out·wards,** toward the outside: *an outward-bound journey; lines diverging ~ from the center;* **out·ward·ly** *adv.* externally. **—out·wear** (–WAIR) *v.* **-wears, -wore, -worn, -wear·ing** **1** of fabrics, etc., last longer than in wearing. **2** wear out; also, become out-of-date: *outworn machinery.* **—out·weigh** (–WAY) *v.* exceed in weight, importance, etc.: *These reasons far ~ the others.* **—out·wit** (–WIT) *v.* **-wits, -wit·ted, -wit·ting** overcome by superior intelligence or cleverness. **—out·work** *n.* a small defensive fortification outside the main one; ***v.*** (–WURK) outdo by working harder, better, etc. **—out·worn** *adj.* worn out; also, out-of-date.

ou·zo (OO·zoh) *n.* **-zos** an unsweetened but flavored Greek cordial.

ova *pl.* of OVUM.

o·val (OH·vl) *n.* & *adj.* (anything) egg-shaped or like an ellipse; **Oval Office** the U.S. President's office; hence, the Presidency. **—o·va·ry** (OH·vuh–) *n.* **-ries** the egg-containing reproductive organ of a female: *A flowering plant's ~ is at the base of its pistil;* **o·var·i·an** (–VAIR–) *adj.* **—o·vate** (OH–) *adj.* egg-shaped, as certain leaves.

o·va·tion (–VAY–) *n.* enthusiastic applause, with clapping or cheering.

ov·en (UV·un) *n.* a chamber in a stove or near a fireplace for baking, heating, etc. **—ov·en·**

bird *n.* a small bird of the wood warbler family with a call like "tea-cher" that builds a domed nest on the ground with a side entrance like that of an oven.

o·ver (OH·vur) *prep.* **1** above: *a roof ~ our heads; Who's ~ you at work?* **2** throughout: *flew ~ the city; that happened ~ a long period.* **3** beyond: *leaped ~ the wall; ~ the hills and far away; lies ~ the ocean; doing ~ 100 m.p.h.* **4** about: *brooding ~ failures.* **5** by means of: *news sent ~ the airwaves.* —***adv.*** [indicating an action as carried across or beyond a place or time]: *Hand it ~ to us; fell ~ on his face; Let's talk it ~; sleeping ~ at his neighbor's; say it* **over and over** *till you know it by heart; not ~* (i.e. very) *tired.* —***adj.:*** *The game is ~* (i.e. at an end); ***prefix.*** [added without a hyphen to adjectives to mean "too" and to nouns and verbs to mean "too much," as in the compounds placed at the foot of the pages; their basic meaning and pronunciation are the same as in the base word in each case.]

o·ver·act (–ACT) *v.* exaggerate in acting a part. —**o·ver·age** (–AGE) *adj.* past the age of usefulness, eligibility, etc.; **o·ver·age** (OH·vuh·rij) *n.* surplus or excess. —**o·ver·all** *adj. & adv.* all-inclusive(ly): *~ expenses; an ~ operating budget; measures 3 ft. ~;* **o·ver·alls** *n.pl.* loose-fitting trousers with an attached piece to cover the chest, worn by workers to protect their clothes. —**o·ver·arm** *adj.* with the arm raised over the shoulder, as in swimming; also, overhand. —**o·ver·awe** (–AW) *v.* **-awes, -awed, -aw·ing** awe into submission; inspire awe in. —**o·ver·bal·ance** (–BAL–) *v.* **-anc·es, -anced, -anc·ing** outweigh; also, cause to lose balance and tip over. —**o·ver·bear·ing** (–BAIR–) *adj.* domineering; dictatorial. —**o·ver·blown** (–BLONE) *adj.* exaggerated; inflated; also, more than full-blown. —**o·ver·board** *adv.* over the side of a ship into the water; **go overboard** *Informal.* act in an overenthusiastic manner. —**o·ver·cast** *adj.* of the sky, cloudy, or dark. —**o·ver·charge** (–CHARJ) *v.* **-charg·es, -charged, -charg·ing** charge too much; also, overload; ***n.*** (OH·vur–) *an ~ of $25.* —**o·ver·clothes** *n.pl.* outerwear. —**o·ver·cloud** (–CLOWD) *v.* cloud over or darken. —**o·ver·coat** *n.* a usu. heavy outer coat worn in cold weather. —**o·ver·come** (–CUM) *v.* **-comes, -came, -com·ing** conquer; also, overpower: *overcome by fatigue.* —**o·ver·do** (–DOO) *v.* **-does, -did, -done, -do·ing** do too much or carry to excess: *She overdid her part; an overdone steak.* —**o·ver·draft** *n.* an overdrawing or the sum overdrawn; **o·ver·draw** (–DRAW) *v.* **-draws, -drew, -drawn, -draw·ing** **1** draw from an account more money than there is in it. **2** exaggerate in drawing or portraying. —**o·ver·dress** (–DRES) *v.* dress too elaborately or showily. —**o·ver·drive** *n.* in a transmission, a higher gear or forward speed available automatically without strain on the engine when the vehicle is cruising at a certain speed in top gear. —**o·ver·due** (–DEW) *adj.* due some time back: *an ~ payment, train, baby* (i.e. not yet born). —**o·ver·es·ti·mate** (–ES–) *v.* **-mates, -mat·ed, -mat·ing** (set or provide) too high an estimate for. —**o·ver·ex·pose** (–POZE) *v.* **-pos·es, -posed, -pos·ing** expose (a photographic film) too long; **o·ver·ex·po·sure** (–POH·zhur) *n.* —**o·ver·flight** *n.* a flight in an aircraft over a territory. —**o·ver·flow** (–FLOH) *v.* flow over: *A river ~s* (its banks) *during a flood; an ~ing cup; hearts ~ing with happiness;* ***n.*** a flood; also, a surplus or excess; ***adj.:*** *an ~ crowd, pipe.* —**o·ver·fly** (–FLY) *v.* **-flies, -flew, -flown, -fly·ing** fly over in an airplane. —**o·ver·grow** (–GROH) *v.* **-grows, -grew, -grown, -grow·ing** grow over, as a wall with ivy; also, outgrow or grow too fast; **o·ver·growth** *n.* —**o·ver·hand** *adj. & adv.* (made) with the hand raised above the elbow, as in playing tennis; also, overarm. —**o·ver·hang** (–HANG) *v.* **-hangs, -hung, -hang·ing** hang or project over; also, hang over in a gloomy or threatening manner: *the ~ing threat of war;* ***n.*** (OH·vur–) a jutting out, as of an upper story over the lower or of the eaves of a roof. —**o·ver·haul** (–HAWL) *v.* **1** examine (machines) thoroughly and repair as necessary; ***n.*** (OH–) an overhauling. **2** overtake. —**o·ver·head** (–HED) *adj. & adv.* (operating or located) above: *cables running ~; a garage's ~ door; an ~ projector to throw images above the lecturer behind him;* ***n.*** (OH–) business expenses such as rent, maintenance, utilities, etc. covering all operations. —**o·ver·hear** (–HEER) *v.* **-hears, -heard, -hear·ing** hear (a speaker or what is spoken) without the speaker's being aware of it. —**o·ver·joy** (–JOY) *v.* fill with great joy; **o·ver·joyed** *adj.* —**o·ver·kill** *n.* (amount of) capacity in excess of what is required to achieve an objective, esp. to kill with nuclear power; excessive killing power; also ***v.*** —**o·ver·land** *adj. & adv.* across, by, or on land: *an ~ route.* —**o·ver·lap**

---

overabundance
overactive
overambitious
overanxious
overbid
overburden
overcareful
overcautious
overconfidence
overconfident
overcook
overcritical
overcrowd
overdevelop
overdue
overeager

(–LAP) *v.* **-laps, -lapped, -lap·ping** lap over; *roof shingles that* ~ (each other); ***n.*** (OH–): *There's an hour's ~ between the day and night shifts.* **—o·ver·lay** (–LAY) *v.* **-lays, -laid, -lay·ing** place over another; also, cover or finish with: *a dome ~d with gold;* ***n.*** (OH–) something laid over: *a map with color ~s showing special features.* **—o·ver·lie** (–LYE) *v.* **-lies, -lay, -lain, -ly·ing** lie on or over: *was ~n* (and killed) *in sleep by its own mother.* **—o·ver·load** *n.* & *v.* (put) too heavy a load (on): *an ~ed truck; air-conditioners ~ing a circuit.* **—o·ver·look** (–LOOK) *v.* **1** look over from above; hence, watch or oversee: *a room ~ing* (i.e. giving a view of) *the harbor.* **2** fail to see: *was not neglected but ~ed in the hurry; a taskmaster who never ~s* (i.e. ignores or excuses) *our shortcomings.* **—o·ver·lord** *n.* one with power over (other) lords. **—o·ver·ly** *adv.* too (much); excessively. **—o·ver·mas·ter** (–MAS–) *v.* overpower; conquer. **—o·ver·much** (–MUCH) *adj., adv.* & *n.* too much. **—o·ver·night** (–NITE) *adj.* during the night: *an ~ stop, telegram, stay, journey;* ***adv.:*** *got ready ~ to start at dawn; a problem difficult to solve ~*(i.e. quickly). **—o·ver·pass** *n.* a crossing at a higher level, as a bridge over a road or railway: *a pedestrian ~.* **—o·ver·play** (–PLAY) *v.* exaggerate the importance of or be overoptimistic about (an advantage one has): *lost his bid by ~ing his hand.* **—o·ver·pow·er** (–POW–) *v.* conquer by superior power; overwhelm. **—o·ver·qual·i·fied** (–KWOL·uh·fide) *adj.* too highly qualified, esp. for a job. **—o·ver·rate** *v.* **-rates, -rat·ed, -rat·ing** rate or value too highly. **—o·ver·reach** (–REECH) *v.* **1** outwit, esp. by cunning. **2** be too clever or crafty; **overreach oneself** fail by being too clever or crafty. **—o·ver·re·act** (–ACT) *v.* react in an unnecessary or uncalled-for manner, as by an outburst. **—o·ver·ride** (–RIDE) *v.* **-rides, -rode, -rid·den, -rid·ing** ride over; also, overrule or prevail over: *to ~ a veto.* **—o·ver·rule** (–ROOL) *v.* **-rules, -ruled, -rul·ing** decide against; set aside: *objection ~d.* **—o·ver·run** (–RUN) *v.* **-runs, -ran, -run, -run·ning** **1** of enemies, weeds, vermin, etc., run over or occupy causing harm. **2** go beyond: *to ~ a time limit;* ***n.*** (OH–): *a 50% ~.* **—o·ver·sea(s)** (–SEEZ) *adv.* abroad; beyond the sea; ***adj.:*** *an overseas territory, assignment, investment.* **—o·ver·see** (–SEE) *v.* **-sees, -saw, -seen, -see·ing** supervise or manage; **o·ver·se·er** (OH·vur·seer) *n.* **—o·ver·sexed** (–SEXT) *adj.* having excessive sexual desire. **—o·ver·shad·ow** (–SHAD–) *v.* be more brilliant than; surpass. **—o·ver·shoe** (OH·vur·shoo) *n.* a galosh or similar outer shoe. **—o·ver·shoot** (–SHOOT) *v.* **-shoots, -shot, -shoot·ing** shoot over or beyond (a target); also, go or pass beyond (a limit): *The aircraft overshot the runway.* **—o·ver·sight** *n.* an act of overlooking; failure to notice: *an error due to (an) ~.* **—o·ver·sim·pli·fy** (–SIM–) *v.* **-fies, -fied, -fy·ing** simplify so much as to distort or misrepresent. **—o·ver·size(d)** *adj.* larger in size than ordinary. **—o·ver·sleep** (–SLEEP) *v.* **-sleeps, -slept, -sleeping** sleep longer than intended. **—o·ver·spread** (–SPRED) *v.* **-spreads, -spread, -spread·ing** spread over; cover *(with).* **—o·ver·state** (–STATE) *v.* **-states, -stat·ed, -stat·ing** exaggerate; **o·ver·state·ment** *n.* **—o·ver·stay** (–STAY) *v.* stay beyond (a time limit, one's welcome, etc.). **—o·ver·step** (–STEP) *v.* **-steps, -stepped, -step·ping** go beyond the limits of; exceed. **—o·ver·stuff** (–STUF) *v.* stuff with too much of something: *spring-filled and ~ed upholstery for extra comfort.*

o·vert (OH–, oh·VURT) *adj.* done or manifested openly: *an ~ act; ~ behavior, hostility;* **o·vert·ly** *adv.*

o·ver·take (–TAKE) *v.* **-takes, -took, -tak·en, -tak·ing** catch up with or pass: *had ~en the school bus while its signals were flashing; Fate overtook the Titanic on its maiden voyage.* **—o·ver-the-coun·ter** *adj.* sold directly: *~ trading* (of securities not listed on a stock exchange); *~ drugs* (i.e. not dispensed by pharmacists). **—o·ver·throw** (–THROH) *v.* **-throws, -threw, -thrown, -throw·ing** **1** throw beyond. **2** defeat or destroy: *charged with plotting to ~ the government;* ***n.*** (OH·vur–) defeat or destruction. **—o·ver·time** *n.* time in excess of what is standard; also, the pay for working overtime: *no ~ for casual labor;* ***adj.*** & ***adv.:*** *a game still tied at the end of two ~ periods; fined for ~ parking; works ~ to double his income.* **—o·ver·tone** *n.* in music, a higher tone heard in harmony with a fundamental note that is sounded; hence, a suggestion or implication: *The air was tense with ~s of rebellion.* **—o·ver·ture** (–chur) *n.* **1** a proposal or offer to negotiate. **2** a musical composition designed as a prelude or introduction esp. to an opera. **—o·ver·turn** (–TURN) *v.* turn (something) over; upset: *an ~ed truck;* ***n.*** (OH–) an overturning. **—o·ver·view** *n.* a brief survey or summary. **—o·ver·ween·ing** (–WEEN–) *adj.* conceited; arrogant: *~ pride, vanity.* **—o·ver·**

---

overeat
overemphasis
overemphasize
overenthusiastic
overexercise
overexert
overheat
overindulge
overindulgence
overindulgent
overload
overpay
overpopulate
overprice

weigh (–WAY) *v.* outweigh; also, weigh down or oppress; **o·ver·weight** (OH–) *n.* & *adj.* (a weight) over the standard or normal weight. —**o·ver·whelm** (–HWELM) *v.* engulf; also, overcome: *~ed by superior forces; an ~ing victory, gratitude, sorrow;* **o·ver·whelm·ing·ly** *adv.* —**o·ver·win·ter** (–WIN–) *v.* pass the winter. —**o·ver·wrought** (–RAWT) *adj.* **1** exhausted by too much work or excitement. **2** too elaborate or ornate.

Ov·id 43 B.C.–A.D. 17, Latin poet.

ov·i·duct (OH·vuh–) *n.* a tube carrying an egg from the ovary to the uterus; a Fallopian tube. —**o·vip·a·rous** (–VIP·uh·rus) *adj.* reproducing by laying eggs, not viviparous; **o·vi·par·i·ty** (–PAIR–) *n.* —**o·void** (OH–) *n.* something egg-shaped; **o·void** or **o·voi·dal** (–VOI–) *adj.* —**o·vu·late** (OH·vyuh–, OV·yuh–) *v.* **-lates, -lat·ed, -lat·ing** produce and discharge eggs from the ovary; **o·vu·la·tion** (–LAY–) *n.* —**o·vule** (OH–) *n.* unfertilized or immature egg or seed; **o·vu·lar** *adj.* —**o·vum** (OH–) *n., pl.* **-va** (–vuh) an unfertilized egg.

owe (OH) *v.* **owes, owed, ow·ing** be in debt for (something) to someone: *I ~ you nothing; We ~ much to our country; Jerry ~s* (i.e. bears) *her a grudge; a borrower always ~ing for something;* **owing to** because of; on account of.

owl *n.* a nocturnal bird of prey with large round eyes and tufts of feathers on the heads of some species resembling horns or ears, characterized by its hooting call; **owl·ish** *adj.;* **owl·ish·ly** *adv.* —**owl·et** *n.* a young or small owl.

own (OHN) *v.* have as one's (property) or as belonging to one: *I only live here, I don't ~ the place; a waif whom his parents would not ~; He ~ed* (i.e. admitted) *he had been misled; ~ed to having lied; would not* **own up** (i.e. confess) *to the theft.* —***adj.*** & ***pron.:*** *my ~ children; your ~ business; to each his ~;* **hold one's own** defend oneself; **of one's own** belonging to oneself; **on one's own** independent. —**own·er** *n.;* **own·er·ship** *n.*

ox *n., pl.* **ox·en** a heavy-bodied, long-tailed, cloven-hoofed, cud-chewing animal such as a cow, buffalo, bison, or yak; esp., a castrated bull used for beef or as a draft animal.

ox·al·ic (–SAL–) **acid** a toxic organic acid found in plants such as the "wood sorrel," used in bleaching and removing stains, rust, etc. —**ox·a·lis** (OX·uh–) *n.* a group of plants with an acidic taste, including the "wood sorrel," mostly used as ornamentals.

ox·blood (–blud) *n.* a deep red color. —**ox·bow** (–boh) *n.* the U-shaped part of a yoke that passes under and around the neck of the draft animal. —**oxen** *pl.* of ox. —**Ox·ford** (–furd) a city of S. England and the site of Oxford University. —**oxford** *n.* **1** a low shoe that is laced over the instep. **2** a cloth of cotton or rayon used for shirts and blouses. —**Oxford gray** a dark gray color.

ox·i·dant (OX·uh·dunt) *n.* oxidizer; ***adj.*** oxidizing. —**ox·i·da·tion** (–DAY–) *n.* an oxidizing or being oxidized; **ox·i·da·tive** *adj.* —**ox·ide** *n.* an oxygen compound. —**ox·i·dize** *v.* **-diz·es, -dized, -diz·ing** combine with oxygen, as metal in rusting or when a substance burns in air; **ox·i·diz·a·ble** *adj.;* **ox·i·diz·er** *n.* —**ox·y·a·cet·y·lene** (ox·ee·uh·SETL·een) *adj.* using an oxygen-acetylene mixture: *the ~ flame of a welding torch.* —**ox·y·gen** (–jun) *n.* a colorless, odorless gaseous element occurring in the atmosphere that is essential to life and for combustion; **ox·y·gen·ic** (–JEN–) *adj.* —**ox·y·gen·ate** *v.* **-ates, -at·ed, -at·ing** treat or combine with oxygen, as in making hydrogen peroxide or in a heart-lung machine that uses an **ox·y·gen·a·tor** (–ay·tur) *n.;* **ox·y·gen·a·tion** (–NAY–) *n.* —**oxygen tent** a hood or canopy put over the bed of a patient to contain an extra supply of oxygen.

oys·ter (OIS–) *n.* a bivalve marine mollusk valued as food and for the pearls found in certain kinds; **oys·ter·man** *n.* **-men.** —**oyster cracker** a salted cracker for eating with oysters. —**oys·ter·ing** *n.* the work of taking oysters from the sea.

oz. ounce(s).

O·zarks (OH–) or **Ozark Mountains** a low mountain range extending across Illinois, Missouri, Arkansas, and Oklahoma.

o·zone (OH–) *n.* a form of oxygen with a sharp odor, formed in air by electric discharges and remaining as a layer in the **o·zon·o·sphere** (–ZON–) of the atmosphere up to 30 mi. (48.28 km) above the earth, shielding it from the sun's ultraviolet rays. —**o·zon·ic** (–ZON–) *adj.*

---

overproduce
overproduction
overrefined
overripe
oversell
oversensitive
overspecialize
overspend
overstimulate
overstock
overstrict
oversupply
overtire
overzealous

P

P or **p** (PEE) *n.* **P's** or **p's** **1** the 16th letter of the English alphabet. **2** something symbolized by P, as the 16th in a series, something shaped like the letter, or its consonant sound. **—mind one's P's and Q's** be very careful about every detail; make no mistakes. **—p** or **p.** page; par; participle; past; pawn; pence; penny; pico-; pint; population; president; pressure; proton. **—P** phosphorus.

pa (PAH, PAW) *n. Informal.* father. **—p.a.** per annum. **—Pa** pascal; protactinium. **—Pa.** or **PA** Pennsylvania. **—P.A.** power of attorney; press agent; private account; public address (system); purchasing agent.

pa·´an·ga (pah·AHNG·uh) *n.* the basic money unit of Tonga, equal to 100 seniti.

Pab·lum *Trademark.* an easily digested cereal food for infants; **pablum** *n.* a food, esp. something simplified or watered down. **—pab·u·lum** (PAB·yuh–) *n.* food; nourishment; pablum: *poor mental ~.*

pac *n.* a larrigan; also, an inner shoe worn with boots in cold weather.

pa·ca (PAH·cuh) *n.* a burrowing South American rodent with a spotted brown coat.

pace *n.* **1** a step in walking; also, one's speed: *It is three ~s from my desk to the door; He's too fast to* **keep pace with;** *an energetic person who* **sets the pace** (for others to keep up with) *at work.* **2** a manner of walking, esp. a horse's ambling gait; **put one through one's paces** test or demonstrate one's abilities. **—v. pac·es, paced, pac·ing:** *The expectant father was ~ing up and down outside; We ~d off the room to measure it.*

pa·ce (PAY·see) *prep. Latin.* without annoyance to: *Let me say this ~ the competition.*

pace·mak·er *n.* a tiny electronic device implanted near the heart to regulate its beat. **—pac·er** *n.* one who sets the pace in a race. **—pace·set·ter** **1** a leader. **2** a pacer.

pach·y·derm (PAK·i–) *n.* a large, thick-skinned mammal, as the elephant, rhinoceros, or hippopotamus. **—pach·y·der·mal** (–DUR–), **-der·ma·tous** or **-der·mous** *adj.* callous; insensitive.

pach·y·san·dra (pak·i·SAN·druh) *n.* a woody, evergreen, low-growing plant often used as ground cover.

Pa·cif·ic (Ocean) (puh·SIF·ic) the ocean between Asia and the Americas. **—Pacific** *adj.* **1** of the Pacific: *the ~ coast* (of America); **Pacific Islands** same as OCEANIA; **Pacific (Standard) time** the clock followed in western North America, including Washington, Oregon, Nevada, California, and British Columbia. **2 pacific** tending to pacify; calm; peaceful. **—pa·cif·i·cal·ly** *adv.* **—pac·i·fi·er** (PAS–) *n.* one that pacifies, esp. something for an infant to suck or chew on. **—pac·i·fism** *n.* opposition to war or military action; **pac·i·fist** *n. & adj.: a ~ approach to a settlement;* also **pac·i·fis·tic** (–FIS–) *adj.* **—pac·i·fy** (PAS·i·fye) *v.* **-fies, -fied, -fy·ing** make peaceful; also, quiet or calm down; **pac·i·fi·ca·tion** (–CAY–) *n.*

pack *n.* **1** things wrapped up and tied together as a bundle for carrying; **pack animal** a load-carrying animal, as a mule **(pack mule),** camel, or **pack·horse,** often equipped with a **pack saddle.** **2** things considered in sets or groups, as a deck of cards: *Cigarettes come in ~s of 20; beer in 6-packs; a year's ~ of salmon* (i.e., caught in one season). **3** something compactly put together, as an ICE PACK (def. 1), or gauze or cloth pad applied in treatments; also, a cosmetic paste. **4** persons, animals, or things grouped together for a common purpose: *a ~ of hunting dogs, wolves, thieves; a ~ of lies; a submarine ~.* **—v.** **1** make, put, or crowd into a pack: *~ everything in two bags; time to* **pack up** *and go home; The refugees were* **packed into** *the train like sardines; ~ the kids off to school after breakfast; The inept were* **sent packing** (i.e. dismissed) *from their jobs.* **2** treat so as to make compact or leak-proof: *A plumber ~s a pipe joint; A road roller ~s the earth; A dentist ~s a bleeding gum.* **3** *Informal.* carry in a pack;

be loaded with; possess: *He ~ed a gun in his guitar case; clouds ~ing a storm; I want a word that ~s more punch.* **4** arrange with corrupt aim; *~ a jury* (with sympathizers). —**pack·er** *n.* —**pack·age** (–ij) *n.* **1** a parcel or bundle. **2** a proposal, plan, offer, etc. containing many items to be accepted as a whole: *a compensation ~* (i.e. salary, bonus, etc.); ***adj.:*** *a ~ deal, tour.* —***v.*** **-ag·es, -aged, -ag·ing:** *~d goods.* — **package store** *U.S.* a store selling liquor in sealed containers; originally, a euphemism for "liquor store." —**pack animal** See PACK, *n.* 1. —**pack·et** *n.* **1** a small parcel, as of mail. **2** a boat plying a regular route carrying passengers, freight, and mail; also **packet boat.** —**pack horse** See PACK, *n.* 1. —**pack ice** same as ICE PACK. —**pack·ing** *n.* **1** material used to prevent or stop a leakage of water, steam, or air. **2** the processing and packing of food, esp. meat, for wholesale, as is done in a **packing house** or **packing plant.** —**pack mule** See PACK, *n.* 1. —**pack rat** **1** any of various North American rodents that carry away small articles and hide them in their nests. **2** one who hoards odd, unnecessary articles. —**pack·sack** *n.* a traveling bag of sturdy material, strapped to one's back. —**pack saddle** See PACK *n.* 1. —**pack·thread** *n.* strong thread for sewing up bags. —**pack·train** *n.* a line of pack animals.

pact *n.* a treaty; agreement; *a peace ~; a ~ of friendship.*

pad *n.* **1** a mass of soft material or a cushion-like container: *a writing ~* (i.e. sheets of paper glued together at one end); *an inked stamp ~* (for a rubber stamp). **2** a frameless flexible saddle. **3** a water plant's floating leaf. **4** the soft under part of fingers and toes, esp. of the feet of animals. **5** launch(ing) pad. **6** *Slang.* one's living quarters, esp. a bed. **7** *Slang.* a bribe collected by policemen for ignoring illegal activities: *That cop is* **on the pad.** —***v.*** **pads, pad·ded, pad·ding** stuff or fill out: *an essay ~d with quotations; a heavily ~d* (i.e. inflated) *expense account; ~ing* (i.e. walking noiselessly) *about on bare feet; a well-~d seat; a* **padded cell** *for violent inmates;* **pad·ding** *n.* material used to pad or fill out.

pad·dle *n.* **1** an oar with a broad, flat blade; also, any other similar implement, as a board of a water wheel or the **paddle wheel** of a steamboat, a table tennis racket, or one used in **paddle ball,** a game similar to squash, and in **paddle tennis,** an outdoor game resembling tennis. **2** an instrument used in stirring, mixing, or beating, shaped like a paddle, as a potter's pallet; also, a handled board used for spanking: *The* **paddlefish** *has a snout like a spatula.* —***v.*** **pad·dles, pad·dled, pad·dling:** *Children ~d* (i.e. splashed about) *in the wading pool; soundly ~d* (i.e. spanked) *for telling a lie; At school Jane* **paddles her own canoe** (i.e. manages all by herself). —**pad·dler** *n.*

pad·dock (–uk) *n.* an enclosure adjoining a stable, for feeding, exercising, or displaying animals, esp. racehorses.

pad·dy (PAD·ee) *n.* **pad·dies** rice in the husk, esp. when standing in the field; also, a field of rice, often called **pad·dy-field.**

Pad·dy *n. Slang.* an Irishman. —**paddy wagon** *U.S.* a patrol wagon.

pad·lock *n.* a lock that can be put on a staple or chain by means of a U-shaped link that snaps shut and stays shut until unlocked. ***v.:*** *I found the door shut and ~ed.*

pa·dre (PAH·dray, –dree) *n.* in Latin countries, a title for a priest; Father.

pae·an (PEE·un) *n.* a song of exultation or triumph.

paed(o)- same as PED(O)-.

pa·gan (PAY·gun) *n.* one who has no recognized religion. —***adj.:*** *~ idols; ~ beliefs.* —**pa·gan·ism** *n.*

¹page *n.* **1** one side of a leaf of a book; also, a leaf: *to tear out a ~.* **2** a record; also, one of a series of events: *an important ~ in our life; in the ~s of history.* —***v.*** **pag·es, paged, pag·ing** **1** arrange into pages; paginate. **2** turn the pages: *to ~ through a volume.*

²page *n.* an attendant or messenger, as at a hotel, theater, or in a legislature. —***v.*** **pag·es, paged, pag·ing** summon by calling the name of.

pag·eant (PAJ·unt) *n.* a spectacular show, parade, or procession, as the "Tournament of Roses" in Pasadena, Calif. —**pag·eant·ry** *n.: mere pomp and ~.*

page boy or **page·boy** *n.* a boy who works as a page; also, a shoulder-length hairdo style.

pag·i·nate (PAJ–) *v.* **-nates, -nat·ed, -nat·ing** arrange into pages; **pag·i·na·tion** (–NAY–) *n.*

pa·go·da (puh·GOH·duh) *n.* a many-storied pyramidal tower of India and the Far East: *A Chinese ~ is eight-sided.*

paid *pt.* & *pp.* of PAY.

pail *n.* **1** a cylindrical vessel, usu. with a handle, for liquids; bucket. **2** the amount a pail will hold; also **pail·ful, -fuls.**

pain *n.* **1** suffering of body or mind: *aches and ~s;* **pain in the neck** nuisance. **2** penalty; **under** (or **on** or **upon**) **pain of:** *told to surrender on ~ of death.* **3** **pains** *pl.* effort; care: *She took great ~s to research her book;* **pains·tak·ing** *n.* & *adj.;* **pains·tak·ing·ly** *adv.* —**pain** *v.* feel or cause pain. —**pain·ful** *adj.;* **pain·ful·ly** *adv.* —**pain·less** *adj.;* **pain·less·ly** *adv.*

Paine, Thomas. 1737–1809, an American writer and revolutionary.

pain·kill·er *n.* something that relieves pain, as a drug; **pain·kill·ing** *adj.*

paint *v.* **1** apply color, as with a **paint·brush;** also, make something in colors, as a picture, or **paint·ing; paint the town red** *Slang.* go on a wild spree. **2** apply (medicine), esp. with a swab. **3** put cosmetics on. —***n.*** a usu. liquid mixture or pigment for coating a surface for decoration or protection; also, such a coating: *two coats of* ~. **—paint·er** *n.*

pair *n.* **1** two persons, animals, or things of the same kind: *a ~ of socks; four ~(s) of gloves; a newly married ~; a ~ of oxen; The animals entered the ark* **in pairs;** *The skating ~s are next on the program.* **2** something with two equal parts: *a ~ of pants; to cut with a ~ of scissors.* **—v.:** *The guests paired off for the dance.*

pai·sa (PYE·sah) *n., pl.* **-se** (–SAY) or **-sas** a money unit of India, Pakistan, and Oman, equal to 1/100 of a rupee, and of Bangladesh (1/100 of a taka).

pais·ley (PAYZ·lee) *n.* a colorful cloth design of curved and swirled figures; also **Paisley.** —*adj.: a ~ shawl.*

Pai·ute (PYE·yoot) *n.* a Shoshonean-speaking Indian, originally of Nevada, California, Utah, and Arizona.

pa·ja·mas (puh·JAM·uz, –JAH–) *n.pl.* a loose-fitting sleeping suit of pants and shirt. **—*adj.:*** *pajama tops, bottoms.*

Pak·i·stan a S. Asian republic to the W. of India; 310,404 sq.mi. (803,943 km²); *cap.* Islamabad. **—Pak·i·stan·i** (–STAN·ee) *adj.* & *n.: ~s speak Urdu besides many ~ dialects.*

pal *n. Informal.* a chum; buddy.

pal·ace (–is) *n.* a large, splendid residence, esp. of a sovereign, archbishop, or other dignitary; also, a similar building for exhibitions, entertainment, etc. **—*adj.*** involving intimacy and influence with persons in power: *~ politics; ~ revolution; a* **palace guard.**

pal·a·din (PAL·uh–) *n.* a knight or champion.

pala(e)o- same as PALEO.

palaestra same as PALESTRA.

pal·an·quin (–un·KEEN) *n.* a covered litter formerly used in Eastern countries, borne on the shoulders of servants by means of poles; also **pal·an·keen.**

pal·at·a·ble (PAL·it·uh·bl) *adj.* tasty; also, agreeable: *~ advice.* **—pal·a·tal** *n.* & *adj.* (a speech sound) formed near the palate: *"ch," "j," and "y" are ~ sounds, or ~s;* **pal·a·tal·ize** *v.* **-iz·es, -ized, -iz·ing:** *"Nyet" has a ~d "n";* **pal·a·tal·i·za·tion** (–ZAY–) *n.* **—pal·ate** (–it) *n.* **1** the sense of taste: *a wine pleasing to the ~.* **2** the roof of the mouth, with the **hard palate** at the front and **soft palate** at the back; **¹pal·a·tine** *adj.: the ~ bones.*

pa·la·tial (puh·LAY·shul) *adj.* of or like a palace: *~ surroundings.*

pa·lat·i·nate (puh·LATN·ate, –it) *n.* the territory of a palatine, as the Upper and Lower **Palatinates** of S.W. Germany until 1620. **—²pal·a·tine** (PAL·uh–) *n.* a lord or count having royal prerogatives; ***adj.*** **1** of a palatine or his territory: *Carolina was a ~ colony; The English "count palatine" had supreme powers.* **2** See PALATE.

pa·lav·er (puh·LAV–) *n.* extended talk, esp. between traders. **—v.** wheedle; cajole.

¹pale *n.* a picket or stake; hence, an enclosed area; (**within, beyond,** or) **outside the pale** (of the law, church, respectability, etc.). **—v. pales, paled, pal·ing** enclose.

²pale *adj.* **pal·er, pal·est** of the face, bloodless; light; weak: *to turn ~ with fear; a ~ blue; a ~* (i.e. poor) *imitation.* **—v. pales, paled, pal·ing:** *~s into insignificance by comparison.* **—pale·ly** *adv.* **—pale·ness** *n.* **—pale·face** *n.* a white person.

paleo- *comb.form.* prehistoric. **—Pa·le·o·cene** (–seen) *n.* the first epoch of the Cenozoic era of the earth, beginning about 65 million years ago; ***adj.:*** *~ rock formations.* **—pa·le·og·ra·phy** (–OG·ruh·fee) *n.* the study of ancient documents; **pa·le·og·ra·pher** *n.;* **pa·le·o·graph·ic** (–GRAPH–) or **-i·cal** *adj.* **—Pa·le·o·lith·ic** (–LITH–) *n.* the earliest part of the Stone Age; ***adj.:*** *a ~ tool chipped out of stone; the ~ Neanderthal man;* also **paleolithic** *adj.* **—pa·le·o·mag·net·ic** (–NET–) *adj.* of ancient rocks, exhibiting magnetism; **pa·le·o·mag·net·i·cal·ly** *adv.;* **pa·le·o·mag·net·ism** (–MAG–) *n.*

paleon(tol). *Abbrev.* for **pa·le·on·tol·o·gy** (–TOL·uh·jee) *n.* the study of fossils as a clue to earlier forms of life; **pa·le·on·tol·o·gist** *n.* **—Pa·le·o·zo·ic** (–ZOE·ic) *n.* the geologic era from 600 million to 225 million years ago; ***adj.:*** *Amphibians and reptiles appear in the ~ era.*

Pa·ler·mo (puh·LUR·moh) capital of Sicily.

Pal·es·tine (PAL·i·stine) the land between the Mediterranean and the Jordan River, the birthplace of Judaism and Christianity, and sacred also to Muslims, presently occupied by Israel: *The* **Palestine Liberation Organization** *composed of Arab groups seeks to govern ~.* **—Pal·es·tin·i·an** (–STIN·ee·un) *n.* & *adj.: Many ~s are ~ Arabs.*

pa·les·tra (puh·LES·truh) *n., pl.* **-trae** (–tree) or **-tras** a theater for athletics, esp. wrestling, in ancient Greece.

pal·ette (–it) *n.* an artist's hand-held board for mixing colors; hence, range of colors: *He paints in a wide ~; A* **palette** (or **pallet**) **knife** *is used to mix and apply colors and by printers to spread ink.*

pal·frey (PAWL·free) *n. Archaic.* a saddle horse, esp. one for a woman to ride.

Pa·li (PAH·lee) *n.* the Indic language of Buddhist scriptures.

pal·imp·sest *n.* a document or writing material such as vellum or parchment bearing evidence of more than one writing, the earlier one(s) having been imperfectly erased.

pal·in·drome *n.* a sentence (as *Madam, I'm Adam*), phrase, or word (as *Malayalam*) that reads the same backward or forward.

pal·ing (PAY·ling) *n.* a pale, picket, or stake; also, a collection of them or a fence made with them.

pal·i·node *n.* a recantation; originally, an ode written to retract something said in an earlier poem.

pal·i·sade *n.* a fortification of stakes or pales; also, one of the stakes used in such a fence. —**v. -sades, -sad·ed, -sad·ing:** *tall cliffs ~ing a shore.* —**palisades** *pl.* a line of cliffs, esp. **the Palisades** on the western bank of the lower Hudson River in New Jersey and New York.

[1]**pall** (PAWL) *v.* **palls, palled, pall·ing** get boring; cloy: *This show is beginning to ~ on me.*

[2]**pall** (PAWL) *n.* a covering, as on a coffin: *A ~ of smoke hangs over the city.* —**pall·bear·er** *n.* one who escorts or helps to carry a coffin at a funeral.

pal·la·di·um (puh·LAY·dee·um) *n.* a silvery-white, metallic chemical element.

pal·let (PAL·it) *n.* **1** a paddlelike wooden tool for mixing and shaping clay in a pottery. **2** same as PALETTE. **3** a low, portable platform for storing or moving objects. **4** a makeshift bed or mattress used on the floor.

pal·li·ate (PAL·ee–) *v.* **-ates, -at·ed, -at·ing** lessen the severity of (a crime, illness, pain, evil, etc). —**pal·li·a·tion** (–AY–) *n.* —**pal·li·a·tive** (–ay·tiv) *n.* & *adj.: a mere ~ and no cure.*

pal·lid (PAL·id) *adj.* pale: *a ~ complexion.* —**pal·lor** (PAL·ur) *n.* paleness.

[1]**palm** (PAHM) *n.* the inner surface of the hand from the wrist to the base of the fingers; also, a part corresponding to this, as of a glove or the blade of a paddle; **grease the palm of** to bribe; **have an itching palm** *Informal.* be greedy for money. —**v.** conceal in the palm, as a card; hence, steal; also, pass off: *The con man* **palmed off** *a false gem on the young lady.*

[2]**palm** (PAHM) *n.* **1** any of various trees having trunks without branches and crowns of pinnate leaves or leaves shaped like a hand, i.e. **pal·mate** or **pal·mat·ed** leaves: *Palms belong to the* **pal·ma·ceous** (–MAY·shus) *family.* **2** a palm leaf as a symbol of victory; **bear** (or **carry off**) **the palm** win; **yield the palm to** accept defeat by; **palm·er** *n.* a pilgrim back from the Holy Land (bearing palm leaves as a token). —**pal·met·to** (pal·MET·oh) *n.* **-to(e)s** a palm with fan-shaped leaves, common in South Carolina ("Palmetto State").

palm·ist (PAH·mist) *n.* one who tells fortunes by reading the lines on a person's palms; **palm·is·try** (–tree) *n.* the palmist's art. —**palm sugar** jaggery. —**Palm Sunday** the Sunday before Easter, commemorating Jesus' triumphal entry into Jerusalem. —**palm·y** (PAH·mee) *adj.* **palm·i·er, -i·est** flourishing; prosperous: *the ~ days of one's youth.* —**pal·my·ra** (–MYE·ruh) *n.* a fan-leaved palm of India and Africa with durable wood, edible fruits, and leaves used for thatching.

pal·o·mi·no (pal·uh·MEE·noh) *n.* **-nos** a light-colored horse with white mane and tail.

pal·pa·ble (PAL·puh·bl) *adj.* **1** that can be felt; hence, obvious: *a ~ advantage;* **pal·pa·bly** *adv.: The story is ~ absurd.* **2** *Med.* that can be examined by feeling, or **pal·pat·ing (-pate, -pates, -pat·ed); pal·pa·tion** (–PAY–) *n.: ~ of the breast to check for lumps.* —**pal·pa·bil·i·ty** (–BIL–) *n.* —**pal·pi·tate** *v.* **-tates, -tat·ed, -tat·ing** throb rapidly, as the heart does under exertion or excitement. —**pal·pi·ta·tion** (–TAY–) *n.: ~ is sometimes a symptom of heart disease or goiter.*

pal·sy (PAWL·zee) *n.* **-sies** **1** paralysis or a disorder characterized by trembling, as Parkinson's disease and St. Vitus's dance. **2** a paralyzing influence. —**v. -sies, -sied, -sy·ing:** *He stood still, ~d by fear.* —**pal·sied** *adj.: a ~ limb; ~ children.*

pal·ter (PAWL–) *v.* trifle; use trickery: *a matter too serious to ~ with;* **pal·ter·er** *n.* —**pal·try** (PAWL·tree) *adj.* **-tri·er, -tri·est** trifling; contemptible: *His contribution was a ~ sum.* —**pal·tri·ly** *adv.* —**pal·tri·ness** *n.*

pam·pas (PAM·puz) *n.pl.* the vast treeless plains of South America, esp. in Argentina. —**pampas grass** a tall South American grass with silvery plumes of flowers. —**pam·pe·an** (–pee·un) *adj.* & *n.: a ~ Indian.*

pam·per *v.* treat with indulgence: *a ~ed child; to ~ one's vanity.* —**pam·per·er** *n.*

pam·phlet (–flit) *n.* an unbound booklet on a current topic. —**pam·phlet·eer** (–TEER) *n.* —**pam·phlet·eer·ing** *n.* the issuing of pamphlets, esp. as propaganda.

pan *n.* **1** a flat, open dish for cooking, as a *frying pan* or *saucepan.* **2** a shallow receptacle, depression, cover, etc., as a *brain pan, salt pan,* or a gold miner's dish for washing gravel or gold ore. —**v. pans, panned, pan·ning** **1** sift; esp., wash gravel for gold. **2** *Informal.* criticize harshly: *a movie ~d by every critic.* **3 pan out** *Informal.* of an enterprise, turn out well: *Our plans did not ~ out.* **4** turn (a movie camera) in a sweeping motion for a panoramic view.

pan- *comb.form.* all: as in *Pan-American, panhuman, pantheism.* —**pan·a·ce·a** (pan·uh·SEE·uh) *n.* a cure-all remedy: *no ~ for man's greed.*

pa·nache (puh·NASH) *n.* an air of confidence and ease; flamboyance.

Pan·a·ma (PAN·uh·mah) a Central American republic; 29,209 sq.mi. (75,650 km^2); *cap.* **Panama City:** *The* **Panama Canal,** *built in the early 1900's, cuts across the neck of land called* **Isthmus of Panama** *and connects the Atlantic with the Pacific;* **Pan·a·ma·ni·an** (–MAY·nee·un) *adj.* & *n.* —**panama (hat)** a straw hat woven from leaves of the palmlike jipijapa plant common in South and Central America.

Pan-A·mer·i·can *adj.* pertaining to the Americas: *~ Games; ~ Highway;* **Pan American Day** April 14; **Pan-A·mer·i·can·ism** *n.* cooperative movement among the nations of North and South America for defense, commerce, and other interests.

pan·a·tel·(l)a (–uh·TEL·uh) *n.* a long, slender cigar.

pan·cake *n.* a thin batter cake cooked on both sides and served hot.

pan·chro·mat·ic (–croh·MAT–) *adj.* of film, sensitive to all colors.

pan·cre·as (–cree·us) *n.* a long, fleshy gland near the stomach that secretes a hormone called insulin and **pan·cre·at·ic** (–AT·ic) **juice** which helps in digestion.

pan·da (–duh) *n.* a black-and-white bearlike animal of China and Tibet, also called the **giant panda:** *The* **lesser panda** *is a smaller, raccoon-like, reddish Asiatic animal.*

pan·dem·ic (–DEM·ic) *n.* an epidemic spread over a wide area. ***—adj.:*** *Influenza was ~ in 1918–1919 and killed about 20 million.* **—pan·de·mo·ni·um** (–MOH·nee–) *n.* wild disorder: *~ broke loose when the teacher was late for class.*

pan·der *n.* a procurer; pimp. ***—v.:*** *movies that ~ to lust.* **—pan·der·er** *n.*

P. and L. profit and loss.

Pan·do·ra (–DOR·uh) *n.* in Greek myth, the first mortal woman, who caused all earthly ills by opening a box against the advice of the gods; **Pandora's box** a source of endless trouble.

pan·dow·dy (–DOW·dee) *n.* **-dies** a deep-dish pie of sliced apples.

pane *n.* a division of a window or door framing a sheet of glass; also, the glass.

pan·e·gyr·ic (–JEER·ic) *n.* a formal eulogy or tribute to a person or event.

pan·el *n.* **1** a usu. rectangular piece, section, or division of a surface such as a ceiling, wall, or door, often at a different level from its surroundings: *an airplane wing ~; ~s of a skirt; an instrument ~.* **2** a number of persons forming a group for a specific purpose: *a jury ~; a ~ of experts in a subject holding a* **panel discussion.** ***—v.*** **pan·els, pan·el(l)ed, pan·el·(l)ing** cover (walls of a room) with panels, which are collectively called **pan·el·(l)ing. —pan·el·ist** *n.* a member of a panel of experts or judges. **—panel truck** a small delivery truck with a fully enclosed body.

pang *n.* a sharp, sudden attack of pain, remorse, hunger, jealousy, or fury.

pan·go·lin (pang·GO–) *n.* an anteater that has scales like an armadillo's; also called "scaly anteater."

pan·han·dle *n.* a strip of territory projecting like the handle of a pan: *the Texas ~ between Oklahoma and New Mexico; the N. and E. ~s of West Virginia, nicknamed the* **Panhandle state.** ***—v.*** **-dles, -dled, -dling** beg on the street; **pan·han·dler** *n.*

pan·ic *n.* a sudden fear, esp. one that spreads, as when a bank fails or a fire breaks out; (**hit, press** or) **push the panic button** react in a panicky manner. ***—v.*** **-ics, -icked, -icking:** *Don't ~, it's only a rumor.* **—pan·ic-strik·en** *adj.: a ~ crowd.* **—pan·ick·y** *adj.*

pan·i·cle *n.* a flower cluster branched as in oats and other grasses. **—pan·i·cled** *adj.*

pan·jan·drum (–JAN–) *n.* [used mockingly] someone who is pretentious or pompous.

pan·(n)ier (–yur) *n.* a basket for carrying loads, esp. one of a pair slung across a pack animal's back.

pan·o·ply (–uh·plee) *n.* **-plies** a complete suit of armor; hence, any bright or splendid covering or array: *waited on by a full ~ of servants.* **—pan·o·plied** (–pleed) *adj.*

pan·o·ra·ma (pan·uh·RAM·uh) *n.* a view in all directions; also, an unlimited, comprehensive, or continuous view: *a ~ of the countryside from a hilltop.* **—pan·o·ram·ic** *adj.*

pan·sy (–zee) *n.* **-sies** **1** a garden plant of the violet family whose velvety flowers have markings suggesting a face. **2** *Slang.* a male homosexual; an effeminate man; sissy.

pant *v.* breathe in gasps, as from exertion; also, yearn desperately: *~ing for a lover's return.* ***—n.*** a gasp or puff of breath. **—pan·ting·ly** *adv.*

pan·ta·loons (PAN·tuh–) *n.pl.* men's loose, baggy trousers, as worn in the 19th century.

pan·the·ism (PAN·thee·izm) *n.* the belief that God is the same as the forces and manifestations of nature; **pan·the·ist** *n.* **—pan·the·is·tic** (–IS–) or **-ti·cal** *adj.* **—pan·the·on** (–THEE·un) *n.* a temple of all the gods; also, the gods themselves: *a ~ of national heroes.*

pan·ther *n.* a large black cat, esp. a leopard; also, a cougar or puma.

pan·tie or **pan·ty** (–tee) *n.* usu. **pan·ties** *pl.* a woman's or child's short underpants.

pan·to·mime (–tuh–) *n.* expression using gestures without words, as in the dramatic art form of the same name; ***v.*** **-mimes, -mimed, -mim·ing:** *Knowing only English, he had to ~ his way through Europe.* **—pan·to·mim·ist** *n.* **—pan·to·mim·ic** (–MIM–) *adj.*

pan·try (–tree) *n.* **-tries** a room or closet for storing food and table accessories such as china and linens.

pants *n.pl. Informal.* trousers; also, panties. — ***adj.*** usu. **pant:** *a pant leg;* **pant·suit** *n.* a woman's jacket-and-trouser outfit. **—with one's pants down** in an embarrassing position.

panty See PANTIE. **—panty hose** *sing. & pl.* a woman's undergarment combining pantie and stockings. **—pan·ty·waist** *n. Slang.* a sissy.

pap *n.* soft food, as for infants: *The book is mere political ~.*

pa·pa (PAH·puh) *n. Informal.* father. **—pa·pa·cy** (PAY·puh·see) *n.* **-cies** **1** a pope's term of office, position, authority, etc.; also, popes collectively. **2** esp. **Papacy,** the system of government of the Roman Catholic Church.

pa·pa·in (puh·PAY·in) *n.* an enzyme extracted from the fruit of the papaya, used esp. as a meat tenderizer.

pa·pal (PAY·pl) *adj.* of the pope: *the ~ succession; a ~ bull;* **the Papal States** territory in C. Italy held by popes till 1870.

pa·pa·raz·zo (pah·puh·RAHT·so) *n., pl.* **-raz·zi** (–see) a journalist who doggedly pursues news stories and pictorial subjects.

pa·paw (PAW·paw, puh·PAW) *n.* same as PAWPAW. **—pa·pa·ya** (puh·PYE·uh) *n.* a tropical tree resembling a palm, bearing a yellowish-orange melonlike fruit; often erroneously called "papaw" or "pawpaw."

pa·per (PAY–) *n.* **1** a thin, pliable sheet material made of pulp prepared from wood or rags and used for writing, printing, wrapping, covering, etc.; also, a piece or sheet of this. **2** something written or printed, as an essay or newspaper: *a scholarly ~ by an academic; lost his admission* **papers** (i.e. documents); *a plan that looks good* **on paper** (i.e. in theory). **—*v.*** cover with paper; **pa·per·er** *n.* **—pa·per·back** *n.* a book with paper covers: *A trade ~ is higher-priced and larger in size than a mass-market ~;* ***adj.:*** *a ~ publisher.* **—pa·per·board** *n.* cardboard; pasteboard. **—paper boy** a newspaper carrier. **—paper clip** a wire or plastic clasp for holding papers together. **—pa·per·hang·er** *n.* one who decorates with wallpaper. **—paper tiger** a threatening but ineffectual person or thing. **—pa·per·weight** *n.* a weight used to keep papers from being blown away. **—pa·per·work** *n.* clerical duties incidental to one's main occupation: *catching up on last week's ~.* **—pa·per·work·er** *n.* a worker in a paper factory. **—pa·per·y** *adj.* thin like paper.

pa·pier-mâ·ché (PAY·pur·muh·SHAY) *n.* a plastic material made of paper pulp mixed with glue and other additives.

pa·pil·la (puh·PIL·uh) *n., pl.* **-pil·lae** (–PIL·ee) a nipplelike projection on a body surface, as on the tongue: *A wart is an overgrowth of a skin ~.* **—pap·il·lar·y** (PAP·uh–) *adj.*

pap·il·lon (PAP·i·lon) *n.* a European toy spaniel with butterflylike ears.

pa·pist (PAY·pist) *n.* [hostile use] a Roman Catholic; also ***adj.;*** **pa·pist·ry** *n.* a papist's beliefs and practices.

pa·poose (pa·POOS) *n.* a North American Indian baby.

pa·pri·ka (pa·PREE·kuh) *n.* a mild seasoning made from some red peppers.

Pap test a test for cancer of the lung, stomach, or cervix using a specimen of mucus, or "Pap smear," from the part concerned. Also **Pap smear.**

Pap·u·a (PAP·yoo·uh) **New Guinea** a Commonwealth country consisting of the E. half of New Guinea and nearby islands; 178,260 sq.mi. (461,691 km²); *cap.* Port Moresby.

pap·ule (PAP·yool) *n.* a non-pus-forming pimple. **—pap·u·lar** *adj.*

pa·py·rus (puh·PYE·rus) *n.* **-rus·es** or **-ri** (–rye) a writing material, document, or scroll of paper made from the pith of an Egyptian reed.

par *n.* **1** standard or equal value: *to sell stocks or shares* **at par, above par, below par;** *The Canadian dollar was* **on a par with** *the U.S. dollar. His performance was not quite* **up to par. 2** in golf, the standard score for a hole or a course.

par. paragraph; parallel; parish.

pa·ra (PAH·ruh) *n.* a money unit equal to 1/100 of the Yugoslavian dinar.

para- *prefix.* alongside; related; accessory: as in *paramedical, parapsychology, paratyphoid.*

par·a·ble (PAIR·uh–) *n.* a simple story with a moral: *the ~ of the "prodigal son."* **—par·a·bol·i·cal** (–BOL–) *adj.: Christ's ~ teachings.*

pa·rab·o·la (puh·RAB·uh·luh) *n.* a curve, as of the path of a ball thrown in the air. **—par·a·bol·ic** (pair·uh·BOL–) *adj.: a ~ surface.*

par·a·chute (PAIR·uh·shoot) *n.* an umbrella-shaped contrivance used for a slow, safe descent from the air to the ground: *A* **drag parachute** *is used as a brake behind a landing plane or a car.* **—*v.* -chutes, -chut·ed, -chut·ing:** *Troops and supplies were ~d into the jungle.* **—par·a·chut·ist** *n.*

Par·a·clete (PAIR·uh·cleet) *n.* the Holy Ghost.

pa·rade (puh·RAID) *n.* a showy display, esp. an organized public procession: *a New Year's Day ~; a military ~; a May Day ~ in Red Square.* **—*v.* -rades, -rad·ed, -rad·ing:** *The rich ~ their wealth; beauties ~ing on a stage; The prisoners were ~d before a jeering crowd.*

par·a·digm (PAIR·uh·dim, –dime) *n.* a model or pattern; esp. in grammar, an example of the complete inflectional forms of a noun, pronoun, or verb, as *ride, rides, riding, rode, ridden.*

par·a·dise (PAIR·uh·dice) *n.* a place of supreme happiness, as heaven or Eden **(Paradise):** *Niagara Falls is a honeymooners' ~.* **—par·a·di·si·a·cal** (–di·SYE·uh·cl) or **-dis·i·ac** (–DIS·ee–) *adj.*

par·a·dox (PAIR·uh–) *n.* a seemingly contradictory statement, situation, or person, as a hippie in a homburg. **—par·a·dox·i·cal** (–DOX–) *adj.: "Hasten slowly" is ~ but makes sense;* **paradoxical sleep** *characterized by rapid eye movements.* **—par·a·dox·i·cal·ly** *adv.*

par·af·fin (PAIR·uh–) *n.* **1** a waxy substance made from petroleum and used for candles, waterproofing the inside of milk cartons, etc. **2** *Brit.* kerosene. **—*v.* -fins, -fined, -fin·ing:** *Wax paper is ~d; so are airtight lids.* **—par·af·fin·ic** (–FIN–) *adj.*

par·a·gon (PAIR·uh–) *n.* a model (*of* virtue, excellence, etc.): *a ~ of a wife.*

par·a·graph (PAIR·uh–) *n.* a subdivision of a written piece, starting a new line; also, a short piece complete in itself, as a news item in a paper. **—*v.:*** *That essay is neatly ~ed.* **—par·a·graph·ic** (–GRAF–) *adj.*

Par·a·guay (PAIR·uh·gwye) a South American republic; 157,048 sq.mi. (406,752 km²); *cap.* Asunción. —**Par·a·guay·an** (–GWYE·un) *n.* & *adj.*

par·a·keet (PAIR·uh–) *n.* a small long-tailed parrot, as a budgie or lovebird.

par·al·lax (PAIR·uh–) *n.* the apparent difference in position of an object viewed from different directions, as when an extended finger is seen with one eye closed and then the other.

par·al·lel (PAIR·uh–) *adj.* in the same direction but an equal distance apart: ~ *lines never meet; two* **parallel bars** *set horizontally on posts for gymnastic exercises.* —***n.:*** **parallels of latitude** *around a globe show distances from the equator; batteries connected* **in parallel** (i.e. negatives together and positives together); *Man's moon-landing is without* ~ (i.e. equal) *in history; The preacher* **drew a parallel** *between Easter and pagan spring festivals;* **par·al·lel·ism** *n.* —***v.*** **-al·lels, -al·lel(l)ed, -al·lel·(l)ing:** *a creative genius* ~*ing Shakespeare.* —**par·al·lel·o·gram** (–LEL·uh–) *n.* a four-sided figure with opposite sides parallel and equal, but usu. not a rectangle.

pa·ral·y·sis (puh·RAL·i–) *n., pl.* **-ses** (–seez) the partial or complete loss of sensation and movement in the body or in an organ; hence, a state of powerlessness. —**par·a·lyt·ic** (–LIT–) *n.* & *adj.: a* ~ *in a wheelchair; a* ~ *stroke.* —**par·a·lyze** (PAIR·uh–) *v.* **-lyz·es, -lyzed, -lyz·ing** cause paralysis in: *Paraplegia* ~*s the lower body; a city* ~*d by a transit strike.* —**par·a·lyz·ing·ly** *adv.*

Par·a·mar·i·bo (–MAIR–) capital of Surinam.

par·a·me·ci·um (pair·uh·MEE·shee·um) *n., pl.* **-ci·a** or **-ci·ums** a one-celled oval-shaped amoebalike animal of fresh waters that swims about by means of hairlike cilia.

par·a·med·ic (PAIR·uh–) *n.* an auxiliary medical worker, as a nurses's aide, lab technician, or midwife. —**par·a·med·i·cal** (–MED–) *adj.: Giving injections, taking X rays, etc. are* ~ *work.*

pa·ram·e·ter (puh·RAM·i–) *n.* a factor; characteristic; feature: *Temperature, pressure, and density are the* ~*s of the atmosphere; to study a problem in all its* ~*s.* —**par·a·met·ric** (–MET–) or **-ri·cal** *adj.*

par·a·mil·i·tar·y (–MIL–) *adj.* auxiliary to a military force: ~ *training; a* ~ *force.*

par·a·mount (PAIR·uh–) *adj.* supreme; primary: *of* ~ *importance.*

par·a·mour (PAIR·uh·moor) *n.* an illicit lover, esp. a mistress.

Pa·ra·ná (pair·uh·NAH) Argentina's main river flowing into the Atlantic near Buenos Aires; **Paraná city** a trading center on the Paraná.

par·a·noi·a (pair·uh·NOY·uh) *n.* a mental disorder characterized by delusions of grandeur, persecution, etc. —**par·a·noi·ac** (–NOY–) or **par·a·noid** (PAIR·uh–) *n.* & *adj.: a paranoid schizophrenic.*

par·a·pet (PAIR·uh–) *n.* a low wall or railing at the edge of a balcony, roof, bridge, or atop a rampart.

par·a·pher·na·li·a (–fur·NAY·lee·uh) *n. sing.* & *pl.* equipment or gear proper to an activity or office.

par·a·phrase (PAIR·uh–) *n.* a restatement of a text to give the meaning, often in simpler form. —***v.*** **-phras·es, -phrased, -phras·ing:** *a poem difficult to* ~.

par·a·ple·gi·a (–PLEE·jee·uh) *n.* paralysis of the lower half of the body. —**par·a·pleg·ic** (–PLEE·jic) *n.* & *adj.*

par·a·pro·fes·sion·al (–FESH–) *n.* a professional's trained assistant.

par·a·psy·chol·o·gy (–COL·uh·jee) *n.* the psychology of psychic phenomena. —**par·a·psy·chol·o·gist** n.

par·a·site (PAIR·uh–) *n.* one that exists at another's expense; sponger: *The mistletoe, tapeworm, and bacteria are biological* ~*s.* —**par·a·sit·ic** (–SIT–) or **-i·cal** *adj.* —**par·a·sit·ism** (PAIR·uh–) *n.* —**par·a·sit·ize** *v.* **-iz·es, -ized, -iz·ing:** *Aphids* ~ *plants.* —**par·a·si·tol·o·gy** (–TOL·uh·jee) *n.;* **par·a·si·tol·o·gist** *n.*

par·a·sol (PAIR·uh·sol) *n.* a woman's umbrella carried as a sunshade.

par·a·sym·pa·thet·ic (pair·uh·sim·puh·THET·ic) **nervous system** a subsystem of the nervous system controlling involuntary activities and working in opposition to the sympathetic nervous system, as in slowing down the heartbeat that sympathetic impulses speed up.

par·a·thi·on (pair·uh·THYE·on) *n.* a poisonous insecticide used against plant lice.

par·a·thy·roid (–THYE–) *adj.* having to do with a **parathyroid (gland),** any of two pairs of glands located near the thyroids and producing hormones that regulate the body's use of calcium and phosphorus.

par·a·troops (PAIR·uh–) *n.pl.* soldiers trained to parachute from airplanes; **par·a·troop·er** *n.*

par·a·ty·phoid (–TYE–) *n.* an intestinal infection caused by food poisoning.

par·boil *v.* boil partially; precook: ~*ed rice.*

par·cel *n.* **1** a wrapped package or bundle. **2** a collection or group of persons, animals, or things: *a* ~ *of liars.* **3** a piece or portion: *a* ~ *of land.* —**part and parcel** an essential part. —***v.*** **-cels, -cel(l)ed, -cel·(l)ing:** *work* ~*d out to free-lancers; goods* ~*d up for shipping.* —**parcel post** a postal service for parcels rather than letters.

parch *v.* to dry, as by the sun's heat: ~*ed throats thirsting for a drink; land* ~*ed by drought;* **parched** (i.e. roasted) **corn.**

parch·ment *n.* fine writing material made from skins, as vellum, or paper specially processed; also, a document on such material, as a diploma.

pard *n.* **1** *Archaic.* leopard. **2** *Regional.* short for **pard·ner,** partner.

par·don (PAR·dn) *n.* **1** forgiveness; **I beg your pardon** a polite formula of apology, as for not hearing something said. **2** release from a penalty of law: *the Nixon* ~. **—*v.*** forgive: ~ *me for interrupting;* ~ *my rudeness;* **par·don·a·ble** *adj.;* **par·don·a·bly** *adv.* **—par·don·er** *n.* formerly, one licensed to raise money by dispensing papal pardons.

pare (PAIR) *v.* **pares, pared, par·ing** **1** clip or cut (the edge) or shave (the surface): ~ *one's nails;* ~ *an apple;* hence **paring knife.** **2** reduce: ~ *down a budget.*

par·e·gor·ic (pair·uh·GOR–) *n.* an opium preparation used to relieve intestinal pain and diarrhea.

par·ent (PAIR·unt) *n.* a father or mother; also, originator or source: *a parent-teacher association; the* ~ *firm of a subsidiary.* **—par·ent·age** (–ij) *n.: a man of noble* ~. **—par·en·tal** (–REN–) *adj.:* ~ *responsibilities.* **—par·ent·hood** *n.*

pa·ren·the·sis (puh·REN·thuh–) *n., pl.* **-ses** (–seez) one of a pair of rounded brackets ( ) used to enclose words, numbers, or other symbols; also, a word or clause inserted within a sentence and set off from it by a pair of such brackets, commas, or dashes, i.e. **(with)in parentheses. —par·en·the·size** *v.* **-siz·es, -sized, -siz·ing. —par·en·thet·ic** (–THET–) or **-i·cal** *adj.;* **par·en·thet·i·cal·ly** *adv.*

pa·re·sis (puh·REE·sis) *n., pl.* **-ses** (–seez) partial paralysis; **general paresis** a brain disease resulting from syphilis. **—pa·ret·ic** (–RET–) *n.* & *adj.*

par ex·cel·lence (–ek·suh·LAHNCE) preeminent(ly): *a writer* ~ *though a poor talker.*

par·fait (–FAY) *n.* a frozen dessert of cream and eggs; also, ice cream in several layers served in a **parfait glass,** a tall, slender glass with a short stem.

pa·ri·ah (puh·RYE·uh) *n.* an outcast.

pa·ri·e·tal (puh·RYE·uh·tl) *adj.* pertaining to walls: **parietal bones** *forming the sides and roof of the skull;* ~ *regulations affect life within college walls.*

par·i-mu·tu·el (pair·ee·MYOO·choo·ul) *n.* a betting system in which the winners share the total amount wagered minus a percentage for the management; also, a machine used to register bets and calculate payoffs.

parings *n. pl.* leavings or shavings.

pa·ri pas·su (PAIR·ee·PASS·oo) *Latin.* at an equal rate.

Par·is (PAIR·is) **1** in Greek legend, the prince of Troy who abducted Helen. **2** capital of France; **Pa·ri·sian** (–RIZH–) *n.* & *adj.* **—Paris green** a bright green powder used on plants as an insecticide.

par·ish (PAIR–) *n.* **1** an administrative division of a diocese, with a priest or minister in charge; also, as in Louisiana, a county. **2** the members of a parish collectively, or **pa·rish·ion·ers** (puh·RISH–).

par·i·ty (PAIR·i·tee) *n.* **-ties** (–teez) equality, esp. in purchasing power: *Firefighters want* ~ *of pay with policemen.*

park *n.* an area of land set aside for public recreation. **—*v.*** **1** put (a vehicle) in a place and leave temporarily. **2** *Informal.* put or leave somewhere: ~ *the kids with Grandma.*

par·ka (PAR·kuh) *n.* a hooded fur jacket for winter wear; also, a similar warm garment of cloth.

parking lot area for parking motor vehicles. **—parking meter** a coin-operated clock device for regulating the use of a parking space.

Par·kin·son's disease a nervous disorder of advancing age characterized by muscular tremors of the hand, face, and other parts of the body; also called **par·kin·son·ism** and "shaking palsy."

Parkinson's Law the satirical observation that work expands to fill the time available.

park·way *n.* a broad boulevard or landscaped highway.

par·lance (–lunce) *n.* style of speech: *In common* ~ *"inebriated" would be "drunk."*

par·lay *n.* a bet or series of bets with a previous wager plus winnings as the next bet. **—*v.:*** *Heinz* ~*ed a pickle and made a fortune.*

par·ley (–lee) *n.* **-leys** a negotiation for coming to terms with an adversary. **—*v.:*** *Israel refused to* ~ *with the P.L.O.* **—par·lia·ment** (PAR·luh–) *n.* a legislative assembly, esp. of Britain and other Commonwealth countries, usu. **Parliament. —par·lia·men·tar·i·an** (–TAIR·ee·un) *n.* an expert in parliamentary practice. **—par·lia·men·ta·ry** (–MEN·tuh·ree) *adj.:* ~ *language, procedure.* **—par·lor** (–lur) *n.* a semiprivate room for social conversation; also, one specially designed for a business: *a beauty* ~*; funeral* ~*;* **parlor car** a railroad car with superior individual accommodation; chair car. Also **par·lour** *Brit.*

par·lous (–lus) *Archaic. adj.* hazardous. **—*adv.*** extremely: *The night is* ~ *cold.* **—par·lous·ly** *adv.*

Par·me·san (PAR·muh·zahn) *n.* a hard, dry cheese with a sharp flavor. **—par·mi·gia·na** (–JAH·nuh) or **par·mi·gia·no** (–JAH·noh) *adj.* prepared with Parmesan; *eggplant* ~.

pa·ro·chi·al (puh·ROH·kee·ul) *adj.* **1** of a parish: ~ *school.* **2** narrow-minded: *very* ~ *in his interests;* **pa·ro·chi·al·ism** *n.* **—pa·ro·chi·al·ly** *adv.*

par·o·dy (PAIR·uh·dee) *n.* **-dies** a satirical imitation; also, a poor imitation; travesty: *a mere* ~ *of a court of justice.* **—*v.*** **-dies, -died, -dy·ing** imitate in a parody of: *The Smiths* ~*d Wordsworth.* **—par·o·dist** *n.* a writer of parodies.

pa·role (puh·ROLE) *n.* the release of a prisoner before his term is fully served: *a convict free* **on parole. —*v.*** **-roles, -roled, -rol·ing:** *He* *was ~d for good conduct.* —**pa•rol•ee** (puh·roh·LEE) *n.*

pa•rot•id (puh·ROT·id) **gland** any of the two salivary glands at the base of each ear.

par•ox•ysm (PAIR·uk·sizm) *n.* a sudden outburst (of rage, despair, laughter, etc.). —**par•ox•ys•mal** (–SIZ·mul) *adj.*

par•quet (–KAY) *n.* **1** the part of a theater's main floor from the orchestra pit to the **parquet circle,** the part beneath the rear balcony. **2** a floor of parquetry. —***v.*** **-quets** (–KAZE), **–quet•ed** (–KADE), **–quet•ing** (–KAY·ing): *wainscoting ~d with cedar.* —**par•quet•ry** (PAR·kit·ree) *n.* **-ries** a mosaic of inlaid wood.

par•ra•keet (PAIR·uh–) same as PARAKEET.

par•ri•cide (PAIR·i–) *n.* a murderer of a parent or other close relative; also, such a murder. —**par•ri•ci•dal** (–SYE·dl) *adj.*

par•rot (PAIR·ut) *n.* one of a family of colorful tropical birds with hooked bills and the ability to mimic speech; hence, one who repeats something without grasping it. —***v.:*** *children ~ing their teachers.* —**parrot fever** a viral lung infection caught from sick birds.

par•ry (PAIR·ee) *v.* **par•ries, par•ried, par•ry•ing** turn aside a blow, as in fencing; hence, evade adroitly: *He ~d reporter's questions with a "No comment."* —***n.,*** *pl.* **par•ries:** *the thrust and ~ of political debates.*

parse *v.* **pars•es, parsed, pars•ing** give a grammatical description of (a sentence, phrase, word, etc.).

par•sec *n.* a unit of astronomical distance equal to 3.26 light-years.

par•si•mony (PAR·si·moh·nee) *n.* stinginess; niggardliness. —**par•si•mo•ni•ous** (–MOH–) *adj.* —**par•si•mo•ni•ous•ly** *adv.* —**par•si•mo•ni•ous•ness** *n.*

pars•ley (–lee) *n.* a plant whose crinkled leaves are used as a garnish.

pars•nip *n.* a vegetable of the carrot family with a long whitish edible root.

par•son (–sun) *n.* a clergyman, usu. a Protestant one; **par•son•age** (–ij) *n.* a parson's residence.

part. participial; participle; particular.

part *n.* **1** a portion, division, or section of something: *Petals are ~s of a flower; I like the music only* **in part** (i.e. not completely); *Her efforts were wasted* **for the most part** (i.e. mostly). **2** a person's share or role in an activity: *You did your ~ well; Jane took her mother's ~ in the family dispute; One of the actors forgot his ~* (i.e. lines); *played the ~* (i.e. role) *of Othello; I didn't* **take part** (i.e. get involved) *in the fight;* **For my part** (i.e. personally) *I like things as they are; There was some hesitation* **on the part of** (i.e. by) *John.* **3 parts** *pl.: a man of ~s* (i.e. abilities); *traveling in foreign ~s* (i.e. regions). **4:** *He took the criticism* **in good part** (i.e. graciously). —***v.*** divide; keep apart; separate: *The referees ~ed the fighting teams; She ~s her hair in the middle; We must* **part company** (i.e. leave each other) *in London; She* **parted from** (i.e. left) *us without saying good-bye; We* **part with** *our earthly goods at death.* —**par•take** (–TAKE) *v.* **-takes, -took, -tak•en** (–TAY·kn), **-tak•ing** take a share or part in: *The whole town partook in the festival; to ~ of a banquet.* —**par•tak•er** *n.*

par•terre (–TAIR) *n.* **1** a garden area of flower beds. **2** same as PARQUET CIRCLE.

par•the•no•gen•e•sis (–JEN·uh–) *n.* reproduction by unfertilized egg, as in honeybees and wasps. —**par•the•no•ge•net•ic** (–NET·ic) *adj.*

par•tial (–shul) *adj.* **1** not total: *a ~ eclipse of the moon.* **2** biased; having a fondness for: *a referee* **partial to** *one side; ~ towards the rich.* —**par•ti•al•i•ty** (–shee·AL·i·tee) *n.* —**par•tial•ly** *adv.* to a certain degree: *a student ~ dependent on his parents.* —**par•ti•ble** *adj.* divisible. —**par•tic•i•pate** (–TIS–) *v.* **-pates, -pat•ed, -pat•ing** take part: *to ~ in social activities.* —**par•tic•i•pant** *n.* & *adj.* —**par•tic•i•pa•tion** (–PAY–) *n.* —**par•tic•i•pa•tor** (–TIS–) *n.;* **par•tic•i•pa•to•ry** *adj.* involving direct or active participation, as of people in a **participatory democracy** and of audience in **participatory theater.** —**par•ti•ci•ple** *n.* a word with characteristics of verb and adjective, as *acting* in "He is acting" and "an acting president." —**par•ti•cip•i•al** (–SIP–) *adj.* —**par•ti•cle** *n.* **1** a tiny bit; smallest unit of matter: *not a ~ of evidence against him; protons, electrons, and other atomic ~s; The betatron and cyclotron are* **particle accelerators; particle board** *made with sawdust or wood ~s.* **2** an uninflected part of speech or an affix, as *in, and, the, bi-,* and *oh.* —**par•ti•col•ored** (–CUL·urd) *adj.* having more than one color: *a ~ marble; ~ thoughts about the future.* —**par•tic•u•lar** (–TIK·yuh·lur) *adj.* **1** relating to an individual person or thing; specific: *This ~ case is an exception to the rule; I like sea food, lobsters* **in particular** (i.e. especially). **2** special; also, exact; careful: *a matter of ~ concern to me; very ~ about her dress.* —***n.*** detail: *She is good in every ~; He was fired, but I won't go into ~s.* —**par•tic•u•lar•i•ty** (–LAIR–) *n.* —**par•tic•u•lar•ize** (–TIK–), **-iz•es, -ized, -iz•ing:** *He condemned the group without ~ing about individual members.* —**par•tic•u•lar•ly** *adv.* especially: *John is ~ good at math.* —**par•tic•u•late** (–lut, –lit) *n.* & *adj.* formed of particles: *airborne ~ fallout; cytoplasmic ~s.* —**part•ing** *n.* separation: *a tearful ~ of lovers; They agreed on a* **parting of the ways** *after 50 years together.* —***adj.*** final: *a dying man's ~ words; a ~ shot from the getaway car.*

par•ti pris (–tee·PREE), *pl.* **-tis pris** (–tee·PREE, –PREEZ) a preconceived opinion; bias.

par•ti•san (–zn, –sn) *n.* a strong supporter of a party, esp. a militant; also, a guerrilla. —***adj.:*** *He's too ~ to serve on this body; ~ politics, propaganda.* —**par•ti•san•ship** *n.* —**par•tite** *adj.* &

comb.form. divided; cleft: *a ~ leaf; a tripartite treaty.* —**par·ti·tion** (–TISH·un) *n.* division; separation: *a ~ between rooms; the ~ of India in 1947.* —**v.:** *The dining area was ~ed off.* —**par·ti·tion·ist** *n.: a nation torn by ~s and secessionists.* —**par·ti·tive** (–tiv) *n.* & *adv. Grammar.* serving to divide: *"Some of us" is a ~ construction; "Some," "few," "any," etc. are ~s;* **par·ti·tive·ly** *adv.* —**par·ti·zan** *n.* & *adj.* same as PARTISAN. —**part·ly** *adv.* in part: *You're ~ right and ~ wrong; He's the culprit, but you're ~ to blame.* —**part·ner** *n.* one who shares in some activity or business with another or others: *an active ~ in my business;* cf. SILENT PARTNER; *a dancing ~; ~s in crime.* —**part·ner·ship** *n.* participation, esp. in a business; also, the business or the business contract itself. —**part of speech** one of the grammatical classes of words, as noun, verb, adjective, etc. —**partook** *pt.* of PARTAKE.

par·tridge (–trij) *n.* any of various plump-bodied game birds such as the quail, pheasant, or grouse.

part-song *n.* a usu. unaccompanied song for several voices. —**part-time** *adj.* & *adv.* for less than the usual time: *working ~ on a ~ job;* **part-tim·er** *n.*

par·tu·ri·tion (–RISH·un) *n.* childbirth.

part·way *adv.* part of the way; partly: *~ through the book, Jim fell asleep.* —**par·ty** (–tee) *n.* **-ties** **1** a group taking part in an organized cause or activity: *a hunting ~; a political ~;* **party politics** *doesn't help the common good.* **2** a gathering for amusement or celebration: *a birthday ~.* **3** a person: *An innocent ~ got hit; Dick would not be a ~ to* (i.e. participant in) *the deal; the opposite ~* (in a legal action); *the ~* (*Informal.* person) *who called yesterday.* —**v. -ties, -tied, -ty·ing** hold or attend parties. —**party line** **1** a telephone circuit with more than one subscriber. **2** a party's policies and principles. —**par·ty-poop(·er)** *n. Slang.* a wet blanket. —**party spirit** social spirit; also, narrow loyalty. —**party wall** a common wall between two properties.

par·ve·nu (PAR·vuh·new) *n.* one not deserving his social position; social upstart.

pas (PAH) *n., pl.* **pas** (PAHZ) a dance step or a series of steps.

Pas·a·de·na (–DEE·nuh) a city of S.W. California.

pas·cal (–CAL) *n.* unit of pressure of one newton per square meter.

pas·chal (PAS·cul) *adj.* of the Passover, or **Pasch** (PASK), or of Easter: *the* **Paschal Lamb** (i.e. Christ).

pa·sha (PAH·shuh) *n.* a title of rank once used after the name of Turkish officers.

Pash·to (PUHSH·toh) *n.* an Iranian language spoken in Afghanistan and N. Pakistan.

pas·qui·nade (–NADE) *n.* a lampoon. —**v. -nades, -nad·ed, -nad·ing** ridicule (someone) with a lampoon.

pass. passenger; passive.

pass *v.* **1** go or cause to go towards and beyond; get to or cause to get to and past; also, proceed; depart: *We ~ed each other on the street; She ~ed by my window; Please ~ (me) the salt; This story ~es belief; Many years have ~ed (by) since my graduation; That was insulting, but let it ~; She ~ed* (i.e. died) *quietly in her sleep.* **2** be or cause to be accepted or approved; succeed, at least minimally: *Jim ~ed the test; The teacher ~ed him with a C grade; A law is ~ed; A bill ~es (the Senate); The judge ~ed sentence; The forger tried to ~ a bad check; Nylon will not ~ for silk.* —**bring to pass** cause to happen or exist: *Space travel has brought to ~ many fancies of former ages.* —**come to pass** happen: *How did this ever come to ~?* —**pass away** (or **on**): *Grandma ~ed away* (i.e. died) *last night.* —**pass off:** *The shopkeeper ~ed off a cheap imitation as the real thing.* —**pass out** **1:** *The teacher ~ed out free tickets for the show.* **2** *Informal: He ~ed out* (i.e. fainted) *on hearing about the tragedy.* —**pass over:** *No one was ~ed over* (i.e. ignored) *at promotion time.* —**pass up:** *Who would ~ up* (i.e. refuse or give up) *a chance of a lifetime?* —**n.** **1** a movement: *A magician makes ~es with a wand; a bomber's ~ over its target; annoyed by strangers making ~es* (i.e. sexual advances) *at her on the street; a forward ~* (i.e. a ball thrown forward) *during play.* **2** a resulting state or condition: *What a pretty ~* (i.e. state of affairs) *we have reached!* **3** something indicating acceptance or allowing progress: *a free ~ to the games; a convoy advancing through a mountain ~.* —**pass·a·ble** (–uh·bl) *adj.: a bridge ~* (i.e. useable) *only in the dry season; a ~* (i.e. adequate) *knowledge of the subject;* **pass·a·bly** *adv.: His French is ~ good.* —**pass·age** (–ij) *n.: I forgot my misfortune with the ~ of time; a ~ to Europe by boat; We were refused ~ without a visa; The bill had a stormy ~ in Congress; a ~* (i.e. quotation or selection) *from Shakespeare; an underground ~;* **pass·age·way** *n.: Hallways and alleys are ~s.* —**pass book** same as BANKBOOK. —**pas·sé** (pa·SAY) *adj.* out-moded; oldish. —**pas·sel** (–sl) *n. Informal.* a group or assortment; parcel. —**pas·sen·ger** (PASS·n·jur) *n.* one being conveyed in a vehicle; also, a traveler. —**passe-par·tout** (pass·par·TOO) *n.* **1** a kind of adhesive tape used for mounting, esp. a frame for a picture. **2** something that serves as a master key for passage everywhere. —**pass·er** *n.* —**pass·er-by** *n., pl.* **-ers-by** a person passing by: *seated atop her car in full view of every ~.*

pass·er·ine (–rine, –rin) *n.* & *adj.* the largest order of birds, including half of all known species such as blackbirds, finches, jays, sparrows, and warblers.

pas·sim *adv. Latin.* here and there (in the book specified).

pass·ing *adj.* getting past; hence, succeeding: *C is the ~ grade; The ~ lane is not for slow driving;*

The hero got only a ~ (i.e. casual) *mention in the press;* **n.:** *The* ~ (i.e. death) *of de Gaulle left a void in France; I spoke to her* **in passing** *before boarding my plane;* **passing bell** death bell.

pas·sion (PASH·un) *n.* **1** strong feeling, esp. of love, lust, hate, anger, or enthusiasm; also, one of these or an outburst of it: *language without* ~; *The child flew into a* ~ *(of rage); She has a* ~ (i.e. enthusiasm) *for pottery; Pride is his ruling* ~. **2** an object of such feeling: *Pottery was one of her early* ~*s.* **3 Passion** Christ's sufferings, from after the Last Supper to the Crucifixion, dramatized in **Passion plays: Passion Sunday** *ushers in* **Passion Week,** *the week before Easter; The* **pas·sion·flow·er** *borne by a woody vine, is thought to symbolize features of the Passion.* —**pas·sion·ate** (–it) *adj.* full of passion: *a* ~ *character; a* ~ *embrace; a* ~ *appeal for mercy;* **pas·sion·ate·ly** *adv.: She is* ~ *fond of the outdoors.* —**pas·sion·less** *adj.: a* ~ *performance of Hamlet;* **pas·sion·less·ly** *adv.* —**pas·sive** (–siv) *adj.* not active but receiving or acted upon: *a* ~ *audience;* ~ (i.e. meek) *submission to authority;* **passive resistance** nonviolent action for a cause, as by work-to-rule or civil disobedience; **pas·siv·ism** *n.;* **pas·siv·ist** *n.* —**passive voice** the verb form used to show that the receiver of the action is the grammatical subject, as in "Paul was hit by Peter"; cf. ACTIVE VOICE. —**pas·sive·ly** *adv.* —**pas·sive·ness** or **pas·siv·i·ty** (–SIV–) *n.*

pass·key *n.* a master key. —**Pass·o·ver** *n.* the commemoration of the deliverance of Israel from slavery in Egypt: ~ *is a Jewish holiday.* —**pass·port** *n.* a government document identifying the bearer's citizenship for purposes of travel abroad; hence, something guaranteeing acceptance or admission: *A university degree is a* ~ *to many careers.* —**pass·word** *n.* a secret identifying word or phrase, as used to pass through a guarded gate. —**past** *adj.* passed by; gone; former: *Night comes after the day is* ~; ~ *achievements; the* ~ *president of a society; "Ran" is the* **past tense** *of "run."* —**n.:** *memories from the* ~; *our country's glorious* ~; *I know something about his* ~. —**prep.** & **adv.** beyond: *It is 10 minutes* ~ *(five); A car sped* ~ *(us); a miracle* ~ *human understanding.*

pas·ta (PAHS·tuh) *n.* dough made into spaghetti, macaroni, ravioli, and other Italian foods; also, a dish made with this paste. —**paste** *n.* **1** a sticky or plastic mixture, as of flour and water or toothpaste; pasta; also, a soft food prepared by pounding and mixing: *anchovy* ~; *tomato* ~; *almond* ~. **2** any soft mixture or substance, as paper adhesives, clay used in pottery, etc.; also, a soft glass, or *strass,* used for making imitation gems; also, such a gem. —**v. pastes, past·ed, past·ing** **1** stick: *a wall* ~*d with posters; A book's endpapers are* **pasted down;** hence **paste·down** *n.* **2** *Slang.* thrash: *He got a sound* **pasting** *for his insolence;* **paste·board** *made of layers of paper pasted together.* —**paste job** *Informal.* a pastiche.

pas·tel (pass·TEL) *n.* a chalklike pigment mixed with gum and made into crayons for painting in soft colors; also, a painting made with such crayons. —**adj.** soft and delicate in color effects: *the pure,* ~ *shades of a Degas.* —**pas·tel·(l)ist** (–TEL–) *n.*

pas·tern *n.* the part of a horse's foot between the hoof and the fetlock.

Pas·teur (pass·TUR), **Louis.** 1822–1895, French bacteriologist, who first used inoculations of specific viruses to develop immunity to diseases; hence **Pasteur treatment** (for rabies). —**pas·teur·ize** (PAS·chuh–) *v.* **-iz·es, -ized, -iz·ing** sterilize, esp. milk, by heating to kill bacteria in an apparatus called **pas·teur·iz·er** *n.;* **pas·teur·i·za·tion** (–ZAY–) *n.*

pas·tiche (–TEESH) *n.* a musical or other artistic composition that is a patchwork of borrowings from various sources; potpourri; also **pas·tic·cio** (–TEE·choh), *pl.* **-tic·ci** (–chee) or **-cios.** Also **v. -tich·es, -tiched, -tich·ing** make into a hodgepodge.—**pas·ties** (PAY·stees) *n.pl.* a pair of adhesive coverings for the nipples, worn by strippers. See also PASTY. —**pas·tille** (–TEEL) *n.* a medicated lozenge or tablet; also, a pellet for fumigation or a crayon of pastel; also **pas·til** (PAS·til).

pas·time *n.* activity pursued as a diversion.

past master an expert or adept (*in* or *of* an art, occupation, etc.).

pas·tor (–tur) *n.* a clergyman heading a parish or congregation. —**pas·to·ral** (–ul) *adj.* **1:** *a priest's* ~ *responsibilities; a bishop's* ~ *letter.* **2** of rural life; hence, idyllic: *Virgil's* ~ *poetry; "As You Like It" is* ~ *drama; a* ~ *scene;* **pas·to·rale** (–RAL) *n.* a musical composition with a pastoral theme. —**pas·tor·ate** (–it) *n.* a pastor's office or term.

past participle a verb form or adjective showing completed action, as in "It is *lost*" or "a *lost* world."

pas·tra·mi (puh·STRAH·mee) *n.* a highly seasoned smoked beef.

pas·try (PAY·stree) *n.* **-tries** sweet baked goods, as pies, tarts, turnovers, etc., baked from flour paste.

past tense See PAST.

pas·ture (–chur) *n.* food for grazing animals; hence, land **(pas·ture·land)** where grass and such vegetation grows; also **pas·tur·age** (–ij). —**v. –tures, –tured, –tur·ing:** *Sheep* ~*ing on a village common; A* **pas·tur·er** ~*s livestock.*

pas·ty (PAY·stee) *adj.* **-ti·er, -ti·est** like paste; sticky and doughy; also, dull and pale: *a* ~ *complexion;* **pas·ti·ness** *n.* —**n.** (PAS–), *pl.* **-ties** a pie with a meat filling.

pat. patent(ed).

pat *n.* **1** a light tap or stroke with a flat surface, as with the palm of the hand; **pat on the back** an expression of encouragement or sympathy. **2** a small flat portion made (as if) by a pat: *a ~ of butter for a toast.* **—v. pats, pat·ted, pat·ting:** *The child ~d her cat; Tim ~d himself on the back* (i.e. congratulated himself) *and decided to try even harder.* **—adj.** & **adv.** prompt(ly): *a resourceful girl with a ~ answer for everything; The book was published ~ on schedule.* —(**have, have down** or) **know pat** *Informal.* know perfectly, esp. from memory. **—stand pat** *Informal.* stand firm, without budging.

patch *n.* **1** a small piece of material that serves to mend, cover, or decorate where it is applied: *a jacket with ~es at the elbows; the general with an eye ~ over his blind eye; a shoulder ~* (i.e. insignia). **2** something similar to a patch in appearance: *a black dog with a ~ of white on its back; a potato or cabbage ~* (i.e. area or plot). —**v.:** *Mother ~ed Jim's torn pants; The lovers soon* **patched up** *their quarrel.* **—patch pocket** one sewn on to the outside of a garment. **—patch test** an allergy test for a substance made by using a pad saturated with it on one's skin. **—patch·work** *n.* a piece of work or a design made up of many patches: *a ~ quilt.* **—patch·y** *adj.* **patch·i·er, -i·est:** *The fog was ~; ~ sunlight;* **patch·i·ly** *adv.;* **patch·i·ness** *n.*

pate *n. Informal.* head; brain; **-pated** *comb.form.* as in *bald-pated, addlepated.*

pâ·té (pah·TAY) *n. French.* a patty; also, paste, esp. **pâté de foie gras** (–duh·fwah·GRAH) a paste made of goose liver, often with truffles.

pa·tel·la (puh·TEL·uh) *n.* **-tel·las** or **-tel·lae** (–TEL·ee) kneecap. **—pat·en** (PATN) *n.* a flat piece of metal, esp. a small plate used for the Eucharistic bread.

pat·ent (PAT·nt, *esp. Brit.* PAY·tnt) *adj.* **1** plain; evident: *a ~ falsehood; It is ~ to everyone.* **2** of a document, public: *letters ~.* **—pat·en·cy** *n.;* **pat·ent·ly** *adv.: a theory that is ~ absurd.* **—patent** *n.* an exclusive right to an invention or process granted to a person, or **pat·en·tee,** by a **pat·en·tor** or government authority, as the U.S. **Patent Office:** *A "Patent Pending" notice on a product discourages imitators.* **—v.:** *A better mousetrap should be ~ed; Mere ideas and principles are not* **pat·ent·a·ble** *adj.;* **pat·ent·a·bil·i·ty** (–BIL–) *n.* **—patent leather** a glossy smooth black leather. **—patent medicine** one protected by a trademark and usu. sold without a prescription; proprietary medicine.

pa·ter (PAY·tur) *n.* **1** *Brit. Informal.* one's father. **2** a paternoster. **—pa·ter·fa·mil·i·as** (–MIL·ee·us) *n.* the father of a household. **—pa·ter·nal** (–TUR·nl) *adj.* of, like, or from a father: *~ affection; one's ~ grandmother; a ~ government;* **pa·ter·nal·ism** *n.* government as by a father; **pa·ter·nal·is·tic** (–LIS–) *adj.;* **pa·ter·nal·is·ti·cal·ly** *adv.* **—pa·ter·ni·ty** (–TUR–) *n.* fatherhood; parentage: *An unwed mother brings a* **paternity suit** *to establish the father's responsibility; A* **paternity test** *compares the blood groups of child, mother, and alleged father.* **—pa·ter·nos·ter** (pah·tur·NAW·stur) *n.* the Lord's Prayer; also **Pater Noster.**

Pat·er·son a city in New Jersey.

path *n.* **1** a track or trail, as in a park, used by people on foot: *a garden ~.* **2** a course or route: *the flight ~ of a satellite.*

path. pathology; pathological. **—pa·thet·ic** (puh·THET–) *adj.* **1** pitiful; pitiable: *a ~ story of starving children.* **2** full of pathos; also, capable of feeling; **pathetic fallacy** a figure of speech attributing feelings to nature, as in "the cruel sea" and "the happy autumn fields." **—pa·thet·ic·al·ly** *adv.*

path·find·er *n.* an explorer; **Pathfinders of America** an organization of young people, founded in 1914. **—path·less** *adj.* wild; trackless.

path·o·gen (–uh·jun) *n.* a disease-causing microorganism or substance; **path·o·gen·ic** (–JEN–) *adj.;* **path·o·gen·e·sis** *n.* the origin and development of a disease; **path·o·ge·net·ic** (–NET–) *adj.* **—path·o·log·i·cal** (–LOJ–) adj. **1** of pathology: *a ~ condition* (caused by a disease). **2** compulsive; *a ~ drinker, liar.* **—path·ol·o·gist** (–THOL–) *n.* a specialist in pathology, who works mostly in a laboratory, performing biopsies, postmortems, etc. **—path·ol·o·gy** (–THOL·uh·jee) *n.* **-gies** the study of the origin, nature, and symptoms of diseases, esp. as affecting body tissues: *the ~ of pneumonia;* **—pa·thos** (PAY–) *n.* the quality of arousing pity and tenderness: *The death of Falstaff is full of ~.*

path·way *n.* path: *"High in his ~ hung the sun."*

-pathy *comb.form.* **1** feeling; emotion: as in *telepathy, antipathy.* **2** disease or treatment: as in *psychopathy, osteopathy.* **—pa·tience** (PAY·shunce) *n.* capacity to endure suffering and put up with inconveniences without complaining: *the ~ of Job; A teacher has to have ~ with slow learners; He has no ~ with latecomers.* **—pa·tient** (–shunt) *adj.: a ~ listener; ~ Griselda;* **pa·tient·ly** *adv.* **—pa·tient** *n.* a person receiving medical care; **pa·tient·hood** *n.*

pat·i·na (PAT·n·uh, puh·TEE·nuh) *n.* **-nas** or **-nae** (–nee) a glossy green film or coating formed on copper, bronze, etc. by oxidation that is considered elegant; also, any surface finish, natural or artificial: *a head of Zeus with a fine ~; a ~ of good manners.*

pa·ti·o (PAT·ee·oh) *n.* **-os** an open courtyard; also, an area adjoining a dwelling, used for outdoor lounging, dining, etc.

pat·ois (PAT·wah) *n., pl.* **-ois** (–wahz) a nonstandard variety of a language, as a provincial dialect or the jargon of an occupational class.

pat. pend. patent pending.

patri- *comb.form.* father: as in *patriarch, patrimony.* **—pa·tri·arch** (PAY·tree·arc) *n.* **1** the head of a tribe or founder of a family, as Abraham, Isaac, and Jacob in the Bible; hence, any venerable male leader or founder, as Joseph Smith in the Mormon Church. **2** a high-ranking bishop of the Eastern Orthodox Church. **—pa·tri·ar·chal** (–AR–) *adj.: It is a ~ custom for a married woman to take her husband's name.* **—pa·tri·ar·chate** (–kit) *n.* **—pa·tri·ar·chy** *n.* **-chies** a social organization in which authority is handed down along the male line; cf. MATRIARCHY. **—pa·tri·cian** (puh·TRISH·un) *n.* aristocrat; cf. PLEBEIAN; also ***adj.:*** *his ~ air.* **—pat·ri·cide** *n.* the murder of one's father; also, the killer himself; **pat·ri·ci·dal** (–SYE·dl) *adj.*

Pat·rick, Saint. A.D. 385?–461? patron saint of Ireland.

pat·ri·mo·ny (–moh·nee) *n.* **-nies** a legacy from one's father or ancestors; **pat·ri·mo·ni·al** (–MOH·nee·ul) *adj.* **—pa·tri·ot** (PAY·tree·ut) *n.* one who loves his country; **pa·tri·ot·ism** *n.* **—pa·tri·ot·ic** (–OT–) *adj.;* **pa·tri·ot·i·cal·ly** *adv.* **—pa·tris·tic** (–TRIS–) *adj.* of the early church fathers: *~ writings;* also **pa·tris·ti·cal.**

pa·trol (puh·TROLE) *v.* **-trols, -trolled, -troll·ing** make a regular circuit of a territory for service, security, etc.; **pa·trol·ler** *n.* ***—n.*** a patrolling person or body of men or a group of patrolling ships, planes, etc.: *highway ~;* **pa·trol·man** *n.* **-men** a policeman on patrol duty. **—patrol wagon** a small, enclosed police truck for transporting prisoners.

pa·tron (PAY·trun) *n.* **1** a special benefactor, guardian, or protector: *a wealthy ~ of the arts; St. George is the* **patron saint** *of England.* **2** a regular customer of a shop, library, or other establishment; *fem.* **pa·tron·ess; —pa·tron·al** *adj.* **—pa·tron·age** (PAY·truh·nij, PAT–) *n.* **1** protection, support, etc. given by a patron; also, the business brought by a customer. **2** the power to grant favors, esp. political; also, such favors, as appointments, contracts, etc. **—pa·tron·ize** *v.* **-iz·es, -ized, -iz·ing** **1** be a patron of: *We don't ~ that store any more.* **2** be condescending toward; **pa·tron·iz·ing** *adj.: a very ~ air;* **pa·tron·iz·ing·ly** *adv.* **—pat·ro·nym·ic** (–NIM–) *adj.* derived from or indicating a father's name: *"Mc" meaning "son" is a ~ prefix.* ***—n.:*** *"Dudding," "Simpson," and "O'Brien"* (i.e. descendant of Brian) *are ~s.* **—pa·troon** (puh–) *n.* a feudal landholder under the Dutch colonial regimes of New York and New Jersey.

pat·sy (–see) *n.* **-sies** *Slang.* one who is easily victimized, imposed upon, etc.; fall guy.

pat·ten (–tn) *n.* a wooden overshoe or a shoe with a platformlike metal framework to keep the wearer's foot above wet ground.

¹pat·ter *n.* quick, light tapping, as of rain on a roof, children's feet on a pavement, etc. ***—v.:*** *The children ~ed down the hallway as the bell rang.*

²pat·ter *n.* **1** the gabble or chatter of a rapid-talking hawker, comedian, or other performer. **2** the special jargon or cant used by a group, as thieves, beggars, etc. ***—v.:*** *The magician ~ed away while we watched.* **—pat·ter·er** *n.*

pat·tern *n.* **1** an ideal, model, or guide: *She was a ~ of domestic virtues; a paper ~ for making a dress.* **2** design with a repeating, hence predictable arrangement of elements: *wallpaper ~; a paisley ~; group behavior following a cultural ~; a winter weather ~; the holding ~ over a busy airport; a series of stranglings with a ~ to them.* — ***v.:*** *Children tend to ~ themselves after their parents.*

pat·ty *n.* **pat·ties** a small, flat, disk-shaped form of chopped or minced meat, fish, or other food: *a hamburger ~; A* **patty shell** *of pastry holds a creamed meat, vegetable, or fruit filling.*

pau·ci·ty (PAW–) *n.* smallness; fewness; lack: *a ~ of good speakers; ~ of evidence in a case.*

Paul (PAWL) **1 Saint Paul** A.D. 5?–67? "Apostle of the Gentiles" whose letters, or "Epistles," are part of the New Testament; **Paul·ine** *adj.* **2 Paul VI,** 1897–1978, Pope from 1963.

Paul Bun·yan (BUN·yun) a giant lumberjack of American folklore.

paunch (PAWNCH) *n.* a potbelly. **—paunch·y** *adj.* **—paunch·i·ness** *n.*

pau·per (PAW–) *n.* a poor person living on public charity. **—pau·per·ism** *n.* **—pau·per·ize** *v.* **-iz·es, -ized, -iz·ing:** *a nation ~d by inflation.*

pause (PAWZ) *n.* a partial stop, esp. in reading or speaking; also, a lengthening of a musical note indicated by 𝄑 or 𝄐 placed over it: *Unforeseen events always* **give one pause** (i.e. make one stop and reflect). ***—v.*** **paus·es, paused, paus·ing:** *Let's ~ and catch our breath.*

pave *v.* **paves, paved, pav·ing** cover or overlay, as a path, street, or an area with asphalt, concrete, tiles, etc.: *negotiations* **paving the way for** *a lasting peace; Their road to ruin was ~d with* (i.e. full of) *good intentions.* **—pave·ment** *n.* **1** a paved surface, esp. of a street; *Brit.* a sidewalk. **2** material used to pave; also **pav·ing. —pav·er** *n.*

pa·vil·ion (puh·VIL·yun) *n.* a tent; also, a light, tentlike open or temporary structure, as for an exhibit, recreational shelter, or as part of a building complex: *a hospital's maternity ~; Expo 67 had 76 national ~s; a band ~ in a park.*

Pav·lov, Ivan Petrovich. 1849–1936, Russian physiologist, noted for his theory of "conditioned reflexes." **—Pav·lov·i·an** (–LOH–) *adj.*

paw *n.* **1** a foot of an animal with claws, distinguished from a HOOF. **2** *Informal.* a human hand. ***—v.*** use the paws (as to kick, touch, etc.), esp. to grasp or handle in a rude manner: *She resented being ~ed on their first date.*

pawl *n.* a pivoted or hinged catch working with a ratchet wheel to drive it forward or to prevent backward rotation, as on a windlass.

pawn *n.* **1** a chessman of the lowest value; hence, one under someone else's control. **2** something given as surety, as jewels held **in pawn** against the payment of a loan. ***—v.:*** *He ~ed his guitar for ten dollars.* **—pawn·bro·ker**

n. a person who lends money in exchange for personal goods left as security; **pawn·shop** *n.* a pawnbroker's place of business.

Paw·nee (–NEE) *n.* (a member of) a confederation of Plains Indian tribes now living on a reservation in Oklahoma.

paw·paw *n.* a North American tree of the custard-apple family that bears small greenish fruit containing pulp with a bananalike flavor.

Pax *n. Latin.* peace, esp. as enforced by a military power, in compounds such as ~ *Romana* (i.e. Roman peace), ~ *Americana.*

pay *n.* money given for work or service; wages; salary: *a writer* **in the pay of** *a corporation.* —***adj.:*** ~ *dirt, telephone, television.* —***v.*** **pays, paid, pay·ing 1** give (money or similar amount) in return for a product or service: *I ~d $8,000 for the car; He ~s rent on his house; a* **pay-as-you-go** (i.e. as the service is received) *system of paying bills or taxes;* **pay·a·ble** *adj.* **2** bring money; be profitable or worthwhile (to): *It ~s to advertise; The business closed because it didn't ~; The job ~s $400 a week.* **3** give (something) that is due, fair, or proper: *Jane* **paid her way** (i.e. expenses) *through college; ~ compliments; ~ attention to a lecture; ~ a visit to someone; ~ a penalty.* —**pay off 1** pay (someone) in full. **2** be profitable; bring returns: *Hard work ~s off in the long run.* **3** *Informal.* to bribe. —**pay out,** *pt.* **payed** let out (a rope) gradually. —**pay the piper** (or **fiddler**) pay for one's pleasure; also, suffer the consequences of one's action. —**pay through the nose** pay excessively. —**pay up** pay fully what is due. —**pay·day** *n.* the day on which wages are paid. —**pay dirt** earth or ore containing enough mineral to make the mining profitable; hence, a profitable find or discovery. —**pay·ee** (pay·EE) *n.* one who receives something paid, or **pay·ment,** from a **pay·er** or **pay·or.** —**pay·load** *n.* the revenue-producing load in a plane, train, truck, etc.; hence, in a spacecraft, the passengers, instruments, etc., as distinguished from fuel and other operational loads; also, a missile's warhead or bomb load. —**pay·mas·ter** *n.* an official in charge of paying wages and salaries. —**pay·off** *n.* a bribe. —**pay·o·la** (–OH·luh) *n. Slang.* bribe. —**pay phone** (or **station**) a coin-operated public telephone. —**pay·roll** *n.* a list of employees and the pay they receive; also, the amount of money needed to pay them in a given period. —**payt.** payment. —**pay-TV** *n.* the system of broadcasters selling program packages to viewers on a subscription basis.

pa·zazz (puh·ZAZ) *n.* same as PIZAZZ.

Pb lead.

PBB "polybrominated biphenyl," a poisonous industrial chemical.

P.B.S. Public Broadcasting Service.

P.B.X. private branch telephone exchange.

p.c. percent; post card. —**P.C.** Peace Corps; Police Constable; Privy Council.

PCB "polychlorinated biphenyl," a cancer-causing industrial chemical.

PCP "phencyclidine," a hallucinogen.

pct. percent.

PCV positive crankcase ventilation (valve).

pd. paid. —**Pd** palladium. —**P.D.** per diem; Police Department.

P.D.Q. or **p.d.q.** pretty damn quick; at once.

P.D.T. Pacific Daylight Time.

P.E. Physical Education; Professional Engineer; Protestant Episcopal.

pea (PEE) *n.* the small, round edible seed borne in the pods of vines of the pulse family; also, any of these vines or a related plant, as the sweet pea or the chickpea. —**as like as two peas** like twins; exactly alike.

peace (PEECE) *n.* a state of calm and quiet; freedom from war; also, an agreement, esp. between nations, to end a war or not to fight; treaty: *You have ~ of mind when* **at peace** *with yourself;* **Hold your peace** (i.e. stay quiet) *when your mother is talking; ordered to* **keep the peace** (i.e. obey the laws) *by a magistrate; Christmas is a good time to* **make (one's) peace** *with enemies; the Paris Peace Conference of 1919.* —**peace·a·ble** or **peace·ful** *adj.: a peaceable man leading a peaceful life;* **peace·a·ble·ness** *n.;* **peace·ful·ness** *n.;* **peace·a·bly** *adv.;* **peace·ful·ly** *adv.* —**Peace Corps** a volunteer organization established by the U.S. government in 1961 for educational, agricultural, and technological work in developing countries. —**peace·keep·ing** *adj.: the U.N.'s ~ role in the Middle East.* —**peace·mak·er** *n.* one who helps settle quarrels: *"Blessed are the ~s."* —**peace·nik** *n.* [disparaging term] a demonstrator for peace. —**peace officer** a civil officer such as a policeman, sheriff, or justice of the peace. —**peace pipe** a pipe smoked ceremonially by North American Indians at a peace conference. —**peace sign** a V-sign made with the fingers of one's palm turned outwards. —**peace·time** *n.* period of peace; ***adj.:*** ~ *efforts.*

peach (PEECH) *n.* **1** a small, roundish, orange-yellow, fleshy fruit of a low-growing, widely cultivated tree. **2** *Slang.* a highly admired person. —**peach·y** *adj.* **1.** *Slang.* fine. **2** peach-colored.

pea·cock (PEE–) *n.* a large Asiatic bird, the male of the **pea·fowl,** having long greenish-blue feathers with tips marked like eyes which it spreads out at the back like a fan in the presence of the female, or **pea·hen:** *"proud as a peacock";* **peacock blue** a greenish blue.

pea jeacket a heavy, woollen, double-breasted outer coat.

[1]**peak** (PEEK) *n.* a pointed top, as of a mountain, a pyramid, or a conical cap; summit; hence, any tapered end or high point: *the ~ of a beard: the ~ of one's career; traffic at the ~ of the rush hour;* ***adj.:*** *Summer is the ~ season for travel; an engine running at ~ efficiency.* —***v.:***

House prices ~ in the spring; **peaked** *adj.: a ~ helmet; a ~ roof.*

²peak (PEEK) *v.* look sickly; waste away: *to ~ and pine;* **peak·ed** (PEE·kid) *adj.* pale and wan.

peal (PEEL) *n.* **1** a long, loud sound, esp. of bells; also, of trumpets, thunder, or laughter. **2** a set of tuned bells; carillon; also, changes rung on it. **—*v.*** ring or sound loudly: *"the ~ing organ"; A carillon ~ed forth the victory anthem.*

pea·nut (PEE–) *n.* **1** a tropical vine of the pulse family whose pods ripen underground, yielding seeds, also called groundnuts and goobers, used in preparations such as **peanut butter, peanut oil,** and **peanut brittle,** a candy. **2** *Slang.* a small or insignificant person; **peanuts** *pl.* a relatively small amount of money. **—*adj.*** petty; cheap: *~ politics; The* **peanut gallery** *of a theater has cheap seating.*

pear (PAIR) *n.* a fleshy, sweet, cone-shaped fruit borne by varieties of trees widely cultivated in temperate regions.

pearl (PURL) *n.* a white or bluish-gray, satiny gem got from oyster shells: *"a ~ of great price";* **cast pearls before swine** to give something valuable to people who cannot appreciate it. **—pearl·y** *adj.* **—pearl gray** bluish gray. **—Pearl Harbor** a U.S. naval base near Honolulu, bombed by Japan on Dec. 7, 1941; hence, a devastating surprise attack.

peas·ant (PEZ·nt) *n.* a tiller of the soil; rustic; also, an uncultured person. **—*adj.:*** *~ labor; ~ girl.* **—peas·ant·ry** (–ree) *n.* peasants as a class: *The ~, led by Wat Tyler, revolted in 1381.*

pease (PEEZ) *Archaic pl.* of PEA, as in **peas(e)·cod,** a pea pod.

pea soup *Informal.* thick fog.

peat (PEET) *n.* partially decayed vegetable matter dug from marshy places and used as fertilizer and, in dried form, as fuel: *Sphagnum, or* **peat moss,** *forms soft, spongy ~.* **—peat·y** *adj.*

peb·ble *n.* a small, smoothly-worn stone, as found on a beach; ***v.*** **peb·bles, peb·bled, peb·bling** cover with pebbles; also, make to look pebbly, as **pebble leather** with a grainy surface. **—peb·bly** *adv.* full of or covered with pebbles or little bumps.

pe·can (pi·CAN, –CAHN) *n.* the oval, edible nut of a type of hickory common in southern U.S.

pec·ca·dil·lo (pec·uh·DIL·oh) *n.* **-dil·lo(e)s** a petty sin.

pec·ca·ry (PEC·uh·ree) *n.* **-ries** a tropical animal related to the wild hog.

pec·ca·vi (pe·CAH·wee) *n.* an acknowledgment of guilt.

¹peck *n.* a unit of dry measure equal to 8 quarts: *"a ~ of pickled peppers"; a pretty ~ of troubles.*

²peck *n.* a quick blow or stroke with a beak or as if made with a beak, as a light, quick kiss. **—*v.:*** *Using two fingers, she ~ed out the note on her typewriter; He's just ~ing at the food, he's not hungry.* **—pecking order** an order of social dominance or precedence, as in a flock of poultry in which a weaker bird will submit to one stronger while dominating others weaker than itself.

pec·tin *n.* a white, colloidal substance found in ripe fruits, used in making jellies because of its solidifying properties. **—pec·tic** or **pec·tin·ous** *adj.*

pec·to·ral (PEC·tuh·rul) *adj.* on the chest or breast: *the ~ cross worn by a bishop; a ~ fin of a fish; The* **pectoral sandpiper** *has streaks on its breast.*

pec·u·late *v.* **-lates, -lat·ed, -lat·ing** embezzle. **—pec·u·la·tion** (–LAY–) *n.* **—pec·u·la·tor** *n.*

pe·cul·iar (pi·CULE·yur) *adj.* particular; special; also, strange; odd: *an item of ~ interest to collectors; a custom* **peculiar to** *certain tribes.* **—pe·cul·iar·ly** *adv.* **—pe·cu·li·ar·i·ty** (–lee·AIR·i·tee) *n.*

pe·cu·ni·ar·y (pi·CUE·nee–) *adj.* relating to money: *a ~ motive.*

ped- *comb.form.* **1** foot: as in *pedicab, pedicure, pedometer.* **2** child: as in *pedagogue, pediatric, pedodontist.* **—ped·a·gog(ue)** (–uh·gog) *n.* a teacher, esp. a pedantic or dogmatic one. **—ped·a·go·gy** (–goh·jee) *n.* the art and science of teaching. **—ped·a·gog·ic** (–GOJ–) or **-i·cal** *adj.* **—ped·a·gog·i·cal·ly** *adv.*

ped·al (PEDL) *adj.* (*also* PEE·dl) relating to the foot or to a **pedal** *n.* a lever worked by the foot, as on musical instruments such as the piano and on machines such as the bicycle and the sewing machine. **—*v.*** **ped·als, –al(l)ed, –al·(l)ing:** *The bicyclists ~d uphill.* **—ped·a·lo** (–uh·loh) *n.* a small boat with a paddle wheel turned by pedals.

ped·ant (–unt) *n.* one who makes a show of his learning, esp. by too much attention to trivial things. **—pe·dan·tic** (–DAN–) *adj.: It's ~ to call a flea "Pulex irritans."* **—ped·ant·ry** (PED·n·tree) *n.* **-ries:** *~ parading as scholarship.*

ped·dle (PEDL) *v.* **ped·dles, ped·dled, ped·dling** sell, esp. small articles, from place to place; also, circulate (gossip, lies, etc.) **—ped·dler** *n.* a hawker: *an influence ~; a ~ of vice.* Also **ped·lar.**

-ped(e) *comb.form.* foot; feet: as in *centipede, quadruped.*

ped·e·rast (PED·uh–) *n.* one who practices **ped·er·as·ty** *n.* anal intercourse with a boy.

ped·es·tal (PED·is·tl) *n.* the supporting base of a column or statue: *A* **pedestal desk** *has a set of drawers supporting its top on one or both sides; To set someone* **on a pedestal** *is to idolize him.* **—pe·des·tri·an** (puh·DES·tree·un) *n.* a walker, esp. one out on a street. **—*adj.*** **1:** *a ~ overpass across a highway; ~ traffic.* **2** commonplace: *a ~ style of writing;* **pe·des·tri·an·ism** *n.* **—pe·des·tri·an·ize** *v.* **-iz·es, -ized,**

-iz·ing convert for pedestrian use: *a street ~d into a shopping mall.*

pedi- See PED-. **—pe·di·at·ric** (pee·dee·AT·ric) *adj.* relating to **pe·di·at·rics** *n.pl.* a branch of medicine dealing with the care of children: *a pediatric hospital ward; pediatric nasal drops.* **—pe·di·a·tri·cian** (–TRISH·un) *n.* a pediatric specialist.

ped·i·cab *n.* a three-wheeled vehicle pedalled like a bicycle, with passengers seated at the back, used as a taxicab in Asian countries. **—ped·i·cure** *n.* treatment of the feet and toenails; **ped·i·cur·ist** *n.* **—ped·i·gree** *n.* ancestry; also, a list or record showing ancestry; hence, purity of breed; **ped·i·gree(d)** *adj.* having a pedigree, as dogs, cattle, horses, poultry, corn, wheat, etc. **—ped·i·ment** *n.* a triangular, gablelike structure over a row of columns, a doorway, etc.

pedlar same as PEDDLER.

pedo- See PED-. **—pe·do·don·tist** (pee·duh·DON–) *n.* a dentist specialized in the care of children's teeth. **—pe·do·phile** *n.* one who prefers a child as his sex object.

pe·dom·e·ter (pi·DOM·i–) *n.* an instrument worn for measuring distances walked. **—pe·dun·cle** (PEE–, pi·DUNG·cl) *n.* the stalk of a flower or fruit, esp. of a cluster, as of the lily of the valley.

peek *n.* a peeping or stealthy look; ***v.:*** *He ~ed over the wall.* **—peek·a·boo** *n.* a game played with infants by covering one's face and then uncovering it saying "Peekaboo!" Also ***adj.*** *Informal.* see-through: *a ~ blouse.*

peel *n.* a skin, rind, or bark. **—*v.*** to skin: *Boiled potatoes ~ easily; ~ a banana to eat it; I'll keep my* **eyes peeled** (*Informal.* be on the alert) *for a job vacancy; An aircraft* **peels off** (i.e. veers away) *from a formation during an aerobatic stunt.* **—peel·ing** *n.* esp. **peelings** *pl.* parts peeled off, as of potatoes.

peen *n.* the rounded or wedgelike end of a hammer head opposite to its face.

¹peep *n.* the high-pitched cry of young birds, mice, etc.; cheep; also, a complaining sound. **—*v.*** utter a peep: *The child wouldn't stop ~ing;* **Peeper** *frogs ~ in early spring.*

²peep *n.* a brief look taken from a hidden position: *the ~ of dawn in the eastern sky; a partition with* **peep·holes** *for the curious passer-by; The* **peep show** *at the circus charged 50¢ a viewing; A marksman adjusts the* **peep sight** *to line up his target and front sight.* **—*v.:*** *a child ~ing through a keyhole; always afraid of a* **peeping Tom** (i.e. voyeur) *under her window.* **—peep·er** *n. Slang.* one who peeps; **peepers** *pl.* one's eyes.

¹peer *v.* **1** look closely, often with narrowed eyes; squint: *She ~ed at him over her glasses.* **2** appear partly or slowly: *the sun ~ing through clouds.*

²peer *n.* **1** an equal in rank, value, ability, etc.: *A child picks up language from his ~s;* **peer·less** *adj.: Toscanini was ~ in his time as a conductor;* **peer·less·ly** *adv.* **2** a British noble; *fem.* **peer·ess.** **—peer·age** (–ij) *n.* the nobility, comprising the titles of duke, marquess, earl, viscount, and baron in descending order.

peeve (PEEV) *n.* an irritation or grudge; also, a bad mood: *He takes out his petty ~s from work on his wife; "Not enough heat" is a pet ~ of hers.* **—*v.* peeves, peeved, peev·ing:** *one easily ~d by loud talkers.* **—pee·vish** *adj.* fretful; also, showing ill temper: *a ~ child; a ~ remark.* **—pee·vish·ly** *adv.* **—pee·vish·ness** *n.*

pee·wee *n.* **1** *Informal.* a tiny person or thing; ***adj.:*** *a ~ baseball league.* **2** same as PEWEE.

peg *n.* **1** a small, often tapered bolt of wood or metal used to fasten, as a tent to the ground, to plug, as a barrel, to hang things, as on a **peg board,** or to tighten, as violin strings: *He's a* **square peg in a round hole** (or vice versa, i.e. He is badly matched with his position). **2** a degree or step: *In the reshuffle, some were* **taken down a peg** *or two* (i.e. humbled); *was moved* **up a peg** *to office manager.* **3** in baseball, a hard throw of the ball aimed at putting out a runner. **—*v.* pegs, pegged, peg·ging** **1** fasten, mark, plug, etc. using pegs. **2** work hard: *She* **pegs away** *at math all year.* **3** hold at a certain mark or level: *Oil was once ~d at $40 a bbl.; a ~d currency.*

Peg·a·sus (PEG·uh–) in Greek myths, a winged horse; also, a constellation in the N. Hemisphere.

peg board See PEG, *n.* 1. **—peg leg** *Informal.* (a person with) a wooden leg.

peg·ma·tite (PEG·muh–) *n.* a coarse-grained crystalline rock occurring in veins and containing quartz and feldspar. **—peg·ma·tit·ic** (–TIT–) *adj.*

peg top a child's spinning top with a metal peg at its base; **peg tops** *pl.* trousers that are narrow at the ankles; also **peg-top trousers.**

P.E.I. Prince Edward Island.

peign·oir (pain·WAHR) *n.* a woman's dressing gown.

Pei·ping (BAY·ping) former name of PEKING.

pe·jo·ra·tive (pi·JOR·uh·tiv) *adj.* tending to make worse or lower: *"Silly" got its present meaning by a ~ change from "blessed."* **—*n.*** a pejorative word, as "egregious" or "knave." **—pe·jo·ra·tive·ly** *adv.*

Pe·king (PEE·KING) capital of China. **—Pe·king·ese** (pee·king·EEZ) *adj.* of Peking or its people. **—*n., pl.* -ese** **1** an inhabitant of Peking; also, the Chinese dialect spoken there. **2** a Chinese breed of dog with long hair, flat face, and curled tail. Also **Pe·kin·ese.**

pe·koe (PEE·koh) *n.* a high grade of black tea from India and Sri Lanka.

pel·age (–ij) *n.* the hair, fur, or wool covering of a mammal.

pe·lag·ic (puh·LAJ–) *adj.* of the oceans, as distinguished from the coast: *~ fauna include crustaceans and whales.*

pelf *n.* [contemptuous use] wealth: *the tyranny of ~ and power.*

pel•i•can (–kun) *n.* a large web-footed bird with an elastic pouch under its long bill for scooping up and storing fish, fabled to feed starving young with its own blood.

pel•la•gra (puh·LAG·ruh, –LAY–) *n.* a chronic disease caused by lack of niacin and protein in the diet, first affecting the skin and mucous membranes. —**pel•la•grous** (–grus) *adj.*

pel•let (PEL·it) *n.* a tiny, well-packed mass or ball, as of medicine or snow; also, a piece of lead shot; bullet; ***v.*** make into or hit with pellets. —**pel•let•al** *adj.* —**pel•let•ize, -iz•es, -ized, -iz•ing:** *~d rat poison.*

pell-mell *adj.* & *adv.* in confusion; recklessly.

pel•lu•cid (puh·LOO·sid) *adj.* clear and transparent: *Addison's ~ prose style.*

¹pelt *v.* hit continuously; strike repeatedly: *hail ~ing a roof; The children ~ed each other with mud; The angry mob ~ed stones at the embassy; Rain is ~ing down.* —***n.*** a pelting: *the ~ of hailstones; The horses ran away* **at full pelt** (i.e. full speed).

²pelt *n.* an untanned or undressed skin of a fox, mink, beaver, etc.; **pelt•ry** (–ree) *n., pl.* **-ries** pelts collectively.

pel•vis *n.* **-vis•es** or **-ves** (–veez) the basinlike framework of bones of the hip. —**pel•vic** *adj.: The* **pelvic girdle** (or **arch**) *supports a vertebrate's hind limbs or* **pelvic fins** *in fish.*

pem•(m)i•can (–cun) *n.* a concentrated food of dried and powdered meat mixed with fat and fruit.

pen. or **Pen.** peninsula. —**P.E.N.** International Association of Poets, Playwrights, Editors, Essayists, and Novelists.

¹pen *n.* an enclosure, esp. one for domestic animals. —***v.*** **pens,** *pt.* & *pp.* **penned** *or* **pent, pen•ning:** *His* **pent-up** (i.e. repressed) *fury was unleashed in violence.*

²pen *n.* **1** an instrument for writing with ink or other fluid. **2** written expression; writing: *"The ~ is mightier than the sword";* **pen pals** (or **pen friends**) *exchange letters by mail.* —***v.*** **pens, penned, pen•ning** write: *a well-penned letter.*

³pen *n. Slang.* a penitentiary. —**pe•nal** (PEE·nl) *adj.* having to do with or liable to punishment: *a ~ offense; the* **penal code** (of laws, crimes, penalties, etc.). —**pe•nal•ize** *v.* **-iz•es, -ized, -iz•ing** punish: *You may not be ~d if you confess; The football team was ~d 10 yards;* **pe•nal•i•za•tion** (–ZAY–) *n.* —**pen•al•ty** (PEN·ul·tee) *n.* **-ties** punishment: *A ~ of $20 for speeding; the death ~; a hockey player sent to the* **penalty box.** —**pen•ance** (–unce) *n.* punishment that is self-imposed or voluntary: *For the crimes of his youth, Paul* **did penance** *for the rest of his life; A sinner receives the sacrament of ~ from a priest* (as in the Roman Catholic Church).

penates See LARES AND PENATES.

pence a *pl.* of the British PENNY.

pen•chant (–chunt) *n.* a strong inclination: *a writer with a ~ for detail.*

pen•cil (–sl) *n.* a drawing, writing, or marking implement or stick of crayon, lead, cosmetic material, etc. —***v.*** **-cils, -cil(l)ed, -cil(l)ing:** *changes ~d on a script.*

pen•dant (–dunt) *n.* a suspended ornament or fixture, as a locket, chandelier, etc.; also **pen•dent.** —***adj.*** **pendent** or **pendant** suspended; hanging: *a balcony ~ over a porch.* —**pend•ing** *adj.* unsettled: *The case is still ~* (in the courts); *patent ~;* ***prep.*** during: *a building closed ~ repairs.* —**pen•du•lar** (PEN·juh·lur) *adj.* relating to a pendulum; **pen•du•lous** (–lus) *adj.* hanging: *Orioles build ~ nests.* —**pen•du•lum** *n.* a freely swinging suspended body, as the bob-and-rod regulating mechanism of a clock: *a swing of the political ~ to the Left.*

Pe•nel•o•pe (puh·NEL·uh·pee) the faithful wife of Ulysses in Homer's *Odyssey.*

pe•ne•plain or **pe•ne•plane** (PEE·nuh–) *n.* an area of land that has been eroded almost to a level surface.

penes a *pl.* of PENIS.

pen•e•trate (PEN·i–) *v.* **-trates, -trat•ed, -trat•ing** force a way into physically or mentally; also, see into: *a wound that has ~d to the bone; a preacher who ~s the hearts of sinners; a jungle too dense to ~.* —**pen•e•trat•ing** *adj.: a ~ odor; a ~ study in sociology; a ~ intellect;* also **pen•e•tra•tive** (–tray·tiv). —**pen•e•tra•tion** (–TRAY–) *n.: an ad campaign's ~ of a market.* —**pen•e•tra•ble** (–truh·bl) *adj.*

pen•guin (PENG·gwin) *n.* a flightless, web-footed, short-legged sea bird of the S. hemisphere with paddlelike flippers instead of wings.

pen•i•cil•lin (–SIL·in) *n.* a powerful antibiotic obtained from molds of the genus **Pen•i•cil•li•um** or synthetically.

pen•in•su•la (puh·NIN·suh·luh) *n.* a land area almost surrounded by water, as Lower California or Florida. —**pen•in•su•lar** (–lur) *adj.: Napoleon's* **Peninsular War** *in Spain and Portugal.*

pe•nis (PEE–) *n.* **-nis•es** or **-nes** (–neez) the erectile male sex organ.

pen•i•tence *n.* repentance; the state of being penitent; **pen•i•tent** *n.* & *adj.* (one) who is sorry for having sinned; **pen•i•ten•tial** (–TEN·shul) *adj.: a Lenten ~ service; King David's ~ psalms;* **pen•i•ten•tial•ly** or **pen•i•tent•ly** *adv.* —**pen•i•ten•tia•ry** (–TEN·shuh·ree) *n.* **-ries** a prison for serious crimes, as the U.S. Penitentiary in Atlanta, Ga.; ***adj.:*** *a ~ offense* (punishable by a jail term).

pen•knife *n.* a small pocket knife. —**pen•light** or **pen•lite** *n.* a small flashlight resembling a fountain pen. —**pen•man** (–mun) *n.* **-men** one skilled in **pen•man•ship** *n.* calligraphy; handwriting.

Penn, William. 1644–1718, English Quaker who founded Pennsylvania. —**Penn., Penna.** Pennsylvania.

pen name a writer's assumed name; pseudonym.

pen·nant (–unt) *n.* a long, tapering flag used for signaling, identification, or as a championship emblem.
pen·ni (PEN·ee) *n., pl.* **pen·ni·a** or **pen·nis** a copper coin equal to 1/100 of the Finnish markka. —**pen·ni·less** (PEN·ee·lis) *adj.* very poor; destitute.
pen·non (PEN·un) *n.* a banner or pennant.
Penn·syl·va·ni·a (–VAY·nee·uh) a Northeastern U.S. state; 45,333 sq.mi. (117,412 km^2); *cap.* Harrisburg. —**Pennsylvania Dutch** the people descended from early German settlers; also, their High German dialect. —**Penn·syl·va·ni·an** *n.* & *adj.;* **Pennsylvanian period** the second half of the Carboniferous.
pen·ny (PEN·ee) *n.* **pen·nies 1** a British money unit equal to 1/100, formerly 1/240, of a pound; **pence** *pl.* [collectively] as in *tenpence, a few pence.* **2** in the U.S. and Canada, a cent. —**cost a pretty penny** cost a good deal. —**turn an honest penny** earn a little money honestly. —**penny ante** a poker game with a penny as the highest bet. —**penny arcade** a coin-operated amusement center. —**penny pincher** *Informal.* a miser; **pen·ny-pinch·ing** *n.* & *adj.* —**pen·ny·roy·al** (–ROY·ul) *n.* a mint with a strongly pungent odor. —**pen·ny·weight** *n.* a unit of weight equal to 24 grains or 1/20 of a troy ounce. —**pen·ny-wise** *adj.* thrifty in minor things: "*~ and pound foolish.*" —**pen·ny·worth** *n.* a small amount, value, or bargain.
pe·nol·o·gy (pee·NOL·uh·jee) *n.* prison management and treatment of offenders.
pen pal See ²PEN.
pen·sion (–shun) *n.* a regular payment made by an employer to a former employee on retirement: *old-age ~; a ~ fund.* —***v.:*** *Some are* **pensioned off** *before 65.* —**pen·sion·a·ble** (–uh·bl) *adj.: a ~ age; ~ disability.* —**pen·sion·er** *n.* one receiving a pension.
pen·sive (–siv) *adj.* thoughtful or melancholic: *a ~ mood.* —**pen·sive·ly** *adv.* —**pen·sive·ness** *n.*
pent a *pt.* & *pp.* of ¹PEN. —***adj.*** shut up; confined.
penta- *comb.form.* five: as in **pen·ta·cle** (–tuh·cl) *n.* a five-pointed star. —**pen·ta·gon** (PEN·tuh–) *n.* a five-sided figure with five angles; **the Pentagon** a pentagon-shaped building in Arlington, Virginia, housing the headquarters of the U.S. Department of Defense; hence, the U.S. military establishment; **pen·tag·o·nal** (–TAG·uh·nl) *adj.* —**pen·ta·gram** *n.* same as PENTACLE. —**pen·tam·e·ter** (–TAM·i·tur) *n.* a verse or verse form with five feet: "*The curfew tolls the knell of parting day*" *is an iambic ~.* —**Pen·ta·teuch** (–tuke) *n.* the first five books of the Bible; Torah. —**pen·tath·lon** (–TATH–) *n.* a modern Olympic contest of five events, viz. horseback riding, fencing, pistol shooting, running, and swimming. —**Pen·te·cost** (PEN·tuh–) *n.* a church festival on the seventh Sunday after Easter, celebrating the descent of the Holy Spirit on Christ's apostles; **Pen·te·cos·tal** (–COS·tl) *adj.: Speaking in various tongues was a ~ gift; "Assemblies of God" is a ~ church;* **Pen·te·cos·tal·ism** *n.*
pent·house *n.* an apartment or structure built on the roof of a tall building: *a ~ suite.*
Pen·to·thal (–tuh·thawl) *Trademark.* a barbiturate used as an anesthetic.
pent-up See ¹PEN.
pe·nu·che (puh·NOO·chee) *n.* a fudge made of brown sugar.
pe·nul·ti·mate (pi·NUL·tuh·mit) *adj.* & *n.* (the one) next to the last.
pe·num·bra (pi·NUM·bruh) *n., pl.* **-brae** (–bree) or **-bras** a partial shadow formed around a totally dark area, or umbra, as in an eclipse.
pen·u·ry (PEN·yuh·ree) *n.* extreme poverty. —**pe·nu·ri·ous** (–NEW·ree·us) *adj.: the ~ years of famine and drought.*
pe·on (PEE·on) *n.* **-ons** or **-on·es** (pay·OH·neez) formerly, a laborer forced to work to pay off a debt. —**pe·on·age** (PEE·uh·nij) *n.* the Latin American system of employing peons, illegal in the U.S. since 1911.
pe·o·ny (PEE·uh·nee) *n.* **-nies** a plant of the buttercup family bearing large red, pink, or white flowers.
peo·ple (PEE·pl) *n.pl.* **1** human beings, esp. of a particular place, group, or nation: *a government of the ~; the ~ of England; my ~ from Peoria.* **2** *pl.* **peoples** a race or social group: *a chosen ~; the ~s of Asia; the ant ~* (i.e. species). **3 people's, a** socialist; communist: *a ~'s democracy;* **b** populist; popular: *the ~'s bible; the ~'s party.* —***v.*** **-ples, -pled, -pling:** *a planet ~d by apes.* —**people mover** a mass-transport system or vehicle. —**people's park** a park without restrictions.
Pe·or·i·a (pee·OR·ee·uh) a city of C. Illinois.
pep *n.* briskness; vigor; energy; **pep pill** *Informal.* a stimulating drug, as an amphetamine. —***v.*** **peps, pepped, pep·ping:** *The coach* **pepped up** *their spirits.* —**pep·per** *n.* **1** a pungent condiment got by grinding the dried berries, or **peppercorns,** of an East Indian vine. **2** capsicum. —***v.*** **1** season with pepper. **2** shower; pelt. —**pepper mill** a hand mill for grinding peppercorns. —**pep·per·mint** *n.* an aromatic mint. —**pep·per·o·ni** (–OH·nee) *n.* **-ni(s)** a highly seasoned Italian sausage. —**pepper shaker** a container for sprinkling powdered pepper. —**pep·per·y** *adj.* **pep·per·i·er, -i·est** pungent; also, hot-tempered; fiery.
pep·py *adj. Informal.* **pep·pi·er, pep·pi·est** full of pep or energy.
pep·sin *n.* an enzyme of the stomach aiding the digestion of proteins.
pep talk one given to raise the morale of a group.

pep·tic *adj.* relating to pepsin or to digestion: **peptic ulcers** *of the stomach and duodenum.*

per *prep.* **1** for each: *traveling at 30 miles ~ hour.* **2** through: *money sent ~ bearer of the letter.* **3** according to: *as ~ your instructions.*

per. period; person. **—Per.** Persia(n).

per·ad·ven·ture (–VEN·chur) *Archaic. adv.* perhaps. **—*n.*:** *beyond a ~* (i.e. beyond doubt).

per·am·bu·late (–AM·byoo–) *v.* **-lates, -lat·ed, -lat·ing** walk (through, over, up and down, etc.); **per·am·bu·la·tion** (–LAY–) *n.* **—per·am·bu·la·tor** *n. Brit.* a baby carriage.

per an·num (–AN·um) each year; annually.

per·cale (–CALE) *n.* a closely woven cotton fabric used for shirts, dresses, pajamas, etc.

per cap·i·ta (–CAP·i·tuh) per person: *$100 ~; a per-capita allowance.*

per·ceive (–SEEV) *v.* **-ceives, -ceived, -ceiv·ing** be aware of through the senses; also, take in by the mind: *By the smoke from the chimney I ~d that the house was occupied; "Ultrasound" is not* **per·ceiv·a·ble** *(adj.) by the human ear;* **per·ceiv·a·bly** *adv.*

per·cent (–SENT) *adj.* & *adv.* per hundred: *a five ~ sales tax;* ***n.*** a hundredth part: *Ten ~ of 1,000 is 100.* **—per·cent·age** (–ij) *n.* a part or portion, esp. of a hundred: *Only a small ~ of pupils was absent.* **—per·cen·tile** *n.* a value or range of distribution of a variable within a series of 100 parts: *A 3% score is in the third ~.*

per·cept (PUR–) *n.* an impression received by the senses, not one conceived in the mind. **—per·cep·ti·ble** (–SEP–) *adj.* capable of being perceived: *Outside the home, the animosity between the brothers was hardly ~.* **—per·cep·ti·bly** *adv.;* **per·cep·ti·bil·i·ty** (–BIL–) *n.* **—per·cep·tion** (–SEP–) *n.* the act or power of perceiving; also, understanding: *Good ~ of depth is important for a pilot; The survivors had no clear ~ of what happened in the crash;* **per·cep·tive** *adj.: Hearing is a ~ faculty; a quiet youth with a keen and ~ mind;* **per·cep·tive·ly** *adv.;* **per·cep·tu·al** (–SEP·choo·ul) *adj.: An optical illusion is a ~ problem;* **per·cep·tu·al·ly** *adv.*

perch *n.* **1** any of a family of spiny freshwater food fishes. **2** a bird's roost; also, a resting place, esp. a high position; vantage point; ***v.*:** *a village ~ed on a mountain height; He ~ed on a tree to watch the parade.*

per·chance (–CHANCE) *adv.* perhaps.

per·cip·i·ent (–SIP·ee·ent) *adj.* discerning. **—per·cip·i·ence** *n.* perception.

per·co·late (PUR·cuh–) *v.* **-lates, -lat·ed, -lat·ing** pass or make (a liquid) pass through a porous medium; filter (through); also, make, esp. coffee, by **per·co·la·tion** (–LAY–) in a **per·co·la·tor** *n.*

per con·tra (–CON·truh) *Latin.* on the contrary.

per·cus·sion (–KUSH·un) *n.* **1** a striking or hitting, as of the **percussion cap** containing powder in the firing mechanism of a gun. **2** a section of a band or orchestra containing **percussion instruments** such as drums, cymbals, xylophone, etc.; **per·cus·sion·ist** *n.* a player of such musical instruments.

per di·em (–DEE·um) by the day. **—*n.*,** *pl.* **per diems** a daily allowance.

per·di·tion (–DISH·un) *n.* damnation; hell.

per·dur·a·ble (–DEW–) *adj.* extremely durable; lasting: *hard and ~ like granite.* **—per·dur·a·bil·i·ty** (–BIL–) *n.*

per·e·grine (PER·uh·grin) *adj.* traveling about; migratory; cosmopolitan, as the **peregrine (falcon)** used in falconry. **—per·e·gri·nate** *v.* **-nates, -nat·ed, -nat·ing** travel around or abroad, esp. on foot; **per·e·gri·na·tion** (–NAY–) *n.*

per·emp·to·ry (–EMP–) *adj.* decisive; absolute; also, dictatorial: *a ~ manner; a juror rejected by a* **peremptory challenge** (with no reasons given). **—per·emp·to·ri·ly** *adv.*

per·en·ni·al (–EN·ee·ul) *adj.* continually recurring; also, lasting from year to year or throughout the year: *a ~ problem; a ~ stream; The iris and the chrysanthemum are* **perennial plants; per·en·ni·al** *n.* **—per·en·ni·al·ly** *adv.*

perf. perfect; perforated. **—per·fect** (PUR·fict) *adj.* **1** flawless; without fault; absolute: *No one is ~; a ~ circle; a ~ stranger.* **2** *Gram.* showing completed action: *a ~ tense; "Having done" is a ~ participle;* ***n.*** a perfect tense or verb form. **—per·fect·ly** *adv.* **—per·fect** (–FECT) *v.: Practice helps ~ a skill;* **per·fect·i·ble** *adj.;* **per·fec·ti·bil·i·ty** (–BIL–) *n.: the ~ of human nature.* **—per·fec·tion** (–FEC–) *n.: It takes years to bring an invention to ~; She does everything* **to perfection** (i.e. perfectly), *but she is not a* **per·fec·tion·ist** *n.* one who demands perfection; **per·fec·tion·ism** *n.;* **per·fec·tion·ist** or **-is·tic** (–NIS–) *adj.* **—per·fec·to** (–FEC–) *n.* **-tos** a cigar tapered at both ends.

per·fi·dy (–fi·dee) *n.* **-dies** (–deez) treachery. **—per·fid·i·ous** (–FID–) *adj.: the ~ Benedict Arnold.*

per·fo·rate (–fuh–) *v.* **-rates, -rat·ed, -rat·ing** bore or punch through, esp. make a line of holes through, as on sheets of postage stamps: *An ulcer may ~ through the duodenal or stomach wall;* **per·fo·ra·tor** *n.* **—per·fo·ra·tion** (–RAY–) *n.*

per·force (–FORCE) *adv.* necessarily.

per·form (–FORM) *v.* carry out (a task, promise, etc.); act (esp., enact a role, piece of music, etc.): *A surgeon ~s an operation; the* **performing arts** *such as drama, dancing, and music.* **—per·form·ance** (–unce) *n.: Promises are meaningless without ~; a beautiful ballet ~; an engine's poor ~ on the highway.* **—per·form·er** *n.*

per·fume (PUR–) *n.* a pleasant odor; also, a sweet-smelling fluid preparation. **—*v.*** (–FUME) **-fumes, -fumed, -fum·ing:** *a temple ~d with incense;* **per·fum·er** *n.* **—per·fum·er·y** (–FEW·muh·ree) *n.* **-er·ies** a perfumer's art, products, or place of business.

per·func·to·ry (–FUNK·tuh·ree) *adj.* done merely routinely; indifferent: *a ~ inspection.* **—per·func·to·ri·ly** *adv.* **—per·func·to·ri·ness** *n.*

per·go·la (–guh·luh) *n.* an arbor or walk having a roof of trellis work with climbing vines.

perh. *Abbrev.* for **per·haps** (–HAPS) *adv.* possibly; maybe.

peri- *prefix.* around; about; near: as in *perimeter, perigee.*

Per·i·cles (–cleez) 495?–429 B.C., Athenian general and statesman.

per·i·cyn·thi·on (–SINTH·ee·un) *n.* the point in a lunar orbit that is nearest to the moon's center. **—per·i·gee** (–jee) *n.* the point in a satellite's orbit that is nearest to the earth's center. **—per·i·he·li·on** (–HEE·lee·un) *n.* **-li·ons** or **-li·a** the point in a solar orbit that is nearest to the sun.

per·il *n.* danger; also, a source of danger: *Enter at your ~; Tax evaders live* **in peril of** *the law; the ~s of flying.* **—*v.*** **-ils, -il(l)ed, -il·(l)ing** imperil. **—per·i·lous** (–lus) *adj.* dangerous; hazardous; **per·i·lous·ly** *adv.*

per·i·lune (–loon) *n.* same as PERICYNTHION. **—pe·rim·e·ter** (puh·RIM·i·tur) *n.* the outer boundary or border of a figure, area, etc.; also, its length. **—per·i·ne·um** (–NEE–) *n., pl.* **-ne·a** (–uh) the area between the genitals and the anus; **per·i·ne·al** *adj.* **—pe·ri·od** (PEER·ee·ud) *n.* **1** a portion of time, esp. one well marked: *a school day divided into eight ~s; The Cambrian ~ began 600 million years ago; the Civil War ~;* ***adj.:*** *~ furniture; a ~ piece.* **2** the menses. **3** a punctuation mark (.) used at the end of a sentence or abbreviation; ***interj.*** used for emphasis: *No more drinks for me, ~!* **4** a well-proportioned sentence, esp. one in which the principal clause is placed at the end. **—pe·ri·od·ic** (–OD·ic) *adj.* occurring at regular intervals: *An engine needs ~ tune-ups; ~ tides;* **pe·ri·od·i·cal** *adj.* periodic; esp., published at regular intervals; ***n.*** a weekly, monthly, yearly, etc. publication. **—pe·ri·od·i·cal·ly** *adv.* **—pe·ri·o·dic·i·ty** (–uh·DIS·i·tee) *n.* **—periodic sentence** same as PERIOD, *n.* 4. **—periodic table** a chart showing the chemical elements arranged according to their atomic numbers and the **periodic law** governing them. **—per·i·o·don·tics** (–DON–) *n.pl.* [takes *sing. v.*] a branch of dentistry that deals with diseases of the bones and tissue around the teeth; **per·i·o·don·tal** *adj.* **—period piece** a work of art or architecture peculiar to a historical period.

per·i·pa·tet·ic (–puh·TET·ic) *adj.* **1** involving walking; itinerant. **2 Peripatetic** having to do with Aristotle or his philosophy; ***n.*** a Peripatetic or itinerant philosopher. **—pe·riph·er·al** (puh·RIF–) *adj.* of a periphery; outer; external; hence, incidental: *~ vision* (outside the area of direct sight); *~ nervous system* (branching out from the central nervous system); ***n.*** an external device or unit connected to a computer, as a keyboard, display, or printer; **pe·riph·er·al·ly** *adv.* **—pe·riph·er·y** (–RIF–) *n.* **-er·ies** an outer boundary or surface; outskirts. **—pe·riph·ra·sis** (puh·RIF·fruh–) *n., pl.* **-ses** (–seez) a roundabout way of speaking; circumlocution; **per·i·phras·tic** (–FRAS–) *adj.*

pe·rique (puh·REEK) *n.* a dark, strong tobacco from Louisiana that is used in blends.

per·i·scope *n.* an optical instrument that enables one to see above or around an obstacle, used esp. in submarines. **—per·i·scop·ic** (–SCOP·ic) *adj.*

per·ish *v.* be destroyed: *Hundreds ~ed in the fire;* **Perish the thought!** [said of something unthinkable]. **—per·ish·a·ble** *adj.* liable to spoil or decay quickly; ***n.:*** *Fruit, vegetables, eggs, etc. are ~s.* **—per·ish·a·bly** *adv.*

per·i·stal·sis (–STAWL·sis) *n., pl.* **-ses** the wavelike contractions of a tubular structure such as the bile duct and the intestines which tends to force its contents forward. **—per·i·stal·tic** *adj.* **—per·i·style** *n.* a row of columns around a building or court; **per·i·sty·lar** (–STYE–) *adj.* **—per·i·to·ne·um** (–tuh·NEE–) *n.* the membrane lining the cavity of the abdomen; **per·i·to·ne·al** *adj.* **—per·i·to·ni·tis** (–NYE·tis) *n.* inflammation of the peritoneum.

per·i·wig *n.* a men's wig, esp. a peruke.

per·i·win·kle *n.* **1** an evergreen plant of the dogbane family whose creeping variety is also called "running myrtle." **2** any of various small snails with conical shells found along the sea coast.

per·jure (–jur) *v.* **-jures, -jured, -jur·ing** usu. **perjure oneself,** give false evidence or withhold a truth after taking an oath; **per·jur·er** *n.* **—per·jur·y** *n.*

¹perk [short form] **1** *v.* percolate: *freshly ~ed coffee;* **2** *n.* perquisite: *A chauffeur-driven car is one of the ~s of the presidency.*

²perk *v.* move, become, or behave in a smart, brisk, lively, or pert manner: *The horse ~ed up an ear at the sound; She's beginning to* **perk up** (i.e. be active) *after her long illness; all* **perked out** *in his Sunday best.* **—perk·y** *adj.* **perk·i·er, -i·est** lively; also, saucy; **perk·i·ly** *adv.;* **perk·i·ness** *n.*

per·lite *n.* a pearly volcanic glass similar to obsidian.

perm *n.* *Brit. Informal.* permanent wave. **—perm.** permanent. **—per·ma·frost** *n.* subsoil that is permanently frozen, as in Greenland and N. regions of the U.S.S.R., Canada, and Alaska. **—per·ma·nent** (–muh–) *adj.* lasting long or indefinitely; not temporary: *the 32 ~ teeth; a ~ home, job;* **permanent press** fabric treated for wrinkle resistance; durable press; **permanent (wave)** a hair wave that lasts through several washings. **—per·ma·nence** or **-nen·cy** *n.* **—per·ma·nent·ly** *adv.*

per·me·a·ble (PUR·mee·uh–) *adj.* capable of being permeated; having pores or openings to allow fluids to pass through, as limestone; **per·me·a·bly** *adv.;* **per·me·a·bil·i·ty** (–BIL–) *n.* —**per·me·ate** *v.* **-ates, -at·ed, -at·ing** seep through; also, pervade: *gases ~ (through) charcoal; The smell of cooking ~d the house;* **per·me·a·tion** (–AY–) *n.*

Per·mi·an (–mee·un) *n.* the last period of the Paleozoic era of the earth, beginning about 275 million years ago; ***adj.:*** *Cone-bearing trees appeared in the ~ period; ~ fossils.*

per·mis·si·ble (–MIS–) *adj.* that may be permitted: *~ evidence;* **per·mis·si·ble·ness** or **-bil·i·ty** (–BIL–) *n.* —**per·mis·sive** (–MIS·iv) *adj.* granting permission; also, indulgent; excessively lenient: *modern ~ society; ~ child discipline;* **per·mis·sive·ly** *adv.;* **per·mis·sive·ness** *n.;* **per·mis·siv·ist** *n.* —**per·mit** v. (–MIT) **-mits, -mit·ted, -mit·ting** allow: *Weather ~ing, we'll eat in the patio; Smoking is not ~d here; An urgent matter* **permits of** *no delay.* —***n.*** (PUR–) **1** permission; license: *a fishing ~.* **2** the pompano fish, esp. the "great pompano."

per·mu·ta·tion (–mew·TAY–) *n.* an arrangement of a set of things in a particular order: *CBA is one of six ~s possible with A, B, C.*

per·ni·cious (–NISH·us) *adj.* severely harmful; deadly: *a ~ habit;* **pernicious anemia.** —**per·ni·cious·ly** *adv.*

per·nick·e·ty (–NIK·i·tee) *adj.* same as PERSNICKETY.

per·o·ra·tion (–uh·RAY–) *n.* the concluding part of a formal discourse.

per·ox·ide (–OX–) *n.* an oxide containing an unusual proportion of oxygen, esp. hydrogen peroxide (H_2O_2). —***v.*** **-ides, -id·ed, -id·ing** bleach (hair) with hydrogen peroxide.

per·pen·dic·u·lar (–DIK·yuh·lur) *adj.* at a 90° angle, esp. upright or vertical: *cliffs rising ~ to the shore;* ***n.:*** *a tower leaning 10° from the ~.* —**per·pen·dic·u·lar·ly** *adv.* —**per·pen·dic·u·lar·i·ty** (–LAIR–) n.

per·pe·trate (PUR·puh–) *v.* **-trates, -trat·ed, -trat·ing** commit, esp. a crime, blunder, or other outrageous act. —**per·pe·tra·tor** *n.* —**per·pe·tra·tion** (–TRAY–) *n.*

per·pet·u·al (–PECH·oo·ul) *adj.* continuing indefinitely; ceaseless: *a ~ nuisance; A* **perpetual calendar** *can be used for many years; A* **perpetual motion** *machine is supposed to run for ever.* —**per·pet·u·al·ly** *adv.* —**per·pet·u·ate** *v.* **-ates, -at·ed, -at·ing:** *Superstitions help ~ myths; elixirs to ~ life;* **per·pet·u·a·tor** *n.* —**per·pet·u·a·tion** (–AY–) *n.* —**per·pet·u·i·ty** (–CHOO·i·tee) *n.* **-ties** indefinite duration: *bequeathed to him and his heirs* **in perpetuity.**

per·plex (–PLEX) *v.* puzzle and worry: *~ed by her change of behavior.* —**per·plexed** *adj.* puzzled; also, complicated: *a ~ issue;* **per·plex·ed·ly** *adv.* —**per·plex·ing** *adj.: torn by ~ doubts;* **per·plex·ing·ly** *adv.* —**per·plex·i·ty** *n.* **-ties:** *the ~s of one's first day in New York.*

per·qui·site (–zit) *n.* a bonus, fringe benefit, or a peculiar privilege, esp. one attached to a position or office, as a salesman's expense account or company car.

pers. person(al); personnel. —**Pers.** Persia(n).

per se (pur·SAY) by or in itself: *Drinking ~, as opposed to drunk driving, is not criminal.*

per·se·cute (PUR·si–) *v.* **-cutes, -cut·ed, -cut·ing** harass, esp. because of one's beliefs; also, annoy constantly; pester: *~d by a hostile press.* —**per·se·cu·tion** (–CUE–) *n.: the Nazi ~ of the Jews; to suffer ~ for justice' sake.* —**per·se·cu·tor** *n.*

per·se·vere (–suh·VEER) *v.* **-veres, -vered, -ver·ing** continue doing, esp. something hard; be steadfast: *to ~ in one's efforts;* **per·se·ver·ance** *n.*

Per·sia (–zhuh) the former name of IRAN. —**Per·sian** *n.* an inhabitant of Persia; an Iranian; also, the chief Iranian language; also ***adj.;*** **Persian cat** a breed of cat with long, silky hair; **Persian Gulf** the sea separating Iran and Arabia; **Persian lamb** the fur of karakul sheep.

per·si·flage (–flahzh) *n.* light banter or writing.

per·sim·mon (–SIM·un) *n.* the pulpy, edible, plumlike fruit of a group of trees of the ebony family.

per·sist (–SIST) *v.* continue being or doing, esp. with stubbornness: *She ~ed in taking her daily walk till the end; mountain snows ~ing till early summer.* —**per·sist·ence** *n.: The continuity of moving pictures is based on ~ of vision.* —**per·sist·ent** *adj.: a ~ cough; a ~ questioner;* **per·sist·ent·ly** *adv.*

per·snick·e·ty (–SNIK·i·tee) *adj.* *Informal.* fussy; extremely fastidious.

per·son *n.* **1** a human being; individual; also, a legal entity having rights and duties: *A* **per·son-to-per·son** *phone call is operator-handled.* **2** an individual physically considered: *She threatened me but didn't touch my ~; The President was here* **in person** (i.e. personally); *found a friend* **in the person of** *a policeman.* **3** any of three pronoun categories: **first person** "I," **second person** "You," **third person** "he," "she," or "it." **4** *comb.form* [as a neutral substitute for "man"] as in *chairperson, person-day, personhood.* —**per·so·na** (–SOH·nuh) *n.* **1** *pl.* **-nae** (–nee) a character in a play or novel; also, the author's voice. **2** *pl.* **-nas** in psychology, a personality assumed by an individual as a mask. —**per·son·a·ble** (–uh·bl) *adj.* pleasing in appearance or personality; **per·son·a·bly** *adv.* —**per·son·age** (–ij) *n.* a person of rank or importance. —**per·son·al** *adj.* pertaining to a particular person; private: *a ~* (i.e. live) *appearance by a movie star; a ~ and confidential letter; a highly ~ remark bordering on slander; ~ hygiene* (i.e. of the body); **personal effects** belongings such as clothing and toiletry; **personal equation** variation in observation or judgment because of one's personality; **per·son·al·ly** *adv.* —**per·son·al·i·ty** (–NAL–) *n.* **-ties** **1** individuality; a person's character; also, the person; *~ problems between* *co-workers; She's a TV ~: a Soviet ~ cult.* **2 personalities** offensive personal remarks: *Let us not indulge in ~s.* —**per·son·al·ize** *v.* **-iz·es, -ized, -iz·ing** make identifiably one person's: *~d greeting cards.* —**personal property** or **per·son·al·ty** *n.* **-ties** chattels, not real estate. —**persona (non) grata,** *pl.* **personae (non) gra·tae** (–GRAH·tee) one who is (not) acceptable. —**per·son·ate** *v.* **-ates, -at·ed, -at·ing** *Law.* impersonate; **per·son·a·tion** (–NAY–) *n.* —**per·son-day** *n.* the duration of a working person's average day. —**per·son·i·fy** (pur·SON–) *v.* **-fies, -fied, -fy·ing:** *the Mississippi ~d as "Ol' Man River"; He looks like strength ~d;* **per·son·i·fi·ca·tion** (–CAY–) *n.* —**per·son·nel** (–NEL) *n.* employees as a body: *Office ~ have their coffee break at 10* A.M.; ***adj.:*** *a ~ department.*

per·spec·tive (–SPEC·tiv) *n.* the look of objects as affected by their dimensions and distance from the viewer: *a picture drawn out of ~; to see events in the right ~; a new ~ of history;* also ***adj.*** —**per·spec·tive·ly** *adv.*

per·spi·ca·cious (–CAY·shus) *adj.* discerning: *a ~ analysis of an obscure issue;* **per·spi·ca·cious·ly** *adv.* —**per·spi·cac·i·ty** (–CAS·i·tee) *n.*

per·spic·u·ous (–SPIC·yoo·us) *adj.* clearly expressed; lucid: *a ~ style.* —**per·spic·u·ous·ly** *adv.;* **perspic·u·ous·ness** *n.* —**per·spi·cu·i·ty** (–CUE·i·tee) *n.*

per·spire (–SPIRE) *v.* **-spires, -spired, -spir·ing** to sweat. —**per·spi·ra·tion** (–RAY–) *n.*

per·suade (–SWADE) *v.* **-suades, -suad·ed, -suad·ing** move or win over to think or act as desired: *She ~d him to stop smoking; Are you ~d that he's lying?* —**per·sua·sion** (–SWAY·zhun) *n.* **1:** *a convincing speaker with great powers of ~.* **2** a group or party with a particular set of beliefs; denomination: *Protestants of all ~s; a Calvinist of the strictest ~.* —**per·sua·sive** (–ziv) *adj.;* **per·sua·sive·ly** *adv.;* **per·sua·sive·ness** *n.*

pert *adj.* **1** saucy or flippant: *a ~ answer.* **2** jaunty; also, lively: *~ as a schoolgirl; feeling ~ and refreshed.* —**pert·ly** *adv.* —**pert·ness** *n.*

PERT Program Evaluation and Review Technique (of computer scheduling).

per·tain (–TAIN) *v.* belong; refer; relate: *fresh evidence* **pertaining to** *the mystery;* **per·ti·nence** (PUR·tn·unce) *n.* relevance; **per·ti·nent** *adj.* relevant; **per·ti·nent·ly** *adv.: a question ~ put at the right moment.*

Perth a city of W. Australia.

per·ti·na·cious (–NAY·shus) *adj.* stubbornly clinging to an opinion or course of action: *a ~ newshound; a lawyer's ~ cross-examination of a witness;* **per·ti·na·cious·ly** *adv.;* **per·ti·nac·i·ty** (–NAS–) *n.: a bill-collector's ~ in dunning his creditors.*

pertinence, pertinent(ly) See PERTAIN.

per·turb (–TURB) *v.* agitate mentally; upset: *easily ~ed by unforeseen events.* —**per·tur·ba·tion** (–BAY–) *n.*

per·tus·sis (–TUSS–) *n.* whooping cough.

Pe·ru (puh·ROO) a South American republic; 496,225 sq.mi. (1,285,216 km²); *cap.* Lima.

pe·ruke (puh–) *n.* a type of men's wig fashionable in the 17th and 18th centuries.

pe·ruse (puh·ROOZ) *v.* **-rus·es, -rused, -us·ing** read, esp. attentively. —**pe·rus·al** *n.*

Pe·ru·vi·an (–ROO–) *n.* & *adj.* (a person) of or from Peru.

per·vade (–VADE) *v.* **-vades, -vad·ed, -vad·ing** spread through all parts of: *The spirit of camaraderie soon ~d the camp.* —**per·va·sive** (–VAY·siv) *adj.: a ~ influence;* **per·va·sive·ly** *adv.;* **per·va·sive·ness** *n.*

per·verse (–VURCE) *adj.* contrary to what is desirable, reasonable, or established as normal: *an obstinate and ~ nature; found a ~ delight in tormenting the weak.* —**per·verse·ly** *adv.;* **per·verse·ness** or **per·ver·si·ty** *n.* **-ties:** *the ~s of human nature.* —**per·ver·sion** (–VUR·zhun) *n.: The translation seems a ~ of the author's original sense; Some sexual ~s are now more acceptable.* —**per·vert** *v.* (–VURT) (cause) to turn (something normal or desirable) to something bad; corrupt; distort; lead astray: *the ~ing influence of TV violence; a verdict that ~s the ends of justice;* ***n.*** (PUR–) a perverted person, esp. a sexual deviate.

pe·se·ta (puh·SAY·tuh) *n.* a silver coin and the basic monetary unit of Spain and Spanish dependencies.

pe·se·wa (puh·SAY·wuh) *n.* a money unit of Ghana, equal to 1/100 of a cedi.

pes·ky (–kee) *adj.* **-ki·er, -ki·est** *Informal.* annoying, as gnats or mosquitoes.

pe·so (PAY·soh) *n.* **-sos** the basic unit of Argentina, Bolivia, Colombia, Cuba, the Dominican Republic, Mexico, the Philippines, and Uruguay. See also CENTAVO, CENTIMO.

pes·si·mism (PES·uh·mizm) *n.* the tendency to expect the worst possible outcome. —**pes·si·mist** *n.* —**pes·si·mis·tic** (–MIS–) *adj.;* **pes·si·mis·ti·cal·ly** *adv.*

pest *n.* a harmful plant or animal, as insects, mice, and weeds; also, an annoying person; nuisance: *Snails and larvae are garden ~s; ~ control by spraying and dusting with insecticides; Rumormongers are ~s of society.* —**pes·ter** *v.* annoy; vex: *Stop ~ing me!* —**pes·ter·er** *n.* —**pest·hole** *n.* a place that helps the spread of disease. —**pest·house** *n.* a hospital for the victims of plague and such pestilential diseases. —**pes·ti·cide** *n.* a chemical or other agent used against harmful plants and animals. —**pes·tif·er·ous** (–TIF·er·us) *adj.* **1** disease-causing. **2** *Informal.* annoying: *~ telephone solicitations.* —**pes·ti·lence** (PES·tl·unce) *n.* any fatal epidemic disease, as the plague: *Man has survived ~, war, and famine;* **pes·ti·lent** or **-len·tial** (–LEN–) *adj.;* **pes·ti·len·tial·ly** *adv.*

pes·tle (PESL) *n.* a club-shaped tool used with a mortar for pounding or grinding.

¹pet *n.* a domesticated animal kept for companionship, as a cat, dog, canary, or goldfish; also, a young person treated by someone with special care; favorite: *a teacher's ~;* **adj.:** *one's ~ peeves; a ~ project; "Bettina" was Beth's ~ name; a ~ rock.* —**v. pets, pet·ted, pet·ting** **1** fondle; caress. **2** *Informal.* make love by caressing: *back-seat ~ing parties.*

²pet *n.* a peevish mood: *She spent all day in a ~.* —**pet·tish** *adj.;* **pet·tish·ly** *adv.;* **pet·tish·ness** *n.*

pet. petroleum. —**Pet.** Peter.

pet·al (PETL) *n.* one of the separate leaflike parts of a flower's corolla. —**pet·al(l)ed** *adj.: the many-~ daisy.*

pe·tard (pi·TARD) *n.* an explosive device: *The schemer was* **hoist with** (or **by**) **his own petard** (i.e. his own victim, like one blown up by his own bomb).

pet·cock *n.* a small valve or faucet for draining radiators, boilers, etc.

pe·ter (PEE–) *v.* esp. in **peter out,** come to an end gradually; be exhausted, as provisions, one's energies, etc. —**Peter, St.** (died c. A.D. 67), chief of Christ's disciples; **rob Peter to pay Paul** satisfy one need by creating another, as by using the rent money to make a car payment. —**Peter I,** 1672–1725, czar of Russia (1682–1725), also called "Peter the Great." —**Peter Principle** the promoting of employees to one level above their competence. —**for Pete's sake** [an oath of entreaty].

pet·i·ole (PET·ee·ole) *n.* a leafstalk; also, a stalklike connecting part between thorax and abdomen, as in the wasp.

pe·tit (PET·ee) *adj. Law.* small or minor; opposed to GRAND: as in **petit jury** (of 12 members), **petit larceny** (i.e. theft of property below a certain value), etc.

pe·tite (puh·TEET) *adj.* of a woman, small and slender in figure.

pe·tit four (pet·ee·FOR) *n., pl.* **petits** (pet·ee) **fours** or **petit fours** a small frosted cake.

pe·ti·tion (puh·TISH·un) *n.* a formal request to someone in authority; also, a document making such a request: *a ~ for retrial; to grant a ~; Parliament's* **Petition of Right** *presented to King Charles I.* —**v.:** *the people's constitutional right to ~ the government; 800 citizens ~ed the mayor for a new hospital.* —**pe·ti·tion·er** *n.*

pet·nap·(p)ing *n.* stealing of pets, esp. for sale to laboratories for use in experiments.

Pe·trarch (PEE·trark), 1304–1374, Italian poet.

pet·rel (PET·rul) *n.* a black-and-white sea bird with long wings, as a shearwater, fulmar, or *storm petrel.*

pet·ri·fy *v.* **-fies, -fied, -fy·ing** make or become like rock; also, stun or daze: *standing motionless, ~d by* (or *with*) *fear;* **petrified forests** *(as in Arizona) made up of tree trunks buried in rock millions of years ago.* —**pet·ri·fac·tion** (–FAC–) or **-fi·ca·tion** (–CAY–) *n.* —**petro-** *comb.form.* **1** having to do with petroleum: as in *petrochemical, petrodollars.* **2** pertaining to rock: as in *petrography, petrology.* —**pet·ro·chem·i·cal** (–KEM–) *n.* a chemical made from crude oil and natural gas and used in plastics, synthetics, fertilizers, etc.; **pet·ro·chem·is·try** *n.* —**pet·ro·dol·lars** (PET·roh–) *n.pl.* excess revenue made by oil-rich countries from increased prices of petroleum. —**pet·ro·glyph** (–glif) *n.* a rock carving. —**pe·trog·ra·phy** (–TROG–) *n.* the science of the description and classification of rocks; **pe·trog·ra·pher** *n.;* **pet·ro·graph·ic** (–GRAPH–) or **-i·cal** *adj.* —**pet·rol** (PET·rul) *n. Brit.* gasoline. —**pet·ro·la·tum** (–LAY–) *n.* a yellowish jellylike substance made from petroleum for use in ointments, dressings, etc.; also **petroleum jelly.** —**pe·tro·le·um** (puh·TROH·lee·um) *n.* a dark, oily, bituminous liquid found in rock strata and yielding paraffin, gasoline, etc.; crude oil; also called "black gold." —**pe·trol·o·gy** (–TROL–) *n.* a branch of geology dealing with rocks; **pe·trol·o·gist** *n.;* **pet·ro·log·ic** (–LOJ–) or **-log·i·cal** *adj.;* **pet·ro·log·i·cal·ly** *adv.*

pet·ti·coat *n.* a woman's under-skirt; **adj.** female; **petticoat government** rule by women.

pet·ti·fog *v.* **-fogs, -fogged, -fog·ging** quibble over trifles, esp. in legal matters; **pet·ti·fog·ger** *n.;* **pet·ti·fog·ger·y** *n.* chicanery; **pet·ti·fog·ging** *adj.* & *n.*

pet·ty *adj.* **pet·ti·er, pet·ti·est** **1** small or unimportant; low in rank: *a ~ detail; ~ grievances;* **petty cash** money for small expenses; **petty jury** same as PETIT JURY; **petty larceny** same as PETIT LARCENY; **petty officer** a naval rank of enlisted men varying from **master chief petty officer** down to **petty officer third class** which is just above seaman. **2** mean; small-minded: *~ partisanship; ~ spite;* **pet·ti·ly** *adv.;* **pet·ti·ness** *n.*

pet·u·lance (PECH·uh·lunce) *n.* petty irritability; peevishness. —**pet·u·lant** *adj.* —**pet·u·lant·ly** *adv.*

pe·tu·ni·a (puh·TUNE·yuh) *n.* a garden plant of the nightshade family with large, velvety, funnel-shaped flowers.

pew *n.* a bench with a back, fixed in rows for seating in churches.

pe·wee (PEE·wee) *n.* a small bird related to the flycatcher; also **pee·wee.**

pew·ter *n.* a silver-gray alloy of tin used for cooking utensils and tableware; also, these articles; **adj.:** *fine ~ ware; a ~ craftsman.*

pe·yo·te (pay·OH·tee) *n.* a psychedelic drug made from a cactus called *mescal;* mescaline; also, this cactus.

pf. pfennig; preferred.

Pfc., PFC private first class.

pfd. preferred.

pfen·nig (FEN·ig) *n.* **pfen·nigs** or **pfen·ni·ge** (–i·guh) a German unit of currency equal to 1/100 of a mark.

pg. page. —**P.G.** postgraduate. —**PG** parental guidance suggested (a movie rating); prostaglandin.

pH (pee·AICH) *n.* a measure of the relative alkalinity and acidity of a solution on a scale from 0 (highest acidity) to 14 (highest alkalinity): *A neutral solution is 7 pH.*

pha·e·ton (FAY·uh·tn) *n.* a light, four-wheeled carriage; also, an early type of automobile or touring car; **Pha·ë·thon** (–thon) in Greek myth, the son of Helios, whose sun chariot he tried to drive unsuccessfully.

phage (FAIJ) *n.* [short form] bacteriophage; **-phage** or **phago-** *comb.form.* destroying: as in **phag·o·cyte** (FAG·uh·site) *n.* a microbe-destroying blood cell.

pha·lanx (FAY–) *n.* **1** *pl.* **-lanx·es** a body of troops in compact formation. **2** *pl.* **-lan·ges** (fuh·LAN·jeez) one of the bones of the fingers or toes.

phal·a·rope (FAL·uh–) *n.* a small wading bird similar to a sandpiper but with lobed toes.

phal·lic (FAL·ic) *adj.* **1** genital, esp. as related to a child's psychosexual development. **2** pertaining to the generative power whose symbol is the penis, or **phal·lus** (FAL·us) *n.* **phal·lus·es** or **phal·li** (–lye).

phan·tasm (FAN·tazm) *n.* a figment of the imagination; specter; phantom; **phan·tas·mal** (–TAZ·ml) or **-mic** *adj.* —**phan·tas·ma·go·ri·a** (–GOR·ee·uh) *n.* a constantly changing scene or succession of images as in a dream. —**phan·ta·sy** (FAN·tuh·see) *n.* **-sies** same as FANTASY. —**phan·tom** (FAN·tum) *n.* a specter; ghost; ***adj.*** illusory; ghostlike: *a ~ ship on the horizon.*

Phar·aoh (FAIR·oh) *n.* a ruler of ancient Egypt; also, a tyrant.

Phar·i·sa·ic (fair·uh·SAY–) *adj.* of the Pharisees; **pharisaic** or **-i·cal** *adj.* self-righteous; hypocritical; **phar·i·sa·i·cal·ly** *adv.* —**Phar·i·see** (FAIR–) *n.* a member of an ancient Jewish sect.

pharm. pharmaceutical; pharmacist; pharmacy. —**phar·ma·ceu·ti·cal** (far·muh·SOO–) *adj.* having to do with pharmacy: *a ~ chemist; The American Pharmaceutical Association;* ***n.*** a medicinal drug; —**phar·ma·ceu·ti·cal·ly** *adv.* —**phar·ma·ceu·tics** *n.pl.* [takes sing. *v.*] the science of preparing and dispensing drugs. —**phar·ma·cist** *n.* druggist. —**pharmaco-** *comb.form.* drug: as in **phar·ma·co·ge·net·ics** (–NET–) *n.pl.* the study of the influence of one's genetic traits in responses to drugs. —**phar·ma·col·o·gy** (–COL·uh·jee) *n.* the science of drugs and their effects, comprising therapeutics, toxicology, etc.; **phar·ma·col·o·gist** *n.;* **phar·ma·co·log·ic** (–LOJ·ic) or **-i·cal** *adj.* —**phar·ma·co·p(o)e·ia** (–PEE·uh) *n.* a book with authoritative information on drugs, their properties, dosages, etc.: *The first U.S. ~ was published in 1778.* —**phar·ma·cy** (FAR·muh–) *n.* **1** the profession dealing with the preparation and dispensing of drugs. **2** a drugstore.

pha·ros (FAIR·os) *n.* a lighthouse or beacon.

phar·ynx (FAIR·inx) *n.* **-ynx·es** or **-yn·ges** (–RIN·jeez) the tract, nearly 4½ in. (11.43 cm) long, connecting the mouth with the esophagus and serving as both a food and air passage. —**pha·ryn·ge·al** (–RIN·jee·ul) *adj.: a ~ muscle;* ***n.*** a pharyngeal speech sound. —**phar·yn·gi·tis** (–JYE·tis) *n.* sore throat.

phase (FAZE) *n.* a particular, esp. changing aspect of something; also, a stage of development: *the ~s of the moon* (as "full moon," "crescent," etc.); *the color ~s of the red fox; the final ~ of a war; Windshield wipers have to work* **in phase** (i.e. in a reciprocal relationship); **out of phase** not synchronized. —***v.*** **phas·es, phased, phas·ing** plan or carry out in stages: *a carefully ~d army withdrawal; An addict is ~d off a drug; Operations were* **phased down** (**phase·down** *n.*) *in Indochina long before the retreat; Innovative changes are* **phased in** *at a plant; An obsolete product line is* **phased out** (i.e. gradually done away with); **phase-out** *n.* —**phase-locked** *adj.* in precise synchronization *(with).*

Ph.D. Doctor of Philosophy.

pheas·ant (FEZ·nt) *n.* any of a group of birds of the same family as the peacock and the domestic fowl, esp. the "ring-necked" and "golden" species.

phe·net·ic (fee·NET–) *adj.* in classification of organisms, based on similarity of characteristics, not hereditary factors.

pheno- *comb.form.* benzene-derived: as in **phe·no·bar·bi·tal** (fee·nuh·BAR·bi·tawl) *n.* a barbiturate used as a sedative. —**phe·nol** (FEE·nole, –nawl) *n.* same as CARBOLIC ACID; **phe·nol·ic** (–NOH–, –NOL–) *adj.* & *n.: A* **phenolic (resin)** *is used in molded plastic products, varnishes, adhesives, etc.*

phe·nom·e·non (fi·NOM·uh·non) *n.* **1** *pl.* **-na** anything observable or apparent: *natural phenomena such as storms, eclipses, and sunsets.* **2** *pl.* **-nons** a remarkable person, thing, or event, as a child prodigy: *The Guinness book is a publishing ~.* —**phe·nom·e·nal** (–nl) *adj.* extraordinary: *a ~ success;* **phe·nom·e·nal·ly** *adv.* —**phe·nom·e·nal·ism** *n.* the philosophical theory that there is no reality beyond what is observable by the senses. —**phe·no·type** (FEE–) *n.* an organism's observable properties collectively; also, a group of organisms with common characteristics.

phen·yl (FEN·il, FEEN–) *n. Chem.* a benzene-derived monovalent radical.

pher·o·mone (FER·uh–) *n.* a scented chemical secretion, usu. in the females of species, esp. insects, for eliciting specific responses in others of the species, as to find food or mates. —**pher·o·mo·nal** (–MOH·nl) *adj.*

phew (FEW) *interj.* expressing impatience, astonishment, etc.

phi (FYE) *n.* the 21st letter of the Greek alphabet (Φ, ϕ).

phi·al (FYE·ul) *n.* same as VIAL.

Phi Be·ta Kap·pa (fye·bay·tuh·CAP·uh) *n.* (a member of) an American honor society of outstanding students, founded in 1776.

phil. philosophy; philology. —**phil-** same as PHILO-. —**Phil.** Philippians (New Testament book). —**Phil·a·del·phi·a** (fil·uh·DEL·fee·uh) a city of S.E. Pennsylvania; **Philadelphia lawyer** a shrewd or tricky lawyer; **Phil·a·del·phi·an** *adj.* & *n.* —**phi·lan·der** (fi·LAN–) *v.* of a man, have love affairs in a casual or frivolous manner; **phi·lan·der·er** *n.* —**phi·lan·thro·py** (fi·LAN·thruh·pee) *n.* **-pies** the desire to help mankind; also, a humanitarian effort, gift, or institution, as the Smithsonian Institution or the Ford Foundation; **phi·lan·thro·pist** *n.* as James Smithson or Henry Ford; **phil·an·throp·ic** (–THROP–) *adj.* —**phi·lat·e·ly** (–LAT·uh·lee) *n.* stamp collecting; **phi·lat·e·list** *n.*; **phil·a·tel·ic** (–TEL–) *adj.* —**-phile** *comb.form.* loving: as in *Anglophile, bibliophile.* —**phil·har·mon·ic** (–MON–) *n.* a symphony orchestra; also, a society sponsoring one; ***adj.*** devoted to music: *a ~ society.* —**phi·lip·pic** (fi·LIP·ic) *n.* a bitter attack; tirade. —**Phil·ip·pine** (FIL·i·peen) *adj.* of the **Phil·ip·pines** (–peenz), or **Philippine Islands,** a republic consisting of over 7,000 islands off the coast of S.E. Asia; 115,831 sq.mi. (300,000 km²); *cap.* Manila. —**phil·is·tine** (FIL·is·teen) *n.* an uncultured person who is hostile to the arts, like the biblical **Phil·is·tines,** a non-Semitic displaced people at war with the Israelites; **phil·is·tin·ism** *n.* —**Phil·lips curve** a curve correlating inflation and rising wages with unemployment in inverse proportion. —**phil·lu·men·ist** (fi·LOO–) *n.* a collector of matchbox labels; the hobby is **phil·lu·me·ny** (–nee) *n.* —**philo-** *comb.form.* loving; lover of: as in *philodendron* (loving trees), *philosopher* (lover of wisdom). —**phil·o·den·dron** (–DEN·drun) *n.* a vine of the arum family, esp. a species with heart-shaped leaves. —**phi·lol·o·gy** (fi·LOL·uh·jee) *n.* study of language; in older use, linguistics, esp. historical and comparative; **phi·lol·o·gist** *n.*; **phil·lo·log·i·cal** (–LOJ–) *adj.* —**philos.** philosopher; philosophy; **phi·los·o·phy** (fi·LOS·uh·fee) *n.* **1** the study of the most fundamental nature and principles of things; also, learning, esp. in the arts and sciences: *a Doctor of Philosophy.* **2** *pl.* **-phies** a system, theory, or the sum total of one's beliefs, esp. as helpful to peace of soul; hence, calmness: *the Epicurean ~; one's ~ of life; sufferings borne with ~;* **phi·los·o·pher** *n.*: *a friend, ~, and guide.* —**phil·o·soph·ic** (–SOF·ic) or **-i·cal** *adj.*: *the ~ mind; a ~ doubt;* **phil·o·soph·i·cal·ly** *adv.* —**phi·los·o·phize** (–LOS–) *v.* **-phiz·es, -phized, -phiz·ing:** *Job ~d on his miseries.* —**phil·ter** or **phil·tre** (FIL·tur) *n.* a magic drink or drug, esp. a love potion.

phleb(o)- *comb.form.* vein: as in **phle·bi·tis** (fli·BYE–) *n.* inflammation of a vein, usu. in the leg. —**phle·bot·o·my** (fli·BOT·uh·mee) *n.* **-mies** an opening of a vein to let out blood in the treatment of disease.

phlegm (FLEM) *n.* **1** thick mucus brought up by coughing. **2** apathy; also, imperturbability; **phleg·mat·ic** (fleg·MAT–) *adj.*: *a ~ temperament; too ~ to get easily excited;* **phleg·mat·i·cal·ly** *adv.*

phlo·em (FLOH·em) *n.* food-conducting tissue of the stems, roots, and leaves of higher plants and trees.

phlox *n.* a group of garden plants with brilliantly-colored flowers, including the sweet William.

Phnom Penh (puh·NOM·pen) capital of Democratic Kampuchea (Cambodia).

-phobe *comb.form.* one who fears or hates (as specified): as in *Anglophobe, xenophobe.* —**pho·bi·a** (FOH·bee·uh) *n.* an irrational and morbid fear or hatred; **-phobia** *comb.form.* as in *agoraphobia, claustrophobia.* —**pho·bic** *adj.*

phoe·be (FEE·bee) *n.* a small North American bird of the flycatcher family.

Phoe·ni·cia (fi·NISH·uh, –NEESH–) an ancient country on the Mediterranean coast in the region of present-day Lebanon, Syria, and Israel; **Phoe·ni·cian** *n.* & *adj.* —**Phoe·nix** (FEE–) capital of Arizona. —**phoe·nix** *n.* a mythical bird, fabled to burn itself after 5,000 years of life, and rise again from its ashes; hence, a symbol of immortality.

phon. phonetics. —**phon** (FON) *n.* the unit of loudness of sounds; **-phone** *comb.form.* sound: as in *megaphone, xylophone.* —**phone** (FONE) **1** *n.* & *v. Informal.* **phones, phoned, phon·ing** same as TELEPHONE. **2** *n.* a speech sound. —**phone-in** *n.* a TV or radio program in which listeners phone the host to air their views on the topic being discussed; call-in. —**pho·neme** (FOH·neem) *n.* a distinctive speech sound of a language: *"Cat," "kit," and "chord" begin with the same ~;* **pho·ne·mic** (–NEE–) *adj.*: *For many people there is no ~ difference between "Mary," "merry," and "marry";* **pho·ne·mics** *n.pl.* the study of the sound systems of languages; **pho·ne·mi·cal·ly** *adv.* —**pho·net·ic** (fuh·NET–) *adj.* pertaining to speech sounds, esp. to **pho·net·ics** *n.pl.* the study of the production and transcription of speech sounds; **pho·ne·ti·cian** (foh·nuh·TISH·un) *n.* an expert in phonetics; **pho·net·i·cal·ly** (–NET–) *adv.*: *The "p" of "pot" is ~ different from that of "spot."*

phoney same as PHONY.

phon·ic (FON–) *adj.* pertaining to speech sounds, esp. to **phon·ics** *n.pl.* a method of teaching reading using the sound values of letters; **phon·i·cal·ly** *adv.* —**pho·no** (FOH–) *n.* **-nos** [short form] phonograph. —**phono-** *comb.form.* sound: as in *phonograph, phonology.* —**pho·no·graph** *n.* a machine that reproduces sound as transcribed in a spiral groove on a cylinder or disk, or **phonograph**

record; **pho·no·graph·ic** (–GRAF–) *adj.;* **pho·no·graph·i·cal·ly** *adv.* —**pho·nol·ogy** (foh·NOL·uh·jee) *n.* the study of the sounds and sound changes of a language; **pho·nol·o·gist** (–jist) *n.;* **pho·no·log·i·cal** (–LOJ–) *adj.* —**pho·no·rec·ord** (FON–) *n.* a phonograph record.

pho·n(e)y (FOH·nee) *adj. Informal.* **-ni·er, -ni·est** not genuine; sham; fake. —**pho·ny** *n.* **-nies** a fake; charlatan: *The new doctor proved to be a ~;* also **pho·ney, -neys.** —**pho·ni·ly** *adv.* —**pho·ni·ness** *n.*

phoo·ey (FOO·ee) *interj.* expressing scorn or disgust.

phosph(o)- *comb.form.* phosphorous: as in **phos·phate** (FOS·fate) *n.* a phosphorus-oxygen compound chemical, occurring naturally in **phosphate rock,** and used in fertilizers, detergents, and soft drinks; hence, any such product; **phos·phat·ic** (–FAT–) *adj.* —**phos·phor(e)** (FOS·fur, –for) *n.* a phosphorescent substance, as used in fluorescent lamps and television tubes: **phosphor bronze** *contains up to 0.5% phosphorus.* —**phos·pho·res·cence** (–RES·unce) *n.* the giving of light with little or no burning or heat, as in fireflies; also, the light produced; **phos·pho·res·cent** *adj.;* **phos·pho·res·cent·ly** *adv.* —**phos·pho·rus** *n.* a nonmetallic easily-burning chemical element occurring in minerals such as apatite and in animal tissue; **phos·pho·rous** (FOS·fuh·rus, fos·FOR–) or **phos·phor·ic** (–FOR–) *adj.:* **phosphoric acid** *forms phosphates;* **phosphorous acid** *forms* **phos·phites.** —**phot.** photograph; photographic; photography. —**phot** (FOHT) *n.* the c.g.s. unit of illumination, equal to 1 lumen per sq. cm. —**pho·tic** (FOH–) *adj.* pertaining to light activity: *the uppermost* **photic zone** *of the ocean penetrated by sunlight.* —**pho·to** (FOH·toh) *n.* **-tos** short for PHOTOGRAPH. —**photo-** *comb.form.* light; photographic: as in *photoelectric, photocopy;* **pho·to·com·po·si·tion** (–ZISH·un) *n.* photographic typesetting. —**pho·to·cop·y** (FOH·tuh–) *n.* a photographic copy, usu. of graphic matter, made with a **pho·to·cop·i·er** *n.;* ***v.*** **-cop·ies, -copied, -cop·y·ing.** —**pho·to·e·lec·tric** (–i·LEC–) *adj.* electrically affected by light: *Automatic doors and burglar alarms are operated by* **photoelectric cells,** also called "electric eyes"; **pho·to·e·lec·tric·al·ly** *adv.* —**pho·to·e·lec·tron** (–LEC–) *n.* an electron emitted by a metal surface exposed to light; hence **pho·to·e·mis·sion** (–MISH·un) *n.;* **pho·to·e·mis·sive** (–siv) *adj.* —**pho·to·en·grav·ing** (–GRAY·ving) *n.* a photographic process for making printing plates, esp. of pictures; also, such a picture or its printing plate; **pho·to·en·grave** *v.* **-graves, -graved, -grav·ing; pho·to·en·grav·er** *n.* —**photo finish** a race finish so close that only a photograph can determine the winner. —**pho·to·flash** *n.* same as FLASHBULB; ***adj.:*** *~ equipment.* —**photog.** photographic; photography. —**pho·to·gen·ic** (–JEN–) *adj.* suitable for being photographed; also, looking good in photographs. —**pho·to·graph** (FOH·tuh·graf) *n.* a picture taken by a camera on light-sensitive film, developed, and printed on paper; the art or process is **pho·tog·ra·phy** (–TOG·ruh·fee) *n.;* **photograph** *v.: She always ~s well* (i.e. looks well in pictures); *a bullet ~ed in flight;* **pho·tog·ra·pher** (–TOG–) *n.;* **pho·to·graph·ic** (–GRAF) *adj.;* **pho·to·graph·i·cal·ly** *adv.* —**pho·to·gra·vure** (–gruh·VYOOR) *n.* photoengraving using an intaglio plate; also, a plate or print made by this process. —**pho·to·li·thog·ra·phy** (–THOG–) *n.* a lithographic process using photography for preparing the printing surface. —**pho·tom·e·ter** (foh·TOM·i·tur) *n.* an instrument for measuring the intensity of light; light meter; **pho·to·met·ric** (–MET–) *adj.;* **pho·tom·e·try** (–TOM–) *n.* —**pho·to·mi·cro·graph** (–MYE·cruh–) *n.* a photograph taken using a microscope. —**pho·to·mu·ral** (–MYOOR·ul) *n.* an enlarged photograph used as a wall decoration. —**pho·ton** (FOH·tahn) *n.* a quantum of electromagnetic energy, as given out in X rays, gamma rays, etc. —**pho·to-off·set** *n.* offset printing using plates prepared by photolithography. —**pho·to·play** *n.* a play filmed as a motion picture. —**pho·to·sen·si·tive** (–SEN–) *adj.* sensitive to light. —**pho·to·sphere** *n.* the innermost part of the atmosphere of the sun or of a star. —**Pho·to·stat** *Trademark.* a photocopying machine; **photostat** *n.* a copy made with such a machine; ***v.*** **-stats, -stat·(t)ed, -stat·(t)ing; pho·to·stat·ic** (–STAT–) *adj.* —**pho·to·syn·the·sis** (–SIN·thuh–) *n.* a chemical process by which green plants make food and give off oxygen by the action of sunlight on carbon dioxide and water; **pho·to·syn·the·size** *v.;* **pho·to·syn·thet·ic** (–THET–) *adj.* —**pho·to·ther·a·py** (–THER·uh·pee) *n.* treatment by use of light. —**pho·tot·ro·pism** (-TOT·ruh-) *n.* the bending of a plant, usu. stalks or leaves, as of the sunflower, toward light or, as some roots, away from light; **pho·to·trop·ic** (-TROP-) *adj.*

phr. *Abbrev.* for **phrase** (FRAZE) *n.* a group of words, esp. as a unit within a sentence; also, a short, pithy expression, as "Peace with honor" or "go the whole hog": *a well-turned ~; a Czech-English* **phrase book** (for tourists); **phras·al** (FRAY·zl) *adj.: "Let (oneself) go" is a ~ verb.* — ***v.*** **phras·es, phrased, phras·ing:** *a well-~d toast; inelegant* **phrasing,** or **phra·se·ol·o·gy** (–OL·uh·jee) *n.* **-gies** style of expression; choice of words.

phre·net·ic (fri·NET–) *adj.* same as FRENETIC. —**phren·ic** (FREN·ic) *adj.* of the diaphragm: *a ~ nerve.* —**phre·nol·o·gy** (fri·NOL·uh·jee) *n.* the science that claims to tell a person's character from the shape of the skull; **phre·**

nol·o·gist *n.* —**phren·o·log·i·cal** (–LOJ–) *adj.: a ~ chart locating one's abilities, emotions, etc. on the skull.*

PHS Public Health Service.

phy·lac·ter·y (fi·LAC·tuh·ree) *n.* **-ter·ies** either of two small, cubical leather cases holding scriptural texts, worn on the forehead and left arm by orthodox Jewish men during prayers.

phy·log·e·ny (–LOJ·uh·nee) *n.* the evolutionary development of a type of animal or plant or of a language stock. —**phy·lum** (FY–) *n., pl.* **-la** a subkingdom in the classification of animals and plants.

phys. physical; physician; physics. —**phys. ed.** physical education. —**phys·ic** (FIZ·ic) *n.* a medicine, esp. a laxative; *v.* **-ics, -icked, -ick·ing** treat with medicine. —**phys·i·cal** *adj.* **1** material: *the ~ universe; Ghosts are not ~ beings; a university's ~ plant; a* **physical science** (as physics, chemistry, astronomy). **2** of the body: *a ~ examination* (or a **physical**) *by a doctor;* **physical education** *promotes ~ fitness;* **physical therapy** same as PHYSIOTHERAPY. **3** having to do with the laws of nature, esp. of matter and energy: *To go back in time is a ~ impossibility; Thawing is a ~ change; ~ chemistry.* **4** of the earth's features: *~ geography.* —**phys·i·cal·ly** *adv.* —**phy·si·cian** (–ZISH·un) *n.* a medical doctor; **phy·si·cian·ly** *adj.* —**phys·ics** (FIZ–) *n.pl.* the science of matter and energy and their interactions; **phys·i·cist** *n.* —**phys·i·og·no·my** (fiz·ee·OG·nuh·mee) *n.* **-mies** external features, esp. of the face, as indicative of character: *the ~ of the moon.* —**phys·i·og·ra·phy** *n.* physical geography; **phys·i·o·graph·ic** (–GRAF–) *adj.* —**physiol.** *Abbrev. for* **phys·i·ol·o·gy** (–OL·uh·jee) *n.* the branch of biology that deals with the vital functions and processes of living organisms; **phys·i·ol·o·gist** *n.;* **phys·i·o·log·ic** (–LOJ–) or **-i·cal** *adj.* —**phys·i·o·ther·a·py** (–THER–) *n.* the treatment of disease by physical means such as massages, exercise, light, heat, etc.; physical therapy; **phys·i·o·ther·a·pist** *n.* —**phy·sique** (fi·ZEEK) *n.* bodily build: *a man of fine ~.*

-phyte or **phyto-** *comb.form.* plant or growth: as in *xerophyte; zoophyte.* —**phy·to·tox·ic** (fye·tuh·TOX–) *adj.* injurious to plants. —**phy·to·tron** (FYE·tuh–) *n.* a laboratory for the study of plant growth.

P.I. Programmed Instruction.

[1]**pi** (PYE) *n.* **pis** (PIZE) the 16th letter of the Greek alphabet; the symbol (π) for the ratio of circumference to its diameter, equal to 3.1416.

[2]**pi** or **pie** (PYE) *n.* **pies** mixed up printing type; *v.* **pies, pied, pi(e)·ing:** *a ~d case of type.*

pi·a·nis·si·mo (pee·uh·NIS·i·moh) *Music. adj.* & *adv.* very soft; more softly than piano. —**pi·an·ist** (–AN–, PEE·uh–) *n.* one who plays the piano. —[1]**pi·an·o** (pee·AH·noh) *adj.* & *adv. Music.* soft(ly): *a ~ passage.* —*n., pl.* **-nos** a passage to be performed softly. —[2]**pi·an·o** (pee·AN·oh) *n.* **-os** same as **pi·an·o·for·te** (–fort) *n.* a large percussion instrument with wire strings that are struck by playing on a keyboard or by a mechanical device in a *player piano.*

pi·as·ter (pee·AS·tur) *n.* 1/100 of a lira or pound in Turkey, Egypt, Lebanon, Sudan, and Syria; *Brit.* **pi·as·tre.**

pi·az·za (pee·AZ·uh) *n.* **1** (*usu.* pee·AT·suh) an open public square in Italy. **2** a verandah.

pi·broch (PEE·broc) *n.* a usu. martial piece of music for the bagpipe.

pic *n.* **pics** or **pix** *Informal.* a picture; also, a movie.

pi·ca (PYE·cuh) *n.* a size of printing type giving six lines to the inch vertically; 12-point type.

pic·a·resque (–uh·RESK) *adj.* of fiction, dealing with roguish heroes and their adventures.

Pi·cas·so (pi·CAH·so), **Pablo.** 1881–1973, Spanish artist.

pic·a·yune (pik·ee·YOON) *adj.* trivial; petty.

pic·ca·lil·li (PIC·uh·lil·ee) *n.* **-lil·lis** a spicy relish of chopped vegetables.

pic·co·lo (PIC·uh·loh) *n.* **-los** a small, high-pitched flute.

pice *n. sing.* & *pl.* same as PAISA.

pick *v.* **1** take up, separate, or pull off with the fingers, beak, or a pointed instrument; also, choose or select: *a little girl ~ing flowers in the garden; A chicken is ~ed* (of its feathers); *~ rags* (i.e. shred them); *to ~ one's teeth or nose* (in order to clean it); *She ~ed* (i.e. chose) *her words carefully before speaking; to ~* (i.e. steal from) *somebody's pocket; a child* **picking at** *food because not hungry.* **2** dig; pierce; open: *Rocky soil is hard to ~; a lock that no thief can ~; a watertight alibi you can't ~ holes in; slowly ~ed her way through the crowd* **3** pluck, as the strings of a banjo or guitar; hence, play. —*n.* **1** a picking or choosing; hence, chosen person or thing; choice; also, best: *These apples are the ~ of the crop.* **2** a pickax. **3** a plectrum. —**pick off** dispose of: *From his ambush, the gunman ~ed off his victims one by one.* —**pick on** tease; nag: *Why do you always ~ on your younger brother?* —**pick out** distinguish; make out; play on a keyboard. —**pick over** handle: *He ~ed over the ties for a long time before buying one.*—**pick up** take; get; also, learn: *a suspect ~ed up by police for questioning; Where did you ~ up your French? We'll ~ up* (i.e. regain) *our trail in the morning; She's slowly ~ing up* (i.e. recovering) *after the operation; a girl he ~ed up* (i.e. persuaded to accompany him) *in Times Square.* —**pick·a·back** *adj.* & *adv.* same as PIGGYBACK.

pic(k)·a·nin·ny *n.* **-nin·nies** [unfavorable term] a black child.

pick·ax(e) *n.* a heavy, T-shaped tool for digging.

pick·er·el *n.* a small North American freshwater fish of the pike family. —**pick·er·el·weed** *n.* a blue-flowered plant of shallow waters with arrow-shaped leaves.

pick·et (–it) *n.* **1** a pointed stake or pale; one of the posts forming a picket fence. **2** one posted as a guard; also, a body of such persons; hence, a striking member of a union stationed outside a place of work, often in a group called a **picket line.** **—*v.*** **1** enclose or secure with a picket: *to* ~ (i.e. tether) *one's horse before going indoors.* **2** post pickets at; also, act as a picket: *to* ~ *a factory;* **pick·et·er** *n.*

pick·ings *n.pl.* what is picked or gathered; hence, returns or profits: *slim* ~ *for so much trouble.*

pick·le *n.* **1** salt water or vinegar for preserving foods in; hence, an article of food thus preserved; ***v.*** **-les, -led, -ling:** *~d onions.* **2** *Informal.* a predicament: *a sad* (or *sorry, pretty, fine,* etc.) *pickle.*

pick·lock *n.* a burglar. **—pick-me-up** *n.* a tonic. **—pick·pock·et** *n.* one who steals from somebody's pocket. **—pick·up** *n.* **1** *Informal.* a casual lover. **2** a light truck with an open body. **3** an electronic device for changing vibrations (as from a phonograph record) or sounds and images (as in radio and TV reception) into electrical energy. **—pick·y** *adj.* **pick·i·er, -i·est** choosy; fussy: *very* ~ *about her clothes.*

pic·nic *n.* **1** an informal meal eaten during an outing; also, such an outing. **2** *Informal.* a pleasant job or experience: **—*v.* -nics, -nicked, -nick·ing; pic·nick·er** *n.* **—pic·nick·y** *adj.: eating on the lawn in* ~ *style.*

pico- *comb.form.* one trillionth of: as in *picocurie, picosecond.* **—pi·cor·na·vi·rus** (–COR·nuh–) *n.* one of a virus group with a small proportion of RNA.

pi·cot (PEE·coh) *n.* one of a series of ornamental loops forming an edging on lace, ribbon, etc.

pic·to·graph (PIC·tuh–) *n.* picture writing, as seen in ancient caves; also, a picture or symbol: *A car and dangling keys is a* ~ *for "auto rental."* **—pic·to·graph·ic** (–GRAF–) *adj.* **—pic·tog·ra·phy** (–TOG·ruh·fee) *n.* **—pic·tor·i·al** (–TOR·ee·ul) *adj.* of or having to do with pictures: *a* ~ *history of the war;* **pic·tor·i·al·ly** *adv.* **—pic·ture** (PIK·chur) *n.* something drawn, painted, or photographed; also, any other visual image or an idea: *She looked the* ~ *of health; Get the* ~ (i.e. idea)? **—*v.* -tures, -tured, -tur·ing:** *Judas ~d as a villain; a ~d urn; I ~d* (i.e. imagined) *myself at death's door.* **—Pic·ture·phone** *Trademark.* a telephone that shows a television picture of the person one is talking to. **—pic·tur·esque** (–chuh·RESK) *adj.: a cottage with a* ~ *setting in the mountains; a* ~ *style of writing;* **pic·tur·esque·ly** *adv.;* **pic·tur·esque·ness** *n.* **—picture tube** a cathode-ray tube displaying a picture, as in TV. **—picture window** a large window giving a wide view of the outside.

pid·dle *v.* **pid·dles, pid·dled, pid·dling** trifle or dawdle: *~ing over petty expenses.* **—pid·dling** *adj.* petty; trifling: *a* ~ *sum as reward.*

pid·gin (PIJ·in) *n.* a trade jargon used as a bridge between languages, with minimal vocabulary and grammar, as **pidgin English** which has Chinese or S. Pacific elements.

¹pie same as ²PI.

²pie *n.* a baked dish of meat, vegetables, or fruit, usu. having a top crust of pastry: *as easy as ~; as American as apple ~.*

³pie *n.* magpie; also, a parti-colored bird or animal; hence **pied:** *the pied-billed grebe; the Pied Piper of Hamelin.* **—pie·bald** (PYE·bawld) *adj.* of two colors, esp. black-and-white; ***n.*** a piebald horse.

piece (PEECE) *n.* **1** a part, portion, or bit of something: *a* ~ *of paper;* **go to pieces** break into pieces; also, collapse; break down; **of a piece with** in keeping with; **piece of one's mind** *Informal.* a scolding; **piece of the action** a share in the business. **2** a single article or amount, often from a larger class or whole: *one ~ of luggage; a ~ of music; a three-~ suit; cloth sold only by the* ~ (i.e. standard length); *a fowling* ~ (i.e. rifle); *I said my ~ and sat down.* **—*v.* piec·es, pieced, piec·ing** make into one piece or whole; patch: ~ *a quilt; a personal account* **pieced out** *by hearsay; odds and ends* **pieced together** *in one volume.* **—pièce de ré·sis·tance** (pee·ES·duh·ray·zees·TAHNCE) the main item or event, esp. a main dish. **—piece goods** cloth sold by the yard from bolts. **—piece·meal** *adv.* piece by piece; ***adj.:*** *carried out a* ~ *operation.* **—piece of eight** an old Spanish peso worth 8 reals. **—piece·work** *n.* work based on the amount produced, not the time taken.

pied See ³PIE.

pied-à-terre (pee·aid·uh·TAIR) *n., pl.* **pieds-** (pee·aid–) an occasional dwelling.

pie-eyed *adj. Slang.* drunk.

pie in the sky a vainly hoped-for reward; a utopian plan.

pie·plant *n.* the rhubarb, used in pies.

pier (PEER) *n.* **1** a bridgelike structure jutting out into the sea for use as a landing place, promenade, or breakwater. **2** a pillar or post supporting an arch or bridge, esp. where two spans meet. **3** a section of a wall between windows: *a* ~ *glass.*

Pierce (PEERCE), **Franklin.** 1804–1869, 14th U.S. President (1853–57).

pierce (PEERCE) *v.* **pierc·es, pierced, pierc·ing** go into or through (something); penetrate: *A nail ~s a tire; a heart ~d with grief; an ear-~ing shriek; a* **pierced earring** *for use in a ~d ear lobe.* **—pierc·ing·ly** *adv.*

pier glass a tall mirror set in a pier (*n.* 3).

Pierre (PEER) capital of South Dakota.

pies *pl.* of ²PI or PIE.

piety See PIOUS.

piezo- *comb.form.* pressure: as in **pi·e·zo·e·lec·tric·i·ty** (pee·aye·zoh·i·lec·TRIS–) (produced by a crystal under pressure); **pi·e·zom·**

e·ter (–uh·ZOM·uh·tur) (for measuring pressure or compressibility).

pif·fle (PIFL) *n. Informal.* trivial talk; also ***v.;*** **pif·fling** *adj.* worthless.

pig *n.* **1** a domesticated animal, raised for pork meat, ham, bacon, etc. and thought of as stupid, filthy, and greedy; swine; hog: *roast ~; too* **pig-head·ed** (i.e. stubborn) *to listen to advice; The place is filthy as a* **pig·sty,** or **pig·pen; pig·gish** *manner of eating;* **pig·gish·ly** *adv.;* **pig·gish·ness** *n.* **2** *Slang.* a policeman or other hated person: *a male chauvinist ~!* **3** a bar into which molten iron is cast; also **pig iron.**

pi·geon (PIJ·un) *n.* **1** one of many species of birds of the dove family, usu. tame, and often trained as homing and carrier pigeons. **2** one considered easy to dupe, gentle, and timid; hence **pi·geon-heart·ed** or **pi·geon-liv·ered** *adj.* —**pi·geon·hole** *n.* a small compartment in a desk or cabinet resembling a pigeon's nesting hole; ***v.*** **-holes, -holed, -hol·ing** classify; shelve: *~d and forgotten.* —**pi·geon·toed** *adj.* having toes or feet pointed inward.

pig·gish *adj.* See PIG, *n.* 1. —**pig·gy** *n.* a little pig; ***adj.*** piggish; **pig·gy·back** *adj.* & *adv.: a child rewarded with a ~ ride (on her dad's back); a truck trailer carried ~ on a railroad flatcar; three ~ commercials during the same break; a spacecraft carrying ~ capsules;* ***v.:*** *I ~ed home on a charter flight after missing my plane;* **pig·gy·bank** *n.* a coin bank in the shape of a piggy. —**pig·head·ed** *adj.* See PIG, *n.* 1. —**pig iron** same as PIG, *n.* 3. —**pig Latin** a coded jargon, as "agicmay ords-way" for "magic words." —**pig·let** *n.* a young pig.

pig·ment *n.* a coloring substance, as added to paints, inks, plastics, etc. or as found in plant and animal tissues, esp. in skin and hair; ***v.:*** *a deeply ~ed tissue;* **pig·men·ta·tion** (–TAY–) *n.: Albinos lack ~.*

Pig·my (–mee) *adj.* & *n.* **-mies** same as PYGMY.

pig·nut *n.* the brown hickory or its nut. —**pig·pen** See PIG, *n.* 1. —**pig·skin** *n.* leather from the skin of a pig; hence, *Informal.* a football. —**pigsty** See PIG, *n.* 1. —**pig·tail** *n.* a tight braid of hair worn at the back of the head.

¹pike *n.* short for TURNPIKE.

²pike *n.* **1** a wooden shaft with a metal head, once carried by foot soldiers, or **pike·men** (*sing.* **-man**). **2** a pointed tip, as of a spear or arrow. **3** any of a large family of freshwater food fishes that have long snouts, including muskellunge and the walleye, or **pike·perch.**

pik·er (PYE·kur) *n. Slang.* a stingy person; cheapskate. —**pike·staff** *n.* **-staves** the shaft of a pike; also, a traveler's spiked staff.

pi·laf(f) (pi·LAHF, PEE–) *n.* a flavored rice dish with meat, fish, etc. boiled together.

pi·las·ter (–LAS–) *n.* a rectangular column that supports a wall, into which it is set, though partially projecting from it; **pi·las·tered** (–tird) *adj.*

Pi·late (PYE·lut), **Pontius.** the Roman governor of Judea, A.D. 26–36, who condemned Jesus to death on the cross.

pi·lau or **pi·law** (–LAW) *n.* same as PILAF.

pil·chard (PIL·churd) *n.* a small salt-water fish of the herring family; the European sardine; also, any related fish, as the California pilchard and Pacific sardines.

¹pile *n.* a heap, as of books, garbage, logs, dishes, etc.: *He had made his ~* (i.e. of wealth) *by the time he was 30.* —***v.*** **piles, piled, pil·ing:** *Five people ~d into the rear seat; telegrams ~ing up on the senator's desk;* **pile-up** *n.: a bad ~* (of vehicles in collison) *on a fogbound expressway.*

²pile *n.* the raised surface of rugs, fabrics such as velvet, etc.; nap; **piled** *adj.: deep-~ carpeting.*

³pile *n.* a heavy post or beam forming a support or foundation for a dock, bridge, etc. or one driven into the earth with a **pile driver** or **pile engine,** a hammering machine.

piles *n.pl.* hemorrhoids.

pil·fer *v.* steal or take away in small amounts; filch. —**pil·fer·age** (–ij) *n.: Store losses by ~ alone amount to $1 million.* —**pil·fer·er** *n.*

pil·grim *n.* **1** a traveler or wanderer, esp. one going on a pilgrimage. **2 Pilgrim (Father)** one of the English Puritans who settled in Plymouth, Massachusetts, in 1620. —**pil·grim·age** (–ij) *n.* a journey to a shrine or sacred place such as Mecca or Jerusalem.

pill *n.* **1** a tiny ball, pellet, or capsule of medicine for swallowing whole; **a bitter pill (to swallow)** something unpleasant to accept or endure. **2 the Pill** *Informal.* an oral contraceptive.

pil·lage (–ij) *v.* **-ag·es, -aged, -ag·ing** to loot or plunder; ***n.*** a pillaging or things pillaged; booty; spoils. —**pil·lag·er** *n.*

pil·lar (PIL·ur) *n.* a vertical, usu. cylindrical supporting structure; column; also, such a pillar set up as a memorial, as the Washington monument: *He was a ~ of strength in time of trouble;* **driven from pillar to post** (i.e. from one resource to another) *in search of employment; the* **pil·lared** (–urd) *majesty of the Parthenon.*

pill·box *n.* **1** a shallow cylindrical container for pills. **2** a small, low, concrete-and-steel gun emplacement.

pil·lion (PIL·yun) *n.* an extra seat behind a horse's saddle or motorcycle seat.

pil·lo·ry (PIL·uh·ree) *n.* **-ries** a wooden post and framework in which an offender's head and hands were locked for exposure to public scorn as punishment in former times; ***v.*** **-ries, -ried, -ry·ing** ridicule publicly: *a play ~d by critics.*

pil·low (PIL·oh) *n.* a cushion to rest the head on when sleeping; ***v.*** *The child slept, softly ~ed on her mother's breast.* —**pil·low·case** or **pil·low·slip** *n.* a removable cover for a pillow. —**pil·low·y** *adj.* soft like a pillow.

pi·lot (PYE·lut) *n.* a person or thing that leads or guides, as the operator of an aircraft, a helmsman working from the **pi·lot·house** of a ship, or an engine sent ahead of a train to see that the line is clear. **—*adj.*** serving to activate, guide, test, etc. **—*v.*** guide or steer: *to ~ a ship through rough seas.* **—pi·lot·age** (–ij) *n.* piloting or the fee paid to a ship's pilot. **—pilot balloon** one sent up to test the wind's direction and velocity; trial balloon. **—pilot film** (or **tape**) a film or tape of a television series for advance viewing by sponsors. **—pi·lot·ing** *n.* navigation, esp. of a ship. **—pilot lamp** (or **light**) a flame kept lit for igniting a main burner when needed; also, an indicator light. **—pi·lot·less** *adj.*

Pil·s(e)ner (PILS·nur, PILZ–) *n.* a light lager beer, usu. served in a tall, conical, footed **Pils(e)ner glass.** Also **pils(e)ner.**

pi-mes·on (PYE·mes–) *n.* same as PION.

pi·m(i)en·to (pi·MEN·toh) *n.* **-tos** **1** allspice; also, an evergreen tree of the myrtle family that yields the spice. **2** a sweet pepper used esp. for stuffing olives.

pimp *n.* a prostitute's agent; pander; also ***v.*** act as a procurer.

pim·per·nel *n.* a small, wild-growing plant of the primrose family with scarlet, white, or blue flowers that close in cloudy weather.

pim·ple *n.* a small, inflamed swelling on the skin; pustule. **—pim·pled** or **pim·ply** (–plee) *adj.: a ~ face.*

pin *n.* **1** a short, stiff piece of wire having a sharp point, used in various designs for fastening papers, cloth, etc. together; also, a peg of wood or metal similar in shape or function: *bobby pin, bowling pin, cotter pin, hair pin, hat pin, safety pin.* **2** an ornament or badge with a pin or clasp. **3 pins** *pl. Informal.* legs. **—*v.* pins, pinned, pin·ning** fasten or hold firmly: *so busy it is hard* **to pin him down** *to a definite time or place of meeting; Jane tried* **to pin the blame on** *someone else; a leader on whom people had* **pinned their hopes.** **—pin·ner** *n.*

pin·a·fore (–uh·for) *n.* a sleeveless garment worn like an apron over a dress or blouse.

pin·ball machine a game machine on which points are scored as a spring-driven ball slides down a board hitting various targets such as pins and bumpers.

pince-nez *n. sing. & pl.* (PANCE·nay, *pl. also* –nayz) a pair of eyeglasses that are clipped to the bridge of the nose. **—pin·cers** *n.pl.* a tool like the claws of a crab that is used for gripping or nipping things and that is worked like a pair of scissors. **—pincer movement** a military maneuver in which the enemy is cut off and attacked by forces closing in on either side. **—pinch** *v.* **1** squeeze between finger and thumb; also, act or suffer in a tightening or pressing manner: *Tight shoes ~; I'm ~ed for time; the look of faces ~ed by famine.* **2** *Slang.: Who's ~ing* (i.e. stealing) *my pencils? ~ed* (i.e. arrested) *on a vagrancy charge.* **3 pinch pennies** be stingy: *never ~es pennies when entertaining friends.* **—*n.:*** *a friendly ~ on the cheek; the ~ of poverty; Take tall tales with* **a pinch of salt** (i.e. with doubts); *a friend who never failed me* **in a pinch** (i.e. hardship or emergency); ***adj.:*** *a ~ hit, homer, runner* (baseball terms). **—pinch·ers** same as PINCERS. **—pinch hit** in baseball, a hit got at a crucial moment; **pinch-hit** *v.* **-hits, -hit, -hit·ting** act as a substitute (*for* someone), as a **pinch-hit·ter** who takes a batter's place at a pressing time.

pin curl a curl of hair held in place by a bobby pin while setting. **—pin·cush·ion** *n.* a small cushion that pins and needles are stuck into for storage.

¹pine *v.* **pines, pined, pin·ing** to long or yearn; also, waste away through grief: *~ing for his wife and family.*

²pine *n.* any of a family of evergreen trees with needlelike leaves and cones; also, its wood; **pin·e·al** (PIN·ee·ul) *adj.* like a pine cone: *The* **pineal body** (or **gland**) *is an organ at the center of the brain.* **—pine·ap·ple** *n.* the juicy fruit, shaped like a pine cone, of a spiny tropical plant. **—pine nut** See PIÑON. **—pine tar** a dark, viscous liquid obtained from pine wood and used in paints, varnishes, disinfectants, etc.

pin·feath·er (–fedh·ur) *n.* a young feather that is just emerging from the skin. **—pin·fire** *v.* treat (an ailing horse) with electric needles.

ping *n.* a sharp ringing sound as of a bullet striking metal; also, the knock in a badly burning gas engine. **—*v.:*** *an auto engine that ~s under load.* **—Ping-Pong** *Trademark.* a table-tennis set; **ping-pong** *n.* table tennis.

pin·head *n.* something tiny or trifling; also, a stupid person; **pin·head·ed** *adj.* **—pin·hold·er** *n.* a holder for cut flowers that has a pin-studded base. **—pin·hole** *n.* a minute hole, as if made by a pin.

¹pin·ion (PIN·yun) *n.* a bird's wing, esp. the outer rear edge having flight-feathers; ***v.*** hamper or restrain, as by cutting off a bird's pinions; also, disable a person by binding his arms to his sides.

²pin·ion (PIN·yun) *n.* a small gear whose teeth mesh with a larger wheel or rack: *a rack and ~ movement.*

pink *n.* **1** any of a group of plants bearing beautiful and fragrant flowers that have reddish petals with crinkled edges, as the carnation and sweet William; **in the pink** in the best condition or state (*of* health, repair, fashion, etc.). **2** a pale red color. **—*adj.*** **1** of the color pink. **2** with red or Communist leanings. **3** emotionally excited: *She was tickled ~ at the suggestion.* **—pink·ish** *adj.* **—*v.*** **1** stab gently; prick. **2** cut with **pinking shears** to make a zigzag pattern; also, decorate with a scalloped edge. **—pink·eye** *n.* reddening of eyes in acute conjunctivitis. **—pink·ie** or **pink·y** *n.* **pink·ies** the little finger. **—pink·o** *n.* [hostile term] a Communist sympathizer. **—pink slip** *Informal.* a notice terminating an employee.

pin money money given or set aside for minor expenses.

pin·nace (PIN·is) *n.* a ship's boat.

pin·na·cle (PIN·uh·cl) *n.* a spire, mountain peak, or other tall, tapering form: *at the ~ of her glory.*

pin·nate (PIN·ate) *adj.* of compound leaves, featherlike in formation, as of the sumac, ash, etc.; **pin·nate·ly** *adv.*

pi·noc(h)·le (PEE·nucl, –nocl) *n.* a card game played with a deck of 48 cards.

pi·ñon (PIN·yun, –yone) *n.* any of several pines of southwestern U.S. bearing edible nuts called **pine nuts.**

pin·point *n.* a tiny thing, esp. a spot precisely marked, as with a pin on a map; ***v.:*** *targets ~ed by radar;* ***adj.:*** *with ~ accuracy.* **—pin·prick** *n.* a prick, as with a pin; also, a petty annoyance. **—pins and needles** a tingling sensation, as in a limb after numbness: *She's been* **on pins and needles** (i.e. anxious) *awaiting her finals.* **—pin·set·ter** *n.* a person who spots and sets up pins in a bowling alley or a mechanical device for this; also **pin·spot·ter; Pinspotter** *Trademark.* **—pin·stripe** *n.* a very narrow stripe on a fabric; also, a suit with such stripes; **pin·striped** *adj.*

pint (PYE–) *n.* a unit of volume or capacity equal to 16 oz.; ½ quart; 0.4732 l. **—pint-size** *adj. Informal.* very small.

pin·to (–toh) *n.* **-tos** one that is spotted or piebald, as a horse or **pinto bean,** a variety of kidney bean.

pin·up *adj.* designed or suitable for putting up, esp. for viewing; ***n.*** a sexy picture of a girl; also **pinup girl.** **—pin·wheel** *n.* a paper toy having vanes pinned down in the middle and revolving like a wheel. **—pin·worm** *n.* a small roundworm.

pinx. *Abbrev.* for **pinx·it** *Latin.* painted: *Giotto ~* (i.e. painted it).

pi·on (PYE·on) *n.* any of three short-lived mesons, existing in positive, negative, and neutral forms, with weights around 270 times that of an electron. **—pi·on·ic** (–ON–) *adj.*

pi·o·neer (pye·uh·NEER) *n.* an explorer; initiator: *a wagon train of ~s headed west;* ***adj.:*** *life in a ~ settlement.* **—*v.*** *The Wright brothers ~ed in aviation; Armstrong and Aldrin ~ed the way to the moon.*

pi·ous (PYE·us) *adj.* **1** showing reverence: *a ~ lady;* **pi·e·ty** *n.* **-ties:** *Almsgiving is an act of ~.* **2** showing false piety: *He's a ~ fraud;* **pi·os·i·ty** (–OS–) *n.* **—pi·ous·ly** *adv.*

¹pip *n.* **1** a dot with a number value, as on dice or dominoes. **2** a small seed, as of the orange or apple. **3** a short, high-pitched signal; also, a blip.

²pip *n.* **1** a disease of chickens, marked by a crust formed on the tongue. **2** *Slang.* any annoying or depressing disease.

pipe *n.* **1** a tube for conveying water, gas, oil, etc. **2** a tube with a small bowl at one end for smoking tobacco, etc. **3** a musical tube blown by air, as in a bagpipe or in a **pipe organ; pipes** *pl.* bagpipe; also, organs of respiration or singing. **—*v.* pipes, piped, pip·ing** **1** play on a pipe; **pipe down** *Slang.* stop talking. **2** convey by pipes. **—pipe dream** *Informal.* a phantasy or vain hope. **—pipe fitter** a mechanic who lays or installs pipes and whose work is **pipe fitting.** **—pipe line** a line of connected pipes; also, any channel or process, as of information, supplies, etc. **—pipe of peace** calumet. **—pip·er** *n.* **pay the piper** See PAY. **—pi·pet(te)** (pye·PET) *n.* a suction tube for measuring or transferring liquids. **—pip·ing** (PYE–) *n.* **1** a system of pipes. **2** pipe music. **3** a pipelike trimming material for edges or seams. **—piping hot** very hot.

pip·it *n.* a small, larklike songbird.

pip·kin *n.* a small pot of metal or earthenware.

pip·pin *n.* a yellowish-green variety of apple with excellent flavor; hence, *Slang.* a highly admired person or thing.

pip·squeak *n.* one considered small or insignificant.

pi·quant (PEEK·unt) *adj.* agreeably pungent, lively, vivid, etc.; *a ~ sauce; ~ wit; the actress's ~ charm;* **pi·quan·cy** *n.;* **pi·quant·ly** *adv.* **—pique** (PEEK) *n.* feeling of hurt vanity or pride: *stomped out of the party in a ~;* also **v. piques, piqued, piqu·ing** **1:** *It ~d her not to be invited.* **2** arouse; excite (interest, curiosity, etc.).

pi·qué (pi·KAY) *n.* a plain or printed fabric of cotton, rayon, or silk, with raised cords usu. running the length of the material.

pi·quet (pik·ET, –AY) *n.* a card game for two, played with 32 cards.

pi·ra·cy (PYE·ruh·see) *n.* **-cies** the action of a pirate: *laws against air ~; TV ~ via satellites.*

pi·ra·nah (puh·RAN·yuh) *n.* a fierce little fish of South American rivers that attacks humans and animals in large groups.

pi·rate (PYE·rit) *n.* a robber of the high seas or a hijacker; also, one who violates a copyright or patent. **—*v.* -rates, -rat·ed, -rat·ing:** *A fake book is a ~d work.* **—pi·rat·i·cal** (–RAT–) *adj.*

pir·ou·ette (–oo·ET) *n.* a whirling around on the toe or on the ball of the foot, as in ballet; ***v.* -ettes, -et·ted, -et·ting.**

pis *pl.* of ¹PI.

pis·ca·to·ri·al (–TOR·ee·ul) *adj.* of fishing or fishermen; also **pis·ca·to·ry** (PIS–). **—Pis·ces** (PYE·seez, PIS·eez) a N. constellation and the 12th sign of the zodiac; also called "the Fishes." **—pisci-** *comb.form.* fish: as in **pis·ci·cul·ture** (fish-raising).

pis·mire *n.* an ant.

piss [vulgar] *n.* urine. **—*v.*** urinate; **pissed off** angry.

pis·ta·chi·o (pi·STASH·ee·oh) *n.* **-os** a tree of warm and dry regions yielding clusters of seeds called **pistachio nuts** or "green almonds" that have an edible kernel.

pis·til *n.* the seed-bearing, female organ of a flower, made up of one or more carpels. **—pis·til·late** *adj.* of a flower, having a pistil, esp. without stamens.

pis·tol *n.* a small firearm that can be fired with one hand. **—pis·tol-whip** *v.* **-whips, -whipped, -whip·ping** beat with the barrel of a pistol.

pis·ton (–tun) *n.* a flat, round device used in pumps and engines, that moves back and forth by the pressure of a fluid inside a cylinder in which it is fitted tightly by **piston rings,** the resulting motion being transmitted by a **piston rod** attached to the piston.

¹pit *n.* the stone of a fruit such as the cherry or plum. **—*v.* pits, pit·ted, pit·ting** remove the pit from: *~d dates.*

²pit *n.* **1** a hole or cavity in the ground, naturally formed or one dug for burial, mining, trapping, etc.: *"He who digs a ~ shall fall into it."* **2** a place or area resembling a pit, as for servicing automobiles during a race, the orchestra's place in front of a stage, a body depression or hollow such as a pock mark, the armpit, or the pit of the stomach, an enclosure for bearbaiting or cockfights, etc. **—pit** *v.* **pits, pit·ted, pit·ting:** *an unequal contest with one man ~d* (i.e. set) *against three; The moon's surface is ~d with craters.*

pi·ta (PEE·tah) *n.* a flat, round bread of the Middle East.

pit-a-pat *n.* a throbbing; pitter-patter; ***adv.:*** *Her heart went ~ when her name was called.*

¹pitch *v.* **1** put up; also, set or fix in a particular manner: *~ a tent; a voice ~ed too low to be heard; hopes ~ed too high; a* **pitched battle** *savagely fought.* **2** throw; toss; hurl: *to ~ hay into a cart with a* **pitch·fork;** *A baseball* **pitch·er** *~es the ball to the batter; a boat ~ing and rolling in the waves; The heckler was ~ed out of the hall.* **—pitch in:** *If everyone ~es in we will finish the work soon.* **—pitch into:** *We ~ed into the food as soon as we were served.* **—pitch on:** *Jones ~ed on me to propose the toast.* **—*n.:*** *a bowler's fast ~; emotion stirred up to a fever ~; the ~ of a voice; A free trip to Florida was included in the sales ~* (*Slang.* talk).

²pitch *n.* a black, sticky substance made from coal tar or petroleum and used for waterproofing, filling cracks, etc. **—pitch-black** *adj.* extremely black or dark; also **pitch-dark. —pitch·blende** (–blend) *n.* a pitchlike mineral ore containing radium, uranium, and actinium.

pitch·er *n.* **1** one who pitches in a baseball game. **2** a large, usu. earthenware jug for liquids, with a handle on one side and a lip for pouring on the other: *A* **pitcher plant** *has pitcher-shaped leaves for trapping insects.*

pitchfork See ¹PITCH, *v.* 2.

pitch·man *n.* **-men** *Informal.* one who makes a sales pitch. **—pitch pipe** a pipe producing a standard tone, used in tuning.

pitch·y *adj.* **pitch·i·er, -i·est** full of or like pitch.

pit·e·ous (PIT·ee·us) *adj.* deserving or causing pity: *O ~ sight!* **pit·e·ous·ly** *adv.*

pit·fall *n.* a concealed pit for catching animals or people; hence, any hidden danger.

pith *n.* the spongy core tissue of plant stems; also, a similar substance lining orange skins, inside a feather's shaft, etc.; hence, the core or gist: *"matters of great pith* (i.e. importance) *and moment."*

pit·head *n.* the entrance to a mine.

pith·e·can·thro·pus (–uh·CAN·thruh–) *n., pl.* **-pi** same as JAVA MAN.

pith·y *adj.* **pith·i·er, -i·est** brief and full of meaning: *Pope's ~ couplets;* **pith·i·ly** *adv.;* **pith·i·ness** *n.*

pit·i·a·ble (PIT·ee·uh–) *adj.* arousing regrettable pity; pathetic: *the ~ condition of starving children;* **pit·i·a·bly** *adv.;* **pit·i·a·ble·ness** *n.* **—pit·i·ful** *adj.* pathetic; also, so scanty or small as to evoke pity: *a ~ minority;* **pit·i·ful·ly** *adv.;* **pit·i·ful·ness** *n.* **—pit·i·less** *adj.*

pi·ton (PEE·tahn) *n.* a spike or wedge that is driven into ice surfaces or fissures in rock for passing ropes through in mountain-climbing.

Pi·tot (PEE·toh) **tube** an L-shaped tube for measuring the pressure and velocity of a flowing gas or liquid.

pit·tance (–unce) *n.* a meager allowance or remuneration.

pit·ter-pat·ter *n.* & *v.* same as PATTER.

Pitts·burgh a city of S.W. Pennsylvania.

pi·tu·i·tar·y (puh·TUE·i·ter·ee) *adj.* & *n.* **-tar·ies** (of) an endocrine gland attached to the brain, that secretes hormones controlling growth and other bodily functions: *~ dwarfism.*

pit viper any of a number of vipers with a deep hollow in the side of the head, as rattlesnakes, copperheads, and water moccasins.

pit·y *n.* **1** sorrow for another's suffering: **have** (or **take**) **pity** *on a poor beggar.* **2** a cause for regret: *What a ~ it's raining!* **—*v.* pit·ies, pit·ied, pity·ing** feel pity (for); **pit·y·ing·ly** *adv.*

piv·ot (–ut) *n.* a shaft or point on which something turns; hence, a person or thing in a key position, as the **pi·vot·man** or center in basketball, ice hockey, etc.; ***v.:*** *His entire life ~s on the king's good pleasure.* **—piv·ot·al** *adj.: a decision of ~ significance to her career.*

pix a *pl.* of PIC.

pix·ie or **pix·y** *n.* **pix·ies** a mischievous fairy; sprite; **pix·y·ish** *adj.: a ~ little girl.*

pi(z)·zazz (puh·ZAZ) *n. Slang.* vigor; style: *accessories to give your car a little ~.*

piz·za (PEET·suh) *n.* a pie consisting of thinly rolled dough baked with tomato, cheese, and spices on it, as made and sold in a **piz·ze·ri·a** (–REE·uh) *n.*

piz·zi·ca·to (pit·si·CAH·toh) *adj. & adv. Music.* played by plucking the strings; ***n.,*** *pl.* **-ti** (–tee) a passage or note so played.

pj's (PEE·jaze) *n.pl. Informal.* pajamas.

pk(s). park(s); peak(s); peck(s). —**pkg.** package(s). —**pkt.** packet.

PKU "phenylketonuria," a genetic disorder.

pkwy. parkway.

pl. place; plate; plural.

plac·ard (–ard, –urd) *n.* a notice posted in a public place; poster; ***v.:*** *The visit of the circus was ~ed in advance; walls ~ed with advertisements.*

pla·cate (PLAY–, PLAC–) *v.* **-cates, -cat·ed, -cat·ing** soothe or satisfy; appease: *a spoilt child hard to ~ with gifts;* **plac·a·ble** *adj.;* **pla·ca·tion** (–CAY–) *n.*

place *n.* **1** a definite portion of occupied space, as a city, a street or court, a building, a home, a particular spot, etc.: *"No ~ like home"; "a ~ for everything and everything in its ~"; A church is a ~ of worship; Who took my ~? dad's ~ at the head of the table;* **go places** *Informal.* start to succeed: *You're going ~s, boy!* **take place** happen. **2** a position, esp. one of rank, office, function, etc.: *a teacher's ~ in society; not my ~ to criticize you, Sir; A servant had to know his ~ or he would be* **put in his place;** *corruption in high ~s; goods returned, though damaged, because they were not ordered* **in the first place;** *In 22.2, each 2 has a different* **place value.** —***v.*** **plac·es, placed, plac·ing:** *He was ~d third in the race; The name is familiar, but I can't ~ his face; to ~ an order for books.*

pla·ce·bo (pluh·SEE·boh) *n.* **-bo(e)s** a preparation, as colored water, given only to humor a patient, without medical effect: *Some arthritis cures have merely a* **placebo effect.**

place card See PLACE SETTING. —**place kick** in football, the kicking of a ball held on the ground; **place-kick** *v.;* **place·kick·er** *n.* —**place mat** See PLACE SETTING. —**placement agency** one that finds jobs for people.

pla·cen·ta (pluh·SEN·tuh) *n.* **-tas** or **-tae** (–tee) a disc-shaped organ attached to the uterus, through which a fetus is nourished by its mother. —**pla·cen·tal** *adj.*

plac·er (PLASS·ur) *n.* an alluvial or glacial deposit containing minerals; **placer mining.**

place setting china and silver for one person at a table, usu. on a **place mat,** sometimes with a **place card** bearing the guest's name. —**place value** See PLACE, *n.* 2.

plac·id (PLAS·id) *adj.* calm; peaceful: *a ~ lake;* **plac·id·ly** *adv.;* **pla·cid·i·ty** (–SID–) *n.*

plack·et *n.* a finished slit at the top of a skirt, shirt, etc. to make it easier to put on and take off: *a shirt with a four-button ~ front.*

pla·gia·rize (PLAY·juh–) *v.* **-riz·es, -rized, -riz·ing** use or pass off another's ideas or writings as one's own. —**pla·gia·rism** *n.* —**pla·gia·rist** *n.*

plague (PLAIG) *n.* an affliction, esp. a deadly epidemic such as the *bubonic plague: She avoids TV* **like the plague.** —***v.*** **plagues, plagued, plagu·ing:** *a society ~d by high taxes and rising prices.*

plaice *n.* a flatfish, as the sole or flounder.

plaid (PLAD) *n.* a pattern of checks or colored stripes crossing at right angles, as on the woolen scarf worn over the shoulder by Scottish Highlanders; also, this garment. —***adj.:*** *a ~ skirt; ~ stamps.*

plain *adj.* **1** easy to see, hear, understand, etc.: *~ to the view; ~ and clear; ~ language.* **2** without ornament, color, seasoning, beauty, etc.: *~ food; a ~ face; a* **plain-spo·ken** *young man; a policeman in ~ clothes;* **plain·clothes·man** *n.* **-men. 3** flat: *~ ground.* —***n.*** level land; **Plains Indian** a North American Indian of a group that lived in the prairie regions; **plains·man** *n.* **-men** an inhabitant of the plains, esp. a frontiersman. —***adv.:*** *just ~ bored;* also **plain·ly.** —**plain·ness** *n.* —**plain sailing** progress that is smooth and easy. —**plain·song** or **plain·chant** *n.* ancient church music sung in unison; Gregorian chant.

plaint *n.* **1** *Poet.* lamentation; **plain·tive** (–tiv) *adj.* mournful; **plain·tive·ly** *adv.;* **plain·tive·ness** *n.* **2** *Law.* complaint; **plain·tiff** *n.* one who brings a lawsuit.

plait *n. & v.* **1** braid. **2** (*also* PLEET) pleat.

plan *n.* a drawing or outline of some action; scheme; program: *a building ~ drawn to scale; summer ~s; a five-year ~.* —***v.*** **plans, planned, plan·ning:** *a ~d economy.* —**plan·ner** *n.*

pla·nar (PLAY·nur) *adj.* lying in one plane: *a ~ surface.* —**plane** *n.* **1** a flat or level surface; hence **plane geometry,** distinguished from SOLID GEOMETRY. **2** a level: *the supernatural ~; a high ~ of achievement.* **3** a carpenter's tool for shaping and smoothing. **4** airplane: *a* **plane·load** *of refugees; the senator's* **plane·side** *chat with the press before boarding.* **5** same as PLANE TREE. —***adj.*** level; flat; **plane·ness** *n.* —***v.*** **planes, planed, plan·ing:** *a surface ~d smooth;* **plan·er** *n.*

plan·et (–it) *n.* a heavenly body revolving around the sun whose light it reflects, esp. Mercury, Venus, Earth, Mars, Jupiter, Saturn, Uranus, Neptune, and Pluto; **plan·e·tar·y** (–ter·ee) *adj.* —**plan·e·tar·i·um** (–TAIR–) *n.* **-ums** or **-i·a** (–ee·uh) an optical device for showing the pattern and movement of the planets, sun, moon, and stars projected inside a dome; also, a building housing this. —**plan·e·tes·i·mal** (–TES–) *n.* one of many minute celestial bodies that unite gradually to form the planets of any system. —**plan·et·oid** *n.* asteroid. —**plan·e·tol·o·gy** (–TOL–) *n.*

-gies the study of planets; **plan·e·tol·o·gist** *n.*

plane tree any of a family of trees including the sycamores, with leaves that are broader than they are long.

plan·gent (–junt) *adj.* resounding, esp. mournfully: *"pulse of ~ water like a knell."* **—plan·gen·cy** *n.*

plank *n.* a board that is at least 2 in. (5.08 cm) thick and 8 in. (20.32 cm) wide, as used in flooring a stage or platform; hence, an item of a political platform: *A higher minimum wage was one of his campaign ~s.* **—v. 1** cover with planks. **2** *Informal: She* **planked down** (i.e. put down with some force) *her dues and strode out of the room.* **3** cook and serve (fish, steak, etc.) on a board. **—plank·ing** *n.: new ~ for a floor.*

plank·ton (–tun) *n.* the mass of tiny, drifting animal and plant life in bodies of water, such as protozoans, jellyfish, algae, etc. **—plank·ton·ic** (–TON–) *adj.*

planned obsolescence designing that makes a product useless or out-of-date after a short time. **—planned parenthood** birth control, esp. as an organized movement.

plant *n.* **1** a living thing that is typically rooted in the ground and nourishes itself with food from air, sunlight, and water; an herb, vine, soft-stemmed shrub, or young tree. **2** a factory or facility used to make a product or provide a service; also, the machinery in it or an apparatus set up for a specific operation: *an automobile ~; a heating ~; the school ~; a college's physical ~.* **—v.** put in the ground, as a sapling or seed; also, set (up); place (forcibly, covertly, etc.): *stood with arms akimbo and feet ~ed wide apart; good habits ~ed early in the young by their parents; The boxer ~ed one on his opponent's left jaw; suspected as an undercover agent ~ed by the C.I.A.* **—plan·tain** (–tin) *n.* **1** a kind of banana plant; also, its fruit. **2** any of various low-growing herbs or weeds, such as the "broadleaf" and "ribgrass"; **plantain lily** a perennial lily with broad leaves and white and blue flowers. **—plan·tar** (–tur) *adj.* having to do with the sole of the foot. **—plan·ta·tion** (–TAY–) *n.* **1** a large estate growing a crop such as cotton, rubber, tobacco, or sugar cane, with the help of laborers who live on the estate. **—plant·er** *n.* one that plants, as a machine, a farmer, or plantation owner; also, a container for house plants. **—plantigrade** See -GRADE. **—plant louse** an aphid.

plaque (PLAK) *n.* a thin, flat piece or formation, as a tablet of wood or metal commemorating some event, an ornamental brooch or badge, a film or deposit on teeth, etc.

plash *n.* & *v.* splash.

plasm (PLAZM) *n.* **1** genetic or cell-forming material; ***comb.form*** as in: *cytoplasm, ectoplasm, protoplasm.* **2** plasma. **—plas·ma** (PLAZ·muh) *n.* **1** the liquid part of blood, lymph, or milk; also, protoplasm. **2** a gas containing equal numbers of positive and negative particles, formed by ionization, as in a **plasma torch** used in melting and vaporizing solids: *A* **plasma jet** *is used in satellites to steer through space;* **plasma physics** *studies ionized gas, esp. in cosmic phenomena and thermonuclear reactions.* **—plas·mat·ic** (–MAT–) or **plas·mic** *adj.*

—plas·ter *n.* a pasty mixture that hardens on drying; used to coat walls, ceilings, etc.; **v.** cover with or as if with plaster: *wet, ~ed-down hair; a wall ~ed with posters;* **plaster of Paris** *made with gypsum is used for statuary, in* **plaster casts** *holding fractured bones, and to make sheets of* **plas·ter·board** *for walls, ceilings, etc.* **—plas·ter·er** *n.;* **plas·ter·y** *adj.* **—plas·tic** *adj.* of substances, having molding, shaping, or pliable qualities; also, changeable in form; hence, artificial; insincere: *Clay, wax, plaster, etc. are ~ substances; the ~* (i.e. easily molded) *mind of a child; sculpture, painting, ceramics, and such* **plastic arts;** *A* **plastic bomb** *is a puttylike explosive; our ~ culture; her ~ smile;* **plastic surgery** *restores deformed or maimed body parts to their original shape.* **—n.** a synthetic, moldable substance such as nylon or vinyl. **—Plas·ti·cine** (–seen) *Trademark.* a modeling paste; also **plas·ti·cene** *n.* **—plas·tic·i·ty** (–TIS–) *n.* **—plas·ti·cize** *v.* **-ciz·es, -cized, -ciz·ing. —plastic money** the credit card used instead of cash. **—plas·tid** *n.* any of various tiny bodies in the cytoplasm of a plant cell, such as chloroplasts.

plat *n.* a plot of land, esp. a building lot; also, a map or plan indicating such plots; **v. plats, plat·ted, plat·ting** make a plat of.

plate *n.* **1** a flat, usu. shaped material or article, as: **a** a shallow, circular dish for serving food; also, food so served or dishes and plated utensils collectively; **b** a sheet of metal, glass, plastic, etc., as for taking photographs, for printing engraved impressions, etc.; also, a print thus made, esp. of a full-page picture in color; **c** a piece of metal or plastic fitted with false teeth; denture; **d** any of various protective pieces of material, such as make up a ship's steel hull or the horny or bony covering of reptiles and fishes. **2** same as HOME PLATE. **—v. plates, plat·ed, plat·ing:** *silver-~d spoons; a book all ~d and ready for printing.* **—pla·teau** (pla·TOH) *n.* **-teaus** or **-teaux** (–TOZE) a flat or level region; tableland; hence, a leveling off in a trend; stable period. **—plate glass** sheet glass for windows, mirrors, etc. **—plat·en** *n.* **1** in a printing press, a plate that presses the paper against the printing surface. **2** the roller of a typewriter. **—plate tectonics** the theory that the earth's crust is made up of huge plates, the friction between which causes earthquakes, mountains, volcanoes, etc. **—plat·form** *n.* an elevated floor, esp. a stage for speakers; hence, a statement of principles and policies of a political party or candidate: **platform tennis** *is played with a rubber ball and paddles on a wooden platform in a wire enclosure.*

—**plat·i·num** *n.* a silver-white, noncorrosive, metallic element: *A* **platinum blonde** *has silver white hair.* —**plat·i·tude** *n.* a solemnly made but well-worn or flat statement, as "Whatever will be, will be"; **plat·i·tu·di·nous** (–TUE·di·nus) *adj.;* **plat·i·tu·di·nous·ly** *adv.*

Pla·to (PLAY·toh) 427?–347? B.C., Greek philosopher. —**Pla·ton·ic** (–TON·ic) *adj.* of love, friendship, etc., purely intellectual or spiritual, with no sexual interest; **pla·ton·i·cal·ly** *adv.*

pla·toon (pluh·TOON) *n.* a military unit forming usu. part of a company; also, a group, esp. of players; ***v.*** in baseball, use alternate players in the same position. —**platoon sergeant** a noncommissioned officer ranking above staff sergeant and below first sergeant.

plat·ter *n.* **1** a usu. oval dish for serving meat or fish. **2** *Slang.* phonograph record. —**on a platter** as if served; (got) without effort.

plat·y·pus *n.* **-pus·es** or **-pi** (–pye) an aquatic, egg-laying mammal of Australia and Tasmania, with a bill like a duck's, webbed feet, and a paddle-shaped tail.

plau·dit (PLAW–) *n.* usu. **plaudits** *pl.* an expression of approval; applause. —**plau·si·ble** (–zuh·bl) *adj.* believable, esp. as (a person, theory, argument, etc.) appears; **plau·si·bil·i·ty** (–BIL–) *n.;* **plau·si·bly** *adv.*

play *n.* **1** amusing or recreational activity; sport; fun; also, the way the activity is carried on or a stage or act in it: *All work and no ~ is a dull life; foul ~; A flying shuttlecock is* **in play.** **2** an organized fun activity, as a game, a drama or similar performance, gambling, etc.: *Shakespeare's ~s.* **3** working, movement, activity, etc., esp. as being free, light, or quick: *the full ~ of a poet's fancy; too much ~ in a steering wheel; the ~ of moonlight on the lake; "The good life depends on the liver" is a* **play on words.** —***v.:*** *Children ~ all day; ~ at doctor and patient; Americans ~ing the Soviet team; The circus ~s southern cities in the winter; to ~ the piano; The officer ~ed his flashlight under the car; not safe to ~ with matches; A journalist* **plays down** (or **up**) *a rumor; Will you* **play back** *my recording now? The salesman* **played upon** *the buyer's inexperience to sell a lemon.* —**play·er** *n.* —**play·ful** *adj.;* **play·ful·ly** *adv.;* **play·ful·ness** *n.*

pla·ya (PLAH·yuh) *n.* a stretch of mud flats that becomes a shallow lake after rains, as in the "Great Basin" region of western U.S.

play·act·ing *n.* acting on the stage; also, pretense. —**play·back** *n.* the replaying of a recording. —**play bill** a theatrical announcement; also, a program. —**play book** a notebook with diagrams of plays for a football team. —**play·boy** or **play·girl** *n.* one given to pleasure-seeking, esp. sexual. —**play-by-play** *n.* & *adj.* detailed (account of an event). —**player piano** a piano played by a mechanical device. —**play·fel·low** *n.* same as PLAYMATE. —**play·go·er** *n.* one who frequents the theater. —**play·ground** *n.* an area for outdoor play. —**play·house** *n.* a theater; also, a building for children to play in. —**play·ing card** one of a set of small rectangular cards used in card games. —**play·let** *n.* a short play. —**play·list** *n.* a list of recordings to be broadcast by radio. —**play·mate** *n.* a companion for playing with. —**play·off** *n.* a contest for breaking a tie or deciding a championship at the end of a tournament. —**play·pen** *n.* a portable enclosure for an infant to play in. —**play·suit** *n.* a play outfit consisting of blouse and shorts. —**play·thing** *n.* a toy. —**play·wright** *n.* the author of a play.

pla·za (PLAH·zuh, PLAZ–) *n.* a public square; also, a commercial area, as a *toll plaza* (containing tollbooths), a *service plaza* (for motorists), or a *shopping plaza* (i.e. shopping center).

plea (PLEE) *n.* **1** an appeal: *a ~ for mercy.* **2** defense, esp. in answer to a charge: *Ignorance of the law is no ~; a reduced charge as a result of* **plea bargaining** *between prosecuting and defending attorneys; A defendant enters a ~ through a lawyer,* or **plead·er** *n.* one qualified to plead. —**plead** *v.* **pleads,** *pt.* & *pp.* **plead·ed** or **pled** *(Regional),* **plead·ing** **1** argue a case; also, answer a charge: *How do you ~—guilty or not guilty?* **2** offer as an excuse: *to ~ insanity when charged with murder.* **3** beg: *He ~ed for more time; She ~ed with her mother to let her go to the movie.* —**plead·ings** *n.pl.* statements made by the lawyers for the plaintiff and the defendant in a suit.

pleas·ant (PLEZ·nt) *adj.* having a pleasing effect: *a ~ time at the party; a medicine ~ to the taste;* **pleas·ant·ly** *adv.: smiles ~ at everyone;* **pleas·ant·ness** *n.* —**pleas·ant·ry** (–ree) *n.* **-ries** fun; joking; also, a joke or a pleasant remark. —**please** (PLEEZ) *v.* **pleas·es, pleased, pleas·ing** be agreeable (to); like; also, as a polite formula; *Come in ~!* **If you please,** *I'd like the door closed; a salesman eager to ~ customers; We're ~d to meet you;* **pleasing** *adj.: His manner was most ~;* **pleas·ing·ly** *adv.* —**pleas·ur·a·ble** (PLEZH–) *adj.* enjoyable; **pleas·ur·a·bly** *adv.* —**pleas·ure** (PLEZH·ur) *n.* the feeling of being pleased; also, something that pleases: *the ~ of your company; secret ~ in a rival's defeat; to mix business with ~ on a trip.*

pleat (PLEET) *n.* a fold, as on a skirt or drapes, stitched flat at the top; also ***v.:*** *a skirt with ~ed ruffles.*

pleb *n.* short for PLEBE, PLEBEIAN. —**plebe** (PLEEB) *n.* a freshman at the U.S. Military Academy or Naval Academy. —**ple·be·ian** (pli·BEE·un) *n.* one of the common people, not a patrician; ***adj.*** vulgar; coarse. —**pleb·i·scite** (–site) *n.* a vote by all the people of a country, esp. to determine their political independence. —**plebs** *n., pl.* **ple·bes** (PLEE·beez) the lowest class of people in ancient Rome; also, the masses.

plec·trum *n.* **-trums** or **-tra** a pick for playing a stringed musical instrument such as a banjo or mandolin.

pled a *pt.* & *pp.* of PLEAD.

pledge *n.* **1** a promise or vow: *a ~ of allegiance to the flag; An alcoholic* **takes the pledge** (not to drink). **2** a person or thing placed as security or guarantee; hostage; also, a member accepted but not yet initiated into a club, fraternity, etc. **3** the condition of being held **in pledge** as a pawn or hostage. **—*v.* pledg·es, pledged, pledg·ing:** *She ~d her jewels to get the loan; The oath ~d him to secrecy; ~d $100 to the Heart Fund.*

-plegia *comb.form.* paralysis: as in *paraplegia, quadriplegia.*

Ple·iad (PLEE·ad) one of a cluster of stars in the constellation Taurus, also called the "Seven Sisters" or **Ple·ia·des** (PLEE·uh·deez) *n.pl.*

Pleis·to·cene (PLY·stuh·seen) *n.* & *adj.* (of) the first epoch of the Quarternary period in the Cenozoic era of the earth, beginning about two million years ago.

ple·na·ry (PLEE·nuh·ree, PLEN·uh–) *adj.* full; complete, esp. in membership: *a ~ session of the council.* **—plen·i·po·ten·ti·ar·y** (–TEN·shee–) *adj.* having full powers or authority; ***n.*** **-ar·ies** such a diplomat, as "ambassador extraordinary and plenipotentiary" (highest rank of diplomat). **—plen·i·tude** *n.* fullness; also, completeness: *in the ~ of his glory.* **—plen·ty** *n.* a large number or amount: *We get ~ of rain; apples* **in plenty; *adj.*** *Informal.* sufficient: *There's ~ food;* ***adv.*** *Informal. I got ~ hungry;* **plen·te·ous** (–tee·us) *adj.*, usu. *Poet.* for **plen·ti·ful:** *a ~ harvest;* **plen·ti·ful·ly** *adv.* **—ple·num** (PLEE–) *n.* **-nums** or **-na** **1** a full space or enclosure; opposed to VACUUM. **2** a full assembly, esp. of a legislative body.

pleth·o·ra (PLETH·uh·ruh) *n.* an overabundance; fullness to excess.

pleu·ri·sy (PLOOR·i·see) *n.* inflammation of the **pleu·ra,** a membrane that covers each lung and lines the chest cavity.

Plex·i·glas *Trademark.* a light but tough acrylic plastic used in aircraft windows, lenses, etc.; also **plex·i·glass** *n.*

plex·us *n.* **-us(·es)** a network of arteries, lymphatics, or nerves, as the SOLAR PLEXUS.

pli·a·ble (PLY·uh·bl) *adj.* flexible; adaptable; also, easy to persuade or influence; **pli·a·bil·i·ty** (–BIL–) *n.* **—pli·ant** (PLY·unt) *adj.;* **pli·an·cy** *n.* **—pli·ers** (PLY·urz) *n. sing.* & *pl.* a tool with a pair of jaws for gripping, bending, cutting wires, etc.

plight (PLITE) *n.* **1** a solemn promise; ***v.:*** *"till death us do part . . . I ~ thee my troth."* **2** an unfortunate condition: *the sad ~ of refugees.*

plinth *n.* the square base of a column, pedestal, statue, vase, a piece of furniture, etc.

Pli·o·cene (PLY·uh·seen) *n.* & *adj.* (of) the last epoch of the Cenozoic era of the earth, beginning about 14 million years ago.

PLO Palestine Liberation Organization.

plod *v.* **plods, plod·ded, plod·ding** walk heavily or with effort; hence, apply oneself steadily to a difficult task. **—plod·der** *n.* **—plod·ding·ly** *adv.*

PL/1 "Programming Language One," a general-purpose computer language.

plop *v.* **plops, plop·ped, plop·ping** set, drop, or throw down, as a stone into water; ***n.*** (the sound of) a plopping.

plot *n.* **1** a small piece of ground, esp. a measured area, as on a ground plan; also, a chart, map, or diagram. **2** the plan of events in a literary work such as a novel or play; also, a secret plan of action to hurt a person, group, or nation: *the Gunpowder Plot.* **—*v.* plots, plot·ted, plot·ting** [corresponding to the *n.* meanings] **1:** *a subdivision ~d out for new housing; to ~ a temperature curve; X and Y coordinates to ~ the position of a ship.* **2:** *a well ~d novel; to ~ the overthrow of a dictator.* **—plot·ter** *n.*

plough *Brit.* plow.

plov·er (PLUV·ur, PLOH–) *n.* any of a group of small, stout shore birds of the lapwing family, with a short body and pointed wings.

plow *n.* **1** a farm implement for turning up the soil that is worked in furrows and drawn by animals or a tractor. **2** snowplow. **—*v.:*** *to ~ a field; He ~s a lonely furrow* (i.e. works all by himself); *Profits are* **plowed back** (i.e. reinvested) *in our business; She* **plows into** *her work at 8 a.m. sharp and is finished before everyone else; a book difficult to* **plow through** *in a week;* **plow·a·ble** *adj.;* **plow·er** *n.* **—plow·man** *n.* **-men** a farm worker. **—plow·share** *n.* the blade of a plow.

ploy *n.* a tactic or device.

pluck *v.* **1** pull off (a bird's feathers, flower or fruit from a tree, etc.). **2** pull; tug (at): *a singer ~ing away at his guitar; Someone in the crowd ~ed at my sleeve; I couldn't* **pluck up** (i.e. summon) *enough courage to protest.* **—*n.*** boldness; courage; **pluck·y** *adj.* **pluck·i·er, -i·est; pluck·i·ly** *adv.*

plug *n.* **1** a small piece of wood or metal used to stop up a hole; also, something similar, as a device with prongs to connect with an electrical outlet or an automobile spark plug. **2** *Informal.* a favorable bit of publicity, esp. on TV or radio. **—*v.* plugs, plugged, plug·ging:** *Wire-tapping was used to ~ the leak of top secret information; An electric kettle is ~d into a wall outlet; French students ~d into a tape player; She* **plugs away** *at her homework till bedtime; a best seller ~d by the networks.* **—plug hat** *Informal.* a man's high silk hat. **—plug·o·la** (–OH·luh) *n.* payola given for a plug (*n.* 2). **—plug tobacco** a cake or piece of chewing tobacco. **—plug-ug·ly** *n.* **-lies** *Slang.* a rowdy or thug.

plum *n.* **1** a smooth-skinned, juicy fruit similar to the cherry or peach; also, the tree it grows on. **2** raisin, as used in plum cakes and puddings; hence, something attractive or desirable: *That job's a real ~; politicians craving for the ~s of office.*

plum·age (PLOO·mij) *n.* a bird's feathers.

plumb (PLUM) *n.* a small weight (**plumb bob**) attached to a line (**plumb line**) to measure the depth of water or to test whether a wall is vertical; **out of** (or **off**) **plumb** not vertical or straight. **—*adj.*** vertical; also, downright; thorough; *a ~ fool;* ***adv.:*** *The post has to be erected ~; She's ~ wrong on that point.* **—*v.:*** *to ~* (the depths of) *a mystery.* **—plumb·er** (PLUM·ur) *n.* one skilled in plumbing; **plumb·ing** (PLUM·ing) *n.* the putting in and repairing of pipes and fixtures for water, gas, sewage, etc.; also, the pipes and fixtures. **—plumb·ism** (–bizm) *n.* lead poisoning.

plume (PLOOM) *n.* **1** a large feather used as an ornament or a tuft of feathers; also, a feathery part, as of a seed, leaf, or insect; hence "plume moth," "plume poppy," "plume hyacinth." **2** a formation like a feather; trail: *a ~ of smoke from a volcano.* **—*v.* plumes, plumed, plum·ing:** *a white-plumed egret; a swan ~ing* (i.e. preening) *its feathers; The boss* **plumed** (i.e. prided) **himself on** *his assistant's achievements.*

plum·met (PLUM·it) *n.* a plumb bob or line. —***v.*** plunge: *I sold my stocks before prices began ~ing.*

plump *adj.* **1** rounded; chubby; pleasantly fat; also **plump·ish; plump·ly** *adv.;* **plump·ness** *n.* **2** direct; blunt: *A ~ "No" was her answer;* ***adv.*** heavily or suddenly: *He dropped himself ~ into the chair.* **—*n.*** a falling or plunging; also, the sound made by it. **—*v.*** [corresponding to the *adj.* senses] **1:** *The child is eating well and gradually ~ing up.* **2:** *She ~ed her books down on the bed; Each teacher seemed to* **plump for** (i.e. champion) *his own pupil.*

plum·y (PLOO·mee) *adj.* **plum·i·er, -i·est** adorned with plumes; also, feathery.

plun·der *v.* rob, esp. on a large scale, as invaders do; pillage; loot; **plun·der·er** *n.* **—*n.:*** *unjust taxation that bordered on ~; a sunken ship loaded with ~.*

plunge (PLUNJ) *v.* **plung·es, plunged, plung·ing** **1** go or send down suddenly into water or as if into water or some other deep place: *He ~d his burned hand into the water; a country ~d into war; ~d in grief by a sudden death; the ~ing neckline of a decolletage.* **2** *Informal.* gamble or speculate rashly. **—*n.:*** *a ~ in the pool; ready to start the business, though hesitant to* **take the plunge;** *a ~ into stocks that left him a pauper.* **—plung·er** *n.* **1** a long-handled suction cup for freeing clogged drains. **2** one who plunges, esp. a rash speculator.

plunk *n.* a metallic or twanging sound, as made by plucking on a stringed musical instrument. **—*v.*** fall or drop heavily; plump: *He* **plunked** *the change* **down** *on the counter.*

plu·per·fect (ploo·PUR–) *adj.* & *n.* (of the) past perfect tense, indicating with the use of "had" an action completed before a specified past time; e.g. "He *had finished* the job when I arrived."

plu·ral (PLOOR·ul) *adj.* being more than one; ***n.*** a word form indicating more than one, as *boys, oxen, fish,* or *women.* **—plu·ral·ism** *n.* a state, condition, or theory that allows or advocates more than one, as holding two church offices at the same time or having several ethnic groups with equal rights in the same society. **—plu·ral·i·ty** (–RAL–) *n.* **-ties** in an election, the number of a winner's votes if less than a majority; also, the excess of such a winner's votes over the nearest rival's. **—plu·ral·ize** *v.* **-iz·es, -ized, -iz·ing:** *"Fish" is ~d in "Fish swim";* **plu·ral·i·za·tion** (–ZAY–) *n.*

plus *n.* **plus·(s)es** the addition sign (+), or **plus sign;** also, something added; hence, an advantage. **—*prep.:*** *Two ~ 2 is 4; aptitude ~ qualifications.* **—*adj.:*** *She got a B ~ in math; a ~ factor; a ~ quantity.* **—*conj.*** *Informal: He's jobless, ~* (i.e. in addition to which) *he's in debt.* **—plus fours** knickers reaching below the knees, used for sports and as country wear.

plush *n.* a fabric like velvet but with a thicker pile; ***adj.*** soft or luxurious: *~ carpeting; a ~ toy; dines in ~* (i.e. luxurious) *surroundings;* also **plush·y, plush·i·er, -i·est; plush·ly** *adv.*

Plu·to (PLOO·toh) *n.* **1** in Greek and Roman myths, the god of the underworld. **2** the outermost planet of the solar system. **—plu·toc·ra·cy** (–TOC–) *n.* **-cies** government by the wealthy; also, the wealthy class; **plu·to·crat** *n.* a member of the plutocracy; **plu·to·crat·ic** (–CRAT–) *adj.* **—plu·ton·ic** (–TAHN–) *adj.* of rocks, water, etc., formed deep down in the earth. **—plu·to·ni·um** (–TOE–) *n.* a radioactive metallic element used in nuclear reactions. **—Plu·tus** (PLOO–) the Greek god of wealth.

plu·vi·al (PLOO·vee·ul) *adj.* relating to rain.

ply *n.* **plies** a layer, fold, or strand of a material such as woven cloth, twisted rope, or plywood: *four ~s of polyester cord; a two-ply paper towel.* —***v.* plies, plied, ply·ing** **1** to twist, mold, or shape. **2** to work (at something or on someone): *a boat ~ing between New York and London; ~ing the same route for 10 years; a cutter ~ing his shears; She ~d the child with toys, then with questions.*

Ply·mouth (PLIM·uth) **Rock** **1** a boulder at Plymouth, Mass., on which the Pilgrims are believed to have first set foot on landing in 1620. **2** an American breed of chicken.

ply·wood *n.* a building material made of sheets of wood glued and pressed together.

pm. premium. **—Pm** promethium. **—P.M.** postmaster; post meridiem (i.e. in the afternoon; also **p.m., PM**); post-mortem (also **p.m.**); prime minister; provost marshal.

P.M.G. paymaster general; postmaster general.

pmk. postmark.

p.n. or **P/N** promissory note.

PNdB Perceived Noise Decibel.

pneu·mat·ic (new·MAT–) *adj.* having to do with air, esp. air under pressure: *a ~ tire; ~ drill; ~ tubes to shoot messages through a plant;* **pneu·mat·ics** *n.pl.* [takes *sing. v.*] the study of the properties of gases; **pneu·mat·ic·al·ly** *adv.* —**pneumo-** *comb. form.* lung; as in **pneu·mo·co·ni·o·sis** (–coh·nee·OH–) *n.* a lung disease caused by inhaling dust of silica, asbestos, etc.; **pneu·mo·nia** (–MOH–) *n.* a disease of the lungs ("double pneumonia" when both lungs affected) usu. caused by viruses or bacteria such as **pneu·mo·coc·cus, -coc·cus·es** or **-coc·ci** (–coc·sye).

Pnom–Penh same as PHNOM PENH.

pnxt. same as PINX.

¹Po polonium.

²Po a river of N. Italy.

P.O. petty officer; postal order; post office.

poach (POHCH) *v.* **1** cook fish, egg without its shell, etc. in a boiling liquid or over steam. **2** take game or fish illegally. —**poach·er** *n.* **1** one who poaches game or fish. **2** a covered pan or baking dish for poaching food.

P.O.B. Post Office Box.

P.O.C. port of call.

pock *n.* an eruption on the skin caused by a disease such as smallpox; also, a pitlike mark or scar left by it.

pock·et *n.* a small bag forming part of one's clothing, for carrying money, handkerchief, etc.; also, a similar hollow space, as an *air pocket, billiard pocket; a ~* (i.e. isolated group) *of primitive life in the jungle; a ~* (i.e. area) *of unemployment;* **in someone's pocket** under someone's control; **out of pocket** short of cash: *have petty cash for out-of-pocket* (i.e. incidental) *expenses.* —**pocket** [in compounds] small; limited; handy; as in **pocket battleship** (of limited size and equipment); **pock·et·book** *n.* purse; also, available money; **pocket book** a book in a small format; **pock·et·knife** *n.* **-knives** a knife with blade(s) folding into the handle. **pocket veto** an indirect veto of a bill by the President's not signing it before Congress adjourns.

pock·mark *n.* the scar left by a pock; **pock·marked** or **pock·y** *adj.* **pock·i·er, -i·est.**

po·co (POH·coh) *adv. Music.* somewhat; **poco a poco** little by little.

po·co·sin (–COH–) *n.* in southeastern U.S., a swampy region.

pod *n.* **1** a seed case or shell, as of beans or peas, that splits open when ripe; also, a cocoon or egg capsule. **2** a detachable container, enclosure, or housing outside a craft for carrying fuel, instruments, etc. —*v.* **pods, pod·ded, pod·ding** to form pods.

P.O.D. pay on delivery; Post Office Department.

-pod *comb. form.* footed: as in *arthropod* ("joint-footed"), *cephalopod* ("head-footed"). —**po·di·a·try** (–DYE·uh·tree) *n.* a branch of medicine dealing with foot ailments; **po·di·a·trist** *n.* —**po·di·um** (POH·dee·um) *n., pl.* **-di·a** a small platform for standing on, as for an orchestra conductor; also, a lectern.

P.O.E. port of embarkation; port of entry.

Poe, Edgar Allan. 1809–1849, American writer and poet.

po·em (POE·um) *n.* a piece of creative writing, usu. in verse form, with emotional and imaginative content; **po·e·sy** *n. Arch.* poetry; **po·et** *n.* one who composes poetry; **po·et·ess** *fem.* [rare]. —**po·et·as·ter** (POE·it·as–) *n.* a second-rate poet. —**po·et·ic** (–ET–) or **–et·i·cal** *adj.:* **Poetic justice** *punishes evil and rewards good;* **poetic license** disregard of a convention for the sake of artistic effect; **po·et·i·cal·ly** *adv.* —**poet laureate** a nation's official poet. —**po·et·ry** (POH·i·tree) *n.* the art of writing poems; also, poems collectively.

po·grom (poh·GROM, POH·grum) *n.* an organized massacre, as of Jews in Czarist Russia.

poi *n.* **poi(s)** a pasty Hawaiian food made from taro root.

poign·ant (POIN·yunt) *adj.* painful to the mind and feelings: *~ sorrow;* **poign·ant·ly** *adv.* —**poign·an·cy** *n.*

poin·ci·a·na (–see·AN·uh) *n.* a flowering tree of the pea family with fernlike leaves and fiery red blossoms.

poin·set·ti·a (–SET·ee·uh) *n.* a tropical plant with yellow flowers and red, petallike leaves.

point *n.* **1** a tapering end, as of a pencil; tip; also, a mark made with a tip; dot; hence, a position in time or space: *The patient was* **at the point of death** *last night; a terminal case past* **the point of no return;** *hope or despair, it depends on your* **point of view. 2** a mark as a unit or measure; degree; score: *the freezing ~ of water; You score 10 ~s for that; 72 ~s make 1 in. of printing type; a decimal ~* (as in 1.5); *a ~ of the compass, as N.N.E.* **3** the chief idea; a single detail, item, or particular; hence, characteristic; purpose; urgency: *Let me answer you ~ by ~; his good and bad ~s as a writer; no ~ in arguing further.* —***v.:*** *Use a sharpener to ~ the pencil; to* **point out** *a place on a map; All the symptoms* **point to** *stomach ulcers; badly written essays that* **point up** *the need for remedial English; a gun ~ed at his head; a* **pointed** *remark that made the listeners uneasy;* **point·ed·ly** *adv.* —**point-blank** *adj. & adv.*: *gunned down at ~ range; a ~ denial of the charge; She refused him ~* (i.e. bluntly). —**point·er** *n.* **1** a person or thing that points, as a rod; also, a breed of hunting dog that sniffs out game and stays pointing to it. **2** an indication; hint: *a few ~s on what to look for in a used car.* —**poin·til·lism** (PWAHN·tl·izm) *n.* painting in small dots of primary color that blend into the desired tones when seen at a distance, as practiced by Seurat, the first pointillist; **poin·til·list** *n. & adj.* —**point·less** *adj.* without a point; also, meaningless; **point·less·ly** *adv.;* **point·less·ness** *n.* —**point·y** *adj.* **point·i·er, -i·est** having many points; also, pointed: *a* *clown's ~ cap.* —**point zero** the place of explosion of an atomic bomb.

poise *n.* self-possession; also, the way one carries oneself; carriage. —***v.*** **pois·es, poised, pois·ing** balance; be balanced: *standing ~d at the brink, ready to dive.*

poi·son (POI·zn) *n.* a substance that causes illness or death in a living organism; hence, anything destructive or harmful: *Chemicals such as cyanide, certain plants, snake bites, and stings of insects are* **poi·son·ous** (–us) *adj.;* **poi·son·ous·ly** *adv.* —***v.:*** *killed by a ~ed arrow; found dead, ~ed by his butler; reading that ~s young minds.* —***adj.*** poisonous; **(poison) hemlock** an herb of the parsley family; **poison ivy** a vine or shrub of the cashew family, related to the **poison sumac,** varieties of both of which are also known as **poison oak.** —**poi·son-pen (letter)** a malicious, harassing letter, usu. by an anonymous writer.

poke *v.* **pokes, poked, pok·ing** prod or jab; push; also, *Informal.* punch: *Someone in the crowd ~d me; She ~d her head in my door to announce the visitor; ~ing around in the bushes for the lost ball; a dawdler ~ing along with his work; You like* **to poke fun at** (i.e. tease) *her.* —***n.*** **1:** *a friendly ~ in the ribs; took a ~ at him* (*Informal.* gave him a punch). **2** *Regional.* bag; sack; **pig in a poke** something to buy or accept sight unseen. —**pok·er** *n.* **1** a metal rod for stirring a fire. **2** a card game in which bets are placed on the value of the cards held; **poker face** *Informal.* an expressionless face, like that of a poker player who wants to keep his hand a secret. —**poke·weed** *n.* any of a family of perennial herbs with juicy purple berries and leaves that turn red in the fall. —**pok·(e)y** *adj.* **-ok·i·er, -i·est** **1** annoyingly slow. **2** dull, dowdy, or stuffy and cramped, as a **pok·(e)y** *n.* **pok·eys** or **pok·ies** *Slang.* a jail. —**pok·i·ly** *adv.;* **pok·i·ness** *n.*

pol *n. Slang* [short form] politician.

Pol. Poland; Polish —**Po·land** (POH·lund) a country in C. Europe; 120,725 sq.mi. (312,677 km²); *cap.* Warsaw.

po·lar (POH·lur) *adj.* **1** of a pole. **2** of the region of the North or South Pole; **polar bear** a large, white-furred bear of the Arctics; **polar circle** same as ARCTIC CIRCLE or ANTARCTIC CIRCLE. —**Po·la·ris** (–LAIR–) the North Star. —**po·lar·i·ty** (–LAIR–) *n.* **-ties** the condition of having opposed poles, as a magnet or a battery, or tendencies, qualities, etc.: *the political ~ between capital and labor.* —**po·lar·ize** *v.* **-iz·es, -ized, -iz·ing** give or get polarity: *~d sunglasses cut out much reflected light; a camera with a ~ing filter; a community ~d* (i.e. badly divided) *by the issue;* **po·lar·i·za·tion** (–ZAY–) *n.* —**Po·lar·oid** *Trademark.* a light-polarizing material, esp. as used in a self-developing and printing portable camera called "Polaroid Land Camera." —**Pole** *n.* a person of or from Poland. —**pole** *n.* **1** a long, slender, and usu. rounded piece of wood or metal, used as a *tent pole, flagpole,* or to propel a boat with; ***v.*** **poles, poled, pol·ing.** **2** either end of an imaginary rotating axis, as of the earth; hence SOUTH POLE, NORTH POLE; also, either of two opposite forces or principles, as of a magnet or the terminals of a battery: *The two sides were* **poles apart** (i.e. widely separated) *when they started talks.* —**pole·ax(e)** *n.* a battle-ax, usu. with a spike or hook opposite its blade.

pole·cat *n.* a weasellike animal of Europe, related to the ferret; also, a skunk.

po·lem·ic (–LEM–) or **po·lem·i·cal** *adj.* having to do with a **po·lem·ic** *n.* controversy, or **po·lem·ics** *n.pl.* [takes *sing. v.*] the art of arguing or debating; **po·lem·i·cist** *n.* one who practices polemics. —**po·le·mol·o·gy** (poh·li·MOL–) *n.* the study of war.

pole·star *n.* the North Star; hence, a guiding principle: *Duty was the ~ of his life.* —**pole vault** an athletic jump over a high crossbar using a flexible pole.

po·lice (puh·LEECE) *n.* **1** a department of government that prevents crime, maintains public peace and safety, enforces laws, etc.; also, its members, one of whom is a **po·lice·man, -men** or **po·lice·wo·man, -men.** **2** any similar private organization providing security services. —***v.*** **-lic·es, -liced, -lic·ing** **1:** *a well-~d neighborhood safe to walk in at night.* **2** keep a military area clean and orderly. —**police dog** a dog trained to help police, esp. a German shepherd. —**police state** one in which social, political, and economic life is repressed, usu. by use of secret police.

pol·i·clin·ic (–CLIN–) *n.* a hospital's outpatient department; cf. POLYCLINIC.

pol·i·cy (–see) *n.* **-cies** **1** a principle, conduct, or plan of action: *"Satisfaction or money back" is our ~; the foreign ~ of peaceful coexistence.* **2** an insurance contract, issued to a **pol·i·cy·hold·er** *n.*

po·li·o (POH·lee·oh) *n.* short form of **po·li·o·my·e·li·tis** (–my·uh·LYE–) *n.* an acute viral infection of the central nervous system, sometimes leading to paralysis; **po·li·o·my·e·lit·ic** (–LIT–) *adj.*

pol·ish *n.* a glossy surface finish, as of glass; also, a substance used to give this finish: *shoe ~; nail ~;* hence, refinement; culture. —***v.:*** *to ~ furniture; highly ~ed manners; He* **polished off** (i.e. finished) *his dinner in no time;* **Polish up** (i.e. practice and improve) *your French before going to Paris.*

Pol·ish (POH·lish) *n.* the Slavic language of the Poles; ***adj.*** of or from Poland: *She's ~; a ~ dialect; a ~ village.*

polit. political; politician. —**Po·lit·bu·ro** (POL·it·byoo–) *n.* a Communist Party's top policy-making group.

po·lite (puh·LITE) *adj.* **-lit·er, -lit·est** **1** correct and proper in one's behavior; not rude: *a ~ young lady; At least be ~ if you can't be friendly.*

2 cultured; polished; elegant: *a man of ~ learning.* —**po·lite·ly** *adv.* —**po·lite·ness** *n.*: *"Punctuality is the ~ of kings."* —**pol·i·tesse** (–TES) *n.* formal politeness; decorousness.

pol·i·tic *adj.* **1** shrewd and tactful: *She thought it ~ not to disagree with her boss.* **2** political: *the* BODY POLITIC. —**po·lit·i·cal** (puh·LIT–) *adj.* having to do with government or politics: *amnesty for ~ prisoners; The Russian sought ~ asylum in the U.S.; a ~ party;* **po·lit·i·cal·ly** *adv.;* **political science** the science of government. —**pol·i·ti·cian** (–TISH·un) *n.* one busy with political affairs, esp. one in political office; also, an opportunist: *just a scheming ~, no statesman.* —**po·lit·i·cize** (–LIT–) *v.* **-ciz·es, -cized, -ciz·ing** make political in character; **po·lit·i·ci·za·tion** (–ZAY–) *n.: the ~ of the Olympics.* —**pol·i·tick** *v.* be busy with political activities. —**po·lit·i·co** (–LIT–) *n.* **-co(e)s** a party politician. —**pol·i·tics** *n.* [takes *sing.* or *pl. v.*] political science; also, political principles or activities; hence, intrigue: *~ is a social science; Office ~ take up too much of his time.* —**pol·i·ty** *n.* **-ties** government or a form of government; also, a state or other political unit.

Polk (POKE), **James Knox.** 1795–1849, 11th U.S. President (1845-49).

pol·ka (POLE·kuh) *n.* a fast Bohemian dance for couples; also, music for this. —**polka dot** a round dot repeated as a pattern on fabric: *a polka-dot design.*

poll (POLE) *n.* **1** voting or the counting of votes; also, the results of a vote: *a light ~ due to bad weather.* **2 polls** *pl.* voting place: *Britain goes to the ~s tomorrow; The ~s close at 8 p.m.* **3** an opinion survey on a specific issue, as a *Gallup poll* or *Harris poll.* **4** the head: *a ~ tax.* —**v. 1:** *The winner ~ed 40% of the votes; a ~ing booth; A random sample of the population was ~ed on the issue.* **2** shear or crop (head hair, wool, horns, etc.). —**poll·er** *n.*

pol·lack (POLL·uk) *n.* a food fish of the cod family.

pol·lard (POLL·urd) *n.* a hornless animal; also, a tree whose branches have been cut away to promote new, dense growth. —**polled** (POLED) *adj.* hornless.

pol·len (POLL·un) *n.* a fine powder produced by flowers for the fertilization of other flowers by the agency of wind, insects, etc.; **pollen count** (or **index**) the estimate of the number of pollen grains in the air for warning hay-fever victims. —**pol·li·nate** *v.* **-nates, -nat·ed, -nat·ing** fertilize by pollen; **pol·li·na·tor** *n.* a pollinating agent; **pol·li·na·tion** (–NAY–) *n.*

pol·li·wog *n.* a tadpole.

poll·ster (POLE·stur) *n.* one who conducts a poll of public opinion.

poll tax a uniform per-head tax, not based on income or property.

pol·lute (puh·LOOT) *v.* **pol·lutes, pol·lut·ed, pol·lut·ing** make unclean; defile, esp. the environment, e.g. air, water, and soil, by **pol·lut·ants** (–LOOT–) such as wastes, exhausts, smoke, noise, etc.; **pol·lu·tion** (–LOO–) *n.* —**pol·lut·er** *n.*

Pol·lux (POL·ux) *n.* the brighter of the twin stars, Castor and Pollux, in the constellation Gemini.

po·lo (POH·loh) *n.* a ball game played on horseback using mallets; also, water polo.

Po·lo (POH·loh), **Marco.** 1254?–1324?, an Italian traveler in China and S. Asia.

po·lo·naise (pol·uh·NAIZ) *n.* a dignified processional dance of Polish origin; also, the music for it.

po·lo·ni·um (puh·LOH·nee·um) *n.* a radioactive metallic element.

polo shirt a short-sleeved, knitted pullover of cotton or jersey.

pol·ter·geist (POLE·tur·guyst) *n.* the supposed spirit behind the phenomena of haunted houses such as fire-raising, stone-throwing, china-smashing, and door-slamming.

pol·troon (–TROON) *n.* a contemptible coward; **pol·troon·er·y** *n.*

poly- *comb.form.* many; much: as in **pol·y·cen·trism** *n.* plurality of independent centers of Communist policy-making, as in Italy, China, Yugoslavia, etc.; **pol·y·cen·trist** *n.* & *adj.* —**pol·y·chro·mat·ic** (–MAT–) *adj.* many-colored; having changing colors. —**pol·y·chlo·ri·nat·ed bi·phen·yl** (–FENL, –FEE·nl) an industrial chemical compound, similar to pesticides, found contaminating the environment and entering the food chain. —**pol·y·clin·ic** (–CLIN–) *n.* a hospital with various specialist departments. —**pol·y·es·ter** (–ES–) *n.* any of a group of synthetic resins used in making paints, fibers, films, plastics, etc. —**pol·y·eth·yl·ene** (–ETH·uh·leen) *n.* any of various thermoplastics used for containers, kitchenware, tubing, etc. —**po·lyg·a·my** (–LIG–) *n.* marriage with more than one spouse at the same time; **po·lyg·a·mist** *n.;* **po·lyg·a·mous** (–mus) *adj.: a ~ tribe; Certain ashes and maples are ~* (i.e. have both bisexual and unisexual flowers). —**pol·y·glass tire** a fiberglass-belted tire made with polyester cord. —**pol·y·glot** *adj.* speaking, writing, or containing several languages: *a ~ edition of the Bible; a ~ population;* **n.** a multilingual person or text. —**pol·y·gon** *n.* a closed plane figure, usu. one with five or more straight sides; **po·lyg·o·nal** (–LIG–) *adj.* —**pol·y·graph** *n.* a lie detector; **v.:** *arrested, thumb-printed, and ~ed.* —**pol·y·he·dron** (–HEE·drun) *n.* a solid figure with five or more plane surfaces; **pol·y·he·dral** *adj.* —**pol·y I:C** (pol·ee·eye·SEE) a synthetic ribonucleic acid that stimulates the production of interferon for protecting the body from viral infections. —**pol·y·math** *n.* a person of wide-ranging knowledge. —**pol·y·mer** *n.* a substance composed of molecules that have combined with each other, as polyethylene which is made by the polymerization of ethylene gas; **pol·y·mer·ic** (–MER–) *adj.;* **po·lym·er·ize** (–LIM–) *v.* **-iz·es, -ized, -iz·ing; po·lym·er·i·za·tion** (–ZAY–) *n.*

Pol·y·ne·sia (–NEE·zhuh) a region of the C. Pacific including Hawaii, Samoa, Tonga, and nearby islands. —**Pol·y·ne·sian** (-zhun) *n.* **1** a member of a group of Caucasoid peoples of Polynesia. **2** a Maori. **3** any of the languages spoken by Polynesians. —***adj.*** of Polynesia, Polynesians, or their language or culture.

pol·y·no·mi·al (–NOH·mee·ul) *n.* an expression with more than two terms, esp. one in algebra or biology, as "x + y – z" or "Populus nigra italica" (Lombardy poplar); ***adj.:*** *a ~ equation; ~ nomenclature.* —**pol·yp** (POL·ip) *n.* a coelenterate, as a hydra, sea anemone, or coral, that has a hollow cylindrical body with one end attached to the sea bottom while the other, equipped with tentacles, acts as its mouth. —**po·lyph·o·ny** (–LIF–) *n.* musical composition of two or more harmonizing melodies; counterpoint; **pol·y·phon·ic** (–FON–) *adj.;* **pol·y·phon·i·cal·ly** *adv.* —**pol·y·pro·ply·ene** (–PROH·puh·leen) *n.* a thermoplastic resin used in packaging, tubing, etc. —**pol·y·ri·bo·some** (–RYE·buh·sohm) *n.* same as **pol·y·some** (–sohm) *n.* a cluster of ribosomes acting in union with messenger RNA to produce proteins. —**pol·y·sty·rene** (–STY·reen) a tough, clear plastic used for housewares, toys, electrical insulation, radio cabinets, etc. —**pol·y·syl·la·ble** *n.* a word that is **pol·y·syl·lab·ic** (–LAB–) *adj.* of many syllables. —**pol·y·tech·nic** (–TEK–) *n.* & *adj.* (a school) providing instruction in many technical subjects. —**pol·y·the·ism** (–THEE–) *n.* a religion with more than one god; **pol·y·the·ist** *n.* & *adj.;* **pol·y·the·is·tic** (–IS–) *adj.* —**pol·y·un·sat·u·rat·ed** *adj.* of a fatty acid or vegetable oil, lacking four or more hydrogen atoms. —**pol·y·u·re·thane** (–YOOR·uh–) *n.* a synthetic rubber used in flexible and rigid forms as foams, molded products, etc. —**pol·y·vi·nyl** (–VYE·nil) **chloride** a thermoplastic material used for imitation leather, phonograph records, etc. —**pol·y·wa·ter** (–WAU–) *n.* a polymer of water, much denser than ordinary water and nonfreezing; also called "anomalous water."

po·made (–MADE, –MAHD) *n.* a scented ointment for the hair; ***v.*** **-mades, -mad·ed, -mad·ing** apply pomade to: *~d hair.*

pome·gran·ate (POM·gran·it) *n.* a round tropical fruit full of seeds with a hard rind and tart, crimson pulp.

Pom·er·a·ni·an (–RAY·nee·un) *n.* a breed of small dog with long, silky hair.

pom·mel (PUM·ul) *n.* a knoblike projection, as on a sword's hilt or the front end of a saddle. —***v.*** **pom·mels, pom·me·(l)ed, pom·mel·(l)ing** to pummel.

pomp *n.* a showy display; *a ceremony full of ~ and pageantry.*

pom·pa·dour (–dore) *n.* a hairdo that rises straight up from the forehead, over a pad or roller in the case of women.

pom·pa·no (–puh·noh) *n.* a food fish of the Atlantic, the largest type of which is the permit or *great pompano.*

Pom·pei·i (pom·PAY·ee, –PAY) an Italian city destroyed by an eruption of Mt. Vesuvius in A.D. 79.

pom-pom *n.* an ornamental tuft or ball of soft material; pompon. —**pom·pon** *n.* pom-pom; also, the small, round flower head of a chrysanthemum or dahlia.

pom·pous (–pus) *adj.* showy; pretentious: *a ~ speech;* **pom·pous·ly** *adv.;* **pom·pous·ness** or **pom·pos·i·ty** (–POS–) *n.*

ponce *n. Slang.* a man who lives off a prostitute's earnings; pimp.

pon·cho (–choh) *n.* **-chos** a cloak resembling a blanket with a hole through it for the wearer's head; also, a similar garment, esp. a raincoat.

pond *n.* a body of water smaller than a lake.

pon·der *v.* weigh mentally; consider deeply: *a philosopher ~ing a truth; ~ing over his future;* **pon·der·er** *n.;* **pon·der·a·ble** *adj.* appreciable. —**pon·der·o·sa (pine)** (–ROH–) a tall pine of W. North America valued as timber. —**pon·der·ous** *adj.* heavy; clumsy; dull: *an elephant's ~ gait; a ~ lecture.*

pone *n.* cornmeal bread in oval loaves, common in southern U.S.

pon·gee (–jee) *n.* a soft, light-brown cloth of Chinese silk.

pon·iard (–yurd) *n.* a dagger.

pon·tiff *n.* a bishop, esp., the **(Supreme) Pontiff,** or Pope. —**pon·tif·i·cal** (–TIF–) *adj.* papal; hence, stately; also, pompous: *~ robes,* or **pontificals** *n.pl.* a pontiff's ceremonial vestments and insignia. —**pon·tif·i·cate** (–kit) *n.* a pontiff's office or term of office; ***v.*** (-cate) **-cates, -cat·ed, -cat·ing** officiate as a pontiff; also, speak pompously.

pon·toon (–TOON) *n.* a flat-bottomed boat; also, one of the floats on some aircraft's landing gear; also **pon·ton** (–tn). —**pontoon bridge** a temporary bridge supported by pontoons.

pon·y (POH·nee) *n.* **-nies** **1** a small horse. **2** a small glass of liqueur. **3** same as CRIB, *n.* 3. —**pony express** a system of mail carried by a relay of riders, once used in western U.S. —**po·ny·tail** *n.* hair tied high behind the head and hanging down like a pony's tail.

pooch *n. Slang.* a dog.

poo·dle *n.* a breed of intelligent dogs with thick curly hair that is clipped or shaved in various styles.

pooh *interj.* indicating impatience or contempt. **—pooh-bah** *n.* a self-important official with much nominal authority. **—pooh-pooh** *v.* treat with contempt; dismiss lightly.

pool *n.* **1** a small body of water, as a *swimming pool;* also, a puddle or small collection of liquid: *The murder victim lay in a ~ of blood.* **2** a form of billiards, played on a six-pocket **pool table,** often in a **pool hall** or **pool room. 3** a group or combination of people or resources for a common purpose, as a *typists' pool, car pool* (to share driving), *football pool* (for betting), or a business combine or cartel (for controlling a market). **—v.** put in a common fund: *We ~ed our talents to make the show a success.*

[1]**poop (deck)** a raised deck at the stern of a ship.

[2]**poop** *Slang.* **1** *v.* be exhausted; **poop out** cease functioning. **2** *n.* inside information: *a* **poop sheet** *handed out to newsmen.*

poor *adj.* needy; lacking in quality or amount; hence, needing pity: *a ~ widow; a ~ showing at the polls; Pity the ~ child;* **the poor** [takes *pl. v.*] needy people. **—poor·ly** *adv.* **—poor·house** *n.* formerly, a publicly supported institution for the poor. **—poor-mouth** *v. Informal.* complain of or plead poverty.

pop. population; popular.

[1]**pop** *n. Informal.* father.

[2]**pop** *adj.* popular in artistic or cultural appeal: *~ culture;* **pops** *n.pl.* pop music: *Boston pops orchestra;* **pop (art)** *or* **Pop (art)** *uses everyday subjects and techniques based on commercial art;* **pop artist** or **pop·ster** *n.*

[3]**pop** *n.* **1** a light explosive sound; esp., a gun shot. **2** a carbonated drink. **3** in baseball, a short, high fly ball; also **pop fly, pop-up. —v. pops, popped, pop·ping** make a popping sound; also, happen, do something, or act with a pop, i.e. suddenly or unexpectedly: *She was waiting for him to* **pop the question** (i.e. to propose); *hippies ~ing* (i.e. swallowing) *pills and blowing marijuana; There's no end to the problems that* **pop up** *at work.* **—pop off** *Slang.* **1** die suddenly. **2** talk or write carelessly. **—pop art** See [2]POP. **—pop·corn** *n.* the white, puffed-out kernels of Indian corn roasted over a fire, usu. in a **pop·per.**

pope *n.* the head of the Roman Catholic Church. **—Pope, Alexander.** 1688–1744, English poet.

pop·eyed *adj.* having protruding eyes. **—pop fly** See [3]POP, *n.* 3. **—pop·gun** *n.* a toy gun that fires a cork or pellets with a popping sound.

pop·in·jay *n.* a vain person; fop.

pop·lar (–lur) *n.* any of a group of fast-growing trees of the willow family such as aspens and cottonwoods.

pop·lin *n.* a tightly woven ribbed fabric with a plain weave.

pop-off *n.* a person who pops off in speech or writing. **—pop·o·ver** (–oh·vur) *n.* a light, puffy muffin that pops over the edge of the pan in which it is baked.

pop·py (POP·ee) *n.* **pop·pies** any of a family of herbs with large, usu. red flowers and a milky juice: **poppy seed** *is used to flavor bakery products.*

pop·py-cock *n. Informal.* nonsense.

popster See [2]POP. **—pop-top** *n.* & *adj.* (a soda or beer container) having a ring for pulling the top open.

pop·u·lace (POP·yuh·lis) *n.* the common people; the masses. **—pop·u·lar** (–lur) *adj.* of or for the common people, esp. appealing to or liked by them: *a ~ government; The President is not chosen by ~ vote; a ~ price; left-wing parties united in a ~ front against fascism;* **pop·u·lar·ly** *adv.;* **pop·u·lar·ize** *v.* **-iz·es, -ized, -iz·ing** make popular; **pop·u·lar·i·ty** (–LAIR–) *n.* **—pop·u·late** *v.* **-lates, -lat·ed, -lat·ing** inhabit; supply with people to inhabit: *a densely ~d area; Animal life existed before humans ~d the earth;* **pop·u·la·tion** (–LAY–) *n.* the people or the number of people of a particular place or group: *the adult male ~; the falling ~ of urban areas; the recent* **population explosion** *due to improved living conditions and faster reproduction.* **—pop·u·list** *n.* a member of a political party devoted to helping the common people as against moneyed interests, as the *Populist Party* active in U.S. politics in the 1890's; **pop·u·lism** *n.* **—pop·u·lous** (–lus) *adj.* thickly populated; **pop·u·lous·ness** *n.*

pop-up See [3]POP, *n.* 3.

P.O.R. pay on return.

por·ce·lain (POR·sl·in) *n.* a fine-grained, white, translucent, glazed ceramic ware; china. **—por·ce·lain·ize** *v.* **-iz·es, -ized, -iz·ing** coat with porcelain: *~d steel.*

porch *n.* a roofed entrance to a building; also, a verandah.

por·cine (–sine, –sin) *adj.* of or like pigs or hogs. **—por·cu·pine** (–kyuh–) *n.* a large rodent with a covering of long, sharp spines for protection.

[1]**pore** *v.* **pores, pored, por·ing** study long and intently; ponder: *She's been ~ing over her books all day.*

[2]**pore** *n.* a tiny opening on leaves, skin, etc. for the absorption or passage of fluids, as when sweating. **—pored** *adj.*

por·gy (–gee) *n.* **-gies** a food fish of the Mediterranean and N. Atlantic waters such as the scup and the sea bream.

pork *n.* the meat of a pig or hog, esp. when cured. **—pork barrel** public funding of local projects for the political benefit of elected representatives: *~-barrel politics.* **—pork·er** *n.* a young hog raised for food. **—pork·y** *adj.* **pork·i·er, -i·est** like pork.

porn or **por·no** *n.* & *adj.* [short form] pornography; pornographic: *hard-core porn; a porno* *movie.* —**por·nog·ra·phy** *n.* writings and pictures meant to arouse sexual desire. —**por·no·graph·ic** (–GRAF–) *adj.*

po·rous (POR·us) *adj.* full of pores; allowing light, air, etc. to pass through; **por·ous·ly** *adv.;* **por·ous·ness** or **po·ros·i·ty** (–ROS–) *n.*

por·phy·ry (POR·fuh·ree) *n.* **-ries** an igneous rock containing large crystals of one kind, as feldspar, in a mass of smaller crystals, as in some granites. —**por·phy·rit·ic** (–RIT–) *adj.*

por·poise (–pus) *n.* **-pois·es** a smaller kind of sea mammal than a whale; also, a dolphin.

por·ridge (POR·ij) *n. Brit.* a soft food of cereal or oatmeal boiled in milk until thick. —**por·rin·ger** (–jur) *n.* a small basin or bowl for serving porridge, soup, etc., esp. to a child.

Port. Portugal; Portuguese.

port *n.* **1** a harbor; also, a harbor city, esp. an official **port of entry** for cargo and people into a country. **2** a strong, dark-red wine of Portugal. **3** a ship's or aircraft's left side for one facing front; ***adj.*** & ***v.:*** *~ the helm* (i.e. turn it to the left). **4** an opening, as in a fortress wall; also, one in a ship's or aircraft's side as a window, or **port·hole.** **5** one's bearing or carriage. —**port·a·ble** (–uh·bl) *adj.* easy to carry or move, as a small TV or typewriter: *a ~ pension plan for employees changing jobs;* ***n.:*** *extra classes housed in ~s;* **port·a·bil·i·ty** (–BIL–) *n.* —**port·age** (–ij) *n.* the carrying (place or route) of boats and provisions overland, as from one river to another; ***v.*** **-ag·es, -aged, -ag·ing:** *riding rapids and ~ing around waterfalls.* —**por·tal** *n.* entrance, esp. an imposing one; **por·tal-to-por·tal** *adj.* relating to a workman's time between entering the employer's premises and leaving it, irrespective of the actual place of work.

Port-au-Prince (–oh–) capital of Haiti.

port·cul·lis (–CULL·is) *n.* an iron grating that is slid down grooves to close the gateway of an ancient fortress. —**porte-co·chere** (–coh·SHARE) *n.* a roofed porch at the entrance to a building for vehicles to stop to let off or take in people.

por·tend (–TEND) *v.* be a warning of (some future event); bode. —**por·tent** (POR–) *n.* a foreboding; omen; **por·ten·tous** (–TEN·tus) *adj.* ominous; also, arousing awe; amazing; hence, pompous; **por·ten·tous·ly** *adv.*

por·ter *n.* any of various servants such as baggage carrier, doorman, or janitor serving in hotels, trains, etc. **2** a heavy, dark-brown beer; **por·ter·house (steak)** a choice cut of beef between sirloin and tenderloin. —**port·fo·li·o** (–FOH·lee·oh) *n.* **-os** **1** a thin, flat, usu. leather case for papers and documents. **2** the office or department of a cabinet minister: *A minister without ~ has general functions.* **3** a list of one's investments such as stocks, bonds, and shares. —**porthole** See PORT, *n.* 4.

—**por·ti·co** (POR·ti·coh) *n.* **-o(e)s** a porch with a row of columns supporting its roof; **por·ti·coed** (–code) *adj.* —**por·tiere** (–TYAIR) *n.* a curtain hung over a doorway.

por·tion *n.* a shared part of a whole, as a serving of food, an inheritance, or a dowry; hence, one's lot in life; fate: *Sorrow was her ~ all life long.* —***v.:*** *The aged farmer ~ed out the land among his sons; squandered the money ~ed to her.* —**por·tion·less** *adj.*

Port·land (–lund) a city of N.W. Oregon. —**portland cement** a fine powder got by burning limestone and clay, used in making concrete that originally had the color of stone from Portland, England.

Port Lou·is (–LOO·is, –ee) capital of Mauritius.

port·ly *adj.* **-li·er, -li·est** fat but stately in bearing. —**port·li·ness** *n.* —**port·man·teau** (–MAN·toh) *n.* **-teaus** or **-teaux** (–toze) a suitcase that opens in to two compartments hinged together; **portmanteau word** one formed by joining two words together, as "motel" (motor + hotel) or "smog" (smoke + fog).

Port Mores·by (–MORZ·bee) seaport and capital of Papua New Guinea. —**port of call** a port where ships stop for repairs, supplies, cargo, etc. —**port of entry** See PORT, *n.* 1. —**Port-of-Spain** capital of Trinidad and Tobago. —**Por·to-No·vo** capital of Benin. —**Por·to Ri·co** former name of PUERTO RICO.

por·trait (–trit, –trait) *n.* a picture or representation; a dramatic or graphic portrayal; **por·trait·ist** *n.* one who paints portraits; **por·trai·ture** (–chur) *n.* the art of portraying; also a portrait or portraits. —**por·tray** (–TRAY) *v.* **1** draw or paint a picture of: *An artist ~s a scene; a book ~ing* (i.e. in words) *pioneer life.* **2** play the role of; enact: *a character hard to ~ on the modern stage;* **por·tray·al** *n.: Burton's ~ of Mark Antony.*

Por·tu·gal (–chuh·gul) a country of S.W. Europe; 35,553 sq. mi. (92,082 km²); *cap.* Lisbon. —**Por·tu·guese** (–GEEZ) *n. sing.* & *pl.* **1** a person of or from Portugal. **2** the language of Portugal and Brazil. Also ***adj.*** —**Portuguese man-of-war** a jellyfish that is a colony of animals attached to a gas-filled float from which hang long tentacles for grasping at fish, stinging, etc.

por·tu·lac·a (–chuh·LAC·uh) *n.* a low-growing fleshy tropical plant of the purslane family bearing brilliant flowers.

pos. position; positive; possessive.

pose (POZE) *v.* **pos·es, posed, pos·ing** **1** assume or make assume a certain position: *Let's ~ for a photograph; a cameraman ~ing a group for a picture.* **2** affect a posture or attitude; also, pretend to be someone else: *gained entry by ~ing as a policeman.* **3** raise a question, esp. a baffling one: *Overpopulation ~s many problems.* —***n.:*** *a temptress in an alluring ~; His piety is a mere ~.*

Po·sei·don (poh·SYE·dn) the Greek god of the sea.

pos·er (POH·zur) *n.* one who poses; also, something baffling. —**po·seur** (poh·ZUR) *n.* one who poses for effect.

posh *adj. Informal.* elegant or luxurious. —**posh·ly** *adv.* —**posh·ness** *n.*

pos·it (POZ–) *v.* put forward as a fact; postulate. —**po·si·tion** (–ZISH·un) *n.* a place or location, esp. in relation to other factors; also, a post of employment; hence, a high rank: *a safe ~ behind a wall; troops moving into ~ before a parade; opposing parties maneuvering for ~* (i.e. of advantage); *one's ~ in society; a clerical ~; men of ~* (i.e. high rank) *in our company; I can't agree with your ~* (i.e. stand) *on the issue;* **v.:** *troops ~ed in readiness for action;* **po·si·tion·al** *adj.* —**pos·i·tive** (POZ·i·tiv) *adj.* actual, real, definite, creative, etc.; not negative: *"Yes" is a ~ answer; a ~ refusal; a battery's ~ terminal from which current flows; a ~ print; 3 is a ~ integer, –3 is negative; not just sure but ~; helpful, ~ criticism; a ~ pregnancy test; "simple" and "much" are ~, "simpler" and "more" are their comparatives;* **n.** something positive. —**pos·i·tive·ly** *adv.* —**pos·i·tive·ness** *n.* —**pos·i·tron** (POZ–) *n.* the positive antiparticle of an electron.

poss. possessive.

pos·se (POS·ee) *n.* a body of persons having legal authority: *a ~ of constables.*

pos·sess (puh·ZES) *v.* **1** own; have (as a natural or acquired quality or skill): *a mendicant who ~es nothing; an orator ~ing great powers of persuasion.* **2** dominate; gain control over: *an apostle ~ed by missionary zeal;* **possessed** *adj.* controlled by an evil spirit: *a ~ woman exorcised by a priest;* **possessed of** in possession of. —**pos·ses·sion** (–ZESH·un) *n.* ownership; also, something owned: *to take ~ of a newly bought house; a will made when in ~ of one's senses; to give away one's material* **possessions;** *Guam is a ~ of the U.S.* —**pos·ses·sive** (–ZES·iv) *adj.: a ~ nature, parent; "My," "his," and "your" are* **possessive adjectives;** *"mine" and "theirs" are* **possessive pronouns.** —**n.** the possessive case; also, a possessive word; **pos·ses·sive·ly** *adv.;* **pos·ses·sive·ness** *n.* —**pos·ses·sor** *n.*

pos·si·ble *adj.* that can exist, happen, or be done: *Reply as soon as ~; It's ~ to beat cancer;* **pos·si·bly** (–blee) *adv.: How could you ~ do such a thing? She's away, ~* (i.e. perhaps) *out of town.* —**pos·si·bil·i·ty** (–BIL–) *n.* **-ties.**

pos·sum (POS·um) *n. Informal.* same as OPOSSUM. —**play possum** act like an opossum which pretends to be dead in order to deceive its enemy.

post- *prefix.* after (in time or space); behind: as in *posterior, postgraduate, postlude.*

post (POHST) *n.* **1** an upright piece of wood or metal supporting or displaying something, as a *lamppost, goalpost, signpost, bedpost.* **2** a place of duty; also, a job: *Stay at your ~s; the ~ of Secretary of State.* **3** esp. *Brit.* the mail. **4** a trading post. —**v.** [corresponding to the *n.* senses] **1:** *We'll ~ it on the bulletin board; Obey ~ed speed limits.* **2:** *sentries ~ed at the gate.* **3:** *a letter ~ed yesterday in London; We'll keep you ~ed* (i.e. informed) *on what happens.* —**post·age** (–ij) *n.* the charge for mailing something, usu. paid by means of **postage stamps** or a **postage meter** that imprints mail and records the charges. —**post·al** *adj.* having to do with the post office: *a* **postal card** *has a stamp printed on it; a picture* **post-card.** —**postal code** the Canadian zip code, as L5C 1S3; **post code** *Brit.* —**Postal Service** same as POST OFFICE. —**post chaise** a four-wheeled closed carriage. —**post·date** (–DATE) *v.* **-dates, -dat·ed, -dat·ing:** *next month's rent paid by a ~d check.* —**post·er** *n.* a placard for posting, as in a public place. —**pos·te·ri·or** (pos·TEER·ee·ur) *adj.* after; behind; not anterior; **n.** the buttocks. —**pos·ter·i·ty** (–TER–) *n.* descendants; generations to follow. —**pos·tern** (POH–) *n.* a back door or gate; **adj.:** *a ~ door.* —**post exchange** a store at a military post. —**post·grad·u·ate** (–GRAJ–) *adj.* after a bachelor's degree: *M.A. and Ph.D. are ~ degrees;* **n.** a postgraduate student. —**post·haste** *adv.* with all speed. —**post·hu·mous** (POS·choo·mus) *adj.* after one's death: *a ~ award received by his widow; her ~ daughter* (born after the father's death); **post·hu·mous·ly** *adv.: a book published ~* (i.e. after the author's death). —**post·hyp·not·ic** (–hip·NOT–) *adj.: a ~ suggestion* (i.e. one made during a trance for carrying out afterwards). —**post·ie** (–tee) *n. Regional.* letter carrier. —**pos·til·(l)ion** (–TIL·yun) *n.* in horse-drawn vehicles, one who guides the team of horses by riding the leading horse. —**post·im·pres·sion·ism** *n.* a school of late 19th-century painting in revolt against impressionism. —**post·lude** (–lood) *n.* a concluding piece of music; also, a final phase. —**post·man** *n.* **-men** mailman. —**post·mark** *n.* a mark stamped on mail by the post office to show the place and date of mailing; **v.** *an envelope ~ed London, Ont.* —**post·mas·ter** *n.* a person in charge of a post office; *fem.* **post·mis·tress; postmaster general** the official who heads a country's postal department. —**post·me·rid·i·an** (–RID–) *adj.* afternoon; **post me·rid·i·em** (–RID–) after noon; P.M. —**post-mor·tem** *n.* & *adj.* (examination of a body) after death. —**post·na·sal** (–NAY·zl) **drip** the dripping of mucus from the sinuses down the back of the throat. —**post·na·tal** (–NAY·tl) *adj.* following childbirth. —**post office** a place where mail is received for distribution, stamps are sold, etc.; **Post Office** or **Postal Service** the government department in charge of the mails. —**post·op·er·a·tive** (–uh·tiv) *adj.* following a surgical operation. —**post·paid** *adj.* & *adv.* with the postage paid by the sender. —**post·par·tum** (–PAR–) *adj.* of the period after childbirth. **—post·pone** (–PONE) *v.* **-pones, -poned, -pon·ing** put off; delay; **post·pone·ment** *n.* **—post road** a road over which mail is or was carried. **—post·script** *n.* something written as an afterthought, added to a letter after signing it, as the last section of a book, etc. **—post time** the scheduled time at which a horse race starts.

pos·tu·lant (POS·chuh·lunt) *n.* a candidate seeking admission to a religious order. **—pos·tu·late** (POS·chuh–) *v.* **-lates, -lat·ed, -lat·ing** assume as a basic truth or axiom; hence, require: *Do natural phenomena ~ the existence of the supernatural?* **—*n.*** a fundamental principle.

pos·tur·al (–chuh·rul) *adj.* having to do with posture. **—pos·ture** (–chur) *n.* **1** a way of holding the body: *a reclining ~; exercises to improve the ~.* **2** state; condition; hence, attitude: *a defensive ~ against the Soviets; a holier-than-thou ~.* **—*v.* -tures, -tured, -tur·ing** assume a posture, esp. for effect; attitudinize.

post·war *adj.* after-the-war: *the ~ population increase.*

po·sy (POH·zee) *n.* **-sies** formerly, same as POESY hence, a motto in verse; also, a bouquet.

pot *n.* **1** a round vessel for domestic use, esp. cooking; **go to pot** go to ruin. **2** *Informal.* in betting, the entire stake; kitty. **3** *Slang.* marijuana. **—*v.* pots, pot·ted, pot·ting** put into a pot for keeping or cooking: *a room full of ~d plants.*

po·ta·ble (POH·tuh·bl) *n.* & *adj.* (something) drinkable; **po·ta·bil·i·ty** (–BIL–) *n.; water of doubtful ~.*

pot·ash *n.* a potassium compound obtained from wood ashes for use mainly as a fertilizer. **—po·tas·si·um** (–TAS·ee·um) *n.* a soft, silver-white metallic chemical element; **potassium bromide** a salt used as a sedative and in photography; **potassium carbonate** used in glass-making, soaps, etc.; **potassium cyanide** a poisonous compound used as an insecticide; **potassium nitrate** a salt used in explosives, to preserve meat, and in medicine.

po·ta·tion (–TAY–) *n.* a drink, esp. of alcoholic liquor.

po·ta·to (–TAY–) *n.* **-toes** the starchy tuber of a widely cultivated plant, round, hard, and with thin skin, eaten also fried crisp in slices called **potato chips. —potato beetle** (or **bug**) same as COLORADO BEETLE.

pot·bel·lied (–leed) *adj.* having a rounded body, as a "potbellied stove." **—pot·bel·ly** *n.* **-bel·lies** a protruding belly. **—pot·boil·er** *n.* a usu. second-rate work, esp. a book written for one's livelihood. **—pot cheese** cottage cheese.

po·ten·cy (–see) *n.* the quality of being **po·tent** (POH–) *adj.* powerful: *a ~ argument; a ~ medicine; a ~ ruler; no longer ~* (i.e. sexually) *after his illness;* **po·tent·ly** *adv.* **—po·ten·tate** *n.* a ruler or sovereign. **—po·ten·tial** (–TEN·shul) *adj.* capable of coming into being: *A coiled spring has ~ energy;* ***n.*** capacity: *a new recruit with great ~ for high positions; A* **po·ten·ti·om·e·ter** (–OM–) *measures electric ~s* (i.e. voltage); **po·ten·tial·ly** *adv.: a ~ explosive situation;* **po·ten·ti·al·i·ty** (–AL–) *n.* **-ties. —po·ten·ti·ate** *v.* **-ates, -at·ed, -at·ing** make more powerful: *alcohol ~d by drugs;* **po·ten·ti·a·tion** (–AY–) *n.*

pot·head *n. Slang.* a habitual marijuana user.

poth·er *n.* & *v.* fuss; bother.

pot·herb *n.* an herb used as a vegetable or in flavoring, as the mustard plant or mint. **—pot·hole** *n.* a rounded hole or depression, as in a rocky river bed or worn-out road surface. **—pot·hook** *n.* a hook for hanging a pot over a fire or for lifting hot pots and lids. **—pothunter** See POTSHOT.

po·tion (POH–) *n.* a drink, esp. one that is medicinal, poisonous, or supposedly magical: *a love ~.*

pot·luck *n.* food that is available as regular fare: *surprise visitors invited to take ~ with the family.*

Po·to·mac (puh·TOH·muc) an eastern U.S. river on which Washington, D.C., is situated.

pot·pie *n.* a meat pie baked in a pot, with only a top crust. **—pot·pour·ri** (poh·poo·REE) *n.* a medley of musical or literary pieces. **—pot·roast** *n.* beef browned and cooked slowly in a closed pot with only a little water. **—pot·sherd** *n.* a broken piece of pottery. **—pot·shot** *n.* a random or casual shot with no regard for rules, as a **pot·hunt·er** does: *The new play seemed an easy target for any critic to* **take potshots at. —pot·tage** (–ij) *n.* a kind of thick soup or stew. **—pot·ter** *v.* same as PUTTER; ***n.*** one who makes pottery. **—pot·ter·y** *n.* **1** pots, dishes, vases, etc. made of clay; also, the potter's art. **2** *pl.* **pot·ter·ies** a potter's workshop.

pouch (POWCH) *n.* a small bag or sack, as for keeping or carrying something: *tobacco ~; mail ~; diplomatic ~* (for documents or messages); also, an animal's baglike body part, as a kangaroo's pocket or the one under a pelican's bill. **—*v.:*** *a pocket gopher ~ing nuts under a tree; Marsupials are ~ed mammals.* **—pouch·y** *adj.* **pouch·i·er, -i·est:** *cheeks ~ with age.*

poult (POHLT) *n.* a young fowl, esp. a turkey. **—poul·ter·er** *n. Brit.* one who deals in poultry.

poul·tice (POLE·tis) *n.* a warm, pulpy mass (as of mustard, herbs, flour, etc.) applied to a painful body part as a dressing; also ***v.* -tic·es, -ticed, -tic·ing.**

poul·try (–tree) *n.* domestic fowls such as chickens, turkeys, ducks, and geese; **poul·try·man** *n.* **-men** a poultry farmer.

pounce *v.* **pounc·es, pounced, pounc·ing** swoop down (*on, upon, at* a person or thing) as if to seize: *greedily ~ing on every opportunity to make some money.*

¹pound (POWND) *n.* an enclosure for confining stray dogs or cattle; also, a trap for fish, forming part of a "pound net."

²pound (POWND) *v.* strike or hit heavily and repeatedly: *Knock once, don't ~ on my door; Use a mortar and pestle to ~ the medication; his heart ~ing with terror;* **pounded out** *the story on his typewriter; the unemployed* **pounding the pavement** (i.e. walking the streets) *looking for work.* **—n.** a pounding or its sound.

³pound (POWND) *n.* **1** the basic money unit of the U.K. and certain African and Middle Eastern countries. **2** a unit of weight equal to 16 oz. avoirdupois (0.4536 kg) or 12 oz. troy (0.3732 kg): *A* **pound cake,** *rich in eggs, used to be made with a pound each of flour, butter, sugar, etc.*

pound·age (–ij) *n.* **1** the weight in pounds; also, the per-pound rate of tax, etc. **2** a confining; also, the fee charged at a pound. **—pound cake** See ³POUND, *n.* 2. **—pound-fool·ish** *adj.* careless about large sums of money: *"penny-wise and ~."*

pour (POR) *v.* flow or cause to flow, as a stream, flood, or heavy rain, freely, copiously, or steadily: *~ me a glass of water; a child ~ing forth his tale of sorrow; Rush-hour crowds ~ out of the subway.*

pour·boire (poor·BWAHR) *n.* tip; gratuity. **—pour·par·ler** (poor·par·LAY) *n.* a discussion prior to formal negotiations.

pout (POWT) *v.* show displeasure by pushing out the lips; sulk; ***n.:*** *continued in a ~ till she had her way.* **—pout·er** *n.*

pov·er·ty *n.* the condition of being poor; want; deficiency: *a ~ of talent; A nonfarm U.S. family of seven with an annual income of $6,983 was at the* **poverty line** *in the early 70's; the* **pov·er·ty-strick·en** *countries of the Third World.*

P.O.W. prisoner of war; also **POW.**

pow·der *n.* a dry material of fine particles such as some cosmetics, medicines, etc.; also, gunpowder: *That fight is not worth* **powder and shot;** *Watch out and* **keep your powder dry;** also ***v.:*** *her ~ed nose; imported ~ed milk.* **—pow·der·y** *adj.* **—powder keg** a potentially explosive situation. **—pow·der-puff** *adj.* of appeal to women: *~ journalism.* **—powder room** women's lavatory.

pow·er *n.* **1** ability; strength; might: "Power corrupts"; **power of attorney** a document authorizing another to act for one in a legal matter. **2** a person or state having authority and strength: *a summit meeting of the Great Powers; The* **powers that be** (i.e. the authorities) *willed otherwise.* **—*v.:*** *a small car ~ed by a big engine.* **—*adj.:*** *a ~ saw; ~ steering; a party's* **power base** *eroded by scandals; The mayor was a* **power broker** *for politicians;* **pow·er·house, power plant,** *or* **power station** *where electricity is generated: the* **power plant** (i.e. engine and related parts) *of an automobile, aircraft, or ship; feminists shaking the* **power structure** *of a male-dominated society; a vice-president jobless after a* **power struggle** *in the company.* **—pow·er·ful** *adj.;* **pow·er·ful·ly** *adv.* **—pow·er·less** *adj.;* **pow·er·less·ly** *adv.*

pow·wow *n.* a conference of or with North American Indians; hence, *Informal.* any conference.

pox *n.* **pox(·es)** a disease such as *chicken pox* or *smallpox* that leaves pock marks on the skin; **the pox** syphilis.

pp. pages; past participle; pianissimo. **—p.p.** or **P.O.** parcel post; postpaid; prepaid.

ppd. postpaid; prepaid.

ppr. or **p.pr.** present participle.

p.p.s. or **P.P.S.** a second postscript (post postscript).

p.q. previous question; **P.Q.** Province of Quebec.

pr. pair(s); present; price; pronoun. **—Pr.** Provençal. **—Pr** praseodymium. **—PR** or **P.R.** payroll; public relations; Puerto Rico.

prac·ti·ca·ble (–cuh·bl) *adj.* that can be put into practice; feasible: *A trip to the moon may be ~ but hardly a practical idea for a holiday;* **prac·ti·ca·bly** *adv.* **—prac·ti·cal** *adj.* **1** having to do with practice rather than theory or thinking: *a scheme full of ~ difficulties; too unwieldy for ~ purposes; a ~ mind; A* **practical joke** *is a trick actually played on the victim.* **2** engaged in practice or work: *a ~ farmer; A* **practical nurse** *helps professional nurses with day-to-day tasks of caring for the sick.* **3** virtual: *Jack is the boss but Jill is in ~ control.* **—prac·ti·cal·ly** *adv.* **—prac·ti·ca·bil·i·ty** (–BIL–) *n.* **—prac·ti·cal·i·ty** (–CAL–) *n.* **—prac·tice** (–tis) *v.* **-tic·es, -ticed, -tic·ing** do, engage in, or work at (something) habitually *(He ~s what he preaches),* customarily *(a ~ing Roman Catholic),* repeatedly *(She ~s the piano daily),* or professionally: *(~ medicine).* **—*n.:*** *a plan difficult to put* **in(to) practice** (i.e. carry out); *superstitious ~s such as fortune-telling and voodoo; She* **makes a practice** *of arriving late in school; He's* **out of practice** *on the violin; "Practice makes perfect"; a flourishing law ~.* **—prac·ticed** (–tist) *adj.* skilled: *a ~ pickpocket; bore it with ~ coolness.* **—prac·ti·tion·er** (–TISH–) *n.* a professional, esp. a physician. **—prac·tise** *esp. Brit. n.* & *v.* practice.

prae·tor (PREE·tor) *n.* a law official of ancient Rome, with rank next below consul. **—Prae·to·ri·an** (–TOR·ee·un) *n.* & *adj.* (a member) of the **Praetorian Guard,** a Roman emperor's bodyguard.

prag·mat·ic or **prag·mat·i·cal** (–MAT–) *adj.* concerned with practical values; matter-of-fact; also, having to do with **prag·ma·tism** (PRAG–) *n.* the philosophy of judging things by how they work rather than by abstract values of truth and goodness; **prag·ma·tist** *n.* & *adj.*

Prague (PRAHG) capital of Czechoslovakia.

Prai·a (PRY·uh) capital of Cape Verde.

prai·rie (PRAIR·ee) *n.* a region of level or rolling land where tall grass grows but few trees, esp. in the Mississippi valley. **—prairie dog** any of various squirrellike rodents of the North American prairies with a shrill doglike bark. **—Prairie Provinces** Alberta, Saskatchewan, and Manitoba. **—prairie schooner** a large covered wagon used by pioneers to travel across the prairies.

praise (PRAYZ) *v.* **prais·es, praised, prais·ing** **1** worship: *God be ~d!* **2** speak of with admiration: *~d by some, hated by others.* **—n.:** *a cook who receives only ~s; The principal's speech was in ~ of his teachers; She bores me by* **singing the praises** *of her children all day long; ~ be to God!* **—praise·wor·thy** (–wur·dhee) *adj.;* **praise·wor·thi·ly** *adv.;* **praise·wor·thi·ness** *n.*

pra·line (PRAY·leen, PRAH–) *n.* a candy made of brown sugar and nuts.

pram *n. Brit.* perambulator.

prance *v.* **pranc·es, pranced, pranc·ing** move about, as a horse does, by springing forward on the hind legs; hence, strut about; swagger; also ***n.*** **—pranc·er** *n.* **—pranc·ing·ly** *adv.*

prank *n.* a mischievous trick played on someone; **prank·ish** *adj.* **—prank·ster** *n.*

pra·se·o·dym·i·um (pray·zee·oh·DIM·ee·um) *n.* a yellowish-white metallic chemical element.

prate *v.* **prates, prat·ed, prat·ing** talk foolishly and at length; also ***n.*** **—prat·er** *n.* **—prat·ing·ly** *adv.*

prat·fall *n. Slang.* a fall on one's buttocks.

pra·tique (prah·TEEK) *n.* quarantine clearance given to a ship at a port of entry.

prat·tle *v.* **prat·tles, prat·tled, prat·tling** prate; also, babble; also ***n.*** **—prat·tler** *n.*

prawn *n.* a crustacean like a shrimp but larger.

pray *v.* **1** worship God; also, ask for a divine favor: *~ (to) God for help; a hopeless case that is past* **praying for. 2** ask humbly; entreat: *He ~ed the policeman not to ticket him.* **3** please: *~ be careful.* **—pray·er** *n.* one who prays. **—prayer** (PRAIR) *n.: She says her ~s every night; the Lord's Prayer; Columbus knelt down in ~; The Book of Common Prayer;* hence **prayer book; prayer·ful** *adj.;* **prayer·ful·ly** *adv.;* **prayer·ful·ness** *n.* **—praying mantis** same as MANTIS.

pre- *prefix.* before (in time, position, etc.); in front of: as in *prearranged, precursor, prefix.*

preach (PREECH) *v.* deliver (a sermon); hence, set forth or urge in a moralistic tone, usu. in a tiresome way: *always ~ing (about) social justice; He likes to ~ in his classes; Stop ~ing and start practicing.* **—preach·er** *n.* **—preach·ment** *n.* an exhortation. **—preach·y** *adj.* **preach·i·er, -i·est.**

pre·am·ble (PREE·am·bl) *n.* an introduction to a constitution, statute, etc. **—pre·ar·range** (–uh·RAINJ) *v.* **-ar·rang·es, -ar·ranged, -ar·rang·ing** arrange beforehand; **pre·ar·range·ment** *n.*

preb·en·dar·y *n.* **-dar·ies** a clergyman supported by a **preb·end** *n.* a portion of the church revenue.

Pre·cam·bri·an (–CAM·bree·un) *n.* & *adj.* (of) the earliest era of geological time, beginning about 4½ billion years ago. **—pre·can·cer·ous** (–CAN·suh·rus) *adj.* of tissue, that may develop into cancer.

pre·car·i·ous (–CAIR·ee·us) *adj.* dependent on chance; uncertain: *a ~ existence in a war-torn country.* **—pre·car·i·ous·ly** *adv.;* **pre·car·i·ous·ness** *n.*

pre·cau·tion (–CAW–) *n.* care taken against danger, failure, etc. or to ensure good results: *a fire-safety ~;* **pre·cau·tion·ar·y** *adj.: ~ measures against guerrillas.* **—pre·cede** (–SEED) *v.* **-cedes, -ced·ed, -ced·ing** be or happen before (in time, position, order, etc.); **preced·ing** *adj.: in the ~ paragraph;* **prec·e·dence** (PRES·i–, pri·SEE–) *n.: The Chief Justice has ~ over the Vice-President of the U.S.; Emergency cases take ~ over routine checkups.* **—pre·ced·ent** *n.* (PRES·i·dunt) a previous case; esp. in law, a case that serves as an example: *Nixon's resignation was without ~ in U.S. history; a judgment based on ~s;* ***adj.*** (pri·SEE-) preceding. **—pre·cen·tor** (–SEN·tur) *n.* one who heads a church choir or congregational singing. **—pre·cept** (PREE–) *n.* instruction; also, a rule of behavior; maxim: *She rules by example rather than ~; A familiar ~ is "Look before you leap";* **pre·cep·tor** (–SEP–) *n.* a teacher. **—pre·ces·sion** (–SESH–) *n.* a forward movement, as the **precession of the equinoxes,** the earlier occurrence of the equinoxes in each successive year caused by the gyration of the earth's rotating axis; **pre·ces·sion·al** *adj.* **—pre·cinct** (PREE·sinct) *n.* **1** a subdivision or district: *a police ~; an election ~.* **2 precincts** *pl.* environs; grounds or enclosure: *school ~s.*

pre·cious (PRESH·us) *adj.* **1** of great value; hence, beloved: *gold, silver, and such ~ metals; ~ gems; ~ qualities; a ~ child;* **pre·cious·ly** *adv.;* **pre·cious·ness** *n.* **2** overstylized; affected: *a beauty queen's ~ manner;* **pre·ci·os·i·ty** (presh·ee·OS–) *n.* **-ties.** **—pre·cious** *adv.* very: *~ little; ~ few.*

prec·i·pice (PRES·uh·pis) *n.* a steep cliff; a vertically falling rock face. **—pre·cip·i·tate** (–SIP–) *v.* **-tates, -tat·ed, -tat·ing** **1** throw down with violence; cause to happen abruptly: *a border incident ~ing a crisis.* **2** cause to fall, as from a solution or from the atmosphere: *Alumina ~s as its solution cools.* **—n.** (–SIP·uh·tate, –tit) a substance, usu. in crystal form, got by precipitating. **—*adj.*** **1** hasty; rash; also **pre·cip·i·tant. 2** falling steeply; also **pre·cip·i·tous:** *a ~ slope;* **pre·cip·i·tous·ly; pre·cip·i·tous·ness** *n.* **—pre·cip·i·ta·tion**

(–TAY–) *n.* **1:** *Snow, rain, and hail are forms of ~; a region of heavy ~.* **2** haste; also **pre•cip•i•tan•cy** (–SIP–) *n.* **-cies.**

pré•cis (pray·SEE, PRAY·see) *n., pl.* **-cis** (–SEEZ, –seez) a summary; a concise statement. **—pre•cise** (pri·SICE) *adj.* correct; exact; also, careful; hence, overcareful; fussy: *a ~ account of the incident; very ~ in her diction; too prim and ~ for my temperament;* **pre•cise•ly** *adv.;* **pre•cise•ness** *n.* **—pre•ci•sian** (–SIZH·un) *n.* one who is strict, esp. about religious observances. **—pre•ci•sion** (–SIZH–) *n.* accuracy: *the ~ of a watch;* ***adj.:*** *A chronometer is a ~ instrument; "~ approach radar" helps pilots make safe landings in fog.* **—pre•ci•sion•ist** *n.* a stickler for precision.

pre•clude (pri·CLOOD) *v.* **-cludes, -clud•ed, -clud•ing** to bar; prevent: *The barbed wire fence ~d all possibility of escape.* **—pre•clu•sion** *n.*

pre•co•cious (pri·COH·shus) *adj.* showing early maturity; *a very ~ child;* **pre•co•cious•ly** *adv.;* **pre•co•cious•ness** *n.* **—pre•coc•i•ty** (–COS–) *n.*

pre•cog•ni•tion (pree·cog·NISH·un) *n.* advance knowledge of an event before it happens; **pre•cog•ni•tive** (–COG·ni·tiv) *adj.: ~ clairvoyance.* **—pre•con•ceive** (pree·cun·SEEV) *v.* **-ceives, -ceived, -ceiv•ing** form (an idea or opinion) beforehand: *our ~d notions;* **pre•con•cep•tion** (–SEP–) *n.* **—pre•con•cert•ed** *adj.* arranged beforehand. **—pre•con•di•tion** (–DISH–) *v.* condition or train beforehand; ***n.*** prerequisite. **—pre•cook** *v.* cook beforehand partially or completely. **—pre•cur•sor** (–CUR·sur) *n.* forerunner; also, predecessor: *"John the Baptist" was Christ's ~;* **pre•cur•so•ry** *adj.*

pred. predicate.

pre•da•cious or **pre•da•ceous** (–DAY·shus) *adj.* predatory.

pre•date (–DATE) *v.* **-dates, -dat•ed, -dat•ing** antedate.

pre•da•tion (–DAY–) *n.* preying or plundering; the way of life of a **pred•a•tor** (–uh·tur) *n.;* **pred•a•to•ry** (PRED·uh–) *adj.: a ~ person; ~ instincts;* **pred•a•to•ri•ly** *adv.;* **pred•a•to•ri•ness** *n.*

pre•de•cease (–SEECE) *v.* **-ceas•es, -ceased, -ceas•ing** die before (someone); **pred•e•ces•sor** (PRED·uh), PREE·duh–) *n.* one who has gone before (someone). **—pre•des•ti•na•tion** (–NAY–) *n.* the theological doctrine that God has predestined certain souls to salvation and others to damnation. **—pre•des•tine** (–DES·tin) *v.* **-tines, -tined, -tin•ing** determined beforehand; foreordain; also **pre•des•ti•nate, -nates, -nat•ed, -nat•ing.** **—pre•de•ter•mine** (–TUR·min) *v.* **-mines, -mined, -min•ing** determine beforehand.

pred•i•ca•ble (–cuh·bl) *adj.* that can be predicated. **—pred•i•cate** *v.* **-cates, -cat•ed, -cat•ing** **1** declare; assert (something of someone): *~ goodness of God.* **2** found (an assertion or statement on something); ***n.*** what is said of a grammatical or logical subject: *In "She is great," "great" is a ~, or a* **pred•i•ca•tive** *adjective;* cf. ATTRIBUTIVE; **pred•i•ca•tion** (–CAY–) *n.* **—pre•dic•a•ment** (–DIC·uh–) *n.* a perplexing situation; also, a difficult one.

pre•dict (–DICT) *v.* foretell; **pre•dic•tion** *n.;* **pre•dict•a•ble** (–uh·bl) *adj.;* **pre•dict•a•bly** (–uh·blee) *adv.* **—pre•di•gest** (–JEST) *v.* treat (food), as with enzymes, to make it easier to digest; **pre•di•ges•tion** (–JES·chun) *n.* **—pre•di•lec•tion** (pree·di·LEC–, pred·i–) *n.* a special liking: *a ~ for spiced foods.* **—pre•dis•pose** (–POZE) *v.* **-pos•es, -posed, -pos•ing** incline in advance; be susceptible: *Military life ~d him to a strict regimen;* **pre•dis•po•si•tion** (–ZISH·un) *n.* **—pre•dom•i•nate** (–DOM–) *v.* **-nates, -nat•ed, -nat•ing** be greater in number, power, influence, etc.; **pre•dom•i•nance** (–nunce) *n.;* **pre•dom•i•nant** (–nunt) *adj.;* **pre•dom•i•nant•ly** *adv.* **—pree•mie** (–mee) *n. Informal.* a prematurely born infant. **—pre•em•i•nent** (–EM–) *adj.* outstanding; surpassing; **pre•em•i•nent•ly** *adv.;* **pre•em•i•nence** *n.* **—pre•empt** (–EMPT) *v.* acquire or appropriate (something) before others; also, in radio and TV, take the place of: *a news special ~ing regular programs;* **pre•emp•tion** *n.;* **pre•emp•tive** (–tiv) *adj.: Congress abolished ~ land rights in 1891; a ~ surprise attack to forestall enemy plans.*

preen *v.* of a bird, clean and smooth (itself or its feathers) with the beak; hence, dress (oneself) carefully; also, pride oneself (*on*): *He ~s himself too much on his sharp business deals.*

pre•ex•ist (–ZIST) *v.* exist before (something or someone); antedate; **pre•ex•is•tence** (–ZIS·tunce) *n.;* **pre•ex•is•tent** *adj.*

pref. preface; preference; preferred; prefix.

pre•fab (PREE·fab) *n. Informal.* a prefabricated building; **pre•fab•ri•cate** (–FAB–) *v.* **-cates, -cat•ed, -cat•ing** to make in sections that can easily be assembled: *a ~d house assembled in two days:* **pre•fab•ri•ca•tion** (–CAY–) *n.*

pref•ace (–is) *n.* a statement at the beginning of a book, speech, etc.; ***v.*** **-ac•es, -aced, -ac•ing:** *The speaker ~d his remarks with a reading from Scripture;* **pref•a•to•ry** (–uh·tor·ee) *adj.: a ~ note by the publisher.*

pre•fect (PREE–) any of various administrative officials, as of ancient Rome, the head of a department in France, etc.; **pre•fec•ture** (–chur) *n.* a prefect's office, territory, or residence.

pre•fer (pri·FUR) *n.* **-fers, -ferred, -fer•ring** **1** like better: *She ~s tea to coffee;* **preferred stock** *has priority over common stock in the sharing of dividends and assets.* **2** promote; advance; **pre•fer•ment** *n.* **3** bring forward (a charge against someone, a claim to something, etc.). **—pref•er•a•ble** (PREF–) *adj.;* **pref•er•a•bly** *adv.;* **pref•er•ence; pref•er•en•tial** (–uh·

REN·shul) *adj.: get ~ treatment; ~ voting to indicate voter's order of preference; a ~ shop favoring union members in hiring; a ~ tariff rate extended to a friendly nation;* **pref·er·en·tial·ly** *adv.* **—pre·fer·rer** *n.*

pre·fig·ure (pree·FIG·yur) *v.* **-ures, -ured, -ur·ing** foreshadow; be a prototype of; also, picture to oneself in advance. **—pre·fix** (PREE–) *n.* a word element used at the beginning of a word, as *pre-, ante-, dis-,* or *ex-;* ***v.*** (PREE–, pree·FIX); *"Ms." may be ~ed to a woman's name.* **—pre·flight** *adj.* preparatory to a flight: *~ instructions.* **—pre·form** *v.* form beforehand; **pre·for·ma·tion** (–MAY–) *n.* **—preg·na·ble** (–nuh·bl) *adj.* open to attack; **preg·na·bil·i·ty** (–BIL–) *n.;* **preg·nant** (–nunt) *adj.* carrying a developing offspring in the uterus; also, fertile or fruitful; hence, filled (with) or rich (in): *"Cocacolonize" is ~ with meaning; a ~* (i.e. significant) *pause.* **preg·nan·cy** (–nun·see) *n.* **-cies.**

pre·heat (PREE–) *v.* heat beforehand: *Place the TV dinner in an oven ~ed to 400° F.*

pre·hen·sile (pree·HEN·sil. –syle) *adj.* that can seize or grasp: *a monkey's ~ tail.*

pre·his·tor·ic (pree·his·TOR–) *adj.* of the time before recorded history, i.e. up to 5,000 years ago: *Dinosaurs are ~ animals; ~ art found in caves;* also **pre·his·tor·i·cal. —pre·ig·ni·tion** (–NISH·un) *n.* in an internal-combustion engine, the ignition of fuel before the piston is ready to receive the power generated. **—pre·in·duc·tion** (–DUC–) *adj.* prior to induction into the military. **—pre·judge** (–JUJ) *v.* **-judg·es, -judged, -judg·ing** judge beforehand or before examining all the evidence; **pre·judg·ment** *n.* **—prej·u·dice** (–uh·dis) *v.* **-dic·es, -diced, -dic·ing 1** harm (a right, claim, etc.): *behavior that ~d his chances of promotion.* **2** cause bias in: *a jury ~d by news reports of the crime.* ***—n.:*** *a statement made* **without prejudice** *to one's existing rights; racial ~ against blacks; popular ~s.* **—prej·u·di·cial** (–DISH·ul) *adj.*

prel·a·cy (–uh·see) *n.* **-cies** office or government of a prelate; also, prelates collectively. **—prel·ate** (–it) *n.* a high-ranking clergyman, as a bishop.

pre·launch *adj.* in preparation for a launch, esp. of spacecraft.

pre·lim (PREE·lim, pri·LIM) *n.* & *adj. Informal.* [short for] **pre·lim·i·nar·y** (–LIM–) *adj.* coming before; introductory: *a judge's ~ hearing on a case; a ~ discussion.* ***—n.,*** *pl.* **-nar·ies:** *competitors eliminated in the ~s* (i.e. rounds of matches).

pre·lit·er·ate (pree·LIT·uh·rit) *adj.* of a society or culture, not yet having a written language.

prel·ude (PREL·yood, PRAY·lood) *n.* an action or event leading to something major; esp. in music, an opening movement of an opera or oratorio; also, a separate concert work; ***v.*** **-udes, -ud·ed, -ud·ing:** *the calm that ~d the storm.*

prem. premium.

pre·mar·i·tal (–MAIR·i·tl) *adj.* before marriage: *~ sex.* **—pre·ma·ture** (–muh·TYOOR, –CHOOR) *adj.* before the proper or usual time, as a baby born more than two weeks early; **pre·ma·ture·ly** *adv.* **—pre·med(·i·cal)** (–MED–) *adj.* preparatory to the study of medicine: *a ~ course; a ~ student or a* **pre·med** *n.* **—pre·med·i·tate** (–MED–) *v.* **-tates, -tat·ed, -tat·ing** think out or consider beforehand: *a ~ murder;* **pre·med·i·ta·tion** (–TAY–) *n.*

pre·mier (prim·YAIR, PREE·mee·ur) *adj.* first in rank or importance, as the **premier danseur** of a ballet; also, earliest. ***—n.*** a prime minister; **pre·mier·ship** *n.* **—pre·miere** (prim·YAIR, prim·EER) *n.* the first public performance or showing, as of a play or movie; **pre·mier(e)** *v.* **-mier(e)s, -miered, -mier·ing:** *The new TV show ~d last night; The star of the show was herself ~ing in it.*

prem·ise (–is) *n.* **1** the logical basis for drawing a conclusion. **2 prem·is·es** *pl.* a piece of land with the buildings on it: *No picnicking on these ~s; office ~s* (i.e. building or a portion of it). ***—v.*** **-mis·es, -mised, -mis·ing** state or imply as a premise.

pre·mi·um (PREE·mee·um) *n.* **1** an incentive bonus or reward; a gift offered as an inducement to buy a product or service; also, an extra payment: *tax loopholes that* **put a premium** (i.e. unusual value) *on dishonesty; theater tickets bought* **at a premium** (i.e. at a high price) *at the last moment.* **2** the fee paid on an insurance policy. ***—adj.*** of high grade: *~ gasoline.*

pre·mo·lar (–MOH·lur) *n.* any of four pairs of bicuspid teeth in front of the molars on either side in both jaws; also ***adj.*** **—pre·mo·ni·tion** (–muh·NISH–) *n.* forewarning; also, foreboding or presentiment; **pre·mon·i·to·ry** (–MON–) *adj.* **—pre·na·tal** (–NAY·tl) *adj.* before birth: *Mothers need ~ care; ~ injury to children.* **—pre·oc·cu·py** *v.* **-pies, -pied, -py·ing 1:** *seats found ~d though reserved for us.* **2** engross: *a pastor of souls ~d with worldly cares;* **pre·oc·cu·pa·tion** (–PAY–) *n.: the ~s of a family man.* **—pre·or·dain** (–DANE) *v.* decree beforehand: *the change of seasons as ~ed by nature.*

prep. preparatory; preposition. **—prep** [short form] *adj.* preparatory: *a ~ school;* ***v.*** **preps, prepped, prep·ping** prepare (a patient for surgery, etc.).

pre·pack·age (–PAK·ij) *v.* **-ag·es, -aged, -ag·ing** package in standard units or grades for sale: *~d foods.*

prep·a·ra·tion (–RAY–) *n.* a preparing or something prepared: *packing up in ~ for a trip; last-minute ~s for a wedding; a ~ for colds sold at drugstores.* **—pre·par·a·to·ry** (pri·PAIR·uh–) *adj.: a countdown* **preparatory to** *takeoff;* **preparatory school** a private school preparing students for college. —**pre·pare** (–PARE) *v.* **-pares, -pared, -par·ing** make or get ready: *Be ~d for emergencies; Who will ~ dinner? layoffs to* **prepare the way** *for automation;* **pre·par·ed·ness** (–PAIR·id–) *n.: an alert to test our ~ for war.*

pre·pay (–PAY) *v.* **-pays, -paid, -pay·ing** pay beforehand: *a ~d ticket;* **pre·pay·ment** *n.*

pre·pon·der·ate (–PON–) *v.* **-ates, -at·ed, -at·ing** be greater than something else in numbers, weight, power, etc.; predominate: *Considerations of charity ~ over the demands of justice;* **pre·pon·der·ant** *adj.: Was sex or ambition the ~ influence of his life?* **pre·pon·der·ance** (–unce) *n.: a ~ of women over men in recent censuses.*

prep·o·si·tion (–ZISH·un) *n.* a word such as "on," "above," or "by" used with a noun or pronoun as object, forming a **prep·o·si·tion·al phrase** as "on top."

pre·pos·sess (–puh·ZES) *v.* prejudice; also, influence in a favorable way: *seemed ~ed by the youth's winning ways;* **pre·pos·sess·ing** *adj.: a girl of ~ charm;* **pre·pos·ses·sion** *n.*

pre·pos·ter·ous (–POS–) *adj.* contrary to reason and common sense; absurd: *making ~ demands on my time and patience;* **pre·pos·ter·ous·ly** *adv.*

pre·pro·gram *v.* **-grams, -gram(m)ed, -gram·(m)ing** of a computer, program in advance.

pre·puce (PREE–) *n.* foreskin.

pre·re·cord (–CORD) *v.* record for later broadcasting. —**pre·req·ui·site** (–REK·wi·zit) *n.* & *adj.* (something) required beforehand.

pre·rog·a·tive (–ROG·uh·tiv) *n.* a special privilege or right: *a lady's ~ to change her mind.*

pres. present; president.

pres·age (PRES·ij) *v.* (*usu.* pri·SAGE) **-ag·es, -aged, -ag·ing** predict; forebode; ***n.*** a sign or omen; also, presentiment.

pres·by·o·pi·a (–OH·pee·uh) *n.* farsightedness characteristic of middle age. —**pres·by·op·ic** (–OP–) *adj.* & *n.*

pres·by·ter (PREZ·bi·tur) *n.* a church elder; also, a priest or minister; **pres·by·ter·y** *n.* **-ter·ies** in the Presbyterian church, an administrative court; also, a church sanctuary; **Pres·by·te·ri·an** (–TEER·ee·un) *n.* & *adj.* (a member) of a Christian denomination or church that is governed by elders and is of Calvinistic persuasion.

pre·school *adj.* before school-going age: *a center for ~ children,* or **pre·school·ers.** —**pre·sci·ence** (PREE·shee·unce, PRESH·ee–) *n.* foreknowledge; **pre·sci·ent** *adj.*

pre·scribe (–SCRIBE) *v.* **-scribes, -scribed, -scrib·ing** order or direct with authority (to use books, medicines, etc. or to follow a course of action). —**pre·script** (PREE–) *n.* & *adj.* (something) prescribed as a direction or rule. —**pre·scrip·tion** (–SCRIP–) *n.* something prescribed, esp. a doctor's order for a medicine; also, the medicine itself: *a ~ drug;* **pre·scrip·tive** (–tiv) *adj.;* **pre·scrip·tive·ly** *adv.*

pres·ence (PREZ–) *n.* a being present; also, one's bearing or personality; esp., an impressive appearance: *a crime committed in the ~ of witnesses; troops to maintain our ~ in Europe; a lady of commanding ~; to act with* **presence of mind** (i.e. calmness) *in a panicky situation.* —**pres·ent** *adj.* being or existing here and now as specified or understood: *All students were ~ yesterday; in the ~ case; The* **present tense** *of "got" is "get(s)"; "getting" is the* **present participle;** *keeping up with* **pres·ent-day** *fashions.* —***n.*** **1** the present time: *She's too busy* **at present;** *a light meal to satisfy you* **for the present.** **2** a gift. **3** a document: *Know ye,* **by these presents,** *that . . .* —***v.*** (pri·ZENT) offer; give; introduce: *graduates* **presented with** *diplomas; a lawyer ~ing arguments in a case; a new diplomat ~ing credentials; to* **present arms** (i.e. a weapon in a deferential way) *in salute; a visiting dignitary ~ed at court.* —**pre·sent·a·ble** (–ZEN–) *adj.* respectable in appearance; **pre·sent·a·bly** *adv.* —**pre·sen·ta·tion** (–TAY–) *n.;* also **pre·sent·ment** (–ZENT–) *n.*

pre·sen·ti·ment (–ZEN–) *n.* a feeling that something, esp. bad, is about to happen; premonition; foreboding.

pres·ent·ly *adv.* at present; also, soon.

pres·er·va·tion (prez·ur·VAY–) *n.* a preserving or being preserved. —**pre·ser·va·tive** (–ZUR·vuh·tiv) *n.* & *adj.* (one) that preserves: *Salt is a food ~; no ~s* (i.e. chemicals) *added; a ~ medium for a photographic solution.* —**pres·er·va·tor** (PREZ·ur–) *n.: an archaeologist appointed ~ of a historic site.* —**pre·serve** (–ZURV) *v.* **-serves, -served, -serv·ing** keep or maintain without danger or harm, or decay: *May God ~ you! Fruits may be ~d by cooking with sugar; laws to ~ our natural resources;* ***n.:*** *strawberry ~s; No poaching on private game ~s* (i.e. grounds). —**pre·serv·er** *n.: Wear a life ~ against drowning.*

pre·set (–SET) *v.* **-sets, -set, -set·ting** set beforehand: *a long-range missile with a ~ guidance system.* —**pre·shrunk** (PREE–) *adj.* of a fabric, shrunk during manufacture to reduce shrinkage in use.

pre·side (–ZIDE) *v.* **-sides, -sid·ed, -sid·ing** have authority or control (*over*), esp. as chairman: *to ~ at a trial; Churchill would not ~ over* (i.e. be responsible for) *the dissolution of the empire.* —**pres·i·dent** (PREZ–) *n.* the chief executive of a republic, as the **President** of the U.S.; also, the chief officer of a company, college, club, etc.; a chairman; **pres·i·den·cy** *n.* **-cies; pres·i·den·tial** (–DEN·shul) *adj.: the ~ oath of office; ~ powers.* —**pre·sid·i·o** (–SID·ee·oh) *n.* **-os** in S.W. United States, a military fort: *Spanish soldiers built California's first ~ in San Diego in 1769;* **pre·sid·i·um** (–ee·um) *n.* **-i·ums** or **-i·a** (–ee·uh) in Communist countries, a permanent executive committee, as the **Presidium** of the Supreme Soviet, whose chairman is U.S.S.R.'s chief of state.

pre·soak (–SOKE) *v.* soak beforehand: *Badly soiled clothes launder better if* ~*ed;* ***n.:*** *Detergents and* ~*s have essentially the same ingredients.* **—pre·spot·ter** *n.* a dry-cleaning worker who removes certain stains before cleaning.

press *v.* **1** act upon with steady force: ~*ed his beloved to his heart;* ~ *the button for help; to* ~ *grapes; fresh juice just* ~*ed; clothes* ~*ed while you wait; Phonograph records, cotton bales, etc. are* ~*ed; candidates* **pressing the flesh** (*Slang.* shaking hands) *all day.* **2** urge: *She* ~*ed him to stay for dinner; politicians* ~*ing the need for reform; an angry public* ~*ing for an inquiry; Women and children were* **pressed into service** *at the height of the war; armies* ~*ing onward to victory; The police decided not to* ~ *charges and dropped the case.* **3** weigh heavily (upon); oppress: *hard* ~*ed for money; too much work* ~*ing on her mind.* ***—n.*** **1:** *elbowed his way through the* ~ *of people on Broadway; driven forward by the* ~ *of ambition; a fabric that keeps its* ~. **2** printing press; hence, newspapers; journalists; publicity: *Morning papers* **go to press** *after midnight; Her candidature will be announced to the* ~ *at tomorrow's* **press conference;** *A* **press agent** *works to ensure a good* ~ *for a celebrity or event.* **—press·er** *n.* **—pressing** *adj.* urgent: *away in Europe on* ~ *business.* **—press box** a space reserved for reporters, esp. at a sports event. **—press·man** *n.* **-men** the operator of a printing press. **—press·room** *n.* where the presses are installed in a printing plant; also, a room for journalists. **—pres·sure** (PRESH·ur) *n.* the action of pressing or the condition of being pressed: *Atmospheric* ~ *decreases with altitude; Hypertension is high blood* ~*; He studies hard under* ~ *of exams; A* **pressure cooker** *cooks fast with steam under* ~. **—pres·sure** *v.* **pres·sures, pres·sured, pres·sur·ing:** *people* ~*d into signing sales contracts;* **pressure group** a group that exerts pressure on governments and legislatures to further its own interests; **pressure suits** *and* **pressurized cabins** *help people remain under normal atmospheric pressure at high altitudes;* **pres·sur·ize** *v.* **-iz·es, -ized, -iz·ing; -i·za·tion** (–ZAY–) *n.* **—pres·sur·iz·er** (–eye·zur) *n.*

pres·ti·dig·i·ta·tion (–dij·i·TAY–) *n.* sleight of hand; legerdemain. **—pres·ti·dig·i·ta·tor** (–DIJ·uh·tay–) *n.* a juggler.

pres·tige (–TEEZH) *n.* reputation based on outstanding achievement. **—pres·ti·gious** (–TEE·jus) *adj.;* **pres·ti·gious·ly** *adv.*

pres·to (–toh) *adj.* & *adv. Music.* very quick(ly). ***—n.,*** *pl.* **-tos** a musical passage in fast tempo. ***—interj.:*** *Hey* ~*! And the rabbit vanished.*

pre·stressed concrete concrete cast around steel cables held under tension by hydraulic jacks.

pre·sume (–ZOOM) *v.* **-sumes, -sumed, -sum·ing** **1** assume: ~*d innocent until proven guilty; Dr. Livingstone, I* ~*?* **2** venture; hence, take liberties: *She* ~*s to advise her parents; a very* **presuming** (i.e. presumptuous) *young man; It would be* **presuming on** *his generosity to ask for another loan.* **—pre·sum·a·ble** (–ZOOM·uh·bl) *adj.;* **pre·sum·a·bly** (–uh·blee) *adv.* **—pre·sump·tion** (–ZUMP–) *n.: only a* ~*, not a proven fact; It was considered* ~ *(i.e. audacity) for women to want to vote;* **pre·sump·tive** (–tiv) *adj.: She was the* ~ *heir till her brother was born; The smoking pistol in his hand seems* ~ *evidence against him.* **—pre·sump·tu·ous** (–choo·us) *adj.* arrogant or excessively forward; presuming; **pre·sump·tu·ous·ly** *adv.*

pre·sup·pose (pree·suh·POZE) *v.* **-sup·pos·es, -sup·posed, -sup·pos·ing** assume beforehand; also, require as a precondition; **pre·sup·po·si·tion** (–ZISH·un) *n.* **—pre·tax** *adj.* before tax: ~ *earnings.* **—pre·teen** (PREE·teen) *n.* a child who is in the 9–12 age range; ***adj.:*** *a* ~ *fashion.*

pre·tence *esp. Brit.* pretense. **—pre·tend** (pri·TEND) *v.* **1** make believe: *Let's* ~ *we're in space.* **2** claim, esp. falsely; profess: *She* ~*ed not to hear; to* ~ *illness as an excuse; The young Stuarts* **pretended to** *the British throne;* **pre·tend·er** *n.* **—pre·tense** (pri·TENCE,PREE–) *n.: begging alms under* ~ *of poverty; gained entry to the club by false* ~*s; a plain-spoken manner free from all* ~ (i.e. phoniness); **pre·ten·sion** *n.: a journalist with no* ~*s to scholarship.* **—pre·ten·tious** (–TEN·shus) *adj.* making undue claims; hence, showy: *She's too* ~ *to be popular; a pompous and* ~ *style of writing;* **pre·ten·tious·ly** *adv.;* **pre·ten·tious·ness** *n.*

pret·er·it(e) (PRET·uh·rit) *adj.* & *n.* (in) the past tense.

pre·ter·nat·u·ral (pree·tur·NACH·uh·rul) *adj.* out of the ordinary; also, supernatural; psychic: *a man of* ~ *strength; miracles and such* ~ *phenomena.* **—pre·ter·nat·u·ral·ly** *adv.*

pre·test (–TEST) *n.* & *v.* test in advance.

pre·text (PREE–) *n.* a false purpose or reason; pretense: *espionage under the* ~ *of missionary work.*

Pre·to·ri·a (pri·TOR·ee·uh) the administrative capital of South Africa.

pret·ty (PRIT·ee) *adj.* **pret·ti·er, pret·ti·est** **1** moderately pleasing and attractive to look at: *a* ~ *little girl.* **2** *Informal.* considerable in amount: *a* ~ *mess you're into; cost me a* ~ *sum.* — ***adv.*** fairly: *She'll be here* ~ *soon;* ~ *much as we expected;* **sitting pretty** in a fairly advantageous position. ***—v.*** **pret·ties, pret·tied, pret·ty·ing:** *a basement room* ~*d up for a party;* also **pret·ti·fy, -fies, -fied, -fy·ing.** **—pret·ti·ly** *adv.* **—pret·ti·ness** *n.*

pret·zel (–sl) *n.* a glazed, salted, brittle biscuit in the form of a loose knot or stick.

prev. previous(ly).

pre·vail (pri·VALE) *v.* be stronger, more usual, common, or effective; hence, succeed: *under* ~*ing conditions; Reason* ~*ed over prejudices; The children* **prevailed on** (or **upon** or **with**) (i.e. persuaded) *their mother to take them to the movie; The* **prevailing** (i.e. generally current) *westerly winds make flying from west to east faster in the N. Hemisphere; youth following the ~ing fashions in dress;* **pre·vail·ing·ly** *adv.* —**prev·a·lent** (PREV·uh–) *adj.* widespread: *a custom ~ among certain tribes;* **prev·a·lence** *n.*

pre·var·i·cate (–VAIR–) *v.* **-cates, -cat·ed, -cat·ing** evade the truth by quibbling or a similar tactic; **pre·var·i·ca·tor** *n.* —**pre·var·i·ca·tion** (–CAY–) *n.*

pre·vent (pri–) *v.* stop from doing or happening; hinder: *measures to ~ a disease; prompt action to ~ a fire from spreading;* **pre·vent·a·ble** or **-i·ble** *adj.;* **pre·ven·tion** *n.:* "*~ is better than cure*"; *~ of cruelty to animals.* —**pre·ven·tive** (–tiv) *adj.* helping to prevent something: *suspects held without bail in ~ detention; Vaccination is ~ medicine;* ***n.*** a preventive measure or agent, as a drug. Also **pre·vent·a·tive** *adj.* & *n.*

pre·view (PREE·vyoo) *n.* an advance showing or viewing of something to come, as a play, movie, or TV program; hence, a foretaste; also ***v.***

pre·vi·ous (PREE·vee·us) *adj.* earlier: *I cannot be at tomorrow's party because of a ~ engagement; a commitment made* **previous to** (i.e. before) *your request.* —**pre·vi·ous·ly** *adv.*

pre·vi·sion (–VIZH–) *n.* foresight; also, a prediction; ***v.*** foresee.

pre·vue (PREE·vyoo) same as PREVIEW. —**pre·war** (PREE·WOR) *adj.* before a (or the) war.

prex·y *n.* **prex·ies** *Slang.* a college president.

prey (PRAY) *n. sing.* an animal hunted for food; hence, a victim: *Vultures are birds* **of prey** (i.e. predators); *He* **fell a prey** *to* (i.e. became a victim of) *loansharks.* —***v.:*** *Larger beasts ~ on smaller ones; Thoughts from the past ~ed (up)on her mind.*

price *n.* the amount of money to be paid to the seller of something; cost; worth: *The President would not agree to peace* **at any price** (i.e. at too heavy a price); *government-imposed* **price controls** *to fight inflation; antitrust laws against* **price-fix·ing; price support** *legislation to help farmers; a* **price(-cutting) war** *among competitors.* —***v.*** **pric·es, priced, pric·ing:** *House builders almost ~d themselves out of the market; ~d too high for my pocket.* —**price·less** *adj.* invaluable: *a ~ gem.*

prick *n.* a little mark or puncture made by a sharp point, as of a pin or thorn; also, the sharp pain thus caused or a pricking: *the* **pricks of conscience.** —***v.:*** *A balloon bursts when ~ed; Thickly growing seedlings are* **pricked out** (i.e. transplanted) *uniformly in larger pans;* **prick up one's ears** listen closely. —**prick·er** *n.* —**prick·le** *n.* a thorn or spine; also, a sharp sensation; ***v.*** **-les, -led, -ling** tingle; **prick·ly** *adv.* **-li·er, -li·est** having sharp points; also, stinging: *the ~ porcupine; the itchy reddish rash of* **prickly heat; prickly pear** a cactus with edible, pear-shaped, prickly fruits.

pride *n.* **1** a sense of one's own worth; hence, pleasure over one's qualities, possessions, or achievements; also, a source of such esteem: *to take ~ in a job well done; David was the ~ and joy of her old age.* **2** false esteem of oneself; hence, contempt of others: "*~ goes before a fall.*" **3** best part; prime: *in the days of her ~; Shakespeare's* **pride of place** *among dramatists.* **4** a group, esp. of lions or peacocks. —***v.*** **prides, prid·ed, prid·ing:** *He* **prides himself** *on his unflappability.* —**pride·ful** *adj.* —**pride·ful·ly** *adv.*

prie-dieu (pree·DYUR) *n.* a small desk for use when kneeling in prayer.

pri·er (PRY·ur) *n.* one who pries; pryer.

priest (PREEST) *n.* a religious official who performs sacrifices and other functions, esp., as in the Roman Catholic Church, a clergyman ranking next below a bishop; *fem.* **priest·ess; priest·hood** *n.;* **priest·ly** *adj.;* **priest·li·ness** *n.*

prig *n.* a rigid and smug observer of morals and manners. —**prig·gish** *adj.: too ~ to dress casually;* **prig·gish·ly** *adv.* —**prim** *adj.* **prim·mer, prim·mest** overprecise or formal; **prim·ly** *adv.;* **prim·ness** *n.*

prim. primary; primitive.

pri·ma·cy (PRY·muh·see) *n.* **-cies** superiority; preeminence; also, the rank or office of a church primate. —**pri·ma don·na** (PREE·muh·DON·uh), *pl.* **prima donnas** the leading woman singer in an opera; hence, a vain or temperamental person. —**pri·ma fa·ci·e** (PRY·muh·FAY·shee·ee) *Law.* of evidence, adequate without further examination. —**pri·mal** (PRY·mul) *adj.* primitive; primeval. —**pri·ma·ry** (PRY·mer·ee) *adj.* first in time, rank, or importance: *"Aborigine" has its* **primary accent** (or **stress**) *on the third syllable; A* **primary cell,** *as used in a flashlight, cannot be recharged;* **primary school** *comprises kindergarten through Grade 3; ~ elections* —***n.,*** *pl.* **-ries:** *the New Hampshire presidential ~.* —**pri·ma·ri·ly** (pry·MER–, PRY·mer–) *adv.* —**pri·mate** (PRY–) *n.* **1** (*also* PRY·mit) an archbishop. **2** any of the highest order of mammals including man, apes, and monkeys.

prime *n.* **1** the earliest or best stage or period: *The year is at its ~ in the spring; the ~ of youth.* **2** a number that is not composed of other numbers, as 1, 2, 3, 5, 7, 11, or 13. —***adj.*** first; hence, chief: *the* **prime meridian** *of 0° longitude passing through Greenwich, England; the* **prime minister** *of a country; the* **prime rate** *of interest charged to a bank's best customers.* —***v.*** **primes, primed, prim·ing** make ready or prepare, as a gun (with powder) for firing, a water pump (by pouring in some water), a painting surface (with a first coat), a witness (with facts), etc.; —**prim·er** *n.* **1** (PRY–) one that prepares, as a device to set off an explosive charge, a first coat of paint, etc. **2** (PRIM–)

a beginner's textbook. **—prime time** on radio and TV, the evening hours from 7 to 11 E.S.T.

pri·me·val (pry·MEE·vul) *adj.* of the earliest times: *earth's ~ uninhabited state; ~ jungles;* **pri·me·val·ly** *adv.* **—prim·i·tive** (–tiv) *adj.* of early times; of the simplest kind; undeveloped: *~ peoples; ~ weapons;* **n.:** *~s such as the Tasmanians or the Bushmen; a ~* (i.e. not trained or sophisticated) *in her artistic leanings;* **prim·i·tive·ly** *adv.;* **prim·i·tive·ness** *n.;* **prim·i·tiv·ism** *n.;* **prim·i·tiv·i·ty** (–TIV–) *n.* **—pri·mo·gen·i·tor** (pry·muh·JEN–) *n.* the earliest ancestor; **pri·mo·gen·i·ture** (–JEN·i·chur) *n.* the fact of being or the right of the eldest. **—pri·mor·di·al** (pry·MOR·dee·ul) *adj.* primeval: *a ~ swamp; the ~ "soup" from which life arose on earth; Did matter originate as a ~ fireball of radiation?* **pri·mor·di·al·ly** *adv.*

primp *v.* dress or groom (oneself) in a finicky way: *~ing for hours before a mirror.*

prim·rose *n.* any of a group of early-flowering ornamental plants, with yellowish flowers in the *common primrose;* **primrose path** (or **way**) path of pleasure.

prin. principal; principle.

prince *n.* a male member of a royal family; also, a small ruler; hence, the chief or excellent one: *a ~ among men;* **prince consort** a reigning queen's husband; **prince·dom** *n.* **—Prince Edward Island** a province of E. Canada; 2,184 sq.mi. (5,657 km²); *cap.* Charlottetown. **—prince·ly** *adj.* **-li·er, -li·est** noble; generous: *paid a ~ sum for the house;* **prince·li·ness** *n.;* **prince·ling** *n.* a petty prince; **prin·cess** (–sis, –ses) *n.* a female member of a royal family. **—prin·ci·pal** (–pul) *adj.* chief: *"Take-took-taken-taking" are the* **principal parts** *of "take";* **n.** the main accomplice in a crime, the chief actor in a play, the head of a school, a capital sum bearing interest, the main body of an estate, etc.; **prin·ci·pal·ly** *adv.;* **prin·ci·pal·ship** *n.* **—prin·ci·pal·i·ty** (–PAL–) *n.* **-ties** a prince's territory, as Andorra or Monaco. **—prin·ci·ple** *n.* a fundamental truth, law, or rule; also, the basis of an action or operation, esp. behavior: *~s of good government; two machines built on the same ~; probable* **in principle** *but impossible in practice; Men of ~ object to things* **on principle;** *a high-* **principled** *woman.*

prink same as PRIMP.

print *n.* **1** a mark made by pressure, as a fingerprint, type impression, design on cloth, etc. **2** a cloth or paper with such marks: *a Japanese color ~.* **3** printed copy; also, a photograph made from a negative: *There are millions of copies of the Bible* **in print;** *it has never gone* **out of print.** **—v.:** *She ~ed her name instead of signing it; ~ed percale;* **print·a·ble** *adj.* **—printed circuit** an electronic circuit in which the connections are printed on an insulated base with a conducting material instead of being wired together. **—print·er** *n.* one that prints; esp., a person whose work or business in printing; **printer's devil** a printer's young helper (on whom printing errors used to be blamed). **—print·ing** *n.* **1** the art or business of producing books, periodicals, etc. with type or plates on a **printing press.** **2** a printing or the copies printed at one time; impression. **—print·out** *n.* a computer's printed output; **v. print out.**

pri·or (PRY·ur) *adj.* earlier in time; preceding in importance or rank: *I must give ~ consideration to business engagements before social visits; He was in farming* **prior to** (i.e. before) *entering politics.* **—n.,** *fem.* **pri·or·ess,** the superior of a **pri·o·ry** (PRY·uh·ree) *n.* **-ries** a monastery. **—pri·or·i·ty** (–OR–) *n.* **-ties** a level, esp. the top level of importance or urgency; also, something that has priority: *top ~ for emergency relief; Different people have different ~s;* **adj.:** *a ~ project; ~ mail.*

prism (PRIZ·um) *n.* a solid with similar, equal, and parallel ends and sides that are parallelograms, esp. a transparent one with triangular ends that breaks up white light into the colors of the rainbow, or **pris·mat·ic** (–MAT–) **colors,** i.e. violet, indigo, blue, green, yellow, orange, and red.

pris·on (PRIZ·un) *n.* a place of confinement, esp. for convicted criminals; **pris·on·er** *n.* a captive; **prisoner of conscience** a political prisoner; **prisoner of war** one taken prisoner in war.

pris·sy (PRIS·ee) *adj.* **pris·si·er, pris·si·est** *Informal.* prim or prudish; **pris·si·ly** *adv.;* **pris·si·ness** *n.*

pris·tine (–teen, –TEEN) *adj.* unspoiled; uncorrupted: *a painting restored to its ~ beauty.*

prith·ee (PRIDH·ee) *interj. Archaic.* I pray thee; please.

pri·va·cy (PRY·vuh·see) *n.* the quality or state of being private; secrecy: *in the ~ of my home; data banks as a threat to ~; the invasion of ~ rights by electronic snooping.* **—pri·vate** (PRY·vit) *adj.* having to do with one person or group; not public: *a ~ office; ~ dealings to serve ~ ends; a ~ school; a* **private eye** (i.e. detective); *the* **private** (i.e. free) **enterprise** *system of capitalist society.* **—n.** **1** a U.S. soldier or marine of the lowest rank: *A* **private first class** *ranks next below a corporal.* **2 privates** *pl.* genitals. **3 in private** privately; not publicly. **—pri·va·teer** (–TEER) *n.* formerly, an armed, privately owned ship in the service of a belligerent government; also, a crew member or commander of such a vessel; **pri·va·teer·ing** *n.: ~ ended about 1865.* **—private parts** genitals. **—pri·va·tism** (PRY·vuh–) *n.* the avoidance of involvements other than for one's private interests; **pri·va·tis·tic** (–TIS–) *adj.*

pri·va·tion (pry·VAY–) *n.* the condition of being deprived of life's ordinary necessities: *the many ~s imposed by war.*

priv•et (–it) *n.* an evergreen shrub widely grown for hedges.

priv•i•lege (PRIV·lij) *n.* a benefit or advantage granted to a particular individual or attached to a certain position; also, a legal right: *the ~s of membership.* —**priv•i•leged** (–lijd) *adj.: a ~ class; a* **privileged communication** *between lawyer and client; a statement ~ in the House but slanderous if repeated outside.*

priv•y (PRIV·ee) *adj.* private: **privy to** privately informed about. —***n.,*** *pl.* **priv•ies** an outhouse, esp. a toilet. —**privy council** a body of advisors appointed by a sovereign. —**privy purse** a ruler's private allowance.

prize *n.* something worth competing for or that is offered to a winner in a competition, lottery, etc.; ***adj.:*** *~ cattle* (i.e. cattle that have won prizes); *~ money.* —***v.*** **priz•es, prized, priz•ing** **1** value highly; also, estimate the value of. **2** force (open) with a lever; pry. —**prize•fight** *n.* a professional boxing match, fought in a **prize ring,** a square enclosure of ropes; **prize•fight•er** *n.* —**prize money** money offered as prize. —**prize•win•ner** *n.;* **prize•win•ning** *adj.: a ~ essay.*

P.R.O. public relations officer.

pro- *comb.form.* **1** forward in place or time: as in *proboscis, prologue.* **2** for; in place of: as in *proconsul; pronoun.* **3** favorable to: *pro-European policies.* —**pro** (PROH) *n.* **pros** **1** *Informal.* [short form] professional: *a football ~; a ~ football player.* **2** something in favor: *the ~s and cons of a question;* ***adj., adv.*** & ***prep.:*** *the ~-and-con arguments; spoke at length ~ and con; arguments ~ and con hanging.* —**pro•ac•tive** (–AC–) *adj.* favoring the first-learned: *~ inhibition.* —**pro-am** *adj.* professional-and-amateur.

prob. probable; probably; problem.

prob•a•ble (PROB·uh·bl) *adj.* likely (because reasonable or logical) to be or to happen: *possible to win $1 million in the draw, though everyone is not a ~ winner; the ~ cause of death;* **prob•a•bly** *adv.;* **prob•a•bil•i•ty** (–BIL–) *n.* **-ties:** *She'll succeed* **in all probability;** *Drowning is one of the ~s of how he died.* —**pro•bate** (PROH–) *n.* in law, the official proving of a will's genuineness; ***adj.:*** *a ~ court;* ***v.*** **-bates, -bat•ed, -bat•ing** legally establish (a will) as genuine and valid. —**pro•ba•tion** (–BAY–) *n.* a trial of a person's conduct or worth: *a new employee confirmed after a month's ~; a first offender given a suspended sentence and placed on ~ for one year under a* **probation officer; pro•ba•tion•al** *adj.;* **pro•ba•tion•ar•y** (–BAY·shuh·ner–) *adj.: a ~ period; a ~ appointment.* —**pro•ba•tion•er** *n.* —**pro•ba•tive** (PROH·buh·tiv) *adj.* serving to test or prove. —**probe** *n.* an investigation; also, an instrument for probing, as a surgeon's slender metal device for exploring a wound or body cavity, or an unmanned rocket or other craft equipped with instruments sent on a space exploration: *a lunar ~;* ***v.*** **probes, probed, prob•ing:** *a committee ~ing charges of corruption; scuba divers ~ing the hull of a sunken ship.* —**pro•bi•ty** (PROH–) *n.* uprightness.

prob•lem (–lum) *n.* a question put forward for solution; hence, a difficult or perplexing situation or person: *a mathematical ~;* ***adj.:*** *a ~ drinker.* —**prob•lem•at•ic** (–MAT–) or **-i•cal** *adj.* puzzling; also, not settled; open to question.

pro•bos•cis (proh·BOS·is) *n.* **-cis•es** a long, flexible snout, such as an elephant's trunk, a butterfly's tubelike organ for sucking nectar, etc.

proc. proceedings.

pro•caine (PROH·cain) *n.* a white powder used as a local anesthetic, esp. by dentists.

pro•ceed (pruh·SEED) *v.* go forward; advance: *Stop and ~ slowly at 5 m.p.h.; She thanked him and ~ed to untie the parcel; to ~* (i.e. legally) *against violators; quarrels ~ing* (i.e. arising) *from old enmities;* **proceedings** *pl.* (record of) the activities of a society; also, legal action: *divorce ~s.* —***n.,*** *pl.* **pro•ceeds** (PROH·seedz) [takes *pl. v.*] returns: *The ~ of this lottery will go to charity.* —**pro•ce•dure** (–SEE·jur) *n.: the ~s to be followed in filing for divorce;* **pro•ce•dur•al** *adj.: a meeting delayed by ~ problems.* —**proc•ess** (PROS·es) *n.* **-ess•es** (–iz) **1** a course or series of actions or their method: *A meeting is* **in process** (i.e. going on); *a manufacturing ~; deported by due ~ of law.* **2** an outgrowth or projecting part, as the appendix of the intestine. Also ***adj.*** made by or involving a special process; **process art** (reflecting the artist's conceptual process); **process camera** (for preparing negatives); **process cheese** (blended from several cheeses); **process engineer** (of an assembly line operation). —**proc•ess** (PROS–) *v.* put through methodically, as an application, order, recruits, etc.; **pro•ces•sion** (–SESH·un) *n.* an orderly, formal movement, esp. of people: *a funeral ~;* **pro•ces•sion•al** *n.* & *adj.* (a hymn book or music) for processions. —**proc•es•sor** (PROS–) *n.* **1** one that processes: *a food ~.* **2** a computer or its part that operates on data.

pro•claim (proh·CLAIM) *v.* announce publicly and officially; also, glorify: *A public holiday ~ed in honor of a returning hero; a full-page ad ~ing the virtues of a new product.* —**proc•la•ma•tion** (–luh·MAY–) *n.: a ~ of amnesty.*

pro•cliv•i•ty (–CLIV–) *n.* **-ties** a natural weakness (*for* or *to* do something considered objectionable).

pro•cras•ti•nate (–CRAS–) *v.* **-nates, -nat•ed, -nat•ing** put off doing something from day to day; **pro•cras•ti•na•tor** *n.* —**pro•cras•ti•na•tion** (–NAY–) *n.: "~ is the thief of time".*

pro•cre•ate (PROH·cree–) *v.* **-ates, -at•ed, -at•ing** beget (offspring). —**pro•cre•a•tive**

(–ay·tiv) *adj.:* ~ *instincts.* **—pro·cre·a·tion** (–AY–) *n.* **—pro·cre·a·tor** (PROH–) *n.*

Pro·crus·te·an (–CRUS·tee·un) *adj.* ruthless in enforcing conformity, like **Pro·crus·tes** (–teez) of Greek myth, who stretched his victims to fit his beds.

proc·tor (–tur) *n.* an administrative official of a college; *v.: graduate students hired to* ~ (i.e. supervise) *an exam;* **proc·to·ri·al** (–TOR·ee·ul) *adj.:* ~ *duties.*

proc·u·ra·tor (PROC·yuh·ray–) *n.* an agent or manager, esp. a financial or legal official. **—pro·cure** (pruh·CURE) *v.* **-cures, -cured, -cur·ing** **1** obtain, esp. by some effort; also, bring about: *to* ~ *votes;* ~ *an abortion;* **pro·cure·ment** (–CURE–) *n.: the* ~ *of military supplies.* **2** get (women for prostitution); **pro·cur·er** *n.* a pimp; *fem.* **pro·cur·ess.**

Pro·cy·on (PROH·see·on) *n.* a star in the constellation Canis Minor.

prod *v.* **prods, prod·ded, prod·ding** poke; hence, urge: *to* ~ *cattle;* ~*d into activity by approaching exams;* ***n.*** a thrust; jab; **prod·der** *n.*

prod·i·gal (–gul) *n.* a wastefully extravagant person; ***adj.:*** *an inheritance depleted by* ~ *spending; the parable of the* ~ *son; Nature's* ~ (i.e. abundant) *resources;* **prod·i·gal·ly** (–guh·lee) *adv.;* **prod·i·gal·i·ty** (–GAL–) *n.* **-ties.**

prod·i·gy (–jee) *n.* **-gies** something amazing or extraordinary, esp. a marvelously talented child: *The child Mozart was a musical* ~. **—pro·di·gious** (–DIJ·us) *adj.: a weight lifter of* ~ *strength;* **pro·di·gious·ly** *adv.;* **pro·di·gious·ness** *n.*

pro·duce (pruh–) *v.* **-duc·es. -duced, -duc·ing** bring or put forward; also, bring into existence (in any of various ways, esp. by manufacturing): *evidence* ~*d in court; Cows* ~ *milk; a method that* ~*s results; Causes* ~ *effects; She* ~*s the plays she directs; books printed and* ~*d abroad.* **—*n.*** (PROD–) what is produced by a farm, esp. fruits and vegetables. **—pro·duc·er** (–DEW·sur) *n.* one who produces commercial goods or services; also, one who produces movies, plays, or shows; **producer goods** raw materials, tools, machinery, etc. for the production of consumer goods. **—prod·uct** (PROD–) *n.* what is produced; result: *farm* ~*s; commercial* ~*s; a* ~ *of genius; 6 is the* ~ *of 2 and 3; the gross national* ~. **—pro·duc·tion** (–DUC–) *n.;* **pro·duc·tive** (tiv) *adj.* producing a lot; also, producing good results; **pro·duc·tive·ly** *adv.;* **pro·duc·tive·ness** or **pro·duc·tiv·i·ty** (–TIV–) *n.*

pro·em (PROH·em) *n.* a prelude or preface.

pro·ette (–ET) *n.* a female golf professional.

Prof. Professor; **prof** *n.* [short form] professor.

pro·fane (pruh·FANE) *adj.* not sacred; also, not showing the reverence due to sacred things: *an expert in sacred and* ~ *music; a* ~ *man's* ~ *language;* **pro·fane·ly** *adv.;* **pro·fane·ness** *n.* **—*v.* -fanes, -faned, -fan·ing:** *temples* ~*d by heathen marauders;* **prof·a·na·tion** (–uh·NAY–) *n.;* **pro·fan·a·to·ry** (–FAN–) *adj.* **—pro·fan·i·ty** (–FAN–) *n.* **-ties** **1** profaneness. **2** vulgar or irreverent speech; also, such an utterance: *a mouthful of* ~*s.*

pro·fess (–FES) *v.* **1** affirm; declare one's faith in: *renounced Christ and* ~*ed (faith in) Islam.* **2** to practice (law, medicine, or other professions). **3** declare; also, claim: *He* ~*es ignorance of what happened; She* ~*es expertise in ESP;* **pro·fessed** *adj.;* **pro·fess·ed·ly** (–FES·id·lee) *adv.* avowedly: *a* ~ *poor piano player;* ~ *a Communist.* **—pro·fes·sion** (–FESH·un) *n.: the Creed as a* ~ *of faith; Law, medicine, and divinity were called the learned* ~*s; the oldest* ~ (i.e. prostitution); *a religious by calling but a teacher by* ~*; a national body's call to the* ~ (i.e. the people practicing a certain profession); **pro·fes·sion·al** (–FESH–) *adj.: a* ~ *boxer, not an amateur; a lawyer's* ~ *ethics; a* ~ *pickpocket; The break-in seemed a* ~ *job;* ***n.:*** *Librarians are* ~*s; an Olympic champion* **turned professional** (to play for pay); **pro·fes·sion·al·ly** *adv.;* **pro·fes·sion·al·ism** *n.* **—pro·fes·sion·al·ize** *v.* **-iz·es, -ized, -iz·ing; -i·za·tion** (–ZAY–) *n.* **—pro·fes·sor** (–FES–) *n.* a teacher, usu. in a college; **pro·fes·so·ri·al** (–SOR·ee·ul) *adj.;* **pro·fes·sor·ship** (–FES–) *n.;* also **pro·fes·sor·ate** (–it).

prof·fer (PROF·ur) *n. Formal.* offer; ***v.*** **prof·fers, prof·fered, prof·fer·ing:** *a night's lodging* ~*d in friendship.*

pro·fi·cient (pruh·FISH·unt) *adj.* skilled: ~ *in cooking, though not an expert;* **pro·fi·cient·ly** *adv.* **—pro·fi·cien·cy** *n.*

pro·file (PROH–) *n.* the side view of a face; also, an outline; hence, an outline biography or sketch: *Her face looks better in* ~*; Kennedy wrote "Profiles in Courage"; a patient's medication* ~*; Keep a* **low profile** (i.e. don't draw attention to yourself) *and avoid talking to the media.* **—*v.* -files, -filed, -fil·ing:** *Washington is* ~*d on the quarter dollar.*

prof·it *n.* financial gain; hence, a valuable benefit or advantage: *business* **profits;** *the* **profit and loss** *statement at the close of a period; repaired, repainted, and sold* **at a profit. —*v.:*** *to* ~ *by one's mistakes.* **—prof·it·a·ble** *adj.* yielding a profit; **prof·it·a·bly** *adv.;* **prof·it·a·bil·i·ty** (–BIL–) *n.* **—prof·i·teer** (–TEER) *n.* one who makes excessive profits in a time of scarcity; ***v.:*** *hoarding of wheat for* ~*ing.* **—prof·it·less** *adj.*

prof·li·gate (–git) *adj.* & *n.* dissipated or extravagant (person); **prof·li·gate·ly** *adv.* **—prof·li·ga·cy** (–guh·see) *n.*

pro for·ma (–FOR·muh) *Latin.* as a matter of form: *a* ~ *invoice* (sent as notice, not to ask for payment).

pro·found (pruh·FOUND) *adj.* deep [in nonmaterial senses]; also, far down; thoroughgoing: *a* ~ *sleep;* ~ *sympathy; a* ~ *thinker; a* ~ *bow;* ~ *changes in society;* **pro·found·ly** *adv.* totally:

~ *deaf.* —**pro·fun·di·ty** (–FUN–) *n.* **-ties:** *the ~ of a philosopher's thought; Confucian ~s.*

pro·fuse (–FYOOS) *adj.* plentiful to excess; also, extravagant in giving or expression: ~ *thanks; too ~ in his praise;* **pro·fuse·ly** *adv.* —**pro·fu·sion** (–FEW·zhun) *n.: Rain fell in ~ after the long drought.*

pro·gen·i·tor (proh·JEN·i·tur) *n.* ancestor; begetter. —**prog·e·ny** (PROJ·uh·nee) *n.* **-nies** offspring.

pro·ges·ter·one (–JES·tuh·rohn) *n.* a steroid sex hormone that prepares the uterus to receive a fertilized ovum. —**pro·ges·to·gen** (–JES·tuh·jun) *n.* a synthetic compound similar to progesterone in its effects.

prog·na·thous (PROG·nuh·thus) *adj.* (having the jaws) projecting.

prog·no·sis (–NOH–) *n., pl.* **-ses** (–seez) an estimate of the course, duration, and effect of a patient's illness. —**prog·nos·tic** (–NOS–) *adj.* & *n.* predictive (sign or symptom): *a ~ weather chart;* **prog·nos·ti·cate** *v.* **-cates, -cat·ed, -cat·ing** foretell from a sign or symptom; **prog·nos·ti·ca·tor** *n.;* **prog·nos·ti·ca·tion** (–CAY–) *n.*

pro·gram or, esp. *Brit.* **pro·gramme** (PROH·gram, –grum) *n.* a list of items or events, as for a performance, or a plan or outline of steps to be taken in a procedure or operation: *a computer ~ for updating customer accounts; a ~ of studies for a degree.* —***v.*** **-gram(me)s, -gram(m)ed, -gram·(m)ing; programmed instruction** instruction, as by teaching machines, in small steps, at each of which the student has to answer a question correctly before proceeding to the next; **pro·gram·(m)a·ble** *adj.: a ~ calculator;* **pro·gram·(m)at·ic** (–MAT–) *adj.* —**pro·gram·(m)er** *n.*

prog·ress (PROG·res) *n.* forward movement; advance: *A meeting is* **in progress;** *the ~ of civilization through the centuries;* ***v.*** (pruh·GRES): *How is the patient ~ing? to ~ towards perfection;* **pro·gres·sion** (–GRESH·un) *n.* —**pro·gress·ive** (–GRES·iv) *adj.* going forward; hence, favoring continual reform, esp. in government: *a ~ party;* **progressive** (or modern) **jazz** *is based on progressions from one chord to another.* —***n.*** one who favors political reform; **pro·gress·ive·ly** *adv.;* **pro·gress·ive·ness** *n.*

pro·hib·it (–HIB–) *v.* forbid by law (*from* doing something): *Smoking ~ed.* —**pro·hi·bi·tion** (–BISH·un) *n.* a prohibiting, esp. of alcoholic liquors, as was in force in the U.S. between 1920 and 1933; **pro·hi·bi·tion·ist** *n.* —**pro·hib·i·tive** (–HIB–) *adj.* preventing (from doing something): ~ *house prices;* **pro·hib·i·tive·ly** *adv.;* **pro·hib·i·to·ry** (–HIB–) *adj.: a ~ order against a publication.*

proj·ect *n.* (PROJ·ect) **1** a proposed or actual undertaking, often on a large scale; scheme: *a highway construction ~; a Grade 9 chemistry ~; Project H.O.P.E.* **2** a group of apartments or houses forming a unit, usu. built and run with public funds; also called *housing project.* —***v.*** (pruh·JECT) **1** propose: *the ~ed tax increase.* **2** (cause to) jut out: *a promontory ~ing into the sea.* **3** extend spatially or in time: *to ~ population increases of the next decade.* **4** cause to appear on a surface; throw forward: *pictures ~ed on a screen; a world map made by mathematically ~ing the globe on a flat surface.* —**pro·jec·tile** (–JEC·tl, –tile) *n.* anything hurled forward, as a missile or rocket. —**pro·jec·tion** (–JEC–) *n.* [besides the *v.* senses] *Psych.* the ascribing or attribution of one's own feelings or motives to other persons or things, often as a defense mechanism. —**pro·jec·tor** (–JEC–) *n.* a machine for projecting pictures, operated by a **pro·jec·tion·ist** from a **projection booth.**

pro·lapse *n.* (proh·LAPS) the downward slipping of an organ from its normal position because of weakness of supporting tissue, as of the rectum or uterus; also ***v.*** **-laps·es, -lapsed, -laps·ing.**

pro·le·gom·e·non (–li·GOM·uh–) *n., pl.* **-na** a preliminary statement, usu. a learned preamble to a treatise.

pro·le·tar·i·an (–roh·li·TAIR·ee·un) *adj.* & *n.* (a member) of the **pro·le·tar·i·at** (–ut) *n.* the industrial working class.

pro-life, -lif·er same as RIGHT-TO-LIFE(R).

pro·lif·er·ate (–LIF–) *v.* **-ates, -at·ed, -at·ing** multiply or grow rapidly, esp. in an uncontrolled manner: *Corals ~ by budding;* **pro·lif·er·a·tion** (–RAY–) *n.: the U.N. nuclear nonproliferation treaty (1968) to control the spread of nuclear weapons;* **pro·lif·er·ous** (–LIF·uh·rus) *adj.: a ~ growth of new tissue.* —**pro·lif·ic** (–LIF–) *adj.* productive; fertile: *Rabbits and hamsters are ~ animals; a ~ writer;* **pro·lif·i·cal·ly** *adv.*

pro·lix (proh·LIX) *adj.* verbose; long-winded. —**pro·lix·i·ty** *n.* —**pro·lix·ly** *adv.*

pro·log(ue) (PROH·log) *n.* an introductory part, as of a play or other literary work; hence, any introductory act or event.

pro·long (pruh·LONG) *v.* make longer, esp. in time: *a visit ~ed into the night.* —**pro·lon·ga·tion** (–long·GAY–) *n.*

prom *n.* a formal dance held by a school or college class. —**prom·e·nade** (–uh·NAID) *n.* **1** a public walk or ride taken for pleasure; also, a public place for walking, as a ship's **promenade deck. 2** a ball or dance. —***v.*** **-nades, -nad·ed, -nad·ing** walk about; hence, parade (someone, as if displaying).

Pro·me·theus (pruh·MEE·thyoos) *n.* a Titan of Greek myth who stole fire from heaven for man's benefit; **Pro·me·the·an** (–thee·un) *adj.* life-bringing; daringly creative. —**pro·me·thi·um** (–thee·um) *n.* a rare-earth metallic chemical element.

prom·i·nence *n.* a being prominent or something prominent: *a paper that gives ~ to sports* *stories; Churchill came* **into prominence** *in World War II; an iceberg noticed as a ~ on the horizon; solar ~s erupting as huge arches of gas.* **—prom·i·nent** *adj.* projecting; hence, conspicuous; distinguished; eminent: *an insect's ~ eyes; a ~ position in public life;* **prom·i·nent·ly** *adv.*

pro·mis·cu·ous (–MIS·cue·us) *adj.* disorderly; hence, indiscriminate; casual, esp. in sexual relationships: *a ~ youth;* **pro·mis·cu·ous·ly** *adv.* **—prom·is·cu·i·ty** (–CUE–) *n.* **-ties;** also **pro·mis·cu·ous·ness** (–MIS–).

prom·ise (–is) *n.* word that binds one to do or not to do something; also, what is promised; hence, an expectation or hope of success: *a great ~ but a poor performance; sued for breach of ~; a land of ~ flowing with milk and honey; a juvenile poem that shows much ~.* **—*v.* -is·es, -ised, -is·ing:** *I ~ you help; the* **Promised Land** (or Canaan); *An honest politician never ~s the moon;* **prom·is·ing** *adj.* likely to give success or good results: *weather that looks ~; a ~ start in life;* **prom·is·ing·ly** *adv.* **—prom·is·so·ry** (–i·sor·ee) *adj.: a* **promissory note** *for $500 due for payment in 60 days.*

pro·mo (PROH·moh) *n.* & *adj. Informal.* promotional (announcement): *those ~s for pink pills and jogging.*

prom·on·to·ry (–un·tor·ee) *n.* **-ries** a headland; cape.

pro·mote (–MOTE) *v.* **-motes, -mot·ed, -mot·ing** **1** raise in rank; also, further the popularity of: *pupils ~d to a higher grade; a new soap well ~d by ads.* **2** help to establish: *to ~ peace and understanding.* **—pro·mo·ta·ble** (–tuh·bl) *adj.: a ~ candidate; "Martin" is more ~ in the English media than "Martineau."* **—pro·mot·er** *n.* **—pro·mo·tion** *n.;* **pro·mo·tion·al** *adj.: a ~ ad campaign.*

prompt *v.* **1** make (someone) do something; also, cause (something) to be: *a gift ~ed by charity; an example that ~ed others to do the same.* **2** remind; supply cues or lines, as a **prompt·er** does during a stage performance with the aid of a **prompt·book,** i.e. annotated script. —***adj.*** performed or acting quickly; also, done without delay: *~ obedience; a ~ reply;* **prompt·ly** *adv.;* **prompt·ness** or **promp·ti·tude** *n.*

prom·ul·gate (PROM–, proh·MUL–) *v.* **-gates, -gat·ed, -gat·ing** put into force officially; hence, make widespread: *a regulation ~d by executive order.* **—prom·ul·ga·tion** (–GAY–) *n.*

pron. pronoun; pronounced; pronunciation.

prone *adj.* **1** liable or inclined: *Man is ~ to error; a nervous and accident-~ driver.* **2** (lying) on one's face: *stretched ~ on the pavement; the ~ glide in swimming;* **prone·ly** *adv.* **—prone·ness** *n.*

prong *n.* a pointed end, as a tine of a fork, fang of a tooth, or the tip of an antler, as of the **prong·horn (antelope),** a North American ruminant with two curved horns, each having a projection. **—pronged** *adj.* & *comb. form.* branched: *a two-~ tuning fork; a three-~ attack.*

pro·noun (PROH–) *n.* a word such as *I, you, he, herself,* or *anybody* that functions like a noun. **—pro·nom·i·nal** (–NOM·i·nl) *adj.*

pro·nounce (pruh·NOUNCE) *v.* **-nounc·es, -nounced, -nounc·ing** **1** declare officially: *carried to the hospital but ~d dead on arrival; I ~ you man and wife; A judge ~s sentence; He was ~d guilty;* **pro·nounce·ment** *n.* **2** give the pronunciation of: *"Poughkeepsie" is ~d* (puh·KIP·see). **—pro·nounce·a·ble** *adj.: "Chomley" is more ~ than "Cholmondeley."* **—pro·nounced** *adj.* marked; decided: *a ~ change in his personality.*

pron·to (PRON·toh) *adv. Informal.* quickly; promptly.

pro·nun·ci·a·men·to (–see·uh·MEN·toh) *n.* **-tos** a public announcement or proclamation. **—pro·nun·ci·a·tion** (–see·AY–) *n.* the way of saying a word, syllable, or sound of a language.

proof *n.* **1** the act or process of proving; test; trial: *"The ~ of the pudding is in the eating"; to put a new bike* **to the proof** (i.e. try it out); **proof coin** one of a trial set of superior quality; *a photographer's or printer's ~* (i.e. trial print); *page ~s of a new book.* **2** something that establishes truth or correctness; evidence: *a postal receipt as ~ of delivery.* **3** the relative strength of an alcoholic liquor: *A* **proof spirit** *is 100 proof, i.e. 50% alcohol by volume.* **—*adj.*** of proven value or strength: *a coat that is* **proof against** *the cold weather;* **-proof** *comb. form: a water-~ watch; a fool-~ plan* (i.e. one sure to succeed). **—proof·read** *v.* **-reads, -read** (–red), **-read·ing** read for errors; **proof·read·er** *n.*

prop. property; proposition; proprietor; proprietary. **—prop** *n.* **1** a support; stay: *a corn plant's ~ roots; The ~ of his old age was an only son;* ***v.*** **props, propped, prop·ping** support something that is falling: *a poor defense* **propped up** *by shady witnesses.* **2** [short form] propeller; stage property.

prop·a·gan·da (–uh·GAN·duh) *n.* ideas or doctrines spread by an interested party; also, such an effort or a plan or method used in this: *war ~; political ~; radio and TV as ~ instruments;* **prop·a·gan·dist** *n.;* **prop·a·gan·dize** *v.* **-diz·es, -dized, -diz·ing. —prop·a·gate** (PROP·uh–) *v.* **-gates, -gat·ed, -gat·ing** spread (breeds, plants, news, etc.) as with seeds or cuttings; reproduce; hence, transmit; publicize: *Trees ~ themselves; insects ~ing diseases; a story ~d on the air waves;* **prop·a·ga·tion** (–GAY–) *n.: sexual ~ of the species; Society for the Propagation of the Faith; the rectilinear ~ of light;* **prop·a·ga·tor** *n.: a malicious ~ of lies.*

pro·pane (PROH–) *n.* a colorless, flammable gas got from petroleum and natural gas for use as a fuel, in refrigeration, etc.

pro·pel (pruh·PEL) *v.* **-pels, -pelled, -pel·ling** drive (something) forward: *a man ~d by ambition; a jet- ~d aircraft.* —**pro·pel·lant** or **pro·pel·lent** *n.* & *adj.: a rocket propellant composed of a fuel and an oxidizer; liquid hydrogen as the propellent fuel.* —**pro·pel·ler** *n.* a revolving device for propelling an aircraft, ship, etc.; also **screw propeller.**

pro·pen·si·ty (pruh·PEN–) *n.* **-ties** an inclination, esp. one inborn: *an unnatural ~ for punning!*

prop·er *adj.* **1** right, correct, or suitable as if belonging or related to: *weather* **proper to** *this time of year; put things back in their ~ places; ~ conduct for a lady; Suburbs are outside the city ~; A* **proper fraction** *has its numerator less than the denominator.* **2** *Informal.* thorough; excellent: *a ~ tongue-lashing from his wife.* **3** designating one, not many; not common: **proper noun** (or **name**), *as "New York" or "the Joneses";* **proper adjective,** *as in "New York office" or "Thermos (bottle)."* —**prop·er·ly** *adv.* —**prop·er·tied** (–teed) *adj.* owning property: *the ~ classes.* —**prop·er·ty** (PROP·ur·tee) *n.* **-ties** what is owned by one, esp. real estate and movable goods; hence, a quality or characteristic: *Get off my ~; This car is not stolen ~; Stage ~s do not include scenery and costumes; Density is one of the ~s of matter; a man* **of property** (i.e. wealthy); **property man** a theater employee in charge of stage properties.

pro·phase (PROH·faze) *n.* the first stage of mitosis when the chromatin gathers into chromosomes before splitting into paired chromatids.

proph·e·cy (PROF·uh·see) *n.* **-cies** a foretelling; also, something prophesied, esp. if divinely inspired; **proph·e·sy** (–sye) *v.* **-sies, -sied, -sy·ing** predict (that something will happen). —**proph·et** (–it) *n.* one who tells the future, esp. if divinely inspired or claimed to be: *The ı atherman is often a poor ~;* **proph·et·ess** (–is) *fem.* —**pro·phet·ic** (pruh·FET–) *adj.: Jeremiah's ~ utterances; a gloom ~ of doom;* **pro·phet·i·cal·ly** *adv.*

pro·phy·lac·tic (proh·fuh·LAC–) *adj.* & *n.* preventive (agent or device): *The Salk vaccine and the condom are ~s.* —**pro·phy·lax·is** (–LAX–) *n.* prevention; protection: *scaling and cleaning as ~ against tooth decay.*

pro·pin·qui·ty (–PING·kwuh·tee) *n.* nearness (in place, time, or relationship); kinship.

pro·pi·ti·ate (–PISH·ee–) *v.* **-ates, -at·ed, -at·ing** win the favor of (someone of influence, esp. if angry); appease; **pro·pi·ti·a·to·ry** *adj.: a ~ offering;* **pro·pi·ti·a·tion** (–AY–) *n.* —**pro·pi·tious** (–PISH·us) *adj.* favorable; auspicious: *The weather was ~ but the flight never arrived.*

prop·jet *n.* same as TURBOPROP.

prop·man *n.* same as PROPERTY MAN.

pro·po·nent (pruh·POH·nunt) *n.* one who proposes or espouses something.

pro·por·tion (pruh·POR–) *n.* **1** the proper relation of things one to another as of parts to a whole: *arms somewhat out of ~ to the body; paid in ~ to work done; cost of living risen out of all ~ to wages; ½ = 3/6 is a ~.* **2** part or share: *your ~ of the work; the ~ of silver in the dollar; a disease of epidemic* **proportions** (i.e. dimensions or size). —***v.:*** *~ your expenses to your earnings; a well-~ed figure.* —**pro·por·tion·al** *adj.* in due proportion: *a typewriter with ~ spacing;* **proportional representation** *of parties in a legislature according to their share of the votes cast;* **pro·por·tion·al·ly** *adv.* —**pro·por·tion·ate** (–it) *adj.;* **pro·por·tion·ate·ly** *adv.*

pro·pose (pruh·POZE) *v.* **-pos·es, -posed, -pos·ing** **1** put forward for consideration or acceptance: *to ~ Jones for mayor; He ~d that we accept the report; She was waiting for him to ~* (marriage). **2** plan; intend: *I ~ to go abroad in the spring.* —**pro·pos·al** (–POH·zl) *n.;* **pro·pos·er** *n.* —**prop·o·si·tion** (–uh·ZISH·un) *n.* **1** a statement, esp. a resolution at a meeting. **2** *Informal.* a proposed deal or something to be dealt with, as a problem or a person: *That's a tough ~.* **3** *Informal.* a proposal, esp. for sexual intercourse; also ***v.;*** **prop·o·si·tion·al** *adj.*

pro·pound (pruh–) *v.* propose (a theory, doctrine, riddle, etc.). —**pro·pound·er** *n.*

pro·pri·e·tor (pruh·PRY·uh·tur) *n.* owner, esp. of a business; **pro·pri·e·tress** *fem.* —**pro·pri·e·tar·y** (–ter·ee) *adj.* pertaining to ownership: *a ~ right; ~ medicine* (i.e. patent medicine); *Delaware, Maryland, and Pennsylvania were* **proprietary colonies** (i.e. controlled by a proprietor under a grant from the king); ***n.*** proprietor; also, proprietary medicine. —**pro·pri·e·tor·ship** *n.*

pro·pri·e·ty (pruh·PRY·uh·tee) *n.* the quality or condition of being proper or fitting, esp. in regard to behavior; **pro·pri·e·ties** *n.pl.* standards or requirements of proper behavior.

pro·pul·sion (pruh·PUL–) *n.* a propelling; also, a propelling force: *jet ~ of rockets.* —**pro·pul·sive** (–PUL·siv) *adj.*

pro ra·ta (proh·RAY·tuh, –RAT·uh) *adj.* & *adv.* proportionate(ly). —**pro·rate** (–RATE) *v.* **-rates, -rat·ed, -rat·ing** divide, distribute, or assess proportionately (to other factors such as share or interest of each). —**pro·ra·tion** (–RAY–) *n.* a prorating, esp. controlling the production of oil or gas for conserving resources; **pro·ra·tion·ing** *n.*

pro·rogue (proh·ROHG) *v.* **-rogues, -rogued, -rogu·ing** formally dismiss (a legislature); adjourn. —**pro·ro·ga·tion** (–GAY–) *n.*

pros. prosody. —**pros** *pl.* of PRO.

pro·sa·ic (proh·ZAY–) *adj.* like prose; prosy; hence, matter-of-fact; dull. —**pro·sa·i·cal·ly** *adv.*

pro·sce·ni·um (proh·SEE·nee·um) *n.* **-ni·ums** or **-ni·a** the front part, esp. the apron of a stage framed by the **proscenium arch** containing the curtain.

pro·scribe (proh–) *v.* **-scribes, -scribed, -scrib·ing** to outlaw; hence, prohibit (a person or practice). —**pro·scrip·tion** (pruh·SCRIP–) *n.*

prose (PROZE) *n.* ordinary language that is not in verse form.

pros·e·cute (PROS·i–) *v.* **-cutes, -cut·ed, -cut·ing** pursue (a claim, an occupation, or a business); esp., bring (an offender) before a court of law: *Trespassers will be ~d; a* **prosecuting attorney** (i.e. government lawyer) or **pros·e·cu·tor** *n.* —**pros·e·cu·tion** (–CUE–) *n.* a carrying out, esp. of a legal action; hence, the prosecuting party, usu. the government; cf. DEFENSE.

pros·e·lyte (–uh·lite) *n.* a convert from one religion to another. —***v.*** **-lytes, -lyt·ed, -lyt·ing** to convert, esp. by inducements; also **pros·e·lyt·ize** (–uh·li–), **-iz·es, -ized, -iz·ing; pros·e·lyt·ism** *n.*

pro·sit (PROH–) *interj.* [used as a toast] to your health!

pros·o·dy (PROS·uh·dee) *n.* verse structure or its study: *Meter, rhyme, etc. are* **pro·sod·ic** (–SOD–) *features;* **pros·o·dist** *n.*

pros·pect *n.* an extensive view or outlook; hence, an expectation of something or someone expected: *a ~ of the countryside from the hilltop; She seems a fine ~ as a client; a job with good* **prospects** (i.e. chances) *for promotion.* —***v.*** search (*for* gold, oil, and such minerals); **pros·pec·tor** *n.* —**pros·pec·tive** (–PEC·tiv) *adj.* hoped for; expected: *a ~ candidate for president; the ~ bride;* **pros·pec·tive·ly** *adv.* —**pros·pec·tus** *n.* an outline, esp. of something proposed, giving its main features, as of a book in preparation, a business, an educational institution, etc.

pros·per *v.* succeed; thrive, esp. financially; **pros·per·ous** (–us) *adj.: a ~ business; ~* (i.e. favorable) *weather for tomatoes;* **pros·per·ous·ly** *adv.* —**pros·per·i·ty** (–PER–) *n.* **-ties:** "*~ makes friends, adversity tries them.*"

pros·ta·glan·din (–GLAN–) *n.* any of about 14 cyclic fatty acids found in animal tissues with active roles in muscle contraction, regulation of blood pressure, reproduction, etc. —**pros·tate** *n.* a male gland surrounding the urethra, which secretes a fluid that mixes with the sperm cells to form semen; also ***adj.*** —**pros·ta·ti·tis** (–TYE·tis) *n.* inflammation of the prostate; its removal is by **pros·ta·tec·to·my** (–TEC–) *n.* **-mies.**

pros·the·sis (PROS·thuh–, –THEE–) *n., pl.* **-ses** (–seez) the replacement of a missing tooth, eye, or limb; also, a replacement part, as a denture or artificial eye, a **pros·thet·ic** (–THET–) device; **pros·thet·ics** *n.pl.* a branch of surgery dealing with artificial body parts; its dental specialty is **pros·tho·don·tics** (–thuh·DON–) *n.pl.*

pros·ti·tute *n.* a woman who provides sex for pay; hence, any person who sells his talents for base purposes; also ***v.*** **-tutes, -tut·ed, -tut·ing.** —**pros·ti·tu·tion** (–TUE–) *n.: the ~ of literary talent for political propaganda.*

pros·trate *v.* **-trates, -trat·ed, -trat·ing** lie stretched out, usu. with the face downward; hence, lay low; also, weaken; exhaust: *A worshiper ~s himself before the altar; ~d* (i.e. exhausted) *by heat.* —***adj.*** lying flat; also, laid low; overcome; **pros·tra·tion** (–TRAY–) *n.: nervous ~* (i.e. breakdown).

pros·y (PROH·see) *adj.* **pros·i·er, -i·est** like prose; also, prosaic.

Prot. Protestant.

pro·tac·tin·i·um (proh·tac·TIN·ee·um) *n.* a radioactive metallic chemical element.

pro·tag·o·nist (–TAG·uh–) *n.* the main character in a play or story; hence, champion; leader.

pro·te·an (PROH·tee·un) *adj.* like the Greek god **Pro·te·us** who could assume any form; hence, changeable; also, versatile: *a ~ artist.*

pro·tect (–TECT) *v.* to guard against harm, esp. with or as if with a cover or barrier: *Roofs ~ us from the elements; tariffs to ~ industries from foreign competition; The whooping crane is a ~ed species.* —**pro·tec·tion** (–TEC–) *n.: ~ of wild life; ~ of domestic industries;* **pro·tec·tion·ism** *is contrary to free trade;* **pro·tec·tion·ist** *n.;* **protection money** money extorted by racketeers or paid as bribes to police to avoid prosecution. —**pro·tec·tive** (–tiv) *adj.: ~ tariffs; camouflage as ~ coloration against the enemy; a drunk kept in ~ custody;* **pro·tec·tive·ly** *adv.* —**pro·tec·tor** *n.;* **pro·tec·tor·ate** (–it) *n.* a state or territory dependent on another for defense, foreign relations, etc., as Solomon Islands (Britain). —**pro·té·gé** (PROH·tuh·zhay) *n.* a person to whom one is patron; *fem.* **pro·té·gée** (–zhay).

pro·tein (PROH·teen) *n.* a complex chemical compound occurring as an essential part of all living things: *Milk, eggs, fish, and lean meat have high ~ value.*

pro tem (proh·TEM) short form of **pro tem·po·re** (proh·TEM·puh·ree) *adj.* & *adv.* temporary; temporarily: *a pro tem committee chairman; appointed president of the Senate pro tempore.*

pro·test (pruh·TEST) *v.* **1** object (to): *minorities ~ing (against) discrimination in hiring.* **2** declare solemnly: *St. Joan died ~ing her innocence;* **prot·es·ta·tion** (–TAY–) *n.* —***n.*** (PROH–): *loud ~s from press and public; an unjust levy paid* **under protest** (i.e. unwillingly). —**pro·test·er** or **-tes·tor** *n.* —**Prot·es·tant** (PROT·is·tunt) *n.* a Christian not of the Roman Catholic or Eastern Orthodox church; ***adj.:*** *The* **Protestant ethic** *considers work as the road to salvation;* **Prot·es·tant·ism** *n.*

pro·tha·la·mi·on (proh·thuh·LAY·mee·un) *n., pl.* **-mi·a** a song celebrating a wedding, as Edmund Spenser's poem of that name.

proto- *comb.form.* first (in time, importance, etc.): as in *protocol, prototype.* **—pro·to·col** (PROH·tuh–) *n.* **1** an initial draft of a document, esp. a treaty. **2** a code of etiquette to be observed on state occasions: *She violated ~ by offering her gloved hand to the Queen.* **—pro·to·mar·tyr** *n.* the first martyr of a cause, as St. Stephen for Christianity. **—pro·ton** (–tahn) *n.* the positively charged elementary particle in the nucleus of all atoms. **—pro·to·plasm** *n.* the essential living matter of all animal and plant cells; **pro·to·plas·mic** (–PLAZ–) *adj.* **—pro·to·type** *n.* the original; the first model; archetype. **—pro·to·zo·an** (–ZOE·un) *n.* a one-celled, microscopic animal, as an amoeba or paramecium: *~s comprise the subkingdom or phylum called* **Pro·to·zo·a** (–ZOE·uh) *n.pl.*

pro·tract (–TRACT) *v.* lengthen; prolong: *a ~ed delay.* **—pro·trac·tion** *n.* **—pro·trac·tor** *n.* an instrument in the form of a semicircular graduated disc used for plotting and measuring angles.

pro·trude (–TROOD) *v.* **-trudes, -trud·ed, -trud·ing** (cause to) jut out: *to ~ one's tongue; a ~ing jaw.* **—pro·tru·sion** (–TROO·zhun) *n.* **—pro·tru·sive** (–SIV) *adj.* **—pro·tu·ber·ant** (–TUE·buh·runt) *adj.* protruding; bulging; **pro·tu·ber·ance** (–unce) *n.* a bulge.

proud *adj.* **1** feeling, arousing, or showing proper pride or self-esteem; hence, glorious: *too ~ to beg; the ~ moment of breaking a world record; a mother* **proud of** *her many children; a ~* (i.e. spirited) *steed.* **2** having or showing too high an opinion of oneself: *~ as a peacock; ~ and arrogant.* **3** *Brit.* standing out: *a ~ edge.* **—do one proud** *Informal.* do one credit; make one feel gratified. **—proud·ly** *adv.* **—proud·ness** *n.* **—proud flesh** overgrown granular tissue around a healed wound.

prov. province, provincial; provisional; provost. **—Prov.** Provençal; Proverbs (Old Testament book).

prove (PROOV) *v.* **proves,** *pt.* **proved,** *pp.* **proved** or **prov·en, prov·ing** **1** establish; demonstrate: *~ that you can lift this weight; Later events ~d my suspicions; a charge that you cannot ~; a ~n car that has sold well for many years; The new recruit ~d herself in 3 days; "The exception ~s the rule" because every rule has some exception.* **2** turn out: *The new recruit ~d to be a good choice; The book ~d interesting.* **—prov·a·ble** *adj.;* **prov·a·bil·i·ty** (–BIL–) *n.*

prov·e·nance (PROV·uh·nunce) *n.* place of origin; source.

Pro·ven·çal (proh·vun·SAHL, prov·un–) *adj.* of or having to do with the Romance language of **Pro·vence** (praw·VAHNCE), a region of S.E. France: *the Provençal troubadours of the Middle Ages.* **—*n.*** the Provençal language or a person of the region.

prov·en·der *n.* **1** hay, corn, oats, and such dry food for livestock. **2** *Informal.* provisions; food.

pro·ve·ni·ence (proh·VEE·nee·unce) *n.* same as PROVENANCE.

prov·erb *n.* a short, wise saying long in use among a people, as contained in the Old Testament book **Proverbs.** **—pro·ver·bi·al** (–VUR·bee·ul) *adj.: Solomon's wisdom is ~;* **pro·ver·bi·al·ly** *adv.: Dogs are ~ faithful animals.*

pro·vide (pruh·VIDE) *v.* **-vides, -vid·ed, -vid·ing** see to or supply (a need or contingency): *I ~ for my family* (i.e. family's needs); *insurance to ~ against accidents and for old age; Sheep ~ us with wool; Rules ~ penalties for infractions;* **pro·vid·er** *n.* **—provided** or **providing** *conj.* on the condition that; if. **—Prov·i·dence** (PROV–) **1** capital of Rhode Island. **2** God's care and help; also, God. **—prov·i·dence** *n.* a being provident; prudent management; **prov·i·den·tial** (–DEN–) *adj.* fortunate; **prov·i·den·tial·ly** *adv.* **—prov·i·dent** *adj.* careful about future needs; hence, frugal; **prov·i·dent·ly** *adv.*

prov·ince (PROV–) *n.* an administrative division of a country, as of Canada; also, a territory or district; hence, a sphere of activity or interest: *Saving souls is outside the ~ of a magistrate.* **—pro·vin·cial** (–VIN·shul) *adj.* of the provinces rather than of cities; hence, rustic; unsophisticated; also, narrow: *a ~ accent; His concerns remained rather ~ even after traveling abroad;* **pro·vin·cial·ism** *n.;* **pro·vin·cial·ly** *adv.*

proving ground a place for the systematic testing of new equipment, theories, etc.

pro·vi·sion (–VIZH·un) *n.* **1** the act of providing. **2** something provided; arrangement: *There is a ~ in the will for gifts to charity.* **3 provisions** *pl.* food supplies or stocks. **—*v.*** supply with provisions. **—pro·vi·sion·al** *adj.* temporary: *the ~ wing of the Irish Republican Army; a ~ government in exile;* **pro·vi·sion·al·ly** *adv.* **—pro·vi·so** (–VYE·zoh) *n.* **-so(e)s** a legal stipulation; provision.

Pro·vo or **pro·vo** (PROH·voh) *n.* **-vos** **1** [short form] provisional (wing of the I.R.A.). **2** a member of a Dutch or German anarchist political group using provocative methods.

prov·o·ca·tion (prov·uh·CAY–) *n.* a provoking or something that provokes: *The police fired under ~; Various ~s were offered to make him fight.* **—pro·voc·a·tive** (–VOC·uh·tiv) *adj.* provoking; also, tending to arouse a feeling or reaction: *a very ~ dress;* **pro·voc·a·tive·ly** *adv.;* **pro·voc·a·tive·ness** *n.* **—pro·voke** (–VOKE) *v.* **-vokes, -voked, -vok·ing** **1** stir up; excite: *a cool-headed man is not easily ~d; She was ~d into saying things she now regrets.* **2** cause: *a thought-~ing speech; artless comments that ~d laughter.* **3** irritate: *very* **provoking** *behavior;* **pro·vok·er** *n.;* **pro·vok·ing·ly** *adv.*

pro·vost (PROH–, PROV·ust) *n.* a high-ranking official, esp. of a college. **—provost** (PROH·voh) **guard** soldiers on police duty under a **provost marshal.**

prow *n.* the front part of a ship, boat, aircraft, etc.

prow·ess *n.* **1** bravery; also, daring acts. **2** extraordinary ability.

prowl *v.* go about cautiously like a beast of prey: *enemy subs ~ing along our coast; prostitutes ~ing the streets;* ***n.:*** *a bear* **on the prowl;** *The police arrived in a* **prowl car** (i.e. squad car) *when a* **prowler** *was reported breaking into the house.*

prox·i·mate (–mit) *adj.* nearest in order, location, or time: *a ~ cause.* **—prox·im·i·ty** (–SIM–) *n.* nearness: *a marriage between first cousins forbidden because of ~ of blood; located in close ~ to a garbage dump;* **proximity fuze** a radar device in a shell or bomb for exploding it when near its target. **—prox·i·mo** *adj. Formal.* of the next month; cf. INSTANT, ULTIMO.

prox·y *n.* **prox·ies** a substitute for another person; also, authority to act for another or a document giving such authority: *Marriage by ~ is not so common as voting by ~, as at business meetings;* ***adj.:*** *The* **proxy statement** *showed the company chairman holding 18,000 shares.*

prude (PROOD) *n.* one who affects excessive modesty in speech and manners; **prud·ish.** *adj.;* **prud·ish·ly** *adv.;* **prud·ish·ness** *n.*

pru·dence (PROO·dnce) *n.* the quality of being **pru·dent** (PROO·dnt) *adj.* cautious and circumspect; also, careful in management: *a ~ and thrifty wife; a ~ investor;* **pru·dent·ly** *adv.* **—pru·den·tial** (–DEN–) *adj.: ~ in buying insurance; a ~ committee with discretionary powers;* **pru·den·tial·ly** *adv.*

prud·er·y (PROO–) *n.* **-er·ies** a being prudish or an instance of it: *Victorian ~ dictated such ~s as saying "limb" for "leg."*

prune (PROON) *n.* a dried sweet plum; also, a plum suitable for drying. **—*v.* prunes, pruned, prun·ing** cut out superfluous or dying parts from (a plant); also, trim: *a wordy essay that needs ~ing;* **prun·er** *n.*

pru·ri·ent (PROO·ree·unt) *adj.* having, showing, or causing lustful desires: *literature catering to ~ interest;* **pru·ri·ence** *n.* **—pru·ri·tus** (–RYE–) *n. Med.* itching.

Prus·sia (PRUSH·uh) a N. European kingdom and empire (1701–1919), in a region now covered by East Germany, Poland, and the U.S.S.R. **—Prus·sian** *n.* & *adj.: The pigment* **Prussian blue** *was discovered in Berlin, 1704.*

pry *v.* **pries, pried, pry·ing** **1** snoop; **prying** *adj.* inquisitive; **pry·ing·ly** *adv.* **2** prize (*v.* 2).**—pry·er** *n.* **—pry** *n.* **pries** **1** a tool for prying, as a lever. **2** an inquisitive person or an act of prying.

Ps. Psalms. **—P.S.** Public School; postscript.

psalm (SAHM) *n.* a sacred song or poem, esp. one from **Psalms,** a book of the Old Testament consisting of 150 psalms, believed to be by King David, the **Psalm·ist** *n.* **—psalm·o·dy** (–uh·dee) *n.* **1** the singing of psalms. **2** *pl.* **-dies** an arrangement of psalms; also, a psalm book. **—Psal·ter** (SAWL–) *n.* Psalms or a collection of psalms for use in worship; also **psalter, psalm book.**

P.S.E. Psychological Stress Evaluator, a type of lie detector based on voiceprints.

pseud. pseudonym. **—pseu·do** (SUE·doh) *adj.* counterfeit; sham; also ***comb.form.*** as in *pseudoscience;* **pseu·do·nym** (–nim) *n.* an assumed name, as "Mark Twain." **—pseu·don·y·mous** (–DON·uh·mus) *adj.: The ~ author of "Tom Sawyer" is really Sam Clemens.*

p.s.f. pounds per square foot.

pshaw (SHAW) *interj.* expressing contempt, disbelief, etc.

p.s.i. pounds per square inch.

psi (SYE) *n.* the 23rd letter of the Greek alphabet (Ψ, ψ). **—psi·lo·cin** (SYE·luh–) *n.* a hallucinogenic drug made from a Mexican mushroom; a derivative of it is **psi·lo·cy·bin** (–SYE·bin) *n.* **—psi·lo·phyte** (SYE·luh·fite) *n.* a Paleozoic order of simple plants that includes the oldest known vascular land plants; **psi·lo·phyt·ic** (–FIT–) *adj.* **—psi particle** an atomic particle discovered in 1974, related to the heavier particles, **psi-prime** and **psi,** discovered later.

psit·ta·co·sis (sit·uh·COH–) *n.* same as PARROT FEVER.

pso·ri·a·sis (suh·RYE·uh–) *n.* a skin disease forming itchy, red patches covered with loose silver-white scales.

psst *interj.* made to attract someone's attention quietly.

P.S.T. Pacific Standard Time.

psych. psychology. **—psych(e)** (SIKE) *v.* **psyches, psyched, psych·ing** *Slang.* **1** get (someone) excited; also, get oneself mentally ready: *a few moments to get ~d up for the dive.* **2** psychoanalyze; probe (someone's) mind; hence, intimidate or be intimidated: *We'll ~ him out with this story;* **psych-out** *n.* **—psy·che** (SYE·kee) *n.* one's soul or mind. **—psy·che·del·ic** (sye·cuh·DEL–) *adj.* relating to hallucinogenic drugs such as LSD or their abnormal effects on the mind; ***n.*** a psychedelic drug or its user. **—psy·chi·a·try** (suh·KYE·uh·tree, sye–) *n.* the branch of medicine dealing with mental and emotional disorders; **psy·chi·a·trist** *n.;* **psy·chi·at·ric** (sye·kee·AT–) *adj.* **—psy·chic** (SYE·kik) *n.* one who is sensitive to forces outside the physical world, as a spiritualistic medium; ***adj.:*** *I don't know what she thinks, I'm not ~;* also **psy·chi·cal:** *~ research into spiritualism, ESP, and such phenomena;* **psychic energizer** an antidepressant drug; **psy·chi·cal·ly** *adv.* **—psy·cho** (SYE·coh) *adj.* & *n.* **-chos** *Informal.* psychopath(ic). **—psych(o)-** *comb.form.* mental: as in *psychoactive, psychiatry.* **—psy·cho·ac·tive** (–AC·tiv) *adj.* acting on the mind: *a ~ drug.* **—psy·cho·a·nal·y·sis** (–uh·NAL–) *n.* the probing of a person's repressed desires, fears, and anxieties for the treatment of his mental and emotional disorders; **psy·cho·an·a·lyt·ic** (–an·uh·LIT·ic) or **-i·cal** *adj.;* **psy·cho·an·a·lyt·i·cal·ly** *adv.;* **psy·cho·an·a·lyst** (–AN·uh·list) *n.;* **psy·cho·an·a·lyze** (–AN·uh·lize) *v.* **-lyz·es, -lyzed, -lyz·ing.** **—psy·cho·chem·i·cal** (–KEM–) *n.* a psychoactive chemical such as LSD or nerve gas; also ***adj.*** **—psy·cho·dra·ma** (–DRAH·muh) *n.* a form of group mental therapy in which patients act out problem situations in order to understand and face them. **—psy·cho·gen·ic** (–JEN–) *adj.* caused by mental or emotional conflicts; origination in the mind.**—psychol.** *Abbrev.* for **psy·chol·o·gy** (–COL·uh·jee) *n.* **-gies** the science of mental processes and behavior of people and animals; **psy·chol·o·gist** *n.;* **psy·cho·log·i·cal** (–LOJ–) *adj.;* **psy·cho·log·i·cal·ly** *adv.* **—psy·cho·path** (SYE·coh–) *n.* a mentally ill person; **psy·cho·path·ic** (–PATH–) *adj.***—psy·cho·sex·u·al** (–SEK·shoo·ul) *adj.* relating to the mental and emotional aspects of one's sex life. **—psy·cho·sis** (–COH·sis) *n., pl.* **-ses** (–seez) a major mental disorder, either functional, as schizophrenia, or with an organic cause such as brain damage; **psy·chot·ic** (–COT–) *n.* & *adj.* (a person) affected by a psychosis; also, having to do with a psychosis. **—psy·cho·so·mat·ic** (–soh·MAT–) *adj.* of a physical disorder, involving both the mind and the body, as certain stomach ulcers, high blood pressure, etc. **—psy·cho·sur·ger·y** (–SUR·juh·ree) *n.* a type of brain surgery for reducing mental illness by destroying specific portions of tissue deep in the brain; **psy·cho·sur·geon** (–jun) *n.* **—psy·cho·ther·a·py** (–THER·uh·pee) *n.* treatment of mental and emotional disorders by psychological rather than physical means; **psy·cho·ther·a·pist** *n.* **—psychotic** See PSYCHOSIS. **—psy·cho·trop·ic** (–TROP–) *n.* & *adj.* (a drug) tending to alter the mind, as a tranquilizer or hallucinogen.

pt. part; past tense; payment; pint; point; port. **—Pt** platinum. **—p.t.** past tense; pro tempore. **—P.T.** Pacific Time; Physical Therapy; physical training.

P.T.A. Parent-Teacher Association.

ptar·mi·gan (TAR·mi·gun) *n.* any of several grouses of mountainous and cold regions that have brown feathers in the summer and white in the winter and completely feathered feet.

PT boat a small fighting ship of the U.S. Navy; "patrol torpedo boat."

pte. private.

pter·o·dac·tyl (ter·uh·DAC·tl) *n.* an extinct winged reptile with wingspans up to 50 ft. (15.24 m) that lived more than 60 million years ago.

ptg. printing.

P.T.O. please turn over.

Ptol·e·my (TOL·uh·mee), **Claudius.** a Greek astronomer of Alexandria, who lived about A.D. 150. **—Ptol·e·ma·ic** (–MAY–) *adj.: In the* **Ptolemaic system,** *the earth was the center of the universe.*

pto·maine (TOH·main) *n.* any of various chemical compounds produced by decaying foods: **ptomaine poisoning** *caused by the bacteria of decaying proteins.*

PTV public television.

Pty. Proprietary.

Pu plutonium.

pub *n. Informal.* same as PUBLIC HOUSE. **—pub.** public; publication; published; publisher; publishing.

pu·ber·ty (PEW–) *n.* the age at which one is capable of sexual reproduction, usu. 12 years for girls and 14 for boys; **pu·ber·tal** *adj.* **—pu·bes** (PEW·beez) *n. sing.* & *pl.* pubic hair or region; **pu·bes·cent** (–BES·nt) *adj.* arriving at or having reached puberty; **pu·bes·cence** (–unce) *n.* **—pu·bic** *adj.* of the genital region; also, of the **pu·bis** (PEW–) *n., pl.* **pu·bes** (–beez) a bone of the pelvis on either side, arching together at the front.

publ. publication; published, publisher. **—pub·lic** *adj.* **1** of the people as a whole: *a survey of ~ opinion; a ~ park;* **in the public domain** everyone's property; not protected by private rights. **2** civic; governmental: *~ assistance, defender, service.* **3** not private; well-known; open: *~ morals; a ~ figure; ~ life.* ***—n.*** the people; also, a section of it: *the reading, traveling, and other ~s; A private company* **goes public** (selling shares on the stock exchange); *a crime committed* **in public; pub·lic·ly** *adv.* **—public address system** an amplification system of microphones and loudspeakers for addressing a large audience. **—pub·li·can** (–cun) *n.* **1** a tax collector of ancient Rome. **2** the keeper of a pub in Britain. **—public assistance** government aid to the needy. **—pub·li·ca·tion** (–CAY–) *n.* a publishing or a thing published; also, the process of publishing, including printing and distribution. **—public defender** an attorney defending the indigent among accused persons at public expense. **—public house** *esp. Brit.* a licensed tavern or bar. **—pub·li·cist** *n.* a press agent; one who publicizes. **—pub·lic·i·ty** (–LIS–) *n.* the state of being known by everyone; hence, public notice and the getting of it; also, articles, announcements, etc. used in the process. **—pub·li·cize** (PUB·luh–) *v.* **-ciz·es, -cized, -ciz·ing** give publicity to.**—public relations** the promotion of a good opinion with the public by means of publicity. **—public school** in the U.S. and Canada, a free school supported by taxes. **—public service** government service. **—pub·lic-spir·it·ed** *adj.* having the good of the public as one's concern. **—public televi-**

sion noncommercial television for public information and instruction. **—public utility** See UTILITY. **—pub·lish** *v.* make known publicly, esp. print and distribute something written or drawn, as books, art, and music, to the public: *a* **pub·lish·a·ble** *book;* **pub·lish·er** *n.*

Puc·ci·ni (poo·CHEE·nee), **Giacomo.** 1858–1924, Italian composer of operas.

puck *n.* **1** the disk used in ice hockey. **2** a mischievous spirit; **puck·ish** *adj.*

puck·a (–uh) *adj.* same as PUKKA.

puck·er *v.* draw into folds or wrinkles; also, become wrinkled: *the ~ed stripes of seersucker; She ~ed up and blew a kiss our way;* also ***n.;*** **puck·er·y** *adj.*

pud·ding (POOD–) *n.* a soft, thick, sweet, cooked dessert, as *rice pudding,* or a baked one, as *plum pudding.*

pud·dle (PUDL) *n.* **1** a small pool of liquid, usu. of muddy water. **2** a pasty mixture of clay and sand for waterproofing; ***v.:*** *to ~ up a hole.* **—pud·dling** *n.* the conversion of pig iron into wrought iron by heating and stirring in a **puddling furnace.**

pu·den·da (pyoo·DEN–) *n. pl.* genital organs of either sex. **—pu·den·dum** *n.* vulva.

pudg·y (PUJ·ee) *adj.* **pudg·i·er, -i·est 1** thickset: *~ fingers.* **2** chubby.

pueb·lo (PWEB–) *n.* **-los 1** an Indian village of S.W. United States, consisting of compactly built, terraced adobe houses; also, one of these houses. **2 Pueblo** an Indian belonging to a tribe inhabiting pueblos.

pu·er·ile (PYOO·uh·rul) *adj.* childish; silly; **pu·er·ile·ly** *adv.* **—pu·er·il·i·ty** (–RIL–) *n.* **-ties:** *name-calling and such ~s.*

pu·er·per·al (pyoo·UR·puh·rul) *adj.* related to childbirth or the period, or **pu·er·pe·ri·um** (–PEER·ee·um), about six weeks, following childbirth.

Puer·to Ri·co (pwer·toh·REE·coh) a self-governing island commonwealth in the Caribbean, associated with the U.S. 3,435 sq. mi. (8,897 km²); *cap.* San Juan. **—Puer·to Ri·can** *n.* & *adj.*

PUFA polyunsaturated fatty acids.

puff *n.* **1** a short, quick blast or draw of air, smoke, or other gas: *~s of steam from an iron; a ~ of breath; punctuated by ~s on his pipe.* **2** a swelling (as if full of air) or something air-filled or fluffy: *hair done in ~s; cream ~s and such ~ pastry; a powder ~* (i.e. pad or ball). **3** overblown praise: *The review was a ~ for the book.* **—*v.*** [corresponding to the *n.* senses] **1:** *smoke ~ing out of a chimney; She ~ed out the candles one by one; He ~s away at his cigar when thinking hard; huffing and ~ing for air.* **2:** *a trumpeter with cheeks ~ed out; a young hero all ~ed up with pride.* **3:** *an ad ~ing a product to the skies;* **puff·er·y** *n.* **—puff·ball** *n.* a mushroom-like, white, round fungus that bursts at the touch releasing a cloud of tiny spores. **—puff·er** *n.* a globe fish that swells up with air and floats with belly upward when disturbed. **—puf·fin** *n.* a black-and-white sea bird with an enormous beak and a puffy body. **—puf·fy** *adj.* **puff·i·er, -i·est** swollen: *a boxer's face ~ with bruises;* **puff·i·ness** *n.*

pug *n.* **1** a small dog with a short turned-up nose and a tail curled up over its back; also, a nose like a pug's. **2** short form of **pu·gil·ist** (PYOO·juh–) *n.* boxer; **pu·gil·is·tic** (–LIS–) *adj.* **—pu·gil·ism** (PYOO–) *n.* boxing.

pug·na·cious (–NAY·shus) *adj.* fond of fighting: *the ~ offspring of a quarrelsome family;* **pug·na·cious·ly** *adv.* **—pug·nac·i·ty** (–NAS–) *n.*

pug-nosed *adj.* having an upturned nose like a pug's.

pu·is·sant (PYOO·i·sunt, PWIS·unt) *adj. Archaic* or *poetic.* powerful; mighty; **pu·is·sant·ly** *adv.* **—pu·is·sance** *n.*

puke *n.* & *v.* **pukes, puked, puk·ing** *Informal.* vomit.

puk·ka or **puck·a** *adj.* first-rate; genuine.

pul (POOL) *n.* **puls** or **pu·li** (–lee) a coin worth 1/100 of an afghani.

pul·chri·tude (PUL·cruh–) *n.* beauty; comeliness; **pul·chri·tu·di·nous** (–TUE–) *adj.*

pule *v.* **pules, puled, pul·ing** cry feebly; whine.

pull *v.* **1** use force to get action in the direction of the force; opposite of PUSH: *Don't ~ that door, push it; She ~ed my hair; a child ~ing at her mother's sleeve; ~ your horse back; Let's ~ this sled uphill; The boat leaks, ~ for the shore.* **2** use or suffer force in various ways: *A dentist ~s* (i.e. extracts) *teeth; She's ~ing* (i.e. plucking) *flowers in the garden; The cat ~ed the paper to shreds; a toy ~ed apart by kids; I ~ed* (i.e. sprained) *a muscle in my leg; He has to ~ on his pipe to think; She stepped on the gas and ~ed ahead of the others; The ball ~ed to the left and missed the pins.* **3** [figurative uses]: *Let's* **pull for** (i.e. support) *the winning team; That was a neat trick he* **pulled off** (i.e. accomplished); *He* **pulls himself together** (i.e. composes himself) *in no time after each defeat; Let's* **pull** (i.e. get) **out** *of here, the house is on fire; Many were taken to hospital, but everyone* **pulled through** *within a week; A car* **pulls up** *at a stoplight;* **pulled up** (i.e. reprimanded) *for being late in school.* **—pull·er** *n.* **—*n.:*** *the ~ of gravity; a hard ~ to the top of the hill; a bell ~* (i.e. a handle to pull the bell by); *a long ~* (i.e. draught) *at the bottle; You need some ~* (i.e. influence) *to get that job.* **—pull date** the date stamped on perishable goods after which they are not to be sold.

pul·let (POOL·it) *n.* a young hen.

pul·ley (POOL·ee) *n.* **pul·leys** a wheel with a grooved rim for driving a belt that transmits power or for running a rope for raising weights.

Pull·man (POOL·mun) *n.* **-mans** a railroad parlor car; also Pullman car.

pull·out *n.* a withdrawal, as of troops; also, something to be pulled out, as a magazine insert. —**pull·o·ver** (–OH–) *n.* & *adj.* (a sweater or shirt) that is put on by being pulled over the head.

pul·mo·nar·y (PUL·muh·ner·ee) *adj.* of the lungs. —**pul·mo·tor** (POOL–) *n.* an early type of resuscitator; **Pulmotor** *Trademark.*

pulp *n.* **1** a soft moist mass, as the juicy part of a fruit, the soft tissue inside a tooth, the ground mixture of **pulp·wood,** rag, etc. from which paper is made, etc. **2** a cheap or sensationalistic magazine, printed on inferior paper made from wood pulp. —**pulp·y** *adj.* **pulp·i·er, -i·est.**

pul·pit (POOL–) *n.* an enclosed raised structure set up in church for preaching from; hence, the clergy.

pulpwood, pulpy See PULP.

pul·sar (PUL·sahr) *n.* a type of celestial objects known by the pulsations of radio, light, and X-ray waves received from them. —**pul·sate** *v.* **-sates, -sat·ed, -sat·ing** beat or throb with a regular rhythm, as the heart or pulse does; **pul·sa·tion** (–SAY–) *n.* —**pulse** *n.* a regular beat, as of the heart pumping blood which is felt in the arteries, esp. at the wrist; hence, an indication of life or feeling: *a Gallup poll reflecting the ~ of the nation;* ***v.*** **puls·es, pulsed, puls·ing:** *traffic ~ing through a city during rush hour.*

pul·ver·ize *v.* **-iz·es, -ized, -iz·ing** reduce to or become powder. —**pul·ver·i·za·tion** (–ZAY–) *n.*

pu·ma (PYOO·muh) *n.* a cougar.

pum·ice (PUM·is) *n.* a lightweight, porous, volcanic rock used as a scouring and polishing powder.

pum·mel (PUM·ul) *v.* **pum·mels, pum·mel(l)ed, pum·mel·(l)ing** pound (on) repeatedly, esp. with the fists.

pump *n.* **1** a machine for forcing fluids in or out of places, esp. by up-and-down action, as of a lever: *a ~-action rifle.* **2** a low-cut slip-on shoe for formal evening wear.—***v.:*** *The flooded basement had to be ~ed out; to ~ up a bicycle tire; a teacher ~ing knowledge into pupils; Hard as the reporters ~ed she would only say "No comment"; a politician kissing babies and ~ing* (i.e. shaking) *hands; Lasers are ~ed* (i.e. excited for energy radiation) *by light, radio waves, electricity, etc.*

pump·er·nick·el *n.* a kind of heavy, dark bread usu. made from whole-meal rye.

pump·kin (PUM·kin) *n.* a large, round, orange-yellow, edible gourdlike fruit, typical of the farm; **pumpkin head** *Slang.* a dolt.

pump-prim·ing *n.* government expenditure on public works, relief, etc. in order to stimulate business and employment during a recession.

pun *n.* & *v.* **puns, pun·ned, pun·ning** play on words, e.g. *"Mr. Dole" is doleful news";* **pun·ner** or **pun·ster** *n.*

punch *v.* **1** strike with the fist: *a boxer practicing on a suspended* **punching bag. 2** cut, stamp, etc. with a quick thrust: *A ticket is inspected and ~ed; workers* **punch in** *and* **punch out** *of a factory by thrusting a timecard into a time clock; coded data is ~ed on a* **punch card** *in a key punch machine.* —**punch·er** *n.* —***n.*** **1** a blow or a thrust of the fist: *a boxer's "one-two punch";* **pull (one's) punches** *Informal.* be ineffective on purpose. **2** a punching device: *a three-hole paper ~.* **3** *Informal.* vigor; force: *a pep talk full of ~; the* **punch line** *of a joke designed to get a laugh.* **4** a sweetened drink mixed in a large **punch bowl** from juices, wines, liquors, etc. and ladled out, as at a party. —**punch-drunk** *adj.* dazed by blows.

pun·cheon (PUNCH·un) *n.* a large cask to hold up to 120 gallons of liquor; also, a liquid measure of 70 gallons.

punching bag See PUNCH, *v.* 1. —**punch line** See PUNCH, *n.* 3. —**punch press** a machine that cuts, shapes, or stamps metal. —**punch-up** *n.* *Brit. Informal.* a brawl. —**punch·y** *adj.* **punch·i·er, -i·est** having vigor or force.

punc·til·i·o (punc·TIL·ee·oh) *n.* **-os** a fine point of conduct or ceremony; hence, formality; **punc·til·i·ous** (–us) *adj.: a diplomat's ~ attention to protocol.* —**punc·tu·al** (PUNK·choo·ul) *adj.* on time, esp. habitually; **punc·tu·al·ly** *adv.;* **punc·tu·al·i·ty** (–choo·AL–) *n.* —**punc·tu·ate** (PUNK·choo–) *v.* **-ates, -at·ed, -at·ing** show pauses, emphases, etc., esp. in written language, using **marks of punc·tu·a·tion** (–AY–), as the comma, question mark, exclamation point, etc.: *a speech ~d* (i.e. interrupted) *by frequent cheers.* —**punc·ture** (PUNK·chur) *n.* & *v.* **-tures, -tured, -tur·ing** (make) a tiny hole, esp. with or as if with a point: *~d pride.*

pun·dit *n.* a learned person; also, a supposed authority: *the weather ~s of Channel 6.*

pun·gent (–junt) *adj.* sharp to the taste and smell; hence, keen; biting: *Horse radish is ~; ~ satire;* **pun·gent·ly** *adv.* —**pun·gen·cy** *n.*

Pu·nic (PYOO–) *adj.* of ancient Carthage: *"~ faith" was treachery to Romans;* ***n.*** a Phoenician dialect.

pun·ish *v.* cause suffering or discomfort, usu. for some offense; penalize: *An offender is ~ed; Thievery used to be ~ed by hanging; The boxer continued to ~* (i.e. hurt) *his fallen opponent;* **pun·ish·a·ble** *adj.: a ~ offense.* —**pun·ish·ment** *n.* **1:** *"The ~ should fit the crime."* **2** *Informal.* rough use: *A taxicab gets a lot of ~.* —**pu·ni·tive** (PYOO·nit·iv) *adj.* related to punishment: *~ laws; ~ damages awarded against a willful wrongdoer;* **pu·ni·tive·ly** *adv.*

punk *n.* **1** a slow-burning, spongy preparation of dried fungi or decayed wood used as tinder; **punk·y** *adj.* smoldering. **2** *Slang.* a hoodlum; also, an inexperienced youngster, as a child hobo. —***adj.*** of poor quality: *the ~est grub I ever had.* —**punk rock** rock'n'roll of the late 1970's characterized by rowdy costumes, language, and performing style.

pun·ster *n.* one fond of making puns.

punt *n.* **1** a flat-bottomed boat propelled with a long pole; ***v.*** travel by, convey by, or propel a punt. **2** kick given to a football dropped from one's hands and before it touches the ground; also ***v.***

pu·ny (PYOO·nee) *adj.* **-ni·er, -ni·est** inferior in size, strength, or importance; petty. —**pu·ni·ness** *n.*

pup *n.* a young dog, fox, wolf, etc.; also, a young seal, whale, or shark. —***v.*** **pups, pupped, pup·ping** bring forth pups.

pu·pa (PYOO·puh) *n., pl.* **-pae** (–pee) or **-pas** an insect in its middle stage of development, between larva and adult, when it is encased in a cocoon; **pu·pal** (–pul) *adj.* —**pu·pil** (PYOO·pl) *n.* **1** a young student, esp. one under a teacher's personal supervision; hence, follower. **2** the black, circular portion inside the iris of the eye. —**pu·pil·lar·y** *adj.* of a pupil. —**pup·pet** (PUP·it) *n.* a doll-like hand-controlled figure of a person or animal used in a puppet show; **pup·pet·eer** (–TEER) *n.;* **pup·pet·ry** *n.*

pup·py *n.* **pup·pies** same as PUP. —**puppy love** juvenile love for one of the opposite sex. —**pup tent** a small, wedge-shaped shelter tent for one or two persons.

pur·blind (PUR·blined) *adj.* partly blind; dim-sighted; hence, obtuse.

pur·chase (PUR·chus) *v.* **-chas·es, -chased, -chas·ing** *Formal.* buy: *The* **purchasing power** *of the dollar goes down with rising prices;* **pur·chas·a·ble** *adj.;* **pur·chas·er** *n.* —***n.*** **1** a purchasing or thing purchased: *the "Louisiana Purchase"* (of territory from France in 1803). **2** a secure hold; also, advantage; leverage.

pur·dah (–duh) *n.* the seclusion of women from public view; also, a veil or curtain used for this, as in India.

pure (PYOOR) *adj.* **1 pur·er, pur·est** free from taint, defects, errors, etc.; unmixed: *~ as snow; "the ~ in heart"; ~ English; a ~ breed;* hence **pure·bred** *n.* & *adj.;* also, usu. of races, **pure·blood** *n.* & *adj.;* **pure-blood·ed** *adj.* **2** sheer; absolute: *by ~ accident; That's ~ nonsense; nonsense* **pure and simple. 3** abstract; theoretical: *~ mathematics.* —**pure·ly** *adv.;* **pure·ness** *n.* —**pu·rée** (pyoo·RAY) *n.* a cooked vegetable that has been rubbed through a sieve and made into a paste or suspension; also, a puréed vegetable soup; also ***v.*** **pu·rées, pu·réed, pu·rée·ing.**

pur·ga·tion (–GAY–) *n.* the act of purging: *the ~ of the soul;* **pur·ga·tive** (PUR·guh·tiv) *n.* a purging agent, as a cathartic; ***adj.:*** *the ~ effect of calomel.* —**pur·ga·to·ry** (PUR·guh–) *n.* **-ries** in Roman Catholic theology, a state of temporary punishment that purifies souls for entry into heaven; **pur·ga·tor·i·al** (–TOR–) *adj.* —**purge** (PURJ) *v.* **purg·es, purged, purg·ing** clear or cleanse by getting rid of something undesired: *souls ~d of sin; a drug that ~s the bowels; to ~ away dross from metal; a political party ~d of undesirable members;* ***n.*** a purging or something that purges. —**pu·ri·fy** (PYOOR·uh·fye) *v.* **-fies, -fied, -fy·ing** make or become pure; **pu·ri·fi·ca·tion** (–CAY–) *n.* —**pu·ri·fi·er** *n.* —**pu·rif·i·ca·to·ry** (–RIF·i·kuh–) *adj.*

Pu·rim (POOR·im) *n.* a Jewish holiday commemorating Esther's deliverance of the Jews from a massacre plotted by Haman.

pu·rine (PYOOR·een) *n.* a colorless crystalline substance that is the parent of compounds of the uric-acid group; also, a derivative of it, as caffeine, adenine, and guanine.

pur·ism (PYOOR–) *n.* the too strict adherence to what is traditionally correct in language matters without regard for the changing nature of vocabulary, usage, etc.; also, an instance of this, as saying "It is I" instead of "It's me" or (core·RECT) for (cuh·RECT); **pur·ist** *n.;* **pu·ris·tic** (–RIS–) *adj.* —**pu·ri·tan** (PYOOR·i·tun) *n.* one who is very strict in matters of religion and morals, as the **Puritan** group of the Church of England in the 16th and 17th centuries; **pu·ri·tan·ism** or **Pu·ri·tan·ism** *n.* —**pu·ri·tan·i·cal** (–TAN–) *adj.* —**pu·ri·ty** (PYOOR–) *n.* the quality or state of being pure; pureness; freedom from dirt, evil, or foreign elements.

purl *v.* **1** knit with inverted stitches so as to produce a ribbed appearance. **2** of a stream, flow with a murmuring sound. Also ***n.***

pur·lieu (PUR·lew) *n.* a bordering or outlying region; **purlieus** *pl.* environs.

pur·loin (–LOIN) *v. Formal.* steal: *a publisher of ~ed manuscripts.*

pur·ple *n.* crimson color, indicative of high rank: *"clothed in ~ and fine linen"; a bishop raised* **to the purple** (i.e. cardinalate). —***adj.*** **1** bluish red. **2** ornate or gaudy in style: *He writes a dull prose except for the occasional* **purple patch** (or **passage**). **3** *Slang.* off-color: *a ~ joke.* —**pur·plish** *adj.* —**Purple Heart** a U.S. decoration for soldiers wounded in battle.

pur·port *v.* (pur·PORT) intend or mean supposedly: *an offer ~ed to be generous.* —***n.*** (PUR·port) general meaning or intent; gist: *the ~ of the message.* —**pur·port·ed·ly** *adv.*

pur·pose (–pus) *n.* intention, esp. with determination: *the ~ of our visit; ignored the letter* **on purpose** (i.e. deliberately) *to snub him; remarks quite* **to the purpose** (i.e. pertinent). —***v.*** **-pos·es, -posed, -pos·ing:** *She ~d* (i.e. intended) *to stay awake but fell asleep.* —**pur·pose·ful** *adj.;* **pur·pose·ful·ly** *adv.: Having mouths to feed helps one work more ~.* —**pur·pose·less** *adj.* —**pur·pose·ly** *adv.* on purpose.

purr *n.* & *v.* **purrs, purred, purr·ing** (make) the low, murmuring sound of a cat at ease or satisfied.

purse *n.* a small bag, originally one with drawstrings; a woman's handbag; also, means;

amount of money: *Beware of ~-snatchers in a crowd; a* **purse-proud** *man* (i.e. proud of his money) *with no education to boast of; a prize fight with a $1 million ~* (i.e. stake); *The accountant retired with a poor pension but a well-lined ~; presented with a gold watch and a ~* (i.e. gift of money); *the girl who controls his* **purse strings.** —***v.*** **purs·es, pursed, purs·ing** pucker: *She ~d her lips in disapproval.* —**purs·er** *n.* an official in charge of money matters on a ship or cabin service on an airliner.

purs·lane (–lin, –lane) *n.* an annual trailing weed, sometimes used in salads.

pur·su·ance (pur·SUE·unce) *n.* a carrying out: *a letter sent* **in pursuance of** *the client's wishes;* **pur·su·ant** *adj.: goods shipped* **pursuant to** (i.e. according to) *a customer's instructions.* —**pur·sue** (–SUE) *v.* **-sues, -sued, -su·ing** **1** follow (someone) in order to catch up: *police ~ing a getaway car; was ~d by reporters whenever she got out of her car.* **2** have as aim, esp. to accomplish (something): *She ~s her studies; She'll ~ a career in politics.* —**pur·su·er** *n.* —**pur·suit** (–SUTE) *n.: man's ~ of happiness; His many pursuits* (i.e. occupations) *include fishing.*

pu·ru·lent (PURE·uh·lunt, –yuh·lunt) *adj.* containing or forming pus. —**pu·ru·lence** *n.*

pur·vey (–VAY) *v.* supply (food); **pur·vey·ance** *n.;* **pur·vey·or** *n.* supplier: *pimps and other ~s of vice.*

pur·view *n.* range or scope of authority or perception.

pus *n.* a thick, yellow discharge from an infected body part. —**pus·sy** *adj.* **pus·si·er, pus·si·est** like or containing pus.

push (POOSH) *v.* **1** press against (a person or thing) so as to move forward: *Pull that door shut but ~ it open; Everyone hates being* **pushed around** (i.e. harassed). **2** *Informal.* promote; also, sell, esp. illegally: *Get the mayor to ~ the lottery; a* **(drug) pusher** *peddling amphetamines.* —***n.:*** *a self-starter who never needs a ~; a good salesman with a lot of ~* (i.e. drive) *but not pushy.* —**push button:** *an elevator operated by ~s; robot-controlled* **push-but·ton** *warfare.* —**push·cart** *n.* a cart that is pushed, as for supermarket shopping.

Push·kin, Alexander. 1799–1837, Russian poet and novelist.

push·o·ver *n. Slang.* one easy to impose upon; also, an easy job.

Push·tu (PUHSH·too) same as PASHTO.

push-up *n.* an exercise done by raising and lowering the body held stiffly extended in a prone position. —**push·y** *adj.* **push·i·er, -i·est** *Informal.* unpleasantly aggressive; **push·i·ly** *adv.;* **push·i·ness** *n.*

pu·sil·lan·i·mous (pew·si·LAN·i·mus) *adj.* faint-hearted; timid. —**pu·sil·la·nim·i·ty** (–NIM–) *n.*

puss (POOS) *n.* a cat; also **[1]puss·y, puss·ies.** —**[2]pus·sy** *adj.* See PUS. —**puss·y·cat** *n.* an agreeable or quiet-going person. —**puss·y·foot** *v. Informal.* be overly cautious and noncommittal. —**puss·y·wil·low** *n.* a small tree with fur-covered grayish-white catkins.

pus·tule (–chool) *n.* a pus-filled pimple.

put (POOT) *v.* **puts, put, put·ting** **1** place, esp. move something onto a position: *Food is ~ on the table.* **2** make (someone or something) be in a certain way; set: *Children are ~ to bed; an idea difficult to ~ into words.* **3** throw: *~ing the shot.* —***n.*** a throw: *shot ~.* —***adj.*** *Informal.* in place: *Stay ~ till I return.* —**put across** convey (an idea) successfully. —**put down** **1** crush: *~ down a revolt.* **2** write down. **3** *Informal.* snub; belittle; **put-down** *n.* an act or statement that belittles, criticizes, etc. —**put in** *Informal.* **1** contribute: *She ~s in a lot of work on holidays.* **2** apply: *He ~ in for a loan.* —**put off** postpone: *Do not ~ it off till tomorrow.* —**put on** **1** apply: *The work is ~ing too much strain on my nerves.* **2** *Informal.* tease: *You're ~ing me on!* **put-on** *n.* a pretense; hoax. —**put out** dismiss; in baseball, retire (a batter or runner); **put-out** *n.* —**put up:** *a house ~ up for sale; He ~ up a good fight; She'll ~ you up for the night; Who ~ him up to this? an unsociable character difficult to ~ up with.* —**put upon** impose upon.

pu·ta·tive (PYOO·tuh·tiv) *adj.* supposed: *an illegitimate child's ~ father.*

put-down, put-on, put-out See PUT.

pu·tre·fy (PYOO·truh·fye) *v.* **-fies, -fied, -fy·ing** be or make putrid; **pu·tre·fac·tion** (–FAC–) *n.;* **pu·tre·fac·tive** (–tiv) *adj.* —**pu·tres·cent** (–TRES–) *adj.;* —**pu·tres·cence** *n.* —**pu·trid** (PYOO–) *adj.* rotting; decayed; hence, corrupt; foul: *the ~ smell of ~ meat; the ~ air of a porno shop;* **pu·trid·ness** or **pu·trid·i·ty** (–TRID–) *n.*

putsch (POOCH) *n.* a secretly plotted attempt to overthrow a government.

putt *v.* strike (a golf ball) across the putting green to try to drop it into the hole. —**putt·er** *n.* one who putts or a club used in putting.

put·tee (puh·TEE, PUTT·ee) *n.* a gaiter or a strip of cloth wound round the calf like a gaiter.

put·ter or **pot·ter** *v.* busy oneself aimlessly *(over, along,* or *around)* something; also, fritter *(away).* —**put·ter·er** or **pot·ter·er** *n.*

put·ty *n.* **put·ties** a doughlike cement used in fixing window panes, to fill holes in wood, etc. —***v.*** **put·ties, put·tied, put·ty·ing.**

puz·zle *v.* **puz·zles, puz·zled, puz·zling** bewilder: *a stranger ~d by local customs; good at* **puzzling out** (i.e. solving) *conundrums; She* **puzzled over** (i.e. tried to think of) *a solution all night.* —***n.*** a problem or task that puzzles or is designed to puzzle: *in a ~ at a crossroads; a jigsaw ~.* —**puz·zle·ment** *n.* the state of being puzzled or a puzzle. —**puz·zler** *n.*

PV polyvinyl; **PVC** polyvinyl chloride.

pvt. or **Pvt.** private.

PW Prisoner of War.
P.W.D. Public Works Department.
pwt. pennyweight.
PX post exchange.
pya (pee·AH) *n.* a Burmese coin worth 1/100 of a kyat.
Pyg·ma·li·on (pig·MAY·lee·un) *n.* in Greek myth, a sculptor who fell in love with a statue he had made.
pyg·my (PIG·mee) *n.* **-mies** a person or thing of small stature like a **Pyg·my,** one of a Negroid people of Africa of short stature. ***—adj.*** dwarfish: *A* **pygmy antelope** *stands 10 in.* (25.4 cm) *tall.*
py·ja·mas (puh·JAM·uz) *n.pl. Brit.* pajamas.
py·lon (PY·lon, –lun) *n.* **1** a gateway of an ancient Egyptian temple, esp. one consisting of two pyramidal towers. **2** a framework of steel used to support overhead cables; also, a post, tower, or conical marker for guiding air or road traffic. **—py·lo·rus** (pye·LOR–) *n., pl.* **-ri** (–rye) the passageway from the stomach into the intestine, controlled by a ring of muscular fibers called the **py·lor·ic sphincter.**
Pyong·yang (PYUNG–) capital of North Korea.
py·or·rhe·a (pye·uh·REE·uh) *n.* a pus-forming disease affecting the roots of the teeth.
pyr·a·mid (PEER·uh–) *n.* **1** any of the huge structures with a square base and triangular sides meeting at the top, built in ancient Egypt for royal tombs; also, any solid figure with a polygonal base and sloping sides that meet at the top. **2** any structure or scheme resembling a pyramid, sometimes inverted. ***—adj.*** **pyr·a·mid** or **py·ram·i·dal** (–RAM–): *a pyramid-fire cooking arrangement at a camp; a pyramidal army tent; a pyramid scheme for raising money* (as by chain letter) *or selling goods.* **—*v.:*** *a financial empire built by ~ing of subsidiaries within a holding company; profits ~ed by speculative buying or selling of stock.*
pyre *n.* a woodpile for burning a dead body.
Pyr·e·nees (PEER·uh·neez) *n.pl.* the mountain range separating France and Spain.
py·re·thrum (pye·REE–) *n.* a group of plants related to chrysanthemums, one of which is used in an insecticide and another as a fever medicine. **—Py·rex** (PYE–) *Trademark.* glassware made to resist heat and chemicals. **—py·rex·i·a** (pye·REX·ee·uh) *n. Med.* fever. **—pyr·i·dine** (PEER·i·deen) *n.* a pungent-smelling liquid base distilled from coal tar; **py·rim·i·dine** (–RIM–) *n.* an organic base or a derivative of it that is a constituent of DNA or RNA. **—py·ri·tes** (puh·RYE·teez) *n.pl.* a sulfur-bearing mineral, esp. the gold-colored iron sulphide, or **py·rite** (PYE–) *n.;* **py·rit·ic** (–RIT–) *adj.* **—pyr(o)-** *comb.form.* fire; heat. **—py·rol·y·sis** (–ROL–) *n.* chemical decomposition by the action of heat. **—py·ro·ma·ni·a** (–MAY·nee·uh) *n.* a compulsive urge to set fire to things; **py·ro·ma·ni·ac** *n.* & *adj.* **—py·rom·e·ter** (–ROM–) *n.* an instrument for measuring the unusually high temperatures of glass, pottery, and metal work. **—py·ro·tech·nics** (–TEK–) *n.pl.* fireworks; also, any brilliant display, as of rhetoric or emotion; **py·ro·tech·nic** or **-ni·cal** *adj.*
Pyr·ric (PEER·ic) *adj.* of a victory, won at heavy cost, esp. of lives.
Py·thag·o·ras (pi·THAG·u·rus) Greek philosopher-mathematician of the 6th c. B.C. **—Py·thag·o·re·an** (–REE·un) *n.* & *adj.*
py·thon (PY·thon, –thun) *n.* a large, nonvenomous snake such as the anaconda or the boa constrictor that crushes its prey within its coils.
pyx (PIX) *n.* a small container for holding a Eucharistic wafer.

Q

Q or **q** (CUE) *n.* **Q's** or **q's** the 17th letter of the English alphabet. —**q.** quart(s); queen; query; question; quire.

Qa·tar (KAH·tar) an emirate on the Persian Gulf; 4,400 sq.mi. (11,400 km^2); *cap.* Doha.

Q.C. Queen's Counsel; **QC** quickchange (aircraft).

Q.E.D. which was to be demonstrated or proved; "quod erat demonstrandum."

q.i.d. four times daily.

qin·tar (kin·TAR) *n.* an Albanian monetary unit equal to 1/100 of a lek.

qi·vi·ut (KEE·vee·oot) *n.* the soft undercoat of the musk ox.

Q.M. Quartermaster; **QMG** Quartermaster General.

qq.v. which things see.

qr. quarter; quire.

QSO quasi-stellar object.

Q-switch *n.* a device for getting a short-duration, high-energy pulse from a crystal laser.

qt. quart, quantity.

q.t. or **Q.T.** *Slang.* usu. **on the q.t.** quietly; in confidence.

qto. quarto.

qty. quantity.

qua (KWAH, KWAY) *adv.* as; in the capacity of: *Men ~ men have certain rights.*

[1]**quack** (KWAK) *n.* a duck's cry; also ***v.***

[2]**quack** (KWAK) *n.* one who pretends to have medical skills; hence, any charlatan; also **quack·sal·ver.** —**quack·er·y** *n.* **-er·ies:** *arthritic victims of ~s.*

quad (KWOD) *n.* short for QUADRANGLE or QUADRUPLET. —**quadr(i)-** *comb.form.* four: as in **quad·ran·gle** (KWOD·rang·gl) *n.* a flat figure with four sides and four angles; also, such a four-sided area surrounded by buildings; **quad·ran·gu·lar** (kwod·RANG·gyuh·lur) *adj.* —**quad·rant** (KWOD·runt) *n.* **1** one quarter of a circle or its circumference; a 90° arc. **2** an instrument for measuring angles to determine altitudes. —**quad·ra·phon·ic** (kwod·ruh·FON·ic) *adj.* relating to sound reproduction that uses four separate channels; cf. STEREOPHONIC. —**quad·rat·ic** (kwod·RAT–) *adj.* in algebra, relating to the square of a number: $ax^2 + bx + c = 0$ *is a* **quadratic equation.** —**quad·ren·ni·al** (kwod·REN·ee·ul) *adj.* happening once every four years; also, lasting four years; **quad·ren·ni·um** (–ee·um) *n.* **-ums** or **-ren·ni·a** a period of four years. —**quad·ri·lat·er·al** (kwod·ruh·LAT·uh·rul) *adj.* having four sides; ***n.*** a four-sided figure; quadrangle. —**qua·drille** (kwuh·DRIL) *n.* a French square dance of the 1800's. —**quad·ril·lion** (kwod·RIL·yun) *n.* in the U.S. and Canada, a billion millions or 1 followed by 15 zeros; in the U.K., 1 followed by 24 zeros. —**quad·ri·par·tite** (–PAR–) *adj.* having four parts; also, involving four persons or groups: *a ~ decision.* —**quad·ri·ple·gi·a** (–PLEE·jee·uh) *n.* paralysis from the neck down, affecting all four limbs; **quad·ri·ple·gic** (–PLEE·jic, –PLEJ·ic) *adj.* & *n.* —**quad·ri·vi·um** (–RIV·ee·um) *n., pl.* **-vi·a** in the Middle Ages, the higher four of the seven liberal arts, i.e. music, geometry, astronomy, and arithmetic; cf. TRIVIUM. **quad·ri·vi·al** *adj.* —**quad·roon** (kwod·ROON) *n.* a person with one-quarter Negro ancestry; child of a mulatto and a white. —**quad·ru·ped** (KWOD·ruh·ped) *n.* & *adj.* four-footed (animal). —**quad·ru·ple** (QWOD–, qwod·ROO–) *v.* **-ples, -pled, -pling** multiply by four; ***adj.*** multiplied by four; also, containing four parts: *a ~ alliance.* —**quad·ru·plet** (KWOD·ruh·plit) *n.* **1** one of four born at a single birth. **2** any group of four: *a ~ of musical notes.* —**quad·ru·pli·cate** *adj.* (kwod·ROO·plik·it) **1** multiplied by four. **2** fourth in a group; ***n.*** any one of the four in a group: *Prepare the contract* **in quadruplicate** (i.e. in four copies); ***v.*** (–cate) **-cates, -cat·ed, -cat·ing** provide four of something; **quad·ru·pli·ca·tion** (–CAY–) *n.*

quaff *v.* drink with zest. —***n.:*** *a hearty ~ of ale.*

quag·mire (KWAG–) *n.* damp ground that yields underfoot; bog.

qua·hog (KWOH–, KWAW–) *n.* a hard-shelled, edible clam of the eastern coast of North America; also **qua·haug.**

[1]**quail** *n.* any of several game birds of the grouse and pheasant families, esp. the bobwhite.

[2]**quail** *v.* lose courage, shrink back in fear: *The lion ~ed under his trainer's whip.*

quaint *adj.* old-fashioned or odd in an interesting or unusual way: *~ manners; a ~ refrain.* **—quaint·ly** *adv.;* **quaint·ness** *n.*

quake *v.* **quakes, quaked, quak·ing** shake violently, usu. from fear or shock: *His heart ~d with fright; the ~ing aspen.* **—*n.*** a shaking or shivering, esp. an earthquake. **—Quak·er** *n.* [not used by members] a member of the religious group called the Society of Friends. **—quak·y** *adj.* **quak·i·er, -i·est.**

qual·i·fy (KWOL·uh·fye) *v.* **-fies, -fied, -fy·ing** **1** make suitable or competent for an occupation, calling, task, etc.: *a well-~d applicant; Our team did not ~ for the finals.* **2** limit or modify; also, moderate; soften: *Adjectives ~ nouns; to ~ a scolding with a smile.* **—qual·i·fi·ca·tion** (–CAY–) *n.: a principal with impressive ~s; an answer accepted without ~.* **—qual·i·fi·er** *n.*

qual·i·ta·tive (KWOL·i·tay·tiv) *adj.* having to do with quality; **qual·i·ta·tive·ly** *adv.* **—qual·i·ty** (KWOL·i·tee) *n.* **-ties** **1** essential nature; characteristic. **2** worth; excellence; high rank: *the fine ~ of his singing; fabric of poor ~; a woman of ~; the ~ of life in North America;* ***adj.:*** *~ ice cream; a ~ newspaper* (i.e. not for the masses).

qualm (KWAHM) *n.* **1** a temporary feeling of sickness or faintness. **2** a feeling of doubt or uneasiness about the rightness of an action: *no ~s about letting her walk home alone.* **—qualm·ish** *adj.: felt ~ as she was about to parachute.* **—qualm·ish·ly** *adv.;* **qualm·ish·ness** *n.*

quan·da·ry (KWON·duh·ree) *n.* **-ries** a state of uncertainty and hesitation: *The unexpected development placed her in a ~.*

quan·ta·some (KWON·tuh·sohm) *n.* a chlorophyll-containing granule inside plant chloroplasts.

quan·ti·fy (KWON·tuh·fye) *v.* **-fies, -fied, -fy·ing** determine or indicate the quantity of. **—quan·ti·ta·tive** (KWON·tuh·tay·tiv) *adj.* having to do with quantity; **quan·ti·ta·tive·ly** *adv.* **—quan·ti·ty** (KWON–) *n.* **-ties** amount; number: *a small ~ of sugar; Stores buy goods* **in quantity** (i.e. in bulk or in large amounts); *Our new teammate is an* **unknown quantity** (i.e. one not yet tried out). **—quan·tize** *v.* **-tiz·es, -tized, -tiz·ing** express or measure (energy) in quanta. **—quan·tum** *n., pl.* **-ta** a specific quantity; esp. in the **quantum theory,** one of the quanta or basic amounts in which energy is given out or absorbed by a substance, not in continuous waves; cf. PHOTON: *Within an atom, electrons make* **quantum jumps** (or **leaps**) *as they change orbits absorbing or giving off energy; The discovery of the wheel was a ~ leap in human progress;* **quantum mechanics** *deals with atomic structures and phenomena in terms of measurable quanta.*

quar·an·tine (KWOR·un·teen) *n.* the detaining of ships, people, animals, etc. in isolation to prevent disease from spreading; also, the place or time in which they are so held. **—*v.* -tines, -tined, -tin·ing:** *a ship ~d for 40 days at a port of entry.*

quark *n.* a hypothetical subatomic particle carrying a fractional electric charge and being the supposed basic constituent of known particles such as protons and neutrons.

quar·rel (KWOR·ul) *n.* an argument or disagreement; also, its cause: *a family ~.* **—*v.* quar·rels, quar·rel(l)ed, quar·rel·(l)ing:** *I must ~ with your decision.* **—quar·rel·some** (–sum) *adj.: a ~ mood.* **—quar·rel·(l)er** *n.*

quar·ry (KWOR·ee) *n.* **quar·ries** **1** an object of pursuit, esp. a hunted animal. **2** a place where rock or limestone is dug from the earth; ***v.* quar·ries, quar·ried, quar·ry·ing.**

quart (KWORT) *n.* one fourth of a gallon; two pints; also, a dry measure equaling 1/8 peck. **—quar·tan** (–tn) *n.* & *adj.* (a fever, esp. malarial) occurring every fourth day counting inclusively. **—quar·ter** *n.* **1** a fourth part, as of an hour (15 minutes), a year (3 months), a dollar (25 cents or the coin), an animal's carcass (one leg and adjacent parts), etc. **2** a region or place; hence, a special district: *the Latin ~ of Paris.* **3** esp. **quarters** *pl.* living space, hence, mercy; compassion: *military ~s; married ~s; Give no ~* (i.e. grant no mercy) *to the enemy; He used his knife when fighting* **at close quarters** (i.e. close together). **—*v.* 1:** *to ~ an apple.* **2** provide with shelter: *~ horses in the stable; soldiers ~ed in barracks.* **—quar·ter·back** *n.* the football player who calls the signals and directs the team's play; ***v.:*** *to ~ the college team.* **—quarter day** the day that begins each quarter of the year and on which rents and other payments fall due. **—quar·ter·deck** *n.* part of a ship's upper deck near the stern. **—quar·ter·fi·nal** *n.* one of a round of matches before the semifinals in a tournament. **—quarter horse** a strong muscular horse originally bred in the U.S. for short races and later used as a range and rodeo horse. **—quar·ter·ly** *n.* **-lies** a publication issued every three months; ***adv.* & *adj.:*** *a report issued ~; a ~ journal.* **—quar·ter·mas·ter** *n.* **1** an army officer who supplies food, clothing, etc. to soldiers. **2** a naval petty officer who looks after a ship's steering, signals, etc. **—quarter note** a musical note held one fourth the time of a whole note. **—quar·ter·staff** *n., pl.* **-staves** a large wooden staff formerly used as a weapon. —**quar·tet(te)** (kwor·TET) *n.* piece of music for four instruments or people; also, the group performing this; hence, any group of four. —**quar·to** (KWOR·toh) *n.* **-tos** the page size, usu. 9 × 12 in. (22.86 × 30.48 cm) resulting from folding one sheet into four leaves; also, a book printed on such pages.

quartz (KWORTS) *n.* a hard mineral, silicon dioxide, which is found in rocks such as sandstone and **quartz·ite** and in crystalline form as in amethyst: *the* **quartz crystal** *of a radio transmitter or electric clock that vibrates with a natural frequency.*

qua·sar (KWAY·sar, –zar) *n.* same as QUASI-STELLAR RADIO SOURCE.

quash *v.* **1** crush; suppress: *~ a rebellion.* **2** to void legally: *a decision ~ed by a higher court.*

qua·si (KWAY·sye, –zye; KWAH·see, –zee) *adj.* & *comb.form.* resembling but not quite; similar: *a ~-humorous situation; to act in a ~-judicial capacity; a ~ contract.* —**qua·si-stel·lar radio source** (or **object**) any of a group of very distant, starlike objects that emit brilliant light and often powerful radio waves.

quas·sia (KWOSH·uh) *n.* a drug made from the wood of a tropical American tree.

Qua·ter·nar·y (kwuh·TUR·nuh·ree) *n.* the second of the two periods of the Cenozoic era; ***adj.:*** *Man developed in the ~ period.* —**quat·rain** (KWAH·train) *n.* a stanza of four lines. —**quat·re·foil** (CAT·ur·foil) *n.* a leaf or flower with four parts or petals; also, a four-lobed architectural ornament.

qua·ver (KWAY–) *v.* tremble; quiver: *His voice ~ed with fright;* also ***n.***

quay (KEE) *n.* wharf.

quean (KWEEN) *n.* a woman of poor reputation.

quea·sy (KWEE·zee) *adj.* **-si·er, -si·est** nauseated; uneasy; troublesome: *a ~ stomach; a ~ problem.* —**quea·si·ly** *adv.* —**quea·si·ness** *n.*

Que. *Abbrev.* for **Que·bec** (kwi·BEC) province of E. Canada; 594,860 sq.mi. (1,540,680 km^2); *cap.* **Quebec (City).** —**Que·bec(k)·er** or **Que·be·cois** (cay·buh·KWAH) *n.*

que·bra·cho (cay·BRAH·choh) *n.* **-chos** a South American tree of the cashew family whose hard wood is used in tanning and dyeing.

Quech·ua (KECH·wah) *n.* a South American Indian language spoken in the Andes region from Colombia to Chile and Argentina; also, an Andean Indian of the Inca empire.

queen *n.* **1** a female sovereign; also, the wife or widow of a king. **2** a woman noted for beauty, power, etc.: *a movie ~;* ***v.:*** *The actress likes to* **queen it** *over* (i.e. act like a queen toward) *her admirers.* **3** a mature egg-laying ant, bee, etc. of a colony. —**queen·ly** *adj.* **-li·er, -li·est** —**queen·li·ness** *n.* —**Queen Anne's lace** a variety of wild carrot with lacy clusters of small white flowers. —**queen consort** wife of a reigning king. —**queen mother** mother of a reigning monarch. —**queen-size** *adj.* of a bed, approx. 60 × 80 in. (1.524 × 2.032 m) —**Queens** a borough of New York City. —**Queens·land** (KWEENZ·land, –lund) a state of N.E. Australia; *cap.* Brisbane.

queer *adj.* unusual; strange, esp. abnormal: *a ~ idea; a ~ sensation in the stomach.* —***v.*** *Slang.* spoil: *Doping ~ed his chances for an Olympic medal.* —***n.*** & ***adj.*** *Slang.* homosexual. —**queer·ly** *adv.* —**queer·ness** *n.*

quell *v.* crush; put an end to: *~ an uprising; ~ one's doubts.*

quench *v.* cool suddenly, esp. something burning: *Steel is tempered by ~ing it while red-hot; Water ~es thirst; The outburst ~ed his fury.*

quer·u·lous (KWER·uh·lus, –yuh·lus) *adj.* complaining; fretful: *a ~ invalid.* —**quer·u·lous·ly** *adv.*

que·ry (KWEER·ee) *n.* **-ries** question; inquiry; also, a question mark, esp. one used to express doubt about an item; ***v.*** **-ries, -ried, -ry·ing:** *The proofreader ~d the author's spelling.* —**quest** *n.* a search; expedition: *man's ~ for happiness; the prospector's ~ for gold;* also ***v.*** —**ques·tion** (KWES·chun) *n.* **1** a sentence asking for information; also, an asking or something asked: *Send your ~s in writing; a ~-and-answer session.* **2** doubt; also, a subject of doubt, discussion, or dispute: *His honesty is* **beyond** (or **without**) **question;** *Age is not* **in question** *for this candidate; but there is some ~ about his competence; The chairman put the ~ to the vote;* **out of the question** impossible. —***v.:*** *Mother ~ed us about the broken glass; I must ~ your claim.* —**ques·tion·a·ble** *adj.;* **ques·tion·a·bly** *adv.* —**ques·tion·er** *n.* —**question mark** the punctuation mark (?) put at the end of a written question. —**ques·tion·naire** (–chuh·NAIR) *n.* a list of questions on a particular subject, as for an opinion survey.

quet·zal (ket·SAHL) *n.* **1** a large Central American bird with bright green and red plumage. **2** *pl. usu.* **-zal·es** (–SAH·les) the basic monetary unit of Guatemala, equal to 100 centavos. —**Quet·zal·co·atl** (ket·SAHL·coh·AH·tl) *n.* the feathered serpent god of the Aztecs.

queue (CUE) *n.* **1** a braid of hair which hangs down the back. **2** a line of people waiting in order of arrival: *a ~ at the cashier's counter.* —***v.*** **queues, queued, queu·ing:** *Eager fans* **queued up** *to buy tickets.*

quib·ble *v.* **quib·bles, quib·bled, quib·bling** make petty distinctions, esp. in order to evade an issue; cavil; also ***n.*** —**quib·bler** *n.*

quiche (Lor·raine) (keesh·law·REN) a custard pie filled with cheese and often bacon, mushrooms, etc.

quick *adj.* fast or prompt, esp. in reacting to a stimulus; live and active: *a ~ response to a call; He is ~ in math* (i.e. in understanding it); *a dog* *with a ~ ear; a* **quick-wit·ted** *retort* (showing a sharp and alert mind); *too* **quick-tem·pered** (i.e. easily angered) *to control himself.* —***n.*** **1** a live or sensitive part: *The child clipped her nails* **to the quick;** *His criticism cut her to the ~* (i.e. hurt her feelings). **2** living persons: *"to judge the ~ and the dead."* —**quick·ly** *adv.* —**quick·ness** *n.* —**quick bread** bread that can be baked immediately after mixing because of a leavening agent such as baking powder. —**quick-change** *adj.* of aircraft, able to be converted quickly from passenger to cargo service. —**quick·en** *v.* make or become more active, alive, or fast: *~ your pace to catch up with him; The pulse ~s under fear; stories that ~ one's imagination; the ~ing felt in the womb as pregnancy advances.* —**quick-freeze** *v.* **-freez·es, -froze, -froz·en, -freez·ing** freeze (food) rapidly in preparation for long-term storing at low temperatures. —**quick·ie** (KWIK·ee) *n.* & *adj. Slang.* (something) done or prepared in a hurry, as a cheap movie: *a ~* (i.e. wildcat) *strike.* —**quick·lime** *n.* unslaked lime. —**quick·lunch** *n.* a place specializing in quickly prepared food; luncheonette. —**quick·sand** *n.* soft, wet sand that yields to pressure and may suck down objects on its surface. —**quick·sil·ver** *n.* mercury. —**quick·step** *n.* **1** lively music for a military march in quick time, a pace of 120 steps a minute. **2** a lively dance step. —**quick-tempered, quick-witted** See QUICK, *adj.*

quid *n.* **1** piece of chewing tobacco. **2** *Brit. Slang.* a pound sterling; sovereign.

quid pro quo something expected or given as a return for something else; a consideration.

qui·es·cent (kwye·ES·nt) *adj.* inactive for a time; quiet; **qui·es·cent·ly** *adv.;* **qui·es·cence** *n.* —**qui·et** (KWY·ut) *adj.* free from agitation or activity; hence, without noise; subdued; calm; peaceful: *a man of ~ disposition; the ~ countryside; a ~ stream; decorated in ~ colors;* also ***n.:*** *the teacher asked for absolute ~; neighbors living in peace and ~;* ***v.:*** *He ~ed the frightened animals; The class ~ed down when the bell rang;* **qui·et·ly** *adv.;* **qui·et·ness** *n.* —**qui·e·tude** *n.* tranquillity; repose. —**qui·e·tus** (kwye·EE·tus) *n.* anything which ends activity, esp. death: *The newspaper story gave the rumors their ~.*

quill *n.* a stiff, hollow, pointed shaft, as a porcupine's spine or the stem of a goose's feather; also, the feather or a pen or other object made from it.

quilt *n.* a padded blanket or coverlet with its filling kept in place by lines of stitching, often in a pattern; ***v.:*** *a ~ed robe; a* **quilting bee** (See BEE).

quin·a·crine (KWIN·uh·creen) *n.* a quinine compound; "quinacrine hydrochloride."

quince *n.* the hard, yellow, acid fruit of a small tree related to apples and pears.

qui·nine (KWY–) *n.* a bitter crystalline substance prepared from cinchona bark and used to treat malaria and other fevers.

quin·sy (KWIN·zee) *n.* a throat inflammation with an abscess near the tonsils.

quint *n.* short for QUINTUPLET.

quin·tal (KWIN·tl) *n.* **1** in the metric system, 100 kilograms. **2** hundredweight.

quin·tes·sence (–TES·nce) *n.* the purest form or best example: *the Good Samaritan as the ~ of charity;* **quin·tes·sen·tial** (–SEN–) *adj.* —**quin·tet(te)** (kwin·TET) *n.* a piece of music for five voices or instruments; hence, a group of five (singers, team of basketball players, etc.). —**quin·til·lion** (kwin·TIL·yun) *n.* in the U.S. and Canada, 1 followed by 18 zeros; in the U.K., 1 followed by 30 zeros. —**quin·tu·ple** (KWIN·tup·ul, kwin·TUE·pl) *v.* **-ples, -pled, -pling** multiply or increase by five; also ***n.:*** *20 is the ~ of 4;* ***adj.*** multiplied by, or consisting of, five. —**quin·tu·plet** (KWIN·tuh·plit, kwin·TUP–) *n.* one of five offspring of a single birth. —**quin·tu·pli·cate** *v.* (kwin·TUE·plic–) **-cates, -cat·ed, -cat·ing** quintuple; ***n.*** (–kit) a set of five copies: *reports typed* **in quintuplicate;** ***adj.*** fivefold.

quip *n.* a pointed, neatly turned remark or retort; ***v.*** **quips, quipped, quip·ping.** —**quip·ster** *n.*

qui·pu (KEE·poo) *n.* a device made of knotted cords used by the ancient Incas for keeping accounts, recording events, and for messages.

quire *n.* a set of 24 or 25 sheets of the same kind of paper.

quirk *n.* a peculiar characteristic; a turn or twist from what is usual: *the ~s of an eccentric character; by some ~ of fate;* **quirk·y** *adj.;* **quirk·i·ness** *n.*

quirt *n.* a short-handled riding whip with a braided leather lash.

quis·ling (KWIZ–) *n.* a traitor, esp. the puppet of a foreign power occupying his country.

quit *v.* **quits,** *pt.* & *pp.* **quit** or **quit·ted, quit·ting** **1** leave (a place or situation); cease (doing something); give up: *He ~ school; She ~ smoking; He ~ all claims for damages.* **2** free oneself of; be rid of: *paid up and ~ his debts; She left the party to be ~ of his company.* —**quits** *adj. Informal.* finished: *After one more game I'll be ~ with you* (i.e. on even terms); *We'll* **call it quits** (*Informal.* stop or give up) *if it rains.* —**quit·claim** *n.* the formal giving up of a claim or title to a property, right, etc.; also, a document to this effect, or **quitclaim deed.**

quite (KWITE) *adv.* completely; also, to a great extent; really: *He's ~ wrong; She's ~ anxious; Micawber is* **quite a** *character;* **quite a few** *Informal.* a good number.

Qui·to (KEE·toh) capital of Ecuador.

quit·tance (–tunce) *n.* **1** release from debt, responsibility, etc. **2** repayment. —**quit·ter** *n. Informal.* one who gives up without trying hard enough.

[1]quiv·er (QUIV·ur) *n.* a trembling; quaver: *a ~ of rage;* ***v.:*** *to ~ with indignation.*
[2]quiv·er (QUIV·ur) *n.* a carrying case for arrows.
qui vive? (kee·VEEV) a French sentry's challenge: *Be* **on the qui vive** (i.e. watchful) *against pickpockets.*
quix·ot·ic (–OT–) *adj.* like DON QUIXOTE: *a ~ adventure;* also **quix·ot·i·cal —quix·ot·i·cal·ly** *adv.*
quiz *n.* **quiz·zes** a series of questions, esp. a test; ***v.*** **quiz·zes, quizzed, quiz·zing:** *Father ~d him about his activities.* **—quiz·zi·cal** *adj.* **1** questioning; puzzled: *a ~ look.* **2** teasing; humorous; **quiz·zi·cal·ly** *adv.*
quoin (COIN, KWOIN) *n.* an external angle or corner of a wall; also, a stone helping to form this; cornerstone.
quoit *n.* a flat metal ring thrown to encircle a peg in the game of **quoits** *pl.* [takes *sing.v.*].
quon·dam (KWON–) *adj.* that once was; former: *a ~ friend, now archenemy.*
Quon·set (KWON·sit) **hut** *Trademark.* a prefabricated building made of corrugated metal and shaped like a half cylinder.
quo·rum (KWOR·um) *n.* the minimum number of a group's members that must be present to transact business legally.
quot. quotation. **—quo·ta** (KWOH·tuh) *n.* that proportion of a total due from or to a person, group, etc.: *a salesman's ~ of business; immigration ~s for ethnic groups.* **—quote** (KWOHT) *v.* **quotes, quot·ed, quot·ing** **1** repeat exactly; give words from: *to ~ a poem; ~ Shakespeare.* **2** present as examples; cite: *I could ~ many instances of his bravery.* **3** state the price of goods or services. Also ***n.*** same as **quo·ta·tion** (–TAY–) *n.: biblical ~s; today's stock market ~s; a pair of* **"quotation marks"** [as used here]; **quo·ta·ble** (–tuh·bl) *adj.* **— quoth** (KWOHTH) *v. Archaic.* said.
quo·tid·i·an (kwoh·TID·ee·un) *adj.* daily: *the ~ chills and fever of malaria.*
quo·tient (KWOH·shunt) *n.* the number that results from dividing one quantity by another, as 3 from 21/7.
qursh (KOORSH) *n. sing.* & *pl.* a coin worth 1/20 of a riyal.
q.v. which see.
qy. query.

R

R or **r** (AHR) *n.* **R's** or **r's** the 18th letter of the English alphabet; **the three R's** reading, writing, and arithmetic, as the basics of education. —**R** restricted (movie rating). —**R.** or **r.** rabbi; radius; railroad; rare; Republican; resistance (electrical); right; river; road; roentgen; rook; runs (baseball).

[1]**Ra** radium. —[2]**Ra** (RAH) the Egyptian sun god and chief diety. —**R.A.** Royal Academy; regular army.

Ra·bat (rah·BAHT) capital of Morocco.

rab·bet (RAB·ut) *n.* a groove cut in or near a board's edge so that another piece can fit into it; ***v.:*** *two boards ~ed together.*

rab·bi (RAB·eye) *n.* **rab·bis** formerly, a teacher of Jewish law; now, the spiritual leader of a Jewish congregation. —**rab·bin·ate** (RAB·i·nit) *n.* the office or tenure of a rabbi. —**rab·bin·ic** (–BIN–) or **-i·cal** *adj.*

rab·bit *n.* a small, long-eared, short-tailed, burrowing animal with soft fur. —**rabbit ears** *Informal.* an indoor television antenna consisting of two adjustable rods. —**rabbit fever** same as TULAREMIA. —**rabbit punch** a sharp blow on the back of the neck.

rab·ble *n.* a disorderly crowd; mob. —**rab·ble-rous·er** *n.* one who tries to arouse a crowd to violent emotions or actions. —**rab·ble-rous·ing** *n.* & *adj.*

Rab·e·lais (RAB·uh·lay), **Francois.** 1494–1553, French satirist; **Rab·e·lai·si·an** (–LAY–) *adj.*

rab·id *adj.* afflicted with rabies; hence, fanatical, violent: *a ~ dog; ~ zeal; a ~ thirst.* —**ra·bies** (RAY·beez) *n.* a serious, infectious disease which attacks the central nervous system of warm-blooded animals and is transmitted by a bite.

rac·coon (rac·OON) *n.* a furry, gray-brown animal with a bushy, ringed tail and black, mask-like hair around its eyes.

[1]**race** *n.* **1** a contest, esp. of speed, to reach a point or achieve an aim: *a boat ~; the ~ for mayor.* **2** a steady, onward movement on a regular course, as of a river, life, etc. —***v.*** **rac·es, raced, rac·ing:** *I'll ~ you to that tree; The ambulance ~d to the hospital; to ~* (i.e. rev) *a car engine;* **rac·er** *n.*

[2]**race** *n.* **1** a major division of mankind, formerly based on skin color, as white, black, and yellow, now on hereditary characteristics, distributed geographically or nationally; also, a subspecies of a plant or animal. **2** any group with similar ancestry or characteristics: *a noble ~ of warriors.* —**ra·cial** *adj.;* **ra·cial·ly** *adv.*

race·course *n.* a usu. oval course laid out for racing horses or dogs. —**race·horse** *n.* a horse bred and trained for racing.

ra·ceme (–SEEM) *n.* a flower cluster with short-stemmed individual flowers at regular intervals on a main stalk.

race·track, race·way same as RACECOURSE.

ra·chi·tis (–KYE–) *n.* same as RICKETS.

ra·cial·ism or **ra·cism** *n.* belief in the superiority of one race or group; also, discrimination based on this belief; **ra·cial·ist** or **ra·cist** *n.* & *adj.* —**ra·cial·is·tic** (–IS–) *adj.*

Ra·cine (–SEEN), **Jean.** 1639–99, French playwright.

racism, racist same as RACIALISM, RACIALIST.

[1]**rack** *n.* **1** a framework for storing or displaying various items: *magazine ~.* **2** a toothed bar that meshes with another toothed structure such as a pinion. **3** an instrument of torture on which limbs are stretched; hence, any torment; **rack and ruin** See WRACK. —***v.*** torture; torment; **rack one's brains** think hard; **rack up** *Slang.* score: *Our team quickly ~ed up 10 points.* —**rack car** a railroad flat car with tiered racks for transporting cars, trucks, etc.

[1]**rack·et** *n.* a long-handled oval frame strung with netting, used in tennis, squash, etc. —**rack·ets** *n.pl.* [takes *sing.v.*] a game similar to tennis, played in a four-walled court.

[2]**rack·et** *n.* **1** loud noise; revelry: *the ~ of a children's party;* **rack·et·y** *adj.* **2** a dishonest scheme or activity, esp. for obtaining money: *a blackmail ~;* **rack·et·eer** (–TEER) *n.;* **rack·et·eer·ing** *n.*

rac·on·teur (–TUR) *n.* a skillful storyteller.

rac·quet (RAK·it) same as RACKET.

ra·cy (RAY·see) *adj.* **-ci·er, -ci·est** having the characteristic flavor, etc. of something; hence, piquant; spicy: *~ fruit; his ~ sense of humor* (suggesting frankness and earthiness); **rac·i·ly** *adv.;* **rac·i·ness** *n.*

rad. *Math.* radical; radius. **—rad** *n.* a unit of absorbed dose of radiation, equal to 100 ergs per gram.

ra·dar (RAY–) *n.* an electronic device for locating faraway objects such as missiles, mountains, and rainstorms by reflecting radio waves and studying the blips of light received on a fluorescent screen, or **ra·dar·scope** *n.*

ra·di·al (RAY·dee·ul) *adj.* branching out like rays from a center; **ra·di·al·ly** *adv.* **—radial engine** internal-combustion engine with cylinders arranged radially. **—radial(-ply) tire** an automobile tire in which ply cords are laid at right angles to the center line of the thread. **—ra·di·an** (RAY–) *n.* an angle of nearly 57.-296° at the center of a circle which corresponds to an arc of length equal to that of a radius. **—ra·di·ant** *adj.* giving off rays, as of light or heat; hence, glowing; happy: *a necklace ~ with diamonds; a ~ bride;* **radiant energy** energy transmitted in waves; **ra·di·ant·ly** *adv.;* **ra·di·ance** *n.* **—ra·di·ate** *v.* **-ates, -at·ed, -at·ing** give out rays (of); hence, spread out from a center: *Spokes ~ from a wheel's center; The sun ~s energy; a salesman ~ing confidence;* **ra·di·a·tor** *n.* **—ra·di·a·tion** (–AY–) *n.;* **radiation sickness** illness caused by overexposure to radioactive matter.

rad·i·cal *adj.* basic or fundamental; also, favoring fundamental changes: *a ~ politician;* ***n.*** **1** a radical politician. **2** two or more atoms acting as one. **3** *Math.* a root, indicated by a **radical sign** as in $\sqrt[3]{9}$ (i.e. cube root of 9). **—rad·i·cal·ly** *adv.* **—rad·i·cal·ism** *n.* **—rad·i·cal·ize** *v.* **-iz·es, -ized, -iz·ing** make politically radical; **rad·i·cal·i·za·tion** (–ZAY–) *n.*

radii a *pl.* of RADIUS. **—ra·di·o** (RAY·dee·oh) *n.* **-os** the sending and receiving of sound and picture signals using electromagnetic waves without connecting wires, as in broadcasting; also, a broadcasting receiving set or broadcasting as a business, medium, etc.; ***adj.:*** *a ~ announcer, engineer, program, wave.* **—*v.* -oes, -oed, -o·ing** communicate with or transmit (a message) by radio. **—radio-** *comb.form.* **1** radio: as in *radiosonde; radiotelephone.* **2** radiant: as in *radiograph, radiology, radiometer.* **3** radioactive: as in *radiocarbon, radiogenic, radioisotope, radiotherapy.* **—ra·di·o·ac·tiv·i·ty** (–TIV–) *n.* the process by which radioactive substances such as radium, thorium, and uranium give off alpha particles, beta particles, or gamma rays; **ra·di·o·ac·tive** (–AC·tiv) *adj.;* **ra·di·o·ac·tive·ly** *adv.* **—radio astronomy** the study of radio waves from heavenly bodies such as the sun, Jupiter, pulsars, quasars, etc. **—ra·di·o·car·bon** (–CAR·bun) *n.* same as CARBON 14. **—radio frequency** an electromagnetic wave frequency above 10,000 hertz that is suitable for broadcasting. **—radio galaxy** one that is a source of radio waves. **—ra·di·o·gen·ic** (–JEN–) *adj.* produced by radioactivity. **—ra·di·o·gram** *n.* a telegram sent by radio. **—ra·di·o·graph** *n.* an X-ray photograph; ***v.*** make a radiograph of; **ra·di·o·graph·ic** (–GRAF–) *adj.;* **ra·di·o·graph·i·cal·ly** *adv.;* **ra·di·og·ra·phy** (–OG–) *n.* **—ra·di·o·i·so·tope** (–EYE·suh–) *n.* a radioactive form of a substance such as iodine or iron used in diagnosis and treatment, esp. of cancer. **—ra·di·ol·o·gy** (–OL–) *n.* a branch of medicine dealing with the use of radiant energy such as X rays in diagnosis and treatment; **ra·di·ol·o·gist** *n.;* **ra·di·o·log·i·cal** (–LOJ–) *adj.* **—ra·di·om·e·ter** (–OM–) *n.* an instrument for measuring radiant energy; **ra·di·om·e·try** (–OM–) *n.;* **ra·di·o·met·ric** (–MET–) *adj.;* **ra·di·o·met·ri·cal·ly** *adv.* **—ra·di·o·phone** same as RADIOTELEPHONE. **—ra·di·o·sonde** (RAY·dee·oh·sond) *n.* a meteorological device consisting of a balloon carrying instruments for recording weather data which are transmitted by radio to ground stations. **—ra·di·o·tel·e·graph** (–TEL–) *n.* wireless telegraphy; **ra·di·o·tel·e·graph·ic** (–GRAF–) *adj.;* **ra·di·o·te·leg·ra·phy** (–LEG–) *n.* **—ra·di·o·tel·e·phone** (–TEL·uh–) *n.* a telephone using radio waves as the transmission medium, as in moving vehicles; **ra·di·o·te·leph·o·ny** (–LEF–) *n.* **—radio telescope** the telescope used in radio astronomy, equipped with an antenna to pick up radio waves from beyond the reach of optical telescopes by means of a giant dishlike reflector. **—ra·di·o·ther·a·py** (–THER–) *n.* therapy using X rays, radium, and other radioactive substances; **ra·di·o·ther·a·pist** *n.*

rad·ish *n.* the usu. white or red and spherical crisp, sharp-tasting, edible root of a plant of the mustard family.

ra·di·um (RAY·dee–) *n.* a very unstable radioactive metallic element, used in luminous paints and in **radium therapy,** esp. of cancer. **—ra·di·us** (RAY·dee–) *n., pl.* **-di·i** (–dee·eye) or **-di·us·es** **1** a straight line from the center to the outside of a circle or sphere. **2** area or distance covered by a radius: *people living within a ~ of 10 miles from downtown.* **—ra·dome** (RAY–) *n.* a dome-shaped housing for a radar antenna. **—ra·don** (RAY–) *n.* a radioactive gaseous element formed when radium breaks down.

R.A.F. Royal Air Force.

raf·fi·a (RAF·ee·uh) *n.* (fiber from) a large-leaved palm tree of Madagascar.

raff·ish (RAF–) *adj.* showy; rakish; disreputable: *a hooker's ~ memoirs;* **raff·ish·ly** *adv.;* **raff·ish·ness** *n.*

raf•fle (RAFL) *n.* the casting of lots for prizes; ***v.* raf•fles, raf•fled, raf•fling** hold a raffle or sell (*off* an article) by a raffle; **raf•fler** *n.*

raft *n.* **1** a floating structure of logs or timbers fastened together; ***v.*** make (logs, boards, etc.) into, send by, or carry on a raft. **2** *Informal.* collection: *charged with a whole ~ of offenses.* —**raft•er** *n.* one of the sloping beams supporting a roof.

rag *n.* **1** a small, valueless, or torn piece of cloth; ***adj.:*** *~ doll, paper, rug;* **rags** *pl.* worn-out clothes. **2** a tune in ragtime. —***v.* rags, ragged, rag•ging** *Slang.* tease or taunt.

ra•ga (RAH·guh) *n.* a melodic pattern in Indian music.

rag•a•muf•fin (RAG·uh–) *n.* a ragged and dirty person, esp. a child. —**rag•bag** *n.* a bag for rags; also, a miscellaneous collection.

rage *n.* **1** (a fit of) fury: *a drunken ~.* **2** a fad or vogue. —***v.* rag•es, raged, rag•ing** be in a rage: *~d at anyone who opposed him; while a storm ~d outside* (i.e. was at its height).

rag•ged (RAG·id) *adj.* **1** tattered or torn; also, wearing rags. **2** shabby or shaggy; also, uneven or jagged. —**rag•ged•ly** *adv.;* **rag•ged•ness** *n.* —**rag•ged•y** *adj.* ragged.

rag•lan (–lun) *adj.* of a sleeve, extending to the collar with slanted underarm seams; ***n.*** an overcoat with raglan sleeves.

ra•gout (–GOO) *n.* a highly seasoned stew of meat and vegetables.

rag•tag *n.* riffraff.

rag•time *n.* a strongly rhythmic style of piano playing, a forerunner of jazz.

rag•weed *n.* a weed with hairy, toothed leaves and long spikes of flowers full of pollen.

rah *interj.* hurrah.

raid *n.* & *v.* (make) a sudden, hostile attack or invasion; **raid•er** *n.*

¹rail *n.* any of a family of marsh birds including coots and gallinules having thin bodies for slipping through reeds and grasses.

²rail *v.* complain bitterly (against or at a person or thing); **rail•ler•y** *n.* **rail•ler•ies.**

³rail *n.* **1** a horizontal bar connecting posts and forming a guard or barrier, as on a fence; ***v.*** fence with rails, or **rail•ing** *n.* **2** either of a pair of parallel connected steel bars forming a track for a train or similar vehicle; hence, a railroad: *travel by ~.* —**rail•road** *n.* a track of rails for locomotives and cars; also, this transportation system; ***v.*** **1** send by railroad. **2** *Informal.* rush (a person, piece of legislation, etc.) through a system without careful consideration. —**rail•road•er** *n.;* **rail•road•ing** *n.* —**rail•way** *n.* **1** a railroad track or a railroad for streetcars or other light vehicles. **2** *Brit.* railroad.

rai•ment *n. Archaic.* clothing.

rain *n.* water falling in drops from the sky; hence, anything resembling it: *a ~ of bullets, kisses, tears;* **rains** *pl.* seasonal rainfalls; **rain•y** *adj.* **rain•i•er, -i•est:** *~ weather;* **rainy day** future time of need. —***v.:*** *It is ~ing outside; They ~ed flowers on the returning hero; tears ~ing down her cheeks; "It never ~s but it pours"* (i.e. things happen in quick succession); *The game was* **rained out** (i.e. postponed because of rain). —**rain•bow** *n.* arch of colorful light seen in mist or spray; **rainbow trout** a brightly colored North American trout with a rosy band along its body on either side. —**rain•check** *n.* a present offer that is extended for a future occasion, as a ticket from a game stopped by rain. —**rain•coat** *n.* a waterproof outer coat. —**rain•drop** *n.* a drop of rain. —**rain•fall** *n.* a fall of rain; also, its amount as measured in a **rain gauge.** —**rain forest** an evergreen tropical forest of equatorial regions characterized by dense growth, with treetops forming a canopy shading the forest floor. —**rain•mak•ing** *n.* the making of rain by artificial means; **rain•mak•er** *n.* —**rain•storm** *n.* a storm with heavy rain. —**rainy day.** See RAIN, *n.*

raise (RAIZ) *v.* **rais•es, raised, rais•ing** **1** move (a person or thing) to a higher level or position: *to ~ a flag; to ~ the standard of living; ~ the dead* (to life); *never ~s* (i.e. increases) *his voice.* **2** bring up; raise; also, get: *to ~ crops, children, funds; ~* (i.e. cause) *a laugh; ~* (i.e. erect) *a monument;* **raise Cain** create a disturbance. **3** end: *~ a siege.* —***n.*** an increase: *a 5% ~ in prices.*

rai•sin (RAY·zn) *n.* a sweet sun-dried grape.

rai•son d'être (ray·zon·DET·ruh) *French.* reason for being (what something is).

ra•ja(h) (RAH·juh) *n.* an Indian prince.

¹rake *n.* **1** a long-handled tool or machine equipped with prongs for gathering leaves or hay, smoothing the ground, etc.; ***v.* rakes, raked, rak•ing:** *to ~ leaves off a lawn; to* **rake in** (i.e. gather quickly and abundantly) *profits; Why* **rake up** *long-forgotten enmities?* **2** a dissolute man; also **rake•hell; rak•ish** *adj.;* **rak•ish•ly** *adv.;* **rak•ish•ness** *n.* —**rake-off** *n. Informal.* an illicit share or commission.

²rake *n.* & *v.* slant or slope, as of a mast or funnel toward the stern, of a floor from the horizontal, etc. —**rak•ish** (RAY–) *adj.* **1** smart or trim, suggesting speed: *a ~ ship.* **2** jaunty or dashing: *a hat set at a ~ angle.* —**rak•ish•ly** *adv.;* **rak•ish•ness** *n.*

Ra•leigh (RAW·lee, RAH–) **1** capital of North Carolina. **2 Sir Walter.** 1552?–1618, English explorer.

¹ral•ly (RAL·ee) *v.* **ral•lies, ral•lied, ral•ly•ing** come or bring together for a united effort: *to ~ round* (or *to the side of*) *a leader; ~d his forces for a renewed attack.* **2** recover (former strength): *Prices ~* (after a drop); *a patient ~ing after an attack.* —***n.,*** *pl.* **ral•lies** a rallying, as of a market or people such as scouts, sports car enthusiasts, or worshipers for a group activity.

²ral·ly *v.* **ral·lies, ral·lied, ral·ly·ing** banter.
ram *n.* a male sheep, usu. with outward-curving horns; also, a battering ram. **—*v.* rams, rammed, ram·ming** butt or strike violently against, down, or into: *Piles are ~d into a river bed; Automobiles ~ into each other in a collision.*
ram·ble *v.* **-bles, -bled, -bling** go about in an aimless or leisurely manner; hence, wander away, as from a subject while talking: *a ~ing vine;* ***n.*** a roaming or excursion: *a ~ in the woods;* **ram·bler** *n.: climbing and ~ roses.*
ram·bunc·tious (–BUNK–) *adj.* boisterous and unruly; **ram·bunc·tious·ness** *n.*
ram·e·kin (RAM·uh–) *n.* a small baking dish or an individual portion cooked in it.
ram·ie (RAM·ee) *n.* (fiber such as bast obtained from) an Asiatic nettle.
ram·i·fy *v.* **-fies, -fied, -fy·ing** branch out; spread out; **ram·i·fi·ca·tion** (–CAY–) *n.* offshoot; hence, consequence.
ramp *n.* a sloped means of access to a different level, as at a highway interchange or the staircase used to board a plane. **—ram·page** *n.* a spell of reckless or violent behavior: *a gang* **on the** (or **on a**) **rampage;** ***v.*** (–PAGE) **–pag·es, –paged, –pag·ing** rush about in a rage; **ram·pa·geous** (–PAY·jus) *adj.* **—ramp·ant** (–unt) *adj.* unchecked in growth or movement: *inflation running ~; ~* (i.e. rank) *vegetation;* **ram·pan·cy** *n.*
ram·part *n.* a defensive barrier, esp. one built around a fort with a parapet on top.
ram·rod *n.* a rod used to ram a charge into a muzzle-loading firearm.
ram·shack·le *adj.* rickety: *a ~ dwelling, vehicle.*
ran *pt.* of RUN.
ranch *n.* **1** a large farm for raising cattle, sheep, or horses; also, a farm with a specialty such as raising chickens, mink, or fruit. **2** a low-roofed one-story dwelling; also **ranch house.** **—*v.*** manage or work on a ranch. **—ranch·er** or, in southwestern U.S., **ran·cher·o** (–CHAIR–) *n.* a ranch owner or worker.
ran·cid *adj.* tasting or smelling like spoiled fat, butter, etc.; **ran·cid·i·ty** (–SID–) *n.* **—ran·cor** (RANG·cur) *n.* bitter or spiteful hatred; **ran·cor·ous** *adj.;* **ran·cor·ous·ly** *adv.*
rand *n. sing.* & *pl.* the basic money unit of South Africa, equal to 100 cents.
R & B rhythm and blues.
R & D research and development.
ran·dom (–dum) *adj.* made or done without a purpose, plan, or aim: *~ shots; ~ samples taken* **at random** *as representative of a large group;* **random access** access to data in a computer memory in the order desired by user; **ran·dom·ly** *adv.* **—ran·dom·ize** *v.* **-iz·es, -ized, -iz·ing:** *a ~d selection of items;* **ran·dom·i·za·tion** (–ZAY–) *n.*
R & R rest and recuperation (leave).
ran·dy *adj.* **-di·er, -di·est** lecherous; vulgar; also, sexually aroused.
ra·nee (RAH–) *n.* a raja's wife; rani.
rang *pt.* of RING.
range (RAINJ) *v.* **rang·es, ranged, rang·ing** **1** vary within a limited area or distance: *pay ~ing from $20,000 to 25,000; a wide-~ing survey; Radar is a ~ing* (i.e. distance-finding) *device; Buffalo once ~d* (i.e. roamed) *our plains.* **2** arrange in rows or groups: *eggs ~d small, medium, and large; ~d themselves with* (i.e. joined) *the invaders.* **—*n.*** **1** distance or extent: *too high a price ~; a wide ~ of vision; within ~ of gunfire.* **2** an area: *a cattle ~* (for pasture); *a rifle ~* (for practicing shooting). **3** row or line: *a mountain ~.* **4** a cooking stove, usu. with oven and storage compartment. **—range finder** a usu. optical distance-measuring device, as in a camera. **—rang·er** *n.* **1** one who patrols or guards a region: *a forest ~.* **2** also **Ranger,** a member of the U.S. Army trained as a commando; also, a special police officer of Texas.
Ran·goon (rang·GOON) capital of Burma.
rang·y (RAIN·jee) *adj.* **rang·i·er, -i·est** able to range about; hence, long-limbed, as cattle or horses; **rang·i·ness** *n.*
ra·ni (RAH·nee) *n.* a raja's wife.
¹rank *adj.* **1** coarse and vigorous in growth, as weeds. **2** bad-smelling: *~ tobacco.* **3** extreme: *~ nonsense, ingratitude.* **—rank·ly** *adv.;* **rank·ness** *n.*
²rank *n.* **1** a row, as of a lineup of soldiers: *join the ~s* (i.e. army); *a general who rose from the ~s* (i.e. of the enlisted); *the ~s of the unemployed.* **2** position according to grade and seniority, esp. of a military officer. **—*v.*:** *Alaska ~s above other states when ~ed according to size; A colonel ~s* (i.e. is higher than) *a major; the* (highest) **ranking** *Republican senator.* **—rank and file** ordinary soldiers; hence, the common people.
ran·kle (RANG–) *v.* **-kles, -kled, -kling** be a source of irritation or soreness (to): *a slight that still ~s* (in her mind).
ran·sack *v.* search (a place) thoroughly, as if to plunder; also, plunder or pillage.
ran·som (–sum) *n.* a price demanded for freeing a person from captivity: *kidnapped and held for ~;* ***v.*** free by paying a ransom: *rescued by police before being ~ed;* **ran·som·er** *n.*
rant *v.* talk wildly and loudly: *~s and raves when drunk;* ***n.*** a noisy or bombastic speech.
rap *n.* **1** a sharp knock; **rap on the knuckles** a mild punishment or reproof. **2** *Slang.* legal punishment or blame: *someone to take the ~; a bum ~; a ~ sheet.* **3** *Slang.* a chat: *a ~ session.* **4** *Informal.* the least bit: *don't care a ~.* **—*v.* raps, rapped, rap·ping** **1** tap or knock sharply, as on a door. **2** *Slang.* talk informally. **—rap·per** *n.*
ra·pa·cious (–PAY–) *adj.* plundering; greedy; grasping: *the ~ wolf; a ~ tyrant;* **ra·pa·cious·ly** *adv.;* **ra·pa·cious·ness** or **ra·pac·i·ty** (–PAS–) *n.*
¹rape *n.* a forcing of one, esp. a woman, to have sexual intercourse; ***v.*** **rapes, raped, rap·ing**

ravish; **rap·ist** (RAY–) *n.* one who has committed rape.

²rape *n.* a plant related to cole, used as fodder and for **rape·seed** oil.

Raph·a·el (RAF·ee·ul, RAY·fee–) 1483–1520, Italian painter.

rap·id *adj.* moving at a swift pace; quick: *a ~ pulse, stream; the ~ growth of weeds; ~-fire questioning; the* **rapid eye movement** *and ~ breathing and heart rates associated with the dreaming phase of sleep; a* **rapid transit** *public transportation system using fast trains.* **—*n.*** usu. **rapids** *pl.* a part of a river with swift currents and rocks beneath the surface: *a shallow boat for shooting the ~s of the Niagara;* **rap·id·ly** *adv.;* **ra·pid·i·ty** (–PID–) *n.*

ra·pi·er (RAY·pee·ur) *n.* a narrow-bladed, pointed dueling sword used for thrusting.

rap·ine (RAP·in) *n.* plundering; pillage. **—rap·ist** See ¹RAPE.

rap·pen (RAH·pun) *n. sing. & pl.* the Swiss centime.

rap·port (–POR) *n.* a close relationship, implying mutual sympathy and harmony.

rap·proche·ment (–PROHSH·mahng) *n.* the establishment of cordial relations.

rap·scal·lion (–SKAL·yun) *n.* rascal; rogue.

rap session *Slang.* an informal group discussion. **—rap sheet** *Slang.* a police record.

rapt *adj.* absorbed or engrossed (in a thought or emotion): *listening with ~ attention; was ~ in thought.* **—rap·ture** (–chur) *n.* the state of being rapt in a feeling of bliss: *a ~ of joy;* **rap·tur·ous** *adj.;* **rap·tur·ous·ly** *adv.*

ra·ra a·vis (rair·uh·AY·vis) a rare or extraordinary person or thing; rarity. **—rare** *adj.* **rar·er, rar·est** **1** not frequent; without many instances or specimens; hence, unusually good: *a ~ event, book; a ~ talent, beauty.* **2** not dense: *the ~ mountain air; the ~er regions of the atmosphere.* **3** of meat, not cooked much: *a ~ steak.* **—rare·ly** *adv.;* **rare·ness** *n.* **—rare·bit** *n.* same as WELSH RAREBIT. **—rare-earth elements** (or **metals**) a series of metallic elements from lanthanum to lutetium with similar properties; also **rare earths.** **—rar·e·fy** (RAIR·uh·fye) *v.* **-fies, -fied, -fy·ing** make or become less dense: *a ~d gas;* **rar·e·fac·tion** (–FAC–) *n.: Sound waves consist of condensations and ~s* (i.e. expansions). Also **rar·i·fy.**

rar·ing (RAIR–) *adj. Informal.* very eager: *~ to go.*

rar·i·ty (RAIR–) *n.* **-ties** rareness; also, an unusual person or thing.

ras·cal (–cul) *n.* a scoundrel; rogue; [used jokingly] a naughty or mischievous person; **ras·cal·ly** *adv.;* **ras·cal·i·ty** (–CAL–) *n.*

¹rash *n.* **1** a skin eruption, often itchy, usu. covering an area of the body in spots or patches, as in measles and prickly heat. **2** sudden appearance in large numbers: *a ~ of accidents on a slippery road.*

²rash *adj.* hasty or thoughtless; precipitate: *a ~ decision, action, person; ~ driving;* **rash·ly** *adv.;* **rash·ness** *n.*

rash·er *n.* a slice of bacon; also, a serving (of several slices).

rasp *n.* a coarse file with a surface of points or teeth; hence, the grating sound made (as) when one is used: *a cricket's ~;* ***v.:*** *voices that ~ one's nerves; He ~s out his orders;* **rasp·y** *adj.*

rasp·ber·ry (RAZ·ber·ee, –buh·ree) *n.* **-ber·ries** **1** a small, round, usu. red or purple fruit of a bush of the rose family. **2** *Slang.* a noise of disapproval made by sticking out the tongue and blowing strongly.

Ras·ta short for **Ras·ta·far·i·an** (–FAIR–) *n. & adj.* (member) of a West Indian cult based on the former Emperor of Ethiopia as God.

rat *n.* **1** a destructive rodent larger than a mouse. **2** *Slang.* a person considered low or mean, as an informer; also **rat·fink.** **—*v.* rats, rat·ted, rat·ting** act in a low way; **rat on** inform on; also, go back on (one's word), **—smell a rat** suspect something tricky. **—rat cheese** *Informal.* cheddar.

ratch·et (RACH·it) *n.* a wheel that is so toothed that it can move in only one direction, working with a pawl; also, the pawl itself or the wheel, also called **ratchet wheel.**

¹rate *v.* **rates, rat·ed, rat·ing** scold; berate.

²rate *n.* **1** a measurement of something variable in proportion to something that is standard: *moving at the ~ of 30 m.p.h.; the postal ~ for first-class mail;* **at any** (or **this, that**) **rate** in any (or this, that) case. **2** class or grade: *a first-~ mind.* **—*v.* rates, rat·ed, rat·ing** **1** rank or be ranked: *She is ~d in the top 5% of her class; The estimator ~d it as worth $1,250.* **2** *Informal.* deserve: *so good he ~s a promotion.*

ratfink See RAT, *n.* 2.

rath·er *adv.* **1** more readily, properly, correctly, etc.: *He would ~ play than work; He was let go, ~, he resigned; I'd ~ you arrive early than be late.* **2** somewhat: *a ~ chilly reception.*

raths·kel·ler (RAHT·skel·ur) *n.* a German-style basement restaurant.

rat·i·fy *v.* **-fies, -fied, -fy·ing** give formal approval of (a treaty, law, etc.), usu. by vote; **rat·i·fi·ca·tion** (–CAY–) *n.* **—rat·ing** (RAY–) *n.* **1** (placement in) a rank or grade; also, *Brit.* an enlisted man in the navy. **2** a comparative estimate: *a fuse wire with a 15 amp. ~; a four-star credit ~; a TV show cancelled because of low ~s* (as determined by popularity surveys). **—ra·tio** (RAY·shoh) *n.* **-tios** the relation in quantity, amount, or degree between two things or this expressed as the quotient of two numbers; proportion: *The length-to-width ~ of the U.S. flag is 1.9 or 19/10.* **—ra·ti·o·ci·nate** (rash·ee·OH·suh·nate) *v.* **-nates, -nat·ed, -nat·ing** go through the formal process of reasoning; **ra·ti·o·ci·na·tion** (–NAY–) *n.* **—ra·tion** (RASH·un, RAY–) *n.* a share or allotment, esp of food; **rations** *pl.* food supply;

provisions; ***v.:*** *Food is ~ed* (to the public) *during a war.* —**ra·tion·al** (RASH–) *adj.* **1** based on reasoning: *a ~ explanation of a mystery.* **2** able to reason: *Man is ~.* —**ra·tion·al·ly** *adv.* —**ra·tion·ale** (–NAL) *n.* the rational basis for something; also, an explanation of underlying reasons. —**ra·tion·al·ism** (RASH–) *n.* the principle or practice of using reason as the ultimate authority for knowledge, as opposed to faith or sense experience; **ra·tion·al·ist** *n.;* **ra·tion·al·is·tic** (–IS–) *adj.* —**ra·tion·al·i·ty** (–NAL–) *n.* —**ra·tion·al·ize** (RASH–) *v.* **-iz·es, -ized, -iz·ing** **1** make rational; also, treat in a rational manner. **2** find a seemingly rational excuse for (one's weakness). —**ra·tion·al·i·za·tion** (–ZAY–) *n.*

rat·lin(e) (RAT·lin) *n.* any of the short ropes across the shrouds of a ship, serving as a ladder.

rat race *Informal.* the frantic struggle for survival in the modern competitive world: *fed up with the 9-to-5 ~.*

rat·tan (–TAN) *n.* the stem of various climbing palms used for wickerwork, furniture, etc.

rat·ter *n.* a rat-catching dog or cat.

rat·tle *n.* a baby's toy that makes noise when shaken; hence, a series of short, sharp sounds; also, the set of loosely-joined horny pieces on the end of a rattlesnake's tail used to give a warning sound. —***v.*** **rat·tles, rat·tled, rat·tling** **1** make the sound of a rattle; hence, talk in an incessant chatter. **2** *Informal.* upset; disturb one's composure. —**rat·tle·brain** *n.* one who is **rat·tle·brained** *adj.* frivolous or giddy. —**rat·tler** or **rat·tle·snake** *n.* a venomous American snake with a rattle on the end of its tail. —**rat·tle·trap** *n.* something rattling or rickety, as an old car. —**rat·tling** *adj.* **1** that rattles. **2** *Informal.* lively; splendid: *a ~ business;* ***adv.:*** *a ~ good time.*

rat·trap *n.* a trap for rats; hence, *Informal.* a run-down building. —**rat·ty** *adj.* **rat·ti·er, rat·ti·est** suggestive of or infested with rats.

rau·cous (RAW·cus) *adj.* rough-sounding or rowdy: *~ voices, parties;* **rau·cous·ly** *adv.;* **rau·cous·ness** *n.*

raun·chy (RAWN·chee) *adj.* **-chi·er, -chi·est** sloppy or slovenly; also, earthy; lustful; vulgar: *a ~ girlie magazine;* **raun·chi·ness** *n.*

rau·wol·fi·a (raw·WOL·fee·uh) *n.* a reserpine-containing plant or shrub of the dogbane family.

rav·age (–ij) *n.* & *v.* **-ag·es, -aged, -ag·ing** (cause) destruction or devastation: *the ~s of war; an area ~d by floods.*

rave *v.* **raves, raved, rav·ing** **1** talk wildly or furiously (*about*), as when delirious. **2** talk with great, often excessive enthusiasm (*about*). —***n.*** *Informal.* enthusiastic praise; ***adj.:*** *~ reviews, notices.* —**rav·ing** *adj.* that raves; hence, *Informal.* making one rave with enthusiasm: *a ~ beauty;* ***adv.:*** *was ~ mad.*

rav·el (RAV·ul) *v.* **-els, -el(l)ed, -el·(l)ing** **1** tangle or confuse. **2** untwist; unravel. —***n.*** a raveled part; also **rav·el·(l)ing** *n.*

rav·en (RAY·vun) *n.* a larger-size species of crow; ***adj.*** black and lustrous like a raven's feathers.

rav·en·ing (RAV–) or **rav·e·nous** *adj.* very hungry; also, rapacious: *~ wolves;* **rav·e·nous·ly** *adv.;* **rav·e·nous·ness** *n.*

ra·vine (–VEEN) *n.* a long, narrow, deep depression in the earth's surface, smaller than a valley or canyon.

ra·vi·o·li (rav·ee·OH·lee) *n.pl.* [takes *sing.v.*] small casings of pasta filled with meat or cheese.

rav·ish *v.* **1** transport with joy; enrapture; also, enchant: *~ed with delight; a ~ing view, beauty.* **2** commit rape on. —**rav·ish·er** *n.;* **rav·ish·ment** *n.*

raw *adj.* **1** in the natural state, as uncooked meat, untreated animal hide, untrained recruits, unprocessed materials, data, etc. **2** rough or harsh: *~ weather, wind, deal; a ~ spot* (on the body with the skin removed by a wound). —**in the raw** in a natural state; also, naked. —**raw·boned** *adj.* lean, gaunt, or gawky, not fat. —**raw·hide** *n.* (a whip made with) untanned cattle hide.

[1]**ray** *n.* a thin line of light radiating from a central source such as the sun; hence, any similar line or a raylike part, as a petal of the daisy or an arm of the starfish: *a ~* (i.e. gleam) *of hope.*

[2]**ray** *n.* any of a group of fishes including manta rays and skates having a flat, disklike body, pectoral fins like large wings, and a whiplike tail.

ray·on *n.* a silklike shiny fabric made from cellulose fiber.

raze *v.* **raz·es, razed, raz·ing** to level (to the ground); demolish.

ra·zor (RAY·zur) *n.* a shaving implement; **ra·zor-back(ed)** *adj.* having a ridged back, as certain hogs; **razor-bill** See AUK.

razz *v.* tease; ridicule. —***n.*** raspberry (*n.* 2).

raz·zle-daz·zle *n.* & *v.* **-daz·zles, -daz·zled, -daz·zling** *Slang.* (bewilder or deceive with) something dazzling or exciting. —**razz·ma·tazz** (RAZ·muh–) *n. Slang.* liveliness or flashiness.

Rb rubidium.

r.b.i. or **RBI** run(s) batted in.

R.C. Red Cross; Roman Catholic.

RCAF Royal Canadian Air Force.

R.C.Ch. Roman Catholic Church.

R.C.M.P. Royal Canadian Mounted Police.

Rd. or **rd.** road; rod; round. —**R.D.** Rural Delivery.

Re rhenium. —**'re** are.

[1]**re** (RAY, REE) *prep.* in the matter of.

[2]**re** (RAY) *n. Music.* the second tone of the diatonic scale.

re- *prefix* [meaning "again" or "anew," as in the compounds placed at the foot of the pages. Their basic meaning and pronunciation are the same as in the base word in each case. A hyphen may be used to emphasize or distinguish, as in *re-cover,* "cover again."].

R.E.A. Railway Express Agency; Rural Electrification Administration.

reach (REECH) *v.* get to a person, place, or thing: *You can ~ me by phoning; His fame ~es far and wide; cannot be ~ed* (i.e. got at or influenced) *by bribes; ~* (i.e. extend) *your hand out of the window; tried to ~* (toward) *the extended hand; quickly ~ed for his gun; ~ me the salt.* **—*n.*:** *Infinity is beyond ~ of man's imagination; in the outer ~es of the atmosphere; Keep drugs out of ~ of children.* **—reach·er** *n.*

re·act (ree·ACT) *v.* **1** act back or in response (*to, on,* or *against* a person or thing): *If I ask for a raise, how will he ~? She ~ed with kindness; People ~ against cruelty.* **2** act chemically: *Carbon ~s with oxygen to produce carbon dioxide; Carbon and oxygen are* **re·act·ants;** *Ohms express electrical* **re·act·ance** (i.e. opposition) *to the flow of alternating current.* **—re·ac·tion** (–AC–) *n.* **1** a response or acting back: *allergic ~ to smoke; the action and ~ of colliding bodies; your ~ to the new tax; A catalyst speeds up a chemical ~.* **2** a political or social tendency to return to a former state of affairs; **re·ac·tion·ar·y** *adj.* & *n.* **-ar·ies** (one) favoring reaction, esp. political. **—re·ac·ti·vate** (–AC–) *v.* **-vates, -vat·ed, -vat·ing** make or become active again: *~ a service, program, disease, fear;* **re·ac·ti·va·tion** (–VAY–) *n.* **—re·ac·tive** (–AC·tiv) *adj.*: *a ~ tendency, impulse;* **reactive dye** one that reacts with a material to make it nonfading. **—re·ac·tor** (–AC–) *n.* **1** one that reacts, esp. positively in a medical test. **2** same as NUCLEAR REACTOR; also, a device or vessel in which a chemical process is carried out.

read (REED) *v.* **reads, read** (RED), **read·ing** **1** get the meaning of, esp. something written: *We ~ English, novels, Braille; I ~* (i.e. follow) *you; You ~ to me* (i.e. aloud) *while I sew; He's ~ing* (i.e. studying) *law.* **2** show, mean, or be: *The clock ~s 10 p.m.; "thimk" should ~ "think."* **—*adj.*** (RED) informed: *He's well ~ in medicine.* **—read between the lines** look for or see a hidden meaning; **read** (something) **into** see something that is not expressed; **read out of** expel from (a party). **—read·a·ble** (REE·duh–) *adj.;* **read·a·ble·ness** or **read·a·bil·i·ty** (–BIL–) *n.* **read·a·bly** (–blee) *adv.* **—read·er** *n.* one who reads; also, a book containing selections for one learning to read; anthology. **—read·er·ship** *n.* **1** a reader's position or office. **2** an audience of readers, as of a magazine. **—read·ing** *n.* the act of one who reads; also, reading material, what a dial shows, or an interpretation. **—read·out** *n.* **1** recorded or displayed data from a computer; also, the process or device used. **2** transmission of data, as from a space vehicle.

read·y (RED·ee) *adj.* **read·i·er, -i·est** **1** prepared or willing to do (as specified or implied) without delay: *Are you ~ to go? always ~* (i.e. apt) *to find fault;* **make ready** prepare. **2** immediately available: *Dinner is ~; ~ cash; a ~ reply for everything; moved up with guns* **(at the) ready.** **—read·i·ly** *adv.;* **read·i·ness** *n.* **—*v.*** **read·ies, read·ied, read·y·ing** make ready, prepare for something immediate. **—read·y-made** *adj.* made ready for use or sale, not made-to-order; hence, lacking individuality; commonplace. **—ready room** a briefing room for aircraft crews before flight. **—read·y-to-wear** *adj.* of clothes, ready-made.

re·a·gent (ree·AY·junt) *n.* a chemical used for its reaction to substances in laboratory testing, industrial manufacture, etc., as bicarbonate of soda and oxalic acid.

¹re·al (REE·ul, ray·AHL) *n.* a former Spanish coin worth ⅛ of a piece of eight.

²re·al (REE·ul, REEL) *adj.* existing in fact, not as appears or is supposed to be; genuine; not imaginary: *Is that diamond ~ or fake? a ~ experience, not a dream; lands, houses, and such ~* (i.e. immovable) *property,* or **real estate;** *A concave lens does not have a ~ focus or form a ~ image that may be projected on a screen;* **for real** *Slang.* real(ly). **—*adv.*** *Informal.* very: *was ~ nice to me.* **—re·al·ism** *n.* philosophy or action based on realities or things as they are, not as they should be, esp. in the artistic portrayal of life; **re·al·ist** *n.;* **re·al·is·tic** (–LIS–) *adj.;* **re·al·is·ti·cal·ly** *adv.* **—re·al·i·ty** (–AL–) *n.* **-ties** the quality of being real; also, a real person or fact; **in reality** in fact. **—re·al·ize** (REE–) *v.* **-iz·es, -ized, -iz·ing** **1** be aware of fully: *didn't ~ I was late.* **2** make real: *to ~ an ambition.* **3** convert into money: *to ~ an investment, bonds, stocks; ~d* (i.e. obtained as money) *very little from the sale.* **—re·al·iz·a·ble** *adj.;* **re·al·i·za·tion** (–ZAY–) *n.* **—re·al·ly** *adv.* actually; ***interj.*** indeed.

realm (RELM) *n.* kingdom; domain; region: *the ~ of fancy, philosophy, science.*

re·al·po·li·tik (ray·AHL·poh·li·teek) *n.* practical politics based on reality. **—real time** instantaneous processing of computer input: *Most process-control systems operate in ~;* **real-time** *adj.*: *Airline bookings must be processed by a ~ system.* **—Re·al·tor** (REE·ul·tur) *Trademark.* a real-estate agent who is a member of the National Association of Real Estate Boards; also **realtor** *n.;* **re·al·ty** (REE·ul·tee) *n.* **-ties** real estate.

---

reabsorb
readapt
readjust
readmit
reaffirm
realign
reanimate
reappear
reapply
reappoint

¹ream (REEM) *n.* **1** 480, 500, or 516 ("perfect ream") sheets of the same size of paper. **2** *Informal.* a large quantity: *~s of unpublished poetry.*

²ream (REEM) *v.* widen a hole or bore using a rotating tool with a ridge or spiral surface; **ream·er** *n.* such a tool; also, a juicer with a ridged surface.

reap (REEP) *v.* cut (grain) or gather (a crop); hence, harvest: *You ~ what you sow.* —**reap·er** *n.* one that reaps, esp. a machine such as a self-binder.

¹rear (REER) *v.* **1** raise: *~ed its head; a ~ing horse* (i.e. rising on its hind legs). **2** bring up (children); breed (livestock); set up (a monument, temple, etc.).

²rear (REER) *n.* & *adj.* (at or in) the back part or position: *the ~ bumper, ~-view mirror of a car;* **bring up the rear** come last in order, as in a procession. —**rear admiral** a naval officer ranking next below a vice admiral. —**rear guard** soldiers guarding the rear of an army. —**rear·most** *adj.* last. —**rear·ward** (–wurd) *adj.* & *adv.* at or toward the rear; also **rear·wards** *adv.*

rea·son (REE·zn) *n.* **1** a motive or occasion that explains something: *resigned for ~s of health; not guilty* **by reason of** *insanity; fired* **with reason** (i.e. justification). **2** thinking and judging capacity: *Animals, infants, etc. have no ~; lost his ~ in his final days.* **3** good sense: *Please listen to ~; It* **stands to reason** (i.e. is logical) *that workers be paid.* —**v.:** *man's capacity to ~; He's too headstrong to ~ with; Let's ~ out a solution based on the evidence we have;* **rea·son·er** *n.;* **rea·son·ing** *n.* —**rea·son·a·ble** (REE–) *adj.* **1** according to reason: *Everyone is rational though not all are ~ in judgment; guilty beyond a ~ doubt.* **2** moderate or fair: *a ~ price, demand, excuse, house* (i.e. in price); **rea·son·a·ble·ness** *n.;* **rea·son·a·bly** *adv.*

re·as·sure (ree·uh·SHOOR) *v.* **-as·sures, -as·sured, -as·sur·ing** assure so as to remove the fears of; restore confidence to: *a ~ing smile;* **re·as·sur·ing·ly** *adv.* —**re·as·sur·ance** *n.*

re·bate (REE–) *n.* & *v.* **-bates, -bat·ed, -bat·ing** (give) a partial refund of payment: *a tax ~.*

reb·el *n.* & *adj.* (having to do with) one that rebels: *famous ~s of history; a ~ army;* **v.** (ri·BEL) **-els, -elled, -el·ling** actively resist or fight against authority: *The Confederates ~d; Everyone ~s at* (i.e. opposes or feels repelled by) *injustices.* —**re·bel·lion** (–BEL·yun) *n.* a defiance of authority, esp. armed resistance to one's government: *~s that have failed;* **re·bel·lious** (–yus) *adj.: ~ troops; children who are ~ by temperament;* **re·bel·lious·ly** *adv.;* **re·bel·lious·ness** *n.*

re·birth (REE–) *n.* a second birth, as in reincarnation; also, a revival or renaissance. —**re·born** (–BORN) *adj.* born again.

re·bound (REE–) *n.* a springing back: *hit the ball* **on the rebound;** *married the first girl he met on the ~* (i.e. after his rejection); **v.** (–BOUND) bounce back; also, recover from a setback or frustration.

re·buff (–BUF) *n.* & *v.* snub or repulse: *offered her a ride but was ~ed.*

re·buke (–BYOOK) *v.* **-bukes, -buked, -buk·ing** blame or reprove sharply; also **n.**

re·bus (REE–) *n.* a riddle composed of pictures, letters, and numbers.

re·but (–BUT) *v.* **-buts, -but·ted, -but·ting** refute by use of arguments, evidence, etc., as in court or in a debate; **re·but·tal** (–BUTL) *n.*

rec. receipt; record(ing); recreation. —**rec** (REK) *n.* [short form] recreation: as in **rec room.**

re·cal·ci·trant (–CAL·si·trunt) *adj.* defiantly resisting control or authority; **re·cal·ci·trance** (–trunce) *n.*

re·call (–CAWL) *v.* **1** call back: *an ambassador ~ed to Washington; defective cars ~ed by a manufacturer.* **2** remember: *I don't ~ your name but recognize your face.* —**n.** (*also* REE–): *Elected judges may be removed by a ~ vote; a retentive memory with almost total ~.*

re·cant (–CANT) *v.* formally withdraw or renounce (a belief, opinion, etc.): *~ed only on his deathbed;* **re·can·ta·tion** (–TAY–) *n.*

re·cap *v.* (–CAP) **-caps, -capped, -cap·ping** **1** retread (a worn tire). **2** *Informal.* recapitulate. —**n.** **1** a recapped tire. **2** a recapitulation. —**re·ca·pit·u·late** (ree·cuh·PICH·uh–) *v.* **-lates, -lat·ed, -lat·ing** sum up; repeat briefly; **re·ca·pit·u·la·tion** (–LAY–) *n.*

recd. or **rec'd.** received.

re·cede (–SEED) *v.* **-cedes, -ced·ed, -ced·ing** (appear to) go backward: *A threat ~s; the ~ing tide, hairline* (of a balding man), *chin* (i.e. that slopes back).

re·ceipt (–SEET) *n.* act of receiving something: *acknowledge ~ of a letter;* **receipts** (i.e. money received) *in the amount of $2 million; Keep your ~s* (i.e. records). —**v.** give a receipt for (goods) or to mark (a bill or invoice) as paid. —**re·ceiv·a·ble** (–SEEV·uh–) *adj.* that may be received or on which (as bills and accounts) payment is to be received; hence **receivables** *n.pl.* —**re·ceive** (–SEEV) *v.* **-ceives, -ceived, -ceiv·ing** **1** take what is offered or delivered: *to ~ a letter, gift, degree; The mind ~s ideas; boats ~ing loads; ~d a crushing blow.* **2** accept:

---

reapportion
reappraise
rearm
rearrange
reascend
reassemble
reassert
reassess
reassign
reassume

a widely ~d opinion; guests ~d (i.e. welcomed) *at the door; to ~ a convert into a church.* —**re·ceiv·er** (–SEE–) *n.* one that receives, as a radio listening set, the listening end of a telephone, a football player who receives a kickoff or punt, the judicial manager of property in a bankruptcy, etc.; **re·ceiv·er·ship** *n.: A bankrupt company goes into ~.* —**receiving line** host, hostess, and guests of honor standing in a row to greet guests.

re·cent (REE·snt) *adj.* of a time just passed: *a ~ event, acquaintance* (made not long ago); **Recent** same as HOLOCENE; **re·cent·ly** *adv.* —**re·cen·cy** or **re·cent·ness** *n.*

re·cep·ta·cle (–SEP·tuh–) *n.* any container or the containerlike base of a flower; also, an electrical outlet to insert a plug in. —**re·cep·tion** (–SEP–) *n.* **1** the receiving of a person or the social function for receiving guests: *a warm ~; the ~ area.* **2** the quality of the sound received in radio or television. —**re·cep·tion·ist** *n.* one employed to receive callers, esp. in an office. —**re·cep·tive** (–SEP·tiv) *adj.* able or ready to receive suggestions, stimuli, etc.; **re·cep·tive·ly** *adv.;* **re·cep·tive·ness** or **re·cep·tiv·i·ty** (–TIV–) *n.* —**re·cep·tor** (–SEP–) *n.* the receiver of a stimulus, as the light-sensitive retina and the nerve endings inside a muscle; sense organ.

re·cess (REE–, –SES) *n.* **1** an inner place, as a niche or alcove; also, a secluded place: *the innermost ~es of one's heart.* **2** a break in an activity for rest or recreation: *a ten-minute ~; the summer ~.* —**v.:** *lighting fixtures ~ed in the ceiling; We ~ for lunch at 1 p.m.* —**re·ces·sion** (–SESH·un) *n.* **1** a going backward; withdrawal; **re·ces·sion·al** *n.* a piece of music for the end of a church service. **2** a temporary decline of business activity, less severe than a depression. —**re·ces·sive** (–siv) *adj.* receding, esp. of a genetic character or trait that is latent, not dominant.

re·cher·ché (ruh·sher·SHAY, –SHER–) *adj.* of manner, diction, etc., studied; excessively refined.

re·cid·i·vism (–SID–) *n.* tendency to relapse (into crime or other behavior or illness pattern); **re·cid·i·vist** *n.* repeater.

recip. reciprocal; reciprocity. —**rec·i·pe** (RES·uh·pee) *n.* a list of ingredients and set of directions for preparing something to eat or drink; hence, a formula or procedure: *a ~ for happiness, peace, success.* —**re·cip·i·ent** (–SIP·ee·unt) *n.* one who receives.

re·cip·ro·cal (–SIP·ruh·cl) *adj.* involving exchange between two parties or a back-and-forth relationship, as when Tom dates Mary and vice versa: *"each other" is a ~ pronoun; Customs unions with mutual tariff concessions start as ~ trade agreements between countries;* **n.:** *a/b is the ~ of b/a;* **re·cip·ro·cal·ly** *adv.* —**re·cip·ro·cate** (–SIP–) *v.* **-cates, -cat·ed, -cat·ing:** *His love for her was not ~d; the ~ing motion of a piston in a ~ing engine;* **re·cip·ro·ca·tion** (–CAY–) *n.* —**rec·i·proc·i·ty** (–PROS–) *n.* **-ties** mutual exchange between two parties: *a relationship that died because of lack of ~.*

re·cit·al (–SYE·tl) *n.* **1** a reciting of facts; account. **2** a performance, as by a musician or group of dancers; **re·cit·al·ist** *n.* —**rec·i·ta·tion** (res·i·TAY–) *n.* a reciting, esp. from memory; also, a lesson or a piece of prose or verse recited. —**rec·i·ta·tive** (–tuh·TEEV) *n.* a portion of an opera's text that is sung in a speechlike style, often with little accompaniment, or in "secco recitative." —**re·cite** (–CITE) *v.* **-cites, -cit·ed, -cit·ing** repeat from memory; also, recount or relate; **re·cit·er** *n.*

reck·less *adj.* very careless and unconcerned about consequences; extremely rash: *~ driving;* **reck·less·ly** *adv.;* **reck·less·ness** *n.*

reck·on (–un) *v.* **1** count or compute: *to ~ the per-unit cost; We ~ed* (i.e. relied) *on your helping us.* **2** consider: *was ~ed peerless in his time; a person who will have to be* **reckoned with** (i.e. taken into consideration). **3** *Regional.* guess; suppose: *I ~ you're right.* —**reck·on·er** *n.* —**reck·on·ing** *n.* **1** calculation: *the ~ of a ship's location.* **2** an account or its settlement: *as the day of ~ drew near.*

re·claim (–CLAIM) *v.* get back what was temporarily given up: *Wasteland is ~ed by irrigation and drainage; processes to ~ rubber, metal, etc. from waste; checked baggage to be ~ed; a ~ed* (i.e. reformed) *sinner;* **re·claim·a·ble** *adj.: recycling of ~ wastes.* —**rec·la·ma·tion** (–MAY–) *n.* —**ré·clame** (ray·CLAHM) *n.* (passion for) publicity.

re·cline (–CLINE) *v.* **-clines, -clined, -clin·ing** (cause) to lie down: *a ~ing figure; ~ your head on the pillow.*

rec·luse (REC·loose, rik·LOOSE) *n.* one living a secluded or cloistered life, as a hermit or monk; **re·clu·sive** (–CLOO·siv) *adj.*

rec·og·ni·tion (–NISH·un) *n.* a recognizing; also, favorable notice: *a scientist who has won worldwide ~; Sigma Xi is a ~ society.* —**re·cog·ni·zance** (–COG·ni·zunce, –CON–) *n.* a legal undertaking entered into before a court: *The accused was released on his own ~* (i.e. without payment of surety). —**rec·og·nize** (REC·ug–) *v.* **-niz·es, -nized, -niz·ing 1** know from memory; identify: *a face difficult to ~.* **2** take notice of formally: *speakers have to be ~d by the chair; The U.N. ~d* (i.e. accepted)

---

reattach
reawake
reawaken
rebaptize
rebroadcast
rebuild
recapitalize
recapture
recharge
recheck

Communist China in 1971. **3** take notice of favorably: *His work was ~d soon after his death.* **—rec·og·niz·a·ble** (REC·ug·nye·zuh·bl) *adj.;* **rec·og·niz·a·bly** *adv.*

re·coil (–COIL) *v.* spring back in reaction, as at an ugly sight or as a gun does when fired; ***n.*** a recoiling or its distance; **re·coil·less** *adj.: a light, small-caliber ~ rifle.*

rec·ol·lect (rec·uh·LECT) *v.* remember (something forgotten); recall (something) hazily: *cannot ~ what happened next;* **rec·ol·lec·tion** (–LEC–) *n.* memory: *no ~ of promising you money; childhood ~s.*

re·com·bi·nant (–COM·buh·nunt) *adj.* combining genes from different sources: *~ DNA;* **re·com·bi·na·tion** (–NAY–) *n.* **—re·com·bine** (ree·cum·BINE) *v.* **-bines, -bined, -bin·ing** combine again or anew.

rec·om·mend (–uh·MEND) *v.* favor or speak favorably (of): *I ~ him for admission; highly ~ed as a scholar; nothing to ~* (i.e. as a cure) *for a cold; died ~ing* (i.e. commending) *his soul to God;* **rec·om·men·da·ble** *adj.;* **rec·om·men·da·to·ry** *adj.: a ~ letter.* **—rec·om·men·da·tion** (–DAY–) *n.: a letter of ~; Good grooming is itself a ~ in a job applicant; ~s for safe driving.*

rec·om·pense (REC·um–) *n.* a return or compensation; requital; ***v.*** **-pens·es, -pensed, -pens·ing:** *was well ~d for his services.*

rec·on·cile (REC·un–) *v.* **-ciles, -ciled, -cil·ing** **1** restore to harmony: *After each fight they are soon ~d; a story difficult to ~* (i.e. make agree) *with the facts.* **2** settle: *to ~ differences; hard to ~ oneself to life in a wheelchair; was at last ~d to his lot.* **—rec·on·cil·a·ble** (–SYE·luh–) *adj.* **—rec·on·cil·i·a·tion** (–AY–) *n.*

rec·on·dite (REC·un–) *adj.* abstruse or obscure: *a ~ subject, style, author.*

re·con·di·tion (–DISH·un) *v.* repair and put in good condition: *a ~ed used car.*

re·con·nais·sance (–CON·uh·sunce) *n.* a military survey to explore or spy for information, esp. about the enemy: *a ~ plane, satellite.* **—rec·on·noi·ter** (–uh·NOY–) *v.* make a reconnaissance of (a place); *Brit.* **rec·on·noi·tre, -tres, -tred, -tring.**

re·con·sid·er (–cun·SID–) *v.* consider again with a view to changing (a decision, view, etc.); **re·con·sid·er·a·tion** (–RAY–) *n.*

re·con·sti·tute (–CON·stuh–) *v.* **-tutes, -tut·ed, -tut·ing** restore (powdered milk, frozen juice, etc.) to its original consistency by adding water.

re·con·struct (–cun·STRUCT) *v.* rebuild in original form using remaining parts, evidence, etc.: *to ~ a city, extinct languages;* **re·con·struc·tion** *n.* a reconstructing or something reconstructed; **Reconstruction** (the period of 1865–1877 marking) the reorganization and reestablishment of the S. states in the Union after the U.S. Civil War.

re·cord (–CORD) *v.* put or register (scientific data, historical events, musical performances, etc.) on paper, magnetic tape, film, phonograph discs, etc.; put (something heard, seen, felt, etc.) in permanent form; hence, to evidence: *Annual rings ~ a tree's age;* ***—n.*** (REC·urd) **1** a recording or being recorded; also, what is recorded, as a document, disc, tape, etc. containing anything written, spoken, sung, etc.; hence, history: *a good driving ~; a ~ of convictions; You're* **on record** *as saying so; It was supposed to be* **off the record** (i.e. not for putting down or publication). **2** the highest, lowest, biggest, etc. in regard to something: *1,069 lb. was the 1978 ~ for a man's weight; ~s broken at the Olympics;* ***adj.:*** *a ~ attendance, heat, height.* **—re·cord·er** (–CORD–) *n.* **1** one that records, esp. an instrument or machine such as a tape recorder. **2** a flutelike wooden musical instrument. **—re·cord·ing** (–CORD–) *n.* what is recorded, as on magnetic tape; also, the device, as a disc, containing it; **re·cord·ist** *n.* one who records. **—record player** a phonograph.

re·count (–COUNT) *v.* **1** narrate; also, enumerate. **2** also **re-count,** count again. ***—n.*** (REE–) a counting again.

re·coup (–COOP) *v.* recover something lost or its equivalent: *to ~ one's losses, health, fortunes.*

re·course (REE–, –CORCE) *n.* a seeking of help or protection; also, a source of aid: *had ~ to legal measures.*

re·cov·er (–CUV–) *v.* get back or regain: *Police ~ stolen property; working harder to ~ lost time; ~ damages* (by process of law); *to ~* (i.e. gain control of) *a fumbled ball, oneself in a fall, consciousness;* **re·cov·er·a·ble** *adj.* **—re·cov·er·y** (–CUV–) *n.* **-er·ies:** *the ~ of stolen vehicles; A quick ~ saved the skidding car; the* **recovery room** *where patients are wheeled in from surgery to recover from the effects of anesthesia.* **—re·cov·er** (–CUV–) *v.* cover again.

rec·re·ant (REC·ree·unt) *n.* & *adj.* (one who is) cowardly or disloyal.

re·cre·ate (ree·cree·ATE) *v.* create anew, as a scene from history; **re·cre·a·tive** *adj.* **—rec·re·a·tion** (–ree·AY–) *n.* (means of) refreshment after work, as games, picnics, and such pleasurable activities: *finds ~ in bird watching;* **rec·re·ate** (REC–) *v.* **-ates, -at·ed, -at·ing:** *Children like to ~ outdoors.* **—rec·re·a·tion·al** (–AY–) or **rec·re·a·tive** (–AY–) *adj.: a*

---

rechristen
recommence
reconquer
reconsecrate
reconsign
reconsult
reconvene
reconvert
recook
recopy

recreational vehicle *such as a trailer or camper.*
re·crim·i·nate (–CRIM–) *v.* **-nates, -nat·ed, -nat·ing** accuse (someone) back; **re·crim·i·na·tion** (–NAY–) *n.: mutual ~s ending in divorce proceedings.* **—re·crim·i·na·tive** or **re·crim·i·na·to·ry** (–CRIM–) *adj.*
re·cru·des·cence (ree·croo·DES–) *n.* a new outbreak (of a disorder) or a worsening, as of a disease; **re·cru·des·cent** *adj.* **—re·cru·desce** (–DES) *v.*
re·cruit (–CROOT) *v.* enlist (new personnel) for an army, navy, or other organization; ***n.*** a newly enlisted soldier, sailor, or member of a group; **re·cruit·er** *n.;* **re·cruit·ment** *n.*
rect. receipt; rectangle; rectified; rector(y).
rec·tal (REC·tl) *adj.* of the rectum; **rec·tal·ly** *adv.* **—rec·tan·gle** (REC–) *n.* a four-sided figure with four right angles, but usu. not a square; **rec·tan·gu·lar** (–TANG·gyuh·lur) *adj.* **—rec·ti·fy** (REC–) *v.* **-fies, -fied, -fy·ing** set right: *to ~ mistakes; ~d* (i.e. purified) *spirits: a ~ing device, or* **rec·ti·fi·er** *to change alternating current to direct current;* **rec·ti·fi·ca·tion** (–CAY–) *n.* **—rec·ti·lin·e·ar** (–LIN·ee·ur) *adj.* having to do with straight lines: *the ~ propagation of light.* **—rec·ti·tude** (REC–) *n.* uprightness of character or conduct. **—rec·to** (–toh) *n.* **-tos** a right-hand page; cf. VERSO. **—rec·tor** (–tur) *n.* a minister or clergyman in charge of a parish; also, the head of a seminary, college, or school; **rec·tor·ate** (–it) *n.;* **rec·to·ri·al** (–TOR–) *adj.;* **rec·to·ry** (REC–) *n.* **-ries** a rector's residence. **—rec·tum** *n.* **-tums** or **-ta** the straight final portion of the intestine leading to the anus.
re·cum·bent (–CUM·bunt) *adj.* lying down or reclining: *the almost horizontal ~ fold in a rock formation.*
re·cu·per·ate (–COO–) *v.* **-ates, -at·ed, -at·ing** regain (health) or recover (losses); **re·cu·per·a·tive** *adj.* **—re·cu·per·a·tion** (–RAY–) *n.*
re·cur (–CUR) *v.* **-curs, -curred, -cur·ring** occur again; also, return: *a ~ing nightmare; a ~ing decimal such as 3.3333 . . .;* **re·cur·rent** *adj.: a ~ spelling mistake;* **re·cur·rence** *n.*
re·cy·cle (ree·SYE–) *v.* **-cles, -cled, -cling** put (waste materials) through a process or treatment for using again: *garbage ~ing; ~d paper;* **re·cy·cla·ble** (–kluh·bl) *adj.: prefers ~ containers to returnable ones.*
red *n.* **1** the color of fresh blood; **in the red** in debt; **see red** get very angry. **2** a political revolutionary; **Red** a Communist or extreme radical. ***—adj.*** **red·der, red·dest** [corresponding to the *n.* senses] **1:** *~ and white blood cells; with ~* (i.e. bloodshot) *eyes;* **red·ly** *adv.;* **red·ness** *n.* **2:** *African nations going ~* (i.e. Communist); *Red China* (i.e. People's Republic of China).
re·dact (–DACT) *v.* prepare a redaction of; also, draw up (a statement, proclamation, etc.); **re·dac·tor** *n.* **—re·dac·tion** (–DAC–) *n.* a revised or rearranged edition, as of parts of the Bible; **re·dac·tion·al** *adj.*
red alga a class of marine algae such as agar, useful as gelatin substitutes. **—red blood cell** (or **corpuscle**) one of the oxygen-rich, hemoglobin-containing cells of the blood; **red-blood·ed** *adj.* vigorous or lusty. **—red·breast** (–brest) *n.* a robin. **—red·bud** *n.* an ornamental tree of the pea family that bears delicate pink blossoms early in the spring before its leaves appear. **—red·cap** *n.* a porter at a bus or railroad station. **—red carpet** an impressive or ceremonial welcome; **red-car·pet** *adj.: ~ treatment.* **—red cedar** a North American tree of the cypress family, esp. a juniper, or "eastern red cedar," and arborvitae, or "western red cedar." **—red clover** a clover much used for pasture and hay and for enriching the soil. **—red·coat** *n.* a red-coated British soldier of the Revolutionary War. **—Red Cross** an international relief organization, identified by its red-cross-on-white emblem, founded in Switzerland in 1863. **—red deer** a large Old World deer related to the elk, with a reddish brown coat and a yellow-to-orange patch on the rump. **—red·den** *v.* make or become red; flush or blush; **red·dish** *adj;* **red·dish·ness** *n.*
re·deem (–DEEM) *v.* get back (something or someone in another's possession) by paying a price: *jewelry ~ed by repaying a loan; The government ~s savings bonds; A mortgage is ~ed* (i.e. paid off); *the ~ing* (i.e. saving) *features of an otherwise poor product; the ~ing of slaves; humanity ~ed from sin by a* **re·deem·er,** or **the Redeemer** Jesus; **re·deem·a·ble** (–DEE·muh–) *adj.* **—re·demp·tion** (–DEMP–) *n.* a redeeming, being redeemed, or something that redeems; **re·demp·tive** (–tiv) or **re·demp·to·ry** *adj.*
red fox a fox with reddish fur. **—Red Guard** a member of any of the militant Maoist groups of students who campaigned in the Chinese "cultural revolution" of the late 1960's. **—red-hand·ed** *adj. & adv.* in the act of committing a crime: *caught ~.* **—red·head** *n.* a red-haired person; **red·head·ed** *adj.* **—red herring** something irrelvant used to distract attention from the main issue. **—red-hot** *adj.* glowing red with heat; hence, very excited; also, very new.

---

recross
recrystallize
recut
redecorate
rededicate
redefine
redeploy
redeposit
redetermine
redevelop

re·dis·trict (–DIS–) *v.* organize into new districts.

red-let·ter day a memorable or happy occasion. —**red light** a warning light or signal, as one requiring traffic to stop; **red-light district** part of a town with many brothels. —**red·lin·ing** (RED·lye·ning) *n.* economic discrimination against poor neighborhoods, as when a bank refuses to grant mortgages or loans. —**red man** a redskin. —**red·neck** *n. Slang.* a white farmer of Southern U.S. considered as bigoted or narrow-minded. —**red oak** an ornamental oak with oblong leaves that turn red in the fall and that have lobes with irregular teeth and bristly points. —**red ochre** earthy variety of hematite used as a pigment.

red·o·lent (REDL·unt) *adj.* smelling (*of*); hence, suggestive (*of*); **red·o·lent·ly** *adv.* —**red·o·lence** *n.*

re·dou·ble (ree·DUBL) *v.* **-bles, -bled, -bling** increase greatly; intensify: *~ one's efforts.*

re·doubt (–DOWT) *n.* a small temporary fortification; **re·doubt·a·ble** *adj.* formidable; **re·doubt·a·bly** *adv.*

re·dound (–DOWND) *v.* have a result or reaction: *actions that ~ to one's credit.*

red pepper a seasoning ground from the fruit or seeds of a red capsicum; also, the plant.

re·dress (–DRES) *v.* set right or repair (a wrong, grievance, etc.); ***n.*** reparation or the means of finding a remedy.

Red Sea the sea between the Arabian peninsula and N.E. Africa. —**red shift** shift in the spectral lines of distant objects such as quasars toward the red end because of movement away from the earth. —**red·skin** *n.* a North American Indian. —**red snapper** a Caribbean species of snapper fish. —**red squirrel** the noisiest of the squirrel family with reddish fur on its back. —**red·start** *n.* an American wood warbler whose male has red markings on its wings and tail. —**red tape** excessive adherence to rules and regulations, as in government service; bureaucratic routine. —**red tide** a red discoloration of sea water due to the sudden increase of certain organisms that kill marine life.

re·duce (–DUCE) *v.* **-duc·es, -duced, -duc·ing** make less, lower, smaller, simpler, etc.: *how to ~ weight, expenses; A heckler is ~d to silence; 3/9 can be ~d to 1/3; hydrogen used to ~ an oxide* (i.e. by removing oxygen) *to metal;* **re·duc·er** *n.;* **re·duc·i·ble** *adj.* —**re·duc·tion** (–DUC–) *n.* a reducing or being reduced; also, something resulting from reducing or the amount reduced.

re·dun·dan·cy (–DUN·dun·see) *n.* **1** a being redundant; also **re·dun·dance.** **2** *pl.* **-cies** an instance of wordiness. —**re·dun·dant** (–dunt) *adj.* superfluous or unnecessary: *Jobs made ~ by automation; ~ expressions such as "exact same"; a ~* (i.e. wordy) *style;* **re·dun·dant·ly** *adv.*

red·wood *n.* a giant evergreen tree of western U.S. of the sequoia group; also called "California redwood."

reed *n.* **1** any tall, slender grass plant with a hollow, jointed stem that is often used for musical pipes, arrows, etc.; also, the stem. **2** a thin piece of wood, metal, or plastic used in the mouthpiece of a **reed instrument** such as a clarinet or oboe to vibrate and produce a sound when blown into. —**reed·y** *adj.* **reed·i·er, -i·est** of or like a reed or sounding like a reed instrument.

¹reef *n.* a ridge of rocks, sand, or coral lying covered near the surface of the water, except at low tide; **reef·y** *adj.*

²reef *n.* the part of a sail that may be rolled up to reduce the area exposed to the wind; ***v.*** reduce the area of (a sail). —**reef·er** *n.* **1** one who reefs (sails); formerly, a midshipman. **2** *Slang.* a marijuana cigarette. **3** *Slang.* a refrigerated van, freight car, etc. for carrying perishable food.

reek *n.* & *v.* (send out) a strong, unpleasant smell: *walked in ~ing of alcohol; a department ~ing with corruption;* **reek·er** *n.;* **reek·y** *adj.*

reel *n.* **1** (film, thread, cable, etc. wound on) a revolving device such as a roller or spool. **2** a whirling motion. **3** a lively folk dance of the Scottish Highlands; also, Virginia reel. —***v.*** **1** wind on a reel; **reel in** pull in (a fish) using a reeled line; **reel off** repeat (a list, text, etc.) with ease and speed; rattle off. **2** lurch, stagger, or feel unsteady: *came out of the bar and ~ed down the street; His head was ~ing after the blow.* —**reel·a·ble** *adj.;* **reel·er** *n.*

re·en·force (ree·en·FORCE) *v.* same as REINFORCE.

re·en·try or **re-en·try** (–EN·tree) *n.* **-tries** a second entry; also, a reentering, as of the earth's atmosphere by a space vehicle.

reeve *v.* **reeves,** *pt.* & *pp.* **reeved** or **rove, reev·ing** pass (a rope) through a ring, block, or cleat.

ref *n.* & *v.* **refs, reffed, ref·fing** [short form] referee. —**ref.** referee; reference; referred.

re·face (ree·FACE) *v.* **-fac·es, -faced, -fac·ing** put a new face or covering on.

re·fec·tion (–FEC–) *n.* food and drink; also, a meal or repast. —**re·fec·to·ry** (–FEC–) *n.* **-ries** a dining hall in a monastery or convent.

re·fer (ri·FUR) *v.* **-fers, -ferred, -fer·ring** **1** take or send (someone or something): *He ~d me to a lawyer; Let's ~ the dispute to a judge.*

---

redigest
redirect
rediscover
redistill
redistribute
redo
redomesticate
redraw
reedit
reeducate

2 direct one's attention: *He ~d to many authorities in the subject; Does this remark ~* (i.e. apply) *to me?* **—ref·er·a·ble** (REF–, ri·FUR–) *adj.;* **re·fer·er** (–FUR–) *n.* **—ref·er·ee** (–uh·REE) *n.* & *v.* **-ees, -eed, -ee·ing** (act as) one to whom a disputable matter is referred for a decision, as an umpire in certain games: *Who is ~ing the basketball match?* **—ref·er·ence** (REF·uh·runce) *n.* **1** a referring, being referred, or thing referred to: *job applications filed for future ~; a scholarly book with many footnote ~s;* **with** (or **in**) **reference** *to your letter of Jan. 30th.* **2** a source of information on a subject: **reference books** *such as dictionaries, atlases, and encyclopedias; May I cite you as a ~? showed me excellent ~s* (i.e. letters of recommendation) *from former employers.* **—ref·er·en·dum** (–REN–) *n.* **-dums** or **-da** a reference, as of legislative measures, to the direct vote of the people; also, such a vote. **—ref·er·ent** (REF–) *n.* a thing referred to, as the animal by the word *horse;* object of a reference; ***adj.:*** *the ~ word.* **—re·fer·ral** (–FUR·ul) *n.* act of officially referring one person to another; also, the person so referred.

re·fill (–FIL) *v.* fill again; ***n.*** (REE–) a refilling, as of a drug prescription, or something used to refill, as in a ball-point pen; **re·fill·a·ble** (–FIL–) *adj.: a ~ container.*

re·fine (–FINE) *v.* **-fines, -fined, -fin·ing** make finer or less coarse; also, purify; **refined** *adj.: ~d petroleum, sugar, language; a woman of ~d manners, tastes; a ~d* (i.e. cultured) *young woman; a ~d* (i.e. subtle) *distinction;* **refine (up)on** improve or improve on (one's methods, notions, inventions, etc.); **re·fin·er** *n.* **—re·fine·ment** *n.* act or result of refining: *wrought iron as a ~ of pig iron; sarcasm as a ~ of cruelty; a man of ~* (i.e. culture). **—re·fin·er·y** (–FYE·nuh·ree) *n.* **-er·ies** a plant for refining raw materials such as oil or sugar.

refl. reflex(ive).

re·fla·tion (–FLAY–) *n.* stimulation of inflation to cure an economic recession.

re·flect (–FLECT) *v.* **1** throw back (light, heat, sound, etc.): *Mirrors ~ light, images, one's face; Editorials ~ views* (i.e. like a mirror); *great deeds ~ing* (i.e. bringing) *credit on their doers; Bad manners often ~ on* (i.e. bring discredit to) *one's parents.* **2** turn one's thoughts back on (a subject); seriously consider: *acted rashly without ~ing; Please ~ on your actions.* **—re·flec·tion** *n.* **1** a reflecting, being reflected, or something reflected; image: *the laterally inverted ~ in a mirror.* **2** thinking or consideration; also, its expression: *Sorel's ~s on violence.* **3** a remark or observation, esp. one casting blame; hence, blame or discredit: *These comments are no ~ on your motives;* **re·flec·tive** (–tiv) *adj.: copper foil as ~ insulation against heat; a ~ mood;* **re·flec·tor** *n.: The parabolic ~ of a searchlight gives a parallel beam; a ~ fire built against a wall.* **—re·flex** (REE–) *n.* a usu. inborn, automatic reaction to a stimulus: *You jerk back your hand from a flame by* **reflex action;** *the conditioned ~ of the mouth watering at the mention of food.* **—*adj.*** **1** coming in reaction: *A ~ action works in a ~ arc* (i.e. nerve path). **2** reflected back: *A* **reflex camera** *is focused by using its ~ image;* **re·flex·ly** *adv.* **—re·flex·ive** (–FLEX·iv) *adj.* referring back to the subject of a sentence; ***n.*** a reflexive verb or pronoun, as *bethink, hurt oneself, myself, yourselves,* etc.; **re·flex·ive·ly** *adv.;* **re·flex·ive·ness** *n.*

re·flux (REE–) *n.* a flowing back; ***v.*** (*also* ri·FLUX) make (a liquid) vaporize, condense, and flow back to source, as in a **reflux condenser** for continued boiling without evaporation.

re·for·est (–FOR–) *v.* plant (land) with trees again, as after a fire; **re·for·est·a·tion** (–TAY–) *n.*

re-form (REE–) *v.* form again; **re-for·ma·tion** (–MAY–) *n.* **—re·form** (–FORM) *v.* make or become better, esp. by removing faults: *a ~ed criminal; the Dutch Reformed Church;* ***n.*** an improvement in conditions: *political and social ~s; a ~ bill;* **re·form·a·ble** (–FOR·muh–) *adj.;* **re·form·a·tive** (–FOR·muh·tiv) *adj.* **—ref·or·ma·tion** (ref·ur·MAY–) *n.* a reforming or being reformed, esp. **Reformation,** the European religious movement of the 1500's leading to the founding of Protestant churches. **—re·form·a·to·ry** (–FOR·muh–) *n.* **-ries** an institution for young offenders; a correctional training school; also **reform school.** **—re·form·er** (–FOR–) *n.* one who works for reform; **Reformer** a leader of the Reformation.

re·fract (–FRACT– *v.* subject to refraction: *Water ~s light;* **re·frac·tion** (–FRAC–) *n.* the bending of waves of light, sound, etc. when passing from one medium to another obliquely; **re·frac·tive** (–tiv) *adj.: Water has a lower ~ index* (i.e. index of refraction) *than glass.* **—re·frac·tor** (–FRAC–) *n.* a refracting or lens telescope, not a reflecting one. **—re·frac·to·ry** (–FRAC–) *adj.* **1** stubbornly resisting control or direction: *a ~ group of people.* **2** able to withstand great heat: *Fireclay is a ~ material;* ***n.:*** *pl.* **-ries** *Silica, graphite, and carbon are ~s;* **re·frac·to·ri·ly** *adv.;* **re·frac·to·ri·ness** *n.*

¹re·frain (–FRAIN) *n.* a phrase or verse that is repeated at intervals in a poem or song, esp. at the end of a stanza; a chorus or burden.

²re·frain (–FRAIN) *v.* hold oneself (*from* doing something one is inclined to do); forbear.

---

reelect
reembark
reembody
reemerge
reemphasize
reemploy
reenact
reenlist

re·fresh (–FRESH) *v.* **1** make or become fresh again: *a few hints to ~ his memory; a* **re·fresh·er course** *for reviewing what we learned some time back; We ~ ourselves with food, drink, a warm bath, etc.; a ~ing breeze, experience* (because new); *to ~* (i.e. replenish) *supplies, glasses after each drink.* —**re·fresh·ment** (–FRESH–) *n.* a refreshing, being refreshed, or that which refreshes; **refreshments** *pl.* food and drink.

refrig. refrigerating; refrigeration. —**re·frig·er·ant** (–FRIJ–) *n.* & *adj.* (a fluid such as ammonia or freon) that refrigerates: *A heat pump is a ~ device;* **re·frig·er·ate** *v.* **-ates, -at·ed, -at·ing** make or keep (food, etc.) cold or keep from perishing, as in a cabinet or room called **re·frig·er·a·tor** *n.;* **re·frig·er·a·tion** (–RAY–) *n.*

re·frin·gent (–FRIN·junt) *adj.* refracting.

ref·uge (REF·yooj) *n.* (a place providing) shelter or protection from danger or trouble: *sought ~ in flight;* **ref·u·gee** (–JEE, REF–) *n.* one who flees from one country to another for protection, as during a war.

re·ful·gent (–FUL–) *adj.* shining or radiant; **re·ful·gent·ly** *adv.;* **re·ful·gence** *n.*

re·fund (–FUND) *v.* pay back (a deposit, an excess payment, the price of an unsatisfactory purchase, etc.); **re·fund·a·ble** *adj.* —***n.*** (REE–) a refunding or a refunded amount: *a tax ~.*

re·fur·bish (–FUR–) *v.* brighten or polish up; renovate; **re·fur·bish·ment** *n.*

re·fuse (–FYOOZ) *v.* **-fus·es, -fused, -fus·ing** decline (*to* do, give, grant, or accept something) directly or bluntly. *She ~d to change her mind; ~d* (i.e. rejected) *the presidency; an offer* (so good) *you can't ~;* ***n.*** (REF·yoos, –yooz) what is rejected; waste; rubbish. —**re·fus·al** (–FEW·zul) *n.*

re·fute (–FYOOT) *v.* **-futes, -fut·ed, -fut·ing** prove (a person or argument) to be wrong by use of evidence, reasoning, etc.; **re·fut·a·ble** *adj.;* **re·fut·er** *n.* —**ref·u·ta·tion** (ref·yuh·TAY–) *n.*

reg. region; register(ed); registrar; registry; regular; regulation.

re·gain (–GAIN) *v.* get back: *to ~ one's health, consciousness, popularity, footing; to ~* (i.e. get back to) *the shore.*

re·gal (REE·gul) *adj.* royal, esp. majestic or splendid as a king is: *~ bearing, dignity, splendor;* **re·gal·ly** *adv.*

re·gale (–GALE) *v.* **-gales, -galed, -gal·ing** entertain (*with* something delightful or delicious); **re·gale·ment** *n.*

re·ga·li·a (–GAY–) *n.pl.* **1** the crown, scepter, and such emblems of royalty; hence, the insignia or emblems of any office or order. **2** finery.

re·gard (–GARD) *v.* consider mentally or with the eyes (in a specified manner, as with favor or respect): *He ~ed her lovingly; a highly ~ed physician; ~ed as of no value;* **as regards** or **regarding** concerning. —***n.*** consideration: *Have some ~ for cleanliness; without ~ to the rights of others; was held in some ~* (i.e. esteem); **in** (or **with**) **regard to** concerning; **regards** *pl.* good wishes; **re·gard·ful** *adj.;* **re·gard·less** *adj.: seemed ~* (i.e. careless) *of the consequences;* ***adv.:*** *Do it* **regardless of** (i.e. in spite of) *the cost; We'll start at dawn, ~* (i.e. whatever the conditions).

re·gat·ta (–GAT·uh) *n.* a boat race or a series of boat races.

regd. registered.

re·gen·cy (REE·jun–) *n.* **-cies** **1** the government of a regent or its period of rule, as the **Regency** (1811–1820) in English history. **2** a body of regents.

re·gen·er·ate (–JEN–) *v.* **-ates, -at·ed, -at·ing** **1** reform completely; be reborn spiritually. **2** regrow (a part, as plants and lower animals): *The human body can ~ hair, nails, etc.* —***adj.*** (–uh·rit) reborn spiritually; reformed. —**re·gen·er·a·tive** (–tiv) *adj.;* **re·gen·er·a·tor** *n.* —**re·gen·er·a·tion** (–RAY–) *n.*

re·gent (REE·junt) *n.* **1** one who rules a country when the monarch is too young, is ill, or absent. **2** a member of a governing body of a school, library, museum, etc.

reg·gae (REG·ay) *n.* a popular form of West Indian music influenced by rock'n'roll.

reg·i·cide (REJ–) *n.* the killer or the killing of a king. —**re·gime** or **ré·gime** (ruh·ZHEEM, ray–) *n.* **1** a system of government; also, a rule or its period: *a democratic ~; during the previous ~.* **2** regimen. —**reg·i·men** (REJ–) *n.* way of living in regard to diet, exercise, etc.; also, a course of treatment. —**reg·i·ment** (REJ–) *n.* a military unit composed of battalions or squadrons; ***v.*** (–MENT) organize (as a school system) in a strict or uniform manner; **reg·i·men·tal** (–MEN·tl) *adj.;* **regimentals** *n.pl.* military uniform; **reg·i·men·ta·tion** (–TAY–) *n.* —**Re·gi·na** (–JYE–) capital of Saskatchewan.

re·gion (REE·jun) *n.* **1** a usu. indefinite area or division but with common characteristics throughout: *the Rocky Mountain ~; the metropolitan ~.* **2** a field or domain; locality: *in the ~ of the lungs; the ~ of art.* —**re·gion·al** *adj.: a ~ dialect, expression; ~ geography, government; a matter of ~, not national interest;* **re·gion·al·ism** *n.;* **re·gion·al·ly** *adv.*

reg·is·ter (REJ–) *n.* **1** a record or recording device: *a hotel ~; a cash ~.* **2** a particular compass or range of voice: *A bass sings in a different ~ from a soprano; "Informal" and*

---

reenter
reequip
reestablish
reevaluate
reexamine
reexchange
reexport
refashion

"Slang" are different ~s (*Brit.* levels of usage). **3** a grille over a hole in a wall or floor to regulate the air from a heating or cooling system. **—v.:** *Births, deaths, etc. are ~ed at the registry; ~ed mail has special protection; Her face ~ed* (i.e. showed) *no surprise;* **registered nurse** one licensed to practise nursing. **—reg·is·trant** *n.* one who registers, as the owner of a trademark; **reg·is·trar** *n.* an official in charge of records. **—reg·is·tra·tion** (–TRAY–) *n.* a registering, an entry in a register, the number of those registered, or a certificate of registering, as of an automobile. **—reg·is·try** (–tree) *n.* **-tries** **1** an office of registration or a register book. **2** registration, esp. of a ship: *a ship of Liberian ~.*

reg·nal (REG·nl) *adj.* of a reign: *Queen Elizabeth's 25th ~ year.* **—reg·nant** (–nunt) *adj.* reigning; predominant; prevalent.

re·gress (–GRES) *v.* go backward; also, cause regression; **re·gress·ive** (–iv) *adj.;* **re·gres·sor** *n.* **—re·gres·sion** (–GRESH·un) *n.* a return to an earlier or more primitive condition, as in daydreaming and such defense mechanisms.

re·gret (–GRET) *n.* & *v.* **-grets, -gret·ted, -gret·ting** (feel) sorrow or dissatisfaction about an action or any unfortunate occurrence: *I ~ to have to say this; She ~s her past; We sent our ~s* (i.e. a polite note) *declining the invitation;* **re·gret·ta·ble** (–GRET–) *adj.;* **re·gret·ful** *adj.: felt regretful about the whole regrettable incident.* **—re·gret·ta·bly** *adv.;* **re·gret·ful·ly** *adv.* **—re·gret·ter** *n.*

re·group (–GROOP) *v.* group again, esp. reorganize (one's forces) for a renewed fight.

regt. regiment.

reg·u·lar (REG·yuh·lur) *adj.* **1** according to rule or custom; normal; usual: *9 to 5 are ~ business hours; "drink-drank-drunk" are not the parts of a ~ verb; ~ or king size? ~ and premium gasolines.* **2** habitual or predictable in doing something: *a ~ customer, subscriber; a ~* (*Informal.* thorough) *nuisance; a ~* (i.e. likeable) *guy.* **3** even; symmetrical; orderly: *~ heartbeats, features, life of a camp.* **4** professional or recognized: *the ~ soldiers of a ~ army* (i.e. not draftees, reserves, etc.); *the ~* (i.e. religious, not secular) *clergy; a ~* (i.e. official) *nominee of the party.* **—n.** **1** a regular soldier, clergyman, or player (i.e. not a substitute). **2** *Informal.* a regular attender (as at church services). **—reg·u·lar·ly** *adv.* **—reg·u·lar·i·ty** (–LAIR–) *n.* **—reg·u·lar·ize** (REG·yuh–) *v.* **-iz·es, -ized, -iz·ing. —reg·u·late** *v.* **-lates, -lat·ed, -lat·ing** control or keep in a controlled state: *signals ~ing the flow of traffic; a well-~d* (i.e. adjusted) *clock;* **reg·u·la·tor** *n.;* **reg·u·la·tive** (–lay·tiv) *adj.: a ~ principle, instrument;* **reg·u·la·to·ry** *adj.: ~ agencies, moves, steps; a ~* (i.e. subject to control) *product.* **—reg·u·la·tion** (–LAY–) *n.* **1** control. **2** a rule for the enforcement of a law: *traffic ~s; military ~s;* ***adj.*** as required by regulations: *the ~ size; a ~ uniform.*

re·gur·gi·tate (–GUR·juh–) *v.* **-tates, -tat·ed, -tat·ing** throw back what is contained inside; vomit; **re·gur·gi·ta·tion** (–TAY–) *n.*

re·ha·bil·i·tate (–BIL–) *v.* **-tates, -tat·ed, -tat·ing** restore (a criminal, patient with a severe illness or disability, run-down neighborhood, etc.) to a good or healthy condition; **re·ha·bil·i·ta·tive** (–tay·tiv) *adj.* **—re·ha·bil·i·ta·tion** (–TAY–) *n.*

re·hash (–HASH) *v.* work up (old material) in a new form without much improvement; ***n.*** (REE–): *a ~ of some leftovers.*

re·hear (–HEER) *v.* **-hears, -heard** (–HURD), **-hear·ing** of a court or tribunal, hear (a case) a second time.

re·hearse (–HURCE) *v.* **-hears·es, -hearsed, -hears·ing** **1** practice (a play, role, concert, etc.) for public performance. **2** recite; tell in detail; enumerate. **—re·hears·al** *n.: a camera ~* (before a TV show); *dress ~.* **—re·hears·er** *n.*

reign (RAIN) *n.* a sovereign's rule or its period; ***v.*** rule as a sovereign; hence, prevail: *Peace ~ed in Jerusalem.*

re·im·burse (ree·im·BURCE) *v.* **-burs·es, -bursed, -burs·ing** pay (a person) for an amount spent; also, repay (the amount spent); **re·im·burs·a·ble** *adj.;* **re·im·burse·ment** *n.*

rein (RAIN) *n.* one of a pair of long, narrow straps or lines connected to the bridle of an animal for its driver or rider to control it; hence, a check or control: *a storyteller* **giving (free) rein to** *his imagination; a party assuming the ~s of government.* **—v.** guide or curb: *to ~ in a horse before dismounting; to ~ (in) one's passions* (i.e. have them under control).

re·in·car·na·tion (ree·in·car·NAY–) *n.* the supposed rebirth of a soul in another body; **re·in·car·nate** (–CAR–) *v.* **-nates, -nat·ed, -nat·ing.**

rein·deer (RAIN–) *n. sing.* & *pl.* a large antlered deer of N. Europe and Asia, used as a beast of burden, esp. to pull sledges, as in Lapland. **—reindeer moss** a type of Arctic lichen eaten by reindeer.

re·in·force (ree·in·FORCE) *v.* **-forc·es, -forced, -forc·ing** strengthen, as a military force with more troops, ships, planes, etc., concrete **(reinforced concrete)** with metal inside it, or a response to a stimulus in a learning process, as by pairing the taste of a food with

---

refasten
refilm
refilter
refinance
refinish
refit
refocus
refold

a sound or tone as added stimulus; **re·in·forc·er** *n.* —**re·in·force·ment** *n.*

re·in·state (ree·in·STATE) *v.* **-states, -stat·ed, -stat·ing** restore to a former position or condition: *~d with full pay and seniority;* **re·in·state·ment** *n.*

re·it·er·ate (ree·IT–) *v.* **-ates, -at·ed, -at·ing** repeat (a request, warning, belief, etc.) insistently; **re·it·er·a·tive** (–ay·tiv) *adj.* —**re·it·er·a·tion** (–AY–) *n.*

re·ject (–JECT) *v.* refuse (to accept, agree to, or submit to) something; also, discard or throw out (something or someone): *a ~ed lover;* ***n.*** (REE–) a rejected person or thing; **re·jec·tion** (–JEC–) *n.: an organism's immunological ~ of a transplanted organ or foreign tissue; a publisher's* **rejection slip** *sent back with an unwanted submission.*

re·joice (–JOICE) *v.* **-joic·es, -joiced, -joic·ing** feel joy or give joy to; gladden; **re·joic·er** *n.;* **re·joic·ing** *n.*

re·join (–JOIN) *v.* **1** join again, esp. go back to a group. **2** reply formally, as to a plaintiff in court; **re·join·der** *n.* such a reply; also, an answer to a reply.

re·ju·ve·nate (–JOO·vuh–) *v.* **-nates, -nat·ed, -nat·ing** make young again or give new vigor to; **re·ju·ve·na·tion** (–NAY–) *n.*

rel. relating; relative.

re·lapse (–LAPS) *v.* **-laps·es, -lapsed, -laps·ing** fall back (*into* a previous condition such as an illness, criminal habits, silence, etc.): *the tick-borne ~ing* (i.e. recurring) *fever of W. United States.* —***n.*** a relapsing.

re·late (–LATE) *v.* **-lates, -lat·ed, -lat·ing** **1** tell or narrate (a story or adventure); **re·lat·er** or **re·la·tor** *n.* **2** connect: *The Smiths are not ~d to the Smythes; "Frail" and "fragile" are ~d; The generation gap makes it hard for children to ~* (i.e. be responsive) *to their parents; interested in what ~s* (i.e. refers) *to ourselves;* **re·lat·ed** *adj.;* **re·lat·ed·ness** *n.* —**re·lat·a·ble** *adj.* —**re·la·tion** (–LAY–) *n.* **1** an account or narration. **2** connection, esp. a relative: *Our friends and ~s were all there; Results should bear some ~ to costs; Bara Yogi is no ~ of Mahesh Yogi; had no ~s* (i.e. sexual) *though married; an expert in international ~s* (i.e. dealings or affairs); **in** (or **with) relation to** concerning; **re·la·tion·al** *adj.;* **re·la·tion·ship** *n.* —**rel·a·tive** (REL·uh·tiv) *n.* one related by blood or marriage; *adj.* related to each other or to something else; comparative: *the ~ merits of coffee and tea; living in ~ comfort* (i.e. compared to others less rich); *"hot" and "cold" are ~* (i.e. variable from person to person); *10 times in 2 days is a higher* **relative frequency** *than 10 times in 3 days;* **relative humidity** percentage of moisture in the air compared to the maximum it can hold at the same temperature; **relative pronoun** a pronoun such as *that, which, what, who, whom,* or *whose* that introduces a relative clause, as in "This is the house *that* Jack built"; **relative to** concerning; **rel·a·tive·ly** *adv.;* **rel·a·tive·ness** *n.* —**rel·a·tiv·ism** *n.* the philosophical theory of notions of right and wrong being relative, not absolute; **rel·a·tiv·ist** *n.;* **rel·a·tiv·is·tic** (–IS–) *adj.* —**rel·a·tiv·i·ty** (–TIV–) *n.* **-ties** relativeness: *the ~ of truth; the* **theory of relativity** *put forward by Einstein showing that our measurements of space and time are relative.*

re·lax (–LAX) *v.* make or become less stiff, tense, or severe: *to ~ one's muscles; Discipline is ~ed at certain times; Sit back and ~* (i.e. rest); **re·lax·er** *n.* —**re·lax·ant** (–unt) *n.* & *adj.* (a drug) that relaxes muscles: *the ~ effect of tranquilizers.* —**re·lax·a·tion** (ree·lak·SAY–) *n.* a relaxing; hence, rest or recreation.

[1]**re·lay** (REE–) *n.* a linking of one stage with the next in a continuous operation, as in a **relay race** run by a team, each member covering only a part of the distance; a conveying: *the ~ of a puck from one player to another; an electrical ~ switch; a ~ satellite for TV and other signals; men working in ~s* (i.e. shifts). —***v.*** **1** convey; pass on: *the ~ing of messages; Men were ~ed* (i.e. supplied in groups) *to fight the fire.* **2** operate or control (electrical circuits) by means of a relay device.

[2]**re·lay** (ree·LAY) *v.* **-lays, -laid, -lay·ing** lay again.

re·lease (–LEECE) *v.* **-leas·es, -leased, -leas·ing** free or let go from a confined or restricted condition: *Prisoners are ~d; a priest ~d from his vows; property ~d* (i.e. legally) *to a claimant; a statement ~d for publication at 3 p.m.* —***n.:*** *a ~ of pressure; ~ from jail; a motion picture awaiting ~* (i.e. to the theaters); *obtained a settlement after signing a ~* (from further claims); *a statement for immediate ~.*

rel·e·gate (REL·uh–) *v.* **-gates, -gat·ed, -gat·ing** **1** put away or assign (to a lower position); hence, exile. **2** hand over (a task or business to be carried out or disposed of); delegate; **rel·e·ga·tion** (–GAY–) *n.*

re·lent (–LENT) *v.* become less stern or more merciful; **re·lent·less** *adj.;* **re·lent·less·ly** *adv.;* **re·lent·less·ness** *n.*

rel·e·vant (REL·uh·vunt) *adj.* having some bearing on (a matter); pertinent (*to*); *testimony ~ to a case;* **rel·e·vant·ly** *adv.* —**rel·e·vance** (–vunce) or **rel·e·van·cy** *n.*

re·li·a·ble (–LYE·uh–) *adj.* of a person or thing, dependable: *a ~ witness, product; ~ information;* **re·li·a·bly** *adv.* —**re·li·a·bil·i·ty** (–BIL–) or **re·li·a·ble·ness** *n.* —**re·li·ance**

---

reformulate
refortify
refreeze
refuel
refurnish
regild
reglue
regrow

(–LYE·unce) *n.* **1** trust or confidence: *didn't place much ~ on miracle cures.* **2** one relied on for support. **—re·li·ant** *adj.* relying; trusting; dependent.

rel·ic *n.* something from the past, as an object kept as a souvenir or keepsake, a part of a saint's body venerated as a memorial, or an ancient custom or practice; **relics** *pl.* ruins; remains; *Archaic.* corpse. **—rel·ict** *n.* & *adj.* (something) residual or remaining unchanged from a previous era, esp. geologic: *a ~ mountain; a Carboniferous ~.*

re·lief (–LEEF) *n.* **1** a removal or lessening of suffering or distress; hence, money, food, clothes, etc. given to the poor; **on relief** receiving public aid; on welfare. **2** a lessening of strain, pressure, obligation, etc.: *comic ~ in Shakespeare's tragedies; a sigh of ~; working long hours without ~* (i.e. replacement); ***adj.:*** *a ~* (baseball) *pitcher.* **3** a figure or design made to stand out from its surface, as "high relief" or "low relief" (BAS-RELIEF); **in relief** distinctly or boldly (*against* something contrasting); **relief map** one showing mountains, valleys, etc. using colors, shading, or with clay. **—re·lieve** (–LEEV) *v.* **-lieves, -lieved, -liev·ing** remove or lessen suffering, pressure, etc.: *to ~ misery; ~d to hear you're safe; You'll be ~d in a few minutes when the next shift arrives; anecdotes to ~ the monotony of a speech;* **re·liev·er** *n.*

relig. religion. **—re·li·gion** (–LIJ–) *n.* **1** the worship of God, gods, or the supernatural; also, belief in or devotion to such worship: *a man of ~.* **2** an organized system of faith and worship: *the Christian ~; makes a ~ of watching baseball.* **—re·li·gion·ist** *n.* **—re·li·gi·os·i·ty** (–OS–) *n.* (affected) religiousness. **—re·li·gious** (–LIJ·us) *adj.* of or devoted to religion; hence, scrupulous or conscientious; ***n.*** *sing.* & *pl.* a monk, nun, or other member of a religious order; **re·li·gious·ly** *adv.;* **re·li·gious·ness** *n.*

re·lin·quish (–LING·kwish) *v.* give up (something one has a claim to or is interested in keeping): *finally ~ed all hope of getting custody of the child;* **re·lin·quish·ment** *n.* **—rel·i·quar·y** (REL·uh·kwer·ee) *n.* **-quar·ies** a small receptacle for a relic. **—rel·ique** (REL·ic, ruh·LEEK) *n. Archaic.* relic.

rel·ish *n.* **1** olives, pickles, sardines, etc. that give one a zest for food; also, a slightly sweet preparation of chopped pickles: *green tomato ~; tart corn ~.* **2** zest or appetite: *has great ~ for foods advertised on TV; shows little ~ for racy humor.* **—*v.*** like the taste of; enjoy: *doesn't ~ the prospect of going on a diet;* **rel·ish·a·ble** *adj.*

re·live (ree·LIV) *v.* **-lives, -lived, -liv·ing** live or undergo (an experience) again mentally.

re·lo·cate (–LOH–, ree·loh·CATE) *v.* **-cates, -cat·ed, -cat·ing** move to a new location; settle in another place; **re·lo·ca·tion** (–CAY–) *n.*

re·luc·tant (–LUC·tunt) *adj.* not inclined (*to* do something); hence, unwilling: *a ~ answer, helper; ~ obedience;* **re·luc·tant·ly** *adv.;* **re·luc·tance** (–tunce) *n.*

re·ly (–LYE) *v.* **-lies, -lied, -ly·ing** have confidence that a person or thing will do or be as expected: *He ~s on weather forecasts; ~ on your assistant to do his duty, but don't depend on him for everything.*

REM (REM) *n.* the "rapid eye movement" or dreaming phase of sleep.

re·main (–MAIN) *v.* continue, keep on, or be left, as when others have departed: *the ~ing members of the once-popular club; ~ standing till the chairman sits; It ~s to be seen if he'll do as told; 3 ~s if you take away 8 from 11.* **—re·main·der** (–MAIN–) *n.* **1** what is left: *The ~ of 11 minus 8 is 3, of 21 divided by 3 is zero.* **2** a copy or the copies of a published book for disposal at a very low price after its sales have dropped off; ***v.:*** *The present edition will be ~ed when the revised one is out.* **—re·mains** (–MAINZ) *n.pl.* **1** what is left of something broken up or ruined, as of a destroyed civilization, a dead writer's unpublished works, etc. **2** [used respectfully] a dead body.

re·mand (–MAND) *v.* order back, esp. judicially: *a prisoner ~ed in custody; a case ~ed to a lower court;* ***n.*** a remanding.

re·mark (–MARK) *n.* a brief comment or casual observation. **—*v.*** **1** comment (*on* or *upon* something); also, make a remark. **2** notice or observe; **re·mark·a·ble** *adj.* worthy of notice; hence, extraordinary: *has a ~ memory;* **re·mark·a·ble·ness** *n.;* **re·mark·a·bly** *adv.*

Rem·brandt (REM·brandt) 1606–69, the greatest Dutch painter.

re·me·di·a·ble (–MEE·dee·uh–) *adj.* that can be remedied; **re·me·di·al** *adj.* serving to remedy or correct: *~ measures, courses, English;* **re·me·di·al·ly** *adv.* **—rem·e·dy** *n.* & *v.* **-dies, -died, -dy·ing** (provide or serve as) a cure or treatment for an illness or some other unhealthy condition such as an evil, loss, etc.

re·mem·ber (–MEM–) *v.* **1** keep in mind or recall: *Please ~ to phone me; don't ~ meeting him; thanks to the rich uncle who ~ed her* (i.e. in his will). **2** mention (someone) as sending greetings (to another): *~ me to your friends.* **—re·mem·brance** (–MEM·brunce) *n.* **1** a remembering or being remembered. **2** a memory; also, a memento or keepsake. **3** a gift; also, a greeting, esp. **remembrances** *pl.* **—re·mind** (–MINED) *v.* put in mind; cause to

---

rehandle
rehear
reheat
reimpose
reinsert
reintegrate
reinterpret
reintroduce

remember; **re·mind·er** *n.* **—rem·i·nisce** (–NIS) *v.* **-nisc·es, -nisced, -nisc·ing** recall or tell about one's past experiences. **—rem·i·nis·cence** *n.* **1** a reminiscing, esp. an account of usu. pleasurable recollections, or **reminiscences** *pl.* **2** something that is reminiscent of another person or thing. **—rem·i·nis·cent** (–NIS·unt) *adj.* **1** that reminds one or is suggestive of. **2** reminiscing: *Grandpa became more and more ~ toward the end.* **—rem·i·nis·cent·ly** *adv.*

re·miss (–MIS) *adj.* careless or negligent (*in* carrying out a task or duty); **re·miss·ly** *adv.;* **re·miss·ness** *n.* **—re·mis·sion** (–MISH·un) *n.* a remitting (defs. 2, 3). **—re·mit** (–MIT) *v.* **-mits, -mit·ted, -mit·ting 1** send (money) as expected or due payment; **re·mit·tance** (–tunce) *n.* **2** let off or free from (punishment, debts, etc.): *power to ~* (i.e. forgive) *sins.* **3** lessen (efforts, pain, symptoms, etc.): *the rising and falling* **re·mit·tent** *fever.* **—re·mit·tal** (–MITL) *n.* remission.

rem·nant (–nunt) *n.* a small remaining part or piece: *broadloom ~s; a ~ sale* (of ends of bolts); *~s of a defeated army.*

re·mod·el (–MODL) *v.* **-els, -el(l)ed, -el·(l)ing** alter the structure or design of (a building, clothes, etc.).

re·mon·strance (–MON·strunce) *n.* an act or instance of remonstrating. **—re·mon·strant** (–strunt) *n.* & *adj.* (person) remonstrating; **re·mon·strant·ly** *adv.* **—re·mon·strate** *v.* **-strates, -strated, -strat·ing** reason or plead (*with* someone *about* something objected to); expostulate; **re·mon·stra·tor** *n.* **re·mon·stra·tion** (–STRAY–) *n.*

rem·or·a (REM·uh·ruh) *n.* a tropical ocean fish that attaches itself to marine animals and ships with a disklike sucking organ on its head.

re·morse (–MORSE) *n.* a torturing sense of guilt; **re·morse·ful** *adj.;* **re·morse·less** *adj.* pitiless; also, persistent.

re·mote (–MOTE) *adj.* **-mot·er, -mot·est** far removed in space or time, esp. from a central point: *a ~ village in the mountains; in the ~ past, future; a ~* (i.e. slight) *possibility; radio-operated* **remote control** *for planes, missiles, garage doors, etc.;* **re·mote·ly** *adv.;* **re·mote·ness** *n.* **—re·move** (–MOOV) *v.* **-moves, -moved, -mov·ing** move or take away: *~d his hat and coat; to ~ stains; impeached, found guilty, and ~d from office; He ~d himself* (i.e. moved away) *to Europe to start a new life; his first cousin once* **removed** (i.e. child of his first cousin); **re·mov·a·ble** *adj.;* **re·mov·al** *n.;* **re·mov·er** *n.* ***—n.*** a moving away; also, an interval or degree of distance: *a few ~s from his old neighborhood.*

re·mu·ner·ate (–MYOO–) *v.* **-ates, -at·ed, -at·ing** *Formal.* pay (someone) for a service or trouble; recompense; **re·mu·ner·a·tion** (–RAY–) *n.* **—re·mu·ner·a·tive** (–MYOO·nuh·ruh·tiv) *adj.;* gainful; profitable; **re·mu·ner·a·tive·ly** *adv.;* **re·mu·ner·a·tive·ness** *n.;* **re·mu·ner·a·tor** *n.;* **re·mu·ner·a·to·ry** *adj.*

ren·ais·sance (REN·uh·sahnce) *n.* rebirth or revival; **Renaissance** the European revival in art and literature from the 14th to the 17th c.

re·nal (REE·nl) *adj.* of or located near kidneys: *~ artery, calculus.*

re·nas·cence (–NAS–, –NAY–) *n.* same as RENAISSANCE; **re·nas·cent** *adj.*

ren·con·tre (–CON·tur) or **ren·count·er** (–COUNT–) *n.* an unforeseen, usu. hostile encounter.

rend *v.* **rends, rent, rend·ing** split or tear apart with violence: *a heart-rending scene of families being torn apart; Shrieks rent the air.*

ren·der *v.* **1** *Formal.* give: *~ aid, services, judgment; to ~ thanks to God; bills payable when ~ed* (i.e. presented); *a city ~ed up* (i.e. surrendered) *to the enemy.* **2** cause to be in a (specified) condition: *people ~ed helpless, homeless, speechless* (as by fright); *to ~* (i.e. melt) *fat for lard.* **3** interpret artistically by painting, acting, singing, or translating: *takes a great actor to ~ Hamlet well; a ~ing of the Psalms into modern English.*

ren·dez·vous (RON·day·voo) *n., pl.* **-vous** (–vooz) a previously agreed-on meeting; also, the meeting place or the agreement to meet; ***v.*** **-vouses** (–vooz), **-voused** (–vood), **-vous·ing** (–voo·ing) meet; also, bring together (people, ships, spacecraft, etc.).

ren·di·tion (–DISH·un) *n.* a rendering (*v.* 3).

ren·e·gade (REN·uh–) *n.* & *v.* **-gades, -gad·ed, -gad·ing** (become) a traitor to one's faith or party; deserter; turncoat; ***adj.*** traitorous; apostate: *a ~ priest.* **—re·nege** (–NIG) *v.* **-neges, -neged, -neg·ing 1** go back (on a promise) or commitment). **2** fail to follow suit (in a card game in violation of rules); **re·neg·er** *n.*

re·new (–NEW) *v.* make (like) new something that has lost its force or effect: *to ~ a contract, subscription, an attack; ~ supplies, efforts, one's enthusiasm;* **re·new·a·ble** *adj.: a ~ resource;* **re·new·al** *n.;* **re·new·er** *n.*

ren·net (REN·it) *n.* a substance containing **ren·nin,** a milk-curdling enzyme found in the stomachs of cud-chewing animals.

Re·no (REE·noh) a city of Nevada.

Re·noir (REN·wahr), **Pierre A.** 1841–1919, French painter.

re·nounce (–NOUNCE) *v.* **-nounc·es, -nounced, -nounc·ing** give up (someone or something that one is attached to): *to ~ one's religion; She ~d worldly pleasures and joined a con-*

reinvest
reinvigorate
reissue
rejudge
rekindle
relearn
relet
relight

vent; ~d all claims to his inheritance; would never ~ his kith and kin; **re·nounce·ment** *n.*

ren·o·vate (REN·uh–) *v.* **-vates, -vat·ed, -vat·ing** restore (a building, painting, etc.) to new condition by cleaning, repairing, etc.; **ren·o·va·tor** (–vay·tur) *n.;* **ren·o·va·tion** (–VAY–) *n.*

re·nown (–NOWN) *n.* great distinction or fame: *men of ~;* **re·nowned** *adj.: a ~ warrior, scientist; ~ for his exploits.*

[1]**rent** *pt. & pp.* of REND. **—*n.* & *adj.*** torn (place in a fabric); split: *a ~ in her gown; a ~ garment.*

[2]**rent** *n. & v.* (get or be let for) regular payment for the use of a piece of property: *rooms* **for rent;** *evicted for nonpayment of ~; a car ~ed at the airport; a tool that ~s for $2 an hour;* **rent·er** *n.* **—rent·al** (REN·tl) *n.* a renting, a piece of property rented out, or the payment for it; ***adj.:*** *a ~ agreement, charge, car; A* **rental library** *charges for books lent.*

re·nun·ci·a·tion (–see·AY–) *n.* a renouncing.

rep. report(er); representative; republic; **Rep.** Republican. **—rep** *n.* **1** a heavy, ribbed fabric, usu. silk, used for neckwear; also **repp. 2** [short form] repertory; representative.

re·pair (–PAIR) *v.* **1** restore, esp. something damaged, to good condition. **2** remedy (a loss, harm, wrong, etc.). **3** betake oneself (*to* a place). **—*n.*** **1** a repairing; also, an instance of repairing: *a body shop for car ~s; ~s costing $2,000.* **2** condition with respect to repairs: *a house kept in (good) ~; was in bad ~ after years of neglect.* **—re·pair·a·ble** *adj.* **—re·pair·man** *n.* **-men. —rep·a·ra·tion** (–uh·RAY–) *n.* (act of making) amends for a wrong: *war ~s levied on a vanquished power.* **—re·par·a·tive** (–PAIR·uh·tiv) *adj.* having to do with reparation or repairs.

rep·ar·tee (–ur·TEE) *n.* (cleverness and skill in making) a witty reply or replies: *good at ~.*

re·past (–PAST) *n.* meal; food and drink.

re·pa·tri·ate (–PAY·tree–) *v.* **-ates, -at·ed, -at·ing** send (prisoners of war) or bring back (what is acquired abroad) to one's own country; ***n.*** a repatriated person; **re·pa·tri·a·tion** (–AY–) *n.*

re·pay (–PAY) *v.* **-pays, -paid, -pay·ing** pay back; make return for or to: *to ~ a loan, lender, kindness; generosity repaid with ingratitude;* **re·pay·a·ble** *adj.;* **re·pay·ment** *n.*

re·peal (–PEEL) *v.* cancel or annul, esp. a law; ***n.*** a repealing; **re·peal·er** *n.*

re·peat (–PEET) *v.* do or say (something) again: *never ~s a mistake; to ~ a lesson* (i.e. recite from memory), *formula* (after someone, as when being sworn in); *a tiresome lecturer who* **repeats himself** (i.e. what he said once); *a* **repeating decimal** *such as 0.333 . . .; a* **repeating firearm** *with a magazine of cartridges that may be fired in succession.* **—*n.*** **1** a repeating or anything repeated, as a rerun television program. **2** in music, a passage to be repeated or a symbol indicting this. **—re·peat·ed** *adj.* occurring again and again; **re·peat·ed·ly** *adv.;* **re·peat·er** *n.*

re·pel (–PEL) *v.* **-pels, -pelled, -pel·ling** force or drive back: *to ~ an attack, an amorous advance; Like (magnetic) poles ~* (each other); *a ~ing* (i.e. disgusting) *appearance, odor, sight.* **—re·pel·lent** (–PEL·unt) *n. & adj.* (something) that repels: *an insect ~* (spray); *a water ~ (surface);* also **re·pel·lant; re·pel·lence** *n.* repulsion.

re·pent (–PENT) *v.* feel sorry for (and seek forgiveness, as a sinner): *He ~ed (of) his past; a choice of successor that he lived to ~* (i.e. regret); **re·pent·ance** (–unce) *n.;* **re·pent·ant** *adj.*

re·per·cus·sion (ree·pur·KUSH·un) *n.* **1** a reaction or effect, often far-reaching, of some action or event. **2** an echo or reverberation. **—re·per·cus·sive** (–CUSS·iv) *adj.*

rep·er·toire (REP·ur·twar) *n.* the stock of plays, parts, etc. that a performer or company has at its command; also **rep·er·to·ry, -ries; repertory theater** a company that has a repertory of prepared plays or operas to put on in rotation during a season. **—rep·er·tor·i·al** (–TOR–) *adj.*

rep·e·ti·tion (–TISH·un) *n.* a repeating or something repeated; **rep·e·ti·tious** (–TISH·us) or **re·pet·i·tive** (–PET·uh·tiv) *adj.* tending to repeat or characterized by repetition; hence, dull or boring; **rep·e·ti·tious·ly** or **re·pet·i·tive·ly** *adv.;* **rep·e·ti·tious·ness** or **re·pet·i·tive·ness** *n.*

re·pine (–PINE) *v.* **-pines, -pined, -pin·ing** be discontented or express discontent; fret; **re·pin·er** *n.*

re·place (–PLACE) *v.* **-plac·es, -placed, -plac·ing** **1** take the place of (someone or something that is gone or no longer usable): *to ~ a (burned-out) light bulb; a highly qualified executive difficult to ~* (i.e. find a substitute for). **2** put back: *to ~ books on a shelf; ordered to ~* (i.e. pay for) *the broken china.* **—re·place·a·ble** *adj.;* **re·place·ment** *n.;* **re·plac·er** *n.*

re·play (–PLAY) *v.* play over or again; ***n.*** (REE–) a playing again; repetition: *the instant ~* (i.e. from videotape) *of an action being filmed.*

re·plen·ish (–PLEN–) *v.* provide a fresh supply for: *to ~ a stock, wardrobe; to ~ supplies, losses;* **re·plen·ish·ment** *n.* **—re·plete** (–PLEET) *adj.* fully supplied; filled: *a book ~ with absurdities;* **re·plete·ness** *n.;* **re·ple·tion** *n.* fullness, often excessive.

rep·li·ca (REP·li·cuh) *n.* a duplicate or copy, esp. one made by the original artist; **rep·li·cate** *v.* **-cates, -cat·ed, -cat·ing** duplicate or

---

reline
reload
remake
remanufacture
remarry
remelt
remigrate
remold

produce an exact copy of; **rep·li·ca·tion** (–CAY–) *n.* —**re·ply** (–PLY) *v.* **-plies, -plied, -ply·ing** answer orally or in writing, usu. in kind or appropriately; ***n.*** an answer or response.

re·port (–PORT) *v.* give information about or an account of what one has seen or done: *a journalist ~ing from the scene of the disaster; a widely ~ed story; to ~ a prowler to the police; UFO's ~ed seen by the villagers; sorry to ~ he is ill; will ~* (i.e. present himself) *for duty at 9 a.m.* —***n.*** **1** a reporting or account. **2** rumor; hence, repute: *an idle ~; as ~ has it; a man of good ~.* **3** a sound, as of a gun or explosion. —**re·port·a·ble** *adj.* —**re·port·age** (–ij) *n.* a reporting; also, reporting in the style of newspapers. —**report card** a report sent periodically from school to parents about a pupil's progress. —**re·port·ed·ly** *adv.* according to report. —**re·port·er** *n.* one who reports, esp. news for a periodical; **rep·or·to·ri·al** (–TOR–) *adj.*

re·pose (–POZE) *v.* **-pos·es, -posed, -pos·ing** **1** put or place (trust, confidence, etc.) in someone or something. **2** (lie at) rest: *~d her head on his shoulder; bodies ~ing in their graves undisturbed;* ***n.*** rest; hence, quietness or peace: *looked serene in ~; the eternal ~ of departed souls; a self-assured ~ of manner;* **re·pose·ful** *adj.* —**re·pos·i·to·ry** (–POZ–) *n.* **-ries** a storage place or container; also, a person or institution to which something is entrusted: *the ~ of her confidences; our ~ of knowledge.*

re·pos·sess (ree·puh·ZES) *v.* take possession of (property, as a seller because of buyer's default in payments); **re·pos·ses·sion** (–ZESH·un) *n.*

re·pous·sé (ruh·poo·SAY) *n.* embossing method used on thin metal by hammering out the design from the back.

repp same as REP, *n.* 1.

rep·re·hend (–HEND) *v.* rebuke or blame; **rep·re·hen·si·ble** *adj.* blameworthy; **rep·re·hen·si·bly** *adv.* —**rep·re·hen·sion** *n.*

rep·re·sent (–ZENT) *v.* **1** stand for as an image, symbol, or example: *Words ~ ideas; a picture ~ing a scene from Scripture; Satan ~s evil.* **2** act or speak in place of another: *Lawyers ~ their clients.* **3** present (as a fact): *was not licensed as ~ed to the public.* —**rep·re·sen·ta·tion** (–TAY–) *n.* **1** a representing or being represented, as a picture or statue. **2** representatives as a group. **3** a formal statement of facts or arguments in support of a demand or viewpoint. —**rep·re·sen·ta·tion·al** *adj.* —**rep·re·sen·ta·tive** (–ZEN·tuh·tiv) *adj.* **1** representing: *a ~ sample, collection; a painting that is ~ of a style.* **2** based on elections: *a ~ form of government; a ~ assembly, institution.* Also ***n.*** one who represents a person or group, as a delegate, salesman, or agent; **Representative** a member of the lower house of a state legislature or Congress. —**rep·re·sen·ta·tive·ly** *adv.;* **rep·re·sen·ta·tive·ness** *n.*

re·press (–PRES) *v.* **1** keep down, as an undesirable impulse or an unpleasant memory from the conscious mind. **2** put down (something developing or seeking an outlet). —**re·pres·sion** (–PRESH·un) *n.;* **re·pres·sive** (–PRES·iv) *adj.*

re·prieve (–PREEV) *v.* **-prieves, -prieved, -priev·ing** give temporary relief (from trouble or danger, esp. from death by execution); ***n.*** a reprieving or being reprieved, esp. a temporary suspension of a sentence of death.

rep·ri·mand (REP·ruh–) *n.* & *v.* (give) a formal or sharp rebuke, often public, as from one in authority.

re·pris·al (–PRY·zl) *n.* (act of) retaliation, esp. in war.

re·prise (–PREEZ) *n.* a renewal or repetition of an action; esp. in music, the return to an original theme.

re·proach (–PROHCH) *v.* find fault with in a resentful manner. —***n.*** a reproaching; also, the cause of it or the resulting discredit or disgrace: *a term of ~; someone thought to be above ~* (i.e. faultless); **re·proach·ful** *adj.;* **re·proach·ful·ly** *adv.;* **re·proach·ful·ness** *n.*

rep·ro·bate (REP·ruh–) *n.* & *adj.* (one who is) depraved or very wicked; **rep·ro·ba·tion** (–BAY–) *n.* censure; condemnation.

re·pro·duce (ree·pruh·DUCE) *v.* **-duc·es, -duced, -duc·ing** produce (copies from an original, sound from a recording, or offspring from egg, by means of spores, etc.); **re·pro·duc·i·ble** (–DEW·suh–) *adj.* —**re·pro·duc·tion** (–DUC–) *n.* what is reproduced; also, the sexual or asexual reproducing of new individuals by a plant or animal; **re·pro·duc·tive** (–tiv) *adj.* —**re·prog·ra·phy** (–PROG·ruh·fee) *n.* duplication of graphic material, as by photocopiers.

re·proof (–PROOF) *n.* a reproving. —**re·prove** (–PROOV) *v.* **-proves, -proved, -prov·ing** express disapproval of; find fault with; **re·prov·er** *n.*

rep·tile (REP·tl, –tile) *n.* a crawling, scaly vertebrate such as a snake, lizard, crocodile, or turtle; **rep·til·i·an** (–TIL·ee·un) *n.* & *adj.*

re·pub·lic (–PUB–) *n.* a state or a form of government headed by an elected president and run by elected representatives, as the U.S., France, India, etc.: *Russia is a "Socialist republic."* —**re·pub·li·can** (–cun) *adj.* of or like a

---

remount
rename
renegotiate
renominate
renumber
reoccupy
reopen
reorder

republic; also, favoring a republic; ***n.*** one who favors a republic; **re·pub·li·can·ism** *n.* —**Republican** *n.* & *adj.* (a member) of the **Republican Party,** one of the two chief political parties of the U.S.

re·pu·di·ate (–PEW·dee–) *v.* **-ates, -at·ed, -at·ing** disown or reject: *to ~ a treaty, charge, doctrine, friend;* **re·pu·di·a·tor** *n.;* **re·pu·di·a·tion** (–AY–) *n.*

re·pug·nance (–PUG·nunce) *n.* the quality or condition of being repugnant; also, a strong dislike or aversion; also **re·pug·nan·cy.** —**re·pug·nant** (–nunt) *adj.* disagreeable or objectionable (*to* one's tastes, ideas, likings, etc.): *Food is ~ to a sick stomach; We think slavery ~;* **re·pug·nant·ly** *adv.*

re·pulse (–PULCE) *v.* **-puls·es, -pulsed, -puls·ing** repel by force, discourtesy, coldness, etc.; rebuff: *to ~ an attack, attacker; a neighbor who ~s offers of friendship; Creeping things don't ~* (i.e. disgust) *some children.* —***n.*** a repulsing or being repulsed; rejection. —**re·pul·sion** *n.* **1** repulse; a being repelled: *magnetic attraction and ~* **2** strong aversion or disgust. —**re·pul·sive** (–siv) *adj.: a ~ sight, creature; ~ forces;* **re·pul·sive·ly** *adv.;* **re·pul·sive·ness** *n.*

rep·u·ta·ble (REP·yuh·tuh–) *adj.* having a good reputation: *a ~ business, dealer, lawyer;* **rep·u·ta·bly** *adv.;* **rep·u·ta·bil·i·ty** (–BIL–) *n.* —**rep·u·ta·tion** (–TAY–) *n.* (good) public estimation of character or quality: *a good ~ as a lawyer; the ~ of a swindler; a witchhunt that destroyed many ~s.* —**re·pute** (–PYOOT) *n.* reputation: *held in high ~; a house of ill ~;* ***v.*** **-putes, -put·ed, -put·ting** consider or account: *~d (to be) the world's richest man;* **reputed** *adj.* supposed: *the ~ father of the orphan; the book's ~ author;* **re·put·ed·ly** *adv.* according to general belief.

req. request; require(d); requisition. —**re·quest** (–KWEST) *v.* ask politely or formally: *to ~ the pleasure of your company; to ~ a favor; Visitors ~ed not to smoke.* —***n.*** a requesting or being requested; also, something requested: *She's here at your ~; a performance repeated* **by request;** *Not all ~s were granted; a ~ item* (for which you have to ask); **re·quest·er** *n.*

Re·qui·em (REK·wee·um, RAY–) *n.* (the musical setting of) a Mass for the repose of departed souls.

re·quire (–KWIRE) *v.* **-quires, -quired, -quir·ing** demand, as by rule or necessity: *We are ~d to stop at a red signal; as ~d by law; ~d reading for history students; Piano playing ~s* (i.e. calls for) *practice;* **re·quire·ment** *n.* something required or needed: *has fulfilled his Ph.D. ~s.* —**req·ui·site** (REK·wuh·zit) *n.* & *adj.* (thing) needed or required: *the quorum ~ for a business meeting; air and water as the prime ~s for survival.* —**req·ui·si·tion** (–ZISH·un) *n.* formal demand for something required, as of military supplies or personnel: *Our only jeep was in constant ~;* ***v.:*** *Help was ~ed from outside the town.*

re·quite (–KWITE) *v.* **-quites, -quit·ed, -quit·ing** make return for (an act) or to (a person); also, retaliate against or avenge; **re·quit·al** (–KWYE·tl) *n.*

rere·dos (REER–, RAIR–) *n.* a decorated wall or screen rising behind an altar.

re·run (REE–) *n.* & *v.* **-runs, -ran, -run, -run·ning** (to make) another showing of a motion picture or television program after the first run.

res. research; reserve; residence; resigned; resolution.

re·sale (REE–) *n.* a selling again of an item to a third party or subsequent buyer; **re·sal·a·ble** (–SAY·luh–) *adj.*

re·scind (–SIND) *v.* annul (a law) or cancel (an order); **re·scis·sion** (–SIZH–) *n.*

re·script (REE–) *n.* an order or decree in answer to a question or petition, as from the pope.

res·cue *v.* **-cues, -cued, -cu·ing** free or save (someone in trouble) by quick action; ***n.*** such a freeing; **res·cu·er** *n.*

re·search (–SURCH, REE–) *n.* a careful search or investigation, esp. an organized scholarly or scientific inquiry; ***v.*** do research into: *scientists ~ing the causes of cancer; a well-~ed thesis;* **re·search·er** *n.*

re·sec·tion (–SEC–) *n.* the surgical removal of a portion of an organ or bone.

re·sem·blance (–ZEM·blunce) *n.* similar appearance, esp. superficial; similarity. —**re·sem·ble** (–ZEM–) *v.* **-bles, -bled, -bling** be similar to in appearance or qualities.

re·sent (–ZENT) *v.* feel or show anger at (something offensive) or toward (an offender); **re·sent·ful** *adj.;* **re·sent·ful·ly** *adv.;* **re·sent·ful·ness** *n.* —**re·sent·ment** *n.* indignation and ill will resulting from an offense.

re·ser·pine (–SUR·pin, –peen) *n.* a tranquilizing drug used to treat high blood pressure.

res·er·va·tion (rez·ur·VAY–) *n.* a reserving or something reserved, as an advance booking of a room at a hotel, public land set aside for a special purpose, as for Indians, or a tacit or expressed condition: *You have our whole-hearted support without ~s.* —**re·serve** (–ZURV) *v.* **-serves, -served, -serv·ing** hold back or keep for a particular person, another occasion, later use, etc.: *to ~ a seat, table, room; film rights ~d by a novelist; wisely ~d his energies till the final act.* —***n.*** **1** a reserved place or thing, as money

---

reorganize
reorient
repack
repaint
rephotograph
rephrase
replant
reprint

kept **in reserve** for later use, public land for forest conservation, a body of trained people, or **re•serv•ists,** ships, or aircraft standing by for military service when needed, etc. **2** the keeping of one's thoughts or feelings to oneself; aloofness; *unburdened his mind without* ~. **—re•served** (–ZURVD) *adj.* set aside; also, restrained in manner; **re•serv•ed•ly** (–vid·lee) *adv.;* **re•serv•ed•ness** *n.* **—res•er•voir** (REZ·urv·wahr) *n.* a large supply or store, esp. of water.

re•side (–ZIDE) *v.* **-sides, -sid•ed, -sid•ing** **1** *Formal:* live, esp. in a settled way (in a place, at a hotel, etc.). **2** exist; be vested: *Power ~s in the people.* **—res•i•dence** (REZ–) *n.* a residing or where one resides; home: *a poet* **in residence** (i.e. on duty as teacher) *at a university.* **—res•i•den•cy** *n.* **-cies** **1** a doctor's period of advanced training at a hospital, following internship; also, this position. **2** a governor-general's or diplomat's official residence. **3** residence: *~ requirement for outsiders to obtain a divorce in some states.* **—res•i•dent** *n.* & *adj.* (one) who lives in a place; also, a doctor in residency or a foreign diplomatic representative; **res•i•den•tial** (–DEN–) *adj.: a ~ hotel, neighborhood;* **res•i•den•tial•ly** *adv.* **—re•sid•u•al** (–ZIJ·oo·ul) *adj.* of or being a residue or remainder: *~ air, estate, product;* ***n.*** **1** remainder. **2** in television, a fee paid to a performer for each rerun of a show or commercial. **—re•sid•u•ar•y** (–ZIJ·oo–) *adj.* having to do with what remains of an estate after bequests are made: *a ~ clause, legacy.* **—res•i•due** (REZ–) *n.* what remains at the end of a process: *the ~ of an estate after settlement of claims; the ~ of salt left after evaporation;* also **re•sid•u•um** (–ZIJ·oo·um), *pl.* **-sid•u•a.**

re•sign (–ZINE) *v.* give up (a job or position): *She ~ed from the board; ~ed as chairman; ~ed his membership; He is ~ed to* (i.e. ready to endure) *a life of mediocrity; had to* **resign himself** (i.e. submit) *to it;* **re•signed** *adj.* submissive; **re•sign•ed•ly** (–nid·lee) *adv.* **—res•ig•na•tion** (–NAY–) *n.* **1** a resigning or a formal notice of it. **2** passive acceptance of suffering or misfortune.

re•sil•i•ence (–ZIL·yunce) *n.* elasticity or buoyancy; also **re•sil•i•en•cy. —re•sil•ient** (–ZIL·yunt) *adj.* springing back to the original form or position, as rubber and springs: *a ~* (i.e. buoyant) *disposition.*

res•in (REZN) *n.* an organic substance such as rosin or shellac that is secreted by plants and trees, esp. firs and pines, and certain insects, much used in paints and varnishes; also, any synthetic plastic material; **res•in•ous** (–us) *adj.*

re•sist (–ZIST) *v.* act against (an attack, enemy, temptation, etc. that is trying to overcome one): *couldn't ~ laughing at his jokes;* ***n.*** a protective coating put on a surface; **re•sist•er** *n.;* **re•sist•i•ble** *adj.* **—re•sist•ance** (–unce) *n.* **1** a resisting or the power to resist (a disease). **2** the opposition offered by a substance to the passage of electricity. **3** secretly conducted opposition to foreign military occupation; often **Resistance. —re•sist•ant** *adj.* **—re•sis•tive** (–tiv) *adj.* tending to resist; **re•sis•tiv•i•ty** (–TIV–) *n.* capacity for resistance, esp. to electricity, as used in locating buried objects and in prospecting. **—re•sis•tor** *n.* a device with electrical resistance used in controlling voltage, to heat furnaces, etc.

res•o•lute (REZ·uh–) *adj.* determined or firm in one's purpose; unwavering; **res•o•lute•ly** *adv.;* **res•o•lute•ness** *n.* **—res•o•lu•tion** (–LOO–) *n.* **1** a resolving or determining; also, the power of determination: *acted with ~.* **2** a solving or breaking up: *the ~ of a dramatic plot; The high ~ of an electron microscope.* **3** what is resolved (upon): *a ~ not to drink; a ~* (i.e. statement) *passed by the city council.* **—re•solve** (–ZOLV) *v.* **-solves, -solved, -solv•ing** **1** decide or determine: *~d to give up smoking;* ***n.:*** *made a firm ~ never to smoke.* **2** solve; dispel; break up: *to ~ a mystery; White light is ~d into the colors of the spectrum; the* **resolving power** *of a telescope or microscope to provide separate images of closely spaced parts of an object;* **re•solv•a•ble** or **re•sol•u•ble** *adj.;* **re•solved** *adj.* firm or resolute.

res•o•nance (REZ·uh·nunce) *n.* a resounding quality; an echoing, strengthening, or prolonging of sound, as by a hollow or cavity: *the ~ box, or resonator, of a guitar or violin; a quartz crystal vibrating in ~ with* (i.e. at the same frequency as) *a generator;* **res•o•nant** *adj.* having resonance: *A ~ voice depends on one's mouth, throat, and nasal cavities; Vowels are more ~ than consonants.* **—res•o•nate** (REZ·uh) *v.* **-nates, -nat•ed, -nat•ing** produce resonance; resound; **res•o•na•tor** *n.;* **res•o•na•tion** (–NAY–) *n.*

re•sort (–ZORT) *v.* **1** go to (a place, esp. habitually): *tourists ~ing to a beach, shrine, spa.* **2** turn to, as for help: *to ~ to violence, tears, trickery.* **—*n.:*** *a seaside ~; the ~ to force; took to drinking* **as the** (or **a**) **last resort** (i.e. means of help).

re•sound (–ZOUND) *v.* sound loudly; reverberate; echo or ring. **—re•sound•ing** *adj.: a ~ success, victory; ~ cheers;* **re•sound•ing•ly** *adv.*

re•source (REE–, –SORCE) *n.* a means or source of help, relief, supply, etc. that may be

---

republish
resay
rescore
rescreen
reseal
reseed
resell
reset

drawn upon when needed: *the earth's natural ~s such as land, water, and minerals; financial ~s; a ~ person, center* (as a library); *a man of ~* (i.e. skill and ability); **re·source·ful** (–SORCE–) *adj.;* **re·source·ful·ly** *adv.;* **re·source·ful·ness** *n.*

resp. respective(ly); respondent.

re·spect (–SPECT) *v.* **1** have or show esteem for: *~ your elders; I ~ your rights though not your way of life; a ~ed member of our club;* **re·spect·er** *n.* **2** refer to; concern: **respecting** *yesterday's deliberations;* **as respects** in regard to. —*n.* **1** esteem or proper regard: *He talks of his teachers with ~; She is held in ~ by her peers; give her my* **respects** (i.e. respectful regards). **2** a point considered; reference; relation: *a great man in many ~s;* **in** (or **with**) **respect to** *the raise you asked for.* —**re·spect·a·ble** (–SPECT–) *adj.* worthy of respect; proper: *a ~ gentleman; ~ society; ~* (i.e. fairly good) *size, record, income;* **re·spect·a·bly** *adv.;* **re·spect·a·bil·i·ty** (–BIL–) *n.* —**re·spect·ful** *adj.* having or showing respect: *~ manner; ~ to old people;* **re·spect·ful·ly** *adv.;* **re·spect·ful·ness** *n.* —**re·spect·ive** (–iv) *adj.* as relates to each individually; **re·spect·ive·ly** *adv.* in order: *I, II, and III are 1, 2, and 3, ~.*

res·pi·ra·tion (–puh·RAY–) *n.* breathing by means of lungs or gills in animals and through leaves and buds in plants; **res·pi·ra·to·ry** (RES·puh·ruh–, ris·PYE·ruh–) *adj.* —**res·pi·ra·tor** (–ray·tur) *n.* **1** an iron lung or other artificial breathing device. **2** a mask worn over the nose and mouth to prevent the breathing in of harmful substances. —**re·spire** (–SPIRE) *v.* **-spires, -spired, -spir·ing** breathe.

res·pite (RES·pit) *n.* a temporary relief (from an exertion or suffering); also, a reprieve: *works without ~ from 9 to 5;* ***v.*** give a respite to; also, reprieve.

re·splend·ent (–SPLEN–) *adj.* full of splendor; shining brightly (with joy, in glory, etc.); **re·splend·ent·ly** *adv.* —**re·splend·ence** *n.*

re·spond (–SPOND) *v.* react, as in answer to a question, letter, appeal, or any stimulus; also, show a favorable reaction (to a medication, kindness, etc.); **re·spond·er** *n.* one that responds, esp. a signal-returning electronic device, as in radar. —**re·spond·ent** *n. Law.* a defendant; ***adj.*** responding. —**re·sponse** (–SPONCE) *n.* a responding, as a reply or any reaction to a stimulus. —**re·spon·si·ble** (–SPON–) *adj.* **1** accountable or answerable (*for* an action or happening, often *to* someone). **2** having or requiring mental and moral qualities: *a ~ official, job; Animals are not ~ beings.* —**re·spon·si·bly** *adv.;* **re·spon·si·bil·i·ty** (–BIL–) *n.* **-ties.** —**re·spon·sive** (–siv) *adj.* reacting favorably (*to* a treatment, an appeal, etc.); **re·spon·sive·ly** *adv.;* **re·spon·sive·ness** *n.*

rest *n.* **1** a break from activity, as for relaxation; pause: *a day of ~ from work; things at ~ and in motion; souls gone to their ~* (i.e. to another world); *a stool as a ~* (i.e. support) *for the feet; a symbol indicating a half ~* (i.e. interval of silence) *between notes in music; the seaman's ~* (i.e. lodging); **at rest** not moving; asleep; dead; **lay to rest** bury. **2** remainder. —***v.*** **1** stop working; (let) be inactive: *He ~s only at night; never ~s his horses; The prosecution ~s* (i.e. from presenting evidence in a case). **2** be at ease; relax: *The patient is ~ing; wouldn't let me ~ till I said "yes."* **3** support or be supported; lean: *a pillow to ~ your head on; a house ~ing on a weak foundation.* **4** remain: *Please ~ assured we'll do our best.* —**rest·ful** *adj.;* **rest·ful·ly** *adv.*

res·tau·rant (RES·tuh·runt, –rahnt) *n.* a commercial eating place. —**res·tau·ra·teur** (–tuh·ruh·TUR) *n.* a restaurant operator; rarely **res·tau·ran·teur.**

rest home an institution for the aged or convalescent.

res·ti·tu·tion (–TUE–) *n.* restoration to the owner of property that he was deprived of; also, the making good of loss or damage.

res·tive (–tiv) *adj.* balky, as a horse; restless or impatient, as if under restraint; **res·tive·ly** *adv.;* **res·tive·ness** *n.* —**rest·less** *adj.* unable to rest; without rest; always busy or moving; impatient: *~ night, sleep, waves, crowd;* **rest·less·ly** *adv.;* **rest·less·ness** *n.*

res·to·ra·tion (–RAY–) *n.* a restoring or being restored; also, something restored. —**re·stor·a·tive** (–STOR·uh·tiv) *n.* & *adj.* (a food, medicine, etc.) that restores health, strength, or consciousness. —**re·store** (–STOR) *v.* **-stores, -stored, -stor·ing** **1** bring back to its original condition (a ruined building, a damaged painting, poor health, etc.). **2** return (order, books to a shelf, property to its owner, etc.). —**re·stor·a·ble** *adj.;* **re·stor·er** *n.*

re·strain (–STRAIN) *v.* keep in check, esp. by use of force or authority: *a leash to ~ a dog from attacking people; ~ your curiosity, temper;* **re·strain·a·ble** *adj.;* **re·strain·er** *n.;* **re·strained** *adj.* controlled; disciplined; **re·strain·ed·ly** *adv.* —**re·straint** *n.* a restraining, being restrained, or means of restraining; also, control or confinement: *rebellious children kept under ~; the social ~s against nudism; spoke with ~, choosing her words carefully.* —**re·strict** (–STRICT) *v.* confine within limits: *student ac-*

---

resettle
resew
reshow
reshuffle
resilver
resmooth
respell
restaff

tivities ~ed to school hours; ~ your speed to 50 m.p.h.; a vocabulary ~ed to 500 words; **re·stric·tion** *n.* —**re·stric·tive** (–tiv) *adj.* restricting: *price fixing, monopolies, and such ~ trade practices; a ~ subordinate clause limiting the meaning of its main clause, as "that Jack built" in "The house that Jack built is for sale";* **re·strict·ive·ly** *adv.*

rest room a public lavatory.

re·sult (–ZULT) *n.* a final effect or consequence of an action, esp. a desired effect: *work to get ~s; All got the same ~* (i.e. answer to the sum); ***v.:*** *Carelessness ~s in accidents; accidents ~ing from carelessness.* —**re·sult·ant** *n.* & *adj.* (something) that results.

re·sume (–ZOOM) *v.* **-sumes, -sumed, -sum·ing** renew (an activity) or return to (one's seat, etc.); **re·sump·tion** (–ZUMP–) *n.* —**ré·su·mé** or **re·su·me** (REZ·oo·may, –MAY) *n.* a summary of qualifications and employment experience.

re·sur·gent (–SUR·junt) *adj.* tending to rise again; **re·sur·gence** *n.: ~ of hopes, spirits, interest, nationalism.*

res·ur·rec·tion (rez·uh·REC–) *n.* a rising from the dead, as Christ's **Resurrection;** also, revival. —**res·ur·rect** (–RECT) *v.: to ~ dead issues, old practices.*

re·sus·ci·tate (–SUS·uh–) *v.* **-tates, -tat·ed, -tat·ing** revive from apparent or near death; bring back to consciousness; **re·sus·ci·ta·tor** (–tay·tur) *n.* a device to force oxygen into the lungs of a person in order to revive him. —**re·sus·ci·ta·tion** (–TAY–) *n.: mouth-to-mouth ~.*

ret. retain; retired; return(ed). —**ret** *v.* **rets, ret·ted, ret·ting** soak (flax or hemp) in water in order to soften.

re·tail (REE–) *n.* the sale of goods in small quantities to consumers; ***v.*** **1** sell at retail: *the ~ing of meat; radios that ~* (i.e. are sold at retail) *at $25 each.* **2** retell or relate (stories, gossip, slander, etc.). —***adj.:*** *a ~ price, store, merchant; the ~ trade;* ***adv.:*** *buys wholesale and sells ~.* —**re·tail·er** *n.*

re·tain (–TAIN) *v.* continue to hold or keep, esp. against opposing forces: *insulated so as to ~ heat; a* **retaining wall** *to hold back a mass of earth, flood waters, or racing cars; a good memory that ~s everything; to ~ a lawyer* (so that his services may be available as needed). —**re·tain·er** *n.* **1** one that retains; also, an employee in a wealthy household. **2** a fee to secure the services of a lawyer or other professional.

re·take (–TAKE) *v.* **-takes, -took, -tak·en, -tak·ing** recapture; also, take again, esp. a photograph; ***n.*** a second photographing or photograph.

re·tal·i·ate (–TAL·ee–) *v.* **-ates, -at·ed, -at·ing** return injury or evil, usu. in kind (against someone): *They ~d with lightning speed;* **re·tal·i·a·to·ry** (–TAL·ee·uh–) *adj.;* **re·tal·i·a·tion** (–AY–) *n.*

re·tard (–TARD) *v.* slow down; check the progress or movement of; **re·tar·da·tion** (–DAY–) *n.;* **re·tard·ed** *adj.* mentally handicapped; **re·tard·ate** *n.* a retarded person. —**re·tard·ant** *n.* & *adj.* (a chemical or other substance) that retards a process or resists an action, as of fire.

ret. retain; retired; returned.

retch *v.* try to vomit.

retd. retained; retired; returned.

re·ten·tion (–TEN–) *n.* a retaining or retaining capacity; **re·ten·tive** (–tiv) *adj.: has a very ~ memory;* **re·ten·tive·ness** *n.*

ret·i·cent *adj.* not speaking freely, esp. from reserve or embarrassment; **ret·i·cent·ly** *adv.;* **ret·i·cence** *n.*

ret·i·na (RETN·uh) *n.* **-nas** or **-nae** (–nee) the light-sensitive back part of the eye on which images are formed; **ret·i·nal** *adj.*

ret·i·nue (RETN·ew) *n.* a body of retainers, attendants, or assistants following an important person.

re·tire (–TIRE) *v.* **-tires, -tired, -tir·ing** **1** of a person, withdraw from work or activity at the end of the day, a career, etc.: *He will ~ at 75; ~s daily* (i.e. to bed) *at 11 p.m.* **2** cause to withdraw (a person from his career, from a game such as basketball or cricket by being put out, bonds, loans, etc. from circulation, etc.). —**re·tire·ment** *n.* —**re·tired** (–TIRED) *adj.* **1** no longer in service. **2** secluded. —**re·tir·ee** (–REE) *n.* one who has retired. —**re·tir·ing** *adj.* shy or reserved.

re·tool (–TOOL) *v.* change over to new tools, dies, and such machinery, as at the beginning of a new production season.

re·tort (–TORT) *n.* **1** a container, usu. of glass, for distilling substances. **2** a quick, sharp, or witty reply; ***v.*** make such a reply.

re·touch (–TUCH) *v.* improve (a photograph, composition, etc.) by slight changes.

re·trace (–TRACE) *v.* **-trac·es, -traced, -trac·ing** go back over (the way one came, past actions, etc.): *to ~ one's steps, a route;* **re·trace·a·ble** *adj.*

re·tract (–TRACT) *v.* draw back or withdraw (a statement, promise, etc.); **re·tract·a·ble** or **re·trac·tile** (–tl) *adj.* that may be drawn back: *a cat's ~ claws;* **re·trac·tion** *n.*

re·tread *v.* (–TRED) **-treads, -tread·ed, -tread·ing** same as RECAP, def. 1. —***n.*** (REE–) a retreaded tire; also, a new tread.

re·treat (–TREET) *n.* **1** a going back or withdrawal, as from battle; also, a temporary withdrawal from regular occupations for religious exercises; ***v.:*** *The enemy ~ed before our advancing*

---

restate
restock
restring
restructure
restudy
restuff
restyle
resubmit

armies; ~ed to the mountains. **2** a signal for a military retreat sounded on a bugle or drum, also played at the end of a working day or when lowering a flag at dusk; **beat a retreat** run away, as a defeated army. **3** a place of seclusion; refuge.

re·trench (–TRENCH) *v.* reduce (expenses, staff, etc. for economy); **re·trench·ment** *n.*

ret·ri·bu·tion (–BEW–) *n.* deserved punishment (for one's actions); **re·trib·u·tive** (–TRIB·yoo·tiv) or **re·trib·u·to·ry** *adj.*

re·trieve (–TREEV) *v.* **-trieves, -trieved, -triev·ing** regain by making an effort, as a dog, or **re·triev·er** trained to fetch killed or wounded game: *to ~ misplaced articles, one's reputation, data from storage;* **re·triev·a·ble** *adj.;* **re·triev·al** *n.*

retro- *comb.form.* back(ward): as in **ret·ro·ac·tive** (–AC·tiv) *adj.* covering a period that is past: *a ~ pay raise, law, tax;* **ret·ro·ac·tive·ly** *adv.* **—ret·ro·fire** *v.* **-fires, -fired, -fir·ing** fire (a retrorocket); ***n.*** such firing. **—ret·ro·fit** *v.* **-fits, -fit·ted, -fit·ting** modify (an aircraft or machinery) by fitting it with newly designed parts or equipment: *an oil furnace ~d with devices to increase efficiency.* **—ret·ro·grade** *adj.* tending to take one backward; hence, not progressive: *~ steps, ideas, policies;* ***v.*** **-grades, -grad·ed, -grad·ing** go backward; hence, decline or deteriorate; **ret·ro·gress** *v.* move backward; **ret·ro·gress·ive** (–GRES·iv) *adj.* retrograde; **ret·ro·gres·sion** *n.* **—ret·ro·rock·et** *n.* on a spacecraft, a small rocket that fires in the direction of flight in order to slow the craft down. **—ret·ro·spect** *n.* survey of the past; **in retrospect** when looking back (at what is past); **ret·ro·spec·tion** (–SPEC–) *n.;* **ret·ro·spec·tive** (–tiv) *adj.;* **ret·ro·spec·tive·ly** *adv.*

ret·si·na or **ret·zi·na** (RET·si·nuh) *n.* a Greek wine flavored with resin.

re·turn (–TURN) *v.* come, go, give, take, or send back: *We ~ home; ~ borrowed books; ~ a visit, compliment, blow; A jury ~s a verdict; a candidate ~ed* (i.e. elected) *to a legislature or office; an enterprise that ~s* (i.e. yields as profit or earnings) *$2 million annually;* **re·turn·er** *n.* ***—n.*** **1** a returning or thing returned: *one favor* **in return** *for another.* **2 returns** *pl.* yield: *a business that folded because of poor ~s.* **3** an official report: *election ~s; an income-tax ~.* ***—adj.:*** *a ~ match; ~ postage, air fare.* **—re·turn·a·ble** (–TURN–) *n.* & *adj.* (a container) that may be returned. **—re·turn·ee** (–NEE) *n.* one who has returned, as from service overseas.

retzina same as RETSINA.

re·un·ion (–YOON·yun) *n.* a uniting again or the state of being reunited.

re-up (–UP) *v.* **-ups, -upped, -up·ping** *Slang.* rejoin the armed services.

rev *n. Informal.* a revolution of a motor; ***v.*** **revs, revved, rev·ving** increase (the speed of a motor), as by pressing the gas pedal of an automobile. **—rev.** revenue; reverse; review(ed); revised; revolution. **—Rev.** Revelation (New Testament book); Reverend; **Revs.** Reverends.

re·vamp (–VAMP) *v.* patch up; hence, reconstruct or revise: *a ~ed project; a dissertation ~ed into a book.*

re·vanche (ruh·VAHNSH) *n. French.* revenge; **re·vanch·ism** (–VANCH–) *n.* the aggressiveness of a defeated nation seeking to recover lost territory.

re·veal (–VEEL) *v.* make known or visible (something that is hidden): *to ~ a secret, a* **revealed religion** *based on revelations, not a natural religion; a very* **revealing** *gown* (that displays the wearer's body); **re·veal·ing·ly** *adv.*

rev·eil·le (REV·uh·lee) *n.* a bugle call for awakening soldiers in the morning.

rev·el (REVL) *v.* **-els, -el(l)ed, -el·(l)ing** take much pleasure (in an activity or state); also, take part in a revel; **rev·el·(l)er** *n.* ***—n.*** a usu. boisterous merrymaking; also **rev·el·ry, -ries.**

rev·e·la·tion (–LAY–) *n.* **1** a revealing or something revealed, esp. something startling and usu. pleasing. **2** God's disclosure of Himself to man; **Revelation(s)** the last book of the New Testament. **—re·vel·a·to·ry** (–VEL·uh–) *adj.*

re·venge (–VENJ) *v.* **-veng·es, -venged, -veng·ing** avenge (a wrong or wronged person) in a retaliatory or malicious spirit; **revenge oneself** or **be revenged** take vengeance (*on* someone); **re·veng·er** *n.* ***—n.*** a revenging; also, a desire or opportunity for taking vengeance; **re·venge·ful** *adj.*

rev·e·nue (REV·uh·new) *n.* **1** income, esp. from an investment. **2** a government's income from taxes (INTERNAL OR INLAND revenue), customs, duties, etc.: *Federal* **revenue sharing** *with state and other local governments;* **rev·e·nu·er** *n.* a tax official.

re·verb (–VURB) [short form] reverberate, reverberation; ***n.*** an echolike sound effect used by musicians. **—re·ver·ber·ate** (–VUR–) *v.* **-ates, -at·ed, -at·ing 1** reecho; hence, resound. **2** reflect heat, as in an open-hearth or **re·ver·ber·a·to·ry** furnace. **—re·ver·ber·a·tor** *n.;* **re·ver·ber·a·tion** (–RAY–) *n.*

Re·vere (–VEER), **Paul.** 1735–1818, American Revolutionary patriot. **—re·vere** (–VEER) *v.* **-veres, -vered, -ver·ing** regard (usu. a person) with great respect and love; **—rev·er·ence** (REV·uh·runce) *n.* love and respect mixed with awe; ***v.*** **-enc·es, -enced, -enc·ing**

---

resurface
resurvey
retell
retest
rethink
retrain
retransmit
retrial

regard (a person's memory, tomb, and such things) with reverence. —**rev·er·end** *adj.* worthy of being revered; **Reverend** [used as title for a member of the clergy] *the ~ Anne Jones; the ~ A. Jones.* —***n.*** *Informal.* a clergyman. —**rev·er·ent** *adj.* feeling or showing reverence; **rev·er·ent·ly** *adv.;* **rev·er·en·tial** (–REN–) *adj.* reverent; **rev·er·en·tial·ly** *adv.*

rev·er·ie or **rev·er·y** (REV·uh·ree) *n.* **-er·ies** (the condition of being lost in) a pleasant daydream.

re·vers (–VEER, –VAIR) *n., pl.* **-vers** (–VEERZ, –VAIRZ) a part of a garment such as a lapel that has been turned back and stitched to show the underside of the material. —**re·ver·sal** (–VUR·sl) *n.* a reversing. —**re·verse** (–VURCE) *n.* **1** the opposite or contrary: *Selling is the ~ of buying.* **2** something that is opposite, esp. in direction: *the obverse and the ~* (i.e. back) *of a coin; to put a car in ~* (gear); *suffered many ~s* (i.e. setbacks or misfortunes) *before reaching his present position;* ***adj.:*** *z, y, x . . . is the ~ alphabetical order; the ~ image in a mirror;* **reverse racism** policy of favoring those traditionally discriminated against, to the prejudice of majority interests; **re·verse·ly** *adv.* —***v.*** **-vers·es, -versed, -vers·ing** turn to the other side or in an opposite direction: *Children often ~ the letter "S"; to ~ a car, policy, trend, judicial decision* (i.e. cancel it); *to ~ the charges* (as of a telephone call so that the recipient, not caller, pays); **re·vers·i·ble** *adj.;* **re·vers·i·bly** *adv.* —**re·ver·sion** (–VUR·zhun) *n.* a reverting; **re·vert** (–VURT) *v.* **1** go back or return, as offspring to an ancestral type or thoughts to a previous subject or something recalled. **2** of property, go back to a prior owner.

re·vet·ment (–VET–) *n.* a facing of stone, concrete, or brick protecting an embankment; also, a retaining wall.

re·view (–VYOO) *n.* **1** a looking at or examination, as of work or events at the end of a period, a higher court's reexamination of a lower court's decision, or the inspection of troops at a parade. **2** a critical evaluation of a new publication; also, a magazine dealing with current affairs, including also book reviews. **3** a revue. —***v.:*** *to ~ a lesson, situation, decision, parade, book, movie;* **re·view·er** *n.*

re·vile (–VILE) *v.* **-viles, -viled, -vil·ing** abuse with words; slander; **re·vile·ment** *n.;* **re·vil·er** *n.*

re·vise (–VIZE) *v.* **-vis·es, vised, -vis·ing** go over (an essay, book, statement, etc.) carefully and change, correct, or improve it: *a ~d estimate, edition; the 1881–85* **Revised Version** *of the King James Bible; the 1946–57* **Revised Standard Version** *of the American Standard Version of the Bible;* —***n.*** a revising or a revision; also, a printer's revised proof. —**re·vi·sion** (–VIZH·un) *n.* a revising; also, a policy of revision, esp. departure from accepted Communist doctrine or policies; **re·vi·sion·ist** *n.* & *adj.* —**re·vis·er** or **re·vi·sor** *n.*

re·vi·tal·ize (–VYE·tl–) *v.* **-iz·es, -ized, -iz·ing** give new vigor or vitality to; **re·vi·tal·i·za·tion** (–ZAY–) *n.*

re·viv·al (–VYE·vl) *n.* **1** a reviving or being revived; also, a revitalization: *the Revival of Learning* (i.e. the Renaissance) *in Europe.* **2** a new presentation of a play, fresh publication of a book, etc. **3** an evangelistic meeting for renewal of religious fervor; **re·viv·al·ism** *n.;* **re·viv·al·ist** *n.* —**re·vive** (–VIVE) *v.* **-vives, -vived, -viv·ing** bring back (a person, idea, hope, practice, activity, etc.) from a lifeless, unconscious, or inactive condition: *Fresh air seemed to ~ her spirits; The news story ~d old memories; Fears of fresh violence ~d* (i.e. came back). —**re·viv·i·fy** (–VIV–) *v.* **-fies, -fied, -fy·ing** give new life or vigor to; (cause) to revive; **re·viv·i·fi·ca·tion** (–CAY–) *n.*

re·voke (–VOKE) *v.* **-vokes, -voked, -vok·ing** cancel by withdrawing (a privilege, trust, grant, licence, etc.) **re·vok·er** *n.* —**rev·o·ca·ble** (REV·uh·cuh–) *adj.;* **rev·o·ca·tion** (–CAY–) *n.*

re·volt (–VOLT) *n.* refusal to submit to established authority; a casting off of allegiance: *the ~ of the colonies;* ***v.:*** *Lucifer ~ed against God; a crime that humanity ~s* (i.e. recoils) *from; a crime that ~s* (i.e. disgusts) *humanity;* **re·volt·ing** *adj.* disgusting; **re·volt·ing·ly** *adv.*

rev·o·lu·tion (–LOO–) *n.* **1** the overthrow of something established, esp. a government; hence, a radical or complete change: *the French Revolution of 1789–99; the Industrial Revolution; the microelectronics ~ of the 1980's.* **2** a going round in an orbit: *the annual ~ of the earth around the sun that causes the ~* (i.e. cycle) *of the seasons; the number of ~s* (i.e. rotations) *per minute made by a motor.* —**rev·o·lu·tion·ar·y** *adj.* & *n.* **-ar·ies** or **rev·o·lu·tion·ist** *n.* & *adj.* —**Revolutionary War** same as AMERICAN REVOLUTION. —**rev·o·lu·tion·ize** *v.* **-iz·es, -ized, -iz·ing** change completely or radically: *Automation has ~d industry;* **rev·o·lu·tion·iz·er** *n.* —**re·volve** (–VOLV) *v.* **-volves, -volved, -volv·ing** **1** (cause to) move in a circle around a center or axis: *Satellites ~ around their planets; a life of leisure ~ing around television; A four-leaved* **revolving door** *helps keep out drafts; credit cards operating on the* **revolving credit** *system that automatically renews credit as bills are paid off.* **2** (cause to) turn over in the mind; reflect upon: *She's ~ing the pros and cons before deciding.* —**re·volv·a·ble** *adj.* —**re·volv·er** *n.* a hand-

---

reunify
reunite
reuse
revaluate
reverify
revictual
revisit
rewarm

gun with five to seven cartridges contained in a revolving cylinder.

re·vue (–VIEW) *n.* a light variety entertainment consisting of songs, skits, chorus dances, etc.

re·vul·sion (–VUL–) *n.* a strong and sudden change of feeling or a feeling of reaction (*against* or *from* something) in disgust or horror.

re·ward (–WORED) *n.* & *v.* (give) something in return for a service, esp. in recognition of merit: *a $10,000 ~ for helping the police; Is virtue its own ~? the intellectual ~s of scholarship; was amply ~ed* (i.e. recompensed) *for his time and effort;* **re·ward·ing** *adj.* satisfying or gratifying: *a ~ experience.*

re·write (–RITE) *v.* **-writes, -wrote, -writ·ten, -writ·ing** revise, esp. to write a news story reported by telephone in a form fit for publication; *n.* a rewritten story, as done by a **rewrite man.**

Rey·kja·vik (RAY·kyuh·veek) capital of Iceland.

R.F. radio frequency; rapid-fire.

R.F.D. Rural Free Delivery.

Rh rhodium. —**r.h.** relative humidity; right hand.

rhap·so·dy (RAP·suh·dee) *n.* **-dies** a highly enthusiastic expression of feeling, esp. of delight; hence, ecstasy or rapture; also, a musical composition such as Liszt's *Hungarian Rhapsodies;* **rhap·sod·ic** (–SOD–) or **rhap·sod·i·cal** *adj.;* **rhap·sod·i·cal·ly** *adv.* —**rhap·so·dist** (RAP–) *n.;* **rhap·so·dize** *v.* **-diz·es, -dized, -diz·ing.**

rhe·a (REE·uh) *n.* a South American bird resembling but smaller than the ostrich.

Rhen·ish (REN–) *n.* & *adj.* (a wine) of the Rhine region.

rhe·ni·um (REE·nee–) *n.* a rare, silvery-white, metallic element used in alloys.

rheo- *comb.form.* flow: as in **rhe·ol·o·gy** (–OL–) *n.* the science of the deformation and flow of matter; **rhe·o·log·i·cal** (–LOJ–) *adj.* —**rhe·o·stat** (REE·uh–) *n.* a resistor for regulating the flow of electric current, as used in dimmer switches; **rhe·o·stat·ic** (–STAT–) *adj.*

rhe·sus (REE·sus) **monkey** a macaque of S.E. Asia in which the Rh factor was discovered in 1940.

rhet·o·ric (RET·uh–) *n.* **1** the art of effective writing and speaking; hence, skill in this; **rhet·o·ri·cian** (–RISH·un) *n.* **2** showy eloquence. —**rhe·tor·i·cal** (–TOR–) *adj.* using rhetoric; oratorical; **rhetorical question** one asked merely for effect, not for an answer, as in "Here was a Caesar! When comes such another?" **rhe·tor·i·cal·ly** *adv.*

rheum (ROOM) *n.* a watery discharge or flow, as mucus or tears; **rheum·y** *adj.* —**rheu·mat·ic** (–MAT–) *adj.* having to do with rheumatism; ***n.*** a rheumatic patient; **rheumatic fever** a disease of children accompanied by fever, painful joints, inflammation in the heart, etc. —**rheu·ma·tism** (ROO·muh–) *n.* any of several diseases affecting the muscles and joints, as rheumatic fever, lumbago, arthritis, and bursitis; **rheu·ma·toid** *adj.* —**rheumatoid arthritis** an often crippling disease characterized by inflammation and stiffness of the joints.

Rh (AR·AICH) **factor** an antigen present in the red blood cells of most people, or **Rh positive** people: *Rh negative people cannot safely receive Rh positive transfusions.*

Rhine (RINE) a river flowing into the North Sea through Switzerland, West Germany, and the Netherlands; **Rhine·land** region bordering the Rhine, esp. in West Germany. —**rhine·stone** *n.* an imitation diamond of cut glass or paste; also, faceted rock crystal, originally from Germany.

rhi·ni·tis (rye·NYE–) *n.* inflammation of the nasal mucous membranes, caused by hay fever, a cold, etc.

rhi·no (RYE·noh) *n.* **-no(s)** short form of **rhi·noc·er·os** (–NOS·uh·rus) *n.* a huge clumsy-looking tropical beast of Asia and Africa characterized by one or two (as in the African species) upward-curving horns projecting from its snout.

rhi·zome (RYE–) *n.* the rootlike but usu. horizontal underground stem of wild ginger, mint, and such perennials; **rhi·zom·a·tous** (–ZOM·uh·tus) *adj.*

Rh negative lacking the Rh factor in the blood.

rho (ROH) *n.* the 17th letter of the Greek alphabet (Ρ, ρ).

Rhode (RODE) **Island** a New England state; 1,214 sq.mi. (3,144 km²); *cap.* Providence.

Rho·de·sia (roh·DEE·zhuh) the former name of Zimbabwe; **Rho·de·sian** *n.* & *adj.*

rhod(o)- *comb.form.* rose: as in **rho·di·um** (ROH–) *n.* a hard, silvery-white metallic element. —**rho·do·den·dron** (–DEN·drun) *n.* any of a group of mostly evergreen woody plants of the heath family bearing spectacular clusters of flowers.

rhom·boid (ROM–) *n.* an oblique-angled parallelogram with opposite sides equal. —***adj.*** shaped like a rhombus or rhomboid; also **rhom·boi·dal** (–BOY·dl). —**rhom·bus** (ROM–) *n.* **-bus·es** or **-bi** (–bye) an oblique-angled parallelogram with all sides equal.

Rhone (RONE) a river flowing into the Mediterranean through Switzerland and France.

Rh positive having the Rh factor in the blood.

---

rewash
rewater
reweave
reweigh
reweld
rewind
reword
rework

rhu·barb (ROO–) *n.* **1** a perennial vegetable with reddish, juicy stalks and large leaves, much used in desserts as pie fillings and sauces. **2** *Slang.* a heated argument.

rhumba same as RUMBA.

rhyme (RIME) *n.* similarity of end sounds between words, as in *beside—decried,* esp. as used at the ends of lines of verse; hence, verse or poetry using this device; ***v.* rhymes, rhymed, rhym·ing** make rhyme(s) or put into rhymes: *"Head" doesn't ~ with "bead"; Blank verse is so called because it is not ~d;* **rhym·er** or **rhyme·ster** *n.* [pejorative] one who makes rhymes; versifier. —**rhy·o·lite** (RYE·uh–) *n.* a fine-grained granite rock showing flow lines of the cooled lava. —**rhythm** (RITHM) *n.* regularly repeated sound forming a pattern suggesting movement, as the tread of marching soldiers, the beating of the heart, the beat of strong and weak syllables, esp. in verse, the duration of musical bars, etc.: *a children's* **rhythm band** *of percussion instruments;* **rhyth·mic** or **rhyth·mi·cal** *adj.;* **rhyth·mi·cal·ly** *adv.* —**rhythm and blues** popular American music influenced by rock'n'roll and blues. —**rhythm method** birth control involving avoidance of intercourse during ovulation.

R.I. or **RI** Rhode Island.

ri·al (ree·AWL, –AHL, RYE·ul) *n.* the basic money unit of Iran and Oman.

rib *n.* **1** one of the 12 pairs of curved bones attached to the backbone and forming a **rib cage,** or chest cavity enclosing the heart, stomach, and other organs. **2** anything like a rib in form or function, as one of the keel-to-deck timbers of a ship's frame, the metal strips supporting an umbrella's cloth, etc. —***v.* ribs, ribbed, rib·bing** **1** form or furnish with ribs. **2** *Informal.* tease, like poking in the ribs; **rib·ber** *n.*

rib·ald (–uld) *adj.* vulgarly or indecently humorous: *~ jokes;* **rib·ald·ry** *n.*

rib·and (–und) *n. Archaic.* for **rib·bon** (–un) *n.* a narrow strip or band of material, as used to tie hair, decorate costumes, packages, etc., as a badge of honor or membership, etc.: *an inked typewriter ~; torn to* **ribbons** (i.e. tatters).

rib cage See RIB, *n.* 1.

ri·bo·fla·vin (RYE·buh·flay–) *n.* a growth-promoting vitamin of the B complex found in liver, milk, eggs, etc. —**ri·bo·nu·cle·ic** (–new·CLEE–) **acid** a nucleic acid that functions in protein synthesis and as a carrier of genetic codes. —**ri·bose** (RYE–) *n.* a sugar present in all animal and plant cells. —**ri·bo·some** (RYE·buh·sohm) *n.* one of the cell structures that are the site of protein synthesis; **ri·bo·so·mal** (–SOH·mul) *adj.*

rice *n.* a cereal grass of warm countries, grown esp. in Asia for food; also, its grains boiled for food; ***v.* ric·es, riced, ric·ing** make (cooked potatoes, etc.) into ricelike grains using a **ric·er** *n.*

rich *adj.* having more resources, esp. money, property, etc. than are required for normal needs: *a ~ banker; Arab nations ~ in oil; a ~ soil, cake, fuel mixture; ~ food, colors, furnishings, tones; that's ~!* (*Informal.* very amusing); **the rich** *n.pl.* wealthy people; **rich·es** *n.pl.* wealth. —**rich·ly** *adv.;* **rich·ness** *n.*

Rich·mond (–mund) capital of Virginia.

Rich·ter (RIK·tur) **scale** a scale of numbers for measuring the strength of an earthquake, 8 or more being the most destructive and 4 and below being hardly noticeable.

rick *n.* an outdoor stack of hay, straw, etc.

rick·ets *n.* a vitamin-deficiency disease affecting esp. children, resulting in bowlegs, knock-knees, etc. from softened bones.

rick·ett·si·a (–KET·see·uh) *n., pl.* **-ae** (–ee) a rod-shaped microorganism responsible for parrot fever, typhus, and other diseases; **rick·ett·si·al** *adj.* —**rick·et·y** *adj.* having rickets; hence, feeble or shaky.

rick·rack *n.* a zigzag braid used as trimming on clothes.

rick·sha(w) (RIK·shaw) *n.* same as JINRIKISHA.

ric·o·chet (RIC·uh·shay) *n.* & *v.* **-chets,** *pt.* & *pp.* **-cheted** (–shayed) or **-chet·ted** (–shet·id), **-chet·ing** (–shay·ing) or **-chet·ting** (–shet·ing) (make) a glancing rebound from a surface, as a bullet off a wall or a flat stone off a water surface: *"ricochet words" such as hodge-podge and super-duper.*

rid *v.* **rids,** *pt.* & *pp.* **rid** or **rid·ded, rid·ding** make free (*of* something undesirable): *to ~ a dog of fleas; longed to be ~ of the nuisance; tried to* **get rid of** (i.e. do away with) *his rich uncle;* **rid·dance** (RID·unce) *n.* a ridding: *thought it* **good riddance** (i.e. welcome relief) *when the noisy party was over.*

ridden *pp.* of RIDE. —***comb.form.*** dominated by: as in *guilt-ridden, disease-ridden.*

¹rid·dle (RIDL) *n.* a puzzling or enigmatical question, usu. phrased as a paradox, and requiring a witty answer, as "What grows bigger the more you take from it?" (A hole); ***v.* rid·dles, rid·dled, rid·dling** talk in riddles; also, solve: *~ me this.*

²rid·dle *n.* a coarse sieve, as for grading potatoes or sifting coal. —***v.* rid·dles, rid·dled, rid·dling** **1** make holes in: *~d with bullets; a department ~d with* (i.e. full of) *corruption.* **2** sift with a riddle.

ride *v.* **rides, rode, rid·den** (RIDN), **rid·ing** **1** sit, usu. astride, and manage (an animal, etc.): *to ~ a horse, bicycle; a child ~ing her father piggyback; a mind ridden* (i.e. dominated) *by fears.* **2** travel or be carried by: *never rode on a train; a ship ~ing the waves; a kite ~ing winds; a car that ~s* (i.e. runs) *smoothly.* **3** *Informal.* tease. —**let ride** *Informal.* let pass or leave undisturbed. —***n.*** a riding or something to ride, as a Ferris wheel; **take for a ride** *Slang.* cheat (someone). —**rid·er** *n.* one who rides; also, something appended to a contract, bill, etc. as an amendment or addition; **rid·er·less** *adj.;* **rid·er·ship** *n.*

ridge (RIJ) *n.* a long and narrow, usu. horizontal line formed by the meeting of two rising surfaces: *the ~ of a mountain range, an animal's back, the nose; the ~s on a corded fabric, on plowed land between furrows, of high pressure on a weather map; the ~ of a roof topped by a* **ridge·pole** *to which the rafters are fastened.* **—*v.* ridg·es, ridged, ridg·ing** form into or extend in ridges: *The floor of the Atlantic ~s in the middle from north to south.* **—ridg·gy** *adj.*

rid·i·cule *n.* & *v.* **-cules, -culed, -cul·ing** (subject someone to) scornful laughter, usu. by verbal means. **—ri·dic·u·lous** (–DIK·yuh·lus) *adj.* arousing laughter; absurd; **ri·dic·u·lous·ly** *adv.;* **ri·dic·u·lous·ness** *n.*

ri·el (ree·EL) *n.* the basic money unit of Cambodia.

rife *adj.* widespread: *Rumor is ~ that John Smith is dead; His hometown was ~ with* (i.e. full of) *rumors of his death.*

riff *n.* a recurring melodic phrase in jazz.

rif·fle (RIFL) *n.* **1** (a choppy stretch of water formed by) a shoal or reef; also, the ripples caused. **2** way of shuffling cards by combining the separate decks into one while their edges are bent and rapidly released against each other; ***v.* rif·fles, rif·fled, rif·fling** shuffle (cards) in this manner; also, rapidly leaf through a book.

riff·raff *n.* & *adj.* worthless or disreputable (people).

ri·fle (RYE·fl) *v.* **-fles, -fled, -fling** **1** cut spiral grooves in (a gun barrel), as of a **rifle** *n.* a long-barreled gun that fires its bullets with a spinning motion; also, a body of riflemen. **2** ransack and rob; **rif·ler** *n.* **—ri·fle·man** *n.* **-men** a soldier armed with a rifle.

rift *n.* a cleft or fissure; hence, a breach of friendship. **—*v.*** split or cleave.

rig *v.* **rigs, rigged, rig·ging** **1** fit out (as a ship) with rigging: *appeared at the party ~d out in her best attire;* **rig·ging** *n.* (ropes, chains, etc. supporting) a ship's masts, sails, etc.; also, the similar network of ropes and chains controlling theater scenery; **rig·ger** *n.* **2** manipulate dishonestly, as the outcome of a prizefight or election, market prices, etc. **—*n.*** **1** the kind and arrangement of a ship's rigging: *a schooner's fore-and-aft ~.* **2** outfit; equipment; machinery: *a drilling ~; a tractor-trailer ~.*

rig·a·ma·role (RIG·uh·muh–) *n.* same as RIGMAROLE.

right (RITE) *adj.* **1** good, true, correct, just, or proper; not wrong: *It is ~ to tell the truth; the ~ clothes for rainy weather.* **2** not left: *He writes with his ~ hand; politically* **Right** (i.e. conservative). **3** straight; not slanting: *a ~ line, angle* (i.e. 90°); *a ~* (circular) *cone.* **—*adv.*** [corresponding to the *adj.* senses] **1:** *You guessed ~; turned out ~ in the end.* **2:** *Turn ~ from north to face east.* **3:** *Let's do it ~ now; Come home* **right away** (or **off**) (i.e. immediately); *(You're)* **right on!** (*Informal.* quite right). **—*n.*** **1** that which is right (*adj.* 1): *Infants can't tell ~ from wrong; our social ~s* (i.e. privileges) *and responsibilities; the ~-to-life movement of anti-abortionists;* **by right(s)** justly. **2** the right side or wing; **Right** in politics, a conservative or reactionary position, person, view, etc. **—*v.*** **1** put (what is wrong) in order: *to ~ a wrong.* **2** make straight (what is slanting or overturned); also, become straight: *The boat ~ed itself.* **—right·eous** (RYE·chus) *adj.* **1** upright; morally blameless, often to the point of intolerance: *a ~ Christian.* **2** justifiable: *~ indignation, zeal;* **right·eous·ly** *adv.;* **right·eous·ness** *n.* **—right·ful** *adj.* according to just claims; by right: *the ~ owner; his ~ rank; a woman's ~ place in society;* **right·ful·ly** *adv.;* **right·ful·ness** *n.* **—right-hand** *adj.* **1** of or having to do with the right side: *on the driver's ~ side; the president's ~* (i.e. trusted) *man.* **2** of or having to do with the right hand: *a ~ glove, blow.* **—right-hand·ed** *adj.* right-hand: *a ~ pitcher, propeller* (i.e. turning clockwise); ***adv.:*** *throws ~;* **right-hand·ed·ly** *adv.;* **right-hand·ed·ness** *n.* **—right·ist** *n.* & *adj.* conservative or reactionary. **—right·ly** *adv.;* **right·ness** *n.* **—right-mind·ed** *adj.* morally or intellectually right: *a ~ citizen, employer.* **—right of way** **1** the right to go first, as of vehicles or pedestrians at a crossing; precedence. **2** (right to use) land owned by another, as to walk through; also, land used by a public utility, railroad, or highway. **—right-to-life** *adj.* opposed to abortions, mercy-killing, and such ways in which life is terminated: *a ~ group, movement;* **right-to-lif·er** *n.* **—right wing** the rightist division of a party; **right-wing** *adj.;* **right-wing·er** *n.*

rig·id (RIJ–) *adj.* stiff or strict; not bending or yielding: *the ~ frame of a ~ airship; ~ economy, rules, disciplinarian;* **rig·id·ly** *adv.;* **rig·id·ness** or **ri·gid·i·ty** (–JID–) *n.*

rig·ma·role (RIG·muh–) *n.* words or action without sense; something too involved or incoherent.

rig·or (RIG·ur) *n.* **1** strictness or exactness: *a life of ~ and discipline; the ~ of his logic.* **2** severity or harshness: *the ~ of military training; the ~s of the Alaskan climate.* **—rig·or·ous** *adj.;* **rig·or·ous·ly** *adv.;* **rig·or·ous·ness** *n.* **—rigor mor·tis** stiffening of the muscles following death. **—rig·our** *Brit.* rigor.

rile *v.* **riles, riled, ril·ing** *Informal.* irritate or anger.

rill *n.* a small brook; rivulet; **rille** (RIL) *n.* a long, narrow, often sinuous valley on the moon.

rim *n.* a circular or curving edge, as the lip of a cup, the spectacle frame around the lenses, or the outer part of a wheel over which a tire is fitted; ***v.* rims, rimmed, rim·ming** form a rim around; also, roll around the rim of, as a basketball before dropping into the basket.

rime *n.* **1** same as RHYME. **2** hoarfrost; **rim·y** *adj.* **—v. rimes, rimed, rim·ing** cover with rime.

rind (RINED) *n.* the outer covering or skin of a fruit such as a lemon, of bacon, or of cheese.

rin·der·pest (RIN·dur–) *n.* an infectious disease of cattle.

¹ring *n.* **1** something curved round like a circle, as the ornamental band worn on a finger. **2** an enclosed area for a circus or prizefight; **the ring** prizefighting or a similar contest: *threw his hat into the ~ as a candidate.* **3** a close group of people working for a selfish or dishonest purpose: *a crime ~;* **ring·lead·er** *n.* **—v. rings, ringed, ring·ing** encircle or move in a ring; also, place or put a ring (as in the nose of an animal or around a tree by cutting away bark); **ring·er** *n.*

²ring *v.* **rings, rang, ring·ing** **1** (cause a bell) to give forth a clear sound: *A phone ~s; Please ~ me at the office; ~ the bell for service; The story ~s true* (like a genuine coin) *but it doesn't* **ring a bell** (i.e. remind me of anything); *Sales clerks* **ring up** *customer's purchases* (on the cash register). **2** resound; be filled (*with* a sound): *a room ~ing with laughter; a neighborhood ~ing with a scandal; her ears still ~ing with the scolding she got.* **—n.** sound of or like ringing; also, its characteristic quality: *The story has the ~ of truth; Give me a ~* (i.e. phone call) *when you're ready.* **—ring·er** *n.* **1** one that rings. **2** *Slang.* impostor; **dead ringer** one who looks exactly like another.

ringleader See ¹RING, *n.* 3. **—ring·let** *n.* a small ring, as a curl of hair. **—ring·mas·ter** *n.* the director of performances in a circus ring. **—ring·side** *n.* a place close to a boxing or circus ring; ***adj.:*** *a ~ seat for a close view of the action.* **—ring·worm** *n.* a contagious fungus infection of the skin that spreads out in a ring.

rink *n.* (a building housing) a smooth floor or surface prepared for ice hockey, roller-skating, curling, etc.

rink·y-dink *n.* & *adj. Slang.* (something) shoddy or cheap.

rinse (RINCE) *v.* **rins·es, rinsed, rins·ing** **1** wash lightly or cleanse thus, as the mouth with water: *~ the soap out of your hair.* **2** dye or tint (hair, fabrics, etc.). **—n.** a rinsing or something used for washing or tinting the hair.

Ri·o de Ja·nei·ro (REE·oh·day·zhuh·NAIR·oh) South America's second largest city and a seaport of Brazil. **—Rio Grande** (REE·oh·GRAND, –GRAN·dee) a river flowing from S. Colorado, forming the border of Texas with Mexico, and emptying into the Gulf of Mexico.

ri·ot (RYE·ut) *n.* **1** a violent outbreak or disturbance by a group of people: *a race ~;* **read the riot act (to)** give official warning of consequences. **2** something wild or unrestrained: *Our garden is a ~ of color; You're a ~!* (*Informal.* extremely funny); **run riot** be wild or unrestrained; grow luxuriantly. **—v.:** *Inmates ~ed at Attica in 1971;* **ri·ot·er** *n.* **—ri·ot·ous** (–us) *adj.;* **ri·ot·ous·ly** *adv.;* **ri·ot·ous·ness** *n.*

R.I.P. (May he, she, or they) rest in peace.

rip *v.* **rips, ripped, rip·ping** **1** tear or split apart quickly, esp. along a joining such as a seam or along the grain of wood, as with a **rip·saw.** **2** *Informal.* rush violently: *came ~ing up the street; ~d out (with)* (i.e. uttered) *blasphemies; mercilessly ~d into* (i.e. attacked) *him;* **rip·per** *n.* **—n.** a tear or rent. **—rip off** *Informal.* **1** steal or rob: *Tax evaders ~ off the government.* **2** exploit: *the public ~d off by big business.* **—rip cord** a cord by which a parachute is pulled open during descent.

ripe *adj.* **rip·er, rip·est** **1** fully developed or mature: *The harvest is ~; ~ tomatoes, wine, cheese, wisdom.* **2** ready (for use, action, etc.): *Time is ~; ~ for change.* **—ripe·ly** *adv.;* **ripe·ness** *n.* **—rip·en** *v.* make or become ripe: *the ~ing of fruit, cheese.*

rip-off *n. Informal.* (an act of) theft or exploitation: *Third World ~ by capitalist countries; a ~ artist.*

ri·post(e) (–POHST) *n.* & *v.* (make) a sharp, quick retort like a fencer's counterattack or thrust following a parry; also, such a thrust.

rip·ple (RIPL) *n.* & *v.* **rip·ples, rip·pled, rip·pling** (make) a series of little waves, as when still water is disturbed: *~s in her hair; a ~ of laughter; sand ~d by the tide; breeze ~ing a field of corn.*

rip-roar·ing *adj. Informal.* boisterous; hilarious. **—ripsaw** See RIP, *v.* 1.

rise (RIZE) *v.* **ris·es, ris·en** (RIZ·un), **ris·ing** go up or get up: *to ~ from bed; ~ing temperatures; Wages and prices ~; her ~ing tone of anger; The Mississippi ~s* (i.e. has its origin) *in Minnesota; The rebels rose against the government; The general rose* (i.e. in his career) *from the ranks; A resourceful person will* **rise to** (i.e. be able to handle) *the occasion.* **—n.** **1** an upward movement, slope, increase, etc. **2** origin; **give rise to** originate; start. **3 get a rise out of** *Slang.* get an emotional response or reaction from. **—ris·er** *n.* **1** one that rises. **2** the vertical part between two steps.

ris·i·ble (RIZ·uh–) *adj.* of or having to do with laughter; funny; **ris·i·bil·i·ty** (–BIL–) *n.* **-ties:** *tickled his ~s* (i.e. sense of humor).

risk *n.* & *v.* (incur or expose, esp. voluntarily, to) the possibility of danger or loss (of something): *You* **run** (or **take**) **a risk** *by stepping into heavy traffic; You ~ your life, health, being killed; Use the bridge at your own ~* (i.e. without claims for accidents, etc.); *rejected for insurance as a poor ~* (i.e. hazard); **risk·y** *adj.* **risk·i·er, -i·est:** *a ~ venture, undertaking;* **risk·i·ness** *n.* **—ris·qué** (–KAY) *adj.* close to being indecent; off-color.

rite *n.* a ceremonial form or act: *the last ~s for the dying; the Eastern Orthodox ~* (i.e. liturgy or church denomination). **—rit·u·al** (RICH·oo·

ul) *n.* a system of rites as established for a usu. religious ceremony; hence, a ceremonial action or procedure: *a church ~; an initiation ~; the ~ of voodoo;* **adj.:** *a ~ dance; ~ laws;* **rit·u·al·ly** *adv.* —**rit·u·al·ism** *n.;* **rit·u·al·ist** *n.;* **rit·u·al·is·tic** (–LIS–) *adj.;* **rit·u·al·is·ti·cal·ly** *adv.*

ritz·y (RIT·see) *adj.* **ritz·i·er, -i·est** *Slang.* high-class; luxurious; plush: *a ~ hotel;* **ritz·i·ness** *n.*

ri·val (RYE·vl) *n.* & *adj.* (being or acting as) one trying to equal or surpass another; competitor: *a ~ computer company; ~s in rental cars;* **v. -vals, -val(l)ed, -val·(l)ing:** *trying harder every day to ~* (i.e. equal or excel) *the leader of the market.* —**ri·val·ry** *n.* **-ries:** *long-standing political ~s; sibling ~.*

rive *v.* **rives,** *pt.* & *pp.* **rived** or **riv·en** (RIVN), **riv·ing** split or tear apart violently. —**riv·er** (RIV·ur) *n.* a natural stream larger than a brook or creek, normally confined within banks, and flowing into a sea, lake, or another river; **riv·er·bank** *n.* —**river basin** the region drained by a river and its tributaries. —**riv·er·bed** *n.* the channel in which a river flows; **riv·er·boat** *n.* —**riv·er·side** *n.* & *adj.* (on) a river's bank. —**Riv·er·side** a city of S. California.

riv·et *n.* & *v.* **-ets, -et·(t)ed, -et·(t)ing** (fasten with) a metal bolt whose plain end is flattened into another head after being passed through the parts to be joined together: *steel beams ~d together; a preacher who can ~ your attention for an hour;* **riv·et·er** *n.*

Riv·i·er·a (riv·ee·AIR·uh) a resort area along the Mediterranean shore of S. France and N.W. Italy including Cannes, Nice, Monaco, and Genoa.

riv·u·let (RIV·yoo·lit) *n.* a small river or stream.

Ri·yadh (ree·YAHD) capital of Saudi Arabia. —**ri·yal** (–YAHL, –YAWL) *n.* the basic money unit of Saudi Arabia, Qatar, and Yemen (Sana); also, 1/5 of a dinar (Iraq).

rm(s). ream(s); room(s).

Rn radon. —**R.N.** Registered Nurse; Royal Navy.

RNA same as RIBONUCLEIC ACID.

roach (ROHCH) *n.* **1** a freshwater European fish of the carp family; rarely, a North American minnow. **2** short form of COCKROACH.

road (RODE) *n.* **1** a usu. public path, way, or course for traveling to a destination: *a traveling salesman* **on the road** *much of the time; the rules of the ~; the royal ~ to success.* **2** a roadstead, often **roads,** as in *Hampton Roads,* Virginia. —**road·a·bil·i·ty** (–BIL–) *n.* the ability of a vehicle to travel safely and smoothly. —**road·bed** *n.* the foundation laid for a highway, railroad, etc. —**road·block** *n.* a barrier placed across a road, as by police; hence, any hindrance. —**road hog** *Informal.* an unmannerly driver, esp. a motorist who drives in the middle of the road. —**road runner** a cuckoo-family bird of the deserts of S.W. North America that is better able to run than fly; also called "chaparral cock." —**road·show** *n.* a touring theatrical show. —**road·side** *n.* & *adj.* (on or at) the side of a road: *a ~ picnic table, park, restaurant.* —**road·stead** (–sted) *n.* a sheltered anchorage for ships near a shore. —**road·ster** *n.* **1** an early open-bodied automobile with a single wide seat. **2** a horse for riding or driving on a road. —**road test** the testing of a vehicle for roadworthiness; also, a test of driving ability. —**road·way** *n.* a road; also, the part of a road used by vehicles. —**road·work** *n.* running exercise for boxers in training. —**road·wor·thy** *adj.* of vehicles, in good condition; **road·wor·thi·ness** *n.*

roam (ROME) *v.* go about (in a large area) without special plan or aim; wander over: *pirates ~ing the seas; ~ed about the country after dropping out of school;* **roam·er** *n.*

roan (RONE) *n.* & *adj.* (a horse or other animal) of a brownish or blackish color sprinkled with white or gray; also, a roan color.

roar (RORE) *n.* & *v.* (make) a loud, full, and rumbling sound, as a lion: *the ~ of thunder;* **roar·er** *n.*

roast (ROHST) *v.* **1** cook by dry or radiant heat in an oven or over an open fire, as meat, coffee beans, metal ore, etc. **2** *Informal.* subject (a person) to ridicule or criticism. —***n.*** **1** roasted meat or meat suitable for roasting. **2** a picnic at which food is roasted: *corn ~; steer ~;* **adj.** roasted: *~ pig, beef.* —**roast·er** *n.*

rob *v.* **robs, robbed, rob·bing** deprive (a person or establishment) of property, good name, etc. by violence, fraud, or any unjust means: *the swindler who ~d the poor widow of her savings; He ~s banks; children ~ing an orchard; ~ing* (i.e. stealing) *apples;* **rob·ber** *n.* —**rob·ber·y** *n.* **rob·ber·ies** theft by violence or any unjust means: *highway ~.*

robe *n.* & *v.* **robes, robed, rob·ing** (clothe with) a long, loose outer garment, as worn wrapped around when lounging or as a *bathrobe,* or a ceremonial one, as worn by a judge; also, a *lap robe.*

rob·in *n.* either or two thrushes, a common American bird with a reddish breast or a smaller European species, also called "redbreast." —**Robin Hood** in English legend, a hero of the common people who robbed the rich to give to the poor. —**Rob·in·son Cru·soe** (–CROO·soh) the title hero of Daniel Defoe's novel about a sailor marooned on a desert island and his faithful servant called Friday.

ro·bot (ROH·bot) *n.* a mechanical man or human automaton; hence, an insensitive, machinelike human being.

ro·bust (roh·BUST, ROH·bust) *adj.* healthy and vigorous in body or mind; **ro·bust·ly** *adv.;* **ro·bust·ness** *n.*

Roch·es·ter (ROCH·es–) a city of W. New York.

¹rock *n.* the hard, firm, solid part of the earth's crust made up of minerals; also, a large mass of this or a piece: *firm as a ~.* **—on the rocks** *Informal.* **1** ruined or bankrupt. **2** of a drink, served with ice cubes. **—rock·y** *adj.* **rock·i·er, -i·est.**

²rock *v.* move back and forth upon a base: *to ~ a baby to sleep; waves ~ing a boat; a building ~ed* (i.e. shaken) *by an explosion;* **n.** **1** a rocking movement. **2** rock'n'roll.

rock-and-roll same as ROCK'N'ROLL.

rock·bound *adj.* of a coast, covered with rocks. **—rock bottom** the very lowest level; **rock-bot·tom** *adj.* the very lowest: *~ prices.* **—rock candy** large, hard sugar crystals.

Rock·e·fel·ler (ROK·uh–), **John D.** either of two U.S. philanthropists, father (1839–1937) and son (1874–1960).

rock·er *n.* a curved piece at the base of a cradle or chair that enables it to be rocked; also, a chair mounted so as to be rocked by its occupant; also **rocking chair; off one's rocker** *Slang.* crazy.

rock·et *n.* (a spacecraft or projectile powered by) a cylinder containing fuel which, when rapidly burned, creates thrust by the force of the escaping gases, as used in shooting fireworks, war missiles, space probes, etc.; **rock·et·ry** *n.* the science of making and using rockets. **—rocket ship** a rocket-propelled spacecraft.

rock-fall *n.* the fall of rock down a slope, as in a cave or mine; also, fallen rock. **—Rock·ford** a city of N.E. Illinois. **—rock garden** a flower garden on rocky ground or among rocks. **—Rock·ies** *Informal.* the Rocky Mountains.

rocking chair See ROCKER. **—rocking horse** a toy horse on rockers for a child to ride.

rock'n'roll a style of popular music and dance based on blues and country-and-western music, and characterized by heavy rhythms, common melodies, and popular lyrics.

rock salt salt that is mined from the earth, not sea salt. **—rock wool** an insulating material made from molten rock by blowing a jet of steam through it. **—rock·y** *adj.* **rock·i·er, -i·est** **1** shaky; also, *Informal.* dizzy or weak. **2** full of rocks; consisting of rocks; also, firm or hard as rock. **—rock·i·ness** *n.* **—Rocky Mountain goat** a goatlike antelope with a dense, shaggy coat, found in the Rocky Mountains; **Rocky Mountains** a mountain system of W. North America, extending from Alaska to New Mexico. **Rocky Mountain sheep** same as BIGHORN.

ro·co·co (ruh·COH·coh) *n.* a highly ornate and elaborate artistic style of the 1700's, more delicate in design than baroque; ***adj.*** overelaborate or quaint.

rod *n.* **1** a thin, straight stick or bar, as used to punish children, to fish with, as a measuring unit (16½ ft. or 5m), or one carried as a symbol of authority: *"Spare the ~* (i.e. punishment) *and spoil the child"; ruled the land with a ~ of iron.* **2** anything rodlike, as one of the light receptors in the retina of the eye or a rod-shaped bacterium. **3** *Slang.* a pistol.

rode *pt.* of RIDE.

ro·dent (ROHD·nt) *n.* any of an order of mammals such as squirrels, beavers, and rats having incisors suited to gnawing.

ro·de·o (ROH·dee·oh, roh·DAY·oh) *n.* **-os** an exhibition of or contest in cowboy skills such as bareback riding, calf roping, steer wrestling, etc.

Ro·din (raw·DAN), **Auguste.** 1840–1917, French sculptor.

roe (ROH) *n.* **1** fish eggs or milt. **2** a small, tailless deer of Europe and Asia whose male, or **roe·buck,** has short, three-tined antlers.

roent·gen (RENT·gun) *n.* the international unit for measuring radiation such as gamma rays and X rays, or **Roentgen rays,** as X rays were called after their discoverer. **—roent·gen·ol·o·gy** (–NOL–) *n.* the branch of radiology dealing with X rays; **roent·gen·ol·o·gist** *n.*

rog·er (ROJ·ur) *interj.* esp. of a radio message, "received and understood"; OK!

rogue (ROHG) *n.* a scoundrel; rascal; **rogue elephant** a savage elephant that lives away from its herd; **rogues' gallery** a collection of pictures of criminals in police files. **—ro·guer·y** *n.* **—ro·guish** *adj.* **1** dishonest. **2** mischievous. **—ro·guish·ly** *adv.;* **ro·guish·ness** *n.*

roil *v.* muddy (water, etc.) by stirring up sediment; hence, vex or irritate; rile; **roil·y** *adj.* **roil·i·er, -i·est** turbid; also, irritated.

roist·er *v.* make merry boisterously; **roist·er·er** *n.*

role *n.* an actor's part; hence, a part or function assumed by one; also **rôle.**

Rolf·ing *n.* a technique of manipulating muscle tissue for promoting more efficient body energy.

roll (ROLE) *v.* **1** (cause to) move or go forward with a turning motion, as a ball, wheel, or something on wheels; revolve: *The years ~ed by; tears ~ing down her cheeks; Heads will ~* (i.e. people will be punished). **2** (cause to) sway from side to side, as a ship tossed by waves; hence, walk with a swagger. **3** have a rising and falling surface: *the ~ing fields, country, plain.* **4** of sounds, have a full or reverberating quality: *the ~ing drum, thunder; to ~ one's r's* (i.e. utter with a trill). **5** flatten by using a roller: *to ~ dough with a rolling pin; to ~ a road surface; ~ed oats.* **—n.** **1** something rolled up: *a ~ of film; cabbage ~s; to call the ~* (i.e. list of names); **strike off the rolls** expel from membership. **2** rolling movement: *walks with the ~ of a sailor.* **3** rising and falling surface: *the ~ of the land.* **4** rolling sound: *the ~ of distant thunder, of drums.* **—roll back** move back, esp. prices to a former level; **roll·back** *n.* such a rolling back. **—roll bar** a metal bar across the roof inside an automobile to protect the driver if the vehicle should roll over. **—roll call** (the time of) the reading aloud of a list of names, as of soldiers, to find out who is absent. —**roll·er** *n.* **1** one that rolls, as a long, swelling waves. **2** a cylinder used to roll a surface or one on which something is rolled. **3** any of a family of jaylike birds whose male has the habit of tumbling in the air to attract the attention of the female. —**roller coaster** an elevated railway with ascents, descents, and abrupt turns, carrying passengers in open cars on amusement rides. —**roller derby** a contest between roller-skating teams; **roller skate** a skate with small wheels instead of a runner for use on floors; **rol·ler-skate** *v.* **-skates, -skat·ed, -skat·ing.**

rol·lick (ROL·ik) *v.* behave in a carefree, frolicsome manner; **rol·lick·ing** *adj.*; **rol·lick·ing·ly** *adv.*

rolling pin a long cylindrical piece of wood or other material for rolling out dough. —**rolling stock** all the wheeled vehicles of a railroad or trucking company. —**roll-top** *adj.* of a desk, having a sliding top that closes and locks over the desk's working surface.

ro·ly-po·ly (roh·lee·POH·lee) *adj.* & *n.* **-lies** (a person or animal that is) short and plump.

Rom. Roman(s); Romance; Romania(n). —**ro·maine** (–MAIN) *n.* a variety of lettuce with a long roll of leaves curled inside each other. —**Ro·man** (ROH·mun) *n.* a person of or from Rome; ***adj.*** having to do with Rome, the Romans, or the Roman Catholic Church; **Roman Candle** a firework that shoots out sparks and balls of fire successively; **Roman Catholic** *n.* & *adj.* (a member) of the Christian church that has the pope as its head; **Roman Catholicism.** —**ro·mance** (–MANCE, ROH–) *n.* **1** a novel of love and adventure involving characters and events somewhat remote from real life, as of medieval knights; hence, this class of literature or a love experience with elements of romance in it. **2** any love story or love affair. **3 Romance** *n.* & *adj.* (of or having to do with) the languages derived from Latin, as Italian, French, Spanish, Portuguese, Provençal, etc. —***v.*** (–MANCE) **-manc·es, -manced, -manc·ing** exaggerate, indulge in fancies, or woo (someone) romantically; **ro·manc·er** *n.* —**Roman Empire** the empire of ancient Rome that lasted from about 27 B.C. to A.D. 392 and covered most of W. Europe and the lands of Asia and Africa around the Mediterranean. —**Ro·ma·ni·a** (–MAY·nee·uh, –MAIN·yuh) a country of S.E. Europe; 91,699 sq.mi. (237,-500 km²); *cap.* Bucharest; **Ro·ma·ni·an** *n.* & *adj.* (a person from or the language) of Romania. —**Roman numerals** numerals written in Roman letters, as I = 1, V = 5, X = 10, L = 50, C = 100, D = 500, and M = 1,000. —**ro·man·tic** (–MAN–) *adj.* **1** of or having to do with romance, esp. love and adventure: *a ~ scene, tale, situation.* **2** impractical or visionary. **3** of or having to do with 19th century romanticism; often **Romantic.** Also ***n.*** a romantic person or a romanticist; **ro·man·ti·cal·ly** *adv.* —**ro·man·ti·cism** (–MAN–) *n.* in literature and the fine arts, a movement or style marking a departure from classicism, based on emotion and inspiration rather than reason and logic and freedom and spontaneity of expression as opposed to restraint and order; **ro·man·ti·cist** *n.* —**ro·man·ti·cize** (–MAN–) *v.* **-ciz·es, -cized, -ciz·ing** make or be romantic: *a highly ~d tale.*

Rom·a·ny (ROM·uh–, ROH·muh–) *adj.* & *n.* **-nies** (a Gypsy or the language) of the Gypsies.

Rome capital of Italy.

Ro·me·o (ROH·mee·oh) the tragic hero of Shakespeare's *Romeo and Juliet;* hence, an ardent lover.

romp *n.* & *v.* (run or jump about in) boisterous play; **romp·er** *n.* **1** one who romps. **2** usu. **rompers** *pl.* a child's playsuit consisting of bloomers and top.

rood (RUDE) *n.* **1** a crucifix or cross. **2** a unit of area equal to ¼ acre (1,011.7 m²).

roof *n.* **roofs** the top covering of a building; also, a similar part, as of a car, the mouth, etc. —***v.*** cover with a roof; **roofed** (ROOFT) *adj.*; **roof·ing** *n.* & *adj.* (material) for roofs: *a ~ tile;* **roof·less** *adj.* —**roof·top** *n.* the top of a building: *You don't shout a private matter from the ~s; a ~ restaurant.* —**roof·tree** *n.* same as RIDGEPOLE.

rook *n.* **1** a chess piece shaped like a castle tower. **2** an Old World bird of the crow family with purplish black feathers, noted for its cunning; ***v.*** cheat or swindle. —**rook·er·y** *n.* **-er·ies** a colony of rooks or their nesting place.

rook·ie (–ee) *n.* *Informal.* an inexperienced recruit or a novice.

room *n.* **1** part of a building set apart by walls or partitions, as for an office or as living quarters; also, the people in it; **room·ful** *n.* **2** unoccupied space: *standing ~ only; much ~* (i.e. scope) *for improvement in your work.* —***v.*** **1** to lodge: *a ~ing house.* **2** occupy lodgings. —**room and board** lodging and meals. —**room·er** *n.* a lodger. —**room·ette** (–MET) *n.* a private compartment in a railroad sleeping car. —**rooming house** a house with furnished rooms for rent. —**room·mate** *n.* one sharing a room or rooms with others. —**room·y** *adj.* **room·i·er, -i·est** spacious; **room·i·ness** *n.*

Roo·se·velt (ROH·zuh–) **1 Franklin D.** 1882–1945, 32nd U.S. President (1933–45). **2 Theodore.** 1858–1919, 26th U.S. President (1901–09).

roost *n.* a perching place for birds, esp. domestic fowls; hence, a resting or sleeping place; **rule the roost** be in charge (of an establishment). —***v.*** perch on a roost; also, settle for the night; **roost·er** *n.* a male domestic fowl; cock.

root *n.* **1** the usu. underground part of a plant that serves as support and draws nourishment from the soil; also, the similar part of a hair, tooth, etc. **2** a source or origin: *the ~ of the trouble; "Root," "wort," and "ramify" have the same Indo-European ~; 3 is the square ~ of 9 and the cube ~ of 27* (9 = 3 × 3; 27 = 3 × 3 × 3) **—*v.*** **1** fix or settle (as in the ground). **2** become fixed or begin growing by sending out roots, or **take root. 3** poke, search, or dig (up), as with the snout; **root out** pull out by the roots; hence, remove or destroy. **4** *Informal.* work hard or cheer (*for* a contestant, team, etc.); **root•er** *n.* **—root beer** a sweetened carbonated drink flavored with extracts of the roots of plants such as sarsaparilla and trees such as sassafras. **—root•let** *n.* a small root. **—root•stock** *n.* same as RHIZOME.

rope *n.* a thick, strong cord or string made of twisted strands of fiber or similar material and traditionally used in a ship's rigging, to tether animals, for hanging people, etc. **—*v.* ropes, roped, rop•ing** tie, catch, mark off an area, etc. with a rope; **rope in** *Slang.* deceive (a person) into doing something. **—give one rope** let one act freely (and reap the consequences). **—know** (or **learn**) **the ropes** *Informal.* know (or learn) about a job or activity.

Roque•fort (ROKE·furt) **cheese** a strong-tasting, mold-ripened cheese made from sheep's milk, originally in Roquefort, France.

Ror•schach (ROR·shahk) **test** a psychological test based on the subject's interpretation of a series of ink-blot designs.

ro•sa•ry (ROH·zuh·ree) *n.* **-ries** (a string of beads used by Roman Catholics to keep count of) a series of prayers to the Virgin Mary.

¹rose (ROZE) *pt.* of RISE.

²rose (ROZE) *n.* (the beautiful, usu. fragrant flower of) any of a large family of shrubs with a prickly stem; also, the flower's commonly reddish color; ***adj.*** of this color. **—ro•sé** (–ZAY) *n.* a light pink wine. **—ro•se•ate** (ROH·zee·it) *adj.* rose-colored. **—rose•bud** *n.* the bud of a rose. **—rose•bush** *n.* a shrubby rose. **—rose-col•ored** *adj.* rosy; also, optimistic. **—rose•mar•y** (–mair·ee) *n.* **-mar•ies** an evergreen mint with fragrant leaves and pale blue flowers. **—ro•sette** (–ZET) *n.* a rose-shaped ornament, as of ribbon or as used in architecture. **—rose water** a watery perfume containing attar of roses. **—rose•wood** *n.* (the dark, reddish-brown wood of) a tropical tree of the pea family.

Rosh Ha•sha•na (ROHSH·huh·SHAH·nuh, ROSH–) the Jewish New Year.

ros•in (ROZN) *n.* the resin of pine trees, used in paints and varnishes and to rub on smooth surfaces to keep them from being slippery.

ros•ter *n.* a list, esp. of personnel on duty.

ros•trum *n.* **-trums** or **-tra 1** a platform or stage for public speaking. **2** a beaklike part or structure.

ros•y (ROH·zee) *adj.* **ros•i•er, -i•est** rose-colored; pinkish red; also, optimistic; **ros•i•ly** *adv.;* **ros•i•ness** *n.*

rot *v.* **rots, rot•ted, rot•ting** decompose; decay. **—*n.*** **1** decay; also, a disease of plants and trees, as "potato rot" and "dry rot," spread by fungi or bacteria. **2** *Slang.* rubbish; also ***interj.***

ro•ta•ry (ROH·tuh·ree) *adj.* & *n.* **-ries** wheel-like, circular, or rotating (machine or setup, esp. a traffic circle): *the cogwheel emblem of a Rotary Club; a ~ engine, press.* **—ro•tate** (ROH–) *v.* **-tates, -tat•ed, -tat•ing** turn around a center or axis, as a wheel or top; also, (cause to) take turns, as work shifts, crops, etc.; **ro•ta•tor** *n.;* **ro•ta•to•ry** *adj.* **—ro•ta•tion** (–TAY–) *n.;* **ro•ta•tion•al** *adj.*

R.O.T.C. Reserve Officers' Training Corps.

rote *n.* a repetitive or routine way of doing something, as memorizing **by rote. —ro•tis•ser•ie** (roh·TIS·uh·ree) *n.* **1** a restaurant or shop featuring roasted meat. **2** a grill with an electrically rotated spit. **—ro•to•gra•vure** (roh·tuh·gruh·VYOOR) *n.* (pictorial section of a newspaper produced by) a printing process using cylinders on which print and pictures have been engraved. **—ro•tor** (ROH·tur) *n.* a rotating part, as the armature of a generator or the system of blades of a helicopter.

rot•ten (ROTN) *adj.* having rotted; hence, spoiled; corrupt; foul-smelling: *~ eggs, smell; ~* (*Slang.* unpleasant) *weather;* **rot•ten•ness** *n.*

Rot•ter•dam a Netherlands seaport.

ro•tund (–TUND) *adj.* plump or rounded out; **ro•tun•di•ty** or **ro•tund•ness** *n.* **—ro•tun•da** (–TUN–) *n.* a round, usu. dome-covered building; also, the room within such a building.

rou•ble (ROO·bl) same as RUBLE.

rou•é (roo·AY) *n.* a dissolute or dissipated man; rake.

rouge (ROOZH) *n.* a reddish powder used as a cosmetic; also, one used for polishing metal, glass, etc. **—*v.* roug•es, rouged, roug•ing** use rouge (on).

rough (RUF) *adj.* not smooth, even, or level; hence, not gentle, pleasant, etc.; harsh, stormy, crude, coarse, severe, etc.: *a ~ ride on a ~ road; ~ weather, manners, work, voices, life, sketch;* ***adv.*** in a rough manner; also **rough•ly; rough•ness** *n.* **—*n.*** **1** a rough or violent person. **2** rough ground, esp. uncleared land along a golf fairway. **3** a rough condition: *to take the ~ with the smooth; a diamond* **in the rough** (i.e. not polished). **—*v.*** **1** treat roughly; subject (a person) to roughness, as in sports. **2** do incompletely; sketch roughly: *a ~ed-in outline.* **—rough it** live a rough life. **—rough•age** (–ih) *n.* coarse material, esp. fibrous foodstuff such as bran eaten for bulk. **—rough-and-read•y** *adj.* effective in a rough and crude way. **—rough-and-tum•ble** *n.* & *adj.*

(a struggle) that is rough and disorderly. —**rough·en** *v.* make or become rough. —**rough-hew** *v.* **-hews,** *pt.* & *pp.* **-hewed** or **-hewn, -hew·ing** hew (stone, timber, etc.) without smoothing; hence, give rough form to. —**rough·house** *n.* & *v.* **-hous·es, -housed, -hous·ing** *Informal.* (take part in or subject to) rough play or fun. —**rough·neck** *n.* **1** *Informal.* a coarse or rowdy person. **2** a workman on a drilling rig. —**rough·shod** *adj.* of horses, with shoes having projecting nail heads; **ride roughshod over** treat (a person, feelings, etc.) roughly.

rou·lette (roo·LET) *n.* **1** a gambling game using a ball rolled over a small revolving wheel with numbers on it, or **roulette wheel. 2** a small toothed wheel used to make a series of dots or perforations; ***v.*** mark or perforate (as sheets of stamps) with a roulette.

Rou·ma·ni·a(n) same as ROMANIA(N).

round *adj.* **1** shaped like a circle, ball, or cylinder: *a ~ table, column; a ~ vowel such as "O"* (pronounced with rounded lips). **2** curved or filled out in form or figure; full or complete: *~ shoulders; a buxom ~ figure; a ~ dozen, sum* (such as 1,000 instead of 998 or 1,006). **3** vigorous: *in ~ terms; a ~ scolding; at a ~ pace.* ***—n.*** **1** something round, as a ball, a rung of a ladder, a cut of beef below the rump, etc.; **in the round** showing all sides: *figures sculptured in the ~* (i.e. not in relief); *a theater-in-the-~* (with stage in center and seats all around). **2** a course or activity that ends where it begins: *a policeman on his ~s; the endless ~ of parties; the earth's yearly ~.* **3** something forming a part of the action in a group or sequence, as a section of a boxing match, one shot from a weapon such as a firearm or the ammunition for it, etc.: *a ~ of applause; "Three Blind Mice" is a ~, or musical canon.* **—*v.*** **1** make or become round. **2** go or turn round. **3** surround or encircle; **round up** drive or gather (animals, etc.) together. ***—adv.*** & ***prep.*** **1** in a circular path (by a place or person, back to one's position, etc.): *just saw her going ~* (the corner); *talked him ~ to vote for us.* **2** on all sides (of a person or place): *gathered ~* (their leader); *showing visitors ~* (the displays). **3** throughout (a place or period); around: *rains all ~ the year; spread the news ~* (the town). —**round·ish** *adj.* somewhat round. —**round·ly** *adv.;* **round·ness** *n.* —**round·a·bout** *adj.* indirect; circuitous: *a ~ route.* —**roun·de·lay** (ROUN·duh–) *n.* (the music for) a simple song with words returning again and again to the opening lines. —**round·house** *n.* a round building for repairing locomotives with a turntable in the center. —**round-shoul·dered** *adj.* with stooping shoulders. —**round table** (a conference by) a group of people meeting as equals or without consideration of precedence, as among King Arthur's "Knights of the Round Table." —**round-the-clock** *adj.* & *adv.* (continuing) day and night. —**round trip** a trip to and back from a place; **round-trip** *adj.* —**round·up** *n.* a rounding up or gathering (of cattle, scattered members of a group, news items for a summary, etc.); also, the men and horses rounding up cattle on a ranch. —**round·worm** *n.* a nematode, esp. one found in the intestines of children.

rouse (ROWZ) *v.* **rous·es, roused, rous·ing** stir, as from sleep; stir up (game from cover or a person to a state of excitement such as anger): *given a ~ing* (i.e. enthusiastic) *welcome.*

Rous·seau (roo·SOH), **Jean J.** 1712–78, French writer.

roust·a·bout (ROUS·tuh–) *n.* a usu. unskilled workman doing odd jobs as a deckhand, longshoreman, or in a circus, taking down tents, etc.

rout **1** *n.* & *v.* (put to) flight; hence, defeat. **2** dig or scoop out, as pigs root out things from the ground. —**route** (ROOT, ROWT) *n.* a regular course or road, as of one making deliveries: *a mail ~; newspaper ~;* ***v.*** **routes, rout·ed, rout·ing** send (goods, traffic, etc.) by a route or arrange the route for; **route·man** *n.* **-men** one covering a route. —**rou·tine** (–TEEN) *n.* a regular series of actions or operations: *our office ~; a computer input ~; a comedy ~* (i.e. act or bit); ***adj.*** habitual; hence, ordinary or dull; **rou·tine·ly** *adv.* —**rou·tin·ize** (–TEEN–) *v.* **-iz·es, -ized, -iz·ing:** *to ~ a process.*

rove (ROHV) a *pt.* of REEVE. ***—v.*** **roves, roved, rov·ing** go about or wander (over), usu. with a purpose: *a ~ing reporter;* **rov·er** *n.*

[1]row (ROH) **1** *n.* a line of persons or things; also, a street lined with houses; **in a row** in succession: *three years in a ~.* **2** *v.* move (a boat) using oars; hence, carry (people or goods) in a rowboat; ***n.*** a trip in a rowboat.

[2]row (ROU) *n.* & *v.* (have) a noisy quarrel; squabble.

row·an (ROH·un, ROW–) *n.* a European species of mountain ash.

row·boat *n.* a boat propelled by oars.

row·dy *n.* & *adj.* **-di·er, -di·est** (one who is) quarrelsome or disorderly; **row·di·ly** *adv.;* **row·di·ness** *n.;* **row·dy·ish** *adj.;* **row·dy·ism** *n.*

row·el *n.* & *v.* **-els, -el(l)ed, -el·(l)ing** (urge a horse with) a small wheel with projections that is attached to the end of a spur.

row (ROH) **house** one of a series of connected houses of identical design.

roy·al (ROY·ul) *adj.* **1** of or having to do with a sovereign, a kingdom, or its government; **roy·al·ist** *n.* & *adj.* **2** kingly; splendid. —**roy·al·ly** *adv.* —**roy·al·ty** *n.* **-ties** **1** royal person(s) or their rank, quality, etc. **2** a share of receipts from a property or creative work paid to its owner, author, composer, etc.

r.p.m. revolutions per minute. —**r.p.s.** revolutions per second.

R.R. railroad; rural route.
R.S. Revised Statues; Royal Society.
R.S.F.S.R. Russian Soviet Federated Socialist Republic.
R.S.V. Revised Standard Version (of the Bible).
R.S.V.P. please reply; also **r.s.v.p.**
rt. right. —**rte.** route. —**Rt.Hon.** Right Honorable. —**Rt.Rev.** Right Reverend.
Ru ruthenium.
rub *v.* **rubs, rubbed, rub·bing** (cause) to move while pressing against something: *His shoulder ~d mine; We ~ hands* (together) *to keep warm; An eraser ~s off writing; to ~ a surface dry; a tire ~ing against the fender.* —***n.*** a rubbing; also, something that rubs or irritates. —**rub down** rub (something) to polish, clean, etc.; also, massage. —**rub the wrong way** irritate (someone).
ru·ba·to (roo·BAH·toh) *adj.* & *adv. Music.* with freedom in performance for greater expression; ***n.*** **-tos** a rubato passage.
rub·ber (RUB·ur) *n.* **1** one that rubs, esp. an eraser. **2** an elastic substance obtained from the latex of certain trees; also, a similar synthetic product. **3 rubbers** *n.pl.* rubber overshoes. **4** (a game that determines the winning majority of) a series of games. —***adj.*** of rubber: *~ shoes, tires;* **rub·ber·y** *adj.* —**rubber band** a circular elastic band to put round things as a fastener. —**rubber cement** an adhesive consisting of rubber in an evaporating solvent. —**rub·ber·ize** *v.* **-iz·es, -ized, -iz·ing** coat with rubber. —**rub·ber·neck** *n. Informal.* one who is considered inquisitive because he stares and gapes; a gawking sightseer; ***v.:*** *traffic jam was due to drivers ~ing at a crash site.* —**rubber plant** a house plant related to the fig, with glossy, rubberlike leaves. —**rubber stamp** a device for stamping dates, signatures, endorsements, etc.; hence, one who routinely approves decisions made by others; also, such approval; **rub·ber-stamp** *v.*
rub·bish *n.* something worthless or discarded; trash; hence, nonsense.
rub·ble *n.* (a mass of) broken stones, bricks, etc.; debris of destroyed buildings.
rub·down *n.* a massage.
rube (ROOB) *n. Slang.* a country fellow.
ru·bel·la (roo·BEL·uh) same as MEASLES, *n.* 2.
Ru·bens (ROO·bunz), **Peter P.** 1577–1640, Flemish painter.
ru·be·o·la (roo·BEE·uh·luh) same as MEASLES, *n.* 1. —**ru·bi·cund** (ROO·buh–) *adj.* ruddy; reddish.
Ru·bi·con (ROO·bi–) a small river that was the N. boundary of ancient Italy and that Julius Caesar had to cross in his march on Rome; **cross the Rubicon** commit oneself irrevocably to a course of action.
ru·bid·i·um (roo·BID–) *n.* a soft, potassiumlike metallic element.
ru·ble (ROO–) *n.* the basic money unit of the U.S.S.R., equal to 100 kopecks.
ru·bric (ROO–) *n.* directions, titles, etc. given in red ink in medieval religious texts; hence, a procedural guide or rule. —**ru·by** (ROO·bee) *n.* **-bies** a red variety of corundum, one of the costliest of gems; also, its usu. deep-red color; ***adj.*** deep-red.
ruck·sack *n.* a knapsack.
ruck·us *n. Informal.* a row or uproar.
rud·der *n.* a hinged piece of wood or metal at the rear end of a boat or aircraft for steering it.
rud·dy *adj.* **rud·di·er, rud·di·est** reddish (in complexion); healthy-looking; **rud·di·ly** *adv.;* **rud·di·ness** *n.*
rude (ROOD) *adj.* **rud·er, rud·est** **1** rough in manner; discourteous: *It's ~ to contradict your elders; fired for being ~ to customers.* **2** of primitive times; barbarous: *a ~ implement; our ~ forefathers.* **3** rough in effect: *a ~ sketch; a ~ shock* (i.e. a violent one). —**rude·ly** *adv.* —**rude·ness** *n.* —**ru·di·ment** (ROO·duh–) *n.* **1** usu. **rudiments** *pl.* basics; elements: *the ~s of algebra.* **2** an incompletely evolved organ or structure. —**ru·di·men·ta·ry** (–MEN–) *adj.: only a ~ knowledge of linguistics; the ~ wings of flightless birds.*
[1]**rue** (ROO) *n.* & *v.* **rues, rued, ru·ing** regret. —**rue·ful** *adj.* sorrowful; **rue·ful·ly** *adv.;* **rue·ful·ness** *n.*
[2]**rue** (ROO) *n.* an evergreen herb formerly used in medicines.
ruff **1** *v.* to trump in a card game; ***n.*** a trumping. **2** *n.* a stiff, crimped or pleated, frill-like collar worn in the 1500's and 1600's by men and women; hence, a similar band of fur or feathers, as around the neck of a species of sandpiper called "ruff" and the **ruffed** (RUFT) **grouse** of North America.
ruf·fi·an (RUF·ee·un) *n.* & *adj.* (one who is) rough or rowdy; **ruf·fi·an·ism** *n.;* **ruf·fi·an·ly** *adv.*
ruf·fle (RUFL) *v.* **ruf·fles, ruf·fled, ruf·fling** **1** make (what is smooth and still) uneven, rough, or disturbed: *to ~ hair, feathers, calm waters, one's temper.* **2** shuffle or flip through (pages, playing cards, etc.). —***n.*** **1** disturbance; ripple. **2** a strip of material with a frilly edge used as trimming on dresses; also, the ruff on a bird's neck.
rug *n.* a piece of fabric used as a floor covering; also, a lap robe.
rug·by (–bee) *n.* the British original of American football, distinguished by continuous play by players wearing little protective gear.
rug·ged (RUG·id) *adj.* **1** of ground, rocky; rough in feature. **2** of people, hardy or sturdy. **3** of weather, stormy. —**rug·ged·ly** *adv.;* **rug·ged·ness** *n.*
Ruhr (ROOR) an industrial region of N. West Germany along the Ruhr river.
ruin (ROO·in) *n.* (state or cause of) complete destruction or damage beyond repair: *the ~ of one's plans; Drinking was his ~; a city lying* **in**

ruins. —*v.* come or bring to ruin: *crops ~ed by frost; The scandal ~ed his career.* **—ru·in·a·tion** (–NAY–) *n.* **—ru·in·ous** (–us) *adj.*; **ru·in·ous·ly** *adv.*; **ru·in·ous·ness** *n.*

rule (ROOL) *n.* **1** the way in which something normally happens or is usu. done: *the ~s of grammar;* **As a rule** *he doesn't work on Sundays.* **2** a regulation or a set of regulations governing life or conduct; also, a (period of) government: *"Drive right" is a ~ of the road; the Benedictine monastic ~; the long ~ of Queen Victoria.* **3** a line or a metal strip used to mark a line; also, a ruler (*n.* 2). **—*v.* rules, ruled, rul·ing** **1** lay down as a rule; make an official decision: *evidence ~d not admissible;* **rule out** exclude. **2** exercise authority over; govern, as if by force: *~d the country with an iron hand.* **3** mark lines on: *~d paper.* **—rule of thumb** a practical though not precise method. **—rul·er** *n.* **1** one who governs; sovereign. **2** a strip of wood, metal, etc. for marking and measuring straight lines. **—rul·ing** *n.* an official decision, as by a court or umpire; ***adj.*** that governs; controlling: *one's ~ passion.*

rum *n.* an alcoholic liquor made from molasses.

Rum. Rumania(n). **—Ru·ma·ni·a(n)** (roo·MAY–) same as ROMANIA(N).

rum·ba (–buh) *n.* a ballroom dance of Cuban origin in quadruple time; also, the music for it.

rum·ble *v.* **-bles, -bled, -bling** (move with or) make a low, heavy rolling sound: *thunder ~ing in the distance;* ***n.*** **1** a rumbling sound. **2** a street fight, as between teenage gangs. **—rumble seat** an outside seat at the back of an early automobile.

ru·mi·nate (ROO·muh–) *v.* **-nates, -nat·ed, -nat·ing** chew the cud; hence, meditate or muse; **ru·mi·nant** (–nunt) *n.* a split-hoofed grazing animal such as a cow, sheep, camel, or giraffe that chews the cud; ***adj.*** cud-chewing; also, meditative; **ru·mi·na·tion** (–NAY–) *n.*

rum·mage (RUM·ij) *v.* **rum·mag·es, rum·maged, rum·mag·ing** search thoroughly through (a drawer, attic, etc.) moving things about; hence, find out or turn up (something) by rummaging; ***n.*** a rummaging; also, miscellaneous articles, as offered at a **rummage sale,** usu. to raise money for charity.

rum·my (RUM·ee) *n.* a card game in which players try to form matching sets and sequences.

ru·mor (ROO·mur) *n.* general talk or a story that is not authentic or verifiable; ***v.*** tell or spread by rumor; *Brit.* **ru·mour.**

rump *n.* **1** buttocks; also, a corresponding cut of beef. **2** a remnant, as of a body of people.

rum·ple *v.* **-ples, -pled, -pling** crush (a sheet of paper, garment, etc.) or tousle (hair); ***n.*** a wrinkle or crease; **rum·ply** *adv.*

rum·pus *n. Informal.* a row or uproar; **rumpus room** a room set apart for noisy activities, parties, etc.

rum-run·ner *n.* one engaged in **rum-run·ning** *n.* transportation of alcoholic liquor illegally across a border.

run *v.* **runs, ran, run·ning** **1** (cause) to move at a pace faster than walking: *He ~s for exercise; is out ~ing his horse.* **2** (cause) to go or move quickly: *left what he was doing and ran for his life; a ship run aground; She ran her eyes over the page; was shot trying to ~ the blockade; He's ~ing* (i.e. contesting) *for mayor.* **3** (cause) to go on or keep going: *a train ~ing between Chicago and New York; a manager to ~ the business; an engine left ~ing.* **4** exist in a specified way: *roads ~ing at right angles to each other; Prices ~ high as demand increases; a talent that ~s in his family.* **5** drop stitches or ravel: *a fabric that will not ~.* **6** publish: *a story they ran in yesterday's editions.* **7** chase: *to ~ a rabbit down.* **8** smuggle: *charged with ~ing guns.* **—*n.*** **1** a running, its duration, or result: *a 12-hour ~; a print ~ of 10,000 copies.* **2** a trip or route: *the New York-Boston ~.* **3** a series or succession of things: *a ~ of bad luck; a ~* (i.e. of withdrawals) *on a bank.* **4** a track or area: *a ski ~; a sheep ~.* **5** a ravel, as in stockings. **—a run for one's money** satisfaction; challenge. **—in the long run** ultimately. **—on the run** (while) running or fleeing. **—run across** (or **into**) meet by chance. **—run down** **1** decline in strength; deteriorate. **2** hunt down; knock down. **3** speak badly of. **—run in** **1** *Informal.* arrest and put in jail. **2** make a brief visit. **—run out** come to an end; **run out of** have no more of. **—run through** spend rapidly; also, go over in review. **—run up** *Informal.* accumulate. **—run·a·bout** *n.* a light, usu. one-seated vehicle. **—run·a·round** *n. Informal.* a being referred from place to place in a frustrating manner. **—run·a·way** *n.* one that runs away; ***adj.*** fugitive: *a ~ slave; ~* (i.e. rapid) *inflation; a ~* (i.e. easy) *victory.* **—run-down** *adj.* not running; declining; deteriorating; **run·down** *n.* a summary.

rune (ROON) *n.* **1** any letter of an ancient Germanic alphabet used in inscriptions. **2** a mystical or obscure poem. **—ru·nic** *adj.*

rung *n.* a crosspiece of a ladder or one joining two legs of a chair. **—*v.*** a *pp.* of RING.

run-in *n. Informal.* a quarrel.

run·let (–lit) or **run·nel** (RUNL) *n.* a small stream.

run·ner *n.* **1** one that runs, as a racer, messenger, a football player carrying the ball, or a *base runner* in baseball. **2** a piece or strip placed along the length of something, as the blade of a skate or a narrow carpet. **3** a horizontally growing stem that takes root at nodes forming new plants, as in the strawberry; also, such a new plant. **—run·ner-up** *n.* **run·ners-up** a competitor who finishes in second place. **—run·ning** *n.* the act of running; **be in** (or **out of**) **the running** have some (or no) chance of winning; ***adj.*** **1** of or involving movement: *a* *train's ~ time between Boston and New York; a ~ leap, knot* (that slides); *A ship or aircraft travels with its* **running lights** *on.* **2** flowing: *washbasins with ~ water; a ~ sore* (discharging pus). **3** continuous or continuing: *$2.50 per ~ foot; a ~ commentary, pattern, script;* ***adv.*** continuously: *hasn't slept for three nights ~.* **—running gear** a vehicle's wheels and axles. **—running mate** a candidate for election on the same ticket as another for a higher office. **—run·ny** *adj.* **run·ni·er, run·ni·est** thin in consistency; also, flowing, as with mucus: *a ~ nose.* **—run·off** *n.* a final contest between the leading candidates in an election. **—run-of-the-mill** *adj.* of a product or specimen, commonplace; ordinary. **—run-on** *n.* & *adj.* (a dictionary entry) that continues from a previous entry in the same paragraph.

runt *n.* a stunted or undersized plant, animal, or [derogatorily] person; **runt·y** *adj.*

run-through *n. Informal.* a rehearsal; also, a rundown. **—run·way** *n.* a special track or way for the movement of people, animals, machines, etc., as the paved strip used by aircraft for takeoffs and landings, or a narrow extension of a stage from its center into the audience.

ru·pee (roo·PEE) *n.* the basic money unit of India, Pakistan, Sri Lanka, Mauritius, etc., equal to 100 paise or cents. **—ru·pi·ah** (–PEE–) *n.* the basic money unit of Indonesia, equal to 100 sen.

rup·ture *n.* & *v.* **-tures, -tured, -tur·ing** (cause or suffer) a break or tear, as of the spleen, or a weakening of the muscular wall, as in hernia; also, a break in relations: *An infected appendix may ~; a ~d bag of waters; a ~ of diplomatic relations.*

ru·ral (ROOR·ul) *adj.* of or having to do with the country, as opposed to the city: *a ~* (mail) *route, scene;* **ru·ral·ism** *n.* **—ru·ral·ly** *adv.*

ruse (ROOZ) *n.* a trick used to mask something, as illness feigned to skip school.

[1]**rush** *v.* **1** move with great speed or haste: *a patient ~ed to the hospital; a sale that was ~ed through; You're ~ing me!* **2** attack with speed and force: *Commandos had to ~ the hijacked plane.* **—*n.*** a rushing or rushed activity: *forgot her hat in the ~; the ~ of modern life.*

[2]**rush** *n.* a grasslike plant with round stems growing in marshy places; **rush·y** *adj.*

rush hour the time of the heaviest traffic during the day, esp. morning or evening.

rusk *n.* a dry and crisp piece of twice-baked bread or cake.

Russ. Russia(n).

rus·set (RUSS·it) *adj.* reddish brown, as the cloth that English peasantry used to wear or a kind of winter apple. **—*n.*** russet cloth or apple.

Rus·sia (RUSH·uh) same as the UNION OF SOVIET SOCIALIST REPUBLICS; **Rus·sian** *n.* & *adj.* (the official language or a person) of the Soviet Union; **Russian roulette** the firing of a revolver as an act of bravado at one's own head without knowing if its only cartridge is in the firing chamber.

rust *n.* **1** a reddish brown coating formed on exposed metal, esp. iron; also, the color. **2** a fungus disease of plants, esp. cereals such as wheat, that leaves spores resembling metal rust. **—*v.*** become covered with rust; hence, deteriorate.

rus·tic *adj.* **1** of the country: *~ charm, simplicity.* **2** crude or unpolished: *~ furniture, manners, humor;* ***n.*** one from the country, esp. an uncouth person. **—rus·ti·cal·ly** *adv.;* **rus·tic·i·ty** (–TIS–) *n.* **—rus·ti·cate** *v.* **-cates, -cat·ed, -cat·ing** **1** send to the country; also, in Britain, punish by suspension from school. **2** lead a rural life. **—rus·ti·ca·tor** *n.* **—rus·ti·ca·tion** (–CAY–) *n.*

rus·tle (RUSL) *n.* the light, clear sound of dry leaves, papers, silk, etc. rubbing lightly together. **—*v.*** **-tles, -tled, -tling** **1** make or move with a rustle. **2** act or move with energy or speed; **rustle up** gather; get (something) ready. **3** steal (cattle, horses, etc.); **rust·ler** *n.*

rust·y *adj.* **rust·i·er, -i·est** coated with rust or rust-colored; also, in need of polishing, as a skill lying unused.

rut *n.* & *v.* **ruts, rut·ted, rut·ting** **1** (make) a track or furrow, as by wheels on a road; hence, a settled, routine, or monotonous way or course of action: *longed to get out of the ~ and do some traveling.* **2** (be in) a period or state of sexual excitement or heat, as the male deer. **—rut·ty** *adj.* **rut·ti·er, rut·ti·est; rut·ti·ness** *n.*

ru·ta·ba·ga (root·uh·BAY·guh) *n.* a yellow turnip of the mustard family.

ru·the·ni·um (–THEE–) *n.* a silver-white metallic chemical element used in alloys.

ruth·less (ROOTH–) *adj.* merciless or cruel; **ruth·less·ly** *adv.;* **ruth·less·ness** *n.*

R.V. Revised Version (of the Bible). **—RV** *n.* **RVs** recreational vehicle.

R value the thermal resistance value of insulation: *Attic insulation to an ~ of "R 30" is recommended for diminishing heat loss through the roof of a house.*

Rwan·da (roo·WAHN·duh) an E.C. African country; 10,169 sq.mi (26,338 km^2); *cap.* Kigali.

Rwy. or **Ry.** Railway.

Rx (AR·EX) *n.* a medical prescription; hence, remedy.

-ry shortened form of -ERY: as in *dentistry, jewelry, mimicry.*

ry·a (REE·uh) *n.* a handmade Swedish rug or spread with long pile.

rye *n.* (the grain of) a cereal grass similar to wheat, used to make bread and liquors; also, a whiskey distilled from rye.

S

S or **s** (ES) *n.* **S's** or **s's** **1** the 19th letter of the English alphabet. **2** anything S-shaped. —**S** sulphur; **S.** Saturday; sea; September; Sunday. —**S.** or **s.** south(ern); saint (*pl.* **SS.** or **ss.**); school. —**s.** second; small; son; substantive. —**s** **1** plural form: as in *boys, girls.* **2** third person singular ending of verbs in the present indicative: as in *loves, kills.* **3** possessive case of nouns: as in *boy's, children's.* **4** contracted form of *is, has, us,* and *does:* as in *It's; He's gone; Let's go; What's it mean?*

S.A. Salvation Army; South Africa; South America.

Saar (SAR, ZAR) the region of the Saar River in Germany near the French border, now a West German state.

Sab·bath (SAB·uth) *n.* a day of rest and worship, Sunday in Christian practice or Saturday for Jews; **Sab·bat·i·cal** (–BAT–) *adj.* —**sabbatical** *n.* a year or a shorter period of leave for rest, study, etc. given, formerly every seven years, usu. to college teachers.

sa·ber or **sa·bre** (SAY·bur) *n.* a heavy cavalry sword for cutting and thrusting, usu. having a curved blade; also, a fencing foil with a guard that curves around the hand to protect the knuckles. —**saber rattling** menacing show of military strength. —**saber saw** a small electric jigsaw.

Sa·bin (SAY–) **vaccine** an oral polio vaccine.

sa·ble (SAY–) *n.* a marten of N. Europe and Asia or its fur which is dark-brown to black; hence, black color; **sables** *pl.* mourning garments.

sab·o·tage (SAB·uh·tahzh) *n.* damage done to property as a vengeful or subversive act, as by enemy agents or striking workers; ***v.* -tag·es, -taged, -tag·ing** commit sabotage on, as a **sab·o·teur** (–TUR) *n.*

sa·bra (SAH·bruh) *n.* a native-born Israeli.

sabre same as SABER.

sac *n.* a baglike, usu. liquid-containing part of an animal or plant, as the bladder in humans.

SAC (SAC) Strategic Air Command.

sac·cha·rin (SAC·uh–) *n.* a very sweet coal-tar product used as a sugar substitute; **sac·cha·rine** (–rin) *adj.* sugary; also, affectedly sweet: *a ~ smile, voice; ~ poetry;* **sac·cha·rin·i·ty** (–RIN–) *n.*

sac·er·do·tal (sas·ur·DOH·tl) *adj.* priestly: *~ ordination, vestments;* **sac·er·do·tal·ly** *adv.;* **sac·er·do·tal·ism** *n.*

sa·chem (SAY·chum) *n.* the chief of some North American Indian tribes.

sa·chet (sa·SHAY) *n.* (a small bag or pad containing) perfumed powder.

sack *n.* **1** a large bag of coarse cloth; **the sack** *Slang.* dismissal. **2** a plundering of a captured city. **3** a dry, white wine popular in the 16th and 17th centuries. —***v.*** **1** fire; dismiss. **2** plunder or pillage.—**sack·cloth** *n.* burlap or other coarse cloth; also **sack·ing; sackcloth and ashes** mourning or penitence. —**sack·ful** *n.* what a sack will hold.

sa·cral (SAY·crul) *adj.* of the sacrum. —**sac·ra·ment** (SAC·ruh–) *n.* a Christian rite or ceremony such as baptism, the Eucharist, and matrimony considered especially sacred; **sac·ra·men·tal** (–MEN–) *adj.* —**Sac·ra·men·to** (–MEN·toh) capital of California. —**sa·cred** (SAY–) *adj.* set apart for or dedicated to someone holy, esp. to the worship of a divine being; holy; inviolable: *a mountain ~ to the Muses; the ~ altar; the ~ writings of the Bible, Koran, etc.; a ~ duty;* **sacred cow** something venerated blindly as above criticism; **sa·cred·ly** *adv.;* **sa·cred·ness** *n.* —**sac·ri·fice** (SAK·ruh–) *n.* an offering or giving up of something valuable (as) to a god; also, the thing so offered: *a lamb killed as a ~ to God; human ~s; the ~ of one's time and energies in the cause of education; a house sold at a ~* (i.e. loss); *a baseball batter's ~ fly or ~ hit* (that advances a base runner while the batter is put out). —***v.* -fic·es, -ficed, -fic·ing** make a sacrifice; give up (something valuable) for the sake of something else: *He ~d his health in the pursuit of wealth; John* (the batter) *~d Jack* (the base runner) *to second base* (i.e. got Jack to second while himself being put out). **—sac·ri·fi·cial** (–FISH·ul) *adj.;* **sac·ri·fi·cial·ly** *adv.* **—sac·ri·lege** (SAC·ruh·lij) *n.* a violation of something sacred; gross irreverence; **sac·ri·le·gious** (–LIJ·us) *adj.;* **sac·ri·le·gious·ly** *adv.* **—sac·ris·tan** (SAC·ris·tun) *n.* an official in charge of a **sac·ris·ty** *n.* **-ties** a place, usu. near the sanctuary, where sacred vessels, vestments, etc. are kept; vestry. **—sa·cro·il·i·ac** (say·croh·IL·ee·ac) *n.* & *adj.* (the joint) between the ilium and the sacrum. **—sac·ro·sanct** (SAC·roh–) *adj.* most sacred; consecrated. **—sa·crum** (SAY–) *n., pl.* **-cra** (–cruh) or **-crums** the lower end of the spinal column.

sad *adj.* **sad·der, sad·dest** full of or causing sorrow; not happy; **sad·ly** *adv.;* **sad·ness** *n.* **—sad·den** *v.* make or become sad.

sad·dle (SADL) *n.* the usu. padded and curved seat for the rider of a horse, bicycle, etc.; also, something shaped like a saddle, as a cut of lamb, mutton, or venison consisting of the loins and the connecting back portion; **in the saddle** in a controlling position. **—v. sad·dles, sad·dled, sad·dling** put a saddle upon; hence, burden. **—sad·dle·bag** *n.* one of a pair of bags hung on each side behind a saddle. **—sad·dle·bow** (–boh) *n.* the arched front part of a saddle. **—saddle horse** a horse for riding. **—saddle shoe** a casual-wear white oxford with a band of contrasting color across the instep.

Sad·du·cee (SAJ·uh–) *n.* a member of a Jewish sect opposed to the Pharisees and accepting only the written law of the Bible; **Sad·du·ce·an** (–SEE–) *adj.*

sad·i·ron (SAD·eye·urn) *n.* a heavy flatiron.

sad·ism (SAD–, SAY–) *n.* the getting of pleasure, esp. sexual, from inflicting pain on another; **sad·ist** *n.* **—sa·dis·tic** (–DIS–) *adj.;* **sa·dis·ti·cal·ly** *adv.* **—sad·o·mas·o·chism** (sad·oh·MAS·uh·kizm, say·doh–) *n.* sadism and masochism in the same person; **sad·o·mas·o·chist** *n.*

sa·fa·ri (suh·FAR·ee) *n.* **-ris** a hunting expedition, esp in Africa; also, the people and animals in it.

safe *adj.* **saf·er, saf·est** free from danger, harm, risk, etc.: *A locked door is ~; a dark but ~ street; The policeman made her feel ~; a ~ guess; a ~* (i.e. reliable) *guide.* **—n.** a place for keeping something safe, esp. a strongbox or steel container. **—safe·ly** *adv.;* **safe·ness** *n.* **—safe-con·duct** *n.* permission to pass safely through hostile territory. **—safe-de·pos·it** *adj.* of a box or vault, for storing valuables, as in a bank; also **safe·ty-de·pos·it.** **—safe·guard** *n.* & *v.* (give) protection. **—safe·keep·ing** *n.* a keeping or being kept safe; custody. **—safe·ty** *n.* **-ties** **1** the state of being safe; security; also, a safety device. **2** in football, a play worth two points for the defensive team when the ball carrier is downed in his own end zone or steps out of his end zone; also, a defensive back close to his team's goal line. Also ***adj.;*** **safety-deposit** same as SAFE-DEPOSIT; *a shatterproof* **safety glass;** *a* **safety match** *that will strike fire only on a prepared surface; A clasplike* **safety pin** *has its point held inside a guard; A* **safety razor** *has its blade between guards for protection; the* **safety valve** *of a steam boiler for release of excessive pressure.*

saf·flow·er (SAF·lou–) *n.* a thistlelike plant with orange flowers whose seeds yield an oil used in medicine and cooking. **—saf·fron** (SAF·run) *n.* a bright orange dyestuff and cooking spice obtained from a crocus.

sag *v.* **sags, sagged, sag·ging** sink or hang down in the middle under weight or pressure, as a stretched rope, horizontal beam, or plank: *a ~ing roof; ~ing spirits, prices;* ***n.*** a sagging (place).

sa·ga (SAH·guh) *n.* a long story of heroic deeds, esp. a medieval Norse historical narrative.

sa·ga·cious (suh·GAY·shus) *adj.* of keen mind and sound practical judgment: *a ~ decision; Guide dogs are ~ animals;* **sa·gac·i·ty** (–GAS–) *n.*

sag·a·more (SAG·uh–) *n.* a subordinate chief among some North American Indians.

sage (SAIJ) **1** *n.* & *adj.* **sag·er, sag·est** (an elderly man who is) wise and discerning: *One of the Seven Sages of Greece said "Know thyself"; ~ advice;* **sage·ly** *adv.* **2** a small shrubby mint of Mediterranean origin whose leaves and stems are used in seasonings; also, the aromatic American **sage·brush** of the composite family.

sag·gy (SAG·ee) *adj.* **sag·gi·er, sag·gi·est** having a tendency to sag; sagging: *~ pants;* **sag·gi·ness** *n.*

Sag·it·ta·ri·us (saj·i·TAIR·ee·us) a S. constellation and the ninth sign of the zodiac.

sa·go (SAY–) *n.* **-gos** the starch or flour from the pith of the East Indian **sago palm.**

sa·gua·ro (suh·GWAH·roh) *n.* **-ros** the giant, candelabra-shaped cactus of Arizona, S.E. California, and N.W. Mexico.

Sa·ha·ra (suh·HAR·uh, –HAIR–) the world's largest desert, stretching across N. Africa, covering about 3 million sq.mi. (8 million km^2); **Sa·har·an** *adj.*

said *pt.* & *pp.* of SAY. ***—adj.*** above-mentioned.

Sai·gon (sye·GON) capital of the former South Vietnam. See HO CHI MINH CITY.

sail *n.* **1** a sheet of cloth spread to catch the wind for power to move a boat; also, the arm of a windmill. **2** sails collectively; also, a ship. **3** voyage. **—v. 1** move upon (a body of water) or be moved forward using sails; also, begin a voyage, or set sail. **2** manage (a vessel). **3** glide smoothly like a ship with outspread sails or under sail; **sail into** *Informal.* attack or criticize. **—sail·boat** *n.* a boat moved by a sail. **—sail·cloth** *n.* canvas or other cloth for sails, tents, etc. —**sail·fish** *n.* a large marlin with a saillike dorsal fin. —**sail·or** *n.* one who sails, esp. an enlisted man in a navy. —**sail·plane** *n.* a glider plane designed for soaring.

saint *n.* a holy person, esp. one officially recognized by a Christian church; **saint·hood** *n.* —**saint·ly** *adj.* **-li·er, -li·est; saint·li·ness** *n.* —**Saint Ber·nard** (–bur·NARD) a large powerful dog originally bred by monks for rescuing lost travelers in the Swiss Alps. —**Saint Valentine's Day** February 14, on which valentines are exchanged. —**Saint Vi·tus** (VYE–) **dance** or **Saint Vi·tus's** (–tus·iz) **dance** See CHOREA.

saith (SETH) *Archaic.* says.

[1]**sake** *n.* **for the sake of; for our** (or **your, God's,** etc.) **sake** in the interest of us (or you, God, etc.).

[2]**sa·ke** or **sa·ki** (SAH·kee) *n.* a Japanese rice wine, usu. served warm.

sa·laam (suh·LAHM) *n.* an Eastern greeting (meaning "peace" in Arabic) made by placing the right palm on the forehead while bowing; ***v.*** greet with or make a salaam.

sal·a·ble (SAY·luh–) *adj.* that can be sold; also **sale·a·ble.**

sa·la·cious (suh·LAY·shus) *adj.* obscene; pornographic; **sa·la·cious·ly** *adv.;* **sa·la·cious·ness** *n.*

sal·ad (SAL·ud) *n.* a cold dish of vegetables and fruit served with a salad dressing or sauce of oil, vinegar, cream, etc.

sal·a·man·der (SAL·uh–) *n.* **1** a lizardlike amphibian that lives in streams and ponds. **2** a mythical reptile said to live in fire.

sa·la·mi (suh·LAH·mee) *n.* a thick, highly seasoned Italian sausage. —**sal·a·ry** (SAL·uh·ree) *n.* **-ries** compensation periodically paid to employees working in offices rather than in factories or shops; **sal·a·ried** (–reed) *adj.: the ~ staff.*

sale *n.* **1** a selling: *used cars* **for sale** (i.e. that can be bought); *a company with annual ~s* (income) *of $10 million; She works in promotion, not ~s* (department). **2** a selling at reduced prices: *spring ~ of winter boots; boots* **on sale** (i.e. selling for less than usual). —**saleable** same as SALABLE.

Sa·lem (SAY–) capital of Oregon.

sales·clerk *n.* one who helps sell goods in a store; also **sales·per·son.** —**sales·man** *n.* **-men** a man who sells goods or services; **sales·wom·an, -wom·en; sales·girl; sales·la·dy, -dies.** —**sales·man·ship** *n.* —**sales slip** a customer's receipt for a purchase. —**sales talk** talk aimed at selling or persuading. —**sales tax** a tax on things sold.

sal·i·cyl·ic (–SIL·ic) **acid** a chemical used in making aspirin.

sa·lient (SAIL·yunt) *adj.* projecting; hence, prominent: *a ~ feature; ~ points, characteristics;* ***n.*** an angle, part of a fortification, etc. that points outward; **sa·lience** *n.*

sa·line (SAY·leen, –line) *adj.* of salt; salty. —***n.*** a saline cathartic or medicinal solution. —**sa·lin·i·ty** (suh·LIN–) *n.*

Salis·bur·y (SAWLZ–) capital of Zimbabwe.

sa·li·va (suh·LYE·vuh) *n.* the digestive juice secreted in the mouth by the **sal·i·var·y** (SAL·uh·ver·ee) glands. —**sal·i·vate** (SAL·uh–) *v.* **-vates, -vat·ed, -vat·ing** produce saliva, esp. excessively; **sal·i·va·tion** (–VAY–) *n.*

Salk (SAWLK) **vaccine** a polio vaccine given as injections.

sal·low (SAL·oh) *adj.* yellowish or sickly in complexion.

sal·ly (SAL·ee) *v.* **sal·lies, sal·lied, sal·ly·ing** go *(forth)* or set *(out)* suddenly (as if) in attack. —***n.*** **1** a sallying forth or sortie. **2** a witty remark. **3** an excursion or jaunt.

salm·on (SAM·un) *n.* any of seven species of large food and game fishes, commonly pink-colored, that swim back from the ocean to spawn in freshwater streams; also, their yellowish pink color.

sal·mo·nel·la (–NEL·uh) *n.* any of a genus of bacteria that cause food poisoning, paratyphoid, etc.

sa·lon (suh·LON) *n.* a reception hall or fashionable gathering place: *a beauty ~.* —**sa·loon** (suh·LOON) *n.* **1** a tavern; **sa·loon·keep·er** *n.* **2** a large room for a specified social purpose: *a dining ~.*

sal·si·fy (SAL·suh·fee, –fye) *n.* **-fies** a garden vegetable whose fleshy roots have an oyster-like flavor.

sal soda same as WASHING SODA.

SALT (SAWLT) Strategic Arms Limitation Talks.

salt (SAWLT) *n.* **1** a white, crystalline substance (sodium chloride) obtained from sea water and mines and widely used as a seasoning and preservative; hence, that which adds piquancy or liveliness to anything; **salt of the earth** the finest of people; **worth one's salt** worth one's pay. **2** a chemical compound resulting from a base neutralizing an acid, as calcium carbonate; **salts** *pl.* a laxative such as *Epsom salts* or a restorative such as "smelling salts" inhaled to relieve faintness, headache, etc. **3** *Informal.* a sailor. —***v.*** season or preserve with salt; **salt away** lay away safely; **salt(·ed)** *adj.* preserved or seasoned with salt: *salted fish, meat; salt beef; salt pork.* —**salt·y** *adj.* **salt·i·er, -i·est; salt·i·ness** *n.* —**salt·box** *n.* a two-story dwelling, as of colonial days, having its roof extended at the back to cover a kitchen annex. —**salt·cel·lar** (–sel·ur) *n.* a salt container used on the table. —**salt·ine** (–TEEN) *n.* a thin salted cracker. —**Salt Lake City** capital of Utah. —**salt lick** rock salt occurring above the ground which animals lick. —**salt·pe·ter** or **salt·pe·tre** (–pee·tur) *n.* naturally occurring potassium nitrate; niter; also, nitrate of sodium or calcium. —**salt·shak·er** (–shay·

kur) *n.* salt container for sprinkling salt on food. —**salt·wa·ter** *adj.* of or living in salty water: ~ *lake, fish.*

sa·lu·bri·ous (–LOO·bree·us) *adj.* healthful or invigorating. —**sal·u·tar·y** (SAL·yoo–) *adj.* healthful or beneficial (even if unpleasant).

sal·u·ta·tion (–yoo·TAY–) *n.* an act or expression of greeting, as a bow, raising the hat, "Dear Sir" at the beginning of a letter, etc. —**sa·lute** (–LOOT) *v.* **-lutes, -lut·ed, -lut·ing** greet, esp. to show honor or respect using a standard gesture such as a bow or a formal act such as raising the right hand or firing cannon; ***n.*** a saluting act or gesture; greeting.

sal·vage (–vij) *n.* **1** the saving of useful property from loss or waste, as ship or cargo from shipwreck, scrap metal, etc.: ***v.*** **-vag·es, -vaged, -vag·ing** save (property) from fire, flood, shipwreck, etc.: *~d wastepaper; escaped with his dignity barely ~d.* **2** property salvaged; also, compensation for salvage work. —**sal·vage·a·ble** *adj.* —**sal·va·tion** (–VAY–) *n.* **1** the saving of a person from damnation; redemption; also, any saving from a great loss or calamity. **2** a person or thing that effects such a saving.

salve (SAV) *v.* **salves, salved, salv·ing** soothe (a wound, sore, one's conscience, ego, etc.); ***n.*** a balm, ointment, or anything that soothes.

sal·ver *n.* a serving tray. —**sal·vo** *n.* **-vo(e)s** simultaneous discharge of guns as a salute or in attack; volley: *a ~ of bombs, cheers, insults.*

Sam. Samuel (Old Testament book). —**SAM** (SAM) *n.* surface-to-air missile.

sa·mar·i·um (–MAIR–) *n.* a rare-earth metallic element.

sam·ba *n.* a Brazilian ballroom dance of African origin in duple time; also, the music for it.

same *adj.* & *pron.* (being) the one referred to or implied: *He sleeps in the ~* (i.e. identical) *bed every day; This is the ~ lunch we ate yesterday* (i.e. same in kind, appearance, amount, etc.); *They are both the ~* (i.e. alike); *Fill in the form and forward ~* (*Nonstandard.* it) *to us.* ***adv.*** in the same manner: *I feel the ~;* **same·ness** *n.*

sam·iz·dat (sah·miz·DAHT) *n.* in the U.S.S.R., secret publication of officially banned writings.

Sa·mo·a (suh·MOH·uh) a group of 16 islands in the S. Pacific; **Sa·mo·an** *n.* & *adj.*

sam·o·var (SAM·uh–) *n.* a metal urn with an internal tube containing burning charcoal, used in Russia to heat water for tea.

sam·pan *n.* an Oriental boat having a small cabin often used as a dwelling and equipped with a sail and propelled by an oar at the stern.

sam·ple *n.* a part or specimen that shows the quality of something: *free ~s of a new toothpaste; a random ~ of the population; a fair ~* (i.e. instance or specimen) *of his wit;* ***v.*** **-ples, -pled, -pling** take as a sample; test a part of. —**sam·pler** *n.* **1** one who samples; also, a collection of samples. **2** a piece of cloth embroidered in various designs for practice or display.

Sam·son (–sn) in the Bible, an Israelite famed for his strength.

Sam·u·el (SAM·yoo–) a prophet of the Old Testament.

sam·u·rai (SAM·uh·rye) *n. sing.* & *pl.* (a member of) a warrior class in feudal Japan.

Sa·na (sah·NAH) capital of the Yemen Arab Republic.

San An·to·ni·o (–TOH·nee·oh) a city of Texas.

san·a·to·ri·um (san·uh·TOR·ee·um) *n.* **-ums** or **-ri·a** **1** an establishment for treating a particular group of patients, as those with tuberculosis or mental illness. **2** a convalescent home.

San Ber·nar·di·no (–bur·nuh·DEE–) a city of California.

sanc·ti·fy (SANK·tuh–) *v.* **-fies, -fied, -fy·ing** make holy; consecrate: *a day ~d by God as the Sabbath; a practice ~d by custom;* **sanc·ti·fi·ca·tion** (–CAY–) *n.* —**sanc·ti·mo·ni·ous** (–MOH·nee·us) *adj.* pious in a showy way; **sanc·ti·mo·ni·ous·ly** *adv.;* **sanc·ti·mo·ny** *n.* pretended piety. —**sanc·tion** (SANK–) *n.* **1** official or authoritative approval. **2** penalty provided by a law for its enforcement: *economic ~s such as trade boycotts and embargoes to force a nation to obey international law.* **—*v.*** approve of officially. —**sanc·ti·ty** *n.* sacredness; **sanctities** *pl.* obligations, feelings, etc. considered as sacred. —**sanc·tu·ar·y** (SANK·choo–) *n.* **-ar·ies** **1** a consecrated place such as a place of worship, esp. the part of a church containing the altar. **2** a place of refuge or protection: *a wild life ~; hijackers given ~ in certain countries.* —**sanc·tum** *n.* a sacred place; also, *Informal.* one's place of seclusion; den.

sand *n.* loose grains of worn-down rock, finer than gravel but coarser than silt, found in river beds, on seashores, etc.; **sands** *pl.* tract of sand. **—*v.*** put sand over or into; also, smooth (a surface), as with sandpaper; **sand·er** *n.*

san·dal (SAN·dl) *n.* a slipper or low shoe with straps joining the sole to the foot.

san·dal·wood *n.* the heavy, straight-grained, fragrant, yellowish wood of several trees of the East Indies that is used for carving and whose oil is used for cosmetics.

sand·bag *n.* a sand-filled bag used for ballast, protection, etc.; ***v.*** **-bags, -bagged, -bag·ging** put sandbags in or around; also, hit (someone) with a sandbag. —**sand·bank** *n.* a shoal, ridge, etc. formed by a deposit of sand, as at the mouth of a river; also **sand·bar.** —**sand·blast** *n.* & *v.* (clean, engrave, etc. with) a blast of air or steam containing sand; **sand·blast·er** *n.* —**sand·box** *n.* a small enclosure filled with sand for children to play in. —**sand·hog** *n.* a laborer working underground or under water, as in a caisson.

San Di·e·go (san·dee·AY–) a seaport of California.

sand·lot *adj.* of sports and games, informal or unorganized: ~ *baseball;* **sand·lot·ter** *n.* —**sand·man** *n.* the folklore genie who makes children sleepy. —**sand·pa·per** *n.* & *v.* (rub with) paper coated with sand for polishing surfaces. —**sand·pip·er** (–pye·pur) *n.* any of a large family of birds including snipes, esp. a small bird with a long, soft-tipped bill seen on seashores. —**sand·stone** *n.* a rock composed of sand particles cemented together by silica, clay, calcium, etc. —**sand·storm** *n.* a desert storm driving clouds of sand through the air.

sand·wich *n.* two slices of bread with a layer of meat, cheese, etc. between them; ***v.*** place or crowd in between other persons or things.

sand·y *adj.* **sand·i·er, -i·est** **1** containing or covered with sand. **2** yellowish-red: ~ *hair.*

sane *adj.* **san·er, san·est** mentally sound; also, sensible; **sane·ly** *adv.*

San·for·ize (SAN·fuh–) *v.* **-iz·es, -ized, -iz·ing** *Trademark.* preshrink cloth by a special process.

San Fran·cis·co (–frun·SIS–) a seaport of California.

sang *pt.* of SING.

sang-froid (–FRWAH) *n.* coolness or composure. —**san·gui·nar·y** (SANG·gwuh·ner·ee) *adj.* bloody or bloodthirsty. —**san·guine** (SANG·gwin) *adj.* disposed to be cheerful and confident; also, ruddy.

sanit. sanitary; sanitation. —**san·i·tar·i·an** (–TAIR–) *n.* a specialist in sanitation. —**san·i·tar·i·um** (–TAIR–) *n.* **-ums** or **-i·a** a health resort; also, a sanatorium. —**san·i·tar·y** *adj.* hygienic; hospital-clean; **sanitary napkin** a disposable absorbent pad to wear during menstruation. —**san·i·ta·tion** (–TAY–) *n.* public health, including sewage disposal, water treatment, pollution control, food processing, etc. —**san·i·tize** *v.* **-tiz·es, -tized, -tiz·ing** make sanitary; also, remove objectionable features from. —**san·i·ty** *n.* mental health; also, soundness of judgment.

San Jo·se (–hoh·ZAY) a city of California. —**San Jo·sé** (–hoh·ZAY) capital of Costa Rica. —**San Juan** (–HWAHN) capital of Puerto Rico.

sank *pt.* of SINK.

San Ma·ri·no (–muh·REE–) world's smallest republic, in E.C. Italy; 24 sq.mi. (61 km²); *cap.* **San Marino.**

sans (SANZ) *prep.* without.

San Sal·va·dor (–SAL·vuh–) capital of El Salvador.

San·skrit *n.* the Indo-European classical language of India, with records from around 1000 B.C.

San·ta Claus (SAN·tuh·clawz) in folklore, a red-suited, white-bearded, jolly old man who brings gifts to children at Christmas. —**Santa Is·a·bel** (–IZ·uh–) former name of MALABO. —**San·ta Fe** (–FAY) capital of New Mexico. —**San·ti·a·go** (sahn·tee·AH·go) capital of Chile. —**San·to Do·min·go** (sahn·toh·doh·MEENG·goh) capital of the Dominican Republic. —**São Pau·lo** (sowng·POW·loo) a city of Brazil. —**São To·mé** (sowng·taw·MAY) **and Prín·ci·pe** (–PREEN·see·puh) an African republic consisting mainly of two islands in the Gulf of Guinea; 372 sq.mi. (964 km²); *cap.* **São Tomé.**

sap *n.* **1** the vital juice that circulates in a plant carrying food and water; hence, health and vigor; **sap·less** *adj.* **2** *Slang.* fool. **3** a trench dug for approaching or undermining an enemy's position. —***v.*** **saps, sapped, sap·ping** dig under; undermine; hence, weaken or wear away: *strength ~d by heat;* **sap·per** *n.* trench-digging soldier.

sa·pi·ent (SAY·pee·unt) *adj.* wise or discerning; **sa·pi·ent·ly** *adv.;* **sa·pi·ence** *n.*

sap·ling *n.* a young tree; also, a young person.

sap·o·dil·la (–DIL–) *n.* a tropical evergreen tree that bears delicious, apple-shaped, rusty-brown fruit and whose latex is used for gum chicle.

sap·phire (SAF·ire) *n.* a variety of corundum valued as a gem; also, its color; ***adj.*** bright-blue.

sap·py (SAP·ee) *adj.* **sap·pi·er, sap·pi·est** full of sap; *Slang.* foolish; **sap·pi·ness** *n.*

sap·ro·phyte (–fite) *n.* an organism that draws nourishment from dead or decaying matter; **sap·ro·phyt·ic** (–FIT–) *adj.*

sap·suck·er *n.* a woodpecker that gets sap out of trees. —**sap·wood** *n.* the light-colored, sap-carrying part of a tree trunk between bark and heartwood.

Sar·a·cen (SAIR·uh·sn) *n.* an Arab or Moslem, esp. at the time of the Crusades; ***adj.*** also **Sar·a·cen·ic** (–SEN–).

sa·ran (suh·RAN) *n.* a synthetic plastic material used as a film or sheet esp. for wrapping, and as a textile fiber for draperies, upholstery, etc.

sar·casm (SAR·caz·um) *n.* an ironical and cutting remark, often used to ridicule; also, this mode of humor; **sar·cas·tic** (–CAS–) *adj.;* **sar·cas·ti·cal·ly** *adv.*

sar·co·ma (–COH–) *n.* **-mas** or **-ma·ta** (–muh·tuh) a cancer of connective tissues, esp. of bones or muscles; cf. CARCINOMA. —**sar·coph·a·gus** (–COF·uh–) *n., pl.* **-gi** (–jye) or **-gus·es** a stone coffin, esp. an inscribed or ornamented one.

sar·dine (–DEEN) *n.* a small herring or pilchard, usu. canned for food or dried and powdered for fish meal. —**Sar·din·i·a** (–DIN·ee–) a Mediterranean island S. of Corsica. —**sar·don·ic** (–DON–) *adj.* scornful or sarcastic: ~ *laughter, humor, expression;* **sar·don·i·cal·ly** *adv.*

sarge *n. Informal.* sergeant.

sa·ri or **sa·ree** (SAR·ee) *n.* a S. Asian, esp. Indian garment of women, consisting of a decorated length of lightweight cloth draped around the body.

sa·rin (SAH–) *n.* a lethal nerve gas.

sa·rong (–RONG) *n.* a colorful piece of cloth worn like a skirt by men and women of the East Indies.

sar·sa·pa·ril·la (sas·uh·puh·RIL·uh, sar·suh–) *n.* (the fragrant root of) a tropical vine of the smilax group, used to flavor carbonated drinks.

sar·to·ri·al (–TOR–) *adj.* of tailoring, esp. of men's clothes: *a ~ masterpiece;* **sar·to·ri·al·ly** *adv.*

sash *n.* **1** a broad strip of cloth worn either as a belt or over one shoulder as a dress accessory or badge. **2** the frame holding the glass in a door or window; also, the sliding frame of a double-hung **sash window.**

sa·shay (–SHAY) *v. Informal.* walk or move in a gliding manner, esp. sideways.

Sask. *Abbrev.* for **Sas·katch·e·wan** (–KACH·uh·wahn) a Prairie Province of Canada; 251,700 sq.mi. (651,900 km²); *cap.* Regina.

sass *n. Informal.* impudent talk; ***v.*** talk to impudently.

sas·sa·fras (SAS·uh–) *n.* (the aromatic root bark of) a North American laurel with pale yellow flowers and irregularly-shaped leaves.

sass·y *adj.* **sass·i·er, -i·est** *Informal.* **1** saucy. **2** fresh; lively; stylish; ***v.*** **sass·ies, sass·ied, sass·y·ing:** *a little car ~d up with a lot of accessories.*

sat *pt.* & *pp.* of SIT. —**sat.** saturate(d); saturation. —**Sat.** Saturday.

Sa·tan (SAY·tn) *n.* the Devil.

sa·tang (suh·TAHNG) *n. sing.* & *pl.* 1/100 of a baht.

sa·tan·ic (–TAN–) *adj.* like Satan.

satch·el (SACH·ul) *n.* a bag for carrying books to school, clothes, etc.

sate *v.* **sates, sat·ed, sat·ing** satisfy (a desire or appetite) so fully that it dies: *~d with food and drink.*

sa·teen (–TEEN) *n.* an imitation satin cloth, usu. all-cotton.

sat·el·lite (SATL–) *n.* a person or thing following another that is more important or larger, as a small planet or man-made object put in an orbit, or one of many nations controlled by a great power: *a communications ~; Soviet ~s such as East Germany and Hungary; ~ cities around a metropolis.*

sa·ti·ate (SAY·shee–) *v.* **-ates, -at·ed, -at·ing** satisfy (a desire or appetite) to excess; glut; surfeit; **sa·ti·a·tion** (–AY–) *n.;* **sa·ti·e·ty** (suh·TYE·uh·tee) *n.*

sat·in (SATN) *n.* & *adj.* (smooth and glossy as) silk or other fabric woven with a lustrous face; **sat·in·y** *adj.* —**sat·in·wood** *n.* (an East Indian tree that has) a yellowish-brown wood with a satiny luster.

sa·tire (SAT–) *n.* the use of irony and sarcasm to expose folly and vice, as in cartoons, comedies of manners, and the literature of Swift and Pope; also, such a work or works collectively or their art; **sat·i·rist** *n.;* **sat·i·rize** *v.* **-riz·es, -rized, -riz·ing** attack using satire. —**sa·tir·i·cal** (–TEER–) *adj.;* **sa·tir·i·cal·ly** *adv.*

sat·is·fac·tion (–FAC–) *n.* a satisfying or something that satisfies, esp. the discharge of a debt or claim, making up for harm done, etc.: *~ guaranteed or your money back;* **sat·is·fac·to·ry** *adj.* satisfying; adequate; **sat·is·fac·to·ri·ly** *adv.* —**sat·is·fy** (SAT–) *v.* **-fies, -fied, -fy·ing** **1** fulfill (a need, desire, hope, demand, claim, condition, etc.). **2** please or convince: *a spoiled child hard to ~; She ~d herself that the insult was not intended.*

sa·to·ri (–TOR·ee) *n.* spiritual awakening that is the goal of Zen Buddhism.

sa·trap (SAY–, SAT–) *n.* a subordinate or petty ruler, as in the ancient Persian Empire.

sat·u·rate (SACH·uh–) *v.* **-rates, -rat·ed, -rat·ing** (cause) to be filled, charged, or soaked to the maximum: *A ~d solution will not dissolve any more of the solute; Air ~d with moisture will condense if cooled;* **sat·u·ra·tion** (–RAY–) *n.*

Sat·ur·day *n.* the day of the week following Friday; the last day of the week; **Saturday night special** a cheap, widely sold handgun. —**Sat·urn** the planet sixth in distance from the sun and the second largest, with three rings around it. —**sat·ur·nine** *adj.* gloomy or forbidding in aspect.

sat·yr (SAY·tur, SAT–) *n.* in Greek myth, a lecherous woodland deity with the lower half of his body like a goat's; **sat·y·ri·a·sis** (–RYE·uh–) *n.* excessive sexual desire in the male.

sauce *n.* **1** a liquid or soft preparation served with food as a relish or as a topping with dessert: *barbecue ~; spaghetti ~; cranberry ~* (i.e. stewed fruit). **2** *Informal.* impudence. —***v.*** **sauc·es, sauced, sauc·ing** **1** season; add flavor to. **2** *Informal.* be saucy to. —**sauce·pan** *n.* a metal cooking pot with a handle. —**sau·cer** *n.* a small, shallow dish for holding a cup. —**sauc·y** *adj.* **sauc·i·er, -i·est** flippant and disrespectful in behavior; **sauc·i·ly** *adv.;* **sauc·i·ness** *n.*

Sa·u·di (SOW·dee, sah·OO–) **Arabia** a kingdom occupying most of the Arabian peninsula; 831,313 sq.mi. (2,153,090 km²); *cap.* Riyadh. —**Sa·u·di** *n.* & *adj.*

sau·er·bra·ten (SOUR·brah·tn) *n.* marinated and cooked beef. —**sau·er·kraut** (SOUR·crowt) *n.* finely cut cabbage fermented in brine.

sau·na (SOW·nuh, SAW–) *n.* (a room used for) a Finnish-style steam bath in which water is thrown on hot stones to produce steam.

saun·ter *n.* & *v.* stroll.

sau·sage (SAW·sij) *n.* chopped and seasoned meat stuffed in a tubular casing.

sau·té (soh·TAY) *v.* **-tés, -té(e)d, -té·ing** fry quickly in a little fat; ***n.*** & ***adj.*** sautéed (food).

sau·terne(s) (soh·TURN) *n.* a sweet white table wine.

sav·age (–ij) *n.* a member of any of the most primitive peoples; hence, one who is fierce, brutal, or rough-mannered; ***adj.*** utterly uncivilized or brutal: *a ~ tribe, dog, attack; a ~* (i.e. fierce) *temper;* ***v.*** **-ag·es, -aged, -ag·ing** attack violently or brutally. **—sav·age·ly** *adv.;* **sav·age·ness** *n.;* **sav·age·ry** *n.*

sa·van·na(h) (suh·VAN·uh) *n.* tropical grassland lying between forests and deserts, as of the Sudan, the veldts of South Africa, and the pampas and llanos of South America. **—Sa·van·nah** a city of Georgia.

sa·vant (suh·VAHNT, SAV·unt) *n.* a learned person.

save *v.* **saves, saved, sav·ing** make or keep free from danger, risk, loss, etc.: *The seatbelt ~d my life; Take a plane to ~ time; Read in the light to ~ your eyes; ~ing money* (i.e. putting it aside) *for a vacation; tips to help you ~; Jesus ~s* (i.e. souls from sin); **sav·er** *n.* ***—n.*** an act, as of a goalkeeper, that prevents an opponent from scoring. ***—conj.*** & ***prep.*** except(ing). **—sav·ings** *pl.* money saved; ***adj.:*** *a* **savings account** *in a* **savings bank;** *a high-interest, fixed-term* **savings certificate;** *a* **savings and loan association** *owned and operated by shareholders.* **—sav·io(u)r** (SAIV·yur) *n.* one who saves, esp. Jesus Christ, **the Savio(u)r.**

sa·voir-faire (sav·wahr·FAIR) *n.* tact or ability to get along well in society. **—sa·vor** (SAY·vur) *n.* & *v.* (have or enjoy) the distinctive taste, smell, or other quality of (something): *the ~ of soy sauce; She ~ed the wine slowly; His style ~s of arrogance.* **—sa·vor·y** *adj.* **-vor·i·er, -i·est** pleasing to the smell and taste; agreeable; ***n.,*** *pl.* **-vor·ies** **1** an hors d'oeuvre or appetizer, usu. served before wines. **2** a European mint, used to flavor foods such as poultry. **—sav·vy** (SAV·ee) *v.* **sav·vies, sav·vied, sav·vy·ing** *Slang.* (have) shrewd understanding (about a subject); grasp: *an aide with political ~.*

saw *pt.* of SEE. **—saw** *n.* **1** a wise saying; maxim. **2** a tool for cutting hard substances, having a metal blade with teeth on a straight or circular edge; ***v.*** **saws,** *pt.* **sawed,** *pp.* **sawed** or **sawn, saw·ing** cut (as if) with a saw. **—saw·bones** *n. Slang.* a surgeon. **—saw·dust** *n.* fine fragments of wood produced in sawing. **—saw·horse** *n.* a frame with four legs for supporting wood being sawn by hand. **—saw·mill** *n.* a factory in which logs are sawn into lumber. **—saw·yer** *n.* one who saws wood.

sax *n.* [short form] saxophone.

Sax·on (SAK·sn) *n.* & *adj.* (a dialect or member) of a Germanic people who settled in Britain in the fifth century; also, Anglo-Saxon.

sax·o·phone (SAX·uh–) *n.* a single-reed wind instrument with a curved body usu. made of brass; **sax·o·phon·ist** (–FOH–) *n.*

say *v.* **says, said** (SED), **say·ing** **1** utter; speak; tell: *Please ~ what is on your mind; He's ~ing his prayers; The clock ~s* (i.e. shows) *12.* **2** state; declare: *hard to ~ whether he's lying; said to be a learned man.* **3** [used parenthetically] let us suppose (as an example, estimate, etc.): *You would make, ~, $20 an hour.* ***—n.*** expression of one's opinion: *a chance to have her ~; The boss has the final ~* (i.e. power of deciding) *in the matter.* **—say·ing** *n.* an act of saying or something said, esp. a commonly heard statement: *the ~s of great men.* **—say-so** *n. Informal.* assertion or assurance; hence, authority.

sb. substantive; **Sb** antimony.

S.C. or **SC** South Carolina. **—sc.** namely; scale; scene; science; screw. **—Sc** scandium; **Sc.** Scotch; Scottish. **—s.c.** small capitals.

scab *n.* **1** a blood clot on the surface of a wound or the crust formed on a healing wound; also, a plant disease producing scablike spots. **2** *Slang.* a worker acting against a striker; also, any scoundrel. ***—v.*** **scabs, scabbed, scab·bing** **1** of a wound, become covered with a scab. **2** *Slang.* act as a scab (worker).

scab·bard (–urd) *n.* a sheath for a sword or dagger.

scab·by *adj.* **scab·bi·er, scab·bi·est** covered with scabs; hence, low or mean. **—sca·bies** (SCAY·beez) *n.* a contagious itching disease of humans caused by a mite; also called "the itch." **—scab·rous** (SCAB·rus, SCAY–) *adj.* **1** rough or scaly; scurfy: *a ~ leaf.* **2** scabby; hence, vile; indelicate; obscene.

scads *n.pl. Informal.* a large amount (*of* money, people, time, etc.).

scaf·fold (SCAF·uld, –oled) *n.* & *v.* (furnish with or put on) a raised framework, usu. of poles and planks, to stand on while working on a building; formerly, a platform from which criminals were hanged; **scaf·fold·ing** *n.* a scaffold for workmen or the poles, planks, etc. forming it.

scal·a·wag (SCAL·uh–) *n. Informal.* a rascal, scamp, or reprobate: *the ~s and carpetbaggers of the Reconstruction period.*

scald (SCAWLD) *v.* burn (as if) with a hot liquid or steam; ***n.*** a burn caused thus.

scale *n.* **1** a series or sequence forming a classifying and measuring system: *the zero-to-100° temperature ~; a $10,000-$15,000 salary ~; the 8-tone musical ~.* **2** relative size or proportion: *a map drawn to ~; a ~ model of an airplane; a ~ of one inch to 10 miles; bribery on a large ~.* **3** any of the thin, flat, horny pieces covering a fish or reptile; also, any layer or piece resembling this. **4** a weighing machine; **scales** *pl.* (the pans, or **scale·pans** of) a balance; **turn the scales** decide or settle. ***—v.*** **scales, scaled, scal·ing** **1** climb up as on a ladder; **scale up** (or **down**) increase (or reduce) in proportion. **2** scrape scales from (fish) or remove in layers or pieces, as bark from trees, tartar from teeth, etc. **3** weigh on a scale. —**scale insect** an insect such as mealybugs that resemble scales as they cluster on the plants on which they feed.

sca·lene (scay·LEEN, SCAY–) *adj.* having the sides all of unequal length: *a* ~ *triangle.*

scal·lion (SCAL·yun) *n.* an onion that has not developed a bulb; also, a leek or green onion.

scal·lop (SCOL·up, SCAL–) *n.* **1** a bivalve mollusk with fanlike rounded and ribbed shells; also, a scallop shell. **2** a scallop-shaped decoration, as on the edge of a dress. —***v.*** **1** bake in a casserole with a milk sauce and bread crumbs. **2** ornament or trim with scallops.

scalp *n.* the hair-covered skin and flesh of the head; ***v.*** **1** tear the scalp from. **2** *Informal.* buy and sell theater tickets, stocks, etc. at a high, often illegal profit; **scalp·er** *n.* —**scal·pel** *n.* a surgeon's dissecting knife.

scal·y (SCAY·lee) *adj.* **scal·i·er, -i·est** having scales; **scaly anteater** same as PANGOLIN.

scam *n. Slang.* a swindling scheme.

scamp *n.* a rascal. —**scamp·er** *n.* run quickly, as small animals or children when scared; ***n.*** a playful running or scurrying.

scam·pi (–pee) *n.pl.* the Norwegian lobster or shrimp, also called "Dublin prawn," cooked in Italian style.

scan *v.* **scans, scanned, scan·ning** **1** look at closely, going over (an object) part by part, as a television camera in transmitting a picture or a radar beam searching an area: *had time only to* ~ (i.e. go quickly over) *the morning's headlines during breakfast.* **2** mark off (lines of verse) into feet. —***n.*** a scanning. —**scan·ner** *n.*

Scan(d). Scandinavia(n).

scan·dal (SCAN·dl) *n.* **1** action or conduct that is shocking and shameful; also, the feeling of general outrage that results from it. **2** slander or evil gossip. —**scan·dal·ize** *v.* **-iz·es, -ized, -iz·ing** outrage the feelings of; **scan·dal·iz·er** *n.* —**scan·dal·mon·ger** (–mung·gur, –mong·gur) *n.* one who spreads slander. —**scan·dal·ous** (–us) *adj.* causing or spreading scandal; **scan·dal·ous·ly** *adv.*

Scan·di·na·vi·a (–NAY·vee·uh) the region of N.W. Europe including usu. Norway, Sweden, Denmark, Iceland, and sometimes Finland; **Scan·di·na·vi·an** *n.* a person of or from Scandinavia; also, any of the Germanic languages spoken there; ***adj.*** of Scandinavia, its peoples, or their languages. —**scan·di·um** *n.* a soft, gray metallic element discovered in Sweden.

scan·sion *n.* metrical scanning of verse.

scant *adj.* falling short of the required size or quantity; barely enough: *with* ~ *regard for truth;* ~ *of breath;* ***v.*** make scant; limit (the supply of).

scant·ling *n.* a small beam or piece of timber, esp. one used as an upright in building.

scant·y *adj.* **scant·i·er, -i·est** falling short; barely enough: ~ *rainfall, bathing suit;* **scant·i·ly** *adv.;* **scant·i·ness** *n.*

scape·goat *n.* one made to take the blame for others. —**scape·grace** *n.* a scamp or rascal.

scap·u·la (SCAP·yoo·luh) *n.* **-las** or **-lae** (–lee) the shoulder blade; **scap·u·lar** *adj.*

scar *n.* & *v.* **scars, scarred, scar·ring** (form or leave) a mark, as of a healed wound or burn.

scar·ab (SCAIR·ub) *n.* (the carved image of) a dung beetle, sacred to the ancient Egyptians.

scarce (SCAIRCE) *adj.* **scarc·er, scarc·est** not easily available: *Water is* ~ *this summer; a* ~ (i.e. rare) *book; likes to* **make himself scarce** (*Informal.* go or stay away) *when help is needed;* **scarce·ly** *adv.* hardly; also, not: *so tired he can* ~ *walk;* **scarce·ness** *n.;* **scar·ci·ty** *n.* **-ties** inadequate supply.

scare *v.* **scares, scared, scar·ing** fill (a timid person or animal) with fear, often so as to put to flight; also, become frightened; ***n.*** fright; **scare up** *Informal.* get together (supplies, etc.) to meet a need. —**scare·crow** *n.* a ragged figure set up in a field to scare birds away from crops.

scarf *n.* **scarfs** or **scarves** a long strip of cloth or a neckerchief worn for ornament or protection around the neck, head, waist, etc.; also, a long and narrow table covering.

scar·i·fy (SCAIR–) *v.* **-fies, -fied, -fy·ing** scratch, cut, or break up a surface, as the skin for vaccination, topsoil in agriculture, etc.; also, hurt (a person) by severe criticism; **scar·i·fi·ca·tion** (–CAY–) *n.*

scar·let *n.* & *adj.* bright red (color), as of the rash in **scarlet fever** or **scar·la·ti·na** (–TEE–) *n.* an infectious disease marked by fever and sore throat.

scarp *n.* & *v.* (make into) a steep slope or escarpment, as of a cuesta.

scar·y (SCAIR·ee) *adj.* **scar·i·er, -i·est** *Informal.* frightening or easily frightened; **scar·i·ly** *adv.;* **scar·i·ness** *n.*

scat *v.* **scats, scat·ted, scat·ting** *Slang.* **1** go away; ***interj.*** used to drive away an animal. **2** in jazz, sing or speak scat; ***n.*** nonsense sounds or syllables.

scath·ing (SCAY·dhing) *adj.* severe or harsh: ~ *criticism, remarks;* **scath·ing·ly** *adv.*

sca·tol·o·gy (scuh·TOL·uh·jee) *n.* obscene literature, esp. dealing with excrement; **scat·o·log·i·cal** (–LOJ–) *adj.*

scat·ter *v.* go or send in different directions, as papers by a wind or a flock when driven. —**scat·ter·brain** *n.* one who cannot concentrate on a subject; **scat·ter·brained** *adj.* —**scatter rug** a small rug.

scav·enge (–inj) *v.* **-eng·es, -enged, -eng·ing** search among or gather (discarded objects); also, feed on rubbish or dead matter, as vultures and hyenas; **scav·eng·er** *n.*

sce·nar·i·o (si·NAIR·ee·oh) *n.* **-os** (an outline of) a sequence of events as planned, imagined, etc., esp. a film director's script containing instructions on camera shots, etc.; **sce·nar·ist** *n.* —**scene** (SEEN) *n.* **1** the place or stage of an action or incident; hence, a sphere of activity or way of life: *the drug ~; the disco ~;* **behind the scenes** behind the stage; hence, not publicly. **2** an act or incident of a play; **make a scene** make an embarrassing display of one's emotions. **3** a view, esp. one that has artistic appeal, as a landscape. —**scen·er·y** (SEEN–) *n.* **-er·ies** **1** the features of a landscape: *paused to admire the ~.* **2** the painted screens and such accessories used on a stage to represent the place of an action. —**sce·nic** (SEE–) *adj.* **1** having fine scenery: *a ~ route, highway.* **2** of natural scenery: *~ artists, effects.* —**sce·ni·cal·ly** *adv.*

scent (SENT) *v.* to smell or suspect; also, perfume: *to ~ game, trouble; a ~ed parlor.* —***n.*** a perfume; also, a smell or the trail left by it: *bloodhounds thrown off a ~ by water; a keen ~* (i.e. sense of smell) *for game;* **scent·less** *adj.*

scep·ter (SEP–) *n.* the staff carried by a sovereign as a symbol of power; hence, sovereignty.

scep·tic (SKEP–) same as SKEPTIC.

scep·tre (SEP·tur) *Brit.* scepter.

schedule (SKEJ·ool) *n.* a list of times for doing things according to a plan: *a publishing ~; a train running behind ~* (i.e. late); ***v.*** **-ules, -uled, -ul·ing** enter in a schedule: *Charters are not ~d flights; a meeting ~d* (i.e. planned) *for 9 a.m.*

scheel·ite (SHEEL–, SHAY–) *n.* a tungsten-ore mineral.

sche·mat·ic (skee·MAT–) *n.* & *adj.* (of or like) a scheme or diagram: **sche·mat·i·cal·ly** *adv.* —**scheme** (SKEEM) *n.* **1** a plan or systematic arrangement: *the rhyme ~ of a sonnet.* **2** a project: *a drainage ~.* **3** an underhand plan; plot; ***v.*** **schemes, schemed, schem·ing** plot or intrigue: *a ~ing politician;* **schem·er** *n.*

scher·zo (SCAIR·tsoh) *n.* **-zos** or **-zi** (–tsee) a lively movement of a symphony or sonata.

Schick (SHIK) **test** a test for immunity to diphtheria.

Schil·ler (SHIL·ur), **Friedrich von.** 1759–1805, German poet.

schil·ling (SHIL–) *n.* the basic money unit of Austria, worth 100 groschen.

schism (SIZM) *n.* division or split within a church, as the Great Schism of the 1300's with rival popes; also, a resulting sect or the offense of causing religious schism; **schis·mat·ic** (–MAT–) *n.* & *adj.* (one) that causes or is guilty of schism. —**schist** (SHIST) *n.* mineral rock that splits easily into layers, as mica and talc; **schist·ose** *adj.* —**schiz·oid** (SKIT·soid) *n.* & *adj.* (one) showing schizophrenic symptoms; **schiz·o·phre·nia** (skit·suh·FREE·nee·uh) *n.* a mental disorder involving a split personality, the emotional side being disturbed, with consequent aggressive and destructive tendencies; **schiz·o·phren·ic** (–FREN–) *n.* & *adj.* (one) who has schizophrenia.

schle·miel (shluh·MEEL) *n. Slang.* a bungler or chump.

schlep(p) (SHLEP) *n. Slang.* an awkward or dull person.

schlock (SHLOK) *n.* & *adj. Slang.* (anything) cheap or trashy.

schmaltz (SHMAHLTS) *n. Slang.* excessive sentimentalism in art, music, etc.; **schmaltz·y** *adj.*

schmo (SHMOH) *n.* **schmo(e)s** *Slang.* a dolt or jerk.

schnapps (SHNAHPS) *n.* a ginlike alcoholic liquor.

schnau·zer (SHNOW–) *n.* a terrierlike German breed of dog.

schnook (SHNOOK) *n. Slang.* a sucker or dupe.

schnozzle (SHNOZL) *n. Slang.* the nose.

schol·ar (SCOL·ur) *n.* **1** a student. **2** a learned person; **schol·ar·ly** *adj.* —**schol·ar·ship** *n.* **1** a grant of money or other aid to help a student. **2** the knowledge or erudition of a learned person; also, a student's level of attainment. —**scho·las·tic** (scuh·LAS–) *adj.* having to do with schools or scholars; also, pedantic; **scho·las·ti·cal·ly** *adv.* —**school** (SCOOL) *n.* **1** a place for teaching and learning; hence, education, an educational course or session, or a particular department of instruction. **2** a situation or experience having training value: *the ~ of adversity, hard knocks.* **3** the group of teachers and taught; also, a group of people who agree in their views, methods, etc. **4** a group of the same kind and size of fish or other water animals swimming together. —***v.*** **1** teach or train; **school·ing** *n.* **2** swim together, as tuna and sardines. —**school board** a local group managing a school system. —**school·book** *n.* a book for use in schools. —**school·boy** *n.* a boy attending school; *fem.* **school·girl.** —**school·fel·low** *n.* schoolmate. —**school·house** *n.* a school building. —**school·marm** or **school·ma'am** (–mahm, –mam) *n. Informal.* **1** a woman schoolteacher. **2** one who is pedantic or priggish. —**school·mas·ter** *n.* [old-fashioned] a schoolteacher; *fem.* **school·mis·tress.** —**school·mate** *n.* one going to the same school as another. —**school·room** *n.* a room in which teaching is done. —**school·teach·er** *n.* one who teaches in a school. —**school·yard** *n.* a piece of ground near or around a school; school playground. —**school year** the September-June period.

schoon·er (SKOON–) *n.* a fore-and-aft-rigged ship with two or more masts.

schtick (SHTIC) *n.* same as SHTICK.

Schu·bert (SHOO–), **Franz P.** 1797–1828, Austrian composer.

Schu·mann (SHOO·mahn), **Robert.** 1810–1856, German composer.

schuss (SHOOSS) *n.* & *v.* (make) a fast run on skis down a slope; **schuss·boom·er** *n.* one who schusses downhill.

schwa (SHWAH) *n.* a neutral vowel sound, as of the A and E of *another;* also, the symbol (ə) used to represent it in a phonetic alphabet.

Schweit·zer (SHWITE·sur), **Albert.** 1875–1965, medical missionary in Africa.

sci. science; scientific.

sci·at·ic (sye·AT–) *adj.* having to do with the hip or hip nerves; **sci·at·i·ca** *n.* inflammation of the large sciatic nerve running down the back of each thigh.

sci·ence (SYE·unce) *n.* **1** systematized knowledge based on observed and tested facts, as distinguished from art; also, a branch of it, as mathematics, logic, and the physical and biological sciences; **sci·en·tist** *n.* **2** a skill or technique: *the ~ of boxing.* **—science fiction** fiction based on imaginative and fantastic applications of science and technology to the future, life on other planets, etc. **—sci·en·tif·ic** (–TIF–) *adj.* dealing with or based on science; **sci·en·tif·i·cal·ly** *adv.* **—sci-fi** (SYE·fye) *n.* [short form] science fiction.

scil. *Abbrev.* for **scil·i·cet** (SIL–) *adv.* namely.

scim·i·tar (SIM·i·tur) *n.* a curved sword of Eastern origin.

scin·til·la (sin·TIL·uh) *n.* spark; a shred or least trace: *not a ~ of evidence, truth;* **scin·til·late** (SIN–) *v.* **-til·lates, -til·lat·ed, -til·lat·ing** sparkle brilliantly, as a diamond; **scin·til·la·tion** (–LAY–) *n.*

sci·on (SYE·un) *n.* **1** a branch or shoot for grafting. **2** a descendant; offspring.

scis·sion (SIZH·un) *n.* a cutting or splitting. **—scis·sor** (SIZ·ur) *n.* & *v.* (cut with) scissors; **scis·sors** (SIZ·urz) *n.pl.* **1** a cutting instrument for cloth, paper, hair, etc. having two pivoted blades that are squeezed against each other by the action of the hand inserted through two rings at one end of the blades. **2** [takes *sing. v.*] a wrestling hold using the legs like scissors; **scissors kick** a swimming kick used with a sidestroke in which the legs are moved like scissors.

scle·ro·sis (scluh·ROH–) *n., pl.* **-ses** (–seez) hardening of tissues, as of the arteries or nerves; **scle·rot·ic** (–ROT–) *adj.*

scoff *v.* mock or jeer (at a person or thing deserving respect); ***n.*** a scoffing; **scoff·law** *n.* one who habitually flouts the law.

scold *v.* find fault (with) or rebuke in an ill-tempered way; ***n.*** one who scolds, esp. a woman. **—scold·ing** *n.* & *adj.*

sconce *n.* a light fixture bracketed to a wall, usu. for a candle.

scone *n.* a quick bread or biscuit made on a griddle or in an oven.

scoop *n.* **1** a shovellike tool or utensil that is used to dig or ladle out a portion of a substance, as various kitchen utensils for taking up sugar, ice cream, mashed potatoes, etc., shovels used in industry for coal, dirt, etc., or a gougelike surgical instrument; also, a scooping or the amount taken up in one scooping. **2** *Informal.* a piece of news published by a paper ahead of its rivals. ***—v.*** **1** take up or hollow out with a scoop. **2** *Informal.* beat (rival newspapers) by publishing a story first.

scoot *v. Informal.* be off swiftly; dart; decamp. **—scoot·er** *n.* **1** a child's two-wheeled vehicle consisting of two tandem wheels connected by a footboard, with a steering post connected to the front wheel. **2** a motor scooter.

scope *n.* **1** extent or range of perception or activity: *matters outside the ~ of an inquiry; The ~ of man's mind is limited; a plan with much ~* (i.e. room or opportunity) *for expansion.* **2** short form of words ending in **-scope** *comb. form.* observing instrument: as in *microscope, stethoscope, telescope.*

sco·pol·a·mine (–POL·uh·meen, –min) *n.* an alkaloid drug used to dilate the pupils for eye examination, as a sedative, and as a truth serum.

scor·bu·tic (–BYOO–) *adj.* having to do with scurvy; **scor·bu·ti·cal** *adj.*

scorch *v.* burn the outside or surface of (cloth, vegetation, etc.) so as to discolor or damage: *the* **scorched earth** *policy of devastating an area before yielding it to invaders.* ***—n.*** a superficial burn.

score *n.* **1** a mark, scratch, or notch, as in keeping tally; hence, a record or account, as of points in a game: *a ~ of 6 to 4 in the deciding game; a baseball box ~; have no regrets on that ~* (i.e. account); **know the score** *Informal.* know the real facts about a situation; **settle** (or **pay off**) **a score** get even for a past offense. **2** a set of 20: *four ~ and seven;* **scores** *of* (i.e. many) *times.* **3** the notation of a musical work containing one or more parts, as for an orchestra. ***—v.*** **scores, scored, scor·ing** **1** make or assign as points; also, keep a record of the number of points. **2** make a mark or line: *The editor ~d through the lines to be deleted.* **3** arrange (a piece of music) in a score. **4** succeed. **—score·less** *adj.;* **scor·er** *n.*

sco·ri·a *n., pl.* **-ri·ae** (–ee) slag or dross, as from the reduction of metal ores; also, a coarse pumice.

scorn *n.* & *v.* (regard with) contempt: *a know-it-all who ~s advice; a scientist who treated laymen with ~;* **scorn·ful** *adj.;* **scorn·ful·ly** *adv.*

Scor·pi·o (–pee·oh) a S. constellation and the eighth sign of the zodiac; also **Scor·pi·us. —scor·pi·on** (–pee·un) *n.* an arachnid with a venomous sting at the end of a curved tail.

Scot. Scotland; Scottish. **—Scot** *n.* a person of or from Scotland. **—Scotch** **1** *n.* & *adj.* [less preferred form] Scots or Scottish. **2** Scotch whisky.

scotch *v.* wound without killing; hence, stamp out or crush: *to ~ a rumor, theory.*

Scotch·man *n.* **-men** [less preferred form] Scotsman. **—Scotch tape** *Trademark.* an adhesive tape; **scotch-tape** *v.* **-tapes, -taped, -tap·**

ing. —**Scotch terrier** same as Scottish terrier. —**Scotch whisky** whiskey distilled in Scotland from malted barley.

scot-free *adj.* unpunished; without loss or injury.

Scot•land (–lund) the N. division of Great Britain; 30,404 sq. mi. (78,772 km²); *Cap.* Edinburgh. —**Scotland Yard** London police (headquarters), esp. its crime investigation department. —**Scots** *n.* & *adj.* Scottish. —**Scots•man** (–mun) *n.* **-men** a person of or from Scotland. —**Scot•tie** or **Scot•ty** *n.* **Scot•ties** *Informal.* **1** Scottish terrier; also **scottie, scotty. 2** Scotsman. —**Scot•tish** *adj.* of Scotland, its people, or their dialect of English; ***n.*** Scottish English; **the Scottish** Scottish people; **Scottish terrier** a strong and plucky, short-legged terrier of Scottish breed with a hard, wiry coat and small upright ears.

scoun•drel (–drul) *n.* a villain or rascal; ***adj.*** villainous or wicked.

scour *v.* **1** clean or polish (pots, pans, etc.) by rubbing with something abrasive, as a **scouring rush,** or horsetail; ***n.*** a scouring; **scours** *pl.* diarrhea in newborn cattle, etc. **2** dig or wear away by the force of something in motion, as a channel by a stream. **3** search (an area, one's memory, etc.) by quickly going over.

scourge (SCURJ) *n.* & *v.* **scourg•es, scourged, scourg•ing** (punish as with) a whip; hence, any large-scale punishment or widespread affliction such as the plague.

[1]**scout** *n.* & *v.* (one sent out) to reconnoiter, survey, or search for something, as a military or police **scout car,** a space vehicle, or a *girl scout* or *boy scout: to ~ for artistic talent, firewood; a ~ing expedition.* —**scout•ing** *n.* activities of scouts, esp. of the Boy Scouts or Girl Scouts. —**scout•mas•ter** *n.* the adult leader of a band of scouts.

[2]**scout** *v.* scoff at or jeer.

scow *n.* a barge used for bulk cargo; also, a sailboat with a square stern and rounded bow.

scowl *n.* an ill-humored or sullen look or frown with contracted eyebrows; ***v.*** look with a scowl; **scowl•er** *n.*

scrab•ble *n.* & *v.* **scrab•bles, scrab•bled, scrab•bling** scrape; scramble; scribble; **scrab•bler** *n.* —**Scrabble** *Trademark.* a word game played on a board with lettered tiles.

scrag•gly *adj.* **scrag•gli•er, scrag•gli•est** irregular or ragged: *a ~ beard.* —**scrag•gy** *adj.* **scrag•gi•er, scrag•gi•est** rugged or scrawny: *~ cliffs; a ~ neck.*

scram *v.* **scrams, scrammed, scram•ming** *Slang.* go away; also ***interj.*** —**scram•ble** *v.* **-bles, -bled, -bling 1** move forward by climbing, crawling, etc.; struggle: *to ~ up a hill; to ~ to get the football, for seats, for a living, power, wealth.* **2** mix or jumble: *~d eggs* (stirred while frying); *a ~d* (i.e. deliberately garbled) *radio or television signal.* —***n.*** a scrambling, esp. a disorderly struggle.

Scran•ton (–tun) a city of Pennsylvania.

scrap *n.* **1** a piece or fragment, as of torn paper, leftover meat, or a brief extract from something written or printed; also, discarded metal or trash: *a* **scrap•book** *for collecting pictures, clippings, etc.; ~ iron.* **2** *Informal.* a fight or struggle. —***v.*** **scraps, scrapped, scrap•ping 1** make into scraps; discard as junk. **2** *Informal.* fight or quarrel. —**scrap•per** *n.* —**scrape** *v.* **scrapes, scraped, scrap•ing 1** rub or scratch against or with something rough or sharp: *to ~ paint off with a knife; fell and ~d her knee; a tire ~ing against a fender.* **2** get by trying very hard: *They ~d together enough money to pay the rent; ~d through the examination with a C grade; managed to ~ along even during the Depression.* —***n.*** **1** a scraping (sound) or a scraped place. **2** a predicament. —**scrap•er** *n.* —**scrap•heap** *n.* a pile of discarded things. —**scrap•py** *adj.* **scrap•pi•er, scrap•pi•est 1** made up of fragments; disconnected. **2** *Informal.* quarrelsome; also, tough or gritty. —**scrap•pi•ly** *adv.;* **scrap•pi•ness** *n.*

scratch *v.* **1** mark, cut, or scrape lightly with something sharp or pointed: *furniture ~ed by movers; ~es his head when lost for words; a ~ing pen* (that writes with a scraping noise). **2** write or draw hurriedly; also, draw a line through as in striking out a name: *a candidate ~ed* (i.e. withdrawn) *from the race.* **3** scrape (money) together. —***n.*** **1** a scratching or a mark or cut made by it: *a* **scratch test** (made on the skin) *for determining a person's allergies.:* **2** a line marking the starting point of a race; **from scratch** from the starting line; without any advantages; **up to scratch** up to the point of readiness; in good condition. —***adj.*** **1** for quick notes: *~ paper, pad.* **2** hastily put together: *a ~ team.* —**scratch•y** *adj.* **scratch•i•er, -i•est; scratch•i•ly** *adv.;* **scratch•i•ness** *n.*

scrawl *v.* write carelessly or hastily; ***n.*** such writing; **scrawl•er** *n.;* **scrawl•y** *adj.*

scraw•ny *adj.* **-ni•er, -ni•est** *Informal.* thin and bony: *a turkey's ~ neck; a ~ youngster;* **scraw•ni•ness** *n.*

scream (SCREEM) **1** *n.* & *v.* (utter) a sharp, shrill cry of pain, fright, etc. **2** *Informal.* a very funny person or thing.

screech *n.* & *v.* (utter) a harsh, shrill, piercing sound or cry; shriek: *heard a ~ of brakes;* **screech•y** *adj.*

screen *n.* **1** a covered frame or something similar put up to hide, protect, or separate: *a painted Japanese ~; a wire mesh ~ to keep out flies; a smoke ~ against enemy observation.* **2** a projection surface for motion pictures, slides, or other images; hence, motion pictures: *stars of the stage and ~.* **3** a sieve or other straining device. —***v.*** **1** shield; protect; partition: *A row of trees ~ed our view; a sheltered life ~ed from* *unhealthy influences.* **2** show (a motion picture) on a theater screen. **3** sift or separate: *candidates carefully* ~*ed for sensitive jobs.* — **screen·play** *n.* the script of a motion picture.

screw *n.* **1** a naillike but spirally threaded metal piece for fastening things by turning a **screw·driv·er** (–dry·vur) in its slotted head; **put the screws on** use pressure on (someone). **2** any mechanical device working like a screw on an advancing spiral, as a jack for lifting loads, the **screw propeller** of a ship or airplane, a corkscrew, thumbscrew, etc. **—*v.*** **1** twist or turn, as a screw; hence, fasten or tighten: *He* ~*ed the lid on tight; had to* ~ *up* (i.e. gather) *some courage to do it.* **2** twist out of shape; contort (one's face); **screw up** *Slang.* mess or foul up (a job, activity, etc.). —**screw·ball** *n.* & *adj. Slang.* eccentric (person); **screw·y** *adj.* **screw·i·er, -i·est** *Slang.* crazy or eccentric.

scrib·ble *n.* & *v.* **scrib·bles, scrib·bled, scrib·bling** (make) marks or writing in a careless or hasty manner: *graffiti* ~*d on walls; an illegible* ~; **scrib·bler** *n.* —**scribe** *n.* a writer, esp. a copyist of manuscripts before the invention of printing.

scrim *n.* a loosely woven cotton fabric used for lining, curtains, etc.; hence, a gauze curtain used on a stage for special effects.

scrim·mage (–mij) *n.* a play in football beginning at the *line of scrimmage* when the ball is snapped back; also, a practice game between a team's players; ***v.*** **scrim·mag·es, scrim·maged, scrim·mag·ing** take part in a scrimmage or struggle.

scrimp *v.* be sparing or niggardly (with food, money, and other resources); **scrim·py** *adj.*

scrim·shaw *n.* a carved or engraved object of ivory, bone, shells, etc., as made by whalers during long voyages; also, such objects collectively or their craft.

scrip *n.* a receipt or certificate of entitlement to a share of stock, land, money, etc. —**script** *n.* **1** handwriting or a type style resembling it. **2** the written text of a motion picture, play, etc. —**scrip·tur·al** (–chuh·rul) *adj.* of or having to do with sacred writings, esp. the Bible; **scrip·tur·al·ly** *adv.* —**Scrip·ture** (–chur) *n.* **1** the Bible; also **the Scriptures** *pl.* **2 scripture** any sacred book. —**scrive·ner** (SCRIV·nur) *n. Archaic.* a scribe or copyist.

scrod *n.* young cod or other fish boned and cut into strips for cooking; ***v.*** **scrods, scrod·ded, scrod·ding** to fillet (a fish) for cooking.

scrof·u·la (–yuh·luh) *n.* a tuberculosis of the lymph nodes, esp. of the neck; **scrof·u·lous** (–lus) *adj.*

scroll (SCROLE) *n.* a usu. written roll of paper or parchment; also, a scroll-shaped ornament as on an Ionic capital or the head of a violin; **scroll·saw** *n.* a fine saw for cutting thin materials into intricate patterns, or **scroll·work** *n.*

Scrooge or **scrooge** (SCROOJ) *n.* a mean and miserly person.

scro·tum (SCROH–) *n., pl.* **-ta** or **-tums** the pouch containing the testicles; **scro·tal** *adj.*

scrounge (SCROUNJ) *v.* **scroung·es, scrounged, scroung·ing** *Slang.* collect by (or to go about) searching, begging, pilfering, etc.; **scroung·er** *n.*

[1]**scrub** *n.* **1** small or stunted trees or shrubs; also, land with such growth. **2** one considered insignificant or inferior; also, a player not on the regular team. —***adj.*** stunted, small, or inferior; **scrub·by** *adj.* **scrub·bi·er, scrub·bi·est:** ~ *growth, land.*

[2]**scrub** *v.* **scrubs, scrubbed, scrub·bing** wash or clean (utensils, hands, floors, etc.) by rubbing hard, usu. with a "scrub(bing) brush"; hence, rub hard; ***n.*** a scrubbing: *the* **scrub nurse** *of an operating room;* **scrub·wom·an** *n.* **-wom·en** cleaning woman.

scruff *n.* the back of an animal's neck, esp. the loose skin covering it; **scruf·fy** *adj.* **scruff·i·er, -i·est** shabby; also, mean.

scrump·tious (–shus) *adj. Informal.* splendid or delicious; **scrump·tious·ly** *adv.*

scrunch *v.* crush or squeeze; ***n.*** scrunching noise.

scru·ple (SCROO–) *n.* **1** in apothecaries' weight, 20 grains (1.296 g); hence, a small amount. **2** (feeling of) uneasiness about doing what may not be right or proper; ***v.*** **-ples, -pled, -pling** hesitate (to do something); have scruples; **scru·pu·lous** (–pyuh·lus) *adj.* conscientious; careful about fine points of morality, accuracy, etc.: *very* ~ *about giving every devil his due; a scholar's* ~ *attention to detail;* **scru·pu·lous·ly** *adv.* —**scru·pu·los·i·ty** (–LOS–) *n.*

scru·ti·nize (SCROO–) *v.* **-niz·es, -nized, -niz·ing** examine carefully with attention to details, as ballots cast; **scru·ti·ny** *n.* **-nies** a careful inspection.

scu·ba (SCOO·buh) *n.* underwater breathing equipment, as used by a diver, or **scuba diver.**

scud *v.* **scuds, scud·ded, scud·ding** move fast, as clouds or a boat driven by wind; ***n.*** a scudding or clouds, etc. driven by wind.

scuff *v.* **1** walk dragging the feet. **2** scratch, scrape, or wear out (shoes, floors, etc.). —***n.*** **1** a rough or worn spot on a surface. **2** a light, heelless house slipper. —**scuf·fle** *n.* & *v.* **scuf·fles, scuf·fled, scuf·fling** **1** (struggle in) a rough, confused fight at close quarters. **2** shuffle.

scull *n.* & *v.* (propel a boat with) a light oar, either one mounted at the stern or one used in pairs by oarsmen in a race; also, a light racing boat.

scul·ler·y *n.* **scul·ler·ies** a dish-washing and cleaning room attached to a kitchen. —**scul·lion** (–yun) *n. Archaic.* a kitchen servant.

sculpt *v.* [short form] sculpture. —**sculp·tor** *n.* one who produces sculpture. —**sculp·ture**

(–chur) *n.* the art of carving out or otherwise making three-dimensional works of art; also, the products of such art collectively or a statue, carving, or other figure carved out, cast, or modeled in clay, wax, etc.; ***v.* -tures, -tured, -tur·ing** carve; also, cover with sculpture.

scum *n.* dross or such refuse that rises to the top of a liquid, as the "green scum" formed by organisms on the surface of a pond: *the* ~ (i.e. despicable people) *of society;* ***v.* scums, scummed, scum·ming** become covered with or form scum; **scum·my** *adj.* **scum·mi·er, scum·mi·est.**

scup *n.* a food fish of the N. Atlantic coast of the U.S.

scup·per *n.* an opening in the side of a ship at deck level for water to run off.

scurf *n.* scaly or flaky dead matter such as dandruff; **scurf·y** *adj.*

scur·ril·ous (SCUR·uh·lus) *adj.* foully abusive or jesting: ~ *language, attacks, writers;* **scur·ril·ous·ly** *adv.* **—scur·ril·i·ty** (–RIL–) *n.* **-ties.**

scur·ry *v.* **scur·ries, scur·ried, scur·ry·ing** scamper; ***n.*** a scamper or hurrying.

scur·vy *adj.* **-vi·er, -vi·est** mean or contemptible; **scur·vi·ly** *adv.* ***—n.*** a disease caused by lack of ascorbic acid, or vitamin C, in the diet.

scutch·eon (–un) *n.* same as ESCUTCHEON.

scut·tle *n.* **1** a metal pail for carrying and pouring coal. **2** a lidded opening in the hull or deck of a ship. **3** a scamper or scurry. **—*v.* scut·tles, scut·tled, scut·tling** **1** sink (a ship) by cutting a hole in it. **2** to scurry or scamper. **—scut·tle·butt** *n.* a ship's drinking fountain; hence, *Informal.* rumor or gossip.

scythe (SIDHE) *n.* an L-shaped mowing and reaping implement with a long curved blade and a handle swung by both hands; ***v.* scythes, scythed, scyth·ing.**

S.D., SD or **S.Dak.** South Dakota.

Se selenium. **—S.E., SE** or **s.e.** southeast(ern).

sea (SEE) *n.* **1** a large body of salt water connected to an ocean; also, the ocean: *the Mediterranean Sea; the landlocked Caspian Sea; The Sea of Galilee is a freshwater lake; freshwater and* ~ *water; an invasion by* ~ *and land.* **2** the ocean in regard to its vastness, storminess, etc.; also, a heavy swell: *blessed with calm* ~*s; a* ~ *of troubles;* **at sea** in the ocean; also, lost or bewildered. ***—adj.*** of the sea; marine: *a* ~ *fish, route; the* ~ *air;* **—sea anemone** an anemonelike polyp with brightly colored tentacles. **—sea·bed** *n.* the floor of a sea. **—sea·bird** a bird that lives on or by the sea, as the albatross or petrel. **—sea·board** *adj.* bordering on the sea; ***n.*** such land: *the Atlantic* ~*;* also **sea·coast.** **—sea·far·er** (–fair·ur) *n.* a traveler of the seas; sailor; **sea·far·ing** *n.* & *adj.* **—sea·food** *n.* saltwater fish and shellfish eaten as food. **—sea·go·ing** *adj.* oceangoing; also, seafaring. **—sea gull** same as GULL, *n.* 1. **—sea horse** a fish of warm waters with a head resembling a horse's and a prehensile tail.

[1]seal (SEEL) *n.* a stamped design, usu. on **sealing wax** made of rosin, shellac, etc. put on a document to make it official or on a letter, bottle, door, etc. to make it secure; also, the stamp or wax used: *the state* ~ *of Texas; the Good Housekeeping* ~ *of approval; negotiations under a* ~ *of secrecy; an Easter* ~ (i.e. decorative paper stamp). ***—v.:*** *a* ~*ed bid for a contract; a* ~*ed jar of preserves; found his lips* ~*ed* (by confidentiality); *Police* **seal off** *an area to investigate a crime; The judge's sentence* ~*ed his fate.*

[2]seal (SEEL) *n.* any of an order of sea animals with four flippers, including fur seals, sea lions, and walruses, that usu. live in coastal waters, esp. in polar regions; also, a seal's pelt; ***v.*** hunt seals; **seal·er** *n.*

Sea·lab (SEE–) *n.* a laboratory or program to study man's ability to live and work under water. **—sea lane** a sea traffic lane or route.

seal·ant (SEEL·unt) *n.* a sealing agent or substance.

sea legs ability to adjust to the rolling of a ship by keeping one's balance, not being seasick, etc. **—sea level** the average level of the surface of the sea, used as a measuring standard for heights and depths on land. **—sea lion** a species of seal with a coat of short, coarse hair and small ears, often trained as a circus performer.

seal·skin (SEEL–) *n.* (a garment made from) the pelt of a seal.

seam (SEEM) *n.* **1** the line formed by the joining of two edges, esp. of cloth sewn together; also, of boards, as of a boat; hence, any mark or line resembling it. **2** a layer or bed of coal or other mineral. ***—v.*** join together forming a seam; mark with seamlike features such as wrinkles, scars, fissures, etc. **—seam·less** *adj.*

sea·man (SEE·mun) *n.* **-men** a sailor, esp. one in a naval rank below petty officer; **sea·man·ship** *n.* skill in handling a boat or ship. **—sea·mount** *n.* a large volcanic mountain under the sea.

seam·stress (SEEM–) *n.* a woman who sews, esp. for a living. **—seam·y** *adj.* **seam·i·er, -i·est** sordid or squalid: *the* ~ *side of life;* **seam·i·ness** *n.*

sé·ance (SAY·ahnce) *n.* a spiritualist session to communicate with the dead.

sea·plane (SEE–) *n.* an airplane with floats for landing or taxiing on water; also, a flying boat. **—sea·port** *n.* a port for seagoing vessels.

sear (SEER) *v.* burn the outside tissue so as to harden, as in branding, cauterizing, or in browning roasts; also, wither or dry up (grain, etc.).

search (SURCH) *v.* look through or examine (a place, person, etc.) to find something: *Police* ~*ed all the baggage for firearms;* ***n.:*** *the* ~ *for a missing child; man* **in search of** *happiness;*

search·er *n.* —**search·ing** *adj.* thorough or penetrating: *a ~ investigation; ~ questions.* —**search·light** (–lite) *n.* (a powerful beam of light from) an apparatus on a swivel for projecting it in any direction. —**search warrant** a document issued by a court authorizing a police search.

sea·scape *n.* (a picture representing) a view of the sea. —**sea·shell** *n.* the shell of a sea mollusk. —**sea·shore** *n.* a place where land and sea meet; seacoast; in law, the ground between high and low tide. —**sea·sick** *adj.* sick (as if) from the rolling motion of a ship; **sea·sick·ness** *n.* nausea. —**sea·side** *n.* & *adj.* (of or at) a seashore or seacoast.

sea·son (SEE·zn) *n.* one of the divisions of the year, i.e. spring, summer, autumn, and winter; hence, any special period: *the rainy ~; Christmas ~; the baseball ~; wears her hat* **in (season) and out of season** (i.e. at all times).—**v.** 1 make (food) tasty with the use of salt, pepper, spices, etc.: *a highly ~ed sauce; ~s her lectures with humor.* 2 to condition; mature; age; also, become conditioned: *~ed lumber does not warp or shrink; a ~ed air traveler;* **sea·son·er** *n.* —**sea·son·a·ble** (–uh·bl) *adj.* happening or suited to the season, occasion, etc.: *normal, ~ temperatures; ~ advice, clothes, gifts;* **sea·son·a·bly** *adv.* —**sea·son·al** *adj.* having to do with or dependent on a season: *~ migrations, blooms, employment, rates;* **sea·son·al·ly** *adv.* —**sea·son·ing** *n.* condiment. —**season ticket** a ticket for a series of games or shows, transportation, etc. that is good for a specified period.

seat (SEET) *n.* 1 a place to sit (on); also, the part of a chair, bench, etc. or the back of a body or garment on which one sits: *a room with ~s for 200; a bucket ~; the padded ~ of his pants.* 2 where one gets a right to sit: *a reserved ~ on a flight; lost his ~ in the last election.* 2 where something is based; center: *the ~ of a government; universities as ~s of learning.* —**v.** cause to sit: *Guests are ~ed first; Please* **be seated;** *This room ~s* (i.e. has seats for) *200 people.* —**seat belt** same as LAP BELT. —**seat·ing** *n.* sitting accommodation, seats, or their arrangement.

SEATO (SEE·toh) Southeast Asia Treaty Organization.

Se·at·tle (see·ATL) a seaport city of Washington.

sea urchin a sea animal related to starfish that has a body enclosed in a hard round shell covered with long, movable spines. —**sea wall** a wall or embankment built to protect a shore from the waves. —**sea·ward** (–wurd) *adj.* 1 coming from the sea. 2 toward the sea; **n.** the direction or side toward the sea; **sea·ward(s)** *adv.* toward the sea. —**sea·way** *n.* an inland waterway with access from the sea for oceangoing ships; also, a sea lane. —**sea·weed** *n.* a sea plant or plants, esp. a marine alga. —**sea·wor·thy** *adj.* of a ship, fit for sailing; **sea·wor·thi·ness** *n.*

se·ba·ceous (–BAY·shus) *adj.* oil-secreting, as the **sebaceous glands** opening into the hair follicles of the skin.

sec. according to; secant; second(s); secondary; secretary; section(s). —**S.E.C.** Securities and Exchange Commission.

se·cede (–SEED) *v.* **-cedes, -ced·ed, -ced·ing** of a group, cut (itself) off as a part (*from* a state, religious body, etc.); **se·ces·sion** (–SESH·un) *n.;* **se·ces·sion·ist** *n.*

se·clude (–CLOOD) *v.* **-cludes, -clud·ed, -clud·ing** shut (oneself) off from others: *the ~d life of a convent; a ~d spot;* **se·clu·sion** (–CLOO·zhun) *n.* isolation; **se·clu·sive** (–siv) *adj.*

sec·ond (SEC·und) *adj.* next after the first: *her ~ child; He is ~ in command; given a ~* (i.e. another) *chance;* **adv.:** *November is the ~ last month; the horse that finished ~;* also **sec·ond·ly** *adv.* —**v.** support: *was proposed and ~ed for election to the office;* **sec·ond·er** *n.* —**n.** 1 a person, thing, or place that is second: *running in ~* (gear); *happened on the ~* (day of the month); **seconds** *and rejects sold cheap.* 2 a 60th part of a minute; hence, a moment or instant. —**sec·ond·ar·y** (–der·ee) *adj.* that is second, subordinate, or inferior: *Punctuation is ~ to correct spelling; the* **secondary accent** (i.e. stress) *on the third syllable of "secondary"; elementary school followed by* **secondary school** (i.e. high school). —**n.,** *pl.* **-ar·ies** a secondary person or thing, as the defensive backfield in football; **sec·ond·ar·i·ly** *adv.* —**sec·ond-class** *adj.: complained of ~ treatment; Newspapers and periodicals qualify as ~ mail for reduced rates;* **adv.:** *travels ~* (i.e. accommodation by train, ship, or air); *mail sent ~.* —**sec·ond-guess** *v. Informal.* use hindsight to criticize someone for something already done. —**sec·ond·hand** *adj.* not new or from the original source: *~ information: ~* (i.e. used) *goods from a ~ dealer.* —**second lieutenant** the lowest rank of commissioned officer in the military. —**second nature** something acquired, esp. a habit, that comes to one naturally. —**second person** a pronoun or verb form referring to the person spoken to, as "you," "yours," "are," etc. —**sec·ond-rate** *adj.* of inferior quality. —**sec·ond-string** *adj. Informal.* in sports, substitute, not of the regular team; **sec·ond-string·er** *n.* —**second thought(s)** reconsideration of a first opinion or judgment. —**second wind** renewal of regular strength, as by regaining one's breath.

se·cre·cy (SEE·cruh·see) *n.* **-cies** a being (kept) secret; also, the tendency to conceal. —**se·cret** (–crit) *adj.* having to do with concealing or keeping from general knowledge or view; *a ~ plot, society, door, police;* **n.** something secret or mysterious: *She can't keep a ~; Scientists unlock the ~s of nature; the ~* (cause) *of his successes;* **se·cret·ly** *adv.* —**sec·re·tar·i·al** (–TAIR–) *adj.* of a secretary. —**sec·re·tar·i·at** (–TAIR·ee·ut) *n.* an administrative staff or unit; also, the office of a secretary. —**sec·re·tar·y** (SEC·ruh·ter·ee) *n.* **-tar·ies** **1** a person who handles the correspondence, keeps records, etc. of a person or organization; also, a company officer with similar duties. **2** the head of a government department, as the U.S. **Secretary of State** (i.e. President's adviser on foreign affairs). **3** a writing desk. —**sec·re·tar·y·ship** *n.* —**se·crete** (–CREET) *v.* **-cretes, -cret·ed, -cret·ing** **1** hide in a secret place; cache. **2** discharge, as from a gland; **se·cre·tion** *n.;* **se·cre·to·ry** *adj.* —**se·cre·tive** (SEE·cruh·tiv, si·CREE–) *adj.* tending to conceal rather than communicate; not frank or open; **se·cre·tive·ly** *adv.;* **se·cre·tive·ness** *n.* —**Secret Service** a branch of government concerned with security: *The U.S.* **Secret Service** *protects the President and other high officials and dignitaries, investigates counterfeiting, etc.*

sect. section. —**sect** *n.* a group, esp. religious, following a particular doctrine or leader, often a dissenting group; religious denomination; **sec·tar·i·an** *n.* & *adj.* (a person) devoted to a sect, esp. in a narrow-minded way; **sec·tar·i·an·ism** *n.;* **sec·ta·ry** (SEK–) *n.* **-ries** a sectarian. —**sec·tion** *n.* a cutting or a cut-off part; hence, a division or part of something larger: *the sports ~ of a newspaper; a city's residential ~; the ~s of a fruit, pie, chapter, bookcase* (to be assembled); *a ~ of a railroad maintained by a* **section gang** *of workers;* **v.** divide into sections or so as to display a section. —**sec·tion·al** *adj.* **1** characteristic of a section; hence, local or regional; **sec·tion·al·ism** *n.* **2** made up of sections; modular: *~ furniture.* —**sec·tion·al·ly** *adv.* —**sec·tor** *n.* **1** part of a circle between two radii. **2** area of operation or activity: *the public and private ~s of industry.*

sec·u·lar (SEC·yuh·lur) *adj.* of the world, not of the church, a religion, or religious life: *~ education, society, clergy* (i.e. not belonging to a religious order); **sec·u·lar·ism** *n.* —**sec·u·lar·ize** *v.* **-iz·es, -ized, -iz·ing** make secular; transfer to civil or lay use or control, as church schools; **sec·u·lar·i·za·tion** (–ZAY–) *n.*

se·cure (–KYOOR) *adj.* protected against danger, harm, risk, fear, worry, etc.; safe: *Lock the doors to feel ~; a nation ~ from attack; a ~ investment; a* (i.e. firm) *knot.* —**v. -cures, -cured, -cur·ing** make secure: *A door is ~d by locking it; tickets ~d long before a rush; Banks ~ their loans by collaterals;* **se·cure·ly** *adv.* —**se·cur·i·ty** *n.* **-ties** **1** protection or the feeling of being protected or secure: *brought up in the ~ of the home; the* **security blanket** *that a child clings to as if for protection; Japanese jailed as ~ risks during the war; the U.N.* **Security Council** *for safeguarding world peace.* **2** something that protects or secures: *His signature is good ~ for a loan;* **securities** *pl.* stocks and bonds.

secy. or **sec'y** secretary.

se·dan (–DAN) *n.* **1** an automobile having an enclosed body with center posts between front and back windows to support the roof; not a hardtop. **2** a covered portable chair carried on poles like a litter but usu. by two men; also **sedan chair.** —**se·date** (–DATE) **1** *adj.* calm and composed in manner; **se·date·ly** *adv.;* **se·date·ness** *n.* **2** *v.* **-dates, -dat·ed, -dat·ing** give a sedative to; **se·da·tion** (–DAY–) *n.;* **sed·a·tive** (SED·uh·tiv) *n.* & *adj.* (a barbiturate, bromide, or other substance) that tends to soothe and calm the nerves. —**sed·en·tar·y** (–ter–) *adj.* involving much sitting: *a ~ occupation, life; ~ habits.*

Se·der (SAY–) *n.* the domestic observance of the beginning of the Jewish Passover, esp. on its first night.

sedge *n.* any of a family of grasslike plants but with triangular, solid stems that grow in marshy places; **sedg·y** *adj.*

sed·i·ment *n.* matter settling at the bottom of a liquid; dregs; also, matter deposited by water, wind, etc., as by a receding flood; **sed·i·men·ta·ry** (–MEN–) *adj.* containing or formed by sediment: *Shale, limestone, and sandstone are ~ rocks;* **sed·i·men·ta·tion** (–TAY–) *n.*

se·di·tion (–DISH–) *n.* (action or speech regarded as) the stirring up of discontent or rebellion against a government. —**se·di·tion·ist** (–DISH–) *n.;* **se·di·tious** *adj.*

se·duce (–DUCE) *v.* **-duc·es, -duced, -duc·ing** persuade to do something wrong or unlawful, esp. to have sexual intercourse; **se·duc·er** *n.; fem.* **se·duc·tress** (–DUC–) . —**se·duc·tion** (–DUC–) *n.;* **se·duc·tive** (–tiv) *adj.*

sed·u·lous (SEJ·oo·lus) *adj.* diligent in pursuing an objective till it is reached: *~ imitation of a model;* **sed·u·lous·ly** *adv.*

S.E. or **s.e.** southeast(ern).

[1]**see** *v.* **sees, saw, seen, see·ing** **1** be aware of through the eyes; also, look at: *You can ~ me; You cannot ~ in the dark; ~ this picture; ~* (i.e. look and find) *who is at the door.* **2** perceive with the mind; understand: *I ~ that you're right.* **3** experience or have knowledge of: *an old house that has seen better times.* **4** visit; also, receive (a visitor): *time to ~ a lawyer; The boss will ~ you now.* **5** make sure; take care: *Please ~ that this is done; ~* (i.e. escort) *the visitor out;* **saw** *her* **off** *at the airport.* **6** consider or judge: *if you ~ fit to do so.* —**see through** **1** understand the real nature of (a person, scheme, etc.); also **see into.** **2** take care of an undertaking or a person through (something) till the end: *I'll ~ you through this crisis; I have to ~ the project through.*

[2]**see** *n.* a bishop's office, authority, or diocese.

seed *n.* **1** the part of a plant from which a new plant will sprout, esp. a grainlike mature ovule; also, a bulb or tuber; **go** (or **run**) **to seed** have finished with flowering and production; hence, deteriorate. **2** sperm or semen. **3** source or origin: *tales that sowed ~s of suspicion in her mind.* **4** descendants: *the ~ of Abraham.* **—v. 1** scatter seeds over (a field); sow (seeds); remove the seeds from (fruit): *Clouds are ~ed with crystals of dry ice and other chemicals to make rain or snow.* **2** rank a player or team according to ability: *Top-seeded players meet last in a tournament.* **—seed·er** *n.* **—seed·less** *adj.* **—seed·ling** *n.* a plant grown from a seed; also, a young tree smaller than a sapling.**—seed money** money for beginning an enterprise. **—seed·time** *n.* the sowing season. **—seed·y** *adj.* **seed·i·er, -i·est** full of seeds; also, gone to seed; hence, shabby-looking; **seed·i·ly** *adv.;* **seed·i·ness** *n.*

see·ing *conj.* considering *(that): got up to go ~ it was late.* **—Seeing Eye (dog)** *Trademark.* a blind person's guide dog.

seek *v.* **seeks, sought, seek·ing** try (to find or get): *to ~ advice, fortune, shelter; We ~ to please; a much sought-after speaker;* **seek·er** *n.*

seem *v.* appear: *She ~s happy; What ~s to be the trouble? I ~ to have lost my way;* **seem·ing** *adj.* apparent but not necessarily real or genuine: *his ~ sincerity;* **seem·ing·ly** *adv.* **—seem·ly** *adj.* **-li·er, -li·est** that looks good or proper: *Clothes should be ~ if not attractive; ~* (i.e. pleasing) *behavior;* **seem·li·ness** *n.* **—seen** *pp.* of [1]SEE.

seep *v.* flow out slowly through cracks (of a ceiling, etc.) or fine pores, as of sand; **seep·age** (–ij) *n.*

seer *n.* one who claims to see into or foretell the future; prophet; *fem.* **seer·ess.**

seer·suck·er *n.* a crinkly, lightweight fabric for dresses, jackets, etc.

see·saw *n.* a plank supported in the middle for children to sit on at opposite ends and ride up and down; hence, an up-and-down movement; ***v.*** move up and down or back and forth, as the lead in a close contest.

seethe (SEEDH) *v.* **seethes, seethed, seeth·ing** be agitated or disturbed, as boiling water: *a nation ~ing with rebellion; ~ing with resentment.*

see-through *n.* & *adj.* (a blouse, dress, etc.) that can be seen through.

seg·ment (–munt) *n.* **1** a natural section or part: *the ~s of an orange, earthworm's body; the various ~s of the population.* **2** *Geom.* a portion of a circle cut off by a plane or that between two parallel planes. **—v.** (-ment) divide into segments; **seg·men·ta·tion** (–TAY–) *n.*

seg·re·gate (SEG·ruh–) *v.* **-gates, -gat·ed, -gat·ing** to separate, esp. as a group and for racial reasons; **seg·re·ga·tion** (–GAY–) *n.* (policy of) separation of racial groups in housing, education, and facilities such as transportation; **seg·re·ga·tion·ist** *n.*

se·gue (SEG·way) *n.* & *v.* **-gues, -gued, -gue·ing** (a musical direction) to proceed without pause *to* or *into* the following movement.

sei·gneur (seen·YUR) *n.* a feudal lord, esp. of French Canada; **sei·gneur·i·al** *adj.* **—sei·gnior** (SEEN·yur) *n.* a gentleman, esp. a feudal lord; **sei·gn(i)o·ri·al** (seen·YOR·ee·ul) *adj.*

Seine (SEN) a river of N. France.

seine (SAIN) *n.* & *v.* **seines, seined, sein·ing** (fish with) a weighted net for encircling and hauling in schools of fish.

seis·mic (SIZE–, SICE–) *adj.* of or caused by an earthquake: *A "tidal wave" is a ~ sea wave;* **seis·mi·cal·ly** *adv.;* **seis·mic·i·ty** (–MIS–) *n.* **—seis·mo·gram** *n.* a record made by a **seis·mo·graph** *n.* an earthquake-recording instrument; **seis·mo·graph·ic** (–GRAF–) *adj.;* **seis·mog·ra·phy** (–MOG–) *n.* **—seis·mol·o·gy** (–MOL–) *n.* the science of earthquakes; **seis·mol·o·gist** *n.;* **seis·mo·log·i·cal** (–LOJ–) *adj.* **—seis·mom·e·ter** (–MOM–) *n.* a seismograph; **seis·mo·met·ric** (–MET–) *adj.*

seize (SEEZ) *v.* **seiz·es, seized, seiz·ing** take hold or possession of suddenly and with force: *~d the food without waiting to be served; contraband ~d by customs; seems to* **seize (up)on** (i.e. understand and use) *every opportunity to annoy her; was ~d* (i.e. stricken) *with remorse soon after the deed; brakes with a tendency to ~* (i.e. stick fast); **sei·zure** (–zhur) *n.* a seizing or being seized.

sel·dom (–dum) *adv.* rarely; not often.

se·lect (–LECT) *v.* choose or pick out of many using care and discrimination: *A jury is ~ed;* ***adj.*** **1** carefully chosen; also, choice: *Only a ~ few were admitted.* **2** careful in choosing; exclusive: *a ~ group of friends.* **—se·lec·tion** (–LEC–) *n.;* **se·lec·tive** (–tiv) *adj.* careful in

---

self-abasement
self-accusation
self-acting
self-adjusting
self-administered
self-advancement
self-aggrandizement
self-aggrandizing
self-analysis
self-appointed
self-asserting
self-assertion
self-assertive
self-awareness
self-betrayal
self-closing
self-command
self-complacent
self-concerned
self-condemned
self-confessed
self-congratulation
self-congratulatory
self-constituted
self-correcting
self-created

selecting; **se·lec·tiv·i·ty** (–TIV–) *n.* —**selective service** system of compulsory military service for men reaching 18 years, based on the classification in which each one falls. —**se·lect·man** *n.* **-men** a member of a board of officers chosen annually to manage the affairs of a New England town. —**se·lec·tor** *n.*

sel·e·nite (SEL·uh–) *n.* a transparent, crystalline variety of gypsum. —**se·le·ni·um** (–LEE–) *n.* a metalloid element used in photoelectric cells, rectifiers, etc. —**sel·e·nog·ra·phy** (–NOG–) *n.* the science of the moon's physical features; **sel·e·nog·ra·pher** *n.*

self *n.* **selves** (SELVZ) one's own person *(his very ~),* nature *(one's former ~),* or interests *(puts ~ above all else);* **pron.:** *a check payable to ~; our noble ~s.* —**self-** *comb.form.* of, by, to, or for oneself or itself [as in the compounds placed at the foot of the pages; their basic meaning and pronunciation are the same as in the base word in each case]

self-ad·dressed (–DREST) *adj.* addressed to oneself: *a ~ envelope.* —**self-as·sur·ance** (–SHOOR–) *n.* confidence in oneself; **self-as·sured** *adj.* —**self-bind·er** *n.* a farm machine that cuts grain and ties it into bundles. —**self-cen·tered** *adj.* selfish; **self-cen·tered·ness** *n.* —**self-com·posed** *adj.* in control of one's emotions; calm and cool. —**self-con·ceit** *n.* too much pride in oneself; vanity. —**self-con·cept** *n.* self-image. —**self-con·fi·dence** *n.* confidence in oneself; **self-con·fi·dent** *adj.* —**self-con·scious** *adj.* (unduly) aware of oneself; hence, ill at ease; **self-con·scious·ly** *adv.;* **self-con·scious·ness** *n.* —**self-con·tained** *adj.* **1** complete within itself; independent. **2** showing self-control; hence, reserved. —**self-con·tra·dic·tion** *n.* a statement containing a contradrication; also, a contradiction of oneself or itself; **self-con·tra·dic·to·ry** *adj.* —**self-con·trol** *n.* control of one's actions, feelings, desires, etc.; **self-con·trolled** *adj.* —**self-de·fense** *n.* defense of oneself, one's rights, actions, etc. —**self-de·ni·al** *n.* sacrifice of one's own desires; **self-de·ny·ing** *adj.* —**self-de·struct** *v.* destroy oneself or itself. —**self-de·ter·mi·na·tion** *n.* freedom to make one's own decision, esp. of a people to determine for themselves what form of government they shall have; **self-de·ter·mined** *adj.* —**self-dis·cov·er·y** *n.* discovering of one's real capabilities, character, motivations, etc. —**self-ed·u·cat·ed** *adj.* educated by oneself, with little formal schooling. —**self-ef·fac·ing** *adj.* minimizing one's own achievements. —**self-es·teem** *n.* a sense of one's own great worth. —**self-ev·i·dent** *adj.* obvious, and needing no explanation. —**self-ex·plan·a·to·ry** *adj.* explaining itself; obvious without explanation. —**self-ex·pres·sion** *n.* expression of oneself, esp. in the arts. —**self-fer·til·i·za·tion** *n.* fertilization of a plant or animal by its own pollen or sperm. —**self-ful·fill·ing** *adj.* becoming fulfilled because predicted or expected: *a ~ prophecy.* —**self-gov·ern·ment** *n.* government by one's own people, esp. elected representatives; **self-gov·ern·ing** *adj.* —**self-im·age** *n.* conception of one's own worth, identity, etc. —**self-im·por·tant** *adj.* showing too high an opinion of oneself; **self-im·por·tance** *n.* —**self-in·ter·est** *n.* the seeking of one's own advantage over the interest of others; selfishness. —**self·ish** *adj.* caring too much for oneself without regard for the rights of others; **self·ish·ly** *adv.;* **self·ish·ness** *n.* —**self·less** *adj.* unselfish; **self·less·ly** *adv.;* **self·less·ness** *n.* —**self-load·er** *n.* a firearm that loads itself again after firing; **self-load·ing** *adj.* —**self-lu·mi·nous** *adj.* luminous by itself, as the sun. —**self-made** *adj.* who has reached his position largely through his own efforts. —**self-med·i·cate** *v.* **-cates, -cat·ed, -cat·ing** administer medicine to oneself without consulting a doctor. —**self-pol·li·na·tion** *n.* pollination of the same flower or another flower of the same plant. —**self-pos·ses·sion** *n.* self-control; **self-pos·sessed** *adj.* —**self-pro·pelled** *adj.* propelled by its own power: *~ artillery, missiles.* —**self-reg·u·lat·ing** *adj.* of machines, regulating itself; automatic. —**self-re·li·ance** *n.* reliance on one's own powers esp. mental; **self-re·li·ant** *adj.* —**self-re·spect** *n.* respect for one's own worth as a person; **self-re·spect·ing** *adj.* —**self-re·straint** *n.* self-control. —**self-right·eous** *adj.* overly

---

self-criticism
self-cultivation
self-deceit
self-deceiving
self-deception
self-defeating
self-delusion
self-depreciation
self-destruction
self-discipline
self-distrust
self-doubt
self-driven
self-employed
self-employment
self-examination
self-explaining
self-forgetful
self-giving
self-help
self-hypnosis
self-imposed
self-improvement
self-incrimination
self-induced
self-indulgence

righteous or moralistic; **self-right·eous·ly** *adv.;* **self-right·eous·ness** *n.* —**self-sac·ri·fice** *n.* sacrifice of one's own interests for the good of others; **self-sac·ri·fic·ing** *adj.* —**self·same** *adj.* identical. —**self-sat·is·fied** *adj.* smugly satisfied with oneself; **self-sat·is·fac·tion** *n.* —**self-seal·ing** *adj.* sealing by itself: *a ~ tire* (i.e. when punctured); *a ~ envelope* (i.e. by pressure). —**self-seek·er** *n.* a seeker of one's own advantage; a selfish person; **self-seek·ing** *n.* & *adj.* —**self-serv·ice** *n.* the practice of customers' serving themselves, as at a gas station, cafeteria, etc.; **self-serv·ing** *adj.* self-seeking; selfish. —**self-start·er** *n.* an electrical device for starting an internal combustion engine without cranking; also, *Informal.* a person with initiative; **self-start·ing** *adj.* —**self-styled** *adj.* so named by oneself without justification. —**self-suf·fi·cient** *adj.* needing no outside help; also, conceited about one's own capabilities; **self-suf·fi·cien·cy** *n.* —**self·taught** taught by oneself without help from others. —**self-willed** *adj.* obstinate; stubborn. —**self-wind·ing** *adj.* of a watch, winding itself automatically.

sell *v.* **sells, sold, sell·ing** **1** exchange (goods, services, etc.) for money or other return: *They ~ cars; in jail for ~ing state secrets to the enemy.* **2** (cause to) be sold or accepted: *Snow tires ~ best in winter; sold his voters on abortion; His excuse just wouldn't ~.* —***n.*** a selling; *Slang.* hoax. —**sell·er** *n.: a* **seller's market** *with scarcity and high prices.* —**sell out** **1** dispose of completely by selling. **2** *Informal.* betray. —**sell·out** *n.* **1** a selling out or a show for which all seats are sold. **2** *Informal.* a betrayal.

Selt·zer (–sur) **water** mineral water; usu. **seltzer water** carbonated water.

sel·vage or **sel·vedge** (–vij) *n.* the edge of a cloth woven so as to prevent raveling.

selves *pl.* of SELF.

se·man·tics (–MAN–) *n.pl.* [takes *sing. v.*] the study of meanings in language; **se·man·tic** *adj.;* **se·man·ti·cal·ly** *adv.* —**sem·a·phore** (SEM·uh·for) *n.* a visual signaling system based on different positions of arms or hand-held flags.

sem·blance (–blunce) *n.* outward appearance; also, resemblance or likeness.

se·men (SEE·mun) *n.* male reproductive fluid containing sperm.

se·mes·ter (–MES–) *n.* one of the two terms into which an academic year is divided; **se·mes·tral** (–trul) *adj.*

semi- *comb.form.* half; partly; incompletely [as in the compounds placed at the foot of the pages; their basic meaning and pronunciation are the same as in the base word in each case]

sem·i·an·nu·al (sem·ee·AN·yoo·ul) *adj.* occurring every half year; also, lasting a half year. —**sem·i·au·to·mat·ic** (sem·ee·aw·tuh·MAT·ic) *n.* & *adj.* (a gun) that is self-loading though not firing like a machine gun. —**sem·i·cir·cle** (SEM·i–) *n.* a half circle; **sem·i·cir·cu·lar** *adj.* —**sem·i·co·lon** (–coh·lun) *n.* the punctuation mark (;). —**sem·i·con·duc·tor** (–DUC–) *n.* a material such as silicon or selenium that conducts electricity better than an insulator but not as well as a conductor, hence used in electronic devices such as transistors, lasers, and solar batteries. —**sem·i·con·scious** (–CON–) *adj.* only partly conscious or awake. —**sem·i·dry·ing** (–DRY–) *adj.* of oils such as cottonseed and sesame, that become thick without hardening when exposed. —**sem·i·fi·nal** (–FYE–) *n.* & *adj.* (a match or round) that is next to the last, as in a tournament. —**sem·i·flu·id** (–FLOO–) *n.* & *adj.* (a substance such as molasses or pitch) that is thick but flowing. —**sem·i·lu·nar** (–LOO–) *adj.* crescent-shaped. —**sem·i·month·ly** (–MUNTH–) *n.* & *adj.* (a periodical) issued twice a month; also ***adv.***

sem·i·nal (SEM·uh·nl) *adj.* of or having to do with seed or semen; hence, containing the seeds of later development: *a ~ idea;* **sem·i·nal·ly** *adv.* —**sem·i·nar** *n.* (a meeting of) a group of students doing research under a professor's guidance. —**sem·i·nary** (SEM·uh·ner·ee) *n.* **-nar·ies** an educational institution for preparing priests, ministers, rabbis, etc.; **sem·i·nar·i·an** (–NAIR–) *n.*

Sem·i·nole *n.* (a member of) an American Indian people of Florida and Oklahoma.

sem·i·per·me·a·ble (–PUR·mee·uh–) *adj.* of a membrane, permeable only to certain substances. —**sem·i·pre·cious** (–PRESH·us) *adj.* of a gemstone, of less value than precious stones, as amethyst or turquoise. —**sem·i·pri·**

---

self-indulgent
self-inflicted
self-limiting
self-love
self-lubricating
self-mastery
self-operating
self-perpetuating
self-portrait
self-possessed
self-possession
self-proclaimed
self-propelled
self-propelling
self-protection
self-realization
self-regard
self-registering
self-reproach
self-rule
self-satisfaction
self-satisfied
self-supporting
self-sustaining

vate (–PRY–) *n.* & *adj.* (a hospital room) that is shared with one other patient. **—sem·i·pro·fes·sion·al** (–FESH–) *n.* a player who gets paid on a part-time basis; also **sem·i·pro;** *adj.: a ~ sport, player.* **—sem·i·skilled** *adj.* partly skilled or requiring limited training. **—sem·i·soft** *adj.* of a cheese, medium soft, as Limburger.

Sem·ite *n.* a person speaking a Semitic language. **—Se·mit·ic** (–MIT–) *n.* & *adj.* (of) the group of languages comprising Hebrew, Arabic, Assyrian, Aramaic, Syrian, Phoenician, etc.

sem·i·trail·er (SEM·eye–) *n.* a cargo-carrying trailer with wheels at the rear, supported at the front by a truck tractor. **—sem·i·trans·par·ent** (–PAIR–) *adj.* only partially transparent. **—sem·i·trop·i·cal** (–TROP–) *adj.* partly tropical. **—sem·i·vow·el** *n.* a consonantlike vowel, esp. "w" and "y." **—sem·i·week·ly** *n.* & *adj.* (a periodical) published twice a week; also ***adv.***

sen *n. sing.* & *pl.* 1/100 of a yen, Brunei dollar, Cambodian riel, or rupiah.

sen. senate; senator; senior. **—sen·ate** (–it) *n.* the upper branch of a legislature; also, a legislative or governing council, as of a university; **sen·a·tor** *n.;* **sena·to·ri·al** (–TOR–) *adj.*

send *v.* **sends, sent, send·ing** **1** cause (a person or thing) to go without oneself going: *children sent to school; Please ~ this message; The wind sent the papers flying.* **2** *Slang.* excite or thrill. **—send for** send a request or messenger for. **—send packing** dismiss without ceremony. **—send·er** *n.* **—send-off** *n. Informal.* a farewell demonstration to honor someone setting out on a new venture, a trip, etc.

se·ne (SAY·nay) *n.* 1/100 of a Western Samoan tala.

Sen·e·ca (SEN·uh–) *n.* (a member of) an Iroquoian-speaking people of W. New York State.

Sen·e·gal (sen·i·GAWL) a country of W. Africa; 75,750 sq.mi. (196,192 km²); *cap.* Dakar; **Sen·e·ga·lese** (–guh·LEEZ) *n.* & *adj., sing.* & *pl.*

se·nile (SEE–) *adj.* typical of old age; hence, weak in mind and body: *too ~ to work;* **se·nil·i·ty** (–NIL–) *n.* **—sen·ior** (SEEN·yur) *n.* **1** a student in a graduating class. **2** one who is older or of higher rank; ***adj.*** older in age, rank, etc.: *John Smith, Sr.* (i.e. father of John Smith, Jr.); *my ~ colleague;* **senior citizen** an elderly, usu. retired person; **senior high school** grades 10, 11, and 12 of high school; **sen·ior·i·ty** (–YOR–) *n.* **-ties** superiority in age; also, priority because of length of service in a job.

sen·i·ti (SEN·uh·tee) *n. sing.* & *pl.* 1/100 of a pa'anga.

sen·na (SEN·uh) *n.* a laxative made from the dried leaves of a cassia plant.

se·ñor (say·NYOR) *n.* **-ño·res** (–res) *Spanish.* a gentleman; [as a title] Mr. or Sir. **—se·ño·ra** (–NYOR·ah) *n. Spanish.* a lady; [as a title] Mrs. or Madam. **—se·ño·ri·ta** (–REE·tah) *n. Spanish.* a young lady; [as a title] Miss.

sen·sa·tion (–SAY–) *n.* **1** sense impression, esp of touch or feeling: *~s of heat and cold; a ~ of giddiness.* **2** (cause of) a widespread feeling of excitement: *The announcement caused a ~; She is a great ~ as a singer;* **sen·sa·tion·al** *adj.* arousing or meant to arouse general excitement; **sen·sa·tion·al·ly** *adv.;* **sen·sa·tion·al·ism** *n.* **—sense** *n.* **1** (power of) feeling or awareness: *the five ~s of sight, hearing, smell, taste, and touch, each with a corresponding* **sense organ** *such as the eye, ear, etc.; a ~ of security;* **one's senses** healthy state of mind: *came to his ~s when told the facts.* **2** understanding or appreciation: *a poor ~ of humor; had the good ~ to say no; your ~ of responsibility.* **3** a particular meaning: *true in every ~ of the word;* **in a sense** to some extent; **make sense** have meaning or be reasonable. **—*v.* sens·es, sensed, sens·ing** be aware of; also, understand. **—sense·less** *adj.;* **sense·less·ly** *adv.* **—sen·si·bil·i·ty** (–BIL–) *n.* **1** ability to sense or perceive. **2** fineness of feeling; **sensibilities** *pl.* sensitive feelings. **—sen·si·ble** *adj.* **1** having good sense; showing good judgment: *a ~ young woman; ~ clothing for a cold day.* **2** perceiving or aware; also, that can be perceived or noticed: *~ phenomena, differences.* **—sen·si·bly** *adv.* **—sen·si·tive** (–tiv) *adj.* **1** able to feel (and be affected) easily or readily: *a ~ skin; ~ to criticism; a ~ thermometer; a* **sensitive plant** *such as mimosa.* **2** keen or perceptive: *a ~ and intelligent boy.* **3** having to do with delicate or secret information: *a ~ position in government.* **—sen·si·tive·ly** *adv.;* **sen·si·tive·ness** *n.;* **sen·si·tiv·i·ty** (–TIV–) *n.;* **sensitivity training** See ENCOUNTER. **—sen·si·tize** *v.* **-tiz·es, -tized, -tiz·ing** make or become sensitive; **sen·si·ti·za·tion**

---

semiarid
semicentennial
semicivilized
semidarkness
semidivine
semiformal
semigloss
semi-independent
semiliquid
semiliterate
semiofficial
semipermanent
semipolitical
semireligious
semiretired
semisweet
semitone
semiyearly

(–ZAY–) *n.* —**sen·si·tom·e·ter** (–TOM–) *n.* an instrument for measuring photographic sensitivity. —**sen·sor** *n.* a sensing device for a physical stimulus such as heat or light; **sen·so·ry** (SEN·suh·ree) *adj.* of the senses or sensation: ~ *nerves.* —**sen·su·al** (–shoo·ul) *adj.* having to do with the gratification of the sense: ~ *pleasure, appetite, lips, music;* **sen·su·al·ist** *n.;* **sen·su·al·ly** *adv.;* **sen·su·al·i·ty** (–AL–) *n.* —**sen·su·ous** (–shoo·us) *adj.* having to do with the enjoyment of sense impressions: ~ *delight, appeal, verse, colors;* **sen·su·ous·ly** *adv.;* **sen·su·ous·ness** *n.*

sent *pt.* & *pp.* of SEND.

sen·tence (–tnce) *n.* **1** a group of words forming a complete statement, question, or command. **2** a decision, as of a judge, esp. on the punishment of a criminal; also, the punishment; ***v.*** **-tenc·es, -tenced, -tenc·ing:** *convicted and ~d to three years in jail.* —**sen·ten·tious** (–TEN–) *adj.* expressed tersely; full of meaning; also, moralistic.

sen·tient (–shunt) *adj.* that can feel; conscious. —**sen·ti·ment** *n.* attitude or disposition of mind influenced or refined by feelings, as patriotism (duty influenced by love of country): *public ~ against porn movies; a speech full of noble ~s;* **sen·ti·men·tal** (–MEN–) *adj.* having to do with sentiment rather than reason: *the ~ behavior of a ~ parent; has more ~ value than commercial;* **sen·ti·men·tal·ly** *adv.;* **sen·ti·men·tal·ism** *n.* **sen·ti·men·tal·ist** *n.;* **sen·ti·men·tal·i·ty** (–TAL–) *n.* **-ties** (expression of) too much sentiment; **sen·ti·men·tal·ize** (–MEN–) *v.* **-iz·es, -ized, -iz·ing** make sentimental; also, indulge in sentiment (about); **sen·ti·men·tal·i·za·tion** (–ZAY–) *n.*

sen·ti·mo (–TEE–) *n.* **-mos** 1/100 of a Philippine peso.

sen·ti·nel (–nl) *n.* a sentry. —**sen·try** (–tree) *n.* **-tries** a member of a military guard; **sentry box** a shelter for a sentry to stand in.

Seoul (SOLE) capital of South Korea.

sep. separate(d).

se·pal (SEE·pl) *n.* one of the usu. green, leaflike parts at the base of a flower or enclosing a bud.

sep·a·ra·ble (SEP·uh·ruh–) *adj.* capable of being separated; **sep·a·ra·bly** *adv.* —**sep·a·rate** (–rit) *adj.* distinct from another; not together: *Keep them ~; seated at ~ tables.* —***n.*** a blouse, skirt, etc. for wearing in different combinations, or **separates** *pl.* —***v.*** (-rate) **-rates, -rat·ed, -rat·ing** (cause to) be apart; divide: *War ~s families; ~d from the group and was lost; a wall ~ing two apartments; The couple ~d* (i.e. decided to live apart). —**sep·a·rate·ly** (–rit–) *adv.;* **sep·a·ra·tion** (–RAY–) *n.;* **sep·a·ra·tor** (–ray–) *n.* —**sep·a·ra·tist** (–ruh–) *n.* a member of a group that wants to withdraw from a large esp. political group; **sep·a·ra·tism** *n.;* **sep·a·ra·tive** (–tiv) *adj.*

se·pi·a (SEE·pee·uh) *n.* & *adj.* dark-brown (pigment or a drawing done in it).

sep·sis *n., pl.* **-ses** (–seez) poisoning caused by disease germs.

Sept. *Abbrev.* for **Sep·tem·ber** (–TEM–) *n.* the ninth month of the year, having 30 days.

sep·tic *adj.* resulting from or causing sepsis: *died of a ~ wound; Sewage decomposes in a* **septic tank** *by bacterial action.* —**sep·ti·ce·mi·a** (–SEE·mee·uh) *n.* blood poisoning.

sep·tu·a·ge·nar·i·an (–juh·NAIR·ee·un) *n.* & *adj.* (a person) in his seventies. —**Sep·tu·a·gint** (SEP·too·uh·jint) *n.* the oldest Greek translation of the Old Testament.

sep·tum *n.* partition, as in the heart or nose.

sep·ul·cher (–cur) *n.* & *v.* (bury in) a tomb; **se·pul·chral** (–PUL·crul) *adj.* having to do with burial or the grave: ~ *gloom, voices* (i.e. hollow and deep). —**sep·ul·ture** (–chur) *n.* burial.

seq. *pl.* **seqq.** the following —**se·quel** (SEE–) *n.* something following or resulting from an earlier happening, as a continuation of a story with the same characters.—**se·quence** (SEE–) *n.* (a series with) a logical or natural connection: *the cause-effect ~ of events; grammatical ~ of tenses in principal and subordinate clauses; Ace, King, and Queen form a ~ in cards; Any set of terms in a specific order is a mathematical ~; a motion picture ~* (i.e. connected episode); **se·quen·tial** (–KWEN–) *adj.;* **se·quen·tial·ly** *adv.* —**se·ques·ter** (–KWES–) *v.* seclude; also, separate, remove, or impound; also **se·ques·trate, -trates, -trat·ed, -trat·ing; se·ques·tra·tion** (–TRAY–) *n.*

se·quin (SEE–) *n.* any of the shiny discs of metal sewn on to dresses, etc. for decoration; spangle; **se·quined** (–kwind) *adj.*

se·quoi·a (–KWOY·uh) *n.* a group of the largest and oldest trees, including the redwood and giant sequoia of W. California.

ser. serial; series.

sera a *pl.* of SERUM.

se·rag·lio (–RAL·yoh) *n.* **-lios** a sultan's palace or its harem.

se·ra·pe (suh·RAH·pee) *n.* a bright-colored woolen shawl used by Latin American men.

ser·aph (SER·uf) *n.* **-aphs** or **-a·phim** an angel of the highest order; **se·raph·ic** (–RAF–) *adj.;* **se·raph·i·cal·ly** *adv.*

Serb (SURB) or **Ser·bi·an** *n.* **1** a person of or from **Ser·bi·a,** a constituent republic of Yugoslavia. **2** Serbo-Croatian. —***adj.*** of Serbia, its people, or their language. —**Ser·bo-Cro·a·tian** (–AY·shun) *n.* the major language of Yugoslavia; ***adj.*** of this language or of the people who speak it.

sere (SEER) *adj. Poet.* dry or withered.

ser·e·nade (–NADE) *n.* music played or sung by a lover under his sweetheart's window; ***v.*** **-nades, -nad·ed, -nad·ing** play or sing a serenade (to).

ser·en·dip·i·ty (–DIP–) *n.* **-ties** **1** gift for making fortunate discoveries when least expecting them. **2** such a discovery. —**ser·en·dip·i·tous** (–tus) *adj.*

se·rene (–REEN) *adj.* **1** calm and clear: *~ skies.* **2** calm and dignified: *a ~ life, smile;* **Serene** [used of or to royalty of certain countries]: *His, Her, Your ~ Highness.* —**se·rene·ly** *adv.;* **se·rene·ness** or **se·ren·i·ty** (–REN–) *n.*

serf (SURF) *n.* a feudal peasant bound to the soil and to the service of his lord; **serf·dom** *n.*

serge (SURJ) *n.* a fabric with a twill weave showing diagonal ridges, used for dresses, suits, etc.

ser·geant (SAR·junt) *n.* a noncommissioned military officer ranking above corporal or airman; also, a police officer ranking above an ordinary policeman; **ser·geant-at-arms** *n.* **ser·geants-** an officer who keeps order in a legislature or court.

se·ri·al (SEER·ee·ul) *n.* & *adj.* (a story or publication) forming a series or succession with others: *a ~ novel; a television ~; the* **serial number** *on a check;* **se·ri·al·ly** *adv.;* **se·ri·al·ist** *n.* —**se·ri·al·ize** *v.* **-iz·es, -ized, -iz·ing; se·ri·al·i·za·tion** (–ZAY–) *n.* —**se·ries** (SEER·eez) *n. sing.* & *pl.* a number of things or events with some connection to each other: *a ~ of accidents, lectures, publications.*

ser·i·graph *n.* an artist's own handmade print using the silk-screen process, or **se·rig·ra·phy** (–RIG–) *n.* —**se·rig·ra·pher** (–RIG–) *n.*

se·ri·ous (SEER·ee·us) *adj.* **1** showing or requiring earnestness: *~ matter, interest; ~ about her work.* **2** important or grave: *a patient in ~ but not critical condition.* —**se·ri·ous·ly** *adv.;* **se·ri·ous·ness** *n.*

ser·mon (SUR·mun) *n.* **1** a religious or moral talk usu. based on Scripture. **2** any moralistic talk; **ser·mon·ize** *v.* **-iz·es, -ized, -iz·ing.** —**Sermon on the Mount** Christ's talk to his disciples containing the Beatitudes, Lord's Prayer, etc.

se·rol·o·gy (–ROL–) *n.* the study of serums and their properties; **se·ro·log·ic** (–LOJ–) or **-log·i·cal** *adj.* —**se·rous** (SEER·us) *adj.* of, producing, or like serum: *a ~ fluid, membrane.* —**se·ro·to·nin** (–TOH–) *n.* a hormone present in the blood, brain, and intestinal tract.

ser·pent (SUR·punt) *n.* a big snake, thought of as sly and treacherous. —**ser·pen·tine** (–teen, –tine) *adj.* like a serpent; twisted, cunning, etc.; ***n.*** (–teen) a magnesium silicate mineral with a layered-sheet structure and mottled like a snake's skin.

ser·rate (SER–) *adj.* having a saw-toothed edge; also **ser·rat·ed; ser·ra·tion** (–RAY–) *n.*

ser·ried (SER·eed) *adj.* in close order: *soldiers in ~ ranks.*

se·rum (SEER–) *n.* **-rums** or **-ra** **1** the clear fluid part of blood left after clotting. **2** blood serum containing antibodies for injection into patients with hepatitis, measles, etc.

ser·vant (SUR·vunt) *n.* **1** a person employed in household work. **2** a person in the service of a government: *a civil ~; public ~.* —**serve** (SURV) *v.* **serves, served, serv·ing** **1** carry out duties (*as* a teacher, *on* a jury, *at* table, etc.); do work (for or in): *Sales people ~ customers; Soldiers ~ in the army; A stick will ~* (i.e. satisfy) *our purpose.* **2** put (ball, shuttlecock, etc.) in play. **3** supply food, needs, etc. (for): *time to ~ coffee; enough food to ~ four people; a community well ~d with health care; Being ticketed for speeding seemed to* **serve him right.** **4** undergo: *~d his term in jail; has to ~ three years as an apprentice.* **5** present (an order, warrant, etc.): *The typist ~d notice* (on her boss) *that she was quitting; was ~d with a summons to appear in court.* —***n.*** a serving of a ball or shuttlecock. —**serv·er** *n.* —**serv·ice** (–is) *n.* **1** what is produced by serving, as work, benefit, etc.: *~ with a smile; guaranteed to give good ~ for five years; telephone ~* (i.e. facility or system); *a marriage ~* (i.e. ceremony); *a bill for* **services** *rendered by a professional; applied to be* **of service** *as a cook.* **2** function or occupation of serving: *was on active ~ in Vietnam; government ~;* **at one's service** ready to serve or be of use. **3** set of dishes, spoons, etc. used for serving food. Also ***v.*** **-ic·es, -iced, -ic·ing** do work on or for: *a car garaged for ~ing.* —**serv·ice·a·ble** *adj.* useful or durable. —**serv·ice·man** *n.* **-men** a man in military service; also, a repairman. —**service mark** the trademark of a service such as a financial or utility company. —**service module** part of a manned spacecraft between landing module and command module containing the propulsion, retrofire, and thrust systems. —**service station** a facility for supplying gas and repair services to motorists. —**ser·vi·ette** (–ET) *n. Brit.* a table napkin. —**ser·vile** *adj.* of or like a slave; hence, cringing or submissive; **ser·vile·ly** *adv.;* **ser·vil·i·ty** (–VIL–) *n.* —**serv·ing** *n.* a portion or helping of food. —**ser·vi·tor** *n.* a servant or attendant. —**ser·vi·tude** *n.* bondage or slavery; also, forced labor as punishment for a crime. —**ser·vo** *n.* **-vos** [short form] servomechanism; servomotor; **ser·vo·mech·a·nism** (–MEC·uh–) *n.* a control system for detecting and correcting errors in an automatic system, as one helping to keep an automatic pilot on course; **ser·vo·mo·tor** *n.* a motor supplying power for moving a servomechanism.

ses·a·me (SES·uh·mee) *n.* an East Indian herb whose seeds yield an oil used in cooking and flavoring.

ses·qui·cen·ten·ni·al (–TEN·ee·ul) *n.* & *adj.* (of) a 150th anniversary. —**ses·qui·pe·da·li·an** (–puh·DAY·lee·un) *adj.* **1** of words, many-syllabled. **2** of a style, using long words; pedantic.

ses·sile (SES·ul) *adj.* fixed to a spot, as barnacles, leaves attached to stem without stalk, etc. —**ses·sion** (SESH·un) *n.* the sitting or assembly of a group of people for a deliberative or similar activity, esp. its duration, as of a court, legislature, school, etc.: *a long morning ~; met in secret ~s; The court is* **in session** *from 10 a.m.;* **ses·sion·al** *adj.* —**set** *v.* **sets, set, set·ting 1** put or place with a purpose, direction, or in a certain manner or condition: *She ~ the flowers on the table; to ~* (i.e. arrange) *a table for dinner; a manner that ~s everyone at ease; What value did you ~ on the missing diamond? a house ~ on fire; styles ~ in Paris; a sonnet ~* (i.e. adapted) *to music; Type is ~ for printing.* **2** (cause) to be firm or settled in position: *Concrete ~s in a mold; hair ~ in a permanent.* **3** go down: *the ~ing sun.* **4** make (a hen) sit on eggs for hatching; also, sit. —***n.*** **1** a group or collection of persons or things belonging together: *the smart ~; a ~ of numbers; a ~ of games in tennis; a dining-room ~* (of furniture); *a dinner ~* (of dishes); *transistor ~* (i.e. assembled equipment). **2** scenery of a play or motion picture. **3** the way in which something is formed or forming: *the ~ of his shoulders; the ~ of public opinion on the subject.* —***adj.*** fixed or established: *a person of ~ views; a ~ time for everything; He is ~* (i.e. intent) *on winning;* **all set** ready or prepared. —**set about** (or **in, to**) begin. —**set aside** put by; also, reject, as a decision by a higher court. —**set forth** make known (views, plans, etc.); also, start, as on a journey. —**set off 1** explode. **2** offset. **3** make more impressive by contrast. **4** start on a journey. —**set on** (or **upon**) attack. —**set up** erect; put up; raise (a cry); establish. —**set·back** *n.* a reversal of or check to progress. —**set·screw** *n.* a screw that is threaded through one metal part and tightened against the surface of another to prevent relative motion between them. —**set·tee** (–TEE) *n.* a benchlike sofa with back and arms. —**set·ter** *n.* a long-haired hunting dog trained like a pointer. —**set·ting** *n.* **1** act of setting; also, what is set, as eggs that a hen sits on for hatching, dishes or silverware for one person at a table, or the music for a poem or other text. **2** what something is set in, as the mounting of a jewel, the time, place, and surroundings of a play or story, etc. —**set·tle** *v.* **set·tles, set·tled, set·tling 1** reach a final decision or agreement (*with* a party, *for* something, *on* a time, place, or plan): *The strikers ~d for a 10% raise; an argument hard to ~; accounts to be ~d* (i.e. paid) *before leaving; property divided and* **settled (up)on** *his children* (i.e. legally). **2** (cause) to take up residence: *Immigrants ~ in a country; are ~d in thinly populated areas; The French ~d* (i.e. colonized) *Quebec;* **set·tler** *n.* **3** establish (oneself or itself): *people ~d in their ways; takes time to ~ into a new job; Marriage helps people* **settle down** (in life). **4** (cause) to be in a more stable, composed, or compact state: *a tranquilizer to ~ your nerves; Rain helps ~ loose earth; A new house ~s* (in its foundation); *Dust ~s* (i.e. comes to rest). —**set·tle·ment** *n.* **1** a settling, as an agreement or its terms, bestowal of property upon someone, etc. **2** a being settled, as a colony or colonization. **3** a social institution or center for improvement of living conditions. —**set-to** (–too) *n.* **-tos** fight or argument. —**set·up** *n.* what is set up, as an arrangement, plan, etc.; also, the act or manner of arranging.

sev·en (SEV·un) *n., adj.* & *pron.* one more than six; the number 7 or VII; **sev·enth** *n., adj.* & *adv.* —**seven seas** all the oceans of the world. —**sev·en·teen** (–TEEN) *n., adj.* & *pron.* seven more than 10; 17; XVII; **sev·en·teenth** *n.* & *adj.* —**sev·en·teen-year** (SEV–) **locust** a kind of cicada that takes up to 17 years to come out of the ground as an adult. —**seventh heaven** a state of bliss or extreme happiness. —**sev·en·ty** *n., adj.* & *pron.* **-ties** seven times 10; 70 or LXX; **sev·en·ti·eth** *n.* & *adj.*

sev·er *v.* cut off; also, part or separate: *a ~ed head, rope, connection, communication line;* **sev·er·ance** *n.;* **severance pay** *given on termination of employment.* —**sev·er·al** (–ul) *adj.* **1** more than two; a few: *~ times, people;* ***pron.*** some: *~ of us were present; saw ~* (of the kind mentioned). **2** separate; different: *went their ~ ways; a joint and ~ liability;* **sev·er·al·ly** *adv.* separately; individually: *makers held jointly and ~ responsible for a product.*

se·vere (–VEER) *adj.* **-ver·er, -ver·est 1** strict or rigorous: *a ~ test of endurance; ~ reasoning, looks.* **2** hard to endure: *a ~ illness, headache, scolding; a ~* (i.e. violent) *storm.* —**se·vere·ly** *adv.;* **se·ver·i·ty** (–VER–) *n.* **-ties.**

Se·ville (–VIL) a city of S.W. Spain.

Sè·vres (SEV·ruh) *n.* a kind of fine porcelain made at a town of the same name in N. France.

sew (SOH) *v.* **sews,** *pt.* **sewed,** *pp.* **sewn** or **sewed, sew·ing** fasten with stitches. —**sew·ing** *n.* something sewn or to be sewn, by hand or with a **sewing machine;** also, the occupation. —**sew up** close with stitches; hence, *Informal.* make certain: *had the game all sewn up by the second quarter.* —**sew·er** *n.*

sew·age (SOO·ij) *n.* waste matter carried in sewers and drains. —**sew·er** *n.* a usu. underground pipe or drain for water and wastes; **sew·er·age** (–ij) *n.* a sewer system; also, sewage.

sex *n.* the male-female distinction and characteristic differences; also, sexual activity, esp. intercourse; **sexed** (SEXT) *adj.;* **sex·less** *adj.*

sex·a·ge·nar·i·an (sex·uh·juh·NAIR·ee·un) *n.* & *adj.* (a person) in his sixties.

sex appeal sexual attractiveness. **—sex chromosome** either of two chromosomes that are alike (XX) in the female and different (XY) in the male, by the pairing of which the sex and sex-linked characteristics of offspring are determined. **—sex hormone** any of the various hormones secreted by the gonads that control the development of sexual organs and characteristics.**—sex·ism** *n.* prejudice or discrimination based on sex, esp. against women; **sex·ist** *n.* & *adj.* **—sex·pot** *n. Slang.* a very sexy woman.

sex·tant (–tunt) *n.* an instrument for measuring angular distance between points, used esp. in navigation. **—sex·tet(te)** (–TET) *n.* a group of six or a musical composition for six voices.

sex·ton (–tun) *n.* a custodian of church property and equipment.

sex·u·al (SEK·shoo·ul) *adj.* of or having to do with sex: ~ *morality, reproduction;* **sexual intercourse** uniting of male and female genitals; **sex·u·al·ly** *adv.;* **sex·u·al·i·ty** (–AL–) *n.* **—sex·y** *adj.* **sex·i·er, -i·est** *Informal.* sexually stimulating or provocative; **sex·i·ly** *adv.;* **sex·i·ness** *n.*

Sey·chelles (say·SHELL, –SHELZ) a republic consisting of about 90 islands off the E. coast of Africa, N.E. of Madagascar; 145 sq.mi. (376 km²); *cap.* Victoria.

sf, s.f. or **S.F.** science fiction.

Sgt. sergeant.

sh *interj.* hush!

shab·by (SHAB·ee) *adj.* **shab·bi·er, shab·bi·est** in a much-worn, poor, or run-down condition: ~ *clothes, interiors; a ~-looking man;* ~ (i.e. unworthy or mean) *treatment;* **shab·bi·ly** *adv.;* **shab·bi·ness** *n.*

shack *n.* a small, crude dwelling; shanty; ***v.*** **shack up** *Slang.* cohabit (*in* a place, *with* a partner).

shack·le *n.* **1** a manacle or fetter; hence, any restraint; ***v.*** **shack·les, shack·led, shack·ling** restrain with shackles. **2** a fastening or coupling device.

shad *n.* a herring-family fish of N. Atlantic waters valued for its flesh and roe.

shade *n.* **1** a place that is not in direct light and heat, esp. of the sun; hence, a partly dark condition or relative obscurity: *the lights and ~s of a picture;* **the shades** (i.e. darkness) *of evening; was* **put in the shade** *by his more brilliant brother.* **2** a device to control light, as of a lamp, or to shut out light, as used over a window. **3** gradation of color; also, a slight difference: *Maroon is a ~ of red; many ~s of meaning; a ~ above normal temperature.* ***—v.*** **shades, shad·ed** (SHAY–), **shad·ing** **1** screen from light; hence, make dark or darker in lighting or coloring. **2** change little by little, as into a different shade. **—shades** *pl. Slang.* sunglasses. **—shad·ing** *n.* **1** use of a shade against light or of a dark color or lines for a shade effect. **2** a slight variation. **—shad·ow** (–oh) *n.* **1** the shade cast by an object blocking the light; hence, anything unsubstantial or ghostlike; also, a follower. **2** a shaded area, as in a picture; hence, darkness or gloom. **3** slight trace: *beyond a ~ of doubt.* Also ***v.*** **1** cast a shadow on. **2** represent faintly. **3** follow, esp. secretly: *~ed by detectives.* **—shad·ow·y** *adj.* **—shad·ow-box** *v.* to box with an imaginary opponent for training or exercise; **shad·ow-box·ing** *n.* **—shad·y** (SHAY–) *adj.* **shad·i·er, -i·est** **1** in the shade or giving shade. **2** *Informal.* dishonest: *a ~ character, deal.*

shaft *n.* **1** a long handle or stem, as of a spear or arrow; also, a dart or similar thrown missile: *~s of ridicule, wit.* **2** a beam (of light). **3** a polelike, round, often hollow bar; also, a structure or passage resembling it: *the ~ of a mine; elevator ~* (in which it moves). ***—v.*** *Slang.* cheat or trick: *He got ~ed in that deal.*

shag *n.* (cloth, carpet, etc. with) long, rough nap; also, a mass of coarse hair, fiber, or finely shredded tobacco. ***—v.*** **shags, shagged, shag·ging** chase after and return a ball when it goes out of play. **—shag·gy** *adj.* **shag·gi·er, shag·gi·est** looking unkempt or needing a shave; also, covered with rough coarse fiber or hair: ~ *eyebrows; a ~ dog.*

shah *n.* a king of Iran.

shake *v.* **shakes, shook, shak·en** (SHAY–), **shak·ing** **1** (cause to) move jerkily up and down or back and forth: ~ *the bottle before use;* ~ (dust from) *a rug; They shook hands on parting; shook her head* (to say "No"); *swore and shook his fists at him.* **2** (cause to) tremble or totter; hence, waver or weaken: *Earthquakes ~ a building; Nothing could ~ his faith in God.* ***—n.:*** *ordered a ~* (i.e. milkshake); *has got* **the shakes** (i.e. a trembling disease); *a fair ~* (*Informal.* deal); **no great shakes** *Informal.* not especially good. **—shake down** **1** get by shaking, as fruit from a tree; *Slang.* extort money (from a victim). **2** cause to settle down; hence, get adjusted or accustomed. **—shake off** get rid of. **—shake·down** *n.* **1** *Slang.* extortion of money, as by graft. **2** a getting adjusted or accustomed, as of new equipment, of people to a new environment, etc.: *a ~ cruise.* **—shak·er** *n.* **1** a device for shaking (cocktails, etc.). **2** one that shakes; **Shaker** a member of the United Society of Believers, a Quaker sect well known for their austere and functional furniture.

Shake·speare (–speer), **William.** 1564–1616, the greatest English poet and playwright; **Shake·spear·e·an** (–SPEER·ee·un) *n.* & *adj.*

shake-up *n.* a drastic reorganization, esp. of personnel. **—shak·y** (SHAY–) *adj.* **shak·i·er, -i·est** weak; not firm; hence, unreliable: *a*

~ *voice, foundation;* **shak·i·ly** *adv.;* **shak·i·ness** *n.*

shak·o (SHAC·oh, SHAY–) *n.* **-os** (–ose) a cylindrical, flat-topped, stiff military hat with an upright plume in front.

shale *n.* a soft sedimentary rock that easily splits into layers; **shale oil** petroleum from bituminous shale.

shall (SHAL) *auxiliary v., pt.* **should** (SHOOD, shud) *Formal.* **1** [expressing future time in the first person]: *I ~ be away on business.* **2** [expressing necessity or obligation]: *You ~ not smoke; She ~ be your boss; They ~ not pass; Should I give up smoking? You should not have done that.*

shal·lop (–lup) *n.* a small, light, open boat.

shal·lot (shuh·LOT) *n.* an onionlike herb with bulbs clustered like garlic, used to flavor cooked foods.

shal·low (SHAL·oh) *adj.* **1** not deep: ~ *water, dish;* **shal·lows** *n.pl.* shallow waters; shoal. **2** superficial; lacking depth of mind or character.

sha·lom (shah·LOME) *n.* & *interj. Hebrew* [used as greeting] peace.

shalt *Archaic* [used with *thou*] shall.

sham *n.* & *adj.* false or fake (person or thing); ***v.*** **shams, shammed, sham·ming** feign or pretend; **sham·mer** *n.*

sha·man (SHAH·mun, SHAY–) *n.* a medicine man.

sham·ble *v.* **-bles, -bled, -bling** walk awkwardly; shuffle; ***n.*** a shambling gait. —**sham·bles** *n.pl.* [takes *sing. v.*] scene of disorder or destruction.

shame *n.* (feeling of) great dishonor or disgrace; also, a cause of such feeling: *What a ~! ~ on you! You're a ~ to womanhood;* **put to shame** make ashamed; hence, surpass. —***v.*** **shames, shamed, sham·ing** make ashamed; hence, disgrace; **shame·ful** *adj.;* **shame·ful·ly** *adv.;* **shame·ful·ness** *n.* —**shame·faced** *adj.* bashful; also, showing shame; **shame·fac·ed·ly** *adv.* —**shame·less** *adj.* not ashamed; brazen: *a ~ liar.*

sham·my (–mee) *n.* **sham·mies** same as CHAMOIS, *n.* 2.

sham·poo (–POO) *n.* a soaplike preparation for washing the hair and scalp; also, a shampooing; ***v.*** **-poos, -pooed, -poo·ing** use shampoo on the hair; also, clean (a rug, etc.) with liquid soap; **sham·poo·er** *n.*

sham·rock *n.* a three-leaved clover or similar plant; Ireland's national emblem.

Shang·hai (–hye) an E. Chinese seaport and the world's largest city. —**shang·hai** *v.* **-hais, -haied, -hai·ing** drug and put on board ship; hence, kidnap or trap in this manner.

shank *n.* **1** part of the human leg between knee and ankle; also, a corresponding part in animals. **2** in a tool, device, etc., a connecting or essential part, usu. straight, as a shaft, stem, or handle: *the ~ of a fish hook;* **the shank** (i.e. early part) **of the evening.**

shan't shall not.

shan·tung *n.* a silky fabric, heavier than pongee, used for curtains, robes, etc.

shan·ty *n.* **-ties** **1** same as CHANTEY; also **shan·tey, -teys.** **2** a shack or hut. —**shan·ty·town** *n.* an area of mostly shacks.

shape *n.* outline or form, esp. of something having mass and bulk; configuration: *the ~ of an S, a pear; a god appearing in different ~s; Ideas* **take shape** *as realities; She's in good ~* (i.e. condition) *for a 60-year-old.* —***v.*** **shapes, shaped, shap·ing:** *a statue ~d out of marble; experiences that ~ one's character; told to* **shape up** (i.e. perform satisfactorily) *or get out.* —**shape·less** *adj.;* **shape·less·ly** *adv.;* **shape·less·ness** *n.* —**shape·ly** *adj.* **-li·er, -li·est** of a woman, having a good figure; **shape·li·ness** *n.*

shard *n.* same as POTSHERD. —**share** *n.* **1** a part or portion of a property or responsibility that belongs to one: *a ~ of the profits; stock certificates showing the number of ~s held by each* **share·hold·er** *of a corporation.* **2** a plowshare. —***v.*** **shares, shared, shar·ing:** *Two girls ~ a room; The prize money was ~d equally among the winners; Everyone ~d in the celebrations.* —**share·crop** *v.* **-crops, -cropped, -crop·ping** work (another's land) for a share of the crop; **share·crop·per** *n.*

shark *n.* **1** a swindler: *a loan ~.* **2** one highly skilled in a particular line: *a card ~.* **3** any of a group of usu. large, meat-eating ocean fishes with graceful, torpedolike bodies, reputed to attack humans. —**shark·skin** *n.* a shark's hide or leather; also, a smooth fabric with steplike twill weave.

sharp *adj.* **1** having a thin cutting edge or fine point: *a ~ knife, pencil, nose* (i.e. pointed), *turn* (i.e. abrupt). **2** pricking or biting: ~ *words, taste, weather* (i.e. cold). **3** shrill or high-pitched: *a ~ cry of pain; a ~ musical note* (half a tone above natural pitch). **4** having qualities of keenness, quickness, smartness, etc.: ~ *ears, desire, lawyer, clothes* (i.e. stylish). **5** clear-cut: *a ~ contrast; in ~ relief.* —***n.*** a musical note or tone raised above its normal pitch by a half step; also, the symbol (#) used to indicate such a note or tone; ***v.*** raise by one half step; also, sound such a note. —***adv.*** in a sharp manner: *at 8 p.m. ~; sing ~; Look ~!* (i.e. watch out!); **sharp·ly** *adv.* —**sharp·ness** *n.* —**sharp·en** *v.* make or become sharp; **sharp·en·er** *n.* —**sharp·er** *n.* a cheat; swindler. —**sharp-eyed** *adj.* keen in sight or watchfulness; also **sharp-sight·ed.** —**sharp·ie** (–ee) *n. Informal.* a clever or cunning person; also, a sharper. —**sharp·shoot·er** *n.* marksman; **sharp·shoot·ing** *n.* —**sharp-tongued** *adj.* harsh or severly critical in speech; **sharp-wit·ted** *adj.* having a keen mind and quick tongue.

shat·ter *v.* break into scattering pieces: *windshields made of safety glass that is* **shat·ter·proof** *adj.*

shave *v.* **shaves,** *pt.* & *pp.* **shaved** or **shav·en, shav·ing** remove hair from the face with a razor; also, cut off (hair), slice (ham, etc.) thin, graze (a surface), or pass very close to. **—*n.:*** *a ~ and a shower in the morning; ~s of beef; escaped with a close ~ though badly shaken.* **—shav·er** *n.* **1** a shaving instrument, esp. an electric razor. **2** *Informal.* a youngster. **—shav·ing** *n.: wood ~s; pencil ~s.*

Shaw, George B. 1856–1950, British dramatist; **Sha·vi·an** (SHAY–) *n.* & *adj.* (an admirer) of Shaw, his works, etc.

shawl *n.* a square or oblong piece of cloth used esp. by women as a covering for the head or shoulders.

Shaw·nee (–NEE) *n.* (member of) an Algonquian Indian people now living in Oklahoma; also, their language.

shay *n. Informal.* chaise.

she (SHEE) *n.* & *pron., objective* HER, *possessive* HERS, *pl.* THEY, *objective* THEM, *possessive* THEIR(S) the female animal or human being (referred to); also, a person or thing thought of as female: *~ is their queen; Is Terry a he or a ~?*

sheaf (SHEEF) *n.* **sheaves** a bundle of cut stalks of grain, arrows in a quiver, or papers.

shear (SHEER) *v.* **shears,** *pt.* & *pp.* **sheared** or **shorn, shear·ing** **1** strip (a sheep) of its wool; hence, deprive of: *shorn wool; Samson shorn of his strength; a dictator shorn of his powers.* **2** cut or break by the action of two forces sliding in opposite directions, as causes materials to split into layers. **—*n.*** a shearing, a shearing force or stress, or a blade of a pair of **shears** *pl.* large scissors: *pinking ~s; tin ~s; sheep ~s.* **—shear·er** *n.* **—shear·wa·ter** *n.* a long-winged ocean bird that skims over waves.

sheath (SHEETH) *n.* **1** a case for the blade of a knife; hence, a similar covering over a cat's claw or the base of a grass's leaf that wraps around its stem. **2** a woman's straight, close-fitting dress. **—sheathe** (SHEEDH) *v.* **sheathes, sheathed, sheath·ing** put into or enclose in a sheath; **sheathing** *n.* the inner layer of boards used under the siding or roofing of a frame house.

sheave (SHIV, SHEEV) *n.* a wheel or pulley with a grooved rim.

she·bang (shuh·BANG) *n. Informal.* outfit; business; affair: **the whole shebang.**

she'd she had; she would.

shed *n.* one-story structure sometimes open on one side, used for shelter or storage. **—*v.*** **sheds, shed, shed·ding** **1** let drop or fall; cast off (skin): *~ tears, Snakes ~ (their skin); ~ your coat.* **2** give forth; send out: *The sun ~s light; She ~s happiness.* **—shed blood** kill violently.

sheen *n.* the shiny quality of satin, silk, etc.; soft luster; **sheen·y** *adj.*

sheep *n. sing.* & *pl.* an animal related to the goat, raised for its wool, milk, and meat (i.e. mutton and lamb); hence, one considered meek or submissive (as sheep being shorn). **—sheep dog** a dog trained to herd and watch sheep. **—sheep·fold** *n.* a pen or shelter for sheep; also **sheep·cote.** **—sheep·ish** *adj.* bashful or embarrassed; **sheep·ish·ly** *adv.;* **sheep·ish·ness** *n.* **—sheep range** land used for grazing sheep. **—sheep·skin** *n.* the skin of a sheep; also, leather or parchment made from it; hence, *Informal.* a diploma. **—sheep·walk** *n.* same as SHEEP RANGE.

sheer *v.* swerve or deviate, as a ship from its course. **—*adj.*** **1** very thin or transparent: *a ~ fabric* (as organdy or chiffon); ***n.*** such a fabric, garment, etc.; **sheers** *pl.* sheer drapes. **2** pure; unmixed: *~ nonsense.* **3** very steep; precipitous: *a ~ drop; ~ cliffs.* **—*adv.*** directly; also, very steeply.

sheet *n.* **1** a rope or chain used to adjust the sails of a ship; **sheets** *pl.* corner spaces at the bow *(foresheets)* and stern *(stern sheets)* of an open boat that are not occupied by thwarts. **2** a broad, thin piece of material or something resembling it: *bed ~s; a ~ of paper, glass, water, ice; broad flashes of* **sheet lightning** *lighting up the sky from beyond the horizon;* **sheet·ing** *n.* cloth for bed sheets; also, wood or metal in sheets for lining surfaces, etc.; **sheet metal** thin-rolled metal in sheets; **sheet music** printed music on unbound sheets of paper.

sheik(h) (SHEEK, SHAKE) *n.* an Arab chief; also, a Muslim title; **sheik(h)·dom** (–dum) *n.*

shek·el *n.* the basic money unit of Israel, equal to 100 agorot.

shelf *n.* **shelves** (SHELVZ) **1** a board attached at a height horizontally to a wall or inside a cabinet for holding things, as books in a bookcase; **on the shelf** put aside as useless or not urgent. **2** a ledge of rocks, esp. one under water. **—shelf life** how long a packaged product will keep if stored.

she'll she will; she shall.

shell *n.* **1** the hard outer covering of oysters, snails, and other mollusks, insects such as beetles, turtles, eggs, seeds, and nuts. **2** a shell-like outer covering, as the framework of a house or ship, a sleeveless pullover blouse, or the case of a pie. **3** a racing rowboat. **4** a hollow artillery projectile; also, a cartridge case for a shotgun or other small arms. **—*v.*** **1** remove the shell or husk of. **2** bombard with artillery shells. **3** **shell out** *Informal.* pay or hand out (an amount).

shel·lac (shuh·LAC) *n.* varnish made of refined lac dried into flakes and dissolved in alcohol; also, lac used in sealing wax and molded articles. **—*v.*** **shel·lacs, shel·lacked,**

shel·lack·ing **1** varnish with shellac. **2** *Informal.* thrash; also, beat decisively; **shel·lack·ing** *n.* a thrashing; also, a decisive defeat. **—shell bean** (the edible seed of) a bean that is shelled for use, as lima bean.

Shel·ley (SHEL·ee), **Percy B.** 1792–1822, English poet.

shell·fire *n.* the firing of artillery shells. **—shell·fish** *n.* an oyster, clam, lobster, etc. that is not a true fish. **—shell shock** same as COMBAT FATIGUE.

shel·ter *n.* (a roof or other cover for) protection from the elements or a specific threat: *Where shall we take ~?* **—v.** protect or provide a shelter for; also, find shelter.

shelves *pl.* of SHELF. **—shelve** *v.* **shelves, shelved, shelv·ing** **1** put (something) on a shelf; hence, put off or put aside. **2** furnish with shelves; **shelv·ing** *n.* boards, posts, etc. for putting up shelves.

she·nan·i·gans (–NAN·i·gunz) *n.pl. Informal.* mischievous, devious, or tricky behavior.

Shen·yang (SHUN·yahng) a city of N.E. China.

shep·herd (SHEP·urd) *n.* & *v.* (to herd or look after as) one who tends sheep; *fem.* **shep·herd·ess** *n.*

sher·bet (SHUR·but) *n.* an ice made with fruit juice, sugar, and low-fat milk or egg white.

sher·iff *n.* the chief law-enforcement officer of a county.

Sher·pa (SHUR·puh) *n.* a member of a Nepalese people famed as porters and guides in the Himalayas.

sher·ry *n.* **sher·ries** a usu. yellowish-to-brown fortified wine.

she's (SHEEZ) she is; she has.

Shet·land (pony) (SHET·lund) the smallest breed of horse having long, thick hair, originally from the **Shetland Islands** N.E. of Scotland.

shew (SHOH) *n.* & *v.* **shews,** *pt.* **shewed,** *pp.* **shewed** or **shewn, shew·ing** *Archaic.* show.

shib·bo·leth (–buh·luth) *n.* a custom or usage, esp. in language, narrowly applied as a criterion of membership in a particular class or faction; a test word or password.

shied *pt.* & *pp.* of SHY.

shield (SHEELD) *n.* & *v.* (protect or defend with or as if with) a piece of armor held in one hand.

shier, shiest See SHY.

shift *v.* change location, position, or direction esp. in a restless or unstable manner: *The wind has ~ed to northeast; kept ~ing in his chair nervously; tried to ~ the blame to his employees; Now you're ~ing your ground* (i.e. the basis of your reasoning); *had to* **shift for himself** *without a home or friends.* **—n.** **1** change: *a ~ in the wind;* **make shift** manage as best one can (with available resources). **2** group or period in which people work in a relay system: *a night ~.* **3** a gearshift. **4** a sheathlike but beltless dress. **—shift·less** *adj.* lazy; **shift·less·ness** *n.* **—shift·y** *adj.* **shift·i·er, -i·est** evasive or tricky: *~ behavior, looks;* **shift·i·ly** *adv.;* **shift·i·ness** *n.*

shill *n. Slang.* a person hired to lure customers into buying, betting, gambling, etc. by posing as a customer himself.

shil·le·lagh (shi·LAY·lee) *n. Irish.* a cudgel.

shil·ling (SHIL·ing) *n.* **1** the basic money unit of Kenya, Somalia, Tanzania, and Uganda, worth 100 cents. **2** a money unit of Rhodesia equal to 1/20 of a pound; formerly, a British money of account equal to 1/20 of a pound.

shil·ly-shal·ly *n.* & *v.* **-shal·lies, -shal·lied, -shal·ly·ing** (show) inability to make up one's mind; dawdle over a decision.

shim *n.* & *v.* **shims, shimmed, shim·ming** (level up or support by use of) a thin wedge or strip of material.

shim·mer *n.* & *v.* (shine with) a wavering or unsteady light; glimmer; **shim·mer·y** *adj.*

shim·my (SHIM·ee) *v.* **shim·mies, shim·mied, shim·my·ing** shake or wobble, as the defective front wheels of an automobile; also, dance the shimmy; ***n.*** a shaking or vibration; also, a jazz dance of the 1920's.

shin *n.* the front of the leg between the knee and the ankle; ***v.*** **shins, shinned, shin·ning** climb (*up* a tree trunk, pole, etc.) using hands and legs; **shin·bone** *n.* the larger of the two bones of the lower leg.

shin·dig *n. Informal.* a noisy social gathering.

shine *v.* **shines, shone, shin·ing** **1** send out or reflect light, as the sun, moon, lights, etc.; hence, be brilliant or conspicuous (in some respect, at some skill, etc.): *a ~ing example of self-sacrifice.* **2** [*pt.* usu. **shined**] make shiny; polish. **—n.** brightness; brilliance; also, gloss; **take a shine to** *Slang.* become fond of. **—shin·er** (SHY·nur) *n.* **1** one that shines, esp. a silvery fish or minnow. **2** *Slang.* a black eye.

shin·gle (SHING·gl) *n.* **1** a flat, thin piece of wood, asbestos, or other material laid in overlapping rows to cover roofs or walls; ***v.*** **-gles, -gled, -gling:** *a ~d roof.* **2** *Informal.* a small sign such as a physician or other professional hangs out at his door. **3** a woman's short haircut tapered at the nape. **4** (a beach covered with) small well-rounded pebbles; **shin·gly** *adj.* **—shingles** *sing.* & *pl.* same as HERPES ZOSTER.

shin·guard *n.* protective padding worn on the shin while playing soccer, baseball, etc. **—shin·ny** *v.* **shin·nies, shin·nied, shin·ny·ing** same as SHIN.

Shin·to (–toh) *n.* the traditional religion of Japan that centers around the worship of ancestors and the basic forces and processes of nature; **Shin·to·ism** *n.*

shin·y (SHY·nee) *adj.* **shin·i·er, -i·est** bright or shining; also, polished; **shin·i·ly** *adv.;* **shin·i·ness** *n.*

-ship *n.suffix.* state or condition: as in *authorship, fellowship;* also, *workmanship* (i.e. skill of a workman); *readership* (i.e. group of readers).

ship *n.* **1** a large seagoing vessel; also, its officers and crew. **2** an aircraft or spacecraft. **—*v.* ships, shipped, ship·ping 1** put on board a ship; hence, transport by sea, rail, road, or air; **ship·per** *n.* **2** take in or install in a ship: *to* ~ *water* (i.e. be flooded) *in a storm; to* ~ *oars, rudder.* **3** go on board a ship to travel, for service, etc.; **ship·board** *n.* & *adj.* (aboard) ship: *a* ~ *riot; happened on* ~. **—ship·build·er** *n.* one whose business is **ship·build·ing** *n.* the designing and construction of ships. **—ship·fit·ter** *n.* one who fits a ship's parts together. **—ship·mate** *n.* a fellow sailor. **—ship·ment** *n.* goods shipped or their shipping. **—ship·ping** *n.* **1** ships of a nation, business, etc. collectively. **2** the transporting of goods; **shipping clerk** one in charge of shipping. **—ship·shape** *adj.* trim and tidy; in good order; also ***adv.*** **—ship·worm** *n.* a clamlike mollusk that bores holes in wood. **—ship·wreck 1** *n.* & *v.* (cause or suffer) the loss or destruction of a ship at sea; hence, ruin or failure. **2** *n.* wreckage or a wrecked ship. **—ship·wright** *n.* a shipbuilder or repairer, esp. a carpenter. **—ship·yard** *n.* an establishment for the building and repair of ships.

shire *n.* in Britain, a county.

shirk *v.* avoid doing one's work or duty; **shirk·er** *n.*

shirr *v.* **1** gather (cloth) together by means of short parallel stitches; ***n.*** such a gathering; also **shirr·ing. 2** bake (shelled eggs) in a shallow dish with butter.

shirt *n.* a garment for the upper part of the body with a front opening, collar, and short or long sleeves, as usu. worn by men; also, an undershirt; **lose one's shirt** *Slang.* lose all one's money or property. **—shirt·dress** *n.* a shirtwaist dress. **—shirt·ing** *n.* cloth for shirts. **—shirt·tail** *n.* the part of a shirt that is usu. tucked inside one's trousers. **—shirt·waist** *n.* a blouse fashioned like a shirt; **shirt·waist·er** *n.* shirtdress.

shish kebab skewered KEBAB.

shiv *n. Slang.* a knife.

Shi·va (SHEE·vuh) same as SIVA.

shiv·er 1 *v.* tremble, as from fear or cold; ***n.*** a shivering or shaking; **shiv·er·y** *adj.* **2** *n.* & *v.* splinter.

shlemiel, shlep(p), shlock, shmaltz, shnook same as SCHLEMIEL, SCHLEP(P), SCHLOCK, SCHMALTZ, SCHNOOK.

shoal (SHOLE) *n.* **1** a large group, esp. a school of fish. **2** (a sandbar or ridge of rocks forming) a shallow place.

shoat (SHOTE) *n.* a weaned young hog.

shock *n.* **1** a sudden violent shake or jolt, as felt when electric current passes through the body or an earthquake strikes: *The news came as a* ~. **2** a failure or collapse of the circulatory system resulting from a serious injury or burn; also, a dazed emotional condition brought on by some disaster or personal loss. **3** a thick bushy mass, esp. of hair; also, a stack of sheaves of grain. **4** [short form] shock absorber. **—*v.*** cause shock to; hence, fill with horror or disgust. **—shock absorber** anything that lessens a shock, esp. a piston device used on automobiles, aircraft landing gears, etc. to reduce the shock of rough rides or impacts. **—shock·er** *n.* a person or thing that shocks, esp. a sensational story. **—shock·ing** *adj.* causing great surprise, disgust, etc.: ~ *language, news.* **—shock·proof** *adj.* protected against shocks: *a* ~ *watch.* **—shock therapy** treatment of severe mental illness using electric current, drugs, etc. to produce convulsions. **—shock troops** troops specially trained to lead attacks.

shod *pt.* & *pp.* of SHOE. **—shod·dy** *n.* **shod·dies** cloth made of woolen waste; hence, anything of inferior quality though looking good; ***adj.*** **shod·di·er, shod·di·est:** ~ *merchandise;* ~ (i.e. shabby) *treatment;* **shod·di·ly** *adv.;* **shod·di·ness** *n.*

shoe (SHOO) *n.* **1** an outer covering for a foot, usu. made of leather. **2** something resembling a shoe in function, position, etc., as a horseshoe, *brake shoe,* ferrule, the outer casing of a pneumatic tire, etc. **—*v.* shoes,** *pt.* & *pp.* **shod** or **shoed, shoe·ing:** *Blacksmiths* ~ *horses; well-shod feet; shod with steel.* **—shoe·horn** *n.* an implement with a curved blade used to ease the heel into a shoe. **—shoe·lace** *n.* a length of string or strap for lacing and tying a shoe. **—shoe·mak·er** *n.* one who makes or repairs shoes. **—shoe·shine** *n.* a cleaning and polishing of a pair of shoes. **—shoe·string** *n.* **1** shoelace. **2** *Informal.* a small or barely adequate amount of capital; ***adj.:*** *a* ~ *operation;* **shoestring catch** in baseball, football, etc., a catch made just before the ball hits the ground. **—shoe tree** a foot-shaped form, usu. of wood, inserted in a shoe to preserve its shape.

sho·gun (SHOH–) *n.* title of the hereditary commander-in-chief and virtual ruler of Japan till 1867.

shone *pt.* of SHINE.

shoo *interj.* [used to drive away birds, flies, etc.] go away! **—*v.* shoos, shooed, shoo·ing** drive away by calling "shoo." **—shoo-in** *n. Informal.* an easy winner.

shook *pt.* of SHAKE; **shook up** *Slang.* upset or agitated.

shoot *v.* **shoots, shot, shoot·ing 1** send forth suddenly and swiftly like a bullet, arrow, or other missile: *He shot two rounds; reporters*

~ing questions; The flames shot up; cars ~ing past spectators; to ~ (i.e. discharge) *a gun; addicts* **shooting up** (*Slang.* injecting) *amphetamines; a canoe for ~ing* (i.e. passing quickly along) *the rapids.* **2** kill or get by shooting: *a robber shot dead; planes shot down; shot three goals; A camera ~s pictures.* **—n.:** *the young ~s of a growing tree; out on a tiger ~; He lost the ~* (i.e. shooting match). **—shooting gallery** an enclosed place with targets for practicing shooting. **—shooting script** a script with scenes arranged in the order required for filming. **—shooting star** a meteor. **—shoot·out** *n. Informal.* a gunfight.

shop *n.* **1** a small retail store; **shop·keep·er** *n.* **2** a place where goods are produced or a service is provided; a workshop or factory: *a carpenter's ~; barber ~;* **talk shop** indulge in or use shoptalk. **—v. shops, shopped, shop·ping** visit stores or buy from (a store); **shop around** search about (for a bargain, better job, etc.); **shop·per** *n.* **—shop·lift·er** *n.* one who steals goods displayed for sale in a store; **shop·lift** *v.;* **shop·lift·ing** *n.* **—shoppe** (SHOP) *n.* [archaic spelling] shop (*n.* 1). **—shopping center** a place with many shops and a parking area. **—shop·talk** *n.* discussion of one's business, as with a colleague, esp. using jargon; also, such jargon. **—shop·worn** *adj.* of articles displayed for sale, soiled or frayed by having been handled or on display; hence, not fresh or attractive.

shore *n.* **1** land along the edge of a sea, lake, etc.; coast. **2** a prop or brace to support a structure, esp. on its side; **v. shores, shored, shor·ing:** *to ~ up a shaky wall.* **—shore bird** a wading bird such as a plover or sandpiper. **—shore·line** *n.* the line formed by a coast; coastline. **—shore patrol** members of the U.S. Navy or Coast Guard carrying out police duties on shore. **—shorn** a *pp.* of SHEAR.

short *adj.* **1** relatively small in extent or duration; not long or tall: *a ~ speech, man; the ~ vowels of "pat," "pet," "pit," "pot," and "put"; has a ~* (i.e. not retentive) *memory.* **2** less than sufficient: *food in ~ supply; We're* **short of** *supplies; nothing ~ of* (i.e. less than) *what was promised; cheats his customers with ~ weight and ~ change; Being ~* (i.e. curt) *didn't help him keep customers.* **3** of pastry and such baked foods, crumbly or flaky. **4** *Finance.* not yet owning (securities, goods, etc. sold). **—adv.:** *stopped ~* (i.e. abruptly) *in the middle of his speech;* **cut short** *his vacation and returned to work; His performance* **fell short** *of expectations; would stop at nothing ~ of murder; sells cotton ~* (i.e. for future delivery). **—n.** something short or shortened, as a short form, item, movie, sale, etc.; also, a short circuit; **shorts** *pl.* short trousers or drawers. **—v.** shortchange or short-circuit. **—short·age** (–ij) *n.* a deficiency or its amount. **—short·bread** *n.* a rich crumbly cake or cookie. **—short·cake** *n.* a pastry cake served with sugared or cooked fruit. **—short·change** *v.* **-chang·es, -changed, -chang·ing** *Informal.* give less than the correct change; hence, deprive of what is due; cheat. **—short circuit** a usu. dangerous high flow of electric current between two points bypassing the main circuit; **short-cir·cuit** *v.* **—short·com·ing** *n.* a failing or fault. **—short·cut** *n.* a way that is shorter than the regular route; hence, any way of saving time or effort. **—short·en** *v.* **1** make or become shorter. **2** make (pastry) crisp and flaky by use of **short·en·ing** *n.* butter, lard, etc. added to doughs and batters. **—short·fall** *n.* a falling short or its amount; shortage. **—short fuse** *Informal.* a quick temper. **—short·hand** *n.* a system of rapid writing using abbreviations and symbols; stenography; **short·hand·ed** *adj.* short of helpers. **—short·horn** *n.* a roan-colored breed of beef cattle having short horns, originally from England. **—short-lived** (–lived, –livd) *adj.* lasting a short time. **—short·ly** *adv.* **1** briefly; also, abruptly or curtly. **2** in a short time; soon. **—short·ness** *n.* **—short order** (an order for) food that can be quickly cooked: *a short-order cook at a lunch counter.* **—short-range** *adj.* having a short range in distance or time; not long-range. **—short shrift** little consideration; curt treatment. **—short·sight·ed** *adj.* nearsighted; also, lacking in foresight; **short·sight·ed·ly** *adv.;* **short·sight·ed·ness** *n.* **—short-spo·ken** *adj.* using few words; hence, curt. **—short·stop** *n.* the infielder or his position between second and third base. **—short story** a compact work of prose fiction, as published in magazines, with a simple plot and limited number of characters. **—short subject** a cartoon, newsreel, or other short item shown between feature films. **—short-tem·pered** *adj.* quickly angered. **—short-term** *adj.* having to do with a relatively short period of time; not long-term. **—short ton** 2,000 lb. (907.18 kg). **—short·wave** *n.* electromagnetic radiation of wavelength less than 100 meters, as used in FM broadcasting. **—short-wind·ed** *adj.* easily getting out of breath; having breathing difficulty.

Sho·sho·ni or **Sho·sho·nee** (–SHOH·nee) *n.* (a member of) an American Indian people now living in Wyoming, Nevada, and Idaho; **Sho·sho·ne·an** *n.* & *adj.*

shot *pt.* & *pp.* of SHOOT. **—adj. 1 shot with** flecked or streaked with: *a sky ~ with patches of cloud; red silk ~ with gold thread; an essay* **shot through with** (i.e. full of) *humor.* **2** *Slang.* worn out or broken, as an automobile part needing replacement. **—n. 1** a shooting or anything like it, as a scoring attempt in a game, an injection or dose of a drug, a pointed remark, or a random guess: *He's a good ~* (i.e. marksman); *warned not to approach within ~* (i.e. range) *of the rifles.* **2** a solid metal ball, esp. a large one for a cannon; also, smaller lead pellets collectively: *bird ~.* **3** a camera picture or film sequence. —**call the shots** give orders. —**shot in the arm** something to stimulate or invigorate. —**shot·gun** *n.* a smooth-bore hunting gun that fires lead pellets: *a* **shotgun wedding** *forced on the bride by pregnancy.* —**shot put** the contest of throwing a heavy metal ball for distance; **shot-put·ter** *n.;* **shot-put·ting** *n.*

should *pt.* of SHALL.

shoul·der (SHOHL–) *n.* **1** where the arm is joined to the trunk; **shoulders** *pl.* the upper part of the back, esp. as bearing burdens; **straight from the shoulder** frankly or directly. **2** a shoulderlike part, esp. the usu. unpaved edge of a road. **—*v.*** push, support, or bear (a burden, blame, etc.) with or as if with a shoulder or shoulders. —**shoulder belt** (or **harness**) an anchored belt worn over one shoulder attached to a lap belt for safety in an automobile. —**shoulder blade** either of the two flat, triangular bones at the back of the shoulder.

shouldn't should not.

shout *n.* & *v.* (utter) a sudden loud cry or call; **shout·er** *n.*

shove (SHUV) *v.* **shoves, shoved, shov·ing** push roughly, often to get a person or thing out of one's way; ***n.*** such a push; **shove off** *Informal.* leave, as by pushing one's boat away from a shore. —**shov·el** *n.* & *v.* **-els, -el(l)ed, -el·(l)ing** (dig out or throw with) an implement with a broad hollowed out blade and handle for scooping out loose material such as earth, coal, and snow; **shov·el·ful** *n.* **-fuls** how much a shovel will hold.

show (SHOH) *v.* **shows,** *pt.* & *pp.* **shown** (SHONE) or **showed, show·ing** **1** (cause to) be seen: *He ~d me a picture; Your slip is ~ing; Children like to* **show off** (i.e. be watched while doing something they are proud of); *He likes to ~ off* (i.e. display) *his new car; Half of those who reserved seats didn't* **show up** (i.e. arrive). **2** explain or demonstrate: *She'll ~ you how it works.* **3** direct or guide: *The hostess ~d us around; ~d us* (i.e. to) *the door.* **—*n.*** **1** a showing: *voting by ~ of hands;* **for show** for attracting attention. **2** a display, exhibition, or performance: *a ~ of temper; a dog ~; The ~ starts at 8; in charge of the whole ~* (i.e. operation). —**show·boat** *n.* formerly, a large boat equipped as a traveling theater. —**show business** the entertainment industry. —**show·case** *n.* a glass case for displaying articles in a store or museum. —**show·down** *n. Informal.* the bringing out of a dispute into the open in order to force a settlement.

show·er (SHOU·ur) *n.* **1** a brief fall of rain or anything similar, as of hail, arrows, stones, meteorites, etc. **2** a party for giving gifts to a woman on a special occasion, as before marriage. **3** (a bathroom fixture for) an overhead spray of water; also, a wash taken under a shower, or **shower bath.** **—*v.*** **1** rain briefly; also come or send in a shower. **2** take a shower bath. —**show·er·y** *adj.*

show·man (SHOH·mun) *n.* **-men** a man skilled in presenting things in an impressive or dramatic manner; also, a producer of shows; **show·man·ship** *n.* —**shown** a *pp.* of SHOW. —**show·off** *n.* one who vainly displays his good points. —**show·piece** *n.* something considered the best of its kind, as fit for display. —**show·place** *n.* a place that is proudly shown to tourists. —**show·room** *n.* a room in which goods are displayed for viewing. —**show window** a shop's outside display window. —**show·y** *adj.* **show·i·er, -i·est** striking or gaudy in appearance; **show·i·ly** *adv.;* **show·i·ness** *n.*

shrank a *pt.* of SHRINK.

shrap·nel (–nl) *n.* the flying fragments from an exploding bomb, shell, or mine; originally, an antipersonnel shell.

shred *v.* **shreds, shred·ded, shred·ding** cut or tear into narrow strips or fragments: *a paper ~ing machine; ~d wheat* (molded into biscuits for use as a breakfast food); ***n.:*** *not a ~* (i.e. bit) *of evidence;* **shred·der** *n.*

Shreve·port (SHREEV–) a city of N.W. Louisiana.

shrew *n.* **1** a bad-tempered scolding woman; **shrew·ish** *adj.* **2** a mouselike insect-eating mammal related to moles.

shrewd (SHROOD) *adj.* sharp and clever in practical matters: *a ~ businessman, observer, guess;* **shrewd·ly** *adv.;* **shrewd·ness** *n.*

shriek (SHREEK) *n.* & *v.* (utter) a sharp, shrill cry of sudden fear or other emotion; screech.

shrift *n. Archaic.* confession or shriving: *was given* SHORT SHRIFT.

shrike *n.* a usu. gray or brownish bird with a shrieking call, noted for its habit of impaling its prey on a thorn with its hooked beak before tearing it apart; also called "butcherbird."

shrill *adj.* of cries and such sounds, high-pitched and sharp, as of a cricket, whistle, etc.; ***v.*** utter with or make such a sound; **shril·ly** *adv.;* **shrill·ness** *n.*

shrimp *n.* a small shellfish related to crabs and lobsters, valued as sea food; also, *Informal.* a small insignificant person.

shrine *n.* **1** a place sacred to the memory of a venerated person. **2** a tomb or reliquary; ***v.*** **shrines, shrined, shrin·ing** enshrine.

shrink (SHRINGK) *v.* **shrinks,** *pt.* **shrank** or **shrunk,** *pp.* **shrunk** or **shrunk·en, shrink·ing** **1** contract in extent, scope, volume, etc., as fabrics when laundered: *~ing fortunes, influence; how to ~ wool* (i.e. make it shrink); **shrink·age** *n.* **2** draw back instinctively (*from* something unpleasant or frightening, as a dog from the whip). **—*n.*** *Slang.* a psychiatrist. —**shrinking violet** a shy or timid person.

shrive *v.* **shrives,** *pt.* **shrove** (SHROHV) or **shrived,** *pp.* **shriv·en** or **shrived, shriv·ing** hear the confession of, as a priest does.

shriv·el *v.* **-els, -el(l)ed, -el·(l)ing** dry up or wither into a wrinkled state, as a leaf or fruit from the heat of the sun.

shroud *n.* **1** (something that covers or veils, as) a burial cloth for a dead body. **2 shrouds** *pl.* the set of ropes supporting a ship's mast. **—v.** cover or hide: *a kidnaping ~ed in mystery.*

Shrove (SHROHV) **Tuesday** the last day before Lent; the eve of Ash Wednesday.

shrub *n.* a woody-stemmed plant smaller than a tree; bush; **shrub·by** *adj.* **—shrub·ber·y** *n.* **1** shrubs collectively. **2** *pl.* **shrub·ber·ies** a place planted with shrubs.

shrug *v.* **shrugs, shrugged, shrug·ging** raise (the shoulders) momentarily to show indifference, doubt, etc.; **shrug off** dismiss (something) as unimportant. **—n.** a shrugging gesture.

shrunk(en) See SHRINK.

shtg. shortage.

shtick *n. Slang.* a comic routine; also, a gimmicky thing or quality.

shuck *n.* a husk, pod, shell, or similar outer covering; also, something of little or no value: *not worth ~s;* **v.** remove the shucks of. **—shucks** *interj.* expressing disgust or disappointment.

shud·der *n.* & *v.* (experience) a sudden shaking or trembling of the body from horror, disgust, etc.: *I ~ to think what might have happened.*

shuf·fle (SHUFL) *v.* **shuf·fles, shuf·fled, shuf·fling** **1** walk or move in a dragging manner. **2** mix and rearrange (a deck of cards); also, disarrange (papers, etc.). **—n.** a shuffling of cards, shuffling movement, dance, action, etc. **—shuf·fle·board** *n.* a game played by pushing disks using a long cue over the scoring areas marked on a narrow, smooth-surfaced court.

shun *v.* **shuns, shunned, shun·ning** avoid (a person or thing) because of aversion or dislike: *a modest man who ~s publicity;* **shun·pike** *n. Informal.* a route taken to avoid a turnpike or expressway; **shun·pik·er** *n.;* **shun·pik·ing** *n.*

shunt *v.* move or turn off to one side; esp., switch (a train) from one track to another; **n.** a shunting; also, *Brit.* a railroad switch.

shush *interj.* & *v.* hush!

shut *v.* **shuts, shut, shut·ting** close so as to keep in or out: *Please ~ the door; Blinds ~ out light; a factory* **shut down** *by a strike; Turn the tap to* **shut off** *the water; people* **shut in** *by a snowstorm;* **shut up** *Informal.* stop talking. **—shut·down** *n.* a shutting down of a factory, usu. temporarily. **—shut·eye** *n. Slang.* sleep. **—shut-in** *n.* & *adj.* (one) confined indoors by illness. **—shut·out** *n.* (a victory resulting from) a preventing of the opposite side from scoring, as in baseball. **—shut·ter** *n.* one that shuts, as a hinged cover for a window or the opening-and-closing device of a camera aperture; **v.** furnish with a shutter or shutters; **shut·ter·bug** *n.* a photography enthusiast.

shut·tle *n.* & *v.* **shut·tles, shut·tled, shut·tling** (something designed) to move back and forth over a course, as the needlelike device carrying threads from side to side in a loom or a vehicle carrying passengers back and forth over a route; **shut·tle·cock** *n.* a light, feathered object, or "bird," that is hit back and forth in badminton.

shy *adj.* **shy·er** or **shi·er, shy·est** or **shi·est** reserved or timid in manner; bashful: *feels ~ to undress in public;* **shy (of)** short (of): *$100 ~ of the target figure.* **—v. shies, shied, shy·ing** **1** shrink or draw back, esp. suddenly, as a horse startled by something in its way. **2** fling (a stone, stick, etc.) sideways at a target. **—shy·ly** *adv.;* **shy·ness** *n.*

shy·lock *n.* a hardhearted moneylender.

shy·ster *n. Informal.* a professional, esp. a lawyer, who uses tricky methods.

Si silicon **—SI** the MKS or metric system of units. **—S.I.** Staten Island.

Si·am (sye·AM) former name of THAILAND; **Si·a·mese** (–MEEZ) *n.* & *adj., sing.* & *pl.* Thai; **Siamese twins** twins born joined together.

Si·ber·i·a (sye·BEER·ee·uh) the cold and isolated N. Asian part of the U.S.S.R.; **Si·be·ri·an** *n.* & *adj.*

sib·i·lant (–lunt) *n.* & *adj.* (a sound such as "s," "sh," "z," or "zh") that has a hissing quality.

sib·ling *n.* a fellow offspring, esp. a brother or sister.

sib·yl (SIBL) *n.* a prophetess of the ancient Greeks and Romans; **sib·yl·line** (–line, –leen) *adj.*

[1]sic *adv. Latin.* thus [used within square brackets to confirm that something that seems questionable, as a spelling error, is faithfully reproduced].

[2]sic *v.* **sics, sicked, sick·ing** incite (a dog) to attack: *She ~d Tiger on the burglar; ~ him, Tiger!*

Sic·i·ly (SIS·uh·lee) an island off the S. tip of Italy; **Si·cil·i·an** (–SIL–) *n.* & *adj.*

[1]sick same as [2]SIC.

[2]sick *adj.* ill; suffering from something bodily or mental: *You look ~; worried ~ about her child; ~ and tired of* (i.e. quite fed up with) *her nagging; ~ at* (or *to*) *his stomach* (i.e. nauseated); *a ~* (i.e. morbid or macabre) *joke; ~* (i.e. longing) *for home; a ~* (i.e. migraine) *headache; Nurses care for* **the sick** (people); **sick·ish** *adj.* **—sick bay** part of a ship used as a hospital. **—sick·bed** *n.* a sick person's bed. **—sick·en** *v.* make or become sick: *~ed and died;* **sick·en·ing** *adj.;* **sick·en·ing·ly** *adv.*

sick·le *n.* a short-handled mowing tool with a curved blade. **—sick·le-cell anemia** a hereditary blood disorder found in people of African origin in which red blood cells change to a sickle shape.

sick·ly *adj.* **-li·er, -li·est** **1** of or having to do with sickness: *a ~ complexion.* **2** frequently sick: *a ~ child.* **—sick·ness** *n.* illness, esp. nausea; also, a particular disease. **—sick-out**

n. the labor tactic of claiming illness as a group, esp. when unable to strike. **—sick·room** *n.* a sick person's room.

side *n.* **1** a boundary surface or line, away from the center, esp. of something considered as not having a front or back: *the four ~s of a square; the two ~s of a street; the ~ of a mountain.* **2** the left or right of something having a front, back, etc.: *the passenger ~ of a car; the ~ door of a house; seated* **side by side** (i.e. next to each other); *She seemed to* **split her sides** *with laughter;* **on the side** in addition to the regular or main thing. **3** a group or party in relation to another: *the opposing ~s of a dispute; the losing ~; Referees shouldn't* **take sides** (i.e. favor one side). **4** either surface of something flat or considered as having only two sides: *the two ~s of a leaf; the dark ~ of the moon; the windward ~.* **—adj.:** *a ~* (i.e. not main) *street, view; a ~* (i.e. not main or central) *issue.* **—v. sides, sid·ed, sid·ing** furnish with sides; **side against** (or **with**) oppose (or favor). **—side·arm** *adj.* & *adv.* of a throw or stroke, not overhand or underhand but made with the arm relatively parallel to the ground; **side arm** a sword, pistol, or other weapon worn at the waist. **—side·board** *n.* a low cabinet that holds dining accessories, its top being used as a side table. **—side·burns** *n.pl.* hair grown down the sides of a man's face. **—side·car** *n.* a small car attached to the side of a motorcycle. **—side dish** a dish of food served along with the main course. **—side effect** a usu. adverse secondary effect or reaction, esp. of a drug. **—side·kick** *n. Slang.* a pal or partner. **—side·light** *n.* incidental bit of information that helps to understand a subject or character. **—side·line** *n.* **1** the side boundary of a playing field or court. **2** a business carried on in addition to one's main business or job. **—side·long** *adj.* & *adv.* (directed) to one side: *a ~ glance.* **—side·man** *n.* **-men** a supporting player, esp. in a jazz band. **—side·piece** *n.* a piece that forms the side of something.

si·de·re·al (sye·DEER·ee·ul) *adj.* of or having to do with the stars: *Astronomers use* **sidereal time** *based on the earth's rotation in reference to the stars.*

sid·er·ite (SID·uh–) *n.* a carbonate ore of iron; also, a meteorite that is mostly iron.

side·sad·dle *n.* & *adv.* (a saddle designed to be used) with both legs of the rider on the same side of the animal. **—side·show** *n.* a small show, as of a circus, that is not part of the main show. **—side·slip** *n.* a sideways slip or skid. **—side·split·ting** *adj.* extremely funny. **—side·step** *v.* **-steps, -stepped, -step·ping** step aside; also, dodge or avoid (a blow, responsibility, etc.) by stepping aside. **—side·stroke** *n.* a swimming stroke executed on the side in combination with a scissors kick. **—side·swipe** *n.* & *v.* **-swipes, -swiped, -swip·ing** (give) a glancing blow or hit. **—side·track** *v.* **1** switch (a train) to a railroad siding; ***n.*** such a siding. **2** distract (someone) or turn aside from the main issue. **—side·walk** *n.* a usu. paved walkway at the side of a street. **—side·wall** *n.* the side of a tire. **—side·ways** *adj.* & *adv.* using a side; also, with a side forward; also **side·wise.** **—side·wind·er** (–wine·dur) *n.* a rattlesnake of S.W. United States and Mexico that moves with sideways loops. **—sid·ing** *n.* **1** boards or shingles covering the outside of a frame house. **2** a short railroad track branching from a main one. **—si·dle** (SYE–) *v.* **-dles, -dled, -dling** move sideways.

SIDS sudden infant death syndrome.

siege (SEEJ) *n.* a surrounding of a place, as a fortress, to force it to surrender; also, the condition of being threatened (as if) from all sides, as by an illness; **lay siege to** besiege.

si·er·ra (see·ER·uh) *n.* a range of mountains with a jagged outline of peaks. **—Sierra Le·one** (–lee·OHN) a W. African republic; 27,-699 sq.mi. (71,740 km²); *cap.* Freetown.

si·es·ta (see·ES·tuh) *n.* a midday nap.

sieve (SIV) *n.* a utensil with holes for straining out the large particles of a mixture or the solid parts of a liquid. **—sift** *v.* pass (as) through a sieve: *~ed flour; to ~* (i.e. carefully examine) *evidence;* **sift·er** *n.*

sig. signal; signature. **—Sig.** Signor; Signore.

sigh (SYE) *n.* & *v.* (make) a long, deep breathing sound, as in relief, sadness, etc.: *breathed a ~ of relief; a lover ~ing* (i.e. yearning) *for his beloved.*

sight (SITE) *n.* **1** the act, power, or range of seeing: *lost his ~ in an accident; came within ~ of land.* **2** something seen: *a lovely ~! the* (interesting) *~s of a city; She's quite a ~* (i.e. looks odd) *in that hat.* **3** a seeing device: *a telescopic ~; a marksman taking a ~* (i.e. aim) *before firing.* **—v.** see or take aim, esp. by use of a seeing device. **—at** (or **on**) **sight** as soon as seen. **—catch sight of** see. **—know by sight** be able to recognize upon seeing. **—not by a long sight** probably not; also, not at all. **—sight unseen** without seeing in advance. **—sight·ed** *adj.* & *comb.form.* having sight (as specified): *a ~ firearm; clear-~;* **sight·less** *adj.* **—sight·ly** *adj.* **-li·er, -li·est** pleasant-looking; **sight·li·ness** *n.* **—sight reading** the skill of performing written music, of reading something in a foreign language, etc. without previous preparation; hence **sight-read** (–reed) *v.* **-reads, -read** (–red), **-read·ing.** **—sight·see·ing** *n.* the visiting of places of interest, as a tourist or other **sight·se·er** (–see·ur) *n.*

sig·ma (SIG·muh) *n.* the 18th letter of the Greek alphabet (Σ, σ, ς).

sign (SINE) *n.* **1** a mark, symbol, gesture, etc. that means or stands for something: *a multiplication ~; dollar ~; ~s of the zodiac; the ~ language of deaf-mutes; a no-parking ~* (i.e. signboard). **2** evidence or indication: *Breathing is* *a ~ of life; ~s of forced entry.* **—v.** to write one's name or signature on (a document); hence, agree legally (to a contract): *authors who* **sign away** *their rights for small payments; A broadcasting station* **signs on** *in the morning and* **signs off** *at the end of the day; a drive to* **sign up** (i.e. enlist) *new members;* **sign·er** *n.* **—sig·nal** (–nl) *n.* **1** a sign with an agreed-on meaning, used to warn, inform, etc.: *a traffic ~; a smoke ~; "SOS" and "Mayday" are distress ~s;* **v. -nals, -nal(l)ed, -nal·(l)ing** give warning, notice, etc. to (someone) by a signal or signals; hence, communicate: *The siren ~d the end of the emergency.* **2** an electrical or electromagnetic transmission that conveys a message, as in telegraphy, radio, and television. **—adj.** remarkable or notable: *a ~ achievement, defeat, discovery;* **sig·nal·ly** *adv.* **—sig·nal·ize** *v.* **-iz·es, -ized, -iz·ing** make remarkable or distinguished: *a year ~d by conquests in space;* **sig·nal·i·za·tion** (–ZAY–) *n.;* **sig·nal·man** *n.* **-men** one who signals or works with signals. **—sig·na·to·ry** (SIG·nuh–) *n.* **-ries** one who has signed (a document) together with others: *~s to the Geneva Convention;* **adj.:** *the ~ nations.* **—sig·na·ture** (SIG·nuh·chur) *n.* **1** an identifying mark, esp. one's name written by oneself. **2** a musical sign placed after the clef to indicate the key or the time, as "3/4." **3** in broadcasting, a musical or visual device used to identify a program, performer, etc. **—sign·board** *n.* a board displaying a notice, sign, etc. **—sig·net** *n.* a small seal, as on a **signet ring** worn on a finger. **—sig·nif·i·cance** (–NIF–) *n.* what is signified, esp. meaning in regard to its suggestiveness, importance, etc.: *a message with a special ~; an event of great ~ in his career.* **—sig·nif·i·cant** *adj.* **1** having a special meaning: *a ~ wink.* **2** important: *the ~ events of the war;* **sig·nif·i·cant·ly** *adv.* **—sig·ni·fi·ca·tion** (–CAY–) *n.* **—sig·ni·fy** *v.* **-fies, -fied, -fy·ing** **1** be a sign of; mean: *A nod ~s agreement.* **2** show by means of a sign. **3** be of consequence or importance. **—sign of the cross** a cross traced on one's person with the hand or fingers. **—sign of the zodiac** one of the 12 equal parts into which the zodiac is divided, each bearing the name of a constellation.

si·gnor (see·NYOR) *n., pl.* **-gno·ri** (–NYOR·ee) *Italian.* a gentleman; [as a title] Mr. **—si·gno·ra** (see·NYOR·ah) *n., pl.* **-re** (–ay) *Italian.* a married woman; [as a title] Mrs. or Madam. **—si·gno·re** (see·NYOR·ay) *n., pl.* **-ri** (–ee) *Italian.* a gentleman; [as a title in direct address] Sir. **—si·gno·ri·na** (see·nyuh·REE·nuh) *n., pl.* **-ne** (–nay) *Italian.* a young lady; [as a title] Miss.

sign·post *n.* a post having a sign on it.

Sikh (SEEK) *n.* & *adj.* (member) of a religion of India combining Hindu and Moslem elements, founded by Guru Nanak (1469–1538); **Sikh·ism** *n.*

Sik·kim a former Himalayan kingdom, an Indian state since 1975.

si·lage (SYE·lij) *n.* slightly fermented green fodder preserved in a silo.

sild *n.* Norwegian canned herring.

si·lence (SYE·lunce) *n.* a keeping still or quiet; hence, absence of any sound or communication: *the ~ of the night; "~ gives consent";* **interj.** Quiet! **—v. -lenc·es, -lenced, -lenc·ing** make silent; also, repress (free speech) or stop (as enemy guns) from firing; **si·lenc·er** *n.* a muffling device used on a gun. **—si·lent** (SYE–) *adj.* still; quiet; also, not talkative; not active: *the ~ atmosphere of a library; the* **silent majority** *of people not actively involved in politics; the ~* (i.e. not pronounced) *"n" of "hymn";* **silent partner** one who helps finance a business without helping to run it; **si·lent·ly** *adv.*

sil·hou·ette (sil·oo·ET) *n.* & *v.* **-ettes, -et·ted, -et·ting** (show in) a solid outline, as of something seen against a light: *a profile in ~* (i.e. solid black on white or the reverse); *a building ~d against the sky.*

sil·i·ca (SIL·i·cuh) *n.* silicon dioxide occurring as quartz, chalcedony, opal, and other minerals and forming about 60% of the earth's crust; **si·li·ceous** (–LISH·us) *adj.* **—sil·i·cate** *n.* a mineral such as mica, asbestos, or feldspar that is a compound of silicon, oxygen, and a metal. **—sil·i·con** *n.* a metalloid that is the most abundant element in the earth's crust next to oxygen and is found in granite, sand, clay, etc. **—sil·i·cone** *n.* an organic silicon compound much used commercially in the form of fluids, resins, and varnishes. **—sil·i·co·sis** (–COH–) *n.* a lung disease caused by prolonged inhaling of silica dust.

silk *n.* a strong, shiny fiber produced by silkworms for cocoons; also, the thread or fabric made from it; **silk·en** or **silk·y** *adj.* **silk·i·er, -i·est.** **—silk screen** a method of printing with stencils of silk or similar material; **silk-screen** *v.* **—silk·worm** *n.* a caterpillar that spins a cocoon of silk, esp. a larva that is raised on mulberry leaves.

sill *n.* **1** a horizontal supporting part or structure, as at the bottom of a door, window, or outside wall. **2** a sheet of igneous rock formed by magma forcing its way between sedimentary rock layers.

sil·ly *adj.* **sil·li·er, sil·li·est** lacking in common sense or judgment; stupid or trivial; **sil·ly** or **sil·li·ly** *adv.;* **sil·li·ness** *n.*

si·lo (SYE–) *n.* **-los** **1** a usu. upright cylindrical tower for storing green fodder; also, a trench, bunker, or box for the same purpose. **2** an underground installation for launching guided missiles.

silt *n.* fine-grained waterborne sediment, as at the bottom of rivers; **v.** obstruct or fill (up) with silt; **silt·a·tion** (–TAY–) *n.;* **silt·y** *adj.* **—silt·stone** *n.* silt hardened as rock.

Si·lu·ri·an (–LOOR–) *n.* & *adj.* (of) the third period of the Paleozoic era of the earth, beginning about 435 million years ago.

sil·ver *n.* a white precious metal used for coins, jewelry, and table utensils, esp. spoons and dishes; hence, money or tableware of silver; also, a lustrous grayish white; ***v.*** cover or plate with silver. —***adj.*** of or plated with silver; also **sil·ver·y.** —**silver bromide, silver chloride, silver iodide, silver nitrate** light-sensitive silver compounds used in photography. —**sil·ver·fish** *n.* a small, silver-colored, wingless insect that eats materials containing starch or glue. —**silver lining** the brighter side of an otherwise depressing situation. —**silver maple** a North American maple whose leaves are silvery white underneath. —**sil·ver·smith** *n.* a craftsman of silver articles. —**sil·ver·ware** *n.* silver or metal tableware.

sim·i·an (SIM·ee·un) *n.* & *adj.* (of) an ape or monkey.

sim·i·lar (SIM·uh·lur) *adj.* nearly alike; of the same kind: *Twins are quite ~ to each other;* **sim·i·lar·ly** *adv.;* **sim·i·lar·i·ty** (–LAIR–) *n.* **-ties** (a point of) likeness. —**sim·i·le** (–uh·lee) *n.* a figure of speech expressing a comparison using *like* or *as,* e.g. "flowing like a river." —**si·mil·i·tude** (–MIL–) *n.* resemblance; also, a comparison.

sim·mer *v.* keep or remain just below the boiling point; hence, be on the point of breaking out, as with anger, laughter, etc.; **simmer down** calm down. —***n.*** a simmering.

si·mo·nize (SYE·muh–) *v.* **-niz·es, -nized, -niz·ing** clean and polish (an automobile, etc.) with wax.

si·mon-pure (SYE·mun–) *adj.* unquestionably authentic or untainted; genuine. —**si·mo·ny** (SYE·muh·nee, SIM–) *n.* the buying or selling of spiritual things, esp. church appointments.

sim·pa·ti·co (–PAH·ti–) *adj.* compatible or likable.

sim·per *n.* a silly or affected smile; ***v.*** smirk.

sim·ple *adj.* **-pler, -plest 1** not complicated or having many parts, frills, etc.: *~ substances and compounds;* **simple interest** *based on the principal amount; a* **simple sentence** *with one clause; ~* (i.e. elementary) *facts; ~* (i.e. plain) *English, truth, food.* **2** of people, unaffected, sincere, or innocent: *a ~ child, soul; not so ~* (i.e. inexperienced) *as to believe everything she hears.* **3** common or lowly: *~ peasant folk.* —***n.*** **1** one who is simple-minded. **2** *Archaic.* a medicinal herb. —**sim·ple-mind·ed** *adj.* inexperienced or stupid; **sim·ple·ton** (–tun) *n.* a fool. —**sim·plic·i·ty** (–PLIS–) *n.* **-ties 1** the state of being simple: *a manner full of ~ and candor; the ~ of her costume; The explanation is ~ itself.* **2** something that is simple: *the ~s* (i.e. basic truths) *of our existence.* —**sim·pli·fy** *v.* **-fies, -fied, -fy·ing** make simple(r); **sim·pli·fi·ca·tion** (–CAY–) *n.* —**sim·plis·tic** (–PLIS–) *adj.* excessively simple; oversimplified: *a ~ explanation, theory;* **sim·plis·ti·cal·ly** *adv.* —**sim·ply** (–plee) *adv.* **1** in a simple manner: *came ~ dressed.* **2** absolutely: *It's ~ wonderful!*

sim·u·late (–YOO–) *v.* **-lates, -lat·ed, -lat·ing** look or act like having or being (something that one is not): *lay still ~ing death; a ~d moon landing by use of models;* **sim·u·la·tor** *n.;* **sim·u·la·tion** (–LAY–) *n.*

si·mul·cast (SYE–) *v.* **-casts,** *pt.* & *pp.* **-cast** or **-cast·ed, -cast·ing** broadcast simultaneously, as over radio and television; ***n.*** such a transmission. —**si·mul·ta·ne·ous** (–TAY·nee·us) *adj.* done or happening at the same time; **si·mul·ta·ne·ous·ly** *adv.*

sin *n.* & *v.* **sins, sinned, sin·ning** (commit) an offense against God, as by breaking a religious or moral law: *Murder is a crime and a ~;* **living in sin** (i.e. adultery) *with various mistresses;* **sin·ful** *adj.;* **sin·ful·ly** *adv.;* **sin·ful·ness** *n.;* **sin·ner** *n.*

Si·nai (SYE·nye), **Mount.** in the Bible, a mountain on which God gave the law to Moses.

since *adv.* & *prep.* from the time mentioned or implied till now: *They fought once but have been friends ever ~; in business ~ 1920.* —***conj.:*** *had no trouble ~ we came to this city; left early ~* (i.e. because) *he didn't want to be late.*

sin·cere (–SEER) *adj.* **-cer·er, -cer·est** of people or their feelings, desires, etc., without deceit; genuine: *a ~ friend; ~ sympathy;* **sin·cere·ly** *adv.;* **sin·cer·i·ty** (–SER–) *n.*

si·ne·cure (SYE·nuh, SIN·uh–) *n.* a position that provides an income without much work or responsibility.

si·ne di·e (SYE·nee·DYE·ee) without a further date being fixed: *adjourned ~.* —**sine qua non** (–kway·NON) an essential condition or prerequisite.

sin·ew *n.* a tendon; hence, muscular power; **sin·ew·y** *adj.*

sing. singular.

sing *v.* **sings,** *pt.* **sang** or **sung,** *pp.* **sung, sing·ing** make pleasant sounds with the voice; utter or tell (something) musically, in verse, etc.: *children ~ing songs; Birds sang in the trees; sang her child to sleep; always ~ing the praises of his children; The poet sang of heaven; while bullets sang* (i.e. whistled) *past us; was murdered before he could ~* (*Slang.* squeal; tell the police); **sing·er** *n.*

Sin·ga·pore (SING·guh–) an island republic at the S. end of the Malay Peninsula; 224 sq.mi. (581 km²); *cap.* **Singapore.**

singe (SINJ) *v.* **sing·es, singed, singe·ing** scorch or burn superficially; also, burn hair, feathers, etc. from; ***n.*** a slight burn.

Sin·gha·lese (sing·guh·LEEZ) same as SINHALESE.

sin·gle (SING·gl) *adj.* one only; not combined or associated with another: *Bachelors are ~ men, not married; a ~ room in a hotel; refused without a ~ reason; Tom and Jerry in ~ combat; ~* (i.e.

without duplicity) *devotion, heart;* ***n.*** **1** a single person or thing: *a bar patronized by* **singles** (i.e. unmarried people). **2 singles** *pl.* a match with one player on either side. **3** a baseball hit that allows the batter to reach first base only. ***—v.*** **-gles, -gled, -gling 1** select (a person *out* of a group). **2** hit a single (baseball hit). **—sin·gle-breast·ed** *adj.* of coats, etc., not double-breasted. **—single file** a line or column of persons or things coming one behind another; also ***adv.:*** *marched* ~. **—sin·gle-hand·ed** *adj.* & *adv.* involving or using only one hand or person; **sin·gle-hand·ed·ly** *adv.* **—sin·gle-mind·ed** *adj.* having only one aim; hence, honest or straightforward. **—sin·gle·ton** (–tun) *n.* something occurring alone, esp. a single card of a suit in a player's hand. **—sin·gle-track** *adj.* one-track; hence, limited in scope. **—sin·gle·tree** *n.* the crossbar to which the traces of a harness are attached. **—sin·gly** (–glee) *adv.* alone; individually.

sing·song *n.* & *adj.* (rising and falling in) an unvarying speech rhythm or tone.

sin·gu·lar (SING·gyuh·lur) *adj.* **1** standing apart from others because strange, extraordinary, unique, etc.: *a woman of* ~ *beauty.* **2** in grammar, referring to one person: *"Deer" is* ~ *and plural;* ***n.*** the singular number or a singular form. **—sin·gu·lar·ly** *adv.* **—sin·gu·lar·i·ty** (–LAIR–) *n.*

Sin·ha·lese (sin·huh·LEEZ) *adj.* of Sri Lanka, its major group of people, or their language; ***n.*** *sing.* & *pl.* a member of the major ethnic group of Sri Lanka; also, the Indic language spoken by this group.

sin·is·ter *adj.* of people, appearances, looks, etc., suggestive of ill will, threatening evil or danger, etc.: *a* ~ *plot, smile, motive.*

sink (SINGK) *v.* **sinks,** *pt.* **sank** or **sunk,** *pp.* **sunk, sink·ing** (make) go down or lower, as under water: *to swim or float without* ~*ing; The boat sprang a leak and sank; was not sunk by torpedoes; The sun* ~*s in the west; sank into the chair too tired to stand up; Her heart sank on hearing the sad news; an example so telling it sank into our minds.* ***—n.*** **1** a basin with a drain leading from it; also, a drain or sewer; hence, place of filth or corruption. **2** a sunken land area in which water collects. **3** also **sink·hole,** a depression in a limestone or karst region through which water enters the ground. **—sink·a·ble** *adj.* **—sink·er** *n.* one that sinks or a weight for sinking. **—sinking fund** a fund accumulated for the paying off of a usu. public debt.

Si·no- (SYE–, SIN·oh) *comb.form.* Chinese: as in *Sino-Soviet;* **Si·nol·o·gy** (–NOL–) *n.* study of Chinese culture.

sin·ter *v.* of particles, fuse together into a mass without melting; ***n.*** a mineral deposit or other substance produced by sintering.

sin·u·ous (SIN·yoo·us) *adj.* **1** of a path or movement, curved or winding; serpentine. **2** devious or crooked. **—sin·u·ous·ly** *adv.;* **sin·u·os·i·ty** (–OS–) *n.* **—si·nus** (SYE–) *n.* a curved hollow or cavity, esp. any of the four groups of hollows in the skull that are connected to the nasal cavity; **si·nus·i·tis** (–SYE–) *n.* inflammation of the sinuses, as during a head cold or because of allergies.

Sioux (SOO) *n.* & *adj.* same as DAKOTA; **Siou·an** (SOO·un) *adj.*

sip *v.* **sips, sipped, sip·ping** drink little by little from a container; ***n.*** a sipping or a sipped amount; **sip·per** *n.*

si·phon (SYE·fun) *n.* **1** a bent-tube device through which a liquid may be drawn up by air pressure and down over a barrier; ***v.:*** *Gasoline was* ~*ed out of the gas tank.* **2** also **siphon bottle,** a bottle from which soda water may be drawn by the pressure of the gas inside.

sir *n.* [a formal term used to address a man, usu. in respect]: *Dear Sir; Your name, Sir?* [as a title] *Sir John (Smith).* **—sire** *n.* **1** *Archaic.* forefather; [as a title of respect] Lord. **2** the male parent of an animal; ***v.*** **sires, sired, sir·ing** beget.

si·ren (SYE–) *n.* **1** a device for producing a wailing sound signal, usu. in warning, as in a fire truck or ambulance. **2** in Greek myth, a sea nymph who would lure sailors to their destruction with her enchanting song; hence, an enchantress.

sir·loin *n.* a choice cut of beef from the loin in front of the rump.

si·roc·co (suh·ROC·oh) *n.* **-roc·cos** a hot desert wind blowing from N. Africa across the Mediterranean into S. Italy.

sir·(r)ee (suh·REE) *interj.* [used after "Yes" or "No" for emphasis] Sir!

sir·up (SEER–, SUR–) *n.* same as SYRUP.

sis *n.* *Informal* [used as a form of address in speech] sister.

si·sal (SYE·sl) *n.* a strong fiber produced by two agave plants with swordlike leaves.

sis·sy (SIS·ee) *n.* **sis·sies** *Informal.* an effeminate or timid boy or man; **sis·si·fied** *adj.* like a sissy. **—sis·ter** *n.* **1** a female offspring of the same parents as one; also, a half sister, a female fellow-member of a closely knit group, etc. **2** a nun; also, a nurse. **—sis·ter·hood** *n.* **—sis·ter-in-law** *n.* **sis·ters-** the sister of one's spouse, wife of one's brother, or wife of one's spouse's brother. **—sis·ter·ly** *adj.*

Sis·y·phus (SIS·uh–) in Greek myth, a king of Corinth condemned in Hades to roll a heavy stone up a steep hill forever.

sit *v.* **sits, sat, sit·ting 1** rest on one's buttocks, as on a chair, in a stable or relaxed condition: *too busy to* **sit down** *for meals;* **sit in (on)** participate (in); **sit on** participate as a member of (a committee, jury, etc.); **sit up** be in a wakeful or alert condition. **2** occupy a place or remain in a position: *a book* ~*ing on a shelf; to* ~ *for a portrait; A hen* ~*s on its eggs (until they are hatched); The coat doesn't* ~ *well on* (i.e. suit) *you;*

The court ~*s* (i.e. is in session) *all day; She* ~*s* (i.e. baby-sits) *for busy housewives; He sat* (i.e. seated) *the young rider on the horse.* —**sit·ter** *n.*
si·tar (si·TAR) *n.* a lutelike instrument of India with six or seven strings on movable frets and up to 20 sympathetic strings that are not plucked.
sit·com *n. Informal.* situation comedy.
sit-down *n.* a strike or demonstration in which the participants occupy a place till their demands are met.
site *n.* location of an activity, structure, etc.
sit-in *n.* a sit-down in a public place. —**sitting** *n.* a session. —**sitting duck** *Informal.* an easy target or victim.
sit·u·ate (SICH·oo–) *v.* **-ates, -at·ed, -at·ing** put in a place; locate. —**sit·u·at·ed** *adj.* **1** located. **2** of people, financially (*well, badly,* etc.) off. —**sit·u·a·tion** (–AY–) *n.* **1** location or site. **2** state of affairs or condition. **3** employment; position: ~ *wanted, vacant.* —**situation comedy** a light play or comedy, esp. as a radio or television series, involving a set of characters in various episodes. —**sit·u·a·tion·al** *adj.*
sit-up *n.* an exercise involving sitting up and lying back using the arms for support. —**sitz bath** a bath taken seated in hot water up to the hips.
Si·va (SEE·vuh) one of the three chief Hindu gods.
six *n., adj. & pron.* one more than five; the number 6 or VI: ~ *boys;* ~ *of them;* **at sixes and sevens** in confusion or disagreement; **sixth** *n. & adj.* —**six-gun** *n.* a six-shooter. —**six-pack** *n.* a package of six (cans, bottles, etc.). —**six·pence** *n.* a British coin worth six pence; **six·pen·ny** *adj.* —**six-shoot·er** *n. Informal.* a six-chambered revolver. —**six·teen** (–TEEN) *n., adj. & pron.* six more than 10; 16 or XVI; **six·teenth** *n. & adj.* —**sixth sense** power of intuition. —**six·ty** *n., adj. & pron.* **-ties** six times ten; 60 or LX; **the sixties** the 10 numbers, years, etc. from 60 through 69; **six·ti·eth** (–ith) *n. & adj.*
siz(e)·a·ble (SYE·zuh–) *adj.* fairly large or bulky; **siz(e)·a·bly** *adv.* —**size** *n.* **1** relative bigness, esp. as measured by length, width, etc.: *hats of all* ~*s;* ~ (i.e. classification) *8 shoes.* **2** a material such as starch, gelatin, or wax added to paper or cloth to impart qualities of smoothness, stiffness, luster, etc.; also **siz·ing.** —***v.*** **siz·es, sized, siz·ing** **1** arrange in sizes. **2** treat (paper, cloth, etc.) with size. —**size up** *Informal.* **1** meet requirements. **2** assess (a person, situation, problem, etc.). —**-size(d)** *comb.form.* of (a specified) size: *a large-*~ *kitchen; a life-*~ *statue.*
siz·zle (SIZL) *n. & v.* **siz·zles, siz·zled, siz·zling** (burn or fry with) a hissing sound, as fat; hence, be very hot; **siz·zler** *n. Informal.* a hot day.
S.J. Society of Jesus.
skate *n.* **1** a flat marine fish of the ray group with winglike spreading fins on the sides of its body and a slender tail. **2** (a shoe fitted with) a metal runner for gliding on ice; ice skate; also, a roller skate; ***v.*** **skates, skat·ed, skat·ing** move along on skates; **skat·er** *n.* —**skate·board** *n.* a narrow oblong board with rollers at each end for riding on hard surfaces; **skate·board·ing** *n.*
ske·dad·dle (ski·DADL) *v.* **-dad·dles, -dad·dled, -dad·dling** *Informal.* run away; scoot.
skeet *n.* trapshooting using clay pigeons that are sprung into the air from two target houses.
skein (SKAIN) *n.* a loosely twisted coil of thread or yarn.
skel·e·ton (–tun) *n.* the framework of bones in an animal's body; hence, any framework, outline, or essential part: *the* ~ *of a novel; working with a* ~ *staff;* **skeleton key** one designed to open many locks; **skel·e·tal** *adj.*
skep·tic *n.* one who questions generally accepted beliefs, esp. religious doctrines; also, an adherent of skepticism; **skep·ti·cal** *adj.;* **skep·ti·cal·ly** *adv.* —**skep·ti·cism** *n.* **1** the philosophical theory that reality is unknowable. **2** a questioning attitude; also, religious unbelief.
sketch *n. & v.* (make) a rough outline or drawing; also, a short, light, prose narrative or essay; **sketch·y** *adj.* **sketch·i·er, -i·est** hastily done or incomplete like a sketch; **sketch·i·ly** *adv.*
skew *n. & adj.* (having) a slant or twist; ***v.*** swerve; slant.
skew·er *n. & v.* (fasten or pierce with) a long pin to hold meat being roasted or broiled.
ski (SKEE) *v.* **skis, skied, ski·ing** glide on snow using long, flat runners attached to the shoes; ***n.*** such a runner; **ski·er** *n.* —**ski·bob** *n.* a bicyclelike vehicle with skis instead of wheels for use on snow-covered slopes.
skid *v.* **skids, skid·ded, skid·ding** slide on a slippery surface, as the wheels of a car, without gripping the road surface. —***n.*** **1** a skidding. **2** a runner that enables an aircraft to skid along while landing; also, a sliding wedge used as a braking device. **3** a track for sliding or rolling a heavy object. **4** a low platform or pallet for holding loads. —**skid·dy** *adj.* **skid·di·er, skid·di·est** slippery. —**on the skids** *Slang.* headed for failure or ruin. —**skid row** the slum section of a city frequented by society's derelicts.
skiff *n.* a small rowboat or sailing ship.
skil·ful same as SKILLFUL.
ski lift a cable system for carrying skiers up a slope.
skill *n.* ability or expertness gained by training and practice, as in languages, diving, or carpentry; hence, an art or craft: *typing and such office* ~*s;* **skilled** *adj.* having or showing skill (*in* something): *a* ~ *workman, job.*
skil·let (–it) *n.* a frying pan.

skil(l)·ful *adj.* having skill; expert; also, done with skill: *a ~ job;* **skil(l)·ful·ly** *adv.;* **skil(l)·ful·ness** *n.*

skim *v.* **skims, skimmed, skim·ming** **1** go lightly over (milk and remove cream, over waves, as gulls and such sea birds, over ice, as a skater, or through reading matter, a book, etc. picking up essential facts). **2** send skimming; skip, as a flat stone over water. —**skim(med) milk** milk with the cream removed. —**skim·mer** *n.* —**skim·ming** *n.* **1** what is skimmed off. **2** the practice of evading tax on gambling profits.

skimp *v. Informal.* scrimp; **skimp·y** *adj.* **skimp·i·er, -i·est** scanty; not ample: *a ~ dress;* **skimp·i·ly** *adv.*

skin *n.* the outer layer of tissue covering an animal's body; hide or pelt; also, something resembling it, as the rind of a fruit, casing of a sausage, etc.; **save one's skin** save oneself; escape unhurt. —***v.*** **skins, skinned, skin·ning** remove the skin of; hence, *Informal.* cheat or swindle; **skin·less** *adj.* —**skin diving** underwater diving by a swimmer equipped with a scuba or other breathing apparatus; **skin-dive** *v.* **-dives, -dived, -div·ing; skin diver.** —**skin·flick** *n. Informal.* a pornographic motion picture.—**skin·flint** *n.* a mean and stingy person. —**skin-graft** *n.* a piece of skin transplanted from another area. —**-skinned** (SKIND) *comb.form.* having skin of a specified kind: as in *dark-~, thick-~.* —**skin·ny** *adj.* **skin·ni·er, skin·ni·est** [unfavorable] lean or thin-looking; **skin·ni·ness** *n.* —**skin·ny-dip** *n.* & *v.* **-dips, -dipped, -dip·ping** *Informal.* (have) a swim in the nude. —**skin·tight** *adj.* tight-fitting.

skip *n.* & *v.* **skips, skipped, skip·ping** (make) a light and quick leap or series of leaps, as a young lamb or child frisking about: *a girl ~ing rope* (held in the hands and revolved under the feet and over the head); *likes to ~ flat stones on the lake; made such progress she was allowed to ~* (i.e. bypass) *a grade; used to ~* (i.e. not attend) *school on flimsy excuses; a ~ing TV picture.*

skip·per *n.* master of a ship.

skir·mish *n.* & *v.* (take part in) a minor engagement or encounter, as between two small groups of soldiers.

skirt *n.* (part of) a garment that hangs from the waist, esp. a woman's outer garment; hence, *Slang.* a woman or girl; ***v.*** form, be, or pass along the border or edge of: *a path ~ing (along) the lake.*

ski run a slope or runway for skiing.

skit *n.* a short, humorous dramatic sketch.

ski touring cross-country skiing. —**ski tow** a cable system for pulling skiers up a slope.

skit·tish *adj.* **1** of a horse, excitable or jumpy. **2** too lively or fickle.

skiv·vy (SKIV·ee) *n.,* usu. **skiv·vies** *pl. Slang.* men's underwear.

ski·wear (SKEE–) *n.* clothes to wear while skiing.

skoal (SKOLE) *interj.* [a toast] to your health!

Skt. Sanskrit.

skul(l)·dug·ger·y (–DUG–) *n. Informal.* trickery.

skulk *v.* move stealthily; sneak or lurk; **skulk·er** *n.*

skull *n.* the bony case enclosing the brain; also, head or mind; **skull·cap** *n.* a close-fitting brimless cap, as a yarmulke.

skunk *n.* **1** a small furry animal of the weasel family, with black and white markings, noted for the evil-smelling liquid it squirts if molested. **2** *Informal.* a despised person. —***v.*** *Slang.* defeat utterly. —**skunk cabbage** a plant of the arum family that gives off an offensive odor.

sky *n.* **skies** the usu. blue upper region of clouds, heavenly bodies, and celestial phenomena; hence, heaven. —**sky·cap** *n.* a porter at an air terminal. —**sky·div·ing** *n.* the sport of jumping from an airplane and executing various maneuvers during the free fall before opening the parachute. —**sky-high** *adj.* & *adv.* very high. —**sky-jack** *v. Informal.* hijack an aircraft; **sky-jack·er** *n.* —**Sky·lab** a U.S. earth satellite designed and equipped as a manned space station or laboratory for engineers and scientists, that remained aloft from 1973 to 1979. —**sky·lark** *n.* the common lark of Europe and Asia noted for the music it showers on the earth as it flies up toward the sky; ***v.*** to frolic boisterously. —**sky·light** *n.* a window that admits light through the roof. —**sky·line** *n.* **1** the visible horizon. **2** an outline, as of a city's buildings, seen against the sky. —**sky·lounge** *n.* a pickup vehicle for airline passengers that is carried from a city terminal to the airport by helicopter. —**sky marshal** a federal plainclothesman who guards against skyjackings. —**sky·rock·et** *n.* a firework rocket; ***v.*** (make) rise rapidly: *~ing prices; a star ~ed to fame by a movie.* —**sky·scrap·er** *n.* a very tall building. —**sky·train** *n.* a cheap airline service. —**sky·ward** (–wurd) *adj.* & *adv.* toward the sky; also **sky·wards** *adv.* —**sky·way** *n.* an air lane; also, an elevated highway or passageway. —**sky·writ·ing** *n.* writing in the sky with smoke from an aircraft; **sky·writ·er** *n.*

slab *n.* a thick, flat, usu. square-cornered piece of stone, wood, or solid food such as meat, cheese, etc.

slack *adj.* **1** not tight, as the loose end of a rope. **2** careless or dull. **3** slow; not brisk: *a ~ pace; a ~ season for business.* —***n.*** a slack end; also, a dull season; inactive condition: *to take up the ~* (of a rope, etc.). —***v.:*** *Don't* **slack off** *as examinations approach; likes to* **slack up** *a little before redoubling his efforts;* **slack·er** *n.;* **slack·ness** *n.* —**slack·en** *v.* make or become slack. —**slacks** *n.pl.* trousers for casual wear.

slag *n.* nonmetallic waste material that rises to the top in the smelting of metal ores; also, volcanic scoria.

slain *pp.* of SLAY.

slake *v.* **slakes, slaked, slak·ing** quench or satisfy (thirst, fire, desire for revenge, etc.); **slaked lime** calcium hydroxide produced by putting water on lime.

sla·lom (SLAH·lum) *n.* skiing down a zigzag course between poles forming a line of obstacles.

slam *n.* **1** (the bang of) a violent impact, as of a door pushed shut. **2** [short form] GRAND SLAM or LITTLE SLAM. **—*v.* slams, slammed, slam·ming:** *She* ~*d the door in his face; a pileup of cars that* ~*d into each other; a book badly* ~*d* (*Informal.* criticized) *by reviewers.* **—slam-bang** *adj.* & *adv.* hurried(ly) or headlong. **—slam·mer** *n. Slang.* jail.

slan·der *n.* & *v.* (make) a false statement to harm another's reputation; **slan·der·er** *n.;* **slan·der·ous** (–us) *adj.*

slang *n.* nonstandard language with a colorful or vigorous quality; ***v.*** use abusive epithets. **—slang·y** *adj.* **slang·i·er, -i·est:** ~ *style, vocabulary.*

slant *n.* & *v.* **1** slope or incline, esp. from the vertical. **2** (express with) a particular or personal bias: ~*ed news reporting.* **—*adj.*** sloping; also **slant·ing; slant·ing·ly** *adv.* **—slant·ways** or **slant·wise** *adj.* & *adv.* oblique(ly); slanting(ly).

slap *n.* & *v.* **slaps, slapped, slap·ping** hit with a flat surface, esp. the open hand: *a* ~ *in the face; a hearty* ~ *on the back; stopped and* ~*d* (i.e. summarily imposed) *a fine on the speeder.* **—slap·dash** *adj.* & *adv.* hurried(ly) or haphazard(ly). **—slap-hap·py** *adj. Slang.* giddy or dazed, as from too many blows. **—slap·stick** *n.* & *adj.* (comedy) characterized by horseplay and broad humor.

slash *n.* & *v.* (make) a sweeping stroke, as with a knife; hence, a resulting gash or slit: *a murder victim found with his throat* ~*ed; a flapless* **slash pocket** *with a slanted opening; Prices are* ~*ed* (i.e. cut down) *the day after Christmas.*

slat *n.* a narrow strip of material, as of a Venetian blind or the bars of a crib.

slate *n.* **1** a rock that splits in layers and is used for roofing tile and flagstone; hence, a slab or the bluish-gray color of slate. **2** a list of candidates. **—*v.* slates, slat·ed, slat·ing** [corresponding to the *n.* senses] **1:** *a* ~*d, not thatched roof.* **2:** *candidates* ~*d for the chairmanship; elections* ~*d* (i.e. scheduled) *for next fall.*

slath·er *v. Informal.* pour or spread generously, as jam, paint, etc.; **slathers** *n.pl.* a large amount or number.

slat·tern *n.* a slovenly woman; slut; **slat·tern·ly** *adj.*

slaugh·ter (SLAW–) *n.* & *v.* massacre; also, butcher(y), as in a **slaugh·ter·house** where animals are killed for food. **—slaugh·ter·er** *n.*

Slav. Slavic. **—Slav** (SLAHV, SLAV) *n.* a member of a Slavic-speaking people such as Russians, Poles, Czechs, Slovaks, Croats, Serbs, Ukrainians, etc. **—slave** *n.* **1** a person owned by another; also, a victim of a habit or one subject to a dominating influence. **2** one who slaves; ***v.*** **slaves, slaved, slav·ing** work like a slave; ***adj.:*** *a* ~ *ant, trader;* ~ *labor;* **slave driver** one in charge of slaves at work; hence, a harsh taskmaster. **—slav·er** *n.* **1** (SLAY–) a slave dealer or his ship. **2** (SLAV–) saliva dribbling from the mouth, as of a dog; ***v.*** slobber. **—slav·er·y** (SLAY–) *n.* the custom or practice of owning slaves; also, their condition; bondage or drudgery. **—Slav·ic** (SLAH–, SLAV–) *n.* a group of Indo-European languages spoken in E. European countries including the U.S.S.R., Yugoslavia, Bulgaria, Czechoslovakia, and Poland; ***adj.*** of the Slavs or their languages. **—slav·ish** (SLAY–) *adj.* of or like slaves; servile; **slav·ish·ly** *adv.;* **slav·ish·ness** *n.* **—Sla·von·ic** (–VON–) *n.* & *adj.* same as SLAVIC.

slaw *n.* [short form] coleslaw.

slay *v.* **slays, slew, slain, slay·ing** [literary use] kill violently; **slay·er** *n.*

sleaze (SLEEZ) *n.* the condition of being sleazy or shabby. **—slea·zy** *adj.* **-zi·er, -zi·est** **1** squalid or disreputable; cheap; shabby: *a* ~ *hotel.* **2** of fabrics, flimsy or thin. **—slea·zi·ly** *adv.;* **slea·zi·ness** *n.*

sled *n.* a vehicle with parallel runners instead of wheels for traveling over snow and ice; ***v.*** **sleds, sled·ded, sled·ding** carry or ride on a sled; **sled·der** *n.*

sledge *n.* & *v.* **sledg·es, sledged, sledg·ing** **1** (carry or ride on) a heavy sled, usu. drawn by a horse. **2** (hit with) a large, heavy hammer, usu. swung with both hands, or **sledge·ham·mer** *n.*

sleek *adj.* & *v.* (make) smooth and glossy: ~ *hair; a* ~ *automobile; a* ~ (i.e. smooth-talking) *young man;* **sleek·ly** *adv.;* **sleek·ness** *n.*

sleep *n.* & *v.* **sleeps, slept, sleep·ing** (be in) a state of natural unconsciousness that provides periodic rest for mind and body: *Infants* ~ *longer than adults; The nuisance ended when the dog was put to* ~ (i.e. killed); *stopped* **sleeping around** (*Informal.* being promiscuous) *after getting married; tried without avail to* **sleep off** (i.e. get over by sleeping) *what was bothering him;* **sleep·less** *adj.;* **sleep·less·ly** *adv.;* **sleep·less·ness** *n.* **—sleep·er** *n.* **1** one that sleeps; also, a railway **sleeping car** for passengers. **2** a supporting horizontal beam laid on the ground. **3** *Informal.* a person or thing that suddenly attains fame or success. **4** a baby's one-piece sleeping garment. **—sleeping bag** a bag for sleeping in outdoors. **—sleeping pill** (or **tablet**) a pill containing a sleep-inducing drug. **—sleeping sickness** any of several coma-inducing fatal diseases spread by insect-bites, esp. an African variety transmitted by the tsetse fly. **—sleep·walk·ing** *n.* a neurotic reaction during which a sleeping person walks or acts as if awake without remembering it on waking up; **sleep·walk·er** *n.* **—sleep·wear** *n.* night clothes.

—**sleep·y** *adj.* **sleep·i·er, -i·est** inclined to sleep; also, quiet or inactive: *a ~ village;* **sleep·y·head** *n.* a sleepy person; **sleep·i·ly** *adv.;* **sleep·i·ness** *n.*

sleet **1** *n.* & *v.* (shower) drops of freezing rain. **2** *n.* a glaze of ice formed by freezing rain. —**sleet·y** *adj.*

sleeve *n.* the arm of a garment; also, a tubelike part fitting around another part, as in engine bearings; **up one's sleeve** kept secretly in reserve; **sleeve·less** *adj.*

sleigh (SLAY) *n.* & *v.* sled or sledge.

sleight (SLITE) **of hand** skill with the hands, as of a magician or juggler; also, a magician's trick(s).

slen·der *adj.* **1** slim and graceful: *a ~ beauty, figure.* **2** slight; scanty; meager: *a ~ income; ~ hopes, means.* —**slen·der·ness** *n.* —**slen·der·ize** *v.* **-iz·es, -ized, -iz·ing** become or make (appear) slender.

slept *pt.* & *pp.* of SLEEP.

sleuth (SLOOTH) *n.* & *v. Informal.* (act as) a detective; **sleuth·hound** *n.* bloodhound.

slew *pt.* of SLAY. —*n.* **1** *Informal.* a large number (of people) or amount; lot. **2** a veer or swing; *v.: The car ~ed into a snowbank.* **3** a swampy inlet.

slice *n.* a thin broad piece (cut from bread, meat, cheese, fruits, etc.); hence, a share or portion (of profits, luck, etc.): *drama as a ~* (i.e. representation) *of life.* —*v.* **slic·es, sliced, slic·ing** **1** cut into slices or cut (*off, into, away*) as a slice. **2** hit (a ball) so that it goes off course or into a backspin. —**slic·er** *n.*

slick *adj.* **1** smooth or slippery, as with oil. **2** facile, clever, or skillful: *~ solutions to a complex problem; a ~ talker, operator, excuse.* —*v.* make smooth or glossy; **slick up** smarten; spruce up. —*n.* an oily spot. —**slick·er** *n.* **1** a raincoat, esp. of oilskin. **2** *Informal.* a wily person: *a city ~.* —**slick·ly** *adv.;* **slick·ness** *n.*

slide *v.* **slides, slid, slid·ing** (cause) to move smoothly in contact with a surface: *Sleds ~ over snow and ice; a ~ing door, drawer; a matter too urgent to* **let slide** (i.e. let drift). —*n.* **1** a sliding, as of rock or snow downhill, something that slides, a sliding surface or chute, as on a children's playground, etc. **2** something that is slid into place for use, as a small glass plate containing an object to be examined under a microscope or a transparency for projection on a screen using a **slide projector.** —**slide fastener** zipper. —**slid·er** (SLY–) *n.* **1** a person or thing that slides. **2** a slightly curving fast pitch in baseball. —**slide rule** a mathematical calculating device in the form of a ruler with a sliding middle section. —**sliding scale** a schedule of taxes, fees, etc. that varies to suit changing conditions such as cost of living.

slier, sliest See SLY.

slight *adj.* small; not considerable: *a ~ difference, excuse: on the ~est pretext; a ~* (i.e. small in build) *girl, figure.* —*v.* treat as insignificant, usu. intentionally: *felt ~ed by his superior manner;* *n.* a humiliation or discourtesy. —**slight·ly** *adv.;* **slight·ness** *n.*

sli·ly same as SLYLY.

slim *adj.* **slim·mer, slim·mest** thin or small: *a ~ woman; ~ chances, attendance;* *v.* **slims, slimmed, slim·ming** make or become slim: *~ing exercises.*

slime *n.* something sticky and filthy, as soft mud, mold on decaying vegetable matter, the mucous coating on snails, fish, etc.; **slim·y** *adj.* **slim·i·er, -i·est.**

slim-jim *n.* & *adj. Slang.* (one that is) very slim.

sling *n.* **1** a device consisting of a strip of leather for throwing a stone held in its loop; hence, a fling or throw. **2** a similar looped device for supporting an arm in a cast, for lifting a load, carrying a rifle, etc. —*v.* **slings, slung, sling·ing** suspend in or throw as with a sling: *a hammock slung between trees; purse slung over her shoulder.* —**sling·shot** *n.* a forked stick with an elastic sling attached for shooting stones, etc.

slink (SLINGK) *v.* **slinks,** *pt.* & *pp.* **slunk** or **slinked, slink·ing** go or move (away, by, etc.) in a stealthy manner, as from fear. —**slink·y** *adj.* **slink·i·er, -i·est** **1** furtive or stealthy. **2** of a woman's clothing, hugging the body; close-fitting: *a ~ evening gown.*

slip *v.* **slips, slipped, slip·ping** **1** (cause) to move smoothly or easily; hence, slide: *She ~d and fell on the ice; ~d off his coat and shoes; tried to ~ out of the room; Secrets* **slip out.** **2** escape (from): *Names ~ (from) my mind; Don't let a good opportunity ~; She* **let slip** *a few epithets in her fury.* **3** err: *liable to* **slip up** *in spelling.* **4** decline: *Polls showed his popularity ~ing.* —*n.* **1** a slipping: *a ~ of the tongue* (i.e. an unintentional error in speech). **2** something that is slipped on, as a pillowcase, a woman's sleeveless undergarment or petticoat, etc. **3** a docking space for ships between wharves or docks. **4** something cut small: *a ~ of paper; a grapevine ~* (i.e. cutting) *for planting; a ~ of a* (i.e. young or slim) *girl.* —**slip·case** *n.* a protective case or container for a book or phonograph record with one edge open. —**slip·cov·er** *n.* a fitted protective cover for a sofa or chair. —**slip·knot** *n.* a running knot, as of a noose (i.e. "slip noose") or lasso. —**slip·page** (–ij) *n.* (extent of) slipping, as in machinery. —**slipped disk** rupture of the disk between two vertebrae causing intense pain in the back and legs. —**slip·per** *n.* a light loose shoe for indoor wear. —**slip·per·y** *adj.* **slip·per·i·er, -i·est** **1** causing slipping: *a wet, ~ road.* **2** slipping away from grasp; hence, unreliable. —**slip·per·i·ness** *n.* —**slip·shod** *adj.* careless in manner or style; slovenly. —**slip·stream** *n.* backward flow of air past a moving object such as an airplane. —**slip-up** *n. Informal.* a mistake or mishap.

slit *n.* & *v.* **slits, slit, slit·ting** (split open by) a straight narrow cut: *a ~ in a door for letters; to ~ open an envelope;* **adj.:** *a ~ trench for protection in warfare; the ~ pupil of a cat's eye; a ~ skirt.*

slith·er *n.* & *v.* (move along in) an unsteady sliding or crawling motion, as a snake; **slith·er·y** *adj.*

sliv·er *v.* cut or split into long, thin pieces; ***n.*** such a piece; splinter.

slob *n. Informal.* a slovenly or stupid person. —**slob·ber** *n.* & *v.* (wet or smear with) saliva running from the mouth; hence, (indulge in) excessive sentimentality (*over* something); **slob·ber·y** *adj.*

sloe (SLOH) *n.* (the small, black, plumlike fruit of) a shrub, also called "blackthorn," used to flavor **sloe gin; sloe-eyed** *adj.* having blue-black or almond-shaped eyes.

slog *v.* **slogs, slogged, slog·ging** work hard or toil (*at* or *away at* something).

slo·gan (SLOH·gun) *n.* a catchy phrase or motto used in promoting a cause or advertising something, as "Peace with honor" or "Satisfaction guaranteed."

sloop *n.* a sailboat with one mast carrying the mainsail and a jib.

slop *n.* **1** something semiliquid or watery, as slush, spilled liquid, gruel, etc. **2** usu **slops** *pl.* liquid waste such as swill or collected urine. —***v.*** **slops, slopped, slop·ping** spill; also, feed slops to (pigs, etc.).

slope *n.* & *v.* **slopes, sloped, slop·ing** (make) an angle, esp. with the horizontal; incline: *a gentle ~; a ~ing roof; coasting down a ~* (i.e. sloping surface).

slop·py *adj.* **slop·pi·er, slop·pi·est** muddy; messy; slovenly; sentimental: *~ habits, work; a ~ eater; ~ reasoning.* —**sloppy Joe** ground beef prepared with sauce and served on a bun. —**slop sink** a sink for slops, as in a hospital.

slosh *v.* splash through or with slush or muddy water. —**slosh·y** *adj.*

slot *n.* & *v.* **slots, slot·ted, slot·ting** **1** (make) a small, narrow depression for inserting something, as for coins to operate a slot machine or for the pin on the bottom of a model racing car, or **slot car,** running in a groove between rails. **2** *Informal.* (place in) position in a series or sequence, as on a program: *filled a two-minute ~ in the evening news.*

sloth (SLAWTH, SLOHTH) *n.* **1** a nocturnal tropical animal with long shaggy hair related to armadillos and living mostly on trees, moving about sluggishly, often upside down, on branches. **2** sluggishness or laziness; **sloth·ful** *adj.;* **sloth·ful·ness** *n.* —**sloth bear** a bear of India with shaggy black hair, noted for its liking for honey; hence called "honey bear."

slot machine a machine operated by inserting a coin in its slot, esp. a gambling device or a vending machine.

slouch *n.* **1** a slovenly or incompetent person. **2** a forward bend or droop of head and shoulders; ***v.*** move, stand, or sit with a slouch. —**slouch·y** *adj.*

slough *n.* **1** (SLOU) a place of deep mud; quagmire; hence, a dejected or despondent condition. **2** (SLOO) a swamp, esp. a backwater or inlet, as a bayou. **3** (SLUF) castoff skin, esp. of a snake; ***v.*** cast off or discard.

Slo·vak (SLOH·vahk, –vak) *n.* & *adj.* (a member or the language) of the Slavic people of E. Czechoslovakia.

slov·en (SLUV·un) *n.* a careless or untidy person; **slov·en·ly** *adj.* **-li·er, -li·est** untidy; slipshod; ***adv.*** in a slovenly manner; **slov·en·li·ness** *n.*

Slo·vene (SLOH·veen) *n.* & *adj.* (a member or the language) of the people of **Slo·ve·ni·a** (sloh·VEE·nee·uh), a constituent republic of Yugoslavia. —**Slo·ve·ni·an** *n.* & *adj.* Slovene.

slow (SLOH) *adj.* taking longer than normal or necessary: *a ~ train* (i.e. not fast), *learner, watch* (i.e. behind in showing the correct time), *fire* (i.e. in burning), *party* (i.e. not lively); *Business is ~* (i.e. slack or sluggish). —***adv.:*** *Drive ~;* also **slow·ly** *adv.;* **slow·ness** *n.* —***v.*** make or become slow(er). —**slow burn** *Informal.* controlled but gradually rising anger, esp. as a dramatic device. —**slow·down** *n.* a slowing down (of a business, operation, etc.). —**slow motion** motion-picture action shown at slower-than-normal speed; **slow-mo·tion** *adj.* —**slow·poke** *n. Informal.* one who moves or does anything slowly. —**slow-wit·ted** *adj.* mentally dull.

SLR single-lens reflex (camera).

sludge *n.* a muddy mixture or slushy deposit, as the sediments resulting from ore refining, sewage treatment, etc.; **sludg·y** *adj.* **sludg·i·er, -i·est** slushy.

slue (SLOO) **1** *n.* same as SLEW. **2** *n.* & *v.* **slues, slued, slu·ing** veer or swing.

slug *n.* **1** a snaillike mollusk without a real shell. **2** a small piece of metal, as a bullet, a disk to use in a slot machine, or a strip of type metal or cast type. **3** *Slang.* a measure of drink. **4** *n.* & *v.* **slugs, slugged, slug·ging** *Informal.* (hit) a hard blow, esp. with the fist or a bat; **slug·ger** *n.* —**slug·gard** *n.* & *adj.* (one who is) lazy or sluggish; **slug·gish** *adj.* slow-moving: *a ~ stream, mind; ~ bowels;* **slug·gish·ly** *adv.;* **slug·gish·ness** *n.*

sluice (SLOOSE) *n.* **1** a gate for controlling a flow of water, as of a dam; also **sluice gate.** **2** a channel controlled by a gate, as the **sluice·way** for surplus water from a dam or a trough for washing gold ore of impurities. —***v.*** **sluic·es, sluiced, sluic·ing** let out (water), wash (gold from ore), send (logs, etc.) by means of a sluice.

slum *n.* an overcrowded, poverty-stricken area, as of a large city; ***v.*** **slums, slum·med, slum·ming** visit the slums; also, visit a place in a socially condescending manner.

slum·ber *n.* & *v.* (pass in) light sleep; doze: *the peaceful ~ of a newborn babe; a ~ing* (i.e. dormant) *volcano;* **slum·ber·ous** *adj.* drowsy; also, reposeful or inactive.
slum·lord *n.* the often absentee owner of slum property.
slump *v.* **1** sink or decline suddenly; ***n.:*** *a stock-market ~.* **2** slouch or droop in posture.
slung *pt.* & *pp.* of SLING.
slunk *pt.* & *pp.* of SLINK.
slur *v.* **slurs, slurred, slur·ring** **1** pass hurriedly or carelessly (*over* syllables or sounds in pronouncing). **2** to slight or disparage. **3** *Music.* glide over (successive notes) without a break. ***—n.*** **1** a slurring. **2** a slighting remark: *a racial ~.* **3** *Music.* slurred notes or a line (⁀ or ∪) connecting such notes.
slurp *n.* & *v. Slang.* (eat or drink with) a sucking noise, as made when sipping: *to ~ soup.*
slur·ry *n.* **slur·ries** a thin, watery mixture of something insoluble, as clay or cement.
slush *n.* watery mud or partly melted snow; **slush·y** *adj.* —**slush fund** a fund for corrupt purposes, esp. for bribing public officials.
slut *n.* a slovenly woman; also, a prostitute; **slut·tish** *adj.*
sly *adj.* **sli·er** or **sly·er, sli·est** or **sly·est** crafty or wily; evasive or furtive: *a ~ wink, maneuver, cat, fox;* **on the sly** in a sly manner; **sly·ly** or **sli·ly** *adv.;* **sly·ness** *n.*
Sm samarium. —**S.M.** Master of Science; Sergeant Major.
smack **1** *n.* & *v.* (have) a slight but distinctive taste, flavor, or suggestion: *the ~ of chicory in coffee; airs that ~ of superiority.* **2** *n.* & *v.* (make) noise with lips, as when chewing food, kissing loudly, or cracking a whip. **3** *v.* slap: *She ~ed him in the face;* ***adv.*** *Informal.* squarely: *hit him ~ in the face; fell ~ on her face.* **4** *n.* a single-masted sailboat. —**smack·er** *n.* **1** one that smacks, as a loud kiss. **2** *Slang.* a dollar.
small (SMAWL) *adj.* **1** relatively not large; of less than the usual size, quantity, importance, etc.: *a ~ car; ~ children;* REGULAR *and* SMALL *capitals; ~ beginnings, businesses* (involving small capital investment). **2** small in mind: *a ~ man, nature* (i.e. mean); **feel small** feel unimportant or shameful. ***—n.*** a small thing: *the ~* (i.e. the narrowest part) *of the back.* —**small·ness** *n.* —**small arms** firearms that are easy to carry and use, not artillery, as revolvers, rifles, etc. —**small fry** offspring or people of little importance. —**small hours** 1, 2, 3, etc. a.m. —**small potatoes** *Slang.* person(s) or thing(s) considered insignificant. —**small·pox** *n.* a highly infectious virus disease characterized by a rash that leaves pock marks all over the face and body. —**small talk** light conversation; chitchat. —**small-time** *adj. Informal.* minor or mediocre; **small-tim·er** *n.*
smart *n.* & *v.* **1** (cause or feel) a sharp pain. **2** (feel) distress of mind: *still ~ing from the injustice.* ***—adj.*** **1** causing sharp pain. **2** lively; clever; stylish: *a ~ pace, youngster, reply; looking ~ and intelligent; the ~* (i.e. fashionable) *set.* —**smart·ly** *adv.;* **smart·ness** *n.* —**smart al·eck** (–AL·ik) *Informal.* a conceited and obnoxious person; **smart-al·eck·y** *adj.* —**smart·en** *v.* make or become smart(er).
smash *v.* **1** break into pieces with violence, as a glass window with a rock. **2** deal a crushing blow to: *to ~ an enemy, an uprising.* **3** crash: *The car ~ed into the wall;* **smash·ing** *adj.: a ~* (i.e. crushing) *defeat; The play was a ~* (i.e. impressive or striking) *success.* ***—n.*** **1** a violent crash or its sound. **2** a crushing blow; ruin. **3** *Informal.* a popular success or great hit; ***adj.:*** *a ~ hit, musical.* —**smash·up** *n.* a wreck; disaster.
smat·ter·ing *n.* **1** slight knowledge (of a subject, language, etc.). **2** a small number or amount: *a major award and a ~ of smaller ones.*
smear (SMEER) *v.* spread or daub with anything greasy, sticky, or dirty; hence, mark or stain; soil (a reputation): *a dress ~ed with paint.* ***—n.*** a blotch, mark, or stain: *a cervical ~ for a cancer test; "Nazi," "Communist," and such* **smear words** *to discredit an opponent.* —**smear·y** *adj.* **smear·i·er, -i·est.** —**smear·case** *n. Regional.* cottage cheese.
smell *n.* **1** sense of perception through the nose; also, the quality perceived; odor or scent. **2** act of smelling. ***—v.*** **smells,** *pt.* & *pp.* **smelled** or **smelt, smell·ing** perceive with the nose; sniff; hence, judge (as if) by smell: *to ~ smoke, trouble, a* RAT; **smelling salts** See SALTS. —**smell·y** *adj.* **smell·i·er, -i·est** having a bad smell.
smelt *n.* a silvery food fish similar to salmon but smaller and with larger scales. ***—v.*** melt (ore) and extract metal; hence, obtain or refine (metal) by this method; **smelt·er** *n.* **1** one who smelts; also, a furnace for smelting. **2** a smelting works, or **smelt·er·y** *n.* **-er·ies.**
smidg·en (SMIJ·un) *n.* *Informal.* a small amount; also **smidg·in, smidg·eon.**
smi·lax (SMYE–) *n.* a woody or herbaceous vine of the lily family bearing clusters of red or bluish-black berries.
smile *n.* & *v.* **smiles, smiled, smil·ing** (make) a relaxed expression of the face, usu. with an upward curving mouth and parted lips, to show amusement, pleasure, etc.; hence, an act of smiling.
smirch *n.* & *v.* soil; stain; smear (one's good name).
smirk *n.* & *v.* (put on) an affected or silly smile; simper.
smite *v.* **smites,** *pt.* **smote,** *pp.* **smit·ten** or **smote, smit·ing** **1** [literary] strike or hit with force to injure or kill: *God smote their enemies.* **2** affect or impress strongly: *smitten with love, curiosity, remorse.*
smith *n.* a worker in metal, esp. a blacksmith. —**Smith, Captain John.** 1580–1631, English

explorer and colonist in Virginia. **—Smith, Joseph.** 1805–44, founder of the Mormon Church.

smith·er·eens (smidh·uh·REENZ) *n.pl. Informal.* small bits or fragments.

smith·y *n.* **smith·ies** a smith's workshop.

smock *n.* a loose outer garment worn to protect the clothes while working. **—*v.*** ornament with smocking; **smock·ing** *n.* a pattern of stitches for gathering the cloth of a smock or dress.

smog *n.* a mixture of fog and smoke polluting the air; **smog·gy** *adj.* **—smoke** *n.* **1** fumes given off by something burning; also, mist, fog, or anything resembling smoke. **2** (a smoking of) a cigar, cigarette, etc. **—*v.*** **smokes, smoked, smok·ing** **1** give off smoke; also, use a cigar, cigarette, pipe, etc. for pleasure. **2** treat with smoke, as in curing meat or fish in a **smoke·house,** in fumigation, blackening glasses, etc.; **smoke out** force to come out, as snakes from a hole; **smok·er** *n.;* **smoke·less** *adj.* **—smoke detector** a home fire-alarm device that is set off photoelectrically or by ionization in the presence of smoke; **smoke jumper** a firefighter who parachutes into a hard-to-reach area. **—smoke·screen** *n.* a thick smoke used to hide troops, ships, etc. from the enemy. **—smoke·stack** *n.* a tall chimney, as of a factory, or the funnel of a ship, locomotive, etc. **—smok·y** *adj.* **smok·i·er, -i·est** **1** giving off smoke, as a fire. **2** filled with smoke, as a room. **3** of or like smoke in appearance, smell, etc. Also **smok·ey. —smok·i·ness** *n.*

smol·der (SMOLE–) *v.* burn and smoke without flame; hence, exist in a suppressed condition: *a ~ing fire, hatred, rebellion;* ***n.*** flameless burning.

smooch *n.* & *v. Slang.* kiss or pet(ting); **smooch·y** *adj.*

smooth *adj.* perfectly even, without roughness; polished: *a ~ surface; stones worn ~; ~ sailing on calm seas; a ~ ride; a ~-bore firearm without rifling; a ~* (i.e. mild-tasting) *wine; a ~* (i.e. deceptive) *sales pitch; a ~-tongued flatterer.* **—*v.*** make smooth(er), easy, or refined: *~ed down her ruffled dress;* **smooth away** get rid of (difficulties); **smooth over** reduce (differences); make (faults, etc.) seem less serious. **—smooth·ie** (–ee) *n. Slang.* a suave, often smooth-tongued man. **—smooth·ly** *adv.;* **smooth·ness** *n.*

smor·gas·bord (–gus–) *n.* a buffet luncheon or supper consisting of a variety of foods spread on a table.

smote *pt.* & a *pp.* of SMITE.

smoth·er (SMUDH–) *v.* cover so as to deprive of air; hence, suffocate: *to ~ a fire with ashes; ~* (i.e. suppress) *one's resentment; a child ~ed* (i.e. overwhelmed) *with kisses; ~ed* (i.e. covered and baked) *chicken.* **—*n.*** something dense and stifling, as smoke, fog, etc.; hence, a confusion or welter.

smoul·der (SMOLE–) *Brit.* smolder.

smudge *n.* **1** a stained or smeared spot. **2** a smoky fire, as from a **smudge pot** or stove used in orchards to protect plants from frost or insects. **—*v.*** **smudg·es, smudged, smudg·ing** **1** smear or stain; **smudg·y** *adj.* **2** protect (an orchard) with smudge.

smug *adj.* **smug·ger, smug·gest** self-satisfied or complacent in a superior or secure manner: *a ~ look; ~ respectability;* **smug·ly** *adv.;* **smug·ness** *n.*

smug·gle *v.* **smug·gles, smug·gled, smug·gling** bring *(into)* or take *(out of)* a country illegally or secretly: *~ing of marijuana through customs;* **smug·gler** *n.*

smut *n.* **1** obscene talk or writing. **2** soot or smudge; also, a parasitic fungus of corn and other cereals that produces black spores resembling particles of soot. **—smut·ty** *adj.* **smut·ti·er, smut·ti·est. —smutch** *n.* & *v.* smudge.

Sn tin.

snack *n.* & *v.* (eat) a light meal; **snack bar** a lunch counter serving snacks.

snaf·fle *n.* a jointed bit for a horse's bridle.

snag *n.* an underwater obstacle, as a tree or branch, that is dangerous to boats; hence, a hidden or unexpected difficulty; ***v.*** **snags, snagged, snag·ging** **1** catch (as if) on a snag: *poachers ~ing fish.* **2** hinder, as if with a snag: *a project ~d by difficulties.* **—snag·gy** *adj.*

snail *n.* a small, soft-bodied, slow-moving mollusk with a spiral shell on its back for coiling into if molested.

snake *n.* **1** a long, scaly, legless reptile with a forked tongue and tapering tail. **2** a sly or deceitful person. **—*v.*** **snakes, snaked, snak·ing** move, wind, or twist like a snake. **—snake·bird** *n.* **1** a swimming bird with a long neck, also called "darter." **2** wry neck. **—snak·y** *adj.* **snak·i·er, -i·est** of or like a snake.

snap *v.* **snaps, snapped, snap·ping** **1** make a sudden, sharp sound, as of a dry twig or taut rope breaking or a finger flicked audibly against the thumb: *to ~ a whip; She ~s at* (i.e. speaks sharply to) *her child when impatient.* **2** make a quick, sharp movement, as an animal snatching food in its jaws: *The best bargains were ~d up by those first to arrive; Each one ~d to attention as his name was called; a football ~d back into play from the scrimmage line; her eyes ~ing* (i.e. flashing) *with fury; tourists ~ing pictures* (i.e. snapshots); **snap out of it** get quickly out of a bad mood or habit. **—*n.*** **1** a quick, cracking sound, as of a whip or a sudden bite; also, a short, sharp utterance. **3** *Informal.* vigor or liveliness. **4** a brief spell of cold weather. **5** a fastener or clasp that closes with a click. **6** a thin, crisp cookie. **7** *Informal.* a snapshot. **8** *Slang.* an easy job; cinch. **—*adj.*** **1** quick: *a ~ decision, vote.* **2** that fastens with a snapping sound. **—snap bean** any stringless bean that is picked when tender and used as a vegetable without shelling; green bean or wax bean. **—snap·drag·on** *n.* a colorful garden flower with long spikes of two-lipped blossoms that snap open like jaws when pressed on their sides. **—snap·per** *n.* one that snaps, esp. a snapping turtle or a tropical food fish with a large mouth and strong teeth. **—snapping turtle** either of two species of North American turtle with powerful jaws. **—snap·pish** *adj.* quick-tempered; irascible. **—snap·py** *adj.* **snap·pi·er, snap·pi·est** **1** inclined to be snappish or ill-tempered. **2** crackling, as a pine fire. **3** smart or lively: *Make it ~!* **—snap·shot** *n.* a casual photograph taken with a hand camera.

snare *n.* **1** a trap made with a noose for catching small birds and animals: *v.* **snares, snared, snar·ing** catch (as) in a snare. **2** a pitfall or trap.

snarl *n.* & *v.* **1** (make) an angry or threatening growling sound, as a dog with its teeth bared. **2** (utter) sharp, angry words. **3** tangle; disorder: *a traffic ~ during rush hour.* **—snarl·y** *adj.* **snarl·i·er, -i·est** snarling; also, tangled.

snatch *v.* seize or grasp roughly or hastily: *He ~ed her purse and ran; a youth ~ed away by death.* **—*n.*** **1** a snatching. **2** a short period or small amount: *~es of conversation, sleep, a show.*

sneak (SNEEK) *v.* move or act in a stealthy or cowardly manner: *~ed away at night; a ~ing* (i.e. secret) *suspicion;* ***n.*** a sneaking or one who sneaks; ***adj.*** stealthy: *a ~ thief, attack;* **sneak·y** *adj.* **sneak·i·er, -i·est. —sneak·er** *n.* canvas shoe with a soft sole. **—sneak preview** an advance showing of a motion picture for testing audience reaction before its release.

sneer *v.* show ill-natured contempt by facial expression, words, tone of voice, etc.; ***n.*** a sneering or its expression.

sneeze *n.* & *v.* **sneez·es, sneezed, sneez·ing** (make) a sudden and violent expulsion of air through the nose and mouth that gets rid of something irritating; **sneeze at** *Informal.* scorn or despise.

snick·er *n.* & *v.* (utter) a sly, half-suppressed laugh.

snide *adj.* slyly critical; also, mean or spiteful.

sniff *v.* **1** draw air quickly and audibly through the nose, as to test something by smelling. **2** express scorn by sniffing. **—*n.*** a sniffing or its sound; also, a breathing in of something. **—snif·fle** (SNIF·ul) *v.* **snif·fles, snif·fled, snif·fling** sniff again and again, as when one has a head cold or is crying; ***n.*** a sniffling (sound); **the sniffles** a head cold with congested nose. **—snif·ter** *n.* a stemmed, bowl-shaped drinking glass with a narrow brim to contain the aroma of the liquor in it.

snig·ger *n.* & *v.* same as SNICKER.

snip *v.* **snips, snipped, snip·ping** cut off or clip, as hair with scissors, in a short, quick stroke; ***n.*** a snipping or snipped piece; **snips** *pl.* hand shears for cutting sheet metal.

snipe *v.* **snipes, sniped, snip·ing** **1** hunt snipe; ***n.*** a long-billed, chunky, black-and-white shorebird of the sandpiper family. **2** shoot at people from a hidden position; also, to direct sly verbal attacks (*at* people); **snip·er** *n.*

snip·pet (–it) *n.* a small piece (of information, writing, etc.) as if snipped from a larger source. **—snip·py** *adj.* **snip·pi·er, snip·pi·est** *Informal.* snappish or haughty; **snip·pi·ly** *adv.*

snitch *v.* *Slang.* **1** pilfer or steal. **2** tattle *(on);* ***n.*** a tattletale.

sniv·el *v.* **-els, -el(l)ed, -el·(l)ing** cry or whine in a sniffling manner; ***n.*** a sniveling; **sniv·el·(l)er** *n.*

snob *n.* one who cares much for rank and wealth and looks down on people he considers socially inferior; **snob·bish** *adj.;* **snob·bishly** *adv.;* **snob·bish·ness** *n.* **—snob·ber·y** *n.* **snob·ber·ies** a snobbish act or quality.

snood *n.* a net worn by women to hold the hair at the back of the head.

snoop *v.* *Informal.* inquire into other people's affairs in a sneaky manner: *~ing with wiretaps;* ***n.*** a snooper. **—snoop·y** *adj.* **snoop·i·er, -i·est** prying or nosy.

snoot *n.* *Informal.* **1** face. **2** nose; **snoot·y** *adj.* **snoot·i·er, -i·est** haughty; snobbish; **snoot·i·ly** *adv.;* **snoot·i·ness** *n.*

snooze *n.* & *v.* **snooz·es, snoozed, snooz·ing** *Informal.* (take) a nap or doze.

snore *n.* & *v.* **snores, snored, snor·ing** (make) a rough, hoarse breathing noise while sleeping.

snor·kel (–kul) *n.* & *v.* (swim under water using) a curved breathing tube projecting above the water.

snort *v.* force air suddenly through the nose, as a horse does or a person showing contempt, anger, etc. **—*n.*** **1** a snorting. **2** *Slang.* a drink of liquor, usu. straight and quickly gulped.

snot *Slang* [vulgar] *n.* nasal mucus; also, one who is **snot·ty** *adj.* **snot·ti·er, snot·ti·est** impudent.

snout *n.* the projecting nose and mouth of a pig, crocodile, certain beetles and butterflies, etc.

snow *n.* (a falling of) white feathery crystals of frozen water vapor from the atmosphere; ***v.*** (cause) to fall in or as snow: *It ~ed on Christmas Day;* **snow in** shut in by snow; **snow under** cover with snow or overwhelm, as with accumulated work; **snow·y** *adj.* **snow·i·er, -i·est. —snow·ball** *n.* a ball of handpacked snow; ***v.*** throw snowballs at; also, increase rapidly like a rolling mass of snow. **—snow·bank** *n.* a mass of heaped snow; snowdrift. **—snow·belt** *n.* a region of heavy snowfall. **—snow·bound** *adj.* shut in or obstructed by snow. **—snow·drift** *n.* snow piled up by the wind. **—snow·drop** *n.* an amaryllis that bears delicate white nodding blossoms in early spring. —**snow·fall** *n.* (amount of) fall of snow. —**snow·fence** *n.* a lath-and-wire fence put up against drifting snow. —**snow·field** *n.* a region or expanse of perennial snow, as at the head of a glacier. —**snow·flake** *n.* a crystal of falling snow. —**snow·man** *n.* **-men** a human figure made with packed snow. —**snow·mo·bile** (–moh·beel) *n.* a vehicle with short skis in front and a wide track driven by an engine for traveling over snow and ice; **snow·mo·bil·er** *n.;* **snow·mo·bil·ing** *n.* —**snow·plow** *n.* a plowlike machine for clearing streets, driveways, etc. of snow. —**snow·shoe** (–shoo) *n.* a light, racketlike wooden frame strung with leather thongs to walk over snow without sinking. —**snow·storm** *n.* a storm with a heavy fall of snow. —**snow·suit** *n.* a warmly lined, usu. hooded winter suit for children to wear outdoors. —**snow tire** a tire with a heavy tread for extra traction over snow and ice.

snub *v.* **snubs, snubbed, snub·bing** **1** slight (a person); treat with contempt. **2** check or stop (an animal or thing in motion). ***—n.*** a slight; scornful treatment; **snub nose** a short nose with upturned tip; **snub-nosed** *adj.*

snuck *Regional* or *Informal.* sneaked.

snuff *v.* **1** draw (air) up the nose; sniff; hence, draw powdered tobacco into the nose. **2** pinch off the burnt wick of (a candle to make it burn brighter); also, put out (a candle); **snuff out** put an end to; kill. ***—n.*** **1** the charred end of a candlewick. **2** powdered tobacco for snuffing; **up to snuff** *Informal.* up to standard; also, sharp or alert. —**snuf·fle** *n.* & *v.* **snuf·fles, snuf·fled, snuf·fling** same as SNIFFLE.

snug *adj.* **snug·ger, snug·gest** warm and sheltered; hence, compact or close-fitting: *a ~ cabin, corner; tucked ~ in bed; lay ~* (i.e. concealed) *till the danger passed; a ~* (i.e. comfortable though small) *income; a ~ fit;* **snug·ly** *adv.* —**snug·gle** *v.* **snug·gles, snug·gled, snug·gling** draw closely to (someone for coziness); nestle.

so. south(ern).

so (SOH) *adv.* **1** in the way (indicated or implied): *I told you ~; talked ~ fast no one could follow; did it ~ as to confuse everyone; did it ~ that everyone was confused.* **2** very (much): *She's ~ sweet; It hurts ~.* **3** likewise: *I live here; ~ does she.* ***—conj.*** with the purpose or result that: *lay down* **so (that)** *I could sleep; was tired, ~ (Informal.* therefore) *I fell asleep.* ***—pron.:*** *a dozen* **or so** (i.e. approximately that). ***—interj.:*** *~, that's how! ~ you're back!* ***—adj.:*** *Is that ~? wants everything just ~* (i.e. in proper order). —**and so on** (or **forth**) and the rest. —**so what?** *Informal.* even if that's true, what does it matter?

soak (SOKE) *v.* make (or become) thoroughly wet by keeping (or remaining) in a liquid: *~ the clothes before washing; Let them ~ in the tub; Water ~s* (i.e. penetrates) *through the clothes; Towels ~ up* (i.e. absorb) *water.* ***—n.*** **1** a soaking, being soaked, or a liquid for soaking something in. **2** *Slang.* a drunkard.

so-and-so *n.* **so-and-sos** *Informal.* an unnamed person or thing.

soap (SOPE) *n.* **1** substance made by the action of alkali on fat or fatty acids, used to cleanse by the suds it forms with water; ***v.*** apply soap to. **2** [short form] soap opera. —**no soap** *Slang.* nothing doing; nothing accomplished. —**soap·box** *n.* an improvised platform, as for addressing a crowd in the street. —**soap opera** a sentimental daytime serial drama on radio or television. —**soap·stone** *n.* a soft rock with a soapy feel, composed mostly of talc, much used in industry as insulating material, etc. —**soap·suds** *n.pl.* lather made by soap in water. —**soap·y** *adj.* **soap·i·er, -i·est** covered with or containing soap; also, smooth or greasy.

soar *v.* rise upward or fly high, as an eagle, glider, or sailplane: *~ing prices, skyscrapers, ambitions.*

s.o.b. or **S.O.B.** son of a bitch.

sob *v.* **sobs, sobbed, sob·bing** weep or cry with short, gasping breaths; also, utter sobbing; ***n.*** a sobbing (sound).

so·ber (SOH–) *adj.* **1** not drunk; hence, temperate; ***v.*** esp. **sober down** or **sober up,** make or become sober. **2** serious or sensible: *a ~ estimate, expression, criticism; ~* (i.e. quiet, not flashy) *colors, clothes.* —**so·ber·ly** *adv.;* **so·ber·ness** *n.* —**so·bri·e·ty** (–BRY·uh–) *n.* the quality or condition of being sober; temperance; seriousness.

so·bri·quet (SOH·bruh·cay) *n.* a fanciful epithet or nickname.

soc. social(ist); society.

so-called *adj.* so-termed, though inaccurately or unjustifiably.

soc·cer (SOK·ur) *n.* the international variety of football, played between teams of 11 players using a round inflated ball.

so·cia·ble (SOH·shuh–) *adj.* liking companionship; also, marked by friendliness: *a ~ woman, occasion;* ***n.*** a social; **so·cia·bly** *adv.;* **so·cia·bil·i·ty** (–BIL–) *n.* —**so·cial** (SOH·shul) *adj.* **1** of or having to do with living and working together: *Man is a ~ being; ants, bees, and such ~ insects; his ~* (i.e. friendly) *nature.* **2** having to do with relationships within human society: *a ~ club; ~ classes, mobility* (between classes, as in a democracy); *a ~ climber* (in fashionable society), *leader.* ***—n.*** a social gathering or party; **so·cial·ly** *adv.* —**social disease** veneral disease. —**so·cial·ism** (–izm) *n.* the theory or system of public ownership of the means of production and distribution brought about by nonrevolutionary changes in the social order; **so·cial·ist** *n.* & *adj.;* —**So·cial·ist** **1** *n.* & *adj.* (member) of a socialist political party. **2** in Communist theory, leading to the Communist ideal: *a ~ gov-*

ernment, republic. —**so·cial·is·tic** (–LIS–) *adj.* —**so·cial·ite** *n.* a prominent member of fashionable society. —**so·cial·ize** *v.* **-iz·es, -ized, -iz·ing** **1** be or make social: *was ~ing too much at work; the ~ing influence of schooling.* **2** make socialistic; also, nationalize: *to ~ industry, public services.* Hence **so·cial·i·za·tion** (–ZAY–) *n.* —**socialized medicine** the providing of hospital and medical care for all through public funds. —**social science** anthropology, economics, history, political science, psychology, sociology, law, etc. as distinguished from the natural sciences and humanities; a discipline practiced by a **social scientist.** —**social security** the government program of aiding those in need because of old age, unemployment, sickness, etc. —**social work** community work involving services such as medical help, family counseling, and aid to the handicapped; also **social service; social worker.** —**so·ci·e·ty** (–SYE·uh–) *n.* **-ties** **1** human beings considered as a social group: *Criminals are a threat to ~.* **2** an organized group of individuals, as a club or association; also, an animal or plant community. **3** a social group with a particular character: *industrial ~; primitive ~; high ~; leaders of ~* (i.e. high-class people); ***adj.*** of high society: *a newspaper's ~ page; ~ gossip, women.* **4** companionship: *enjoys her ~.* —**so·ci·e·tal** (–tl) *adj.* —**Society of Friends** a Christian group founded about 1650, practicing simplicity in religious worship and devoted to humanitarian work, education, etc., cf. QUAKER. —**socio-** *comb.form.* social; society. —**sociol.** sociology. —**so·ci·ol·o·gy** (soh·see·OL·uh·jee, –shee–) *n.* the science of human relationships among individuals and groups; **so·ci·ol·o·gist** *n.;* **so·ci·o·log·i·cal** (–LOJ–) *adj.* —**so·ci·o·path** *n.* an aggressively antisocial mentally ill person.

sock *n.* **1** a short stocking. **2** *Slang.* a hard or vigorous blow; ***v.*** punch or hit hard, esp. **sock it to one.** —**socked in** *Informal.* closed, as an airport, or grounded, as planes, by bad weather.

sock·et (–it) *n.* a hollow part into which something fits, as of the eye, a joint, or an electric bulb.

sock·eye *n.* a small Pacific salmon, also called "red salmon."

Soc·ra·tes (–ruh·teez) 470?–399 B.C., Greek philosopher; **So·crat·ic** (–CRAT–) *n.* & *adj.*

sod *n.* the surface layer of earth held together by roots of grass, etc.; also, a piece of this; ***v.*** **sods, sod·ded, sod·ding** cover with sod; turf.

so·da (SOH·duh) *n.* **1** [short form] soda pop or soda water. **2** same as SODIUM BICARBONATE and SODIUM CARBONATE. —**soda biscuit** a biscuit leavened with baking soda and sour milk or buttermilk; **soda cracker** a light cracker made without sugar or shortening. —**soda fountain** a counter at which soft drinks are served. —**soda pop** a carbonated and sweetened soft drink; **soda water** carbonated water.

sod·den (SODN) *adj.* **1** soaked through; drenched; also, stupefied, as if drunk. **2** of baked things, soggy or doughlike: *~ biscuits, bread.*

so·di·um (SOH·dee–) *n.* an alkaline metallic element. —**sodium bicarbonate** a white crystalline salt; bicarbonate of soda or baking soda. —**sodium carbonate** a salt much used industrially, occurring as a white powder ("soda ash") or as crystals ("sal soda"); washing soda. —**sodium chloride** common salt. —**sodium hydroxide** a corrosive alkali, also called "caustic soda"; lye. —**sodium nitrate** a salt used in explosives, fertilizers, etc.; niter; saltpeter. —**sodium pentothal** a drug used by surgeons, psychiatrists, etc. to relieve anxiety; also used as a truth serum. —**sodium thi·o·sul·fate** (–thigh·oh·SUL–) *n.* same as HYPO.

Sod·om (–um) **and Go·mor·rah** (guh·MOR·uh) in the Bible, two sinful cities destroyed by fire from heaven. —**sod·om·y** *n.* sexual intercourse considered abnormal or bestial, esp. anal intercourse, between men; **sod·om·ite** *n.*

so·ev·er (–EV·ur) *adv.* & *suffix.* in any way; also, of any kind; at all: *how good ~; what~.*

so·fa (SOH·fuh) *n.* a usu. upholstered couch or long seat with back and arms; **sofa bed** a sofa that can be opened into a double bed.

So·fi·a (soh·FEE·uh, SOH–) capital of Bulgaria.

soft (SAWFT) *adj.* **1** not hard or rough to the senses, esp. touch; yielding to pressure; smooth: *~ fur, breeze; Talc is the ~est* (i.e. relatively) *of minerals; ~ in the head* (i.e. silly). **2** not sharp, loud, or glaring: *~ music, shadows, colors.* **3** easy and gentle to the feelings: *a ~ and luxurious life; a ~ job; a ~* (i.e. kind) *heart, spot.* **4** opposed to "hard": *~ drugs* (such as marijuana, amphetamines, and hallucinogens); **soft-core** *pornography* (without explicit sex); *the ~ "c" of "city," "g" of "gem," "ch" of "chip."* —***adv.*** in a soft manner; **soft·ly** *adv.;* **soft·ness** *n.* —**soft·ball** *n.* a game similar to baseball but played on a smaller field and with a larger ball which is pitched underhand. —**soft-boiled** *adj.* of eggs, boiled without the yolk becoming hard. —**soft·bound** or **soft·cov·er** *n.* & *adj.* paperback. —**soft coal** bituminous coal. —**soft drink** a sweetened and flavored, usu. carbonated, nonalcoholic drink, as cola. —**sof·ten** (SOFN) *v.* make or become soft(er); **sof·ten·er** *n.* —**soft·heart·ed** *adj.* kind and gentle. —**soft landing** the gentle setting down of a spacecraft without damage to its contents. —**soft-line** *adj.* conciliatory; accommodating. —**soft palate** See PALATE. —**soft-ped·al** *v.* **-als, -al(l)ed, -al·(l)ing** *Informal.* play down or tone down, as in playing a piano using the "soft pedal" for reducing volume. —**soft sell** a selling method using suggestion or persuasion instead of pressure. —**soft soap** *Informal.* flattery; **soft-soap** *v.* —**soft·ware** *n.* operational directions, procedures, accessory materials, etc. of any system or equipment, esp. the programs that come with a computer. —**soft·wood** *n.* wood of coniferous trees such as pines and firs that is easy to work or finish. —**soft·y** *n.* **soft·ies** *Informal.* one who is weak emotionally or physically; also **soft·ie.**

sog·gy *adj.* **sog·gi·er, sog·gi·est** esp. of ground, soaked or damp; also, sodden: ~ *bread;* **sog·gi·ly** *adv.;* **sog·gi·ness** *n.*

soi·gné (swah·NYAY) *adj.* *French.* well-groomed; also, well-maintained; *fem.* **soi·gnée** (–NYAY).

soil *n.* **1** the earth's surface or ground, esp. as supporting growth and development: *good* ~ *for crops; barren* ~*; methods of* ~ *conservation; a son of* **the soil** (i.e. a farmer); *set foot on Canadian* ~ (i.e. land). **2** stain or spot; also, foul matter; ***v.*** make or become dirty: ~*ed linen, hands, reputation.*

soi·ree or **soi·rée** (swah·RAY) *n.* an evening party.

so·journ (SOH·jurn) *n.* a temporary stay in a place; ***v.*** (*also* soh·JURN): *used to* ~ *abroad in the summer.*

sol. soluble; solution. —**Sol.** Solicitor; Solomon.

sol (SOLE) *n.* **1** *Music.* the fifth tone of the diatonic scale. **2** a money unit of Peru, equal to 100 centavos. **3** (*also* SOL) a colloid in a liquid solution. **4 Sol** (SOL) in Roman myth, the sun god.

sol·ace (–is) *n.* consolation or relief; ***v.*** **-ac·es, -aced, -ac·ing** to comfort or console.

so·lar (SOH·lur) *adj.* of or coming from the sun: *our* ~ *day, year;* **solar flares** *of hydrogen gas; the* **solar wind** *of electrically charged particles; electric power from* **solar energy** *captured by means of a* **solar battery** *made of* ~ *cells, as on an orbiting satellite.* —**so·lar·i·um** (–LAIR–) *n.* **-i·ums** or **-i·a** (–ee·uh) a glass-enclosed room for sunning, as in a sanitarium. —**solar plexus** the radiating network of nerves behind the stomach. —**solar system** the sun and the celestial objects such as planets, meteoroids, dust particles, etc. revolving around it.

sold *pt.* & *pp.* of SELL.

sol·der (SOD·ur) *n.* an alloy used melted by the heat of a **soldering iron** to patch or join metal parts; ***v.*** join with solder.

sol·dier (SOLE·jur) *n.* a member of an army, usu. not an officer. —***v.*** **1** work as a soldier. **2** *Informal.* shirk one's duty. —**sol·dier·ly** *adj.* & *adv.* —**soldier of fortune** a mercenary. —**sol·dier·y** *n.* **-dier·ies** **1** (a body of) soldiers. **2** military science or training.

¹sole *n.* **1** the bottom surface of the foot; also, the bottom of a shoe or other footwear; ***v.*** **soles, soled, sol·ing:** *to* ~ *a shoe; rubber*~*d slippers.* **2** a flat fish of warm seas used as food.

²sole *adj.* one and only: *my* ~ *purpose; the* ~ *survivor;* ~ (i.e. exclusive) *publication rights;* **sole·ly** *adv.* alone; also, exclusively.

sol·e·cism (SOL·uh–) *n.* a departure from accepted grammar, usage, etiquette, etc., as "between you and I" (instead of "me").

sol·emn (–um) *adj.* **1** serious in an impressive or awe-inspiring way: *a* ~ *occasion, oath, responsibility, face* (i.e. one without levity). **2** formal or ceremonious; religious: *a* ~ *curse, high mass, procession.* —**sol·emn·ly** *adv.* —**so·lem·ni·ty** (–LEM·nuh–) *n.* **-ties** the quality of being solemn; also, a solemn ceremony. —**sol·em·nize** (SOL·um·nize) *v.* **-niz·es, -nized, -niz·ing** observe (a festival) or perform (a wedding or other ceremony) with solemnity; **sol·em·ni·za·tion** (–ZAY–) *n.*

so·le·noid (SOH·luh–, SOL–) *n.* a cylindrical coil of wire working as an electrically induced magnet to actuate switches and other devices.

so·lic·it (suh·LIS–) *v.* **1** ask earnestly and respectfully: *to* ~ *funds for charity; to* ~ *the membership for donations.* **2** entreat or accost for something immoral: *prostitutes charged with* ~*ing.* —**so·lic·i·ta·tion** (–TAY–) *n.* —**so·lic·i·tor** (–LIS–) *n.* **1** one who solicits. **2** *Brit.* a lawyer qualified only to advise clients and prepare cases for barristers. **3** a legal official of a state or city; **solicitor general,** *pl.* **solicitors general** or **solicitor generals** a law officer ranking next below the attorney general. —**so·lic·i·tous** (–LIS·uh·tus) *adj.* showing care, concern, or solicitude; **so·lic·i·tous·ly** *adv.* —**so·lic·i·tude** (–LIS–) *n.* **1** care or worry, as about the future. **2** care in a concerned or protective manner: *parental* ~.

sol·id *n.* **1** a substance that is not a liquid or gas. **2** a three-dimensional object, as a cube or sphere, dealt with in solid geometry. —***adj.*** **1** not liquid or gaseous: ~ *fuels; frozen* ~. **2** not hollow but filled entirely and uniformly; dense in consistency or texture; hard and firm: *bars of* ~ *gold; a* ~ *structure of* ~ *brick; waited one* ~ *hour; in* ~ *colors, not patterned; "Icebox" is written* ~*, unlike "ice-skating" and "ice pick."* **3** having qualities of soundness, strength, genuineness, dependability, etc.: *a* ~ *citizen, build, character, treatise.* **4** three-dimensional, not flat: *a* ~ *figure.* Hence **so·lid·i·ty** (–LID–) *n.* —**sol·id·ly** *adv.;* **sol·id·ness** *n.* —**sol·i·dar·i·ty** (–DAIR–) *n.* unity of purpose, interests, feelings, etc., as of a closely knit group. —**so·lid·i·fy** (–LID–) *v.* **-fies, -fied, -fy·ing** make or become solid, as water by freezing; **so·lid·i·fi·ca·tion** (–CAY–) *n.* —**sol·id-state** *adj. Physics.* having to do with the physical properties of solids, as used in electronic devices such as semiconductors, transistors, and integrated circuits that have no moving parts, gases, heated filaments, etc.

so·lil·o·quy (suh·LIL·uh·kwee) *n.* **-quies** the act of talking to oneself; also, a dramatic device or speech in which an actor thinks aloud for the benefit of the audience; **so·lil·o·quize** (–kwize) *v.* **-quiz·es, -quized, -quiz·ing:** *Hamlet ~ing on death.* —**sol·i·taire** *n.* **1** a card game for one person. **2** a gem set by itself. —**sol·i·tar·y** (–ter·ee) *adj.* living or existing away from others; alone and isolated: *a prisoner in ~ confinement; a hermit's ~ life; ~ bees and wasps* (that are not social); *a ~* (i.e. lonely) *place.* —**sol·i·tude** *n.* a lonely place or condition; seclusion. —**so·lo** (SOH–) *n.* **-los** **1** a musical piece for one voice or instrument; ***v.*** perform a solo; **so·lo·ist** *n.* **2** any performance by one person. —***adj.*** & ***adv.*** alone: *She flew ~; a ~ dance.*

Sol·o·mon (–uh·mun) a king of Israel famous for his wisdom.

So·lon (SOH·lun, –lon) 638?–558? B.C., Athenian sage and lawgiver; **solon** *n.* a wise lawmaker.

so long *Informal.* good-bye.

sol·stice (–stis) *n.* the time of the year when the sun appears at its farthest point north or south, i.e. about June 21 (**summer solstice** in the Northern Hemisphere) and December 22 **(winter solstice); sol·sti·tial** (–STISH–) *adj.*

sol·u·ble (SOL·yoo–) *adj.* that can be dissolved or solved; **sol·u·bly** *adv.;* **sol·u·bil·i·ty** (–BIL–) *n.* —**sol·ute** (SOL·yoot, SOH·loot) *n.* & *adj.* (the substance) dissolved or in solution. —**so·lu·tion** (–LOO–) *n.* **1** (a mixture formed by) the dissolving or dispersion of one substance in another, esp. a solid in a liquid. **2** the solving of a problem; also, the resulting explanation or answer: *the ~ of a mystery, crime.* —**solve** (SOLV) *v.* **solves, solved, solv·ing** find the answer to (a problem, puzzle, mystery, etc.); **solv·a·ble** *adj.;* **solv·er** *n.* —**sol·vent** *adj.* **1** able to pay all one's debts; **sol·ven·cy** *n.* **2** dissolving; ***n.*** a substance such as water or turpentine that can dissolve other substances.

So·ma·li·a (–MAH·lee·uh) a republic of N.E. Africa; 246,200 sq.mi. (637,657 km²); *cap.* Mogadishu; **So·ma·li** *adj.* & *n.* **-lis.** —**So·ma·li·land** See DJIBOUTI.

so·mat·ic (–MAT–) *adj.* of the body; **somatic cell** an animal or plant cell that is not a germ cell; **so·mat·i·cal·ly** *adv.*

som·ber *adj.* gloomy or melancholy; cheerless: *~ mood, tones, colors;* also **som·bre** *Brit.;* **som·ber·ly** *adv.*

som·bre·ro (–BRAIR·oh) *n.* **-ros** a wide-brimmed felt or straw hat of Spanish origin.

-some **1** *comb.form.* body: as in *chromosome, ribosome.* **2** *adj. suffix* [denoting a condition or quality]: as in *cumbersome, quarrelsome.* **3** *n.suffix.* group of: as in *twosome, foursome.*

some (SUM) *adj.* of an indefinite number, amount, or quantity: *happened ~ days back; had ~ sleep; in ~* (i.e. certain) *countries; in ~* (i.e. a) *country I can't remember; consult ~* (i.e. any) *lawyer; That was ~* (*Informal.* a remarkable or wonderful) *game!* —***adv.:*** *happened ~* (i.e. about or nearly) *10 days back; I slept ~* (*Informal.* somewhat). —***pron.*** **1** certain people or things: *~ are good, ~ are bad.* **2** a few: *I know ~ of them;* **and then some** *Slang.* and a good deal more than that. —**some·bod·y** (–bod·ee, –bud·ee) *pron.* some person; ***n.,*** *pl.* **-bod·ies** a person of importance. —**some·day** *adv.* at some future time. —**some·how** *adv.* by some means. —**some·one** same as SOMEBODY. —**some·place** *adv. Informal.* somewhere.

som·er·sault (SUM·ur–) *n.* & *v.* (perform) a complete roll of the body with the heels turning over the head; also **som·er·set** *n.* & *v.*

some·thing *n.* an unspecified thing, amount, or part: *There's ~ in that bottle; He's ~* (i.e. a bit or little) *of a jack-of-all-trades; She's ~* (*Informal.* a person of importance) *in the F.B.I.* **something else** *Slang.* one that is remarkably special. —***adv.*** somewhat: *~ like $20,000.* —**some·time** *adv.* at an unspecified time: *See you ~ tomorrow; happened ~ back;* ***adj.*** former: *~ professor of law;* **some·times** *adv.* now and then; occasionally. —**some·way** *adv.* by some means. —**some·what** *adv.* to some extent or degree; ***n.*** something: *She's ~ of a poet.* —**some·where** *adv.* at some place: *saw him ~; would place it ~ in the 1950's; ~* (i.e. approximately) *around $100.*

som·nam·bu·lism (–NAM·byoo–) *n.* sleepwalking; **som·nam·bu·list** *n.* —**som·no·lent** (–nuh–) *adj.* sleepy or drowsy; also, causing sleep; **som·no·lence** *n.*

son (SUN) *n.* a male offspring, esp. a boy or man in relation to his parent.

so·nar (SOH–) *n.* a radar device that uses reflected sound waves to find water depth, detect submarines, etc.

so·na·ta (suh·NAH–) *n.* an instrumental composition with three or four movements contrasting in rhythm but related in thought; **so·na·ti·na** (–nuh·TEE–) *n.* a short or simplified sonata.

sonde (SOND) *n.* same as RADIOSONDE.

song *n.* **1** a piece of music for singing; also, a short poem whether set to music or not. **2** a singing or a sound like it, as of a bird, boiling kettle, etc.; **for a song** for a small payment; cheaply. —**song·bird** *n.* a bird that has a musical call, as most caged birds, larks, warblers, etc. —**song·fest** *n.* an informal gathering for singing songs. —**song·ster** *n.* a singer or songwriter; *fem.* **song·stress** (–stris).

son·ic *adj.* having to do with sound waves: *a ~ depth finder; the explosive* **sonic boom** *produced by a supersonic aircraft breaking the* **sonic** (or **sound**) **barrier** *of sharply rising aerodynamic drag as the craft approaches the speed of sound.*

son–in–law *n.* **sons–** a daughter's husband.

son·net (–it) *n.* a rhymed poem in 14 lines of iambic pentameter.

son·ny *n.* **son·nies** [endearing term] son or boy.

so·no·rous (suh·NOR·us, SON·uh–) *adj.* resonant; also, having a full, rich, or impressive sound: ~ *voices, phrases; a* ~ *style;* **so·nor·i·ty** (–NOR–) *n.*

soon *adv.* in a short time: *I'll be back* ~*; arrived* ~*er than expected; to be done as* ~ *as possible; She would as* ~ (or *would* ~*er,* i.e. rather) *die fighting than yield;* **sooner or later** sometime; eventually.

soot *n.* black unburned carbon seen as smoke and found sticking to the sides of chimneys; **soot·y** *adj.* **soot·i·er, -i·est:** *a* ~ *chimney; the* ~ (i.e. blackish) *mold.*

sooth *Archaic, n.* truth; ***adj.*** true. **—soothe** (SOODH) *v.* **soothes, soothed, sooth·ing** to comfort or relieve: *to* ~ *a child;* ~ *pain; a* ~*ing lotion;* ~*ing* (i.e. pleasing) *flattery;* **sooth·er** *n.;* **sooth·ing** *adj.* tending to soothe; **sooth·ing·ly** *adv.* **—sooth·say·er** *n.* one who foretells the future; **sooth·say·ing** *n.*

sop *v.* **sops, sopped, sop·ping** dip or soak (as if) by dipping: *to* ~ *up a spill with a sponge; came in from the rain* **sopping wet. *—n.*** something given to appease, as bread dipped in milk to a child; hence, a bribe or concession: *as a* ~ *to his conscience.*

S.O.P. standard (or standing) operating procedure.

soph·ism (SOF–) *n.* a clever but logically invalid argument; **soph·ist** *n.;* **so·phis·tic** (–FIS–) or **-ti·cal** *adj.* **—so·phis·ti·cate** (–FIS–) *v.* **-cates, -cat·ed, -cat·ing** make experienced or worldly-wise by loss of natural simplicity; **so·phis·ti·cat·ed** *adj.: a* ~ *young lady;* ~ *tastes; modern* ~ (i.e. highly developed) *equipment, weapons;* **so·phis·ti·ca·tion** (–CAY–) *n.* **—soph·is·try** (SOF·is·tree) *n.* **-tries** a sophism or sophistical reasoning.

Soph·o·cles (SOF·uh·cleez) 496?–406 B.C., Greek dramatist.

soph·o·more (SOF·uh–) *n.* a second-year university student or one in Grade 10 of high school; **soph·o·mor·ic** (–MOR–) *adj.* of or like a sophomore; hence, immature and overconfident. **—-sophy** *comb.form.* knowledge or science: as in *philosophy, theosophy.*

sop·o·rif·ic (–RIF–) *n.* & *adj.* (a drug such as a barbiturate) that induces sleep.

sop·py *adj.* **sop·pi·er, sop·pi·est** soaked or wet through.

so·pra·no (suh·PRAH–) *n.* **-nos** (a singer with) the highest singing voice of women and boys; also, a soprano part; ***adj.*** of or for a soprano.

sorb. *v.* absorb or adsorb.

sor·cer·y (SOR·suh·ree) *n.* **-cer·ies** witchcraft, esp. by use of charms, spells, etc. **—sor·cer·er** *n., fem.* **sor·cer·ess.**

sor·did *adj.* dirty or filthy; hence, wretched, base, or mean: *the* ~ *life of the slums; the* ~ *details of a crime;* **sor·did·ly** *adv.;* **sor·did·ness** *n.*

sore *adj.* **sor·er, sor·est** causing or feeling pain: *a* ~ *throat, heart; feels* ~ (i.e. vexed) *at being slighted; a* ~ *point; in* ~ (i.e. grievous) *need.* ***—n.*** a sore spot on the body, esp. an infected wound. ***—adv.*** *Archaic.* greatly; **sore·ly** *adv.;* **sore·ness** *n.* **—sore·head** *n. Informal.* one who easily gets angry, disgruntled, etc.

sor·ghum (SOR·gum) *n.* a tropical cereal plant resembling corn but having flowers in branched clusters bearing edible, starchy seeds used also for syrup, forage, etc.

so·ror·i·ty (–ROR–) *n.* **-ties** a group of women organized as a society, esp. for fellowship, as among university students.

sorp·tion *n.* a sorbing or being sorbed; **sorp·tive** (–tiv) *adj.*

sor·rel *n.* **1** a reddish brown (horse); ***adj.*** reddish-brown. **2** an herb of the buckwheat family with pungent, sour leaves used in salads, for flavoring, etc. **3** a tree of the heath family with sour-tasting leaves.

sor·row (–oh) *n.* sadness or grief of a prolonged nature, as from a beloved's death; ***v.*** grieve; **sor·row·ful** *adj.;* **sor·row·ful·ly** *adv.* **—sor·ry** *adj.* **sor·ri·er, sor·ri·est** **1** feeling sorrow, regret, pity, etc.: *I'm* ~ *to disappoint you; feel* ~ *for her.* **2** poor; pitiful; worthless: *a* ~ *state of affairs, excuse, sight.* **—sor·ri·ly** *adv.;* **sor·ri·ness** *n.*

sort *n.* **1** a group of individuals of the same general kind: *all* ~*s of people, plants, cars; this* ~ *of trouble.* **2** a particular class, rank, quality, character, etc.: *said something of the* ~*; I don't like his* ~ (of people); **of sorts** or **of a sort** of mediocre quality; **out of sorts** slightly ill or in low spirits; **sort of** *Informal.* somewhat: ~ *of disappointed.* ***—v.*** arrange according to kind or character: *letters are* ~*ed (out) in the post office.*

sor·tie (–tee) *n.* a sally or sudden attack; also, a combat plane's flight into enemy territory, as for bombing.

SOS (es·oh·ES) *n.* a distress signal, as used in wireless telegraphy.

so-so *adj.* & *adv.* fairly or passably (good).

sot *n.* a habitual drunkard; **sot·tish** *adj.*

sot·to vo·ce (SOT·oh·VOH·chee) in a low voice; also, aside.

sou·brette (soo·BRET) *n.* a pert or lively young woman, usu. a maidservant, in a role subsidiary to that of her mistress, as in musical comedies.

souf·flé (soo·FLAY) *n.* & *adj.* (a baked dish) made light and puffy by the use of beaten egg whites before baking: *vegetable* ~*; chocolate* ~.

sough (SOW, SUF) *n.* & *v.* (make) a soft sighing or murmuring sound.

sought *pt.* & *pp.* of SEEK.

soul (SOLE) *n.* **1** the spiritual part of a person as distinguished from the body and thought of as immortal and the source of inner strength, inspiration, etc.; hence, essence or spirit: *We eat to keep body and ~ together; puts his heart and ~ into his work; did a lot of* **soul-search·ing** *before they decided to break up; Not a ~* (i.e. person) *was in sight.* **2** an emotional and spiritual quality felt to be characteristic of black American culture, esp. black music; ***adj.*** characteristically black; **soul brother** a fellow black; **soul food** food traditionally popular among American blacks. —**soul·ful** *adj.* full of or expressing deep feeling; **soul·ful·ly** *adv.;* **soul·ful·ness** *n.* —**soul music** jazz developed from blues and gospel music.

¹sound *n.* a channel wider than a strait, linking two bodies of water or separating an island from the mainland; also, a narrow coastal inlet. —***v.*** **1** (use a sounding device) to measure the depth of (water); fathom; hence, inquire or try to find out the views, feelings, etc. of: *Let's ~ him out on the new proposal.* **2** dive down suddenly, as a whale does. —**sound·er** *n.*

²sound *adj.* **1** free from defect; good, healthy, or strong: *a will made while of ~ mind, enjoying ~ health; ~ advice, views; a ~ foundation.* **2** heavy; thorough: *~ sleep, thrashing;* ***adv.*** thoroughly: *was ~ asleep;* **sound·ly** *adv.;* **sound·ness** *n.*

³sound *n.* what is or can be heard: *the ~ of music, voices, fighting, machinery; vowel and consonant ~s; came within ~* (i.e. earshot) *of the guns.* —***v.:*** *to ~ a horn; a voice that ~s strange;* **sound off** *Informal.* talk freely or loudly, as to complain, boast, etc.; **sound·less** *adj.* —**sound barrier** same as SONIC BARRIER. —**sounding board** or **sound·board** *n.* a structure or device for increasing or directing sound, as in a violin or piano. —**sound·proof** *adj.* insulated against sound: *a ~ studio, ceiling.* —**sound track** record of the sounds of a motion picture made along one edge of the film.

soup (SOOP) *n.* **1** a liquid food made with meat, fish, or vegetables, eaten with a large-bowled **soup·spoon.** **2** *Informal.* something thick or heavy, as fog; **in the soup** in a hard plight. —***v.*** **soup up** *Slang.* increase the power of (an engine, etc.).

soup·çon or **soup·con** (soop·SOHNG) *n.* a slight trace or flavor (*of* a taste or quality).

soup·y (SOO·pee) *adj.* **soup·i·er, -i·est** like soup in thickness; hence, *Informal.* foggy.

sour *adj.* **1** having the sharp, acid taste of fruits such as lemon. **2** having the acid or rancid taste of foods such as milk gone bad; hence, unpleasant: *~ breath; ~ wine; ~* (i.e. acid) *soil; ~* (i.e. impure) *gasoline.* **3** of people, turned disagreeable: *a ~ employee, face.* —***v.*** make or become sour. —**sour·ly** *adv.;* **sour·ness** *n.*

source (SORCE) *n.* where something rises or originates: *the ~ of the Mississippi; a reliable ~ of information; light from a remote ~; a ~ of trouble.*

sour·dough (–doh) *n.* **1** fermented dough used as leaven. **2** a lone prospector or pioneer, as in Alaska and N.W. Canada; also, an experienced hand or old-timer. —**sour grapes** scorning of something because it is beyond one's grasp. —**sour·puss** (–poos) *n. Slang.* a sullen person.

souse (SOWCE) *v.* **sous·es, soused, sous·ing** **1** pickle; hence, soak or plunge. **2** *Slang.* make or become drunk. —***n.*** **1** a pickling or soaking, brine for pickling, or pickled pork, fish, etc. **2** *Slang.* a habitual drunk.

south *n.* **1** the direction to the right of one facing the rising sun. **2** a region lying in this direction, as **the South,** i.e. southern states of the U.S., south of Pennsylvania, the Ohio River, and Missouri. —***adj.*** in, to, or from the south. —***adv.*** toward the south. —**South Africa** a southern African country; 471,445 sq. mi. (1,221,037 km²); *capitals:* Cape Town and Pretoria; **South African.** —**South America** the continent of the Western Hemisphere S. of Panama; **South American.** —**South Asia** the region comprising India, Pakistan, Sri Lanka, and Bangladesh. —**South Bend** a city of N. Indiana. —**South Car·o·li·na** (-cair·uh·LYE·nuh) a S. state of the U.S.; 31,055 sq. mi. (80,432 km²); *cap.* Columbia; **South Car·o·lin·i·an** (–LIN·ee·un). —**South China Sea** the sea S. of China and Taiwan, W. of the Philippines, N. of Indonesia, and E. of the Malay Peninsula. —**South Dakota** (–duh·COH·tuh) a Midwestern U.S. state; 77,047 sq.mi. (199,551 km²); *cap.* Pierre; **South Dakotan.** —**south·east** *n.* & *adj.* (in, toward, or from) a direction or place halfway between south and east; ***adv.*** toward the southeast; **the Southeast** southeastern U.S.; **Southeast Asia** the region comprising the peninsula E. of India and S. of China, the Philippines, Malaysia, and W. Indonesia; **south·east·er·ly** *adj.* & *adv.;* **south·east·ern** *adj.;* **south·east·ward** (–wurd) *adj.* & *adv.;* **south·east·wards** *adv.* —**south·er·ly** (SUDH–) *adj.* & *adv.* toward or from the south. —**south·ern** (SUDH–) *adj.* of, from, or toward the south; **Southern** of the South; **south·ern·er** *n.* a person of or from the south; **Southern Hemisphere** the half of the earth S. of the equator; **southern lights** same as AURORA AUSTRALIS; **south·ern·most** *adj.* farthest south. —**South Korea** See KOREA. —**south·paw** *n. Slang.* a left-handed person, esp. a baseball pitcher. —**South Pole** the earth's southernmost point. —**South Sea Islands** the islands of the S. Pacific. —**South Vietnam** See VIETNAM. —**south·ward** (–wurd) *adj.* & *adv.* toward the south; **south·wards** *adv.* —**south·west** *n.* & *adj.* (in, toward, or from) a direction or region halfway between south and west; ***adv.*** in, toward, or from the southwest; **the Southwest** southwestern U.S.; **South West Africa** same as NAMIBIA; **south·west·er·ly** *adj.* & *adv.;* **south·west·ern** *adj.;* **south·west·ward** (–wurd) *adj.* & *adv.;* **south·west·wards** *adv.* —**South Yemen** See YEMEN (ADEN).

sou·ve·nir (soo·vuh·NEER) *n.* an article given, bought, kept, etc. as a reminder of a person, place, or occasion.
sov·er·eign (SOV·run, –uh·rin) *n.* **1** a supreme ruler or monarch. **2** a British gold coin worth one pound. ***—adj.*** **1** supreme and independent: *a ~ state.* **2** great in excellence, importance, etc.: *a ~ remedy; of ~ importance.* **—sov·er·eign·ty** *n.* **-ties** **1** supreme and independent authority. **2** a sovereign's status or power. **3** a sovereign state.
so·vi·et (SOH·vee·it, –et) *n.* in the U.S.S.R., an elected legislative body: *a village ~; town ~s; the Supreme Soviet of the U.S.S.R.;* **so·vi·et·ism** *n.* **—Soviet** *adj.* of the Soviet Union; **Soviet Union** same as UNION OF SOVIET SOCIALIST REPUBLICS.
1**sow** *n.* an adult female swine.
2**sow** (SOH) *v.* **sows,** *pt.* **sowed,** *pp.* **sown** (SONE) or **sowed, sow·ing** to plant (seed); hence, spread or scatter: *Reap what you ~; to ~ wheat, a field* (with wheat); *to ~ discord;* **sow·er** *n.*
sow bug woodlouse.
sox *Informal.* a *pl.* of SOCK, *n.* 1.
soy (sauce) a sauce made from fermented soybeans. **—soy·bean** *n.* a plant of the pea family yielding protein-rich seeds; also, the seed.
Sp. Spain; Spanish. **—S.P.** Shore Patrol. **—sp.** special(ist); species; specific; spelling; spirit.
spa (SPAH) *n.* (a health resort having) a mineral spring.
space *n.* **1** the boundless expanse or extent which physical objects may occupy: *exploration of ~; visitors from (outer) ~.* **2** an area or volume limited by objects; room or interval between objects: *parking ~s; not enough ~ for a bed; wide open ~s; ~s between lines; to book ~* (i.e. accommodation) *in a hotel; in the ~* (i.e. interval) *of an hour.* ***—v.*** **spac·es, spaced, spac·ing** divide into or separate by spaces. **—space·craft** *n. sing.* & *pl.* a vehicle such as a satellite or rocket designed for travel in space. **—spaced-out** *adj. Slang.* under the influence of a narcotic. **—space fiction** fiction dealing with life and travel in outer space. **—space·flight** *n.* flight into outer space. **—space heater** a portable unit for warming up a room or other small area. **—Space·lab** *n.* a manned laboratory module for carrying into orbit in a space shuttle. **—space·man** *n.* **-men** a male member of the crew of a spaceship; *fem.* **space·wom·an. —space medicine** See BIOASTRONAUTICS. **—space·ship** *n.* a vehicle for traveling in outer space. **—space shuttle** a recoverable and reusable space vehicle to link up with a space station. **—space station** a manned earth satellite in a fixed orbit for use in space experiments, as a stopping or launching place for spaceships, etc. **—space·suit** *n.* a spaceman's pressurized garment. **—space·walk** *n.* & *v.* (engage in) movement outside a spaceship. **—spa·cial** (SPAY–) *adj.* same as SPATIAL. **—spa·cious** (SPAY·shus) *adj.* large in extent or scope: *~ accommodation; a ~ life of ease;* **spa·cious·ly** *adv.;* **spa·cious·ness** *n.*
spade **1** *n.* & *v.* **spades, spad·ed, spad·ing** (dig with) a sharp, pointed shovel for turning the soil by pressing its blade into the ground; **spade·ful** *n.* **2** a black figure (♠) marking a suit of playing cards; also, a card of this suit. **—spade·work** *n.* the hard preliminary work involved in starting a project.
spa·dix (SPAY–) *n.* **-dix·es** or **-di·ces** (–duh·seez) the spike of flowers enclosed in a spathe, as in the jack-in-the-pulpit.
spa·ghet·ti (spuh·GET·ee) *n.* slender sticks of pasta boiled and served in long, thin strings.
Spain a country of S.W. Europe; 194,885 sq.mi. (504,750 km^2); *cap.* Madrid.
spake *Archaic pt.* of SPEAK.
span *n.* **1** the extent or distance between two linked points such as the ends of a bridge; also, one of its individual parts between pillars or supports: *the ~ of an arch bridge; a bridge with 10 ~s; our brief ~ of life; a child's attention ~* (i.e. length of concentration). **2** the maximum distance between the tips of the little finger and the thumb. ***—v.*** **spans, spanned, span·ning** extend across; also, measure, as by the span of one's hand.
Span. Spanish.
span·dex *n.* an elastic synthetic fiber used for girdles, etc.
span·gle (SPANG–) *v.* **-gles, -gled, -gling** decorate (as if) with spangles: *a star-~d sky;* ***n.*** a small disk of glittering material sewn on fabrics for decoration. **—span·gly** *adj.*
Span·iard (–yurd) *n.* a person of or from Spain. **—span·iel** (–yul) *n.* a breed of sporting dog with a long, silky coat, large, round eyes, and drooping ears. **—Span·ish** *adj.* of Spain, its people, or their language; ***n.*** the Spanish language; **the Spanish** the people of Spain; **Spanish America** the parts of Latin America in which Spanish is the chief language; **Spanish American. —Spanish fly** same as CANTHARIS and CANTHARIDES. **—Spanish moss** a tropical air plant that hangs from trees in long, beardlike masses.
spank *v.* strike (one to be punished) on the buttocks with the palm, a slipper, etc.; ***n.*** such a blow. **—spank·ing** *adj.* rapid or strong: *a ~ breeze;* ***adv.*** very: *a ~ good time; looks ~ new.*
spar *v.* **spars, sparred, spar·ring** make the motions of boxing (*at* someone); hence, dispute or wrangle (*with* someone). ***—n.*** a pole supporting a sail, as a mast, boom, or gaff. **—SPAR** or **Spar** a member of the U.S. Coast Guard Women's Reserve.
spare *v.* **spares, spared, spar·ing** **1** relieve (someone) from having to undergo something: *She ~d him some embarrassment; They ate out to ~ her the trouble of cooking; alive because ~d* (i.e. from death) *by providence.* **2** give up or do without (something useful or needed): *"~ the rod and spoil the child"; We have time enough and to ~; ~s no expense when helping friends; Can*

you ~ the time? **—adj. spar·er, spar·est** **1** extra; free: *~ time, tires, rooms, parts.* **2** thin or lean; also, meager or scanty: *a ~ figure, build; a ~ diet, meal.* **—n.** **1** something extra or in reserve, as a spare tire. **2** in bowling, the knocking down of all 10 pins with the first two balls. **—spare·ly** *adv.;* **spare·ness** *n.* **—spare·ribs** *n.pl.* ribs of pork with closely trimmed meat. **—spar·ing** *adj.* frugal or careful; also, scanty or meager; **spar·ing·ly** *adv.*

spark *n.* a particle of fire given off when flint is struck with steel or electricity jumps across a gap, as in the **spark plug** of an automobile engine; hence, any particle or flash: *not a ~ of life in the body;* **v.** give off sparks; also, stir up or stimulate: *The comment ~ed a heated discussion.* **—spar·kle** *v.* **-kles, -kled, -kling** send out sparks; also, shine or glitter as if giving off sparks: *~ing gems, wit; ~ing* (i.e. bubbling) *wines;* **n.:** *the ~ of light playing on a fountain: the ~* (i.e. liveliness) *of her eyes;* **spar·kler** *n.* one that sparkles, as a firework or diamond.

spar·row (SPAIR·oh) *n.* a small, plain-looking, usu. brownish bird of the finch family. **—spar·row·hawk** *n.* any of various small hawks or falcons.

sparse *adj.* **spars·er, spars·est** thinly scattered; not dense: *~ vegetation, population, hair;* **sparse·ly** *adv.;* **sparse·ness** or **spar·si·ty** *n.*

Spar·ta (–tuh) a city-state of ancient Greece noted for its military power. **—Spar·tan** *adj.* of ancient Sparta or like its people: *the ~ virtues of frugality, courage, stern discipline, etc.;* **n.** a person of Sparta.

spasm (SPAZ·um) *n.* **1** a sudden, involuntary, painful contraction of a muscle or muscles, as a cramp or convulsion. **2** a brief burst of energy or excitement. **—spas·mod·ic** (–MOD–) *adj.* having to do with or characterized by spasms: *a ~ cough; ~ efforts;* **spas·mod·i·cal·ly —spas·tic** *adj.* of or having to do with spasms; *~ colitis, paralysis;* **n.** a person with spastic paralysis.

spat a *pt.* & *pp.* of SPIT. **—n.** **1** the young of oysters and other shellfish. **2** usu. **spats** *pl.* gaiters covering the instep and ankle. **3** *Informal.* a petty quarrel; **v. spats, spat·ted, spat·ting.**

spate *n.* a large number or outpouring: *a ~ of words, new books.*

spathe (SPAIDH) *n.* the bract enclosing a spadix, as in the calla lily.

spa·tial (SPAY·shul) *adj.* of or having to do with space; **spa·tial·ly** *adv.*

spat·ter *v.* to splash (liquid) in drops or splash (a person or thing with mud, etc.); **n.** a spattering or a spot made by it.

spat·u·la (SPACH·uh·luh) *n.* a small paddle-like implement for spreading or mixing paints, drugs, etc.; **spat·u·late** *adj.*

spav·in *n.* a disease of horses affecting the hock joint and often causing lameness; **spav·ined** (–ind) *adj.* lame.

spawn *n.* eggs or offspring in large numbers, as of fish, frogs, shellfish, etc.; **v.** produce spawn; hence, bring forth in great numbers: *porno shops ~ed by the sex revolution.*

spay *v.* remove the ovaries of (an animal).

S.P.C.A. Society for the Prevention of Cruelty to Animals. **—S.P.C.C.** Society for the Prevention of Cruelty to Children.

speak (SPEEK) *v.* **speaks, spoke, spo·ken** (SPOH·kn), **speak·ing** utter or express something using language: *Animals don't ~; She ~s English; was invited to ~* (i.e. make a speech) *at the graduation; seats that are already spoken for* (i.e. reserved); *dissidents who* **speak out** *on human rights; Good students* **speak well for** *their school; got his dander up,* **so to speak. —speak·eas·y** (–ee·zee) *n.* **-eas·ies** *Slang.* a place where liquor is sold illegally under prohibition. **—speak·er** *n.* **1** one who speaks; also, a loudspeaker. **2** the chairman of a deliberative assembly.

spear (SPEER) *n.* **1** a thrusting or throwing weapon with a long wooden shaft and a pointed head of metal or stone. **2** a sprout or young shoot of a plant, as of grass. **—v.** pierce or stab with or as with a spear: *to ~ trout; a hockey player penalized for ~ing.* **—spear·head** (–hed) *n.* the pointed head of spear; hence, the first attacker (in an assault) or leader (of a movement); **v.** act as the spearhead of (an assault, undertaking, etc.). **—spear·man** *n.* **-men** a soldier armed with a spear. **—spear·mint** *n.* a mint with erect stems bearing tapering spikes of flowers and smooth leaves used in flavoring.

spec. special; specifically. **—spe·cial** (SPESH·ul) *adj.* of a different or particular kind: *as a ~ favor; ~ permission to watch a late movie; a ~ edition; an extra charge for* **special delivery** *by postal messenger;* **special education** *for handicapped children; Green Berets are* **Special Forces** *soldiers trained in guerrilla warfare; lobbying by* **spe·cial-in·ter·est groups** *trying to influence legislation in their favor;* **n.** a special person, train, edition of a newspaper, produce on sale, television program, etc.; **spe·cial·ly** *adv.* **—spe·cial·ist** *n.* one specializing in a particular subject or line of work. **—spe·cial·ize** *v.* **-iz·es, -ized, -iz·ing** concentrate one's work or study in a particular area: *After four years of general studies they ~; She's ~ing in plastic surgery; This restaurant ~s in sea food; Wings are forelimbs ~d* (i.e. adapted) *for flying;* **spe·cial·i·za·tion** (–ZAY–) *n.* **—spe·cial·ty** *n.* **-ties** a special feature, study, or article: *Greek drama is his ~; hardware, jewelry, and such ~ stores.* **—spe·cie** (SPEE·shee) *n.* coins, as opposed to paper money: *payment* **in specie; spe·cies** (–sheez) *n. sing.* & *pl.* a kind, esp. a biological grouping (under GENUS) of varieties of plants and animals or races whose members can interbreed: *the female of* **the species** (i.e. human race). **—specif.** specifically; **spe·cif·ic** (–SIF–) *adj.*

1 of a definite kind: *Give ~ reasons; the ~ differences* (i.e. as different species of genus "Panthera") *between lions, tigers, and leopards.* **2** curing a particular disease; ***n.*** a specific drug or cure, as quinine for malaria. **—spe·cif·i·cal·ly** (–SIF–) *adv.* **—spec·i·fi·ca·tion** (–CAY–) *n.* something specified; usu. **specifications** *pl.* detailed description of materials, measurements, etc. for a project or undertaking. **—specific gravity** relative density of a substance compared to a standard, as water: *Mercury has a ~ of 13.6;* **spec·i·fic·i·ty** (–FIS–) *n.* **—spec·i·fy** *v.* **-fies, -fied, -fy·ing** mention explicitly; also, describe in detail. **—spec·i·men** (–mun) *n.* a sample taken for a close or comparative study: *botanical ~s; a urine ~; a poor ~* (i.e. representative) *of humanity.* **—spe·cious** (SPEE·shus) *adj.* good, true, correct, etc. in appearance only: *a ~ excuse, argument, resemblance;* **spe·cious·ly** *adv.*

speck *n.* a small mark, spot, or bit: *a ~ of dust;* ***v.*** mark with specks: *a ~ed apple.* **—speck·le** *n.* a small speck, esp. a natural or distinctive marking; ***v.*** **-les, -led, -ling:** *Most trout are ~d.*

specs *n.pl. Informal.* **1** eyeglasses; spectacles. **2** specifications. **—spec·ta·cle** (–tuh–) *n.* **1** a sight or display that attracts public attention: *a fine ~; made a ~ of herself by getting drunk; a movie ~* (with great scenery, large cast, etc.). **2 spectacles** *pl.* eyeglasses. **—spec·tac·u·lar** (–TAC·yuh–) *n.* & *adj.* (a motion picture or television show) that is impressive or striking in visual impact: *a ~ performance; a ~ three-alarm fire;* **spec·tac·u·lar·ly** *adv.* **—spec·ta·tor** (SPEC·tay·tur) *n.* one who watches without taking part, as at a sports event; **spectator sport** baseball, racing, etc. as distinguished from hunting or fishing. **—spec·ter** *n.* a ghost or spirit; *Brit.* **spec·tre. —spec·tral** (–trul) *adj.* having to do with a specter or spectrum. **—spec·tro·gram** *n.* a trace, graph, or photograph made by a **spec·tro·graph** *n.* an instrument for photographing a spectrum; **spec·tro·graph·ic** (–GRAF–) *adj.;* **spec·tro·graph·i·cal·ly** *adv.* **—spec·trom·e·ter** (–TROM–) *n.* a type of spectroscope for measuring spectral wavelengths; **spec·tro·met·ric** (–MET–) *adj.* **—spec·tro·scope** *n.* an optical instrument for separating light into its constituent wavelengths as seen in a spectrum; **spec·tro·scop·ic** (–SCOP–) *adj.;* **spec·tros·co·py** (–TROS·cuh–) *n.* **—spec·trum** *n., pl.* **-tra** or **-trums** **1** a series of colored bands representing wavelengths resulting from the diffraction of white light into its constituents. **2** range or array: *people representing a wide ~ of opinions; a broad-~ antibiotic* (for a variety of diseases). **—spec·u·late** *v.* **-lates, -lat·ed, -lat·ing** **1** reflect (upon or about a subject on which there is insufficient evidence); hence, conjecture or guess. **2** trade (in stocks, commodities, land, etc.) hoping to profit from future price changes. **—spec·u·la·tion** (–LAY–) *n.* **—spec·u·la·tive** (SPEC·yuh·luh·tiv) *adj.;* **spec·u·la·tive·ly** *adv.;* **spec·u·la·tor** (–lay·tur) *n.*

speech *n.* **1** what is spoken, the manner of speaking, the power to speak, or a particular language: *freedom of ~; the faculty of ~; the ~ of the natives.* **2** words spoken to an audience: *an after-dinner ~; a farewell ~.* **—speech·less** *adj.* dumb or silent; also, unable to speak, as from shock.

speed *n.* **1** rate of movement: *maximum ~ of 60 m.p.h.; a transmission with four ~s* (i.e. gears); *was dispatched with ~* (i.e. swiftness); **at speed** rapidly. **2** *Slang.* a methamphetamine. **—*v.*** **speeds,** *pt.* & *pp.* **sped** or **speed·ed, speed·ing** **1** move fast, esp. over a speed limit; **speed·er** *n.;* **speed·ing** *n.* **2** cause to go fast; hence, help succeed: *airmail to ~ a letter on its way; workers told to* **speed up** *production.* **—speed·boat** *n.* a fast motorboat or launch. **—speed·om·e·ter** (spi·DOM–) an instrument that shows the speed at which a vehicle is moving. **—speed·ster** *n.* a speeding person or a vehicle designed for speed, as a racing car. **—speed·way** *n.* a racing track for motorcycles or cars. **—speed·well** *n.* a weedy herb of the figwort family with small, usu. blue flowers. **—speed·y** *adj.* **speed·i·er, -i·est** swift; also, prompt: *a ~ recovery, reply;* **speed·i·ly** *adv.*

spe·le·ol·o·gy (spee·lee·OL–) *n.* the scientific study of caves; **spe·le·ol·o·gist** *n.*

spell *n.* **1** (magic influence of) an incantation or words used as a charm; **cast a spell on** bewitch; also, fascinate; **under a spell** bewitched; also, fascinated. **2** a brief period (of a specified type of weather, an activity, illness or depression, etc.), as one's turn in rotation with others; also, the relieving of one worker by another. **—*v.*** **spells, spelled, spell·ing** **1** relieve (a person) for a while at work or duty. **2** *pt.* & *pp.* also **spelt,** write or say the letters making up a word: *How is your name ~d? Red often ~s* (i.e. means) *danger;* **spell out** read (letter by letter) or explain (a message) carefully; **spell·er** *n.* **—spell·bind** (–bined) *v.* **-binds, -bound, -bind·ing** hold as if under a spell; also, fascinate; **spell·bind·er** *n.* a fascinating speaker; **spell·bound** *adj.: listening ~ for two hours.* **—spell·down** or **spelling bee** a spelling contest in which players who make spelling errors are eliminated. **—spell·ing** *n.* the act of spelling or the way a word is spelled. **—spelt** See SPELL, *v.* 2.

spe·lunk·er (spi·LUNK–) *n.* one whose hobby is exploring caves, or **spe·lunk·ing** *n.*

spend *v.* **spends, spent, spending** use (a resource such as money, time, effort, thought, etc. on or for something); hence, consume or use up: *a storm that has ~t its fury.* **—spend·thrift** *n.* one who spends money wastefully; ***adj.*** wasteful; prodigal. **—spent** *adj.* exhausted or used up: *a ~ bullet, horse.*

sperm *n.* the male generative fluid; also, a spermatozoon; **sper·mat·o·zo·on** (–mat·uh·ZOH–) *n.,pl.* **-zo·a** (–ZOH·uh) a male germ cell. —**sperm whale** the best-known of the whales, a thickset animal with paddlelike flippers and an enormous blunt-snouted head that yields **sperm oil** used for lubricating.

spew *v.* vomit or cast forth.

sp·gr. specific gravity.

sphag·num (SFAG–) *n.* a soft moss of swampy places that forms peat when decomposed.

sphere (SFEER) *n.* **1** a perfectly round solid body; also, a globular body such as a star or planet. **2** an imagined hollow globe with the earth at its center and the heavenly bodies revolving around it in fixed concentric shells; hence, the range or domain of an activity or quality: *one's ~ of activity, interest, influence.* —**spher·i·cal** (SFER–, SFEER–) *adj.;* **spher·i·cal·ly** *adv.* —**spher·oid** (SFEER–) *n.* a body that is a slightly flattened or elongated sphere, as the earth or a football; **sphe·roid·al** (–ROY–) *adj.*

sphinc·ter (SFINGK–) *n.* a ringlike muscle controlling a body opening, as of the anus or vagina. —**sphinx** (SFINGKS) *n.* a statue with a lion's body and human head, which in its Greek version was a monster who would strangle every passer-by unable to solve a riddle; hence, an enigmatic or puzzling character.

sphyg·mo·ma·nom·e·ter (–muh·NOM–) *n.* See MANOMETER.

spice *n.* a food seasoning made from a plant, as pepper, ginger, and mace; hence, something that adds flavor: *"Variety is the ~ of life"*; ***v.*** **spic·es, spiced, spic·ing** season with spice or add zest to; **spic·y** *adj.* **spic·i·er, -i·est:** *~ humor; ~* (i.e. slightly racy) *stories.* —**spice·bush** *n.* an aromatic shrub of the laurel family with small yellow flowers and red fruit.

spick-and-span *adj.* fresh or spotlessly clean.

spic·ule *n.* **1** one of the thousands of jets of gas rising from the sun's chromosphere. **2** a tiny, needlelike body of bony material. —**spic·u·lar** *adj.*

spi·der (SPY–) *n.* **1** an eight-legged, insectlike creature that spins webs of silk. **2** a cast-iron frying pan, originally with short legs. —**spi·der·y** *adj.*

spiel (SPEEL) *n. Slang.* a voluble or glib persuasive talk, as of a circus barker; also ***v.***

spiff·y *adj.* **spiff·i·er, -i·est** *Slang.* smart or dapper. —**spiff·i·ly** *adv.*

spig·ot (–ut) *n.* a faucet; also, a plug or peg for stopping the vent of a barrel or cask.

spike *n.* **1** a usu. large nail or metal point, as those forming the top of an iron fence or the projections on the soles of shoes for preventing slipping. **2** a long, pointed cluster of flowers or an ear of grain. —***v.*** **spikes, spiked, spik·ing** **1** connect with spikes, as a rail to a tie; also, provide with spikes, as shoes, or impale on a spike. **2** prevent or thwart (a scheme or attempt). **3** *Informal.* add alcoholic liquor to (a drink). —**spike·nard** *n.* an East Indian plant yielding a costly perfume.

spill *v.* **spills,** *pt. & pp.* **spilled** or **spilt, spill·ing** **1** (let a liquid or a substance in loose particles) flow over accidentally from a container: *~d milk, salt; a narrow neck to prevent ~ing; to ~* (i.e. be guilty of shedding) *blood.* **2** *Informal.* throw off or out: *The horse ~d him.* —***n.*** **1** a spilling or something spilled. **2** *Informal.* a fall from a horse or vehicle. **3** also **spill·way,** a channel for overflowing water, as from a reservoir.

spin *v.* **spins, spun, spin·ning** **1** turn or revolve rapidly, as a top, wheel, etc.; also, shape by turning, as on a lathe or wheel: *her head ~ing from the dance; good at ~ing* (i.e. telling) *yarns.* **2** make (thread) by drawing out and twisting cotton, wool, etc.; also, make something with thread, as a web, or threadlike from glass, gold, or sugar (i.e. "cotton candy"). **3** move along smoothly and rapidly on a wheeled vehicle. —***n.*** **1** a spinning motion, as of a plane coming down out of control. **2** a ride in an automobile, on a bicycle, etc. —**spin·ner** *n.*

spin·ach (–ich) *n.* a garden vegetable with a thick cluster of leaves rich in vitamins and minerals.

spi·nal (SPY·nl) *adj.* of the spinal column or spinal cord; **spinal column** a column or series of jointed or fused bones called vertebrae supporting the back; backbone; **spinal cord** a cord of nerve tissue extending from the brain through the spinal column.

spin·dle *n.* a short, round, or smooth stick or rod with tapered ends for spinning yarn into thread; also, anything resembling it in form or function, as a turned wooden piece for a baluster or the back of a chair. —**spin·dly** *adj.* **-dlier, -dli·est** long and very thin or frail, as legs; also **spin·dling.** —**spin·drift** *n.* spray from the sea, as during a gale.

spine *n.* **1** a stiff, sharp-pointed, protective growth, as on a cactus or porcupine. **2** the spinal column or anything resembling it, as the hinged back of a book; also, backbone or courage; **spine·less** *adj.* —**spi·nel** (–NEL) *n.* a hard, crystalline mineral whose red variety is used as a gem called "spinel ruby." —**spin·et** (–it) *n.* a pianolike early keyboard instrument on which the harpsichord is based.

spin·na·ker (SPIN·uh–) *n.* a large, triangular sail used with the mainsail for added speed when running before the wind.

spin·ner·et *n.* the organ with which a spider or caterpillar spins silk. —**spinning jenny** a multiple-spindled spinning machine invented about 1764. —**spinning wheel** a device for spinning thread or yarn with a spindle driven by a large wheel operated by hand or foot. —**spin-off** *n.* a benefit, product, etc. derived or resulting from a larger enterprise, as abridged editions of a reference work. —**spin·ster** *n.* a woman who has never married; **spin·ster·hood** *n.*

spin·y (SPY·nee) *adj.* **spin·i·er, -i·est** having spines; **spiny lobster** a kind of lobster with a spiny body and no large claws.

spi·ra·cle (SPY·ruh–) *n.* a body opening for breathing, as those along the sides of an insect's body, a fish's gill slit, or a whale's nasal opening.

spiraea same as SPIREA.

spi·ral (SPY·rul) *n.* & *adj.* (a curve or coil) winding in widening circles like the hairspring of a watch or helically like a screw: *a* ~ (i.e. circular) *staircase; an inflationary* ~ (of rising prices and wages). **—*v.* -rals, -ral(l)ed, -ral·(l)ing** make or move in a spiral. —**spi·ral·ly** *adv.*

spi·rant (SPY·runt) *n.* & *adj.* (a consonant such as "f," "s," "sh," or "th") uttered with audible friction of the breath.

spire *n.* **1** a tapering and pointed structure, as the top of a church steeple or a tapering stalk of grass. **2** the top part of a univalve shell, as of a conch.

spi·r(a)e·a (spy·REE·uh) *n.* an ornamental plant of the rose family bearing small clusters of white or pink flowers on slender stalks.

spir·it (SPEER–) *n.* **1** an animating principle, as the soul to the body; the moral, religious, or emotional aspect of something: *The* ~ *is willing though the body is weak; the* ~ *of our founders; Obey the letter and* ~ *of the law; a noble* ~ (i.e. person); **spir·it·u·al** (–choo·ul) *adj.;* **spir·it·u·al·ly** *adv.;* **spir·it·u·al·i·ty** (–choo·AL–) *n.* **2** a bodiless or supernatural being, as God, fairies, ghosts, etc. **3** disposition, mood, or state of mind: *in good* **spirits;** *team* ~; *the* ~ *of 76; Put some* ~ (i.e. enthusiasm) *into it.* **4** usu. **spirits** *pl.* a distilled liquid: ~*s of turpentine, camphor; a teetotaler who shuns* ~*s* (i.e. alcohol). —***v.*** carry (a person *away*) secretly. —**spir·it·ed** *adj.* lively; energetic; **spir·it·less** *adj.* —**spir·it·u·al·ism** *n.* belief in the souls of the dead communicating with the living; **spir·it·u·al·ist** *n.;* **spir·it·u·al·is·tic** (–LIS–) *adj.* —**spir·it·u·al·ize** *v.* **-iz·es, -ized, -iz·ing** make spiritual. —**spir·it·u·ous** (–choo·us) *adj.* containing alcohol got by distilling.

spi·ro·chete (SPY·ruh·keet) *n.* a spiral-shaped, slender bacterium such as causes syphilis, yaws, or relapsing fever.

[1]spit *n.* **1** small point of land projecting into water. **2** a pointed rod or bar on which meat is roasted over a fire; ***v.*** **spits, spit·ted, spit·ting** pierce (as if) with a spit.

[2]spit *v.* **spits,** *pt.* & *pp.* **spit** or **spat, spit·ting** eject (saliva) from the mouth; hence, throw out (something) or make a sound like spitting, as a cat when angry or fat when frying: *guns* ~*ing fire;* ***n.*** a spitting; also, saliva spat out; **spit and polish** *Informal.* (much or excessive attention to) neatness and orderliness, esp. of a superficial kind. —**spit·ball** *n.* **1** a ball of chewed up paper used as a missile. **2** a baseball pitch delivered after the ball has been moistened with spit or sweat.

spite *n.* petty ill will with a tendency to annoy or irritate; **in spite of** notwithstanding. —***v.*** **spites, spit·ed, spit·ing** show spite toward; annoy or irritate. —**spite·ful** *adj.;* **spite·ful·ly** *adv.*

spit·tle (SPITL) *n.* saliva. —**spit·tle·bug** *n.* a hopping insect whose larvae secrete a frothy substance for protection from enemies. —**spit·toon** (spi·TOON) *n.* a container to spit into.

splash *v.* dash (water, mud, etc.) so as to make it scatter in drops: *Do not* ~ *when painting; passing cars* ~*ing pedestrians; a coat* ~*ed with mud; children* ~*ing in the pool;* ~*ing across a flooded street;* ***n.*** a splashing or a spot or noise made by splashing; **make a splash** *Informal.* make a sensation; attract much attention. —**splash·down** *n.* the landing of a spacecraft on water. —**splash·y** *adj.* **splash·i·er, -i·est** *Informal.* showy or sensational.

splat *n.* a vertical center rail or slat in the back of certain chairs.

splat·ter *n.* & *v.* spatter.

splay *v.* spread out or flare (a window or other opening) as with a beveled jamb; ***n.*** such a flare or beveled surface. —**splay·foot** *n.* **-feet** a broad flat foot that is turned outward; **splay·foot·ed** *adj.* having splayfeet; hence, clumsy.

spleen *n.* a large glandlike organ lying between the stomach and the diaphragm that acts as a blood filter but was once believed the cause of bad temper; hence, spite or ill temper.

splen·did *adj.* brilliant and impressive: *a* ~ *palace, victory; a* ~ (*Informal.* excellent) *idea;* **splen·did·ly** *adv.* —**splen·dor** (–dur) *n.* brilliance; pomp; magnificence; also **splen·dour** *Brit.*

sple·net·ic (spli·NET–) *adj.* **1** of the spleen; also **splen·ic** (SPLEN–, SPLEE–). **2** bad-tempered or peevish; **sple·net·i·cal·ly** *adv.*

splice *v.* **splic·es, spliced, splic·ing** **1** join (ropes, etc.) without knotting by weaving untwisted ends together; also, join together (pieces of timber, etc.) by overlapping. **2** fasten together (tape, film, etc.) by cutting and gluing. —***n.*** a joint made by splicing.

splint *n.* **1** a thin strip of wood or other flexible material for weaving or braiding into baskets, chair seats, etc. **2** a thin strip of wood, a plaster cast, or other device for keeping an injured body part in position while healing. —**splin·ter** *n.* a long, thin, sharp piece of broken glass, bone, wood, etc.: *a new party formed by a* ~ (i.e. fractional) *group;* ***v.*** break into splinters. —**split** *v.* **splits, split, split·ting** **1** separate lengthwise or along a natural line of division, as along the grain of wood or into layers of slate. **2** cut or divide into parts: *The* *bag ~ at the seams; the ~ing up of land into housing lots; the ~ing of the atom; a* **splitting** (i.e. severe) *headache.* **3** *Slang.* leave a place. ***—n.*** a splitting, crack, division, etc. ***—adj.:*** *a ~* (i.e. not unanimous) *decision; two telecast scenes shown side by side on a ~ screen;* **split-lev·el** *n.* & *adj.* (a house) with an intermediate level about half a floor above or below the others built adjacently; **split personality** a personality with conflicting patterns of behavior; also, *Informal.* schizophrenia.

splotch *n.* an irregular or blotchy spot or stain; ***v.*** mark with a splotch or splotches; **splotch·y** *adj.*

splurge *n.* & *v.* **splurg·es, splurged, splurg·ing** *Informal.* (make) a showy or extravagant display or spend money extravagantly (*on* an automobile, etc.).

splut·ter *v.* make a sputtering sound, esp. speak in an excited and confused manner; ***n.*** a spluttering.

spoil *v.* **spoils,** *pt.* & *pp.* **spoiled** or **spoilt, spoil·ing** **1** destroy the usefulness or value of; damage: *"Too many cooks ~ the broth"; a ~d* (i.e. pampered) *child; methods to preserve food from ~ing* (i.e. beginning to rot); *Bad weather ~d the picnic.* **2 be spoiling for** *Informal.* be eager for (a fight, etc.). **3** *Archaic.* rob or plunder; ***n.*** usu. **spoils** *pl.* loot or booty: *the ~s of war.* **—spoil·age** (–ij) *n.* **—spoil·er** *n.* **1** one that spoils or loots. **2** a plate that acts as an air brake, as on an airplane wing or racing car. **—spoil·sport** *n.* one who spoils the enjoyment of others. **—spoils system** the political practice of rewarding supporters with public offices when a party assumes power.

Spo·kane (–KAN) a city of E. Washington.

[1]spoke *n.* any of the radial bars extending from the hub of a wheel to its rim.

[2]spoke *pt.* of SPEAK. **—spoken** *pp.* of SPEAK. —***adj.*** & ***comb.form.*** uttered: *the ~ word; plain-~; soft-~.* **—spokes·man** *n.* **-men** a person expressing the views of another or of a group; *fem.* **spokes·wom·an, -wom·en.**

spo·li·a·tion (spoh·lee·AY–) *n.* robbery or plundering, esp. in war; **spo·li·a·tor** *n.*

sponge (SPUNJ) *n.* **1** a water animal with a porous skeleton that resembles a plant in being attached to the bottom of the sea or to other objects; also, a porous or spongelike mass or rubber, or **sponge rubber,** or other synthetic material used for cleansing, washing, etc.; hence, a washing or wiping with a sponge. **2** *Informal.* a parasite; also **spong·er.** ***—v.*** **spong·es, sponged, spong·ing** wipe, rub, wash, etc. with a sponge. **—sponge bath** a cleaning of the body using a wet sponge. **—sponge·cake** *n.* a light spongy cake made without shortening. **—spon·gy** *adj.* **-gi·er, -gi·est** like a sponge; full of holes.

spon·sor (–sur) *n.* an endorser or supporter, as a godparent, the promoter of a legislative proposal, or one paying for a radio or television program by buying commercial advertising; ***v.*** act as sponsor for. **—spon·sor·ship** *n.*

spon·ta·ne·i·ty (–tuh·NEE–) *n.* **-ties** the quality or an instance of being spontaneous. **—spon·ta·ne·ous** (–TAY·nee·us) *adj.* caused or happening naturally, without planning or premeditation: *~ laughter; a ~ outburst, abortion* (i.e. miscarriage); **spontaneous combustion** the catching fire of something from heat produced by chemical action within itself, as in a pile of oily rags; **spon·ta·ne·ous·ly** *adv.*

spoof *Informal. n.* a hoax or trick; also, a parody or takeoff; ***v.*** ridicule or parody.

spook *n.* *Informal.* a ghost; *Slang.* a spy; ***v.*** frighten; **spook·y** *adj.*

spool *n.* cylinder or reel on which thread, wire, film, ribbon, etc. is wound.

spoon *n.* **1** a utensil consisting of a shallow bowl at one end of a handle for eating, stirring, etc.; ***v.*** take up with a spoon. **2** something spoon-shaped, as a fishing lure. **—spoon·ful** *n.* **-fuls.** **—spoon·bill** *n.* an ibislike wading bird with a spoon-shaped bill.

spoon·er·ism *n.* the interchanging of sounds in running words with comic effect, as in "kinkering congs" for "conquering kings."

spoon·feed *v.* **-feeds, -fed, -feed·ing** feed with a spoon, as a child; hence, help (someone) in such a way as to prevent him from thinking or acting for himself.

spoor *n.* the trail or track of a wild animal.

spo·rad·ic (spuh·RAD–) *adj.* occurring in scattered or isolated instances: *~ cases of a disease; ~ gunfire;* **spo·rad·i·cal·ly** *adv.*

spore *n.* in algae, fungi, ferns, and such lower forms of life, a tiny one-celled body capable of giving rise to a new individual; ***v.*** **spores, spored, spor·ing** form spores.

sport *n.* **1** a pastime requiring physical exertion and skill, as baseball, bowling, etc. **2** fun or amusement; also, an object of fun; plaything: *said it* **for** (or **in**) **sport;** *They liked to* **make sport** *of his accent; He soon became the ~ of the class.* **3** *Informal.* a good fellow: *Be a ~!* **4** *Informal.* a flashy fellow. **5** a mutant. ***—v.*** **1** to play or jest. **2** *Informal.* to display: *~ing a new jacket.* ***—adj.*** **1** of or for sports. **2** for casual wear: *a ~(s) shirt.* **—sport·ing** *adj.* of or having to do with sports: *the ~ public; a ~* (i.e. sportsmanlike) *offer, a ~* (*Informal.* fair) *chance;* **sport·ing·ly** *adv.* **—sport·ive** (–iv) *adj.* full of or done in fun; **sport·ive·ly** *adv.* **—sports car** a small, low-slung fast car with a light, sleek body and a powerful engine. **—sports·cast** *n.* a broadcast of a sporting event; **sports·cast·er** *n.* **—sports·man** *n.* **-men** **1** a man who takes part in sports such as hunting and fishing. **2** one who plays fair; **sports·man·like** *adj.;* **sports·man·ship** *n.* **—sports·wom·an** *n.* **-wom·en.** **—sports·writ·er** *n.* a journalist who writes about sports events. **—sport·y** *adj.*

sport·i·er, -i·est *Informal.* good for sport; also, flashy or showy.

spot *n.* **1** a small extent of space: *a clear ~ in the jungle; the exact ~ where he landed.* **2** a small, distinguishable area or mark: *the leopard's ~s; a ~* (i.e. stain) *remover; a clear skin without ~s* (i.e. blemishes). **3 in a (bad) spot** *Slang.* in trouble; **on the spot** then and there; **put on the spot** *Slang.* place in a difficult or embarrassing situation. **—v. spots, spot·ted, spot·ting** **1** mark or become marked with spots; also, to stain: *the ~d sandpiper; a page ~d with smudges.* **2** locate; also, see or recognize: *couldn't ~ him in the crowd.* **—adj.** happening, done, etc. on the spot: *~ news coverage of a fire; ~ transactions; a 30-second ~ commercial; a* **spot-check** *by police;* **spot-check** *v.* make a random, on-the-spot check. **—spot·light** *n.* a bright light thrown on a spot requiring illumination, as on the stage; hence, the focus of public attention; **v.** light up with a spotlight; hence, put in public view. **—spot·ter** *n.* **1** one who removes spots before cleaning clothes. **2** one who locates, identifies, or keeps watch on people, targets, etc. **—spot·ty** *adj.* **spot·ti·er, spot·ti·est** spotted; uneven; irregular: *~ appearance, work.*

spouse *n.* one's wife or husband.

spout *n.* a jet or stream, as of water, from a pipe, nozzle, or projecting tube, as of a kettle; also, a projecting part or a pipe, as for rainwater from a roof; **v.** shoot out, as water from a spout or fountain; also, *Informal.* utter or speak in a vehement or declamatory manner.

sprain *v.* stretch or tear the ligaments of (a body joint) accidentally; **n.** such an injury.

sprang a *pt.* of SPRING.

sprat *n.* a small herringlike sea fish.

sprawl *v.* lie on one's back with limbs loosely spread out: *bodies ~ed on a beach;* **n.** a sprawling or a spread-out condition: *halting urban ~.*

spray *n.* **1** (an ornament shaped like) a small cluster of leaves, flowers, or fruit. **2** a mist or jet of tiny drops, as from a breaking wave or a spray gun. **—v.:** *insecticide ~ed on trees; the enemy ~ed with bullets;* **spray·er** *n.* **—spray can** an aerosol container; **spray gun** a device like an airbrush for applying paints, lacquers, etc.

spread (SPRED) *v.* **spreads, spread, spread·ing** (cause) to cover a large(r) area; extend or stretch out; also, scatter: *A bird ~s its wings; to ~ a rug on the lawn; ~ jam on toast; to ~ seed, news, contagious diseases; payments ~ over many years; to ~* (i.e. lay) *the table for dinner.* **—n.** a spreading, what is spread, or its expanse or extent: *the ~ of civilization; the ~ of an eagle's wings; ~s* (i.e. covers) *for tables, beds, etc.; a tasty sandwich ~; an ad designed as a two-page ~.* **—spread·er** *n.*

spree *n.* an uninhibited activity or indulgence in something: *a shopping ~; spending ~; the hangover following a ~* (i.e. drinking bout).

sprig *n.* a small twig or spray: *a ~ of mistletoe.*

spright·ly (SPRITE) *adj.* **-li·er, -li·est** lively or spirited: *a ~ lad;* **adv.** gaily; **spright·li·ness** *n.*

spring *v.* **springs,** *pt.* **sprang** or **sprung,** *pp.* **sprung, spring·ing** **1** move, esp. rise suddenly and lightly: *to ~ out of bed; weeds ~ing up on a lawn; He sprang to her defense; He's sprung of* (or *from*) *noble blood.* **2** of a wall, door, etc., give way to pressure and crack, warp, etc. **3** cause to spring: *a trap that is easily sprung; wanted to ~ the news on* (i.e. make it known suddenly to) *her parents; The boat* **sprang a leak** *and sank; was sprung from jail* (*Slang.* released) *by paying bail.* **—n.** **1** a springing: *a sudden ~.* **2** an elastic device or quality: *cars with coil ~s and leaf ~s; the ~ of her step.* **3** the growing season, following winter. **4** a natural stream rising from under the ground: *mineral ~s.* **5** source or origin; also, motive. **—adj.** [corresponding to the *n.* senses] **2:** *a ~ device, lock.* **3:** *~ cleaning, rains.* **4:** *fresh ~ water.* **—spring·board** *n.* a flexible board to jump from with a springing motion, as at a swimming pool. **—spring fever** a feeling of restlessness during the change from the cold of winter to the warmth of spring. **—Spring·field** **1** a city of S.W. Massachusetts. **2** capital of Illinois. **3** a city of S.W. Missouri. **—spring tide** either of the two higher-than-normal tides occurring during new moon and full moon because of the combined pull of the sun and the moon. **—spring·time** *n.* the spring season. **—spring·y** *adj.* **spring·i·er, -i·est** elastic or resilient: *a ~ step, mattress;* **spring·i·ly** *adv.;* **spring·i·ness** *n.*

sprin·kle (SPRING·kl) *v.* **-kles, -kled, -kling** fall or scatter in small drops or particles: *to ~ salt on food; to ~ a lawn* (with water); *It's ~ing outside* (i.e. raining slightly); **n.** a sprinkling; also, a light rain; **sprin·kler** *n.;* **sprin·kling** *n.* a small number or quantity.

sprint *n.* & *v.* (run) a relatively short race, up to 400 meters (444 yds.) in track and field; dash; **sprint·er** *n.*

sprite *n.* an elf or fairy.

sprock·et (–it) *n.* one of the teeth on a wheel rim that engage with the links of a chain going over it, as in a bicycle; also, the wheel, or **sprocket wheel.**

sprout *n.* a young shoot, as from a seed in the ground; also, a bud; **v.** cause or begin to grow; germinate.

spruce (SPROOSE) *n.* an evergreen tree related to the firs but with cones hanging downwards. **—adj. spruc·er, spruc·est** neat and smart; **v. spruc·es, spruc·ed, spruc·ing:** *He ~d himself up for the party.*

sprung *pp.* & a *pt.* of SPRING.

spry *adj.* **spri·er** or **spry·er, spri·est** or **spry·est** esp. of the elderly, vigorous and active; **spry·ly** *adv.;* **spry·ness** *n.*

spud *n.* *Informal.* potato.

spume (SPYOOM) *n.* & *v.* **spumes, spumed, spum·ing** foam or froth. —**spu·mo·ni** (spuh·MOH·nee) *n.* an Italian-style ice cream; also **spu·mo·ne.**

spun *pt.* & *pp.* of SPIN.

spunk *n. Informal.* pluck or spirit; **spunk·y** *adj.* **spunk·i·er, -i·est.**

spur *n.* **1** a pricking device with a sharp point or rowel, worn on a rider's heel for urging a horse forward; hence, a stimulus or incentive; **on the spur of the moment** suddenly and impulsively. **2** something spurlike, as the small projection on the leg of a cock, a lateral ridge extending from a mountain, or a railroad siding. ***—v.*** **spurs, spurred, spur·ring** urge on or incite, as with spurs.

spurge *n.* (any of) a large family of shrubs, trees, and usu. poisonous plants yielding a milky juice, including cassava, castor oil, poinsettia, and rubber.

spu·ri·ous (SPYOOR·ee·us) *adj.* not genuine or authentic: *a ~ signature, document;* **spu·ri·ous·ly** *adv.;* **spu·ri·ous·ness** *n.*

spurn *v.* refuse or reject with disdain: *to ~ a lover; ~ed his attentions.*

spurt *v.* (cause) to gush out suddenly, as blood from a wound; also, show a short and sudden burst of energy, as near the finish in a race; ***n.:*** *~s of flame; a ~ of activity in the stock market.*

sput·nik *n.* an earth satellite orbited by the U.S.S.R.

sput·ter *n.* & *v.* (make) a popping and spitting noise, as of fat when frying; also, spit out (drops or bits of food) or talk in excitement and confusion. —**spu·tum** (SPEW–) *n., pl.* **-ta** (–tuh) saliva and mucus that is spat out.

spy *v.* **spies, spied, spy·ing** **1** keep secret watch (*on* a person or search out information *for* a nation) for hostile purposes, as in wartime; ***n.,*** *pl.* **spies** one who spies. **2** catch sight of, as with a **spy glass,** a small telescope.

sq. squadron; square. —**sqq.** the following ones.

squab (SKWOB) *n.* a young pigeon; ***adj.*** short and stout.

squab·ble (SKWOBL) *n.* & *v.* **squab·bles, squab·bled, squab·bling** (have) a petty and noisy quarrel.

squab·by *adj.* **squab·bi·er, squab·bi·est** short and stout.

squad (SKWOD) *n.* the smallest military unit, composed of 10 or 12 soldiers; hence, a small group of people working together; **squad car** a police cruiser or patrol car. —**squad·ron** (–run) *n.* an organized military unit, esp. in an air force; hence, any organized multitude: *~s of birds, flies.*

squal·id (SKWOL–) *adj.* filthy, as from neglect; also, morally bad; sordid: *~ slums, poverty, existence, conditions.*

squall (SQUAWL) **1** *n.* a sudden rise in the wind, esp. at sea, often accompanied by rain, hail, or thunder; **squall·y** *adj.* **2** *n.* & *v.* (utter) a loud, harsh cry or scream.

squal·or (SKWOL·ur) *n.* the state of being squalid; wretchedness; sordidness.

squa·mous (SKWAY·mus) *adj.* formed of scales; also, scalelike; also **squa·mose.**

squan·der (SKWON–) *v.* spend (wealth, resources, etc.) wastefully or extravagantly.

square *n.* **1** a plane figure with four equal sides and angles. **2** anything in this shape, as a city block, a public place enclosed by streets on all sides, an instrument in the shape of an L or T to make or measure right angles, etc. **3** the product of a quantity multiplied by itself: *49 is the ~ of 7; 7 is the* **square root** *of 49.* **4** *Slang.* an old-fashioned person; one who is not hip. ***—adj.*** **squar·er, squar·est** **1** like a square in shape: *a ~ room; a room 20 feet ~* (i.e. 20 ft. long on all sides); *within [~] brackets; ~ jaws, shoulders.* **2** suggesting evenness, balance, straightness, etc.: *fair and ~* (i.e. honest) *dealings; ~* (i.e. balanced) *accounts; a ~* (i.e. substantial) *meal; a ~* (i.e. straightforward) *refusal.* **3** *Slang.* not hip; old-fashioned. ***—v.*** **squares, squared, squar·ing:** *~d graph paper; ~d timber* (with rectangular edges); *to ~* (i.e. settle) *accounts; performance that does not ~* (i.e. agree) *with promises; 7 ~d is 49;* **square off** *Informal.* get ready to fight, as in boxing; **square oneself** *Informal.* make up for a wrong. ***—adv.*** in a square shape or manner; also **square·ly; square·ness** *n.* —**square dance** a folk dance in groups of four couples in a square formation performing various figures; **square-dance** *v.* —**square measure** a unit or system for measuring areas. —**square one** the starting point, as in games. —**square-rigged** *adj.* with four-sided sails fastened horizontally on yards slung across masts, not fore and aft; **square-rig·ger** *n.* a square-rigged ship. —**square root** See SQUARE, *n.* 3. —**squar·ish** *adj.* nearly square.

squash (SKWOSH) *v.* **1** squeeze, crush, or beat into a flat mass or pulp; hence, give a crushing blow to; suppress (a riot) or silence (an adversary). **2** produce or move with a splashing sound. ***—n.*** **1** a squashing fall or its soft, heavy sound; also, a squashed mass; **squash·y** *adj.* **2** a gourd of the New World related to pumpkins, used as a vegetable and in pies. **3** a game like handball but played with rackets in a walled court, in full **squash racquets,** distinguished from **squash tennis** played in a similar court with larger rackets and an inflated ball.

squat *v.* **squats, squat·ted, squat·ting** **1** crouch or sit on the heels with bent knees; ***n.*** squatting posture. **2** settle on land without original legal right; **squat·ter** *n.: ~s' rights to public land recognized by an 1841 law; Millions live in ~ settlements* (i.e. shanty towns) *in developing countries.* ***—adj.*** **squat·ter, squat·test** **1**

crouching. **2** short and thick in stature, as a toad or puffin; dumpy: *a* ~ *little man;* also **squat·ty.**

squaw *n.* [disparaging use] a North American Indian married woman.

squawk *n.* & *v.* (utter) a loud, harsh, complaining cry; hence, *Informal.* protest or complain raucously. **—squeak** (SQUEEK) *n.* & *v.* (utter) the sharp, high-pitched cry of a mouse or the sound of a door hinge that needs oiling: *too choked even to* ~ *for help; The bill managed to* **squeak through** *the legislature with a narrow margin; a* **narrow squeak** (i.e. escape); **squeak·y** *adj.* **squeak·i·er, -i·est:** ~ *shoes, floor boards; a* ~ *voice; hair washed* **squeak·y-clean.** **—squeal** (SQUEEL) *n.* & *v.* **1** (make) a long squeaking cry or sound, as a pig when hurt or faulty brakes. **2** (act as) an informer; **squeal·er** *n.*

squeam·ish (SQUEEM–) *adj.* **1** prudish or scrupulous. **2** queasy or easily nauseated. **—squeam·ish·ness** *n.*

squee·gee (–jee) *n.* a tool with a rubber-edged blade set crosswise on a handle, as used for window-washing; also, any similar device. Also *v.* **—squeeze** *v.* **squeez·es, squeezed, squeez·ing** **1** press from the sides, as in extracting juice from a fruit, hugging someone, or forcing a way through a crowd. **2** put pressure on (a victim) or get (money, etc.) by pressure; hence, oppress. ***—n.*** a squeezing or being squeezed: *a* ~ (i.e. restraint) *on bank loans to fight inflation; a plastic* **squeeze bottle** *for sprays; a* **squeeze play** *with the batter bunting the ball and the runner scoring from third base.*

squelch *n.* & *v. Informal.* **1** (silence or put down with) a rebuke, stare, etc. **2** (slosh or splash through mud, etc. making) a sucking sound.

squib *n.* **1** a short witty or satirical piece. **2** a small firecracker that makes a fizzing noise.

squid *n.* a sea mollusk with 10 arms similar to an octopus's.

squig·gle *n.* a wavy twist or curve; ***v.*** **squig·gles, squig·gled, squig·gling** move with or make squiggles; also, write as a squiggle; **squig·gly** (–glee) *adj.*

squint *v.* **1** look with the eyes partly closed; peer. **2** look sideways; also, be cross-eyed. ***—n.*** **1** a peering. **2** cross-eye; also, a sidelong glance.

squire *v.* **squires, squired, squir·ing** act as a squire (to). ***—n.*** **1** a woman's escort. **2** a justice of the peace. **3** in Britain, a country gentleman, esp. the chief landowner of a district; formerly, a knight's personal attendant or armor-bearer.

squirm *n.* & *v.* wriggle or writhe; hence, show great embarrassment. **—squirm·y** *adj.*

squir·rel (SKWUR·ul) *n.* any of a family of esp. tree-dwelling rodents related to the chipmunk, valued for their fur.

squirt *v.* eject (a liquid) in a thin stream, as through a small pump or syringe; ***n.*** **1** a jet of liquid; also, a squirting device such as a "water pistol," or **squirt gun.** **2** *Informal.* an impudent youngster.

squish *n.* & *v.* (make) a soft splashing or squashing (*v.* 2) sound; **squish·y** *adj.*

Sr. Senior; Sister; **Sr** strontium.

Sri Lan·ka (sree·LAHNG·kuh) an island republic off S.E. India; 25,332 sq.mi. (65,610 km²); *cap.* Colombo; **Sri Lan·kan** *n.* & *adj.*

S.R.O. standing room only.

S.S. steamship.

S.S.E. south-southeast.

S.S.R. Soviet Socialist Republic.

SST supersonic transport.

S.S.W. south-southwest.

St. Saint; Strait; Street. **—st.** stanza; stet; stone; street. **—s.t.** short ton.

sta. station(ary).

stab *n.* (wound made by) a thrust with a pointed weapon such as a dagger; also, the pain caused; **stab in the back** a treacherous attack or betrayal. ***—v.*** **stabs, stabbed, stab·bing** pierce or wound (a person) with or as if with a pointed weapon; **stab·ber** *n.*

sta·bil·i·ty (stuh·BIL–) *n.* a being stable; firmness; steadiness; permanence. **—sta·bi·lize** (STAY–) *v.* **-liz·es, -lized, -liz·ing** make stable or steady: ~ *fluctuating prices;* ~ *a ship using a gyroscope;* ~ *an airplane with a horizontal* **sta·bi·liz·er** *in its tail assembly;* **sta·bi·li·za·tion** (–ZAY–) *n.* **—sta·ble** (STAY·bl) *adj.* **-bler, -blest** not likely to give way or be overturned: *a* ~ (i.e. firm) *government; a* ~ (i.e. steady) *job, personality; a* ~ (i.e. lasting) *design, chemical compound.* ***—n.*** a building in which domestic animals are housed and fed; hence, such animals, esp. racehorses collectively: *a publisher with a* ~ *of authors.* ***—v.*** **-bles, -bled, -bling** to lodge or be kept in a stable.

stac·ca·to (stuh·CAH·toh) *adj.* & *adv.* in a broken or disconnected manner: ~ *speech; music played* ~ (i.e. with successive notes detached).

stack *n.* a neatly arranged or orderly pile, as a haystack, rifles put up in a pyramid arrangement, etc.; also, a smokestack; **stacks** *pl.* where books are stored in a library, esp. the main collection. ***—v.*** **1** pile or arrange in a stack. **2** arrange (cards) so as to cheat. **—stack up** measure up or compare (*with* or *against* a standard); **stack·up** *n.* aircraft in a holding pattern.

sta·di·um (STAY·dee–) *n.* a large structure of tiers of seats, often domed, built around a playing field or arena.

staff *n., pl.* also **staves** (for defs. 1 & 3). **1** a supporting stick or pole, as used when walking or for hoisting a flag; hence, one that supports or sustains: *Bread is the* ~ *of life; an only son, the* ~ *of her old age.* **2** a group of assistant workers or officers: *office* ~; *a military chief of* ~; ***v.***

supply with a staff. **3** the set of five lines on which music is written. **—staff•er** *n.* a member of a staff, as distinguished from casual employees. **—staff sergeant** in the U.S. Air Force, Army, and Marine Corps, a noncommissioned officer ranking above a sergeant.

stag *n.* an adult male deer. ***—adj.*** for men only: *a ~ party, movie;* **go stag** esp. of men, attend (a party) unaccompanied by a date.

stage *n.* **1** a step or degree of advance in a process: *the pupa ~ of a butterfly; completed it* **by easy stages** (i.e. slowly). **2** one of the independently powered sections of a long-range rocket or missile that are jettisoned successively after burning their fuel. **3** a stagecoach. **4** a theater platform; hence, a scene of action; also, theater or drama: *a career* **on the stage** (i.e. in acting); ***v.*** **stag•es, staged, stag•ing** present (as) on a stage: *to ~ a play; to ~* (i.e. organize and carry out) *a protest.* **—stage•coach** *n.* a horse-drawn coach that served a regular route carrying passengers and mail. **—stage•hand** *n.* one who helps with the arrangements on a theater stage. **—stage-struck** *adj.* having an intense desire to join the acting profession.

stag•fla•tion (–FLAY–) *n.* a condition in which business activity is stagnant and inflation grows.

stag•ger (STAG·ur) *v.* **1** move unsteadily, as on weak feet, faltering or swaying from side to side: *seemed to ~ under the heavy load; The news dealt a ~ing blow to his hopes.* **2** arrange in a zigzag way or alternately: *to plant in ~ed rows; ~ed working hours help ease traffic congestion.* **—staggers** *n.pl.* [takes *sing. v.*] a nervous disease, esp. of horses, characterized by lack of muscle coordination.

stag•ing *n.* the moving forward of personnel or equipment in stages: *a military ~ area; ~ facilities for handling the refugee exodus.*

stag•nant (–nunt) *adj.* not flowing or active as in normal conditions: *~ water, air; a ~ pond; a ~* (i.e. sluggish) *market.* **—stag•nate** *v.* **-nates, -nat•ed, -nat•ing** make or become stagnant; **stag•na•tion** (–NAY–) *n.*

stag•y *adj.* **stag•i•er, -i•est** theatrical; also, artificial.

staid *Archaic pt. & pp.* of [1]STAY, *v.* 1. ***—adj.*** settled or steady in one's behavior; also, sedate or sober; **staid•ly** *adv.*

stain *n.* **1** a color or spot that soils; hence, a blemish or dishonor; **stain•less** *adj.* **2** a penetrating dye or pigment, as used to color wood, glass for ornamental windows of **stained glass,** and substances for examination under a microscope. **—stainless steel** a chromium alloy of steel that resists rust and corrosion.

stair *n.* one of a series of steps, or **stairs** *pl.* **—stair•case** or **stair•way** *n.* a series of stairs (with supporting structure, handrails, etc.). **—stair•well** *n.* a vertical open space or shaft containing stairs.

stake *n.* **1** a stick or post that is pointed at one end for driving into the ground to mark a boundary, tie a vine to, etc.: *Joan was burnt at* **the stake** *as a witch;* **pull up stakes** *Informal.* leave a place where one is established; move. **2** a share or interest in an undertaking; also, a grubstake. **3 stakes** *pl.* something risked; hence, a reward or prize: *high ~s; Soldiers put their lives* **at stake.** ***—v.*** **stakes, staked, stak•ing 1** mark with stakes: *Gold hunters ~ (out) a claim* (by marking off boundaries); **stake out** assign (a policeman) for surveillance; also, put (a place or suspect) under surveillance; **stake•out** *n.* **2** gamble (money, etc.); wager; also, *Informal.* furnish (a person) with money or resources; grubstake.

sta•lac•tite (stuh·LAC–) *n.* an iciclelike hanging formation of calcium deposited by water dripping from the roof of a cave; the corresponding formation rising from the floor is a **sta•lag•mite** (–LAG–) *n.*

stale *adj.* **stal•er, stal•est** not fresh or new: *~ food, news; ~* (i.e. flat) *soda; ~* (i.e. uninteresting) *jokes;* ***v.*** **stales, staled, stal•ing** make or become stale. **—stale•mate** *n. & v.* **-mates, -mat•ed, -mat•ing** (bring to) a deadlock or standstill.

Sta•lin (STAH–), **Joseph.** 1879–1953, Soviet premier and party head.

stalk (STAWK) *v.* **1** approach or pursue (game, a victim, etc.) without being seen or heard. **2** walk stiffly, esp. haughtily. ***—n.*** **1** a stalking (stride). **2** a connecting part such as the stem of a flower, leaf, wine glass, etc.; **stalked** *adj.*

stall (STAWL) *n.* **1** a compartment accommodating one individual or group, as for an animal in a stable, a booth or cubicle at a fair, a church pew, etc. **2** a stop or standstill, esp. one due to a malfunction; also, the condition of an airplane or wing losing its lift. ***—v.*** **1** put or keep in a stall. **2** bring or come to a standstill; stop running or functioning: *The car ~ed.* **3** *Informal.* use a delaying tactic or ruse; *to ~ off creditors.*

stal•lion (STAL·yun) *n.* a male horse used for breeding.

stal•wart (STAWL·wurt) *adj.* strong and sturdy, esp. steadfast in loyalty or staunch in support; ***n.*** a stalwart or loyal supporter.

sta•men (STAY·mun) *n.* in flowers, the long, slender, threadlike male reproductive organ having a pollen-containing sac, or anther, at its tip.

Stam•ford (–furd) a city of S.W. Connecticut.

stam•i•na *n.* **1** vigor or endurance. **2** a *pl.* of STAMEN.

stam•mer *v.* speak haltingly with breaks in or between words; stutter; ***n.*** a stammering; **stam•mer•er** *n.*

stamp *n.* **1** a small gummed paper label bearing an official design used as a token of payment of postage or revenue; also, any similar seal: *a trading ~.* **2** an official mark or seal of approval, quality, etc.; hence, a kind or type: *men of that ~.* **3** (a device for impressing) a design or message on anything: *a rubber ~; a date ~; the ~* (i.e. imprint) *of genius in her works.* **4** a stamping, as with one's foot. **—*v.* 1** strike down on with force, so as to pound or crush: *She ~ed the floor in anger; ~ed his foot* (i.e. on the ground) *in impatience; He ~ed on her toes in the crowd;* **stamp out** put out or end, as by stamping: *to ~ out a fire, corruption, rebellion.* **2** put a stamp on; imprint: *a self-addressed, ~ed envelope; events indelibly ~ed in his memory; Her accent ~s* (i.e. characterizes) *her as British.* **—stam·pede** (–PEED) *n.* a confused, headlong flight, as of a frightened herd; also, a general rush (*to* a place); ***v.* -pedes, -ped·ed, -ped·ing** flee, put to flight, or make a rush. **—stamping ground** *Informal.* a habitual gathering place or favorite haunt.

stance *n.* a way of standing, esp. in regard to position of the feet; hence, posture or attitude.

stanch (STAWNCH, STAHNCH, STANCH) *v.* same as STAUNCH. **—stan·chion** (–chun) *n.* **1** an upright supporting bar, as the mullion of a window. **2** a framework in which the head of a cow is secured in its stall.

stand *v.* **stands, stood, stand·ing 1** be or remain erect or upright on one's feet: *Please sit down, don't ~; has to ~ to touch the ceiling; He ~s 6 feet; She ~s* (i.e. ranks) *first in her class.* **2** (cause) to be in a specified position or condition: *No parking or ~ing near an intersection; The bookcase stood near the entrance; He ~s accused; a ~ing order* (continuing in effect). **3** bear or undergo: *couldn't ~ the heat; ordered to ~ trial; Will you ~ us* (*Informal.* bear the expense of) *a drink?* **—*n.* 1** an act of standing; also, a stop. **2** place of standing: *a taxi ~; A witness* **takes the stand** *in court; shouting from the* **stands** (i.e. tiered seats for spectators); *a ~* (i.e. growth) *of trees; takes a ~* (i.e. position) *on every issue.* **—stand by** be near so as to help or be ready for action. **—stand for 1** represent. **2** *Informal.* put up with. **—stand in 1** act as a stand-in. **2** be associated or friendly (with someone). **—stand off** keep away; also, *Informal.* put off or stall (a creditor, etc.). **—stand out** project; also, be prominent or outstanding. **—stand pat** be steadfast; resist change. **—stand up 1** rise to one's feet. **2** remain intact: *a statement that won't ~ up in court;* **stand up for** support or defend; **stand up to** challenge or face boldly. **—stand·ard** (–urd) *n.* **1** a flag or military banner, esp. of a ruler or leader, as a rallying point; hence, a model or principle of comparison: *a school's admission ~s; the gold ~.* **2** an upright support, as of a lamp. **—*adj.*** uniformly accepted: *~ English; a ~* (i.e. recognized) *textbook on the subject.* **—stand·ard-bear·er** *n.* the leader of a movement. **—stand·ard·ize** *v.* **-iz·es, -ized, -iz·ing** make standard; **stand·ard·i·za·tion** (–ZAY–) *n.* **—standard of living** the level of use of goods and services to satisfy one's material needs and desires: *The U.S.A. and Sweden have the highest ~s of living.* **—standard time** the uniform official time adopted throughout a country or time zone. **—stand·by** *n.* **-bys** a person or thing to be relied on; one held in reserve for use when necessary. **—stand·ee** (–DEE) *n. Informal.* one who stands, not having a seat (in a bus, theater, etc.). **—stand-in** *n.* a substitute person, esp. one taking the place of an actor or actress in routine roles. **—stand·ing** *n.* **1** status or rank: *in good ~; high ~.* **2** duration: *of long ~.* **—*adj.* 1** from an upright position: *a ~ jump.* **2** that stands: *a ~ tree; ~* (i.e. permanent) *orders; ~* (i.e. stagnant) *water.* **—stand·off** *n.* a tie or draw; **stand·off·ish** *adj.* aloof. **—stand·out** *n.* something outstanding. **—stand·pipe** *n.* a high reservoir or vertical pipe used in a water-supply system. **—stand·point** *n.* point of view. **—stand·still** *n.* a complete stop or halt. **—stand-up** *adj.* having to do with standing: *a ~ lunch counter, comedian* (performing alone, without costume, stage properties, etc.).

stank a *pt.* of STINK.

stan·za (–zuh) *n.* group of lines of verse forming a division of a poem.

sta·pes (STAY·peez) *n.* the innermost bone of the middle ear.

staph *n.* short form of **staph·y·lo·coc·cus** (staf·uh·loh·COC·us) *n., pl.* **-coc·ci** (–COC·sye) a round bacterium that grows in grapelike clusters and causes food poisoning, impetigo, boils, etc.

sta·ple (STAY–) *n.* **1** the chief marketable commodity or material produced in a place: *Coffee is the ~ of their economy;* ***adj.*** chief: *~ industries; a ~ food, subject of conversation.* **2** textile fiber in regard to its length: *cotton of short ~.* **3** a U-shaped piece of wire with sharp ends used to fasten things together; ***v.* sta·ples, sta·pled, sta·pling:** *papers ~d together;* **sta·pler** *n.*

star *n.* **1** any of the heavenly bodies seen at night as bright points of light, including planets, and held by astrologers to influence human events; hence, fortune; destiny; fate: *your lucky ~.* **2** a figure with five or six points, as an asterisk; also, a star-shaped medal or military decoration. **3** a brilliant or leading performer or singer; also, one distinguished in his field, as an athlete; **star·dom** (–dum) *n.* **—*v.* stars, starred, star·ring 1** mark with an asterisk; also, adorn with stars. **2** present (an actor, singer, etc.) in a leading role or perform in one. **—*adj.*:** *a ~ performer.*

star·board (–burd, –bord) *n.* & *adj.* (of or on) the right side of a ship or plane facing forward.
starch *n.* a white, odorless, tasteless food substance found in potatoes, rice, etc.; also, a form of this used to stiffen cloth or size paper; ***v.*** stiffen with starch; **starch·y** *adj.* **starch·i·er, -i·est:** ~ *foods; a* ~ (i.e. stiff or formal) *manner.*
stare *v.* **stares, stared, star·ing** look long and directly with wide-open eyes, as a child out of curiosity; ***n.:*** *a rude* ~; **star·er** *n.*
star·fish *n.* a sea animal usu. having five arms in the shape of a star. —**star·gaze** *v.* **-gaz·es, -gazed, -gaz·ing** **1** gaze at the stars, as an astronomer. **2** daydream.
stark *adj.* **1** utter; complete: ~ *nonsense, contrast, madness.* **2** stiff in death; also, bare; *a* ~ *landscape.* ***—adv.*** utterly: *lay* ~ *naked;* **stark-nak·ed** *adj.* —**stark·ly** *adv.;* **stark·ness** *n.*
star·let (–lit) *n.* a young actress being promoted as a future star. —**star·light** *n.* the light given by the stars.
star·ling *n.* any of a family of black, aggressive songbirds including mynas, some with iridescent feathers.
star·lit *adj.* lighted by the stars: *a* ~ *sky.* —**star·ry** *adj.* **star·ri·er, star·ri·est** lighted by stars; bright; **star·ry-eyed** *adj.* dreamy or visionary: ~ *youth, optimism.* —**Stars and Stripes** the U.S. flag. —**star-span·gled** *adj.* dotted with stars; **Star-Spangled Banner** the U.S. flag; also, the U.S. national anthem.
start *v.* **1** begin moving or acting, as by taking a first step: *to* ~ *on a journey; to* ~ *a fire with a match; to* ~ *an engine, a discussion; to* ~ (i.e. flush) *game; to* ~ (i.e. loosen) *a seam, bolts; to* ~ (i.e. enter) *a horse in a race.* **2** move suddenly, as if surprised or frightened. ***—n.*** **1** a beginning; also, a starting point or time. **2** an opportunity or chance; also, a lead over others; advantage. **3** a sudden movement or jerk; also, a spurt of energy: *by fits and* ~*s.* —**star·tle** *v.* **-tles, -tled, -tling** surprise or frighten so as to make one move suddenly: *slammed the door,* ~*ing the sleeping child; so nervous he* ~*s easily; a* **startling** *discovery.*
starve *v.* **starves, starved, starv·ing** (cause to) suffer from continued lack of food; also, kill or subdue with hunger: *Hundreds* ~*d to death during the famine; were* ~*d into surrendering; neglected children* ~*ing for affection; I'm* ~*ing* (*Informal.* hungry); **star·va·tion** (–VAY–) *n.* —**starve·ling** *n.* one that is thin from being ill-fed or starved.
stash *v. Informal.* hide or store (money, supplies, etc.) secretly; ***n.*** what is hidden away; also, a hiding place.
stat. statute.
state *n.* **1** condition or mode of existence, without reference to its cause: *the* ~ *of the world; a* ~ *of mind; solid, liquid, and gaseous* ~*s of matter; a* ~ *of emergency; an undeclared* ~ *of war.* **2** a civil or political government or its territory: *separation of church and* ~*; affairs of* ~*;* ~ *secrets; a police* ~*; an independent, sovereign* ~ (i.e. nation); *the U.S.* **State Department** (of foreign affairs); *He's from* **the States** (i.e. U.S.A.); **state·hood** *n.* **3** rank or station in life: *a humble* ~*; in great* ~ (i.e. dignity); *A body* **lies in state** (i.e. in a public place of honor). ***—v.*** **states, stat·ed, stat·ing** say formally or carefully; ~ *your reasons; as the law* ~*s; at the* ~*d* (i.e. indicated) *price.* —**state·craft** *n.* practical statesmanship. —**state·house** *n.* a state legislative building; **State·house** *n.* a U.S. state capitol. —**state·less** *adj.* having no nationality. —**state·ly** *adj.* **-li·er, -li·est** majestic; also, haughty; **state·li·ness** *n.* —**state·ment** *n.* a stating or something stated, as a declaration, assertion, a financial summary, or invoice. —**state of the art** the level of development attained in a field or industry at a given time; **state-of-the-art** *adj.* —**state·room** *n.* a private cabin on a ship; formerly, such a room on a railroad car. —**state·side** *Informal. adj.* of, from, or in the U.S., as viewed from abroad; ***adv.*** in or to the continental U.S. —**states·man** *n.* **-men** a wise, experienced, or skilled leader in public, esp. international affairs; **states·man·like** *adj.;* **states·man·ship** *n.*
stat·ic *adj.* **1** of or having to do with rest or equilibrium, not motion: ~ *balancing of a wheel; the* ~ *pressure of a column of liquid; a* ~ *existence without progress or change; the* **static** (i.e. not flowing) **electricity** *on a comb run through the hair.* **2** of or having to do with static. ***—n.*** **1** an electrical atmospheric disturbance such as interferes with radio or television reception: *FM radio has no* ~. **2** *Slang.* hostile criticism. —**stat·i·cal·ly** *adv.*
sta·tion (STAY–) *n.* **1** an assigned place of duty: *Return to your* ~*s;* ***v.:*** *guards* ~*ed at entrances.* **2** a stopping place: *a bus* ~. **3** a place where a service is provided: *gas* ~*; police* ~*; postal* ~*; television* ~. **4** social position or rank: *of all walks and* ~*s in life.* —**sta·tion·ar·y** (–er·ee) *adj.* fixed; not moving; also, unchanging in condition: *a* ~ *vehicle, weather front.* —**station break** a periodic pause in a broadcast or telecast, usu. for station identification. —**sta·tion·er** *n.* one who sells stationery; **sta·tion·er·y** *n.* writing paper and envelopes; also, writing materials. —**station wagon** an automobile with a body extended at the back to allow additional room for passengers or goods, and having a tailgate. —**sta·tis·tics** (–TIS–) *n.pl.* **1** [takes *sing.v.*] the science of gathering and analyzing numerical facts or data. **2** such data collectively; **statistic** *n.* a statistical item; **sta·tis·ti·cal** *adj.;* **sta·tis·ti·cal·ly** *adv.;* **stat·is·ti·cian** (–TISH–) *n.* —**stat·u·ar·y** (STACH·oo·er·ee) *n.* **-ar·ies** a collection of statues or the art of making them; **stat·ue** (STACH·oo) *n.* a three-dimensional image of a person or animal that is cast, modeled, or carved; **stat·u·esque** (–ESK)

adj. like a statue in being well-proportioned or stately; **stat·u·ette** (–ET) *n.* a small statue. —**stat·ure** (STACH·ur) *n.* height reached or development attained by a person: *a man of short ~; of great moral ~.* —**sta·tus** (STAY–, STAT–) *n.* **-tus·es** state or condition according to some standard: *the (legal) ~ of a minor; her marital ~; people of some* (i.e. high) *~; a ~ seeker;* **status quo** (–KWOH) an unchanged state of affairs; **status symbol** something regarded as a mark of high social status, as an expensive automobile. —**stat·ute** (STACH·oot) *n.* a law enacted by a legislative body; **statute of limitations** a law setting a time limit for prosecutions except in serious crimes such as murder; **stat·u·tor·y** *adj.* having to do with or fixed by statute: *Common law and ~ law; Intercourse with a minor girl is a ~ offense called* **statutory rape.**

staunch (STAWNCH, STAHNCH) *adj.* **1** strong or steadfast: *a ~ supporter, friendship, defense.* **2** watertight: *a ~ ship;* ***v.*** stop the flow of (blood) or of blood from (a wound); stanch. —**staunch·ly** *adv.;* **staunch·ness** *n.*

stave *n.* **1** one of the curved strips of wood making up the walls of a barrel or cask. **2** a pole or staff; also, a musical staff. **3** a stanza. —***v.*** **staves,** *pt.* & *pp.* **staved** or **stove** (STOHV), **stav·ing** make a break or hole in (the sides of a cask, boat, etc.); **stave off** prevent or ward off (something troublesome). —**staves** a *pl.* of STAFF, defs. 1 & 3; also, *pl.* of STAVE.

[1]**stay** *v.* **1** remain: *Please ~ for a while; ~ed the night with friends;* **stay put** *Informal.* remain at one's place or where stationed. **2** dwell, esp. as a guest for a short while. **3** wait: *"Time and tide ~ for no man."* **4** hold back; check: *to ~ an execution; snacks to ~ him* (i.e. his hunger) *till dinner time.* **5** of a runner, horse, etc., endure or last (to the end, for a period or distance, etc.). —***n.:*** *a pleasant ~ at a hotel; a ~ of execution pending an appeal.*

[2]**stay** *n.* **1** a prop, brace, or support; **stays** *pl.* corset; ***v.*** **stays, stayed, stay·ing** prop or hold up; **staying power** endurance or stamina. **2** a steadying rope or wire, as for a ship's mast; guy.

std. standard. —**S.T.D.** Doctor of Sacred Theology.

Ste. Saint (female).

stead (STED) *n.* **in (one's) stead** instead of; as a substitute for; **stand in good stead** be of service or advantage to: *Your French will stand you in good ~ in your travels.* —**stead·fast** (STED–) *adj.* firm; fixed; unwavering: *her ~ loyalty; his ~ gaze;* **stead·fast·ly** *adv.;* **stead·fast·ness** *n.* —**stead·y** *adj.* **stead·i·er, -i·est** stable or regular in movement or behavior: *a ~ heartbeat, progress, job* (i.e. without interruption), *ship* (i.e. upright in a rough sea), *worker* (i.e. reliable), *nerves* (i.e. calm), *friendship* (i.e. steadfast); *wanted to* **go steady** (*Informal.* date each other exclusively) *before getting married.* —***n., pl.*** **stead·ies** *Informal.* one's regular and exclusive date. —***v.*** **stead·ies, stead·ied, stead·y·ing** make or become steady. —***adv.*** in a steady manner; also **stead·i·ly** *adv.;* **stead·i·ness** *n.* —**stead·y-state theory** the theory that the universe will maintain its present state, as it always has, without the big bang with which it is supposed to renew itself.

steak (STAKE) *n.* a fleshy slice of meat, esp. beef; also, any slice of meat or fish that is broiled or fried like beefsteak.

steal (STEEL) *v.* **steals, stole, sto·len** (STOH·lun), **steal·ing** take or get (something) in a secret, sly, or unexpected manner: *Thieves ~; A starving man may ~ food; Lovers ~ looks, kisses; A baby ~s your heart; A runner tries to ~* (i.e. reach) *a base by catching the opposing team off guard; A feeling of shame stole over her; He stole* (i.e. sneaked) *out of the house when she was asleep.* —***n.*** *Informal.* a stealing or something stolen, esp. an unusual bargain. —**stealth** (STELTH) *n.* secrecy or furtiveness; **by stealth** secretly or slyly; **stealth·y** *adj.* **stealth·i·er, -i·est** sly or secret in manner; **stealth·i·ly** *adv.;* **stealth·i·ness** *n.*

steam (STEEM) *n.* **1** the vapor given off by boiling water; also, this condensed, as from evaporation inside a heated automobile. **2** (the power of) hot steam under pressure, as used to drive the piston in the cylinder of a **steam engine; let off steam** *Informal.* get rid of excess energy or pent-up feelings. —***v.:*** *a ~ing cup of soup, kettle; a ~ed-up car window; to ~ open a sealed envelope.* —**steam·y** *adj.* —**steam·boat** *n.* a small steamship. —**steam·er** *n.* one that uses steam, as a cooker, cleaning appliance, or a steamship. —**steam fitter** a worker who installs and maintains pipes in heating and cooling systems; **steam fitting.** —**steam·roll·er** *n.* a steam-driven roller for road surfaces; ***v.*** crush (opposition) or force (one's way *into* or legislation *through*) as with a steamroller; also **steam·roll.** —**steam·ship** *n.* a ship driven by steam power. —**steam shovel** an excavating machine powered by steam.

steed *n.* [literary] a riding horse.

steel *n.* **1** a hard and tough alloy of iron and carbon. **2** a steel instrument or weapon. **3** steellike hardness and strength. —***adj.:*** *a ~ bar; ~ blue;* **steel·y** *adj.* —***v.*** make with or like steel: *~ed himself to face the ordeal.* —**steel band** a percussion band using steel oil drums of varying pitches. —**steel wool** hairlike shavings of steel used in a ball or pad for scouring, smoothing, etc. —**steel·yard** *n.* a weighing scale with a long arm carrying an adjustable weight to balance the object to be weighed which is hung from the end of the shorter arm.

steep *v.* (let) soak, as by immersion, esp. for extracting the essence of something; hence, immerse (*oneself* in a subject of study);

steeped in filled or pervaded with: *~ed in misery.* **—adj.** 1 sharply sloping: *a ~ hill;* **n.** a steep climb or slope. 2 *Informal.* excessive or exaggerated: *~ demands, prices.* **—steep·en** *v.* make or become steep(er). **—steep·ly** *adv.;* **steep·ness** *n.* **—stee·ple** *n.* a tall tower, usu. topped by a spire, on a church building; also, a spire; **stee·pled** *adj.* **—stee·ple·chase** *n.* a cross-country race on horseback or a footrace over an obstacle course. **—stee·ple·jack** *n.* one who works on steeples, smokestacks, etc.

steer *n.* a young castrated ox raised for beef.

steer *v.* 1 direct the course of (a vehicle using a wheel, rudder, or other device). 2 direct one's way or follow a course: *~ for home; always* **steers clear** *of trouble.* **—steer·a·ble** *adj.* **—steer·age** (–ij) *n.* 1 the act of steering or the response of a ship to the helm. 2 formerly, a section of a ship for passengers paying the lowest fares. **—steers·man** *n.* **-men** helmsman.

steg·o·sau·rus (–uh·SOR–) *n., pl.* **-ri** (–rye) a dinosaur with two staggered rows of large, triangular, bony plates along its back; also **steg·o·saur.**

stein (STINE) *n.* a beer mug, originally of earthenware. **—Stein·beck** (STINE–), **John.** 1902–68, American novelist.

stel·lar (–ur) *adj.* of a star: *~ light, magnitudes; a ~ role* (i.e. of chief performer); *~* (i.e. excellent) *performance.*

stem *n.* 1 the main part or trunk, as of a tree, plant, etc. from which branches grow: *"Kind" is the ~ of the word "unkindnesses"; wineglasses and such* **stem·ware** (having a stem connecting bowl and base) *for serving cold beverages and desserts.* 2 the prow of a ship; **from stem to stern** from one end to the other; throughout. **—v. stems, stemmed, stem·ming** 1 derive or develop: *problems ~ing from lack of education.* 2 stop or check: *to ~ the tide of heresy.*

stench *n.* an offensive odor; stink.

sten·cil *n.* a sheet of paper, metal, etc. on which designs, letters, etc. are cut for transferring them to a surface by laying the sheet on it and applying ink or color; also, a letter or design so made; **v. -cils, -cil(l-ed, -cil·(l)ing:** *a ~d address.*

sten·o *n.* **-os** [short form] stenographer; stenography. **—ste·nog·ra·pher** (–NOG–) *n.* one skilled in shorthand; **ste·nog·ra·phy** *n.* shorthand; **sten·o·graph·ic** (–GRAF–) *adj.*

sten·to·ri·an (–TOR–) *adj.* of a voice or tone, loud and powerful.

step *n.* 1 a lifting of the foot and setting it down in walking, running, dancing, etc.; also, its distance, style, sound, or print; **step by step** slowly; **in** (or **out of) step** in (or out of) rhythm (*with* another marcher or dancer). 2 a stair or rung: *the ~s of a ladder.* 3 a stage or degree in a movement forward or upward: *What's the next ~? a ~ closer to a settlement; A major is a ~ above a captain;* **take steps** take the necessary measures. **—v. steps, stepped, step·ping** 1 put a foot down: *She ~d on a nail;* **step on it** *Informal.* go faster, as by pressing the accelerator. 2 walk: *to ~ across a street; Please ~ in* (the house) *for a minute; just ~d out for some fresh air; to* **step down** *voltage using a transformer; to* **step off** (i.e. pace off) *a distance;* **step up** 1 *Informal.* came forward. 2 increase (an activity or amount). **—step-** *prefix.* by remarriage: as in **step·broth·er** (–brudh–) *n.* son of a stepparent; **step·child** *n.* child of one's spouse by a former marriage, i.e. **step·daugh·ter** or **step·son; step·par·ent** (–pair–) *n.* a parent (**step·moth·er** or **step·fa·ther)** acquired by the remarriage of one's mother or father. **—step·lad·der** *n.* a short ladder with flat steps instead of rungs and hinged to a supporting frame.

steppe (STEP) *n.* one of the prairielike treeless plains of the U.S.S.R. extending from S. Ukraine to central Asia.

step·ping·stone *n.* a stone to step on when crossing a stream, mounting, ascending, etc.; hence, a means of advancement. **—step·sis·ter** *n.* the daughter of one's stepparent; **step·son** (–sun) *n.* a son by the former marriage of one's spouse. **—step-up** *n.* a stepping up or increase in amount, intensity, etc.

-ster *n.suffix.* one who does or is associated with (something specified): as in *mobster, punster, trickster.*

stere (STEER) *n.* a unit of volume equal to one cubic meter.

stereo- *comb.form.* solid; three-dimensional; **ster·e·o** (STER·ee·oh, STEER–) *n.* **-os** 1 a record player or sound system that is stereophonic. 2 a picture or system that is stereoscopic. **—ster·e·o·phon·ic** (–FON–) *adj.* using two or more channels of sound recording and reproduction for a realistic effect; **ster·e·o·phon·i·cal·ly** *adv.* **—ster·e·o·scope** *n.* an optical instrument having two eyepieces for a three-dimensional view of an object; **ster·e·o·scop·ic** (–SCOP–) *adj.;* **ster·e·o·scop·i·cal·ly** *adv.;* **ster·e·os·co·py** (–OS·cuh·pee) *n.* (the science of) the viewing of things in three dimensions. **—ster·e·o·type** *n.* a printing plate cast from a mold of type set separately; hence, a fixed or rigid mental impression; **v. -types, -typed, -typ·ing** make a stereotype of; **ster·e·o·typed** *adj.* lacking originality or objectivity: *~ thinking, impressions, characters.*

ster·ile (–ul) *adj.* 1 unable to bear offspring, produce crops, seed, results, etc.: *a ~ woman, husband; ~ land, plants, efforts.* 2 sterilized. **—ste·ril·i·ty** (–RIL–) *n.* **—ster·i·lize** *v.* **-liz·es, -lized, -liz·ing** 1 to free from living microorganisms: *~d surgical instruments.* 2 make incapable of reproduction. **—ster·i·liz·er** *n.;* **ster·i·li·za·tion** (–ZAY–) *n.*

ster·ling (STUR–) *n.* & *adj.* **1** (of or payable in) British money with the pound as the basic unit. **2** (made of) silver that is at least 92.5% pure; hence, genuinely excellent: *~ qualities, character.*

[1]stern *adj.* severe or strict in manner or looks: *a ~ disciplinarian, face; ~ measures;* **stern·ly** *adv.;* **stern·ness** *n.*

[2]stern *n.* the rear end of a ship, aircraft, etc.; opposed to BOW. **—stern sheets** *pl.* See SHEETS. **—ster·num** (STUR–) *n.* **-nums** or **-na** a bone down the front of the chest to which the uppermost seven pairs of ribs are attached; breastbone; **ster·nal** *adj.*

ster·oid (STEER–, STER–) *n.* any of a class of organic chemical compounds including sex hormones, adrenal hormones, bile acids, and cholesterol.

ster·to·rous (STUR·tuh·rus) *adj.* of a breathing sound, like snoring.

stet *n.* in proofreading, "let it stand" or "do not delete"; ***v.*** **stets, stet·ted, stet·ting** mark with a "stet."

steth·o·scope *n.* an instrument used by physicians to listen to the sounds produced by the heart, lungs, etc.

ste·ve·dore (STEE·vuh–) *n.* one who loads and unloads ships.

stew *n.* a dish of meat and vegetables made by slow boiling; ***v.*** cook by slow boiling; hence, worry or fret.

stew·ard (–urd) *n.* **1** one who manages another's estate or finances. **2** a labor union representative. **3** a racetrack official. **4** one in charge of food service on a ship or airplane or in a club; **stew·ard·ess** *n.* an airline hostess. **—stew·ard·ship** *n.*

stick *n.* **1** a long and slender twig broken off from a tree; also, any long, thin piece: *a ~ of candy, dynamite, gum.* **2** a specially shaped piece or an implement: *a walking ~; hockey ~s; the carrot and the ~* (i.e. threat of punishment). **3** *Informal.* an awkward or stupid person; **the sticks** *Informal.* backwoods. ***—v.*** **sticks, stuck, stick·ing** **1** pierce or thrust (into, out, etc.): *a corpse with a knife stuck in its back; Do not ~ your head out of the window; with a kerchief ~ing* (i.e. protruding) *from his pocket.* **2** be or make fixed or immovable: *A stamp is stuck on an envelope; We were out of gas and got stuck on the road; enough evidence to make a charge ~* (i.e. be valid); *People ~* (i.e. cling) *together when in trouble; was told to* **stick around** (*Informal.* wait) *while her car was being serviced; She would always* **stick by** (i.e. remain loyal to) *her friends; a matter of honor to* **stick to** *one's word; If you're loyal, the boss will* **stick up for** (*Informal.* defend) *you.* **3** *Slang.* cheat or defraud: *was stuck by phony salesmen; We seem to be stuck* (i.e. saddled) *with this lemon.* **4** hesitate: *a swindler who ~s at nothing.* **—stick·er** *n.* a gummed label, bur, etc. that sticks: *the* **sticker price** *of a new automobile from which discounts are calculated.* **—stick insect** an insect that resembles a twig. **—stick-in-the-mud** *n. Informal.* one who resists progress.

stick·le·back *n.* a small scaleless fish that has a row of spines in front of its dorsal fin.

stick·ler *n.* one who is strict in the observance of something: *a ~ for precision, discipline, punctuality.*

stick·pin *n.* an ornamental pin worn on a necktie.

stick shift a lever for changing gears in an automobile. **—stick-to-it·ive·ness** *n. Informal.* persistence or tenacity. **—stick·up** *n. Slang.* an armed robbery; holdup. **—stick·y** *adj.* **stick·i·er, -i·est** **1** that sticks; adhesive; also, thick or viscous. **2** *Informal.* disagreeable or troublesome: *a ~ problem, valve; ~* (i.e. hot and humid) *weather.*

stiff *adj.* **1** that resists bending or moving: *~ joints; a ~ back, bow; a ~* (i.e. hard to stir) *paste; a ~* (i.e. hard to work) *soil.* **2** hard or strong: *~ resistance, penalties, a ~ breeze, drink* (i.e. strong in alcohol); *~ manners* (i.e. formal); ***adv.:*** *was scared ~.* **—stiff·ly** *adv.;* **stiff·ness** *n.* **—stiff-arm** *v.* same as STRAIGHT-ARM. **—stiff·en** *v.* make or become stiff(er); **stiff·en·er** *n.* **—stiff-necked** (–nect) *adj.* stubborn.

sti·fle (STY–) *v.* **-fles, -fled, -fling** **1** stop the breath of; hence, kill. **2** make or become unable to breathe; also, become unconscious: *firemen ~d by smoke; the ~ing heat of the Sahara.* **3** suppress: *to ~ a yawn, cry; freedom of speech ~d by restrictions.* **—sti·fling·ly** *adv.*

stig·ma (–muh) *n.* **-mas** **1** the pollen-receiving part of a flower's pistil. **2** *pl.* **-ma·ta** (–MAH·tuh, –muh·tuh) marks resembling the five wounds of the crucified Christ. **3** a mark of disgrace, as once put on evil-doers, slaves, etc.: *the ~ of being born illegitimate;* **stig·ma·tize** (STIG·muh–) *v.* **-tiz·es, -tized, -tiz·ing:** *people unjustly ~d by reason of birth, color, creed, etc.* **—stig·mat·ic** (–MAT–) *adj.*

stile *n.* step(s) for people to climb over a fence or wall but keep out animals; also, a turnstile.

sti·let·to (sti·LET·oh) *n.* **-to(e)s** a narrow-bladed dagger.

still *adj.* **1** at rest; motionless: *Stand ~;* "*~ waters run deep*"*; a ~* (i.e. not bubbling) *wine.* **2** quiet; silent: *Be ~; a ~ night; the ~ small voice* (of conscience). ***—v.*** make quiet or motionless. ***—adv.*** **1** without moving: *to sit ~ (for a picture).* **2** even to the (specified or implied) time: *He's ~ sick; They were ~ undecided yesterday; She'll ~ be here tomorrow.* **3** even: *Her brother is ~ taller;* ***conj.*** yet: *She has hurt you; ~ you have to forgive her.* ***—n.*** **1** a photograph, esp. a frame from a motion picture. **2** stillness: *the ~ of the night.* **3** an apparatus for making alcoholic liquor; also, a distillery. **—still·ness** *n.* **—still·birth** *n.* (birth of) a child born dead;

still·born *adj.* born dead. **—still life,** *pl.* **still lifes** a picture of inanimate objects such as fruits, flowers, pottery, etc.

stilt *n.* **1** one of a pair of poles with supports for the feet at a height, used for walking across water or for amusement. **2** one of a set of piles or posts supporting a building raised above water or swampland. **—stilt·ed** *adj.* stiffly formal: *a ~ style, expression.*

stim·u·lant (STIM·yuh·lunt) *n.* & *adj.* (anything) that stimulates, as nicotine, caffeine, amphetamines, etc. **—stim·u·late** *v.* **-lates, -lat·ed, -lat·ing** make active; also, increase the activity of; excite: *to ~ public interest in the arts; tax refunds to ~ the economy; laser action by ~d emission of radiation;* **stim·u·la·tion** (–LAY–) *n.;* **stim·u·la·tive** (–lay·tiv) *adj.* **—stim·u·lus** *n., pl.* **-li** (–lye) something that excites one to (increased) activity: *behavior as responses to stimuli.*

sting *v.* **stings, stung, sting·ing** cause sharp pain (to), as with the pricking organ of a bee, mosquito, or wasp: *Nettles ~; the ~ing taste of ginger; stung by insults; stung into action by their taunts;* **sting·er** *n.* **—n.** a stinging, the wound or pain caused by it, or the stinging organ of an insect or plant. **—sting·ray** *n.* a fish of the ray group with venomous spines on its whiplike tail.

stin·gy (STIN·jee) *adj.* **-gi·er, -gi·est** miserly; not generous: *too ~ to give to charity; a ~ allowance;* **stin·gi·ly** *adv.;* **stin·gi·ness** *n.*

stink (STINGK) *n.* & *v.* **stinks,** *pt.* **stank** or **stunk,** *pp.* **stunk, stink·ing** (give off) a bad smell. **—stink·bug** *n.* any bug that gives off a bad odor. **—stink·er** *n.* **1** one that stinks. **2** *Informal.* someone or something difficult or disagreeable.

stint *v.* restrict oneself or one's consumption of or expenditure on something: *never ~ed on charity.* **—n.** **1** limitation or restraint. **2** a share of work or a brief assignment: *~s of teaching overseas.*

sti·pend (STY–) *n.* a fixed payment regularly made for a professional's services.

stip·ple *v.* **stip·ples, stip·pled, stip·pling** paint, engrave, or apply (paint, etc.) in dots instead of lines: *a ~d ceiling design;* **n.** stippled work, its method, or effect.

stip·u·late (STIP·yuh–) *v.* **-lates, -lat·ed, -lat·ing** specify as a necessary condition: *as ~d in the contract; The terms ~d delivery in two years; The parties had ~d for it* (i.e. demanded it as a condition); **stip·u·la·tor** *n.;* **stip·u·la·tion** (–LAY–) *n.*

stir (STUR) *v.* **stirs, stirred, stir·ring** move so as to disturb or activate: *A wind ~s the leaves; noticed someone ~ing in the shadows; ~d the fire into a blaze; to ~* (i.e. mix) *sugar into coffee; The picture ~d memories; a story likely to ~ up trouble; His speech ~d them up to mutiny;* **stir·rer** *n.* **—n.** a stirring or a state of activity, excitement, etc.: *a ~ in the audience.* **—stir·ring** *adj.* rousing or exciting: *a ~ speech; ~ times.*

stir·rup (STUR–) *n.* a rider's footrest hanging from the saddle as a loop or ring.

stitch (STICH) *n.* **1** one complete movement of a threaded needle, as in sewing or embroidering: *10 ~es* (with a surgical needle) *to close a wound; basting, running, and hemming ~es* (i.e. methods of stitching); *without a ~* (i.e. least bit of clothing) *on him.* **2** a sharp pain, esp. in the side; **in stitches** *Informal.* laughing uncontrollably. **—v.** make a stitch or series of stitches (in). **—stitch·er·y** *n.* needlework.

St. John's **1** chief town of Antigua. **2** capital of Newfoundland. **—St. Law·rence River** Canada's largest river, beginning from Lake Ontario and flowing into the Gulf of St. Lawrence, including the **St. Lawrence Seaway** from Montreal to the mouth of Lake Ontario by which oceangoing ships travel to the Great Lakes from the Atlantic. **—St. Lou·is** (–LOO·is) largest city of Missouri.

stoat (STOHT) *n.* a short-tailed weasel, esp. in its brown summer coat.

stock *n.* **1** a collection or supply, as of goods for sale, the repertoire of plays with a *stock company, rolling stock,* or *livestock;* **in** (or **out of**) **stock** available (or not); **take stock** to inventory or assess. **2** a supporting base: *The barrel of a firearm is fitted into a wooden ~; meat and vegetable juices as ~s for soups and gravies; rags and wood pulp as ~* (i.e. raw material) *for paper; a book printed on heavy ~* (i.e. paper); *A scion grows best when grafted to a rooted ~* (i.e. stem); *a stupid ~* (i.e. blockhead); *slaves punished in* **the stocks** (i.e. wooden frame with holes for locking limbs in). **3** invested capital, as of a company, or a part of it owned by a shareholder: *too level-headed to* **take** (or **put**) **stock in** (*Informal.* trust) *the rumors going round.* **4** a race or group with a common descent: *English is of Indo-European ~.* **—adj.** **1** available; in common use: *a ~ size, car; a ~* (i.e. commonplace) *answer, joke.* **2** having to do with livestock: *a ~ breeder, farm, train.* **3** having to do with stocks: *a ~ clerk working in a ~ room; a ~* (i.e. shares) *certificate.* **—v.** keep a supply of or provide with stock; also, lay in a supply of, as for the winter.

stock·ade (–CADE) *n.* an enclosure of stakes driven into the ground for confinement or defense.

stock·bro·ker *n.* a broker dealing in stocks and bonds. **—stock car** a standard passenger car modified or rebuilt for racing. **—stock company** **1** a corporation whose capital is held in shares. **2** a theatrical company that puts on a stock of prepared plays at a theater. **—stock exchange** an organized marketplace for the buying and selling of securities. **—stock·hold·er** *n.* an owner of stock in a company; shareholder.

Stock·holm (–home, –hohlm) capital of Sweden.

stock·i·net(te) (–NET) *n.* an elastic, machine-knit cloth; also, a knitting stitch. **—stock·ing** *n.* a close-fitting knitted covering for the foot and leg.

stock market a stock exchange; also, market activity in securities. **—stock·pile** *n.* & *v.* **-piles, -piled, -pil·ing** (accumulate) a reserve supply, as of commodities, raw materials, or nuclear weapons. **—stock·still** *adj.* motionless. **—stock·y** *adj.* **stock·i·er, -i·est** short but sturdy in build. **—stock·yard** *n.* a yard for livestock, esp. one connected with a meatpacking operation.

stodg·y (STOJ·ee) *adj.* **stodg·i·er, -i·est** dull or heavy: *~ reading, food; a ~ newspaper;* **stodg·i·ly** *adv.;* **stodg·i·ness** *n.*

sto·gie or **sto·gy** (STOH·gee) *n.* **-gies** a long, thing, usu. inexpensive cigar.

Sto·ic (STOH–) *n.* & *adj.* (a member) of an ancient Greek school of philosophy that taught calm resignation and the pursuit of virtue as the highest good; **stoic** *n.* one who is stoical; **sto·i·cal** *adj.* able to endure suffering with calm, being indifferent to pleasure and pain; **sto·i·cal·ly** *adv.;* **sto·i·cism** *n.*

stoke *v.* **stokes, stoked, stok·ing** tend and feed a fire; also, work as a stoker; **stok·er** *n.* one who tends a furnace or boiler; also, a machine for feeding solid fuel into a furnace.

STOL (STOLE) *n.* an aircraft that requires only a short distance for takeoff and landing.

stole *pt.* of STEAL. **—*n.*** **1** a woman's scarf worn around the shoulders with its ends hanging down in front. **2** a similar narrow strip of cloth worn by a clergyman during a ceremony. **—stolen** *pp.* of STEAL.

stol·id *adj.* unemotional; not sensitive; **stol·id·ly** *adv.;* **sto·lid·i·ty** (–LID–) *n.*

sto·lon (STOH–) *n.* a runner (*n.* 3).

stom·ach (STUM·uk) *n.* **1** the saclike digestive organ into which food is received from the mouth; hence, appetite or inclination: *no ~ for a walk after dinner.* **2** abdomen or belly. **—*v.*** relish or swallow; hence, put up with or endure: *couldn't ~ the insult.* **—stom·ach·ache** *n.* pain in the stomach or abdomen. **—stom·ach·er** *n.* an ornamental front-piece formerly worn by women under the lacing of the bodice. **—sto·mach·ic** (–MAC–) *adj.* of the stomach; ***n.*** a stomach medicine.

stomp *n.* **1** (jazz music for) a dance of the 1930's characterized by rhythmic stomping. **2** a stomping; ***v.*** stamp heavily with the feet.

stone *n.* **1** (a piece of) hard, solid mineral such as granite or marble; hence, something resembling it, as a gem, a kidney stone or gallstone, the hard seed of a drupe such as the cherry or peach, etc. **2** *sing.* & *pl.* a British unit of weight equal to 14 pounds. **—*v.*** **stones, stoned, ston·ing** throw stones at or remove the stone from (a fruit). **—stone-** *comb.form.* completely: as in *stone-blind, stone-broke, stone-deaf.* **—Stone Age** the earliest stage of human culture when tools were made out of stone. **—stoned** *adj. Slang.* under the influence of (alcohol or a drug): *~ on speed.* **—stone's throw** a short distance. **—stone·wall** *v. Informal.* refuse to cooperate with; also, obstruct (an investigation). **—ston·y** *adj.* **ston·i·er, -i·est** **1** full of stones. **2** like stone; hard or cold: *a ~ heart, stare, face.* **—ston·i·ly** *adv.;* **ston·i·ness** *n.*

stood *pt.* of STAND.

stooge (STOOJ) *n. Informal.* one who serves another's low purpose, as the butt of a vaudeville comedian's jokes; ***v.*** **stoog·es, stooged, stoog·ing** act as a stooge (*for* someone).

stool *n.* **1** a seat without a back or arms; also, a footstool. **2** feces. **—stool pigeon** *Slang.* an informer or decoy; also **stool·ie** (–lee), **-ies.**

stoop *v.* **1** bend forward and downward, as the head and shoulders of an aged man. **2** lower or degrade oneself. **—*n.*** **1** a stooping carriage or posture; also, a bending forward. **2** a flight of steps at the entrance to a house. **—stoop labor** work involving stooping, as picking strawberries.

stop *v.* **stops, stopped, stop·ping** **1** keep (one) from moving or acting: *to ~ at a traffic signal; ~ the thief!* **2** bring (a movement or action) to an end: *Please ~ shouting; to ~ a leak; Strikes ~ work; a boxer ~d* (i.e. knocked out) *in the second round; a cork to* **stop up** (i.e. close) *a bottle.* **3** press down on (a violin string, finger hole of a wind instrument, etc.) to produce a desired tone or pitch. **4** stay: *We ~d with friends on our way to London; They had to* **stop over** *in Bombay before flying to Manila.* **5** **stop by** drop in for a visit; also **stop in.** **—*n.*** **1** a stopping or ending; also, a stopping place: *a bus ~;* **put a stop to** end. **2** a stopping device such as a camera's shutter or a lever or key for changing the pitch or tone of a musical instrument, esp. an organ; **pull out all the stops** make a great effort. **3** a consonant such as "p," "t," and "k" pronounced with stopping of the breath. **—stop·cock** *n.* a cock or valve to regulate the flow from a container. **—stop·gap** *n.* a temporary expedient; makeshift. **—stop·light** *n.* a traffic light, esp. when red; also, a rear light of a vehicle that comes on when the brakes are applied. **—stop·o·ver** *n.* a brief stay in the course of a journey. **—stop·page** (–ij) *n.* an act of stopping or the condition of being stopped; also, a block or obstruction. **—stop·per** *n.* a plug or similar device to close an opening; also, one that causes a stoppage. **—stop·ple** *n.* & *v.* **stop·ples, stop·pled, stop·pling** (close a bottle, etc. with) a plug or other stopper. **—stop·watch** *n.* a watch that can be stopped and started as desired for timing races, etc.

stor·age (–ij) *n.* the act of storing goods, as in a warehouse, space for storing, or the cost of storing; **storage battery** a battery of cells that produces electricity by chemical action and that may be recharged. **—store** *v.* **stores, stored, stor·ing** put aside in a safe place for future use; also, stock (a place *with* something). ***—n.*** **1** a stock or supply (of something useful): *a good ~ of food; what the future may have* **in store** *for us; Children* **set** (or **put** or **lay**) **great** (or **much, little,** etc.) **store by** (i.e. value) *what teachers tell them;* **stores** *pl.* supplies for the regular needs of an establishment or operation: *military ~s.* **2** a place where goods are sold: *a grocery ~.* **3** a storehouse. **—store·front** *n.* the front of a store; also, a room to which the public has access for buying goods and services; ***adj.:*** *a ~ clinic, office, operation.* **—store·house** *n.* a building in which goods are stored; also, a person or place having a large supply: *a ~ of knowledge, information.* **—store·keep·er** *n.* a store owner or operator. **—store·room** *n.* a room for storing supplies.

sto·rey (STOR·ee) *n.* **-reys** *Brit.* same as STORY, *n.* 4.**—sto·ried** (STOR·eed) *adj.* **1** celebrated in stories or history. **2** ornamented with designs based on history or legend: *a ~ urn.* **3** having stories or floors: *a ~ house; a three-~ building.*

stork *n.* any of a family of large wading birds with long legs, necks, and bills, esp. the white stork that builds its nest on rooftops and chimneys.

storm *n.* **1** a disturbance of the atmosphere marked by strong winds, rain, snow, or hail. **2** any strong disturbance, or a violent outburst or attack. ***—v.*** blow hard; hence, rage or rush violently: *She ~ed out of the room in a huff; ~ed their way into the hall; a fort ~ed* (i.e. attacked) *by the enemy.* **—storm door** (or **window**) an outer door (or window) as added protection against the weather. **—storm·y** *adj.* **storm·i·er, -i·est** characterized by a storm or similar disturbance: *a ~ night, meeting, scene;* **storm(y) petrel** a petrel thought to be a sign of a coming storm; **storm·i·ly** *adv.;* **storm·i·ness** *n.*

sto·ry (STOR·ee) *n.* **-ries** **1** an account or narrative; also, a newspaper report. **2** a made-up account with literary qualities, esp. a short story; hence, *Informal.* a falsehood. **3** the plot of a novel or play. **4** one of the horizontal divisions of a building; floor. **—sto·ry·book** *n.* a book of stories, esp. for children; ***adj.*** fairy-tale or romantic. **—sto·ry·tell·er** *n.* one who tells stories; **sto·ry·tell·ing** *n.*

sto·tin·ka (–TING–) *n., pl.* **-ki** (–kee) 1/100 of a Bulgarian lev.

stoup (STOOP) *n.* a basin for holy water at the entrance of a church.

stout *adj.* **1** strong in resisting strain; having endurance: *a ~ rope, heart; offered ~ resistance.* **2** thickset or bulky: *a ~ figure, woman.* ***—n.*** a dark beer with the flavor of malt and hops. **—stout·ly** *adv.;* **stout·ness** *n.*

stove a *pt.* & *pp.* of STAVE. ***—n.*** a closed heating or cooking apparatus; **stove·pipe** *n.* a pipe connecting a stove to a chimney.

stow (STOH) *v.* pack (things) closely in a place; **stow away** hide on board a ship or aircraft so as to get transport; **stow·a·way** *n.* one who stows away. **—stow·age** (–ij) *n.* a stowing; also, room for storing.

STP standard temperature and pressure; ***n.*** a psychedelic drug.

St. Paul capital of Minnesota. **—St. Pe·ters·burg** (–PEE·turz–) a city of Florida.

stra·bis·mus (struh·BIZ–) *n.* a focusing disorder of the eyes; squint, cross-eye, or walleye.

strad·dle *v.* **strad·dles, strad·dled, strad·dling** **1** stand across (a ditch), sit on (a fence, animal's back, etc.); also, stand with the legs wide apart. **2** appear to favor both sides of (an issue). ***—n.*** a straddling. **—strad·dler** *n.*

strafe *v.* **strafes, strafed, straf·ing** of aircraft, attack with machine-gun fire while flying low.

strag·gle *v.* **strag·gles, strag·gled, strag·gling** **1** spread in an irregular manner, as vines. **2** stray from the main group. **—strag·gler** *n.* **—strag·gly** *adj.: a ~ beard, plant.*

straight (STRAIT) *adj.* **1** without curves, bends, angles, etc.; hence, direct: *a ~* (i.e. honest or upright) *citizen; to put the record ~* (i.e. correct); *votes the ~ Republican ticket* (i.e. for no other party); *a ~* (i.e. reliable) *tip; ~* (i.e. undiluted) *liquor.* **2** *Slang.* of people, conservative or conventional; not a drug addict, homosexual, etc. ***—adv.*** accurately; directly; upright; continuously; without delay; **straight away** (or **off**) at once. ***—n.*** **1** the condition of being straight; also, something straight. **2** *Slang.* a square person. **3** (a poker hand containing) five cards in sequence (as 4, 5, 6, 7, 8) but not all of the same suit. **—straight·ness** *n.* **—straight-arm** *v.* in football, push away (a tackler) with the arm extended stiffly. **—straight arrow** *Slang.* a stodgily proper or upright person. **—straight·a·way** *n.* & *adj.* (in) a straight or direct course; ***adv.*** straightway. **—straight·edge** (–ej) *n.* a piece or strip with a perfectly straight edge for testing or marking lines and surfaces. **—straight·en** *v.* make or become straight; **straighten out** make or become straight in thinking or behavior. **—straight face** a face showing no sign of merriment or other emotion; **straight-faced** *adj.* **—straight·for·ward** (–FOR·wurd) *adj.* direct; also, candid or frank; also ***adv.*** **—straightjacket, straight laced** same as STRAITJACKET, STRAITLACED. **—straight man** See FOIL. **—straight time** (rate of pay for) regular working hours, not overtime. —**straight·way** *adv.* at once.

strain *v.* **1** stretch or exert to the utmost: *a dog ~ing at his leash to get away; In poor light you have to ~ your eyes; Their* **strained** *relations led to separation; had to ~ every nerve* (i.e. try one's hardest) *to get top grades.* **2** filter (a liquid) through a strainer; also, filter out (solids); **strain·er** *n.* ***—n.*** **1** a stretching force or its effect: *Stress causes ~* (i.e. deformation) *in materials; A wrong step may cause a muscle ~.* **2** manner or style: *speaks in a mournful ~.* **3 strains** *pl.* snatches of music or singing. **4** an inherited quality or tendency: *the ~ of weakness in his character; a good ~* (i.e. breed) *of wheat.*

strait *n.* a narrow channel connecting two large bodies of water, as at Gibraltar; **straits** *pl.* difficulty or need: *in dire ~s.* ***—adj.*** *Archaic.* narrow; hence, strict. —**strait·en** *v.* make narrow; also, restrict; **in straitened circumstances** in poverty or need. —**strait·jack·et** *n.* a jacket-like garment designed to restrain a person physically. —**strait·laced** *adj.* severely strict in regard to religion and morals.

strand *n.* **1** one of the threads or wires that are twisted together to make a rope, cable, etc.: *a ~* (i.e. string) *of pearls; the ~s of melody in a composition.* **2** the shore or beach of a sea, lake, or river; ***v.*** be or put in a helpless position, as a ship run aground: *The last flight had left and he was ~ed.*

strange (STRAINJ) *adj.* **strang·er, strang·est** not familiar or accustomed: *The voice sounded ~; ~ visitors from space; felt ~ like a fish out of water; a northerner ~ to southern ways;* **strange·ly** *adv.* **strange·ness** *n.* —**strang·er** *n.* a person who is new in a place or unaccustomed (to a group or situation): *Dogs bark at ~s; gave hospitality to ~s; a ~ to luxury.*

stran·gle (STRANG·gl) *v.* **-gles, -gled, -gling** kill by squeezing the throat; hence, choke; also, stifle or suppress; **stran·gler** *n.* —**stran·gle·hold** *n.* a wrestling hold that would choke one's opponent; hence, a deadly grip. —**stran·gu·late** (STRANG·gyuh–) *v.* **-lates, -lat·ed, -lat·ing** constrict or tighten so as to block circulation, as in a loop of intestine caught in a hernia; **stran·gu·la·tion** (–LAY–) *n.: death by ~.*

strap *n.* & *v.* **straps, strapped, strap·ping** (bind or fasten with) a narrow strip of flexible material, as of a belt or wristwatch: *The victim was found ~d to a chair; the shoulder ~ of a purse, camera, uniform* (showing rank); *Pupils used to be ~d* (i.e. punished by beating with a strap); *a* **strap·less** *brassiere, gown.* —**strapped** *adj.* having straps; also, *Informal.* short of: *~ for funds, cash.* —**strap·ping** *adj. Informal.* robust or sturdy: *a ~ girl, youth.*

strass *n.* See PASTE, *n.* 2.

stra·ta (STRAY·tuh, STRAT–) a *pl.* of STRATUM.

strat·a·gem (–uh·jum) *n.* a carefully laid plan or scheme to entrap or outwit an opponent: *a military or political ~.* —**strat·e·gy** (–uh·jee) *n.* **-gies** the science or art of planning and directing military operations; hence, the resourceful management of any affair or operation: *the ~ of a game;* **strat·e·gist** *n.* —**stra·te·gic** (struh·TEE·jic) *adj.;* **stra·te·gi·cal·ly** *adv.*

strat·i·fy *v.* **-fies, -fied, -fy·ing** form (into) strata or layers: *Shale, sandstone, etc. are ~d rocks; the social classes of a ~d society;* **strat·i·fi·ca·tion** (–CAY–) *n.* —**strat·o·sphere** (–uh·sfeer) *n.* the usu. cloudless layer of the earth's atmosphere from about 10 miles (16.093 km) to about 30 miles (48.28 km) up. —**strat·um** (STRAY–, STRAT–) *n., pl.* **-ta** or **-tums** a horizontal or parallel layer, as of sedimentary rock, the atmosphere, social or cultural levels, etc. —**stra·tus** (STRAY–) *n., pl.* **-ti** (–tye) a layer-like or sheetlike formation of low clouds.

Strauss (STROUS), **Johann.** 1825–99, Austrian composer.

Stra·vin·sky (struh·VIN·skee), **Igor.** 1882–1971, Russian-born U.S. composer.

straw *n.* **1** the dried hollow stalks or stems of grains after threshing, used as bedding for animals and to make hats, baskets, etc.; also, one such stem or a similar tube used for sucking up beverages. **2** something trifling or worthless: *didn't care a ~.* ***—adj.:*** *a ~ hat; ~* (i.e. yellowish) *color.* —**straw·ber·ry** *n.* **-ber·ries** (the red, pulpy fruit of) a low-growing vinelike plant of the rose family. —**straw boss** *Informal.* an occasional supervisor with little authority. —**straw man** an imaginary opponent. —**straw·flow·er** *n.* (an annual herb bearing) a yellow, orange, red, or white flower that can be kept dried for use in winter boquets, etc.; also called "everlasting flower." —**straw vote** an unofficial vote to find out a general trend.

stray *v.* wander from the usual or regular path; hence, go wrong: *sheep ~ing from the fold; ~ed from the path of virtue;* ***adj.:*** *a ~ dog; ~ bullets; ~* (i.e. isolated) *cases;* ***n.*** a strayed child or domestic animal: *waifs and ~s.*

streak (STREEK) *n.* a long, thin mark such as is made in the sky by a shooting star; hence, a brief period or spell: *the ~ of dawn in the eastern sky; fat and lean ~s* (i.e. layers) *in bacon; the mean ~* (i.e. strain) *in his character; a ~* (i.e. period) *of luck.* ***—v.*** make streaks; also, move swiftly: *A popular prank was ~ing* (i.e. running naked in public); **streak·er** *n.* —**streak·y** *adj.*

stream (STREEM) *n.* a small river or brook; hence, a steady flow or unbroken series: *a ~ of tears, letters, visitors;* ***v.:*** *eyes ~ing with tears; ~ing eyes; blood ~ing from a wound; flags ~ing* (i.e. waving) *in the wind;* **stream·er** *n.* a long, narrow, flowing strip, esp. a pennant or banner. —**stream·let** *n.* a small stream. —**stream·line** *v.* **-lines, -lined, -lin·ing** organize (an operation) for greater speed and efficiency; make streamlined. —**stream·lined** *adj.* **1** having a smoothly flowing shape for swift movement through air or water: *a ~ automobile body.* **2** efficiently organized: *a ~ office.*

street *n.* a usu. paved public road lined with buildings, as in a town or city; also, the people living or working there; **street·car** *n.* a public passenger vehicle moving on rails laid on the streets; **street railway** (company operating) a streetcar line; **street theater** same as GUERRILLA THEATER; **street·walk·er** *n.* a prostitute.

strength *n.* inherent capacity for action; quality of being strong: *A weight-lifter is a man of great* (physical) *~; the ~ of one's character; ~ to endure suffering; There's ~ in numbers; 40% alcoholic ~; trusted her* **on the strength of** *your reference;* **strength·en** *v.* make or become strong(er); **strength·en·er** *n.*

stren·u·ous (–yoo·us) *adj.* demanding much strength or energy: *the ~ life of an athlete; ~ efforts; a ~ day;* **stren·u·ous·ly** *adv.;* **stren·u·ous·ness** *n.;* **stren·u·os·i·ty** (–OS–) *n.*

strep *n.* [short form] streptococcus. —**strep throat** *Informal.* a sore throat and fever caused by a streptococcus infection. —**strep·to·coc·cus** (–COC–) *n., pl.* **-coc·ci** (–COC·sye) any of a group of spherical bacteria that grow together in chains, some causing scarlet fever, septicemia, strep throat, etc. —**strep·to·my·cin** (–MY·sin) *n.* a powerful antibiotic derived from a mold.

stress *n.* **1** pressure or force that tends to strain or deform the body subjected to it: *Compressive ~ tends to shorten a body; He broke under the combined ~ of loss of job and family troubles.* **2** emphasis: *lays great ~ on punctuality; "Indecision" has its ~* (i.e. accent) *on the third syllable.* —**v.:** *He ~ed each point by thumping the table; The French seem to ~ words on the last syllable.*

stretch *v.* draw out or extend: *a clothesline ~ed across the yard; She ~ed out a helping hand; walks around his desk to ~ his limbs; reached too high and ~ed* (i.e. strained) *a muscle; socks that ~ to fit several sizes; a desert ~ing to the horizon; to ~ a point, the truth, one's patience.* —**n.** a stretching or being stretched; also, an extent of area or time: *works for hours at a ~; A ~ of the imagination takes you to fairyland; an endless ~ of ocean; the two ~es of a racecourse.* —**adj.** that stretches easily: *~ socks, pants.* —**stretch·a·ble** *adj.* —**stretch·y** *adj.* —**stretch·er** *n.* a device for carrying a disabled or sick person, usu. a light frame with canvas stretched across it borne by two **stretch·er-bear·ers.**

strew (STROO) *v.* **strewed,** *pt.* & *pp.* **strewed** or **strewn, strew·ing** scatter or cover by scattering: *a park ~ed with litter.*

stri·at·ed (STRY·ay·tid) *adj.* streaked or striped in parallel lines, as the fibers making up the **striated muscle** of an external organ, not a "smooth" muscle, as of an internal organ.

strick·en a *pp.* of STRIKE. —**adj.** wounded; also, afflicted (*by* trouble, sorrow, disease, etc.).

strict *adj.* **1** careful in enforcing rules: *a ~ teacher, parent.* **2** carefully observed; exact or precise: *a ~ rule; the ~ sense of a word; in the ~est confidence.* —**strict·ly** *adv.;* **strict·ness** *n.* —**stric·ture** (STRIK·chur) *n.* a narrowing or restricting; hence, a restriction or a censure: *~s on sex before marriage.*

stride *v.* **strides, strode, strid·den, strid·ing** walk with long steps, as from vigor or enthusiasm: *He strode into the room; kept her feet dry by ~ing over the stream.* —**n.** **1** a long step or the distance covered by it: **takes** *successes and failures* **in his stride** (i.e. as a matter of course; without getting upset). **2** usu. **strides** *pl.* progress: *the rapid ~s made by the computer industry.*

stri·dent (STRY·dnt) *adj.* loud in a harsh, grating, or obtrusive manner: *a ~ voice; the ~ tone of his petition;* **stri·dent·ly** *adv.* —**stri·den·cy** *n.*

strife *n.* a fighting or quarrel, esp. a struggle between opposing sides: *bitter ~ between factions; industrial ~* (between labor and management).

strike *v.* **strikes,** *pt.* **struck,** *pp.* **struck** or **strick·en, strik·ing** **1** hit, esp. aim or deal a blow with the hand or a weapon: *lost his patience and struck (out at) the bully; The invaders struck* (i.e. attacked) *without warning; A disease ~s a population; lit a fire by ~ing a match; The lightning struck him dead; A bright idea struck her; How does our plan ~* (i.e. impress) *you? A clock ~s* (i.e. sounds) *the hours; They struck* (i.e. advanced) *across the trackless desert; They struck* (i.e. engaged in a strike) *for more pay.* **2** effect or produce something by or as if by striking: *After some digging they struck oil; stories that ~ terror into young minds; A plant ~s roots as it grows in a place; They haggled a lot before ~ing* (i.e. agreeing on) *a bargain; He often ~s the pose of a concerned citizen;* **strike up** begin (an acquaintance, conversation, etc.) or begin playing (a song, etc.). —**n.** **1** a striking, esp. an attack. **2** a stoppage of work by employees to force their employer to agree to higher pay or better working conditions: *Workers go on ~.* **3** in baseball, any of four ways in which a failure may be called against a batter. **4** in bowling, a knocking down of all the pins with the first ball. **5** a discovery (of an oil deposit). —**strike·break·er** *n.* one hired to replace a striking worker. —**strike·out** *n.* a baseball batter's being put out as a result of three strikes. —**strik·ing** *adj.* very impressive: *a ~ personality, performance;* **strik·ing·ly** *adv.*

string *n.* **1** a cord or wire that is thicker than a thread, as for tying up a parcel, working a puppet, keeping a bow taut, etc.: *a ~ of pearls* (i.e. pearls on a string); *a ~* (i.e. series) *of lies;* **strings** *pl.* stringed instruments, as of an orchestra, or their players collectively. **2**

something resembling a string or cord, as a nerve or the fiber connecting the halves of a bean pod. **3** *Informal.* a condition attached to an offer; hence, a means of control; **pull strings** exert influence secretly. **—*v.* strings,** *pt.* & *pp.* **strung** or **stringed, string·ing:** *to ~ beads; to ~ a racket* (i.e. provide with strings); *a carcass strung up* (i.e. hung) *by its legs; a line strung* (i.e. stretched) *between two posts; to ~* (i.e. tune) *a violin; highly strung* (i.e. taut) *nerves; Bean pods are ~ed* (i.e. cleaned of strings); *the violin, guitar, and such* **stringed instruments. — string bean** a bean whose pods are eaten as a vegetable after their strings are removed, not one that is shelled for use; also, a snap bean.

strin·gent (–junt) *adj.* strictly or severely binding: *~ regulations; a ~* (i.e. tight) *market;* **strin·gen·cy** *n.*

string·er *n.* **1** a connecting or supporting timber, esp. a horizontal piece. **2** a part-time correspondent of a newspaper. **—string·y** *adj.* **string·i·er, -i·est** having or forming strings; also, sinewy or wiry in build.

strip *v.* **strips, stripped, strip·ping 1** undress; also, remove the covering of (a fruit). **2** deprive (of what belongs to one by taking it off completely or forcibly): *a general ~d of his powers; a stolen car ~d of its accessories; to ~* (i.e. remove) *old paint off furniture.* **3** damage or break the thread of (a screw) or teeth of (a gear). **—*n.*** a long, narrow piece: *~s of cloth, cardboard, land; a landing ~* (i.e. air strip). **—stripe** *n.* **1** a long, narrow band of contrasting color: *a tiger's ~s; a dark suit with chalk ~s; the stars and ~s of the U.S. flag;* ***v.* stripes, striped, strip·ing:** *the ~d bass, skunk.* **2** usu. **stripes** *pl.* a strip of braid or a chevron worn on the sleeve of a uniform to show the wearer's rank or length of service. **3** sort or type. **—strip·ling** *n.* a youth who has not yet attained maturity. **—strip mine** an "open-pit" mine for removing coal or other mineral from the surface of the earth; **strip-mine** *v.* **—strip-tease** (–teez) *n.* a stage show in which a woman takes off her clothes one by one with suggestive dancing and accompanying music; **strip-teas·er** or **strip·per** *n.*

strive *v.* **strives,** *pt.* **strove** (STROHV) or **strived,** *pp.* **striv·en, striv·ing** make great efforts or try hard (to accomplish something, for an effect, against a difficulty, etc.).

strobe (light) an electronic device emitting brilliant flashes, used in photography, in the stroboscope, etc.; **stro·bo·scope** (STROH·buh–, STROB·uh–) *n.* an instrument for studying rapid motion, using flashes of light that are synchronized with the speed of the moving object.

strode *pt.* of STRIDE.

stroke *v.* **strokes, stroked, strok·ing** pass the hand caressingly over (a pet, person, etc.). **—*n.* 1** a stroking. **2** a striking or blow, esp. one dealt suddenly or sharply: *a sword ~; killed by a ~ of lightning; a ~ of misfortune, luck; at the ~ of 12* (o'clock); *died of a ~* (i.e. apoplexy). **3** an effort, esp. a vigorous or successful one: *a ~ of genius; didn't do one ~ of work all day.* **4** an action or movement that is repeated rhythmically: *a swimming ~; the ~s of a piston; up and down ~s of the pen.*

stroll (STROLE) *n.* & *v.* (take) a leisurely walk: *a ~ in the park; a ~ing* (i.e. wandering) *troupe of players; She ~s* (i.e. along or through) *the streets.* **—stroll·er** *n.* one who strolls; also, a light carriage for a sitting child.

strong *adj.* **1** having great power to act or resist, not weak; powerful: *~ muscles, mind, will, reasons, drink, temptation, winds.* **2** of a specified number: *We are 10 ~.* **3** ill-smelling; foul: *~ cheese, breath, smell.* **4** of a verb, not regular in conjugation, as "sink–sank–sunk." **—strong·ly** *adv.* **—strong-arm** *adj. Informal.* using undue force: *a ~ method;* ***v.*** use coercion or violence against. **—strong·box** *n.* a securely built box or safe for valuables. **—strong·hold** *n.* a fortress; also, a place in which a party or cause has strong support: *a Republican ~.* **—strong·man** *n.* **-men** a despot or dictator. **—strong-mind·ed** *adj.* mentally strong or unyielding. **—strong·room** *n.* a room that is built safe against fire, burglary, etc.; also **strong room.**

stron·ti·um (–shee–, –tee–) *n.* a metallic chemical element; **strontium 90** a radioactive isotope of strontium found in atomic fallout.

strop *n.* & *v.* **strops, stropped, strop·ping** (sharpen a razor on) a leather strap. **—stro·phe** (STROH·fee) *n.* a stanza, esp. of a choral ode; **stroph·ic** (STROF–) *adj.*

strove *pt.* of STRIVE.

struck *pt.* or a *pp.* of STRIKE. **—*adj.*** affected by a labor strike: *~ businesses.*

struc·ture (–chur) *n.* **1** anything constructed of parts; a building. **2** the manner of arrangement of parts in a system: *the ~ of society; sentence ~; a wage ~.* **—*v.* -tures, -tured, -tur·ing** organize with differentiated parts: *a ~d curriculum;* **struc·tur·al** *adj.: ~ steel* (used in building); *~ defects, differences;* **struc·tur·al·ly** *adv.*

stru·del (STROO·dl) *n.* a rolled-up pastry with a filling of fruit or cheese.

strug·gle *n.* **1** great effort or exertion: *the ~ for survival.* **2** strife or conflict. **—*v.* strug·gles, strug·gled, strug·gling** make great efforts, as against contending forces: *She ~d to free herself; ~d for breath; ~d out of his arms.*

strum *v.* **strums, strummed, strum·ming** play (a guitar, *on* the piano, a tune, etc.) in a casual or unskillful manner.

strum·pet (–pit) *n.* a prostitute.

strung *pt.* & *pp.* of STRING.

strut *v.* **struts, strut·ted, strut·ting** walk in a jaunty and self-important manner: *a stripper ~ing her stuff on the stage.* **—*n.* 1** a strutting walk or gait. **2** a brace or support, as under the rafters of a roof.

strych·nine (STRIC·nin, –nine, –neen) *n.* a bitter, poisonous drug prepared from an East Indian plant.

stub *n.* a short piece remaining after its main part is used up or broken off: *the ~ of a cigarette, pencil, tooth, tree* (i.e. stump), *ticket* or *check* (kept as a record); ***v.*** **stubs, stubbed, stub·bing:** *to ~* (i.e. hurt by striking) *one's toe* (against a hard surface); *to ~ a cigar* (i.e. put it out by rubbing on a surface). **—stub·ble** *n.* **1** stumps left projecting from the ground after harvesting. **2** a short, bristly growth, as of hair on the face. Hence **stub·bly** *adj.* **—stub·born** (STUB·urn) *adj.* determined not to change one's way; unyielding: *a ~ disposition, child, resistance, cough, soil* (that is hard to work); **stub·born·ly** *adv.;* **stub·born·ness** *n.* **—stub·by** *adj.* **stub·bi·er, stub·bi·est** **1** short and thick: *~ fingers.* **2** covered with stubs or stumps: *a ~ field.*

stuc·co (STUC·oh) *n.* **stuc·co(e)s** a plaster-like material for coating outside walls; ***v.*** **stuc·co(e)s, stuc·coed, stuc·co·ing** coat or decorate with stucco.

stuck *pt.* of STICK. **—stuck-up** *adj. Informal.* conceited.

stud *n.* **1** a male animal kept for breeding, esp. a stallion, or **stud·horse. 2** one of the upright timbers inside a wall frame to which the boards or panels are nailed. **3** a knoblike head, as used to ornament a leather surface, or a small, two-headed button used on dress shirts; ***v.*** **studs, stud·ded, stud·ding** decorated or dotted (as if) with studs: *a star-~d sky; ~d with gems; a ~d snow tire for better traction over ice.* **—stud·book** *n.* a register of purebred racehorses or dogs. **—stud·ding** *n.* a wall's studs or their material.

stu·dent (STEW·dnt) *n.* one who studies (a subject) or attends a school. **—studhorse** See STUD, *n.* 1. **—stud·ied** (–eed) *adj.* deliberate: *a ~ insult; ~ courtesy; a ~* (i.e. carefully prepared) *reply;* **stud·ied·ly** *adv.* **—stu·di·o** (STEW·dee·oh) *n.* **-os** an artist's or photographer's workroom; also, a broadcasting room or a place where motion pictures are produced; **studio couch** a backless and armless couch that can be made into a bed. **—stu·di·ous** (–dee·us) *adj.* **1** devoted to study: *~ habits.* **2** diligent: *~ care, efforts; attention.* Hence **stu·di·ous·ly** *adv.* **—stud·y** *n.* **stud·ies** **1** concentration of the mind on a subject in an effort to learn it; also, any earnest "mental" effort. **2** a detailed examination of a subject, the subject itself, or a work or treatise discussing it; **studies** *pl.* education: *a man of ~s.* **3** a room for study. **—*v.*** **stud·ies, stud·ied, stud·y·ing:** *She's ~ing medicine; works days and ~s nights; ~d* (i.e. carefully considered) *the pros and cons of marrying.*

stuff *n.* **1** substance or material that something is made of or for making something: *woolen ~; the ~* (i.e. basic qualities) *of genius; He knows his ~* (i.e. subject of specialty). **2** thing(s): *What's that ~ you're drinking? Get rid of the ~; ~* (i.e. trash) *and nonsense!* **—*v.*** fill or pack: *a pillow ~ed with feathers; a ~ed-up nose* (from a cold); *a ~ed ballot box* (containing fraudulent votes); *A turkey is ~ed with bread crumbs, seasoning, etc. for roasting; That bear is only ~ed though it looks live; ~ed (himself) too full with cake;* **stuffed shirt** *Slang.* one who is pretentious or pompous. **—stuff·ing** *n.* **1** padding used in upholstery. **2** a filling of bread crumbs, seasoning, etc. for roast fowl. **—stuf·fy** *adj.* **stuf·fi·er, stuf·fi·est:** *a ~* (i.e. not airy) *room; a ~* (i.e. congested) *nose; a ~* (i.e. straitlaced) *clergyman; a ~* (i.e. dull) *sermon.*

stul·ti·fy *v.* **-fies, -fied, -fy·ing** make (an action) seem foolish; also, render futile or ineffectual: *a ~ing experience;* **stul·ti·fi·ca·tion** (–CAY–) *n.*

stum·ble *v.* **-bles, -bled, -bling** take a wrong step in walking or running, trip accidentally, or falter because of age or weakness: *~d and fell in the dark; ~d through his performance; ~d upon* (i.e. happened to find) *what he was looking for;* ***n.*** a stumbling; also, a mistake or wrong act; **stum·bler** *n.* **—stumbling block** a hindrance or obstacle.

stump *n.* **1** the part of a tree trunk remaining in the ground after the tree has been felled; hence, something resembling it, as an amputated limb; stub; **stumps** *pl. Slang.* legs. **2** a political campaigner's speaking platform, as a tree stump. **—*v.*** **1** walk stiffly, as if on wooden legs. **2** make political speeches (in): *went ~ing (the country) for votes.* **3** *Informal.* perplex or confound; floor: *was ~ed by the strange events.* **—stump·y** *adj.* short and thick.

stun *v.* **stuns, stunned, stun·ning** make dizzy, as (if) by a blow: *was ~d by the news.*

stung *pt.* & *pp.* of STING.

stunk a *pt.* & *pp.* of STINK.

stun·ning *adj.* bewildering; also, *Informal.* strikingly attractive: *a ~ blonde;* **stun·ning·ly** *adv.*

stunt *v.* **1** check (growth or development): *a ~ed tree; factors ~ing growth.* **2** do a stunt; ***n.*** a feat to attract attention or show one's daring, as at a circus.

stu·pe·fy (STEW·puh–) *v.* **-fies, -fied, -fy·ing** stun or cause stupor in; hence, bewilder: *~d with drink, drugs; the ~ing effect of a disaster;* **stu·pe·fac·tion** (–FAC–) *n.* **—stu·pen·dous** (–PEN·dus) *adj.* astonishing, esp. by immensity or greatness: *a ~ marvel, achievement;* **stu·pen·dous·ly** *adv.* **—stu·pid** (STEW–) *adj.* showing lack of intelligence; silly: *a ~ child, idea; ~ behavior;* **stu·pid·ly** *adv.;* **stu·pid·i·ty** (–PID–) *n.* **-ties. —stu·por** (–pur) *n.* a dazed condition; numbness; **stu·por·ous** (–us) *adj.*

stur·dy *adj.* **-di·er, -di·est** strong and hardy, esp. in build or growth: *a ~ oak; ~ limbs; a ~ race, defender; ~ common sense;* **stur·di·ly** *adv.;* **stur·di·ness** *n.*

stur·geon (–jun) *n.* any of a family of large food fishes that yield caviar and isinglass.

stut·ter *n.* & *v.* stammer, esp. by repeating the first sound of a word; **stut·ter·er** *n.*

St. Vi·tus's (–VYE·tus·iz) **dance** See CHOREA.

sty *n.* **sties** **1** a pen for pigs; hence, any filthy place. **2** also **stye,** *pl.* **sties** a small pus-filled inflammation on the rim of an eyelid.

Styg·i·an (STIJ·ee·un) *adj.* **1** of the Styx. **2** dark or gloomy; also **stygian.**

style *n.* **1** a distinctive fashion or mode in one's way of living, esp. dress, indicative of taste or excellence: *a hat that is out of ~; He dresses and lives in ~* (i.e. good style); *She lacks ~.* **2** a distinctive manner of artistic expression or design: *a flowery ~ of writing; Shakespeare's ~; built in the Byzantine ~; Too many rules* **cramp one's style** (*Informal.* limit one's freedom). **3** a formal manner or mode: *the ~ of addressing clergy; a publisher's house ~* (i.e. rules for spelling, punctuation, etc.). **4** a pointed device or structure, as a stylus, a phonograph needle, or the stem of a flower's pistil with the stigma at its top. **—*v.* styles, styled, styl·ing** **1** make or design according to a style: *clothes ~d for comfort;* **styl·ing** *n.* style imparted to something. **2** call or name: *~d himself "emperor."* **—styl·ish** *adj.* according to the prevailing fashion; fashionable; **styl·ish·ly** *adv.;* **styl·ish·ness** *n.* **—styl·ist** *n.* one who is concerned with or is an expert in artistic style, esp. of written expression; **sty·lis·tic** (–LIS–) *adj.;* **sty·lis·ti·cal·ly** *adv.* **—styl·ize** *v.* **-iz·es, -ized, -iz·ing** put (something) in a particular style of design: *The fleur-de-lis is a ~d flower* (i.e. not realistic). **—sty·lus** *n.* **-lus·es** or **-li** (–lye) a pointed instrument, as for engraving, cutting the grooves in or playing a phonograph record, etc.

sty·mie (–mee) *n.* formerly in golf, the situation when a ball to be putted is blocked by another ball closer to the hole; ***v.* -mies, -mied, -mie·ing** block or thwart. Also **sty·my, -mies, -mied, -my·ing.**

styp·tic (STIP–) *adj.* helping to stop bleeding; astringent; **styptic pencil** a stick of medication containing an astringent.

Sty·ro·foam (STY·ruh·fome) *Trademark.* a lightweight polystyrene; also **styrofoam** *n.*

Styx (STIKS) in Greek myth, a river that dead souls had to cross on their way to Hades.

suave (SWAHV) *adj.* polished and gracious in manner; **suave·ly** *adv.;* **suave·ness** or **suav·i·ty** *n.*

sub *n.* [short form] submarine; substitute; subordinate; ***v.* subs, subbed, sub·bing** *Informal.* substitute (for someone). **—sub.** subscription; substitute; suburb(an). **—sub-** *prefix.* **1** lower or under; hence, further divided or secondary: as in

subagent	**subindex**
subaqueous	**subkingdom**
subbasement	**suborder**
subclass	**subphylum**
subentry	**subregion**
subfamily	**subroutine**
subfreezing	**subsection**
subgenus	**subspecies**
subgroup	**subsystem**
subhead(ing)	**subtopic**

2 near(ly); somewhat: as in

subacute	**sublethal**
subarctic	**subsaturated**
subclinical	**subtemperate**
subhuman	

sub·al·pine *adj.* of or in the lower slopes of the Alps; hence, below the timberline: *the ~ forests of the Rockies; the ~ larch.* **—sub·al·tern** (–AWL–) *n.* & *adj.* subordinate. **—sub·as·sem·bly** (–SEM–) *n.* an assembled unit that is a component of a larger unit. **—sub·a·tom·ic** (–TOM–) *adj.* smaller than the atom. **—sub·branch** *n.* a division of a branch. **—sub·com·mit·tee** (SUB·cuh–) *n.* a small committee under a larger one. **—sub·com·pact** (–COM–) *n.* an automobile smaller than a compact. **—sub·con·scious** (–CON–) *adj.* of thoughts and feelings, existing in the mind but not fully recognized; ***n.* the subconscious** the realm of subconscious mental processes; **sub·con·scious·ly** *adv.* **—sub·con·ti·nent** (–CON–) *n.* a subdivision of a continent, as the Indian peninsula. **—sub·con·tract** (–CON–) *n.* a contract for carrying out part of a main contract; ***v.:*** *A building contractor ~s plumbing, heating, and other installations;* **sub·con·trac·tor** *n.* **—sub·cul·ture** *n.* a social group within a larger one exhibiting a culture of its own, as of teenagers. **—sub·cu·ta·ne·ous** (–cue·TAY·nee·us) *adj.* under the skin: *a ~ injection; ~ fat.* **—sub·dea·con** (–DEE·cun) *n.* a cleric next below a deacon. **—sub·deb** *n.* short form of **sub·deb·u·tante** (–DEB·yuh·tahnt) *n.* a girl about to become a debutante. **—sub·di·vide** *v.* **-vides, -vid·ed, -vid·ing** divide further, as land into small lots; **sub·di·vis·ion** (–VIZH–) *n.*

sub·due (–DEW) *v.* **-dues, -dued, -du·ing** **1** overpower; hence, bring under control: *was ~d after a brief struggle; to ~ one's passions.* **2** soften or tone down: *in a ~d light; ~d tones.* **—sub·head** *n.* a subordinate heading or division; also **sub·head·ing.** **—subj.** subject; subjunctive. **—sub·ject** *n.* (–jict) **1** theme or topic of a conversation, study, etc.: *Don't change the ~; Algebra is his favorite ~.* **2** a person owing allegiance to a king or to his government. **3** one undergoing an investigation; also, one chosen for artistic representation. **4** in grammar, a word or term representing the one about whom something is said, as "John" in "John loves Mary," "John is here," and "John is loved by Mary." ***—adj.*** under another's rule; not independent: *a ~ people;* **subject to 1** owing obedience to: *You're ~ to the laws of your country.* **2** prone or liable to: *Humans are ~ to error.* **3** conditional upon: *an arrangement ~ to approval.* ***—v.*** (–JECT) **subject to 1** bring under (a rule or power). **2** cause to undergo (a treatment) or experience (something). **—sub·jec·tion** (–JEC–) *n.;* **sub·jec·tive** (–tiv) *adj.* relating to the person thinking, not to the object thought of; personal: *a purely ~ opinion;* **sub·jec·tive·ly** *adv.;* **sub·jec·tiv·i·ty** (–TIV–) *n.* **—subject matter** content, not form or style. **—sub·join** (–JOIN) *v.* append. **—sub ju·di·ce** (–JOO·di·see) *Latin.* before a court; awaiting judgment. **—sub·ju·gate** (SUB·juh–) *v.* **-gates, -gat·ed, -gat·ing** bring under slavish subjection; **sub·ju·ga·tion** (–GAY–) *n.* **—sub·junc·tive** (–JUNK·tiv) *n.* & *adj.* (a verb mood) expressing a possibility rather than an actuality, as in "I suggest he *be* present," or "If I *were* you. . . ." **—sub·lease** *n.* a lease granted by a lessee; ***v.*** (–LEECE) **-leas·es, -leased, -leas·ing** grant or obtain a sublease of. **—sub·let** (–LET) *v.* **-lets, -let, -let·ting** let rented or leased property to another; also, subcontract (work). **—sub·li·mate** (SUB·luh–) *v.* **-mates, -mat·ed, -mat·ing** purify or refine, as by vaporizing and condensing a solid such as sulfur: *Sexual energy may be ~d into religious activity;* **sub·li·ma·tion** (–MAY–) *n.;* **sub·lime** (suh·BLIME) *v.* **-limes, -limed, -lim·ing** sublimate; also, go through the sublimation process; ***adj.*** so elevated or noble as to inspire awe and wonder: *~ virtue, beauty, devotion, heights;* **sub·lim·i·ty** (–LIM–) *n.;* **sub·lim·i·nal** (–LIM–) *adj.* of stimuli, learning processes, etc., barely perceived: *toy commercials containing ~ suggestions to buy; the ~* (i.e. subconscious) *self.* **—sub·lu·nar·y** (SUB·loo–, –LOO–) *adj.* terrestrial or mundane. **—sub·ma·chine** (–muh·SHEEN) **gun** a lightweight automatic or semiautomatic weapon with rapid-firing action. **—sub·mar·gin·al** (–MAR–) *adj.* **1** below the margin in standards, productivity, etc. **2** near the margin (of a wing, etc.). **—sub·ma·rine** (–muh·REEN) *adj.* underwater; ***n.*** a warship designed for underwater operation; **submarine sandwich** same as HERO SANDWICH. **—sub·merge** (–MURJ) *v.* **-merg·es, -merged, -merg·ing** put or sink under water; hence, sink below a level, as of poverty; **sub·mer·gence** *n.* Also **sub·merse, -mers·es, -mersed, -mers·ing; sub·mer·sion** *n.;* **sub·mers·i·ble** *n.* & *adj.* (a diving vessel or other vehicle) that can operate under water. **—sub·mi·cro·scop·ic** (–my·cruh·SCOP–) *adj.* too tiny to be seen with an ordinary microscope. **—sub·min·i·a·ture** (–MIN·ee·uh·chur, –MIN·uh–) *adj.* smaller than miniature size. **—sub·mis·sion** (–MISH·un) *n.* a submitting or something submitted; also, obedience; **sub·mis·sive** (–siv) *adj.;* **sub·mit** (–MIT) *v.* **-mits, -mit·ted, -mit·ting 1** give way or yield (to a treatment, situation, etc.). **2** present as to a higher authority: *to ~ a report; I ~* (i.e. claim or affirm) *that you are mistaken.* **—sub·nor·mal** (–NOR·mul) *adj.* below normal; **sub·nor·mal·i·ty** (–MAL–) *n.* **—sub·or·bit·al** (–OR·bitl) *adj.* involving less than a full orbit: *a ~ space flight.* **—sub·or·di·nate** (–BOR·duh·nit) *n.* & *adj.* (a person or thing) that is below another in rank; (one) that is dependent: *was kind to her ~s; "If," "since," "whether," etc. start* **subordinate clauses** *in complex sentences;* ***v.*** (–nate) **-nates, -nat·ed, -nat·ing** make subordinate or subservient *(to);* **sub·or·di·na·tion** (–NAY–) *n.* **—sub·orn** (suh·BORN) *v.* induce (a witness, etc.) to commit perjury; **sub·or·na·tion** (–NAY–) *n.* **—sub·plot** *n.* a secondary or subordinate plot in a story. **—sub·poe·na** (suh·PEE·nuh) *n.* a legal written order requiring a person to appear or documents to be submitted in court; ***v.*** **-naes, -naed, -nae·ing:** *Watergate tapes were ~d.* **—sub·pro·fes·sion·al** (–FESH–) *n.* same as PARAPROFESSIONAL. **—sub ro·sa** (–ROH·zuh) secretly; in confidence. **—sub·scribe** (–SCRIBE) *v.* **-scribes, -scribed, -scrib·ing 1** pay or pledge (a sum of money) to a cause, fund, etc.; also, (agree to) take a periodical: *to ~ to charities, magazines.* **2** sign one's name at the bottom of (a document); hence, give consent or approval (to a measure, opinion, etc.). Hence **sub·scrib·er** *n.* **—sub·script** *n.* & *adj.* (something) written low on the line, as the "2" of H_2O or underneath a character, as the cedilla of "ç"; **sub·scrip·tion** (–SCRIP–) *n.* a subscribing or the payment made; also, a sum of money raised. **—sub·se·quent** *adj.* coming after: *~ developments; ~ to his arrest;* **sub·se·quent·ly** *adv.* **—sub·ser·vi·ent** (–SUR–) *adj.* slavishly serving; obsequious; subordinate *(to);* **sub·ser·vi·ence** *n.* **—sub·side** (–SIDE) *v.* **-sides, -sid·ed, -sid·ing 1** sink to a lower or more normal level, as receding flood waters, loose earth, etc. **2** of anything agitated or rising, become tranquil or quiet; abate: *A fever, storm, anger ~s.* Hence **sub·sid·ence** (SUB–) *n.* **—sub·sid·i·ar·y** (–SID·ee·er·ee) *adj.* **1** auxiliary or secondary *(to).* **2** allied in a subordinate capacity, as a corporation controlled by a parent or "holding" company; ***n.:*** *the Canadian ~ of an American company.* **—sub·si·dize** *v.* **-diz·es, -dized, -diz·ing** help with a subsidy; **sub·si·di·za·tion** (–ZAY–) *n.;* **sub·si·dy** *n.* **-dies** money or other aid given by a government to farmers, schools, airlines, etc. **—sub·sist** (–SIST) *v.* continue to be or keep alive (*on* food or *by* some means); **sub·sist·ence** *n.* existence; sustenance; livelihood; ***adj.:*** *a ~ diet; ~ wages; the ~ economy of primitives;*

~ *farming with no surpluses for sale.* —**sub·soil** *n.* the infertile two or three feet of soil beneath the topsoil. —**sub·son·ic** (–SON–) *adj.* slower than the speed of sound: ~ *travel, aircraft.* —**sub·stance** (–stunce) *n.* **1** what something consists of; material: *Margarine is a butterlike ~; the ~ of what he said; I agree with him* **in substance** (i.e. in essentials). **2** solid quality; body; hence, richness: *ate nothing of ~ for 10 days; a man of some ~* (i.e. wealth or property). —**sub·stand·ard** (–STAN·durd) *adj.* below standard: ~ *living conditions, English.* —**sub·stan·tial** (–STAN–) *adj.* **1** having substance: *a ~ meal, structure; a ~* (i.e. considerable) *improvement; nothing ~ about a dream.* **2** in essentials: *two versions in ~ agreement.* Hence **sub·stan·tial·ly** (–STAN–) *adv.* —**sub·stan·ti·ate** (–STAN·shee–) *v.* **-ates, -at·ed, -at·ing** give substance to; hence, establish by giving evidence: *to ~ a charge, claim, opinion;* **sub·stan·ti·a·tion** (–AY–) *n.;* **sub·stan·tive** (–stun·tiv) *n.* a word or phrase used as a noun, not adjective, as in "to feed *the poor*"; ***adj.*** dealing with essentials; also, substantial; **sub·stan·ti·val** (–TYE·vul) *adj.* —**sub·sta·tion** *n.* a branch station, esp. of a post office.

sub·sti·tute *n.* & *adj.* (a person or thing) that takes the place of another: *a ~ teacher; a sugar ~;* ***v.*** **-tutes, -tut·ed, -tut·ing:** *coffee ~d with chicory; Margarine ~s for butter;* **sub·sti·tu·tion** (–TUE–) *n.*

sub·stra·tum (–stray–, –strat–) *n., pl.* **-ta** or **-tums** a supporting lower layer or stratum. —**sub·struc·ture** *n.* a supporting structure or part, as a building's foundation. —**sub·sume** (–SOOM) *v.* **-sumes, -sumed, -sum·ing** bring (an idea, example, etc.) *under* something larger, as a class, rule, etc. —**sub·sur·face** (–SUR·fis) *n.* & *adj.* (earth material), lying near the surface. —**sub·teen** *n.* a child approaching the age of 13. —**sub·ten·ant** (–TEN·unt) *n.* one who rents property from a tenant; **sub·ten·an·cy** *n.* —**sub·ter·fuge** (–fyooj) *n.* (deception by means of) a trick or stratagem. —**sub·ter·ra·ne·an** (–RAY–) *adj.* in the earth or underground; hence, secret or hidden.

sub·tile (SUTL) *adj.* **-til·er, -til·est** delicate or rare, not dense; subtle.

sub·ti·tle *n.* **1** a secondary or explanatory title, as of a book. **2** printed matter such as translated dialogue shown on a television or motion-picture screen. Also ***v.*** **-tles, -tled, -tling.**

sub·tle (SUTL) *adj.* **-tler, -tlest** **1** difficult to perceive by mind or sense because fine or delicate: *a ~ distinction, flavor, joke.* **2** having or showing a keen or clever mind: *a ~ observer, design; a ~* (i.e. tricky) *scheme.* —**sub·tle·ty** *n.;* **sub·tly** *adv.*

sub·to·tal *n.* a total to be added to others for a complete or "grand" total. —**sub·tract** (–TRACT) *v.* take away one number from another; **sub·trac·tion** *n.* —**sub·tra·hend** (SUB·truh–) *n.* a number to be subtracted from another. —**sub·trop·i·cal** (–TROP–) *adj.* bordering on the tropics; hence, nearly tropical; also **sub·trop·ic.** —**sub·urb** *n.* a town, district, or community on the outskirts of a city; **the suburbs** *pl.* a city's residential outskirts; **sub·ur·ban** (–BUR·bun) *adj.;* **sub·ur·ban·ite** *n.* one living in a suburb; **sub·ur·bi·a** (–bee·uh) *n.* suburbs or suburbanites collectively. —**sub·ven·tion** (–VEN–) *n.* a subsidy or endowment. —**sub·vert** (–VURT) *v.* upset or overthrow (something established); hence, undermine (morality, etc.); **sub·vers·ion** *n.;* **sub·ver·sive** (–siv) *adj.* —**sub·way** *n.* an underground railway or its tunnel; also, an underground passage.

suc·ceed (suk·SEED) *v.* **1** come after or follow, as in an office: *to ~ to the throne; Carter ~ed Ford as President.* **2** be successful (in one's purpose): *~ed in overthrowing his opponents.* —**suc·cess** (–SES) *n.* **1** wished-for result or outcome, esp. good fortune: *to meet with ~; had great ~ in life.* **2** a person or thing that is successful: *The play was a ~.* —**suc·cess·ful** (–SES–) *adj.* having success; hence, prosperous or fortunate; **suc·cess·ful·ly** *adv.* —**suc·ces·sion** (–SESH·un) *n.* **1** the act of succeeding or the right to succeed another. **2** a coming, one after another, of people or events: *It snowed for three days* **in succession** (i.e. in a row); *a ~* (i.e. series) *of calamities.* —**suc·ces·sive** (–SES·iv) *adj.* coming one after another in series; **suc·ces·sive·ly** *adv.* —**suc·ces·sor** *n.* one that succeeds another (to an office, ownership of property, etc.).

suc·cinct (suc·SINCT) *adj.* concise and compact in expression: *a ~ summary, style, writer;* **suc·cinct·ly** *adv.;* **suc·cinct·ness** *n.*

suc·cor (SUC·ur) *n.* & *v.* help or aid in time of need.

suc·co·tash (SUC·uh–) *n.* kernels of sweet corn and lima beans cooked together.

suc·cu·lent (SUC·yuh–) *adj.* juicy or fleshy; ***n.*** a fleshy plant adapted for storing water, as cactuses and agaves; **suc·cu·lence** or **suc·cu·len·cy** *n.*

suc·cumb (suh·CUMB) *v.* yield or give way, as from weakness (to temptation, etc.): *soon ~ed to his injuries* (i.e. died).

such *adj.* of the kind (specified or suggested): *Shakespeare, Milton, and ~ poets; poets* **such as** *Milton; was ~ a great poet;* **such and such** a certain but not specified (person or thing). —***adv.*** to that degree: *a man of ~ fine manners.* —***pron.*** such a one or ones: *Take ~* (i.e. books) *as you can read in one day; ~ was not my intention; A debtor,* **as such,** *owes money; no admission to Communists, fellow travelers, and ~.* —**such·like** *pron.* & *adj.* (people or things) of such a kind.

suck *v.* draw in a fluid, esp. a liquid, (as by) using the lips: *An infant ~s (milk from) its mother's breast; She ~s oranges; the ~ing action of* *a pump; A vacuum cleaner ~s in dust; Sponges ~ up moisture; likes to ~ on his pipe;* ***n.*** the act of sucking; suction. —**suck·er** *n.* **1** one that sucks, as a family of fishes with thick lips; also, a sucking organ, as the roots of a parasitic plant, or a disk-shaped clinging organ, as on the tentacles of an octupus. **3** a lollipop. **4** *Slang.* one who is easily cheated or fooled. —**suck·le** *v.* **-les, -led, -ling** feed at the breast or udder; hence, nourish or rear; **suck·ling** *n.* & *adj.* (a child or animal) that is not yet weaned: *a ~ infant, pig.*

su·cre (SOO·cray) *n.* the basic money unit of Ecuador, worth 100 centavos. —**Su·cre** (SOO·cray) the judicial capital of Bolivia.

su·crose (SOO–) *n.* common table sugar, obtained from sugar cane and beets.

suc·tion *n.* a sucking; also, the process by which a fluid is drawn up, as through a drinking straw, or by which a concave pad or disk sticks to a surface: *Lift pumps are ~ pumps;* **suc·tion·al** *adj.*

Su·dan (soo·DAN) the largest country of Africa; 967,500 sq.mi. (2,505,813 km^2); *cap.* Khartoum; **Su·da·nese** (–NEEZ) *n.* & *adj.*

sud·den (SUDN) *adj.* happening, met with, done, etc. unexpectedly or hastily: *came to a ~ stop; a ~ decision on the eve of the wedding; a ~ rush of wind; a ~ turn, descent;* **all of a sudden** suddenly; **sudden death** in games, an overtime period that ends as soon as one side has scored or reached a predetermined score; **sud·den·ly** *adv.;* **sud·den·ness** *n.*

suds (SUDZ) *n.pl.* soapy water; also, the bubbles formed on it; **suds·y** *adj.*

sue (SOO) *v.* **sues, sued, su·ing** **1** take legal action (against): *He ~d his doctor; ~d for malpractice; ~d for $2 million.* **2** plead or solicit respectfully (*for* a favor, peace, etc.).

suede or **suède** (SWADE) *n.* soft leather for shoes, coats, etc. made by raising a velvety nap on the flesh side of tanned animal hide.

su·et (SOO·it) *n.* hard fat around the kidneys and loins of sheep and cattle.

Su·ez (soo·EZ) a city at the S. end of the **Suez Canal** connecting the Mediterranean with the Red Sea.

suff. sufficient; suffix.

suf·fer (SUF·ur) *v.* undergo pain, harm, loss, or anything hard to bear: *had to ~ much because of the strike; Businesses ~ed; They ~ed great losses; ~ed harm, insults; ~ing from malaria;* "*Suffer* (i.e. allow) *the little children to come unto me*"; **suf·fer·er** *n.* —**suf·fer·ance** (–unce) *n.* **1** passive toleration: *an unwanted employee kept* **on sufferance** (instead of being fired). **2** suffering capacity. —**suf·fer·ing** *n.* the bearing of pain, harm, loss, etc.; also, what is suffered: *the ~s of the poor.*

suf·fice (suh·FICE) *v.* **suf·fic·es, suf·ficed, suf·fic·ing** **1** be sufficient or enough: *$100 will ~ for expenses.* **2** satisfy the appetite of. —**suf·fi·cient** (–FISH·unt) *adj.* of a quantity or scope that satisfies needs; enough: *not ~ evidence to lay charges;* **suf·fi·cient·ly** *adv.;* **suf·fi·cien·cy** *n.*

suf·fix *n.* an affix added to the end of a word to form derivatives, as *-ly, -ness,* and *-y;* also, an inflectional ending such as *-ed, -ing,* or *-s.*

suf·fo·cate (SUF·uh–) *v.* **-cates, -cat·ed, -cat·ing** choke or stifle without sufficient oxygen or fresh air: *A drowning person ~s; was ~d by carbon monoxide fumes; found city life quite ~ing;* **suf·fo·ca·tion** (–CAY–) *n.*

suf·fra·gan (SUF·ruh·gun) *n.* a bishop subordinate to an archbishop; also, an assistant bishop; ***adj.*** diocesan; also, assistant: *a ~ see, bishop.* —**suf·frage** (SUF·rij) *n.* the right to vote; franchise; also, assent or approval: *adult ~;* **suf·fra·gist** (–fruh·jist) *n.* —**suf·fra·gette** (–JET) *n.* a woman advocating the franchise for women.

suf·fuse (suh·FYOOZ) *v.* **suf·fus·es, suf·fused, suf·fus·ing** fill (a face, the sky, etc.) with a spreading color, light, moisture, etc.; **suf·fu·sion** (–FYOO·zhun) *n.* an overspreading.

sug·ar (SHOOG·ur) *n.* a sweet carbohydrate made by green plants, esp. sucrose obtained from the tall tropical grass called **sugar cane** or from the **sugar beet** of temperate climates used as a sweetener of foods; **sug·ar·coat** *v.* cover, esp. something unpleasant, with sugar: *a ~ed pill;* **sugar maple** a North American maple whose sweet sap is the chief source of *maple sugar* and *maple syrup;* **sug·ar·plum** *n.* a round piece of candy; **sug·ar·y** *adj.*

sug·gest (sug·JEST, suh–) *v.* **1** put forward an idea or proposal, as for consideration: *I ~ we eat now.* **2** bring to mind, as by association of ideas: *the appropriate action ~ed by the circumstances; the alternatives that seemed to ~ themselves.* —**sug·gest·i·ble** (–JES–) *adj.* easily influenced by suggestion from outside the mind; **sug·gest·i·bil·i·ty** (–BIL–) *n.* —**sug·ges·tion** (–JES·chun) *n.* a suggestion or what is suggested; also, a hint or trace; **sug·ges·tive** (–tiv) *adj.* **1** tending to suggest: *a ~ reading list.* **2** suggesting something indecent: *a ~ dance; ~ pictures;* **sug·ges·tive·ly** *adv.;* **sug·ges·tive·ness** *n.*

su·i·cide (SOO·uh–) *n.* the act of killing oneself intentionally; also, one who commits suicide; **su·i·cid·al** (–SYE·dl) *adj.* leading to suicide; also, disastrous to oneself. —**su·i ge·ne·ris** (SOO·ee·JEN·uh·ris) *Latin.* in a class by itself, himself, etc.; unique.

suit (SOOT) *n.* **1** a set of outer clothes for wearing together, as coat and trousers. **2** a suing or legal action: *to bring ~ for damages.* **3** any of the four sets of playing cards; **follow suit** play a card of the same suit as the previous player's; hence, follow the example set. **4** an entreaty or pleading, as for a woman's hand; hence, courtship; **suit·or** *n.* ***—v.*** be suitable for or make fit: *a speech that ~s the occasion; She*

~ed her vocabulary to the children's level; Nine o'-clock will ~ me fine; ~ yourself! (i.e. Do as you please!). **—suit·a·ble** *adj.* proper or appropriate; **suit·a·bly** *adv.;* **suit·a·bil·i·ty** (–BIL–) *n.* **—suit·case** *n.* a flat-sided rectangular traveling bag for clothes. **—suite** (SWEET) *n.* **1** a group attending on an important person; retinue. **2** a set of rooms forming a unit, as in a hotel. **3** (*also* SOOT) a set of matched furniture, as for a bedroom or living room. **4** in music, a group of instrumental pieces of varying character with related themes, as Tchaikovsky's "Nutcracker Suite." **—suit·ing** *n.* fabric for suits.

su·ki·ya·ki (soo·kee·YAH·kee) *n.* a Japanese dish of sliced meat and vegetables, often cooked in a skillet at the table.

Suk·kot(h) (SOOK·ote, –us) *n.* a Jewish festival commemorating the wanderings of the Israelites in the desert.

sul·fa (SUL·fuh) *adj.* of or relating to a group of chemical compounds used against bacterial infections; ***n.*** a sulfa drug, esp. the basic **sul·fa·nil·a·mide** (–NIL·uh–); **sul·fon·a·mide** (–FON–) *n.* any of the group of sulfa drugs including sulfanilamide, **sul·fa·di·a·zine** (–DYE·uh·zeen), etc. **—sul·fate** *n.* a salt or ester of sulfuric acid; **sul·fide** *n.* a compound of sulfur with another element or radical; **sul·fite** *n.* a salt or ester of sulfurous acid. **—sul·fur** *n.* a pale-yellow, nonmetallic element that burns with a stifling odor; **sulfur dioxide** a pungent, poisonous gas and industrial pollutant produced by burning metallic compounds of sulfur; **sul·fur·ic** (–FYOOR–) *adj.* of or containing sulfur, as **sulfuric acid,** a heavy, oily, highly corrosive acid much used in industry, esp. in making fertilizers and in refining petroleum. **—sul·fu·rous** (SUL·fur·us) *adj.* **1** like burning sulfur in stench or heat: *~ fumes, fires of hell.* **2** (*usu.* –FYOOR·us) of or containing sulfur: *~ acid.*

sulk *v.* be sulky; ***n.*** a sulky spell: *He's in a ~ before breakfast; having* **the sulks. —sulk·y** *adj.* **sulk·i·er, -i·est** moody and ill-humored: *a ~ scowl, silence, refusal;* ***n.,*** *pl.* **sulk·ies** a light, two-wheeled racing carriage seating one person; **sulk·i·ly** *adv.;* **sulk·i·ness** *n.*

sul·len *adj.* gloomy and silent: *a ~ disposition, resentment, silence; ~ looks, skies;* **sul·len·ly** *adv.;* **sul·len·ness** *n.*

sul·ly *v.* **sul·lies, sul·lied, sul·ly·ing** soil or defile the purity of (one's reputation, character, etc.).

sul·phur (–fur) same as SULFUR.

sul·tan (–tn) *n.* a Moslem ruler. **—sul·tan·a** (–TAN·uh) *n.* **1** a sultan's wife, mother, sister, or daughter. **2** a seedless variety of raisin with a distinctive flavor. **—sul·tan·ate** (SUL·tn–) *n.* a sultan's position, authority, or rule.

sul·try (–tree) *adj.* **-tri·er, -tri·est** sweltering; hot and moist: *~ weather, days of summer.* **2** hot or fiery: *a ~ sun; a ~* (i.e. passionate) *glance.*

sum *n.* **1** an amount of money: *a large ~ (of money); a lump ~ payment.* **2** the total amount or quantity: *The ~ of 4, 5, and 6 is 15; the ~* (i.e. height) *of happiness, folly;* **the sum and substance** (i.e. gist) *of what she said;* **in sum** in brief. **3** an arithmetical problem: *good at ~s.* **—*v.* sums, summed, sum·ming** find the total of; **sum up** summarize.

su·mac(h) (SHOO·mac, SOO–) *n.* any of a group of trees and shrubs of the cashew family with narrow, pinnate leaves, whose nonpoisonous species bear erect clusters of red berries while the poisonous ones have drooping clusters, usu. white in the *poison sumac.*

Su·ma·tra (soo·MAH·truh) the second largest island of Indonesia; **Su·ma·tran** (–trun) *n.* & *adj.*

sum·ma·rize (SUM·uh–) *v.* **-riz·es, -rized, -riz·ing** be or make a summary of. **—sum·ma·ry** (SUM·uh–) *n.* **-ries** a brief statement giving the main points (of a book, speech, etc.); ***adj.*** **1** brief and comprehensive: *a ~ account.* **2** carried out without formalities, delays, etc.; prompt: *~ action, dismissal, trial.* **—sum·ma·ri·ly** (–MER·uh·lee, SUM·uh·ruh·lee) *adv.* **—sum·ma·tion** (–MAY–) *n.* a summing up, as of arguments in a trial.

sum·mer *n.* & *adj.* (of or for) the warmest season of the year; ***v.*** spend the summer (*in* or *at* a place); **sum·mer·y** *adj.* **—sum·mer·house** *n.* a roofed but usu. not walled structure, as in a garden, to rest in during warm weather; **summer house** a cottage for use in the summer. **—summer sausage** a smoked or dried sausage that keeps without spoiling in warm weather. **—summer squash** a quick-growing nontrailing squash such as zucchini that is harvested and used in the summer. **—sum·mer·time** *n.* the summer season.

sum·mit *n.* the highest point, level, or state: *the ~ of a mountain;* **summit meeting** a meeting of heads of state; **sum·mit·ry** (–tree) *n.* international diplomacy by means of summit meetings.

sum·mon (–mun) *v.* **1** call formally or with authority, as to appear in court; also, order (an assembly) to convene: *relatives ~ed to the dying man's bedside.* **2** call forth by an act of the will; *to ~ (up) strength, courage, energy.* **—sum·mon·er** *n.* **—sum·mons** (–unz) *n., pl.* **sum·mons·es** a summoning, esp. to appear in court on a charge: *a traffic ~ for careless driving; a ~ for help;* ***v.*** *Informal.* serve a summons on.

su·mo (wrestling) (SOO·moh) a Japanese form of wrestling.

sump *n.* pit or pool in which drained water collects, as in a cellar.

sump·tu·ous (SUMP·choo·us) *adj.* lavishly provided or richly furnished: *a ~ meal; ~ clothes;* **sump·tu·ous·ly** *adv.*

sum total everything added up.

sun *n.* **1** the bright heavenly body around which the earth and other planets revolve; hence, any star with planets orbiting around it. **2** the light or heat of the sun; hence, anything that is a source of light, warmth, glory, etc. —*v.* **suns, sunned, sun·ning** to warm or dry (oneself) in sunlight: *lay ~ing himself by the pool.* —**sun·less** *adj.* —**Sun.** Sunday. —**sun·bath** *n.* exposure of the body to sunlight or a sunlamp; **sun·bathe** (–baidh) *v.* **-bathes, -bathed, -bath·ing.** —**sun·beam** *n.* a ray or beam of sunlight. —**Sun·belt** *n.* the southern third of the U.S. plus S. California as a region of great growth. —**sun·bon·net** *n.* a wide-brimmed bonnet for shading the face and neck from the sun. —**sun·burn** *n.* a burning of the skin by overexposure to the sun's rays; *v.* **-burns,** *pt.* & *pp.* **-burned** or **-burnt, -burn·ing** (cause to) get a sunburn. —**sun·burst** *n.* sunlight bursting through a break in the clouds; also, a decoration with spreading rays around a center. —**sun·dae** (–dee, –day) *n.* ice cream with a topping of nuts, syrup, etc. —**Sun·day** (–dee, –day) *n.* the first day of the week, the Christian Sabbath.

sun·der *v.* [literary] put asunder; sever; tear apart.

sun·di·al (–dye·ul) *n.* an ancient time-telling device consisting of a horizontal dial that is read by the position of the shadow cast on it by an erect pointer in its center. —**sun·down** *n.* sunset.

sun·dries (–dreez) *n.pl.* sundry things; **sun·dry** (–dree) *adj.* miscellaneous (people or things); **all and sundry** everyone.

sun·fish *n.* a brightly colored freshwater food and game fish with a roundish body; also, an ocean fish with a silvery body seen on the surface in sunny weather. —**sun·flow·er** *n.* a large flower with rays of yellow petals around a central disk of tiny brown, yellow, or purple flowers yieldir · oily edible seeds.

sung *pp.* & a *pt.* of SING.

sun·glass·es *n.pl.* tinted eyeglasses to protect the eyes from the sun.

sunk *pp.* & a *pt.* of SINK. —**sunk·en** *adj.* **1** submerged: *~ ships, treasures.* **2** below the general level: *a ~ living room, ~* (i.e. hollow) *cheeks; ~* (i.e. depressed) *spirits.*

sun·lamp *n.* a lamp giving off ultraviolet rays, esp. one used therapeutically. —**sun·light** *n.* the light of the sun; **sun·lit** *adj.* lighted by the sun. —**sun·ny** *adj.* **sun·ni·er, sun·ni·est** full of sunshine; also bright or cheerful: *a ~ day, meadow, smile;* **sunny side** the more cheerful aspect (of a situation); **sunny side up** of eggs, served fried on one side only, with the yolk on top. —**sun·rise** *n.* (the time of) the sun's coming up above the horizon; —**sun·roof** *n.* an automobile roof that is openable in part. —**sun·seek·er** *n.* one who travels to a warmer and sunnier place in the winter. —**sun·set** *n.* **1** the sun's going down below the horizon, esp. the light and color accompanying it. **2** the end of the day marked by the sunset; **sunset law** a law providing for the termination of government agencies, bylaws, etc. that are considered unjustified or wasteful of resources. —**sun·shade** *n.* a parasol, awning, etc. used as protection against the sun's rays; **sunshades** *pl. Slang.* sunglasses. —**sun·shine** *n.* the light and heat from the sun; also, cheerfulness; **sun·shin·y** *adj.* —**sunshine law** a law requiring government agencies to conduct their business with openness, as by allowing the public to attend their meetings. —**sun·spot** *n.* any of the dark spots appearing occasionally on the sun's surface. —**sun·stroke** *n.* a heatstroke caused by overexposure to the sun or other source of heat, marked by high fever and a dry skin. —**sun·suit** *n.* a play outfit consisting of short pants with shoulder straps and a bib front. —**sun·tan** *n.* a tanning of the skin by exposure to the sun. —**sun·up** *n.* the time of sunrise.

Sun Yat-sen (SOON·YAHT·SEN) 1866–1925, Chinese leader considered the father of modern China.

sup *v.* **sups, supped, sup·ping** **1** have supper (*on* soup and crackers, etc.). **2** take sips or spoonfuls of (a food). —*n.* a sip or mouthful.

sup. superior; supplement(ary); supply; supra.

su·per (SOO–) *n. Informal.* **1** a supernumerary actor. **2** the superintendent of an apartment building. —*adj.* superior in fineness, excellence, sophistication, or quality: *~ clothes for ~ kids; a ~ secret;* **adv.** very: *This is ~ secret; something ~ special.* —**super-** *prefix.* **1** over or above; hence, superior (in rank, quality, degree, etc.): as in

superagency	**supersecret**
superblock	**superstar**
superbomb	**superstate**
supergalaxy	**superstratum**
superindividual	**supersystem**
superliner	**superwoman**
supersalesman	

2 extra or added; hence, in excess: as in

superadd	**superphysical**
superfine	**supersize**
superheat	**supersubtle**
supernormal	**supertax**
superpatriot	

su·per·a·bun·dant (–uh·BUN·dunt) *adj.* more than enough; **su·per·a·bun·dance** *n.* —**su·per·an·nu·at·ed** (–AN·yoo–) *adj.* retired and pensioned; also, too old for work or service. —**su·perb** (soo·PURB) *adj.* of the highest excellence, magnificence, or splendor: *a ~ view, performance, display;* **su·perb·ly** *adv.* —**su·per·car·go** (SOO–, –CAR–) *n.* **-go(e)s** an officer in charge of commercial and business affairs on a merchant ship. —**su·per·charge** *v.* **-charg·es, -charged, -charg·ing** increase the power of (an internal-combustion engine) with a **su·per·charg·er,** a device for compressing extra air into the engine cylinders, as used in high-altitude aircraft and racing cars. —**su·per·cil·i·ous** (–SIL·ee·us) *adj.* contemptuous in a haughty way. —**su·per·cit·y** *n.* **-cit·ies** same as MEGALOPOLIS. —**su·per·con·duc·tiv·i·ty** (–TIV–) *n.* absence of electrical resistance in metals such as lead and tin at temperatures near absolute zero. —**su·per-du·per** (SOO·pur·DOO·pur) *adj. Slang.* excellent. —**su·per·e·go** (–EE·goh) *n.* **-gos** in psychoanalytic theory, the part of the psyche that exercises a moral control on the ego. —**su·per·em·i·nent** (–EM–) *adj.* eminent in an extraordinary or remarkable way. —**su·per·er·o·ga·tion** (–GAY–) *n.* the doing of more than what duty requires; **su·per·e·rog·a·to·ry** (–ROG·uh–) *adj.* nonessential; superfluous. —**su·per·fi·cial** (–FISH·ul) *adj.* of the surface only; hence, shallow: *a ~ burn, wound; ~ knowledge, education;* **su·per·fi·cial·ly** *adv.;* **su·per·fi·ci·al·i·ty** (–AL–) *n.* **-ties.** —**su·per·flu·ous** (–PUR·floo·us) *adj.* surplus or unnecessary; **su·per·flu·i·ty** (–FLOO–) *n.* **-ties.** —**su·per·high·way** *n.* a freeway with four or more lanes. —**su·per·hu·man** (–HEW–) *adj.* exceeding normal human power or capacity: *~ efforts, strength; a ~* (i.e. spiritual) *being.* —**su·per·im·pose** (–POZE) *v.* **-pos·es, -posed, -pos·ing** lay on top of something else, as different scenes blended on a television screen; **su·per·im·po·si·tion** (–ZISH–) *n.* —**su·per·in·tend** (–TEND) *v.* act as superintendent of; **su·per·in·tend·ence** *n.;* **su·per·in·ten·dent** *n.* a custodian or director, as of an educational body; also, a maintenance supervisor of a building. —**su·pe·ri·or** (–PEER·ee·ur) *adj.* higher in excellence, quality, rank, etc.: *~ ability, performance, forces; Grade A eggs are ~ to Grade B; proved herself ~ to* (i.e. above) *petty jealousies; his ~* (i.e. haughty) *manners;* ***n.*** **1** a person or thing that is superior. **2** the head of a religious community. —**su·pe·ri·or·i·ty** (–OR–) *n.* —**Lake Superior** the largest of the Great Lakes. —**su·per·jet** *n.* a supersonic jet airplane. —**superl.** *Abbrev.* for **su·per·la·tive** (–PUR·luh·tiv) *adj.* of the highest kind or degree: *~ praise, wisdom; a ~ adjective such as "best," "wisest," or "most beautiful";* ***n.*** one that is superlative or of the highest degree: *regular ~s with "-est" endings; tends to speak in ~s* (i.e. exaggerated praise); **su·per·la·tive·ly** *adv.* —**su·per·man** *n.* **-men** a man with superhuman powers. —**su·per·mar·ket** *n.* a large, self-service retail store, esp. one of a chain of food stores. —**su·per·nal** (–PUR·nl) *adj.* heavenly; exalted. —**su·per·nat·u·ral** (–NACH·uh·rul) *adj.* not explainable by the laws of nature; spiritual or divine: *a ~ being such as an angel or devil;* **su·per·nat·u·ral·ly** *adv.* —**su·per·no·va** (–NOH·vuh) *n.* **-vae** (–vee) or **-vas** a nova of unusual brilliance. —**su·per·nu·mer·ar·y** (–NEW–) *adj.* & *n.* **-ar·ies** (one) that is more than the required number; extra. —**su·per·pose** (–POZE) *v.* **-pos·es, -posed, -pos·ing** same as SUPERIMPOSE: **su·per·po·si·tion** (–ZISH·un) *n.* —**su·per·pow·er** *n.* any of the two or three most powerful nations. —**su·per·sat·u·rate** (–SACH–) *v.* **-rates, -rat·ed, -rat·ing** saturate (a solution) to excess using heat; **su·per·sat·u·ra·tion** (–RAY–) *n.* —**su·per·scribe** *v.* **-scribes, -scribed, -scrib·ing** write above or on top of; **su·per·scrip·tion** (–SCRIP–) *n.;* **su·per·script** *n.* & *adj.* (a figure or symbol) written raised above a letter or line, as the "2" in "x^2y." —**su·per·sede** (–SEED) *v.* **-sedes, -sed·ed, -sed·ing** succeed or take the place of, as being better or more modern. —**su·per·son·ic** (–SON–) *adj.* faster than sound: *~ flight, speed, transport;* **su·per·son·ics** *n.pl.* the science of supersonic phenomena, esp. sound waves. —**su·per·star** *n.* an exceptionally successful star in sports or entertainment. —**su·per·sti·tion** (–STISH·un) *n.* a belief or practice considered irrational, as knocking on wood for good luck or spilling salt as a bad omen: *One man's religion is another's ~;* **su·per·sti·tious** *adj.* —**su·per·struc·ture** *n.* a structure built on top of another; also, the part of a building above its foundation. —**su·per·tank·er** *n.* a very large oil tanker. —**su·per·vene** (–VEEN) *v.* **-venes, -vened, -ven·ing** of a condition or process, succeed or take place unexpectedly; **su·per·ven·tion** (–VEN–) *n.* —**su·per·vise** (–vize) *v.* **-vis·es, -vised, -vis·ing** direct or oversee (people or their work); **su·per·vi·sion** (–VIZH·un) *n.;* **su·per·vi·sor** *n.;* **su·per·vi·so·ry** *adj.*

su·pine (soo·PINE) *adj.* flat on the back; hence, passive or indolent: *a ~ attitude.*

supp(l). supplement; supplementary.

sup·per *n.* an evening meal; the last meal of the day; **supper club** a nightclub; **sup·per·time** *n.*

sup·plant (suh·PLANT) *v.* replace (as if) by use of force or fraud: *a king ~ed by a courtier; workers ~ed by machinery.*

sup·ple *adj.* easily bending or flexing without damage or strain: *a ~ vine; ~ as leather; a gymnast's ~ limbs; a ~ mind, prose style;* **sup·ple·ness** *n.;* **sup·ply** *adv.*

sup·ple·ment (–luh·munt) *n.* an addition that makes something better or fuller: *vitamins added as food ~s; annual ~s to update an encyclopedia; an advertising ~ of a newspaper;* ***v.*** (–MENT): *Spare-time jobs ~ his income;* **sup·ple·men·tal** (–MEN–) *adj.;* **sup·ple·men·ta·ry** *n.* & *adj.*

sup·pli·ant (–lee·unt) *n.* & *adj.* (one) who supplicates; also **sup·pli·cant; sup·pli·cate** *v.* **-cates, -cat·ed, -cat·ing** pray for or ask a favor of humbly: *The prisoners ~d the king for mercy;* **sup·pli·ca·tion** (–CAY–) *n.*

sup·ply (suh·PLY) *v.* **sup·plies, sup·plied, sup·ply·ing** give or provide: *to ~ food to the hungry; ~d them with food; a need that is hard to ~* (i.e. satisfy); *likes to ~* (i.e. fill in as a substitute) *in place of absent colleagues.* —***n.,*** *pl.* **sup·**

plies a supplying or a quantity of a needed item supplied; **supplies** *pl.* stores or provisions: *office ~s.* —**sup·pli·er** *n.*

sup·port (suh·PORT) *v.* **1** hold up; hence, maintain or provide for: *staves to ~ a tomato plant; oxygen required to ~ life; enough money to ~ a wife and two children.* **2** back up: *A seconder ~s a motion; a charge not ~ed by evidence; a star and ~ing actors* (in subordinate roles). **3** bear or endure. —***n.*** a supporting, one that supports, or a means of support: *The move lacked ~; demonstrations in ~ of strikers' demands; The breadwinner is the ~ of a family.* —**sup·port·a·ble** *adj.;* **sup·port·er** *n.;* **sup·port·ive** (–iv) *adj.* giving support: *~ evidence; professional and ~ staff.*

sup·pose (suh·POZE) *v.* **sup·pos·es, sup·posed, sup·pos·ing** assume; take for granted: *Let's ~ the earth is flat; Who do you ~ this is? Do creatures ~ a creator? You're not ~d* (i.e. allowed) *to smoke here;* **sup·posed** *adj.: the ~ injustice; more ~ than real;* **sup·pos·ed·ly** (–id·lee) *adv.;* **sup·pos·ing** *conj.* assuming: *~ there was life on Mars;* **sup·po·si·tion** (–ZISH–) *n.* —**sup·pos·i·to·ry** (–POZ–) *n.* **-ries** a small cone or cylinder of a medicated substance put into a body cavity such as the rectum or vagina.

sup·press (suh·PRES) *v.* put down by force; keep under; keep back: *to ~ a yawn, riot, newspaper; to ~ freedom of speech, the truth; consciously to ~ memories, thoughts, or desires;* **sup·pres·si·ble** *adj.;* **sup·pres·sion** (–PRESH·un) *n.* —**sup·pres·sant** (–sunt) *n.: Codeine is a cough ~.* —**sup·pres·sive** *adj.*

sup·pu·rate (SUP·yoo–) *v.* **-rates, -rat·ed, -rat·ing** form or discharge pus; **sup·pu·ra·tion** (–RAY–) *n.*

su·pra (SOO·pruh) *adv.* above or earlier. —**supra-** *prefix.* above; beyond: as in **su·pra·na·tion·al** (–NASH–) *adj.* above the level of individual nations: *a ~ organization, authority.*

su·prem·a·cist (–PREM·uh–) *n.* one who believes in the supremacy of (a specified group): *a white ~ government;* **su·prem·a·cy** *n.* **-cies** the state of being supreme; also, supreme power: *the ~ of state over church; papal ~.* —**su·preme** (suh·PREEM) *adj.* **1** highest in authority or power: *God as* **Supreme Being;** *the* **Supreme Court** *of a state or of the U.S.; the* **Supreme Soviet** *of the U.S.S.R.* **2** highest in degree or quality: *the ~ sacrifice* (of one's life); *~ ignorance.* —**su·preme·ly** *adv.;* **su·preme·ness** *n.*

Supt. Superintendent.

sur- *prefix.* **1** super-: as in *surcharge, surname.* **2** sub-: as in *surreptitious, surrogate.* —**sur·cease** (SUR·seece) *n. Archaic.* end or cessation. —**sur·charge** *v.* **-charg·es, -charged, -charg·ing** **1** overburden (with a feeling). **2** charge extra; also, overprint (as a postage stamp) with an extra charge. —***n.*** **1** an extra charge: *a ~ for home delivery; a stamp bearing a ~ of 5¢.* **2** an excessive burden (of grief, etc.). —**sur·cin·gle** *n.* a band or strap around a horse's body to secure a saddle, pack, etc.

sure (SHOOR) *adj.* **sur·er, sur·est** **1** free from doubt: *He is ~ the watch is accurate; Please make ~ of your facts; She is ~* (i.e. bound; certain) *to come.* **2** reliable or unerring: *A smoking pistol is ~ evidence of firing; a good marksman with a ~ aim; a ~ remedy.* —***adv.*** *Informal.* surely; **for sure** without doubt: *That's for ~;* **sure enough** *Informal.* in fact; certainly. —**sure-fire** *adj. Informal.* sure to succeed; definite. —**sure-foot·ed** *adj.* not likely to stumble or err. —**sure·ly** *adv.* certainly; also, without stumbling or failing; **sure·ness** *n.* —**sure·ty** *n.* **-ties** **1** security or assurance (against loss, failure, etc.). **2** one legally responsible for another's performance according to an agreement or obligation, as guaranteed by a **surety bond.**

surf *n.* waves of the sea breaking on the shore; also, the foam and the thundering sound produced; ***v.*** ride the waves on a surfboard in the sport of **surf·ing** *n.;* **surf·er** *n.*

sur·face (SUR·fis) *n.* **1** the outside of anything, as any of the faces of a solid figure, the top of a liquid, etc. **2** outward features or appearance. —***adj.*** **1** of or by the surface: *~ mail* (by land or water); *~ transit; a ~-to-air missile.* **2** external: *a ~ impression; mere ~* (i.e. superficial) *friendships.* —***v.*** **-fac·es, -faced, -fac·ing** **1** provide with a (smooth) surface: *to ~ a road.* **2** rise to the surface of the water, as a submarine.

surf·board *n.* the long, narrow, light-weight board used in surfing.

sur·feit (–fit) *n.* an excess of anything good, esp. food or drink; also, the resulting feeling of nausea; ***v.:*** *~ed with food, riches.*

surg. surgeon; surgery; surgical.

surge (SURJ) *v.* **surg·es, surged, surg·ing** move powerfully and suddenly in or like a swelling wave: *the ~ing flood waters; a crowd ~ing forward;* ***n.*** a rushing wave or its onrush: *the ~ of the sea; the ~ of passion.*

sur·geon (–jun) *n.* a physician specialized in surgery; **sur·ger·y** (–juh·ree) *n.* **-ger·ies** the branch of medicine dealing with operations performed on the body to treat disease, injuries, and deformities; also, a surgeon's work or a place where operations are done; **sur·gi·cal** (–cl) *adj.;* **sur·gi·cal·ly** *adv.*

Su·ri·nam (soor·i·NAHM) a country on the N.E. coast of South America; 63,037 sq.mi. (163,265 km²); *cap.* Paramaribo; **Su·ri·nam·er** *n.*

sur·ly *adj.* **-li·er, -li·est** ill-tempered or rude; **sur·li·ly** *adv.;* **sur·li·ness** *n.*

sur·mise (–MIZE) *n.* & *v.* **-mis·es, -mised, -mis·ing** guess or conjecture. —**sur·mount** (–MOUNT) *v.* **1** be or rise above: *a church spire ~ed by a cross.* **2** get over; hence, overcome (difficulties). —**sur·mount·a·ble** *adj.* —**sur·name** *n.* last name or family name.

—**sur·pass** (–PASS) *v.* go beyond or be superior to (someone in some quality): *None* ~*ed Samson in strength; This* ~*es* (i.e. defies) *description;* **sur·pass·ing·ly** *adv.* —**sur·plice** (–plis) *n.* a loose, white, usu. knee-length outer vestment worn in church by clergy and choir. —**sur·plus** *n.* **1** a quantity or amount left over after meeting needs: *farm* ~*es of crops and livestock.* **2** excess of assets over liabilities; ***adj.:*** *a* ~ (i.e. not deficit) *budget.* —**sur·prise** *v.* **-pris·es, -prised, -pris·ing** come upon suddenly and unexpectedly: *was* ~*d in the act of stealing;* ~*d* (i.e. attacked when off guard) *by enemy troops; Your behavior* ~*s* (i.e. astonishes) *me;* ***n.*** an act of or the feeling of being surprised; also, something unexpected: *The party was a* ~*;* **sur·pris·ing** *adj.;* **sur·pris·ing·ly** *adv.* —**sur·re·al·ism** (–REE·ul–) *n.* a movement in the art and literature of the 1920's to depict reality in unnatural and fantastic forms and images, as products of the unconscious mind; **sur·re·al·ist** *n.* & *adj.;* **sur·re·al·is·tic** (–LIS–) *adj.* —**sur·ren·der** (–REN–) *v.* give up or yield (a possession or right to something); hence, abandon or relinquish: *to* ~ *a fort to the enemy; refused to* ~ *(himself) to the police;* ~*ed his insurance policy for its cash value;* ***n.*** a surrendering. —**sur·rep·ti·tious** (–TISH·us) *adj.* accomplished in a secret or stealthy manner: ~ *entry through a window; a* ~ *glance;* **sur·rep·ti·tious·ly** *adv.*

sur·rey (SUR·ee) *n.* **sur·reys** a four-wheeled, doorless, usu. flat-topped, two-seated pleasure carriage.

sur·ro·gate (SUR·uh–, –git) *n.* **1** a substitute or deputy. **2** in certain states, a probate court judge. —**sur·round** (suh·ROUND) *v.* encircle or cause to be encircled: *Police* ~*ed the house; a star* ~*ed by admirers;* ~*ed with luxuries;* **sur·round·ings** *n.pl.* things that surround; environment. —**sur·tax** *n.* an extra tax on something already taxed, as on incomes above a certain level. —**sur·tout** (–TOO) *n.* an overcoat or frock-coat of the 19th century. —**surv.** survey; surveying; surveyor. —**sur·veil·lance** (–VAY·lunce) *n.* close watch kept over a subject. —**sur·vey** (–VAY) *v.* look over or examine as a whole, as a tract of land by a **sur·vey·or** using geometrical principles of **sur·vey·ing.** —***n.*** (SUR–) a broad overall study or examination, as in surveying a tract of land, a field of study, public opinion on a subject, a situation, etc.; also, a record or map of a surveying. —**sur·vive** (–VIVE) *v.* **-vives, -vived, -viv·ing** continue in existence (after someone or something); outlive or outlast: *Children normally* ~ *their parents; None* ~*d (the disaster);* **sur·vi·val** (–vul) *n.: the* **survival of the fittest** *in the process of natural selection; an airman's* **survival kit** *containing food and emergency equipment;* **sur·vi·vor** (–vur) *n.*

sus·cep·ti·ble (–SEP–) *adj.* easily acted on or influenced: *Wax is susceptible of impressions; inexperienced youth* **susceptible to** *the temptations of a big city; has a* ~ *nature though sensitive and intelligent;* **sus·cep·ti·bil·i·ty** (–BIL–) *n.* **-ties.** —**sus·pect** (–PECT) *v.* **1** assume to be the truth; surmise: *She* ~*s he's lying;* ~*s him of cheating;* ~*s adultery; She has more brains than he* ~*ed.* **2** doubt or distrust: *She* ~*s the truth of his stories;* ~*s his truthfulness;* ***n.*** & ***adj.*** (SUS–) (one) that is suspected, as of a crime: *a lineup of* ~*s; His reasons are* ~ (i.e. regarded with suspicion). —**sus·pend** (–PEND) *v.* **1** hang (as if) from a support: *Chandeliers are* ~*ed from ceilings; dust particles* ~*ed in air.* **2** stop (an activity or operation) for a time: *Work was* ~*ed in protest; to* ~ *payments, rules, judgment; a body in* **suspended animation** *without vital signs, as in drowning, trances, etc.* **3** remove for a while from duties or privileges: *was* ~*ed with pay pending an investigation.* —**sus·pend·ers** *n.pl.* a pair of shoulder straps to hold up trousers; also, *Brit.* garters. —**sus·pense** (–SPENCE) *n.* a state of uncertainty or anxiety about an outcome: *a story full of* ~*; keeps you in* ~ *till the end;* **sus·pense·ful** *adj.* —**sus·pen·sion** (–SPEN–) *n.* **1** an act of suspending, the state of being suspended, or a suspending device: *A* **suspension bridge** *hangs from cables supported by towers on either end.* **2** a mixture such as milk, smoke, or a colloidal substance in which particles are suspended or dispersed without being dissolved. —**sus·pen·sive** *adj.;* **sus·pen·so·ry** *adj.* —**sus·pi·cion** (–SPISH·un) *n.* **1** a suspecting or being suspected: *arrested* **on suspicion** *of murder; a mind full of* ~*;* **above suspicion** not to be suspected. **2** a slight trace or soupçon: *a* ~ *of jealousy in her voice.* —**sus·pi·cious** (–SPISH·us) *adj.* arousing, showing, or feeling suspicion: ~ *of people's motives;* ~ *behavior;* **sus·pi·cious·ly** *adv.* —**sus·tain** (–STAIN) *v.* **1** support actively so as to keep from failing: *strong enough to* ~ *any weight; an atmosphere too rare to* ~ *life; Objection* ~*ed* (i.e. upheld), *declared the judge; made a* ~*ed* (i.e. continuous) *effort to stay awake.* **2** suffer or endure: *wounds* ~*ed in war;* ~*ed great losses in the fire.* —**sus·te·nance** (SUS·tuh·nunce) *n.* **1** nourishment or food to sustain life. **2** a means of livelihood.

sut·ler *n.* one selling provisions to soldiers at a camp.

su·tra (SOO·truh) *n.* an ancient Hindu maxim; also, a Buddhist sermon.

su·ture (SOO·chur) *n.* a joining together (as) by sewing: *the zigzag* ~*s of the skull bones; surgical incisions closed by means of* ~*s* (i.e. stitches); *The* ~*s* (i.e. catgut, silk, wire, etc.) *are taken out as the wound heals.*

Su·va (SOO·vuh) a seaport and the capital of Fiji.

su·ze·rain (SOO·zuh–, –rin) *n.* **1** a feudal lord. **2** a state with political control, or **su·ze·rain·ty,** over another.

s.v. under the word or entry.

svelte (SVELT) *adj.* **svelt·er, svelt·est** suave; of women, slender or lithe.

S.W. or **s.w.** southwest(ern). —**Sw.** Sweden; Swedish.

swab (SWOB) *n.* **1** a cleaning mop. **2** a bit of cotton or other absorbent material at the end of a stick for removing discharged matter from or applying medicine to a body part. **3** *Slang.* a sailor; gob; also, a lout. —***v.*** **swabs, swabbed, swab·bing** use a swab on.

swad·dle (SWODL) *v.* **swad·dles, swad·dled, swad·dling** bind or wrap (a newborn baby) in long, narrow strips of cloth, or **swad·dling clothes.**

swag *n.* **1** a festoon or garland hung in a curve, esp. such a decorative design. **2** *Slang.* loot or stolen goods.

swage *n.* a metalworking tool for shaping and forming objects; ***v.*** **swag·es, swaged, swag·ing** shape or form with a swage.

swag·ger (SWAG·ur) *v.* walk with a superior or insolent bearing; also, brag or boast; ***n.*** a swaggering manner; **swagger stick** a short cane carried by an army officer.

Swa·hi·li (swah·HEE·lee) *n.* a Bantu language used widely in E. Africa from Somalia to Mozambique; also, a Swahili speaker.

swain *n.* a rustic youth or shepherd; also, a lover or suitor.

¹swallow (SWOL·oh) *v.* **1** take from the mouth into the stomach, as food. **2** accept or take in like swallowed food: *so gullible he'll ~ any story; to ~ an insult* (meekly); *a body ~ed up* (i.e. engulfed) *by the waves.* **3** take back or suppress: *It hurt his pride to ~ his words; had to ~ his pride and apologize.* —***n.*** a swallowing or the amount swallowed at one time.

²swal·low (SWOL·oh) *n.* any of a family of small, insect-eating birds with powerful wings and a forked tail; **swal·low·tail** *n.* a tailcoat; **swal·low-tailed** *adj.*

swam *pt.* of SWIM.

swa·mi (SWAH·mee) *n.* a Hindu religious teacher.

swamp (SWOMP) *n.* a tract of low-lying marshy land. —***v.*** **1** sink in as in a swamp. **2** overwhelm or deluge: *The heavy seas ~ed our boat; a switchboard ~ed with phone calls; ~ed by debts, backlogs.* —**swamp buggy** a vehicle designed for use on swampy ground or in shallow water. —**swamp fever** malaria. —**swamp·land** *n.* swamp. —**swamp·y** *adj.*

swan (SWON, SWAWN) *n.* a graceful, long-necked, usu. snow-white water bird related to the geese.

swank (SWANGK) *n.* *Informal.* dash or style; also, swagger; ***adj.*** dashing; stylish in a showy manner; also **swank·y, swank·i·er, -i·est** —***v.*** swagger.

swan's-down *n.* **1** the soft down of swan. **2** a fine, soft cloth of cotton or wool used for baby clothes; also **swans·down.** —**swan song** a person's last performance or work, like the fabled swan's dying song.

swap (SWOP, SWAWP) *n.* & *v.* **swaps, swapped, swap·ping** *Informal.* exchange or barter; **swap·per** *n.*

sward (SWORD) *n.* grassy surface; turf.

swarm (SWORM) *n.* **1** a large group of honeybees flying away to form a new colony; also, a settled colony of bees. **2** a large dense crowd or throng: *a ~ of school children.* —***v.*** **1** of bees, migrate in a swarm. **2** be present or fly about in large numbers: *Shoppers ~ed into the store; a place ~ing* (i.e. teeming) *with mosquitoes, locusts.*

swart (SWORT) or **swarth** same as **swarth·y** (SWOR–) *adj.* **swarth·i·er, -i·est** dark-complexioned.

swash (SWOSH) *v.* dash or splash (water, etc.); ***n.*** the sound or action of water washing over something. —**swash·buck·ler** *n.* a swaggering soldier or bully; **swash·buck·ling** *adj.*

swas·ti·ka (SWOS·ti·kuh) *n.* an ancient design or symbol in the form of a cross with arms bent at right angles in the same direction: *The clockwise ~ was the Nazi emblem.*

swat (SWOT) *n.* & *v.* **swats, swat·ted, swat·ting** *Informal.* (hit with) a quick, sharp blow: *to ~ a fly;* **swat·ter** *n.*

swatch (SWOCH) *n.* a sample piece of cloth: *a ~ book of suitings.*

swath (SWOTH, SWAWTH) *n.* a space cleared by one passage of a mower or cut of a scythe; also, the row of grass or grain left cut; **cut a wide swath** attract much attention. Also **swathe** (SWAIDH).

swathe (SWAIDH) *v.* **swathes, swathed, swath·ing** wrap up in a long strip or bandage; hence, envelop: *~d in a bath towel.*

sway *v.* swing sideways (from an upright position): *tall grasses ~ing in the wind; They ~ed to the rhythm of the music; would not be ~ed* (i.e. influenced) *by his feelings;* ***n.*** a swaying; also, influence or control: *under the ~ of Communism; when Rome held ~ over Europe.* —**sway·back(ed)** *adj.* having a sagging back, as some horses; **sway·back** *n.* a curvature of the spine, as of a swaybacked horse.

Swa·zi·land (SWAH·zee–) a monarchy in southern Africa; 6,704 sq.mi. (17,363 km²); *cap.* Mbabane.

swear (SWARE) *v.* **swears, swore, sworn, swear·ing** **1** declare, promise, etc. solemnly, calling God to witness; take an oath: *Witnesses ~ to tell the truth; They* **swear by** *the Bible; Judges* **swear in** *public officials* (to their offices); *sworn evidence;* **swear off** renounce or give up; **swear out** get (a warrant) by swearing that what is charged is true. **2** curse; utter (an oath): *She never ~s; He ~s at people when mad.* —**swear·word** *n.* word or phrase used in cursing; an oath or obscenity.

sweat (SWET) *n.* **1** moisture formed on the skin, esp. after strenuous exercise; perspiration; also, anything resembling it, as moisture condensed on a cold surface. **2** a state or spell of sweating induced by fear, anxiety, etc.: *found the frightened child* **in a cold sweat;** *The crew was in a* ~ (*Informal.* impatient) *for the plane to take off; all the* ~ (i.e. drudgery) *you pour into writing a book.* **—v. sweats,** *pt.* & *pp.* **sweat** or **sweat·ed, sweat·ing:** *You* ~ *freely in a sauna bath; Cold water pipes* ~ *on a hot and humid day; Hides, tobacco leaves, etc. are* ~*ed in being processed; She* ~ *blood* (i.e. worked like a slave) *to write that book; The passengers had to* **sweat it out** (*Informal.* wait anxiously) *while help was on the way.* **—sweat·er** *n.* a knitted or crocheted pullover or jacket. **—sweat shirt** a loose pullover of heavy cotton jersey. **—sweat·shop** *n.* a place of work characterized by low pay, long hours, etc. **—sweat·y** *adj.* **sweat·i·er, -i·est** sweating or causing sweat.

Swed. Sweden; Swedish. **—Swede** (SWEED) *n.* a native or inhabitant of Sweden. **—Swe·den** (SWEE·dn) a country of N. Europe; 173,649 sq.mi. (449,750 km²); *cap.* Stockholm. **—Swe·dish** *n.* & *adj.* (the people or the Germanic language) of Sweden.

sweep *v.* **sweeps, swept, sweep·ing** pass swiftly and smoothly over: *A wind* ~*s over a meadow; fingers* ~*ing the keys of a piano; to* ~ (i.e. clean) *the floor with a broom; Long skirts* ~ *the ground; She swept out of the room* (with dignity); *The flood waters swept away the bridge; Excitement swept the nation on election day; They swept the series* (i.e. won all the games); *The highway* ~*s* (i.e. stretches without a break) *along the coast.* **—n. 1** a sweeping: *Give the floor a good* ~*; cut it off with one* ~ *of the sword; made a clean* ~ (i.e. capture) *of all the prizes; the* ~ *of the highway round the hill; a lovely* ~ (i.e. stretch) *of meadow; stars beyond the* ~ (i.e. range) *of our telescopes.* **2** one who cleans chimneys, or "chimney sweep." **—sweep·er** *n.* **—sweep·ing** *adj.: a* ~ *victory, change, generalization;* **sweep·ing·ly** *adv.;* **sweep·ings** *n.pl.* things swept up from a floor. **—sweep-sec·ond hand** the hand of a timepiece sweeping over the entire dial once every minute showing seconds. **—sweep·stakes** *n. sing.* & *pl.* a lottery or horse race in which the participants put up the money that is divided as prizes; also **sweep·stake.**

sweet *adj.* **1** like sugar in taste; hence, agreeable or pleasing: *as* ~ *as honey; Roses smell* ~*;* ~ *music, praise, smiles, temper; a* ~ *little child.* **2** not sour: ~ *milk, soil;* ~ (i.e. fresh) *butter.* **—n.** one that is sweet, as a darling; *Brit.* dessert; **sweets** *pl.* sweet things, esp. candy. **—sweet·ly** *adv.;* **sweet·ness** *n.* **—sweet·bread** *n.* the thymus or pancreas of a calf, lamb, etc. used for food. **—sweet·bri·er** or **sweet·bri·ar** (–bry·ur) *n.* same as EGLANTINE. **—sweet cider** See CIDER. **—sweet clover** a cloverlike herb grown for hay, forage, and green manure. **—sweet corn** a variety of corn that has sweet kernels when unripe. **—sweet·en** *v.* make sweet or pleasant; **sweet·en·er** *n.* a sweetening agent, as sugar or saccharin; **sweet·en·ing** *n.* **—sweet fern** a small North American shrub with sweet-smelling fernlike leaves. **—sweet·heart** *n.* a loved one; darling: *an underhand* **sweetheart contract** (or **deal** or **agreement**) *made by an employer in collusion with a union leader against labor interests.* **—sweet·meat** *n.* a candy. **—sweet pea** a pea-family plant grown for its beautiful, fragrant flowers. **—sweet pepper** a mild-flavored capsicum; green pepper. **—sweet potato** the thick, fleshy, sweet, yellow or reddish root of a plant of the morning-glory family. **—sweet-talk** *v. Informal.* flatter or coax; cajole. **—sweet tooth** *Informal.* fondness for sweet foods. **—sweet William** (or **william**) a garden plant of the pink family bearing dense, round velvety clusters of flowers in many shades.

swell *v.* **swells,** *pt.* **swelled,** *pp.* **swelled** or **swol·len** (SWOH·lun), **swell·ing** grow or make bigger than normal in volume, size, etc., as because of pressure from within; (cause to) bulge out: *a swollen ankle; A wind* ~*s the sails; a river swollen by rains; New members have* ~*ed our ranks; He's* ~*ing* (i.e. filled) *with pride.* **—n. 1** something swollen, as a large, rising wave or a rounded hill. **2** a swelling sound, as of the organ, or a device to control volume in an organ or harpsichord. **3** *Informal.* a stylish or fashionable person; **adj.** *Informal.* stylish; fashionable; also, *Slang.* excellent: *a* ~ *guy, time.* **—swelled head** *Informal.* self-conceit; **swell·head** *n.* a conceited person; **swell·head·ed** *adj.* **—swell·ing** *n.* a swollen part of the body; also, a swollen condition or increase in size.

swel·ter *v.* be oppressed by heat; **swel·ter·ing** *adj.* hot and sultry.

swept *pt.* & *pp.* of SWEEP. **—swept·back** *adj.* of an aircraft's wings, slanted backward.

swerve *v.* **swerves, swerved, swerv·ing** turn aside from the direction of motion or from a course of action; **n.** a swerving.

swift *adj.* fast or rapid, esp. in a smooth and easy manner: *a* ~ *pace; a* ~*-footed messenger;* ~ *retaliation; a* ~ *flight, transition;* ~ *to anger;* **swift·ly** *adv.;* **swift·ness** *n.* **—n.** a swallowlike swift-flying bird. **—Swift, Jonathan.** 1667–1745, British satirist who wrote *Gulliver's Travels.*

swig *n. Informal.* a deep draft, esp. of liquor. —**v. swigs, swigged, swig·ging** take deep drafts of.

swill *n.* kitchen refuse mixed with liquids, as fed to pigs; slops; **v.** feed (pigs) on swill; also, guzzle or drink greedily.

swim *v.* **swims, swam, swum, swim·ming 1** move through water using one's limbs, fins, or tail: *Animals* ~ *instinctively; You either sink or* ~*; She* ~*s the Channel;* **swimming** *as a sport; a portable, above-ground, backyard* **swimming pool. 2** move or be in a condition like swimming: *eyes* ~*ing with tears; Her head swam* (i.e. was whirling). **—n.** an act or period of swimming; **in the swim** involved with what is going on around one. —**swim·mer** *n.* —**swim·suit** *n.* a garment to wear for swimming.

swin·dle *v.* **-dles, -dled, -dling** cheat (a trusting person) of money or property; ***n.*** a swindling; fraudulent scheme; **swin·dler** *n.*

swine *n. sing. & pl.* a pig; also, a person considered contemptible or disgusting; **swin·ish** (SWY–) *adj.*

swing *v.* **swings, swung, swing·ing** **1** hang or move to and fro like a pendulum: *She ~s her arms when walking; a hammock swung between trees.* **2** move in a curve with force and freedom: *Tarzan ~s from tree to tree; A batter ~s at the ball to hit it; The gate swung open; to ~* (*Informal.* manage successfully) *a business deal, election; music that ~s* (i.e. has a lively, relaxed jazz beat). **3** *Slang.* to be free and uninhibited in pursuing pleasure, following the latest in fashions and ways of life. —***n.*** **1** a swinging or its manner or amount; also, a swinging blow, gait, rhythm, etc. **2** activity or progress: *Classes are* **in full swing.** **3** a seat suspended by a rope or chain to sit in and swing for pleasure. **4** a trip or tour. **5** jazz music with a happy, relaxed beat and freedom to improvise, as played by big bands in the 1930's and 40's. —**swing·er** *n.* one that swings, esp. *Slang.* one who is ultrafashionable and uninhibited in his sex life, as in exchanging wives. —**swing shift** *Informal.* the work shift between the day and night shifts, usu. from 4 p.m. to midnight.

swipe *Informal. n.* a strong, sweeping blow; ***v.*** **swipes, swiped, swip·ing** hit with a sweeping stroke; also, *Slang.* pilfer, as by snatching.

swirl *v.* whirl or eddy; ***n.*** a swirling motion; also, a curl or whorl; **swirl·y** *adj.*

swish *v.* (cause) to move with a light hissing or brushing sound, as of a whip cutting the air; ***n.*** a swishing movement or sound.

Swiss *n. sing. & pl.* a native or inhabitant of Switzerland; ***adj.*** of Switzerland or its people: *The* **Swiss Guards** *work as papal bodyguards and sentries in the Vatican;* **Swiss (cheese)** a firm, pale-yellow cheese with large holes; **Swiss chard** same as CHARD; **Swiss steak** steak prepared by pounding the meat with flour and braising it with seasonings and sauce.

switch *n.* **1** a device for controlling a connection: *the on-and-off electric ~; Trains change tracks by means of a railroad ~ consisting of short movable rails; a ~* (i.e. change or shift) *of plans.* **2** a slender rod made from a flexible twig to use for whipping; also, a lash or whip. **3** a tress of detached hair worn as part of a coiffure. —***v.*** **1** turn (a light off or on). **2** shift (a train) to a different track; also, shift or change (plans, positions, topics, hats, etc.). **3** strike with a switch; also, jerk or swing sharply: *A horse ~es its tail to drive away flies.* —**switch·er** *n.* —**switch·back** *n.* a zigzag course, esp. a railroad for gradually climbing a steep hill. —**switch·blade** *n.* a pocketknife whose blade springs open when a button on the handle is pressed. —**switch·board** *n.* a panel controlling a system of electric circuits, as in a telephone exchange. —**switch-hit** *v.* in baseball, (to be able) to bat from either side of the plate; **switch-hit·ter** *n.* —**switch·man** *n.* **-men** one in charge of railroad switches.

Switz. *Abbrev.* for **Switz·er·land** (SWIT·sur–) a country of C. Europe; 15,941 sq.mi. (41,288 km²); *cap.* Bern.

swiv·el *n.* a coupling device that allows free turning of one part on another, as used in a **swivel chair** with rotating seat. —***v.*** **-els, -el(l)ed, -el·(l)ing** (cause) to turn as on a swivel; hence, swing around.

swiz·zle stick a small stirrer for a mixed drink.

swob *n. & v.* **swobs, swobbed, swob·bing** same as SWAB.

swol·len a *pp.* of SWELL. —***adj.*** bulging or blown up.

swoon *n. & v.* faint; lose consciousness.

swoop *n.* a sweeping down or swift descent, as of a kite seizing its prey: *at one fell ~;* ***v.*** make a swift attack; seize swiftly: *commandoes ~ed down on the hijackers; ~ed her up and rushed to hospital.*

sword (SORD) *n.* a metal weapon consisting of a long blade set in a hilt; **cross swords** fight; **put to the sword** kill with a sword. —**sword·fish** *n.* a large ocean fish that has its upper jaw elongated into a sword. —**sword of Damocles** imminent danger, like the sword hung by a hair over the head of Damocles of ancient Sicily. —**sword·play** *n.* the art or skill of using a sword; also, fighting with swords. —**swords·man** (–mun) *n.* **-men** one skilled in the use of a sword; also, one using a sword in fencing, fighting, etc. —**sword·tail** *n.* a tropical fish whose male has a swordlike extension on its tail fin.

swore *pt.* of SWEAR. —**sworn** *pp.* of SWEAR; ***adj.*** bound by or promised with an oath: *~ enemies; ~ to secrecy.*

swum *pp.* of SWIM.

swung *pp.* of SWING.

syb·a·rite (SIB·uh–) *n.* a lover of luxury and sensuality; **syb·a·rit·ic** (–RIT–) *adj.*

syc·a·more (SIC·uh–) *n.* a North American shade tree with reddish-brown wood and bark that breaks off in scales; also, an Old World maple or fig tree.

syc·o·phant (SIC·uh·funt) *n.* a servile flatterer; toady; **syc·o·phan·cy** *n.* —**syc·o·phan·tic** (–FAN–) *adj.*

Syd·ney (SID·nee) a seaport of S.E. Australia.

syl(l). syllable. —**syl·lab·i·cate** (si·LAB–) *v.* **-cates, -cat·ed, -cat·ing** syllabify; **syl·lab·i·ca·tion** (–CAY–) *n.* —**syl·lab·i·fy** (–LAB–) *v.* **-fies, -fied, -fy·ing** form or divide into syllables; **syl·lab·i·fi·ca·tion** (–CAY–) *n.* —**syl·la·ble** (SIL·uh–) *n.* (a part of) a word pronounced as an uninterrupted unit, usu. consisting of a vowel with or without consonants:

"Syllable" has 3 ~s in it; He didn't utter a ~ (i.e. said nothing); **syl·lab·ic** (–LAB–) *adj.: "l" and "n" are ~ consonants in "bottle"* (BOTL) *and "button"* (BUTN).

syl·la·bus (SIL·uh–) *n., pl.* **-bi** (–bye) or **-bus·es** an outline or summary, esp. of a course of study.

syl·lo·gism (SIL·uh·jizm) *n.* a form of reasoning with two premises and a logical conclusion, as "A = B; and B = C; therefore A = C"; **syl·lo·gis·tic** (–JIS–) *adj.*

sylph (SILF) *n.* **1** an elemental spirit of the air. **2** a slender, graceful woman.

syl·van (SIL·vun) *adj.* of or living in the woods; also, wooded; full of trees.

sym. symbol; symmetrical.

sym·bi·o·sis (sim·bye·OH–, –bee–) *n., pl.* **-ses** (–seez) the living together of two different organisms, esp. for mutual benefit, as nitrogen-fixing bacteria inhabiting leguminous plants; **sym·bi·ot·ic** (–OT–) *adj.*

sym·bol (SIM·bl) *n.* a letter, sign, or object that represents an idea or quality by natural association or by convention, as H (hydrogen), the six-pointed star (Judaism), and the dove (peace); **sym·bol·ic** (–BOL–) or **-i·cal** *adj.;* **sym·bol·i·cal·ly** *adv.* —**sym·bol·ism** (SIM·bl·izm) *n.* symbolic representation, symbolic meaning, or a system of symbols. —**sym·bol·ize** *v.* **-iz·es, -ized, -iz·ing** represent by symbols or stand as a symbol of; **sym·bol·i·za·tion** (–ZAY–) *n.*

sym·me·try (SIM·uh·tree) *n.* **-tries** (a pleasing balance of form resulting from) correspondence of opposite parts in regard to size, shape, and position: *The human body has ~; A potato lacks ~;* **sym·met·ri·cal** (–MET–) *adj.;* **sym·met·ri·cal·ly** *adv.*

sym·pa·thet·ic (–THET–) *adj.* **1** kind toward others; agreeing or agreeable; harmonious. **2** having to do with the part of the autonomic nervous system that produces responses opposite to those of the parasympathetic nervous system, as slowing down gland activity. **3** of sounds and vibrations, produced in one body by transmission in the same frequency from another body. —**sym·pa·thet·i·cal·ly** *adv.* —**sym·pa·thize** *v.* **-thiz·es, -thized, -thiz·ing** feel or show sympathy in feeling or thought: *I ~ with you in your suffering; I don't ~* (i.e. agree) *with your aims;* **sym·pa·thiz·er** *n.* —**sym·pa·thy** (SIM·puh·thee) *n.* **-thies** **1** understanding and sharing of another's feelings; compassion: *Children turn to their parents for ~.* **2** agreement (with a person or his plan, proposal, views, etc.).

sym·pho·ny (SIM·fuh·nee) *n.* **-nies** **1** an elaborate musical composition for an orchestra, usu. in sonata form. **2** a large orchestra that plays symphonies; also **symphony orchestra.** **3** a symphony-orchestra concert. **4** harmony, esp. of sounds. —**sym·phon·ic** (–FON–) *adj.*

sym·po·si·um (–POH·zee–) *n.* **-si·ums** or **-si·a** a conference to discuss a given subject; also, a collection of opinions or essays on a subject.

symp·tom (SIMP·tum) *n.* a change in a body organ or function that indicates a disease, as a rash or headache; hence, a sign or indication of a disorder; **symp·to·mat·ic** (–tuh·MAT–) *adj.* —**symp·tom·ize** *v.* **-iz·es, -ized, -iz·ing** be a symptom of; also **symp·tom·a·tize.**

syn. synonym; synonymous; synonymy. —**syn-** *prefix.* together; at the same time: as in *synopsis, syntax, synthesis.* —**syn·a·gog(ue)** (SIN·uh·gog) *n.* (the place of worship of) a Jewish congregation; **syn·a·gog·al** (–GOG–) *adj.* —**syn·apse** (SIN·aps, suh·NAPS) *n.* the place where one nerve cell is linked to another. —**sync(h)** (SINK) *n.* & *v.* short form of SYNCHRONIZE, SYNCHRONIZATION. —**syn·chro·mesh** (SING·cruh–) *n.* in automobiles, a gear-changing system designed to work smoothly by means of a friction clutch that synchronizes the speed of one gear with that of another. —**syn·chro·nize** (SING·cruh–) *v.* **-niz·es, -nized, -niz·ing** (make) agree in time or rate: *Watches tell the same time when ~d; lip movements ~d with the voice;* **syn·chro·ni·za·tion** (–ZAY–) *n.;* **syn·chro·niz·er** *n.;* **syn·chro·nous** (–nus) *adj.: a satellite in a ~* (i.e. geostationary) *orbit.* —**syn·cline** (SING–) *n.* a basin-shaped fold in rock. —**syn·co·pate** (SING·cuh–) *v.* **-pates, -pat·ed, -pat·ing** **1** shorten, as by omitting a sound or syllable in the middle of a word, as in *heav'n.* **2** in music such as jazz, shift or anticipate the accent to a normally weak beat or off-beat. Hence **syn·co·pa·tion** (–PAY–) *n.* —**syn·di·cate** *n.* (–kit) **1** a group of organized gangsters. **2** an agency selling the same features, articles, pictures, etc. to many periodicals. **3** a joint selling venture or agency, as of the members of a cartel. —***v.*** (–cate) **-cates, -cat·ed, -cat·ing** form into or sell through a syndicate: *a ~d cartoon strip, column, columnist;* **syn·di·ca·tor** *n.;* **syn·di·ca·tion** (–CAY–) *n.* —**syn·drome** (SIN·drome, –drum) *n.* the combination or pattern of a number of symptoms occurring together that is characteristic of an ailment or abnormality: *the sudden infant death ~ or "crib death"; a drug withdrawal ~.* —**syn·er·gism** (SIN·ur·jizm) *n.* the working together of two or more substances, muscles, or drugs to produce an effect that is greater than that of the sum of their individual effects; **syn·er·gist** *n.;* **syn·er·gis·tic** (–JIS–) *adj.;* **syn·er·gis·ti·cal·ly** *adv.* —**syn·fu·el** *n.* a synthetic liquid fuel made from coal, oil shale, tar sands, etc. —**syn·od** (SIN·ud) *n.* an assembly or council of church officials called to discuss matters of faith and morals; **syn·od·al** *adj.;* also **syn·od·ic** (–NOD–) or **-i·cal** *adj.* —**syn·o·nym** (SIN·uh·nim) *n.* a word with (nearly) the same meaning as another in one or more senses:

"Hit" is a close ~ of "strike"; **syn·on·y·mous** (–NON·uh·mus) *adj.* —**syn·on·y·my** (–NON·uh·mee) *n.* **-mies** **1** sameness of meaning, as between two words. **2** a listing of synonyms with meanings discriminated. —**syn·op·sis** (suh·NOP–) *n., pl.* **-ses** (–seez) a summary or outline (of a story, treatise, etc.); **syn·op·tic** (–NOP–) *adj.* presenting a comprehensive view; also **syn·op·ti·cal.** —**syn·tax** (SIN–) *n.* the arrangement of words in phrases, clauses, and sentences; **syn·tac·tic** (–TAC–) or **-ti·cal** *adj.* —**syn·the·sis** (SIN·thuh–) *n., pl.* **-ses** (–seez) the combining of parts into a whole: *the ~ of ideas* (into a philosophy), *races* (into a nation), *elements* (into a compound); **syn·the·size** *v.* **-siz·es, -sized, -siz·ing; syn·the·siz·er** *n.* —**syn·thet·ic** (–THET–) *adj.* **1** involving synthesis. **2** produced by chemical combination; hence, artificial: *~ rubber, smiles.* Also **syn·thet·i·cal; syn·thet·i·cal·ly** *adv.* —**syn·thet·ics** *n.pl.* man-made materials.

syph·i·lis (SIF–) *n.* a bacterium-caused venereal disease usu. transmitted by sexual contact; **syph·i·lit·ic** (–LIT–) *n.* & *adj.* (a person) having syphilis.

sy·phon (SYE·fun) same as SIPHON.

Syr·a·cuse (SEER·uh–) a city of central New York.

Syr·i·a (SEER·ee·uh) a country of S.W. Asia; 71,498 sq.mi. (185,180 km²); *cap.* Damascus; **Syr·i·an** *n.* & *adj.*

sy·ringe (suh·RINJ, SEER·inj) *n.* a device consisting of a narrow tube equipped with a rubber bulb or piston for injecting fluids into the body, cleansing wounds, etc.; ***v.*** **-ring·es, -ringed, -ring·ing** inject or cleanse with a syringe.

syr·up (SEER–, SUR–) *n.* a thick, sugary liquid: *corn ~; maple ~; cough ~* (i.e. medication); **syr·up·y** *adj.*

syst. *Abbrev.* for **sys·tem** (SIS·tum) *n.* **1** a related or organized whole composed of many individual parts: *a school ~; the solar ~; a ~ of philosophy; the digestive ~; Too much sleep is bad for the ~* (i.e. body); *Radicals wish to overturn the ~* (i.e. social order). **2** a complex or elaborate method: *the pronunciation ~ of a dictionary; a classification ~; a computer ~ for handling a payroll; Some work by a ~, others without ~* (i.e. orderliness); **sys·tem·at·ic** (–MAT–) or **-i·cal** *adj.* organized, methodical, and thorough; **sys·tem·at·i·cal·ly** *adv.* —**sys·tem·a·tize** *v.* **-tiz·es, -tized, -tiz·ing** make systematic. —**sys·tem·ic** (–TEM–) *adj.* of the system or the body as a whole, not localized: *~ circulation, poison;* ***n.*** a pesticide that is injected into a plant or animal. —**systems analysis** the analysis of a system or operation into its parts in order to determine how to use a computer to run it most efficiently; **systems analyst.**

sys·to·le (SIS·tuh·lee) *n.* the contracting phase of the heartbeat during which blood is pumped out; cf. DIASTOLE; **sys·tol·ic** (–TOL–) *adj.*

T or **t** (TEE) *n.* **T's** or **t's** **1** the 20th letter of the English alphabet. **2 to a T** exactly; to perfection: *The nickname suits him to a ~.* —**T** temperature (absolute); time (of firing or launching); tritium. —**t.** teaspoon(s); temperature; tenor; tense; time. —**T.** tablespoon(s); Testament; Tuesday. —**T.** or **t.** tenor; territory; ton(s). —**t** tonne.

Ta tantalum.

tab *n.* **1** a small extension or piece projecting from a garment, filing card, etc.; **keep (a) tab on** or **keep tabs on** *Informal.* keep watch on. **2** *Informal.* bill or check: *She picked up the ~ for the whole party.* —***v.*** **tabs, tabbed, tab·bing** put a tab on; also, label or identify.

Ta·bas·co (tuh·BAS–) *Trademark.* a kind of hot sauce made from red peppers.

tab·by (TAB·ee) *n.* **tab·bies** a gray or brown cat with dark stripes; also, any female domestic cat.

tab·er·nac·le (TAB·ur·nacl) *n.* **1** a temporary dwelling. **2** a synagogue; **Tabernacle** a tent carried by the Israelites as a place of worship during their travels. **3** a small cabinet or container for the consecrated host in the center of the altar.

tab·la (TAB·luh) *n.* a pair of small hand drums used by musicians of India.

ta·ble (TAY·bl) *n.* **1** a piece of furniture with a flat horizontal top and legs supporting it, esp. one to eat at: *to put food on the ~; She provides a good ~* (i.e. fare); *spoke to the whole ~* (i.e. group around the table). **2** a tabulated list: *a ~ of contents; the multiplication ~s.* **3** tableland. **4** inscribed tablet: *the* **tables** *of the law.* **5 turn the tables** reverse a situation to an opponent's disadvantage. —***v.*** **-bles, -bled, -bling** put off consideration of (a legislative bill) indefinitely; *Brit.* put on the agenda. —**tab·leau** (–loh) *n., pl.* **-leaux** (–loze) or **-leaus** **1** a graphic or dramatic picture. **2** a dramatic scene posed by silent actors in costume. —**ta·ble·cloth** *n.* covering for a table, as at meals. —**ta·ble d'hôte** (TAH·bl·DOTE), *pl.* **ta·bles d'hôte** (–blz–) in restaurants, a complete meal at a fixed price; cf. À LA CARTE. —**ta·ble-hop** *v.* **-hops, -hopped, -hop·ping** leave one's table in a restaurant to chat with friends at other tables. —**ta·ble·land** *n.* plateau. —**ta·ble·spoon** *n.* a large serving spoon or a spoon for eating soup; also, tablespoonful; **ta·ble·spoon·ful** *n.* **-fuls** a measuring unit equal to three teaspoonfuls or ½ fl. oz. (1.4786 cl). —**tab·let** (–lit) *n.* **1** a flat, thin piece of material for writing on, as in ancient times; also, a slab bearing an inscription put at the head of a grave or used as a plaque. **2** pad of sheets of writing paper glued together at one end. **3** a small, flat cake of medicine, as of aspirin. —**table tennis** a tennislike game played on a table with a light, hollow plastic ball. —**ta·ble·top** *n.* the flat horizontal top of a table. —**ta·ble·ware** *n.* dishes, glasses, spoons, knives, etc. for use at meals. —**tab·loid** *n.* a usu. half-size newspaper giving news in condensed form with many pictures and sensational headlines; ***adj.*** condensed or summarized.

ta·boo (tuh·BOO, tab–) *adj.* **1** prohibited because obscene or harmful, as four-letter words. **2** not to be touched because sacred or cursed as among certain tribes; ***n.*** such a prohibition or the custom. —***v.*** **-boos, -booed, -boo·ing** prohibit or put under taboo. Also **ta·bu.**

ta·bor (TAY·bur) *n.* a small drum used as accompaniment by one playing on a pipe, as in the Middle Ages.

tabu same as TABOO.

tab·u·lar (–yuh·lur) *adj.* **1** having to do with lists or tables: *data in ~ form; ~ value, computations.* **2** flat like a tabletop: *~ rock, structure, surface.* —**tab·u·late** *v.* **-lates, -lat·ed, -lat·ing** arrange (data) in lists or tabular form; **tab·u·la·tor** *n.;* **tab·u·la·tion** (–LAY–) *n.*

TAC Tactical Air Command. —**TACAN** Tactical Air Navigation.

ta·chom·e·ter (tuh·COM·uh·tur) *n.* an instrument that measures the speed of a rotating wheel or shaft, usu. in revolutions per minute.

—**tach·y·car·di·a** (tak·i·CAR·dee·uh) *n.* abnormally rapid beating of the heart.

tac·it (TAS–) *adj.* unspoken; also, implied, not expressed: ~ *approval, understanding;* **tac·it·ly** *adv.;* **tac·it·ness** *n.* —**tac·i·turn** (TAS–) *adj.* inclined by nature to be silent; uncommunicative; **tac·i·tur·ni·ty** (–TUR–) *n.*

tack *n.* **1** a flat-headed, sharp-pointed nail: *carpet ~s.* **2** a temporary stitch. **3** in sailing, a zigzag course or one of the movements in such a course; also, the direction of the ship's movement in relation to the position of the sails: *port ~; starboard ~.* **4** course of action or policy: *try a different ~.* —**v. 1** fasten with tacks. **2** attach or append (to something). **3** move along in a zigzag course, as in sailing. **4** change one's attitude or policy.

tack·le *n.* **1** gear or equipment, as a ship's ropes and pulleys: *fishing ~* (i.e. rod, line, etc.). **2** (method of) tackling an opponent, as in football. **3** in football, an offensive or defensive lineman next to the end. —**v. -les, -led, -ling 1** lay hold of (an opponent); hence, try to deal with (a problem, etc.). **2** in football, seize or throw (the ball carrier) to the ground; **tack·ler** *n.*

tack·y *adj.* **tack·i·er, -i·est 1** sticky. **2** *Informal.* shabby; gaudy; dowdy; **tack·i·ness** *n.*

ta·co (TAH·coh) *n.* **-cos** a rolled or folded tortilla with a filling of meat, etc.

Ta·co·ma (tuh·COH·muh) a seaport of Washington.

tac·o·nite (TAC·uh–) *n.* a hard rock containing about 30% iron ore.

tact *n.* delicate skill in handling people and difficult situations; **tact·ful** *adj.;* **tact·ful·ly** *adv.;* **tact·ful·ness** *n.;* **tact·less** *adj.;* **tact·less·ly** *adv.* —**tac·tic** *n.* a skillful move or maneuver; **tac·ti·cal** *adj.;* **tac·ti·cian** (–TISH·un) *n.* —**tac·tics** *pl.* **1** [takes *sing. v.*] the art or science of conducting a battle. **2** methods of gaining advantage: *cheap ~s; scare ~s.* —**tac·tile** (TAC·tl, –tile) *adj.* relating to the sense of touch: *a ~ impression, organ, stimulus;* **tac·til·i·ty** (–TIL–) *n.*

tad *n.* **1** a little boy. **2** a little bit.

ta-dah (tuh·DAH) *interj.* uttered when presenting a surprise.

tad·pole *n.* a frog or toad of the larva stage with gills and tail.

taf·fe·ta (TAF·uh·tuh) *n.* a fine, stiff, lustrous fabric of silk, rayon, etc.

taff·rail *n.* the rail around a ship's stern.

taf·fy (TAF·ee) *n.* **taf·fies** a chewy candy prepared from molasses or brown sugar.

Taft, William H. 1857–1930, 27th U.S. President (1909–13).

tag *n.* **1** a small hanging piece or end. **2** the metal binding on the end of a shoelace. **3** a small piece of card or leather attached as a label: *a price ~.* **4** an epithet. **5** a quotation or saying used for effect at the end of a speech or story; also **tag line. 6** a game in which a child chases his playmates till he touches one. —**v. tags, tagged, tag·ging 1** furnish with a tag or label. **2** follow closely; trail (along or after). **3** to touch, as in the game of tag; hence, select or choose; **tag·ger** *n.*

Ta·ga·log (tah·GAH–) *n.* a member of the chief native people of the Philippines; also, their language.

tag line same as TAG, *n.* 5. —**tag sale** garage sale.

Ta·hi·ti (tuh·HEE·tee) the largest island of the French Polynesian group; 402 sq.mi. (1,041 km²); *cap.* Papeete; **Ta·hi·tian** (–HEE·shun) *n.* & *adj.*

tai chi (TYE·jee) a Chinese martial art characterized by slow movements; in full "t'ai-chi ch'uan."

tai·ga (TYE·guh) *n.* the swampy coniferous forest land of Siberia between the tundra and the steppes.

tail *n.* **1** the backward extension of an animal's body; hence, a similar part: *the ~ of an airplane, comet, procession;* **turn tail** *Informal.* run away in fear. **2** *Informal.* one who shadows another, as a detective. —***adj.*** at or from the rear: *a ~ wind.* —**v.** furnish with a tail; also, follow close behind. —**tails** *n.pl.* **1** the reverse side of a coin. **2** tailcoat; hence, full-dress attire. —**tailed** *adj.;* **tail·less** *adj.* —**tail·coat** *n.* a man's full-dress coat that is cut away in front and divided and tapered at the back like a swallow's tail. —**tail·gate** *n.* the gate that opens into the back of a truck, station wagon, etc.; **v. -gates, -gat·ed, -gat·ing** drive too close behind (another vehicle). —**tail·light** *n.* a red warning light at the rear of a vehicle.

tai·lor (TAY·lur) *n.* one who makes or repairs clothes; **v.** work as a tailor; also, make by tailor's work: *a suit ~ed to measure; a text ~ed* (i.e. adapted) *to the needs of the young student.*

tail·pipe *n.* an automobile exhaust pipe leading out of the muffler. —**tail·spin** *n.* **1** same as SPIN, *n.* 1. **2** *Informal.* state of mental confusion. —**tail wind** a wind in the direction in which a craft is going.

taint *n.* a trace of corruption or contamination; **v.** contaminate; corrupt; spoil: *~ed food, money, reputation.*

Tai·pei (TYE·PAY) capital of the Republic of China. —**Tai·wan** (TYE·WAHN) island off S.E. China forming the Republic of China; 13,885 sq.mi. (35,961 km²).

ta·ka (TAH·kuh) *n. sing.* & *pl.* the basic money unit of Bangladesh, equal to 100 paise.

take *v.* **takes, took, tak·en, tak·ing 1** get or seize by force or skill: *was ~n prisoner; Who took the game?* **2** get, obtain, or assume: *He's out ~ing the air: I don't ~* (i.e. subscribe to) *the Tribune; She'll ~ office tomorrow.* **3** get by choice: *Please ~ a seat; You can ~ it or leave it.* **4** get from a source: *a passage ~n from the Bible; to ~ notes of a lecture.* **5** get or receive as offered or due: *can't ~ a joke; She's ~ing rest.* **6** understand or feel: *What shall I ~ this to mean? didn't ~ notice of her.* **7** do, perform, or execute: *He ~s a walk after dinner; took a swipe at him.* **8** move or remove: *Where does this road ~ us? 7 remains if you ~ 5 from 12.* **—n.** a taking, what is taken, an amount taken, etc.: *the many ~s of a movie scene; an evening's ~ at the box office;* **on the take** *Slang.* accepting money illicitly. **—take after** be or act like (someone). **—take down** pull down; also, write down. **—take for** consider to be. **—take in:** *has to ~ in laundry to pay her debts; took in the sights of the town on the last visit; a dress that needs to be ~n in* (i.e. reduced) *at the waist; too sharp to be easily ~n in* (i.e. deceived). **—take it** *Slang.* endure (something hard to bear). **—take off:** *An aircraft ~s off* (on a flight); *He ~s off* (*Informal.* mimics) *celebrities to entertain audiences; Everyone ~s off* (*Informal.* leaves) *for home after school.* **—take on** **1** engage or employ. **2** undertake (to deal with). **3** acquire (a look, appearance, etc.). **—take over** take charge or control of. **—take place** happen or occur. **—take to** accept quickly; become fond of. **—take up** **1** begin (to do or learn). **2** fill or occupy (a place or time). **3** tighten; make shorter: *~ up the slack on a rope.* **—take•off** *n.* **1** a taking off, as in flight. **2** *Informal.* a burlesque or parody. **—take•out** *adj.* in ordering food, for consumption away from the premises. **—take•o•ver** *n.* the taking over of a power in a government or organization. **—tak•ing** *adj.* attractive; captivating; ***n.*** seizure; **takings** *pl.* profits or receipts.

ta•la (TAH·luh) *n.* the basic money unit of Western Samoa, worth 100 senes.

talc *n.* the softest of minerals, hence used in **tal•cum powder** made of perfumed white talc for use on the skin.

tale *n.* **1** a made-up story, esp. a long one. **2** falsehood; also, gossip or scandal; **tell tales** spread gossip. **3** a tally or count. **—tale•bear•er** *n.* one who spreads gossip; also, a telltale.

tal•ent *n.* **1** a natural ability or aptitude (for some activity or skill). **2** persons with talent: *recruiting new ~.* **3** a unit of weight or money among the ancient Greeks. **—tal•ent•ed** *adj.* gifted.

ta•ler (TAH·lur) *n. sing. & pl.* a large German silver coin replaced by the mark in 1891.

tales•man *n.* **-men** one called to jury duty from among those who happen to be present in court.

tal•is•man *n.* **-mans** an object such as an inscribed ring which by its presence is supposed to bring good luck; charm or amulet.

talk (TAWK) *v.* **1** communicate with spoken words; speak: *Teachers ~ to their classes; Parents ~ with teachers; was ~ing nonsense after drinking; Some birds ~; No ~ing in the library.* **2** tell; relate: *Police know how to make him ~; gossips ~ing behind her back.* **—n.** a talking; informal conversation or speech: *much ~ and little action; a little ~ about cleanliness; There's ~ of prices coming down; summit ~s in Paris; Their divorce is the ~ of the town* (i.e. subject of gossip). **—talk back** *Informal.* answer impertinently. **—talk down** to speak to in a superior manner. **—talk out** discuss openly. **—talk over** **1** discuss (something) together. **2** persuade (someone). **—talk•er** *n.* **—talk•a•tive** (–uh·tiv) *adj.* fond of talking; **talk•a•tive•ly** *adv.;* **talk•a•tive•ness** *n.* **—talking book** a sound recording of a book for the blind. **—talk•ing-to** *n. Informal.* a scolding or lecture. **—talk show** a television or radio show featuring interviews. **—talk•y** *adj.* talkative.

tall (TAWL) *adj.* **1** of people and things, having considerable height: *a ~ structure; ~ people, stature; 6 feet ~* (i.e. high). **2** *Informal.* extravagant, exaggerated, or difficult: *a ~ price, tale, order* (i.e. requirement or proposal). **—tall•ness** *n.*

Tal•la•has•see (tal·uh·HAS·ee) capital of Florida.

tal•low (TAL·oh) *n.* a hard, white substance got by melting suet and such animal fat, used chiefly in making candles, soap, etc.

tal•ly *n.* **tal•lies** **1** formerly, a notched stick as a reckoning device or either half of it split lengthwise for each of the two parties to a deal; hence, a counterpart or duplicate; also, (a record for) a score or reckoning. **2** a ticket or tag for identification. **3** a group forming a unit in counting; lot. **—v. tal•lies, tal•lied, tal•ly•ing:** *Votes for each side were ~d up; two accounts that don't ~; Your total doesn't ~ with mine.*

tal•ly•ho (tal·ee·HOH) *n. & interj.* **1** a huntsman's cry on sighting the fox. **2** a coach drawn by four horses.

Tal•mud (TAHL·mood, TAL·mud) *n.* the body of early Jewish law and ethics; **Tal•mud•ic** (–MEW–) *adj.*

tal•on (–un) *n.* a claw of a bird of prey or animal; also, a clawlike finger or hand.

tam *n.* same as TAM-O'-SHANTER.

tamable same as TAMEABLE.

ta•ma•le (tuh·MAH·lee) *n.* a Mexican preparation of steamed corn meal mixed with highly seasoned pork or chicken.

tam•a•rack *n.* the North American "eastern larch" tree or its wood.

tam•a•rind (TAM·uh–) *n.* a tropical tree of the pea family bearing plump pods containing an acid pulp used in foods.

tam•ba•la (–BAH–) *n.* 1/100 of a Malawi kwacha.

tam•bou•rine (tam·buh·REEN) *n.* a shallow hand drum with jingles attached to the frame, played by shaking it or hitting it with the hand.

tame *adj.* **tam•er, tam•est** **1** of animals, domesticated, not wild; made docile. **2** dull or insipid: *a ~ show, ending.* **—v. tames, tamed, tam•ing** make tame or docile: *to ~ a* *bear, river.* —**tam(e)·a·ble** *adj.;* **tame·ly** *adv.;* **tame·ness** *n.;* **tam·er** *n.*

Tam·il *n.* a Dravidian language of S. India and N. Sri Lanka; also, a speaker of Tamil.

tam-o'-shan·ter *n.* a Scottish bonnet with a flat crown and a pompom in the center.

tamp *v.* pack (earth) down by a series of blows or taps.

Tam·pa a seaport of W. Florida.

tam·per *v.* interfere with the working of: *Do not ~ with your watch; a will that had been ~ed with; a lawyer charged with ~ing* (i.e. influencing) *a jury.*

tam·pon *n.* a plug inserted into a wound or a body cavity to absorb a flow.

tan *n.* **1** a yellowish brown color, as the skin color resulting from sunning. **2** a tannin-containing liquid; also, tanbark. ***—adj.*** **tan·ner, tan·nest** yellowish-brown. ***—v.*** **tans, tanned, tan·ning** **1** make or become tan. **2** change (hide) into leather by soaking in tannin. **3** *Informal.* whip or thrash.

tan·a·ger (TAN·uh·jur) *n.* a small songbird related to the finches, brilliantly colored in the male.

Ta·na·na·rive (tah·nah·nah·REEV) capital of Madagascar.

tan·bark *n.* a tannin-rich bark, as of the oak or sumac.

tan·dem *adv.* one behind the other: *riding ~;* ***adj.*** harnessed or arranged tandem: *a ~ arrangement, bicycle* (with two sets of pedals). ***—n.*** **1** a tandem arrangement or harness: *husband and wife working in ~.* **2** a tandem carriage, bicycle, or trailer.

tang *n.* **1** the projecting part of a knife or file that is held inside its handle. **2** a sharp flavor or odor, as of garlic; **tang·y** *adj.*

tan·ge·lo (TAN·juh–) *n.* **-los** a fruit that is a cross between a tangerine and a "pomelo" (grapefruit).

tan·gent (–junt) *n.* & *adj.* (a line, curve, or surface) that touches without cutting; **fly** (or **go**) **off at a tangent** go away suddenly from one line of thought or action; **tan·gen·tial** (–JEN–) *adj.;* **tan·gen·tial·ly** *adv.*

tan·ge·rine (–juh·REEN) *n.* a delicate, loose-skinned kind of orange with segments that separate easily.

tan·gi·ble (TAN·juh–) *adj.* that can be felt by touching; hence, real or definite: *show ~ improvement; ~ property* (i.e. that can be appraised); ***n.*** a material asset or property; **tan·gi·bil·i·ty** (–BIL–) *n.* —**tan·gi·bly** *adv.*

tan·gle *v.* **-gles, -gled, -gling** of threads, hair, etc., twist together or become involved or entangled: *a ~d mass of hair; a ~d web of passions; Don't ~* (*Informal.* quarrel or fight) *with neighbors;* ***n.*** a complicated or confused mass (of material) or condition: *a ~ of red tape; a political ~.*

tan·go (TANG·goh) *n.* **-gos** a ballroom dance of South American origin characterized by long, gliding steps and intricate poses; ***v.*** **-gos, -goed, -go·ing** dance the tango.

tank *n.* **1** a cistern or large container for storing a fluid: *an automobile's gas ~; a railroad ~ car;* **tank·ful** *n.* **2** an armored vehicle moving on endless tracks and equipped with guns. —**tank·ard** (–urd) *n.* a large drinking cup with a handle and hinged cover. —**tank·er** *n.* **1** a ship for transporting oil or similar cargo; also a railroad car or a truck for the same purpose. **2** an aircraft for refueling other planes in flight. —**tank top** a sleeveless, collarless top with shoulder straps like those of a one-piece bathing suit, or **tank suit.** —**tank town** a small town where trains stop for water. —**tank truck** a truck built as a tanker.

tan·ner *n.* one who tans hides, working in a **tan·ner·y** *n.* **tan·ner·ies.** —**tan·nic acid** or **tan·nin** *n.* a bitter substance produced in the galls of trees by insect larvae, used esp. in dyeing leather.

tan·sy (–zee) *n.* **-sies** a bitter-tasting aromatic herb related to the thistle that yields an oil used in medicine.

tan·ta·lize (TAN·tuh–) *v.* **-liz·es, -lized, -liz·ing** torment or tease, as **Tan·ta·lus** of Greek myth, punished by continual disappointment whenever he tried to eat or drink what was placed within his reach; **tan·ta·liz·ing** *adj.: a ~ vision of water in the desert;* **tan·ta·liz·ing·ly** *adv.* —**tan·ta·lum** (TAN·tuh–) *n.* a rare, corrosion-resistant, metallic element.

tan·ta·mount (TAN·tuh–) *adj.* equal in force or effect: *The "friendly" warning was ~ to a threat.*

tan·tra (TUN·truh, TAHN–) *n.* Hindu scriptures dealing with spells, rituals, and symbols; **tan·tric** *adj.*

tan·trum *n.* an outburst of bad temper.

Tan·za·ni·a (–zuh·NEE·uh) an E. African country consisting of Tanganyika and several offshore islands, chiefly Zanzibar; 364,900 sq.mi. (945,087 km²); *cap.* Dar es Salaam; **Tan·za·ni·an** (–NEE·un) *n.* & *adj.*

Tao·ism (TOW·izm, DOW–) *n.* a Chinese religion based on a philosophy developed as a reaction to Confucianism; **Tao·ist** *n.* & *adj.*

¹tap *n.* **1** a device for controlling an outflow, as a water faucet or the stopper of a cask; **on tap** ready for use: *beer on ~; free advice on ~.* **2** a fluid drawn out, esp. liquor of a particular quality: *spinal ~* (i.e. sample of spinal fluid for diagnosis). **3** a plug-in multiple electrical outlet; also, a wiretap. **4** a tool for cutting an internal screw thread, as of a nut. ***—v.*** **taps, tapped, tap·ping:** *Latex, maple sap, etc. are ~d from trees; to ~ a beer barrel; phone lines suspected of being ~d; sources of energy waiting to be ~d.* —**tap·per** *n.*

²tap *v.* **taps, tapped, tap·ping** **1** rap or strike lightly, as on a door or on one's back for attention: *He ~d out his message in code.* **2** choose (someone) *for* a post, membership, etc. ***—n.*** a light, rapid blow. —**tap dance** a dance performed with rhythmic tapping of the floor wearing specially soled shoes; **tap-dance** *v.* **-danc·es, -danced, -danc·ing; tap-danc·er** *n.* —**tap·per** *n.*

tape *n.* a narrow strip or band of fabric, paper, or light, flexible metal, as for measuring distances, binding or sticking, recording messages in sound or video, etc.; ***v.* tapes, taped, tap·ing:** *broken pieces ~d together; a ~d, not live show.* —**tape deck** the recording and playback unit of a hi-fi system with separate amplifier and speaker; also, a tape player. —**tape measure** a measuring tape marked off in units of length. —**tape player** a playback machine for tape recordings or cassettes.

ta·per (TAY–) *n.* **1** a long wick or slender candle for lighting lamps, fires, etc. **2** a gradual decrease; ***v.:*** *A church spire ~s* (i.e. decreases in size) *toward the top; Rain will* **taper off** *after midnight.*

tape recorder a machine that records and plays back sound on magnetic tape; **tape-re·cord** (–CORD) *v.;* **tape-re·cord·ing** *n.*

tap·es·try (TAP·is·tree) *n.* **-tries** a decorative fabric woven in colorful designs and pictures for use as wall hangings, draperies, etc.

tape·worm *n.* a ribbonlike parasitic worm found in the intestines of humans and animals.

tap·house *n.* a tavern.

tap·i·o·ca (–ee·OH·cuh) *n.* a food starch obtained from the roots of the cassava.

ta·pir (TAY–) *n.* a piglike animal of South America and Malaya with an extended snout or short trunk.

tap·pet (–it) *n.* in machines, a collar or arm for imparting intermittent motion, as to open and close a valve in an engine.

tap·room *n.* a barroom.

tap·root *n.* the main root growing vertically downward from a tree or plant and sprouting smaller roots sideways.

taps *n.pl.* the last bugle call at night signaling "lights out," originally a drum signal.

tap·ster *n.* one who taps and serves liquor in a tavern.

tar **1** a thick, black, sticky substance obtained from coal, fats, and other organic matter and used in making asphalt, chemicals such as phenol, etc. **2** *Informal.* sailor. ***—v.* tars, tarred, tar·ring** cover or smear with tar.

ta·ran·tu·la (tuh·RAN·choo·luh) *n.* a large, hairy, ferocious-looking spider of warm climates, esp. the "wolf spider" of S. Italy, the "bird spider" of South America, and the "trap-door spider" of S. United States.

tar·dy *adj.* **tar·di·er, -di·est** slow or late, as because of sluggishness: *~ reply, progress, students;* **tar·di·ly** *adv.;* **tar·di·ness** *n.*

tare *n.* **1** vetch; also, in the Bible, a weed, possibly the darnel. **2** (deduction of) the weight of a container or conveyance from the gross weight to get the net weight of the goods carried in it; ***v.* tares, tared, tar·ing** ascertain the tare of (a container, etc.).

tar·get (–gut) *n.* a mark or other object that is aimed at in shooting; hence, an object of attack; also, a goal or objective: *a ~ for ridicule; the ~ date for completing a project;* ***v.:*** *a book ~ed for fall publication.*

tar·iff (TAIR–) *n.* a schedule or system of charges, rates, etc., esp. for taxing exports and imports; also, any such tax, esp. import duty.

tar·mac *n. Brit.* a paved area, as on an airfield.

tarn *n.* a small mountain lake or pool.

tar·nish *v.* dull the brightness of (polished metal); hence, sully or stain (a reputation, etc.); ***n.*** a tarnishing or stain; **tar·nish·a·ble** *adj.*

ta·ro (TAH·roh) *n.* **-ros** a tropical plant of the arum family whose large underground stems are used as food.

tar·ot (TAIR·oh) *n.* one of a set of 22 playing cards, sometimes used for fortune-telling.

tar·pau·lin (–PAW–, TAR·puh–) *n.* waterproofed canvas used as a protective cover for exposed objects.

tar·pon (–pun) *n.* a large game fish common off the S. Atlantic coast of the U.S.

tar·ra·gon (TAIR·uh–) *n.* a European herb related to the sagebrushes, used in salads and as flavoring for foods.

tar·ry **1** (TAIR·ee) *v.* **tar·ries, tar·ried, tar·ry·ing** delay; linger; also, put off departure. **2** (TAR·ee) *adj.* **tar·ri·er, tar·ri·est** of or covered with tar.

tar·sal (–sul) *adj.* of the tarsus; **tar·sus** *n., pl.* **-si** (–sye) the group of small bones, including the heel bone, at the ankle.

tar sands sands containing oil.

tart *adj.* **1** agreeably sour or acid, as some applies. **2** caustic or sharp: *a ~ reply;* **tart·ly** *adv.;* **tart·ness** *n.*—***n.*** **1** a small, sweet pie with a filling of fruit, jam, or custard. **2** *Informal.* a prostitute.

tar·tan (–tn) *n.* & *adj.* (made of) a plaid woolen cloth, as worn by Scottish clansmen: *a ~ kilt.*

Tar·tar (–tur) *n.* a member of a Turkic-speaking people of the U.S.S.R.; also, a member of a Mongolian group that invaded W. Asia and E. Europe during the Middle Ages. —**tar·tar** (–tur) *n.* **1** a potassium salt deposited as a crust in wine casks, purified into "cream of tartar" for use in medicine and cooking. **2** a crusty deposit on teeth formed by saliva. —**tar·tar·ic** (–TAIR–, –TAR–) *adj.* —**tar·tar(e)** (–tur) **sauce** a fish sauce made with mayonnaise, pickles, parsley, etc.

task *n.* (a piece of) usu. difficult work assigned to or demanded of someone: *home ~s set by teachers;* **take to task** scold or reprove; **task force** a group, as in the military, organized for a specific operation; **task·mas·ter** *n.* one who sets tasks of a demanding nature.

Tas·ma·ni·a (–MAY·nee·uh) an island state of Australia; 26,383 sq.mi. (68,332 km²); **Tas·ma·ni·an** *n.* & *adj.*

tas·sel (–ul) *v.* **tas·sels, tas·sel(l)ed, tas·sel·(l)ing** put on or adorn with tassels. **—*n.*** a hanging bunch of loose threads or cords, used as an ornament at the edge of a curtain, cushion, etc.; also, a tassellike tuft of flowers at the top of a cornstalk.

taste (TAIST) **1** what is sensed by the organs of the mouth, as sweet, sour, bitter, etc.: *Water has no ~.* **2** a small quantity or sample; a tasting: *the first ~ of winter.* **3** sense of perception of various tastes. **4** ability to perceive what is artistically good; also, artistic style: *a woman of excellent ~; ~s* (i.e. likes) *differ; a pun that is not* **in good taste** (i.e. somewhat improper or offensive). **—*v.* tastes, tast·ed, tast·ing** have a flavor; also, have or try the flavor of (something): *Sugar ~s sweet; He ~s wines for a living; The jailbird ~d* (i.e. experienced) *freedom only briefly;* **taste of** experience; also, have the flavor of: *a reply that ~s of arrogance.* **—taste·less** *adj.;* **tast·er** *n.* **—taste bud** any of the papillae on the tongue that act as taste receptors. **—taste·ful** *adj.* having or showing good artistic taste; **taste·ful·ly** *adv.* **—tast·y** *adj.* **tast·i·er, -i·est** that tastes good; **tast·i·ness** *n.*

tat *v.* **tats, tat·ted, tat·ting** make (lace) by tatting; **tat·ting** *n.* a fine lace or the process of making it by hand with loops and knots of thread wound around a shuttle.

ta·ta·mi (tuh·TAH·mee) *n.* a Japanese floor covering or mat of straw.

Ta·tar (TAH·tur) *n.* same as TARTAR.

tat·ter *n.* a torn strip left loose on a garment; also, a shred or scrap (of paper, etc.); **tat·ters** *pl.* torn and ragged clothes. **—*v.*** make or become ragged; **tat·tered** *adj.* **—tat·ter·de·mal·ion** (–MAIL·yun) *n.* a person in tattered clothes; ragamuffin.

tat·ter·sall (TAT·ur·sawl) *n.* a check pattern of colored lines on a light background.

tatting See TAT.

tat·tle *n.* idle talk; gossip; ***v.*** **tat·tles, tat·tled, tat·tling** gossip; tell tales or secrets; also, reveal (a secret) by tattling; **tat·tler** *n.* **—tat·tle·tale** *n. Informal.* a telltale or informer.

tat·too (–TOO) *n.* **tat·toos** **1** a bugle or drum signal calling soldiers, etc. to their quarters at night; hence, a rhythmic rapping or tapping. **2** a colored design put on the skin by pricking it; ***v.*** **tat·tooes, tat·tooed, tat·too·ing** mark (the skin) or put (a design) on it in this way: *~d skin, ship design, sailors.*

tau (TAW, TOW) *n.* the 19th letter of the Greek alphabet (T, τ).

taught *pt.* & *pp.* of TEACH.

taunt (TAWNT, TAHNT) *v.* jeer at or mock repeatedly so as to provoke: *to ~ a boy about his big ears; was ~ed into a fight;* ***n.*** such jeering, or a taunting remark.

taupe (TOPE) *n.* a brownish gray, as of moleskin.

Tau·rus (TOR–) the second sign of the zodiac and a N. constellation.

taut *adj.* tightly stretched; hence, strained or tense: *~ ropes, muscles, nerves; a ~* (i.e. tidy) *ship with ~ sails;* **taut·ly** *adv.;* **taut·ness** *n.*

tau·tol·o·gy (–TOL·uh·jee) *n.* **-gies** (an instance of) the saying of a thing over again without added clarity or force, as in "was seen naked with nothing on"; **tau·to·log·i·cal** (–LOJ–) *adj.;* **tau·to·log·i·cal·ly** *adv.*

tav·ern (TAV·urn) *n.* an establishment where alcoholic liquor is served; also, formerly, an inn.

taw *n.* a shooting marble or the line from which players shoot; also, the game of marbles.

taw·dry (–dree) *adj.* **-dri·er, -dri·est** cheap and showy: *a ~ dress, ornament.*

taw·ny (–nee) *adj.* **-ni·er, -ni·est** brownish-yellow: *the lion's ~ coat; the ~ eagle of Africa.*

tax *n.* a charge levied on incomes, properties, or businesses by a government; hence, a strain or burden. **—*v.*** **1** levy a tax on (incomes, purchases, etc.). **2** be a strain on; put a burden on: *complaints that ~ one's patience.* **3** accuse or charge: *~ed with neglecting duty.* **4** check or evaluate: *The client had his lawyer's bill ~ed.* **—tax·a·ble** *adj.;* **tax·a·tion** (–AY–) *n.*

tax·i (–see) *n.* **-is** [short form] taxicab. **—*v.* -is** or **-ies, -ied, -i·ing** or **-y·ing** **1** go in a taxicab. **2** of an airplane, move along the ground or on water in preparation for takeoff or after landing. **—tax·i·cab** *n.* a chauffeured automobile for hire, usu. equipped with a taximeter.

tax·i·der·my *n.* the art of stuffing and mounting the skins of animals for a lifelike look; **tax·i·der·mist** *n.*

tax·i·me·ter (–mee·tur) *n.* the fare-registering device attached to a taxicab. **—tax·i·way** *n.* any of the paved strips or lanes that aircraft use to taxi to and from the runways.

tax·on·o·my (–SON·uh·mee) *n.* biological classification of plants and animals; **tax·on·o·mist** *n.;* **tax·o·nom·ic** (–NOM–) *adj.*

tax·pay·er *n.* one who has to pay a tax. **—tax shelter** a means of reducing one's income tax, as a financial investment.

Tay·lor (TAY·lur), **Zachary.** 1784–1850, 12th U.S. President (1849–50).

TB, T.B. or **t.b.** tuberculosis. **—Tb** terbium. **—t.b.** trial balance.

T-bar lift a ski lift consisting of a motor-driven endless cable from which metal bars in the shape of an upside-down "T" are suspended for pulling up two skiers at a time. **—T-bone steak** a small beefsteak consisting of a T-shaped bone with some tenderloin.

tbs. or **tbsp.** tablespoon(s).

Tc technetium.

Tchai·kov·sky (chye·KAWF·skee), **Peter.** 1840–93, Russian composer.

Te tellurium.

tea (TEE) *n.* **1** a yellowish-brown, slightly bitter beverage made with the cured leaves of an evergreen Asiatic shrub steeped in boiling water; also, the plant or the leaves prepared for use. **2** any tealike drink made with plant leaves or roots. **3** tea and refreshments served in the afternoon; also, a reception or party; *Brit.* a late-afternoon meal at which tea is drunk. **—tea·ber·ry** (TEE·ber·ee) *n.* **-ber·ries** (the fruit of) the wintergreen.

teach (TEECH) *v.* **teach·es, taught** (TAWT), **teach·ing** help to learn (a subject, to do something, etc.); give lessons to (a class, students, etc.): *She ~es (school) for a living; That will ~ you* (to do as expected)! **teach·a·ble** *adj.;* **teach·er** *n.;* **teach·ing** *n.* a teacher's profession or practice; also, what is taught: *Christ's* **teachings; teaching machine** a device with a corrective "right"-or-"wrong" feedback for use in programmed instruction.

tea·cup (TEE–) *n.* a cup for drinking tea; **tea·cup·ful** *n.* **-fuls.**

teak (TEEK) *n.* the strong and durable yellowish-brown wood of an East Indian tree.

tea·ket·tle (TEE–) *n.* a kettle with handle and spout.

teal (TEEL) *n.* a kind of small duck, esp. the "green-winged" and "blue-winged" species of North America.

team (TEEM) *n.* a group of draft animals harnessed to the same plow; hence, a group of workers or players; ***v.*** join (individuals) together in a team; also, combine as a team: *Everyone ~ed up against him;* ***adj.:*** *~ spirit, play, teaching* (with several teachers for the same group of students). **—team·mate** *n.* a fellow member of one's team. **—team·ster** *n.* one who hauls loads with a team or truck: *The* **Teamster's Union** *includes workers ranging from truck drivers to public service employees.* **—team·work** *n.* the coordinated effort of a closely knit group.

tea·pot *n.* a pot with spout and handle for brewing and serving tea.

[1]tear (TARE) *v.* **tears, tore, torn, tear·ing** pull apart (a material) by force, leaving rough or jagged edges: *She tore the letter open; Her dress tore on a nail; a group torn by factions; felt torn between conflicting loyalties; couldn't ~ herself away from her family; Demolition crews* **tear down** *buildings; Critics mercilessly* **tore into** (i.e. attacked) *her when the book appeared.* ***—n.*** a tearing; also, a torn place or rent.

[2]tear (TEER) *n.* a drop, or **tear·drop** of the salty liquid shed by glands through the eyes, esp. when one cries; **in tears** weeping; **tear·ful** *adj.;* **tear·ful·ly** *adv.;* **tear·y** *adj.* **—tear gas** a gas used in dispersing people by irritating their eyes and causing tears to flow. **—tear-jerk·er** *n. Slang.* a highly sentimental play or motion picture.

tea·room *n.* a small restaurant serving tea, coffee, light meals, etc.

tease (TEEZ) *v.* **teas·es, teased, teas·ing** **1** worry or annoy by repeated irritating actions or remarks: *doesn't like to be ~d by his playmates; continued to ~* (i.e. beg) *her parents after being refused; likes to ~ men* (without gratifying them) *with her charms.* **2** card or comb so as to fluff (wool, flax, hair by combing it toward the scalp, etc.); also, raise a nap on (cloth) by using a teasel. ***—n.*** a teasing or one who teases. **—tea·sel** (TEE·zl) *n.* a thistlelike herb with stiff bracts surrounding its ripened flower heads, which are traditionally used to raise the nap in fulling cloth.

tea·spoon (TEE–) *n.* a small spoon such as is used to stir tea; also, a teaspoonful; **tea·spoon·ful** *n.* **-fuls** a measuring unit equal to 1/6 fl.oz. (0.4928 cl).

teat (TEET) *n.* the nipple on an udder or breast.

tea·zel or **tea·zle** (TEE–) same as TEASEL.

tech. technical(ly); technician; technology. **—tech·ne·ti·um** (tek·NEE·shee–) *n.* the first man-made element, obtained as a byproduct in atomic fission. **—tech·nic** (TEK–) *adj.* technical; ***n.*** (*also* tek·NEEK) technique. **—tech·ni·cal** *adj.* **1** having to do with the practical or skilled aspect of an art or science: *a ~ school, expert; ~ assistance to developing countries.* **2** specialized: *a ~ book; ~ language, terms.* **3** in a legal or formal sense: *a ~ difference, foul, knockout* (of a boxer judged too tired to go on fighting). **—tech·ni·cal·ly** *adv.* **—tech·ni·cal·i·ty** (–CAL–) *n.* **-ties** **1** quality or state of being technical. **2** a technical term, point, detail, etc. **—tech·ni·cian** (–NISH·un) *n.* one skilled in the techniques of a craft or occupation; a skilled craftsman. **—Tech·ni·col·or** *Trademark.* a process of making colored motion pictures; **tech·ni·col·or** *n.* vivid colors. **—tech·nique** (–NEEK) *n.* artistic skill or ability required to achieve an effect; also, a method or manner of execution. **—tech·noc·ra·cy** (–NOC·ruh·see) *n.* management by technical experts; **tech·no·crat** (TEK–) *n.;* **tech·no·crat·ic** (–CRAT–) *adj.* **—tech·nol·o·gy** (–NOL–) *n.* **-gies** science as applied to man's needs, esp. in industry; also, a technical method or process; **tech·nol·o·gist** *n.;* **tech·no·log·i·cal** (–LOJ–) *adj.;* **tech·no·log·i·cal·ly** *adv.* **—tec·ton·ics** (–TON–) *n.pl.* [with *sing.v.*] the study of the earth's crust; **tec·ton·ic** *adj.*

ted·dy (TED·ee) **bear** a stuffed toy bear.

te·di·ous (TEE·dee·us) *adj.* long and tiresome; wearisome: *~ work, processes, lecturers;* **te·di·um** *n.* the condition or quality of being tedious; boredom.

tee *n.* a small peg on which a golf ball is placed for driving; also, the small area or "teeing ground" from which play is begun at each hole of a golf course; ***v.*** **tees, teed, tee·ing** place (a ball) on a tee; **tee off** begin play; **teed off** *Slang.* fed up.

teem *v.* swarm or be full of something: *~ing with fish, mosquitoes.*

teen *n.* **1** a teenager. **2 teens** *pl.* the years or numbers from 13 to 19. —**teen-age** *adj.* **1** of people in their teens: *a ~ club.* **2** in one's teens: *a ~ daughter;* also **teen-aged.** —**teen·ag·er** *n.*

tee·ny (–nee) *adj.* **-ni·er, -ni·est** *Informal.* tiny; also **teen·sy(-ween·sy), tee·ny-wee·ny.** —**teen·y-bop·per** *n. Slang.* a teenager, esp. one following a hippie's lifestyle.

tee·pee (TEE–) *n.* same as TEPEE.

tee shirt same as T-SHIRT.

tee·ter *v.* move unsteadily; waver; also, teeter-totter; ***n.*** teeter-totter. —**tee·ter-tot·ter** *n.* & *v.* seesaw.

teeth *pl.* of TOOTH. —**teethe** (TEEDH) *v.* **teethes, teethed, teeth·ing** grow teeth, as an infant; **teething ring** a ring for infants to bite on while teething. —**teeth·ridge** *n.* the gums along the inside of the upper front teeth.

tee·to·tal·er (–TOH·tl·ur) *n.* one pledged to drink no alcoholic liquor; **tee·to·tal** *adj.;* **tee·to·tal·ism** *n.*

Tef·lon *Trademark.* a tough, heat- and corrosion-resistant plastic used in nonstick utensils, as an insulator, etc.

Te·gu·ci·gal·pa (–goo·see·GAHL·pah) capital of Honduras.

Teh·ran or **Te·her·an** (teh·HRAHN) capital of Iran.

tek·tite *n.* a tiny glassy globule of a meteoric kind.

tel telegram; telegraph; telephone.

Tel A·viv (–uh·VEEV) a seaport and the largest city of Israel.

tele- *comb.form.* afar or distant; also, television. —**tel·e·cast** (TEL·uh–) *n.* & *v.* **-casts,** *pt.* & *pp.* **-cast** or **-cast·ed, -cast·ing** broadcast by television; **tel·e·cast·er** *n.* —**tel·e·com·mu·ni·ca·tion** (–mew·nuh·CAY–) *n.* communication by radio, telephone, telegraph, etc. —**tel·e·film** *n.* a motion picture produced for television. —**teleg.** telegram; telegraph(y). —**tel·e·gen·ic** (–JEN–) *adj.* of a person, that looks attractive on television. —**tel·e·gram** *n.* a telegraphed message. —**tel·e·graph** *v.* **-graphs, -graphed, -graph·ing** send (a message) to (a person) by telegraph; ***n.*** a system or apparatus for sending messages by wire or radio using electrical impulses; **te·leg·ra·pher** (–LEG·ruh–) or **te·leg·ra·phist** *n.;* **te·leg·ra·phy** (–LEG·ruh·fee) *n.;* **tel·e·graph·ic** (–GRAF–) *adj.* —**tel·e·ki·ne·sis** (–kuh·NEE–) *n.* the moving of objects by psychic power without touching them. —**tel·e·me·ter** (TEL·uh·mee–) *n.* an apparatus for measuring and transmitting data from a distance, as used in weather balloons and spacecraft; **te·lem·e·try** (–LEM·uh·tree) *n.;* **tel·e·met·ric** (–MET–) *adj.* —**te·lep·a·thy** (–LEP·uh·thee) *n.* communication between persons by thought alone, without sensory means; **tel·e·path·ic** (–PATH–) *adj.;* **tel·e·path·i·cal·ly** *adv.* —**tel·e·phone** *v.* **-phones, -phoned, -phon·ing** speak to (someone) or communicate (a message) using the telephone; ***n.*** system or apparatus for the transmission of speech sounds over wires using electrical impulses; **tel·e·phon·ic** (–FON–) *adj.;* **te·leph·o·ny** (–LEF·uh–) *n.* —**tel·e·pho·to** (–FOH·toh) *adj.* of a camera or lens, producing a large image of a distant object; **tel·e·pho·to·graph** (–FOH–) *n.* a picture taken with a telephoto lens; also, a picture sent by wire or radio; ***v.*** take or transmit (telephotographs); **tel·e·pho·tog·ra·phy** (–TOG·ruh·fee) *n.* —**tel·e·play** *n.* a play produced for television. —**tel·e·print·er** *n.* teletypewriter. —**tel·e·prompt·er** *n.* an electronic device for giving a speaker on television a line-by-line view of his script; **TelePrompTer** *Trademark.* —**tel·e·scope** *n.* an instrument for observing distant objects, esp. celestial bodies; ***v.*** **-scopes, -scoped, -scop·ing** slide into one another like the sections of a collapsible telescope; **tel·e·scop·ic** (–SCOP–) *adj.;* **tel·e·scop·i·cal·ly** *adv.* —**tel·e·text** *n.* the broadcasting of printed information for reception on video terminals. —**tel·e·thon** *n.* a long television program for a special purpose such as to raise funds for charity. —**Tel·e·type** *Trademark.* teletypewriter; **tel·e·type** *v.* **-types, -typed, -typ·ing** send (a message) by teletypewriter; **tel·e·type·writ·er** (–TYPE·rye·tur) *n.* a form of telegraph in which messages to be sent are typed out and are reproduced by means of an automatic typewriter at the receiving end; **tel·e·typ·ist** *n.* —**tel·e·view** *v.* watch by television. —**tel·e·vise** (–vize) *v.* **-vis·es, -vised, -vis·ing** broadcast by television; **tel·e·vi·sion** (TEL·uh·vizh·un̆) *n.* the radio transmission of images by converting light signals into electrical signals and back into images on a screen at the receiving end; also, a television receiving set. —**Tel·ex** *Trademark.* a teletypewriter system operated by dialing subscribers' numbers; also **tel·ex** *n.* & *v.*

tell *v.* **tells, told, tell·ing** **1** make known in words; say or inform: *to ~ a story; ~ them the truth; a secret you're not supposed to ~* (i.e. reveal); *She's ~ing her beads; It's hard to ~ them apart* (i.e. distinguish them). **2** have a marked effect: *Every blow ~s; Inflation ~s heavily on our buying power.* —**tell off** count off (from a group); also, *Informal.* rebuke or scold. —**tell on** *Informal.* inform on. —**tell·er** *n.* **1** one who tells. **2** one who counts votes, money, etc., esp. a bank cashier who receives and pays out money. —**tell·ing** *adj.* effective; striking: *a ~ blow, argument, impression;* **tell·ing·ly** *adv.* —**tell·tale** *adj.* revealing: *a ~ blush, sign;* ***n.*** one who informs on others; tattletale.

tel·lu·ri·um (–LOOR·ee–) *n.* a metalloid element similar to selenium.

tel·ly *n. Brit. Informal.* television.

Tel·star *n.* a U.S. communications satellite, first launched in 1962, for relaying telephone calls, television programs, etc. across the Atlantic.

Tel·u·gu (–uh·goo) *n.* a Dravidian language of S.E. India or its speaker.

tem·blor *n.* an earthquake.

te·mer·i·ty (–MER–) *n.* rashness or boldness.

temp. temperature; temporary; in the time of. —**tem·per** *n.* **1** emotional nature or state of mind in regard to anger: *in a bad* ~; *a* ~ *tantrum; never loses her* ~ (i.e. calmness of mind). **2** degree of hardness, strength, and toughness given to a material such as steel or glass by a heating-and-cooling process. —**v. 1** soften or mitigate: *justice* ~*ed with mercy.* **2** bring to the proper condition, esp. of toughness: ~*ed steel; sheet of* ~*ed safety glass; Clay is* ~*ed by moistening, mixing, kneading, etc.* —**tem·per·a** (–puh·ruh) *n.* a painting method using colors mixed with egg whites, yolks, etc. instead of oil as the medium to produce an opaque effect. —**tem·per·a·ment** *n.* **1** the nature of a person as shown in his behavior, tendencies, and aspirations: *an artistic* ~; *a restless* ~. **2** an excitable or moody nature. —**tem·per·a·men·tal** (–MEN–) *adj.* —**tem·per·ance** (–unce) *n.* moderation in indulging the pleasures of the senses, esp. partial or total abstinence from alcoholic liquor. —**tem·per·ate** (–it) *adj.* **1** deliberately self-restrained: ~ *language, reply, manners.* **2** moderate in climate; neither very hot nor very cold: *California has a* ~ *climate; the* **Temperate Zones** *between the tropics and the polar circles.* **3** moderate or abstemious in regard to alcoholic drinks. —**tem·per·a·ture** (–uh·chur) *n.* degree of heat or cold: *the* ~ *of boiling water; Normal body* ~ *is 98.6°F (37°C); a patient running a* ~ (i.e. fever). —**tem·pered** (–purd) *adj.* properly conditioned: ~ *steel, clay;* ***comb. form.*** having a (specified) emotional nature: as in *hot-*~, *sweet-*~. —**tem·pest** (–pist) *n.* a violent windstorm, often with rain, snow, or hail; **tem·pes·tu·ous** (–PES·choo·us) *adj.;* **tem·pes·tu·ous·ly** *adv.*

tem·plate (–plit) *n.* a pattern, usu. a thin metal plate, from which an exact copy may be made; also, any of various guides for cutting tools, or a routing or locating device.

tem·ple *n.* **1** a building dedicated to the worship of a god or gods; also, a Jewish, Christian, or Mormon place of worship. **2** either side of the head between forehead and ear; also, the hinged arm of a spectacle frame.

tem·plet (–plit) *n.* same as TEMPLATE.

tem·po (–poh) *n., pl.* **-pi** (–pee) or **-pos 1** *Music.* (characteristic) speed of movement. **2** pace of activity: *the fast* ~ *of city life.* —**tem·po·ral** (–puh·rul) *adj.* **1** of earthly life, not eternal or spiritual; secular or worldly: *man's* ~ *affairs.* **2** of the temples of the head: *the* ~ *bones.* —**tem·po·rar·y** *adj.* lasting only for a time; not permanent: *a* ~ *appointment;* ~ *quarters;* **tem·po·rar·i·ly** (–RAIR–, –rer–) *adv.* —**tem·po·rize** *v.* **-riz·es, -rized, -riz·ing** delay a decision or answer so as to gain time; **tem·po·riz·er** *n.*

tempt *v.* entice or try to make (a person) do something not necessarily good for him: *felt* ~*ed to accept it; Daredevils like to* ~ (i.e. risk or defy) *fate;* **temp·ta·tion** (–TAY–) *n.;* **tempt·er** *n.;* **tempt·ing** *adj.: a very* ~ *offer;* **tempt·ress** (–tris) *n. fem.*

tem·pu·ra (TEM·puh·rah, –POOR·uh) *n.* a Japanese dish of fish or vegetables fried in batter.

ten *n., adj. & pron.* one more than nine; 10 or X.

ten·a·ble (–uh·bl) *adj.* that can be held or defended, as against attack: *a* ~ *theory, position;* **ten·a·bil·i·ty** (–BIL–) *n.* —**te·na·cious** (–NAY–) *adj.* firmly holding, clinging, etc.; hence, stubborn or resolute: *a* ~ *grip, memory, glue:* ~ *of his rights;* ~ *courage; a* ~ *salesman;* **te·na·cious·ly** *adv.;* **te·nac·i·ty** (–NAS–) *n.* —**ten·an·cy** (TEN·un·see) *n.* **-cies** (the period of) occupancy of a tenant. —**ten·ant** (–unt) *n.* one paying rent to a landlord for the occupancy and use of land or a building; hence, an occupant: *Sharecropping is a form of* **tenant farming.** —**v.** occupy as a tenant: *rooms* ~*ed by students.* —**ten·ant·ry** *n.* **-ries** group of tenants.

Ten Commandments in the Bible, ten moral and religious rules given to Moses by God.

tend *v.* **1** incline or have a tendency (to): *Old people* ~ *to forget things; leftist views* ~*ing toward Communism; The road* ~*s east from there.* **2** attend to; take care of: *Shepherds* ~ *sheep; someone to* ~ *the store.* —**tend·en·cy** *n.* **-cies** a natural inclination or disposition; leaning: *a* ~ *to fall asleep; the upward* ~ *of prices.* —**ten·den·tious** (–DEN·shus) *adj.* one-sided or biased: *a* ~ *statement, report;* ~ *writings;* **ten·den·tious·ly** *adv.;* **ten·den·tious·ness** *n.*

ten·der *n.* **1** one that attends to or serves, as a boat or small ship attending a larger vessel to carry supplies and passengers or the car attached to a locomotive to carry a supply of coal or water. **2** a formal offer, proposal, or bid: *a* ~ *of marriage; sealed* ~*s for a contract; legal* ~ (i.e. money); **v.** present: *to* ~ *one's resignation, apologies, thanks.* —***adj.*** soft or delicate: *the* ~ *loving care of parents; a* ~ *heart, wound, conscience, subject; at a* ~ (i.e. early) *age;* **ten·der·ly** *adv.;* **ten·der·ness** *n.* —**ten·der·foot** *n.* **-foots** or **-feet** a newcomer to a life of hardship, as in pioneer country; also, a novice scout. —**ten·der·heart·ed** *adj.* easily moved to pity or compassion. —**ten·der·ize** *v.* **-iz·es, -ized, -iz·ing** make (meat) tender by pounding or by using enzymes; **ten·der·iz·er** *n.* —**ten·der·loin** *n.* a tender part of a loin of beef or pork; **Tenderloin** the district of a city noted for vice and corruption. —**ten·der·om·e·ter** (–ROM–) *n.* an instrument for measuring the tenderness of foods. —**ten·don** (–dun) *n.* a strong, fibrous band or cord attaching muscles to bones or cartilages: *the* ~ *of Achilles;* **ten·di·**

nous (–nus) *adj.* **—ten·dril** *n.* the threadlike clinging organ of a climbing plant.

ten·e·ment *n.* a dwelling house, esp. one divided into units for several families; hence, a living unit or apartment; **tenement house** an overcrowded and run-down dwelling, as in the slums. **—ten·et** (–it) *n.* a doctrine or belief held in common by a group or profession: *Anglican ~s; the ~s of socialism.*

ten·fold *adj.* & *adv.* ten times. **—ten-gal·lon hat** the wide-brimmed, soft-crowned cowboy hat.

10-4 (TEN·for) in radio communications, "OK"; "message received."

Tenn. *Abbrev.* for **Ten·nes·see** (ten·uh·SEE) an east-central state of the U.S.; 42,244 sq.mi. (109,411 km²); *cap.* Nashville; **Ten·nes·se·an** (–SEE–) *n.* & *adj.*

ten·nis *n.* a game played between two or two pairs of players on a rectangular court divided by a net using rackets to hit a pressurized ball back and forth; **tennis shoe** a sneaker.

Ten·ny·son (TEN·uh·sn), **Alfred.** 1809–92, English poet.

ten·on (–un) *n.* the shaped projecting end of a piece of wood that fits into the hollow of another to make a "mortise joint." **—ten·or** (–ur) *n.* **1** the general direction or tendency; drift: *the ~ of a conversation; Nothing disturbs the even ~ of her life.* **2** the highest regular adult male voice; also, a part for or a singer with such a voice, an instrument with a tenor range, etc.

ten·pen·ny *adj.* worth 10 British pennies; **tenpenny nail** a nail 3 in. (7.62 cm) long. **—ten·pin** *n.* a bottle-shaped bowling pin, as used in the commonest form of bowling, or **ten·pins.**

tense *n.* the form of a verb showing time: *past, present, and future ~s.* **—*adj.* tens·er, tens·est** **1** stretched tight; taut: *a ~ muscle, rope.* **2** showing or feeling nervous tension; hence, anxious: *~ nerves; a ~ atmosphere, moment.* **—*v.* tens·es, tensed, tens·ing** make or become tense. **—tense·ly** *adv.;* **tense·ness** or **ten·si·ty** *n.* **—ten·sile** (–sl, –sile) *adj.* of or having to do with tension: *Steel has the greatest* **tensile strength** (i.e. breaking limit). **—ten·sion** *n.* **1** a stretched or strained condition; hence, stress: *the ~ of a violin string; Chewing gum helps relieve (nervous) ~; a hostile meeting in an atmosphere of ~.* **2** gas pressure; also, voltage: *a high-~ wire.*

tent *n.* **1** a light, portable shelter made usu. of canvas stretched over supporting poles, as used when camping; also, a tepee or wigwam. **2** a tentlike canopy such as an *oxygen tent.* **—*v.*** live in, cover with, or lodge in a tent.

ten·ta·cle (–tuh·cl) *n.* a slender flexible arm of an animal used for capturing food, as in anemones and octopuses, used as feelers, as in mollusks, or for protection, as in the jellyfish. **—ten·ta·tive** (–tuh·tiv) *adj.* done or made as a trial or first step; provisional: *a ~ plan, proposal, refusal, acceptance; a ~* (i.e. hesitant) *smile;* **ten·ta·tive·ly** *adv.*

ten·ter·hook *n.* **on tenterhooks** in a state of anxious suspense.

tenth *adj.* next after the ninth; ***n.*** a tenth person or thing; also, a 1/10 part, as of a gallon.

ten·u·ous (–yoo·us) *adj.* extremely thin or fine: *the ~ spider web; a ~ fabric, distinction, the ~* (i.e. rare) *mountain air; a ~* (i.e. flimsy or weak) *claim;* **ten·u·ous·ly** *adv.;* **ten·u·ous·ness** *n.*

ten·ure (–yur) *n.* the act, right, period, or manner of holding an office or position; **ten·ured** *adj.* having permanent tenure: *a ~ position, professor.*

te·o·sin·te (tee·uh·SIN·tee) *n.* a cornlike fodder grass native to Central America.

te·pee (TEE–) *n.* the cone-shaped tent used by Plains Indians.

tep·id *adj.* lukewarm; hence, lacking fervor or enthusiasm; **te·pid·i·ty** (–PID–) *n.*

te·qui·la (–KEE·luh) *n.* a Mexican liquor distilled from the juice of an agave plant.

ter. terrace; territory.

ter·bi·um *n.* a rare-earth chemical element.

ter·cen·te·nar·y (–TEN·uh·ree, –SEN·tuh–) *adj.* & *n.* **-nar·ies** a 300th anniversary (celebration); also **ter·cen·ten·ni·al** (–TEN–).

te·re·do (–REE·doh) *n.* **-dos** a shipworm.

term *n.* **1** a word or expression with a definite function or precise meaning: *a legal ~ such as "escrow"; "nigger," "honkie" and such opprobrious ~s; spoke in flattering* **terms;** *the three algebraic ~s in "$x^2 + y^2 + 2xy$";* **in terms of** as regards; concerning. **2** a set or fixed period: *a four-year ~ of office; the ~ of a lease; a school ~; born at full ~* (of childbearing). **3 terms** *pl.* conditions of agreement: *the ~s of a treaty, lease, contract; They're not on speaking ~s* (i.e. relations); *Let us* **come to terms** *or they'll* **bring** (i.e. force) *us* **to terms. —*v.*** name or call by a term: *Ethelred, ~ed "the unready."*

ter·ma·gant (–muh·gunt) *n.* & *adj.* quarrelsome or scolding (woman).

ter·mi·na·ble (–nuh·bl) *adj.* that can be terminated. **—ter·mi·nal** (–muh·nl) *adj.* **1** having to do with (the end of) a fixed period or term: *~ examinations, accounts.* **2** having to do with an end part or final stage: *~ buds;* **terminal leave** *before discharge from the army; a ~ outpost; a ~ illness* (ending in death). **—*n.*** **1** an end or extremity of a transportation or communication line: *the keyboard of a computer ~; a bus ~* (i.e. station); *the observation deck of an air ~.* **2** a point of electrical connection: *battery ~s.* **—ter·mi·nal·ly** *adv.* **—ter·mi·nate** *v.* **-nates, -nat·ed, -nat·ing** put or come to an end: *to ~ a job, employee, partnership, pregnancy* (by abortion); *plurals ~ing in "-es";* **ter·mi·na·ble** *adj.;* **term·mi·na·tion** (–NAY–) *n.* **—ter·mi·nol·o·gy** (–NOL–) *n.* **-gies** (system of) terms used in a branch of study or line of work: *legal ~;* **ter·mi·no·log·i·cal** (–LOJ–)

adj. **—term insurance** life insurance providing temporary protection for a specified period. **—ter·mi·nus** (–muh–) *n., pl.* **-ni** (–nye) or **-nus·es** the final point or place where something terminates: *the ~ of a pipeline, railroad, busline.*

ter·mite *n.* an antlike social insect that is very destructive to wooden structures.

tern *n.* a sea bird of the gull family but smaller and with a long forked tail.

ter·nar·y (–nuh·ree) *adj.* triple or threefold: *~ steel alloy; a ~ system* (of three components).

terp·si·cho·re·an (–suh·cuh·REE·un) *adj.* having to do with dancing.

terr. terrace; territory. **—ter·race** (–is) *n.* **1** an open courtyard adjoining a house, sometimes overlooking a garden. **2** the flat roof of an Oriental or Spanish house. **3** one of a series of levels bounded by ridges made on sloping land for irrigation and to prevent erosion. **4** a row of houses along a slope above street level. **—v. ter·rac·es, ter·raced, ter·rac·ing** form into terraces or make terraces in: *~d cultivation of hillsides.* **—ter·ra cot·ta** (TER·uh·COT·uh) a hard, durable, high-quality clay or earthenware or a figure made with it. **—terra fir·ma** (–FIR·muh) solid ground. **—ter·rain** (tuh·RAIN, TER–) *n.* a stretch of land with regard to its natural features or fitness for a use such as warfare. **—terra in·cog·ni·ta** (–COG·nuh·tuh, –NEE·tuh), *pl.* **ter·rae** (–ee) **in·cog·ni·tae** (–tee) unexplored territory.

ter·ra·pin (TER·uh–) *n.* a North American turtle, esp. the "diamondback terrapin."

ter·rar·i·um (–RAIR·ee–) *n.* **-i·ums** or **-i·a** (–ee·uh) an indoor miniature garden in a covered glass container. **—ter·raz·zo** (tuh·RAZ·oh, –RAHT·soh) *n.* a mosaic flooring of marble chips set in cement. **—ter·res·tri·al** (–RES·tree·ul) *adj.* **1** of the earth, not celestial: *our ~ globe; ~ magnetism; ~ rocket guidance system; Mercury, Venus, and Mars are ~ planets (like the earth).* **2** of the ground or land: *sediments of ~ origin* (i.e. not from the air or water); *a ~* (i.e. not arboreal) *animal; ~* (i.e. not aerial or aquatic) *plants.*

ter·ri·ble (TER·uh–) *adj.* **1** causing terror or extreme fear: *a ~ crime; ~* (i.e. extreme) *anxiety.* **2** *Informal.* extremely bad: *a ~ dinner, joke.* **—ter·ri·bly** *adv.*

ter·ri·er (–ee·ur) *n.* a breed of usu. small, active watchdogs, originally used to drive game out of burrows in the ground.

ter·rif·ic (tuh·RIF–) *adj.* **1** causing great fear; terrifying. **2** *Informal.* extraordinary; astounding: *a ~ speed, achievement; a ~* (i.e. magnificent) *view.* **—ter·ri·fy** (–fye) *v.* **-fies, -fied, -fy·ing** fill with terror; frighten overwhelmingly; **ter·ri·fy·ing** *adj.;* **ter·ri·fy·ing·ly** *adv.*

ter·ri·to·ri·al (–TOR–) *adj.* having to do with territory or a particular area: *a country's ~ ambitions; ~ government; a nation's rights over its* **territorial waters** (i.e. off its coast but not high seas). **—ter·ri·to·ry** (TER·uh–) *n.* **-ries** an area or region in regard to jurisdiction or control over it: *A ~ has less self-government than a province or state; India used to be British ~; Most animals defend their ~ aggressively; a ~ assigned to a door-to-door salesman; Religion is outside the ~ of science.*

ter·ror (TER·ur) *n.* great fear or the cause of it: *The murders struck ~ into their hearts; the reign of ~ during the French Revolution; ~ tactics of guerrillas; That child is a ~* (*Informal.* nuisance) *to his parents.* **—ter·ror·ism** *n.* the policy of using killings, bombings, kidnapings, etc. as a political means by repressive governments, guerrillas, etc.; **ter·ror·ist** *n.* & *adj.* **—ter·ror·ize** *v.* **-iz·es, -ized, -iz·ing** terrify, esp. as a means of coercion: *a people ~d into submission.*

ter·ry *n.* a cotton cloth with a pile of uncut loops for absorbency, as used for towels, sweaters, etc.; also **terry cloth.**

terse *adj.* **ters·er, ters·est** concise and elegant in expression: *a ~ statement, style, writer;* **terse·ly** *adv.;* **terse·ness** *n.*

ter·ti·ar·y (TUR·shee·er·ee, –shuh·ree) *adj.* **1** third; following secondary: *a ~ order of monks, nuns, and lay people; a ~ color* (got by mixing secondary colors). **2 Tertiary** of the earlier of the two periods of the Cenozoic era of the earth; ***n.*** the Tertiary period.

tes·sel·late (TES·uh–) *v.* **-lates, -lat·ed, -lat·ing** pave in a checkered pattern of small squares: *a ~d floor, pavement;* **tes·sel·la·tion** (–LAY–) *n.*

Test. Testament. **—test.** testator; testimony.

test *n.* an examination or trial for comparison with a standard: *a ~ of intelligence; a driving ~; a blood ~ for sugar; tabulation of ~s* (i.e. results); ***v.*** put to test; also, score or rate on tests; **test·er** *n.*

tes·ta·ment (TES·tuh–) *n.* **1** either part of the Bible, the Old Testament or the New Testament. **2** a statement of beliefs. **3** *Law.* a will disposing of one's property. **—tes·ta·men·ta·ry** (–MEN–) *adj.* **—tes·tate** *n.* & *adj.* (one) who has left a valid will; **tes·ta·cy** *n.;* **tes·ta·tor** (–tay–) *n.* the maker of a will; *fem.* **tes·ta·trix** (–TAY–). **—tes·ti·cle** *n.* either of the pair of sperm-producing glands in male mammals. **—tes·ti·fy** *v.* **-fies, -fied, -fy·ing** bear witness (to); also, serve as evidence of: *facts ~ing to his honesty.* **—tes·ti·mo·ni·al** (–MOH·nee·ul) *n.* a letter of recommendation or appreciation; also, a dinner, gift, or other tribute in honor of someone. **—tes·ti·mo·ny** *n.* **-nies** **1** statement made in court by a witness under oath. **2** evidence or proof. **—tes·tis** *n., pl.* **-tes** (–teez) same as TESTICLE. **—tes·tos·ter·one** (–TOS·tuh·rohn) *n.* a male sex hormone.

test tube a glass container in the shape of a tube closed at one end for use in experiments:

a **test-tube baby** *born in 1978 from an ovum fertilized in a laboratory vessel called "Petri dish" in Oldham, England.* **—tes·ty** *adj.* **-ti·er, -ti·est** irritable; quickly angered; **tes·ti·ly** *adv.*

tet·a·nus (TETN·us) *n.* an infectious disease characterized by stiffening of the voluntary muscles, esp. lockjaw; **tet·a·nal** or **te·tan·ic** (–TAN–) *adj.*

tetch·y *adj.* **tetch·i·er, -i·est** irritable or peevish.

tête-à-tête (TAIT·uh·tait) *n.* a close private talk between two people; ***adj.*** & ***adv.*** (in) private.

teth·er *n.* a line by which an animal is tied so as to restrict its range of movement; **at the end of one's tether** at the limit of one's endurance. **—*v.*** fasten with a tether.

tetra- *comb.form.* four. **—tet·ra·cy·cline** (TET·ruh·sye·clin) *n.* any of a group of antibiotics effective against many bacteria, some viruses, and rickettsial germs. **—tet·ra·eth·yl** (tet·ruh·ETH·ul) **lead** an antiknock added to gasoline. **—tet·ra·he·dron** (–HEE·drun) *n.* a solid figure with four triangular faces; **tet·ra·he·dral** *adj.* **—te·tram·e·ter** (–TRAM·uh–) *n.* a line of verse with four feet or measures.

Teut. Teuton(ic). **—Teu·ton·ic** (tew·TON–) *adj.* Germanic; **Teu·ton** (TEW·tn) *n.* one speaking German or a Germanic language.

Tex. *Abbrev.* for **Tex·as** (–us) a S.W. state of the U.S.; 267,338 sq.mi. (692,402 km²); *cap.* Austin; **Tex·an** (–un) *n.* & *adj.*

text *n.* **1** the main body of a work or the original words of an author, as distinguished from notes, illustrations, appendices, etc.: *reconstructing the ~ of the Bible; a ~ corrupted by copyists.* **2** a topic or subject: *The preacher chose for his ~ "Blessed are the meek."* **3** a textbook: *your history ~.* **—tex·tu·al** (–choo·ul) *adj.* **—text·book** *n.* a standard or authoritative book for the study of a subject. **—tex·tile** *adj.* having to do with fabrics and fibers; also, woven: *~ industries, fabrics;* ***n.*** a cloth or fabric, esp. woven or knit; also, textile material such as fiber and yarn. **—tex·ture** (–chur) *n.* a woven, hence surface characteristic, as given by the arrangement and size of threads, esp. as can be seen and felt: *Burlap has a coarse ~, not fine; the granular ~ of igneous rocks; Brick imparts ~ to an interior; the (surface) ~ of a poem, painting, society;* **tex·tur·al** *adj.;* **tex·tured** *adj.: a ~, not plain surface; ~ vegetable protein spun from soybean fibers and made to look like beef, ham, etc.*

T-group *n.* a sensitivity-training group.

Th. Thursday; **Th** thorium. **—-th** *suffix.* **1** contracted form of -ETH. **2** forming ordinal numbers: as in *sixth, fiftieth.*

Thai (TYE) *n.* the Sino-Tibetan language of Thailand; also, a Thai speaker; ***adj.*** of Thailand or its people. **—Thai·land** (TYE–) a country of S.E. Asia; 198,457 sq.mi. (514,000 km²); *cap.* Bangkok.

thal·a·mus (THAL·uh–) *n., pl.* **-mi** (–mye) the coordinating and distribution center of sensations in the forepart of the brain.

tha·lid·o·mide (thuh·LID·uh–) *n.* a sedative drug used in the 1960's and found to cause deformities of the fetus if taken in early pregnancy.

thal·li·um *n.* a soft, white, poisonous metallic element. **—thal·lo·phyte** (THAL·uh·fite) *n.* a simple plant such as an alga, fungus, or bacterium that has no roots, stems, or leaves.

Thames (TEMZ) a river of S. England flowing through London into the North Sea.

than *conj.* [used to introduce the second term of a comparison]: *Jack is taller ~ Jill; would rather fight ~ argue; none other ~ his wife; She's shorter ~ him (Informal.* he is).

thane *n.* an Anglo-Saxon lord's retainer or knight.

thank *v.* express gratitude to: *(I) ~ you for your kindness; has only himself to ~* (i.e. blame) *for his misfortune;* **thank·ful** *adj.* grateful; also, glad; **thank·ful·ly** *adv.;* **thank·less** *adj.* ungrateful; also, unappreciated; **thank·less·ly** *adv.* **—thanks** *n.pl.* (expression of) gratitude: *Our sincere ~; (It's)* **thanks to** (i.e. because of) *her seatbelt she was saved;* ***interj.*** *thank you!;* **thanks·giv·ing** (–GIV–) *n.* formal expression of gratitude, esp. to God, as on the annual **Thanksgiving** holiday in the U.S. (4th Thursday in November) and Canada (2nd Monday in October), originally a fall harvest festival.

that (DHAT) *pron.* **1** *pl.* **those** (DHOZE) a person or thing already mentioned or implied, esp. as farther from the speaker than another, or this: *Do you like this color or ~? ~ is my friend;* ***adj.:*** *~ boy; those girls;* **at that** *Informal.* even so; **in that** because; **that is** repeating; in other words. **2** [used as a relative pronoun] who; whom; which: *the house ~ Jack built.* **—*conj.:*** *He's happy ~ he's won; ~ he's bald is obvious; Oh,* (I wish) *~ it were spring!* **—*adv.*** to that extent: *He's ~ happy he's crying.*

thatch *n.* **1** material such as straw or leaves for roofing; also, a roof covered with thatch. **2** *Informal.* head hair. **—*v.*** cover as with thatch.

thaw *v.* **1** of frozen things, (cause) to become warmer so as to melt: *It's ~ing, not raining outside; Do not refreeze a ~ed TV dinner.* **2** of people or their manner, become less cold. **—*n.:*** *A ~ is forecast; spring ~.*

T.H.C. the intoxicant chemical in hashish, "*t*etra*h*ydro*c*annabinol."

Th.D. Doctor of Theology.

the (dhuh; *before vowels:* dhee) *def. art.* **1** [referring to a certain person or things]: *~ man I meant; went in ~ house.* **2** [referring to a unique person or thing]: *He was ~ greatest; ~ sun and ~ moon; ~ top of your head; ~ United States; ~ definite article.* **3** [referring to a whole class or something generalized as representative of a class]: *our neighbors, ~ Smiths;*

~ grammatical articles; ~ rich and ~ poor; ~ good and ~ true; in bed with (~) flu; to play ~ piano; 10 miles to ~ gallon. **—adv.** [used with comparatives] in that degree: *Start early ~ more surely to catch your plane; ~* (i.e. in what degree) *earlier ~ better.*

the·a·ter or **the·a·tre** (THEE·uh·tur) *n.* **1** a building or place with rows of seats for viewing a play, motion picture, or other dramatic performance or action: *a lecture ~; an operation ~; a ~ of operations* (i.e. scene of battle) *during the war.* **2** drama: *Greek ~; "Hamlet" is good ~.* **—the·a·ter-in-the-round** same as ARENA THEATER. **—the·at·ri·cal** (thee·AT–) *adj.* **1** having to do with the theater or drama: *a ~ effect, company.* **2** showy; affected; also, melodramatic: *a ~ manner, behavior, style.* Hence **the·at·ri·cals** (–AT–) *n.pl.* amateur performances; also, dramatics. **—the·at·ri·cal·ly** *adv.* **—the·at·rics** *n.pl.* [takes *sing.* or *pl. v.*] the art of the theater; also, histrionics.

thee See THOU.

theft *n.* stealing or an instance of it.

their (DHAIR) *adj. possessive of* THEY; of or by them: *~ houses, actions.* **—theirs** (DHAIRZ) *pron.* their one(s): *The child is ~.*

the·ism (THEE–) *n.* belief in God, a god, or gods; **the·ist** *n.;* **the·is·tic** (–IS–) *adj.*

them (DHEM) *pron.* **1** *obj. case* of THEY: *He loves ~.* **2** *Nonstandard.* those: *~ hills; in ~ houses.*

theme (THEEM) *n.* **1** a topic or subject; also, a short essay. **2** a recurrent melody, as elaborated in a composition; also, a **theme song,** an identifying melody or signature, as at the opening of a television feature or one repeated throughout a motion picture; **the·mat·ic** (–MAT–) *adj.;* **the·mat·i·cal·ly** *adv.*

them·selves (dhem·SELVZ) *pron.* emphatic or reflexive of THEY, THEM: *They ~ did it; talking among ~.*

then (DHEN) *adv.* **1** at that time: *She wasn't born ~; the ~ reigning queen; He paid up* **then and there;** ***n.*** that time: *by ~; since ~;* ***adj.:*** *the ~ queen of England.* **2** after that: *I shaved, ~ I showered; Now it's my turn, ~ yours; the man, his wife, and ~ the children.* **3** in that case; therefore: *If you don't pay, ~ you can't have it;* **but then** (i.e. but on the other hand) *where's the money?* **—thence** (DHENCE) *adv.* from that; from there; from then: *a few yards ~; a few months ~; ~* (i.e. therefore) *it follows that. . . .* **—thence·forth** *adv.* from then on; also **thence·for·ward(s).**

the·oc·ra·cy (thee·OC·ruh·see) *n.* **-cies** a state based on religious authority; government by priests, as of the Israelites; **the·o·crat·ic** (–CRAT–) *adj.* **—the·o·lo·gian** (thee·uh·LOH·jun) *n.* a specialist in theology; **the·ol·o·gy** (–OL–) *n.* **-gies** **1** study of God or religion. **2** a system of beliefs about God. **—the·o·log·i·cal** (–LOJ–) *adj.*

the·o·rem (THEE·uh–) *n.* a statement or proposition that can be proved from axioms or postulates; hence, an established principle. **—the·o·ret·i·cal** (–RET–) *adj.* based on theory; hence, not based on fact; not practical; also **the·o·ret·ic; the·o·ret·i·cal·ly** *adv.* **—the·o·rize** (THEE·uh–) *v.* **-riz·es, -rized, -riz·ing** form a theory; speculate; **the·o·rist** or **the·o·re·ti·cian** (–TISH·un) *n.* **—the·o·ry** (THEE·uh·ree, THEER·ee) *n.* **-ries** **1** the principles of an art or science, as opposed to practice: *teaches musical ~.* **2** a reasoned-out and tested explanation of facts or phenomena: *the ~ of evolution.* **3** an opinion based on conjecture or speculation; guess: *~s about the assassination.* **—theory of games** same as GAME THEORY.

the·os·o·phy (thee·OS·uh·fee) *n.* **-phies** a religious system based on supposed mystical insight into the nature of God and the universe rather than on reason or sense experience; **the·os·o·phist** *n.;* **the·o·soph·ic** (–SOF–) or **-i·cal** *adj.;* **the·o·soph·i·cal·ly** *adv.*

ther·a·peu·tic (–uh·PEW–) *adj.* having to do with curing illness or preserving health: *Drugs are ~ agents; a ~ bath, abortion* (for saving the mother); **ther·a·peu·ti·cal·ly** *adv.* **—ther·a·peu·tics** *n.pl.* [takes *sing. v.*] branch of medicine dealing with the treatment of disease; **ther·a·py** *n.* **-pies** treatment of disease: *physical, occupational, group, shock ~;* **ther·a·pist** *n.*

there (DHAIR) *adv.* **1** at, in, or to that place: *He's ~, not here; went ~ yesterday;* ***n.*** that place: *He's in ~.* **2** in that matter: *We agree with you ~.* **3** [used impersonally with *be, seem, appear,* etc.]: *~ is no time left; ~ seems to be a way out; ~ were many reasons.* **—interj.:** *~, now! I told you so; ~, ~! Don't cry.* **—there·a·bouts** (DHAIR·uh) *adv.* near that place, time, amount, etc.: *$2,000 or ~; in Chicago or ~;* also **there·a·bout. —there·af·ter** (–AF–) *adv.* afterward; after that. **—there·at** (–AT) *adv. Archaic.* at that place or time; hence, because of that. **—there·by** (–BY) *adv.* by that means or in that way; also, by that place or in that connection: *~ hangs a tale.* **—there·for** (–FOR) *adv.* for that (purpose); **there·fore** (DHAIR·for) *adv.* for that reason; hence. **—there·from** (–FRUM) *adv.* from that. **—there·in** (–IN) *adv. Formal.* in (to) that place; also, in that respect. **—there·of** (–OV) *adv. Formal.* of that or from that. **—there·on** (–ON) *adv. Archaic.* on that; also, thereupon. **—there·to** (–TOO) *adv. Formal.* to that place or thing; also **there·un·to** (–UN·too) *adv.* **—there·to·fore** *adv. Formal.* before that time. **—there·up·on** (–ON) *adv.* **1** immediately after that; also, because of that. **2** *Archaic.* upon that (subject). **—there·with** (–WIDH) *adv.* along with that; also, *Archaic.* then. **—there·with·al** (–awl) *adv. Archaic.* besides.

therm(o)- *comb.form.* heat; temperature: as in *thermometer, thermostat.* **—ther·mal** (THUR·

mul) *adj.* having to do with heat: ~ *air currents, springs, underwear* (made of specially knit insulating material); **thermal pollution** pollution of a lake or river by discharge of heated industrial water that kills animal and plant life. **—therm·is·tor** *n.* an electronic resistor whose resistance varies with temperature, used esp. to measure temperature differences. **—ther·mo·dy·nam·ics** (–NAM–) *n.pl.* [takes *sing. v.*] a branch of physics that studies heat energy and its conservation; **ther·mo·dy·nam·ic** *adj.;* **ther·mo·dy·nam·i·cal·ly** *adv.* **—ther·mom·e·ter** (–MOM–) *n.* an instrument for measuring temperature, usu. by observing the expansion or contraction of mercury or alcohol in a graduated glass tube; **ther·mo·met·ric** (–MET–) *adj.;* **ther·mo·met·ri·cal·ly** *adv.* **—ther·mo·nu·cle·ar** (–NEW·clee·ur) *adj.* having to do with the fusion of atoms at very high temperatures and the release of nuclear energy, as in the hydrogen bomb: *a* ~ *bomb, reaction, reactor, war* (using thermonuclear weapons). **—ther·mo·plas·tic** (–PLAS–) *adj.* that can be heated and molded again after cooling and hardening, as nylon, polystyrene, and other plastics; ***n.*** such a plastic; **ther·mo·plas·tic·i·ty** (–TIS–) *n.* **—ther·mos** (THUR–) *n.* a vacuum bottle. **—ther·mo·sphere** *n.* the uppermost region of the atmosphere from about 50 mi. (80 km) to about 280 mi. (450 km); **ther·mo·spher·ic** (–SFEER–, –SFER–) *adj.* **—ther·mo·stat** *n.* an automatic device for regulating temperature in heating and cooling systems, as in a stove or air conditioner; **ther·mo·stat·ic** (–STAT–) *adj.;* **ther·mo·stat·i·cal·ly** *adv.*

the·sau·rus (thi·SOR–) *n., pl.* **-ri** (–rye) or **-rus·es** a dictionary of synonyms and antonyms; also, a treasury or collection of information.

these *pl.* of THIS.

The·seus (THEE·soos, –see·us) in Greek myth, a great king of Athens who killed the Minotaur.

the·sis (THEE–) *n., pl.* **-ses** (–seez) **1** a proposition put forward for exposition and defense. **2** a research paper prepared by a candidate for an academic degree.

Thes·pi·an (THES·pee·un) *adj.* having to do with the dramatic art; ***n.*** an actor or actress. Also **thespian.**

the·ta (THAY·tuh, THEE–) *n.* the 8th letter of the Greek alphabet (Θ, θ).

thews *n.pl.* sinews or muscles.

they (DHAY) *pron., pl.* of HE, SHE, or IT; *objective* THEM, *possessive* THEIR(S). **1** the persons, animals, or things previously mentioned or referred to. **2** *Informal.* people in general: ~ *say prices will come down.* **—they'd** (DHAID) they had; then would. **—they'll** (DHAIL) they will; they shall. **—they're** (DHAIR) they are. **—they've** (DHAVE) they have.

thi·a·mine (THIGH·uh·meen, –min) *n.* a vitamin of the B complex found in whole-grain cereals whose lack in diet causes beriberi; also **thiamin** (–min).

thick *adj.* **1** with relatively much space between opposite sides or surfaces; not thin: *a* ~ *slice, sheet, wall;* ~ *skin, rope, fingers; an inch* ~ (as measured between opposite surfaces). **2** crowded or closely set; dense; firm or stiff in consistency: *a* ~ *growth, smoke, soup;* ~ (*Informal.* intimate) *friends.* **3** not clear: ~ *weather, gloom, voice; a* ~ (i.e. stupid) *head.* **4** *Informal.* too much to endure. ***—adv.*** thickly; **lay it on thick** *Slang.* praise or blame too much. ***—n.*** thickest or hardest part; **through thick and thin** through good times and bad. **—thick·ly** *adv.;* **thick·ness** *n.* **—thick·en** *v.* make or become thick(er); **thick·en·ing** *n.* **—thick·et** (–it) *n.* a dense growth of shrubs or small trees. **—thick·set** *adj.* **1** having a thick body; stocky. **2** thickly or closely planted: *a* ~ *hedge.* **—thick-skinned** *adj.* having a thick skin; hence, not easily offended by criticism, insults, etc.

thief (THEEF) *n.* **thieves** (THEEVZ) one who steals in a secret and nonviolent manner. **—thieve** (THEEV) *v.* **thieves, thieved, thiev·ing** be a thief or steal (something); **thiev·ish** *adj.* **—thiev·er·y** *n.* **-er·ies** the practice of stealing; also, a theft.

thigh (THYE) *n.* the part of the leg between the knee and the hip; **thigh·bone** *n.* the bone of the thigh; femur.

thim·ble *n.* a small cap used while sewing to protect the finger that pushes the needle; **thim·ble·ful** *n.*

Thim·phu (–poo) capital of Bhutan; also **Thimbu.**

thin *adj.* **thin·ner, thin·nest** **1** with relatively little space between opposite sides or surfaces; not thick: *a* ~ *sheet, wire; a* ~ *wall only a few inches thick.* **2** having little flesh or fat; not dense, crowded, or substantial: ~ *build, hair, mist,* ~ *mountain air.* **3** weak; not strong: *a* ~ *soup, blood; a* ~ (i.e. flimsy) *excuse, disguise; a* ~ *voice.* ***—v.*** **thins, thinned, thin·ning** make or become thin(ner): *His hair is* ~*ing on top; its strength* ~*d down with water; Emigration* ~*s out a population.* **—thin·ly** *adv.;* **thin·ness** *n.*

thine (DHINE) *pron.* & *adj. Archaic. possessive of* THOU; your(s): ~ *eyes;* ~ *is the kingdom.*

thing *n.* **1** any object, matter, circumstance, opinion, etc.: *the* ~ *called soul; the proper* ~ *to say; the latest* ~ *in sleepwear; a box full of sewing* ~*s; attends to* ~*s of the soul on Sunday. Do your own* ~ (*Informal.* what interests you). **2** a creature; also, a person considered with pity, affection, contempt, etc.: *poor little* ~*; miserable* ~. **3** *Informal.* an irrational fear or prejudice: *has a* ~ *about spilling salt.* **—see things** have hallucinations.

think (THINGK) *v.* **thinks, thought** (THAWT), **think·ing** use the mind to form images and ideas, consider things, have opinions, hopes, judgments, etc.: *He's ~ing about taking the job; ~s himself qualified; ~s of her with high regard; was rebuffed when he thought to help her; likes to* **think aloud** (i.e. utter his thoughts) *when alone; will* **think twice** (i.e. consider carefully) *before making the same mistake; had to* **think up** *an excuse for his absence;* **think•er** *n.* —**think tank** an organization for studying the problems of governments and societies and proposing solutions and policies; also **think factory.**

thin•ner *adj. comp.* of THIN. —***n.*** a liquid, esp. a volatile one such as turpentine, used to thin paints, etc. —**thin-skinned** *adj.* having a thin skin; hence, sensitive to criticism, etc.

thi•o•pen•tal (thigh·oh·PEN–) **sodium** same as SODIUM PENTOTHAL.

third *adj.* next after the second; ***n.*** one that is third; also, any of the three equal parts of something. —***adv.*** in third place; also **third•ly.** —**third-class** *adj.* **1** of a class of accommodations that is usu. the lowest: *a ~ ticket.* **2** of a class of mail that includes printed matter other than periodicals, small articles, etc. weighing less than 16 oz. (453.59 g); ***adv.*** by third class. —**third degree** *Informal.* mental or bodily torture as a means of forcing a prisoner to talk; **third-de•gree burn** injury resulting in charred skin and destruction of tissue. —**third dimension** the quality of depth or solidity that makes an object or scene seem real; **third-di•men•sion•al** *adj.* —**third person** a pronoun or verb form such as *he, she, it, they,* or *goes* that refers to the one(s) spoken of. —**third-rate** *adj.* lowest-rated; hence, poor or inferior. —**Third World** the countries of Asia, Africa, and Latin America that are industrially less developed than other nations.

thirst *n.* discomfort caused by the need to drink; hence, a craving or strong desire; ***v.*** be thirsty or desire ardently: *~ing for adventure, knowledge, revenge.* —**thirst•y** *adj.* **thirst•i•er, -i•est** having or causing thirst: *felt ~; a land ~ for rain;* **thirst•i•ly** *adv.;* **thirst•i•ness** *n.*

thir•teen (–TEEN) *n., adj. & pron.* three more than ten; 13 or XIII; **thir•teen•th** *n. & adj.* —**thir•ty** *adj. & n.* **-ties** three times ten; 30 or XXX; **the thirties** the numbers or years from 30 through 39; **thir•ti•eth** (–ith) *n. & adj.*

this (DHIS) *pron., pl.* **these** (DHEEZ) a person or thing that is present or referred to as nearer to the speaker than another, or *that: ~ is your book, that is mine;* ***adj.:*** *~ book; these books; Now ~* (i.e. a certain) *man had three sons;* ***adv.*** to this extent: *~ big, much, far.*

this•tle (THIS·ul) *n.* any of a group of weeds with prickly leaves and soft, silky, purplish flowers that bear seeds equipped with down; **this•tle•down** *n.*

thith•er *adv.* to that place; ***adj.*** on that side; **thith•er•ward(s)** *adv.* toward that place.

tho' (DHOH) *conj. & adv.* though.

thole *n.* either of a pair of pegs on the gunwale of a boat between which the oar is held in rowing; also **thole•pin.**

thong *n.* a narrow strip of leather or plastic, esp. one used as a strap or lace.

Thor in Norse myth, the god of thunder.

tho•rax (THOR–) *n.* **-rax•es** or **-ra•ces** (–uh·seez) the segment of an insect's body between head and abdomen; also, the human chest; **tho•rac•ic** (–RAS–) *adj.: the ~ cavity containing the heart and lungs.*

Thor•eau (THOR·oh, thuh·ROH), **Henry D.** 1817–62, U.S. writer and philosopher.

tho•ri•um (THOR·ee–) *n.* a radioactive metallic element used as fuel in nuclear reactors.

thorn *n.* a short, hard, sharp-pointed protective outgrowth on a plant stem, as in the hawthorn and locust; hence, a source of trouble or annoyance: *She's a ~ in his flesh; He's a ~ in her side;* **thorn•y** *adj.*

thor•ough (THUR·oh) *adj.* painstaking; marked by great attention to detail: *a ~ search, scholar, grasp of the subject; a ~* (i.e. complete) *scoundrel;* **thor•ough•ly** *adv.;* **thor•ough•ness** *n.* —**thor•ough•bred** *n. & adj.* (an animal) of pure stock; **Thoroughbred** a breed of race horses descended from three Arabian stallions. —**thor•ough•fare** *n.* a public street open at both ends with free flow of traffic. —**thor•ough•go•ing** *adj.* very thorough; also, out-and-out.

thorp *n. Archaic.* village.

those *pl.* of THAT.

¹thou (DHOW) *pron., possessive* THY OR THINE, *objective* THEE; *pl.* YOU OR YE, *possessive* YOUR(S), *objective* YOU OR YE. *Archaic.* the one spoken to; you.

²thou (THOW) *n. Slang.* thousand.

though (DHOH) *conj.* **1** in spite of the fact that; although: *likes to work ~ ill; good to take an umbrella ~* (i.e. even if) *it may not rain; looks as ~* (i.e. as if) *it may not rain.* **2** nevertheless: *They get along, ~ not like friends;* ***adv.*** however: *They get along; not like friends, ~.*

thought *pt.* of THINK. —***n.*** **1** mental consideration of a subject or an expression of it: *seems lost in ~; acted without ~; a mother full of ~ for her children's future; had no ~* (i.e. intention) *of hurting; a book of ~s* (i.e. quotations); *Chaucer reflects medieval ~* (i.e. thinking). **2** a little bit: *Be a ~ more considerate of others.* —**thought•ful** *adj.;* **thought•ful•ly** *adv.;* **thought•ful•ness** *n.* —**thought•less** *adj.* not thinking; also, not considerate; **thought•less•ly** *adv.;* **thought•less•ness** *n.*

thous•and (THOW·znd) *n.* ten times 100; 1,000 or M: *three ~ people; ~s* (i.e. a large number) *of people;* **thou•sandth** *n. & adj.*

thrall (THRAWL) *n.* a slave; also, slavery or **thral(l)•dom** (–dum) *n.*

thrash *v.* beat repeatedly, as in threshing grain with a flail: *In his frustration, he ~ed the donkey soundly; children ~ing about in the water; They*

thrashed over *the problem for many hours; It took all evening to* **thrash out** (i.e. arrive at) *a solution.* **—thrash·er** *n.* one that thrashes; also, a New World bird with a down-curved bill and loud, varied songs, that thrashes its tail up and down when excited.

thread (THRED) *n.* **1** a fine cord made of cotton, flax, etc. spun out and twisted together; also, anything fine and continuous like thread, as the filaments made by a spider or silkworm: *the ~* (i.e. main subject) *of a conversation, narrative; Death occurred when one of the Fates cut the ~ of life;* **threads** *pl. Slang.* clothes. **2** the continuous spiral ridge around a screw or inside a nut. **—v. 1** pass a thread through (a needle, beads, etc.). **2** pass through like a thread: *She ~ed her way through the crowd; red silk ~ed with gold; to ~ a roll of film into a camera.* **3** form a screw thread on or in (a bolt or nut); also, form a thread, as syrup of a certain thickness when dropped from a spoon. **—thread·bare** *adj.* badly worn out: *a ~ carpet; a ~ person* (in worn-out clothes), *argument* (i.e. hackneyed). **—thread·y** *adj.* **thread·i·er, -i·est** stringy; also, not strong and full: *a ~ voice.*

threat (THRET) *n.* expression of one's intention to hurt; also, possibility or cause of something evil or harmful happening: *a ~ of rain; Drunk drivers are a ~ to public safety.* **—threat·en** *v.* **1** utter a threat against (someone): *was ~ed with death.* **2** be a threat to: *An epidemic ~s a country.* **3** be a sign of: *Clouds ~ rain.* **—threat·en·ing** *adj.;* **threat·en·ing·ly** *adv.*

three *n., pron. & adj.* one more than two; 3 or III. **—3-D** (THREE·DEE) *adj.* three-dimensional: *a ~ picture, movie.* **—three·fold** *adj.* having three parts or three times as much or as many: *a ~ increase;* **adv.** three times. **—three·pence** (THREP–, THRIP–) *n.* (a coin worth) three British pennies. **—three R's** reading, writing, and arithmetic, as the basics of elementary education. **—three·score** *adj.* sixty. **—three·some** (–sum) *n.* a group of three.

thren·o·dy (THREN·uh·dee) *n.* **-dies** a song of lamentation; dirge.

thresh *v.* separate (grain) from wheat by beating; also, beat out (wheat, etc.) with a flail or machine; hence, thrash.

thresh·old *n.* **1** the sill of a doorway as a point of entry; hence, entrance or starting point: *the ~ of a career, discovery, new era.* **2** the point at which a stimulus or sensation becomes perceptible: *below the ~ of consciousness; factors influencing a patient's allergic ~* (i.e. reaction).

threw *pt.* of THROW.

thrice *adv.* three times (as many or as much).

thrift frugality in expenditure; careful management of money or resources; **thrift shop** a shop selling secondhand clothes and housewares, usu. for charity. **—thrift·y** *adj.* **thrift·i·er, -i·est** economical, esp. in saving; **thrift·i·ly** *adv.;* **thrift·less** *adj.*

thrill *n.* a surge of excited feeling: *the ~ of a discovery; a ~ of joy; does it for ~s;* **v.** have or cause a thrill: *~ed us with horror and suspense;* **thrill·er** *n.;* **thrill·ing** *adj.: a ~ motion picture;* **thrill·ing·ly** *adv.*

thrips *n. sing. & pl.* a small, slender insect, usu. with two pairs of wings fringed with hairs, destructive to plants and grain.

thrive *v.* **thrives,** *pt.* **thrived** or **throve** (THROHV), *pp.* **thrived** or **thriv·en** (THRIV·un), **thriv·ing** prosper or flourish; develop or grow vigorously.

throat *n.* **1** the air-and-food passage from the back of the mouth to the esophagus: *a sore ~ from a cold.* **2** the front part of the neck. **3** a narrow passage or part. **—throat·y** *adj.* **throat·i·er, -i·est** produced in the throat; guttural or husky: *a ~ voice;* **throat·i·ly** *adv.;* **throat·i·ness** *n.*

throb *v.* **throbs, throbbed, throb·bing** palpitate or pulsate: *the ~ing of the heart; a wound ~ing with pain;* **n.** a throbbing or strong beat.

throe (THROH) *n.* a pang or spasm: *in the* **throes** (i.e. struggle or agony) *of finishing a task on time; the ~s of revolution.*

throm·bo·sis (–BOH–) *n., pl.* **-ses** (–seez) the blocking of a blood vessel by a **throm·bus** *n., pl.* **-bi** (–bye) blood clot; **throm·bot·ic** (–BOT–) *adj.*

throne *n.* **1** the chair of state of a king; also, a similar chair used on ceremonial occasions by a bishop, etc. **2** a sovereign or ruler; also, sovereignty.

throng *n.* a crowd of people, esp. a moving and jostling one; also, a multitude; **v.:** *Admirers ~ed round the star; ~ed the theater on opening night.*

throt·tle *n.* a valve regulating the fuel flowing into an engine, as of an automobile, or the mechanism controlling it, as the accelerator pedal. **—v. throt·tles, throt·tled, throt·tling** **1** choke or strangle; hence, suppress. **2** reduce the fuel flowing into an engine; hence, lessen speed. **—throt·tler** *n.*

through (THROO) *prep.* **1** in at one side of (something) and out at the other; from beginning to end of (a period): *Come in ~ the door; slept ~ the night; Monday ~* (i.e. including) *Friday; ticketed for driving ~ a red light* (i.e. without stopping); *when you are ~* (i.e. finished with) *eating.* **2** by reason of: *failed ~ neglect; found out ~* (i.e. by the agency of) *a friend.* **—adv.:** *slept the night ~; read the book ~; a train going ~* (i.e. nonstop) *to New York;* **wet through and through** (i.e. completely). **—adj. 1** finished: *Are you ~?* **2** involving no stopping: *~ trains, flights, traffic; a ~ ticket to Paris.* **—through·out** *adv. & prep.* **1** in every part (of): *~ the country; well decorated ~.* **2** during the whole (of): *was absent ~ the day.* **—through·put** *n.* processing capacity or the amount processed, as by a computer. **—through·way** *n.* an expressway.

throve a *pt.* of THRIVE.

throw (THROH) *v.* **throws, threw** (THROO), **thrown** (THRONE), **throw·ing** **1** cause to move rapidly or with force, usu. through the air: *to ~ a ball; a rider ~n by a horse; was ~n* (i.e. put) *into prison; to ~ a switch* (by moving a lever to "on" or "off" position). **2** shed, drop, or toss casually or routinely: *to ~ off a disguise; Snakes ~ their skin; He threw a six* (in dice); *Domestic animals ~* (i.e. bring forth) *their young.* **3** *Informal.* give: *to ~ a party; He threw the fight* (i.e. gave it up intentionally). **4** fashion or shape by turning or twisting, as on a potter's wheel or lathe: *Thrown silk is stronger than raw silk.* ***—n.*** a throwing, a distance covered by throwing, or what is thrown, as a scarf or furniture covering. **—throw in** add as a free gift or bargain. **—throw off** give off (sparks) or get rid of (a burden). **—throw out** expel (an intruder or undesirable person), reject (a proposal), put forth (a signal, challenge, etc.), or put out (a base runner in baseball). **—throw up** give up (a job or game); also, *Informal.* vomit. **—throw·a·way** *n.* & *adj.* (a pamphlet, disposable container, etc.) designed to be thrown away after use. **—throw·back** *n.* a reversion to an earlier type or an example of it. **—throw rug** a small rug.

thru (THROO) *Informal.* through.

thrum *v.* **thrums, thrummed, thrum·ming** same as STRUM.

thrush *n.* any of a family of songbirds that are usu. plain brown or have a spotted white breast as in the "wood thrush."

thrust *v.* **thrusts, thrust, thrust·ing** push with force and suddenness: *She ~ the letter into my hands; ~ her hands into her pockets; ~ himself into her presence; ~ at him with the sword; an election ~ on an unwilling candidate;* ***n.:*** *the ~ of a sword, an argument or speech, an attacking enemy; the supporting ~ of an arch; Jet engines and propellers produce ~ for a plane to move forward overcoming drag; the upward ~ of a rocket in reaction to the flow of exhaust gas.* **—thrust·er** or **thrus·tor** *n.*

thru·way (THROO–) *n. Informal.* throughway.

Thu·cyd·i·des (thoo·SID·uh·deez) 460?–400? B.C., Greek historian.

thud *n.* & *v.* **thuds, thud·ded, thud·ding** (move or hit making) a dull sound, as of something heavy falling on soft ground.

thug *n.* a hoodlum or ruffian.

thu·li·um (THOO·lee–) *n.* a rare-earth chemical element used in portable X-ray equipment.

thumb (THUM) *n.* the short, thick opposable digit of the hand; **all thumbs** very clumsy or awkward; **turn thumbs down on** disapprove of; **under one's thumb** under one's power. ***—v.*** turn, handle, soil, etc. with the thumb: *She ~ed through the pages looking for pictures; a badly ~ed book; a hiker trying to ~ a ride* (by gesturing with the thumb); *She ~ed her nose* (as a gesture of contempt) *at him.* **—thumb index** a set of lettered notches cut in the fore edge of a reference book to help the reader locate its contents. **—thumb·nail** *n.* the nail of a thumb; **thumbnail sketch** brief and concise word-picture. **—thumb·screw** *n.* a screw that can be turned with the thumb and forefingers. **—thumb·tack** *n.* a wide-headed tack that can be pressed into a board with the thumb.

thump *n.* a heavy blow with something thick such as a fist; also, the sound made by such a blow or fall; ***v.:*** *The speaker ~ed the table for attention; heartily ~ed his back in encouragement; a* **thump·ing** (*Informal.* very large or whopping) *victory.*

thun·der *n.* the loud sound usu. heard after a flash of lightning; also, a similar sound, as of a great waterfall or resounding applause; ***v.:*** *It often ~s when it rains; the ~ing Niagara Falls; Cannons ~ed in salute; The train ~ed past the station;* **thun·der·ous** *adj.;* **thun·der·ous·ly** *adv.* **—thun·der·bolt** *n.* a flash or shaft of lightning with a **thund·er·clap** *n.* a loud crash. **—thun·der·cloud** *n.* a cumulonimbus cloud that gathers before a thunderstorm; also **thun·der·head.** **—thun·der·show·er** *n.* a shower with thunder and lightning. **—thun·der·storm** *n.* a storm with thunder and lightning. **—thun·der·struck** *adj.* overcome with astonishment; also **thun·der·strick·en.**

Thur(s). *Abbrev.* for **Thurs·day** (THURZ·dee, –day) *n.* the fifth day of the week.

thus (DHUS) *adv.* in this or that manner; to this or that degree or extent; so; therefore; **thus·ly** *adv. Informal.* thus.

thwack *n.* & *v.* whack, esp. with something flat or heavy: *the ~ of a ball on gut.*

thwart (THWORT) *n.* & *adj.* (a seat) placed across a boat. ***—v.*** obstruct, esp. by blocking the way: *to ~ one's plans; to ~ one in his ambitions.*

thy (DHYE) *adj., Archaic. possessive* of THOU; your: *~ kingdom.*

thyme (TIME) *n.* an aromatic garden herb of the mint family that yields an oil; **thy·mol** (THY–) a drug made from thyme, used as an antiseptic and in perfumes. **—thy·mine** (THYE·min, –meen) *n.* one of the pyrimidine bases of DNA. **—thy·mus** *n.* a glandlike lymphoid organ located behind the breastbone that helps to provide immunity in childhood; also **thymus gland.**

thy·roid *n.* **1** a large ductless gland in the neck that produces the hormone **thy·rox·in(e)** (–ROX·in, –een) regulating growth and metabolism. **2** a synthetic hormone used in treating goiter. ***—adj.*** having to do with the thyroid.

thy·self (dhy·SELF) *pron. Archaic.* reflexive or emphatic of THOU; yourself.

Ti titanium. **—ti** (TEE) *n. Music.* the seventh tone of the diatonic scale.

ti·ar·a (tee·AIR·uh, –AHR–) *n.* **1** a crownlike ornamental headband worn by women. **2** the pope's triple crown.

Ti·ber (TYE–) a river of C. Italy flowing through Rome.

Ti·bet (ti·BET) a country north of the Himalayas, now part of China; 471,700 sq.mi.

(1,221,700 km²); *cap.* Lhasa; **Ti·bet·an** *n.* & *adj.*

tib·i·a (TIB·ee·uh) *n., pl.* **-i·ae** (–i·ee) or **-i·as** the shinbone.

tic *n.* a habitual nervous twitching of muscles of the face; also, a similar shrugging of the shoulder or other repeated movement of a body part.

tick **1** *n.* & *v.* (make) a light, clicking sound, as a clock; hence, *Informal.* make (something) run. **2** *n.* & *v.* (mark with) a check mark. **3** *n.* a small, blood-sucking, parasitic insect related to mites, some of which transmit "tick fever." **4** *n.* the cloth case that is filled to make a pillow or mattress; **tick·ing** *n.* a closely woven cotton fabric for making ticks. **5** *n. Informal.* credit or trust. —**tick·er** *n.* **1** a ticking instrument, esp. a telegraph machine that prints out news, stock-market reports, etc. on paper tape, or **ticker tape.** **2** *Slang.* the heart.

tick·et (–it) *n.* **1** a card or piece of paper: *a price ~* (i.e. tag); *to buy theater ~s* (for admission to a show); *a police speeding ~* (i.e. summons). **2** a list of candidates for election; slate. ***—v.:*** *prices as ~ed on each article; was ~ed for a parking violation.*

tick·le *v.* **-les, -led, -ling** feel or cause a tingling or thrilling sensation in (a person, body part, etc.) by stroking lightly, as the sole of the foot with a feather: *had to ~ him to make him laugh; a ~ing sensation in the throat; stories that ~ your curiosity;* ***n.*** an act of tickling or the sensation caused. —**tick·ler** *n.* **1** one that tickles. **2** a memorandum book or other aid to memory. —**tick·lish** *adj.* sensitive or delicate: *a ~ subject that requires tact; a ~ situation, problem;* **tick·lish·ly** *adv.;* **tick·lish·ness** *n.*

tic(k)-tac(k)-toe *n.* a game played by two persons making "naughts and crosses" on a square of nine spaces alternately till either player gets his symbol in a row of three. —**tick·tock** *n.* the ticking sound of a clock.

t.i.d. *Medicine.* three times a day.

tid·al (TYE·dl) *adj.* having to do with tides: *a ~ bore in a river; a ~ inlet;* **tidal wave** a tidelike destructive ocean wave caused by an undersea earthquake or by a hurricane, as one that struck the coast of Bangladesh in 1970 killing over 200,000 people; hence, a great outburst, as of public indignation.

tid·bit *n.* a choice morsel of food, gossip, etc.

tid·dly·winks (TID·lee–) *n.* a game in which small disks are snapped by their edges using larger disks into a container.

tide *n.* the rise and fall of ocean waters from the gravitational pull of the moon; also, the resulting outward and inward flow in estuaries, rivers, etc.; hence, a trend, as of public opinion, events, etc.: *waiting for a turn of the ~* (i.e. from one condition to its opposite). **2** *comb.form.* season or time: as in *Christmastide, Eastertide, Whitsuntide.* ***—v.*** **tides, tid·ed, tid·ing** (help) get through or survive: *Savings* **tided** *her* **over** *the long illness.* —**tide·land** *n.* submerged coast land; also, land regularly covered by high tide. —**tide·wa·ter** *n.* **1** water that is brought in or that is affected by the tide. **2** an area affected by the tide, as the Tidewater costal plain of E. Virginia. —**ti·dings** (TYE–) *n.pl.* news: *glad ~.* —**ti·dy** (TYE·dee) *adj.* **-di·er, -di·est** **1** neat or orderly; **ti·di·ness** *n.* **2** *Informal.* relatively large: *a ~ sum of money.* ***—v.*** **-dies, -died, -dy·ing** make tidy: *~ up your room.* ***—n.,*** *pl.* **-dies** a small protective cover for the back, arms, or headrest of a chair or sofa. —**tid·i·ly** *adv.;* **tid·i·ness** *n.*

tie (TYE) *v.* **ties, tied, ty·ing** **1** fasten or secure with a string, cord, rope, etc. that can be knotted: *to ~ up a parcel; ~ your shoes; She ~d* (i.e. made) *a bow in her hair.* **2** connect or link: *two countries ~d by common interests; evidence that* **ties in with** (i.e. relates to) *suspected motives.* **3** restrict or confine: *He's* **tied down** *by family responsibilities; was too* **tied up** *to answer phone calls; road construction ~ing up traffic.* **4** equal (another team) in score. ***—n.*** **1** anything that ties or unites, as a cord, a necktie, a knot, crosspieces to which railroad tracks are fastened, etc.: *family ~s; ~s of friendship.* **2** equality of scores between teams; also, a contest resulting in such a tie or draw; ***adj.:*** *a ~ score; a game played as a* **tie-break·er.** —**tie·back** *n.* (a curtain with) a band or strap to tie it to one side. —**tie-dye** *n.* method of producing patterns on cloth by tying small portions of it by string before dyeing: ***v.*** **-dyes, -dyed, -dye·ing.** —**tie-in** *n.* a connection (with something else), as of a book with a motion picture based on it.

Tien·tsin (TIN·tsin) a seaport of N. China.

tier (TEER) *n.* one of a series of rows, as of seats in a stadium, arranged one above another.

tie rod a connecting member, esp. one connecting a front wheel of an automobile to the steering mechanism. —**tie-up** *n.* **1** a temporary suspension of work in progress, traffic, etc. **2** a connection or relation.

tiff *n.* & *v.* (have) a petty quarrel.

ti·ger (TYE·gur) *n.* a large, tawny-coated, black-striped, flesh-eating Asiatic animal of the cat family; **ti·ger·ish** *adj.* fierce or cruel.

tight (TITE) *adj.* **1** going round and binding without looseness or slack: *a ~ knot, grip; ~* (or **tight·fit·ting**) *clothes; a ~* (i.e. taut) *rope; An aerialist is a* **tight·rope** *artist.* **2** closed firmly against leaks or losses: *water-~ container; a ~ roof, schedule; Money is ~* (i.e. not easy to borrow); *a ~* (*Informal.* stingy) *moneylender;* **tight·fist·ed** *adj.* stingy; **tight-lipped** (–lipt) *adj.* secretive. **3** *Slang.* intoxicated. ***—adv.*** closely or firmly: *decided to* **sit tight** *on his job and watch developments; sleep ~* (i.e. soundly); **tight·ly** *adv.;* **tight·ness** *n.* —**tight·en** *v.* make or become tight(er); **tight·en·er** *n.* —**tight-**

fisted, tightfitting tight-lipped, tightrope See TIGHT, *adj.* 1, 2. **—tights** *n.pl.* a skintight garment for the hips and legs, as worn by acrobats, dancers, etc. **—tight•wad** *n. Slang.* a stingy person.

ti•glon (TYE–) *n.* the offspring of a tiger and a lioness; also **ti•gon.** **—ti•gress** (TYE·gris) *n.* a female tiger.

Ti•gris (TYE–) a river that rises in E. Turkey and joins the Euphrates in Iraq to flow into the Persian Gulf.

Ti•jua•na (tee·WAH·nuh) a city of Mexico lying near the U.S. border.

til•de (–duh) *n.* a diacritical mark (˜) placed over a palatal "n," as in Spanish *cañon,* and over nasalized vowels, as in Portuguese *São.*

tile *n.* **1** a thin slab or piece of baked clay, stone, or synthetic material for covering roofs, paving floors, etc. **2** a section of an earthenware drainage or sewage pipe. **—*v.* tiles, tiled, til•ing** cover with tiles; **til•er** *n.;* **til•ing** *n.* tiles collectively.

till *prep.* & *conj.* until **—*v.*** cultivate land by plowing, sowing, etc. **—*n.*** a drawer in which money is kept behind a counter: *caught with his hand in the* ~ (i.e. stealing). **—till•age** (–ij) *n.* the tilling of land; also, cultivated land. **—till•er** *n.* **1** one who tills. **2** an offshoot or sprout from the base of a plant such as rice or wheat. **3** the handle of a boat's rudder.

tilt *v.* **1** (cause) to slope or slant: *A table with uneven legs ~s; Cups, barrels, dump trucks, etc. are ~ed to empty them.* **2** charge or attack, as in the medieval lists: *Knights used to ~ on horseback; Don Quixote ~ed at a windmill thinking it a giant.* **—*n.*** **1** a slope or slant. **2** the medieval contest of knights trying to unhorse each other with lances while charging at speed; **(at) full tilt** at full speed.

tilth *n.* tillage or the state of being tilled.

tilt-top *adj.* of a table, having a top that can be tilted to a vertical position and stored flat against a wall.

tim•bal (–bl) *n.* a kettledrum. **—tim•bale** (–bl) *n.* a custardlike dish of meat, etc. baked in a mold; also, a small fried pastry shell or mold with a timbale filling.

tim•ber *n.* **1** wood prepared for use, as for building; also, a wooden beam. **2** trees bearing wood suitable for use. **—*v.*** cover, support, or furnish with timbers; **tim•bered** (–burd) *adj.;* **tim•ber•ing** *n.* timbers or timber work. **—tim•ber•line** *n.* the latitude or upper limit above which it is too cold for trees to grow. **—timber wolf** the gray North American wolf.

tim•bre (TAM·bur, TIM–) *n.* the characteristic tone of a voice or instrument, regardless of the pitch or volume of sounds. **—tim•brel** *n.* a small tambourine or drumlike musical instrument.

time *n.* **1** the continuous period that includes the past, present, and future: *God transcends ~ and space.* **2** a period of definite duration: *in the ~ of Christ; Precambrian ~; It took me a long ~; He beat ~* (i.e. rhythm or rate of movement) *with his feet while she sang; earns double ~* (i.e. rate of pay) *on holidays.* **2** a particular point or occasion in time: *Clocks tell ~; Better luck next ~; harvest ~; ~ to go to bed.* **4** a period as used or experienced: *having a good ~; hard ~s; no ~ to waste.* **5** a system of measuring time: *solar ~; daylight saving ~.* **—*v.* times, timed, tim•ing** **1** set the time or speed of: *to ~ one's activities; ~ a program.* **2** measure the time or duration of: *to ~ a race, runner.* **—*adj.*** having to do with time: *a test with a ~ limit; a ~ loan repayable at a specified time.* **—against time** trying to finish in a given time. **—ahead of time** before the due time. **—do** (or **serve**) **time** *Informal.* serve a prison term. **—in time** **1** eventually. **2** without being late. **3** keeping the right rhythm or tempo. **—make time** compensate for lost time by going faster than normal; also, save time this way. **—mark time** appear to be active but without making progress, as when moving the feet up and down without marching forward. **—on time** **1** at the right time. **2** on credit. **—time bomb** one that is set to go off at a definite time. **—time clock** a clock device for recording employees' hours of work. **—time deposit** deposit of money for a fixed time. **—time-hon•ored** (–on·urd) *adj.* long-existing: *~ customs.* **—time•keep•er** *n.* one who keeps account of hours worked, time elapsed, etc. **—time•less** *adj.* eternal; also, not limited by time in regard to value or usefulness; **time•less•ly** *adv.;* **time•less•ness** *n.* **—time lock** one that can be opened only at a fixed time. **—time•ly** *adj.* **-li•er, -li•est** happening or done at a suitable or useful time: *a ~ reminder;* **time•li•ness** *n.* **—time•out** *n.* a brief suspension of play, as in basketball or football. **—time•piece** *n.* a clock, watch, or other time-measuring instrument. **—tim•er** *n.* a clock device for indicating the passage of a period of time; also, an automatic device for starting and stopping the operation of a machine. **—times** *prep.* multiplied by: *3 ~ 5 is 15.* **—time•serv•er** *n.* one who servilely seeks to please those in power or changes his principles to suit the times; **time•serv•ing** *n.* & *adj.* **—time sharing** system enabling several people to use the time of the same computer in various functions. **—time sheet** a record of the hours worked by an employee or employees. **—times sign** the symbol × as in 7 × 8 = 56. **—time•ta•ble** *n.* a schedule of the hours at which work is started and stopped, buses, planes, etc. arrive and depart, etc. **—time•worn** *adj.* worn out or hackneyed: *a ~ practice, expression.* **—time zone** any of the 24 longitudinal divisions of the world in each of which the same standard time is used regardless of local time.

tim·id *adj.* lacking in the self-confidence required to assert oneself; too cautious and fearful; **tim·id·ly** *adv.;* **ti·mid·i·ty** (–MID–) *n.*

tim·ing (TYE·ming) *n.* regulation of the speed, duration, etc. or choice of the right moment of an action for maximum effect; also, time measurement.

tim·or·ous (TIM·uh·rus) *adj.* full of fear and apprehension; **tim·or·ous·ly** *adv.;* **tim·or·ous·ness** *n.*

tim·o·thy (TIM·uh·thee) *n.* a tall grass with spikes of tightly packed flowers grown for hay.

tim·pa·ni (–puh·nee) *n.pl.* a set of kettle drums played by one performer, or **tim·pa·nist** in an orchestra.

tin *n.* **1** a light, bluish-white, malleable, corrosion-resistant metal used in alloys. **2** a container made of tin plate. **—v. tins, tinned, tin·ning** plate with tin; also, *Brit.* to can: *~d salmon.* **—tin can** a packaging container made of tin.

tinct. *Abbrev.* for **tinc·ture** (TINK·chur) *n.* **1** a medication dissolved in alcohol: *~ of iodine.* **2** a tinge or trace; **v. -tures, -tured, -tur·ing** tinge *(with);* also, tint.

tin·der *n.* a material that catches fire easily or that is used to start a fire; **tin·der·box** *n.* a potential source of a fire or flare-up, as a box containing tinder, flint, and steel formerly used to kindle a fire.

tine *n.* a prong, esp. of a fork.

tin·foil *n.* a thin sheeting of tin used as wrapping.

tinge (TINJ) *n.* & *v.* **ting·es, tinged, ting(e)·ing** (modify with) a slight coloring, flavor, taste, etc.: *Ivory gets a yellowish ~; a voice ~d with sadness.*

tin·gle (TING·gl) *n.* & *v.* **-gles, -gled, -gling** (have or cause) a slight prickling or stinging sensation, as from cold, excitement, etc. **—tin·gly** *adj.*

tin·ker (TING–) *n.* one who goes around mending pots, pans, etc.; hence, an unskilled or amateur worker; **v.** repair or work in an unskilled way (at or with something); **tin·ker·er** *n.*

tin·kle (TING–) *n.* & *v.* **-kles, -kled, -kling** (make or cause to make) a short, light ringing sound, as of little bells, esp. a series of such sounds.

tin·ny (TIN·ee) *adj.* **tin·ni·er, tin·ni·est** **1** like tin in appearance, value, sound, etc.: *a ~* (i.e. thin or metallic) *voice; a ~* (i.e. not well-made) *car.* **2** of or containing tin: *a ~ alloy, lode.* **—tin·ni·ly** *adv.;* **tin·ni·ness** *n.* **—tin plate** tin-coated sheets of iron or steel, as used for roofing, food containers, etc.

tin·sel (–sl) *n.* glittering material used for decoration in thin sheets, threads, etc., as on Christmas trees; also, anything showy, gaudy, and cheap.

tin·smith *n.* a worker in tin plate; a repairer of tinware.

tint *n.* & *v.* (color with) a light shade or hue: *Pink is a ~ of red; ~ed window glass, hair.*

tin·tin·nab·u·la·tion (–LAY–) *n.* the tinkling of bells.

tin·ware *n.* articles made of tin plate.

ti·ny (TYE·nee) *adj.* **-ni·er, -ni·est** very small; minute; **tin·i·ness** *n.*

-tion *n. suffix.* act, state, or result of (something): as in *narration, perfection, ambition.* **—-tious** *adj. suffix.* as in *ambitious, contentious, vexatious.*

tip *n.* **1** an end part, esp. a pointed or tapering end: *the ~ of the tongue, nose, toe.* **2** a light stroke or glancing blow; tap. **3** a piece of secret information; also, a useful hint or suggestion. **4** a small gift of money; gratuity. **5** a tilt or slope. **—v. tips, tipped, tip·ping** [corresponding to the *n.* senses] **1:** *a cane ~d with brass; a filter-~d cigarette.* **2:** *The ball was ~d into the basket.* **3:** *was* **tipped off** *by an anonymous phone call;* **tip one's hand** *Slang.* reveal one's intentions, usu. accidentally. **4:** *never forgot to ~ the waiter;* **tip·per** *n.* **5:** *the habit of ~ing his hat to ladies; A boat ~s over when loaded unevenly; She* **tips the scales at** (i.e. weighs) *110 lb.* **—tip-off** *n.* a tipping off; warning. **—tip·pet** (–it) *n.* a scarflike garment with ends hanging down in front.

tip·ple *v.* **tip·ples, tip·pled, tip·pling** drink (alcoholic liquor) habitually and excessively; **tip·pler** *n.*

tip·ster *n. Informal.* one who supplies secret information, usu. for pay, as about horse races.

tip·sy (–see) *adj.* **-si·er, -si·est** intoxicated; hence, unsteady; **tip·si·ly** *adv.;* **tip·si·ness** *n.* **—tip·toe** *v.* **-toes, -toed, -toe·ing** walk on the tips of one's toes; **n.** the tip of a toe; **on tiptoe** on one's tiptoes; silently; also, eagerly. **—tip-top** *n.* the highest point; **adj. & adv.** at the very top; hence, *Informal.* excellent.

ti·rade (TYE–, –RAID) *n.* a long, vehement or scolding speech; harangue.

Ti·ra·na (–RAH·nuh) or **Ti·ra·në** (–nuh) capital of Albania.

[1]tire *n.* a usu. hollow casing of rubber with a grooved tread, fixed to the rim of a wheel for a smooth ride.

[2]tire *v.* **tires, tired, tir·ing** make or become weary or bored; **tired** *adj.* fatigued; also, worn-out or hackneyed; **—tire·less** *adj.* never getting tired; hence, ceaseless: *a ~ worker; ~ energy, efforts;* **tire·less·ly** *adv.;* **tire·less·ness** *n.* **—tire·some** (–sum) *adj.* that tires or bores; **tire·some·ly** *adv.;* **tire·some·ness** *n.*

Tir·ol (tuh·ROLE, TYE–) an Alpine region of W. Austria and N. Italy; **Ti·ro·le·an** (–ROH–) *n.* & *adj.*

'tis (TIZ) it is.

tis·sue (TISH·oo) *n.* **1** the body substance of animals and plants consisting of cells: *muscular ~; connective ~; nervous ~.* **2** web or network: *a ~ of lies; a ~ of twaddle.* **3** a fine, sheer cloth or gauze. **4** soft absorbent paper: *facial ~; toilet ~;* **tissue paper** a thin, lightweight paper used for wrapping, paper napkins, etc.

tit *n.* **1** a titmouse. **2** a nipple; **tits** *pl. Vulgar.* breasts.

ti·tan (TYE·tn) *n.* a giant, like the **Titans,** the first gods of Greek myth, including Atlas and Prometheus; **ti·tan·ic** (–TAN–) *adj.* giantlike in size or strength. **—ti·ta·ni·um** (–TAY–) *n.* a lightweight, silver-gray, corrosion-resistant metal.

tit·bit *n.* same as TIDBIT. **—tit for tat** retaliation; blow for blow.

tithe (TIDHE) *n.* & *v.* **tithes, tithed, tith·ing** (pay) a tenth part of one's income, as traditionally given to the church; **tith·er** *n.*

ti·tian (TISH·un) *n.* a golden red; **Ti·tian** 1489?–1576, Venetian painter.

tit·il·late (TITL·ate) *v.* **-il·lates, -il·lat·ed, -il·lat·ing** excite or stimulate, as if by tickling; **tit·il·la·tion** (–AY–) *n.*

tit·i·vate (TIT·uh–) *v.* **-vates, -vat·ed, -vat·ing** *Informal.* dress up; spruce up.

ti·tle (TYE–) *n.* **1** the name of a literary or artistic product, as put on the **title page** of a book; **titles** *pl.* credits, subtitles, etc. appearing on a television or motion-picture screen. **2** a name giving a person's rank or occupation, as Mister, Miss, Lord, Doctor, Supervisor, etc.; also, a championship: *the world heavyweight ~; a ~ bout.* **3** a legal right to ownership; also, a deed or other document showing ownership of property. **—*v.* -tles, -tled, -tling** give a title to; **ti·tled** *adj.* having a title of rank or nobility. **—ti·tle·hold·er** *n.* the holder of a championship. **—title role** the character in a play or motion picture after whom it is named.

tit·mouse *n., pl.* **-mice** any of a family of small songbirds with long, soft feathers.

tit·ter *n.* & *v.* giggle.

tit·tle (TITL) *n.* a particle or dot. **—tit·tle-tat·tle** *n.* gossip; idle chatter.

tit·tiv·ate *v.* same as TITIVATE.

tit·u·lar (TICH·uh·lur) *adj.* **1** of or bearing a title: *~ role, rank.* **2** nominal: *a ~ bishop* (of a nonexistent jurisdiction).

tiz·zy *n.* **tiz·zies** *Informal.* state of nervous excitement; dither.

tk. tank; truck.

TKO or **T.K.O.** technical knockout.

tkt. ticket.

Tl thallium.

TLC tender loving care.

Tm thulium. **—TM** Trademark; Transcendental Meditation.

T-man *n.* **-men** an investigator of the U.S. Treasury Department.

T.M.O. telegraph money order.

tn. ton(s); town. **—TN** Tennessee.

TNT or **T.N.T.** a powerful explosive used in shells and bombs; "trinitrotoluene."

to (TOO, tuh) *prep.* **1** [indicating the direction of an action or movement or its result]: *He goes ~ school; with his back ~ the wall; came ~ our rescue; put ~ sleep; torn ~ pieces.* **2** [indicating a limit]: *count ~ 100; It is five minutes ~ six; faithful ~ the end.* **3** [indicating a relationship]: *a score of 10 ~ one; dances ~ every tune; kind ~ animals; gives ~ charity; talks ~ himself.* **4** [used before verbs to indicate the infinitive]: *She likes ~ sing; Go if you want ~ (go).* **—*adv.*** [indicating the direction of an action or movement toward something implied]: *came ~* (consciousness) *soon after fainting; As soon as served they fell ~ (eating); A door swings ~* (the shut position); *wearing his hat wrong end ~* (forward); **to and fro** forward and back; back and forth.

t.o. turn over. **—T.O.** Telegraph Office.

toad (TODE) *n.* a froglike but less aquatic animal with a darker, drier, and usu. warty body. **—toad·stool** *n.* a poisonous mushroom. **—toad·y** *n.* **toad·ies** a servile flatterer; sycophant; ***v.* toad·ies, toad·ied, toad·y·ing** be a toady (to a superior).

toast (TOHST) *n.* **1** (a slice of) bread browned by heat, as in a toaster. **2** a drink or an invitation to drink in honor of a person or thing: *to propose a ~ to the bride; was the ~* (i.e. celebrity or popular hero) *of the town on her return from the Olympics.* **—*v.* 1** brown (as bread) or warm (one's body) in the sun or before a fire. **2** propose or drink a toast to. **—toast·er** *n.* an applicance for toasting bread; also, one who proposes a toast. **—toast·mas·ter** *n.* one who presides at a banquet introducing speakers, proposing toasts, etc.; *fem.* **toast·mis·tress.**

to·bac·co (tuh·BACK·oh) *n.* **-bac·cos** a broad-leaved plant of the nightshade family; also, products such as cigarettes and snuff prepared from its leaves; **to·bac·co·nist** *n.* a tobacco dealer, esp. retail.

to·bog·gan (tuh·BOG·un) *n.* & *v.* (coast downhill on) a small sled without runners whose front end curves upward; also, decline rapidly in value.

toc·sin *n.* an alarm bell or other warning sound.

to·day (tuh·DAY) *n.* & *adv.* **1** (on or for) this day. **2** (at) the present time; (in) this day or age: *~'s youth.*

tod·dle *v.* **tod·dles, tod·dled, tod·dling** walk with short uncertain steps, as a young child, or **tod·dler** *n.*

tod·dy (TOD·ee) *n.* **tod·dies** an alcoholic drink mixed with hot water, sugar, spices, etc.; also, the fermented sap of an E. Indian palm.

to-do (tuh·DOO) *n.* **-dos** (–DOOZ) fuss or commotion.

toe (TOH) *n.* one of the five fingerlike parts of the human foot; also, the forepart of a foot or hoof. **—*v.* toes, toed, toe·ing** touch or reach with the toes, as the starting line of a race: *Members of a party are expected to* **toe the line** (i.e. conform to policy, rules, etc.); *Some ~* (i.e.

turn the toes) *in, others ~ out when walking;* **toed** (TODE) *adj.* (secured by nails) driven obliquely; ***comb.form.*** as in *three-~* (i.e. having three toes). **—on one's toes** *Informal.* alert and ready. **—toe dance** a dance performed on the toes, as in ballet; **toe-dance** *v.* **-danc·es, -danced, -danc·ing; toe-danc·er** *n.* **—toe·hold** *n.* a narrow footing, as on a ledge; hence, a slight advantage. **—toe·nail** *n.* the nail of a toe.

tof·fee or **tof·fy** (TOF·ee, TAW·fee) *n.* **tof·fees** or **tof·fies** taffy or caramel.

tog *v.* **togs, togged, tog·ging** *Informal.* clothe or dress; **togs** *n.pl.* clothes.

to·ga (TOH·guh) *n.* the loose outer garment of citizens in ancient Rome; **to·gaed** (–gud) *adj.*

to·geth·er (tuh·GEDH·ur) *adv.* **1** in or into one place or group: *Lovers like to be ~; working ~; The two ~ weigh 300 lb.; the man* **together with** *his wife.* **2** at the same time: *heard them singing ~; was missing for days ~* (i.e. continuously). ***—adj.*** *Slang.* self-possessed; well-integrated: *a young, happy ~ couple;* **to·geth·er·ness** *n.* closeness of relationship.

tog·ger·y *n. Informal.* clothing; togs.

tog·gle *n.* a device that hangs or pulls crosswise, as a T-head crosspiece passed through a loop, or a **toggle bolt** that has a winged nut that spreads out crosswise to lock the bolt in position; **toggle switch** the common electric switch with a lever.

To·go (TOH–) a W. African country; 21,622 sq.mi. (56,000 km²); *cap.* Lomé.

[1]toil *n.* work that is long and laborious: *after years of ~ and sweat;* ***v.:*** *Farmers ~ in the fields; a tractor-trailer ~ing* (i.e. moving laboriously) *up a hill;* **toil·er** *n.*

[2]toil *n.* usu. **toils** *pl.* meshes or a netlike trap. **—toi·let** *n.* **1** the bowl-shaped plumbing fixture for receiving body wastes; also, a washroom equipped with a toilet. **2** the process of washing, dressing, and grooming oneself. **—toilet paper** (or **tissue**) soft paper for wiping oneself after using the toilet. **—toi·let·ry** *n.* usu. **toi·let·ries** *pl.* articles such as soap and cosmetics used in washing and grooming. **—toilet training** training of a child to use the toilet and control bladder and bowel movements. **—toi·lette** (twah·LET, toi–) *n.* toilet (*n.* 2); also, costume or attire. **—toilet water** cologne or similar perfumed liquid.

toil·some (–sum) *adj.* laborious or wearisome; **toil·worn** *adj.* wearied by toil.

To·kay (toh·KAY) *n.* a golden-colored sweet wine of Hungarian origin.

toke *n.* & *v.* **tokes, toked, tok·ing** *Slang.* (puff on) a marijuana cigarette. **—to·ken** (TOH·kn) *n.* **1** a gift, souvenir, or other article that serves as a sign or indication of an inner quality, feeling, etc.: *as a ~ of our gratitude;* **in token of** as evidence of; **by the same token** for the same reason. **2** a coinlike piece of metal serving as an admission ticket: *a subway ~.* **—*adj.*** serving as a token; partial; hence, nominal: *a ~ payment to acknowledge a debt; a ~ gesture;* **to·ken·ism** *n.* the policy of making merely nominal concessions to a demand, as for racial equality.

To·ky·o (TOH·kee·oh) capital of Japan; **To·ky·o·ite** *n.*

tol·bu·ta·mide (–BEW·tuh–) *n.* an oral drug used in mild cases of diabetes.

told *pt.* & *pp.* of TELL.

tole *n.* lacquered or enameled tin plate used for trays, lampshades, etc.

To·le·do (tuh·LEE·doh) a city and port of Ohio on Lake Erie.

tol·er·a·ble *adj.* bearable or endurable; hence, fairly good; **tol·er·a·bly** *adv.* **—tol·er·ance** (–unce) *n.* **1** the quality of being tolerant; also, resistance to a drug's ill effects: *~ increases with addiction.* **2** the allowable variation from a standard dimension, weight, or fineness, as in minting coins. **—tol·er·ant** (–unt) *adj.* willing to let others live according to their own beliefs, practices, etc. **—tol·er·ate** *v.* **-ates, -at·ed, -at·ing** **1** put up with or bear: *to ~ rowdyism; a character difficult to ~* (i.e. work or live with). **2** resist the ill effects of (a drug, etc.). **—tol·er·a·tion** (–RAY–) *n.*

toll (TOLE) *n.* **1** a charge or fee, as for using a bridge or turnpike, making a long-distance telephone call, or **toll call,** etc. **2** loss or damage suffered: *The earthquake took a heavy ~ of lives.* **3** a tolling sound. ***—v.*** ring (a bell) in slow, measured strokes; hence, announce (the hour of day, a death, etc.) or summon by tolling. **—toll·booth** *n.* a booth at which a toll is collected; **toll·gate** *n.* the point where tollbooths are located on a bridge, turnpike, etc.; **toll·house** *n.* a building from which tolls are taken. **—toll road** a turnpike.

Tol·stoy, Leo. 1828–1910, Russian novelist and social thinker.

tol·u·ene (TOL·yoo·een) *n.* a benzenelike coal-tar product used in industrial chemicals, esp. explosives, antiknock, etc.

tom *adj.* & *comb.form.* male: as in *tomcat, tomcod, tomboy; ~ turkey.* **—Tom** *Informal.* same as UNCLE TOM.

tom·a·hawk *n.* & *v.* (strike, kill, etc. with) a light, axlike tool and weapon of North American Indians.

to·ma·to (tuh·MAY·toh, –MAH–) *n.* **-toes** a usu. large, pulpy, round, red or yellow fruit used as a vegetable; also, the plant it grows on.

tomb (TOOM) *n.* a burial place for a dead body, as a grave, vault, or other chamber; also, an above-ground structure such as a cenotaph or mausoleum; **the tomb** death.

tom·boy *n.* a girl who is romping and boisterous; **tom·boy·ish** *adj.*

tomb·stone (TOOM–) *n.* a stone marking a tomb or grave.

tom·cat *n.* a male cat. **—Tom Collins** a cocktail made with gin and lemon juice.

tome *n.* a learned or heavy volume.

tom·fool·er·y (–FOO–) *n.* **-er·ies** silly or nonsensical behavior. **—tom·my** (TOM·ee) **gun** or **Tommy gun** *Informal.* a submachine gun trademarked "Thompson submachine gun"; **tom·my-gun** *v.* **-guns, -gunned, -gun·ning** shoot with a tommy gun.

to·mog·ra·phy (tuh·MOG·ruh·fee) *n.* technique of X-raying body tissue in isolated planes or sections.

to·mor·row (tuh·MOR·oh) *n.* & *adv.* (on) the day after today.

tom·tit *n.* a titmouse. **—tom-tom** *n.* any of various usu. hand-beaten drums used in India and by African and Amerindian tribes.

-tomy *comb.form.* surgical operation: as in *lobotomy, hysterotomy.*

ton (TUN) *n.* either of two units of weight, *short ton* (2,000 lb./907.18 kg) or *long ton* (2,240 lb./1,016.05 kg). See also TONNE.

to·nal·i·ty (toh·NAL–) *n.* **-ties** the relationship of tones to the keynote of a musical composition; hence, tonal character. **—tone** *n.* **1** the sound of a voice or musical instrument, esp. as to its character or quality: *in angry ~s; in a low ~ of voice; the solemn ~s of an organ.* **2** a musical sound of a particular pitch: *Chinese, Bantu, and other ~ languages differentiate meaning by pitch; Do and re are a whole ~* (i.e. note or step) *apart.* **3** manner of expression; also, style: *a high moral ~.* **4** vigor and tension, as of a muscle; also, responsiveness or resilience, as of rubber. **5** the relative lightness or darkness of a color: *Rose is a ~ of red blended with gray; decorated in ~s* (i.e. shades) *of blue.* **—*v.* tones, toned, ton·ing** give a tone to; also, moderate: *was too excited to* **tone down** *his remarks.* **—ton·al** *adj.*; **ton·al·ly** *adv.* **—tone arm** the movable arm containing the pickup of a record player. **—tone-deaf** *adj.* unable to distinguish musical tones. **—tone row** an arrangement of the 12 tones of the chromatic scale without key signatures or scales, as in Arthur Shönberg's works. **—ton·ey** (TOH–) *adj.* **ton·i·er, -i·est** same as TONY.

tong *n.* a Chinese club or secret society.

Ton·ga (TONG·guh) a Polynesian country consisting of about 150 islands; 270 sq. mi. (699 km²); *cap.* Nukualofa; **Ton·gan** *n.* & *adj.*

tongs *n.pl.* a device for grasping or lifting chunks of coal, sugar, ice, etc., having two arms pivoted or hinged together at one end or in the middle.

tongue (TUNG) *n.* **1** the fleshy movable structure in the mouth that is used for tasting and speaking; also, something similar in shape or use, as a strip of land projecting into water, the striking piece inside a bell, or the flap under the lacing of a shoe. **2** the power of speech, a language, or the manner of its use: *your mother ~; a nasty ~;* **hold one's tongue** be silent; **speak in tongues** have GLOSSOLALIA. **—*v.* tongues, tongued, tongu·ing** lick with the tongue; also, play (a flute, cornet, etc.) by using the tongue; **tongued** *adj.* & *comb. form.* as in *golden-~ orator, ~ lightning.* **—tongue-and-groove joint** a joint made by the lip of one board fitting with the groove on another, as in floors and sidings. **—tongue-in-cheek** *adj.* & *adv.* ironical(ly) or satirical(ly). **—tongue-lash·ing** *n. Informal.* a severe scolding. **—tongue-tied** *adj.* unable to speak properly because of shortness of the membrane under the tongue; also, speechless from embarrassment. **—tongue twister** a phrase or sentence that is difficult to say fast, as "She sells seashells beside the seashore."

ton·ic *n.* & *adj.* **1** (a drug, medicine, etc.) that is invigorating or bracing: *"Tonic (water)" is a carbonated quinine-flavored mix.* **2** (of or based on) a keynote. **—ton·i·cal·ly** *adv.*

to·night (tuh·NITE) *n.* & *adv.* (on) the present or the coming night.

ton·nage (TUN·ij) *n.* total weight in tons (as carried by a ship) or total amount of a country's shipping; also, a shipping duty based on tonnage. **—tonne** (TUN) *n.* a metric ton of 1,000 kg.

ton·neau (tuh·NOH) *n.* **ton·neaus** or **ton·neaux** (–NOZE) the part of an automobile body that contains the rear seats.

ton·sil (–sl) *n.* either of two masses of lymphoid tissue on the sides at the back of the mouth; **ton·sil·(l)ar** *adj.*; **ton·sil·lec·to·my** (–LEC·tuh·mee) *n.* **-mies** surgical removal of the tonsils; **ton·sil·li·tis** (–LYE–) *n.* inflammation of the tonsils.

ton·so·ri·al (–SOR·ee·ul) *adj.* having to do with haircutting. **—ton·sure** (–shur) *n.* the ritual shaving of the crown of the head, as before entering the priesthood; also, the shaven part; ***v.* -sures, -sured, -sur·ing:** *a ~d cleric, monk.*

ton·y (TOH·nee) *adj.* **ton·i·er, -i·est** *Slang.* stylish or elegant; also, swanky.

too *adv.* **1** more than enough: *sleeps ~ long.* **2** also: *You ~ can be rich; I like her ~.* **3** *Informal.* very: *was only ~ glad to die; not feeling ~ well.* **4** so; indeed: *"I didn't do it"; "You did ~."*

took *pt.* of TAKE.

tool *n.* **1** a hand implement such as is used in carpentry, gardening, etc.: *the ~s of one's trade.* **2** a working part of a machine that drills, planes, grinds, etc.; also, such a machine, or "machine tool." **3** one that serves as a means; hence, a stooge or dupe. **—*v.*** **1** form or finish (an article) with a tool. **2** equip (a plant) with tools or machinery: *~ing up for the new production season.*

toot *v.* sound (a horn) in short blasts; ***n.*** such a blast. **—toot·er** *n.*

tooth *n., pl.* **teeth** **1** any of the hard bony structures in the jaws, used for biting, chewing, etc.; also, a toothlike part of a saw, gear wheel, comb, rake, etc. **2** taste or liking. **3** *pl.* effectiveness: *laws with teeth.* **—in the teeth of** in the face of; in defiance of. **—fight tooth and nail** fight with all one's strength.

—**toothed** *adj.*; **tooth·less** *adj.* —**tooth·ache** *n.* a pain in a tooth. —**tooth·brush** *n.* a brush for cleaning the teeth. —**tooth powder** or **tooth·paste** *n.* a powder or paste for cleaning the teeth. —**tooth·pick** *n.* a small sliver of wood or similar slender instrument for cleaning between the teeth. —**tooth·some** (–sum) *adj.* tasty; also, attractive or comely. —**tooth·y** *adj.* **tooth·i·er, -i·est** having or showing prominent teeth: *a ~ smile, grin;* **tooth·i·ly** *adv.*

top *n.* **1** a cone-shaped toy for spinning with a string wound around it. **2** the highest or upper(most) point or part: *from the ~ of the building; the ~* (i.e. surface) *of a table; seated at the ~* (i.e. head) *of the table; shouted at the ~ of her voice; The ~* (i.e. best) *of the morning to you! a pajama ~; bikini ~s; collects bottle ~s* (i.e. caps); (above-ground) *beet ~s; was at the ~* (i.e. acme) *of his career; would never* **blow his top** (*Slang.* lose his temper). —**on top of** **1** besides. **2** in control or mastery of. —***v.*** **tops, topped, top·ping** **1** trim the top of (a plant). **2** provide (a bottle, box, etc.) with a cap or lid; also, crown or be at the top of. **3** reach the top of; also, rise above; be or do better than: *try to ~ this.* **4** **top off** complete (*with* something) as a finishing touch. —***adj.*** highest or foremost: *~ drawer, man, speed.* —**top·per** *n.*

to·paz (TOH–) *n.* a hard silicate mineral valued as a gem, esp. in its yellow, pink, and brown varieties.

top brass high officials or officers.

top·coat *n.* a lightweight overcoat. —**top-draw·er** *adj. Informal.* of the highest rank or importance. —**top-dress** *v.* put or scatter material on the surface of (land); **top-dress·ing** *n.* fertilizer, gravel, etc. that is spread on the surface without being worked in.

tope *v.* **topes, toped, top·ing** drink (alcoholic liquor) to excess; **top·er** *n.*

To·pe·ka (tuh·PEE·kuh) capital of Kansas.

top-flight *adj. Informal.* of the highest rank; first-rate. —**top hat** a man's tall cylindrical hat worn in formal dress. —**top-heav·y** (–hev–) *adj.* unstable because too heavy at the top.

top·ic *n.* **1** a theme or subject for an essay, conversation, discussion, etc. **2** a subject of general interest: *the ~s of the day.* —**top·i·cal** *adj.* **1** having to do with topics. **2** of current or local interest: *a ~ story, discussion.* **2** *Medicine.* local: *a ~ anesthetic, remedy.* —**top·i·cal·ly** *adv.* —**top·i·cal·i·ty** (–CAL–) *n.*

top·knot *n.* a tuft of hair or feathers that is either worn or is growing on the top of the head. —**top·less** *adj.* not wearing a top to cover the breasts: *a ~ waitress, dancer, restaurant* (featuring topless women); **top·less·ness** *n.* —**top-lev·el** *adj.* of the highest level of authority or rank: *a ~ meeting.* —**top·mast** *n.* the second section of a ship's mast above its deck. —**top·most** *adj.* highest or uppermost. —**top-notch** *adj. Informal.* first-rate; excellent.

topog. *Abbrev.* for **to·pog·ra·phy** (tuh·POG·ruh·fee) *n.* **-phies** description or representation of the surface features of a region; also, such features as hills, lakes, rivers, cities, etc.; **to·pog·ra·pher** *n.* —**top·o·graph·ic** (–GRAF–) or **-i·cal** *adj.*

top·ping *n.* something that forms the top or is put on top of something else: *a pie ~.* —**top·ple** *v.* **top·ples, top·pled, top·pling** fall (over, down, etc.) because top-heavy; also, overturn or overthrow. —**tops** *adj.* topmost; preeminent. —**top·sail** (–sl, –sail) *n.* a sail next above the lowest sail or one set above a gaff. —**top-se·cret** *adj.* of the highest secrecy; extremely confidential: *~ information.* —**top·side** *adj.* & *adv.* on or to a ship's main deck or an upper deck; ***n.*** also **top·sides** *n.pl.* the part of a ship above the waterline. —**top·soil** *n.* the humus-rich upper layer of soil in which plants are rooted. —**top·sy-tur·vy** *adj.* & *adv.* upside down; hence, in disorder or confusion.

toque (TOKE) *n.* a small, close-fitting, usu. brimless hat; also, a knitted woolen cap.

tor *n.* a crag or high rocky hill.

To·rah or **to·rah** (TOR·uh) *n.* **1** the Jewish Bible, same as the Pentateuch; also, the scroll in which it is preserved in synagogues. **2** the entire oral and written body of Jewish laws, customs, and ceremonies.

torch *n.* **1** a flaming light, esp. one carried in the hand in former times, as by a **torch·bear·er;** hence, a source of enlightenment: *the ~ of civilization, learning.* **2** a device such as a blowtorch for shooting a very hot flame. **3** *Brit.* a flashlight. —**torch·light** *n.* & *adj.* (done by) the light of a torch or torches: *a ~ procession, rally.* —**torch song** a sentimental song of unrequited or lost love.

tore *pt.* of TEAR.

tor·e·a·dor (TOR·ee·uh–) *n.* a bullfighter. —**to·re·ro** (tuh·RAIR·oh) *n.* **-ros** a matador or bullfighter.

tor·ment *n.* great pain or agony; also, its cause or source; tormentor. —***v.*** (–MENT) inflict pain or suffering continuously or by repeated acts: *~ed by mosquitoes, jealousy, annoying questions;* **tor·men·tor** (–tur) or **tor·ment·er** *n.*

torn *pp.* of TEAR.

tor·na·do (–NAY–doh) *n.* **-do(e)s** a destructive windstorm or cyclone characterized by a funnel-shaped cloud moving along a narrow path.

To·ron·to (tuh·RON·toh) capital of Ontario.

tor·pe·do (–PEE·doh) *n.* & *v.* **-does** (-doze), **-doed, -do·ing** (attack or destroy with) a cigar-shaped, self-propelling underwater missile filled with explosives; **torpedo boat** a small, fast war vessel carrying torpedoes; PT boat. —**tor·pid** *adj.* dormant, sluggish, or inactive, as a hibernating animal. —**tor·por** (–pur)

adj. the state of being torpid; sluggishness; dullness; apathy.
torque (TORK) *n.* a rotating or twisting force exerted around an axis; ***v.*** **torques, torqued, torqu·ing** impart a torque to.
Tor·rance (–unce) a city of S.W. California.
tor·rent (–unt) *n.* a swift and violent flow or downpour: *rain in ~s; a ~ of abuse, words;* **tor·ren·tial** (–REN–) *adj.* **—tor·rid** *adj.* parched or scorching; hence, ardent or passionate; **Torrid Zone** the geographical region lying north and south of the equator extending to the tropics of Cancer and Capricorn; also called "the tropics."
tor·sion *n.* a twisting or being twisted, as when a taut wire or rod fixed at one end is turned left or right; also, the stress so produced: *Some automobiles have a* **torsion bar** *suspension instead of coil springs;* **tor·sion·al** *adj.;* **tor·sion·al·ly** *adv.*
tor·so *n.* **-sos** (–soze) or **–si** (–see) the trunk of a human statue or body, esp. as separate from head and limbs.
tort *n. Law.* a wrongful act arising from a breach of duty other than under contract, as in an automobile accident, which is liable to a civil suit for damages.
torte (TORT) *n., pl.* **tortes** or **tort·en** a rich cake made with eggs, crumbs, and chopped nuts. **—tor·til·la** (–TEE·uh) *n.* a round thin cake of unleavened cornmeal, a staple Mexican food.
tor·toise (–tus) *n.* a land or freshwater turtle; **tortoise shell** the shell of the "hawksbill" turtle used in making ornamental objects; **tor·toise-shell** *adj.* yellowish-brown and mottled.
tor·to·ni (–TOH·nee) *n.* an ice cream made with heavy cream, almonds, maraschino cherries, and often flavored with rum.
tor·tu·ous (TOR·choo·us) *adj.* marked by twists and turns; hence, devious or crooked: *a ~ trail; ~ logic, policy.* **—tor·ture** (–chur) *n.* **1** infliction of severe pain to punish, force a confession, etc. **2** severe physical pain or mental agony. **—*v.* -tures, -tured, -tur·ing** inflict severe pain on; also, twist or distort: *~d with rheumatism; ~d by his captors; language ~d out of its meaning;* **tor·tur·er** *n.*
To·ry (TOR·ee) *n.* **-ries** **1** formerly, an extreme conservative in regard to allegiance to the established church and the British throne, as the loyalists during the American Revolution. **2** a member of the British or Canadian Conservative party. *—n. & adj.* also **tory,** (one who is) conservative or reactionary.
toss *n.* a tossing or being tossed. **—*v.*** throw in a light, easy, or careless manner: *beauties ~ing beach balls; a ship ~ed by the waves; ~ing about in bed sleeplessly; She ~ed her head* (in contempt or indifference); *a facile writer who could* **toss off** *a story in no time; agreed to* **toss up** (i.e. flip a coin) *to break the tie;* **toss-up** *n.* a flipping of a coin to decide something; hence, *Informal.* an even chance.
tot *n.* **1** a little child. **2** esp. *Brit.* a small amount or portion, as a shot of alcoholic liquor. **—*v.* tots, tot·ted, tot·ting** esp. *Brit.* total (up). **—to·tal** (TOH·tl) *n.* a complete amount; sum; ***adj.*** whole or complete: *the ~ amount, a ~ eclipse, loss;* **total war** (i.e. all-out, not limited war); *~ abstinence, expenses, recall* (of everything from memory); ***v.*** **-tals, -tal(l)ed, -tal·(l)ing** add (figures); also, amount to: *expenses ~ing (to) $18,000.* **—to·tal·ly** *adv.* **—to·tal·i·tar·i·an** (–TAIR·ee·un) *adj.* of a government, exercising absolute power over the people, often under a dictator; ***n.*** one favoring such a system, or **to·tal·i·tar·i·an·ism** *n.* **—to·tal·i·ty** (toh·TAL–) *n.* **-ties** a total amount; hence, whole or entirety. **—to·tal·i·za·tor** (TOH·tl·i·zay·tur) *n.* a pari-mutuel machine; also **to·tal·i·sa·tor, to·tal·i·zer.**
tote *v.* **totes, tot·ed, tot·ing** *Informal.* **1** carry as a load: *a gun-~ing robber.* **2** total. **—*n.*** **1** [short form] totalizator: *a ~ board.* **2** a large handbag with pockets and shoulder strap; also **tote bag.**
to·tem (TOH–) *n.* a tribal or family symbol among N.W. American Indians in the shape of an animal, bird, or other natural object; **totem pole** a post with a series of totem symbols carved, painted, and placed one on top of another.
tot·ter *v.* stand or move in an unsteady manner, as if about to fall; hence, stagger.
tou·can (TOO–) *n.* a brilliantly colored tropical American bird with an enormous bill.
touch (TUCH) *v.* **1** make physical contact or strike lightly with the hand or some other part of the body: *Things feel hot, cold, rough, hard, etc. when ~ed; Skyscrapers seem to ~ the sky; Teetotalers won't ~* (i.e. use) *liquor; Ships ~ (at) many ports; Her talk ~ed (up)on* (i.e. dealt with or referred to) *many questions; a friend whom he can ~* (*Slang.* ask) *for a loan now and then.* **2** affect: *She was ~ed by his sad plight; something that ~es your interests; flowers and fruits ~ed* (i.e. damaged) *by frost; a manner ~ed with envy.* **—*n.*** **1** a touching or contact: *cold to the ~; pods that burst open at the slightest ~; Let's keep in ~ by letters; has lost ~ with Latin.* **2** a skillful or artistic stroke: *the deft ~es of an artist's brush; poetic ~es in her writings; a finishing ~.* **3** the sense of feeling or what is felt: *senses of taste and ~; the soft ~ of a baby's skin; typewriter keys with a light ~.* **4** a slight tinge or trace: *a ~ of frost in the autumn air; a ~ of irony; a ~* (i.e. slight attack) *of the flu.* **—touch down** of an aircraft or spacecraft, to land. **—touch off** start (an action or process) suddenly or violently, as by touching an explosive charge with a match. **—touch up** improve (a painting, literary composition, etc.) by slight changes. **—touch and go** a risky situation; **touch-and-go** *adj.* risky or precarious. **—touch·down** *n.* **1** (the moment of) landing of an aircraft or spacecraft. **2** in football, (a score of six points made by) possession of

the ball on or past the opponent's goal line. **—tou·ché** (too·SHAY) *interj.* [as in fencing to acknowledge a hit] score! **—touched** *adj.* emotionally moved; also, mentally unbalanced. **—touch football** an informal variety of football with tackling substituted by touching of the ball carrier. **—touch·ing** *adj.* moving; producing sympathy: *a ~ appeal.* **—touch·stone** *n.* a test of genuineness, as by a former method of testing precious metals by rubbing them on a siliceous stone. **—touch·type** *v.* **-types, -typed, -typ·ing** type without looking at the keys. **—touch·y** *adj.* **touch·i·er, -i·est** easily offended; hence, risky: *a ~ situation, subject;* **touch·i·ly** *adv.;* **touch·i·ness** *n.*

tough (TUF) *n.* a rough or violent person; ruffian. **—*adj.*** **1** so hard, firm, etc. in texture and consistency as not to be easily torn or broken: *Leather is ~; ~ meat, putty.* **2** hard to deal with; stiff: *a ~ customer, fight, opposition, job; ~* (i.e. hard to bear) *luck; a ~* (i.e. unruly) *neighborhood.* **—tough·en** *v.* make or become tough(er); **tough·en·er** *n.* **—tough·ly** *adv.;* **tough·ness** *n.*

tou·pee (too·PAY) *n.* a small hairpiece to cover a bald spot.

tour (TOOR) *n.* **1** a period or shift of work on an assignment or at a specific place: *a ~ of duty overseas.* **2** a going round visiting or inspecting: *a guided ~ of New York; a fact-finding ~; a circus that is always* **on tour** (i.e. touring); ***v.*** go on a tour through (a place). **—tour de force** (-duh·FORCE) *n.* **tours** (toor-) **de force** a feat of strength or skill. **—tour·ism** *n.* traveling for pleasure; also, the industry serving travelers; **tour·ist** *n.* one traveling for recreation; ***adj.:*** *a ~ resort, ticket, trap;* **tourist class** the least expensive class of travel accommodation.

tour·ma·line (TOOR·muh·lin, -leen) *n.* a mineral whose transparent varieties are valued as gems.

tour·na·ment (TOOR·nuh-, TUR-) *n.* **1** a series of athletic contests or games in competition for a championship. **2** formerly, a series of military exercises or contests, esp. between knights, as jousting and tilting; also **tour·ney** (-nee), **-neys.**

tour·ni·quet (TOOR·nuh·kit, TUR-) *n.* a device to check bleeding from a wound, usu. a bandage tightened around the affected limb.

tou·sle (TOW·zl) *v.* **-sles, -sled, -sling** dishevel (hair, etc.); muss.

tout *v. Informal.* publicize or puff; hence, solicit (business, customers, votes, etc.); also, solicit bets on (racehorses); ***n.*** one who touts.

tow (TOH) *v.* pull along behind, as with a rope or chain. **—*n.*** **1** a towing or being towed; **in tow** being towed; also, in one's care or charge. **2** a boat, barge, or other vehicle being towed; also, the line used.

to·ward (TORD, tuh·WORD) *prep.* **1** in the direction of: *turned ~ his wife; progress ~ peace; ~* (i.e. approaching or near) *the end of his life.* **2** with respect to: *attitude ~ a settlement; feelings ~ us; contributions ~* (i.e. for) *helping the poor.* Also **to·wards.**

tow·a·way (TOH·uh-) *n.* & *adj.* (the action) of towing away automobiles: *a ~ zone during snow emergencies.* **—tow·boat** (TOH·bote) *n.* a tugboat.

tow·el *n.* & *v.* **-els, -el(l)ed, -el·(l)ing** (wipe or dry with) an absorbent cloth or paper; **throw in the towel** give up the fight; **tow·el·(l)·ing** *n.* fabric such as terry cloth used for making towels.

tow·er *n.* a structure that is tall relative to its width, rising above its surroundings: *a church ~; an observation ~; airport control ~; a fortress ~;* **tower of strength** one looked up to for protection or leadership. **—*v.*** rise high like a tower; **tow·er·ing** *adj.: the ~ skyscrapers; a ~* (i.e. very high) *achievement, ambition; in a ~* (i.e. violent) *rage.*

tow·head (TOH·hed) *n.* (a person with) a head of flaxen hair; **tow·head·ed** *adj.*

tow·hee (TOH-, TOU-) *n.* a small bird of the finch family, related to the sparrows.

tow·line (TOH-) *n.* a line or rope for towing.

town *n.* **1** a community or settlement larger than a village and smaller than a city; also, townspeople: *The whole ~ was talking about it.* **2** in New England, a township. **3** the business and entertainment center of a city; **go to town** *Slang.* act with energy and enthusiasm; also, achieve success; **on the town** *Informal.* on a spree; out for a good time. **—town crier** formerly, one who made public announcements through the streets. **—town hall** a building containing the administrative offices of a town. **—town house** a row house, usu. of two or three stories. **—town meeting** a meeting of a town's inhabitants; also, a meeting of the voters of a New England township. **—towns·folk** *n.pl.* townspeople. **—town·ship** *n.* **1** (a division of a county forming) a unit of local government. **2** in U.S. land surveys, a unit of 36 square miles. **—towns·man** (-mun) *n.* **-men** **1** one who lives in or was raised in a town. **2** a fellow inhabitant of a town. **—towns·peo·ple** *n.pl.* town-bred people; also, the people of a town.

tow·path (TOH-) *n.* a path along a canal traveled by men or animals towing boats. **—tow rope** a rope used for towing. **—tow truck** a truck equipped for towing automobiles.

tox·e·mi·a (-SEE·mee·uh) *n.* illness due to toxic substances in the circulating blood, as from food poisoning. **—tox·ic** *adj.* poisonous; of or caused by a toxin; **tox·ic·i·ty** (-SIS-) *n.;* **tox·i·col·o·gy** (-COL-) *n.* the study of poisons and their control; **tox·i·col·o·gist** *n.* **—tox·in** *n.* a poison produced by a living organism such as a bacterium or fungus; also, a poison secreted by a plant or animal.

toy *n.* an object for a child to play with; a trifle or trinket; also, anything of small size; ***adj.:*** *a*

~ soldier, balloon; a **toy dog** *such as a chihuahua, Pekingese, or Pomeranian.* **—v.** play idly (*with* an article meant for other uses, as a pencil, or an idea, plan, etc.).

tpk. turnpike.

tr. translated; transpose; treasurer.

trace *n.* **1** either of a pair of straps or chains connecting an animal to the vehicle it pulls; **kick over the traces** become unruly or reckless. **2** a mark or other evidence of an occurrence or presence, as an animal's tracks in the snow: *vanished without a ~.* **3** a barely perceptible or measurable amount: *~s of poison, precipitation; a* **trace element** *such as magnesium or iodine required in minute amounts for proper nutrition.* **—v. trac·es, traced, trac·ing 1** follow a track or trail (*to* its origin or originator): *to ~ game, criminals, the origin of a word; He ~d his ancestry back to African forebears; phobias that may be ~d back to childhood experiences.* **2** draw; also, copy (an original) using transparent paper. **—trace·a·ble** *adj.;* **trac·er** *n.* **—trac·er·y** *n.* **-er·ies** an intricate decorative pattern of lines, circles, and other shapes filling a window or other opening. **—trac·ing** *n.* something traced, as a copy (of a map or drawing) on transparent paper, a recording made by an instrument such as a cardiograph, etc.

tra·che·a (TRAY·kee·uh) *n., pl.* **-che·ae** (–kee·ee) or **-che·as** the windpipe; **tra·che·al** *adj.* **—tra·che·ot·o·my** (–OT·uh·mee) *n.* **-mies** a surgical cutting into the trachea to relieve suffocation. **—tra·cho·ma** (truh·COH–) *n.* a contagious tropical disease of the eyelids that may affect the cornea and lead to blindness.

track *n.* the path of something moving, a course to travel over, or the marks left, as the footprints of an animal, ruts made by wheels, the set of parallel rails on which a train moves, a path beaten through a forest, a course laid around a field for running or racing, the path of a hurricane, the groove of a phonograph record, etc.: *Tanks, bulldozers, and tractors move on endless ~s* (i.e. belts or treads); *was shot dead* **in his tracks** (i.e. right where he was); **keep** (or **lose) track of** keep (or fail to be) informed about; **on** (or **off) the track** on (or off) the right course; **track·less** *adj.* **—v. 1** follow the track of: *to ~ an animal; to* **track down** (i.e. find) *game; an obscure quotation that is hard to ~ down* (in books); *Radio signals help ~ a satellite from* **tracking stations** *on the earth.* **2** make tracks on or with: *to ~ up a polished floor; to ~ mud into a house* (i.e. bring it on one's feet or shoes). **—track and field** (sports) events consisting of races, hurdles, etc. around a track and jumps, throws, etc. in the center of the field; **track-and-field** *adj.* **—track record** a record of achievements in a field of endeavor.

tract *n.* **1** a stretch or extent, esp. of land; a usu. large area. **2** a pathway or continuous system of bodily organs with a special function: *The respiratory ~ consists of the nose, throat, larynx, trachea, bronchi, and lungs.* **3** a pamphlet or small treatise on a religious or political subject. **—trac·ta·ble** (TRAC·tuh–) *adj.* easy to manage or handle: *Be ~ if not docile; a ~* (i.e. malleable) *metal.* **—trac·tate** *n.* a treatise, esp. a contentious one. **—trac·tion** *n.* a pulling or drawing, a being pulled, or pulling power: *A broken leg is put in ~* (i.e. pulled by weights over a pulley) *to keep the parts in position while healing; The first tractors, driven by steam, were called* **traction engines;** *snow tires for better ~* (i.e. moving without slipping) *on snow and ice:* **trac·tion·al** *adj.;* **trac·tive** (–tiv–) *adj.* **—trac·tor** (–tur) *n.* **1** a powerful motor vehicle for pulling or pushing farm machines, snow plows, etc. **2** the cab-and-engine unit that pulls a freight trailer, or **trac·tor-trail·er.**

trade *n.* **1** the buying and selling of goods and services; commerce: *retail ~; foreign ~; the tourist ~* (i.e. market); *caters chiefly to the rush-hour ~* (i.e. clientele or customers). **2** an exchange or swap; also, a bargain. **3** a skilled occupation or craft, not a business or profession; also, the people in a trade: *the book ~; rumors circulating in the ~; a ~ school.* **—v. trades, trad·ed, trad·ing 1** buy and sell; do business: *no ~ing with the enemy; They ~ in stocks;* **trade (up)on** use or exploit to one's advantage. **2** swap or exchange: *Let's ~ seats; People* **trade in** *a used car* (in part payment) *when buying a new one;* **trade-in** *n.* **3** be a customer (*at* a store, *with* a merchant, etc.). **—trade book** one for general sale, not a textbook. **—trade·mark** *n.* a brand name, slogan, symbol, or device used by a company to identify its product or service; **v.** register as a trademark: *"finger-licking good" is ~ed.* **—trade name** brand name or trademark; also, a company's business name. **—trade-off** *n.* an exchanging of something one owns for another benefit; also, a balancing of two factors or elements. **—trade paperback** See PAPERBACK. **—trad·er** *n.* a merchant; also, a merchant ship. **—trade school** one teaching skilled trades. **—trades·man** *n.* **-men** a retailer or shopkeeper; also, *Regional.* a craftsman. **—trades·people** *n.pl.* people engaged in trade. **—trade union** a workers' union; labor union. **—trade wind** any of a system of winds blowing towards the equator with great regularity throughout the year because of pressure differences between the tropics and the polar regions. **—trading post** a store at a frontier or outpost selling supplies, esp. to Indians in exchange for furs, jewelry, etc. **—trading stamp** a stamplike label given as a bonus to retail customers with cash purchases for them to collect and exchange for gifts.

tra·di·tion (–DISH–) *n.* the oral handing down of beliefs, laws, customs, legends, etc. from generation to generation; also, a body of such beliefs, etc. or something received by tradition, as the observance of Thanksgiving: *in the*

Jewish ~; ~ has greater force than customs; **tra·di·tion·al** *adj.;* **tra·di·tion·al·ly** *adv.*

tra·duce (truh·DEWCE) *v.* **-duc·es, -duced, -duc·ing** bring (a person) into disrepute unjustly; vilify or defame; **tra·duc·er** *n.*

traf·fic *n.* **1** the movement of people and vehicles, esp. in a public place such as a street or highway: *Signals regulating the flow of ~; a ~ jam at an intersection; air ~ controllers; the ~ pattern determined by furniture arrangement in a living area.* **2** business done by a transportation or communications company; volume of passengers, freight, telegrams, etc. **3** commercial activity; buying and selling: *Charge the highest price that the ~ will bear; no ~ with criminals; the ~ in illicit drugs;* ***v.*** **traf·fics, traf·ficked, traf·fick·ing** carry on trade or traffic, esp. illicitly. **—traffic circle** an intersection at which all traffic moves in the same direction in a circle, often around a **traffic island,** instead of stopping for cross-traffic to pass. **—traffic light** (or **signal**) a set of red, green, and amber lights regulating traffic at an intersection.

tra·ge·di·an (truh·JEE·dee·un) *n.* a writer of or actor in tragedies; *fem.* **tra·ge·di·enne** (–EN); **trag·e·dy** (TRAJ·uh·dee) *n.* **-dies** a serious drama or play with a sad ending; also, any sad or terrible happening; **trag·ic** (TRAJ–) *adj.: ~ drama, actor, writer, events;* **trag·i·cal·ly** *adv.*

trail *v.* **1** follow closely, as in one's tracks: *police ~ing a suspect.* **2** drag, tow, or bring after oneself: *a child ~ing a toy truck; the ~ing skirt of a wedding gown; the* **trailing** (i.e. rear, not front or "leading") **edge** *of an airplane's wing; The hurt runner began to ~* (i.e. lag behind). **3** move in a casual or aimless manner: *The children ~ed along behind their mother; smoke ~ing from a chimney; creeping plants that ~ along the ground or over walls.* **4** become weaker: *The voice on the phone ~ed off.* **—*n.*** something that trails (as dust or smoke); also, what is left behind, as a scent, trace, or track: *the ~ of misery left by a war; the exhaust ~ of an aircraft; an Indian ~; Pioneers blazed ~s through the wilderness by marking trees.* **—trail bike** a light motorcycle for rough, cross-country riding. **—trail·blaz·er** *n.* a pioneer or explorer; **trail·blaz·ing** *n.* & *adj.* **—trail·er** *n.* **1** a wheeled vehicle designed to be hauled, either a wagon or closed van carrying cargo, usu. pulled by a tractor, or one for recreational travel and camping, equipped as temporary living quarters; also, a mobile home. **2** a creeping plant such as an ivy. **—trailer park** (or **camp** or **court**) a site equipped with water, electricity, etc. for a community of mobile homes. **—trailing arbutus** same as ARBUTUS. **—trail-ski·ing** *n.* cross-country skiing.

train *n.* **1** a connected series of railroad cars pulled by a locomotive; hence, a chain or sequence: *a freight ~; a ~ of events, thought; A war brings misery in its ~.* **2** a line or group of people, animals, vehicles, etc. moving along together: *a wagon ~; a ~* (i.e. caravan) *of camels; a king and his ~* (i.e. retinue). **3** a trailing part: *the ~ of a wedding gown, peacock, comet.* **—*v.*** **1** teach, instruct, or practice in order to develop a faculty or skill: *Educators ~ minds; a ~ed acrobat; a seal ~ed to do tricks; She's ~ing for the Olympics.* **2** guide or direct physically: *a shrub ~ed to grow on a trellis; Spotlights were kept ~ed on the stage.* **—train·ee** (–NEE) *n.* one being trained. **—train·er** *n.* **—train·ing** *n.* **—train·load** *n.* what a full railroad train carries: *a ~ of refugees.* **—train·man** *n.* **-men** a member of the crew of a railroad train.

traipse *v.* **traips·es, traipsed, traips·ing** *Informal.* wander or walk about aimlessly.

trait *n.* a distinguishing feature or quality of a person: *the characteristic ~s of a people.*

trai·tor (–ur) *n.* one who betrays or is disloyal (to his faith, country, friends, etc.); *fem.* **trai·tress** (–tris); **trai·tor·ous** (–us) *adj.*

tra·jec·to·ry (truh·JEC·tuh·ree) *n.* **-ries** the curved path of an object moving under a gravitational or other force, as planets, space vehicles, bullets, and other projectiles.

tram *n.* a car or carrier for loads, as in mines; also, *Brit.* a streetcar.

tram·mel (TRAM·ul) *n.* & *v.* **tram·mels, tram·mel(l)ed, tram·mel·(l)ing** (entangle or confine as in) shackles or the meshes of a net: *the ~s of tradition.*

tramp *v.* **1** walk with heavy steps; also, trample. **2** go around on foot, esp. wearily, as in search of a home or work; wander as a tramp. **—*n.*** **1** the sound of heavy steps, as of marching soldiers; also, a hike or march. **2** a person without a fixed home, esp. one who lives by doing odd jobs; also, *Slang.* a streetwalker or prostitute. **3** a cargo ship without regular trade routes or schedules, available for hire as needed. **—tram·ple** *v.* **-ples, -pled, -pling** stamp or tread heavily (on); hence, crush; also, treat ruthlessly: *age-old customs ~d under foot by tyrants;* ***n.*** a trampling (sound). **—tram·po·line** (–puh·leen, –lin) *n.* a bouncing table for gymnastic use consisting of a sturdy sheet or net stretched over a frame.

trance *n.* **1** a partly conscious state without voluntary movement, as in deep hypnosis, catalepsy, or the condition of a spiritualistic medium. **2** a trancelike state of absorption; also, a daze or stupor.

tran·quil (TRANG–) *adj.* peaceful and quiet in a deep or settled way; also, undisturbed or serene: *a ~ life;* **tran·quil·ly** *adv.;* **tran·quil·(l)i·ty** (–QUIL–) *n.;* **tran·quil·(l)ize** *v.* **-(l)iz·es, -(l)iz·ed, -(l)iz·ing** make or become tranquil; **tran·quil·(l)iz·er** *n.* a drug used to relieve anxiety, soothe nervous tension, or reduce high blood pressure.

trans. transitive; translated; translation; translator; transportation. **—trans-** *prefix.* across; over; beyond: as in *trans-Alaska, transplant.*

—trans·act (–SACT, –ZACT) *v.* conduct or carry on (business with someone); **trans·ac·tion** (–AC–) *n.* a business deal; **transactions** *pl.* report of the proceedings of a learned society. **—trans·at·lan·tic** (–LAN–) *adj.* across or beyond the Atlantic: *a ~ flight, cable; a ~ nation.* **—trans·ceiv·er** (–SEE·vur) *n.* a combined radio transmitter-receiver. **—tran·scend** (–SEND) *v.* be above the limits of (human powers, experience, etc.); hence, surpass: *philanthropy that ~s national boundaries;* **tran·scend·ent** *adj.;* **tran·scen·den·tal** (–DEN–) *adj.* spiritual; also, abstract; **transcendental meditation** concentration of the mind away from material things in order to achieve peace of mind; **tran·scen·den·tal·ism** *n.* philosophy of knowledge through intuition rather than sense experience. **—trans·con·ti·nen·tal** (–NEN–) *adj.* across a continent: *~ railroad.* **—tran·scribe** (–SCRIBE) *v.* **-scribes, -scribed, -scrib·ing** make a transcript or transcription of: *Secretaries ~ shorthand notes; The recording was put through a ~ing machine for playing back;* **tran·script** (TRANS–) *n.* a copy, esp. official, of something recorded, as a speech, academic grades, etc. **—tran·scrip·tion** (–SCRIP–) *n.* **1** a recording made for broadcasting. **2** a musical arrangement. **3** a transcribing or transcript. **—trans·duc·er** (–DEW·sur) *n.* a device such as a phonograph pickup or a microphone that converts electric waves into mechanical vibrations or vice versa. **—tran·sept** *n.* either of the arms of a cross-shaped church. **—trans·fer** (–FUR) *v.* **-fers, -ferred, -fer·ring** **1** move (someone) or convey (something) from one place or person to another: *managers ~d from New York to Chicago; A property is ~d from vendor to buyer.* **2** change from one place, position, etc. to another: *Students ~ from school to school; ~ at the next stop to Route 18.* **—n.** (TRANS–) a transferring, being transferred, something transferred, as a design or drawing from one surface to another, a ticket allowing a passenger to transfer to another route, or a transferring point on a route. **—trans·fer·a·ble** (–FUR·uh–) *adj.;* **trans·fer·al** (–FUR–) or **trans·fer·ence** (–FUR–) *n.* **—trans·fig·ure** (–FIG·yur) *v.* **-ures, -ured, -ur·ing** change the form or appearance of; also, transform so as to glorify or exalt; **trans·fig·u·ra·tion** (–RAY–) *n.* **—trans·fix** (–FIX) *v.* pierce through, as with a pointed weapon; hence, hold motionless, as if impaled. **—trans·form** (–FORM) *v.* **1** change the shape, appearance, or nature of a person or thing fundamentally. **2** change from one form to another, as electricity to a different voltage, one mathematical expression to another, or the active to the passive voice. **—trans·form·er** (–FORM–) *n.* one that transforms, esp. a voltage-changing device. **—trans·for·ma·tion** (–MAY–) *n.* **—trans·fuse** (–FEWZ) *v.* **-fus·es, -fused, -fus·ing** **1** transfer (a liquid) from one vessel to another; esp., inject blood from one person into the circulatory system of another; **trans·fu·sion** (–FEW–) *n.* **2** infuse or inspire. **—trans·gress** (–GRES) *v.* go beyond (a limit); hence, break (a law or command); sin against; **trans·gres·sion** (–GRESH–) *n.;* **trans·gres·sor** (–GRES·ur) *n.* **—tran·ship** same as TRANSSHIP. **—tran·sient** (–shunt) *adj.* short in duration or stay; passing or fleeting; ***n.*** a temporary lodger, worker, etc.; **tran·sient·ly** *adv.;* **tran·sience** or **tran·sien·cy** *n.* **—tran·sis·tor** (–ZIS–, –SIS–) *n.* an electronic device like a vacuum tube in controlling the flow of electricity in a circuit but more compact and durable, hence much used in radios, computers, etc.; **tran·sis·tor·ize** *v.* **-iz·es, -ized, -iz·ing** equip (a device) with transistors. **—trans·it** *n.* **1** passage or conveyance: *goods lost* **in transit** *between New York and Boston.* **2** a local public transportation system using buses, trains, etc. **3** a surveying instrument with a telescope on a tripod to measure angles. **—tran·si·tion** (–ZISH–) *n.* a passing from one condition, stage, etc. to another: *a period of ~; a smooth ~;* **tran·si·tion·al** *adj.* **—tran·si·tive** (–suh·tiv) *n.* & *adj.* (a verb such as *give* or *love*) that has a direct object; **tran·si·tive·ly** *adv.;* **tran·si·tive·ness** *n.;* **tran·si·tiv·i·ty** (–TIV–) *n.* **—tran·si·to·ry** *adj.* of things, transient by nature; short-lived, not permanent: *the ~ things of this world; ~ pleasures.*

Trans·kei (–KAY, –KYE) a homeland of the Xhosa people of South Africa; 16,070 sq.mi. (41,620 km²); *cap.* Umtata.

transl. translated; translation. **—trans·late** (–LATE) *v.* **-lates, -lat·ed, -lat·ing** change from one place or condition to another: *a word that is difficult to ~* (into another or one's own language); *to ~ a philosophy into action; Enoch was ~d* (i.e. conveyed) *to heaven;* **trans·lat·a·ble** *adj.;* **trans·la·tor** *n.;* **trans·la·tion** *n.* a translating or a translated version. **—trans·lit·er·ate** (–LIT–) *v.* **-ates, -at·ed, -at·ing** write (words, letters, etc.) in the characters of another language, as the Greek epsilon with English "e." **—trans·lu·cent** (–LOO·snt) *adj.* partly transparent, as frosted glass; **trans·lu·cent·ly** *adv.;* **trans·lu·cence** or **-cen·cy** *n.* **—trans·mi·grate** (–MY–) *v.* **-grates, -grat·ed, -grat·ing** of the soul, pass from one body after its death into another; **trans·mi·gra·tion** (–GRAY–) *n.* **—trans·mis·si·ble** (–MIS–) *adj.* capable of being transmitted. **—trans·mis·sion** (–MISH·un) *n.* **1** a transmitting or being transmitted, as radio waves. **2** in a vehicle, the assembly of parts, esp. a set of gears, that transmits power from engine to drive shaft. **—trans·mit** (–MIT) *v.* **-mits, -mit·ted, -mit·ting** pass along as an agent or medium; pass on; let through: *Germs ~ diseases; to ~ a message by* radio; *The sun* ~*s heat and light (through the air)*; **trans·mit·tal** or **-mit·tance** *n.*; **trans·mit·ter** *n.* one that transmits, esp. a set of broadcasting equipment for radio or television signals; **trans·mit·ti·ble** (–tuh·bl) or **-mit·ta·ble** *adj.* same as TRANSMISSIBLE. —**trans·mog·ri·fy** (–MOG–) *v.* **-fies, -fied, -fy·ing** transform, esp. in a bewildering manner or with grotesque effect. —**trans·mute** *v.* **-mutes, -mut·ed, -mut·ing** change the nature or substance of (a base metal, etc.) into something better or higher; **trans·mu·ta·tion** (–TAY–) *n.* a change, as in alchemy: *the* ~ *of elements using atom-smashers.* —**trans·na·tion·al** (–NASH–) *adj.* going beyond national boundaries. —**trans·o·ce·an·ic** (–shee·AN·ic) *adj.* across or beyond the ocean: *a* ~ *flight;* ~ *travel, transport.* —**tran·som** (–sum) *n.* a horizontal crossbar, as at the top of a window or door; lintel; also, a narrow window above a door. —**tran(s)·son·ic** (–SON–) *adj.* between subsonic and supersonic in speed: *the* ~ *zone* (i.e. sound barrier). —**transp.** transportation. —**trans·pa·cif·ic** (–puh·SIF–) *adj.* across or beyond the Pacific. —**trans·par·en·cy** *n.* **-cies** transparent quality; also, something transparent, as a slide for an overhead projector: *color* ~*s;* **trans·par·ent** (–PAIR·unt) *adj.* that can be seen through, as glass; a ~ (i.e. sheer) *fabric; a* ~ *lie; her* ~ (i.e. frank) *sincerity;* **trans·par·ent·ly** *adj.* —**tran·spire** (–SPIRE) *v.* **-spires, -spired, -spir·ing** give off water vapor, as through the pores of a plant's leaves; hence, leak out or become known; also, happen or occur; **tran·spi·ra·tion** (–spuh·RAY–) *n.* —**trans·plant** (–PLANT) *v.* remove (an organ or tissue, people, etc. as in digging up plants) from one place to plant or resettle in another; ***n.*** a transplanting or something transplanted: *a hair* ~*; tissue* ~*s; heart* ~*s;* **trans·plan·ta·tion** (–TAY–) *n.* —**trans·po·lar** (–POH·lur) *adj.* across a pole or polar region. —**tran·spon·der** (–SPON–) *n.* a radio device that automatically transmits a response signal, as used to identify approaching planes on a radar screen. —**trans·port** (–PORT) *v.* **1** carry or convey, esp. in a vehicle. **2** carry away; enrapture: ~*ed with joy.* —***n.*** (TRANS–) **1** (means of) transporting: *road* ~*; air* ~. **2** strong emotion, esp. rapture: *in a* ~ (or *in* ~*s*) *of joy, rage.* —**trans·por·ta·tion** (–TAY–) *n.* a transporting or being transported; also, a means of transporting or the transporting business: *public* ~*; sentenced to* ~ *for life* (i.e. life in a penal colony); **trans·port·er** *n.* —**trans·pose** (–POZE) *v.* **-pos·es, -posed, -pos·ing** **1** change the normal position of, esp. interchange, as letters or sounds in a word. **2** in music, change the key of, as in playing a composition. Hence **trans·po·si·tion** (–ZISH·un) *n.* —**trans·sex·u·al** (–SEK·shoo·ul) *n.* a person with a psychological urge to change sex; also, one who has had a sex change by surgery; ***adj.:*** *a* ~ *operation.* —**trans·ship** (–SHIP) *v.* **-ships, -shipped, -ship·ping** transfer from one ship or vehicle to another for further shipment; **trans·ship·ment** *n.* —**tran·sub·stan·ti·a·tion** (–AY–) *n.* the Roman Catholic doctrine that the Eucharistic bread and wine are changed into Christ's body and blood during Mass. —**trans·verse** (–VURCE) *adj.* set crosswise; ***n.*** (*also* TRANS-) a transverse beam, axis, etc. —**trans·ves·tite** (–VES–) *n.* a person, usu. a male, who gets sexual pleasure from dressing like one of the opposite sex; also ***adj.;*** **trans·ves·tism** *n.*

trap *n.* **1** a device for capturing an animal; hence, a device, stratagem, or ambush for catching someone off guard: *fell into his own* ~*; a speed* ~ *set up by police to catch speeders.* **2** a U-shaped bend in a drainpipe to hold water to prevent the return of sewer gas. **3** a light, two-wheeled carriage with springs. **4** a spring device used in skeet and trapshooting for throwing clay pigeons; also **trap house. 5** in a golf course, a pit filled with sand as a hazard. **6 traps** *pl.* the percussion devices in a jazz band or orchestra. **7** a dark-colored, igneous rock such as basalt; also **trap·rock. 8 traps** *pl. Informal.* belongings. —***v.*** **traps, trapped, trap·ping** **1** trap animals; also, catch as in a trap; snare; **trap·per** *n.* **2** adorn or equip with trappings; caparison. —**trap·door** *n.* (a hinged or sliding door covering) an opening in a floor, ceiling, or roof.

trap·eze (–PEEZ) *n.* a short bar hung horizontally by two ropes on which an aerialist, or **trapeze artist,** performs in a circus. —**trap·e·zoid** (TRAP·uh–) *n.* a four-sided plane figure with two sides parallel; **trap·e·zoi·dal** (–ZOY–) *adj.*

trap house same as TRAP, *n.* 4. —**trap·pings** *n.pl.* ornamental coverings, as of a caparisoned horse; hence, accessories or accouterments: *all the* ~*s of high office.* —**trap·rock** same as TRAP, *n.* 7. —**trap·shoot·ing** *n.* the sport of shooting at clay pigeons sprung from a trap.

trash *n.* worthless or discarded stuff; rubbish; also, a worthless person or riffraff; ***v.*** *Slang.* vandalize; destroy; discard as trash; **trash·y** *adj.* **trash·i·er, -i·est** worthless.

trau·ma (TRAW·muh) *n.* **-mas** or **-ma·ta** (–muh·tuh) an unpleasant emotional experience such as may cause neurotic symptoms; also, a wound or injury sometimes called "physical trauma"; **trau·mat·ic** (–MAT–) *adj.* —**trau·ma·tize** (TRAW–) *v.* **-tiz·es, -tized, -tiz·ing** subject to a physical or psychic trauma.

trav·ail (TRAV–, truh·VAIL) *n.* & *v.* [literary] toil or labor. —**trav·el** *n.* a journey; traveling: *the* **travels** *of Sinbad;* ***v.*** **-els, -el(l)ed, -el·(l)ing** **1** go from one place to another; journey; also, be transmitted, as light or sound. **2** journey over or through; traverse; **trav·el·(l)er** *n.* —**trav·e·log(ue)** (–log) *n.* a motion picture or an illustrated lecture on travels.

trav·erse *v.* (–VURCE) **-ers·es, -ersed, -ers·ing** travel or move across (something extensive, as a desert or sky); also, move diagonally across (a slope, as a skier). ***—n.*** & ***adj.*** (TRAV–) (something) lying or extending across; transverse: *the* **traverse rod** *on which a curtain slides.*

trav·er·tine (–teen, –tin) *n.* a porous, whitish limestone found along springs and streams.

trav·es·ty *n.* **-ties** a ridiculous imitation, parody, or burlesque: *The trial was a ~ of justice;* ***v.*** **-ties, -tied, -ty·ing** make a travesty of.

trawl *n.* & *v.* **1** (fish or catch cod, shrimp, etc. with) a huge bag-shaped net that is dragged along in the water by a boat, or **trawl·er** *n.* **2** (fish or catch with) a long line called a **trawl line** or "setline" from which short lines with baited hooks are hung.

tray *n.* a flat open receptacle with a low rim for holding or carrying food, etc.

treach·er·ous (TRECH·uh·rus) *adj.* not to be trusted, as one likely to be disloyal; also, not reliable, as ice too thin to skate on: *~ driving conditions;* **treach·er·ous·ly** *adv.* —**treach·er·y** *n.* **-er·ies** (an act of) betrayal.

trea·cle (TREE–) *n.* *Brit.* molasses; **trea·cly** *adj.* **-cli·er, -cli·est** sweet and cloying, as sentimentality.

tread (TRED) *v.* **treads,** *pt.* **trod,** *pp.* **trod·den** (TRODN) or **trod, tread·ing** step on or walk: *where angels fear to ~; to ~ on a flower bed; to ~* (i.e. crush with feet) *grapes for making wine; to ~ out a fire; a path trodden* (i.e. formed by walking) *through a lawn;* **tread water** *pt.* **tread·ed** keep one's head above water by moving the legs up and down. ***—n.*** **1** the act, sound, or a way of treading: *the heavy ~ of soldiers marching.* **2** a part that treads or is trodden on, as the horizontal part of a step, the grooved surface of a tire, the sole of a shoe, etc. —**trea·dle** (TREDL) *n.* a lever or pedal, as of a sewing machine, that is worked by the foot. —**tread·mill** (TRED–) *n.* a machine worked by treading on an endless belt going over wheels.

treas. treasurer; treasury.

trea·son (TREE·zn) *n.* open disloyalty to one's country, as by joining with or helping an enemy; **trea·son·a·ble** or **-son·ous** (–us) *adj.*

treas·ure (TREZH·ur) *n.* **1** wealth stored or put away, as money, jewels, etc. **2** a person or thing of great value: *art ~s.* ***—v.*** **-ures, -ured, -ur·ing** hoard as treasure; also, value or cherish protectively: *a ~d gift, friendship, memory.* —**treas·ur·er** *n.* an official in charge of funds, revenues, or finances, as of a treasury. —**treas·ure-trove** (–trohv) *n.* treasure found hidden, esp. one of unknown ownership; hence, a valuable discovery. —**treas·ur·y** *n.* **-ur·ies** **1** a place where a treasure or funds are kept; hence, funds; also, a rich storehouse: *a ~ of information.* **2** **Treasury** a government department in charge of financial affairs.

treat (TREET) *v.* **1** deal with: *She ~s employees with kindness; Doctors ~ ailments; ~ patients* (for their ailments); *a poem that ~s (of) the vanity of things; Don't ~ it as a joke; refused to ~* (i.e. negotiate) *with terrorists.* **2** subject to a process: *metal ~ed with acid.* **3** entertain or provide with: *She ~ed them to a lunch.* ***—n.*** an entertainment, gift, or something special that gives pleasure: *"trick or ~?"* —**trea·tise** (–is) *n.* a book, article, etc. containing a systematic discussion: *a ~ on poetry.* —**treat·ment** *n.* a treating of someone or something; also, a medicine or method used. —**treat·y** *n.* **-ties** a formal agreement between nations, as for peace, trade, etc.; also, a document setting forth the terms of such an agreement.

tre·ble (TREB·ul) *n.* in music, the highest or soprano part that is sung by women or boys and played on instruments such as the violin and clarinet. ***—adj.*** **1** of or having to do with the treble; also, high-pitched; **treble clef** the sign (𝄞) showing that the pitch of the notes on a staff is above middle C. **2** triple; ***v.*** **-bles, -bled, -bling** make or become triple.

tree *n.* a large perennial plant with a woody stem and branches starting at a height from the ground; also, a family tree or shoe tree; ***v.*** **trees, treed, tree·ing** chase up a tree; also, put in a shoe tree; **treed** *adj.* wooded: *a ~ lot;* **tree·less** *adj.* —**tree farm** an area in which trees are grown for timber and other forest products. —**tree line** same as TIMBERLINE. —**tree of heaven** same as AILANTHUS. —**tree surgery** the care of trees by pruning, spraying, removing decayed wood, etc.

tre·foil (TREE–) *n.* **1** a leaf with three parts, as of the clover and other plants of the lotus group; also, this group of plants. **2** a decorative design like a threefold leaf.

trek *v.* **treks, trekked, trek·king** travel slowly or laboriously, as by wagon; also, *Informal.* go on foot; ***n.*** a journey or migration. —**trek·ker** *n.*

trel·lis *n.* & *v.* (train a vine on) a frame of latticework.

trem·a·tode (TREM·uh–) *n.* any of a class of parasitic flatworms including flukes.

trem·ble *v.* **-bles, -bled, -bling** shake, as from fear, cold, etc.; also, quake: *a ~ing voice; The ground ~d from the earthquake;* ***n.*** a trembling; also, tremor. —**tre·men·dous** (tri·MEN·dus) *adj.* awe-inspiring because great or gigantic; also, *Informal.* excellent; very great: *a ~ achievement;* **tre·men·dous·ly** *adv.* —**trem·o·lo** (TREM·uh–) *n.* **-los** a tremulous or vibrating effect of repeated sound in singing or playing; also, an organ stop for producing such an effect. —**trem·or** (–ur) *n.* a trembling or shaking, as in palsy: *a low-intensity earth* ~ (i.e. quake). —**trem·u·lous** (–yuh·lus) *adj.* marked by trembling or quivering; hence, fearful; **trem·u·lous·ly** *adv.;* **trem·u·lous·ness** *n.*

trench *n.* a long, narrow ditch, as dug for laying pipes or to protect soldiers in warfare; ***v.*** dig trenches in or protect (troops) with trenches. —**trench·ant** (–unt–) *adj.* cutting; clear-cut; effective: *a ~ policy, style, wit;* **trench·an·cy** *n.* —**trench coat** a military-style belted raincoat. —**trench·er** *n.* a wooden platter used formerly for serving and carving food; **trench·er·man** *n.* **-men** a hearty eater. —**trench foot** a foot disease with symptoms like those of frostbite, which attacked soldiers exposed to the cold and dampness of the trenches in World War I. —**trench mouth** a bacterial infection of the mouth characterized by sores and ulcers.

trend *n.* & *v.* (have) a general direction or drift, as of events, opinions, fashions, etc.; also, a current style or vogue; **trend·y** *adj.* **trend·i·er, -i·est** *Informal.* following the latest fashions; swinging; **trend·i·ly** *adv.*

Tren·ton (–tun) capital of New Jersey.

tre·pan (tri·PAN) *n.* & *v.* **-pans, -panned, -pan·ning** [earlier form] trephine; **trep·a·na·tion** (–NAY–) *n.* —**tre·phine** (tri·FINE, –FEEN) *n.* a surgical instrument for making small openings in the skull; ***v.*** **-phines, -phined, -phin·ing** operate on with a trephine; **treph·i·na·tion** (–NAY–) *n.*

trep·i·da·tion (–DAY–) *n.* fear or apprehension marked by trembling.

tres·pass (–pus, –pass) *v.* intrude unlawfully on another's property or rights; transgress: *a "No Trespassing" sign; sorry to ~ on your time;* ***n.*** a trespassing; also, a moral transgression; sin; **tres·pass·er** *n.*

tress *n.* a lock or curl of hair; **tress·es** *pl.* a woman's or girl's long flowing hair.

tres·tle (TRES·ul) *n.* a framework supporting a platform, table top, bridge, etc.

trey *n.* a die, domino, etc. with three spots. —**tri-** *prefix.* three or third: as in *triangle, triceps, triennial.* —**tri·ad** (TRY–) *n.* a group or set of three.

tri·age (tree·AHZH, TREE–) *n.* a selecting or sorting, as of wounded in battle to determine order of treatment.

tri·al (TRY·ul) *n.* **1** a trying or attempt to find out something: *Wrestling is a ~ of strength; hired* **on trial** *for three months: A case is brought to ~* (in court); *~ by jury; Animals learn by* **trial and error;** *the* **tri·al-and-err·or** *method of picking a hat of the right size.* **2** (cause of) hardship or annoyance: *the ~s and tribulations of life; was a ~ to his parents.* ***—adj.:*** *a ~ marriage, model of a vehicle; a ~ judge, court;* **trial balloon** a proposal or announcement made for testing reactions, as a balloon used in weather forecasting.

tri·an·gle (TRY·ang·gl) *n.* a plane figure with three straight sides and angles; hence, anything resembling this, as a percussion instrument made of a steel rod bent into a triangle; **tri·an·gu·lar** (–ANG·gyuh·lur) *adj.;* **tri·an·gu·lar·ly** *adv.* —**tri·an·gu·late** (–ANG·gyuh–) *v.* **-lates, -lat·ed, -lat·ing** in surveying, divide into triangles for computing a distance or position; **tri·an·gu·la·tion** (–LAY–) *n.*

Tri·as·sic (try·AS–) *n.* & *adj.* (of) the first period of the Mesozoic era of the earth, beginning about 225 million years ago.

trib. tributary.

tribe *n.* **1** a group of people with a common way of life, speaking the same language, obeying a chief or elders, and usu. of the same ancestry: *the 12 ~s of Israel; an Indian ~.* **2** group of people, animals, or plants of the same kind: *the rose ~; a new ~ of journalists.* —**trib·al** (TRY·bul) *adj.;* **tribes·man** *n.*

tri·bol·o·gy (try·BOL·uh·jee) *n.* the study of friction, wear, and lubrication of sliding surfaces.

trib·u·la·tion (–LAY–) *n.* great misery or affliction; also, the cause of it.

tri·bu·nal (try·BEW·nl, tri–) *n.* court of justice; also, a judgment seat. —**trib·une** (TRIB·yoon, trib·YOON) *n.* a public defender, as an official of ancient Rome elected to protect the rights of plebeians.

trib·u·tar·y (TRIB·yoo·ter·ee) *adj.* **1** paying tribute; subject: *a ~ state.* **2** contributing to a larger stream: *a ~ river.* ***—n.,*** *pl.* **-tar·ies** a tributary nation or river. —**trib·ute** (TRIB·yoot) *n.* **1** a payment or levy exacted by a ruler from a subject. **2** something said or given as a mark of gratitude, respect, etc.: *made speeches to* **pay tribute** *to the retiring president.*

trice *n.* **in a trice** in an instant.

tri·cen·ten·ni·al (–TEN·ee·ul) *n.* a 300th anniversary; ***adj.*** happening once every 300 years. —**tri·ceps** (TRY–) *n.* **-ceps·es** or **-ceps** a muscle along the back of the upper arm. —**tri·cer·a·tops** (–SER·uh–) *n.* a plant-eating dinosaur with three pointed horns, one above each eye and a short one on the nose.

tri·chi·na (tri·KYE·nuh) *n., pl.* **-nae** (-nee) or **-nas** a roundworm that enters the human body through pork meat and causes **trich·i·no·sis** (trik·uh·NOH–) *n.*

trick *n.* **1** a skillfully deceptive action such as a prank or fraud; also, a feat or illusion: *a card ~; the "~* (i.e. prank) *or treat" greeting of children on their Halloween rounds;* **do** (or **turn**) **the trick** achieve the desired result. **2** knack: *to learn the ~s* (i.e. devices or expedients) *of the trade.* **3** a peculiar habit or mannerism. **4** a round of play in a card game. **5** a shift or tour of duty. ***—v.*** **1** deceive or cheat: *was ~ed into buying the lemon.* **2** adorn or deck *(out).* —**trick·er·y** *n.* **-er·ies.** —**trick·ish** *adj.* tricky.

trick·le *v.* **-les, -led, -ling** fall in drops; also, flow or move slowly, as a brook; ***n.*** a small flow.

trick·ster *n.* one who tricks or deceives. —**trick·y** *adj.* **trick·i·er, -i·est** **1** using tricks; deceptive: *a ~ politician.* **2** intricate; difficult to handle: *a ~ job, situation.* —**trick·i·ly** *adv.*

tri·col·or (TRY·cul·ur) *adj.* having three colors; ***n.*** such a flag, as of France.

tri·cot (TREE·coh) *n.* a plain knitted fabric used for underwear and shirts.

tri·cy·cle (TRY·si–) *n.* a child's three-wheeled vehicle worked by pedals. —**tri·dent** (TRIDE·nt) *n.* a three-pronged spear.

tried *pt.* & *pp.* of TRY. —***adj.*** tested or proved; hence, trustworthy: *a ~ and true formula.*

tri·en·ni·al (try·EN·ee·ul) *adj.* happening every three years; also, lasting three years; **tri·en·ni·al·ly** *adv.*

Tri·este (tree·EST) a seaport of N.E. Italy.

tri·fle (TRY–) *n.* something of small value; also, a small amount of money; **a trifle** to a slight degree: *a ~ annoyed, late.* —***v.*** **-fles, -fled, -fling** talk or act in a frivolous or disrespectful manner: *Don't ~ with holy things; to ~ away* (i.e. waste) *precious time;* **tri·fler** *n.* —**tri·fling** *adj.* frivolous; trivial: *no ~ matter.*

tri·fo·cals (TRY·foh·clz) *n.pl.* eyeglasses with lenses having sections for near, far, and middle distances. —**tri·fo·li·ate** (try·FOL·ee–) *adj.* having three leaflets, as clover.

trig *adj.* stylish or smart-looking. —***n.*** [short form] trigonometry.

trig·ger (TRIG·ur) *n.* & *v.* (fire or set off by or as if by) a lever that is pulled back by the forefinger, or **trigger finger,** to activate the firing mechanism of a gun: *Stimuli ~ responses; a prison riot ~ed by a beating incident.*

trig·o·nom·e·try (–NOM·uh·tree) *n.* a branch of mathematics dealing with relations between the sides and angles of triangles; **trig·o·no·met·ric** (–nuh·MET–) or **-ri·cal** *adj.*

trill *n.* a tremulous or vibrating sound, as made by rapidly tapping the teethridge with the tip of the tongue while expelling air or by the rapid alternation of two musical notes that are a tone or semitone apart; also, a warble; ***v.*** sing, speak, or play (a musical note) with a trill: *the ~ed "r" of Spanish.*

tril·lion (TRIL·yun) *n.* a thousand billion; in Britain, a billion billion (1 followed by 18 zeros); **tril·lionth** *n.* & *adj.* —**tril·li·um** (TRIL·ee–) *n.* a wild flower of the lily family having stems bearing three leaves each and one three-petaled flower. —**tril·o·gy** (TRIL·uh·jee) *n.* **-gies** a unified series of three plays, novels, etc.

trim *v.* **trims, trimmed, trim·ming** **1** clip or cut away unwanted parts from (a hedge, beard, etc.) so as to make neat and tidy. **2** decorate (a Christmas tree, dress, etc.). **3** balance the weight of (a vehicle or craft) so that it can move forward without tilting; also, balance (an aircraft) for level flight. **4** adjust (the sails of a boat) to make full use of the wind; hence, change (views) or take a position that suits prevailing views, as a politician. **5** *Informal.* defeat; thrash; also, cheat, or swindle. —***adj.*** **trim·mer, trim·mest** shapely, well-proportioned, or efficient-looking: *a ~ figure, ship, lawn, haircut;* **trimly** *adv.;* **trim·ness** *n.* —***n.*** **1** orderly condition: *found everything in good ~.* **2** what a dress, furniture, automobile, etc. are ornamented with, as lace, handles, chrome, etc.

tri·ma·ran (TRY·muh–) *n.* a boat similar to a catamaran but with three hulls.

tri·mes·ter (try·MES–, TRY–) *n.* any of the three terms into which an academic year is sometimes divided; also, a three-month period: *abortions during the first ~* (of pregnancy). —**trim·e·ter** (TRIM·uh–) *n.* a line of verse with three metrical feet.

trim·ming *n.* **1** ornament or decoration. **2** **trimmings** *pl.* trimmed-off parts; also, garnishings and such food accessories: *turkey with all the ~s.* **3** *Informal.* a beating; also, a fleecing.

tri·month·ly (try·MUNTH·lee) *adj.* occurring or appearing every three months.

tri·nal (TRY·nl) or **trine** *adj.* threefold; triple.

Trin·i·dad (TRIN·uh–) **and To·ba·go** (toh·BAY–) a West Indian country consisting of two islands; 1,980 sq.mi. (5,128 km²); *cap.* Port-of-Spain; **Trin·i·dad·i·an** (–DAY–, –DAD–) *n.* & *adj.*

Trin·i·tar·i·an (–TAIR–) *n.* a believer in the doctrine of the Trinity; **Trin·i·tar·i·an·ism** *n.*

tri·ni·tro·tol·u·ene (try·nye·truh·TOL·yoo·een) *n.* a derivative of toluene; same as TNT.

trin·i·ty *n.* **-ties** a set of three; **Trinity** the union of Father, Son, and Holy Ghost in one Godhead.

trin·ket (TRING·kit) *n.* a small ornament or piece of personal jewelry; also, a trifle or toy.

tri·o (TREE·oh) *n.* **-os** a group of three performing a dance, musical composition, etc. together; also, a composition for three voices or instruments. —**tri·ode** (TRY–) *n.* an electron tube with three electrodes including a grid controlling the flow of electrons from cathode to anode.

trip *n.* **1** a journey, esp. a short excursion, as for pleasure: *a honeymoon ~; a round-~ fare; a ~ to the kitchen during the commercial break.* **2** *Slang.* a drug-induced visionary experience or similar excursion: *an acid ~; an ego ~; a power ~.* **3** a light, quick stepping. **4** a slip or stumble; also, a causing of a person to fall by catching his foot. **5** a catching device, as a pawl. —***v.*** **trips, tripped, trip·ping** **1** (cause) to stumble or slip up: *He ~d and fell down the stairs; was so sure of his facts, no one could ~ him up.* **2** move with quick, light steps, as a child. **3** operate or activate (a mechanism), esp. by releasing a catching device, as in a trip-hammer. —**trip·per** *n.*

tri·par·tite (try·PAR–) *adj.* having three parts; also, made between three parties, as a treaty.

tripe *n.* **1** the lining of the second and third stomachs of beef animals used as food. **2** *Slang.* talk, writing, etc. considered worthless; trash.

trip·ham·mer *n.* a heavy, power-driven hammer that is operated by tripping a catching device when raised and ready to fall.

tri·ple (TRIP·ul) *adj.* three times as much, as many, as large, etc.; also, threefold: *a ~ alliance, jump* (i.e. "hop, skip, and jump"), *threat* (i.e. football player good at passing, running, and kicking), *time* (with three beats to the measure). ***—n.*** a triple amount, group, etc.; also, a baseball hit that enables the batter to reach third base; ***v.*** **-ples, -pled, -pling** make a threefold increase; also, hit a triple. **—tri·plet** (TRIP·lit) *n.* one of three born at a single birth; also, a group of three musical notes or lines of verse. **—tri·plex** (TRIP·lex) *n.* & *adj.* (something) that is triple or threefold: *a ~ apartment.* **—trip·li·cate** (–luh·kit) *n.* one of three identical copies; **in triplicate** in three copies; ***adj.*** threefold, as invoices; also, third: *the ~ carbon copy;* ***v.*** (–kate) **-cates, -cat·ed, -cat·ing** triple, esp. in copies. **—tri·pod** (TRY–) *n.* a three-legged stand, stool, etc.; **trip·o·dal** (TRIP·uh·dl) or **tri·pod·ic** (–POD–) *adj.* **—tri·ply** (TRIP·lee) *adv.* in a triple manner.

Trip·o·li (–uh·lee) **1** one of Libya's two capitals. **2** a city of N. W. Lebanon.

trip·tych (–tic) *n.* a picture or altarpiece in three side-by-side panels. **—tri·reme** (TRY·reem) *n.* an ancient Greek or Roman warship with three banks of oars. **—tri·sect** (TRY–, –SECT) *v.* divide into three equal parts; **tri·sec·tion** (–SEC–) *n.*

trite *adj.* **trit·er, trit·est** worn out by constant use; hackneyed: *a ~ expression, quotation;* **trite·ly** *adv.;* **trite·ness** *n.*

trit·i·um (TRIT·ee–, TRISH–) *n.* a radioactive isotope of hydrogen three times as heavy as ordinary hydrogen. **—Tri·ton** (TRY·tn) the Greek demigod of the sea, represented carrying a three-pronged spear and a trumpet made of a conical sea shell; **triton (shell)** (shell of) a marine gastropod.

tri·umph (TRY–) *n.* a glorious or decisive victory or its celebration; ***v.*** win or celebrate a triumph (over an enemy, opposition, etc.); also, succeed or prevail; **tri·um·phal** (–UM–) *adj.: a ~ procession, arch.* **—tri·um·phant** (–UM–) *adj.* victorious or rejoicing: *a ~ army; ~ shouts, fans;* **tri·um·phant·ly** *adv.*

tri·um·vir (try·UM·vur) *n.* **-virs** or **-vir·i** (–vuh·rye) a member of a **tri·um·vi·rate** (–UM·vuh·rit) *n.* a group of three forming a government. **—triv·et** (TRIV·it) *n.* a three-legged wrought-iron stand for utensils near or on the fire; also, a metal stand with short feet to hold hot dishes on the table.

triv·i·a (TRIV·ee·uh) *n.pl.* unimportant things; trivialities; also, *pl.* of TRIVIUM. **—triv·i·al** (TRIV·ee·ul) *adj.* insignificant; trifling; **triv·i·al·ly** *adv.;* **triv·i·al·i·ty** (–AL–) *n.* **-ties** trivial quality; also, a trifle. **—triv·i·um** (TRIV·ee–) *n., pl.* **triv·i·a** course of studies consisting of the first three liberal arts of a classical education, i.e. grammar, rhetoric, and logic.

-trix *n. suffix.* feminine of agent nouns ending in *-tor,* as *aviatrix.*

tri-week·ly *adj.* & *adv.* thrice a week; also, every three weeks.

tro·che (TROH·kee) *n.* a usu. round medicinal lozenge. **—tro·chee** (TROH·kee) *n.* a metrical foot of one accented and one unaccented syllable, as in "Mary had a little lamb"; **tro·cha·ic** (–KAY–) *adj.*

trod *pt.* and a *pp.* of TREAD; **trod·den** a *pp.* of TREAD.

trog·lo·dyte (TROG·luh–) *n.* **1** a cave man or unsocial person; also, a brutish person. **2** an anthropoid ape.

troi·ka (TROY·kuh) *n.* a team of three administrators or horses; also, a Russian carriage or sleigh drawn by three horses abreast.

Tro·jan (TROH·jun) *n.* an inhabitant of Troy; also, one noted for courage and endurance; ***adj.*** of Troy or its people; **Trojan horse** a person or thing with a hidden destructive or subversive capacity, like a large wooden horse filled with enemy soldiers that the Trojans received as a gift during their war **(Trojan War)** with the Greeks.

troll (TROLE) *n.* **1** in Scandinavian folklore, a dwarfish monster with magical powers. **2** a fishing line with lure or bait used for trolling. **3** a round such as "Three Blind Mice." ***—v.*** **1** sing heartily or in a full, rolling voice; also, sing the parts of (a round) in succession. **2** draw (a fishing line) behind a moving boat; also, fish (in water) in this way: *to ~ for bass.* **—trol·ley** *n.* **trol·leys** **1** a pulley ("trolley wheel") rolling at the end of a pole ("trolley pole") against an electrified overhead wire that powers a streetcar or bus; also, a streetcar **(trolley car)** or bus **(trolley bus)** so powered. **2** a wheeled basket or carriage running suspended from an overhead track, as in a store. **—trol·lop** (–up) *n.* a slovenly woman or slut; also, a prostitute. **—trol·ly** *n.* **trol·lies** same as TROLLEY.

trom·bone (TROM–, –BONE) *n.* a brass wind instrument with a long twice-bent tube ending in a trumpet-shaped bell and having a sliding section for changing tones; **trom·bon·ist** *n.*

tromp *v.* same as TRAMP.

troop *n.* a collection of people or animals, esp. an organized unit, as the subdivision of a cavalry regiment, a Boy Scout unit, etc.; **troops** *pl.* soldiers. ***—v.*** go (*out, off,* etc.) as a group; also, gather (*around* someone) in a group. **—troop·er** *n.* a cavalryman, mounted policeman, or a state policeman. —**troop·ship** *n.* a ship for carrying troops.

trope *n.* the figurative use of a word; figure of speech. —**tro·phy** (TROH·fee) *n.* **-phies** **1** something captured in war, displayed as a memorial, or kept as evidence of some exploit, as the mounted head of an animal killed. **2** a prize awarded for victory in a contest. —**trop·ic** *n.* either of the two parallels of latitude, the **Tropic of Cancer,** 23½°N. or the **Tropic of Capricorn,** 23½°S. of the equator; **tropics** or **Tropics** *pl.* the region lying between about 30°N. and 30°S. of the equator; **trop·ic** or **-i·cal** *adj.* of or having to with the tropics; also, very hot; torrid: *the ternlike* **tropic bird;** *tropical fish; the tropical rain forest;* **trop·i·cal·ly** *adv.* —**tro·pism** (TROH–) *n.* a tendency of living things, as in GEOTROPISM or PHOTOTROPISM, to bend in response to a stimulus such as gravity or light. —**trop·o·sphere** (TROP·uh–, TROH·puh–) *n.* the layer of the atmosphere up to about 10 mi. (16.093 km) from the earth's surface, characterized by weather phenomena; **trop·o·spher·ic** (–SFER–, –SFEER–) *adj.*

trot *n.* the gait of a horse, etc. that is faster than a walk, with the legs moving in diagonal pairs; also, a person's jogging gait; ***v.*** **trots, trot·ted, trot·ting** ride, go, etc. at a trot or brisk pace; **trot out** *Informal.* bring out, as a horse for inspection or approval; **trot·ter** *n.*

troth (TRAWTH, TROHTH) *n. Archaic.* word of promise, as to marry, be loyal, etc.; bethrothal: *to pledge* (or *plight*) *one's* ~.

trou·ba·dour (TROO·buh·dor) *n.* a poet-musician of S. France who composed and sang love songs in Provençal from the 11th to the 13th century.

trou·ble (TRUB·ul) *n.* **1** worry; distress; pain; difficulty: *a world full of ~ and sorrow; The ~ is you can't have it both ways; without money you're* **in trouble;** *heart* ~ (i.e. disease). **2** an instance or cause of pain or worry: *Our ~s are over with death; He is a ~ to society; racial ~s.* **3** inconvenience or exertion: *Walking to work is no ~ to her; takes the ~ to be on time.* —***v.*** **-bles, -bled, -bling** cause trouble to; bother: *Nightmares ~ children; ~d* (i.e. agitated) *waters; May I ~* (i.e. inconvenience) *you for a favor? Don't ~ (yourself) to pick up the glove.* —**trou·ble·mak·er** *n.* one who causes trouble to others; **trou·ble·shoot·er** *n.* one who can trace a malfunction or other trouble to its source and help to get rid of it; hence **trou·ble·shoot** *v.;* **trou·ble·shoot·ing** *n.* —**trou·ble·some** (–sum) *adj.* causing trouble: *~ people, ailments;* **trou·blous** (–blus) *adj.* [literary] unsettled; also, troublesome.

trough (TRAWF) *n.* a long, narrow, open container, as for holding water or food for animals, a channel to carry away water from eaves, etc.; also, something similar in shape, as the depressions alternating with the crests of a wave or a low-pressure area that gives rise to a hurricane.

trounce *v.* **trounc·es, trounced, trounc·ing** thrash or beat; *Informal.* defeat in a game; **trounc·er** *n.*

troupe (TROOP) *n.* a company or group of actors, singers, etc.; ***v.*** **troupes, trouped, troup·ing** travel with a troupe; **troup·er** *n.*

trou·sers (TROW·zurz) *n.pl.* a two-legged outer garment extending from the waist to the ankles, as usu. worn by men.

trous·seau (TROO·soh) *n., pl.* **trous·seux** (–soze) or **trous·seaus** a bride's personal outfit of clothes, etc.

trout *n.* a freshwater food and game fish related to the salmon; **trout lily** same as DOGTOOTH VIOLET.

trove short form of TREASURE-TROVE.

trow (TROH, TROW) *v. Archaic.* believe or suppose.

trow·el (–ul) *n.* a hand tool with a broad flat blade for spreading and smoothing plaster or mortar; also, a similar garden tool but with a curved blade; ***v.*** **-els, -el(l)ed, -el·(l)ing** spread, smooth, or dig with a trowel.

Troy a legendary city of Asia Minor made famous by the Trojan War waged by the Greeks to get back Queen Helen, abducted by the Trojan prince, Paris. —**troy** *adj.* relating to a system of weighing gold, silver, etc. developed at Troyes, France, based on a pound of 12 ounces of 480 grains each.

tru·ant (TROO·unt) *n.* one who stays away from school without permission; also, one who shirks duty; ***adj.*** errant; straying; **tru·an·cy** *n.* **-cies.**

truce *n.* a temporary ceasing of hostilities by agreement between the fighting parties; hence, a respite from conflict, pain, etc.

truck *n.* **1** an automotive vehicle for carrying loads, having a rear portion that is either open, as in a *dump truck,* pickup, etc., or closed, as in a tractor-and-trailer unit or a *panel truck.* **2** a swiveling, wheeled frame used at the end of a railroad car, locomotive, etc. **3** goods for the market, esp. vegetables, as grown on a **truck farm.** **4** small articles; odds and ends; also, *Informal.* trash. **5** dealings; exchange; business: *would have no ~ with Communists.* —***v.*** **1** drive trucks or carry (a load) on a truck; **truck·er** *n.* **2** exchange or barter. —**truck·le** *v.* **-les, -led, -ling** be servile; submit tamely *(to);* **truckle (bed)** trundle bed.

truc·u·lent (–yuh·lunt) *adj.* pugnacious or defiant; also, savage or fierce; **truc·u·lent·ly** *adv.;* **truc·u·lence** *n.*

trudge *v.* **trudg·es, trudged, trudg·ing** walk wearily (over); ***n.*** a weary walk.

true (TROO) *adj.* **tru·er, tru·est** **1** agreeing with a norm or standard, esp. ethical; not false: *a ~ story; was ~ to his word; a ~ Christian; the ~* (i.e. rightful) *heir; prophecies that* **come true** (i.e. are realized). **2** agreeing with standards of correctness or accuracy: *The geographic, not magnetic north is ~ north; Floating ribs are not ~ ribs; a portrait that is ~ to life;* **out of true** not correctly positioned; ***v.*** **trues, trued, true·ing** make or put in the correct position: *to ~ up a door frame.* ***—adv.:*** *a story that rings ~; a plant that breeds ~ to type; That 2 and 2 are 4 holds ~ under most conditions.* ***—n.*** that which is true: *the ~, the good, and the beautiful.* **—true bill** a bill of indictment endorsed by a grand jury. **—true-blue** *adj.* very loyal and staunch: *a ~ Conservative.* **—true-heart·ed** *adj.* very loyal and sincere: *a ~ follower.*

truf·fle *n.* a fungus that grows underground in clusters and is prized as a food delicacy.

tru·ism (TROO–) *n.* a statement that is self-evident and superfluous. **—tru·ly** (TROO·lee) *adv.* in a true manner; really; sincerely; truthfully; faithfully.

Tru·man (TROO·mun), **Harry S.** 1884–1972, 33rd U.S. President (1945–53).

trump *n.* a playing card of a suit that ranks higher than others during the play of a hand: *Spades are ~s;* ***v.*** play a trump or take (a trick or card) with a trump; **trump up** bring forward falsely; **trumped-up** *adj.: a ~ charge, excuse.* **—trump·er·y** *n.* **-er·ies** something showy and valueless; rubbish.

trum·pet (–pit) *n.* **1** a loud-sounding brass wind instrument with a looped tube and flared bell; also, a sound like a trumpet's. **2** a trumpetlike hearing aid, or "ear trumpet." ***—v.*** blow a trumpet or proclaim loudly; **trum·pet·er** *n.*

trun·cate (TRUNG–) *v.* **-cates, -cat·ed, -cat·ing** cut off a part, esp. the apex of; lop: *a ~d pyramid, quotation.* ***—adj.*** of a feather or leaf, having a blunt top. **—trun·ca·tion** (–CAY–) *n.* **—trun·cheon** (–chun) *n.* a club or staff of authority, as a nightstick or drum major's baton.

trun·dle *v.* **-dles, -dled, -dling** roll (*along, down,* etc.) on wheels; **trun·dler** *n.* **—trundle bed** a low bed on casters, as for a child, that is rolled under another bed when not in use.

trunk *n.* **1** the main stem, as opposed to branches, of a tree or treelike structure such as a system of nerves or blood vessels. **2** a main transportation or telephone line; also **trunk line. 3** a human or animal body without head or limbs; also, the long snout of an elephant. **4** a large reinforced box for a traveler's clothing, etc.; also, the luggage compartment of a car. **5 trunks** *pl.* very short trousers worn by men for swimming and athletics.

truss *n.* **1** a supporting framework of beams, bars, etc. under a roof or bridge. **2** a support worn to keep in an inguinal hernia. **3** a bundle or pack. ***—v.*** **1** support (a roof, bridge, etc.) with a truss. **2** bind or tie (a person) up so that he cannot move; also, bind the wings or legs of (a fowl) for cooking.

trust *n.* **1** firm assurance or belief that a person or thing will be as good as hoped or expected: *the implicit ~ of children in their parents; God was her sole ~* (i.e. trusted person); *goods sold and bought* **on trust** (i.e. credit); *We take many things around us on ~* (i.e. without proof). **2** something entrusted to a person's care or responsibility; also, the condition of being so trusted and the responsibility or obligation resulting from it: *A treasurer is in a position of ~; a property held* **in trust** *for a minor; was accused of betraying a ~.* **3** an illegal business organization that controls other organizations for fixing prices, eliminating competition, etc. — ***v.*** have trust (in): *He ~s everyone to do his duty; I ~ you are fine; The premier expects people to ~ in him as in God; Libraries ~ patrons to return books; books ~ed* (i.e. entrusted) *to your care; Never* **trust to** (i.e. rely on) *luck to wake up at an unusual hour.* **—trus·tee** (–TEE) *n.* one to whom property is legally committed in trust; also, a member of the governing body ("board of trustees") of a school, hospital, etc.; **trus·tee·ship** *n.* **—trust·ful** *adj.* full of trust; ready to confide; not suspicious; **trust·ful·ly** *adv.;* **trust·ful·ness** *n.* **—trust fund** money or other property held in trust for another by a bank or "trust company." **—trust·ing** *adj.* trustful. **—trust territory** one of the 11 territories established after World War II to be administered by different countries, as New Guinea by Australia, supervised by the U.N. Trusteeship Council. **—trust·wor·thy** (–wur·dhee) *adj.* worthy of trust; reliable; **trust·wor·thi·ness** *n.* **—trust·y** *adj.* **trust·i·er, -i·est** of proven trustworthiness: *a ~ steed, sword, servant.* ***—n.,*** *pl.* **trust·ies** a well-behaved prison inmate granted special privileges.

truth (TROOTH) *n.* **1** that which is true; also, the quality or state of being true, exact, honest, loyal, etc.: *Speak the ~; The ~ will make you free; The ~ of the matter is, I forgot;* **in truth** truly; in fact. **2** a fact, belief, etc. accepted as true: *a religious ~; the ~s of science.* **—truth·ful** *adj.* telling the truth; also, factual: *a ~ child, account;* **truth·ful·ly** *adv.;* **truth·ful·ness** *n.* **—truth serum** a drug such as sodium pentothal that is used in lie-detector tests since it tends to lull the mind of the subject and throw him off his guard.

try *v.* **tries, tried, try·ing** **1** make an effort to do something: *I'll ~ and* (*Informal.* try to) *be on time.* **2** test or put to the proof: *Have you ~d this sauce? fired for ~ing the boss's patience; Don't ~* (i.e. attempt) *impossible things; was ~d* (i.e. in court) *for murder but acquitted; Blubber is ~d out* (i.e. rendered) *to extract oil; Customers* **try on** *suits* (i.e. put them on to check the fit) *before buying; They* **try out** *new employees* (i.e. evaluate their work) *before confirming them; She's ~ing out* (i.e. to determine fitness) *for the lead role.* ***—n.,*** *pl.* **tries** attempt: *Give it a ~; It's worth a ~.* **—try·ing** *adj.* that tries one's patience; hard to endure: *a ~ person, period.* —**try·out** *n. Informal.* a testing of fitness (of a candidate) or of reaction, as of the audience to a play.

tryst *n.* an appointed time, place, or meeting, as between lovers.

tsar (TSAR, ZAR) same as CZAR; *fem.* **tsa·ri·na** (–REE–).

tset·se (TSET·see, TSEET–) *n.* a bloodsucking, two-winged African fly that is the carrier of sleeping sickness; also **tsetse fly.**

T.Sgt. technical sergeant.

T-shirt *n.* a collarless, short-sleeved, close-fitting pullover shirt, as worn by men for sports or underwear.

tsp. teaspoon(s); teaspoonful(s).

T square a T-shaped ruler for making parallel lines.

tsu·na·mi (tsoo·NAH·mee) *n.* a tidal wave caused by an undersea earthquake or volcanic eruption; **tsu·na·mic** *adj.*

tub *n.* a large open container with a wide top, as for washing clothes; also, a bathtub; **tub·by** *adj.* **tub·bi·er, tub·bi·est** fat and short like a washtub.

tu·ba (TUE·buh) *n.* the lowest-pitched and largest of brass wind instruments, also called "bass horn." —**tu·bal** *adj.* of or in a tube, esp. a Fallopian tube: *sterilization by ~ ligation; ~ pregnancy.* —**tube** *n.* **1** a usu. long hollow cylinder, as for conveying fluids; pipe: *the ~s of a boiler; pneumatic ~s worked by air pressure; the Eustachian ~.* **2** a railroad tunnel; *Brit.* subway. **3** a container made of a short tube closed at one end: *a test ~; a ~ of toothpaste, paint, etc.* (with soft metal covering and screw-on cap). **4** [short form] inner tube; electron tube; vacuum tube; **the tube** *Informal.* television. —**tube·less** *adj.: the ~ tire, without an inner tube.*

tu·ber (TUE–) *n.* the thickened underground stem of plants such as the potato; **tu·ber·ous** (–us) *adj.* —**tu·ber·cle** (TUE–) *n.* a small, rounded swelling or lump on a body surface or organ, as caused by the **tubercle bacillus,** the bacterial agent in tuberculosis. —**tu·ber·cu·lar** (–BUR·kyuh·lur) *adj.* of or having to do with tuberculosis: *a ~ patient; ~ symptoms;* **tu·ber·cu·late(d)** *adj.* having tubercles. —**tu·ber·cu·lin** (–BUR–) *n.* an extract from tubercle bacilli used in a skin test to diagnose tuberculosis. —**tu·ber·cu·lo·sis** (–LOH–) *n.* an infectious disease, esp. of the lungs, characterized by tubercles in body tissue; **tu·ber·cu·lous** (–BUR·kyuh·lus) *adj.* tubercular.

tube·rose *n.* a plant of the agave family with a tubelike rootstock and a slender stem bearing waxy-white flowers with a heavy odor that are used in perfumes; **tu·ber·ose** (TUE·buh–) *adj.* having tubers; tuberous.

tub·ing (TUE·bing) *n.* a length of tube, material in tube form, or a system of tubes. —**tu·bu·lar** (TUE·byuh·lur) *adj.* consisting of or having the form of a tube; also, made with tubes. —**tu·bule** (–byool) *n.* a small tube or tubular structure.

tuck *v.* **1** thrust into a place snugly or compactly: *Children are ~ed in bed at night; to ~ one's shirt in* (the trousers); *old clothes ~ed away in trunks; could* **tuck away** (or **in**) (*Slang.* finish off) *a whole cake.* **2** pull up in a fold or folds; also, make tucks in (a garment): *She ~ed up her skirt and waded across;* ***n.*** a fold sewed in a garment, esp. to shorten it.

tuck·er *v. Informal.* weary or tire (out).

Tuc·son (TOO·sahn, too·SAHN) a city of S. Arizona.

-tude *n. suffix.* indicating state or condition: as in *attitude, pulchritude, solitude.*

Tue(s). *Abbrev.* for **Tues·day** (TOOZ·dee, –day, TYOOZ–) *n.* the third day of the week, following Monday.

tu·fa (TUE·fuh) *n.* a soft limestone similar to travertine; **tu·fa·ceous** (–FAY·shus) *adj.* —**tuff** *n.* a soft, porous rock formed by compacted volcanic ash or dust; **tuff·a·ceous** (–FAY–) *adj.*

tuft *n.* a bunch, cluster, clump, etc. that is attached at the base: *a ~ of hair; a rug made of ~s of pile; ~s of grass; the ~* (i.e. crest) *of a titmouse;* ***v.*** provide or secure with tufts: *A mattress is ~ed at intervals to keep its padding in place;* **tuft·ed** *adj.: a ~ed carpet.*

tug *v.* **tugs, tugged, tug·ging** pull hard (*at* something); also, move by tugging; haul, as with a tugboat; ***n.*** a hard pull; also, a tugboat; **tug·boat** *n.* a small powerful boat used for towing and pushing ocean liners in and out of harbors, barges along rivers, etc. —**tug of war** or **tug-of-war** *n.* **tugs-** a contest in which two teams pull at the opposite ends of a rope till one crosses a central line; hence, a power struggle.

tu·grik (TOO–) *n.* the basic money unit of the Mongolian People's Republic, worth 100 mongos.

tu·i·tion (tue·ISH·un) *n.* (payment for) instruction, as at a college.

tu·la·re·mi·a (tue·luh·REE·mee·uh) *n.* an infectious disease caught by humans from rabbits, squirrels, rats, etc.

tu·lip (TUE–) *n.* a bulbous herb of the lily family with large, cup-shaped flowers in brilliant colors. —**tulip tree** a tall broadleaf tree of the magnolia family with tuliplike flowers.

tulle (TOOL) *n.* a sheer netting of silk, rayon, etc. used for bridal veils, scarfs, etc.

Tul·sa (TUL·suh) a city of Oklahoma.

tum·ble *v.* **-bles, -bled, -bling** **1** fall headlong, esp. head over heels, as in a somersault; also, move (*out* of a place, *in* bed, etc.) in a disorderly manner: *clothes ~ing in a dryer.* **2** cause to tumble; upset; turn over. —***n.*** a headlong fall; hence, confusion or disorder. —**tumb·le·down** *adj.* dilapidated; ready to collapse: *a ~ house.* —**tum·bler** *n.* **1** one who tumbles, does handsprings, somersaults, etc.; also, a breed of pigeon that does acrobatics in the air. **2** a drinking glass with no stem or handle. **3** a lock mechanism in which levers must be raised to an exact height to move the bolt. **4** a drying machine for clothes. —**tum·ble·weed** *n.* a thistlelike plant with a round shape that breaks off when dry and is tumbled about by the wind.

tum·brel or **tum·bril** *n.* a two-wheeled cart that can be tilted for dumping its load.

tu·mid (TUE–) *adj.* swollen or enlarged, as by a tumor; hence, overblown or inflated in style: *~ prose;* **tu·mid·i·ty** (–MID–) *n.*

tum·my *n.* **tum·mies** [child's word] stomach.

tu·mor (TUE·mur) *n.* swelling in a body part from an abnormal growth of tissue, either benign, as a cyst, or malignant, as cancer; **tu·mor·ous** (–us) *adj.;* also **tu·mour** *Brit.* —**tu·mult** (TUE–) *n.* commotion, disturbance, or confusion, as during a storm or battle; also, an excited state of mind; **tu·mul·tu·ous** (–MUL·choo·us) *adj.: a ~ welcome, mob; ~ passions;* **tu·mul·tu·ous·ly** *adv.*

tun *n.* a large cask; also, a unit of liquid measure equal to 252 gal. (954 liters).

tu·na (TUE·nuh) *n.* (the flesh of) a large swift ocean fish of the mackerel family valued as food, including bonitos and albacores; also **tuna fish.**

tun·dra (–druh) *n.* the vast, treeless, swampy plains of the arctic.

tune (TOON, TYOON) *n.* **1** a melody or air, esp. one that is simple and popular. **2** the correct musical pitch: *to sing in ~; a misfit who is out of ~* (i.e. not well-adjusted) *with society;* **change one's tune** assume a different style or tone of expression; **to the tune of** to the amount of (a huge sum of money). —***v.* tunes, tuned, tun·ing** **1** adjust (a musical instrument) to the proper pitch; also, put (a motor or engine) in the best working condition; also **tune up.** **2** attune *(to)* or be in tune *(with);* **tune in** adjust (a radio or television set) for best reception: *to* **tune in** *to a station;* **tune out** turn off (a broadcast or program); also, turn away from what is happening or ignore (a command, etc.); **tun·er** *n.* —**tune·ful** *adj.* melodious; pleasant to hear: *~ melodies;* **tune·ful·ly** *adv.* —**tune-up** or **tune·up** *n.* the checking and adjusting of the parts of an engine to put it in proper working condition.

tung·sten (–stun) *n.* a hard, silver-white metallic element with a high melting point, used in making a very hard steel, or **tungsten steel.**

tu·nic (TUE–) *n.* a loose, gownlike, usu. belted, knee-length garment, as worn by ancient Greeks and Romans; also, a blouse: *maternity tops in ~ style.*

tuning fork a two-pronged metal instrument that gives a fixed tone when struck.

Tu·nis (TUE–) a seaport and the capital of Tunisia. —**Tu·ni·sia** (–NEE·zhuh) a country of N. Africa; 63,170 sq.mi. (163,610 km^2); **Tu·ni·sian** *n.* & *adj.*

tun·nel (TUNL) *n.* an excavated underground passageway for a road, sewer, etc.; also, a tunnellike passage, as in a mine; ***v.* tun·nels, tun·nel(l)ed, tun·nel·(l)ing** make a tunnel (*through* a mountain, *under* the sea, etc.): *a cave ~d by the action of a river;* **tun·nel·(l)er** *n.* —**tunnel vision** the defect of not having peripheral vision; hence, narrow-mindedness.

tun·ny *n.* **tun·nies** same as TUNA.

tuque (TUKE) *n.* a knitted woolen cap with a tapered end hanging by the side when worn.

tur·ban (–bun) *n.* a man's headdress of Persian origin, consisting of a scarf wound round the head; also, a close-fitting, brimless hat worn by women.

tur·bid *adj.* **1** cloudy or disturbed, as by stirring up sediment: *~ waters, feelings.* **2** dense or thick: *~ clouds, smoke.* —**tur·bid·ly** *adv.;* **tur·bid·ness** *n.;* **tur·bid·i·ty** (–BID–) *n.* —**tur·bine** (–bin, –bine) *n.* an engine consisting of a wheel turned by the force of water, steam, or gas. —**turbo-** *comb.form.* turbine-driven: as in **tur·bo·e·lec·tric** (–LEC–) *adj.* using electricity produced by turbine generators; **tur·bo·fan** *n.* (a jet engine having) a fan driven by a turbine; **tur·bo·jet** *n.* (an airplane powered by) a jet engine with a turbine-driven air compressor; **tur·bo·prop** *n.* (an airplane powered by) a turbojet engine with a turbine-driven propeller; **tur·bo·train** *n.* a high-speed passenger train powered by turbines.

tur·bot (–but) *n.* a large flatfish of European coastal waters, related to flounders.

tur·bu·lent (–byuh·lunt) *adj.* causing or marked by a disturbance; also, tempestuous: *a ~ mob, sea, period of life; ~ passions;* **tur·bu·lent·ly** *adv.;* **tur·bu·lence** *n.*

tu·reen (tuh·REEN, tyuh–) *n.* a deep, usu. lidded bowl for serving soup or sauce.

turf *n.* **1** sod. **2** peat or a piece of it for fuel. **3 the turf** horse racing; also, a track for horse racing. **4** *Slang.* one's territory or domain. —***v.*** cover with turf; sod. —**turf·y** *adj.*

tur·gid (–jid) *adj.* enlarged or bloated, as an organ by excess of blood; hence, disorderly or unrestrained in style: *a ~ narrative;* **tur·gid·i·ty** (–JID–) *n.*

Tu·rin (TOOR·in, –RIN, tyoor–) a city of N.W. Italy.

Turk. Turkey; Turkish. —**Turk** *n.* a person of or from Turkey. —**Tur·key** a W. Asian country; 301,382 sq.mi. (780,576 km^2); *cap.* Ankara. —**tur·key** *n.* (the flesh of) a large North American poultry bird related to the pheasant; **talk turkey** *Informal.* talk bluntly or seriously; **turkey buzzard** (or **vulture**) a species of New World vulture. —**Tur·kic** *n.* & *adj.* (of) a group of languages of Turkey and S. Central Asia including the Turkish and Tatar branches; **Turk·ish** *n.* & *adj.* (the language) of the Turks;

Turkish bath a hot-air or steam bath with massage and cold shower; **Turkish towel** a thick terry-cloth towel.

tur·mer·ic (TUR·muh–) *n.* (a yellow dyestuff or seasoning obtained from) a S. Asian plant of the ginger family.

tur·moil *n.* a confused or disorderly state.

turn *v.* **1** (cause) to revolve or rotate: *A wheel ~s; to ~ a key in a lock;* **2** form (something) by revolving: *a rod ~ed on a lathe; a well-~ed* (i.e. gracefully formed) *ankle, compliment.* **3** change in position: *to ~ the pages of a book; so gruesome it ~s your stomach.* **4** change the movement or course (of): *~ your steps home; He ~s his dog out at night.* **5** change the direction or trend (of): *Let's ~ our attention to the environment; Friends ~ed against him; ~ left at the lights.* **6** change nature or condition: *Milk ~s sour if kept; Can you ~ this into French? Success ~ed his head* (i.e. unsettled him or made him vain). **—turn color** become a different color; also, blush or grow pale. **—turn down 1** refuse (an offer). **2** lower (volume of sound, degree of heat, etc.). **—turn in** hand over or hand in; also, *Informal.* go to bed. **—turn loose** set free (to go without restraint). **—turn off 1** shut off (water, gas, electricity, etc.) or put out (a light). **2** *Informal.* (cause) to lose interest. **—turn on 1** start (water, gas, etc.) flowing or switch on (a light). **2** *Informal.* (cause) to become interested or excited as by taking a narcotic drug. **—turn out 1** turn off (lights), drive out (people), produce (books, scholars, etc.). **2** happen or come to be: *Things ~ out well in the end.* **—turn up 1** raise the volume or intensity of (sound, heat, etc.). **2** appear or be found; also, happen. ***—n.*** **1** a rotation, as of a wheel; also, a form or style: *a ~ of expression; roasts done* **to a turn** (i.e. just right). **2** (place of) a change of direction; a bend or curve; **at every turn** constantly. **3** a change in conditions, circumstances, etc.: *His illness took a ~ for the worse.* **4** moment or duration of action in regular order: *We* **take turns** (i.e. alternate) *doing chores; your ~ at cooking; "One good ~* (i.e. deed) *deserves another";* **in** (or **out of**) **turn** in (or out of) proper order. **5** natural inclination; bent. **6** a short walk, ride, or drive. **—turn·a·bout** (TUR·nuh–) *n.* a reversal of position, policy, allegiance, etc.; rarely, retaliation: "*~ is fair play.*" **—turn·a·round** *n.* an area in which a vehicle can be turned around; also **turnabout. —turn·buck·le** *n.* a coupling with internal screw threads at either end for receiving the threaded ends of two rods to be held together. **—turn·coat** *n.* a renegade. **—turn·er** *n.* one that turns; also, one who turns things on a lathe; **turn·er·y** *n.* **-er·ies** a turner's workshop; also, a turner's work or products. **—turn·ing** *n.* act of one that turns; a bend, as in a road; also, the use of the lathe; **turning point** a moment of decisive change.

tur·nip *n.* a plant of the cabbage family of which the leaves and the enlarged upper part of the root are used as vegetables.

turn·key *n.* a jailer. ***—adj.*** of a product or service, delivered so completely finished that starting to use it is as simple as turning a key. **—turn·off** *n.* a ramp or road where one turns off from a highway. **—turn·out** *n.* **1** a gathering of people, as at a function or event; also, the way one is dressed or something is equipped. **2** a widened place in a road where vehicles can pass; also, a railroad siding. **—turn·o·ver** *n.* **1** a turning over or upset; also, a pastry or small pie whose crust has been folded over the filling. **2** rate of replacement of employees. **3** amount of goods sold or business done in a given period. **—turn·pike** *n.* a highway on which tolls are charged; also, a tollgate. **—turn·stile** *n.* a gateway with a rotating device for letting in people one by one or counting their numbers. **—turn·ta·ble** *n.* a round platform, as for turning locomotives around or playing a phonograph record.

tur·pen·tine *n.* a pungent inflammable oil distilled from the resinous sap of pine trees, used as a solvent and paint thinner; also called "spirits (or oil) of turpentine."

tur·pi·tude *n.* inherent wickedness or depravity.

turps *n.* [short form] turpentine.

tur·quoise (–kois, –kwois) *n.* a greenish-blue mineral valued as a gem or its brilliant greenish-blue color; also ***adj.***

tur·ret (TUR·ut) *n.* **1** a towerlike ornamental structure, as at the four corners of a tower. **2** a revolving structure housing guns on a battleship, tank, or airplane. **3** the rotating multiple-sided toolholder of a lathe. **—tur·ret·ed** *adj.* having turrets.

tur·tle *n.* a slow-moving reptile with stumpy, clublike limbs (or flippers in "sea turtles") and a rounded body encased in a protective shell; **turn turtle** turn upside down. **—tur·tle·dove** (–duv) *n.* a small European dove with a mournful cooing note. **—tur·tle·neck** *n.* (a sweater with) a high, close-fitting, turned-down collar.

Tus·ca·ro·ra (–cuh·ROR·uh) *n.* (a member of) a tribe of Iroquoian Indians, now living in parts of New York State and Ontario.

tusk *n.* a long, enlarged, pointed tooth projecting on either side of the mouth in the elephant, walrus, boar, etc.; **tusked** *adj.* **—tusk·er** *n.* a tusked animal, esp. a male elephant.

tus·sle (TUS·ul) *n.* & *v.* **tus·sles, tus·sled, tus·sling** wrestle or scuffle; also, struggle.

tus·sock (TUS·uk) *n.* a thick tuft or clump of growing grass or hair, as along the back of the **tussock moth.**

Tut·ankh·a·men (too·tung·KAH·mun) an Egyptian king of the 14th century B.C. whose tomb and its treasures were discovered in 1922; also **Tut·ankh·a·mun, King Tut.**

tu·te·lage (TUE·tl·ij) *n.* the state of being in the charge of a guardian or tutor; also, guardianship or instruction. —**tu·te·lar** (–ur) *adj.* tutelary; **tu·te·lar·y** (–ler·ee) *adj.* (of a) guardian: *a ~ spirit, saint; ~ authority.* —**tu·tor** (TUE–) *n.* a private teacher; ***v.*** act as a tutor to; **tu·to·ri·al** (–TOR–) *adj.*

tut·ti-frut·ti (TOOT·ee·FROOT·ee) *n.* an ice cream, candy, preserve, etc. containing a variety of fruits or flavors.

tu·tu (TOO·too) *n.* the usu. very short stiff skirt worn by a ballerina.

tux *n.* short form of **tux·e·do** (tuk·SEE·doh) *n.* **-dos** (a man's semiformal suit with) a tailless black jacket.

TV *n.* **TV's** or **TVs** television (receiving set).

TVA Tennessee Valley Authority.

TV dinner a frozen dinner packaged in a tray for quick heating and serving.

twad·dle (TWODL) *n.* empty talk or writing. Also ***v.*** **twad·dles, twad·dled, twad·dling.**

twain *n., pron. & adj. Archaic.* two; pair. —**Twain, Mark** See CLEMENS.

twang *n.* **1** the sharp, vibrating sound of a plucked string. **2** a sharp, nasal tone of voice. —***v.*** **1** (cause) to make a twang, as on a stringed instrument. **2** speak with a nasal twang. —**twang·y** *adj.* **twang·i·er, -i·est:** *a ~ drawl.*

'twas (TWUZ, TWOZ) it was.

tweak (TWEEK) *v.* pinch and twist (a nose, ears, etc.); ***n.*** a sharp pinch and twist.

tweed *n.* a rough, heavy woolen cloth with a hairy surface, usu. woven of fibers in two colors; **tweeds** *pl.* clothes of tweed, esp. a suit; **tweed·y** *adj.* **tweed·i·er, -i·est** of or like tweed; also, informal-looking.

'tween *prep. Archaic.* between.

tweet *n., v. & interj.* (make) the thin chirp of a small bird. —**tweet·er** *n.* the speaker of a hi-fi that reproduces only the high-frequency sounds.

tweeze *v.* **tweez·es, tweezed, tweez·ing** *Informal.* pluck with tweezers. —**tweez·ers** *n.pl.* small pincers for handling tiny objects, esp. for plucking hairs.

twelfth *adj.* following the eleventh; 12th; ***n.*** one that is 12th in order; also, one of 12 equal parts; 1/12; **Twelfth Night** the 12th night after Christmas; Epiphany. —**twelve** (TWELV) *n., adj. & pron.* two more than 10; 12 or XII; **twelve-tone** *adj.* relating to the technique of TONE ROW in modern music.

twen·ty *n.* **-ties** two times 10; 20 or XX; **the twenties** numbers or years from 20 through 29; **twen·ty-one** *n.* same as BLACKJACK, *n.* 2; **twen·ty-twen·ty** (or **20/20**) **vision** normal eyesight, i.e. the ability to read characters that a person with normal eyesight can read from 20 feet away; 6/6 (in the metric system); **twen·ti·eth** *n. & adj.*

twerp *n. Slang.* an undesirable or contemptible person.

twice *adv.* two times.

twid·dle (TWIDL) *n.* a twirl or twist; ***v.*** **twid·dles, twid·dled, twid·dling** toy or play with idly; **twiddle one's thumbs** be unoccupied; have nothing to do; **twid·dler** *n.*

twig *n.* a slender shoot or branch; **twig·gy** *adj.* slender or thin like a twig.

twi·light (TWYE–) *n.* the faint light of the period just before sunrise or just after sunset; hence, a period of fading light or decline: *in the ~ of his career, life;* ***adj.:*** *a drug-induced semiconscious* **twilight sleep;** *a* **twilight zone** (i.e. gray area) *of morality.*

twill *n.* (a fabric with) a weave that produces diagonal ribs, as in drills, serge, gabardine, etc.; **twilled** *adj.* —**twin** *n.* either of two offspring born at the same birth; hence, one of two closely related or similar individuals or things; **the Twins** same as GEMINI. —***adj.:*** *his ~ sister; ~* (i.e. two single) *beds; the ~ cities of Minneapolis and St. Paul; a ~ bill* (i.e. doubleheader). —***v.*** **twins, twinned, twin·ning** bring forth twins; also, to couple or pair (*with* another). —**twine** *n.* a strong thread or cord made of two or more strands twisted together; also, an entwining or tangle; ***v.*** **twines, twined, twin·ing** **1** twist together (*into* or as something). **2** wrap or wind (*around* something). **3** meander or extend in a winding manner. —**twinge** (TWINJ) *n. & v.* **twing·es, twinged, twing·ing** (give or feel) a sudden shooting pain: *~s of rheumatism; a ~ of toothache, remorse.* —**twi-night** (TWYE–) *adj.* of a doubleheader, that continues from late afternoon into the evening; **twi-night·er** *n.* a twi-night doubleheader.

twin·kle (TWING–) *v.* **-kles, -kled, -kling** **1** (cause) to shine with a flickering light: *Stars ~ in the sky.* **2** move quickly and lightly: *has ~ing* (i.e. sparkling) *eyes; Her eyes ~d* (i.e. lit up) *with joy; the ~ing feet of dancers; vanished in the* **twinkling** *of an eye* (i.e. in an instant). —***n.*** a gleam or sparkle; also, a wink or blink.

twirl *v.* spin or whirl with dexterity: *a baton-~ing majorette; to ~ one's mustache, a hula hoop around the hips;* ***n.:*** *a ~* (i.e. curl) *of hair; the ~s and flourishes of a signature.*

twist *v.* **1** to wind or turn, as on an axis: *threads ~ed together into a string; a column with a ~ed design; ~ed her head to look over her shoulder; ~ed* (i.e. broke) *off a piece of dough.* **2** bend or force out of shape or position; distort or wrench: *a rope ~ed into a knot; bodies ~ing about in pain; a ~ed* (i.e. sprained) *ankle; a ~ed tale of intrigue; words ~ed out of their meaning.* **3** send (a ball) spinning in a curved path. —***n.*** **1** bend or curve: *a road with many ~s and turns; a board with a slight ~* (i.e. warp). **2** something twisted: *a ~ of bread; a ~* (i.e. braid) *of tobacco; a ~ of lemon* (peel for flavoring a drink). **3** distortion or wrenching; also, a kink or quirk: *an unexpected ~ in a plan; a queer mental ~.* **4** spin given to a ball in tennis, baseball, bowling, etc. **5** a vigorous dance of the 1960's with twisting hip and leg movements.

—twist·er *n.* one that twists, as a ball sent with a twisting motion, a tornado, or a waterspout.

twit *v.* **twits, twit·ted, twit·ting** taunt or tease (a person with or about a weakness).

twitch *n.* a sudden involuntary jerk, as of a facial muscle; also, a sharp tug or pull; ***v.*** pull or jerk suddenly or spasmodically: *to ~ a fishing line; ~ing fingers.*

twit·ter *v.* **1** chirp or chatter, as birds; also, titter or giggle. **2** tremble with excitement; flutter. ***—n.:*** *the ~ of swallows; Wedding day found them all in a ~.*

'twixt *prep. Archaic.* between. **—two** (TOO) *n., adj. & pron.* one more than one; 2 or II; **in two** in two parts. **—two bits** *Slang.* a quarter of a dollar; 25 cents; **two-bit** *Slang.* cheap. **—two-by-four** *n.* a piece of lumber 4 in. wide and 2 in. thick (10.16 × 5.08 cm) before trimming. **—two-edged** *adj.* cutting both ways: *a ~ sword, argument.* **—two-faced** *adj.* having two faces; hence, deceitful or insincere. **—two·fer** (TOO·fur) *n. Informal.* a discounted item of which one can buy "two for" the price of one, esp. a cut-rate theater ticket. **—two-fis·ted** *adj. Informal.* vigorous or strong. **—two·fold** *adj. & adv.* double; doubly. **—2,4-D** *n.* an organic herbicide or weedkiller. **—two·pence** (TUP·unce) *n.* two pence; **two·pen·ny** (TUP·uh·nee) *adj.* worth or costing two pence. **—two-ply** *adj.* having two thicknesses, strands, etc. **—two·some** (–sum) *n.* (a golf match for) two people. **—two-step** *n. & v.* **-steps, -stepped, -step·ping** dance with a series of sliding steps in march or polka rhythm. **—two-time** *v.* **-times, -timed, -tim·ing** *Slang.* be unfaithful to (a spouse or lover). **—two-way** *adj.* involving two directions or parties: *a ~ street, radio, race* (between two contestants); **two-way TV** a modified home television set that may be used by the viewer for shopping, banking, participating in opinion polls, requesting information from data banks, etc.

twp. township.

TWX teletypewriter exchange.

TX Texas.

-ty same as -ITY.

ty·coon (tye·COON) *n.* **1** a wealthy businessman. **2** the title by which foreigners referred to the shogun of Japan.

tying *pres. part.* of TIE.

tyke *n. Informal.* a small child considered as mischievous, helpless, etc.

Ty·ler (TYE–), **John.** 1790–1862, 10th U.S. President (1841–45).

tym·pa·ni (TIM·puh·nee) *n.pl.* same as TIMPANI; **tym·pa·nist** *n.* **—tym·pan·ic** (tim·PAN–) **membrane** the eardrum. **—tym·pa·num** (TIM·puh–) *n.* **-nums** or **-na** (–nuh) the middle ear; also, eardrum; **tym·pan·ic** (–PAN–) *adj.*

type *n.* **1** a person or thing considered as belonging to a group or category because similar to others; hence, a category, sort, or kind: *He's the strong, silent ~; a fine ~ of woman; don't like this ~ of novel* (*Informal:* this type novel); *a plant variety that is true to ~* (i.e. the original); *dramatic characters that are ~s rather than individuals.* **2** a printing block with raised letters or characters; hence, printed letters: *Gutenberg printed from movable ~; The book is* **in type** *ready to print; italic ~.* ***—v.*** **types, typed, typ·ing** **1** classify as to type; typecast; also, typify: *to ~ one's blood as A, B, AB, or O.* **2** write with a typewriter. **—-type** *comb.form.* as in *archetype, prototype, stereotype.* **—type·cast** *v.* **-casts, -cast, -cast·ing** cast (an actor) repeatedly in the same type of role: *was ~ as a villain; the ~ing of women as sex objects.* **—type·face** *n.* a set of type of one design; also, the design: *same ~, though a different size.* **—type·found·er** *n.* one who designs or produces metal printing type; **type·found·ing** *n.* **—type·script** *n.* typewritten matter. **—type·set** *v.* **-sets, -set, -set·ting** set (matter) in type; compose; **type·set·ter** *n.;* **type·set·ting** *n.* **—type·write** *v.* **-writes, -wrote, -writ·ten, -writ·ing** type (def. 2); **type·writ·er** *n.* a keyboard machine that produces printed characters on paper; **type·writ·ing** *n.*

ty·phoid (TYE·foid) *n.* a serious infectious disease spread by a bacillus that enters the body through contaminated food or water; also **typhoid fever.**

ty·phoon (tye·FOON) *n.* a destructive tropical cyclone of the W. Pacific.

ty·phus (TYE·fus) *n.* any of various rickettsial diseases often caused by the bite of infected lice, fleas, ticks, etc.; also **typhus fever.** **—ty·phous** (–fus) *adj.*

typ·i·cal (TIP·i·cl) *adj.* having the characteristics of a type or class: *a ~ soap opera; Sentimentality is ~* (i.e. characteristic) *of soaps;* **typ·i·cal·ly** *adv.;* **typ·i·cal·ness** or **-cal·i·ty** (–CAL–) *n.* **—typ·i·fy** (TIP–) *v.* **-fies, -fied, -fy·ing** **1** to be a symbol of; prefigure or foreshadow. **2** have the characteristics of; exemplify: *Johnny Appleseed ~s the pioneer planter.* **—typ·ist** (TYE–) *n.* one who uses a typewriter. **—ty·po** (TYE–) *n. Informal.* a typing or typesetting error of a mechanical kind. **—ty·pog·ra·pher** (–POG·ruh–) *n.* an expert in typography; **ty·pog·ra·phy** *n.* the art of printing with type; also, the arrangement or appearance of typeset matter; **ty·po·graph·ic** (–GRAF–) *adj.;* **ty·po·graph·i·cal** *adj.;* **ty·po·graph·i·cal·ly** *adv.* **—ty·pol·o·gy** (tye·POL–) *n.* classification by types based on similar characteristics, as of languages considered as "analytic" (Chinese, English, etc.), "synthetic" (Sanskrit, Greek, etc.), and "agglutinative" (Turkish, Korean, etc.); **ty·po·log·i·cal** (–LOJ–) *adj.*

ty·ran·ni·cal (tuh·RAN–) *adj.* of or like a tyrant; cruel and unjust; also **ty·ran·nic; ty·ran·ni·cal·ly** *adv.* **—tyr·an·nize** (TEER·uh–) *v.* **-niz·es, -nized, -niz·ing** act or rule as a tyrant or despot; oppress: *the rich ~ing (over)* *the poor;* **tyr·an·niz·er** *n.* —**ty·ran·no·saur** (–RAN–) or **ty·ran·no·saur·us** (–SOR–) *n.* the largest of the flesh-eating dinosaurs. —**tyr·an·nous** (TEER·uh·nus) *adj.* tyrannical; **tyr·an·nous·ly** *adv.;* **tyr·an·ny** (–nee) *n.* **-an·nies** a tyrant's rule or authority; also, a cruel and unjust act or use of power: *the ~ of the majority.* —**ty·rant** (TYE·runt) *n.* an absolute ruler or despot; also, a cruel or oppressive person in authority.

tyre *Brit.* same as [1]TIRE.

ty·ro (TYE–) *n.* **-ros** (–roze) an inexperienced and amateurish beginner in a field of activity.

Tyr·ol (tuh·ROLE, TYE–) same as TIROL; **Ty·ro·le·an** *n.* & *adj.*

tzar (TSAR, ZAR) same as CZAR; *fem.* **tza·ri·na** (–REE–).

U

U or **u** (YOO) *n.* **U's** or **u's** the 21st letter of the English alphabet. —**U** **1** uranium. **2** *n.* something shaped like a "U": *a 360° U-turn; the U-tube used in chemistry experiments.* **3** *adj. Informal.* in Britain, upper-class. —**U** or **U.** Union; University. —**U, U., u** or **u.** unit(s).

U.A.R. United Arab Republic.

U.A.W. United Automobile Workers.

u·biq·ui·tous (yoo·BIK·wuh·tus) *adj.* seeming to be present or occurring everywhere: *the ~, omnivorous common crow;* **u·biq·ui·tous·ly** *adv.;* **u·biq·ui·ty** *n.*

U-boat *n.* a German submarine.

ud·der (UD·ur) *n.* a pendulous, milk-secreting organ with two or more teats, as in the cow or goat.

UFO *n.* **UFO's** an unidentified flying object; flying saucer. —**u·fol·o·gist** (yoo·FOL–) *n.* one who studies UFO's; **u·fol·o·gy** *n.*

U·gan·da (yoo·GAN·duh, –GAHN–) a country of E.C. Africa; 91,134 sq.mi. (236,036 km^2); *cap.* Kampala; **U·gan·dan** *n.* & *adj.*

ugh (uh, uk, etc.) *interj.* expressing disgust or horror.

ug·li (–lee) *n.* **-li(e)s** a Jamaican fruit similar to the tangelo. —**ug·ly** (–lee) *adj.* **-li·er, -li·est** hideous or repulsive in appearance: *an ~ toad; an ~* (i.e. dangerous) *gaping wound; gave me an ~* (i.e. ill-natured) *look; the loud-mouthed and boorish* **Ugly American** *type; the* **ugly duckling** *who grew into a graceful swan;* **ug·li·ness** *n.*

uh *interj.* expressing surprise, contempt, or a question; also, a sound prolonged while thinking or searching for a word; **uh-huh** *interj.* indicating that one is receptive to what is being said; **uh-uh** *interj.* indicating disagreement.

UHF or **uhf** ultrahigh frequency.

U.K. United Kingdom.

u·kase (YOO·case, –CAZE) *n.* an edict or decree, as of a czar.

U·krain·i·an (yoo·CRAY·nee·un) *n.* & *adj.* (the Slavic language or a native or inhabitant) of the Ukraine; **the U·kraine** (yoo·CRAIN, YOO·crain) same as the **Ukrainian Soviet Socialist Republic,** a constituent republic of the U.S.S.R.; *cap.* Kiev.

u·ku·le·le (yoo·kuh·LAY·lee) *n.* a small, four-stringed Hawaiian guitar.

U.L. Underwriters' Laboratories.

U·lan Ba·tor (OO·lahn·BAH·tor) capital of the Mongolian People's Republic.

ul·cer (UL·sur) *n.* an open, usu. inflamed sore on the skin or on a mucous membrane, as in *stomach* (or *peptic*) *ulcers;* **ul·cer·ous** (–us) *adj.* —**ul·cer·ate** *v.* **-ates, -at·ed, -at·ing** make or become ulcerous; **ul·cer·a·tion** (–RAY–) *n.;* **ul·cer·a·tive** (–uh·tiv) *adj.*

ull·age (–ij) *n.* amount by which a liquid container falls short of being full: *A small* **ullage rocket** *is used to force liquid propellants into position for firing the rocket engine of a space vehicle.*

ul·na *n.,pl.* **-nae** (–nee) or **-nas** the larger of the two bones of the forearm; **ul·nar** *adj.*

ul·ster *n.* a long, loose, heavy, usu. belted overcoat; **Ul·ster** See NORTHERN IRELAND.

ult. ultimate(ly). —**ul·te·ri·or** (–TEER·ee·ur) *adj.* lying on the farther side; hence, hidden: *an ~ motive.* —**ul·ti·mate** (–tuh·mit) *adj.* remotest, beyond which it is impossible to go: *the ~ origin of the universe; in the ~ analysis; God, the Ultimate Reality;* ***n.*** an ultimate point, result, fact, etc.; **ul·ti·mate·ly** *adv.* —**ul·ti·ma·tum** (–tuh·MAY–) *n.* **-tums** or **-ta** (–tuh) a final offer or demand threatening consequences if rejected. —**ul·ti·mo** (UL·tuh–) *adj.* of last month: *your letter of the 30th ~.* —**ul·tra** (–truh) *n.* an extremist; ***adj.*** & ***prefix.*** going beyond the usual; extreme(ly): *too ~ in his politics;* **ul·tra·con·serv·a·tive** (–SUR·vuh·tiv) *adj.* extremely conservative. —**ul·tra·fash·ion·a·ble** (–FASH–) *adj.* extremely fashionable. —**ul·tra·fiche** (–feesh) *n.* extremely reduced microfiche. —**ul·tra·high** *adj.* exceedingly high; **ultrahigh frequency** a radio-wave frequency between 300 and 3,000 megahertz. —**ul·tra·ma·rine** (–muh·REEN) *adj.* **1** situated beyond the sea. **2** brilliant-blue, as a pigment made from lapis lazuli; ***n.*** this color. —**ul·tra·mi·cro·scope** (–MY·cruh–) *n.* a microscope that uses scattered light to see extremely minute objects such as bacteria and colloidal particles suspended in liquid or air;

ul·tra·mi·cro·scop·ic (–SCOP–) *adj.* too tiny to be seen with an ordinary microscope. —**ul·tra·min·i·a·ture** (–MIN–) *adj.* same as SUBMINIATURE. —**ul·tra·mod·ern** (–MOD–) *adj.* extremely modern in style, trend, ideas, etc. —**ul·tra·mon·tane** (–MON–) *adj.* situated south of the mountains, i.e. Alps; hence, favoring papal authority over national and diocesan; **ul·tra·mon·ta·nism** (–MON·tuh–) *n.* —**ul·tra·short** *adj.* of a wavelength below 10 meters. —**ul·tra·son·ic** (–SON–) *adj.* beyond human hearing range; having to do with ultrasound; **ul·tra·son·ics** *n.* the science of ultrasonic sound waves and their applications in science and industry; **ul·tra·sound** *n.* sound of more than 20,000 vibrations per second, too high-pitched for human hearing. —**ul·tra·vi·o·let** (–VYE·uh–) *adj.* beyond the violet end of the visible light range: ~ *light, radiation, lamps* (yielding radiations of wavelengths between visible light and X rays). —**ultra vi·res** (–VYE·reez) *adj.* & *adv. Latin.* beyond one's legal power or authority.

ul·u·late (UL·yuh–, YOOL–) *v.* **-lates, -lat·ed, -lat·ing** make a prolonged sound, as in wailing or howling; **ul·u·la·tion** (–LAY–) *n.*

U·lys·ses (yoo·LIS·eez) the legendary Greek hero of the Trojan War and king of Ithaca, whose wanderings on his way back home from Troy are described in Homer's *Odyssey;* Odysseus.

um·bel *n.* an umbrellalike flower cluster, as of the carrot, parsley, etc. of the **um·bel·lif·er·ous** (–LIF–) family of plants.

um·ber *n.* a brown mineral pigment or its color; ***adj.*** of the brown color of "raw umber" or the deep reddish brown of "burnt umber."

um·bil·i·cal (–BIL–) *adj.* of the navel: *The* **umbilical cord** *connects the navel of an unborn child to the placenta of its mother's uterus for nutrition and waste removal;* **um·bil·i·cus** *n.* navel.

um·bra (–bruh) *n.,pl.* **-brae** (–bree) or **-bras** a dark spot or shadow, esp. the darker region of shadow cast by the sun in which a "total eclipse" is experienced; **um·bral** *adj.* —**um·brage** (–brij) *n.* **1 take umbrage at** take offense at. **2** shade or shady foliage. —**um·brel·la** (–BREL·uh) *n.* **1** a circular cover of cloth on a folding frame of hinged ribs sliding on a center pole, carried for protection against sun or rain. **2** a protective organization, device, etc.: *an air ~ of military aircraft; the ~ group for Palestinian guerrillas.*

u·mi·ak (OO·mee–) *n.* a large, open Eskimo boat made with sealskin stretched over a wooden frame for carrying 10 to 12 people.

um·laut (OOM·lowt) *n.* in Germanic languages, the change of a vowel sound because of another vowel following it, as in the German "Hände," *pl.* of "Hand"; also, the diacritical mark placed over the changed vowel, as in ä, ö, and ü.

ump short form of **um·pire** *n.* & *v.* **-pires, -pired, -pir·ing** (act as) a judge or referee in a contest or dispute, esp. an official administering the rules in sports such as baseball or hockey, sometimes assisting a referee, as in tennis and volleyball: *to ~ a game.*

ump·teen *adj. Slang.* an indefinitely large number of: *I've told you ~ times;* **ump·teenth** (–TEENTH) *adj.: for the ~ time.*

UMT Universal Military Training.

U.M.W. United Mine Workers.

UN or **U.N.** United Nations.

un- [A prefix freely added to words, using a hyphen before a capital letter, to mean "not" when added to adjectives and adverbs, "the opposite of" when added to nouns, and an opposite action when a verb is formed. The more common of such compounds, whose basic meaning and pronunciation are the same as in the base word in each case, are placed at the bottom of this and the following pages.]

un·a·bridged *adj.* not abridged; also, comprehensive or compendious: *an ~ dictionary.* —**un·ac·count·a·ble** *adj.* **1** that cannot be accounted for; strange. **2** not responsible. —**un·ac·cus·tomed** *adj.* not accustomed *(to);* also, unusual or strange. —**un·ad·vised** *adj.* without guidance or advice; hence, rash or indiscreet. —**un-A·mer·i·can** *adj.* considered as contrary to U.S. customs, traditions, goals, etc.

u·nan·i·mous (yoo·NAN·uh·mus) *adj.* in complete agreement; with the agreement of all;

---

unabashed
unable
unaccented
unaccompanied
unacknowledged
unacquainted
unadorned
unadvertised
unaffected
unafraid
unaided
unalterable
unannounced
unanswerable
unappetizing
unapproachable
unashamed
unasked
unassailable
unassisted
unattainable
unattended
unattested
unattractive
unauthentic
unauthorized
unavailable
unavoidable
unbearable
unbeaten

u·nan·i·mous·ly *adv.;* **u·na·nim·i·ty** (–nuh·NIM–) *n.*

un·armed *adj.* having no weapons; also, not armored. —**un·as·sum·ing** (–SOO–) *adj.* modest; not pretentious or forward. —**un·at·tached** *adj.* not attached, esp. in regard to marriage; **unmarried** or **unengaged.** —**un·a·vail·ing** *adj.* being of no avail; futile; **un·a·vail·ing·ly** *adv.* —**un·a·ware** *adj.* not aware; **un·a·wares** (–WAIRZ) *adv.* by surprise; unexpectedly; also, unintentionally. —**un·backed** *adj.* not backed or supported; also, having no back or backing. —**un·bal·anced** *adj.* not balanced; also, mentally unstable. —**un·bar** *v.* **-bars, -barred, -bar·ring** unbolt or open (a gate, etc.); hence, open up (a closed channel, field, etc.). —**un·be·com·ing** *adj.* not appropriate to one's appearance or character: ~ *clothes, conduct;* **un·be·com·ing·ly** *adv.* —**un·be·known** (–NOHN) *adj.* unknown (*to* one); also **un·be·knownst.** —**un·be·lief** *n.* doubt or lack of belief, esp. in something religious; **un·be·liev·er** *n.;* **un·be·liev·a·ble** *adj.;* **un·be·liev·a·bly** *adv.* —**un·bend** *v.* **-bends, -bent, -bend·ing** straighten; also, relax from formality, tension, etc.; **un·bend·ing** *adj.* stiff or resolute; also, stubborn: *an* ~ *attitude.* —**un·bid·den** *adj.* not invited; also, without being ordered. —**un·blush·ing** *adj.* not blushing; also, shameless; **un·blush·ing·ly** *adv.* —**un·bolt** *v.* draw back the bolts of (a door, etc.); **un·bolt·ed** *adj.* **1** not bolted, as a door. **2** not sifted: ~ *flour.* —**un·born** *adj.* not yet born: *an* ~ *fetus;* ~ (i.e. future) *generations.* —**un·bos·om** *v.* reveal one's feelings, secrets, thoughts, etc., esp. **unbosom oneself** (*to* someone). —**un·bound·ed** *adj.* without limits; boundless; also, not kept within limits; unrestrained. —**un·bri·dled** *adj.* not bridled, esp. uncontrolled: ~ *anger, insolence.* —**un·bur·den** *v.* to free from a burden; also, relieve (oneself, one's heart, conscience, etc.) by confession (to someone) or disclosing (guilt, etc.). —**un·called-for** *adj.* not called for; unnecessary: ~ *impertinence, remarks.* —**un·can·ny** *adj.* mysterious or weird; also, so remarkable as to seem superhuman: *an* ~ *instinct for guessing the right answer; an* ~ *feeling of something wrong.* —**un·cer·e·mo·ni·ous** *adj.* not ceremonious; hence, abrupt or discourteous: *an* ~ *exit, rebuke.* —**un·cer·tain** *adj.* **1** not certain or sure: *feel* ~ *about the future; a word of* ~ *origin; told him in no* ~ (i.e. vague) *terms.* **2** changeable or varying: ~ *weather, temper, health.* —**un·cer·tain·ly** *adv.* —**un·cer·tain·ty** *n.* **-ties** an uncertain state; also, something that is uncertain: *the* ~*s of a hand-to-mouth existence.* —**un·char·i·ta·ble** *adj.* harsh or severe, as in judging others: *an* ~ *imputation of motive;* **un·char·i·ta·bly** *adv.* —**un·chart·ed** *adj.* of places, not shown on a map; hence, not mapped; unexplored: ~ *seas.* —**un·chris·tian** *adj.* not Christian; hence, *Informal.* outrageous or unusual: *charges* ~ *prices.*

un·ci·al (UN·shee·ul, –shul) *n.* & *adj.* (a letter or manuscript) in the all-capital, noncursive lettering style with large rounded characters used by scribes between A.D. 300 and 900.

un·cir·cum·cised *adj.* not circumcised; also, non-Jewish; gentile; heathen.

un·cle (UNG·cl) *n.* the brother of one's father or mother; also, one's aunt's husband. —**Uncle Sam** *Informal.* the U.S. government or nation, personified as a long-haired man in a tall hat and costume decorated with stars and stripes. —**Uncle Tom** *Informal.* a black man who is servile to whites.

un·cloak *v.* remove a cloak or cover from; hence, unmask or expose. —**un·clothe** *v.* **-clothes, -clothed, -cloth·ing** to strip of clothes; also, uncover or divest. —**un·coil** *v.* unwind. —**un·com·fort·a·ble** *adj.* feeling or causing discomfort: *The baby seems* ~; *an* ~ *chair; an* ~ (i.e. uneasy) *silence;* **un·com·fort·a·bly** *adv.* —**un·com·mit·ted** *adj.* **1** not committed or pledged, as to a particular allegiance, undertaking, etc.; neutral. **2** not committed to an institution. —**un·com·mon** *adj.* rare or unusual; also, remarkable or outstanding; **un·com·mon·ly** *adv.* —**un·com·mu·ni·ca·tive** *adj.* talking little; reserved. —**un·com·pro·mis·ing** *adj.* unyielding or inflexible: *an* ~ *attitude; a man of* ~ *devotion to duty.* —**un·con·cern** *n.* lack of concern, care,

---

unbefitting
unbiased
unbind
unbleached
unblemished
unbreakable
unbroken
unburned
unbutton
uncap
uncared-for
uncaught
unceasing
uncensored
unchallenged
unchanged
unchaperoned
unchecked
uncivil
uncivilized
unclaimed
unclassified
unclean
unclear
unclothed
uncontrollable
unconventional
uncooked
uncorrected
uncorroborated

or solicitude, as from selfishness or insensitiveness; indifference; **un·con·cerned** *adj.* not concerned, anxious, or solicitous. —**un·con·di·tion·al** *adj.* without conditions attached: ~ *surrender, rejection, offer.* —**un·con·scion·a·ble** *adj.* contrary to what the conscience dictates; unreasonable or excessive: *took an* ~ *time; an* ~ (i.e. unscrupulous) *villain;* **un·con·scion·a·bly** *adv.* —**un·con·scious** *adj.* not conscious or aware: *lay bleeding and* ~ *from his wounds; was* ~ *of having offended her; an* ~ *habit, prejudice, tendency;* ***n.*** **the unconscious** the part of the mind containing thoughts, ideas, feelings, etc. that one is not fully aware of or that have been repressed; **un·con·scious·ly** *adv.;* **un·con·scious·ness** *n.* —**un·con·sti·tu·tion·al** *adj.* not according to the constitution (of an organization); **un·con·sti·tu·tion·al·ly** *adv.;* **un·con·sti·tu·tion·al·i·ty** (–NAL–) *n.* —**un·cork** *v.* pull the cork out of (a bottle). —**un·count·ed** *adj.* not counted; too numerous to be counted; innumerable. —**un·cou·ple** *v.* **-ples, -pled, -pling** disconnect (something coupled together). —**un·couth** (–COOTH) *adj.* awkward or clumsy-looking; also, unrefined or crude. —**un·cov·er** *v.* **1** remove the cover from; hence, disclose or expose. **2** bare one's head in respect.

UNCTAD U.N. Conference on Trade and Development.

unc·tion (UNK–) *n.* **1** an anointing with oil (as in church rites) or with ointment (as in medical treatment); also, the oil or salve used. **2** anything that soothes or comforts; also, this quality: *preaches with great* ~. **3** unctuousness. —**unc·tu·ous** (–CHOO·us) *adj.* too suave or smooth; **unc·tu·ous·ly** *adv.;* **unc·tu·ous·ness** *n.*

un·cut *adj.* not cut or abridged: *an* ~ *version; a rough,* ~ (i.e. not shaped and polished) *diamond.* —**un·daunt·ed** *adj.* not daunted or disheartened. —**un·de·ceive** *v.* **-ceives, -ceived, -ceiv·ing** free (someone) from error or deception; disabuse. —**un·de·cid·ed** *adj.* not having come to a decision; also, not decided or settled, as a contest. —**un·de·mon·stra·tive** *adj.* not demonstrative (*adj.* 2); **un·de·mon·stra·tive·ly** *adv.* —**un·de·ni·a·ble** *adj.* that cannot be disputed; hence, excellent in regard to value or genuineness; **un·de·ni·a·bly** *adv.*

un·der *prep.* **1** directly below: *Look* ~ *the table; a boulder* ~ *the* (surface of) *water; wears a shirt* ~ *his jacket; priced* ~ (i.e. less than) *a dollar; 15 is* ~ *the voting age.* **2** subject or subordinate to: *a country* ~ *a dictatorship; testified* ~ *oath; was* ~ *a wrong impression; working* ~ *a contract; "Beauty" is listed* ~ (the heading) *"B"; was excused* ~ (i.e. because of) *the circumstances.* — ***adv.:*** *The boat sprang a leak and went* ~*; priced $100 and* ~*; snowed* ~ *by unanswered mail; Companies* **go under** *by bankruptcy.* —***adj.*** lower in position or authority; also, hold in control: *to keep wages and prices* ~. —***comb.form*** [as in the following compounds whose basic meaning and pronunciation are the same as in the base word in each case]

undercook
underdose
undereducated
underemployed
underpay
underpopulated
underpriced
underripe
undersexed
undersized

un·der·a·chieve *v.* **-chieves, -chieved, -chiev·ing** do less well in school than expected for one's level of ability; **un·der·a·chiev·er** *n.* —**un·der·act** *v.* act (a dramatic part) with less than the required emphasis; underplay. —**un·der·age** *adj.* below the required or full age. —**un·der·arm** *adj.* **1** of the armpit: ~ *wetness.* **2** *adj.* & *adv.* underhand (def. 1): *an* ~ *throw.* —**un·der·bel·ly** *n.* the underside of an animal's body; hence, a weak or vulnerable part. —**un·der·bid** *v.* **-bids, -bid, -bid·ding** **1** bid less than what is justified, as by the cards in one's hand. **2** bid lower than (another person). —**un·der·brush** *n.* low shrubs, small trees, etc. under the large trees of a forest. —**un·der·car·riage** *n.* **1** the supporting frame or structure of an automobile or other thing on wheels. **2** landing gear of an airplane. —**un·der·charge** *v.* **-charg·es, -charged, -charg·ing** **1** charge (a buyer) less than the usual price. **2** load (a

---

uncultivated
uncultured
undamaged
undecipherable
undeclared
undefeated
undefended
undefiled
undefined
undemocratic
undependable
undeserved
undesirable
undeveloped
undifferentiated
undisciplined
undiscovered
undisguised
undisputed
undistinguished
undisturbed
undivided
undone
undraped
unearned
uneconomic
uneducated
unemotional
unending
unenforceable

gun, battery, etc.) insufficiently; ***n.*** (UN–) such a charge. **—un·der·class** *n.* the poor and underpriviledged of a society; **un·der·class·man** (–CLASS–) *n.* a freshman or sophomore. **—un·der·clothes** *n.pl.* underwear; also **un·der·cloth·ing** (–CLOH–) *n.* **—un·der·coat (·ing)** *n.* **1** a coating of a tarlike substance given to the underside of an automobile for protection against rust. **2** a coat of paint applied to a wall, furniture, etc. before the final coat. **—*v.*** apply an undercoat to. **—un·der·cov·er** *adj.* (done in) secret, as spying: *an ~ agent, investigation; ~ work, payments.* **—un·der·cur·rent** *n.* a current below the surface, esp. in an opposite direction, as an undertow: *a ~ of resentment.* **—un·der·cut** *v.* **-cuts, -cut, -cut·ting** **1** cut away the underpart, as at the bottom of a coal bed for easy shattering by explosives or on the side of a tree trunk to make it fall toward a particular side. **2** sell or work for less than (a competitor). **3** hit (a ball) so as to give it a backspin, as in tennis, billiards, or golf. **—un·der·de·vel·oped** *adj.* of countries, not advanced industrially and hence poor in standard of living, education, health care, etc. **—un·der·dog** *n.* **1** one in a state of subjection. **2** the predicted loser in a contest. **—un·der·done** *adj.* not cooked enough. **—un·der·es·ti·mate** *n.* & *v.* **-mates, -mat·ed, -mat·ing** (form) too low an estimate of (a person's strength, costs of a project, etc.). **—un·der·foot** *adj.* & *adv.* under the foot or feet; also, in the way of one walking. **—un·der·gar·ment** *n.* a piece of underwear. **—un·der·go** *v.* **-goes, -went, -gone, -go·ing** go through (a painful, unpleasant, or dangerous experience). **—un·der·grad·u·ate** *n.* a college student who has not yet received his first degree. **—un·der·ground** *adj.* & *adv.* **1** beneath the surface of the ground: *an ~ installation, passage; ~ testing of atomic bombs; Moles live ~.* **2** in(to) hiding; away from public knowledge; *went ~ to escape from the police; ~ resistance to enemy occupation; dissident publications of the ~ press; an avant-garde ~ movie.* **—*n.*** **1** an underground region or political movement. **2** *Brit.* a subway. **—un·der·growth** *n.* underbrush. **—un·der·hand** *adj.* & *adv.* **1** with the hand swung forward below the level of the elbow or shoulder: *an ~ throw, serve; to pitch a ball ~.* **2** underhanded(ly). **—un·der·hand·ed** *adj.* sly or deceitful; not open or honest; **un·der·hand·ed·ly** *adv.;* **un·der·hand·ed·ness** *n.* **—un·der·lie** *v.* **-lies, -lay, -lain, -ly·ing** **1** lie or be situated under. **2** form the basis or foundation of (a doctrine, etc.). **—un·der·line** *v.* **-lines, -lined, -lin·ing** draw a line under; hence, stress or emphasize; ***n.*** a line under a word, passage, etc. **—un·der·ling** *n.* a servile follower or subordinate. **—un·der·ly·ing** *adj.* **1** lying under: *~ strata.* **2** basic or fundamental: *~ principles, motives, reasons.* **—un·der·mine** (–MINE) *v.* **-mines, -mined, -min·ing** **1** dig under or wear away from under: *to ~ a foundation; flood waters ~ing river banks.* **2** weaken or impair gradually, as by insidious means: *rumors that ~ a person's reputation; health ~d* (i.e. sapped) *by a chronic illness.* **—un·der·most** *adj.* & *adv.* lowest. **—un·der·neath** (–NEETH) *prep.* & *adv.* below or beneath, esp. in a hidden place: *carried a knife ~* (his cloak). **—un·der·nour·ished** *adj.* not getting sufficient nourishment. **—un·der·pants** *n.pl.* long or short pants worn as underwear. **—un·der·pass** *n.* a road passing under a railroad or highway. **—un·der·pin·ning** *n.* masonry support or prop under a structure; **underpinnings** *pl. Slang.* a person's legs. **—un·der·play** *v.* underact; also, play down; treat as not very important. **—un·der·priv·i·leged** *adj.* not enjoying the rights and privileges of other people, as the poor or minority groups of a society. **—un·der·pro·duce** (–DOOS, –DYOOS) *v.* **-duc·es, -duced, -duc·ing** produce less than is needed or normal; **un·der·pro·duc·tion** (–DUC–) *n.* **—un·der·rate** *v.* **-rates, -rat·ed, -rat·ing** to rate too low; underestimate. **—un·der·score** *n.* & *v.* **-scores, -scored, -scor·ing** same as UNDERLINE. **—un·der·sea** *adj.* & *adv.* beneath the surface of the sea; also **un·der·seas** *adv.* **—un·der·sec·re·tar·y** *n.* **-tar·ies** an assistant secretary of a government department.**—un·der·sell** (–SEL) *v.* **sells, -sold, -sell·ing** sell (an article) at a lower price than (a competitor). **—un·der·shirt** *n.* a vest

---

unenlightened
unenviable
unethical
uneventful
unexceptional
unexciting
unexpired
unexplained
unexplored
unexpressed
unexpurgated
unfair
unfasten
unfathomable
unfavorable
unfettered
unfinished
unfit
unflagging
unflattering
unforeseen
unforgivable
unfulfilled
unfurnished
ungentlemanly
ungrateful
unhampered
unhandy

or similar undergarment worn under a shirt. **—un·der·shorts** *n.pl.* shorts worn by men and boys as underwear. **—un·der·shot** *adj.* **1** with the lower jaw projecting beyond the upper jaw or teeth when the mouth is closed. **2** of a water wheel, turned by water flowing underneath. **—un·der·side** *n.* the lower side or surface, as of a leaf. **—un·der·signed** *adj.* (whose name is) signed at the end (of a document); **the undersigned** the person or persons whose signatures are at the bottom of the document or letter. **—un·der·staffed** *adj.* having fewer people on the staff than required. **—un·der·stand** (–STAND) *v.* **-stands, -stood, -stand·ing** **1** get the meaning or significance of: *words that are difficult to ~; tried to make himself understood in French; Spouses ~ each other; Parents ~ children; Please ~* (i.e. get the meaning; also, be sympathetic). **2** learn or infer: *I ~ you are in hospital; I understood her to say she'd be late; When you say "or else," the rest is understood.* **—un·der·stand·a·ble** (–STAND–) *adj.;* **un·der·stand·a·bly** *adv.* **—un·der·stand·ing** *n.* **1** (power of) comprehension or knowledge: *a vocabulary within her ~; man's limited ~.* **2** agreement or mutual harmony: *Let's come to an ~.* **—adj.:** *an ~ parent, wink, heart.* **—un·der·state** (–STATE) *v.* **-states, -stat·ed, -stat·ing** **1** state weakly or less than adequately. **2** state in a very restrained manner. **—un·der·state·ment** *n.* **—un·der·stud·y** *n.* **-stud·ies** one trained to substitute for another, esp. in a theatrical role; ***v.*** **-stud·ies, -stud·ied, -stud·y·ing** to study (a role or part) or act as understudy to (an actor, etc.). **—un·der·take** (–TAKE) *v.* **-takes, -took, -tak·en, -tak·ing** take upon oneself (a task or to do something); also, promise or guarantee (that); **un·der·tak·er** *n.* [less favored term] funeral director; **un·der·tak·ing** *n.* a task or enterprise; also, a guarantee. **—un·der-the-count·er** *adj. Informal.* of dealings, secret or illicit; also **un·der-the-ta·ble.** **—un·der·things** *n.pl. Informal.* women's underwear. **—un·der·tone** *n.* a subdued tone of voice or color; also, an underlying quality: *an ~ of melancholy.* **—un·der·tow** (–toh) *n.* an undercurrent of water beneath the surface in the opposite direction, as the backward flow of waves breaking on a beach. **—un·der·wa·ter** *adj. & adv.* under the surface of the water: *an ~ demolition team; ~ diving, photography, research.* **—un·der·wear** *n.* clothing worn under other clothes, esp. next to the skin, as panties, briefs, shorts, etc. **—un·der·weight** *adj.* below the normal, required, or allowed weight. **—un·der·whelm** *v. Informal.* fail to overwhelm. **—un·der·world** *n.* **1** the lower world; Hades. **2** the part of society composed of criminals. **—un·der·write** *v.* **-writes, -wrote, -writ·ten, -writ·ing** assume financial liability, as in insuring against loss or risk, in agreeing to buy up unsold stocks and bonds of a particular issue, to finance an enterprise or meet the expenses of educating someone, etc.; **un·der·writ·er** *n.* **—un·dies** (–deez) *n.pl.* underthings.

un·do *v.* **-does, -did, -done, -do·ing** **1** untie (a knot, string, parcel, etc.) or open or unfasten (a button, blouse, etc.). **2** annul or cancel the effect of (what is done, a spell, etc.); also, bring to ruin; **un·do·ing** *n.* (cause of) ruin; **un·done** *adj.* not done; unfinished; also, ruined. **—un·doubt·ed** *adj.* certain beyond a doubt: *a man of ~ integrity;* **un·doubt·ed·ly** *adv.* **—un·dreamed-of** (–DREMD–) or **un·dreamt-of** (–DREMT–) *adj.* never even dreamed of; inconceivable or unexpected: *an ~ good fortune; ~ discoveries.* **—un·dress** *v.* take off one's clothes or the clothes of; disrobe; ***n.*** ordinary or informal dress; also, nakedness. **—un·due** *adj.* improper or excessive: *with ~ haste; ~ importance given to minor stories; accused of exerting ~ influence in his own favor.*

un·du·lant (UN·joo·lunt, –dyoo–) *adj.* undulating; **undulant fever** an infectious disease characterized by fever that varies from time to time; **un·du·late** *v.* **-lates, -lat·ed, -lat·ing** have a wavy form or move in waves: *a lake surface ~ing in the breeze; ~ing* (i.e. rolling) *prairie land;* **un·du·la·tion** (–LAY–) *n.*

un·du·ly (–DEW–) *adv.* improperly or excessively. **—un·dy·ing** *adj.* deathless or eternal: *her ~ devotion, beauty, fame.* **—un·earth** *v.* bring to light, as from a hidden condition; dig up, as

---

unharmed
unhealthful
unheeded
unheralded
unhitch
unhook
unhurried
unhurt
unidentified
unimaginative
unimpaired
unimportant
unimpressive
unimproved
unincorporated
uninformed
uninhabited
uninhibited
uninitiated
uninjured
uninspired
uninsured
unintelligent
unintended
unintentional
uninteresting
uninterrupted
uninvited

from the earth: *to ~ fresh evidence, new facts, plots.* —**un·earth·ly** *adj.* **1** not of this world; hence, strange or weird. **2** *Informal.* preposterous or absurd: *rang our doorbell at an ~ hour.* —**un·eas·y** *adj.* **-eas·i·er, -eas·i·est** marked by lack of ease in mind or body: *an ~ sleep, laugh, peace; ~ in the presence of strangers;* **un·eas·i·ly** *adv.;* **un·eas·i·ness** *n.* —**un·em·ployed** *adj.* **1** without a job: *an ~ worker.* **2** not in use: *~ skills, hours.* —**un·em·ploy·ment** *n.* —**un·e·qual** *adj.* **1** not equal in amount, value, etc. **2** not well matched or even. **3** not adequate (to a task). —**un·e·qual(l)ed** *adj.* unparalleled; unmatched. —**un·e·quiv·o·cal** *adj.* not equivocal; clear; **un·e·quiv·o·cal·ly** *adv.* —**un·err·ing** *adj.* making no errors; unfailing; exact: *~ aim, blows, precision;* **un·err·ing·ly** *adv.*

UNESCO (yoo·NES·coh) U.N. Educational, Scientific, and Cultural Organization.

un·e·ven *adj.* **1** not even, level, or uniform: *an ~ road surface, handwriting, performance.* **2** unequal: *an ~ match.* **3** odd: *1, 3, 5 are ~ numbers.* —**un·e·ven·ly** *adv.* —**un·ex·am·pled** (–AM–) *adj.* unprecedented; unparalleled. —**un·ex·cep·tion·a·ble** *adj.* that cannot be found fault with; quite admirable; **un·ex·cep·tion·a·bly** *adv.* —**un·ex·cep·tion·al** *adj.* not forming an exception; ordinary. —**un·ex·pect·ed** *adj.* not expected; unforeseen; **un·ex·pect·ed·ly** *adv.* —**un·fail·ing** *adj.* **1** never failing in loyalty or constancy; reliable. **2** never coming to an end: *~ patience.* **3** sure or infallible. —**un·faith·ful** *adj.* disloyal or adulterous; also, not true or accurate: *~ to the original.* —**un·fa·mil·iar** *adj.* not well known *(to);* also, not acquainted *(with).* —**un·feel·ing** *adj.* lacking feeling or sensation; also, cruel or hardhearted; **un·feel·ing·ly** *adv.* —**un·feigned** *adj.* genuine. —**un·flap·pa·ble** *adj. Informal.* not easily excited; self-assured. —**un·flinch·ing** *adj.* resolute; fearless; —**un·fold** *v.* open up or develop; also, reveal: *as the story ~s; to ~ plans.* —**un·for·get·ta·ble** *adj.* never to be forgotten; **un·for·get·ta·bly** *adv.* —**un·for·tu·nate** *adj.* not lucky; also, regrettable: *an ~ incident;* ***n.*** one considered to have had bad luck, as a fallen woman or social outcast; **un·for·tu·nate·ly** *adv.* —**un·found·ed** *adj.* baseless; not factual: *an ~ allegation.* —**un·friend·ly** *adj.* hostile or unfavorable. —**un·frock** *v.* remove from the priesthood; deprive (a cleric) of his rank. —**un·gain·ly** *adj.* awkward or clumsy. —**un·god·ly** *adv.* sinful or irreligious; also, *Informal.* outrageous. —**un·gov·ern·a·ble** *adj.* incapable of being restrained or directed; unruly: *an ~ temper.* —**un·gra·cious** *adj.* not gracious; rude or unpleasant. —**un·guard·ed** *adj.* not protected; also, thoughtless or careless: *an ~ moment.*

un·guent (UNG·gwunt) *n.* an ointment or salve.

un·gu·late (UNG·gyuh–) *adj.* hoofed; ***n.*** a hoofed herbivorous mammal such as a horse, rhinoceros, deer, elephant, or pig.

un·hand *v.* remove the hand from; let go of. —**un·hap·py** *adj.* **-hap·pi·er, -hap·pi·est** sorrowful; also, unfortunate or inappropriate; **un·hap·pi·ly** *adv.;* **un·hap·pi·ness** *n.* —**un·health·y** *adj.* **-health·i·er, -i·est** **1** not healthy or healthful: *an ~ child, climate, habit.* **2** morally harmful; unwholesome: *an ~ influence, atmosphere.* —**un·heard** *adj.* not heard or given a hearing; **un·heard-of** *adj.* never heard of; unprecedented; also, outrageous. —**un·hinge** *v.* **-hing·es, -hinged, -hing·ing** **1** remove from the hinges; hence, dislodge. **2** unsettle; make unstable, esp. mentally. —**un·ho·ly** *adj.* **-li·er, -li·est** **1** not sacred; also, wicked. **2** *Informal.* outrageous; unreasonable. —**un·horse** *v.* **-hors·es, -horsed, -hors·ing** unseat, (as) from a horse.

uni- *comb.form.* single: as in *unicorn, uniform;* **u·ni·cam·er·al** (yoo·nuh·CAM–) *adj.* having only one chamber or body of legislators: *a ~ legislature.*

UNICEF (YOO·nuh·sef) U.N. International Children's (Emergency) Fund.

u·ni·corn (YOO·nuh–) *n.* a horselike mythical animal with a single horn on its forehead. —**u·ni·cy·cle** (YOO·nuh–) *n.* a vehicle consisting of a wheel and pedals worked by a rider seated on top. —**u·ni·form** (YOO·nuh–) *adj.* unvarying in form or character throughout the parts of a substance, series, etc.: *the ~ body*

---

unjustifiable
unknowing
unlace
unlatch
unleaded
unleavened
unlicensed
unlimited
unlisted
unmanageable
unmanned
unmannerly
unmarked
unmarred
unmarried
unmatched
unmindful
unmixed
unmolested
unmoved
unnameable
unnamed
unnecessary
unnoticeable
unnoticed
unobserved
unobstructed
unobtrusive

temperature of a warm-blooded animal; ~ (i.e. same) *laws, standards, taxes;* ***n.*** clothes distinctive of a particular group such as soldiers or nurses; **u·ni·form·ly** *adv.;* **u·ni·form·i·ty** (–FORM–) *n.* —**u·ni·fy** (YOO–) *v.* **-fies, -fied, -fy·ing** make or become united; **u·ni·fi·ca·tion** (–CAY–) *n.* —**u·ni·lat·er·al** (–LAT–) of or involving one side only; one-sided; not bilateral or reciprocal: *the ~ repudiation of an agreement;* **u·ni·lat·er·al·ly** *adv.*

un·im·peach·a·ble *adj.* that cannot be doubted or questioned; also, blameless: ~ *authority, honesty.* —**un·in·ter·est·ed** *adj.* having or showing no interest; indifferent: *an ~ listener.*

un·ion (YOON·yun) *n.* **1** a joining together or the state of being joined together, usu. permanently, as one unit: *matrimonial ~; "~ is strength."* **2** a group or whole resulting from joining together: *a labor ~;* **the Union** the United States of America: *the President's State of the ~ message to Congress.* **3** the part of a flag bearing a union emblem, as the blue rectangle with stars in the American flag. **4** a coupling or similar connecting device. —**un·ion·ize** *v.* **-iz·es, -ized, -iz·ing** form into a labor union. —**union jack** a flag consisting of a union emblem, as the **Union Jack** of the U.K. —**Union of Soviet Socialist Republics** a country of E. Europe and N. Asia consisting of 15 constituent republics; 8,649,500 sq.mi. (22,402,000 km²); *cap.* Moscow. —**u·nique** (yoo·NEEK) *adj.* having no like or equal; one of a kind: *a ~ achievement; This is absolutely ~ (Informal.* extraordinary); **u·nique·ly** *adv.;* **u·nique·ness** *n.* —**u·ni·sex** (YOO·nuh–) *adj. Informal.* designed to suit both sexes: ~ *clothing; the ~ look* (not distinguishable as to sex); **u·ni·sex·u·al** (–SEK·shoo·ul) *adj.* of one sex; not bisexual; also, **unisex.** —**u·ni·son** (YOO·nuh·sun, –zun) *n.* agreement in pitch or sound: *Plainsong is sung in ~* (not harmony); *They spoke* **in unison** (i.e. the same words at the same time). —**u·nit** (YOO–) *n.* **1** an individual thing or group with specific characteristics, as part of a complex whole: *the family as a social ~; The dollar and pound are basic money ~s; metric ~s of weight; a military ~ such as the battalion or platoon; the pickup ~ of a record player; an easy-to-assemble wall ~ with shelves, cabinets, etc.* **2** the least whole number; one. —**U·ni·tar·i·an** (yoo·nuh·TAIR–) *n.* & *adj.* (a member) of a Christian church that rejects the doctrine of the Trinity and believes that God is a single person. —**u·ni·tar·y** (YOO·nuh·ter·ee) *adj.* characterized by centralization; unified, not divided: *Britain has a ~ system of government, not federal.* —**u·nite** (yoo·NITE) *v.* **-nites, -nit·ed, -nit·ing** join together; also, become one entity; combine as one whole: *We stand ~d; a ~d effort, front.* —**United Arab Emirates** a federation of seven states on the Persian Gulf; 32,000 sq.mi. (82,800 km²); *cap.* Abu Dhabi. —**United Kingdom** a country of W. Europe consisting of Great Britain and Northern Ireland; 94,226 sq.mi. (244,044 km²); *cap.* London. —**United Nations** a world organization of nations dedicated to peace and security, with over 150 members. —**United States (of America)** a country of North America comprising 50 states, including Alaska and Hawaii; 3,615,122 sq.mi. (9,363,123 km²); *cap.* Washington, D.C. —**u·nit·ize** (YOO–) *v.* **-iz·es, -ized, -iz·ing** making into one unit; also, divide into units. —**unit pricing** labeling of articles with their prices per pound, liter, or other standard unit to help shoppers compare prices. —**u·ni·ty** (YOO–) *n.* **-ties** **1** the oneness of purpose, spirit, etc. of a complex whole: *artistic ~ in variety: the ~ of dramatic action or plot; the ~ of design achieved by artistic arrangement of lines, shapes, and colors; to live together in ~* (i.e. harmony). **2** a quantity or magnitude considered as equal to 1 in calculations. —**Univ.** University. —**u·ni·valve** (YOO·nuh–) *n.* a snail, limpet, or other mollusk with a one-piece shell; also, such a shell. —**u·ni·ver·sal** (yoo·nuh·VUR·sl) *adj.* applying to every individual or case within a class or category: *Death is a ~ phenomenon; ~ adult suffrage, literacy, conscription, rejoicing; Type O blood is a ~ donor* (because safe for any recipient); *Esperanto as a ~ language; a* **universal motor** *for A.C. or D.C. current; The wristlike action of a* **universal joint** (or **coupling**) *lets an automobile ride over bumps without breaking the drive shaft;* **u·ni·**

---

unoccupied
unofficial
unopened
unorthodox
unpaid
unpalatable
unpardonable
unpaved
unperturbed
unpin
unplanned
unpleasing
unplowed
unpolished
unpolluted
unpracticed
unpredictable
unprejudiced
unpremeditated
unprepared
unpretentious
unprocessed
unprofitable
unpromising
unprotected
unproven
unprovoked
unpublished

ver·sal·ly *adv.;* **u·ni·ver·sal·i·ty** (–SAL–) *n.* **—u·ni·ver·sal·ize** (–VUR–) *v.* **-iz·es, -ized, -iz·ing** make universally applicable. **—universal product code** a small square of black bars and numbers representing price information imprinted on articles for scanning by automatic checkout systems. **—u·ni·verse** (YOO·uh–) *n.* all reality; the cosmos; everything in space, esp. the world of human beings. **—u·ni·ver·si·ty** (–VUR–) *n.* **-ties** an educational institution of the highest level for instruction in many branches of study.

un·just *adj.* not just or right; **un·just·ly** *adv.* **—un·kempt** (–KEMPT) *adj.* not combed; also, not well cared-for: *an ~ lawn, house.* **—un·kind** *adj.* not kind, esp. harsh or inconsiderate; **un·kind·ly** *adj.* & *adv.;* **un·kind·ness** *n.* **—un·known** *n.* & *adj.* (one) that is unfamiliar, strange, or unidentified: *dedicated to the ~ soldiers killed in the war; a letter representing an ~ quantity in an algebraic equation; Our new teammate is an* **unknown quantity** (i.e. one not yet tried out). **—un·law·ful** *adj.* not lawful; illegal; also, immoral; **un·law·ful·ly** *adv.;* **un·law·ful·ness** *n.* **—un·lead·ed** (–LED–) *adj.* of gasoline, containing no tetraethyl lead-additive. **—un·learn** *v.* get rid of or forget (something learned, as ideas or habits); **un·learn·ed** *adj.* **1** (–LUR·nid) lacking learning; ignorant: *an ~ scholar, remark.* **2** (–LURND) that has not been learned: *an ~ habit, lesson.* **—un·leash** *v.* free (as if) from a leash: *to ~ an animal, one's fury.*

un·less (–LES) *conj.* except when; if not; *no pay ~ you work.*

un·let·tered *adj.* not educated, esp. not able to read and write. **—un·like** *adj.* & *prep.* different (from): *The twins are quite ~ (each other);* **un·like·ly** *adj.* not likely: *an ~ event; searched in the most ~* (i.e. unpromising) *places;* **un·like·li·hood** *n.* **—un·lim·ber** (–LIM–) *v.* get ready for action, as by detaching a field gun from its vehicle. **—un·load** *v.* **1** take or remove a load from (one's back, a vehicle, etc.) or a charge from (a firearm). **2** get rid or dispose of (unwanted goods, company stocks, etc.); also, unburden (feelings, troubles, etc. on someone). **—un·lock** *v.* **1** to open (a door, etc.) by releasing a lock. **2** release or disclose as if by unlocking: *to ~ nature's mysteries, one's heart, a flood of tears.* **—un·looked-for** *adj.* not looked for or expected. **—un·loose** *v.* **-loos·es, -loosed, -loos·ing** set free; also, loosen; also **un·loos·en.** **—un·luck·y** *adj.* **-luck·i·er, -i·est** not lucky; unfortunate; ill-fated; **un·luck·i·ly** *adv.* **—un·make** *v.* **-makes, -made, -mak·ing** ruin or destroy (something made, as a reputation); also, depose from a position, rank, etc. **—un·man** *v.* **-mans, -manned, -man·ning** deprive of manly courage; weaken the spirit of; **un·man·ly** *adj.* **—un·mask** *v.* remove a mask *(from);* hence, disclose the true nature *(of).* **—un·mean·ing** (–MEE–) *adj.* without meaning; also, vacant or expressionless. **—un·men·tion·a·ble** *adj.* not fit to be referred to in public; **unmentionables** *n.pl.* [jocular] underwear. **—un·mit·i·gat·ed** *adj.* not lessened or modified: *~ horror; an ~ liar.* **—un·mor·al** *adj.* amoral; nonmoral. **—un·nat·u·ral** *adj.* not natural or normal; hence, artificial, depraved, etc.; **un·nat·u·ral·ly** *adv.* **—un·nec·es·sar·y** *adj.* needless; **un·nec·es·sar·i·ly** *adv.* **—un·nerve** *v.* **-nerves, -nerved, -nerv·ing** cause to lose one's self-control or power to act. **—un·num·bered** *adj.* innumerable; uncounted. **—un·or·gan·ized** *adj.* not organized into a system, organism, labor union, etc. **—un·pack** *v.* remove (something) from a package; also, remove the contents of (a trunk, suitcase, etc.). **—un·par·al·leled** *adj.* that has no parallel or match. **—un·pleas·ant** *adj.* not pleasant; disagreeable; **un·pleas·ant·ly** *adv.;* **un·pleas·ant·ness** *n.* **—un·plumbed** *adj.* of unknown depth; hence, not fully understood. **—un·pop·u·lar** *adj.* not generally liked; **un·pop·u·lar·i·ty** (–LAIR–) *n.* **—un·prec·e·dent·ed** (–PRES·uh–) *adj.* without precedent; unheard-of. **—un·prin·ci·pled** (–PRIN–) *adj.* lacking moral principles. **—un·print·a·ble** *adj.* not fit to be printed, esp. because obscene. **—un·pro·fes·sion·al** *adj.* not ethical. **—un·qual·i·fied** *adj.* not qualified; also, absolute or not restricted. **—un·ques·tion·a·ble** *adj.* not to be questioned or doubted; also, beyond doubt; **un·ques·tion·a·bly** *adv.* **—un·quote**

---

unpunished
unquestioned
unquiet
unrealistic
unrecorded
unrelated
unreliable
unrelieved
unrepentant
unrequited
unrestricted
unrighteous
unripe
unsafe
unsaid
unsalable
unsanitary
unsatisfactory
unsatisfied
unsaturated
unscheduled
unscientific
unseasoned
unseeing
unseen
unselfish
unserviceable
unshackle

[used to end a quotation]: *She said, quote, He is a saint, unquote.* —**un•rav•el** *v.* **-els, -el(l)ed, -el•(l)ing** separate the threads of (something woven); also, solve (a mystery). —**un•read** (–RED) *adj.* not read, as a book; also, uneducated. —**un•re•al** *adj.* not real; imaginary or fanciful. —**un•rea•son•a•ble** *adj.* not reasonable; also, excessive or immoderate; **un•rea•son•a•bly** *adv.;* **un•rea•son•ing** *adj.* not reasoning or guided by reason; irrational. —**un•re•con•struct•ed** *adj.* holding to outmoded practices, attitudes, etc.; not reconciled to changed conditions. —**un•re•gen•er•ate** (–it) *adj.* not born again spiritually; hence, obstinate or unrepentant. —**un•re•lent•ing** *adj.* not softening (in harshness, cruelty, etc.); not showing pity or kindness. —**un•re•mit•ting** *adj.* not ceasing or slackening; incessant; **un•re•mit•ting•ly** *adv.* —**un•re•served** *adj.* not reserved in speech; also, not limited or restricted; **un•re•serv•ed•ly** (–vid·lee) *adv.* —**un•rest** *n.* state of restlessness; also, a social condition verging or revolt: *social ~; labor ~; ~ on campus.* —**un•ri•val(l)ed** *adj.* having no rival or equal. —**un•roll** *v.* **1** open (something rolled up); also, become unrolled. **2** display or be displayed: *a scene ~ing before our eyes.*

UNRRA (UN·ruh) U.N. Relief and Rehabilitation Agency.

un•ruf•fled *adj.* not ruffled; hence, calm and serene. —**un•rul•y** *adj.* **-rul•i•er, -i•est** disorderly or disobedient: *an ~ crowd, child;* **un•rul•i•ness** *n.*

UNRWA U.N. Relief and Works Agency.

un•sad•dle *v.* **-sad•dles, -sad•dled, -sad•dling** take the saddle off (a horse, etc.) —**un•sa•vor•y** *adj.* unpleasant to the taste or smell; also, morally unpleasant. —**un•scathed** (–SCAY–) *adj.* uninjured. —**un•schooled** *adj.* not educated or trained; hence, not disciplined. —**un•scram•ble** *v.* **-bles, -bled, -bling** restore to original condition from being scrambled or confused: *to ~* (i.e. decode) *a message.* —**un•screw** *v.* detach or take off by turning or by removing screws: *to ~ a light bulb, fixture, jar* (i.e. its top). —**un•scru•pu•lous** *adj.* defying moral principles. —**un•seal** *v.* remove the seal of; hence, open. —**un•sea•son•a•ble** *adj.* not usual for the season; hence, coming at the wrong time: *~ cold weather; arrived at an ~ hour;* **un•sea•son•a•bly** *adv.* —**un•seat** *v.* displace from a seat; hence, remove from office. —**un•seem•ly** *adj.* not seemly or becoming. —**un•set•tle** *v.* **-set•tles, -set•tled, -set•tling** move from a settled position; also, make or become unstable or disturbed: *an ~ing bit of news;* **un•set•tled** *adj.: ~ weather conditions, issues, debts* (i.e. not paid), *territory* (i.e. uninhabited). —**un•sheathe** *v.* **-sheathes, -sheathed, -sheath•ing** draw (a sword, etc.) from a sheath or as from a sheath. —**un•sight•ly** *adj.* not pleasing to the eye; ugly. —**un•skilled** *adj.* **1** of persons, not skilled or trained in a line of work. **2** of work, not requiring skill. —**un•skill•ful** *adj.* having no skill or training; also, awkward or clumsy. —**un-snap** *v.* **-snaps, -snapped, -snap•ping** unfasten the snaps of. —**un•snarl** *v.* untangle. —**un•so•phis•ti•cat•ed** *adj.* lacking worldly wisdom or experience. —**un•sound** *adj.* not sound: *an ~ argument, structure, undertaking; of ~ mind.* —**un•spar•ing** *adj.* not sparing; liberal; also, merciless or severe (in criticism, of praise, etc.). —**un•speak•a•ble** *adj.* that cannot be expressed or described: *her ~ joy, beauty; ~ horrors.* **un•speak•a•bly** *adv.* —**un•sta•ble** *adj.* not stable: *an ~ government, person, mind, equilibrium, chemical compound, nuclear particle.* —**un•stead•y** *adj.* not steady or firm: *an ~ hand, pulse, voice; ~ market conditions, winds.* —**un•stop** *v.* **-stops, -stopped, -stop•ping** remove the stopper from (a bottle, etc.); free (a pipe, etc.) of an obstruction. —**un•strung** *adj.* in a nervous condition; also, with the strings (of a guitar, racket, etc.) loosened or removed. —**un•stuck** *adj.* loosened or unfastened: *stamps that come ~ before the letter is mailed.* —**un•stud•ied** *adj.* of behavior, not artificial; natural and spontaneous. —**un•sub•stan•tial** *adj.* not having substance; flimsy; visionary. —**un•sung** *adj.* not celebrated or praised: *an ~ hero.* —**un•tan•gle** *v.* **-gles, -gled, -gling** free from a snarled or entangled condition; disentangle: *to ~ a mess, knots, mix-ups.* —**un•taught** *adj.* not educated; also, naturally acquired or learned. —**un•think•a•ble** *adj.* that cannot be thought of as possible; un-

---

unshakable
unshaven
unshod
unshorn
unsifted
unsightly
unsinkable
unsociable
unsoiled
unsold
unsolicited
unsought
unspoiled
unstinting
unstructured
unsubstantiated
unsuccessful
unsuitable
unsullied
unsupported
unsurpassed
unsuspected
unsweetened
unswerving
unsympathetic
unsystematic
untainted
untamed

imaginable; inconceivable; **un·think·ing** *adj.* thoughtless or heedless: *in one of those ~ moments; an ~ remark.* —**un·tie** *v.* **-ties, -tied, -ty·ing** or **-tie·ing** to free (something tied, knotted, etc.) or as from a restraint; unfasten; disentangle.

un·til *prep.* & *conj.* up to the time of or when; till: *Please wait ~ noon; Don't go ~ you've eaten.*

un·time·ly *adj.* & *adv.* premature(ly); inopportune(ly); **un·time·li·ness** *n.*

un·to (UN·too) *prep. Archaic.* to or till: *what you do ~ others; was faithful ~ death.*

un·told *adj.* **1** uncounted; innumerable; also, vast or immense: *~ wealth, misery; ~ thousands of people.* **2** not told or revealed: *an ~ tale of intrigue.* —**un·touch·a·ble** *adj.* that cannot or must not be touched; ***n.*** a member of the lowest caste of Hindus, formerly shunned by Brahmins; an "outcaste." —**un·to·ward** (–TOH·urd, –TORD) *adj.* unfavorable: *~ circumstances; an ~* (i.e. willful) *child; an ~* (i.e. improper or unseemly) *remark.* —**un·truth** *n.* falsity; also, a falsehood; **un·truth·ful** *adj.* —**un·tu·tored** *adj.* untaught; uneducated. —**un·twist** *v.* unravel or loosen (something twisted); also, become untwisted, —**un·used** *adj.* not used; also, unaccustomed (*to* something). —**un·u·su·al** *adj.* not usual; rare; **un·u·su·al·ly** *adv.* —**un·ut·ter·a·ble** *adj.* inexpressible. —**un·var·nished** *adj.* not varnished; hence, plain and simple: *an ~ account; the ~ truth.* —**un·veil** *v.* **1** reveal or display for the first time: *~d his plan; to ~ a statue.* **2** remove one's veil. —**un·voiced** *adj.* not expressed in words; unspoken. —**un·well** *adj.* **1** sick or ill. **2** menstruating. —**un·whole·some** *adj.* **1** harmful to body, mind, or morals. **2** not of sound health. —**un·wield·y** *adj.* hard to handle or deal with because of large size, weight, shape, etc. —**un·will·ing** *adj.* not willing; reluctant: *was ~ to go; an ~ partner in the crime;* **un·will·ing·ly** *adv.;* **un·will·ing·ness** *n.* —**un·wind** (–WINED) *v.* **-winds, -wound, -wind·ing** **1** uncoil (something wound up, as a ball or spool). **2** untangle. **3** relax. —**un·wise** *adj.* not wise; imprudent. —**un·wit·ting** *adj.* unaware; also, inadvertent or unintentional; **un·wit·ting·ly** *adv.* —**un·wont·ed** (–WUN–, –WONE–, –WAUN–) *adj.* not usual or habitual: *left in ~ haste.* —**un·wor·thy** *adj.* **-thi·er, -thi·est** not worthy: *~* (i.e. shameful) *conduct; conduct ~ of* (i.e. unbecoming) *a hero; was deemed ~* (i.e. undeserving) *of an award;* **un·wor·thi·ness** *n.* —**un·wrap** *v.* **-wraps, -wrapped, -wrap·ping** take off the wrapping of. —**un·writ·ten** *adj.* not written down; hence, customary or traditional: *Britain's ~ constitution; the ~ common law.*

up *adv.* **1** to a higher position, degree, etc.; not down: *went ~ to the top floor; Prices go ~; Please speak ~* (i.e. louder); **up to** till (a limit of time or extension); about or planning to do (something); at the disposition of (someone): *What are you ~ to? What happens now is ~ to you.* **2** to a vertical or active position: *get ~ in the morning; stand ~ on your feet; He stirs ~ trouble;* **up against** *Informal.* faced with (a problem or difficulty). **3** to the point of completeness or finality: *to keep ~ a practice; to tie ~ a package; ate it all ~.* **4** in games, ahead or leading; also, at bat in baseball: *a score of 10 ~* (i.e. apiece). —***prep.:*** *to go ~ the stairs; rowed her boat ~ the river; drove ~* (i.e. along) *the street.* —***adj.:*** *Prices are ~ again; the ~ elevator; What's ~* (i.e. happening)? *She's* **up and around** (or **about**) *after her recent illness;* **up and doing** busy or active. —***n.*** an upward movement or condition; also, one that is up: *the* **ups and downs** *of fortune, mood.* —***v.*** **ups, upped, up·ping** raise: *to ~ prices;* **up and** *Informal.* abruptly or unexpectedly: *She ~s and walks out of the party.* —**up-and-com·ing** *adj.* likely to succeed; promising.

U·pan·i·shad (oo·PAN–) any of a group of philosophical treatises forming the latest part of the Vedas.

up·beat (–beet) *n.* in music, an unaccented beat or the upward gesture of the conductor's hand indicating it; hence, an upswing or upturn; ***adj.*** cheerful or optimistic. —**up·braid** (–BRAID) *v.* to reprimand or censure, usu. with justification. —**up·bring·ing** *n.* the bringing up or raising of a child.

UPC universal product code.

up·chuck *n.* & *v. Slang.* vomit. —**up·com·ing** *adj.* forthcoming; coming soon. —**up·coun·try** *n., adj.* & *adv.* (of, in, or toward) the interior, esp. isolated part of a country or region. —**up·date** (–DATE) *v.* **-dates, -dat·ed, -dat·**

---

untarnished
untasted
untenable
untested
unthankful
untidy
untiring
untitled
untouched
untraceable
untrained
untravel(l)ed
untried
untrimmed
untroubled
untrue
unverified
unvisited
unwanted
unwarranted
unwary
unwashed
unwavering
unwed
unworkable
unworldly
unyielding
unzip

ing make up-to-date; ***n.*** (UP–) an updating or something that updates, as a piece of information. —**up·draft** *n.* an upward draft of air or other gas. —**up·end** (–END) *v.* set or stand on end; overturn. —**up·front** *adj. Informal.* **1** forthright or direct. **2** as advance payment or front money. —**up·grade** *n.* an upward slope; also, a rise or increase; ***adj.*** & ***adv.*** upward; uphill; ***v.*** **-grades, -grad·ed, -grad·ing** raise to a higher grade or rating, as a job, employee, etc. —**up·growth** *n.* upward growth or development. —**up·heav·al** (–HEE·vul) *n.* a heaving up, as of the earth's crust by an earthquake; hence, a sudden or violent change: *social* ~. —**up·hill** *adj.* going up, as on a hill; hence, tiring or laborious: *an ~ task, fight;* ***adv.:*** *to drive* ~. —**up·hold** (–HOLED) *v.* **-holds, -held, -hold·ing** **1** give moral support to (a person, cause, etc.); also, maintain: *to ~ a great tradition, principle.* **2** confirm by higher authority: *a judgment upheld on appeal.* —**up·hol·ster** (–HOLE–) *v.* furnish (a chair, seat, etc.) with upholstery; **up·hol·ster·er** *n.;* **up·hol·ster·y** *n.* **-ster·ies** materials such as fabrics, springs, and padding used to make soft coverings for furniture; also, the upholsterer's craft.

U.P.I. United Press International.

up·keep *n.* the keeping up or maintaining (of a house, garden, dependents, etc.); also, its cost or the state of maintenance. —**up·land** *n.* & *adj.* (of) the higher land of a region, above valleys or plains: *~ meadows; Finland's ~ district.* —**up·lift** *n.* a lifting up, esp. a movement for social, moral, or spiritual improvement. —**up·man·ship** *n.* same as ONE-UPMANSHIP. —**up·most** *adj.* same as UPPERMOST. —**up·on** (uh·PON) *prep.* & *adv.* on: *once ~ a time.* —**up·per** *adj.* higher in position, rank, etc.: *the ~ jaw; the ~ house of a bicameral legislature; the ~ crust of society; a river's ~ reaches; Upper Egypt* (i.e. Nile valley S. of 30° N.); *Michigan's Upper* (i.e. northern) *Peninsula; the Upper* (i.e. later) *Cambrian Period;* ***n.*** **1** the part of a shoe or boot above the sole. **2** *Slang.* a stimulant drug such as caffeine, cocaine, or an amphetamine. —**upper case** capital letters; **up·per-case** *adj.* & *v.* **-cas·es, -cased, -cas·ing** (set up) in capital letters. —**upper class** the class of society above the middle class; **up·per-class** *adj.;* **up·per·class·man** (–mun) *n.* **-men** a junior or senior in a high school or college. —**upper crust** the highest social class. —**up·per·cut** *n.* in boxing, a short, swinging blow directed upward from the waist level. —**upper hand** a position of advantage; mastery. —**up·per·most** *adj.* & *adv.* first or highest in place, authority, etc. —**Upper Vol·ta** (–VOL·tuh) a W. African country; 105,869 sq.mi. (274,200 km²); *cap.* Ouagadougou. —**up·pish** or **up·pi·ty** *adj. Informal.* haughty or arrogant. —**up·raise** (–RAIZ) *v.* **-rais·es, -raised, -rais·ing** lift up; elevated. —**up·rear** (–REER) *v.* lift up or raise; also, rise or be lifted up. —**up·right** *adj.* **1** vertically erect. **2** morally straight: *a just and ~ man.* —***n.*** something that is upright; also, an upright or vertical position. —***adv.*** in an upright position; also **up·right·ly.** —**up·right·ness** *n.* —**upright piano** the commonest type of piano, with strings set up vertically. —**up·ris·ing** *n.* a small rebellion or outbreak against a government. —**up·riv·er** *adj.* & *adv.* toward the source of a river. —**up·roar** *n.* a noisy disturbance or commotion; **up·roar·i·ous** (–ROR–) *adj.* noisy or boisterous: *~ welcome, laughter; an ~* (i.e. extremely funny) *joke;* **up·roar·i·ous·ly** *adv.* —**up·root** (–ROOT) *v.* remove by or as if by pulling up by the roots: *people ~ed from their ancestral homes.* —**up·rush** *n.* an upward rush (of a liquid or gas).

UPS United Parcel Service.

up·set (–SET) *v.* **-sets, -set, -set·ting** topple or unsettle from a stable condition: *A flat-bottomed boat does not ~ easily; to ~ a vase, schedule, favored candidate* (in an election); *to ~ plans, nerves; emotionally ~.* —***n.*** (UP–) an upsetting, an unexpected defeat, or a disturbance: *a stomach ~;* ***adj.*** tipped over; defeated; disturbed or disordered. —**up·shift** *v.* shift (an automobile) to a higher gear. —**up·shot** *n.* outcome or general effect: *the ~ of the matter.* —**up·side** *n.* the upper side; **upside down** inverted; in(to) confusion or disorder; **up·side-down** *adj.*

up·si·lon (YOOP·suh–) *n.* the 20th letter of the Greek alphabet (Υ,υ).

up·stage *adj.* & *adv.* at or toward the rear of a stage; ***v.*** draw attention to oneself to the disadvantage of (someone else); *Informal.* steal the show from; snub. —**up·stairs** *n.* an upper floor; ***adj. & adv.:*** *She is ~; went ~; an ~ window.* —**up·stand·ing** *adj.* upright in carriage or character. —**up·start** *n.* & *adj.* (of or like) one who has recently acquired wealth or position, hence is haughty or self-assertive. —**up·state** *n., adj.* & *adv.* (in, to, or from) the more N. part of a state, away from its principal city: *the Upstate Medical Center in Syracuse, N.Y.* —**up·stream** *adj.* & *adv.* against the current of a stream. —**up·stroke** *n.* an upward stroke of a pen, brush, etc. —**up·surge** *n.* a sudden surging up or increase. —**up·swing** *n.* an upward swinging movement, as of a golf club; hence, an upward trend. —**up·take** *n.* a taking up by the mind; absorption: (*slow* or) *quick* **on the uptake** (i.e. in understanding). —**up·tight** (–TITE) *adj. Slang.* tense or nervous (*about* something); **up·tight·ness** *n.* —**up-to-date** *adj.* extending to the present time: *a new and ~ edition; an ~* (i.e. modern) *fashion, style;* **up-to-date·ness** *n.* —**up·town** *n., adj.* & *adv.* (in, of, or toward) the upper part of a city or town, away from downtown. —**up·turn** *n.* an upward turn or improving trend, as after a recession; ***v.*** turn up or over; overturn; **up·turned** *adj.*

—**up·ward** (–wurd) *adj.* & *adv.* in or toward a higher place, position, etc.; up or above: *move* ~; *the* **upward mobility** *of the middle class; 18 years and* ~; *aged* **upward of** (i.e. more than) *17;* also **up·wards** *adv.;* **up·ward·ly** *adv.* —**up·wind** *adj.* & *adv.* into or against the wind; to windward.

u·ra·cil (YOOR·uh–) *n.* the RNA base replacing the thymine of DNA in protein synthesis.

U·rals (YOOR·ulz) the mountain range in the U.S.S.R. separating Asia and Europe; also **Ural Mountains.**

u·ra·ni·um (yoo·RAY·nee–) *n.* a heavy, radioactive metallic chemical element that is the chief source of atomic energy; **u·ran·ic** (–RAN–) *adj.;* **u·ra·nous** (–RAY·nus) *adj.* —**U·ra·nus** (YOOR·uh–) the seventh planet from the sun.

urb *n.* an urban area, not a suburb. —**ur·ban** (UR·bun) *adj.* of or having to do with a city or cities: *the demolition of slums for* **urban renewal** *and rebuilding.* —**ur·bane** (–BANE) *adj.* refined or smoothly polite in manner; **ur·ban·i·ty** (–BAN–) *n.* —**ur·ban·ize** (UR·buh–) *v.* **-iz·es, -ized, -iz·ing** make or become urban or citylike; **ur·ban·i·za·tion** (–ZAY–) *n.* —**ur·ban·ol·o·gy** (–OL–) *n.* the study of cities and their problems; **ur·ban·ol·o·gist** *n.* —**urban sprawl** city congestion spreading into the countryside.

ur·chin *n.* a youngster considered as pert or mischievous.

Ur·du (–doo) *n.* the Indo-European official language of Pakistan, widely used also in N. India.

-ure *n. suffix.* state or result: as in *failure, seizure, judicature.*

u·re·a (yoo·REE·uh) *n.* an organic nitrogen compound that is the chief constituent of urine; **u·re·mi·a** (–REE·mee·uh) *n.* poisoning of the blood by body wastes because of defective functioning of the kidneys. —**u·re·ter** (–REE–) *n.* tube carrying urine from a kidney into the bladder; **u·re·thra** (–thruh) *n.,pl.* **-thrae** (–three) or **-thras** the canal through which urine is expelled from the bladder, used also for discharge of semen in males; **u·re·thri·tis** (–THRYE–) *n.* inflammation of the urethra.

urge *v.* **urg·es, -urged, -urg·ing** **1** force or drive forward; spur: *He* ~*d his horses forward with the whip.* **2** ask, plead, or argue earnestly (for): *was strongly* ~*d to buy now and pay later; a lawyer* ~*ing a claim in court; sterner measures were* ~*d; did it at the* ~*ing of friends.* —***n.*** an urging; also, an impulse or inner drive. —**ur·gent** (UR·junt) *adj.* requiring immediate attention: *an* ~ *message, request; in* ~ *need of help; an* ~ (i.e. insistent) *petitioner;* **ur·gen·cy** *n.;* **ur·gent·ly** *adv.*

u·ric (YOOR–) *adj.* of or having to do with urine; **uric acid** an acid found in blood and urine. —**u·ri·nal** (YOOR·uh·nl) *n.* a place for urinating; also, a plumbing fixture, or **urine receptacle.** —**u·ri·nal·y·sis** (–NAL–) *n.* examination of the urine by microscope or chemical tests. —**u·ri·nar·y** (YOOR·uh–) *adj.* of or having to do with urine or its secretion or discharge: *the* ~ *bladder, system, tract.* —**u·ri·nate** *v.* **-nates, -nat·ed, -nat·ing** discharge urine from the body; **u·ri·na·tion** (–NAY–) *n.* —**u·rine** (YOOR·in) *n.* the yellowish liquid containing waste products that is produced by the kidneys, collected in the **urinary bladder** and expelled through the urethra.

urn *n.* a footed vase or one with a pedestal, used to hold the ashes of the dead in ancient Rome; also, a closed vessel with a spigot for making tea or coffee.

u·ro·gen·i·tal (yoor·oh·JEN–) *adj.* of the urinary and genital organs. —**u·rol·o·gy** (–ROL–) *n.* the branch of medicine concerned with the urinary system and male genitals; **u·rol·o·gist** *n.*

Ur·sa (UR·suh) **Ma·jor** the most prominent of the N. constellations; also called "Great Bear." —**Ursa Minor** a N. constellation; also called "Little Bear." —**ur·sine** (UR–) *adj.* of or like a bear.

ur·ti·car·i·a (ur·tuh·CAIR–) *n.* same as HIVES.

U·ru·guay (YOOR·uh·gway, –gwye) a country of S.E. South America; 68,536 sq.mi. (177,508 km²); *cap.* Montevideo.

us objective case of WE. —**U.S.** United States; **U.S.A.** United States of America; United States Army.

us(e)·a·ble (YOO·zuh·bl) *adj.* fit for use; **us(e)·a·bil·i·ty** (–BIL–) *n.*

U.S.A.F. United States Air Force.

us·age (YOO·sij, –zij) *n.* **1** act or manner of using; treatment: *submitted to ill* ~*; damaged by rough* ~. **2** long-established practice: *Standard English* ~ *as established by good writers; customs sanctified by* ~.

U.S.C.G. United States Coast Guard. —**U.S.D.A.** United States Department of Agriculture.

use (YOOZ) *v.* **us·es, used, us·ing** put into action or service; employ for a purpose: *When it rains* ~ *an umbrella; She* ~*s* (i.e. consumes) *too much sugar; The sugar is (all)* **used up;** *an ill-*~*d* (i.e. treated) *child; She is* **used to** (i.e. accustomed to) *walking to work;* ~*d to live* (i.e. formerly lived) *in the country.* —***n.*** (YOOSE) **1** a using or being used: *the* ~*s of an automobile; No smoking when oxygen is* **in use;** *Obsolete words are* **out of use.** **2** purpose, benefit, or advantage of using; usefulness: *makes good* ~ *of his time; no* ~ *crying over spilled milk; She* **has no use for** (i.e. dislikes) *latecomers.* **3** ability to use: *lost the* ~ *of both eyes in an accident; gets the* ~ *of* (i.e. permission to use) *her car on weekends.* **4** customary practice; habit. —**us·er** *n.* —**used** (YOOZD) *adj.* not new; second-hand: *a* ~ *car.* —**use·ful** *adj.* serviceable; helpful; **use·ful·ly** *adv.;* **use·ful·ness** *n.* —**use·less** (YOOS·lis) *adj.;* **use·less·ly** *adv.;* **use·less·ness** *n.*

USES United States Employment Service.
ush·er *n.* an official who escorts people to their seats in a church, theater, etc. **—*v.*** go before (someone) showing the way; conduct or escort: *to ~ a patron to his seat; celebrations to* **usher in** *the New Year.* **—ush·er·ette** (–RET) *n.* a female usher.
U.S.I.A. United States Information Agency. **—U.S.M.** United States Mail. **—U.S.M.C.** United States Marine Corps. **—U.S.N.** United States Navy. **—U.S.O.** United Service Organizations. **—U.S.P.** United States Pharmacopoeia. **—U.S.S.** United States Ship.
U.S.S.R. Union of Soviet Socialist Republics.
usu. usual(ly). **—u·su·al** (YOO·zhoo·ul) *adj.* commonly seen or experienced; ordinary; customary: *the ~ office hours; his ~ cheerful self; appeared cheerful* **as usual** (i.e. in the usual manner); **u·su·al·ly** *adv.* **—u·su·fruct** (YOO·zyuh–) *n.* legal right to use and enjoy another's property without damaging or altering it. **—u·su·rer** (YOO·zhuh·rur) *n.* one who practices usury; **u·su·ri·ous** (–ZHOOR–) *adj.* **—u·surp** (yoo·SURP, –ZURP) *v.* seize and hold (a throne, power, authority, etc.) by force or without right; **u·surp·er** *n.;* **u·sur·pa·tion** (–PAY–) *n.* **—u·su·ry** (YOO·zhuh·ree) *n.* (the lending of money at) an excessive rate of interest.
UT or **Ut.** *Abbrev.* for **U·tah** (YOO·taw, –tah) a W. state of the U.S.; 84,916 sq.mi. (219,931 km²); *cap.* Salt Lake City. **—Ute** (YOOT) *n.* (a member of) an Amerindian people now living in Utah and Colorado; also, their language.
u·ten·sil (yoo·TEN–) *n.* an implement or container for domestic use, usu. worked by hand: *pots, pans, and such kitchen ~s; writing ~s.*
u·ter·us (YOO·tuh–) *n., pl.* **-ter·i** (–tuh·rye) the hollow, muscular organ in the pelvis of female mammals in which the young are carried till birth; womb; **u·ter·ine** *adj.*
u·tile (YOO·tl) *dj.* having utility. **—u·til·i·tar·i·an** (yoo·til·uh·TAIR–) *adj.* of or having to do with usefulness rather than beauty, truth, etc.; ***n.*** one who believes in utilitarianism; **u·til·i·tar·i·an·ism** *n.* a philosophy that stresses the greatest happiness of the greatest number as the criterion of the rightness of actions. **—u·til·i·ty** (–TIL–) *n.* **-ties** **1** a service that is essential to the public, as transportation, communications, electricity, water, gas, garbage disposal, etc.; also, a company, or **public utility,** that provides such a service; **utilities** *pl.* company shares issued by a public utility. **2** usefulness; ***adj.*** having various uses; *a ~ table, knife, airport* (for small nonjet aircraft); **utility beef** (of the lowest grade); **utility player** (who can substitute for absent players in several positions); **utility room** (used for laundry, heating and maintenance equipment, etc.). **—u·ti·lize** *v.* **-liz·es, -lized, -liz·ing** put to practical or profitable use: *how to ~ spare time, solar energy; Garbage can be ~d by recycling;* **u·ti·li·za·tion** (–ZAY–) *n.*
ut·most *n.* & *adj.* farthest or greatest that is possible: *a question of the ~ importance; the ~ limit of endurance; the ~ we could do.*
U·to·pi·a or **u·to·pi·a** (yoo·TOH·pee·uh) *n.* an imaginary place of ideal social conditions, as in Thomas More's *Utopia;* hence, a perfect society or any visionary scheme; **U·to·pi·an** or **u·to·pi·an** *adj.*
ut·ter *adj.* total; absolute: *~ destruction, surprise, misery;* **ut·ter·ly** *adv.* **—*v.*** **1** give forth (a vocal sound, cry, sigh, spell, oath, etc.) audibly; hence, speak out or express (thoughts, sentiments, the truth, etc.). **2** deliver or put (counterfeit money, forged notes, etc.) into circulation. **—ut·ter·ance** *n.* an act of uttering vocally, or what is uttered; also, a manner or style of speaking. **—ut·ter·most** *n.* & *adj.* same as UTMOST.
U-turn *n.* a 360-turn made by a vehicle.
u·vu·la (YOO·vyuh·luh) *n.* **-las** or **-lae** (–lee) a small fleshy part hanging down from the soft palate; **u·vu·lar** *n.* & *adj.* (a speech sound) produced with the uvula.
ux·o·ri·ous (uk·SOR·ee·us, ug·ZOR–) *adj.* excessively fond of or submissive to one's wife.

V

V or **v** (VEE) *n.* **V's** or **v's** **1** the 22nd letter of the English alphabet. **2** something shaped like a "V." **3** the Roman numeral for 5. **—V** vanadium. **—V.** or **v.** velocity; verb(al); versus; volt(s); voltage; volume. **—v** volt(s).

V.A. Veterans Administration; Vicar Apostolic; Vice Admiral. **—VA** or **Va.** Virginia.

va·can·cy (VAY·cun–) *n.* **-cies** a being vacant or unoccupied; also, vacant space or an unoccupied position, quarters, apartment for rent, etc.: *Sorry, no ~s; time spent daydreaming and staring into ~* (i.e. empty space). **—va·cant** (VAY·kunt) *adj.* not occupied or filled: *a ~ lot; a want ad headed "Situations ~"; a ~* (i.e. blank) *stare, mind; too much ~* (i.e. free or idle) *time on her hands since retirement;* **va·cant·ly** *adv.* **—va·cate** (vay·CATE) *v.* **-cates, -cat·ed, -cat·ing** **1** make vacant: *ordered to ~ the premises.* **2** cancel or make void: *had his conviction ~d under a new law.* **—va·ca·tion** (–CAY–) *n.* & *v.* (take) a period of rest from work, study, etc.; **va·ca·tion·er** or **va·ca·tion·ist** *n.;* **va·ca·tion·land** *n.* an area providing recreational facilities, tourist attractions, etc.

vac·ci·nate (VAC·suh–) *v.* **-nates, -nat·ed, -nat·ing** inoculate with or administer a vaccine to (someone *against* smallpox, etc.); **vac·ci·na·tion** (–NAY–) *n.* **—vac·cine** (vac·SEEN, VAC–) *n.* a preparation of bacteria or viruses of a particular disease injected into the body to build up resistance or immunity to the disease, originally a preparation of the cowpox virus given to prevent smallpox; **vac·ci·nee** (vac·suh·NEE) *n.* one who has been vaccinated; **vac·cin·i·a** (–SIN–) *n.* cowpox.

vac·il·late (VAS·uh–) *v.* **-il·lates, -il·lat·ed, -il·lat·ing** shift back and forth or waver (in an opinion, resolution, feelings, etc.) in an indecisive manner; **vac·il·la·tion** (–LAY–) *n.*

va·cu·i·ty (–CUE–) *n.* **-ties** emptiness, esp. of mind; also, a senseless or inane remark, action, etc. **—vac·u·ole** (VAC·yoo–) *n.* a fluid-containing cavity in a plant cell. **—vac·u·ous** (–yoo·us) *adj.* senseless or inane; also, idle; **vac·u·ous·ly** *adv.;* **vac·u·ous·ness** *n.* **—vac·u·um** (VAC·yoo–, –yoom) *n.* **vac·u·ums** or **vac·u·a** (–yoo·uh) an empty space or void without even air in it, usu. an enclosed space from which all air has been removed; ***v.*** clean with a vacuum cleaner; ***adj.*** of or producing a vacuum; **vacuum bottle** (or **flask** or **jug**) a double-walled bottle with an insulating vacuum between the walls, which are also heat-reflecting, for keeping liquids hot or cold for up to 24 hours; **vacuum cleaner** a machine that cleans floors, carpets, etc. by suction; **vac·u·um-packed** *adj.* packed airtight or in an airtight container; **vacuum tube** an electron tube.

va·de me·cum (VAY·dee·MEE–) a handbook or manual for constant use.

Va·duz (VAH·doots) capital of Liechtenstein.

vag·a·bond (VAG·uh–) *n.* a drifter, esp. one who leads a carefree, roaming life; ***adj.:*** *the ~ life of gypsies; a ~ poet;* **vag·a·bond·age** (–ij) *n.* **—va·gar·y** (vuh·GAIR·ee, VAY·guh·ree) *n.* **-gar·ies** an erratic or unpredictable departure or change from the usual or normal: *the ~s of weather, fashion, the market, politics.*

va·gi·na (vuh·JYE·nuh) *n.* **-nas** or **-nae** (–nee) the canal leading from the vulva to the uterus in female mammals, functioning also as part of the birth canal; **vag·i·nal** (VAJ·uh·nl) *adj.;* **vag·i·ni·tis** (vaj·uh·NYE–) *n.* inflammation of the vagina.

va·grant (VAY·grunt) *n.* a beggar or similar person who wanders from place to place without a regular occupation, esp. one likely to become a public menace; ***adj.:*** *a ~ life; ~* (i.e. wandering) *thoughts, melodies;* **va·gran·cy** *n.* **-cies.**

vague (VAIG) *adj.* **va·guer, va·guest** not clear or distinct: *a ~ rumor, answer, idea; was ~ and uncertain about his intentions; the ~ outlines of a flying object; a ~ feeling of something wrong;* **vague·ly** *adv.;* **vague·ness** *n.*

vain *adj.* **1** having or showing too high a regard for one's self; conceited: *She's ~ about her good looks.* **2** lacking in value; worthless or empty: *a ~ boast; ~ pomp, pursuits.* **3** unavailing; useless: *a ~ attempt, endeavor; All her efforts were* **in vain** (i.e. without result). **—vain·ly** *adv.;* **vain·ness** *n.* **—vain·glo·ry** *n.* too high an esteem of oneself as shown by boasting or showing off; **vain·glo·ri·ous** *adj.;* **vain·glo·ri·ous·ness** *n.*

val valuation; value(d).

val·ance (VAL·unce, VAY–) *n.* a short curtain or curtainlike decorative strip of wood, hung from the top of a window, the canopy of a bed, or from an edge, as of a shelf.

vale *n. Poetic.* valley.

val·e·dic·tion (val·uh·DIC–) *n.* a bidding farewell; also, a farewell utterance. **—val·e·dic·to·ri·an** (–TOR–) *n.* a student, usu. the highest ranked, who delivers the valedictory at graduation; **val·e·dic·to·ry** (–DIC–) *adj.* & *n.* **-ries** (a speech) bidding farewell.

va·lence (VAY·lunce) *n.* the capacity of an element to combine with other elements: *Oxygen has a ~ of 2 and hydrogen 1, as in* H_2O *(water);* also **va·len·cy.**

Va·len·ci·a (vuh·LEN·shuh) a seaport of E. Spain.

Va·len·ci·ennes (vuh·len·see·ENZ) *n.* a fine lace in which the design is woven together with the background to give an even texture.

val·en·tine (VAL·un–) *n.* a sweetheart chosen on Saint Valentine's Day, February 14, and greeted with a card; also, the card.

val·et (VAL·it, –ay) *n.* a male servant performing personal services for a man, as a hotel employee who cleans and presses clothes; ***v.*** serve as a valet.

Val·let·ta (vuh·LET·uh) capital of Malta.

val·e·tu·di·nar·i·an (–tue·duh·NAIR–) *n.* & *adj.* (a person) of weak health, or unduly worried about his state of health; **val·e·tu·di·nar·i·an·ism** *n.*

Val·hal·la (–HAL·uh) in Norse myth, Odin's great hall in which slain warriors are received.

val·i·ant (VAL·yunt) *n.* & *adj.* brave or courageous (person): *a ~ hero, deed,* **val·i·ant·ly** *adv.* **—val·id** *adj.* having the force of law, reason, or evidence: *a ~ objection, contract, ticket;* **val·id·ly** *adv.;* **val·id·ness** *n.* **—val·i·date** *v.* **-dates, -dat·ed, -dat·ing** make or show to be valid, as a claim; **val·i·da·tion** (–DAY–) *n.;* **va·lid·i·ty** (–LID–) *n.*

va·lise (vuh·LEECE) *n.* a bag in which to carry clothes, etc. when traveling.

Val·i·um (VAL·ee–) *Trademark.* diazepam, a tranquilizer.

Val·kyr·ie (val·KEER·ee, VAL·kuh·ree) *n.* in Norse myth, one of the goddess-maidens who choose the heroes to be slain in battle and conduct them to Odin.

val·ley (VAL·ee) *n.* **val·leys** a long, narrow depression between hills or mountains, esp. the low land through which a river flows; also, a valleylike dip or channel, as between two slopes of a roof. **—Valley Forge** a village of S.E. Pennsylvania where George Washington camped in the winter of 1777–78 during the Revolutionary War.

val·or (–ur) *n.* courage or bravery, as in battle; *Brit.* **val·our; val·or·ous** *adj.;* **val·o·ri·za·tion** (–ZAY–) *n.* price support for a commodity by government subsidies.

Val·pa·rai·so (–puh·RYE·zoh, –rah·EE·soh) chief seaport of Chile.

valse (VAHLS) same as WALTZ.

val·u·a·ble (VAL·yoo·uh–, –yoo·bl) *adj.* having great value or usefulness: *a ~ help, gem;* **valuables** *n.pl.* jewelry and such articles of great value. **—val·u·a·tion** (–AY–) *n.* a determining of the value of an asset; also, the estimated value or worth; **val·u·a·tor** (VAL·yoo·ay·tur) *n.* an appraiser. **—val·ue** (VAL·yoo) *n.* **1** what something is worth because of its usefulness or importance: *a story of some news ~; the ~ of education, vitamins and minerals, the Canadian dollar; a keepsake treasured for its sentimental ~; a thing of no commercial ~; the traditional* **values** (i.e. ideals, standards, etc.) *of North American society; avoidance of subjective* **value judgments** *about people and their actions; The consumer wants ~* (i.e. adequate return) *for his money.* **2** what a symbol or letter is equivalent to: *The ~ of L is 50; ½ and 3/6 have the same ~; "x" has the ~ "ks."* **3** a relative quality, as the degree of lightness or darkness of a color, duration of a note or rest in music, etc. **—*v.*** **-ues, -ued, -u·ing** **1** think highly of: *to ~ someone's advice; a* **valued** *friend.* **2** estimate; rate: *to ~ health above riches; assets ~d at $200,000.* **—val·ue·less** *adj.* **—val·ue-add·ed tax** a government tax on a product or service based on the difference between the producer's sale price and his cost of materials and expenses.

valve (VALV) *n.* **1** an opening and closing device that controls a flow, as in the heart, water faucets, and wind instruments such as the trumpet and French horn for changing musical pitch. **2** a hinged part of the shell of a bivalve mollusk or clam; also, one of the parts into which a capsule or pod separates on bursting open. **3** *Brit.* electron tube. **—valved** *adj.;* **valve·less** *adj.* **—val·vu·lar** (–vyuh·lur) *adj.* having valves or the form of a valve.

va·moose (vuh·MOOSE) *v.* **-moos·es, -moosed, -moos·ing** *Slang.* leave quickly (from).

¹vamp *n.* **1** the upper front covering of a shoe or boot. **2** a patched-up article, as a shoe repaired with a new vamp; also, a quickly improvised musical accompaniment. **—*v.*** **1** patch up or repair (as) with a new vamp: *to* **vamp up** *an excuse, a publication* (to look like a new one). **2** *Music.* improvise or play a vamp.

²vamp *n.* a woman who seduces and exploits men unscrupulously; adventuress. **—vam·pire** *n.* **1** a ghost of folklore that sucks the blood of sleeping people; hence, one who preys on others, as a blackmailer or adventuress. **2** short form of **vampire bat,** a tropical American bat that sucks the blood of fowl and livestock, and sometimes attacks sleeping people.

van *n.* **1** a large closed truck or wagon for transporting livestock, merchandise, etc. **2** the vanguard of an advancing army, fleet, etc.

va·na·di·um (vuh·NAY·dee–) *n.* a ductile metallic element used in steel and other alloys.

Van Al·len (radiation) belt (van·AL·un–) a part of the earth's magnetosphere that contains large numbers of charged particles that could be dangerous to space travelers.

Van Bu·ren (–BYOOR·un), **Martin.** 1782–1862, 8th U.S. President (1837–41).

Van·cou·ver (–COO–) largest city of British Columbia.

van·dal (VAN·dl) *n.* one who willfully or ignorantly destroys valuable property; **Vandal** *n.* a member of a barbaric Germanic tribe that sacked Rome in A.D. 455; **van·dal·ism** *n.* —**van·dal·ize** *v.* **-iz·es, -ized, -iz·ing** destroy or damage (property) maliciously.

Van·dyke (–DIKE) **beard** a pointed, closely trimmed beard.

vane *n.* **1** a blade of a rotating device as in a turbine or windmill on which the force of water, wind, etc. acts; also, a weather vane. **2** the feather of an arrow; also, a plate or strip of metal attached to a rocket or missile to give it stability in flight.

van Gogh (–GOH), **Vincent.** 1853–90, Dutch painter.

van·guard (VAN·gard) *n.* the front part of an advancing army; hence, the leadership or leading position in a movement.

va·nil·la (vuh·NIL·uh) *n.* (a flavoring made from) the capsules, or **vanilla beans** of a climbing orchid; also, the plant.

van·ish *v.* disappear suddenly and completely, often mysteriously: *The fairy ~ed from sight; Hopes ~; Endangered species may ~* (i.e. cease to exist) *unless protected;* **van·ish·er** *n.* —**van·i·ty** *n.* **-ties** **1** the quality of being vain; self-conceit; also, what one is vain about, as one's beauty or achievements. **2** worthlessness or something considered as of no real value. **3** a mirror and table for a woman to sit at while making up; also, a storage cabinet fitted under a washroom sink; ***adj.:*** *a ~ stool, mirror; a* **vanity case** *for cosmetics and toilet articles while traveling; a* **vanity press** *that publishes at authors' expense.*

van·quish (VANG–) *v.* defeat utterly; get the mastery of, as in single combat: *a ~ed foe; ~ed fears.*

van·tage (–tij) *n.* a position of strategic advantage or commanding view; also **vantage point.**

van·ward (–wurd) *adj.* & *adv.* in or toward the vanguard; forward.

vap·id *adj.* having lost freshness or flavor; hence, flat, dull, or boring; **vap·id·ness** *n.;* **va·pid·i·ty** (–PID–) *n.* **-ties** something vapid, as a dull remark. —**va·por** (VAY·pur) *n.* the gaseous state of a normally solid or liquid substance; also, a gas: *Water ~ seen as steam, fog, etc. condenses as dew, rain, and snow; Sulfur ~ sublimes into a powder; the ~s* (i.e. fantastic notions) *of a feverish mind;* ***v.*** (cause) to rise as vapor; also, give off vapor; **va·por·ings** *n.pl.* boastful talk. —**va·por·ish** (VAY–) *adj.* full of or like vapor; also, of low spirits or depressing. —**va·por·ize** (VAY–) *v.* **-iz·es, -ized, -iz·ing** change into vapor; **va·por·iz·er** *n.* a device for vaporizing a medicated liquid or steaming a room. —**vapor lock** blockage of fuel flow into an internal-combustion engine because of vapor bubbles formed by engine heat. —**va·por·ous** (VAY·puh·rus) *adj.* full of or like vapor; foggy or misty; also, volatile or fanciful; **va·por·ous·ly** *adv.;* **va·por·ous·ness** *n.* —**vapor pressure** (or **tension**) the pressure of a vapor in contact with its solid or liquid form in an enclosed space. —**vapor trail** same as CONTRAIL. —**va·por·y** *adj.* vaporous. —**va·pour** *Brit.* vapor.

va·que·ro (vah·CAIR·oh) *n.* **-ros** a ranchhand or cowboy of S.W. United States.

var. variable; variant(s); variation; variety; various. —**var·i·a** (VAIR·ee·uh) *n.pl.* a miscellany. —**var·i·a·ble** (VAIR·ee·uh–) *adj.* likely to vary or change: *~ winds, standards, moods; the "variable toad" with ~ green coloring; a curtain rod of ~* (i.e. adjustable) *length; a* **variable star** *with changing brightness, as a pulsar or nova; the ~* (not constant) *value of letters used in algebra;* ***n.*** something variable or changeable; **var·i·a·ble·ness** *n.;* **var·i·a·bly** *adv.;* **var·i·a·bil·i·ty** (–BIL–) *n.* —**var·i·ance** *n.* **1** difference or disagreement: *They are often* **at variance** *on matters of opinion.* **2** a deviation or departure: *a ~* (i.e. license) *to set up business in a residential area.* —**var·i·ant** (–unt) *adj.* varying from a standard or others of its kind; ***n.:*** *"Humor" and "humour" are American and British spelling ~s; a pronunciation ~.* —**var·i·a·tion** (–AY–) *n.* a change in form, position, condition, etc.: *temperature ~s from the normal; musical ~s on a theme by altering the accompaniment, harmonies, etc.; ~s between individuals, as in color of eyes, because of genetic differences and environmental factors.* —**var·i·col·ored** (VAIR–) *adj.* of various colors, as a parrot or marble; variegated in color.

var·i·cose (VAIR–) *adj.* abnormally swollen: *~ veins;* **var·i·cos·i·ty** (–COS–) *n.* **-ties** a varicose condition, vein, or lesion.

var·ied (VAIR·eed) *adj.* changed; also, diverse; of various kinds: *a man of ~ interests; a ~ style;* **var·ied·ly** *adv.* —**var·i·e·gat·ed** (VAIR·ee·uh·gay–, VAIR·ee·gay–) *adj.* marked with different colors, spots, etc.: *~ Easter eggs;* **var·i·e·ga·tion** (–GAY–) *n.* —**va·ri·e·tal** (–RYE·uh–) *n.* & *adj.* (a wine) made from a particular variety of grape; **va·ri·e·tal·ly** *adv.* —**va·ri·e·ty** (–RYE·uh–) *n.* **-ties** **1** variation; diversity: *artistic ~ in unity; a wide ~ of* (i.e. collection of different) *goods.* **2** kind or sort: *many ~s of goods; ~s* (i.e. subspecies or cultivars) *of roses.* **3** *Brit.* a variety show. —**variety meats** nonflesh meats, esp. organs, as sweetbreads, tripe, etc. —**variety show** an entertainment or show with songs, dances, skits, etc. —**variety store** a retail store selling a variety of small items. —**var·i·o·rum** (–OR–) *n.* an edition or text with critical notes by many. —**var·i·ous** (VAIR·ee·us) *adj.* different or diverse; also, many: *for ~ reasons;* **var·i·ous·ly** *adv.*

var·let (–lit) *n. Archaic.* a knave or scoundrel.

var·mint (–munt) *n.* a person or animal regarded as contemptible; also **var·ment.**

var·nish *n.* & *v.* (cover with or as with) a resinous preparation applied to wood, metal, etc. to give a hard, glossy surface; also, the glossy appearance; hence, surface polish or outside show.

var·si·ty *n.* **-ties** the main team representing a college, school, or club in a sports competition.

var·y (VAIR·ee) *v.* **var·ies, var·ied, var·y·ing** differ or make different; change or undergo change: *Customs ~ from place to place; ~ your cruising speed to avoid monotony; Visual acuity ~s inversely as size of letters read.*

vas·cu·lar (–kyuh·lur) *adj.* containing or having to do with vessels carrying blood, sap, etc.: *Mosses and liverworts are not* **vascular plants** (having xylem and phloem tissue). —**vas def·er·ens** (–DEF–) the duct through which semen passes from testicles to penis. —**vase** (VACE, VAZE) *n.* a decorative rounded vessel of pottery, etc. used esp. to hold flowers. —**vas·ec·to·my** (–SEC·tuh–) *n.* **-mies** surgical cutting of the vas deferens for producing sterility.

Vas·e·line (–uh·leen) *Trademark.* petrolatum; petroleum jelly.

vas·o·con·stric·tor (vas·oh·cun·STRIC·tur) *n.* & *adj.* (a nerve or drug) causing constriction of the blood vessels, as when turning pale; **vas·o·di·la·tor** (–dye·LAY–) *n.* & *adj.* (a nerve or drug) causing expansion of the blood vessels, as in blushing; **vas·o·mo·tor** (–MOH–) *adj.* influencing the narrowing or widening of blood vessels.

vas·sal (VAS·ul) *n.* a feudal tenant owing homage and allegiance to his lord; hence, a subordinate or servant. —**vas·sal·age** (–ij) *n.* a vassal's condition of servitude, the homage and service required of him, or the lands held.

vast *adj.* very great in extent or range: *the ~ Sahara; a ~ amount of money;* **vast·ly** *adv.;* **vast·ness** *n.* —*n. Poetic.* vast space; **vast·y** *adj.*

vat *n.* a large tub, barrel, or similar vessel to hold a liquid, esp. in an industrial process; **vat dye** a colorfast dye, esp. indigo, originally made in vats. —**VAT** value-added tax.

vat·ic *adj.* prophetic; oracular.

Vat·i·can (VAT·uh·cun) papal headquarters, authority, or government: *an appeal to* **the Vatican; Vatican City** world's smallest independent state, an enclave of 1/6 sq.mi. (0.4 km²) in Rome.

vaude·ville (VODE·vil, VAWD–, –uh·vil) *n.* a variety show featuring songs, dances, acrobatics, etc. that was popular as theatrical entertainment before the advent of motion pictures.

vault *n.* **1** (a chamber or structure with) an arched roof or ceiling, esp. one underground, usu. for a special purpose: *a storage ~; buried in the family ~; a bank ~ for the safekeeping of valuables; beneath the ~ of heaven* (i.e. sky). **2** a leaping or vaulting. —***v.*** **1** to arch like a vault; also, cover with or build as a vault; **vault·ed** *adj.: a ~ dome.* **2** to leap upward (over a barrier, from or onto a horse, etc.) supported by the hands or using a pole; **vault·er** *n.;* **vault·ing** *adj.: his ~* (i.e. overzealous) *ambition;* **vaulting horse** same as HORSE, *n.* 2.

vaunt *n.* & *v.* boast or brag; **vaunt·ed** *adj.: her ~* (i.e. boasted-about) *popularity.*

vb. verb; verbal.

V.C. Viet Cong.

V.D. venereal disease.

V-Day *n.* day of victory.

VDT video display terminal.

veal (VEEL) *n.* a young calf or its flesh used for food.

vec·tor (–tur) *n.* **1** a mathematical quantity or line segment with magnitude and direction. **2** the carrier or transmitter of a disease-causing organism or agent, as the mosquito carrying the malarial parasite.

Ve·da (VAY·duh, VEE–) *n.* any of the four ancient Sanskrit scriptures of the Hindus; **Ve·dic** *adj.* —**Ve·dan·ta** (–DAN–) *n.* a philosophical system based on the Vedas.

Veep or **veep** *n. Informal.* vice-president.

veer *v.* change direction, as under an external force; ***n.*** change of direction.

veer·y *n.* **veer·ies** a tawny brown thrush of N.E. United States.

veg·e·ta·ble (VEJ·uh·tuh–, VEJ·tuh–) *n.* & *adj.* (having to do with) a plant, esp. a plant part, as of the lettuce, beet, or tomato, that is used for food: *the ~ kingdom; They sell fruits and ~s; the ~ existence* (i.e. without mental activity) *of a terminally ill patient on a life-support system;* **veg·e·tal** (–tul) *adj.* vegetable or vegetative. —**veg·e·tar·i·an** (–TAIR–) *n.* one who eats no meat: *a strict ~ who has no use for fish and dairy products;* ***adj.:*** *a ~ diet, restaurant;* **veg·e·tar·i·an·ism** *n.* —**veg·e·tate** *v.* **-tates, -tat·ed, -tat·ing** grow as plants; also, exist like plants with very little physical or mental activity; **veg·e·ta·tive** (–tay·tiv) *adj.: a ~ organ, process such as growth or decay, existence.* —**veg·e·ta·tion** (–TAY–) *n.* **1** plant life or growth: *the luxuriant ~ of the jungle.* **2** the act or state of vegetating. —**veg·e·ta·tion·al** (–TAY–) *adj.*

ve·he·mence (VEE·uh–) *n.* the state or quality of being vehement; **ve·he·ment** *adj.* intense in feeling; passionate: *~ desires, utterances; a ~* (i.e. violent) *wind;* **ve·he·ment·ly** *adv.*

—**ve·hi·cle** (VEE·uh–) *n.* **1** a carriage or conveyance used on land or in space: *motor ~s; space ~s.* **2** a medium: *pigments in ~s such as oils, resins, latex, etc.; a drug given in an inert ~ such as syrup; language as the ~ of thought and feeling.* —**ve·hic·u·lar** (–HIK·yuh·lur) *adj.: ~ traffic, tunnels.*

V-8 *n.* & *adj.* (an engine) having eight cylinders in two rows set at an angle; also, a vehicle with such an engine.

veil (VAIL) *n.* a piece of sheer fabric or net used to hide or protect a woman's head or face, as a curtain, etc.: *a bridal ~; a ~ of secrecy, clouds;* **take the veil** become a nun; **v.** put a veil over: *a ~ed beauty, widow; the moon ~ed by clouds; a* **veiled** (i.e. hidden or implied) *threat;* **veil·ing** *n.* a veil or a sheer fabric such as lace or chiffon.

vein (VAIN) *n.* **1** a channel carrying blood, sap, etc.: *the ~s and arteries of the circulatory system; the vascular network of ~s on a leaf; the ~s on an insect's wing; a ~* (i.e. seam or lode) *of mineral ore deposited by ground water in rock fissures.* **2** a streak or marking, as in marble: *the ~* (i.e. streak) *of melancholy running through her work; in a serious ~* (i.e. mood). —**v.** mark with veins; **veined** *adj.;* **vein·ing** *n.;* **vein·y** *adj.*

ve·lar (VEE·lur) *n.* & *adj.* (a sound) made at the back of the mouth near the velum or soft palate, as a hard "g."

veld(t) (VELT) *n.* the treeless grasslands of South Africa whose lower regions are often scrub-covered.

vel·lum (VEL·um) *n.* a fine parchment, as used for binding expensive books; also, a strong paper with a smooth finish imitating vellum, used for diplomas, etc.

ve·loc·i·pede (vuh·LOS·uh·peed) *n.* an early form of bicycle or tricycle; also, a child's tricycle. —**ve·loc·i·ty** (–LOS–) *n.* **-ties** swiftness or speed, esp. of inanimate things: *the ~ of a bullet, light, sound.*

ve·lour(s) (vuh·LOOR) *n., pl.* **-lours** (–LOORZ) a velvetlike fabric used for coats, upholstery, etc.

ve·lum (VEE–) *n.,pl.* **-la** (–luh) the soft back portion of the palate.

ve·lure (vuh·LOOR) *n.* & *v.* **-lures, -lured, -lur·ing** (brush a hat, etc. with) a velvety pad. —**vel·vet** (–vut) *n.* & *adj.* (made of, covered with, or suggesting) a fabric of silk, rayon, etc. with a soft downy surface; also, something resembling it, as the furry covering of a deer's growing antlers: *seductive black ~; the ~ touch of soft skin; "an iron hand in a ~ glove"* (i.e. softness masking ruthlessness); **vel·vet·y** *adj.* —**vel·vet·een** (–TEEN) *n.* a cotton fabric resembling velvet.

Ven. Venerable.

ve·nal (VEE·nl) *adj.* open to bribes or influenced by bribery; corrupt: *~ politicians, practices, conduct;* **ve·nal·ly** *adv.;* **ve·nal·i·ty** (–NAL–) *n.* —**vend** *v.* sell, esp. peddle or hawk; **vend·ee** (–DEE) *n.* buyer. —**vend·er** *n.* same as VENDOR.

ven·det·ta (–DET·uh) *n.* a family feud in which injuries are avenged with violence and bloodshed; also, any prolonged feud.

vending machine a coin-operated machine, esp. one selling candy, cigarettes, etc. —**ven·dor** *n.* one that vends; seller.

ve·neer (vuh·NEER)*n.* a layer of wood, brick, etc. used to cover something inferior: *furniture with an oak ~; exterior walls of brick ~; could see through his ~ of urbanity;* **v.** cover with a veneer.

ven·er·a·ble (VEN·uh·ruh–) *adj.* worthy of respect or reverence because of age, dignity, sanctity, etc.; **ven·er·a·bil·i·ty** (–BIL–) *n.* —**ven·er·ate** *v.* **-ates, -at·ed, -at·ing** regard with deep reverence; revere; **ven·er·a·tion** (–RAY–) *n.*

ve·ne·re·al (–NEER·ee·ul) *adj.* of or transmitted by sexual intercourse: *~ diseases;* **ve·ne·re·al·ly** *adv.*

Ve·ne·tian (–NEE–) *n.* & *adj.* (a native or inhabitant) of Venice. —**Venetian blind** a window blind made of slats that can be opened and closed to regulate lighting.

Ven·e·zue·la (ven·iz·WAY·luh) a South American country; 352,145 sq.mi. (912,050 km²); *cap.* Caracas; **Ven·e·zue·lan** (–lun) *n.* & *adj.*

venge·ance (VEN·junce) *n.* punishment in return for a wrong; revenge; **with a vengeance** in a vehement or excessive way: *started dieting with a ~.* —**venge·ful** (VENJ–) *adj.* seeking vengeance; revengeful; vindictive; **venge·ful·ly** *adv.*

ve·ni·al (VEE·nee·ul, –nyul) *adj.* pardonable or excusable: *~ sin;* **ve·ni·al·ly** *adv.*

ven·i·punc·ture (–PUNK–) *n.* the puncturing of a vein to take a blood sample or give an injection.

Ven·ice (–is) a seaport of N. Italy.

ve·ni·re (vuh·NYE·ree) *n.* a writ summoning a jury; also, a list of persons from which to draw a jury, one of whom is a **ve·ni·re·man** (–mun).

ven·i·son (VEN·i·sn, –zn) *n.* the flesh of a deer used as food.

ven·om (–um) *n.* the poison of a snake or spider; also, malice; **ven·om·ous** (–us) *adj.* poisonous; also, spiteful or malicious: *a ~ letter;* **ven·om·ous·ly** *adv.*

ve·nous (VEE·nus) *adj.* of or having to do with veins: *~ blood.*

vent *n.* **1** an outlet or opening for a gas to escape through, for air to be drawn in for ventilation, as in an automobile, etc.: *a* **vent pipe** *for the escape of sewer gas; She* **gave vent** (i.e. free expression) *to her feelings by getting up and shouting;* **v.:** *He ~ed his anger on everyone he met; Sinks,* *toilets, etc. are ~ed through the roof.* **2** a vertical slit at the edge of a garment: *a jacket with side ~s.* **—ven·ti·late** *v.* **-lates, -lat·ed, -lat·ing** **1** let fresh air into; hence, oxygenate (blood in lungs, etc.): *a well-~d room.* **2** furnish with a vent, outlet, etc.; also, submit (a grievance, question, etc.) to public discussion. **—ven·ti·la·tion** (–LAY–) *n.* **—ven·ti·la·tor** *n.* an opening or a device such as a fan for ventilating a place.

ven·tral (–trul) *adj.* of or near the belly; cf. DORSAL; hence, lower; **ven·tral·ly** *adv.* **—ven·tri·cle** *n.* either of the two lower chambers of the heart. **—ven·tril·o·quism** (–TRIL·uh–) *n.* the art of talking without moving the lips so that the voice seems to come from a source outside the speaker such as a puppet held in the hand; **ven·tril·o·quist** *n.*

ven·ture (VEN·chur) *n.* an enterprise or undertaking involving risk but with a chance for profit, as in buying stocks: *a speculative ~;* **venture capital** *not secured by collateral for investment in stocks;* **at a venture** taking a risk; without much deliberation. **—*v.* -tures, -tured, -tur·ing** expose (lives, etc.) to risk; dare (to do something risky or hazardous): *if I may ~ an opinion; wouldn't ~* (to step) *outside in the storm.* **—ven·ture·some** (–sum) *adj.* daring; also, hazardous; also **ven·tur·ous** (–us); **ven·ture·some·ly** *adv.;* **ven·ture·some·ness** *n.;* **ven·tur·ous·ly** *adv.;* **ven·tur·ous·ness** *n.* **—ven·ue** (VEN·yoo) *n.* **1** the locality of the commission of a crime, or the place of jury selection or trial: *requested a change of ~ because of adverse publicity.* **2** the appointed meeting place for a gathering or event: *the ~ of the Olympic Games.*

Ve·nus (VEE–) **1** the Roman goddess of love and beauty. **2** the planet closest to the earth and appearing brighter than any star. **—Venus' fly·trap** a swamp plant with two-lobed hairy leaves that can trap and digest insects; also **Ve·nus's-fly·trap.** **—Ve·nu·sian** (–NEW·zhun) *n.* & *adj.* (an imaginary inhabitant) of the planet Venus.

ve·ra·cious (–RAY·shus) *adj.* truthful; **ve·ra·cious·ly** *adv.;* **ve·rac·i·ty** (–RAS–) *n.* habitual truthfulness; also, truth or accuracy, as of a report.

ve·ran·da(h) (–RAN·duh) *n.* an outside corridor or covered gallery of a building; also, a porch.

verb (VURB) *n.* a part of speech or word expressing action, being, or happening. **—ver·bal** (–bul) *adj.* **1** having to do with words: *a ~ distinction, aptitude test; ~ imagery; a ~* (i.e. oral) *assurance; a ~* (i.e. word-for-word or literal) *translation.* **2** having to do with verbs: *"-ed," "-ing," and such ~ endings;* **verbal auxiliary** same as AUXILIARY VERB. **—ver·bal·ize** *v.* **-iz·es, -ized, -iz·ing** **1** express (an idea or experience) in words; also, be verbose or wordy. **2** change (a noun) into a verb. **—ver·bal·i·za·tion** (–ZAY–) *n.* **—ver·bal·ly** *adv.* **—verbal noun** an infinitive ("To fly without wings is impossible") or gerund ("Flying is fun") used as a noun. **—ver·ba·tim** (–BAY–) *adj.* & *adv.* word for word: *The speech was reported ~; a ~ report.*

ver·be·na (–BEE·nuh) *n.* a group of mostly tropical plants bearing flat heads of phloxlike flowers.

ver·bi·age (VUR·bee·ij) *n.* use of too many words; verbosity; wordiness. **—ver·bose** (–BOSE) *adj.* using more words than are necessary: *a ~ speaker, style;* **ver·bose·ly** *adv.;* **ver·bos·i·ty** (–BOS–) *n.*

ver·bo·ten (–BOH·tun) *adj. German.* forbidden or prohibited.

ver·dant (VURD·nt) *adj.* green: *~ grass, meadows; ~* (i.e. immature) *youth;* **ver·dant·ly** *adv.*

Ver·di (VER·dee), **Giuseppe.** 1813–1901, Italian composer of operas.

ver·dict (VUR–) *n.* a formal decision or finding, as of a jury at the end of a trial.

ver·di·gris (VUR·duh·greece, –gris) *n.* a greenish deposit on exposed brass, bronze, or copper; also, a poisonous pigment that is an acetate of copper. **—ver·dure** (–jur) *n.* green vegetation or the green color of growing things.

verge (VURJ) *n.* & *v.* **verg·es, verged, verg·ing** (be on) the brink or extreme edge of something: *on the ~ of a roof, cliff; on the ~ of bankruptcy, tears, being exposed; spelling so poor it ~s on illiteracy; ~ing* (i.e. inclining) *toward old age.* **—verg·er** *n.* a caretaker of a church; sexton.

Ver·gil (VUR·jul) same as VIRGIL.

ver·i·fy *v.* **-fies, -fied, -fy·ing** prove the correctness or truth of (a statement, piece of information, etc.) by checking with a standard or authority; also, confirm or bear out: *suspicions ~d by later events;* **ver·i·fi·a·ble** *adj.;* **ver·i·fi·ca·tion** (–CAY–) *n.* **—ver·i·ly** *adv. Archaic.* truly; in truth. **—ver·i·si·mil·i·tude** (–MIL–) *n.* the quality of seeming to be true or real. **—ver·i·ta·ble** (–tuh–) *adj.* truly so termed: *a ~ gold mine, heaven on earth.* **—ver·i·ty** *n.* **-ties** the quality of being true or real; also, a fundamental or universal truth; *the eternal ~s of all creeds and philosophies.*

ver·meil (VUR·mul) *n.* **1** (*also* vur·MAY) gilded silver. **2** vermilion. **—ver·mi·cel·li** (–SEL·ee, –CHEL–) *n.* pasta in finer strings than spaghetti, used in soups, etc. **—ver·mic·u·lite** (–MIK·yuh–) a micalike mineral that expands greatly when heated to form a lightweight cellular material that is much used in insulation, packaging, etc. **—ver·mi·form** *adj.* wormlike in shape; **vermiform appendix** same as APPENDIX, *n.* 2. **—ver·mi·fuge** *n.* a medicine for killing worms in the intestines. **—ver·mil·ion** (–MIL·yun) *n.* a bright-red pigment; also, a bright red; ***adj.*** bright-red. **—ver·min** *n. sing.* & *pl.* (any of various) insects or small animals that are pests, as fleas, rats, etc.; also, a contemptible person; **ver•min•ous** (–us) *adj.*

Ver•mont (vur·MONT) a New England state; 9,609 sq.mi. (24,887 km²); *cap.* Montpelier; **Ver•mont•er** *n.*

ver•mouth (–MOOTH) *n.* a white wine flavored with herbs.

ver•nac•u•lar (–NAK·yuh·lur) *n.* the native language of a people or place, esp. its everyday, spoken variety, as distinguished from a literary or learned language; also, the idiom of a group or class; ***adj.:*** *Italian, French, etc. started as ~ forms of Latin; "Venus' flytrap" is the ~ name for "Dionaea muscipula."*

ver•nal (VUR·nl) *adj.* of or like spring: *~ flowers, equinox* (around March 21); **ver•nal•ize** *v.* **-iz•es, -ized, -iz•ing** chill (a seed or plant) in order to induce rapid growth as in the spring season; **ver•nal•i•za•tion** (–ZAY–) *n.* **—ver•nal•ly** *adv.*

ver•ni•er (VUR·nee·ur) *n.* a small scale or ruler that is slid alongside a larger one for fractional readings of length and angle measurements; also **vernier scale.**

Ve•ron•i•ca (–RON–) *n.* same as SPEEDWELL.

Ver•sailles (–SYE, –SAILZ) a city near Paris.

ver•sa•tile (VUR·suh·tl) *adj.* **1** having the skills or aptitude for many different activities: *a ~ genius, mind.* **2** able to turn or swing freely: *a ~ anther; an insect's ~ antennae.* **—ver•sa•til•i•ty** (–TIL–) *n.* **—verse** *n.* **1** a line of poetry; also, a stanza or poem. **2** language in verses; poetry. **3** a sentence from a chapter of the Bible. **—versed** *adj.* skilled; experienced; learned: *a scholar well ~ in his specialty.* **—ver•si•cle** *n.* a short verse or sentence as one of a series recited by a clergyman alternately with responses from the congregation. **—ver•si•fy** *v.* **-fies, -fied, -fy•ing** turn into verse form; also, write verse; **ver•si•fi•er** *n.;* **ver•si•fi•ca•tion** (–CAY–) *n.* **—ver•sion** *n.* a particular form or variant, esp. an account or description from one point of view; also, a translation of the Bible: *the Revised Version.* **—vers li•bre** (vair·LEE·bruh) *French.* free verse. **—ver•so** *n.* **-sos** a left-hand page of a book. **—ver•sus** *prep.* against; also, in contrast with. **—ver•te•bra** (–tuh·bruh) *n., pl.* **-brae** (–bree) or **-bras** one of the segments of the backbone; **ver•te•bral** *adj.* **—ver•te•brate** (–brit, –brate) *n.* & *adj.* (an animal such as a fish, amphibian, bird, reptile, or mammal) that has a backbone.

ver•tex *n.* **-tex•es** or **-ti•ces** (–seez) **1** the topmost point; apex; zenith: *the ~* (i.e. point farthest from the base) *of a pyramid.* **2** the meeting point of two sides, as of a triangle. **—ver•ti•cal** (–cul) *adj.* **1** of or at the vertex; directly overhead. **2** perpendicular to the horizontal; upright or erect; ***n.*** a vertical line, plane, part, etc. **—ver•ti•cal•ly** *adv.* **—ver•ti•cal•i•ty** (–CAL–) *n.* **—ver•tig•i•nous** (–TIJ·uh·nus) *adj.* of or having to do with **ver•ti•go** (VUR·tuh–) *n.* **-ti•goes** or **-tig•i•nes** (–TIJ·uh·neez) dizziness or giddiness felt when one's sense of balance is disturbed, as in diseases of the inner ear.

ver•vain *n.* any of a family of plants and trees including the verbena, teak, etc.

verve *n.* vigorous energy or enthusiasm; vivacity.

ver•y *adj.* **ver•i•er, -i•est** **1** [used for emphasis before nouns]: *at that ~* (i.e. same) *moment; The ~* (i.e. mere) *idea is revolting; as I told you from the ~* (i.e. extreme) *beginning.* **2** *Archaic.* real or genuine: *in ~ truth; A ~er fool was never seen.* ***—adv.*** [used for emphasis before adverbs, adjectives, and participles except participles with clearly verbal meaning]: *a ~ great idea; at ~ much reduced prices; at the ~ least; treated the child as his ~ own.* **—very high frequency** a radio frequency between 30 and 300 megahertz. **—very low frequency** a radio frequency below 30 kilohertz.

ves•i•cant (–kunt) *n.* & *adj.* (a substance such as mustard gas) that causes blistering. **—ves•i•cle** *n.* a fluid-filled membranous cavity; a small blister; cyst; **ve•sic•u•lar** (–SIC–) *adj.;* **ve•sic•u•late** (–lit) *adj.*

ves•per *adj.* of or having to do with the evening or vespers; **ves•pers** or **Ves•pers** *n.pl.* an evening church service. **—ves•per•tine** (–tin, –tine) *adj.* of the evening; also, active in the evening (as bats and owls) or opening in the evening (as some flowers).

Ves•puc•ci (–POO·chee), **Amerigo.** 1451?–1512, Italian explorer after whom America was named.

ves•sel (VES·ul) *n.* **1** a hollow utensil for holding esp. liquids, as a bowl, barrel, bottle, etc.; also, in the Bible, a person considered as filled with a particular quality, influence, etc.: *~s of wrath.* **2** a ship or large boat. **3** a duct or tube of the body: *blood ~s.*

vest *n.* a short sleeveless garment worn under one's suit jacket; also, *Brit.* undershirt. ***—v.*** **1** clothe, as in vestments: *a priest ~ed for Mass; An official is ~ed* (i.e. invested or endowed) *with authority.* **2** put (authority, rights, etc.) in the possession of a person: *by the powers ~ed in Congress; powers that ~* (i.e. reside) *in Congress; a ~ed interest.*

ves•tal (–tl) *adj.* chaste or pure, as a **vestal virgin,** a priestess of the Roman goddess **Ves•ta.** ***—n.*** a chaste woman; virgin.

vested interest an economic or political privilege enjoyed by a group or organization that may be lost by change; also, such a group or its selfish concern.

vest•ee (–TEE) *n.* a vestlike front or trimming worn by women under a bodice.

ves•ti•bule (VES·tuh–) *n.* a room, hall, or passage serving as an entrance or antechamber; **ves•tib•u•lar** (–TIB·yuh–) *adj.*

ves•tige (–tij) *n.* a remaining part or remnant of something that is no longer in existence:

~*s of an ancient civilization; not a* ~ (i.e. least bit) *of evidence; The appendix, wisdom teeth, etc. are* ~*s from an earlier stage of evolution;* **ves·tig·i·al** (–TIJ–) *adj.;* **ves·tig·i·al·ly** *adv.*

vest·ing *n.* the conferring of a fixed right, as when an employee may retain his pension regardless of changing circumstances. **—vest·ment** *n.* a ceremonial outer garment or robe, as worn by a clergyman at religious services. **—vest-pock·et** *adj.* very small: *a* ~ *dictionary.* **—ves·try** (–tree) *n.* **-tries** **1** a sacristy, as in Protestant churches. **2** in the Episcopal Church, a committee managing church business; **ves·try·man** *n.* **-men** a member of a vestry. **—ves·ture** *n.* clothing or covering; garments.

Ve·su·vi·us (–SOO·vee–) an active volcano near Naples, Italy.

vet *n.* [short form] **1** veterinarian; veterinary. **2** veteran; also ***adj.*** **—vet.** veteran; veterinarian; veterinary.

vetch *n.* a plant of the pea family valued as cattle food and green manure.

vet·er·an (–un) *n.* **1** a former member of the armed forces, esp. an old soldier, sailor, etc. **2** a person with long experience in his occupation; ***adj.:*** *a* ~ *soldier, farmer, journalist;* ~ *benefits.* **—Veterans Day** a day honoring veterans of the U.S. armed services, usu. the fourth Monday in October.

vet·er·i·nar·i·an (–NAIR·ee·un) *n.* one who practices veterinary medicine. **—vet·er·i·nar·y** (VET·uh·ruh–) *adj.* having to do with the medical and surgical treatment of animals; ***n., pl.*** **-nar·ies** a veterinarian.

ve·to (VEE·toh) *n.* **-toes** (the exercise of) the right to prohibit an act, as of the U.S. President not to approve a bill passed by both houses of Congress; ***v.*** **-toes, -toed, -to·ing** forbid or prohibit (an action) by special right; also, prevent (a bill) from becoming law.

vex *v.* irritate or annoy in a worrying manner; also, plague or afflict (with a disorder); **vexed question** much disputed question; **vex·a·tion** (–SAY–) *n.;* **vex·a·tious** (–shus) *adj.;* **vex·a·tious·ly** *adv.;* **vex·a·tious·ness** *n.*

V.F.W. Veterans of Foreign Wars of the United States.

VHF or **vhf** very high frequency.

v.i. intransitive verb. **—V.I.** Virgin Islands.

vi·a (VYE·uh, VEE–) *prep.* by (way of): ~ *the Panama Canal;* ~ *airmail.*

vi·a·ble (VYE·uh–) *adj.* **1** capable of surviving, as a fetus outside the womb. **2** feasible or practicable: *a* ~ *plan, alternative, economy.* **—vi·a·bly** *adv.;* **vi·a·bil·i·ty** (–BIL–) *n.* **—vi·a·duct** (VYE·uh-) *n.* a bridge on tall supports for carrying a railroad track or road over another road or track, valley, etc.

vi·al (VYE·ul) *n.* a small bottle to hold medicines and other liquids.

vi·and (VYE·und) *n.* an article of food, usu. **viands** *pl.* **—vi·at·i·cum** (–AT–) *n.* **1** the Eucharist given to a dying person. **2** food or money for a journey, as in ancient Rome.

vibes *n.pl.* **1** *Slang.* vibrations (*n.* 3). **2** vibraphone. **—vi·bra·harp** (VYE·bruh–) *n.* same as VIBRAPHONE. **—vi·brant** (VYE·brunt) *adj.* **1** vibrating; hence, resonant. **2** vigorous or energetic: *a* ~ *personality.* **—vi·brant·ly** *adv.;* **vi·bran·cy** *n.* **—vi·bra·phone** (VYE·bruh–) *n.* an instrument resembling a xylophone with metal bars and electrically operated resonators; **vi·bra·phon·ist** *n.* **—vi·brate** (VYE–) *v.* **-brates, -brat·ed, -brat·ing** **1** set or be in rapid back-and-forth motion, as a taut string when plucked; also, oscillate, as a pendulum. **2** respond sympathetically; thrill; also, resound or echo, as a sound in the ears. **—vi·bra·tion** (–BRAY–) *n.* **1** a trembling, as caused by an earthquake or felt in a vehicle because of a wheel that is not properly balanced. **2** oscillation. **3 vibrations** *pl.* instinctive reactions or feelings about a person or thing. **—vi·bra·tion·al** *adj.* **—vi·bra·to** (vee·BRAH·toh) *n.* **-tos** a tremulous effect produced by slight and rapid vibrations in pitch in singing or in playing stringed instruments. **—vi·bra·tor** (VYE·bray·tur) *n.* one that vibrates, as an electrical massaging device; **vi·bra·to·ry** (–bruh–) *adj.*

vi·bur·num (vye·BUR–) *n.* a shrub of the honeysuckle family bearing fragrant clusters of white or pink flowers.

vic·ar (VIC·ur) *n.* **1** a minister or clergyman in charge of a parish or a parish chapel. **2** a deputy or representative of a higher church official, as **vicar apostolic,** a bishop representing the pope, and **vi·car-gen·er·al,** *pl.* **vi·cars-gen·er·al** a bishop's deputy. **—vi·car·age** (VIC·uh·rij) *n.* the residence or benefice of a vicar. **—vi·car·i·al** (–CAIR–) *adj.* of a vicar; delegated; **vi·car·i·ate** *n.* the office or authority of a vicar. **—vi·car·i·ous** (–CAIR–) *adj.* acting for or as by another: ~ (i.e. delegated) *authority; the* ~ *pleasure felt in another's enjoyment; nosebleed as* ~ *menstruation;* **vi·car·i·ous·ly** *adv.;* **vi·car·i·ous·ness** *n.*

¹vice *n.* **1** a moral fault; an immoral habit or tendency: *virtues and* ~*s; drunkenness, gambling, and such* ~*s; a police* **vice squad** *raiding a brothel.* **2** a trick or bad habit of a horse or other domestic animal, as shying. **3** *Brit.* vise.

²vi·ce (VYE·see) *prep.* in the place of: *was appointed* ~ *John Smith.* ***—prefix.*** (VICE) as in *vice-president, vice-regent;* **vice admiral** a naval officer ranking below admiral and above rear admiral; **vice·ge·rent** (–JEER·unt) *n.* a ruler's deputy; **vice·ge·ren·cy** *n.*

vi·cen·ni·al (vye·SEN·ee·ul) *adj.* lasting for or happening every 20 years.

vice-pres·i·dent *n.* an executive ranking next below a president: *the* **Vice-Pres·i·dent** *of the United States;* **vice-pres·i·den·cy** *n.* **-cies;** **vice-pres·i·den·tial** (–DEN–) *adj.* **—vice·re·gal** (–REE·gul) *adj.* of a viceroy; **vice·roy** *n.*

a ruler representing a sovereign, as in the Spanish and British empires; **vice·roy·al·ty** *n.* **—vi·ce ver·sa** (VYE·see·VUR·suh, VICE–) in the reverse order.

vi·chys·soise (vish·ee·SWAHZ, vee·shee–) *n.* a thick soup made with leeks, cream, potatoes, etc. and usu. served cold. **—Vich·y** (VISH·ee) **water** water from the mineral springs at Vichy, France; also, any mineral water.

vic·i·nage (VIS·uh·nij) *n.* a vicinity or neighborhood; **vic·i·nal** (–nl) *adj.* **—vi·cin·i·ty** (–SIN–) *n.* **-ties** nearness or proximity: *in close ~ to the church; in the ~ of $200 a day; London and ~* (i.e. surrounding area).

vi·cious (VISH·us) *adj.* **1** characterized by vice; wicked: *~ habits, lies; gave me a ~ look; a ~* (i.e. unruly) *horse; a ~* (i.e. severe) *blow.* **2** involving interaction of cause and effect: *the ~ spiral of rising wages and prices;* **vicious circle** a situation in which the solution of a problem results in a new problem similar to the original one; also, the fallacy of basing an argument on the very thing to be proved. **—vi·cious·ly** *adv.;* **vi·cious·ness** *n.*

vi·cis·si·tudes (vuh·SIS·uh–) *n.pl.* unpredictable and sudden changes usu. bringing hardship; ups and downs: *the* **vicissitudes** *of life.*

vic·tim *n.* one who suffers injury, harm, loss, etc.: *a lamb killed and placed on the altar as the sacrificial ~; the ~ of a crime, accident, disease, swindle;* **vic·tim·ize** *v.* **-iz·es, -ized, -iz·ing** make a victim of; **vic·tim·iz·er** *n.;* **vic·tim·i·za·tion** (–ZAY–) *n.* **—vic·tim·less** *adj.: a ~ crime such as drug-trafficking, gambling, or prostitution.*

vic·tor (–tur) *n.* the winner or conqueror in a battle, struggle, etc. **—Vic·to·ri·a** (–TOR–) **1** 1819–1901, queen of Britain (1837–1901). **2** capital of British Columbia. **3** capital of Seychelles. **—vic·to·ri·a** *n.* a low, four-wheeled carriage with a folding top covering a seat at the rear for passengers; also, a similar early automobile. **—Vic·to·ri·an** *adj.* of or characteristic of the period of Queen Victoria's reign, usu. associated with prudery, bigotry, etc.; ***n.*** a writer of the Victorian period; **Vic·to·ri·an·ism** *n.* **—vic·to·ri·ous** (–TOR–) *adj.* conquering; also, marked by victory; **vic·to·ri·ous·ly** *adv.* **—vic·to·ry** (VIC·tuh·ree, –tree) *n.* **-ries** success in a struggle, esp. in battle or war.

vic·tuals (VIT·lz) *n.pl. Informal* or *Regional.* food supplies; articles of food; ***v.*** **-tuals, -tual(l)ed, -tual.(l)ing** supply with victuals; **vic·tual·(l)er** *n.*

vi·cu·ña (vye·COON·yuh, vi–) *n.* (the fine, soft, and expensive wool of) an Andean animal of the camel family, related to the alpaca and llama.

vide (VYE·dee) *v. Latin.* please see (page, book, etc. referred to). **—vi·de·li·cet** (vi·DEL–) *adv. Latin.* namely; that is to say.

—vid·e·o (VID·ee·oh) *n.* television, esp. the picture as distinguished from the sound; ***adj.:*** *~ signals; a* **video cassette** (or **cartridge**) *for storing and playback of recordings on film or videotape; A* **vid·e·o·disc,** *like a phonograph record, plays back pictures and sounds recorded on it;* **videodisc player;** *a computer's* **video display terminal** *with a TV-like screen; a* **video game** *played by manipulating points of light on a television screen; the* **vid·e·o·phone** *for seeing the person you are phoning.* **—vid·e·o·tape** *n.* & *v.* **-tapes, -taped, -tap·ing** (record a television production on) magnetic tape: *A* **videotape recorder** *can be plugged into a television set for recording programs on a cassette for later viewing.* **—vid·e·o·tex** *n.* a computer service that supplies subscribers with information displayed on a video terminal or television screen.

vie (VYE) *v.* **vies, vied, vy·ing** contend or compete (*with* another *for* something).

Vi·en·na (vee·EN·uh) capital of Austria; **Vi·en·nese** (–uh·NEEZ) *n.* & *adj., sing.* & *pl.*

Vien·tiane (vyen·TYAHN) capital of Laos.

Vi·et Cong (VEE·ut·CONG) *sing.* & *pl.* (a member of) the Communist guerrilla force that fought against South Vietnamese and U.S. forces for unification of Vietnam; also **Vi·et·cong.** **—Vi·et·nam** (VEE·ut·NAHM) the reunited Socialist Republic of Vietnam formed in 1976 with Hanoi as capital; formerly North Vietnam, 61,300 sq.mi. (158,750 km²), *cap.* Hanoi, and South Vietnam, 67,293 sq.mi. (174,289 km²), *cap.* Ho Chi Minh City (*formerly* Saigon); **Vi·et·nam·ese** (–nuh·MEEZ) *n.* & *adj., sing.* & *pl.*

view (VYOO) *n.* **1** what is seen by someone looking from a certain position: *structures that spoil our ~; a breathtaking ~; came within ~* (i.e. range of sight); *the ~* (i.e. picture) *hanging on the wall; exhibits* **on view; in view** in sight or as an aim. **2** a personal opinion or judgment: *your ~s on the matter;* **in view of** because of. **3** intention or purpose: *came* **with a view** *to discussing matters.* **—*v.*** look at; inspect; consider (in a particular manner, from a standpoint, with a feeling, etc.); **view·er** *n.* one that views, esp. an optical device for looking at slides. **—view·find·er** *n.* in a camera, a reflecting or direct-vision device for sighting the subject to be photographed. **—view·point** *n.* point of view or attitude.

vi·ges·i·mal (vye·JES·uh·mul) *adj.* based on 20; also, twentieth.

vig·il (VIJ–) *n.* **1** a staying awake; watch: *to keep ~ over a patient needing constant attention.* **2** the eve of a solemn religious festival; **vigils** *pl.* devotions or prayers.**—vig·i·lance** (–lunce) *n.* watchfulness or alertness against danger or trouble, as by a **vigilance committee,** or self-appointed group of citizens to enforce laws; **vig·i·lant** (–lunt) *adj.* watchful or alert. **—vig·i·lan·te** (–LAN·tee) *n.* a member of a vigilance committee, as in pioneer days:

the U.S. Navy's Vigilante reconnaissance bomber; **vig·i·lan·tism** *n.;* **vig·i·lant·ly** (VIJ–) *adv.*

vi·gnette (vin·YET) *n.* **1** a short literary sketch, as of a personal experience or incident. **2** a picture or photograph that shades off at the edges without definite borders. **—*v.* -gnettes, -gnet·ted, -gnet·ting** make a vignette of (an incident, picture, etc.). **—vi·gnet·tist** *n.*

vig·or (–ur) *n.* active force; strength or vitality; also, effectiveness: *the ~ of youth; a plant growing with ~; acted with ~ and resolution;* also **vig·our** *Brit.;* **vig·or·ous** (–us) *adj.;* **vig·or·ous·ly** *adv.;* **vig·or·ous·ness** *n.*

Vi·king (VYE–) *n.* a Scandinavian pirate or explorer of the groups active between the 8th and 10th centuries A.D.; Norseman; also **vi·king.**

vile *adj.* **vil·er, vil·est** disgustingly foul, low, or depraved: *~ language, odors, habits; ~* (i.e. bad) *weather;* **vile·ly** *adv.;* **vile·ness** *n.* **—vil·i·fy** *v.* **-fies, -fied, -fy·ing** use abusive language about (a person); calumniate or slander; **vil·i·fi·er** *n.;* **vil·i·fi·ca·tion** (–CAY–) *n.*

vil·la (VIL·uh) *n.* a suburban or country residence or estate. **—vil·lage** (–ij) *n.* a community smaller than a town, esp. one chartered as a municipality; also, the people of a village; **vil·lag·er** *n.* **—vil·lain** (VIL·un) *n.* **1** a wicked person or scoundrel, esp. as a dramatic character in opposition to the hero: *the ~ of the piece.* **2** [used jokingly] rascal. **—vil·lain·ous** (–us) *adj.;* **vil·lain·ous·ly** *adv.;* **vil·lain·ous·ness** *n.* **—vil·lain·y** *n.* **vil·lain·ies** wickedness or a wicked act.

-ville *comb.form* [used in slang coinages to suggest a condition as specified]: as in *dullsville, weirdsville.*

vil·lein (VIL·un, –ain) *n.* a feudal serf with some rights of a freeman. **—vil·lein·age** (–ij) *n.;* also **vil·len·age** *n.*

vil·lous (–us) *adj.* having or covered with villi. **—vil·lus** *n., pl.* **vil·li** (–eye) one of the small hairlike projections lining the small intestine and helping to absorb food.

Vil·ni·us (VIL·nee–) capital of Lithuania.

vim *n.* vitality or energy.

vin·ai·grette (vin·uh·GRET) *n.* a small ornamental box containing smelling salts or a sponge soaked in vinegar and lavender.

Vin·ci (VIN·chee), **Leonardo da.** 1452–1519, noted Italian artist and scientist.

vin·ci·ble *adj.* conquerable.

vin·di·cate *v.* **-cates, -cat·ed, -cat·ing** prove (one's innocence under attack) or establish (a disputed claim, judgment, etc.) by evidence, testimony, a verdict, etc.: *felt ~d when things turned out as he had predicted;* **vin·di·ca·tor** *n.;* **vin·di·ca·tion** (–CAY–) *n.* **—vin·dic·tive** (–DIC·tiv) *adj.* seeking vengeance; unforgiving: *~ feelings, acts, people;* **vin·dic·tive·ly** *adv.;* **vin·dic·tive·ness** *n.*

vine *n.* the grapevine; also, any plant with a flexible stem, as cucumbers that creep along the ground or an ivy that climbs trellises, etc. using tendrils. **—vin·e·gar** (VIN·uh·gur) *n.* a sour liquid used as a seasoning and preservative and made by fermentation and oxidation of fruit juices or other liquids containing sugar; **vin·e·gar·y** *adj.* **—vine·yard** (VIN·yurd) *n.* a grapevine plantation. **—vin rosé** same as ROSÉ. **—vi·nous** (VYE·nus) *adj.* of or having to do with wine: *~ liquids, disorders.* **—vin·tage** (–tij) *n.* **1** a grape harvest, esp. of a particular year or the wine made from it: *a wine label showing ~; of the ~ of 1955.* **2** a make (as of an automobile, costume, piano, etc.) with reference to its year or age: *of prewar ~; an early ~ camera.* **—*adj.*** superior in quality: *a ~ wine, crop; 1947 and 1955 were ~ years* (i.e. for vintage wines); *~ Americana; a ~* (i.e. old) *typewriter.* **—vint·ner** *n.* a wine maker or wine merchant. **—vi·nyl** (VYE·nl) *n.* a stiff, flexible plastic material used in making a wide range of products; **vinyl chloride** a cancer-producing chemical used in the manufacture of vinyl plastics.

vi·ol (VYE·ul) *n.* an early stringed instrument played with a bow that gave way to the violin family of instruments. **—vi·o·la** (vee·OH·luh) *n.* a stringed instrment of larger size and lower pitch than the violin.

vi·o·la·ble (VYE·uh·luh–) *adj.* capable of being violated; **vi·o·late** *v.* **-lates, -lat·ed, -lat·ing** go against or treat with contempt: *to ~ a law, agreement, sanctuary, the Sabbath; to ~ someone's privacy, rights; ~* (i.e. rape) *a woman;* **vi·o·la·tor** *n.;* **vi·o·la·tion** (–LAY–) *n.* a violating or being violated, as an infringement, disturbance of the peace, desecration, or rape. **—vi·o·lence** (VYE·uh·lunce) *n.* (use of) physical force that causes injury, damage, etc.: *a crime of ~; a strike marred by ~; the ~ of a hurricane; sex and ~ in TV shows; the ~ done to a text by a bad translation;* **vi·o·lent** *adj.* involving great, excessive, or unlawful force: *writhing in ~ pain; a ~ assault; a ~ death by murder, suicide, etc.; a ~ temper; a ~ attack using ~ language; colors in ~* (i.e. striking) *contrast;* **vi·o·lent·ly** *adv.*

vi·o·let (VYE·uh–) *n.* any of a large family of low-growing plants bearing five-petaled, typically bluish-purple flowers in early spring: *shy as a ~;* ***n.*** & ***adj.*** bluish-purple.

vi·o·lin (vye·uh·LIN) *n.* a four-stringed, high-pitched musical instrument played with a bow; **vi·o·lin·ist** (–LIN–) *n.* **—vi·ol·ist** *n.* **1** (VYE·uh–) a viol player. **2** (vee·OH–) a viola player. **—vi·o·lon·cel·lo** (vye·uh·lun·CHEL·oh, vee·uh–) *n.* same as CELLO; **vi·o·lon·cel·list** *n.*

V.I.P. *Informal.* very important person.

vi·per (VYE–) *n.* any of a family of poisonous snakes with fangs, including Old World adders and pit vipers. —**vi·per·ous** (–us) *adj.* of or like a viper; venomous; hence, spiteful or malicious; also **vi·per·ine.**

vi·ra·go (–RAY–, –RAH–) *n.* **-go(e)s** a scolding or overbearing woman.

vi·ral (VYE·rul) *adj.* of or caused by a virus: ~ *pneumonia, hepatitis.*

vir·e·o (VEER·ee·oh) *n.* **-os** a small, olive-green North American songbird.

Vir·gil (–jul) 70–19 B.C., the Roman poet who wrote the *Aeneid.*

vir·gin (–jin) *n.* one who has never had sexual intercourse, esp. a young woman; **the Virgin** mother of Jesus. —***adj.*** of or like a virgin, esp. in being pure, untouched, etc.: ~ *forests, soil, snow, modesty.* —**vir·gi·nal** (VUR·juh·nul) **1** *adj.* virgin: ~ *beauty, purity;* **vir·gi·nal·ly** *adv.* **2** *n.* a harpsichord with a rectangular case. —**Vir·gin·ia** (–JIN·yuh) a S. state of the U.S.; 40,817 sq. mi. (105,716 km²); *cap.* Richmond; **Vir·gin·ian** *n.* & *adj.* —**Virginia creeper** a North American woody vine with dark-blue berries and leaves that turn red in the fall. —**Virginia reel** an American reel danced by couples in double-line formation. —**Virgin Islands** a group of West Indian islands, half of which are controlled by the U.S. and the others by Britain. —**vir·gin·i·ty** (–JIN–) *n.* **-ties** the condition of a virgin; maidenhood; also, celibacy or spinsterhood. —**Virgin Mary** the mother of Jesus. —**Vir·go** the sixth sign of the zodiac and a constellation near the equator.

vir·gule (VIR·gyool) *n.* a diagonal line used as in 1/3, to separate alternatives as in "and/or," to mean *per* as in "km/h," etc.

vir·i·des·cent (–uh·DES–) *adj.* greenish or turning green.

vir·ile (VEER·ul) *adj.* manly in being robust, potent, etc.; **vi·ril·i·ty** (–RIL–) *n.*

vi·ri·on (VYE·ree·on) *n.* a fully-formed, matured virus. —**vi·rol·o·gy** (–ROL–) *n.* the study of viruses and virus diseases; **vi·rol·o·gist** *n.;* **vi·ro·log·i·cal** (–LOJ–) *adj.*

vir·tu (–TOO) *n.* a rare, curious, or skillfully done quality; also, art objects having such a quality or the taste for them. —**vir·tu·al** (VIR·choo·ul) *adj.* being such practically or in effect though not formally: *in ~ isolation; a ~ impossibility; the ~ boss; The* **virtual image** *behind a mirror is not real;* **vir·tu·al·ly** *adv.* —**vir·tue** (–choo) *n.* **1** moral excellence; also, a particular moral quality: "~ *is its own reward"; ~s and vices; a woman of easy ~* (i.e. chastity); *thought to* **make a virtue of necessity** *by fasting when he was being starved.* **2** power or efficacy; also, a particular quality or worth: *a wonder drug with little ~ in it; the ~s of dieting;* **in** (or **by**) **virtue of** because of; on the strength of. —**vir·tu·o·so** (–OH·soh) *n.* **-o·sos** or **-o·si** (–see) an artist with great technical skill; **vir·tu·os·i·ty** (–OS–) *n.* —**vir·tu·ous** (–us) *adj.* of or having moral virtue: *a ~ life; ~* (i.e. chaste) *women;* **vir·tu·ous·ly** *adv.;* **vir·tu·ous·ness** *n.*

vir·u·lent (VEER·yuh·lunt) *adj.* deadly or dangerous like poison: ~ *infection, disease, hatred, language;* **vir·u·lent·ly** *adv.;* **vir·u·lence** *n.* —**vi·rus** (VYE–) *n.* a microorganism that is smaller than bacteria, causing diseases such as influenza, measles, and chickenpox; also, any poisonous or harmful influence.

vi·sa (VEE·zuh) *n.* permission granted to enter or stay in a country, as endorsed on a passport; ***v.*** **-sas, -saed, -sa·ing:** *a ~d passport, tourist.* —**vis·age** (VIZ·ij) *n.* facial appearance or aspect; **vis·aged** (–ijd) *comb.form.* as in *grim-~, square-~, stern-~.* —**vis-a-vis** (vee·zuh·VEE) *prep.* considered in relation to; ***adj.*** & ***adv.*** face-to-face: *a ~ position; sat ~;* ***n.*** a vis-a-vis person or thing.

vis·cer·a (VIS·uh·ruh) *n.pl.* internal organs, esp. the intestines; **vis·cer·al** *adj.* of the viscera; also, instinctive or intuitive rather than intellectual: ~ *reactions;* **vis·cer·al·ly** *adv.*

vis·cid (VIS·id) *adj.* viscous or sticky: *a ~ secretion, leaf.* —**vis·cose** *n.* a viscous solution of cellulose from wood, cotton, etc. treated with chemicals, as in making rayon, cellophane, etc. —**vis·cos·i·ty** (–COS–) *n.* **-ties** the viscous quality of fluids that depends on molecular interaction and temperature: *motor oils of high and low ~s.*

vis·count (VYE–) *n.* a peer ranking below an earl or count and above a baron; *fem.* **vis·count·ess.**

vis·cous (–cus) *adj.* having a sticky or syrupy quality: *The more ~ a fluid the more slowly it flows, as pitch and molasses;* **vis·cous·ly** *adv.*

vis·cus *n. sing.* of VISCERA.

vise (VICE) *n.* a device for firmly holding an object being worked on, consisting of parallel jaws closed and opened by a screw with a handle.

vi·sé (VEE·zay) *n.* & *v.* **-sés, -séed, -sé·ing** same as VISA.

Vish·nu (–noo) the second member of the Hindu trinity, or "the Preserver" appearing in incarnations such as Rama and Krishna.

vis·i·bil·i·ty (–BIL–) *n.* **-ties** a being visible or its condition, degree, range, etc.: ~ *increases with height; poor ~ because of fog.* —**vis·i·ble** (VIZ–) *adj.* that can be seen; apparent: *the ~ spectrum; a vagrant with no ~ means of support; a highly ~* (i.e. conspicuous) *public figure;* **vis·i·bly** *adv.* —**vis·ion** (VIZH·un) *n.* **1** power of seeing or perceiving: *test your ~; the field of ~* (i.e. sight) *of an optical instrument; a man of great ~* (i.e. foresight or imagination); *poetic ~.* **2** something seen, esp. by the mind or imagination: *a ~ of heavenly glory; the beatific ~; The ~ raised its head;* ***v.*** see (as) in a vision; envision. —**vi·sion·ar·y** *n.* **-ar·ies** one who sees visions; hence, a dreamer or impractical person; ***adj.:*** *a ~ idea, scheme.* **—vis·it** (VIZ–) *v.* **1** go or come to see for pleasure; also, be a guest or stay with: *to ~ the zoo, Europe; ~ing (with) relatives; too much ~ing* (i.e. chatting) *on the phone.* **2** go or come to see officially or professionally, as a doctor, inspector, supervisor, etc. **3** inflict or afflict: *was ~ed with calamities; the sufferings God ~ed on Job.* ***—n.*** a visiting; also, a stay as a guest. **—vis·it·a·ble** *adj.* **—vis·i·tant** (–tunt) *n.* a visitor. **—vis·i·ta·tion** (–TAY–) *n.* **1** an official visit, esp. for inspection. **2** reward or punishment sent by God. **—visiting nurse** a nurse whose work is visiting patients in their homes and who takes part in public-health projects. **—vis·i·tor** *n.* one who visits on business or for pleasure, as a tourist. **—vi·sor** (VYE·zur) *n.* a part that shields the face or eyes, as the movable front part of a helmet, a cap's brim, or a shade attached to a windshield for protection from glare; **vi·sored** (–zurd) *adj.* **—vis·ta** *n.* a long narrow view as between rows of trees; hence, an extended or comprehensive mental view or prospect: *a discovery that opened up new ~s of knowledge.*

VISTA (VIS·tuh) Volunteers in Service to America, an antipoverty program administered by the U.S. government.

vis·u·al (VIZH·oo·ul) *adj.* having to do with seeing or sight: *~ impressions; ~ education using* **visual aids** *such as films, charts, and slides; painting, sculpture, ceramics, etc. as* **visual arts;** *the brain's ~ cortex* (i.e. seeing part); *20/20 vision means normal* **visual acuity;** *~ aphasia* (i.e. alexia) *of seeing without understanding words; a* **visual binary** *star that appears single to the unaided eye;* **vis·u·al·ly** *adv.* **—vis·u·al·ize** *v.* **-iz·es, -ized, -iz·ing** form a mental picture (of something abstract, forgotten, etc.); **vis·u·al·iz·er** *n.;* **vis·u·al·i·za·tion** (–ZAY–) *n.*

vi·ta (VEE·tuh, VYE–) *n., pl.* **-tae** (VEE·tye, VYE·tee) a brief biography or curriculum vitae. **—vi·tal** (VYE·tl) *adj.* **1** having to do with life; important for life: *Heart, liver, lungs, brain, etc. are ~ organs; a ~* (i.e. fatal) *wound; Temperature, pulse, and respiration are the* **vital signs;** *the lung's* **vital** (i.e. inhaling) **capacity;** *a ~* (i.e. lively) *personality.* **2** essential; very important: *one of the ~ issues of our times; ~ to the success of the mission.* **—vi·tal·ly** *adv.;* **vi·tal·i·ty** (–TAL–) *n.* **-ties** physical vigor; capacity to survive; also, mental vigor or energy; liveliness. **—vi·tal·ize** *v.* **-iz·es, -ized, -iz·ing** give life, vigor, or liveliness to; **vi·tal·iz·er** *n.;* **vi·tal·i·za·tion** (–ZAY–) *n.* **—vi·tals** *n.pl.* vital organs, parts, or elements. **—vital statistics** data about births, deaths, marriages, etc.; also, *Informal.* a woman's bust-waist-hip measurements. **—vi·ta·min** (VYE·tuh–) *n.* a complex organic substance essential to the body's health and growth which is supplied by foods and whose deficiency causes rickets, scurvy, and such diseases: *Vitamins include* **vitamin A** *essential for growth, resistance to infection, good vision, etc.;* **vitamin B** *a complex of more than 15 ~s including* **B_1** (thiamine), **B_2** (riboflavin), *niacin, and* **B_6** *and* **B_{12}** *needed for the nervous system, red blood cells, etc.;* **B_{17}** See LAETRILE; *Vitamin* **C** *essential for bones, teeth, tissues, healing processes, etc.;* **D** *needed to supply calcium and phosphorus, prevents rickets, and formed by the action of sunlight;* **E** *needed for heart and skeletal muscles, thought to help the reproductive system;* **K** *needed to prevent hemorrhaging by clotting of blood.*

vi·ti·ate (VISH·ee–) *v.* **-ates, -at·ed, -at·ing** make faulty, ineffective, etc.: *the original text ~d* (i.e. corrupted) *by corrections and changes; a technicality that ~d* (i.e. invalidated) *a legal document;* **vi·ti·a·tor** *n.;* **vi·ti·a·tion** (–AY–) *n.*

vit·i·cul·ture (VIT·uh–) *n.* cultivation of grapes; **vit·i·cul·tur·ist** (–CUL–) *n.*

vit·re·ous (VIT·ree·us) *adj.* of or like glass: *the ~ luster of a mineral; ~ rocks;* **vitreous humor** (or **body**) the transparent, jellylike substance filling the eyeball cavity behind the lens. **—vit·ri·fy** *v.* **-fies, -fied, -fy·ing** fuse into glass or glasslike condition by heat: *nonporous ~d ceramics; ~d bricks don't absorb water;* **vit·ri·fi·ca·tion** (–CAY–) *n.* **—vi·trine** (–TREEN) *n.* a glass-covered display case. **—vit·ri·ol** (–ree·ul) *n.* **1** a sulfate that has glassy crystals, as of copper, or **blue vitriol,** of iron, or **green vitriol,** and of zinc, or **white vitriol;** also, sulfuric acid. **2** sharp or bitter feelings, criticism, etc.; **vit·ri·ol·ic** (–OL–) *adj.*

vit·tles *n.pl. Regional.* victuals.

vi·tu·per·ate (vye·TUE–, vuh–) *v.* **-ates, -at·ed, -at·ing** abuse; revile; **vi·tu·per·a·tive** (–tiv) *adj.;* **vi·tu·per·a·tive·ly** *adv.;* **vi·tu·per·a·tor** *n.;* **vi·tu·per·a·tion** (–RAY–) *n.*

vi·va (VEE·vah) *interj. Italian.* long live (person specified)! **—vi·va·ce** (vee·VAH·chay) *adj.* & *adv. Music.* in a brisk, lively manner. **—vi·va·cious** (–VAY·shus) *adj.* lively and buoyant: *a ~ youth, girl;* **vi·va·cious·ly** *adv.;* **vi·va·cious·ness** *n.;* **vi·vac·i·ty** (–VAS–) *n.* **—vi·var·i·um** (–VAIR–) *n.* **-i·ums** or **-i·a** (–ee·uh) a glass-sided enclosure for keeping small pets. **—viva vo·ce** (VYE·vuh·VOH·see) *adj.* & *adv.* oral(ly): *a ~ examination; voted ~.* **—viv·id** *adj.* **1** lively: *a ~ description, imagination, personality.* **2** brilliant or brightly colored: *~ colors; a ~ blue.* **3** clear and distinct: *a ~ memory, recollection.* **—viv·id·ly** *adv.;* **viv·id·ness** *n.* **—viv·i·fy** *v.* **-fies, -fied, -fy·ing** impart energy or freshness to; also, give new vitality to; **viv·i·fi·er** *n.;* **viv·i·fi·ca·tion** (–CAY–) *n.* **—vi·vip·a·rous** (–VIP·uh·rus) *adj.* giving birth to living young, not oviparous or egg-laying: *Mammals, some snakes, and fishes such as the guppy are ~;* **viv·i·par·i·ty** (–PAIR–) *n.* **—viv·i·sec·tion** (–SEC–) *n.* dissection of a living animal for study; hence **viv·i·sect** (VIV–) *v.;* **viv·i·sec·tion·ist** (–SEC–) *n.*

vix·en (VIX·un) *n.* a female fox; also, an ill-tempered woman; **vix·en·ish** *adj.;* **vix·en·ish·ly** *adv.*

viz. namely; that is.

viz·ard (–urd) *n.* a mask or disguise.

vi·zi(e)r (vuh·ZEER) *n.* in some Moslem countries, a minister of state: *The "grand vizier" was a sultan's prime minister.*

viz·or (VYE·zur) *n.* same as VISOR.

VLF very low frequency.

V.O.A. Voice of America.

vocab. *Abbrev.* for **vo·cab·u·lar·y** (–CAB·yuh·ler·ee) *n.* **-lar·ies** **1** a list of words, as in a glossary: *A dictionary's* **vocabulary entries** *include words, affixes, abbreviations, phrasal entries, idioms, and inflections, as shown in boldface in this dictionary.* **2** the stock of words used by a person (his "active vocabulary") or only understood by him ("passive vocabulary"); also, the word-stock of a language, words used in a branch of learning, profession, etc.: *how to improve your ~; the expanding English ~; scientific ~; the ~* (i.e. movements) *of ballet.* **—vo·cal** (VOH·cl) *adj.* having (to do with) voice: *the ~ organs of the mouth and larynx; Glottis muscles vibrate two bands of tissue called* **vocal cords** *to produce sounds; ~* (i.e. sung, not instrumental) *music; Be ~* (i.e. outspoken) *about your grievances; Vowels are ~ sounds;* ***n.*** a vocal sound, as a vowel; also, a vocal solo; **vo·cal·ly** *adv.* **—vo·cal·ic** (–CAL–) *adj.* having to do with a vowel or vowels. **—vo·cal·ist** (VOH·cuh–) *n.* a singer, not an instrumentalist; **vo·cal·ize** *v.* **-iz·es, -ized, -iz·ing** use the voice or utter; speak, sing, or shout; **vo·cal·i·zer** *n.;* **vo·cal·i·za·tion** (–ZAY–) *n.* **—vo·ca·tion** (–CAY–) *n.* an occupation, profession, or trade in which one works; also, an occupation one is specially suited or called to: *Plan a career when choosing your ~; a ~ to religious life;* **vo·ca·tion·al** *adj.;* **vo·ca·tion·al·ism** *n.* **—voc·a·tive** (–uh·tiv) *n.* & *adj.* (a grammatical case) showing the person or thing directly spoken to, as in *"John,* come here!" **—vo·cif·er·ate** (voh·SIF–) *v.* **-ates, -at·ed, -at·ing** shout or utter loudly; **vo·cif·er·a·tion** (–RAY–) *n.;* **vo·cif·er·ous** (–SIF–) *adj.* noisy and unrestrained: *a ~ group; ~ in their demands;* **vo·cif·er·ous·ly** *adv.;* **vo·cif·er·ous·ness** *n.*

vod·ka (–kuh) *n.* an unflavored alcoholic liquor distilled from potatoes, rye, barley, etc.

vogue (VOHG) *n.* (something that is in) fashion or popularity at a particular time; also, the period of popularity: *when minis were in ~; "input," "interface," "phase out," and such* **vogue words** *of the electronic age;* **vogu·ish** *adj.*

voice *n.* **1** a sound communicating thoughts or feelings, esp. of a person speaking, crying, etc.: *The human ~ is highly developed; the larynx or* **voice box;** *has temporarily lost her ~ because of laryngitis; a singer not* **in voice** (i.e. in proper condition to sing) *till she is well; talks in a loud ~; listen to the ~ of conscience; the people's ~* (i.e. right to be heard) *in a democratic regime; a measure approved* **with one voice** (i.e. unanimously) *by the legislators.* **2** a singer, as in a choir, or the part of a musical composition for one singer or instrument. **3** the active or passive form of a verb. ***—v.*** **voic·es, voiced, voic·ing** give expression to in spoken or written form: *~d his strong disapproval;* **-voiced** *comb.form.* as in *soft-~, deep-~;* **voice·less** *adj.;* **voice·less·ly** *adv.;* **voice·less·ness** *n.* **—voice-o·ver** *n.* a narration or announcement without the speaker being shown, as in motion pictures. **—voice·print** *n.* pattern of sound waves characteristic of a person's voice, as recorded by a "sound spectrograph," used like the fingerprint for identification purposes.

void *n.* an empty space; hence, emptiness or a gap: *The death of a loved one leaves a ~ in our hearts.* ***—adj.*** **1** empty or vacant: *~ space; language that is* **void of** (i.e. devoid of) *meaning.* **2** legally invalid: *a ~ ballot, contract.* ***—v.*** make empty or void; also, empty out or evacuate (the bladder); **void·a·ble** *adj.;* **void·er** *n.*

voi·là (vwah·LAH) *interj. French.* behold! there!

voile (VOIL) *n.* a sheer fabric of plain weave used for veils, curtains, dresses, etc.

vol. volume; volunteer.

vol·a·tile (VOL·uh·tl) *adj.* easily changing into vapor at relatively low temperature, as gasoline or alcohol. **2** easily changeable in disposition or mood; fickle. **—vol·a·til·i·ty** (–TIL–) *n.;* **vol·a·til·ize** *v.* **-iz·es, -ized, -iz·ing** evaporate.

vol·can·ic (–CAN–) *adj.* of or like a volcano; hence, violent and explosive: *~ eruption, temperaments; crystalline* **volcanic rock** *formed by cooled lava;* **volcanic glass** *such as obsidian formed by rapid cooling of lava.* **—vol·ca·nism** (VOL·cuh–) *n.* volcanic phenomena including geysers and fumaroles. **—vol·ca·no** (–CAY–) *n.* **-no(e)s** (a cone-shaped mountain with) a funnel-shaped crater spewing lava, ashes, and gases; **vol·ca·nol·o·gy** (–NOL–) *n.* the science concerned with volcanic phenomena; **vol·ca·nol·o·gist** *n.*

vole *n.* a mouselike rodent found in fields and meadows.

Vol·ga (VOL·guh, VOLE–) a river of the western U.S.S.R. and the longest in Europe, flowing into the Caspian Sea.

vo·li·tion (–LISH·un) *n.* an act of the will or the power of willing; **vo·li·tion·al** *adj.;* **vol·i·tive** (VOL·uh·tiv) *adj.*

vol·ley (VOL·ee) *n.* **1** the simultaneous discharge of many weapons; hence, a shower of missiles: *a ~ of shots, oaths, cheers, questions.* **2** in tennis, etc., a return of the ball before it hits the playing surface. ***—v.*** **vol·leys, vol·leyed, vol·ley·ing** **1** discharge or be discharged as in a volley. **2** return (a ball or shuttlecock) before it hits the ground. —**vol·ley·ball** *n.* a team game played by hitting an inflated ball back and forth over a high net without letting it touch the ground; also, the ball.

vol·plane *v.* **-planes, -planed, -plan·ing** glide down, as in an airplane; ***n.*** such a glide.

volt (VOHLT) *n.* the MKS unit of electromotive force; **volt·age** (–ij) *n.* —**vol·ta·ic** (–TAY–) *adj.* having to do with electricity produced by chemical action: *the* **voltaic cells** *of an automobile battery.*

Vol·taire (–TAIR) 1694–1778, French philosopher and satirist.

volte-face (volt·FAHS) *n.* an about-face in policy, attitude, etc.

volt·me·ter (VOHLT·mee–) *n.* a voltage-measuring instrument.

vol·u·ble (VOL·yoo–) *adj.* talking much and unendingly; **vol·u·bly** *adv.;* **vol·u·bil·i·ty** (–BIL–) *n.* —**vol·ume** (VOL·yum) *n.* **1** cubic capacity or the solid content of something three-dimensional; hence, quantity: *~s of smoke; the daily ~ of output; turn down the ~* (of sound) *of the radio.* **2** a bound book; also, a book as one of a set or series: *a dictionary in two ~s;* **speak volumes** be very expressive. —**vol·u·met·ric** (–MET–) *adj.* involving measurement of volume: *~ analysis.* —**vo·lu·mi·nous** (–LOO·muh·nus) *adj.* large in content, output, size, etc.: *a ~ treatise, writer, output;* **vo·lu·mi·nous·ly** *adv.*

vol·un·ta·rism (VOL·un·tuh–) *n.* a system or theory of belief that stresses the role of the will over that of reason. —**vol·un·tar·y** *adj.* done of one's own free will or by choice: *the ~ contributions and services supporting a ~* (i.e. not state-supported) *church or school; Walking, talking, etc. are ~* (i.e. not reflex) *actions carried out by use of ~ muscles; went into ~ bankruptcy to be free of debts and start afresh.* —***n.*** solo organ music, as played at a church service; **vol·un·tar·i·ly** *adv.;* **vol·un·tar·y·ism** *n.* principle or system of running a church, school, or other service by voluntary contributions without state aid. —**vol·un·teer** (–TEER) *n.* a person who is in military service of his own free will; also, an unpaid worker; ***adj.:*** *a ~ fireman;* ***v.:*** *to ~ for the army; ~ed to help; ~ed her services as a social worker.*

vo·lup·tu·ar·y (–LUP·choo·er·ee) *n.* **-ar·ies** one who leads a luxurious and sensual life; **vo·lup·tu·ous** (–us) *adj.* having to do with sensual pleasure: *~ fancies, music; a ~* (i.e. sexy) *woman;* **vo·lup·tu·ous·ly** *adv.;* **vo·lup·tu·ous·ness** *n.*

vo·lute (–LOOT) *n.* something in spiral form or shape, as the scroll of an Ionic column or a marine snail with a spiral shell.

vom·it *v.* discharge with force from within, as the contents of the stomach through the mouth; throw up; ***n.*** what is vomited; also, a vomiting.

voo·doo (VOO–) *n.* **-doos** **1** sorcery as practiced by African tribes, including the cult of guardian spirits who possess devotees and the vicarious injuring of enemies by sticking pins into images of wax. **2** one who practices voodoo; also, a charm or fetish used in voodoo. —**voo·doo·ism** *n.* the religion or practice of voodoo.

vo·ra·cious (–RAY·shus) *adj.* devouring or insatiable: *a ~ appetite, shark, reader;* **vo·ra·cious·ly** *adv.;* **vo·ra·cious·ness** *n.;* **vo·rac·i·ty** (–RAS–) *n.*

vor·tex *n.* **-tex·es** or **-ti·ces** (–tuh·seez) **1** a whirling phenomenon or formation such as a whirlpool, whirlwind, or the eye of a cyclone. **2** a vortexlike situation or condition: *the ~ of war; sucked into the ~ of politics.* —**vor·ti·cal** *adj.*

vo·ta·ry (VOH·tuh–) *n.* **-ries** a devout worshiper or devoted follower; devotee: *a ~ of Zeus, peace, yoga.* —**vote** *n.* **1** a choice, as between candidates for office, or a formal expression of it, as by ballot. **2** a ballot; also, the right to vote. **3** a majority expression of feeling: *a ~ of thanks;* **vote of confidence** *in a government.* **4** votes collectively: *the Jewish ~.* —***v.*** **votes, vot·ed, vot·ing** **1** give a vote (to): *~d for the Republicans; ~s the Democratic ticket.* **2** decide, ratify, etc. by vote: *to ~ a candidate to the Senate; to* **vote in** *a candidate to office; to* **vote out** *an incumbent mayor; to* **vote down** *a bill in Congress instead of ~ing it through; The function was ~d* (i.e. adjudged) *a success.* —**vot·er** *n.* —**vo·tive** (VOH·tiv) *adj.* having to do with a vow: *a ~ pilgrimage, prayer, candle.*

vouch *v.* give a guarantee or serve as evidence (*for* the truth of a statement, someone's qualities, etc.); **vouch·er** *n.* one that vouches, esp. a document or other piece of evidence of a business transaction, as a canceled check, coupon, etc. —**vouch·safe** (–SAFE) *v.* **-safes, -safed, -saf·ing** grant as a special favor; deign (*to* do or give): *to ~ an answer to* (or *to answer*) *our prayers.*

vow *n.* & *v.* (make) a solemn promise, esp. to God: *to ~ obedience, secrecy, revenge; ~ed never to drink again; marriage ~s* (of fidelity); *A religious* **takes vows** (usu. of poverty, chastity, and obedience).

vow·el *n.* (a letter such as *a, e, i, o,* and *u* representing) a vocal sound made with more or less open mouth and no obstruction of breath as in forming consonants. —**vox po·pu·li** (–POP·yuh·lye) *Latin.* the voice of the people; public opinion.

voy·age (–ij) *n.* & *v.* **-ag·es, -aged, -ag·ing** (make) a relatively long journey by water, air, or in space: *an Atlantic ~; a ~ of exploration; a ~ to the moon; when the Vikings ~d across the ocean;* **voy·ag·er** *n.* —**vo·ya·geur** (vwah·yah·ZHUR) *n.* a French Canadian boatman, esp. one who worked for a fur-trading company.

vo·yeur (vwah·YUR) *n.* one who gets sexual pleasure from watching sex acts, etc., esp. from hiding; peeping Tom; **vo·yeur·ism** *n.;* **vo·yeur·is·tic** (–RIS–) *adj.*

V.P. Vice-President.

vroom *n.* the sound of a speeding sports car.

vs. versus; **v.s.** see above. —**vss.** verses; versions.

V/STOL vertical short takeoff and landing (aircraft).

VT or **Vt.** Vermont. —**v.t.** transitive verb.

VTOL vertical takeoff and landing (aircraft).

VTR videotape recorder.

Vul·can (VUL·kn) the Roman god of fire and metalworking; **vul·can·ism** same as VOLCANISM. —**vul·can·ite** *n.* a hard, vulcanized rubber. —**vul·can·ize** *v.* **-iz·es, -ized, -iz·ing** treat (crude rubber or similar material) with sulphur and heat to give it greater strength, elasticity, etc.; **vul·can·i·zer** *n.;* **vul·can·i·za·tion** (–ZAY–) *n.*

Vulg. Vulgate. —**vul·gar** (–gur) *adj.* **1** showing lack of refinement or good taste: *a ~ expression; ~ manners, display of wealth.* **2** of the common people or general public: *~ errors, superstitions; the ~ masses.* —**vul·gar·ly** *adv.* —**vul·gar·i·an** (–GAIR–) *n.* a vulgar person, esp. one who is rich. —**vul·gar·ism** *n.* a coarse or uneducated expression, as "irregardless"; also, vulgarity. —**vul·gar·i·ty** (–GAIR–) *n.* **-ties** the quality or condition of being vulgar; also, a vulgar or coarse action, habit, or usage. —**vul·gar·ize** *v.* **-iz·es, -ized, -iz·ing** make common, popular, etc.; hence, debase or degrade; **vul·gar·iz·er** *n.;* **vul·gar·i·za·tion** (–ZAY–) *n.* —**Vulgar Latin** the nonclassical Latin spoken by the common people of ancient Rome which gave rise to the modern Romance languages. —**Vul·gate** *n.* a Latin translation of the Bible used as the official text in the Roman Catholic Church; **vulgate** *n.* a popular text or version; also, vernacular speech.

vul·ner·a·ble (VUL·nuh·ruh–) *adj.* that can be wounded; also, open to attack: *The heel was Achilles' ~ spot; a ~ argument, position; ~ to* (i.e. affected by) *criticism, ridicule;* **vul·ner·a·bly** *adv.;* **vul·ner·a·bil·i·ty** (–BIL–) *n.*

vul·pine *adj.* of or like a fox; cunning or sly.

vul·ture (–chur) *n.* a large, carrion-eating bird of prey of a family that includes buzzards, condors, and Old World species of the hawk family; also, a greedy or ruthless person; **vul·tur·ous** *adj.*

vul·va (–vuh) *n., pl.* **-vae** (–vee) or **-vas** the external genital organ of the female including the labia and the vaginal opening; **vul·val** or **vul·var** *adj.*

v.v. vice versa.

vying *pres. part.* of VIE.

W

W or **w** (DUB·ul·yoo) *n.* **W's** or **w's** the 23rd letter of the English alphabet. —**W** tungsten; watt(s); west(ern); work. —**W.** or **w.** watt(s); west(ern); weight; width. —**w.** week(s); wide; wife; with. —**W.** Wales, Wednesday; Welsh.

WA Washington (state). —**W.A.** West Africa; Western Australia.

wab·ble (WOB·ul) *v.* **wab·bles, wab·bled, wab·bling** same as WOBBLE; **wab·bler** *n.*

Wac *n.* a member of the WAC; **WAC** Women's Army Corps.

wack·y *adj.* **wack·i·er, -i·est** *Slang.* eccentric or unconventional in behavior.

wad (WOD) *n.* a small lump of soft material: *a ~ of cotton to plug the ears; a ~ of chewing tobacco; a ~* (i.e. disk) *of felt used in a shotgun cartridge; a ~* (*Slang.* large bundle) *of money;* ***v.*** **wads, wad·ded, wad·ding** press or roll up into a wad; also, to plug with a wad or **wad·ding,** soft material.

wad·dle (WODL) *v.* **wad·dles, wad·dled, wad·dling** walk with short steps, swaying from side to side, as a duck or penguin; ***n.*** such a gait; **wad·dler** *n.* —**wade** *v.* **wades, wad·ed, wad·ing** **1** walk through a medium such as water, snow, or mud that hinders free movement; also, make one's way (*through* dull reading, etc.). **2** cross (a stream) by wading. **3 wade into** *Informal.* attack (a person, task, etc.) with vigor. —***n.*** a wading. —**wad·er** *n.* one that wades, as a **wading bird** (shore birds, cranes, etc. with long legs and bills adapted to probing the water for food); **waders** *pl.* a waterproof garment with attached boots, as used by anglers.

wa·di (WAH·dee) *n.* **-di(e)s** a watercourse or ravine, as in the Sahara and Arabian deserts, that is dry except in the rainy season.

Waf. *n.* a member of the **WAF,** or "Women in the Air Force."

wa·fer (WAY–) *n.* a thin, crisp cracker or cake, as used in the Eucharist; also, an adhesive seal or a disk of silicon carrying an integrated circuit.

waf·fle (WOF·ul) *n.* a batter cake made on a waffle iron. —***v.*** **waf·fles, waf·fled, waf·fling** be vague or indecisive. —**waffle iron** a metal utensil with two hinged plates between which a waffle is cooked.

waft *v.* move or carry lightly (as) by a breeze or wave; ***n.*** an odor or sound thus carried; also, a slight breeze or wafting movement.

wag *v.* **wags, wagged, wag·ging** shake or swing back and forth, up and down, etc., as a dog's tail: *A scandal makes tongues ~* (i.e. gossip). —***n.*** **1** a wagging. **2** a joker or jester; **wag·ger·y** *n.* **wag·ger·ies; wag·gish** *adj.*

wage *n.* periodic compensation paid for manual or physical work; also **wag·es** *pl.: Her ~s were $200 a week; the minimum ~* (rate) *fixed by government; inflationary ~ and price increases; "The ~s of sin is death"; the* **wage earners** *of a family.* —***v.*** **wag·es, waged, wag·ing** carry on (a war, battle, compaign, etc. with an adversary). —**wag·er** (WAY·jur) *n.* & *v.* bet; gamble.

wag·gle *n.* & *v.* **wag·gles, wag·gled, wag·gling** wag or shake; **wag·gly** *adj.*

Wag·ner (VAHG–), **Richard.** 1813–83, German composer; **Wag·ne·ri·an** (–NEER–) *n.* & *adj.*

wag·on (–un) *n.* a four-wheeled vehicle or cart for hauling loads; also, a *station wagon* or *patrol wagon;* **on the wagon** *Slang.* abstaining from alcoholic liquor; formerly, "on the water wagon"; **wag·on·er** *n.* —**wag·on·ette** (–NET) *n.* a four-wheeled carriage with two lengthwise seats facing each other. —**wag·on-lit** (vah·gawn·LEE) *n.* **-lits** (–LEE) a European railroad sleeping car. —**wagon train** a caravan of wagons on a journey.

wag·tail *n.* any of a group of Old World birds that wag their tails up and down.

wa·hi·ne (wah·HEE·nay, –nee) *n.* a Polynesian woman; also, a female surfer.

wa·hoo (WAH–) *n.* a large tropical food and game fish of the mackerel family.

waif *n.* a homeless or neglected child; also, a stray animal or something discarded.

wail *n.* & *v.* (make) a loud and long cry of grief, pain, or hunger: *the* **Wailing Wall** *of Jerusalem at which Jews pray and seek consolation;* **wail·ful** *adj.* sorrowful; plaintive; **wail·ful·ly** *adv.*

wain *n. Regional.* a large or heavy farm wagon. —**wain·scot** *n.* wood paneling on the interior wall of a room, esp. on its lower part; also, the lower part of an interior wall finished differently from the top; ***v.*** **-scots, -scot·ed, -scot·ing** line (a wall) with wood, or **wain·scot·(t)ing** *n.* —**wain·wright** *n.* one who builds wagons.

waist *n.* **1** the usu. narrow part of the abdomen just above the hips; also, a similar narrowed middle part of a violin, ship's deck between forecastle and quarterdeck, etc. **2** a bodice or blouse. —**waist·band** *n.* a band around the waist at the top of a skirt or trousers. —**waist·coat** *n. Brit.* a man's vest. —**waist·line** *n.* **1** the line of the waist or the measurement around it, as showing fatness. **2** the dividing line between the waist and skirt of a dress, usu. at the waist.

wait *v.* **1** stay expecting something; keep from moving or doing anything; continue in a place (*for* or *till* a specified time): *Please ~ for the next bus; ~ till noon; a matter so urgent it can't ~; used to* **wait up** *all night for her errant husband; had to ~* (*Informal.* delay) *dinner for a late arrival.* **2** await: *Join the line and ~ your turn.* **3** serve: *Waiters* **wait at** (or **on**) *tables; Waiters* **wait table;** *Store clerks* **wait (up)on** *customers.* ***—n.*** a waiting or its duration; **lie in wait for** stay concealed, ready to attack. —**wait·er** *n.* a man who serves customers seated at tables as in a restaurant; also, a salver or tray for food. —**wait·ing** *n.* act or period of waiting; **in waiting** in attendance. —**waiting game** the strategy of waiting till one has an advantage over the opposite side or party. —**waiting list** a list of people waiting to obtain something. —**waiting room** room in which people wait for a service. —**wait·ress** (–ris) *n.* a female waiter.

waive *v.* **waives, waived, waiv·ing** **1** give up (a right or claim); **waiv·er** *n.* a waiving or a document to that effect. **2** dispense with (a rule, formalities, etc.). **3** defer or dismiss.

wake *v.* **wakes,** *pt.* **woke** or **waked,** *pp.* **waked** or **wo·ken, wak·ing** awaken; also, rouse: *Please ~ me when you ~ up; Hibernating animals can ~ themselves up; were quick to ~ up to* (i.e. realize) *the possibility of danger.* ***—n.*** **1** a watch or vigil, as over a dead body before burial. **2** the track left in the water by a moving craft; **in the wake of** following; hence, as a consequence of. —**wake·ful** *adj.* sleepless or restless; also, watchful or alert; **wake·ful·ly** *adv.;* **wake·ful·ness** *n.* —**wak·en** (WAY·kun) *v.* to wake. —**wake-rob·in** *n.* same as TRILLIUM.

Wal·dorf (WALL–) **salad** a salad of diced apples, celery, nuts, and mayonnaise.

wale *n.* a ridge made on the skin by a stroke of a whip or stick; wheal; weal; also, a woven ridge on cloth such as corduroy; hence, texture; ***v.*** **wales, waled, wal·ing** mark (the skin) or weave (cloth, wickerwork, etc.) with wales.

Wales the land of the Welsh, a peninsula on the W. coast of Great Britain; 8,017 sq.mi. (20,764 km²); *cap.* Cardiff.

walk (WAWK) *v.* **1** go on foot without running; *She ~s to school; Don't ~ on the grass; The ghost may ~* (i.e. appear) *tonight; a lady ~ing* (i.e. taking out) *her dog; She ~s (through) the streets; ~ed* (i.e. accompanied) *his date home.* **2** conduct oneself: *to ~ in peace; ~ in the ways of the Lord.* **3** in baseball, receive a base on balls; also, give a base on balls to (a batter). ***—n.*** **1** a walking, as for exercise; stroll or hike; also, one's manner of walking: *You know him from his ~; an hour's ~* (i.e. walking distance). **2** a place for walking, as a path laid out in a park: *a letter carrier's ~* (i.e. route). **3** in baseball, a going to first base on four balls. —**walk off** (or **away**) **with** win easily; also, steal. —**walk out** go on strike or quit suddenly; **walk·out** *n.;* **walk out on** *Informal.* desert. —**walk·er** *n.* —**walk·a·way** (WAUK·uh–) *n.* an easy victory. —**walk·ie-talk·ie** *n.* a small, portable radio transmitter-receiver. —**walk-in** *n. Informal.* a sure win; ***adj.*** that may be walked into: *a large ~ safe, refrigerator, closet.* —**walking papers** *Informal.* dismissal from a job, etc.; **walking stick** a stick or cane used in walking. —**walk of life** calling or occupation. —**walk-on** *n.* (actor playing) a bit part that involves little speaking. —**walk-o·ver** *n. Informal.* an easy victory. —**walk·up** *n.* (an apartment in) a building without an elevator, usu. only a few stories high; ***adj.:*** *a ~ apartment.* —**walk·way** *n.* a passage for walking.

wall (WAWL) *n.* an upright enclosing, dividing, or protective structure of stone, wood, etc., as of a house; also, a side of a room or hollow structure: *the muscular ~ of the stomach;* **drive** (or **push**) **to the wall** put in an extreme or desperate situation. ***—v.:*** *to ~ in a garden; to ~ off a part of the house; to ~ up an unused fireplace;* **walled** *adj.*

wal·la·by (WOL·uh·bee) *n.* **-bies** any of various small kangaroos.

wall·board *n.* a large sheet molded of wood fiber, plaster and paper, or asbestos and cement for covering walls and ceilings.

wal·let (WOL·ut, WALL–) *n.* a pocketbook for carrying paper money, cards, etc.

wall·eye *n.* **1** a disorder in which one or both eyes are turned outward, showing much white. **2** a pike or pike perch with large eyes; also **wall·eyed pike.**

wall·flow·er *n. Informal.* a woman who is too shy or not attractive enough as a dancing partner.

Wal·loon (wah·LOON) *n.* a dialect of French spoken in S. Belgium; also, a Belgian of Celtic descent who speaks Walloon.

wal·lop (WOL·up) *n.* & *v. Informal.* (a very hard blow or the power) to hit very hard: *the* ~ (i.e. impact) *of a hard-hitting editorial; was* ~*ed* (i.e. trounced) *in the third round;* **wal·lop·ing** *n., adj.* & *adv.: was given a good* ~*; a* ~ *(big) lie.*

wal·low (WOL·oh) *v.* roll oneself about (in mud, as a hog, or in wealth, luxury, etc.); ***n.*** a wallowing or a place of mud or dust in which animals wallow.

wall·pa·per *n.* & *v.* (cover or paste with) colored decorative paper to put on walls. —**Wall Street** the financial center of the U.S.; the New York street and district with major banks, stock exchange, etc.; hence, U.S. financiers collectively.

wal·nut (WAWL–) *n.* a forest tree valued for its wood, esp. the "black walnut," and for its edible nuts; also, a nut or the dark brown wood.

wal·rus (WAWL–) *n.* a large seal-like mammal with two tusks growing downward from the mouth and feet flattened into flippers, valued for its blubber, hide, and ivory.

waltz (WAULTS) *n.* (music for) a gliding ballroom dance in 3/4 time; ***v.*** dance a waltz; also, move easily, nimbly, or successfully (*through* a place).

wam·ble (WOM·ul, WAM–, –bl) *v.* **-bles, -bled, -bling** **1** stagger or reel. **2** feel nausea.

wam·pum (WOM–) *n.* beads of shell often strung together, once used as money by North American Indians.

wan (WON, WAWN) *adj.* **wan·ner, wan·nest** pale or emaciated, as from illness: *a* ~ *expression, look;* **wan·ly** *adv.;* **wan·ness** *n.*

wand (WOND) *n.* **1** a slender rod, as used by a magician; baton; also, a staff of authority or scepter. **2** a tool or implement: *a* ~ *used in optical scanning of price tags; the cleaning* ~ (like a vacuum cleaner's) *that is moved back and forth over a surface.*

wan·der (WON·dur) *v.* move about in an aimless manner; also, stray or meander: *a* ~*ing tribe;* ~*ed from the path of virtue; a mind that* ~*s from one thing to another; the* ~*ing course of a river;* **wan·der·er** *n.;* **wandering Jew** a trailing plant with purplish striped leaves. —**wan·der·lust** *n.* the urge to travel or wander.

wane *v.* **wanes, waned, wan·ing** become smaller after reaching fullness, as the moon; hence, decline in intensity, power, influence, etc.; become weaker; ***n.*** the process or period of waning; **on the wane** waning or declining.

wan·gle (WANG·gl) *v.* **-gles, -gled, -gling** *Informal.* manage to get by influence, manipulation, persuasion, etc.; finagle.

Wan·kel (WAHNG·kl, WANG–) **engine** an internal-combustion engine that works in a continuous cycle using a rotor instead of a four-stroke piston and has fewer moving parts than the conventional automobile engine.

want (WONT, WAUNT) *v.* **1** desire or wish for (something worth having or necessary): *He* ~*s a new car; The child felt not* ~*ed by his parents; a murder suspect* ~*ed by police; The dog* ~*s out* (*Informal.* wants to get out). **2** lack; need; require: *The shirt* ~*s a button; "Waste not,* ~ *not"* (life's necessities); *A contented man* **wants for** *nothing.* —***n.:*** *Does advertising create* ~*s* (i.e. desires) *or help supply needs? an invention that supplies a long-felt* ~ (i.e. need); *a second-rate product for* ~ (i.e. lack) *of something better; state aid for people in* ~ (of food, shelter, clothing, etc.); **want ad** *Informal.* a brief advertisement for an employee, service, goods, etc. wanted by someone. —**want·ing** *adj.* lacking (in some essential): *Students found* **wanting in** *math are not promoted;* ***prep.*** lacking; also, minus.

wan·ton (WON·tun, WAUN–) *adj.* **1** lacking in restraint; frolicsome: *a* ~ *child;* ~ *winds; in* ~ *profusion; a* ~ (i.e. loose) *woman;* ~ (i.e. sensual) *thoughts.* **2** unprovoked; unjustified: *a* ~ *insult, attack;* ~ *damage, mischief;* ~ (i.e. merciless) *cruelty.* —***n.*** a morally loose person, esp. a woman; ***v.*** behave licentiously (*with* another); also, squander. —**wan·ton·ly** *adv.;* **wan·ton·ness** *n.*

wap·i·ti (WOP·uh·tee) *n.* the North American elk with many-pronged antlers and a whitish rump.

war (WORE) *n.* an open, armed, usu. prolonged conflict, as between nations; hence, any struggle; strife: *England* **at war** *with France; a national program of* ~ *on poverty; the art of* ~*; the strategy, tactics, and logistics of* ~*; won a few battles but lost the* ~*;* ***v.*** **wars, warred, war·ring** be in conflict; fight.

war·ble (WOR·bl) *v.* **-bles, -bled, -bling** sing (a song) with trills, quavers, etc., as a songbird, esp. a small, active, insect-eating **war·bler.** —***n.*** **1** a warbling (song or sound). **2** a painful swelling under an animal's skin, as caused by the larva of a **warble fly.**

war bonnet a ceremonial headdress of skin and feathers worn by American Indians. —**war bride** the bride of a soldier on active service during a war. —**war chest** a fund to support a political campaign, protracted strike, etc. —**war crime** a violation of international rules of warfare, as genocide, inhumane treatment of prisoners, etc. —**war cry** a slogan or rallying cry used in fighting for a cause.

-ward(s) *adj.* & *adv. suffix.* in the direction (specified): as in *backward(s), earthward, homeward, toward(s).* —**ward** (WORED) *v.* usu. **ward off,** turn aside (a blow, weapon, etc.) or keep away (danger, evil, enemies). —***n.*** **1** an administrative division of a municipality, prison, hospital, etc. **2** one under the care of a guardian or law court; hence, guardianship or custody.

war dance a dance performed by primitive tribes when preparing for war or to celebrate a victory.

war·den (WOR·dn) *n.* an administrative official in charge of a prison, one enforcing game laws ("game warden"), governing a school or hospital in the U.K., etc.; also, a churchwarden. —**ward·er** *n.* a watchman or guard. —**ward heeler** *Informal.* a heeler or hanger-on of a political boss in his constituency or ward. —**ward·robe** *n.* one's collection or stock of clothes; also, a cabinet or closet for clothes. —**ward·room** *n.* the eating and lounging place of commissioned officers on a warship. —**ward·ship** *n.* guardianship.

ware *n.* **1** usu. **wares** *pl.* manufactured articles for sale. **2** pottery. ***—comb.form.*** (specified) kind of goods: as in *hardware, ironware, tinware.* —**ware·house** *n.* & *v.* **-hous·es, -housed, -hous·ing** (store in) a building or room where goods for sale are kept; **ware·house·man** *n.* **-men.** —**ware·room** *n.* a room used for displaying goods for sale.

war·fare *n.* the waging of a war; struggle or conflict.

war·fa·rin (WOR·fuh–) *n.* an anticoagulant drug, also used as a rat poison.

war game a simulated military exercise for studying tactics.

war·head *n.* the explosive-containing front part of a torpedo or other missile. —**war·horse** *n. Informal.* a veteran of many wars or struggles; also, a hackneyed bit of theater, music, or ballet.

war·i·ly (WAIR–) *adv.* in a wary manner; **war·i·ness** *n.*

war·like *adj.* having to do with war; also, bellicose: *a ~ people, demonstration; ~ music, supplies.*

war·lock *n.* a sorcerer or wizard.

war·lord *n.* a military commander-in-chief with supreme power over a region, as in China between 1912 and 1928.

warm *adj.* **1** having or providing comfortable heat; not cold: *a ~ fire, room; a ~-air heating system; ~ clothing; ~ colors such as red, orange, and yellow.* **2** somewhat hot; heated: *a ~ discussion; ~ from running; a ~* (i.e. fresh) *scent; getting ~* (i.e. close to the object sought); *quit his job when they made it ~* (*Informal.* unpleasant) *for him.* **3** marked by sympathy and cordiality: *a ~ welcome, smile.* ***—v.*** make or become warm: *to ~ up a room;* **warm to** become more enthusiastic about (a subject, as one proceeds with it); **warm to(ward)** become friendly or sympathetic to (a person); **warm up** loosen one's muscles, etc. before a physical activity: *exercises for ~ing up before jogging.* —**warm·ish** *adj.;* **warm·ly** *adv.* —**warm-blood·ed** *adj.* having a body temperature that does not vary with the environment, as mammals and birds; not cold-blooded. —**warmed-o·ver** *adj.* of foods, stale but reheated; hence, not fresh or new. —**warm·heart·ed** *adj.* cordial; sympathetic; **warm·heart·ed·ness** *n.* —**warming pan** a long-handled covered pan containing hot coals used to warm beds.

war·mon·ger (–mung·gur, –mong–) *n.* one who likes to stir up wars; **war·mon·ger·ing** *n.* & *adj.*

warmth *n.* the quality or state of being warm. —**warm-up** *n.* **1** a warming up using exercises before starting a physical activity. **2** the idling of an engine till normal operating efficiency is reached.

warn *v.* give advance notice to (as if) against a danger or penalty: *young people ~ed of the risks of hitchhiking; were ~ed not to hitchhike; a sign to* **warn off** *trespassers.* —**warn·ing** *n.* & *adj.* (an act or thing) that warns; **warn·ing·ly** *adv.*

warp *v.* twist or bend out of shape, as a wooden board out of its plane when drying; hence, distort or deform: *Plywood doesn't ~ easily; a mind ~ed by prejudices.* ***—n.*** **1** a twist or distortion, as in a wooden board because of shrinkage. **2** the lengthwise threads, crossed by the woof or weft, in a woven fabric or loom.

war paint paint put on the face by American Indian warriors when on the warpath; **on the war·path** setting out for battle; ready to fight. —**war·plane** *n.* a military airplane, esp. one used in war.

war·rant (–unt) *n.* **1** official or legal authorization; also, justification or reasonable grounds: *acted without ~.* **2** a document such as a legal writ authorizing an arrest, search, etc.; also, a voucher for payment. **3** a certificate of appointment issued to a noncommissioned military officer, or **warrant officer.** —***v.*** **1** authorize; also, justify: *a conclusion that is ~ed by the evidence.* **2** guarantee or assure: *a diamond ~ed to be genuine; I'll ~ (you) he'll keep his word.* —**war·ran·ty** *n.* **-ties** a guarantee (*n.* 1).

war·ren (WAUR·un, WOR–) *n.* a system of burrows inhabited by rabbits; hence, a crowded tenement or slum area.

war·ri·or (WAUR·ee·ur, WOR–) *n.* a soldier or fighter experienced in battle.

War·saw capital of Poland.

war·ship *n.* a ship used in warfare, as a battleship, destroyer, submarine, etc.

wart (WORT) *n.* a small, hard growth on the skin, caused by a virus; also, a similar protuberance on a plant; **warts and all** exposing even blemishes; **wart·y** *adj.* —**wart hog** an African pig with pairs of wartlike bumps between its eyes and well-developed tusks.

war·time *n.* & *adj.* (having to do with) the duration of a war.

war·y (WAIR·ee) *adj.* **war·i·er, -i·est** careful or cautious, as if suspicious of danger or trouble: *a fox's ~ movements; keeping a ~ eye for muggers;* **wary of** cautious against; **war·i·ly** *adv.*

was (WOZ, WUZ, wuz) *1st and 3rd person sing. pt.* of BE.

Wash. Washington (state).

wash (WAUSH, WOSH) *v.* **1** clean with water or other liquid: *to ~ the dishes after dinner; He shaves and ~s* (i.e. himself) *in the morning; to* **wash up** (i.e. hands and face) *before dinner; a stain you can ~ out* (i.e. remove) *with soap and water; a fabric that ~es* (i.e. is cleaned, esp. without damage) *well in cold water; an excuse that won't ~* (*Informal.* is too weak). **2** wet, flow over, or cover with (a liquid): *a deck ~ed by waves; houses ~ed white outside.* **3** carry (by the action of waves, etc.): *driftwood ~ed ashore; a section of railroad ~ed away by the flood;* needed several drinks to **wash down** what he swallowed. ***—n.*** **1** a washing or being washed, as by waves. **2** what is (to be) washed, as laundry. **3** a piece of land sometimes covered by the sea; also, a dry river bed, as in a canyon. **4** a liquid for washing, as for the hair, mouth, or eyes; also, a thin coat of color or paint applied with long strokes. **5** a weak or watery liquid; liquid garbage; hogwash. **6** an eddy made in water or air by a moving craft. ***—adj.*** washable without damage: *a ~ dress.* **—wash·a·ble** *n. & adj.* (a fabric or garment) that may be washed without damage: *a ~ ink* (removable by washing). **—wash-and-wear** *adj.* needing little or no ironing after washing; durable-press. **—wash·ba·sin** or **wash·bowl** *n.* a bathroom fixture in which to wash one's face and hands. **—wash·board** *n.* a ridged board on which to scrub dirt out of clothes. **—wash·cloth** or **wash·rag** *n.* a piece of cloth used for washing one's face and body. **—wash drawing** a watercolor picture done in washes of black and gray. **—washed-out** *adj.* faded from washing; also, *Informal.* feeling or looking tired. **—washed-up** *adj. Informal.* exhausted; also, finished. **—wash·er** *n.* **1** one that washes, as a washing machine. **2** a flat disk of metal or rubber with a hole in it used with a nut or bolt to ensure tightness or prevent leakage. **—wash·er·wom·an** *n.* **-wom·en** a woman whose work is washing clothes; laundress. **—wash·house** *n.* a building in which clothes are washed. **—wash·ing** *n.* the act of washing, material obtained by washing, a thin coating of metal, or clothes washed or to be washed; **washing machine** a machine for washing clothes. **—washing soda** sodium carbonate used in washing and bleaching.

Wash·ing·ton **1 George.** 1732–99, 1st U.S. President (1789–97). **2** a N.W. state of the U.S.; 68,192 sq.mi. (176,616 km²); *cap.* Olympia. **3** capital of the U.S., forming the District of Columbia. **—Wash·ing·to·ni·an** (–TOH–) *n. & adj.*

wash·out *n.* **1** the washing away of earth by flowing water. **2** *Slang.* a failure. **—wash·room** *n.* a room with washing and toilet facilities. **—wash·stand** *n.* a stand or table on which a washbowl is set. **—wash·tub** *n.* a tub for soaking and washing clothes; also called "laundry tub." **—wash·wom·an** *n.* same as WASHERWOMAN. **—wash·y** *adj.* **wash·i·er, -i·est** **1** of liquids, watery or weak. **2** of colors, pale. **3** lacking in vigor; feeble.

was·n't (WUZ·nt, WOZ–) was not.

WASP or **Wasp** (WOSP, WAUSP) *n.* a white Anglo-Saxon Protestant, as a member of the most privileged class in an English-speaking country; **Wasp·ish** *adj.*

wasp (WOSP, WAUSP) *n.* a slender-bodied, winged stinging insect related to the bees and ants; **wasp·ish** *adj.* **1** snappish or irritable. **2** of or like a wasp, esp. in build; **wasp waist** a slender waist.

was·sail (WOSL, WOS·ail) *n.* a toast to someone's health formerly used in England; also, a liquor drunk on joyous occasions; hence, a drinking party; revelry; ***v.*** drink a wassail to (someone); also, carouse; **was·sail·er** *n.*

Was·ser·mann (WOS·ur·mun) **test** a blood test for syphilis.

wast (WOST) *Archaic.* the form of WERE used with *thou.*

wast·age (WAIS·tij) *n.* loss by use, leakage, decay, etc.; also, the amount wasted. **—waste** *v.* **wastes, wast·ed, wast·ing** **1** spend or be spent uselessly: *to ~ time, money, energy; to ~* (i.e. not use) *an opportunity; Water is ~ing* (from the leaking faucet). **2** wear down gradually: *Tuberculosis is a ~ing disease; Starving people ~ away.* **3** ravage; day waste. ***—n.*** **1** a wasting or something wasted: *a mere ~ of time; body ~s;* **go to waste** be wasted. **2** an unused expanse of water, snow-covered land, desert, etc. **3** a gradual wearing down, as of bodily tissue: *the processes of ~ and repair.* **4** a bunch of cotton or wool material used for cleaning, wiping, etc. ***—adj.*** **1** discarded as useless or unused: *~ matter, water, energy;* **waste pipe** for carrying off waste water, etc. **2** desolate; ruined: ~ land; **lay waste** devastate. **—waste·ful** *adj.;* **waste·ful·ly** *adv.;* **waste·ful·ness** *n.;* **wast·er** *n.* **—waste·bas·ket** *n.* a basket or other receptacle for wastepaper. **—waste·land** *n.* barren land; hence, unproductive effort. **—waste·pa·per** *n.* useless or discarded paper; also **waste paper.** **—waste product** a useless by-product of a manufacturing or bodily process.

wast·rel (WAY·strul) *n.* a spendthrift; also, a good-for-nothing.

watch *v.* **1** follow (a person or thing) with one's eyes; look at or observe steadily: *to ~ a game; a suspect being ~ed by police; was beaten up while everyone ~ed* (i.e. looked on); *He's ~ing* (i.e. waiting) *(for) a chance to pop the question;* **watch it** *Informal.* be careful; **watch out** *Informal.* be on one's guard; also **watch oneself.** **2** stay awake or alert: *a mother ~ing at a sick child's bedside.* ***—n.*** **1** a timepiece to carry on one's person, as a wristwatch, stopwatch, etc. **2** a state or attitude of attention: *Keep ~ over my house; Be* **on the watch** *for prowlers.* **3** a guard or his period of duty: *the night ~.*

4 a usu. four-hour period of duty on shipboard; also, the crew on duty during such a period. —**watch·band** *n.* the band or bracelet of a wristwatch. —**watch·case** *n.* the metal covering of the works of a watch. —**watch·dog** *n.* a dog kept to guard property; hence, a guardian. —**watch·ful** *adj.* keeping careful guard; vigilant; **watch·ful·ly** *adv.;* **watch·ful·ness** *n.* —**watch·mak·er** *n.* one who makes or repairs watches; **watch·mak·ing** *n.* —**watch·man** (–mun) *n.* **-men** one who keeps watch over property, esp. at night. —**watch night** a New Year's eve service held at midnight in some churches. —**watch·tow·er** *n.* a lookout tower. —**watch·word** *n.* **1** a guiding principle as embodied in a motto or slogan. **2** a secret password.

wa·ter (WAU–, WOT–) *n.* **1** the colorless, odorless, tasteless, and transparent liquid that falls as rain and fills lakes, rivers, etc.; also, a waterlike substance or product such as tears, urine, saliva, *soda water, rose water,* etc. **2** a body of water such as a sea or lake; also, the state of the tide: *at high ~; low ~;* **waters** *pl.* flowing or moving water: *territorial ~s; taking the* (mineral) *~s at a spa.* **3** the degree of transparency and brilliance of a precious stone; also, the wavy, lustrous finish given to silk, linen, metal surfaces, etc.; **of the first** (or **purest**) **water** of the highest degree of perfection; **hold water** of a theory, argument, etc., prove sound. —***v.*** **1** supply with water: *to ~ a lawn; to ~ cattle; land ~ed by rivers; ~ed* (i.e. diluted) *wine, milk, soup;* **water down** weaken. **2** drink or take in water: *cattle ~ing at a stream; a ship docked for ~ing.* **3** give out water or a waterlike substance: *Mouths ~ in the presence of food; Her eyes ~ed from the wind.* —***adj.:*** *Ocean birds are ~ birds; a ~ heater; ~ pressure, safety, supplies, vapor.* —**water ballet** dancelike synchronized swimming. —**Water Bearer** same as AQUARIUS. —**water bed** a bed with a water-filled mattress. —**wa·ter·borne** *adj.* carried by water: *~ cargo, diseases.* —**water buffalo** See BUFFALO. —**Wa·ter·bur·y** a city of Connecticut. —**water chestnut** **1** a European water plant with nutlike fruits. **2** a Chinese sedge with an edible tuber. —**water closet** a toilet or lavatory. —**wa·ter·col·or** *n.* a pigment that is mixed with water for painting; also, a painting done with watercolors. —**wa·ter·cooled** *adj.* cooled by circulating water, as an engine. —**water cooler** a machine that dispenses cold drinking water, as used in offices. —**wa·ter·course** *n.* a stream, river, or artificial channel; also, its bed. —**wa·ter·craft** *n. sing.* & *pl.* a ship, boat, or similar craft for transport on or in water. —**wa·ter·cress** *n.* a water plant whose leaves are used in salads, etc. —**wa·ter·fall** *n.* a stream flowing down a height; cascade. —**water flea** a tiny freshwater shellfish with a transparent body and flealike hopping movement. —**wa·ter·fowl** *n.* a water bird such as the duck, grebe, loon, or shearwater; **waterfowl** *pl.* swimming game birds. —**wa·ter·front** *n.* the section of a city fronting on a body of water; harbor area. —**water gap** a narrow gorge cut by a river through a mountain ridge. —**water gas** a fuel gas manufactured by passing steam over hot coke. —**Wa·ter·gate** *n.* a political scandal involving high government officials acting criminally, as the burglary of U.S. Democratic Party headquarters in 1972 that led to the resignation of President Nixon. —**water glass** **1** a drinking glass. **2** a water-soluble compound of silicon, sodium, and oxygen used in fireproofing, waterproofing, and as an adhesive. —**water hole** a small pond or pool. —**watering place** **1** a place at which animals drink from a river, lake, etc. **2** a spa with mineral springs. —**wa·ter·lil·y** *n.* **-lil·ies** a plant related to the lotus bearing large white or pink flowers and leaves that float on the surface of the water; also called "pond lily." —**wa·ter·line** *n.* the varying line along which the water surface touches the side of a ship or boat, depending on the load it is carrying. —**wa·ter·logged** *adj.* filled or soaked with water, as a boat or fields; hence, bogged down. —**Wa·ter·loo** a Belgian town and the site of the battle in which Napoleon was finally defeated in 1815; ***n.*** a crushing defeat. —**water main** a large pipe carrying water. —**wa·ter·mark** *n.* an identifying design impressed on paper during manufacturing that is visible only when held against light; ***v.*** mark (paper) with a watermark. —**wa·ter·mel·on** (–un) *n.* a large green melon with a delicious red or yellow pulp. —**water moccasin** a large, venomous water snake of the southern U.S. —**water ou·zel** (–OO·zul) a small, thrushlike bird of W. North America that dives under water for insects; also called "dipper." —**water pipe** **1** a hookah. **2** a pipe carrying water. —**water polo** a team game played in a swimming pool using a large inflated ball. —**water power** the power of moving water used to drive machinery. —**wa·ter·proof** *adj.* that will not let water through, as coats, hats, etc. treated with rubber; ***v.*** make waterproof; ***n.*** a waterproof material or raincoat; **wa·ter·proof·ing** *n.* —**wa·ter-re·pel·lent** *adj.* that repels water though not waterproof; also **wa·ter-re·sist·ant.** —**wa·ter·shed** *n.* **1** a dividing ridge between two areas drained by different river systems; hence, a turning point. **2** river basin. —**wa·ter·side** *n.* the shore of a river, lake, sea, etc. —**wa·ter-ski** *v.* **-skis, -skied, -ski·ing** glide over water towed by a speedboat, wearing **wa·ter·skis** that are similar to, though wider than, snow skis. —**wa·ter·spout** *n.* **1** a tornado over the ocean. **2** something that spouts water, as a pipe that drains water from a roof. —**water strider** an insect seen on ponds and streams gliding about on the water surface on long spiderlike legs. **—water table** the level of underground water, as seen in a well. **—wa·ter·tight** *adj.* **1** so tight as not to let in or let out water: *a ship's ~ compartments.* **2** having no loopholes or flaws: *a ~ argument, contract, plan.* **—wa·ter·way** *n.* a navigable river, canal, etc. **—wa·ter·wheel** (–hweel) *n.* a wheel, as of a mill, that is turned by flowing water. **—water wings** two air-filled bags worn on the shoulders to keep one afloat when learning to swim. **—wa·ter·works** *n.pl.* the system of reservoirs, pipes, pumps, etc. for supplying a town with water. **—wa·ter·y** *adj.* **1** of, like, or full of water: *~ clouds, eyes, soil: a ~ discharge; a ~ grave under the ocean.* **2** diluted; hence, weak: *a ~ soup; a ~ color;* **wa·ter·i·ness** *n.*

WATS (WOTS) Wide Area Telephone Service.

watt (WOT) *n.* the MKS unit of electrical power; **watt·age** (–ij) *n.*

wat·tle (WOTL) *n.* **1** a woven material of rods intertwined with twigs, used for walls, fences, and roofs. **2** an Australian acacia tree or shrub. **3** the fleshy fold of skin hanging from the throat of a turkey, chicken, etc. **—wat·tled** *adj.* **1** made of wattle (*n.* 1). **2** having wattles, as a bird.

Wave *n.* a member of the **WAVES,** the women's branch of the U.S. Navy.

wave *n.* **1** a moving ridge of water as on the sea, that swells and breaks on the shore; hence, any similar movement: *invaders attacking in ~s; a ~* (i.e. surge) *of enthusiasm; a heat ~;* **make waves** *Informal.* disturb the prevailing state of affairs. **2** an up-and-down motion or undulation: *natural ~s in hair; a permanent ~; a ~ of the hand, flag; Sound travels in ~s.* **—*v.* waves, waved, wav·ing:** *corn ~ing in the wind; people ~ing flags; They ~d to us* (i.e. greeted us) *from the balcony; All objections were ~d aside* (i.e. dismissed). **—wave band** a range of radio-wave frequencies. **—wave·length** *n.* the distance between the crests or troughs of a wave in its line of advance: *a secretary* **on the same wavelength** *as* (i.e. in harmony with) *her boss.* **—wave·let** *n.* a ripple or little wave. **—wa·ver** (WAY–) *v.* **1** hesitate after making a decision or seem to want to go back on it: *never ~s in his resolution, promises; to ~ between two courses.* **2** move to and fro; become unsteady: *a ~ing flame, voice.* **—*n.*** a wavering. **—wa·ver·er** *n.* **—wa·ver·ing·ly** *adv.* **—wav·y** (WAY·vee) *adj.* **wav·i·er, -i·est** moving in or having waves: *~ hair, line, seas;* **wav·i·ness** *n.*

wax *n.* a fatty plastic substance, as made by bees for their cells, distilled from petroleum, etc. and applied to furniture surfaces and floors for protection and polish. **—*v.*** **1** rub or treat with wax. **2** become or grow (as specified): *She ~ed eloquent about her child's accomplishments; The moon ~es* (i.e. grows bigger) *from new moon to full moon before waning.* **—wax bean** a variety of string bean with yellow pods. **—wax·en** *adj.* made of wax; also, like wax in smoothness. **—wax museum** a museum of waxworks. **—wax myrtle** an ornamental evergreen shrub of eastern U.S. with berries that yield a wax used for candles. **—wax paper** a kind of wax-coated, moisture-proof paper. **—wax·wing** *n.* a small crested bird with a yellow band across the end of its tail and waxy shiny red beads on its wings. **—wax·work** *n.* a figure made of wax; **wax·works** *n.pl.* [with *sing. v.*] an exhibition of such figures. **—wax·y** *adj.* **wax·i·er, -i·est** like wax, pale yellow, soft and pliable, or shiny; **wax·i·ness** *n.*

way *n.* **1** a road or route for getting from one place to another: *the ~ home; lost our ~ in the woods; Please lead the ~; She went that ~* (i.e. direction); *our neighbors living across the ~* (i.e. street); *out our ~* (i.e. in our neighborhood); *It's a long ~* (i.e. distance) *off; quite a* **ways** (*Nonstandard.* distance) *from here.* **2** manner or mode of doing something: *"Where there's a will there's a ~"; the right ~ to use your knife and fork; so willful he wants his own ~ all the time; the ~ she goes about her duties; Let's do it the democratic ~; In some ~s* (i.e. respects) *yours is a better plan; The patient is in a bad ~* (i.e. condition). **3** **ways** *pl.* structures to support a ship under construction. **—*adv.*** *Informal.* far: *~ back in the 1920's; ~ out in the woods.* **—by the way** during a journey; hence, incidentally. **—by way of** through; also, for the purpose of: *told it by ~ of example.* **—give way** yield; also, collapse or fail: *The dam gave ~.* **—go out of one's way** make a special effort (*to* do something); **make way** clear the way (*for* another person). **—out of the way** unusual or strange: *saw nothing out of the ~; an out-of-the-way experience.* **—under way** in motion; hence, in progress. **—way·bill** *n.* a list of goods being shipped, showing the route, charges, etc. **—way·far·er** (–fair–) *n.* a traveler, esp. one going on foot; **way·far·ing** *n.* & *adj.* **—way·lay** (–LAY) *v.* **-lays, -laid, -lay·ing** lie in wait for and attack; also, stop (someone) on his way. **—way-out** *adj. Informal.* far-out. **—-ways** *adv. suffix.* in the (specified) way: as in *endways, lengthways, sideways.* **—ways and means** methods and resources for achieving an end, esp. for raising revenue; also, a committee for this. **—way·side** *n.* the side of a road or path. **—way station** a station between main stations on a railroad or bus route. **—way·ward** (–wurd) *adj.* willful or disobedient; also, erratic or freakish; **way·ward·ly** *adv.;* **way·ward·ness** *n.* **—way·worn** *adj.* wearied by travel.

W.C. water closet; without charge.

W.C.T.U. Women's Christian Temperance Union.

we (WEE) *pron., pl.* of I; *objective* US, *possessive* OUR(s) **1** the first person plural of I; a group that includes the speaker. **2** a sovereign or other person speaking as the representative of a group; also, this use: *the royal ~; editorial ~.*

weak (WEEK) *adj.* lacking in physical, mental, or moral strength; not strong: *~ muscles, health, character, arguments; a student who is ~ in math; a ~ verb inflected by adding "-ed" for past tense and past participle;* **weak·en** *v.* make or become weak(er); **weak·en·er** *n.* —**weak·fish** *n.* a food fish with an easily torn mouth found along the E. and Gulf coasts of the U.S. —**weak-kneed** *adj.* lacking in courage or the ability to stand firm and resolute. —**weak·ling** *n.* one that lacks physical or moral strength. —**weak·ly** *adj.* **-li·er, -li·est** feeble or weak; ***adv.*** in a weak manner. —**weak·ness** *n.* **1** lack of strength; also, a weak point or defect. **2** fondness or liking that is considered a sign of being weak: *a ~ for cigars; Cigars are his ~* (i.e. weak point).

weal (WEEL) *n.* **1** same as WALE. **2** well-being; prosperity: *the public ~; in ~ and woe.*

weald (WEELD) *n.* a wooded area, as **the Weald** of England that includes Sussex, Kent, and Surrey.

wealth (WELTH) *n.* **1** abundance of money, property, etc.; hence, abundance: *a ~ of detail, words, imagery.* **2** material goods and resources that have money value. —**wealth·y** *adj.* **wealth·i·er, -i·est** rich in material resources: *a ~ family;* **wealth·i·ness** *n.*

wean (WEEN) *v.* accustom (an infant, young animal, etc.) to food other than its mother's milk; hence, withdraw (a person) *from* a habit, company, occupation, etc.; **weaned on** raised or trained on: *But Jones, ~d on stickball, grew up to be a baseball player.*

weap·on (WEP·un) *n.* any instrument used for fighting, as an arrow, sword, gun, club, etc.; hence, anything used as a means of defense or attack; **weap·on·ry** (–ree) *n.* weapons collectively; also, their design and production.

wear (WAIR) *v.* **wears, wore, worn, wear·ing** **1** have on one's person or show in one's appearance: *to ~ clothes, perfume, jewelry, weapons, a beard, a smile.* **2** make (a hole, path, etc.) or become (damaged) by use: *shoes worn at the heels; an excuse that has worn thin.* **3** last or endure (*well, badly,* etc. as specified). **4** pass or go gradually: *as the years wore on* (or *away*); *when the effects of the drug* **wear off.** **5** tire or exhaust: *a face worn with care; They* **wear out** *her patience; to* **wear down** *her resistance.* —***n.*** **1** a wearing or being worn. **2** clothes: *children's ~.* **3** damage from use: *The shoes show ~.* **4** wearing capacity: *a lot of ~ still left in those shoes.* —**wear·a·ble** *adj.;* **wear·er** *n.* —**wear and tear** normal loss or damage from use.

wea·ri·some (WEER·ee·sum) *adj.* causing weariness; tiresome; **wea·ri·some·ly** *adv.;* **wea·ri·some·ness** *n.* —**wea·ry** (WEER·ee) *adj.* **-ri·er, -ri·est** **1** worn out; exhausted: *feet ~ with walking; grown ~ of city life.* **2** showing tiredness: *a ~ sigh.* **3** causing tiredness: *a ~ climb.* —***v.*** **-ries, -ried, -ry·ing** make or become weary; tire; **wea·ri·ly** *adv.;* **wea·ri·ness** *n.*

wea·sand (WEE·znd) *n. Archaic.* windpipe.

wea·sel (WEE·zl) *n.* a small, furry, short-legged, flesh-eating animal with an agile and slender body; ***v.*** be evasive or misleading; **weasel word** an evasive or meaningless expression, like an egg sucked out by a weasel but left outwardly intact; **wea·sel·ly** *adj.*

weath·er (WEDH·ur) *n.* the condition of the atmosphere in regard to temperature, precipitation, cloudiness, winds, etc.: *fine ~; flew into ~* (i.e. stormy conditions) *over Bermuda;* **under the weather** *Informal.* out of sorts; ill. —***adj.*** windward: *on the ~ side.* —***v.*** **1** expose to the action of weather: *Soil results from the ~ing of rocks.* **2** become changed in color or worn by exposure to the weather. **3** pass through (a storm, etc.) safely. **4** sail to the windward of (a cape, etc.). —**weath·er·a·bil·i·ty** (–BIL–) *n.* resistance to weathering. —**weath·er-beat·en** *adj.* seasoned, hardened, etc. by exposure to the weather: *a ~ sailor, face.* —**weath·er·board** *n.* & *v.* same as CLAPBOARD; **weath·er·board·ing** *n.* clapboards. —**weath·er-bound** *adj.* staying indoors, unable to proceed, etc. because of bad weather. —**weath·er·cock** *n.* a weather vane with the figure of a cock on top; hence, one that is inconstant or changeable. —**weather eye** alertness to signs of change: *The police are* **keeping a weather eye** (i.e. close watch) **on** (or **open for** or **out for**) *the escapees.* —**weath·er·glass** *n.* a barometer. —**weath·er·ing** *n.* the gradual breaking down of rocks by the action of wind, rain, heat and cold, bacteria, etc. —**weath·er·ize** *v.* **-iz·es, -ized, -iz·ing** insulate so as to keep out the cold and save heating fuel. —**weath·er·man** *n.* **-men** one who reports on weather conditions, as in a news broadcast. —**weath·er·proof** *adj.* able to withstand exposure to the weather without damage; ***v.*** make weatherproof. —**weath·er·strip** *v.* **-strips, -stripped, -strip·ping** fit or seal with weatherstripping. —**weath·er·strip(·ping)** *n.* material such as strips of metal, wood, or felt for sealing the gaps around doors and windows to keep out drafts. —**weather vane** a device with an arrow on top that turns freely to point in the direction from which the wind is blowing. —**weath·er-wise** *adj.* skilled in predicting changes in the weather, public opinion, etc. —**weath·er·worn** *adj.* weather-beaten.

weave (WEEV) *v.* **weaves,** *pt.* **wove** (WOHV) or **weaved,** *pp.* **wo·ven** (WOH–) or **wove, weav·ing** **1** interlace (threads, strips, etc.) *into* a fabric or an article such as a basket or hat; hence, make (a fabric, hat, web, etc.) *from* threads, straw, or wicker: *She ~s* (i.e. cloth) *on a loom; to ~ a wreath of flowers.* **2** construct (a story, poem, musical composition, etc.) as if by weaving, *from* strands of plot, melody, etc.; also, weave (plots, melodies, etc.) *into* a story or composition. **3** *pt.* usu. **weaved,** make one's way *through* or drive (a car, etc.) in and out of traffic: *changing lanes to ~ through traffic.* **—n.** a form or pattern of weaving, as plain, twill, and satin. **—weav·er** *n.* **—web** *n.* **1** something woven, esp. the network spun by a spider; also, any network: *a ~ of lies, intrigue, railroads; the ~ of life seen in nature by the interdependence of humans, animals, and plants.* **2** connecting material or tissue, as the membrane joining the toes of swimming birds. **3** a large reel of newsprint, as used on a rotary "web-press." **—v. webs, webbed, web·bing** join by a web; also, ensnare or trap, as in a web; **webbed** *adj.* ; **web·bing** *n.* a tough fabric woven in tape form for use in upholstery, belts, etc. **—web·foot** *n., pl.* **-feet** a foot with webbed toes; **web-foot·ed** or **web·toed** *adj.*

Web·ster **1 Daniel.** 1782–1852, American statesman and orator. **2 Noah.** 1758–1843, American lexicographer.

Wed. Wednesday. **—we'd** (WEED) we had; we should; we would. **—wed** *v.* **weds,** *pt.* **wed·ded,** *pp.* **wed·ded** or **wed, wed·ding** give, take, or join in marriage; also, unite closely, firmly, intimately, etc.: *~ed bliss;* **wedded to** devoted to (an occupation, opinion, etc.). **—wed·ding** *n.* a marriage ceremony and festivities; also, a marriage anniversary: *silver ~.*

wedge (WEJ) *n.* a piece of wood, metal, etc. tapering to a thin edge, used for splitting wood, raising weights, etc.; also, something wedge-shaped, as a triangular piece of pie; **v. wedg·es, wedged, wedg·ing:** *to ~* (i.e. split) *open a log; to ~ up* (i.e. chock) *a tipping cabinet; to ~* (i.e. squeeze) *one's way into a car; was ~d in* (i.e. stuck) *between two people in the crowded bus.*

wed·lock *n.* the state of being married; matrimony.

Wednes·day (WENZ·dee) *n.* the fourth day of the week.

wee *adj.* **we·er, we·est** very small or tiny: *the ~* (i.e. very early) *hours of the morning.*

weed *n.* **1** a plant of no value or one that is harmful, esp. when growing in a cultivated field: *a noxious ~;* **the weed** *Informal.* tobacco; **v.** take weeds out (of): *to* **weed out** *troublesome elements; to ~ out a herd to improve the breed;* **weed·er** *n.* **2 weeds** *pl.* mourning garments, as of a widow. **—weed·y** *adj.* **weed·i·er, -i·est** **1** full of weeds, as a garden. **2** rank in growth like weeds. **3** lanky or scrawny.

week *n.* **1** seven successive days, esp. the calendar period from Sunday through Saturday. **2** the working part of the calendar week: *He doesn't drink during the ~;* **week·day** *n.* any day of the workweek, esp. Monday through Friday. **—week·end** or **week-end** *n.* the period from the close of one working week till the beginning of the next, usu. Saturday and Sunday; **v.** spend the weekend (*at* or *in* a place, *with* a person, etc.). **—week·ly** *adj.* of or happening once a week: *a ~ pay check, publication, visit;* also **adv. —n.,** *pl.* **-lies** a weekly publication.

ween *v. Archaic.* imagine; suppose.

wee·nie (–nee) *n. Informal.* a wiener.

wee·ny (WEE·nee) *adj. Informal.* very tiny or small; also **ween·sy.**

weep *v.* **weeps, wept, weep·ing** shed tears; also, shed or exude drops of water or other liquid: *Cold pipes ~ on a hot day; wept tears of joy; to ~ bitter tears; ~ing* (i.e. mourning) *for her beloved.* **—weep·ing** *adj.* that weeps; also, having drooping branches, as the **weeping willow. —weep·y** *adj.* **weep·i·er, -i·est** *Informal.* inclined to weep; tearful.

wee·vil (–vl) *n.* any of a family of long-snouted beetles whose larvae damage crops, grain, and fruit; **wee·vil·(l)y** *adj.*

weft *n.* the threads of a fabric or loom running crosswise to the warp; woof.

weigh (WAY) *v.* **1** measure (the weight of): *to ~ luggage; The cook ~s out the ingredients for a cake; He ~s 120 lb.; Boxers, jockeys, etc. have to* **weigh in** *before a contest; They must ~ in at the declared weights.* **2** bend (as if) with weight; bear down: *a tree* **weighed down** *by fruit; minds ~d down with worries; His conscience seemed to* **weigh (up)on** *him, or ~ him down* (i.e. worry him). **3** consider carefully: *~ed the pros and cons of giving up her job.* **4 weigh anchor** of a ship, lift the anchor before sailing; **under weigh** progressing or advancing. **5** have importance or significance: *Experience seems to ~ more with employers than education.* **—weight** (WAIT) *n.* **1** how heavy an object is: *His ~ is 178 lb.; ~ depends on gravitational pull and the mass of an object; Sugar is sold* **by weight,** *not volume;* **pull one's weight** do one's share. **2** system or unit of weight. **3** something heavy, as the disks at the ends of a barbell, a "pound," "gram," or other standard piece used in weighing, a quantity weighed out, or an object used to keep papers in place. **4** a burden or load to be supported: *The animal collapsed under the ~; That's a ~ off my mind.* **5** importance; influence: *a man of ~; public opinion carrying ~;* **throw one's weight around** be overbearing or overassertive. **—v.** put weight on; hence, burden: *a stick with a ~ed tip; a mind ~ed down with worries.* **—weight·less** *adj.* having little weight or gravitational pull; **weight·less·ly** *adv.;* **weight·less·ness** *n.* **—weight lifting** the competitive sport of lifting barbells. **—weight·y** *adj.* **weight·i·er, -i·est** very important or serious: *a ~ announcement, argument, speaker; ~ matters of state, responsibilities;* **weight·i·ly** *adv.*

weir (WEER) *n.* an obstruction erected across a stream or river for diverting the water, as a milldam, a fence of stakes or brush for catching fish, etc.

weird (WEERD) *adj.* **1** mysterious in an unearthly way: *a ~ shriek from the dark.* **2** *Informal.* strange or fantastic: *a ~ sense of humor;* **weird·o** *n.* **-os** *Slang.* an eccentric person or thing; also **weird·ie** (–dee). —**weird·ly** *adv.;* **weird·ness** *n.*

welch same as WELSH.

wel·come (–cum) *adj.* received with pleasure: *a ~ visitor; ~ news; Contributions are always ~; You're* **welcome to** (i.e. permitted to) *use our kitchen;* **You're welcome** [in response to an expression of thanks] You are under no obligation. ***—n.*** a cordial reception; ***interj.*** you are welcome: *~ back!* ***—v.*** **-comes, -comed, -com·ing** greet or receive cordially: *was ~d with a hug; We ~ suggestions.*

weld *v.* join (pieces of metal) by heating to the melting point and fusing, hammering, or pressing together; hence, unite closely or intimately; **weld·er** *n.* ***—n.*** a welding or welded joint. —**weld·ment** *n.* a unit formed of pieces welded together.

wel·fare *n.* **1** the condition of being healthy, happy, prosperous, etc. **2** the provision of food and such necessities to the needy, as by government programs of public assistance. **3** government aid given to the poor and needy; **on welfare** receiving such aid. —**welfare state** a state or social system in which the government finances and often provides free social services such as medical treatment, education, housing, and pensions.

wel·kin *n. Archaic.* the sky or upper air.

we'll (WEEL) we will; we shall.

[1]**well** *n.* **1** a hole or shaft dug in the ground to get water, oil, gas, etc.; also, a spring or fountain of water: *an artesian ~; a ~ of information.* **2** a shaft resembling a well, as a *stairwell.* **3** a reservoir: *the ~ of a fountain pen.* ***—v.*** flow out, rise up, etc. as water from a spring or well.

[2]**well** *adv., comp.* **bet·ter,** *superl.* **best** in a good or satisfactory manner: *a job ~ done; He eats ~; a ~-liked person; ~-polished shoes; Shake ~ before use; It is ~ past noon; We might ~ make the deadline;* **as well (as)** **1** in addition (to). **2** equally (with). ***—adj.*** good or satisfactory: *All's ~ that ends well; It's ~ that he asked my permission; You look ~* (i.e. in good health); *came out of the hospital a ~ man.* ***—interj.*** expressing surprise, agreement, doubt, etc.: *~, what did I tell you? ~, no!* —**well-ad·vised** *adj.* prudent; also, based on wise counsel: *a ~ rest.* —**well-ap·point·ed** *adj.* well equipped or furnished. —**well-bal·anced** *adj.* rightly balanced; also, healthy. —**well-be·ing** *n.* welfare (*n.* 1). —**well·born** *adj.* born in a good family. —**well-bred** *adj.* **1** having good manners. **2** of good stock. —**well-de·fined** *adj.* clearly distinguishable; distinct. —**well-dis·posed** *adj.* favorably disposed (toward a person or thing). —**well-done** *adj.* **1** skillfully performed. **2** cooked thoroughly. —**well-fa·vored** *adj.* good-looking; handsome. —**well-fed** *adj.* plump; fat. —**well-fixed** *adj. Informal.* rich. —**well-found·ed** *adj.* based on good evidence, reasoning, judgment, etc. —**well-groomed** *adj.* neat in appearance; *a ~ candidate, lawn; a ~* (i.e. cleaned, curried, etc.) *horse.* —**well-ground·ed** *adj.* having a good foundation (*in* a subject); also, well-founded. —**well·head** *n.* the source of an oil well or spring. —**well-heeled** *adj. Informal.* well-to-do; rich. —**well-in·formed** *adj.* having considerable general knowledge.

Wel·ling·ton (–tun) capital of New Zealand.

well-in·ten·tioned *adj.* having or showing good intentions. —**well-knit** *adj.* well constructed; of a person, sturdily built. —**well-known** *adj.* famous; also, familiar. —**well-man·nered** *adj.* having good manners. —**well-mean·ing** *adj.* well-intentioned; also, intended well though ineffective; also **well-meant.** —**well-nigh** *adv.* almost; very nearly. —**well-off** *adj.* well-to-do; prosperous. —**well-or·dered** *adj.* well-arranged; orderly. —**well-pre·served** *adj.* of an old person, now showing signs of age. —**well-read** (–red) *adj.* having read much. —**well-round·ed** *adj.* comprehensive; multi-faceted; shapely (as a figure). —**well-spo·ken** *adj.* **1** well-uttered. **2** impressive in speech and manner.

well·spring *n.* a spring; also, a never-failing source.

well-thought-of *adj.* having a good reputation. —**well-timed** *adj.* timely; opportune. —**well-to-do** *adj..* sufficiently rich or prosperous. —**well-turned** *adj.* gracefully formed or expressed: *~ verses.* —**well-wish·er** *n.* one who wishes another, a cause, etc. well; **well-wish·ing** *n.* & *adj.* —**well-worn** *adj.* much worn; also, too much used or trite.

welsh (WELSH, WELCH) *v. Slang.* evade an obligation, as a bookmaker who fails to pay a bet; cheat: *~ed on his promise;* **welsh·er** *n.* —**Welsh** *n.* & *adj.* (of) the Celtic people or language of Wales; **Welsh·man** *n.* **-men; Welsh·wom·an, -wom·en.** —**Welsh cor·gi** (–COR·gee) either of two varieties of small dogs of Welsh origin having short legs and foxlike head and tail. —**Welsh rabbit** a dish of melted, often seasoned cheese served on toast or crackers; also **Welsh rarebit.**

welt *n.* **1** a reinforcing strip or border, as used at the joining of a shoe's sole and upper, at the edge of a garment of upholstery, etc. **2** a ridge or wale on the skin; hence, a slash or blow that would raise a welt; ***v.*** *Informal.* thrash severely.

wel·ter *v.* wallow; also, be soaked (in blood, etc.). ***—n.*** a chaotic rolling or tumbling; also,

a confused mass or jumble (of papers, data, etc.).
wel·ter·weight *n.* a boxer weighing between 136 and 147 lb. (61 and 67 kg for Olympics).
wen *n.* a cyst formed on the scalp, back, etc. by the clogging up of oil glands of the skin; sebaceous cyst.
wench *n.* [derogatory] a young woman; also, *Archaic.* a female servant.
wend *v.* go on (one's way).
went *pt.* of GO.
wept *pt.* of WEEP.
were (WUR) past second pers. *sing.*, past *pl.*, and past subjunctive of BE: *as if I ~ a millionaire;* **as it were** so to speak. **—we're** (WEER) we are. **—weren't** were not.
were·wolf (WEER·woolf, WUR–, WAIR–) *n.* **-wolves** (–woolvz) in folklore, a person who changes into a wolf; also **wer·wolf.**
wert (WURT) *Archaic.* the form of WERE used with *thou.*
wes·kit *n. Informal.* waistcoat.
Wes·ley (–lee), **John.** 1703–91, the founder of Methodism; **Wes·ley·an** *n.* & *adj.*
west *n.* **1** where the sun sets; the direction opposite east. **2** a region or countries lying west. **—the West 1** W. United States, esp. W. of the Mississippi. **2** the countries of Europe and America as distinguished from Asia; also, non-Communist countries of W. Europe and the Americas. ***—adj.*** & ***adv.*** in or toward the west. **—West Berlin** See BERLIN. **—west·er·ly** *adj.* & *adv.* toward or from the west; ***n.,*** *pl.* **-lies** a wind from the west. **—west·ern** *adj.* of, toward, or from the west; ***n.*** a story of the western U.S. featuring cowboy life; **Western** *adj.* of the West; **west·ern·er** or **West·ern·er** *n.* **—Western Hemisphere** the half of the earth that includes North and South America. **—west·ern·ize** *v.* **-iz·es, -ized, -iz·ing** give a western character to. **—Western Samoa** a country of two main islands in the S. Pacific; 1,097 sq.mi. (2,842 km²); *cap.* Apia. **—West Germany** See GERMANY. **—West Indies** Caribbean islands consisting of the Bahamas and the Antilles groups; **West Indian.** **—West Point** (the site of) the U.S. Military Academy in S.E. New York. **—West Virginia** a S.E. state of the U.S.; 24,181 sq.mi. (62,628 km²); *cap.* Charleston; **West Virginian** **—west·ward** (–wurd) *adj.* & *adv.* toward the west; **west·ward·ly** *adj.* & *adv.* Also **west·wards** *adv.*
wet *adj.* **wet·ter, wet·test 1** covered or soaked with water or another liquid, not dry: *~ hands, sponge; came in soaking ~ from the pool; ~* (i.e. rainy) *weather; ~* (i.e. not yet dry) *paint, ink;* **all wet** *Slang.* wrong or mistaken. **2** against prohibition of liquor; permitting alcoholic drinks: *a ~ county, candidate.* ***—n.*** **1** that which makes wet; liquid or moisture. **2** rainy weather. **3** one opposed to prohibition. ***—v.*** **wets, wet·ted, wet·ting** make or become wet; **wet·ter** *n.* **—wet·ly** *adv.;* **wet·ness** *n.* **—wet·back** *n. Informal.* an illegal immigrant from Mexico, as one who swims across the Rio Grande. **—wet bar** a bar or counter equipped with running water. **—wet blanket** one who dampens enthusiasm or lessens the gaiety of others.
weth·er (WEDH·ur) *n.* a male sheep castrated when young.
wet·land *n.* usu. **wetlands** *pl.* swamps, marshes, or bogs. **—wet nurse** a woman hired to suckle another's infant; **wet-nurse** *v.* **-nurs·es, -nursed, -nurs·ing.** **—wet suit** a heat-retaining garment of porous material such as foam rubber used by skin divers, etc. **—wetting agent** a chemical substance that lowers the surface tension of a liquid, as used in developing film.
we've (WEEV) we have.
whack (HWAK) *n. Informal.* **1** a sharp, resounding blow or its sound. **2** a portion or share. **3 at a** (or **one**) **whack** in one attempt; **have** (or **take**) **a whack at** aim a blow at; also, make an attempt at; **out of whack** not in proper condition. ***—v.*** *Informal.* strike (with) a sharp, resounding blow; **whack up** divide into shares; **whack·er** *n.* **—whack·ing** *adj. Informal.* very large. **—whack·y** *adj.* **whack·er, -i·est** same as WACKY.
whale (HWAIL) *n.* a fishlike but air-breathing, warm-blooded sea mammal that is the largest of animals; **a whale of a** *Informal.* great or impressive (party, good time, job, difference, etc.). ***—v.*** **whales, whaled, whal·ing 1** hunt whales, as a whaler. **2** *Informal.* thrash. **—whale·boat** *n.* a long narrow rowboat or motorboat. **—whale·bone** *n.* a horny, elastic plate attached to the upper jaw of "baleen whales," used for straining out food and formerly for corset stays. **—whal·er** *n.* a person or ship engaged in whaling; also, a whaleboat. **—whal·ing** *n.* the hunting and processing of whales.
wham (HWAM) *n.* & *v.* **whams, whammed, wham·ming** *Informal.* (strike with) a hard impact or solid blow; ***interj.*** a sound imitating this.
wham·my (HWAM·ee) *n.* **wham·mies** *Slang.* a jinx; hex; evil eye: *hit with a double ~.*
wharf (HWORF) *n.* **wharves** or **wharfs** a rectangular structure projecting from the shore along which ships dock for loading and unloading; **wharf·age** (–ij) *n.* the use or charge for using a wharf; **wharf·in·ger** (–jur) *n.* a wharf operator.
what (HWOT, HWUT) *pron.* **1** [used in questions]: *~ is the time?* **what about** what do you think concerning; **what for?** why? for what purpose? **2** that which: *I heard ~ you said; Do ~ you like;* **what have you** *Informal.* other similar things. ***—adj.*** **1** [used in questions]: *on ~ date?* **2** that or those which: *Get ~ help you can; She sent me ~ books she could*

borrow. **3** [used in exclamations]: ~ *an idea! ~ fools we are!* **—adv.** in what respect? how much?: ~ *does it matter?* **what with** on account of: ~ *with inflation and rising prices, poor people are suffering;* [used in exclamations] ~ *woeful neglect!* **—what·ev·er** (–EV·ur) *pron.* **1** no matter what: *He'll get it,* ~ *the cost.* **2** [used for emphasizing *what*]: *She'll agree with* ~ *you say;* ~ *is the matter with you? furniture, groceries, stationery,* **or whatever** (*Informal.* anything at all). **—adj.** **1** no matter what: *He'll get it at* ~ *cost to himself.* **2** [used for emphasizing *what*]: *Get* ~ *books you need.* **3** [used after its noun] at all: *Get any book* ~. **—what·not** *n.* a set of open shelves for books, curios, etc. **—what·so·ev·er** (–EV·ur) *adj.* & *pron.* [emphatic form] whatever.

wheal (HWEEL) *n.* a temporarily swollen and itching patch on the skin, as from an allergy or insect bite; also, a weal or welt.

wheat (HWEET) *n.* a cereal grass of temperate climates, the most widely cultivated of food-grain crops, used for bread flour, breakfast foods, pasta, etc.; **wheat·en** *adj.* made of wheat; **wheat germ** the vitamin-rich embryo of a wheat kernel.

whee·dle (HWEE–) *v.* **-dles, -dled, -dling** use flattery, coaxing, etc. to persuade or influence (a person *into* doing something); also, get (something *out* of someone) by wheedling; **whee·dler** *n.*

wheel (HWEEL) *n.* **1** a circular disk or frame with a central axis on which it turns; also, anything shaped or moving like a wheel: *the potter's ~; a roulette ~; the ~ of fortune; the steering ~ of an automobile, ship;* **at the wheel** in control, as the driver of a motor vehicle or a helmsman. **2 wheels** *pl.* moving force or machinery: *the ~s of government, progress; Slang.* an automobile; **wheels within wheels** intricate machinery, motives, influences, etc. **3** *Slang.* a boss; a big shot. **4** a bicycle. **5** a turning movement of troops or ships without change of alignment and position. **—v.** **1** turn; revolve; rotate. **2** circle; also, move on wheels or in a wheeled vehicle; **wheel and deal** *Slang.* make deals aggressively and unscrupulously. **—wheel·bar·row** (–bair·oh) *n.* a small vehicle for moving loads, having a box mounted on a wheel and attached to two shafts that are held in the hands and pushed forward. **—wheel·base** *n.* the distance between the front and rear axles of a motor vehicle. **—wheel·chair** *n.* a chair mounted on wheels, used by invalids. **—wheeled** *adj.* having wheels. **—wheel·er** *n.* **1** one that wheels or has wheels: *a two-~.* **2** wheelhorse (*n.* 1). **—wheel·er-deal·er** *n. Slang.* a shrewd and aggressive operator in business, politics, etc. **—wheel·horse** *n.* **1** a horse harnessed nearest the vehicle. **2** *Informal.* a steady and hard worker. **—wheel·house** *n.* same as PILOTHOUSE. **—wheel·ie** (–ee) *n.* the stunt of balancing a wheeled vehicle momentarily on its rear wheel(s). **—wheel·wright** (–rite) *n.* one whose work is making and repairing wheels and wheeled vehicles.

wheeze (HWEEZ) *v.* **wheez·es, wheezed, wheez·ing** breathe or utter with a whistling sound, as an asthmatic; ***n.*** a wheezing (sound); **wheez·y** *adj.* **wheez·i·er, -i·est** inclined to wheeze; also, wheezing; **wheez·i·ness** *n.*

whelk (HWELK) *n.* a usu. edible marine snail with a spiral shell.

whelm (HWELM) *v.* submerge; engulf; overwhelm.

whelp (HWELP) *n.* one of the young of a flesh-eating animal, esp. of a dog, wolf, bear, lion, tiger, leopard, etc.; ***v.*** bring forth (whelps).

when (HWEN) *adv.* at what time? **—conj.** **1** at the time that: *Call me ~ you wake up; limps ~ he walks; We were fast asleep, ~ I heard a knock on the door.* **2** although; considering that: *continues to work ~ he can retire on a fat pension.* **—pron.** what or which time: *Since ~ have you been an expert?* **—n.** time; date; occasion: *the ~ and where of the happening; the ~ and how of it.* **—whence** (HWENCE) *adv.* & *conj.* from what place, source, or cause: ~ *does the need arise?* ~ (i.e. wherefore) *it follows that the earth is round.* **—when·ev·er** (–EV·ur) *adv.* & *conj.* at whatever time; when; **when·so·ev·er** (–EV·ur) *adv.* & *conj.* [in emphatic uses] whenever.

where (HWAIR) *adv.* in, at, to, or from what place? ~ *is the boy?* ~ *did he get the money? the hotel* ~ (i.e. in which) *I stayed;* ~ (i.e. in what respect) *did I go wrong?* **—conj.** in the place in which: *found it just ~ I left it; ~ there's smoke there's fire; I go* ~ (i.e. to the place to which) *business takes me; born in Chicago,* ~ (i.e. in which place) *he lived 20 years.* **—pron.** what or which place: *asked us ~ we are from; ~ we were going to; ~ you seem to have gone wrong.* **—n.** the place or scene (*of* a happening). **—where·a·bouts** (–uh·bouts) *adv.* & *conj.* about where; ***n.*** place where a person or thing is: *Her ~ is unknown;* rarely also **where·a·bout.** **—where·as** (–AZ) *conj.* **1** in view of the fact that; since. **2** while; on the contrary. **—where·at** (–AT) *adv.* & *conj.* at or in consequence of which. **—where·by** (–BY) *adv.* & *conj.* by or through which. **—where·fore** *adv.* for what reason? ***conj.*** for which reason; ***n.*** the reason: *the why and the ~ of it.* **—where·from** (–FROM, –FRUM) *conj.* from which. **—where·in** (–IN) *adv.* in what (respect)? ***conj.*** in which; during which; in what way. **—where·of** (–OV) *adv.* & *conj.* of what, which, or whom. **—where·on** (–ON) *conj.* on which. **—where·so·ev·er** (–EV·ur) *conj.* [in emphatic uses] wherever. **—where·to** (–TOO) *adv.* to what place? ***conj.*** to which. **—where·up·on** (–ON) *conj.* upon which; at which. **—wher·ev·er** (–EV·ur) *adv.* [emphatic form] where? ***conj.*** in, at, or to whatever place: ~ *you are.* **—where·with** (–WIDH) *adv.* with what? ***conj.*** with which.

—where·with·al (–awl) *n.* the necessary money or means: *the ~ to finance the project.*
wher·ry (HWER·ee) *n.* **wher·ries** a light rowboat or barge with sharp stem and stern.
whet (HWET) *v.* **whets, whet·ted, whet·ting** sharpen (a knife, ax, etc.) by rubbing on or with a stone; hence, make keen or stimulate (appetite, curiosity, desires, etc.). **—whet·ter** *n.*
wheth·er (HWEDH·ur) *conj.* [posing a choice between alternatives, expressed by "or" or merely implied]: *It is yours ~ you like it or not; Please cable back ~ my son survived the crash; It's doubtful ~* (i.e. if) *she will agree.*
whet·stone (HWET–) *n.* a stone for whetting knives, etc.
whew (HYOO) *interj.* expressing relief, surprise, etc.
whey (HWAY) *n.* the liquid part of milk left after the curd separates.
which (HWICH) *pron.* **1** [used in questions to distinguish between several persons or things]: *~ is your dog? ~ of them is yours?* **Which is which** which is one and which the other. **2** [used in subordinate clauses to refer to something already mentioned]: *the car in ~ he drives to work; The book, ~ is still being written, will be published next year; I'm hungry, ~ means it's time to eat.* ***—adj.:*** *~dog is yours? "Modern English," ~ book is still being written, will be published next year.* **—which·ev·er** (–EV·ur) *pron.* & *adj.* any (of two or more): *Work the day you like, ~ it is; Work ~ day you like;* **which·so·ev·er** (–EV·ur) *pron.* & *adj.* [emphatic form] whichever.
whick·er (HWICK–) *n.* & *v.* neigh; whinny.
whiff (HWIF) *n.* **1** a slight puff or breath: *a ~ of fresh air; a ~ of smoke.* **2** a slight smell or trace: *a ~ of garlic, scandal.* ***—v.*** blow or puff lightly.
whif·fle·tree (HWIF–) *n.* same as SINGLETREE.
whig (HWIG) *n.* **1** a member of a British political party between the late 1600's and the 1850's that opposed royal power and the Tories; also, an American who supported the Revolutionary War. **2** a member of an American political party (1834–54) opposed to the Democratic Party.
while (HWILE) *n.* a period of time: *for a short ~; a long ~;* **once in a while** occasionally; **worth one's while** worth one's time or effort. ***—conj.*** **1** during the time that: *She works ~ he plays.* **2** whereas; although: *She's a Democrat ~ he's a Republican.* ***—v.*** **whiles, whiled, whil·ing** usu. **while away,** spend (time) in a leisurely way. **—whi·lom** (HWYE·lum) *adj.* & *adv. Archaic.* former(ly). **—whilst** (HWYE–) *conj. Regional.* while.
whim (HWIM) *n.* a sudden fanciful idea or desire: *a childish ~.*
whim·per (HWIM–) *v.* cry with whining, broken sounds; also, utter in this manner; ***n.*** a whimpering.
whim·sey (HWIM·zee) *n.* **-seys** same as WHIMSY. **—whim·si·cal** (–zi·cl) *adj.* full of whims; capricious; also, odd or fanciful: *a ~ idea, expression;* **whim·si·cal·ly** *adv.;* **whim·si·cal·i·ty** (–CAL–) *n.* **—whim·sy** (–zee) *n.* **-sies** caprice or whim; also, a fanciful or quaint quality, esp. of humor.
whine (HWINE) *n.* the weak, nasal tone of a complaining child; also, a complaint or cry made in this tone; ***v.*** **whines, whined, whin·ing** utter with or make a whine. **—whin·ny** (HWIN·ee) *n.* & *v.* **whin·nies, whin·nied, whin·ny·ing** (make) a low and gentle neigh.
whip (HWIP) *n.* **1** a stick with a lash attached as an instrument of punishment or for urging animals forward; also, a blow using a whip or a whipping or lashing motion. **2** one who drives or uses a whip, as a coachman, one in charge of a hunting pack, or a party official helping the floor leader in a legislature in discipline, attendance during voting, etc. **3** a dessert made by beating egg white with fruit and sugar. ***—v.*** **whips, whipped, whip·ping** **1** beat with a whip; lash; hence, move suddenly or quickly like the lash of a whip: *to ~ a horse; with the rain ~ing her face; flags ~ing in the wind; ~d out his knife and attacked us; a team ~d* (i.e. defeated) *in the finals;* **whip into shape** *Informal.* bring into proper condition by vigorous action; **whip up** rouse (enthusiasm, interest, etc.); also, prepare (a meal, etc.) quickly. **2** wind or wrap (a stick, rope, etc.) closely with cord for strength or protection. **3** beat (cream, etc.) until stiff, as in making **whipped cream** topping for desserts. **—whip·cord** *n.* **1** a thin, tightly twisted cord, as used for the lashes of whips. **2** a twilled cloth made of hard-twisted yarns. **—whip hand** control or advantage (*over* or *of* an opponent). **—whip·lash** *n.* **1** the lash of a whip. **2** injury to the neck caused by a severe jolt as in an automobile collision; also **whiplash injury.** **—whip·per·snap·per** *n.* an insignificant but presumptuous person. **—whip·pet** (–it) *n.* a racing dog resembling a small greyhound. **—whipping boy** a scapegoat, like a boy formerly used to take the punishment for a prince's faults. **—whip·ple·tree** *n.* same as SINGLETREE.
whip·poor·will (HWIP·ur–) *n.* a North American insect-eating bird that flies mostly by night, named in imitation of its call.
whip·saw *n.* a two-handled saw or a cross-cut saw operated by two persons; ***v.*** cut with a whipsaw; also, *Informal.* cheat or be worsted by the joint action of two or in two ways at the same time.
whir(r) (HWUR) *n.* & *v.* **whir(r)s, whirred, whir·ring** (vibrate, fly, operate, etc. with) a buzzing sound, as of a small machine.
whirl (HWURL) *n.* **1** a rapidly revolving motion, as by the force of wind or water; also, something that whirls or a condition of dizziness, confusion, etc.: *Her head was in a ~; the social ~* (i.e. round) *of parties and dances.* **2** *Informal.* a try or attempt: *Give it a ~.* ***—v.***

swing round and round rapidly and continuously, as leaves caught in a wind or a car gone out of control: *dancers ~ing about the room; and ~ed her away in his new sports car; Her head ~ed* (i.e. She felt dizzy). **—whirl·i·gig** (HWURL–) *n.* a whirling or spinning toy; also, a merry-go-round. **—whirl·pool** *n.* a spinning mass of water caused by opposing currents or by wind; a vortex or eddy of water; **whirlpool bath** a therapeutic bath of swirling warm water. **—whirl·wind** *n.* a whirling column of air, as seen in deserts; ***adj.*** *Informal.* fast or hurried: *a ~ tour.* **—whirl·y·bird** *n. Informal.* a helicopter.

whish (HWISH) *n.* & *v.* (move with) a swish or soft rushing sound.

whisk (HWISK) *v.* **1** move or sweep with a light, quick, brushing movement, as with a small bunch of straw, twigs, feathers, etc. used for brushing dust, etc. off clothes; ***n.*** such a sweeping movement or the brush used; also **whisk broom. 2** beat or whip (eggs, creams, etc.) to a froth using a whisk; ***n.*** a kitchen utensil made of looped wires. **—whisk·er** *n.* **1** one of the long, bristly hairs growing above the mouth of a cat, rat, bird, insect, etc.; **whiskered** *adj.* **2** one of the hairs growing on the sides of a man's face; **whiskers** *pl.* the beard on a man's face other than the mustache.

whis·key (HWIS·kee) *n.* **-keys** or **-kies** a strong alcoholic liquor distilled from grain and malt, including bourbon, rye, and Scotch; also **whis·ky, -kies** *Brit.*

whis·per (HWIS–) *v.* **1** speak or say in a very low voice; also, tell very privately, as a secret. **2** make a rustling sound, as leaves or wind. **—*n.*** **1** a whispering or something whispered. **2** a rustling sound.

whist (HWIST) *n.* a card game from which bridge developed.

whis·tle (HWISL) *v.* **-tles, -tled, -tling** make a shrill, clear sound by forcing breath through pursed lips; also, make a similar sound, as a bird, wind, steam engine, or with a whistle; **whistle for** *Informal.* expect in vain to get (something). **—*n.*** a whistling (sound); also, a device for producing such a sound, as used by policemen, sports officials, etc.; **blow the whistle on** *Slang.* inform on; expose. **—whis·tler** *n.* **—whistle stop 1** a brief stop at a small town in a political campaign tour. **2** a small town along a railroad route at which a train stops only be request.

whit (HWIT) *n.* the least bit; iota: *not a ~ of truth; not a ~ worried.*

white (HWITE) *adj.* **whit·er, whit·est 1** having the color of fresh snow or milk; light-colored or pale; not black: *a ~ horse; the ~ matter of the brain* (surrounding the gray matter); *a ~* (i.e. albino) *mouse; ~* (i.e. snowy) *Christmas; ~* (i.e. gray) *hair; a ~-haired* (i.e. blond) *boy* (*Informal.* favorite); *the ~* (i.e. Caucasoid) *race;* hence: *~ Australia policy; ~ supremacy.* **2** denoting the absence of color: *incandescent ~ heat of metals; turned ~ with fear, fury; ~ meat* (such as pork, poultry, rabbit, and veal); *~ wine; ~ blood cells; ~* (i.e. not green) *creme de menthe; ~* (i.e. unprinted) *space on a page; a ~* (i.e. reactionary) *political faction.* **3** symbolic of goodness, peace, etc.; often "not black": *~ as a lily; a ~* (i.e. harmless) *lie, magic, witch; ~ flag* (of truce or surrender). **—*n.*** **1** white color or pigment. **2** something that is white: *dressed in ~* (clothes); *the ~* (i.e. albumen) *of an egg; the ~ of the eyes* (around the iris); *an uncrowded page with plenty of ~* (space). **3** a Caucasoid. **4** a member of a reactionary group. **—white ant** same as TERMITE. **—white·bait** *n. sing.* & *pl.* small fish or the young of herring, sprat, etc. used whole as food. **—white blood cell** one of the colorless corpuscles of the blood that help defend the body against infection; leucocyte. **—white·cap** *n.* the foamy crest of a breaking wave. **—white-col·lar** *adj.* of a job or worker, clerical or professional, not blue-collar; **white-collar crime** a crime such as fraud, embezzlement, and theft of various kinds committed by people in white-collar occupations. **—white corpuscle** a white blood cell. **—white dwarf** a small star of extremely high density that shines with a white light. **—white elephant** something useless and expensive to maintain, like an albino elephant that is not put to work in some S.E. Asian countries because considered sacred. **—white-faced** *adj.* of cattle, horses, etc., having a white patch on the face, as a Hereford. **—white feather** esp. **show the white feather,** show cowardice. **—white·fish** *n.* any of a family of freshwater food fishes related to the salmons and trouts. **—white flag** See WHITE, *adj.* 3. **—white·fly** *n.* **-flies** a sap-sucking plant pest that resembles a tiny moth and is covered with a white powder. **—white gasoline** a gasoline without any lead additive. **—white gold** a platinumlike alloy of gold and nickel, zinc, etc. used in jewelry. **—white goods** white household linens; also, household appliances such as refrigerators, washers, etc., usu. white-enameled. **—White·hall** *n.* the British government. **—white·head** *n.* a form of acne. **—white heat** the temperature at which metals, etc. appear white when heated beyond the red-hot stage; **white-hot** *adj.* **—white hope** a person or thing expected to bring glory to a group, as a white boxer recovering a title from a black. **—White·horse** capital of Yukon Territory. **—the White House** the official residence of the U.S. President in Washington, D.C.; hence, the executive branch of the U.S. government. **—white lead** a poisonous lead carbonate used as a paint pigment in the form of a white powder. **—white lie** a harmless lie, as one told out of politeness or kindness. **—white matter** whitish tissue consisting of nerve fibers surrounding the gray matter of the brain. **—whit·en** (HWYE–) *v.* make or become white(r); **whit·en·er** *n.;* **whit·en·ing** *n.;* **white·ness** *n.* **—white pine** a pine with soft, light-colored wood and five needles to the cluster. **—white race** the Caucasoid race. **—white room** a sterilized and pressurized "clean" room for laboratory work. **—White Russia** same as BYELORUSSIA. **—white sale** a sale of household linens. **—white slave** a female, esp. white, forced to be a prostitute; **white slavery. —white·tail** *n.* a deer with a tail that is white underneath and antlers curving forward; also **white-tailed deer. —white·wall** *n.* & *adj.* (an automobile tire) having a white band on the outer sidewall. **—white·wash** *n.* **1** a mixture of lime and water for coating walls, woodwork, etc.; hence, a covering up of faults or defects as if by use of whitewash. **2** *Informal.* a defeat that is a complete shutout. ***—v.*** **1** cover or conceal with whitewash. **2** *Informal.* defeat with a shutout. **—white·wood** *n.* (a tree such as the basswood or tulip tree that has) a soft, light-colored wood. **—whit·ey** (HWYE·tee) *n.* [derogatory slang] the white man or white society.

whith·er (HWIDH·ur) *adv.* to what place, result, condition, etc.? ***—conj.*** to which place, etc. **—whith·er·so·ev·er** (–EV·ur) *adv.* & *conj.* to whatever place.

whit·ing (HWYE–) *n.* **1** powdered chalk as used in the manufacture of paint, putty, etc. **2** a kind of silvery lake. **—whit·ish** (HWYE–) *adj.* somewhat white. **—whit·low** (HWIT·loh) *n.* bacterial infection around a toenail or fingernail.

Whit·man (HWIT·mun), **Walt.** 1819–92, American poet.

Whit·ney (HWIT·nee), **Mount.** a peak of the Sierra Nevada Mts. in E. California, the highest in the U.S. outside of Alaska.

Whit·sun·day (HWIT–) *n.* same as PENTECOST.

whit·tle (HWITL) *v.* **whit·tles, whit·tled, whit·tling** pare or cut shavings from (wood, etc.) with a knife; hence, shape or carve (an object); also, reduce: *Inflation ~s away our purchasing power; to ~ down expenses;* **whit·tler** *n.*

whiz(z) HWIZ) *n.* **whiz·zes** **1** the hissing sound of an arrow, ball, etc. rushing through the air. **2** *Slang.* an expert or skilled person; wizard: *a ~ at electronics; a ~ kid.* ***—v.*** **whiz·zes, whizzed, whiz·zing** make a whiz; also, speed past making this sound.

WHO World Health Organization.

who (HOO) *pron., objective* WHOM, *possessive* WHOSE **1** [used in questions about persons]: *~ is the president? ~ are these people? ~ did you say is coming to dinner?* **2** the person(s) that: *the man ~ called yesterday; those ~ smoke; don't know ~* (more correctly: *whom*) *to trust anymore.*

whoa (HWOH) *interj.* [to a horse, etc.] stop!

who·dun·it (–DUN–) *n. Informal.* a story, play, etc. dealing with crime detection. **—who·ev·er** (hoo·EV·ur) *pron.* **1** no matter who; any person who: *~ owes money is a debtor.* **2** [emphasizing *who*]: *~ is that guy?*

whole (HOLE) *adj.* with no part taken away or left out; entire: *a ~ roast pig; herring salted ~; the ~ neighborhood; came out alive and ~* (i.e. unhurt); *~ blood* (with all its components); *a ~* (i.e. not half) *brother; a ~ number* (i.e. not a fraction); *the ~ person* (i.e. physical, emotional, etc.). ***—n.*** complete or entire thing, unit, system, etc.: *a ~ and its parts; a complex ~;* **as a whole** as one complete unit, not in parts; **on the whole** considering everything; in general; **whole·ness** *n.* **—whole-heart·ed** *adj.* with all one's enthusiasm; not half-hearted. **—whole-meal** *adj.* made of the entire kernel (of wheat): *~ flour.* **—whole milk** milk with no butterfat, etc. removed. **—whole note** the standard unit of time in music notation, indicated as an open oval shape without stem. **—whole number** same as INTEGER. **—whole·sale** *n.* the selling of goods in large quantities and at lower prices, usu. to retailers. ***—adj.*** **1** (selling) in large quantities: *the ~ price; a ~ dealer.* **2** general; indiscriminate: *~ slaughter, condemnation.* ***—adv.:*** *Retailers buy ~; a plan rejected ~.* ***—v.*** **-sales, -saled, -sal·ing** sell at wholesale; **whole·sal·er** *n.* **—whole·some** (–sum) *adj.* **1** healthful: *a ~ climate; ~ foods, environments; ~* (i.e. healthy and vigorous) *youth.* **2** beneficial for mind and soul: *~ movies, reading; ~* (i.e. prudent) *fear of the law.* **—whole·some·ness** *n.* **—whole step** one tone or interval in a musical scale. **—whole-wheat** *adj.* ground from entire kernels of wheat: *~ flour for making ~ bread.*

who'll (HOOL) who shall; who will.

whol·ly (HOH·lee, HOLE–) *adv.* to the whole extent; entirely; solely.

whom (HOOM) *pron.* objective case of WHO: *the woman to ~ you are married; ~* (*Formal* for "who") *are you married to?* **—whom·ev·er** (–EV·ur) objective case of WHOEVER; **whom·so·ev·er** (–EV·ur) objective case of WHOSOEVER.

whoop (HOOP, HWOOP) *n.* **1** an excited long cry or shout, as of joy; also, the hoot of an owl, the cry of a crane, etc. **2** a long and loud drawing in of the breath following a paroxysm of coughing in *whooping cough.* ***—v.*** shout or call loudly; also, hoot as an owl; **whoop it up** *Slang.* make merry noisily. **—whoop·ee** *interj.* expressing great joy; ***n.*** noisy fun. **—whoop·er** *n.* whooping crane. **—whooping cough** a highly contagious bacterial disease, esp. of children, marked by coughing spells followed by whoops (*n.* 2). **—whooping crane** a large, white, nearly extinct North American crane with a loud, deep call. **—whoop·la** *n.* same as HOOPLA. **—whoops** *interj.* uttered when suddenly realizing one's error or wrong step.

whoosh (HWOOSH) *n.* & *v.* (make) a loud noise, as of rushing air.

whop·per (HWOP·ur) *n. Informal.* something huge, esp. a lie. —**whop·ping** *adj. Informal.* extraordinarily huge; colossal.
whore (HORE) *n.* a prostitute; **whor·ish** *adj.;* **whore·house** *n.* a brothel.
whorl (HWORL, HWURL) *n.* a whirling or circular shape or formation, as a ring of leaves or flowers around a point on an axis, one of the turns in a univalve spiral shell, or a fingerprint pattern of circles; **whorled** *adj.: the ~ arrangement of the parts of a flower.*
who's (HOOZ) who is; who has; —**whose** (HOOZ) *pron.* possessive case of WHICH and WHO: *~ is this child? ~ are these?* **adj.:** *~ child is this? a flower ~ smell is sweet;* **who·so** (HOO·soh) *pron.* whoever; **who·so·ev·er** (–EV·ur) *pron.* [emphatic form] whoever. —**who's who** a compilation of short biographies.
whr. watt-hour.
why (HWY) *adv.* for what reason, cause, or purpose? *~ go to school?* —**conj.:** *Everyone knows ~ we eat; These are the reasons ~ I resigned.* —**n.,** *pl.* **whys:** *the how and ~ of our existence; the ~s and the wherefores.* —**interj.** expressing surprise, etc.: *~, I thought it was Sunday! ~, what's wrong with that?*
WI Wisconsin. —**W.I.** West Indies; West Indian.
Wich·i·ta (–taw) a city of S. Kansas.
wick *n.* (a piece of) cord or tape for drawing up and burning the fuel in an oil lamp, stove, or candle.
wick·ed (–id) *adj.* **1** bad in a willful or immoral way: *a ~ and disobedient child; a ~ witch; a thoroughly ~ old man.* **2** roguish; mischievous: *a ~ joke, look.* **3** *Informal.* skillfully executed or dealt; formidable: *a ~ blow; performance.* —**wick·ed·ly** *adv.;* **wick·ed·ness** *n.*
wick·er *n.* a thin, flexible twig or strip of osier, rattan, etc. used for weaving into baskets, furniture, etc.; also, such woven material or objects made with it. —**wick·er·work** *n.* wicker material or objects made of wicker.
wick·et (–it) *n.* a small gate or opening, as a box-office window, a small door set in a large gate, a wire arch or hoop through which balls are hit in croquet, the set of three wooden stumps put up at either end of a cricket "pitch," etc.
wick·i·up (WICK·ee–) *n.* a simple hut made of brush and matting, used as shelter by nomadic tribes of American Indians.
wide *adj.* **wid·er, wid·est** **1** having a relatively large measurement from side to side; not narrow: *a ~ doorway, margin, aperture, gap; ~* (i.e. fully open) *eyes; a door 4 ft. ~* (i.e. in width). **2** extensive; of great range: *the ~ world; a ~ selection of shoes; a man of ~ interests.* **3 wide of** far from (the mark, target, truth, etc.). **4 -wide** *comb. form.* throughout: as in *nationwide, countrywide.* —**adv. 1** over a relatively large area or extent; extensively: *was ~ awake; a ~ open mouth; travels far and ~.* **2** away from the target; *The bullet went ~.* —**wide·ly** *adv.;* **wide·ness** *n.* —**wide-an·gle** *adj.* having a relatively wide angle of view that takes in a large area of a scene: *a ~ lens, shot.* —**wide-a·wake** *adj.* fully awake; also, alert. —**wide-eyed** *adj.* with wide-open eyes; hence, amazed; also, simple or naive: *a ~ admirer;* **wide-mouthed** *adj.: a ~ jar, channel; stared in ~ astonishment.* —**wid·en** (WYE·dn) *v.* make or become wide(r); broaden. —**wide·spread** *adj.* widely spread out; also, widely prevalent: *~ belief, fear.*
widg·eon (WIJ·un) *n.* a North American wild duck usu. called "baldpate" because of the male's white head; also, a European species. Also **wi·geon.**
wid·ow (–oh) *n.* a woman after her husband's death but before remarriage; **v.** cause to become a widow; **wid·ow·hood** *n.* —**wid·ow·er** *n.* a man after his wife's death but before remarriage.
width *n.* measurement from side to side of something; breadth; also, a piece of a certain width.
wield (WEELD) *v.* handle (a tool, weapon, etc.) skillfully and effectively: *to ~ an ax, the pen, sword; ~* (i.e. exercise) *power, influence;* **wield·er** *n.*
wie·ner (WEE·nur) *n.* a frankfurter of shorter size; also called "Vienna sausage" or **wie·ner·wurst.**
wife *n.* **wives** a female spouse; also, any married woman; **wife·hood** *n.;* **wife·less** *adj.;* **wife·ly** *adj.*
wig *n.* a head covering of false hair; **wigged** (WIGD) *adj.* wearing a wig: *a ~ judge.* —**v. wigs, wigged, wig·ging** *Slang.* thrill or excite; also, be thrilled, excited, etc.: *teeny-boppers ~ing out over their idol.*
wigeon See WIDGEON.
wig·gle *v.* **wig·gles, wig·gled, wig·gling** move with quick, side-to-side movements: *to ~ one's toes;* **n.** a wiggling movement; **wig·gler** *n.;* **wig·gly** *adj.* **wig·gli·er, wig·gli·est** wiggling, as a worm; also, wavy: *~ underlining.*
wight (WITE) *n. Archaic.* a human being; also, a creature.
wig·let (–lit) *n.* a small wig.
wig·wag *v.* **-wags, -wagged, -wag·ging** **1** move to and fro; wag. **2** signal (a message) by waving a flag, light, etc. according to a code; **n.** the wigwagging of messages; also, such a message.
wig·wam (–wom) *n.* a usu. dome-shaped dwelling of North Ameican Indians made of a framework of poles covered with bark or woven mats.
wild (WILED) *adj.* **1** of animals, plants, etc., not tamed or cultivated: *the ~ boar of Europe and Asia; the ~ rose; ~ honey; a ~ region.* **2** not civilized; hence, not restrained or orderly: *~ tribes; the ~ and woolly* (i.e. barbarous) *West; ~ laughter; a ~* (i.e. erratic) *pitch* (in baseball); *a ~ card* (i.e. playing card with arbi-

trary rank or value). **3** crazy; frantic: *a ~ scheme; ~ speculation; ~ with rage; a ~* (i.e. violent) *storm.* **—adv.:** *weeds growing ~; children allowed to* **run wild** *on the streets.* **—n.** a wild region or condition: *return to the ~; plants growing in the ~; in the ~s of Africa; the call of the ~* (i.e. "Nature"). **—wild·ly** *adv.;* **wild·ness** *n.* **—wild·cat** *n.* **1** any of the smaller wild animals of the cat family, esp. a lynx or bobcat; also, a fierce fighter. **2** a risky or reckless undertaking, as the unstable banks and currencies existing before the U.S. Bank Act was passed in 1863, a gas or oil well drilled in an unproved area, etc.; ***adj.*** unauthorized; illicit; illegal: *~ operations, stocks, strikes;* ***v.* -cats, -cat·ted, -cat·ting** drill for gas or oil in an unproved area; **wild·cat·ter** *n.* **—wil·de·beest** (WIL·duh–) *n.* same as GNU. **—wil·der·ness** (WIL–) *n.* an uninhabited region without tracks or trails, as a forest or desert. **—wild-eyed** *adj.* staring in an angry or deranged manner; hence, irrational or foolish: *~ notions.* **—wild·fire** *n.* a fast-spreading forest fire. **—wild·fowl** *n.* a game bird such as a wild duck, quail, or pheasant. **—wild-goose chase** a foolish or futile pursuit, endeavor, etc. **—wild·life** *n.* animals, birds, fishes, etc. in their natural state; ***adj.:*** *~ conservation, management, sanctuary.* **—wild oat(s)** a wild grass resembling oats; **sow one's wild oats** esp. of males, be promiscuous in youth. **—wild rice** a tall North American grass that grows wild in shallow waters; also, its grain that is used like rice. **—Wild West** the W. United States of pioneer days. **—wild·wood** *n.* a forest in its natural state.

wile *n.* a sly trick, esp. one used to ensnare someone: *the ~s of the serpent who tricked Eve; a woman's* **wiles** (i.e. coquettish or playful tricks). **—v. wiles, wiled, wil·ing** lure or entice; **wile away** same as WHILE AWAY.

wil·ful same as WILLFUL. **—will** *n.* **1** the mental power to make and carry out a decision: *the ~ to succeed; a patient's ~ to live; "Where there's a ~ there's a way."* **2** wish or choice: *elected to carry out the ~ of the people; hires and fires* **at will** (i.e. as he likes); *servants to* **do his will** (i.e. obey him) *round the clock.* **3** (document containing) a statement of how a person wants his property to be disposed of after death: *died without making his ~; her last ~ and testament.* **4** feeling or disposition toward another: *good ~; ill ~.* **—v. 1** decide or determine: *~ing is more important than wishing; but God ~ed otherwise.* **2** influence by mental power: *psychic power to ~ a rock to move itself.* **3** bequeath (a property to someone). **4** wish; desire: *Do as you ~.* **5** *auxiliary v., pt.* **would** (WOOD) expressing futurity *(The world ~ end),* willingness or determination *(I ~ marry her),* capability, likelihood, habit, or custom *("Boys ~ be boys"; That ~ be the mailman),* command *(You ~ do as I say; That ~ be all).* **—will·ful** *adj.* **1** obstinate or stubborn: *a ~ child.* **2** intentional: *~ disobedience, murder.* **—will·ful·ly** *adv.;* **will·ful·ness** *n.*

Wil·liam I (WIL·yum), 1027?–87, king of England (1066–87); also called "William the Conqueror."

wil·lies (WIL·eez) *n.pl. Slang.* jitters.

will·ing *adj.* **1** ready or consenting: *~ to marry him; She is ~.* **2** ready and prompt: *~ workers, hands, ears.* **3** voluntary: *~ obedience, sacrifice.* **—will·ing·ly** *adv.;* **will·ing·ness** *n.*

wil·li·waw (WIL·ee·waw) *n.* a sudden violent wind or squall blowing into the sea from mountains along a coast; hence, a state of turmoil or confusion. **—will-o'-the-wisp** (wil·uh·dhuh·WISP) *n.* **1** a light sometimes seen hovering over marshes, believed to be marsh gas igniting itself; also called "jack-o'-lantern." **2** an elusive and misleading hope or goal.

wil·low (WIL·oh) *n.* any of a family of trees with long, narrow leaves and slender, pliable branches, often used in weaving baskets; also, its wood; **willow pattern** a blue-on-white Chinese landscape design featuring willows, pagodas, etc. and used on china called **wil·low·ware. —wil·low·y** *adj.* slender, lithe, etc. like a willow.

will·pow·er *n.* strength of will or determination; resoluteness. **—wil·ly-nil·ly** *adj. & adv.* (happening, existing, etc.) whether one wants it or not.

Wil·son (–sn), **Woodrow.** 1856–1924, 28th U.S. President (1913–21).

wilt *v.* (cause) to droop or become weak, as a plant from heat or lack of water. **—n. 1** a wilting. **2** a disease caused by fungi, bacteria, or viruses that makes plants wilt and die.

Wil·ton (rug or **carpet)** a carpet made on a Jacquard loom with velvet cut pile.

wi·ly (WYE·lee) *adj.* **-li·er, -li·est** full of wiles; sly, as a fox; **wi·li·ness** *n.*

wim·ble *n.* a boring tool such as a gimlet, auger, or brace and bit.

wim·ple *n.* a head covering of women in the Middle Ages, as worn by nuns, exposing only the face; ***v.* -ples, -pled, -pling** cover or veil (as if) with a wimple; also, cause to ripple.

win *v.* **wins, won** (WUN), **win·ning** succeed in achieving (a desired aim) by effort, as the result of competition, etc.: *Which team won (the race)? to ~ a war, scholarship, mountain summit, reputation, wife, audience; would give anything to ~* (i.e. gain) *her favor; Persevering people* **win out** *in the end; took much persuasion to* **win over** *the hostile crowd to his view.* **—n.** *Informal.* victory or success, esp. in a contest or race.

wince *v.* **winc·es, winced, winc·ing** shrink back or flinch involuntarily; ***n.*** a wincing movement or expression.

winch *n.* a crank for imparting rotary motion; also, a crank device as used in a crane to lift and lower loads.

[1]wind (WINED) *v.* **winds, wound** (WOWND), **wind·ing** **1** (cause) to move in a curving or twisting manner: *a river ~ing* (its way) *through the plain; a ~ing* (i.e. spiral) *staircase; gradually wound* (i.e. insinuated) *herself into his affections.* **2** wrap or coil: *A vine ~s around its support; with a shawl wound round his neck; a body wrapped in a* **winding sheet** *for burial.* **3** roll into a ball, as yarn, or on a spool or reel, as thread, tape, etc. **4** tighten the spring of (a clock or other mechanism) for power to operate: *a self- ~ing automatic watch;* ***n.*** a winding or turn. **—wind up** **1** make very tense or nervous. **2** of a baseball pitcher, swing the arm to throw the ball. **3** conclude (an activity or business); also, *Informal.* come to an end; end up: *wound up in jail.* **—wind·er** *n.*

[2]wind *n.* **1** air in motion, esp. a strong current: *Gale-force ~s whipped the waves; a cold winter ~; changing ~s* (i.e. trends) *of public opinion; Politicians find out* **which way** (or **how**) **the wind blows** *before taking a stand on an issue;* **get** (or **have** or **catch**) **wind of** learn about, as if by a wind-borne scent; **in the wind** about to happen; astir; **the four winds** the four directions or points of the compass. **2** gas from the stomach or bowels. **3** breathing power: *The jogger stopped to recover his ~; mere ~* (i.e. empty talk). **4 winds** *pl.* wind instruments of an orchestra, or the players. ***—v.*** **1** get the scent of; follow (a hunted animal, etc.) by scent. **2** put out of breath (*by* running, *from* a climb, etc.). **3** *pt.* **wind·ed** or **wound** (WOWND) blow (a horn); hence, sound (a signal or blast). **—wind·age** (–ij) *n.* deflecting power of the wind on a missile in flight. **—wind·bag** *n. Informal.* one who talks much but communicates little of importance. **—wind·blown** (–blone) *adj.* blown by the wind: *~ hair, trees.* **—wind·break** *n.* a growth of trees, etc. for breaking the force of the wind. **—wind-bro·ken** *adj.* of horses, having the heaves. **—wind·burn** *n.* skin irritation caused by exposure to the wind. **—wind·chill** or **wind chill** an estimate of how cold one feels because of the added effect of a wind blowing at a certain speed; also **windchill factor. —wind·fall** *n.* an unexpected piece of good fortune, esp. financial profit, like ripe fruit blown down by the wind. **—wind·flow·er** *n.* same as ANEMONE. **—wind gap** a water gap after the stream has dried up. **—wind·hov·er** (–huv–, –hov–) *n. Brit.* a kestrel.

wind·ing (WINE–) *n.* a continuous coil of conducting wire in an electrical generator, motor, etc.; also, the way the coil is wound. **—winding sheet** See [1]WIND, *v.* 2.

wind instrument a musical instrument in which air is the vibrating medium, including woodwinds and brasses, as flutes, saxophones, trumpets, and trombones. **—wind·jam·mer** *n. Informal.* a large sailing ship (as distinguished from a steamship); also, one of its crew.

wind·lass (–lus) *n.* a winch cranked by hand, as once much used to hoist water from wells.

wind·mill *n.* a mill or machine moved by the power of the wind acting on a wheel of vanes or sails mounted on top of a tower. **—win·dow** (–doh) *n.* **1** an opening in a wall for letting in light and air or for looking through; also, a framework having panes of glass, etc. that closes it: *a church ~; car ~; shop ~.* **2** a windowpane. **—window dressing** a display that seeks to impress favorably, as of goods in a store window; **win·dow-dress** *v.;* **window dresser. —win·dow·pane** *n.* a pane of glass in a window. **—win·dow-shop** *v.* **-shops, -shopped, -shop·ping** look at goods displayed in shop windows without going inside to buy; **win·dow-shop·per** *n.* **—win·dow·sill** *n.* the sill across the bottom of a window. **—wind·pipe** *n.* the air passage between the throat and the lungs, extending from the larynx to the bronchi: **—wind·proof** *adj.* protecting from the wind: *a ~ jacket.* **—wind·row** (–roh) *n.* a row of leaves, etc. formed by wind action; also, a row of hay or grain made for drying. **—wind·shield** (–sheeld) *n.* the screen of glass above the dashboard of an automobile, train, etc.; *Brit.* **wind·screen. —wind·sock** *n.* an open cone of cloth flown at the top of a pole to show wind direction, as at an airport; also **wind sleeve.**

Wind·sor (–zur) a port of S.E. Ontario at the U.S. border. **—Windsor knot** a wide or double knot used in a necktie.

wind·storm *n.* a storm with high wind but little precipitation. **—wind·surf·ing** *n.* the sport of riding a **wind·surf·er,** a surfboard equipped with a mast and sail; **Windsurfing** *Trademark.* **—wind·swept** *adj.* swept (as if) by wind. **—wind tunnel** a tunnel with air forced through it at various speeds for testing airplanes, automobiles, missiles, etc.

wind·up (WINED–) *n.* **1** the close or conclusion of an activity or business. **2** the swinging of a baseball pitcher's arm before the delivery.

wind vane same as WEATHER VANE. **—wind·ward** (–wurd) *n.* the side or direction from which the wind is blowing: *An anchor is cast to ~* (for security); **to windward (of)** in(to) an advantageous position in respect to. ***—adj.*** *the ~ and leeward sides of an island; a ~ tide* (i.e. against the wind); ***adv.*** toward the wind. **—Windward Islands** a group of islands of the West Indies; See ANTILLES. **—wind·y** *adj.* **wind·i·er, -i·est** having much wind: *a ~ day; the ~ city* (i.e. Chicago), *prairies; ~* (i.e. empty) *talk; a ~* (i.e. voluble) *talker;* **wind·i·ly** *adv.;* **wind·i·ness** *n.*

wine *n.* an alcoholic drink made from the fermented juice of grapes; also, a drink similarly made from the juice of other fruits and plants: *dandelion ~.* ***—v.*** **wines, wined, win·ing** drink wine; also, entertain with wine, esp. **wine and**

dine, treat to food and drink. —**wine-col·ored** *adj.* dark purplish-red. —**win·er·y** *n.* **-er·ies** a wine-making establishment.

wing *n.* **1** one of the paired organs of flight in birds, bats, insects, etc.: *the penguin's paddlelike ~s* (once used for flying); **under one's wing** under one's protection. **2** a structure similar to a bird's wing in function, as the vanes of a windmill, feathers of an arrow, etc.: *the ~s of an aircraft; The seeds of the maple, pine, ash, etc. have ~s.* **3** a side structure or extension: *the maternity ~ of a hospital; an unseen figure shouting from the ~s* (of the stage); *the ~s of a* **wing chair** *that has a high back with sidepieces projecting forwards.* **4** a section or unit of an organization such as an air force: *the left and right ~s of a political party.* **5** any of various side positions or players in hockey, football, soccer, etc. **6** means or manner of flight; **on the wing** in flight; on the fly; **take wing** fly away; **wings** *pl.* insignia earned by a qualified pilot, navigator, etc. in an air force. **—v. 1** fly: *geese ~ing (their way) north after the winter.* **2** cause to go fast. **3** to wound in the wing. **4** provide with wings; **winged** (WINGD, *rarely* WING·id) *adj.: the ~ messenger of the gods; the ~-T formation;* **wing·less** *adj.* —**wing chair** See WING, *n.* 3. —**wing·ding** *n. Slang.* a wild party or celebration; also, a humdinger. —**wing·span** *n.* the distance between the wing tips of an aircraft; —**wing·spread** *n.* the distance between the tips of the outspread wings of a bird, insect, etc.

wink *v.* **1** close and open one eye as a signal or hint. **2** twinkle the eyes; also, twinkle or flicker, as stars in the sky. **3 wink at** ignore; blink at (violations, irregularities, etc.). **4 wink back** (or **away**) **tears** remove tears by blinking. **—n.** a winking or the instant it lasts: *vanished in a ~; didn't sleep a ~; "forty winks" (Informal.* a short nap). —**wink·er** *n.* one that winks; also, *Informal.* an eyelash.

win·kle *n.* a periwinkle (*n.* 2).

win·ner *n.* one that wins. —**win·ning** *n.* a victory; **winnings** *pl.* money won. **—adj. 1** victorious or successful. **2** attractive or charming: *her ~ ways, smile;* **win·ning·ly** *adv.*

Win·ni·peg capital of Manitoba.

win·now (WIN·oh) *v.* blow the chaff from (grain); also, blow away (chaff); hence, sort out or sift: *to ~ wheat; to ~ out the chaff; to ~ out facts from falsehoods.*

win·o (WYE·noh) *n.* **-os** *Informal.* a wine-drinking alcoholic.

win·some (–sum) *adj.* sweet and charming: *her ~ manner, smile;* **win·some·ly** *adv.;* **win·some·ness** *n.*

Win·ston-Sa·lem (WIN·stun·SAY·lum) a city of N.W. North Carolina.

win·ter *n.* the coldest part of the year; the season following autumn; also, a period of inactivity, decline, or distress; **adj.:** *~ carnival; ~ Olympics for winter sports such as skiing, skating, and bobsledding.* **—v.** pass the winter (*in* a place); also, feed (*on* food) or maintain (cattle, etc.) during the winter. —**win·ter·green** *n.* a hardy, low-growing evergreen shrub of the heath family with glossy oval leaves, urn-shaped pink flowers, and bright red berries that yield the aromatic **oil of wintergreen** used as a flavoring and in medicines. —**win·ter·ize** *v.* **-iz·es, -ized, -iz·ing** to ready (an automobile, house, etc.) for use in the winter. —**win·ter·kill** *n.* & *v.* (cause) the death of a plant or animal from exposure to winter weather. —**win·ter·tide** *n. Archaic.* wintertime; **win·ter·time** *n.* the winter season. —**winter wheat** wheat that is planted in the fall and harvested in the spring or summer. —**win·try** (–tree) *adj.* **-tri·er, -tri·est** of or like winter; hence, cold, cheerless, etc.: *~ weather, winds, welcome;* also **win·ter·y.**

win·y (WYE·nee) *adj.* **win·i·er, -i·est** like wine; exhilarating; also, vinous.

wipe *v.* **wipes, wiped, wip·ing** clean, dry, etc. by rubbing with a handkerchief, towel, hand, etc.: *washed and ~d the dishes; ~d away her tears; had to ~ up the mess on the floor; ~d his feet on the mat; ~d* (i.e. applied) *dirt on the rug;* **wipe out** destroy completely: *The whole population was ~d out by the epidemic.* **—n. 1** an act of wiping; also, something to wipe with; **wip·er** *n.* **2** in motion pictures, a special effect by which a new scene displaces another by gradually expanding and occupying the whole frame.

wire *n.* **1** metal drawn out into a slender rod or thread; also, a length of this. **2** anything made or woven of wire: *barbed ~;* **adj.:** *~ netting, gauze, ropes.* **3** telegraph; also, a telegram or cablegram. **4 pull wires** *Informal.* exert secret influence as if manipulating puppets. **5** the finish line of a horse race; **under the wire** barely on time. **—v. wires, wired, wir·ing:** *a house ~d for electricity; broken pieces ~d together; Students ~* (i.e. telegraph) *home; ~ parents for money; ~d congratulations.* —**wire·drawn** *adj.* drawn out into a wire; also, tenuous or overrefined: *a ~ argument.* —**wire·hair** *n.* a fox terrier with wiry hair; also **wire-haired (fox) terrier.** —**wire·less** *adj.* operating by radio waves; **n. 1** wireless telegraphy or telephony. **2** *Brit.* radio. —**Wire·pho·to** *Trademark.* a picture sent by wire or radio using electrical signals. —**wire·pull·ing** *n. Informal.* the use of secret influence; **wire·pull·er** *n.* —**wire recorder** an early form of recording sound magnetically on steel wire. —**wire service** a commercial agency that gathers and distributes news and pictures to subscribing papers using Teletype and facsmile machines. —**wire·tap** *v.* **-taps, -tapped, -tap·ping** tap a telephone line secretly to get information; **n.** a wiretapping (device). —**wire·worm** *n.* a long and slender larva of the "click beetle" that damages corn, wheat, and other crops. —**wir·ing** *n.* a system of wires, as for distributing electricity through a house. —**wir·y** *adj.* **wir·i·er, -i·est 1** of or like wire: *~ hair.*

2 lean and strong: *a man of ~ build.* **—wir·i·ness** *n.*

Wis. or **Wisc.** *Abbrev.* for **Wis·con·sin** (–CON–) a Midwestern state of the U.S.; 56,154 sq. mi. (145,438 km²); *cap.* Madison; **Wis·con·sin·ite** *n.*

wis·dom (WIZ·dum) *n.* the quality of being wise, having knowledge and judgment, etc.; also, wise sayings: *a man of ~; the ~ of the ancients;* **wisdom tooth** any of the four teeth, one at the back of each jaw on either side, that appear in early adulthood. **—wise** (WIZE) *n.* way or manner: *in no ~; in this ~;* **-wise** *comb.form.* **1** in the manner specified: as in *clockwise, lengthwise, likewise.* **2** with regard to: as in *healthwise, saleswise, usagewise.* **—wise** (WIZE) *adj.* **wis·er, wis·est** **1** having or showing good sense, prudence, judgment, etc.; also, learned. **2** shrewd or crafty. **3** aware or informed: *seemed none the ~r after being told;* **get wise** *Slang.* find out; realize; **wise to** *Slang.* aware of; **wise·ly** *adv.* **—wise·a·cre** (WYE·zay·cur) *n.* one who pretends to be wise. **—wise·crack** *n.* & *v. Slang.* (make) a clever or flippant remark. **—wise guy** *Slang.* one who is conceited or pretentious.

wish *v.* **1** like and want (to have or do something): *Some ~ health, others riches; Do you ~ me to speak to your boss? Do as you ~.* **2** desire (*for* something or to be in some condition): *had everything she could ~ for; ~ed she didn't have to go to work; ~ed herself back home; ~ed she were a bird.* **3** have or express a hope for: *~ you good luck, good night; ~es no one ill.* **4** **wish on** *Informal.* foist or impose on: *a job so tough I wouldn't ~ it on anyone.* **—n.** a desire or want, or an expression of it: *granted her every~; best ~es for the holidays.* **—wish·bone** *n.* a forked bone in front of the breastbone of a bird, considered a token of wish-fulfillment by some. **—wish·ful** *adj.* longing; desirous; **wishful thinking** belief based on hope or desire rather than on reality; **wish·ful·ly** *adv.;* **wish·ful·ness** *n.* **—wish·y-wash·y** *adj. Informal.* thin or watery; also, weak or indecisive: *~ excuses, people;* **wish·y-wash·i·ness** *n.*

wisp *n.* a small bunch (of straw, hay, etc.); hence, one that is small or slight: *a ~ of air, smoke; a ~ of a girl, smile;* **wisp·y** *adj.* **wisp·i·er, -i·est.**

wist *Archaic pt.* & *pp.* of WIT.

wis·te·ri·a (–TEER–) *n.* a twining vine of the pea family that bears large drooping clusters of bluish flowers; also **wis·tar·i·a** (–TAIR–).

wist·ful *adj.* pensively longing or yearning: *a ~ gaze; ~ eyes; in a ~ mood;* **wist·ful·ly** *adv.;* **wist·ful·ness** *n.*

wit *n.* **1** mental power marked by quickness in perceiving unusual relationships between things; also, a person with such a mind or an often entertaining expression of such a mind: *Bernard Shaw was a famous ~; conversation sparkling with ~; Shakespeare's ~ and humor.* **2** intelligence or understanding: *has a quick ~;* **at one's wit's end** at the end of one's mental resources; at a loss what to do next. **—v.** *pres.* (I, he, she, it) **wot,** *pt.* & *pp.* **wist, wit·ting** *Archaic.* know; **to wit** that is to say; namely. **—wit·an** (WITN) *n. pl.* the members of the WITENAGEMOT.

witch (WICH) *n.* **1** a woman supposed to have supernatural power, usu. evil; sorceress; also, any hag or shrew. **2** *Informal.* a charming or betwitching woman. **—v.** bewitch. **—witch·craft** *n.* a witch's power or practices; sorcery. **—witch doctor** one who practices primitive or tribal medicine using magic. **—witch·er·y** *n.* **-er·ies** (an act of) witchcraft; also, charm or fascination. **—witch hazel** a shrub or small tree bearing clusters of four-petaled yellow flowers in late fall after its leaves have died; also, an astringent and antiseptic lotion made from its bark and leaves. **—witch-hunt** *n.* the searching out and harassing of political opponents, as of persons suspected of witchcraft in former times. **—witch·ing** *adj.* bewitching.

wit·e·na·ge·mot (WITN·uh·guh·mote) *n.* a council of advisers of Anglo-Saxon kings.

with (WIDH, WITH) *prep.* **1** [indicating the relationship of an action to its object]; *I agree ~ you; He is fighting ~ her; to swim ~* (i.e. in the direction of) *the current.* **2** [indicating a person or thing as having something]: *a man ~ a beard; a book ~ covers; tea ~ cream and sugar; She is ~ child* (i.e. pregnant). **3** [indicating the use of something as a means or instrument]: *shoot ~ a gun; a pen to write ~.* **4** [indicating the agreement of one action in regard to the time, direction, degree, etc. of another]: *Temperature varies ~ time of day; The day ends ~ sunset;* **with that** (i.e. thereupon) *he got up and left.* **5** [indicating cause]: *shivering ~ cold; wet ~ tears.* **6** [indicating the manner of an action]: *handle ~ care; singing~ joy.* **7** [indicating association or relationship]: *Your relations ~ people; Down ~ tyrants! To hell ~ it;* **with it** *Slang.* up-to-date; progressive. **8** despite; notwithstanding: *~ all that effort, he achieved little.* **—with-** *prefix.* **1** against: as in *withstand.* **2** away: as in *withdraw.* **—with·al** (–AWL) *adv. Archaic.* besides; also, despite that. **—with·draw** (–DRAW) *v.* **-draws, -drew** (–DROO), **-drawn, -draw·ing** **1** take back: *instinctively withdrew her hand from the fire; to ~ money from a bank; was asked to ~ his remark.* **2** remove oneself: *The candidate withdrew from the contest.* **—with·draw·al** (–DRAW·ul) *n.* **1** a withdrawing. **2** the giving up of a drug that one is addicted to; ***adj.:*** *~ illness, syndrome.* **—with·drawn** (–DRAWN) *adj.* **1** retiring or reserved. **2** secluded; isolated.

withe (WITH, WIDHE) *n.* a tough, flexible twig, as of a willow or osier, that is used for tying bundles of firewood, plaiting, etc.

with·er (WIDH·ur) *v.* (cause) to dry up, as something growing that loses vitality: *Tea proc-*

essing starts with the ~ing of leaves; She ~ed him with a look.

with·ers (WIDH–) *n.pl.* the ridge between the shoulder bones of a horse, ox, etc.

with·hold (–HOLED) *v.* **-holds, -held, -hold·ing** hold back; keep back: *to ~ permission; Employees have taxes withheld from their paychecks; The* **withholding tax** *collected by employers is remitted to the I.R.S.* **—with·in** (–IN) *prep.* & *adv.* (in) to the interior; inside: *Enquire ~; ~ the house; ~ reach, sight, call; Stay ~ limits; return ~ three days; makes you feel good ~* (i.e. inwardly); ***n.:*** *Civil wars start from ~.* **—with-it** *adj. Slang.* up-to-date or modish; hip. **—with·out** (–OUT) *prep.* & *adv.* **1** lacking; not having: *had to go ~ food and water; is used to going ~; left ~ saying good-bye; ~ question* (i.e. beyond doubt). **2** outside (of): *within and ~ the building; well decorated within and ~;* ***n.:*** *as seen from ~.* **—with·stand** (–STAND) *v.* **-stands, -stood, -stand·ing** stand against; oppose or resist (an attack, etc.) successfully.

with·y *n.* **with·ies** same as WITHE.

wit·less (–lis) *adj.* lacking wit or sense; foolish: *a ~ observation;* **wit·less·ly** *adv.;* **wit·less·ness** *n.*

wit·ness (–nis) *n.* **1** a person who sees something happen and can say so under oath; eyewitness: *the ~ of an accident; Third-party ~es attest a document signed in their presence.* **2** testimony, as given by a witness in court; evidence: *perjured himself by giving false ~; One may not* **bear witness** (i.e. testify) *against himself.* ***—v.*** be a witness of; testify to: *those who ~ed the accident; a properly ~ed* (i.e. attested) *will; actions ~ing a guilty mind; Martyrs ~ their faith.* **—wit·ted** *comb.form.* having intelligence (of the specified kind): as in *dull-~, quick-~.* **—wit·ti·cism** (WIT·uh–) *n.* a witty remark. **—wit·ting** *adj.* intentional; **wit·ting·ly** *adv.* **—wit·ty** *adj.* **wit·ti·er, wit·ti·est** having or showing wit; amusing: *a ~ retort, speaker;* **wit·ti·ly** *adv.;* **wit·ti·ness** *n.*

wive *v.* **wives, wived, wiv·ing** *Archaic.* take as a wife; also, marry a woman. **—wives** *pl.* of wife.

wiz·ard (–urd) *n.* **1** a magician or sorcerer. **2** *Informal.* one highly gifted in or skilled (*at* an activity): *a financial ~.* **—wiz·ard·ry** *n.* magic; sorcery.

wiz·ened (WIZ·nd) *adj.* withered; shriveled: *a ~ face.*

wk(s). week(s); work(s).

wkly. weekly.

W.N.W. west-northwest.

W.O. Warrant Officer. **—w/o** without.

woad (WODE) *n.* an herb of the mustard family with small, four-petaled yellow flowers and lance-shaped leaves that yield a blue dye; also, the dyestuff.

wob·ble *v.* **wob·bles, wob·bled, wob·bling** **1** (cause) to shake from side to side in an unstable manner, as a table on uneven legs; also, walk or move unsteadily. **2** waver; vacillate. ***—n.*** a wobbling movement. **—wob·bly** *adj.* **wob·bli·er, wob·bli·est** shaky; unsteady; **wob·bli·ness** *n.*

woe (WOH) *n.* misery or grief of a desperate nature; also, a cause of such grief: *tales of ~; poverty, war, and other ~s of mankind;* ***interj.:*** *~* (be) *to you! ~ is me* (i.e. Alas)! **—woe·be·gone** (–bi·gawn) *adj.* miserable or dismal in appearance. **—woe·ful** *adj.* full of woe; wretched; pitiful: *a ~ expression; his ~ ignorance;* **woe·ful·ly** *adv.;* **woe·ful·ness** *n.*

wok *n.* a bowl-shaped pan used in cooking Chinese foods.

woke a *pt.* of WAKE. **—woken** a *pp.* of WAKE.

wold *n.* an upland or rolling country without woods.

wolf (WOOLF) *n.* **wolves** (WOOLVZ) **1** a doglike wild animal with short, upright ears and a long, bushy tail, that hunts game, often in packs; **cry wolf** give a false alarm. **2** one who is greedy or rapacious; *Slang.* a sexually aggressive male; **wolf·ish** *adj.* ***—v.*** eat greedily: *~s down his food.* **—wolf·hound** *n.* any of several breeds of hunting dogs including the "borzoi" and the "Scottish deerhound."

wolf·ram (WOOL·frum) *n.* same as TUNGSTEN; **wolf·ram·ite** *n.* tungsten ore.

wolfs·bane (WOOLFS–) *n.* a species of aconite; monkshood. **—wol·ve·rine** (wool·vuh·REEN) *n.* a vicious, destructive hunting animal of northern regions that is related to skunks but resembles a bear and has dark, shaggy hair. **—wolves** *pl.* of WOLF.

wom·an (WOOM·un) *n., pl.* **wom·en** (WIM·un) **1** an adult female human being. **2** the female human being; also, women collectively; womankind: *~'s place in society.* **3** feminine nature or qualities; womanliness. **4** formerly, a female attendant. **—wom·an·hood** *n.* **1** the state or condition of being a woman. **2** women's qualities. **3** women as a group; womankind. **—wom·an·ish** *adj.* like a woman, esp. in regards to weaknesses; also, effeminate. **—wom·an·ize** *v.* **-iz·es, -ized, -iz·ing** **1** make effeminate. **2** *Informal.* philander; **wom·an·iz·er** *n.* **—wom·an·kind** (–kined) *n.* women in general. **—wom·an·like** *adj.* womanly; **wom·an·ly** *adj.* being or having the qualities suitable and becoming in a mature woman: *her ~ dignity, ~ compassion, modesty;* **wom·an·li·ness** *n.*

womb (WOOM) *n.* the uterus; hence, a place of development or generation: *events in the ~ of time.*

wom·bat *n.* a small bearlike burrowing marsupial of Australia.

women *pl.* of WOMAN. **—wom·en·folk** (WIM·un–) *n.pl. Informal.* womankind; also **wom·en·folks.** **—women's lib(eration)** the movement for establishing women's rights on an equal footing with those of men; feminism; **women's lib·ber** *Informal.* feminist.

won *pt.* & *pp.* of WIN. —**won** (WAWN, WAHN) *n. sing.* & *pl.* the basic money unit of North and South Korea.

won·der (WUN–) *n.* **1** feeling of surprise and astonishment aroused by something great or unusual: *gazed in wide-eyed* ~. **2** a person or thing considered as marvelous: *The pyramids of Egypt are one of the* ~*s of the world; It's a* ~ (i.e. miracle) *he survived the crash; was wearing a seatbelt:* **no wonder** *she survived; a drug that* **does** (or **works**) **wonders** *for your system.* —**v.** **1** feel wonder: *We* ~ *at the marvels of nature.* **2** be curious (about): *I* ~ *who's at the door.* —**wonder drug** a drug such as an antibiotic that works quickly and effectively against disease. —**won·der·ful** *adj.* **1** marvelous; astonishing. **2** *Informal.* excellent; admirable. —**won·der·ful·ly** *adv.;* **won·der·ful·ness** *n.* —**won·der·land** *n.* a land of wonders, as in fairy tales, also, a place of great beauty or tourist interest. —**won·der·ment** *n.* astonishment; amazement; also, a thing of wonder. —**won·drous** (–drus) *adj.* [literary] wonderful; ***adv.*** [with adjectives]: *was* ~ *sad, happy, good;* **won·drous·ly** *adv.;* **won·drous·ness** *n.*

won't (WOHNT) will not.

wont (WOHNT, WAUNT) *adj.* accustomed: *was* ~ *to rise early;* **n.** habit or usual practice: *as was her* ~; **wont·ed** *adj.* accustomed; usual; habitual: *in his* ~ *style.*

won ton (WAHN·tahn) **1** a Chinese dish of meat-filled noodle casings. **2** a soup containing won ton; also **won-ton soup.**

woo *v.* **woos, wooed, woo·ing** **1** court (a woman); seek to marry. **2** seek to win (fame, wealth, success, etc.); also, try to persuade (a person); **woo·er** *n.*

wood *n.* **1** the hard fibrous substance beneath the bark of a tree or shrub; also, lumber or timber. **2** usu. **woods** *pl.* a thick growth of trees, usu. smaller than a forest; **out of the woods** *Informal.* out of a dangerous or difficult situation. **3** something made of wood, as a golf club, cask, or woodcut. —***adj.*** wooden; also, growing in woods. —**wood alcohol** a poisonous industrial chemical used as a solvent and in fuels and antifreezes; methanol. —**wood·bine** *n.* **1** a honeysuckle. **2** the Virginia creeper. —**wood·block** *n.* a block of wood; also, a woodcut. —**wood·carv·ing** *n.* an art object carved out of wood; also, the art; **wood·carv·er** *n.* —**wood·chop·per** *n.* one whose work is chopping down trees. —**wood·chuck** *n.* an animal of the squirrel family that hibernates in its burrow in the winter; groundhog. —**wood coal** **1** charcoal. **2** lignite. —**wood·cock** *n.* a bird related to the snipes that lives in damp woods digging earthworms, etc. from the ground with its long bill. —**wood·craft** *n.* skill in hunting, trapping, etc. required for living in the woods; also, woodworking skill. —**wood·cut** *n.* an engraving made on a block of wood to print from; also, the picture or design so printed; **wood·cut·ter** *n.* one who chops wood or cuts down trees. —**wood·ed** *adj.* covered with trees. —**wood·en** *adj.* **1** made of wood. **2** stiff like wood: *a* ~ *smile;* ~ (i.e. clumsy) *gestures; a* ~ (i.e. lifeless) *and insensitive expression.* —**wood·en·ly** *adv.;* **wood·en·ness** *n.* —**wood·en·ware** *n.* salad bowls, spoons, etc. of wood. —**wood·land** *n.* land covered with woods; ***adj.:*** ~ *scenery, caribou; the* ~ *culture of Woodlands Indians.* —**wood·lot** *n.* a small area of forest maintained for firewood, timber, etc. —**wood·louse** *n.* a crustacean that lives in the bark of trees, old wood, etc. and can roll itself into a ball if disturbed; sow bug; also called "pill bug." —**wood·man** *n.* **-men** same as WOODSMEN. —**wood·note** *n.* the call of a bird in the woods. —**wood nymph** a mythical nymph of the forest; dryad. —**wood·peck·er** *n.* any of a large family of birds noted for their habit of climbing tree trunks, often perching crosswise, and drumming on them with their beaks and making holes to search for insects. —**wood·pile** *n.* a pile of firewood. —**wood·ruff** *n.* an aromatic herb used to flavor wine drinks. —**wood·screw** *n.* a metal screw for use in wood. —**wood·shed** *n.* a shed for storing firewood. —**woods·man** *n.* **-men** one who lives or works in the woods, as a lumberman; also, one skilled in hunting, trapping, etc. —**woods·y** (–zee) *adj.* **woods·i·er, -i·est** of or like the woods; sylvan: ~ *surroundings;* **woods·i·ness** *n.* —**wood·wind** *n.* a wind instrument such as the flute, oboe, clarinet, and saxophone, originally made of wood. —**wood·work** *n.* things made of wood, esp. stairs, doors, moldings, etc. inside a house; **the woodwork** *Informal.* hiding place; **wood·work·ing** *n.* the craft of making things from wood, including carpentry, wood carving, etc. —**wood·y** *adj.* **wood·i·er, -i·est** **1** tree-covered; wooded. **2** forming or consisting of wood: ~ *stem, tissue.* **3** like or suggesting wood: *a* ~ *flavor,* smell. —**wood·i·ness** *n.*

woof *n.* same as WEFT. —**woof·er** *n.* a loudspeaker reproducing low-pitched sounds in a hi-fi system.

wool *n.* **1** the soft, warm, curly hair covering the body of a sheep; also, anything that resembles or feels like wool, as *steel wool.* **2** yarn, cloth, or clothing of wool. —**wool·(l)en** (–un) *adj.* **1** made of wool. **2** relating to woolen products: ~ *manufacture.* —***n.*** cloth made of wool; **wool(l)ens** *pl.* woolen fabrics or clothes. —**wool·gath·er·ing** *n.* daydreaming. —**wool·ly** *adj.* **wool·li·er, wool·li·est** *adj.* **1** like, consisting of, or covered with wool: ~ *clouds; the* **woolly bear** *caterpillar of the "tiger moth."* **2** indistinct, confused, or hazy: ~ *notions; the wild and* ~ (i.e. barbarous) *American West.* Also **wool·y.** —***n.,*** usu. **wool·lies** *pl. Informal.* a garment of wool, esp. underwear. —**wool·sack** *n.* **1** a bag of wool. **2** the office of the Lord Chancellor of Britain whose official seat as speaker of the House of Lords is a large red bag of wool.

wooz·y *adj.* **wooz·i·er, -i·est** *Informal.* befuddled; dizzy or weak, as from drinking; **wooz·i·ness** *n.*

wop *n. Slang* [disparaging] an Italian.

Worces·ter (WOOS·tur) a city of C. Massachusetts.

word (WURD) *n.* **1** a spoken or written unit of language conveying an idea and consisting of speech sounds, as *oh, word,* etc.; also, a unit of information in a computer memory; **in a word** briefly; **in so many words** exactly in those words; **word for word** exact(ly); literal(ly). **2** information; news: *Any ~ of the missing child?* **3** talk, esp. a brief one: *May I have a ~ with you? a ~ of advice; They had* **words** (i.e. a quarrel). **4** what is spoken or written as an order, promise, secret code, etc.: *His ~ is law around here; She'll keep her ~* (i.e. promise); *Give the ~* (i.e. password) *to the sentry;* **the Word** the Bible. **—*v.*** express in words; phrase: *a politely ~ed letter.* **—word·age** (–ij) *n.* **1** number or quantity of words. **2** verbosity. **3** wording. **—word·book** *n.* a word list or dictionary. **—word·ing** *n.* the way something is worded; phrasing. **—word of mouth** spoken words; **word-of-mouth** *adj.* oral. **—word of honor** a solemn promise. **—word·play** *n.* play on words, as in punning; also, repartee; verbal wit. **—word processing** secretarial and editorial work using typewriters, editing keyboards, printout units, etc.; **word processor.**

Words·worth (–wurth), **William.** 1770–1850, English poet.

word·y *adj.* **word·i·er, -i·est** using too many words; verbose; **word·i·ness** *n.*

wore *pt.* of WEAR.

work (WURK) *n.* **1** effort or exertion required to do or produce something: *Digging is hard ~; intellectual ~;* **make short work of** finish (a task, meal, etc.) quickly. **2** employment; occupation: *looking for ~ because* **out of work;** *phone me at ~* (i.e. place of employment). **3** usu. **works** *pl.* factory: *iron ~s; gas ~s;* **in the works** in preparation; being worked on. **4** something being worked on or in the process of being produced: *Take your ~ home; A vise has jaws for holding ~.* **5** a product or result of work: *statues, paintings, poems, and such* **works of art;** *Faith without (good) ~s is dead; ~s of mercy* (i.e. charitable acts); *~ measured in joules or foot-pounds based on force applied and distance moved.* **6 works** *pl.* operating parts, as of a clock; also, operations and structures: *a public ~s department in charge of highways, dams, bridges, buildings, etc.;* **the works** *Slang.* everything possible, necessary, available, etc.; often **the whole works:** *Loan sharks threatened to give him the ~s* (i.e. use extreme measures) *if he went to the police; ordered a hamburger with the ~s.* **—*adj.*** used at or in work: *~ clothes, elephants, routines, songs;* ***comb.form.*** as in *clockwork, needlework, nightwork.* **—*v.*** **works,** *pt.* & *pp.* **worked** or **wrought** (RAWT), **work·ing** **1** do physical or mental work: *She ~s three days a week; students ~ing at their tasks; an author ~ing on a book.* **2** function or operate as planned, designed, etc.: *a good idea, but will it ~? a gadget that doesn't ~.* **3** cause to work or function: *She ~s herself to death.* **4** get or produce by working: *a drug that ~s wonders; The storm ~ed havoc.* **5** control or manage: *Sales representatives ~their territories.* **6** (cause) to get into a new condition gradually: *A screw sometimes ~s loose; ~ your way up the corporate ladder.* **7** make or shape (clay, dough, etc.) by kneading, mixing, etc. **8** (cause) to move in an agitated way: *Yeast is used to ~ beer; his features ~ing with emotion.* **—work off** get rid of (a debt, bad feelings, etc.) by working, doing something, etc. **—work (up)on** influence; also, try to persuade. **—work out** **1** solve (a problem, etc.). **2** develop (something new). **3** accomplish (something by resolving difficulties). **4** prove effective or successful, as a plan. **5** have a workout. **—work up** **1** produce by work or effort: *to ~ up a sweat, enthusiasm.* **—work·a·ble** (WUR·kuh–) *adj.* that can be worked; hence, feasible or practicable; **work·a·ble·ness** *n.* **—work·a·day** *adj.* everyday; ordinary: *the ~ world.* **—work·a·hol·ic** (–uh·HOL–) *n.* one who is addicted to the work habit. **—work·bag** *n.* a bag for holding working materials such as needlework; **work basket** a basket for holding needlework. **—work·bench** *n.* a table at which mechanical work such as carpentry is done. **—work·book** *n.* **1** a book designed to be used with a textbook, containing questions, exercises, etc. **2** a workman's handbook. **—work·box** *n.* a box for tools and materials used in work. **—work·day** *n.* **1** the part of the day during which work is done. **2** a day of work. **—work·er** *n.* **1** one who works, esp. as an employee. **2** in a colony of ants, bees, wasps, etc., a sexually underdeveloped insect that does the work of providing food, defending the colony, etc. **—work ethic** the attitude or belief that work is ennobling. **—work farm** a farm on which minor offenders serve their terms. **—work·horse** *n.* **1** a horse that is used for work, as on a farm. **2** one that may be depended on to work hard and long. **—work·house** *n.* **1** a house of correction for petty criminals. **2** *Brit.* a poorhouse. **—work·ing** *adj.* that works, used in working, or for working with: *the ~ classes of society; ~ hours, clothes; a ~ majority* (sufficient for carrying on work); *a ~ knowledge of a foreign language; ~ capital* (for running a business); ***n.*** operation or action, as of a machine; **work·ing·man** *n.* **-men** a manual or industrial worker; **work·ing·wom·an** *n.* **-wom·en.** **—work·load** (–lode) *n.* the amount of work that a worker has to do in a given period.

—work·man *n.* **-men** **1** a workingman. **2** a skilled craftsman. **—work·man·like** *adj.* skillful; well-done; ***adv.*** skillfully; well. **—work·man·ly** *adj.* & *adv.* workmanlike. **—work·man·ship** *n.* the skill or quality of work seen in something finished; craftsmanship. **—work·out** *n.* **1** an exercise or series of exercises for maintaining physical fitness. **2** a test or trial of performance. **—work·room** *n.* a room in which manual work is done. **—work·sheet** a sheet of paper on which school exercises are to be done; also, one serving as a work schedule or one on which something is worked out tentatively. **—work·shop** *n.* **1** an establishment where light manufacturing work is done. **2** a session at which ideas and methods of applying one's knowledge in some field are discussed. **—work·ta·ble** *n.* a table for working at, having drawers, etc. for holding materials and implements. **—work·up** *n.* a complete diagnostic survey of a patient. **—work·week** *n.* the portion of a week spent in work: *a 30-hour, four-day ~.*

world (WURLD) *n.* **1** the earth as the home of man: *a trip round the ~; the nations of the ~; other ~s to conquer;* **out of this world** *Informal.* wonderful; excellent. **2** people and their affairs; also, any domain or sphere of activity: *a man of the ~; led a life apart from the ~; the ~ of letters, fashion; the end of the ~; the ~ to come* (after death). **3** the universe; everything: *wouldn't give up her house for* **all the world;** *What* **in the world** (i.e. whatever) *do you mean? a ~* (i.e. great deal) *of good, of troubles.* **—world-beat·er** *n. Informal.* one that breaks previous records. **—world·ling** *n.* one who is busy with secular or worldly pursuits. **—world·ly** *adj.* **-li·er, -li·est** of this world; not religious or otherworldly: *~ pleasures, pursuits, wealth; He's too* **world·ly-mind·ed** *for a religious;* **world·li·ness** *n.* **—world·ly-wise** *adj.* prudent or experienced in the ways of advancing one's worldly interests. **—world war** a war involving much of the world, as **World War I** (1914–18) or **World War II** (1939–45). **—world·wide** *adj.* existing throughout the world.

worm (WURM) *n.* **1** a small, slender, soft-bodied, legless, creeping or crawling animal such as an earthworm or a leech; also, a wormlike larva, mollusk, or other animal. **2** a small, contemptible person; wretch. **3** something wormlike in shape or movement, as the thread of a screw: *The ~ of conscience gnawed at his soul.* **4 worms** *pl.* infection of a body part, esp. the intestine, by parasitic worms. **—*v.*** **1** move like a worm or make (one's way) by creeping or crawling; insinuate: *~ed their way through the bushes; ~ed himself into a position of influence; secrets ~ed* (i.e. got) *out of her confidants.* **2** purge (a dog, etc.) of intestinal worms. **—worm·y** *adj.* **—worm-eat·en** *adj.* burrowed by worms, as wood; hence, antiquated or worn-out. **—worm gear** a gear for transmitting rotary motion, made up of a toothed wheel meshing at right angles with an endless screw on a shaft. **—worm·hole** *n.* a hole burrowed by a worm in timber, etc. **—worm·wheel** *n.* the toothed wheel of a worm gear. **—worm·wood** *n.* **1** any of a group of bitter or aromatic plants of the thistle family, as a European herb yielding an oil used in making absinthe and vermouth, the shrubby American sagebrush, etc. **2** something bitter or unpleasant.

worn *pp.* of WEAR; ***adj.*** damaged by wear; also, exhausted or tired; **worn-out** *adj.* used up by wear; also, tired out.

wor·ri·ment (WUR–) *n.* (a cause of) anxiety or worry. **—wor·ri·some** (–sum) *adj.* causing worry; also, tending to worry; **wor·ri·some·ly** *adv.* **—wor·ry** (WUR–) *v.* **wor·ries, wor·ried, wor·ry·ing** to bother or trouble physically or mentally in a harassing manner; be uneasy or anxious: *Cats and dogs like to ~ their victims into submission; Children tend to ~ their loose teeth with the tongue; to be ~d about the future; Parents ~ over their children; Most people ~* (i.e. manage to struggle) *through life.* **—*n.,*** *pl.* **wor·ries** (cause of) trouble or anxiety; **wor·ri·er** *n.* **—worry beads** a string of beads that are fingered for release from nervous tension. **—wor·ry·wart** (–wort) *n. Informal.* one who worries a lot.

worse (WURSE) *adj. comp.* of BAD & ILL: *bad grammar and ~ spelling; ~ than anyone else; feel ~ after taking the medicine.* **—*adv.*** *comp.* of BADLY & ILL: *He was badly shaken by the accident but others fared ~; They were* **worse off.** **—*n.:*** *Things went from bad to ~; a change* **for the worse.** **—wors·en** (WUR·sn) *v.* make or become worse.

wor·ship (WUR–) *n.* **1** great reverence, as for a deity; also, a religious service or rite: *Sunday as a day of ~; hero ~; freedom of ~* (i.e. religion); *the ~* (i.e. extraordinary respect) *of the almighty dollar.* **2** *Brit.* a title of respect for magistrates, mayors, etc.: *Your* (or *His*) *Worship.* **—*v.*** **-ships, -ship(p)ed, -ship·(p)ing** **1** show great reverence, as to a divine being; also, idolize or adore. **2** attend religious services: *Where do you ~?* **—wor·ship·(p)er** *n.* **—wor·ship·ful** *adj.* **1** *Brit.* a title of respect for certain officials; also used in titles of guilds, lodges, etc.: *the Worshipful Company of Goldsmiths.* **2** full of veneration: *her ~ eyes.* **—wor·ship·ful·ly** *adv.*

worst (WURST) *adj. superl.* of BAD & ILL: *the ~ winter in living memory;* ***adv.*** *superl.* of BADLY & ILL: *did ~ in geography.* **—*n.:*** *The ~ of the winter was in January; a punster at his ~; Be ready for the ~; will get only a small fine* **at (the) worst.** **—*v.*** defeat.

wor·sted (WOOS·tid, WUR–) *n.* a smooth compact woolen fabric made of yarn from long fibers; also, such yarn or thread.

wort (WURT) *n.* **1** the mixture of grains and water before it is boiled and fermented into beer, ale, etc. **2** *comb.form.* plant: as in *figwort, liverwort, milkwort.*

worth (WURTH) *n.* value, as because of intrinsic merit: *Trash is of little ~; a book of some ~; a customer demanding his money's ~; a dollar's ~* (i.e. quantity) *of nuts; a person's net ~* (i.e. assets minus liabilities). ***—adj.*** [governing *n.* like *prep.*] **1** having value estimated at: *a painting ~ millions; an heiress ~* (i.e. having property valued at) *$1 billion; money that's not ~ the paper it's printed on.* **2** deserving of: *a book ~ reading; not ~ your while to complain; Is it ~ the trouble?* **—worth·less** *adj.* valueless; useless; also, despicable; **worth·less·ness** *n.* **—worth·while** *adj.* worth the time or effort spent; of some value: *a ~ undertaking, occupation.* **—wor·thy** (WUR·dhee) *adj.* **-thi·er, -thi·est** having value or merit; also, deserving (of something): *a ~ charity; ~ of your consideration.* ***—n.,*** *pl.* **-thies** a person of outstanding merit; **worth·i·ly** *adv.;* **worth·i·ness** *n.*

wot *v.* pres. tense of WIT.

would (WOOD, wud) *pt.* of WILL, def. 5: *said he ~ marry her; he ~ if he could; They ~* (i.e. used to) *talk for hours about their love; ~* (i.e. I wish) *that it were possible! if you ~* (i.e. please) *be so good.* **—would-be** *adj.* wishing, intended, or pretending to be: *a ~ poet.* **—would·n't** (WOOD·nt) would not. **—wouldst** (WOODST) *Archaic.* the form of WOULD used with *thou.*

wound (WOOND) *n.* **1** an injury to tissue below the skin: *to stitch up an open ~; a surgical ~.* **2** injury to one's feelings or good name. ***—v.*** **1** inflict a wound or wounds; hurt or injure. **2** (WOWND) *pt.* & *pp.* of [1]WIND or a *pt.* & *pp.* of [2]WIND, *v.* 3.

wove a *pt.* & *pp.* of WEAVE. **—woven** a *pp.* of WEAVE.

wow *interj.* expressing surprise and admiration. ***—v.*** *Slang.* overwhelm with delight; arouse enthusiasm in. ***—n.*** *Slang.* **1** a great success; hit. **2** rise and fall of pitch because of faulty sound reproduction.

WP word processing.

wpm or **WPM** words per minute.

wrack (RAK) *n.* **1** wreck or destruction, esp. **(w)rack and ruin.** **2** a tidewater plant, also called "eelgrass"; also, a seaweed cast up ashore, or a species of brown algae.

wraith (RAITH) *n.* an apparition of a dying or dead person; ghost.

wran·gle (RANG·gl) *v.* **-gles, -gled, -gling** **1** argue or quarrel noisily about or over something. **2** herd or tend (cattle, horses, etc.) on the range. ***—n.*** an angry or noisy quarrel or dispute. **—wran·gler** *n.*

wrap (RAP) *v.* **wraps,** *pt.* & *pp.* **wrapped** or **wrapt, wrap·ping** **1** cover or enclose by winding or folding around: *paper for ~ing gifts; ~d herself in a blanket; sat ~d in thought; too much* **wrapped up** (i.e. engrossed) **in** *his studies;* **wrap up** dress warmly; also, *Informal.* conclude or settle: *Let's ~ it up and go home.* **2** wind or put around, as a shawl around the neck or a bandage around a limb. ***—n.*** an outer covering, as a shawl, cloak, or coat; **under wraps** secret: *plans kept under ~s.* **—wrap·a·round** *n.* & *adj.* (a garment or other article) shaped so as to curve around a body or follow a contour: *a ~ robe, windshield; ~ sunglasses; a room with a ~ view.* **—wrap·per** *n.* **1** one that wraps, as a woman's dressing gown. **2** that in which something is wrapped, as the dust jacket of a book or the wrapping in which a magazine is mailed: *in a plain ~;* also **wrap·ping.** **—wrap-up** *n. Informal.* a summary that concludes a report, statement, etc.

wrasse (RAS) *n.* any of a family of fishes of warm seas with thick lips, large scales, and usu. brilliant coloring, noted for picking and eating the parasites off larger fish.

wrath (RATH) *n.* [literary use] great anger, as attributed to God, that seeks to punish the wrong-doer; hence, punishment or vengeance; **wrath·ful** *adj.;* **wrath·ful·ly** *adv.;* **wrath·ful·ness** *n.*

wreak (REEK) *v.* **1** work off or give vent to (one's anger, malice, etc.). **2** cause or inflict (havoc, vengeance, etc. *on* someone, *among* a group, etc.)

wreath (REETH) *n.* **wreaths** (REEDHZ) a ring twisted of boughs, flowers, etc.: *a ~ laid at a grave; ~s* (i.e. curls) *of smoke.* **—wreathe** (REEDH) *v.* **wreathes, wreathed, wreath·ing** **1** make into a wreath; encircle; adorn: *to ~ flowers into a garland; happy faces* **wreathed in smiles.** **2** of smoke, etc., coil or circle; spiral (upward, etc.).

wreck (REK) *v.* ruin or destroy as by a crash or shattering blow; also, be destroyed. ***—n.*** a wrecking, being wrecked, or what remains after destruction, as a shipwreck; also, one who has lost health or money: *~s towed off after a highway crash; the ~ of our hopes; He's a nervous ~;* **wreck·age** (–ij) *n.* (the remains of) a wrecking: *The ~ of the aircraft littered the runway.* **—wreck·er** *n.* one that wrecks, as one whose work is tearing down buildings; also, one that removes or salvages wrecks.

wren (REN) *n.* any of a family of small, active, insect-eating birds noted for their short, erect tail.

wrench (RENCH) *n.* **1** a sudden twisting or jerking movement, as sometimes causes back injury. **2** an injury, grief, or distortion (as of meaning) caused as if by a wrenching pull: *Leaving home was a ~.* **3** a tool for gripping and turning a nut or bolt. ***—v.:*** *She ~ed her hand away from his grip; ~ed the gun out of his hand; ~ed her ankle while playing; words ~ed out of their context.*

wrest (REST) *v.* to force or wrench something, esp. from another's possession, sometimes with deftness or skill: *He ~ed the gun from his attacker's hand; to ~ a living from the harsh envi-*

ronment; usurpers who ~ed power from the prince; ***n.*** a wresting or forcible twist. **—wres·tle** (RESL) *v.* **-tles, -tled, -tling** contend or grapple (*with* an opponent) in hand-to-hand combat, as in the sport of **wres·tling;** hence, struggle (*with* a task, problem, temptation, etc.); ***n.*** a struggle; **wres·tler** *n.*

wretch (RECH) *n.* a miserable, unhappy, or despised person; **wretch·ed** *adj.* utterly poor or miserable: *the ~ existence of the poor; ~ slums, food; felt ~ when forsaken by friends;* **wretch·ed·ly** *adv.;* **wretch·ed·ness** *n.*

wrig·gle (RIGL) *v.* **wrig·gles, wrig·gled, wrig·gling** twist and turn, as a worm does; squirm; also, move or make one's way (as if) by wriggling: *the ~ing eel; ~d away from her grasp; to ~out of* (i.e. escape by devious means from) *a difficulty;* ***n.*** a wriggling; **wrig·gler** *n.* the larva of a mosquito; **wrig·gly** *adj.*

-wright *comb.form.* maker: as in *playwright, shipwright, wheelwright.*

wring (RING) *v.* **wrings, wrung, wring·ing** **1** twist and squeeze with force: *to ~ wet clothes; to ~ out the water; to ~ a bird's neck* (i.e. kill it); *to ~* (i.e. force) *a confession, the truth, a promise, etc. from someone; She wrung her hands* (i.e. together) *in agony; a sad tale that wrung* (i.e. pained) *our hearts.* **2** clasp or squeeze (someone's *hands* in friendship). ***—n.*** a wringing. **—wring·er** *n.* one that wrings, esp. a machine for squeezing out water from washed clothes.

wrin·kle (RING·kl) *n.* **1** a small ridge or crease on a normally smooth surface: *~s on the forehead; ~s on an aging skin; to iron the ~s out of a newly washed fabric.* **2** a difficulty or problem to be ironed out, as in an agreement. **3** *Informal.* development; gimmick; device; innovation: *a new ~ in home movies.* ***—v.*** **-kles, -kled, -kling** get wrinkles, as fabrics; also, make wrinkles in; crease. **—wrin·kly** *adj.* **-kli·er, -kli·est** wrinkled.

wrist (RIST) *n.* the joint that connects hand and arm; **slap on the wrist** *Informal.* a light punishment or rebuke; **wrist·band** *n.* the part of a sleeve or cuff that goes around the wrist; also, a band or strap, as of a wristwatch; **wrist·let** *n.* a bracelet; also, a knitted band worn around the wrist for warmth; **wrist·watch** *n.* a watch worn on a strap or bracelet about the wrist.

writ (RIT) *n.* something written, esp. a court order: *a ~ of habeas corpus; Holy Writ* (i.e. the Bible). ***—v.*** *Archaic.* a *pt.* & *pp.* of WRITE.

—write (RITE) *v.* **writes,** *pt.* **wrote** or **writ,** *pp.* **writ·ten** (RITN) or **writ, writ·ing** **1** make letters so as to form words, etc. using a pen, pencil, etc.: *learn to read and ~; She ~s a steady hand; a pencil that doesn't ~ well; Print, don't ~ your name; Please* **write down** *what you hear.* **2** communicate by letter: *She ~s (to) her parents every month; too trivial a matter* **to write home about.** **3** produce (a document, record, literary or artistic work, etc.) by writing: *to ~ checks, prescriptions, music, news stories, plays; to ~ for a living, for the stage, for the media.* **4** be evident or obvious: *Suspicion was written on his face;* **writ large** clearly evident. **—write in** add (an unlisted candidate's name) to a ballot; hence, vote for (someone) thus. **—write off** cancel or forget (a bad debt, loss, etc.), depreciate (capital expenditures), or ignore (a person or thing as of no account). **—write out** write fully or completely. **—write up** write an account of, as for publication. **—write-in** *n.* a candidate written in by a voter. **—write-off** *n.* something written off. **—writ·er** *n.* one who writes, esp. an author; **writer's cramp** a muscle spasm of the hand, as may afflict those writing much. **—write-up** *n. Informal.* a usu. favorable report or account (of a person, event, etc.).

writhe (RIDHE) *v.* **writhes, writhed, writh·ing** (cause) to twist or turn about, as with pain; hence, suffer or squirm in agony, under an insult, etc.

writ·ing (RITE–) *n.* **1** the act of one that writes: *put it in ~* (i.e. written form); *at this ~* (i.e. at the time this is being written). **2** something written: *legible ~; the ~s of the ancients; makes a living by ~* (as an occupation). ***—adj.*** used to write with or on: *~ implements, materials, paper.* **—written** *pp.* of WRITE.

wrong (RONG) *adj.* not right, esp. morally; also, not just, correct, proper, presentable, desirable, etc.: *Cheating is ~; ~ spelling; a child with shoes on the ~ feet; caught driving the ~ way on a one-way street; Something is ~ with a car that won't start; You get a* **wrong number** (or unwanted person) *by dialing incorrectly.* ***—n.:*** *Infants don't know right from ~; confessed to having done much ~; "Two ~s don't make a right"; soon realized he was* **in the wrong.** ***—adv.*** [used at the end of a phrase] wrongly; **get** (someone or something) **wrong** *Informal.* misunderstand; **go wrong** turn out badly; also, depart from virtue. ***—v.*** do wrong to; treat unjustly; harm or injure; **wrong·do·er** *n.;* **wrong·do·ing** *n.* **—wrong·ful** *adj.* unjust; also, unlawful; **wrong·ful·ly** *adv.;* **wrong·ful·ness** *n.* **—wrong·head·ed** *adj.* stubborn or obstinate in a wrong opinion or judgment; perverse; **wrong·head·ed·ly** *adv.;* **wrong·head·ed·ness** *n.* **—wrong·ly** *adv.* [used esp. before a *pp.*]: *was ~ accused, spelled; was refused, whether rightly or ~.* **—wrong·o** *n.* **-o(e)s** *Slang.* a bad person or error.

wrote a *pt.* of WRITE.

wroth (RAWTH) *adj.* wrathful; angry.

wrought (RAWT) *v. Archaic.* a *pt.* & *pp.* of WORK: *What hath God ~!* ***—adj.*** formed or shaped, as metals by hammering: *~* (i.e. manufactured) *silk;* **wrought iron** iron that has been forged or rolled so as to make it malleable, tougher, and more durable than cast iron; **wrought-up** *adj.* very much excited or agitated.

wrung *pt.* & *pp.* of WRING.
wry (RYE) *adj.* **wri·er, wri·est** twisted; distorted; contorted: *a ~ face, mouth* (i.e. grimace); *a ~ smile* (of disappointment); ~ (i.e. ironic) *humor;* **wry·ly** *adv.;* **wry·ness** *n.* —**wry·neck** *n.* **1** a congenital or rheumatic disorder in which the head is continually pulled to one side. **2** a bird of the woodpecker family that twists its head like a snake when disturbed; snakebird.
W.S.W. west-southwest.
wt. weight.
Wu·han (WOO·hahn) a city of E. China.
wurst *n.* a sausage.
W.Va. or **WV** West Virginia.
WW I World War I; **WW II** World War II.
WY or **Wyo.** *Abbrev.* for **Wy·o·ming** (wye·OH–) a W. state of the U.S.; 97,912 sq.mi. (253,596 km²); *cap.* Cheyenne.

X

X or **x** (EKS) *n.* **X's** or **x's** **1** the 24th letter of the English alphabet. **2** something shaped like an "X." **3** the Roman numeral for 10. **4** an unknown quantity or one whose identity is withheld. —**X** **1** symbol for Christ, as in *Xmas.* **2** rating of the motion pictures to which those under 17 years are not admitted. —**x** multiplication symbol; ***v.*** **x-es** or **x's,** *pt.* & *pp.* **x-ed** or **x'd, x-ing** or **x'ing** cross *out* with an x or series of x's.

Xan·thip·pe (zan·TIP·ee) wife of Socrates; the proverbial scold or nagging wife; also **Xan·tip·ee.**

x-ax·is *n.* the horizontal axis on a chart or graph.

X chromosome See SEX CHROMOSOME.

Xe symbol for **xe·non** (ZEE–) *n.* a colorless, odorless, tasteless gaseous element. —**xeno-** *comb.form.* strange; foreign; as in **xen·o·phobe** (ZEN·uh·fobe) *n.* one who hates and fears foreigners; **xen·o·pho·bi·a** (–FOH–) *n.* fear or hatred of foreigners; **xen·o·pho·bic** *adj.*

xer(o)- *comb.form.* dry: as in **xer·ic** (ZEER–) *adj. Botany.* deficient in moisture. —**xe·rog·ra·phy** (zuh·ROG·ruh·fee) *n.* a dry photographic printing process that uses electrically charged particles fused by heat; **xe·ro·graph·ic** (–GRAF–) *adj.* —**xe·ro·phyte** (ZEER·uh·fite) *n.* a plant adapted to a dry climate, esp. a desert plant; **xe·ro·phyt·ic** (–FIT–) *adj.* —**Xe·rox** (ZEER–) *Trademark.* xerographic copying (machine); **xe·rox** *v.* make xerographic copies (of).

Xer·xes (ZURK·seez) 519?–465? B.C., a famous king of Persia.

Xho·sa (KOH·sah) *n.* a group of Bantu-speaking agricultural tribes of South Africa; also, a member of this group.

xi (ZYE) *n.* the 14th letter of the Greek alphabet (Ξ, ξ).

XL extra large.

Xmas (KRIS·mus) *n.* Christmas. —**Xn.** Christian; **Xnty.** Christianity.

X-ra·di·a·tion (–ray·dee·AY–) *n.* X-ray treatment; also, X rays.

X-rat·ed (–ray·tid) *adj.* rated X (*no.* 2); *Informal.* pornographic or obscene.

X ray an electromagnetic ray of extremely short wavelength, capable of penetrating opaque substances, much used in medical diagnosis and treatment. —**X-ray** **1** *v.* examine or treat with X rays. **2** *adj.: an ~ examination, photograph;* **X-ray astronomy** the study of **X-ray stars,** stars that give off X rays; **X-ray tube** a cathode-ray tube for producing X rays.

xy·li·tol (ZYE·luh·tole) *n.* a sugar substitute.

xyl(o)- *comb.form.* wood: as in **xy·lem** (ZYE·lum) *n.* the woody central tissue of a vascular plant, that conducts water and minerals upward and gives mechanical support. —**xy·lo·phone** (ZYE·luh–) *n.* a percussion instrument consisting of wooden bars that are struck with two small wooden hammers to sound the musical scale; **xy·lo·phon·ist** (–foh–) *n.*

Y

Y or **y** (WYE) *n.* **Y's** or **y's** **1** the 25th letter of the English alphabet. **2** anything shaped like a "Y." —**Y** (WYE) **1** yttrium. **2** *n.* [short form] Y.M.C.A.; Y.W.C.A.; Y.M.H.A.; Y.W.H.A. —**-y** *suffix.* **1** forming adjectives: as in *funny, salty, sleepy, sticky.* **2** forming nouns: as in *expiry, perjury, treaty.* **3** same as -IE.

yacht (YOT) *n.* & *v.* (sail) a small ship used for cruising and racing; **yacht·ing** *n.* the sport of sailing a yacht; **yachts·man** (–mun) *n.* **-men.**

ya·hoo (YAH–, YAY–) *n.* a coarse or uncouth person, like the **Yahoos** of Swift's *Gulliver's Travels.*

Yah·we(h) (YAH·way) the Hebrew name of God; Jehovah; also **Yah·ve(h).**

yak *n.* **1** a long-haired ox of Tibet and C. Asia. **2** *Slang.* idle, endless, or noisy chatter; also ***v.*** **yaks, yakked, yak·king.**

yam *n.* the thick root of a vine similar to the sweet potato, grown for food in tropical countries; also, a juicy variety of sweet potato grown in the U.S.

yam·mer *n.* & *v.* whimper; whine; also, loud or voluble chatter; **yam·mer·er** *n.*

yang *n.* in Chinese thought, the masculine, active force or principle of life and being, complementary to YIN.

Yang·tze (YANG·see) the longest river of China, flowing into the Yellow Sea.

yank *n.* & *v.* *Informal.* (pull with) a sudden hard jerk.

Yank *n.* *Slang.* a Yankee, esp. an American soldier of World War I or II. —**Yan·kee** (YANG–) *n.* **1** a person from the U.S. **2** a person from New England or N. United States; ***adj.*** of or typical of the Yankees. —**Yan·qui** (YAHNG·kee) *n.* a Yankee (*n.* 1) as distinguished from a Latin American.

Ya·oun·dé (yah·oon·DAY) capital of Cameroon.

yap *n.* & *v.* **yaps, yapped, yap·ping** *Slang.* bark; yelp; chatter; **yap·per** *n.*

^{1}**yard** *n.* **1** a unit of length equal to 3 feet (0.9144 m). **2** a slender pole or spear fastened across a mast to support a sail.

^{2}**yard** *n.* **1** a piece of ground, as around a house, church, or farm; also, an enclosed area or pen for poultry, livestock, etc. **2** a place covered with railroad tracks where cars are stored, switched, etc.

yard·age (–ij) *n.* length in yards; also, an extent or distance covered in yards. —**yard·arm** *n.* either end of a yard supporting a square sail. —**yard goods** textiles sold by the yard.

yard·man (–mun) *n.* **-men** a man who works in a railroad yard. —**yard·mas·ter** *n.* a man in charge of a railroad yard.

yard·stick *n.* a graduated measuring stick one yard in length; hence, a standard or criterion of value.

yar·mul·ke (YAR·mul·kuh) *n.* a skullcap worn esp. ceremonially by Jewish men and boys; also **yar·mel·ke.**

yarn *n.* **1** a fiber spun into strands for wearing, knitting, etc. **2** *Informal.* a tall tale or story; ***v.*** tell stories, esp. **spin a yarn.**

yar·row (YAIR·oh) *n.* a perennial herb with finely cut aromatic leaves and flat-topped clusters of small white, yellow, or pink flowers.

yaw *n.* movement about a vertical axis, as when an airplane's nose turns right or left; ***v.*** of a ship, airplane, space vehicle, projectile, etc., turn right or left in its course.

yawl *n.* a small, two-masted, fore-and-aft-rigged ship like a ketch but with the shorter mast nearer the stern; also, a dinghy or rowboat.

yawn *n.* an involuntary taking in of breath with wide-open mouth, usu. because of fatigue; ***v.*** open wide, as the mouth during a yawn.

yawp *v.* *Informal.* complain noisily; squawk; **yawp·er** *n.*

yaws *n.pl.* [takes *sing.v.*] a contagious tropical skin eruption of small sores in clusters.

y-ax·is *n., pl.* **-ax·es** the vertical axis on a chart or graph.

Yb ytterbium. —**Y.B.** yearbook.

Y chromosome See SEX CHROMOSOME.

y·clept or **y-clept** (i·CLEPT) *pp.* *Archaic.* called or named.

yd(s). yard(s).

ye *Archaic.* **1** (YEE) *pron.* you. **2** (*popularly* YEE, *more correctly* as "the") same as THE: "*Ye Olde Candle Shoppe.*"

yea (YAY) *adv.* yes; indeed.**—*n.*** an affirmative vote(r); aye. **—yeah** (YAH) *adv. Informal.* yes: *Oh, ~?* (i.e. I doubt it).

year (YEER) *n.* **1** the period of about 365¼ days that the earth takes to go once around the sun; also called "solar year." **2** an annual period such as a "calendar year" (Jan. 1 through Dec. 31 in the Gregorian calendar), the usu. Sept.-June "school year," etc.: *in the ~ 1492; the ~ 300 B.C.; the 1978–79 school ~.* **3** any 12-month period: *the fiscal ~; a taxation ~; was given five ~s (in jail).* **4 years** *pl.: advanced in ~s* (i.e. age); *~s* (i.e. a long time) *from now.* **—year after year** or **year in, year out** every year. **—year·book** *n.* an annual publication or reference book reporting on people and events of the preceding year, as of a graduating class. **—year·ling** (YEER–, YUR–) *n.* & *adj.* one-year-old (animal). **—year·long** *adj.* lasting through a year. **—year·ly** *adj.* & *adv.* once a year; every year; annual(ly).

yearn (YURN) *v.* be filled with tender feeling (of eager longing *for* someone or something that is missed or desired, of pity *for* someone in trouble, *to* do or get something, etc.); **yearn·ing** *n.* a tender longing.

year-round *adj.* & *adv.* throughout the year, not seasonal(ly): *a ~ publication, resort; complaints heard ~.*

yeast (YEEST) *n.* **1** a yellowish frothy moist substance consisting of one-celled fungi that cause dough to rise, sugars to ferment, etc., used in baking and brewing; also, one of the fungi. **2** a dried form of yeast sold in granules, cake form, etc. **3** foam or froth; spume; hence, ferment; agitation; **yeast·y** *adj.* **yeast·i·er, -i·est** containing yeast; also, frothy, light, or frivolous.

yegg *n. Slang.* a burglar, esp. one who breaks open safes; also **yegg·man, -men.**

yell *n.* **1** a loud cry or shout expressing fear, joy, etc. **2** a cheer given in unison to encourage teams at school athletic events.**—*v.*** utter or say with a yell.

yel·low (YEL·oh) *n.* the color of gold, egg yolk, etc.; hence, the yolk of an egg; also, a yellow pigment, dye, cloth, clothes, etc. **—*adj.* 1** yellow-colored, as paper by age. **2** having a yellowish skin, as the Mongoloid peoples, or **yellow race. 3** envious or jealous. **4** *Informal.* cowardly. **5** sensational and vulgar: *~ journalism.* **—*v.*** make or become yellow; **yel·low·ish** *adj.* **—yellow fever** an acute, infectious, tropical virus disease carried by mosquitoes that damages the liver; also **yellow jack. —yellow jacket** a small wasp with yellow stripes. **—Yel·low·knife** capital of Northwest Territories. **—Yellow Pages** (section of) a telephone directory usu. printed on yellow paper with classified listings and advertisements of businesses, professions, etc. **—Yellow River** a river that rises in N. China and flows into the Yellow Sea; **Yellow Sea** the inland extension of the Pacific Ocean between Korea and E. China.

yelp *n.* & *v.* (utter or say with) a short, sharp cry or bark, as of a dog.

Yem·en (–un) **1 Yemen (Aden)** "People's Democratic Republic of Yemen" in S. Arabia; also called "South Yemen"; 111,075 sq.mi. (287,683 km²); *cap.* Aden. **2 Yemen (Sana)** "Yemen Arab Republic" in the S.W. corner of Arabia; 75,290 sq.mi. (195,000 km²); *cap.* Sana. **—Yem·e·ni** (–nee) *n.* & *adj.*

yen *n.* **1** *pl.* **yen** the basic money unit of Japan, equal to 100 sen. **2** a craving, as for a narcotic; also, a strong desire or urge (*to* do something).

yeo·man (YOH·mun) *n.* **-men 1** a petty officer of the U.S. Navy with clerical duties. **2** formerly, a servant in a royal household; **yeoman of the guard** a ceremonial bodyguard of the British sovereign. **3** a member of a group of small landowners and farmers of medieval England, noted for patriotism; **yeoman('s) service** good and faithful service; **yeo·man·ly** *adj.* & *adv.;* **yeo·man·ry** *n.* yeomen collectively.

yes *adv.* [expressing agreement, confirmation, etc.] aye; yea: *~, dinner's ready; Is that you? ~; willing, ~* (i.e. and what is more), *anxious to help.* **—*n., pl.*** **yes·es** an affirmative reply; ***v.*** **yes·es, yessed, yess·ing** say yes (to).

Ye·shi·va (yuh·SHEE·vuh) *n.* a Jewish school; also, a rabbinical seminary.

yes-man *n.* **-men** *Informal.* one who agrees with everything his superiors say.

yester- *comb.form. Archaic.* of yesterday: as in *yestereve(ning), yestermorn, yesternight.* **—yes·ter·day** (–dee, –day) *n.* & *adv.* **1** (on) the day before today. **2** (in) the recent past: *heroes of ~; She was not born ~.* **—yes·ter·eve(·ning)** (–EEV, –EEV–) *n.* & *adv. Archaic.* (on) the evening of yesterday. **—yes·ter·year** *Archaic. n.* last year; also, the recent past; **of yesteryear** of yore.

yet *adv.* **1** [in negative and doubtful contexts] up to the (specified or implied) time: *It's not ~ time; She had not ~ arrived at midnight; Isn't she home ~? Is she home ~?* **as yet** up to now. **2** [in affirmative contexts, sometimes with intensive force] still: *She is waiting ~; while there is ~ time; makes things ~ more difficult; He may make it ~* (i.e. eventually; sometime). **3** nevertheless; however: *strange, ~ true;* ***conj.:*** *A strange story, ~ it is true.*

Ye·ti (YET·ee) *n.* same as ABOMINABLE SNOWMAN.

yew (YOO) *n.* an evergreen tree or shrub with rich, dark-green leaves and scarlet, berrylike seeds, esp. the "Pacific (or western) yew" valued for its fine-grained wood and the "American yew" whose boughs are used in Christmas decorations.

Yid·dish *n.* a German-derived language spoken esp. by E. European Jews and usu. written in Hebrew characters; **adj.:** ~ *folklore, literature.*

yield (YEELD) *v.* **1** give, as from within, in response to one's efforts or by cultivation: *Land ~s crops, trees ~ fruit, mines ~ ore, investments ~ profits.* **2** give in, give up, give way, etc. *to* someone, as by right, by persuasion, entreaty, or force of circumstances: ~ *right of way to pedestrians; graciously ~ed the floor to his critic; refused to* ~ (i.e. grant) *the point (of the argument); ~ed* (i.e. surrendered) *to the rapist; to ~ to temptation, treatment; ~s* (superiority) *to none in performance.* **3** give way (to physical pressure) and bend, break, etc. ***—n.*** amount or quantity yielded. **—yield·ing** *adj.* submissive; also, flexible.

yin *n.* in Chinese thought, the female, passive force or principle of life and being, complementary to YANG.

yip *n.* & *v.* **yips, yipped, yip·ping** *Informal.* yelp.

yip·pee *interj.* expressing great joy.

yip·pie (YIP·ee) *n. Slang.* a member of a radical group of hippies.

Y.M.C.A. Young Men's Christian Association. **—Y.M.H.A.** Young Men's Hebrew Association.

yo·del (YOH·dl) *v.* **-dels, -del(l)ed, -del·(l)ing** sing with abrupt changes from the normal tone to high falsetto and back, as practiced by the mountain peoples of the Alps; ***n.*** such singing; **yo·del·(l)er** *n.*

yo·ga (YOH·guh) *n.* a Hindu school of thought or a system of self-discipline developed by it consisting of physical exercises, control of the senses, and meditation for purifying one's soul. **—yo·gi** (–gee) *n.* **-gis** one who practices yoga; also **yo·gin.**

yo·g(h)urt (YOH–) *n.* a semisolid acid food made by fermenting milk.

yoke *n.* **1** a wooden frame to which a pair of draft animals are harnessed: *two* ~ (i.e. pairs) *of oxen.* **2** a yokelike frame fitted to the shoulders of a person carrying a load at either end. **3** anything like a yoke in form or function, as the shoulder-piece of a shirt, blouse, etc. or the waist-piece of a skirt supporting gathered parts, the wheel by which an airplane pilot controls ailerons and elevator, or an assembly of magnetic coils around the neck of a cathode-ray tube for deflection of electron beams. **4** a coupling, clamp, or tie: *the ~ of matrimony.* **5** bondage; servitude; also, tyrannic rule: *to throw off the ~ of slavery; under the ~ of a dictator.* ***—v.*** **yokes, yoked, yok·ing** **1** couple (as) with a yoke; join together. **2** harness (an animal) to (a plow, etc.).

yo·kel (YOH·kl) *n.* a bumpkin.

Yo·ko·ha·ma (yoh·kuh·HAH·muh) largest seaport of Japan, S. of Tokyo.

yolk (YOKE) *n.* **1** the yellow, inner part of an egg serving as nourishment for the young before hatching; also, the corresponding part of an ovum or egg cell in mammals. **2** the lanolin-containing oily film covering sheep's wool. **—yolked** *adj.*

Yom Kip·pur (–KIP·ur) a Jewish holiday observed as a day of atonement for sins.

yon *adj.* & *adv. Archaic.* yonder. **—yon·der** *adj.* [literary use] **1** (seen) over there: ~ *hills;* **adv.:** *Look* ~. **2** more distant; farther: *the ~ side of the mountains.*

Yon·kers (YONG–) a city of S.E. New York.

yore *n.* time long past: *in days of ~.* ***—adv.*** *Obsolete.* long ago.

you (YOO) *pron. sing.* & *pl.* **1** the person(s) spoken to; **y'all** *Southern.* you all (as a group); also, you (as one of a group). **2** any person; one: ~ *feel lost in a jungle;* ~ *never know.* **—you'd** you had; you would; **you'll** you will; you shall.

young (YUNG) *adj.* **young·er** (–gur), **young·est** (–gist) in an early period of one's life; not old: *a ~ lady; too ~ to drive; in the morning when the day is still ~;* [condescending style] *How are you, ~ man? old in years but* ~ (i.e. not experienced) *in the business; books for* **young adults** (i.e. teen-agers); **young and old** everyone. ***—n.*** **1** young offspring; **with young** of an animal, pregnant. **2** young persons: *books for* **the young. —young·ish** *adj.* somewhat young. **—young blood** young people; also, youthful energy, vigor, etc. **—young·ling** *n.* & *adj.* (one) that is young. **—young·ster** *n.* a child; also, a young person. **—Youngs·town** a city of N.E. Ohio. **—youn·ker** (YUNG·kur) *n. Rare.* a young fellow.

your (YOOR, YOR) *adj.* possessive case of YOU: ~ *children, country;* [suggesting familiarity] ~ *average customer;* [in titles] *Your Honor, Lordship, Majesty.* **—you're** you are. **—yours** (YOORZ, YORZ) *pron.* one(s) belonging to you: *This is ~; my books and ~; a book* **of yours;** [used in complimentary close of letter, before signature] ~ *sincerely; Sincerely ~.* **—your·self** (–SELF) *pron.* **-selves** reflexive or emphatic of YOU(R): *Help ~; (You) said it ~; You don't seem to be* ~ (i.e. well as usual) *today.* **—yours truly** complimentary phrase used before the signature in letters; hence, *Informal.* I; me. — **yous(e)** (YOOZ) *pron. Regional* [usu. *pl.*] you.

youth (YOOTH) *n.* **youths** (YOODHZ, YOOTHS) **1** the fact, quality, or period of being young, esp. the period between childhood and adulthood: *the vigor of ~; in her ~.* **2** a young person, esp. a man. **3** *pl.* young people. **—youth·ful** *adj.* young, esp. having to do with a young person's qualities: ~ *audiences, enthusiasm, hopes, impatience, indiscretions, pranks, vigor;* **youth·ful·ly** *adv.;* **youth·ful·ness** *n.* **—youth hostel** See HOSTEL.

you've (YOOV) you have.

yowl *n.* & *v.* (utter) a loud, long, complaining cry or howl, as of a dog in pain.

yo-yo (YOH·yoh) *n.* **-yos** **1** a toy consisting of a spool with a string wound around it, whose free end is held in the hand and manipulated so as to make the spool rise and fall by the unwinding and rewinding of the string. **2** *Slang.* a stupid or gullible person. ***—adj.*** going back and forth or up and down; fluctuating; ***v.*** fluctuate; vacillate.

yr. year(s); your. **—yrs.** years; yours.

Y.T. Yukon Territory.

yt·ter·bi·um (i·TUR–) *n.* a soft, silvery rare-earth metallic element. **—yt·tri·um** (IT·ree–) *n.* a silvery metallic element used in electronics.

yu·an (yoo·AHN) *n. sing. & pl.* the basic money unit of the People's Republic of China, equal to 10 chiao.

yuc·ca (YUC·uh) *n.* an evergreen desert plant of the agave family with stiff, sword-shaped leaves growing in a cluster; also, its whitish bell-like flower borne in a cluster from the center of the leaves.

Yu·go·sla·vi·a (yoo·goh·SLAH·vee·uh) a Balkan country on the Adriatic; 98,766 sq.mi. (255,804 km²); *cap.* Belgrade; **Yu·go·slav** (–SLAHV) or **Yu·go·sla·vi·an** (–SLAH–) *n. & adj.*

yuk·ky *adj.* **yuk·ki·er, yuk·ki·est** [child's word] bad-tasting.

Yu·kon (YOO–) **1 Yukon River** a river that rises in the Yukon Territory, flows across Alaska, and falls into the Bering Sea. **2 Yukon Territory** a territory of N.W. Canada; 207,076 sq.mi. (536,324 km²); *cap.* Whitehorse.

yule (YOOL) *n.* Christmas; **Yule log** a large log traditionally used to start the Christmas Eve fire; **yule·tide** *n.* Christmastide.

yum·my *adj.* **yum·mi·er, yum·mi·est** *Slang. n. & adj.* (something) very tasty, delicious, or delightful.

yurt (YOORT) *n.* a domed tentlike dwelling of C. Asian nomads.

Y.W.C.A. Young Women's Christian Association. **—Y.W.H.A.** Young Women's Hebrew Association.

Z

Z or **z** (ZEE, *Brit.* ZED) *n.* **Z's** or **z's** the last letter of the English alphabet. —**Z** atomic number; zenith. —**z** zero; zone.

Za·greb (ZAH–) a city of N.W. Yugoslavia.

Za·ire (zah·EER) a country of C. Africa; 905,-568 sq.mi. (2,345,409 km^2); *cap.* Kinshasa. —**za·ire** *n. sing.* & *pl.* the basic money unit of Zaire, equal to 100 makuta. —**Za·ir·e·an** or **Za·ir·i·an** (–EER–) *n.* & *adj.*

Zam·bi·a a country of S.C. Africa; 290,586 sq.mi. (752,614 km^2); *cap.* Lusaka; **Zam·bi·an** *n.* & *adj.*

za·ny (ZAY–) *n.* **-nies** a clown or buffoon; also, a silly person. —***adj.*** **-ni·er, -ni·est** like a zany; funny; also, silly or crazy; **za·ni·ly** *adv.;* **za·ni·ness** *n.*

Zan·zi·bar (ZAN·zuh–) capital of a Tanzanian island of the same name off the coast of Africa.

zap *v.* **zaps, zapped, zap·ping** *Slang.* strike or kill with a sudden blow; also, zoom or zip; ***n.*** zip; pep; vigor; ***interj.*** expressing swiftness of action, sudden surprise, etc.

zeal (ZEEL) *n.* enthusiastic devotion to a cause and untiring activity in pursuing it: *a missionary's ~ for the salvation of souls.* —**zeal·ot** (ZEL·ut) *n.* one who is zealous in a fanatic or partisan way; **zeal·ous** (ZEL·us) *adj.* full of or characterized by zeal: *~ workers, efforts; ~ for reform;* **zeal·ous·ly** *adv.;* **zeal·ous·ness** *n.*

ze·bra (ZEE·bruh) *n.* a horselike wild animal of Africa with black and white stripes.

ze·bu (ZEE·byoo) *n.* a domesticated ox, originally from India, characterized by a large hump and dewlap.

zed *n. Brit.* same as **zee** *n.* the letter Z.

Zeit·geist (ZITE·guyst) *n.* the intellectual and moral climate of an era; the prevailing spirit of the times.

Zen the Japanese form of Buddhism that stresses enlightenment through intuition.

ze·na·na (zuh·NAH·nuh) *n.* the women's section of a Muslim household in E. countries.

Zend-A·ves·ta same as AVESTA.

ze·nith (ZEE–) *n.* the point of the sky directly overhead; hence, the highest point (of one's career, fortunes, etc.); **ze·nith·al** *adj.*

ze·o·lite (ZEE·uh–) *n.* a silicate mineral widely used as a water softener; **ze·o·lit·ic** (–LIT–) *adj.*

zeph·yr (ZEF·ur) *n.* a soft breeze; light wind; also, a yarn, fabric, or garment of soft or light material.

zep·pe·lin (ZEP·uh–) *n.* a rigid airship having a cigar-shaped body supported by internal gas cells, as used in aviation before World War II.

ze·ro (ZEER·oh) *n.* **-ro(e)s** **1** naught or nothing; also, the symbol 0, or cipher, representing it. **2** the beginning or lowest point on a graduated scale, as 0°C. —***adj.*** having zero value. —***v.*** **-roes, -roed, -ro·ing** adjust to zero point: *to* **zero in** *a rifle* (at center of target); **zero in on** aim directly at (a target), as by adjusting the sights of a firearm; hence, focus on. —**zero-base(d) budgeting** reassessing of every expenditure from the beginning instead of dealing only with proposed increases; **zero gravity** weightlessness; **zero hour** preset time for starting an operation, as when a countdown reaches zero; hence, crucial or critical point; **zero population growth** condition of births not exceeding deaths in a given population; **ze·ro-ze·ro** *adj.* of weather conditions, with visibility reduced to nil horizontally and vertically.

zest *n.* **1** keen enjoyment; relish; gusto: *eats with ~; ~ for life.* **2** a stimulating quality: *Lemon gratings add ~ to a dish.* —**zest·ful** *adj.;* **zest·ful·ly** *adv.;* **zest·ful·ness** *n.*

ze·ta (ZAY·tuh) *n.* the sixth letter of the Greek alphabet (Z, ζ).

Zeus (ZOOS) the supreme god of the ancient Greeks.

zig·zag *n.* (a design, line, etc. in) a series of short, sharp turns from one side to the other; ***adj.*** having a zigzag form, as "forked" lightning; ***v.*** **-zags, -zagged, -zag·ging** form or move in a zigzag.

zilch *n. Slang.* zero; nil.

zil·lion (ZIL·yun) *n. Informal.* a very large number.

Zim·ba·bwe (–BAH·bway) a S. African country; 150,804 sq.mi. (390,580 km²); *cap.* Salisbury; **Zim·ba·bwe·yan** *n.* & *adj.*

zinc (ZINGK) *n.* a bluish-white, rust-resistant metallic element used in alloys and for galvanizing iron and steel. **—*v.* zincs, zin(c)ked, zin(c)k·ing** galvanize (*v.* 2). **—zinc ointment** an ointment made with zinc oxide and petrolatum for soothing skin ailments, burns, insect bites, etc.; **zinc oxide** a white powdery substance used in making pigments, cosmetics, plastics, soaps, ointments, etc.

zing *n. Slang.* **1** a sharp. shrill sound, as of bullets whistling past; **zing·er** *n.* a punchline or witty retort. **2** liveliness; zest; vigor; **zing·y** *adj.* **zing·i·er, -i·est:** *the ~est show in town.*

zin·ni·a (ZIN·ee·uh, ZEEN·yuh) *n.* a garden plant of the composite family with stiff, hairy stems, leaves arranged opposite each other, and showy flower heads in a wide variety of colors.

zi·on (ZYE·un) **1** a hill in ancient Jerusalem that was the site of Solomon's temple; hence, the seat of Jewish worship. **2** the Israelites or their homeland. **3** in Christian usage, the heavenly city or the church of God. **—Zi·on·ism** *n.* the Jewish national movement starting in 1897 that resulted in the establishment of Israel in 1948 and continues to provide worldwide support for Israel; **Zi·on·ist** *n.* & *adj.*

zip *n.* **1** *Informal.* brisk energy; vim; zing; also, a zinging sound; ***v.* zips, zipped, zip·ping** proceed with zip; also, make a zinging sound. **2** *Slang.* (a score of) zero. **—zip code** or **Zip Code** a five-digit number identifying a U.S. postal delivery area. **—Zip gun** an improvised pistol for firing .22 caliber cartridges. **—zip·per** *n.* a fastener consisting of two interlocking rows of teeth; **zip·pered** *adj.* **—zip·py** *adj.* **zip·pi·er, zip·pi·est** *Informal.* full of energy; brisk; snappy.

zir·ca·loy (ZUR·cuh–) *n.* a zirconium alloy. **—zir·con** (ZUR–) *n.* a zirconium silicate mineral, esp. the transparent variety used as a gem. **—zir·co·ni·um** (–COH–) *n.* a grayish-white, corrosion-resistant metallic element used in alloys, nuclear reactors, high-temperature furnaces, etc.

zith·er *n.* a musical instrument consisting of 30 to 40 strings stretched across a flat, shallow sound box, and played with the fingertips and a plectrum.

zlo·ty (LAW·tee) *n., pl.* **-ty(s)** the basic money unit of Poland, equal to 100 groszy.

Zn zinc.

zo·di·ac (ZOH·dee–) *n.* an imaginary belt across the sky extending 8° on either side of the sun's yearly path, through which the moon and planets move from east to west; it is divided into 12 houses, each named for a constellation, or *sign of the zodiac,* as Aries, Taurus, Gemini, etc.; also, a circular diagram representing this; **zo·di·a·cal** (–DYE·uh·cl) *adj.*

zom·bi(e) (–bee) *n.* **1** in voodoo belief, a corpse reanimated by a supernatural power; also, this power. **2** *Informal.* a person who behaves as though he is in a trance, dead to the life around him.

zon·al (ZOH·nl) *adj.* having to do with or divided into zones; zoned; **zon·al·ly** *adv.* **—zone** *n.* **1** an area or region divided in the form of a belt or band: *the Torrid, Temperate, and Frigid ~s of the earth; a time ~;* **zone melting and refining** *of metals using ring-shaped heaters that melt away impurities in narrow bands.* **2** an area having a special characteristic or restricted use or purpose: *a combat ~* (where fighting is going on); *demilitarized ~; the erogenous ~s of the body; postal ~s; danger ~; residential ~.* **—*v.* zones, zoned, zon·ing** form or divide into zones, as a city into commercial, residential, and industrial districts; **zoned** *adj.;* **zon·ing** *n.;* **zo·na·tion** (–NAY–) *n.*

zonked (ZONGKT) *adj. Slang.* stupefied, as by drink; also, high, as from a drug; also **zonked-out.**

zoo- *comb.form.* animal(s): as in *zoology.* **—zoo** *n.* **zoos** a place where wild animals are kept for display. **—zo·o·ge·og·ra·phy** (zoh·oh·jee·OG–) *n.* the science of the relationship of animals to the regions and environments in which they live; **zo·o·ge·og·ra·pher** *n.;* **zo·o·ge·o·graph·ic** (–GRAF–) or **-i·cal** *adj.* **—zool.** zoological; zoology; **zoological garden** zoo; **zo·ol·o·gy** (zoh·OL·uh·jee) *n.* the scientific study of animal life; **zo·ol·o·gist** *n.;* **zo·o·log·i·cal** (zoh·uh·LOJ–) *adj.*

zoom *v.* **1** (cause) to move with a hum or buzz. **2** of an airplane, climb suddenly upward; also of prices, etc. **3** focus a camera using a **zoom lens,** or **zoom·er,** a photographic device for taking quick close-up shots without adjusting the focus. **—*n.*** a zooming in on a scene.

zo·o·mor·phism (zoh·uh·MOR·fizm) *n.* attribution of animal form or characteristics to a god or other nonanimal being, **zo·o·mor·phic** *adj.* **—zo·o·phyte** (ZOH·uh·fite) *n.* an invertebrate animal such as a coral or sponge that resembles a plant in being flowerlike and fixed in position. **—zo·o·plank·ton** (–PLANK·tun) *n.* the floating and drifting animal life of the plankton. **—zo·o·spore** *n.* a spore, as of an alga or fungus, equipped with flagella.

Zo·ro·as·ter (zoh·roh·AS–) a Persian prophet who lived around 600 B.C. and founded **Zo·ro·as·tri·an·ism** (–AS·tree–) *n.* a religion that has the Avesta for its Bible and has influenced Judaism, Christianity, and Islam; **Zo·ro·as·tri·an** *n.* & *adj.*

zoster same as HERPES ZOSTER.

Zou·ave (zoo·AHV) *n.* a member of a French military regiment originally made up of Algerians wearing a colorful costume and with a quick, spirited style of drill; also, a member of a regiment adopting the same uniform and drill, as during the U.S. Civil War.

zounds *interj. Archaic.* A mild oath, originally "by God's wounds!"

zow·ie (–ee) *interj.* expressing enthusiasm, approval, etc.

zoy·si·a (ZOY·see·uh) *n.* a creeping grass with wiry leaves, used for lawns in warm, humid regions.

ZPG zero population growth.

Zr zirconium.

zuc·chet·to (zoo·KET·oh) *n.* **-chet·tos** a skullcap worn by Roman Catholic ecclesiastics.

zuc·chi·ni (zoo·KEE·nee) *n.* a summer squash resembling a cucumber.

Zu·lu (ZOO·loo) *n.* a member of a South African people or their language; also ***adj.*** **—Zu·lu·land** the home of the Zulus in Natal province, South Africa; 10,375 sq.mi. (26,871 km^2).

Zu·ni (ZOO·nee) or **Zu·ñi** (ZOON·yee) *n.* a member of a Pueblo Indian people of New Mexico or their language; also ***adj.***

Zur·ich (ZOOR·ic) a city of N. Switzerland.

zwie·back (SWEE–, SWYE–, ZWYE–) *n.* a rusklike bread or cake toasted in slices.

Zwing·li (–glee), **Ulrich.** 1484–1531, Swiss Protestant reformer; **Zwing·li·an** (ZWING·lee·un, –glee–) *n.* & *adj.*

zy·gote (ZYE·goht) *n.* a cell formed by the union of two gametes; a fertilized egg; **zy·got·ic** (–GOT–) *adj.*

zym(o)- *comb.form.* leavening: as in **zy·mase** *n.* an enzyme present in yeast; **zy·mo·sis** (–MOH–) *n.* fermentation; **zy·mur·gy** (ZYE–) *n.* the chemistry of fermentation processes, as in brewing and wine-making.

THE NEW YORK TIMES BRIEF STYLE MANUAL

"*The New York Times* Brief Style Manual" is designed to resolve questions of usage and answer uncertainties in choosing the correct expression quickly. While the dictionary *describes* current oral and written usage as it exists, the style manual *prescribes* guidelines for correct usage. Taken together, the dictionary and the style manual provide the means to speaking and writing with greater precision.

The materials included in the "Brief Style Manual" are adapted from:

The New York Times *Manual of Style and Usage:*
A Desk Book of Guidelines for Writers and Editors.

Revised and Edited by Lewis Jordan,
News Editor, *The New York Times*

USAGE

abbreviations. Commonly used abbreviations are listed within the dictionary.

Points are usually used in abbreviations of the names of governmental bureaus and agencies, well-known organizations, companies, etc.: *F.C.C., N.A.M.* But to avoid inconsistencies, points are omitted in abbreviations of the names of the broadcasting networks and their subsidiaries.

If an abbreviation has become a recognized word and is pronounced as a word, the points are omitted and the word may be set either caps and lowercase (the usual style for an acronym formed from a company name) or all caps: *NATO, UNESCO.* To avoid confusion, points are required in the cases of some abbreviations that spell actual words: *WHO, CAB, AID.*

In company and corporation names, points should be omitted when an abbreviation that formerly required points has been adopted without points as the official name: *the RCA Corporation.*

When letters within a single word are used as an abbreviation, they are capitalized but do not take points: *DDT, TB, TV.* But *V.D.* requires the points because it stands for two words.

In the context of an extremely formal invitation or announcement in which even dates are spelled out, avoid abbreviations.

Freer use of abbreviations is permitted in tabular matter to conserve space and keep listings within one line so far as possible. All the standard abbreviations may be used, as well as coined contractions, provided the item can be understood.

The main considerations in using abbreviations in writing are to avoid obscure contractions like *N.R.D.G.A.* (National Retail Dry Goods Association) and to avoid creating a typographical mess by excessive use of abbreviations. There is no reason to inflict on the reader a sentence like this: *The U.A.W. and the U.M.W. supported the complaints made by the W.H.O., UNICEF and the F.A.O., but AFL-CIO leaders did not.*

adverb placement. An adverb used with a compound verb should normally be placed between elements of the verb, as it is a few words back in this sentence and in the following example: *He will usually take the opposing side.* The split infinitive (which see) is another matter.

articles. See **a, an** and **the** in Difficult Words section. Avoid the faddish practice of dropping *A* or *The* when it begins a sentence. If several consecutive paragraphs begin with the same article, recast enough of the first sentences of the paragraphs to break up the monotony.

The article should appear before each of the coordinate nouns in a series or a pair: *He was helped by a policeman, a fireman and a doctor. The hero and the heroine received medals.* An exception is made if the nouns convey a single idea: *They found a bow and arrow.*

capitalization. Capitalize the first word of a sentence. Capitalize all proper nouns and adjectives: *Germans, Chicago,* etc.

Capitalize geographic directions when they refer to specific regions: *the Middle East,* but do not capitalize merely directional parts of states or compass points indicating direction: *eastern New Jersey, The road led north.*

Capitalize the main words (nouns, verbs, adjectives, adverbs), as well as the initial word of the titles of books, articles, plays, musical compositions, etc.: *Tropic of Cancer, St. Louis Blues.*

clichés. They are all things to all men. Many are beneath contempt, but some are all to the good; they lend a helping hand and add insult to injury. But they are, regrettably, never in short supply. They come in two categories: the ones that have attained a ripe old age, like those already mentioned here, and the overnight stars, like *ambience, charisma, dialogue, dichotomy, game plan, life style, orchestration, polarization, scenario, stonewalling* and *think tank,* to name a few of the many that truly need no introduction.

Some of the oldies assay as golden, and the language would be poorer if they were proscribed. They have survived not only because they are apt, but also because they have flavor and style that consciously devised replacements cannot match. It is hard to improve on *labor of love, sour grapes, dog in the manger, Achilles' heel, spill the beans, tip of the iceberg* and even *foregone conclusion* if they are properly used. But *armed to the teeth, crying need, flat denial, floral tribute, last sad rites, in this day and age, leaps and bounds, wee small hours* and even a single word like *massive* in some contexts are better left unsaid.

As for the overnight stars, they do have this distinction: They require virtually no time at all to become timeworn and trite. That is because faddishness, in writing as in raiment, is so hard to resist. But it must be resisted, just as clichés with older and more respectable qualifications must be carefully examined to determine whether their use can be justified. Most often the answer will be no.

compound words are listed separately within the dictionary. To avoid confusion, and sometimes absurdities, compound nouns that are usually solid words should be separated when the first part of the compound is modified by an adjective: *businessman, small-business man; sailmaker, racing-sail maker.*

The usefulness of the hyphen in forming compounds that serve as adjectives before nouns is demonstrated in the entries **ill-** and **well-.** An example: *He wore a well-tailored gray suit.* But the hyphen is omitted when the words follow the noun they modify: *The suit was well tailored.*

fused participles. They should be defused. For example: *The police tried to prevent him jumping* should be changed to *prevent him from jumping* or *prevent his jumping.*

genus and species. A biological species is a group of individuals capable of interbreeding and producing fertile offspring. The name of a species is always preceded by the name of the genus, or larger category, of which it is a subdivision. Only the genus name is capitalized: Homo sapiens.

In second references, names may in some contexts be abbreviated: E. coli for Escherichia coli. If a subspecies name is used, it must be accompanied by genus and species names: Homo sapiens neanderthalensis.

The more comprehensive taxonomic classifications of plants and animals are, in ascending order, family, order, class, phylum and kingdom. Capitalize the names of all such classifications except kingdom: the phylum Protozoa. But nouns and adjectives derived from such classifications are not capitalized: protozoan (n. and adj.).

italicizing. In general writing, italics are used to indicate emphasis or that a word or phrase is foreign. To refer to an expression, word, letter or number as such, either italics or quotation marks may be used: New Yorkers often use the adjective *wonderful. The present participle ends in "ing".*

number of subject and verb. After a *neither-nor* construction, if the subjects are both singular, use a singular verb: *Neither Jack nor Jill was happy.* If the subjects are both plural, use a plural verb: *Neither the Yankees nor the Athletics were hitting.* If one subject is singular and the other plural, use the number of the one after the *nor: Neither the man nor his horses were ever seen again.*

A copulative verb takes the number of the noun preceding it, which is the subject: *What was remarkable was the errors made on both sides.*

When the verb is far removed from the subject, and especially if another noun intervenes, mistakes like this one may occur: *The value of all of Argentina's exports to the United States* are *given as 183 million pesos.*

Improper identification of subject also causes trouble: *Natalie Gibbs is one of those women who goes in for fantastic dress.* The verb should be *go,* since its subject is *who,* which refers to the plural *women.*

Sums of money are usually construed as singular: *Ten dollars buys less now than five did then.* The thought here is of a sum, not of individual bills or coins. But the plural is used when the idea of individual items is suggested: *Three hundred parcels of food were shipped.*

Total of or *number of* may take either a plural or a singular verb; in general, when the expression is preceded by *a* it is plural: *A total of 102 persons were injured. A number of people were injured.* When the expression is preceded by *the,* it is usually singular: *The total of all department budgets is $187 million. The number of passengers injured was later found to be 12.*

If *couple* conveys the idea of two persons, it should be construed as a plural: *The couple were married.* But: *Each couple was asked to give $10.*

percent, percentage. *Percent* is one word with no point, and a preceding number is expressed in figures (except when the number begins a sentence): *80 percent, 8 percent, one-half of 1 percent.* But: *five percentage points, 12 percentage points.* The symbol *%* may be used with the figure in tabular matter: *5% Raise, 93%.* Do not use the abbreviation *pct.* in general writing. It may be used in tabular and other special matter.

Do not use *percent* when *percentage point* is meant: If an interest rate rises to 11 percent from 10 percent, it is a rise of one percentage point, but it is an increase of 10 percent.

plurals of abbreviations, letters and figures. These plurals are usually formed by adding *'s,* as in *M.D.'s, C.P.A.'s, A B C's, p's and q's, size 8's.* But shortened word forms do not take the apostrophe: *co-ops, vets.*

plurals of combined words and compounds. These are variously formed. The plurals of military titles are for the most part formed by adding *s* to the second word, which is usually the more important element of the compound: *major generals, lieutenant colonels,* etc. But the *s* is added to the first word in *sergeants major, adjutants general* and *inspectors general.* In civilian titles the *s* is added to the first word, usually the more important element: *attorneys general, postmasters general,* etc. The *s* is also added to the more important element in words like *courtsmartial* and *rights of way.* When compounds are written as one word, the plurals are formed in the normal way. This guide applies also to such words as *cupfuls, handfuls, tablespoonfuls, breakthroughs.*

plurals of common nouns. Ordinarily the plurals are formed by the addition of *s* or *es: hammers, saws, churches, boxes, gases.* Words ending in *o* preceded by a vowel take the *s: folios, taboos.* Words ending in *o* preceded by a consonant usually take *es: echoes, embargoes, mosquitoes, Negroes* (always capitalized), *potatoes.*

Words ending in *y* preceded by a vowel take the *s* only: *alloys, attorneys, days.* When words end in *y* preceded by a consonant, the *y* is changed to *i* and *es* is added: *armies, ladies, skies.* For exceptions, see **plurals of proper names.**

Some words are the same in the plural as in the singular: *chassis, deer, sheep, swine, fowl,* etc. The collective plural of *fish* is the same as the singular, but *fishes* may be used in the sense of specific kinds: *certain fishes.*

The original plurals of some nouns of foreign derivation are to be used: *data, phenomena,* etc. The plurals of some other nouns of foreign derivation are sometimes formed in the English manner: *memorandums, curriculums, formulas,* etc.

plurals of proper names. The plurals of proper names are formed by adding *s* or *es: Cadillacs, Harolds, Joneses, Charleses.* In forming the plurals of proper names ending in *y,* the *y* is not changed to *ie* as it is in some common nouns: *Harrys, Kennedys, Germanys, Kansas Citys.* There are some exceptions, like *Alleghenies, Rockies, Sicilies.*

possessives. See **apostrophe** in the Punctuation section.

prepositions. The prepositions that may be used after certain words are a matter of idiom. Some of those words that precede the prepositions in such idioms are listed in the illustrative phrases that accompany definitions within the dictionary and also in the Difficult Words section of this guide. See, for example, **forbid** and **prohibit.** The listings should not be taken to mean that such words are invariably followed by prepositions.

pronouns and missing antecedents. Pronouns require nouns or pronouns as antecedents. An adjective will not serve: *The bitterness of the German resistance indicated their awareness of the danger.* But *the Germans' resistance* gives *their* its needed antecedent.

quotations. Direct quotations, in which words are spoken in direct discourse, require quotation marks at their beginning and end: *John said, "I am overjoyed to see you."*

Indirect quotations, commonly introduced by the word *that,* require no quotation marks: *John said that he was overjoyed to see you.*

When two persons are quoted in succession, the second quotation should begin a new paragraph, preceded by the identification of the speaker, to make it immediately clear to the reader that the speaker has changed.

If a quotation begins with a sentence fragment, do not go on to quote one or more full sentences. Instead, close the quotation marks at the end of the fragment and introduce the full sentences as a separate, further quotation, preferably beginning a new paragraph, as follows:

The President said the ceremony represented "the beginning of the difficult task of administering clemency."

"Instead of signing these decisions in a routine way," he continued, "I want to underline the commitment of my Administration to an even-handed policy of clemency."

If a quotation comprises several sentences, the attribution should either precede the quotation or follow the first sentence; if the first sentence is long, the attribution may be interpolated between phrases of it. In other words, a quotation should not go beyond a phrase or a brief sentence before the reader is told who is speaking.

A long quotation, especially one consisting of several sentences, should not hang from a stubby or abrupt introduction, such as *He said,* at the beginning of the paragraph. Instead, the attribution should be expanded and run into the preceding paragraph, or should be moved down to follow the first phrase or sentence of the quotation.

When attribution introduces a quoted sentence fragment or a single quoted sentence, a comma should precede the quotation marks; if the quotation is longer than one sentence, it should be introduced with a colon.

See also **quotation marks** in the Punctuation section.

sequence of tenses. In writing in which the governing verb is generally in the past tense, for precision's sake the tenses of other verbs in a sentence must be properly related to it. The following examples are offered as a guide:

He said he was sick. He was sick at the time he said so.

He pointed out that the earth is round. The *is* is right because the earth is always round.

He said he had been sick. He was sick at some time before the saying.

He said he was sick on July 4. Here a *had* is not needed to put the sickness back in time before the saying; *July 4* does that.

Mr. Jones is a sick man, Dr. Manley said, and cannot work. This means that Jones was sick when the doctor so reported. The *said* is not the governing verb, but merely a parenthetical interpolation and thus *is* and *cannot* are correct. They would change to *was* and *could not* if the sentence read *Dr. Manley said that Mr. Jones, etc.*

Mr. Jones was a sick man, Dr. Manley said, and could not work. Here the meaning is that Jones was sick at some time in the past before the doctor spoke.

split infinitive. It should generally be avoided, but can sometimes be justified. For instance: *He was obliged to more than double the price.* But *to clearly show* is poor usage. A compound verb, however, should usually be separated when it is used with an adverb. See **adverb placement.**

PUNCTUATION

accent marks are to be used in ordinary reading matter in certain words of languages developed from the Latin and in German words. Some words are sometimes written without their accents in English: *cafe, facade,* etc.

The most frequently used accents are the grave accent *(è),* the acute accent *(é)* and the circumflex *(â): cause célèbre, raison d'être.*

The cedilla *(ç),* used in French and other languages to denote a soft *c,* should be used in words requiring it: *garçon, François, français,* etc.

The tilde *(ñ),* which in Spanish and Portuguese has a marked effect upon the pronunciation, should also be used when required: *vicuña, mañana, São Paulo.*

The German umlaut *(ä),* is sometimes represented by an *e* added to the vowel when the umlaut is omitted.

In the Latin languages, the dieresis, also consisting of two dots, is used to indicate that two adjacent vowels are pronounced separately *(Citroën, Noël)* or that a normally silent final consonant is pronounced *(Saint-Saëns).*

In general, do not use the accent marks in other languages—the Scandinavian languages and Hungarian, for example—whose accenting systems are so unfamiliar as to invite error.

apostrophe. The apostrophe is used to indicate the possessive case of a noun *(man's),* to denote a contraction or omission of letters or numerals *(it's* for *it is, '64* for *1964)* and to form the plurals of letters or numerals *(p's and q's, size 7's, B-52's).*

The singular possessive is formed with *'s (boy's coat)* and the plural with *s' (boys' coats, the Manleys' car).*

For a plural that does not end in *s (women, children),* the possessive is formed with *'s: women's, children's.*

Sometimes a singular idea is expressed in words that are technically plural; in such a case, the plural form of the possessive is used: *United States', General Motors', Lehman Brothers'.* Never *United States's,* etc.

Almost all singular words ending in *s* require another *s* as well as the apostrophe to form the possessive: *James's, Charles's, The Times's.* But the *s* after the apostrophe is dropped when two or more sibilant sounds precede the apostrophe: *Kansas' Governor, Moses' behalf.* It is also dropped in certain expressions in which the word following the apostrophe begins with *s: for conscience' sake, for appearance' sake, for goodness' sake.*

When a name ends with a sibilant letter that is silent, the possessive is formed with *'s: Arkansas's, Duplessis's, Malraux's.* By custom, however, the possessive of an ancient classical name is formed with an apostrophe only: *Achilles' heel, Euripides' dramas.*

The apostrophe is used in expressions like *60 days' notice* and *20 years' confinement.* But: *a 60-day warning period, a 20-year sentence, a sentence of 20 years.* Also:

a million dollars' worth of publicity, two cents' worth. But, with figures: *$5 million worth.*

Apostrophes are omitted in names of many organizations: *Citizens Union, Doctors Hospital, Teachers College,* etc. But if the word is plural before the addition of an *s,* the apostrophe is used: *Young Men's Christian Association, Children's Court.* Also: *The Ladies' Home Journal.*

In contractions that have come into common usage, the apostrophe is not used: *cello, cellist, copter, chutist, phone, plane.* The apostrophe is used in abbreviations and contractions like *O.K.'d.*

colon. The colon is used as a mark of introduction to a word, phrase, sentence, passage, list, tabulation, text, textual excerpts, etc. It is also used in giving clock times *(10:30 A.M.)* and, in sports, the times of races *(2:55, 4:10:23).*

As a mark of punctuation within the sentence the colon can be effective: *Today is the dead center of the year, or as near dead center as one can conveniently get: 182 days gone by, 182 to come.*

In ordinary writing, the first word after a colon is not capitalized if what follows is not a complete sentence: *There were three considerations: expense, time and feasibility.* But: *He promised this: The company will make good all the losses.*

While a comma suffices to introduce a direct quotation of one sentence that remains within the paragraph, the colon should be used to introduce longer quotations.

Do not use a dash with a colon.

comma. In general, use a comma when the elements of a series are separated by semicolons: *Jack Jones, the manager; Jeff Stone, the coach; Dick Smith, a player, and Harry Roberts, an umpire, were arrested.* Use a comma in sentences like this to avoid confusion: *A martini is made of gin and dry vermouth, and a chilled glass is essential.*

Commas are also to be used in compound sentences before *and, but* and *for: They left early, and their mother said they would arrive before lunch. The track was slow, but the betting was fast. He was impatient, for his dismissal was due any day.* When the clauses are exceptionally short, however, the comma may be omitted: *Nero fiddled and Rome burned.* Also: *The comma is small but mighty.*

Use commas to set off a nonrestrictive clause: *The house, which was 100 years old, was still in good condition.* Do not use the comma after an identifying noun used in the restrictive sense: *The painter Van Gogh had a hard struggle.* The absence of commas in *His brother George was best man* means that the bridegroom has more than one brother. If there is only one brother, *George* should be set off by commas. Thus a monogamous society must be well supplied with commas: *His wife, Nancy, was not there.*

Between adjectives in a series or a pair, use a comma if the adjectives are of equal significance—that is, if they could sensibly be connected by *and: a tired, disillusioned politician; quick, easy solutions.* But: *a gray iron cot; a wiry old carpenter.*

The comma may also be used to introduce a quotation: *He said, "I will be back."* For quotations of more than one sentence use the colon (which see). In attributing quoted matter, put the comma before the quotation mark: *"I am ready," he said.*

A comma may also introduce a paraphrase similar in form to a quotation but lacking quotation marks: *The question is, How high will prices rise? He said, Yes, he would accept the job.* But: *He said yes. She said no.*

In general, use the comma when giving figures in thousands *(1,250 miles, $12,416.22).* But do not use it in designations of years, street numbers, box numbers, room numbers or telephone numbers.

In financial matter, precise use of the comma is often needed to avoid confusion: *The stock advanced 3 points, to 21.* The comma makes it clear that the range of advance was not between 3 and 21, but from 18 upward.

Do not use a comma before an *of* indicating place or position: *George H. Brown of Brooklyn. President John P. Manley of Ghana.* In ages, heights, distances, times, etc., expressed in the following form, the comma is omitted: *4 years 9 months 21 days; 6 feet 3 inches tall; 2 hours 15 minutes 10 seconds.*

Commas are used in names like these: *John P. Manley, Jr.* (or *Sr.*), *John P. Manley, 3d.*

Commas are used when constructions like this cannot be avoided: *the Salem, Oregon, public schools; a Columbus, Ohio, newspaper.* (But *public schools of Salem, Oregon,* is preferred.) In proper names, use parentheses to indicate that what is enclosed is not part of the name: *The Columbus (Ohio) Citizen.* See **parentheses and brackets.**

In dates giving the month and the year but not the day, the comma should not be used between month and year: *He said he left Boston in April 1975 and never returned.* But when the day is given, a comma is used between day and year, and a comma or some other punctuation mark must always be used after the year. A construction like this is not acceptable: *He said that May 5, 1969 was not a happy day for him.*

dash. The dash is often misused for the comma: *John—who was badly hurt last year—was pronounced fit today. His friends—Mr. and Mrs. Jones—were late.* But the dash is properly used when what follows is a series punctuated by commas: *The Administration will face many problems—unemployment, school segregation, declining revenue and rising Government costs—during the present session of Congress.* Here the dash is also needed to avoid confusion: *The costs—taxes and lawyers' fees—were higher than expected.*

Another use of the dash is to mark an abrupt change in continuity of expression: "*The balance of payments is—but you know all that.*" A sudden interruption in dialogue or Q. and A. matter should be marked by a two-em dash:

"*Your Honor,*" *she said,* "*please let me finish my——.*"

"*Overruled!*" *the judge shot back.*

But a quotation that trails off indecisively is treated differently. See **quotations.**

The dash may also precede *namely, viz., i.e.* and similar words or abbreviations. Do not use a dash together with a comma, a semicolon or a colon.

elipsis. When textual excerpts are used, ellipsis should be indicated in important statements or documents if confusion or unfairness may result from the absence of such indication.

Use three points (not asterisks) to indicate an omission in the interior of a sentence, and four points for an omission at the end of a sentence. To indicate the omission of an entire paragraph or more, use a centered line of three points between paragraphs.

exclamation mark. When ending a sentence, clause, phrase, or even a single word that indicates vigorous emotion or feeling, use the exclamation mark: *"Hang him!" the crowd shouted. "That is a monstrous lie!" he roared. "Resign! Resign!" came the cry from the opposition.* Omission of the mark in such cases would vitiate the intended effect. Depending on context, the mark is also properly used, inside quotation marks or not, in instances like these: *"Oh, what a vicious thing to say!" "Ouch!" How unfair was history's verdict! How ridiculous to call him "a second Babe Ruth"!*

hyphen. Many compounds are formed with the hyphen as a connector, but as such words become established the hyphen is often dropped in favor of the solid form.

The hyphen is used in constructions like these: *three-mile hike, 30-car train.* It is also used to avoid confusion in words like *re-form* (meaning to form again).

Hyphens should not be used in constructions like the following if the meaning is clear without them: *sales tax bill, foreign aid plan.* But: *pay-as-you-go plan.* The hyphen is not needed in these forms: *navy blue skirt, dark green paint.*

In many compounds, the hyphen should be used to avoid ambiguity or absurdity: *small-business man,* not *small businessman* (note separation of solid compound; see **compound words in the Usage section);** *unfair-practices charge,* not *unfair practices charge.*

The usefulness of the hyphen in forming compounds that serve as adjectives before nouns is demonstrated in the dictionary entries **ill-** and **well-**. An example: *He wore a well-tailored gray suit.* But the hyphen is omitted when the words follow the noun they modify: *The suit was well tailored.*

Do not use the hyphen to connect an adverb ending in *ly* with a participle in such phrases as *newly married couple, elegantly furnished house.* But adjectives ending in *ly* are another matter: *a gravelly-voiced, grizzly-maned statesman of the old school.*

Hyphens are not used in titles like these: *commander in chief, director general, editor in chief, secretary general.* Do use the hyphen in titles like *secretary-treasurer.*

The suspensive hyphen is a useful device: *On successive days there were three-, five- and nine-inch snowfalls.*

Street numbers in some areas take the hyphen: 107-71 111th Street.

Use the hyphen in such expressions as *Italian-American, Japanese-American.* But: *French Canadian.*

parentheses and brackets. In general, parentheses are used to indicate an interpolation by a writer in his own copy: *Cardinal Manley cited the encyclical "Pacem in Terris" ("Peace on Earth").* Or: *In 1962, the painting sold for £100 ($280).*

A nickname interpolated in an actual name should be enclosed in parentheses: *Anthony (Tough Tony) Anastasia.* The parentheses should also be used in making a differentiation such as this in proper names: *the Springfield (Massachusetts) General Hospital,* indicating that *Massachusetts* is not part of the name. But use commas in *a Springfield, Massachusetts, hospital.* See **comma**.

When a clause in parentheses comes at the end of a sentence and is part of it, put the period outside the parentheses: *The witness did not identify the automobile (a Cadillac, according to earlier testimony).* If the parenthesized matter is independent of the sentence and requires a period, the period is placed inside the closing mark: *The university was not identified. (It developed later that he was speaking of Harvard.)*

Do not place a comma before a parenthesis mark; if a comma is indicated after the sentence or phrase preceding the parenthesis, the comma should be placed outside the closing parenthesis mark: *The university (Harvard), he said, was not involved.*

Do not use a dash and parentheses together.

Brackets, in general, are used to enclose an interpolation from another place. Bracketed matter should be paragraphed and indented unless it is merely a phrase or a short sentence that may be interpolated without making the original paragraph cumbersome.

In quoted matter, the brackets are used in place of the parentheses to indicate that the person quoted did not make the interpolation: *"Then," he said, "I went to see Manley [Attorney General John P. Manley].*" Bracketing into a quotation should, however, be a last resort. A writer should make every effort to adjust the introductory or surrounding language so that the quotation can stand on its own.

In bracketed matter that is more than one paragraph long, place a bracket at the beginning of each paragraph and at the end of the last paragraph only.

parenthetical attribution. The interpolated phrase of attribution is often misused: *In Laos the State Department announced that two attachés were missing.* The phrase *the State Department announced* is a parenthesis, and does not govern the tense of the verb that follows. It should be set off by punctuation: *In Laos, the State Department announced, two attachés are missing.* Another example: *While the building was being renovated Mr. Brown said that the document had been found in a closet.* It should read: *While the building was being renovated, Mr. Brown said, the document was found in a closet.* Ignorance of a parenthesis may result in ambiguity: *In 1973 the witness testified that he never saw the defendant.* Note the difference commas can make: *In 1973, the witness testified, he never saw the defendant.*

period. An important thing to remember about the period is that it is used to end a sentence and that the insertion of one can often mean two easy-to-read sentences instead of one cumbersome sentence.

Do not use the period after *percent;* Roman numerals; serial references such as *(1)* and *(a);* sums of money in dollar denominations (write *$50* unless cents are added: *$50.69*).

question mark. It is used to indicate a direct query: *What are the problems facing the country?* Indirect questions do not require the mark: *They asked if he could attend.*

Requests cast in the form of questions also take the period rather than the question mark: *Will you please register at the desk. May I take your coat.* See **quotation marks.**

quotation marks. Quoted matter, spoken or written, is enclosed in double (outside) or single (inside) quotation marks: *"I do not know the meaning you attach to 'workweek,' " he said. "Please tell me."*

The period and the comma should be placed inside the quotation marks, as in the foregoing example. The colon and the semicolon are placed outside: *He defined "workweek": the average number of hours worked weekly by the men in his factory.* Question marks and exclamation marks may come before or after the quotation marks, depending on the meaning: *The crowd shouted, "Long live the King!" Just imagine, he was afraid of "elephants without trunks"! "Who are these 'economic royalists'?" he asked. Have you read "Lord Jim"?*

If an expression in a foreign language is quoted, any parenthetical translation should also be quoted: *"Pacem in Terris" ("Peace on Earth").*

In continuous quoted matter that is more than one paragraph long, place a quotation mark at the beginning of each of the paragraphs and at the end of the last paragraph only.

In general, the use of slang words should be justified by the context and should not require quotation marks. But the marks should be used with words or phrases employed in an arbitrary or opposite sense, as in *That sad day was the only "happy" one he could recall.*

semicolon. The semicolon is used principally as a mark of division in sentences containing statements that are closely related but require a separation more emphatic than a comma: *Peace is indivisible; if any European country is menaced, all are menaced. The contestants were ready; the timekeeper was not. The assignment was difficult; still, he carried it out.*

The semicolon is also used in a series of three or more things that includes defining matter: *Those present were Thomas A. Jones, a banker; Harriet G. Smith, a lawyer; Harold I. Abbot, a tax consultant, and John Trenton, a principal stockholder.* (Note the comma before the *and.*)

If a semicolon and a closing quotation mark or a closing parenthesis appear together in a sentence, the semicolon should follow the other mark: *He said it was "bills, bills, bills"; she said he was stingy.*

slash mark. Use a slash mark to indicate alternative expressions: *he/she, and/or,* etc. Use this device sparingly. The slash mark is also used to indicate the end of a line in quoting verse: *In Xanadu did Kubla Khan/A stately pleasure dome decree.*

DIFFICULT WORDS

a, an. The indefinite article *a* is used before words beginning with a consonant sound, including the aspirate *h: a car, a hotel, a historical.* It is also used before words like *union, euphonious, unit.* The indefinite article *an* is used before words beginning with a vowel sound: *onion, uncle, honor.* The choice of article before an abbreviation or a numeral or other symbol also depends upon the sound: *an N.Y.U. student, an 11-year-old girl.* See **articles,** in Usage section, and **the.**

affect, effect. The verb *affect* means to influence, change or otherwise have effect *(Her attitude affected the outcome);* to like to do, wear or use *(He affected cowboy boots and spurs);* to pretend *(He affects erudition that few scholars can match).* The verb *effect* means to accomplish, complete, cause, make possible, carry out *(They effected changes in important statutes).* The noun is almost invariably *effect (One effect was a hurried rewriting of the textbooks). Affect* as a noun is another, psychological matter; it is rarely used.

after is almost always better than the preposition *following* as in *He went home after the game.*

allude, refer. To allude to something is to speak of it without direct mention; to refer to it is to mention directly.

among, between. In general, *between* applies to two things, and *among* to more than two. But *between* is correct in reference to more than two when the items are related severally and individually: *The talks between the three powers ended in agreement to divide the responsibility among them.*

as if is preferred, but *as though* is not incorrect.

as much as. Write *as much as if not more than,* not *as much if not more than.* Even better: *He earns as much as an Army colonel, if not more.*

averse (unwilling to or reluctant to), **adverse** (opposed to or unfavorable to).

a while, awhile. *He plans to stay for a while. He plans to stay awhile.*

beside (at the side of), **besides** (in addition to).

biannual, biennial. *Biannual* means twice a year; so do *semiannual* and *semiyearly.* Every two years is *biennial.* To aid comprehension, avoid the prefix forms when possible and write *twice a year* or *every two years.*

bring, take. *Bring* denotes movement toward the speaker or writer; *take* denotes movement away from the speaker or writer, or any other movement that is not toward him. Thus it would be incorrect, when writing from any city except Detroit, to state that the Canadian Prime Minister was *bringing* a group of industrialists to a conference in Detroit.

canvas (cloth), **canvass** (to survey, poll or solicit).

careen, career. *Careen* means to tilt or be tilted or to heel over (as a ship). The verb *career* means to move at high speed, to rush wildly.

charge. Use preposition *with.* (But after *accuse,* use *of.*) In writing about arrests and criminal proceedings, the word *charge* should be used with care: Ideally it is the formal allegation submitted to a court by a prosecutor or (in the case of an indictment for a serious crime) by a grand jury; at a minimum, *charge* may refer to the official allegation lodged by the police at the time of booking.

collide, collision. There is a collision only when both bodies are in motion. If the phrase *collided with* seems to fix blame, it can be avoided by using this construction: *An automobile and a bus collided.* The phrase *were in collision* accomplishes the same purpose, but is stilted and should be avoided.

compare. Use preposition *to* or *with.* In the sense of likening, use *to: He compared the quarterback's role to that of a company's vice president for operations.* Use *with* in the sense of examining for similarities or differences: *They compared Mrs. Jones's record as a forecaster with Mr. Smith's, and found Mrs. Jones's more accurate.*

comprise means to include or contain; the whole comprises the parts: *The system comprises 35 formerly independent rail and bus lines.* Not: *Thirty-five lines comprise the system.* And not *comprised of.*

convince, persuade. Convince should be followed by an *of* phrase or a *that* clause, but not by the infinitive *to. Persuade* may be followed by any of them.

defect (n.). Use preposition *in* (for a defect in a thing), but *of* for a person's shortcoming, as: *A defect of perception led him astray.*

different from, different than. You can't go wrong with *different from;* you can, and almost always will, with *different than.*

dilemma does not mean simply a problem; it involves a choice between two alternatives, both unattractive.

due to is properly used in the sense of *caused by* or *resulting from* when *due* is an adjective modifying a noun: *His dismissal was due to that single escapade.* (The modified noun is *dismissal.*) But *due to* should not be used when there is no modified noun: *He was dismissed due to that single escapade.* In this instance, *because of* solves the problem.

each other, one another. Two persons look at *each other;* more than two look at *one another.*

emigrate, immigrate. *Emigrate* (with preposition *from*) refers to leaving a country. *Immigrate* (with preposition *to* or *into*) refers to arriving in a country.

ended, ending. Use *ended* for the past, *ending* for the future: *the period ended* [last] *Jan. 15, the period ending* [next] *June 15.*

enormity, enormousness. *Enormity* refers to horror or great wickedness; *enormousness* refers to size: *the enormity of the crime, the enormousness of the national debt.*

everyone, every one. It is a solid word as a pronoun used in the sense of every person or everybody. But it is two words in the sense of every or each one (modified noun) of a group named: *Every one of his predictions came true. Every one of the defendants was heard.* But: *Everyone was there.* Also note that *everyone* (like *everybody*) is singular in form: *He wanted everyone to be a New Yorker.* Not: *to be New Yorkers.*

fewer, less. Use *fewer* in reference to a number of individual persons or things: *Fewer than 100 members voted for the proposal.* If the number is one, write *one vote* *fewer,* not *one fewer votes* or *one fewer vote.* Use *less* in reference to quantity: *Most shoppers are buying less sugar this year.* Also use *less* when, although a number is specified, it suggests rather a quantity or sum: The police recovered less than $1,500.

flaunt, flout. To flaunt is to make an ostentatious or defiant display; to flout is to show contempt for.

forbear (avoid, shun), **forebear** (ancestor).

forbid. Use preposition *to.* But after *prohibit*, use *from.*

founder, flounder. To founder is to sink or collapse; to flounder is to stumble or flail awkwardly.

heretofore is stilted and should normally be replaced by *until now.* On the rare occasions when *heretofore* is appropriate—perhaps for a formal effect—it should not be confused with *theretofore,* which means *until then.*

include is usually used to introduce a number of names or items that do not constitute a complete listing: *His softball team includes two Ph.D.'s. The cost of the trip included $100 for food and lodging.* See **comprise.**

jibe. It has two meanings. One is to accord; the other, which is nautical, is to shift. Do not use in the sense of taunt; use *gibe* for that.

lay, lie. *Lay* means in general to place, to put, to deposit; it requires a direct object. *Lie* means in general to be in a reclining position, to be situated; it thus does not take an object. Some examples of correct use follow:

LAY: *He always lays his hat on the hall table. He laid his hat on the table. At this time, I imagine, he is laying his hat on the table. He had already laid his hat on the table.*

LIE: *Massachusetts lies to the north and New York to the west. He lay quietly, waiting for her return. The demonstrators spent the next three hours lying in the street. Having lain there for three hours, they decided it was futile to remain.*

But consider the hen: She not only *lays eggs;* she also just *lays* (no object stated; eggs understood)—if, that is, she is a *laying* hen.

leave alone (to leave in solitude); **let alone (to refrain from disturbing).**

like, as. The day may come when *like* will be fully accepted as a conjunction. But meanwhile do not so use it *(He runs like a fish swims—with no apparent effort)* except in very informal contexts or when it introduces a noun not followed by a verb *(He deals cards like a riverboat gambler).*

In the following examples, *like* and *as* are correctly used: *Tom, like his father, is a fierce competitor. This gingersnap tastes good, as a cookie should. The piano sounded as if it had been properly tuned. She treated him like a slave. He treated her as a loyal subject treats a monarch. You can easily build one, as I did. You can build one exactly like the one I built.*

loan. Avoid as a verb; use *lend.* And *lent,* rather than *loaned.*

loath (unwilling), **loathe** (to hate).

mantel (shelf), **mantle** (cloak).

masterful (overpowering), **masterly** (skillful).

mean, median. In statistics, a *mean* is an average; a *median* is a figure that ranks midway in a list of numbers arranged in ascending or descending order. For example, in a discussion of the varying wages of 51 workers, the mean is the total of their pay divided by 51. The median is a wage that is higher than 25 of the wages and lower than the remaining 25. If the total of items listed is an even number—50, say, instead of 51—the median is the average of the two numbers in the middle of the listing. In other words, if the 25th number in a listing of 50 is 200 and the 26th is 220, the median is 210.

not only, but also (and similar constructions). The parallel in such constructions is often destroyed by misplacement of words: *It would not only be unwieldy but also unworkable.* Make it: *It would be not only unwieldy but also unworkable.* Sometimes the *also* after the *but* is omitted, but that omission often impairs the balance of the sentence. Balance may in some cases be achieved by some other word or words, properly placed: *It would be not only unwieldy but unworkable as well.*

none. Construe as a plural unless it is desired to emphasize the idea of *not one* or *no one*—and then it is often better to use *not one* or *no one* instead of *none.*

O, oh. The vocative *O* is always capitalized, whether occurring at the beginning of a sentence or at some intermediate point: *For Thee, O Lord. Oh* is capitalized only when occurring at the beginning of a sentence: *Oh, what a shame! But, oh, how glad we were!* The form *O* is virtually obsolete as far as ordinary usage is concerned and is found principally in quotations from poetry, in classical references and in religious matter.

only. Place it next to the word it modifies: *He ate only a sandwich,* not *He only ate a sandwich.* See **not only, but also.**

oral, verbal. Use *oral* to convey the idea of words that are spoken. *Verbal* is less precise; its chief meaning is words used in any manner—spoken, written or printed.

palate (part of mouth), **palette** (artist's paint board), **pallet** (bed; also, portable platform).

people, persons. In general, use *people* for round numbers and groups (the larger the group, the better *people* sounds), and *persons* for precise or quite small numbers: *One million people were notified. He notified 1,316 persons. He said 30 people had been asked to volunteer. Only two persons showed up. Seventeen persons were injured.* The important thing is to avoid the ridiculous: *As we all know, persons are funny.*

persuade, convince. Either may be followed by an *of* phrase or a *that* clause, but only *persuade* may be followed by the infinitive *to.* Thus: *They persuaded him to leave.* Never *convinced him to leave.*

prohibit. Use preposition *from.* And after *forbid,* use *to.*

principal, principle. *Principal* is basically either a noun meaning a chief person or thing, or an adjective meaning first in rank, importance or degree. *Principle* means, basically, a fundamental truth, doctrine or law, or a guiding rule or code of conduct, or method of operation.

prone (lying face down), **supine** (face up).

proved, proven. In general, *proved* is preferred: *The prosecutor had proved the defendant's guilt.* But as an adjective preceding a noun, *proven* is better: *a proven remedy, proven oil reserves.* And the Scottish legal verdict is *not proven.*

ready. Avoid using as a verb. In a sentence like *City Hall was readied for the inauguration,* it is usually possible to substitute a more natural verb, such as *prepare.*

rebut, refute. *Rebut* means to respond to a statement or speaker, taking issue; *refute* means to prove the statement or speaker wrong or false. Unless the intention is to say that one side demolished the other's argument, use *rebut, dispute, deny* or *reject,* not *refute.*

record, new. The redundant *new* should not be used in a context like this: *He set a new record in the high jump.* But this is all right: *The new record exceeded the old by two inches.*

serve, service. As verbs meaning to provide a service, they are not interchangeable. People are *served,* individually or in groups (a club, a town, a nation). Inanimate objects or systems that are maintained, inspected, supplied, repaired, etc., are *serviced.* A newspaper *serves* its readers; mechanics *service* the presses. A company or an institution is *served* by its employees or its supporters. And a horse at stud *services* a mare.

signature, signing. Use *signing* for the act or ceremony of endorsing a treaty or a document: *the signing of the cease-fire agreement.* Reserve *signature* for the actual name written at the end of a document.

spell out, in the sense of explaining or detailing, is overworked and should be replaced whenever possible with synonyms like *detail, enumerate, explain, list, specify.* Above all, avoid the redundant *spell out in detail.* But *spell out* is fine in the sense of actually rendering letter by letter. And so is *spell.*

staunch (adj.). Use *staunch* in the sense of steadfast or resolute. Use *stanch* (v.) for stopping the flow of a liquid—blood, for instance—and in similar contexts.

take, bring. *Take* denotes movement away from the speaker or writer, or any other movement that is not toward him; *bring* denotes motion toward the speaker or writer.

that (conj.). After a verb like *said, disclosed, announced,* etc., it is often possible to omit *that* for conciseness: *He said* [*that*] *he was tired.* But if the words after *said* (or after any other verb) can be mistaken for its direct object, the reader may be momentarily led down a false trail, and the *that* must be retained: *The Mayor announced that his party's tax program would be introduced shortly.*

When a time element follows the verb, the conjunction *that* is always needed to make quickly clear whether the time element applies to the material preceding or following: *Governor Manley announced today that he would sign the income tax bill.*

Often a sentence with two parallel clauses requires the expression *and that* in the second part; then the *that* should be kept in the first part also, for balance: *The Mayor said that he might run again and that if he did, Joan Manley would be his campaign manager.*

that, which. *That* is preferred in restrictive clauses: *The university that he admires most is Harvard.* In nonrestrictive clauses, *which* is mandatory: *Harvard, which is not his alma mater, is first in his affections.*

the. Capitalize when an integral part of a name: *The Hague, The New York Times.* But: *the Netherlands.* See **a** and **an** above, and **articles** in the Usage section.

usage, use. *Usage* refers to habitual or preferred practice in such fields as grammar, law, etiquette and diplomacy. *Use* is the preferred noun in references to employment of an object or consumption of a commodity: *the use of energy, gasoline use, automobile use, drug use.*

who, whom. Use *who* in the sense of *he* or *she* or *they: John P. Manley, who was appointed to fill the vacancy. . . .* (*He* was appointed.) Use *whom* in the sense of *him* or *her* or *them: Joan Manley, whom the board recommended, was finally appointed.* (The board recommended *her.*)

Do not be misled by the verb in a parenthetical phrase between the pronoun and its verb, as in: *John P. Manley, whom the police said is the mastermind. . . .* (It must be *who,* as removal of the parenthetical *the police said* will demonstrate. Or, to put it another way: The police are saying that *he* is the mastermind.) But *whom* is correct here: *John P. Manley, whom the police described as. . . .* (They described *him.*)

within, without. A simple *in* is often much better than *within,* which is pretentious in sentences like this: *He had no enemies within the party.* As for *without,* there are many instances in which it is either unclear or not idiomatic, as in: *His critics within and without the industry were seldom silent.* Make it: . . . *in* [or *inside*] *and outside the industry.* On rare occasions when more dramatic phrasing is justified, the expression *within and without* is appropriate: *The President denounced enemies within and without.*

TABLE OF METRIC WEIGHTS AND MEASURES

Weight

10 milligrams (mg)	= 1 centigram (cg)
10 centigrams	= 1 decigram (dg) = 100 milligrams
10 decigrams	= 1 gram (g) = 1 000 milligrams
10 grams	= 1 dekagram (dag)
10 dekagrams	= 1 hectogram (hg) = 100 grams
10 hectograms	= 1 kilogram (kg) = 1 000 grams
1 000 kilograms	= 1 metric ton (t)

Linear Measure

10 millimeters (mm)	= 1 centimeter (cm)
10 centimeters	= 1 decimeter (dm) = 100 millimeters
10 decimeters	= 1 meter (m) = 1 000 millimeters
10 meters	= 1 dekameter (dam)
10 dekameters	= 1 hectometer (hm) = 100 meters
10 hectometers	= 1 kilometer (km) = 1 000 meters

Area Measure

100 sq millimeters (mm^2)	= 1 sq centimeter (cm^2)
10 000 sq centimeters	= 1 sq meter (m^2) = 1 000 000 sq millimeters
100 sq meters	= 1 are (a)
100 ares	= 1 hectare (ha) = 10 000 sq meters
100 hectares	= 1 sq kilometer (km^2) = 1 000 000 sq meters

Volume Measure

10 milliliters (mL)	= 1 centiliter (cL)
10 centiliters	= 1 deciliter (dL) = 100 milliliters
10 deciliters	= 1 liter (L) = 1 000 milliliters
10 liters	= 1 dekaliter (daL)
10 dekaliters	= 1 hectoliter (hL) = 100 liters
10 hectoliters	= 1 kiloliter (kL) = 1 000 liters

Cubic Measure

1 000 cu millimeters (mm^2)	= 1 cu centimeter (cm^2)
1 000 cu centimeters	= 1 cu decimeter (dm^3) = 1 000 000 cu millimeters
1 000 cu decimeters	= 1 cu meter (m^3)
1 000 000 cu centimeters	= 1 000 000 000 cu millimeters

Standard Proofreading Marks

Mark	Meaning
∧	Make correction indicated in margin.
Stet	Retain crossed-out word or letter; let it stand.
Stet (dotted)	Retain words under which dots appear; write "Stet" in margin.
×	Appears battered; examine.
≡	Straighten lines.
√√√	Unevenly spaced; correct spacing.
//	Line up; i.e., make lines even.
run in	Make no break in the reading; no paragraph.
no ¶	No paragraph; sometimes written "run in."
out see copy	Here is an omission; see copy.
¶	Make a paragraph here.
tr	Transpose words or letters as indicated.
ℯ	Take out matter indicated; delete.
ℯ (with close-up marks)	Take out character indicated and close up.
¢	Line drawn through a cap means lowercase.
9	Upside down; reverse.
⁀‿	Close up; no space.
#	Insert a space here.
⊥	Push down this space.
□	Indent line one em.
[	Move this to the left.
]	Move this to the right.
⌐¬	Raise to proper position.
⌞⌟	Lower to proper position.
////	Hair space letters.
w.f.	Wrong font; change to proper font.
Qu?	Is this right?
l.c.	Put in lowercase.
s.c.	Put in small capitals.
Caps	Put in capitals.
C+s.C.	Put in caps and small caps.
rom	Change to roman.
ital	Change to italic.
≡	Under letter or word, means caps.
=	Under letter or word, means small caps.
—	Under letter or word, means italic.
∿∿	Under letter or word, means boldface.
,/	Insert comma.
;/	Insert semicolon.
:/	Insert colon.
⊙	Insert period.
/?/	Insert question mark.
/!/	Insert exclamation mark.
/=/	Insert hyphen.
∨'	Insert apostrophe.
∨"∨"	Insert quotation marks.
∨e	Insert superior letter or figure.
∧1	Insert inferior letter or figure.
[/]	Insert brackets.
(/)	Insert parentheses.
1/M	One-em dash.
2/M	Two-em parallel dash.

Sample of a Marked Proof

By JOHN P. MANLEY *bold*
Special to The New York Times

l.c. HOUSTON, Monday, Jul 21—Men have landed and *y/a*
walked on the Moon.

spell Two Americans, astronauts of Appollo (Eleven) steered *⅜/figs*
their fragile 4-legged lunar module safely and smoothly to *w.f.*
the historic landing yesterday at 4:17:40

(P.M., Eastern daylight time.) *⊙*

less # Neil A. ✓ Armstrong, the 38-year old civilian Comman- *c/=/=/ l.c.*
der, radioed to earth and the control mission room here: *tr.*
A "Houston, Tranquillity Base here. The *Eagle* has landed." *rom*
tr The first men to reach the moon, Mr. Armstrong and his *⅟m*
⊙ co-pilot, Colonel Edwin E. Aldrin Jr. of the Air Force—
brought their ship to rest on a level, rock-strewn plain near *2̸*
the Southwestern shore of the arid Sea of Tranquility. *l.c./#/ l*

Footprints on the Moon

a About six and half hours later, Mr. Armstrong opened the *bold/e.*
landing crafts hatch stepped slowly down the ladder and *×/×*
declared as he planted the 1st human footprint on the lunar *tr./⌃*
crust: *spell/@*

"/ Thats one small step for man, one giant leap for mankind."

METRIC CONVERSION CHART—APPROXIMATIONS

Symbol	When You Know	Multiply By	To Find	Symbol
		Mass (weight)		
g	grams	0.035	ounces	oz
kg	kilograms	2.2	pounds	lb
t	tonnes (1 000 kg)	1.1	short tons	
		Length		
mm	millimeters	0.04	inches	in
cm	centimeters	0.4	inches	in
m	meters	3.3	feet	ft
m	meters	1.1	yards	yd
km	kilometers	0.6	miles	mi
		Volume		
mL	milliliters	0.03	fluid ounces	fl oz
L	liters	2.1	pints	pt
L	liters	1.06	quarts	qt
L	liters	0.26	gallons	gal
m^3	cubic meters	35	cubic feet	ft^3
m^3	cubic meters	1.3	cubic yards	yd^3
		Temperature (exact)		
°C	Celsius temp.	9/5 (°C) +32	Fahrenheit temp.	°F
°F	Fahrenheit temp.	5/9 (°F) −32	Celsius temp.	°C
		Mass (weight)		
oz	ounces	28	grams	g
lb	pounds	0.45	kilograms	kg
	short tons (2 000 lb)	0.9	tonnes	t
		Length		
in	inches	*2.5	centimeters	cm
ft	feet	30	centimeters	cm
yd	yards	0.9	meters	m
mi	miles	1.6	kilometers	km
		Volume		
tsp	teaspoons	5	milliliters	mL
tbsp	tablespoons	15	milliliters	mL
fl oz	fluid ounces	30	milliliters	mL
c	cups	0.24	liters	L
pt	pints	0.47	liters	L
qt	quarts	0.95	liters	L
gal	gallons	3.8	liters	L
ft^3	cubic feet	0.03	cubic meters	m^3
yd^3	cubic yards	0.76	cubic meters	m^3

*in = 2.54 cm exactly